William F. Maag Library
Youngstown State University

ST/ESA/STAT/SER.X/25, Part I

Department of Economic and Social Affairs
Statistics Division

NATIONAL ACCOUNTS STATISTICS: MAIN AGGREGATES AND DETAILED TABLES, 1996-1997
PART I

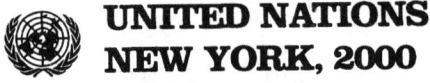
**UNITED NATIONS
NEW YORK, 2000**

NOTE

Symbols of United Nations documents are composed of capital letters combined with figures. The first 14 editions of the Yearbook were issued without series symbols.

ST/ESA/STAT/SER.X/25. PART I

UNITED NATIONS PUBLICATION
Sales No. E.00.XVII.11

ISBN 92-1-161425-2

Inquiries should be directed to:
SALES SECTION
UNITED NATIONS
NEW YORK, NY 10017

Copyright © United Nations, 2000
All rights reserved
Printed by the United Nations Reproduction Section, New York

CONTENTS

Introduction v
I. System of National Accounts ix
II. Country Tables 1

Albania	3	Dominica	519
Algeria	6	Dominican Republic	521
Angola	9	Ecuador	526
Anguilla	13	Egypt	576
Argentina	17	El Salvador	580
Australia	20	Equatorial Guinea	589
Austria	74	Estonia	591
Azerbaijan	137	Ethiopia	611
Bahamas	146	Ethiopia (Former)	613
Bahrain	154	Fiji	616
Bangladesh	158	Finland	624
Barbados	167	France	696
Belarus	169	French Guiana	766
Belgium	176	French Polynesia	770
Belize	219	Gabon	774
Bermuda	222	Gambia	775
Bhutan	224	Georgia	778
Bolivia	228	Germany	784
Botswana	251	Germany, Federal Republic (Former)	825
Brazil	258	Ghana	890
Brunei Darussalam	262	Greece	891
Bulgaria	264	Grenada	917
Burundi	273	Guadeloupe	919
Cambodia	275	Guatemala	923
Cameroon	278	Guinea-Bissau	928
Canada	281	Guyana	930
Cayman Islands	354	Haiti	932
Chad	358	Honduras	935
Chile	360	Hungary	941
China	366	Iceland	961
China, Hong Kong SAR	368	India	1016
Colombia	388	Indonesia	1068
Comoros	422	Iran, Islamic Republic of	1072
Costa Rica	424	Iraq	1082
Cote d'Ivoire	433	Ireland	1087
Croatia	438	Israel	1113
Cuba	440	Italy	1129
Cyprus	443	Jamaica	1177
Czech Republic	464	Japan	1179
Denmark	470	Jordan	1238

INTRODUCTION

This is the fortieth issue of *National Accounts Statistics: Main Aggregates and Detailed Tables* 1/ showing detailed national accounts estimates for 165 countries and areas. Like the previous issues, it has been prepared by the Statistics Division of the Department for Economic and Social Affairs of the United Nations Secretariat with the generous co-operation of national statistical services. It is issued in accordance with the request of the Statistical Commission 2/ that the most recent available data on national accounts for as many countries and areas as possible is published regularly.

SCOPE OF PUBLICATION

National accounts estimates in terms of the United Nations System of National Accounts (SNA) are shown, where available, for each of the following tables:

Part I. Summary information

1.1 Expenditures on the gross domestic product (current prices)

1.2 Expenditures on the gross domestic product (constant prices)

1.3 Cost components of the gross domestic product

1.4 General government current receipts and expenditures, summary

1.5 Current income and outlay of corporate and quasi-corporate enterprises, summary

1.6 Current income and outlay of households and non-profit institutions, summary

1.7 External transactions on current account, summary

1.8 Capital transactions of the nation, summary.

1.9 Gross domestic product by institutional sector of origin

1.10 Gross domestic product by kind of activity (current prices)

1.11 Gross domestic product by kind of activity (constant prices)

1.12 Relations among national accounting aggregates

Part 2. Final expenditures on gross domestic product: detailed breakdowns and supporting tables

2.1 General government final consumption expenditure by function (current prices)

2.2 General government final consumption expenditure by function (constant prices)

2.3 Total government outlays by function and type (current prices)

2.4 Composition of general government social security benefits and social assistance grants to households

2.5 Private final consumption expenditure by type (current prices)

2.6 Private final consumption expenditure by type (constant prices)

2.7 Gross capital formation by type of good and owner (current prices)

2.8 Gross capital formation by type of good and owner (constant prices)

2.9 Gross capital formation by kind of activity of owner, ISIC major divisions (current prices)

2.10 Gross capital formation by kind of activity of owner, ISIC major divisions (constant prices)

2.11 Gross fixed capital formation by kind of activity of owner, ISIC divisions (current prices)

2.12 Gross fixed capital formation by kind of activity of owner, ISIC divisions (constant prices)

2.13 Stocks of reproducible fixed assets, by type of good and owner (current prices)

2.14 Stocks of reproducible fixed assets, by type of good and owner (constant prices)

2.15 Stocks of reproducible fixed assets by kind of activity (current prices)

2.16 Stocks of reproducible fixed assets by kind of activity (constant prices)

2.17 Exports and imports of goods and services, detail

Part 3. Institutional sector accounts: detailed flow accounts

1. General government

3.11 Production account: total and subsectors

3.12 Income and outlay account: total and subsectors

3.13 Capital accumulation account: total and subsectors

3.14 Capital finance account: total and subsectors

3.15 Balance sheet: total and subsectors

2. Corporate and quasi-corporate enterprises

3.21 Production account: total and sectors

3.22 Income and outlay account: total and sectors

3.23 Capital accumulation account: total and sectors

3.24 Capital finance account: total and sectors

3.25 Balance sheet: total and sectors

3.26 Financial transactions of financial institutions: detail

3. Households and private unincorporated enterprises

3.31 Production account: total and subsectors

3.32 Income and outlay account: total and subsectors

3.33 Capital accumulation account: total and subsectors

3.34 Capital finance account: total and subsectors

3.35 Balance sheet

4. Private non-profit institutions serving households

3.41 Production account

3.42 Income and outlay account

3.43 Capital accumulation account

3.44 Capital finance account

5. External transactions

3.51 Current account, detail

3.52 Capital accumulation account

3.53 Capital finance account

Part 4. Production by kind of activity: detailed breakdowns and supporting tables

4.1 Derivation of value added by kind of activity (current prices)

4.2 Derivation of value added by kind of activity (constant prices)

4.3 Cost components of value added

CONCEPTUAL REFERENCES

The form and concepts of the statistical tables in the present publication generally conform to the recommendations in A System of National Accounts 3/, Studies in Methods, Series F. No. 2, Rev.3. 1968, except where noted. A summary of the conceptual framework, their classifications and definitions of transactions is provided in chapter I of the present publication.

COMPILATION OF DATA

To compile the large volume of national accounts data, the Statistics Division each year sends to countries or areas pre-filled SNA questionnaire. The recipients are requested to update the questionnaire with the latest available national accounts estimates and to indicate where the scope and coverage of the country estimates differ for conceptual or statistical reasons from the definitions and classifications recommended in SNA. Data obtained from these replies are supplemented by information gathered from correspondence with the national statistical services and from national source publications.

In the present publication, the data for each country or area are presented in separate chapters, as far as possible, under uniform table headings and classifications of SNA. Differences in definition and coverage of specific items are indicated in footnotes to the relevant tables.

Country data in chapter II are presented in alphabetical order. Unless otherwise stated, the data in the country tables relate to the calendar year against which they are shown.

COMPARABILITY OF THE NATIONAL ESTIMATES

Every effort has been made to present the estimates of the various countries or areas in a form designed to facilitate international comparability. To this end, important differences in concept, scope, coverage and classification have been described in the notes, which precede and accompany the country tables. Such differences should be taken into account if misleading comparison among countries or areas are to be avoided.

REVISIONS

The figures shown are the most recent estimates and revisions available at the time of compilation. In general, figures for the most recent year are to be regarded as provisional. For more up to date information, reference is made to selected issues of the United Nations Monthly Bulletin of Statistics 4/.

NOMENCLATURE

The information for the countries and areas shown in this publication reflect what is available to the Statistics Division of the United Nations as of October 1999.

Designations, which have changed in recent years, are as follows:

Hong Kong - Pursuant to a Joint Declaration signed on 19 December 1994, the United Kingdom re-stored Hong Kong to the People's Republic of China with effect from 1 July 1997; the People's Republic of China resumed the exercise of sovereignty over the territory with effect from that date.

Zaire - All data for the former Zaire are shown under the country name of Democratic Republic of the Congo.

Czech Republic, Slovakia - Data for Czech Republic and Slovakia are shown separately under the appropriate country name. For period prior to 1 January 1993, data for the former Czechoslovakia are shown under the country name Czechoslovakia (Former)

Yugoslavia (Former) - All data for Yugoslavia prior to 1 January 1992 refer to the Socialist Federal Republic of Yugoslavia which was composed of six republics. After that date, when available, data for the republics, Bosnia and Herzegovina, Croatia, Slovenia, The Former Yugoslav Republic of Macedonia and Yugoslavia which is composed of two republics (Serbia and Montenegro) are shown separately.

USSR (Former) - In 1991, the Union of Soviet Socialist Republics formally dissolved into fifteen independent republics (Armenia, Azerbaijan, Belarus, Georgia, Kazakstan, Kyrgyzstan, Latvia, Lithuania, Republic of Moldova, Russian Federation, Tajikistan, Turkmenistan, Ukraine and Uzbekistan). When available, data are shown for the individual republics. All data for the former USSR are shown under the country name USSR (Former)

Germany - On October 1990, the Federal Republic of Germany and the German Democratic Republic united to form one sovereign State under the designation Germany.

Yemen - In May 1990, Yemen and Democratic Yemen united to form a single State. Since that date they have been represented as one country with the name "Yemen".

EXPLANATION OF SYMBOLS

The following symbols have been employed:
Data not available ....
Category not applicable ....
Magnitude nil or less than half of the unit employed .... -
Decimal figures are always preceded by a point (.)

When a series is not homogeneous, it is indicated by presenting the data in separate rows.

Decimals in tables do not necessarily add to totals shown because of rounding.

GENERAL DISCLAIMER

The designations employed and the presentation of material in this publication do not imply the expression of any opinion whatsoever on the part of the Secretariat of the United Nations concerning the legal status of any country, territory, city or area or of its authorities, or concerning the delimitation of its frontiers and boundaries.

Where the designation "country or area" appears in the headings of tables, it covers countries, territories, cities or areas. In prior issues of this publication. where the designation "country" appears in the headings of tables, it covers countries, territories, cities or areas

In some tables, the designations "developed" and "developing" economies are intended for statistical convenience and do not, necessarily, express a judgment about the stage reached by a particular country or area in the development process.

1/ United Nations publication. The first 25 editions of this publication were issued under the title Yearbook of National Accounts Statistics under the following sales number:
1957, 58.XVII.3; 1958, 59.XVII.3; 1959, 60.XVII.3; 1960, 61.XVII.4; 1961, 62.XVII.2; 1962, 63.XVII.2; 1963, 64.XVII.4; 1964, 65.XVII.2; 1965, 66.XVII.2; 1966, 67.XVII.14; 1967, E.69.XV11.6; 1968, vol.I, E.70.XV11.2, vol.II, E.70.XVll.3: 1969, vol.I, E.71.XVII.2. vol.II, E.71.XVII.3; 1970, (2 volumes), E.72.XVII.3; 1971, (3 volumes), E.73.XVII.3; 1972, (3 volumes), E.74.XVII.3:1973, (3 volumes), E.75.XVII.2; 1974, (3 volumes), E.75.XVII.5; 1975, (3 volumes), E.76.XVII.2 .1976, (2 volumes), E.77.XVII.2; 1977, (2 volumes), E.78.XVII.2; 1978, (2 volumes), E.79.XVII.8; 1979, (2 volumes), E.80.XVII.11; 1980, (2 volumes), E.82.XVII.6; 1981, (2 volumes), E.83.XV11.3;
Beginning with the twenty-sixth edition, this publication replaced Volume 1. Individual Country Data of the Yearbook and it was issued under the following sales number:
1982, E.85.XVll.3; 1983, E.86.XV11.3; 1984, E.86,XV11.26; 1985, E.87.XVII.l0; 1986. E.89.XV11.7 (Parts I and II); 1987, E.90.XVII.2 (Parts I and II); 1988, E.90.XVII.18 (Parts I and II): 1989, E.91 XVII.16 (Parts I and II); 1990, E.93.XIll.3 (Parts I and II); 1991, E.94.XVII.5 (Parts I and II):1992, E.95.XVII.4 (Parts I and II); 1993, E.96.XVII.5 (Parts I and II); 1994, E.97.XVII.6 (Parts I and II); 1999, E.99.XVII.7 (Parts I and II).

2/ See Official Records of the Economic and Social Council, First Year, Second Session, (E/39), annex III, chap. IV.

3/ United Nations publication, Sales No. E.69.XVII.3. The first addition of the report, published in 1953 was prepared by an expert committee appointed by the Secretary-General of the United Nations.

4/ United Nations publication, ST/ESA/STAT/SER.Q.

I. SYSTEM OF NATIONAL ACCOUNTS (SNA)

The System of National Accounts (SNA) was adopted by the Statistical Commission at its fifteenth session 1/ for the use of national statistical authorities and in the international reporting of comparable national accounting data. The System 2/ is a revision and extension of the former SNA, which was first formulated in 1952. In 1993, the Statistical Commission at its twenty-seventh session adopted the revised System of National Accounts. The revised System 3/ is expected to be fully implemented by the year 1999. The summary of concepts provided in this chapter refers to the 1968 SNA.

A. STRUCTURE OF SNA

SNA provides a comprehensive and detailed framework for the systematic and integrated recording of transaction flows in an economy. It brings together into an articulated and coherent system data ranging in degree of aggregation from consolidated accounts of the nation to detailed input-output and flow-of-funds tables. It includes production and goods and services and outlay and capital finance accounts for institutional sectors and subsectors.

The country tables are divided into four parts. These are listed in the above introduction. Part 1 contains summary but comprehensive information, at current and, where appropriate, constant prices. This part includes not only the basic gross domestic product (final expenditures and cost composition) but also summary information on government receipts and disbursements, enterprise and household income and outlay, and external transactions, a summary capital transactions account, information on gross product by institutional sector of origin and kind of activity and, finally, a table showing the relation among the aggregate concepts used in the revised SNA and also commonly in national statistical systems. Tables 1.1, 1.3, 1.4, 1.5, 1.6, 1.7 and 1.8 form a simple, closed and balancing set of flow accounts, drawn from the much more complex and elaborate standard accounts of SNA; these tables can therefore be used not only to provide an overview of the operation of the economic system but also as a guide to the more detailed data that follow and as a framework to enforce conceptual and statistical consistency.

Part 2 shows detailed breakdowns of the final expenditure components on gross domestic product (consumption, capital formation, imports and exports), in current and constant prices, together with supporting tables giving additional information on government outlays and capital stock. This part also shows tables relating to stocks of reproducible tangible assets at current and constant prices.

Part 3 shows detailed institutional sector accounts. For each sector and subsector, five accounts are given: a production account, an income and outlay account, a capital formation account, a capital finance account, and a balance sheet. The latter four are standard SNA accounts, as shown in annex 8.3 to *A System of National Accounts* 2/ and in annex 8.2 to *Provisional Guidelines on National and Sector Balance Sheets and Reconciliation Accounts of the System of National Accounts* 4/.

The SNA standard accounts do not include institutional sector production accounts, but provision is made for this information in the supporting tables.

The sectors and subsectors distinguished in part 3 are: general government (central, state or provincial, local, social security funds), corporate and quasi-corporate enterprises (non-financial, financial), households and private unincorporated enterprises (farm entrepreneurial, other farm, non-farm entrepreneurial, non-farm wage earner, other) and nonprofit institutions serving households.

Part 4 contains kind-of-activity breakdowns. Two levels of detail are employed. All of the information is asked for at the major division (1-digit) level of the International Standard Industrial Classification of All Economic Activities 5/ (ISIC). In some cases, data are also asked for at the ISIC division (2-digit) level, with a very small amount of further breakdown to the 3-digit level. Where appropriate, both current and constant prices are specified. The tables show the derivation of value added (gross output less intermediate consumption), the cost components of value added, and employment.

B. STANDARD CLASSIFICATIONS OF THE SNA

Detailed discussions of definitions and classifications are to be found in *A System of National Accounts* 2/ and in the other publications on SNA cited above. SNA distinguishes between transactor and transaction classifications. Below is a short summary of the main characteristics of each of the classifications used by the system.

I. Classifications of transactors

1. Kind of activity

The kind-of-activity classification employed is the major division (1-digit) level or, in some tables the division (2-digit) level of ISIC.

In SNA, this classification is intended to be applied to establishment-type units, defined as the smallest units for which separate production accounts can be compiled. SNA also employs a much broader kind of activity classification, which divides producers into industries, and three categories of other producers. Industries are, broadly, establishments whose activities are intended to be self-sustaining, whether through production for the market or for own use, and it is to this category that the ISIC breakdown is generally applied.

All establishments falling into ISIC major divisions 1-8 should be classed as industries. Producers of government services, private non-profit services to households, and domestic services are classed as other producers; all of these should fall into ISIC category 9 "Community, social and personal services". ISIC category 9 also may, of course, include some establishments classed as industries. Where countries consider, however, that some establishments classed as other producers should appear in ISIC categories other than 9, the nature of the exceptions would be specified in footnotes to tables 1.10 and 1.11.

2. Institutional sectors

The basic SNA institutional sectoring is given in *A System of National Accounts* 2/, table 5.1.

Institutional sectoring, in SNA, is intended to be applied to enterprise-type units, that is, units for which complete accounts can be compiled, as opposed to the establishment-type units employed in the kind-of-activity classification. This distinction is applicable mainly to the corporate and quasi-corporate enterprise sector.

The sectoring and subsectoring employed in the institutional sector accounts in part 3 is as follows:

General government

    Central

    State or provincial

    Local

    Social security funds

Corporate and quasi-corporate enterprises

    Non-financial

    Financial

Households and private unincorporated enterprises

    Farm entrepreneurial

    Other farm

    Non-farm entrepreneurial

    Non-farm wage earner

    Other

Non-profit institutions serving households

Rest of the world

(a) General government. This sector includes (1) producers of government services, all bodies, departments and establishments of any level of government that engage in administration, defense, regulation of the public order and health, cultural, recreational and other social services and social security arrangements that are furnished but not normally sold to the public; and (2) industries of government, ancillary departments and establishments mainly engaged in supplying goods and services to other units of government, such as printing plants, central transport pools and arsenals, and agencies mainly selling goods and services to the public but operating on a small scale and financially integrated with general government, such as government restaurant facilities in public buildings. Non-profit institutions which, while not an official part of any organ of government, are wholly or mainly financed and controlled by it should be included in producers of government services. Ancillary agencies may occur in any kind of activity. Producers of government services normally occur only in major division 9 (which of course may also include ancillary agencies).

Provision is made for four subsectors of general government, all of which may include the two components noted above. However, it is not intended that artificial distinctions should be introduced where they do not exist in the institutions of a particular country. It will, for instance, usually be desirable to separate state or provincial government from local government only in countries in which state or provincial governments exercise a considerable degree of autonomy. Similarly, social security funds should in general be distinguished separately only where they are organized separately from the other activities of general government and exercise substantial autonomy in their operations.

(b) Corporate and quasi-corporate enterprises. SNA defines this sector to include enterprises which meet any one of the following criteria: (1) they are incorporated; (2) they are owned by a non-resident; (3) they are relatively large partnerships or proprietorships with complete income statements and balance sheets; (4) they are non-profit institutions mainly serving business and financed and controlled by business; or (5) they are engaged in financial activities. Because of the difficulty that may be encountered in compiling separate production account data for incorporated and unincorporated units, a combined production account for these two sectors has also been provided for.

(c) Households and private unincorporated enterprises. This sector includes all private unincorporated enterprises not classed as quasi-corporations. SNA also includes in this sector private non-profit institutions serving households that employ less than the equivalent of two full-time persons.

The criterion for classifying the subsectors of the household sector in these tables differs slightly from that tentatively proposed in SNA. There, the subsectoring is based on the occupational status of the person designated "head of household". Here, the classification is based on the most important source of household income, taking all household members into account. It is considered that this criterion more accurately reflects both changing social views and changing labour force participation practices; it also responds to recent directives relating to the elimination of sex-based stereotypes.

(d) Private non-profit institutions serving households. This sector includes institutions, not mainly financed and controlled by general governments and employing the equivalent of two or more persons, that furnish educational, health, cultural, recreational and other social and community services to households free of charge or at prices that do not fully cover their costs of production.

As in the case of general government, SNA includes two components in this sector: (1) producers of private non-profit services to households, which engage in the activities enumerated above, and (2) commercial activities of these institutions, such as owning and letting dwellings, operating eating and lodging facilities, and publishing and selling books, for which it is possible to compile separate production accounts but not complete separate financial accounts. (Where separate financial accounts can be compiled, such activities would be classed as ordinary quasi-corporations.) In SNA, these commercial activities are considered to be industries and should be classed in the appropriate ISIC categories, whereas the non-profit services proper will all fall into ISIC category 9.

II. Classifications of transactions

1. Classification of the functions of government

Table 5.3 of A System of National Accounts 2/ contains a classification of the purposes of government, the l-digit level of which was used in previous publications for classifying general government outlays. This classification has now been superseded by the Classification of the Functions of Government 6/.

2. Household consumption expenditure

Table 6.1 of SNA provides a classification of household goods and services. The classification used in the present publication is a slightly condensed version of the second level of this classification, in which some second-level categories have been combined.

3. Purposes of private non-profit bodies serving households

This classification appears in table 5.4 of SNA. It is used for classifying the final consumption expenditures of private non-profit institutions serving households.

4. Gross capital formation

Table 6.2 of SNA classifies stocks according to type, and table 6.3 classifies gross fixed capital formation according to type. These classifications are used in the present publication in slightly modified form, calling for less detail in some arena and slightly more detail in others (specifically, transport equipment).

5. Exports and imports of goods and services

This classification is given in table 6.4 of SNA.

6. Transfers

Table 7.1 of SNA contains a classification of unrequired current transfers, including direct taxes. This classification is not employed directly in the present publication but it is the source of the definitions of a number of flows, and will be referred to in that connection.

7. Financial assets and liabilities

Table 7.2 of SNA gives a classification of items appearing in the capital finance account.

8. Balance sheet categories

Classifications of the various types of assets not included in the previous classification are given in tables 5.1 and 5.2 of Provisional Guidelines on National and Sector Balance Sheets and Reconciliation Accounts of the System of National Accounts, 4/ which deal respectively, with stocks and fixed assets, and non-reproducible tangible assets. These classifications are used in the capital stock tables in part 2 and the balance sheet tables in part 3 of the present publication.

C. DEFINITIONS OF FLOWS

The following section briefly defines the content of the flows appearing in the SNA tables of chapter III of the present publication.

I. Total supply of goods and services

1. Gross output of goods and services

Gross output of goods and services covers both the value of goods and services produced for sale and the value of goods and services produced for own use. It includes (a) the domestic production of goods and services which are either for sale or for transfer to others, (b) net additions to work in progress valued at cost and to stocks of finished goods valued in producers' prices; (c) products made on own account for government or private consumption or for gross fixed capital formation; and (d) rents received on structures, machinery and equipment (but not on land) and imputed rent for owner-occupied dwellings.

Production for own consumption of households includes all own-account production of primary products (agricultural, fishing, forestry, mining and quarrying), own-account production of such items as butter, flour, wine, cloth or furniture made from primary products, and other goods and services that are also commonly sold. Gross output of the distributive trades is defined as the difference between sales and purchase values of goods sold. Gross output of banks and similar financial institutions is defined at the sum of actual service charges and imputed service charges; the latter is equal to the excess of property income received over interest paid out on deposits. For casualty insurance companies, gross output is defined as the excess of premiums received over claims paid, and for life insurance schemes it is the excess of premiums received over the sum of claims paid and net additions to actuarial reserves, excluding the accrued interest of the policy holders in these reserves. Gross output of general government includes the market value of sales and goods and services produced for own use. The latter should be valued at cost, that is, the sum of net purchases of goods and services for intermediate consumption (at purchasers prices), consumption of fixed capital, compensation of employees and any indirect taxes paid.

The concept of gross output appears in the tables in both part 3 and part 4. In part 3, each sector production account aggregates to its gross output. In part 4, gross output of various kind-of-activity sectors appears in tables 4.1-4.2 and 4.5-4.10. In the sector production accounts (tables 3.11, 3.21, 3.31 and 3.41) and the supply tables (4.5, 4.6, 4.9 and 4.10), gross output is divided into marketed and non-marketed components. The marketed component includes all output offered for sale (whether or not a buyer is actually found) or valued on the basis of a market transaction, even if it reaches the ultimate recipient through a transfer.

2. Imports of goods and services

Imports of goods and services include broadly the equivalent of general imports of merchandise as defined in external trade statistics, plus imports of services and direct purchases abroad made by resident households and by the government on current account. Transfer of migrants household and personal effects and gifts between households are also included. The following additions and deductions are required, however, to move from the general trade concept to the national accounting concept. Additions required include (1) the value of purchases of bankers, stores and ballast for ships, aircraft, etc., (2) fish and salvage purchased from foreign vessels, and (3) purchases from abroad of gold ore and gold for industrial uses. Deductions required include (4) goods imported solely for improvement or repair and subsequently re-exported; and (5) leased or rented machinery, equipment and other goods; the value of the repairs or leasing and rental services is included, however. The valuation of imports is c.i.f. In principle, transactions should be recorded at the moment the transfer of ownership takes place and not when goods physically enter the domestic territory, but in practice the time of recording used in the national accounts usually must follow that used in the external trade statistics.

Total imports of goods and services appear in tables 1.1, 1.2, 1.7 and 3.51. A detailed breakdown is given in table 2.17.

II. Disposition of total supply: intermediate and final uses

1. Intermediate consumption

Intermediate consumption covers non-durable goods and services used up in production, including repair and maintenance, research and development and exploration costs. It also includes indirect outlays on financing capital formation, such as flotation costs for loans and transfer costs involved in the purchase and sale of intangible assets and financial claims. Intermediate consumption is, as far as possible, valued in purchasers? prices at the moment of use. For producers of government services and private non-profit services to households, intermediate consumption includes (1) purchases of goods and services on current account less sales of similar second-hand goods and scraps and wastes, (2) value of goods in kind received as transfers or gifts from foreign governments, except those received for distribution to households without renovation or alteration, (3) durable goods acquired primarily for military purposes, and (4) goods and services paid for by government but furnished by private suppliers to individuals (e.g., medical services), provided that the individuals have no choice of supplier. However, intermediate consumption of these producers does not include (1) goods and services acquired for use in constructing capital assets, such as roads or buildings, (2) goods and services paid for by government but furnished by private suppliers to individuals, when the individuals can choose the supplier and (3) purchases of strategic materials for government stockpiles.

Intermediate consumption appears in each institutional sector production account in part 3, and in tables 4.1-4.2 by kind of activity. In addition to the flow numbers assigned in SNA, flow numbers have been introduced for two categories of intermediate consumption not separately numbered in A System of National Accounts 2/. The first is imputed bank service charges. The imputed bank service charge is defined as the excess of property income accruing to banks and similar financial institutions from the investment of deposits over the interest accruing to their depositors. This imputation is made because of the view that banks perform services for depositors for which no explicit payment is made, in return for the use of the deposits as earning assets. It is not possible to allocate the imputation to specific recipients of the services, however, so that it cannot be included, as would be desirable, as part of the intermediate consumption of each reception. It is therefore deducted as a lump-sum adjustment. The adjustment appears in the tables showing kind-of-activity breakdowns of value added or intermediate consumption, including tables 1.10, 1.11 and 4.1-4.2. The second addition is intermediate consumption of industries of government, required for constructing a production account for general government (table 3.11).

2. Government final consumption expenditure

Government final consumption expenditure is equal to the service produced by general government for its own use. Since these services are not sold, they are valued in the gross domestic product at their cost to the government. This cost is defined as the sum of (1) intermediate consumption, (2) compensation of employees, (3) consumption of fixed capital and (4) payments of indirect taxes, less (5) the value of own account production of fixed assets, and less (6) sales of goods and services.

The latter item, government sales, includes all payments made by individuals for services received (whether nominal or full cost) and it also includes the provision of second-hand goods from government stores as transfers in kind to foreign governments. Sales of such items as timber from forest preserves, seeds from agricultural experiment stations and government publications would also appear here. Compensation of employees, consumption of fixed capital and indirect taxes paid (if any) should preferably relate to all general government activity, with inter-governmental purchases and sales of goods and services eliminated in order to avoid double counting. With this treatment, there will be no operating surplus for any general government unit. Where countries consider that ancillary agencies and/or unincorporated government enterprises selling to the general public are operated on commercial principles and that the prices charged reflect market values, treatment of these entities on a net basis is an acceptable alternative. In this treatment, their sales to other government agencies will appear as intermediate consumption of the latter, and their operating surplus wilt appear as an item of general government income. This treatment has a number of disadvantages: the boundary between ancillary agencies and other government agencies is very difficult to specify precisely, and variations in treatment are likely to lead to incomparability among countries. Also, the net treatment makes it impossible to obtain figures for such flows as total compensation of general government employees. Finally, the level of gross domestic product will vary when the governments internal transfer prices are altered, a result that is somewhat incongruous.

Total government consumption expenditures appear in tables 1.1, 1.2, 4.7 and 4.8. A breakdown by government subsectors appears in table 3.12. Tables 2.1-2.2 show detailed breakdowns by function

3. Private final consumption expenditure

Private consumption expenditure measures the final consumption expenditure of all resident non-governmental units. Thus, it is the sum of final consumption expenditure of households and that of private non-profit institutions serving households.

(a) Private non-profit institutions serving households. Final consumption expenditure of these units, as in the case of government, is equal to services they produce for their own use and is valued at cost. Cost includes purchases and the value (in purchasers prices) of transfers of goods and services received in kind, compensation of employees, consumption of fixed capital, and indirect taxes paid by these institutions, less their sales of goods and services. The definitions of purchases and sales on current account are much the same as those for general government. Private non-profit institutions serving households are defined to include units employing the equivalent of two or more full-time persons and providing educational, health, cultural, recreational, and other social and community services to households free of charge or at prices that are not intended to cover the full costs of their production. Units mainly financed and controlled by general government, however, are included in general government rather than here. Units primarily serving business, such as trade associations, are included with corporate and quasi-corporate enterprises.

In applying these definitions, some judgment is required, and it will often be necessary to examine intent, as well as outcome. A normally profit-making unit that sustains a loss does not thereby become a non-profit institution.

Final expenditures of private non-profit institutions serving households appear in tables 1.1, 1.2 and 3.42, and a breakdown by purpose appears in tables 2.5 and 2.6. Definitions of the purpose categories are given in SNA classification 5.4

(b) Resident households. What is wanted as a component of the final uses of gross domestic product is the final consumption expenditure of resident households. What are most commonly available in the statistics, however, are not expenditure of resident units but expenditure in the domestic market. To adjust expenditure in the domestic market to expenditure of resident units, purchases abroad and net gifts in kind received from abroad have been added, and subtracted are purchases in the domestic market of non-resident units. Corresponding adjustments are made to exports (to ensure that they include purchases of non-residents in the domestic market) and to imports (to ensure that they include purchases of residents abroad). These adjustments include expenditures by tourists, ships crews, border and seasonal workers and diplomatic and military personnel on goods and services, including local transportation, but they exclude expenditures reimbursable as travel expenses (which are counted as intermediate consumption). These adjustments are shown in tables 2.5 and 2.6.

Household final consumption expenditure includes outlays on non-durable and durable goods and services, less sales of second-hand goods and of scraps and wastes. In addition to market purchases, household final consumption expenditure includes the imputed gross rent of owner-occupied dwellings, food and other items produced on own account and consumed, and items provided as wages and salaries in kind by an employer, such as food, shelter or clothing and other fringe benefits included in compensation of employees, except those considered to add to household saving. The imputed gross rent of owner-occupied dwellings should, in principle, be valued at the rent of similar facilities on the market but has been approximated by costs, including operating maintenance and repair charges, depreciation, mortgage interest, and interest on the owners equity. Other non-marketed output included in final consumption is valued at producers prices. Total resident final consumption expenditure appears in tables 1.1, 1.2, 1.6 and 1.12. It is broken down by institutional subsectors in tables 3.32, and in tables 4.7 and 4.8 it is broken down by industrial origin. A detailed breakdown by type of good is shown in tables 2.5 and 2.6. The type of good categories is defined in SNA classification 6.1.

4. Gross capital formation

Gross capital formation is the sum of the increase in stocks and gross fixed capital formation, defined below. It appears in tables 1.1, 1.2 and 1.8. Breakdowns of gross capital formation appear in tables 2.7-2.12, 4.7 and 4.8. Gross capital formation of individual institutional sectors appears in tables 3.13, 3.23, 3.33 and 3.43.

(a) Increase in stocks. This flow includes the value of the physical change in (a) stocks of raw materials, work in progress and finished goods held by private producers, and (b) stocks of strategic materials held by the government. Work put in place on buildings and other structures, roads and other construction projects is treated as gross fixed capital formation rather than increase in stocks but is distinguished separately there to facilitate analysis. Increases in livestock raised for slaughter should be included in the increase in stocks, but breeding and draft animals, dairy cattle, and animals raised for wool clips are treated as fixed capital. The physical change in stocks during a period of account should be valued at average purchasers prices during the period. In some cases, the available data relate to the change in the value of stocks held rather than the value of the physical change.

A classification of the increase in stocks by type is given in tables 2.7 and 2.8, and defined in SNA classification 6.2. The increase in stocks by kind of activity of owner is shown in tables 2.9 and 2.10.

(b) Gross capital formation. This flow is defined to include purchases and own-account production of new producers durable goods, reduced by net sales to the rest of the world of similar second-hand or scrapped goods. Outlays of producers of government services for military purposes (except on land and certain civilian-type items, such as schools, hospitals, family-type housing and, in some cases, roads when for civilian use) are, however, considered to be current expenditures. Military purposes are here construed in terms of final expenditures: they include the military airport, but not the bulldozer used in constructing the airport. Gross fixed capital formation includes outlays on reclamation and improvement of land and development and extension of timber tracts, mines, plantations, orchards, vineyards etc., and on breeding and dairy cattle, draft animals, and animals raised for wool. Outlays on alteration or extension of fixed assets, which significantly extend their life or increase their productivity, are included, but outlays on repair and maintenance to keep fixed assets in good working order are not. All costs are included that are directly connected with the acquisition and installation of the fixed assets, such as customs duties and other indirect taxes, transport, delivery and installation charges, site clearing, planning and designing costs, legal fees and other transfer costs with respect to transactions in land, mineral deposits, timber tracts etc. However, the costs of financing, such as flotation costs, underwriters commissions and the cost of advertising bond issues, are excluded; these items are included in intermediate consumption. The acquisition of fixed assets is to be recorded at the moment that the ownership of the goods passes to the buyer. In the case of construction projects, this is taken to be the time that the work is put in place but, as noted above, uncompleted construction projects are shown separately from completed ones.

A classification of fixed assets by type is given in tables 1.7 and 2.8, and the categories are defined in SNA classification 6.3. A classification by kind of activity of purchaser is given in tables 2.9, 2.10, 2.11 and 3.12, and a classification by producing industry is given in tables 4.7 and 4.8. Breakdowns by institutional sector are given in tables 3.13, 3.23, 3.33 and 3.43.

5. Exports of goods and services

Exports of goods and services are defined to be parallel to the definition of imports given above, and they are shown in the same tables and classifications. Exports are, however, valued f.o.b., whereas imports are valued c.i.f.

III. Cost components and income shares

1. Value added and gross domestic product

The value added of industries at producers Prices is equal to the gross output of the industries at producers prices less the value of their intermediate consumption at purchasers prices. Value added for the total of all domestic producers plus import duties and value added tax which are not included in the value added of any domestic producer, and less imputed bank service charges (which are deducted in a single line) is equal to the gross domestic product is shown in tables I.9-1.11, and 4.1-4.2. Gross domestic product may be defined alternatively as the sum of final expenditures in the domestic economy (tables 1.1 and 1.2) or as the sum of incomes received in the domestic economy (tables 1.3, 1.9 and 4.3). In principle, all three methods should yield the same result but in statistical practice there are likely to be small discrepancies. Such statistical discrepancies are shown where they exist.

2. Compensation of employees

Compensation of employees appears in SNA as a domestic concept and as a national concept. Table 1.3 employs the domestic concept, that is, compensation of employees paid by resident producers. This includes payments to non-resident employees working in the country but excludes payments to resident employees temporarily working abroad. In order to show the relation of this concept to compensation received by resident households (shown in tables 1.6 and 3.32) and compensation paid to the rest of the world (shown in tables 1.7 and 3.51), the two components are shown separately in table 1.3. Each component includes (a) wages and salaries, (b) employers contributions to social security schemes and (c) employers contributions to private pension, insurance and similar schemes. The national concept of compensation of employees is shown in the household sector income and outlay account (tables 1.6 and 3.31), where compensation received by resident households from domestic producers and that received from the rest of the world are gathered together. The portion paid by resident producers appears in table 1.3; that paid by the rest of the world appears in table 1.7.

Wages and salaries include all payments to employees for their labour, whether in cash or in kind before deduction of employee contributions to social security schemes, withholding taxes and the like. They include commissions, bonuses and tips, and cost of living, vacation and sick leave allowances paid directly by the employers to the employee but exclude reimbursement for travel and other expenses incurred by employees for business purposes which is included in intermediate consumption. The pay and allowances of members of incorporated enterprises and the fees of ministers of religion are included. Wages and salaries in kind are valued at their cost to the employer and include goods and services furnished to employees free of charge or at markedly reduced cost that are clearly and primarily of benefit to the employees as consumers.

Employers contributions to social security schemes include all social security contributions that employers make on behalf of their employees, but not the employees own share of such contributions. Social security contributions may be broader than payments to social security funds, since not all social security arrangements are funded.

Employers contributions to pension, insurance and similar schemes include paid and imputed contributions by employers on behalf of their employees to private funds, reserves or other schemes for providing pensions, family allowances, lay-off and severance pay, maternity leave, workmen's compensation, health and other casualty insurance, life insurance and the like. Where employers make payments to employees for such benefits without the establishment of a formal fund for this purpose, the contributions that would be required to support such a fund are imputed both here and subsequently as an imputed transfer from households to their employers, since of course the employees do not control the use of the fund.

3. Operating surplus

Operating surplus is the balancing item in the SNA production account. For an individual establishment it is defined as the excess of value added over the sum of compensation of employees, consumption of fixed capital, and net indirect taxes. The operating surplus of all types of establishments - corporate, quasi-corporate, and unincorporated, public and private - is included in the figure shown in table 1.3. Operating surplus for each of the institutional sectors individually is shown in tables 3.11, 3.21 and 3.31; its breakdown by kind of activity is incurred by employees for business purposes, which shown in table 4.3. It is also included in the totals for property and entrepreneurial income shown in tables1.4, 1.5 and 1.6.

4. Consumption of fixed capital

Consumption of fixed capital includes allowances for normal wear and tear, foreseen obsolescence and probable (normally expected) accidental damage to fixed capital not made good by repair, all valued at current replacement cost. Unforeseen obsolescence, damages due to calamities, and depletion of natural resources are not included, since these are capital losses and should appear as changes in the balance sheet. Also not included is the revaluation of past allowances for consumption of fixed capital due to changes in the current replacement cost of fixed assets; this also will appear as part of the change in accumulated allowances shown in the balance sheet. Total consumption of fixed capital appears in tables 1.3, 1.8 and 1.12, consumption of fixed capital of individual institutional sectors in tables 3.11, 3.21, 3.31 and 3.41, and consumption of fixed capital by kind of activity in table 4.3. The accumulated consumption of fixed capital for specific types of assets and kind-of-activity sectors appears as the difference between the gross and net capital stock in tables 2.13-2.16, and for individual institutional sectors it appears in tables 3.15, 3.25, 3.35 and 3.45.

5. Indirect taxes

Indirect taxes are defined as taxes chargeable to the cost of production or sale of goods and services. They include (a) import and export duties, (b) excise, sales, entertainment and turnover taxes, (c) real state, and land taxes, unless they are merely an administrative device for collecting income tax, (d) levies on value added and the employment of labour (but not social security contributions), (e) motor-vehicle, driving-test, license, airport and passport fees, when paid by producers, and (f) the operating surplus of government fiscal monopolies on such items as alcoholic beverages and tobacco (in principle reduced by the normal profit margin of similar business units). In the present publication, indirect taxes paid and subsidies received from supranational organizations (e.g., the European Economic Community) are shown separately. Also, the net treatment of value added taxes recommended by the European Economic Community has been employed.

Unlike all other indirect taxes, SNA does not al-locate import duties among producers in tables by kind of activity. Indirect taxes are only allocated to a particular kind of activity where they are levied directly on the output of that activity (e.g., excise duties) or on the process of producing that output (e.g., employment taxes). Import duties, however, are levied on the output of foreign rather than domestic producers, and are therefore shown separately in tables by kind of activity, including tables 1.10, 1.11, 4.1, 4.2, 4.3, 4.5 and 4.6.

Total indirect taxes appear in table 1.3. Indirect taxes paid by individual institutional sectors appear in tables 3.11, 3.21, 3.31, and 3.41. Indirect taxes paid to supranational organizations appear in tables 1.7 and 1.12.

Indirect taxes retained by government are shown in table 3.12.

6. Subsidies

Subsidies are grants on current account by the government to (a) private enterprises and public corporations, or (b) unincorporated public enterprises when clearly intended to compensate for losses resulting from the price policies of government. Total subsidies, including those paid by supranational organizations, as well as by government, appear in table 1.3; subsidies paid by supranational organizations in tables 1.7 and 1.12; and those paid by government in tables 1.4 and 3.12. Subsidies received by individual institutional sectors appear in tables 3.21, 3.31 and 3.41.

7. Withdrawals from quasi-corporations

Withdrawals from the entrepreneurial income of quasi-corporations consist of the actual payments made to the proprietors of quasi-corporations from the entrepreneurial income of these units. Entrepreneurial income of quasi-corporations is equal to their income from production (net operating surplus) plus their net income (receipts less payments) from property. In some cases, the whole of the entrepreneurial income will be treated as if paid out to the proprietors; in other cases, some of it is retained as net saving within the quasi-corporation. Withdrawals from quasi-corporations also include withdrawals from foreign branches of domestic companies or from domestic branches of foreign companies, since both of these categories are treated as quasi-corporations. The withdrawals may be negative, since proprietors may provide funds to the enterprises to compensate for losses. SNA assigns separate flow numbers to withdrawals as they appear in the paying sectors (flow 4.4) and in the receiving sectors (flow 4.5). As disbursements they appear in table 3.22 and as part of a larger total in table 1.5. As receipts, they appear in tables 3.12, 3.22, 3.32 and 3.42, and as parts of the larger total in tables 1.4. 1.5 and 1.6.

8. Property income

Property income consists of payments of interest, dividends and land rents and royalties, all of which are assigned separate SNA flow numbers, both as payments and as receipts. Interest is defined as income payable and receivable on financial claims, such as bank and other deposits, bills and bonds, including public debt, and the equity of households in life insurance actuarial reserves and pension funds. Dividends consist of income payable and receivable on corporate equity securities and other forms of participation in the equity of private incorporated enterprises, public corporations and cooperatives. Rent payments include, in addition to net land rent, royalty payments for concessions to exploit mineral deposits or for the use of patents, copyrights, trademarks and the like. They exclude rent payments on machinery and equipment or buildings, which are treated as the purchase of a service rather than property income and appear in gross output of the seller and intermediate consumption of the purchaser. Payments of land rent are always treated as a domestic flow since foreign owners are, for national accounting purposes, dealt with as residents of the country in which the land is located. When it is not possible to separate rent of buildings and rent of the land on which the buildings stand, the whole flow is attributed to the buildings, that is, excluded from property income and included in intermediate consumption.

Property income paid and received by individual institutional sectors is shown in tables 3.12, 3.22, 3.32 and 3.42. As part of a larger total it appears in the summary tables 1.4, 1.5 and 1.6.

IV. Taxes and unrequited transfers

The categories of taxes and unrequited transfers are classified and defined in SNA classification 7.1. SNA does not provide the full articulation of the to-whom from- whom relationships of these flows, but assigns flow numbers to the various combinations of them used in specific standard tables and accounts. In order to define less ambiguously the flows used in the present publication, a somewhat fuller listing of individual flow components is used.

1. Casualty insurance transactions

Casualty insurance transactions refer to health, accident, fire, theft, unemployment and similar insurance schemes. The total of net premiums for the economy as a whole is equal to the total premiums payable less an imputed service charge which in turn is defined to be equal to the difference between premiums and claims. As a consequence, for the economy as a whole, net premiums and claims are equal. However, the total service charge is distributed to sectors of receipt and disbursement in proportion to the total (not net) premiums paid, so that net premiums and claims are not necessarily equal for each sector. In the former SNA, these insurance transactions were considered to be in part capital items, and this practice continues in the accounts of a number of countries. In the revised SNA, however, all casualty insurance transactions, including compensation for capital losses, are considered to be current flows. They are shown in detail in tables 3.12, 3.22, 3.32 and 3.42.

2. Taxes and other government receipts

Taxes and other government receipts include direct taxes, compulsory fees, fines and penalties, social security contributions, and other current transfers received by general government.

Direct taxes include two components. Direct taxes on income cover levies by public authorities at regular intervals (except social security contributions) on income from employment, property, capital gains or any other source. Real estate and land taxes are included only if they are merely administrative procedures for the assessment and collection of income tax. Other direct taxes cover levies by public authorities at regular intervals on the financial assets and the net of total worth of enterprises, private non-profit institutions and households, and on the possession or use of goods by households. Direct taxes received are shown in tables 1.4 and 3.2; payments of other sectors are shown in tables 3.22, 3.32 and 3.42.

Compulsory fees are payments to public authorities by households for services that are obligatory and unavoidable in the only circumstances in which they are useful. Examples of such fees are payments by households for driving tests and licenses, airport and court fees and the like. Similar payments by business units are treated as indirect taxes. Fines and penalties, however, include not only those paid by households but also those paid by corporate and quasi-corporate enterprises and private non-profit institutions serving households. They appear in the same tables as direct taxes.

Social security contributions consist of contributions for the account of employees, whether made by employees or by employers on their behalf, to the social security arrangements that are imposed, controlled or financed by the government for the purpose of providing social security benefits for the community or large sections of the community. They appear as receipts in tables 1.4 and 3.12. and as payments in tables 1.6 and 3.32.

Current transfers n.e.c. received by general government consist primarily of transfers received from the rest of the world and imputed employee welfare contributions. Transfers from the rest of the world include grants between governments to finance military outlays, outlays for health and educational purposes, and similar transfers in kind of military equipment, food, clothing etc. Payments and assessments and other periodic contributions to international organizations are also included. In addition to actual transfers, this item also includes imputed transfers arising from the obligation of the government as an employer to pay directly to its employees pensions, family allowances, severance and lay-off pay and other welfare benefits when there is no special fund, reserve or insurance for these purposes. In these circumstances, SNA provides for the establishment of an imputed fund to which imputed contributions are made, of a magnitude sufficient to support the unfounded benefit payments. The imputed contributions are included in compensation of employees, as an addition to actual payments, and are then shown as an imputed payment by the employees back to the government as an employer. These transfers appear in table 1.4 as an aggregate, and in table 3.12 in more detail.

3. Household transfer receipts

Household transfer receipts include social security benefits, social assistance grants, and unfounded employee welfare benefits. These flows, in varying detail, are shown in tables 1.6, 2.4 and 3.32.

Social security benefits are payments to individuals under the social security arrangements described above. The payments are often made out of a special fund and may be related to the income of individuals from employment or to contributions to social security arrangements made on their behalf. Examples are unemployment insurance benefits, old age, disability and survivors pensions, family allowances and reimbursements for medical and hospital expenses. It may be difficult to distinguish social security benefits from social assistance grants, on the one hand, and insurance benefits, on the other. The main criterion is method of finance; the actual content will vary from country to country. Medical services, for instance, may be supplied as social assistance, as a part of social security, as a casualty insurance benefit, or as a free government service.

Social assistance grants are cash grants to individuals and households, except social security benefits and unfounded employee welfare benefits. They may be made by public authorities, private non-profit institutions, or corporate and quasi-corporate enterprises. Examples are relief payments; widows, guardians and family allowances and payments of medical and dental expenses which are not part of social insurance schemes; war bonuses, pensions and service grants; and scholarships, fellowships and maintenance allowances for educational, training and similar purposes. They include payments made by public authorities for services provided by business enterprises and private non-profit institutions directly and individually to persons, whether these payments are made to the individuals or directly to the providers of the services that the persons are considered to have purchased. They exclude, however, transfers to persons or households as indemnities for property losses during floods, wars and similar calamities; these are considered to be capital items.

Unfunded employee welfare benefits are pensions, family allowances, severance and lay-off pay, maternity leave pay, workmen's and disability compensation and reimbursements for medical expenses and other casualties which employers pay directly to their former or present employees when there is no special fund, reserve or insurance for these purposes.

4. Transfers received by private non-profit institutions

Transfers received by private non-profit institutions serving households include grants and gifts, in cash and in kind, to non-profit institutions serving households which are intended to cover partially the cost of the provision of services by these institutions. They also include membership dues paid to political organizations, fraternal bodies and the like. They appear as a receipt in table 3.42, and as payments sometimes as part of a larger total, in tables 3.12, 3.22 and 3.32.

5. Other current transfers n.e.c.

Other current transfers n.e.c. include transfers to and from resident sectors that are not specifically included in any other flows. They may include migrants remittances, transfers of immigrants personal and household goods, and transfers between resident and non-resident households, in cash and in kind. They include allowances for bad debts.

V. Finance of gross accumulation

1. Net saving

Net saving is the balancing item in the SNA income and outlay account. It is defined as the difference between current receipts and current disbursements. Net saving for the nation as a whole appears in tables 1.8 and 1.12. Net saving for individual institutional sectors appears in tables 3.12, 3.13, 3.22, 3.23, 3.32, 3.33, 3.42 and 3.43.

2. Surplus of the nation on current transactions

The surplus of the nation on current transactions is the balancing item in the external transactions current accounts (tables 1.7 and 3.51). It also appears in table 1.8, the capital transactions account, in table 1.12, the table showing relationships among the national accounting aggregates, and table 3.52, the external transactions capital accumulation account.

3. Purchases of land, net

Purchases of land, net, include purchases less sales of land, subsoil deposits, forests and inland waters, including any improvements that are an integral part of these assets except buildings and other structures. The purchases and sales are valued at the transaction (sales) price of the land, forests etc., not including the transfer costs involved; such transfer costs are included in gross capital formation. Purchases and sales are assumed to take place when the legal title to the land is passed. They are considered to take place between resident institutions only. Where the land is purchased by a non-resident, a nominal resident institution is considered to be the owner of the land. The foreign owner is assigned equity in the resident institution equivalent to the purchase price of the land. The value recorded in the flow is the same for both the buyer and the seller. For the country as a whole, therefore, purchases and sales will cancel out. If the sales value of the structures situated on the land cannot be separated from the sales value of the land itself, the entire transaction should he recorded as a purchase and sale of structures (i.e., of second-hand assets), unless the structures are intended for immediate demolition. Purchases of land appear in the capital accumulation accounts of the individual institutional sectors, (tables 3.13, 3.23, 3.33 and 3.43)

4. Purchases of intangible assets, net

Purchases of intangible assets, net, are defined as purchases, less sales, of exclusive rights to mineral, fishing and other concessions and of patents, copyrights etc. These transactions involve the once-and-for-all relinquishment and acquisition of the exclusive rights, although they may be paid for over a period of years; they do not include concessions, leases, licenses to use patents and permission to publish copyrighted materials which involve the periodic payment of royalties or rents, with eventual reversion of the rights to the seller. The purchases and sales are valued at the transaction (sales) value of the mineral concession, lease, patent, etc., not including any transfer costs involved. (The transfer costs are included in gross capital formation.) Purchases of intangible assets appear in the individual institutional sector capital accumulation accounts (tables 3.13, 3.23, 3.33 and 3.43) as a part of gross accumulation. Purchases from the rest of the world appear in table 3.52.

5. Capital transfers

Capital transfers are defined as unrequited transfers, in cash or in kind, which are used for purposes of capital formation or other forms of capital accumulation, are made out of wealth, or are non-recurrent. Examples of capital transfers are grants from one government to another to finance deficits in external trade, investment grants, unilateral transfers of capital goods, legacies, death duties and inheritance taxes, migrants transfers of financial assets and indemnities in respect of calamities. Mixed transfers, considered by one party to the transaction as capital and the other as current, are treated as capital. Capital transfers appear in tables 3.13, 3.23, 3.33, 3.43 and 3.52.

6. Net lending

Net lending is defined as the excess of the sources of finance of accumulation (i.e., net saving, consumption of fixed capital and capital transfers received) over the uses of these funds for gross capital formation, net purchases of land and intangibles, and capital transfers paid. It appears in the capital accumulation accounts of the individual institutional sectors (tables 3.13, 3.23, 3.33 and 3.43), and in the external transactions capital accumulation account (table 3.52). Net lending is also equal to the difference between a sectors net acquisition of financial liabilities; it thus also appears in the institutional sector capital finance accounts (tables 3.14, 3.24, 3.34, 3.44 and 3.53). Although not for all countries, net lending derived in these two different ways are statistically identical.

VI. Financial assets and liabilities

Net acquisition of financial assets is defined as the difference between, on the one hand, acquisitions or purchases and, on the other, relinquishment or sales by given transactors of financial claims of second parties. Net incurrence of liabilities is equal to the issue or sale less redemption or payment or financial claims of second parties. A classification and definitions of financial assets and liabilities is given in SNA classifications 7.2.

Changes in financial assets and liabilities for individual institutional sectors appear in the capital finance accounts (tables 3.14, 3.24, 3.34, 3.44, and 3.53). Their total amount is shown in the sector balance sheets (tables 3.15, 3.25, 3.35 and 3.45).

VII. Other assets

1. Reproducible tangible assets

Reproducible tangible assets are classified and defined in table 5.1 of the Provisional Guidelines of National and Sector Balance Sheets and Reconciliation Accounts of the System of National Accounts 4/. They appear, classified by type of asset and broad sector, in tables 2.13 and 2.14, by kind of activity in tables 2.15 and 2.16 and for individual institutional sectors, in the sector balance sheets in tables 3.15, 3.25, 3.35 and 3.45.

2. Non-reproducible tangible assets

Non-reproducible tangible assets are classified and defined in table 5.2 of the Provisional Guidelines (see above). Only the total appears in the tables, in the sector balance sheets (tables 3.15, 3.25 and 3.45).

3. Non-financial intangible assets

Non-financial intangible assets include the mineral, fishing and other concessions, leases, patents, copyrights etc., the purchase and sale of which is recorded in the capital accumulation account. These intangible assets are created at the time of the purchase or sale, that is, when a once-and-for-all lump sum payment has been made for the lease, concession, patent or copyright. They appear in the sector balance sheets (tables 3.15, 3.25, 3.35 and 3.45).

1/ Official records of the Economic and Social Council. Forty-fourth session. Supplement No. 10, (E/4471), paras. 8-24.
2/ The system is published in A System of National Accounts, Studies in Methods, Series F, No. 2, Rev. 3 (United Nations publications, Sales No. E.69.XVII.3).
3/ System of National Accounts 1993 (United Nations publication, Sales No. E.94.XVII.4).
4/ Statistical Papers, Series M, No. 60 United Nations publication, Sales No. 77.XVII.10.
5/ Statistical Papers, Series M, No. 4, Rev. 2, Add. I (United Nations publication, Sales No. E.71.XVII.8).
6/ Statistical Papers, Series M, No. 70 (United Nations publication, Sales No. 80.XVII.17).

II. COUNTRY TABLES

Albania

Source

Reply to the United Nations National Accounts Questionnaire from the Statistical Directory of the Ministry of Economy, Tirana.

General note

The estimates shown in the following tables have been prepared in accordance with the United Nations System of National Accounts so far as the existing data would permit.

1.1 Expenditure on the gross domestic product, in current prices

Million leks

	1986	1987	1988	1989	1990	1991	1992	1993	1994	1995	1996	1997
1 Government final consumption expenditure	1612	1663	1608	1645	1715	...	...	...	...	...	...	...
2 Private final consumption expenditure	10345	10785	10764	11392	12227	...	...	...	...	...	...	...
3 Gross capital formation	5456	4817	4971	5926	4108	...	...	...	...	...	...	...
A Increase in stocks	–	–685	–447	72	–1702	...	...	...	...	...	...	...
B Gross fixed capital formation	5456	5502	5418	5854	5810	...	...	...	...	...	...	...
4 Exports of goods and services	–30	–19	–342	–289	–1239	...	...	...	...	...	...	...
5 less: Imports of goods and services						...	...	...	...	...	...	...
equals: Gross domestic product	17383[a]	17246[a]	17001[a]	18674[a]	16812[a] 16813	16404	50697	125334	184393	229793	280998	...

a For the years 1986-1990, prices have been unchanged, therefore the estimates in the current prices table are equal to those shown in the constant price table.

1.2 Expenditure on the gross domestic product, in constant prices

Million leks

	1986	1987	1988	1989	1990	1991	1992	1993	1994	1995	1996	1997
	At constant prices of: 1986 / 1990											
1 Government final consumption expenditure	1612	1663	1608	1645	1715	...	...	...	...	...	...	...
2 Private final consumption expenditure	10345	10785	10764	11392	12227	...	...	...	...	...	...	...
3 Gross capital formation	5456	4817	4971	5926	4108	...	...	...	...	...	...	...
A Increase in stocks	–	–685	–447	72	–1702	...	...	...	...	...	...	...
B Gross fixed capital formation	5456	5502	5418	5854	5810	...	...	...	...	...	...	...
4 Exports of goods and services	–30	–19	–342	–289	–1239	...	...	...	...	...	...	...
5 less: Imports of goods and services						...	...	...	...	...	...	...
equals: Gross domestic product	17383[a]	17246[a]	17001[a]	18674[a]	16812[a] 16813	12105	11235	12309	13331	15107	16482	...

a For the years 1986-1990, prices have been unchanged, therefore the estimates in the current prices table are equal to those shown in the constant price table.

Albania

1.3 Cost components of the gross domestic product

Million leks

	1986	1987	1988	1989	1990	1991	1992	1993	1994	1995	1996	1997
1 Indirect taxes, net	...	...	...	...	...	...	...	...	...	...	...	...
2 Consumption of fixed capital	2100	2146	2089	2198	2238	...	...	...	...	...	...	...
3 Compensation of employees paid by resident producers to ..	8894	9091	9058	9684	10399	...	...	...	...	...	...	...
4 Operating surplus	6389	6009	5854	6792	4175	...	...	...	...	...	...	...
equals: Gross domestic product ..	17383	17246	17001	18674	16812	...	...	...	...	...	...	...

1.10 Gross domestic product by kind of activity, in current prices

Million leks

	1986	1987	1988	1989	1990	1991	1992	1993	1994	1995	1996	1997
1 Agriculture, hunting, forestry and fishing	...	...	...	...	6762	6967	27491	68484	100755	125435	148318	...
2 Mining and quarrying	...	...	...	...	6252	5260	8548	17362	23112	26943	35137	...
3 Manufacturing	...	...	...	...	...	...	...	...	...	...	...	...
4 Electricity, gas and water	...	...	...	...	...	...	...	...	...	...	...	...
5 Construction	...	...	...	...	1114	1085	3867	11344	17721	23621	32107	...
6 Wholesale and retail trade, restaurants and hotels [a]	...	...	...	...	2135	2554	9271	24268	36592	45677	56210	...
7 Transport, storage and communication	...	...	...	...	550	537	1520	3876	6213	8118	9226	...
8 Finance, insurance, real estate and business services	...	...	...	...	...	...	...	...	...	...	...	...
9 Community, social and personal services	...	...	...	...	...	...	...	...	...	...	...	...
Total, Industries	...	...	...	...	...	...	...	...	...	...	...	...
Producers of government services	...	...	...	...	...	...	...	...	...	...	...	...
Other producers	...	...	...	...	...	...	...	...	...	...	...	...
Subtotal	...	...	...	...	...	...	...	...	...	...	...	...
less: Imputed bank service charge	...	...	...	...	...	...	...	...	...	...	...	...
plus: Import duties	...	...	...	...	...	...	...	...	...	...	...	...
plus: Value added tax	...	...	...	...	...	...	...	...	...	...	...	...
plus: Other adjustments	...	...	...	...	...	...	...	...	...	...	...	...
equals: Gross domestic product ..	17383	17246	17001	18674	16812 16813	16404	50697	125334	184393	229793	280998	...

[a] Includes items "Finance, insurance, real estate and business services", "Community, social and personal services", "Producers of Government Services and "Other Services".

Albania

1.11 Gross domestic product by kind of activity, in constant prices

Million leks

	1986	1987	1988	1989	1990	1991	1992	1993	1994	1995	1996	1997
	At constant prices of: 1986 / 1990											
1 Agriculture, hunting, forestry and fishing	...	...	...	...	6762	5141	6092	6726	7284	8246	8494	...
2 Mining and quarrying	...	...	...	...	6252	3882	1894	1705	1671	1771	2013	...
3 Manufacturing	...	...	...	...	...	...	...	...	...	...	...	...
4 Electricity, gas and water	...	...	...	...	...	...	...	...	...	...	...	...
5 Construction	...	...	...	...	1114	801	857	1114	1281	1553	1840	...
6 Wholesale and retail trade, restaurants and hotels [a]	...	...	...	...	2135	1885	2055	2383	2646	3003	3608	...
7 Transport, storage and communication	...	...	...	...	550	396	337	381	449	534	529	...
8 Finance, insurance, real estate and business services	...	...	...	...	...	...	...	...	...	...	...	...
9 Community, social and personal services	...	...	...	...	...	...	...	...	...	...	...	...
Total, Industries	...	...	...	...	...	...	...	...	...	...	...	...
Producers of government services	...	...	...	...	...	...	...	...	...	...	...	...
Other producers	...	...	...	...	...	...	...	...	...	...	...	...
Subtotal	...	...	...	...	...	...	...	...	...	...	...	...
less: Imputed bank service charge	...	...	...	...	...	...	...	...	...	...	...	...
plus: Import duties	...	...	...	...	...	...	...	...	...	...	...	...
plus: Value added tax	...	...	...	...	...	...	...	...	...	...	...	...
plus: Other adjustments	...	...	...	...	...	...	...	...	...	...	...	...
equals: Gross domestic product	17383	17246	17001	18674	16812 / 16813	12105	11235	12309	13331	15107	16482	...

[a] Includes items "Finance, insurance, real estate and business services", "Community, social and personal services", "Producers of Government Services and "Other Services".

Algeria

Source

Official estimates are published in *Comptes Economiques* by the Direction des Statistiques et de la Comptabilité Nationale, Secrétariat d'Etat au Plan, Alger.

General note

The estimates shown in the following tables have been prepared in accordance with the United Nations System of National Accounts so far as the existing data would permit.

1.1 Expenditure on the gross domestic product, in current prices

Million Algerian dinars

	1986	1987	1988	1989	1990	1991	1992	1993	1994	1995	1996	1997
1 Government final consumption expenditure	52891	57996	65139	70615	89890	128236	184543	221019	263752	...	...	...
2 Private final consumption expenditure	156414	154882	214094	262877	312320	413551	540727	646117	835293	...	...	...
3 Gross capital formation	99333	93880	98040	127798	162198	265346	322172	339643	467205	...	...	...
A Increase in stocks	−2000	1000	6297	12970	18854	50955	41837	15508	59660	...	...	...
B Gross fixed capital formation	101333	92880	91743	114828	143344	214391	280335	324135	407545	...	...	...
4 Exports of goods and services	38714	45834	49898	77792	129220	246533	266290	251846	341900	...	...	...
5 less: Imports of goods and services	50801	39886	79453	121066	139110	198354	241235	269126	424503	...	...	...
equals: Gross domestic product [a]	296551	312706	347717	418016	554518	855311	1072496	1189499	1483646	...	...	...

a All data revised according to "Statistical Yearbooks of Algeria" published by the National Board of Statistics, Algeria.

1.3 Cost components of the gross domestic product

Million Algerian dinars

	1986	1987	1988	1989	1990	1991	1992	1993	1994	1995	1996	1997
1 Indirect taxes, net	55561	62009	67808	76488	106177	154630	189319	199686	273343	...	...	...
2 Consumption of fixed capital	31660	32525	33215	33215	40280	57019	59886	102068	124336	...	...	...
3 Compensation of employees paid by resident producers to ..	120091	125754	137504	154162	179338	263536	339764	407558	465339	...	...	...
A Resident households	120091	125754	137648	156145	...	...	...	...	...	...	...	...
B Rest of the world	...	...	...	...	...	...	...	...	...	...	...	...
4 Operating surplus	89240	92418	109848	154151	228723	380126	483527	480187	620628	...	...	...
equals: Gross domestic product [a]	296551	312706	347717	418016	554518	855311	1072496	1189499	1483646	...	...	...

a All data revised according to "Statistical Yearbooks of Algeria" published by the National Board of Statistics, Algeria.

1.7 External transactions on current account, summary

Million Algerian dinars

	1986	1987	1988	1989	1990	1991	1992	1993	1994	1995	1996	1997
Payments to the rest of the world												
1 Imports of goods and services	50833	39962	79453	121066	139110	198354	241235	269126	424503	...	...	...
A Imports of merchandise, c.i.f.	43393	34153	66427	107427	123294	171644	208694	239571	385447	...	...	...

Algeria

Million Algerian dinars	1986	1987	1988	1989	1990	1991	1992	1993	1994	1995	1996	1997
B Other	7440	5809	4789	20972	15816	26710	32541	29554	39056	...	...	...
2 Factor income to rest of the world	7583	7953	12360	14274	19466	42528	49734	44205	62535	...	...	...
A Compensation of employees	...	...	...	...	...	...	...	...	...	...	...	...
B Property and entrepreneurial income	7583	7953	12360	14274	19466	42528	49734	44205	62535	...	...	...
3 Current transfers to the rest of the world	719	539	513	500	619	996	3077	4228	4376	...	...	...
4 Surplus of the nation on current transactions	−15271	963	−10367	−7913	18940	53571	30818	−1058	−40223	...	...	...
Payments to the rest of the world and surplus of the nation on current transfers [a]	43862	49416	81959	127926	178135	295449	324864	316500	451191	...	...	...
Receipts from the rest of the world												
1 Exports of goods and services	38714	49898	49898	77792	129220	246533	266290	251846	341900	...	...	...
A Exports of merchandise, f.o.b.	35391	41986	45421	71937	122279	233589	249145	236966	321095	...	...	...
B Other	3323	3848	3698	5855	6941	12944	17145	14880	20805	...	...	...
2 Factor income from rest of the world	1012	685	615	1096	916	1809	2908	3944	5026	...	...	...
A Compensation of employees	...	...	...	...	...	...	...	...	...	...	...	...
B Property and entrepreneurial income	1012	685	615	1096	916	1809	2908	3944	5026	...	...	...
3 Current transfers from rest of the world	4137	2897	31447	49038	48000	47108	55666	60711	104265	...	...	...
Receipts from the rest of the world on current transactions [a]	43862	49416	81959	127926	178135	295449	324864	316500	451191	...	...	...

[a] All data revised according to "Statistical Yearbooks of Algeria" published by the National Board of Statistics, Algeria.

1.10 Gross domestic product by kind of activity, in current prices

Million Algerian dinars	1986	1987	1988	1989	1990	1991	1992	1993	1994	1995	1996	1997
1 Agriculture, hunting, forestry and fishing	26278	31787	38785	51633	62725	87307	128416	131102	145615	...	...	...
2 Mining and quarrying	45154	51020	57209	80066	149296	269325	294740	294397	383588	...	...	...
3 Manufacturing	39541	38423	42793	40845	42929	60211	76047	81044	103801	...	...	...
4 Electricity, gas and water	3161	3449	3464	3886	4514	6506	10812	11212	13673	...	...	...
5 Construction	44316	42600	41708	50153	57185	78528	102149	121496	151781	...	...	...
6 Wholesale and retail trade, restaurants and hotels	43965	42903	49707	61877	71500	110355	138023	179927	237722	...	...	...
7 Transport, storage and communication	16245	16466	18357	21688	27484	41890	57480	65439	70460	...	...	...
8 Finance, insurance, real estate and business services	2702	2857	3898	4262	7926	10725	16704	19904	25833	...	...	...
9 Community, social and personal services	4851	5300	6419	7774	9007	11201	14960	17555	22179	...	...	...
Total, Industries	226212	234805	262339	322184	432568	676047	839332	922078	1154652	...	...	...
Producers of government services	...	...	...	...	...	...	...	...	...	...	...	...
Other producers	...	...	...	...	...	...	...	...	...	...	...	...
Subtotal	226212	234805	262339	322184	432568	676047	839332	922078	1154652	...	...	...
less: Imputed bank service charge	...	...	...	...	...	...	...	...	...	...	...	...

Algeria

Million Algerian dinars

	1986	1987	1988	1989	1990	1991	1992	1993	1994	1995	1996	1997
plus: Import duties	5081	7036	8500	12200	19000	42000	36300	35500	48700	...	...	...
plus: Value added tax	...	...	...	...	...	...	...	...	...	...	...	...
plus: Other adjustments	...	...	...	...	...	...	...	...	...	...	...	...
equals: Gross domestic product [a]	296551	312706	347717	418016	554518	855311	1072496	1189499	1483646	...	...	...

a All data revised according to "Statistical Yearbooks of Algeria" published by the National Board of Statistics, Algeria.

1.12 Relations among national accounting aggregates

Million Algerian dinars

	1986	1987	1988	1989	1990	1991	1992	1993	1994	1995	1996	1997
Gross domestic product [a]	296552	312706	347717	418016	554518	855311	1072496	1189499	1483646	...	...	...
plus: Net factor income from the rest of the world	−6571	−7268	−11745	−13178	...	...	...	...	...	...	...	...
Factor income from rest of the world	1012	685	615	1096	...	...	...	...	...	...	...	...
less: Factor income to the rest of the world	7583	7953	12360	14274	...	...	...	...	...	...	...	...
equals: Gross national product	292700	316100	337700	408700	537100	803600	1000900	1120600	1414500	1874000	...	...
less: Consumption of fixed capital	31660	32525	33215	32558	40280	57019	59886	102068	124336	...	...	...
equals: National income	261040	283575	304485	376142	496820	746581	941014	1018532	1290164	...	...	...
plus: Net current transfers from the rest of the world	3418	2358	2068	3850	...	...	...	...	...	...	...	...
Current transfers from rest of the world	4137	2897	2581	333492	402211	541786	725269	867136	1099045	...	...	...
less: Current transfers to the rest of the world	719	539	513	500	619	996	3077	4228	4376	...	...	...
equals: National disposable income	261707	275195	334348	420161	543068	803686	1018373	1103653	1401690	...	...	...
less: Final consumption	209305	212878	279233	333502	...	...	...	...	...	...	...	...
equals: Net saving	52401	62317	51716	86669	140857	261899	293104	236517	302645	...	...	...
less: Surplus of the nation on current transactions	−15271	963	−10367	−7913	...	...	...	...	...	...	...	...
equals: Net capital formation	67674	61355	64825	95240	121918	208328	262286	237575	342868	...	...	...

a Gross National Income data received by facsimile dated 18 October 1996 from the Permanent Mission of Algeria to the United Nations.

Angola

Source

Reply to the United Nations National Accounts Questionnaire from the Instituto Nacional de Estatística. The official estimates are published in *Contas Nacionais de Angola* by the Secretaria de Estado do Planeamento, Departamento de Contas Nacionais. Detailed description of the sources and methods used for the national accounts estimates is found in *Metodologia de Contas Nacionais de Republica Popular de Angola* published in 1989 by the Ministerio do Plano.

General note

The estimates shown in the following tables have been prepared in accordance with the United Nations System of National Accounts so far as the existing data would permit.

1.1 Expenditure on the gross domestic product, in current prices

Million Angolan kwanza

	1986	1987	1988	1989	1990	1991	1992	1993	1994	1995	1996	1997
1 Government final consumption expenditure	68980	73169	78949	80605	87814	...	...	...	...	...	...	...
2 Private final consumption expenditure	94195	93203	108946	134383	137768	...	...	...	...	...	...	...
3 Gross capital formation	34972	40815	34810	33898	35958	...	...	...	...	...	...	...
A Increase in stocks	1252	2509	−58	2547	1792	...	...	...	...	...	...	...
B Gross fixed capital formation	33720	38306	34868	31351	34166	...	...	...	...	...	...	...
Residential buildings	14573	17376	16086	15667	15886	...	...	...	...	...	...	...
Non-residential buildings						...	...	...	...	...	...	...
Other construction and land improvement, etc.						...	...	...	...	...	...	...
Other	19147	20930	18782	15684	18280	...	...	...	...	...	...	...
4 Exports of goods and services	44324	72783	78674	94308	119851	...	...	...	...	...	...	...
5 less: Imports of goods and services	49710	58002	61739	64328	73329	...	...	...	...	...	...	...
equals: Gross domestic product	192761	221968	239640	278866	308062	...	...	...	...	...	...	...

1.2 Expenditure on the gross domestic product, in constant prices

Million Angolan kwanza

	1986	1987	1988	1989	1990	1991	1992	1993	1994	1995	1996	1997
At constant prices of: 1987												
1 Government final consumption expenditure	70173	73169	77325	72879	73362	...	...	...	...	...	...	...
2 Private final consumption expenditure	96086	93202	92971	101449	98615	...	...	...	...	...	...	...
3 Gross capital formation	35565	40815	30775	28589	30798	...	...	...	...	...	...	...
A Increase in stocks	1003	2509	−510	2708	2888	...	...	...	...	...	...	...
B Gross fixed capital formation	34562	38306	31285	25881	27910	...	...	...	...	...	...	...
Residential buildings	14774	17376	13908	12750	12807	...	...	...	...	...	...	...
Non-residential buildings						...	...	...	...	...	...	...
Other construction and land improvement, etc.						...	...	...	...	...	...	...

Angola

Million Angolan kwanza

	1986	1987	1988	1989	1990	1991	1992	1993	1994	1995	1996	1997
At constant prices of: 1987												
Other	19788	20930	17377	13131	15103	...	...	...	...	...	...	...
4 Exports of goods and services	57125	72783	92116	90505	94064	...	...	...	...	...	...	...
5 less: Imports of goods and services	51502	58002	58849	58176	62639	...	...	...	...	...	...	...
equals: Gross domestic product	207446	221968	234338	235246	234200	...	...	...	...	...	...	...

1.3 Cost components of the gross domestic product

Million Angolan kwanza

	1986	1987	1988	1989	1990	1991	1992	1993	1994	1995	1996	1997
1 Indirect taxes, net	11010	12324	14244	18182	22741	...	...	...	...	...	...	...
A Indirect taxes	15873	17018	17561	19861	23486	...	...	...	...	...	...	...
B less: Subsidies	4863	4694	3317	1679	745	...	...	...	...	...	...	...
2 Consumption of fixed capital	...	...	...	...	...	...	...	...	...	...	...	...
3 Compensation of employees paid by resident producers to	91542	96521	103428	108592	119913	...	...	...	...	...	...	...
4 Operating surplus	90209	113123	121968	152092	165408	...	...	...	...	...	...	...
equals: Gross domestic product	192761	221968	239640	278866	308062	...	...	...	...	...	...	...

1.7 External transactions on current account, summary

Million Angolan kwanza

	1986	1987	1988	1989	1990	1991	1992	1993	1994	1995	1996	1997
Payments to the rest of the world												
1 Imports of goods and services	49710	58002	61739	64328	73329	...	...	...	...	...	...	...
A Imports of merchandise, c.i.f.	40010	47594	48182	47417	54615	...	...	...	...	...	...	...
B Other	9700	10408	13557	16911	18714	...	...	...	...	...	...	...
2 Factor income to rest of the world	9670	9005	27088	29874	38707	...	...	...	...	...	...	...
A Compensation of employees	2124	2064	1885	1047	300	...	...	...	...	...	...	...
B Property and entrepreneurial income	7546	6941	25203	28827	38407	...	...	...	...	...	...	...
3 Current transfers to the rest of the world	1539	240	5799	5564	14768	...	...	...	...	...	...	...
4 Surplus of the nation on current transactions	−11479	7541	−14247	−3783	−4561	...	...	...	...	...	...	...
Payments to the rest of the world and surplus of the nation on current transfers	49440	74788	80379	95983	122243	...	...	...	...	...	...	...
Receipts from the rest of the world												
1 Exports of goods and services	44324	72783	78674	94308	119851	...	...	...	...	...	...	...
A Exports of merchandise, f.o.b.	39312	67365	73256	89039	114432	...	...	...	...	...	...	...
B Other	5012	5418	5418	5269	5419	...	...	...	...	...	...	...
2 Factor income from rest of the world	359	209	419	568	430	...	...	...	...	...	...	...
A Compensation of employees	−	−	−	−	−	...	...	...	...	...	...	...
B Property and entrepreneurial income	359	209	419	568	430	...	...	...	...	...	...	...
3 Current transfers from rest of the world	4757	1795	1286	1107	1962	...	...	...	...	...	...	...
Receipts from the rest of the world on current transactions	49440	74788	80379	95983	122243	...	...	...	...	...	...	...

Angola

1.10 Gross domestic product by kind of activity, in current prices

Million Angolan kwanza	1986	1987	1988	1989	1990	1991	1992	1993	1994	1995	1996	1997
1 Agriculture, hunting, forestry and fishing	27362	28402	37981	53187	55067	...	...	...	...	...	...	...
2 Mining and quarrying	34394	63067	64137	81866	100657	...	...	...	...	...	...	...
3 Manufacturing	20768	16152	19673	17065	15354	...	...	...	...	...	...	...
4 Electricity, gas and water	457	530	463	443	380	...	...	...	...	...	...	...
5 Construction	9239	11449	9695	8988	9003	...	...	...	...	...	...	...
6 Wholesale and retail trade, restaurants and hotels [a]	25405	25926	27648	31354	32827	...	...	...	...	...	...	...
7 Transport, storage and communication	9629	8768	8195	8389	9822	...	...	...	...	...	...	...
8 Finance, insurance, real estate and business services [b]	2533	619	1074	1543	214	...	...	...	...	...	...	...
9 Community, social and personal services [ab]	8049	9087	9880	10051	12526	...	...	...	...	...	...	...
Total, Industries	137836	164000	178746	212887	235849	...	...	...	...	...	...	...
Producers of government services	51023	53881	57936	63189	69982	...	...	...	...	...	...	...
Other producers						...	...	...	...	...	...	...
Subtotal	188860	217881	236682	276076	305831	...	...	...	...	...	...	...
less: Imputed bank service charge	793	–722	364	326	–478	...	...	...	...	...	...	...
plus: Import duties	4694	3365	3322	3116	1753	...	...	...	...	...	...	...
plus: Value added tax	...	...	...	...	...	...	...	...	...	...	...	...
plus: Other adjustments												
equals: Gross domestic product	192761	221968	239640	278866	308062	...	...	...	...	...	...	...

[a] Restaurants and hotels are included in item "Community, social and personal services".

[b] Item "Finance, insurance, real estate and business services" includes finance and insurance only. Real estate and business services are included in item "Community, social and personal services".

1.11 Gross domestic product by kind of activity, in constant prices

Million Angolan kwanza	1986	1987	1988	1989	1990	1991	1992	1993	1994	1995	1996	1997
At constant prices of: 1987												
1 Agriculture, hunting, forestry and fishing	27579	28402	27606	28648	28554	...	...	...	...	...	...	...
2 Mining and quarrying	44624	63067	75371	79186	81018	...	...	...	...	...	...	...
3 Manufacturing	21643	16152	17953	14740	12301	...	...	...	...	...	...	...
4 Electricity, gas and water	474	530	483	437	370	...	...	...	...	...	...	...
5 Construction	9549	11449	8567	7271	7169	...	...	...	...	...	...	...
6 Wholesale and retail trade, restaurants and hotels [a]	25975	25926	25298	27674	27335	...	...	...	...	...	...	...
7 Transport, storage and communication	10002	8768	8217	7537	8098	...	...	...	...	...	...	...
8 Finance, insurance, real estate and business services [b]	2614	619	1113	1396	165	...	...	...	...	...	...	...
9 Community, social and personal services [ab]	8421	9087	9506	8173	8896	...	...	...	...	...	...	...
Total, Industries	150881	164000	174114	175063	173906	...	...	...	...	...	...	...
Producers of government services	52534	53881	57436	56998	58214	...	...	...	...	...	...	...
Other producers						...	...	...	...	...	...	...
Subtotal	2 03415	217881	231550	232061	232120	...	...	...	...	...	...	...

Angola

Million Angolan kwanza

	1986	1987	1988	1989	1990	1991	1992	1993	1994	1995	1996	1997
	At constant prices of: 1987											
less: Imputed bank service charge	780	–722	372	–361	–572	...	...	...	...	...	...	...
plus: Import duties	4810	3365	3160	2823	1508	...	...	...	...	...	...	...
plus: Value added tax	...	...	...	...	...	...	...	...	...	...	...	...
plus: Other adjustments	...	...	...	...	...	...	...	...	...	...	...	...
equals: Gross domestic product	207445	221968	234338	235245	234200	...	...	...	...	...	...	...

a Restaurants and hotels are included in item "Community, social and personal services".

b Item "Finance, insurance, real estate and business services" includes finance and insurance only. Real estate and business services are included in item "Community, social and personal services".

1.12 Relations among national accounting aggregates

Million Angolan kwanza

	1986	1987	1988	1989	1990	1991	1992	1993	1994	1995	1996	1997
Gross domestic product	192761	221968	239640	278866	308062	...	...	...	...	...	...	...
plus: Net factor income from the rest of the world	–9311	–8796	–26669	–29306	–38277	...	...	...	...	...	...	...
Factor income from rest of the world	359	209	419	568	430	...	...	...	...	...	...	...
less: Factor income to the rest of the world	9670	9005	27088	29874	38707	...	...	...	...	...	...	...
equals: Gross national product	183450	213172	212971	249560	269785	...	...	...	...	...	...	...
less: Consumption of fixed capital	...	...	...	...	...	...	...	...	...	...	...	...
equals: National income	183450	213172	212971	249560	269785	...	...	...	...	...	...	...
plus: Net current transfers from the rest of the world	3218	1555	–4513	–4457	–12806	...	...	...	...	...	...	...
Current transfers from rest of the world	4757	1795	1286	1107	1962	...	...	...	...	...	...	...
less: Current transfers to the rest of the world	1539	240	5799	5564	14768	...	...	...	...	...	...	...
equals: National disposable income	186668	214728	208458	245103	256979	...	...	...	...	...	...	...
less: Final consumption	163175	166372	187895	214988	225582	...	...	...	...	...	...	...
equals: Net saving	23493	48356	20563	30115	31397	...	...	...	...	...	...	...
less: Surplus of the nation on current transactions	–11479	7541	–14247	–3783	–4561	...	...	...	...	...	...	...
equals: Net capital formation	34972	40815	34810	33898	35958	...	...	...	...	...	...	...

Anguilla

Source

The official estimates are published in *Anguilla—National Accounts Statistics – National Accounts Statistics, 1984-1987* by the Ministry of Finance and Economic Development on May 1988.

General note

The estimates shown in the following tables have been prepared in accordance with the United Nations System of National Accounts so far as the existing data would permit.

1.1 Expenditure on the gross domestic product, in current prices

Thousand East Caribbean dollars

	1986	1987	1988	1989	1990	1991	1992	1993	1994	1995	1996	1997
1 Government final consumption expenditure	9219	11984	14737	17648	19671	22971	24792	27526	31347	34638	38548	44683
2 Private final consumption expenditure	37350	50160	58061	68031	73400	79220	109108	117924	117873	157808	176232	165057
3 Gross capital formation	37277	50934	42929	57162	59999	52563	57756	48584	52981	58546	62239	60086
A Increase in stocks	–	–	–	–	–	–	–	–	–	–	–	–
B Gross fixed capital formation	37277	50934	42929	57162	59999	52563	57756	48584	52981	58546	62239	60086
4 Exports of goods and services	46600	51750	82530	101610	111170	117080	123210	147240	170380	153390	154120	172820
5 less: Imports of goods and services	52820	67190	91786	111975	117220	121000	150620	162140	172360	201920	217270	205100
Statistical discrepancy	–10826	–14988	...	...	...	–6	...	–6	–4	28	–4	–2
equals: Gross domestic product	66800	82650	106471	132476	147020	150828	164246	179128	200217	202490	213865	237544

1.4 General government current receipts and disbursements

Thousand East Caribbean dollars

	1986	1987	1988	1989	1990	1991	1992	1993	1994	1995	1996	1997
Receipts												
1 Operating surplus	...	...	...	...	...	...	...	...	...	...	...	...
2 Property and entrepreneurial income	1136	780	1778	1791	1171	604	2272	705	2938	1517	2373	4646
3 Taxes, fees and contributions	11276	14811	18346	24315	24710	28201	30526	33370	39762	44206	44980	51440
A Indirect taxes	9993	12846	15776	21169	21055	24060	26406	28738	33767	37620	38115	45494
B Direct taxes	64	109	132	44	84	127	64	108	129	339	291	267
C Social security contributions	1219	1856	2438	3102	3571	4014	4056	4524	5866	6247	6574	5679
D Compulsory fees, fines and penalties	...	...	...	...	...	...	...	...	...	...	...	...
4 Other current transfers	1872	1749	1521	1400	1988	2223	2942	3057	3430	3656	4035	3824
Total current receipts of general government	14284	17340	21645	27506	27869	31028	35740	37132	46129	49379	51388	59910
Disbursements												
1 Government final consumption expenditure	9219	11984	14737	17648	19671	22971	24792	27526	31347	34638	38548	44683
A Compensation of employees	8386	9886	13102	14895	16896	18429	19167	20274	21848	22394	26171	28085

Anguilla

Thousand East Caribbean dollars

	1986	1987	1988	1989	1990	1991	1992	1993	1994	1995	1996	1997
B Consumption of fixed capital	...	...	...	...	...	...	...	...	...	...	...	...
C Purchases of goods and services, net	3398	2098	1635	2753	2775	4542	5625	7252	9499	12244	12377	16598
D less: Own-account fixed capital formation	...	...	...	...	...	...	...	...	...	...	...	...
E Indirect taxes paid, net	...	...	...	...	...	...	...	...	...	...	...	...
2 Property income	–	61	135	397	290	322	349	411	477	587	738	511
3 Subsidies	15	...	...	...	...	...	...	...	...	...	...	...
4 Other current transfers	1334	1547	1829	2101	2444	2630	3234	3093	3815	4314	5200	6168
A Social security benefits	109	182	259	292	405	442	578	780	1022	1060	1261	1586
B Social assistance grants	...	...	...	...	...	...	...	...	...	...	...	...
C Other	1225	1365	1570	1809	2039	2188	2656	2313	2793	3254	3939	4582
5 Net saving	3716	3748	4944	7360	5464	5105	7365	6102	10490	9346	6902	8548
Total current disbursements and net saving of general government	14284	17340	21645	27506	27869	31028	35740	37132	46129	49379	51388	59910

1.10 Gross domestic product by kind of activity, in current prices

Thousand East Caribbean dollars

	1986	1987	1988	1989	1990	1991	1992	1993	1994	1995	1996	1997
1 Agriculture, hunting, forestry and fishing	2990	3130	4160	5440	6650	5130	6760	6040	7170	6430	7060	7370
2 Mining and quarrying	770	890	800	750	660	1160	1350	1170	1150	1320	1780	1960
3 Manufacturing	540	770	780	810	920	1070	1150	1120	1270	1330	1580	1640
4 Electricity, gas and water	1530	1250	2290	2030	2440	2520	3970	5580	5790	6470	5610	7170
5 Construction	11690	15840	14900	19840	24490	21680	24770	21450	21450	23170	26700	28610
6 Wholesale and retail trade, restaurants and hotels	19950	24450	35350	45680	48490	50110	51450	60880	71680	71230	14020	15050
7 Transport, storage and communication	8180	10760	13660	14410	15150	17220	18650	21390	24110	23280	25360	30920
8 Finance, insurance, real estate and business services	6430	8230	10800	15110	17980	19570	18830	21610	23830	23830	32300	30670
9 Community, social and personal services [a]	940	1290	1380	1930	2090	2290	2410	2560	2730	2840	...	...
Total, Industries	53020	66610	84120	106000	118870	120750	129340	141800	159180	159900	114410	123390
Producers of government services	8400	9900	13120	14910	16900	18270	19240	20380	22560	23040	24836	26250
Other producers	...	...	...	...	...	...	...	...	...	...	...	...
Subtotal [b]	61420	76510	97240	120910	135770	139020	148580	162180	181740	182940	235440	260420
less: Imputed bank service charge	3200	4280	6530	9580	10290	12440	11280	12490	16230	17810	21570	22880
plus: Import duties	...	...	...	...	...	...	...	...	...	...	...	...
plus: Value added tax	...	...	...	...	...	...	...	...	...	...	...	...
plus: Other adjustments [c]	9978	12831	15761	21146	21040	23728	26406	28818	33767	37620	...	...
equals: Gross domestic product	68198	85061	106471	132476	146520	150308	163706	178508	200220	202490	213870	237540

a Item "Other producers" is included in item "Community, social and personal services".
b Gross domestic product in factor values.
c Item "Other adjustments" refers to indirect taxes net of subsidies.

Anguilla

1.11 Gross domestic product by kind of activity, in constant prices

Thousand East Caribbean dollars

	1986	1987	1988	1989	1990	1991	1992	1993	1994	1995	1996	1997
	At constant prices of: 1984				1990							
1 Agriculture, hunting, forestry and fishing	2850	2910	5120	6010	6650	4850	6340	5780	6530	5800	5830	6170
2 Mining and quarrying	740	840	1110	970	660	960	1120	950	930	1070	1330	1460
3 Manufacturing	470	610	810	820	920	1030	1090	1140	1180	1260	1300	1340
4 Electricity, gas and water	820	690	1950	2250	2440	2510	2880	3870	4040	3670	3120	3910
5 Construction	8190	9500	15440	20580	24490	18170	21140	17980	17980	19060	21970	22850
6 Wholesale and retail trade, restaurants and hotels	16620	18080	47280	48530	47990	48260	50190	57780	66660	61960	58960	66920
7 Transport, storage and communication	7470	9400	13650	14110	15150	17950	19280	21710	22580	21860	22690	27890
8 Finance, insurance, real estate and business services	5580	6100	13690	15440	17980	18490	17620	19280	20800	20770	27710	26030
9 Community, social and personal services [a]	900	1210	1520	1970	2090	2190	2250	2310	2380	2440	...	...
Statistical discrepancy [a]	...	...	...	...	...	...	...	...	...	...	−36580	−38600
Total, Industries	43640	49340	100570	110680	118370	114410	121910	130800	143080	137890	106330	117970
Producers of government services	6650	7290	15760	16050	16900	17970	18160	19230	20430	20580	22540	23430
Other producers	...	...	...	...	...	...	...	...	...	...	...	...
Subtotal	50290	56630	116330	126730	135270	132380	140070	150030	163510	158470	128870	141400
less: Imputed bank service charge	2830	3680	8350	9570	10290	12050	10930	11510	14720	16150	19550	20740
plus: Import duties	...	...	...	...	...	...	...	...	...	...	...	...
plus: Value added tax	...	...	...	...	...	...	...	...	...	...	...	...
plus: Other adjustments	...	...	...	...	...	...	...	...	...	...	...	...
equals: Gross domestic product [b]	47460	52950	107980	117160	124980	120330	129140	138520	148790	142320	148420	162140

a Item "Other producers" is included in item "Community, social and personal services".
b Gross domestic product in factor values.

2.1 Government final consumption expenditure by function, in current prices

Thousand East Caribbean dollars

	1986	1987	1988	1989	1990	1991	1992	1993	1994	1995	1996	1997
1 General public services	1691	3166	3772	4030	3880	6085	6486	7950	8728	11465	11809	14971
2 Defence	...	...	...	...	...	...	...	...	...	...	...	...
3 Public order and safety	1213	1394	1798	2162	2469	2727	2992	3067	3438	3518	3974	4395
4 Education	2149	2817	3314	4201	4742	5210	5351	5725	5937	6271	7228	8022
5 Health	1456	1531	2116	2945	3150	3587	3701	4679	5066	5682	6758	7998
6 Social security and welfare	343	359	362	370	480	584	614	605	770	832	925	910
7 Housing and community amenities	735	880	978	1288	1471	1576	1828	1076	1712	1714	1987	2351
8 Recreational, cultural and religious affairs	...	...	...	...	...	...	...	...	...	...	...	...
9 Economic services	506	1056	713	1691	2388	1986	2403	3318	4150	4142	3978	4304
A Fuel and energy	...	...	...	...	...	...	...	...	...	...	...	...

Anguilla

Thousand East Caribbean dollars

	1986	1987	1988	1989	1990	1991	1992	1993	1994	1995	1996	1997
B Agriculture, hunting, forestry and fishing	232	263	417	489	...	486	518	579	599	620	692	976
C Mining (except fuels), manufacturing and construction	...	...	...	...	...	...	...	...	...	...	...	...
D Transportation and communication	227	700	432	767	...	1221	1356	1686	2334	2493	2598	2555
E Other economic affairs	47	93	95	662	...	279	529	1053	1217	1029	688	773
10 Other functions	1126	781	1684	961	1091	1216	1417	1106	1546	1508	1889	1731
Total government final consumption expenditures	9219	11984	14970	17875	19671	22971	24792	27526	31347	35132	38548	44683

Argentina

General note

The preparation of national accounts statistics in Argentina is undertaken by Banco Central de la República Argentina, Buenos Aires. The official estimates are published on a quarterly basis in the *Economic Reports*. In 1975, the publication *Sistema de Cuentas del Producto e Ingreso de la Argentina* was presented. Volume I *Metodologia y Fuentes* contains a detailed description of the sources and methods used for the national accounts estimation. Volume II *Cuadros Estadísticos* presents estimates for the period 1950–1973, in accordance with the United Nations System of National Accounts (1968 SNA). On 1 June 1983, the peso Argentino equal to 10,000 pesos, was introduced. On 4 June 1985, a new currency called the austral was introduced. One austral is equivalent to 1,000 peso Argentinos. On 1 January 1992, the peso Argentino equal to 10,000 australes was introduced. The following tables have been prepared from successive replies to the United Nations National Accounts Questionnaire. When the scope and coverage of the estimates differ for conceptual or statistical reasons from the definitions and classifications recommended in SNA, a footnote is indicated to the relevant tables.

Gross domestic product

Gross domestic product is estimated mainly through the production approach.

Expenditures on the gross domestic product

The expenditure approach is used to estimate government final consumption expenditure, increase in stocks, investment in construction, and exports and imports of goods and services. The commodity-flow approach is used to estimate the current value of gross investment other than for construction. Private final consumption expenditure is taken as a residual. Government final consumption expenditure, consisting of compensation of employees and net purchases of goods and services, is obtained from government accounts. Investment in construction is estimated through the use of accounting data for the public sector, agricultural census data for the agricultural sector, and construction licenses and miscellaneous sources for the urban private construction. The estimation of domestically produced capital goods is done on the basis of the industrial censuses.

For the years between censuses, the data are updated through a combination of indexes of physical output and price indexes.

Data on exports and imports of goods and services are obtained from the balance of payments accounts. Constant values of government consumption expenditures are obtained through extrapolating wages and salaries by the number of persons employed and through deflating purchases of goods and services by the wholesale price index for non-agricultural goods. Private consumption expenditure at constant prices is obtained as a residual. The current values of construction are deflated by indexes of construction costs or extrapolated by input volumes. Domestic machinery and equipment products are deflated by index of producer prices or extrapolated by volume of production. Imported machinery and equipment are deflated by price indexes. Price deflation is used for exports and imports of goods and services.

Cost structure of the gross domestic product

The estimates of compensation of employees are based on employment data, remuneration data and collective wage agreement data. Intercensal estimates are rough, except for those activities for which accounting data are available. Operating surplus is, in general, obtained as a residual. Consumption of fixed capital is calculated on the basis of accounting data from public enterprises, capital stock data in the case of private construction, gross investment data and estimated depreciation rates in the case of durable production equipment. Information on indirect taxes is obtained by type of government authority.

Gross domestic product by kind of activity

The table of gross domestic product by kind of economic activity is prepared in factor values. The production approach is used to estimate value added of most industries. The basic statistics on agricultural production are obtained from the Secretaría de Agricultura y Ganadería de la Nación. The production is valued at farmers' prices, which are obtained by subtracting transportation costs and commercial mark-ups from wholesale prices. Production estimates for beef, mutton and pork, are defined as the value of sales for slaughter, adjusted for changes in stocks and exports of live animal. Own-account consumption of agricultural products and meat is included in the estimates. Since no annual information is available, indirect indicators are used to estimate the value of intermediate consumption. For mining, information on quantities and prices is obtained from the government authorities concerned. Input data are supplied by state companies and balance sheets of a representative sample of mining enterprises.

The general method used in estimating industrial production is by interpolating prices and quantities between census years. After the latest industrial census of 1963, extrapolation is used, based on changes in the production volume. Information on prices is obtained from the wholesale price index and miscellaneous sources for products not included in that index. Data on the number of construction permits issued are used to estimate the

Argentina

value of construction in the private sector. The data are converted into value figures by using the cost of construction index. Intermediate consumption is estimated from analysis of budgets, surveys, etc. For the public sector, data are obtained from the accounts of official organizations and state enterprises. Intermediate consumption is estimated on the basis of coefficients obtained from a study of records in the field of public works. Gross output of the trade sector is estimated through applying gross percentage mark-up rates to the value of goods recorded as entering the various marketing channels. Input values are based on information from balance sheets of joint stock companies and other inquiries. Value added in the transport sector is estimated from financial statements and accounts data, direct information or from survey data. For financial intermediaries the data used is based on the financial statements of all credit institutions in the country. The data needed to calculate value added of insurance services is provided by the Superintendencia de Seguros de la Nación. The value of rents paid is calculated on the basis of the population censuses and the rent component of the consumer price index. In the case of owner-occupied dwellings, the average gross rent for rented dwellings is applied.

The value added of the producers of government, provincial government and local government services is based on the accounts and budget data of the concerned authorities. Business services and other professional services are estimated through population census data and income data. The value of domestic services is obtained by multiplying the number of employees by their average compensation. For the estimates in constant prices, extrapolation of the base year value by indexes of production volume or output quantity and occasionally of employment data are used for all sectors except public construction, in which case the current values are deflated by an index of construction costs.

1.1 Expenditure on the gross domestic product, in current prices

Million Argentine pesos

	1986	1987	1988	1989	1990	1991	1992	1993	1994	1995	1996	1997
1 Government final consumption expenditure	8	19	87	2531	55326	151531	192261	...	...	...	...	...
2 Private final consumption expenditure								...	...	...	...	...
3 Gross capital formation	2	5	21	503	9647	26478	37854	...	...	...	...	...
4 Exports of goods and services	1	2	11	424	7140	13884	14954	...	...	...	...	...
5 less: Imports of goods and services	1	2	7	213	3192	10995	18432	...	...	...	...	...
equals: Gross domestic product	10	23	111	3244	68922	180898	226638	...	...	...	...	...

1.2 Expenditure on the gross domestic product, in constant prices

Thousand Argentine pesos

	1986	1987	1988	1989	1990	1991	1992	1993	1994	1995	1996	1997
	At constant prices of: 1986											
1 Government final consumption expenditure	8119	8255	7907	7425	7347	8399	9519	10062	10754	10093	...	...
2 Private final consumption expenditure											...	...
3 Gross capital formation	1701	1921	1853	1453	1232	1621	2164	2511	3057	2560	...	...
4 Exports of goods and services	821	792	941	1011	1181	1121	1144	1172	1358	1667	...	...
5 less: Imports of goods and services	651	726	659	551	547	960	1599	1813	2221	1965	...	...
equals: Gross domestic product	9989	10242	10042	9338	9213	10180	11229	11931	12948	12355	...	...

1.10 Gross domestic product by kind of activity, in current prices

Million Argentine pesos

	1986	1987	1988	1989	1990	1991	1992	1993	1994	1995	1996	1997
1 Agriculture, hunting, forestry and fishing	1	2	10	312	5599	12420	13577	...	...	...	...	...
2 Mining and quarrying	–	–	3	103	1972	3733	4067	...	...	...	...	...
3 Manufacturing	3	6	31	1004	18464	44115	49541	...	...	...	...	...
4 Electricity, gas and water	–	–	2	66	1328	2924	3826	...	...	...	...	...
5 Construction	1	2	7	201	3064	8422	12107	...	...	...	...	...

Argentina

Million Argentine pesos

	1986	1987	1988	1989	1990	1991	1992	1993	1994	1995	1996	1997
6 Wholesale and retail trade, restaurants and hotels	2	4	17	550	10750	28725	34929	...	...	...	...	...
7 Transport, storage and communication	–	1	6	138	3614	9429	11719	...	...	...	...	...
8 Finance, insurance, real estate and business services	2	4	17	418	10239	27675	38133	...	...	...	...	...
9 Community, social and personal services	2	4	19	479	14679	44876	59022	...	...	...	...	...
Total, Industries	10	23	111	3270	69709	182050	226920	...	...	...	...	...
Producers of government services	...	...	...	...	...	...	...	...	...	...	...	...
Other producers	...	...	...	...	...	...	...	...	...	...	...	...
Subtotal	10	23	111	3270	69709	182050	226920	...	...	...	...	...
less: Imputed bank service charge	–	–	–	26	786	1152	283	...	...	...	...	...
plus: Import duties	...	...	...	...	...	...	...	...	...	...	...	...
plus: Value added tax	...	...	...	...	...	...	...	...	...	...	...	...
plus: Other adjustments	...	...	...	...	...	...	...	...	...	...	...	...
equals: Gross domestic product	10	23	111	3244	68922	180898	226638	...	...	...	...	...

1.11 Gross domestic product by kind of activity, in constant prices

Thousand Argentine pesos

	1986	1987	1988	1989	1990	1991	1992	1993	1994	1995	1996	1997
At constant prices of: 1986												
1 Agriculture, hunting, forestry and fishing	781	757	820	750	813	847	839	865	896	917	...	...
2 Mining and quarrying	202	217	229	227	234	241	267	294	320	341	...	...
3 Manufacturing	2738	2764	2640	2439	2384	2619	2888	3036	3224	3000	...	...
4 Electricity, gas and water	195	205	191	182	195	202	220	242	265	280	...	...
5 Construction	597	683	663	501	420	526	615	685	788	703	...	...
6 Wholesale and retail trade, restaurants and hotels	1627	1638	1565	1454	1444	1665	1905	1985	2153	1983	...	...
7 Transport, storage and communication	469	485	476	471	456	503	568	599	657	658	...	...
8 Finance, insurance, real estate and business services	1522	1542	1515	1394	1319	1515	1661	1814	2052	2047	...	...
9 Community, social and personal services	1857	1926	1924	1903	1886	1948	2068	2195	2358	2308	...	...
Total, Industries	9987	10219	10025	9321	9151	10067	11030	11715	12710	12237	...	...
Producers of government services	...	...	...	...	...	...	...	...	...	...	...	...
Other producers	...	...	...	...	...	...	...	...	...	...	...	...
Subtotal	9987	10219	10025	9321	9151	10067	11030	11715	12710	12237	...	...
less: Imputed bank service charge	180	185	170	144	95	133	193	241	331	345	...	...
plus: Import duties	182	208	187	161	157	246	392	457	569	463	...	...
plus: Value added tax	...	...	...	...	...	...	...	...	...	...	...	...
plus: Other adjustments	...	...	...	...	...	...	...	...	...	...	...	...
equals: Gross domestic product	9989	10242	10042	9338	9213	10180	11229	11931	12948	12355	...	...

Australia

General note

The preparation of national accounts statistics in Australia is undertaken by the Australian Bureau of Statistics (ABS), Canberra. The Australian National Accounts System corresponds closely to the United Nations System of National Accounts. Detailed descriptions of the concepts, definitions, sources and methods used are published in *Australian National Accounts, Concepts, Sources and Methods*. Preliminary annual estimates for the latest financial year are published about 6 to 7 weeks after the end of the financial year in the Commonwealth Budget Paper *National Income and Expenditure* while quarterly estimates are released usually about eight weeks after the end of the quarter in the quarterly publication *Australian National Accounts, National Income and Expenditure* (5206.0). The most comprehensive national accounts publication is *Australian National Accounts, National Income and Expenditure* (5204.0) which is released annually. In addition to these national income and expenditure publications, input-output tables have been published for the years 1958–59, 1962–63, 1968–69, 1974–75, 1986–87 and annually from 1977–78 to 1983–84 in *Australian National Accounts, Input-Output Tables* (5209.0).

Annual estimates of gross product at constant prices and indexes of gross product at constant prices per person employed and per hour worked, by industry, are published in *Australian National Accounts, Gross Product, Employment and Hours Worked* (5211.0) until 1989–90. From 1990–91 these estimates are included in 5204.0. Quarterly estimates of gross product at constant prices, by industry, are published in *Australian National Accounts: Gross Product, Employment and Hours Worked* (5222.0).

The following tables have been prepared from successive replies to the United Nations national accounts questionnaire. When the scope and coverage of the estimates differ for conceptual or statistical reasons from the definitions and classifications recommended in SNA, a footnote is placed on the relevant tables. Estimates relate to the fiscal year beginning 1 July. All data at constant prices are at average 1984–85 prices. Data in all tables (except table 4.4) are expressed in millions of dollars. In table 4.4, data on number of persons are in units of thousand persons, while hours worked data are shown in units of millions of hours. More detailed employment data have become available from 1983–84 (see table 4.4). This has resulted in some industry reclassifications which are explained in the footnotes to this table.

Gross domestic product

Gross domestic product is estimated using both the income and expenditure approaches. The difference between the two approaches is shown as statistical discrepancy and by convention, recorded on the expenditure side of the account.

Expenditures on the gross domestic product

Government final consumption expenditure and public gross fixed capital formation are estimated from the accounting records of the government sector. Private final consumption expenditure on goods is mainly derived from information collected in retail censuses (held every five years) as well as data on production, imports and exports, and motor vehicle registrations. The results of a monthly survey of retail sales are used to interpolate between census benchmarks and to extrapolate for the period since the last retail census. Benchmarks for dwellings rent are derived from population census data collected every five years. The consumer price index is used in conjunction with a perpetual inventory model of the stock of dwellings to interpolate between census year estimates and extrapolate from the most recent census. Estimates of expenditure on other services are based mainly on revenue or earnings data. Increase in stocks is based on book value levels of stocks reported in ABS economic censuses, taxation statistics and quarterly ABS surveys of stocks (less the stock valuation adjustment).

Estimates of private gross fixed capital expenditure are obtained from a quarterly collections of building and engineering construction statistics and from a quarterly survey of new capital expenditure by private businesses on plant and equipment. Exports and imports of goods are estimated from customs data while exports and imports of services are derived from transportation survey data and from data obtained as a by-product of the administration of foreign exchange transactions. Constant price estimates are derived quarterly with annual estimates obtained by summing the quarterly series. Government consumption expenditures are deflated by composite wage rate and material price indexes. Substantial use is made of data from consumer price index in the revaluation of private final consumption expenditure. Estimates of gross fixed capital expenditure are revalued using (output) building price indexes for building; composite wage material price indexes for engineering construction; domestic and overseas producer price indexes (including the computer equipment price index produced by the United States Bureau of Economic Analysis) and import price indexes for equipment; and quantity revaluation for real estate transfer expenses.

For exports and imports, considerable use is made of the quantity revaluation technique with the remainder deflated using price indexes (including the BEA index). Increase in stocks estimates are derived using detailed price indexes to revalue book value levels.

Australia

Cost structure of the gross domestic product

The components of indirect taxes (net) are estimated from government accounting records. Estimates of gross operating surplus are mainly based on taxation statistics. Estimates of the consumption of fixed capital are derived at current replacement cost using the perpetual inventory method. Since December quarter 1981, the compensation of employees data have been based on a quarterly survey of employers—prior to that quarter, estimates were mainly based on payroll tax data.

Gross domestic product by kind of activity

The table of gross domestic product by kind of economic activity is prepared at market prices. Constant price estimates of gross product for agriculture, mining and gas industries are derived using double deflation. Estimates for finance, property and business services, and public administration and defence are derived by extrapolating the base year value of gross product using hours worked estimates. Estimates for the community services are derived by extrapolating the base year value of gross product using the sum of the relevant components of government and private final consumption expenditure. Estimates for the remaining industries are derived using the gross output method.

1.1 Expenditure on the gross domestic product, in current prices

Million Australian dollars — Fiscal year beginning 1 July

	1986	1987	1988	1989	1990	1991	1992	1993	1994	1995	1996	1997
1 Government final consumption expenditure	49043	52497	56662	61482	66602	71598	74492	76838	79341	83437	86419	...
2 Private final consumption expenditure	157324	175657	196364	218314	231700	244229	256737	269502	286830	306369	318480	...
3 Gross capital formation	62727	72874	88590	94786	79920	75313	83213	89729	100507	102525	104124	...
A Increase in stocks	−1633	574	3501	5203	−1549	−2177	482	1233	2581	2239	−1410	...
B Gross fixed capital formation	64360	72300	85089	89583	81469	77490	82731	88496	97926	100286	105534	...
Residential buildings	11859	13422	18520	20009	18578	18637	21418	23715	25625	22687	22596	...
Non-residential buildings	20659	23356	25438	29127	26923	23538	22001	22001	23928	26556	29866	...
Other construction and land improvement, etc.												...
Other	31842	35522	41131	40447	35968	35315	39312	42780	48373	51043	53072	...
4 Exports of goods and services	44031	51468	55110	60625	65988	69753	76465	82531	87090	98528	104601	...
5 less: Imports of goods and services	47894	52578	60734	67007	65220	67439	77400	83496	95680	99107	101691	...
Statistical discrepancy	−656	−276	3889	3271	1771	−3987	−5555	−2668	2203	361	4373	...
equals: Gross domestic product	264575	299642	339881	371471	380761	389467	407952	432436	460291	492113	516306	...

1.2 Expenditure on the gross domestic product, in constant prices

Million Australian dollars — Fiscal year beginning 1 July

	1986	1987	1988	1989	1990	1991	1992	1993	1994	1995	1996	1997
At constant prices of: 1989												
1 Government final consumption expenditure	56731	58351	59540	61482	63132	65106	66071	67367	69666	71743	72844	...
2 Private final consumption expenditure	194063	200727	209062	218314	220424	226400	233317	241178	253544	263754	269954	...
3 Gross capital formation [a]	74557	82100	93546	94786	79250	74611	80972	85697	96004	97705	102005	...
A Increase in stocks [a]	−2061	676	3698	5203	−1169	−2319	676	989	2254	1664	−2186	...
B Gross fixed capital formation [a]	76618	81424	89848	89583	80419	76930	80296	84708	93750	96041	104191	...
Residential buildings	16347	17423	20693	20011	17957	17970	20677	22564	23941	20730	...	...
Non-residential buildings	25508	26910	27354	29091	26288	22974	21510	21476	22832	24497	...	...
Other construction and land improvement, etc.	...	...	...	...	...	...	...	...	...	...	...	...
Other [b]	34877	37124	41851	40374	36102	35794	37227	40285	46369	48323	...	...
4 Exports of goods and services	52421	56719	57459	60625	67623	73730	78194	85908	89555	99254	109257	...

Australia

Million Australian dollars   Fiscal year beginning 1 July

	1986	1987	1988	1989	1990	1991	1992	1993	1994	1995	1996	1997
At constant prices of: 1989												
5 less: Imports of goods and services	46658	51349	63646	67007	63409	65800	70746	76214	89957	95525	107298	...
Statistical discrepancy	−775	−279	4162	3271	1719	−3799	−5217	−2485	2026	333	3813	...
equals: Gross domestic product	330339	346269	360123	371471	368739	370248	382591	401451	420838	437264	450575	...

a Livestock is excluded from items "Increase in Stocks" and "Gross Fixed Capital Formation".   b Item "Statistical discrepancy" in tables 2.7 and 2.8 refers to real estate transfer expenses and the expenses are included in item "other" in tables 1.1 and 1.2.

1.3 Cost components of the gross domestic product

Million Australian dollars   Fiscal year beginning 1 July

	1986	1987	1988	1989	1990	1991	1992	1993	1994	1995	1996	1997
1 Indirect taxes, net	31646	36987	41201	44418	44640	44183	45539	50717	56170	60639	63308	...
A Indirect taxes	36367	41532	45817	49056	50410	50188	51895	57198	62403	66806	70369	...
B less: Subsidies	4721	4545	4616	4638	5770	6005	6356	6481	6233	6167	7061	...
2 Consumption of fixed capital	42592	46733	51372	55997	58294	59814	62779	65166	66799	69530	72407	...
3 Compensation of employees paid by resident producers to ..	133478	146826	163744	182279	190386	194510	201523	211947	225705	241374	257597	...
A Resident households	133299	146616	163465	181873	189957	194184	201212	211664	225316	240916	257058	...
B Rest of the world	179	210	279	406	429	326	311	283	389	458	539	...
4 Operating surplus	56859	69096	83564	88777	87441	90960	98111	104606	111617	120570	122994	...
A Corporate and quasi-corporate enterprises	22186	28747	34784	36035	34964	36990	41322	46753	50399	52896	52754	...
B Private unincorporated enterprises	34673	40349	48780	52742	52477	53970	56789	57853	61218	67674	70240	...
C General government	...	...	...	...	...	...	...	...	...	...	...	...
equals: Gross domestic product	264575	299642	339881	371471	380761	389467	407952	432436	460291	492113	516306	...

1.4 General government current receipts and disbursements

Million Australian dollars   Fiscal year beginning 1 July

	1986	1987	1988	1989	1990	1991	1992	1993	1994	1995	1996	1997
Receipts												
1 Operating surplus	–	–	–	–	–	–	–	–	–	–	–	...
2 Property and entrepreneurial income	9615	9875	11144	12947	14033	14520	14018	16012	15253	16546	18189	...
3 Taxes, fees and contributions	83355	94695	106384	115693	119478	116104	119198	127016	139998	153345	164690	...
A Indirect taxes	36367	41532	45817	49056	50410	50188	51895	57198	62403	66806	70369	...
B Direct taxes	45432	51367	58541	64303	66666	63058	64239	66383	73888	82590	90425	...
C Social security contributions	...	...	...	...	...	...	...	...	...	...	...	...
D Compulsory fees, fines and penalties	1556	1796	2026	2334	2402	2858	3064	3435	3707	3949	3896	...
4 Other current transfers	–	–	–	–	–	–	–	–	–	–	–	...
Total current receipts of general government	92970	104570	117528	128640	133511	130624	133216	143028	155251	169891	182879	...
Disbursements												
1 Government final consumption expenditure	49043	52497	56662	61482	66602	71598	74492	76838	79341	83437	86419	...
A Compensation of employees	33786	36373	39675	42168	45056	47611	...	...	...	...	...	...
B Consumption of fixed capital	5407	5688	6031	6492	6825	6974	...	...	...	...	...	...
C Purchases of goods and services, net	...	...	...	...	...	...	...	...	...	...	...	...

Australia

Million Australian dollars	1986	1987	1988	1989	1990	1991	1992	1993	1994	1995	1996	1997
D less: Own-account fixed capital formation	...	...	...	...	...	...	...	...	...	...	...	...
E Indirect taxes paid, net	...	...	...	...	...	...	...	...	...	...	...	...
2 Property income	11181	12149	13999	16737	16320	15379	14863	16177	18036	18458	17428	...
A Interest	11181	12149	13999	16737	16320	15379	14863	16177	18036	18458	17428	...
B Net land rent and royalties	–	–	–	–	–	–	–	–	–	–	–	...
3 Subsidies	4721	4545	4616	4638	5770	6005	6356	6481	6233	6167	7061	...
4 Other current transfers	29179	32341	34373	37988	43160	48955	53396	57866	60851	65522	68574	...
A Social security benefits	...	...	...	...	...	...	...	...	...	...	...	...
B Social assistance grants	24852	27739	29328	32370	37262	42351	46076	49667	51820	55705	58566	...
C Other	4327	4602	5045	5618	5898	6604	7320	8199	9031	9817	10008	...
5 Net saving	−1154	3038	7878	7795	1659	−11313	−15891	−14334	−9210	−3693	3397	...
Total current disbursements and net saving of general government	92970	104570	117528	128640	133511	130624	133216	143028	155251	169891	182879	...

1.5 Current income and outlay of corporate and quasi-corporate enterprises, summary

Million Australian dollars	1986	1987	1988	1989	1990	1991	1992	1993	1994	1995	1996	1997
Receipts												
1 Operating surplus	22186	28747	34784	36035	34964	36990	41322	46753	50399	52896	52754	...
2 Property and entrepreneurial income received	27142	28639	36412	44465	44590	37739	36113	35039	40640	46925	42971	...
3 Current transfers	–	–	–	333	150	–	–	–	–	–	–	...
Total current receipts	49328	57386	71196	80833	79704	74729	77435	81792	91039	99821	95725	...
Disbursements												
1 Property and entrepreneurial income	42957	44340	55458	67399	67408	56955	51076	49913	59698	67348	68109	...
2 Direct taxes and other current payments to general government	6646	8737	10211	13264	15410	15334	15885	15020	18428	21066	23162	...
3 Other current transfers	1009	999	985	1708	1170	1150	991	1178	1333	1451	1386	...
4 Net saving	−1284	3310	4542	−1538	−4284	1290	9483	15681	11580	9956	3068	...
Total current disbursements and net saving	49328	57386	71196	80833	79704	74729	77435	81792	91039	99821	95725	...

1.6 Current income and outlay of households and non-profit institutions

Million Australian dollars	1986	1987	1988	1989	1990	1991	1992	1993	1994	1995	1996	1997
Receipts												
1 Compensation of employees	133450	146776	163690	182243	190389	194639	201709	212175	225867	241526	257736	...
A From resident producers	133299	146616	163465	181873	189957	194184	201212	211664	225316	240916	257058	...
B From rest of the world	151	160	225	370	432	455	497	511	551	610	678	...
2 Operating surplus of private unincorporated enterprises	34673	40349	48780	52742	52477	53970	56789	57853	61218	67674	70240	...
3 Property and entrepreneurial income	27955	28250	35267	42803	41190	31819	26900	24078	32505	36509	34663	...
4 Current transfers	31811	35245	37718	41282	46926	52648	55239	59918	63268	68977	72451	...
A Social security benefits	...	...	...	...	...	...	...	...	...	...	...	...
B Social assistance grants	24852	27739	29328	32370	37262	42351	46076	49667	51820	55705	58566	...
C Other	6959	7506	8390	8912	9664	10297	9163	10251	11448	13272	13885	...
Total current receipts	227889	250620	285455	319070	330982	333076	340637	354024	382858	414686	435090	...

Australia

Million Australian dollars

	1986	1987	1988	1989	1990	1991	1992	1993	1994	1995	1996	1997
Disbursements												
1 Private final consumption expenditure	157324	175657	196364	218314	231700	244229	256737	269502	286830	306369	318480	...
2 Property income	19163	20431	26833	33522	33788	27230	24595	22777	26652	31028	28551	...
3 Direct taxes and other current transfers n.e.c. to general government	39556	43607	49459	52265	52558	49688	50591	54005	58341	64552	70174	...
A Social security contributions	...	...	...	...	...	...	...	...	...	...	...	...
B Direct taxes	38000	41811	47433	49931	50156	46830	47527	50570	54634	60603	66278	...
C Fees, fines and penalties	1556	1796	2026	2334	2402	2858	3064	3435	3707	3949	3896	...
4 Other current transfers	1311	1376	1385	1372	1553	1492	1425	1706	1898	1902	2036	...
5 Net saving	10535	9549	11414	13597	11383	10437	7289	6034	9137	10835	15849	...
Total current disbursements and net saving	227889	250620	285455	319070	330982	333076	340637	354024	382858	414686	435090	...

1.7 External transactions on current account, summary

Million Australian dollars

	1986	1987	1988	1989	1990	1991	1992	1993	1994	1995	1996	1997
Payments to the rest of the world												
1 Imports of goods and services	47894	52578	60734	67007	65220	67439	77400	83496	95680	99107	101691	...
A Imports of merchandise, c.i.f.	40157	43538	50457	54746	52846	54702	63682	68693	79578	82040	83719	...
B Other	7737	9040	10277	12261	12374	12737	13718	14803	16102	17067	17972	...
2 Factor income to rest of the world	10577	12141	15780	20747	21449	19326	17508	17508	19635	22105	22914	...
A Compensation of employees	179	210	279	406	429	326	311	283	389	458	539	...
B Property and entrepreneurial income	10398	11931	15501	20341	21020	19000	17197	17225	19246	21647	22375	...
By general government	2288	2962	3160	3906	4282	3930	3402	3748	5080	5134	4980	...
By corporate and quasi-corporate enterprises	8110	8969	12341	16435	16738	15070	13795	13477	14166	16513	17395	...
By other	...	...	...	...	...	...	...	...	...	...	...	...
3 Current transfers to the rest of the world	1873	2161	2296	2467	2524	2461	2566	2961	3013	2769	2688	...
A Indirect taxes to supranational organizations	...	...	...	...	...	...	...	...	...	...	...	...
B Other current transfers	1873	2161	2296	2467	2524	2461	2566	2961	3013	2769	2688	...
4 Surplus of the nation on current transactions	−11382	−9968	−17273	−21735	−14639	−11098	−13998	−14514	−24404	−16258	−13776	...
Payments to the rest of the world and surplus of the nation on current transfers	48962	56912	61537	68486	74554	78128	83476	89451	93924	107723	113517	...
Receipts from the rest of the world												
1 Exports of goods and services	44031	51468	55110	60625	65988	69753	76465	82531	87090	98528	104601	...
A Exports of merchandise, f.o.b.	36487	41903	44187	48927	52568	55427	60634	64419	67000	76038	80814	...
B Other	7544	9565	10923	11698	13420	14326	15831	18112	20090	22490	23787	...
2 Factor income from rest of the world	1960	1935	2259	3268	3749	3969	4191	3998	3809	5403	4788	...
A Compensation of employees	151	160	225	370	432	455	497	511	551	610	678	...
B Property and entrepreneurial income	1809	1775	2034	2898	3317	3514	3694	3487	3258	4793	4110	...
By general government	47	48	62	113	118	25	17	32	23	19	13	...

Australia

Million Australian dollars	1986	1987	1988	1989	1990	1991	1992	1993	1994	1995	1996	1997
By corporate and quasi-corporate enterprises	1762	1727	1972	2785	3199	3489	3677	3455	3235	4774	4097	...
By other	–	–	–	–	...	...	...	...	...	...	...	...
3 Current transfers from rest of the world	2971	3509	4168	4593	4817	4406	2820	2922	3025	3792	4128	...
A Subsidies from supranational organisations	...	...	...	...	...	...	...	...	...	...	...	...
B Other current transfers	2971	3509	4168	4593	4817	4406	2820	2922	3025	3792	4128	...
Receipts from the rest of the world on current transactions	48962	56912	61537	68486	74554	78128	83476	89451	93924	107723	113517	...

1.8 Capital transactions of the nation, summary

Million Australian dollars	1986	1987	1988	1989	1990	1991	1992	1993	1994	1995	1996	1997
Finance of gross capital formation												
Gross saving	50689	62630	75206	76322	67052	60228	63660	72547	78306	86628	94721	...
1 Consumption of fixed capital	42592	46733	51372	55997	58294	59814	62779	65166	66799	69530	72407	...
A General government	5495	5783	6119	6585	6983	7213	7417	7588	7760	8053	8307	...
B Corporate and quasi-corporate enterprises	22090	24187	26017	28279	29874	30909	32729	33872	34680	36145	37766	...
Public	6817	7250	7750	8435	8809	9051	9269	9186	9219	8929	8962	...
Private	15273	16937	18267	19844	21065	21858	23460	24686	25461	27216	28804	...
C Other	15007	16763	19236	21133	21437	21692	22633	23706	24359	25332	26334	...
2 Net saving	8097	15897	23834	20325	8758	414	881	7381	11507	17098	22314	...
A General government	–1154	3038	7878	7795	1659	–11313	–15891	–14334	–9210	–3693	3397	...
B Corporate and quasi-corporate enterprises	–1284	3310	4542	–1538	–4284	1290	9483	15681	11580	9956	3068	...
C Other	10535	9549	11414	14068	11383	10437	7289	6034	9137	10835	15849	...
less: Surplus of the nation on current transactions	–11382	–9968	–17273	–21735	–14639	–11098	–13998	–14514	–24404	–16258	–13776	...
Statistical discrepancy	656	276	–3889	–3271	–1771	3987	5555	2668	–2203	–361	–4373	...
Finance of gross capital formation	62727	72874	88590	94786	79920	75313	83213	89729	100507	102525	104124	...
Gross capital formation												
Increase in stocks	–1633	574	3501	5203	–1549	–2177	482	1233	2581	2239	–1410	...
Gross fixed capital formation	64360	72300	85089	89583	81469	77490	82731	88496	97926	100286	105534	...
1 General government	7669	7454	7484	8638	8873	8939	9435	9080	9462	9507	9945	...
2 Corporate and quasi-corporate enterprises	35623	38596	43028	47281	42785	39054	39590	42654	48888	53878	56714	...
A Public	11317	9933	10407	13128	12177	11789	10355	9587	11447	10788	9285	...
B Private	24306	28663	32621	34153	30608	27265	29235	33067	37441	43090	47429	...
3 Other	21068	26250	34577	33664	29811	29497	33706	36762	39576	36901	38875	...
Gross capital formation	62727	72874	88590	94786	79920	75313	83213	89729	100507	102525	104124	...

1.9 Gross domestic product by institutional sectors of origin

Million Australian dollars	1986	1987	1988	1989	1990	1991	1992	1993	1994	1995	1996	1997
Domestic factor incomes originating												
subtotal: Domestic factor incomes	190337	215922	247308	271056	277827	285470	299634	316553	337322	361944	380591	...
Indirect taxes, net	31646	36987	41201	44418	44640	44183	45539	50717	56170	60639	63308	...

Australia

Million Australian dollars	1986	1987	1988	1989	1990	1991	1992	1993	1994	1995	1996	1997
A Indirect taxes	36367	41532	45817	49056	50410	50188	51895	57198	62403	66806	70369	...
B less: Subsidies	4721	4545	4616	4638	5770	6005	6356	6481	6233	6167	7061	...
Consumption of fixed capital	42592	46733	51372	55997	58294	59814	62779	65166	66799	69530	72407	...
Gross domestic product	264575	299642	339881	371471	380761	389467	407952	432436	460291	492113	516306	...

1.10 Gross domestic product by kind of activity, in current prices

Million Australian dollars	1986	1987	1988	1989	1990	1991	1992	1993	1994	1995	1996	1997
1 Agriculture, hunting, forestry and fishing	10326	12403	14636	14860	12617	11783	12984	13876	12917	16497	16387	...
2 Mining and quarrying	13528	14199	13019	15716	17878	16308	16827	16423	17127	18091	18673	...
3 Manufacturing	43272	48115	52603	56307	55769	55429	58100	62484	66749	70512	72296	...
4 Electricity, gas and water	9752	10396	11571	12534	12859	13665	13836	13935	13897	13970	13854	...
5 Construction	18345	20111	23899	26754	25707	24056	23917	25733	28544	29498	30458	...
6 Wholesale and retail trade, restaurants and hotels	50729	57519	67270	72731	73794	75900	78949	85721	91657	99252	103789	...
7 Transport, storage and communication	20728	24049	27037	28071	29221	31424	32158	33761	37269	38526	40475	...
8 Finance, insurance, real estate and business services	53102	65870	78328	86415	94369	99047	106924	111927	116865	126789	135364	...
9 Community, social and personal services	36320	40295	44747	49451	53440	57095	60613	63696	67369	72090	76167	...
Total, Industries	256102	292957	333110	362839	375654	384707	404308	427556	452394	485225	507463	...
Producers of government services	10616	11651	12389	12673	13417	14414	15118	16266	17025	18235	20204	...
Other producers	...	...	...	...	...	...	...	...	...	...	...	...
Subtotal	266718	304608	345499	375512	389071	399121	419426	443822	469419	503460	527667	...
less: Imputed bank service charge	5382	8599	9372	7993	11634	13004	14807	14609	12600	14471	14499	...
plus: Import duties	3239	3633	3754	3952	3324	3350	3333	3223	3472	3124	3138	...
plus: Value added tax	...	...	...	...	...	...	...	...	...	...	...	...
plus: Other adjustments	...	...	...	...	...	...	...	...	...	...	...	...
equals: Gross domestic product	264575	299642	339881	371471	380761	389467	407952	432436	460291	492113	516306	...

1.11 Gross domestic product by kind of activity, in constant prices

Million Australian dollars	1986	1987	1988	1989	1990	1991	1992	1993	1994	1995	1996	1997
At constant prices of: 1989												
1 Agriculture, hunting, forestry and fishing	14318	13703	13726	14860	15925	15145	15980	16320	13122	16020	18218	...
2 Mining and quarrying	12414	14073	14570	15716	16410	16669	16831	17067	17809	18715	19307	...
3 Manufacturing	50204	53619	56702	56307	55347	53936	54826	57581	59820	60463	61138	...
4 Electricity, gas and water [a]	10846	11396	11932	12534	12808	12944	13184	13642	14018	14065	14271	...
5 Construction	21989	23733	26151	26754	25011	22691	23563	25157	26708	27048	28177	...
6 Wholesale and retail trade, restaurants and hotels [b]	62254	65693	70735	72731	68821	69374	70020	74199	80931	84675	85893	...
7 Transport, storage and communication	23596	25263	26929	28071	28862	30381	31986	34577	37886	40642	42959	...
8 Finance, insurance, real estate and business services	73319	77953	81003	86415	88594	88397	92641	95677	100118	103225	107178	...
9 Community, social and personal services [b]	43372	45453	47589	49451	50645	51784	53728	55418	57219	59765	60023	...
Total, Industries	312314	330885	349336	362839	362423	361319	372758	389637	407630	424617	437164	...

Australia

Million Australian dollars	1986	1987	1988	1989	1990	1991	1992	1993	1994	1995	1996	1997
At constant prices of: 1989												
Producers of government services	12092	12758	12925	12673	12881	13439	13767	14341	14939	15547	15471	...
Other producers	...	...	...	...	...	...	...	...	...	...	...	...
Subtotal	324406	343643	362261	375512	375303	374758	386525	403978	422568	440164	452636	...
less: Imputed bank service charge	6135	6460	7044	7993	8233	7921	7730	7602	8286	9319	9844	...
plus: Import duties	2669	2969	3825	3952	3793	3901	4258	4524	5304	5425	5935	...
plus: Value added tax	...	...	...	...	...	...	...	...	...	...	...	...
plus: Other adjustments	9399	6117	1081	–	–2125	–490	–462	551	1251	994	1849	...
equals: Gross domestic product	330339	346269	360123	371471	368739	370248	382591	401451	420838	437264	450575	...

a Item "Electricity, gas and water" includes sewage services.   b Restaurants and hotels are included in item "Community, social and personal services".

1.12 Relations among national accounting aggregates

Million Australian dollars	1986	1987	1988	1989	1990	1991	1992	1993	1994	1995	1996	1997
Gross domestic product	264575	299642	339881	371471	380761	389467	407952	432436	460291	492113	516306	...
plus: Net factor income from the rest of the world	–8617	–10206	–13521	–17329	–17550	–15357	–13317	–13510	–15826	–16702	–18126	...
Factor income from rest of the world	1960	1935	2259	3418	3899	3969	4191	3998	3809	5403	4788	...
less: Factor income to the rest of the world	10577	12141	15780	20747	21449	19326	17508	17508	19635	22105	22914	...
equals: Gross national product	255958	289436	326360	354142	363211	374110	394635	418926	444465	475411	498180	...
less: Consumption of fixed capital	42592	46733	51372	55997	58294	59814	62779	65166	66799	69530	72407	...
equals: National income	213366	242703	274988	298145	304917	314296	331856	353760	377666	405881	425773	...
plus: Net current transfers from the rest of the world	1098	1348	1872	1976	2143	1945	254	–39	12	1023	1440	...
Current transfers from rest of the world	2971	3509	4168	4443	4667	4406	2820	2922	3025	3792	4128	...
less: Current transfers to the rest of the world	1873	2161	2296	2467	2524	2461	2566	2961	3013	2769	2688	...
equals: National disposable income	214464	244051	276860	300121	307060	316241	332110	353721	377678	406904	427213	...
less: Final consumption	206367	228154	253026	279796	298302	315827	331229	346340	366171	389806	404899	...
equals: Net saving	8097	15897	23834	20325	8758	414	881	7381	11507	17098	22314	...
less: Surplus of the nation on current transactions	–11382	–9968	–17273	–21735	–14639	–11098	–13998	–14514	–24404	–16258	–13776	...
Statistical discrepancy	656	276	–3889	–3271	–1771	3987	5555	2668	–2203	–361	–4373	...
equals: Net capital formation	20135	26141	37218	38789	21626	15499	20434	24563	33708	32995	31717	...

2.1 Government final consumption expenditure by function, in current prices

Million Australian dollars	1986	1987	1988	1989	1990	1991	1992	1993	1994	1995	1996	1997
1 General public services	6743	7989	8027	8262	9092	10488	11027	11982	12010	12515	13290	...
2 Defence	6683	6617	7381	7850	7923	8608	9059	9320	9230	9136	8720	...
3 Public order and safety	3252	3535	3946	4532	4810	5134	5352	5486	5823	6312	6744	...
4 Education	11056	11498	12295	13021	14208	15264	15732	16018	16456	16930	18111	...
5 Health	8654	9457	10608	11447	12222	12766	13145	13244	13996	15225	15981	...
6 Social security and welfare	1945	2153	2218	2635	3340	3688	3927	4126	4459	4827	4994	...
7 Housing and community amenities	782	871	895	1049	1169	1214	1241	1258	1538	1843	1997	...

Australia

Million Australian dollars	1986	1987	1988	1989	1990	1991	1992	1993	1994	1995	1996	1997
8 Recreational, cultural and religious affairs	2096	2228	2487	2561	2739	2840	2890	3050	3268	3580	3590	...
9 Economic services	7888	8258	8922	10003	11062	11542	11823	11851	12139	12625	12473	...
A Fuel and energy	166	178	175	216	176	200	296	223	259	260	277	...
B Agriculture, hunting, forestry and fishing	1663	1740	1856	2021	2214	2083	1938	1977	1857	1947	2082	...
C Mining (except fuels), manufacturing and construction	384	424	507	541	563	586	554	548	610	640	629	...
D Transportation and communication	4003	4265	4602	5304	5873	6158	6024	6061	6106	6368	6535	...
E Other economic affairs	1672	1651	1781	1920	2236	2515	3011	3042	3307	3410	2951	...
10 Other functions	−56	−109	−117	122	37	54	296	503	422	444	519	...
Total government final consumption expenditures	49043	52497	56662	61482	66602	71598	74492	76838	79341	83437	86419	...

2.3 Total government outlays by function and type

Million Australian dollars — Fiscal year beginning 1 July

1986

	Final consumption expenditures — Total	Compensation of employees	Other	Subsidies	Other current transfers and property income	Total current disbursements	Gross capital formation	Other capital outlays	Total outlays
1 General public services	6743	...	...	39	800	7582	823	−	8405
2 Defence	6683	...	...	−	60	6743	−	−	6743
3 Public order and safety	3252	...	...	−	51	3303	391	1	3695
4 Education	11056	...	...	9	2419	13484	1040	51	14575
5 Health	8654	...	...	55	5062	13771	570	7	14348
6 Social security and welfare	1945	...	...	44	19919	21908	103	123	22134
7 Housing and community amenities	782	...	...	285	77	1144	456	740	2340
8 Recreational, cultural and religious affairs	2096	...	...	23	181	2300	869	102	3271
9 Economic services	7888	...	...	4253	2088	14229	3361	142	17732
A Fuel and energy	166	...	...	614	2	782	−39	78	821
B Agriculture, hunting, forestry and fishing	1663	...	...	464	6	2133	362	−16	2479
C Mining (except fuels), manufacturing and construction	384	...	...	399	3	786	29	22	837
D Transportation and communication	4003	...	...	2333	1732	8068	2851	49	10968
E Other economic affairs	1672	...	...	443	345	2460	158	9	2627
10 Other functions	−56	...	...	13	9703	9660	10	−30	9640
Total	49043	...	...	4721	40360	94124	7623	1136	102883

1987

	Final consumption expenditures — Total	Compensation of employees	Other	Subsidies	Other current transfers and property income	Total current disbursements	Gross capital formation	Other capital outlays	Total outlays
1 General public services	7989	...	...	29	818	8836	708	−242	9302
2 Defence	6617	...	...	−	61	6678	1	−	6679
3 Public order and safety	3535	...	...	−	52	3587	426	6	4019
4 Education	11498	...	...	2	2767	14267	966	53	15286

Australia

1987

	Final consumption expenditures Total	Compensation of employees	Other	Subsidies	Other current transfers and property income	Total current disbursements	Gross capital formation	Other capital outlays	Total outlays
5 Health	9457	...	...	4	5667	15128	596	33	15757
6 Social security and welfare	2153	...	...	24	21872	24049	127	138	24314
7 Housing and community amenities	871	...	...	187	99	1157	465	793	2415
8 Recreational, cultural and religious affairs	2228	...	...	31	250	2509	1047	29	3585
9 Economic services	8258	...	...	4250	2782	15290	3160	148	18598
A Fuel and energy	178	...	...	711	4	893	29	35	957
B Agriculture, hunting, forestry and fishing	1740	...	...	624	6	2370	279	−19	2630
C Mining (except fuels), manufacturing and construction	424	...	...	377	4	805	33	13	851
D Transportation and communication	4265	...	...	2015	2444	8724	2676	98	11498
E Other economic affairs	1651	...	...	523	324	2498	143	21	2662
10 Other functions	−109	...	...	18	10122	10031	−41	−37	9953
Total	52497	...	...	4545	44490	101532	7455	921	109908

1988

	Final consumption expenditures Total	Compensation of employees	Other	Subsidies	Other current transfers and property income	Total current disbursements	Gross capital formation	Other capital outlays	Total outlays
1 General public services	8027	...	...	8	927	8962	494	133	9589
2 Defence	7381	...	...	−	61	7442	−	−6	7436
3 Public order and safety	3946	...	...	−	79	4025	607	9	4641
4 Education	12295	...	...	1	3076	15372	1086	35	16493
5 Health	10608	...	...	3	6239	16850	626	22	17498
6 Social security and welfare	2218	...	...	27	23028	25273	131	175	25579
7 Housing and community amenities	895	...	...	212	137	1244	410	707	2361
8 Recreational, cultural and religious affairs	2487	...	...	31	257	2775	687	−115	3347
9 Economic services	8922	...	...	4311	3710	16943	3199	273	20415
A Fuel and energy	175	...	...	422	4	601	28	58	687
B Agriculture, hunting, forestry and fishing	1856	...	...	649	9	2514	272	−26	2760
C Mining (except fuels), manufacturing and construction	507	...	...	368	−	875	4	22	901
D Transportation and communication	4602	...	...	2253	3534	10389	2704	146	13239
E Other economic affairs	1781	...	...	619	163	2563	191	73	2827
10 Other functions	−117	...	...	23	10858	10764	210	−53	10921
Total	56662	...	...	4616	48372	109650	7450	1180	118280

Australia

1989

	Final consumption expenditures Total	Compensation of employees	Other	Subsidies	Other current transfers and property income	Total current disbursements	Gross capital formation	Other capital outlays	Total outlays
1 General public services	8262	...	...	25	1063	9350	921	40	10311
2 Defence	7850	...	...	–	74	7924	1	–19	7906
3 Public order and safety	4532	...	...	2	83	4617	600	25	5242
4 Education	13021	...	...	15	3425	16461	1350	58	17869
5 Health	11447	...	...	3	7017	18467	789	35	19291
6 Social security and welfare	2635	...	...	33	25292	27960	151	213	28324
7 Housing and community amenities	1049	...	...	375	212	1636	500	1053	3189
8 Recreational, cultural and religious affairs	2561	...	...	35	224	2820	691	107	3618
9 Economic services	10003	...	...	4037	4873	18913	3533	610	23056
A Fuel and energy	216	...	...	484	34	734	30	36	800
B Agriculture, hunting, forestry and fishing	2021	...	...	485	26	2532	311	–47	2796
C Mining (except fuels), manufacturing and construction	541	...	...	450	1	992	31	55	1078
D Transportation and communication	5304	...	...	2082	4604	11990	2986	428	15404
E Other economic affairs	1920	...	...	536	208	2664	175	138	2977
10 Other functions	122	...	...	113	12462	12697	167	29	12893
Total	61482	...	...	4638	54725	120845	8703	2151	131699

1990

	Final consumption expenditures Total	Compensation of employees	Other	Subsidies	Other current transfers and property income	Total current disbursements	Gross capital formation	Other capital outlays	Total outlays
1 General public services	9092	...	...	11	1001	10104	1098	42	11244
2 Defence	7923	...	...	–	93	8016	–	–72	7944
3 Public order and safety	4810	...	...	–	90	4900	685	1	5586
4 Education	14208	...	...	20	3809	18037	1497	89	19623
5 Health	12222	...	...	25	7643	19890	878	46	20814
6 Social security and welfare	3340	...	...	6	29321	32667	144	136	32947
7 Housing and community amenities	1169	...	...	500	196	1865	482	1011	3358
8 Recreational, cultural and religious affairs	2739	...	...	30	269	3038	617	119	3774
9 Economic services	11062	...	...	5050	4988	21100	3260	893	25253
A Fuel and energy	176	...	...	529	61	766	29	90	885
B Agriculture, hunting, forestry and fishing	2214	...	...	1676	12	3902	232	–48	4086
C Mining (except fuels), manufacturing and construction	563	...	...	338	3	904	37	4	945
D Transportation and communication	5873	...	...	1978	4585	12436	2757	602	15795
E Other economic affairs	2236	...	...	529	327	3092	205	245	3542
10 Other functions	37	...	...	128	12070	12235	286	77	12598
Total	66602	...	...	5770	59480	131852	8947	2342	143141

Australia

1991

	Final consumption expenditures Total	Compensation of employees	Other	Subsidies	Other current transfers and property income	Total current disbursements	Gross capital formation	Other capital outlays	Total outlays
1 General public services	10488	...	...	12	1173	11673	1350	58	13081
2 Defence	8608	...	...	–	75	8683	–	–8	8675
3 Public order and safety	5134	...	...	–	88	5222	629	36	5887
4 Education	15264	...	...	30	4317	19611	1376	135	21122
5 Health	12766	...	...	48	8176	20990	808	73	21871
6 Social security and welfare	3688	...	...	5	34034	37727	253	205	38185
7 Housing and community amenities	1214	...	...	603	112	1929	542	970	3441
8 Recreational, cultural and religious affairs	2840	...	...	41	273	3154	649	109	3912
9 Economic services	11542	...	...	4853	4699	21094	3015	1027	25136
A Fuel and energy	200	...	...	569	11	780	18	64	862
B Agriculture, hunting, forestry and fishing	2083	...	...	1226	19	3328	251	5	3584
C Mining (except fuels), manufacturing and construction	586	...	...	356	11	953	23	6	982
D Transportation and communication	6158	...	...	1953	4192	12303	2565	636	15504
E Other economic affairs	2515	...	...	749	466	3730	158	316	4204
10 Other functions	54	...	...	413	11387	11854	353	138	12345
Total	71598	...	...	6005	64334	141937	8975	2743	153655

1992

	Final consumption expenditures Total	Compensation of employees	Other	Subsidies	Other current transfers and property income	Total current disbursements	Gross capital formation	Other capital outlays	Total outlays
1 General public services	11027	...	...	20	1265	12312	987	30	13329
2 Defence	9059	...	...	–	78	9137	–	–1	9136
3 Public order and safety	5352	...	...	–	108	5460	454	1	5915
4 Education	15732	...	...	52	4611	20395	1709	125	22229
5 Health	13145	...	...	59	9031	22235	860	80	23175
6 Social security and welfare	3927	...	...	–1	36918	40844	186	200	41230
7 Housing and community amenities	1241	...	...	433	173	1847	530	1033	3410
8 Recreational, cultural and religious affairs	2890	...	...	54	280	3224	814	49	4087
9 Economic services	11823	...	...	5476	4294	21593	3656	780	26029
A Fuel and energy	296	...	...	610	9	915	30	83	1028
B Agriculture, hunting, forestry and fishing	1938	...	...	1011	30	2979	235	6	3220
C Mining (except fuels), manufacturing and construction	554	...	...	351	20	925	29	20	974
D Transportation and communication	6024	...	...	1931	3541	11496	3209	567	15272
E Other economic affairs	3011	...	...	1573	694	5278	153	104	5535
10 Other functions	296	...	...	263	11501	12060	294	77	12431
Total	74492	...	...	6356	68259	149107	9490	2374	160971

Australia

1993

	Final consumption expenditures Total	Compensation of employees	Other	Subsidies	Other current transfers and property income	Total current disbursements	Gross capital formation	Other capital outlays	Total outlays
1 General public services	11982	...	...	30	1368	13380	1107	38	14525
2 Defence	9320	...	...	–	80	9400	–	–14	9386
3 Public order and safety	5486	...	...	–	153	5639	401	12	6052
4 Education	16018	...	...	45	4850	20913	1677	69	22659
5 Health	13244	...	...	91	9839	23174	934	57	24165
6 Social security and welfare	4126	...	...	4	40121	44251	148	145	44544
7 Housing and community amenities	1258	...	...	410	151	1819	557	1113	3489
8 Recreational, cultural and religious affairs	3050	...	...	71	308	3429	870	–215	4084
9 Economic services	11851	...	...	5556	4256	21663	3372	990	26025
A Fuel and energy	223	...	...	587	8	818	5	53	876
B Agriculture, hunting, forestry and fishing	1977	...	...	1064	52	3093	220	5	3318
C Mining (except fuels), manufacturing and construction	548	...	...	311	18	877	33	2	912
D Transportation and communication	6061	...	...	2044	3583	11688	2910	778	15376
E Other economic affairs	3042	...	...	1550	595	5187	204	152	5543
10 Other functions	503	...	...	274	12917	13694	98	–13	13779
Total	76838	...	...	6481	74043	157362	9164	2182	168708

1994

	Final consumption expenditures Total	Compensation of employees	Other	Subsidies	Other current transfers and property income	Total current disbursements	Gross capital formation	Other capital outlays	Total outlays
1 General public services	12010	...	...	12	1427	13449	973	23	14445
2 Defence	9230	...	...	–	79	9309	–	–17	9292
3 Public order and safety	5823	...	...	–	161	5984	496	4	6484
4 Education	16456	...	...	26	5120	21602	1741	135	23478
5 Health	13996	...	...	107	10661	24764	914	35	25713
6 Social security and welfare	4459	...	...	4	41436	45899	195	133	46227
7 Housing and community amenities	1538	...	...	452	169	2159	732	1171	4062
8 Recreational, cultural and religious affairs	3268	...	...	71	362	3701	818	–313	4206
9 Economic services	12139	...	...	5356	4995	22490	3574	966	27030
A Fuel and energy	259	...	...	787	2	1048	4	69	1121
B Agriculture, hunting, forestry and fishing	1857	...	...	1246	41	3144	174	5	3323
C Mining (except fuels), manufacturing and construction	610	...	...	297	26	933	34	92	1059
D Transportation and communication	6106	...	...	1781	3981	11868	3064	763	15695
E Other economic affairs	3307	...	...	1245	945	5497	298	37	5832
10 Other functions	422	...	...	205	14477	15104	120	–19	15205
Total	79341	...	...	6233	78887	164461	9563	2118	176142

Australia

1995

	Final consumption expenditures			Subsidies	Other current transfers and property income	Total current disburse-ments	Gross capital formation	Other capital outlays	Total outlays
	Total	Compen-sation of employ-ees	Other						
1 General public services	12515	...	...	79	1479	14073	768	3	14844
2 Defence	9136	...	...	–	116	9251	2	–	9253
3 Public order and safety	6312	...	...	–	171	6483	531	3	7017
4 Education	16930	...	...	6	5538	22474	1850	74	24398
5 Health	15225	...	...	160	11585	26970	908	42	27920
6 Social security and welfare	4827	...	...	–2	44253	49078	166	105	49349
7 Housing and community amenities	1843	...	...	355	197	2395	561	1191	4147
8 Recreational, cultural and religious affairs	3580	...	...	98	409	4087	840	98	5025
9 Economic services	12625	...	...	5433	4641	22699	3906	743	27348
A Fuel and energy	260	...	...	1049	2	1311	43	54	1408
B Agriculture, hunting, forestry and fishing	1947	...	...	1262	38	3247	212	4	3463
C Mining (except fuels), manufacturing and construction	640	...	...	256	21	917	29	–23	923
D Transportation and communication	6368	...	...	1872	3127	11367	3332	694	15393
E Other economic affairs	3410	...	...	994	1453	5857	290	14	6161
10 Other functions	444	...	...	39	15591	16074	111	–14	16171
Total	83437	...	...	6167	83980	173584	9643	2245	185472

1996

	Final consumption expenditures			Subsidies	Other current transfers and property income	Total current disburse-ments	Gross capital formation	Other capital outlays	Total outlays
	Total	Compen-sation of employ-ees	Other						
1 General public services	13290	...	...	–6	1386	14670	652	78	15400
2 Defence	8720	...	...	–	73	8792	51	21	8864
3 Public order and safety	6744	...	...	–	218	6962	515	12	7489
4 Education	18111	...	...	31	5663	23805	2037	122	25964
5 Health	15981	...	...	197	12157	28335	1136	65	29536
6 Social security and welfare	4994	...	...	14	47032	52040	194	145	52379
7 Housing and community amenities	1997	...	...	681	170	2848	368	1084	4300
8 Recreational, cultural and religious affairs	3590	...	...	72	476	4138	1236	157	5531
9 Economic services	12473	...	...	5894	4244	22611	3373	907	26891
A Fuel and energy	277	...	...	977	–	1254	85	50	1389
B Agriculture, hunting, forestry and fishing	2082	...	...	1204	59	3345	161	–21	3485
C Mining (except fuels), manufacturing and construction	629	...	...	219	29	877	29	4	910
D Transportation and communication	6535	...	...	2353	3130	12018	2959	835	15812
E Other economic affairs	2951	...	...	1141	1026	5118	139	39	5296
10 Other functions	519	...	...	179	14583	15281	–10	546	15817
Total	86419	...	...	7061	86002	179482	9552	3137	192171

Australia

2.4 Composition of general government social security benefits and social assistance grants to households

Million Australian dollars — Fiscal year beginning 1 July

	1986 SSB	1986 SAG	1987 SSB	1987 SAG	1988 SSB	1988 SAG	1989 SSB	1989 SAG	1990 SSB	1990 SAG	1991 SSB	1991 SAG
1 Education benefits	...	954	...	1216	...	1371	...	1519	...	1772	...	2061
A Pre-primary and primary	...	4	...	15	...	16	...	73	...	9	...	8
B Secondary	...	157	...	290	...	339	...	417	...	456	...	576
C Tertiary	...	436	...	505	...	545	...	598	...	747	...	914
D Other	...	357	...	406	...	471	...	431	...	560	...	563
2 Health benefits	...	4526	...	5355	...	5864	...	6562	...	7121	...	7570
A Hospital	...	774	...	1175	...	1327	...	1445	...	1573	...	1616
B Clinics and practitioners	...	2895	...	3144	...	3426	...	3841	...	4284	...	4623
C Public health	...	14	...	1	...	–	...	1	...	1	...	11
D Medicaments, etc.	...	843	...	1035	...	1111	...	1275	...	1263	...	1320
3 Social security and welfare benefits	...	19121	...	20893	...	21874	...	23864	...	27905	...	32321
A Social security	...	18992	...	20742	...	21674	...	23644	...	27660	...	32070
Temporary sickness	...	429	...	511	...	553	...	611	...	651	...	445
Old age and permanent disability	...	8109	...	9093	...	9820	...	10648	...	12157	...	13326
Unemployment	...	3454	...	3375	...	3136	...	3068	...	4561	...	6736
Family assistance	...	2809	...	3094	...	3908	...	4762	...	5320	...	6362
Other	...	4191	...	4669	...	4257	...	4555	...	4971	...	5201
B Welfare	...	129	...	151	...	200	...	220	...	245	...	251
4 Housing and community amenities	...	60	...	70	...	92	...	185	...	158	...	91
5 Recreation and cultural benefits	...	3	...	3	...	3	...	4	...	4	...	6
6 Other	...	188	...	202	...	124	...	236	...	302	...	302
Total	...	24852	...	27739	...	29328	...	32370	...	37262	...	42351

	1992 SSB	1992 SAG	1993 SSB	1993 SAG	1994 SSB	1994 SAG	1995 SSB	1995 SAG	1996 SSB	1996 SAG	1997 SSB	1997 SAG
1 Education benefits	...	2233	...	2278	...	2339	...	2561	...	2457	...	...
A Pre-primary and primary	...	9	...	9	...	1	...	15	...	–	...	...
B Secondary	...	606	...	625	...	597	...	624	...	597	...	...
C Tertiary	...	1016	...	1054	...	1108	...	1241	...	1247	...	...
D Other	...	602	...	590	...	633	...	681	...	613	...	...
2 Health benefits	...	8340	...	9016	...	9732	...	10582	...	11044	...	...
A Hospital	...	1690	...	1706	...	1805	...	2001	...	2167	...	...
B Clinics and practitioners	...	5063	...	5441	...	5795	...	6139	...	6264	...	...
C Public health	...	3	...	1	...	2	...	4	...	3	...	...
D Medicaments, etc.	...	1584	...	1868	...	2130	...	2438	...	2610	...	...
3 Social security and welfare benefits	...	34935	...	37858	...	39027	...	41631	...	44333	...	...
A Social security	...	34774	...	37681	...	38828	...	41403	...	44057	...	...
Temporary sickness	...	370	...	426	...	413	...	354	...	144	...	...
Old age and permanent disability	...	14296	...	15867	...	16209	...	17156	...	18496	...	...
Unemployment	...	7491	...	7675	...	7418	...	6615	...	6868	...	...
Family assistance	...	7396	...	8383	...	9287	...	11486	...	12747	...	...
Other	...	5221	...	5330	...	5501	...	5792	...	5802	...	...
B Welfare	...	161	...	177	...	199	...	228	...	276	...	...

Australia

	1992 Social security benefits	1992 Social assistance grants	1993 Social security benefits	1993 Social assistance grants	1994 Social security benefits	1994 Social assistance grants	1995 Social security benefits	1995 Social assistance grants	1996 Social security benefits	1996 Social assistance grants	1997 Social security benefits	1997 Social assistance grants
4 Housing and community amenities	...	164	...	136	...	145	...	152	...	85	...	...
5 Recreation and cultural benefits	...	4	...	4	...	10	...	11	...	12	...	...
6 Other	...	400	...	375	...	567	...	768	...	635	...	...
Total	...	46076	...	49667	...	51820	...	55705	...	58566	...	...

2.5 Private final consumption expenditure by type and purpose, in current prices

Million Australian dollars — Fiscal year beginning 1 July

	1986	1987	1988	1989	1990	1991	1992	1993	1994	1995	1996	1997
Final consumption expenditure of resident households												
1 Food, beverages and tobacco	35047	37908	41056	44930	47611	49764	52098	55362	59925	65374	66877	...
A Food	24705	26513	28947	31623	33223	34966	36544	38573	41947	45928	47452	...
B Non-alcoholic beverages												...
C Alcoholic beverages	7342	8148	8554	9329	10039	10329	10520	11440	12480	13253	13209	...
D Tobacco	3000	3247	3555	3978	4349	4469	5034	5349	5498	6193	6216	...
2 Clothing and footwear	10470	11606	12450	12914	13104	13846	14069	14325	14943	15383	15021	...
3 Gross rent, fuel and power	31248	35340	40280	45138	48980	51539	53824	56198	59024	62292	65406	...
A Fuel and power	3681	3926	4216	4659	5008	5268	5665	5771	6116	6295	6495	...
B Other	27567	31414	36064	40479	43972	46271	48159	50427	52908	55997	58911	...
4 Furniture, furnishings and household equipment and operation	11573	12923	14109	15373	15292	16023	16647	17776	18984	19643	20024	...
5 Medical care and health expenses	10687	12032	13530	14921	16528	18066	19274	20350	21564	22689	23423	...
6 Transport and communication	22258	24892	28309	32295	33927	35258	37735	39014	41642	44207	46236	...
A Personal transport equipment	5233	5734	7561	9149	8629	8451	9329	9793	11241	11857	12387	...
B Other	17025	19158	20748	23146	25298	26807	28406	29221	30401	32350	33849	...
7 Recreational, entertainment, education and cultural services	14461	16180	18386	20669	22438	24371	26043	27980	30804	33850	35644	...
A Education	2508	2802	3359	4067	4572	5052	5416	5876	6354	6884	7456	...
B Other	11953	13378	15027	16602	17866	19319	20627	22104	24450	26966	28188	...
8 Miscellaneous goods and services	21549	25340	29224	32436	34786	37061	39291	41991	44668	48481	51673	...
Total final consumption expenditure in the domestic market by households, of which	157293	176221	197344	218676	232666	245928	258981	272996	291554	311919	324304	...
plus: Direct purchases abroad by resident households	2934	3472	3944	4753	4887	4647	4926	4927	5380	5854	6259	...
less: Direct purchases in the domestic market by non-resident households	2903	4036	4924	5115	5853	6346	7170	8421	10104	11404	12083	...
equals: Final consumption expenditure of resident households	157324	175657	196364	218314	231700	244229	256737	269502	286830	306369	318480	...

Australia

2.6 Private final consumption expenditure by type and purpose, in constant prices

Million Australian dollars — Fiscal year beginning 1 July

At constant prices of: 1989

Final consumption expenditure of resident households

	1986	1987	1988	1989	1990	1991	1992	1993	1994	1995	1996	1997
1 Food, beverages and tobacco [a]	43488	44296	44107	44930	45600	46220	46933	48327	50757	52829	52519	...
A Food	30554	31170	30960	31623	32348	33292	34297	35469	37553	39662	39740	...
B Non-alcoholic beverages												...
C Alcoholic beverages	8858	9048	9111	9329	9378	9294	9255	9723	10241	10365	10098	...
D Tobacco	4076	4077	4037	3978	3873	3635	3381	3135	2963	2801	2681	...
2 Clothing and footwear [b]	12652	13031	13093	12914	12547	13049	13147	13486	14051	14379	13976	...
3 Gross rent, fuel and power	40812	41948	43417	45138	46452	47613	49085	50540	52448	53989	55313	...
A Fuel and power	4257	4279	4386	4659	4746	4794	4974	4954	5218	5329	5441	...
B Other	36555	37668	39031	40479	41706	42819	44111	45586	47230	48660	49872	...
4 Furniture, furnishings and household equipment and operation [b]	13121	13826	14538	15373	15013	15659	16304	17255	18263	19024	19599	...
5 Medical care and health expenses	13093	13574	14402	14921	15369	16100	16902	17629	18512	19297	19609	...
6 Transport and communication	27709	28303	30308	32295	32405	33255	34920	35772	37993	39342	41185	...
A Personal transport equipment	6610	6468	7898	9149	8609	8061	8632	8631	9536	9750	10645	...
B Other	21098	21835	22409	23146	23796	25195	26289	27140	28456	29592	30540	...
7 Recreational, entertainment, education and cultural services	17774	18451	19496	20669	21173	22070	22887	24217	26049	27707	28515	...
A Education	2921	3133	3537	4067	4294	4557	4820	5196	5561	5909	6256	...
B Other	14853	15318	15959	16602	16879	17513	18067	19021	20488	21798	22259	...
8 Miscellaneous goods and services	25957	28351	30667	32437	32920	34271	35776	37816	40370	42674	44751	...
Total final consumption expenditure in the domestic market by households, of which	194605	201779	210028	218676	221478	228237	235954	245041	258442	269241	275468	...
plus: Direct purchases abroad by resident households	2810	3327	4153	4582	4308	3964	...	...	...	...	...	...
less: Direct purchases in the domestic market by non-resident households	3361	4338	4948	4777	5149	5437	...	...	...	...	...	...
equals: Final consumption expenditure of resident households [c]	194063	200727	209062	218314	220424	226400	233317	241178	253544	263754	269954	...

a Item "Food, beverages and tobacco" includes food, beverages and tobacco consumed in institutions except hospitals and nursing homes.
b Drapery is included in item "Clothing and footwear".
c Item "Final consumption expenditure of resident households" includes consumption expenditure of private non-profit institutions serving households.

2.7 Gross capital formation by type of good and owner, in current price

Million Australian dollars — Fiscal year beginning 1 July

	1986				1987				1988			
	Total	Total private	Public enterprises	General government	Total	Total private	Public enterprises	General government	Total	Total private	Public enterprises	General government
Increase in stocks, total	−1633	−1217	−370	−46	574	1307	−734	1	3501	3420	115	−34
1 Goods producing industries	1109	1109	...	...	1928	1928	...	...	1972	1972	...	...
2 Wholesale and retail trade	640	1154	−514	...	2002	2413	−411	...	3352	2955	397	...
3 Other, except government stocks	542	542	...	...	253	253	...	...	268	268	...	...
4 Government stocks	163	...	209	−46	137	...	136	1	−32	...	2	−34

Australia

Million Australian dollars — Fiscal year beginning 1 July

	1986 Total	1986 Total private	1986 Public enterprises	1986 General government	1987 Total	1987 Total private	1987 Public enterprises	1987 General government	1988 Total	1988 Total private	1988 Public enterprises	1988 General government
Statistical discrepancy	−4087	−4022	−65	...	−3746	−3287	−459	...	−2059	−1775	−284	...
Gross fixed capital formation, total	64360	45374	11317	7669	72300	54913	9933	7454	85089	67198	10407	7484
1 Residential buildings	11859	10734	1012	113	13422	12468	802	152	18520	17595	753	172
2 Non-residential buildings	20659	9554	4983	6122	23356	12663	4952	5741	25438	14505	5439	5494
3 Other construction												
4 Land improvement and plantation and orchard development												
5 Producers' durable goods	28652	21896	5322	1434	30615	24875	4179	1561	34183	28150	4215	1818
6 Breeding stock, dairy cattle, etc.	...	...	...	...	...	...	...	...	...	...	...	...
Statistical discrepancy	3190	3190	...	...	4907	4907	...	...	6948	6948	...	...
Total gross capital formation	62727	44157	10947	7623	72874	56220	9199	7455	88590	70618	10522	7450

	1989 Total	1989 Total private	1989 Public enterprises	1989 General government	1990 Total	1990 Total private	1990 Public enterprises	1990 General government	1991 Total	1991 Total private	1991 Public enterprises	1991 General government
Increase in stocks, total	5203	1977	3161	65	−1549	−2711	1088	74	−2177	−1671	−542	36
1 Goods producing industries	1734	1734	...	...	−993	−993	...	...	−556	−556	...	...
2 Wholesale and retail trade	4051	1739	2312	...	−217	−747	530	...	−515	−254	−261	...
3 Other, except government stocks	749	749	...	...	604	604	...	...	−230	−230	...	...
4 Government stocks	143	...	78	65	−315	...	−389	74	−97	...	−133	36
Statistical discrepancy	−1474	−2245	771	...	−628	−1575	947	...	−779	−631	−148	...
Gross fixed capital formation, total	89583	67817	13128	8638	81469	60419	12177	8873	77490	56762	11789	8939
1 Residential buildings	20009	18633	1214	162	18578	17227	1177	174	18637	17505	859	273
2 Non-residential buildings	29127	16768	6391	5968	26923	14400	6434	6089	23538	11335	6058	6145
3 Other construction												
4 Land improvement and plantation and orchard development												
5 Producers' durable goods	35283	27252	5523	2508	31428	24252	4566	2610	30649	23256	4872	2521
6 Breeding stock, dairy cattle, etc.	...	...	...	...	...	...	...	...	...	...	...	...
Statistical discrepancy	5164	5164	...	...	4540	4540	...	...	4666	4666	...	...
Total gross capital formation	94786	69794	16289	8703	79920	57708	13265	8947	75313	55091	11247	8975

	1992 Total	1992 Total private	1992 Public enterprises	1992 General government	1993 Total	1993 Total private	1993 Public enterprises	1993 General government	1994 Total	1994 Total private	1994 Public enterprises	1994 General government
Increase in stocks, total	482	305	122	55	1233	1277	−128	84	2581	3974	−1494	101
1 Goods producing industries	1016	1016	...	...	−441	−441	...	...	2943	2943	...	...
2 Wholesale and retail trade	1030	727	303	...	3134	2442	692	...	2582	3724	−1142	...
3 Other, except government stocks	307	307	...	...	−193	−193	...	...	−147	−147	...	...
4 Government stocks	−312	...	−367	55	−37	...	−121	84	147	...	46	101
Statistical discrepancy	−1559	−1745	186	...	−1230	−531	−699	...	−2944	−2546	−398	...
Gross fixed capital formation, total	82731	62941	10355	9435	88496	69829	9587	9080	97926	77017	11447	9462
1 Residential buildings	21418	20085	1149	184	23715	22806	761	148	25625	24447	891	287
2 Non-residential buildings	22001	10238	5216	6547	22001	10694	4939	6368	23928	11805	5445	6678
3 Other construction												

Australia

	1992				1993				1994			
	Total	Total private	Public enterprises	General government	Total	Total private	Public enterprises	General government	Total	Total private	Public enterprises	General government
4 Land improvement and plantation and orchard development												
5 Producers' durable goods	34404	27710	3990	2704	36993	30542	3887	2564	42805	35197	5111	2497
6 Breeding stock, dairy cattle, etc.	...	...	...	...	...	...	...	...	...	...	...	...
Statistical discrepancy	4908	4908	...	...	5787	5787	...	...	5568	5568	...	...
Total gross capital formation	83213	63246	10477	9490	89729	71106	9459	9164	100507	80991	9953	9563

	1995				1996				1997			
	Total	Total private	Public enterprises	General government	Total	Total private	Public enterprises	General government	Total	Total private	Public enterprises	General government
Increase in stocks, total	2239	3271	−1168	136	−1410	1114	−2131	−393	...	...	...	...
1 Goods producing industries	2156	2156	...	...	−435	−435	...	...	...	...	...	...
2 Wholesale and retail trade	−296	176	−472	...	101	782	−681	...	...	...	...	...
3 Other, except government stocks	463	463	...	...	636	636	...	...	...	...	...	...
4 Government stocks	−810	...	−946	136	−2337	...	−1944	−393	...	...	...	...
Statistical discrepancy	726	476	250	...	625	131	494	...	...	...	...	...
Gross fixed capital formation, total	100286	79991	10788	9507	105534	86304	9285	9945	...	...	...	...
1 Residential buildings	22687	21715	839	133	22596	21981	620	−5	...	...	...	...
2 Non-residential buildings	26556	14844	4913	6799	29866	17844	4602	7420	...	...	...	...
3 Other construction									...	...	...	...
4 Land improvement and plantation and orchard development												
5 Producers' durable goods	45560	37949	5036	2575	46957	40364	4063	2530	...	...	...	...
6 Breeding stock, dairy cattle, etc.	...	...	...	...	...	...	...	...	...	...	...	...
Statistical discrepancy	5483	5483	...	...	6115	6115	...	...	...	...	...	...
Total gross capital formation	102525	83262	9620	9643	104124	87418	7154	9552	...	...	...	...

2.8 Gross capital formation by type of good and owner, in constant prices

Million Australian dollars

Fiscal year beginning 1 July

	1986				1987				1988			
	Total	Total private	Public enterprises	General government	Total	Total private	Public enterprises	General government	Total	Total private	Public enterprises	General government
At constant prices of: 1989												
Increase in stocks, total [a]	−2061	−1566	−430	−65	676	1543	−868	1	3698	3473	262	−37
1 Goods producing industries [a]	−525	−525	...	...	460	460	...	...	983	983	...	...
2 Wholesale and retail trade	−2097	−1371	−726	...	−56	980	−1037	...	2658	2398	260	...
3 Other, except government stocks	626	331	295	...	272	103	169	...	95	93	2	...
4 Government stocks	−65	...	...	−65	1	...	...	1	−37	...	...	−37
Gross fixed capital formation, total [a]	76618	54766	13087	8765	81424	62116	11150	8158	89848	70943	11031	7873
1 Residential buildings	16347	14865	1326	156	17423	16258	974	191	20693	19685	820	188
2 Non-residential buildings	25508	11772	6194	7542	26910	14568	5725	6617	27354	15549	5805	6000
3 Other construction												
4 Land improvement and plantation and orchard development												
5 Producers' durable goods	29925	23162	5579	1184	30969	25149	4419	1401	34758	28606	4403	1749

Australia

Million Australian dollars — Fiscal year beginning 1 July

	1986 Total	1986 Total private	1986 Public enterprises	1986 General government	1987 Total	1987 Total private	1987 Public enterprises	1987 General government	1988 Total	1988 Total private	1988 Public enterprises	1988 General government
At constant prices of: 1989												
6 Breeding stock, dairy cattle, etc.	...	...	...	...	...	...	...	...	...	...	...	...
Statistical discrepancy [b]	4952	4952	...	...	6155	6155	...	...	7093	7093	...	...
Total gross capital formation [a]	74557	53200	12657	8700	82100	63659	10282	8159	93546	74416	11293	7836

	1989 Total	1989 Total private	1989 Public enterprises	1989 General government	1990 Total	1990 Total private	1990 Public enterprises	1990 General government	1991 Total	1991 Total private	1991 Public enterprises	1991 General government
At constant prices of: 1989												
Increase in stocks, total [a]	5203	1977	3161	65	−1169	−2575	1329	77	−2319	−1541	−826	47
1 Goods producing industries [a]	850	850	...	...	−1349	−1349	...	...	−643	−643	...	...
2 Wholesale and retail trade	3611	528	3083	...	190	−1542	1731	...	−1339	−688	−651	...
3 Other, except government stocks	677	599	78	...	−87	316	−403	...	−385	−210	−175	...
4 Government stocks	65	...	...	65	77	...	...	77	47	...	...	47
Gross fixed capital formation, total [a]	89583	67817	13128	8638	80419	59874	11857	8688	76930	56639	11465	8827
1 Residential buildings	20011	18633	1216	162	17957	16760	1025	172	17970	16830	872	268
2 Non-residential buildings	29091	16768	6316	6007	26288	14097	6189	6002	22974	11399	5840	5735
3 Other construction												
4 Land improvement and plantation and orchard development												
5 Producers' durable goods	35206	27252	5494	2460	30751	23834	4521	2396	29913	22553	4750	2610
6 Breeding stock, dairy cattle, etc.	...	...	...	...	...	...	...	...	...	...	...	...
Statistical discrepancy [b]	5168	5168	...	...	5351	5351	...	...	5881	5881	...	...
Total gross capital formation [a]	94786	69794	16289	8703	79250	57299	13186	8765	74611	55098	10639	8874

	1992 Total	1992 Total private	1992 Public enterprises	1992 General government	1993 Total	1993 Total private	1993 Public enterprises	1993 General government	1994 Total	1994 Total private	1994 Public enterprises	1994 General government
At constant prices of: 1989												
Increase in stocks, total [a]	676	355	264	57	989	1137	−265	117	2254	3795	−1599	58
1 Goods producing industries [a]	510	510	...	...	−748	−748	...	...	1344	1344	...	...
2 Wholesale and retail trade	323	−321	644	...	1926	2022	−96	...	1148	2774	−1626	...
3 Other, except government stocks	−213	166	−379	...	−306	−137	−169	...	−296	−323	27	...
4 Government stocks	57	...	...	57	117	...	...	117	58	...	...	58
Gross fixed capital formation, total [a]	80296	61116	9903	9277	84708	66492	9256	8959	93750	73259	11147	9343
1 Residential buildings	20677	19320	1176	181	22564	21898	523	143	23941	22740	914	287
2 Non-residential buildings	21510	10457	4916	6137	21476	10780	4954	5742	22832	11702	5248	5882
3 Other construction												
4 Land improvement and plantation and orchard development												
5 Producers' durable goods	31291	24928	3809	2554	33720	27533	3728	2459	40020	32541	4990	2489
6 Breeding stock, dairy cattle, etc.	...	...	...	...	...	...	...	...	...	...	...	...
Statistical discrepancy [b]	5936	5936	...	...	6565	6565	...	...	6349	6349	...	...
Total gross capital formation [a]	80972	61471	10167	9334	85697	67629	8991	9076	96004	77054	9548	9401

Australia

	1995				1996				1997			
	Total	Total private	Public enter-prises	General govern-ment	Total	Total private	Public enter-prises	General govern-ment	Total	Total private	Public enter-prises	General govern-ment
	At constant prices of: 1989											
Increase in stocks, total [a]	1664	2905	–1390	149	–2186	619	–2372	–433	...	...	...	...
1 Goods producing industries [a]	2359	2359	...	...	–588	–588	...	...	...	...	...	...
2 Wholesale and retail trade	–228	180	–407	...	475	946	–471	...	...	...	...	...
3 Other, except government stocks	–616	366	–983	...	–1640	261	–1901	...	...	...	...	...
4 Government stocks	149	...	...	149	–433	...	...	–433	...	...	...	...
Gross fixed capital formation, total [a]	96041	76257	10438	9347	104191	85505	8983	9702	...	...	...	...
1 Residential buildings	20730	19808	850	72	...	...	...	...	...	...	...	...
2 Non-residential buildings	24497	14485	4422	5590	...	...	...	...	...	...	...	...
3 Other construction					...	...	...	...	...	...	...	...
4 Land improvement and plantation and orchard development					...	...	...	...	...	...	...	...
5 Producers' durable goods	42561	34574	5081	2906	...	...	...	...	...	...	...	...
6 Breeding stock, dairy cattle, etc.	...	...	...	...	...	...	...	...	...	...	...	...
Statistical discrepancy [b]	5762	5762	...	...	...	...	...	...	...	...	...	...
Total gross capital formation [a]	97705	79162	9048	9496	102005	86124	6611	9269	...	...	...	...

a Livestock is excluded from items "Increase in Stocks" and "Gross Fixed Capital Formation".
b Item "Statistical discrepancy" in tables 2.7 and 2.8 refers to real estate transfer expenses and the expenses are included in item "other" in tables 1.1 and 1.2.

2.17 Exports and imports of goods and services, detail

Million Australian dollars

Fiscal year beginning 1 July

	1986	1987	1988	1989	1990	1991	1992	1993	1994	1995	1996	1997
Exports of goods and services												
1 Exports of merchandise, f.o.b.	36487	41903	44187	48927	52568	55427	60634	64419	67000	76038	80814	...
2 Transport and communication	3158	3605	3834	4105	4593	4738	5290	5974	6086	6634	6763	...
3 Insurance service charges	96	89	95	124	196	244	412	508	556	748	820	...
4 Other commodities	1324	1766	1994	2272	2692	2910	2870	3122	3256	3612	4025	...
5 Adjustments of merchandise exports to change-of-ownership basis	–	–	–	–	–	–	–	–	–	...	...	...
6 Direct purchases in the domestic market by non-residential households	2903	4036	4924	5115	5853	6346	7170	8421	10104	11404	12083	...
7 Direct purchases in the domestic market by extraterritorial bodies	63	69	76	82	86	88	89	87	88	92	96	...
Total exports of goods and services	44031	51468	55110	60625	65988	69753	76465	82531	87090	98528	104601	...
Imports of goods and services												
1 Imports of merchandise, c.i.f.	40157	43538	50457	54746	52846	54702	63682	68693	79578	82040	83719	...
A Imports of merchandise, f.o.b.	37370	40640	47232	51326	49681	51469	59934	64863	75218	77635	79346	...
B Transport of services on merchandise imports	2763	2874	3201	3396	3141	3209	3724	3806	4336	4381	4349	...
By residents	...	...	...	...	...	...	...	...	...	...	...	...
By non-residents	2763	2874	3201	3396	3141	3209	3724	3806	4336	4381	4349	...
C Insurance service charges on merchandise imports	24	24	24	24	24	24	24	24	24	24	24	...
By residents	...	...	...	...	...	...	...	...	...	...	...	...

Australia

Million Australian dollars	1986	1987	1988	1989	1990	1991	1992	1993	1994	1995	1996	1997
By non-residents	24	24	24	24	24	24	24	24	24	24	24	...
2 Adjustments of merchandise imports to change-of-ownership basis	–	–	–	–	–	–	–	–	–	–	–	...
3 Other transport and communication	1634	1989	2331	2469	2369	2627	2593	3095	3998	4177	4158	...
4 Other insurance service charges	296	284	288	312	384	556	796	1012	1040	1044	1124	...
5 Other commodities	2458	2875	3308	4232	4260	4400	4825	5206	5146	5423	5912	...
6 Direct purchases abroad by government	2934	3472	3944	4753	4887	4647	4926	4927	5380	5854	6259	...
7 Direct purchases abroad by resident households	415	420	406	495	474	507	578	563	538	569	519	...
Total imports of goods and services	47894	52578	60734	67007	65220	67439	77400	83496	95680	99107	101691	...
Balance of goods and services	–3863	–1110	–5624	–6382	768	2314	–935	–965	–8590	–579	2910	...
Total imports and balance of goods and services	44031	51468	55110	60625	65988	69753	76465	82531	87090	98528	104601	...

3.12 General government income and outlay account: total and subsectors

Fiscal year beginning 1 July

Million Australian dollars	1986					1987				
	Total government	Central government	State or provincial government	Local government	Social security funds	Total government	Central government	State or provincial government	Local government	Social security funds
Receipts
1 Operating surplus	–	–	...	–	...	–	–	...	–	...
2 Property and entrepreneurial income	9615	6663	...	5408	...	9875	6128	...	6257	...
A Withdrawals from public quasi-corporations	3300	2796	...	504	...	2685	2106	...	579	...
B Interest	5342	3587	...	4208	...	6098	3652	...	4955	...
C Dividends	1	1	...	–	...	8	5	...	3	...
D Net land rent and royalties	972	279	...	696	...	1084	365	...	720	...
3 Taxes, fees and contributions	83355	67115	...	16240	...	94695	75587	...	19108	...
A Indirect taxes	36367	21532	...	14835	...	41532	24028	...	17504	...
B Direct taxes	45432	45432	...	...	...	51367	51367	...	...	...
Income	45432	45432	...	...	...	51367	51367	...	...	...
Other	...	...	...	...	...	...	...	...	...	...
C Social security contributions	...	...	...	...	...	...	...	...	...	...
D Fees, fines and penalties	1556	151	...	1405	...	1796	192	...	1604	...
4 Other current transfers	–	24	...	19426	...	–	29	...	20826	...
A Casualty insurance claims	...	...	...	...	...	...	...	...	...	...
B Transfers from other government subsectors	–	24	...	19426	...	–	29	...	20826	...
C Transfers from rest of the world	...	...	...	...	...	...	...	...	...	...
D Other transfers, except imputed	–	...	...	–	...	–	...	...	–	...
E Imputed unfunded employee pension and welfare contributions	...	...	...	...	...	...	...	...	...	...
Total current receipts	92970	73802	...	41074	...	104570	81744	...	46191	...

Australia

Million Australian dollars — Fiscal year beginning 1 July

Disbursements

	1986 Total government	1986 Central government	1986 State or provincial government	1986 Local government	1986 Social security funds	1987 Total government	1987 Central government	1987 State or provincial government	1987 Local government	1987 Social security funds
1 Government final consumption expenditure	49043	16340	...	32703	...	52497	16957	...	35540	...
2 Property income	11181	7963	...	5674	...	12149	7651	...	7008	...
A Interest	11181	7963	...	5674	...	12149	7651	...	7008	...
B Net land rent and royalties	–	...	...	...	...	–	...	...	...	...
3 Subsidies	4721	1938	...	2783	...	4545	1804	...	2741	...
4 Other current transfers	29179	45740	...	2889	...	32341	49989	...	3207	...
A Casualty insurance premiums, net	...	...	...	...	...	...	...	...	...	...
B Transfers to other government subsectors	...	19426	...	24	...	...	20826	...	29	...
C Social security benefits	...	...	...	...	...	...	...	...	...	...
D Social assistance grants	24852	24042	...	810	...	27739	26785	...	954	...
E Unfunded employee welfare benefits	–	–	...	–	...	–	–	...	–	...
F Transfers to private non-profit institutions serving households	3145	1090	...	2055	...	3236	1012	...	2224	...
G Other transfers n.e.c.	...	...	...	...	...	...	...	...	...	...
H Transfers to rest of the world	1182	1182	...	–	...	1366	1366	...	–	...
Net saving	–1154	1821	...	–2975	...	3038	5343	...	–2305	...
Total current disbursements and net saving	92970	73802	...	41074	...	104570	81744	...	46191	...

Receipts

	1988 Total government	1988 Central government	1988 State or provincial government	1988 Local government	1988 Social security funds	1989 Total government	1989 Central government	1989 State or provincial government	1989 Local government	1989 Social security funds
1 Operating surplus	–	–	...	–	...	–	–	...	–	...
2 Property and entrepreneurial income	11144	4914	...	8704	...	12947	4713	...	10775	...
A Withdrawals from public quasi-corporations	1605	721	...	884	...	1880	865	...	1015	...
B Interest	8375	3762	...	7087	...	9846	3535	...	8787	...
C Dividends	7	5	...	2	...	17	15	...	2	...
D Net land rent and royalties	1157	426	...	731	...	1204	299	...	971	...
3 Taxes, fees and contributions	106384	84186	...	22198	...	115693	91542	...	24151	...
A Indirect taxes	45817	25417	...	20400	...	49056	26975	...	22081	...
B Direct taxes	58541	58541	...	...	...	64303	64303	...	...	...
Income	58541	58541	...	...	...	64303	64303	...	...	...
Other	...	...	...	...	...	...	...	...	...	...
C Social security contributions	...	...	...	...	...	...	...	...	...	...
D Fees, fines and penalties	2026	228	...	1798	...	2334	264	...	2070	...
4 Other current transfers	–	15	...	21192	...	–	30	...	22885	...
A Casualty insurance claims	...	...	...	...	...	...	...	...	...	...
B Transfers from other government subsectors	–	15	...	21192	...	–	30	...	22885	...
C Transfers from rest of the world	...	...	...	...	...	...	...	...	...	...

Australia

	1988					1989				
	Total govern-ment	Central govern-ment	State or provincial govern-ment	Local govern-ment	Social security funds	Total govern-ment	Central govern-ment	State or provincial govern-ment	Local govern-ment	Social security funds
D Other transfers, except imputed	–	...	...	–	...	–	...	...	–	...
E Imputed unfunded employee pension and welfare contributions	...	...	...	...	...	...	...	...	...	...
Total current receipts	117528	89115	...	52094	...	128640	96285	...	57811	...

Disbursements

1 Government final consumption expenditure	56662	18378	...	38284	...	61482	19125	...	42357	...
2 Property income	13999	7465	...	9008	...	16737	7361	...	11917	...
A Interest	13999	7465	...	9008	...	16737	7361	...	11917	...
B Net land rent and royalties	–	...	...	...	...	–	...	...	...	...
3 Subsidies	4616	1776	...	2840	...	4638	1911	...	2727	...
4 Other current transfers	34373	52061	...	3519	...	37988	56832	...	4071	...
A Casualty insurance premiums, net	...	...	...	...	...	...	...	...	...	...
B Transfers to other government subsectors	...	21192	...	15	...	...	22885	...	30	...
C Social security benefits	...	...	...	...	...	...	...	...	...	...
D Social assistance grants	29328	28272	...	1056	...	32370	31148	...	1222	...
E Unfunded employee welfare benefits	–	–	...	–	...	–	–	...	–	...
F Transfers to private non-profit institutions serving households	3632	1184	...	2448	...	4035	1216	...	2819	...
G Other transfers n.e.c.	...	...	...	...	...	...	...	...	...	...
H Transfers to rest of the world	1413	1413	...	–	...	1583	1583	...	–	...
Net saving	7878	9435	...	–1557	...	7795	11056	...	–3261	...
Total current disbursements and net saving	117528	89115	...	52094	...	128640	96285	...	57811	...

	1990					1991				
	Total govern-ment	Central govern-ment	State or provincial govern-ment	Local govern-ment	Social security funds	Total govern-ment	Central govern-ment	State or provincial govern-ment	Local govern-ment	Social security funds

Receipts

1 Operating surplus	–	–	...	–	...	–	–	...	–	...
2 Property and entrepreneurial income	14033	4928	...	11580	...	14520	5609	...	11137	...
A Withdrawals from public quasi-corporations	2521	1145	...	1376	...	4303	2422	...	1881	...
B Interest	10062	3380	...	9069	...	8985	3038	...	8099	...
C Dividends	18	15	...	3	...	17	13	...	4	...
D Net land rent and royalties	1432	389	...	1132	...	1215	137	...	1153	...
3 Taxes, fees and contributions	119478	93629	...	25849	...	116104	88394	...	27710	...
A Indirect taxes	50410	26731	...	23679	...	50188	25097	...	25091	...
B Direct taxes	66666	66666	...	...	...	63058	63058	...	...	...
Income	66666	66666	...	...	...	63058	63058	...	...	...
Other	...	...	...	...	...	...	...	...	...	...
C Social security contributions	...	...	...	...	...	...	...	...	...	...
D Fees, fines and penalties	2402	232	...	2170	...	2858	239	...	2619	...
4 Other current transfers	–	55	...	24195	...	–	42	...	25856	...

Australia

	1990					1991				
	Total govern-ment	Central govern-ment	State or provincial govern-ment	Local govern-ment	Social security funds	Total govern-ment	Central govern-ment	State or provincial govern-ment	Local govern-ment	Social security funds
A Casualty insurance claims..	...	...	...	...	...	...	...	...	...	...
B Transfers from other government subsectors	–	55	...	24195	...	–	42	...	25856	...
C Transfers from rest of the world	...	...	...	...	...	...	...	...	...	...
D Other transfers, except imputed	–	...	...	–	...	–	...	...	–	...
E Imputed unfunded employee pension and welfare contributions	...	...	...	...	...	...	...	...	...	...
Total current receipts	133511	98612	...	61624	...	130624	94045	...	64703	...

Disbursements

1 Government final consumption expenditure	66602	20783	...	45819	...	71598	22536	...	49062	...
2 Property income	16320	6189	...	12606	...	15379	5748	...	11857	...
A Interest	16320	6189	...	12606	...	15379	5748	...	11857	...
B Net land rent and royalties ..	–	...	...	...	...	–	...	...	...	...
3 Subsidies	5770	2833	...	2937	...	6005	2479	...	3526	...
4 Other current transfers	43160	62885	...	4525	...	48955	69860	...	4993	...
A Casualty insurance premiums, net	...	...	...	...	...	...	...	...	...	...
B Transfers to other government subsectors	...	24195	...	55	...	...	25856	...	42	...
C Social security benefits	...	...	...	...	...	...	...	...	...	...
D Social assistance grants	37262	35924	...	1338	...	42351	40927	...	1424	...
E Unfunded employee welfare benefits	–	–	...	–	...	–	–	...	–	...
F Transfers to private non-profit institutions serving households	4339	1207	...	3132	...	5103	1576	...	3527	...
G Other transfers n.e.c.	...	...	...	...	...	...	...	...	...	...
H Transfers to rest of the world	1559	1559	...	–	...	1501	1501	...	–	...
Net saving	1659	5922	...	–4263	...	–11313	–6578	...	–4735	...
Total current disbursements and net saving	133511	98612	...	61624	...	130624	94045	...	64703	...

	1992					1993				
	Total govern-ment	Central govern-ment	State or provincial govern-ment	Local govern-ment	Social security funds	Total govern-ment	Central govern-ment	State or provincial govern-ment	Local govern-ment	Social security funds

Receipts

1 Operating surplus	–	–	...	–	...	–	–	...	–	...
2 Property and entrepreneurial income	14018	5682	...	10303	...	16012	6770	...	10861	...
A Withdrawals from public quasi-corporations	4939	3009	...	1930	...	7243	4463	...	2780	...
B Interest	7816	2535	...	7183	...	7458	2117	...	6897	...
C Dividends	36	27	...	9	...	29	23	...	6	...
D Net land rent and royalties ..	1227	111	...	1181	...	1282	166	...	1178	...
3 Taxes, fees and contributions .	119198	89693	...	29505	...	127016	94549	...	32467	...
A Indirect taxes	51895	25233	...	26662	...	57198	27920	...	29278	...
B Direct taxes	64239	64239	...	...	...	66383	66383	...	...	...
Income	64239	64239	...	...	...	66383	66382	...	...	...
Other	...	...	...	...	...	...	...	...	...	...

Australia

	1992					1993				
	Total government	Central government	State or provincial government	Local government	Social security funds	Total government	Central government	State or provincial government	Local government	Social security funds
C Social security contributions	...	...	...	...	...	...	...	...	...	...
D Fees, fines and penalties	3064	221	...	2843	...	3435	246	...	3189	...
4 Other current transfers	–	41	...	27049	...	–	44	...	28467	...
A Casualty insurance claims	...	...	...	...	...	...	...	...	...	...
B Transfers from other government subsectors	–	41	...	27049	...	–	44	...	28467	...
C Transfers from rest of the world	...	...	...	...	...	...	...	...	...	...
D Other transfers, except imputed	–	...	...	–	...	–	...	...	–	...
E Imputed unfunded employee pension and welfare contributions	...	...	...	...	...	...	...	...	...	...
Total current receipts	133216	95416	...	66857	...	143028	101363	...	71795	...

Disbursements

1 Government final consumption expenditure	74492	23826	...	50666	...	76838	24784	...	52054	...
2 Property income	14863	5413	...	11417	...	16177	6630	...	11166	...
A Interest	14863	5413	...	11417	...	16177	6630	...	11166	...
B Net land rent and royalties	–	...	...	...	...	–	...	...	...	...
3 Subsidies	6356	2499	...	3857	...	6481	2742	...	3739	...
4 Other current transfers	53396	75045	...	5441	...	57866	80344	...	6033	...
A Casualty insurance premiums, net	...	...	...	...	...	...	...	...	...	...
B Transfers to other government subsectors	...	27049	...	41	...	...	28467	...	44	...
C Social security benefits	...	...	...	...	...	...	...	...	...	...
D Social assistance grants	46076	44535	...	1541	...	49667	48078	...	1589	...
E Unfunded employee welfare benefits	–	–	...	–	...	–	–	...	–	...
F Transfers to private non-profit institutions serving households	5760	1901	...	3859	...	6411	2011	...	4400	...
G Other transfers n.e.c.	...	...	...	...	...	...	...	...	...	...
H Transfers to rest of the world	1560	1560	...	–	...	1788	1788	...	–	...
Net saving	–15891	–11367	...	–4524	...	–14334	–13137	...	–1197	...
Total current disbursements and net saving	133216	95416	...	66857	...	143028	101363	...	71795	...

	1994					1995				
	Total government	Central government	State or provincial government	Local government	Social security funds	Total government	Central government	State or provincial government	Local government	Social security funds

Receipts

1 Operating surplus	–	–	...	–	...	–	–	...	–	...
2 Property and entrepreneurial income	15253	4763	...	12007	...	16546	5386	...	12381	...
A Withdrawals from public quasi-corporations	5529	2634	...	2895	...	7219	3572	...	3647	...
B Interest	8251	1880	...	7831	...	7704	1497	...	7382	...
C Dividends	119	19	...	100	...	111	26	...	85	...
D Net land rent and royalties	1354	230	...	1181	...	1512	291	...	1267	...
3 Taxes, fees and contributions	139998	106037	...	33961	...	153345	116888	...	36457	...

Australia

	1994					1995				
	Total govern-ment	Central govern-ment	State or provincial govern-ment	Local govern-ment	Social security funds	Total govern-ment	Central govern-ment	State or provincial govern-ment	Local govern-ment	Social security funds
A Indirect taxes	62403	31835	...	30568	...	66806	33956	...	32850	...
B Direct taxes	73888	73888	...	...	...	82590	82590	...	...	...
Income	73888	73888	...	...	...	82590	82590	...	...	...
Other	...	...	...	...	...	...	...	...	...	...
C Social security contributions	...	...	...	...	...	...	...	...	...	...
D Fees, fines and penalties	3707	314	...	3393	...	3949	342	...	3607	...
4 Other current transfers	–	63	...	30207	...	–	92	...	31702	...
A Casualty insurance claims	...	...	...	...	...	...	...	...	...	...
B Transfers from other government subsectors	–	63	...	30207	...	–	92	...	31702	...
C Transfers from rest of the world	...	...	...	...	...	...	...	...	...	...
D Other transfers, except imputed	...	...	...	–	...	–	...	...	–	...
E Imputed unfunded employee pension and welfare contributions	...	...	...	...	...	...	...	...	...	...
Total current receipts	155251	110863	...	76175	...	169891	122366	...	80540	...

Disbursements

1 Government final consumption expenditure	79341	25505	...	53836	...	83437	26296	...	57141	...
2 Property income	18036	8164	...	11389	...	18458	9293	...	10386	...
A Interest	18036	8164	...	11389	...	18458	9293	...	10386	...
B Net land rent and royalties	–	...	...	...	...	–	...	...	...	...
3 Subsidies	6233	2774	...	3459	...	6167	2982	...	3185	...
4 Other current transfers	60851	84534	...	6587	...	65522	90269	...	7047	...
A Casualty insurance premiums, net	...	...	...	...	...	...	...	...	...	...
B Transfers to other government subsectors	...	30207	...	63	...	...	31702	...	92	...
C Social security benefits	...	...	...	...	...	...	...	...	...	...
D Social assistance grants	51820	50054	...	1766	...	55705	53864	...	1841	...
E Unfunded employee welfare benefits	–	–	...	–	...	–	–	...	–	...
F Transfers to private non-profit institutions serving households	7235	2477	...	4758	...	8209	3095	...	5114	...
G Other transfers n.e.c.	...	...	...	...	...	...	...	...	...	...
H Transfers to rest of the world	1796	1796	...	–	...	1608	1608	...	–	...
Net saving	–9210	–10114	...	904	...	–3693	–6474	...	2781	...
Total current disbursements and net saving	155251	110863	...	76175	...	169891	122366	...	80540	...

	1996					1997				
	Total govern-ment	Central govern-ment	State or provincial govern-ment	Local govern-ment	Social security funds	Total govern-ment	Central govern-ment	State or provincial govern-ment	Local govern-ment	Social security funds

Receipts

1 Operating surplus	–	–	...	–	...	...	...	...	...	...
2 Property and entrepreneurial income	18189	5221	...	13853	...	...	...	...	...	...
A Withdrawals from public quasi-corporations	9192	3645	...	5547	...	...	...	...	...	...

Australia

	1996					1997				
	Total government	Central government	State or provincial government	Local government	Social security funds	Total government	Central government	State or provincial government	Local government	Social security funds
B Interest	7308	1168	...	6970	...	...	...	...	...	...
C Dividends	36	19	...	17	...	...	...	...	...	...
D Net land rent and royalties	1653	388	...	1319	...	...	...	...	...	...
3 Taxes, fees and contributions	164690	125962	...	38728	...	...	...	...	...	...
A Indirect taxes	70369	35143	...	35226	...	...	...	...	...	...
B Direct taxes	90425	90425	...	...	...	...	...	...	...	...
Income	90425	90425	...	...	...	...	...	...	...	...
Other	...	...	...	...	...	...	...	...	...	...
C Social security contributions	...	...	...	...	...	...	...	...	...	...
D Fees, fines and penalties	3896	394	...	3502	...	...	...	...	...	...
4 Other current transfers	–	101	...	32574	...	...	...	...	...	...
A Casualty insurance claims	...	...	...	...	...	...	...	...	...	...
B Transfers from other government subsectors	–	101	...	32574	...	...	...	...	...	...
C Transfers from rest of the world	...	...	...	...	...	...	...	...	...	...
D Other transfers, except imputed	–	...	...	–	...	...	...	...	...	...
E Imputed unfunded employee pension and welfare contributions	...	...	...	...	...	...	...	...	...	...
Total current receipts	182879	131284	...	85155	...	...	...	...	...	...

Disbursements

	Total government	Central government	State or provincial government	Local government	Social security funds	Total government	Central government	State or provincial government	Local government	Social security funds
1 Government final consumption expenditure	86419	25909	...	60510	...	...	...	...	...	...
2 Property income	17428	9626	...	8687	...	...	...	...	...	...
A Interest	17428	9626	...	8687	...	...	...	...	...	...
B Net land rent and royalties	–	...	...	...	...	...	...	...	...	...
3 Subsidies	7061	3156	...	3905	...	...	...	...	...	...
4 Other current transfers	68574	93619	...	7630	...	...	...	...	...	...
A Casualty insurance premiums, net	...	...	...	...	...	...	...	...	...	...
B Transfers to other government subsectors	...	32574	...	101	...	...	...	...	...	...
C Social security benefits	...	...	...	...	...	...	...	...	...	...
D Social assistance grants	58566	56671	...	1895	...	...	...	...	...	...
E Unfunded employee welfare benefits	...	–	...	–	...	...	...	...	...	...
F Transfers to private non-profit institutions serving households	8585	2951	...	5634	...	...	...	...	...	...
G Other transfers n.e.c.	...	...	...	...	...	...	...	...	...	...
H Transfers to rest of the world	1423	1423	...	–	...	...	...	...	...	...
Net saving	3397	–1026	...	4423	...	...	...	...	...	...
Total current disbursements and net saving	182879	131284	...	85155	...	...	...	...	...	...

Australia

3.13 General government capital accumulation account: total and subsectors

Million Australian dollars — Fiscal year beginning 1 July

	1986					1987				
	Total govern-ment	Central govern-ment	State or provincial govern-ment	Local govern-ment	Social security funds	Total govern-ment	Central govern-ment	State or provincial govern-ment	Local govern-ment	Social security funds

Finance of gross accumulation

1 Gross saving	4341	2412	...	1929	...	8821	5978	...	2843	...
A Consumption of fixed capital	5495	591	...	4904	...	5783	635	...	5148	...
B Net saving	−1154	1821	...	−2975	...	3038	5343	...	−2305	...
2 Capital transfers	299	—	...	3599	...	234	1	...	3322	...
A From other government subsectors	125	...	...	3425	...	21	...	...	3110	...
B From other resident sectors	174	—	...	174	...	213	1	...	212	...
C From rest of the world	...	...	...	...	...	...	...	...	...	...
Finance of gross accumulation	4640	2412	...	5528	...	9055	5979	...	6165	...

Gross accumulation

1 Gross capital formation	7623	1152	...	6471	...	7455	1189	...	6266	...
A Increase in stocks	−46	−35	...	−11	...	1	1	...	—	...
B Gross fixed capital formation	7669	1187	...	6482	...	7454	1188	...	6266	...
2 Purchases of land, net	−135	−85	...	−50	...	−541	−393	...	−148	...
3 Purchases of intangible assets, net	...	...	...	...	...	...	...	...	...	...
4 Capital transfers	1271	3659	...	912	...	1462	3492	...	1059	...
A To other government subsectors	790	3308	...	782	...	849	3100	...	838	...
B To other resident sectors	481	351	...	130	...	613	392	...	221	...
C To the rest of the world	...	...	...	...	...	...	...	...	...	...
Net lending	−4119	−2314	...	−1805	...	679	1691	...	−1012	...
Gross accumulation	4640	2412	...	5528	...	9055	5979	...	6165	...

	1988					1989				
	Total govern-ment	Central govern-ment	State or provincial govern-ment	Local govern-ment	Social security funds	Total govern-ment	Central govern-ment	State or provincial govern-ment	Local govern-ment	Social security funds

Finance of gross accumulation

1 Gross saving	13997	10128	...	3869	...	14380	11707	...	2673	...
A Consumption of fixed capital	6119	693	...	5426	...	6585	651	...	5934	...
B Net saving	7878	9435	...	−1557	...	7795	11056	...	−3261	...
2 Capital transfers	229	1	...	3321	...	345	24	...	3877	...
A From other government subsectors	27	...	...	3120	...	17	...	...	3573	...
B From other resident sectors	202	1	...	201	...	328	24	...	304	...
C From rest of the world	...	...	...	...	...	...	...	...	...	...
Finance of gross accumulation	14226	10129	...	7190	...	14725	11731	...	6550	...

Gross accumulation

1 Gross capital formation	7450	1011	...	6439	...	8703	1378	...	7325	...
A Increase in stocks	−34	−19	...	−15	...	65	7	...	58	...
B Gross fixed capital formation	7484	1030	...	6454	...	8638	1371	...	7267	...

Australia

	1988					1989				
	Total government	Central government	State or provincial government	Local government	Social security funds	Total government	Central government	State or provincial government	Local government	Social security funds
2 Purchases of land, net	–469	–72	...	–397	...	26	86	...	–60	...
3 Purchases of intangible assets, net	...	...	...	...	...	...	...	...	...	...
4 Capital transfers	1649	3532	...	1210	...	2125	3946	...	1735	...
A To other government subsectors	907	3118	...	882	...	1468	3570	...	1454	...
B To other resident sectors	742	414	...	328	...	657	376	...	281	...
C To the rest of the world	...	...	...	...	...	...	...	...	...	...
Net lending	5596	5658	...	–62	...	3871	6321	...	–2450	...
Gross accumulation	14226	10129	...	7190	...	14725	11731	...	6550	...

	1990					1991				
	Total government	Central government	State or provincial government	Local government	Social security funds	Total government	Central government	State or provincial government	Local government	Social security funds

Finance of gross accumulation

1 Gross saving	8642	6619	...	2023	...	–4100	–5858	...	1758	...
A Consumption of fixed capital	6983	697	...	6286	...	7213	720	...	6493	...
B Net saving	1659	5922	...	–4263	...	–11313	–6578	...	–4735	...
2 Capital transfers	191	2	...	4546	...	172	–	...	3893	...
A From other government subsectors	15	...	...	4372	...	–	...	...	3721	...
B From other resident sectors	176	2	...	174	...	172	–	...	172	...
C From rest of the world	...	...	...	...	...	...	...	...	...	...
Finance of gross accumulation	8833	6621	...	6569	...	–3928	–5858	...	5651	...

Gross accumulation

1 Gross capital formation	8947	1346	...	7601	...	8975	1555	...	7420	...
A Increase in stocks	74	3	...	71	...	36	–15	...	51	...
B Gross fixed capital formation	8873	1343	...	7530	...	8939	1570	...	7369	...
2 Purchases of land, net	–106	–44	...	–62	...	–68	46	...	–114	...
3 Purchases of intangible assets, net	...	...	...	...	...	...	...	...	...	...
4 Capital transfers	2448	4854	...	1951	...	2811	4346	...	2186	...
A To other government subsectors	1974	4601	...	1730	...	2152	4047	...	1826	...
B To other resident sectors	474	253	...	221	...	659	299	...	360	...
C To the rest of the world	...	...	...	...	...	...	...	...	...	...
Net lending	–2456	465	...	–2921	...	–15646	–11805	...	–3841	...
Gross accumulation	8833	6621	...	6569	...	–3928	–5858	...	5651	...

	1992					1993				
	Total government	Central government	State or provincial government	Local government	Social security funds	Total government	Central government	State or provincial government	Local government	Social security funds

Finance of gross accumulation

1 Gross saving	–8474	–10612	...	2138	...	–6746	–12379	...	5633	...
A Consumption of fixed capital	7417	755	...	6662	...	7588	758	...	6830	...
B Net saving	–15891	–11367	...	–4524	...	–14334	–13137	...	–1197	...
2 Capital transfers	190	1	...	5418	...	318	7	...	4100	...

Australia

	1992					1993				
	Total govern-ment	Central govern-ment	State or provincial govern-ment	Local govern-ment	Social security funds	Total govern-ment	Central govern-ment	State or provincial govern-ment	Local govern-ment	Social security funds
A From other government subsectors	45	...	...	5274	...	54	...	...	3843	...
B From other resident sectors	145	1	...	144	...	264	7	...	257	...
C From rest of the world	...	...	...	...	...	...	...	...	...	...
Finance of gross accumulation	−8284	−10611	...	7556	...	−6428	−12372	...	9733	...
Gross accumulation										
1 Gross capital formation	9490	1064	...	8426	...	9164	934	...	8230	...
A Increase in stocks	55	6	...	49	...	84	−22	...	106	...
B Gross fixed capital formation	9435	1058	...	8377	...	9080	956	...	8124	...
2 Purchases of land, net	−292	−15	...	−277	...	−568	−201	...	−367	...
3 Purchases of intangible assets, net	...	...	...	...	...	...	...	...	...	...
4 Capital transfers	2666	5571	...	2324	...	2750	4033	...	2506	...
A To other government subsectors	2081	5318	...	1992	...	2279	3832	...	2236	...
B To other resident sectors	585	253	...	332	...	471	201	...	270	...
C To the rest of the world	...	...	...	...	...	...	...	...	...	...
Net lending	−20148	−17231	...	−2917	...	−17774	−17138	...	−636	...
Gross accumulation	−8284	−10611	...	7556	...	−6428	−12372	...	9733	...

	1994					1995				
	Total govern-ment	Central govern-ment	State or provincial govern-ment	Local govern-ment	Social security funds	Total govern-ment	Central govern-ment	State or provincial govern-ment	Local govern-ment	Social security funds
Finance of gross accumulation										
1 Gross saving	−1450	−9337	...	7887	...	4360	−5684	...	10044	...
A Consumption of fixed capital	7760	777	...	6983	...	8053	790	...	7263	...
B Net saving	−9210	−10114	...	904	...	−3693	−6474	...	2781	...
2 Capital transfers	280	−	...	3388	...	527	−	...	3556	...
A From other government subsectors	27	...	...	3135	...	9	...	...	3038	...
B From other resident sectors	253	−	...	253	...	518	−	...	518	...
C From rest of the world	...	...	...	...	...	...	...	...	...	...
Finance of gross accumulation	−1170	−9337	...	11275	...	4887	−5684	...	13600	...
Gross accumulation										
1 Gross capital formation	9563	782	...	8781	...	9643	963	...	8680	...
A Increase in stocks	101	−36	...	137	...	136	4	...	132	...
B Gross fixed capital formation	9462	818	...	8644	...	9507	959	...	8548	...
2 Purchases of land, net	−438	−80	...	−358	...	−237	−30	...	−207	...
3 Purchases of intangible assets, net	...	...	...	...	...	...	...	...	...	...
4 Capital transfers	2556	3394	...	2270	...	2482	3199	...	2312	...
A To other government subsectors	2097	3229	...	1976	...	1984	3048	...	1965	...
B To other resident sectors	459	165	...	294	...	498	151	...	347	...
C To the rest of the world	...	...	...	...	...	...	...	...	...	...
Net lending	−12851	−13433	...	582	...	−7001	−9816	...	2815	...
Gross accumulation	−1170	−9337	...	11275	...	4887	−5684	...	13600	...

Australia

	1996					1997				
	Total government	Central government	State or provincial government	Local government	Social security funds	Total government	Central government	State or provincial government	Local government	Social security funds

Finance of gross accumulation

1 Gross saving	11704	−220	...	11924	...	...	...	...	...	...
A Consumption of fixed capital	8307	806	...	7501	...	...	...	...	...	...
B Net saving	3397	−1026	...	4423	...	...	...	...	...	...
2 Capital transfers	591	—	...	3084	...	...	...	...	...	...
A From other government subsectors	49	...	...	2542	...	...	...	...	...	...
B From other resident sectors	542	—	...	542	...	...	...	...	...	...
C From rest of the world	...	...	...	...	...	...	...	...	...	...
Finance of gross accumulation	12295	−220	...	15008	...	...	...	...	...	...

Gross accumulation

1 Gross capital formation	9552	679	...	8873	...	...	...	...	...	...
A Increase in stocks	−393	−11	...	−382	...	...	...	...	...	...
B Gross fixed capital formation	9945	690	...	9255	...	...	...	...	...	...
2 Purchases of land, net	20	40	...	−20	...	...	...	...	...	...
3 Purchases of intangible assets, net	...	...	...	...	...	...	...	...	...	...
4 Capital transfers	3117	3552	...	2058	...	...	...	...	...	...
A To other government subsectors	2557	3398	...	1652	...	...	...	...	...	...
B To other resident sectors	560	154	...	406	...	...	...	...	...	...
C To the rest of the world	...	...	...	...	...	...	...	...	...	...
Net lending	−394	−4491	...	4097	...	...	...	...	...	...
Gross accumulation	12295	−220	...	15008	...	...	...	...	...	...

3.14 General government capital finance account: total and subsectors

Million Australian dollars   *Fiscal year beginning 1 July*

	1988					1989				
	Total government	Central government	State or provincial government	Local government	Social security funds	Total government	Central government	State or provincial government	Local government	Social security funds

Acquisition of financial assets

1 Gold and SDRs	...	...	...	...	...	...	...	...	...	...
2 Currency and transferable deposits	−832	...	...	...	...	961	...	...	...	...
3 Other deposits	...	...	...	...	...	...	...	...	...	...
4 Bills and bonds, short-term	−3108	...	...	...	...	−1496	...	...	...	...
A Corporate and quasi-corporate enterprises, resident	−3101	...	...	...	...	−1415	...	...	...	...
B Other government subsectors	−7	...	...	...	...	−81	...	...	...	...
C Rest of the world	...	...	...	...	...	...	...	...	...	...
5 Bonds, long-term	926	...	...	...	...	1815	...	...	...	...
A Corporations	864	...	...	...	...	1667	...	...	...	...
B Other government subsectors	62	...	...	...	...	148	...	...	...	...
C Rest of the world	...	...	...	...	...	...	...	...	...	...

Australia

Million Australian dollars   **Fiscal year beginning 1 July**

	1988					1989				
	Total government	Central government	State or provincial government	Local government	Social security funds	Total government	Central government	State or provincial government	Local government	Social security funds
6 Corporate equity securities	49	...	...	...	...	267	...	...	...	...
7 Short-term loans, n.e.c.	...	...	...	...	...	...	...	...	...	...
8 Long-term loans, n.e.c.	6833	...	...	...	...	1260	...	...	...	...
9 Other receivables	...	...	...	...	...	...	...	...	...	...
10 Other assets	1857	...	...	...	...	836	...	...	...	...
Total aquisition of financial assets	5725	...	...	...	...	3643	...	...	...	...

Incurrence of liabilities

1 Currency and transferable deposits	...	...	...	...	...	...	...	...	...	...
2 Other deposits	28	...	...	...	...	38	...	...	...	...
3 Bills and bonds, short-term	−5516	...	...	...	...	−192	...	...	...	...
4 Bonds, long-term	16	...	...	...	...	98	...	...	...	...
5 Short-term loans, n.e.c.	471	...	...	...	...	460	...	...	...	...
6 Long-term loans, n.e.c.	...	...	...	...	...	...	...	...	...	...
7 Other payables	...	...	...	...	...	...	...	...	...	...
8 Other liabilities	1694	...	...	...	...	499	...	...	...	...
Total incurrence of liabilities	−3307	...	...	...	...	903	...	...	...	...
Statistical discrepancy	3435	...	...	...	...	−1131	...	...	...	...
Net lending	5597	...	...	...	...	3871	...	...	...	...
Incurrence of liabilities and net worth	5725	...	...	...	...	3643	...	...	...	...

	1990					1991				
	Total government	Central government	State or provincial government	Local government	Social security funds	Total government	Central government	State or provincial government	Local government	Social security funds

Acquisition of financial assets

1 Gold and SDRs	...	...	...	...	...	...	...	...	...	...
2 Currency and transferable deposits	−912	...	...	...	...	−1086	...	...	...	...
3 Other deposits	...	...	...	...	...	...	...	...	...	...
4 Bills and bonds, short-term	677	...	...	...	...	−29	...	...	...	...
A Corporate and quasi-corporate enterprises, resident	659	...	...	...	...	−56	...	...	...	...
B Other government subsectors	18	...	...	...	...	27	...	...	...	...
C Rest of the world	...	...	...	...	...	...	...	...	...	...
5 Bonds, long-term	−495	...	...	...	...	−643	...	...	...	...
A Corporations	−431	...	...	...	...	−415	...	...	...	...
B Other government subsectors	−64	...	...	...	...	−228	...	...	...	...
C Rest of the world	...	...	...	...	...	...	...	...	...	...
6 Corporate equity securities	523	...	...	...	...	−2013	...	...	...	...
7 Short-term loans, n.e.c.	...	...	...	...	...	...	...	...	...	...
8 Long-term loans, n.e.c.	5184	...	...	...	...	3566	...	...	...	...
9 Other receivables	...	...	...	...	...	...	...	...	...	...
10 Other assets	1060	...	...	...	...	−742	...	...	...	...
Total aquisition of financial assets	6037	...	...	...	...	−947	...	...	...	...

Incurrence of liabilities

Australia

	1990					1991				
	Total govern-ment	Central govern-ment	State or provincial govern-ment	Local govern-ment	Social security funds	Total govern-ment	Central govern-ment	State or provincial govern-ment	Local govern-ment	Social security funds
1 Currency and transferable deposits	...	...	...	...	...	...	...	...	...	...
2 Other deposits	14	...	...	...	...	20	...	...	...	...
3 Bills and bonds, short-term	6082	...	...	...	...	7066	...	...	...	...
4 Bonds, long-term	1922	...	...	...	...	8204	...	...	...	...
5 Short-term loans, n.e.c.	−1829	...	...	...	...	−3034	...	...	...	...
6 Long-term loans, n.e.c.	...	...	...	...	...	...	...	...	...	...
7 Other payables	...	...	...	...	...	...	...	...	...	...
8 Other liabilities	484	...	...	...	...	271	...	...	...	...
Total incurrence of liabilities	6673	...	...	...	...	12527	...	...	...	...
Statistical discrepancy	1820	...	...	...	...	2172	...	...	...	...
Net lending	−2456	...	...	...	...	−15646	...	...	...	...
Incurrence of liabilities and net worth	6037	...	...	...	...	−947	...	...	...	...

	1992					1993				
	Total govern-ment	Central govern-ment	State or provincial govern-ment	Local govern-ment	Social security funds	Total govern-ment	Central govern-ment	State or provincial govern-ment	Local govern-ment	Social security funds

Acquisition of financial assets

1 Gold and SDRs	...	...	...	...	...	...	...	...	...	...
2 Currency and transferable deposits	2553	...	...	...	...	−1109	...	...	...	...
3 Other deposits	...	...	...	...	...	...	...	...	...	...
4 Bills and bonds, short-term	1160	...	...	...	...	2012	...	...	...	...
A Corporate and quasi-corporate enterprises, resident	1142	...	...	...	...	1867	...	...	...	...
B Other government subsectors	18	...	...	...	...	145	...	...	...	...
C Rest of the world	...	...	...	...	...	...	...	...	...	...
5 Bonds, long-term	1481	...	...	...	...	−113	...	...	...	...
A Corporations	1485	...	...	...	...	−607	...	...	...	...
B Other government subsectors	−4	...	...	...	...	494	...	...	...	...
C Rest of the world	...	...	...	...	...	...	...	...	...	...
6 Corporate equity securities	−1440	...	...	...	...	−2864	...	...	...	...
7 Short-term loans, n.e.c.	...	...	...	...	...	...	...	...	...	...
8 Long-term loans, n.e.c.	−703	...	...	...	...	−2193	...	...	...	...
9 Other receivables	...	...	...	...	...	...	...	...	...	...
10 Other assets	−285	...	...	...	...	49	...	...	...	...
Total aquisition of financial assets	2766	...	...	...	...	−4218	...	...	...	...

Incurrence of liabilities

1 Currency and transferable deposits	...	...	...	...	...	...	...	...	...	...
2 Other deposits	28	...	...	...	...	52	...	...	...	...
3 Bills and bonds, short-term	4574	...	...	...	...	−560	...	...	...	...
4 Bonds, long-term	14979	...	...	...	...	20265	...	...	...	...
5 Short-term loans, n.e.c.	−130	...	...	...	...	364	...	...	...	...
6 Long-term loans, n.e.c.	...	...	...	...	...	...	...	...	...	...
7 Other payables	...	...	...	...	...	...	...	...	...	...
8 Other liabilities	−570	...	...	...	...	−74	...	...	...	...

Australia

	1992					1993				
	Total govern-ment	Central govern-ment	State or provincial govern-ment	Local govern-ment	Social security funds	Total govern-ment	Central govern-ment	State or provincial govern-ment	Local govern-ment	Social security funds
Total incurrence of liabilities	18881	...	...	...	...	20047	...	...	...	...
Statistical discrepancy	4033	...	...	...	...	−6491	...	...	...	...
Net lending	−20148	...	...	...	...	−17774	...	...	...	...
Incurrence of liabilities and net worth	2766	...	...	...	...	−4218	...	...	...	...

	1994					1995				
	Total govern-ment	Central govern-ment	State or provincial govern-ment	Local govern-ment	Social security funds	Total govern-ment	Central govern-ment	State or provincial govern-ment	Local govern-ment	Social security funds
Acquisition of financial assets										
1 Gold and SDRs	...	...	...	...	...	...	...	...	...	...
2 Currency and transferable deposits	1953	...	...	...	...	−2112	...	...	...	...
3 Other deposits	...	...	...	...	...	...	...	...	...	...
4 Bills and bonds, short-term	1298	...	...	...	...	−299	...	...	...	...
5 Bonds, long-term	−1340	...	...	...	...	−1737	...	...	...	...
A Corporations	−844	...	...	...	...	−1737	...	...	...	...
B Other government subsec-tors	−496	...	...	...	...	−	...	...	...	...
C Rest of the world	...	...	...	...	...	...	...	...	...	...
6 Corporate equity securities	−956	...	...	...	...	−14316	...	...	...	...
7 Short-term loans, n.e.c.	...	...	...	...	...	...	...	...	...	...
8 Long-term loans, n.e.c.	1392	...	...	...	...	−4305	...	...	...	...
9 Other receivables	...	...	...	...	...	...	...	...	...	...
10 Other assets	1035	...	...	...	...	−1766	...	...	...	...
Total aquisition of financial assets	3382	...	...	...	...	−24535	...	...	...	...
Incurrence of liabilities										
1 Currency and transferable deposits	...	...	...	...	...	...	...	...	...	...
2 Other deposits	102	...	...	...	...	74	...	...	...	...
3 Bills and bonds, short-term	−1765	...	...	...	...	−6898	...	...	...	...
4 Bonds, long-term	18274	...	...	...	...	1370	...	...	...	...
5 Short-term loans, n.e.c.	−436	...	...	...	...	880	...	...	...	...
6 Long-term loans, n.e.c.	...	...	...	...	...	...	...	...	...	...
7 Other payables	...	...	...	...	...	...	...	...	...	...
8 Other liabilities	1677	...	...	...	...	−1923	...	...	...	...
Total incurrence of liabilities	17852	...	...	...	...	−6497	...	...	...	...
Statistical discrepancy	−1619	...	...	...	...	−11037	...	...	...	...
Net lending	−12851	...	...	...	...	−7001	...	...	...	...
Incurrence of liabilities and net worth	3382	...	...	...	...	−24535	...	...	...	...

	1996					1997				
	Total govern-ment	Central govern-ment	State or provincial govern-ment	Local govern-ment	Social security funds	Total govern-ment	Central govern-ment	State or provincial govern-ment	Local govern-ment	Social security funds
Acquisition of financial assets										
1 Gold and SDRs	...	...	...	...	...	...	...	...	...	...
2 Currency and transferable deposits	3175	...	...	...	...	...	...	...	...	...
3 Other deposits	...	...	...	...	...	...	...	...	...	...

Australia

	1996					1997				
	Total govern-ment	Central govern-ment	State or provincial govern-ment	Local govern-ment	Social security funds	Total govern-ment	Central govern-ment	State or provincial govern-ment	Local govern-ment	Social security funds
4 Bills and bonds, short-term	−480	...	...	...	...	...	...	...	...	...
5 Bonds, long-term	−336	...	...	...	...	...	...	...	...	...
A Corporations	−336	...	...	...	...	...	...	...	...	...
B Other government subsectors	−	...	...	...	...	...	...	...	...	...
C Rest of the world	...	...	...	...	...	...	...	...	...	...
6 Corporate equity securities	−10460	...	...	...	...	...	...	...	...	...
7 Short-term loans, n.e.c.	...	...	...	...	...	...	...	...	...	...
8 Long-term loans, n.e.c.	−407	...	...	...	...	...	...	...	...	...
9 Other receivables	...	...	...	...	...	...	...	...	...	...
10 Other assets	−119	...	...	...	...	...	...	...	...	...
Total aquisition of financial assets	−8627	...	...	...	...	...	...	...	...	...

Incurrence of liabilities

	1996					1997				
1 Currency and transferable deposits	...	...	...	...	...	...	...	...	...	...
2 Other deposits	64	...	...	...	...	...	...	...	...	...
3 Bills and bonds, short-term	−1429	...	...	...	...	...	...	...	...	...
4 Bonds, long-term	−2908	...	...	...	...	...	...	...	...	...
5 Short-term loans, n.e.c.	−103	...	...	...	...	...	...	...	...	...
6 Long-term loans, n.e.c.	...	...	...	...	...	...	...	...	...	...
7 Other payables	...	...	...	...	...	...	...	...	...	...
8 Other liabilities	−951	...	...	...	...	...	...	...	...	...
Total incurrence of liabilities	−5327	...	...	...	...	...	...	...	...	...
Statistical discrepancy	−2906	...	...	...	...	...	...	...	...	...
Net lending	−394	...	...	...	...	...	...	...	...	...
Incurrence of liabilities and net worth	−8627	...	...	...	...	...	...	...	...	...

3.22 Corporate and quasi-corporate enterprise income and outlay account: total and sectors

Million Australian dollars   Fiscal year beginning 1 July

	1986			1987			1988			1989		
	Total	Non-financial	Financial	Total	Non-financial	Financial	Total	Non-financial	Financial	Total	Non-financial	Financial

Receipts

1 Operating surplus	22186	29521	−7335	28747	36290	−7543	34784	42052	−7268	36035	45144	−9109
2 Property and entrepreneurial income	27142	8153	42811	28639	7962	46858	36412	10301	59331	44465	11717	71229
A Withdrawals from quasi-corporate enterprises	...	...	...	...	...	...	...	...	...	...	...	...
B Interest	26274	7107	41195	28099	7199	44894	35865	9337	56670	43710	10765	67678
C Dividends	607	745	1616	288	470	1964	325	700	2661	527	681	3551
D Net land rent and royalties	261	301	−	252	293	−	222	264	−	228	271	−
3 Current transfers	−	−	−	−	−	−	−	−	−	333	183	150
A Casualty insurance claims	−	−	−	−	−	−	−	−	−	−	−	−
B Casualty insurance premiums, net, due to be received by insurance companies	...	...	...	...	...	...	...	...	...	...	...	...
C Current transfers from rest of the world	−	−	−	−	−	−	−	−	−	333	183	150
D Other transfers except imputed	...	...	...	...	...	...	...	...	...	...	...	...

Australia

Million Australian dollars — Fiscal year beginning 1 July

	1986 Total	1986 Non-financial	1986 Financial	1987 Total	1987 Non-financial	1987 Financial	1988 Total	1988 Non-financial	1988 Financial	1989 Total	1989 Non-financial	1989 Financial
E Imputed unfunded employee pension and welfare contributions	...	...	...	...	...	...	...	...	...	...	...	...
Total current receipts	49328	37674	35476	57386	44252	39315	71196	52353	52063	80833	57044	62270

Disbursements

	1986 Total	1986 Non-financial	1986 Financial	1987 Total	1987 Non-financial	1987 Financial	1988 Total	1988 Non-financial	1988 Financial	1989 Total	1989 Non-financial	1989 Financial
1 Property and entrepreneurial income	42957	30914	35865	44340	34096	36425	55458	42541	46137	67399	50837	55043
A Withdrawals from quasi-corporations	3300	330	2970	2685	437	2248	1605	516	1089	1880	912	968
Public	3300	330	2970	2685	437	2248	1605	516	1089	1880	912	968
Private	...	...	...	...	...	...	...	...	...	...	...	...
B Interest	34815	24789	32056	35875	26782	33027	46321	33336	42893	56410	38517	52603
C Dividends	3064	3977	841	3622	4678	1090	5451	6566	1921	6591	8847	1449
D Net land rent and royalties	1778	1818	−2	2158	2199	60	2081	2123	234	2518	2561	23
2 Direct taxes and other current transfers n.e.c. to general government	6646	5613	1033	8737	7076	1661	10211	8063	2148	13264	10341	2923
A Direct taxes	6646	5613	1033	8737	7076	1661	10211	8063	2148	13264	10341	2923
On income	6646	5613	1033	8737	7076	1661	10211	8063	2148	13264	10341	2923
Other	...	...	...	...	...	...	...	...	...	...	...	...
B Fines, fees, penalties and other current transfers n.e.c.	−	−	...	−	−	...	−	−	...	−	−	...
3 Other current transfers	1009	1009	−	999	999	−	985	985	−	1708	1054	654
A Casualty insurance premiums, net	823	823	−	799	799	−	730	730	−	654	654	−
B Casualty insurance claims liability of insurance companies	...	...	...	...	...	...	...	...	...	...	...	654
C Transfers to private non-profit institutions	186	186	...	200	200	...	255	255	...	318	318	...
D Unfunded employee pension and welfare benefits	...	...	...	...	...	...	...	...	...	...	...	...
E Social assistance grants	...	...	...	...	...	...	...	...	...	...	...	...
F Other transfers n.e.c.	...	...	...	...	...	...	...	...	...	...	...	...
G Transfers to rest of the world	...	...	...	...	...	...	...	...	...	...	...	...
Net saving	−1284	138	−1422	3310	2081	1229	4542	764	3778	−1538	−5188	3650
Total current disbursements and net saving	49328	37674	35476	57386	44252	39315	71196	52353	52063	80833	57044	62270

	1990 Total	1990 Non-financial	1990 Financial	1991 Total	1991 Non-financial	1991 Financial	1992 Total	1992 Non-financial	1992 Financial	1993 Total	1993 Non-financial	1993 Financial

Receipts

	1990 Total	1990 Non-financial	1990 Financial	1991 Total	1991 Non-financial	1991 Financial	1992 Total	1992 Non-financial	1992 Financial	1993 Total	1993 Non-financial	1993 Financial
1 Operating surplus	34964	43705	−8741	36990	45572	−8582	41322	47869	−6547	46753	53038	−6285
2 Property and entrepreneurial income	44590	10899	72703	37739	8653	59322	36113	7407	53644	35039	7111	50221
A Withdrawals from quasi-corporate enterprises	...	...	...	...	...	...	...	...	...	...	...	...
B Interest	43797	9857	68630	36869	7379	55884	34840	5745	49786	33489	4983	45954
C Dividends	577	778	4073	616	973	3438	920	1260	3858	1165	1695	4267
D Net land rent and royalties	216	264	−	254	301	−	353	402	−	385	433	−
3 Current transfers	150	−	150	−	−	−	−	−	−	−	−	−
A Casualty insurance claims	...	...	...	...	...	...	...	...	...	...	...	...
B Casualty insurance premiums, net, due to be received by insurance companies	...	...	...	...	...	...	...	...	...	...	...	...

Australia

	1990 Total	1990 Non-financial	1990 Financial	1991 Total	1991 Non-financial	1991 Financial	1992 Total	1992 Non-financial	1992 Financial	1993 Total	1993 Non-financial	1993 Financial
C Current transfers from rest of the world	150	–	150	–	–	–	–	–	–	–	–	–
D Other transfers except imputed	...	...	...	...	...	...	...	...	...	...	...	...
E Imputed unfunded employee pension and welfare contributions	...	...	...	...	...	...	...	...	...	...	...	...
Total current receipts	79704	54604	64112	74729	54225	50740	77435	55276	47097	81792	60149	43936

Disbursements

	1990 Total	1990 Non-financial	1990 Financial	1991 Total	1991 Non-financial	1991 Financial	1992 Total	1992 Non-financial	1992 Financial	1993 Total	1993 Non-financial	1993 Financial
1 Property and entrepreneurial income	67408	52679	53741	56955	44967	42224	51076	39102	36912	49913	37910	34296
A Withdrawals from quasi-corporations	2521	1438	1083	4303	1800	2503	4939	1909	3030	7243	3388	3855
Public	2521	1438	1083	4303	1800	2503	4939	1909	3030	7243	3388	3855
Private	...	...	...	...	...	...	...	...	...	...	...	...
B Interest	54913	38675	50907	43409	32069	37704	36169	25753	31080	31792	22221	26959
C Dividends	7277	9823	1728	6687	8496	1986	7468	8893	2773	8191	9568	3420
D Net land rent and royalties	2697	2743	23	2556	2602	31	2500	2547	29	2687	2733	62
2 Direct taxes and other current transfers n.e.c. to general government	15410	11983	3427	15334	11711	3623	15885	12028	3857	15020	11944	3076
A Direct taxes	15410	11983	3427	15334	11711	3623	15885	12028	3857	15020	11944	3076
On income	15410	11983	3427	15334	11711	3623	15885	12028	3857	15020	11944	3076
Other	...	...	...	...	...	...	...	...	...	...	...	...
B Fines, fees, penalties and other current transfers n.e.c.	–	–	...	–	–	...	–	–	...	–	–	...
3 Other current transfers	1170	1170	–	1150	1150	–	991	991	–	1178	1178	–
A Casualty insurance premiums, net	819	819	–	750	750	–	623	623	–	789	789	–
B Casualty insurance claims liability of insurance companies	...	...	...	...	...	...	...	...	...	...	...	...
C Transfers to private non-profit institutions	351	351	...	400	400	...	368	368	...	389	389	...
D Unfunded employee pension and welfare benefits	...	...	...	...	...	...	...	...	...	...	...	...
E Social assistance grants	...	...	...	...	...	...	...	...	...	...	...	...
F Other transfers n.e.c.	...	...	...	...	...	...	...	...	...	...	...	...
G Transfers to rest of the world	...	...	...	...	...	...	...	...	...	...	...	...
Net saving	−4284	−11228	6944	1290	−3603	4893	9483	3155	6328	15681	9117	6564
Total current disbursements and net saving	79704	54604	64112	74729	54225	50740	77435	55276	47097	81792	60149	43936

	1994 Total	1994 Non-financial	1994 Financial	1995 Total	1995 Non-financial	1995 Financial	1996 Total	1996 Non-financial	1996 Financial	1997 Total	1997 Non-financial	1997 Financial

Receipts

	1994 Total	1994 Non-financial	1994 Financial	1995 Total	1995 Non-financial	1995 Financial	1996 Total	1996 Non-financial	1996 Financial	1997 Total	1997 Non-financial	1997 Financial
1 Operating surplus	50399	58260	−7861	52896	62035	−9139	52754	61991	−9237	...	...	...
2 Property and entrepreneurial income	40640	7593	56074	46925	9757	63824	42971	7209	62041	...	...	...
A Withdrawals from quasi-corporate enterprises	...	...	...	...	...	...	...	...	...	...	...	...
B Interest	39417	5715	51941	44255	6297	58295	40991	4823	55718	...	...	...
C Dividends	789	1384	4133	2203	2927	5529	1477	1827	6323	...	...	...
D Net land rent and royalties	434	494	–	467	533	–	503	559	–	...	...	...
3 Current transfers	–	–	–	–	–	–	–	–	–	...	...	...

Australia

	1994			1995			1996			1997		
	Total	Non-financial	Financial	Total	Non-financial	Financial	Total	Non-financial	Financial	Total	Non-financial	Financial
A Casualty insurance claims ..	...	...	...	...	...	...	...	...	...	...	...	...
B Casualty insurance premiums, net, due to be received by insurance companies	...	...	...	...	...	...	...	...	...	...	...	...
C Current transfers from rest of the world	–	–	–	–	–	–	–	–	–	...	...	...
D Other transfers except imputed	...	...	...	...	...	...	...	...	...	...	...	...
E Imputed unfunded employee pension and welfare contributions	...	...	...	...	...	...	...	...	...	...	...	...
Total current receipts	91039	65853	48213	99821	71792	54685	95725	69200	52804	...	...	...
Disbursements												
1 Property and entrepreneurial income	59698	41537	41188	67348	47786	46218	68109	50439	43949	...	...	...
A Withdrawals from quasi-corporations	5529	3455	2074	7219	4718	2501	9192	6578	2614	...	...	...
Public	5529	3455	2074	7219	4718	2501	9192	6578	2614	...	...	...
Private	...	...	...	...	...	...	...	...	...	...	...	...
B Interest	39740	22729	35164	43595	24645	39234	42268	24273	37488	...	...	...
C Dividends	11616	12487	3857	13504	15337	4420	13430	16318	3785	...	...	...
D Net land rent and royalties ..	2813	2866	93	3030	3086	63	3219	3270	62	...	...	...
2 Direct taxes and other current transfers n.e.c. to general government	18428	13527	4901	21066	16202	4864	23162	16324	6838	...	...	...
A Direct taxes	18428	13527	4901	21066	16202	4864	23162	16324	6838	...	...	...
On income	18428	13527	4901	21066	16202	4864	23162	16324	6838	...	...	...
Other	...	...	...	...	...	...	...	...	...	...	...	...
B Fines, fees, penalties and other current transfers n.e.c.	–	–	...	–	–	...	–	–	...	...	...	...
3 Other current transfers	1333	1333	–	1451	1451	–	1386	1386	–	...	...	...
A Casualty insurance premiums, net	986	986	–	1059	1059	–	1096	1096	–	...	...	...
B Casualty insurance claims liability of insurance companies	...	...	...	...	...	...	...	...	...	...	...	...
C Transfers to private non-profit institutions	347	347	...	392	392	...	290	290	...	...	...	...
D Unfunded employee pension and welfare benefits	...	...	...	...	...	...	...	...	...	...	...	...
E Social assistance grants	...	...	...	...	...	...	...	...	...	...	...	...
F Other transfers n.e.c.	...	...	...	...	...	...	...	...	...	...	...	...
G Transfers to rest of the world	...	...	...	...	...	...	...	...	...	...	...	...
Net saving	11580	9456	2124	9956	6353	3603	3068	1051	2017	...	...	...
Total current disbursements and net saving	91039	65853	48213	99821	71792	54685	95725	69200	52804	...	...	...

Australia

3.23 Corporate and quasi-corporate enterprise capital accumulation account: total and sectors

Million Australian dollars
Fiscal year beginning 1 July

	1986 Total	1986 Non-financial	1986 Financial	1987 Total	1987 Non-financial	1987 Financial	1988 Total	1988 Non-financial	1988 Financial	1989 Total	1989 Non-financial	1989 Financial
Finance of gross accumulation												
1 Gross saving	20806	20552	254	27497	24405	3092	30559	24726	5833	26741	20773	5968
A Consumption of fixed capital	22090	20414	1676	24187	22324	1863	26017	23962	2055	28279	25961	2318
B Net saving	−1284	138	−1422	3310	2081	1229	4542	764	3778	−1538	−5188	3650
2 Capital transfers	887	887	–	1029	1026	3	1350	1339	11	1700	1695	5
A From resident sectors	887	887	–	1029	1026	3	1350	1339	11	1700	1695	5
B From rest of the world	...	...	...	...	...	...	...	...	...	...	...	...
Finance of gross accumulation	21693	21439	254	28526	25431	3095	31909	26065	5844	28441	22468	5973
Gross accumulation												
1 Gross capital formation	34298	31268	3030	38890	35164	3726	45812	39514	6298	52486	45667	6819
A Increase in stocks	−1325	−1240	−85	294	325	−31	2784	2796	−12	5205	5376	−171
B Gross fixed capital formation	35623	32508	3115	38596	34839	3757	43028	36718	6310	47281	40291	6990
2 Purchases of land, net	135	45	90	541	505	36	469	427	42	−26	37	−63
3 Purchases of intangible assets, net	...	...	...	...	...	...	...	...	...	...	...	...
4 Capital transfers	125	125	–	21	21	–	27	27	–	17	17	–
A To resident sectors	125	125	–	21	21	–	27	27	–	17	17	–
B To the rest of the world	...	...	...	...	...	...	...	...	...	...	...	...
Net lending	−12865	−9999	−2866	−10926	−10259	−667	−14399	−13903	−496	−24036	−23253	−783
Gross accumulation	21693	21439	254	28526	25431	3095	31909	26065	5844	28441	22468	5973

	1990 Total	1990 Non-financial	1990 Financial	1991 Total	1991 Non-financial	1991 Financial	1992 Total	1992 Non-financial	1992 Financial	1993 Total	1993 Non-financial	1993 Financial
Finance of gross accumulation												
1 Gross saving	25590	16182	9408	32199	24749	7450	42212	33184	9028	49553	40239	9314
A Consumption of fixed capital	29874	27410	2464	30909	28352	2557	32729	30029	2700	33872	31122	2750
B Net saving	−4284	−11228	6944	1290	−3603	4893	9483	3155	6328	15681	9117	6564
2 Capital transfers	2225	1985	240	2561	2305	256	2464	2405	59	2565	2427	138
A From resident sectors	2225	1985	240	2561	2305	256	2464	2405	59	2565	2427	138
B From rest of the world	...	...	...	...	...	...	...	...	...	...	...	...
Finance of gross accumulation	27815	18167	9648	34760	27054	7706	44676	35589	9087	52118	42666	9452
Gross accumulation												
1 Gross capital formation	41640	37916	3724	36885	32630	4255	40263	37202	3061	43530	40870	2660
A Increase in stocks	−1145	−951	−194	−2169	−2034	−135	673	795	−122	876	893	−17
B Gross fixed capital formation	42785	38867	3918	39054	34664	4390	39590	36407	3183	42654	39977	2677
2 Purchases of land, net	106	229	−123	68	114	−46	292	300	−8	568	616	−48
3 Purchases of intangible assets, net	...	...	...	...	...	...	...	...	...	...	...	...
4 Capital transfers	15	15	–	–	–	–	45	45	–	54	54	–
A To resident sectors	15	15	–	–	–	–	45	45	–	54	54	–
B To the rest of the world	...	...	...	...	...	...	...	...	...	...	...	...
Net lending	−13946	−19993	6047	−2193	−5690	3497	4076	−1958	6034	7966	1126	6840
Gross accumulation	27815	18167	9648	34760	27054	7706	44676	35589	9087	52118	42666	9452

Australia

	1994 Total	1994 Non-financial	1994 Financial	1995 Total	1995 Non-financial	1995 Financial	1996 Total	1996 Non-financial	1996 Financial	1997 Total	1997 Non-financial	1997 Financial
Finance of gross accumulation												
1 Gross saving	46260	41433	4827	46101	39802	6299	40834	36064	4770	...	...	...
A Consumption of fixed capital	34680	31977	2703	36145	33449	2696	37766	35013	2753	...	...	...
B Net saving	11580	9456	2124	9956	6353	3603	3068	1051	2017	...	...	...
2 Capital transfers	2487	2463	24	1999	1982	17	2512	2448	64	...	...	...
A From resident sectors	2487	2463	24	1999	1982	17	2512	2448	64	...	...	...
B From rest of the world	...	...	...	...	...	...	...	...	...	...	...	...
Finance of gross accumulation	48747	43896	4851	48100	41784	6316	43346	38512	4834	...	...	...
Gross accumulation												
1 Gross capital formation	50209	47733	2476	55616	53648	1968	55404	54048	1356	...	...	...
A Increase in stocks	1321	1547	–226	1738	2579	–841	–1310	547	–1857	...	...	...
B Gross fixed capital formation	48888	46186	2702	53878	51069	2809	56714	53501	3213	...	...	...
2 Purchases of land, net	438	502	–64	237	309	–72	–20	18	–38	...	...	...
3 Purchases of intangible assets, net	...	...	...	...	...	...	...	...	...	...	...	...
4 Capital transfers	27	27	–	9	9	–	49	49	–	...	...	...
A To resident sectors	27	27	–	9	9	–	49	49	–	...	...	...
B To the rest of the world	...	...	...	...	...	...	...	...	...	...	...	...
Net lending	–1927	–4366	2439	–7762	–12182	4420	–12087	–15603	3516	...	...	...
Gross accumulation	48747	43896	4851	48100	41784	6316	43346	38512	4834	...	...	...

3.32 Household and private unincorporated enterprise income and outlay account

Million Australian dollars — Fiscal year beginning 1 July

	1986	1987	1988	1989	1990	1991	1992	1993	1994	1995	1996	1997
Receipts												
1 Compensation of employees	133450	146776	163690	182243	190389	194639	201709	212175	225867	241526	257736	...
2 Operating surplus of private unincorporated enterprises	34673	40349	48780	52742	52477	53970	56789	57853	61218	67674	70240	...
3 Property and entrepreneurial income	27955	28250	35267	42803	41190	31819	26900	24078	32505	36509	34663	...
A Withdrawals from private quasi-corporations	...	...	...	...	...	...	...	...	...	...	...	...
B Interest	26236	26324	32758	40114	38300	28948	23452	20148	26558	29700	28595	...
C Dividends	1614	1846	2384	2554	2781	2752	3330	3818	5807	6674	5921	...
D Net land rent and royalties	105	80	125	135	109	119	118	112	140	135	147	...
4 Current transfers	31811	35245	37718	41753	46926	52648	55239	59918	63268	68977	72451	...
A Casualty insurance claims	1443	1380	1232	1224	1407	1282	1042	1322	1667	1800	1867	...
B Social security benefits	...	...	...	...	...	...	...	...	...	...	...	...
C Social assistance grants	24852	27739	29328	32370	37262	42351	46076	49667	51820	55705	58566	...
D Unfunded employee pension and welfare benefits	...	...	...	...	...	...	...	...	...	...	...	...
E Transfers from general government	3331	3436	3887	4353	4690	5503	6128	6800	7582	8601	8875	...
F Transfers from rest of the world	2185	2690	3271	3335	3567	3512	1993	2129	2199	2871	3143	...
G Other transfers n.e.c.	–	–	–	471	–	–	–	–	–	–	–	...
Total current receipts	227889	250620	285455	319541	330982	333076	340637	354024	382858	414686	435090	...

Australia

Million Australian dollars	1986	1987	1988	1989	1990	1991	1992	1993	1994	1995	1996	1997
Disbursements												
1 Final consumption expenditure	157324	175657	196364	218314	231700	244229	256737	269502	286830	306369	318480	...
A Market purchases	...	...	...	...	...	...	...	...	...	...	...	...
B Gross rents of owner-occupied housing	20853	23548	26706	...	...	...	...	...	...	...	...	...
C Consumption from own-account production	...	...	...	...	...	...	...	...	...	...	...	...
2 Property income	19163	20431	26833	33522	33788	27230	24595	22777	26652	31028	28551	...
A Interest	18942	20221	26560	33222	33493	26928	24289	22461	26297	30656	28179	...
Consumer debt	4538	4500	5900	8073	7183	5077	3866	3192	3683	4324	4499	...
Mortgages	8064	8441	10386	12660	13195	11797	12077	11811	14940	18131	15707	...
Other	6340	7280	10274	12489	13115	10054	8346	7458	7674	8201	7973	...
B Net land rent and royalties	221	210	273	300	295	302	306	316	355	372	372	...
3 Direct taxes and other current transfers n.e.c. to general government	39556	43607	49459	52265	52558	49688	50591	54005	58341	64552	70174	...
A Social security contributions	...	...	...	...	...	...	...	...	...	...	...	...
B Direct taxes	38000	41811	47433	49931	50156	46830	47527	50570	54634	60603	66278	...
Income taxes	38000	41811	47433	49931	50156	46830	47527	50570	54634	60603	66278	...
Other	...	...	...	...	...	...	...	...	...	...	...	...
C Fees, fines and penalties	1556	1796	2026	2334	2402	2858	3064	3435	3707	3949	3896	...
4 Other current transfers	1311	1376	1385	1372	1553	1492	1425	1706	1898	1902	2036	...
A Net casualty insurance premiums	620	581	502	488	588	532	419	533	681	741	771	...
B Transfers to private non-profit institutions serving households	...	...	...	...	...	...	...	...	...	...	...	...
C Transfers to rest of the world	691	795	883	884	965	960	1006	1173	1217	1161	1265	...
D Other current transfers, except imputed	...	...	...	...	...	...	...	...	...	...	...	...
E Imputed employee pension and welfare contributions	...	...	...	...	...	...	...	...	...	...	...	...
Net saving	10535	9549	11414	14068	11383	10437	7289	6034	9137	10835	15849	...
Total current disbursements and net saving	227889	250620	285455	319541	330982	333076	340637	354024	382858	414686	435090	...

3.33 Household and private unincorporated enterprise capital accumulation account

Million Australian dollars	1986	1987	1988	1989	1990	1991	1992	1993	1994	1995	1996	1997
Finance of gross accumulation												
1 Gross saving	25542	26312	30650	35201	32820	32129	29922	29740	33496	36167	42183	...
A Consumption of fixed capital	15007	16763	19236	21133	21437	21692	22633	23706	24359	25332	26334	...
Owner-occupied housing	7444	8509	10458	11802	11908	12061	12518	13278	13953	14834	15656	...
Other unincorporated enterprises	7563	8254	8778	9331	9529	9631	10115	10428	10406	10498	10678	...
B Net saving	10535	9549	11414	14068	11383	10437	7289	6034	9137	10835	15849	...
2 Capital transfers	447	502	540	500	402	472	429	361	356	378	452	...
A From resident sectors	447	502	540	500	402	472	429	361	356	378	452	...
B From rest of the world	...	...	...	...	...	...	...	...	...	...	...	...
Total finance of gross accumulation	25989	26814	31190	35701	33222	32601	30351	30101	33852	36545	42635	...

Australia

Million Australian dollars	1986	1987	1988	1989	1990	1991	1992	1993	1994	1995	1996	Fiscal year beginning 1 July 1997
Gross accumulation												
1 Gross capital formation	20806	26529	35328	33597	29333	29453	33460	37035	40735	37266	39168	...
A Increase in stocks	–262	279	751	–67	–478	–44	–246	273	1159	365	293	...
B Gross fixed capital formation	21068	26250	34577	33664	29811	29497	33706	36762	39576	36901	38875	...
2 Purchases of land, net	...	...	...	...	...	...	...	...	...	...	...	...
3 Purchases of intangibles, net	...	...	...	...	...	...	...	...	...	...	...	...
4 Capital transfers	237	282	443	403	355	394	372	440	540	413	389	...
A To resident sectors	237	282	443	403	355	394	372	440	540	413	389	...
B To the rest of the world	...	...	...	...	...	...	...	...	...	...	...	...
Net lending	4946	3	–4581	1701	3534	2754	–3481	–7374	–7423	–1134	3078	...
Total gross accumulation	25989	26814	31190	35701	33222	32601	30351	30101	33852	36545	42635	...

3.34 Household and private unincorporated enterprise capital finance account

Million Australian dollars	1986	1987	1988	1989	1990	1991	1992	1993	1994	1995	1996	Fiscal year beginning 1 July 1997
Acquisition of financial assets												
1 Gold	...	...	...	...	...	...	...	...	...	...	...	...
2 Currency and transferable deposits	...	...	...	16951	4144	5576	8184	12680	4181	13539	14799	...
3 Other deposits	...	...	...	...	...	...	...	...	...	...	...	...
4 Bills and bonds, short-term	...	...	...	217	1298	–5111	–2099	1415	2119	204	–1179	...
A Corporate and quasi-corporate	...	...	...	215	1293	–5116	–2088	1410	2114	210	–1176	...
B Government	...	...	...	2	5	5	–11	5	5	–6	–3	...
C Rest of the world	...	...	...	...	...	...	...	...	...	...	...	...
5 Bonds, long-term	...	...	...	–133	1340	–4857	–3871	–1305	833	1663	–1277	...
A Corporate	...	...	...	2004	1720	–3388	–4053	–1430	769	1611	–1074	...
B Government	...	...	...	–2137	–380	–1469	182	125	64	52	–203	...
C Rest of the world	...	...	...	...	...	...	...	...	...	...	...	...
6 Corporate equity securities	...	...	...	–210	–4887	4718	12069	6753	2160	8702	4785	...
7 Short-term loans, n.e.c.	...	...	...	1568	–91	–330	–480	819	–720	800	1946	...
8 Long-term loans, n.e.c.	...	...	...	...	...	...	...	...	...	...	...	...
9 Trade credits and advances	...	...	...	...	...	...	...	...	...	...	...	...
10 Net equity of households in life insurance and pension fund reserves	...	...	...	16960	13423	14056	8559	12535	8939	18039	25293	...
11 Proprietors' net additions to the accumulation of quasi-corporations	...	...	...	...	...	...	...	...	...	...	...	...
12 Other	...	...	...	...	...	...	...	...	...	...	...	...
Total acquisitions of financial assets	...	...	...	35353	15227	14052	22362	32897	17512	42947	44367	...
Incurrence of liabilities												
1 Short-term loans, n.e.c.	...	...	...	298	–414	1130	–28	241	–252	–758	–574	...
2 Long-term loans, n.e.c.	...	...	...	19366	8917	7181	7832	27226	26080	31785	27869	...
3 Trade credits and advances	...	...	...	...	...	...	...	...	...	...	...	...
4 Other accounts payable	...	...	...	...	...	...	...	...	...	...	...	...
5 Other liabilities	...	...	...	...	...	...	...	...	...	...	...	...
Total incurrence of liabilities	...	...	...	19664	8503	8311	7804	27467	25828	31027	27295	...
Statistical discrepancy	...	...	...	13988	3190	2987	18039	12804	–893	13054	13994	...

Australia

Million Australian dollars	1986	1987	1988	1989	1990	1991	1992	1993	1994	1995	1996	Fiscal year beginning 1 July 1997
Net lending	...	...	...	1701	3534	2754	–3481	–7374	–7423	–1134	3078	...
Incurrence of liabilities and net lending	...	...	...	35353	15227	14052	22362	32897	17512	42947	44367	...

3.51 External transactions, current account: detail

Million Australian dollars	1986	1987	1988	1989	1990	1991	1992	1993	1994	1995	1996	Fiscal year beginning 1 July 1997
Payments to the rest of the world												
1 Imports of goods and services	47894	52578	60734	67007	65220	67439	77400	83496	95680	99107	101691	...
A Imports of merchandise, c.i.f.	40157	43538	50457	54746	52846	54702	63682	68693	79578	82040	83719	...
B Other	7737	9040	10277	12261	12374	12737	13718	14803	16102	17067	17972	...
2 Factor income to rest of the world	10577	12141	15780	20747	21449	19326	17508	17508	19635	22105	22914	...
A Compensation of employees	179	210	279	406	429	326	311	283	389	458	539	...
B Property and entrepreneurial income	10398	11931	15501	20341	21020	19000	17197	17225	19246	21647	22375	...
By general government	2288	2962	3160	3906	4282	3930	3402	3748	5080	5134	4980	...
By corporate and quasi-corporate enterprises	8110	8969	12341	16435	16738	15070	13795	13477	14166	16513	17395	...
By other	...	...	...	...	...	...	...	...	...	...	...	...
3 Current transfers to the rest of the world	1873	2161	2296	2467	2524	2461	2566	2961	3013	2769	2688	...
A Indirect taxes by general government to supranational organizations	...	...	...	...	...	...	...	...	...	...	...	...
B Other current transfers	1873	2161	2296	2467	2524	2461	2566	2961	3013	2769	2688	...
By general government	1182	1366	1413	1583	1559	1501	1560	1788	1796	1608	1423	...
By other resident sectors	691	795	883	884	965	960	1006	1173	1217	1161	1265	...
4 Surplus of the nation on current transactions	–11382	–9968	–17273	–21735	–14639	–11098	–13998	–14514	–24404	–16258	–13776	...
Payments to the rest of the world and surplus of the nation on current transfers	48962	56912	61537	68486	74554	78128	83476	89451	93924	107723	113517	...
Receipts from the rest of the world												
1 Exports of goods and services	44031	51468	55110	60625	65988	69753	76465	82531	87090	98528	104601	...
A Exports of merchandise, f.o.b.	36487	41903	44187	48927	52568	55427	60634	64419	67000	76038	80814	...
B Other	7544	9565	10923	11698	13420	14326	15831	18112	20090	22490	23787	...
2 Factor income from rest of the world	1960	1935	2259	3268	3749	3969	4191	3998	3809	5403	4788	...
A Compensation of employees	151	160	225	370	432	455	497	511	551	610	678	...
B Property and entrepreneurial income	1809	1775	2034	2898	3317	3514	3694	3487	3258	4793	4110	...
By general government	47	48	62	113	118	25	17	32	23	19	13	...
By corporate and quasi-corporate enterprises	1762	1727	1972	2785	3199	3489	3677	3455	3235	4774	4097	...
By other	...	...	...	...	...	...	...	...	...	...	...	...
3 Current transfers from rest of the world	2971	3509	4168	4593	4817	4406	2820	2922	3025	3792	4128	...
A Subsidies to general government from supranational organizations	...	...	...	...	...	...	...	...	...	...	...	...
B Other current transfers	2971	3509	4168	4593	4817	4406	2820	2922	3025	3792	4128	...
To general government	786	819	897	1108	1100	894	827	793	826	921	985	...

Australia

Million Australian dollars	1986	1987	1988	1989	1990	1991	1992	1993	1994	1995	1996	1997
To other resident sectors	2185	2690	3271	3485	3717	3512	1993	2129	2199	2871	3143	...
Receipts from the rest of the world on current transfers	48962	56912	61537	68486	74554	78128	83476	89451	93924	107723	113517	...

3.52 External transactions, capital accumulation account

Million Australian dollars	1986	1987	1988	1989	1990	1991	1992	1993	1994	1995	1996	1997
Finance of gross accumulation												
1 Surplus of the nation on current transactions	−11382	−9968	−17273	−21735	−14639	−11098	−13998	−14514	−24404	−16258	−13776	...
2 Capital transfers from rest of the world	...	...	...	...	...	...	...	...	...	...	...	...
Total finance of gross accumulation	−11382	−9968	−17273	−21735	−14639	−11098	−13998	−14514	−24404	−16258	−13776	...
Gross accumulation												
1 Capital transfers to the rest of the world	...	...	...	...	...	...	...	...	...	...	...	...
2 Purchases of intangible assets, n.e.c., net, from rest of the world	...	...	...	...	...	...	...	...	...	...	...	...
Net lending to the rest of the world	−11382	−9968	−17273	−21735	−14639	−11098	−13998	−14514	−24404	−16258	−13776	...
Total gross accumulation	−11382	−9968	−17273	−21735	−14639	−11098	−13998	−14514	−24404	−16258	−13776	...

3.53 External transactions, capital finance account

Million Australian dollars	1986	1987	1988	1989	1990	1991	1992	1993	1994	1995	1996	1997
Acquisition of foreign financial assets												
1 Gold and SDRs	3394	3924	1845	4154	2133	−3300	−1586	−1426	−1967	4041	6153	...
2 Currency and transferable deposits	...	...	...	...	...	...	...	...	...	...	...	...
3 Other deposits	...	...	...	...	...	...	...	...	...	...	...	...
4 Bills and bonds, short-term	...	...	...	...	...	...	...	...	...	...	...	...
5 Bonds, long-term	...	...	...	...	...	...	...	...	...	...	...	...
6 Corporate equity securities	7822	7498	6568	1493	−53	8412	4742	6088	−454	7193	6812	...
A Subsidiaries abroad	4229	7586	2520	3093	−3354	4036	4706	1445	105	4229	2533	...
B Other	3593	−88	4048	−1600	3301	4376	36	4643	−559	2964	4279	...
7 Short-term loans, n.e.c.	...	...	−	−	−	−	−	−	−	−	320	...
A Subsidiaries abroad	...	...	...	...	...	...	...	...	...	...	...	...
B Other	...	...	−	−	−	−	−	−	−	−	320	...
8 Long-term loans	−515	2388	4273	2451	57	2006	1882	5130	−884	7059	767	...
A Subsidiaries abroad	−1341	198	2836	−359	−769	391	−86	1167	−434	699	307	...
B Other	826	2190	1437	2810	826	1615	1968	3963	−450	6360	460	...
9 Proprietors' net additions to accumulation of quasi-corporate, non-resident enterprises	428	143	−	−	−	−	−	−	−	−	−	...
10 Trade credits and advances	349	679	1126	225	159	−972	−11	1483	−818	624	1867	...
11 Other	214	−521	−	−	−	−	−	−	−3747	−1949	−914	...
Total acquisitions of foreign financial assets	11692	14111	13812	8323	2296	6146	5027	11275	−7870	16968	15005	...

Australia

Million Australian dollars — Fiscal year beginning 1 July

	1986	1987	1988	1989	1990	1991	1992	1993	1994	1995	1996	1997
Incurrence of foreign liabilities												
1 Currency and transferable deposits	...	...	...	...	...	...	...	...	...	...	...	...
2 Other deposits	18	−8	335	2738	168	409	575	1724	−78	580	3720	...
3 Bills and bonds, short-term	...	...	4932	4834	4854	6771	4953	−3938	1944	2737	321	...
4 Bonds, long-term	...	...	9304	9840	1834	−844	1362	10021	8758	19052	11703	...
5 Corporate equity securities	6170	4164	9256	5713	8470	6381	9166	16330	6451	13203	8517	...
A Subsidiaries of non-resident incorporated units	1949	1827	7125	4140	5252	5304	5153	1692	1521	6487	5915	...
B Other	4221	2337	2131	1573	3218	1077	4013	14638	4930	6716	2602	...
6 Short-term loans, n.e.c.	...	...	–	–	–	–	–	–	–	–	1848	...
A Subsidiaries of non-residents	...	...	...	...	...	...	...	...	...	...	...	...
B Other	...	...	–	–	–	–	–	–	–	–	1848	...
7 Long-term loans	15064	20069	6522	6008	1175	4067	2091	−1635	1848	−1159	2117	...
A Subsidiaries of non-residents	1429	2344	5219	3508	−2547	1403	1447	323	−377	−372	633	...
B Other	13635	17725	1303	2500	3722	2664	644	−1958	2225	−787	1484	...
8 Non-resident proprietors' net additions to accumulation of resident quasi-corporate enterprises	...	...	...	...	...	...	...	...	...	...	...	...
9 Trade credits and advances	235	80	1315	−556	337	504	460	1399	518	736	−129	...
10 Other	−302	−29	−20	177	60	43	−66	97	−3164	−1876	1700	...
Total incurrence of liabilities	21596	25746	31644	28754	16898	17331	18541	23998	16277	33273	29797	...
Statistical discrepancy	1567	−1825	−559	1304	37	−87	484	1791	257	−47	−1016	...
Net lending	−11471	−9810	−17273	−21735	−14639	−11098	−13998	−14514	−24404	−16258	−13776	...
Total incurrence of liabilities and net lending	11692	14111	13812	8323	2296	6146	5027	11275	−7870	16968	15005	...

4.3 Cost components of value added

Million Australian dollars — Fiscal year beginning 1 July

	1986						1987					
	Compensation of employees	Capital consumption	Net operating surplus	Indirect taxes	less: Subsidies received	Value added	Compensation of employees	Capital consumption	Net operating surplus	Indirect taxes	less: Subsidies received	Value added
All producers												
1 Agriculture, hunting, forestry and fishing	2257	3243	4505	813	492	10326	2538	3413	5720	1066	334	12403
2 Mining and quarrying	3877	2740	4715	2489	293	13528	3900	3070	5093	2480	344	14199
3 Manufacturing	25452	5600	7801	5221	802	43272	27654	6006	9422	5774	741	48115
4 Electricity, gas and water	3704	3248	2414	546	160	9752	3833	3445	2785	560	227	10396
5 Construction	10877	1317	5668	502	19	18345	11596	1481	6451	606	23	20111
6 Wholesale and retail trade, restaurants and hotels	22699	4097	9743	14334	144	50729	25304	4547	11930	16031	293	57519
A Wholesale and retail trade	19777	3385	9093	14230	118	46367	22017	3724	11226	15883	264	52586
B Restaurants and hotels	2922	712	650	104	26	4362	3287	823	704	148	29	4933
7 Transport, storage and communication	10334	6775	4981	946	2308	20728	11004	7274	6901	1094	2224	24049
A Transport and storage	7299	5364	3664	759	2260	14826	7727	5781	4545	873	2177	16749
B Communication	3035	1411	1317	187	48	5902	3277	1493	2356	221	47	7300
8 Finance, insurance, real estate and business services	16052	11469	19675	6076	170	53102	18954	13124	26117	7753	78	65870
A Financial institutions	7086	1710	253	2354	128	11275	8639	1905	3696	2904	59	17085

Australia

Million Australian dollars   **Fiscal year beginning 1 July**

	1986						1987					
	Compensation of employees	Capital consumption	Net operating surplus	Indirect taxes	less: Subsidies received	Value added	Compensation of employees	Capital consumption	Net operating surplus	Indirect taxes	less: Subsidies received	Value added
B Insurance	...	...	...	...	...	...	...	...	...	...	...	...
C Real estate and business services	8966	9759	19422	3722	42	41827	10315	11219	22421	4849	19	48785
Real estate, except dwellings	8966	1938	6450	991	42	18303	10315	2280	7323	1219	19	21118
Dwellings	...	7821	12972	2731	...	23524	...	8939	15098	3630	...	27667
9 Community, social and personal services	28745	2994	2739	2123	281	36320	31644	3217	3276	2407	249	40295
A Sanitary and similar services	...	...	...	...	...	...	...	...	...	...	...	...
B Social and related community services	22848	2313	1279	432	260	26612	24945	2462	1386	517	223	29087
Educational services	11380	1238	–62	202	72	12686	12137	1320	–62	242	62	13575
Medical, dental, other health and veterinary services	11468	1075	1341	230	188	13926	12808	1142	1448	275	161	15512
C Recreational and cultural services	1901	367	969	1576	15	4798	2259	412	1332	1723	17	5709
D Personal and household services	3996	314	491	115	6	4910	4440	343	558	167	9	5499
Total, Industries	123997	41483	62241	33050	4669	256102	136427	45577	77695	37771	4513	292957
Producers of government services	9481	1109	–	78	52	10616	10399	1156	–	128	32	11651
Other producers	...	...	...	...	...	...	...	...	...	...	...	...
Total	133478	42592	62241	33128	4721	266718	146826	46733	77695	37899	4545	304608
less: Imputed bank service charge	...	...	5382	...	...	5382	...	...	8599	...	...	8599
Import duties	...	...	...	3239	...	3239	...	...	...	3633	...	3633
Value added tax	...	...	...	...	...	...	...	...	...	...	...	...
Other adjustments	...	...	...	...	...	...	...	...	...	...	...	...
Total	133478	42592	56859	36367	4721	264575	146826	46733	69096	41532	4545	299642

Of which general government:

1 Agriculture, hunting, forestry and fishing	214	99	...	...	...	313	222	103	...	...	...	325
2 Mining and quarrying	25	...	...	...	...	25	25	...	...	...	...	25
3 Manufacturing	473	56	...	...	...	529	463	58	...	...	...	521
4 Electricity, gas and water	514	20	...	...	...	534	576	21	...	...	...	597
5 Construction	2272	82	...	...	...	2354	2220	85	...	...	...	2305
6 Wholesale and retail trade, restaurants and hotels	37	4	...	...	...	41	47	4	...	...	...	51
7 Transport, storage and communication	667	2155	...	...	...	2822	694	2284	...	...	...	2978
8 Finance, insurance, real estate and business services	1230	62	...	...	...	1292	1267	70	...	...	...	1338
9 Community, social and personal services	18722	1908	...	...	...	20630	20366	2001	...	...	...	22367
Total, industries of general government	24154	4386	...	...	...	28540	25880	4627	...	...	...	30507
Producers of government services	9670	1070	...	78	51	10767	10659	1111	...	128	31	11867
Total, general government	33980	5415	...	78	51	39422	36594	5685	...	128	31	42376

                                          1988   1989

Australia

	Compensation of employees	Capital consumption	Net operating surplus	Indirect taxes	less: Subsidies received	Value added	Compensation of employees	Capital consumption	Net operating surplus	Indirect taxes	less: Subsidies received	Value added
All producers												
1 Agriculture, hunting, forestry and fishing	2971	3530	7425	1099	389	14636	3175	3701	7253	1197	466	14860
2 Mining and quarrying	4083	3374	4310	1635	383	13019	4845	3641	5940	1738	448	15716
3 Manufacturing	30269	6214	10593	6199	672	52603	32599	6537	11375	6508	712	56307
4 Electricity, gas and water	4005	3658	3504	611	207	11571	4014	3885	4263	660	288	12534
5 Construction	13128	1629	8428	742	28	23899	15073	1765	9071	873	28	26754
6 Wholesale and retail trade, restaurants and hotels	29112	4916	15283	18215	256	67270	33111	5263	14260	20270	173	72731
A Wholesale and retail trade	25400	3967	14148	18068	221	61362	28732	4192	12866	20100	139	65751
B Restaurants and hotels	3712	949	1135	147	35	5908	4379	1071	1394	170	34	6980
7 Transport, storage and communication	11921	7693	8103	1559	2239	27037	12666	8347	7271	1783	1996	28071
A Transport and storage	8347	6089	5339	1236	2192	18819	8828	6568	4430	1418	1955	19289
B Communication	3574	1604	2764	323	47	8218	3838	1779	2841	365	41	8782
8 Finance, insurance, real estate and business services	21995	15682	31541	9183	73	78328	26575	17777	33244	8912	93	86415
A Financial institutions	9865	2113	5699	3189	55	20811	11189	2399	3819	3415	70	20752
B Insurance	...	...	...	...	...	...	...	...	...	...	...	...
C Real estate and business services	12130	13569	25842	5994	18	57517	15386	15378	29425	5497	23	65663
Real estate, except dwellings	12130	2601	8860	1347	18	24920	15386	2988	10009	1489	23	29849
Dwellings	...	10968	16982	4647	...	32597	...	12390	19416	4008	...	35814
9 Community, social and personal services	35084	3458	3749	2724	268	44747	38897	3757	4093	3069	365	49451
A Sanitary and similar services	...	...	...	...	...	...	...	...	...	...	...	...
B Social and related community services	27705	2623	1513	563	239	32165	30409	2829	1647	614	335	35164
Educational services	13043	1413	−73	263	66	14580	14589	1531	−88	286	92	16226
Medical, dental, other health and veterinary services	14662	1210	1586	300	173	17585	15820	1298	1735	328	243	18938
C Recreational and cultural services	2560	457	1576	1995	20	6568	2950	504	1742	2262	20	7438
D Personal and household services	4819	378	660	166	9	6014	5538	424	704	193	10	6849
Total, Industries	152568	50154	92936	41967	4515	333110	170955	54673	96770	45010	4569	362839
Producers of government services	11176	1218	−	96	101	12389	11324	1324	−	94	69	12673
Other producers	...	...	...	...	...	...	...	...	...	...	...	...
Total	163744	51372	92936	42063	4616	345499	182279	55997	96770	45104	4638	375512
less: Imputed bank service charge	...	...	9372	...	...	9372	...	...	7993	...	...	7993
Import duties	...	...	...	3754	...	3754	...	...	...	3952	...	3952
Value added tax	...	...	...	...	...	...	...	...	...	...	...	...
Other adjustments	...	...	...	...	...	...	...	...	...	...	...	...
Total	163744	51372	83564	45817	4616	339881	182279	55997	88777	49056	4638	371471
Of which general government:												
1 Agriculture, hunting, forestry and fishing	232	109	...	...	...	341	240	117	...	...	...	357
2 Mining and quarrying	16	...	...	...	...	16	13	...	...	...	...	13
3 Manufacturing	560	61	...	...	...	621	436	66	...	...	...	502
4 Electricity, gas and water	785	22	...	...	...	807	788	23	...	...	...	811

Australia

	1988						1989					
	Compensation of employees	Capital consumption	Net operating surplus	Indirect taxes	less: Subsidies received	Value added	Compensation of employees	Capital consumption	Net operating surplus	Indirect taxes	less: Subsidies received	Value added
5 Construction	2016	90	...	...	...	2106	2071	97	...	...	...	2168
6 Wholesale and retail trade, restaurants and hotels	44	5	...	...	...	49	54	5	...	...	...	59
7 Transport, storage and communication	876	2420	...	...	...	3296	971	2578	...	...	...	3549
8 Finance, insurance, real estate and business services	1336	81	...	...	...	1417	1580	91	...	...	...	1672
9 Community, social and personal services	22051	2113	...	...	...	24164	23900	2283	...	...	...	26183
Total, industries of general government	27916	4901	...	...	...	32817	30053	5261	...	...	...	35314
Producers of government services	11782	1168	...	96	99	12947	12168	1267	...	94	68	13461
Total, general government	40147	6011	...	96	99	46155	42649	6478	...	94	68	49153

	1990						1991					
	Compensation of employees	Capital consumption	Net operating surplus	Indirect taxes	less: Subsidies received	Value added	Compensation of employees	Capital consumption	Net operating surplus	Indirect taxes	less: Subsidies received	Value added
All producers												
1 Agriculture, hunting, forestry and fishing	3043	3709	4528	1827	490	12617	2897	3644	4629	1316	703	11783
2 Mining and quarrying	5006	3844	7624	1894	490	17878	4768	4027	7487	626	600	16308
3 Manufacturing	33156	6818	9839	6539	583	55769	32484	6980	10249	6412	696	55429
4 Electricity, gas and water	4101	3972	4344	725	283	12859	4170	3969	4972	824	270	13665
5 Construction	15288	1866	7769	801	17	25707	13726	1934	7673	753	30	24056
6 Wholesale and retail trade, restaurants and hotels	34851	5496	14178	20405	1136	73794	35679	5626	14097	20996	498	75900
A Wholesale and retail trade	30033	4339	12692	20175	1107	66132	30348	4419	12948	20695	468	67942
B Restaurants and hotels	4818	1157	1486	230	29	7662	5331	1207	1149	301	30	7958
7 Transport, storage and communication	13181	8838	7195	2017	2010	29221	13936	9281	8035	2132	1960	31424
A Transport and storage	9092	6934	3866	1570	1981	19481	9702	7253	3769	1625	1930	20419
B Communication	4089	1904	3329	447	29	9740	4234	2028	4266	507	30	11005
8 Finance, insurance, real estate and business services	27352	18362	39337	9508	190	94369	28073	18777	42412	10277	492	99047
A Financial institutions	11536	2560	7665	3797	173	25385	11850	2656	9488	4174	444	27724
B Insurance	...	...	...	...	...	...	...	...	...	...	...	...
C Real estate and business services	15816	15802	31672	5711	17	68984	16223	16121	32924	6103	48	71323
Real estate, except dwellings	15816	3263	9629	1600	17	30291	16223	3412	9476	1723	48	30786
Dwellings	...	12539	22043	4111	...	38693	...	12709	23448	4380	...	40537
9 Community, social and personal services	42412	3989	4261	3303	525	53440	45834	4138	4410	3409	696	57095
A Sanitary and similar services	...	...	...	...	...	...	...	...	...	...	...	...
B Social and related community services	33407	2982	1898	730	467	38550	35586	3060	1993	796	648	40787
Educational services	15676	1620	−83	311	92	17432	16760	1666	−69	315	126	18546
Medical, dental, other health and veterinary services	17731	1362	1981	419	375	21118	18826	1394	2062	481	522	22241
C Recreational and cultural services	3111	539	1594	2373	46	7571	3597	571	1569	2380	42	8075

Australia

	1990						1991					
	Compensation of employees	Capital consumption	Net operating surplus	Indirect taxes	less: Subsidies received	Value added	Compensation of employees	Capital consumption	Net operating surplus	Indirect taxes	less: Subsidies received	Value added
D Personal and household services	5894	468	769	200	12	7319	6651	507	848	233	6	8233
Total, Industries	178390	56894	99075	47019	5724	375654	181567	58376	103964	46745	5945	384707
Producers of government services	11996	1400	–	67	46	13417	12943	1438	–	93	60	14414
Other producers	...	...	...	...	...	...	...	...	...	...	...	...
Total	190386	58294	99075	47086	5770	389071	194510	59814	103964	46838	6005	399121
less: Imputed bank service charge	...	...	11634	...	...	11634	...	...	13004	...	...	13004
Import duties	...	...	...	3324	...	3324	...	...	...	3350	...	3350
Value added tax	...	...	...	...	...	...	...	...	...	...	...	...
Other adjustments	...	...	...	...	...	...	...	...	...	...	...	...
Total	190386	58294	87441	50410	5770	380761	194510	59814	90960	50188	6005	389467

Of which general government:

	Comp.	Capital	Net op.	Indirect	Subsidies	Value added	Comp.	Capital	Net op.	Indirect	Subsidies	Value added
1 Agriculture, hunting, forestry and fishing	251	121	...	...	...	372	236	121	...	...	...	357
2 Mining and quarrying	13	...	...	...	...	13	3	...	...	...	...	3
3 Manufacturing	413	70	...	...	...	483	261	72	...	...	...	333
4 Electricity, gas and water	822	24	...	...	...	846	844	24	...	...	...	868
5 Construction	2226	102	...	...	...	2328	2231	104	...	...	...	2335
6 Wholesale and retail trade, restaurants and hotels	64	5	...	...	...	69	64	6	...	...	...	70
7 Transport, storage and communication	1012	2740	...	...	...	3752	1098	2847	...	...	...	3945
8 Finance, insurance, real estate and business services	1722	96	...	...	...	1818	1713	101	...	...	...	1815
9 Community, social and personal services	25902	2425	...	...	...	28327	27930	2499	...	...	...	30429
Total, industries of general government	32425	5583	...	...	...	38008	34380	5775	...	...	...	40155
Producers of government services	13024	1336	...	100	57	14403	14287	1373	...	111	53	15718
Total, general government	45692	6868	...	100	57	52603	48801	7132	...	111	53	55991

	1992						1993					
	Compensation of employees	Capital consumption	Net operating surplus	Indirect taxes	less: Subsidies received	Value added	Compensation of employees	Capital consumption	Net operating surplus	Indirect taxes	less: Subsidies received	Value added

All producers

1 Agriculture, hunting, forestry and fishing	2942	3764	5680	1251	653	12984	3174	3871	6237	1349	755	13876
2 Mining and quarrying	4860	4380	7532	627	572	16827	5033	4681	6728	617	636	16423
3 Manufacturing	33682	7425	11295	6473	775	58100	34959	7705	13634	6874	688	62484
4 Electricity, gas and water	3988	4017	5450	851	470	13836	3750	3903	5709	878	305	13935
5 Construction	14009	2045	7143	764	44	23917	14894	2175	7909	852	97	25733
6 Wholesale and retail trade, restaurants and hotels	37348	5869	14226	21823	317	78949	39541	6118	15652	24741	331	85721
A Wholesale and retail trade	31741	4606	13225	21486	285	70773	33577	4804	14634	24434	266	77183
B Restaurants and hotels	5607	1263	1001	337	32	8176	5964	1314	1018	307	65	8538
7 Transport, storage and communication	13984	9828	8227	2000	1881	32158	14600	10030	9179	2083	2131	33761
A Transport and storage	9526	7632	4159	1497	1856	20958	10074	7702	4899	1550	2099	22126
B Communication	4458	2196	4068	503	25	11200	4526	2328	4280	533	32	11635

Australia

	1992						1993					
	Compensation of employees	Capital consumption	Net operating surplus	Indirect taxes	less: Subsidies received	Value added	Compensation of employees	Capital consumption	Net operating surplus	Indirect taxes	less: Subsidies received	Value added
8 Finance, insurance, real estate and business services	29047	19587	48266	10894	870	106924	31177	20583	48760	12199	792	111927
A Financial institutions	11685	2810	14298	4494	788	32499	12421	2874	14799	5094	714	34474
B Insurance	...	...	...	...	...	...	...	...	...	...	...	...
C Real estate and business services	17362	16777	33968	6400	82	74425	18756	17709	33961	7105	78	77453
Real estate, except dwellings	17362	3584	9700	1693	82	32257	18756	3732	9065	1839	78	33314
Dwellings	...	13193	24268	4707	...	42168	...	13977	24896	5266	...	44139
9 Community, social and personal services	48110	4362	5099	3746	704	60613	50230	4556	5407	4198	695	63696
A Sanitary and similar services	...	...	...	...	...	...	...	...	...	...	...	...
B Social and related community services	37580	3191	2271	823	647	43218	39286	3327	2489	859	643	45318
Educational services	18220	1726	−63	335	127	20091	19185	1780	−58	358	143	21122
Medical, dental, other health and veterinary services	19360	1465	2334	488	520	23127	20101	1547	2547	501	500	24196
C Recreational and cultural services	3578	617	1876	2640	51	8660	3784	646	2091	3077	39	9559
D Personal and household services	6952	554	952	283	6	8735	7160	583	827	262	13	8819
Total, Industries	187970	61277	112918	48429	6286	404308	197358	63622	119215	53791	6430	427556
Producers of government services	13553	1502	—	133	70	15118	14589	1544	...	184	51	16266
Other producers	...	...	...	...	...	...	...	...	...	...	...	...
Total	201523	62779	112918	48562	6356	419426	211947	65166	119215	53975	6481	443822
less: Imputed bank service charge	...	...	14807	...	...	14807	...	...	14609	...	...	14609
Import duties	...	...	...	3333	...	3333	...	...	...	3223	...	3223
Value added tax	...	...	...	...	...	...	...	...	...	...	...	...
Other adjustments	...	...	...	...	...	...	...	...	...	...	...	...
Total	201523	62779	98111	51895	6356	407952	211947	65166	104606	57198	6481	432436
Of which general government:												
1 Agriculture, hunting, forestry and fishing	185	122	...	...	...	307	198	124	...	...	...	322
2 Mining and quarrying	—	...	...	...	...	—	—	...	...	...	...	—
3 Manufacturing	266	76	...	...	...	342	203	78	...	...	...	281
4 Electricity, gas and water	815	24	...	...	...	839	760	25	...	...	...	785
5 Construction	2195	108	...	...	...	2303	2412	111	...	...	...	2523
6 Wholesale and retail trade, restaurants and hotels	49	6	...	...	...	55	45	7	...	...	...	52
7 Transport, storage and communication	1029	2878	...	...	...	3907	869	2914	...	...	...	3783
8 Finance, insurance, real estate and business services	1764	108	...	...	...	1872	1762	111	...	...	...	1873
9 Community, social and personal services	29124	2593	...	...	...	31717	30388	2674	...	...	...	33062
Total, industries of general government	35427	5915	...	...	...	41342	36637	6044	...	...	...	42681
Producers of government services	14811	1440	...	175	71	16355	...	...	...	...	...	...
Total, general government	50398	7354	...	175	71	57856	...	...	...	...	...	...

Australia

	1994						1995					
	Compensation of employees	Capital consumption	Net operating surplus	Indirect taxes	less: Subsidies received	Value added	Compensation of employees	Capital consumption	Net operating surplus	Indirect taxes	less: Subsidies received	Value added

All producers

1 Agriculture, hunting, forestry and fishing	3496	3906	5007	1442	934	12917	3604	3901	8503	1457	968	16497
2 Mining and quarrying	5085	4870	7364	658	850	17127	5560	5156	7492	685	802	18091
3 Manufacturing	36991	7778	14949	7619	588	66749	39090	8025	15883	8143	629	70512
4 Electricity, gas and water	3505	3881	5806	936	231	13897	3430	4043	5640	1214	357	13970
5 Construction	16279	2216	9181	893	25	28544	17396	2298	8872	956	24	29498
6 Wholesale and retail trade, restaurants and hotels	41779	6219	16791	27162	294	91657	45075	6407	17979	29987	196	99252
A Wholesale and retail trade	35044	4859	15410	26819	269	81863	38010	4972	16439	29621	190	88852
B Restaurants and hotels	6735	1360	1381	343	25	9794	7065	1435	1540	366	6	10400
7 Transport, storage and communication	16024	10341	10565	2319	1980	37269	17097	10733	10279	2393	1976	38526
A Transport and storage	11226	7834	5734	1754	1955	24593	11409	7950	5093	1798	1932	24318
B Communication	4798	2507	4831	565	25	12676	5688	2783	5186	595	44	14208
8 Finance, insurance, real estate and business services	34642	21292	48471	12985	525	116865	37751	22330	53773	13435	500	126789
A Financial institutions	13088	2840	11475	5595	469	32529	14046	2850	12956	5839	444	35247
B Insurance	...	...	...	...	...	...	...	...	...	...	...	...
C Real estate and business services	21554	18452	36996	7390	56	84336	23705	19480	40817	7596	56	91542
Real estate, except dwellings	21554	3749	10832	1970	56	38049	23705	3861	12606	2091	56	42207
Dwellings	...	14703	26164	5420	...	46287	...	15619	28211	5505	...	49335
9 Community, social and personal services	52679	4708	6083	4667	768	67369	56013	4986	6620	5149	678	72090
A Sanitary and similar services	...	...	...	...	...	...	...	...	...	...	...	...
B Social and related community services	40570	3437	2745	873	649	46976	43075	3619	2691	938	543	49780
Educational services	19704	1821	–41	364	93	21755	20414	1903	–90	386	80	22533
Medical, dental, other health and veterinary services	20866	1616	2786	509	556	25221	22661	1716	2781	552	463	27247
C Recreational and cultural services	4401	678	2240	3494	107	10706	4470	748	2347	3887	123	11329
D Personal and household services	7708	593	1098	300	12	9687	8468	619	1582	324	12	10981
Total, Industries	210480	65211	124217	58681	6195	452394	225016	67879	135041	63419	6130	485225
Producers of government services	15225	1588	...	250	38	17025	16358	1651	...	263	37	18235
Other producers	...	...	...	...	...	...	...	...	...	...	...	...
Total	225705	66799	124217	58931	6233	469419	241374	69530	135041	63682	6167	503460
less: Imputed bank service charge	...	...	12600	...	...	12600	...	...	14471	...	...	14471
Import duties	...	...	...	3472	...	3472	...	...	...	3124	...	3124
Value added tax	...	...	...	...	...	...	...	...	...	...	...	...
Other adjustments	...	...	...	...	...	...	...	...	...	...	...	...
Total	225705	66799	111617	62403	6233	460291	241374	69530	120570	66806	6167	492113

Of which general government:

1 Agriculture, hunting, forestry and fishing	210	126	...	...	...	336	231	131	...	...	...	362
2 Mining and quarrying	–	...	...	...	...	–	2	...	...	...	...	2
3 Manufacturing	158	81	...	...	...	239	149	84	...	...	...	233

Australia

	1994						1995					
	Compensation of employees	Capital consumption	Net operating surplus	Indirect taxes	less: Subsidies received	Value added	Compensation of employees	Capital consumption	Net operating surplus	Indirect taxes	less: Subsidies received	Value added
4 Electricity, gas and water	718	25	...	...	...	743	724	26	...	...	...	750
5 Construction	2198	114	...	...	...	2312	2387	118	...	...	...	2505
6 Wholesale and retail trade, restaurants and hotels	42	7	...	...	...	49	47	7	...	...	...	54
7 Transport, storage and communication	799	2962	...	...	...	3761	696	3044	...	...	...	3740
8 Finance, insurance, real estate and business services	1621	119	...	...	...	1741	1773	123	...	...	...	1896
9 Community, social and personal services	30733	2737	...	...	...	33470	31789	2869	...	...	...	34658
Total, industries of general government	36479	6172	...	...	...	42651	37798	6402	...	...	...	44200
Producers of government services	...	...	...	...	...	...	...	...	...	...	...	...
Total, general government	...	...	...	...	...	...	...	...	...	...	...	...

	1996						1997					
	Compensation of employees	Capital consumption	Net operating surplus	Indirect taxes	less: Subsidies received	Value added	Compensation of employees	Capital consumption	Net operating surplus	Indirect taxes	less: Subsidies received	Value added
All producers												
1 Agriculture, hunting, forestry and fishing	3747	3869	8358	1430	1017	16387	...	...	...	...	...	...
2 Mining and quarrying	6059	5446	7290	732	854	18673	...	...	...	...	...	...
3 Manufacturing	40990	8259	15020	8641	614	72296	...	...	...	...	...	...
4 Electricity, gas and water	3373	4195	5796	1062	572	13854	...	...	...	...	...	...
5 Construction	18034	2397	9033	1030	36	30458	...	...	...	...	...	...
6 Wholesale and retail trade, restaurants and hotels	47821	6665	18057	31373	127	103789	...	...	...	...	...	...
A Wholesale and retail trade	40239	5154	16599	30978	113	92857	...	...	...	...	...	...
B Restaurants and hotels	7582	1511	1458	395	14	10932	...	...	...	...	...	...
7 Transport, storage and communication	17938	11152	11273	2583	2471	40475	...	...	...	...	...	...
A Transport and storage	11952	8364	6157	1955	2415	26013	...	...	...	...	...	...
B Communication	5986	2788	5116	628	56	14462	...	...	...	...	...	...
8 Finance, insurance, real estate and business services	41904	23460	55806	14589	395	135364	...	...	...	...	...	...
A Financial institutions	15112	2926	13026	6300	318	37046	...	...	...	...	...	...
B Insurance	...	...	...	...	...	...	...	...	...	...	...	...
C Real estate and business services	26792	20534	42780	8289	77	98318	...	...	...	...	...	...
Real estate, except dwellings	26792	4062	12860	2432	77	46069	...	...	...	...	...	...
Dwellings	...	16472	29920	5857	...	52249	...	...	...	...	...	...
9 Community, social and personal services	59464	5257	6860	5512	926	76167	...	...	...	...	...	...
A Sanitary and similar services	...	...	...	...	...	...	...	...	...	...	...	...
B Social and related community services	45812	3794	2768	1018	820	52572	...	...	...	...	...	...
Educational services	21540	1980	−95	412	113	23724	...	...	...	...	...	...
Medical, dental, other health and veterinary services	24272	1814	2863	606	707	28848	...	...	...	...	...	...
C Recreational and cultural services	4992	812	2366	4142	92	12220	...	...	...	...	...	...

Australia

	1996						1997					
	Compensation of employees	Capital consumption	Net operating surplus	Indirect taxes	less: Subsidies received	Value added	Compensation of employees	Capital consumption	Net operating surplus	Indirect taxes	less: Subsidies received	Value added
D Personal and household services	8660	651	1726	352	14	11375	...	...	...	...	...	...
Total, Industries	239330	70700	137493	66952	7012	507463	...	...	...	...	...	...
Producers of government services	18267	1707	...	279	49	20204	...	...	...	...	...	...
Other producers	...	...	...	...	...	...	...	...	...	...	...	...
Total	257597	72407	137493	67231	7061	527667	...	...	...	...	...	...
less: Imputed bank service charge	...	...	14499	...	...	14499	...	...	...	...	...	...
Import duties	...	...	...	3138	...	3138	...	...	...	...	...	...
Value added tax	...	...	...	...	...	...	...	...	...	...	...	...
Other adjustments	...	...	...	...	...	...	...	...	...	...	...	...
Total	257597	72407	122994	70369	7061	516306	...	...	...	...	...	...

Of which general government:

1 Agriculture, hunting, forestry and fishing	241	135	...	...	...	376	...	...	...	...	...	...
2 Mining and quarrying	11	...	...	...	...	11	...	...	...	...	...	...
3 Manufacturing	78	86	...	...	...	164	...	...	...	...	...	...
4 Electricity, gas and water	658	27	...	...	...	685	...	...	...	...	...	...
5 Construction	1852	121	...	...	...	1973	...	...	...	...	...	...
6 Wholesale and retail trade, restaurants and hotels	55	7	...	...	...	62	...	...	...	...	...	...
7 Transport, storage and communication	284	3105	...	...	...	3389	...	...	...	...	...	...
8 Finance, insurance, real estate and business services	1555	127	...	...	...	1682	...	...	...	...	...	...
9 Community, social and personal services	33812	2992	...	...	...	36804	...	...	...	...	...	...
Total, industries of general government	38546	6600	...	...	...	45146	...	...	...	...	...	...
Producers of government services	...	...	...	...	...	...	...	...	...	...	...	...
Total, general government	...	...	...	...	...	...	...	...	...	...	...	...

Austria

General note

The preparation of annual national accounts statistics in Austria is undertaken by the Austrian Central Statistical Office, Vienna. The official estimates are published annually in Oesterreichs Volkseinkommen (Austrian Central Statistical Office, Beitrage zur Osterreichischen Statistik). The concepts, definitions, sources of basic statistics and methods of estimation are described in the 1964–1977 and 1970–1980 issue of the above mentioned publication. The estimates are generally in accordance with the classifications and definitions recommended in the United Nations System of National Accounts (SNA). Input-output tables have been published for the years 1961, 1964 and 1976. The following tables have been prepared from successive replies to the United Nations national accounts questionnaire. When the scope and coverage of the estimates differ for conceptual or statistical reasons from the definitions and classifications recommended in SNA, a footnote is indicated to the relevant tables.

Gross domestic product

Gross domestic product is estimated mainly through the production approach.

Expenditures on the gross domestic product

The estimates of government final consumption expenditure are derived from production accounts compiled on the basis of the accounting records of the various authorities. The values of private expenditure on goods are mostly obtained by means of the commodity flow method, either by multiplying the quantity data by average consumer prices or by adding distributive margins and turnover tax and indirect taxes to the value of goods produced domestically or imported. The sources of data include statistics on agricultural produce, industrial output data by commodities, data on energy and foreign trade by commodities, motor vehicle registration statistics, closed accounts for public transportation enterprises, communication, insurance and others. For price data the consumer price index is largely referred to. In addition, decennial household surveys provide benchmark information on average prices. Own-account consumption is valued at producers' prices, for use of owner-occupied dwellings the corresponding market rents are imputed. For private expenditure on services, the estimates are mostly based on value added tax statistics. The data on increase in stocks are based on regular stock surveys covering almost all branches, those that are not covered are included in statistical discrepancy.

For gross fixed capital formation in machinery and electrical equipment, the value of domestic production plus imports minus exports is adjusted to include transport costs, trade margins, customs duties, etc. The estimates of transport equipment are based on registration statistics and are obtained by multiplying the quantity by the current prices. For construction, the gross value is derived from data on characteristic gross output, with additions for material supplied, non-characteristic construction (including own-account construction, e.g. residential buildings). The estimates of exports and imports of goods and services are based on foreign trade statistics and the balance of payments.

Constant price estimates of government final consumption expenditure are based on deflation for intermediate consumption and non-commodity sales. Compensation of employees is in certain activities also deflated, for others quantum indicators are used. For private consumption expenditure, direct revaluation at base-year prices is used where information is available on quantities of commodities consumed. Otherwise, the current estimates are deflated by appropriate price indexes. This same method is used for increase in stocks, exports and imports of goods and services and for gross fixed capital formation.

Cost structure of the gross domestic product

Estimates of compensation of employees are based on contributions paid by employers to government funds and wage statistics. Direct information is available on compensation of government employees. Operating surplus is basically derived as a residual item. Further breakdown is based on income tax statistics for unincorporated enterprises, independent professions and property. Corporate balance sheets and tax statistics are used for undistributed profits of corporations: for agriculture and forestry income is derived from the production account. In the case of the public sector, data are obtained from the accounting records of public bodies. Depreciation estimates of stocks are obtained either by using the perpetual inventory concept or, in some instances, are extrapolated by net output at constant prices and inflated by national accounts' price index for fixed capital formation. Indirect taxes and subsidies are obtained directly from the records of the various governments.

Gross domestic product by kind of activity

The table of gross domestic product by kind of economic activity is prepared at market prices, i.e. producers' values. The production approach is used to estimate value added of nearly all industries. The income approach is used to estimate value added of public administration and defence. The value added of agriculture is obtained by deducting the cost of all non-factor inputs from the gross value of production, which include an imputation for produce consumed on the farms. The calculations are based on production statistics for quantities, and on agricultural price surveys.

Mining and quarrying, electricity, gas and water as well as large-scale manufacturing are surveyed by annual overall censuses while small-scale manufacturing is surveyed annually by samples. Benchmark estimates have been prepared for 1964, 1971, 1976 and 1983. When necessary extrapolation is based on output statistics, sample survey and turnover statistics. For construction, census type data on gross output and input have been available annually since 1968, own-account construction is imputed for housing and agriculture. The estimates of turnover in retail and wholesale trade are based on the 1964, 1976 and 1983 census of non-agricultural establishments, the 1971 census of turnover and, since 1973, an annual sample survey. Estimates of restaurants and hotels are based on the 1964 industrial census and on a special survey in 1972, and 1976 and 1983 censuses. For the intermediate years, value added tax and turnover tax statistics as well as other suitable indicators (private accommodation) are used. For railways and air transportation and communication, value added is derived from the accounts of concerned enterprises. For the other activities of the transport sector, benchmark data have been provided by the 1964, 1976 and 1983 industrial censuses, extrapolated by various indicators. From 1973 onward, value added tax statistics provide the output indicators for most transportation other than large enterprises mentioned before.

For the financial institutions, value added is derived from accounting records for banking, and other financial institutions from statistics of the supervisory board for insurance. Data on real estate are obtained from decennial housing censuses and micro-census data on housing and rents. In the case of owner-occupied dwellings, rents paid for comparable dwellings are applied. The value added of government services is estimated by adding the cost items obtained from accounting records. The estimates of other services are based on annual turnover statistics, value added tax statistics and various net to gross ratios obtained from the 1964 and 1976 census of non-agricultural establishments. The value of domestic and health services is calculated by means of VAT, social security and wage statistics.

For the constant price estimates, double deflation is used, but not invariably, for agriculture, electricity, gas and water, construction, transportation and ownership of dwellings. In manufacturing, a combination of double deflation and fixed net ratios is applied. The turnover of wholesale and retail trade is deflated by appropriate price indexes. For the producers of government services, partly quantum indicators, partly suitable price (wage) indexes are used. For most of the remaining activities, value added is mostly calculated by deflation.

1.1 Expenditure on the gross domestic product, in current prices

Million Austrian schillings

	1986	1987	1988	1989	1990	1991	1992	1993	1994	1995	1996	1997
1 Government final consumption expenditure	281858	292480	302489	319601	338117	367799	398258	429574	454957	469322	478304	...
2 Private final consumption expenditure	813986	843921	886040	943288	1012961	1073004	1147677	1194057	1254605	1310245	1375415	...
A Households	793414	822108	863268	919359	986375	1043736	1115792	1160149	1218044	1271569	1335662	...
B Private non-profit institutions serving households	20572	21813	22772	23929	26586	29268	31885	33908	36561	38676	39753	...
3 Gross capital formation	330496	352247	369042	397565	438967	488312	491685	487812	534181	564390	580911	...
A Increase in stocks [a]	21388	24434	14930	11505	16978	22027	8245	2713	833	10320	4120	...
B Gross fixed capital formation [b]	309108	327813	354112	386060	421989	466285	483440	485099	533348	554070	576791	...
Residential buildings	65011	68838	76351	78609	79771	88302	100971	109442	122164	140447	149084	...
Non-residential buildings	90353	99971	104980	118534	138490	156926	162069	166588	182378	174832	183308	...
Other construction and land improvement, etc.	...	...	...	...	...	...	...	...	...	...	...	...
Other	133024	137895	149984	165011	179674	195091	192392	179179	197277	204438	212438	...
4 Exports of goods and services [c]	516675	522948	590759	669618	728312	774706	791618	786507	838841	900905	988783	...
5 less: Imports of goods and services [c]	503971	517471	582559	653395	704875	757999	771967	772607	842963	910504	1001790	...
Statistical discrepancy	–	–	–	–	–	–	–	–	–	...	...	...
equals: Gross domestic product	1439044	1494125	1565771	1676677	1813482	1945822	2057271	2125343	2239621	2334358	2421623	...

a Item "Increase in stocks" includes breeding stock, draught animals and a statistical discrepancy.
b Item "Gross fixed capital formation" includes value added tax on investments of investors not entitled to deduct invoiced value added tax. This component is not included in the sub-items.
c The estimates on transit trade are on a net basis.

Austria

1.2 Expenditure on the gross domestic product, in constant prices

Million Austrian schillings

	1986	1987	1988	1989	1990	1991	1992	1993	1994	1995	1996	1997
	At constant prices of: 1983											
1 Government final consumption expenditure	244897	245396	248184	251700	254878	260585	265839	273091	279845	279716	280037	...
2 Private final consumption expenditure	736639	758116	783196	812020	842503	866473	892211	898484	914198	940481	963244	...
A Households	718758	738906	764628	793072	822776	846121	870902	877498	892448	918541	941002	...
B Private non-profit institutions serving households	17881	19210	18568	18948	19727	20352	21309	20986	21750	21940	22242	...
3 Gross capital formation	309144	320142	335227	344203	371043	394680	384957	384207	419824	430963	430840	...
A Increase in stocks [a]	21248	19629	14151	3014	7355	8037	−2163	4812	8585	11785	1405	...
B Gross fixed capital formation [b]	287896	300513	321076	341189	363688	386643	387120	379395	411239	419178	429435	...
Residential buildings	61447	62866	67626	67359	65547	68398	75071	78735	84949	96130	100528	...
Non-residential buildings	84311	91280	93882	102304	117143	125559	124575	124292	132347	122432	124224	...
Other construction and land improvement, etc.	...	...	...	...	...	...	...	...	...	...	...	...
Other	124434	128833	140797	152252	162141	172707	166385	154475	171480	176794	183266	...
4 Exports of goods and services	494230	509558	561617	625271	674460	714435	726344	716915	757289	806323	881553	...
5 less: Imports of goods and services	485858	512321	565483	612847	657837	700276	712850	708212	766903	820226	891628	...
equals: Gross domestic product	1299052	1320891	1362741	1420347	1485047	1535897	1556501	1564485	1604253	1637257	1664046	...

a Item "Increase in stocks" includes breeding stock, draught animals and a statistical discrepancy.

b Item "Gross fixed capital formation" includes value added tax on investments of investors not entitled to deduct invoiced value added tax. This component is not included in the sub-items.

1.3 Cost components of the gross domestic product

Million Austrian schillings

	1986	1987	1988	1989	1990	1991	1992	1993	1994	1995	1996	1997
1 Indirect taxes, net	186678	196282	206622	222946	236348	245317	262945	272375	305768	316944	334013	...
A Indirect taxes	234044	245154	254887	271413	287880	305779	325823	340005	356603	367337	387463	...
B less: Subsidies	47366	48872	48265	48467	51532	60462	62878	67630	50835	50393	53450	...
2 Consumption of fixed capital	176195	183870	194114	205630	218486	235159	252567	270078	288691	306784	324700	...
3 Compensation of employees paid by resident producers to	765733	797421	826879	879607	949140	1030150	1098620	1145579	1189018	1230698	1244973	...
A Resident households	761254	792734	821189	873612	942809	1023590	1091938	1139989	1182733	1224321	1238596	...
B Rest of the world	...	...	5690	5995	6331	6560	6682	5590	6285	6377	6377	...
4 Operating surplus	310438	316552	338156	368494	409508	435196	443139	437311	456144	479932	517937	...
Statistical discrepancy	–	–	–	–	–	–	–	–	–	...	...	...
equals: Gross domestic product	1439044	1494125	1565771	1676677	1813482	1945822	2057271	2125343	2239621	2334358	2421623	...

1.4 General government current receipts and disbursements

Million Austrian schillings

	1986	1987	1988	1989	1990	1991	1992	1993	1994	1995	1996	1997
Receipts												
1 Operating surplus	...	...	...	...	...	...	...	...	...	...	...	...
2 Property and entrepreneurial income	25909	29436	30382	32886	37920	40616	49795	45508	46051	50700	41837	...
3 Taxes, fees and contributions	617660	635784	665260	694568	752338	816876	890141	938292	962475	990871	1057773	...
A Indirect taxes	234044	245154	254887	271413	287880	305779	325823	340005	356603	341394	360193	...

Austria

Million Austrian schillings

	1986	1987	1988	1989	1990	1991	1992	1993	1994	1995	1996	1997
B Direct taxes	203767	203357	214461	214465	238931	267125	296940	312658	299237	327687	363481	...
C Social security contributions	175993	183339	191817	204269	220619	238882	262302	280022	300523	315815	327835	...
D Compulsory fees, fines and penalties	3856	3934	4095	4421	4908	5090	5076	5607	6112	5975	6264	...
4 Other current transfers	38508	40491	42019	44422	47055	51104	54265	57401	55666	65271	59187	...
Total current receipts of general government	682077	705711	737661	771876	837313	908596	994201	1041201	1064192	1106842	1158797	...

Disbursements

	1986	1987	1988	1989	1990	1991	1992	1993	1994	1995	1996	1997
1 Government final consumption expenditure	270655	280436	288203	302691	319460	348274	375155	404966	425932	440275	446446	...
A Compensation of employees	182910	191440	195816	205391	218514	237013	255618	273863	287375	298369	301617	...
B Consumption of fixed capital	11310	11561	11803	12218	12770	13502	13809	14468	15053	15704	16246	...
C Purchases of goods and services, net	73568	74525	77670	81729	84604	93908	101630	111995	118764	121240	123751	...
D less: Own-account fixed capital formation	...	...	...	...	...	...	...	...	...	...	...	...
E Indirect taxes paid, net	2867	2910	2914	3353	3572	3851	4098	4640	4740	4962	4832	...
2 Property income	51880	58355	61603	66147	73398	81898	87451	91950	91058	102392	106811	...
A Interest	51880	58355	61603	66147	73398	81898	87451	91950	91058	102392	106811	...
B Net land rent and royalties	...	...	...	...	...	...	...	...	...	...	...	...
3 Subsidies	48393	49872	49199	49407	52504	61539	64027	68765	58246	63130	64793	...
4 Other current transfers	295527	316037	323595	338030	363129	391272	423994	472364	503832	527139	545054	...
A Social security benefits	151079	161466	167759	176423	188672	199860	212479	229572	247261	262160	274109	...
B Social assistance grants	80442	87039	85223	86354	94142	103715	117149	142328	150709	148760	148785	...
C Other	64006	67532	70613	75253	80315	87697	94366	100464	105862	116219	122160	...
5 Net saving	15622	1011	15061	15601	28822	25613	43574	3156	−14876	−26094	−4307	...
Total current disbursements and net saving of general government	682077	705711	737661	771876	837313	908596	994201	1041201	1064192	1106842	1158797	...

1.6 Current income and outlay of households and non-profit institutions

Million Austrian schillings

	1986	1987	1988	1989	1990	1991	1992	1993	1994	1995	1996	1997

Receipts

	1986	1987	1988	1989	1990	1991	1992	1993	1994	1995	1996	1997
1 Compensation of employees	765733	797421	832569	885602	955471	1036710	1105302	1151169	1195303	1237075	1251350	...
A From resident producers	761254	792734	820045	872478	937951	1018631	1086666	1132301	1172654	...	...	...
B From rest of the world	...	...	7586	7993	8442	8746	8938	8949	9493	...	...	...
2 Operating surplus of private unincorporated enterprises	...	...	...	...	...	...	...	...	...	...	...	...
3 Property and entrepreneurial income	268276	276370	289897	314271	362892	391652	397286	382010	399772	427889	474870	...
4 Current transfers	333552	360631	365163	381912	407362	439009	469467	526186	567328	585461	616937	...
A Social security benefits	151079	161466	167759	176423	188672	199860	212479	229572	247261	262160	274109	...
B Social assistance grants	80442	87039	85223	86354	94142	103715	117149	142328	150709	148760	148785	...
C Other	102031	112126	112181	119135	124548	135434	139839	154286	169358	174541	194043	...
Total current receipts	1367561	1434422	1487629	1581785	1725725	1867371	1972055	2059365	2162403	2250425	2343157	...

Disbursements

	1986	1987	1988	1989	1990	1991	1992	1993	1994	1995	1996	1997
1 Private final consumption expenditure	813986	843921	886040	943288	1012961	1073004	1147677	1194057	1254605	1310245	1375415	...
2 Property income	15729	17274	19174	22735	30213	38826	42816	43333	43839	44074	43237	...

Austria

Million Austrian schillings

	1986	1987	1988	1989	1990	1991	1992	1993	1994	1995	1996	1997
3 Direct taxes and other current transfers n.e.c. to general government	368643	376483	396592	406117	447559	490959	540345	578090	601458	637347	671855	...
A Social security contributions	175993	183339	191817	204269	220619	238882	262302	280022	300523	315815	327835	...
B Direct taxes	177591	177166	186394	180517	203375	227462	249864	267853	265798	286510	305898	...
C Fees, fines and penalties	15059	15978	18381	21331	23565	24615	28179	30215	35137	35022	38122	...
4 Other current transfers	73920	80099	86262	92335	93812	101636	111357	123939	127420	128921	142342	...
5 Net saving	95284	116646	99562	117310	141181	162947	129860	119946	135081	129838	110308	...
Total current disbursements and net saving	1367562	1434423	1487630	1581785	1725726	1867372	1972055	2059365	2162403	2250425	2343157	...

1.7 External transactions on current account, summary

Million Austrian schillings

	1986	1987	1988	1989	1990	1991	1992	1993	1994	1995	1996	1997
Payments to the rest of the world												
1 Imports of goods and services [a]	503971	517471	582559	653395	704875	757999	771967	772607	842963	910504	1001790	...
A Imports of merchandise, c.i.f. [a]	404818	408767	445222	509269	551254	585907	588666	562313	623314	648180	704104	...
B Other	99153	108704	137337	144126	153621	172092	183301	210294	219649	262324	297686	...
2 Factor income to rest of the world	70336	70190	75379	97154	107508	118089	112732	117437	110394	122970	143300	...
A Compensation of employees [b]	–	–	1896	1998	2111	2186	2256	3359	3323	3421	3580	...
B Property and entrepreneurial income	70414	70266	73483	95156	105397	115903	110476	114078	107071	119549	139720	...
By general government [c]	7348	7423	6898	8489	8779	10189	10315	12096	13311	17397	17881	...
By corporate and quasi-corporate enterprises	...	...	...	...	...	...	...	...	...	...	...	...
By other	...	...	...	...	...	...	...	...	...	...	...	...
3 Current transfers to the rest of the world [b]	14028	12717	15640	18312	19080	23313	28671	30275	31334	59921	67255	...
A Indirect taxes to supranational organizations	...	...	...	...	...	...	...	...	...	25943	27270	...
B Other current transfers	14028	12717	15640	18312	19080	23313	28671	30275	31334	33978	39985	...
4 Surplus of the nation on current transactions	3384	–2440	–2942	3277	13635	820	–1628	–8245	–20617	–41316	–49840	...
Payments to the rest of the world and surplus of the nation on current transfers	591719	597938	670636	772138	845098	900221	911742	912074	964074	1052079	1162505	...
Receipts from the rest of the world												
1 Exports of goods and services [a]	516675	522948	590759	669618	728312	774706	791618	786507	838841	900905	988783	...
A Exports of merchandise, f.o.b. [a]	339842	343280	375072	427938	467800	479309	486038	468277	512989	567557	623273	...
B Other	176833	179668	215687	241680	260512	295397	305580	318230	325852	333348	365510	...
2 Factor income from rest of the world	58403	57287	66912	88239	100230	104997	103072	108008	102157	115346	135686	...
A Compensation of employees [b]	–	–	7586	7993	8442	8746	8938	8949	9608	9798	9957	...
B Property and entrepreneurial income	58448	57361	59326	80246	91788	96251	94134	99059	92549	105548	125729	...
3 Current transfers from rest of the world [b]	16641	17703	12965	14281	16556	20518	17052	17559	23076	35828	38036	...
A Subsidies from supranational organisations	...	...	...	...	...	...	...	...	...	7178	9323	...
B Other current transfers	16641	17703	12965	14281	16556	20518	17052	17559	23076	28650	28713	...

Austria

Million Austrian schillings

	1986	1987	1988	1989	1990	1991	1992	1993	1994	1995	1996	1997
Receipts from the rest of the world on current transactions	591719	597938	670636	772138	845098	900221	911742	912074	964074	1052079	1162505	...

a The estimates on transit trade are on a net basis.
b Item "Compensation of employees" is included in current transfers to/from the rest of the world.
c Only central government data are included in the general government estimates.

1.8 Capital transactions of the nation, summary

Million Austrian schillings

	1986	1987	1988	1989	1990	1991	1992	1993	1994	1995	1996	1997
Finance of gross capital formation												
Gross saving	333880	349807	366100	400842	452602	489132	490057	479567	513564	523074	531071	...
1 Consumption of fixed capital	176195	183870	194114	205630	218486	235159	252567	270078	288691	306784	324700	...
A General government	10032	10359	10696	11118	11621	12287	12566	13166	13698	14291	14784	...
B Corporate and quasi-corporate enterprises	166163	173511	183418	194512	206865	222872	240001	256912	274993	292493	309916	...
C Other	...	...	...	...	...	...	...	...	...	...	...	...
2 Net saving	157685	165937	171986	195212	234116	253973	237490	209489	224873	216290	206371	...
A General government	16649	2011	15995	16541	29794	26690	44723	4291	−7465	−6179	16359	...
B Corporate and quasi-corporate enterprises	45752	47280	56429	61361	63141	64336	62907	85252	97257	92631	79704	...
C Other	95284	116646	99562	117310	141181	162947	129860	119946	135081	129838	110308	...
less: Surplus of the nation on current transactions	3384	−2440	−2942	3277	13635	820	−1628	−8245	−20617	−41316	−49840	...
Finance of gross capital formation	330496	352247	369042	397565	438967	488312	491685	487812	534181	564390	580911	...
Gross capital formation												
Increase in stocks [a]	21388	24434	14930	11505	16978	22027	8245	2713	833	10320	4120	...
Gross fixed capital formation [b]	309108	327813	354112	386060	421989	466285	483440	485099	533348	554070	576791	...
1 General government	52092	50728	50676	55192	57293	63043	67726	67493	70459	68065	66905	...
2 Corporate and quasi-corporate enterprises	...	...	...	...	...	...	...	...	...	...	...	...
3 Other	...	...	...	...	...	...	...	...	...	...	...	...
Gross capital formation	330496	352247	369042	397565	438967	488312	491685	487812	534181	564390	580911	...

a Item "Increase in stocks" includes breeding stock, draught animals and a statistical discrepancy.
b Item "Gross fixed capital formation" includes value added tax on investments of investors not entitled to deduct invoiced value added tax. This component is not included in the sub-items.

Austria

1.9 Gross domestic product by institutional sectors of origin

Million Austrian schillings

	1986	1987	1988	1989	1990	1991	1992	1993	1994	1995	1996	1997
Domestic factor incomes originating
1 General government	182910	191440	195816	205391	218514	237013	255494	273775	287823	...	...	...
2 Corporate and quasi-corporate enterprises	...	...	...	...	...	...	...	...	...	...	...	...
3 Households and private unincorporated enterprises	...	...	...	...	...	...	...	...	...	...	...	...
4 Non-profit institutions serving households	9250	9724	9766	10104	10860	11644	12682	13342	13975	...	...	...
subtotal: Domestic factor incomes	1076171	1113973	1165035	1248101	1358648	1465346	1541759	1582890	1645162	1710630	1762910	...
Indirect taxes, net	186678	196282	206622	222946	236348	245317	262945	272375	305768	316944	334013	...
A Indirect taxes	234044	245154	254887	271413	287880	305779	325823	340005	356603	367337	387463	...
B less: Subsidies	47366	48872	48265	48467	51532	60462	62878	67630	50835	50393	53450	...
Consumption of fixed capital	176195	183870	194114	205630	218486	235159	252567	270078	288691	306784	324700	...
Statistical discrepancy	–	–	–	–	–	–	–	–	–	...	...	...
Gross domestic product	1439044	1494125	1565771	1676677	1813482	1945822	2057271	2125343	2239621	2334358	2421623	...

1.10 Gross domestic product by kind of activity, in current prices

Million Austrian schillings

	1986	1987	1988	1989	1990	1991	1992	1993	1994	1995	1996	1997
1 Agriculture, hunting, forestry and fishing	47114	48473	49023	52304	56629	52992	50035	47322	50446	35897	34685	...
2 Mining and quarrying	10679	9052	9248	9498	9250	9236	8832	8638	8258	8601	8751	...
3 Manufacturing	335912	339417	358702	379725	410956	436350	442359	435682	455605	468490	480495	...
4 Electricity, gas and water	45430	48395	45637	48014	49215	52630	56758	60349	60750	63319	67130	...
5 Construction	85763	90854	95554	102950	114911	130173	140027	149493	165295	169483	179845	...
6 Wholesale and retail trade, restaurants and hotels	252175	260440	273946	294327	319462	339703	359698	363780	377630	405934	416336	...
7 Transport, storage and communication	87190	92318	99940	106954	116394	126961	139444	142490	148078	150677	154559	...
8 Finance, insurance, real estate and business services	234320	249388	267568	297240	324789	353711	386747	417882	429607	467777	498975	...
9 Community, social and personal services	49645	55111	59614	65319	70046	75555	85249	92730	99541	109959	117914	...
Total, Industries	1148227	1193447	1259231	1356331	1471651	1577310	1669149	1718366	1795210	1880137	1958690	...
Producers of government services	192802	201559	206399	217047	230698	250728	269888	289094	303574	314119	318021	...
Other producers	28640	30237	31570	32847	36378	39974	43732	46544	50333	52992	54618	...
Subtotal	1369669	1425243	1497200	1606225	1738727	1868012	1982769	2054004	2149117	2247248	2331329	...
less: Imputed bank service charge	68277	74942	79691	88193	94097	101766	109773	123908	109487	116815	119361	...
plus: Import duties	8996	9861	10631	11507	12026	12642	13269	13122	13903	12860	14690	...
plus: Value added tax	128655	133962	137630	147138	156825	166933	171006	182125	186088	191065	194965	...
plus: Other adjustments	–	–	–	–	–	–	–	–	–	...	...	...
equals: Gross domestic product	1439043	1494124	1565770	1676677	1813481	1945821	2057271	2125343	2239621	2334358	2421623	...

Austria

1.11 Gross domestic product by kind of activity, in constant prices

Million Austrian schillings

	1986	1987	1988	1989	1990	1991	1992	1993	1994	1995	1996	1997
	At constant prices of: 1983											
1 Agriculture, hunting, forestry and fishing	44638	44657	46539	46211	48118	44937	43569	43512	45666	44074	44955	...
2 Mining and quarrying	12133	10746	11427	11671	10897	10679	10177	9979	9139	9514	9278	...
3 Manufacturing	316205	314632	326592	341217	357345	370947	368290	359803	371494	374994	379974	...
4 Electricity, gas and water	42596	44833	43308	45301	46604	48379	51251	52225	51500	52161	52204	...
5 Construction	80812	81737	84061	87618	91959	97958	100678	103162	111008	110827	113981	...
6 Wholesale and retail trade, restaurants and hotels	236406	242339	253369	265053	281474	292750	296805	294743	297204	311215	312717	...
7 Transport, storage and communication	78439	83463	86838	92443	97871	102065	105722	109821	116229	121857	126993	...
8 Finance, insurance, real estate and business services	199504	204975	212293	226115	235881	249120	262096	274287	269480	281880	289980	...
9 Community, social and personal services	42458	45142	47213	49510	51851	53059	54227	55891	56857	58828	61014	...
Total, Industries	1053191	1072523	1111639	1165138	1222000	1269894	1292815	1303423	1328577	1365350	1391096	...
Producers of government services	167654	169520	171143	172533	175837	179219	183848	188580	192745	194021	194271	...
Other producers	25181	25660	26154	26284	27541	28577	29827	29190	30440	30531	30910	...
Subtotal	1246026	1267703	1308936	1363955	1425378	1477690	1506490	1521193	1551762	1589902	1616277	...
less: Imputed bank service charge	60103	63672	65589	69117	70170	75606	82165	92193	82013	87633	88154	...
plus: Import duties	8992	9573	10214	11021	11239	11257	11094	10972	11377	10571	12009	...
plus: Value added tax	104137	107286	109179	114487	118600	122556	121082	124513	123127	124417	123914	...
plus: Other adjustments	...	...	...	...	...	...	...	...	...	...	...	...
equals: Gross domestic product	1299052	1320890	1362740	1420346	1485047	1535897	1556501	1564485	1604253	1637257	1664046	...

1.12 Relations among national accounting aggregates

Million Austrian schillings

	1986	1987	1988	1989	1990	1991	1992	1993	1994	1995	1996	1997
Gross domestic product	1439043	1494124	1565770	1676677	1813481	1945821	2057271	2125343	2239621	2334358	2421623	...
plus: Net factor income from the rest of the world	−11933	−12903	−8467	−8915	−7278	−13092	−9660	−9429	−8237	−7624	−7614	...
Factor income from rest of the world	58403	57287	66912	88239	100230	104997	103072	108008	102157	115346	135686	...
less: Factor income to the rest of the world	70336	70190	75379	97154	107508	118089	112732	117437	110394	122970	143300	...
equals: Gross national product	1427110	1481221	1557303	1667762	1806203	1932729	2047611	2115914	2231384	2326734	2414009	...
less: Consumption of fixed capital	176195	183870	194114	205630	218486	235159	252567	270078	288691	306784	324700	...
equals: National income	1250915	1297351	1363189	1462132	1587717	1697570	1795044	1845836	1942693	2019950	2089309	...
plus: Net current transfers from the rest of the world	2613	4986	−2675	−4031	−2524	−2795	−11619	−12716	−8258	−24093	−29219	...
Current transfers from rest of the world	16641	17703	12965	14281	16556	20518	17052	17559	23076	35828	38036	...
less: Current transfers to the rest of the world	14028	12717	15640	18312	19080	23313	28671	30275	31334	59921	67255	...
equals: National disposable income	1253528	1302337	1360514	1458101	1585193	1694775	1783425	1833120	1934435	1995857	2060090	...
less: Final consumption	1095844	1136401	1188529	1262889	1351078	1440803	1545935	1623631	1709562	1779567	1853719	...
equals: Net saving	157685	165937	171986	195212	234116	253973	237490	209489	224873	216290	206371	...
less: Surplus of the nation on current transactions	3384	−2440	−2942	3277	13635	820	−1628	−8245	−20617	−41316	−49840	...
equals: Net capital formation	154301	168377	174928	191935	220481	253153	239118	217734	245490	257606	256211	...

Austria

2.1 Government final consumption expenditure by function, in current prices

Million Austrian schillings

	1986	1987	1988	1989	1990	1991	1992	1993	1994	1995	1996	1997
1 General public services	44066	45237	45842	47734	50434	59377	63250	68167	71755	73327	...	...
2 Defence	18094	16954	16516	18333	17877	18192	18521	19322	20096	20345	...	...
3 Public order and safety	13086	13359	13245	13783	14592	15887	16951	18265	19728	21023	...	...
4 Education	59870	62678	64061	67228	71385	77479	83748	90885	96657	100151	...	...
5 Health	64081	69754	72715	76852	82695	88751	98967	108112	115539	119941	...	...
6 Social security and welfare	49387	50001	53047	55269	58455	64613	69237	74213	74673	78261	...	...
7 Housing and community amenities	558	577	445	641	−302	9	−377	−473	−855	−1766	...	...
8 Recreational, cultural and religious affairs	5116	5352	5512	5963	6400	7265	7912	8655	9276	9659	...	...
9 Economic services	16397	16524	16820	16888	17923	16701	16946	17820	19063	19334	...	...
A Fuel and energy	–	1	–	1	2	3	–	5	1	3	...	...
B Agriculture, hunting, forestry and fishing	1769	1849	1943	1983	1932	702	747	832	1028	1464	...	...
C Mining (except fuels), manufacturing and construction	7498	7922	8373	8488	8991	9732	10084	11011	11293	11402	...	...
D Transportation and communication	6706	6340	6081	6062	6651	5910	5736	5604	6025	5914	...	...
E Other economic affairs	424	412	423	354	347	354	379	368	716	551	...	...
10 Other functions	–	–	–	–	–	–	–	–	–	–	...	...
Total government final consumption expenditures	270655	280436	288203	302691	319459	348274	375155	404966	425932	440275	446446	...

2.2 Government final consumption expenditure by function, in constant prices

Million Austrian schillings

	1986	1987	1988	1989	1990	1991	1992	1993	1994	1995	1996	1997
At constant prices of: 1983												
1 General public services	38431	38616	38515	38674	39457	44114	45199	46936	...	...	...	...
2 Defence	15540	14116	13373	14647	13897	13362	13056	13021	...	...	...	...
3 Public order and safety	11537	11518	11263	11197	11233	11566	11906	12367	...	...	...	...
4 Education	52568	53146	53716	54120	55135	55925	57430	59295	...	...	...	...
5 Health	55395	57689	58012	58313	59247	59611	61100	62723	...	...	...	...
6 Social security and welfare	42980	42262	43447	43341	44333	45974	47478	49163	...	...	...	...
7 Housing and community amenities	486	487	366	506	−222	6	−255	−306	...	...	...	...
8 Recreational, cultural and religious affairs	4488	4597	4627	4829	5003	5418	5676	5994	...	...	...	...
9 Economic services	14227	14163	14050	13614	14004	12461	12195	12383	...	...	...	...
A Fuel and energy	–	1	–	1	2	2	–	3	...	...	...	...
B Agriculture, hunting, forestry and fishing	1533	1579	1624	1590	1488	463	479	522	...	...	...	...
C Mining (except fuels), manufacturing and construction	6513	6796	6992	6854	7048	7324	7314	7703	...	...	...	...
D Transportation and communication	5812	5431	5082	4881	5189	4399	4121	3893	...	...	...	...
E Other economic affairs	369	356	352	288	277	273	281	262	...	...	...	...
10 Other functions	–	–	–	–	–	–	–	–	...	...	...	...
Total government final consumption expenditures	235652	236594	237369	239241	242087	248437	253785	261576	267437	...	...	...

Austria

2.3 Total government outlays by function and type

Million Austrian schillings

1986

	Final consumption expenditures Total	Compensation of employees	Other	Subsidies	Other current transfers and property income	Total current disbursements	Gross capital formation	Other capital outlays	Total outlays
1 General public services	44066	30850	13216	308	2592	46966	...	...	...
2 Defence	18094	9059	9035	–	117	18211	...	...	...
3 Public order and safety	13086	12864	222	3	97	13186	...	...	...
4 Education	59870	47944	11926	410	3338	63618	...	...	...
5 Health	64081	24633	39448	5717	2433	72231	...	...	...
6 Social security and welfare	49387	43483	5904	2562	279717	331666	...	...	...
7 Housing and community amenities	558	2252	–1694	803	2446	3807	...	...	...
8 Recreational, cultural and religious affairs	5116	2798	2318	2125	1556	8797	...	...	...
9 Economic services	16397	9027	7370	34119	3222	53738	...	...	...
A Fuel and energy	–	–	–	24	11	35	...	...	...
B Agriculture, hunting, forestry and fishing	1769	1539	230	13855	438	16062	...	...	...
C Mining (except fuels), manufacturing and construction	7498	3691	3807	3088	1728	12314	...	...	...
D Transportation and communication	6706	3778	2928	15696	520	22922	...	...	...
E Other economic affairs	424	19	405	1456	525	2405	...	...	...
10 Other functions	–	–	–	–	51880	51880	...	...	...
Total	270655	182910	87745	48393	347407	666455	52092	30245	748792

1987

	Final consumption expenditures Total	Compensation of employees	Other	Subsidies	Other current transfers and property income	Total current disbursements	Gross capital formation	Other capital outlays	Total outlays
1 General public services	45237	32074	13163	302	2702	48241	...	...	...
2 Defence	16954	9103	7851	–	40	16994	...	...	...
3 Public order and safety	13359	13115	244	3	105	13467	...	...	...
4 Education	62678	50572	12106	496	3870	67044	...	...	...
5 Health	69754	27380	42374	5547	2628	77929	...	...	...
6 Social security and welfare	50001	44571	5430	1972	299274	351247	...	...	...
7 Housing and community amenities	577	2359	–1782	884	2647	4108	...	...	...
8 Recreational, cultural and religious affairs	5352	2977	2375	2153	1748	9253	...	...	...
9 Economic services	16524	9289	7235	36024	3023	55571	...	...	...
A Fuel and energy	1	–	1	41	12	54	...	...	...
B Agriculture, hunting, forestry and fishing	1849	1578	271	16540	501	18890	...	...	...
C Mining (except fuels), manufacturing and construction	7922	3810	4112	2552	1389	11863	...	...	...
D Transportation and communication	6340	3885	2455	15618	531	22489	...	...	...
E Other economic affairs	412	16	396	1273	590	2275	...	...	...
10 Other functions	–	–	–	–	58355	58355	...	...	...
Total	280436	191440	88996	49872	374392	704700	50728	28048	783476

Austria

1988

	Final consumption expenditures			Subsidies	Other current transfers and property income	Total current disburse-ments	Gross capital formation	Other capital outlays	Total outlays
	Total	Compen-sation of employ-ees	Other						
1 General public services	45842	32537	13305	−121	2887	48608	...	...	...
2 Defence	16516	9253	7263	1	37	16554	...	...	...
3 Public order and safety	13245	13186	59	3	110	13358	...	...	...
4 Education	64061	51543	12518	427	3825	68313	...	...	...
5 Health	72715	27938	44777	5717	2543	80975	...	...	...
6 Social security and welfare	53047	46515	6532	1331	306221	360599	...	...	...
7 Housing and community amenities	445	2345	−1900	1031	2925	4401	...	...	...
8 Recreational, cultural and religious affairs	5512	3113	2399	2503	1798	9813	...	...	...
9 Economic services	16820	9386	7434	34187	3249	54256	...	...	...
A Fuel and energy	–	–	–	58	16	74	...	...	...
B Agriculture, hunting, forestry and fishing	1943	1660	283	15508	571	18022	...	...	...
C Mining (except fuels), manufacturing and construction	8373	3883	4490	2809	1533	12715	...	...	...
D Transportation and communication	6081	3825	2256	14663	496	21240	...	...	...
E Other economic affairs	423	18	405	1149	633	2205	...	...	...
10 Other functions	–	–	–	–	61603	61603	...	...	...
Total	288203	195816	92387	49199	385198	722600	50676	29122	802398

1989

	Final consumption expenditures			Subsidies	Other current transfers and property income	Total current disburse-ments	Gross capital formation	Other capital outlays	Total outlays
	Total	Compen-sation of employ-ees	Other						
1 General public services	47734	33954	13780	25	2946	50705	...	...	...
2 Defence	18333	9373	8960	2	35	18370	...	...	...
3 Public order and safety	13783	13752	31	1	121	13905	...	...	...
4 Education	67228	54884	12344	476	4033	71737	...	...	...
5 Health	76852	29478	47374	6343	3152	86347	...	...	...
6 Social security and welfare	55269	49084	6185	1242	319726	376237	...	...	...
7 Housing and community amenities	641	2440	−1799	966	3023	4630	...	...	...
8 Recreational, cultural and religious affairs	5963	3399	2564	2187	1964	10114	...	...	...
9 Economic services	16888	9746	7142	33867	3030	53785	...	...	...
A Fuel and energy	1	–	1	267	29	297	...	...	...
B Agriculture, hunting, forestry and fishing	1983	1688	295	14337	600	16920	...	...	...
C Mining (except fuels), manufacturing and construction	8488	4133	4355	2489	1185	12162	...	...	...
D Transportation and communication	6062	3908	2154	15444	454	21960	...	...	...
E Other economic affairs	354	17	337	1330	762	2446	...	...	...
10 Other functions	–	–	–	–	66147	66147	...	...	...
Total	302691	205391	97300	49407	404177	756275	55192	24289	835756

Austria

1990

	Final consumption expenditures			Subsidies	Other current transfers and property income	Total current disbursements	Gross capital formation	Other capital outlays	Total outlays
	Total	Compensation of employees	Other						
1 General public services	50434	36161	14273	144	3585	54163	...	...	...
2 Defence	17877	9543	8334	2	43	17922	...	...	...
3 Public order and safety	14592	14672	–80	–3	159	14748	...	...	...
4 Education	71385	57320	14065	617	4407	76409	...	...	...
5 Health	82695	32128	50567	6941	3469	93105	...	...	...
6 Social security and welfare	58455	52255	6200	1202	343047	402704	...	...	...
7 Housing and community amenities	–302	2534	–2836	921	2780	3399	...	...	...
8 Recreational, cultural and religious affairs	6400	3649	2751	2685	2147	11232	...	...	...
9 Economic services	17923	10252	7671	35345	3492	56760	...	...	...
A Fuel and energy	2	–	2	87	16	105	...	...	...
B Agriculture, hunting, forestry and fishing	1932	1766	166	14135	751	16818	...	...	...
C Mining (except fuels), manufacturing and construction	8991	4369	4622	2975	1408	13374	...	...	...
D Transportation and communication	6651	4102	2549	16761	444	23856	...	...	...
E Other economic affairs	347	15	332	1387	873	2607	...	...	...
10 Other functions	–	–	–	–	73398	73398	...	...	...
Total	319459	218514	100946	52504	436527	808491	57293	28355	894138

1991

	Final consumption expenditures			Subsidies	Other current transfers and property income	Total current disbursements	Gross capital formation	Other capital outlays	Total outlays
	Total	Compensation of employees	Other						
1 General public services	59377	39403	19974	36	4256	63669	...	...	...
2 Defence	18192	10476	7716	–	52	18244	...	...	...
3 Public order and safety	15887	15948	–61	1	146	16034	...	...	...
4 Education	77479	62591	14888	618	5077	83174	...	...	...
5 Health	88751	34499	54252	7454	3902	100107	...	...	...
6 Social security and welfare	64613	56158	8455	1622	368947	435182	...	...	...
7 Housing and community amenities	9	2825	–2816	1191	2994	4194	...	...	...
8 Recreational, cultural and religious affairs	7265	4141	3124	2708	2449	12422	...	...	...
9 Economic services	16701	10972	5729	47909	3449	68059	...	...	...
A Fuel and energy	3	–	3	87	43	133	...	...	...
B Agriculture, hunting, forestry and fishing	702	1853	–1151	16801	802	18305	...	...	...
C Mining (except fuels), manufacturing and construction	9732	4726	5006	10122	1306	21160	...	...	...
D Transportation and communication	5910	4376	1534	18703	395	25008	...	...	...
E Other economic affairs	354	17	337	2196	903	3453	...	...	...
10 Other functions	–	–	–	–	81898	81898	...	...	...
Total	348274	237013	111261	61539	473170	882983	63043	27880	973906

Austria

1992

	Final consumption expenditures Total	Compensation of employees	Other	Subsidies	Other current transfers and property income	Total current disbursements	Gross capital formation	Other capital outlays	Total outlays
1 General public services	63250	42112	21138	417	4846	68513	...	...	...
2 Defence	18521	10633	7888	–	37	18558	...	...	...
3 Public order and safety	16951	17015	–64	1	141	17093	...	...	...
4 Education	83748	67823	15925	860	5266	89874	...	...	...
5 Health	98967	38419	60548	7963	4771	111701	...	...	...
6 Social security and welfare	69237	60392	8845	1866	398135	469238	...	...	...
7 Housing and community amenities	–377	3037	–3414	1195	3523	4341	...	...	...
8 Recreational, cultural and religious affairs	7912	4522	3390	3176	2767	13855	...	...	...
9 Economic services	16946	11665	5281	48549	4508	70003	...	...	...
A Fuel and energy	–	–	–	83	48	131	...	...	...
B Agriculture, hunting, forestry and fishing	747	1938	–1191	17944	1043	19734	...	...	...
C Mining (except fuels), manufacturing and construction	10084	5153	4931	9217	1992	21293	...	...	...
D Transportation and communication	5736	4555	1181	19486	429	25651	...	...	...
E Other economic affairs	379	19	360	1819	996	3194	...	...	...
10 Other functions	–	–	–	–	87451	87451	...	...	...
Total	375155	255618	119537	64027	511445	950627	67726	28133	1046486

1993

	Final consumption expenditures Total	Compensation of employees	Other	Subsidies	Other current transfers and property income	Total current disbursements	Gross capital formation	Other capital outlays	Total outlays
1 General public services	68167	45008	23159	398	5147	73712	...	...	...
2 Defence	19322	10993	8329	–	67	19389	...	...	...
3 Public order and safety	18265	18284	–19	1	131	18397	...	...	...
4 Education	90885	73093	17792	704	6251	97840	...	...	...
5 Health	108112	41495	66617	7284	5154	120550	...	...	...
6 Social security and welfare	74213	64721	9492	1827	442232	518272	...	...	...
7 Housing and community amenities	–473	3272	–3745	2426	3969	5922	...	...	...
8 Recreational, cultural and religious affairs	8655	4905	3750	3611	3122	15388	...	...	...
9 Economic services	17820	12092	5728	52514	6291	76625	...	...	...
A Fuel and energy	5	–	5	82	65	152	...	...	...
B Agriculture, hunting, forestry and fishing	832	1995	–1163	18092	1150	20074	...	...	...
C Mining (except fuels), manufacturing and construction	11011	5453	5558	10756	3612	25379	...	...	...
D Transportation and communication	5604	4625	979	21272	455	27331	...	...	...
E Other economic affairs	368	19	349	2312	1009	3689	...	...	...
10 Other functions	–	–	–	–	91950	91950	...	...	...
Total	404966	273863	131103	68765	564314	1038045	67493	36995	1142533

Austria

1994

	Final consumption expenditures – Total	Compensation of employees	Other	Subsidies	Other current transfers and property income	Total current disbursements	Gross capital formation	Other capital outlays	Total outlays
1 General public services	71755	47425	24330	419	6417	78591	...	...	...
2 Defence	20096	11465	8631	2	91	20189	...	...	...
3 Public order and safety	19728	19715	13	1	156	19885	...	...	...
4 Education	96657	77249	19408	693	6473	103823	...	...	...
5 Health	115539	44259	71280	7363	5509	128411	...	...	...
6 Social security and welfare	74673	66982	7691	1730	470401	546804	...	...	...
7 Housing and community amenities	−855	3490	−4345	3182	4244	6571	...	...	...
8 Recreational, cultural and religious affairs	9276	5291	3985	3316	3380	15972	...	...	...
9 Economic services	19063	11499	7564	41540	7161	67764	...	...	...
A Fuel and energy	1	–	1	85	108	194	...	...	...
B Agriculture, hunting, forestry and fishing	1028	2053	−1025	16625	1758	19411	...	...	...
C Mining (except fuels), manufacturing and construction	11293	5546	5747	6137	3804	21234	...	...	...
D Transportation and communication	6025	3729	2296	17290	449	23764	...	...	...
E Other economic affairs	716	171	545	1403	1042	3161	...	...	...
10 Other functions	–	–	–	–	91058	91058	...	...	...
Total	425932	287375	138557	58246	594890	1079068	70459	37568	1187095

1995

	Final consumption expenditures – Total	Compensation of employees	Other	Subsidies	Other current transfers and property income	Total current disbursements	Gross capital formation	Other capital outlays	Total outlays
1 General public services	73327	48751	24576	1095	11575	85997	...	...	...
2 Defence	20345	11758	8587	2	88	20435	...	...	...
3 Public order and safety	21023	20665	358	1	157	21181	...	...	...
4 Education	100151	80039	20112	744	7070	107965	...	...	...
5 Health	119941	46616	73325	7438	6082	133461	...	...	...
6 Social security and welfare	78261	69337	8924	1656	486480	566397	...	...	...
7 Housing and community amenities	−1766	3658	−5424	3350	4430	6014	...	...	...
8 Recreational, cultural and religious affairs	9659	5539	4120	3445	3503	16607	...	...	...
9 Economic services	19334	12006	7328	45399	7754	72487	...	...	...
A Fuel and energy	3	–	3	77	75	155	...	...	...
B Agriculture, hunting, forestry and fishing	1464	2274	−810	21707	1321	4492	...	...	...
C Mining (except fuels), manufacturing and construction	11402	5846	5556	4852	4894	21148	...	...	...
D Transportation and communication	5914	3809	2105	17165	404	23383	...	...	...
E Other economic affairs	551	77	474	15					
10 Other functions	–	–	–	–			...		
Total	440275	298369	141906	63130	629531				

Austria

	1996								
	Final consumption expenditures			Subsidies	Other current transfers and property income	Total current disburse-ments	Gross capital formation	Other capital outlays	Total outlays
	Total	Compensation of employ-ees	Other						
Total	446446	301617	144829	64793	651865	1163104	66905	38131	1268140

2.4 Composition of general government social security benefits and social assistance grants to households
Million Austrian schillings

	1986		1987		1988		1989		1990		1991	
	Social security benefits	Social assistance grants	Social security benefits	Social assistance grants	Social security benefits	Social assistance grants	Social security benefits	Social assistance grants	Social security benefits	Social assistance grants	Social security benefits	Social assistance grants
1 Education benefits	4	3193	4	3712	3	3664	3	3866	3	4203	3	4869
2 Health benefits	354	1857	375	2046	384	1999	394	2499	407	2813	341	3253
3 Social security and welfare benefits	149464	67684	160241	72943	166372	70753	175434	70783	187605	77279	198735	85060
4 Housing and community amenities	...	2446	...	2646	...	2924	...	3021	...	2779	...	2993
5 Recreation and cultural benefits	...	1545	...	1739	...	1789	...	1949	...	2131	...	2431
6 Other	1257	3718	846	3953	1000	4094	592	4236	657	4937	781	5109
Total	151079	80442	161466	87039	167759	85223	176423	86354	188672	94142	199860	103715

	1992		1993		1994		1995		1996		1997	
	Social security benefits	Social assistance grants	Social security benefits	Social assistance grants	Social security benefits	Social assistance grants	Social security benefits	Social assistance grants	Social security benefits	Social assistance grants	Social security benefits	Social assistance grants
1 Education benefits	4	5035	4	5965	4	6198	4	6811	...	...	...	...
2 Health benefits	379	3943	312	4320	270	4812	340	5198	...	...	...	...
3 Social security and welfare benefits	210496	96100	226158	118972	244239	125282	257830	122644	...	...	...	...
4 Housing and community amenities	...	3522	...	3885	...	4081	...	4243	...	...	...	...
5 Recreation and cultural benefits	...	2747	...	3087	...	3347	...	3485	...	...	...	...
6 Other	1600	5802	3098	6099	2748	6989	3986	6379	...	...	...	...
Total	212479	117149	229572	142328	247261	150709	262160	148760	274109	148785	...	...

2.5 Private final consumption expenditure by type and purpose, in current prices
Million Austrian schillings

	1986	1987	1988	1989	1990	1991	1992	1993	1994	1995	1996	1997
Final consumption expenditure of resident households
1 Food, beverages and tobacco	179826	181545	185497	193726	204088	213950	222579	225663	226255	228313	229050	...
A Food	136348	137772	140961	148330	157581	166080	172633	175640	175692	174937	172917	...
B Non-alcoholic beverages	5074	5498	5624	5880	6573	7049	7904	7842	8017	8682	8371	...
C Alcoholic beverages	18358	18247	18954	19590	19390	19303	20353	20822	20019	22752	25595	...
D Tobacco	20045	20028	19958	19926	20545	21518	21689	21359	22527	21943	22167	...
2 Clothing and footwear	86678	89228	89737	94638	100056	104178	105680	105562	104941	100965	100918	...
3 Gross rent, fuel and power	149535	152916	153699	163395	178090	188199	200164	212427	229582	250505	274075	...
A Fuel and power	43195	42558	39786	40228	42893	48052	46770	49063	48466	52711	58658	...
B Other	106340	110358	113913	123167	135197	140147	153394	163364	181116	197794	215417	...
4 Furniture, furnishings and household equipment and operation	61081	64051	74875	78666	85433	88495	94033	99065	104831	107330	110665	...

Austria

Million Austrian schillings

	1986	1987	1988	1989	1990	1991	1992	1993	1994	1995	1996	1997
A Household operation	14535	14479	15227	15881	16811	18364	19439	20771	22192	23201	24107	...
B Other	46546	49572	59648	62785	68622	70131	74594	78294	82639	84129	86558	...
5 Medical care and health expenses	31610	34320	36348	42290	45815	49564	55405	59509	64094	68523	74160	...
6 Transport and communication	123570	125403	133393	152103	164173	178078	188588	188839	192170	200536	222595	...
A Personal transport equipment	33162	32259	37489	42981	48595	52877	58002	53463	53337	53344	64462	...
B Other	90408	93144	95904	109122	115578	125201	130586	135376	138833	147192	158133	...
7 Recreational, entertainment, education and cultural services	54965	60566	73293	78902	84925	91890	97975	101131	107919	109615	110589	...
A Education	3112	3531	4165	4600	5310	5860	6083	6620	6470	6777	6567	...
B Other	51853	57035	69128	74302	79615	86030	91892	94511	101449	102838	104022	...
8 Miscellaneous goods and services	149057	154567	163048	174411	188358	203875	222768	233546	235734	240342	242091	...
A Personal care	21974	22977	24516	25921	28218	30166	31950	32810	33848	33973	34381	...
B Expenditures in restaurants, cafes and hotels	110086	112322	117244	125634	133823	144478	156638	161552	163952	165625	164252	...
C Other	16997	19268	21288	22856	26317	29231	34180	39184	37934	40744	43458	...
Total final consumption expenditure in the domestic market by households, of which	836322	862596	909891	978130	1050939	1118230	1187191	1225742	1265526	1306129	1364143	...
A Durable goods	91498	94933	117067	122294	133660	140418	150275	148957	153238	155477	169437	...
B Semi-durable goods	104345	107383	109075	115348	122958	127186	129793	130626	130762	126248	126585	...
C Non-durable goods	271965	273601	277262	293508	311380	331049	341074	347276	348521	358262	369739	...
D Services	368514	386680	406487	446980	482940	519576	566049	598882	633006	666142	698382	...
plus: Direct purchases abroad by resident households	58654	67615	73429	77611	82322	79943	88241	91927	102701	112492	119770	...
less: Direct purchases in the domestic market by non-resident households	101562	108103	120052	136382	146886	154437	159640	157520	150183	147052	148251	...
equals: Final consumption expenditure of resident households [a]	793414	822108	863268	919359	986375	1043736	1115792	1160149	1218044	1271569	1335662	...

Final consumption expenditures by private non-profit organisations serving households

	1986	1987	1988	1989	1990	1991	1992	1993	1994	1995	1996	1997
1 Research and science	...	...	...	...	...	...	...	...	...	...	...	...
2 Education	...	...	...	...	...	...	...	...	...	...	...	...
3 Medical and other health services	...	...	...	...	...	...	...	...	...	...	...	...
4 Welfare services	...	...	...	...	...	...	...	...	...	...	...	...
5 Recreational and related cultural services	...	...	...	...	...	...	...	...	...	...	...	...
6 Religious organisations	...	...	...	...	...	...	...	...	...	...	...	...
7 Professional and labour organisations serving households	...	...	...	...	...	...	...	...	...	...	...	...
8 Miscellaneous	...	...	...	...	...	...	...	...	...	...	...	...
equals: Final consumption expenditures by private non-profit organisations serving households	20572	21813	22772	23929	26586	29268	31885	33908	36561	38676	39753	...
Private final consumption expenditure	813986	843921	886040	943288	1012961	1073004	1147677	1194057	1254605	1310245	1375415	...

a Item "Final consumption expenditure of resident households" includes consumption expenditure of private non-profit institutions serving households.

2.6 Private final consumption expenditure by type and purpose, in constant prices

Million Austrian schillings

	1986	1987	1988	1989	1990	1991	1992	1993	1994	1995	1996	1997
At constant prices of: 1983												

Final consumption expenditure of resident households

	1986	1987	1988	1989	1990	1991	1992	1993	1994	1995	1996	1997
1 Food, beverages and tobacco	163441	164050	166928	172876	177780	179717	181260	180507	178193	183299	181908	...
A Food	125585	126432	129740	134933	139070	140529	142219	142359	140329	143715	141250	...
B Non-alcoholic beverages	4747	5140	5262	5489	6136	6287	6713	6553	6700	7175	6694	...
C Alcoholic beverages	15984	15616	15718	16620	16288	16066	15848	15625	14796	16905	18830	...
D Tobacco	17125	16861	16208	15834	16287	16836	16480	15971	16368	15503	15135	...
2 Clothing and footwear	77879	78642	76755	78211	79793	79929	78061	75169	72328	68602	69104	...
3 Gross rent, fuel and power	132336	135168	134141	139363	143605	149263	150093	153910	157795	165346	170758	...
A Fuel and power	41904	44209	42441	43003	44480	49036	47064	49571	48806	52957	56534	...
B Other	90432	90959	91700	96359	99125	100227	103030	104339	108989	112388	114224	...
4 Furniture, furnishings and household equipment and operation	55320	57443	66206	67884	71547	72129	74470	75533	77962	78619	80772	...
A Household operation	13128	12835	13205	13478	13773	14413	14616	14943	15438	15763	16157	...
B Other	42192	44608	53001	54406	57774	57716	59854	60590	62524	62856	64615	...
5 Medical care and health expenses	27153	28527	29990	33821	35523	36778	38233	39319	39809	40567	42266	...
6 Transport and communication	116710	117436	122305	135451	142624	151984	156385	152852	151697	154249	165242	
A Personal transport equipment	29372	27776	31457	35202	38941	41121	44170	39358	38404	38039	45275	...
B Other	87338	89660	90848	100249	103683	110863	112215	113494	113293	116210	119967	...
7 Recreational, entertainment, education and cultural services	49628	53965	64354	65756	70123	73179	74914	74320	74503	76422	76431	
A Education	2740	2918	3291	3251	3573	3711	3633	3636	3229	3147	2865	...
B Other	46888	51047	61063	62505	66550	69468	71281	70684	71274	73275	73566	...
8 Miscellaneous goods and services	133272	136502	141179	148451	156125	163716	172029	172539	167977	167417	165717	...
A Personal care	20060	21228	22522	23585	25648	26953	27959	27698	27602	27228	27135	...
B Expenditures in restaurants, cafes and hotels	97745	98168	100206	105617	109088	113411	118100	115881	114197	112758	109835	...
C Other	15467	17106	18451	19249	21389	23352	25970	28960	26178	27431	28747	...
Total final consumption expenditure in the domestic market by households, of which	755740	771731	801858	841813	877120	906696	925445	924148	920264	934520	952197	...
A Durable goods	83051	86222	105730	108072	116015	119465	125134	120313	121081	122073	131743	...
B Semi-durable goods	94026	94996	94086	96441	99620	99317	97579	94819	92341	88220	89067	...
C Non-durable goods	256266	260604	264731	276743	285027	295869	295040	296852	292935	302271	305826	...
D Services	322397	329909	337312	360558	376458	392045	407692	412165	413907	421955	425561	...
plus: Direct purchases abroad by resident households	54919	63969	68433	69224	69511	65223	70027	71092	80219	87543	90942	...
less: Direct purchases in the domestic market by non-resident households	91901	96794	105663	117965	123855	125798	124570	117742	108035	103522	102137	...
equals: Final consumption expenditure of resident households	718758	738906	764628	793072	822776	846121	870902	877498	892448	918541	941002	...

Final consumption expenditures by private non-profit organisations serving households

	1986	1987	1988	1989	1990	1991	1992	1993	1994	1995	1996	1997
1 Research and science	...	...	...	...	...	...	...	...	...	...	...	...
2 Education	...	...	...	...	...	...	...	...	...	...	...	...
3 Medical and other health services	...	...	...	...	...	...	...	...	...	...	...	...

Austria

Million Austrian schillings

	1986	1987	1988	1989	1990	1991	1992	1993	1994	1995	1996	1997
	At constant prices of: 1983											
4 Welfare services	...	...	...	...	...	...	...	...	...	...	...	...
5 Recreational and related cultural services	...	...	...	...	...	...	...	...	...	...	...	...
6 Religious organisations	...	...	...	...	...	...	...	...	...	...	...	...
7 Professional and labour organisations serving households	...	...	...	...	...	...	...	...	...	...	...	...
8 Miscellaneous	...	...	...	...	...	...	...	...	...	...	...	...
equals: Final consumption expenditures by private non-profit organisations serving households	17881	19210	18568	18948	19727	20352	21309	20986	21750	21940	22242	...
Private final consumption expenditure	736639	758116	783196	812020	842503	866473	892211	898484	914198	940481	963244	...

2.7 Gross capital formation by type of good and owner, in current price

Million Austrian schillings

	1986				1987				1988			
	Total	Total private	Public enterprises	General government	Total	Total private	Public enterprises	General government	Total	Total private	Public enterprises	General government
Increase in stocks, total [a]	21388	...	...	...	24434	...	...	...	14930	...	...	...
1 Goods producing industries	625	...	...	...	−4522	...	...	...	−1808	...	...	...
A Materials and supplies	−126	...	...	...	1310	...	...	...	1363	...	...	...
B Work in progress	−2222	...	...	...	−2538	...	...	...	−1573	...	...	...
C Livestock, except breeding stocks, dairy cattle, etc.	−412	...	...	...	−194	...	...	...	−738	...	...	...
D Finished goods	1707	...	...	...	−3104	...	...	...	−1010	...	...	...
2 Wholesale and retail trade	1729	...	...	...	3133	...	...	...	8187	...	...	...
3 Other, except government stocks [b]	−76	...	...	...	396	...	...	...	206	...	...	...
4 Government stocks	...	...	...	...	...	...	...	...	...	...	...	...
Statistical discrepancy [c]	18698	...	...	...	25233	...	...	...	7607	...	...	...
Gross fixed capital formation, total	309108	...	...	46122	327813	...	...	45482	354112	...	...	44323
1 Residential buildings	65011	...	...	1606	68838	...	...	1938	76351	...	...	1956
2 Non-residential buildings	90353	...	...	16093	99971	...	...	14817	104980	...	...	14354
3 Other construction	...	...	...	18308	...	...	...	18970	...	...	...	17923
4 Land improvement and plantation and orchard development	...	...	...	...	...	...	...	...	...	...	...	...
5 Producers' durable goods	133024	...	...	5858	137895	...	...	5610	149984	...	...	6169
A Transport equipment [d]	23269	...	...	−	23774	...	...	−	26769	...	...	−
Passenger cars	10822	...	...	...	10753	...	...	...	12464	...	...	...
Other	12447	...	...	...	13021	...	...	...	14305	...	...	...
B Machinery and equipment	109755	...	...	5858	114121	...	...	5610	123215	...	...	6169
6 Breeding stock, dairy cattle, etc.	...	...	...	...	...	...	...	...	...	...	...	...
Statistical discrepancy [e]	20720	...	...	4257	21109	...	...	4147	22797	...	...	3921
Total gross capital formation	330496	...	...	46122	352247	...	...	45482	369042	...	...	44323

	1989				1990				1991			
	Total	Total private	Public enterprises	General government	Total	Total private	Public enterprises	General government	Total	Total private	Public enterprises	General government
Increase in stocks, total [a]	11505	...	...	...	16978	...	...	...	22027	...	...	...
1 Goods producing industries	6193	...	...	...	14322	...	...	...	3456	...	...	...

Austria

	1989 Total	1989 Total private	1989 Public enterprises	1989 General government	1990 Total	1990 Total private	1990 Public enterprises	1990 General government	1991 Total	1991 Total private	1991 Public enterprises	1991 General government
A Materials and supplies	2323	...	...	...	3447	...	...	...	−1209	...	...	...
B Work in progress	3244	...	...	...	5877	...	...	...	4412	...	...	...
C Livestock, except breeding stocks, dairy cattle, etc.	309	...	...	...	−123	...	...	...	−331	...	...	...
D Finished goods	1008	...	...	...	4029	...	...	...	1400	...	...	...
2 Wholesale and retail trade	8497	...	...	...	4185	...	...	...	6407	...	...	...
3 Other, except government stocks [b]	117	...	...	...	884	...	...	...	−28	...	...	...
4 Government stocks	...	...	...	...	...	...	...	...	...	...	...	...
Statistical discrepancy [c]	−2992	...	...	...	−2537	...	...	...	11861	...	...	...
Gross fixed capital formation, total	386060	...	...	48666	421989	...	...	50260	466285	...	...	56804
1 Residential buildings	78609	...	...	2012	79771	...	...	1721	88302	...	...	2351
2 Non-residential buildings	118534	...	...	15599	138490	...	...	15373	156926	...	...	...
3 Other construction	...	...	...	19460	...	...	...	19759	...	...	...	...
4 Land improvement and plantation and orchard development	...	...	...	...	...	...	...	...	...	...	...	...
5 Producers' durable goods	165011	...	...	7579	179674	...	...	9040	195091	...	...	...
A Transport equipment [d]	29753	...	...	−	32256	...	...	−	39009	...	...	...
Passenger cars	14802	...	...	...	16176	...	...	...	19124	...	...	...
Other	14951	...	...	...	16080	...	...	...	19885	...	...	...
B Machinery and equipment	135258	...	...	7579	147418	...	...	9040	156082	...	...	...
6 Breeding stock, dairy cattle, etc.	...	...	...	...	...	...	...	...	...	...	...	...
Statistical discrepancy [e]	23906	...	...	4016	24054	...	...	4367	25966	...	...	54453
Total gross capital formation	397565	...	...	48666	438967	...	...	50260	488312	...	...	56804

	1992 Total	1992 Total private	1992 Public enterprises	1992 General government	1993 Total	1993 Total private	1993 Public enterprises	1993 General government	1994 Total	1994 Total private	1994 Public enterprises	1994 General government
Increase in stocks, total [a]	8245	...	...	...	2713	...	...	...	833	...	...	...
1 Goods producing industries	−2225	...	...	...	−3998	...	...	...	1935	...	...	...
A Materials and supplies	−57	...	...	...	−1979	...	...	...	1050	...	...	...
B Work in progress	3823	...	...	...	211	...	...	...	1429	...	...	...
C Livestock, except breeding stocks, dairy cattle, etc.	−1067	...	...	...	276	...	...	...	−213	...	...	...
D Finished goods	−2769	...	...	...	−2069	...	...	...	−1234	...	...	...
2 Wholesale and retail trade	−637	...	...	...	−2641	...	...	...	−2917	...	...	...
3 Other, except government stocks [b]	130	...	...	...	150	...	...	...	−741	...	...	...
4 Government stocks	...	...	...	...	...	...	...	...	...	...	...	...
Statistical discrepancy [c]	9910	...	...	...	9478	...	...	...	2343	...	...	...
Gross fixed capital formation, total	483440	...	...	61790	485099	...	...	...	533348	...	...	...
1 Residential buildings	100971	...	...	2100	109442	...	...	...	122164	...	...	...
2 Non-residential buildings	162069	...	...	...	166588	...	...	...	182378	...	...	...
3 Other construction	...	...	...	...	...	...	...	...	...	...	...	...
4 Land improvement and plantation and orchard development	...	...	...	...	...	...	...	...	...	...	...	...
5 Producers' durable goods	192392	...	...	...	179179	...	...	...	197277	...	...	...
A Transport equipment [d]	41876	...	...	...	37632	...	...	...	38787	...	...	...
Passenger cars	20795	...	...	...	19144	...	...	...	19902	...	...	...
Other	21081	...	...	...	18488	...	...	...	18885	...	...	...

Austria

	1992				1993				1994			
	Total	Total private	Public enter-prises	General govern-ment	Total	Total private	Public enter-prises	General govern-ment	Total	Total private	Public enter-prises	General govern-ment
B Machinery and equipment	150516	...	...	...	141547	...	...	...	158490	...	...	...
6 Breeding stock, dairy cattle, etc.	...	...	...	...	...	...	...	...	...	...	...	...
Statistical discrepancy [e]	28008	...	...	59690	29890	...	...	...	31529	...	...	...
Total gross capital formation	491685	...	...	61790	487812	...	...	...	534181	...	...	...

	1995				1996				1997			
	Total	Total private	Public enter-prises	General govern-ment	Total	Total private	Public enter-prises	General govern-ment	Total	Total private	Public enter-prises	General govern-ment
Increase in stocks, total [a]	10320	...	...	...	4120	...	...	...	...	...	...	...
Gross fixed capital formation, total	554070	...	...	...	576791	...	...	...	...	...	...	...
1 Residential buildings	140447	...	...	...	149084	...	...	...	...	...	...	...
2 Non-residential buildings	174832	...	...	...	183308	...	...	...	...	...	...	...
3 Other construction	...	...	...	...	...	...	...	...	...	...	...	...
4 Land improvement and plantation and orchard development	...	...	...	...	...	...	...	...	...	...	...	...
5 Producers' durable goods	204438	...	...	...	212438	...	...	...	...	...	...	...
A Transport equipment [d]	42643	...	...	...	44035	...	...	...	...	...	...	...
Passenger cars	21418	...	...	...	23140	...	...	...	...	...	...	...
Other	21225	...	...	...	20895	...	...	...	...	...	...	...
B Machinery and equipment	161795	...	...	...	168403	...	...	...	...	...	...	...
6 Breeding stock, dairy cattle, etc.	...	...	...	...	...	...	...	...	...	...	...	...
Statistical discrepancy [e]	34353	...	...	...	31961	...	...	...	...	...	...	...
Total gross capital formation	564390	...	...	...	580911	...	...	...	...	...	...	...

a Item "Increase in stocks" includes breeding stock, draught animals and a statistical discrepancy.
b Item "Other, except government stocks" refers to transport only.
c Item "Statistical discrepancy" relates to the difference between the estimate of GDP through industrial origin approach and that of expenditure approach.
d Item "Transport equipment" refers to registered motor vehicles.
e Item "Gross fixed capital formation" includes value added tax on investments of investors not entitled to deduct invoiced value added tax. This component is not included in the sub-items.

Austria

2.8 Gross capital formation by type of good and owner, in constant prices

Million Austrian schillings

	1986 Total	1986 Total private	1986 Public enterprises	1986 General government	1987 Total	1987 Total private	1987 Public enterprises	1987 General government	1988 Total	1988 Total private	1988 Public enterprises	1988 General government
At constant prices of: 1983												
Increase in stocks, total	21248	...	...	...	19629	...	...	...	14151	...	...	...
1 Goods producing industries	414	...	...	...	–4254	...	...	...	–1360	...	...	...
A Materials and supplies	322	...	...	...	1118	...	...	...	1916	...	...	...
B Work in progress	–2079	...	...	...	–2436	...	...	...	–1580	...	...	...
C Livestock, except breeding stocks, dairy cattle, etc.	–412	...	...	...	–222	...	...	...	–767	...	...	...
D Finished goods	1895	...	...	...	–2251	...	...	...	–1430	...	...	...
2 Wholesale and retail trade	1618	...	...	...	3102	...	...	...	7699	...	...	...
3 Other, except government stocks	–63	...	...	...	404	...	...	...	164	...	...	...
4 Government stocks	...	...	...	...	...	...	...	...	...	...	...	...
Statistical discrepancy	18867	...	...	...	20155	...	...	...	6881	...	...	...
Gross fixed capital formation, total	287896	...	...	42732	300513	...	...	41247	321076	...	...	39378
1 Residential buildings	61447	...	...	1513	62866	...	...	1772	67626	...	...	1737
2 Non-residential buildings	84311	...	...	15168	91280	...	...	13716	93882	...	...	12924
3 Other construction	...	...	...	17522	...	...	...	17625	...	...	...	16370
4 Land improvement and plantation and orchard development	...	...	...	...	...	...	...	...	...	...	...	...
5 Producers' durable goods	124434	...	...	5554	128833	...	...	5277	140797	...	...	5696
A Transport equipment	18819	...	...	–	20783	...	...	–	22539	...	...	–
Passenger cars	9752	...	...	...	9425	...	...	...	10624	...	...	...
Other	9067	...	...	...	11358	...	...	...	11915	...	...	...
B Machinery and equipment	105615	...	...	5554	108050	...	...	5277	118258	...	...	5696
6 Breeding stock, dairy cattle, etc.	...	...	...	...	...	...	...	...	...	...	...	...
Statistical discrepancy	17704	...	...	2975	17534	...	...	2857	18771	...	...	2651
Total gross capital formation	309144	...	...	42732	320142	...	...	41247	335227	...	...	39378

	1989 Total	1989 Total private	1989 Public enterprises	1989 General government	1990 Total	1990 Total private	1990 Public enterprises	1990 General government	1991 Total	1991 Total private	1991 Public enterprises	1991 General government
At constant prices of: 1983												
Increase in stocks, total	3014	...	...	...	7355	...	...	...	8037	...	...	...
1 Goods producing industries	6284	...	...	...	12657	...	...	...	2677	...	...	...
A Materials and supplies	2106	...	...	...	3260	...	...	...	–1565	...	...	...
B Work in progress	3138	...	...	...	4965	...	...	...	3818	...	...	...
C Livestock, except breeding stocks, dairy cattle, etc.	281	...	...	...	–144	...	...	...	–324	...	...	...
D Finished goods	1358	...	...	...	3916	...	...	...	1400	...	...	...
2 Wholesale and retail trade	7827	...	...	...	4001	...	...	...	5410	...	...	...
3 Other, except government stocks	112	...	...	...	794	...	...	...	41	...	...	...
4 Government stocks	...	...	...	...	...	...	...	...	...	...	...	...
Statistical discrepancy	–10928	...	...	...	–10240	...	...	...	–415	...	...	...
Gross fixed capital formation, total	341189	...	...	41923	363688	...	...	41903	386643	...	...	45600
1 Residential buildings	67359	...	...	1717	65547	...	...	1409	68398	...	...	1813

Austria

	1989				1990				1991			
	Total	Total private	Public enterprises	General government	Total	Total private	Public enterprises	General government	Total	Total private	Public enterprises	General government
At constant prices of: 1983												
2 Non-residential buildings	102304	...	...	13516	117143	...	...	12765	125559	...	...	...
3 Other construction	...	...	...	17262	...	...	...	17019	...	...	...	...
4 Land improvement and plantation and orchard development	...	...	...	...	...	...	...	...	...	...	...	...
5 Producers' durable goods	152252	...	...	6805	162141	...	...	7919	172707	...	...	...
A Transport equipment	24540	...	...	–	25678	...	...	–	30017	...	...	...
Passenger cars	12250	...	...	...	13053	...	...	...	14895	...	...	...
Other	12290	...	...	...	12625	...	...	...	15122	...	...	...
B Machinery and equipment	127712	...	...	6805	136463	...	...	7919	142690	...	...	...
6 Breeding stock, dairy cattle, etc.	...	...	...	...	...	...	...	...	...	...	...	...
Statistical discrepancy	19274	...	...	2623	18857	...	...	2791	19979	...	...	43787
Total gross capital formation	344203	...	...	41923	371043	...	...	41903	394680	...	...	45600

	1992				1993				1994			
	Total	Total private	Public enterprises	General government	Total	Total private	Public enterprises	General government	Total	Total private	Public enterprises	General government
At constant prices of: 1983												
Increase in stocks, total	–2163	...	...	...	4812	...	...	...	8585	...	...	...
1 Goods producing industries	–21	...	...	...	–4582	...	...	...	2295	...	...	...
A Materials and supplies	803	...	...	...	–1705	...	...	...	1483	...	...	...
B Work in progress	3648	...	...	...	–40	...	...	...	1236	...	...	...
C Livestock, except breeding stocks, dairy cattle, etc.	–1105	...	...	...	256	...	...	...	–195	...	...	...
D Finished goods	–1736	...	...	...	–2718	...	...	...	–572	...	...	...
2 Wholesale and retail trade	–1176	...	...	...	–2123	...	...	...	–1621	...	...	...
3 Other, except government stocks	117	...	...	...	122	...	...	...	–726	...	...	...
4 Government stocks	...	...	...	...	...	...	...	...	...	...	...	...
Statistical discrepancy	–2187	...	...	...	11650	...	...	...	8443	...	...	...
Gross fixed capital formation, total	387120	...	...	48161	379395	...	...	...	411239	...	...	...
1 Residential buildings	75071	...	...	1572	78735	...	...	...	84949	...	...	...
2 Non-residential buildings	124575	...	...	...	124292	...	...	...	132347	...	...	...
3 Other construction	...	...	...	...	...	...	...	...	...	...	...	...
4 Land improvement and plantation and orchard development	...	...	...	...	...	...	...	...	...	...	...	...
5 Producers' durable goods	166385	...	...	...	154475	...	...	...	171480	...	...	...
A Transport equipment	30060	...	...	...	25703	...	...	...	25854	...	...	...
Passenger cars	14288	...	...	...	12622	...	...	...	12640	...	...	...
Other	15772	...	...	...	13081	...	...	...	13214	...	...	...
B Machinery and equipment	136325	...	...	...	128772	...	...	...	145626	...	...	...
6 Breeding stock, dairy cattle, etc.	...	...	...	...	...	...	...	...	...	...	...	...
Statistical discrepancy	21089	...	...	46589	21893	...	...	...	22463	...	...	...
Total gross capital formation	384957	...	...	48161	384207	...	...	...	419824	...	...	...

Austria

	1995				1996				1997			
	Total	Total private	Public enterprises	General government	Total	Total private	Public enterprises	General government	Total	Total private	Public enterprises	General government
	At constant prices of: 1983												
Increase in stocks, total	11785	...	...	...	1405	...	...	...	...	...	...	...
Statistical discrepancy	5471	...	...	...	...	...	...	...	...	...	...	...
Gross fixed capital formation, total	419178	...	...	...	429435	...	...	...	...	...	...	...
1 Residential buildings	96130	...	...	...	100528	...	...	...	...	...	...	...
2 Non-residential buildings	122432	...	...	...	124224	...	...	...	...	...	...	...
3 Other construction	...	...	...	...	...	...	...	...	...	...	...	...
4 Land improvement and plantation and orchard development	...	...	...	...	...	...	...	...	...	...	...	...
5 Producers' durable goods	176794	...	...	...	183266	...	...	...	...	...	...	...
A Transport equipment	28240	...	...	...	28838	...	...	...	...	...	...	...
Passenger cars	13291	...	...	...	14067	...	...	...	...	...	...	...
Other	14949	...	...	...	14771	...	...	...	...	...	...	...
B Machinery and equipment	148554	...	...	...	154428	...	...	...	...	...	...	...
6 Breeding stock, dairy cattle, etc.	...	...	...	...	...	...	...	...	...	...	...	...
Statistical discrepancy	23822	...	...	...	21417	...	...	...	...	...	...	...
Total gross capital formation	430963	...	...	...	430840	...	...	...	...	...	...	...

2.9 Gross capital formation by kind of activity of owner, ISIC major divisions, in current prices

Million Austrian schillings

	1986			1987			1988			1989		
	Total gross capital formation	Increase in stocks	Gross fixed capital formation	Total gross capital formation	Increase in stocks	Gross fixed capital formation	Total gross capital formation	Increase in stocks	Gross fixed capital formation	Total gross capital formation	Increase in stocks	Gross fixed capital formation
	All producers											
1 Agriculture, hunting, forestry and fishing	16863	1677	15186	15191	4	15187	15731	150	15581	15296	-692	15988
2 Mining and quarrying	3486	105	3382	5309	-142	5450	2406	-73	2479	1516	-213	1728
3 Manufacturing	49116	-2656	51772	44721	-5869	50590	54933	-1342	56275	64458	8044	56414
4 Electricity, gas and water	20264	250	20015	16120	89	16031	16372	408	15964	17214	-230	17444
5 Construction	12005	1661	10344	12205	1590	10615	11950	-213	12163	11512	-1026	12538
6 Wholesale and retail trade, restaurants and hotels	29351	1729	27622	34261	3133	31128	43558	8187	35371	48075	8497	39578
7 Transport, storage and communication	37424	-44	37468	38807	358	38449	41650	226	41424	43797	100	43697
8 Finance, insurance, real estate and business services	98552	-10	98562	107490	-17	107507	121767	7	121760	125503	15	125488
9 Community, social and personal services	8593	-22	8615	9958	55	9903	12447	-27	12474	11669	2	11667
Total industries	275655	2690	272965	284062	-799	284861	320814	7323	313491	339040	14497	324542
Producers of government services	43592	...	43592	39766	...	39766	39265	...	39265	41666	...	41666
Private non-profit institutions serving households	4135	...	4135	4389	...	4389	4597	...	4597	4818	...	4818
Statistical discrepancy [a,b]	7114	18698	-11584	24030	25233	-1203	4366	7607	-3241	12042	-2992	15034
Total	330496	21388	309108	352247	24434	327813	369042	14930	354112	397566	11505	386060

Austria

	1990			1991			1992			1993		
	Total gross capital formation	Increase in stocks	Gross fixed capital formation	Total gross capital formation	Increase in stocks	Gross fixed capital formation	Total gross capital formation	Increase in stocks	Gross fixed capital formation	Total gross capital formation	Increase in stocks	Gross fixed capital formation

All producers

1 Agriculture, hunting, forestry and fishing	19646	1092	18554	17884	−816	18700	15314	−2156	17470	16836	−436	17272
2 Mining and quarrying	1865	−8	1873	1877	40	1837	1778	−85	1863	1899	−66	1965
3 Manufacturing	81107	12724	68382	73758	3919	69839	68268	−988	69256	55034	−4667	59701
4 Electricity, gas and water	19017	102	18915	17808	−502	18311	21903	1037	20867	20179	697	19482
5 Construction	14730	534	14196	15500	1147	14353	15800	1034	14766	15579	199	15380
6 Wholesale and retail trade, restaurants and hotels	46696	4185	42511	53060	6407	46653	46254	−637	46891	43402	−2641	46043
7 Transport, storage and communication	51185	522	50663	55970	248	55722	59740	54	59686	61910	2	61908
8 Finance, insurance, real estate and business services	126706	53	126653	142421	−42	142463	161780	−15	161795	169309	−47	169356
9 Community, social and personal services	13081	309	12772	14069	−234	14303	16298	91	16207	16655	195	16460
Total industries	374033	19514	354519	392346	10165	382181	407136	−1665	408801	400803	−6765	407567
Producers of government services	44057	...	44057	47974	...	47974	49233	...	49233	52826	...	52826
Private non-profit institutions serving households	5249	...	5249	5793	...	5793	6320	...	6320	6739	...	6739
Statistical discrepancy	15628[a,b]	−2537[a,b]	18164[a,b]	42199[a,b]	11861[a,b]	30337[a,b]	28997[a,b]	9910[a,b]	19086[a,b]	27444	9478[a,b]	17967
Total	438967	16977	421989	488312	22026	466285	491686	8245	483440	487812	2713	485099

	1994			1995			1996			1997		
	Total gross capital formation	Increase in stocks	Gross fixed capital formation	Total gross capital formation	Increase in stocks	Gross fixed capital formation	Total gross capital formation	Increase in stocks	Gross fixed capital formation	Total gross capital formation	Increase in stocks	Gross fixed capital formation

All producers

1 Agriculture, hunting, forestry and fishing	18369	903	17466	...	...	16483	...	...	18052	...	...	...
2 Mining and quarrying	2291	87	2203	...	...	...	...	...	...	...	...	...
3 Manufacturing	57895	−659	58554	...	...	...	...	...	...	...	...	...
4 Electricity, gas and water	20400	−178	20578	...	...	...	...	...	...	...	...	...
5 Construction	18589	1994	16595	...	...	...	...	...	...	...	...	...
6 Wholesale and retail trade, restaurants and hotels	48809	−2917	51726	...	...	...	...	...	...	...	...	...
7 Transport, storage and communication	56479	−798	57277	...	...	...	...	...	...	...	...	...
8 Finance, insurance, real estate and business services	185327	14	185313	...	...	209860	...	...	...	...	...	...
9 Community, social and personal services	17613	44	17569	...	...	19282	...	...	19838	...	...	...
Total industries	425771	−1510	427280	...	...	...	...	...	...	...	...	...
Producers of government services	53708	...	53708	...	...	...	...	...	...	...	...	...
Private non-profit institutions serving households	7273	...	7273	...	...	...	...	...	...	...	...	...
Statistical discrepancy	47430	2343[a,b]	45087	...	...	...	...	...	...	...	...	...
Total	534182	833	533348	...	...	...	...	...	...	...	...	...

a Item "Gross fixed capital formation" includes value added tax on investments of investors not entitled to deduct invoiced value added tax. This component is not included in the sub-items.

b Item "Statistical discrepancy" relates to the difference between the estimate of GDP through industrial origin approach and that of expenditure approach.

Austria

2.10 Gross capital formation by kind of activity of owner, ISIC major divisions, in constant prices

Million Austrian schillings

	1986 Total gross capital formation	1986 Increase in stocks	1986 Gross fixed capital formation	1987 Total gross capital formation	1987 Increase in stocks	1987 Gross fixed capital formation	1988 Total gross capital formation	1988 Increase in stocks	1988 Gross fixed capital formation	1989 Total gross capital formation	1989 Increase in stocks	1989 Gross fixed capital formation
At constant prices of: 1983												
All producers												
1 Agriculture, hunting, forestry and fishing	14759	688	14071	13150	−463	13613	14140	501	13639	13146	−598	13744
2 Mining and quarrying	3346	116	3230	5209	−153	5362	2260	−78	2337	1345	−221	1566
3 Manufacturing	45842	−1838	47680	41350	−4895	46245	49118	−1363	50481	57221	8297	48924
4 Electricity, gas and water	18950	277	18672	14515	−52	14566	14767	553	14214	14550	−537	15086
5 Construction	11217	1583	9634	11235	1530	9704	10792	−206	10999	10081	−938	11020
6 Wholesale and retail trade, restaurants and hotels	27932	1618	26314	32671	3102	29569	40976	7699	33277	44358	7827	36531
7 Transport, storage and communication	34296	−31	34327	34885	373	34512	36405	175	36230	37087	91	36995
8 Finance, insurance, real estate and business services	92774	−10	92784	98460	−20	98480	109273	7	109266	109939	17	109923
9 Community, social and personal services	8025	−22	8047	9163	51	9111	11267	−18	11285	10300	4	10296
Total industries	257141	2381	254760	260636	−527	261163	288997	7270	281728	298027	13942	284085
Producers of government services	40454	...	40454	36341	...	36341	35371	...	35371	36624	...	36624
Private non-profit institutions serving households	3858	...	3858	4046	...	4046	4163	...	4163	4253	...	4253
Statistical discrepancy	7691	18867	−11176	19118	20155	−1037	6695	6881	−186	5299	−10928	16226
Total	309144	21248	287896	320141	19628	300513	335226	14151	321076	344203	3014	341188

	1990 Total gross capital formation	1990 Increase in stocks	1990 Gross fixed capital formation	1991 Total gross capital formation	1991 Increase in stocks	1991 Gross fixed capital formation	1992 Total gross capital formation	1992 Increase in stocks	1992 Gross fixed capital formation	1993 Total gross capital formation	1993 Increase in stocks	1993 Gross fixed capital formation
At constant prices of: 1983												
All producers												
1 Agriculture, hunting, forestry and fishing	16037	660	15377	14141	−653	14794	11596	−1631	13227	12248	−375	12623
2 Mining and quarrying	1642	−4	1646	1610	10	1600	1560	−55	1615	1623	−40	1663
3 Manufacturing	68847	11232	57615	60354	3216	57138	55642	524	55118	40279	−5795	46075
4 Electricity, gas and water	16417	434	15984	14481	−591	15072	18137	1330	16806	16494	1208	15286
5 Construction	12644	479	12165	12867	1018	11849	12724	916	11808	12127	165	11962
6 Wholesale and retail trade, restaurants and hotels	41785	4001	37784	45490	5410	40079	37693	−1176	38869	35376	−2123	37498
7 Transport, storage and communication	42588	487	42100	46113	267	45846	47692	63	47629	48285	17	48268
8 Finance, insurance, real estate and business services	107404	58	107347	115164	−46	115210	126619	−17	126636	128904	−50	128954
9 Community, social and personal services	11166	249	10917	11754	−180	11935	13250	71	13180	13015	155	12860
Total industries	318530	17596	300935	321974	8452	313522	324913	24	324889	308351	−6838	315189
Producers of government services	37397	...	37397	39089	...	39089	38561	...	38561	39938	...	39938
Private non-profit institutions serving households	4440	...	4440	4719	...	4719	4988	...	4988	5194	...	5194
Statistical discrepancy	10675	−10240	20915	28899	−415	29314	16494	−2187	18681	30725	11650	19074

Austria

	1990			1991			1992			1993		
	Total gross capital formation	Increase in stocks	Gross fixed capital formation	Total gross capital formation	Increase in stocks	Gross fixed capital formation	Total gross capital formation	Increase in stocks	Gross fixed capital formation	Total gross capital formation	Increase in stocks	Gross fixed capital formation
At constant prices of: 1983												
Total	371042	7356	363687	394681	8037	386644	384956	–2163	387119	384208	4812	379395

	1994			1995			1996			1997		
	Total gross capital formation	Increase in stocks	Gross fixed capital formation	Total gross capital formation	Increase in stocks	Gross fixed capital formation	Total gross capital formation	Increase in stocks	Gross fixed capital formation	Total gross capital formation	Increase in stocks	Gross fixed capital formation

At constant prices of: 1983

All producers

1 Agriculture, hunting, forestry and fishing	12891	342	12549	...	...	11623	...	...	12580	...	...	...
2 Mining and quarrying	1897	61	1835	...	...	...	...	...	...	...	...	...
3 Manufacturing	45688	1034	44654	...	...	...	...	...	...	...	...	...
4 Electricity, gas and water	15269	–663	15932	...	...	...	...	...	...	...	...	...
5 Construction	14407	1715	12692	...	...	...	...	...	...	...	...	...
6 Wholesale and retail trade, restaurants and hotels	40509	–1621	42131	...	...	...	...	...	...	...	...	...
7 Transport, storage and communication	43952	–775	44727	...	...	...	...	...	...	...	...	...
8 Finance, insurance, real estate and business services	137805	15	137791	...	...	152611	...	...	...	...	...	...
9 Community, social and personal services	13604	34	13569	...	...	14555	...	...	14716	...	...	...
Total industries	326022	142	325879	...	...	...	...	...	...	...	...	...
Producers of government services	39939	...	39939	...	...	...	...	...	...	...	...	...
Private non-profit institutions serving households	5552	...	5552	...	...	...	...	...	...	...	...	...
Statistical discrepancy	48311	8443	39868	...	...	...	...	...	...	...	...	...
Total	419824	8585	411238	...	...	...	...	...	...	...	...	...

2.11 Gross fixed capital formation by kind of activity of owner, ISIC divisions, in current prices

Million Austrian schillings

	1986	1987	1988	1989	1990	1991	1992	1993	1994	1995	1996	1997
All producers												
1 Agriculture, hunting, forestry and fishing	15186	15187	15581	15988	18554	18700	17470	17272	17466	16483	18052	...
A Agriculture and hunting	14759	14772	15150	15536	18084	18134	17049	16850	17044	16009	...	...
B Forestry and logging	427	415	431	452	470	566	421	422	422	474	...	...
C Fishing	...	...	...	...	...	...	...	...	...	...	...	...
2 Mining and quarrying	3382	5450	2479	1728	1873	1837	1863	1965	2203	...	...	...
A Coal mining	194	147	181	108	94	46	56	57	38	...	...	...
B Crude petroleum and natural gas production	2410	4504	1231	635	538	842	949	1001	955	...	...	...
C Metal ore mining	92	74	53	178	189	38	31	7	23	...	...	...
D Other mining	685	725	1014	807	1052	911	827	900	1187	...	...	...
3 Manufacturing	51772	50590	56275	56414	68382	69839	69256	59701	58554	...	...	...
A Manufacturing of food, beverages and tobacco	6367	6951	7845	7799	8127	8334	8716	9821	9301	...	...	...
B Textile, wearing apparel and leather industries	3208	2916	3015	3183	3988	4050	2786	2286	2167	...	...	...

Austria

Million Austrian schillings

	1986	1987	1988	1989	1990	1991	1992	1993	1994	1995	1996	1997
C Manufacture of wood and wood products, including furniture	2362	2619	3659	3443	4477	4123	4097	4015	4189	...	...	...
D Manufacture of paper and paper products, printing and publishing	7495	7812	5439	6656	10683	9803	7597	6325	5386	...	...	...
E Manufacture of chemicals and chemical petroleum, coal, rubber and plastic products	9060	7919	8051	8405	9729	9869	10433	8329	7656	...	...	...
F Manufacture of non-metallic mineral products, except products of petroleum and coal	3738	3923	4689	4531	5921	5672	5914	4884	5375	...	...	...
G Basic metal industries	7082	5708	8792	8447	9498	9879	9503	7537	8495	...	...	...
H Manufacture of fabricated metal products, machinery and equipment	11255	11371	12891	12245	14146	16169	18098	14315	13923	...	...	...
I Other manufacturing industries	1205	1372	1895	1704	1814	1941	2113	2189	2061	...	...	...
4 Electricity, gas and water	20015	16031	15964	17444	18915	18311	20867	19482	20578	...	...	...
A Electricity, gas and steam	18904	14700	14658	16145	17438	16898	19451	17804	18987	...	...	...
B Water works and supply	1111	1331	1306	1299	1476	1413	1415	1678	1591	...	...	...
5 Construction	10344	10615	12163	12538	14196	14353	14766	15380	16595	...	...	...
6 Wholesale and retail trade, restaurants and hotels	27622	31128	35371	39578	42511	46653	46891	46043	51726	...	...	...
A Wholesale and retail trade	19184	21378	24363	27278	29288	32218	32506	31604	35317	...	...	...
B Restaurants and hotels	8438	9750	11008	12300	13223	14435	14385	14439	16409	...	...	...
Restaurants	2234	2546	2867	3208	3401	3700	3668	3675	4259	...	...	...
Hotels and other lodging places	6204	7204	8141	9092	9822	10735	10717	10764	12150	...	...	...
7 Transport, storage and communication	37468	38449	41424	43697	50663	55722	59686	61908	57277	...	...	...
A Transport and storage	25068	25680	27290	28977	32900	34988	38513	41066	36111	...	...	...
B Communication	12400	12769	14134	14720	17763	20734	21173	20842	21166	...	...	...
8 Finance, insurance, real estate and business services	98562	107507	121760	125488	126653	142463	161795	169356	185313	209860	...	...
A Financial institutions	5769	6081	6715	8357	9223	8260	10995	10854	11532	12169	12579	...
B Insurance	1970	2211	2655	2537	2581	2606	2709	2758	2742	2873	3170	...
C Real estate and business services	90823	99215	112390	114594	114849	131597	148091	155744	171039	194818	...	...
Real estate, except dwellings	16156	19893	24413	24199	24038	31386	32565	31024	32191	34559	...	...
Dwellings	74667	79322	87977	90395	90811	100211	115526	124720	138848	160259	168271	...
9 Community, social and personal services	8615	9903	12474	11667	12772	14303	16207	16460	17569	19282	19838	...
Total industries [a]	272965	284861	313491	324542	354519	382181	408801	407567	427280	...	...	...
Producers of government services	43592	39766	39265	41666	44057	47974	49233	52826	53708	...	...	...
Private non-profit institutions serving households	4135	4389	4597	4818	5249	5793	6320	6739	7273	...	...	...
Statistical discrepancy [b]	−11584	−1203	−3241	15034	18164	30337	19086	17967	45087	...	...	...
Total	309108	327813	354112	386060	421989	466285	483440	485099	533348	...	...	...

a Item "Private non-profit institutions serving households" is included with various industries above.

b Item "Gross fixed capital formation" includes value added tax on investments of investors not entitled to deduct invoiced value added tax. This component is not included in the sub-items.

Austria

2.12 Gross fixed capital formation by kind of activity of owner, ISIC divisions, in constant prices

Million Austrian schillings

At constant prices of: 1983

All producers

	1986	1987	1988	1989	1990	1991	1992	1993	1994	1995	1996	1997
1 Agriculture, hunting, forestry and fishing	14071	13613	13639	13744	15377	14794	13227	12623	12549	11623	12580	...
2 Mining and quarrying	3230	5362	2337	1566	1646	1600	1615	1663	1835	...	...	...
3 Manufacturing	47680	46245	50481	48924	57615	57138	55118	46075	44654	...	...	...
4 Electricity, gas and water	18672	14566	14214	15086	15984	15072	16806	15286	15932	...	...	...
5 Construction	9634	9704	10999	11020	12165	11849	11808	11962	12692	...	...	...
6 Wholesale and retail trade, restaurants and hotels	26314	29569	33277	36531	37784	40079	38869	37498	42131	...	...	...
7 Transport, storage and communication	34327	34512	36230	36995	42100	45846	47629	48268	44727	...	...	...
8 Finance, insurance, real estate and business services	92784	98480	109266	109923	107347	115210	126636	128954	137791	152611	...	...
9 Community, social and personal services	8047	9111	11285	10296	10917	11935	13180	12860	13569	14555	14716	...
Total industries	254760	261163	281728	284085	300935	313522	324889	315189	325879	...	...	...
Producers of government services	40454	36341	35371	36624	37397	39089	38561	39938	39939	...	...	...
Private non-profit institutions serving households	3858	4046	4163	4253	4440	4719	4988	5194	5552	...	...	...
Statistical discrepancy	−11176	−1037	−186	16226	20915	29314	18681	19074	39868	...	...	...
Total	287896	300513	321076	341188	363687	386644	387119	379395	411238	...	...	...

2.17 Exports and imports of goods and services, detail

Million Austrian schillings

	1986	1987	1988	1989	1990	1991	1992	1993	1994	1995	1996	1997
Exports of goods and services												
1 Exports of merchandise, f.o.b. [a]	339842	343280	375072	427938	467800	479309	486038	468277	512989	567557	623273	...
2 Transport and communication	41293	44649	55358	64443	73073	82323	92487	99755	108410	110393	...	...
3 Insurance service charges	...	...	...	...	...	...	...	...	...	...	...	...
4 Other commodities	41293	44649	55358	64443	73073	82323	92487	99755	108410	111003	127306	...
5 Adjustments of merchandise exports to change-of-ownership basis	...	...	...	...	...	...	...	...	...	...	...	...
6 Direct purchases in the domestic market by non-residential households	101562	108103	120052	136382	146886	154437	159640	157520	150183	147052	148251	...
7 Direct purchases in the domestic market by extraterritorial bodies	...	...	...	...	...	...	...	...	...	...	...	...
Statistical discrepancy [b]	33978	26916	40277	40855	40553	58637	53453	60955	67259	75293	89953	...
Total exports of goods and services [a]	516675	522948	590759	669618	728312	774706	791618	786507	838841	900905	988783	...
Imports of goods and services												
1 Imports of merchandise, c.i.f. [a]	404818	408767	445222	509269	551254	585907	588666	562313	623314	648180	704104	...
2 Adjustments of merchandise imports to change-of-ownership basis	...	...	...	...	...	...	...	...	...	...	...	...
3 Other transport and communication	32236	32767	42878	50632	57696	66238	68064	67623	72134	78186	...	...

Austria

Million Austrian schillings

	1986	1987	1988	1989	1990	1991	1992	1993	1994	1995	1996	1997
4 Other insurance service charges	...	...	...	...	...	...	...	...	...	...	...	...
5 Other commodities	32236	32767	42878	50632	57696	66238	68064	67623	72134	76047	92600	...
6 Direct purchases abroad by government	59926	72738	76757	81129	86053	83566	92240	86093	107356	117479	...	...
7 Direct purchases abroad by resident households	59926	72738	76757	81129	86053	83566	92240	96093	107356	117547	125152	...
Statistical discrepancy [b]	6991	3199	17702	12365	9872	22288	22997	46578	40159	68730	79934	...
Total imports of goods and services [a]	503971	517471	582559	653395	704875	757999	771967	772607	842963	910504	1001790	...
Balance of goods and services	12704	5477	8200	16223	23437	16707	19651	13900	−4122	−9599	−13007	...
Total imports and balance of goods and services [a]	516675	522948	590759	669618	728312	774706	791618	786507	838841	900905	988783	...

[a] The estimates on transit trade are on a net basis.

[b] Item "Statistical discrepancy" refers to exports/imports of commodities not yet identified as merchandise or services. Before 1979, also including item "Adjustments of merchandise export/import to change of ownership basis".

3.11 General government production account: total and subsectors

Million Austrian schillings

	1986					1987				
	Total government	Central government	State or provincial government	Local government	Social security funds	Total government	Central government	State or provincial government	Local government	Social security funds
Gross output
1 Sales	53260	10579	14098	25690	2893	55675	11285	14588	26732	3070
2 Services produced for own use	270655	101203	59268	52374	57810	280436	101987	62233	55187	61029
3 Own account capital formation	...	...	...	...	...	...	...	...	...	...
Gross output [a]	323915	111782	73366	78064	60703	336111	113272	76821	81919	64099
Gross input
Intermediate consumption	126828	34122	16009	27883	48814	130200	32523	16411	29529	51737
subtotal: Value added	197087	77660	57357	50181	11889	205911	80749	60410	52390	12362
1 Indirect taxes, net	2867	1444	866	557	−	2910	1436	905	569	−
A Indirect taxes	2867	1444	866	557	...	2910	1436	905	569	...
B less: Subsidies	...	...	...	...	...	...	...	...	...	...
2 Consumption of fixed capital	11310	2564	1741	6590	415	11561	2621	1780	6736	424
3 Compensation of employees	182910	73652	54750	43034	11474	191440	76692	57725	45085	11938
4 Net operating surplus	...	...	...	...	...	...	...	...	...	...
Gross input [a]	323915	111782	73366	78064	60703	336111	113272	76821	81919	64099

	1988					1989				
	Total government	Central government	State or provincial government	Local government	Social security funds	Total government	Central government	State or provincial government	Local government	Social security funds
Gross output
1 Sales	60148	11811	15381	29691	3265	63674	12656	16122	31399	3497
2 Services produced for own use	288356	104332	64345	54860	64819	302881	109004	67975	57818	68084
3 Own account capital formation	...	...	...	...	...	...	...	...	...	...
Gross output [a]	348351	115990	79726	84551	68084	366365	121470	84097	89217	71581
Gross input
Intermediate consumption	137818	33623	18041	30884	55270	145403	35021	19209	32767	58406
subtotal: Value added	210533	82367	61685	53667	12814	220962	86449	64888	56450	13175
1 Indirect taxes, net	2914	1423	916	575	−	3353	1776	967	610	−

Austria

	1988					1989				
	Total government	Central government	State or provincial government	Local government	Social security funds	Total government	Central government	State or provincial government	Local government	Social security funds
A Indirect taxes	2914	1423	916	575	...	3353	1776	967	610	...
B less: Subsidies	...	...	...	...	...	...	...	...	...	...
2 Consumption of fixed capital	11803	2676	1817	6878	432	12218	2770	1881	7119	448
3 Compensation of employees	195816	78268	58952	46214	12382	205391	81903	62040	48721	12727
4 Net operating surplus	...	...	...	...	...	...	...	...	...	...
Gross input [a]	348351	115990	79726	84551	68084	366365	121470	84097	89217	71581

	1990					1991				
	Total government	Central government	State or provincial government	Local government	Social security funds	Total government	Central government	State or provincial government	Local government	Social security funds

Gross output

1 Sales	68337	13548	17709	33519	3561	71771	12536	19362	36087	3786
2 Services produced for own use	319888	113723	71467	62445	72253	348415	124280	78242	70504	75389
3 Own account capital formation	...	...	...	...	...	...	...	...	...	...
Gross output [a]	387797	126843	89176	95964	75814	420045	136675	97604	106591	79175

Gross input

Intermediate consumption	152941	35645	20280	35254	61762	165679	37358	22077	40515	65729
subtotal: Value added	234856	91198	68896	60710	14052	254366	99317	75527	66076	13446
1 Indirect taxes, net	3572	1883	1027	662	–	3851	1990	1121	740	–
A Indirect taxes	3572	1883	1027	662	...	3851	1990	1121	740	...
B less: Subsidies	...	...	...	...	...	...	...	...	...	...
2 Consumption of fixed capital	12770	2895	1966	7441	468	13502	3061	2078	7868	495
3 Compensation of employees	218514	86420	65903	52607	13584	237013	94266	72328	57468	12951
4 Net operating surplus	...	...	...	...	...	...	...	...	...	...
Gross input [a]	387797	126843	89176	95964	75814	420045	136675	97604	106591	79175

	1992					1993				
	Total government	Central government	State or provincial government	Local government	Social security funds	Total government	Central government	State or provincial government	Local government	Social security funds

Gross output

1 Sales	78636	13885	20392	40285	4074	85438	14791	22051	44035	4561
2 Services produced for own use	374804	131194	85227	75398	82985	404541	140825	91255	82068	90393
3 Own account capital formation	...	...	...	...	...	...	...	...	...	...
Gross output [a]	453791	144931	106044	115683	87133	490404	155537	113703	126103	95061

Gross input

Intermediate consumption	180266	39143	24011	44189	72923	197433	42472	25141	49605	80215
subtotal: Value added	273525	105788	82033	71494	14210	292971	113065	88562	76498	14846
1 Indirect taxes, net	4098	2068	1216	814	–	4640	2310	1315	1015	–
A Indirect taxes	4098	2068	1216	814	...	4640	2310	1315	1015	...
B less: Subsidies	...	...	...	...	...	...	...	...	...	...
2 Consumption of fixed capital	13809	3130	2126	8047	506	14468	3280	2227	8431	530
3 Compensation of employees	255618	100590	78691	62633	13704	273863	107475	85020	67052	14316
4 Net operating surplus	...	...	...	...	...	...	...	...	...	...
Gross input [a]	453791	144931	106044	115683	87133	490404	155537	113703	126103	95061

Austria

	1994					1995				
	Total govern-ment	Central govern-ment	State or provincial govern-ment	Local govern-ment	Social security funds	Total govern-ment	Central govern-ment	State or provincial govern-ment	Local govern-ment	Social security funds
Gross output										
1 Sales	94312	16287	24436	48156	5433	100541	16007	25893	53299	5342
2 Services produced for own use	426323	148374	96212	84875	96862	...	...	...	...	...
3 Own account capital formation	...	...	...	...	...	...	...	...	...	...
Gross output [a]	520244	164384	119715	134213	101932	540816	169797	124786	139832	106401
Gross input										
Intermediate consumption	213076	46420	26614	53182	86860	221781	48179	27807	55192	90603
subtotal: Value added	307168	117964	93101	81031	15072	319035	121618	96979	84640	15798
1 Indirect taxes, net	4740	2347	1368	1025	—	4962	2501	1426	1035	...
A Indirect taxes	4740	2347	1368	1025	...	4962	2501	1426	1035	...
B less: Subsidies	...	...	...	...	...	...	...	...	...	...
2 Consumption of fixed capital	15053	3412	2317	8772	552	15704	3560	2417	9151	576
3 Compensation of employees	287375	112205	89416	71234	14520	298369	115557	93136	74454	15222
4 Net operating surplus	...	...	...	...	...	...	...	...	...	...
Gross input [a]	520244	164384	119715	134213	101932	540816	169797	124786	139832	106401

	1996					1997				
	Total govern-ment	Central govern-ment	State or provincial govern-ment	Local govern-ment	Social security funds	Total govern-ment	Central govern-ment	State or provincial govern-ment	Local govern-ment	Social security funds
Gross output										
1 Sales	107364	17468	26900	57636	5360	...	...	...	...	...
2 Services produced for own use	...	...	...	...	...	...	...	...	...	...
3 Own account capital formation	...	...	...	...	...	...	...	...	...	...
Gross output [a]	553810	171704	127465	144027	110614	...	...	...	...	...
Gross input										
Intermediate consumption	231115	49519	29190	58004	94402	...	...	...	...	...
subtotal: Value added	322695	122185	98275	86023	16212	...	...	...	...	...
1 Indirect taxes, net	4832	2324	1450	1058	...	...	...	...	...	...
A Indirect taxes	4832	2324	1450	1058	...	...	...	...	...	...
B less: Subsidies	...	...	...	...	...	...	...	...	...	...
2 Consumption of fixed capital	16246	3683	2500	9467	596	...	...	...	...	...
3 Compensation of employees	301617	116178	94325	75498	15616	...	...	...	...	...
4 Net operating surplus	...	...	...	...	...	...	...	...	...	...
Gross input [a]	553810	171704	127465	144027	110614	...	...	...	...	...

[a] Column "State or Provincial Government" includes chambers.

3.12 General government income and outlay account: total and subsectors

Million Austrian schillings

	1986					1987				
	Total govern-ment	Central govern-ment	State or provincial govern-ment	Local govern-ment	Social security funds	Total govern-ment	Central govern-ment	State or provincial govern-ment	Local govern-ment	Social security funds
Receipts										
1 Operating surplus	...	...	...	...	...	...	...	...	...	...
2 Property and entrepreneurial income [a]	25909	18834	2798	2233	2044	29436	22424	2881	2136	1995

Austria

Million Austrian schillings

	1986					1987				
	Total government	Central government	State or provincial government	Local government	Social security funds	Total government	Central government	State or provincial government	Local government	Social security funds
A Withdrawals from public quasi-corporations	6756	7074	−129	−193	4	8190	8508	−103	−219	4
B Interest	10509	3850	2484	2314	1861	12805	6392	2450	2215	1748
C Dividends	6070	5692	350	28	–	6003	5607	381	15	–
D Net land rent and royalties	1768	1768	93	...	–	1112	1112	153	...	–
3 Taxes, fees and contributions	617660	299941	67927	82568	167224	635784	306520	70570	84929	173765
A Indirect taxes	234044	164043	26233	43768	...	245154	173131	27038	44985	...
B Direct taxes	203767	128008	39112	36647	...	203357	125037	40739	37581	...
Income	164138	93495	34634	36009	...	163988	91330	35889	36769	...
Other	39629	34513	4478	638	...	39369	33707	4850	812	...
C Social security contributions	175993	5111	2093	1576	167213	183339	5570	2284	1732	173753
D Fees, fines and penalties	3856	2779	489	577	11	3934	2782	509	631	12
4 Other current transfers	38508	25012	46330	19579	49662	40491	25859	48972	20867	56957
A Casualty insurance claims	260	180	40	40	–	270	185	42	43	–
B Transfers from other government subsectors	...	5125	37095	11922	47933	...	5001	39153	12855	55155
C Transfers from rest of the world	661	289	1	...	371	665	310	1	...	354
D Other transfers, except imputed	...	...	...	...	...	...	...	...	...	...
E Imputed unfunded employee pension and welfare contributions	37587	19418	9194	7617	1358	39556	20363	9776	7969	1448
Total current receipts [b]	682077	343787	117055	104380	218930	705711	354803	122423	107932	232717

Disbursements

	1986					1987				
1 Government final consumption expenditure	270655	101203	59268	52374	57810	280436	101987	62233	55187	61029
2 Property income	51880	42679	3486	5691	24	58355	49383	3367	5539	66
A Interest	51880	42679	3486	5691	24	58355	49383	3367	5539	66
B Net land rent and royalties	...	...	...	...	...	...	...	...	...	...
3 Subsidies	48393	38767	2298	1697	5631	49872	39948	2758	1638	5528
4 Other current transfers	295527	187246	28616	24477	159023	316037	203303	30602	25539	169543
A Casualty insurance premiums, net	260	180	40	40	–	270	185	42	43	–
B Transfers to other government subsectors	...	87607	4879	7673	3676	...	96347	5029	7852	3722
C Social security benefits [cd]	151079	...	...	...	151079	161466	...	...	...	161466
D Social assistance grants [e]	80442	62143	12396	5903	...	87039	67352	13457	6230	...
E Unfunded employee welfare benefits	59909	36319	11287	10861	1442	63406	38397	12060	11413	1536
F Transfers to private non-profit institutions serving households	...	...	...	...	...	...	...	...	...	...
G Other transfers n.e.c.	...	...	...	...	...	...	...	...	...	...
H Transfers to rest of the world	3837	997	14	–	2826	3856	1022	14	1	2819
Net saving	15622	−26108	23387	20141	−3558	1011	−39818	23463	20029	−3449
Total current disbursements and net saving [b]	682077	343787	117055	104380	218930	705711	354803	122423	107932	232717

Austria

	1988					1989				
	Total govern-ment	Central govern-ment	State or provincial govern-ment	Local govern-ment	Social security funds	Total govern-ment	Central govern-ment	State or provincial govern-ment	Local govern-ment	Social security funds

Receipts

1 Operating surplus	...	...	...	...	...	...	...	...	...	...
2 Property and entrepreneurial income [a]	30382	22731	3417	2213	2021	32886	24436	3529	2425	2496
A Withdrawals from public quasi-corporations	10915	11215	–103	–201	4	11253	11578	–88	–245	8
B Interest	11099	4578	2544	2212	1765	13703	6248	2764	2474	2217
C Dividends	6065	5268	782	15	–	5826	5140	661	25	–
D Net land rent and royalties	1144	1144	194	...	–	289	289	192	...	–
3 Taxes, fees and contributions	665260	338879	59896	84651	181834	694568	349864	61998	89428	193278
A Indirect taxes	254887	178821	28471	47595	...	271413	190116	29957	51340	...
B Direct taxes	214461	151379	28506	34576	...	214465	150249	28853	35363	...
Income	170014	108421	27829	33764	...	167394	104407	28170	34817	...
Other	44447	42958	677	812	...	47071	45842	683	546	...
C Social security contributions	191817	5810	2387	1797	181823	204269	6430	2609	1964	193266
D Fees, fines and penalties	4095	2869	532	683	11	4421	3069	579	761	12
4 Other current transfers	42019	27669	51837	21082	59534	44422	30270	53627	22455	61516
A Casualty insurance claims	290	200	45	45	–	367	247	60	60	–
B Transfers from other government subsectors	...	6201	41504	12764	57634	...	7660	42628	13687	59471
C Transfers from rest of the world	618	259	2	...	357	636	238	2	...	396
D Other transfers, except imputed	...	...	...	...	...	...	...	...	...	...
E Imputed unfunded employee pension and welfare contributions	41111	21009	10286	8273	1543	43419	22125	10937	8708	1649
Total current receipts [b]	737661	389279	115150	107946	243389	771876	404570	119154	114308	257290

Disbursements

1 Government final consumption expenditure	288203	104179	64345	54860	64819	302691	108814	67975	57818	68084
2 Property income	61603	52884	3299	5305	115	66147	57728	3046	5200	173
A Interest	61603	52884	3299	5305	115	66147	57728	3046	5200	173
B Net land rent and royalties	...	...	...	...	...	...	...	...	...	...
3 Subsidies	49199	38797	2673	2028	5701	49407	38401	2821	1858	6327
4 Other current transfers	323595	211609	32014	26218	176746	338030	213602	34925	27753	186511
A Casualty insurance premiums, net	290	200	45	45	–	367	247	60	60	–
B Transfers to other government subsectors	...	105548	5317	7909	4218	...	105454	6073	8388	4846
C Social security benefits [cd]	167759	...	...	...	167759	176423	...	...	...	176423
D Social assistance grants [e]	85223	64805	13958	6460	...	86354	64288	15222	6844	...
E Unfunded employee welfare benefits	66026	39918	12673	11804	1631	70137	42391	13546	12460	1740
F Transfers to private non-profit institutions serving households	...	...	...	...	...	...	...	...	...	...
G Other transfers n.e.c.	...	...	...	...	...	...	...	...	...	...
H Transfers to rest of the world	4297	1138	21	–	3138	4749	1222	24	1	3502
Net saving	15061	–18190	12819	19535	–3992	15601	–13975	10387	21679	–3805
Total current disbursements and net saving [b]	737661	389279	115150	107946	243389	771876	404570	119154	114308	257290

Austria

	1990					1991				
	Total government	Central government	State or provincial government	Local government	Social security funds	Total government	Central government	State or provincial government	Local government	Social security funds

Receipts

1 Operating surplus	...	...	...	...	...	...	...	...	...	...
2 Property and entrepreneurial income [a]	37920	27419	4484	2863	3154	40616	28954	4428	3700	3534
A Withdrawals from public quasi-corporations	12416	12726	−48	−273	11	12155	12434	−18	−268	7
B Interest	15585	6496	3340	2944	2805	17625	7485	3744	3208	3188
C Dividends	7523	6618	866	39	–	8069	7625	403	41	–
D Net land rent and royalties	266	266	326	...	–	335	335	299	...	–
3 Taxes, fees and contributions	752338	378245	67327	98083	208683	816876	408620	75569	106780	225907
A Indirect taxes	287880	201184	31880	54816	...	305779	213197	34014	58568	...
B Direct taxes	238931	166744	31932	40255	...	267125	184525	37779	44821	...
Income	190237	119087	31474	39676	...	215256	133709	37146	44401	...
Other	48694	47657	458	579	...	51869	50816	633	420	...
C Social security contributions	220619	6958	2842	2138	208681	238882	7521	3046	2411	225904
D Fees, fines and penalties	4908	3359	673	874	2	5090	3377	730	980	3
4 Other current transfers	47055	31751	57414	23438	64326	51104	37231	63365	24588	67829
A Casualty insurance claims	387	257	65	65	–	400	260	70	70	–
B Transfers from other government subsectors	...	7793	45816	14118	62147	...	11114	50773	14605	65417
C Transfers from rest of the world	679	251	2	...	426	887	405	1	...	481
D Other transfers, except imputed	...	...	...	...	...	...	...	...	...	...
E Imputed unfunded employee pension and welfare contributions	45989	23450	11531	9255	1753	49817	25452	12521	9913	1931
Total current receipts [b]	837313	437415	129225	124384	276163	908596	474805	143362	135068	297270

Disbursements

1 Government final consumption expenditure	319460	113295	71467	62445	72253	348274	124139	78242	70504	75389
2 Property income	73398	64617	3219	5291	271	81898	72820	3365	5375	338
A Interest	73398	64617	3219	5291	271	81898	72820	3365	5375	338
B Net land rent and royalties	...	...	...	...	...	...	...	...	...	...
3 Subsidies	52504	39849	3421	2313	6921	61539	48021	3645	2446	7427
4 Other current transfers	363129	228161	36854	29346	199782	391272	250087	40765	32841	213414
A Casualty insurance premiums, net	387	257	65	65	–	400	260	70	70	–
B Transfers to other government subsectors	...	110959	5813	8833	5409	...	121444	7114	10259	7018
C Social security benefits [cd]	188672	...	...	...	188672	199860	...	...	...	199860
D Social assistance grants [e]	94142	70295	16566	7281	...	103715	77486	17967	8262	...
E Unfunded employee welfare benefits	74454	45024	14373	13164	1893	80827	48924	15567	14249	2087
F Transfers to private non-profit institutions serving households	...	...	...	...	...	...	...	...	...	...
G Other transfers n.e.c.	...	...	...	...	...	...	...	...	...	...
H Transfers to rest of the world	5474	1626	37	3	3808	6470	1973	47	1	4449
Net saving	28822	−8507	14264	24989	−3064	25613	−20262	17345	23902	702
Total current disbursements and net saving [b]	837313	437415	129225	124384	276163	908596	474805	143362	135068	297270

Austria

	1992					1993				
	Total govern-ment	Central govern-ment	State or provincial govern-ment	Local govern-ment	Social security funds	Total govern-ment	Central govern-ment	State or provincial govern-ment	Local govern-ment	Social security funds

Receipts

1 Operating surplus	...	...	...	...	...	...	...	...	...	...
2 Property and entrepreneurial income [a]	49795	33361	4685	8194	3555	45508	29882	4675	8076	2875
A Withdrawals from public quasi-corporations	17242	13254	–30	4009	9	18318	14250	–49	4111	6
B Interest	17675	6686	4201	3720	3068	16385	6603	4090	3260	2432
C Dividends	11332	10870	413	49	–	7850	7284	477	89	–
D Net land rent and royalties	263	263	101	...	–	219	219	157	...	–
3 Taxes, fees and contributions	890141	445821	79551	116138	248631	938292	464774	85664	122399	265455
A Indirect taxes	325823	229040	34666	62117	...	340005	236863	37948	65194	...
B Direct taxes	296940	205571	40853	50516	...	312658	216067	43398	53193	...
Income	238828	148956	40127	49745	...	250592	160328	42797	47467	...
Other	58112	56615	726	771	...	62066	55739	601	5726	...
C Social security contributions	262302	7888	3299	2486	248629	280022	8297	3539	2734	265452
D Fees, fines and penalties	5076	3322	733	1019	2	5607	3547	779	1278	3
4 Other current transfers	54265	41205	70021	28846	67825	57401	45031	74257	30060	79177
A Casualty insurance claims	420	270	75	75	–	424	272	76	76	–
B Transfers from other government subsectors	...	13490	56732	18142	65268	...	15640	60138	18862	76484
C Transfers from rest of the world	728	229	4	...	495	717	213	4	...	500
D Other transfers, except imputed	...	...	...	...	...	...	...	...	...	...
E Imputed unfunded employee pension and welfare contributions	53117	27216	13210	10629	2062	56260	28906	14039	11122	2193
Total current receipts [b]	994201	520387	154257	153178	320011	1041201	539687	164596	160535	347507

Disbursements

1 Government final consumption expenditure	375155	131046	85652	75398	83059	404966	140746	91652	82068	90500
2 Property income	87451	78266	3422	5346	417	91950	82832	3223	5470	425
A Interest	87451	78266	3422	5346	417	91950	82832	3223	5470	425
B Net land rent and royalties	...	...	...	...	...	...	...	...	...	...
3 Subsidies	64027	49487	4056	2644	7840	68765	54178	4241	3247	7099
4 Other current transfers	423994	266708	44626	35328	231714	472364	307052	49433	38873	248780
A Casualty insurance premiums, net	420	270	75	75	–	424	272	76	76	–
B Transfers to other government subsectors	...	125422	7040	10739	11181	...	140033	8061	12670	11010
C Social security benefits [cd]	212479	...	...	...	212479	229572	...	...	...	229572
D Social assistance grants [e]	117149	86885	20956	9308	...	142328	108335	23671	10322	...
E Unfunded employee welfare benefits	85946	52006	16509	15206	2225	91492	55748	17578	15804	2362
F Transfers to private non-profit institutions serving households	...	...	...	...	...	...	...	...	...	...
G Other transfers n.e.c.	...	...	...	...	...	...	...	...	...	...
H Transfers to rest of the world	8000	2125	46	–	5829	8548	2664	47	1	5836
Net saving	43574	–5120	16501	34462	–3019	3156	–45121	16047	30877	703
Total current disbursements and net saving [b]	994201	520387	154257	153178	320011	1041201	539687	164596	160535	347507

Austria

	1994					1995				
	Total government	Central government	State or provincial government	Local government	Social security funds	Total government	Central government	State or provincial government	Local government	Social security funds

Receipts

1 Operating surplus	...	...	...	...	...	...	...	...	...	...
2 Property and entrepreneurial income [a]	46051	31919	4214	7545	2373	50700	36554	4505	7578	2063
A Withdrawals from public quasi-corporations	20869	16612	–41	4289	9	20879	16786	–67	4158	2
B Interest	14211	6080	3498	2697	1936	18455	10694	3447	2623	1691
C Dividends	8285	7600	600	84	1	8166	7341	738	84	3
D Net land rent and royalties	249	249	157	...	–	218	218	387	...	...
3 Taxes, fees and contributions	962475	471957	83394	125455	281669	990871	488473	81714	125982	294702
A Indirect taxes	356603	245079	37085	74439	...	341394	229875	34190	77329	...
B Direct taxes	299237	211118	41661	46458	...	327687	241265	42392	44030	...
Income	240600	154738	41566	44296	...	266354	180683	42343	43328	...
Other	58637	56380	95	2162	...	61333	60582	49	702	...
C Social security contributions	300523	11987	3809	3061	281666	315815	13461	4397	3259	294698
D Fees, fines and penalties	6112	3773	839	1497	3	5975	3872	735	1364	4
4 Other current transfers	55666	42235	78735	32203	89140	65271	55609	81354	33894	95087
A Casualty insurance claims	445	285	80	80	–	400	260	70	70	–
B Transfers from other government subsectors	...	15561	64207	20589	86290	...	19787	66618	22045	92223
C Transfers from rest of the world	803	334	1	...	468	9249	8869	7	...	373
D Other transfers, except imputed	...	...	...	...	...	...	...	...	...	...
E Imputed unfunded employee pension and welfare contributions	54418	26055	14447	11534	2382	55622	26693	14659	11779	2491
Total current receipts [b]	1064192	546111	166343	165203	373182	1106842	580636	167573	167454	391852

Disbursements

1 Government final consumption expenditure	425932	148097	95279	86057	96499	440275	153790	98893	86533	101059
2 Property income	91058	82059	2980	5460	559	102392	91834	3400	6252	906
A Interest	91058	82059	2980	5460	559	102392	91834	3400	6252	906
B Net land rent and royalties	...	...	...	...	...	...	...	...	...	...
3 Subsidies	58246	41945	5372	3765	7164	63130	47304	4400	4017	7409
4 Other current transfers	503832	326936	55096	41339	266558	527139	340660	60762	43750	283636
A Casualty insurance premiums, net	445	285	80	80	–	400	260	70	70	–
B Transfers to other government subsectors	...	151257	10010	13974	10856	...	159775	14443	15137	12314
C Social security benefits [c,d]	247261	...	...	...	247261	262160	...	...	...	262160
D Social assistance grants [e]	150709	112949	26690	11070	...	148760	109884	27135	11741	...
E Unfunded employee welfare benefits	95970	58944	18256	16213	2557	100520	61995	19056	16801	2668
F Transfers to private non-profit institutions serving households	...	...	...	...	...	...	...	...	...	...
G Other transfers n.e.c.	...	...	...	...	...	...	...	...	...	...
H Transfers to rest of the world	9447	3501	60	2	5884	15299	8746	58	1	6494
Net saving	–14876	–52926	7616	28582	2402	–26094	–52952	118	26902	–1158
Total current disbursements and net saving [b]	1064192	546111	166343	165203	373182	1106842	580636	167573	167454	391852

Austria

	1996					1997				
	Total government	Central government	State or provincial government	Local government	Social security funds	Total government	Central government	State or provincial government	Local government	Social security funds

Receipts

1 Operating surplus	...	...	...	...	...	...	...	...	...	...
2 Property and entrepreneurial income [a]	41837	29413	4149	6445	1830	...	...	...	...	...
A Withdrawals from public quasi-corporations	7288	3894	–71	3460	5	...	...	...	...	...
B Interest	15665	8745	3100	2300	1520	...	...	...	...	...
C Dividends	8251	7341	820	85	5	...	...	...	...	...
D Net land rent and royalties	8623	8623	300	...	...	...	...	...	...	...
3 Taxes, fees and contributions	1057773	528777	90294	135288	303414	...	...	...	...	...
A Indirect taxes	360193	243461	36600	80132	...	...	...	...	...	...
B Direct taxes	363481	264975	48234	50272	...	...	...	...	...	...
Income	301578	204283	48191	49104	...	...	...	...	...	...
Other	61903	60692	43	1168	...	...	...	...	...	...
C Social security contributions	327835	16237	4705	3484	303409	...	...	...	...	...
D Fees, fines and penalties	6264	4104	755	1400	5	...	...	...	...	...
4 Other current transfers	59187	50426	84855	35096	103964	...	...	...	...	...
A Casualty insurance claims	500	300	100	100	...	...	...	...	...	...
B Transfers from other government subsectors	...	20854	70100	23200	101000	...	...	...	...	...
C Transfers from rest of the world	5191	4781	10	...	400	...	...	...	...	...
D Other transfers, except imputed	...	...	...	...	...	...	...	...	...	...
E Imputed unfunded employee pension and welfare contributions	53496	24491	14645	11796	2564	...	...	...	...	...
Total current receipts [b]	1158797	608616	179298	176829	409208	...	...	...	...	...

Disbursements

1 Government final consumption expenditure	446446	154236	100565	86391	105254	...	...	...	...	...
2 Property income	106811	95351	3810	6850	800	...	...	...	...	...
A Interest	106811	95351	3810	6850	800	...	...	...	...	...
B Net land rent and royalties	...	...	...	...	...	...	...	...	...	...
3 Subsidies	64793	48493	4700	4300	7300	...	...	...	...	...
4 Other current transfers	545054	357916	62507	45613	294666	...	...	...	...	...
A Casualty insurance premiums, net	500	300	100	100	...	...	...	...	...	...
B Transfers to other government subsectors	...	173448	15200	16000	11000	...	...	...	...	...
C Social security benefits [cd]	274109	...	...	...	274109	...	...	...	...	...
D Social assistance grants [e]	148785	108485	27800	12500	...	...	...	...	...	...
E Unfunded employee welfare benefits	103331	64214	19350	17010	2757	...	...	...	...	...
F Transfers to private non-profit institutions serving households	...	...	...	...	...	...	...	...	...	...
G Other transfers n.e.c.	...	...	...	...	...	...	...	...	...	...
H Transfers to rest of the world	18329	11469	57	3	6800	...	...	...	...	...
Net saving	–4307	–47380	7716	33675	1188	...	...	...	...	...
Total current disbursements and net saving [b]	1158797	608616	179298	176829	409208	...	...	...	...	...

Austria

	1996					1997				
	Total government	Central government	State or provincial government	Local government	Social security funds	Total government	Central government	State or provincial government	Local government	Social security funds

a The item "Property and entrepreneurial income" is greater than the sum of its sub-items. The difference being the unspecified items.
b Column "State or Provincial Government" includes chambers.
c Item "Social security benefits" includes social security funds only.
d Item "Transfers to private non-profit institutions serving households" is included in item "Social assistance grants".
e Item "Social assistance grants" includes unemployment benefits.

3.13 General government capital accumulation account: total and subsectors

Million Austrian schillings

	1986					1987				
	Total government	Central government	State or provincial government	Local government	Social security funds	Total government	Central government	State or provincial government	Local government	Social security funds
Finance of gross accumulation										
1 Gross saving	26932	–23544	25128	26731	–3143	12572	–37197	25243	26765	–3025
A Consumption of fixed capital	11310	2564	1741	6590	415	11561	2621	1780	6736	424
B Net saving	15622	–26108	23387	20141	–3558	1011	–39818	23463	20029	–3449
2 Capital transfers [a]	–28057	–25193	–5747	3327	54	–27319	–23973	–6268	3486	10
A From other government subsectors	...	–5883	98	6228	55	...	–5552	–310	6425	11
B From other resident sectors	–27524	–18778	–5845	–2900	–1	–26798	–17898	–5960	–2939	–1
C From rest of the world	–533	–532	–	–1	–	–521	–523	2	–	–
Finance of gross accumulation [b]	–1125	–48737	19381	30058	–3089	–14747	–61170	18975	30251	–3015
Gross accumulation										
1 Gross capital formation	52092	17716	6404	25952	2020	50728	14864	7318	27748	798
A Increase in stocks	...	...	...	...	...	...	...	...	...	...
B Gross fixed capital formation	52092	17716	6404	25952	2020	50728	14864	7318	27748	798
2 Purchases of land, net	2188	789	229	854	316	729	583	–230	367	9
3 Purchases of intangible assets, net	...	...	...	...	...	...	...	...	...	...
4 Capital transfers	...	...	...	...	...	...	...	...	...	...
Net lending	–55405	–67242	12748	3252	–5425	–66204	–76617	11887	2136	–3822
Gross accumulation [b]	–1125	–48737	19381	30058	–3089	–14747	–61170	18975	30251	–3015

	1988					1989				
	Total government	Central government	State or provincial government	Local government	Social security funds	Total government	Central government	State or provincial government	Local government	Social security funds
Finance of gross accumulation										
1 Gross saving	26864	–15514	14636	26413	–3560	27819	–11205	12268	28798	–3357
A Consumption of fixed capital	11803	2676	1817	6878	432	12218	2770	1881	7119	448
B Net saving	15061	–18190	12819	19535	–3992	15601	–13975	10387	21679	–3805
2 Capital transfers [a]	–28492	–40555	6731	8327	10	–23692	–35688	5894	7779	20
A From other government subsectors	...	–21285	12846	11428	16	...	–21785	11874	11587	21
B From other resident sectors	–27348	–18126	–6115	–3101	–6	–23048	–13260	–5980	–3807	–1
C From rest of the world	–1144	–1144	–	–	–	–644	–643	–	–1	–
Finance of gross accumulation [b]	–1628	–56069	21367	34740	–3550	4127	–46893	18162	36577	–3337
Gross accumulation										
1 Gross capital formation	50676	14772	6925	27728	1251	55192	14998	7227	31336	1631

Austria

	1988					1989				
	Total govern-ment	Central govern-ment	State or provincial govern-ment	Local govern-ment	Social security funds	Total govern-ment	Central govern-ment	State or provincial govern-ment	Local govern-ment	Social security funds
A Increase in stocks	...	...	...	...	...	...	...	...	...	...
B Gross fixed capital formation	50676	14772	6925	27728	1251	55192	14998	7227	31336	1631
2 Purchases of land, net	630	420	−394	680	−76	597	406	374	−136	−47
3 Purchases of intangible assets, net	...	...	...	...	...	...	...	...	...	...
4 Capital transfers	...	...	...	...	...	...	...	...	...	...
Net lending	−52934	−71261	14836	6332	−4725	−51662	−62297	10561	5377	−4921
Gross accumulation [b]	−1628	−56069	21367	34740	−3550	4127	−46893	18162	36577	−3337

	1990					1991				
	Total govern-ment	Central govern-ment	State or provincial govern-ment	Local govern-ment	Social security funds	Total govern-ment	Central govern-ment	State or provincial govern-ment	Local govern-ment	Social security funds

Finance of gross accumulation

1 Gross saving	41592	−5612	16230	32430	−2596	39115	−17201	19423	31770	1197
A Consumption of fixed capital	12770	2895	1966	7441	468	13502	3061	2078	7868	495
B Net saving	28822	−8507	14264	24989	−3064	25613	−20262	17345	23902	702
2 Capital transfers [a]	−27669	−38800	5554	6477	21	−27365	−39324	5900	3157	21
A From other government subsectors	...	−23271	12721	11450	21	...	−26345	14081	9361	22
B From other resident sectors	−26872	−14739	−7164	−4969	–	−26345	−12010	−8134	−6200	−1
C From rest of the world	−797	−790	−3	−4	–	−1020	−969	−47	−4	–
Finance of gross accumulation [b]	13923	−44412	21784	38907	−2575	11750	−56525	25323	34927	1218

Gross accumulation

1 Gross capital formation	57293	16390	7594	32517	792	63043	16686	8307	36931	1119
A Increase in stocks	...	...	...	...	...	...	...	...	...	...
B Gross fixed capital formation	57293	16390	7594	32517	792	63043	16686	8307	36931	1119
2 Purchases of land, net	686	−358	288	701	55	515	108	343	112	−48
3 Purchases of intangible assets, net	...	...	...	...	...	...	...	...	...	...
4 Capital transfers	...	...	...	...	...	...	...	...	...	...
Net lending	−44056	−60444	13902	5689	−3422	−51808	−73319	16673	−2116	147
Gross accumulation [b]	13923	−44412	21784	38907	−2575	11750	−56525	25323	34927	1218

	1992					1993				
	Total govern-ment	Central govern-ment	State or provincial govern-ment	Local govern-ment	Social security funds	Total govern-ment	Central govern-ment	State or provincial govern-ment	Local govern-ment	Social security funds

Finance of gross accumulation

1 Gross saving	57383	−1990	18627	42509	−2513	17624	−41841	18274	39308	1233
A Consumption of fixed capital	13809	3130	2126	8047	506	14468	3280	2227	8431	530
B Net saving	43574	−5120	16501	34462	−3019	3156	−45121	16047	30877	703
2 Capital transfers [a]	−28093	−41201	7623	3712	302	−35780	−43877	7062	−1135	269
A From other government subsectors	...	−28292	16111	10670	40	...	−29839	17099	10804	35
B From other resident sectors	−26916	−11760	−8482	−6936	262	−34579	−12844	−10036	−11933	234
C From rest of the world	−1177	−1149	−6	−22	–	−1201	−1194	−1	−6	–
Finance of gross accumulation [b]	29290	−43191	26250	46221	−2211	−18156	−85718	25336	38173	1502

Austria

	1992					1993				
	Total govern-ment	Central govern-ment	State or provincial govern-ment	Local govern-ment	Social security funds	Total govern-ment	Central govern-ment	State or provincial govern-ment	Local govern-ment	Social security funds

Gross accumulation

1 Gross capital formation	67726	15843	9475	41231	1177	67493	15713	10585	39953	1242
A Increase in stocks	...	...	...	...	...	...	...	...	...	...
B Gross fixed capital formation	67726	15843	9475	41231	1177	67493	15713	10585	39953	1242
2 Purchases of land, net	40	−669	−619	1303	25	1215	−	−801	1958	58
3 Purchases of intangible assets, net	...	...	...	...	...	...	...	...	...	...
4 Capital transfers	...	...	...	...	...	...	...	...	...	...
Net lending	−38476	−58365	17394	3687	−3413	−86864	−101431	15552	−3738	202
Gross accumulation [b]	29290	−43191	26250	46221	−2211	−18156	−85718	25336	38173	1502

	1994					1995				
	Total govern-ment	Central govern-ment	State or provincial govern-ment	Local govern-ment	Social security funds	Total govern-ment	Central govern-ment	State or provincial govern-ment	Local govern-ment	Social security funds

Finance of gross accumulation

1 Gross saving	177	−49514	9933	37354	2954	−10390	−49392	2535	36053	−582
A Consumption of fixed capital	15053	3412	2317	8772	552	15704	3560	2417	9151	576
B Net saving	−14876	−52926	7616	28582	2402	−26094	−52952	118	26902	−1158
2 Capital transfers [a]	−35087	−43203	8545	−2071	−337	−41879	−51145	9406	−3028	961
A From other government subsectors	...	−30577	18324	10236	38	...	−32814	20631	10212	44
B From other resident sectors	−33915	−11464	−9779	−12297	−375	−41145	−17554	−11273	−13235	917
C From rest of the world	−1172	−1162	−	−10	−	−734	−777	48	−5	−
Finance of gross accumulation [b]	−34910	−92717	18478	35283	2617	−52269	−100537	11941	33025	379

Gross accumulation

1 Gross capital formation	70459	15741	10151	43290	1277	68065	14634	9093	42863	1475
A Increase in stocks	...	...	...	...	...	...	...	...	...	...
B Gross fixed capital formation	70459	15741	10151	43290	1277	68065	14634	9093	42863	1475
2 Purchases of land, net	2481	551	393	1472	65	−4024	96	−3005	−1088	−27
3 Purchases of intangible assets, net	...	...	...	...	...	...	...	...	...	...
4 Capital transfers	...	...	...	...	...	...	...	...	...	...
Net lending	−107850	−109009	7934	−9479	1275	−116310	−115267	5853	−8750	−1069
Gross accumulation [b]	−34910	−92717	18478	35283	2617	−52269	−100537	11941	33025	379

	1996					1997				
	Total govern-ment	Central govern-ment	State or provincial govern-ment	Local govern-ment	Social security funds	Total govern-ment	Central govern-ment	State or provincial govern-ment	Local govern-ment	Social security funds

Finance of gross accumulation

1 Gross saving	11939	−43697	10216	43142	1784	...	...	...	...	...
A Consumption of fixed capital	16246	3683	2500	9467	596	...	...	...	...	...
B Net saving	−4307	−47380	7716	33675	1188	...	...	...	...	...
2 Capital transfers [a]	−38053	−50088	9124	495	350	...	...	...	...	...
A From other government subsectors	...	−33699	21083	10500	50	...	...	...	...	...
B From other resident sectors	−37175	−15466	−12009	−10000	300	...	...	...	...	...

Austria

	1996					1997				
	Total govern-ment	Central govern-ment	State or provincial govern-ment	Local govern-ment	Social security funds	Total govern-ment	Central govern-ment	State or provincial govern-ment	Local govern-ment	Social security funds
C From rest of the world	−878	−923	50	−5	...	...	...	...	...	...
Finance of gross accumulation [b]	−26114	−93785	19340	43637	2134	...	...	...	...	...
Gross accumulation										
1 Gross capital formation	66905	13862	9259	42484	1300	...	...	...	...	...
A Increase in stocks	...	...	...	...	...	...	...	...	...	...
B Gross fixed capital formation	66905	13862	9259	42484	1300	...	...	...	...	...
2 Purchases of land, net	78	−562	200	500	−60	...	...	...	...	...
3 Purchases of intangible assets, net	...	...	...	...	...	...	...	...	...	...
4 Capital transfers	...	...	...	...	...	...	...	...	...	...
Net lending	−93097	−107085	9881	653	894	...	...	...	...	...
Gross accumulation [b]	−26114	−93785	19340	43637	2134	...	...	...	...	...

a Capital transfers received are recorded net of capital transfers paid.　　　b Column "State or Provincial Government" includes chambers.

3.32 Household and private unincorporated enterprise income and outlay account

Million Austrian schillings

	1986	1987	1988	1989	1990	1991	1992	1993	1994	1995	1996	1997
Receipts												
1 Compensation of employees	765733	797421	832569	885602	955471	1036710	1105302	1151169	1195303	1237075	1251350	...
A Wages and salaries	626799	652636	680152	723612	782248	849607	903421	937139	972962	1008959	1021746	...
B Employers' contributions for social security	138934	144785	152417	161990	173223	187103	201881	214030	222341	228116	229604	...
C Employers' contributions for private pension and welfare plans	...	...	...	...	...	...	...	...	...	...	...	...
2 Operating surplus of private unincorporated enterprises	...	...	...	...	...	...	...	...	...	...	...	...
3 Property and entrepreneurial income	268276	276370	289897	314271	362892	391652	397286	382010	399772	427889	474870	...
4 Current transfers	333552	360631	365163	381912	407362	439009	469467	526186	567328	585461	616937	...
A Casualty insurance claims	26142	31682	33808	35353	34217	34976	37569	45952	51115	54620	67190	...
B Social security benefits	151079	161466	167759	176423	188672	199860	212479	229572	247261	262160	274109	...
C Social assistance grants	80442	87039	85223	86354	94142	103715	117149	142328	150709	148760	148785	...
D Unfunded employee pension and welfare benefits	59909	63406	66026	70137	74454	80827	85946	91492	95970	100520	103331	...
E Transfers from general government	...	...	...	...	...	...	...	...	...	...	...	...
F Transfers from rest of the world	15980	17038	12347	13645	15877	19631	16324	16842	22273	19401	23522	...
G Other transfers n.e.c.	...	...	...	...	...	...	...	...	...	...	...	...
Total current receipts	1367561	1434422	1487629	1581785	1725725	1867371	1972055	2059365	2162403	2250425	2343157	...
Disbursements												
1 Final consumption expenditure	813986	843921	886040	943288	1012961	1073004	1147677	1194057	1254605	1310245	1375415	...
A Market purchases	739915	767415	808307	858120	921546	978300	1045274	1084812	1136268	1178674	1232413	...
B Gross rents of owner-occupied housing	68161	70476	72175	79413	85476	88972	97022	104144	113268	127521	139186	...
C Consumption from own-account production	5910	6030	5558	5755	5939	5732	5381	5101	5069	4049	3815	...
2 Property income	15729	17274	19174	22735	30213	38826	42816	43333	43839	44074	43237	...

Austria

Million Austrian schillings

	1986	1987	1988	1989	1990	1991	1992	1993	1994	1995	1996	1997
A Interest	15729	17274	19174	22735	30213	38826	42816	43333	43839	...	...	...
Consumer debt	15729	17274	19174	22735	30213	38826	42816	43333	43839	...	...	...
Mortgages	...	...	...	...	...	...	...	...	...	...	...	...
Other	...	...	...	...	...	...	...	...	...	...	...	...
B Net land rent and royalties	...	...	...	...	...	...	...	...	...	...	...	...
3 Direct taxes and other current transfers n.e.c. to general government	368643	376483	396592	406117	447559	490959	540345	578090	601458	637347	671855	...
A Social security contributions	175993	183339	191817	204269	220619	238882	262302	280022	300523	315815	327835	...
B Direct taxes	177591	177166	186394	180517	203375	227462	249864	267853	265798	286510	305898	...
Income taxes	177591	177166	186394	180517	203375	227462	249864	267853	265798	286510	305898	...
Other	...	...	...	...	...	...	...	...	...	...	...	...
C Fees, fines and penalties	15059	15978	18381	21331	23565	24615	28179	30215	35137	35022	38122	...
4 Other current transfers	73920	80099	86262	92335	93812	101636	111357	123939	127420	128921	142342	...
A Net casualty insurance premiums	26142	31682	33808	35353	34217	34976	37569	45952	51115	54620	67190	...
B Transfers to private non-profit institutions serving households	...	...	...	...	...	...	...	...	...	...	...	...
C Transfers to rest of the world	10191	8861	11343	13563	13606	16843	20671	21727	21887	18679	21656	...
D Other current transfers, except imputed	...	...	...	...	...	...	...	...	...	...	...	...
E Imputed employee pension and welfare contributions	37587	39556	41111	43419	45989	49817	53117	56260	54418	55622	53496	...
Net saving	95284	116646	99562	117310	141181	162947	129860	119946	135081	129838	110308	...
Total current disbursements and net saving	1367562	1434423	1487630	1581785	1725726	1867372	1972055	2059365	2162403	2250425	2343157	...

3.41 Private non-profit institutions serving households: production account

Million Austrian schillings

	1986	1987	1988	1989	1990	1991	1992	1993	1994	1995	1996	1997
Gross output												
Gross output	12414	12919	13199	13748	14645	15820	16891	17851	18689	...	...	...
Gross input												
Intermediate consumption	13726	14581	15521	16377	18245	20038	21836	23147	25164	26755	27462	...
subtotal: Value added	24289	25947	27240	28689	32243	35607	39262	41882	45520	48023	49500	...
1 Indirect taxes, net	−179	−159	−164	−170	−173	−190	−319	−188	−192	...	...	...
2 Consumption of fixed capital	1070	1041	1133	1193	1246	1341	1452	1552	1663	1772	1871	...
3 Compensation of employees	9250	9724	9766	10104	10860	11644	12682	13342	13975	...	...	...
4 Net operating surplus	...	...	...	...	...	...	...	...	...	...	...	...
Gross input	14796	15622	16654	17570	19491	21379	23288	24699	26827	28527	29333	...

Austria

3.51 External transactions, current account: detail

Million Austrian schillings

	1986	1987	1988	1989	1990	1991	1992	1993	1994	1995	1996	1997
Payments to the rest of the world												
1 Imports of goods and services [a]	503971	517471	582559	653395	704875	757999	771967	772607	842963	910504	1001790	...
A Imports of merchandise, c.i.f. [a]	404818	408767	445222	509269	551254	585907	588666	562313	623314	648180	704104	...
B Other	99153	108704	137337	144126	153621	172092	183301	210294	219649	262324	297686	...
2 Factor income to rest of the world	70336	70190	75379	97154	107508	118089	112732	117437	110394	122970	143300	...
A Compensation of employees [b]	–	–	1896	1998	2111	2186	2256	3359	3323	3421	3580	...
B Property and entrepreneurial income	70414	70266	73483	95156	105397	115903	110476	114078	107071	119549	139720	...
By general government [c]	7348	7423	6898	8489	8779	10189	10315	12096	13311	17397	17881	...
By corporate and quasi-corporate enterprises	...	...	...	...	...	...	...	...	...	...	...	...
By other	...	...	...	...	...	...	...	...	...	...	...	...
3 Current transfers to the rest of the world [b]	14028	12717	15640	18312	19080	23313	28671	30275	31334	59921	67255	...
A Indirect taxes by general government to supranational organizations	...	...	...	...	...	...	...	...	...	25943	27270	...
B Other current transfers	14028	12717	15640	18312	19080	23313	28671	30275	31334	33978	39985	...
By general government	3837	3856	4297	4749	5474	6470	8000	8548	9447	15299	18329	...
By other resident sectors	10191	8861	11343	13563	13606	16843	20671	21727	21887	18679	21656	...
4 Surplus of the nation on current transactions	3384	–2440	–2942	3277	13635	820	–1628	–8245	–20617	–41316	–49840	...
Payments to the rest of the world and surplus of the nation on current transfers	591719	597938	670636	772138	845098	900221	911742	912074	964074	1052079	1162505	...
Receipts from the rest of the world												
1 Exports of goods and services [a]	516675	522948	590759	669618	728312	774706	791618	786507	838841	900905	988783	...
A Exports of merchandise, f.o.b. [a]	339842	343280	375072	427938	467800	479309	486038	468277	512989	567557	623273	...
B Other	176833	179668	215687	241680	260512	295397	305580	318230	325852	333348	365510	...
2 Factor income from rest of the world	58403	57287	66912	88239	100230	104997	103072	108008	102157	115346	135686	...
A Compensation of employees [b]	–	–	7586	7993	8442	8746	8938	8949	9608	9798	9957	...
B Property and entrepreneurial income	58448	57361	59326	80246	91788	96251	94134	99059	92549	105548	125729	...
3 Current transfers from rest of the world [b]	16641	17703	12965	14281	16556	20518	17052	17559	23076	35828	38036	...
A Subsidies to general government from supranational organizations	...	...	...	...	...	...	...	...	...	7178	9323	...
B Other current transfers	16641	17703	12965	14281	16556	20518	17052	17559	23076	28650	28713	...
To general government	661	665	618	636	679	887	728	717	803	9249	5191	...
To other resident sectors	15980	17038	12347	13645	15877	19631	16324	16842	22273	19401	23522	...
Receipts from the rest of the world on current transfers	591719	597938	670636	772138	845098	900221	911742	912074	964074	1052079	1162505	...

a The estimates on transit trade are on a net basis.
b Item "Compensation of employees" is included in current transfers to/from the rest of the world.
c Only central government data are included in the general government estimates.

Austria

3.52 External transactions, capital accumulation account

Million Austrian schillings

	1986	1987	1988	1989	1990	1991	1992	1993	1994	1995	1996	1997
Finance of gross accumulation												
1 Surplus of the nation on current transactions	3384	−2440	−2942	3277	13635	820	−1628	−8245	−20617	−41316	−49840	...
2 Capital transfers from rest of the world	...	...	...	...	...	...	...	...	...	...	...	...
Total finance of gross accumulation	3384	−2440	−2942	3277	13635	820	−1628	−8245	−20617	−41316	−49840	...
Gross accumulation												
1 Capital transfers to the rest of the world	...	...	...	...	...	...	...	...	...	...	...	...
2 Purchases of intangible assets, n.e.c., net, from rest of the world	...	...	...	...	...	...	...	...	...	...	...	...
Net lending to the rest of the world	3384	−2440	−2942	3277	13635	820	−1628	−8245	−20617	−41316	−49840	...
Total gross accumulation	3384	−2440	−2942	3277	13635	820	−1628	−8245	−20617	−41316	−49840	...

4.1 Derivation of value added by kind of activity, in current prices

Million Austrian schillings

	1986			1987			1988			1989		
	Gross output	Intermediate consumption	Value added	Gross output	Intermediate consumption	Value added	Gross output	Intermediate consumption	Value added	Gross output	Intermediate consumption	Value added
All producers												
1 Agriculture, hunting, forestry and fishing	71495	24381	47114	72273	23800	48473	73232	24209	49023	77122	24818	52304
A Agriculture and hunting	59592	12478	...	60625	12152	...	60884	11861	...	62415	10111	...
B Forestry and logging	11903	11903	...	11648	11648	...	12348	12348	...	14707	14707	...
C Fishing	...	...	...	...	...	...	...	...	...	...	...	...
2 Mining and quarrying	25327	14648	10679	20417	11365	9052	19943	10695	9248	19907	10409	9498
A Coal mining	2224	664	1560	2047	648	1399	1654	462	1192	1455	434	1021
B Crude petroleum and natural gas production	15966	10599	5367	11331	7480	3851	11167	6936	4231	11406	6590	4816
C Metal ore mining	1533	674	859	1265	499	766	1106	394	712	1069	416	653
D Other mining	5604	2711	2893	5774	2738	3036	6016	2903	3113	5977	2969	3008
3 Manufacturing	854430	518518	335912	854319	514902	339417	901614	542912	358702	972642	592917	379725
A Manufacture of food, beverages and tobacco	160992	107543	53449	161036	105532	55504	161757	106657	55100	165906	109250	56656
B Textile, wearing apparel and leather industries	64759	38755	26004	62947	36944	26003	62567	37269	25298	63862	37804	26058
C Manufacture of wood and wood products, including furniture	40158	25468	14690	41927	26731	15196	45061	28545	16516	49697	32356	17341
D Manufacture of paper and paper products, printing and publishing	65941	39822	26119	68110	42662	25448	73993	45272	28721	79221	48322	30899
E Manufacture of chemicals and chemical petroleum, coal, rubber and plastic products [a]	126443	78850	47593	127966	81895	46071	134698	85377	49321	141734	92827	48907

Austria

Million Austrian schillings

	1986 Gross output	1986 Intermediate consumption	1986 Value added	1987 Gross output	1987 Intermediate consumption	1987 Value added	1988 Gross output	1988 Intermediate consumption	1988 Value added	1989 Gross output	1989 Intermediate consumption	1989 Value added
F Manufacture of non-metallic mineral products, except products of petroleum and coal	49402	27345	22057	50537	27247	23290	54100	29653	24447	56572	31062	25510
G Basic metal industries	127508	75834	51674	114453	66978	47475	129797	73529	56268	144861	85105	59756
H Manufacture of fabricated metal products, machinery and equipment	191393	109807	81586	197610	110821	86789	208146	119646	88500	236619	137646	98973
I Other manufacturing industries	27834	15094	12740	29733	16092	13641	31495	16964	14531	34170	18545	15625
4 Electricity, gas and water	98539	53109	45430	100315	51920	48395	96940	51303	45637	101220	53206	48014
A Electricity, gas and steam	95210	52043	43167	96780	50780	46000	93240	50081	43159	97419	51929	45490
B Water works and supply	3329	1066	2263	3535	1140	2395	3700	1222	2478	3801	1277	2524
5 Construction	166694	80931	85763	177874	87020	90854	188789	93235	95554	204752	101802	102950
6 Wholesale and retail trade, restaurants and hotels	390457	138282	252175	406818	146378	260440	432256	158310	273946	463749	169422	294327
A Wholesale and retail trade	286642	92014	194628	299670	98520	201150	321328	108766	212562	344420	116366	228054
B Restaurants and hotels	103815	46268	57547	107148	47858	59290	110928	49544	61384	119329	53056	66273
Restaurants	126	62	64	129	63	66	133	62	71	146	68	78
Hotels and other lodging places	103689	46206	57483	107019	47795	59224	110795	49482	61313	119183	52988	66195
7 Transport, storage and communication	183645	96455	87190	194342	102025	92318	210969	111029	99940	223247	116292	106954
A Transport and storage	145510	91673	53836	154031	97538	56493	167094	105738	61356	177261	110898	66363
B Communication	38135	4782	33353	40311	4486	35825	43875	5291	38584	45986	5395	40591
8 Finance, insurance, real estate and business services	323121	88801	234320	346002	96614	249388	373178	105610	267568	412237	114997	297240
A Financial institutions	81954	14971	66983	91086	18442	72644	98072	20237	77835	111004	22886	88118
B Insurance	32564	7546	25018	34506	7953	26553	38328	9702	28626	40736	9622	31114
C Real estate and business services	205163	65400	139763	216726	69270	147456	232702	74541	158161	256129	81342	174787
Real estate, except dwellings	118742	35475	83267	126611	38429	88182	139896	42876	97020	155287	48103	107184
Dwellings	86421	29925	56496	90115	30841	59274	92806	31665	61141	100842	33239	67603
9 Community, social and personal services	70709	21064	49645	77740	22629	55111	84586	24972	59614	91603	26284	65319
A Sanitary and similar services	...	...	...	...	...	...	...	...	...	...	...	...
B Social and related community services [b]	35287	9354	25933	37193	9914	27279	40358	10718	29640	42610	11370	31240
Educational services	...	...	...	...	...	...	...	...	...	...	...	...
Medical, dental, other health and veterinary services [b]	35287	9354	25933	37193	9914	27279	40358	10718	29640	42610	11370	31240
C Recreational and cultural services [bc]	22719	9097	13622	27405	10107	17298	30447	11040	19407	34558	12250	22308
D Personal and household services [bd]	17440	5752	11688	18451	5768	12683	19624	6023	13601	20917	6354	14563
Total, Industries	2184416	1036189	1148227	2250100	1056652	1193447	2381506	1122275	1259231	2566478	1210147	1356331
Producers of government services	321511	128709	192802	332589	131030	201559	344847	138448	206399	364009	146962	217047
Other producers [d]	42366	13726	28640	44818	14581	30237	47091	15521	31570	49224	16377	32847
Total	2548293	1178624	1369669	2627507	1202263	1425243	2773444	1276244	1497200	2979711	1373486	1606225
less: Imputed bank service charge	...	−68277	68277	...	−74942	74942	...	−79691	79691	...	−88193	88193
Import duties	8996	...	8996	9861	...	9861	10631	...	10631	11507	...	11507

Austria

Million Austrian schillings

	1986			1987			1988			1989		
	Gross output	Intermediate consumption	Value added	Gross output	Intermediate consumption	Value added	Gross output	Intermediate consumption	Value added	Gross output	Intermediate consumption	Value added
Value added tax	128655	...	128655	133962	...	133962	137630	...	137630	147138	...	147138
Other adjustments	...	...	–10	...	...	–10	...	...	–	...	...	–
Total	2685944	1246901	1439043	2771330	1277205	1494124	2921705	1355935	1565770	3138356	1461679	1676677

	1990			1991			1992			1993		
	Gross output	Intermediate consumption	Value added	Gross output	Intermediate consumption	Value added	Gross output	Intermediate consumption	Value added	Gross output	Intermediate consumption	Value added
All producers												
1 Agriculture, hunting, forestry and fishing	82170	25541	56629	78475	25483	52992	76049	26014	50035	73580	26258	47322
A Agriculture and hunting	65784	9155	...	66979	13987	...	64275	14240	...	63691	16369	...
B Forestry and logging	16386	16386	...	11496	11496	...	11774	11774	...	9889	9889	...
C Fishing	...	...	...	...	...	...	...	...	...	...	...	...
2 Mining and quarrying	21550	12300	9250	22306	13070	9236	21370	12538	8832	21973	13335	8638
A Coal mining	1624	601	1023	1582	603	979	1591	657	934	1453	584	869
B Crude petroleum and natural gas production	12335	8104	4231	13109	8929	4180	11995	8206	3789	12687	9045	3642
C Metal ore mining	906	399	507	703	354	349	641	315	326	434	170	264
D Other mining	6685	3196	3489	6912	3184	3728	7143	3360	3783	7399	3536	3863
3 Manufacturing	1043151	632195	410956	1095293	658943	436350	1099779	657420	442359	1072253	636571	435682
A Manufacture of food, beverages and tobacco	173578	113293	60285	182217	118461	63756	188496	119177	69319	190427	120142	70285
B Textile, wearing apparel and leather industries	68477	41277	27200	67806	40633	27173	66853	39572	27281	61773	35939	25834
C Manufacture of wood and wood products, including furniture	57232	36609	20623	57386	35490	21896	58701	36018	22683	56858	34087	22771
D Manufacture of paper and paper products, printing and publishing	84999	51843	33156	90512	55685	34827	90100	56089	34011	85706	52540	33166
E Manufacture of chemicals and chemical petroleum, coal, rubber and plastic products [a]	148613	96491	52122	153668	95503	58165	148923	89907	59016	144251	85724	58527
F Manufacture of non-metallic mineral products, except products of petroleum and coal	59156	32222	26934	63211	33897	29314	63703	33929	29774	64688	35073	29615
G Basic metal industries	149294	86763	62531	147683	86733	60950	145263	86913	58350	136817	82179	54638
H Manufacture of fabricated metal products, machinery and equipment	268572	155800	112772	294473	172512	121961	297178	174692	122486	291251	169920	121331
I Other manufacturing industries	33230	17897	15333	38337	20029	18308	40562	21123	19439	40482	20967	19515
4 Electricity, gas and water	108976	59761	49215	117942	65312	52630	121680	64922	56758	126540	66191	60349
A Electricity, gas and steam	104925	58273	46652	113624	63733	49891	116997	63234	53763	120990	64221	56769
B Water works and supply	4051	1488	2563	4318	1579	2739	4683	1688	2995	5550	1970	3580
5 Construction	225384	110473	114911	249577	119404	130173	267724	127697	140027	280628	131135	149493
6 Wholesale and retail trade, restaurants and hotels	502524	183062	319462	534018	194315	339703	562344	202646	359698	568618	204838	363780
A Wholesale and retail trade	375598	126074	249524	397046	132850	264196	414114	135741	278373	415632	138085	277547
B Restaurants and hotels	126926	56988	69938	136972	61465	75507	148230	66905	81325	152986	66753	86233
Restaurants	150	69	81	196	90	106	191	87	104	180	79	101
Hotels and other lodging places	126776	56919	69857	136776	61375	75401	148039	66818	81221	152806	66674	86132

Austria

	1990			1991			1992			1993		
	Gross output	Intermediate consumption	Value added	Gross output	Intermediate consumption	Value added	Gross output	Intermediate consumption	Value added	Gross output	Intermediate consumption	Value added
7 Transport, storage and communication	242068	125674	116394	262010	135049	126961	285914	146469	139444	295701	153211	142490
A Transport and storage	193097	120218	72879	210164	129474	80690	230843	140310	90532	236784	146537	90247
B Communication	48971	5457	43515	51846	5575	46271	55071	6159	48912	58917	6674	52243
8 Finance, insurance, real estate and business services	451406	126617	324789	492234	138523	353711	536615	149868	386747	578185	160303	417882
A Financial institutions	120164	25327	94837	129948	27808	102140	138902	28323	110579	157463	31271	126192
B Insurance	44365	10681	33684	49123	10949	38174	53491	12589	40902	57061	13889	43172
C Real estate and business services	282123	89339	192784	307916	98439	209477	338523	107463	231060	357531	113503	244028
Real estate, except dwellings	173856	54007	119849	193849	60115	133734	213728	67116	146612	224376	70503	153873
Dwellings	108267	35332	72935	114067	38324	75743	124795	40347	84448	133155	43000	90155
9 Community, social and personal services	99260	29214	70046	107478	31923	75555	119154	33905	85249	128199	35469	92730
A Sanitary and similar services	...	...	...	...	...	...	...	...	...	...	...	...
B Social and related community services [b]	45303	12106	33197	49665	13363	36302	56375	15424	40951	62521	17128	45393
Educational services	...	...	...	...	...	...	...	...	...	...	...	...
Medical, dental, other health and veterinary services [b]	45303	12106	33197	49665	13363	36302	56375	15424	40951	62521	17128	45393
C Recreational and cultural services [bc]	39340	14366	24974	43020	16548	26472	46397	16418	29979	47856	17796	30060
D Personal and household services [bd]	21878	6500	15378	23588	6808	16780	26183	7434	18749	28093	7667	20426
Total, Industries	2776489	1304837	1471651	2959332	1382021	1577310	3090628	1421479	1669149	3145677	1427311	1718366
Producers of government services	385137	154439	230698	417977	167249	250728	452903	183015	269888	488892	199798	289094
Other producers [d]	54623	18245	36378	60012	20038	39974	65568	21836	43732	69691	23147	46544
Total	3216249	1477521	1738727	3437321	1569308	1868012	3609099	1626330	1982769	3704260	1650256	2054004
less: Imputed bank service charge	...	−94097	94097	...	−101766	101766	...	−109773	109773	...	−123908	123908
Import duties	12026	...	12026	12642	...	12642	13269	...	13269	13122	...	13122
Value added tax	156825	...	156825	166933	...	166933	171006	...	171006	182125	...	182125
Other adjustments	...	...	...	...	...	...	...	...	...	...	...	...
Total	3385100	1571618	1813481	3616896	1671074	1945821	3793374	1736103	2057271	3899507	1774164	2125343

	1994			1995			1996			1997		
	Gross output	Intermediate consumption	Value added	Gross output	Intermediate consumption	Value added	Gross output	Intermediate consumption	Value added	Gross output	Intermediate consumption	Value added

All producers

1 Agriculture, hunting, forestry and fishing	77526	27080	50446	61968	26071	35897	61235	26550	34685	...	...	...
A Agriculture and hunting	64897	14451	...	49217	13320	...	48791	14106	...	...	...	...
B Forestry and logging	12629	12629	...	12751	12751	...	12444	12444	...	...	...	...
C Fishing	...	...	...	...	...	...	...	...	...	...	...	...
2 Mining and quarrying	21082	12824	8258	20445	11844	8601	20593	11842	8751	...	...	...
A Coal mining	1208	553	655	1032	436	596	974	420	554	...	...	...
B Crude petroleum and natural gas production	11419	8342	3077	10825	7467	3358	10901	7397	3504	...	...	...
C Metal ore mining	310	116	194	342	131	211	316	122	194	...	...	...
D Other mining	8145	3813	4332	8246	3810	4436	8402	3903	4499	...	...	...

Austria

	1994			1995			1996			1997		
	Gross output	Intermediate consumption	Value added	Gross output	Intermediate consumption	Value added	Gross output	Intermediate consumption	Value added	Gross output	Intermediate consumption	Value added
3 Manufacturing	1124261	668656	455605	1167096	698606	468490	1189284	708789	480495	...	...	...
A Manufacture of food, beverages and tobacco	191394	120872	70522	169271	113695	55576	177110	118621	58489	...	...	...
B Textile, wearing apparel and leather industries	60409	35949	24460	58313	34926	23387	58242	34971	23271	...	...	...
C Manufacture of wood and wood products, including furniture	60428	36953	23475	63934	38918	25016	66049	39748	26301	...	...	...
D Manufacture of paper and paper products, printing and publishing	91504	56111	35393	102939	63170	39769	99657	60465	39192	...	...	...
E Manufacture of chemicals and chemical petroleum, coal, rubber and plastic products [a]	150641	89103	61538	161848	95721	66127	166975	98622	68353	...	...	...
F Manufacture of non-metallic mineral products, except products of petroleum and coal	69363	37220	32143	68803	37061	31742	70104	37367	32737	...	...	...
G Basic metal industries	147899	88183	59716	167417	97717	69700	164112	95120	68992	...	...	...
H Manufacture of fabricated metal products, machinery and equipment	310673	182181	128492	329691	193871	135820	343050	200889	142161	...	...	...
I Other manufacturing industries	41950	22084	19866	44880	23527	21353	43985	22986	20999	...	...	...
4 Electricity, gas and water	126677	65927	60750	135232	71913	63319	143392	76262	67130	...	...	...
A Electricity, gas and steam	120905	63874	57031	129310	69865	59445	137240	74168	63072	...	...	...
B Water works and supply	5772	2053	3719	5922	2048	3874	6152	2094	4058	...	...	...
5 Construction	309334	144039	165295	317412	147929	169483	334492	154647	179845	...	...	...
6 Wholesale and retail trade, restaurants and hotels	583486	205856	377630	613703	207769	405934	624680	208344	416336	...	...	...
A Wholesale and retail trade	427774	140642	287132	456438	143033	313405	468525	145311	323214	...	...	...
B Restaurants and hotels	155712	65214	90498	157265	64736	92529	156155	63033	93122	...	...	...
Restaurants	174	76	98	185	79	106	191	80	111	...	...	...
Hotels and other lodging places	155538	65138	90400	157080	64657	92423	155964	62953	93011	...	...	...
7 Transport, storage and communication	305583	157505	148078	293636	142959	150677	290994	136435	154559	...	...	...
A Transport and storage	243023	149890	93133	229195	134695	94499	224555	127495	97060	...	...	...
B Communication	62560	7615	54945	64441	8263	56178	66439	8940	57500	...	...	...
8 Finance, insurance, real estate and business services	602246	172639	429607	655048	187271	467777	703405	204430	498975	...	...	...
A Financial institutions	145901	31987	113914	152686	34238	118448	159333	37331	122002	...	...	...
B Insurance	57969	15687	42282	64158	17080	47078	68005	18857	49148	...	...	...
C Real estate and business services	392224	123158	269066	431443	133986	297457	468914	146085	322829	...	...	...
Real estate, except dwellings	244799	76494	168305	267320	82738	184582	291506	90351	201155	...	...	...
Dwellings	147425	46664	100761	164123	51248	112875	177408	55734	121674	...	...	...
9 Community, social and personal services	137075	37534	99541	149891	39932	109959	160244	42330	117914	...	...	...
A Sanitary and similar services	...	...	...	...	...	...	...	...	...	...	...	...
B Social and related community services [b]	67946	18717	49229	...	...	...	...	...	...	...	...	...
Educational services	...	...	...	...	...	...	...	...	...	...	...	...

Austria

	1994			1995			1996			1997		
	Gross output	Intermediate consumption	Value added	Gross output	Intermediate consumption	Value added	Gross output	Intermediate consumption	Value added	Gross output	Intermediate consumption	Value added
Medical, dental, other health and veterinary services [b]	67946	18717	49229	...	...	...	...	...	...	...	...	...
C Recreational and cultural services [bc]	50232	18937	31295	...	...	...	...	...	...	...	...	...
D Personal and household services [bd]	30233	8122	22111	...	...	...	...	...	...	...	...	...
Total, Industries	3287270	1492060	1795210	3414430	1534293	1880137	3528319	1569628	1958690	...	...	...
Producers of government services	520374	216800	303574	539435	225316	314119	552999	234978	318021	...	...	...
Other producers [d]	75497	25164	50333	79747	26755	52992	82080	27462	54618	...	...	...
Total	3883141	1734024	2149117	4033612	1786364	2247248	4163398	1832068	2331329	...	...	...
less: Imputed bank service charge	...	−109487	109487	...	−116815	116815	...	−119361	119361	...	...	...
Import duties	13903	...	13903	12860	...	12860	14690	...	14690	...	...	...
Value added tax	186088	...	186088	191065	...	191065	194965	...	194965	...	...	...
Other adjustments	...	...	...	...	...	...	...	...	...	...	...	...
Total	4083132	1843511	2239621	4237537	1903179	2334358	4373053	1951429	2421623	...	...	...

a Item "Crude petroleum and natural gas production" is included in item "Manufacture of chemicals and chemical petroleum, coal, rubber and plastic products."
b Non-governmental only.
c Item "Educational services" is included in item "Recreational and cultural services."
d Item "Sanitary and similar services" is included in item "Personal and household services" which excludes domestic services and caretakers that are included in item "Other producers".

4.2 Derivation of value added by kind of activity, in constant prices

Million Austrian schillings

	1986			1987			1988			1989		
	Gross output	Intermediate consumption	Value added	Gross output	Intermediate consumption	Value added	Gross output	Intermediate consumption	Value added	Gross output	Intermediate consumption	Value added

At constant prices of: 1983

All producers

1 Agriculture, hunting, forestry and fishing	69042	24404	44638	69258	24601	44657	70957	24418	46539	71191	24980	46211
2 Mining and quarrying	27444	15311	12133	23200	12454	10746	23423	11996	11427	22691	11020	11671
A Coal mining	1999	623	1376	1885	715	1170	1555	515	1040	1420	522	898
B Crude petroleum and natural gas production	19142	11464	7678	15084	8581	6503	15731	8298	7433	15316	7322	7994
C Metal ore mining	1318	643	675	1095	489	606	924	387	537	891	396	495
D Other mining	4985	2581	2404	5136	2669	2467	5213	2796	2417	5064	2780	2284
3 Manufacturing	827926	511721	316205	839749	525117	314632	875722	549130	326592	922220	581003	341217
A Manufacture of food, beverages and tobacco	149473	99963	49510	149344	98584	50760	148595	99182	49413	149512	99548	49964
B Textile, wearing apparel and leather industries	58246	35206	23040	56242	34500	21742	54452	33878	20574	54739	34215	20524
C Manufacture of wood and wood products, including furniture	38078	24220	13858	39167	25155	14012	41286	26446	14840	44154	28904	15250
D Manufacture of paper and paper products, printing and publishing	62811	39519	23292	65644	42934	22710	70720	46107	24613	73213	47234	25979
E Manufacture of chemicals and chemical petroleum, coal, rubber and plastic products	147452	95390	52062	158522	107275	51247	167766	112199	55567	173138	115889	57249

Austria

Million Austrian schillings

	1986 Gross output	1986 Intermediate consumption	1986 Value added	1987 Gross output	1987 Intermediate consumption	1987 Value added	1988 Gross output	1988 Intermediate consumption	1988 Value added	1989 Gross output	1989 Intermediate consumption	1989 Value added
At constant prices of: 1983												
F Manufacture of non-metallic mineral products, except products of petroleum and coal	46100	25831	20269	46366	26253	20113	48176	27848	20328	49671	28719	20952
G Basic metal industries	123985	73916	50069	117515	71067	46448	130278	77794	52484	140156	86415	53741
H Manufacture of fabricated metal products, machinery and equipment	174875	103420	71455	177902	104105	73797	184530	109943	74587	205830	124408	81422
I Other manufacturing industries	26906	14256	12650	29047	15244	13803	29919	15733	14186	31807	15671	16136
4 Electricity, gas and water	96346	53750	42596	101151	56318	44833	100225	56917	43308	104678	59377	45301
A Electricity, gas and steam	93182	52751	40431	97822	55269	42553	96801	55807	40994	101498	58237	43261
B Water works and supply	3164	999	2165	3329	1049	2280	3424	1110	2314	3180	1140	2040
5 Construction	156876	76064	80812	162698	80961	81737	168108	84047	84061	175834	88216	87618
6 Wholesale and retail trade, restaurants and hotels	366339	129933	236406	378839	136500	242339	398040	144671	253369	418755	153702	265053
A Wholesale and retail trade	273378	87391	185987	284626	93008	191618	302403	100119	202284	318166	105910	212256
B Restaurants and hotels	92961	42542	50419	94213	43492	50721	95637	44552	51085	100589	47792	52797
Restaurants	111	59	52	111	59	52	112	58	54	119	62	57
Hotels and other lodging places	92850	42483	50367	94102	43433	50669	95525	44494	51031	100470	47730	52740
7 Transport, storage and communication	169099	90660	78439	178872	95409	83463	188767	101929	86838	195896	103454	92443
A Transport and storage	133853	86225	47628	142228	91250	50978	150645	97276	53369	156354	98817	57538
B Communication	35246	4435	30811	36644	4159	32485	38122	4653	33469	39542	4637	34905
8 Finance, insurance, real estate and business services	279736	80232	199504	290171	85196	204975	303287	90994	212293	322826	96711	226115
A Financial institutions	72142	13621	58521	77387	16435	60952	80718	17629	63089	86993	19627	67366
B Insurance	28265	6923	21342	29026	7127	21899	30372	8473	21899	30654	8267	22387
C Real estate and business services	176387	58877	117510	180728	60784	119944	189085	63905	125180	202056	67832	134224
Real estate, except dwellings	102711	32123	70588	106210	34272	71938	114124	37560	76564	122838	41117	81721
Dwellings	73676	26754	46922	74518	26512	48006	74961	26345	48616	79218	26715	52503
9 Community, social and personal services	62087	19629	42458	66026	20884	45142	69709	22496	47213	72906	23396	49510
Total, Industries	2054895	1001704	1053191	2109964	1037440	1072523	2198237	1086598	1111639	2306997	1141858	1165138
Producers of government services	280711	113057	167654	281206	111686	169520	285538	114395	171143	289923	117390	172533
Other producers	37345	12163	25181	38081	12421	25660	38871	12717	26154	39510	13226	26284
Total	2372951	1126924	1246026	2429251	1161547	1267703	2522646	1213710	1308936	2636430	1272474	1363955
less: Imputed bank service charge	...	–60103	60103	...	–63672	63672	...	–65589	65589	...	–69117	69117
Import duties	8992	...	8992	9573	...	9573	10214	...	10214	11021	...	11021
Value added tax	104137	...	104137	107286	...	107286	109179	...	109179	114487	...	114487
Other adjustments	...	...	...	...	...	...	...	...	...	...	...	...
Total	2486080	1187027	1299052	2546110	1225219	1320890	2642039	1279299	1362740	2761938	1341591	1420346

Austria

	1990			1991			1992			1993		
	Gross output	Intermediate consumption	Value added	Gross output	Intermediate consumption	Value added	Gross output	Intermediate consumption	Value added	Gross output	Intermediate consumption	Value added

At constant prices of: 1983

All producers

1 Agriculture, hunting, forestry and fishing	73720	25602	48118	70061	25124	44937	68890	25321	43569	69107	25595	43512
2 Mining and quarrying	22997	12100	10897	23918	13239	10679	22465	12288	10177	23506	13527	9979
A Coal mining	1585	693	892	1594	754	840	1625	810	815	1504	737	767
B Crude petroleum and natural gas production	15285	8148	7137	16211	9188	7023	14736	8219	6517	15914	9491	6423
C Metal ore mining	737	366	371	552	310	242	500	268	232	331	153	178
D Other mining	5390	2893	2497	5561	2987	2574	5604	2991	2613	5757	3146	2611
3 Manufacturing	971184	613839	357345	1008133	637186	370947	1005606	637316	368290	980185	620382	359803
A Manufacture of food, beverages and tobacco	153164	101840	51324	157597	104704	52893	158097	103082	55015	156568	102352	54216
B Textile, wearing apparel and leather industries	57646	37350	20296	55594	36777	18817	53531	35280	18251	48565	32609	15956
C Manufacture of wood and wood products, including furniture	49577	31866	17711	49915	30874	19041	50594	31465	19129	49816	30497	19319
D Manufacture of paper and paper products, printing and publishing	78463	51294	27169	81803	54409	27394	83123	55998	27125	82315	55371	26944
E Manufacture of chemicals and chemical petroleum, coal, rubber and plastic products	177188	118079	59109	185822	120202	65620	186421	118134	68287	184187	116191	67996
F Manufacture of non-metallic mineral products, except products of petroleum and coal	50334	28941	21393	51349	29443	21906	50575	28410	22165	50770	28571	22199
G Basic metal industries	146922	89520	57402	147486	91145	56341	148079	94234	53845	139065	88311	50754
H Manufacture of fabricated metal products, machinery and equipment	227217	139074	88143	243301	151890	91411	238912	152224	86688	232599	148164	84435
I Other manufacturing industries	30673	15875	14798	35266	17742	17524	36274	18489	17785	36300	18316	17984
4 Electricity, gas and water	111782	65178	46604	119314	70935	48379	118287	67036	51251	122115	69890	52225
A Electricity, gas and steam	108570	63880	44690	116214	69608	46606	114953	65666	49287	118435	68345	50090
B Water works and supply	3212	1298	1914	3100	1327	1773	3334	1370	1964	3680	1545	2135
5 Construction	186364	94405	91959	196394	98436	97958	202756	102078	100678	205544	102382	103162
6 Wholesale and retail trade, restaurants and hotels	443282	161808	281474	460063	167313	292750	466141	169336	296805	462991	168248	294743
A Wholesale and retail trade	339306	113248	226058	351894	116827	235067	353736	116792	236944	352314	116598	235716
B Restaurants and hotels	103976	48560	55416	108169	50486	57683	112405	52544	59861	110677	51650	59027
Restaurants	118	61	57	148	77	71	137	71	66	122	63	59
Hotels and other lodging places	103858	48499	55359	108021	50409	57612	112268	52473	59795	110555	51587	58968
7 Transport, storage and communication	205369	107497	97871	213473	111408	102065	223308	117586	105722	227939	118118	109821
A Transport and storage	163772	102950	60822	169780	106855	62925	178192	112693	65499	179242	112998	66244
B Communication	41596	4547	37049	43694	4553	39141	45116	4893	40223	48697	5120	43577
8 Finance, insurance, real estate and business services	339349	103468	235881	358546	109426	249120	376025	113929	262096	391223	116936	274287
A Financial institutions	89608	21338	68270	96544	22869	73675	103968	22478	81490	117161	24280	92881
B Insurance	32301	8947	23354	34475	8982	25493	35751	9983	25768	36636	10700	25936
C Real estate and business services	214179	72118	142061	224101	76485	147616	232777	80284	152493	233798	80691	153107

Austria

	1990			1991			1992			1993		
	Gross output	Intermediate consumption	Value added	Gross output	Intermediate consumption	Value added	Gross output	Intermediate consumption	Value added	Gross output	Intermediate consumption	Value added

At constant prices of: 1983

Real estate, except dwellings	132565	44854	87711	142046	48501	93545	148476	52194	96282	148330	52385	95945
Dwellings	81614	27264	54350	82055	27984	54071	84301	28090	56211	85468	28306	57162
9 Community, social and personal services	77263	25412	51851	80121	27062	53059	81946	27719	54227	84044	28153	55891
Total, Industries	2431309	1209309	1222000	2530023	1260129	1269894	2565423	1272608	1292815	2566653	1263230	1303423
Producers of government services	294277	118440	175837	301529	122310	179219	309346	125498	183848	319208	130628	188580
Other producers	41167	13626	27541	42543	13966	28577	44466	14639	29827	43352	14162	29190
Total	2766753	1341375	1425378	2874095	1396405	1477690	2919235	1412745	1506490	2929213	1408020	1521193
less: Imputed bank service charge	...	−70170	70170	...	−75606	75606	...	−82165	82165	...	−92193	92193
Import duties	11239	...	11239	11257	...	11257	11094	...	11094	10972	...	10972
Value added tax	118600	...	118600	122556	...	122556	121082	...	121082	124513	...	124513
Other adjustments	...	...	...	...	...	...	...	...	...	...	...	...
Total	2896592	1411545	1485047	3007908	1472011	1535897	3051411	1494910	1556501	3064698	1500213	1564485

	1994			1995			1996			1997		
	Gross output	Intermediate consumption	Value added	Gross output	Intermediate consumption	Value added	Gross output	Intermediate consumption	Value added	Gross output	Intermediate consumption	Value added

At constant prices of: 1983

All producers

1 Agriculture, hunting, forestry and fishing	71811	26145	45666	69281	25207	44074	69627	24672	44955	...	...	...
2 Mining and quarrying	22193	13054	9139	22134	12620	9514	21621	12343	9278	...	...	...
A Coal mining	1250	680	570	1052	528	524	982	503	479	...	...	...
B Crude petroleum and natural gas production	14370	8845	5525	14370	8486	5884	13848	8178	5670	...	...	...
C Metal ore mining	230	102	128	250	113	137	232	104	128	...	...	...
D Other mining	6343	3427	2916	6462	3493	2969	6559	3558	3001	...	...	...
3 Manufacturing	1015062	643568	371494	1036285	661291	374994	1053188	673214	379974	...	...	...
A Manufacture of food, beverages and tobacco	157132	102227	54905	147022	101695	45327	149630	103499	46131	...	...	...
B Textile, wearing apparel and leather industries	47122	31930	15192	44914	30219	14695	44688	30205	14483	...	...	...
C Manufacture of wood and wood products, including furniture	51959	32664	19295	53114	33087	20027	54663	34115	20548	...	...	...
D Manufacture of paper and paper products, printing and publishing	86405	58588	27817	91391	62682	28709	89646	61134	28512	...	...	...
E Manufacture of chemicals and chemical petroleum, coal, rubber and plastic products	191210	120185	71025	199792	123924	75868	204235	127193	77042	...	...	...
F Manufacture of non-metallic mineral products, except products of petroleum and coal	53307	29770	23537	51786	28944	22842	52386	29329	23057	...	...	...
G Basic metal industries	146879	92800	54079	155859	98450	57409	158192	100228	57964	...	...	...
H Manufacture of fabricated metal products, machinery and equipment	244126	156667	87459	254136	162866	91270	262506	168612	93894	...	...	...
I Other manufacturing industries	36922	18737	18185	38271	19424	18847	37242	18899	18343	...	...	...

Austria

	1994			1995			1996			1997		
	Gross output	Intermediate consumption	Value added	Gross output	Intermediate consumption	Value added	Gross output	Intermediate consumption	Value added	Gross output	Intermediate consumption	Value added
	At constant prices of: 1983											
4 Electricity, gas and water	121173	69673	51500	127726	75565	52161	131626	79422	52204	...	...	...
A Electricity, gas and steam	117525	68095	49430	124166	74022	50144	128028	77863	50165	...	...	...
B Water works and supply	3648	1578	2070	3560	1543	2017	3598	1559	2039	...	...	...
5 Construction	220222	109214	111008	219294	108467	110827	226098	112117	113981	...	...	...
6 Wholesale and retail trade, restaurants and hotels	466162	168958	297204	482460	171245	311215	485347	172630	312717	...	...	...
A Wholesale and retail trade	356737	117974	238763	374387	120739	253648	379860	123293	256567	...	...	...
B Restaurants and hotels	109425	50984	58441	108073	50506	57567	105487	49337	56150	...	...	...
Restaurants	114	60	54	118	63	55	119	63	56	...	...	...
Hotels and other lodging places	109311	50924	58387	107955	50443	57512	105368	49274	56094	...	...	...
7 Transport, storage and communication	236239	120010	116229	229774	107917	121857	228531	101538	126993	...	...	...
A Transport and storage	184947	114285	70662	176488	101829	74659	174230	95028	79201	...	...	...
B Communication	51292	5725	45567	53286	6088	47198	54301	6510	47792	...	...	...
8 Finance, insurance, real estate and business services	392053	122573	269480	410337	128457	281880	426213	136233	289980	...	...	...
A Financial institutions	109289	24324	84965	114544	25495	89049	117676	27110	90566	...	...	...
B Insurance	35177	11920	23257	37867	12719	25148	40018	13774	26244	...	...	...
C Real estate and business services	243743	84956	158787	253805	88778	165027	264181	93775	170406	...	...	...
Real estate, except dwellings	154754	55127	99627	161723	57524	104199	170317	60868	109449	...	...	...
Dwellings	88989	29829	59160	92082	31254	60828	93864	32907	60957	...	...	...
9 Community, social and personal services	85979	29122	56857	88953	30125	58828	92474	31460	61014	...	...	...
Total, Industries	2630894	1302317	1328577	2686244	1320893	1365350	2734725	1343629	1391096	...	...	...
Producers of government services	329558	136813	192745	332082	138061	194021	335017	140746	194271	...	...	...
Other producers	45181	14741	30440	45341	14810	30531	45901	14991	30910	...	...	...
Total	3005633	1453871	1551762	3063667	1473764	1589902	3115643	1499366	1616277	...	...	...
less: Imputed bank service charge	...	−82013	82013	...	−87633	87633	...	−88154	88154	...	...	...
Import duties	11377	...	11377	10571	...	10571	12009	...	12009	...	...	...
Value added tax	123127	...	123127	124417	...	124417	123914	...	123914	...	...	...
Other adjustments	...	...	...	...	...	...	...	...	...	...	...	...
Total	3140137	1535884	1604253	3198655	1561397	1637257	3251566	1587520	1664046	...	...	...

4.3 Cost components of value added

Million Austrian schillings

	1986						1987					
	Compensation of employees	Capital consumption	Net operating surplus	Indirect taxes	less: Subsidies received	Value added	Compensation of employees	Capital consumption	Net operating surplus	Indirect taxes	less: Subsidies received	Value added
	All producers											
1 Agriculture, hunting, forestry and fishing	...	15328	...	273	2551	47114	...	16160	...	812	3276	48473
2 Mining and quarrying	...	683	...	444	274	10679	...	632	...	446	237	9052
A Coal mining	...	39	...	...	...	1560	...	17	...	...	...	1399
B Crude petroleum and natural gas production	...	489	...	...	...	5367	...	523	...	...	...	3851

Austria

Million Austrian schillings

	1986						1987					
	Compensation of employees	Capital consumption	Net operating surplus	Indirect taxes	less: Subsidies received	Value added	Compensation of employees	Capital consumption	Net operating surplus	Indirect taxes	less: Subsidies received	Value added
C Metal ore mining	...	18	...	...	...	859	...	9	...	...	...	766
D Other mining	...	137	...	...	...	2893	...	83	...	...	...	3036
3 Manufacturing	...	44705	...	38969	16402	335912	...	47083	...	41088	15817	339417
A Manufacture of food, beverages and tobacco	...	5489	...	...	...	53449	...	6467	...	...	...	55504
B Textile, wearing apparel and leather industries	...	2768	...	...	...	26004	...	2706	...	...	...	26003
C Manufacture of wood and wood products, including furniture	...	2040	...	...	...	14690	...	2435	...	...	...	15196
D Manufacture of paper and paper products, printing and publishing	...	6479	...	...	...	26119	...	7283	...	...	...	25448
E Manufacture of chemicals and chemical petroleum, coal, rubber and plastic products [a]	...	7828	...	...	...	47593	...	7376	...	...	...	46071
F Manufacture of non-metallic mineral products, except products of petroleum and coal	...	3221	...	...	...	22057	...	3643	...	...	...	23290
G Basic metal industries	...	6118	...	...	...	51674	...	5319	...	...	...	47475
H Manufacture of fabricated metal products, machinery and equipment	...	9723	...	...	...	81586	...	10579	...	...	...	86789
I Other manufacturing industries	...	1039	...	...	...	12740	...	1275	...	...	...	13641
4 Electricity, gas and water	...	12939	...	1135	1076	45430	...	13201	...	1179	949	48395
A Electricity, gas and steam	...	12224	...	...	...	43167	...	12106	...	...	...	46000
B Water works and supply	...	715	...	...	...	2263	...	1095	...	...	...	2395
5 Construction	...	5190	...	3600	1211	85763	...	5978	...	3828	1285	90854
6 Wholesale and retail trade, restaurants and hotels	...	19048	...	26527	4852	252175	...	18905	...	27486	6608	260440
A Wholesale and retail trade	...	15519	...	19942	4032	194628	...	15649	...	20114	5783	201150
B Restaurants and hotels	...	3529	...	6585	820	57547	...	3256	...	7372	825	59290
Restaurants	...	...	...	...	...	64	...	...	...	...	...	66
Hotels and other lodging places	...	...	...	...	...	57483	...	...	...	...	...	59224
7 Transport, storage and communication	...	18860	...	3350	14893	87190	...	19459	...	3383	15048	92318
A Transport and storage	...	10761	...	...	...	53836	...	11582	...	...	...	56493
B Communication	...	8099	...	...	...	33353	...	7877	...	...	...	35825
8 Finance, insurance, real estate and business services	...	46546	...	13716	2531	234320	...	49290	...	14379	1922	249388
A Financial institutions	...	...	...	...	...	66983	...	...	...	...	...	72644
B Insurance	...	...	...	...	...	25018	...	...	...	...	...	26553
C Real estate and business services	...	...	...	...	...	139763	...	...	...	...	...	147456
Real estate, except dwellings	...	...	...	...	...	83267	...	...	...	...	...	88182
Dwellings	...	...	...	...	...	56496	...	...	...	...	...	59274
9 Community, social and personal services	...	1793	...	5468	2034	49645	...	1765	...	5773	2032	55111
A Sanitary and similar services	...	...	...	...	...	...	...	...	...	...	...	...
B Social and related community services [b]	...	...	...	...	...	25933	...	...	...	...	...	27279

Austria

Million Austrian schillings

	1986					1987				
	Compensation of employees	Capital consumption	Net operating surplus	Indirect taxes	less: Subsidies received	Value added	Compensation of employees	Capital consumption	Net operating surplus	Indirect taxes	less: Subsidies received	Value added

	Comp.	Cap. cons.	Net op. surplus	Indirect taxes	less: Subsidies	Value added	Comp.	Cap. cons.	Net op. surplus	Indirect taxes	less: Subsidies	Value added
Educational services	...	...	...	...	...	...	...	...	...	...	...	...
Medical, dental, other health and veterinary services [b]	...	...	...	...	...	25933	...	...	...	...	...	27279
C Recreational and cultural services [bc]	...	...	...	...	...	13622	...	...	...	...	...	17298
D Personal and household services [bd]	...	...	...	...	...	11688	...	...	...	...	...	12683
Total, Industries	...	165093	...	93482	45824	1148227	...	172470	...	98374	47174	1193447
Producers of government services	...	10032	...	2867	—	192802	...	10359	...	2910	—	201559
Other producers [d]	...	1070	...	48	227	28640	...	1041	...	49	208	30237
Total	765733	176195	378715	96393	47366	1369669	797421	183870	391494	101331	48872	1425243
less: Imputed bank service charge	...	...	68277	...	...	68277	...	...	74942	...	...	74942
Import duties	...	...	...	8996	...	8996	...	...	...	9861	...	9861
Value added tax	...	...	...	128655	...	128655	...	...	...	133962	...	133962
Other adjustments	...	...	...	...	...	—	...	...	...	...	...	—
Total	765733	176195	310438	234044	47366	1439043	797421	183870	316552	245154	48872	1494124

	1988					1989				
	Compensation of employees	Capital consumption	Net operating surplus	Indirect taxes	less: Subsidies received	Value added	Compensation of employees	Capital consumption	Net operating surplus	Indirect taxes	less: Subsidies received	Value added

All producers

	Comp.	Cap. cons.	Net op. surplus	Indirect taxes	less: Subsidies	Value added	Comp.	Cap. cons.	Net op. surplus	Indirect taxes	less: Subsidies	Value added
1 Agriculture, hunting, forestry and fishing	...	16509	...	855	3678	49023	...	16735	...	1102	3968	52304
2 Mining and quarrying	...	717	...	445	197	9248	...	742	...	473	332	9498
A Coal mining	...	52	...	...	...	1192	...	46	...	...	...	1021
B Crude petroleum and natural gas production	...	357	...	...	...	4231	...	274	...	...	...	4816
C Metal ore mining	...	15	...	...	...	712	...	77	...	...	...	653
D Other mining	...	293	...	...	...	3113	...	345	...	...	...	3008
3 Manufacturing	...	48934	...	43643	14114	358702	...	51744	...	44697	13196	379725
A Manufacture of food, beverages and tobacco	...	6817	...	...	...	55100	...	7142	...	...	...	56656
B Textile, wearing apparel and leather industries	...	2623	...	...	...	25298	...	2918	...	...	...	26058
C Manufacture of wood and wood products, including furniture	...	3182	...	...	...	16516	...	3153	...	...	...	17341
D Manufacture of paper and paper products, printing and publishing	...	4726	...	...	...	28721	...	6113	...	...	...	30899
E Manufacture of chemicals and chemical petroleum, coal, rubber and plastic products [a]	...	7006	...	...	...	49321	...	7712	...	...	...	48907
F Manufacture of non-metallic mineral products, except products of petroleum and coal	...	4070	...	...	...	24447	...	4149	...	...	...	25510
G Basic metal industries	...	7650	...	...	...	56268	...	7762	...	...	...	59756
H Manufacture of fabricated metal products, machinery and equipment	...	11212	...	...	...	88500	...	11237	...	...	...	98973

Austria

	1988						1989					
	Compensation of employees	Capital consumption	Net operating surplus	Indirect taxes	less: Subsidies received	Value added	Compensation of employees	Capital consumption	Net operating surplus	Indirect taxes	less: Subsidies received	Value added
1 Other manufacturing industries	...	1648	...	...	...	14531	...	1558	...	...	...	15625
4 Electricity, gas and water	...	14266	...	1195	769	45637	...	15120	...	1290	942	48014
A Electricity, gas and steam ...	...	13099	...	...	...	43159	...	13996	...	...	...	45490
B Water works and supply	...	1167	...	...	...	2478	...	1124	...	...	...	2524
5 Construction	...	5595	...	4088	1240	95554	...	5794	...	4463	1302	102950
6 Wholesale and retail trade, restaurants and hotels	...	21003	...	27846	6663	273946	...	22404	...	29368	6404	294327
A Wholesale and retail trade ..	...	17195	...	20762	5933	212562	...	18338	...	21776	5664	228054
B Restaurants and hotels	...	3808	...	7084	730	61384	...	4066	...	7592	740	66273
Restaurants	...	...	...	...	...	71	...	...	...	...	...	78
Hotels and other lodging places	...	...	...	...	...	61313	...	...	...	...	...	66195
7 Transport, storage and communication	...	20961	...	3562	14354	99940	...	22283	...	3756	14815	106954
A Transport and storage	...	12965	...	...	...	61356	...	13782	...	...	...	66363
B Communication	...	7996	...	...	...	38584	...	8501	...	...	...	40591
8 Finance, insurance, real estate and business services	...	52386	...	16145	1812	267568	...	56474	...	18227	1873	297240
A Financial institutions	...	...	...	...	...	77835	...	...	...	...	...	88118
B Insurance	...	...	...	...	...	28626	...	...	...	...	...	31114
C Real estate and business services	...	...	...	...	...	158161	...	...	...	...	...	174787
Real estate, except dwellings	...	...	...	...	...	97020	...	...	...	...	...	107184
Dwellings	...	...	...	...	...	61141	...	...	...	...	...	67603
9 Community, social and personal services	...	1914	...	5862	2041	59614	...	2019	...	6027	2036	65319
A Sanitary and similar services	...	...	...	...	...	...	...	...	...	...	...	...
B Social and related community services [b]	...	...	...	...	...	29640	...	...	...	...	...	31240
Educational services	...	...	...	...	...	...	...	...	...	...	...	...
Medical, dental, other health and veterinary services [b]	...	...	...	...	...	29640	...	...	...	...	...	31240
C Recreational and cultural services [bc]	...	...	...	...	...	19407	...	...	...	...	...	22308
D Personal and household services [bd]	...	...	...	...	...	13601	...	...	...	...	...	14563
Total, Industries	...	182285	...	103666	44865	1259231	...	193319	...	109368	44886	1356331
Producers of government services	...	10696	...	2914	—	206399	...	11118	...	3353	—	217047
Other producers [d]	...	1133	...	49	213	31570	...	1193	...	51	221	32847
Total	826879	194114	417847	106626	48265	1497200	879607	205630	456687	112768	48467	1606225
less: Imputed bank service charge	...	...	79691	...	...	79691	...	...	88193	...	...	88193
Import duties	...	...	...	10631	...	10631	...	...	...	11507	...	11507
Value added tax	...	...	...	137630	...	137630	...	...	...	147138	...	147138
Other adjustments	...	...	...	...	...	—	...	...	...	...	...	...
Total	826879	194114	338156	254887	48265	1565770	879607	205630	368494	271413	48467	1676677

Austria

	1990						1991					
	Compensation of employees	Capital consumption	Net operating surplus	Indirect taxes	less: Subsidies received	Value added	Compensation of employees	Capital consumption	Net operating surplus	Indirect taxes	less: Subsidies received	Value added
	All producers											
1 Agriculture, hunting, forestry and fishing	...	17619	...	1302	4714	56629	...	18384	...	1752	5365	52992
2 Mining and quarrying	...	761	...	499	337	9250	...	790	...	480	315	9236
A Coal mining	...	37	...	...	...	1023	...	20	...	...	...	979
B Crude petroleum and natural gas production	...	220	...	...	...	4231	...	369	...	...	...	4180
C Metal ore mining	...	77	...	...	...	507	...	16	...	...	...	349
D Other mining	...	427	...	...	...	3489	...	385	...	...	...	3728
3 Manufacturing	...	54875	...	46256	14407	410956	...	58829	...	48166	18214	436350
A Manufacture of food, beverages and tobacco	...	6505	...	...	...	60285	...	7018	...	...	...	63756
B Textile, wearing apparel and leather industries	...	3203	...	...	...	27200	...	3415	...	...	...	27173
C Manufacture of wood and wood products, including furniture	...	3593	...	...	...	20623	...	3469	...	...	...	21896
D Manufacture of paper and paper products, printing and publishing	...	8584	...	...	...	33156	...	8269	...	...	...	34827
E Manufacture of chemicals and chemical petroleum, coal, rubber and plastic products [a]	...	7807	...	...	...	52122	...	8317	...	...	...	58165
F Manufacture of non-metallic mineral products, except products of petroleum and coal	...	4744	...	...	...	26934	...	4766	...	...	...	29314
G Basic metal industries	...	7624	...	...	...	62531	...	8322	...	...	...	60950
H Manufacture of fabricated metal products, machinery and equipment	...	11359	...	...	...	112772	...	13627	...	...	...	121961
I Other manufacturing industries	...	1456	...	...	...	15333	...	1626	...	...	...	18308
4 Electricity, gas and water	...	16208	...	1385	854	49215	...	17504	...	1367	1039	52630
A Electricity, gas and steam	...	14945	...	...	...	46652	...	16157	...	...	...	49891
B Water works and supply	...	1263	...	...	...	2563	...	1347	...	...	...	2739
5 Construction	...	6069	...	4955	1538	114911	...	6192	...	4926	1648	130173
6 Wholesale and retail trade, restaurants and hotels	...	23586	...	30830	5604	319462	...	25587	...	31220	6718	339703
A Wholesale and retail trade	...	19345	...	22869	4782	249524	...	20961	...	22642	5904	264196
B Restaurants and hotels	...	4241	...	7961	822	69938	...	4626	...	8578	814	75507
Restaurants	...	...	...	...	...	81	...	...	...	...	...	106
Hotels and other lodging places	...	...	...	...	...	69857	...	...	...	...	...	75401
7 Transport, storage and communication	...	23688	...	3873	16122	116394	...	25694	...	4564	17886	126961
A Transport and storage	...	14651	...	...	...	72879	...	15892	...	...	...	80690
B Communication	...	9037	...	...	...	43515	...	9802	...	...	...	46271
8 Finance, insurance, real estate and business services	...	60691	...	20306	2046	324789	...	66260	...	21376	2413	353711
A Financial institutions	...	...	...	...	...	94837	...	...	...	...	...	102140
B Insurance	...	...	...	...	...	33684	...	...	...	...	...	38174
C Real estate and business services	...	...	...	...	...	192784	...	...	...	...	...	209477

Austria

	1990						1991					
	Compensation of employees	Capital consumption	Net operating surplus	Indirect taxes	less: Subsidies received	Value added	Compensation of employees	Capital consumption	Net operating surplus	Indirect taxes	less: Subsidies received	Value added
Real estate, except dwellings	...	...	...	...	...	119849	...	...	...	...	...	133734
Dwellings	...	...	...	...	...	72935	...	...	...	...	...	75743
9 Community, social and personal services	...	2122	...	5999	2089	70046	...	2287	...	8442	2674	75555
A Sanitary and similar services	...	...	...	...	...	...	...	...	...	...	...	...
B Social and related community services [b]	...	...	...	...	...	33197	...	...	...	...	...	36302
Educational services	...	...	...	...	...	...	...	...	...	...	...	...
Medical, dental, other health and veterinary services [b]	...	...	...	...	...	33197	...	...	...	...	...	36302
C Recreational and cultural services [bc]	...	...	...	...	...	24974	...	...	...	...	...	26472
D Personal and household services [bd]	...	...	...	...	...	15378	...	...	...	...	...	16780
Statistical discrepancy	...	...	...	...	...	...	...	...	...	...	4445	...
Total, Industries	...	205619	...	115401	47627	1471651	...	221531	...	122295	60634	1577310
Producers of government services	...	11621	...	3572	_	230698	...	12287	...	3851	_	250728
Other producers [d]	...	1246	...	53	226	36378	...	1341	...	58	248	39974
Total	949140	218486	503605	119029	51532	1738727	1030150	235159	536962	126204	60462	1868012
less: Imputed bank service charge	...	...	94097	...	...	94097	...	...	101766	...	...	101766
Import duties	...	...	...	12026	...	12026	...	...	...	12642	...	12642
Value added tax	...	...	...	156825	...	156825	...	...	...	166933	...	166933
Other adjustments	...	...	...	...	...	_	...	...	...	...	...	_
Total	949140	218486	409508	287880	51532	1813481	1030150	235159	435196	305779	60462	1945821

	1992						1993					
	Compensation of employees	Capital consumption	Net operating surplus	Indirect taxes	less: Subsidies received	Value added	Compensation of employees	Capital consumption	Net operating surplus	Indirect taxes	less: Subsidies received	Value added

All producers

1 Agriculture, hunting, forestry and fishing	...	19101	...	1373	8675	50035	...	19582	...	2013	7708	47322
2 Mining and quarrying	...	852	...	491	276	8832	...	894	...	489	314	8638
A Coal mining	...	25	...	...	...	934	...	25	...	...	...	869
B Crude petroleum and natural gas production	...	439	...	...	...	3789	...	462	...	...	...	3642
C Metal ore mining	...	14	...	...	...	326	...	3	...	...	...	264
D Other mining	...	374	...	...	...	3783	...	404	...	...	...	3863
3 Manufacturing	...	64146	...	53795	17094	442359	...	68860	...	53562	19034	435682
A Manufacture of food, beverages and tobacco	...	8075	...	...	...	69319	...	11331	...	...	...	70285
B Textile, wearing apparel and leather industries	...	2579	...	...	...	27281	...	2632	...	...	...	25834
C Manufacture of wood and wood products, including furniture	...	3794	...	...	...	22683	...	4629	...	...	...	22771
D Manufacture of paper and paper products, printing and publishing	...	7049	...	...	...	34011	...	7303	...	...	...	33166

Austria

	1992						1993					
	Compensation of employees	Capital consumption	Net operating surplus	Indirect taxes	less: Subsidies received	Value added	Compensation of employees	Capital consumption	Net operating surplus	Indirect taxes	less: Subsidies received	Value added
E Manufacture of chemicals and chemical petroleum, coal, rubber and plastic products [a]	...	9665	...	...	...	59016	...	9606	...	...	...	58527
F Manufacture of non-metallic mineral products, except products of petroleum and coal	...	5449	...	...	...	29774	...	5614	...	...	...	29615
G Basic metal industries	...	8803	...	...	...	58350	...	8692	...	...	...	54638
H Manufacture of fabricated metal products, machinery and equipment	...	16776	...	...	...	122486	...	16529	...	...	...	121331
I Other manufacturing industries	...	1956	...	...	...	19439	...	2524	...	...	...	19515
4 Electricity, gas and water	...	19187	...	1497	969	56758	...	20672	...	1562	1036	60349
A Electricity, gas and steam	...	17885	...	...	...	53763	...	18891	...	...	...	56769
B Water works and supply	...	1302	...	...	...	2995	...	1781	...	...	...	3580
5 Construction	...	6838	...	5499	1968	140027	...	7221	...	5826	2201	149493
6 Wholesale and retail trade, restaurants and hotels	...	28053	...	38134	8168	359698	...	30285	...	38324	8829	363780
A Wholesale and retail trade	...	23009	...	30893	7137	278373	...	24843	...	31372	7819	277547
B Restaurants and hotels	...	5044	...	7241	1031	81325	...	5442	...	6952	1010	86233
Restaurants	...	...	...	...	...	104	...	...	...	...	...	101
Hotels and other lodging places	...	...	...	...	...	81221	...	...	...	...	...	86132
7 Transport, storage and communication	...	28118	...	4511	19038	139444	...	30325	...	4719	21404	142490
A Transport and storage	...	17391	...	...	...	90532	...	18756	...	...	...	90247
B Communication	...	10727	...	...	...	48912	...	11569	...	...	...	52243
8 Finance, insurance, real estate and business services	...	69768	...	23426	5770	386747	...	74862	...	24624	7004	417882
A Financial institutions	...	...	...	...	...	110579	...	...	...	...	...	126192
B Insurance	...	...	...	...	...	40902	...	...	...	...	...	43172
C Real estate and business services	...	...	...	...	...	231060	...	...	...	...	...	244028
Real estate, except dwellings	...	...	...	...	...	146612	...	...	...	...	...	153873
Dwellings	...	...	...	...	...	84448	...	...	...	...	...	90155
9 Community, social and personal services	...	2483	...	8634	3080	85249	...	2660	...	8903	3014	92730
A Sanitary and similar services	...	...	...	...	...	...	...	...	...	...	...	...
B Social and related community services [b]	...	...	...	...	...	40951	...	...	...	...	...	45393
Educational services	...	...	...	...	...	...	...	...	...	...	...	...
Medical, dental, other health and veterinary services [b]	...	...	...	...	...	40951	...	...	...	...	...	45393
C Recreational and cultural services [bc]	...	...	...	...	...	29979	...	...	...	...	...	30060
D Personal and household services [bd]	...	...	...	...	...	18749	...	...	...	...	...	20426
Total, Industries	...	238549	...	137360	64917	1669149	...	255360	...	140025	70309	1718366
Producers of government services	...	12566	...	4121	–	269888	...	13166	...	4666	–	289094
Other producers [d]	...	1452	...	65	384	43732	...	1552	...	69	257	46544
Total	1098620	252567	552912	141548	62878	1982769	1145579	270078	561219	144758	67630	2054004

Austria

	1992						1993					
	Compensation of employees	Capital consumption	Net operating surplus	Indirect taxes	less: Subsidies received	Value added	Compensation of employees	Capital consumption	Net operating surplus	Indirect taxes	less: Subsidies received	Value added
less: Imputed bank service charge	...	...	109773	...	...	109773	...	...	123908	...	...	123908
Import duties	...	...	...	13269	...	13269	...	...	...	13122	...	13122
Value added tax	...	...	...	171006	...	171006	...	...	...	182125	...	182125
Other adjustments	...	...	...	...	...	–	...	...	...	...	...	–
Total	1098620	252567	443139	325823	62878	2057271	1145579	270078	437311	340005	67630	2125343

	1994						1995					
	Compensation of employees	Capital consumption	Net operating surplus	Indirect taxes	less: Subsidies received	Value added	Compensation of employees	Capital consumption	Net operating surplus	Indirect taxes	less: Subsidies received	Value added

All producers

1 Agriculture, hunting, forestry and fishing	...	19740	...	1433	9827	50446	...	19898	...	1582	24753	35897
2 Mining and quarrying	...	942	...	580	311	8258	...	987	...	...	...	8601
A Coal mining	...	27	...	...	...	655	...	28	...	...	...	596
B Crude petroleum and natural gas production	...	486	...	...	...	3077	...	510	...	...	...	3358
C Metal ore mining	...	4	...	...	...	194	...	4	...	...	...	211
D Other mining	...	425	...	...	...	4332	...	445	...	...	...	4436
3 Manufacturing	...	73985	...	57871	17471	455605	...	78925	...	...	...	468490
A Manufacture of food, beverages and tobacco	...	12175	...	...	...	70522	...	12987	...	...	...	55576
B Textile, wearing apparel and leather industries	...	2828	...	...	...	24460	...	3016	...	...	...	23387
C Manufacture of wood and wood products, including furniture	...	4974	...	...	...	23475	...	5306	...	...	...	25016
D Manufacture of paper and paper products, printing and publishing	...	7847	...	...	...	35393	...	8371	...	...	...	39769
E Manufacture of chemicals and chemical petroleum, coal, rubber and plastic products [a]	...	10320	...	...	...	61538	...	11009	...	...	...	66127
F Manufacture of non-metallic mineral products, except products of petroleum and coal	...	6031	...	...	...	32143	...	6434	...	...	...	31742
G Basic metal industries	...	9339	...	...	...	59716	...	9963	...	...	...	69700
H Manufacture of fabricated metal products, machinery and equipment	...	17759	...	...	...	128492	...	18946	...	...	...	135820
I Other manufacturing industries	...	2712	...	...	...	19866	...	2893	...	...	...	21353
4 Electricity, gas and water	...	22286	...	1832	1021	60750	...	23642	...	...	...	63319
A Electricity, gas and steam	...	20366	...	...	...	57031	...	21605	...	...	...	59445
B Water works and supply	...	1920	...	...	...	3719	...	2037	...	...	...	3874
5 Construction	...	7637	...	7178	2220	165295	...	7948	...	...	...	169483
6 Wholesale and retail trade, restaurants and hotels	...	32708	...	42444	9100	377630	...	35223	...	...	...	405934
A Wholesale and retail trade	...	26834	...	34786	8084	287132	...	28865	...	...	...	313405
B Restaurants and hotels	...	5874	...	7658	1016	90498	...	6358	...	...	...	92529
Restaurants	...	...	...	...	...	98	...	...	...	...	...	106
Hotels and other lodging places	...	...	...	...	...	90400	...	...	...	...	...	92423

Austria

	1994						1995				
	Compensation of employees	Capital consumption	Net operating surplus	Indirect taxes	less: Subsidies received	Value added	Compensation of employees	Capital consumption	Net operating surplus	Indirect taxes	less: Subsidies received	Value added
7 Transport, storage and communication	...	32724	...	5135	17258	148078	...	34966	...	...	...	150677
A Transport and storage	...	20240	...	...	...	93133	...	21627	...	...	...	94499
B Communication	...	12484	...	...	...	54945	...	13339	...	...	...	56178
8 Finance, insurance, real estate and business services	...	80456	...	27203	1159	429607	...	86094	...	...	...	467777
A Financial institutions	...	...	...	...	...	113914	...	...	...	...	...	118448
B Insurance	...	...	...	...	...	42282	...	...	...	...	...	47078
C Real estate and business services	...	...	...	...	...	269066	...	...	...	...	...	297457
Real estate, except dwellings	...	...	...	...	...	168305	...	...	...	...	...	184582
Dwellings	...	...	...	...	...	100761	...	...	...	...	...	112875
9 Community, social and personal services	...	2852	...	9624	2987	99541	...	3038	...	...	...	109959
A Sanitary and similar services	...	...	...	...	...	...	...	...	...	...	...	...
B Social and related community services [b]	...	...	...	...	...	49229	...	...	...	...	...	...
Educational services	...	...	...	...	...	...	...	...	...	...	...	...
Medical, dental, other health and veterinary services [b]	...	...	...	...	...	49229	...	...	...	...	...	...
C Recreational and cultural services [bc]	...	...	...	...	...	31295	...	...	...	...	...	...
D Personal and household services [bd]	...	...	...	...	...	22111	...	...	...	...	...	...
Total, Industries	...	273330	...	153594	60876	1795210	...	290721	...	...	...	1880137
Producers of government services	...	13698	...	4799	–	303574	...	14291	...	...	...	314119
Other producers [d]	...	1663	...	73	265	50333	...	1772	...	...	...	52992
Total	1189018	288691	565631	156612	50835	2149117	1230698	306784	596747	163412	50393	2247248
less: Imputed bank service charge	...	...	109487	...	...	109487	...	...	116815	...	...	116815
Import duties	...	...	...	13903	...	13903	...	...	...	12860	...	12860
Value added tax	...	...	...	186088	...	186088	...	...	...	191065	...	191065
Other adjustments	...	...	...	...	...	–	...	...	...	...	...	...
Total	1189018	288691	456144	356603	50835	2239621	1230698	306784	479932	367337	50393	2334358

	1996						1997					
	Compensation of employees	Capital consumption	Net operating surplus	Indirect taxes	less: Subsidies received	Value added	Compensation of employees	Capital consumption	Net operating surplus	Indirect taxes	less: Subsidies received	Value added
All producers												
1 Agriculture, hunting, forestry and fishing	...	20107	...	2099	22840	34685	...	...	...	...	...	...
2 Mining and quarrying	...	1026	...	...	...	8751	...	...	...	...	...	...
A Coal mining	...	17	...	...	...	554	...	...	...	...	...	...
B Crude petroleum and natural gas production	...	450	...	...	...	3504	...	...	...	...	...	...
C Metal ore mining	...	11	...	...	...	194	...	...	...	...	...	...
D Other mining	...	548	...	...	...	4499	...	...	...	...	...	...
3 Manufacturing	...	83823	...	...	...	480495	...	...	...	...	...	...
A Manufacture of food, beverages and tobacco	...	13301	...	...	...	58489	...	...	...	...	...	...

Austria

		1996					1997					
		Compensation of employees	Capital consumption	Net operating surplus	Indirect taxes	less: Subsidies received	Value added	Compensation of employees	Capital consumption	Net operating surplus	Indirect taxes	less: Subsidies received	Value added
B	Textile, wearing apparel and leather industries	...	3103	...	...	...	23271	...	...	...	...	...	...
C	Manufacture of wood and wood products, including furniture	...	6004	...	...	...	26301	...	...	...	...	...	...
D	Manufacture of paper and paper products, printing and publishing	...	7717	...	...	...	39192	...	...	...	...	...	...
E	Manufacture of chemicals and chemical petroleum, coal, rubber and plastic products [a]	...	10978	...	...	...	68353	...	...	...	...	...	...
F	Manufacture of non-metallic mineral products, except products of petroleum and coal	...	7660	...	...	...	32737	...	...	...	...	...	...
G	Basic metal industries	...	12154	...	...	...	68992	...	...	...	...	...	...
H	Manufacture of fabricated metal products, machinery and equipment	...	19954	...	...	...	142161	...	...	...	...	...	...
I	Other manufacturing industries	...	2952	...	...	...	20999	...	...	...	...	...	...
4	Electricity, gas and water	...	25365	...	...	...	67130	...	...	...	...	...	...
A	Electricity, gas and steam	...	23180	...	...	...	63072	...	...	...	...	...	...
B	Water works and supply	...	2185	...	...	...	4058	...	...	...	...	...	...
5	Construction	...	8386	...	...	...	179845	...	...	...	...	...	...
6	Wholesale and retail trade, restaurants and hotels	...	37437	...	...	...	416336	...	...	...	...	...	...
A	Wholesale and retail trade	...	30713	...	...	...	323214	...	...	...	...	...	...
B	Restaurants and hotels	...	6724	...	...	...	93122	...	...	...	...	...	...
	Restaurants	...	...	...	...	...	111	...	...	...	...	...	...
	Hotels and other lodging places	...	...	...	...	...	93011	...	...	...	...	...	...
7	Transport, storage and communication	...	37348	...	...	...	154559	...	...	...	...	...	...
A	Transport and storage	...	23100	...	...	...	97060	...	...	...	...	...	...
B	Communication	...	14248	...	...	...	57500	...	...	...	...	...	...
8	Finance, insurance, real estate and business services	...	91253	...	...	...	498975	...	...	...	...	...	...
A	Financial institutions	...	...	...	...	...	122002	...	...	...	...	...	...
B	Insurance	...	...	...	...	...	49148	...	...	...	...	...	...
C	Real estate and business services	...	...	...	...	...	322829	...	...	...	...	...	...
	Real estate, except dwellings	...	...	...	...	...	201155	...	...	...	...	...	...
	Dwellings	...	...	...	...	...	121674	...	...	...	...	...	...
9	Community, social and personal services	...	3300	...	...	...	117914	...	...	...	...	...	...
	Total, Industries	...	308045	...	...	...	1958690	...	...	...	...	...	...
	Producers of government services	...	14784	...	...	...	318021	...	...	...	...	...	...
	Other producers [d]	...	1871	...	...	...	54618	...	...	...	...	...	...
	Total	1244973	324700	637298	177808	53450	2331329	...	...	...	...	...	...
	less: Imputed bank service charge	...	...	119361	...	...	119361	...	...	...	...	...	...
	Import duties	...	...	...	14690	...	14690	...	...	...	...	...	...
	Value added tax	...	...	...	194965	...	194965	...	...	...	...	...	...

Austria

	1996						1997					
	Compensation of employees	Capital consumption	Net operating surplus	Indirect taxes	less: Subsidies received	Value added	Compensation of employees	Capital consumption	Net operating surplus	Indirect taxes	less: Subsidies received	Value added
Other adjustments	...	...	...	...	...	...	...	...	...	...	...	...
Total	1244973	324700	517937	387463	53450	2421623	...	...	...	...	...	...

a Item "Crude petroleum and natural gas production" is included in item "Manufacture of chemicals and chemical petroleum, coal, rubber and plastic products."
b Non-governmental only.
c Item "Educational services" is included in item "Recreational and cultural services".
d Item "Sanitary and similar services" is included in item "Personal and household services" which excludes domestic services and caretakers that are included in item "Other producers".

Azerbaijan

Source

Reply to the United Nations National Accounts Questionnaire from the State Committee of Republic of Azerbaijan on Statistics.

General note

The estimates shown in the following tables have been prepared in accordance with the United Nations System of National Accounts (SNA) so far as the existing data would permit.

1.1 Expenditure on the gross domestic product, in current prices

Ten million Azerbaijan Manat

	1986	1987	1988	1989	1990	1991	1992	1993	1994	1995	1996	1997
1 Government final consumption expenditure	...	...	...	...	26	52	427	4732	44048	136500	164200	182870
2 Private final consumption expenditure	...	...	...	...	77	136	1539	10314	143217	899900	1198000	1204360
A Households	...	...	...	...	77	135	1536	10243	141784	891700	1184840	1188950
B Private non-profit institutions serving households	...	...	...	...	–	1	3	71	1433	8200	13160	15410
3 Gross capital formation	...	...	...	...	39	8	–17	3422	28689	253700	396210	587090
A Increase in stocks	...	...	...	...	9	–22	–542	132	–20507	86800	–1470	7070
B Gross fixed capital formation	...	...	...	...	30	31	526	3290	49196	166900	397680	580020
Residential buildings	...	...	...	...	...	...	...	...	1089	15830	37720	...
Non-residential buildings	...	...	...	...	...	...	...	...	8061	71630	170660	...
Other construction and land improvement, etc.	...	...	...	...	...	...	...	...	24204	39220	93060	...
Other	...	...	...	...	...	...	...	...	15841	40220	96240	...
4 Exports of goods and services	...	...	...	...	64	122	2078	9022	119671	346600	340600	439600
5 less: Imports of goods and services	...	...	...	...	58	110	1316	11936	148287	569800	764040	859960
Statistical discrepancy	...	...	...	...	–2	60	–301	155	–	–	31350	–18740
equals: Gross domestic product	...	...	...	...	147	267	2410	15708	187339	1066900	1366320	1535220

Azerbaijan

1.2 Expenditure on the gross domestic product, in constant prices

Ten million Azerbaijan Manat

	1986	1987	1988	1989	1990	1991	1992	1993	1994	1995	1996	1997
At constant prices of:			1992 1993 1994 1995 1996									
1 Government final consumption expenditure	...	...	...	...	...	...	427	372 4732	4495 44048 136500	42980 135770 164200	134290
2 Private final consumption expenditure	...	...	...	...	...	...	1539	1150 10314	7579 143217 899900	139040 984860 1198000	1109600
A Households	...	...	...	...	...	...	1536	10243	7498 141784 891700	138040 976640 1184840	1101270
B Private non-profit institutions serving households	...	...	...	...	...	...	3	71 1433	81 1000 8200	8220 13160	8330
3 Gross capital formation	...	...	...	...	...	...	−17	344 3422	4982 28689 253700	44520 536330 396210	895560
A Increase in stocks	...	...	...	...	...	...	−542	23 132	−1236 −20507 86800	4180 −1470	...
B Gross fixed capital formation	...	...	...	...	...	...	526	321 3290	6218 49196 166900	40340 397680	...
Residential buildings	...	...	...	...	...	...	...	...	1089 15830 37720		...
Non-residential buildings	...	...	...	...	...	...	...	...	8061 71630 170660		...
Other construction and land improvement, etc.	...	...	...	...	...	...	...	...	24204 39220 93060		...
Other	...	...	...	...	...	...	...	...	15841 40220 96240		...
4 Exports of goods and services	...	...	...	...	...	...	2078	1014 9022	9694 119671 346600	114650 350270 340600	486970

Azerbaijan

Ten million Azerbaijan Manat

	1986	1987	1988	1989	1990	1991	1992	1993	1994	1995	1996	1997
At constant prices of: 1992												
1993												
1994												
1995												
1996												
5 less: Imports of goods and services	...	...	...	...	...	...	1316	1416	12968	174680	785640	
								11936	148287		764040	953280
									569800			
Statistical discrepancy	...	...	...	...	...	...	−301	388	−1161	−1310	−141310	−529420
								155			31350	
equals: Gross domestic product	...	...	...	...	...	...	2410	1853	12621	165200	1080280	1143720
								15708	187339	1066900	1366320	

1.3 Cost components of the gross domestic product

Ten million Azerbaijan Manat

	1986	1987	1988	1989	1990	1991	1992	1993	1994	1995	1996	1997
1 Indirect taxes, net	...	...	...	...	17	17	215	973	4982	84600	150000	...
A Indirect taxes	...	...	...	...	27	31	322	2252	11844	107000	173740	...
B less: Subsidies	...	...	...	...	10	14	107	1279	6862	22400	23740	...
2 Consumption of fixed capital	...	...	...	...	20	33	307	2130	26125	150000	152240	...
3 Compensation of employees paid by resident producers to	...	...	...	...	77	140	956	8371	52857	242600	263060	...
A Resident households	...	...	...	...	...	...	...	...	52666	241300	256590	...
B Rest of the world	...	...	...	...	...	...	...	...	190	1300	6470	...
4 Operating surplus	...	...	...	...	52	110	1240	6364	129690	740900	959730	...
A Corporate and quasi-corporate enterprises	...	...	...	...	31	60	851	2501	71213	452600	553430	...
B Private unincorporated enterprises	...	...	...	...	21	44	396	3638	53295	274600	393100	...
C General government	...	...	...	...	1	6	−8	225	5183	13700	13200	...
Statistical discrepancy	...	...	...	...	−20	−33	−307	−2130	−26316	−151200	−158710	...
equals: Gross domestic product	...	...	...	...	147	267	2410	15708	187339	1066900	1366320	1535220

1.4 General government current receipts and disbursements

Ten million Azerbaijan Manat

	1986	1987	1988	1989	1990	1991	1992	1993	1994	1995	1996	1997
Receipts												
1 Operating surplus	...	...	...	...	1	6	−8	225	5183	13700	13200	...
2 Property and entrepreneurial income	...	...	...	...	–	1	17	43	218	400	4650	...
3 Taxes, fees and contributions	...	...	...	...	47	75	669	5914	36990	170800	310450	...
A Indirect taxes	...	...	...	...	27	31	322	2252	11844	107000	173740	...
B Direct taxes	...	...	...	...	11	22	197	1818	13944	56200	83980	...
C Social security contributions	...	...	...	...	9	22	150	1844	11201	7600	52730	...
D Compulsory fees, fines and penalties	...	...	...	...	...	...	...	...	...	...	...	...
4 Other current transfers	...	...	...	...	–	1	1	21	10973	15600	53450	...

Azerbaijan

Ten million Azerbaijan Manat

	1986	1987	1988	1989	1990	1991	1992	1993	1994	1995	1996	1997
Total current receipts of general government	...	...	...	...	48	83	678	6203	53363	200600	381750	...

Disbursements

	1986	1987	1988	1989	1990	1991	1992	1993	1994	1995	1996	1997
1 Government final consumption expenditure	...	...	...	...	26	52	427	4732	44048	136500	164200	...
A Compensation of employees	...	...	...	...	23	42	316	2284	23112	61200	81640	...
B Consumption of fixed capital	...	...	...	...	3	4	31	356	3030	13700	13200	...
C Purchases of goods and services, net	...	...	...	...	–1	6	81	2092	17906	61600	69360	...
D less: Own-account fixed capital formation	...	...	...	...	...	...	...	...	...	...	...	...
E Indirect taxes paid, net	...	...	...	...	–	–	–	–	–	–	–	...
2 Property income	...	...	...	...	2	3	18	12	22	400	1980	...
3 Subsidies	...	...	...	...	10	14	107	1279	6862	22400	23740	...
4 Other current transfers	...	...	...	...	12	35	171	2281	17957	61000	102860	...
A Social security benefits	...	...	...	...	12	35	167	2278	17957	54100	78260	...
B Social assistance grants	...	...	...	...	...	...	...	...	...	...	...	...
C Other	...	...	...	...	–	–	4	2	–	6900	24600	...
5 Net saving	...	...	...	...	–1	–20	–45	–2100	–15525	–19700	88970	...
Total current disbursements and net saving of general government	...	...	...	...	48	83	678	6203	53363	200600	381750	...

1.5 Current income and outlay of corporate and quasi-corporate enterprises, summary

Ten million Azerbaijan Manat

	1986	1987	1988	1989	1990	1991	1992	1993	1994	1995	1996	1997

Receipts

	1986	1987	1988	1989	1990	1991	1992	1993	1994	1995	1996	1997
1 Operating surplus	...	...	...	...	31	60	851	2501	71213	452600	553430	...
2 Property and entrepreneurial income received	...	...	...	...	1	–	–	87	4879	700	950	...
3 Current transfers	...	...	...	...	3	1	5	41	1602	86600	19760	...
Total current receipts	...	...	...	...	34	62	876	2693	76504	537400	579650	...

Disbursements

	1986	1987	1988	1989	1990	1991	1992	1993	1994	1995	1996	1997
1 Property and entrepreneurial income	...	...	...	...	1	3	60	1140	14971	16300	18170	...
2 Direct taxes and other current payments to general government	...	...	...	...	6	16	151	1300	8969	29900	67770	...
3 Other current transfers	...	...	...	...	3	4	58	234	4004	41400	32030	...
4 Net saving	...	...	...	...	23	38	606	19	48559	449800	461680	...
Total current disbursements and net saving	...	...	...	...	34	62	876	2693	76504	537400	579650	...

1.6 Current income and outlay of households and non-profit institutions

Ten million Azerbaijan Manat

	1986	1987	1988	1989	1990	1991	1992	1993	1994	1995	1996	1997

Receipts

	1986	1987	1988	1989	1990	1991	1992	1993	1994	1995	1996	1997
1 Compensation of employees	...	...	...	...	77	140	956	8371	52849	238500	256680	...
2 Operating surplus of private unincorporated enterprises	...	...	...	...	21	44	396	3638	53295	274600	393100	...

Azerbaijan

Ten million Azerbaijan Manat

	1986	1987	1988	1989	1990	1991	1992	1993	1994	1995	1996	1997
3 Property and entrepreneurial income	...	...	...	...	3	5	2	58	566	1100	5860	...
4 Current transfers	...	...	...	...	12	36	183	2635	19789	92300	94260	...
A Social security benefits	...	...	...	...	12	35	167	2278	18406	55300	84870	...
B Social assistance grants	...	...	...	...	–	–	15	357	1383	37000	9390	...
C Other	...	...	...	...	...	...	...	...	...	...	...	...
Total current receipts	...	...	...	...	113	224	1536	14703	126478	605900	744880	...

Disbursements

	1986	1987	1988	1989	1990	1991	1992	1993	1994	1995	1996	1997
1 Private final consumption expenditure	...	...	...	...	77	136	1539	10314	143217	899900	1198000	1204360
2 Property income	...	...	...	...	–	–	2	34	–	6200	70	...
3 Direct taxes and other current transfers n.e.c. to general government	...	...	...	...	14	28	194	2265	14039	62300	75660	...
A Social security contributions	...	...	...	...	9	22	150	1844	11201	49700	53110	...
B Direct taxes	...	...	...	...	5	6	44	421	2838	12600	22550	...
C Fees, fines and penalties	...	...	...	...	...	...	...	...	...	...	...	...
4 Other current transfers	...	...	...	...	1	1	2	92	603	1900	1710	...
5 Net saving	...	...	...	...	21	60	–198	2069	–29948	–356200	–517400	...
Total current disbursements and net saving	...	...	...	...	113	224	1536	14703	126478	605900	744880	...

1.7 External transactions on current account, summary

Ten million Azerbaijan Manat

	1986	1987	1988	1989	1990	1991	1992	1993	1994	1995	1996	1997

Payments to the rest of the world

	1986	1987	1988	1989	1990	1991	1992	1993	1994	1995	1996	1997
1 Imports of goods and services	...	...	...	...	58	110	1316	11936	148287	569800	764040	859960
A Imports of merchandise, c.i.f.	...	...	...	...	58	110	1316	11936	124000	435315	574559	548250
B Other	...	...	...	...	...	...	...	...	24287	134485	189481	311710
2 Factor income to rest of the world	...	...	...	...	...	...	...	23	28	1300	–22100	...
3 Current transfers to the rest of the world	...	...	...	...	...	...	...	–	1328	8200	23880	...
4 Surplus of the nation on current transactions	...	...	...	...	5	71	461	–2479	–17700	–176200	–362080	...
Payments to the rest of the world and surplus of the nation on current transfers	...	...	...	...	...	...	...	...	...	...	...	...

Receipts from the rest of the world

	1986	1987	1988	1989	1990	1991	1992	1993	1994	1995	1996	1997
1 Exports of goods and services	...	...	...	...	64	122	2078	9022	119671	346600	340600	439600
A Exports of merchandise, f.o.b.	...	...	...	...	64	122	2078	9022	99300	270500	276488	322236
B Other	...	...	...	...	...	...	...	...	20371	76100	64112	117364
2 Factor income from rest of the world	...	...	...	...	...	...	...	16	219	400	–9400	...
A Compensation of employees	...	...	...	...	...	...	...	...	...	...	...	...
B Property and entrepreneurial income	...	...	...	...	...	...	...	16	219	400	940	...
3 Current transfers from rest of the world	...	...	...	...	...	...	...	274	12252	57100	52530	...
Receipts from the rest of the world on current transactions	...	...	...	...	...	...	...	...	...	...	...	...

Azerbaijan

1.8 Capital transactions of the nation, summary

Ten million Azerbaijan Manat

	1986	1987	1988	1989	1990	1991	1992	1993	1994	1995	1996	1997
Finance of gross capital formation												
Gross saving	...	...	...	...	44	80	444	943	10989	77500	34130	...
1 Consumption of fixed capital	...	...	...	...	20	33	307	2130	26125	150000	152240	...
A General government	...	...	...	...	3	4	31	356	3030	13700	13200	...
B Corporate and quasi-corporate enterprises	...	...	...	...	17	29	276	1774	23093	136300	139040	...
Public	...	...	...	...	16	28	266	1719	21965	134300	119040	...
Private	...	...	...	...	1	1	10	55	1128	2000	20000	...
C Other	...	...	...	...	...	...	...	...	...	...	...	...
2 Net saving	...	...	...	...	23	46	137	−1187	−15137	−72500	−118110	...
A General government	...	...	...	...	−5	−25	−76	−2456	−18550	−33400	−75770	...
B Corporate and quasi-corporate enterprises	...	...	...	...	28	71	213	1269	3413	−39100	−42340	...
Public	...	...	...	...	7	11	380	−849	34773	326400	348500	...
Private	...	...	...	...	21	61	−167	2118	−31359	−365500	542370	...
C Other	...	...	...	...	...	...	...	...	...	...	...	...
less: Surplus of the nation on current transactions	...	...	...	...	5	71	461	−2479	−17700	−176200	−362080	...
Finance of gross capital formation	...	...	...	...	39	8	−17	3422	28689	253700	396210	...
Gross capital formation												
Increase in stocks	...	...	...	...	9	−22	−542	132	−20507	86800	−1470	7070
Gross fixed capital formation	...	...	...	...	30	31	526	3290	49196	166900	397680	580020
Gross capital formation	...	...	...	...	39	8	−17	3422	28689	253700	396210	587090

1.9 Gross domestic product by institutional sectors of origin

Ten million Azerbaijan Manat

	1986	1987	1988	1989	1990	1991	1992	1993	1994	1995	1996	1997
Domestic factor incomes originating												
1 General government	...	...	...	...	21	43	277	2158	25309	61700	81940	...
2 Corporate and quasi-corporate enterprises	...	...	...	...	73	133	1292	8029	88420	519200	631310	...
A Non-financial	...	...	...	...	73	132	1247	7068	78904	493800	621090	...
B Financial [a]	...	...	...	...	−	−	45	961	9516	25400	10220	...
3 Households and private unincorporated enterprises	...	...	...	...	20	42	387	3605	52447	272000	369050	...
4 Non-profit institutions serving households	...	...	...	...	−	−	1	22	515	3000	8260	...
subtotal: Domestic factor incomes	...	...	...	...	114	219	1957	13814	166691	855900	1090560	...
Indirect taxes, net	...	...	...	...	17	17	215	973	4982	84600	150000	...
A Indirect taxes	...	...	...	...	27	31	322	2252	11844	107000	173740	...
B less: Subsidies	...	...	...	...	10	14	107	1279	6862	22400	23740	...
Consumption of fixed capital	...	...	...	...	20	33	307	2130	26125	150000	152240	...
Statistical discrepancy	...	...	...	...	−5	−2	−69	−1209	−10460	−23600	−26480	...
Gross domestic product	...	...	...	...	147	267	2410	15708	187339	1066900	1366320	...

a Gross Value Added - Financial Intermediation Services Indirectly Measured (FISIM)

Azerbaijan

1.10 Gross domestic product by kind of activity, in current prices

Ten million Azerbaijan Manat

	1986	1987	1988	1989	1990	1991	1992	1993	1994	1995	1996	1997
1 Agriculture, hunting, forestry and fishing	...	...	...	...	39	82	629	4265	60677	269200	338590	308740
2 Mining and quarrying	...	...	...	...	32	63	707	3903	38145	290700	353000	380610
3 Manufacturing	...	...	...	...								
4 Electricity, gas and water	...	...	...	...								
5 Construction	...	...	...	...	12	16	173	1144	13661	39700	127190	211430
6 Wholesale and retail trade, restaurants and hotels	...	...	...	...	4	7	100	577	7240	50800	71250	84080
7 Transport, storage and communication	...	...	...	...	12	16	125	1253	23005	185200	139850	182800
8 Finance, insurance, real estate and business services	...	...	...	...	–	1	57	1128	10495	28100	12050	14400
9 Community, social and personal services	...	...	...	...	21	35	355	2359	24839	96200	157310	179430
Total, Industries	...	...	...	...	120	221	2147	14629	178062	959900	1199240	1361490
Producers of government services	...	...	...	...	10	24	69	942	9602	26900	28710	32740
Other producers	...	...	...	...	4	8	48	374	5153	19100	14850	14220
Subtotal	...	...	...	...	134	252	2264	15944	192817	1005900	1242800	1408450
less: Imputed bank service charge	...	...	...	...	–	–	61	1004	9138	21600	13980	10070
plus: Import duties	...	...	...	...	...	...	...	...	...	...	...	...
plus: Value added tax	...	...	...	...	...	...	...	...	...	...	...	...
plus: Other adjustments	...	...	...	...	13	15	207	768	3660	82600	137500	136840
equals: Gross domestic product	...	...	...	...	147	267	2410	15708	187339	1066900	1366320	1535220

1.11 Gross domestic product by kind of activity, in constant prices

Ten million Azerbaijan Manat

	1986	1987	1988	1989	1990	1991	1992	1993	1994	1995	1996	1997
At constant prices of: 1994												
1 Agriculture, hunting, forestry and fishing	...	...	...	...	...	...	...	...	60677	56360	...	...
2 Mining and quarrying	...	...	...	...	...	...	...	...	38145	30040	...	...
3 Manufacturing	...	...	...	...	...	...	...	...			...	...
4 Electricity, gas and water	...	...	...	...	...	...	...	...			...	...
5 Construction	...	...	...	...	...	...	...	...	13661	14890	...	...
6 Wholesale and retail trade, restaurants and hotels	...	...	...	...	...	...	...	...	7240	4200	...	...
7 Transport, storage and communication	...	...	...	...	...	...	...	...	23005	17830	...	...
8 Finance, insurance, real estate and business services	...	...	...	...	...	...	...	...	10611	10590	...	...
9 Community, social and personal services	...	...	...	...	...	...	...	...	24839	23700	...	...
Total, Industries	...	...	...	...	...	...	...	...	178177	157610	...	...
Producers of government services	...	...	...	...	...	...	...	...	9602	9600	...	...
Other producers	...	...	...	...	...	...	...	...	5038	3950	...	...
Subtotal	...	...	...	...	...	...	...	...	192817	171160	...	...
less: Imputed bank service charge	...	...	...	...	...	...	...	...	9138	9140	...	...
plus: Import duties	...	...	...	...	...	...	...	...	...	...	...	...

Azerbaijan

Ten million Azerbaijan Manat

	1986	1987	1988	1989	1990	1991	1992	1993	1994	1995	1996	1997
At constant prices of: 1994												
plus: Value added tax	...	...	...	...	...	...	...	...	...	...	...	...
plus: Other adjustments	...	...	...	...	...	...	...	...	3660	3270	...	...
equals: Gross domestic product	...	...	...	...	...	...	...	...	187339	165290	...	...

1.12 Relations among national accounting aggregates

Ten million Azerbaijan Manat

	1986	1987	1988	1989	1990	1991	1992	1993	1994	1995	1996	1997
Gross domestic product	...	...	...	...	147	267	2410	15708	187339	1066900	1366320	1535220
plus: Net factor income from the rest of the world					...	...	...	−6	192	−900	12700	...
Factor income from rest of the world								16	219	400	−9400	...
less: Factor income to the rest of the world					...	...	...	23	28	1300	−22100	...
equals: Gross national product	...	...	...	...	147	267	2410	15702	187530	1066000	1379020	...
less: Consumption of fixed capital					20	33	307	2130	26125	150000	152240	...
equals: National income	...	...	...	...	126	234	2103	13572	161405	916000	1226780	...
plus: Net current transfers from the rest of the world								274	10924	48900	28650	...
Current transfers from rest of the world								274	12252	57100	52530	...
less: Current transfers to the rest of the world					...	...	...	−	1328	8200	23880	...
equals: National disposable income	...	...	...	...	126	234	2103	13846	172329	964900	1255430	...
less: Final consumption	...	...	...	...	103	188	1966	15046	187265	1036400	1362200	1387230
Statistical discrepancy	...	...	...	...	...	...	...	12	−201	−1000	−11340	...
equals: Net saving	...	...	...	...	23	46	137	−1187	−15137	−72500	−118110	...
less: Surplus of the nation on current transactions	...	...	...	...	5	71	461	−2479	−17700	−176200	−362080	...
equals: Net capital formation	...	...	...	...	18	−25	−324	1292	2564	103700	243970	...

2.1 Government final consumption expenditure by function, in current prices

Ten million Azerbaijan Manat

	1986	1987	1988	1989	1990	1991	1992	1993	1994	1995	1996	1997
1 General public services	...	...	...	...	9	22	145	1820	19019	58075	66500	73970
2 Defence	...	...	...	...	...	...	...	...	...	...	...	...
3 Public order and safety	...	...	...	...	...	...	...	...	...	...	...	...
4 Education	...	...	...	...	7	14	148	1269	9523	30493	21830	24360
5 Health	...	...	...	...	3	8	64	791	4320	12300	30710	34270
6 Social security and welfare	...	...	...	...	−	−	−	−	−	−	−	...
7 Housing and community amenities	...	...	...	...	2	3	26	245	680	8454	20420	22830
8 Recreational, cultural and religious affairs	...	...	...	...	−	2	14	190	1479	4925	6010	6690
9 Economic services	...	...	...	...	2	2	4	137	8013	9599	8670	9610
A Fuel and energy	...	...	...	...	...	...	...	...	...	...	...	...
B Agriculture, hunting, forestry and fishing	...	...	...	...	2	2	4	137	8013	9599	8670	9610
C Mining (except fuels), manufacturing and construction	...	...	...	...	...	...	...	...	...	...	...	...

Azerbaijan

Ten million Azerbaijan Manat

	1986	1987	1988	1989	1990	1991	1992	1993	1994	1995	1996	1997
D Transportation and communication	...	...	...	...	...	...	...	...	...	...	...	...
E Other economic affairs	...	...	...	...	...	...	...	...	...	...	...	...
10 Other functions	...	...	...	...	2	2	25	280	1015	12601	10060	11140
Total government final consumption expenditures	...	...	...	...	26	52	427	4732	44048	136500	164200	182870

2.2 Government final consumption expenditure by function, in constant prices

Ten million Azerbaijan Manat

	1986	1987	1988	1989	1990	1991	1992	1993	1994	1995	1996	1997
At constant prices of: 1994												
1 General public services	...	...	...	...	...	...	...	...	19000	19000	...	...
2 Defence	...	...	...	...	...	...	...	...	...	...	...	...
3 Public order and safety	...	...	...	...	...	...	...	...	...	...	...	...
4 Education	...	...	...	...	...	...	...	...	9500	8700	...	...
5 Health	...	...	...	...	...	...	...	...	4300	4100	...	...
6 Social security and welfare	...	...	...	...	...	...	...	...	...	...	...	...
7 Housing and community amenities	...	...	...	...	...	...	...	...	700	700	...	...
8 Recreational, cultural and religious affairs	...	...	...	...	...	...	...	...	1500	1500	...	...
9 Economic services	...	...	...	...	...	...	...	...	8500	8500	...	...
A Fuel and energy	...	...	...	...	...	...	...	...	...	...	...	...
B Agriculture, hunting, forestry and fishing	...	...	...	...	...	...	...	...	8500	8500	...	...
C Mining (except fuels), manufacturing and construction	...	...	...	...	...	...	...	...	...	...	...	...
D Transportation and communication	...	...	...	...	...	...	...	...	...	...	...	...
E Other economic affairs	...	...	...	...	...	...	...	...	...	...	...	...
10 Other functions	...	...	...	...	...	...	...	...	500	500	...	...
Total government final consumption expenditures	...	...	...	...	...	...	...	...	44000	43000	...	...

Bahamas

Source

Reply to the United Nations National Accounts Questionnaire from the Department of Statistics, Nassau. Official estimates are published in a series of reports entitled *Expenditure on Gross Domestic Product*.

General note

The estimates shown in the following tables have been prepared in accordance with the United Nations System of National Accounts (1968 SNA) so far as the existing data would permit.

1.1 Expenditure on the gross domestic product, in current prices

Million Bahamian dollars

	1986	1987	1988	1989	1990	1991	1992	1993	1994	1995	1996	1997
1 Government final consumption expenditure	...	...	...	409	428	443	448	...	...	...	...	...
2 Private final consumption expenditure	...	...	...	2302	2323	2381	2269	...	...	...	...	...
A Households	...	...	...	2302	2323	2381	2269	...	...	...	...	...
B Private non-profit institutions serving households	...	...	...					...	...	...	...	...
3 Gross capital formation	...	...	...	725	696	633	639	...	...	...	...	...
A Increase in stocks	...	...	...	13	24	−11	5	...	...	...	...	...
B Gross fixed capital formation	...	...	...	712	671	644	635	...	...	...	...	...
Residential buildings	...	...	...	90	86	82	77	...	...	...	...	...
Non-residential buildings	...	...	...	160	143	133	142	...	...	...	...	...
Other construction and land improvement, etc.	...	...	...					...	...	...	...	...
Other	...	...	...	462	443	429	416	...	...	...	...	...
4 Exports of goods and services	...	...	...	1424	1516	1416	1405	...	...	...	...	...
5 less: Imports of goods and services	...	...	...	1789	1840	1761	1689	...	...	...	...	...
Statistical discrepancy	...	...	...	−64	11	−21	−13	...	...	...	...	...
equals: Gross domestic product	...	...	...	3006	3134	3090	3059	...	...	...	...	...

1.3 Cost components of the gross domestic product

Million Bahamian dollars

	1986	1987	1988	1989	1990	1991	1992	1993	1994	1995	1996	1997
1 Indirect taxes, net	...	...	...	381	411	388	430	...	...	...	...	...
A Indirect taxes	...	...	...	381	411	388	430	...	...	...	...	...
B less: Subsidies	...	...	...	...	...	...	...	...	...	...	...	...
2 Consumption of fixed capital	...	...	...	...	...	...	...	...	...	...	...	...
3 Compensation of employees paid by resident producers to	...	...	...	1534	1624	1572	1587	...	...	...	...	...
4 Operating surplus [a]	...	...	...	1027	1110	1109	1029	...	...	...	...	...
Statistical discrepancy	...	...	...	64	−11	21	13	...	...	...	...	...
equals: Gross domestic product	...	...	...	3006	3134	3090	3059	...	...	...	...	...

a Gross operating surplus.

Bahamas

1.4 General government current receipts and disbursements

Million Bahamian dollars

	1986	1987	1988	1989	1990	1991	1992	1993	1994	1995	1996	1997
Receipts												
1 Operating surplus	–	–	–	...	...	...	...	...	...	...	...	...
2 Property and entrepreneurial income	48	41	39	55	50	59	56	...	...	...	...	...
3 Taxes, fees and contributions	401	412	473	480	523	503	568	...	...	...	...	...
A Indirect taxes	328	341	393	381	411	388	430	...	...	...	...	...
B Direct taxes	8	8	7	21	26	33	50	...	...	...	...	...
C Social security contributions	50	50	55	59	66	63	61	...	...	...	...	...
D Compulsory fees, fines and penalties	16	14	18	19	19	18	28	...	...	...	...	...
4 Other current transfers	9	10	12	12	17	15	16	...	...	...	...	...
Total current receipts of general government	458	463	524	547	590	577	641	...	...	...	...	...
Disbursements												
1 Government final consumption expenditure	306	334	370	409	428	443	448	...	...	...	...	...
A Compensation of employees	227	251	276	303	325	327	336	...	...	...	...	...
B Consumption of fixed capital	7	7	6	5	5	4	5	...	...	...	...	...
C Purchases of goods and services, net	73	76	88	100	98	111	107	...	...	...	...	...
D less: Own-account fixed capital formation	...	...	...	...	...	...	...	...	...	...	...	...
E Indirect taxes paid, net	–	–	–	...	...	...	...	...	...	...	...	...
2 Property income	47	40	46	54	62	70	68	...	...	...	...	...
A Interest	47	40	46	54	62	70	68	...	...	...	...	...
B Net land rent and royalties	...	...	...	...	...	...	...	...	...	...	...	...
3 Subsidies	5	6	6	...	...	...	...	...	...	...	...	...
4 Other current transfers	49	51	59	45	46	48	56	...	...	...	...	...
A Social security benefits	24	26	28	31	34	37	40	...	...	...	...	...
B Social assistance grants	7	8	8	8	9	8	9	...	...	...	...	...
C Other	17	17	23	6	4	4	7	...	...	...	...	...
5 Net saving	51	33	42	40	53	16	69	...	...	...	...	...
Total current disbursements and net saving of general government	458	463	524	547	590	577	641	...	...	...	...	...

Bahamas

1.7 External transactions on current account, summary

Million Bahamian dollars

	1986	1987	1988	1989	1990	1991	1992	1993	1994	1995	1996	1997
Payments to the rest of the world												
1 Imports of goods and services	...	...	...	1789	1840	1761	1689	...	...	...	...	...
A Imports of merchandise, c.i.f.	...	...	...	1329	1304	1243	1234	...	...	...	...	...
B Other	...	...	...	460	536	518	454	...	...	...	...	...
2 Factor income to rest of the world	...	...	...	169	150	182	161	...	...	...	...	...
A Compensation of employees	...	...	...	...	...	...	...	...	...	...	...	...
B Property and entrepreneurial income	...	...	...	169	150	182	161	...	...	...	...	...
By general government	...	...	...	9	10	11	10	...	...	...	...	...
By corporate and quasi-corporate enterprises	...	...	...	44	38	42	36	...	...	...	...	...
By other	...	...	...	115	102	129	115	...	...	...	...	...
3 Current transfers to the rest of the world	...	...	...	21	14	11	18	...	...	...	...	...
4 Surplus of the nation on current transactions	...	...	...	–517	–448	–492	–419	...	...	...	...	...
Payments to the rest of the world and surplus of the nation on current transfers	...	...	...	1461	1556	1462	1448	...	...	...	...	...
Receipts from the rest of the world												
1 Exports of goods and services	...	...	...	1424	1516	1416	1405	...	...	...	...	...
A Exports of merchandise, f.o.b.	...	...	...	155	190	217	194	...	...	...	...	...
B Other	...	...	...	1269	1326	1199	1210	...	...	...	...	...
2 Factor income from rest of the world	...	...	...	16	15	15	12	...	...	...	...	...
A Compensation of employees	...	...	...	...	...	...	...	...	...	...	...	...
B Property and entrepreneurial income	...	...	...	16	15	15	12	...	...	...	...	...
By general government	...	...	...	–	–	–	–	...	...	...	...	...
By corporate and quasi-corporate enterprises	...	...	...	–	–	1	–	...	...	...	...	...
By other	...	...	...	16	15	14	11	...	...	...	...	...
3 Current transfers from rest of the world	...	...	...	22	25	31	31	...	...	...	...	...
Receipts from the rest of the world on current transactions	...	...	...	1461	1556	1462	1447	...	...	...	...	...

1.10 Gross domestic product by kind of activity, in current prices

Million Bahamian dollars

	1986	1987	1988	1989	1990	1991	1992	1993	1994	1995	1996	1997
1 Agriculture, hunting, forestry and fishing	...	...	...	69	82	104	89	...	...	...	...	...
2 Mining and quarrying	...	...	...	98	86	103	105	...	...	...	...	...
3 Manufacturing	...	...	...					...	...	...	...	...
4 Electricity, gas and water	...	...	...	63	67	77	88	...	...	...	...	...
5 Construction	...	...	...	115	109	104	91	...	...	...	...	...
6 Wholesale and retail trade, restaurants and hotels	...	...	...	844	929	800	705	...	...	...	...	...

Bahamas

Million Bahamian dollars	1986	1987	1988	1989	1990	1991	1992	1993	1994	1995	1996	1997
7 Transport, storage and communication	...	...	...	199	229	205	227	...	...	...	...	...
8 Finance, insurance, real estate and business services	...	...	...	547	573	601	610	...	...	...	...	...
9 Community, social and personal services	...	...	...	286	290	305	310	...	...	...	...	...
Statistical discrepancy	...	...	...	64	−11	21	13	...	...	...	...	...
Total, Industries	...	...	...	2385	2354	2320	2238	...	...	...	...	...
Producers of government services	...	...	...	297	324	327	336	...	...	...	...	...
Other producers	...	...	...	43	45	54	55	...	...	...	...	...
Subtotal	...	...	...	2625	2723	2701	2629	...	...	...	...	...
less: Imputed bank service charge	...	...	...	...	...	...	...	...	...	...	...	...
plus: Import duties	...	...	...	290	289	266	268	...	...	...	...	...
plus: Value added tax	...	...	...	...	...	...	...	...	...	...	...	...
plus: Other adjustments [a]	...	...	...	92	122	122	162	...	...	...	...	...
equals: Gross domestic product	...	...	...	3006	3134	3090	3059	...	...	...	...	...

a Item "other adjustments" refers to other indirect taxes.

1.12 Relations among national accounting aggregates

Million Bahamian dollars	1986	1987	1988	1989	1990	1991	1992	1993	1994	1995	1996	1997
Gross domestic product	...	...	...	3006	3134	3090	3059	...	...	...	...	...
plus: Net factor income from the rest of the world	...	...	...	−153	−135	−167	−149	...	...	...	...	...
Factor income from rest of the world	...	...	...	16	15	15	12	...	...	...	...	...
less: Factor income to the rest of the world	...	...	...	169	150	182	161	...	...	...	...	...
equals: Gross national product	...	...	...	2853	2999	2923	2910	...	...	...	...	...
less: Consumption of fixed capital	...	...	...	...	...	...	...	...	...	...	...	...
equals: National income	...	...	...	...	...	...	...	...	...	...	...	...
plus: Net current transfers from the rest of the world	...	...	...	1	11	20	13	...	...	...	...	...
Current transfers from rest of the world	...	...	...	22	25	31	31	...	...	...	...	...
less: Current transfers to the rest of the world	...	...	...	21	14	11	18	...	...	...	...	...
equals: National disposable income	...	...	...	...	...	...	...	...	...	...	...	...
less: Final consumption	...	...	...	2711	2751	2824	2717	...	...	...	...	...
equals: Net saving	...	...	...	...	...	...	...	...	...	...	...	...
less: Surplus of the nation on current transactions	...	...	...	−517	−448	−492	−419	...	...	...	...	...
equals: Net capital formation	...	...	...	...	...	...	...	...	...	...	...	...

2.1 Government final consumption expenditure by function, in current prices

Million Bahamian dollars	1986	1987	1988	1989	1990	1991	1992	1993	1994	1995	1996	1997
1 General public services	37	41	37	66	73	73	80	...	...	...	...	...
2 Defence	11	12	17	17	19	18	18	...	...	...	...	...

Bahamas

Million Bahamian dollars

	1986	1987	1988	1989	1990	1991	1992	1993	1994	1995	1996	1997
3 Public order and safety	39	42	51	52	56	60	60	...	...	...	...	...
4 Education	84	92	92	97	99	99	105	...	...	...	...	...
5 Health	62	67	83	87	83	83	80	...	...	...	...	...
6 Social security and welfare	8	8	15	17	18	21	23	...	...	...	...	...
7 Housing and community amenities	–	–	1	6	7	6	7	...	...	...	...	...
8 Recreational, cultural and religious affairs	4	4	6					...	...	...	...	...
9 Economic services	63	68	71	67	73	84	76	...	...	...	...	...
A Fuel and energy	...	...	...	...	...	...	...	...	...	...	...	...
B Agriculture, hunting, forestry and fishing	7	7	8	7	8	11	10	...	...	...	...	...
C Mining (except fuels), manufacturing and construction [a]	34	38	39	35	39	51	42	...	...	...	...	...
D Transportation and communication	18	20	22	21	23	19	21	...	...	...	...	...
E Other economic affairs	4	4	3	3	3	3	3	...	...	...	...	...
10 Other functions	...	...	...	...	...	...	...	...	...	...	...	...
Total government final consumption expenditures	306	334	370	409	428	443	448	...	...	...	...	...

[a] Item "Mining, manufacturing and construction, except fuel and energy" refers to tourism.

2.3 Total government outlays by function and type

Million Bahamian dollars

	1986 Final consumption expenditures Total	Compensation of employees	Other	Subsidies	Other current transfers and property income	Total current disbursements	Gross capital formation	Other capital outlays	Total outlays
1 General public services	37	31	6	5	15	57	1	5	63
2 Defence	11	5	5	...	–	11	–	...	11
3 Public order and safety	39	33	6	...	–	39	–	...	39
4 Education	84	76	8	...	11	95	2	–	97
5 Health	62	47	15	...	–	62	1	...	63
6 Social security and welfare	8	5	2	...	20	27	1	–	28
7 Housing and community amenities	–	–	–	...	–	1	–	...	1
8 Recreational, cultural and religious affairs	4	3	1	...	–	4	–	...	4
9 Economic services	62	27	36	–	3	65	4	1	70
A Fuel and energy	...	...	...	...	...	...	...	...	...
B Agriculture, hunting, forestry and fishing	7	5	1	...	–	7	1	...	8
C Mining (except fuels), manufacturing and construction [a]	34	8	26	...	–	34	–	...	34
D Transportation and communication	18	10	8	...	–	18	3	1	22
E Other economic affairs	4	4	–	...	3	7	–	–	7
10 Other functions	–	–	–	...	47	47	–	...	47
Total		227	80	5	95	407	8	6	421

Bahamas

1987

	Final consumption expenditures			Subsidies	Other current transfers and property income	Total current disburse-ments	Gross capital formation	Other capital outlays	Total outlays
	Total	Compensation of employees	Other					
1 General public services	41	34	6	6	14	60	1	5	66
2 Defence	12	6	6	...	–	12	–	...	12
3 Public order and safety	42	36	6	...	–	43	–	...	43
4 Education	92	84	8	...	10	102	2	–	103
5 Health	67	52	15	...	–	67	–	...	68
6 Social security and welfare	8	6	2	...	19	27	–	–	27
7 Housing and community amenities	–	–	–	...	1	1	–	...	1
8 Recreational, cultural and religious affairs	4	3	1	...	–	4	–	...	4
9 Economic services	68	30	38	–	6	74	3	1	78
A Fuel and energy	...	...	...	...	...	...	...	...	...
B Agriculture, hunting, forestry and fishing	7	6	1	...	–	8	1	...	8
C Mining (except fuels), manufacturing and construction [a]	37	9	28	...	–	37	–	...	37
D Transportation and communication	20	11	9	...	3	23	2	1	26
E Other economic affairs	4	4	–	...	3	7	–	–	7
10 Other functions	–	–	–	...	40	40	–	...	40
Total	334	251	83	6	91	430	6	6	442

1988

	Final consumption expenditures			Subsidies	Other current transfers and property income	Total current disburse-ments	Gross capital formation	Other capital outlays	Total outlays
	Total	Compensation of employees	Other					
1 General public services	37	36	1	6	15	58	3	6	66
2 Defence	17	12	5	...	1	17	–	...	17
3 Public order and safety	51	41	11	...	1	52	3	...	55
4 Education	92	80	11	...	9	101	7	1	109
5 Health	83	61	22	...	–	83	6	...	89
6 Social security and welfare	15	11	4	...	32	47	–	1	49
7 Housing and community amenities	1	1	–	...	–	1	–	...	1
8 Recreational, cultural and religious affairs	6	4	1	...	–	6	–	–	7
9 Economic services	70	31	40	–	–	71	15	3	88
A Fuel and energy	...	...	...	...	...	...	...	...	...
B Agriculture, hunting, forestry and fishing	8	6	1	...	–	8	1	...	9
C Mining (except fuels), manufacturing and construction [a]	38	10	28	...	–	38	–	...	38
D Transportation and communication	22	12	10	...	–	22	14	–	36
E Other economic affairs	3	3	–	...	–	3	–	3	6
10 Other functions	–	–	–	...	46	46	–	...	46
Total	370	276	94	6	105	481	34	11	527

Bahamas

1989

	Final consumption expenditures			Subsidies	Other current transfers and property income	Total current disburse- ments	Gross capital formation	Other capital outlays	Total outlays
	Total	Compen- sation of employ- ees	Other						
1 General public services	66	50	16	–	3	70	9	–	79
2 Defence	17	13	4	...	–	17	1	...	17
3 Public order and safety	52	42	10	...	–	52	4	...	56
4 Education	97	86	11	...	6	103	6	–	108
5 Health	87	66	21	...	–	88	6	...	93
6 Social security and welfare	17	10	7	...	35	52	1	–	52
7 Housing and community amenities	6	5	2	...		7	–	...	7
8 Recreational, cultural and religious affairs									
9 Economic services	67	32	35	–	–	67	18	–	84
A Fuel and energy	...	...	...	...	...	...	...	...	...
B Agriculture, hunting, forestry and fishing	7	6	1	...	–	7	1	...	8
C Mining (except fuels), manufacturing and construction [a]	35	11	24	...	–	35	–	...	35
D Transportation and communication	21	12	9	...	–	21	17	–	38
E Other economic affairs	3	3	–	...	–	3	–	–	3
10 Other functions	–	–	–	...	54	54	–	...	54
Total	409	303	106	–	99	508	43	–	551

1990

	Final consumption expenditures			Subsidies	Other current transfers and property income	Total current disburse- ments	Gross capital formation	Other capital outlays	Total outlays
	Total	Compen- sation of employ- ees	Other						
1 General public services	73	57	16	...	3	76	1	...	78
2 Defence	19	15	4	...	–	19	–	...	19
3 Public order and safety	56	48	9	...	–	56	1	...	57
4 Education	99	88	11	...	6	105	2	...	107
5 Health	83	63	19	...	–	83	5	...	88
6 Social security and welfare	18	11	7	...	37	55	1	...	55
7 Housing and community amenities	7	5	1	...	–	7	–	...	7
8 Recreational, cultural and religious affairs									
9 Economic services	73	36	37	...	–	73	9	...	82
A Fuel and energy	...	...	...	...	...	...	...	...	...
B Agriculture, hunting, forestry and fishing	8	7	1	...	–	8	–	...	8
C Mining (except fuels), manufacturing and construction [a]	39	13	26	...	–	39	–	...	39
D Transportation and communication	23	14	10	...	–	23	9	...	32
E Other economic affairs	3	3	–	...	–	3	–	...	3
10 Other functions	...	...	...	...	62	62	–	...	62
Total	428	325	103	...	108	536	19	...	555

Bahamas

1991

	Final consumption expenditures			Subsidies	Other current transfers and property income	Total current disbursements	Gross capital formation	Other capital outlays	Total outlays
	Total	Compensation of employees	Other						
1 General public services	73	57	16	...	3	77	2	...	79
2 Defence	18	15	3	...	–	18	–	...	18
3 Public order and safety	60	50	10	...	–	60	1	...	60
4 Education	99	89	9	...	5	103	6	...	109
5 Health	83	64	18	...	–	83	2	...	85
6 Social security and welfare	21	13	8	...	39	60	–	...	60
7 Housing and community amenities	6	5	1	...	–	6	–	...	6
8 Recreational, cultural and religious affairs									
9 Economic services	84	34	50	...	–	84	6	...	90
A Fuel and energy	...	...	...	...	...	...	...	...	...
B Agriculture, hunting, forestry and fishing	11	6	4	...	–	11	1	...	11
C Mining (except fuels), manufacturing and construction [a]	51	13	38	...	–	51	–	...	51
D Transportation and communication	19	12	8	...	–	19	5	...	24
E Other economic affairs	3	3	–	...	–	3	–	...	3
10 Other functions	...	...	...	...	70	70	–	...	70
Total	443	327	115	...	118	561	16	...	578

1992

	Final consumption expenditures			Subsidies	Other current transfers and property income	Total current disbursements	Gross capital formation	Other capital outlays	Total outlays
	Total	Compensation of employees	Other						
1 General public services	80	59	21	...	6	86	3	...	89
2 Defence	18	15	3	...	–	18	–	...	18
3 Public order and safety	60	51	10	...	–	60	–	...	60
4 Education	105	93	11	...	4	109	5	...	114
5 Health	80	64	16	...	–	80	1	...	80
6 Social security and welfare	23	15	8	...	45	68	1	...	69
7 Housing and community amenities	7	5	1	...	1	8	–	...	8
8 Recreational, cultural and religious affairs									
9 Economic services	76	34	42	...	–	76	6	...	82
A Fuel and energy	...	...	...	...	...	...	...	...	...
B Agriculture, hunting, forestry and fishing	10	6	4	...	–	10	...	...	11
C Mining (except fuels), manufacturing and construction [a]	42	13	29	...	–	42	–	...	42
D Transportation and communication	21	12	9	...	...	21	6	...	27
E Other economic affairs	3	3	–	...	...	3	–	...	3
10 Other functions	...	...	...	...	68	68	...	...	68
Total	448	336	112	...	124	571	17	...	588

a Item "Mining, manufacturing and construction, except fuel and energy" refers to tourism.

Bahrain

Source

The estimates are published in *National Accounts of Bahrain* by the Ministry of Finance and National Economy.

General note

The estimates shown in the following tables have been prepared by the Statistics Department in accordance with the United Nations System of National Accounts (1968 SNA) so far as the existing data would permit.

1.1 Expenditure on the gross domestic product, in current prices

Million Bahraini dinars

	1986	1987	1988	1989	1990	1991	1992	1993	1994	1995	1996	1997
1 Government final consumption expenditure	284	311	340	357	380	404	425	441	446	456	428	...
2 Private final consumption expenditure	336	362	411	471	488	510	574	554	537	501	494	...
3 Gross capital formation	368	299	279	383	302	572	582	350	623	394	391	...
A Increase in stocks [a]	−64	−43	−48	19	−77	130	84	−195	34	−143	−56	...
B Gross fixed capital formation	432	342	327	364	379	442	497	545	590	537	448	...
4 Exports of goods and services [b]	1133	1306	1327	1433	1838	1769	1867	2018	1798	2131	2437	...
5 less: Imports of goods and services [b]	973	1112	1077	1270	1501	1659	1780	1616	1577	1582	1735	...
equals: Gross domestic product	1148	1166	1280	1374	1506	1595	1667	1748	1828	1900	2016	...

a Includes net errors and omissions.　　b Non-factor services.

1.2 Expenditure on the gross domestic product, in constant prices

Million Bahraini dinars

	1986	1987	1988	1989	1990	1991	1992	1993	1994	1995	1996	1997
At constant prices of: 1989												
1 Government final consumption expenditure	310	319	345	357	377	394	413	411	413	422	397	...
2 Private final consumption expenditure	336	334	380	471	482	499	563	530	508	459	436	...
3 Gross capital formation	342	310	352	383	341	557	602	313	516	379	443	...
A Increase in stocks [a]	27	28	27	19	−41	113	114	−192	–	−78	52	...
B Gross fixed capital formation	316	282	325	364	382	442	488	505	516	457	391	...
4 Exports of goods and services [b]	1289	1375	1423	1433	1548	1556	1740	2045	1907	2071	2113	...
5 less: Imports of goods and services [b]	1070	1108	1158	1270	1310	1501	1698	1545	1552	1497	1498	...
equals: Gross domestic product	1208	1231	1342	1374	1438	1503	1620	1754	1796	1834	1891	...

a Includes net errors and omissions.　　b Non-factor services.

Bahrain

1.7 External transactions on current account, summary

Million Bahraini dinars

	1986	1987	1988	1989	1990	1991	1992	1993	1994	1995	1996	1997
Payments to the rest of the world												
1 Imports of goods and services	973	1112	1077	1270	1501	1659	1780	1616	1677	1582	1735	...
A Imports of merchandise, c.i.f.	904	1020	975	1177	1396	1547	1603	1451	1514	...	...	...
B Other	69	91	101	93	105	112	177	165	162	...	...	...
2 Factor income to rest of the world	358	326	412	402	440	465	436	430	409	482	...	...
3 Current transfers to the rest of the world	...	...	...	...	...	...	...	...	...	...	...	...
4 Surplus of the nation on current transactions	−58	−9	−29	−108	−24	...	...	...	...	...	...	...
Payments to the rest of the world and surplus of the nation on current transfers [a]	1274	1428	1460	1564	1917	...	...	...	...	...	...	...
Receipts from the rest of the world												
1 Exports of goods and services	1133	1306	1327	1433	1838	1769	1867	2018	1798	2131	2437	...
A Exports of merchandise, f.o.b.	827	914	907	1064	1414	1321	1303	1400	...	...	...	...
B Other	306	392	420	368	424	448	564	618	...	...	...	...
2 Factor income from rest of the world	240	214	205	205	182	160	195	190	88	122	...	...
A Compensation of employees	...	...	...	...	...	...	...	...	...	...	...	...
B Property and entrepreneurial income	240	214	205	205	182	160	195	190	88	122	...	...
3 Current transfers from rest of the world [b]	−100	−92	−73	−75	...	...	...	...	...	...	...	...
A Subsidies from supranational organisations	...	...	...	...	...	...	...	...	...	...	...	...
B Other current transfers	−100	−92	−73	−75	...	...	...	...	...	...	...	...
Receipts from the rest of the world on current transactions [a]	1274	1428	1460	1564	1917	...	...	...	...	...	...	...

a Estimates are derived from Balance of Payment Accounts, therefore are not strictly comparable to those in other tables.

b Current transfers from the rest of the world is net of current transfers to the rest of the world.

1.10 Gross domestic product by kind of activity, in current prices

Million Bahraini dinars

	1986	1987	1988	1989	1990	1991	1992	1993	1994	1995	1996	1997
1 Agriculture, hunting, forestry and fishing	16	16	15	16	14	15	17	18	18	20	22	...
2 Mining and quarrying	213	210	181	227	314	283	281	294	287	319	396	...
3 Manufacturing	164	191	236	232	252	266	252	257	322	418	394	...
4 Electricity, gas and water	21	22	23	28	29	28	30	31	30	34	36	...
5 Construction	103	87	90	88	94	92	101	105	110	107	99	...
6 Wholesale and retail trade, restaurants and hotels	109	118	136	137	148	169	201	197	208	203	207	...
7 Transport, storage and communication	148	140	147	152	140	193	190	199	216	164	184	...
8 Finance, insurance, real estate and business services	267	216	290	290	273	275	324	369	366	335	372	...
9 Community, social and personal services	61	64	70	70	79	77	82	88	94	101	105	...
Total, Industries	1102	1064	1187	1239	1343	1396	1477	1559	1653	1702	1815	...

Bahrain

Million Bahraini dinars

	1986	1987	1988	1989	1990	1991	1992	1993	1994	1995	1996	1997
Producers of government services	261	271	288	300	316	332	345	354	356	370	374	...
Other producers	...	...	...	...	...	...	...	...	...	...	...	...
Subtotal	1364	1335	1475	1539	1658	1728	1821	1914	2009	2071	2188	...
less: Imputed bank service charge	216	169	195	165	152	133	154	166	181	171	173	...
plus: Import duties	...	...	...	...	...	...	...	...	...	...	...	...
plus: Value added tax	...	...	...	...	...	...	...	...	...	...	...	...
plus: Other adjustments	...	...	...	...	...	...	...	...	...	...	...	...
equals: Gross domestic product	1148	1166	1280	1374	1506	1595	1667	1748	1827	1900	2016	...

1.11 Gross domestic product by kind of activity, in constant prices

Million Bahraini dinars

	1986	1987	1988	1989	1990	1991	1992	1993	1994	1995	1996	1997
	At constant prices of: 1989											
1 Agriculture, hunting, forestry and fishing	17	17	14	16	15	15	16	18	18	22	24	...
2 Mining and quarrying	255	217	225	227	230	225	258	288	287	292	311	...
3 Manufacturing	210	239	241	232	257	261	300	366	383	400	402	...
4 Electricity, gas and water	19	20	22	28	28	28	32	35	39	42	46	...
5 Construction	76	78	91	88	89	87	91	90	94	92	81	...
6 Wholesale and retail trade, restaurants and hotels	108	127	139	137	151	165	196	192	194	188	195	...
7 Transport, storage and communication	141	133	143	152	152	175	175	185	187	179	200	...
8 Finance, insurance, real estate and business services	312	291	333	290	280	266	297	316	317	322	320	...
9 Community, social and personal services	55	66	68	70	76	72	69	77	89	94	96	...
Total, Industries	1192	1187	1277	1240	1277	1293	1434	1568	1608	1631	1676	...
Producers of government services	260	279	293	300	313	324	326	328	328	340	346	...
Other producers	...	...	...	...	...	...	...	...	...	...	...	...
Subtotal	1452	1466	1570	1539	1590	1617	1761	1895	1936	1972	2022	...
less: Imputed bank service charge	245	236	228	165	152	114	140	141	140	137	130	...
plus: Import duties	...	...	...	...	...	...	...	...	...	...	...	...
plus: Value added tax	...	...	...	...	...	...	...	...	...	...	...	...
plus: Other adjustments	...	...	...	...	...	...	...	...	...	...	...	...
equals: Gross domestic product	1208	1231	1342	1374	1438	1503	1620	1754	1796	1834	1891	...

1.12 Relations among national accounting aggregates

Million Bahraini dinars

	1986	1987	1988	1989	1990	1991	1992	1993	1994	1995	1996	1997
Gross domestic product	1148	1166	1280	1374	1506	1595	1667	1748	1828	1900	2016	...
plus: Net factor income from the rest of the world	−118	−111	−207	−197	−258	−305	−244	−240	−321	−280	−324	...
Factor income from rest of the world	240	214	205	205	182	...	...	...	...	...	...	...
less: Factor income to the rest of the world	358	326	412	402	440	...	...	...	...	...	...	...
equals: Gross national product	1030	1055	1073	1177	1248	1290	1423	1508	1507	1621	1692	...
less: Consumption of fixed capital	210	209	226	225	229	...	...	...	...	...	...	...

Bahrain

Million Bahraini dinars

	1986	1987	1988	1989	1990	1991	1992	1993	1994	1995	1996	1997
equals: National income	820	846	848	953	1018	...	...	...	...	...	...	...
plus: Net current transfers from the rest of the world	−100	−92	−73	−75	−102	...	...	...	...	...	...	...
equals: National disposable income	720	754	774	878	916	...	...	...	...	...	...	...
less: Final consumption	620	673	751	828	868	913	998	995	983	957	922	...
Statistical discrepancy	...	...	46	−19	77	...	...	...	...	...	...	...
equals: Net saving	100	80	69	31	125	...	...	...	...	...	...	...
less: Surplus of the nation on current transactions	−58	−9	−29	−108	−24	...	...	...	...	...	...	...
equals: Net capital formation	158	89	98[a]	140[a]	149[a]	...	...	...	...	...	...	...

a Data for this table have not been revised, therefore, data for some years are not comparable with those of other tables.

Bangladesh

Source

Reply to the United Nations National Accounts Questionnaire from the Statistics Division, Dhaka.

General note

The estimates shown in the following tables have been prepared by the Bureau of Statistics in accordance with the United Nations System of National Accounts so far as the existing data would permit.

1.1 Expenditure on the gross domestic product, in current prices

Million Bangladesh taka — Fiscal year beginning 1 July

	1986	1987	1988	1989	1990	1991	1992	1993	1994	1995	1996	1997
1 Government final consumption expenditure	61245	69969	90455	103218	114732	124937	134304	147280	160798	177655	198225	227584
2 Private final consumption expenditure	458991	509429	551725	614255	685204	728632	747703	806319	913049	1026129	1099406	1191606
3 Gross capital formation	69490	74306	80710	94427	95955	109851	133890	142614	194651	221200	242427	250507
A Increase in stocks	...	...	14720	–12853	8735	–2889	13100	–12012	10841	...	...	...
B Gross fixed capital formation	69490	74306	65990	107280	87220	112740	120790	154626	183810	221200	242427	250507
Residential buildings	19167	22322	...	...	...	...	...	...	...	...	...	...
Non-residential buildings	2953	3215	...	...	...	...	...	...	...	...	...	...
Other construction and land improvement, etc.	13860	15605	...	...	...	...	...	...	...	...	...	...
Other	33510	33164	...	...	...	...	...	...	...	...	...	...
4 Exports of goods and services [a]	37587	45015	51185	61422	73634	90696	104169	121892	165705	184359	216723	258948
5 less: Imports of goods and services [b]	88112	101583	118958	135751	135133	147614	173325	187740	263133	310913	325591	360595
Statistical discrepancy	...	...	4481	...	...	...	1324	...	–809	3170	–28145	–27127
equals: Gross domestic product	539201	597136	659598	737571	834392	906502	948065	1030365	1170261	1301600	1403045	1540923 [c]

a Item "Exports of goods and services" refers to exports of goods and non-factor services.
b Item "Imports of goods and services" refers to imports of goods and non-factor services.
c Data for 1997 are preliminary estimates.

1.2 Expenditure on the gross domestic product, in constant prices

Million Bangladesh taka — Fiscal year beginning 1 July

	1986	1987	1988	1989	1990	1991	1992	1993	1994	1995	1996	1997
At constant prices of: 1984												
1 Government final consumption expenditure	50457	52482	61450	64150	67095	69611	71614	76220	97717	84289	90110	98919
2 Private final consumption expenditure	356070	372376	405382	425355	434003	433942	440785	460560	487063	516317	556497	590547
3 Gross capital formation	61563	57988	60189	61460	58112	63476	75471	87467	107942	118371	124776	124575
A Increase in stocks	...	...	...	...	...	...	...	...	...	...	...	...
B Gross fixed capital formation	61563	57988	60189	61460	58112	63476	75471	87467	107942	118371	124776	124575
4 Exports of goods and services	48764	52313	53681	63230	61275	74671	81682	92799	125032	138616	158365	183261

Bangladesh

Million Bangladesh taka	1986	1987	1988	1989	1990	1991	1992	1993	1994	1995	1996	1997
	At constant prices of: 1984											Fiscal year beginning 1 July
5 less: Imports of goods and services	74507	80024	109457	118819	100974	92103	98318	97695	134512	157027	159650	171745
Statistical discrepancy	...	...	−4642	2151	−5069	−13408	−11005	−35511	−73449	−58125	−89892	−107430
equals: Gross domestic product	442347	455135	466603	497527	514442	536189	560229	583840	609793	642441	680206	718127[a]

a Data for 1997 are preliminary estimates.

1.3 Cost components of the gross domestic product

Million Bangladesh taka	1986	1987	1988	1989	1990	1991	1992	1993	1994	1995	1996	1997
1 Indirect taxes, net	30082	32695	37601	41807	50070	57492	65589	73150	88073	97990	109800	131220
2 Consumption of fixed capital	36665	41247	46485	51641	58860	63882	68239	74942	83508	93521	100788	110089
3 Compensation of employees paid by resident producers to	...	...	...	...	...	...	...	...	...	...	...	...
4 Operating surplus	...	...	...	...	...	...	...	...	...	...	...	...
equals: Gross domestic product	539201	597136	659598	737571	834392	906502	948065	1030365	1170261	1301600	1403045	1540923[a]

a Data for 1997 are preliminary estimates.

1.8 Capital transactions of the nation, summary

Million Bangladesh taka	1986	1987	1988	1989	1990	1991	1992	1993	1994	1995	1996	1997
Finance of gross capital formation												
Gross saving	...	...	61801	67629	90632	117960	136882	153807	187868	185520	207921	228598
1 Consumption of fixed capital	...	...	46485	51641	58860	63882	68239	74942	83508	93521	100788	110089
2 Net saving	...	...	15316	15988	31772	54078	68643	78865	104360	91999	107133	118509
less: Surplus of the nation on current transactions	...	...	−14428	−26798	−5323	8109	4316	11193	−7592	−32510	−62651	−49036
Statistical discrepancy	...	...	4481	...	...	...	1324	...	−809	3170	−28145	−27127
Finance of gross capital formation	...	...	80710	94427	95955	109851	133890	142614	194651	221200	242427	250507[a]
Gross capital formation												
Increase in stocks	...	...	14720	−12853	8735	−2889	13100	−12012	10841	...	...	...
Gross fixed capital formation	...	...	65990	107280	87220	112740	120790	154626	183810	...	...	...
Gross capital formation	...	...	80710	94427	95955	109851	133890	142614	194651	221200	242427	250507[a]

a Data for 1997 are preliminary estimates.

1.10 Gross domestic product by kind of activity, in current prices

Million Bangladesh taka	1986	1987	1988	1989	1990	1991	1992	1993	1994	1995	1996	1997
1 Agriculture, hunting, forestry and fishing	219761	231623	245392	271790	300596	312438	288842	305888	361367	389986	411632	444797
2 Mining and quarrying	4	3	4	89	112	134	160	190	209	282	365	457
3 Manufacturing	47631	50437	55608	64506	72801	82571	92009	101463	112739	124411	130496	145115
4 Electricity, gas and water	3545	4597	6719	8824	11201	14011	17002	20534	23646	28630	30318	32918
5 Construction	28839	34602	39262	43110	47261	53590	56717	60395	69209	76599	82863	91544
6 Wholesale and retail trade, restaurants and hotels	48028	53073	58103	65251	72309	78282	78306	86156	100548	117461	124996	137433
7 Transport, storage and communication	61901	65945	71774	75061	97697	108672	122466	129221	139049	148238	161161	172946
8 Finance, insurance, real estate and business services	54960	66188	78442	87897	97229	104754	106985	118814	129996	150940	163618	176882

Bangladesh

Million Bangladesh taka	1986	1987	1988	1989	1990	1991	1992	1993	1994	1995	1996	1997
9 Community, social and personal services	53665	65933	75091	88279	96995	108644	136368	152664	171190	194311	217646	247254
Total, Industries	518334	572401	630395	704807	796201	863096	898855	975325	1107953	1230858	1323095	1449346
Producers of government services	20867	24735	29203	32764	38191	43406	49210	55040	62308	70742	79950	91577
Other producers	...	...	...	...	...	...	...	...	...	...	...	...
Subtotal	539201	597136	659598	737571	834392	906502	948065	1030365	1170261	1301600	1403045	1540923
less: Imputed bank service charge	...	...	...	...	...	...	...	...	...	...	...	...
plus: Import duties	...	...	...	...	...	...	...	...	...	...	...	...
plus: Value added tax	...	...	...	...	...	...	...	...	...	...	...	...
plus: Other adjustments	...	...	...	...	...	...	...	...	...	...	...	...
equals: Gross domestic product	539201	597136	659598	737571	834392	906502	948065	1030365	1170261	1301600	1403045	1540923[a]

a Data for 1997 are preliminary estimates.

1.11 Gross domestic product by kind of activity, in constant prices

Million Bangladesh taka	1986	1987	1988	1989	1990	1991	1992	1993	1994	1995	1996	1997
At constant prices of: 1984												
1 Agriculture, hunting, forestry and fishing	176250	174901	173037	190354	193421	197662	201230	201915	199822	207126	220456	227325
2 Mining and quarrying	4	2	3	66	80	94	107	121	137	174	222	278
3 Manufacturing	44403	44682	45927	49256	50423	54117	59033	63665	69165	72823	75401	81480
4 Electricity, gas and water	3217	3743	4822	5561	6704	7876	8933	10184	11339	12460	12668	13403
5 Construction	24469	27475	28816	29749	31087	32471	34032	36074	38593	40146	42098	44708
6 Wholesale and retail trade, restaurants and hotels	41845	43311	45423	46853	48712	50615	50631	53284	58669	64544	68797	73069
7 Transport, storage and communication	52341	54293	56611	59024	60840	63349	66416	70089	74203	77889	82949	88506
8 Finance, insurance, real estate and business services	46323	47873	49334	50862	52585	54354	52499	54455	56547	58682	60953	63331
9 Community, social and personal services	36304	40302	42791	45439	48256	51467	61108	65569	70356	75064	80318	85940
Total, Industries	425156	436582	446764	477164	492108	512005	533989	555356	578831	608908	643862	678040
Producers of government services	17191	18553	19839	20363	22334	24184	26240	28484	30962	33533	36344	40087
Other producers	...	...	...	...	...	...	...	...	...	...	...	...
Subtotal	442347	455135	466603	497527	514442	536189	560229	583840	609793	642441	680206	718127
less: Imputed bank service charge	...	...	...	...	...	...	...	...	...	...	...	...
plus: Import duties	...	...	...	...	...	...	...	...	...	...	...	...
plus: Value added tax	...	...	...	...	...	...	...	...	...	...	...	...
plus: Other adjustments	...	...	...	...	...	...	...	...	...	...	...	...
equals: Gross domestic product	442347	455135	466603	497527	514442	536189	560229	583840	609793	642441	680206	718127[a]

a Data for 1997 are preliminary estimates.

1.12 Relations among national accounting aggregates

Million Bangladesh taka	1986	1987	1988	1989	1990	1991	1992	1993	1994	1995	1996	1997
Gross domestic product	539201	597136	659598	737571	834392	906502	948065	1030365	1170261	1301600	1403045	1540923[a]
plus: Net factor income from the rest of the world	15548	20457	22529	22266	26513	33851	38798	48637	55671	60032	71028	75386
equals: Gross national product	554749	617593	682127	759837	860905	940353	986863	1079002	1225932	1361632	1474073	1616309

Bangladesh

Million Bangladesh taka	1986	1987	1988	1989	1990	1991	1992	1993	1994	1995	1996	1997
less: Consumption of fixed capital	36665	41247	46485	51641	58860	63882	68239	74942	83508	93521	100788	110089
equals: National income	518084	576346	635642	708196	802045	876471	918624	1004060	1142424	1268111	1373285	1506220
plus: Net current transfers from the rest of the world	23560	25786	21854	25265	29663	31176	32026	28404	35783	27672	31479	31479
equals: National disposable income	541644	602132	657496	733461	831708	907647	950650	1032464	1178207	1295783	1404764	1537699
less: Final consumption	520236	579398	642180	717473	799936	853569	882007	953599	1073847	1203784	1297631	1419190
equals: Net saving	21408	22734	15316	15988	31772	54078	68643	78865	104360	91999	107133	118509
less: Surplus of the nation on current transactions	−11417	−10325	−14428	−26798	−5323	8109	1668	11193	−7592	−32510	−62651	−49036
Statistical discrepancy	...	...	4481	...	...	...	−1324	...	−809	3170	−28145	−27127
equals: Net capital formation	32825	33059	34225	42786	37095	45969	65651	67672	111143	127679	141639	140418

a Data for 1997 are preliminary estimates.

2.1 Government final consumption expenditure by function, in current prices

Million Bangladesh taka	1986	1987	1988	1989	1990	1991	1992	1993	1994	1995	1996	1997
1 General public services	10481	11855	12972	17441	18211	23430	24565	25912	23708	...	...	...
2 Defence	6677	7510	9242	10192	10307	11900	15729	15043	16797	...	...	...
3 Public order and safety	3517	4287	4494	4856	5557	6500	7784	8022	8329	...	...	...
4 Education	4698	5533	9602	7346	7172	8424	9955	10689	11512	...	...	...
5 Health	2505	3626	3978	4550	5150	6557	8364	7520	8405	...	...	...
6 Social security and welfare	382	383	519	541	526	587	720	1103	1208	...	...	...
7 Housing and community amenities	1078	1466	1645	2396	2049	2450	2607	2299	2154	...	...	...
8 Recreational, cultural and religious affairs	179	211	216	339	265	250	249	399	383	...	...	...
9 Economic services	6150	7864	12984	17385	14355	14337	17879	19530	20185	...	...	...
A Fuel and energy	1170	936	1109	1821	1514	1789	4597	3612	3023	...	...	...
B Agriculture, hunting, forestry and fishing	2662	4345	7162	8837	6301	5866	5745	7674	9377	...	...	...
C Mining (except fuels), manufacturing and construction	1246	1444	1793	2586	3340	2507	2396	1489	1959	...	...	...
D Transportation and communication	852	897	2636	3831	2850	3766	4621	6215	5243	...	...	...
E Other economic affairs	220	242	284	310	350	409	520	540	583	...	...	...
10 Other functions	25578	27234	34803	38172	51140	50502	46452	56763	68117	...	...	...
Total government final consumption expenditures	61245	69969	90455	103218	114732	124937	134304	147280	160798	...	...	...

2.3 Total government outlays by function and type

Million Bangladesh taka — Fiscal year beginning 1 July

1986

	Final consumption expenditures Total	Compensation of employees	Other	Subsidies	Other current transfers and property income	Total current disbursements	Gross capital formation	Other capital outlays	Total outlays
1 General public services	10481	...	...	697	2394	13572	133	−	13705
2 Defence	6677	...	...	−	2	6679	580	−	7259
3 Public order and safety	3517	...	...	−	1	3518	417	−	3935
4 Education	4698	...	...	−	3386	8084	1164	33	9281

Bangladesh

Million Bangladesh taka — Fiscal year beginning 1 July

1986

	Total (Final consumption)	Compensation of employees	Other	Subsidies	Other current transfers and property income	Total current disbursements	Gross capital formation	Other capital outlays	Total outlays
5 Health	2505	...	...	12	34	2551	850	1	3402
6 Social security and welfare	382	...	...	–	36	418	151	21	590
7 Housing and community amenities	1078	...	...	–	19	1097	1433	7	2537
8 Recreational, cultural and religious affairs	179	...	...	–	205	384	1	–	385
9 Economic services	6150	...	...	53	1611	7814	28374	130	36318
A Fuel and energy	1170	...	...	39	488	1697	13362	29	15088
B Agriculture, hunting, forestry and fishing	2662	...	...	7	266	2935	2536	34	5505
C Mining (except fuels), manufacturing and construction	1246	...	...	7	324	1577	6649	62	8288
D Transportation and communication	852	...	...	–	73	925	5827	5	6757
E Other economic affairs	220	...	...	–	460	680	–	–	680
10 Other functions	25578	...	...	–	–	25578	114	5	25697
Total	61245	...	...	762	7688	69695	33217	197	103109

1987

	Total (Final consumption)	Compensation of employees	Other	Subsidies	Other current transfers and property income	Total current disbursements	Gross capital formation	Other capital outlays	Total outlays
1 General public services	11855	...	...	824	3555	16234	241	4	16479
2 Defence	7510	...	...	–	–	7510	652	–	8162
3 Public order and safety	4287	...	...	–	–	4287	299	–	4586
4 Education	5533	...	...	209	3746	9488	1433	2	10923
5 Health	3626	...	...	–	3	3629	1066	2	4697
6 Social security and welfare	383	...	...	2	48	433	269	33	735
7 Housing and community amenities	1466	...	...	–	17	1483	2261	64	3808
8 Recreational, cultural and religious affairs	211	...	...	–	178	389	7	–	396
9 Economic services	7864	...	...	76	3387	11327	25989	359	37675
A Fuel and energy	936	...	...	22	1709	2667	11378	93	14138
B Agriculture, hunting, forestry and fishing	4345	...	...	50	399	4794	4177	175	9146
C Mining (except fuels), manufacturing and construction	1444	...	...	3	622	2069	3399	88	5556
D Transportation and communication	897	...	...	1	224	1122	6993	3	8118
E Other economic affairs	242	...	...	–	433	675	42	–	717
10 Other functions	27234	...	...	–	6	27240	54	–	27294
Total	69969	...	...	1111	10940	82020	32271	464	114755

Bangladesh

1988

	Final consumption expenditures Total	Compensation of employees	Other	Subsidies	Other current transfers and property income	Total current disbursements	Gross capital formation	Other capital outlays	Total outlays
1 General public services	12972	...	...	7049	6045	26066	243	6	26315
2 Defence	9242	...	...	–	–	9242	803	–	10045
3 Public order and safety	4494	...	...	15	5	4514	595	–	5109
4 Education	9602	...	...	2	244	9848	1435	8	11291
5 Health	3978	...	...	14	66	4058	1451	4	5513
6 Social security and welfare	519	...	...	2	–	521	328	36	885
7 Housing and community amenities	1645	...	...	–	62	1707	1408	36	3151
8 Recreational, cultural and religious affairs	216	...	...	–	181	397	2	–	399
9 Economic services	12984	...	...	1651	4759	19394	25600	582	45576
A Fuel and energy	1109	...	...	33	3121	4263	8790	99	13152
B Agriculture, hunting, forestry and fishing	7162	...	...	1586	474	9222	3231	460	12913
C Mining (except fuels), manufacturing and construction	1793	...	...	32	280	2105	4425	21	6551
D Transportation and communication	2636	...	...	–	119	2755	9154	2	11911
E Other economic affairs	284	...	...	–	765	1049	–	–	1049
10 Other functions	34803	...	...	–	3	34806	39	–	34845
Total	90455	...	...	8733	11365	110553	31904	672	143129

1989

	Final consumption expenditures Total	Compensation of employees	Other	Subsidies	Other current transfers and property income	Total current disbursements	Gross capital formation	Other capital outlays	Total outlays
1 General public services	17441	...	...	7916	1408	26765	178	4	26947
2 Defence	10192	...	...	–	3	10195	885	–	11080
3 Public order and safety	4856	...	...	278	4	5138	698	–	5836
4 Education	7346	...	...	4	4408	11758	1744	4	13506
5 Health	4550	...	...	–	43	4593	1646	–	6239
6 Social security and welfare	541	...	...	–	64	605	222	12	839
7 Housing and community amenities	2396	...	...	17	63	2476	2367	202	5045
8 Recreational, cultural and religious affairs	339	...	...	–	118	457	3	–	460
9 Economic services	17385	...	...	2066	3309	22760	27909	451	51120
A Fuel and energy	1821	...	...	36	1049	2906	10486	96	13488
B Agriculture, hunting, forestry and fishing	8837	...	...	2028	1087	11952	4563	248	16763
C Mining (except fuels), manufacturing and construction	2586	...	...	2	319	2907	4242	99	7248
D Transportation and communication	3831	...	...	–	262	4093	8618	8	12719
E Other economic affairs	310	...	...	–	592	902	–	–	902
10 Other functions	38172	...	...	1	–	38173	27	–	38200
Total	103218	...	...	10282	9420	122920	35679	673	159272

Bangladesh

1990

	Final consumption expenditures Total	Compensation of employees	Other	Subsidies	Other current transfers and property income	Total current disbursements	Gross capital formation	Other capital outlays	Total outlays
1 General public services	18211	...	...	7618	5238	31067	270	2	31339
2 Defence	10307	...	...	–	3	10310	895	–	11205
3 Public order and safety	5557	...	...	–	–	5557	373	–	5930
4 Education	7172	...	...	9	4569	11750	775	3	12528
5 Health	5150	...	...	–	46	5196	1951	–	7147
6 Social security and welfare	526	...	...	–	70	596	268	42	906
7 Housing and community amenities	2049	...	...	6	1	2056	2082	14	4152
8 Recreational, cultural and religious affairs	265	...	...	–	237	502	2	–	504
9 Economic services	14355	...	...	1518	3143	19016	32436	256	51708
A Fuel and energy	1514	...	...	20	909	2443	9648	33	12124
B Agriculture, hunting, forestry and fishing	6301	...	...	1494	749	8544	5793	208	14545
C Mining (except fuels), manufacturing and construction	3340	...	...	4	803	4147	7529	15	11691
D Transportation and communication	2850	...	...	–	135	2985	9466	–	12451
E Other economic affairs	350	...	...	–	547	897	–	–	897
10 Other functions	51140	...	...	–	–	51140	103	–	51243
Total	114732	...	...	9151	13307	137190	39155	317	176662

1991

	Final consumption expenditures Total	Compensation of employees	Other	Subsidies	Other current transfers and property income	Total current disbursements	Gross capital formation	Other capital outlays	Total outlays
1 General public services	23430	...	...	5716	1675	30821	563	–	31384
2 Defence	11900	...	...	–	3	11903	1034	–	12937
3 Public order and safety	6500	...	...	–	–	6500	417	–	6917
4 Education	8424	...	...	17	5380	13821	1105	46	14972
5 Health	6557	...	...	3	80	6640	1661	–	8301
6 Social security and welfare	587	...	...	–	79	666	281	18	965
7 Housing and community amenities	2450	...	...	–	–	2450	2782	222	5454
8 Recreational, cultural and religious affairs	250	...	...	–	281	531	2	–	533
9 Economic services	14337	...	...	1624	3886	19847	36712	510	57069
A Fuel and energy	1789	...	...	35	2238	4062	11347	79	15488
B Agriculture, hunting, forestry and fishing	5866	...	...	1579	367	7812	6673	388	14873
C Mining (except fuels), manufacturing and construction	2507	...	...	10	430	2947	5237	41	8225
D Transportation and communication	3766	...	...	–	234	4000	13454	2	17456
E Other economic affairs	409	...	...	–	617	1026	1	–	1027
10 Other functions	50502	...	...	–	–	50502	65	–	50567
Total	124937	...	...	7360	11384	143681	44622	796	189099

Bangladesh

1992

	Final consumption expenditures Total	Compensation of employees	Other	Subsidies	Other current transfers and property income	Total current disbursements	Gross capital formation	Other capital outlays	Total outlays
1 General public services	24565	...	...	3128	1099	28792	1028	–	29820
2 Defence	15729	...	...	–	–	15729	126	–	15855
3 Public order and safety	7784	...	...	–	2	7786	354	–	8140
4 Education	9955	...	...	–	6708	16663	375	6	17044
5 Health	8364	...	...	–	84	8448	2879	29	11356
6 Social security and welfare	720	...	...	–	115	835	171	–	1006
7 Housing and community amenities	2607	...	...	–	51	2658	955	268	3881
8 Recreational, cultural and religious affairs	249	...	...	–	–	249	1	–	250
9 Economic services	17879	...	...	1431	4787	24097	38338	1870	64305
A Fuel and energy	4597	...	...	115	1948	6660	17541	175	24376
B Agriculture, hunting, forestry and fishing	5745	...	...	414	760	6919	8546	1394	16859
C Mining (except fuels), manufacturing and construction	2396	...	...	6	690	3092	5474	153	8719
D Transportation and communication	4621	...	...	896	418	5935	6770	148	12853
E Other economic affairs	520	...	...	–	971	1491	7	–	1498
10 Other functions	46452	...	...	–	–	46452	120	–	46572
Total	134304	...	...	4559	12846	151709	44347	2173	198229

1993

	Final consumption expenditures Total	Compensation of employees	Other	Subsidies	Other current transfers and property income	Total current disbursements	Gross capital formation	Other capital outlays	Total outlays
1 General public services	25912	...	...	2416	1525	29853	506	–	30359
2 Defence	15043	...	...	–	4	15047	1308	–	16355
3 Public order and safety	8022	...	...	–	2	8024	542	–	8566
4 Education	10689	...	...	1842	7471	20002	3875	78	23955
5 Health	7520	...	...	3382	119	11021	3149	–	14170
6 Social security and welfare	1103	...	...	–	132	1235	411	135	1781
7 Housing and community amenities	2299	...	...	–	7	2306	2323	166	4795
8 Recreational, cultural and religious affairs	399	...	...	–	414	813	12	–	825
9 Economic services	19530	...	...	34	8753	28317	47852	3665	79834
A Fuel and energy	3612	...	...	7	5388	9007	17283	98	26388
B Agriculture, hunting, forestry and fishing	7674	...	...	7	896	8577	6959	960	16496
C Mining (except fuels), manufacturing and construction	1489	...	...	7	374	1870	5149	112	7131
D Transportation and communication	6215	...	...	13	955	7183	18447	2495	28125
E Other economic affairs	540	...	...	–	1140	1680	14	–	1694
10 Other functions	56763	...	...	12	–	56775	140	–	56915
Total	147280	...	...	7686	18427	173393	60118	4044	237555

Bangladesh

	1994 Total (Final consumption)	Compensation of employees	Other	Subsidies	Other current transfers and property income	Total current disbursements	Gross capital formation	Other capital outlays	Total outlays
1 General public services	23708	...	...	1726	1535	26969	1796	16	28781
2 Defence	16797	...	...	–	4	16801	1460	–	18261
3 Public order and safety	8329	...	...	–	2	8331	538	–	8869
4 Education	11512	...	...	2339	7839	21690	6124	80	27894
5 Health	8405	...	...	5164	129	13698	1918	–	15616
6 Social security and welfare	1208	...	...	13	380	1601	767	153	2521
7 Housing and community amenities	2154	...	...	–	3	2157	2365	565	5087
8 Recreational, cultural and religious affairs	383	...	...	–	295	678	13	–	691
9 Economic services	20185	...	...	23	6625	26833	49004	4269	80106
A Fuel and energy	3023	...	...	8	3207	6238	14870	78	21186
B Agriculture, hunting, forestry and fishing	9377	...	...	–	1015	10392	8569	1441	20402
C Mining (except fuels), manufacturing and construction	1959	...	...	15	454	2428	6243	451	9122
D Transportation and communication	5243	...	...	–	575	5818	19309	2299	27426
E Other economic affairs	583	...	...	–	1374	1957	13	–	1970
10 Other functions	68117	...	...	13	–	68130	211	5	68346
Total	160798	...	...	9278	16812	186888	64196	5088	256172

Barbados

Source

Reply to the United Nations National Accounts Questionnaire from the Barbados Statistical Service, Garrison, St. Michael. Information on concepts, sources and methods of estimation utilized, are published by the same service in *National Income and Product*.

General note

The estimates shown in the following tables have been prepared in accordance with the United Nations System of National Accounts (1968 SNA) so far as the existing data would permit.

1.1 Expenditure on the gross domestic product, in current prices

Million Barbados dollars

	1986	1987	1988	1989	1990	1991	1992	1993	1994	1995	1996	1997
1 Government final consumption expenditure	469	498	537	614	694	642	640	732	707	759	...	...
2 Private final consumption expenditure	1692	1934	2004	2145	2188	2262	1993	1977	2142	2543	...	...
3 Gross capital formation	424	467	543	656	648	580	301	420	465	520	...	...
A Increase in stocks	−4	7	8	11	−3	30	−49	14	23	13	...	...
B Gross fixed capital formation	427	460	535	645	651	551	350	440	442	508	...	...
4 Exports of goods and services	1496	1340	1510	1724	1689	1610	1587	1709	1812	1894	...	...
5 less: Imports of goods and services	1435	1325	1495	1725	1780	1701	1344	1537	1651	1951	...	...
equals: Gross domestic product	2646	2914	3099	3414	3440	3393	3177	3301	3474	3765	...	...

1.10 Gross domestic product by kind of activity, in current prices

Million Barbados dollars

	1986	1987	1988	1989	1990	1991	1992	1993	1994	1995	1996	1997
1 Agriculture, hunting, forestry and fishing	146	172	173	153	160	161	153	162	150	203	...	...
2 Mining and quarrying	17	18	17	18	20	19	17	15	17	18	...	...
3 Manufacturing	229	224	240	233	238	231	203	207	208	216	...	...
4 Electricity, gas and water	72	81	85	92	92	100	105	106	102	109	...	...
5 Construction	131	144	170	197	194	162	113	121	134	150	...	...
6 Wholesale and retail trade, restaurants and hotels	720	800	863	942	928	891	816	869	924	1009	...	...
7 Transport, storage and communication	198	225	227	228	244	254	249	255	270	291	...	...
8 Finance, insurance, real estate and business services	311	313	358	425	433	436	453	437	472	506	...	...
9 Community, social and personal services	94	97	99	106	109	110	108	111	122	132	...	...
Total, Industries	1918	2074	2232	2393	2417	2363	2216	2282	2398	2635	...	...
Producers of government services	379	425	435	503	549	530	487	509	523	539	...	...
Other producers	...	...	...	...	...	...	...	...	...	...	...	...
Subtotal [a]	2297	2499	2668	2896	2965	2893	2703	2791	2921	3173	...	...

Barbados

Million Barbados dollars

	1986	1987	1988	1989	1990	1991	1992	1993	1994	1995	1996	1997
less: Imputed bank service charge	...	...	...	...	...	...	...	...	...	...	...	...
plus: Import duties	...	...	...	...	...	...	...	...	...	...	...	...
plus: Value added tax	...	...	...	...	...	...	...	...	...	...	...	...
plus: Other adjustments [b]	349	415	432	518	475	500	474	510	553	592	...	...
equals: Gross domestic product	2646	2914	3099	3414	3440	3393	3177	3301	3474	3765	...	...

a Gross domestic product in factor values.   b Item "Other adjustments" refers to indirect taxes net of subsidies.

1.11 Gross domestic product by kind of activity, in constant prices

Million Barbados dollars

	1986	1987	1988	1989	1990	1991	1992	1993	1994	1995	1996	1997
At constant prices of: 1974												
1 Agriculture, hunting, forestry and fishing	79	70	66	60	65	62	56	54	53	50	...	...
2 Mining and quarrying	8	7	7	6	6	6	6	6	7	7	...	...
3 Manufacturing	86	80	86	90	88	83	76	74	79	85	...	...
4 Electricity, gas and water	23	24	25	26	26	27	28	28	29	30	...	...
5 Construction	54	57	62	67	60	56	51	54	54	57	...	...
6 Wholesale and retail trade, restaurants and hotels	260	284	300	316	299	277	262	270	288	296	...	...
7 Transport, storage and communication	61	64	65	69	63	68	65	66	68	70	...	...
8 Finance, insurance, real estate and business services	145	146	150	156	151	148	140	141	144	148		
9 Community, social and personal services											...	...
Total, Industries	715	732	760	790	760	726	684	692	722	743	...	...
Producers of government services	112	116	117	119	120	118	108	112	112	113	...	...
Other producers	...	...	...	...	...	...	...	...	...	...	...	...
Subtotal [a]	827	848	878	909	881	844	792	804	834	857	...	...
less: Imputed bank service charge	...	...	...	...	...	...	...	...	...	...	...	...
plus: Import duties	...	...	...	...	...	...	...	...	...	...	...	...
plus: Value added tax	...	...	...	...	...	...	...	...	...	...	...	...
plus: Other adjustments	...	...	...	...	...	...	...	...	...	...	...	...
equals: Gross domestic product	...	...	...	...	...	...	...	...	...	...	...	...

a Gross domestic product in factor values.

Belarus

Source

Reply to the United Nations National Accounts Questionnaire from the State Committee of the Republic of Belarus on Statistics and Analysis.

General note

The estimates shown in the following tables have been prepared in accordance with the United Nations System of National Accounts (SNA) so far as existing data would permit.

1.1 Expenditure on the gross domestic product, in current prices

Thousand million roubles

	1986	1987	1988	1989	1990	1991	1992	1993	1994	1995	1996	1997
1 Government final consumption expenditure	...	...	...	...	10	18	142	1751	3581	23157	36627	...
2 Private final consumption expenditure	...	...	...	...	20	40	468	5723	10717	72356	109603	...
A Households	...	...	...	...	19	38	443	5479	10135	68635	104226	...
B Private non-profit institutions serving households	...	...	...	...	1	2	25	244	581	3721	5377	...
3 Gross capital formation	...	...	...	...	12	25	294	4043	5860	30047	45119	...
A Increase in stocks	...	...	...	...	2	6	61	703	−58	63	4681	...
B Gross fixed capital formation	...	...	...	...	10	19	233	3340	5918	29984	40438	...
4 Exports of goods and services	...	...	...	...	20	32	548	6515	12644	59890	88875	...
5 less: Imports of goods and services	...	...	...	...	19	29	535	8172	14988	65637	96050	...
equals: Gross domestic product	...	...	...	...	43	87	917	9859	17815	119813	184174	...

1.2 Expenditure on the gross domestic product, in constant prices

Thousand million roubles

	1986	1987	1988	1989	1990	1991	1992	1993	1994	1995	1996	1997
At constant prices of: 1990												
1991												
1992												
1993												
1994												
1995												
1 Government final consumption expenditure	...	...	...	...	10	10						...
						18	15					
							142	135				
								1751	165			
									3581	3477		
										23156	23118	
2 Private final consumption expenditure	...	...	...	...	20	19						...
						40	37					
							468	461				
								5723	491			
									10717	9468		
										72357	75486	

Belarus

Thousand million roubles

	1986	1987	1988	1989	1990	1991	1992	1993	1994	1995	1996	1997
At constant prices of:	1990											
	1991											
	1992											
	1993											
	1994											
	1995											
A Households	...	...	...	...	19	18						...
						38						
							35					
							443	436				
								5479	468			
									10135	8890		
										68636	71724	
B Private non-profit institutions serving households	...	...	...	...	12	12						...
						2	2					
							25	25				
								244	23			
									581	578		
										3721	3762	
3 Gross capital formation	...	...	...	...	12	13						...
						25	21					
							294	276				
								4043	285			
									5860	4181		
										30047	32218	
A Increase in stocks	...	...	...	...	2	3						...
						6	6					
							61	60				
								703	−3			
									−58	13		
										63	3165	
B Gross fixed capital formation	...	...	...	...	10	10						...
						19	16					
							233	216				
								3340	288			
									5918	4168		
										29984	29053	
4 Exports of goods and services	...	...	...	...	20	20						...
						32	21					
							548	340				
								6515	653			
									12644	9104		
										59890	65038	
5 less: Imports of goods and services	...	...	...	...	19	19						...
						29	17					
							535	364				
								8172	733			
									14988	10260		
										65637	72665	
equals: Gross domestic product	...	...	...	...	43	42						...
						87	78					
							917	847				
								9859	862			
									17815	15970		
										119813	123195	

1.3 Cost components of the gross domestic product

Thousand million roubles

	1986	1987	1988	1989	1990	1991	1992	1993	1994	1995	1996	1997
1 Indirect taxes, net	...	...	...	...	3	4	74	963	2147	16497	27217	...
A Indirect taxes	...	...	...	...	10	12	177	1986	3253	22589	34649	...
B less: Subsidies	...	...	...	...	7	7	103	1023	1106	6091	7432	...
2 Consumption of fixed capital	...	...	...	...	6	12	153	2033	3485	19873	...	...
3 Compensation of employees paid by resident producers to ..	...	...	...	...	20	36	383	5119	7904	52340	81976	...
A Resident households	...	...	...	...	20	36	383	5119	7904	52340	81976	...

Belarus

Thousand million roubles

	1986	1987	1988	1989	1990	1991	1992	1993	1994	1995	1996	1997
B Rest of the world	...	...	...	...	...	...	...	...	...	...	...	...
4 Operating surplus	...	...	...	...	14	34	306	1744	4279	31103	74981	...
A Corporate and quasi-corporate enterprises	...	...	...	...	12	29	213	742	2701	18821	...	...
B Private unincorporated enterprises	...	...	...	...	2	5	93	1001	1572	12223	...	...
C General government	...	...	...	...	...	...	...	2	6	59	...	...
equals: Gross domestic product	...	...	...	...	43	87	917	9859	17815	119813	184174	...

1.4 General government current receipts and disbursements

Thousand million roubles

	1986	1987	1988	1989	1990	1991	1992	1993	1994	1995	1996	1997
Receipts												
1 Operating surplus	...	...	...	...	...	...	...	2	6	59	...	...
2 Property and entrepreneurial income	...	...	...	...	–	–	14	–	1	10	...	...
3 Taxes, fees and contributions	...	...	...	...	15	24	366	4630	7539	48052	...	...
A Indirect taxes	...	...	...	...	10	12	177	1986	3253	22589	...	...
B Direct taxes	...	...	...	...	3	8	98	1324	2465	11705	...	...
C Social security contributions	...	...	...	...	2	4	91	1321	1821	13758	...	...
D Compulsory fees, fines and penalties	...	...	...	...	...	...	...	...	...	...	...	...
4 Other current transfers	...	...	...	...	–	–	25	217	220	1502	...	...
Total current receipts of general government	...	...	...	...	15	24	406	4849	7765	49624	...	...
Disbursements												
1 Government final consumption expenditure	...	...	...	...	10	18	142	1751	3581	23157	...	...
A Compensation of employees	...	...	...	...	4	8	67	880	1606	11436	...	...
B Consumption of fixed capital	...	...	...	...	1	1	13	186	336	2221	...	...
C Purchases of goods and services, net	...	...	...	...	6	9	60	680	1630	9366	...	...
D less: Own-account fixed capital formation	...	...	...	...	...	...	...	...	...	...	...	...
E Indirect taxes paid, net	...	...	...	...	...	...	–	4	10	133	...	...
2 Property income	...	...	...	...	–	2	6	48	26	80	...	...
A Interest	...	...	...	...	–	2	6	48	26	80	...	...
B Net land rent and royalties	...	...	...	...	–	–	–	–	...	...	...	...
3 Subsidies	...	...	...	...	7	7	103	1023	1106	6091	...	...
4 Other current transfers	...	...	...	...	4	9	99	1358	2402	18353	...	...
A Social security benefits	...	...	...	...	4	8	77	1087	1645	14184	...	...
B Social assistance grants	...	...	...	...	...	...	...	...	...	...	...	...
C Other	...	...	...	...	–	–	22	270	756	4169	...	...
5 Net saving	...	...	...	...	–6	–12	56	670	650	1944	...	...
Total current disbursements and net saving of general government	...	...	...	...	15	24	406	4849	7765	49624	...	...

Belarus

1.5 Current income and outlay of corporate and quasi-corporate enterprises, summary

Thousand million roubles

	1986	1987	1988	1989	1990	1991	1992	1993	1994	1995	1996	1997
Receipts												
1 Operating surplus	...	...	...	...	12	29	213	742	2701	18821	...	...
2 Property and entrepreneurial income received	...	...	...	...	...	3	36	1209	2645	13463	...	...
3 Current transfers	...	...	...	...	1	1	8	135	360	1877	...	...
Total current receipts	...	...	...	...	13	33	257	2087	5705	34160	...	...
Disbursements												
1 Property and entrepreneurial income	...	...	...	...	–	2	47	1225	2837	15847	...	...
2 Direct taxes and other current payments to general government	...	...	...	...	2	6	78	1094	2057	8818	...	...
3 Other current transfers	...	...	...	...	2	4	48	644	2327	8244	...	...
4 Net saving	...	...	...	...	8	20	84	–877	–1516	1251	...	...
Total current disbursements and net saving	...	...	...	...	13	33	257	2087	5705	34160	...	...

1.6 Current income and outlay of households and non-profit institutions

Thousand million roubles

	1986	1987	1988	1989	1990	1991	1992	1993	1994	1995	1996	1997
Receipts												
1 Compensation of employees	...	...	...	...	20	36	383	5119	7904	52340	...	...
A From resident producers	...	...	...	...	20	36	383	5119	7904	52340	...	...
B From rest of the world	...	...	...	...	...	...	...	...	...	...	...	...
2 Operating surplus of private unincorporated enterprises	...	...	...	...	2	5	93	1001	1572	12223	...	...
3 Property and entrepreneurial income	...	...	...	...	–	1	4	70	196	2406	...	...
4 Current transfers	...	...	...	...	5	13	145	1932	4467	25932	...	...
A Social security benefits	...	...	...	...	4	9	79	1137	1715	14792	...	...
B Social assistance grants	...	...	...	...	...	...	...	...	...	...	...	...
C Other	...	...	...	...	2	4	66	795	2752	11139	...	...
Total current receipts	...	...	...	...	28	54	625	8122	14140	92901	...	...
Disbursements												
1 Private final consumption expenditure	...	...	...	...	20	40	468	5723	10717	72356	...	...
2 Property income	...	...	...	...	...	...	...	1	4	4	...	...
3 Direct taxes and other current transfers n.e.c. to general government	...	...	...	...	3	6	116	1632	2364	17798	...	...
A Social security contributions	...	...	...	...	2	4	93	1370	1890	14367	...	...
B Direct taxes	...	...	...	...	1	2	22	262	473	3431	...	...
C Fees, fines and penalties	...	...	...	...	...	...	...	...	...	...	...	...
4 Other current transfers	...	...	...	...	–	–	4	44	214	736	...	...
5 Net saving	...	...	...	...	4	7	37	721	841	2007	...	...
Total current disbursements and net saving	...	...	...	...	28	54	625	8122	14140	92901	...	...

Belarus

1.8 Capital transactions of the nation, summary

Thousand million roubles

	1986	1987	1988	1989	1990	1991	1992	1993	1994	1995	1996	1997
Finance of gross capital formation												
Gross saving	...	...	...	...	12	28	330	2547	3460	25075	38592	...
1 Consumption of fixed capital	...	...	...	...	6	12	153	2033	3485	19873	...	...
A General government	...	...	...	...	1	1	13	186	336	2221	...	...
B Corporate and quasi-corporate enterprises	...	...	...	...	5	10	134	1779	2963	16300	...	...
C Other	...	...	...	...	–	1	6	68	186	1351	...	...
2 Net saving	...	...	...	...	6	16	177	515	–25	5203	...	...
A General government	...	...	...	...	–6	–12	56	670	650	1944	...	...
B Corporate and quasi-corporate enterprises	...	...	...	...	8	20	84	–877	–1516	1251	...	...
C Other	...	...	...	...	4	7	37	721	841	2007	...	...
less: Surplus of the nation on current transactions	...	...	...	...	1	3	36	–1496	–2314	–4888	–5831	...
Statistical discrepancy	...	...	...	...	...	...	...	...	86	84	696	...
Finance of gross capital formation	...	...	...	...	12	25	294	4043	5860	30047	45119	...
Gross capital formation												
Increase in stocks	...	...	...	...	2	6	61	703	–58	63	4681	...
Gross fixed capital formation	...	...	...	...	10	19	233	3340	5918	29984	40438	...
1 General government	...	...	...	...	1	2	21	553	702	3408	...	...
2 Corporate and quasi-corporate enterprises	...	...	...	...	7	14	181	2137	3837	21937	...	...
3 Other	...	...	...	...	2	4	31	649	1379	4640	...	...
Gross capital formation	...	...	...	...	12	25	294	4043	5860	30047	45119	...

1.10 Gross domestic product by kind of activity, in current prices

Thousand million roubles

	1986	1987	1988	1989	1990	1991	1992	1993	1994	1995	1996	1997
1 Agriculture, hunting, forestry and fishing	...	...	...	...	10	18	208	1690	2418	19104	...	...
2 Mining and quarrying	...	...	...	...	–	–	1	11	18	117	...	...
3 Manufacturing	...	...	...	...	16	35	353	2861	4975	33922	...	...
4 Electricity, gas and water	...	...	...	...							...	...
5 Construction	...	...	...	...	3	6	64	777	992	6563	...	...
6 Wholesale and retail trade, restaurants and hotels	...	...	...	...	2	5	55	1034	2542	12463	...	...
7 Transport, storage and communication	...	...	...	...	3	5	80	1287	2204	15310	...	...
8 Finance, insurance, real estate and business services	...	...	...	...	–	2	19	914	1429	5844	...	...
9 Community, social and personal services	...	...	...	...	5	10	90	1263	2127	14494	...	...
Total, Industries	...	...	...	...	40	81	868	9836	16706	107816	...	...
Producers of government services	...	...	...	...	2	4	19	230	616	4237	...	...
Other producers	...	...	...	...	–	–	1	11	14	112	...	...
Subtotal	...	...	...	...	42	84	888	10077	17337	112165	...	...
less: Imputed bank service charge	...	...	...	...	...	1	16	829	1196	4128	...	...

Belarus

Thousand million roubles

	1986	1987	1988	1989	1990	1991	1992	1993	1994	1995	1996	1997
plus: Import duties	...	...	...	...	1	4	44	611	1674	11777	...	...
plus: Value added tax	...	...	...	...							...	...
plus: Other adjustments	...	...	...	...	...	...	...	...	...	...	...	...
equals: Gross domestic product	...	...	...	...	43	87	917	9859	17815	119813	...	...

1.11 Gross domestic product by kind of activity, in constant prices

Thousand million roubles

	1986	1987	1988	1989	1990	1991	1992	1993	1994	1995	1996	1997
At constant prices of:	1990											
	1991											
	1992											
	1993											
	1994											
1 Agriculture, hunting, forestry and fishing	...	...	...	...	10	10					...	...
						18	15					
							208	210				
								1690	144			
									2418	2355		
2 Mining and quarrying	...	...	...	...	–	–					...	...
							1	1				
								11	1			
									18	17		
3 Manufacturing	...	...	...	...	16	17					...	...
						35	33					
							353	318				
								2861	231			
									4975	4470		
4 Electricity, gas and water	...	...	...	...	...	...	...	...	...	...	...	...
										663		
5 Construction	...	...	...	...	3	3					...	...
						6	6					
							64	49				
								777	61			
									992			
6 Wholesale and retail trade, restaurants and hotels	...	...	...	...	2	2					...	...
						5	4					
							55	48				
								1034	109			
									2542	1964		
7 Transport, storage and communication	...	...	...	...	3	3					...	...
						5	4					
							80	70				
								1287	108			
									2204	1977		
8 Finance, insurance, real estate and business services	...	...	...	...	–	–					...	...
						2	2					
							19	21				
								914	113			
									1429	1668		
9 Community, social and personal services	...	...	...	...	5	5					...	...
						10	10					
							90	87				
								1263	125			
									2127	2071		
Total, Industries	...	...	...	...	40	40					...	...
						81	73					
							868	805				
								9836	891			
									16706	15184		

Belarus

Thousand million roubles

	1986	1987	1988	1989	1990	1991	1992	1993	1994	1995	1996	1997
At constant prices of:					1990	1991	1992	1993	1994			
Producers of government services	...	...	...	...	2	2					...	...
						4	2	18				
							19	230	21			
									616	604		
Other producers	...	...	...	...	–	–					...	...
							–	1	1			
							1	11	14	1		
										13		
Subtotal	...	...	...	...	42	41					...	...
						84	76	823	914			
							888	10077	17337	15802		
less: Imputed bank service charge	...	...	...	...	...	1	1	18	103	1405	...	...
							16	829	1196			
plus: Import duties	...	...	...	...	1	1	4	42	51	1574	...	...
						4	44	611	1674			
plus: Value added tax	...	...	...	...	...	...	...	...	...	...	...	...
plus: Other adjustments	...	...	...	...	...	...	...	...	...	...	...	...
equals: Gross domestic product	...	...	...	...	43	42					...	...
						87	78	847	862			
							917	9859	17815	15970		

175

Belgium

Source

Reply to the United Nations National Accounts Questionnaire from the Institut National de Statistique, Brussels. The official estimates are published annually by the Institut National in the July–August issue of the *Bulletin de Statistique*.

General note

The estimates shown in the following tables have been prepared in accordance with the United Nations System of National Accounts (1968 SNA) so far as the existing data would permit.

1.1 Expenditure on the gross domestic product, in current prices

Million Belgian francs

	1986	1987	1988	1989	1990	1991	1992	1993	1994	1995	1996	1997
1 Government final consumption expenditure	852550	856475	857185	884036	917652	987397	1027608	1088344	1139453	1181921	1205417	1251591
2 Private final consumption expenditure	3324731	3477779	3633172	3919071	4166130	4423563	4629464	4714894	4924045	5071235	5282002	5488027
3 Gross capital formation	766269	862124	1029814	1198250	1325093	1298388	1355391	1322488	1373088	1462779	1471325	1542766
A Increase in stocks [a]	−29543	8397	16148	19599	−2889	5737	7431	1403	24020	32567	21513	2822
B Gross fixed capital formation	795812	853727	1013666	1178651	1327982	1292651	1347960	1321085	1349068	1430212	1449812	1539944
Residential buildings	150684	169586	221446	272544	308633	282262	308327	322063	351200	385444	368047	389351
Non-residential buildings	275264	282235	318848	325666	348582	382831	411693	406501	413835	422229	414635	454735
Other construction and land improvement, etc.												
Other	369864	401906	473372	580441	670767	627558	627940	592521	584033	622539	667130	695858
4 Exports of goods and services	3293100	3322100	3758100	4347600	4464400	4573000	4677800	4591700	5042600	5394600	5649400	6326400
5 less: Imports of goods and services	3151800	3199800	3588800	4181600	4318900	4413400	4461700	4312200	4710300	5042400	5303000	5933300
equals: Gross domestic product	5084850	5318678	5689471	6167357	6554375	6868948	7228563	7405226	7768886	8068135	8305144	8675484

a Item "Increase in stocks" includes the statistical adjustment concerning gross capital formation.

1.2 Expenditure on the gross domestic product, in constant prices

Million Belgian francs

	1986	1987	1988	1989	1990	1991	1992	1993	1994	1995	1996	1997
At constant prices of: 1990												
1 Government final consumption expenditure	938690	939874	931249	922345	917652	937685	941027	952791	968825	975164	988750	996997
2 Private final consumption expenditure	3696948	3780484	3902833	4046881	4166130	4285205	4380880	4322356	4392581	4430343	4510223	4603343
3 Gross capital formation	852270	948217	1114704	1228822	1325093	1272215	1294865	1239772	1256441	1303016	1295474	1342605
A Increase in stocks [a]	−27082	13783	27406	17691	−2889	6491	12508	3336	21338	16328	2391	−20484
B Gross fixed capital formation	879352	934434	1087298	1211131	1327982	1265724	1282357	1236436	1235103	1286688	1293083	1363089
Residential buildings	176012	187710	239673	280503	308633	277462	289921	295249	312128	335418	314782	328218
Non-residential buildings	302607	311576	344135	334941	348582	376812	394173	381593	378412	378312	368969	400478
Other construction and land improvement, etc.												
Other	400733	435148	503490	595687	670767	611450	598263	559594	544563	572958	609332	634393

Belgium

Million Belgian francs

	1986	1987	1988	1989	1990	1991	1992	1993	1994	1995	1996	1997
	At constant prices of: 1990											
4 Exports of goods and services	3473300	3625200	3955900	4280900	4464400	4605000	4765500	4734100	5130800	5437900	5556600	5953300
5 less: Imports of goods and services	3232200	3429500	3763600	4117500	4318900	4440900	4623700	4589300	4917600	5155700	5270100	5602700
equals: Gross domestic product	5729008	5864275	6141086	6361448	6554375	6659205	6758572	6659719	6831047	6990723	7080947	7293545

a Item "Increase in stocks" includes the statistical adjustment concerning gross capital formation.

1.3 Cost components of the gross domestic product

Million Belgian francs

	1986	1987	1988	1989	1990	1991	1992	1993	1994	1995	1996	1997
1 Indirect taxes, net	421176	481763	513767	590934	614804	630214	684087	723355	800861	796019	853015	935140
A Indirect taxes	603799	653943	689439	749421	801449	832827	876474	918707	988660	992125	1052710	1111240
B less: Subsidies	182623	172180	175672	158487	186645	202613	192387	195352	187799	196106	199695	176100
2 Consumption of fixed capital	478624	508423	565642	602702	657487	681115	732112	738276	769176	808029	820769	863694
3 Compensation of employees paid by resident producers to	2786859	2857477	2974232	3124942	3389242	3639760	3827573	3919667	4058039	4179692	4256213	4391557
A Resident households	2778959	2849277	2965332	3114242	3376942	3624260	3808673	3898967	4036639	4157392	4231113	4364257
B Rest of the world	7900	8200	8900	10700	12300	15500	18900	20700	21400	22300	25100	27300
4 Operating surplus	1398191	1471015	1635830	1848779	1892842	1917859	1984791	2023928	2140810	2284395	2375147	2485093
A Corporate and quasi-corporate enterprises	501867	525414	615059	722388	704154	670492	671017	661395	721757	822213	861381	922141
B Private unincorporated enterprises	894703	943713	1019155	1125507	1189823	1247391	1311724	1360198	1416744	1457967	1508875	1558125
C General government	1621	1888	1616	884	−1135	−24	2050	2335	2309	4215	4891	4827
equals: Gross domestic product	5084850	5318678	5689471	6167357	6554375	6868948	7228563	7405226	7768886	8068135	8305144	8675484

1.4 General government current receipts and disbursements

Million Belgian francs

	1986	1987	1988	1989	1990	1991	1992	1993	1994	1995	1996	1997
	Receipts											
1 Operating surplus	1621	1888	1616	884	−1135	−24	2050	2335	2309	4215	4891	4827
2 Property and entrepreneurial income	57383	53186	54517	69447	78889	89601	81919	80668	64148	68329	80778	61819
3 Taxes, fees and contributions	2355328	2479362	2570535	2687516	2884546	3021848	3192019	3317956	3565339	3686919	3802165	4007852
A Indirect taxes	603799	653943	689439	749421	801449	832827	876474	918707	988660	992125	1052710	1111240
B Direct taxes	965490	991024	1016722	1021654	1098502	1122955	1175244	1209157	1366815	1453333	1492766	1595240
C Social security contributions	786039	834395	864374	916441	984595	1066066	1140301	1190092	1209864	1241461	1256689	1301372
D Compulsory fees, fines and penalties	...	...	...	...	...	...	...	...	...	...	...	...
4 Other current transfers [a]	131066	132447	137952	135944	145474	160006	169119	186277	193107	203767	214988	220687
Total current receipts of general government	2545398	2666883	2764620	2893791	3107774	3271431	3445107	3587236	3824903	3963230	4102822	4295185
	Disbursements											
1 Government final consumption expenditure	852550	856475	857185	884036	917652	987397	1027608	1088344	1139453	1181921	1205417	1251591
2 Property income	560573	557485	568195	629120	685512	691568	771125	793804	778540	719114	704472	679423
A Interest	560573	557485	568195	629120	685512	691568	771125	793804	778540	719114	704472	679423
B Net land rent and royalties	−	−	−	−	−	−	−	−	−	−	−	−
3 Subsidies	137996	129379	143543	133125	143689	150878	149961	155512	147168	154833	165716	142766
4 Other current transfers	1344633	1408491	1451636	1535897	1622295	1772321	1883836	1953739	2019886	2097910	2176528	2257565
A Social security benefits	1001473	1044116	1063835	1115419	1181986	1287841	1375822	1428863	1462304	1527552	1582216	1621204

Belgium

Million Belgian francs

	1986	1987	1988	1989	1990	1991	1992	1993	1994	1995	1996	1997
B Social assistance grants	122830	126881	136793	155528	164307	170943	182760	182929	197043	205576	210712	221306
C Other	220330	237494	251008	264950	276002	313537	325254	341947	360539	364782	383600	415055
5 Net saving	–350354	–284947	–255939	–288387	–261374	–330733	–387423	–404163	–260144	–190548	–149311	–36160
Total current disbursements and net saving of general government	2545398	2666883	2764620	2893791	3107774	3271431	3445107	3587236	3824903	3963230	4102822	4295185

a Item "Other current transfers" includes item "Fees, fines and penalties".

1.5 Current income and outlay of corporate and quasi-corporate enterprises, summary

Million Belgian francs

	1986	1987	1988	1989	1990	1991	1992	1993	1994	1995	1996	1997
Receipts												
1 Operating surplus	501867	525414	615059	722388	704154	670492	671017	661395	721757	822213	861381	922141
2 Property and entrepreneurial income received	1248802	1261101	1405190	1748840	1923141	1999179	2118434	2383070	2212897	2367223	2434781	2534398
3 Current transfers	247378	266390	286407	320426	392539	383120	374723	401167	375278	390427	416762	420274
Total current receipts	1998047	2052905	2306656	2791654	3019834	3052791	3164174	3445632	3309932	3579863	3712924	3876813
Disbursements												
1 Property and entrepreneurial income	1382335	1397819	1581994	1952566	2180774	2305085	2441079	2667097	2490467	2650879	2719415	2829464
2 Direct taxes and other current payments to general government	139975	143831	157067	173848	160158	165853	155479	180808	213112	251633	265894	305840
3 Other current transfers	242402	259451	281421	308510	371870	367440	366852	393381	366516	382167	407159	410613
4 Net saving	233335	251804	286174	356730	307032	214413	200764	204346	239837	295184	320456	330896
Total current disbursements and net saving	1998047	2052905	2306656	2791654	3019834	3052791	3164174	3445632	3309932	3579863	3712924	3876813

1.6 Current income and outlay of households and non-profit institutions

Million Belgian francs

	1986	1987	1988	1989	1990	1991	1992	1993	1994	1995	1996	1997
Receipts												
1 Compensation of employees	2849159	2924077	3046532	3201242	3469542	3723760	3917273	4014767	4160339	4287492	4364013	4500457
A From resident producers	2778959	2849277	2965332	3114242	3376942	3624260	3808673	3898967	4036639	4157392	4231113	4364257
B From rest of the world	70200	74800	81200	87000	92600	99500	108600	115800	123700	130100	132900	136200
2 Operating surplus of private unincorporated enterprises	894703	943713	1019155	1125507	1189823	1247391	1311724	1360198	1416744	1457967	1508875	1558125
3 Property and entrepreneurial income	668650	685716	741774	848705	943831	1035913	1134717	1193933	1186066	1151253	1133304	1154534
4 Current transfers	1458920	1531235	1594620	1693260	1810972	1956475	2093135	2173535	2221091	2322037	2401704	2481073
A Social security benefits	1001473	1044116	1063835	1115419	1181986	1287841	1375822	1428863	1462304	1527552	1582216	1621204
B Social assistance grants	122830	126881	136793	155528	164307	170943	182760	182929	197043	205576	210712	221306
C Other	334617	360238	393992	422313	464679	497691	534553	561743	561744	588909	608776	638563
Statistical discrepancy	8975	9403	12932	15317	13087	14931	10703	15222	23657	27757	35392	36663
Total current receipts	5880407	6094144	6415013	6884031	7427255	7978470	8467552	8757655	9007897	9246506	9443288	9730852
Disbursements												
1 Private final consumption expenditure	3324731	3477779	3633172	3919071	4166130	4423563	4629464	4714894	4924045	5071235	5282002	5488027
2 Property income	126027	130499	142292	172606	193975	212840	226966	233470	220004	217312	207176	209664
3 Direct taxes and other current transfers n.e.c. to general government	1647834	1723788	1776669	1817987	1981379	2087028	2231286	2293561	2440077	2522429	2568892	2679167

Belgium

Million Belgian francs

	1986	1987	1988	1989	1990	1991	1992	1993	1994	1995	1996	1997
A Social security contributions	822319	876595	917014	970181	1043035	1129926	1211521	1265212	1286374	1320729	1342020	1389767
B Direct taxes	825515	847193	859655	847806	938344	957102	1019765	1028349	1153703	1201700	1226872	1289400
C Fees, fines and penalties	...	...	...	...	...	...	...	...	...	...	...	...
4 Other current transfers [a]	314726	325865	348475	362652	415649	434637	457924	487437	497217	532466	570973	570264
5 Net saving	467089	436213	514405	611715	670122	820402	921912	1028293	926554	903064	814245	783730
Total current disbursements and net saving	5880407	6094144	6415013	6884031	7427255	7978470	8467552	8757655	9007897	9246506	9443288	9730852

a Item "Other current transfers" includes item "Fees, fines and penalties".

1.7 External transactions on current account, summary

Million Belgian francs

	1986	1987	1988	1989	1990	1991	1992	1993	1994	1995	1996	1997
Payments to the rest of the world												
1 Imports of goods and services	3151800	3199800	3588800	4181600	4318900	4413400	4461700	4312200	4710300	5042400	5303000	5933300
A Imports of merchandise, c.i.f.	2754900	2774400	3116100	3626300	3766400	3800900	3836000	3650800	3942700	4383400	4614300	5182400
B Other	396900	425400	472700	555300	552500	612500	625700	661400	767600	659000	688700	750900
2 Factor income to rest of the world	697400	664500	789000	1143000	1284900	1466200	1679400	1618400	1716900	1700300	1451000	1329600
A Compensation of employees	7900	8200	8900	10700	12300	15500	18900	20700	21400	22300	25100	27300
B Property and entrepreneurial income	689500	656300	780100	1132300	1272600	1450700	1660500	1597700	1695500	1678000	1425900	1302300
3 Current transfers to the rest of the world	157682	169182	185850	191985	231088	247081	246281	253109	259746	287590	326742	341903
A Indirect taxes to supranational organizations	64613	77013	75711	80718	83257	91933	88738	84572	89616	89177	83644	89131
B Other current transfers	93069	92169	110139	111267	147831	155148	157543	168537	170130	198413	243098	252772
4 Surplus of the nation on current transactions	62425	49369	80468	84510	48174	86809	111974	244264	302335	352950	334834	399394
Payments to the rest of the world and surplus of the nation on current transfers	4069307	4082851	4644118	5601095	5883062	6213490	6499355	6427973	6989281	7383240	7415576	8004197
Receipts from the rest of the world												
1 Exports of goods and services	3293100	3322100	3758100	4347600	4464400	4573000	4677800	4591700	5042600	5394600	5649400	6326400
A Exports of merchandise, f.o.b.	2731600	2713500	3089300	3585400	3658800	3680900	3770400	3656900	3969500	4494000	4728000	5302700
B Other	561500	608600	668800	762200	805600	892100	907400	934800	1073100	900600	921400	1023700
2 Factor income from rest of the world	665600	645300	770300	1132000	1250800	1465400	1665000	1676800	1793300	1807600	1576600	1470700
A Compensation of employees	70200	74800	81200	87000	92600	99500	108600	115800	123700	130100	132900	136200
B Property and entrepreneurial income	595400	570500	689100	1045000	1158200	1365900	1556400	1561000	1669600	1677500	1443700	1334500
3 Current transfers from rest of the world	110607	115451	115718	121495	167862	175090	156555	159473	153381	181040	189576	207097
A Subsidies from supranational organisations	44627	42801	32129	25362	42956	51735	42426	39840	40631	41273	33979	33334
B Other current transfers	65980	72650	83589	96133	124906	123355	114129	119633	112750	139767	155597	173763
Receipts from the rest of the world on current transactions	4069307	4082851	4644118	5601095	5883062	6213490	6499355	6427973	6989281	7383240	7415576	8004197

Belgium

1.8 Capital transactions of the nation, summary

Million Belgian francs

	1986	1987	1988	1989	1990	1991	1992	1993	1994	1995	1996	1997
Finance of gross capital formation												
Gross saving	828694	911493	1110282	1282760	1373267	1385197	1467365	1566752	1675423	1815729	1806159	1942160
1 Consumption of fixed capital	478624	508423	565642	602702	657487	681115	732112	738276	769176	808029	820769	863694
A General government	16606	18176	19582	21672	22168	23447	24284	24880	25540	26209	26549	27028
B Corporate and quasi-corporate enterprises	332755	356315	402650	432660	476547	493047	534442	535511	558667	589639	598175	633094
C Other	129263	133932	143410	148370	158772	164621	173386	177885	184969	192181	196045	203572
2 Net saving	350070	403070	544640	680058	715780	704082	735253	828476	906247	1007700	985390	1078466
A General government	−350354	−284947	−255939	−288387	−261374	−330733	−387423	−404163	−260144	−190548	−149311	−36160
B Corporate and quasi-corporate enterprises	233335	251804	286174	356730	307032	214413	200764	204346	239837	295184	320456	330896
C Other	467089	436213	514405	611715	670122	820402	921912	1028293	926554	903064	814245	783730
less: Surplus of the nation on current transactions	62425	49369	80468	84510	48174	86809	111974	244264	302335	352950	334834	399394
Finance of gross capital formation	766269	862124	1029814	1198250	1325093	1298388	1355391	1322488	1373088	1462779	1471325	1542766
Gross capital formation												
Increase in stocks [a]	−29543	8397	16148	19599	−2889	5737	7431	1403	24020	32567	21513	2822
Gross fixed capital formation	795812	853727	1013666	1178651	1327982	1292651	1347960	1321085	1349068	1430212	1449812	1539944
1 General government	111847	103699	110904	85990	83878	92443	100565	111881	122131	116304	99617	120499
2 Corporate and quasi-corporate enterprises	439610	477700	566750	692797	802683	793367	803202	753880	739900	794832	837832	875557
3 Other	244355	272328	336012	399864	441421	406841	444193	455324	487037	519076	512363	543888
Gross capital formation	766269	862124	1029814	1198250	1325093	1298388	1355391	1322488	1373088	1462779	1471325	1542766

a Item "Increase in stocks" includes the statistical adjustment concerning gross capital formation.

1.9 Gross domestic product by institutional sectors of origin

Million Belgian francs

	1986	1987	1988	1989	1990	1991	1992	1993	1994	1995	1996	1997
Domestic factor incomes originating												
1 General government	671181	668457	672898	710298	749089	805632	841804	896917	944223	988151	1008184	1040407
2 Corporate and quasi-corporate enterprises	3513869	3660035	3937164	4263423	4532995	4751987	4970560	5046678	5254626	5475936	5623176	5836243
A Non-financial	3469128	3594827	3862612	4183677	4468122	4673035	4870122	4952620	5139196	5363642	5518924	5723338
B Financial	44741	65208	74552	79746	64873	78952	100438	94058	115430	112294	104252	112905
3 Households and private unincorporated enterprises	...	...	...	...	...	...	...	...	...	...	...	...
4 Non-profit institutions serving households	...	...	...	...	...	...	...	...	...	...	...	...
subtotal: Domestic factor incomes	4185050	4328492	4610062	4973721	5282084	5557619	5812364	5943595	6198849	6464087	6631360	6876650
Indirect taxes, net	421176	481763	513767	590934	614804	630214	684087	723355	800861	796019	853015	935140
A Indirect taxes	603799	653943	689439	749421	801449	832827	876474	918707	988660	992125	1052710	1111240
B less: Subsidies	182623	172180	175672	158487	186645	202613	192387	195352	187799	196106	199695	176100
Consumption of fixed capital	478624	508423	565642	602702	657487	681115	732112	738276	769176	808029	820769	863694
Gross domestic product	5084850	5318678	5689471	6167357	6554375	6868948	7228563	7405226	7768886	8068135	8305144	8675484

Belgium

1.10 Gross domestic product by kind of activity, in current prices

Million Belgian francs

	1986	1987	1988	1989	1990	1991	1992	1993	1994	1995	1996	1997
1 Agriculture, hunting, forestry and fishing	107903	103403	107067	132978	119607	124135	119675	114623	113230	96505	96086	98222
2 Mining and quarrying	...	...	...	...	...	...	...	...	...	...	...	...
3 Manufacturing	1084310	1086153	1194676	1301680	1363421	1328340	1353091	1349559	1438724	1526391	1507105	1594328
4 Electricity, gas and water [a]	222568	223514	229423	239633	255573	268132	285264	298172	314832	330591	354231	369157
5 Construction	256439	257442	298049	326709	348489	358403	387626	378784	393325	409908	406353	432724
6 Wholesale and retail trade, restaurants and hotels [b]	859783	918881	965528	1021728	1154772	1239954	1319985	1345143	1388894	1396684	1471080	1515410
7 Transport, storage and communication	379142	405805	452207	488516	524569	555905	577817	582423	633597	656145	666122	713442
8 Finance, insurance, real estate and business services	298381	317910	324498	331126	305981	336545	365307	366770	397218	413478	456580	446111
9 Community, social and personal services [c]	1004315	1081117	1169440	1281429	1360848	1456390	1555948	1636849	1727880	1837342	1938122	2021871
Statistical discrepancy	−46699	−28866	−37995	−21546	−23662	−13291	2108	10903	−50150	−41734	−32022	−49234
Total, Industries	4166142	4365359	4702893	5102253	5409598	5654513	5966821	6083226	6357550	6625310	6863657	7142031
Producers of government services	678353	676982	682657	722151	760731	818377	863275	918649	966666	1009168	1028940	1061339
Other producers [d]	50667	50564	50584	50661	52419	54588	57284	58880	59945	60719	62500	64330
Subtotal	4895162	5092905	5436134	5875065	6222748	6527478	6887380	7060755	7384161	7695197	7955097	8267700
less: Imputed bank service charge	207845	204228	200496	196064	184038	198480	211798	215917	220727	237016	285624	261519
plus: Import duties	42012	51354	48578	53723	55699	60421	58173	56162	58011	60039	59798	69115
plus: Value added tax	355521	378647	405255	434633	459966	479529	494808	504226	547441	549915	575873	600188
plus: Other adjustments	...	...	...	...	...	...	...	...	...	...	...	...
equals: Gross domestic product [e]	5084850	5318678	5689471	6167357	6554375	6868948	7228563	7405226	7768886	8068135	8305144	8675484
memorandum item: Mineral fuels and power	221876	221893	228399	243902	264003	...	...	...	...	...	...	...

a Item "Electricity, gas and water" includes also other energy products.
b Including repairs and recovery.
c Item "Community, social and personal services" refers to health services only. All other market services are included in item "Finance, insurance, real estate and business services".
d Item "Other producers" refers to domestic services only. All other non-marketed services are included in item "Finance, insurance, real estate and business services".
e The breakdown by kind of economic activity used in this table is according to the classification NACE/CLIO.

1.11 Gross domestic product by kind of activity, in constant prices

Million Belgian francs

	1986	1987	1988	1989	1990	1991	1992	1993	1994	1995	1996	1997
At constant prices of: 1990												
1 Agriculture, hunting, forestry and fishing	122888	115209	121229	123635	119607	127101	140214	147118	137787	141801	138656	138158
2 Mining and quarrying	...	...	...	...	...	...	...	...	...	...	...	...
3 Manufacturing	1190376	1184568	1249591	1330256	1363421	1355724	1343585	1307149	1364767	1400256	1395118	1465801
4 Electricity, gas and water [a]	223490	239482	250409	253890	255573	263061	267681	267649	273571	285348	295827	294918
5 Construction	272918	278878	315250	328699	348489	354740	366110	352099	356011	364040	356221	375109
6 Wholesale and retail trade, restaurants and hotels [b]	1085498	1091034	1116830	1121263	1154772	1196425	1215432	1203225	1214996	1215738	1226299	1251276
7 Transport, storage and communication	408243	426988	461752	492961	524569	539092	549158	537605	561742	569221	570635	595259
8 Finance, insurance, real estate and business services	269166	296131	313979	327584	305981	333291	358695	365456	387274	405127	435659	439627
9 Community, social and personal services [c]	1130392	1178439	1247966	1328543	1360848	1387800	1407477	1403002	1432855	1482171	1517492	1562849
Statistical discrepancy	−57174	−31348	−29880	−59873	−23662	−46051	−47929	−64117	−60214	−34755	65	6300

Belgium

Million Belgian francs

	1986	1987	1988	1989	1990	1991	1992	1993	1994	1995	1996	1997
	At constant prices of: 1990											
Total, Industries	4645797	4779381	5047126	5246958	5409598	5511183	5600423	5519186	5668789	5828947	5935972	6129297
Producers of government services	749069	746442	744909	755985	760731	773265	785784	797091	814098	824165	837640	837274
Other producers [d]	55677	54450	53631	52444	52419	52805	53455	53100	53061	53372	54472	55225
Subtotal	5450543	5580273	5845666	6055387	6222748	6337253	6439662	6369377	6535948	6706484	6828084	7021796
less: Imputed bank service charge	152239	161099	173247	183532	184038	200244	214076	231970	233660	254950	295504	295872
plus: Import duties	40933	43835	48235	52524	55699	56757	59375	58985	62661	64889	66170	70236
plus: Value added tax	389771	401266	420432	437069	459966	465439	473611	463327	466098	474300	482197	497385
plus: Other adjustments	...	...	...	...	...	...	...	...	...	...	...	...
equals: Gross domestic product [e]	5729008	5864275	6141086	6361448	6554375	6659205	6758572	6659719	6831047	6990723	7080947	7293545

a Item "Electricity, gas and water" includes also other energy products.
b Including repairs and recovery.
c Item "Community, social and personal services" refers to health services only. All other market services are included in item "Finance, insurance, real estate and business services".
d Item "Other producers" refers to domestic services only. All other non-marketed services are included in item "Finance, insurance, real estate and business services".
e The breakdown by kind of economic activity used in this table is according to the classification NACE/CLIO.

1.12 Relations among national accounting aggregates

Million Belgian francs

	1986	1987	1988	1989	1990	1991	1992	1993	1994	1995	1996	1997
Gross domestic product	5084850	5318678	5689471	6167357	6554375	6868948	7228563	7405226	7768886	8068135	8305144	8675484
plus: Net factor income from the rest of the world	–31800	–19200	–18700	–11000	–34100	–800	–14400	58400	76400	107300	125600	141100
Factor income from rest of the world	665600	645300	770300	1132000	1250800	1465400	1665000	1676800	1793300	1807600	1576600	1470700
less: Factor income to the rest of the world	697400	664500	789000	1143000	1284900	1466200	1679400	1618400	1716900	1700300	1451000	1329600
equals: Gross national product	5053050	5299478	5670771	6156357	6520275	6868148	7214163	7463626	7845286	8175435	8430744	8816584
less: Consumption of fixed capital	478624	508423	565642	602702	657487	681115	732112	738276	769176	808029	820769	863694
equals: National income	4574426	4791055	5105129	5553655	5862788	6187033	6482051	6725350	7076110	7367406	7609975	7952890
plus: Net current transfers from the rest of the world	–47075	–53731	–70132	–70490	–63226	–71991	–89726	–93636	–106365	–106550	–137166	–134806
Current transfers from rest of the world	110607	115451	115718	121495	167862	175090	156555	159473	153381	181040	189576	207097
less: Current transfers to the rest of the world	157682	169182	185850	191985	231088	247081	246281	253109	259746	287590	326742	341903
equals: National disposable income	4527351	4737324	5034997	5483165	5799562	6115042	6392325	6631714	6969745	7260856	7472809	7818084
less: Final consumption	4177281	4334254	4490357	4803107	5083782	5410960	5657072	5803238	6063498	6253156	6487419	6739618
equals: Net saving	350070	403070	544640	680058	715780	704082	735253	828476	906247	1007700	985390	1078466
less: Surplus of the nation on current transactions	62425	49369	80468	84510	48174	86809	111974	244264	302335	352950	334834	399394
equals: Net capital formation	287645	353701	464172	595548	667606	617273	623279	584212	603912	654750	650556	679072

2.5 Private final consumption expenditure by type and purpose, in current prices

Million Belgian francs

	1986	1987	1988	1989	1990	1991	1992	1993	1994	1995	1996	1997
Final consumption expenditure of resident households												
1 Food, beverages and tobacco	695800	704608	713911	736656	774571	805448	813984	797911	823992	831436	844755	879162
A Food	578798	584393	593316	612062	638632	666469	665198	648349	668311	667042	673693	699447
B Non-alcoholic beverages	15036	16351	17545	20340	22568	22587	24467	23657	26289	27121	26602	28016
C Alcoholic beverages	46331	49235	47341	47028	55193	55629	58878	58939	59122	60576	63202	68189

Belgium

Million Belgian francs

	1986	1987	1988	1989	1990	1991	1992	1993	1994	1995	1996	1997
D Tobacco	55635	54629	55709	57226	58178	60763	65441	66966	70270	76697	81258	83510
2 Clothing and footwear	243628	255040	268560	285430	316967	328721	344743	348501	351512	348357	341403	354316
3 Gross rent, fuel and power	648985	663823	680681	719661	761575	817179	860783	915372	959537	1001429	1058429	1082965
A Fuel and power	183016	167473	154974	161598	171911	189446	187058	195295	195986	202714	227144	223537
B Other	465969	496350	525707	558063	589664	627733	673725	720077	763551	798715	831285	859428
4 Furniture, furnishings and household equipment and operation	333424	353665	377820	401437	431713	459431	470643	458799	468447	478572	492183	514437
A Household operation	44753	46928	47420	50769	53432	55798	56810	56412	57391	59942	62940	63513
B Other	288671	306737	330400	350668	378281	403633	413833	402387	411056	418630	429243	450924
5 Medical care and health expenses	342924	362612	386114	414201	442066	484883	525112	555077	571447	611787	648356	655356
6 Transport and communication	393860	414466	446920	486872	531909	555032	588732	570083	610468	613849	660380	687173
A Personal transport equipment	133657	143572	161655	176936	203521	209822	224563	195812	210289	196230	221652	226987
B Other	260203	270894	285265	309936	328388	345210	364169	374271	400179	417619	438728	460186
7 Recreational, entertainment, education and cultural services	211522	225778	241800	254882	274243	283574	284051	288186	303450	316852	328291	347932
A Education	...	...	...	...	...	...	...	...	...	...	...	...
B Other	211522	225778	241800	254882	274243	283574	284051	288186	303450	316852	328291	347932
8 Miscellaneous goods and services	435900	473231	502996	547273	589096	625794	681418	693752	738156	755284	801339	849064
A Personal care	54347	55274	57044	58802	61601	65072	69631	81524	82137	84177	84781	85718
B Expenditures in restaurants, cafes and hotels	233929	245956	263346	287843	318371	341762	382832	382085	403422	420626	440142	467920
C Other	147624	172001	182606	200628	209124	218960	228955	230143	252597	250481	276416	295426
Statistical discrepancy	−12212	−10744	−27230	26659	−6510	6801	−7702	19313	24136	27369	13566	23722
Total final consumption expenditure in the domestic market by households, of which	3293831	3442479	3591572	3873071	4115630	4366863	4561764	4646994	4851145	4984935	5188702	5394127
plus: Direct purchases abroad by resident households	99900	113600	129400	127600	138600	146600	160900	171400	196700	201800	219800	224100
less: Direct purchases in the domestic market by non-resident households	69000	78300	87800	81600	88100	89900	93200	103500	123800	115500	126500	130200
equals: Final consumption expenditure of resident households [a]	3324731	3477779	3633172	3919071	4166130	4423563	4629464	4714894	4924045	5071235	5282002	5488027

a Item "Final consumption expenditure of resident households" includes consumption expenditure of private non-profit institutions serving households.

2.6 Private final consumption expenditure by type and purpose, in constant prices

Million Belgian francs

	1986	1987	1988	1989	1990	1991	1992	1993	1994	1995	1996	1997

At constant prices of: 1990

Final consumption expenditure of resident households

	1986	1987	1988	1989	1990	1991	1992	1993	1994	1995	1996	1997
1 Food, beverages and tobacco	717693	725654	729483	728271	753208	749092	760977	748840	758979	765191	764972	780179
A Food	581730	590209	594843	596926	617269	616232	626248	618639	627465	627564	624374	635690
B Non-alcoholic beverages	15980	16821	17931	20634	22568	22095	23286	22025	24019	25208	24642	25867
C Alcoholic beverages	52367	55283	52547	49983	55193	51960	54104	54855	55202	57631	60298	63908
D Tobacco	67616	63341	64162	60728	58178	58805	57339	53321	52293	54788	55658	54714
2 Clothing and footwear	278976	278564	283357	292819	316967	317644	324381	320972	317873	310688	302520	311834
3 Gross rent, fuel and power	707263	723014	728722	743288	761575	791346	800680	812498	820055	836849	863295	865205
A Fuel and power	170815	174235	167037	167679	171911	186700	187431	190116	189751	196536	213842	205425
B Other	536448	548779	561685	575609	589664	604646	613249	622382	630304	640313	649453	659780

Belgium

Million Belgian francs

	1986	1987	1988	1989	1990	1991	1992	1993	1994	1995	1996	1997
At constant prices of: 1990												
4 Furniture, furnishings and household equipment and operation	361123	373966	393715	410864	431713	446783	447024	427625	430697	435869	445464	463252
A Household operation	47436	48624	49493	51612	53432	54543	52292	50617	51289	53585	55824	56011
B Other	313687	325342	344222	359252	378281	392240	394732	377008	379408	382284	389640	407241
5 Medical care and health expenses	399080	411267	431147	449493	442066	472298	486344	485564	484089	497952	511968	511861
6 Transport and communication	438408	455060	482528	503512	531909	542885	559714	525089	540693	537300	559117	566566
A Personal transport equipment	156015	162303	175698	184474	203521	206796	215628	180639	186947	173364	193254	195446
B Other	282393	292757	306830	319038	328388	336089	344086	344450	353746	363936	365863	371120
7 Recreational, entertainment, education and cultural services	223068	233197	247377	258529	274243	278895	280696	283356	296935	305423	315642	336524
A Education	...	...	...	...	...	...	...	...	...	...	...	...
B Other	223068	233197	247377	258529	274243	278895	280696	283356	296935	305423	315642	336524
8 Miscellaneous goods and services	512059	538491	560430	589893	610459	622153	642589	627220	648209	650876	676075	704549
A Personal care	60723	59302	59538	60034	61601	62800	62748	63051	61708	62614	62053	62025
B Expenditures in restaurants, cafes and hotels	285857	293955	307969	324252	339734	345685	360952	350191	358957	366497	375257	390486
C Other	165479	185234	192923	205607	209124	213668	218889	213978	227544	221765	238765	252038
Statistical discrepancy	23578	1571	274	21612	−6510	10309	11875	24592	20451	−305	−27330	−33527
Total final consumption expenditure in the domestic market by households, of which	3661248	3740784	3857033	3998281	4115630	4231405	4314280	4255756	4317981	4339843	4411723	4506443
plus: Direct purchases abroad by resident households	115400	127900	142400	134900	138600	138900	148700	155300	178200	185200	200200	199500
less: Direct purchases in the domestic market by non-resident households	79700	88200	96600	86300	88100	85100	82100	88700	103600	94700	101700	102600
equals: Final consumption expenditure of resident households [a]	3696948	3780484	3902833	4046881	4166130	4285205	4380880	4322356	4392581	4430343	4510223	4603343

[a] Item "Final consumption expenditure of resident households" includes consumption expenditure of private non-profit institutions serving households.

2.11 Gross fixed capital formation by kind of activity of owner, ISIC divisions, in current prices

Million Belgian francs

	1986	1987	1988	1989	1990	1991	1992	1993	1994	1995	1996	1997
All producers												
1 Agriculture, hunting, forestry and fishing	18871	20246	19803	20788	24731	18715	22874	15807	15169	14463	16961	18400
2 Mining and quarrying	...	...	...	...	...	...	...	...	...	...	...	...
3 Manufacturing	177605	189235	235291	297158	356888	348102	328840	266390	264382	299074	327375	338419
A Manufacturing of food, beverages and tobacco	24223	25863	33331	36935	45176	50337	52037	44089	39640	38773	41854	42182
B Textile, wearing apparel and leather industries	14600	18150	19209	18442	20250	17861	17005	16029	20303	16008	13430	18001
C Manufacture of wood and wood products, including furniture	...	...	...	...	...	...	...	...	...	...	...	...
D Manufacture of paper and paper products, printing and publishing	17905	18825	21195	26447	27220	36388	35228	23980	31437	29180	29172	27647
E Manufacture of chemicals and chemical petroleum, coal, rubber and plastic products	38108	40133	67262	87943	120758	101486	91215	81135	76125	102551	127310	137878

Belgium

Million Belgian francs

	1986	1987	1988	1989	1990	1991	1992	1993	1994	1995	1996	1997
F Manufacture of non-metallic mineral products, except products of petroleum and coal	11783	16501	17449	19738	28521	22933	19332	20946	19784	23166	18607	18596
G Basic metal industries	14608	15499	19751	30472	26499	30428	29611	23152	24682	25106	25330	23844
H Manufacture of fabricated metal products, machinery and equipment	47266	42273	46471	64839	75068	77008	75639	49101	42975	56063	61685	58179
I Other manufacturing industries [a]	9112	11991	10623	12342	13396	11661	8773	7958	9436	8227	9987	12092
4 Electricity, gas and water [b]	43208	38575	39738	51410	58683	55923	82787	85961	76114	73438	78870	80670
5 Construction	15153	15230	22966	25366	29754	27455	25038	22891	24170	26978	26047	28368
6 Wholesale and retail trade, restaurants and hotels	94531	110897	135526	151262	168069	173304	173613	163722	163524	160282	162649	174043
A Wholesale and retail trade [c]	82414	94892	116275	131510	148045	150444	149305	139695	141340	140802	143861	155818
B Restaurants and hotels	12117	16005	19251	19752	20024	22860	24308	24027	22184	19480	18788	18225
7 Transport, storage and communication	71429	80590	77516	89584	103355	99449	104868	128839	121744	138192	144379	148325
A Transport and storage	49520	58975	57586	62191	73384	68187	70958	84047	81951	99909	93030	101884
B Communication	21909	21615	19930	27393	29971	31262	33910	44792	39793	38283	51349	46441
8 Finance, insurance, real estate and business services	30628	30471	33074	36575	35287	29845	27175	22894	21233	21130	23377	30528
A Financial institutions	30628	30471	33074	36575	35287	29845	27175	22894	21233	21130	23377	30528
B Insurance	...	...	...	...	...	...	...	...	...	...	...	...
C Real estate and business services	...	...	...	...	...	...	...	...	...	...	...	...
Real estate, except dwellings	...	...	...	...	...	...	...	...	...	...	...	...
Dwellings	163835	183567	230438	288362	322701	...	...	...	...	...	...	...
9 Community, social and personal services [d]	232540	264784	338848	420518	467337	447415	482200	502700	540601	580351	570538	600692
Total industries	683965	750028	902762	1092661	1244104	1200208	1247395	1209204	1226937	1313908	1350196	1419445
Producers of government services	111847	103699	110904	85990	83878	92443	100565	111881	122131	116304	99616	120499
Private non-profit institutions serving households	–	–	–	–	–	–	–	–	–	–	–	...
Total [e]	795812	853727	1013666	1178651	1327982	1292651	1347960	1321085	1349068	1430212	1449812	1539944

a Item "Manufacture of wood and wood products, including furniture" is included in item "Other manufacturing industries".
b Item "Electricity, gas and water" includes also other energy products.
c Including repairs and recovery.
d Business services and real estate except dwellings are included in item "Community, social and personal services".
e The breakdown by kind of economic activity used in this table is according to the classification NACE/CLIO.

2.12 Gross fixed capital formation by kind of activity of owner, ISIC divisions, in constant prices

Million Belgian francs

	1986	1987	1988	1989	1990	1991	1992	1993	1994	1995	1996	1997
At constant prices of: 1990												
All producers												
1 Agriculture, hunting, forestry and fishing	21167	22580	21569	21587	24731	18500	22420	15445	14096	13227	15092	16413
2 Mining and quarrying	...	...	...	...	...	...	...	...	...	...	...	...
3 Manufacturing	190233	203022	249018	303940	356888	340308	315235	252580	247806	275840	299173	309098
A Manufacturing of food, beverages and tobacco	26071	27836	35425	37808	45176	49215	49837	41757	37038	35636	38128	38363
B Textile, wearing apparel and leather industries	15629	19466	20322	18859	20250	17460	16299	15198	18999	14751	12268	16424

Belgium

Million Belgian francs

	1986	1987	1988	1989	1990	1991	1992	1993	1994	1995	1996	1997
At constant prices of: 1990												
C Manufacture of wood and wood products, including furniture	...	...	...	...	...	...	...	...	...	...	...	...
D Manufacture of paper and paper products, printing and publishing	19158	20190	22398	27044	27220	35592	33793	22741	29499	26927	26667	25250
E Manufacture of chemicals and chemical petroleum, coal, rubber and plastic products	40752	42968	71097	89892	120758	99207	87456	77002	71427	94692	116437	126105
F Manufacture of non-metallic mineral products, except products of petroleum and coal	12635	17717	18507	20220	28521	22394	18506	19812	18543	21361	17005	16973
G Basic metal industries	15546	16565	20856	31136	26499	29754	28426	22000	23228	23244	23222	21883
H Manufacture of fabricated metal products, machinery and equipment	50615	45340	49134	66325	75068	75298	72537	46554	40265	51673	56348	53101
I Other manufacturing industries [a]	9827	12940	11279	12656	13396	11388	8381	7516	8807	7556	9098	10999
4 Electricity, gas and water [b]	47140	42247	42564	52749	58683	54851	79170	81037	70276	66331	70700	71561
5 Construction	16484	16636	24550	26107	29754	26722	23771	21556	22464	24743	23758	25874
6 Wholesale and retail trade, restaurants and hotels	104719	122410	146349	156101	168069	168896	164317	152834	150567	145994	147004	156861
A Wholesale and retail trade [c]	91432	104821	125625	135801	148045	146457	141077	130271	130147	128417	130186	140722
B Restaurants and hotels	13287	17589	20724	20300	20024	22439	23240	22563	20420	17577	16818	16139
7 Transport, storage and communication	78319	88211	82953	92198	103355	96974	100083	122179	113634	126931	132056	135026
A Transport and storage	55028	65167	61947	64223	73384	66403	67628	79644	76295	91586	85134	92576
B Communication	23291	23044	21006	27975	29971	30571	32455	42535	37339	35345	46922	42450
8 Finance, insurance, real estate and business services	33139	33094	35298	37461	35287	29226	26051	21656	19800	19373	21255	27662
A Financial institutions	33139	33094	35298	37461	35287	29226	26051	21656	19800	19373	21255	27662
B Insurance	...	...	...	...	...	...	...	...	...	...	...	...
C Real estate and business services	...	...	...	...	...	...	...	...	...	...	...	...
9 Community, social and personal services [d]	266065	292474	366034	432983	467337	439168	455376	464278	485366	510454	495695	515340
Total industries	757266	820674	968335	1123126	1244104	1174645	1186423	1131565	1124009	1182893	1204733	1257835
Producers of government services	122086	113760	118963	88005	83878	91079	95934	104871	111094	103795	88350	105254
Private non-profit institutions serving households	–	–	–	–	–	–	–	–	–	–	–	–
Total [e]	879352	934434	1087298	1211131	1327982	1265724	1282357	1236436	1235103	1286688	1293083	1363089

a Item "Manufacture of wood and wood products, including furniture" is included in item "Other manufacturing industries".
b Item "Electricity, gas and water" includes also other energy products.
c Including repairs and recovery.
d Business services and real estate except dwellings are included in item "Community, social and personal services".
e The breakdown by kind of economic activity used in this table is according to the classification NACE/CLIO.

2.17 Exports and imports of goods and services, detail

Million Belgian francs

	1986	1987	1988	1989	1990	1991	1992	1993	1994	1995	1996	1997
Exports of goods and services												
1 Exports of merchandise, f.o.b.	2731600	2713500	3089300	3585400	3658800	3680900	3770400	3656900	3969500	4494000	4728000	5302700
2 Transport and communication	492500	530300	581000	680600	717500	802200	814200	831300	949300	785100	794900	893500
3 Insurance service charges												
4 Other commodities												

Belgium

Million Belgian francs

	1986	1987	1988	1989	1990	1991	1992	1993	1994	1995	1996	1997
5 Adjustments of merchandise exports to change-of-ownership basis	...	...	...	...	...	...	...	...	...	...	...	...
6 Direct purchases in the domestic market by non-residential households	69000	78300	87800	81600	88100	89900	93200	103500	123800	115500	126500	130200
7 Direct purchases in the domestic market by extraterritorial bodies	...	...	...	...	...	...	...	...	...	...	...	...
Total exports of goods and services	3293100	3322100	3758100	4347600	4464400	4573000	4677800	4591700	5042600	5394600	5649400	6326400

Imports of goods and services

	1986	1987	1988	1989	1990	1991	1992	1993	1994	1995	1996	1997
1 Imports of merchandise, c.i.f.	2754900	2774400	3116100	3626300	3766400	3800900	3836000	3650800	3942700	4383400	4614300	5182400
2 Adjustments of merchandise imports to change-of-ownership basis	...	...	...	...	...	...	...	...	...	...	...	...
3 Other transport and communication	297000	311800	343300	427700	413900	465900	464800	490000	570900	457200	468900	526800
4 Other insurance service charges												
5 Other commodities												
6 Direct purchases abroad by government	...	...	...	...	...	...	...	...	...	...	...	...
7 Direct purchases abroad by resident households	99900	113600	129400	127600	138600	146600	160900	171400	196700	201800	219800	224100
Total imports of goods and services	3151800	3199800	3588800	4181600	4318900	4413400	4461700	4312200	4710300	5042400	5303000	5933300
Balance of goods and services	141300	122300	169300	166000	145500	159600	216100	279500	332300	352200	346400	393100
Total imports and balance of goods and services	3293100	3322100	3758100	4347600	4464400	4573000	4677800	4591700	5042600	5394600	5649400	6326400

3.11 General government production account: total and subsectors

Million Belgian francs

	1986 Total government	1986 Central government	1986 State or provincial government	1986 Local government	1986 Social security funds	1987 Total government	1987 Central government	1987 State or provincial government	1987 Local government	1987 Social security funds
Gross output										
1 Sales	...	...	...	...	...	...	...	...	...	...
2 Services produced for own use	852550	568540	...	231537[a]	52473	856475	573714	...	229193[a]	53568
3 Own account capital formation	...	...	...	...	...	...	...	...	...	...
Gross output	862498	570425	...	238584[a]	53489	867814	576026	...	237269[a]	54519
Gross input										
Intermediate consumption	205074	150281	...	38403[a]	16390	211977	154905	...	39108[a]	17964
subtotal: Value added	687787	438426	...	211933[a]	37428	686633	439957	...	209749[a]	36927
1 Indirect taxes, net	6862	6862	...	–[a]	–	6823	6823	...	–[a]	–
A Indirect taxes	6862	6862	...	–[a]	–	6823	6823	...	–[a]	–
B less: Subsidies	–	–	...	–[a]	–	–	–	...	–[a]	–
2 Consumption of fixed capital	16606	11447	...	4786[a]	373	18176	12500	...	5300[a]	376
3 Compensation of employees	662698	420019	...	206020[a]	36659	659746	420017	...	203383[a]	36346
4 Net operating surplus	1621	98	...	1127[a]	396	1888	617	...	1066[a]	205
Gross input	892861	588707	...	250336[a]	53818	898610	594862	...	248857[a]	54891

Belgium

	1988					1989				
	Total govern-ment	Central govern-ment	State or provincial govern-ment	Local govern-ment	Social security funds	Total govern-ment	Central govern-ment	State or provincial govern-ment	Local govern-ment	Social security funds
Gross output										
1 Sales	...	...	...	...	...	...	...	...	...	...
2 Services produced for own use	857185	567545	...	234607[a]	55033	884036	583801	...	249685[a]	50550
3 Own account capital formation	...	...	...	...	...	...	...	...	...	...
Gross output	872062	573495	...	242620[a]	55947	905223	594588	...	259070[a]	51565
Gross input										
Intermediate consumption	210418	151685	...	41335[a]	17398	197956	138100	...	42135[a]	17721
subtotal: Value added	692480	440021	...	213521[a]	38938	731970	468447	...	229336[a]	34187
1 Indirect taxes, net	7225	7225	...	–[a]	–	7906	7906	...	–[a]	–
A Indirect taxes	7225	7225	...	–[a]	–	7906	7906	...	–[a]	–
B less: Subsidies	–	–	...	–[a]	–	–	–	...	–[a]	–
2 Consumption of fixed capital .	19582	13211	...	5974[a]	397	21672	14434	...	6789[a]	449
3 Compensation of employees ...	664057	419394	...	206416[a]	38247	701508	446250	...	221282[a]	33976
4 Net operating surplus	1616	191	...	1131[a]	294	884	–143	...	1265[a]	–238
Gross input	902898	591706	...	254856[a]	56336	929926	606547	...	271471[a]	51908

	1990					1991				
	Total govern-ment	Central govern-ment	State or provincial govern-ment	Local govern-ment	Social security funds	Total govern-ment	Central govern-ment	State or provincial govern-ment	Local govern-ment	Social security funds
Gross output										
1 Sales	...	...	...	...	...	...	...	...	...	...
2 Services produced for own use	917652	608611	...	257286[a]	51755	987397	655569	...	276536[a]	55292
3 Own account capital formation	...	...	...	...	...	...	...	...	...	...
Gross output	941036	620054	...	268228[a]	52754	1015484	672168	...	286356[a]	56960
Gross input										
Intermediate consumption	205657	136448	...	51773[a]	17436	219609	146781	...	54813[a]	18015
subtotal: Value added	771257	495266	...	239950[a]	36041	829079	533704	...	256021[a]	39354
1 Indirect taxes, net	10577	10577	...	–[a]	–	9481	9481	...	–[a]	–
A Indirect taxes	10577	10577	...	–[a]	–	9481	9481	...	–[a]	–
B less: Subsidies	–	–	...	–[a]	–	–	–	...	–[a]	–
2 Consumption of fixed capital .	22168	14713	...	7000[a]	455	23447	15307	...	7535[a]	605
3 Compensation of employees ...	739647	472673	...	231515[a]	35459	796175	511099	...	247000[a]	38076
4 Net operating surplus	–1135	–2697	...	1435[a]	127	–24	–2183	...	1486[a]	673
Gross input	976914	631714	...	291723[a]	53477	1048688	680485	...	310834[a]	57369

	1992					1993				
	Total govern-ment	Central govern-ment	State or provincial govern-ment	Local govern-ment	Social security funds	Total govern-ment	Central govern-ment	State or provincial govern-ment	Local govern-ment	Social security funds
Gross output										
1 Sales	...	...	...	...	...	...	...	...	...	...
2 Services produced for own use	1027608	679277	...	290580[a]	57751	1088344[a]	713921[a]	...	313559[a]	60864[a]
3 Own account capital formation	...	...	...	...	...	...	...	...	...	...
Gross output	1058306	697821	...	301077[a]	59408	1116260	733543	...	319107[a]	63610
Gross input										
Intermediate consumption	218017	140692	...	57755[a]	19570	225645[a]	144082[a]	...	61394[a]	20169[a]
subtotal: Value added	866088	557580	...	268134[a]	40374	921797[a]	590067[a]	...	288645[a]	43085[a]

Belgium

	1992					1993				
	Total government	Central government	State or provincial government	Local government	Social security funds	Total government	Central government	State or provincial government	Local government	Social security funds
1 Indirect taxes, net	–	–	...	–[a]	–	–[a]	–[a]	...	–[a]	–[a]
A Indirect taxes	–	–	...	–[a]	–	–[a]	–[a]	...	–[a]	–[a]
B less: Subsidies	–	–	...	–[a]	–	–[a]	–[a]	...	–[a]	–[a]
2 Consumption of fixed capital	24284	15744	...	7927[a]	613	24880[a]	15943[a]	...	8269[a]	668[a]
3 Compensation of employees	839754	541836	...	258474[a]	39444	894582[a]	574124[a]	...	278643[a]	41815[a]
4 Net operating surplus	2050	–	...	1733[a]	317	2335[a]	–	...	1733[a]	602[a]
Gross input	1084105	698272	...	325889[a]	59944	1147442[a]	734149[a]	...	350039[a]	63254[a]

	1994					1995				
	Total government	Central government	State or provincial government	Local government	Social security funds	Total government	Central government	State or provincial government	Local government	Social security funds
Gross output										
1 Sales	...	...	...	...	...	...	...	...	...	...
2 Services produced for own use [a]	1139453	746082	...	330282	63089	1181921	775393	...	340489	66039
3 Own account capital formation	...	...	...	...	...	...	...	...	...	...
Gross output	1168294	766802	...	333998[a]	67494	...	...	...	...	...
Gross input										
Intermediate consumption [a]	229088	144664	...	63365	21059	229832	145372	...	64204	20256
subtotal: Value added [a]	969763	622485	...	303086	44192	1014360	649731	...	317105	47524
1 Indirect taxes, net [a]	–	–	...	–	–	–75	–75	...	–	–
A Indirect taxes [a]	–	–	...	–	–	–	–	...	–	–
B less: Subsidies [a]	–	–	...	–	–	75	75	...	–	–
2 Consumption of fixed capital [a]	25540	16239	...	8655	646	26209	16376	...	9182	651
3 Compensation of employees [a]	941914	606246	...	292656	43012	984011	633423	...	305090	45498
4 Net operating surplus [a]	2309	–	...	1775	534	4215	7	...	2833	1375
Gross input [a]	1198851	767149	...	366451	65251	1244192	795103	...	381309	67780

	1996					1997				
	Total government	Central government	State or provincial government	Local government	Social security funds	Total government	Central government	State or provincial government	Local government	Social security funds
Gross output										
1 Sales	...	...	...	...	...	...	...	...	...	...
2 Services produced for own use [a]	1205417	782840	...	354123	68454	1251591	815261	...	366323	70007
3 Own account capital formation	...	...	...	...	...	...	...	...	...	...
Gross output	...	...	...	...	...	...	...	...	...	...
Gross input										
Intermediate consumption [a]	243301	151921	...	70415	20965	253348	159472	...	72628	21248
subtotal: Value added [a]	1034733	658040	...	327463	49230	1067435	678486	...	338449	50500
1 Indirect taxes, net [a]	–262	–262	...	–	–	29	–102	...	...	...
A Indirect taxes [a]	–	–	...	–	–	–	–	...	...	...
B less: Subsidies [a]	262	262	...	–	–	–29	102	...	...	...
2 Consumption of fixed capital [a]	26549	16414	...	9482	653	27028	16598	...	9774	656
3 Compensation of employees [a]	1003555	641653	...	314700	47202	1035551	661990	...	325092	48469
4 Net operating surplus [a]	4891	235	...	3281	1375	4827	–	...	3583	1375
Gross input [a]	1278034	809961	...	397878	70195	1320783	837958	...	411077	71748

a   State or Provincial government is included in local government.

Belgium

3.12 General government income and outlay account: total and subsectors

Million Belgian francs

	1986					1987				
	Total government	Central government	State or provincial government	Local government	Social security funds	Total government	Central government	State or provincial government	Local government	Social security funds
Receipts											
1 Operating surplus	1621	98	...	1127	396	1888	617	...	1066	205
2 Property and entrepreneurial income	57383	22436	...	19411	26355	53186	19448	...	21067	23969
A Withdrawals from public quasi-corporations	3515	9	...	3506	–	3624	624	...	3000	–
B Interest	36471	18831	...	2161	26298	26795	11626	...	2560	23907
C Dividends	14114	2912	...	11145	57	19065	6137	...	12866	62
D Net land rent and royalties	3283	684	...	2599	–	3702	1061	...	2641	–
3 Taxes, fees and contributions	2355328	1466487	...	116607	772234	2479362	1537311	...	119305	822746
A Indirect taxes	603799	571967	...	14150	17682	653943	619440	...	16283	18220
B Direct taxes	965490	867650	...	94621	3219	991024	891430	...	96698	2896
C Social security contributions	786039	26870	...	7836	751333	834395	26441	...	6324	801630
D Fees, fines and penalties	...	...	...	...	...	...	...	...	...	...
4 Other current transfers	131066	140124	...	234717	289697	132447	139365	...	226075	250502
A Casualty insurance claims	459	201	...	258	–	506	222	...	284	–
B Transfers from other government subsectors	...	1620	...	203558	283667	...	1734	...	194000	244960
C Transfers from rest of the world	690	45317	...	–	–	1030	43831	...	–	–
D Other transfers, except imputed	26327[a]	17719	...	4147	4461	23418[a]	14591	...	4900	3927
E Imputed unfunded employee pension and welfare contributions	103590	75267	...	26754	1569	107493	78987	...	26891	1615
Total current receipts	2545398[b]	1629145	...	371862	1088682	2666883[b]	1696741	...	367513	1097422
Disbursements											
1 Government final consumption expenditure	852550	568540	...	231537	52473	856475	573714	...	229193	53568
2 Property income	560573	504727	...	59414	7251	557485	505539	...	57036	6208
A Interest	560573	504727	...	59414	7251	557485	505539	...	57036	6208
B Net land rent and royalties	–	–	...	–	–	–	–	...	–	–
3 Subsidies	137996	174213	...	5649	2761	129379	161424	...	5948	4808
4 Other current transfers	1344633	790197	...	58337	984944	1408491	760145	...	59053	1029987
A Casualty insurance premiums, net	642	281	...	361	–	689	302	...	387	–
B Transfers to other government subsectors	...	487225	...	1620	–	...	438960	...	1734	–
C Social security benefits	1001473	19673	...	–	981800	1044116	19811	...	–	1024305
D Social assistance grants	122830[c]	105358	...	17472	–	126881[c]	107707	...	19174	–
E Unfunded employee welfare benefits	111426	75267	...	34590	1569	113817	78987	...	33215	1615
F Transfers to private non-profit institutions serving households	–[c]	–	...	–	–	–[c]	–	...	–	–
G Other transfers n.e.c.	29650	23781	...	4294	1575	31966	23356	...	4543	4067
H Transfers to rest of the world	78612	78612	...	–	–	91022	91022	...	–	–

Belgium

Million Belgian francs

	1986					1987				
	Total govern-ment	Central govern-ment	State or provincial govern-ment	Local govern-ment	Social security funds	Total govern-ment	Central govern-ment	State or provincial govern-ment	Local govern-ment	Social security funds
Net saving	−350354	−408532	...	16925	41253	−284947	−304081	...	16283	2851
Total current disbursements and net saving	2545398[b]	1629145	...	371862	1088682	2666883[b]	1696741	...	367513	1097422

	1988					1989				
	Total govern-ment	Central govern-ment	State or provincial govern-ment	Local govern-ment	Social security funds	Total govern-ment	Central govern-ment	State or provincial govern-ment	Local govern-ment	Social security funds

Receipts

1 Operating surplus	1616	191	...	1131	294	884	−143	...	1265	−238
2 Property and entrepreneurial income	54517	17347	...	24617	24389	69447	30138	...	25905	25960
A Withdrawals from public quasi-corporations	2888	387	...	2501	−	2640	11	...	2629	−
B Interest	26383	10177	...	3691	24351	30307	12940	...	4005	25918
C Dividends	21656	6182	...	15436	38	32325	16023	...	16260	42
D Net land rent and royalties	3590	601	...	2989	−	4175	1164	...	3011	−
3 Taxes, fees and contributions	2570535	1592527	...	119854	858154	2687516	1665037	...	118184	904295
A Indirect taxes	689439	654802	...	15585	19052	749421	713923	...	16375	19123
B Direct taxes	1016722	911928	...	98457	6337	1021654	923339	...	96692	1623
C Social security contributions	864374	25797	...	5812	832765	916441	27775	...	5117	883549
D Fees, fines and penalties	...	...	...	...	...	...	...	...	...	...
4 Other current transfers	137952	130224	...	218270	276519	135944	122360	...	243857	274593
A Casualty insurance claims	531	233	...	298	−	600	263	...	337	−
B Transfers from other government subsectors	...	1531	...	182244	271157	...	1845	...	208333	269326
C Transfers from rest of the world	989	33118	...	−	−	693	26055	...	−	−
D Other transfers, except imputed	22828[a]	13538	...	5645	3645	14964[a]	5756	...	5795	3413
E Imputed unfunded employee pension and welfare contributions	113604	81804	...	30083	1717	119687	88441	...	29392	1854
Total current receipts	2764620[b]	1740289	...	363872	1159356	2893791[b]	1817392	...	389211	1204610

Disbursements

1 Government final consumption expenditure	857185	567545	...	234607	55033	884036	583801	...	249685	50550
2 Property income	568195	519840	...	54181	6010	629120	585223	...	50235	6218
A Interest	568195	519840	...	54181	6010	629120	585223	...	50235	6218
B Net land rent and royalties	−	−	...	−	−	−	−	...	−	−
3 Subsidies	143543	166680	...	4122	4870	133125	151082	...	3194	4211
4 Other current transfers	1451636	796959	...	62211	1047398	1535897	855304	...	61688	1098409
A Casualty insurance premiums, net	747	327	...	420	−	842	369	...	473	−
B Transfers to other government subsectors	...	453401	...	1531	−	...	477659	...	1845	−
C Social security benefits	1063835	20104	...	−	1043731	1115419	21059	...	−	1094360
D Social assistance grants	136793[c]	116982	...	19811	−	155528[c]	135421	...	20107	−
E Unfunded employee welfare benefits	119416	81804	...	35895	1717	124804	88441	...	34509	1854
F Transfers to private non-profit institutions serving households	−[c]	−	...	−	−	−[c]	−	...	−	−

Belgium

	1988					1989				
	Total government	Central government	State or provincial government	Local government	Social security funds	Total government	Central government	State or provincial government	Local government	Social security funds
G Other transfers n.e.c.	33205	26701	...	4554	1950	41549	34600	...	4754	2195
H Transfers to rest of the world	97640	97640	...	–	–	97755	97755	...	–	–
Net saving	−255939	−310735	...	8751	46045	−288387	−358018	...	24409	45222
Total current disbursements and net saving	2764620[b]	1740289	...	363872	1159356	2893791[b]	1817392	...	389211	1204610

	1990					1991				
	Total government	Central government	State or provincial government	Local government	Social security funds	Total government	Central government	State or provincial government	Local government	Social security funds

Receipts

1 Operating surplus	−1135	−2697	...	1435	127	−24	−2183	...	1486	673
2 Property and entrepreneurial income	78889	32789	...	27670	31448	89601	44698	...	28762	31600
A Withdrawals from public quasi-corporations	2602	3	...	2599	–	2349	49	...	2300	–
B Interest	35503	12593	...	4584	31344	33399	13189	...	4267	31402
C Dividends	36688	19092	...	17492	104	50391	31003	...	19190	198
D Net land rent and royalties	4096	1101	...	2995	–	3462	457	...	3005	–
3 Taxes, fees and contributions	2884546	1789441	...	122910	972195	3021848	1840380	...	140117	1041351
A Indirect taxes	801449	760255	...	19972	21222	832827	801893	...	20423	10511
B Direct taxes	1098502	1000010	...	97727	765	1122955	1007730	...	114556	669
C Social security contributions	984595	29176	...	5211	950208	1066066	30757	...	5138	1030171
D Fees, fines and penalties	...	...	...	...	...	...	...	...	...	...
4 Other current transfers	145474	147540	...	244034	249889	160006	167326	...	258942	234546
A Casualty insurance claims	732	321	...	411	–	700	307	...	393	–
B Transfers from other government subsectors	...	1321	...	207594	244118	...	1468	...	219401	228204
C Transfers from rest of the world	656	43612	...	–	–	925	52660	...	–	–
D Other transfers, except imputed	18559[a]	8555	...	6099	3905	19629[a]	9009	...	6200	4420
E Imputed unfunded employee pension and welfare contributions	125527	93731	...	29930	1866	138752	103882	...	32948	1922
Total current receipts	3107774[b]	1967073	...	396049	1253659	3271431[b]	2050221	...	429307	1308170

Disbursements

1 Government final consumption expenditure	917652	608611	...	257286	51755	987397	655569	...	276536	55292
2 Property income	685512	652955	...	39766	5809	691568	662757	...	39528	4742
A Interest	685512	652955	...	39766	5809	691568	662757	...	39528	4742
B Net land rent and royalties	–	–	...	–	–	–	–	...	–	–
3 Subsidies	143689	179744	...	3211	3690	150878	195658	...	3062	3893
4 Other current transfers	1622295	848011	...	63055	1164262	1772321	885373	...	67259	1268762
A Casualty insurance premiums, net	1032	452	...	580	–	1012	443	...	569	–
B Transfers to other government subsectors	...	451712	...	1321	–	...	447605	...	1468	–
C Social security benefits	1181986	22468	...	–	1159518	1287841	24451	...	–	1263390
D Social assistance grants	164307[c]	143363	...	20944	–	170943[c]	149136	...	21807	–
E Unfunded employee welfare benefits	130738	93731	...	35141	1866	143890	103882	...	38086	1922

Belgium

	1990					1991				
	Total government	Central government	State or provincial government	Local government	Social security funds	Total government	Central government	State or provincial government	Local government	Social security funds
F Transfers to private non-profit institutions serving households	_c	_	...	_	_	_c	_	...	_	_
G Other transfers n.e.c.	44754	36807	...	5069	2878	54814	46035	...	5329	3450
H Transfers to rest of the world	99478	99478	...	_	_	113821	113821	...	_	_
Net saving	−261374	−322248	...	32731	28143	−330733	−349136	...	42922	−24519
Total current disbursements and net saving	3107774[b]	1967073	...	396049	1253659	3271431[b]	2050221	...	429307	1308170

	1992					1993				
	Total government	Central government	State or provincial government	Local government	Social security funds	Total government	Central government	State or provincial government	Local government	Social security funds

Receipts

1 Operating surplus	2050	_	...	1733	317	2335	_	...	1733	602
2 Property and entrepreneurial income	81919	38489	...	30736	29864	80668	34395	...	33193	29728
A Withdrawals from public quasi-corporations	2338	38	...	2300	_	2300	_	...	2300	_
B Interest	28058	11506	...	4128	29594	29802	13069	...	3946	29435
C Dividends	48199	26625	...	21304	270	45292	21060	...	23939	293
D Net land rent and royalties	3324	320	...	3004	_	3274	266	...	3008	_
3 Taxes, fees and contributions	3192019	1926492	...	151714	1113813	3317956	1993205	...	144135	1180616
A Indirect taxes	876474	843154	...	21783	11537	918707	869003	...	23329	26375
B Direct taxes	1175244	1049890	...	124939	415	1209157	1091658	...	115566	1933
C Social security contributions	1140301	33448	...	4992	1101861	1190092	32544	...	5240	1152308
D Fees, fines and penalties	...	...	...	...	...	...	...	...	...	...
4 Other current transfers	169119	167491	...	267004	267032	186277	173429	...	288121	253999
A Casualty insurance claims	725	318	...	407	_	792	347	...	445	_
B Transfers from other government subsectors	...	4718	...	225641	259623	...	1653	...	242158	245621
C Transfers from rest of the world	979	43405	...	_	_	2623	42463	...	_	_
D Other transfers, except imputed	20808[a]	9346	...	6193	5269	24026[a]	11555[a]	...	6246[a]	6225[a]
E Imputed unfunded employee pension and welfare contributions	146607	109704	...	34763	2140	158836	117411	...	39272	2153
Total current receipts	3445107[b]	2132472	...	451187	1411026	3587236[b]	2201029[b]	...	467182[b]	1464945[b]

Disbursements

1 Government final consumption expenditure	1027608	679277	...	290580	57751	1088344	713921	...	313559	60864
2 Property income	771125	743052	...	40594	4649	793804	764420	...	42587	3445
A Interest	771125	743052	...	40594	4649	793804	764420	...	42587	3445
B Net land rent and royalties	_	_	...	_	_	_	_	...	_	_
3 Subsidies	149961	185324	...	2895	4168	155512	187946	...	3246	4160
4 Other current transfers	1883836	943038	...	74489	1356291	1953739	956349	...	77617	1409205
A Casualty insurance premiums, net	1009	442	...	567	_	1093	479	...	614	_
B Transfers to other government subsectors	...	485264	...	4718	_	...	487779	...	1653	_
C Social security benefits	1375822	25598	...	_	1350224	1428863	27271	...	_	1401592
D Social assistance grants	182760[c]	159029	...	23731	_	182929[c]	158303[c]	...	24626[c]	_c

Belgium

	1992					1993				
	Total government	Central government	State or provincial government	Local government	Social security funds	Total government	Central government	State or provincial government	Local government	Social security funds
E Unfunded employee welfare benefits	151599	109704	...	39755	2140	164076	117411	...	44512	2153
F Transfers to private non-profit institutions serving households	—[c]	—	...	—	—	—[c]	—[c]	...	—[c]	—[c]
G Other transfers n.e.c.	58485	48840	...	5718	3927	59129	47457	...	6212	5460
H Transfers to rest of the world	114161	114161	...	—	—	117649	117649	...	—	—
Net saving	−387423	−418219	...	42629	−11833	−404163	−421607	...	30173	−12729
Total current disbursements and net saving	3445107[b]	2132472	...	451187	1411026	3587236[b]	2201029[b]	...	467182[b]	1464945[b]

	1994					1995				
	Total government	Central government	State or provincial government	Local government	Social security funds	Total government	Central government	State or provincial government	Local government	Social security funds

Receipts

1 Operating surplus	2309	—	...	1775	534	4215	7	...	2833	1375
2 Property and entrepreneurial income	64148	21992	...	34341	25149	68329	24912	...	35807	26920
A Withdrawals from public quasi-corporations	2300	—	...	2300	—	1872	1	...	1871	—
B Interest	20345	8831	...	3941	24907	20164	8893	...	3661	26920
C Dividends	38354	13025	...	25087	242	43020	15738	...	27282	—
D Net land rent and royalties	3149	136	...	3013	—	3273	280	...	2993	—
3 Taxes, fees and contributions	3565339	2122881	...	167524	1274934	3686919	2180085	...	193518	1313316
A Indirect taxes	988660	908996	...	25830	53834	992125	888192	...	24556	79377
B Direct taxes	1366815	1179088	...	137131	50596	1453333	1252490	...	164478	36365
C Social security contributions	1209864	34797	...	4563	1170504	1241461	39403	...	4484	1197574
D Fees, fines and penalties	...	...	...	...	...	...	...	...	...	...
4 Other current transfers	193107	181807	...	300791	257969	203767	195149	...	306584	255994
A Casualty insurance claims	787	345	...	442	—	814	357	...	457	—
B Transfers from other government subsectors	...	1911	...	254635	250283	...	5912	...	259709	247066
C Transfers from rest of the world	2370	43001	...	—	—	3807	45080	...	—	—
D Other transfers, except imputed [a]	22919	11199	...	6386	5334	25923	10662	...	8841	6420
E Imputed unfunded employee pension and welfare contributions	167031	125351	...	39328	2352	173223	133138	...	37577	2508
Total current receipts [b]	3824903	2326680	...	504431	1558586	3963230	2400153	...	538742	1597605

Disbursements

1 Government final consumption expenditure	1139453	746082	...	330282	63089	1181921	775393	...	340489	66039
2 Property income	778540	748998	...	41282	5594	719114	692916	...	39204	6304
A Interest	778540	748998	...	41282	5594	719114	692916	...	39204	6304
B Net land rent and royalties	—	—	...	—	—	—	—	...	—	—
3 Subsidies	147168	180630	...	2887	4282	154833	185991	...	6096	4019
4 Other current transfers	2019886	1003544	...	82009	1441162	2097910	1020610	...	86948	1503039
A Casualty insurance premiums, net	1091	478	...	613	—	1129	495	...	634	—
B Transfers to other government subsectors	...	502911	...	1911	2007	...	504856	...	5912	1919

Belgium

	1994					1995				
	Total government	Central government	State or provincial government	Local government	Social security funds	Total government	Central government	State or provincial government	Local government	Social security funds
C Social security benefits	1462304	28774	...	–	1433530	1527552	30240	...	–	1497312
D Social assistance grants [c]	197043	168258	...	28785	–	205576	174471	...	31105	–
E Unfunded employee welfare benefits	171594	125351	...	43891	2352	177707	133138	...	42061	2508
F Transfers to private non-profit institutions serving households [c]	–	–	...	–	–	–	–	...	–	–
G Other transfers n.e.c.	59488	49406	...	6809	3273	63256	54720	...	7236	1300
H Transfers to rest of the world	128366	128366	...	–	–	122690	122690	...	–	–
Net saving	–260144	–352574	...	47971	44459	–190548	–274757	...	66005	18204
Total current disbursements and net saving [b]	3824903	2326680	...	504431	1558586	3963230	2400153	...	538742	1597605

	1996					1997				
	Total government	Central government	State or provincial government	Local government	Social security funds	Total government	Central government	State or provincial government	Local government	Social security funds

Receipts

1 Operating surplus	4891	235	...	3281	1375	4827	–131	...	3583	1375
2 Property and entrepreneurial income	80778	34225	...	38869	24720	61819	14118	...	39761	23720
A Withdrawals from public quasi-corporations	2463	1	...	2462	–	2430	–	...	2430	–
B Interest	19778	9224	...	2870	24720	17609	6749	...	2920	23720
C Dividends	55385	24986	...	30399	–	38620	7360	...	31260	–
D Net land rent and royalties	3152	14	...	3138	–	3160	9	...	3151	–
3 Taxes, fees and contributions	3802165	2253377	...	194627	1354161	4007852	2374996	...	204472	1428384
A Indirect taxes	1052710	921820	...	28633	102257	1111240	932361	...	30051	148828
B Direct taxes	1492766	1291837	...	161760	39169	1595240	1402646	...	170835	21759
C Social security contributions	1256689	39720	...	4234	1212735	1301372	39989	...	3586	1257797
D Fees, fines and penalties	...	...	...	...	...	...	...	...	...	...
4 Other current transfers	214988	194576	...	309570	257796	220687	199480	...	308374	250394
A Casualty insurance claims	860	377	...	483	–	859	377	...	482	–
B Transfers from other government subsectors	...	3641	...	260803	248531	...	3707	...	260422	240098
C Transfers from rest of the world	4317	38296	...	–	–	3803	37137	...	–	–
D Other transfers, except imputed [a]	28655	11754	...	10181	6720	29220	11732	...	9668	7820
E Imputed unfunded employee pension and welfare contributions	181156	140508	...	38103	2545	186805	146527	...	37802	2476
Total current receipts [b]	4102822	2482413	...	546347	1638052	4295185	2588463	...	556190	1703873

Disbursements

1 Government final consumption expenditure	1205417	782840	...	354123	68454	1251591	815261	...	366323	70007
2 Property income	704472	672408	...	43562	5538	679423	649544	...	39780	5879
A Interest	704472	672408	...	43562	5538	679423	649544	...	39780	5879
B Net land rent and royalties	–	–	...	–	–	–	–	...	–	–
3 Subsidies	165716	188407	...	6562	4726	142766	165390	...	5997	4713
4 Other current transfers	2176528	1041065	...	90362	1558076	2257565	1076526	...	95828	1589438
A Casualty insurance premiums, net	1193	523	...	670	–	1191	522	...	669	–

Belgium

	1996					1997				
	Total government	Central government	State or provincial government	Local government	Social security funds	Total government	Central government	State or provincial government	Local government	Social security funds
B Transfers to other government subsectors	...	506516	...	3641	2818	...	497636	...	3707	2884
C Social security benefits	1582216	30803	...	_	1551413	1621204	42426	...	_	1578778
D Social assistance grants [c]	210712	175221	...	35491	_	221306	180097	...	41209	_
E Unfunded employee welfare benefits	185390	140508	...	42337	2545	190391	146527	...	41388	2476
F Transfers to private non-profit institutions serving households [c]	_	_	...	_	_	_	_	...	_	_
G Other transfers n.e.c.	60325	50802	...	8223	1300	73970	59815	...	8855	5300
H Transfers to rest of the world	136692	136692	...	_	_	149503	149503	...	_	_
Net saving	−149311	−202307	...	51738	1258	−36160	−118258	...	48262	33836
Total current disbursements and net saving [b]	4102822	2482413	...	546347	1638052	4295185	2588463	...	556190	1703873

a Item "Other current transfers" includes item "Fees, fines and penalties".
b State or Provincial government is included in local government.
c Item "Transfers to private non-profit institutions serving households" is included in item "Social assistance grants".

3.13 General government capital accumulation account: total and subsectors

Million Belgian francs

	1986					1987				
	Total government	Central government	State or provincial government	Local government	Social security funds	Total government	Central government	State or provincial government	Local government	Social security funds
Finance of gross accumulation										
1 Gross saving	−333748	−397085	...	21711	41626	−266771	−291581	...	21583	3227
A Consumption of fixed capital	16606	11447	...	4786	373	18176	12500	...	5300	376
B Net saving	−350354	−408532	...	16925	41253	−284947	−304081	...	16283	2851
2 Capital transfers	38815	14897	...	18686	5232	40643	16214	...	19185	5244
A From other government subsectors	_	70	...	18686	5232	_	468	...	19185	5244
B From other resident sectors	38602	14614	...	_	_	40598	15701	...	_	_
C From rest of the world	213	213	...	_	_	45	45	...	_	_
Finance of gross accumulation	−294933[a]	−382188	...	40397	46858	−226128[a]	−275367	...	40768	8471
Gross accumulation										
1 Gross capital formation	111847	79694	...	31599	554	103699	60567	...	42557	575
A Increase in stocks	_	_	...	_	_	_	_	...	_	_
B Gross fixed capital formation	111847	79694	...	31599	554	103699	60567	...	42557	575
2 Purchases of land, net	4850	3319	...	1531	_	5815	3689	...	2126	_
3 Purchases of intangible assets, net	_	_	...	_	_	_	_	...	_	_
4 Capital transfers	65905	64817	...	1088	_	70418	68806	...	1612	_
A To other government subsectors	23988	23918	...	70	_	24897	24429	...	468	_
B To other resident sectors	57207	32201	...	1018	_	60114	34073	...	1144	_
C To the rest of the world	8698	8698	...	_	_	10304	10304	...	_	_
Net lending	−477535	−530018	...	6179	46304	−406060	−408429	...	−5527	7896
Gross accumulation	−294933[a]	−382188	...	40397	46858	−226128[a]	−275367	...	40768	8471

Belgium

	1988					1989				
	Total government	Central government	State or provincial government	Local government	Social security funds	Total government	Central government	State or provincial government	Local government	Social security funds

Finance of gross accumulation

1 Gross saving	−236357	−297524	...	14725	46442	−266715	−343584	...	31198	45671
A Consumption of fixed capital	19582	13211	...	5974	397	21672	14434	...	6789	449
B Net saving	−255939	−310735	...	8751	46045	−288387	−358018	...	24409	45222
2 Capital transfers	38334	16889	...	17443	4002	41938	22732	...	15796	3410
A From other government subsectors	–	54	...	17443	4002	–	53	...	15796	3410
B From other resident sectors	38191	16692	...	–	–	41874	22615	...	–	–
C From rest of the world	143	143	...	–	–	64	64	...	–	–
Finance of gross accumulation	−198023[a]	−280635	...	32168	50444	−224777[a]	−320852	...	46994	49081

Gross accumulation

1 Gross capital formation	110904	61262	...	48970	672	85990	44580	...	40741	669
A Increase in stocks	–	–	...	–	–	–	–	...	–	–
B Gross fixed capital formation	110904	61262	...	48970	672	85990	44580	...	40741	669
2 Purchases of land, net	6595	3622	...	2973	–	2212	1020	...	1192	–
3 Purchases of intangible assets, net	–	–	...	–	–	–	–	...	–	–
4 Capital transfers	68977	66788	...	2189	–	65717	64219	...	1498	–
A To other government subsectors	21499	21445	...	54	–	19259	19206	...	53	–
B To other resident sectors	57993	34359	...	2135	–	54540	33836	...	1445	–
C To the rest of the world	10984	10984	...	–	–	11177	11177	...	–	–
Net lending	−384499	−412307	...	−21964	49772	−378696	−430671	...	3563	48412
Gross accumulation	−198023[a]	−280635	...	32168	50444	−224777[a]	−320852	...	46994	49081

	1990					1991				
	Total government	Central government	State or provincial government	Local government	Social security funds	Total government	Central government	State or provincial government	Local government	Social security funds

Finance of gross accumulation

1 Gross saving	−239206	−307535	...	39731	28598	−307286	−333829	...	50457	−23914
A Consumption of fixed capital	22168	14713	...	7000	455	23447	15307	...	7535	605
B Net saving	−261374	−322248	...	32731	28143	−330733	−349136	...	42922	−24519
2 Capital transfers	37608	18612	...	15528	3468	42934	22056	...	17338	3540
A From other government subsectors	–	10	...	15528	3468	–	34	...	17338	3540
B From other resident sectors	37561	18555	...	–	–	42844	21932	...	–	–
C From rest of the world	47	47	...	–	–	90	90	...	–	–
Finance of gross accumulation	−201598[a]	−288923	...	55259	32066	−264352[a]	−311773	...	67795	−20374

Gross accumulation

1 Gross capital formation	83878	42426	...	40760	692	92443	47597	...	44404	442
A Increase in stocks	–	–	...	–	–	–	–	...	–	–
B Gross fixed capital formation	83878	42426	...	40760	692	92443	47597	...	44404	442
2 Purchases of land, net	1409	−854	...	2263	–	621	−672	...	1293	–
3 Purchases of intangible assets, net	–	–	...	–	–	–	–	...	–	–
4 Capital transfers	68362	66855	...	1507	–	70664	69260	...	1404	–

Belgium

	1990					1991				
	Total govern-ment	Central govern-ment	State or provincial govern-ment	Local govern-ment	Social security funds	Total govern-ment	Central govern-ment	State or provincial govern-ment	Local govern-ment	Social security funds
A To other government sub-sectors	19006	18996	...	10	–	20912	20878	...	34	–
B To other resident sectors	52288	31785	...	1497	–	55630	35931	...	1370	–
C To the rest of the world	16074	16074	...	–	–	15034	15034	...	–	–
Net lending	–355247	–397350	...	10729	31374	–428080	–427958	...	20694	–20816
Gross accumulation	–201598[a]	–288923	...	55259	32066	–264352[a]	–311773	...	67795	–20374

	1992					1993				
	Total govern-ment	Central govern-ment	State or provincial govern-ment	Local govern-ment	Social security funds	Total govern-ment	Central govern-ment	State or provincial govern-ment	Local govern-ment	Social security funds

Finance of gross accumulation

1 Gross saving	–363139	–402475	...	50556	–11220	–379283	–405664	...	38442	–12061
A Consumption of fixed capital	24284	15744	...	7927	613	24880	15943	...	8269	668
B Net saving	–387423	–418219	...	42629	–11833	–404163	–421607	...	30173	–12729
2 Capital transfers	44433	23422	...	16378	4633	51046	28286	...	19631	3129
A From other government subsectors	–	67	...	16378	4633	–	41	...	19631	3129
B From other resident sectors	44353	23275	...	–	–	51017	28216	...	–	–
C From rest of the world	80	80	...	–	–	29	29	...	–	–
Finance of gross accumulation	–318706[a]	–379053	...	66934	–6587	–328237[a]	–377378[a]	...	58073[a]	–8932[a]

Gross accumulation

1 Gross capital formation	100565	51822	...	48216	527	111881	41445	...	70138	298
A Increase in stocks	–	–	...	–	–	–	–	...	–	–
B Gross fixed capital formation	100565	51822	...	48216	527	111881	41445	...	70138	298
2 Purchases of land, net	3222	–94	...	3316	–	3577	1756	...	1821	–
3 Purchases of intangible assets, net	–	–	...	–	–	–	–	...	–	–
4 Capital transfers	80806	79421	...	1385	–	90719	89302	...	1417	–
A To other government sub-sectors	20328	20261	...	67	–	21713	22760	...	41	–
B To other resident sectors	63340	42385	...	1318	–	73636	49367	...	1376	–
C To the rest of the world	17466	17466	...	–	–	17083	17083	...	–	–
Net lending	–503299	–510202	...	14017	–7114	–534414	–509881	...	–15303	–9230
Gross accumulation	–318706[a]	–379053	...	66934	–6587	–328237[a]	–377378[a]	...	58073[a]	–8932[a]

	1994					1995				
	Total govern-ment	Central govern-ment	State or provincial govern-ment	Local govern-ment	Social security funds	Total govern-ment	Central govern-ment	State or provincial govern-ment	Local govern-ment	Social security funds

Finance of gross accumulation

1 Gross saving	–234604	–336335	...	56626	45105	–164339	–258381	...	75187	18855
A Consumption of fixed capital	25540	16239	...	8655	646	26209	16376	...	9182	651
B Net saving	–260144	–352574	...	47971	44459	–190548	–274757	...	66005	18204
2 Capital transfers	86202	54427	...	23031	8744	58931	30284	...	27727	920
A From other government subsectors	–	166	...	23031	8744	–	150	...	27727	920
B From other resident sectors	85501	53560	...	–	–	58925	30478	...	–	–
C From rest of the world	701	701	...	–	–	6	6	...	–	–
Finance of gross accumulation [a]	–148402	–281908	...	79657	53849	–105408	–228097	...	102914	19775

Belgium

	1994					1995				
	Total govern-ment	Central govern-ment	State or provincial govern-ment	Local govern-ment	Social security funds	Total govern-ment	Central govern-ment	State or provincial govern-ment	Local govern-ment	Social security funds
Gross accumulation										
1 Gross capital formation	122131	43034	...	78206	891	116444	52362	...	63621	461
A Increase in stocks	–	–	...	–	–	140	–	...	–	–
B Gross fixed capital formation	122131	43034	...	78206	891	116304	52362	...	63621	461
2 Purchases of land, net	4644	2774	...	1870	–	–4474	–6421	...	1947	–
3 Purchases of intangible assets, net	–	–	...	–	–	–	–	...	–	–
4 Capital transfers	101042	99468	...	1574	–	99802	98392	...	1410	–
A To other government subsectors	21718	31572	...	166	–	21385	26073	...	150	–
B To other resident sectors	85541	48745	...	1408	–	84222	60482	...	1390	–
C To the rest of the world	15501	15501	...	–	–	15580	15580	...	–	–
Net lending	–376219	–427184	...	–1993	52958	–317180	–372430	...	35936	19314
Gross accumulation [a]	–148402	–281908	...	79657	53849	–105408	–228097	...	102914	19775

	1996					1997				
	Total govern-ment	Central govern-ment	State or provincial govern-ment	Local govern-ment	Social security funds	Total govern-ment	Central govern-ment	State or provincial govern-ment	Local govern-ment	Social security funds
Finance of gross accumulation										
1 Gross saving	–122762	–185893	...	61220	1911	–9132	–101660	...	58036	34492
A Consumption of fixed capital	26549	16414	...	9482	653	27028	16598	...	9774	656
B Net saving	–149311	–202307	...	51738	1258	–36160	–118258	...	48262	33836
2 Capital transfers	60893	34744	...	25229	920	78182	49381	...	27601	1200
A From other government subsectors	...	412	...	25229	920	...	...	...	27601	1200
B From other resident sectors	60786	33639	...	–	–	62348	...	...	–	–
C From rest of the world	107	107	...	–	–	15834	15834	...	–	–
Finance of gross accumulation [a]	–61869	–151149	...	86449	2831	69050	–52279	...	85637	35692
Gross accumulation										
1 Gross capital formation	99445	39820	...	59303	322	120550	51748	...	68289	513
A Increase in stocks	–172	–	...	–	–	51	–	...	–	–
B Gross fixed capital formation	99617	39820	...	59303	322	120499	51748	...	68289	513
2 Purchases of land, net	–5338	–7205	...	1867	–	2736	844	...	1892	–
3 Purchases of intangible assets, net	–	–	...	–	–	...	–	...	–	–
4 Capital transfers	98888	96174	...	2714	–	107403	104548	...	2855	–
A To other government subsectors	...	24521	...	412	–	...	...	...	...	–
B To other resident sectors	93708	72848	...	1390	–	102160	...	...	...	–
C To the rest of the world	5180	5180	...	–	–	5243	5243	...	–	–
Net lending	–254864	–279938	...	22565	2509	–161639	–209419	...	12601	35179
Gross accumulation [a]	–61869	–151149	...	86449	2831	69050	–52279	...	85637	35692

a State or Provincial government is included in local government.

Belgium

3.21 Corporate and quasi-corporate enterprise production account: total and sectors

Million Belgian francs

	1986				1987				1988			
	\multicolumn{3}{c|}{Corporate and quasi-corporate enterprises}	Addendum: total including unincorporated	\multicolumn{3}{c|}{Corporate and quasi-corporate enterprises}	Addendum: total including unincorporated	\multicolumn{3}{c|}{Corporate and quasi-corporate enterprises}	Addendum: total including unincorporated
	Total	Non-financial	Financial		Total	Non-financial	Financial		Total	Non-financial	Financial	
Gross output												
1 Output for sale	...	...	...	...	...	...	...	...	...	...	...	...
2 Imputed bank service charge	...	...	207845	207845	...	...	204227	204227	...	...	200495	200495
3 Own-account fixed capital formation	...	...	...	...	...	...	...	...	...	...	...	...
Gross output	...	...	418116	3927355	...	...	447490	4114400	...	...	455160	4435621
Gross input												
Intermediate consumption	...	...	321270	...	...	...	325104	...	...	...	321879	...
1 Imputed bank service charge	...	...	207845	207845	...	...	204227	204227	...	...	200495	200495
2 Other intermediate consumption	...	...	113425	...	...	...	120877	...	...	...	121384	...
subtotal: Value added	...	...	96846	3902684	...	...	122386	4079658	...	...	133281	4409877
1 Indirect taxes, net	...	...	19203	−2422	...	...	22765	22174	...	...	23474	29235
A Indirect taxes	...	...	28278	171120	...	...	30898	186221	...	...	32597	195784
B less: Subsidies	...	...	9075	173542	...	...	8133	164047	...	...	9123	166549
2 Consumption of fixed capital	...	...	26040	435978	...	...	27590	462657	...	...	28030	518030
3 Compensation of employees	...	...	188055	1936106	...	...	197454	2000277	...	...	203061	2107114
4 Net operating surplus	...	...	−136452	1533022	...	...	−125423	1594550	...	...	−121284	1755498
Gross input	...	...	418116	3902684	...	...	447490	4079658	...	...	455160	4409877

	1989				1990				1991			
	\multicolumn{3}{c|}{Corporate and quasi-corporate enterprises}	Addendum: total including unincorporated	\multicolumn{3}{c|}{Corporate and quasi-corporate enterprises}	Addendum: total including unincorporated	\multicolumn{3}{c|}{Corporate and quasi-corporate enterprises}	Addendum: total including unincorporated
	Total	Non-financial	Financial		Total	Non-financial	Financial		Total	Non-financial	Financial	
Gross output												
1 Output for sale	...	...	...	...	...	...	...	...	...	...	...	...
2 Imputed bank service charge	...	...	196064	196064	...	...	184036	184036	...	...	198479	198479
3 Own-account fixed capital formation	...	...	...	...	...	...	...	...	...	...	...	...
Gross output	...	...	466123	4826115	...	...	436572	5149232	...	...	477588	5383870
Gross input												
Intermediate consumption	...	...	319633	...	...	...	300477	...	...	...	326087	...
1 Imputed bank service charge	...	...	196064	196064	...	...	184036	184036	...	...	198479	198479
2 Other intermediate consumption	...	...	123569	...	...	...	116441	...	...	...	127608	...
subtotal: Value added	...	...	146490	4800541	...	...	136175	5131278	...	...	151522	5348397
1 Indirect taxes, net	...	...	27548	67124	...	...	28795	59767	...	...	31209	49574
A Indirect taxes	...	...	36144	217015	...	...	37472	237735	...	...	40248	243148
B less: Subsidies	...	...	8596	149891	...	...	8677	177968	...	...	9039	193574
2 Consumption of fixed capital	...	...	31290	549740	...	...	31930	603389	...	...	31880	625788
3 Compensation of employees	...	...	210711	2212723	...	...	224298	2425297	...	...	234080	2609505
4 Net operating surplus	...	...	−123059	1970954	...	...	−148848	2042825	...	...	−145647	2063530
Gross input	...	...	466123	4800541	...	...	436652	5131278	...	...	477609	5348397

Belgium

	1992				1993				1994			
	\multicolumn{3}{c|}{Corporate and quasi-corporate enterprises}	Addendum: total including unincorporated	\multicolumn{3}{c|}{Corporate and quasi-corporate enterprises}	Addendum: total including unincorporated	\multicolumn{3}{c|}{Corporate and quasi-corporate enterprises}	Addendum: total including unincorporated
	Total	Non-financial	Financial		Total	Non-financial	Financial		Total	Non-financial	Financial	
Gross output												
1 Output for sale	...	...	...	...	...	...	...	...	...	...	...	...
2 Imputed bank service charge	...	...	211797	211797	...	...	215917	215917	...	...	220727	220727
3 Own-account fixed capital formation	...	...	...	...	...	...	...	...	...	...	...	...
Gross output	...	...	516624	5688981	...	...	517429	5800438	...	...	536906	6065079
Gross input												
Intermediate consumption	...	...	350156	...	...	...	352349	...	...	...	368986	...
1 Imputed bank service charge	...	...	211797	211797	...	...	215917	215917	...	...	220727	220727
2 Other intermediate consumption	...	...	138359	...	...	...	136432	...	...	...	148259	...
subtotal: Value added	...	...	166546	5642948	...	...	165554	5757487	...	...	189110	6004561
1 Indirect taxes, net	...	...	34021	97085	...	...	37086	125881	...	...	37788	157621
A Indirect taxes	...	...	45257	278236	...	...	48440	309879	...	...	49075	334133
B less: Subsidies	...	...	11236	181151	...	...	11354	183998	...	...	11287	176512
2 Consumption of fixed capital	...	...	32087	675741	...	...	34410	678986	...	...	35892	707744
3 Compensation of employees	...	...	240157	2747662	...	...	259196	2765889	...	...	267540	2848585
4 Net operating surplus	...	...	–139719	2122460	...	...	–165138	2186731	...	...	–152110	2290611
Gross input	...	...	516702	5642948	...	...	517903	5757487	...	...	558096	6004561

	1995				1996				1997			
	\multicolumn{3}{c|}{Corporate and quasi-corporate enterprises}	Addendum: total including unincorporated	\multicolumn{3}{c|}{Corporate and quasi-corporate enterprises}	Addendum: total including unincorporated	\multicolumn{3}{c|}{Corporate and quasi-corporate enterprises}	Addendum: total including unincorporated
	Total	Non-financial	Financial		Total	Non-financial	Financial		Total	Non-financial	Financial	
Gross output												
1 Output for sale	...	...	...	...	...	...	...	...	...	...	...	...
2 Imputed bank service charge	...	...	237016	237016	...	...	285624	285624	...	...	261518	261518
3 Own-account fixed capital formation	...	...	...	...	...	...	...	...	...	...	...	...
Gross output	...	...	...	...	...	...	...	...	...	...	...	...
Gross input												
Intermediate consumption	...	...	394723	...	...	...	456681	...	...	...	430634	...
1 Imputed bank service charge	...	...	237016	237016	...	...	285624	285624	...	...	261518	261518
2 Other intermediate consumption	...	...	157707	...	...	...	171057	...	...	...	169116	...
subtotal: Value added	...	...	188851	6254970	...	...	185157	6449583	...	...	201423	6737323
1 Indirect taxes, net	...	...	38621	147519	...	...	41945	175661	...	...	47729	218079
A Indirect taxes	...	...	49819	332352	...	...	50452	366587	...	...	53140	388797
B less: Subsidies	...	...	11198	184833	...	...	8507	190926	...	...	5411	170718
2 Consumption of fixed capital	...	...	38011	743809	...	...	39222	754998	...	...	40760	795906
3 Compensation of employees	...	...	276222	2919459	...	...	281456	2971202	...	...	290402	3065604
4 Net operating surplus	...	...	–164003	2444183	...	...	–177466	2547722	...	...	–177468	2657734
Gross input	...	...	583574	6254970	...	...	641838	6449583	...	...	632057	6737323

Belgium

3.22 Corporate and quasi-corporate enterprise income and outlay account: total and sectors

Million Belgian francs

	1986 Total	1986 Non-financial	1986 Financial	1987 Total	1987 Non-financial	1987 Financial	1988 Total	1988 Non-financial	1988 Financial	1989 Total	1989 Non-financial	1989 Financial
Receipts												
1 Operating surplus	501867	638319	−136452	525414	650837	−125423	615059	736343	−121284	722388	845447	−123059
2 Property and entrepreneurial income	1248802	...	1248802	1261101	...	1261101	1405190	...	1405190	1748840	...	1748840
A Withdrawals from quasi-corporate enterprises	...	...	...	...	...	...	...	...	...	...	...	...
B Interest	1225138	...	1225138	1238014	...	1238014	1374189	...	1374189	1711888	...	1711888
C Dividends	23639	...	23639	23062	...	23062	30971	...	30971	36922	...	36922
D Net land rent and royalties	25	...	25	25	...	25	30	...	30	30	...	30
3 Current transfers	247378	110055	137323	266390	120483	145907	286407	129697	156710	320426	141178	179248
A Casualty insurance claims	57412	36942	20470	63290	41845	21445	66943	43723	23220	194285	51212	143073
B Casualty insurance premiums, net, due to be received by insurance companies	111473	...	111473	118822	...	118822	127685	...	127685	30160	...	30160
C Current transfers from rest of the world	...	...	...	...	...	...	...	...	...	...	...	...
D Other transfers except imputed	...	...	...	...	...	...	...	...	...	...	...	...
E Imputed unfunded employee pension and welfare contributions	78493	73113	5380	84278	78638	5640	91779	85974	5805	95981	89966	6015
Total current receipts	1998047	748374	1249673	2052905	771320	1281585	2306656	866040	1440616	2791654	986625	1805029
Disbursements												
1 Property and entrepreneurial income	1382335[a]	362699	1019636	1397819[a]	369307	1028512	1581994[a]	411438	1170556	1952566[a]	444226	1508340
A Withdrawals from quasi-corporations	200	...	200	238	...	238	268	...	268	38354	...	38354
B Interest	1296973	345306	951667	1308092	349097	958995	1487048	389549	1097499	1845584	414276	1431308
C Dividends	67769	...	67769	69279	...	69279	72789	...	72789	38678	...	38678
D Net land rent and royalties	17393	17393	...	20210	20210	...	21889	21889	...	29950	29950	...
2 Direct taxes and other current transfers n.e.c. to general government	139975	107065	32910	143831	110094	33737	157067	118564	38503	173848	140607	33241
A Direct taxes	139975	107065	32910	143831	110094	33737	157067	118564	38503	173848	140607	33241
B Fines, fees, penalties and other current transfers n.e.c.	...	...	...	...	...	...	...	...	...	...	...	...
3 Other current transfers	242402	111998	130404	259451	120820	138631	281421	132478	148943	308510	143442	165068
A Casualty insurance premiums, net	51945	38885	13060	55827	42182	13645	61374	46504	14870	69541	53476	16065
B Casualty insurance claims liability of insurance companies	111473	...	111473	118822	...	118822	127685	...	127685	142413	...	142413
C Transfers to private non-profit institutions	...	...	...	...	...	...	...	...	...	...	...	...
D Unfunded employee pension and welfare benefits	78493	73113	5380	84278	78638	5640	91779	85974	5805	95981	89966	6015
E Social assistance grants	...	...	...	...	...	...	...	...	...	...	...	...
F Other transfers n.e.c.	491[b]	...	491	524[b]	...	524	583[b]	...	583	575[b]	...	575
G Transfers to rest of the world	...	...	...	...	...	...	...	...	...	...	...	...
Net saving	233335	166612	66723	251804	171099	80705	286174	203560	82614	356730	258350	98380
Total current disbursements and net saving	1998047	748374	1249673	2052905	771320	1281585	2306656	866040	1440616	2791654	986625	1805029

Belgium

	1990 Total	1990 Non-financial	1990 Financial	1991 Total	1991 Non-financial	1991 Financial	1992 Total	1992 Non-financial	1992 Financial	1993 Total	1993 Non-financial	1993 Financial
Receipts												
1 Operating surplus	704154	853002	–148848	670492	816139	–145647	671017	810736	–139719	661395	826533	–165138
2 Property and entrepreneurial income	1923141	...	1923141	1999179	...	1999179	2118434	...	2118434	2383070	...	2383070
A Withdrawals from quasi-corporate enterprises	...	...	...	...	...	...	...	...	...	...	...	...
B Interest	1885342	...	1885342	1961300	...	1961300	2082349	...	2082349	2341543	...	2341543
C Dividends	37764	...	37764	37839	...	37839	36045	...	36045	41482	...	41482
D Net land rent and royalties	35	...	35	40	...	40	40	...	40	45	...	45
3 Current transfers	392539	161751	230788	383120	158950	224170	374723	164180	210543	401167	176098	225069
A Casualty insurance claims	244468	65205	179263	234376	58401	175975	231362	58709	172653	249879	65795	184084
B Casualty insurance premiums, net, due to be received by insurance companies	45100	...	45100	41695	...	41695	31210	...	31210	33785	...	33785
C Current transfers from rest of the world	...	...	...	...	...	...	...	...	...	...	...	...
D Other transfers except imputed	...	...	...	...	...	...	...	...	...	...	...	...
E Imputed unfunded employee pension and welfare contributions	102971	96546	6425	107049	100549	6500	112151	105471	6680	117503	110303	7200
Total current receipts	3019834	1014753	2005081	3052791	975089	2077702	3164174	974916	2189258	3445632	1002631	2443001
Disbursements												
1 Property and entrepreneurial income	2180774[a]	471719	1709055	2305085[a]	540856	1764229	2441079[a]	567914	1873165	2667097[a]	539727[a]	2127370[a]
A Withdrawals from quasi-corporations	41183	...	41183	46339	...	46339	50013	...	50013	54358	...	54358
B Interest	2067279	450360	1616919	2181734	518213	1663521	2320547	553903	1766644	2536808	520555	2016253
C Dividends	50953	...	50953	54369	...	54369	56508	...	56508	56759	...	56759
D Net land rent and royalties	21359	21359	...	22643	22643	...	14011	14011	...	19172	19172	...
2 Direct taxes and other current transfers n.e.c. to general government	160158	126424	33734	165853	131782	34071	155479	117579	37900	180808	148500	32308
A Direct taxes	160158	126424	33734	165853	131782	34071	155479	117579	37900	180808	148500	32308
B Fines, fees, penalties and other current transfers n.e.c.	...	...	...	...	...	...	...	...	...	...	...	...
3 Other current transfers	371870	164855	207015	367440	164150	203290	366852	165872	200980	393381	178497	214884
A Casualty insurance premiums, net	89824	68309	21515	84546	63601	20945	82181	60401	21780	91979	68194	23785
B Casualty insurance claims liability of insurance companies	178458	...	178458	175205	...	175205	171858	...	171858	183214	...	183214
C Transfers to private non-profit institutions	...	...	...	...	...	...	...	...	...	...	...	...
D Unfunded employee pension and welfare benefits	102971	96546	6425	107049	100549	6500	112151	105471	6680	117503	110303	7200
E Social assistance grants	...	...	...	...	...	...	...	...	...	...	...	...
F Other transfers n.e.c.	617[b]	...	617	640[b]	...	640	662[b]	...	662	685[b]	...	685[b]
G Transfers to rest of the world	...	...	...	...	...	...	...	...	...	...	...	...
Net saving	307032	251755	55277	214413	138301	76112	200764	123551	77213	204346	135907	68439
Total current disbursements and net saving	3019834	1014753	2005081	3052791	975089	2077702	3164174	974916	2189258	3445632	1002631	2443001

Belgium

	1994 Total	1994 Non-financial	1994 Financial	1995 Total	1995 Non-financial	1995 Financial	1996 Total	1996 Non-financial	1996 Financial	1997 Total	1997 Non-financial	1997 Financial
Receipts												
1 Operating surplus	721757	873867	–152110	822213	986216	–164003	861381	1038847	–177466	922141	1099609	–177468
2 Property and entrepreneurial income	2212897	...	2212897	2367223	...	2367223	2434781	...	2434781	2534398	...	2534398
A Withdrawals from quasi-corporate enterprises	...	...	...	...	...	...	...	...	...	...	...	...
B Interest	2167771	...	2167771	2320640	...	2320640	2366754	...	2366754	2476133	...	2476133
C Dividends	45086	...	45086	46533	...	46533	67977	...	67977	58215	...	58215
D Net land rent and royalties	40	...	40	50	...	50	50	...	50	50	...	50
3 Current transfers	375278	171823	203455	390427	176708	213719	416762	184582	232180	420274	183512	236762
A Casualty insurance claims	227205	60030	167175	233503	59049	174454	254951	64756	190195	264228	69791	194437
B Casualty insurance premiums, net, due to be received by insurance companies	29030	...	29030	31850	...	31850	35315	...	35315	36105	...	36105
C Current transfers from rest of the world	...	...	...	...	...	...	...	...	...	...	...	...
D Other transfers except imputed	...	...	...	...	...	...	...	...	...	...	...	...
E Imputed unfunded employee pension and welfare contributions	119043	111793	7250	125074	117659	7415	126496	119826	6670	119941	113721	6220
Total current receipts	3309932	1045690	2264242	3579863	1162924	2416939	3712924	1223429	2489495	3876813	1283121	2593692
Disbursements												
1 Property and entrepreneurial income [a]	2490467	533525	1956942	2650879	545959	2104920	2719415	599714	2119701	2829464	577296	2252168
A Withdrawals from quasi-corporations	55284	...	55284	58965	...	58965	62526	...	62526	66857	...	66857
B Interest	2355875	512993	1842882	2509324	524407	1984917	2562354	581762	1980592	2667722	562636	2105086
C Dividends	58776	...	58776	61038	...	61038	76583	...	76583	80225	...	80225
D Net land rent and royalties	20532	20532	...	21552	21552	...	17952	17952	...	14660	14660	...
2 Direct taxes and other current transfers n.e.c. to general government	213112	179235	33877	251633	209134	42499	265894	216655	49239	305840	250128	55712
A Direct taxes	213112	179235	33877	251633	209134	42499	265894	216655	49239	305840	250128	55712
B Fines, fees, penalties and other current transfers n.e.c.	...	...	...	...	...	...	...	...	...	...	...	...
3 Other current transfers	366516	170738	195778	382167	178783	203384	407159	188607	218552	410613	187779	222834
A Casualty insurance premiums, net	80410	58945	21465	82709	61124	21585	90571	68781	21790	96333	74058	22275
B Casualty insurance claims liability of insurance companies	166355	...	166355	173654	...	173654	189340	...	189340	193562	...	193562
C Transfers to private non-profit institutions	...	...	...	...	...	...	...	...	...	...	...	...
D Unfunded employee pension and welfare benefits	119043	111793	7250	125074	117659	7415	126496	119826	6670	119941	113721	6220
E Social assistance grants	...	...	...	...	...	...	...	...	...	...	...	...
F Other transfers n.e.c. [b]	708	...	708	730	...	730	752	...	752	777	...	777
G Transfers to rest of the world	...	...	...	...	...	...	...	...	...	...	...	...
Net saving	239837	162192	77645	295184	229048	66136	320456	218453	102003	330896	267918	62978
Total current disbursements and net saving	3309932	1045690	2264242	3579863	1162924	2416939	3712924	1223429	2489495	3876813	1283121	2593692

a Property and entrepreneurial income paid by non-financial corporate and quasi-corporate enterprises is net of property income received.

b Item "Other current transfers" includes item "Fees, fines and penalties".

Belgium

3.23 Corporate and quasi-corporate enterprise capital accumulation account: total and sectors

Million Belgian francs

	1986 Total	1986 Non-financial	1986 Financial	1987 Total	1987 Non-financial	1987 Financial	1988 Total	1988 Non-financial	1988 Financial	1989 Total	1989 Non-financial	1989 Financial
Finance of gross accumulation												
1 Gross saving	566090	473327	92763	608119	499824	108295	688824	578180	110644	789390	659720	129670
A Consumption of fixed capital	332755	306715	26040	356315	328725	27590	402650	374620	28030	432660	401370	31290
B Net saving	233335	166612	66723	251804	171099	80705	286174	203560	82614	356730	258350	98380
2 Capital transfers	28175	27668	507	29822	28898	924	29729	27639	2090	26868	24547	2321
Finance of gross accumulation	594265	500995	93270	637941	528722	109219	718553	605819	112734	816258	684267	131991
Gross accumulation												
1 Gross capital formation	408695	378067	30628	486537	456066	30471	581432	548358	33074	709648	673073	36575
A Increase in stocks	−30915	−30915	...	8837	8837	...	14682	14682	...	16851	16851	...
B Gross fixed capital formation	439610	408982	30628	477700	447229	30471	566750	533676	33074	692797	656222	36575
2 Purchases of land, net	2322	2336	−14	2376	2498	−122	4370	3813	557	4989	4094	895
3 Purchases of intangible assets, net	...	...	...	...	...	...	...	...	...	...	...	...
4 Capital transfers	311	359	−48	8613	294	8319	469	352	117	5714	195	5519
Net lending	182937	120233	62704	140415	69864	70551	132282	53296	78986	95907	6905	89002
Gross accumulation	594265	500995	93270	637941	528722	109219	718553	605819	112734	816258	684267	131991

	1990 Total	1990 Non-financial	1990 Financial	1991 Total	1991 Non-financial	1991 Financial	1992 Total	1992 Non-financial	1992 Financial	1993 Total	1993 Non-financial	1993 Financial
Finance of gross accumulation												
1 Gross saving	783579	696372	87207	707460	599468	107992	735206	625906	109300	739857	637008	102849
A Consumption of fixed capital	476547	444617	31930	493047	461167	31880	534442	502355	32087	535511	501101	34410
B Net saving	307032	251755	55277	214413	138301	76112	200764	123551	77213	204346	135907	68439
2 Capital transfers	23739	21270	2469	24565	22132	2433	32379	29520	2859	39018	36906	2112
Finance of gross accumulation	807318	717642	89676	732025	621600	110425	767585	655426	112159	778875	673914	104961
Gross accumulation												
1 Gross capital formation	798112	762825	35287	799363	769518	29845	810547	783372	27175	755097	732203	22894
A Increase in stocks	−4571	−4571	...	5996	5996	...	7345	7345	...	1217	1217	...
B Gross fixed capital formation	802683	767396	35287	793367	763522	29845	803202	776027	27175	753880	730986	22894
2 Purchases of land, net	4536	4400	136	4838	4691	147	4835	4745	90	6395	6295	100
3 Purchases of intangible assets, net	...	...	...	...	...	...	...	...	...	...	...	...
4 Capital transfers	−1637	111	−1748	−883	−15	−868	266	25	241	−307	143	−450
Net lending	6307	−49694	56001	−71293	−152594	81301	−48063	−132716	84653	17690	−64727	82417
Gross accumulation	807318	717642	89676	732025	621600	110425	767585	655426	112159	778875	673914	104961

Belgium

	1994			1995			1996			1997		
	Total	Non-financial	Financial	Total	Non-financial	Financial	Total	Non-financial	Financial	Total	Non-financial	Financial

Finance of gross accumulation

1 Gross saving	798504	684967	113537	884823	780676	104147	918631	777406	141225	963990	860252	103738
A Consumption of fixed capital	558667	522775	35892	589639	551628	38011	598175	558953	39222	633094	592334	40760
B Net saving	239837	162192	77645	295184	229048	66136	320456	218453	102003	330896	267918	62978
2 Capital transfers	44289	42443	1846	89312	40524	48788	70109	48616	21493	72665	50682	21983
Finance of gross accumulation	842793	727410	115383	974135	821200	152935	988740	826022	162718	1036655	910934	125721

Gross accumulation

1 Gross capital formation	762131	740898	21233	826527	805397	21130	858411	835034	23377	877426	846898	30528
A Increase in stocks	22231	22231	...	31695	31695	...	20579	20579	...	1869	1869	...
B Gross fixed capital formation	739900	718667	21233	794832	773702	21130	837832	814455	23377	875557	845029	30528
2 Purchases of land, net	5186	5071	115	14383	14255	128	14544	14403	141	5795	5599	196
3 Purchases of intangible assets, net	...	...	...	...	...	...	...	...	...	...	...	...
4 Capital transfers	23714	15315	8399	94458	48754	45704	38958	20915	18043	31738	16934	14804
Net lending	51762	−33874	85636	38767	−47206	85973	76827	−44330	121157	121696	41503	80193
Gross accumulation	842793	727410	115383	974135	821200	152935	988740	826022	162718	1036655	910934	125721

3.32 Household and private unincorporated enterprise income and outlay account

Million Belgian francs

	1986	1987	1988	1989	1990	1991	1992	1993	1994	1995	1996	1997

Receipts

1 Compensation of employees	2849159	2924077	3046532	3201242	3469542	3723760	3917273	4014767	4160339	4287492	4364013	4500457
A Wages and salaries	2160071	2185043	2257403	2360060	2565175	2740818	2878537	2935007	3062766	3161039	3218465	3322901
B Employers' contributions for social security	470725	505063	531106	571774	617429	673281	708758	728301	734989	748888	752565	782415
C Employers' contributions for private pension and welfare plans	218363	233971	258023	269408	286938	309661	329978	351459	362584	377565	392983	395141
2 Operating surplus of private unincorporated enterprises	894703	943713	1019155	1125507	1189823	1247391	1311724	1360198	1416744	1457967	1508875	1558125
3 Property and entrepreneurial income	668650	685716	741774	848705	943831	1035913	1134717	1193933	1186066	1151253	1133304	1154534
A Withdrawals from private quasi-corporations	200	238	268	300	333	364	396	401	430	432	432	445
B Interest	416784	414827	425887	450553	507376	560842	608738	647781	621638	591066	568926	572189
C Dividends	246828	265769	310796	393028	431537	469826	520620	540559	558658	554376	558386	576280
D Net land rent and royalties	4838	4882	4823	4824	4585	4881	4963	5192	5340	5379	5560	5620
4 Current transfers	1458920	1531235	1594620	1693260	1810972	1956475	2093135	2173535	2221091	2322037	2401704	2481073
A Casualty insurance claims	55452	59856	63001	69581	82146	82469	87139	93652	90258	87431	91974	90452
B Social security benefits	1001473	1044116	1063835	1115419	1181986	1287841	1375822	1428863	1462304	1527552	1582216	1621204
C Social assistance grants	122830	126881	136793	155528	164307	170943	182760	182929	197043	205576	210712	221306
D Unfunded employee pension and welfare benefits	217224	230892	250903	259208	279062	299868	324267	341477	343490	354292	361825	362064
E Transfers from general government	29650	31966	33205	41549	44754	54814	58485	59129	59488	63256	60325	73970
F Transfers from rest of the world	31800	37000	46300	51400	58100	59900	64000	66800	67800	83200	93900	111300
G Other transfers n.e.c.	491	524	583	575	617	640	662	685	708	730	752	777
Statistical discrepancy	8975	9403	12932	15317	13087	14931	10703	15222	23657	27757	35392	36663
Total current receipts	5880407	6094144	6415013	6884031	7427255	7978470	8467552	8757655	9007897	9246506	9443288	9730852

Belgium

Million Belgian francs

Disbursements

	1986	1987	1988	1989	1990	1991	1992	1993	1994	1995	1996	1997
1 Final consumption expenditure	3324731	3477779	3633172	3919071	4166130	4423563	4629464	4714894	4924045	5071235	5282002	5488027
2 Property income	126027	130499	142292	172606	193975	212840	226966	233470	220004	217312	207176	209664
A Interest	121074	125500	137338	167627	188918	207800	221850	228131	214507	211762	201566	203994
B Net land rent and royalties	4953	4999	4954	4979	5057	5040	5116	5339	5497	5550	5610	5670
3 Direct taxes and other current transfers n.e.c. to general government	1647834	1723788	1776669	1817987	1981379	2087028	2231286	2293561	2440077	2522429	2568892	2679167
A Social security contributions	822319	876595	917014	970181	1043035	1129926	1211521	1265212	1286374	1320729	1342020	1389767
B Direct taxes	825515	847193	859655	847806	938344	957102	1019765	1028349	1153703	1201700	1226872	1289400
C Fees, fines and penalties	...	...	...	...	...	...	...	...	...	...	...	...
4 Other current transfers	314726	325865	348475	362652	415649	434637	457924	487437	497217	532466	570973	570264
A Net casualty insurance premiums	57816	61576	66064	73420	87092	88807	91558	96472	91824	89546	96266	94698
B Transfers to private non-profit institutions serving households	...	...	...	...	...	...	...	...	...	...	...	...
C Transfers to rest of the world	48500	49100	54200	58600	81500	80400	86800	90600	96400	118700	138400	139600
D Other current transfers, except imputed [a]	26327	23418	22828	14964	18559	19629	20808	24026	22919	25923	28655	29220
E Imputed employee pension and welfare contributions	182083	191771	205383	215668	228498	245801	258758	276339	286074	298297	307652	306746
Net saving	467089	436213	514405	611715	670122	820402	921912	1028293	926554	903064	814245	783730
Total current disbursements and net saving	5880407	6094144	6415013	6884031	7427255	7978470	8467552	8757655	9007897	9246506	9443288	9730852

[a] Item "Other current transfers" includes item "Fees, fines and penalties".

3.33 Household and private unincorporated enterprise capital accumulation account

Million Belgian francs

	1986	1987	1988	1989	1990	1991	1992	1993	1994	1995	1996	1997
Finance of gross accumulation												
1 Gross saving	596352	570145	657815	760085	828894	985023	1095298	1206178	1111523	1095245	1010290	987302
A Consumption of fixed capital	129263	133932	143410	148370	158772	164621	173386	177885	184969	192181	196045	203572
B Net saving	467089	436213	514405	611715	670122	820402	921912	1028293	926554	903064	814245	783730
2 Capital transfers	5794	6266	7695	9519	11628	12160	13361	14464	12915	64106	40380	36906
Total finance of gross accumulation	602146	576411	665510	769604	840522	997183	1108659	1220642	1124438	1159351	1050670	1024208
Gross accumulation												
1 Gross capital formation	245727	271888	337478	402612	443103	406582	444279	455510	488826	519808	513469	544790
A Increase in stocks	1372	−440	1466	2748	1682	−259	86	186	1789	732	1106	902
B Gross fixed capital formation	244355	272328	336012	399864	441421	406841	444193	455324	487037	519076	512363	543888
2 Purchases of land, net	−7172	−8191	−10965	−7201	−5945	−5459	−8057	−9972	−9830	−9909	−9206	−8531
3 Purchases of intangibles, net	...	...	...	...	...	...	...	...	...	...	...	...
4 Capital transfers	14303	15754	16686	16901	20192	22815	23759	28523	30049	30328	33262	32846
Net lending	349288	296960	322311	357292	383172	573245	648678	746581	615393	619124	513145	455103
Total gross accumulation	602146	576411	665510	769604	840522	997183	1108659	1220642	1124438	1159351	1050670	1024208

Belgium

3.51 External transactions, current account: detail

Million Belgian francs

	1986	1987	1988	1989	1990	1991	1992	1993	1994	1995	1996	1997
Payments to the rest of the world												
1 Imports of goods and services	3151800	3199800	3588800	4181600	4318900	4413400	4461700	4312200	4710300	5042400	5303000	5933300
A Imports of merchandise, c.i.f.	2754900	2774400	3116100	3626300	3766400	3800900	3836000	3650800	3942700	4383400	4614300	5182400
B Other	396900	425400	472700	555300	552500	612500	625700	661400	767600	659000	688700	750900
2 Factor income to rest of the world	697400	664500	789000	1143000	1284900	1466200	1679400	1618400	1716900	1700300	1451000	1329600
A Compensation of employees	7900	8200	8900	10700	12300	15500	18900	20700	21400	22300	25100	27300
B Property and entrepreneurial income	689500	656300	780100	1132300	1272600	1450700	1660500	1597700	1695500	1678000	1425900	1302300
3 Current transfers to the rest of the world	157682	169182	185850	191985	231088	247081	246281	253109	259746	287590	326742	341903
A Indirect taxes by general government to supranational organizations	64613	77013	75711	80718	83257	91933	88738	84572	89616	89177	83644	89131
B Other current transfers	93069	92169	110139	111267	147831	155148	157543	168537	170130	198413	243098	252772
By general government	13999	14009	21929	17037	16221	21888	25423	33077	38750	33513	53048	60372
By other resident sectors	79070	78160	88210	94230	131610	133260	132120	135460	131380	164900	190050	192400
4 Surplus of the nation on current transactions	62425	49369	80468	84510	48174	86809	111974	244264	302335	352950	334834	399394
Payments to the rest of the world and surplus of the nation on current transfers	4069307	4082851	4644118	5601095	5883062	6213490	6499355	6427973	6989281	7383240	7415576	8004197
Receipts from the rest of the world												
1 Exports of goods and services	3293100	3322100	3758100	4347600	4464400	4573000	4677800	4591700	5042600	5394600	5649400	6326400
A Exports of merchandise, f.o.b.	2731600	2713500	3089300	3585400	3658800	3680900	3770400	3656900	3969500	4494000	4728000	5302700
B Other	561500	608600	668800	762200	805600	892100	907400	934800	1073100	900600	921400	1023700
2 Factor income from rest of the world	665600	645300	770300	1132000	1250800	1465400	1665000	1676800	1793300	1807600	1576600	1470700
A Compensation of employees	70200	74800	81200	87000	92600	99500	108600	115800	123700	130100	132900	136200
B Property and entrepreneurial income	595400	570500	689100	1045000	1158200	1365900	1556400	1561000	1669600	1677500	1443700	1334500
3 Current transfers from rest of the world	110607	115451	115718	121495	167862	175090	156555	159473	153381	181040	189576	207097
A Subsidies to general government from supranational organizations	44627	42801	32129	25362	42956	51735	42426	39840	40631	41273	33979	33334
B Other current transfers	65980	72650	83589	96133	124906	123355	114129	119633	112750	139767	155597	173763
To general government	690	1030	989	693	656	925	979	2623	2370	3807	4317	3803
To other resident sectors	65290	71620	82600	95440	124250	122430	113150	117010	110380	135960	151280	169960
Receipts from the rest of the world on current transfers	4069307	4082851	4644118	5601095	5883062	6213490	6499355	6427973	6989281	7383240	7415576	8004197

Belgium

3.52 External transactions, capital accumulation account

Million Belgian francs

	1986	1987	1988	1989	1990	1991	1992	1993	1994	1995	1996	1997
Finance of gross accumulation												
1 Surplus of the nation on current transactions	62425	49369	80468	84510	48174	86809	111974	244264	302335	352950	334834	399394
2 Capital transfers from rest of the world	963	916	1073	1170	2132	2097	2808	2676	4102	3341	5454	21009
A By general government	213	45	143	64	47	90	80	29	701	6	107	15834
B By other resident sectors	750	871	930	1106	2085	2007	2728	2647	3401	3335	5347	5175
Total finance of gross accumulation	63388	50285	81541	85680	50306	88906	114782	246940	306437	356291	340288	420403
Gross accumulation												
1 Capital transfers to the rest of the world	8698	10304	10984	11177	16074	15034	17466	17083	15501	15580	5180	5243
A By general government	8698	10304	10984	11177	16074	15034	17466	17083	15501	15580	5180	5243
B By other resident sectors	...	...	...	...	...	...	...	...	...	...	...	...
2 Purchases of intangible assets, n.e.c., net, from rest of the world	...	...	...	...	...	...	...	...	...	...	...	...
Net lending to the rest of the world	54690	39981	70557	74503	34232	73872	97316	229857	290936	340711	335108	415160
Total gross accumulation	63388	50285	81541	85680	50306	88906	114782	246940	306437	356291	340288	420403

4.3 Cost components of value added

Million Belgian francs

	1986						1987					
	Compensation of employees	Capital consumption	Net operating surplus	Indirect taxes	less: Subsidies received	Value added	Compensation of employees	Capital consumption	Net operating surplus	Indirect taxes	less: Subsidies received	Value added
All producers												
1 Agriculture, hunting, forestry and fishing	6053	...	...	−3652	...	107903	6586	...	...	−3606	...	103403
2 Mining and quarrying	...	...	...	...	...	6542	...	...	...	...	...	4071
A Coal mining [a]	...	...	...	...	...	6542	...	...	...	...	...	4071
B Crude petroleum and natural gas production	...	...	...	...	...	...	...	...	...	...	...	...
C Metal ore mining	...	...	...	...	...	...	...	...	...	...	...	...
D Other mining	...	...	...	...	...	...	...	...	...	...	...	...
3 Manufacturing	716273	...	...	16208	...	1084310	727022	...	...	15622	...	1086153
A Manufacture of food, beverages and tobacco	78936	...	...	23890	...	175814	81052	...	...	22382	...	175678
B Textile, wearing apparel and leather industries	62581	...	...	−1385	...	90287	63565	...	...	−1087	...	90604
C Manufacture of wood and wood products, including furniture [b]	...	...	...	...	...	45616	...	...	...	...	...	48906
D Manufacture of paper and paper products, printing and publishing	52127	...	...	−279	...	65083	54484	...	...	−408	...	67968
E Manufacture of chemicals and chemical petroleum, coal, rubber and plastic products	113897	...	...	−1266	...	215324[c]	118427	...	...	−1485	...	198985[c]

Belgium

Million Belgian francs

		1986					1987				
	Compen-sation of employ-ees	Capital consump-tion	Net operating surplus	Indirect taxes	less: Subsidies received	Value added	Compen-sation of employ-ees	Capital consump-tion	Net operating surplus	Indirect taxes	less: Subsidies received	Value added
F Manufacture of non-metallic mineral products, except products of petro-leum and coal	37075	...	...	38	...	57058[d]	38820	...	...	–73	...	61604[d]
G Basic metal industries	72420	...	...	–230	...	98709	68773	...	...	–526	...	93720
H Manufacture of fabricated metal products, machinery and equipment	266298	...	...	–4349	...	322155	268514	...	...	–3092	...	335318
I Other manufacturing indus-tries	32939	...	...	–211	...	59880[b]	33387	...	...	–89	...	62276[b]
4 Electricity, gas and water	77813	...	...	50522	...	222568[c]	77349	...	...	54794	...	223514[c]
5 Construction	132540	...	...	635	...	256439	136322	...	...	617	...	257442
6 Wholesale and retail trade, restaurants and hotels	402322	...	...	–15097	...	859783	433528	...	...	–14983	...	918881
A Wholesale and retail trade	368990	...	...	–15132	...	729610[e]	398390	...	...	–15131	...	780517[e]
B Restaurants and hotels	33332	...	...	35	...	130173	35138	...	...	148	...	138364
7 Transport, storage and com-munication	233598	...	...	–79607	...	379142	236846	...	...	–69898	...	405805
A Transport and storage	176299	...	...	–67162	...	292761	182153	...	...	–58788	...	311394
B Communication	57299	...	...	–12445	...	86381	54693	...	...	–11110	...	94411
8 Finance, insurance, real estate and business services	179270	...	...	19330	...	298381	190882	...	...	22946	...	317910
A Financial institutions	179270	...	...	19330	...	298381	190882	...	...	22946	...	317910
B Insurance	...	...	...	...	...	...	...	...	...	...	...	...
C Real estate and business services	...	...	...	...	...	...	...	...	...	...	...	...
9 Community, social and per-sonal services	287267	...	...	35304	...	1004315[f]	312729	...	...	46270	...	1081117[f]
Educational services	...	...	...	...	...	...	...	...	...	...	...	...
Medical, dental, other health and veterinary ser-vices	...	...	...	...	...	205892	...	...	...	...	...	217005
Statistical discrepancy	38826	...	...	–	...	–46699	26388	...	...	–	...	–28866
Total, Industries	2073962	...	...	23643	...	4166142	2147652	...	...	51762	...	4365359
Producers of government ser-vices	662230	...	...	...	...	678353	659261	...	...	...	...	676982
Other producers	50667	...	...	...	...	50667	50564	...	...	...	...	50564
Total	2786859	...	...	23643	...	4895162	2857477	...	...	51762	...	5092905
less: Imputed bank service charge	...	...	...	...	...	207845	...	...	...	...	...	204228
Import duties	...	...	...	42012	...	42012	...	...	...	51354	...	51354
Value added tax	...	...	...	355521	...	355521	...	...	...	378647	...	378647
Other adjustments	...	...	...	...	...	...	...	...	...	...	...	...
Total	2786859	471497	1324660	421176	...	5084850[gh]	2857477	497015	1384784	481763	...	5318678[gh]

Of which general government:

1 Agriculture, hunting, forestry and fishing	...	...	...	...	...	...	...	...	...	...	...	...
2 Mining and quarrying	...	...	...	...	...	...	...	...	...	...	...	...
3 Manufacturing	...	...	...	...	...	...	...	...	...	...	...	...
4 Electricity, gas and water	...	...	...	...	...	...	...	...	...	...	...	...
5 Construction	...	...	...	...	...	...	...	...	...	...	...	...
6 Wholesale and retail trade, restaurants and hotels	...	...	...	...	...	...	...	...	...	...	...	...

Belgium

Million Belgian francs

	1986						1987					
	Compensation of employees	Capital consumption	Net operating surplus	Indirect taxes	less: Subsidies received	Value added	Compensation of employees	Capital consumption	Net operating surplus	Indirect taxes	less: Subsidies received	Value added
7 Transport, storage and communication	...	...	...	...	...	...	...	...	...	...	...	...
8 Finance, insurance, real estate and business services	...	...	...	...	...	...	...	...	...	...	...	...
9 Community, social and personal services	...	...	...	...	...	...	...	...	...	...	...	...
Total, industries of general government	538	...	...	...	...	2544	555	...	...	...	...	2281
Producers of government services	...	...	...	...	...	...	...	...	...	...	...	...
Total, general government	...	...	...	...	...	...	...	...	...	...	...	...

	1988						1989					
	Compensation of employees	Capital consumption	Net operating surplus	Indirect taxes	less: Subsidies received	Value added	Compensation of employees	Capital consumption	Net operating surplus	Indirect taxes	less: Subsidies received	Value added
All producers												
1 Agriculture, hunting, forestry and fishing	7369	...	...	−4937	...	107067	8004	...	...	−5299	...	132978
2 Mining and quarrying	...	...	...	...	...	1185	...	...	...	...	...	1405
A Coal mining [a]	...	...	...	...	...	1185	...	...	...	...	...	1405
B Crude petroleum and natural gas production	...	...	...	...	...	...	...	...	...	...	...	...
C Metal ore mining	...	...	...	...	...	...	...	...	...	...	...	...
D Other mining	...	...	...	...	...	...	...	...	...	...	...	...
3 Manufacturing	750665	...	...	12858	...	1194676	801936	...	...	11436	...	1301680
A Manufacture of food, beverages and tobacco	83004	...	...	19326	...	174133	88984	...	...	24586	...	194308
B Textile, wearing apparel and leather industries	64596	...	...	−1095	...	83254	68338	...	...	−795	...	93503
C Manufacture of wood and wood products, including furniture [b]	...	...	...	...	...	51579	...	...	...	...	...	58521
D Manufacture of paper and paper products, printing and publishing	53602	...	...	−480	...	78720	58794	...	...	−540	...	82348
E Manufacture of chemicals and chemical petroleum, coal, rubber and plastic products	127197	...	...	−1062	...	223332[c]	131711	...	...	−877	...	233738[c]
F Manufacture of non-metallic mineral products, except products of petroleum and coal	40982	...	...	−8	...	68140[d]	45015	...	...	86	...	75421[d]
G Basic metal industries	71302	...	...	−898	...	128391	74783	...	...	−685	...	153555
H Manufacture of fabricated metal products, machinery and equipment	275818	...	...	−2832	...	371044	298572	...	...	−10090	...	396648
I Other manufacturing industries	34164	...	...	−93	...	67662[b]	35739	...	...	−249	...	72159[b]
4 Electricity, gas and water	74213	...	...	58475	...	229423[c]	76630	...	...	64563	...	239633[c]
5 Construction	151659	...	...	728	...	298049	168660	...	...	825	...	326709
6 Wholesale and retail trade, restaurants and hotels	457640	...	...	−5596	...	965528	492927	...	...	15657	...	1021728
A Wholesale and retail trade	417697	...	...	−5756	...	816578[e]	448971	...	...	15508	...	857915[e]
B Restaurants and hotels	39943	...	...	160	...	148950	43956	...	...	149	...	163813

Belgium

	1988						1989					
	Compensation of employees	Capital consumption	Net operating surplus	Indirect taxes	less: Subsidies received	Value added	Compensation of employees	Capital consumption	Net operating surplus	Indirect taxes	less: Subsidies received	Value added
7 Transport, storage and communication	242361	...	...	–77030	...	452207	253648	...	...	–73959	...	488516
A Transport and storage	186173	...	...	–67399	...	351977	195344	...	...	–64708	...	381720
B Communication	56188	...	...	–9631	...	100230	58304	...	...	–9251	...	106796
8 Finance, insurance, real estate and business services	195093	...	...	23688	...	324498	207501	...	...	27769	...	331126
A Financial institutions	195093	...	...	23688	...	324498	207501	...	...	27769	...	331126
B Insurance	...	...	...	...	...	...	...	...	...	...	...	...
C Real estate and business services	...	...	...	...	...	...	...	...	...	...	...	...
9 Community, social and personal services	336329	...	...	51748	...	1169440[f]	371888	...	...	61586	...	1281429[f]
Educational services	...	...	...	...	...	...	...	...	...	...	...	...
Medical, dental, other health and veterinary services	...	...	...	...	...	229004	...	...	...	...	...	246664
Statistical discrepancy	44777	...	...	–	...	–37995	–7912	...	...	–	...	–21546
Total, Industries	2260106	...	...	59934	...	4702893	2373282	...	...	102578	...	5102253
Producers of government services	663542	...	...	...	...	682657	700999	...	...	...	...	722151
Other producers	50584	...	...	...	...	50584	50661	...	...	...	...	50661
Total	2974232	...	...	59934	...	5436134	3124942	...	...	102578	...	5875065
less: Imputed bank service charge	...	...	...	...	...	200496	...	...	...	...	...	196064
Import duties	...	...	...	48578	...	48578	...	...	...	53723	...	53723
Value added tax	...	...	...	405255	...	405255	...	...	...	434633	...	434633
Other adjustments	...	...	...	...	...	...	...	...	...	...	...	...
Total	2974232	550515	1545640	513767	...	5689471[gh]	3124942	583961	1749376	590934	...	6167357[gh]

Of which general government:

1 Agriculture, hunting, forestry and fishing	...	...	...	...	...	...	...	...	...	...	...	...
2 Mining and quarrying	...	...	...	...	...	...	...	...	...	...	...	...
3 Manufacturing	...	...	...	...	...	...	...	...	...	...	...	...
4 Electricity, gas and water	...	...	...	...	...	...	...	...	...	...	...	...
5 Construction	...	...	...	...	...	...	...	...	...	...	...	...
6 Wholesale and retail trade, restaurants and hotels	...	...	...	...	...	...	...	...	...	...	...	...
7 Transport, storage and communication	...	...	...	...	...	...	...	...	...	...	...	...
8 Finance, insurance, real estate and business services	...	...	...	...	...	...	...	...	...	...	...	...
9 Community, social and personal services	...	...	...	...	...	...	...	...	...	...	...	...
Total, industries of general government	595	...	...	...	...	2509	613	...	...	...	...	2172
Producers of government services	...	...	...	...	...	...	...	...	...	...	...	...
Total, general government	...	...	...	...	...	...	...	...	...	...	...	...

Belgium

	1990						1991					
	Compensation of employees	Capital consumption	Net operating surplus	Indirect taxes	less: Subsidies received	Value added	Compensation of employees	Capital consumption	Net operating surplus	Indirect taxes	less: Subsidies received	Value added
All producers												
1 Agriculture, hunting, forestry and fishing	8807	...	...	–10189	...	119607	9422	...	...	–6223	...	124135
2 Mining and quarrying	...	...	...	...	...	1151	...	...	...	...	...	...
A Coal mining [a]	...	...	...	...	...	1151	...	...	...	...	...	...
B Crude petroleum and natural gas production	...	...	...	...	...	...	...	...	...	...	...	...
C Metal ore mining	...	...	...	...	...	...	...	...	...	...	...	...
D Other mining	...	...	...	...	...	...	...	...	...	...	...	...
3 Manufacturing	857676	...	...	10831	...	1363421	901447	...	...	18388	...	1328340
A Manufacture of food, beverages and tobacco	97207	...	...	18959	...	202297	101036	...	...	24080	...	213295
B Textile, wearing apparel and leather industries	69747	...	...	–884	...	101817	70347	...	...	–1908	...	98381
C Manufacture of wood and wood products, including furniture [b]	...	...	...	...	...	61626	...	...	...	...	...	...
D Manufacture of paper and paper products, printing and publishing	66440	...	...	–576	...	89194	68684	...	...	–606	...	88265
E Manufacture of chemicals and chemical petroleum, coal, rubber and plastic products	139994	...	...	–1565	...	237992[c]	157384	...	...	–1774	...	246584[c]
F Manufacture of non-metallic mineral products, except products of petroleum and coal	48277	...	...	–92	...	77813[d]	49604	...	...	142	...	75304[d]
G Basic metal industries	79871	...	...	–563	...	131881	78703	...	...	–76	...	103652
H Manufacture of fabricated metal products, machinery and equipment	319200	...	...	–4085	...	444841	337184	...	...	–1086	...	424160
I Other manufacturing industries	36940	...	...	–363	...	77586[b]	38505	...	...	–384	...	78699[b]
4 Electricity, gas and water	76516	...	...	73433	...	255573[c]	77800	...	...	80800	...	268132[c]
5 Construction	191210	...	...	500	...	348489	206511	...	...	687	...	358403
6 Wholesale and retail trade, restaurants and hotels	533143	...	...	18925	...	1154772	586480	...	...	–3103	...	1239954
A Wholesale and retail trade	484437	...	...	19059	...	972538[e]	534882	...	...	–2985	...	1042800[e]
B Restaurants and hotels	48706	...	...	–134	...	182234	51598	...	...	–118	...	197154
7 Transport, storage and communication	273593	...	...	–80436	...	524569	299268	...	...	–86695	...	555905
A Transport and storage	209911	...	...	–70194	...	409869	228878	...	...	–75768	...	435406
B Communication	63682	...	...	–10242	...	114700	70390	...	...	–10927	...	120499
8 Finance, insurance, real estate and business services	218633	...	...	29064	...	305981	229571	...	...	31500	...	336545
A Financial institutions	218633	...	...	29064	...	305981	229571	...	...	31500	...	336545
B Insurance	...	...	...	...	...	...	...	...	...	...	...	...
C Real estate and business services	...	...	...	...	...	...	...	...	...	...	...	...
9 Community, social and personal services	418553	...	...	57011	...	1360848[f]	476256	...	...	54910	...	1456390[f]
Educational services	...	...	...	...	...	...	...	...	...	...	...	...
Medical, dental, other health and veterinary services	...	...	...	...	...	265719	...	...	...	...	...	...
Statistical discrepancy	19569	...	...	–	...	–23662	2781	...	...	–	...	–13291

Belgium

	1990						1991					
	Compensation of employees	Capital consumption	Net operating surplus	Indirect taxes	less: Subsidies received	Value added	Compensation of employees	Capital consumption	Net operating surplus	Indirect taxes	less: Subsidies received	Value added
Total, Industries	2597700	...	...	99139	...	5409598	2789536	...	...	90264	...	5654513
Producers of government services	739123	...	...	...	...	760731	795636	...	...	...	...	818377
Other producers	52419	...	...	...	...	52419	54588	...	...	...	...	54588
Total	3389242	...	...	99139	...	6222748	3639760	...	...	90264	...	6527478
less: Imputed bank service charge	...	...	...	...	...	184038	...	...	...	...	...	198480
Import duties	...	...	...	55699	...	55699	...	...	...	60421	...	60421
Value added tax	...	...	...	459966	...	459966	...	...	...	479529	...	479529
Other adjustments	...	...	...	...	...	...	...	...	...	...	...	...
Total	3389242	643413	1799921	614804	...	6554375 [gh]	3639760	658518	1822041	630214	...	6868948 [gh]

Of which general government:

1 Agriculture, hunting, forestry and fishing	...	...	...	...	...	...	...	...	...	...	...	...
2 Mining and quarrying	...	...	...	...	...	...	...	...	...	...	...	...
3 Manufacturing	...	...	...	...	...	...	...	...	...	...	...	...
4 Electricity, gas and water	...	...	...	...	...	...	...	...	...	...	...	...
5 Construction	...	...	...	...	...	...	...	...	...	...	...	...
6 Wholesale and retail trade, restaurants and hotels	...	...	...	...	...	...	...	...	...	...	...	...
7 Transport, storage and communication	...	...	...	...	...	...	...	...	...	...	...	...
8 Finance, insurance, real estate and business services	...	...	...	...	...	...	...	...	...	...	...	...
9 Community, social and personal services	...	...	...	...	...	...	...	...	...	...	...	...
Total, industries of general government	652	...	...	...	...	3433	...	...	...	...	...	...
Producers of government services	...	...	...	...	...	...	...	...	...	...	...	...
Total, general government	...	...	...	...	...	...	...	...	...	...	...	...

	1992						1993					
	Compensation of employees	Capital consumption	Net operating surplus	Indirect taxes	less: Subsidies received	Value added	Compensation of employees	Capital consumption	Net operating surplus	Indirect taxes	less: Subsidies received	Value added

All producers

1 Agriculture, hunting, forestry and fishing	10367	...	...	−4814	...	119675	10769	...	...	−9667	...	114623
2 Mining and quarrying	...	...	...	...	...	...	...	...	...	...	...	...
3 Manufacturing	912567	...	...	23578	...	1353091	905559	...	...	25538	...	1349559
A Manufacture of food, beverages and tobacco	102690	...	...	24734	...	218848	103758	...	...	22648	...	218732
B Textile, wearing apparel and leather industries	69340	...	...	−701	...	100890	65278	...	...	−752	...	100048
C Manufacture of wood and wood products, including furniture	...	...	...	...	...	...	...	...	...	...	...	...
D Manufacture of paper and paper products, printing and publishing	71987	...	...	−642	...	89498	72047	...	...	−466	...	90674
E Manufacture of chemicals and chemical petroleum, coal, rubber and plastic products	161352	...	...	−538	...	258521 [c]	166541 [c]	...	...	−308 [c]	...	244033 [c]

Belgium

	1992						1993					
	Compensation of employees	Capital consumption	Net operating surplus	Indirect taxes	less: Subsidies received	Value added	Compensation of employees	Capital consumption	Net operating surplus	Indirect taxes	less: Subsidies received	Value added
F Manufacture of non-metallic mineral products, except products of petroleum and coal	52358	...	...	229	...	86007[d]	51641[d]	...	...	303[d]	...	85483[d]
G Basic metal industries	79122	...	...	243	...	107495	81509	...	...	683	...	97204
H Manufacture of fabricated metal products, machinery and equipment	336677	...	...	680	...	416081	321203	...	...	3792	...	438323
I Other manufacturing industries	39041	...	...	−427	...	75751[b]	43582[b]	...	...	−362[b]	...	75062[b]
4 Electricity, gas and water	78940	...	...	96495	...	285264[c]	79912[c]	...	...	107677[c]	...	298172[c]
5 Construction	226012	...	...	609	...	387626	225040	...	...	840	...	378784
6 Wholesale and retail trade, restaurants and hotels	625828	...	...	1652	...	1319985	636364	...	...	24206	...	1345143
A Wholesale and retail trade	568889	...	...	1787	...	1094681[e]	576988[e]	...	...	24222[e]	...	1117648[e]
B Restaurants and hotels	56939	...	...	−135	...	225304	59376	...	...	−16	...	227495
7 Transport, storage and communication	321950	...	...	−80388	...	577817	330155	...	...	−88966	...	582423
A Transport and storage	246191	...	...	−70025	...	453384	251001	...	...	−78183	...	451065
B Communication	75759	...	...	−10363	...	124433	79154	...	...	−10783	...	131358
8 Finance, insurance, real estate and business services	239078	...	...	34354	...	365307	258098	...	...	37430	...	366770
A Financial institutions	239078	...	...	34354	...	365307	258098	...	...	37430	...	366770
B Insurance	...	...	...	...	...	...	...	...	...	...	...	...
C Real estate and business services	...	...	...	...	...	...	...	...	...	...	...	...
9 Community, social and personal services	510958	...	...	59620	...	1555948[f]	542114[f]	...	...	65909[f]	...	1636849[f]
Statistical discrepancy	4835	...	...	–	...	2108	−21806	...	...	–	...	10903
Total, Industries	2930535	...	...	131106	...	5966821	2966205	...	...	162967	...	6083226
Producers of government services	839754	...	...	...	...	863275	894582	...	...	...	...	918649
Other producers	57284	...	...	...	...	57284	58880	...	...	...	...	58880
Total	3827573	...	...	131106	...	6887380	3919667	...	...	162967	...	7060755
less: Imputed bank service charge	...	...	...	...	...	211798	...	...	...	...	...	215917
Import duties	...	...	...	58173	...	58173	...	...	...	56162	...	56162
Value added tax	...	...	...	494808	...	494808	...	...	...	504226	...	504226
Other adjustments	...	...	...	...	...	...	...	...	...	...	...	...
Total	3827573	692589	1901197	684087	...	7228563[gh]	3919667[gh]	702658[gh]	1955199[gh]	723355[gh]	...	7405226[gh]

	1994						1995					
	Compensation of employees	Capital consumption	Net operating surplus	Indirect taxes	less: Subsidies received	Value added	Compensation of employees	Capital consumption	Net operating surplus	Indirect taxes	less: Subsidies received	Value added

All producers

1 Agriculture, hunting, forestry and fishing	11471	...	...	−14537	...	113230	12298	...	...	−11573	...	96505
2 Mining and quarrying	...	...	...	...	...	...	...	...	...	...	...	...
3 Manufacturing	906073	...	...	24894	...	1438724	916363	...	...	26441	...	1526391
A Manufacture of food, beverages and tobacco	105707	...	...	21482	...	230985	106433	...	...	22737	...	240054
B Textile, wearing apparel and leather industries	64223	...	...	−893	...	104048	61531	...	...	−852	...	101767

Belgium

	1994						1995					
	Compensation of employees	Capital consumption	Net operating surplus	Indirect taxes	less: Subsidies received	Value added	Compensation of employees	Capital consumption	Net operating surplus	Indirect taxes	less: Subsidies received	Value added
C Manufacture of wood and wood products, including furniture	...	...	...	...	...	...	...	...	...	...	...	...
D Manufacture of paper and paper products, printing and publishing	71584	...	...	−278	...	95380	74466	...	...	−287	...	104911
E Manufacture of chemicals and chemical petroleum, coal, rubber and plastic products [c]	163758	...	...	−21	...	269318	165409	...	...	20	...	310845
F Manufacture of non-metallic mineral products, except products of petroleum and coal [d]	53539	...	...	389	...	91118	55028	...	...	452	...	97440
G Basic metal industries	81762	...	...	526	...	108816	81743	...	...	557	...	121074
H Manufacture of fabricated metal products, machinery and equipment	322093	...	...	3941	...	463664	327463	...	...	4061	...	470812
I Other manufacturing industries [b]	43407	...	...	−252	...	75395	44290	...	...	−247	...	79488
4 Electricity, gas and water [c]	82916	...	...	118408	...	314832	87362	...	...	122155	...	330591
5 Construction	233740	...	...	1206	...	393325	227722	...	...	1301	...	409908
6 Wholesale and retail trade, restaurants and hotels	639198	...	...	34108	...	1388894	658054	...	...	30014	...	1396684
A Wholesale and retail trade [e]	576183	...	...	33932	...	1148165	591764	...	...	29794	...	1145359
B Restaurants and hotels	63015	...	...	176	...	240729	66290	...	...	220	...	251325
7 Transport, storage and communication	331223	...	...	−86073	...	633597	344733	...	...	−93984	...	656145
A Transport and storage	250188	...	...	−78101	...	491697	259376	...	...	−82248	...	504733
B Communication	81035	...	...	−7972	...	141900	85357	...	...	−11736	...	151412
8 Finance, insurance, real estate and business services	266401	...	...	38136	...	397218	275064	...	...	38894	...	413478
A Financial institutions	266401	...	...	38136	...	397218	275064	...	...	38894	...	413478
B Insurance	...	...	...	...	...	...	...	...	...	...	...	...
C Real estate and business services	...	...	...	...	...	...	...	...	...	...	...	...
9 Community, social and personal services [f]	573361	...	...	79267	...	1727880	609397	...	...	72817	...	1837342
Statistical discrepancy	11797	...	...	−	...	−50150	3969	...	...	−	...	−41734
Total, Industries	3056180	...	...	195409	...	6357550	3134962	...	...	186065	...	6625310
Producers of government services	941914	...	...	...	...	966666	984011	...	...	...	...	1009168
Other producers	59945	...	...	...	...	59945	60719	...	...	...	...	60719
Total	4058039	...	...	195409	...	7384161	4179692	...	...	186065	...	7695197
less: Imputed bank service charge	...	...	...	...	...	220727	...	...	...	...	...	237016
Import duties	...	...	...	58011	...	58011	...	...	...	60039	...	60039
Value added tax	...	...	...	547441	...	547441	...	...	...	549915	...	549915
Other adjustments	...	...	...	...	...	...	...	...	...	...	...	...
Total [g,h]	4058039	...	...	800861	...	7768886	4179692	...	...	796019	...	8068135

Belgium

	1996						1997					
	Compensation of employees	Capital consumption	Net operating surplus	Indirect taxes	less: Subsidies received	Value added	Compensation of employees	Capital consumption	Net operating surplus	Indirect taxes	less: Subsidies received	Value added
All producers												
1 Agriculture, hunting, forestry and fishing	12587	...	...	−13271	...	96086	...	...	...	−13324	...	98222
2 Mining and quarrying	...	...	...	...	...	...	...	...	...	...	...	...
3 Manufacturing	928207	...	...	20744	...	1507105	...	...	...	25813	...	1594328
A Manufacture of food, beverages and tobacco	107407	...	...	18587	...	243892	...	...	...	22938	...	263882
B Textile, wearing apparel and leather industries	58832	...	...	−817	...	94979	...	...	...	−854	...	99402
C Manufacture of wood and wood products, including furniture	...	...	...	...	...	...	...	...	...	...	...	...
D Manufacture of paper and paper products, printing and publishing	74650	...	...	−286	...	101451	...	...	...	−280	...	102957
E Manufacture of chemicals and chemical petroleum, coal, rubber and plastic products [c]	169242	...	...	−328	...	309680	...	...	...	−114	...	343156
F Manufacture of non-metallic mineral products, except products of petroleum and coal [d]	55283	...	...	249	...	94741	...	...	...	331	...	99372
G Basic metal industries	79012	...	...	215	...	108203	...	...	...	179	...	112819
H Manufacture of fabricated metal products, machinery and equipment	339822	...	...	3416	...	475771	...	...	...	3846	...	493189
I Other manufacturing industries [b]	43959	...	...	−292	...	78388	...	...	...	−233	...	79551
4 Electricity, gas and water [c]	84411	...	...	129640	...	354231	...	...	...	135571	...	369157
5 Construction	218433	...	...	887	...	406353	...	...	...	1165	...	432724
6 Wholesale and retail trade, restaurants and hotels	663161	...	...	53560	...	1471080	...	...	...	58322	...	1515410
A Wholesale and retail trade [e]	594553	...	...	53572	...	1206684	...	...	...	58187	...	1232282
B Restaurants and hotels	68608	...	...	−12	...	264396	...	...	...	135	...	283128
7 Transport, storage and communication	352442	...	...	−98001	...	666122	...	...	...	−81920	...	713442
A Transport and storage	270399	...	...	−82799	...	504912	...	...	...	−78442	...	542713
B Communication	82043	...	...	−15202	...	161210	...	...	...	−3478	...	170729
8 Finance, insurance, real estate and business services	282024	...	...	41763	...	456580	...	...	...	47548	...	446111
A Financial institutions	282024	...	...	41763	...	456580	...	...	...	47548	...	446111
B Insurance	...	...	...	...	...	...	...	...	...	...	...	...
C Real estate and business services	...	...	...	...	...	...	...	...	...	...	...	...
9 Community, social and personal services [f]	639913	...	...	82022	...	1938122	...	...	...	92662	...	2021871
Statistical discrepancy	8980	...	...	−	...	−32022	...	...	...	−	...	−49234
Total, Industries	3190158	...	...	217344	...	6863657	...	...	...	265837	...	7142031
Producers of government services	1003555	...	...	...	...	1028940	...	...	...	...	...	1061339
Other producers	62500	...	...	...	...	62500	...	...	...	...	...	64330
Total	4256213	...	...	217344	...	7955097	...	...	...	265837	...	8267700
less: Imputed bank service charge	...	...	...	...	...	285624	...	...	...	...	...	261519
Import duties	...	...	...	59798	...	59798	...	...	...	69115	...	69115

Belgium

	1996						1997					
	Compensation of employees	Capital consumption	Net operating surplus	Indirect taxes	less: Subsidies received	Value added	Compensation of employees	Capital consumption	Net operating surplus	Indirect taxes	less: Subsidies received	Value added
Value added tax	...	...	...	575873	...	575873	...	...	...	600188	...	600188
Other adjustments	...	...	...	...	...	...	...	...	...	...	...	...
Total [gh]	4256213	...	...	853015	...	8305144	...	...	...	935140	...	8675484

[a] Agglomeration and briquettes of coal are included in item "Coal mining".
[b] Item "Other manufacturing industries" includes item "Manufacture of wood and paper products".
[c] Item "Manufacture of chemicals and chemical petroleum, etc." excludes energy products which are included in item "Electricity, gas and water".
[d] Item "Manufacture of non-metallic mineral products, etc." includes "Other mining".
[e] Including repairs and recovery.
[f] Business services and real estate except dwellings are included in item "Community, social and personal services".
[g] Column "Indirect taxes" includes subsidies received.
[h] The breakdown by kind of economic activity used in this table is according to the classification NACE/CLIO.

Belize

Source

Reply to the United Nations National Accounts Questionnaire from the Central Planning Unit, Ministry of Finance and Economic Planning, Belize. Official estimates are published in *National Accounts Statistics*. Information on sources and methods of estimation can be found in *National Accounts Statistics—Sources and Methods* and in *Economic Accounts of the Public Sector*.

General note

The estimates shown in the following tables have been prepared in accordance with the United Nations System of National Accounts (1968 SNA) so far as the existing data would permit.

1.1 Expenditure on the gross domestic product, in current prices

Million Belize dollars

	1986	1987	1988	1989	1990	1991	1992	1993	1994	1995	1996	1997
1 Government final consumption expenditure	103	127	132	146	155	167	176	...	...	...	...	...
2 Private final consumption expenditure	260	287	328	390	344	571	603	...	...	...	...	...
3 Gross capital formation	93	121	160	220	226	260	290	...	...	...	...	...
A Increase in stocks	13	2	−2	21	18	15	12	...	...	...	...	...
B Gross fixed capital formation	80	119	162	199	208	245	278	...	...	...	...	...
4 Exports of goods and services	398	468	572	619	710	609	644	...	...	...	...	...
5 less: Imports of goods and services	398	450	562	650	642	745	775	...	...	...	...	...
equals: Gross domestic product	456	553	630	726	793	861	936	...	...	...	...	...

1.2 Expenditure on the gross domestic product, in constant prices

Million Belize dollars

	1986	1987	1988	1989	1990	1991	1992	1993	1994	1995	1996	1997
At constant prices of: 1984												
1 Government final consumption expenditure	98	119	120	130	134	136	138	...	...	...	...	...
2 Private final consumption expenditure	199	223	256	273	226	362	370	...	...	...	...	...
3 Gross capital formation	90	116	148	195	195	212	229	...	...	...	...	...
A Increase in stocks	13	2	−2	19	16	12	9	...	...	...	...	...
B Gross fixed capital formation	77	113	150	176	180	200	219	...	...	...	...	...
4 Exports of goods and services	440	461	529	588	664	590	617	...	...	...	...	...
5 less: Imports of goods and services	381	422	510	578	554	608	612	...	...	...	...	...
equals: Gross domestic product	446	498	542	608	665	692	742	...	...	...	...	...

Belize

1.3 Cost components of the gross domestic product

Million Belize dollars

	1986	1987	1988	1989	1990	1991	1992	1993	1994	1995	1996	1997
1 Indirect taxes, net	63	74	98	113	118	134	143	...	...	...	...	...
2 Consumption of fixed capital	30	37	41	45	50	55	59	...	...	...	...	...
3 Compensation of employees paid by resident producers to ..	362	443	490	568	626	672	734					
4 Operating surplus								...	...	...	...	...
equals: Gross domestic product ..	456	553	630	726	793	861	936	...	...	...	...	...

1.10 Gross domestic product by kind of activity, in current prices

Million Belize dollars

	1986	1987	1988	1989	1990	1991	1992	1993	1994	1995	1996	1997
1 Agriculture, hunting, forestry and fishing	82	109	118	131	148	145	160	152	...	...	...	...
2 Mining and quarrying	2	2	2	3	4	6	6	7	...	...	...	...
3 Manufacturing	61	89	98	106	106	112	109	111	...	...	...	...
4 Electricity, gas and water	13	15	17	16	15	19	24	29	...	...	...	...
5 Construction	20	27	34	46	54	59	63	70	...	...	...	...
6 Wholesale and retail trade, restaurants and hotels	62	73	87	109	127	132	140	147	...	...	...	...
7 Transport, storage and communication	41	48	49	61	73	84	94	107	...	...	...	...
8 Finance, insurance, real estate and business services	40	40	49	65	64	76	88	94	...	...	...	...
9 Community, social and personal services	38	39	42	44	46	48	51	53	...	...	...	...
Total, Industries	360	442	495	580	638	682	735	770	...	...	...	...
Producers of government services	45	52	57	63	70	76	94	95	...	...	...	...
Other producers	...	...	...	...	...	...	...	...	...	...	...	...
Subtotal [a]	405	494	552	644	708	759	829	865	...	...	...	...
less: Imputed bank service charge	12	14	21	30	32	32	36	38	...	...	...	...
plus: Import duties	...	...	...	...	...	...	...	...	...	...	...	...
plus: Value added tax	...	...	...	...	...	...	...	...	...	...	...	...
plus: Other adjustments [b]	63	74	98	113	118	134	143	168	...	...	...	...
equals: Gross domestic product ..	456	553	630	726	793	861	936	995	...	...	...	...

a Gross domestic product in factor values.   b Item "Other adjustments" refers to indirect taxes net of subsidies.

1.11 Gross domestic product by kind of activity, in constant prices

Million Belize dollars

	1986	1987	1988	1989	1990	1991	1992	1993	1994	1995	1996	1997
	At constant prices of: 1984											
1 Agriculture, hunting, forestry and fishing	74	89	90	95	107	110	123	122	...	...	...	...
2 Mining and quarrying	2	2	2	3	4	5	5	6	...	...	...	...
3 Manufacturing	76	82	80	89	97	94	105	104	...	...	...	...
4 Electricity, gas and water	7	8	8	9	10	12	14	16	...	...	...	...
5 Construction	20	26	29	37	41	44	46	49	...	...	...	...
6 Wholesale and retail trade, restaurants and hotels	60	68	79	97	110	108	110	113	...	...	...	...

Belize

Million Belize dollars

	1986	1987	1988	1989	1990	1991	1992	1993	1994	1995	1996	1997
At constant prices of: 1984												
7 Transport, storage and communication	37	41	51	64	72	80	91	100	...	...	...	...
8 Finance, insurance, real estate and business services	42	46	50	50	54	54	57	59	...	...	...	...
9 Community, social and personal services	38	39	40	42	43	44	45	46	...	...	...	...
Total, Industries	355	402	430	485	536	552	595	616	...	...	...	...
Producers of government services	43	45	46	48	51	53	55	56	...	...	...	...
Other producers	...	...	...	...	...	...	...	...	...	...	...	...
Subtotal [a]	398	447	475	533	586	605	650	672	...	...	...	...
less: Imputed bank service charge	14	16	18	19	20	20	21	22	...	...	...	...
plus: Import duties	...	...	...	...	...	...	...	...	...	...	...	...
plus: Value added tax	...	...	...	...	...	...	...	...	...	...	...	...
plus: Other adjustments [b]	62	66	85	94	98	108	114	...	...	...	...	...
equals: Gross domestic product	446	498	542	608	665	692	742	...	...	...	...	...

a Gross domestic product in factor values.　　　b Item "Other adjustments" refers to indirect taxes net of subsidies.

Bermuda

Source

Reply to the United Nations National Accounts Questionnaire from the Statistical Department of Bermuda, Hamilton.

General note

The estimates shown in the following tables have been prepared in accordance with the United Nations System of National Accounts (1968 SNA) so far as the existing data would permit.

1.1 Expenditure on the gross domestic product, in current prices

Million Bermuda dollars — Fiscal year beginning 1 April

	1986	1987	1988	1989	1990	1991	1992	1993	1994	1995	1996	1997
1 Government final consumption expenditure	141	157	173	192	208	217	218	220	244	249	268	...
2 Private final consumption expenditure	837	927	1019	1094	1157	1191	1230	1270	1327	1373	1413	...
A Households	823	913	1003	1078	1140	1174	1205	1245	1301	1347	1386	...
B Private non-profit institutions serving households	14	14	15	16	17	18	25	25	26	26	27	...
3 Gross capital formation	187	228	295	257	237	226	236	239	234	258	315	...
A Increase in stocks	...	...	...	...	...	...	...	...	...	...	...	...
B Gross fixed capital formation	187	228	295	257	237	226	236	239	234	258	315	...
Residential buildings	51	57	63	68	76	62	49	37	39	...	...	...
Non-residential buildings	45	61	82	38	43	58	60	...	...	...	...	...
Other construction and land improvement, etc.	2	12	21	3	3	4	3	...	...	...	...	...
Other	89	97	129	148	116	102	124	...	...	...	...	...
4 Exports of goods and services	822	874	905	963	993	956	989	1116	1164	1211	1300	...
5 less: Imports of goods and services	690	772	890	915	960	884	953	982	1054	1007	1103	...
equals: Gross domestic product	1296	1415	1502	1592	1635	1705	1720	1864	1914	2083	2194	...

1.2 Expenditure on the gross domestic product, in constant prices

Million Bermuda dollars — Fiscal year beginning 1 April

At constant prices of: 1975

	1986	1987	1988	1989	1990	1991	1992	1993	1994	1995	1996	1997
1 Government final consumption expenditure	54	57	59	62	62	61	60	59	64	63	66	...
2 Private final consumption expenditure	380	403	420	427	422	416	418	421	430	438	447	...
3 Gross capital formation	85	97	117	96	84	76	78	78	74	79	95	...
A Increase in stocks	...	...	...	...	...	...	...	...	...	...	...	...
B Gross fixed capital formation	85	97	117	96	84	76	78	...	74	79	95	...
4 Exports of goods and services	340	345	338	343	337	312	316	342	352	347	363	...
5 less: Imports of goods and services	362	384	414	406	402	355	384	388	404	376	404	...
equals: Gross domestic product	498	518	520	521	502	510	489	512	515	551	567	...

Bermuda

1.7 External transactions on current account, summary

Million Bermuda dollars	1986	1987	1988	1989	1990	1991	1992	1993	1994	1995	1996	1997
Payments to the rest of the world												
1 Imports of goods and services	690	772	890	915	960	884	953	982	1054	1007	1103	...
A Imports of merchandise, c.i.f.	426	475	500	512	576	481	520	554	582	550	569	...
B Other	264	297	391	403	384	403	433	428	472	457	534	...
2 Factor income to rest of the world	25	22	26	46	53	59	47	55	53	65	...	...
3 Current transfers to the rest of the world	61	67	73	81	81	73	89	81	75	70	52	...
Payments to the rest of the world and surplus of the nation on current transfers	...	...	...	...	...	...	...	...	...	...	...	...
Receipts from the rest of the world												
1 Exports of goods and services	822	874	905	963	993	956	989	1116	1164	1211	1300	...
2 Factor income from rest of the world	57	57	35	63	59	61	74	87	77	...	...	...
3 Current transfers from rest of the world	...	7	7	8	8	10	11	10	15	9	–	...
Receipts from the rest of the world on current transactions	...	...	...	...	...	...	...	...	...	...	...	...

1.12 Relations among national accounting aggregates

Million Bermuda dollars	1986	1987	1988	1989	1990	1991	1992	1993	1994	1995	1996	1997
Gross domestic product	1296	1415	1502	1592	1635	1705	1720	1864	1914	2083	2194	...
plus: Net factor income from the rest of the world	32	35	9	17	6	2	15	40	22	64	66	...
Factor income from rest of the world	57	57	35	63	59	61	74	87	77	117	131	...
less: Factor income to the rest of the world	25	22	26	46	53	59	59	47	55	53	65	...
equals: Gross national product	1328	1450	1510	1609	1641	1707	1735	1904	1936	2147	2260	...
less: Consumption of fixed capital	...	...	...	...	...	...	...	...	...	...	...	...
equals: National income	...	...	...	...	...	...	...	...	...	...	...	...
plus: Net current transfers from the rest of the world	...	...	...	...	...	...	...	...	...	...	...	...
equals: National disposable income	...	...	...	...	...	...	...	...	...	...	...	...
less: Final consumption	...	...	...	...	...	...	...	...	...	...	...	...
equals: Net saving	...	...	...	...	...	...	...	...	...	...	...	...
less: Surplus of the nation on current transactions	...	...	...	...	...	...	...	...	...	...	...	...
equals: Net capital formation	...	...	...	...	...	...	...	...	...	...	...	...

Bhutan

Source

Reply to the United Nations National Accounts Questionnaire from the Central Statistical Office. The official estimates are published in *Revised Series on Gross Domestic Product of Bhutan*: and *National Accounts Statistics*.

General note

The estimates shown in the following tables have been prepared in accordance with the United Nations System of National Accounts (1968 SNA) so far as the existing data would permit.

1.1 Expenditure on the gross domestic product, in current prices

Million ngultrum

	1986	1987	1988	1989	1990	1991	1992	1993	1994	1995	1996	1997
1 Government final consumption expenditure	576	634	641	879	783	1015	1215	1383	2106	2727	3445	...
2 Private final consumption expenditure	1838	2321	2605	2495	2718	3229	3745	3411	3136	3147	4224	...
3 Gross capital formation	1135	1088	1519	1453	1683	1711	2948	3297	4100	4572	5204	...
A Increase in stocks	32	–162	10	–121	–34	–71	351	102	229	156	157	...
B Gross fixed capital formation	1103	1250	1509	1574	1717	1782	2597	3399	3871	4416	5046	...
Residential buildings	645	744	724	830	917	856	1214	1412	1556	1953	2404	...
Non-residential buildings												...
Other construction and land improvement, etc.												...
Other	458	506	784	743	800	926	1383	1987	2315	2463	2642	...
4 Exports of goods and services	550	838	1109	1256	1408	1829	2079	2264	2508	3712	3973	...
5 less: Imports of goods and services	1298	1286	1940	1701	1609	2281	3634	3163	3349	4190	5133	...
Statistical discrepancy	...	13	...	...	...	...	...	...	...	...	...	...
equals: Gross domestic product	2802	3608	3934	4382	4983	5501	6354	7192	8501	9968	11714	13892

1.2 Expenditure on the gross domestic product, in constant prices

Million ngultrum

	1986	1987	1988	1989	1990	1991	1992	1993	1994	1995	1996	1997
At constant prices of: 1980												
1 Government final consumption expenditure	...	...	...	...	...	...	...	...	...	...	...	...
2 Private final consumption expenditure	...	...	...	...	...	...	...	...	...	...	...	...
3 Gross capital formation	574	563	789	671	727	725	1148	1000	1259	1147	1293	...
A Increase in stocks	22	–90	5	–54	–9	–17	113	–30	74	50	44	...
B Gross fixed capital formation	551	653	784	724	736	742	1035	1030	1185	1097	1250	...
Residential buildings	244	320	297	298	316	279	360	389	462	471	579	...
Non-residential buildings	...	...	...	...	...	...	...	...	...	...	...	...
Other construction and land improvement, etc.	...	...	...	...	...	...	...	...	...	...	...	...

Bhutan

Million ngultrum	1986	1987	1988	1989	1990	1991	1992	1993	1994	1995	1996	1997
	At constant prices of: 1980											
Other	307	333	487	426	420	464	674	641	723	626	670	...
4 Exports of goods and services	...	...	...	...	...	...	...	...	...	...	...	...
5 less: Imports of goods and services	...	...	...	...	...	...	...	...	...	...	...	...
equals: Gross domestic product	1674	1973	1994	2087	2225	2303	2407	2553	2716	2918	3095	3300

1.3 Cost components of the gross domestic product

Million ngultrum	1986	1987	1988	1989	1990	1991	1992	1993	1994	1995	1996	1997
1 Indirect taxes, net [a]	43	77	83	74	134	159	176	185	351	358	308	...
2 Consumption of fixed capital	192[b]	331[b]	362	399	451	504	591	670	837	1126	1329	...
3 Compensation of employees paid by resident producers to	2567	3200	3489	3909	4397	4839	5587	6337	7313	8484	10077	
4 Operating surplus												...
equals: Gross domestic product	2802	3608	3934	4382	4983	5501	6354	7192	8501	9968	11714	...

[a] Item "Net indirect taxes" excludes excise refunds from the government of India.
[b] The sharp increase in 1987 for "Consumption of fixed capital" is due to the operation of the Chukha Hydel Project.

1.7 External transactions on current account, summary

Million ngultrum	1986	1987	1988	1989	1990	1991	1992	1993	1994	1995	1996	1997
Payments to the rest of the world												
1 Imports of goods and services	1298	1286	2006	1788	1609	2281	3634	3163	3349	4190	5133	...
A Imports of merchandise, c.i.f.	1205	1208	1838	1678	1920	2170	...	...	...	...	...	...
B Other	92	78	168	110	105	111	...	...	...	...	...	...
2 Factor income to rest of the world	524	420	374	343	455	574	862	929	805	1428	1590	...
A Compensation of employees	518	412	353	303	420	522	773	942	564	1195	1386	
B Property and entrepreneurial income	6	8	21	40	35	51	89	286	241	232	204	...
3 Current transfers to the rest of the world	–	...	...	...	...	...	...	...	...	...	...	
4 Surplus of the nation on current transactions	–1080	–635	–990	–539	–291	–640	–1953	–1272	–1072	–1272	–2117	...
Payments to the rest of the world and surplus of the nation on current transfers	742	1071	1390	1592	1773	2215	2543	2819	3083	4345	4606	
Receipts from the rest of the world												
1 Exports of goods and services	550	838	1101	1239	1408	1829	2079	2264	2508	3712	3973	...
A Exports of merchandise, f.o.b.	427	782	973	1115	1308	1718	...	...	...	...	...	...
B Other	123	56	128	124	97	111	...	...	...	...	...	
2 Factor income from rest of the world	57	70	30	171	129	82	128	194	171	220	194	...
A Compensation of employees	–	–	–	–	–	–	–	–	–	–	–	...
B Property and entrepreneurial income	57	70	30	171	129	82	128	194	171	220	194	
3 Current transfers from rest of the world	135	149	170	190	236	304	336	360	404	413	438	...
Statistical discrepancy	...	13	88	–8	...	...	...	...	...	...	...	
Receipts from the rest of the world on current transactions	742	1070	1390	1592	1773	2215	2543	2819	3083	4345	4606	...

Bhutan

1.10 Gross domestic product by kind of activity, in current prices

Million ngultrum

	1986	1987	1988	1989	1990	1991	1992	1993	1994	1995	1996	1997
1 Agriculture, hunting, forestry and fishing	1399	1624	1746	1924	2095	2305	2460	2802	3427	3898	4538	5109
2 Mining and quarrying	37	37	33	42	45	90	99	102	172	193	467	584
3 Manufacturing	137	205	226	302	397	500	647	752	875	1089	1393	1742
4 Electricity, gas and water [a]	97	377	388	391	385	384	445	561	574	1059	1102	1608
5 Construction	268	350	309	365	399	360	595	617	787	931	1040	1206
6 Wholesale and retail trade, restaurants and hotels	234	248	258	282	322	383	480	551	647	731	904	1021
7 Transport, storage and communication	114	126	181	236	347	398	471	587	638	688	856	1018
8 Finance, insurance, real estate and business services	171	210	264	307	378	409	439	458	468	503	442	495
9 Community, social and personal services [b]	351	416	508	525	540	564	609	709	751	1014	1216	...
Total, Industries	2808	3593	3914	4375	4848	5342	6178	7007	8150	9611	11405	13583
Producers of government services	...	...	...	...	...	...	...	...	...	...	...	...
Other producers	...	...	...	...	...	...	...	...	...	...	...	...
Subtotal [c]	2808	3593	3914	4375	4848	5342	6178	7007	8150	9611	11405	13583
less: Imputed bank service charge	49	62	63	67	58	52	68	68	−148	−231	−350	−417
plus: Import duties	...	...	...	...	...	...	...	...	...	...	...	...
plus: Value added tax	...	...	...	...	...	...	...	...	...	...	...	...
plus: Other adjustments [d]	43	77	83	74	134	159	176	185	351	358	308	308
equals: Gross domestic product	2802	3608	3934	4382	4983	5501	6354	7192	8501	9968	11714	13892

a The sharp increase beginning 1986 for item "Electricity, gas and water" is the result of the completion of Chukha Hydel Project.
b Item "Producers of government services" is included in item "Community, social and personal services".
c Gross domestic product in factor values.
d Item "Other adjustments" refers to indirect taxes net of subsidies.

1.11 Gross domestic product by kind of activity, in constant prices

Million ngultrum

	1986	1987	1988	1989	1990	1991	1992	1993	1994	1995	1996	1997
At constant prices of: 1980												
1 Agriculture, hunting, forestry and fishing	881	926	940	963	993	1025	1004	1040	1081	1124	1196	1244
2 Mining and quarrying	22	22	19	22	19	27	24	26	33	35	46	52
3 Manufacturing	71	105	110	129	158	187	209	219	233	270	314	360
4 Electricity, gas and water	60[a]	229[a]	225	222	204	200	210	232	259	325	343	361
5 Construction	142	152	129	136	137	116	169	178	222	243	243	258
6 Wholesale and retail trade, restaurants and hotels	143	142	129	134	135	145	161	164	178	203	211	...
7 Transport, storage and communication	84	91	122	142	172	182	192	235	242	245	275	305
8 Finance, insurance, real estate and business services	126	136	141	163	212	209	215	238	245	263	256	279
9 Community, social and personal services [b]	169	200	210	217	223	233	252	267	293	330	335	358
Total, Industries	1698	2003	2025	2128	2254	2324	2435	2598	2777	3013	3211	3427
Producers of government services	...	...	...	...	...	...	...	...	...	...	...	...
Other producers	...	...	...	...	...	...	...	...	...	...	...	...
Subtotal	1698	2003	2025	2128	2254	2324	2435	2598	2777	3013	3211	3417
less: Imputed bank service charge	24	30	32	41	29	21	28	45	61	95	116	127

Bhutan

Million ngultrum

	1986	1987	1988	1989	1990	1991	1992	1993	1994	1995	1996	1997
At constant prices of: 1980												
plus: Import duties	...	...	...	...	...	...	...	...	...	...	...	...
plus: Value added tax	...	...	...	...	...	...	...	...	...	...	...	...
plus: Other adjustments	...	...	...	...	...	...	...	...	...	...	...	...
equals: Gross domestic product [c]	1674	1973	1994	2087	2225	2303	2407	2553	2716	2918	3095	3300

a The sharp increase beginning 1986 for item "Electricity, gas and water" is the result of the completion of Chukha Hydel Project.
b Item "Producers of government services" is included in item "Community, social and personal services".
c Gross domestic product in factor values.

1.12 Relations among national accounting aggregates

Million ngultrum

	1986	1987	1988	1989	1990	1991	1992	1993	1994	1995	1996	1997
Gross domestic product	2802	3608	3934	4382	4983	5501	6354	7192	8501	9968	11714	13892
plus: Net factor income from the rest of the world	−467	−350	−344	−172	−326	−491	−734	−734	−634	−1208	−1396	−1605
Factor income from rest of the world	57	70	30	171	129	82	128	194	171	220	194	...
less: Factor income to the rest of the world	524	420	374	343	455	574	862	929	805	1428	1590	...
equals: Gross national product	2335	3258	3589	4210	4657	5010	5620	6458	7867	8760	10318	12286
less: Consumption of fixed capital	192	331	362	399	451	504	591	670	837	1127	1329	1329
equals: National income	2143	2928	3227	3811	4206	4507	5029	5788	7030	7634	8989	10958
plus: Net current transfers from the rest of the world	135	149	138	164	236	304	336	360	405	413	438	...
Current transfers from rest of the world	135	...	...	...	...	...	...	...	...	...	...	...
less: Current transfers to the rest of the world	−	...	...	...	...	...	...	...	...	...	...	...
equals: National disposable income	2278	3077	3365	3975	4442	4811	5364	6149	7430	8048	9426	...
less: Final consumption	2414	2955	3246	3374	3501	4244	4960	4794	5242	5874	7669	...
equals: Net saving	−136	122	120	601	940	567	404	1355	2189	2174	1757	...
less: Surplus of the nation on current transactions	−1080	−635	−1036	−452	−291	−640	−1953	−1272	−1072	−1272	−2117	...
equals: Net capital formation	944	758	1156	1053	1232	1207	2358	2627	3263	3445	3875	...

Bolivia

General note

The preparation of national accounts statistics in Bolivia is undertaken by the Instituto Nacional de Estadística, La Paz. The official estimates together with methodological notes are published in a series of publications entitled *Boletín de Cuentas Nacionales*. The most detailed description of the sources and methods used for the national accounts estimation is found in *Cuentas Nacionales, 1958–1966, Planeamiento*. On 1 January 1987, the Bolivian pesos was re-denominated from pesos to bolivianos. One boliviano is equivalent to one million pesos. The estimates are generally in accordance with the classifications and recommendations recommended in the United Nations System of National Accounts (1968 SNA). Input-output table for 1958 has been published in *La Matriz de Transacciones Intersectoriales de Bienes Nacionales e Importados*. The following tables have been prepared from successive replies to the United Nations national accounts questionnaire. When the scope and coverage of the estimates differ for conceptual or statistical reasons from the definitions and classifications recommended in SNA, a footnote is indicated to the relevant tables.

Gross domestic product

Gross domestic product is estimated mainly through the production approach.

Expenditures on the gross domestic product

All components of gross domestic product by expenditure type are estimated through the expenditure approach except private final consumption expenditure which is obtained as a residual. The estimates of the government final consumption expenditure are based on the annual government accounts furnished by the respective government agencies. Increase in stocks estimates are based on information obtained from the enterprises. For public capital information, estimates are obtained from financial statements of the public institutions. The estimates are classified by type of goods and subdivisions of the public sector. For the estimates of private capital formation, the Instituto Nacional de Estadística requests detailed information from the enterprises. The estimates of imported machinery and equipment are based on c.i.f. import values classified by use or economic destination. Trade margins and transport expenses are then added.

The estimation of domestically produced capital goods is done on the basis of annual industrial statistics. Data on exports of goods and services are obtained from the balance of payments accounts. The value of non-monetary gold export is added to the f.o.b. figures while imports are estimated by the Banco Central. For the constant price estimates, government expenditure on wages and salaries are revalued at base-year prices while purchases of goods and services are deflated by implicit price or cost-of-living indexes. The estimates of private consumption expenditure is obtained as a residual. For the remaining items, price deflation is used.

Cost structure of the gross domestic product

The cost structure of the gross domestic product has not been estimated since 1969.

Gross domestic product by kind of activity

The table of gross domestic product by kind of economic activity is prepared at market prices, i.e. producers' values. The production approach is used to estimate value added of most industries, but due to lack of information on intermediate consumption, value added coefficients established from the input-output table of 1958 have been utilized. The income approach is used to estimate value added of public administration and defence and some private industries. For agriculture, information relating to production volume is used, estimated on the basis of information on areas sown and production yields prepared by the Ministerio de Asuntos Campensinos y Agropecuarios and by special institutions. The gross value of production is estimated by using data on physical volumes and producer prices. Estimates of livestock production is based on existing livestock, information on meat cutting for domestic consumption and export data. The mining sector consists of the Corporación Minera de Bolivia (COMIBOL), and of medium and small mines. The basic statistics are obtained from the accounts of COMIBOL, from Ministerio de Minería, from financial statements of medium-sized mines and from export statistics for small mines.

The estimates for the manufacturing sector are based on information obtained from the annual industrial statistics published by the Instituto Nacional de Estadística supplemented by statistics from private and public institutions and other studies. Information on electricity is obtained from the Direccion Nacional de Electricidad which controls all the public and private enterprises. The sources used for the construction estimates are the accounts of public institutions permits issued by municipalities and financial statements submitted by the construction enterprises. The value of production of private construction, which is based on permits issued and classified by surface area, is adjusted by a percentage for planned unfulfilled work. Information on trade margins and trade volumes is furnished by various concerned institutions. The gross trade margins are estimated from the price differences between the wholesale and producers prices as well as the consumer and wholesale prices for all the agricultural products and a sample of manufactured and imported goods

Bolivia

entering the distribution channels. Restaurants and hotels estimates are based on a sample survey of the principal establishments in La Paz, blown-up to cover the whole country by using the number of establishments as indicators. The estimates of railway transport are based on the accounts of the public railway enterprise. The gross value of production for urban passenger transport is estimated on the basis of the number of buses in operation, mileage, passenger volumes and average tariffs. Air transport estimates are based on the accounting statements of the national airline as well as taxes charged on foreign airlines. The accounting statements of the financial institutions are used for the financial sector.

For ownership of dwellings, census information on population and housing is used supplemented by statistics on real estate. For public administration and defense, the main source is the annual financial statement requested by the Banco Central de Bolivia. Estimates for private services are obtained from concerned entities and institutions. For constant price estimates, value added for agriculture, mining and quarrying, manufacturing and transport sectors is extrapolated by quantity index for output. Value added of construction is estimated by multiplying the annual authorized construction volume by the base year prices. For the remaining industries, value added is deflated by appropriate price indexes.

1.1 Expenditure on the gross domestic product, in current prices

Million bolivianos

	1986	1987	1988	1989	1990	1991	1992	1993	1994	1995	1996	1997
1 Government final consumption expenditure	705	942	1230	1516	1815	2310	2833	3270	3750	4302	4939	...
2 Private final consumption expenditure	6214	7440	8537	9791	11870	14891	17489	19413	21441	24140	28275	...
3 Gross capital formation	1194	1514	1511	1471	1935	2980	3677	4051	3971	4799	5589	...
A Increase in stocks	234	368	138	−51	−4	209	86	−25	−133	−130	−50	...
B Gross fixed capital formation	959	1146	1372	1522	1939	2771	3592	4076	4104	4929	5639	...
Residential buildings	...	...	209	268	324	395	503	...	...	...	...	...
Non-residential buildings	...	...	94	108	155	214	298	...	...	...	...	...
Other construction and land improvement, etc.	...	...	496	548	601	777	975	...	...	...	...	...
Other	...	...	573	598	859	1385	1816	...	...	...	...	...
4 Exports of goods and services	2587	2494	2028	2856	3517	4109	4413	4667	5987	6249	7137	...
5 less: Imports of goods and services	1775	2211	2500	2939	3695	5159	6398	6943	7516	8005	9745	...
equals: Gross domestic product	8924	10178	10805	12694	15443	19132	22014	24459	27603	31485	36194	...

1.2 Expenditure on the gross domestic product, in constant prices

Thousand bolivianos

	1986	1987	1988 [a]	1989	1990	1991	1992	1993	1994	1995	1996	1997
At constant prices of:	1980				1990							
1 Government final consumption expenditure	12	14	13 1801	1817	1815	1876	1945	1995	2057	2083	2131	...
2 Private final consumption expenditure	82	85	87 11281	11482	11870	12264	12700	13123	13500	13929	14463	...
3 Gross capital formation	18	20	15 1937	1645	1935	2502	2635	2624	2354	2666	2936	...
A Increase in stocks	4	5	− 195	−62	−4	193	47	−22	−89	−93	−33	...
B Gross fixed capital formation	15	15	16 1742	1707	1939	2309	2588	2656	2443	2759	2971	...
4 Exports of goods and services	30	28	30 2541	3167	3517	3774	3816	4018	4625	4504	4927	...
5 less: Imports of goods and services	33	35	30 3341	3352	3695	4160	4573	4540	4510	4474	5012	...
equals: Gross domestic product	109	112	115 14220	14759	15443	16256	16524	17229	18025	18709	19446	...

a Beginning 1988, the estimates are in millions.

Bolivia

1.3 Cost components of the gross domestic product

Million bolivianos

	1986	1987	1988	1989	1990	1991	1992	1993	1994	1995	1996	1997
1 Indirect taxes, net	921	...	924	1104	1326	1787	2294	...	...	...	...	...
A Indirect taxes	923	...	931	1105	1326	1787	2294	...	...	...	...	...
B less: Subsidies	3	...	6	1	–	–	–	...	...	...	...	...
2 Consumption of fixed capital	...	...	...	...	...	...	...	...	...	...	...	...
3 Compensation of employees paid by resident producers to ..	2153	...	3793	4566	5386	6764	7983	...	...	...	...	...
A Resident households	2148	...	3781	4547	5364	6743	7952	...	...	...	...	...
B Rest of the world	5	...	12	19	22	21	31	...	...	...	...	...
4 Operating surplus	5850	...	6088	7024	8731	10581	11736	...	...	...	...	...
A Corporate and quasi-corporate enterprises	1591	...	...	...	...	...	...	...	...	...	...	...
B Private unincorporated enterprises	4259	...	...	...	...	...	...	...	...	...	...	...
C General government	...	...	...	...	...	...	...	...	...	...	...	...
equals: Gross domestic product ..	8924	...	10805	12694	15443	19132	22014	...	...	...	...	...

1.5 Current income and outlay of corporate and quasi-corporate enterprises, summary

Million bolivianos

	1986	1987	1988	1989	1990	1991	1992	1993	1994	1995	1996	1997
Receipts												
1 Operating surplus	601	...	938	1016	1307	1879	2171	...	...	...	...	...
2 Property and entrepreneurial income received	3	...	20	33	37	41	44	...	...	...	...	...
3 Current transfers	1	...	6	7	21	28	56	...	...	...	...	...
Statistical discrepancy	3	...	4	5	5	7	14	...	...	...	...	...
Total current receipts [a]	607	...	967	1062	1370	1956	2285	...	...	...	...	...
Disbursements												
1 Property and entrepreneurial income	53	...	591	553	810	1110	1018	...	...	...	...	...
2 Direct taxes and other current payments to general government	2	...	11	31	28	33	49	...	...	...	...	...
3 Other current transfers	4	...	10	8	4	8	7	...	...	...	...	...
Statistical discrepancy	3	...	7	11	12	15	24	...	...	...	...	...
1 Net saving [b]	545	...	348	458	517	790	1187	...	...	...	...	...
Total current disbursements and net saving [a]	607	...	967	1062	1370	1956	2285	...	...	...	...	...

a All data in this table exclude private non-financial corporations, and also exclude public and private financial corporations (banks, insurance and pension schemes).
b Excluding consumption of fixed capital.

1.6 Current income and outlay of households and non-profit institutions

Million bolivianos

	1986	1987	1988	1989	1990	1991	1992	1993	1994	1995	1996	1997
Receipts												
1 Compensation of employees	...	...	3793	4561	5380	6757	7976	...	...	...	...	...
2 Operating surplus of private unincorporated enterprises	...	...	5177	6138	7592	8899	9802	...	...	...	...	...

Bolivia

Million bolivianos

	1986	1987	1988	1989	1990	1991	1992	1993	1994	1995	1996	1997
3 Property and entrepreneurial income	...	...	472	465	731	957	1306	...	...	...	...	...
4 Current transfers	...	...	307	582	679	797	1067	...	...	...	...	...
A Social security benefits	...	...	187	352	392	527	792	...	...	...	...	...
B Social assistance grants	...	...	15	11	19	44	50	...	...	...	...	...
C Other	...	...	105	218	267	226	225	...	...	...	...	...
Statistical discrepancy	...	...	291	252	405	416	1403	...	...	...	...	...
Total current receipts [a]	...	...	10039	11998	14786	17826	21553	...	...	...	...	...

Disbursements

	1986	1987	1988	1989	1990	1991	1992	1993	1994	1995	1996	1997
1 Private final consumption expenditure	...	...	8537	9791	11870	14891	17489	...	...	...	...	...
2 Property income	...	...	1034	1092	1507	1947	3390	...	...	...	...	...
3 Direct taxes and other current transfers n.e.c. to general government	...	...	352	409	569	847	889	...	...	...	...	...
A Social security contributions	...	...	243	304	396	586	623	...	...	...	...	...
B Direct taxes	...	...	103	98	163	248	232	...	...	...	...	...
C Fees, fines and penalties	...	...	6	7	10	14	33	...	...	...	...	...
4 Other current transfers	...	...	16	15	21	46	44	...	...	...	...	...
5 Net saving [a,b]	...	...	100	690	819	95	−259	...	...	...	...	...
Total current disbursements and net saving	...	...	10039	11998	14786	17826	21553	...	...	...	...	...

a All data in this table also include private non-financial corporations.   b Excluding consumption of fixed capital.

1.7 External transactions on current account, summary

Million bolivianos

	1986	1987	1988	1989	1990	1991	1992	1993	1994	1995	1996	1997
Payments to the rest of the world												
1 Imports of goods and services	1775	...	2500	2939	3695	5159	6398	...	...	...	...	...
A Imports of merchandise, c.i.f.	1510	...	1381	1658	2226	3532	4348	...	...	...	...	...
B Other	265	...	1119	1281	1469	1627	2051	...	...	...	...	...
2 Factor income to rest of the world	330	...	666	731	783	863	850	...	...	...	...	...
A Compensation of employees	5	...	12	19	22	27	31	...	...	...	...	...
B Property and entrepreneurial income	325	...	654	712	761	836	818	...	...	...	...	...
3 Current transfers to the rest of the world	40	...	13	7	23	12	13	...	...	...	...	...
4 Surplus of the nation on current transactions	666	...	−821	−386	−437	−1309	−2133	...	...	...	...	...
Payments to the rest of the world and surplus of the nation on current transfers	2812	...	2358	3292	4064	4725	5128	...	...	...	...	...
Receipts from the rest of the world												
1 Exports of goods and services	2587	...	2028	2856	3517	4109	4413	...	...	...	...	...
A Exports of merchandise, f.o.b.	2418	...	1310	2052	2724	2889	2623	...	...	...	...	...
B Other	168	...	717	804	793	1221	1790	...	...	...	...	...
2 Factor income from rest of the world	30	...	49	73	70	100	84	...	...	...	...	...
A Compensation of employees	5	...	12	13	16	20	24	...	...	...	...	...

Bolivia

Million bolivianos

	1986	1987	1988	1989	1990	1991	1992	1993	1994	1995	1996	1997
B Property and entrepreneurial income	25	...	37	59	54	80	60	...	...	...	...	...
3 Current transfers from rest of the world	195	...	281	363	477	515	631	...	...	...	...	...
Receipts from the rest of the world on current transactions	2812	...	2358	3292	4064	4725	5128	...	...	...	...	...

1.8 Capital transactions of the nation, summary

Million bolivianos

	1986	1987	1988	1989	1990	1991	1992	1993	1994	1995	1996	1997
Finance of gross capital formation												
Gross saving	1860	...	690	1085	1498	1671	1544	...	...	...	...	...
1 Consumption of fixed capital	–	...	–	...	...	...	...	...	...	...	...	...
2 Net saving	1860	...	690	1085	1498	1671	1544	...	...	...	...	...
less: Surplus of the nation on current transactions	666	...	–821	–386	–437	–1309	–2133	...	...	...	...	...
Finance of gross capital formation	1194	...	1511	1471	1935	2980	3677	...	...	...	...	...
Gross capital formation												
Increase in stocks	234	...	138	–51	–4	209	86	...	...	...	...	...
Gross fixed capital formation	959	...	1372	1522	1939	2771	3592	...	...	...	...	...
1 General government	238	...	336	448	526	793	1099	...	...	...	...	...
2 Corporate and quasi-corporate enterprises	393	...	991	1011	1343	1918	2381	...	...	...	...	...
A Public	242	...	606	616	649	871	1039	...	...	...	...	...
B Private	151	...	385	395	693	1046	1342	...	...	...	...	...
3 Other	328	...	46	63	71	61	112	...	...	...	...	...
Gross capital formation	1194	...	1511	1471	1935	2980	3677	...	...	...	...	...

1.9 Gross domestic product by institutional sectors of origin

Million bolivianos

	1986	1987	1988	1989	1990	1991	1992	1993	1994	1995	1996	1997
Domestic factor incomes originating												
1 General government	484	...	1037	1307	1553	1949	2412	...	...	...	...	...
2 Corporate and quasi-corporate enterprises	2275	...	8844	10283	12565	15396	17307	...	...	...	...	...
A Non-financial	2227	...	8781	10286	12573	15396	17279	...	...	...	...	...
Public	747	...	1260	1529	1953	2672	3302	...	...	...	...	...
Private	1480	...	7520	8757	10620	12725	13977	...	...	...	...	...
B Financial	47	...	63	–3	–8	–	28	...	...	...	...	...
3 Households and private unincorporated enterprises	5245	...	...	...	...	...	...	...	...	...	...	...
4 Non-profit institutions serving households	...	...	...	...	...	...	...	...	...	...	...	...
subtotal: Domestic factor incomes	8003	...	9881	11590	14117	17345	19720	...	...	...	...	...
Indirect taxes, net	921	...	924	1104	1326	1787	2294	...	...	...	...	...
A Indirect taxes	923	...	931	1105	1326	1787	2294	...	...	...	...	...
B less: Subsidies	3	...	6	1	–	–	–	...	...	...	...	...
Consumption of fixed capital	...	...	...	...	...	...	...	...	...	...	...	...
Gross domestic product	8924	...	10805	12694	15443	19132	22014	...	...	...	...	...

Bolivia

1.10 Gross domestic product by kind of activity, in current prices

Million bolivianos

	1986	1987	1988	1989	1990	1991	1992	1993	1994	1995	1996	1997
1 Agriculture, hunting, forestry and fishing	2450	...	1700	1937	2371	2974	3171	3583	4217	4461	4871	...
2 Mining and quarrying	890	...	941	1265	1582	1495	1602	1268	1361	1674	1774	...
3 Manufacturing	1184	...	1926	2156	2620	3392	3774	4127	4577	5497	6670	...
4 Electricity, gas and water	96	...	120	171	248	379	580	786	947	1145	1349	...
5 Construction	255	...	379	401	474	589	684	821	867	958	1119	...
6 Wholesale and retail trade, restaurants and hotels	970	...	1291	1549	1875	2320	2545	2799	3150	3636	4318	...
7 Transport, storage and communication	1056	...	863	1075	1439	1895	2315	2712	2988	3184	3149	...
8 Finance, insurance, real estate and business services	778	...	1278	1370	1569	1967	2274	2578	2904	3317	3960	...
9 Community, social and personal services	636	...	449	514	593	674	786	932	1058	1213	1407	...
Total, Industries	8315	...	8946	10438	12771	15684	17731	19606	22069	25085	28617	...
Producers of government services	484	...	1037	1307	1553	1949	2412	2805	3168	3675	4237	...
Other producers	50	...	67	79	93	113	128	145	160	184	211	...
Subtotal	8849	...	10050	11824	14416	17746	20272	22556	25397	28944	33065	...
less: Imputed bank service charge	66	...	144	200	253	346	486	613	816	988	1225	...
plus: Import duties	141	...	188	191	208	224	290	302	368	456	652	...
plus: Value added tax	...	...	349	410	458	681	1093	1288	1575	1753	2063	...
plus: Other adjustments	...	...	362	469	613	826	845	929	1077	1320	1638	...
equals: Gross domestic product	8924	...	10805	12694	15443	19132	22014	24458	27602	31485	36193	...

1.11 Gross domestic product by kind of activity, in constant prices

Thousand bolivianos

	1986	1987	1988 [a]	1989	1990	1991	1992	1993	1994	1995	1996	1997
At constant prices of:	1980				1990							
1 Agriculture, hunting, forestry and fishing	24	25	26 / 2302	2267	2371	2605	2495	2598	2775	2814	2906	...
2 Mining and quarrying	12	12	15 / 1284	1470	1582	1617	1639	1735	1799	1949	1924	...
3 Manufacturing	14	14	15 / 2315	2430	2619	2746	2748	2860	3003	3138	3265	...
4 Electricity, gas and water	1	1	1 / 222	235	248	266	278	321	356	385	418	...
5 Construction	3	3	3 / 437	462	474	502	559	591	599	624	706	...
6 Wholesale and retail trade, restaurants and hotels	15	16	15 / 1676	1777	1875	1995	2035	2097	2179	2244	2360	...
7 Transport, storage and communication	9	10	10 / 1268	1365	1439	1533	1604	1675	1773	1853	1944	...
8 Finance, insurance, real estate and business services	15	14	14 / 1529	1528	1569	1626	1729	1846	1999	2111	2221	...
9 Community, social and personal services	4	4	4 / 550	576	593	616	646	677	699	712	735	...
Total, Industries	97	99	103 / 11583	12110	12770	13506	13733	14400	15182	15830	16479	...
Producers of government services	10	10	10 / 1549	1570	1553	1565	1629	1678	1723	1749	1797	...
Other producers	1	1	1 / 88	91	93	94	96	98	101	102	104	...

Bolivia

Thousand bolivianos

	1986	1987	1988[a]	1989	1990	1991	1992	1993	1994	1995	1996	1997
At constant prices of:			1980 1990									
Subtotal	108	110	114 13220	13778	14416	15165	15458	16176	17006	17681	18380	...
less: Imputed bank service charge	1	1	1 194	234	253	280	333	387	484	533	603	...
plus: Import duties	2	2	2 177	184	208	247	265	261	255	257	292	
plus: Value added tax	...	...	432	443	458	481	499	518	535	556	598	...
plus: Other adjustments	...	...	586	575	613	642	636	661	711	748	780	...
equals: Gross domestic product	109	112	115 14220	14759	15443	16256	16524	17229	18025	18709	19446	...

a Beginning 1988, the estimates are in millions.

1.12 Relations among national accounting aggregates

Million bolivianos

	1986	1987	1988	1989	1990	1991	1992	1993	1994	1995	1996	1997
Gross domestic product	8924	...	10805	12694	15443	19132	22014	...	...	...	...	...
plus: Net factor income from the rest of the world	–300	...	–616	–658	–713	–763	–766	...	...	...	...	...
Factor income from rest of the world	30	...	49	73	70	100	84	...	...	...	...	...
less: Factor income to the rest of the world	330	...	666	731	783	863	850	...	...	...	...	...
equals: Gross national product	8624	...	10189	12036	14730	18369	21248	...	...	...	...	...
less: Consumption of fixed capital	–	...	...	...	...	...	...	...	...	...	...	...
equals: National income	8624	...	10189	12036	14730	18369	21248	...	...	...	...	...
plus: Net current transfers from the rest of the world	155	...	268	356	454	503	618	...	...	...	...	...
Current transfers from rest of the world	195	...	281	363	477	515	631	...	...	...	...	...
less: Current transfers to the rest of the world	40	...	13	7	23	12	13	...	...	...	...	...
equals: National disposable income	8779	...	10457	12392	15184	18873	21866	...	...	...	...	...
less: Final consumption	6919	...	9767	11307	13685	17201	20322	...	...	...	...	...
equals: Net saving	1860	...	690	1085	1498	1671	1544	...	...	...	...	...
less: Surplus of the nation on current transactions	666	...	–821	–386	–437	–1309	–2133	...	...	...	...	...
equals: Net capital formation	1194	...	1511	1471	1935	2980	3677	...	...	...	...	...

2.1 Government final consumption expenditure by function, in current prices

Million bolivianos

	1986	1987	1988	1989	1990	1991	1992	1993	1994	1995	1996	1997
1 General public services	...	...	921	1138	1343	1727	2160	2481	...	...	...	...
2 Defence	...	...	–	–	–	–	–	–	...	...	...	...
3 Public order and safety	...	...	...	...	...	...	...	...	...	...	...	...
4 Education	...	...	102	111	134	178	230	295	...	...	...	...
5 Health	...	...	1	1	–	1	1	1	...	...	...	...
6 Social security and welfare	...	...	50	32	26	44	54	79	...	...	...	...
7 Housing and community amenities	...	...	2	2	3	3	4	6	...	...	...	...
8 Recreational, cultural and religious affairs	...	...	2	2	3	3	4	6	...	...	...	...

Bolivia

Million bolivianos

	1986	1987	1988	1989	1990	1991	1992	1993	1994	1995	1996	1997
9 Economic services	...	...	53	70	78	97	84	83	...	...	...	...
A Fuel and energy	...	...	...	...	...	...	...	...	...	...	...	...
B Agriculture, hunting, forestry and fishing	...	...	3	3	4	4	12	22	...	...	...	...
C Mining (except fuels), manufacturing and construction	...	...	2	1	3	4	2	–	...	...	...	...
D Transportation and communication	...	...	48	66	70	89	70	61	...	...	...	...
E Other economic affairs	...	...	...	...	...	...	...	...	...	...	...	...
10 Other functions	...	...	100	160	228	257	297	320	...	...	...	...
Total government final consumption expenditures	...	...	1230	1516	1815	2310	2833	3270	...	...	...	...

2.5 Private final consumption expenditure by type and purpose, in current prices

Million bolivianos

	1986	1987	1988	1989	1990	1991	1992	1993	1994	1995	1996	1997
Final consumption expenditure of resident households												
1 Food, beverages and tobacco	2965	...	3233	3625	4393	5408	6242	6854	7583	8858	10260	...
A Food	2764	...	2861	3243	3943	4844	5586	6117	6737	7581	9102	...
B Non-alcoholic beverages	62	...	140	149	171	221	267	608	703	818	966	...
C Alcoholic beverages	70	...	191	179	210	254	280					...
D Tobacco	69	...	41	54	68	88	109	129	143	159	192	...
2 Clothing and footwear	203	...	602	690	815	1001	1105	1268	1436	1589	1820	...
3 Gross rent, fuel and power	498	...	998	1105	1292	1616	1846	...	...	...	...	...
A Fuel and power	54	...	143	180	255	354	495	588	738	910	1113	...
B Other	444	...	855	925	1037	1263	1351	...	...	...	...	...
4 Furniture, furnishings and household equipment and operation	416	...	627	712	846	1064	1301	...	...	...	...	...
A Household operation	55	...	75	96	102	129	166	...	...	...	...	...
B Other	361	...	552	616	744	934	1135	...	...	...	...	...
5 Medical care and health expenses	156	...	257	308	345	414	490	...	...	...	...	...
6 Transport and communication	1026	...	1206	1427	1909	2567	3086	2441	2685	2918	3163	...
A Personal transport equipment	173	...	92	94	185	256	268	...	...	...	...	...
B Other	854	...	1114	1334	1724	2311	2818	...	...	...	...	...
7 Recreational, entertainment, education and cultural services	260	...	603	737	885	1087	1328	...	...	...	...	...
A Education	74	...	309	381	470	570	697	...	...	...	...	...
B Other	187	...	294	356	415	517	631	...	...	...	...	...
8 Miscellaneous goods and services	663	...	929	1098	1290	1612	1935	...	...	...	...	...
A Personal care	19	...	15	20	20	26	31	...	...	...	...	...
B Expenditures in restaurants, cafes and hotels	570	...	780	927	1102	1379	1607	1794	1971	2334	2754	...
C Other	73	...	135	151	169	208	297	...	...	...	...	...
Statistical discrepancy	...	...	98	111	125	161	201	...	...	...	...	...
Total final consumption expenditure in the domestic market by households, of which	6187	...	8553	9812	11901	14930	17533	19360	21337	24063	28197	...

Bolivia

Million bolivianos

	1986	1987	1988	1989	1990	1991	1992	1993	1994	1995	1996	1997
plus: Direct purchases abroad by resident households	26	...	–16	–22	–31	–39	–45	–53	–74	–77	–77	
less: Direct purchases in the domestic market by non-resident households												...
equals: Final consumption expenditure of resident households [a]	6214	...	8537	9791	11870	14891	17489	19413	21411	24140	28275	...

a Item "Final consumption expenditure of resident households" includes consumption expenditure of private non-profit institutions serving households.

2.6 Private final consumption expenditure by type and purpose, in constant prices

Thousand bolivianos

	1986	1987	1988 [a]	1989	1990	1991	1992	1993	1994	1995	1996	1997
At constant prices of:			1980									
					1990							

Final consumption expenditure of resident households

	1986	1987	1988	1989	1990	1991	1992	1993	1994	1995	1996	1997
1 Food, beverages and tobacco	37	...		4230	4215	4393	4581	4739	...	...	...	...
A Food	34	...		3735	3778	3943	4101	4246	...	...	...	...
B Non-alcoholic beverages	1	...		168	166	171	178	183	...	...	...	...
C Alcoholic beverages	1	...		266	205	210	232	235	...	...	...	...
D Tobacco	1	...		60	66	68	70	75	...	...	...	...
2 Clothing and footwear	4	...		839	840	815	785	766	...	...	...	...
3 Gross rent, fuel and power	12	...		1244	1264	1292	1321	1343	...	...	...	...
A Fuel and power	1	...		232	243	255	265	273	...	...	...	...
B Other	11	...		1012	1021	1037	1056	1070	...	...	...	...
4 Furniture, furnishings and household equipment and operation	6	...		810	834	846	863	916	...	...	...	...
A Household operation	1	...		91	106	102	106	115	...	...	...	...
B Other	5	...		719	727	744	757	801	...	...	...	...
5 Medical care and health expenses	4	...		324	347	346	354	370	...	...	...	...
6 Transport and communication	11	...		1710	1768	1909	1991	2044	...	...	...	...
A Personal transport equipment	1	...		116	106	185	217	191	...	...	...	...
B Other	9	...		1595	1662	1724	1774	1853	...	...	...	...
7 Recreational, entertainment, education and cultural services	4	...		815	860	885	908	947	...	...	...	...
A Education	2	...		425	451	470	478	491	...	...	...	...
B Other	2	...		390	410	415	430	457	...	...	...	...
8 Miscellaneous goods and services	4	...		1330	1381	1416	1494	1608	...	...	...	...
A Personal care	–	...		17	22	20	21	21	...	...	...	...
B Expenditures in restaurants, cafes and hotels	3	...		1030	1069	1102	1155	1206	...	...	...	...
C Other	1	...		283	290	294	318	380	...	...	...	...

Bolivia

Thousand bolivianos

	1986	1987	1988 [a]	1989	1990	1991	1992	1993	1994	1995	1996	1997
	At constant prices of:	1980										
		1990										
Total final consumption expenditure in the domestic market by households, of which	81	...	11303	11508	11901	12297	12734	...	...	...	...	...
plus: Direct purchases abroad by resident households	–	...	–22	–26	–31	–32	–33	...	...	...	...	...
less: Direct purchases in the domestic market by non-resident households	...	...	...	...	...	...	...	...	...	...	...	...
equals: Final consumption expenditure of resident households	82	...	11281	11482	11870	12264	12700	...	...	...	...	...

a Beginning 1988, the estimates are in millions.

2.7 Gross capital formation by type of good and owner, in current price

Million bolivianos

	1988				1989				1990			
	Total	Total private	Public enterprises	General government	Total	Total private	Public enterprises	General government	Total	Total private	Public enterprises	General government
Increase in stocks, total	138	85	53	–	–51	–158	107	–	–4	–93	89	–
Gross fixed capital formation, total	1372	431	606	336	1522	458	616	448	1939	764	649	526
1 Residential buildings	209	209	...	...	268	268	...	...	324	324	...	...
2 Non-residential buildings	94	67	14	13	108	72	18	17	155	86	3	66
3 Other construction	496	8	280	208	548	10	285	254	601	12	286	303
4 Land improvement and plantation and orchard development	...	...	...	...	...	...	...	...	...	...	...	...
5 Producers' durable goods	503	94	309	100	513	45	307	161	730	247	356	126
A Transport equipment	87	38	21	27	90	18	40	32	218	147	19	52
B Machinery and equipment	416	56	288	73	424	27	267	130	512	100	338	74
6 Breeding stock, dairy cattle, etc.	71	53	3	15	85	63	6	16	129	95	4	30
Total gross capital formation	1511	516	659	336	1471	300	723	448	1935	671	739	526

	1991				1992				1993			
	Total	Total private	Public enterprises	General government	Total	Total private	Public enterprises	General government	Total	Total private	Public enterprises	General government
Increase in stocks, total	209	22	188	–	86	–137	222	–	...	...	...	...
Gross fixed capital formation, total	2771	1107	871	793	3592	1454	1039	1099	...	...	...	...
1 Residential buildings	395	395	...	...	503	503	...	...	...	...	...	...
2 Non-residential buildings	214	105	21	87	298	138	32	128	...	...	...	...
3 Other construction	777	14	393	370	975	18	346	611	...	...	...	...
4 Land improvement and plantation and orchard development	...	...	...	...	...	...	...	...	...	...	...	...
5 Producers' durable goods	1225	469	448	307	1644	698	655	291	...	...	...	...
A Transport equipment	302	220	37	45	453	392	39	22	...	...	...	...
B Machinery and equipment	923	249	412	262	1191	305	616	269	...	...	...	...
6 Breeding stock, dairy cattle, etc.	160	123	9	28	172	98	5	68	...	...	...	...
Total gross capital formation	2980	1129	1059	793	3677	1318	1261	1099	...	...	...	...

Bolivia

4.1 Derivation of value added by kind of activity, in current prices

Million bolivianos

	1986 Gross output	1986 Intermediate consumption	1986 Value added	1987 Gross output	1987 Intermediate consumption	1987 Value added	1988 Gross output	1988 Intermediate consumption	1988 Value added	1989 Gross output	1989 Intermediate consumption	1989 Value added
All producers												
1 Agriculture, hunting, forestry and fishing	2785	335	2450	...	...	...	2244	544	1700	2547	609	1937
A Agriculture and hunting	2237	246	1991	...	...	...	...	...	...	...	...	...
B Forestry and logging	469	77	392	...	...	...	...	...	...	...	...	...
C Fishing	79	11	67	...	...	...	...	...	...	...	...	...
2 Mining and quarrying	1099	209	890	...	...	...	1283	342	941	1700	435	1265
A Coal mining	...	...	...	...	...	...	...	...	...	...	...	...
B Crude petroleum and natural gas production	883	108	775	...	...	...	551	207	345	681	246	435
C Metal ore mining	216	100	115	...	...	...	732	136	596	1020	189	830
D Other mining	...	...	...	...	...	...	...	...	...	...	...	...
3 Manufacturing	3030	1846	1184	...	...	...	4983	3057	1926	5898	3742	2156
A Manufacture of food, beverages and tobacco	1686	1101	585	...	...	...	2551	1733	817	2966	2044	922
B Textile, wearing apparel and leather industries	171	107	63	...	...	...	521	291	230	577	338	239
C Manufacture of wood and wood products, including furniture	141	57	84	...	...	...	329	214	115	348	236	112
D Manufacture of paper and paper products, printing and publishing	38	22	15	...	...	...	156	90	66	187	107	80
E Manufacture of chemicals and chemical petroleum, coal, rubber and plastic products	648	384	265	...	...	...	913	438	475	1101	568	532
F Manufacture of non-metallic mineral products, except products of petroleum and coal	106	60	46	...	...	...	183	78	105	237	106	131
G Basic metal industries	168	85	83	...	...	...	147	101	46	264	193	71
H Manufacture of fabricated metal products, machinery and equipment	45	23	21	...	...	...	112	71	41	136	94	42
I Other manufacturing industries	28	6	22	...	...	...	71	40	31	81	55	26
4 Electricity, gas and water	133	37	96	...	...	...	202	82	120	267	96	171
5 Construction	461	206	255	...	...	...	800	421	379	919	518	401
6 Wholesale and retail trade, restaurants and hotels	1613	642	970	...	...	...	2302	1011	1291	2728	1179	1549
A Wholesale and retail trade	...	...	...	...	...	...	1455	525	930	1724	604	1119
B Restaurants and hotels	...	...	...	...	...	...	847	486	361	1004	575	430
7 Transport, storage and communication	1664	608	1056	...	...	...	1652	789	863	1996	921	1075
A Transport and storage	1586	574	1012	...	...	...	1472	703	769	1766	818	949
B Communication	78	34	44	...	...	...	180	86	94	229	104	125
8 Finance, insurance, real estate and business services	900	123	778	...	...	...	1537	259	1278	1708	337	1370
A Financial institutions	...	...	...	...	...	...	291	75	216	338	129	209
B Insurance	...	...	...	...	...	...						

Bolivia

Million bolivianos

	1986			1987			1988			1989		
	Gross output	Intermediate consumption	Value added	Gross output	Intermediate consumption	Value added	Gross output	Intermediate consumption	Value added	Gross output	Intermediate consumption	Value added
C Real estate and business services	...	...	...	...	...	...	1245	184	1061	1370	208	1161
Real estate, except dwellings	...	...	...	...	...	...	418	136	282	494	153	341
Dwellings	...	...	...	...	...	...	828	48	780	876	55	821
9 Community, social and personal services	923	288	636	...	...	...	741	293	449	850	336	514
Total, Industries	12609	4294	8315	...	...	...	15744	6798	8946	18612	8174	10438
Producers of government services	768	284	484	...	...	...	1407	370	1037	1773	466	1307
Other producers	50	–	50	...	...	...	67	–	67	79	...	79
Total	13426	4577	8849	...	...	...	17218	7167	10050	20465	8640	11824
less: Imputed bank service charge	...	–66	66	...	...	...	...	–144	144	...	–200	200
Import duties	141	...	141	...	...	...	188	...	188	191	...	191
Value added tax	...	...	...	...	...	...	349	...	349	410	...	410
Other adjustments	...	...	...	...	...	...	362	...	362	469	...	469
Total	13567	4643	8924	...	...	...	18117	7311	10805	21534	8840	12694

	1990			1991			1992			1993		
	Gross output	Intermediate consumption	Value added	Gross output	Intermediate consumption	Value added	Gross output	Intermediate consumption	Value added	Gross output	Intermediate consumption	Value added

All producers

1 Agriculture, hunting, forestry and fishing	3089	718	2371	3932	959	2974	4210	1039	3171	4776	5668	6081
2 Mining and quarrying	2139	558	1582	2208	713	1495	2445	843	1602	2219	2403	2872
A Coal mining	...	...	...	...	...	...	...	...	...	...	...	...
B Crude petroleum and natural gas production	973	309	664	1032	391	641	1100	460	639	...	...	...
C Metal ore mining	1167	249	918	1176	322	854	1345	383	963	...	...	...
D Other mining	...	...	...	...	...	...	...	...	...	...	...	...
3 Manufacturing	7438	4819	2620	9346	5953	3392	10462	6688	3774	5382	2373	2880
A Manufacture of food, beverages and tobacco	3726	2537	1189	4597	3136	1461	5041	3449	1591	981	1186	1433
B Textile, wearing apparel and leather industries	723	416	307	880	561	319	956	618	338	1073	1187	1447
C Manufacture of wood and wood products, including furniture	508	327	181	611	406	205	670	465	205	752	867	947
D Manufacture of paper and paper products, printing and publishing	221	130	91	280	172	109	322	195	128	362	409	465
E Manufacture of chemicals and chemical petroleum, coal, rubber and plastic products	1347	796	551	1805	878	927	2011	955	1055	467	493	662
F Manufacture of non-metallic mineral products, except products of petroleum and coal	289	130	158	368	157	211	501	209	292	586	659	772
G Basic metal industries	316	276	40	353	319	34	448	392	56	544	669	578
H Manufacture of fabricated metal products, machinery and equipment	171	118	53	217	165	52	241	196	45	267	323	339

Bolivia

	1990			1991			1992			1993		
	Gross output	Intermediate consumption	Value added	Gross output	Intermediate consumption	Value added	Gross output	Intermediate consumption	Value added	Gross output	Intermediate consumption	Value added
1 Other manufacturing industries	137	88	49	234	160	73	273	209	64	350	461	471
4 Electricity, gas and water	374	125	248	542	163	379	775	195	580	1025	1234	1477
5 Construction	1087	613	474	1380	791	589	1721	1037	684	1985	2119	2369
6 Wholesale and retail trade, restaurants and hotels	3352	1477	1875	4246	1926	2320	4826	2281	2545	5365	6064	6874
A Wholesale and retail trade	2152	781	1371	2744	1053	1691	3097	1264	1833	3441	3963	4396
B Restaurants and hotels	1200	696	504	1501	873	629	1729	1017	712	1924	2101	2478
7 Transport, storage and communication	2591	1151	1439	3465	1570	1895	4184	1868	2315	4806	5365	5807
A Transport and storage	2287	1025	1262	3097	1410	1687	3695	1652	2044	4187	4587	4802
B Communication	304	126	177	368	160	207	489	217	272	619	778	1005
8 Finance, insurance, real estate and business services	1973	403	1569	2466	499	1967	2920	646	2274	3398	3853	4456
A Financial institutions	421	159	262	555	193	362	815	281	535	...	...	...
B Insurance										...	...	...
C Real estate and business services	1552	244	1307	1912	306	1606	2105	366	1739	...	...	...
Real estate, except dwellings	576	183	393	722	236	486	848	283	565	...	...	...
Dwellings	975	61	914	1190	71	1119	1256	83	1174	...	...	...
9 Community, social and personal services	1002	409	593	1190	517	674	1405	619	786	1639	1867	2124
Total, Industries	23044	10273	12771	28776	13092	15684	32949	15218	17731	...	...	...
Producers of government services	2130	577	1553	2690	740	1949	3273	860	2412			
Other producers	93	–	93	113	–	113	128	–	128			
Total	25267	10850	14416	31579	13832	17746	36350	16078	20272	...	...	...
less: Imputed bank service charge	...	−253	253	...	−346	346	...	−486	486			
Import duties	208	...	208	224	...	224	290	...	290			
Value added tax	458	...	458	681	...	681	1093	...	1093			
Other adjustments	613	...	613	826	...	826	845	...	845			
Total	26546	11103	15443	33310	14178	19132	38578	16564	22014	...	...	...

	1994			1995			1996			1997		
	Gross output	Intermediate consumption	Value added	Gross output	Intermediate consumption	Value added	Gross output	Intermediate consumption	Value added	Gross output	Intermediate consumption	Value added

All producers

1 Agriculture, hunting, forestry and fishing	1194	1451	1620	3583	4217	4461	4791	2236	7027	...	...	...
2 Mining and quarrying	950	1042	1199	1268	1361	1674	2206	1915	4120	...	...	...
3 Manufacturing	3435	1409	1690	1949	964	1190	1190	1690	2880	...	...	...
A Manufacture of food, beverages and tobacco	542	631	763	439	555	670	670	763	1433	...	...	...
B Textile, wearing apparel and leather industries	693	778	927	381	409	520	520	927	1447	...	...	...
C Manufacture of wood and wood products, including furniture	525	600	648	227	268	299	299	648	947	...	...	...
D Manufacture of paper and paper products, printing and publishing	219	248	268	143	162	197	197	268	465	...	...	...

Bolivia

	1994 Gross output	1994 Intermediate consumption	1994 Value added	1995 Gross output	1995 Intermediate consumption	1995 Value added	1996 Gross output	1996 Intermediate consumption	1996 Value added	1997 Gross output	1997 Intermediate consumption	1997 Value added
E Manufacture of chemicals and chemical petroleum, coal, rubber and plastic products	268	291	370	199	202	291	291	370	662	...	...	...
F Manufacture of non-metallic mineral products, except products of petroleum and coal	243	283	341	343	375	431	431	341	772	...	...	...
G Basic metal industries	490	621	511	54	47	67	67	511	578	...	...	...
H Manufacture of fabricated metal products, machinery and equipment	216	240	253	51	84	86	86	253	339	...	...	...
I Other manufacturing industries	239	277	287	112	184	184	184	287	471	...	...	...
4 Electricity, gas and water	239	287	333	786	947	1145	1145	333	1477	...	...	...
5 Construction	1164	1251	1408	821	867	960	960	1408	2369	...	...	...
6 Wholesale and retail trade, restaurants and hotels	2567	2914	3241	2798	3150	3633	3634	3241	6874	...	...	...
A Wholesale and retail trade	1431	1610	1727	2010	2353	2669	2669	1727	4396	...	...	...
B Restaurants and hotels	1136	1304	1514	788	797	964	965	1514	2478	...	...	...
7 Transport, storage and communication	2094	2377	2622	2711	2988	3184	3184	2622	5807	...	...	...
A Transport and storage	1831	2071	2244	2355	2516	2557	2557	2244	4802	...	...	...
B Communication	263	306	378	356	472	627	627	378	1005	...	...	...
8 Finance, insurance, real estate and business services	820	949	1140	2578	2904	3317	3317	1140	4456	...	...	...
9 Community, social and personal services	707	809	911	932	1058	1213	789	473	1262	...	...	...
Total, Industries	...	...	...	...	...	...	...	...	...	...	...	...
Producers of government services	...	...	...	...	...	...	...	...	...	...	...	...
Other producers	...	...	...	...	...	...	...	...	...	...	...	...
Total	...	...	...	...	...	...	...	...	...	...	...	...
less: Imputed bank service charge	...	...	...	...	...	...	...	...	...	...	...	...
Import duties	...	...	...	...	...	...	...	...	...	...	...	...
Value added tax	...	...	...	...	...	...	...	...	...	...	...	...
Other adjustments	...	...	...	...	...	...	...	...	...	...	...	...
Total	...	...	...	...	...	...	...	...	...	...	...	...

4.2 Derivation of value added by kind of activity, in constant prices

Million bolivianos

	1986 Gross output	1986 Intermediate consumption	1986 Value added	1987 Gross output	1987 Intermediate consumption	1987 Value added	1988 Gross output	1988 Intermediate consumption	1988 Value added	1989 Gross output	1989 Intermediate consumption	1989 Value added
At constant prices of: 1990 **All producers**												
1 Agriculture, hunting, forestry and fishing	...	...	...	...	...	...	2992	690	2302	2953	686	2267
2 Mining and quarrying	...	...	...	...	...	...	1758	474	1284	1990	520	1470
3 Manufacturing	...	...	...	...	...	...	6522	4207	2315	6840	4410	2430
A Manufacture of food, beverages and tobacco	...	...	...	...	...	...	3332	2267	1065	3474	2365	1109

Bolivia

Million bolivianos

	1986			1987			1988			1989		
	Gross output	Intermediate consumption	Value added	Gross output	Intermediate consumption	Value added	Gross output	Intermediate consumption	Value added	Gross output	Intermediate consumption	Value added
At constant prices of: 1990													
B Textile, wearing apparel and leather industries	...	...	...	...	...	...	711	413	298	672	384	287
C Manufacture of wood and wood products, including furniture	...	...	...	...	...	...	419	279	139	428	279	149
D Manufacture of paper and paper products, printing and publishing	...	...	...	...	...	...	193	113	79	200	117	83
E Manufacture of chemicals and chemical petroleum, coal, rubber and plastic products	...	...	...	...	...	...	1242	729	513	1319	773	546
F Manufacture of non-metallic mineral products, except products of petroleum and coal	...	...	...	...	...	...	235	108	127	271	122	148
G Basic metal industries	...	...	...	...	...	...	154	138	15	227	202	25
H Manufacture of fabricated metal products, machinery and equipment	...	...	...	...	...	...	147	101	46	159	109	50
I Other manufacturing industries	...	...	...	...	...	...	91	58	32	92	60	32
4 Electricity, gas and water	...	...	...	...	...	...	337	115	222	353	118	235
5 Construction	...	...	...	...	...	...	1000	563	437	1051	588	462
6 Wholesale and retail trade, restaurants and hotels	...	...	...	...	...	...	3048	1372	1676	3167	1391	1777
A Wholesale and retail trade	...	...	...	...	...	...	1911	712	1199	1987	717	1270
B Restaurants and hotels	...	...	...	...	...	...	1137	660	477	1181	674	507
7 Transport, storage and communication	...	...	...	...	...	...	2322	1054	1268	2456	1090	1365
A Transport and storage	...	...	...	...	...	...	2070	942	1128	2173	970	1203
B Communication	...	...	...	...	...	...	252	113	139	283	120	163
8 Finance, insurance, real estate and business services	...	...	...	...	...	...	1879	350	1529	1918	390	1528
A Financial institutions	...	...	...	...	...	...	394	111	284	396	154	242
B Insurance	...	...	...	...	...	...	...	...	...	...	...	...
C Real estate and business services	...	...	...	...	...	...	1484	239	1245	1522	236	1286
Real estate, except dwellings	...	...	...	...	...	...	533	180	352	559	178	382
Dwellings	...	...	...	...	...	...	952	59	893	962	58	904
9 Community, social and personal services	...	...	...	...	...	...	938	388	550	967	391	576
Total, Industries	...	...	...	...	...	...	20795	9213	11582	21695	9585	12111
Producers of government services	...	...	...	...	...	...	2056	507	1549	2124	554	1570
Other producers	...	...	...	...	...	...	88	...	88	91	...	91
Total	...	...	...	...	...	...	22939	9720	13219	23910	10139	13772
less: Imputed bank service charge	...	...	...	...	...	...	...	−194	194	...	−234	234
Import duties	...	...	...	...	...	...	177	...	177	184	...	184
Value added tax	...	...	...	...	...	...	432	...	432	443	...	443
Other adjustments	...	...	...	...	...	...	586	...	586	595	...	595
Total	...	...	...	...	...	...	24135	9915	14220	25132	10373	14759

Bolivia

	1990 Gross output	1990 Intermediate consumption	1990 Value added	1991 Gross output	1991 Intermediate consumption	1991 Value added	1992 Gross output	1992 Intermediate consumption	1992 Value added	1993 Gross output	1993 Intermediate consumption	1993 Value added

At constant prices of: 1990

All producers

	Gross output 1990	Int. cons. 1990	Value added 1990	Gross output 1991	Int. cons. 1991	Value added 1991	Gross output 1992	Int. cons. 1992	Value added 1992	Gross output 1993	Int. cons. 1993	Value added 1993
1 Agriculture, hunting, forestry and fishing	3089	718	2371	3417	812	2605	3270	776	2495	3422	824	2598
2 Mining and quarrying	2139	558	1582	2189	571	1617	2218	579	1639	2343	608	1735
A Coal mining	...	...	...	...	...	...	...	...	...	...	...	...
B Crude petroleum and natural gas production	...	...	...	980	311	669	989	314	675	...	...	...
C Metal ore mining	...	...	...	1209	260	949	1229	265	964	...	...	...
D Other mining	...	...	...	...	...	...	...	...	...	...	...	...
3 Manufacturing	7438	4819	2620	7911	5165	2746	7887	5139	2748	...	...	...
A Manufacture of food, beverages and tobacco	3726	2537	1189	4005	2726	1279	3920	2671	1249	1169	726	443
B Textile, wearing apparel and leather industries	723	416	307	752	447	306	758	441	317	782	455	328
C Manufacture of wood and wood products, including furniture	508	327	181	509	335	174	498	325	173	517	336	188
D Manufacture of paper and paper products, printing and publishing	221	130	91	232	137	96	239	141	98	249	146	103
E Manufacture of chemicals and chemical petroleum, coal, rubber and plastic products	1347	796	551	1365	815	550	1335	794	541	322	178	144
F Manufacture of non-metallic mineral products, except products of petroleum and coal	289	130	158	299	135	164	347	157	189	377	171	206
G Basic metal industries	316	276	40	346	302	44	368	329	39	436	390	46
H Manufacture of fabricated metal products, machinery and equipment	171	118	53	190	132	58	189	131	58	200	139	61
I Other manufacturing industries	137	88	49	212	136	76	233	149	84	264	171	94
4 Electricity, gas and water	374	125	248	401	135	266	419	141	278	484	163	321
5 Construction	1087	613	474	1151	648	502	1282	723	559	1356	766	591
6 Wholesale and retail trade, restaurants and hotels	3352	1477	1875	3577	1582	1995	3660	1625	2035	3780	1683	2097
A Wholesale and retail trade	2152	781	1371	2311	850	1461	2340	869	1472	2412	898	1514
B Restaurants and hotels	1200	696	504	1266	732	534	1320	757	563	1368	785	583
7 Transport, storage and communication	2591	1151	1439	2759	1226	1533	2885	1280	1604	3013	1338	1675
A Transport and storage	2287	1025	1262	2438	1093	1345	2504	1122	1382	2583	1159	1423
B Communication	304	126	177	321	133	188	380	158	222	430	179	252
8 Finance, insurance, real estate and business services	1973	403	1569	2039	413	1626	2198	469	1729	2380	535	1846
A Financial institutions	421	159	262	450	160	290	560	203	357	...	...	...
B Insurance	...	...	...	...	...	...	...	...	...	...	...	...
C Real estate and business services	1552	244	1307	1589	253	1336	1638	266	1372	...	...	...
Real estate, except dwellings	576	183	393	599	190	409	633	200	433	...	...	...
Dwellings	975	61	914	990	63	926	1005	66	939	...	...	...
9 Community, social and personal services	1002	409	593	1042	426	616	1096	449	646	1150	473	677
Total, Industries	23044	10273	12771	24486	10979	13507	24914	11181	13733	...	...	...

Bolivia

	1990			1991			1992			1993		
	Gross output	Intermediate consumption	Value added	Gross output	Intermediate consumption	Value added	Gross output	Intermediate consumption	Value added	Gross output	Intermediate consumption	Value added
At constant prices of: 1990													
Producers of government services	2130	577	1553	2185	619	1565	2249	620	1629	2319	641	1678
Other producers	93	...	93	94	–	94	96	–	96	...	...	...
Total	25267	10850	14416	26765	11598	15167	27259	11801	15458	...	...	...
less: Imputed bank service charge	...	−253	253	...	−280	280	...	−333	333	...	...	...
Import duties	208	...	208	247	...	247	265	...	265	...	...	...
Value added tax	458	...	458	481	...	481	499	...	499	...	...	...
Other adjustments	613	...	613	642	...	642	636	...	636	...	...	...
Total	26546	11103	15443	28134	11878	16256	28659	12134	16524	...	...	...

	1994			1995			1996			1997		
	Gross output	Intermediate consumption	Value added	Gross output	Intermediate consumption	Value added	Gross output	Intermediate consumption	Value added	Gross output	Intermediate consumption	Value added

At constant prices of: 1990

All producers

1 Agriculture, hunting, forestry and fishing	3677	902	2775	3741	927	2814	3880	974	2906	...	...	...
2 Mining and quarrying	2438	639	1800	2636	687	1949	2606	683	1924	...	...	...
3 Manufacturing	...	...	...	...	...	...	...	...	...	...	...	...
A Manufacture of food, beverages and tobacco	781	399	381	865	442	423	936	479	457	...	...	...
B Textile, wearing apparel and leather industries	806	474	332	897	527	370	972	571	401	...	...	...
C Manufacture of wood and wood products, including furniture	550	359	191	538	352	187	502	328	174	...	...	...
D Manufacture of paper and paper products, printing and publishing	258	152	106	248	146	102	202	119	83	...	...	...
E Manufacture of chemicals and chemical petroleum, coal, rubber and plastic products	322	179	142	367	205	162	417	232	184	...	...	...
F Manufacture of non-metallic mineral products, except products of petroleum and coal	392	180	212	235	200	435	436	200	236	...	...	...
G Basic metal industries	451	404	46	345	309	35	321	288	33	...	...	...
H Manufacture of fabricated metal products, machinery and equipment	222	155	67	216	151	65	203	142	61	...	...	...
I Other manufacturing industries	299	194	105	281	183	98	254	165	89	...	...	...
4 Electricity, gas and water	541	185	356	584	199	385	635	217	418	...	...	...
5 Construction	1381	782	600	1438	814	624	1627	921	706	...	...	...
6 Wholesale and retail trade, restaurants and hotels	3955	1776	2179	4081	1837	2244	4285	1925	2360	...	...	...
A Wholesale and retail trade	2542	959	1583	2600	981	1619	2745	1035	1710	...	...	...
B Restaurants and hotels	1413	817	596	1481	856	625	1540	890	650	...	...	...
7 Transport, storage and communication	3195	1422	1773	3813	1641	2172	3498	1556	1944	...	...	...
A Transport and storage	2721	1224	1497	2808	1263	1545	2914	1311	1604	...	...	...
B Communication	474	198	276	1005	378	627	584	245	340	...	...	...

Bolivia

	1994			1995			1996			1997		
	Gross output	Intermediate consumption	Value added	Gross output	Intermediate consumption	Value added	Gross output	Intermediate consumption	Value added	Gross output	Intermediate consumption	Value added
At constant prices of: 1990												
8 Finance, insurance, real estate and business services	2580	582	1991	2743	631	2111	2900	679	2221	...	...	...
A Financial institutions	1192	494	699	...	...	...	...	...	...	...	...	...
B Insurance	...	...	...	...	...	...	...	...	...	...	...	...
C Real estate and business services	...	...	...	...	...	...	...	...	...	...	...	...
9 Community, social and personal services	...	...	...	1216	504	713	1256	520	735	...	...	...
Total, Industries	...	...	...	...	...	...	...	...	...	...	...	...
Producers of government services	2363	640	1723	2399	649	1749	2464	667	1797	...	...	...
Other producers	...	...	...	...	...	...	...	...	...	...	...	...
Total	...	...	...	...	...	...	...	...	...	...	...	...
less: Imputed bank service charge	...	...	...	...	...	...	...	...	...	...	...	...
Import duties	...	...	...	...	...	...	...	...	...	...	...	...
Value added tax	...	...	...	...	...	...	...	...	...	...	...	...
Other adjustments	...	...	...	...	...	...	...	...	...	...	...	...
Total	...	...	...	...	...	...	...	...	...	...	...	...

4.3 Cost components of value added

Million bolivianos

	1986						1987					
	Compensation of employees	Capital consumption	Net operating surplus	Indirect taxes	less: Subsidies received	Value added	Compensation of employees	Capital consumption	Net operating surplus	Indirect taxes	less: Subsidies received	Value added
All producers												
1 Agriculture, hunting, forestry and fishing	377	...	2073	–	...	2450	...	...	...	...	...	...
A Agriculture and hunting	288	...	1703	–	...	1991	...	...	...	...	...	...
B Forestry and logging	84	...	307	–	...	392	...	...	...	...	...	...
C Fishing	4	...	63	–	...	67	...	...	...	...	...	...
2 Mining and quarrying	115	...	362	413	...	890	...	...	...	...	...	...
A Coal mining	...	...	...	...	...	...	...	...	...	...	...	...
B Crude petroleum and natural gas production	16	...	371	387	...	775	...	...	...	...	...	...
C Metal ore mining	99	...	–9	26	...	115	...	...	...	...	...	...
D Other mining	...	...	...	...	...	...	...	...	...	...	...	...
3 Manufacturing	240	...	695	249	...	1184	...	...	...	...	...	...
A Manufacture of food, beverages and tobacco	121	...	366	97	...	585	...	...	...	...	...	...
B Textile, wearing apparel and leather industries	41	...	21	1	...	63	...	...	...	...	...	...
C Manufacture of wood and wood products, including furniture	13	...	70	1	...	84	...	...	...	...	...	...
D Manufacture of paper and paper products, printing and publishing	6	...	9	1	...	15	...	...	...	...	...	...

Bolivia

Million bolivianos

	1986						1987					
	Compensation of employees	Capital consumption	Net operating surplus	Indirect taxes	less: Subsidies received	Value added	Compensation of employees	Capital consumption	Net operating surplus	Indirect taxes	less: Subsidies received	Value added
E Manufacture of chemicals and chemical petroleum, coal, rubber and plastic products	23	...	100	142	...	265	...	...	...	...	...	...
F Manufacture of non-metallic mineral products, except products of petroleum and coal	16	...	28	1	...	46	...	...	...	...	...	...
G Basic metal industries	8	...	68	7	...	83	...	...	...	...	...	...
H Manufacture of fabricated metal products, machinery and equipment	6	...	15	1	...	21	...	...	...	...	...	...
I Other manufacturing industries	5	...	17	–	...	22	...	...	...	...	...	...
4 Electricity, gas and water	28	...	51	17	...	96	...	...	...	...	...	...
5 Construction	59	...	196	–	...	255	...	...	...	...	...	...
6 Wholesale and retail trade, restaurants and hotels	139	...	757	74	...	970	...	...	...	...	...	...
7 Transport, storage and communication	310	...	738	8	...	1056	...	...	...	...	...	...
A Transport and storage	288	...	720	3	...	1012	...	...	...	...	...	...
B Communication	21	...	18	5	...	44	...	...	...	...	...	...
8 Finance, insurance, real estate and business services	126	...	643	9	...	778	...	...	...	...	...	...
9 Community, social and personal services	226	...	401	8	...	636	...	...	...	...	...	...
Total, Industries [ab]	1619	...	5916	780	...	8315	...	...	...	...	...	...
Producers of government services	484	...	...	–	...	484	...	...	...	...	...	...
Other producers	50	...	...	...	...	50	...	...	...	...	...	...
Total [ab]	2153	...	5916	780	...	8849	...	...	...	...	...	...
less: Imputed bank service charge	...	...	66	...	...	66	...	...	...	...	...	...
Import duties	...	...	...	141	...	141	...	...	...	...	...	...
Value added tax	...	...	...	...	...	...	...	...	...	...	...	...
Other adjustments	...	...	...	...	...	...	...	...	...	...	...	...
Total [ab]	2153	...	5850	921	...	8924	...	...	...	...	...	...

	1988						1989					
	Compensation of employees	Capital consumption	Net operating surplus	Indirect taxes	less: Subsidies received	Value added	Compensation of employees	Capital consumption	Net operating surplus	Indirect taxes	less: Subsidies received	Value added

All producers

1 Agriculture, hunting, forestry and fishing	319	...	1381	–	...	1700	362	...	1576	–	...	1937
2 Mining and quarrying	199	...	743	–1	...	941	252	...	1011	1	...	1265
A Coal mining	...	...	...	...	...	...	...	...	...	...	...	...
B Crude petroleum and natural gas production	53	...	293	–2	...	345	83	...	350	1	...	435
C Metal ore mining	145	...	450	1	...	596	169	...	661	–	...	830
D Other mining	...	...	...	...	...	...	...	...	...	...	...	...
3 Manufacturing	646	...	1278	2	...	1926	753	...	1398	5	...	2156
A Manufacture of food, beverages and tobacco	272	...	544	2	...	817	343	...	577	2	...	922
B Textile, wearing apparel and leather industries	132	...	98	1	...	230	137	...	102	1	...	239

Bolivia

	1988						1989					
	Compensation of employees	Capital consumption	Net operating surplus	Indirect taxes	less: Subsidies received	Value added	Compensation of employees	Capital consumption	Net operating surplus	Indirect taxes	less: Subsidies received	Value added
C Manufacture of wood and wood products, including furniture	58	...	57	–	...	115	58	...	53	–	...	112
D Manufacture of paper and paper products, printing and publishing	35	...	31	–	...	66	39	...	41	–	...	80
E Manufacture of chemicals and chemical petroleum, coal, rubber and plastic products	57	...	420	–2	...	475	73	...	458	1	...	532
F Manufacture of non-metallic mineral products, except products of petroleum and coal	50	...	55	–	...	105	57	...	73	–	...	131
G Basic metal industries	12	...	33	–	...	46	15	...	56	–	...	71
H Manufacture of fabricated metal products, machinery and equipment	18	...	23	–	...	41	18	...	24	–	...	42
I Other manufacturing industries	13	...	18	–	...	31	13	...	13	–	...	26
4 Electricity, gas and water	31	...	89	–	...	120	41	...	130	–	...	171
5 Construction	206	...	172	1	...	379	209	...	192	1	...	401
6 Wholesale and retail trade, restaurants and hotels	425	...	855	11	...	1291	492	...	1045	11	...	1549
A Wholesale and retail trade	300	...	620	10	...	930	341	...	767	11	...	1119
B Restaurants and hotels	125	...	235	1	...	361	151	...	278	1	...	430
7 Transport, storage and communication	448	...	413	2	...	863	557	...	516	2	...	1075
A Transport and storage	397	...	370	1	...	769	493	...	455	1	...	949
B Communication	50	...	43	–	...	94	64	...	61	–	...	125
8 Finance, insurance, real estate and business services	182	...	1086	10	...	1278	238	...	1120	12	...	1370
A Financial institutions	89	...	118	9	...	216	127	...	70	12	...	209
B Insurance												
C Real estate and business services	93	...	968	1	...	1061	111	...	1050	1	...	1161
Real estate, except dwellings	93	...	189	1	...	282	111	...	229	1	...	341
Dwellings	–	...	780	–	...	780	–	...	821	–	...	821
9 Community, social and personal services	234	...	214	1	...	449	276	...	237	1	...	514
Total, Industries [ab]	2689	...	6232	25	...	8946	3180	...	7224	34	...	10438
Producers of government services	1037	...	–	–	...	1037	1307	...	...	...	...	1307
Other producers	67	...	–	–	...	67	79	...	...	...	...	79
Total [ab]	3793	...	6232	25	...	10050	4566	...	7224	34	...	11824
less: Imputed bank service charge	...	...	144	...	...	144	...	...	200	...	...	200
Import duties	...	...	...	188	...	188	...	...	...	191	...	...
Value added tax	...	...	...	349	...	349	...	...	...	410	...	...
Other adjustments	...	...	...	362	...	362	...	...	...	469	...	...
Total [ab]	3793	...	6088	924	...	10805	4566	...	7024	1104	...	12694

Bolivia

	1990						1991					
	Compensation of employees	Capital consumption	Net operating surplus	Indirect taxes	less: Subsidies received	Value added	Compensation of employees	Capital consumption	Net operating surplus	Indirect taxes	less: Subsidies received	Value added
All producers												
1 Agriculture, hunting, forestry and fishing	353	...	2018	–	...	2371	438	...	2535	–	...	2974
2 Mining and quarrying	292	...	1287	3	...	1582	344	...	1147	4	...	1495
A Coal mining	...	...	...	...	...	...	...	...	...	...	...	...
B Crude petroleum and natural gas production	109	...	554	1	...	664	148	...	491	2	...	641
C Metal ore mining	...	...	...	...	...	...	196	...	657	2	...	854
D Other mining	...	...	...	...	...	...	...	...	...	...	...	...
3 Manufacturing	886	...	1727	7	...	2620	1112	...	2270	10	...	3392
A Manufacture of food, beverages and tobacco	407	...	779	3	...	1189	511	...	946	4	...	1461
B Textile, wearing apparel and leather industries	143	...	163	1	...	307	180	...	138	1	...	319
C Manufacture of wood and wood products, including furniture	82	...	99	–	...	181	105	...	99	1	...	205
D Manufacture of paper and paper products, printing and publishing	41	...	50	–	...	91	46	...	62	–	...	109
E Manufacture of chemicals and chemical petroleum, coal, rubber and plastic products	92	...	457	2	...	551	114	...	811	3	...	927
F Manufacture of non-metallic mineral products, except products of petroleum and coal	63	...	95	–	...	158	82	...	129	–	...	211
G Basic metal industries	16	...	23	–	...	40	18	...	15	1	...	34
H Manufacture of fabricated metal products, machinery and equipment	22	...	30	–	...	53	26	...	26	–	...	52
I Other manufacturing industries	20	...	29	–	...	49	30	...	44	–	...	73
4 Electricity, gas and water	56	...	192	1	...	248	81	...	298	1	...	379
5 Construction	240	...	233	1	...	474	267	...	321	2	...	589
6 Wholesale and retail trade, restaurants and hotels	600	...	1263	12	...	1875	763	...	1540	17	...	2320
A Wholesale and retail trade	411	...	948	11	...	1371	533	...	1142	16	...	1691
B Restaurants and hotels	189	...	314	1	...	504	229	...	398	1	...	629
7 Transport, storage and communication	708	...	729	2	...	1439	975	...	917	3	...	1895
A Transport and storage	628	...	632	2	...	1262	875	...	810	2	...	1687
B Communication	80	...	97	–	...	177	100	...	107	1	...	207
8 Finance, insurance, real estate and business services	288	...	1264	18	...	1569	357	...	1594	17	...	1967
A Financial institutions	159	...	86	17	...	262	197	...	149	16	...	362
B Insurance												
C Real estate and business services	129	...	1178	1	...	1307	160	...	1445	1	...	1606
Real estate, except dwellings	129	...	264	1	...	393	160	...	326	1	...	486
Dwellings	–	...	914	–	...	914	–	...	1119	–	...	1119
9 Community, social and personal services	319	...	273	1	...	593	366	...	306	1	...	674
Total, Industries [a,b]	3741	...	8984	46	...	12771	4702	...	10927	55	...	15684

Bolivia

	1990						1991					
	Compensation of employees	Capital consumption	Net operating surplus	Indirect taxes	less: Subsidies received	Value added	Compensation of employees	Capital consumption	Net operating surplus	Indirect taxes	less: Subsidies received	Value added
Producers of government services	1553	...	...	...	...	1553	1949	...	...	...	...	1949
Other producers	93	...	...	...	...	93	113	...	...	...	...	113
Total [a,b]	5386	...	8984	46	...	14416	6764	...	10927	55	...	17746
less: Imputed bank service charge	...	...	253	...	...	253	...	...	346	...	...	346
Import duties	...	...	...	208	...	...	...	...	...	224	...	...
Value added tax	...	...	...	458	...	...	...	...	...	681	...	...
Other adjustments	...	...	...	613	...	...	...	...	...	826	...	...
Total [a,b]	5386	...	8731	1326	...	15443	6764	...	10581	1787	...	19132

	1992						1993					
	Compensation of employees	Capital consumption	Net operating surplus	Indirect taxes	less: Subsidies received	Value added	Compensation of employees	Capital consumption	Net operating surplus	Indirect taxes	less: Subsidies received	Value added
All producers												
1 Agriculture, hunting, forestry and fishing	471	...	2699	1	...	3171	...	...	...	...	...	...
2 Mining and quarrying	415	...	1183	4	...	1602	...	...	...	...	...	...
A Coal mining	...	...	...	...	...	...	...	...	...	...	...	...
B Crude petroleum and natural gas production	173	...	464	2	...	639	...	...	...	...	...	...
C Metal ore mining	242	...	719	2	...	963	...	...	...	...	...	...
D Other mining	...	...	...	...	...	...	...	...	...	...	...	...
3 Manufacturing	1268	...	2495	11	...	3774	...	...	...	...	...	...
A Manufacture of food, beverages and tobacco	582	...	1005	5	...	1591	...	...	...	...	...	...
B Textile, wearing apparel and leather industries	206	...	131	1	...	338	...	...	...	...	...	...
C Manufacture of wood and wood products, including furniture	111	...	93	1	...	205	...	...	...	...	...	...
D Manufacture of paper and paper products, printing and publishing	52	...	75	–	...	128	...	...	...	...	...	...
E Manufacture of chemicals and chemical petroleum, coal, rubber and plastic products	134	...	919	3	...	1055	...	...	...	...	...	...
F Manufacture of non-metallic mineral products, except products of petroleum and coal	101	...	190	1	...	292	...	...	...	...	...	...
G Basic metal industries	22	...	34	1	...	56	...	...	...	...	...	...
H Manufacture of fabricated metal products, machinery and equipment	30	...	14	–	...	45	...	...	...	...	...	...
I Other manufacturing industries	30	...	34	–	...	64	...	...	...	...	...	...
4 Electricity, gas and water	98	...	482	1	...	580	...	...	...	...	...	...
5 Construction	328	...	354	2	...	684	...	...	...	...	...	...
6 Wholesale and retail trade, restaurants and hotels	812	...	1714	20	...	2545	...	...	...	...	...	...
A Wholesale and retail trade	575	...	1240	19	...	1833	...	...	...	...	...	...
B Restaurants and hotels	237	...	474	2	...	712	...	...	...	...	...	...
7 Transport, storage and communication	1186	...	1126	3	...	2315	...	...	...	...	...	...

Bolivia

	1992						1993					
	Compensation of employees	Capital consumption	Net operating surplus	Indirect taxes	less: Subsidies received	Value added	Compensation of employees	Capital consumption	Net operating surplus	Indirect taxes	less: Subsidies received	Value added
A Transport and storage	1057	...	984	3	...	2044	...	...	...	...	...	...
B Communication	129	...	142	1	...	272	...	...	...	...	...	...
8 Finance, insurance, real estate and business services	445	...	1807	22	...	2274	...	...	...	...	...	...
A Financial institutions	265	...	249	20	...	535	...	...	...	...	...	...
B Insurance							...	...	...	...	...	...
C Real estate and business services	180	...	1558	1	...	1739	...	...	...	...	...	...
Real estate, except dwellings	180	...	384	1	...	565	...	...	...	...	...	...
Dwellings	–	...	1173	–	...	1174	...	...	...	...	...	...
9 Community, social and personal services	421	...	364	2	...	786	...	...	...	...	...	...
Total, Industries [a,b]	5443	...	12223	66	...	17731	...	...	...	...	...	...
Producers of government services	2412	...	...	...	...	2412	...	...	...	...	...	...
Other producers	128	...	...	...	...	128	...	...	...	...	...	...
Total [a,b]	7983	...	12223	66	...	20272	...	...	...	...	...	...
less: Imputed bank service charge	...	...	486	...	...	486	...	...	...	...	...	...
Import duties	...	...	...	...	...	...	...	...	...	...	...	...
Value added tax	...	...	...	...	...	...	...	...	...	...	...	...
Other adjustments	...	...	...	...	...	...	...	...	...	...	...	...
Total [a,b]	7983	...	11736	2294	...	22014	...	...	...	...	...	...

a Column 4 refers to indirect taxes less subsidies received.
b Column "Consumption of fixed capital" is included in column "Net operating surplus".

Botswana

General note

The preparation of national accounts statistics in Botswana is undertaken by the Central Statistics Office of the Ministry of Finance and Development Planning, Gaborone. Official estimates together with methodological notes are published in a series of reports entitled *National Accounts of Botswana* the most detailed description of the sources and methods used for the national accounts estimation is found in the fifth edition of this report published in 1976 for the fiscal year 1973/74. The estimates are generally in accordance with the classifications and definitions recommended in the United Nations System of National Accounts (1968 SNA). The following tables have been prepared from the successive replies to the United Nations national accounts questionnaire. The estimates relate to fiscal year beginning 1 July. When the scope and coverage of the estimates differ for conceptual or statistical reasons from the definitions and classifications recommended in SNA, a footnote is indicated to the relevant tables.

Gross domestic product

Gross domestic product is estimated mainly through the production approach.

Expenditures on the gross domestic product

All components of gross domestic product by expenditure type are estimated through the expenditure approach except private final consumption expenditure which is obtained as a residual. The estimates of the government final consumption expenditure are based on annual statements of the accounts of central and local governments. Changes in stocks is estimated on the basis of Census of Production and Distribution (CPD) for all the sectors of the economy. Gross fixed capital formation of the government sector is estimated from the government accounts and of the private sector from the CPD. Included in the capital formation estimates are the cost of land clearings and imputed values of new huts. The estimates of imports and exports of goods and services are based on balance-of-payments data. Exports and imports of goods have to be adjusted for duty content, in accordance with the Southern African Customs Union agreement.

Cost structure of the gross domestic product

Estimates of compensation of employees are obtained from the Census of Production and Distribution (CPD). Data on payment of wages and salaries are distinguished whether paid to residents or to non-residents and are also classified by type. The main source for estimating consumption of fixed capital formation in the private sector is the CPD. For government assets, straight—line depreciation is applied, the constant percentage varying for different types of assets. Indirect taxes are extracted from the Accountant General's annual statements of accounts, the CPD and the Trade Statistics Unit.

Gross domestic product by kind of activity

The table of gross domestic product by kind of economic activity is prepared at market prices, i.e. producers' values. The production approach is used to estimate value added of almost all industries. The income approach is used for some sub-groups of private services and for producers of government services. For the traditional farming of the agricultural sector, the main source used for crops is the annual agricultural sample survey and for cattle, the sources used include Household Income and Expenditures Surveys (HIESs) and annual reports of Botswana Meat Commission. The method has been to obtain quantities of production from the above mentioned sources and apply unit values. Data from the 1985/86 and 1993/94 HIESes also provided information on milk production for own use and the value of meat consumed. From the two surveys, detailed input-output activity analysis of the traditional farming sector has been conducted. For the freehold farmers, the main source has been the CPD and to some extent the annual agricultural survey. For the non-respondents, a grossing-up is made by reference to other farms of the same type.

The estimates for the mining sector are obtained from the Census of Manufacturing and Construction (CMC) which covers all the primary industries. For the manufacturing sector which is dominated by about three sub-industries, the source is the CMC and quarterly Survey of Industrial Production. The two above mentioned sources cover all the primary industries, whilst the rest of the sectors are covered by the CPD. This came into effect in 1989. Both the CMC and the CPD gives information for estimating the cost of intermediate consumption. All the government industries go to their respective sectors. For construction, the private contractors and brigades are covered by the CMC. Estimates of construction outlays for sites and services are supplied by city and town councils whilst rural huts construction estimates are imputed on the basis of the HIES data. Estimates of construction carried out by the government departments are derived from the analysis of government accounts.

The main source of information for the trade sector is the CPD. The data obtained from this source is grossed-up to allow for under-coverage. Gross margins are estimated as the difference between sales and purchases of goods for resale. Taxes levied on imported goods are treated as indirect taxes collected by the trade sector. As far as the transport sector is concerned, the source of data is the CPD. The major contributor is post and telecommunication (30 to 40 per cent of value added). Gross

Botswana

output of financial institutions is made up of the actual sales of services and an imputed service charge. Estimates for producers of government services are based on the Annual Statements of Accounts of the central and local governments. For the constant price estimates, the CPD data are deflated by a cost-of-living index.

1.1 Expenditure on the gross domestic product, in current prices

Million Botswana pula — Fiscal year beginning 1 July

	1986	1987	1988	1989	1990	1991	1992	1993	1994	1995	1996	1997
1 Government final consumption expenditure	723	1052	1258	1558	1846	2016	2595	3173	3507	4121	4833	...
2 Private final consumption expenditure	987	1116	1468	2109	2604	3198	3528	3638	4130	4386	5124	...
A Households	972	1096	1380	2011	2492	3072	3377	3471	3943	4168	4869	...
B Private non-profit institutions serving households	15	20	88	98	112	126	150	167	187	218	255	...
3 Gross capital formation	688	278	1889	2465	2687	2460	2545	2838	3531	3775	4661	...
A Increase in stocks	19	−804	196	384	322	−13	157	107	478	252	512	...
B Gross fixed capital formation	670	1082	1693	2081	2365	2473	2388	2731	3053	3523	4149	...
Residential buildings	36	120	97	272	...	458	342	...	...	...	...	...
Non-residential buildings	92	178	318	317	...	429	546	...	...	...	...	...
Other construction and land improvement, etc.	177	214	304	321	...	523	455	...	...	...	...	...
Other	364	570	974	1171	...	1063	1045	...	...	...	...	...
4 Exports of goods and services [a]	1839	3119	3702	3658	4107	4347	4083	5414	5990	7510	10153	...
5 less: Imports of goods and services [b]	1428	1769	2480	3254	3769	3648	3625	3947	4629	5160	6756	...
Statistical discrepancy [c]	–	–	–	1	–	–	–	−1	1	−1	–	...
equals: Gross domestic product	2810	3796	5837	6537	7475	8373	9126	11115	12530	14631	18015	...

a Item "Exports of goods and services" includes exports of goods and services.
b Item "Imports of goods and services" includes imports of goods plus net imports of services.
c The discrepancy is due to the rounding off of numbers to discard the decimal places

1.2 Expenditure on the gross domestic product, in constant prices

Million Botswana pula — Fiscal year beginning 1 July

	1986	1987	1988	1989	1990	1991	1992	1993	1994	1995	1996	1997
At constant prices of: 1985												
1 Government final consumption expenditure	649	869	912	1026	1050	1089	1284	1342	1351	1460	1487	...
2 Private final consumption expenditure	902	941	1067	1420	1573	1724	1659	1511	1558	1504	1585	...
A Households	888	922	1011	1361	1509	1656	1584	1440	1486	1427	1506	...
B Private non-profit institutions serving households	14	19	56	59	64	68	74	70	72	77	79	...
3 Gross capital formation	578	162	1215	1488	1477	1180	1181	1216	1353	1332	1460	...
A Increase in stocks	16	−629	129	234	194	−7	73	49	176	103	172	...
B Gross fixed capital formation	562	791	1086	1254	1283	1188	1108	1167	1177	1229	1288	...
Residential buildings	30	89	62	165	...	223	159	...	...	...	...	...

Botswana

Million Botswana pula	1986	1987	1988	1989	1990	1991	1992	1993	1994	1995	1996	1997
At constant prices of: 1985												
Non-residential buildings	77	132	205	192	...	209	257	...	...	...	...	...
Other construction and land improvement, etc.	150	159	196	195	...	255	231	...	...	...	...	...
Other	305	411	623	702	...	501	461	...	...	...	...	...
4 Exports of goods and services	1729	2352	2348	2189	2336	2348	2020	2290	2308	2661	3125	...
5 less: Imports of goods and services	1210	1461	1882	2221	2311	1966	1794	1630	1771	1752	2092	...
Statistical discrepancy	−11	175	43	9	127	146	166	−28	49	−20	−21	...
equals: Gross domestic product	2636	3039	3703	3911	4252	4522	4516	4700	4847	5185	5544	...

1.3 Cost components of the gross domestic product

Million Botswana pula	1986	1987	1988	1989	1990	1991	1992	1993	1994	1995	1996	1997
1 Indirect taxes, net	216	232	301	373	577	881	1043	925	897	1028	1188	...
A Indirect taxes	226	251	340	413	619	924	1087	958	942	1097	1251	...
B less: Subsidies	11	19	39	40	42	43	44	33	45	69	63	...
2 Consumption of fixed capital	432	576	765	879	829	1157	1195	1496	1653	1944	2432	...
3 Compensation of employees paid by resident producers to ..	850	1052	1383	1698	2100	2571	3066	3306	3610	4035	4563	...
A Resident households	850	1052	1728	...	...	...	...	...	...	...	...	...
B Rest of the world	−	−	...	...	...	...	...	...	...	...	...	...
4 Operating surplus	1312	1936	3388	3587	3969	3764	3822	5388	6370	7624	9832	...
A Corporate and quasi-corporate enterprises	1206	...	...	...	...	...	...	...	...	...	...	...
B Private unincorporated enterprises	106	...	...	...	...	...	...	...	...	...	...	...
C General government	−	...	...	...	...	...	...	...	...	...	...	...
equals: Gross domestic product	2810	3796	5837	6537	7475	8372	9126	11115	12530	14631	18015	...

1.10 Gross domestic product by kind of activity, in current prices

Million Botswana pula	1986	1987	1988	1989	1990	1991	1992	1993	1994	1995	1996	1997
1 Agriculture, hunting, forestry and fishing	144	268	277	308	333	366	444	495	521	563	617	...
2 Mining and quarrying	1230	1702	2969	2896	3075	3126	3042	3932	4086	4859	6487	...
3 Manufacturing	168	192	289	324	362	412	449	500	594	693	853	...
4 Electricity, gas and water	72	107	116	129	152	169	207	239	270	271	314	...
5 Construction	132	185	319	473	552	645	610	694	757	858	988	...
6 Wholesale and retail trade, restaurants and hotels	181	461	613	835	1060	1287	1441	1707	2094	2489	3017	...
7 Transport, storage and communication	59	98	138	162	208	255	320	363	437	504	622	...
8 Finance, insurance, real estate and business services	167	191	400	453	557	645	861	1149	1398	1613	1886	...

Botswana

Million Botswana pula — Fiscal year beginning 1 July

	1986	1987	1988	1989	1990	1991	1992	1993	1994	1995	1996	1997
9 Community, social and personal services	29	35	204	236	286	343	410	479	551	622	695	...
Total, Industries	2182	3308	5252	5816	6585	7248	7783	9559	10707	12473	15479	...
Producers of government services	428	563	713	866	1051	1308	1565	1847	2159	2544	2998	...
Other producers	53	–	...	...	...	...	...	...	...	...	...	...
Subtotal	2663	3871	5965	6682	7636	8556	9348	11405	12866	15018	18477	...
less: Imputed bank service charge	57	74	128	145	159	183	222	290	336	387	462	...
plus: Import duties	203	248	...	...	...	...	...	...	...	...	...	...
plus: Value added tax	...	...	...	...	...	...	...	...	...	...	...	...
plus: Other adjustments	...	–1	...	–	–2	...	...	...	...	...	...	...
equals: Gross domestic product	2810	3796	5837	6537	7475	8372	9126	11115	12530	14631	18015	...

1.11 Gross domestic product by kind of activity, in constant prices

Million Botswana pula — Fiscal year beginning 1 July

At constant prices of: 1985

	1986	1987	1988	1989	1990	1991	1992	1993	1994	1995	1996	1997
1 Agriculture, hunting, forestry and fishing	123	203	187	193	199	203	201	198	189	189	188	...
2 Mining and quarrying	1226	1260	1500	1450	1585	1577	1504	1579	1555	1709	1809	...
3 Manufacturing	146	190	242	254	270	288	285	281	293	312	329	...
4 Electricity, gas and water	64	73	78	80	86	91	106	115	122	121	127	...
5 Construction	111	132	211	264	283	296	252	254	258	265	280	...
6 Wholesale and retail trade, restaurants and hotels	158	394	494	559	607	699	699	733	790	848	938	...
7 Transport, storage and communication	66	103	130	140	161	178	194	191	204	216	245	...
8 Finance, insurance, real estate and business services	146	156	250	320	347	361	419	459	494	521	558	...
9 Community, social and personal services	42	98	153	178	190	200	207	215	224	234	246	...
Total, Industries	2082	2609	3246	3438	3728	3892	3865	4026	4130	4416	4720	...
Producers of government services	392	491	553	572	619	728	753	788	836	893	960	...
Other producers	32	–	...	...	...	...	...	...	...	...	...	...
Subtotal	2506	3100	3799	4010	4347	4620	4619	4814	4966	5309	5680	...
less: Imputed bank service charge	52	61	95	97	95	98	103	113	119	124	135	...
plus: Import duties	183	–	...	...	...	...	...	...	...	...	...	...
plus: Value added tax	...	...	...	...	...	...	...	...	...	...	...	...
plus: Other adjustments	...	...	–1	–2	...	...	...	...	...	...	...	...
equals: Gross domestic product	2636	3039	3703	3911	4252	4522	4516	4700	4847	5185	5544	...

Botswana

1.12 Relations among national accounting aggregates

Million Botswana pula — Fiscal year beginning 1 July

	1986	1987	1988	1989	1990	1991	1992	1993	1994	1995	1996	1997
Gross domestic product	2810	3796	5837	6537	7475	8373	9126	11115	12530	14631	18015	...
plus: Net factor income from the rest of the world	−252	−465	−467	−317	...	62	81	...	...	...	...	...
Factor income from rest of the world	226	309	434	540	...	1137	1223	...	...	...	...	...
less: Factor income to the rest of the world	478	774	901	857	...	1075	1142	...	...	...	...	...
equals: Gross national product	2558	3331	5370	6220	...	8435	9207	...	...	...	...	...
less: Consumption of fixed capital	432	576	765	879	829	1157	1195	1496	1653	1944	2432	...
equals: National income	2125	2755	4605	5341	...	7278	8012	...	...	...	...	...
plus: Net current transfers from the rest of the world	44	−118	68	66	...	131	−58	...	...	...	...	...
Current transfers from rest of the world	123	115	164	212	...	834	583	...	...	...	...	...
less: Current transfers to the rest of the world	79	233	98	146	...	703	641	...	...	...	...	...
equals: National disposable income	2170	2637	4673	5407	...	7409	7954	...	...	...	...	...
less: Final consumption	1710	2168	2726	3667	...	5214	6123	...	...	...	...	...
Statistical discrepancy [a]	−	−	...	...	...	...	...	...	...	...	...	...
equals: Net saving	460	468	1947	1740	...	2195	1831	...	...	...	...	...
less: Surplus of the nation on current transactions	204	766	...	...	...	...	...	...	...	...	...	...
Statistical discrepancy [b]	−	−	...	...	...	...	...	...	...	...	...	...
equals: Net capital formation	256	−298	...	...	...	...	...	...	...	...	...	...

a Item "Statistical discrepancy" refers to discrepancy in income and outlay account.
b Item "Statistical discrepancy" refers to discrepancy in capital finance account.

4.3 Cost components of value added

Million Botswana pula — Fiscal year beginning 1 July

	1986 Compensation of employees	1986 Capital consumption	1986 Net operating surplus	1986 Indirect taxes	1986 less: Subsidies received	1986 Value added	1987 Compensation of employees	1987 Capital consumption	1987 Net operating surplus	1987 Indirect taxes	1987 less: Subsidies received	1987 Value added
All producers												
1 Agriculture, hunting, forestry and fishing	51	8	86	−	...	144	58	10	200	−	...	268
2 Mining and quarrying	93	109	1025	2	...	1230	103	120	1479	−	...	1702
3 Manufacturing	54	18	87	8	...	168	67	24	106	−5	...	192
4 Electricity, gas and water	23	60	−11	−	...	72	46	69	−8	−	...	107
5 Construction	83	6	43	−	−	132	102	13	71	−	1	185
6 Wholesale and retail trade, restaurants and hotels	55	21	102	3	...	181	83	26	104	248	...	461
7 Transport, storage and communication	36	34	−9	−2	...	59	49	52	−4	1	...	98
8 Finance, insurance, real estate and business services	102	30	36	−1	...	167	126	49	26	−10	...	191

Botswana

Million Botswana pula — Fiscal year beginning 1 July

	1986							1987						
	Compen-sation of employ-ees	Capital consump-tion	Net operating surplus	Indirect taxes	less: Subsidies received	Value added	Compen-sation of employ-ees	Capital consump-tion	Net operating surplus	Indirect taxes	less: Subsidies received	Value added
9 Community, social and personal services	12	3	13	1	...	29	55	11	37	–	...	103
Total, Industries	510	288	1372	12[a]	–	2182	650	367	1990	–14[a]	1	2992
Producers of government services	290	139	–	–	...	428	362	201	–	–	...	563
Other producers	50	5	–3	–	...	53	40	7	21	–	...	68
Total	850	433	1369	12[a]	–[a]	2663[a]	1052	576	2010	–14[a]	1[a]	3622[a]
less: Imputed bank service charge	...	...	57	...	...	57	...	...	74	...	...	74
Import duties	...	...	...	203	...	203	...	...	...	248	...	248
Value added tax	...	...	...	...	...	...	...	...	...	...	...	...
Other adjustments	...	...	...	...	...	...	...	...	...	...	...	...
Total [a]	850	432	1312	215	–	2810	1052	576	1936	233	1	3796

	1988							1989						
	Compen-sation of employ-ees	Capital consump-tion	Net operating surplus	Indirect taxes	less: Subsidies received	Value added	Compen-sation of employ-ees	Capital consump-tion	Net operating surplus	Indirect taxes	less: Subsidies received	Value added

All producers

1 Agriculture, hunting, forestry and fishing	73	12	192	...	...	277	89	14	204	1	...	308
2 Mining and quarrying	116	169	2681	3	...	2969	157	178	2555	6	...	2896
3 Manufacturing	104	33	149	3	...	289	132	37	149	6	...	324
4 Electricity, gas and water	51	86	7	–28	...	116	59	83	15	–28	...	129
5 Construction	145	17	149	8	...	319	187	21	258	7	...	473
6 Wholesale and retail trade, restaurants and hotels	111	36	153	313	...	613	137	39	284	375	...	835
7 Transport, storage and communication	91	80	–33	1	...	139	110	100	–50	2	...	162
8 Finance, insurance, real estate and business services	153	65	133	...	...	351	177	69	204	3	...	453
9 Community, social and personal services	79	15	84	1	...	179	103	22	110	1	...	236
Total, Industries	923	513	3515	301[a]	...	5252	1151	563	3729	373[a]	...	5816
Producers of government services	460	253	...	...	...	713	549	317	...	...	...	866
Other producers	...	...	...	...	...	...	...	...	...	...	...	...
Total	1383	766	3515	301	...	5965	1700	880	3729	373	...	6682
less: Imputed bank service charge	...	...	–128	...	...	–128	...	...	–145	...	...	–145
Import duties	...	...	...	...	...	...	...	...	...	...	...	...
Value added tax	...	...	...	...	...	...	...	...	...	...	...	...
Other adjustments	...	...	...	...	...	...	...	...	...	...	...	...
Total	1383	766	3387	301	...	5837	1700	880	3584	373	...	6537

	1990							1991						
	Compen-sation of employ-ees	Capital consump-tion	Net operating surplus	Indirect taxes	less: Subsidies received	Value added	Compen-sation of employ-ees	Capital consump-tion	Net operating surplus	Indirect taxes	less: Subsidies received	Value added

All producers

1 Agriculture, hunting, forestry and fishing	...	...	...	...	...	...	115	21	230	...	...	366
2 Mining and quarrying	...	...	...	...	...	...	199	157	2763	7	...	3126
3 Manufacturing	...	...	...	...	...	...	207	65	144	–4	...	412

Botswana

	1990						1991					
	Compensation of employees	Capital consumption	Net operating surplus	Indirect taxes	less: Subsidies received	Value added	Compensation of employees	Capital consumption	Net operating surplus	Indirect taxes	less: Subsidies received	Value added
4 Electricity, gas and water	...	...	...	...	...	...	45	58	65	1	...	169
5 Construction	...	...	...	...	...	...	361	53	216	15	...	645
6 Wholesale and retail trade, restaurants and hotels	...	...	...	...	...	...	213	45	199	830	...	1287
7 Transport, storage and communication	...	...	...	...	...	...	127	120	1	7	...	255
8 Finance, insurance, real estate and business services	...	...	...	...	...	...	283	91	270	1	...	645
9 Community, social and personal services	...	...	...	...	...	...	209	22	109	3	...	343
Total, Industries	...	...	...	...	...	...	1759	632	3997	860[a]	...	7248
Producers of government services	...	...	...	...	...	...	812	475	...	21	...	1308
Other producers	...	...	...	...	...	...	...	...	...	...	...	...
Total	...	...	...	...	...	...	2571	1107	3997	881	...	8556
less: Imputed bank service charge	...	...	...	...	...	...	...	...	−183	...	...	−183
Import duties	...	...	...	...	...	...	...	...	...	...	...	...
Value added tax	...	...	...	...	...	...	...	...	...	...	...	...
Other adjustments	...	...	...	...	...	...	...	...	...	...	...	...
Total	...	...	...	...	...	...	2571	1107	3997	907	...	8373

	1992						1993					
	Compensation of employees	Capital consumption	Net operating surplus	Indirect taxes	less: Subsidies received	Value added	Compensation of employees	Capital consumption	Net operating surplus	Indirect taxes	less: Subsidies received	Value added

All producers

1 Agriculture, hunting, forestry and fishing	139	24	282	−1	...	444	...	...	...	...	...	...
2 Mining and quarrying	345	157	2534	6	...	3042	...	...	...	...	...	...
3 Manufacturing	228	67	144	10	...	449	...	...	...	...	...	...
4 Electricity, gas and water	75	60	72	...	...	207	...	...	...	...	...	...
5 Construction	359	58	160	33	...	610	...	...	...	...	...	...
6 Wholesale and retail trade, restaurants and hotels	243	44	195	959	...	1441	...	...	...	...	...	...
7 Transport, storage and communication	151	147	15	7	...	320	...	...	...	...	...	...
8 Finance, insurance, real estate and business services	281	92	489	−1	...	861	...	...	...	...	...	...
9 Community, social and personal services	232	22	153	4	...	411	...	...	...	...	...	...
Total, Industries	2053	671	4044	1017[a]	...	7785	...	...	...	...	...	...
Producers of government services	1014	525	...	26	...	1565	...	...	...	...	...	...
Other producers	...	...	...	...	...	...	...	...	...	...	...	...
Total	3067	1196	4044	1043	...	9350	...	...	...	...	...	...
less: Imputed bank service charge	...	...	−222	...	...	−222	...	...	...	...	...	...
Import duties	...	...	...	...	...	...	...	...	...	...	...	...
Value added tax	...	...	...	...	...	...	...	...	...	...	...	...
Other adjustments	...	...	...	...	...	...	...	...	...	...	...	...
Total	3067	1196	3820	1043	...	9126	...	...	...	...	...	...

a Column 4 refers to indirect taxes less subsidies received.

Brazil

Source

Reply to the United Nations National Accounts Questionnaire from the Instituto Brasileiro de Geografia e Estatística, Departamento de Contas Nacionais (DECNA), Rio de Janeiro. The official estimates are shown in a series of publications entitled *Conjuntura Economica*. On 28 February 1986, the cruzado, equal to 1,000 cruzeiros, was introduced. On 15 January 1989, the new cruzado, equal to 1,000 old cruzado, was introduced. On 16 March 1990, the cruzeiro, equal to 1 new cruzado, was introduced. On 1 August 1993, the cruzeiro real, equal to 1,000 cruzeiros, was introduced. On July 1, 1994 the real, equal to 2,750 cruzeiros reais was introduced. However, the estimates are in cruzeiros reais.

General note

The estimates shown in the following tables have been prepared in accordance with the United Nations System of National Accounts so far as the existing data would permit.

1.1 Expenditure on the gross domestic product, in current prices

cruzeiros reais

	1986	1987	1988	1989	1990 [a]	1991	1992	1993	1994	1995	1996	1997
1 Government final consumption expenditure	142	510	3951	65948	2	9	90	2296	57666	110482	...	...
2 Private final consumption expenditure	903	2612	18607	265284	6	36	391	8792	228362	429753	...	...
3 Gross capital formation	254	936	7151	114498	2	11	117	2714	70877	126644	...	...
A Increase in stocks	–	–	–	–	–	–	–	–	–	–	...	...
B Gross fixed capital formation	254	936	7151	114498	2	11	117	2714	70877	126644	...	...
Residential buildings	179	672	4800	81510	...	...	...	...	...	...	...	...
Non-residential buildings					...	...	...	...	...	...	...	...
Other construction and land improvement, etc.					...	...	...	...	...	...	...	...
Other	75	264	2351	32988	...	...	...	...	...	...	...	...
4 Exports of goods and services	117	397	3427	38004	1	5	65	1378	30087	46311	...	...
5 less: Imports of goods and services	85	260	1792	23243	1	4	43	1064	26073	55049	...	...
equals: Gross domestic product	1332	4195	31344	460490	11	57	620	14116	360919	658141	...	...

[a] Data prior to 1990 are in units of Reais; beginning 1990, the estimates are in millions.

1.3 Cost components of the gross domestic product

cruzeiros reais

	1986	1987	1988	1989	1990 [a]	1991	1992	1993	1994	1995	1996	1997
1 Indirect taxes, net	147	420	3028	40724	1	7	74	1788	52243	96361	...	...
A Indirect taxes	166	486	3412	49603	2	8	88	1944	56173	102741	...	...
B less: Subsidies	20	67	384	8878	–	1	14	156	3930	6380	...	...
2 Consumption of fixed capital	...	...	...	...	...	...	...	...	...	...	...	...

Brazil

cruzeiros reais	1986	1987	1988	1989	1990 [a]	1991	1992	1993	1994	1995	1996	1997
3 Compensation of employees paid by resident producers to ..	1185	3776	28316	419766	9	50	547	12272	304402	561780	...	...
4 Operating surplus											...	...
equals: Gross domestic product	1332	4195	31344	460490	11	57	619	14116	360919	658141	...	...

a Data prior to 1990 are in units of Reais; beginning 1990, the estimates are in millions.

1.4 General government current receipts and disbursements

cruzeiros reais	1986	1987	1988	1989	1990 [a]	1991	1992	1993	1994	1995	1996	1997
Receipts												
1 Operating surplus	...	...	...	...	...	...	...	...	...	...	...	...
2 Property and entrepreneurial income	...	...	...	...	...	...	...	...	...	...	...	...
3 Taxes, fees and contributions .	338	979	6861	101045	3	15	161	3653	100830	182525	...	...
A Indirect taxes	166	486	3412	49603	2	8	88	1944	56173	102741	...	...
B Direct taxes	172	493	3449	51442	2	7	73	1709	44657	79784	...	...
C Social security contributions	...	...	...	...	...	...	...	...	...	...	...	...
D Compulsory fees, fines and penalties	...	...	...	...	...	...	...	...	...	...	...	...
4 Other current transfers	−22	74	855	19141	−	2	18	982	9152	21983	...	...
Total current receipts of general government	316	1053	7716	120186	4	17	179	4635	109982	204507	...	...
Disbursements												
1 Government final consumption expenditure	142	510	3951	65948	2	9	90	2296	57666	110483	...	...
A Compensation of employees	...	...	...	...	1	5	55	1274	33471	70154	...	...
B Consumption of fixed capital	...	...	...	...	...	...	...	...	...	...	...	...
C Purchases of goods and services, net	...	...	...	...	1	3	35	1022	24195	40329	...	...
D less: Own-account fixed capital formation	...	...	...	...	...	...	...	...	...	...	...	...
E Indirect taxes paid, net	...	...	...	...	...	...	...	...	...	...	...	...
2 Property income	...	...	...	...	2	2	61	2028	38873	39521	...	...
A Interest	...	...	...	...	2	2	61	2028	38873	39521	...	...
B Net land rent and royalties ..	...	...	...	...	...	...	...	...	...	...	...	...
3 Subsidies	20	67	384	8878	−	1	14	156	3930	6380	...	...
4 Other current transfers	248	734	7312	137737	1	5	58	1546	38440	78120	...	...
5 Net saving	−95	−257	−3931	−92377	−1	−	−44	−1391	−28927	−29996	...	...
Total current disbursements and net saving of general government	316	1053	7716	120186	4	17	179	4635	109982	204507	...	...

a Data prior to 1990 are in units of Reais; beginning 1990, the estimates are in millions.

Brazil

1.7 External transactions on current account, summary

cruzeiros reais

	1986	1987	1988	1989	1990 [a]	1991	1992	1993	1994	1995	1996	1997
Payments to the rest of the world												
1 Imports of goods and services	85	260	1792	23243	1	4	43	1064	26073	55049	...	...
2 Factor income to rest of the world	66	173	1356	15679	–	2	19	458	8960	16267	...	...
A Compensation of employees	–	1	12	128	–	–	–	5	122	200	...	...
B Property and entrepreneurial income	66	171	1344	15551	–	2	18	453	8838	16067	...	...
3 Current transfers to the rest of the world	–	1	4	21	–	–	–	3	105	230	...	...
4 Surplus of the nation on current transactions	–26	–20	401	1057	–	–	10	–25	–1087	–16290	...	...
Payments to the rest of the world and surplus of the nation on current transfers	125	413	3552	40000	1	6	72	1501	34051	55255	...	...
Receipts from the rest of the world												
1 Exports of goods and services	117	397	3427	38004	1	5	65	1378	30087	46311	...	...
2 Factor income from rest of the world	7	14	112	1725	–	–	3	65	2195	5075	...	...
A Compensation of employees	–	–	1	5	–	–	–	1	38	57	...	...
B Property and entrepreneurial income	7	14	112	1720	–	–	3	64	2157	5018	...	...
3 Current transfers from rest of the world	1	2	13	271	–	–	4	58	1769	3869	...	...
Receipts from the rest of the world on current transactions [a]	125	413	3552	40000	1	6	72	1501	34051	55255	...	...

[a] Data prior to 1990 are in units of Reais; beginning 1990, the estimates are in millions.

1.10 Gross domestic product by kind of activity, in current prices

cruzeiros reais

	1986	1987	1988	1989	1990 [a]	1991	1992	1993	1994	1995	1996	1997
1 Agriculture, hunting, forestry and fishing	132	378	2878	35927	1	6	66	1532	43977	68290	...	...
2 Mining and quarrying	32	84	545	6577	–	1	10	221	3489	5867	...	...
3 Manufacturing	391	1207	8807	124533	3	13	140	3098	73142	123821	...	...
4 Electricity, gas and water	28	123	790	10212	–	2	17	378	9086	14198	...	...
5 Construction	85	319	2275	38636	1	4	42	985	25635	45124	...	...
6 Wholesale and retail trade, restaurants and hotels	103	305	2296	32791	1	4	41	937	22302	38037	...	...
7 Transport, storage and communication	60	197	1544	23267	1	3	31	756	17466	30701	...	...
8 Finance, insurance, real estate and business services	208	979	7670	151333	2	10	129	2945	62698	100625	...	...
9 Community, social and personal services	139	434	3451	53728	1	7	86	2235	56826	104296	...	...
Total, Industries	1178	4026	30257	477003	9	49	562	13087	314621	500959	...	...
Producers of government services	97	326	2484	44748	1	5	55	1274	33471	70154	...	...

Brazil

cruzeiros reais	1986	1987	1988	1989	1990 [a]	1991	1992	1993	1994	1995	1996	1997
Other producers	...	...	...	...	...	...	...	...	...	...	...	...
Subtotal	1275	4352	32740	521751	11	55	617	14361	348092	571113	...	...
less: Imputed bank service charge	90	576	4424	101985	1	4	71	2023	39416	39333	...	...
plus: Import duties	...	...	...	...	...	...	...	...	...	...	...	...
plus: Value added tax	...	...	...	...	...	...	...	...	...	...	...	...
plus: Other adjustments [b]	147	420	3028	40724	1	7	73	1778	52243	126361	...	...
equals: Gross domestic product	1332	4195	31344	460490	11	57	619	14116	360919	658141	...	...

a Data prior to 1990 are in units of Reais; beginning 1990, the estimates are in millions.
b Item "Other adjustments" refers to indirect taxes net of subsidies.

1.12 Relations among national accounting aggregates

cruzeiros reais	1986	1987	1988	1989	1990 [a]	1991	1992	1993	1994	1995	1996	1997
Gross domestic product	1332	4195	31344	460490	11	57	620	14039	355567	...	...	...
plus: Net factor income from the rest of the world	−59	−159	−1244	−13954	−	−2	−16	−393	−6800	...	...	...
Factor income from rest of the world	7	14	112	1725	−	−	3	65	2157	...	...	...
less: Factor income to the rest of the world	66	173	1356	15679	−	2	19	458	8958	...	...	...
equals: Gross national product [a]	1272	4037	30101	446536	11	55	605	13646	348766	...	...	...
less: Consumption of fixed capital	...	...	...	...	...	...	...	...	...	...	...	...
equals: National income [b]	1272	4037	30101	446536	...	...	...	...	...	...	...	...
plus: Net current transfers from the rest of the world	−	1	9	249	...	...	...	...	...	...	...	...
Current transfers from rest of the world	1	2	13	271	...	...	...	...	...	...	...	...
less: Current transfers to the rest of the world	−	1	4	21	...	...	...	...	...	...	...	...
equals: National disposable income [c]	1273	4037	30110	446786	...	...	...	...	...	...	...	...
less: Final consumption	1045	3122	22558	331232	...	...	...	...	...	...	...	...
equals: Net saving [d]	228	915	7552	115554	...	...	...	...	...	...	...	...
less: Surplus of the nation on current transactions	−26	−20	401	1057	...	...	...	...	...	...	...	...
equals: Net capital formation [e] ...	254	936	7151	114498	...	...	...	...	...	...	...	...

a Data prior to 1990 are in units of Reais; beginning 1990, the estimates are in millions.
b Item "National income" includes consumption of fixed capital.
c Item "National disposable income" includes consumption of fixed capital.
d Item "Net saving" includes consumption of fixed capital.
e Includes consumption of fixed capital.

Brunei Darussalam

Source

Reply to the United Nations National Accounts Questionnaire from the Statistics Division, Economic Planning Unit, Ministry of Finance.

General note

The estimates shown in the following tables have been prepared by the Government of Brunei in accordance with the United Nations System of National Accounts (1968 SNA) so far as the existing data would permit.

1.10 Gross domestic product by kind of activity, in current prices

Million Brunei dollars

	1986	1987	1988	1989	1990	1991	1992	1993	1994	1995	1996	1997
1 Agriculture, hunting, forestry and fishing	99	112	120	144	154	160	166	174	180	...	...	...
2 Mining and quarrying	2286	2653	2045	2209	2645	3096	2836	2626	2455	...	...	...
3 Manufacturing	533	583	547	558	585					...	...	...
4 Electricity, gas and water	31	33	43	54	59	62	64	67	70	...	...	...
5 Construction	170	183	195	255	277	303	316	334	364	...	...	...
6 Wholesale and retail trade, restaurants and hotels	630	686	708	769	818	845	794	806	795	...	...	...
7 Transport, storage and communication	123	233	245	266	281	297	310	318	338	...	...	...
8 Finance, insurance, real estate and business services	260	288	321	361	411	439	453	477	508	...	...	...
9 Community, social and personal services	1090	1127	1293	1349	1421	1568	1783	1948	2152	...	...	...
Total, Industries	5223	5899	5517	5966	6650	6770	6722	6749	6862	...	...	...
Producers of government services	...	...	...	...	...	...	...	...	...	...	...	...
Other producers	...	...	...	...	...	...	...	...	...	...	...	...
Subtotal	5223	5899	5517	5966	6650	6770	6722	6749	6862	...	...	...
less: Imputed bank service charge	87	98	103	121	142	149	156	164	176	...	...	...
plus: Import duties	...	...	...	...	...	...	...	...	...	...	...	...
plus: Value added tax	...	...	...	...	...	...	...	...	...	...	...	...
plus: Other adjustments	...	...	...	...	...	...	...	...	...	...	...	...
equals: Gross domestic product	5136	5801	5414	5845	6509	6620	6565	6585	6686	...	...	...

1.11 Gross domestic product by kind of activity, in constant prices

Million Brunei dollars

	1986	1987	1988	1989	1990	1991	1992	1993	1994	1995	1996	1997
At constant prices of: 1974												
1 Agriculture, hunting, forestry and fishing	46	49	50	56	56	57	58	59	60	...	...	...
2 Mining and quarrying	2077	1959	1889	1760	1786	2198	2072	2028	1996	...	...	...
3 Manufacturing	217	286	285	288	304					...	...	...
4 Electricity, gas and water	17	18	23	28	31	31	32	32	33	...	...	...
5 Construction	80	80	80	99	102	105	106	109	115	...	...	...

Brunei Darussalam

Million Brunei dollars

	1986	1987	1988	1989	1990	1991	1992	1993	1994	1995	1996	1997
	At constant prices of: 1974											
6 Wholesale and retail trade, restaurants and hotels	305	350	364	389	406	375	373	373	384	...	...	...
7 Transport, storage and communication	57	106	110	116	121	119	122	126	140	...	...	...
8 Finance, insurance, real estate and business services	121	129	139	151	166	167	172	179	188	...	...	...
9 Community, social and personal services	595	606	683	704	720	792	872	927	990	...	...	...
Total, Industries	3514	3584	3624	3591	3692	3844	3808	3832	3907	...	...	...
Producers of government services	...	...	...	...	...	...	...	...	...	...	...	...
Other producers	...	...	...	...	...	...	...	...	...	...	...	...
Subtotal	3514	3584	3624	3591	3692	3844	3808	3832	3907	...	...	...
less: Imputed bank service charge	74	75	77	82	87	93	98	104	111	...	...	...
plus: Import duties	...	...	...	...	...	...	...	...	...	...	...	...
plus: Value added tax	...	...	...	...	...	...	...	...	...	...	...	...
plus: Other adjustments	...	...	...	...	...	...	...	...	...	...	...	...
equals: Gross domestic product	3440	3508	3547	3509	3605	3751	3709	3728	3796	...	...	...

Bulgaria

Source

Reply to the United Nations National Accounts Questionnaire from the National Statistical Institute, Sofia. Official estimates and descriptions are published annually by the same Institute in *Statisticheski Godishnik* (Statistical Yearbook).

General note

The estimates, shown in the tables up to 1990 are prepared by adjusting the net material product estimates to the System of National Accounts concept. Since 1991, the estimates are developed according to the 1993 SNA. Sector accounts from production account to capital account are compiled. The estimates up to 1991 and after 1991 are not methodologically consistent. The previous year is assumed as a base year for the estimates at constant prices. The branches are formed on the base of the existing national classification CBNE 86.

1.1 Expenditure on the gross domestic product, in current prices

Hundred million Bulgarian leva

	1986	1987	1988	1989	1990	1991	1992	1993	1994	1995	1996	1997
1 Government final consumption expenditure [a]	30	27	27	28	33	104	177	251	435	681	995	10480
2 Private final consumption expenditure	212	227	234	252	303	888	1549	2509	4360	6885	14816	135889
A Households [b]	184	192	199	215	253	732	1312	2189	3876	6188	13674	124558
B Private non-profit institutions serving households [c]	29	35	35	37	50	156	237	320	483	696	1142	11331
3 Gross capital formation	124	120	132	131	138	307	399	457	494	1378	1469	20250
A Increase in stocks	31	22	29	28	41	60	74	70	−230	35	−916	934
B Gross fixed capital formation	93	98	103	103	97	246	326	387	723	1343	2385	19316
4 Exports of goods and services	−21	−9	−10	−15	−20	590	946	1142	2368	3932	11000	104783
5 less: Imports of goods and services						532	1063	1370	2401	4072	10458	95295
Statistical discrepancy	...	...	...	...	...	–	–	–	–	–	–	−2602
equals: Gross domestic product	344	365	383	396	454	1357	2008	2989	5256	8803	17487	171034

a Government consumption expenditure on collective goods.
b Household consumption includes the consumption of goods and services of resident and non-resident units in the country, without adjustments with purchases abroad and net gifts in kind, received from abroad. The imputed rent of owner-occupied dwellings.
c Including government consumption expenditure on individual goods.

Bulgaria

1.2 Expenditure on the gross domestic product, in constant prices

Million Bulgarian leva

	1986	1987	1988	1989	1990	1991	1992	1993	1994	1995	1996	1997
At constant prices of:				1989								
				1991								
				1992								
				1993								
				1994								
1 Government final consumption expenditure [a]	...	...	...	2819	2909	10441	9470				...	...
							17661	16024				
								25143	23730			
									43480	42565		
2 Private final consumption expenditure	...	...	...	25180	25258	88813	86709				...	...
							154929	150418				
								250879	239920			
									435997	423225		
A Households	...	...	...	21454	21128	73164	73903				...	...
							131195	130249				
								218927	213149			
									387650	380746		
B Private non-profit institutions serving households [b]	...	...	...	3725	4130	15649	12806				...	...
							23734	20169				
								31952	26771			
									48347	42479		
3 Gross capital formation	...	...	...	13105	9812	30665	27294				...	...
							39937	31859				
								45678	41055			
									49360	81274		
A Increase in stocks	...	...	...	2776	1397	6030	4464				...	...
							7360	4967				
								6956	1921			
									−22967	2606		
B Gross fixed capital formation	...	...	...	10328	8415	24635	22830				...	...
							32577	26892				
								38722	39134			
									72327	78668		
4 Exports of goods and services	...	...	...	−1524	−2009	58976					...	...
							94630					
								114210				
									236770			
5 less: Imports of goods and services	...	...	...	...	...	53184					...	...
							106325					
								136976				
									240055			
equals: Gross domestic product	...	...	...	39579	35970	135711	125869				...	...
							200832	197859				
								298934	304369			
									525552	536470		

a Government consumption expenditure on collective goods.   b Including government consumption expenditure on individual goods.

Bulgaria

1.3 Cost components of the gross domestic product

Hundred million Bulgarian leva

	1986	1987	1988	1989	1990	1991	1992	1993	1994	1995	1996	1997
1 Indirect taxes, net	...	...	...	...	...	103	175	280	664	1090	...	...
A Indirect taxes	...	...	...	...	...	130	211	367	735	1197	...	...
B less: Subsidies	...	...	...	...	...	27	36	87	70	107	...	...
2 Consumption of fixed capital	48	53	59	56	64	190	260	397	536	769	...	...
3 Compensation of employees paid by resident producers to ..	175	183	192	203	244	561	1064	1559	2387	3643	...	...
4 Operating surplus [a]	121	130	132	137	147	714	644	917	2044	3722	...	...
A Corporate and quasi-corporate enterprises	...	...	...	...	...	513	279	189	656	1302	...	...
B Private unincorporated enterprises	...	...	...	...	...	200	365	728	1387	2420	...	...
C General government	...	...	...	...	...	–	–	–	–	–	...	...
Statistical discrepancy [b]	...	...	...	...	...	211	–135	–164	–375	–547		
equals: Gross domestic product ..	344	365	383	396	454	1357	2008	2989	5256	8677	...	...

a Upto 1990, it includes net indirect taxes and operating surplus. Since 1991, includes operating surplus and mixed income.

b Adjustments - including import duties on goods, financial intermediation services indirectly measured.

1.4 General government current receipts and disbursements

Hundred million Bulgarian leva

	1986	1987	1988	1989	1990	1991	1992	1993	1994	1995	1996	1997
Receipts												
1 Operating surplus	...	...	...	...	...	–	–	–	–	–	...	...
2 Property and entrepreneurial income	...	...	...	...	...	1	8	8	23	41	...	...
3 Taxes, fees and contributions .	...	...	...	...	...	572	820	1139	2175	3284	...	...
A Indirect taxes	...	...	...	...	...	130	211	367	735	1197	...	...
B Direct taxes	...	...	...	...	...	306	293	334	723	1041	...	...
C Social security contributions	...	...	...	...	...	136	316	438	718	1046	...	...
D Compulsory fees, fines and penalties	...	...	...	...	...	...	...	...	...	...	...	...
4 Other current transfers	...	...	...	...	...	35	26	36	62	102	...	...
Total current receipts of general government	...	...	...	...	...	608	855	1183	2260	3427	...	...
Disbursements												
1 Government final consumption expenditure	...	...	...	...	...	258	408	564	903	1344	...	...
2 Property income	...	...	...	...	...	223	129	280	766	1242	...	...
A Interest	...	...	...	...	...	223	129	280	766	1242	...	...
B Net land rent and royalties ..	...	...	...	...	...	...	...	...	...	...	...	...
3 Subsidies	...	...	...	...	...	27	36	87	70	107	...	...
4 Other current transfers	...	...	...	...	...	210	306	468	716	959	...	...
A Social security benefits	...	...	...	...	...	124	199	326	509	699	...	...
B Social assistance grants	...	...	...	...	...	67	93	131	181	233	...	...
C Other	...	...	...	...	...	20	14	12	26	27	...	...
5 Net saving	...	...	...	...	...	–110	–24	–216	–196	–225	...	...
Total current disbursements and net saving of general government	...	...	...	...	...	608	855	1183	2260	3427	...	...

Bulgaria

1.5 Current income and outlay of corporate and quasi-corporate enterprises, summary

Hundred million Bulgarian leva

	1986	1987	1988	1989	1990	1991	1992	1993	1994	1995	1996	1997
Receipts												
1 Operating surplus	...	...	...	...	...	513	279	189	656	1302	...	...
2 Property and entrepreneurial income received	...	...	...	...	...	561	964	1558	3795	4956	...	...
3 Current transfers	...	...	...	...	...	30	33	44	62	91	...	...
Total current receipts	...	...	...	...	...	1104	1276	1791	4513	6348	...	...
Disbursements												
1 Property and entrepreneurial income	...	...	...	...	...	588	1097	1685	4151	5188	...	...
2 Direct taxes and other current payments to general government	...	...	...	...	...	255	182	179	470	642	...	...
3 Other current transfers	...	...	...	...	...	26	34	55	93	151	...	...
Statistical discrepancy	...	...	...	...	...	211	135	164	375	547	...	...
4 Net saving	...	...	...	...	...	25	−173	−291	−576	−179	...	...
Total current disbursements and net saving	...	...	...	...	...	1104	1276	1791	4513	6348	...	...

1.6 Current income and outlay of households and non-profit institutions

Hundred million Bulgarian leva

	1986	1987	1988	1989	1990	1991	1992	1993	1994	1995	1996	1997
Receipts												
1 Compensation of employees	...	...	...	...	...	561	1064	1559	2387	3643	...	...
A From resident producers	...	...	...	...	...	561	1064	1559	2387	3643	...	...
B From rest of the world	...	...	...	...	...	...	...	...	...	...	...	...
2 Operating surplus of private unincorporated enterprises	...	...	...	...	...	200	365	728	1387	2420	...	...
3 Property and entrepreneurial income	...	...	...	...	...	123	232	375	1066	1208	...	...
4 Current transfers	...	...	...	...	...	197	298	469	777	1012	...	...
A Social security benefits	...	...	...	...	...	124	199	326	509	700	...	...
B Social assistance grants	...	...	...	...	...	67	93	131	181	233	...	...
C Other	...	...	...	...	...	6	6	12	86	80	...	...
Total current receipts	...	...	...	...	...	1082	1959	3131	5617	8283	...	...
Disbursements												
1 Private final consumption expenditure	...	...	...	...	...	734	1318	2197	3891	6101	...	...
2 Property income	...	...	...	...	...	13	10	30	75	62	...	...
3 Direct taxes and other current transfers n.e.c. to general government	...	...	...	...	...	187	427	593	970	1445	...	...
A Social security contributions	...	...	...	...	...	136	316	438	718	1046	...	...
B Direct taxes	...	...	...	...	...	51	111	155	253	399	...	...
C Fees, fines and penalties	...	...	...	...	...	...	...	...	...	...	...	...
4 Other current transfers	...	...	...	...	...	4	17	25	79	87	...	...
5 Net saving	...	...	...	...	...	143	187	286	601	588	...	...
Total current disbursements and net saving	...	...	...	...	...	1082	1959	3131	5617	8283	...	...

Bulgaria

1.7 External transactions on current account, summary

Hundred million Bulgarian leva

	1986	1987	1988	1989	1990	1991	1992	1993	1994	1995	1996	1997
Payments to the rest of the world												
1 Imports of goods and services	...	...	...	...	...	532	1063	1370	2401	3897	...	...
A Imports of merchandise, c.i.f.	...	...	...	...	...	514	961	1214	2094	3558	...	...
B Other	...	...	...	...	...	18	102	156	306	339	...	...
2 Factor income to rest of the world	...	...	...	...	...	147	62	79	155	390	...	...
A Compensation of employees	...	...	...	...	...	...	...	...	...	...	...	...
B Property and entrepreneurial income	...	...	...	...	...	147	62	79	155	390	...	...
3 Current transfers to the rest of the world	...	...	...	...	...	4	2	3	37	25	...	...
4 Surplus of the nation on current transactions	...	...	...	...	...	−117	−32	−53	−96	−278	...	...
Payments to the rest of the world and surplus of the nation on current transfers	...	...	...	...	...	35	33	28	86	137	...	...
Receipts from the rest of the world												
1 Exports of goods and services	...	...	...	...	...	590	946	1142	2368	3877	...	...
A Exports of merchandise, f.o.b.	...	...	...	...	...	574	915	1029	2162	3577	...	...
B Other	...	...	...	...	...	16	31	113	206	300	...	...
2 Factor income from rest of the world	...	...	...	...	...	9	29	26	86	137	...	...
A Compensation of employees	...	...	...	...	...	...	...	...	...	...	...	...
B Property and entrepreneurial income	...	...	...	...	...	9	29	26	47	103	...	...
3 Current transfers from rest of the world	...	...	...	...	...	25	3	3	39	33	...	...
A Subsidies from supranational organisations	...	...	...	...	...	...	...	...	...	...	...	...
B Other current transfers	...	...	...	...	...	25	3	3	39	32	...	...
Receipts from the rest of the world on current transactions	...	...	...	...	...	35	33	28	86	137	...	...

1.8 Capital transactions of the nation, summary

Hundred million Bulgarian leva

	1986	1987	1988	1989	1990	1991	1992	1993	1994	1995	1996	1997
Finance of gross capital formation												
Gross saving	...	...	...	...	...	248	251	176	365	953	...	...
1 Consumption of fixed capital	...	...	...	...	...	190	260	397	536	769	...	...
A General government	...	...	...	...	...	15	24	32	29	45	...	...
B Corporate and quasi-corporate enterprises	...	...	...	...	...	159	192	286	368	506	...	...
C Other	...	...	...	...	...	16	44	79	139	219	...	...
2 Net saving	...	...	...	...	...	58	−9	−221	−171	184	...	...
A General government	...	...	...	...	...	−110	−24	−216	−196	−225	...	...
B Corporate and quasi-corporate enterprises	...	...	...	...	...	25	−173	−291	−576	−179	...	...
C Other	...	...	...	...	...	143	187	286	601	588	...	...
less: Surplus of the nation on current transactions	...	...	...	...	...	−117	−32	−53	−96	−278	...	...

Bulgaria

Hundred million Bulgarian leva

	1986	1987	1988	1989	1990	1991	1992	1993	1994	1995	1996	1997
Finance of gross capital formation	...	...	...	...	...	365	282	229	461	1231	...	...
Gross capital formation												
Increase in stocks	...	...	...	...	...	60	74	70	–230	15	...	...
Gross fixed capital formation	...	...	...	...	...	246	326	387	723	1236	...	...
1 General government	...	...	...	...	...	30	53	67	93	75	...	...
2 Corporate and quasi-corporate enterprises	...	...	...	...	...	211	233	259	469	865	...	...
3 Other	...	...	...	...	...	...	...	...	...	...	...	...
Gross capital formation	...	...	...	...	...	365	282	229	461	1231	...	...

1.9 Gross domestic product by institutional sectors of origin

Hundred million Bulgarian leva

	1986	1987	1988	1989	1990	1991	1992	1993	1994	1995	1996	1997
Domestic factor incomes originating												
1 General government	...	...	...	...	...	105	220	349	530	816	...	...
2 Corporate and quasi-corporate enterprises	...	...	...	...	...	969	1079	1275	2285	3804	...	...
A Non-financial	...	...	...	...	...	753	945	1122	1914	3358	...	...
Public	...	...	...	...	...	728	897	1019	162	2598	...	...
Private	...	...	...	...	...	25	48	103	262	760	...	...
B Financial	...	...	...	...	...	215	134	153	372	446	...	...
Public	...	...	...	...	...	209	127	145	349	366	...	...
Private	...	...	...	...	...	6	6	8	23	80	...	...
3 Households and private unincorporated enterprises	...	...	...	...	...	200	407	848	1609	2728	...	...
A Owner-occupied housing	...	...	...	...	...	83	142	315	512	863	...	...
B Subsistence production	...	...	...	...	...	15	37	61	114	187	...	...
C Other	...	...	...	...	...	103	227	473	983	1679	...	...
4 Non-profit institutions serving households	...	...	...	...	...	1	2	4	6	16	...	...
subtotal: Domestic factor incomes	...	...	...	...	...	1275	1708	2476	4430	7365	...	...
Indirect taxes, net	...	...	...	...	...	103	175	280	664	1090	...	...
A Indirect taxes	...	...	...	...	...	130	211	367	735	1197	...	...
B less: Subsidies	...	...	...	...	...	27	36	87	70	107	...	...
Consumption of fixed capital	...	...	...	...	...	190	260	397	536	769	...	...
Statistical discrepancy [a]	...	...	...	...	...	211	135	164	375	547	...	...
Gross domestic product	...	...	...	...	...	1357	2008	2989	5256	8677	...	...

a Adjustments - including import duties on goods, financial intermediation services indirectly measured.

1.10 Gross domestic product by kind of activity, in current prices

Hundred million Bulgarian leva

	1986	1987	1988	1989	1990	1991	1992	1993	1994	1995	1996	1997
1 Agriculture, hunting, forestry and fishing	44	43	44	43	83	209	233	297	604	1114	2160	2537
2 Mining and quarrying	193	195	203	204	200	475	667	816	1323	2311	4609	40607
3 Manufacturing												
4 Electricity, gas and water												
5 Construction	27	29	30	31	32	64	117	162	251	416	734	4222
6 Wholesale and retail trade, restaurants and hotels	13	26	26	30	35	118	180	266	529	1018	1785	12828

Bulgaria

Hundred million Bulgarian leva

	1986	1987	1988	1989	1990	1991	1992	1993	1994	1995	1996	1997
7 Transport, storage and communication	20	54	29	34	33	90	125	187	340	497	1139	11249
8 Finance, insurance, real estate and business services	47	49	51	53	72	228	154	228	511	2987	6077	43583
9 Community, social and personal services [a]						260	462	836	1343	2162	...	...
Total, Industries	344	365	383	396	455	1443	1938	2791	4901	8344	16504	152362
Producers of government services	...	...	...	...	...	...	...	...	...	...	...	...
Other producers	...	...	...	...	...	...	...	...	...	...	...	...
Subtotal	344	365	383	396	455	1443	1938	2791	4901	8344	16504	152362
less: Imputed bank service charge	...	...	...	...	...	211	135	164	375	547	...	...
plus: Import duties	...	...	...	...	...	10	40	91	85	214	363	13115
plus: Value added tax	...	...	...	...	...	...	...	...	310	670	...	...
plus: Other adjustments	...	...	...	...	−1[b]	114	166	271	269	245	620	5557
equals: Gross domestic product	344	365	383	396	454	1357	2008	2989	5256	8803	17487	171034

a Including item "Producers of government services".   b Referring to statistical discrepancy.

1.11 Gross domestic product by kind of activity, in constant prices

Million Bulgarian leva

	1986	1987	1988	1989	1990	1991	1992	1993	1994	1995	1996	1997
At constant prices of:				1989								
					1991							
						1992						
							1993					
								1994				
1 Agriculture, hunting, forestry and fishing	...	...	...	4331	4170	20885	17803				...	...
							23329	16279				
									32506			
										69110		
2 Mining and quarrying	...	...	...	20444	17934	47543	43293				...	...
							66741	62727				
									87420			
										123290		
3 Manufacturing	...	...	...								...	...
4 Electricity, gas and water	...	...	...								...	...
5 Construction	...	...	...	3063	2625	6403	7201				...	...
							11676	10820				
									16114			
										25645		
6 Wholesale and retail trade, restaurants and hotels	...	...	...	3009	2344	11807	9540				...	...
							17965	18039				
									28668			
										50771		
7 Transport, storage and communication	...	...	...	3412	2857	8966	9302				...	...
							12495	13546				
									19189			
										46948		

Bulgaria

Million Bulgarian leva

	1986	1987	1988	1989	1990	1991	1992	1993	1994	1995	1996	1997
At constant prices of:			1989									
			1991									
			1992									
			1993									
			1994									
8 Finance, insurance, real estate and business services	...	...	...	5320	6040	22788	6694				...	...
							15362	14559				
									26251			
										41416		
9 Community, social and personal services [a]	...	...	...	...	...	25954	25299				...	...
								46183	46412			
										72989		
										131450		
Total, Industries	...	...	...	39579	35970	144346	119132				...	...
								193751	182382			
										283137		
										488630		
Producers of government services	...	...	...	...	...	...	...	...	...	...	...	...
Other producers	...	...	...	...	...	...	...	...	...	...	...	...
Subtotal	...	...	...	39579	35970	144346	119132				...	...
								193751	182382			
										283137		
										488630		
less: Imputed bank service charge	...	...	...	...	...	21072	6068				...	...
								13453	10480			
										19085		
										34146		
plus: Import duties	...	...	...	...	...	1036	2541				...	...
								3965	6037			
										8221		
										18018		
plus: Value added tax	...	...	...	...	...	...	...	...	17217		...	...
										39300		
plus: Other adjustments	...	...	...	...	...	11401					...	...
							16569	19920				
									14879			
										24668		
equals: Gross domestic product	...	...	...	39579	35970	135711	125869				...	...
								200832	197859			
										304369		
										536470		

a Including item "Producers of government services".

Bulgaria

1.12 Relations among national accounting aggregates

Hundred million Bulgarian leva

	1986	1987	1988	1989	1990	1991	1992	1993	1994	1995	1996	1997
Gross domestic product	...	...	...	...	...	1357	2008	2989	5256	8803	17487	171034
plus: Net factor income from the rest of the world	...	...	...	...	...	−138	−33	−53	−108	−286	−692	...
Factor income from rest of the world	...	...	...	...	...	9	29	26	47	103	324	...
less: Factor income to the rest of the world	...	...	...	...	...	147	62	79	155	390	1016	...
equals: Gross national product	...	...	...	...	...	1219	1975	2936	5147	8517	16795	...
less: Consumption of fixed capital	...	...	...	...	...	190	260	397	536	768	1433	...
equals: National income	...	...	...	...	...	1029	1715	2539	4612	7749	15363	...
plus: Net current transfers from the rest of the world	...	...	...	...	...	21	1	–	12	8	170	...
Current transfers from rest of the world	...	...	...	...	...	25	3	3	39	33	408	...
less: Current transfers to the rest of the world	...	...	...	...	...	4	2	3	27	25	237	...
equals: National disposable income	...	...	...	...	...	1051	1717	2539	4624	7757	15533	...
less: Final consumption	...	...	...	...	...	...	...	...	...	...	...	...
equals: Net saving	...	...	...	...	...	...	...	...	...	...	...	...
less: Surplus of the nation on current transactions	...	...	...	...	...	...	...	...	...	...	...	...
equals: Net capital formation	...	...	...	...	...	...	...	...	...	...	...	...

Burundi

Source

Reply to the United Nations National Accounts Questionnaire from the Département des Etudes et Statistiques, Bujumbura.

General note

The estimates shown in the following tables have been prepared in accordance with the United Nations System of National Accounts (1968 SNA) so far as the existing data would permit.

1.1 Expenditure on the gross domestic product, in current prices

Million Burundi francs

	1986	1987	1988	1989	1990	1991	1992	1993	1994	1995	1996	1997
1 Government final consumption expenditure	24252	28570	31491	36547	38343	36113	35212	...	...	...	...	...
2 Private final consumption expenditure	104340	107015	114298	135449	163216	177692	187784	...	...	...	...	...
3 Gross capital formation	22107	24876	21672	29362	31058	37264	48784	...	...	...	...	...
A Increase in stocks	3247	3763	−4029	3247	−1177	−1043	1005	...	...	...	...	...
B Gross fixed capital formation	18860	21114	25701	26115	32235	38307	47779	...	...	...	...	...
4 Exports of goods and services	15625	13015	17298	15697	15641	21231	20309	...	...	...	...	...
5 less: Imports of goods and services	25482	29886	31852	37507	51602	60402	65705	...	...	...	...	...
equals: Gross domestic product	140842	143590	152907	179548	196656	211898	226384	...	...	...	...	...

1.3 Cost components of the gross domestic product

Million Burundi francs

	1986	1987	1988	1989	1990	1991	1992	1993	1994	1995	1996	1997
1 Indirect taxes, net	17724	15638	17834	24393	21557	...	...	...	...	...	...	...
A Indirect taxes	18096	16117	18515	25368	24533	...	...	...	...	...	...	...
B less: Subsidies	372	479	681	976	2976	...	...	...	...	...	...	...
2 Consumption of fixed capital	4110	5038	5898	9075	8206	...	...	...	...	...	...	...
3 Compensation of employees paid by resident producers to ..	28319	30107	33255	38139	47979	...	...	...	...	...	...	...
4 Operating surplus	90689	92807	95921	107942	118914	...	...	...	...	...	...	...
A Corporate and quasi-corporate enterprises	6328	...	...	...	...	...	...	...	...	...	...	...
B Private unincorporated enterprises	84201	...	...	...	...	...	...	...	...	...	...	...
C General government	160	...	...	...	...	...	...	...	...	...	...	...
equals: Gross domestic product	140842	143590	152907	179548	196656	...	...	...	...	...	...	...

Burundi

1.10 Gross domestic product by kind of activity, in current prices

Million Burundi francs

	1986	1987	1988	1989	1990	1991	1992	1993	1994	1995	1996	1997
1 Agriculture, hunting, forestry and fishing	71872	70447	72852	82609	100602	...	...	...	...	...	...	...
2 Mining and quarrying [a]	923	1425	1470	2020	1583	...	...	...	...	...	...	...
3 Manufacturing	17405	23451	24630	32505	32306	...	...	...	...	...	...	...
4 Electricity, gas and water	...	...	...	...	...	...	...	...	...	...	...	...
5 Construction	5047	3899	4287	5773	6588	...	...	...	...	...	...	...
6 Wholesale and retail trade, restaurants and hotels	18182	15261	19209	18973	9474	...	...	...	...	...	...	...
7 Transport, storage and communication	3732	3918	3918	5718	5989	...	...	...	...	...	...	...
8 Finance, insurance, real estate and business services	134	138	139	224	470	...	...	...	...	...	...	...
9 Community, social and personal services	1943	2341	2734	3451	3858	...	...	...	...	...	...	...
Total, Industries	119238	120880	129239	151273	160870	...	...	...	...	...	...	...
Producers of government services	17363	18074	19828	24354	31180	...	...	...	...	...	...	...
Other producers	594	583				...	...	...	...	...	...	...
Subtotal	137195	139537	149067	175627	192050	...	...	...	...	...	...	...
less: Imputed bank service charge	...	...	...	...	...	...	...	...	...	...	...	...
plus: Import duties	3647	4054	3841	3921	4606	...	...	...	...	...	...	...
plus: Value added tax	...	...	...	...	...	...	...	...	...	...	...	...
plus: Other adjustments	...	...	...	...	...	...	...	...	...	...	...	...
equals: Gross domestic product	140842	143590	152908	179549	196656	...	...	...	...	...	...	...

a Item "Electricity, gas and water" is included in item "Mining and Quarrying".

Cambodia

Source

Reply to the United Nations National Accounts Questionnaire from the Insitut National de la Statistique et des Recherches Economiques, Ministère du Plan, Phnom-penh. The official estimates, together with information on concepts, sources and methods of estimation, are published by the Ministère in *Comptes Economiques du Cambodge*.

General note

The estimates shown in the tables below have been prepared in accordance with the United Nations System of National Accounts (SNA) so far as the existing data would permit.

1.1 Expenditure on the gross domestic product, in current prices

Million riels

	1986	1987	1988	1989	1990	1991	1992	1993	1994	1995	1996	1997
1 Government final consumption expenditure	...	...	...	...	...	...	...	306000	492600	413300	506600	...
2 Private final consumption expenditure	...	...	...	...	...	...	...	5991200	6002200	6799500	7444400	...
A Households	...	...	...	...	...	...	...	5991200	6002200	6799500	7444400	...
B Private non-profit institutions serving households	...	...	...	...	...	...	...	...	...	...	...	...
3 Gross capital formation	...	...	...	...	...	...	...	562800	757000	974300	1261700	...
A Increase in stocks	...	...	...	...	...	...	...	5000	57400	17800	146100	...
B Gross fixed capital formation	...	...	...	...	...	...	...	557800	699600	956500	1115600	...
Residential buildings	...	...	...	...	...	...	...	192800	63500	118600	126000	...
Non-residential buildings	...	...	...	...	...	...	...	36500	7100	63700	124000	...
Other construction and land improvement, etc.	...	...	...	...	...	...	...	234100	413800	511100	482700	...
Other	...	...	...	...	...	...	...	94500	215300	263000	382900	...
4 Exports of goods and services	...	...	...	...	...	...	...	1193500	1412300	2406700	2137300	...
5 less: Imports of goods and services	...	...	...	...	...	...	...	1657900	2384300	3589100	3597400	...
Statistical discrepancy	...	...	...	...	...	...	...	−311100	−79000	580200	548800	...
equals: Gross domestic product	...	...	...	...	...	...	...	6084500	6201000	7585000	8301300	...

1.2 Expenditure on the gross domestic product, in constant prices

Million riels

	1986	1987	1988	1989	1990	1991	1992	1993	1994	1995	1996	1997
At constant prices of: 1993												
1 Government final consumption expenditure	...	...	...	...	...	...	...	306000	466500	379600	430800	...
2 Private final consumption expenditure	...	...	...	...	...	...	...	5991200	6194200	6464300	6781900	...
A Households	...	...	...	...	...	...	...	5991200	6194200	6464300	6781900	...
B Private non-profit institutions serving households	...	...	...	...	...	...	...	...	...	...	...	...
3 Gross capital formation	...	...	...	...	...	...	...	562800	693800	857100	1155500	...

Cambodia

Million riels

	1986	1987	1988	1989	1990	1991	1992	1993	1994	1995	1996	1997
At constant prices of: 1993												
A Increase in stocks	...	...	...	...	...	...	...	5000	61300	16300	151800	...
B Gross fixed capital formation	...	...	...	...	...	...	...	557800	632500	840800	1003700	...
Residential buildings	...	...	...	...	...	...	...	192800	...	...	...	...
Non-residential buildings	...	...	...	...	...	...	...	36500	...	...	...	...
Other construction and land improvement, etc.	...	...	...	...	...	...	...	234100	...	...	...	...
Other	...	...	...	...	...	...	...	94500	...	...	...	...
4 Exports of goods and services	...	...	...	...	...	...	...	1193500	1584600	2241000	1823300	...
5 less: Imports of goods and services	...	...	...	...	...	...	...	1657900	2045600	3340300	2916200	...
Statistical discrepancy	...	...	...	...	...	...	...	−311100	−570300	142400	−34700	...
equals: Gross domestic product	...	...	...	...	...	...	...	6084500	6323200	6744100	7240600	...

1.10 Gross domestic product by kind of activity, in current prices

Million riels

	1986	1987	1988	1989	1990	1991	1992	1993	1994	1995	1996	1997
1 Agriculture, hunting, forestry and fishing	...	42707	109548	125862	333107	666463	1198300	2741971 / 2556400	2614100	3495200	3397500	...
2 Mining and quarrying	...	20168	30132	2500	3124	4689	8500	2500 / 11000	11100	11600	12900	...
3 Manufacturing	...	1563	1953	18022	31355	71005	126900	285525 / 489600	522200	580100	865800	...
4 Electricity, gas and water	...	522	588	600	2155	6966	16300	38525 / 24100	30800	39500	40100	...
5 Construction	...	7924	11785	16000	30115	79001	178200	403130 / 231700	242200	355200	403000	...
6 Wholesale and retail trade, restaurants and hotels	...	14169	28653	29351	58407	173640	327100	638000 / 1147600	1106000	1257600	1446700	...
7 Transport, storage and communication	...	3228	4224	6500	22547	43155	86100	173061 / 367400	385700	423200	494700	...
8 Finance, insurance, real estate and business services	...	7535	8870	15500	40950	92800	172200	311620 / 645800	478700	559900	623200	...
9 Community, social and personal services	...	7073	8400	15400	41763	113762	206400	416058 / 166800	159800	157600	162400	...
Total, Industries	...	104889	204153	229735	563523	1251481	2320000	5010390 / 5640400	5550600	6879900	7446300	...
Producers of government services	...	...	...	9300	28301	62487	108400	215960 / 140300	222200	233700	265300	...
Other producers	...	...	...	...	...	...	...	124300	111000	149100	172200	...
Subtotal	...	...	...	239035	589824	1313968	2428400	5240000 / 5905000	5883800	7262700	7883800	...
less: Imputed bank service charge	...	...	...	...	...	...	...	15000	17200	73000	64200	...
plus: Import duties	...	...	...	1874	8812	22000	79600	174000 / 194500	334400	395300	481700	...
plus: Value added tax	...	...	...	...	...	...	...	...	...	...	...	...
plus: Other adjustments	...	...	...	...	...	...	...	...	...	...	...	...
equals: Gross domestic product	...	98890	195560	240909	598636	1335968	2508000	5414000 / 6084500	6201000	7585000	8301300	...

Cambodia

1.11 Gross domestic product by kind of activity, in constant prices

Million riels

	1986	1987	1988	1989	1990	1991	1992	1993	1994	1995	1996	1997
At constant prices of:				1989				1993				
1 Agriculture, hunting, forestry and fishing	...	106805	106163	125862	127358	135937	138514	137100 / 2556400	2615700	2812200	2848100	...
2 Mining and quarrying	...	2066	2273	2500	2750	3025	3176	3430 / 11000	11800	12200	11600	...
3 Manufacturing	...	13606	17977	18022	17247	18419	18972	20489 / 489600	513500	568800	811800	...
4 Electricity, gas and water	...	566	612	600	541	467	630	668 / 24100	25900	35500	35800	...
5 Construction	...	15459	20064	16000	15972	17642	22935	27087 / 231700	236800	331100	361300	...
6 Wholesale and retail trade, restaurants and hotels	...	27646	48780	29351	26894	30954	32265	34093 / 1147600	1168200	1205300	1261400	...
7 Transport, storage and communication	...	6256	6505	6500	6411	7000	8050	8855 / 367400	404300	404600	426800	...
8 Finance, insurance, real estate and business services	...	14700	15100	15500	15900	16300	17441	18836 / 645800	506900	561600	575200	...
9 Community, social and personal services	...	13800	14300	15400	16234	17100	18755	20443 / 166800	167500	155800	163500	...
Total, Industries	...	200904	231774	229735	229307	246844	260108	271001 / 5640400	5650600	6087100	6495500	...
Producers of government services	...	6943	9760	9300	10995	10980	10980	11529 / 140300	210400	214600	225600	...
Other producers	...	...	...	...	...	...	...	124300	128600	153300	172200	...
Subtotal	...	...	...	239035	240122	257824	271088	282530 / 5905000	5989600	6455000	6893300	...
less: Imputed bank service charge	...	...	...	...	...	...	...	15000	18200	67000	54600	
plus: Import duties	...	...	...	1874	3582	4369	8907	9577 / 194500	351700	356300	401900	...
plus: Value added tax	...	...	...	...	...	...	...	...	...	...	...	...
plus: Other adjustments	...	...	...	...	...	...	...	...	...	...	...	...
equals: Gross domestic product	...	207873	241534	240909	243704	262193	280625	292107 / 6084500	6323200	6744100	7240600	...

1.12 Relations among national accounting aggregates

Million riels

	1986	1987	1988	1989	1990	1991	1992	1993	1994	1995	1996	1997
Gross domestic product	...	...	...	...	...	...	...	6084500	6201000	7585000	8301300	...
plus: Net factor income from the rest of the world	...	...	...	...	...	...	...	306000	492600	413300	506600	...
equals: Gross national product	...	...	...	...	...	...	...	5778500	5708400	7171700	7794700	...
less: Consumption of fixed capital	...	...	...	...	...	...	...	...	...	...	...	...
equals: National income	...	...	...	...	...	...	...	...	...	...	...	...
plus: Net current transfers from the rest of the world	...	...	...	...	...	...	...	...	...	...	...	...
equals: National disposable income	...	...	...	...	...	...	...	...	...	...	...	...
less: Final consumption	...	...	...	...	...	...	...	6297200	6494800	7212800	7951000	...
equals: Net saving	...	...	...	...	...	...	...	...	...	...	...	...
less: Surplus of the nation on current transactions	...	...	...	...	...	...	...	...	...	...	...	...
equals: Net capital formation	...	...	...	...	...	...	...	...	...	...	...	...

Cameroon

Source

Reply to the United Nations National Accounts Questionnaire from the Direction de la Statistique et de la Comptabilité Nationale, Ministère de l'Economie et du Plan, Yaounde. The official estimates are published annually in *Comptes de la Nation*.

General note

The estimates shown in the following tables have been prepared in accordance with the United Nations System of National Accounts (1968 SNA) so far as the existing data would permit.

1.1 Expenditure on the gross domestic product, in current prices

Hundred million CFA francs — Fiscal year beginning 1 July

	1986	1987	1988	1989	1990	1991	1992	1993	1994	1995	1996	1997
1 Government final consumption expenditure	4767	3910	3784	3700	3501	...	...	...	...	...	...	...
2 Private final consumption expenditure	26307	24893	24309	23663	23538	...	...	...	...	...	...	...
3 Gross capital formation	9687	7617	6006	5812	5616	...	...	...	...	...	...	...
A Increase in stocks	64	41	–376	–	–	...	...	...	...	...	...	...
B Gross fixed capital formation	9623	7576	6382	5812	5616	...	...	...	...	...	...	...
Residential buildings	3051	2545	2281	...	...	...	...	...	...	...	...	...
Non-residential buildings				...	...	...	...	...	...	...	...	...
Other construction and land improvement, etc.	3179	2646	1631	...	...	...	...	...	...	...	...	...
Other	3392	2385	2470	...	...	...	...	...	...	...	...	...
4 Exports of goods and services	6356	5738	6672	7328	7215	...	...	...	...	...	...	...
5 less: Imports of goods and services	7898	5714	5641	6294	5634	...	...	...	...	...	...	...
equals: Gross domestic product [a]	39219	36445	35130	34209	34236	...	...	...	...	...	...	...

a Data in this table have not been revised, therefore they are not comparable with the data in other tables.

1.2 Expenditure on the gross domestic product, in constant prices

Hundred million CFA francs — Fiscal year beginning 1 July

	1986	1987	1988	1989	1990	1991	1992	1993	1994	1995	1996	1997
At constant prices of: 1980												
1 Government final consumption expenditure	2134	2055	1923	1962	...	...	...	...	...	...	...	...
2 Private final consumption expenditure	14075	13900	12834	13116	...	...	...	...	...	...	...	...
3 Gross capital formation	5602	4900	4709	4775	...	...	...	...	...	...	...	...
A Increase in stocks	153	95	156	109	...	...	...	...	...	...	...	...
B Gross fixed capital formation	5449	4805	4553	4666	...	...	...	...	...	...	...	...
4 Exports of goods and services	3891	2999	2852	2904	...	...	...	...	...	...	...	...
5 less: Imports of goods and services	2953	2750	2480	2502	...	...	...	...	...	...	...	...
equals: Gross domestic product	22747	21104	19838	20255	...	...	...	...	...	...	...	...

Cameroon

1.10 Gross domestic product by kind of activity, in current prices

Hundred million CFA francs	1986	1987	1988	1989	1990	1991	1992	1993	1994	1995	1996	1997
1 Agriculture, hunting, forestry and fishing	9407	8726	8961	8279	8574	...	...	...	...	...	...	...
2 Mining and quarrying	3268	3197	3108	3200	3107	...	...	...	...	...	...	...
3 Manufacturing	5005	4802	4936	4850	4655	...	...	...	...	...	...	...
4 Electricity, gas and water	468	475	492	595	593	...	...	...	...	...	...	...
5 Construction	2654	1848	1639	1444	1307	...	...	...	...	...	...	...
6 Wholesale and retail trade, restaurants and hotels	5850	5630	5299	5196	5266	...	...	...	...	...	...	...
7 Transport, storage and communication	2315	2576	2133	2381	2485	...	...	...	...	...	...	...
8 Finance, insurance, real estate and business services	4907	4357	4063	3890	3770	...	...	...	...	...	...	...
9 Community, social and personal services	563	502	497	485	475	...	...	...	...	...	...	...
Total, Industries	34437	32113	31128	30320	30232	...	...	...	...	...	...	...
Producers of government services	3250	2997	2969	2824	3010	...	...	...	...	...	...	...
Other producers	500	496	417	454	452	...	...	...	...	...	...	...
Subtotal	38187	35606	34514	33598	33694	...	...	...	...	...	...	...
less: Imputed bank service charge	278	226	198	181	180	...	...	...	...	...	...	...
plus: Import duties	1310	1065	814	792	722	...	...	...	...	...	...	...
plus: Value added tax	...	...	...	...	...	...	...	...	...	...	...	...
plus: Other adjustments	...	...	...	...	...	...	...	...	...	...	...	...
equals: Gross domestic product	39219	36445	35130	34209	34236	...	...	...	...	...	...	...

1.11 Gross domestic product by kind of activity, in constant prices

Hundred million CFA francs	1986	1987	1988	1989	1990	1991	1992	1993	1994	1995	1996	1997
At constant prices of: 1980												
1 Agriculture, hunting, forestry and fishing	5372	4889	5417	5347	5635	...	...	...	...	...	...	...
2 Mining and quarrying	2730	2523	2442	2473	1969	...	...	...	...	...	...	...
3 Manufacturing	3244	3396	3378	3202	3073	...	...	...	...	...	...	...
4 Electricity, gas and water	279	264	269	327	326	...	...	...	...	...	...	...
5 Construction	1205	748	654	595	539	...	...	...	...	...	...	...
6 Wholesale and retail trade, restaurants and hotels	7694	7070	6355	5700	5722	...	...	...	...	...	...	...
7 Transport, storage and communication						...	...	...	...	...	...	...
8 Finance, insurance, real estate and business services						...	...	...	...	...	...	...
9 Community, social and personal services	1793	1656	1627	1558	1661	...	...	...	...	...	...	...
Total, Industries	...	...	...	...	...	...	...	...	...	...	...	...
Producers of government services	...	...	...	...	...	...	...	...	...	...	...	...
Other producers	...	...	...	...	...	...	...	...	...	...	...	...
Subtotal	22317	20546	20142	19202	18924	...	...	...	...	...	...	...
less: Imputed bank service charge	...	...	...	...	...	...	...	...	...	...	...	...
plus: Import duties	1094	903	756	649	693	...	...	...	...	...	...	...

Cameroon

Hundred million CFA francs   **Fiscal year beginning 1 July**

	1986	1987	1988	1989	1990	1991	1992	1993	1994	1995	1996	1997
	At constant prices of: 1980											
plus: Value added tax	...	...	...	...	...	...	...	...	...	...	...	...
plus: Other adjustments	...	...	...	...	...	...	...	...	...	...	...	...
equals: Gross domestic product	23412	21449	20898	19851	19616	...	...	...	...	...	...	...

Canada

General note

The preparation of national accounts statistics in Canada is undertaken by Statistics Canada, in Ottawa, Ontario, Canada. Official estimates are published quarterly and annually in *National Income and Expenditure Accounts*, Statistics Canada Catalogue 13-001 and 13-201. A detailed description of the sources and methods used for the national accounts estimation is found in *Guide to the Income and Expenditure Accounts*, Statistics Canada Catalogue 13-603E (English) and 13-603F (French), published in November, 1990. The estimates are generally in accordance with the classifications and definitions recommended in the United Nations System of National Accounts (SNA). Annual input-output tables at current and constant prices are published in *The Input-Output Structure of the Canadian Economy*, Statistics Canada Catalogue 15-201. Quarterly statistics on flows of funds are published in *Financial Flow Accounts* catalogue 13-014 and annual estimates of balance sheets are published in *National Balance Sheet Accounts* catalogue 13-214. Detailed sources and methods are published in *A Guide to the Financial Flow and National Balance Sheet Accounts* catalogue 13-585e (English) and 13-585f (French). The following tables have been prepared from successive replies to the United Nations National Accounts Questionnaire. When the scope and coverage of the estimates differ for conceptual or statistical reasons from the definitions and classifications recommended in SNA, a footnote is indicated to the relevant tables.

Gross domestic product

All components of gross domestic production by expenditure type are estimated through the expenditure approach.

Expenditures on the gross domestic product

Government final consumption expenditure is based on public accounts and financial records and statements of the government bodies. At the federal and provincial levels, the figures are derived by eliminating from total government budgetary expenditure on all outlays that are not made directly to purchase new goods and services. At the local level, the estimates are built up directly on a gross basis from the data sources, subtracting revenues from sales of goods and services. Benchmark estimates of consumption expenditure are based on the censuses of merchandising and services conducted in 1951, 1961, 1966, and 1971 and on the retail commodity survey of 1974 and 1989 as well as the Family Expenditure Surveys (most recently in 1986, 1990 and 1992). These estimates are first adjusted to include commodities purchased through non-retail trade outlets and then broken down into trade groupings. For the non-census years, the benchmark estimates of each trade group rare interpolated or projected by using the movement of sales of equivalent kind-of-business groupings. For non-retail trade groups, surveys of wholesale trade and service industries are used. Estimates of consumer expenditure on services such as transport, health care and education are based on annual surveys or published reports. Comprehensive figures on the quantities of physical stocks held on farms and grains in commercial channels are available from the Agriculture Division of Statistics Canada. Inventories held by government agencies are obtained from government records. Estimates of inventory book values of non-farm business are based on annual censuses or sample surveys. The estimates of gross fixed capital investment are based on the results of annual surveys which are published in *Private and Public Investment in Canada: Outlook* reports. Data are available separately for non-residential construction and machinery and equipment. Residential construction are derived from housing starts as counted by Canada Mortgage and Housing Corporation, building permit values and quarterly work-put-in-place coefficients. The estimates of exports and imports of goods and services are based on information available in the balance of payments. For merchandise, the import and export figures are obtained from customs entries while for services, the estimates draw upon a number of sources such as surveys of business firms and Statistics Canada's international travel surveys. Constant dollar values of government consumption expenditure are obtained through extrapolating base-year wages and salaries by employment data and through deflating other current expenditure by base-weighted price indexes. Price deflation is also used for private final consumption expenditure, non-farm stocks, non-residential construction and machinery and equipment, and exports and imports of goods and services. The constant price series for farm inventories is derived by valuing the physical quantities of stocks in prices from the base period chosen. For residential construction, the estimates are derived by deflating current dollar component estimates with price indexes. Exports and imports of merchandise are each revalued by specially constructed current-weighted indexes.

Cost structure of the gross domestic product

The general method used in the preparation of the labour income estimates consists of calculating the payments made on labour account by the various industrial groups and summing the results. The estimates are based on monthly and annual samples of full-coverage surveys conducted by Statistics Canada, decennial or quinquennial censuses and published statements of governments. A principal benchmark source of information is the tabulation of total wages and salaries submitted by employers with respect to employees' earnings. Undertaken by the Revenue Canada—Taxation in connection with the administration of the Income Tax Act. The estimates of corporation profits are ob-

Canada

tained from the publication *Financial Statistics for Enterprises*. Estimates of interest and miscellaneous investment income are based on information obtained from various sources such as Revenue Canada—Taxation, the Bank of Canada, accounts and financial statements of governments and others. For unincorporated business, estimates are obtained either through direct inquiry, projections from benchmark data, subtracting expenses from gross income or through applying the ratio of net to gross income based on survey or income tax data. The estimates of depreciation are calculated on an original cost valuation basis with a close link to the figures of book depreciation reported in the accounting records of business firms. For the government sector, capital consumption allowances are imputed while for the agricultural and housing sectors, replacement cost estimates of capital consumption are prepared from estimates of fixed reproducible capital at market values. The estimates of indirect taxes are based on accounting records of the various levels of government. Subsidies consist of federal and provincial production subsidies.

Gross domestic product by kind of activity

The table of gross domestic product of economic activity is prepared in factor values. The income approach is used to estimate the value added of the various industries, except in the case of agriculture, for which the income approach is combined with the activity. The components of GDP at factor cost are classified by industry on the basis of establishment data. Wages, salaries and supplementary labour income as well as net incomes of farms and non-farm unincorporated businesses, corporation profits and capital consumption allowances are built up by assembling data on an industry-by-industry basis. Certain imputations are made to include non-market activities. They are allocated to their appropriate industry of origin. For the estimates at constant prices, double deflation is used for agriculture, manufacturing, electricity and railway and air transport. Price deflation is used for non-residential and other engineering construction, road transport and advertising services. For producers of government services and producers of private non-profit services to households, various indicators are used to extrapolate or deflate value added. For the remaining industries, value added is extrapolated by various quantity indicators or indexes.

1.1 Expenditure on the gross domestic product, in current prices

Million Canadian dollars

		1986	1987	1988	1989	1990	1991	1992	1993	1994	1995	1996	1997
1	Government final consumption expenditure	111482	117964	127982	138578	151546	162311	168806	170251	169130	170570	168356	167907
2	Private final consumption expenditure	282936	306047	331304	358140	377860	390135	402705	419405	435062	449018	466108	493322
3	Gross capital formation [a]	105972	121061	137129	149739	138336	124461	120483	126008	139992	143506	142221	165822
	A Increase in stocks [a]	2655	2651	3467	4063	−2660	−5882	−6562	561	2142	8164	1043	7256
	B Gross fixed capital formation	103317	118410	133662	145676	140996	130343	127045	125447	137850	135342	141178	158566
	Residential buildings	31068	39209	42852	47246	42247	37353	40387	39783	42267	36430	40211	46091
	Non-residential buildings	15800	18671	21029	24211	24203	21044	18416	16595	17017	17390	18399	19182
	Other construction and land improvement, etc.	21327	21084	24020	24861	27533	28584	25082	26957	31904	32063	31729	34075
	Other [b]	35122	39446	45761	49358	47013	43362	43160	42112	46662	49459	50839	59218
4	Exports of goods and services [c]	141562	148823	162800	167739	174438	170995	188586	218885	260483	300849	319456	342066
5	less: Imports of goods and services [c]	137228	142723	158577	168139	174019	175401	191673	219462	252998	277529	288356	328276
	Statistical discrepancy	−572	−1304	1795	387	20	13	−1532	−1774	−1187	595	−210	583
	equals: Gross domestic product	504152	549868	602433	646444	668181	672514	687375	713313	750482	787009	807575	841424

a Increase in stocks of gross capital formation includes stocks of breeding stocks, draught animals, dairy cattle, etc. Stocks of commodities internally processed are valued at cost.

b Producers durable goods of gross fixed capital formation includes domestic progress payments on uncompleted heavy machinery and equipment.

c Excludes financial intermediation.

Canada

1.2 Expenditure on the gross domestic product, in constant prices

Million Canadian dollars

	1986	1987	1988	1989	1990	1991	1992	1993	1994	1995	1996	1997
At constant prices of: 1992												
1 Government final consumption expenditure	143739	145782	152481	156740	162464	167079	168806	168366	165414	164725	162562	162456
2 Private final consumption expenditure	353004	367195	383120	396248	401276	395628	402705	410195	422887	429955	439924	458085
3 Gross capital formation [abc]	110329	122040	133110	142813	131466	122876	120483	123857	135045	135860	135534	156877
A Increase in stocks [a]	2853	3028	2452	4388	−1926	−5806	−6562	437	2918	7459	942	6982
B Gross fixed capital formation [b]	107476	119012	130658	138425	133392	128682	127045	123420	132127	128401	134592	149895
Residential buildings	40048	45876	46955	48861	43975	37769	40387	38704	40064	34349	38056	43038
Non-residential buildings	19114	21228	22396	24195	23591	21163	18416	16557	16569	16439	17134	17504
Other construction and land improvement, etc.	23651	23022	25150	25422	27020	28348	25082	26572	30526	30362	30323	32171
Other [c]	28732	33099	39194	42618	41025	41894	43160	41587	44968	47251	49079	57182
4 Exports of goods and services [d]	141997	146900	161127	162897	170790	174729	188586	211345	236463	258298	273182	295160
5 less: Imports of goods and services [d]	133655	141207	160787	170894	174784	180379	191673	207271	226319	241531	253944	288086
Statistical discrepancy	4318	4289	7297	4912	3223	1241	−1532	−1750	−1155	553	−198	540
equals: Gross domestic product [e]	619732	644999	676348	692716	694435	681174	687375	704742	732335	747860	757060	785032

a Increase in stocks of gross capital formation includes stocks of breeding stocks, draught animals, dairy cattle, etc. Stocks of commodities internally processed are valued at cost.
b Prior to 1992, the differences between the sum of directly rebased components and their aggregates are shown as adjusting entries.
c Producers durable goods of gross fixed capital formation includes domestic progress payments on uncompleted heavy machinery and equipment.
d Excludes financial intermediation.
e The period beginning 1961-1997 was deflated in five segments, 1961-1971, 1971-1981, 1981-1986, 1986-1992 and 1992 to date, with price indexes based on prices of 1961, 1971, 1981 and 1986 and 1992 respectively. The five series are then linked arithmetically at the major group, component and total gross domestic product levels to a 1992 base. Differences between the sum of directly rebased components and their aggregates are shown as adjusting entries (statistical discrepancy).

1.3 Cost components of the gross domestic product

Million Canadian dollars

	1986	1987	1988	1989	1990	1991	1992	1993	1994	1995	1996	1997
1 Indirect taxes, net	57560	64938	73409	82689	86363	89654	94265	98898	102925	106571	109944	114501
A Indirect taxes	68734	75966	84020	92507	96415	102508	106588	109386	112351	115208	117686	122574
B less: Subsidies	11174	11028	10611	9818	10052	12854	12323	10488	9426	8637	7742	8073
2 Consumption of fixed capital	61237	64627	68592	73742	79701	83019	86424	90279	95323	100737	105935	110722
3 Compensation of employees paid by resident producers to	272755	296442	325248	350743	368891	379091	387788	395047	405163	419096	429601	445804
A Resident households	272755	296442	325248	350743	368891	379091	387788	395047	405163	419096	429601	445804
B Rest of the world	...	...	...	...	...	...	...	...	...	...	...	...
4 Operating surplus	112028	122556	136979	139658	133246	120764	117365	127314	145884	161200	161884	170981
Statistical discrepancy	572	1305	−1795	−388	−20	−14	1533	1775	1187	−595	211	−584
equals: Gross domestic product	504152	549868	602433	646444	668181	672514	687375	713313	750482	787009	807575	841424

1.4 General government current receipts and disbursements

Million Canadian dollars

	1986	1987	1988	1989	1990	1991	1992	1993	1994	1995	1996	1997
Receipts												
1 Operating surplus	...	...	...	...	...	...	...	...	...	...	...	...
2 Property and entrepreneurial income	28748	29449	32431	36391	38317	37434	37618	38418	40546	42625	43368	44989

Canada

Million Canadian dollars

	1986	1987	1988	1989	1990	1991	1992	1993	1994	1995	1996	1997
3 Taxes, fees and contributions	173224	192780	213851	229347	247073	255406	263091	266897	279102	293746	306532	326300
A Indirect taxes	68734	75966	84020	92507	96415	102508	106588	109386	112351	115208	117686	122574
B Direct taxes	77874	87500	96832	103333	114732	113683	113376	113125	119945	130042	140381	152629
C Social security contributions	23229	25665	28971	29089	33079	35926	39553	40637	42867	44451	44411	47031
D Compulsory fees, fines and penalties	3387	3649	4028	4418	2847	3289	3574	3749	3939	4045	4054	4066
4 Other current transfers	...	...	...	...	...	...	...	...	...	...	...	...
Total current receipts of general government	201972	222229	246282	265738	285390	292840	300709	305315	319648	336371	349900	371289

Disbursements

	1986	1987	1988	1989	1990	1991	1992	1993	1994	1995	1996	1997
1 Government final consumption expenditure	111482	117964	127982	138578	151546	162311	168806	170251	169130	170570	168356	167907
A Compensation of employees	71472	76049	80991	87316	95492	103270	108922	110424	110174	110483	107595	105536
B Consumption of fixed capital	10293	10887	11700	12645	13542	13532	13904	14395	15189	16001	16373	16825
C Purchases of goods and services, net	29717	31028	35291	38617	42512	45509	45980	45432	43767	44086	44388	45546
D less: Own-account fixed capital formation	...	...	...	...	...	...	...	...	...	...	...	...
E Indirect taxes paid, net	...	...	...	...	...	...	...	...	...	...	...	...
2 Property income	43222	46279	50806	58285	64286	64526	65241	66513	69308	77085	75594	74927
A Interest	43222	46279	50806	58285	64286	64526	65241	66513	69308	77085	75594	74927
B Net land rent and royalties	...	...	...	...	...	...	...	...	...	...	...	...
3 Subsidies	11174	11028	10611	9818	10052	12854	12323	10488	9426	8637	7742	8073
4 Other current transfers	57893	62652	67225	72292	80627	92234	101930	106696	107553	108238	109060	109535
A Social security benefits	33678	36650	39453	42626	47131	54068	58214	59299	58563	57915	59334	59189
B Social assistance grants	18678	19653	20725	22367	26170	30082	35222	38900	40550	41761	40797	41036
C Other	5537	6349	7047	7299	7326	8084	8494	8497	8440	8562	8929	9310
5 Net saving	−21799	−15694	−10342	−13235	−21121	−39085	−47591	−48633	−35769	−28159	−10852	10847
Total current disbursements and net saving of general government	201972	222229	246282	265738	285390	292840	300709	305315	319648	336371	349900	371289

1.5 Current income and outlay of corporate and quasi-corporate enterprises, summary

Million Canadian dollars

	1986	1987	1988	1989	1990	1991	1992	1993	1994	1995	1996	1997
Receipts												
1 Operating surplus	97443	107821	122430	123557	117768	103720	96534	104937	124148	140691	138309	149074
2 Property and entrepreneurial income received	28911	30424	32696	38396	43167	41605	40551	39544	40612	46816	45865	45127
3 Current transfers	5436	6137	7259	10143	11937	10689	8414	7067	7359	9723	9134	7431
Total current receipts	131790	144382	162385	172096	172872	156014	145499	151548	172119	197230	193308	201632
Disbursements												
1 Property and entrepreneurial income	103459	105189	118870	134157	150271	140834	134426	130158	134894	146559	147101	147225
2 Direct taxes and other current payments to general government	14573	16990	17586	18566	16834	15015	14517	14618	18403	22201	24202	29092
3 Other current transfers	464	492	486	590	483	501	494	600	662	699	746	911
4 Net saving	13294	21711	25443	18783	5284	−336	−3938	6172	18160	27771	21259	24404
Total current disbursements and net saving	131790	144382	162385	172096	172872	156014	145499	151548	172119	197230	193308	201632

Canada

1.6 Current income and outlay of households and non-profit institutions

Million Canadian dollars

	1986	1987	1988	1989	1990	1991	1992	1993	1994	1995	1996	1997
Receipts												
1 Compensation of employees	272755	296442	325248	350743	368891	379091	387788	395047	405163	419096	429601	445804
A From resident producers	272755	296442	325248	350743	368891	379091	387788	395047	405163	419096	429601	445804
B From rest of the world	...	...	...	...	...	...	...	...	...	...	...	...
2 Operating surplus of private unincorporated enterprises	32423	32834	36376	36818	37609	38665	41128	44493	45886	48691	52948	54400
3 Property and entrepreneurial income	54380	56688	63423	75008	86968	82320	76282	71914	71346	78552	77266	72662
4 Current transfers	56907	61400	65735	71015	79220	90785	100622	105842	107063	108109	108778	109458
A Social security benefits	33678	36650	39453	42626	47131	54068	58214	59299	58563	57915	59334	59189
B Social assistance grants	18678	19653	20725	22367	26170	30082	35222	38900	40550	41761	40797	41036
C Other	4551	5097	5557	6022	5919	6635	7186	7643	7950	8433	8647	9233
Total current receipts	416465	447364	490782	533584	572688	590861	605820	617296	629458	654448	668593	682324
Disbursements												
1 Private final consumption expenditure	282936	306047	331304	358140	377860	390135	402705	419405	435062	449018	466108	493322
2 Property income	5436	6137	7259	10143	11937	10689	8414	7067	7359	9723	9134	7431
3 Direct taxes and other current transfers n.e.c. to general government	88234	98602	110567	116729	132097	136369	140410	141244	146650	154633	162245	171888
A Social security contributions	23229	25665	28971	29089	33079	35926	39553	40637	42867	44451	44411	47031
B Direct taxes	61618	69288	77568	83222	96171	97154	97283	96858	99844	106137	113780	120791
C Fees, fines and penalties	3387	3649	4028	4418	2847	3289	3574	3749	3939	4045	4054	4066
4 Other current transfers	615	650	749	828	764	836	910	962	1042	1079	1109	1166
5 Net saving	39244	35928	40903	47744	50030	52832	53381	48618	39345	39995	29997	8517
Total current disbursements and net saving	416465	447364	490782	533584	572688	590861	605820	617296	629458	654448	668593	682324

1.7 External transactions on current account, summary

Million Canadian dollars

	1986	1987	1988	1989	1990	1991	1992	1993	1994	1995	1996	1997
Payments to the rest of the world												
1 Imports of goods and services	137228	142723	158577	168139	174019	175401	191673	219462	252998	277529	288356	328276
A Imports of merchandise, c.i.f.	117498	121510	135156	141594	143300	142863	157202	181508	212842	235405	243529	282430
B Other	19730	21213	23421	26545	30719	32538	34471	37954	40156	42124	44827	45846
2 Factor income to rest of the world	28659	28699	34853	36640	40666	38003	38415	39175	44334	48716	48445	51329
A Compensation of employees	...	...	...	...	...	...	...	...	...	...	...	...
B Property and entrepreneurial income	28659	28699	34853	36640	40666	38003	38415	39175	44334	48716	48445	51329
By general government	6667	7617	8758	10143	11165	12196	13521	15362	16927	18149	16981	16121
By corporate and quasi-corporate enterprises	21992	21082	26095	26497	29501	25807	24894	23813	27407	30567	31464	35208
By other	...	...	...	...	...	...	...	...	...	...	...	...
3 Current transfers to the rest of the world	2979	3384	3777	3790	3882	4177	4236	4106	4072	4020	4222	4274
A Indirect taxes to supranational organizations	...	...	...	...	...	...	...	...	...	...	...	...

Canada

Million Canadian dollars

	1986	1987	1988	1989	1990	1991	1992	1993	1994	1995	1996	1997
B Other current transfers	2979	3384	3777	3790	3882	4177	4236	4106	4072	4020	4222	4274
4 Surplus of the nation on current transactions	−12852	−11880	−16123	−23480	−24482	−28058	−29142	−26023	−20559	−4352	4539	−12499
Payments to the rest of the world and surplus of the nation on current transfers	156014	162926	181084	185089	194085	189523	205182	236720	280845	325913	345562	371380

Receipts from the rest of the world

	1986	1987	1988	1989	1990	1991	1992	1993	1994	1995	1996	1997
1 Exports of goods and services	141562	148823	162800	167739	174438	170995	188586	218885	260483	300849	319456	342066
A Exports of merchandise, f.o.b.	125172	131484	143534	146963	152056	147669	163464	190383	227895	264940	280570	301649
B Other	16390	17339	19266	20776	22382	23326	25122	28502	32588	35909	38886	40417
2 Factor income from rest of the world	11855	11891	15554	14710	16692	15623	13496	14496	16786	21247	21622	24448
A Compensation of employees	...	...	...	...	...	...	...	...	...	...	...	...
B Property and entrepreneurial income	11855	11891	15554	14710	16692	15623	13496	14496	16786	21247	21622	24448
By general government	243	472	1072	1374	1403	1477	1208	690	752	1273	1412	1535
By corporate and quasi-corporate enterprises	10194	9861	12475	10971	12177	10896	9128	10509	12381	16062	16625	18814
By other	1418	1558	2007	2365	3112	3250	3160	3297	3653	3912	3585	4099
3 Current transfers from rest of the world	2597	2212	2730	2640	2955	2905	3100	3339	3576	3817	4484	4866
A Subsidies from supranational organisations	...	...	...	...	...	...	...	...	...	...	...	...
B Other current transfers	2597	2212	2730	2640	2955	2905	3100	3339	3576	3817	4484	4866
Receipts from the rest of the world on current transactions	156014	162926	181084	185089	194085	189523	205182	236720	280845	325913	345562	371380

1.8 Capital transactions of the nation, summary

Million Canadian dollars

	1986	1987	1988	1989	1990	1991	1992	1993	1994	1995	1996	1997

Finance of gross capital formation

	1986	1987	1988	1989	1990	1991	1992	1993	1994	1995	1996	1997
Gross saving	91976	106572	124596	127034	113894	96430	88276	96436	117059	140344	146339	154490
1 Consumption of fixed capital	61237	64627	68592	73742	79701	83019	86424	90279	95323	100737	105935	110722
A General government	10293	10887	11700	12645	13542	13532	13904	14395	15189	16001	16373	16825
B Corporate and quasi-corporate enterprises	36002	37437	39437	42175	46132	48198	50546	52730	55972	59678	63330	66748
Public	4341	4484	4569	4674	4779	5031	5315	5786	5907	5959	6030	6176
Private	31661	32953	34868	37501	41353	43167	45231	46944	50065	53719	57300	60572
C Other	14942	16303	17455	18922	20027	21289	21974	23154	24162	25058	26232	27149
2 Net saving	30739	41945	56004	53292	34193	13411	1852	6157	21736	39607	40404	43768
A General government	−21799	−15694	−10342	−13235	−21121	−39085	−47591	−48633	−35769	−28159	−10852	10847
B Corporate and quasi-corporate enterprises [a]	13294	21711	25443	18783	5284	−336	−3938	6172	18160	27771	21259	24404
Public [a]	1745	2433	2733	2077	1147	1285	2143	1931	2881	2811	2470	2452
Private [a]	11549	19278	22710	16706	4137	−1621	−6081	4241	15279	24960	18789	21952
C Other	39244	35928	40903	47744	50030	52832	53381	48618	39345	39995	29997	8517
less: Surplus of the nation on current transactions	−12852	−11880	−16123	−23480	−24482	−28058	−29142	−26023	−20559	−4352	4539	−12499
Statistical discrepancy	572	1305	−1795	−388	−20	−14	1533	1775	1187	−595	211	−584
Finance of gross capital formation	105400	119757	138924	150126	138356	124474	118951	124234	138805	144101	142011	166405

Gross capital formation

	1986	1987	1988	1989	1990	1991	1992	1993	1994	1995	1996	1997
Increase in stocks	2655	2651	3467	4063	−2660	−5882	−6562	561	2142	8164	1043	7256

Canada

Million Canadian dollars

	1986	1987	1988	1989	1990	1991	1992	1993	1994	1995	1996	1997
Gross fixed capital formation	103317	118410	133662	145676	140996	130343	127045	125447	137850	135342	141178	158566
1 General government	14089	14658	15699	17712	19246	19209	18836	18459	20056	20105	19271	18241
2 Corporate and quasi-corporate enterprises	56400	64195	73262	79286	76485	70739	65787	63378	70885	73305	76759	90470
3 Other	32828	39557	44701	48678	45265	40395	42422	43610	46909	41932	45148	49855
Statistical discrepancy	−572	−1304	1795	387	20	13	−1532	−1774	−1187	595	−210	583
Gross capital formation	105400	119757	138924	150126	138356	124474	118951	124234	138805	144101	142011	166405

a All inventory valuation adjustments have been allocated to private corporate enterprises.

1.9 Gross domestic product by institutional sectors of origin

Million Canadian dollars

	1986	1987	1988	1989	1990	1991	1992	1993	1994	1995	1996	1997
Domestic factor incomes originating												
1 General government	71499	76079	81021	87351	95522	103303	108962	110465	110217	110525	107631	105575
2 Corporate and quasi-corporate enterprises	275179	303982	338198	358934	360949	349323	345882	357709	384896	410583	419036	444313
3 Households and private unincorporated enterprises	38105	38937	43008	44116	45666	47229	50309	54187	55934	59188	64818	66897
A Owner-occupied housing [a]	9710	10071	10262	10341	10408	11010	12035	13240	14002	15119	16123	17399
B Subsistence production [a]	196	197	195	194	195	185	189	217	230	221	221	221
C Other	28199	28670	32551	33581	35063	36034	38085	40730	41702	43848	48474	49277
4 Non-profit institutions serving households	...	...	...	...	...	...	...	...	...	...	...	...
subtotal: Domestic factor incomes	384783	418998	462227	490401	502137	499855	505153	522361	551047	580296	591485	616785
Indirect taxes, net	57560	64938	73409	82689	86363	89654	94265	98898	102925	106571	109944	114501
A Indirect taxes	68734	75966	84020	92507	96415	102508	106588	109386	112351	115208	117686	122574
B less: Subsidies	11174	11028	10611	9818	10052	12854	12323	10488	9426	8637	7742	8073
Consumption of fixed capital	61237	64627	68592	73742	79701	83019	86424	90279	95323	100737	105935	110722
Statistical discrepancy	572	1305	−1795	−388	−20	−14	1533	1775	1187	−595	211	−584
Gross domestic product	504152	549868	602433	646444	668181	672514	687375	713313	750482	787009	807575	841424

a owner occupied housing is net imputed rent. Subsistence productions is income-in-kind

1.10 Gross domestic product by kind of activity, in current prices

Million Canadian dollars

	1986	1987	1988	1989	1990	1991	1992	1993	1994	1995	1996	1997
1 Agriculture, hunting, forestry and fishing	15288	14706	15407	16066	16228	15008	15316	16760	...	...	...	...
2 Mining and quarrying	22269	24741	25339	25369	27073	22642	23054	24033	...	...	...	...
3 Manufacturing	85563	93717	104835	107869	103758	96672	96184	102884	...	...	...	...
4 Electricity, gas and water	15835	16588	17823	18135	18445	20668	21686	22834	...	...	...	...
5 Construction [a]	28301	32735	36541	40912	41308	38324	37112	36031	...	...	...	...
6 Wholesale and retail trade, restaurants and hotels	64555	70823	77879	84017	86068	83296	82117	84068	...	...	...	...
7 Transport, storage and communication	34464	36386	37705	39439	40147	41171	42294	43125	...	...	...	...
8 Finance, insurance, real estate and business services	81918	89975	100078	109262	115195	122322	125358	131715	...	...	...	...
9 Community, social and personal services	54744	59054	64964	69942	75829	81381	86028	88365	...	...	...	...
Total, Industries	402936	438725	480572	511012	524051	521483	529148	549815	...	...	...	...
Producers of government services	49924	52948	56170	60642	65727	70057	72977	73979	...	...	...	...

Canada

Million Canadian dollars

	1986	1987	1988	1989	1990	1991	1992	1993	1994	1995	1996	1997
Other producers	1373	1494	1636	1847	1994	2046	2154	2229	...	...	...	...
Subtotal [b]	454233	493167	538378	573502	591772	593585	604279	626023	...	...	...	...
less: Imputed bank service charge	7644	8238	9352	9746	9954	10725	11169	11607	...	...	...	...
plus: Import duties	4169	4220	4644	4494	4237	3742	4125	3368	...	...	...	...
plus: Value added tax	...	...	...	...	...	17379	17786	18153	...	...	...	...
plus: Other adjustments [c]	53391	60718	68765	78195	82126	68533	72354	77377	...	...	...	...
equals: Gross domestic product	504149	549867	602435	646444	668181	672515	687375	713314	...	...	...	...

a The construction industry is defined on an activity basis. It includes all contract and own-account construction put in place.
b Gross domestic product at factor cost.
c Other adjustment includes indirect taxes, excluding import duties and goods and services tax (V.A.T.), less subsidies.

1.11 Gross domestic product by kind of activity, in constant prices

Million Canadian dollars

	1986	1987	1988	1989	1990	1991	1992	1993	1994	1995	1996	1997
	At constant prices of: 1992											
1 Agriculture, hunting, forestry and fishing	16676	15728	15265	16329	16789	16100	15317	16424	16879	17053	17432	17289
2 Mining and quarrying	19742	20824	22646	21500	21480	22406	23054	23745	25200	26223	27002	28175
3 Manufacturing	94829	99215	105126	106612	102570	94999	96181	101877	108403	113740	114942	121999
4 Electricity, gas and water	21214	21925	22230	21794	20724	21849	21685	22485	23402	23499	23957	23934
5 Construction [a]	38241	40146	41244	43288	43503	40165	37112	35541	37293	35397	36412	39062
6 Wholesale and retail trade, restaurants and hotels	75528	80010	83594	86488	85535	81172	82116	83941	89658	90888	92441	99147
7 Transport, storage and communication	34866	37294	39656	41022	41660	41192	42294	42445	44669	46392	47919	50960
8 Finance, insurance, real estate and business services	104657	111097	117067	121231	122252	124300	125359	130267	134856	138372	143203	149295
9 Community, social and personal services	75108	76748	80052	82331	83555	84880	86028	87580	88771	91106	91683	93126
Statistical discrepancy	−580	112	104	−169	−593	−1072	...	...	...	...	...	...
Total, Industries	480281	503099	526984	540426	537475	525991	529146	544305	569131	582670	594991	622987
Producers of government services	66754	67278	68530	70099	71604	72490	72977	72653	71685	70156	68009	66350
Other producers	1746	1823	1896	1968	2085	2065	2154	2236	2247	2262	2277	2288
Subtotal [bc]	548405	569537	594891	607564	609231	600004	604275	619194	643063	655088	665277	691625
less: Imputed bank service charge	8843	9361	9828	10861	11029	11073	11169	11381	11885	12449	12670	13151
plus: Import duties	...	...	...	...	...	...	...	...	...	...	...	...
plus: Value added tax	...	...	...	...	...	...	...	...	...	...	...	...
plus: Other adjustments	80170	84823	91285	96013	96233	92243	94269	96929	101157	105221	104453	106558
equals: Gross domestic product	619732	644999	676348	692716	694435	681174	687377	704742	732335	747860	757060	785032

a The construction industry is defined on an activity basis. It includes all contract and own-account construction put in place.
b Gross domestic product in factor values.
c The period beginning 1961-1997 was deflated in five segments, 1961-1971, 1971-1981, 1981-1986, 1986-1992 and 1992 to date, with price indexes based on prices of 1961, 1971, 1981 and 1986 and 1992 respectively. The five series are then linked arithmetically at the major group, component and total gross domestic product levels to a 1992 base. Differences between the sum of directly rebased components and their aggregates are shown as adjusting entries (statistical discrepency).

1.12 Relations among national accounting aggregates

Million Canadian dollars

	1986	1987	1988	1989	1990	1991	1992	1993	1994	1995	1996	1997
Gross domestic product	504152	549868	602433	646444	668181	672514	687375	713313	750482	787009	807575	841424
plus: Net factor income from the rest of the world	−16804	−16808	−19299	−21930	−23974	−22380	−24919	−24679	−27548	−27469	−26823	−26881

Canada

Million Canadian dollars

	1986	1987	1988	1989	1990	1991	1992	1993	1994	1995	1996	1997
Factor income from rest of the world	11855	11891	15554	14710	16692	15623	13496	14496	16786	21247	21622	24448
less: Factor income to the rest of the world	28659	28699	34853	36640	40666	38003	38415	39175	44334	48716	48445	51329
equals: Gross national product	487348	533060	583134	624514	644207	650134	662456	688634	722934	759540	780752	814543
less: Consumption of fixed capital	61237	64627	68592	73742	79701	83019	86424	90279	95323	100737	105935	110722
equals: National income [a]	425539	467128	516337	551160	564526	567129	574499	596580	626424	659398	674606	704405
plus: Net current transfers from the rest of the world	−382	−1172	−1047	−1150	−927	−1272	−1136	−767	−496	−203	262	592
Current transfers from rest of the world	2597	2212	2730	2640	2955	2905	3100	3339	3576	3817	4484	4866
less: Current transfers to the rest of the world	2979	3384	3777	3790	3882	4177	4236	4106	4072	4020	4222	4274
equals: National disposable income	425157	465956	515290	550010	563599	565857	573363	595813	625928	659195	674868	704997
less: Final consumption	394418	424011	459286	496718	529406	552446	571511	589656	604192	619588	634464	661229
equals: Net saving	30739	41945	56004	53292	34193	13411	1852	6157	21736	39607	40404	43768
less: Surplus of the nation on current transactions	−12852	−11880	−16123	−23480	−24482	−28058	−29142	−26023	−20559	−4352	4539	−12499
Statistical discrepancy	1144	2609	−3590	−775	−40	−27	3065	3549	2374	−1190	421	−1167
equals: Net capital formation [b]	44735	56435	68537	75996	58635	41441	34060	35730	44669	42769	36287	55099

[a] Item "National income" includes a statistical discrepancy.
[b] Increase in stocks of gross capital formation includes stocks of breeding stocks, draught animals, dairy cattle, etc. Stocks of commodities internally processed are valued at cost.

2.5 Private final consumption expenditure by type and purpose, in current prices

Million Canadian dollars

	1986	1987	1988	1989	1990	1991	1992	1993	1994	1995	1996	1997
Final consumption expenditure of resident households												
1 Food, beverages and tobacco	48533	51232	53477	56794	59526	62590	62777	63919	62987	64854	66783	68650
A Food [a]	34619	36670	37951	39793	41975	43446	43427	44985	45728	47202	48512	50074
B Non-alcoholic beverages												
C Alcoholic beverages	7480	7887	8275	8676	8782	8690	8873	8968	9267	9619	9695	9906
D Tobacco	6434	6675	7251	8325	8769	10454	10477	9966	7992	8033	8576	8670
2 Clothing and footwear	18031	19195	20162	21130	21592	21474	21446	22125	23360	23965	23891	25268
3 Gross rent, fuel and power	63315	67802	74454	82008	88575	95226	100604	105761	110147	114054	117861	121582
4 Furniture, furnishings and household equipment and operation	27275	29333	31963	33827	34644	34471	35226	36335	38062	38326	39070	41342
5 Medical care and health expenses	10905	11893	12328	13590	14897	16043	16945	17882	18459	19517	20040	20456
6 Transport and communication	47706	51891	56664	60152	62210	61239	62169	64081	67838	70563	75537	83961
A Personal transport equipment	17347	18858	20911	21592	20673	19716	20380	20479	22489	23618	26324	32127
B Other	30359	33033	35753	38560	41537	41523	41789	43602	45349	46945	49213	51834
7 Recreational, entertainment, education and cultural services	26024	28499	32483	34513	35544	36119	37649	39704	43310	45882	47947	51400
A Education	2819	2892	3234	3408	3625	3936	4321	4834	5102	5343	5653	5950
B Other	23205	25607	29249	31105	31919	32183	33328	34870	38208	40539	42294	45450
8 Miscellaneous goods and services	41092	44946	48303	53331	55891	57579	60173	64512	68345	70600	74083	79772
A Personal care	7881	8298	9065	9771	10230	10726	10792	11287	11741	12107	12546	13046
B Expenditures in restaurants, cafes and hotels	20556	21962	24264	27083	27911	27816	28855	30023	31566	32521	33188	34815
C Other	12655	14686	14974	16477	17750	19037	20526	23202	25038	25972	28349	31911

Canada

Million Canadian dollars

	1986	1987	1988	1989	1990	1991	1992	1993	1994	1995	1996	1997
Total final consumption expenditure in the domestic market by households, of which	282881	304791	329834	355345	372879	384741	396989	414319	432508	447761	465212	492431
A Durable goods	41014	44733	49434	52042	50837	48417	48808	49937	53862	55682	58500	66132
B Semi-durable goods	30766	33017	35118	36977	37870	37739	38129	39269	41749	42691	43117	45734
C Non-durable goods	80810	84914	90009	96047	101896	106685	108307	111608	112206	114545	118720	122494
D Services	130291	142127	155273	170279	182276	191900	201745	213505	224691	234843	244875	258071
plus: Direct purchases abroad by resident households	6402	7569	8377	10039	12742	13210	13788	13901	12759	12926	13796	14405
less: Direct purchases in the domestic market by non-resident households	6347	6313	6907	7244	7761	7816	8072	8815	10205	11669	12900	13514
equals: Final consumption expenditure of resident households [b]	282936	306047	331304	358140	377860	390135	402705	419405	435062	449018	466108	493322

a Including item "Non-alcoholic beverages"
b Item "Final consumption expenditure of resident households" includes consumption expenditure of private non-profit institutions serving households.

2.6 Private final consumption expenditure by type and purpose, in constant prices

Million Canadian dollars

	1986	1987	1988	1989	1990	1991	1992	1993	1994	1995	1996	1997
At constant prices of: 1992												

Final consumption expenditure of resident households

	1986	1987	1988	1989	1990	1991	1992	1993	1994	1995	1996	1997
1 Food, beverages and tobacco [a]	62008	62268	62704	63376	63263	62893	62777	62543	64840	66204	67326	67619
A Food [b]	39944	40486	41009	41747	42380	42901	43427	44040	44612	45226	45867	46652
B Non-alcoholic beverages												
C Alcoholic beverages	10200	10227	10027	10073	9679	9113	8873	8833	9131	9360	9216	9231
D Tobacco	13509	12908	12982	12671	11938	11256	10477	9670	11097	11618	12243	11736
2 Clothing and footwear	23497	23930	23848	24033	23828	21648	21446	21944	23034	23926	23931	24904
3 Gross rent, fuel and power	80436	83234	87857	92064	95357	98047	100604	103664	105806	108088	110908	113593
4 Furniture, furnishings and household equipment and operation	33336	34567	36146	36621	36542	34619	35226	36171	37855	37600	37859	39634
5 Medical care and health expenses	14676	15104	14820	15416	16190	16592	16945	17345	17687	18285	18742	19140
6 Transport and communication [a]	56630	59969	63945	64965	63871	61558	62169	62709	64931	65254	67151	72703
A Personal transport equipment	20096	21493	22807	22246	21154	20557	20380	19659	20267	20173	21616	25766
B Other	36934	38843	41466	43018	42895	41017	41789	43050	44664	45081	45535	46937
7 Recreational, entertainment, education and cultural services [a]	31761	33401	36316	37180	37069	36202	37649	38921	41580	43467	44950	47713
A Education	4309	4251	4491	4468	4362	4242	4321	4565	4555	4526	4538	4539
B Other	27774	29344	31939	32656	32638	31949	33328	34356	37025	38941	40412	43174
8 Miscellaneous goods and services [a]	52428	54681	56381	59470	59528	57825	60173	62957	66182	67356	69583	73319
A Personal care	9894	9931	10499	10932	10996	10845	10792	11094	11452	11887	12371	12691
B Expenditures in restaurants, cafes and hotels	27807	28422	29883	31731	31222	28299	28855	29647	30704	30847	31036	32040
C Other	15121	16591	16398	17236	17681	18747	20526	22216	24026	24622	26176	28588
Statistical discrepancy [c]	−1819	−1292	−877	−441	87	152	...	...	...	...	...	...
Total final consumption expenditure in the domestic market by households, of which [a]	352953	365862	381140	392684	395735	389536	396989	406254	421915	430180	440450	458625
A Durable goods	45069	48095	51396	51968	50522	48467	48808	49254	51647	52508	54465	61020
B Semi-durable goods	39216	40269	40802	41207	41044	37892	38129	39117	41434	42550	42816	44606
C Non-durable goods	102635	103100	105954	108039	107941	107122	108307	109540	113146	114419	116773	117922

Canada

Million Canadian dollars

	1986	1987	1988	1989	1990	1991	1992	1993	1994	1995	1996	1997
At constant prices of: 1992												
D Services	165720	173881	182254	190889	195956	195982	201745	208343	215688	220703	226396	235077
plus: Direct purchases abroad by resident households	7137	8342	9624	11468	13874	14099	13788	12550	10640	10460	10959	11069
less: Direct purchases in the domestic market by non-resident households	8269	7870	8452	8373	8403	7888	8072	8609	9668	10685	11485	11609
equals: Final consumption expenditure of resident households [d]	353004	367195	383120	396248	401276	395628	402705	410195	422887	429955	439924	458085

a The directly rebased components do not add up to the rebased aggregate. The difference should be considered as an adjusting entry/statistical discrepency.
b Including item "Non-alcoholic beverages"
c Differences between the sum of directly rebased components and their aggregates are shown as adjusting entries.
d Item "Final consumption expenditure of resident households" includes consumption expenditure of private non-profit institutions serving households.

2.7 Gross capital formation by type of good and owner, in current price

Million Canadian dollars

	1986 Total	1986 Total private	1986 Public enterprises	1986 General government	1987 Total	1987 Total private	1987 Public enterprises	1987 General government	1988 Total	1988 Total private	1988 Public enterprises	1988 General government
Increase in stocks, total [ab]	2655	2690	...	−35	2651	2689	...	−38	3467	3403	...	64
1 Goods producing industries	−128	−128	...	...	−1067	−1067	...	...	1355	1355	...	...
2 Wholesale and retail trade	2851	2851	...	...	3678	3678	...	...	2008	2008	...	...
3 Other, except government stocks	−33	−33	...	...	78	78	...	...	40	40	...	...
4 Government stocks	−35	...	...	−35	−38	...	...	−38	64	...	...	64
Gross fixed capital formation, total [bc]	103317	89228	...	14089	118410	103752	...	14658	133662	117963	...	15699
1 Residential buildings	31068	30761	...	307	39209	38883	...	326	42852	42447	...	405
2 Non-residential buildings	15800	11921	...	3879	18671	14140	...	4531	21029	16415	...	4614
3 Other construction	21327	14628	...	6699	21084	14728	...	6356	24020	17202	...	6818
4 Land improvement and plantation and orchard development	...	...	...	...	...	...	...	...	...	...	...	...
5 Producers' durable goods [c]	35122	31918	...	3204	39446	36001	...	3445	45761	41899	...	3862
A Transport equipment	9225	8641	...	584	11167	10586	...	581	13601	12969	...	632[d]
Passenger cars	4269	4138	...	131	5399	5198	...	201	5597	5407	...	190
Other	4956	4503	...	453	5768	5388	...	380	8004	7562	...	442
B Machinery and equipment [e]	25897	23277	...	2620	28279	25415	...	2864	32160	28930	...	3230
6 Breeding stock, dairy cattle, etc.	...	...	...	...	...	...	...	...	...	...	...	...
Total gross capital formation [be]	105972	91918	...	14054	121061	106441	...	14620	137129	121366	...	15763

	1989 Total	1989 Total private	1989 Public enterprises	1989 General government	1990 Total	1990 Total private	1990 Public enterprises	1990 General government	1991 Total	1991 Total private	1991 Public enterprises	1991 General government
Increase in stocks, total [ab]	4063	4066	...	−3	−2660	−2727	...	67	−5882	−5845	...	−37
1 Goods producing industries	1626	1626	...	...	−1382	−1382	...	...	−4006	−4006	...	...
2 Wholesale and retail trade	2312	2312	...	...	−1340	−1340	...	...	−1588	−1588	...	...
3 Other, except government stocks	128	128	...	...	−5	−5	...	...	−251	−251	...	...
4 Government stocks	−3	...	...	−3	67	...	...	67	−37	...	...	−37
Gross fixed capital formation, total [bc]	145676	127964	...	17712	140996	121750	...	19246	130343	111134	...	19209
1 Residential buildings	47246	46848	...	398	42247	41776	...	471	37353	36821	...	532
2 Non-residential buildings	24211	18859	...	5352	24203	18273	...	5930	21044	14802	...	6242
3 Other construction	24861	17315	...	7546	27533	19107	...	8426	28584	20593	...	7991

Canada

	1989				1990				1991			
	Total	Total private	Public enter-prises	General govern-ment	Total	Total private	Public enter-prises	General govern-ment	Total	Total private	Public enter-prises	General govern-ment
4 Land improvement and plantation and orchard development	...	...	...	...	...	...	...	...	...	...	...	...
5 Producers' durable goods [c]	49358	44942	...	4416	47013	42594	...	4419	43362	38918	...	4444
A Transport equipment	13698	13002	...	696[d]	11926	11335	...	591[d]	9601	9035	...	566[d]
Passenger cars	5465	5283	...	182	4843	4656	...	187	3508	3368	...	140
Other	8233	7719	...	514	7083	6679	...	404	6093	5667	...	426
B Machinery and equipment [e]	35660	31940	...	3720	35087	31259	...	3828	33761	29883	...	3878
6 Breeding stock, dairy cattle, etc.	...	...	...	...	...	...	...	...	...	...	...	...
Total gross capital formation [be]	149739	132030	...	17709	138336	119023	...	19313	124461	105289	...	19172

	1992				1993				1994			
	Total	Total private	Public enter-prises	General govern-ment	Total	Total private	Public enter-prises	General govern-ment	Total	Total private	Public enter-prises	General govern-ment
Increase in stocks, total [ab]	−6562	−6522	...	−40	561	565	...	−4	2142	2143	...	−1
1 Goods producing industries	−4247	−4247	...	...	−203	−203	...	...	−30	−30	...	...
2 Wholesale and retail trade	−2280	−2280	...	...	563	563	...	...	2383	2383	...	...
3 Other, except government stocks	5	5	...	...	205	205	...	...	−210	−210	...	...
4 Government stocks	−40	...	...	−40	−4	...	...	−4	−1	...	...	−1
Gross fixed capital formation, total [bc]	127045	108209	...	18836	125447	106988	...	18459	137850	117794	...	20056
1 Residential buildings	40387	39903	...	484	39783	39479	...	304	42267	42023	...	244
2 Non-residential buildings	18416	11727	...	6689	16595	10214	...	6381	17017	10194	...	6823
3 Other construction	25082	17927	...	7155	26957	19969	...	6988	31904	23759	...	8145
4 Land improvement and plantation and orchard development	...	...	...	...	...	...	...	...	...	...	...	...
5 Producers' durable goods [c]	43160	38652	...	4508	42112	37326	...	4786	46662	41818	...	4844
A Transport equipment	10770	10194	...	576[d]	10254	9676	...	578[d]	11908	11317	...	591[d]
Passenger cars	4024	3864	...	160	4944	4780	...	164	5488	5305	...	183
Other	6746	6330	...	416	5310	4896	...	414	6420	6012	...	408
B Machinery and equipment [e]	32390	28458	...	3932	31858	27650	...	4208	34754	30501	...	4253
6 Breeding stock, dairy cattle, etc.	...	...	...	...	...	...	...	...	...	...	...	...
Total gross capital formation [be]	120483	101687	...	18796	126008	107553	...	18455	139992	119937	...	20055

	1995				1996				1997			
	Total	Total private	Public enter-prises	General govern-ment	Total	Total private	Public enter-prises	General govern-ment	Total	Total private	Public enter-prises	General govern-ment
Increase in stocks, total [ab]	8164	8134	...	30	1043	1045	...	−2	7256	7251	...	5
1 Goods producing industries	3956	3956	...	...	715	715	...	...	1026	1026	...	...
2 Wholesale and retail trade	3900	3900	...	...	264	264	...	...	6203	6203	...	...
3 Other, except government stocks	278	278	...	...	66	66	...	...	22	22	...	...
4 Government stocks	30	...	...	30	−2	...	...	−2	5	...	...	5
Gross fixed capital formation, total [bc]	135342	115237	...	20105	141178	121907	...	19271	158566	140325	...	18241
1 Residential buildings	36430	36270	...	160	40211	40083	...	128	46091	45965	...	126
2 Non-residential buildings	17390	10500	...	6890	18399	12013	...	6386	19182	13220	...	5962
3 Other construction	32063	23624	...	8439	31729	23424	...	8305	34075	26010	...	8065
4 Land improvement and plantation and orchard development	...	...	...	...	...	...	...	...	...	...	...	...
5 Producers' durable goods [c]	49459	44843	...	4616	50839	46387	...	4452	59218	55130	...	4088

Canada

	1995				1996				1997			
	Total	Total private	Public enterprises	General government	Total	Total private	Public enterprises	General government	Total	Total private	Public enterprises	General government
A Transport equipment	12895	12277	...	618[d]	13901	13269	...	632[d]	16779	16125	...	654[d]
Passenger cars	5393	5216	...	177	5919	5726	...	193	6638	6423	...	215
Other	7502	7061	...	441	7982	7543	...	439	10141	9702	...	439
B Machinery and equipment [c]	36564	32566	...	3998	36938	33118	...	3820	42439	39005	...	3434
6 Breeding stock, dairy cattle, etc.	...	...	...	...	...	...	...	...	...	...	...	...
Total gross capital formation [bc]	143506	123371	...	20135	142221	122952	...	19269	165822	147576	...	18246

a Increase in stocks of gross capital formation includes stocks of breeding stocks, draught animals, dairy cattle, etc. Stocks of commodities internally processed are valued at cost.
b Column "Public enterprises" is included in column "Total private".
c Producers durable goods of gross fixed capital formation includes domestic progress payments on uncompleted heavy machinery and equipment.
d From 1981, the methodology has been changed in order to derive estimates in greater detail.
e Producers durable goods of gross fixed capital formation includes domestic progress payments on uncompleted heavy machinery and equipment.

2.8 Gross capital formation by type of good and owner, in constant prices

Million Canadian dollars

	1986				1987				1988			
	Total	Total private	Public enterprises	General government	Total	Total private	Public enterprises	General government	Total	Total private	Public enterprises	General government
At constant prices of: 1992												
Increase in stocks, total [ab]	2853	2893	...	−40	3028	3070	...	−42	2452	2381	...	71
1 Goods producing industries	−397	−397	...	...	−808	−808	...	...	621	621	...	...
2 Wholesale and retail trade	3106	3106	...	...	4046	4046	...	...	2224	2224	...	...
3 Other, except government stocks	−34	−34	...	...	66	66	...	...	47	47	...	...
4 Government stocks	−40	...	...	−40	−42	...	...	−42	71	...	...	71
Statistical discrepancy	218	218	...	...	−234	−234	...	...	−511	−511	...	...
Gross fixed capital formation, total [bcd]	107476	93779	...	13697	119012	104799	...	14213	130658	115783	...	14875
1 Residential buildings	40048	39670	...	378	45876	45518	...	358	46955	46539	...	416
2 Non-residential buildings	19114	14475	...	4639	21228	16067	...	5161	22396	17406	...	4990
3 Other construction	23651	16422	...	7229	23022	16103	...	6919	25150	18008	...	7142
4 Land improvement and plantation and orchard development	...	...	...	...	...	...	...	...	...	...	...	...
5 Producers' durable goods [d]	28732	26595	...	2137	33099	30696	...	2403	39194	36411	...	2783
A Transport equipment	9676	9045	...	631	11694	11067	...	627	14164	13496	...	668
Passenger cars	4215	4086	...	129	5317	5120	...	197	5422	5239	...	183
Other	5461	4959	...	502	6377	5947	...	430	8742	8257	...	485
B Machinery and equipment [d]	24478	22284	...	2194	26702	24263	...	2439	30765	27993	...	2772
6 Breeding stock, dairy cattle, etc.	...	...	...	...	...	...	...	...	...	...	...	...
Statistical discrepancy	−4069	−3383	...	−686	−4213	−3585	...	−628	−3037	−2581	...	−456
Total gross capital formation [bd]	110329	96672	...	13657	122040	107869	...	14171	133110	118164	...	14946

Canada

	1989				1990				1991			
	Total	Total private	Public enterprises	General government	Total	Total private	Public enterprises	General government	Total	Total private	Public enterprises	General government
At constant prices of: 1992												
Increase in stocks, total [a,b]	4388	4389	...	−1	−1926	−1999	...	73	−5806	−5769	...	−37
1 Goods producing industries	1693	1693	...	...	−1157	−1157	...	...	−4364	−4364	...	...
2 Wholesale and retail trade	2350	2350	...	...	−1307	−1307	...	...	−1433	−1433	...	...
3 Other, except government stocks	129	129	...	...	−5	−5	...	...	−222	−222	...	...
4 Government stocks	−1	...	...	−1	73	...	...	73	−37	...	...	−37
Statistical discrepancy	217	217	...	...	470	470	...	...	250	250	...	...
Gross fixed capital formation, total [b,c,d]	138425	121883	...	16542	133392	115727	...	17665	128682	109783	...	18899
1 Residential buildings	48861	48480	...	381	43975	43527	...	448	37769	37231	...	538
2 Non-residential buildings	24195	18790	...	5405	23591	17816	...	5775	21163	14907	...	6256
3 Other construction	25422	17775	...	7647	27020	18758	...	8262	28348	20307	...	8041
4 Land improvement and plantation and orchard development	...	...	...	...	...	...	...	...	...	...	...	...
5 Producers' durable goods [d]	42618	39216	...	3402	41025	37476	...	3549	41894	37678	...	4216
A Transport equipment	13755	13047	...	708	11625	11044	...	581	9944	9359	...	585
Passenger cars	5036	4869	...	167	4398	4229	...	169	3550	3409	...	141
Other	8719	8178	...	541	7227	6815	...	412	6394	5950	...	444
B Machinery and equipment [d]	34087	30839	...	3248	33302	29971	...	3331	33971	30147	...	3824
6 Breeding stock, dairy cattle, etc.	...	...	...	...	...	...	...	...	...	...	...	...
Statistical discrepancy	−2671	−2378	...	−293	−2219	−1850	...	−369	−492	−340	...	−152
Total gross capital formation [b,d]	142813	126272	...	16541	131466	113728	...	17738	122876	104014	...	18862

	1992				1993				1994			
	Total	Total private	Public enterprises	General government	Total	Total private	Public enterprises	General government	Total	Total private	Public enterprises	General government
At constant prices of: 1992												
Increase in stocks, total [a,b]	−6562	−6522	...	−40	437	440	...	−3	2918	2919	...	−1
1 Goods producing industries	−4247	−4247	...	...	−293	−293	...	...	860	860	...	...
2 Wholesale and retail trade	−2280	−2280	...	...	552	552	...	...	2257	2257	...	...
3 Other, except government stocks	5	5	...	...	181	181	...	...	−198	−198	...	...
4 Government stocks	−40	...	...	−40	−3	...	...	−3	−1	...	...	−1
Gross fixed capital formation, total [b,c,d]	127045	108209	...	18836	123420	104976	...	18444	132127	112397	...	19730
1 Residential buildings	40387	39903	...	484	38704	38401	...	303	40064	39820	...	244
2 Non-residential buildings	18416	11727	...	6689	16557	10188	...	6369	16569	9915	...	6654
3 Other construction	25082	17927	...	7155	26572	19615	...	6957	30526	22515	...	8011
4 Land improvement and plantation and orchard development	...	...	...	...	...	...	...	...	...	...	...	...
5 Producers' durable goods [d]	43160	38652	...	4508	41587	36772	...	4815	44968	40147	...	4821
A Transport equipment	10770	10194	...	576	9942	9381	...	561	11049	10504	...	545
Passenger cars	4024	3864	...	160	4846	4685	...	161	5180	5007	...	173
Other	6746	6330	...	416	5096	4696	...	400	5869	5497	...	372
B Machinery and equipment [d]	32390	28458	...	3932	31645	27391	...	4254	33919	29643	...	4276
6 Breeding stock, dairy cattle, etc.	...	...	...	...	...	...	...	...	...	...	...	...
Total gross capital formation [b,d]	120483	101687	...	18796	123857	105416	...	18441	135045	115316	...	19729

Canada

	1995				1996				1997			
	Total	Total private	Public enterprises	General government	Total	Total private	Public enterprises	General government	Total	Total private	Public enterprises	General government
At constant prices of: 1992
Increase in stocks, total [a,b]	7459	7429	...	30	942	944	...	–2	6982	6977	...	5
1 Goods producing industries	3791	3791	...	...	751	751	...	...	1619	1619	...	...
2 Wholesale and retail trade	3393	3393	...	...	135	135	...	...	5342	5342	...	...
3 Other, except government stocks	245	245	...	...	58	58	...	...	16	16	...	...
4 Government stocks	30	...	...	30	–2	...	...	–2	5	...	...	5
Gross fixed capital formation, total [b,c,d]	128401	108914	...	19487	134592	115819	...	18773	149895	132135	...	17760
1 Residential buildings	34349	34189	...	160	38056	37928	...	128	43038	42912	...	126
2 Non-residential buildings	16439	9947	...	6492	17134	11217	...	5917	17504	12093	...	5411
3 Other construction	30362	22244	...	8118	30323	22364	...	7959	32171	24544	...	7627
4 Land improvement and plantation and orchard development	...	...	...	...	...	...	...	...	...	...	...	...
5 Producers' durable goods [d]	47251	42534	...	4717	49079	44310	...	4769	57182	52586	...	4596
A Transport equipment	11233	10697	...	536	11716	11182	...	534	13768	13237	...	531
Passenger cars	4805	4647	...	158	4976	4813	...	163	5487	5309	...	178
Other	6428	6050	...	378	6740	6369	...	371	8281	7928	...	353
B Machinery and equipment [d]	36018	31837	...	4181	37363	33128	...	4235	43414	39349	...	4065
6 Breeding stock, dairy cattle, etc.	...	...	...	...	...	...	...	...	...	...	...	...
Total gross capital formation [b,d]	135860	116343	...	19517	135534	116763	...	18771	156877	139112	...	17765

a Increase in stocks of gross capital formation includes stocks of breeding stocks, draught animals, dairy cattle, etc. Stocks of commodities internally processed are valued at cost.

b Column "Public enterprises" is included in column "Total private".

c The period beginning 1961-1997 was deflated in five segments, 1961-1971, 1971-1981, 1981-1986, 1986-1992 and 1992 to date, with price indexes based on prices of 1961, 1971, 1981 and 1986 and 1992 respectively. The five series are then linked arithmetically at the major group, component and total gross domestic product levels to a 1992 base. Differences between the sum of directly rebased components and their aggregates are shown as adjusting entries (statistical discrepancy).

d Producers durable goods of gross fixed capital formation includes domestic progress payments on uncompleted heavy machinery and equipment.

2.9 Gross capital formation by kind of activity of owner, ISIC major divisions, in current prices

Million Canadian dollars

	1986			1987			1988			1989		
	Total gross capital formation	Increase in stocks	Gross fixed capital formation	Total gross capital formation	Increase in stocks	Gross fixed capital formation	Total gross capital formation	Increase in stocks	Gross fixed capital formation	Total gross capital formation	Increase in stocks	Gross fixed capital formation
All producers
1 Agriculture, hunting, forestry and fishing	3894	409	3485	3030	–531	3561	3188	–351	3539	4018	455	3563
2 Mining and quarrying [a]	8851	–68	8919	7805	–788	8593	10459	–230	10689	8096	–666	8762
3 Manufacturing	11571	–679	12250	13046	35	13011	16446	1384	15062	19728	1707	18021
4 Electricity, gas and water	6434	129	6305	6644	11	6633	8182	475	7707	9174	8	9166
5 Construction	1695	81	1614	1989	206	1783	2165	77	2088	2425	122	2303
6 Wholesale and retail trade, restaurants and hotels	7092	2851	4241	8457	3678	4779	7348	2008	5340	8286	2312	5974
7 Transport, storage and communication	6779	–42	6821	7504	25	7479	10218	13	10205	11618	116	11502
8 Finance, insurance, real estate and business services [b]	42469	9	42460	54262	53	54209	59181	27	59154	64555	12	64543
9 Community, social and personal services [b]	3133	...	3133	3704	...	3704	4179	...	4179	4130	...	4130
Total industries	91918	2690	89228	106441	2689	103752	121366	3403	117963	132030	4066	127964

Canada

Million Canadian dollars

	1986			1987			1988			1989		
	Total gross capital formation	Increase in stocks	Gross fixed capital formation	Total gross capital formation	Increase in stocks	Gross fixed capital formation	Total gross capital formation	Increase in stocks	Gross fixed capital formation	Total gross capital formation	Increase in stocks	Gross fixed capital formation
Producers of government services	14054	−35	14089	14620	−38	14658	15763	64	15699	17709	−3	17712
Private non-profit institutions serving households	...	...	...	...	...	...	...	...	...	...	...	...
Total [c]	105972	2655	103317	121061	2651	118410	137129	3467	133662	149739	4063	145676

	1990			1991			1992			1993		
	Total gross capital formation	Increase in stocks	Gross fixed capital formation	Total gross capital formation	Increase in stocks	Gross fixed capital formation	Total gross capital formation	Increase in stocks	Gross fixed capital formation	Total gross capital formation	Increase in stocks	Gross fixed capital formation

All producers

1 Agriculture, hunting, forestry and fishing	3844	654	3190	2749	−172	2921	2153	−860	3013	4875	1101	3774
2 Mining and quarrying [a]	8815	−213	9028	7440	−1554	8994	5843	−1011	6854	9036	−932	9968
3 Manufacturing	14923	−2108	17031	12849	−2146	14995	9324	−2167	11491	10858	−260	11118
4 Electricity, gas and water	11455	390	11065	12731	−17	12748	11745	−204	11949	9883	3	9880
5 Construction	2158	−105	2263	1772	−117	1889	1972	−5	1977	2006	−115	2121
6 Wholesale and retail trade, restaurants and hotels	4299	−1340	5639	3783	−1588	5371	3743	−2280	6023	6863	563	6300
7 Transport, storage and communication	11857	61	11796	12019	−179	12198	12810	−41	12851	10568	51	10517
8 Finance, insurance, real estate and business services [b]	57856	−66	57922	49395	−72	49467	50868	46	50822	49341	154	49187
9 Community, social and personal services [b]	3816	...	3816	2551	...	2551	3229	...	3229	4123	...	4123
Total industries	119023	−2727	121750	105289	−5845	111134	101687	−6522	108209	107553	565	106988
Producers of government services	19313	67	19246	19172	−37	19209	18796	−40	18836	18455	−4	18459
Private non-profit institutions serving households	...	...	...	...	...	...	...	...	...	...	...	...
Total [c]	138336	−2660	140996	124461	−5882	130343	120483	−6562	127045	126008	561	125447

	1994			1995			1996			1997		
	Total gross capital formation	Increase in stocks	Gross fixed capital formation	Total gross capital formation	Increase in stocks	Gross fixed capital formation	Total gross capital formation	Increase in stocks	Gross fixed capital formation	Total gross capital formation	Increase in stocks	Gross fixed capital formation

All producers

1 Agriculture, hunting, forestry and fishing	4285	−229	4514	4832	278	4554	5315	515	4800	3622	−1417	5039
2 Mining and quarrying [a]	14697	−1511	16208	16992	4	16988	15856	−220	16076	19463	230	19233
3 Manufacturing	16025	1329	14696	20617	3702	16915	18959	542	18417	23333	2280	21053
4 Electricity, gas and water	9241	245	8996	8674	7	8667	8389	−134	8523	8651	−87	8738
5 Construction	2262	136	2126	1938	−35	1973	2114	12	2102	2342	20	2322
6 Wholesale and retail trade, restaurants and hotels	9055	2383	6672	10696	3900	6796	7413	264	7149	14066	6203	7863
7 Transport, storage and communication	11883	−262	12145	12713	401	12312	13278	−22	13300	16461	−81	16542
8 Finance, insurance, real estate and business services [b]	47622	52	47570	42373	−123	42496	46216	88	46128	54927	103	54824
9 Community, social and personal services [b]	4867	...	4867	4536	...	4536	5412	...	5412	4711	...	4711
Total industries	119937	2143	117794	123371	8134	115237	122952	1045	121907	147576	7251	140325
Producers of government services	20055	−1	20056	20135	30	20105	19269	−2	19271	18246	5	18241

Canada

	1994			1995			1996			1997		
	Total gross capital formation	Increase in stocks	Gross fixed capital formation	Total gross capital formation	Increase in stocks	Gross fixed capital formation	Total gross capital formation	Increase in stocks	Gross fixed capital formation	Total gross capital formation	Increase in stocks	Gross fixed capital formation
Private non-profit institutions serving households	...	...	...	...	...	...	...	...	...	...	...	...
Total [c]	139992	2142	137850	143506	8164	135342	142221	1043	141178	165822	7256	158566

a Includes gold.
b For column "Increase in stocks", item "Community, social and personal services" is included in item "Finance, insurance, real estate and business services".
c Increase in stocks of gross capital formation includes stocks of breeding stocks, draught animals, dairy cattle, etc. Stocks of comodities internally processed are valued at cost

2.11 Gross fixed capital formation by kind of activity of owner, ISIC divisions, in current prices

Million Canadian dollars

	1986	1987	1988	1989	1990	1991	1992	1993	1994	1995	1996	1997
All producers												
1 Agriculture, hunting, forestry and fishing	3485	3561	3539	3563	3190	2921	3013	3774	4514	4554	4800	5039
2 Mining and quarrying	8919	8593	10689	8762	9028	8994	6854	9968	16208	16988	16076	19233
3 Manufacturing	12250	13011	15062	18021	17031	14995	11491	11118	14696	16915	18417	21053
4 Electricity, gas and water	6305	6633	7707	9166	11065	12748	11949	9880	8996	8667	8523	8738
5 Construction	1614	1783	2088	2303	2263	1889	1977	2121	2126	1973	2102	2322
6 Wholesale and retail trade, restaurants and hotels	4241	4779	5340	5974	5639	5371	6023	6300	6672	6796	7149	7863
7 Transport, storage and communication	6821	7479	10205	11502	11796	12198	12851	10517	12145	12312	13300	16542
8 Finance, insurance, real estate and business services	42460	54209	59154	64543	57922	49467	50822	49187	47570	42496	46128	54824
9 Community, social and personal services	3133	3704	4179	4130	3816	2551	3229	4123	4867	4536	5412	4711
Total industries	89228	103752	117963	127964	121750	111134	108209	106988	117794	115237	121907	140325
Producers of government services	14089	14658	15699	17712	19246	19209	18836	18459	20056	20105	19271	18241
Private non-profit institutions serving households	...	...	...	...	...	...	...	...	...	...	...	...
Total	103317	118410	133662	145676	140996	130343	127045	125447	137850	135342	141178	158566

2.17 Exports and imports of goods and services, detail

Million Canadian dollars

	1986	1987	1988	1989	1990	1991	1992	1993	1994	1995	1996	1997
Exports of goods and services												
1 Exports of merchandise, f.o.b.	125172	131484	143534	146963	152056	147669	163464	190383	227895	264940	280570	301649
2 Transport and communication	2587	2842	2938	3446	3720	3825	4076	4748	5122	5515	5899	6276
3 Insurance service charges	...	...	...	...	...	...	...	...	...	...	...	...
4 Other commodities	6996	7695	8845	9396	10064	10751	11992	13933	16269	17649	18894	19477
5 Adjustments of merchandise exports to change-of-ownership basis	...	...	...	...	...	...	...	...	...	...	...	...
6 Direct purchases in the domestic market by non-residential households	6806	6802	7484	7935	8598	8749	9054	9822	11197	12745	14093	14664
7 Direct purchases in the domestic market by extraterritorial bodies	...	...	...	...	...	...	...	...	...	...	...	...
Total exports of goods and services	141562	148823	162800	167739	174438	170995	188586	218885	260483	300849	319456	342066

Canada

Million Canadian dollars

	1986	1987	1988	1989	1990	1991	1992	1993	1994	1995	1996	1997
Imports of goods and services												
1 Imports of merchandise, c.i.f.	117498	121510	135156	141594	143300	142863	157202	181508	212842	235405	243529	282430
A Imports of merchandise, f.o.b.	115195	119324	132715	139216	141000	140658	154430	177593	208593	231206	239578	278463
B Transport of services on merchandise imports	2303	2186	2441	2378	2300	2205	2772	3915	4249	4199	3951	3967
C Insurance service charges on merchandise imports	...	...	...	...	...	...	...	...	...	...	...	...
2 Adjustments of merchandise imports to change-of-ownership basis	...	...	...	...	...	...	...	...	...	...	...	...
3 Other transport and communication	1298	1358	1574	1849	2075	2214	2642	2946	3313	3445	3660	3860
4 Other insurance service charges	9559	9669	10722	11995	12554	13208	14050	16799	19461	20687	21882	21959
5 Other commodities												
6 Direct purchases abroad by government	966	928	847	868	962	1022	951	877	735	730	747	739
7 Direct purchases abroad by resident households	7908	9257	10279	11833	15128	16094	16830	17331	16647	17262	18538	19287
Total imports of goods and services	137228	142723	158577	168139	174019	175401	191673	219462	252998	277529	288356	328276
Balance of goods and services	4334	6100	4223	–400	419	–4406	–3087	–577	7485	23320	31100	13790
Total imports and balance of goods and services	141562	148823	162800	167739	174438	170995	188586	218885	260483	300849	319456	342066

3.12 General government income and outlay account: total and subsectors

Million Canadian dollars

	1986					1987				
	Total government	Central government	State or provincial government	Local government	Social security funds	Total government	Central government	State or provincial government	Local government	Social security funds
Receipts										
1 Operating surplus	...	...	...	...	...	...	...	...	...	...
2 Property and entrepreneurial income	28748	8959	13793	1513	4483	29449	9369	13781	1571	4728
A Withdrawals from public quasi-corporations	...	...	...	...	...	...	...	...	...	...
B Interest	22010	6562	9535	1430	4483	23024	7015	9802	1479	4728
C Dividends [a]	2599	2397	119	83	...	2541	2354	95	92	...
D Net land rent and royalties [b]	4139	...	4139	...	...	3884	...	3884	...	...
3 Taxes, fees and contributions	173224	82802	66504	17673	6245	192780	91363	74995	19291	7131
A Indirect taxes	68734	21413	29865	17456	...	75966	23921	33008	19037	...
B Direct taxes	77874	49883	27991	...	...	87500	55229	32271	...	...
Income	77874	49883	27991	...	...	87500	55229	32271	...	...
Other	...	...	...	...	...	...	...	...	...	...
C Social security contributions	23229	11484	5500	...	6245	25665	12190	6344	...	7131
D Fees, fines and penalties	3387	22	3148	217	...	3649	23	3372	254	...
4 Other current transfers	...	290	22174	19230	...	...	317	23800	20267	...
A Casualty insurance claims	...	...	...	...	...	...	...	...	...	...
B Transfers from other government subsectors	...	290	22174	19230	...	...	317	23800	20267	...
C Transfers from rest of the world	...	...	...	...	...	...	...	...	...	...

Canada

Million Canadian dollars

	1986					1987				
	Total govern-ment	Central govern-ment	State or provincial govern-ment	Local govern-ment	Social security funds	Total govern-ment	Central govern-ment	State or provincial govern-ment	Local govern-ment	Social security funds
D Other transfers, except imputed	...	...	...	...	...	...	...	...	...	...
E Imputed unfunded employee pension and welfare contributions	...	...	...	...	...	...	...	...	...	...
Total current receipts	201972	92051	102471	38416	10728	222229	101049	112576	41129	11859

Disbursements

	Total	Central	State/prov	Local	SS funds	Total	Central	State/prov	Local	SS funds
1 Government final consumption expenditure	111482	24384	55277	31663	158	117964	25171	59053	33561	179
2 Property income	43222	26216	13693	3313	...	46279	27883	15056	3340	...
A Interest	43222	26216	13693	3313	...	46279	27883	15056	3340	...
B Net land rent and royalties	...	...	...	...	...	...	...	...	...	...
3 Subsidies	11174	5741	4797	636	...	11028	6263	4090	675	...
4 Other current transfers	57893	57401	33669	1062	7455	62652	60540	35999	1169	9328
A Casualty insurance premiums, net	...	...	...	...	...	...	...	...	...	...
B Transfers to other government subsectors	...	22185	19386	123	...	...	23899	20361	124	...
C Social security benefits	33678	23542	2721	...	7415	36650	24375	2998	...	9277
D Social assistance grants	18678	7274	10465	939	...	19653	7260	11348	1045	...
E Unfunded employee welfare benefits	...	...	...	...	...	...	...	...	...	...
F Transfers to private non-profit institutions serving households	...	...	...	...	...	...	...	...	...	...
G Other transfers n.e.c. [c]	3314	2217	1097	...	...	3743	2451	1292	...	...
H Transfers to rest of the world	2223	2183	...	...	40	2606	2555	...	...	51
Net saving	−21799	−21691	−4965	1742	3115	−15694	−18808	−1622	2384	2352
Total current disbursements and net saving	201972	92051	102471	38416	10728	222229	101049	112576	41129	11859

	1988					1989				
	Total govern-ment	Central govern-ment	State or provincial govern-ment	Local govern-ment	Social security funds	Total govern-ment	Central govern-ment	State or provincial govern-ment	Local govern-ment	Social security funds

Receipts

	Total	Central	State/prov	Local	SS funds	Total	Central	State/prov	Local	SS funds
1 Operating surplus	...	...	...	...	...	...	...	...	...	...
2 Property and entrepreneurial income	32431	10669	14939	1769	5054	36391	11819	17000	2204	5368
A Withdrawals from public quasi-corporations	...	...	...	...	...	...	...	...	...	...
B Interest	24562	7451	10392	1665	5054	27318	8102	11752	2096	5368
C Dividends [a]	3987	3218	665	104	...	5064	3717	1239	108	...
D Net land rent and royalties [b]	3882	...	3882	...	...	4009	...	4009	...	...
3 Taxes, fees and contributions	213851	99707	85215	20993	7936	229347	106121	91114	23311	8801
A Indirect taxes	84020	26057	37277	20686	...	92507	28922	40615	22970	...
B Direct taxes	96832	60046	36786	...	...	103333	64807	38526	...	...
Income	96832	60046	36786	...	...	103333	64807	38526	...	...
Other	...	...	...	...	...	...	...	...	...	...
C Social security contributions	28971	13585	7450	...	7936	29089	12360	7928	...	8801
D Fees, fines and penalties	4028	19	3702	307	...	4418	32	4045	341	...
4 Other current transfers	...	354	26011	21797	...	...	382	26753	23038	...

299

Canada

	1988					1989				
	Total government	Central government	State or provincial government	Local government	Social security funds	Total government	Central government	State or provincial government	Local government	Social security funds
A Casualty insurance claims ..	...	...	...	...	...	...	...	...	...	...
B Transfers from other government subsectors	...	354	26011	21797	...	...	382	26753	23038	...
C Transfers from rest of the world	...	...	...	...	...	...	...	...	...	...
D Other transfers, except imputed	...	...	...	...	...	...	...	...	...	...
E Imputed unfunded employee pension and welfare contributions	...	...	...	...	...	...	...	...	...	...
Total current receipts	246282	110730	126165	44559	12990	265738	118322	134867	48553	14169

Disbursements

	Total	Central	State/prov	Local	Social	Total	Central	State/prov	Local	Social
1 Government final consumption expenditure	127982	26498	65052	36239	193	138578	28187	70934	39246	211
2 Property income	50806	31711	15730	3365	...	58285	37424	17366	3495	...
A Interest	50806	31711	15730	3365	...	58285	37424	17366	3495	...
B Net land rent and royalties ..	...	...	...	...	...	...	...	...	...	...
3 Subsidies	10611	5357	4533	721	...	9818	4579	4465	774	...
4 Other current transfers	67225	64673	38696	1256	10762	72292	67555	41461	1358	12091
A Casualty insurance premiums, net	...	...	...	...	...	...	...	...	...	...
B Transfers to other government subsectors	...	26132	21903	127	...	...	27016	23049	108	...
C Social security benefits	39453	25582	3170	...	10701	42626	27163	3442	...	12021
D Social assistance grants	20725	7466	12130	1129	...	22367	7760	13357	1250	...
E Unfunded employee welfare benefits	...	...	...	...	...	...	...	...	...	...
F Transfers to private non-profit institutions serving households	...	...	...	...	...	...	...	...	...	...
G Other transfers n.e.c. [c] ...	4172	2679	1493	...	...	4514	2901	1613	...	...
H Transfers to rest of the world	2875	2814	...	...	61	2785	2715	...	...	70
Net saving	−10342	−17509	2154	2978	2035	−13235	−19423	641	3680	1867
Total current disbursements and net saving	246282	110730	126165	44559	12990	265738	118322	134867	48553	14169

	1990					1991				
	Total government	Central government	State or provincial government	Local government	Social security funds	Total government	Central government	State or provincial government	Local government	Social security funds

Receipts

1 Operating surplus	...	...	...	...	...	...	...	...	...	...
2 Property and entrepreneurial income	38317	12683	17570	2462	5602	37434	13072	16471	2263	5628
A Withdrawals from public quasi-corporations	...	...	...	...	...	...	...	...	...	...
B Interest	28653	8762	11950	2339	5602	29515	9466	12289	2132	5628
C Dividends [a]	5099	3921	1055	123	...	3863	3606	126	131	...
D Net land rent and royalties [b]	4565	...	4565	...	...	4056	...	4056	...	...
3 Taxes, fees and contributions .	247073	113225	98527	25204	10117	255406	118748	98855	26956	10847
A Indirect taxes	96415	27160	44407	24848	...	102508	30367	45559	26582	...
B Direct taxes	114732	70805	43927	...	...	113683	70445	43238	...	...
Income	114732	70805	43927	...	...	113683	70445	43238	...	...
Other	...	...	...	...	...	...	...	...	...	...

Canada

	1990					1991				
	Total government	Central government	State or provincial government	Local government	Social security funds	Total government	Central government	State or provincial government	Local government	Social security funds
C Social security contributions	33079	15226	7736	...	10117	35926	17896	7183	...	10847
D Fees, fines and penalties	2847	34	2457	356	...	3289	40	2875	374	...
4 Other current transfers	...	256	28145	25793	...	...	461	29135	27790	...
A Casualty insurance claims	...	...	...	...	...	...	...	...	...	...
B Transfers from other government subsectors	...	256	28145	25793	...	...	461	29135	27790	...
C Transfers from rest of the world	...	...	...	...	...	...	...	...	...	...
D Other transfers, except imputed	...	...	...	...	...	...	...	...	...	...
E Imputed unfunded employee pension and welfare contributions	...	...	...	...	...	...	...	...	...	...
Total current receipts	285390	126164	144242	53459	15719	292840	132281	144461	57009	16475

Disbursements

	Total government	Central government	State or provincial government	Local government	Social security funds	Total government	Central government	State or provincial government	Local government	Social security funds
1 Government final consumption expenditure	151546	31140	77178	43011	217	162311	31803	83749	46534	225
2 Property income	64286	41880	18684	3722	...	64526	41053	19587	3886	...
A Interest	64286	41880	18684	3722	...	64526	41053	19587	3886	...
B Net land rent and royalties	...	...	...	...	...	...	...	...	...	...
3 Subsidies	10052	4293	4866	893	...	12854	6604	5307	943	...
4 Other current transfers	80627	73408	46111	1851	13451	92234	81204	50686	2831	14899
A Casualty insurance premiums, net	...	...	...	...	...	...	...	...	...	...
B Transfers to other government subsectors	...	28466	25590	138	...	...	29276	27979	131	...
C Social security benefits	47131	29824	3938	...	13369	54068	35278	3982	...	14808
D Social assistance grants	26170	9173	15284	1713	...	30082	10107	17275	2700	...
E Unfunded employee welfare benefits	...	...	...	...	...	...	...	...	...	...
F Transfers to private non-profit institutions serving households	...	...	...	...	...	...	...	...	...	...
G Other transfers n.e.c. [c]	4357	3058	1299	...	...	4907	3457	1450	...	...
H Transfers to rest of the world	2969	2887	...	...	82	3177	3086	...	...	91
Net saving	–21121	–24557	–2597	3982	2051	–39085	–28383	–14868	2815	1351
Total current disbursements and net saving	285390	126164	144242	53459	15719	292840	132281	144461	57009	16475

	1992					1993				
	Total government	Central government	State or provincial government	Local government	Social security funds	Total government	Central government	State or provincial government	Local government	Social security funds

Receipts

	Total government	Central government	State or provincial government	Local government	Social security funds	Total government	Central government	State or provincial government	Local government	Social security funds
1 Operating surplus	...	...	...	...	...	...	...	...	...	...
2 Property and entrepreneurial income	37618	13382	16599	2145	5492	38418	12893	17903	2179	5443
A Withdrawals from public quasi-corporations	...	...	...	...	...	...	...	...	...	...
B Interest	29860	10163	12199	2006	5492	30642	10714	12448	2037	5443
C Dividends [a]	3734	3219	376	139	...	2737	2179	416	142	...
D Net land rent and royalties [b]	4024	...	4024	...	...	5039	...	5039	...	...
3 Taxes, fees and contributions	263091	123272	99234	28960	11625	266897	122200	102624	29864	12209

Canada

	1992					1993				
	Total govern-ment	Central govern-ment	State or provincial govern-ment	Local govern-ment	Social security funds	Total govern-ment	Central govern-ment	State or provincial govern-ment	Local govern-ment	Social security funds
A Indirect taxes	106588	30998	47025	28565	...	109386	30997	48952	29437	...
B Direct taxes	113376	71613	41763	...	...	113125	69972	43153	...	...
Income	113376	71613	41763	...	...	113125	69972	43153	...	...
Other	...	...	...	...	...	...	...	...	...	...
C Social security contributions	39553	20600	7328	...	11625	40637	21179	7249	...	12209
D Fees, fines and penalties	3574	61	3118	395	...	3749	52	3270	427	...
4 Other current transfers	...	523	31232	30573	...	...	524	32880	30993	...
A Casualty insurance claims	...	...	...	...	...	...	...	...	...	...
B Transfers from other government subsectors	...	523	31232	30573	...	...	524	32880	30993	...
C Transfers from rest of the world	...	...	...	...	...	...	...	...	...	...
D Other transfers, except imputed	...	...	...	...	...	...	...	...	...	...
E Imputed unfunded employee pension and welfare contributions	...	...	...	...	...	...	...	...	...	...
Total current receipts	300709	137177	147065	61678	17117	305315	135617	153407	63036	17652

Disbursements

1 Government final consumption expenditure	168806	32525	86694	49352	235	170251	33331	86686	49996	238
2 Property income	65241	39558	21594	4089	...	66513	39276	23097	4140	...
A Interest	65241	39558	21594	4089	...	66513	39276	23097	4140	...
B Net land rent and royalties	...	...	...	...	...	...	...	...	...	...
3 Subsidies	12323	4587	6541	1195	...	10488	3714	5531	1243	...
4 Other current transfers	101930	87632	56267	3555	16804	106696	91838	56872	4024	18359
A Casualty insurance premiums, net	...	...	...	...	...	...	...	...	...	...
B Transfers to other government subsectors	...	31496	30687	145	...	...	33377	30899	121	...
C Social security benefits	58214	37424	4091	...	16699	59299	37071	3980	...	18248
D Social assistance grants	35222	11893	19919	3410	...	38900	14518	20479	3903	...
E Unfunded employee welfare benefits	...	...	...	...	...	...	...	...	...	...
F Transfers to private non-profit institutions serving households	...	...	...	...	...	...	...	...	...	...
G Other transfers n.e.c. [c]	5298	3728	1570	...	...	5501	3987	1514	...	...
H Transfers to rest of the world	3196	3091	...	...	105	2996	2885	...	...	111
Net saving	−47591	−27125	−24031	3487	78	−48633	−32542	−18779	3633	−945
Total current disbursements and net saving	300709	137177	147065	61678	17117	305315	135617	153407	63036	17652

Canada

	1994					1995				
	Total government	Central government	State or provincial government	Local government	Social security funds	Total government	Central government	State or provincial government	Local government	Social security funds

Receipts

1 Operating surplus	...	...	...	...	...	...	...	...	...	...
2 Property and entrepreneurial income	40546	13666	19340	2214	5326	42625	15140	19799	2311	5375
A Withdrawals from public quasi-corporations	...	...	...	...	...	...	...	...	...	...
B Interest	30838	11457	11995	2060	5326	32205	12053	12622	2155	5375
C Dividends [a]	2777	2209	414	154	...	3592	3087	349	156	...
D Net land rent and royalties [b]	6931	...	6931	...	...	6828	...	6828	...	...
3 Taxes, fees and contributions	279102	126108	109996	30067	12931	293746	132418	116601	30271	14456
A Indirect taxes	112351	30482	52266	29603	...	115208	30762	54623	29823	...
B Direct taxes	119945	73038	46907	...	...	130042	79436	50606	...	...
Income	119945	73038	46907	...	...	130042	79436	50606	...	...
Other	...	...	...	...	...	...	...	...	...	...
C Social security contributions	42867	22562	7374	...	12931	44451	22201	7794	...	14456
D Fees, fines and penalties	3939	26	3449	464	...	4045	19	3578	448	...
4 Other current transfers	...	557	31590	31268	...	...	729	32951	31382	...
A Casualty insurance claims	...	...	...	...	...	...	...	...	...	...
B Transfers from other government subsectors	...	557	31590	31268	...	...	729	32951	31382	...
C Transfers from rest of the world	...	...	...	...	...	...	...	...	...	...
D Other transfers, except imputed	...	...	...	...	...	...	...	...	...	...
E Imputed unfunded employee pension and welfare contributions	...	...	...	...	...	...	...	...	...	...
Total current receipts	319648	140331	160926	63549	18257	336371	148287	169351	63964	19831

Disbursements

1 Government final consumption expenditure	169130	32826	85582	50480	242	170570	33152	86313	50855	250
2 Property income	69308	40155	24929	4224	...	77085	46281	26510	4294	...
A Interest	69308	40155	24929	4224	...	77085	46281	26510	4294	...
B Net land rent and royalties	...	...	...	...	...	...	...	...	...	...
3 Subsidies	9426	3189	5031	1206	...	8637	3026	4399	1212	...
4 Other current transfers	107553	89116	58086	4085	19681	108238	89323	59478	3875	20624
A Casualty insurance premiums, net	...	...	...	...	...	...	...	...	...	...
B Transfers to other government subsectors	...	32065	31219	131	...	...	33499	31432	131	...
C Social security benefits	58563	35182	3815	...	19566	57915	33511	3900	...	20504
D Social assistance grants	40550	14857	21739	3954	...	41761	15241	22776	3744	...
E Unfunded employee welfare benefits	...	...	...	...	...	...	...	...	...	...
F Transfers to private non-profit institutions serving households	...	...	...	...	...	...	...	...	...	...
G Other transfers n.e.c. [c]	5543	4230	1313	...	...	5763	4393	1370	...	...
H Transfers to rest of the world	2897	2782	...	...	115	2799	2679	...	...	120
Net saving	−35769	−24955	−12702	3554	−1666	−28159	−23495	−7349	3728	−1043

Canada

	1994					1995				
	Total government	Central government	State or provincial government	Local government	Social security funds	Total government	Central government	State or provincial government	Local government	Social security funds
Total current disbursements and net saving	319648	140331	160926	63549	18257	336371	148287	169351	63964	19831

	1996					1997				
	Total government	Central government	State or provincial government	Local government	Social security funds	Total government	Central government	State or provincial government	Local government	Social security funds

Receipts

1 Operating surplus	...	...	...	...	...	...	...	...	...	...
2 Property and entrepreneurial income	43368	15499	20697	2137	5035	44989	15964	22249	2036	4740
A Withdrawals from public quasi-corporations	...	...	...	...	...	...	...	...	...	...
B Interest	32344	12641	12689	1979	5035	32353	13014	12723	1876	4740
C Dividends [a]	3954	2858	938	158	...	4196	2950	1086	160	...
D Net land rent and royalties [b]	7070	...	7070	...	...	8440	...	8440	...	...
3 Taxes, fees and contributions	306532	138553	122693	30525	14761	326300	149864	130107	30718	15611
A Indirect taxes	117686	31290	56309	30087	...	122574	33430	58862	30282	...
B Direct taxes	140381	85637	54744	...	...	152629	93314	59315	...	...
Income	140381	85637	54744	...	...	152629	93314	59315	...	...
Other	...	...	...	...	...	...	...	...	...	...
C Social security contributions	44411	21607	8043	...	14761	47031	23097	8323	...	15611
D Fees, fines and penalties	4054	19	3597	438	...	4066	23	3607	436	...
4 Other current transfers	...	592	28733	30758	...	...	584	24926	30011	...
A Casualty insurance claims	...	...	...	...	...	...	...	...	...	...
B Transfers from other government subsectors	...	592	28733	30758	...	...	584	24926	30011	...
C Transfers from rest of the world	...	...	...	...	...	...	...	...	...	...
D Other transfers, except imputed	...	...	...	...	...	...	...	...	...	...
E Imputed unfunded employee pension and welfare contributions	...	...	...	...	...	...	...	...	...	...
Total current receipts	349900	154644	172123	63420	19796	371289	166412	177282	62765	20351

Disbursements

1 Government final consumption expenditure	168356	32786	84720	50586	264	167907	31780	85205	50593	329
2 Property income	75594	44907	26465	4222	...	74927	44293	26433	4201	...
A Interest	75594	44907	26465	4222	...	74927	44293	26433	4201	...
B Net land rent and royalties	...	...	...	...	...	...	...	...	...	...
3 Subsidies	7742	2425	4101	1216	...	8073	2601	4252	1220	...
4 Other current transfers	109060	85477	58828	3122	21716	109535	81001	58365	2938	22752
A Casualty insurance premiums, net	...	...	...	...	...	...	...	...	...	...
B Transfers to other government subsectors	...	29172	30773	138	...	...	25174	30209	138	...
C Social security benefits	59334	33607	4140	...	21587	59189	32677	3899	...	22613
D Social assistance grants	40797	15410	22403	2984	...	41036	15839	22397	2800	...
E Unfunded employee welfare benefits	...	...	...	...	...	...	...	...	...	...
F Transfers to private non-profit institutions serving households	...	...	...	...	...	...	...	...	...	...

Canada

	1996					1997				
	Total government	Central government	State or provincial government	Local government	Social security funds	Total government	Central government	State or provincial government	Local government	Social security funds
G Other transfers n.e.c. [c]	5972	4460	1512	...	...	6418	4558	1860	...	...
H Transfers to rest of the world	2957	2828	...	...	129	2892	2753	...	...	139
Net saving	–10852	–10951	–1991	4274	–2184	10847	6737	3027	3813	–2730
Total current disbursements and net saving	349900	154644	172123	63420	19796	371289	166412	177282	62765	20351

a Item "Dividends" refers to remitted profits of government business enterprises.
b Item "Net land rent and royalties" refers to royalties only.
c Item "Other transfers n.e.c" represents the Public service (employee) pension benifits.

3.13 General government capital accumulation account: total and subsectors

Million Canadian dollars

	1986					1987				
	Total government	Central government	State or provincial government	Local government	Social security funds	Total government	Central government	State or provincial government	Local government	Social security funds
Finance of gross accumulation										
1 Gross saving	–11506	–19759	–309	5447	3115	–4807	–16755	3268	6328	2352
A Consumption of fixed capital	10293	1932	4656	3705	...	10887	2053	4890	3944	...
B Net saving	–21799	–21691	–4965	1742	3115	–15694	–18808	–1622	2384	2352
2 Capital transfers [a]	–4086	–2556	–1212	–318	...	–3370	–2079	–990	–301	...
A From other government subsectors	...	...	...	...	...	...	...	...	...	...
B From other resident sectors	–4080	–2550	–1212	–318	...	–3337	–2046	–990	–301	...
C From rest of the world	–6	–6	...	...	...	–33	–33	...	...	...
Finance of gross accumulation	–15592	–22315	–1521	5129	3115	–8177	–18834	2278	6027	2352
Gross accumulation										
1 Gross capital formation	14054	2350	6485	5219	...	14620	2466	6381	5773	...
A Increase in stocks	–35	–35	...	...	...	–38	–38	...	...	...
B Gross fixed capital formation	14089	2385	6485	5219	...	14658	2504	6381	5773	...
2 Purchases of land, net [b]	418	56	57	305	...	277	122	–10	165	...
3 Purchases of intangible assets, net	...	...	...	...	...	...	...	...	...	...
4 Capital transfers	...	...	...	...	...	...	...	...	...	...
Net lending	–30064	–24721	–8063	–395	3115	–23074	–21422	–4093	89	2352
Gross accumulation	–15592	–22315	–1521	5129	3115	–8177	–18834	2278	6027	2352

	1988					1989				
	Total government	Central government	State or provincial government	Local government	Social security funds	Total government	Central government	State or provincial government	Local government	Social security funds
Finance of gross accumulation										
1 Gross saving	1358	–15321	7391	7253	2035	–590	–17065	6262	8346	1867
A Consumption of fixed capital	11700	2188	5237	4275	...	12645	2358	5621	4666	...
B Net saving	–10342	–17509	2154	2978	2035	–13235	–19423	641	3680	1867
2 Capital transfers [a]	–4265	–3112	–894	–259	...	–2995	–1841	–853	–301	...
A From other government subsectors	...	...	...	...	...	...	...	...	...	...
B From other resident sectors	–4092	–2939	–894	–259	...	–2781	–1627	–853	–301	...

Canada

	1988					1989				
	Total government	Central government	State or provincial government	Local government	Social security funds	Total government	Central government	State or provincial government	Local government	Social security funds
C From rest of the world	−173	−173	...	...	...	−214	−214	...	...	...
Finance of gross accumulation	−2907	−18433	6497	6994	2035	−3585	−18906	5409	8045	1867
Gross accumulation										
1 Gross capital formation	15763	2935	6390	6438	...	17709	3333	7263	7113	...
A Increase in stocks	64	64	...	...	...	−3	−3	...	...	...
B Gross fixed capital formation	15699	2871	6390	6438	...	17712	3336	7263	7113	...
2 Purchases of land, net [b]	134	−8	−244	386	...	428	27	−162	563	...
3 Purchases of intangible assets, net	...	...	...	...	...	...	...	...	...	...
4 Capital transfers	...	...	...	...	...	...	...	...	...	...
Net lending	−18804	−21360	351	170	2035	−21722	−22266	−1692	369	1867
Gross accumulation	−2907	−18433	6497	6994	2035	−3585	−18906	5409	8045	1867

	1990					1991				
	Total government	Central government	State or provincial government	Local government	Social security funds	Total government	Central government	State or provincial government	Local government	Social security funds
Finance of gross accumulation										
1 Gross saving	−7579	−22035	3396	9009	2051	−25553	−25897	−8929	7922	1351
A Consumption of fixed capital	13542	2522	5993	5027	...	13532	2486	5939	5107	...
B Net saving	−21121	−24557	−2597	3982	2051	−39085	−28383	−14868	2815	1351
2 Capital transfers [a]	−3463	−2285	−874	−304	...	−3356	−2225	−836	−295	...
A From other government subsectors	...	...	...	...	...	...	...	...	...	...
B From other resident sectors	−2791	−1613	−874	−304	...	−3229	−2098	−836	−295	...
C From rest of the world	−672	−672	...	...	...	−127	−127	...	...	...
Finance of gross accumulation	−11042	−24320	2522	8705	2051	−28909	−28122	−9765	7627	1351
Gross accumulation										
1 Gross capital formation	19313	3301	7944	8068	...	19172	3263	8059	7850	...
A Increase in stocks	67	67	...	...	...	−37	−37	...	...	...
B Gross fixed capital formation	19246	3234	7944	8068	...	19209	3300	8059	7850	...
2 Purchases of land, net [b]	460	−16	−185	661	...	823	6	−40	857	...
3 Purchases of intangible assets, net	...	...	...	...	...	...	...	...	...	...
4 Capital transfers	...	...	...	...	...	...	...	...	...	...
Net lending	−30815	−27605	−5237	−24	2051	−48904	−31391	−17784	−1080	1351
Gross accumulation	−11042	−24320	2522	8705	2051	−28909	−28122	−9765	7627	1351

	1992					1993				
	Total government	Central government	State or provincial government	Local government	Social security funds	Total government	Central government	State or provincial government	Local government	Social security funds
Finance of gross accumulation										
1 Gross saving	−33687	−24609	−17949	8793	78	−34238	−29908	−12540	9155	−945
A Consumption of fixed capital	13904	2516	6082	5306	...	14395	2634	6239	5522	...
B Net saving	−47591	−27125	−24031	3487	78	−48633	−32542	−18779	3633	−945
2 Capital transfers [a]	−2490	−1526	−629	−335	...	−2044	−1210	−535	−299	...

Canada

	1992					1993				
	Total govern-ment	Central govern-ment	State or provincial govern-ment	Local govern-ment	Social security funds	Total govern-ment	Central govern-ment	State or provincial govern-ment	Local govern-ment	Social security funds
A From other government subsectors	...	...	...	...	...	...	...	...	...	...
B From other resident sectors	−2369	−1405	−629	−335	...	−1716	−882	−535	−299	...
C From rest of the world	−121	−121	...	...	...	−328	−328	...	...	...
Finance of gross accumulation	−36177	−26135	−18578	8458	78	−36282	−31118	−13075	8856	−945
Gross accumulation										
1 Gross capital formation	18796	3554	7289	7953	...	18455	3856	6919	7680	...
A Increase in stocks	−40	−40	...	...	...	−4	−4	...	...	...
B Gross fixed capital formation	18836	3594	7289	7953	...	18459	3860	6919	7680	...
2 Purchases of land, net [b]	737	20	148	569	...	−36	21	−347	290	...
3 Purchases of intangible assets, net	...	...	...	...	...	...	...	...	...	...
4 Capital transfers	...	...	...	...	...	...	...	...	...	...
Net lending	−55710	−29709	−26015	−64	78	−54701	−34995	−19647	886	−945
Gross accumulation	−36177	−26135	−18578	8458	78	−36282	−31118	−13075	8856	−945

	1994					1995				
	Total govern-ment	Central govern-ment	State or provincial govern-ment	Local govern-ment	Social security funds	Total govern-ment	Central govern-ment	State or provincial govern-ment	Local govern-ment	Social security funds
Finance of gross accumulation										
1 Gross saving	−20580	−22099	−6199	9384	−1666	−12158	−20526	−568	9979	−1043
A Consumption of fixed capital	15189	2856	6503	5830	...	16001	2969	6781	6251	...
B Net saving	−35769	−24955	−12702	3554	−1666	−28159	−23495	−7349	3728	−1043
2 Capital transfers [a]	−1954	−1516	−56	−382	...	−2217	−1270	−489	−458	...
A From other government subsectors	...	...	...	...	...	...	...	...	...	...
B From other resident sectors	−1901	−1463	−56	−382	...	−1967	−1020	−489	−458	...
C From rest of the world	−53	−53	...	...	...	−250	−250	...	...	...
Finance of gross accumulation	−22534	−23615	−6255	9002	−1666	−14375	−21796	−1057	9521	−1043
Gross accumulation										
1 Gross capital formation	20055	3924	7621	8510	...	20135	3608	7248	9279	...
A Increase in stocks	−1	−1	...	...	...	30	30	...	...	...
B Gross fixed capital formation	20056	3925	7621	8510	...	20105	3578	7248	9279	...
2 Purchases of land, net [b]	−369	18	−356	−31	...	195	27	98	70	...
3 Purchases of intangible assets, net	...	...	...	...	...	...	...	...	...	...
4 Capital transfers	...	...	...	...	...	...	...	...	...	...
Net lending	−42220	−27557	−13520	523	−1666	−34705	−25431	−8403	172	−1043
Gross accumulation	−22534	−23615	−6255	9002	−1666	−14375	−21796	−1057	9521	−1043

Canada

	1996					1997				
	Total govern-ment	Central govern-ment	State or provincial govern-ment	Local govern-ment	Social security funds	Total govern-ment	Central govern-ment	State or provincial govern-ment	Local govern-ment	Social security funds
Finance of gross accumulation											
1 Gross saving	5521	–7967	4928	10744	–2184	27672	9754	10091	10557	–2730
A Consumption of fixed capital	16373	2984	6919	6470	...	16825	3017	7064	6744	...
B Net saving	–10852	–10951	–1991	4274	–2184	10847	6737	3027	3813	–2730
2 Capital transfers [a]	–3607	–2633	–497	–477	...	–1700	–702	–521	–477	...
A From other government subsectors	...	...	...	...	...	...	...	...	...	...
B From other resident sectors	–3437	–2463	–497	–477	...	–1567	–569	–521	–477	...
C From rest of the world	–170	–170	...	...	...	–133	–133	...	...	...
Finance of gross accumulation	1914	–10600	4431	10267	–2184	25972	9052	9570	10080	–2730
Gross accumulation											
1 Gross capital formation	19269	3569	7006	8694	...	18246	2832	6536	8878	...
A Increase in stocks	–2	–2	...	...	...	5	5	...	...	...
B Gross fixed capital formation	19271	3571	7006	8694	...	18241	2827	6536	8878	...
2 Purchases of land, net [b]	–1288	–1464	7	169	...	208	–19	27	200	...
3 Purchases of intangible assets, net	...	...	...	...	...	...	...	...	...	...
4 Capital transfers	...	...	...	...	...	...	...	...	...	...
Net lending	–16067	–12705	–2582	1404	–2184	7518	6239	3007	1002	–2730
Gross accumulation	1914	–10600	4431	10267	–2184	25972	9052	9570	10080	–2730

a Capital transfers are presented on a net basis (capital transfers from other sectors less capital transfers to other sectors.   b Includes "net purchases of tangable assets".

3.14 General government capital finance account: total and subsectors

Million Canadian dollars

	1986					1987				
	Total govern-ment	Central govern-ment	State or provincial govern-ment	Local govern-ment	Social security funds	Total govern-ment	Central govern-ment	State or provincial govern-ment	Local govern-ment	Social security funds
Acquisition of financial assets											
1 Gold and SDRs	...	...	...	...	...	...	...	...	...	...
2 Currency and transferable deposits [a]	–2419	–3169	940	–190	...	2743	2467	–68	344	...
3 Other deposits											
4 Bills and bonds, short-term	–871	–3	–1369	501	...	4135	–17	3750	402	...
5 Bonds, long-term	5206	–150	2588	288	2480	2302	–8	240	281	1789
A Corporations	165	–2	167	...	...	239	–4	297	–54	...
B Other government subsectors	5041	–148	2421	288	2480	2063	–4	–57	335	1789
C Rest of the world	...	...	...	...	...	...	...	...	...	...
6 Corporate equity securities [b]	480	–63	543	...	...	–9	–481	472	...	...
7 Short-term loans, n.e.c. [c]	3465	2080	1399	–14	...	1004	670	334	...	...
8 Long-term loans, n.e.c. [c]	–544	–288	–256	...	...	–421	–120	–301	...	...
A Mortgages	–544	–288	–256	...	...	–421	–120	–301	...	...
B Other	...	...	...	...	...	...	...	...	...	...
9 Other receivables	155	–57	239	–27	...	332	74	117	141	...
10 Other assets	5224	–959	5807	–259	635	9381	2869	5519	430	563

Canada

Million Canadian dollars

	1986					1987				
	Total govern-ment	Central govern-ment	State or provincial govern-ment	Local govern-ment	Social security funds	Total govern-ment	Central govern-ment	State or provincial govern-ment	Local govern-ment	Social security funds
Total aquisition of financial assets	10696	–2609	9891	299	3115	19467	5454	10063	1598	2352

Incurrence of liabilities

1 Currency and transferable deposits [a]	251	61	190	...	...	352	164	188	...	...
2 Other deposits	...	...	...	...	...	5708	4350	1275	83	...
3 Bills and bonds, short-term	16227	11425	4806	–4	...	5708	4350	1275	83	...
4 Bonds, long-term	20831	10416	9426	989	...	28859	20615	7134	1110	...
5 Short-term loans, n.e.c. [c]	–1759	–1299	–440	–20	...	1197	458	510	229	...
6 Long-term loans, n.e.c. [c]	13	...	13	...	...	7	...	7	...	...
7 Other payables	2383	–22	2418	–13	...	2483	–22	2251	254	...
8 Other liabilities	–207	–3518	2998	313	...	3571	–845	4180	236	...
Total incurrence of liabilities	37739	17063	19411	1265	...	42177	24720	15545	1912	...
Statistical discrepancy [d]	3021	5049	–1457	–571	...	364	2156	–1389	–403	...
Net lending	–30064	–24721	–8063	–395	3115	–23074	–21422	–4093	89	2352
Incurrence of liabilities and net worth	10696	–2609	9891	299	3115	19467	5454	10063	1598	2352

	1988					1989				
	Total govern-ment	Central govern-ment	State or provincial govern-ment	Local govern-ment	Social security funds	Total govern-ment	Central govern-ment	State or provincial govern-ment	Local govern-ment	Social security funds

Acquisition of financial assets

1 Gold and SDRs	...	...	...	...	...	...	...	...	...	...
2 Currency and transferable deposits [a]	–891	–385	–475	–31	...	959	–81	741	299	...
3 Other deposits										
4 Bills and bonds, short-term	5113	71	3881	1161	...	6615	100	5225	1290	...
5 Bonds, long-term	1224	131	160	–569	1502	2505	–108	1614	–220	1219
A Corporations	163	4	295	–136	...	134	9	306	–181	...
B Other government subsectors	1061	127	–135	–433	1502	2371	–117	1308	–39	1219
C Rest of the world	...	...	...	...	...	...	...	...	...	...
6 Corporate equity securities [b]	1432	519	913	...	...	488	–652	1140	...	...
7 Short-term loans, n.e.c. [c]	478	392	69	17	...	173	–317	438	52	...
8 Long-term loans, n.e.c. [c]	–78	–118	40	...	...	17	–211	228	...	...
A Mortgages	–78	–118	40	...	...	17	–211	228	...	...
B Other	...	...	...	...	...	...	...	...	...	...
9 Other receivables	362	–101	418	45	...	595	26	258	311	...
10 Other assets	17815	6946	9992	344	533	2318	–2129	2614	1185	648
Total aquisition of financial assets	25455	7455	14998	967	2035	13670	–3372	12258	2917	1867

Incurrence of liabilities

1 Currency and transferable deposits [a]	469	113	356	...	...	731	350	381	...	...
2 Other deposits	...	...	...	...	...	...	...	...	...	...
3 Bills and bonds, short-term	18841	19918	–1047	–30	...	26133	23351	2641	141	...
4 Bonds, long-term	19281	10337	8235	709	...	2696	–3464	5263	897	...
5 Short-term loans, n.e.c. [c]	–1143	–1453	145	165	...	721	–325	75	971	...
6 Long-term loans, n.e.c. [c]	–33	...	–33	...	...	–4	...	–4	...	...
7 Other payables	3103	36	2808	259	...	4503	–38	3627	914	...

Canada

	1988					1989				
	Total govern-ment	Central govern-ment	State or provincial govern-ment	Local govern-ment	Social security funds	Total govern-ment	Central govern-ment	State or provincial govern-ment	Local govern-ment	Social security funds
8 Other liabilities	3856	−1075	4913	18	...	−2540	−5660	3222	−102	...
Total incurrence of liabilities	44374	27876	15377	1121	...	32240	14214	15205	2821	...
Statistical discrepancy [d]	−115	939	−730	−324	...	3152	4680	−1255	−273	...
Net lending	−18804	−21360	351	170	2035	−21722	−22266	−1692	369	1867
Incurrence of liabilities and net worth	25455	7455	14998	967	2035	13670	−3372	12258	2917	1867

	1990					1991				
	Total govern-ment	Central govern-ment	State or provincial govern-ment	Local govern-ment	Social security funds	Total govern-ment	Central govern-ment	State or provincial govern-ment	Local govern-ment	Social security funds

Acquisition of financial assets

1 Gold and SDRs	...	...	...	...	...	...	...	...	...	...
2 Currency and transferable deposits [a]	932	500	499	−67	...	−1039	−802	54	−291	...
3 Other deposits										
4 Bills and bonds, short-term	−4330	−117	−4702	489	...	857	145	996	−284	...
5 Bonds, long-term	2682	−77	1395	650	714	3085	−50	1517	398	1220
A Corporations	414	4	229	181	...	685	5	614	66	...
B Other government subsectors	2268	−81	1166	469	714	2400	−55	903	332	1220
C Rest of the world	...	...	...	...	...	...	...	...	...	...
6 Corporate equity securities [b]	2842	136	2706	...	...	2549	218	2331	...	...
7 Short-term loans, n.e.c. [c]	647	−221	907	−39	...	635	47	625	−37	...
8 Long-term loans, n.e.c. [c]	−574	−72	−502	...	...	27	−727	754	...	...
A Mortgages	−574	−72	−502	...	...	27	−727	754	...	...
B Other	...	...	...	...	...	...	...	...	...	...
9 Other receivables	578	16	367	195	...	550	25	285	240	...
10 Other assets	4659	−4937	7362	897	1337	8343	−12	6127	2097	131
Total aquisition of financial assets	7436	−4772	8032	2125	2051	15007	−1156	12689	2123	1351

Incurrence of liabilities

1 Currency and transferable deposits [a]	259	130	129	...	...	225	44	181	...	...
2 Other deposits	...	...	...	...	...	...	...	...	...	...
3 Bills and bonds, short-term	16473	14480	1832	161	...	9654	10028	−293	−81	...
4 Bonds, long-term	15334	6917	7300	1117	...	46137	19955	23695	2487	...
5 Short-term loans, n.e.c. [c]	1259	57	−29	1231	...	390	83	205	102	...
6 Long-term loans, n.e.c. [c]	20	...	20	...	...	−87	...	−87	...	...
7 Other payables	4273	63	3879	331	...	4161	−15	4015	161	...
8 Other liabilities	1361	525	1038	−202	...	6226	58	5488	680	...
Total incurrence of liabilities	38979	22172	14169	2638	...	66706	30153	33204	3349	...
Statistical discrepancy [d]	−728	661	−900	−489	...	−2795	82	−2731	−146	...
Net lending	−30815	−27605	−5237	−24	2051	−48904	−31391	−17784	−1080	1351
Incurrence of liabilities and net worth	7436	−4772	8032	2125	2051	15007	−1156	12689	2123	1351

Canada

	1992					1993				
	Total govern-ment	Central govern-ment	State or provincial govern-ment	Local govern-ment	Social security funds	Total govern-ment	Central govern-ment	State or provincial govern-ment	Local govern-ment	Social security funds

Acquisition of financial assets

1 Gold and SDRs	...	...	...	...	...	...	...	...	...	...
2 Currency and transferable deposits [a]	–405	–752	71	276	...	1429	741	679	9	...
3 Other deposits										
4 Bills and bonds, short-term	–972	–102	118	–988	...	–766	–3	–855	92	...
5 Bonds, long-term	1670	48	454	603	565	701	–11	1798	–113	–973
A Corporations	175	...	98	77	...	–376	1	–249	–128	...
B Other government subsectors	1495	48	356	526	565	1077	–12	2047	15	–973
C Rest of the world	...	...	...	...	...	...	...	...	...	...
6 Corporate equity securities [b]	1215	41	1174	...	...	710	–162	872	...	...
7 Short-term loans, n.e.c. [c]	625	7	551	67	...	798	–84	881	1	...
8 Long-term loans, n.e.c. [c]	–554	–816	262	...	...	–974	–328	–646	...	...
A Mortgages	–554	–816	262	...	...	–974	–328	–646	...	...
B Other	...	...	...	...	...	...	...	...	...	...
9 Other receivables	304	21	167	116	...	369	21	260	88	...
10 Other assets	–2167	–5623	1380	2563	–487	11748	1094	7858	2768	28
Total aquisition of financial assets	–284	–7176	4177	2637	78	14015	1268	10847	2845	–945

Incurrence of liabilities

1 Currency and transferable deposits [a]	124	84	40	...	...	282	209	73	...	...
2 Other deposits	...	...	...	...	...	...	...	...	...	...
3 Bills and bonds, short-term	16626	12714	4096	–184	...	13719	12864	729	126	...
4 Bonds, long-term	35464	12529	21218	1717	...	49095	21970	25261	1864	...
5 Short-term loans, n.e.c. [c]	746	–125	321	550	...	806	58	287	461	...
6 Long-term loans, n.e.c. [c]	67	...	67	...	...	–3	...	–3	...	...
7 Other payables	4683	37	4425	221	...	4656	56	4560	40	...
8 Other liabilities	2818	631	1628	559	...	1213	597	598	18	...
Total incurrence of liabilities	60528	25870	31795	2863	...	69768	35754	31505	2509	...
Statistical discrepancy [d]	–5102	–3337	–1603	–162	...	–1052	509	–1011	–550	...
Net lending	–55710	–29709	–26015	–64	78	–54701	–34995	–19647	886	–945
Incurrence of liabilities and net worth	–284	–7176	4177	2637	78	14015	1268	10847	2845	–945

	1994					1995				
	Total govern-ment	Central govern-ment	State or provincial govern-ment	Local govern-ment	Social security funds	Total govern-ment	Central govern-ment	State or provincial govern-ment	Local govern-ment	Social security funds

Acquisition of financial assets

1 Gold and SDRs	...	...	...	...	...	...	...	...	...	...
2 Currency and transferable deposits [a]	565	629	–153	89	...	4168	4098	–287	357	...
3 Other deposits	...	...	...	...	...	...	...	...	...	...
4 Bills and bonds, short-term	4993	1	4908	84	...	–63	21	–332	248	...
5 Bonds, long-term	1010	23	2083	–15	–1081	1626	–9	1418	1543	–1326
A Corporations	–308	12	–312	–8	...	–73	–10	–303	240	...
B Other government subsectors	1318	11	2395	–7	–1081	1699	1	1721	1303	–1326
C Rest of the world	...	...	...	...	...	...	...	...	...	...

Canada

	1994					1995				
	Total government	Central government	State or provincial government	Local government	Social security funds	Total government	Central government	State or provincial government	Local government	Social security funds
6 Corporate equity securities [b]	3054	−29	3083	...	...	−2275	−3068	793	...	...
7 Short-term loans, n.e.c. [c]	2369	674	1695	...	...	1117	456	651	10	...
8 Long-term loans, n.e.c. [c]	−2054	−1593	−461	...	...	−822	−664	−158	...	...
A Mortgages	−2054	−1593	−461	...	...	−822	−664	−158	...	...
B Other	...	...	...	...	...	...	...	...	...	...
9 Other receivables	−50	−33	−57	40	...	98	74	−19	43	...
10 Other assets	−1624	−2046	−1307	2314	−585	10542	362	10322	−425	283
Total acquisition of financial assets	8263	−2374	9791	2512	−1666	14391	1270	12388	1776	−1043

Incurrence of liabilities

	1994					1995				
1 Currency and transferable deposits [a]	171	−24	195	...	...	252	72	180	...	...
2 Other deposits	...	...	...	...	...	...	...	...	...	...
3 Bills and bonds, short-term	−8833	−8017	−907	91	...	−2907	−892	−2038	23	...
4 Bonds, long-term	55443	34216	20149	1078	...	42242	25711	15964	567	...
5 Short-term loans, n.e.c. [c]	1100	−155	797	458	...	772	−14	791	−5	...
6 Long-term loans, n.e.c. [c]	−14	...	−14	...	...	−13	...	−13	...	...
7 Other payables	2013	34	1959	20	...	5505	142	5265	98	...
8 Other liabilities	4987	1444	3461	82	...	5244	4257	870	117	...
Total incurrence of liabilities	54867	27498	25640	1729	...	51095	29276	21019	800	...
Statistical discrepancy [d]	−4384	−2315	−2329	260	...	−1999	−2575	−228	804	...
Net lending	−42220	−27557	−13520	523	−1666	−34705	−25431	−8403	172	−1043
Incurrence of liabilities and net worth	8263	−2374	9791	2512	−1666	14391	1270	12388	1776	−1043

	1996					1997				
	Total government	Central government	State or provincial government	Local government	Social security funds	Total government	Central government	State or provincial government	Local government	Social security funds

Acquisition of financial assets

1 Gold and SDRs	...	...	...	...	...	...	...	...	...	...
2 Currency and transferable deposits [a]	−999	−2294	445	850	...	2607	3300	−996	303	...
3 Other deposits	...	...	...	...	...	...	...	...	...	...
4 Bills and bonds, short-term	−4062	−95	−3242	−725	...	982	10	33	939	...
5 Bonds, long-term	2510	−29	3861	148	−1470	888	−33	1693	798	−1570
A Corporations	5	−24	−32	61	...	69	−5	37	37	...
B Other government subsectors	2505	−5	3893	87	−1470	819	−28	1656	761	−1570
C Rest of the world	...	...	...	...	...	...	...	...	...	...
6 Corporate equity securities [b]	193	36	157	...	...	539	22	517	...	...
7 Short-term loans, n.e.c. [c]	−858	−1655	819	−22	...	320	607	−238	−49	...
8 Long-term loans, n.e.c. [c]	−437	−310	−127	...	...	−203	−208	5	...	...
A Mortgages	−437	−310	−127	...	...	−203	−208	5	...	...
B Other	...	...	...	...	...	...	...	...	...	...
9 Other receivables	46	10	−14	50	...	22	−14	−19	55	...
10 Other assets	21037	5560	14496	1695	−714	7750	−1454	10923	−559	−1160
Total acquisition of financial assets	17430	1223	16395	1996	−2184	12905	2230	11918	1487	−2730

Incurrence of liabilities

1 Currency and transferable deposits [a]	602	610	−8	...	...	129	105	24	...	...

Canada

	1996					1997				
	Total govern-ment	Central govern-ment	State or provincial govern-ment	Local govern-ment	Social security funds	Total govern-ment	Central govern-ment	State or provincial govern-ment	Local govern-ment	Social security funds
2 Other deposits	...	...	...	...	...	...	...	...	...	...
3 Bills and bonds, short-term	–21949	–20777	–1251	79	...	–27069	–25041	–2062	34	...
4 Bonds, long-term	42934	31336	11205	393	...	22359	17293	4730	336	...
5 Short-term loans, n.e.c. [c]	845	22	828	–5	...	612	–7	262	357	...
6 Long-term loans, n.e.c. [c]	9	...	9	...	...	–18	...	–18	...	...
7 Other payables	6437	–675	6972	140	...	2850	–18	2698	170	...
8 Other liabilities	4114	1935	2211	–32	...	6483	1870	4568	45	...
Total incurrence of liabilities	32992	12451	19966	575	...	5346	–5798	10202	942	...
Statistical discrepancy [d]	505	1477	–989	17	...	41	1789	–1291	–457	...
Net lending	–16067	–12705	–2582	1404	–2184	7518	6239	3007	1002	–2730
Incurrence of liabilities and net worth	17430	1223	16395	1996	–2184	12905	2230	11918	1487	–2730

a Including item "Other deposits".
b Investment in short-term papers, bonds and corporate equity securities of the rest of the world cannot be split between long-term and short-term by purchasers, the total investment has been allocated to the item "Corporate equity securities".
c Loans other than mortgages are included in item "Short-term loans, n.e.c.".
d The statistical discrepancy equals the difference between net lending in the Income and Expenditure Accounts and net acquisition of financial assets in the Financial Flow Accounts (change in financial assets less change in liabilities).

3.15 General government balance sheet: total and subsectors

Million Canadian dollars

	1986					1987				
	Total general govern-ment	Central govern-ment	State or provincial govern-ment	Local govern-ment	Social security funds	Total general govern-ment	Central govern-ment	State or provincial govern-ment	Local govern-ment	Social security funds
Assets										
Non-financial assets	256763	30592	123633	102538	...	267123	31363	127546	108214	...
1 Tangible assets	256763	30592	123633	102538	...	267123	31363	127546	108214	...
A Stocks	372	372	...	...	...	312	312	...	...	...
B Reproducible fixed assets	207904	25074	99911	82919	...	216150	25773	102943	87434	...
C Land and other non-reproducible tangible assets	48487	5146	23722	19619	...	50661	5278	24603	20780	...
2 Intangible assets	...	...	...	...	...	...	...	...	...	...
Financial assets	231686	48011	121998	16510	45167	259345	59326	133822	17394	48803
1 Gold and SDRs	...	...	...	...	...	...	...	...	...	...
2 Currency and transferable deposits [a]	10752	2055	4829	3868	...	13637	4873	4666	4098	...
3 Other deposits	...	...	...	...	...	...	...	...	...	...
4 Bills and bonds, short-term	9298	49	7330	1919	...	13046	53	11072	1921	...
5 Bonds, long-term	70887	140	34893	3801	32053	74702	205	36453	4202	33842
A Corporate	2357	27	1887	443	...	2580	12	2179	389	...
B Other government subsectors	68530	113	33006	3358	32053	72122	193	34274	3813	33842
C Rest of the world	...	...	...	...	...	...	...	...	...	...
6 Corporate equity securities [b]	4377	1046	3331	...	...	3996	213	3783	...	...
7 Short-term loans, n.e.c. [c]	9041	4926	4091	24	...	10688	6244	4420	24	...
8 Long-term loans, n.e.c. [c]	7710	1166	6544	...	...	6695	982	5713	...	...
A Mortgages	7710	1166	6544	...	...	6695	982	5713	...	...
B Other	...	...	...	...	...	...	...	...	...	...
9 Other receivables	2449	–	1769	680	...	2821	115	1885	821	...
10 Other assets	117172	38629	59211	6218	13114	133760	46641	65830	6328	14961
Total assets	488449	78603	245631	119048	45167	526468	90689	261368	125608	48803

Canada

Million Canadian dollars

	1986					1987				
	Total general government	Central government	State or provincial government	Local government	Social security funds	Total general government	Central government	State or provincial government	Local government	Social security funds

Liabilities and net worth

Liabilities	428367	240466	152105	35796	...	471681	270889	163177	37615	...
1 Currency and transferable deposits [a]	2388	1484	904	...	...	2705	1648	1057	...	...
2 Other deposits	...	...	...	...	...	...	...	...	...	...
3 Bills and bonds, short-term	82329	70990	11087	252	...	88251	75591	12333	327	...
4 Bonds, long-term	284368	147426	109472	27470	...	312764	168142	116069	28553	...
5 Short-term loans, n.e.c. [c]	14089	2844	8016	3229	...	14604	2830	8316	3458	...
6 Long-term loans, n.e.c. [c]	1400	...	1400	...	...	1405	...	1405	...	...
7 Other payables	7681	489	4662	2530	...	7096	710	3602	2784	...
8 Other liabilities	36112	17233	16564	2315	...	44856	21968	20395	2493	...
Net worth	60082	−161863	93526	83252	45167	54787	−180200	98191	87993	48803
Total liabilities and net worth	488449	78603	245631	119048	45167	526468	90689	261368	125608	48803

	1988					1989				
	Total general government	Central government	State or provincial government	Local government	Social security funds	Total general government	Central government	State or provincial government	Local government	Social security funds

Assets

Non-financial assets	285283	33792	134955	116536	...	307114	37068	143760	126286	...
1 Tangible assets	285283	33792	134955	116536	...	307114	37068	143760	126286	...
A Stocks	375	375	...	...	...	368	368	...	...	...
B Reproducible fixed assets	230540	27761	108724	94055	...	247916	30540	115549	101827	...
C Land and other non-reproducible tangible assets	54368	5656	26231	22481	...	58830	6160	28211	24459	...
2 Intangible assets	...	...	...	...	...	...	...	...	...	...
Financial assets	280164	64035	147283	17965	50881	291402	64194	152632	21525	53051
1 Gold and SDRs	...	...	...	...	...	...	...	...	...	...
2 Currency and transferable deposits [a]	11866	3732	4172	3962	...	13308	3748	4894	4666	...
3 Other deposits	...	...	...	...	...	...	...	...	...	...
4 Bills and bonds, short-term	18132	106	14944	3082	...	24229	187	20170	3872	...
5 Bonds, long-term	77160	338	37535	3943	35344	79467	228	38824	3852	36563
A Corporate	2733	16	2464	253	...	2868	26	2770	72	...
B Other government subsectors	74427	322	35071	3690	35344	76599	202	36054	3780	36563
C Rest of the world	...	...	...	...	...	...	...	...	...	...
6 Corporate equity securities [b]	5577	872	4705	...	...	6524	696	5828	...	...
7 Short-term loans, n.e.c. [c]	11253	6579	4633	41	...	12132	6969	5070	93	...
8 Long-term loans, n.e.c. [c]	7214	1363	5851	...	...	7175	1097	6078	...	...
A Mortgages	7214	1363	5851	...	...	7175	1097	6078	...	...
B Other	...	...	...	...	...	...	...	...	...	...
9 Other receivables	3171	–	2305	866	...	3740	–	2563	1177	...
10 Other assets	145791	51045	73138	6071	15537	144827	51269	69205	7865	16488
Total assets	565447	97827	282238	134501	50881	598516	101262	296392	147811	53051

Liabilities and net worth

Liabilities	513639	301209	174058	38372	...	552685	319672	191913	41100	...
1 Currency and transferable deposits [a]	3168	1755	1413	...	...	3905	2111	1794	...	...
2 Other deposits	...	...	...	...	...	...	...	...	...	...

Canada

	1988					1989				
	Total general government	Central government	State or provincial government	Local government	Social security funds	Total general government	Central government	State or provincial government	Local government	Social security funds
3 Bills and bonds, short-term	107944	96345	11310	289	...	135806	121338	14050	418	...
4 Bonds, long-term	329763	177901	122955	28907	...	340701	174955	136022	29724	...
5 Short-term loans, n.e.c.[c]	13073	1045	8405	3623	...	13011	117	8300	4594	...
6 Long-term loans, n.e.c.[c]	1412	...	1412	...	...	1405	...	1405	...	...
7 Other payables	7994	612	4339	3043	...	9609	579	5073	3957	...
8 Other liabilities	50285	23551	24224	2510	...	48248	20572	25269	2407	...
Net worth	51808	−203382	108180	96129	50881	45831	−218410	104479	106711	53051
Total liabilities and net worth	565447	97827	282238	134501	50881	598516	101262	296392	147811	53051

	1990					1991				
	Total general government	Central government	State or provincial government	Local government	Social security funds	Total general government	Central government	State or provincial government	Local government	Social security funds
Assets										
Non-financial assets	326083	39083	151414	135586	...	325534	38370	150207	136957	...
1 Tangible assets	326083	39083	151414	135586	...	325534	38370	150207	136957	...
A Stocks	443	443	...	...	...	404	404	...	...	...
B Reproducible fixed assets	263057	32175	121671	109211	...	262141	31595	120378	110168	...
C Land and other non-reproducible tangible assets	62583	6465	29743	26375	...	62989	6371	29829	26789	...
2 Intangible assets	...	...	...	...	...	...	...	...	...	...
Financial assets	300606	61666	161051	22882	55007	319679	64932	172912	25030	56805
1 Gold and SDRs	...	...	...	...	...	...	...	...	...	...
2 Currency and transferable deposits[a]	14221	4106	5344	4771	...	14087	3918	5347	4822	...
3 Other deposits	...	...	...	...	...	...	...	...	...	...
4 Bills and bonds, short-term	20054	70	15923	4061	...	20522	230	15915	4377	...
5 Bonds, long-term	83495	132	43276	2810	37277	86871	93	44873	3408	38497
A Corporate	3274	30	2991	253	...	4046	26	3701	319	...
B Other government subsectors	80221	102	40285	2557	37277	82825	67	41172	3089	38497
C Rest of the world	...	...	...	...	...	...	...	...	...	...
6 Corporate equity securities[b]	9319	833	8486	...	...	11267	549	10718	...	...
7 Short-term loans, n.e.c.[c]	13658	7627	5977	54	...	13708	7695	5996	17	...
8 Long-term loans, n.e.c.[c]	6501	936	5565	...	...	7810	1493	6317	...	...
A Mortgages	6501	936	5565	...	...	7810	1493	6317	...	...
B Other	...	...	...	...	...	...	...	...	...	...
9 Other receivables	4300	–	2928	1372	...	4884	59	3213	1612	...
10 Other assets	149058	47962	73552	9814	17730	160530	50895	80533	10794	18308
Total assets	626689	100749	312465	158468	55007	645213	103302	323119	161987	56805
Liabilities and net worth										
Liabilities	587850	343370	200691	43789	...	646057	368267	230711	47079	...
1 Currency and transferable deposits[a]	4164	2241	1923	...	...	4389	2285	2104	...	...
2 Other deposits	...	...	...	...	...	...	...	...	...	...
3 Bills and bonds, short-term	152963	136522	15882	559	...	163671	147644	15589	438	...
4 Bonds, long-term	356637	182110	143614	30913	...	403581	202079	168121	33381	...
5 Short-term loans, n.e.c.[c]	13943	1	8117	5825	...	14348	1	8420	5927	...
6 Long-term loans, n.e.c.[c]	1424	...	1424	...	...	1334	...	1334	...	...
7 Other payables	9991	18	5685	4288	...	10941	16	6476	4449	...
8 Other liabilities	48728	22478	24046	2204	...	47793	16242	28667	2884	...
Net worth	38839	−242621	111774	114679	55007	−844	−264965	92408	114908	56805

Canada

	1990					1991				
	Total general government	Central government	State or provincial government	Local government	Social security funds	Total general government	Central government	State or provincial government	Local government	Social security funds
Total liabilities and net worth	626689	100749	312465	158468	55007	645213	103302	323119	161987	56805

	1992					1993				
	Total general government	Central government	State or provincial government	Local government	Social security funds	Total general government	Central government	State or provincial government	Local government	Social security funds

Assets

Non-financial assets	333417	39909	152189	141319	...	340061	40793	154102	145166	...
1 Tangible assets	333417	39909	152189	141319	...	340061	40793	154102	145166	...
A Stocks	371	371	...	...	...	366	366	...	...	...
B Reproducible fixed assets	268221	32903	121774	113544	...	273391	33706	123145	116540	...
C Land and other non-reproducible tangible assets	64825	6635	30415	27775	...	66304	6721	30957	28626	...
2 Intangible assets	...	...	...	...	...	...	...	...	...	...
Financial assets	317186	58507	174821	26904	56954	332556	62949	184697	28206	56704
1 Gold and SDRs	...	...	...	...	...	...	...	...	...	...
2 Currency and transferable deposits [a]	13378	3019	5370	4989	...	15186	4087	6089	5010	...
3 Other deposits	...	...	...	...	...	...	...	...	...	...
4 Bills and bonds, short-term	19246	127	14530	4589	...	16911	132	11598	5181	...
5 Bonds, long-term	88035	139	44823	4011	39062	87620	128	45305	4098	38089
A Corporate	4119	24	3699	396	...	3414	26	3120	268	...
B Other government subsectors	83916	115	41124	3615	39062	84206	102	42185	3830	38089
C Rest of the world	...	...	...	...	...	...	...	...	...	...
6 Corporate equity securities [b]	12168	372	11796	...	...	11076	281	10795	...	...
7 Short-term loans, n.e.c. [c]	13202	6571	6547	84	...	14284	6771	7428	85	...
8 Long-term loans, n.e.c. [c]	9538	2962	6576	...	...	8156	2787	5369	...	...
A Mortgages	9538	2962	6576	...	...	8156	2787	5369	...	...
B Other	...	...	...	...	...	...	...	...	...	...
9 Other receivables	5161	53	3380	1728	...	5486	29	3641	1816	...
10 Other assets	156458	45264	81799	11503	17892	173837	48734	94472	12016	18615
Total assets	650603	98416	327010	168223	56954	672617	103742	338799	173372	56704

Liabilities and net worth

Liabilities	708614	398727	259860	50027	...	791432	443064	296075	52293	...
1 Currency and transferable deposits [a]	4513	2369	2144	...	...	4796	2579	2217	...	...
2 Other deposits	...	...	...	...	...	...	...	...	...	...
3 Bills and bonds, short-term	180045	160396	19439	210	...	193112	172479	20349	284	...
4 Bonds, long-term	441487	214615	191645	35227	...	495616	236846	221870	36900	...
5 Short-term loans, n.e.c. [c]	15002	95	8430	6477	...	16125	25	9162	6938	...
6 Long-term loans, n.e.c. [c]	1443	...	1443	...	...	1442	...	1442	...	...
7 Other payables	12449	14	7765	4670	...	14325	11	9604	4710	...
8 Other liabilities	53675	21238	28994	3443	...	66016	31124	31431	3461	...
Net worth	−58011	−300311	67150	118196	56954	−118815	−339322	42724	121079	56704
Total liabilities and net worth	650603	98416	327010	168223	56954	672617	103742	338799	173372	56704

Canada

	1994					1995				
	Total general govern-ment	Central govern-ment	State or provincial govern-ment	Local govern-ment	Social security funds	Total general govern-ment	Central govern-ment	State or provincial govern-ment	Local govern-ment	Social security funds

Assets

Non-financial assets	353090	43487	158069	151534	...	371211	46992	162738	161481	...
1 Tangible assets	353090	43487	158069	151534	...	371211	46992	162738	161481	...
A Stocks	337	337	...	...	...	361	361	...	...	...
B Reproducible fixed assets	283663	35953	126177	121533	...	297668	38760	129669	129239	...
C Land and other non-reproducible tangible assets	69090	7197	31892	30001	...	73182	7871	33069	32242	...
2 Intangible assets	...	...	...	...	...	...	...	...	...	...
Financial assets	339870	60665	195297	28814	55094	352949	61976	206027	30405	54541
1 Gold and SDRs	...	...	...	...	...	...	...	...	...	...
2 Currency and transferable deposits [a]	15062	4135	5925	5002	...	19056	8232	5779	5045	...
3 Other deposits	...	...	...	...	...	...	...	...	...	...
4 Bills and bonds, short-term	22411	134	17212	5065	...	22988	122	18153	4713	...
5 Bonds, long-term	93385	150	52144	4083	37008	93366	141	51917	5626	35682
A Corporate	3889	39	3590	260	...	3932	28	3404	500	...
B Other government subsectors	89496	111	48554	3823	37008	89434	113	48513	5126	35682
C Rest of the world	...	...	...	...	...	...	...	...	...	...
6 Corporate equity securities [b]	14106	248	13858	...	...	15693	990	14703	...	...
7 Short-term loans, n.e.c. [c]	16973	7773	9115	85	...	19182	9319	9768	95	...
8 Long-term loans, n.e.c. [c]	6757	1960	4797	...	...	5464	813	4651	...	...
A Mortgages	6757	1960	4797	...	...	5464	813	4651	...	...
B Other	...	...	...	...	...	...	...	...	...	...
9 Other receivables	5501	61	3584	1856	...	5598	135	3564	1899	...
10 Other assets	165675	46204	88662	12723	18086	171602	42224	97492	13027	18859
Total assets	692960	104152	353366	180348	55094	724160	108968	368765	191886	54541

Liabilities and net worth

Liabilities	852314	470806	327403	54105	...	900344	499571	345949	54824	...
1 Currency and transferable deposits [a]	4967	2555	2412	...	...	5219	2627	2592	...	...
2 Other deposits	...	...	...	...	...	...	...	...	...	...
3 Bills and bonds, short-term	184964	165199	19442	323	...	181924	164230	17404	290	...
4 Bonds, long-term	554473	271328	245032	38113	...	597613	296569	262389	38655	...
5 Short-term loans, n.e.c. [c]	17722	4	10322	7396	...	18890	4	11495	7391	...
6 Long-term loans, n.e.c. [c]	1345	...	1345	...	...	1340	...	1340	...	...
7 Other payables	15108	63	10315	4730	...	15554	76	10650	4828	...
8 Other liabilities	73735	31657	38535	3543	...	79804	36065	40079	3660	...
Net worth	−159354	−366654	25963	126243	55094	−176184	−390603	22816	137062	54541
Total liabilities and net worth	692960	104152	353366	180348	55094	724160	108968	368765	191886	54541

	1996					1997				
	Total general govern-ment	Central govern-ment	State or provincial govern-ment	Local govern-ment	Social security funds	Total general govern-ment	Central govern-ment	State or provincial govern-ment	Local govern-ment	Social security funds

Assets

Non-financial assets	375818	46310	164746	164762	...	381023	45762	165618	169643	...
1 Tangible assets	375818	46310	164746	164762	...	381023	45762	165618	169643	...
A Stocks	362	362	...	...	...	367	367	...	...	...
B Reproducible fixed assets	300873	38113	131041	131719	...	304867	37575	131669	135623	...

Canada

	1996					1997				
	Total general govern- ment	Central govern- ment	State or provincial govern- ment	Local govern- ment	Social security funds	Total general govern- ment	Central govern- ment	State or provincial govern- ment	Local govern- ment	Social security funds
C Land and other non-reproducible tangible assets	74583	7835	33705	33043	...	75789	7820	33949	34020	...
2 Intangible assets	...	...	...	...	...	...	...	...	...	...
Financial assets	348961	65684	198526	31495	53256	351492	72144	196432	32146	50770
1 Gold and SDRs	...	...	...	...	...	...	...	...	...	...
2 Currency and transferable deposits [a]	17363	5496	6301	5566	...	19879	8936	5306	5637	...
3 Other deposits	...	...	...	...	...	...	...	...	...	...
4 Bills and bonds, short-term	19640	26	14926	4688	...	19326	54	14684	4588	...
5 Bonds, long-term	97078	114	56978	5774	34212	97209	82	58175	6310	32642
A Corporate	3922	5	3356	561	...	3915	5	3392	518	...
B Other government subsectors	93156	109	53622	5213	34212	93294	77	54783	5792	32642
C Rest of the world	...	...	...	...	...	...	...	...	...	...
6 Corporate equity securities [b]	16769	1026	15743	...	...	17714	1539	16175	...	...
7 Short-term loans, n.e.c. [c]	21585	10924	10588	73	...	24403	14007	10350	46	...
8 Long-term loans, n.e.c. [c]	5456	885	4571	...	...	5245	514	4731	...	...
A Mortgages	5456	885	4571	...	...	5245	514	4731	...	...
B Other	...	...	...	...	...	...	...	...	...	...
9 Other receivables	5666	166	3551	1949	...	5648	113	3531	2004	...
10 Other assets	165404	47047	85868	13445	19044	162068	46899	83480	13561	18128
Total assets	724779	111994	363272	196257	53256	732515	117906	362050	201789	50770
Liabilities and net worth									
Liabilities	922828	510765	356770	55293	...	920395	511829	352647	55919	...
1 Currency and transferable deposits [a]	5821	3237	2584	...	...	5968	3342	2626	...	...
2 Other deposits	...	...	...	...	...	...	...	...	...	...
3 Bills and bonds, short-term	158586	142128	16153	305	...	131168	116782	14091	295	...
4 Bonds, long-term	640024	328268	272740	39016	...	661686	346400	276231	39055	...
5 Short-term loans, n.e.c. [c]	19641	7	12323	7311	...	20704	414	12589	7701	...
6 Long-term loans, n.e.c. [c]	1346	...	1346	...	...	1329	...	1329	...	...
7 Other payables	16187	43	11176	4968	...	18511	200	13173	5138	...
8 Other liabilities	81223	37082	40448	3693	...	81029	44691	32608	3730	...
Net worth	−198049	−398771	6502	140964	53256	−187880	−393923	9403	145870	50770
Total liabilities and net worth	724779	111994	363272	196257	53256	732515	117906	362050	201789	50770

a Including item "Other deposits".
b Investment in short-term papers, bonds and corporate equity securities of the rest of the world cannot be split between long-term and short-term by purchasers, the total investment has been allocated to the item "Corporate equity securities".
c Loans other than mortgages are included in item "Short-term loans, n.e.c.".

3.23 Corporate and quasi-corporate enterprise capital accumulation account: total and sectors

Million Canadian dollars

	1986			1987			1988			1989		
	Total	Non-financial	Financial	Total	Non-financial	Financial	Total	Non-financial	Financial	Total	Non-financial	Financial
Finance of gross accumulation												
1 Gross saving	49296	42576	6720	59148	51783	7365	64880	56209	8671	60958	51653	9305
A Consumption of fixed capital	36002	34499	1503	37437	35802	1635	39437	37609	1828	42175	40147	2028
B Net saving	13294	8077	5217	21711	15981	5730	25443	18600	6843	18783	11506	7277
2 Capital transfers [a]	3833	3833	...	3121	3121	...	3864	3864	...	2429	2429	...

Canada

Million Canadian dollars

	1986 Total	1986 Non-financial	1986 Financial	1987 Total	1987 Non-financial	1987 Financial	1988 Total	1988 Non-financial	1988 Financial	1989 Total	1989 Non-financial	1989 Financial
A From resident sectors	3833	3833	...	3121	3121	...	3864	3864	...	2429	2429	...
B From rest of the world	...	...	...	...	...	...	...	...	...	...	...	...
Finance of gross accumulation [b]	53129	46409	6720	62269	54904	7365	68744	60073	8671	63387	54082	9305

Gross accumulation

	Total	Non-financial	Financial	Total	Non-financial	Financial	Total	Non-financial	Financial	Total	Non-financial	Financial
1 Gross capital formation	58476	56705	1771	67110	65547	1563	77089	75268	1821	82939	80410	2529
A Increase in stocks	2076	2294	−218	2915	3568	−653	3827	4547	−720	3653	4127	−474
B Gross fixed capital formation	56400	54411	1989	64195	61979	2216	73262	70721	2541	79286	76283	3003
2 Purchases of land, net [c]	−3034	−3155	121	−3526	−4021	495	−4289	−4783	494	−4810	−5630	820
3 Purchases of intangible assets, net	...	...	...	...	...	...	...	...	...	...	...	...
4 Capital transfers	...	...	...	...	...	...	...	...	...	...	...	...
Net lending	−2313	−7141	4828	−1315	−6622	5307	−4056	−10412	6356	−14742	−20698	5956
Gross accumulation [b]	53129	46409	6720	62269	54904	7365	68744	60073	8671	63387	54082	9305

	1990 Total	1990 Non-financial	1990 Financial	1991 Total	1991 Non-financial	1991 Financial	1992 Total	1992 Non-financial	1992 Financial	1993 Total	1993 Non-financial	1993 Financial

Finance of gross accumulation

1 Gross saving	51416	45155	6261	47862	42078	5784	46608	43364	3244	58902	52028	6874
A Consumption of fixed capital	46132	43904	2228	48198	45814	2384	50546	48151	2395	52730	50220	2510
B Net saving	5284	1251	4033	−336	−3736	3400	−3938	−4787	849	6172	1808	4364
2 Capital transfers [a]	2439	2439	...	2692	2692	...	1996	1996	...	1490	1490	...
A From resident sectors	2439	2439	...	2692	2692	...	1996	1996	...	1490	1490	...
B From rest of the world	...	...	...	...	...	...	...	...	...	...	...	...
Finance of gross accumulation [b]	53855	47594	6261	50554	44770	5784	48604	45360	3244	60392	53518	6874

Gross accumulation

1 Gross capital formation	73287	71089	2198	64898	62570	2328	59817	58266	1551	63023	61917	1106
A Increase in stocks	−3198	−2601	−597	−5841	−5098	−743	−5970	−4734	−1236	−355	1450	−1805
B Gross fixed capital formation	76485	73690	2795	70739	67668	3071	65787	63000	2787	63378	60467	2911
2 Purchases of land, net [c]	−5916	−7309	1393	−5143	−5743	600	−5126	−6143	1017	−4179	−4450	271
3 Purchases of intangible assets, net	...	...	...	...	...	...	...	...	...	...	...	...
4 Capital transfers	...	...	...	...	...	...	...	...	...	...	...	...
Net lending	−13516	−16186	2670	−9201	−12057	2856	−6087	−6763	676	1548	−3949	5497
Gross accumulation [b]	53855	47594	6261	50554	44770	5784	48604	45360	3244	60392	53518	6874

	1994 Total	1994 Non-financial	1994 Financial	1995 Total	1995 Non-financial	1995 Financial	1996 Total	1996 Non-financial	1996 Financial	1997 Total	1997 Non-financial	1997 Financial

Finance of gross accumulation

1 Gross saving	74132	65189	8943	87449	76642	10807	84589	70318	14271	91152	74641	16511
A Consumption of fixed capital	55972	53141	2831	59678	56739	2939	63330	60175	3155	66748	63311	3437
B Net saving	18160	12048	6112	27771	19903	7868	21259	10143	11116	24404	11330	13074
2 Capital transfers [a]	1754	1754	...	1827	1827	...	1673	1673	...	1066	1066	...
A From resident sectors	1754	1754	...	1827	1827	...	1673	1673	...	1066	1066	...
B From rest of the world	...	...	...	...	...	...	...	...	...	...	...	...
Finance of gross accumulation [b]	75886	66943	8943	89276	78469	10807	86262	71991	14271	92218	75707	16511

Gross accumulation

1 Gross capital formation	73052	71155	1897	81319	78279	3040	77391	73884	3507	98623	94956	3667

Canada

	1994			1995			1996			1997		
	Total	Non-financial	Financial	Total	Non-financial	Financial	Total	Non-financial	Financial	Total	Non-financial	Financial
A Increase in stocks	2167	3309	−1142	8014	8262	−248	632	810	−178	8153	8153	...
B Gross fixed capital formation	70885	67846	3039	73305	70017	3288	76759	73074	3685	90470	86803	3667
2 Purchases of land, net [c]	−4138	−5632	1494	−3758	−5202	1444	−2148	−1578	−570	−4736	−4747	11
3 Purchases of intangible assets, net	...	...	...	...	...	...	...	...	...	...	...	...
4 Capital transfers	...	...	...	...	...	...	...	...	...	...	...	...
Net lending	6972	1420	5552	11715	5392	6323	11019	−315	11334	−1669	−14502	12833
Gross accumulation [b]	75886	66943	8943	89276	78469	10807	86262	71991	14271	92218	75707	16511

a Capital transfers are presented on a net basis (capital transfers from other sectors less capital transfers to other sectors).
b Tables 3.22 and 3.23 cover corporate and government business enterprises only.
c Includes "net purchases of tangable assets".

3.24 Corporate and quasi-corporate enterprise capital finance account: total and sectors

Million Canadian dollars

	1986			1987			1988			1989		
	Total	Non-financial	Financial	Total	Non-financial	Financial	Total	Non-financial	Financial	Total	Non-financial	Financial
Acquisition of financial assets
1 Gold and SDRs	881	...	881	5175	...	5175	10172	...	10172	816	...	816
2 Currency and transferable deposits [a]	8628	2495	6133	5359	5776	−417	2946	4517	−1571	2548	3056	−508
3 Other deposits	...	...	...	...	...	...	...	...	...	...	...	...
4 Bills and bonds, short-term	18291	2758	15533	4979	4020	959	15652	2096	13556	12574	2700	9874
5 Bonds, long-term	11726	660	11066	13216	262	12954	9012	1367	7645	12548	654	11894
A Corporate, resident	5625	−46	5671	1777	−56	1833	4594	931	3663	5588	213	5375
B Government	6101	706	5395	11439	318	11121	4418	436	3982	6960	441	6519
C Rest of the world	...	...	...	...	...	...	...	...	...	...	...	...
6 Corporate equity securities [b]	10166	974	9192	3172	724	2448	2811	1088	1723	9851	607	9244
7 Short-term loans, n.e.c. [c]	−4737	183	−4920	13941	683	13258	21931	1021	20910	20133	1388	18745
8 Long-term loans, n.e.c. [c]	23225	−166	23391	30168	115	30053	32969	127	32842	37790	494	37296
A Mortgages	23225	−166	23391	30168	115	30053	32969	127	32842	37790	494	37296
B Other	...	...	...	...	...	...	...	...	...	...	...	...
9 Trade credits and advances	9642	2623	7019	18771	8813	9958	16429	6520	9909	13982	5252	8730
A Consumer credit	6730	...	6730	9710	...	9710	9920	...	9920	8258	...	8258
B Other	2912	2623	289	9061	8813	248	6509	6520	−11	5724	5252	472
10 Other receivables	...	...	...	...	...	...	...	...	...	...	...	...
11 Other assets	36950	16277	20673	26248	8474	17774	22199	15046	7153	40085	20604	19481
Total acquisitions of financial assets	114772	25804	88968	121029	28867	92162	134121	31782	102339	150327	34755	115572
Incurrence of liabilities
1 Currency and transferable deposits [a]	28623	...	28623	29147	...	29147	46130	...	46130	52031	...	52031
2 Other deposits	...	...	...	...	...	...	...	...	...	...	...	...
3 Bills and bonds, short-term	10557	7095	3462	9310	6907	2403	13672	11729	1943	9874	7468	2406
4 Bonds, long-term	12995	7288	5707	7218	4315	2903	14776	6649	8127	13407	10234	3173
5 Corporate equity securities	30652	12852	17800	25629	10527	15102	6039	3846	2193	22576	10626	11950
6 Short-term loans, n.e.c. [c]	−238	−804	566	9075	5444	3631	17639	10994	6645	22547	13709	8838
7 Long-term loans, n.e.c. [c]	3112	3263	−151	6006	5686	320	8907	8986	−79	11174	10947	227
8 Net equity of households in life insurance and pension fund reserves	18337	...	18337	17824	...	17824	21286	...	21286	24399	...	24399

Canada

Million Canadian dollars

	1986 Total	1986 Non-financial	1986 Financial	1987 Total	1987 Non-financial	1987 Financial	1988 Total	1988 Non-financial	1988 Financial	1989 Total	1989 Non-financial	1989 Financial
9 Proprietors' net additions to the accumulation of quasi-corporations [d]	12870	6364	6506	12182	3343	8839	13102	4742	8360	8027	5314	2713
10 Trade credits and advances	–166	–308	142	3777	3706	71	826	943	–117	1713	1712	1
11 Other accounts payable	...	...	...	...	...	...	...	...	...	...	...	...
12 Other liabilities	5943	2063	3880	4165	–3639	7804	3010	–2835	5845	2816	–3291	6107
Total incurrence of liabilities	122685	37813	84872	124333	36289	88044	145387	45054	100333	168564	56719	111845
Statistical discrepancy [e]	–5600	–4868	–732	–1989	–800	–1189	–7210	–2860	–4350	–3495	–1266	–2229
Net lending	–2313	–7141	4828	–1315	–6622	5307	–4056	–10412	6356	–14742	–20698	5956
Incurrence of liabilities and net lending	114772	25804	88968	121029	28867	92162	134121	31782	102339	150327	34755	115572

	1990 Total	1990 Non-financial	1990 Financial	1991 Total	1991 Non-financial	1991 Financial	1992 Total	1992 Non-financial	1992 Financial	1993 Total	1993 Non-financial	1993 Financial
Acquisition of financial assets												
1 Gold and SDRs	1246	...	1246	–2103	...	–2103	–5750	...	–5750	1206	...	1206
2 Currency and transferable deposits [a]	1495	2275	–780	5313	846	4467	5570	8831	–3261	587	4175	–3588
3 Other deposits	...	...	...	...	...	...	...	...	...	...	...	...
4 Bills and bonds, short-term	9671	1200	8471	6668	–2123	8791	3973	1055	2918	21167	1649	19518
5 Bonds, long-term	14319	1206	13113	25724	618	25106	23866	1298	22568	35397	–704	36101
A Corporate, resident	4524	587	3937	4479	191	4288	4672	296	4376	3811	331	3480
B Government	9795	619	9176	21245	427	20818	19194	1002	18192	31586	–1035	32621
C Rest of the world	...	...	...	...	...	...	...	...	...	...	...	...
6 Corporate equity securities [b]	11280	615	10665	18060	–434	18494	17724	32	17692	25587	843	24744
7 Short-term loans, n.e.c. [c]	12742	1849	10893	8552	2178	6374	11120	295	10825	3177	2005	1172
8 Long-term loans, n.e.c. [c]	30585	120	30465	25928	496	25432	27520	–668	28188	19562	673	18889
A Mortgages	30585	120	30465	25928	496	25432	27520	–668	28188	19562	673	18889
B Other	...	...	...	...	...	...	...	...	...	...	...	...
9 Trade credits and advances	9676	3774	5902	7201	4983	2218	5703	4780	923	14437	9414	5023
A Consumer credit	5394	...	5394	1713	...	1713	456	...	456	4719	...	4719
B Other	4282	3774	508	5488	4983	505	5247	4780	467	9718	9414	304
10 Other receivables	...	...	...	...	...	...	...	...	...	...	...	...
11 Other assets	33104	16809	16295	29777	21212	8565	32162	16467	15695	31826	23185	8641
Total acquisitions of financial assets	124118	27848	96270	125120	27776	97344	121888	32090	89798	152946	41240	111706
Incurrence of liabilities												
1 Currency and transferable deposits [a]	37236	...	37236	20398	...	20398	29093	...	29093	7226	...	7226
2 Other deposits	...	...	...	...	...	...	...	...	...	...	...	...
3 Bills and bonds, short-term	2083	2673	–590	–9272	–7178	–2094	–11977	–12278	301	5640	5321	319
4 Bonds, long-term	13941	8869	5072	26182	16680	9502	12951	7164	5787	14979	6024	8955
5 Corporate equity securities	16628	6507	10121	30456	8445	22011	25923	9138	16785	54775	14968	39807
6 Short-term loans, n.e.c. [c]	11738	12944	–1206	8948	4395	4553	7983	5905	2078	–3530	–2398	–1132
7 Long-term loans, n.e.c. [c]	9329	9287	42	7537	7480	57	7693	8093	–400	3236	3688	–452
8 Net equity of households in life insurance and pension fund reserves	26747	...	26747	27021	...	27021	27464	...	27464	24591	...	24591
9 Proprietors' net additions to the accumulation of quasi-corporations [d]	11916	6642	5274	17346	10535	6811	9742	9845	–103	10251	8180	2071
10 Trade credits and advances	1408	1392	16	2275	2153	122	1513	1366	147	6447	6079	368
11 Other accounts payable	...	...	...	...	...	...	...	...	...	...	...	...

Canada

	1990			1991			1992			1993		
	Total	Non-financial	Financial	Total	Non-financial	Financial	Total	Non-financial	Financial	Total	Non-financial	Financial
12 Other liabilities	9395	–1342	10737	9342	781	8561	8901	5560	3341	31475	3431	28044
Total incurrence of liabilities	140421	46972	93449	140233	43291	96942	119286	34793	84493	155090	45293	109797
Statistical discrepancy [e]	–2787	–2938	151	–5912	–3458	–2454	8689	4060	4629	–3692	–104	–3588
Net lending	–13516	–16186	2670	–9201	–12057	2856	–6087	–6763	676	1548	–3949	5497
Incurrence of liabilities and net lending	124118	27848	96270	125120	27776	97344	121888	32090	89798	152946	41240	111706

	1994			1995			1996			1997		
	Total	Non-financial	Financial	Total	Non-financial	Financial	Total	Non-financial	Financial	Total	Non-financial	Financial

Acquisition of financial assets

1 Gold and SDRs	–491	...	–491	3776	...	3776	7497	...	7497	–3390	...	–3390
2 Currency and transferable deposits [a]	8878	3342	5536	13854	8189	5665	32059	18248	13811	28468	17822	10646
3 Other deposits	...	...	...	...	...	...	...	...	...	...	...	...
4 Bills and bonds, short-term	613	–1837	2450	5064	3112	1952	5899	–551	6450	5299	1811	3488
5 Bonds, long-term	35276	970	34306	21353	64	21289	25267	–174	25441	33618	–223	33841
A Corporate, resident	3309	–4	3313	6792	339	6453	4883	420	4463	9210	–304	9514
B Government	31967	974	30993	14561	–275	14836	20384	–594	20978	24408	81	24327
C Rest of the world	...	...	...	...	...	...	...	...	...	...	...	...
6 Corporate equity securities [b]	26105	–312	26417	23801	1079	22722	49888	966	48922	40191	582	39609
7 Short-term loans, n.e.c. [c]	19078	4329	14749	10406	–528	10934	10544	–378	10922	28027	2282	25745
8 Long-term loans, n.e.c. [c]	15474	181	15293	10733	–374	11107	17206	–797	18003	18037	23	18014
A Mortgages	15474	181	15293	10733	–374	11107	17206	–797	18003	18037	23	18014
B Other	...	...	...	...	...	...	...	...	...	...	...	...
9 Trade credits and advances	14544	7164	7380	19129	11905	7224	17651	9253	8398	20027	10793	9234
A Consumer credit	7049	...	7049	6718	...	6718	7275	...	7275	9429	...	9429
B Other	7495	7164	331	12411	11905	506	10376	9253	1123	10598	10793	–195
10 Other receivables	...	...	...	...	...	...	...	...	...	...	...	...
11 Other assets	59029	25563	33466	48620	22236	26384	75161	14516	60645	101204	32869	68335
Total acquisitions of financial assets	178506	39400	139106	156736	45683	111053	241172	41083	200089	271481	65959	205522

Incurrence of liabilities

1 Currency and transferable deposits [a]	35447	...	35447	25759	...	25759	35680	...	35680	44511	...	44511
2 Other deposits	...	...	...	...	...	...	...	...	...	...	...	...
3 Bills and bonds, short-term	2680	–311	2991	6041	1977	4064	12239	4599	7640	27042	7132	19910
4 Bonds, long-term	17538	8909	8629	16569	10580	5989	5561	1824	3737	25081	10765	14316
5 Corporate equity securities	44822	16806	28016	24986	10042	14944	73907	20425	53482	85062	23028	62034
6 Short-term loans, n.e.c. [c]	15009	11616	3393	6095	2995	3100	4411	603	3808	14964	8887	6077
7 Long-term loans, n.e.c. [c]	565	–460	1025	–1732	–1713	–19	259	386	–127	1276	1050	226
8 Net equity of households in life insurance and pension fund reserves	21704	...	21704	22800	...	22800	16407	...	16407	25817	...	25817
9 Proprietors' net additions to the accumulation of quasi-corporations [d]	17738	10112	7626	14211	9074	5137	21771	625	21146	27604	10107	17497
10 Trade credits and advances	5640	5733	–93	6012	5993	19	4573	4485	88	10349	10601	–252
11 Other accounts payable	...	...	...	...	...	...	...	...	...	...	...	...
12 Other liabilities	11587	–5774	17361	17215	167	17048	52070	5002	47068	23462	8930	14532
Total incurrence of liabilities	172730	46631	126099	137956	39115	98841	226878	37949	188929	285168	80500	204668
Statistical discrepancy [e]	–1196	–8651	7455	7065	1176	5889	3275	3449	–174	–12018	–39	–11979
Net lending	6972	1420	5552	11715	5392	6323	11019	–315	11334	–1669	–14502	12833
Incurrence of liabilities and net lending	178506	39400	139106	156736	45683	111053	241172	41083	200089	271481	65959	205522

Canada

	1994			1995			1996			1997		
	Total	Non-financial	Financial	Total	Non-financial	Financial	Total	Non-financial	Financial	Total	Non-financial	Financial

a Including item "Other deposits".
b Investment in short-term papers, bonds and corporate equity securities of the rest of the world cannot be split between long-term and short-term by purchasers, the total investment has been allocated to the item "Corporate equity securities".
c Loans other than mortgages are included in item "Short-term loans, n.e.c.".
d Item "Proprietors' net additions to the accumulation of quasi-corporations" consists of corporate and government claims on their associated enterprises.
e The statistical discrepancy equals the difference between net lending in the Income and Expenditure Accounts and net acquisition of financial assets in the Financial Flow Accounts (change in financial assets less change in liabilities).

3.25 Corporate and quasi-corporate enterprise balance sheet: total and sectors

Million Canadian dollars

	1986			1987			1988			1989		
	Total	Non-financial	Financial	Total	Non-financial	Financial	Total	Non-financial	Financial	Total	Non-financial	Financial
Assets												
Non-financial assets	733878	701498	32380	783941	749293	34648	846796	808286	38510	912336	869326	43010
1 Tangible assets	733878	701498	32380	783941	749293	34648	846796	808286	38510	912336	869326	43010
A Stocks	91410	91410	...	98166	98166	...	105402	105402	...	110193	110193	...
B Reproducible fixed assets	533564	506738	26826	567680	538985	28695	612343	580501	31842	659565	624022	35543
C Land and other non-reproducible tangible assets	108904	103350	5554	118095	112142	5953	129051	122383	6668	142578	135111	7467
2 Intangible assets	...	...	...	...	...	...	...	...	...	...	...	...
Financial assets	1223939	305515	918424	1349070	337165	1011905	1479493	370800	1108693	1641659	409252	1232407
1 Gold and SDRs	5653	...	5653	10658	...	10658	19317	...	19317	19455	...	19455
2 Currency and transferable deposits [a]	99194	43466	55728	103314	49158	54156	103129	53074	50055	104140	55574	48566
3 Other deposits	...	...	...	...	...	...	...	...	...	...	...	...
4 Bills and bonds, short-term	84005	13047	70958	91564	18604	72960	109185	20375	88810	125556	25079	100477
5 Bonds, long-term	151951	3895	148056	164677	4135	160542	176382	5283	171099	198430	6250	192180
A Corporate, resident	39206	552	38654	40360	481	39879	46131	1167	44964	53933	1419	52514
B Government	112745	3343	109402	124317	3654	120663	130251	4116	126135	144497	4831	139666
C Rest of the world	...	...	...	...	...	...	...	...	...	...	...	...
6 Corporate equity securities [b]	102429	6632	95797	114135	7934	106201	118421	8199	110222	131744	8787	122957
7 Short-term loans, n.e.c. [c]	170395	6990	163405	176310	7237	169073	188448	6833	181615	203268	7097	196171
8 Long-term loans, n.e.c. [c]	187736	5827	181909	218934	6007	212927	251689	6312	245377	288875	6755	282120
A Mortgages	187736	5827	181909	218934	6007	212927	251689	6312	245377	288875	6755	282120
B Other	...	...	...	...	...	...	...	...	...	...	...	...
9 Trade credits and allowances	156540	91411	65129	173672	98787	74885	189138	104908	84230	203770	110549	93221
A Consumer credit	64725	1700	63025	74239	1700	72539	83693	1700	81993	91993	1700	90293
B Other	91815	89711	2104	99433	97087	2346	105445	103208	2237	111777	108849	2928
10 Other receivables	...	...	...	...	...	...	...	...	...	...	...	...
11 Other assets	266036	134247	131789	295806	145303	150503	323784	165816	157968	366421	189161	177260
Total assets	1957817	1007013	950804	2133011	1086458	1046553	2326289	1179086	1147203	2553995	1278578	1275417
Liabilities and net worth												
Liabilities	1784127	839514	944613	1942198	901576	1040622	2106321	972500	1133821	2315899	1051331	1264568
1 Currency and transferable deposits [a]	420529	...	420529	446888	...	446888	488828	...	488828	540562	...	540562
2 Other deposits	...	...	...	...	...	...	...	...	...	...	...	...
3 Bills and bonds, short-term	38783	26635	12148	48293	33191	15102	61813	45631	16182	70909	52186	18723
4 Bonds, long-term	145430	117061	28369	151798	121440	30358	161813	123939	37874	172431	132777	39654
5 Corporate equity securities	419744	297497	122247	465577	323942	141635	499055	348125	150930	538309	372012	166297
6 Short-term loans, n.e.c. [c]	142818	120922	21896	148260	125193	23067	155195	132002	23193	176093	145462	30631
7 Long-term loans, n.e.c. [c]	37305	36669	636	43024	42085	939	51489	50530	959	61869	60820	1049

Canada

Million Canadian dollars

	1986			1987			1988			1989		
	Total	Non-financial	Financial	Total	Non-financial	Financial	Total	Non-financial	Financial	Total	Non-financial	Financial
8 Net equity of households in life insurance and pension fund reserves	208371	...	208371	232898	...	232898	257081	...	257081	295715	...	295715
9 Proprietors' net equity in quasi-corporations [d]	195404	113204	82200	217907	121709	96198	234793	134997	99796	249032	146902	102130
10 Trade credits and advances	82051	81311	740	89682	88837	845	93460	92719	741	98749	97955	794
11 Other accounts payable	...	...	...	...	...	...	...	...	...	...	...	...
12 Other liabilities	93692	46215	47477	97871	45179	52692	102794	44557	58237	112230	43217	69013
Net worth	173690	167499	6191	190813	184882	5931	219968	206586	13382	238096	227247	10849
Total liabilities and net worth	1957817	1007013	950804	2133011	1086458	1046553	2326289	1179086	1147203	2553995	1278578	1275417

	1990			1991			1992			1993		
	Total	Non-financial	Financial	Total	Non-financial	Financial	Total	Non-financial	Financial	Total	Non-financial	Financial
Assets												
Non-financial assets	958195	911906	46289	965292	916957	48335	974045	923088	50957	1000358	947815	52543
1 Tangible assets	958195	911906	46289	965292	916957	48335	974045	923088	50957	1000358	947815	52543
A Stocks	107303	107303	...	102106	102106	...	101930	101930	...	105193	105193	...
B Reproducible fixed assets	700477	662153	38324	707959	668053	39906	713696	671685	42011	730891	687656	43235
C Land and other non-reproducible tangible assets	150415	142450	7965	155227	146798	8429	158419	149473	8946	164274	154966	9308
2 Intangible assets	...	...	...	...	...	...	...	...	...	...	...	...
Financial assets	1762917	433555	1329362	1873732	448645	1425087	1998280	469124	1529156	2156944	501413	1655531
1 Gold and SDRs	21551	...	21551	19529	...	19529	15135	...	15135	16881	...	16881
2 Currency and transferable deposits [a]	108683	58976	49707	113328	60125	53203	119727	68363	51364	120853	73526	47327
3 Other deposits	...	...	...	...	...	...	...	...	...	...	...	...
4 Bills and bonds, short-term	133701	25276	108425	138505	20872	117633	135205	17384	117821	153750	17368	136382
5 Bonds, long-term	210435	6707	203728	237293	7477	229816	262098	8233	253865	296203	7382	288821
A Corporate, resident	57737	2084	55653	61410	2407	59003	66747	2661	64086	73617	3069	70548
B Government	152698	4623	148075	175883	5070	170813	195351	5572	189779	222586	4313	218273
C Rest of the world	...	...	...	...	...	...	...	...	...	...	...	...
6 Corporate equity securities [b]	142524	9066	133458	161544	8020	153524	182195	7751	174444	218552	7272	211280
7 Short-term loans, n.e.c. [c]	212645	9008	203637	214737	9879	204858	220257	12556	207701	213618	12182	201436
8 Long-term loans, n.e.c. [c]	318684	6794	311890	343467	6546	336921	370785	6507	364278	389197	7223	381974
A Mortgages	318684	6794	311890	343467	6546	336921	370785	6507	364278	389197	7223	381974
B Other	...	...	...	...	...	...	...	...	...	...	...	...
9 Trade credits and allowances	212158	113481	98677	219145	117740	101405	224793	122601	102192	238387	130990	107397
A Consumer credit	96767	1700	95067	98986	1700	97286	99371	1700	97671	104179	1700	102479
B Other	115391	111781	3610	120159	116040	4119	125422	120901	4521	134208	129290	4918
10 Other receivables	...	...	...	...	...	...	...	...	...	...	...	...
11 Other assets	402536	204247	198289	426184	217986	208198	468085	225729	242356	509503	245470	264033
Total assets	2721112	1345461	1375651	2839024	1365602	1473422	2972325	1392212	1580113	3157302	1449228	1708074
Liabilities and net worth												
Liabilities	2463176	1101653	1361523	2611171	1149401	1461770	2764767	1187552	1577215	2953663	1239499	1714164
1 Currency and transferable deposits [a]	580138	...	580138	597985	...	597985	634369	...	634369	643951	...	643951
2 Other deposits	...	...	...	...	...	...	...	...	...	...	...	...
3 Bills and bonds, short-term	70473	52747	17726	60250	45127	15123	46611	32552	14059	54610	39450	15160
4 Bonds, long-term	190339	141016	49323	215709	157721	57988	233363	167437	65926	253020	175837	77183
5 Corporate equity securities	559897	383889	176008	596886	393579	203307	637820	403727	234093	705517	424197	281320
6 Short-term loans, n.e.c. [c]	184842	155901	28941	190134	157592	32542	195773	163065	32708	185090	155692	29398
7 Long-term loans, n.e.c. [c]	71108	69969	1139	77947	76572	1375	86300	84732	1568	89351	88199	1152

Canada

	1990			1991			1992			1993		
	Total	Non-financial	Financial	Total	Non-financial	Financial	Total	Non-financial	Financial	Total	Non-financial	Financial
8 Net equity of households in life insurance and pension fund reserves	322248	...	322248	351993	...	351993	379893	...	379893	411879	...	411879
9 Proprietors' net equity in quasi-corporations [d]	263145	155612	107533	274593	162140	112453	280655	167954	112701	283897	169643	114254
10 Trade credits and advances	101235	100353	882	106951	105942	1009	111320	110197	1123	119714	118226	1488
11 Other accounts payable	...	...	...	...	...	...	...	...	...	...	...	...
12 Other liabilities	119751	42166	77585	138723	50728	87995	158663	57888	100775	206634	68255	138379
Net worth	257936	243808	14128	227853	216201	11652	207558	204660	2898	203639	209729	–6090
Total liabilities and net worth	2721112	1345461	1375651	2839024	1365602	1473422	2972325	1392212	1580113	3157302	1449228	1708074

	1994			1995			1996			1997		
	Total	Non-financial	Financial	Total	Non-financial	Financial	Total	Non-financial	Financial	Total	Non-financial	Financial

Assets

Non-financial assets	1049148	995156	53992	1085139	1029417	55722	1105153	1047584	57569	1147301	1085965	61336
1 Tangible assets	1049148	995156	53992	1085139	1029417	55722	1105153	1047584	57569	1147301	1085965	61336
A Stocks	114745	114745	...	124890	124890	...	127262	127262	...	134593	134593	...
B Reproducible fixed assets	761361	716964	44397	781239	735484	45755	793443	746220	47223	822302	771801	50501
C Land and other non-reproducible tangible assets	173042	163447	9595	179010	169043	9967	184448	174102	10346	190406	179571	10835
2 Intangible assets	...	...	...	...	...	...	...	...	...	...	...	...
Financial assets	2357573	549672	1807901	2522990	602756	1920234	2771952	648501	2123451	3031728	683075	2348653
1 Gold and SDRs	17486	...	17486	20766	...	20766	28202	...	28202	25704	...	25704
2 Currency and transferable deposits [a]	134013	78631	55382	144078	86149	57929	174852	104424	70428	196576	116418	80158
3 Other deposits	...	...	...	...	...	...	...	...	...	...	...	...
4 Bills and bonds, short-term	155883	16504	139379	161483	18774	142709	157828	17209	140619	162422	18542	143880
5 Bonds, long-term	336369	10832	325537	366361	10950	355411	396154	9558	386596	429385	10250	419135
A Corporate, resident	76566	3222	73344	83708	3773	79935	91664	4063	87601	97655	3371	94284
B Government	259803	7610	252193	282653	7177	275476	304490	5495	298995	331730	6879	324851
C Rest of the world	...	...	...	...	...	...	...	...	...	...	...	...
6 Corporate equity securities [b]	256807	7354	249453	289631	8195	281436	348728	9057	339671	396482	10074	386408
7 Short-term loans, n.e.c. [c]	229955	14340	215615	238228	14459	223769	244318	14233	230085	264410	15144	249266
8 Long-term loans, n.e.c. [c]	404415	7954	396461	416151	7997	408154	432413	7845	424568	449272	7724	441548
A Mortgages	404415	7954	396461	416151	7997	408154	432413	7845	424568	449272	7724	441548
B Other	...	...	...	...	...	...	...	...	...	...	...	...
9 Trade credits and allowances	252292	137613	114679	267128	146505	120623	284404	156423	127981	300777	162005	138772
A Consumer credit	110955	1700	109255	116312	1700	114612	122771	1700	121071	133424	1700	131724
B Other	141337	135913	5424	150816	144805	6011	161633	154723	6910	167353	160305	7048
10 Other receivables	...	...	...	...	...	...	...	...	...	...	...	...
11 Other assets	570353	276444	293909	619164	309727	309437	705053	329752	375301	806700	342918	463782
Total assets	3406721	1544828	1861893	3608129	1632173	1975956	3877105	1696085	2181020	4179029	1769040	2409989

Liabilities and net worth

Liabilities	3179527	1321536	1857991	3373640	1380113	1993527	3661030	1447087	2213943	3996937	1524978	2471959
1 Currency and transferable deposits [a]	678224	...	678224	704204	...	704204	739229	...	739229	785080	...	785080
2 Other deposits	...	...	...	...	...	...	...	...	...	...	...	...
3 Bills and bonds, short-term	58644	39161	19483	64329	41365	22964	73851	44528	29323	99673	52669	47004
4 Bonds, long-term	273192	187090	86102	284640	193696	90944	295670	198828	96842	320333	205599	114734
5 Corporate equity securities	763255	453899	309356	818881	485343	333538	913356	519901	393455	1002800	557430	445370
6 Short-term loans, n.e.c. [c]	195745	164689	31056	198771	166342	32429	200195	166507	33688	206539	172732	33807
7 Long-term loans, n.e.c. [c]	89468	87881	1587	87418	86075	1343	87538	86401	1137	88773	87388	1385

Canada

	1994			1995			1996			1997		
	Total	Non-financial	Financial	Total	Non-financial	Financial	Total	Non-financial	Financial	Total	Non-financial	Financial
8 Net equity of households in life insurance and pension fund reserves	446615	...	446615	484824	...	484824	519351	...	519351	577097	...	577097
9 Proprietors' net equity in quasi-corporations [d]	314561	185873	128688	330307	190550	139757	362602	197283	165319	401947	209319	192628
10 Trade credits and advances	126979	125472	1507	136055	134482	1573	144202	142574	1628	147357	145926	1431
11 Other accounts payable	...	...	...	...	...	...	...	...	...	...	...	...
12 Other liabilities	232844	77471	155373	264211	82260	181951	325036	91065	233971	367338	93915	273423
Net worth	227194	223292	3902	234489	252060	−17571	216075	248998	−32923	182092	244062	−61970
Total liabilities and net worth	3406721	1544828	1861893	3608129	1632173	1975956	3877105	1696085	2181020	4179029	1769040	2409989

a Including item "Other deposits".
b Investment in short-term papers, bonds and corporate equity securities of the rest of the world cannot be split between long-term and short-term by purchasers, the total investment has been allocated to the item "Corporate equity securities".
c Loans other than mortgages are included in item "Short-term loans, n.e.c.".
d Item "Proprietors' net additions to the accumulation of quasi-corporations" consists of corporate and government claims on their associated enterprises.

3.26 Financial transactions of financial institutions: detail

Million Canadian dollars

	1986				1987				
	All financial institutions	Central bank	Other monetary institutions	Insurance	Other financial institutions	All financial institutions	Central bank	Other monetary institutions	Insurance	Other financial institutions
Acquisition of financial assets										
1 Gold and SDRs	881	881	–	–	–	5175	5175	–	–	–
A Gold	1012	1012	–	–	–	5200	5200	–	–	–
B Net acquisitions of SDRs	−131	−131	–	–	–	−25	−25	–	–	–
2 Currency and transferable deposits [a]	6133	–	4448	396	1289	−417	–	−4241	416	3408
A Liability of resident institutions	3677	–	1873	382	1422	2642	–	312	−106	2436
B Liability of rest of the world	2456	–	2575	14	−133	−3059	–	−4553	522	972
3 Other deposits	–	–	–	–	–	–	–	–	–	–
A Liability of resident institutions	–	–	–	–	–	–	–	–	–	–
B Liability of rest of the world	–	–	–	–	–	–	–	–	–	–
4 Bills and bonds, short-term	15533	3895	4672	2511	4455	959	1708	−5463	4032	682
A Corporate and quasi-corporate, resident	–	–	–	–	–	–	–	–	–	–
B Government	–	–	–	–	–	–	–	–	–	–
C Rest of the world	–	–	–	–	–	–	–	–	–	–
5 Bonds, long-term	11066	−1276	183	10482	1677	12954	112	871	10756	1215
6 Corporate equity securities [b]	9192	–	−419	2915	6696	2448	–	−1090	915	2623
7 Short-term loans, n.e.c. [c]	−4920	−2676	−4053	−61	1870	13258	95	9732	123	3308
A Liability of resident sectors	–	–	–	–	–	–	–	–	–	–
B Liability of rest of the world	–	–	–	–	–	–	–	–	–	–
8 Long-term loans, n.e.c. [c]	23391	–	18713	4140	538	30053	–	24394	4170	1489
A Mortgages	23391	–	18713	4140	538	30053	–	24394	4170	1489
B Other	–	–	–	–	–	–	–	–	–	–
9 Trade credits and advances	7019	–	5447	310	1262	9958	–	8751	237	970
A Consumer credit	6730	–	5447	–	1283	9710	–	8751	7	952
B Other	289	–	–	310	−21	248	–	–	230	18
10 Other assets	20673	−13	8479	743	11464	17774	−8	1743	822	15217
Total acquisitions of financial assets	88968	811	37470	21436	29251	92162	7082	34697	21471	28912

Canada

Million Canadian dollars

	1986					1987				
	All financial institutions	Central bank	Other monetary institutions	Insurance	Other financial institutions	All financial institutions	Central bank	Other monetary institutions	Insurance	Other financial institutions

Incurrence of liabilities

1 Currency and transferable deposits [a]	28623	1232	26875	–	516	29147	2034	26803	–	310
2 Other deposits	–	–	–	–	–	–	–	–	–	–
3 Bills and bonds, short-term	3462	–	59	–	3403	2403	–	–25	–	2428
4 Bonds, long-term	5707	–	1711	–	3996	2903	–	–1439	–	4342
5 Corporate equity securities	17800	–	2598	517	14685	15102	–	2323	391	12388
6 Short-term loans, n.e.c. [c]	566	–	–2023	363	2226	3631	–	478	65	3088
7 Long-term loans, n.e.c. [c]	–151	–	–31	5	–125	320	–	8	206	106
8 Net equity of households in life insurance and pension fund reserves [d]	18337	–	–	18337	–	17824	–	–	17824	–
9 Other liabilities	10528	–619	5067	1891	4189	16714	4398	3770	2924	5622
Total incurrence of liabilities	84872	613	34256	21113	28890	88044	6432	31918	21410	28284
Statistical discrepancy [e]	732	–	853	–	–121	1189	–	1943	–	–754
Net lending	4828	198	4067	323	240	5307	650	4722	61	–126
Incurrence of liabilities and net lending	88968	811	37470	21436	29251	92162	7082	34697	21471	28912

	1988					1989				
	All financial institutions	Central bank	Other monetary institutions	Insurance	Other financial institutions	All financial institutions	Central bank	Other monetary institutions	Insurance	Other financial institutions

Acquisition of financial assets

1 Gold and SDRs	10172	10172	–	–	–	816	816	–	–	–
A Gold	9087	9087	–	–	–	732	732	–	–	–
B Net acquisitions of SDRs	1085	1085	–	–	–	84	84	–	–	–
2 Currency and transferable deposits [a]	–1571	–	–3425	–888	2742	–508	–	–774	252	14
A Liability of resident institutions	660	–	–747	–402	1809	–544	–	–683	181	–42
B Liability of rest of the world	–2231	–	–2678	–486	933	36	–	–91	71	56
3 Other deposits	–	–	–	–	–	–	–	–	–	–
A Liability of resident institutions	–	–	–	–	–	–	–	–	–	–
B Liability of rest of the world	–	–	–	–	–	–	–	–	–	–
4 Bills and bonds, short-term	13556	173	8828	5248	–693	9874	1131	6896	–653	2500
A Corporate and quasi-corporate, resident	–	–	–	–	–	–	–	–	–	–
B Government	–	–	–	–	–	–	–	–	–	–
C Rest of the world	–	–	–	–	–	–	–	–	–	–
5 Bonds, long-term	7645	142	–1049	8293	259	11894	–652	–2489	13137	1898
6 Corporate equity securities [b]	1723	–	–2039	4068	–306	9244	–	1678	6641	925
7 Short-term loans, n.e.c. [c]	20910	–478	17862	309	3217	18745[b]	–173[b]	17840[b]	19[b]	1059[b]
A Liability of resident sectors	–	–	–	–	–	–	–	–	–	–
B Liability of rest of the world	–	–	–	–	–	–	–	–	–	–
8 Long-term loans, n.e.c. [c]	32842	–	27981	4582	279	37296	–	29385	6310	1601
A Mortgages	32842	–	27981	4582	279	37296	–	29385	6310	1601
B Other	–	–	–	–	–	–	–	–	–	–
9 Trade credits and advances	9909	–	8973	68	868	8730	–	6778	410	1542
A Consumer credit	9920	–	8973	51	896	8258	–	6778	13	1467
B Other	–11	–	–	17	–28	472	–	–	397	75

Canada

	1988					1989				
	All financial institutions	Central bank	Other monetary institutions	Insurance	Other financial institutions	All financial institutions	Central bank	Other monetary institutions	Insurance	Other financial institutions
10 Other assets	7153	−36	−8656	2018	13827	19481	−22	1448	196	17859
Total acquisitions of financial assets	102339	9973	48475	23698	20193	115572	1100	60762	26312	27398

Incurrence of liabilities

	All financial institutions	Central bank	Other monetary institutions	Insurance	Other financial institutions	All financial institutions	Central bank	Other monetary institutions	Insurance	Other financial institutions
1 Currency and transferable deposits [a]	46130	971	44263	–	896	52031	716	51268	–	47
2 Other deposits	–	–	–	–	–	–	–	–	–	–
3 Bills and bonds, short-term	1943	–	−4	–	1947	2406	–	5	–	2401
4 Bonds, long-term	8127	–	3102	–	5025	3173	–	460	–	2713
5 Corporate equity securities	2193	–	1651	421	121	11950	–	2743	356	8851
6 Short-term loans, n.e.c. [c]	6645	–	484	−370	6531	8838	–	−1058	467	9429
7 Long-term loans, n.e.c. [c]	−79	–	25	−87	−17	227	–	−5	226	6
8 Net equity of households in life insurance and pension fund reserves [d]	21286	–	–	21286	–	24399[c]	–[c]	–[c]	24399[c]	–[c]
9 Other liabilities	14088	8281	−2320	2231	5896	8821	−92	3740	1892	3281
Total incurrence of liabilities	100333	9252	47201	23481	20399	111845	624	57153	27340	26728
Statistical discrepancy [e]	4350	–	4068	–	284	2229	–	1502	–	727
Net lending	6356	721	5340	217	78	5956	476	5111	−1028	1397
Incurrence of liabilities and net lending	102339	9973	48475	23698	20193	115572	1100	60762	26312	27398

	1990					1991				
	All financial institutions	Central bank	Other monetary institutions	Insurance	Other financial institutions	All financial institutions	Central bank	Other monetary institutions	Insurance	Other financial institutions

Acquisition of financial assets

1 Gold and SDRs	1246	1246	–	–	–	−2103	−2103	–	–	–
A Gold	1271	1271	–	–	–	−2238	−2238	–	–	–
B Net acquisitions of SDRs	−25	−25	–	–	–	135	135	–	–	–
2 Currency and transferable deposits [a]	−780	–	−354	209	−635	4467	–	3640	266	561
A Liability of resident institutions	−1084	–	−333	181	−932	2636	–	1755	220	661
B Liability of rest of the world	304	–	−21	28	297	1831	–	1885	46	−100
3 Other deposits	–	–	–	–	–	–	–	–	–	–
A Liability of resident institutions	–	–	–	–	–	–	–	–	–	–
B Liability of rest of the world	–	–	–	–	–	–	–	–	–	–
4 Bills and bonds, short-term	8471	−568	5967	1775	1297	8791	2571	5788	−4166	4598
A Corporate and quasi-corporate, resident	–	–	–	–	–	–	–	–	–	–
B Government	–	–	–	–	–	–	–	–	–	–
C Rest of the world	–	–	–	–	–	–	–	–	–	–
5 Bonds, long-term	13113	−258	1702	9926	1743	25106	−474	9276	13223	3081
6 Corporate equity securities [b]	10665	–	2718	6900	1047	18494	–	−609	15258	3845
7 Short-term loans, n.e.c. [bc]	10893	159	8972	−74	1836	6374	703	4154	241	1276
A Liability of resident sectors	–	–	–	–	–	–	–	–	–	–
B Liability of rest of the world	–	–	–	–	–	–	–	–	–	–
8 Long-term loans, n.e.c. [c]	30465	–	21788	6201	2476	25432	–	17764	3346	4322
A Mortgages	30465	–	21788	6201	2476	25432	–	17764	3346	4322
B Other	–	–	–	–	–	–	–	–	–	–
9 Trade credits and advances	5902	–	4682	635	585	2218	–	1758	692	−232

Canada

	1990					1991				
	All financial institutions	Central bank	Other monetary institutions	Insurance	Other financial institutions	All financial institutions	Central bank	Other monetary institutions	Insurance	Other financial institutions
A Consumer credit	5394	–	4682	156	556	1713	–	1758	181	–226
B Other	508	–	–	479	29	505	–	–	511	–6
10 Other assets	16295	–8	4111	2805	9387	8565	23	–5797	1107	13232
Total acquisitions of financial assets	96270	571	49586	28377	17736	97344	720	35974	29967	30683

Incurrence of liabilities

1 Currency and transferable deposits [a]	37236	489	36369	–	378	20398	1863	18259	–	276
2 Other deposits	–	–	–	–	–	–	–	–	–	–
3 Bills and bonds, short-term	–590	–	–	–	–590	–2094	–	–	–	–2094
4 Bonds, long-term	5072	–	1590	1	3481	9502	–	3051	–4	6455
5 Corporate equity securities	10121	–	1379	506	8236	22011	–	2658	812	18541
6 Short-term loans, n.e.c. [c]	–1206	–	–101	–104	–1001	4553	–	1416	–130	3267
7 Long-term loans, n.e.c. [c]	42	–	5	17	20	57	–	13	–9	53
8 Net equity of households in life insurance and pension fund reserves [cd]	26747	–	–	26747	–	27021	–	–	27021	–
9 Other liabilities	16027	–488	7253	1822	7440	15494	–1857	7589	1965	7797
Total incurrence of liabilities	93449	1	46495	28989	17964	96942	6	32986	29655	34295
Statistical discrepancy [e]	–151	–	126	–	–277	2454	–	742	–	1712
Net lending	2670	570	3217	–612	–505	2856	714	3730	312	–1900
Incurrence of liabilities and net lending	96270	571	49586	28377	17736	97344	720	35974	29967	30683

	1992					1993				
	All financial institutions	Central bank	Other monetary institutions	Insurance	Other financial institutions	All financial institutions	Central bank	Other monetary institutions	Insurance	Other financial institutions

Acquisition of financial assets

1 Gold and SDRs	–5750	–5750	–	–	–	1206	1206	–	–	–
A Gold	–5693	–5693	–	–	–	1256	1256	–	–	–
B Net acquisitions of SDRs	–57	–57	–	–	–	–50	–50	–	–	–
2 Currency and transferable deposits [a]	–3261	–	–4994	–225	1958	–3588	–	–5593	901	1104
A Liability of resident institutions	242	–	–1132	–187	1561	–1251	–	–3410	830	1329
B Liability of rest of the world	–3503	–	–3862	–38	397	–2337	–	–2183	71	–225
3 Other deposits	–	–	–	–	–	–	–	–	–	–
A Liability of resident institutions	–	–	–	–	–	–	–	–	–	–
B Liability of rest of the world	–	–	–	–	–	–	–	–	–	–
4 Bills and bonds, short-term	2918	1575	472	–659	1530	19518	2296	3469	6929	6824
A Corporate and quasi-corporate, resident	–	–	–	–	–	–	–	–	–	–
B Government	–	–	–	–	–	–	–	–	–	–
C Rest of the world	–	–	–	–	–	–	–	–	–	–
5 Bonds, long-term	22568	–1304	7793	11224	4855	36101	–1351	19612	11469	6371
6 Corporate equity securities [b]	17692	–	50	13366	4276	24744	–	–169	9112	15801
7 Short-term loans, n.e.c. [b]	10825	–950	9335	100	2340	1172	33	–878	177	1840
A Liability of resident sectors	–	–	–	–	–	–	–	–	–	–
B Liability of rest of the world	–	–	–	–	–	–	–	–	–	–
8 Long-term loans, n.e.c. [c]	28188	–	18702	2431	7055	18889	–	9674	–271	9486
A Mortgages	28188	–	18702	2431	7055	18889	–	9674	–271	9486

Canada

	1992					1993				
	All financial institutions	Central bank	Other monetary institutions	Insurance	Other financial institutions	All financial institutions	Central bank	Other monetary institutions	Insurance	Other financial institutions
B Other	–	–	–	–	–	–	–	–	–	–
9 Trade credits and advances	923	–	283	319	321	5023	–	4636	446	–59
A Consumer credit	456	–	283	–114	287	4719	–	4636	177	–94
B Other	467	–	–	433	34	304	–	–	269	35
10 Other assets	15695	–96	9152	808	5831	8641	–6	–4131	–2177	14955
Total acquisitions of financial assets	89798	–6525	40793	27364	28166	111706	2178	26620	26586	56322

Incurrence of liabilities

1 Currency and transferable deposits [a]	29093	457	28355	–	281	7226	1488	5181	–	557
2 Other deposits	–	–	–	–	–	–	–	–	–	–
3 Bills and bonds, short-term	301	–	–	–	301	319	–	–	–	319
4 Bonds, long-term	5787	–	–1171	–	6958	8955	–	1746	174	7035
5 Corporate equity securities	16785	–	1505	599	14681	39807	–	1157	305	38345
6 Short-term loans, n.e.c. [c]	2078	–	615	258	1205	–1132	–	–525	353	–960
7 Long-term loans, n.e.c. [c]	–400	–	–5	–52	–343	–452	–	–8	–138	–306
8 Net equity of households in life insurance and pension fund reserves [c]	27464	–	–	27464	–	24591	–	–	24591	–
9 Other liabilities	3385	–8181	8339	950	2277	30483	–1107	15988	1782	13820
Total incurrence of liabilities	84493	–7724	37638	29219	25360	109797	381	23539	27067	58810
Statistical discrepancy [e]	–4629	–	390	–	–5019	3588	–	1377	–	2211
Net lending	676	1199	3545	–1855	–2213	5497	1797	4458	–481	–277
Incurrence of liabilities and net lending	89798	–6525	40793	27364	28166	111706	2178	26620	26586	56322

	1994					1995				
	All financial institutions	Central bank	Other monetary institutions	Insurance	Other financial institutions	All financial institutions	Central bank	Other monetary institutions	Insurance	Other financial institutions

Acquisition of financial assets

1 Gold and SDRs	–491	–491	–	–	–	3776	3776	–	–	–
A Gold	–381	–381	–	–	–	3346	3346	–	–	–
B Net acquisitions of SDRs	–110	–110	–	–	–	430	430	–	–	–
2 Currency and transferable deposits [a]	5536	–	6879	624	–1967	5665	–	4592	39	1034
A Liability of resident institutions	1376	–	2044	533	–1201	1883	–	1206	70	607
B Liability of rest of the world	4160	–	4835	91	–766	3782	–	3386	–31	427
3 Other deposits	–	–	–	–	–	–	–	–	–	–
A Liability of resident institutions	–	–	–	–	–	–	–	–	–	–
B Liability of rest of the world	–	–	–	–	–	–	–	–	–	–
4 Bills and bonds, short-term	2450	2022	2508	–1253	–827	1952	–640	–1651	–1635	5878
A Corporate and quasi-corporate, resident	–	–	–	–	–	–	–	–	–	–
B Government	–	–	–	–	–	–	–	–	–	–
C Rest of the world	–	–	–	–	–	–	–	–	–	–
5 Bonds, long-term	34306	–693	13384	14389	7226	21289	–637	7835	14045	46
6 Corporate equity securities [b]	26417	–	1376	7975	17066	22722	–	3011	12284	7427
7 Short-term loans, n.e.c. [b]	14749	625	9296	258	4570	10934	–337	7917	93	3261
A Liability of resident sectors	–	–	–	–	–	–	–	–	–	–
B Liability of rest of the world	–	–	–	–	–	–	–	–	–	–

Canada

	1994					1995				
	All financial institutions	Central bank	Other monetary institutions	Insurance	Other financial institutions	All financial institutions	Central bank	Other monetary institutions	Insurance	Other financial institutions
8 Long-term loans, n.e.c. [c]	15293	–	11394	351	3548	11107	–	10391	–263	979
A Mortgages	15293	–	11394	351	3548	11107	–	10391	–263	979
B Other	–	–	–	–	–	–	–	–	–	–
9 Trade credits and advances	7380	–	6688	580	112	7224	–	6214	644	366
A Consumer credit	7049	–	6688	266	95	6718	–	6214	252	252
B Other	331	–	–	314	17	506	–	–	392	114
10 Other assets	33466	–76	18272	–1741	17011	26384	227	10671	–1126	16612
Total acquisitions of financial assets	139106	1387	69797	21183	46739	111053	2389	48980	24081	35603

Incurrence of liabilities

1 Currency and transferable deposits [a]	35447	791	34174	–	482	25759	319	25297	–	143
2 Other deposits	–	–	–	–	–	–	–	–	–	–
3 Bills and bonds, short-term	2991	–	38	–	2953	4064	–	1	–	4063
4 Bonds, long-term	8629	–	2582	132	5915	5989	–	415	382	5192
5 Corporate equity securities	28016	–	1114	156	26746	14944	–	–796	178	15562
6 Short-term loans, n.e.c. [c]	3393	–	230	–201	3364	3100	–	–153	108	3145
7 Long-term loans, n.e.c. [c]	1025	–	–3	–78	1106	–19	–	1	2	–22
8 Net equity of households in life insurance and pension fund reserves [c]	21704	–	–	21704	–	22800	–	–	22800	–
9 Other liabilities	24894	–554	20557	529	4362	22204	1814	18913	1397	80
Total incurrence of liabilities	126099	237	58692	22242	44928	98841	2133	43678	24867	28163
Statistical discrepancy [e]	–7455	–	–4900	–	–2555	–5889	–	848	–	–6737
Net lending	5552	1150	6205	–1059	–744	6323	256	6150	–786	703
Incurrence of liabilities and net lending	139106	1387	69797	21183	46739	111053	2389	48980	24081	35603

	1996					1997				
	All financial institutions	Central bank	Other monetary institutions	Insurance	Other financial institutions	All financial institutions	Central bank	Other monetary institutions	Insurance	Other financial institutions

Acquisition of financial assets

1 Gold and SDRs	7497	7497	–	–	–	–3390	–3390	–	–	–
A Gold	7424	7424	–	–	–	–4038	–4038	–	–	–
B Net acquisitions of SDRs	73	73	–	–	–	648	648	–	–	–
2 Currency and transferable deposits [a]	13811	–	6820	299	6692	10646	–	6	–839	11479
A Liability of resident institutions	5652	–	259	278	5115	15559	–	4538	–738	11759
B Liability of rest of the world	8159	–	6561	21	1577	–4913	–	–4532	–101	–280
3 Other deposits	–	–	–	–	–	–	–	–	–	–
A Liability of resident institutions	–	–	–	–	–	–	–	–	–	–
B Liability of rest of the world	–	–	–	–	–	–	–	–	–	–
4 Bills and bonds, short-term	6450	–655	–7212	580	13737	3488	–3352	–598	–3781	11219
A Corporate and quasi-corporate, resident	–	–	–	–	–	–	–	–	–	–
B Government	–	–	–	–	–	–	–	–	–	–
C Rest of the world	–	–	–	–	–	–	–	–	–	–
5 Bonds, long-term	25441	2671	10184	9233	3353	33841	5002	–4015	21229	11625
6 Corporate equity securities [b]	48922	–	15405	10885	22632	39609	–	5778	13601	20230
7 Short-term loans, n.e.c. [b]	10922	9	3192	482	7239	25745	–191	11456	–376	14856

Canada

	1996					1997				
	All financial institutions	Central bank	Other monetary institutions	Insurance	Other financial institutions	All financial institutions	Central bank	Other monetary institutions	Insurance	Other financial institutions
A Liability of resident sectors	–	–	–	–	–	–	–	–	–	–
B Liability of rest of the world	–	–	–	–	–	–	–	–	–	–
8 Long-term loans, n.e.c. [c]	18003	–	19319	–509	–807	18014	–	11649	–1555	7920
A Mortgages	18003	–	19319	–509	–807	18014	–	11649	–1555	7920
B Other	–	–	–	–	–	–	–	–	–	–
9 Trade credits and advances	8398	–	6395	1180	823	9234	–	3059	–161	6336
A Consumer credit	7275	–	6395	103	777	9429	–	3059	100	6270
B Other	1123	–	–	1077	46	–195	–	–	–261	66
10 Other assets	60645	–134	29187	1548	30044	68335	116	43128	5725	19366
Total acquisitions of financial assets	200089	9388	83290	23698	83713	205522	–1815	70463	33843	103031

Incurrence of liabilities

1 Currency and transferable deposits [a]	35680	479	35723	–	–522	44511	998	43187	–	326
2 Other deposits	–	–	–	–	–	–	–	–	–	–
3 Bills and bonds, short-term	7640	–	13	–	7627	19910	–	1	–	19909
4 Bonds, long-term	3737	–	2351	311	1075	14316	–	–537	45	14808
5 Corporate equity securities	53482	–	–13	142	53353	62034	–	2418	1891	57725
6 Short-term loans, n.e.c. [c]	3808	–	1501	394	1913	6077	–	1961	962	3154
7 Long-term loans, n.e.c. [c]	–127	–	–1	–130	4	226	–	2	–18	242
8 Net equity of households in life insurance and pension fund reserves [c]	16407	–	–	16407	–	25817	–	–	25817	–
9 Other liabilities	68302	8722	37102	3934	18544	31777	–2812	22632	3484	8473
Total incurrence of liabilities	188929	9201	76676	21058	81994	204668	–1814	69664	32181	104637
Statistical discrepancy [e]	174	–	985	–	–811	11979	–	7600	–	4379
Net lending	11334	187	7599	2640	908	12833	–1	8399	1662	2773
Incurrence of liabilities and net lending	200089	9388	83290	23698	83713	205522	–1815	70463	33843	103031

a Including item "Other deposits".
b Investment in short-term papers, bonds and corporate equity securities of the rest of the world cannot be split between long-term and short-term by purchasers, the total investment has been allocated to the item "Corporate equity securities".
c Loans other than mortgages are included in item "Short-term loans, n.e.c.'.
d The "Insurance" sub-sector includes "Pension Funds".
e The statistical discrepancy equals the difference between net lending in the Income and Expenditure Accounts and net acquisition of financial assets in the Financial Flow Accounts (change in financial assets less change in liabilities).

3.32 Household and private unincorporated enterprise income and outlay account

Million Canadian dollars

	1986	1987	1988	1989	1990	1991	1992	1993	1994	1995	1996	1997
Receipts												
1 Compensation of employees	272755	296442	325248	350743	368891	379091	387788	395047	405163	419096	429601	445804
A Wages and salaries	247343	268756	294840	318716	333460	338525	343069	347468	356174	366870	376811	391218
B Employers' contributions for social security	12263	13691	15448	15747	17538	18862	21355	21914	23295	24408	24811	25931
C Employers' contributions for private pension and welfare plans	13149	13995	14960	16279	17893	21705	23364	25665	25695	27818	27980	28655
2 Operating surplus of private unincorporated enterprises [a]	32423	32834	36376	36818	37609	38665	41128	44493	45886	48691	52948	54400
3 Property and entrepreneurial income	54380	56688	63423	75008	86968	82320	76282	71914	71346	78552	77266	72662
A Withdrawals from private quasi-corporations	...	...	...	...	...	...	...	...	...	...	...	...

Canada

Million Canadian dollars

	1986	1987	1988	1989	1990	1991	1992	1993	1994	1995	1996	1997
B Interest	45794	47003	53616	66039	78341	74727	68665	63880	62889	69530	66413	60711
C Dividends	8586	9685	9807	8969	8627	7593	7617	8034	8457	9022	10853	11951
D Net land rent and royalties	...	...	...	...	...	...	...	...	...	...	...	...
4 Current transfers	56907	61400	65735	71015	79220	90785	100622	105842	107063	108109	108778	109458
A Casualty insurance claims	...	...	...	...	...	...	...	...	...	...	...	...
B Social security benefits	33678	36650	39453	42626	47131	54068	58214	59299	58563	57915	59334	59189
C Social assistance grants	18678	19653	20725	22367	26170	30082	35222	38900	40550	41761	40797	41036
D Unfunded employee pension and welfare benefits	...	...	...	...	...	...	...	...	...	...	...	...
E Transfers from general government	...	...	...	...	...	...	...	...	...	...	...	...
F Transfers from rest of the world	914	990	1052	1095	1228	1391	1524	1690	1878	2113	2085	2120
G Other transfers n.e.c. [b]	3637	4107	4505	4927	4691	5244	5662	5953	6072	6320	6562	7113
Total current receipts	416465	447364	490782	533584	572688	590861	605820	617296	629458	654448	668593	682324

Disbursements

	1986	1987	1988	1989	1990	1991	1992	1993	1994	1995	1996	1997
1 Final consumption expenditure	282936	306047	331304	358140	377860	390135	402705	419405	435062	449018	466108	493322
2 Property income	5436	6137	7259	10143	11937	10689	8414	7067	7359	9723	9134	7431
A Interest	5436	6137	7259	10143	11937	10689	8414	7067	7359	9723	9134	7431
Consumer debt	5436	6137	7259	10143	11937	10689	8414	7067	7359	9723	9134	7431
Mortgages	...	...	...	...	...	...	...	...	...	...	...	...
Other	...	...	...	...	...	...	...	...	...	...	...	...
B Net land rent and royalties	...	...	...	...	...	...	...	...	...	...	...	...
3 Direct taxes and other current transfers n.e.c. to general government	88234	98601	110567	116729	132097	136369	140410	141244	146650	154633	162245	171888
A Social security contributions	23229	25665	28971	29089	33079	35926	39553	40637	42867	44451	44411	47031
B Direct taxes	61618	69288	77568	83222	96171	97154	97283	96858	99844	106137	113780	120791
Income taxes	61618	69288	77568	83222	96171	97154	97283	96858	99844	106137	113780	120791
Other	...	...	...	...	...	...	...	...	...	...	...	...
C Fees, fines and penalties	3387	3649	4028	4418	2847	3289	3574	3749	3939	4045	4054	4066
4 Other current transfers	615	650	749	828	764	836	910	962	1042	1079	1109	1166
A Net casualty insurance premiums	...	...	...	...	...	...	...	...	...	...	...	...
B Transfers to private non-profit institutions serving households	...	...	...	...	...	...	...	...	...	...	...	...
C Transfers to rest of the world	615	650	749	828	764	836	910	962	1042	1079	1109	1166
D Other current transfers, except imputed	...	...	...	...	...	...	...	...	...	...	...	...
E Imputed employee pension and welfare contributions	...	...	...	...	...	...	...	...	...	...	...	...
Net saving	39244	35928	40903	47744	50030	52832	53381	48618	39345	39995	29997	8517
Total current disbursements and net saving	416465	447363	490782	533584	572688	590861	605820	617296	629458	654448	668593	682324

a Item "Operating surplus of private unincorporated enterprises" refers to net income of unincorporated business including net rent.

b Includes "public service pension benifits"

Canada

3.33 Household and private unincorporated enterprise capital accumulation account

Million Canadian dollars

	1986	1987	1988	1989	1990	1991	1992	1993	1994	1995	1996	1997
Finance of gross accumulation												
1 Gross saving	54186	52231	58358	66666	70057	74121	75355	71772	63507	65053	56229	35666
A Consumption of fixed capital	14942	16303	17455	18922	20027	21289	21974	23154	24162	25058	26232	27149
B Net saving	39244	35928	40903	47744	50030	52832	53381	48618	39345	39995	29997	8517
2 Capital transfers [a]	2076	3966	5220	6047	7227	7074	9068	11259	10443	7179	10010	8243
A From resident sectors	247	216	228	352	352	537	373	226	147	140	1764	501
B From rest of the world	1829	3750	4992	5695	6875	6537	8695	11033	10296	7039	8246	7742
Total finance of gross accumulation	56262	56197	63578	72713	77284	81195	84423	83031	73950	72232	66239	43909
Gross accumulation												
1 Gross capital formation	33442	39331	44277	49091	45736	40391	41870	44530	46885	42052	45561	48953
A Increase in stocks	614	−226	−424	413	471	−4	−552	920	−24	120	413	−902
B Gross fixed capital formation	32828	39557	44701	48678	45265	40395	42422	43610	46909	41932	45148	49855
2 Purchases of land, net [b]	2616	3249	4155	4382	5456	4320	4389	4215	4507	3563	3436	4528
3 Purchases of intangibles, net	...	...	...	...	...	...	...	...	...	...	...	...
4 Capital transfers	...	...	...	...	...	...	...	...	...	...	...	...
Net lending	20204	13617	15146	19240	26092	36484	38164	34286	22558	26617	17242	−9572
Total gross accumulation	56262	56197	63578	72713	77284	81195	84423	83031	73950	72232	66239	43909

a Capital transfers are presented on a net basis (capital transfers from other sectors less capital transfers to other sectors.   b Includes "net purchases of tangable assets".

3.34 Household and private unincorporated enterprise capital finance account

Million Canadian dollars

	1986	1987	1988	1989	1990	1991	1992	1993	1994	1995	1996	1997
Acquisition of financial assets												
1 Gold	...	...	...	...	...	...	...	...	...	...	...	...
2 Currency and transferable deposits [a]	28497	16135	43055	48760	29098	20554	24075	9510	21002	20556	14605	−1305
3 Other deposits	...	...	...	...	...	...	...	...	...	...	...	...
4 Bills and bonds, short-term	6976	3376	2551	15569	7572	−11569	−3251	−10251	−12740	−609	−4229	−7639
5 Bonds, long-term	−5800	12606	8083	−16798	−2023	16286	4696	−2839	21773	7522	1906	3990
A Corporate	−1588	−1140	3337	−1242	2554	10751	1199	6328	12468	779	−5631	−1138
B Government	−4212	13746	4746	−15556	−4577	5535	3497	−9167	9305	6743	7537	5128
C Rest of the world	...	...	...	...	...	...	...	...	...	...	...	...
6 Corporate equity securities [b]	8947	13214	3214	6869	2233	21980	17541	39810	18731	15264	36940	48197
7 Short-term loans, n.e.c.	...	...	...	...	...	...	...	...	...	...	...	...
8 Long-term loans, n.e.c. [c]	1192	1848	1690	1533	823	148	2612	1408	2123	1536	691	1735
A Mortgages	1192	1848	1690	1533	823	148	2612	1408	2123	1536	691	1735
B Other	...	...	...	...	...	...	...	...	...	...	...	...
9 Trade credits and advances	...	...	...	...	...	...	...	...	...	...	...	...
10 Net equity of households in life insurance and pension fund reserves	18304	17790	21250	24361	26707	26981	27417	24556	21664	22761	16363	25778
11 Proprietors' net additions to the accumulation of quasi-corporations	...	...	...	...	...	...	...	...	...	...	...	...
12 Other	−5521	−6952	−18767	−22813	−6144	−9781	−8070	1054	−15042	−16766	−21675	−45254

Canada

Million Canadian dollars

	1986	1987	1988	1989	1990	1991	1992	1993	1994	1995	1996	1997
Total acquisitions of financial assets	52595	58017	61076	57481	58266	64599	65020	63248	57511	50264	44601	25502

Incurrence of liabilities

	1986	1987	1988	1989	1990	1991	1992	1993	1994	1995	1996	1997
1 Short-term loans, n.e.c. [c]	2132	4979	3896	3270	3266	635	2433	4435	3279	4853	5909	5597
2 Long-term loans, n.e.c. [c]	20648	25520	25702	28112	21470	18739	21802	16832	14939	13455	17192	18186
A Mortgages	20648	25520	25702	28112	21470	18739	21802	16832	14939	13455	17192	18186
B Other	...	...	...	...	...	...	...	...	...	...	...	...
3 Trade credits and advances	7790	12730	12086	9097	5995	223	−328	5946	7164	7318	4345	7536
A Consumer credit	6730	9710	9920	8258	5394	1713	456	4719	7049	6718	7275	9429
B Other	1060	3020	2166	839	601	−1490	−784	1227	115	600	−2930	−1893
4 Other accounts payable	...	...	...	...	...	...	...	...	...	...	...	...
5 Other liabilities	...	...	...	...	...	...	...	...	...	...	...	...
Total incurrence of liabilities	30570	43229	41684	40479	30731	19597	23907	27213	25382	25626	27446	31319
Statistical discrepancy [d]	1821	1171	4246	−2238	1443	8518	2949	1749	9571	−1979	−87	3755
Net lending	20204	13617	15146	19240	26092	36484	38164	34286	22558	26617	17242	−9572
Incurrence of liabilities and net lending	52595	58017	61076	57481	58266	64599	65020	63248	57511	50264	44601	25502

a Including item "Other deposits".
b Investment in short-term papers, bonds and corporate equity securities of the rest of the world cannot be split between long-term and short-term by purchasers, the total investment has been allocated to the item "Corporate equity securities".
c Loans other than mortgages are included in item "Short-term loans, n.e.c.'.
d The statistical discrepancy equals the difference between net lending in the Income and Expenditure Accounts and net acquisition of financial assets in the Financial Flow Accounts (change in financial assets less change in liabilities).

3.35 Household and private unincorporated enterprise balance sheet

Million Canadian dollars

	1986	1987	1988	1989	1990	1991	1992	1993	1994	1995	1996	1997
Assets												
Non-financial assets	807503	897775	992192	1089301	1125200	1173392	1219494	1283623	1344628	1371519	1409921	1462427
1 Tangible assets	807503	897775	992192	1089301	1125200	1173392	1219494	1283623	1344628	1371519	1409921	1462427
A Stocks of household enterprises	13821	13640	13734	14330	14588	13427	13719	15876	16085	15891	16683	17649
B Dwellings	361018	408592	453384	489619	516276	539592	567783	599475	627849	643192	658040	680801
C Other reproducible fixed assets of unincorporated enterprises	213514	228500	249115	266957	274188	276683	278942	287393	297147	303003	309833	319727
D Land and other non-reproducible tangible assets	219150	247043	275959	318395	320148	343690	359050	380879	403547	409433	425365	444250
2 Intangible assets	...	...	...	...	...	...	...	...	...	...	...	...
Financial assets	829387	904690	995843	1094239	1158812	1237385	1324327	1419459	1510507	1594779	1695975	1790819
1 Gold	...	...	...	...	...	...	...	...	...	...	...	...
2 Currency and transferable deposits [a]	282460	295880	343216	392029	419567	437816	465496	475591	491076	516132	531489	536565
3 Other deposits	...	...	...	...	...	...	...	...	...	...	...	...
4 Bills and bonds, short-term	19878	21507	23115	36300	43262	34295	36041	31190	17719	15158	15637	5259
5 Bonds, long-term	68141	78038	86923	70565	70597	85940	87390	88557	91383	91707	94328	91253
A Corporate	6844	4844	9629	5783	11663	22347	23117	28488	37762	34687	30414	29223
B Government	61297	73194	77294	64782	58934	63593	64273	60069	53621	57020	63914	62030
C Rest of the world	...	...	...	...	...	...	...	...	...	...	...	...
6 Corporate equity securities [b]	205037	234780	243864	257860	268305	289435	309375	357027	391025	406173	457897	508626
7 Short-term loans, n.e.c.	...	...	...	...	...	...	...	...	...	...	...	...
8 Long-term loans, n.e.c. [c]	11379	12589	14266	15558	16415	17435	19246	21524	24299	24622	25021	27200
A Mortgages	11379	12589	14266	15558	16415	17435	19246	21524	24299	24622	25021	27200
B Other	...	...	...	...	...	...	...	...	...	...	...	...
9 Trade credits and advances	385	385	385	385	385	385	385	385	385	385	385	385

Canada

Million Canadian dollars

	1986	1987	1988	1989	1990	1991	1992	1993	1994	1995	1996	1997
10 Net equity in life insurance and pension fund reserves	209351	233843	257989	296585	323140	352783	380635	412587	447282	485452	519934	577642
11 Proprietors' equity in quasi-corporations	...	...	...	...	...	...	...	...	...	...	...	...
12 Other	32756	27668	26085	24957	17141	19296	25759	32598	47338	55150	51284	43889
Total assets	1636890	1802465	1988035	2183540	2284012	2410777	2543821	2703082	2855135	2966298	3105896	3253246
memorandum item: Consumer durable goods	179756	195580	216521	234245	241967	246225	248998	256814	265356	270579	276927	286424

Liabilities and net worth

	1986	1987	1988	1989	1990	1991	1992	1993	1994	1995	1996	1997
Liabilities	269334	311689	351446	390777	423815	440976	464527	487603	512449	533594	564150	596110
1 Short-term loans, n.e.c. [c]	31152	37476	40591	42913	47659	44706	45565	46707	48770	52325	58013	62881
2 Long-term loans, n.e.c. [c]	168843	194456	220841	248836	269455	289839	312170	328409	344973	357782	374300	391905
A Mortgages	168843	194456	220841	248836	269455	289839	312170	328409	344973	357782	374300	391905
B Other	...	...	...	...	...	...	...	...	...	...	...	...
3 Trade credits and advances	69339	79757	90014	99028	106701	106431	106792	112487	118706	123487	131837	141324
A Consumer credit	65110	74624	84078	92378	97152	99371	99756	104564	111340	116697	123156	133809
B Other	4229	5133	5936	6650	9549	7060	7036	7923	7366	6790	8681	7515
4 Other accounts payable	...	...	...	...	...	...	...	...	...	...	...	...
5 Other liabilities	...	...	...	...	...	...	...	...	...	...	...	...
Net worth	1367556	1490776	1636589	1792763	1860197	1969801	2079294	2215479	2342686	2432704	2541746	2657136
Total liabilities and net worth	1636890	1802465	1988035	2183540	2284012	2410777	2543821	2703082	2855135	2966298	3105896	3253246

a Including item "Other deposits".
b Investment in short-term papers, bonds and corporate equity securities of the rest of the world cannot be split between long-term and short-term by purchasers, the total investment has been allocated to the item "Corporate equity securities".
c Loans other than mortgages are included in item "Short-term loans, n.e.c.".

3.51 External transactions, current account: detail

Million Canadian dollars

	1986	1987	1988	1989	1990	1991	1992	1993	1994	1995	1996	1997
Payments to the rest of the world												
1 Imports of goods and services	137228	142723	158577	168139	174019	175401	191673	219462	252998	277529	288356	328276
A Imports of merchandise, c.i.f.	117498	121510	135156	141594	143300	142863	157202	181508	212842	235405	243529	282430
B Other	19730	21213	23421	26545	30719	32538	34471	37954	40156	42124	44827	45846
2 Factor income to rest of the world	28659	28699	34853	36640	40666	38003	38415	39175	44334	48716	48445	51329
A Compensation of employees	...	...	...	...	...	...	...	...	...	...	...	...
B Property and entrepreneurial income	28659	28699	34853	36640	40666	38003	38415	39175	44334	48716	48445	51329
By general government	6667	7617	8758	10143	11165	12196	13521	15362	16927	18149	16981	16121
By corporate and quasi-corporate enterprises	21992	21082	26095	26497	29501	25807	24894	23813	27407	30567	31464	35208
By other	...	...	...	...	...	...	...	...	...	...	...	...
3 Current transfers to the rest of the world	2979	3384	3777	3790	3882	4177	4236	4106	4072	4020	4222	4274
A Indirect taxes by general government to supranational organizations	...	...	...	...	...	...	...	...	...	...	...	...
B Other current transfers	2979	3384	3777	3790	3882	4177	4236	4106	4072	4020	4222	4274
By general government	2223	2606	2875	2785	2969	3177	3196	2996	2897	2799	2957	2892
By other resident sectors	756	778	902	1005	913	1000	1040	1110	1175	1221	1265	1382
4 Surplus of the nation on current transactions	−12852	−11880	−16123	−23480	−24482	−28058	−29142	−26023	−20559	−4352	4539	−12499

Canada

Million Canadian dollars	1986	1987	1988	1989	1990	1991	1992	1993	1994	1995	1996	1997
Payments to the rest of the world and surplus of the nation on current transfers	156014	162926	181084	185089	194085	189523	205182	236720	280845	325913	345562	371380
Receipts from the rest of the world												
1 Exports of goods and services	141562	148823	162800	167739	174438	170995	188586	218885	260483	300849	319456	342066
A Exports of merchandise, f.o.b.	125172	131484	143534	146963	152056	147669	163464	190383	227895	264940	280570	301649
B Other	16390	17339	19266	20776	22382	23326	25122	28502	32588	35909	38886	40417
2 Factor income from rest of the world	11855	11891	15554	14710	16692	15623	13496	14496	16786	21247	21622	24448
A Compensation of employees	...	...	...	...	...	...	...	...	...	...	...	...
B Property and entrepreneurial income	11855	11891	15554	14710	16692	15623	13496	14496	16786	21247	21622	24448
By general government	243	472	1072	1374	1403	1477	1208	690	752	1273	1412	1535
By corporate and quasi-corporate enterprises	10194	9861	12475	10971	12177	10896	9128	10509	12381	16062	16625	18814
By other	1418	1558	2007	2365	3112	3250	3160	3297	3653	3912	3585	4099
3 Current transfers from rest of the world	2597	2212	2730	2640	2955	2905	3100	3339	3576	3817	4484	4866
A Subsidies to general government from supranational organizations	...	...	...	...	...	...	...	...	...	...	...	...
B Other current transfers	2597	2212	2730	2640	2955	2905	3100	3339	3576	3817	4484	4866
To general government	1683	1222	1678	1545	1727	1514	1576	1649	1698	1704	2399	2746
To other resident sectors	914	990	1052	1095	1228	1391	1524	1690	1878	2113	2085	2120
Receipts from the rest of the world on current transfers	156014	162926	181084	185089	194085	189523	205182	236720	280845	325913	345562	371380

3.52 External transactions, capital accumulation account

Million Canadian dollars	1986	1987	1988	1989	1990	1991	1992	1993	1994	1995	1996	1997
Finance of gross accumulation												
1 Surplus of the nation on current transactions	–12852	–11880	–16123	–23480	–24482	–28058	–29142	–26023	–20559	–4352	4539	–12499
2 Capital transfers from rest of the world [a]	1823	3717	4819	5481	6203	6410	8574	10705	10243	6789	8076	7609
A By general government	–6	–33	–173	–214	–672	–127	–121	–328	–53	–250	–170	–133
B By other resident sectors	1829	3750	4992	5695	6875	6537	8695	11033	10296	7039	8246	7742
Total finance of gross accumulation	–11029	–8163	–11304	–17999	–18279	–21648	–20568	–15318	–10316	2437	12615	–4890
Gross accumulation												
1 Capital transfers to the rest of the world	...	...	...	...	...	...	...	...	...	...	...	...
2 Purchases of intangible assets, n.e.c., net, from rest of the world	...	...	...	...	...	...	...	...	...	...	...	...
Net lending to the rest of the world	–11028	–8163	–11304	–17999	–18279	–21648	–20568	–15318	–10316	2437	12615	–4890
Total gross accumulation	–11028	–8163	–11304	–17999	–18279	–21648	–20568	–15318	–10316	2437	12615	–4890

a Capital transfers are presented on a net basis (capital transfers from other sectors less capital transfers to other sectors).

Canada

3.53 External transactions, capital finance account

Million Canadian dollars

	1986	1987	1988	1989	1990	1991	1992	1993	1994	1995	1996	1997
Acquisition of foreign financial assets												
1 Gold and SDRs [a]	881	5175	10172	816	1246	–2103	–5750	1206	–491	3776	7497	–3390
2 Currency and transferable deposits [b]	6160	–4906	–1954	833	112	2022	–4183	–3351	10402	1326	15273	–6552
3 Other deposits	...	...	...	...	...	...	...	...	...	...	...	...
4 Bills and bonds, short-term	...	...	...	...	...	...	...	...	...	...	...	...
5 Bonds, long-term	...	...	...	...	...	...	...	...	...	...	...	...
6 Corporate equity securities	...	...	...	...	...	...	...	...	...	...	...	...
7 Short-term loans, n.e.c. [c]	–2457	3697	4967	2057	–259	600	1261	1793	104	3155	4274	5547
8 Long-term loans	...	...	...	...	...	...	...	...	...	...	...	...
9 Proprietors' net additions to accumulation of quasi-corporate, non-resident enterprises [d]	11357	9724	989	9831	10528	–1428	7300	1381	22547	25158	12327	30346
10 Trade credits and advances	–426	1210	488	119	–273	1245	2305	–1346	2941	188	–344	1203
11 Other	3907	3247	4040	7097	8902	14642	15445	26109	14067	7240	26394	27359
Total acquisitions of foreign financial assets	19422	18147	18702	20753	20256	14978	16378	25792	49570	40843	65421	54513
Incurrence of foreign liabilities												
1 Currency and transferable deposits [b]	328	356	–465	1328	6082	–2183	–4206	–7369	15575	–11241	5890	8318
2 Other deposits	...	...	...	...	...	...	...	...	...	...	...	...
3 Bills and bonds, short-term [e]	2388	2528	9197	1249	5643	4426	4899	9209	981	–1258	–7318	1331
4 Bonds, long-term	22694	7953	15738	17848	14297	27224	18183	30815	14922	28310	18812	8944
5 Corporate equity securities	1877	6640	–2379	3884	–1735	–990	1037	12057	6411	–4243	8277	7644
6 Short-term loans, n.e.c. [c]	–1050	4003	2950	8289	2615	1386	678	–471	–1955	3352	5753	–1627
7 Long-term loans [c]	–100	–62	–5	–58	–15	86	–16	69	–53	263	...	–125
8 Non-resident proprietors' net additions to accumulation of resident quasi-corporate enterprises [f]	4506	1945	–87	1900	10960	10572	14003	997	9668	8266	7304	22898
9 Trade credits and advances	–216	1097	–288	855	1149	153	2166	897	3264	–204	–2686	1889
10 Other	1926	4913	4834	5263	1571	–3886	–3269	1450	9456	10884	13502	17186
Total incurrence of liabilities	32353	29373	29495	40558	40567	36788	33475	47654	58269	34129	49534	66458
Statistical discrepancy	–1902	–3063	511	–1806	–2032	–162	3471	–6544	1617	4277	3272	–7055
Net lending	–11029	–8163	–11304	–17999	–18279	–21648	–20568	–15318	–10316	2437	12615	–4890
Total incurrence of liabilities and net lending	19422	18147	18702	20753	20256	14978	16378	25792	49570	40843	65421	54513

a Item "Gold and SDRs" refers to official international reserves.
b Includes item "Other deposits".
c Loans other than mortgages are included in item "Short-term loans, n.e.c.".
d Item "Proprietors net additions to accumulation of quasi-corporate, non-resident enterprises" relates to claims on associated enterprises aboard.
e Includes only "Bills".
f Item "Non-resident proprietors net additions to accumulation of resident quasi-corporate enterprises" relates to liabilities to associated enterprises abroad.

Canada

4.1 Derivation of value added by kind of activity, in current prices

Million Canadian dollars

	1986 Gross output	1986 Intermediate consumption	1986 Value added	1987 Gross output	1987 Intermediate consumption	1987 Value added	1988 Gross output	1988 Intermediate consumption	1988 Value added	1989 Gross output	1989 Intermediate consumption	1989 Value added
All producers												
1 Agriculture, hunting, forestry and fishing	...	...	15288	...	...	14706	...	...	15407	...	...	16066
A Agriculture and hunting	...	...	11285	...	...	9691	...	...	9926	...	...	10582
B Forestry and logging	...	...	3085	...	...	3898	...	...	4365	...	...	4483
C Fishing	...	...	918	...	...	1117	...	...	1117	...	...	1001
2 Mining and quarrying	...	...	22269	...	...	24741	...	...	25339	...	...	25369
A Coal mining	...	...	965	...	...	991	...	...	1086	...	...	922
B Crude petroleum and natural gas production	...	...	13830	...	...	14831	...	...	12199	...	...	12705
C Metal ore mining	...	...	3990	...	...	5431	...	...	7640	...	...	7818
D Other mining	...	...	3484	...	...	3488	...	...	4414	...	...	3924
3 Manufacturing	...	...	85563	...	...	93717	...	...	104835	...	...	107869
A Manufacture of food, beverages and tobacco	...	...	12110	...	...	13151	...	...	13570	...	...	14063
B Textile, wearing apparel and leather industries	...	...	5346	...	...	5658	...	...	5743	...	...	5934
C Manufacture of wood and wood products, including furniture	...	...	6243	...	...	7305	...	...	7092	...	...	7425
D Manufacture of paper and paper products, printing and publishing	...	...	12781	...	...	14938	...	...	16878	...	...	16952
E Manufacture of chemicals and chemical petroleum, coal, rubber and plastic products	...	...	10953	...	...	11317	...	...	13944	...	...	13346
F Manufacture of non-metallic mineral products, except products of petroleum and coal	...	...	2912	...	...	3432	...	...	3641	...	...	3621
G Basic metal industries	...	...	5922	...	...	7052	...	...	8574	...	...	7834
H Manufacture of fabricated metal products, machinery and equipment	...	...	27093	...	...	28456	...	...	32623	...	...	35772
I Other manufacturing industries	...	...	2203	...	...	2409	...	...	2771	...	...	2922
4 Electricity, gas and water	...	...	15835	...	...	16588	...	...	17823	...	...	18135
A Electricity, gas and steam	...	...	15033	...	...	15754	...	...	16932	...	...	17173
B Water works and supply	...	...	802	...	...	834	...	...	891	...	...	962
5 Construction [a]	...	...	28301	...	...	32735	...	...	36541	...	...	40912
6 Wholesale and retail trade, restaurants and hotels	...	...	64555	...	...	70823	...	...	77879	...	...	84017
A Wholesale and retail trade	...	...	52677	...	...	58254	...	...	64055	...	...	68391
B Restaurants and hotels	...	...	11878	...	...	12569	...	...	13824	...	...	15627
7 Transport, storage and communication	...	...	34464	...	...	36386	...	...	37705	...	...	39439
A Transport and storage	...	...	22619	...	...	24014	...	...	24623	...	...	25557
B Communication	...	...	11845	...	...	12372	...	...	13082	...	...	13882
8 Finance, insurance, real estate and business services	...	...	81918	...	...	89975	...	...	100078	...	...	109262

Canada

Million Canadian dollars

	1986			1987			1988			1989		
	Gross output	Intermediate consumption	Value added	Gross output	Intermediate consumption	Value added	Gross output	Intermediate consumption	Value added	Gross output	Intermediate consumption	Value added
A Financial institutions [b]	...	...	32066	...	...	35060	...	...	38135	...	...	41012
B Insurance	...	...	5641	...	...	6140	...	...	6984	...	...	6971
C Real estate and business services [b]	...	...	44211	...	...	48775	...	...	54959	...	...	61278
Real estate, except dwellings	...	...	16911	...	...	19350	...	...	22807	...	...	25517
Dwellings	...	...	27300	...	...	29425	...	...	32152	...	...	35761
9 Community, social and personal services	...	...	54744	...	...	59054	...	...	64964	...	...	69942
A Sanitary and similar services	...	...	443	...	...	545	...	...	626	...	...	616
B Social and related community services	...	...	36098	...	...	38941	...	...	42314	...	...	46037
Educational services	...	...	20569	...	...	21820	...	...	23528	...	...	25424
Medical, dental, other health and veterinary services	...	...	15530	...	...	17122	...	...	18785	...	...	20613
C Recreational and cultural services	...	...	6546	...	...	6878	...	...	7860	...	...	7997
D Personal and household services	...	...	11657	...	...	12690	...	...	14163	...	...	15291
Statistical discrepancy	...	...	−580	...	...	112	...	...	104	...	...	−169
Total, Industries	...	...	402936	...	...	438725	...	...	480572	...	...	511012
Producers of government services	...	...	49924	...	...	52948	...	...	56170	...	...	60642
Other producers	...	...	1373	...	...	1494	...	...	1636	...	...	1847
Total [c]	...	...	454233	...	...	493167	...	...	538378	...	...	573502
less: Imputed bank service charge	...	...	7644	...	...	8238	...	...	9352	...	...	9746
Import duties	...	...	4169	...	...	4220	...	...	4644	...	...	4494
Value added tax	...	...	...	...	...	...	...	...	...	...	...	...
Other adjustments [d]	...	...	53391	...	...	60718	...	...	68765	...	...	78195
Total	...	...	504152	...	...	549868	...	...	602433	...	...	646444

	1990			1991			1992			1993		
	Gross output	Intermediate consumption	Value added	Gross output	Intermediate consumption	Value added	Gross output	Intermediate consumption	Value added	Gross output	Intermediate consumption	Value added
All producers													
1 Agriculture, hunting, forestry and fishing	...	...	16228	...	...	15008	...	...	15316	...	...	16760
A Agriculture and hunting	...	...	11226	...	...	10383	...	...	10260	...	...	10760
B Forestry and logging	...	...	3982	...	...	3627	...	...	4030	...	...	4964
C Fishing	...	...	1021	...	...	998	...	...	1027	...	...	1036
2 Mining and quarrying	...	...	27073	...	...	22642	...	...	23054	...	...	24033
A Coal mining	...	...	1054	...	...	1000	...	...	797	...	...	981
B Crude petroleum and natural gas production	...	...	15672	...	...	12619	...	...	14001	...	...	15517
C Metal ore mining	...	...	6540	...	...	5257	...	...	4994	...	...	3891
D Other mining	...	...	3807	...	...	3766	...	...	3262	...	...	3644
3 Manufacturing	...	...	103758	...	...	96672	...	...	96184	...	...	102884
A Manufacture of food, beverages and tobacco	...	...	15049	...	...	16244	...	...	16607	...	...	16185
B Textile, wearing apparel and leather industries	...	...	5632	...	...	5226	...	...	5025	...	...	5146

Canada

	1990			1991			1992			1993		
	Gross output	Intermediate consumption	Value added	Gross output	Intermediate consumption	Value added	Gross output	Intermediate consumption	Value added	Gross output	Intermediate consumption	Value added
C Manufacture of wood and wood products, including furniture	...	...	6854	...	...	5719	...	...	6535	...	...	8591
D Manufacture of paper and paper products, printing and publishing	...	...	16214	...	...	13608	...	...	13112	...	...	13266
E Manufacture of chemicals and chemical petroleum, coal, rubber and plastic products	...	...	13657	...	...	14103	...	...	13062	...	...	13747
F Manufacture of non-metallic mineral products, except products of petroleum and coal	...	...	3292	...	...	2669	...	...	2547	...	...	2591
G Basic metal industries	...	...	6150	...	...	5444	...	...	5293	...	...	6014
H Manufacture of fabricated metal products, machinery and equipment	...	...	33981	...	...	30652	...	...	31061	...	...	34295
I Other manufacturing industries	...	...	2929	...	...	3006	...	...	2942	...	...	3049
4 Electricity, gas and water	...	...	18445	...	...	20668	...	...	21686	...	...	22834
A Electricity, gas and steam	...	...	17388	...	...	19547	...	...	20498	...	...	21617
B Water works and supply	...	...	1057	...	...	1121	...	...	1188	...	...	1217
5 Construction [a]	...	...	41308	...	...	38324	...	...	37112	...	...	36031
6 Wholesale and retail trade, restaurants and hotels	...	...	86068	...	...	83296	...	...	82117	...	...	84068
A Wholesale and retail trade	...	...	69710	...	...	67847	...	...	66154	...	...	67472
B Restaurants and hotels	...	...	16357	...	...	15449	...	...	15963	...	...	16596
7 Transport, storage and communication	...	...	40147	...	...	41171	...	...	42294	...	...	43125
A Transport and storage	...	...	25534	...	...	25728	...	...	26078	...	...	27137
B Communication	...	...	14613	...	...	15442	...	...	16216	...	...	15988
8 Finance, insurance, real estate and business services	...	...	115195	...	...	122322	...	...	125358	...	...	131715
A Financial institutions [b]	...	...	41274	...	...	45148	...	...	46143	...	...	48193
B Insurance	...	...	7805	...	...	7783	...	...	7654	...	...	8457
C Real estate and business services [b]	...	...	66117	...	...	69391	...	...	71560	...	...	75065
Real estate, except dwellings	...	...	27366	...	...	27829	...	...	27782	...	...	29279
Dwellings	...	...	38751	...	...	41562	...	...	43779	...	...	45787
9 Community, social and personal services	...	...	75829	...	...	81381	...	...	86028	...	...	88365
A Sanitary and similar services	...	...	630	...	...	632	...	...	685	...	...	717
B Social and related community services	...	...	50633	...	...	55309	...	...	59153	...	...	60731
Educational services	...	...	27571	...	...	29985	...	...	32033	...	...	32886
Medical, dental, other health and veterinary services	...	...	23062	...	...	25325	...	...	27120	...	...	27846
C Recreational and cultural services	...	...	8534	...	...	8917	...	...	9312	...	...	9643
D Personal and household services	...	...	16032	...	...	16523	...	...	16878	...	...	17274
Statistical discrepancy	...	...	−593	...	...	−1072	...	...	–	...	...	–
Total, Industries	...	...	524051	...	...	521483	...	...	529148	...	...	549815

Canada

	1990 Gross output	1990 Intermediate consumption	1990 Value added	1991 Gross output	1991 Intermediate consumption	1991 Value added	1992 Gross output	1992 Intermediate consumption	1992 Value added	1993 Gross output	1993 Intermediate consumption	1993 Value added
Producers of government services	...	...	65727	...	...	70057	...	...	72977	...	...	73979
Other producers	...	...	1994	...	...	2046	...	...	2154	...	...	2229
Total [c]	...	...	591772	...	...	593585	...	...	604279	...	...	626023
less: Imputed bank service charge	...	...	9954	...	...	10725	...	...	11169	...	...	11607
Import duties	...	...	4237	...	...	3742	...	...	4125	...	...	3368
Value added tax	...	...	...	...	...	17379	...	...	17786	...	...	18153
Other adjustments [d]	...	...	82126	...	...	68533	...	...	72354	...	...	77377
Total	...	...	668181	...	...	672514	...	...	687375	...	...	713313

a The construction industry is defined on an activity basis. It includes all contract and own-account construction put in place.
b "Real estate" is included in "Financial institutions".
c Gross domestic product at factor cost.
d Other adjustment includes indirect taxes, excluding import duties and goods and services tax (V.A.T.), less subsidies.

4.2 Derivation of value added by kind of activity, in constant prices

Million Canadian dollars

	1986 Gross output	1986 Intermediate consumption	1986 Value added	1987 Gross output	1987 Intermediate consumption	1987 Value added	1988 Gross output	1988 Intermediate consumption	1988 Value added	1989 Gross output	1989 Intermediate consumption	1989 Value added

At constant prices of: 1992

All producers

	1986	1987	1988	1989
1 Agriculture, hunting, forestry and fishing	16676	15728	15265	16329
A Agriculture and hunting	10528	9610	8827	9887
B Forestry and logging	4457	5274	5360	5127
C Fishing	1072	909	1019	1123
2 Mining and quarrying	19742	20824	22646	21500
A Coal mining	773	890	1055	956
B Crude petroleum and natural gas production	10918	11466	12384	11931
C Metal ore mining	4278	4875	5200	5061
D Other mining	3927	3778	4141	3582
3 Manufacturing	94829	99215	105126	106612
A Manufacture of food, beverages and tobacco	16334	16528	16595	16157
B Textile, wearing apparel and leather industries	6363	6504	6349	6216
C Manufacture of wood and wood products, including furniture	6905	7675	7740	7606
D Manufacture of paper and paper products, printing and publishing	14212	14700	15016	14852
E Manufacture of chemicals and chemical petroleum, coal, rubber and plastic products	11495	12342	13003	13403
F Manufacture of non-metallic mineral products, except products of petroleum and coal	3238	3576	3642	3473
G Basic metal industries	4909	5266	5534	5487

Canada

Million Canadian dollars

	1986 Gross output	1986 Intermediate consumption	1986 Value added	1987 Gross output	1987 Intermediate consumption	1987 Value added	1988 Gross output	1988 Intermediate consumption	1988 Value added	1989 Gross output	1989 Intermediate consumption	1989 Value added
At constant prices of: 1992												
H Manufacture of fabricated metal products, machinery and equipment	...	...	29611	...	...	30613	...	...	34080	...	...	35689
I Other manufacturing industries	...	...	2819	...	...	3001	...	...	3277	...	...	3175
4 Electricity, gas and water	...	...	21214	...	...	21925	...	...	22230	...	...	21794
A Electricity, gas and steam	...	...	20146	...	...	20844	...	...	21128	...	...	20653
B Water works and supply	...	...	1060	...	...	1070	...	...	1092	...	...	1136
5 Construction [a]	...	...	38241	...	...	40146	...	...	41244	...	...	43288
6 Wholesale and retail trade, restaurants and hotels	...	...	75528	...	...	80010	...	...	83594	...	...	86488
A Wholesale and retail trade	...	...	59213	...	...	63207	...	...	66382	...	...	68561
B Restaurants and hotels	...	...	16429	...	...	16777	...	...	17191	...	...	18204
7 Transport, storage and communication	...	...	34866	...	...	37294	...	...	39656	...	...	41022
A Transport and storage	...	...	23826	...	...	25165	...	...	26406	...	...	26476
B Communication	...	...	10567	...	...	11406	...	...	12466	...	...	13982
8 Finance, insurance, real estate and business services	...	...	104657	...	...	111097	...	...	117067	...	...	121231
A Financial institutions [b]	...	...	40607	...	...	42291	...	...	43014	...	...	43725
B Insurance	...	...	6512	...	...	6705	...	...	6672	...	...	6703
C Real estate and business services [b]	...	...	54626	...	...	58612	...	...	62872	...	...	66588
Real estate, except dwellings	...	...	22614	...	...	24990	...	...	27435	...	...	28694
Dwellings	...	...	33581	...	...	34521	...	...	36610	...	...	38591
9 Community, social and personal services	...	...	75108	...	...	76748	...	...	80052	...	...	82331
A Sanitary and similar services	...	...	631	...	...	719	...	...	716	...	...	674
B Social and related community services	...	...	51579	...	...	52484	...	...	53732	...	...	55460
Educational services	...	...	29044	...	...	29276	...	...	29665	...	...	30364
Medical, dental, other health and veterinary services	...	...	22269	...	...	23077	...	...	24102	...	...	24997
C Recreational and cultural services	...	...	9049	...	...	9060	...	...	9421	...	...	9156
D Personal and household services	...	...	13986	...	...	14642	...	...	16234	...	...	16955
Statistical discrepancy	...	...	−580	...	...	112	...	...	104	...	...	−169
Total, Industries	...	...	480281	...	...	503099	...	...	526984	...	...	540426
Producers of government services	...	...	66754	...	...	67278	...	...	68530	...	...	70099
Other producers	...	...	1746	...	...	1823	...	...	1896	...	...	1968
Total [c]	...	...	548405	...	...	569537	...	...	594891	...	...	607564
less: Imputed bank service charge	...	...	8843	...	...	9361	...	...	9828	...	...	10861
Import duties	...	...	...	...	...	...	...	...	...	...	...	...
Value added tax	...	...	...	...	...	...	...	...	...	...	...	...
Other adjustments [d]	...	...	80170	...	...	84823	...	...	91285	...	...	96013
Total	...	...	619732	...	...	644999	...	...	676348	...	...	692716

| 1990 | 1991 | 1992 | 1993 |

Canada

	Gross output	Intermediate consumption	Value added	Gross output	Intermediate consumption	Value added	Gross output	Intermediate consumption	Value added	Gross output	Intermediate consumption	Value added
At constant prices of: 1992												
All producers												
1 Agriculture, hunting, forestry and fishing	...	...	16789	...	...	16100	...	...	15317	...	...	16424
A Agriculture and hunting	...	...	11383	...	...	11443	...	...	10260	...	...	11148
B Forestry and logging	...	...	4533	...	...	3959	...	...	4031	...	...	4218
C Fishing	...	...	1260	...	...	1116	...	...	1026	...	...	1058
2 Mining and quarrying	...	...	21480	...	...	22406	...	...	23054	...	...	23745
A Coal mining	...	...	1016	...	...	1020	...	...	797	...	...	881
B Crude petroleum and natural gas production	...	...	11941	...	...	12648	...	...	14001	...	...	14571
C Metal ore mining	...	...	4953	...	...	5187	...	...	4994	...	...	4598
D Other mining	...	...	3539	...	...	3442	...	...	3262	...	...	3695
3 Manufacturing	...	...	102570	...	...	94999	...	...	96181	...	...	101877
A Manufacture of food, beverages and tobacco	...	...	16218	...	...	16181	...	...	16607	...	...	16653
B Textile, wearing apparel and leather industries	...	...	5754	...	...	5228	...	...	5025	...	...	5109
C Manufacture of wood and wood products, including furniture	...	...	7016	...	...	6161	...	...	6535	...	...	7000
D Manufacture of paper and paper products, printing and publishing	...	...	14473	...	...	13457	...	...	13112	...	...	13252
E Manufacture of chemicals and chemical petroleum, coal, rubber and plastic products	...	...	13425	...	...	12457	...	...	13062	...	...	14202
F Manufacture of non-metallic mineral products, except products of petroleum and coal	...	...	3196	...	...	2639	...	...	2547	...	...	2604
G Basic metal industries	...	...	5126	...	...	5083	...	...	5293	...	...	6015
H Manufacture of fabricated metal products, machinery and equipment	...	...	34028	...	...	30794	...	...	31059	...	...	34053
I Other manufacturing industries	...	...	2982	...	...	2990	...	...	2941	...	...	2989
4 Electricity, gas and water	...	...	20724	...	...	21849	...	...	21685	...	...	22485
A Electricity, gas and steam	...	...	19561	...	...	20687	...	...	20497	...	...	21185
B Water works and supply	...	...	1166	...	...	1159	...	...	1188	...	...	1300
5 Construction [a]	...	...	43503	...	...	40165	...	...	37112	...	...	35541
6 Wholesale and retail trade, restaurants and hotels	...	...	85535	...	...	81172	...	...	82116	...	...	83941
A Wholesale and retail trade	...	...	68108	...	...	65414	...	...	66154	...	...	67486
B Restaurants and hotels	...	...	18423	...	...	15905	...	...	15962	...	...	16455
7 Transport, storage and communication	...	...	41660	...	...	41192	...	...	42294	...	...	42445
A Transport and storage	...	...	26402	...	...	24758	...	...	26078	...	...	26523
B Communication	...	...	15121	...	...	15664	...	...	16216	...	...	15922
8 Finance, insurance, real estate and business services	...	...	122252	...	...	124300	...	...	125359	...	...	130267
A Financial institutions [b]	...	...	44172	...	...	45695	...	...	46144	...	...	47723
B Insurance	...	...	7088	...	...	7367	...	...	7654	...	...	7918
C Real estate and business services [b]	...	...	68917	...	...	70493	...	...	71561	...	...	74626

Canada

	1990 Gross output	1990 Intermediate consumption	1990 Value added	1991 Gross output	1991 Intermediate consumption	1991 Value added	1992 Gross output	1992 Intermediate consumption	1992 Value added	1993 Gross output	1993 Intermediate consumption	1993 Value added
At constant prices of: 1992												
Real estate, except dwellings	...	...	29272	...	...	29112	...	...	27782	...	...	29288
Dwellings	...	...	40398	...	...	42540	...	...	43779	...	...	45338
9 Community, social and personal services	...	...	83555	...	...	84880	...	...	86028	...	...	87580
A Sanitary and similar services	...	...	665	...	...	670	...	...	685	...	...	692
B Social and related community services	...	...	57050	...	...	58127	...	...	59152	...	...	60009
Educational services	...	...	30992	...	...	31355	...	...	32033	...	...	32649
Medical, dental, other health and veterinary services	...	...	25951	...	...	26559	...	...	27119	...	...	27360
C Recreational and cultural services	...	...	9213	...	...	9218	...	...	9312	...	...	9541
D Personal and household services	...	...	16551	...	...	16805	...	...	16879	...	...	17338
Statistical discrepancy	...	...	−593	...	...	−1072	...	...	...	...	...	...
Total, Industries	...	...	537475	...	...	525991	...	...	529146	...	...	544305
Producers of government services	...	...	71604	...	...	72490	...	...	72977	...	...	72653
Other producers	...	...	2085	...	...	2065	...	...	2154	...	...	2236
Total [c]	...	...	609231	...	...	600004	...	...	604275	...	...	619194
less: Imputed bank service charge	...	...	11029	...	...	11073	...	...	11169	...	...	11381
Import duties	...	...	...	...	...	...	...	...	...	...	...	...
Value added tax	...	...	...	...	...	...	...	...	...	...	...	...
Other adjustments [d]	...	...	96233	...	...	92243	...	...	94269	...	...	96929
Total	...	...	694435	...	...	681174	...	...	687377	...	...	704742

	1994 Gross output	1994 Intermediate consumption	1994 Value added	1995 Gross output	1995 Intermediate consumption	1995 Value added	1996 Gross output	1996 Intermediate consumption	1996 Value added	1997 Gross output	1997 Intermediate consumption	1997 Value added
At constant prices of: 1992												
All producers												
1 Agriculture, hunting, forestry and fishing	...	...	16879	...	...	17053	...	...	17432	...	...	17289
A Agriculture and hunting	...	...	11705	...	...	11830	...	...	12277	...	...	12264
B Forestry and logging	...	...	4247	...	...	4422	...	...	4304	...	...	4132
C Fishing	...	...	927	...	...	801	...	...	851	...	...	893
2 Mining and quarrying	...	...	25200	...	...	26223	...	...	27002	...	...	28175
A Coal mining	...	...	917	...	...	948	...	...	981	...	...	999
B Crude petroleum and natural gas production	...	...	15340	...	...	16047	...	...	16499	...	...	17065
C Metal ore mining	...	...	4353	...	...	4718	...	...	4925	...	...	4784
D Other mining	...	...	4590	...	...	4510	...	...	4597	...	...	5327
3 Manufacturing	...	...	108403	...	...	113740	...	...	114942	...	...	121999
A Manufacture of food, beverages and tobacco	...	...	17325	...	...	17502	...	...	17858	...	...	18244
B Textile, wearing apparel and leather industries	...	...	5345	...	...	5506	...	...	5349	...	...	5777
C Manufacture of wood and wood products, including furniture	...	...	7390	...	...	7467	...	...	7860	...	...	8596

Canada

	1994 Gross output	1994 Intermediate consumption	1994 Value added	1995 Gross output	1995 Intermediate consumption	1995 Value added	1996 Gross output	1996 Intermediate consumption	1996 Value added	1997 Gross output	1997 Intermediate consumption	1997 Value added
At constant prices of: 1992												
D Manufacture of paper and paper products, printing and publishing	...	...	13569	...	...	13631	...	...	13469	...	...	13928
E Manufacture of chemicals and chemical petroleum, coal, rubber and plastic products	...	...	14990	...	...	15636	...	...	15965	...	...	16943
F Manufacture of non-metallic mineral products, except products of petroleum and coal	...	...	2701	...	...	2791	...	...	2847	...	...	3051
G Basic metal industries	...	...	6127	...	...	6307	...	...	6523	...	...	6753
H Manufacture of fabricated metal products, machinery and equipment	...	...	37739	...	...	41493	...	...	41602	...	...	45108
I Other manufacturing industries	...	...	3217	...	...	3407	...	...	3469	...	...	3599
4 Electricity, gas and water	...	...	23402	...	...	23499	...	...	23957	...	...	23934
A Electricity, gas and steam	...	...	22097	...	...	22233	...	...	22767	...	...	22810
B Water works and supply	...	...	1305	...	...	1266	...	...	1190	...	...	1124
5 Construction [a]	...	...	37293	...	...	35397	...	...	36412	...	...	39062
6 Wholesale and retail trade, restaurants and hotels	...	...	89658	...	...	90888	...	...	92441	...	...	99147
A Wholesale and retail trade	...	...	72312	...	...	73381	...	...	74842	...	...	80753
B Restaurants and hotels	...	...	17346	...	...	17507	...	...	17599	...	...	18394
7 Transport, storage and communication	...	...	44669	...	...	46392	...	...	47919	...	...	50960
A Transport and storage	...	...	27707	...	...	28172	...	...	28253	...	...	29645
B Communication	...	...	16962	...	...	18220	...	...	19666	...	...	21315
8 Finance, insurance, real estate and business services	...	...	134856	...	...	138372	...	...	143203	...	...	149295
A Financial institutions [b]	...	...	49280	...	...	48965	...	...	50424	...	...	52153
B Insurance	...	...	8088	...	...	8039	...	...	8108	...	...	8167
C Real estate and business services [b]	...	...	77488	...	...	81368	...	...	84671	...	...	88975
Real estate, except dwellings	...	...	30782	...	...	33460	...	...	35750	...	...	38837
Dwellings	...	...	46706	...	...	47908	...	...	48921	...	...	50138
9 Community, social and personal services	...	...	88771	...	...	91106	...	...	91683	...	...	93126
A Sanitary and similar services	...	...	784	...	...	779	...	...	783	...	...	812
B Social and related community services	...	...	60518	...	...	62032	...	...	62264	...	...	62945
Educational services	...	...	32696	...	...	32808	...	...	32851	...	...	32681
Medical, dental, other health and veterinary services	...	...	27822	...	...	29224	...	...	29413	...	...	30264
C Recreational and cultural services	...	...	9853	...	...	10241	...	...	10480	...	...	10879
D Personal and household services	...	...	17616	...	...	18054	...	...	18156	...	...	18490
Total, Industries	...	...	569131	...	...	582670	...	...	594991	...	...	622987
Producers of government services	...	...	71685	...	...	70156	...	...	68009	...	...	66350
Other producers	...	...	2247	...	...	2262	...	...	2277	...	...	2288
Total [c]	...	...	643063	...	...	655088	...	...	665277	...	...	691625

Canada

	1994			1995			1996			1997		
	Gross output	Intermediate consumption	Value added	Gross output	Intermediate consumption	Value added	Gross output	Intermediate consumption	Value added	Gross output	Intermediate consumption	Value added
At constant prices of: 1992											
less: Imputed bank service charge	...	...	11885	...	...	12449	...	...	12670	...	...	13151
Import duties	...	...	...	...	...	...	...	...	...	...	...	...
Value added tax	...	...	...	...	...	...	...	...	...	...	...	...
Other adjustments [d]	...	...	101157	...	...	105221	...	...	104453	...	...	106558
Total	...	...	732335	...	...	747860	...	...	757060	...	...	785032

a The construction industry is defined on an activity basis. It includes all contract and own-account construction put in place.
b "Real estate" is included in "Financial institutions".
c Gross domestic product in factor values.
d Other adjustment includes indirect taxes, excluding import duties and goods and services tax (V.A.T.), less subsidies.

4.3 Cost components of value added

Million Canadian dollars

	1986						1987					
	Compensation of employees	Capital consumption	Net operating surplus	Indirect taxes	less: Subsidies received	Value added	Compensation of employees	Capital consumption	Net operating surplus	Indirect taxes	less: Subsidies received	Value added

All producers

1 Agriculture, hunting, forestry and fishing	4376	...	10912[a]	...	3985	15288	4771	...	9936[a]	...	3435	14706
A Agriculture and hunting	1999	...	9286[a]	...	3934	11285	2099	...	7592[a]	...	3391	9691
B Forestry and logging	2244	...	841[a]	...	24	3085	2514	...	1383[a]	...	27	3898
C Fishing	133	...	785[a]	...	26	918	157	...	961[a]	...	17	1117
2 Mining and quarrying	6283	...	15986[a]	...	102	22269	6042	...	18700[a]	...	133	24741
A Coal mining	444	...	521[a]	...	38	965	426	...	566[a]	...	21	991
B Crude petroleum and natural gas production	1905	...	11925[a]	...	14	13830	1793	...	13038[a]	...	12	14831
C Metal ore mining	1843	...	2147[a]	...	40	3990	1774	...	3657[a]	...	60	5431
D Other mining	2092	...	1392[a]	...	10	3484	2049	...	1439[a]	...	40	3488
3 Manufacturing	55497	...	30066[a]	...	699	85563	58986	...	34731[a]	...	759	93717
A Manufacture of food, beverages and tobacco	6720	...	5390[a]	...	281	12110	7019	...	6132[a]	...	291	13151
B Textile, wearing apparel and leather industries	3769	...	1577[a]	...	25	5346	3951	...	1707[a]	...	20	5658
C Manufacture of wood and wood products, including furniture	4455	...	1788[a]	...	14	6243	5098	...	2207[a]	...	17	7305
D Manufacture of paper and paper products, printing and publishing	8243	...	4539[a]	...	31	12781	8690	...	6247[a]	...	47	14938
E Manufacture of chemicals and chemical petroleum, coal, rubber and plastic products	5832	...	5122[a]	...	177	10953	6122	...	5194[a]	...	133	11317
F Manufacture of non-metallic mineral products, except products of petroleum and coal	1717	...	1195[a]	...	4	2912	1870	...	1562[a]	...	7	3432
G Basic metal industries	4432	...	1490[a]	...	17	5922	4602	...	2450[a]	...	29	7052
H Manufacture of fabricated metal products, machinery and equipment	18647	...	8447[a]	...	142	27093	19933	...	8523[a]	...	207	28456
I Other manufacturing industries	1683	...	519[a]	...	8	2203	1701	...	708[a]	...	9	2409
4 Electricity, gas and water	3813	...	12021[a]	...	598	15835	3954	...	12633[a]	...	617	16588

Canada

Million Canadian dollars

	1986						1987					
	Compensation of employees	Capital consumption	Net operating surplus	Indirect taxes	less: Subsidies received	Value added	Compensation of employees	Capital consumption	Net operating surplus	Indirect taxes	less: Subsidies received	Value added
A Electricity, gas and steam ...	3346	...	11686[a]	...	598	15033	3476	...	12278[a]	...	617	15754
B Water works and supply	467	...	335[a]	...	...	802	478	...	356[a]	...	...	834
5 Construction[b]	20106	...	8195[a]	...	7	28301	23533	...	9201[a]	...	4	32735
6 Wholesale and retail trade, restaurants and hotels	47024	...	17531[a]	...	207	64555	52292	...	18531[a]	...	149	70823
A Wholesale and retail trade ..	38326	...	14351[a]	...	174	52677	42897	...	15358[a]	...	130	58254
B Restaurants and hotels	8699	...	3180[a]	...	32	11878	9395	...	3174[a]	...	19	12569
7 Transport, storage and communication	20791	...	13673[a]	...	3082	34464	21578	...	14808[a]	...	3409	36386
A Transport and storage	14313	...	8306[a]	...	2756	22619	14815	...	9199[a]	...	3101	24014
B Communication	6479	...	5367[a]	...	326	11845	6763	...	5609[a]	...	307	12372
8 Finance, insurance, real estate and business services	31132	...	50786[a]	...	1879	81918	35560	...	54415[a]	...	1994	89975
A Financial institutions[c]	15968	...	16098[a]	...	1219	32066	18452	...	16607[a]	...	1355	35060
B Insurance	3768	...	1873[a]	...	...	5641	4028	...	2112[a]	...	1	6140
C Real estate and business services[c]	11397	...	32815[a]	...	660	44211	13079	...	35695[a]	...	638	48775
Real estate, except dwellings	11397	...	5514[a]	...	431	16911	13079	...	6270[a]	...	385	19350
Dwellings	...	...	27300[a]	...	229	27300	...	...	29425[a]	...	253	29425
9 Community, social and personal services	40613	...	14131[a]	...	616	54744	43932	...	15122[a]	...	530	59054
A Sanitary and similar services	254	...	189[a]	...	2	443	330	...	215[a]	...	2	545
B Social and related community services	28349	...	7749[a]	...	183	36098	30512	...	8429[a]	...	264	38941
Educational services	19372	...	1196[a]	...	1	20569	20550	...	1270[a]	...	2	21820
Medical, dental, other health and veterinary services	8977	...	6553[a]	...	182	15530	9962	...	7159[a]	...	261	17122
C Recreational and cultural services	4219	...	2327[a]	...	427	6546	4567	...	2311[a]	...	261	6878
D Personal and household services	7791	...	3866[a]	...	5	11657	8523	...	4168[a]	...	3	12690
Total, Industries	229636	...	173300[a]	...	11174	402936	250648	...	188077[a]	...	11029	438725
Producers of government services	41873	...	8051[a]	...	...	49924	44438	...	8510[a]	...	...	52948
Other producers	1245	...	128[a]	...	...	1373	1356	...	139[a]	...	...	1494
Total[d]	272755	...	181478[a]	...	11174	454233	296442	...	196726[a]	...	11029	493167
less: Imputed bank service charge	...	...	7644[a]	...	...	7644	...	...	8238[a]	...	...	8238
Import duties	...	...	...	...	...	4169	...	...	...	...	...	4220
Value added tax	...	...	...	...	...	...	...	...	...	...	...	...
Other adjustments[e]	...	...	−572[a]	...	...	53391	...	...	−1305[a]	...	...	60718
Total	272755	...	173262[a]	...	11174	504149	296442	...	187183[a]	...	11029	549867

	1988						1989					
	Compensation of employees	Capital consumption	Net operating surplus	Indirect taxes	less: Subsidies received	Value added	Compensation of employees	Capital consumption	Net operating surplus	Indirect taxes	less: Subsidies received	Value added

All producers

1 Agriculture, hunting, forestry and fishing	4952	...	10455[a]	...	3407	15407	5243	...	10823[a]	...	2953	16066
A Agriculture and hunting	2177	...	7749[a]	...	3349	9926	2337	...	8245[a]	...	2892	10582
B Forestry and logging	2589	...	1776[a]	...	39	4365	2695	...	1788[a]	...	40	4483

Canada

	1988						1989					
	Compensation of employees	Capital consumption	Net operating surplus	Indirect taxes	less: Subsidies received	Value added	Compensation of employees	Capital consumption	Net operating surplus	Indirect taxes	less: Subsidies received	Value added
C Fishing	186	...	931[a]	...	19	1117	211	...	791[a]	...	22	1001
2 Mining and quarrying	6710	...	18629[a]	...	92	25339	6953	...	18416[a]	...	151	25369
A Coal mining	462	...	624[a]	...	12	1086	515	...	407[a]	...	13	922
B Crude petroleum and natural gas production	2022	...	10177[a]	...	8	12199	2157	...	10549[a]	...	9	12705
C Metal ore mining	2007	...	5633[a]	...	39	7640	2253	...	5565[a]	...	101	7818
D Other mining	2218	...	2196[a]	...	33	4414	2028	...	1895[a]	...	29	3924
3 Manufacturing	64675	...	40161[a]	...	575	104835	68389	...	39481[a]	...	716	107869
A Manufacture of food, beverages and tobacco	7450	...	6121[a]	...	255	13570	7634	...	6430[a]	...	263	14063
B Textile, wearing apparel and leather industries	4162	...	1581[a]	...	12	5743	4238	...	1696[a]	...	20	5934
C Manufacture of wood and wood products, including furniture	5472	...	1620[a]	...	12	7092	5711	...	1714[a]	...	15	7425
D Manufacture of paper and paper products, printing and publishing	9551	...	7327[a]	...	31	16878	10230	...	6723[a]	...	43	16952
E Manufacture of chemicals and chemical petroleum, coal, rubber and plastic products	6775	...	7169[a]	...	84	13944	7162	...	6185[a]	...	108	13346
F Manufacture of non-metallic mineral products, except products of petroleum and coal	1998	...	1643[a]	...	6	3641	2070	...	1552[a]	...	8	3621
G Basic metal industries	5048	...	3526[a]	...	23	8574	5227	...	2607[a]	...	35	7834
H Manufacture of fabricated metal products, machinery and equipment	22280	...	10343[a]	...	143	32623	24018	...	11753[a]	...	208	35772
I Other manufacturing industries	1939	...	831[a]	...	10	2771	2100	...	822[a]	...	17	2922
4 Electricity, gas and water	4288	...	13536[a]	...	631	17823	4732	...	13404[a]	...	454	18135
A Electricity, gas and steam	3784	...	13148[a]	...	631	16932	4197	...	12977[a]	...	454	17173
B Water works and supply	503	...	388[a]	...	...	891	536	...	427[a]	...	...	962
5 Construction [b]	26714	...	9827[a]	...	3	36541	29899	...	11013[a]	...	4	40912
6 Wholesale and retail trade, restaurants and hotels	57767	...	20112[a]	...	125	77879	62650	...	21367[a]	...	135	84017
A Wholesale and retail trade	47521	...	16534[a]	...	110	64055	51118	...	17273[a]	...	108	68391
B Restaurants and hotels	10246	...	3579[a]	...	15	13824	11533	...	4094[a]	...	27	15627
7 Transport, storage and communication	22920	...	14784[a]	...	3323	37705	24044	...	15395[a]	...	3111	39439
A Transport and storage	15756	...	8866[a]	...	2970	24623	16522	...	9034[a]	...	2839	25557
B Communication	7164	...	5918[a]	...	353	13082	7521	...	6360[a]	...	271	13882
8 Finance, insurance, real estate and business services	40400	...	59678[a]	...	1954	100078	44503	...	64759[a]	...	1705	109262
A Financial institutions [c]	20591	...	17544[a]	...	1320	38135	22340	...	18672[a]	...	1207	41012
B Insurance	4414	...	2570[a]	...	2	6984	4596	...	2376[a]	...	5	6971
C Real estate and business services [c]	15395	...	39564[a]	...	632	54959	17567	...	43711[a]	...	493	61278
Real estate, except dwellings	15395	...	7412[a]	...	446	22807	17567	...	7950[a]	...	424	25517
Dwellings	...	...	32152[a]	...	187	32152	...	...	35761[a]	...	70	35761
9 Community, social and personal services	48344	...	16620[a]	...	501	64964	51889	...	18053[a]	...	589	69942
A Sanitary and similar services	376	...	250[a]	...	3	626	377	...	239[a]	...	1	616

Canada

	1988						1989					
	Compensation of employees	Capital consumption	Net operating surplus	Indirect taxes	less: Subsidies received	Value added	Compensation of employees	Capital consumption	Net operating surplus	Indirect taxes	less: Subsidies received	Value added
B Social and related community services	33245	...	9068[a]	...	283	42314	36070	...	9967[a]	...	337	46037
Educational services	22162	...	1366[a]	...	2	23528	23940	...	1484[a]	...	3	25424
Medical, dental, other health and veterinary services	11083	...	7702[a]	...	281	18785	12130	...	8483[a]	...	334	20613
C Recreational and cultural services	5277	...	2583[a]	...	213	7860	5280	...	2717[a]	...	247	7997
D Personal and household services	9445	...	4718[a]	...	3	14163	10161	...	5131[a]	...	4	15291
Total, Industries	276770	...	203802[a]	...	10611	480572	298302	...	212711[a]	...	9818	511012
Producers of government services	46991	...	9179[a]	...	...	56170	50758	...	9885[a]	...	...	60642
Other producers	1489	...	148[a]	...	...	1636	1683	...	164[a]	...	...	1847
Total [d]	325250	...	213128[a]	...	10611	538378	350743	...	222759[a]	...	9818	573502
less: Imputed bank service charge	...	...	9352[a]	...	...	9352	...	...	9746[a]	...	...	9746
Import duties	...	...	...	...	...	4644	...	...	...	...	...	4494
Value added tax	...	...	...	...	...	...	...	...	...	...	...	...
Other adjustments [e]	...	...	1795[a]	...	...	68765	...	...	388[a]	...	...	78195
Total	325250	...	205571[a]	...	10611	602435	350743	...	213401[a]	...	9818	646444

	1990						1991					
	Compensation of employees	Capital consumption	Net operating surplus	Indirect taxes	less: Subsidies received	Value added	Compensation of employees	Capital consumption	Net operating surplus	Indirect taxes	less: Subsidies received	Value added

All producers

1 Agriculture, hunting, forestry and fishing	5240	...	10989[a]	...	2774	16228	5398	...	9610[a]	...	3856	15008
A Agriculture and hunting	2418	...	8808[a]	...	2701	11226	2526	...	7857[a]	...	3761	10383
B Forestry and logging	2590	...	1391[a]	...	33	3982	2638	...	989[a]	...	43	3627
C Fishing	232	...	789[a]	...	41	1021	234	...	764[a]	...	52	998
2 Mining and quarrying	7128	...	19945[a]	...	76	27073	7679	...	14963[a]	...	79	22642
A Coal mining	485	...	568[a]	...	5	1054	503	...	496[a]	...	5	1000
B Crude petroleum and natural gas production	2181	...	13491[a]	...	6	15672	2546	...	10073[a]	...	7	12619
C Metal ore mining	2303	...	4237[a]	...	36	6540	2375	...	2882[a]	...	38	5257
D Other mining	2159	...	1649[a]	...	29	3807	2254	...	1512[a]	...	29	3766
3 Manufacturing	68580	...	35177[a]	...	815	103758	67385	...	29287[a]	...	863	96672
A Manufacture of food, beverages and tobacco	7747	...	7301[a]	...	288	15049	7930	...	8314[a]	...	274	16244
B Textile, wearing apparel and leather industries	4144	...	1488[a]	...	20	5632	3894	...	1332[a]	...	28	5226
C Manufacture of wood and wood products, including furniture	5608	...	1246[a]	...	15	6854	5088	...	631[a]	...	28	5719
D Manufacture of paper and paper products, printing and publishing	10562	...	5653[a]	...	55	16214	10582	...	3026[a]	...	90	13608
E Manufacture of chemicals and chemical petroleum, coal, rubber and plastic products	7512	...	6145[a]	...	104	13657	7483	...	6619[a]	...	59	14103
F Manufacture of non-metallic mineral products, except products of petroleum and coal	2048	...	1243[a]	...	5	3292	1901	...	768[a]	...	8	2669

Canada

	1990						1991					
	Compensation of employees	Capital consumption	Net operating surplus	Indirect taxes	less: Subsidies received	Value added	Compensation of employees	Capital consumption	Net operating surplus	Indirect taxes	less: Subsidies received	Value added
G Basic metal industries	5006	...	1145[a]	...	77	6150	5125	...	319[a]	...	37	5444
H Manufacture of fabricated metal products, machinery and equipment	23799	...	10182[a]	...	230	33981	23215	...	7437[a]	...	315	30652
I Other manufacturing industries	2155	...	774[a]	...	21	2929	2167	...	839[a]	...	24	3006
4 Electricity, gas and water	5145	...	13301[a]	...	344	18445	5720	...	14948[a]	...	268	20668
A Electricity, gas and steam	4558	...	12830[a]	...	344	17388	5099	...	14448[a]	...	268	19547
B Water works and supply	587	...	471[a]	...	...	1057	621	...	500[a]	...	...	1121
5 Construction[b]	31178	...	10130[a]	...	4	41308	29362	...	8962[a]	...	164	38324
6 Wholesale and retail trade, restaurants and hotels	64973	...	21095[a]	...	129	86068	64427	...	18869[a]	...	539	83296
A Wholesale and retail trade	52928	...	16782[a]	...	104	69710	52822	...	15026[a]	...	437	67847
B Restaurants and hotels	12045	...	4313[a]	...	25	16357	11606	...	3843[a]	...	101	15449
7 Transport, storage and communication	25119	...	15028[a]	...	3022	40147	25958	...	15212[a]	...	3412	41171
A Transport and storage	17131	...	8403[a]	...	2805	25534	17367	...	8361[a]	...	3201	25728
B Communication	7988	...	6625[a]	...	217	14613	8591	...	6851[a]	...	211	15442
8 Finance, insurance, real estate and business services	47351	...	67844[a]	...	2104	115195	50043	...	72279[a]	...	2678	122322
A Financial institutions[c]	23194	...	18080[a]	...	1450	41274	24610	...	20538[a]	...	1998	45148
B Insurance	5015	...	2790[a]	...	5	7805	5454	...	2329[a]	...	9	7783
C Real estate and business services[c]	19143	...	46974[a]	...	649	66117	19979	...	49412[a]	...	671	69391
Real estate, except dwellings	19143	...	8223[a]	...	521	27366	19979	...	7850[a]	...	559	27829
Dwellings	...	...	38751[a]	...	129	38751	...	...	41562[a]	...	112	41562
9 Community, social and personal services	57193	...	18636[a]	...	782	75829	61700	...	19681[a]	...	995	81381
A Sanitary and similar services	393	...	237[a]	...	4	630	457	...	175[a]	...	9	632
B Social and related community services	39963	...	10670[a]	...	525	50633	43744	...	11565[a]	...	657	55309
Educational services	25979	...	1592[a]	...	3	27571	28395	...	1589[a]	...	9	29985
Medical, dental, other health and veterinary services	13984	...	9078[a]	...	523	23062	15349	...	9976[a]	...	648	25325
C Recreational and cultural services	5741	...	2793[a]	...	239	8534	5989	...	2929[a]	...	221	8917
D Personal and household services	11096	...	4937[a]	...	14	16032	11510	...	5013[a]	...	109	16523
Total, Industries	311906	...	212145[a]	...	10051	524051	317672	...	203811[a]	...	12854	521483
Producers of government services	55162	...	10564[a]	...	...	65727	59546	...	10511[a]	...	...	70057
Other producers	1822	...	171[a]	...	...	1994	1874	...	172[a]	...	...	2046
Total[d]	368891	...	222881[a]	...	10051	591772	379092	...	214493[a]	...	12854	593585
less: Imputed bank service charge	...	...	9954[a]	...	...	9954	...	...	10725[a]	...	...	10725
Import duties	...	...	...	...	...	4237	...	...	...	...	...	3742
Value added tax	...	...	...	...	...	...	...	...	...	...	...	17379
Other adjustments[e]	...	...	20[a]	...	...	82126	...	...	14[a]	...	...	68533
Total	368891	...	212947[a]	...	10051	668181	379092	...	203782[a]	...	12854	672515

Canada

		1992						1993					
		Compensation of employees	Capital consumption	Net operating surplus	Indirect taxes	less: Subsidies received	Value added	Compensation of employees	Capital consumption	Net operating surplus	Indirect taxes	less: Subsidies received	Value added
	All producers												
1	Agriculture, hunting, forestry and fishing	5579	...	9737[a]	...	4132	15316	5892	...	10868[a]	...	2642	16760
	A Agriculture and hunting	2658	...	7602[a]	...	4055	10260	2761	...	7999[a]	...	2561	10760
	B Forestry and logging	2701	...	1329[a]	...	38	4030	2895	...	2069[a]	...	52	4964
	C Fishing	220	...	807[a]	...	38	1027	236	...	800[a]	...	29	1036
2	Mining and quarrying	7314	...	15740[a]	...	49	23054	7124	...	16909[a]	...	43	24033
	A Coal mining	454	...	343[a]	...	3	797	479	...	502[a]	...	2	981
	B Crude petroleum and natural gas production	2545	...	11456[a]	...	4	14001	2230	...	13287[a]	...	6	15517
	C Metal ore mining	2291	...	2703[a]	...	24	4994	2093	...	1798[a]	...	24	3891
	D Other mining	2024	...	1238[a]	...	19	3262	2322	...	1322[a]	...	12	3644
3	Manufacturing	68423	...	27761[a]	...	868	96184	69902	...	32983[a]	...	898	102884
	A Manufacture of food, beverages and tobacco	8515	...	8092[a]	...	222	16607	8547	...	7638[a]	...	180	16185
	B Textile, wearing apparel and leather industries	3698	...	1327[a]	...	19	5025	3737	...	1408[a]	...	24	5146
	C Manufacture of wood and wood products, including furniture	5273	...	1261[a]	...	20	6535	5689	...	2902[a]	...	21	8591
	D Manufacture of paper and paper products, printing and publishing	10548	...	2563[a]	...	98	13112	10577	...	2689[a]	...	109	13266
	E Manufacture of chemicals and chemical petroleum, coal, rubber and plastic products	7673	...	5389[a]	...	59	13062	7981	...	5766[a]	...	75	13747
	F Manufacture of non-metallic mineral products, except products of petroleum and coal	1823	...	724[a]	...	6	2547	1797	...	794[a]	...	7	2591
	G Basic metal industries	5186	...	107[a]	...	30	5293	5191	...	823[a]	...	41	6014
	H Manufacture of fabricated metal products, machinery and equipment	23606	...	7455[a]	...	396	31061	24291	...	10004[a]	...	417	34295
	I Other manufacturing industries	2100	...	842[a]	...	19	2942	2092	...	958[a]	...	23	3049
4	Electricity, gas and water	5959	...	15726[a]	...	245	21686	6472	...	16362[a]	...	205	22834
	A Electricity, gas and steam	5298	...	15200[a]	...	245	20498	5808	...	15808[a]	...	205	21617
	B Water works and supply	661	...	526[a]	...	...	1188	663	...	554[a]	...	...	1217
5	Construction[b]	28330	...	8782[a]	...	74	37112	27496	...	8535[a]	...	85	36031
6	Wholesale and retail trade, restaurants and hotels	65084	...	17033[a]	...	271	82117	65952	...	18115[a]	...	276	84068
	A Wholesale and retail trade	52959	...	13195[a]	...	217	66154	53359	...	14113[a]	...	211	67472
	B Restaurants and hotels	12124	...	3838[a]	...	54	15963	12593	...	4002[a]	...	64	16596
7	Transport, storage and communication	26644	...	15650[a]	...	3484	42294	27048	...	16077[a]	...	3256	43125
	A Transport and storage	17851	...	8227[a]	...	3297	26078	18399	...	8738[a]	...	3105	27137
	B Communication	8793	...	7423[a]	...	186	16216	8648	...	7340[a]	...	151	15988
8	Finance, insurance, real estate and business services	50776	...	74582[a]	...	2250	125358	52819	...	78897[a]	...	2055	131715
	A Financial institutions[c]	25397	...	20746[a]	...	1582	46143	26028	...	22164[a]	...	1430	48193
	B Insurance	5418	...	2236[a]	...	4	7654	5673	...	2785[a]	...	5	8457
	C Real estate and business services[c]	19961	...	51599[a]	...	664	71560	21118	...	53948[a]	...	620	75065

Canada

	1992						1993					
	Compensation of employees	Capital consumption	Net operating surplus	Indirect taxes	less: Subsidies received	Value added	Compensation of employees	Capital consumption	Net operating surplus	Indirect taxes	less: Subsidies received	Value added
Real estate, except dwellings	19961	...	7820[a]	...	528	27782	21118	...	8161[a]	...	576	29279
Dwellings	...	...	43779[a]	...	136	43779	...	...	45787[a]	...	44	45787
9 Community, social and personal services	65437	...	20591[a]	...	950	86028	67377	...	20987[a]	...	1028	88365
A Sanitary and similar services	474	...	211[a]	...	13	685	473	...	245[a]	...	9	717
B Social and related community services	46953	...	12200[a]	...	582	59153	48470	...	12261[a]	...	661	60731
Educational services	30393	...	1639[a]	...	5	32033	31187	...	1699[a]	...	5	32886
Medical, dental, other health and veterinary services	16560	...	10560[a]	...	576	27120	17284	...	10562[a]	...	657	27846
C Recreational and cultural services	6128	...	3184[a]	...	274	9312	6332	...	3311[a]	...	277	9643
D Personal and household services	11882	...	4996[a]	...	81	16878	12102	...	5171[a]	...	81	17274
Total, Industries	323546	...	205601[a]	...	12324	529148	330082	...	219733[a]	...	10489	549815
Producers of government services	62262	...	10715[a]	...	...	72977	62914	...	11065[a]	...	...	73979
Other producers	1980	...	174[a]	...	...	2154	2052	...	177[a]	...	...	2229
Total [d]	387788	...	216490[a]	...	12324	604279	395047	...	230975[a]	...	10489	626023
less: Imputed bank service charge	...	...	11169[a]	...	...	11169	...	...	11607[a]	...	...	11607
Import duties	...	...	...	...	...	4125	...	...	...	...	...	3368
Value added tax	...	...	...	...	...	17786	...	...	...	...	...	18153
Other adjustments [e]	...	...	−1533[a]	...	...	72354	...	...	−1775[a]	...	...	77377
Total	387788	...	203788[a]	...	12324	687375	395047	...	217593[a]	...	10489	713314

a Column "Consumption of fixed capital" is included in column "Net operating surplus".
b The construction industry is defined on an activity basis. It includes all contract and own-account construction put in place.
c "Real estate" is included in "Financial institutions".
d Gross domestic product at factor cost.
e Other adjustment includes indirect taxes, excluding import duties and goods and services tax (V.A.T.), less subsidies.

Cayman Islands

Source

Reply to the United Nations National Accounts Questionnaire from the Government Statistics Office, Grand Cayman. The official estimates are published in *National Income Estimates of the Cayman Islands*.

General note

The estimates shown in the following tables have been prepared by the Government Statistics Office in accordance with the United Nations System of National Accounts (1968 SNA) so far as the existing data would permit.

1.1 Expenditure on the gross domestic product, in current prices

Million Cayman Islands dollars

	1986	1987	1988	1989	1990	1991	1992	1993	1994	1995	1996	1997
1 Government final consumption expenditure	44	53	60	67	84	93	...	...	...	...	...	...
2 Private final consumption expenditure	181	215	268	308	369	385	...	...	...	...	...	...
A Households	181	215	268	308	369	385	...	...	...	...	...	...
B Private non-profit institutions serving households	...	...	...	...	...	...	...	...	...	...	...	...
3 Gross capital formation	67	74	105	110	126	134	...	...	...	...	...	...
A Increase in stocks	...	...	...	...	...	...	...	...	...	...	...	...
B Gross fixed capital formation	67	74	105	110	126	134	...	...	...	...	...	...
4 Exports of goods and services	200	243	261	285	378	363	...	...	...	...	...	...
5 less: Imports of goods and services	204	246	295	326	345	325	...	...	...	...	...	...
Statistical discrepancy [a]	2	–	15	30	–22	–34	...	...	...	...	...	...
equals: Gross domestic product	290	339	414	474	590	616	...	...	...	...	...	...

[a] Item "Statistical discrepancy" relates to the difference between the estimate of GDP through industrial origin approach and that of expenditure approach.

1.2 Expenditure on the gross domestic product, in constant prices

Million Cayman Islands dollars

	1986	1987	1988	1989	1990	1991	1992	1993	1994	1995	1996	1997
	At constant prices of: 1986											
1 Government final consumption expenditure	44	50	53	56	63	68	...	...	...	...	...	...
2 Private final consumption expenditure	181	201	235	256	279	283	...	...	...	...	...	...
A Households	181	201	235	256	279	283	...	...	...	...	...	...
B Private non-profit institutions serving households	...	...	...	...	...	...	...	...	...	...	...	...
3 Gross capital formation	67	70	92	92	95	98	...	...	...	...	...	...
A Increase in stocks	...	...	...	...	...	...	...	...	...	...	...	...
B Gross fixed capital formation	67	70	92	92	95	98	...	...	...	...	...	...
4 Exports of goods and services	200	227	229	237	286	267	...	...	...	...	...	...

Cayman Islands

Million Cayman Islands dollars

	1986	1987	1988	1989	1990	1991	1992	1993	1994	1995	1996	1997
At constant prices of: 1986												
5 less: Imports of goods and services	204	230	259	271	261	239	...	...	...	...	...	...
Statistical discrepancy	2	–1	12	24	–16	–25	...	...	...	...	...	...
equals: Gross domestic product	290	317	362	394	446	452	...	...	...	...	...	...

1.9 Gross domestic product by institutional sectors of origin

Million Cayman Islands dollars

	1986	1987	1988	1989	1990	1991	1992	1993	1994	1995	1996	1997
Domestic factor incomes originating												
1 General government	29	34	40	45	58	63	...	...	...	...	...	...
2 Corporate and quasi-corporate enterprises [a]	165	199	250	300	347	365	...	...	...	...	...	...
3 Households and private unincorporated enterprises [b]	25	29	37	41	46	52	...	...	...	...	...	...
4 Non-profit institutions serving households	...	...	...	...	...	...	...	...	...	...	...	...
subtotal: Domestic factor incomes	219	262	327	386	451	480	...	...	...	...	...	...
Indirect taxes, net	48	57	67	72	82	90	...	...	...	...	...	...
A Indirect taxes	49	59	70	75	83	91	...	...	...	...	...	...
B less: Subsidies	1	2	3	3	1	1	...	...	...	...	...	...
Consumption of fixed capital	23	28	34	38	42	47	...	...	...	...	...	...
Statistical discrepancy	–	–8	–14	–22	15	–1	...	...	...	...	...	...
Gross domestic product	290	339	414	474	590	616	...	...	...	...	...	...

a Item "Corporate and quasi-corporate enterprises" includes private unincorporated enterprises.   b Only domestic servants and rental of dwellings are included in item "Households and private unincorporated enterprises".

1.10 Gross domestic product by kind of activity, in current prices

Million Cayman Islands dollars

	1986	1987	1988	1989	1990	1991	1992	1993	1994	1995	1996	1997
1 Agriculture, hunting, forestry and fishing	2	2	2	2	2	2	...	...	...	...	...	...
2 Mining and quarrying	1	2	3	3	2	2	...	...	...	...	...	...
3 Manufacturing	6	7	8	9	9	9	...	...	...	...	...	...
4 Electricity, gas and water	7	9	12	15	18	19	...	...	...	...	...	...
5 Construction	27	29	40	52	56	55	...	...	...	...	...	...
6 Wholesale and retail trade, restaurants and hotels	60	72	92	116	142	138	...	...	...	...	...	...
7 Transport, storage and communication	38	36	48	52	63	65	...	...	...	...	...	...
8 Finance, insurance, real estate and business services [a]	86	110	134	153	197	210	...	...	...	...	...	...
9 Community, social and personal services	20	22	25	27	34	42	...	...	...	...	...	...
Total, Industries	247	290	364	429	522	542	...	...	...	...	...	...
Producers of government services	30	34	40	45	58	63	...	...	...	...	...	...
Other producers	...	...	...	...	...	...	...	...	...	...	...	...
Subtotal	277	323	404	473	580	605	...	...	...	...	...	...
less: Imputed bank service charge	7	8	12	15	26	30	...	...	...	...	...	...
plus: Import duties	22	28	34	37	42	41	...	...	...	...	...	...

Cayman Islands

Million Cayman Islands dollars

	1986	1987	1988	1989	1990	1991	1992	1993	1994	1995	1996	1997
plus: Value added tax	...	...	...	...	...	...	...	...	...	...	...	...
plus: Other adjustments	–2	–4	–12	–21	–6	–	...	...	...	...	...	...
equals: Gross domestic product	290	339	414	474	590	616	...	...	...	...	...	...

a Item "Finance, insurance, real estate and business services" excludes banks and insurance companies registered in Cayman Islands but with no physical presence in the Islands.

1.11 Gross domestic product by kind of activity, in constant prices

Million Cayman Islands dollars

	1986	1987	1988	1989	1990	1991	1992	1993	1994	1995	1996	1997
At constant prices of: 1986												
1 Agriculture, hunting, forestry and fishing	2	1	1	1	1	2	...	...	...	...	...	...
2 Mining and quarrying	1	2	3	3	2	2	...	...	...	...	...	...
3 Manufacturing	6	7	7	8	7	6	...	...	...	...	...	...
4 Electricity, gas and water	7	8	10	11	13	14	...	...	...	...	...	...
5 Construction	27	27	36	42	44	41	...	...	...	...	...	...
6 Wholesale and retail trade, restaurants and hotels	60	68	79	95	114	107	...	...	...	...	...	...
7 Transport, storage and communication	38	36	43	49	52	54	...	...	...	...	...	...
8 Finance, insurance, real estate and business services [a]	86	100	118	122	132	135	...	...	...	...	...	...
9 Community, social and personal services	20	21	22	25	31	38	...	...	...	...	...	...
Total, Industries	247	270	319	356	396	399	...	...	...	...	...	...
Producers of government services	30	32	34	37	43	46	...	...	...	...	...	...
Other producers	...	...	...	...	...	...	...	...	...	...	...	...
Subtotal	277	302	353	393	439	445	...	...	...	...	...	...
less: Imputed bank service charge	7	7	10	14	28	33	...	...	...	...	...	...
plus: Import duties	22	26	30	33	42	44	...	...	...	...	...	...
plus: Value added tax	...	...	...	...	...	...	...	...	...	...	...	...
plus: Other adjustments	–2	–4	–11	–18	–7	–4	...	...	...	...	...	...
equals: Gross domestic product	290	317	362	394	446	452	...	...	...	...	...	...

a Item "Finance, insurance, real estate and business services" excludes banks and insurance companies registered in Cayman Islands but with no physical presence in the Islands.

1.12 Relations among national accounting aggregates

Million Cayman Islands dollars

	1986	1987	1988	1989	1990	1991	1992	1993	1994	1995	1996	1997
Gross domestic product	290	339	414	474	590	616	...	...	...	...	...	...
plus: Net factor income from the rest of the world	–19	–30	–40	–51	–61	–58	...	...	...	...	...	...
Factor income from rest of the world	8	7	8	9	9	7	...	...	...	...	...	...
less: Factor income to the rest of the world	27	37	48	60	70	65	...	...	...	...	...	...
equals: Gross national product	271	309	374	423	529	558	...	...	...	...	...	...
less: Consumption of fixed capital	23	28	34	38	42	47	...	...	...	...	...	...
equals: National income	248	281	340	385	487	511	...	...	...	...	...	...
plus: Net current transfers from the rest of the world	7	9	11	13	15	15	...	...	...	...	...	...

Cayman Islands

Million Cayman Islands dollars

	1986	1987	1988	1989	1990	1991	1992	1993	1994	1995	1996	1997
equals: National disposable income	255	290	351	398	502	526	...	...	...	...	...	...
less: Final consumption	225	268	329	376	453	478	...	...	...	...	...	...
equals: Net saving	30	22	22	22	49	48	...	...	...	...	...	...
less: Surplus of the nation on current transactions	−30	−42	−86	−106	−43	−35	...	...	...	...	...	...
Statistical discrepancy	−16	−18	−37	−56	−8	4	...	...	...	...	...	...
equals: Net capital formation	44	46	71	72	84	87	...	...	...	...	...	...

Chad

Source

Reply to the United Nations National Accounts Questionnaire from the Sous-Direction de la Statistique, Direction du Plan et du Développement, Ministère des Finances, de l'Economie et du Plan, Ndjamena.

General note

The official estimates have been adjusted by the Sous-Direction de la Statistique in accordance with the United Nations System of National Accounts (1968 SNA) so far as the existing data would permit.

1.1 Expenditure on the gross domestic product, in current prices

Thousand million CFA francs

	1986	1987	1988	1989	1990	1991	1992	1993	1994	1995	1996	1997
1 Government final consumption expenditure	38	66	63	73	61	66	62	70	59	...	...	...
2 Private final consumption expenditure	259	224	238	262	265	269	265	242	258	...	...	...
3 Gross capital formation	24	23	25	29	25	26	31	23	45	...	...	...
A Increase in stocks	–	–	–	–	–	–	–	–	–	...	...	...
B Gross fixed capital formation	24	23	25	29	25	26	31	23	45	...	...	...
4 Exports of goods and services	51	55	67	63	65	66	62	58	105	...	...	...
5 less: Imports of goods and services	111	123	83	105	83	55	69	102	6	...	...	...
equals: Gross domestic product	260	246	311	323	333	373	351	292	461	...	...	...

1.10 Gross domestic product by kind of activity, in current prices

Thousand million CFA francs

	1986	1987	1988	1989	1990	1991	1992	1993	1994	1995	1996	1997
1 Agriculture, hunting, forestry and fishing	96	91	128	112	108	90	103	81	102	...	...	...
2 Mining and quarrying	1	1	1	1	1	1	1	1	1	...	...	...
3 Manufacturing	45	40	48	60	68	57	54	47	62	...	...	...
4 Electricity, gas and water	2	2	2	2	2	2	2	2	3	...	...	...
5 Construction	3	3	3	4	3	3	4	3	5	...	...	...
6 Wholesale and retail trade, restaurants and hotels	86	78	92	98	99	106	102	85	139	...	...	...
7 Transport, storage and communication										...	...	...
8 Finance, insurance, real estate and business services										...	...	...
9 Community, social and personal services										...	...	...
Total, Industries	232	214	273	277	282	259	266	218	313	...	...	...
Producers of government services	18	19	20	27	30	32	32	33	35	...	...	...
Other producers	...	...	...	...	...	...	...	...	...	...	...	...
Subtotal	250	234	293	304	312	292	297	251	348	...	...	...

Chad

Thousand million CFA francs

	1986	1987	1988	1989	1990	1991	1992	1993	1994	1995	1996	1997
less: Imputed bank service charge	...	...	...	...	...	...	...	...	...	...	...	...
plus: Import duties	...	...	...	...	...	...	...	...	...	...	...	...
plus: Value added tax	...	...	...	...	...	...	...	...	...	...	...	...
plus: Other adjustments	10	12	17	18	21	81	53	41	113	...	...	...
equals: Gross domestic product	260	246	311	323	333	373	351	292	461	...	...	...

1.11 Gross domestic product by kind of activity, in constant prices

Thousand million CFA francs

	1986	1987	1988	1989	1990	1991	1992	1993	1994	1995	1996	1997
At constant prices of: 1977												
1 Agriculture, hunting, forestry and fishing	70	67	83	79	67	90	103	81	102	...	...	...
2 Mining and quarrying	–	–	–	–	–	–	1	–	–	...	...	...
3 Manufacturing	24	22	25	30	34	29	28	25	24	...	...	...
4 Electricity, gas and water	1	1	1	1	1	1	1	1	1	...	...	...
5 Construction	2	2	2	2	2	2	2	2	2	...	...	...
6 Wholesale and retail trade, restaurants and hotels	54	50	57	59	59	61	64	55	57	...	...	...
7 Transport, storage and communication										...	...	...
8 Finance, insurance, real estate and business services										...	...	...
9 Community, social and personal services										...	...	...
Total, Industries	151	143	168	173	164	184	200	164	187	...	...	...
Producers of government services	16	19	20	22	21	21	21	21	21	...	...	...
Other producers	...	...	...	...	...	...	...	...	...	...	...	...
Subtotal [a]	168	162	188	194	185	205	221	185	208	...	...	...
less: Imputed bank service charge	...	...	...	...	...	...	...	...	...	...	...	...
plus: Import duties	...	...	...	...	...	...	...	...	...	...	...	...
plus: Value added tax	...	...	...	...	...	...	...	...	...	...	...	...
plus: Other adjustments [b]	7	8	9	11	...	...	...	...	...	...	...	...
equals: Gross domestic product	175	170	196	205	...	...	...	...	...	...	...	...

a Gross domestic product in factor values.   b Item "Other adjustments" refers to indirect taxes net of subsidies.

Chile

General note

The preparation of national accounts statistics in Chile is undertaken by Banco Central de Chile, Santiago. The official estimates are published in *Cuentas Nacionales de Chile*. The following presentation of sources and methods is mainly based on a detailed description received by the United Nations from ODEPLAN. However, descriptions can also be found in *Cuentas Nacionales de Chile, 1960-1975*. The estimates are generally in accordance with the classifications and definitions recommended in the United Nations System of National Accounts (1968 SNA). The following tables have been prepared from successive replies to the United Nations national accounts questionnaire. When the scope and coverage of the estimates differ for conceptual or statistical reasons from the definitions and classifications recommended in SNA, a footnote is indicated to the relevant tables.

Gross domestic product

Gross domestic product is estimated mainly through the production approach.

Expenditures on the gross domestic product

The expenditure approach is used to estimate government final consumption expenditure, increase in stocks, exports and imports of goods and services and capital formation in new construction. The commodity-flow approach is used to estimate other construction. Private final consumption expenditure is estimated as a residual. Data on government consumption expenditure is obtained, that is through special inquiries and direct information from the concerned authorities. Values of locally produced and imported capital goods are adjusted by coefficients by type of capital goods to arrive at purchasers' values. Estimates of exports and imports of goods and services are obtained from the balance of payments statements prepared by the Central Bank. To arrive at constant prices, value added of government services is deflated by index of wages and salaries. Purchases of goods and services are deflated by the wholesale price index and the price index of intermediate imported goods. For private consumption expenditure most domestically produced items are deflated by appropriate components of the consumer price index. Imported goods are deflated by the price index of imported consumer goods. For gross fixed capital formation, buildings and other construction are devalued using double deflation. Base year estimates of transport equipment, machinery and equipment are extrapolated by a quantity index for each industrial group, except for imports which are deflated by price indexes of imported capital goods. Price deflation is used for exports and imports of goods and services.

Cost structure of the gross domestic product

Wages and salaries are in most cases estimated from company accounts and/or direct information from the enterprises. Employers' contributions to social security schemes as well as wages and salaries in kind are included in the estimates. Operating surplus is obtained as a residual. Depreciation data are obtained from accounting statements of enterprises or computed from data of fixed assets by type of capital and useful life time. For indirect taxes, published fiscal statements by type of tax, are used.

Gross domestic product by kind of activity

This table is prepared at market prices, that is, producers' values. The production approach is used to estimate value added of most industries. The income approach is however used for government services, business services and domestic services. The general method of estimating gross value of agricultural production involves the use of physical quantities of production together with the respective wholesale or producers' prices. Quantities of livestock production are obtained from published data and directly from Instituto Nacional de Estadística (INE). The estimates include both marketed and non-marketed production. The inputs into agriculture and forestry are based on information from the suppliers of input products. The estimates for the mining and quarrying sector are mainly based on data on sales and change in stocks, but in some cases on physical production valued at average sales price or on expenditure data in the construction and industrial sectors. For manufacturing, the required statistics for companies with 1 to 49 employees are found in their annual industrial declarations. For units with 50 or more employees, the industrial yearbook of INE is used.

The gross value of construction in the public sector is obtained from accounts of the respective institutions. For the private sector the construction expenditure on all buildings is calculated on the basis of the municipal building permits. In order to estimate intermediate consumption and the components of value added, cost-structure by type of construction are applied to the gross value of production. Estimates of private sector trade is made on the basis of a continuous survey. For public enterprises, information provided in their accounting statements and in their budget statements is used. For transport, information is based on accounts, sales data and on the stock of motor vehicles. The production and input estimates for financial institutions and corporations, real estate and insurance are made possible through data from the Superintendencia de Bancos. Benchmark estimates for actual rents paid and imputed rent for owner-occupied dwellings have been made on the basis of the housing censuses in 1960 and 1970. These estimates are projected annually by a value

Chile

index which combines the increase in physical stock with a price index for rent. For public administration and defense, budgets and accounts provide the required basic data. For the constant price estimates, double deflation is used in the agricultural sector, the output value is extrapolated by quantity indexes by product, whereas intermediate inputs are deflated by an index of input prices.

Value added of fishing, mining and quarrying, manufacturing and electricity is extrapolated by quantity indexes of production. Double deflation is used for construction, current gross values are deflated by price indexes for each type of construction. For intermediate consumption, input structures are used. For trade, value added of the base year is extrapolated by a quantity index. Double deflation is used for the transport and financing, insurance, real estate and business services sector. For transport, current output is deflated separately for different uses and types of transport. For financial institutions, output is deflated by an implicit price index for expenditure. Output of ownership of dwellings is extrapolated by an index based on the change in the housing stock, whereas inputs are deflated by the value index for repairs. For community, social and personal services, double deflation is used.

1.1 Expenditure on the gross domestic product, in current prices

Ten million Chilean pesos

	1986	1987	1988	1989	1990	1991	1992	1993	1994	1995	1996	1997
1 Government final consumption expenditure	43017	49410	61334	74179	90187	116960	146902	180352	212854	254335	290626[a]	...
2 Private final consumption expenditure	223875	290618	354535	442196	571956	766086	989373	1184675	1382907	1618713	1862595[a]	...
3 Gross capital formation	64570	100998	134740	184936	232168	272891	361500	476408	515569	667380	759830[a]	...
A Increase in stocks	5968	12837	14586	11588	18208	31690	20996	28453	17536	49670	51024[a]	...
B Gross fixed capital formation	58602	88161	120154	173348	213960	241201	340504	447954	498033	617710	708806[a]	...
Residential buildings	10839	15317	21648	29901[b]	37399[b]	46359[b]	64151[b]	93762[b]	98517[b]	123160[b]	135595[ab]	...
Non-residential buildings	3962	4747	7758	9757	13249	17704	23580	35793	42460	49189	59829[a]	...
Other construction and land improvement, etc.	19685	25925	30799	41260	59863	62095	88529	106048	127651	142127	179978[a]	...
Other	24116	42171	59948	92431	103449	115043	164244	212351	229405	303233	333403[a]	...
4 Exports of goods and services	99463	137430	204560	263880	320092	401193	465460	494313	626953	790495	804120[a]	...
5 less: Imports of goods and services	89004	124399	163382	229819	289852	347082	444691	538256	598764	743350	863552[a]	...
equals: Gross domestic product	341921	454056	591788	735373	924550	1210047	1518544	1797492	2139518	2587573	2853619[a]	...

a Provisional data
b Corresponds to private dwellings.

1.2 Expenditure on the gross domestic product, in constant prices

Ten million Chilean pesos

	1986	1987	1988	1989	1990	1991	1992	1993	1994	1995	1996	1997
	At constant prices of: 1986											
1 Government final consumption expenditure	43017	41909	43414	45046	45420	47044	49675	51817	52822	55027	56709	...
2 Private final consumption expenditure	223875	240057	256930	282998	289201	314853	358272	384885	416354	457226	497249	...
3 Gross capital formation	64570	81902	91408	115743	121955	122796	149545	181109	182511	244944	263335	...
A Increase in stocks	5968	10576	9987	9898	13445	14479	15204	22646	14246	37137	35522	...
B Gross fixed capital formation	58602	71326	81421	105846	108510	108317	134341	158463	168265	207807	227813	...
Residential buildings	10839	12316	14669	17767	18185	19468	25321	31275	27322	32294	33747	...
Non-residential buildings	3962	3896	5338	5983	6538	7341	9916	12220	12138	13325	15160	...
Other construction and land improvement, etc.	19685	22134	21613	25249	29069	24972	25723	29257	33527	34380	40920	...
Other	24116	32980	39802	56847	54718	56536	73380	85712	95279	127807	137987	...
4 Exports of goods and services	99463	106168	118436	137517	149367	167939	191327	198089	221122	245409	270029	...
5 less: Imports of goods and services	89004	105567	119073	148886	157535	168487	205231	234336	258048	322511	357124	...
equals: Gross domestic product	341921	364468	391115	432418	448407	484145	543588	581565	614761	680095	730197	...

Chile

1.3 Cost components of the gross domestic product

Ten million Chilean pesos

	1986	1987	1988	1989	1990	1991	1992	1993	1994	1995	1996	1997
1 Indirect taxes, net	...	...	...	87952	117961	154022	205318	263113	295506	348823	397115	...
2 Consumption of fixed capital	...	...	...	74126	94339	119272	143257	169269	195727	226978	256909	...
3 Compensation of employees paid by resident producers to ..	...	...	...	236773	312344	413523	535600	658209	779160	925904	1055339	...
4 Operating surplus	...	...	...	336522	399906	523230	634369	706901	869125	1095868	1144255	...
equals: Gross domestic product ..	...	...	...	735373	924550	1210047	1518544	1797492	2139518	2587573	2853619	...

1.4 General government current receipts and disbursements

Ten million Chilean pesos

	1986	1987	1988	1989	1990	1991	1992	1993	1994	1995	1996	1997
Receipts												
1 Operating surplus	...	...	...	...	−12	–	−6	148	–	–	...	...
2 Property and entrepreneurial income	...	...	...	...	38772	32428	31303	31765	35267	69514	...	...
3 Taxes, fees and contributions .	...	...	...	...	181330	246354	329019	409980	468348	562791	...	...
A Indirect taxes	...	...	...	...	123710	162956	214105	272412	305648	361413	...	...
B Direct taxes	...	...	...	...	37446	58860	79242	96982	115478	148172	...	...
C Social security contributions	...	...	...	...	18240	21911	31588	36241	41635	46834	...	...
D Compulsory fees, fines and penalties	...	...	...	...	1935	2627	4084	4345	5586	6371	...	...
4 Other current transfers	...	...	...	...	8138	13435	8388	11680	14024	13090	...	...
Statistical discrepancy	...	...	...	...	2	9	5	–	2	...	...	...
Total current receipts of general government	...	...	...	...	228230	292226	368709	453573	517642	645395	...	...
Disbursements												
1 Government final consumption expenditure	...	...	...	...	90187	116960	146902	180352	212854	254335	...	...
2 Property income	...	...	...	...	37268	41530	39757	43895	48288	55752	...	...
A Interest	...	...	...	...	37268	41530	39757	43895	48288	55752	...	...
B Net land rent and royalties ..	...	...	...	...	...	...	...	...	...	...	...	...
3 Subsidies	...	...	...	...	5749	8934	8787	9299	10142	12589	...	...
4 Other current transfers	...	...	...	...	59283	78469	100476	115537	137225	157514	...	...
A Social security benefits	...	...	...	...	52587	67922	86149	101585	116881	132132	...	...
B Social assistance grants	...	...	...	...	...	1325	1476	1775	1895	2006	...	...
C Other	...	...	...	...	6695	9222	12850	12177	18449	23375	...	...
Statistical discrepancy	...	...	...	...	...	1	–	–	2	–	...	...
5 Net saving	...	...	...	...	35743	46333	72788	104490	109131	165204	...	...
Total current disbursements and net saving of general government	...	...	...	...	228230	292226	368709	453573	517642	645395	...	...

Chile

1.7 External transactions on current account, summary

Ten million Chilean pesos

	1986	1987	1988	1989	1990	1991	1992	1993	1994	1995	1996	1997
Payments to the rest of the world												
1 Imports of goods and services	89004	124399	163382	229819	289852	347082	444691	538256	598764	743350	863552	...
2 Factor income to rest of the world	40810	41278	51565	59550	68467	88570	89852	89215	130965	145339	160516	...
3 Current transfers to the rest of the world	961	948	689	681	4785	6614	5739	8727	4983	6936	5853	...
Statistical discrepancy	818	2931	–935	–5526	–6666	...	...	...	...	...	...	...
4 Surplus of the nation on current transactions	–25105	–22649	–2946	–13348	–17425	–3408	–34352	–99966	–65162	–51175	–165626	...
Payments to the rest of the world and surplus of the nation on current transfers	106488	146906	211754	276702	345679	438859	505930	536232	669550	844449	864295	...
Receipts from the rest of the world												
1 Exports of goods and services	99463	137430	204560	263880	320092	401193	465460	494313	626953	790495	804120	...
2 Factor income from rest of the world	4399	3991	4533	6385	14824	20130	20216	20246	23738	34699	33664	...
3 Current transfers from rest of the world	2672	3489	5018	6436	10764	17536	20254	21672	18860	19255	26511	...
Statistical discrepancy	–47	1997	–2357	–7274	–9441	...	...	...	...	...	...	...
Receipts from the rest of the world on current transactions	106488	146906	211754	276702	345679	438859	505930	536232	669550	844449	864295	...

1.8 Capital transactions of the nation, summary

Ten million Chilean pesos

	1986	1987	1988	1989	1990	1991	1992	1993	1994	1995	1996	1997
Finance of gross capital formation												
Gross saving	39465	78348	131794	171588	214744	269483	327148	376442	450407	616204	594204	690412
1 Consumption of fixed capital	...	...	...	74126	94339	119272	143257	169269	195727	226978	256909	...
2 Net saving	...	...	...	...	...	...	...	...	...	...	...	...
less: Surplus of the nation on current transactions	–25105	–22650	–2946	–13348	–17425	–3408	–34352	–99966	–65162	–51175	–165626	–178633
Finance of gross capital formation	64570	100998	134740	184936	232168	272891	361500	476408	515569	667380	759830	869045
Gross capital formation												
Increase in stocks	5968	12837	14586	11588	18208	31690	20996	28453	17536	49670	51024	56132
Gross fixed capital formation	58602	88161	120154	173348	213960	241201	340504	447954	498033	617710	708806	812914
Gross capital formation	64570	100998	134740	184936	232168	272891	361500	476408	515569	667380	759830	869045

1.10 Gross domestic product by kind of activity, in current prices

Ten million Chilean pesos

	1986	1987	1988	1989	1990	1991	1992	1993	1994	1995	1996	1997
1 Agriculture, hunting, forestry and fishing	29301	39928	50194	61073	76151	112005	139794	144404	160511	181209	189601	...
2 Mining and quarrying	34285	51675	91487	104030	116163	122730	114662	103264	157188	228743	200917	...
3 Manufacturing	61093	79497	106869	132624	171153	230833	288327	346400	411615	500692	549003	...
4 Electricity, gas and water	9176	11349	15056	20239	23695	35797	44949	56304	67093	78939	84255	...
5 Construction	16355	21863	30385	36716	51557	62870	87554	123078	146864	176030	210836	...

Chile

Ten million Chilean pesos

	1986	1987	1988	1989	1990	1991	1992	1993	1994	1995	1996	1997
6 Wholesale and retail trade, restaurants and hotels	48280	70088	79559	106281	128581	171354	217198	251025	278941	335053	367750	...
7 Transport, storage and communication	21693	27633	35574	47706	62272	82967	107022	125107	148086	168768	195346	...
8 Finance, insurance, real estate and business services	41832	51956	60175	76634	91037	106907	143621	182931	230872	273323	312400	...
9 Community, social and personal services	49854	61282	75067	92186	122598	162119	212494	265797	323302	386692	449784	...
Total, Industries	311868	415272	544367	677488	843205	1087582	1355621	1598309	1924473	2329450	2559892	...
Producers of government services	14974	17569	21453	25524	31231	40641	51636	61869	73199	86901	100507	...
Other producers	...	...	...	...	...	...	...	...	...	...	...	...
Subtotal	326842	432841	565820	703012	874436	1128223	1407257	1660178	1997672	2416351	2660398	...
less: Imputed bank service charge	23443	29834	28952	34385	41909	36775	46340	62905	79873	91268	102529	...
plus: Import duties	27175	34955	36328	27357	32454	33513	40244	48141	54787	63827	72735	...
plus: Value added tax	11347	16093	18592	39389	59569	85087	117383	152077	166932	198663	223014	...
plus: Other adjustments	...	...	...	...	...	...	...	...	...	...	...	...
equals: Gross domestic product	341921	454056	591788	735373	924550	1210047	1518544	1797492	2139518	2587573	2853619	...

1.11 Gross domestic product by kind of activity, in constant prices

Ten million Chilean pesos

	1986	1987	1988	1989	1990	1991	1992	1993	1994	1995	1996	1997
At constant prices of: 1986												
1 Agriculture, hunting, forestry and fishing	29301	32092	35787	38023	41487	42494	47595	49081	52783	56434	58611	58485
2 Mining and quarrying	34285	34173	36848	39720	40088	45053	44404	44332	48275	52780	59622	64427
3 Manufacturing	61093	64317	69985	77650	78416	82601	92029	98706	102735	110475	114327	119402
4 Electricity, gas and water	9176	9677	10223	9421	8600	10918	13929	14605	15511	16694	16897	18502
5 Construction	16355	17849	19383	21541	23701	23338	26523	32751	32404	35618	38837	41483
6 Wholesale and retail trade, restaurants and hotels	48280	53540	56384	65297	68314	74884	88034	94421	99261	113312	123925	134083
7 Transport, storage and communication	21693	23768	25855	29539	31867	34549	40536	42887	45196	51831	57288	64667
8 Finance, insurance, real estate and business services	41832	45179	49302	55915	56994	65397	72788	77820	83358	91506	98118	105395
9 Community, social and personal services	49854	50831	52310	53628	54965	56808	59630	61692	63905	65901	68356	71092
Total, Industries	311868	331427	356077	390734	404432	436042	485467	516295	543428	594551	635981	677536
Producers of government services	14974	14726	14793	14746	14916	15165	15605	15895	16068	16293	16516	16740
Other producers	...	...	...	...	...	...	...	...	...	...	...	...
Subtotal	326842	346152	370870	405479	419348	451207	501073	532190	559496	610844	652497	694276
less: Imputed bank service charge	23443	24974	27329	30091	31174	33481	36869	39192	40970	44453	47653	51220
plus: Import duties	27175	13945	15746	20891	22413	24865	31661	36600	40475	52017	58024	66939
plus: Value added tax	11347	29345	31829	36138	37820	41554	47723	51965	55760	61687	67330	71772
plus: Other adjustments	...	...	...	...	...	...	...	...	...	...	...	...
equals: Gross domestic product	341921	364468	391115	432418	448407	484145	543588	581565	614761	680095	730197	781767

Chile

1.12 Relations among national accounting aggregates

Ten million Chilean pesos

	1986	1987	1988	1989	1990	1991	1992	1993	1994	1995	1996	1997
Gross domestic product	341921	454056	591788	735373	924550	1210047	1518544	1797492	2139518	2587573	2853619	...
plus: Net factor income from the rest of the world	−37384	−38440	−48456	−53165	−56818	−68440	−69640	−68970	−107230	−110640	−126850	...
equals: Gross national product	304537	415616	543332	682208	867732	1141608	1448904	1728522	2032289	2476933	2726769	...
less: Consumption of fixed capital	...	...	...	...	...	...	...	...	...	...	...	...
equals: National income	...	...	...	...	...	...	...	...	...	...	...	...
plus: Net current transfers from the rest of the world	1820	2760	4332	5756	6071	11870	15634	15544	14265	14085	...	...
equals: National disposable income	...	...	...	...	...	...	...	...	...	...	...	...
less: Final consumption	266891	340028	415870	526869	651522	859719	1112157	1356586	1573384	1888887	...	...
equals: Net saving	...	...	...	...	...	...	...	...	...	...	...	...
less: Surplus of the nation on current transactions	−25105	−22650	−2946	−13353	−18849	−5287	−31066	−89241	−31278	5951	...	...
equals: Net capital formation	...	...	...	...	...	...	...	...	...	...	...	...

China

Source

Reply to the United Nations National Accounts Questionnaire and communication from the State Statistical Bureau of the People's Republic of China, Beijing.

General note

The estimates shown in the following table have been prepared in accordance with the System of National Accounts (SNA) so far as the existing data would permit.

1.1 Expenditure on the gross domestic product, in current prices

Million Yuan Renminbi

	1986	1987	1988	1989	1990	1991	1992	1993	1994	1995	1996	1997
1 Government final consumption expenditure	136700	149000	172700	203300	225200	283000	349230	449970	598620	669050	785160	865040
2 Private final consumption expenditure	517500	596120	763310	852350	911320	1031590	1245980	1568240	2123000	2783890	3318790	3723440
3 Gross capital formation	384600	432200	549500	609500	644400	751700	963600	1499800	1926060	2387700	2686720	2856400
A Increase in stocks	74800	58000	87100	175600	171200	157700	131900	201800	240430	357650	353110	286600
B Gross fixed capital formation	309800	374200	462400	433900	473200	594000	831700	1298000	1685630	2030050	2333610	2569800
4 Exports of goods and services	−25520	1150	−15110	−18550	51030	61750	27560	−67950	63410	99850	145930	274500
5 less: Imports of goods and services												
Statistical discrepancy	6940	17780	22430	44320	22840	33740	77440	13380	−35150	−92680	−148140	−130480
equals: Gross domestic product	1020220	1196250	1492830	1690920	1854790	2161780	2663810	3463440	4675940	5847810	6788460	7477240

1.10 Gross domestic product by kind of activity, in current prices

Million Yuan Renminbi

	1986	1987	1988	1989	1990	1991	1992	1993	1994	1995	1996	1997
1 Agriculture, hunting, forestry and fishing	276390	320430	383100	422800	501700	528860	580000	688210	945720	1199300	1384420	1396880
2 Mining and quarrying	396700	458580	577720	648400	685800	808710	1028450	1414380	1935960	2471830	2908260	3175230
3 Manufacturing												
4 Electricity, gas and water												
5 Construction	52570	66580	81000	79400	85940	101510	141500	228470	301260	381960	453030	501800
6 Wholesale and retail trade, restaurants and hotels	94320	115930	161800	168700	141970	208700	273500	309070	405040	493230	556030	628150
7 Transport, storage and communication	47560	54490	66100	78600	114750	140970	168180	212320	268590	305470	349400	452550
8 Finance, insurance, real estate and business services	58150	73650	94460	144740	155980	165630	212210	269770	363750	454140	516670	588890
9 Community, social and personal services	94530	106590	128650	148280	168650	207400	259970	341220	455620	541880	620650	733740
Total, Industries	1020220	1196250	1492830	1690920	1854790	2161780	2663810	3463440	4675940	5847810	6788460	7477240
Producers of government services	...	...	...	...	...	...	...	...	...	...	...	...
Other producers	...	...	...	...	...	...	...	...	...	...	...	...
Subtotal	1020220	1196250	1492830	1690920	1854790	2161780	2663810	3463440	4675940	5847810	6788460	7477240

China

Million Yuan Renminbi	1986	1987	1988	1989	1990	1991	1992	1993	1994	1995	1996	1997
less: Imputed bank service charge	...	...	...	...	...	...	...	...	...	...	...	...
plus: Import duties	...	...	...	...	...	...	...	...	...	...	...	...
plus: Value added tax	...	...	...	...	...	...	...	...	...	...	...	...
plus: Other adjustments	...	...	...	...	...	...	...	...	...	...	...	...
equals: Gross domestic product	1020220	1196250	1492830	1690920	1854790	2161780	2663810	3463440	4675940	5847810	6788460	7477240

1.12 Relations among national accounting aggregates

Million Yuan Renminbi	1986	1987	1988	1989	1990	1991	1992	1993	1994	1995	1996	1997
Gross domestic product	1020220	1196250	1492830	1690920	1854790	2161780	2663810	3463440	4675940	5847810	6788460	7477240
plus: Net factor income from the rest of the world	−80	−800	−600	860	5050	4470	1380	−7390	−8940	−98320	−103410	−131990
equals: Gross national product	1020140	1195450	1492230	1691780	1859840	2166250	2665190	3456050	4667000	5749490	6685050	7345250
less: Consumption of fixed capital	102000	118900	134300	159200	182000	215800	250600	363100	...	...	...	...
equals: National income	918140	1076550	1357930	1532580	1677840	1950450	2414590	3092950	...	...	...	...
plus: Net current transfers from the rest of the world	1300	800	1600	1400	1400	4500	6400	6800	...	...	...	...
equals: National disposable income	919440	1077350	1359530	1533980	1679240	1954950	2420990	3099750	...	...	...	...
less: Final consumption	654200	745120	936010	1055650	1136520	1314590	1595210	2018210	2721620	3452940	4103950	4588480
equals: Net saving	265240	332230	423520	478330	542720	640360	825780	1081540	...	...	...	...
less: Surplus of the nation on current transactions	−16410	19120	8320	26740	74950	104790	112730	−63550	...	...	...	...
Statistical discrepancy	950	190	_	−1290	−5370	330	−50	−8390	...	...	...	...
equals: Net capital formation	282600	313300	415200	450300	462400	535900	713000	1136700	...	...	...	...

China, Hong Kong Special Administrative Region

General note

The preparation of national accounts statistics in Hong Kong SAR is undertaken by the Census and Statistics Department, Hong Kong. The official estimates together with methodological notes of the estimates have been published in a series of publications entitled *Estimates of Gross Domestic Product*, issued annually since 1973. The estimates are generally in accordance with the definitions and classifications recommended in the United Nations System of National Accounts (1968 SNA) so far as the existing data would permit. When the scope and coverage of the estimates differ for conceptual or statistical reasons from the definitions and classifications recommended in SNA, a footnote is indicated to the relevant tables.

Gross domestic product

Gross domestic product is estimated mainly through the expenditure approach.

Expenditures on the gross domestic product

The expenditure approach is used to estimate government final consumption expenditure and exports and imports of goods and services. The commodity-flow approach is used for private final consumption expenditure and gross capital formation supplemented by the expenditure approach. Government consumption expenditure data up to 1972 were obtained from the annual reports of the Accountant-General which provided data on the actual expenditure of each department by financial year ending 31 March. Since 1973, quarterly figures have been available from the Treasury and adjustment to a calendar year basis is no longer required. The estimates relate to current expenditure on goods and services by government departments not engaged in trading activities. For the large proportion of the commodities included in private consumption expenditure which is imported, adequate and detailed trade statistics are available. Trade statistics of retained imports are supported and complemented by data from the household expenditure surveys, censuses/surveys of manufacturing establishments, sample surveys on sales of business establishments, administrative statistics and other sources. Foodstuffs produced domestically for local consumption are compiled from the annual output estimates made by the Agriculture and Fisheries Department and other government departments concerned. Imported and domestically produced commodities are reported in importers' and producers' values, respectively, and the retail value is arrived at by adding transport expenses and distributors' profit margins. Estimates of changes in inventories of distributors and manufacturers have been compiled based on results of the censuses/surveys of manufacturing establishments and distributive trades from 1973 onwards. Prior to 1973, token estimates on changes in inventories were made based on the ratio of the 1980 GDP estimates with and without adjustment for changes in inventories. Information on quantities of hydrocarbon oils kept in stock by oil companies are obtained from the Industry Department. For gross fixed capital formation, investment in machinery and equipment is based mainly on the value of retained imports of capital goods, with a percentage added to allow for profit, transport, assembly charges and installation expenses. Estimates of domestically manufactured machinery and equipment locally purchased are calculated from results of the censuses/surveys of manufacturing establishments. Private sector investment in building and construction prior to 1979 is based on the monthly statistical returns of the Building Ordinance Office. From 1979 it is based on the results of annual Survey of Building, Construction and Real Estate Sectors while investment in the government sector is obtained from an analysis of the accounts of government departments.

The estimates of exports and imports of merchandise are obtained from detailed external trade statistics. For port and airport charges and expenditure of non-residents in Hong Kong and that of Hong Kong residents abroad, the main sources of data are the surveys conducted by the Hong Kong Tourist Association, surveys on expenditure of Hong Kong residents abroad, and government accounts. The estimates of other items of imports and exports of services were not available prior to 1978. From 1978 onwards, an annual survey of imports and exports of services has been conducted to provide estimates in respect of the other items of services. Token estimates were made for years prior to 1978 based on benchmark information obtained from the annual survey.

For the constant price estimates, price deflation is used for most of the expenditure items. The current values are deflated by various price indexes such as specially constructed salary rate index, consumer price indexes, tourist price index, cost index of building and construction, overall index of unit values of exports and imports, etc. For changes in inventories, unit value index of imports as well as the consumer price index of appropriate commodity groups are used.

Cost structure of the gross domestic product

The main components of the table: compensation of employees and operating surplus are complied using the production approach. Data, available since 1980, are based on information collected from economic censuses/surveys conducted for the various major economic sectors.

China, Hong Kong SAR

Gross domestic product by kind of activity

The estimates are compiled using the production approach. Data available since 1980 are based on information collected from economic censuses/surveys conducted for the various major economic sectors.

1.1 Expenditure on the gross domestic product, in current prices

Million Hong Kong dollars

	1986	1987	1988	1989	1990	1991	1992	1993	1994	1995	1996	1997
1 Government final consumption expenditure	22887	25722	30008	36253	43283	51470	64070	72620	83658	94236	104385	114161
2 Private final consumption expenditure	189159	219315	254682	287677	330459	391098	451670	514239	592665	654496	722098	802715
A Households	177077	205602	238398	267722	306122	362671	421326	480246	553627	610511	673874	748718
B Private non-profit institutions serving households	12082	13713	16284	19955	24337	28427	30344	33993	39038	43985	48224	53997
3 Gross capital formation	73941	101458	130261	139667	159504	181827	221995	247481	322375	375234	383063	469364
A Increase in stocks [a]	6183	9746	14132	3463	5728	4098	8187	2299	21263	45656	10322	1594
B Gross fixed capital formation	67758	91712	116129	136204	153776	177729	213808	245182	301112	329578	372741	467770
Residential buildings [b]	11667	12868	17390	19911	23475	23826	24517	25725	28708	28322	35472	49832
Non-residential buildings	6832	9931	12042	16433	20311	23339	22088	21744	24201	27914	32199	42561
Other construction and land improvement, etc. [c]	8687	11797	14166	20020	21824	27226	34368	45605	58442	58656	72224	81922
Other	40572	57116	72531	79840	88166	103338	132835	152108	189761	214686	232846	293455
4 Exports of goods and services	348345	470306	604051	697656	782195	926973	1114304	1261827	1410681	1609762	1690675	1749322
5 less: Imports of goods and services	321771	432313	563980	637392	732892	882856	1072704	1198704	1398494	1656583	1707612	1796468
equals: Gross domestic product	312561	384488	455022	523861	582549	668512	779335	897463	1010885	1077145	1192609	1339094

a Refer to "Changes in inventories".
b Item "Residential buildings" includes also combined residential and non-residential buildings.
c Item "other construction and land improvement" includes also transfer costs of land and buildings.

1.2 Expenditure on the gross domestic product, in constant prices

Million Hong Kong dollars

	1986	1987	1988	1989	1990	1991	1992	1993	1994	1995	1996	1997
At constant prices of: 1990												
1 Government final consumption expenditure	36185	37598	39005	41035	43283	46617	52789	53935	56057	57857	60146	61613
2 Private final consumption expenditure	253618	279138	302329	312682	330459	359019	386519	415618	443571	450450	471766	503348
A Households	233512	258327	280710	290017	306122	333542	361847	390796	417869	424086	444482	474867
B Private non-profit institutions serving households	20106	20811	21619	22665	24337	25477	24672	24822	25702	26364	27284	28481
3 Gross capital formation	120090	139504	151772	145580	159504	172140	191933	192483	240229	283903	279754	316998
A Increase in stocks [a]	7095	10464	14317	3376	5728	4081	8453	2224	20058	40103	9608	3703
B Gross fixed capital formation	112995	129040	137455	142204	153776	168059	183480	190259	220171	243800	270146	313295
Residential buildings [b]	21083	19834	21645	21519	23475	22576	23024	23785	25953	24083	27646	34079
Non-residential buildings	12372	15248	15191	18005	20311	22034	20502	20098	21541	23040	24109	28601
Other construction and land improvement, etc. [c]	17635	21141	20392	21330	21824	24529	27250	32889	39840	40002	45991	44127
Other	61905	72817	80227	81350	88166	98920	112704	113487	132837	156675	172400	206488
4 Exports of goods and services	415496	536680	662009	721293	782195	899622	1064219	1199006	1316878	1461273	1538603	1618378

China, Hong Kong SAR

Million Hong Kong dollars

	1986	1987	1988	1989	1990	1991	1992	1993	1994	1995	1996	1997
At constant prices of: 1990												
5 less: Imports of goods and services	374978	484157	605813	657222	732892	865382	1045113	1170819	1329229	1497651	1559869	1668223
equals: Gross domestic product	450411	508763	549302	563368	582549	612016	650347	690223	727506	755832	790400	832114

a Refer to "Changes in inventories".
b Item "Residential buildings" includes also combined residential and non-residential buildings.
c Item "other construction and land improvement" includes also transfer costs of land and buildings.

1.3 Cost components of the gross domestic product

Million Hong Kong dollars

	1986	1987	1988	1989	1990	1991	1992	1993	1994	1995	1996	1997
1 Indirect taxes, net [a]	15212	20445	21450	25390	29614	36323	48777	53278	56286	52974	62442	...
2 Consumption of fixed capital	...	...	...	...	...	...	...	...	...	...	...	...
3 Compensation of employees paid by resident producers to ..	155954	184569	216828	252498	290838	326002	369292	418032	463764	521206	574723	...
4 Operating surplus [b]	140054	182226	221427	246437	268608	305512	362826	412137	486408	494910	555907	...
Statistical discrepancy [c]	1341	−2752	−4684	−465	−6511	675	−1562	14016	4427	8056	−463	...
equals: Gross domestic product ..	312561	384488	455022	523861	582549	668512	779335	897463	1010885	1077145	1192609	...

a Refers to taxes on production and imports.
b Item "Operating surplus" includes consumption of fixed capital.
c The estimates shown refers to the difference between production estimate and expenditure estimate.

1.4 General government current receipts and disbursements

Million Hong Kong dollars

	1986	1987	1988	1989	1990	1991	1992	1993	1994	1995	1996	1997
1 Government final consumption expenditure	22887	25722	30008	36253	43283	51470	64070	72620	83658	94236	104385	114161
A Compensation of employees	17028	19108	21964	26072	31241	38273	48579	54965	63123	71312	80015	86935
B Consumption of fixed capital	...	...	...	...	...	...	...	...	...	...	...	...
C Purchases of goods and services, net	7110	8080	9724	12015	14313	16030	18812	21578	25142	28497	30819	34482
D less: Own-account fixed capital formation	1251	1466	1680	1834	2271	2833	3321	3923	4607	5573	6449	7256
E Indirect taxes paid, net	...	...	...	...	...	...	...	...	...	...	...	...
2 Property income	...	...	...	...	...	...	...	...	...	...	...	...
3 Subsidies	...	...	...	...	...	...	...	...	...	...	...	...
4 Other current transfers	...	...	...	...	...	...	...	...	...	...	...	...
Total current disbursements and net saving of general government	...	...	...	...	...	...	...	...	...	...	...	...

1.10 Gross domestic product by kind of activity, in current prices

Million Hong Kong dollars

	1986	1987	1988	1989	1990	1991	1992	1993	1994	1995	1996	1997
1 Agriculture, hunting, forestry and fishing	1308	1334	1417	1386	1432	1441	1468	1612	1596	1453	1444	...
2 Mining and quarrying	346	257	229	224	210	222	205	197	249	317	311	...
3 Manufacturing	66836	80713	90035	96170	98352	97223	99764	92582	87354	84770	82769	...
4 Electricity, gas and water	8385	9691	10199	10860	12612	13521	15637	17591	22175	23578	26989	...
5 Construction	14253	17024	20658	25738	30220	34659	37337	43089	46325	54761	65058	...
6 Wholesale and retail trade, restaurants and hotels	66020	89249	109793	124749	140722	163284	190760	224462	249167	270520	301277	...
7 Transport, storage and communication	24192	31693	40005	44654	52927	60604	71227	78993	92109	102199	111087	...

China, Hong Kong SAR

Million Hong Kong dollars

		1986	1987	1988	1989	1990	1991	1992	1993	1994	1995	1996	1997
8	Finance, insurance, real estate and business services	80340	101566	126229	148831	172384	212169	259864	304412	370005	382918	432084	...
9	Community, social and personal services	21450	23521	27202	29966	32444	35472	41125	50693	59886	71700	81843	...
	Statistical discrepancy [a]	...	–2752	–4684	–465	–6511	675	–1562	14016	4427	8056	–463	...
	Total, Industries	283130	352296	425767	482578	541303	618595	717387	813631	928866	992216	1102862	...
	Producers of government services	17028	19108	21964	26072	31241	38273	48579	54965	63123	71312	80015	...
	Other producers	8928	10382	11836	14085	17643	20548	20999	24750	28284	32944	37109	...
	Subtotal [b]	309086	381786	459567	522735	590187	677416	786965	893346	1020273	1096472	1219986	...
	less: Imputed bank service charge [c]	13079	17743	21313	23800	30741	45902	54846	63177	70101	80358	89356	...
	plus: Import duties	...	...	...	...	...	...	...	...	...	...	...	...
	plus: Value added tax	1341	...	...	...	...	...	...	...	...	...	...	...
	plus: Other adjustments [d]	15212	20445	21450	25390	29614	36323	48777	53278	56286	52974	62442	...
	equals: Gross domestic product	312561	384488	455022	523861	582549	668512	779335	897463	1010885	1077145	1192609	...

a The estimates shown refers to the difference between production estimate and expenditure estimate.
b Gross domestic product in factor values.
c FISIM
d Refers to taxes on production and imports.

2.5 Private final consumption expenditure by type and purpose, in current prices

Million Hong Kong dollars

		1986	1987	1988	1989	1990	1991	1992	1993	1994	1995	1996	1997
	Final consumption expenditure of resident households												
1	Food, beverages and tobacco	38219	42124	46752	51114	57451	63276	68008	73342	83747	94814	104240	106800
	A Food	34454	37782	41629	45787	51491	56864	60776	66608	76685	87028	95473	98184
	B Non-alcoholic beverages												
	C Alcoholic beverages	2083	2527	2944	2603	2927	3157	3341	3274	3601	3651	4320	4759
	D Tobacco	1682	1815	2179	2724	3033	3255	3891	3460	3461	4135	4447	3857
2	Clothing and footwear [a]	36526	45328	55895	61529	69778	78318	95670	115498	126616	131572	151775	166466
3	Gross rent, fuel and power	28386	31951	37018	42784	49182	56749	66154	75149	90460	106842	123885	139774
4	Furniture, furnishings and household equipment and operation	21800	27387	33029	35040	36871	47890	57714	62501	72007	78655	78950	79936
	A Household operation	3007	3350	3900	4472	5074	5618	6364	7063	7635	8635	9475	10282
	B Other	18793	24037	29129	30568	31797	42272	51350	55438	64372	70020	69475	69654
5	Medical care and health expenses	11180[b]	12901[b]	9567	9996	12032	14132	17065	19282	24804	29966	34504	36544
6	Transport and communication	13367	16032	20173	22390	27127	33722	44312	47785	52969	54504	57757	68286
7	Recreational, entertainment, education and cultural services	16841	20016	23370	26266	28626	33424	35877	45538	50882	57934	66377	68248
	A Education	2335	2654	3003	3496	4079	4576	5056	5823	7075	8173	9457	10657
	B Other	14506	17362	20367	22770	24547	28848	30821	39715	43807	49761	56920	57591
8	Miscellaneous goods and services	15336	19552	26346	32004	35813	41214	49556	56048	61571	64752	69126	77483
	A Personal care	...	...	4686	5443	6219	7758	7993	10061	12421	14917	15729	14557
	B Expenditures in restaurants, cafes and hotels	...	...	...	...	...	...	...	...	...	...	...	...
	C Other	...	...	...	...	...	...	...	...	...	...	...	...
	Total final consumption expenditure in the domestic market by households, of which	181655	215291	252150	281123	316880	368725	434356	495143	563056	619039	686614	743537
	plus: Direct purchases abroad by resident households	14712	17523	21997	26383	31823	37803	41522	47628	56189	67422	72819	78059

China, Hong Kong SAR

Million Hong Kong dollars

	1986	1987	1988	1989	1990	1991	1992	1993	1994	1995	1996	1997
less: Direct purchases in the domestic market by non-resident households	19290	27212	35749	39784	42581	43857	54552	62525	65618	75950	85559	72878
equals: Final consumption expenditure of resident households	177077	205602	238398	267722	306122	362671	421326	480246	553627	610511	673874	748718

Final consumption expenditures by private non-profit organisations serving households

	1986	1987	1988	1989	1990	1991	1992	1993	1994	1995	1996	1997
1 Research and science	...	...	...	...	...	...	...	...	...	...	...	...
2 Education	...	...	...	...	...	...	...	...	...	...	...	...
3 Medical and other health services	...	...	...	...	...	...	...	...	...	...	...	...
4 Welfare services	...	...	...	...	...	...	...	...	...	...	...	...
5 Recreational and related cultural services	...	...	...	...	...	...	...	...	...	...	...	...
6 Religious organisations	...	...	...	...	...	...	...	...	...	...	...	...
7 Professional and labour organisations serving households	...	...	...	...	...	...	...	...	...	...	...	...
8 Miscellaneous	...	...	...	...	...	...	...	...	...	...	...	...
equals: Final consumption expenditures by private non-profit organisations serving households	12082	13713	16284	19955	24337	28427	30344	33993	39038	43985	48224	53997
Private final consumption expenditure	189159	219315	254682	287677	330459	391098	451670	514239	592665	654496	722098	802715

a Personal effects are included in item "Clothing and footwear". b Personal care is included in "Medical care and health expenses".

2.6 Private final consumption expenditure by type and purpose, in constant prices

Million Hong Kong dollars

	1986	1987	1988	1989	1990	1991	1992	1993	1994	1995	1996	1997
At constant prices of: 1990												

Final consumption expenditure of resident households

	1986	1987	1988	1989	1990	1991	1992	1993	1994	1995	1996	1997
1 Food, beverages and tobacco	50923	53275	54711	54635	57451	56901	57080	58600	64045	66841	69367	69803
A Food	45623	47580	48219	48313	51491	51770	52049	54234	59153	62302	64458	65113
B Non-alcoholic beverages												
C Alcoholic beverages	2883	3242	3691	3040	2927	2959	2762	2563	3012	2433	2748	2907
D Tobacco	2417	2453	2801	3282	3033	2172	2269	1803	1880	2106	2161	1783
2 Clothing and footwear [a]	47880	55318	63229	65337	69778	73141	83157	94363	96136	93142	102077	107050
3 Gross rent, fuel and power	34882	38027	42622	46500	49182	51072	54045	57218	59860	63050	66479	69183
4 Furniture, furnishings and household equipment and operation	26198	31278	35431	36260	36871	46185	53899	57222	63768	67686	66123	65128
A Household operation	4302	4484	4748	4925	5074	5222	5436	5719	5683	5991	6275	6534
B Other	21896	26794	30683	31335	31797	40963	48463	51503	58085	61695	59848	58594
5 Medical care and health expenses	15022	16484	11470	11122	12032	12914	14105	14681	17165	19099	20351	19865
6 Transport and communication	17974	20470	24327	24748	27127	30395	38033	38959	40381	38864	40347	47651
7 Recreational, entertainment, education and cultural services	25036	27541	28707	28884	28626	30299	29597	33977	34752	35826	38253	36366
A Education	4314	4384	4255	4194	4079	3895	3691	3653	3795	3754	3825	3870
B Other	20722	23157	24452	24690	24547	26404	25906	30324	30957	32072	34428	32496
8 Miscellaneous goods and services	22634	27304	33585	36088	35463	37239	41243	44172	45959	45321	46796	51531
A Personal care	...	...	5442	5869	6219	7198	6925	8395	9930	11308	11434	10170
B Expenditures in restaurants, cafes and hotels	...	...	...	...	...	...	...	...	...	...	...	...

China, Hong Kong SAR

Million Hong Kong dollars

	1986	1987	1988	1989	1990	1991	1992	1993	1994	1995	1996	1997
At constant prices of: 1990												
C Other	...	...	...	...	...	...	...	...	...	...	...	...
Total final consumption expenditure in the domestic market by households, of which	240549	269697	294082	303574	316880	338146	371159	399192	422066	429829	449793	466577
plus: Direct purchases abroad by resident households	19697	22840	27422	28858	31823	36831	38705	43077	45423	48566	51397	54145
less: Direct purchases in the domestic market by non-resident households	26734	34210	40794	42415	42581	41435	48017	51473	49620	54309	56708	45855
equals: Final consumption expenditure of resident households	233512	258327	280710	290017	306122	333542	361847	390796	417869	424086	444482	474867
Final consumption expenditures by private non-profit organisations serving households												
1 Research and science	...	...	...	...	...	...	...	...	...	...	...	...
2 Education	...	...	...	...	...	...	...	...	...	...	...	...
3 Medical and other health services	...	...	...	...	...	...	...	...	...	...	...	...
4 Welfare services	...	...	...	...	...	...	...	...	...	...	...	...
5 Recreational and related cultural services	...	...	...	...	...	...	...	...	...	...	...	...
6 Religious organisations	...	...	...	...	...	...	...	...	...	...	...	...
7 Professional and labour organisations serving households	...	...	...	...	...	...	...	...	...	...	...	...
8 Miscellaneous	...	...	...	...	...	...	...	...	...	...	...	...
equals: Final consumption expenditures by private non-profit organisations serving households	20106	20811	21619	22665	24337	25477	24672	24822	25702	26364	27284	28481
Private final consumption expenditure	253618	279138	302329	312682	330459	359019	386519	415618	443571	450450	471766	503348

a Personal effects are included in item "Clothing and footwear".

2.7 Gross capital formation by type of good and owner, in current price

Million Hong Kong dollars

	1986				1987				1988			
	Total	Total private	Public enterprises	General government	Total	Total private	Public enterprises	General government	Total	Total private	Public enterprises	General government
Increase in stocks, total [a]	6183	6183	...	...	9746	9746	...	...	14132	14132	...	...
Gross fixed capital formation, total	67758	59013	...	8745	91712	80717	...	10995	116129	102668	...	13461
1 Residential buildings [b]	11667	9347	...	2320	12868	9719	...	3149	17390	13123	...	4267
2 Non-residential buildings	6832	5177	...	1655	9931	8133	...	1798	12042	10130	...	1912
3 Other construction [c]	18224	14157	...	4067	26690	21519	...	5171	34967	29005	...	5962
4 Land improvement and plantation and orchard development	...	...	...	...	...	...	...	...	...	...	...	...
5 Producers' durable goods	31035	30332	...	703	42223	41346	...	877	51730	50410	...	1320
A Transport equipment	4485	4166	...	319	7448	7046	...	402	6329	5755	...	574
B Machinery and equipment	26550	26166	...	384	34775	34300	...	475	45401	44655	...	746
6 Breeding stock, dairy cattle, etc.	...	...	...	...	...	...	...	...	...	...	...	...
Statistical discrepancy	...	...	...	—	...	...	...	—	...	...	...	—
Total gross capital formation [d]	73941	65196	...	8745	101458	90463	...	10995	130261	116800	...	13461

China, Hong Kong SAR

	1989				1990				1991			
	Total	Total private	Public enterprises	General government	Total	Total private	Public enterprises	General government	Total	Total private	Public enterprises	General government
Increase in stocks, total [a]	3463	3463	...	...	5728	5728	...	...	4098	4098	...	...
Gross fixed capital formation, total	136204	118606	...	17598	153776	134006	...	19770	177729	157189	...	20540
1 Residential buildings [b]	19911	14685	...	5226	23475	18375	...	5100	23826	18929	...	4897
2 Non-residential buildings	16433	13016	...	3417	20311	16158	...	4153	23339	19133	...	4206
3 Other construction [c]	44458	37172	...	7286	50179	41290	...	8889	59607	50164	...	9443
4 Land improvement and plantation and orchard development	...	...	...	...	...	...	...	...	...	...	...	...
5 Producers' durable goods	55402	53733	...	1669	59811	58183	...	1628	70957	68963	...	1994
A Transport equipment	8035	7177	...	858	8468	8043	...	425	10295	9835	...	460
B Machinery and equipment	47367	46556	...	811	51343	50140	...	1203	60662	59128	...	1534
6 Breeding stock, dairy cattle, etc.	...	...	...	...	...	...	...	...	...	...	...	...
Statistical discrepancy	...	...	...	−	...	...	...	−	...	...	...	−
Total gross capital formation [d]	139667	122069	...	17598	159504	139734	...	19770	181827	161287	...	20540

	1992				1993				1994			
	Total	Total private	Public enterprises	General government	Total	Total private	Public enterprises	General government	Total	Total private	Public enterprises	General government
Increase in stocks, total [a]	8187	8187	...	...	2299	2299	...	...	21263	21263	...	...
Gross fixed capital formation, total	213808	191493	...	22315	245182	212118	...	33064	301112	261123	...	39989
1 Residential buildings [b]	24517	18935	...	5582	25725	20326	...	5399	28708	23471	...	5237
2 Non-residential buildings	22088	18425	...	3663	21744	17145	...	4599	24201	21559	...	2642
3 Other construction [c]	78978	67809	...	11169	102438	82102	...	20336	133327	104951	...	28376
4 Land improvement and plantation and orchard development	...	...	...	...	...	...	...	...	...	...	...	...
5 Producers' durable goods	88225	86324	...	1901	95275	92545	...	2730	114876	111142	...	3734
A Transport equipment	13153	12445	...	708	14044	13512	...	532	14725	13674	...	1051
B Machinery and equipment	75072	73879	...	1193	81231	79033	...	2198	100151	97468	...	2683
6 Breeding stock, dairy cattle, etc.	...	...	...	...	...	...	...	...	...	...	...	...
Statistical discrepancy	...	...	...	−	...	...	...	−	...	...	...	−
Total gross capital formation [d]	221995	199680	...	22315	247481	214417	...	33064	322375	282386	...	39989

	1995				1996				1997			
	Total	Total private	Public enterprises	General government	Total	Total private	Public enterprises	General government	Total	Total private	Public enterprises	General government
Increase in stocks, total [a]	45656	45656	...	...	10322	10322	...	...	1594	1594	...	...
Gross fixed capital formation, total	329578	277084	...	52494	372741	308856	...	63885	467770	405033	...	62737
1 Residential buildings [b]	28322	21741	...	6581	35472	26740	...	8732	49832	39798	...	10034
2 Non-residential buildings	27914	23891	...	4023	32199	27004	...	5195	42561	36225	...	6336
3 Other construction [c]	116565	80451	...	36114	140577	98984	...	41593	191212	154431	...	36781
4 Land improvement and plantation and orchard development	...	...	...	...	...	...	...	...	...	...	...	...
5 Producers' durable goods	156777	151001	...	5776	164493	156128	...	8365	184165	174579	...	9586
A Transport equipment	30214	28917	...	1297	29918	28306	...	1612	19138	17230	...	1908
B Machinery and equipment	126563	122084	...	4479	134575	127822	...	6753	165027	157349	...	7678
6 Breeding stock, dairy cattle, etc.	...	...	...	...	...	...	...	...	...	...	...	...
Total gross capital formation [d]	375234	322740	...	52494	383063	319178	...	63885	469364	406627	...	62737

China, Hong Kong SAR

a Refer to "Changes in inventories".
b Item "Residential buildings" includes also combined residential and non-residential buildings.
c Item "other construction" includes transfer costs of land and buildings and real estate developer's margin.
d Column "Public Enterprises" is included in column "General Government".

2.8 Gross capital formation by type of good and owner, in constant prices

Million Hong Kong dollars

	1986 Total	1986 Total private	1986 Public enterprises	1986 General government	1987 Total	1987 Total private	1987 Public enterprises	1987 General government	1988 Total	1988 Total private	1988 Public enterprises	1988 General government
At constant prices of: 1990												
Increase in stocks, total [a]	7095	7095	...	...	10464	10464	...	...	14317	14317	...	...
Gross fixed capital formation, total	112995	97600	...	15395	129040	112419	...	16621	137455	120969	...	16486
1 Residential buildings [b]	21083	16911	...	4172	19834	14978	...	4856	21645	16520	...	5125
2 Non-residential buildings	12372	9374	...	2998	15248	12462	...	2786	15191	12791	...	2400
3 Other construction [c]	41945	34569	...	7376	46035	38045	...	7990	45255	37705	...	7550
4 Land improvement and plantation and orchard development	...	...	...	...	...	...	...	...	...	...	...	...
5 Producers' durable goods	37595	36746	...	849	47923	46934	...	989	55364	53953	...	1411
A Transport equipment	5443	5062	...	381	8456	8010	...	446	6779	6163	...	616
B Machinery and equipment	32152	31684	...	468	39467	38924	...	543	48585	47790	...	795
6 Breeding stock, dairy cattle, etc.	...	...	...	...	...	...	...	...	...	...	...	...
Total gross capital formation [d]	120090	104695	...	15395	139504	122883	...	16621	151772	135286	...	16486

	1989 Total	1989 Total private	1989 Public enterprises	1989 General government	1990 Total	1990 Total private	1990 Public enterprises	1990 General government	1991 Total	1991 Total private	1991 Public enterprises	1991 General government
At constant prices of: 1990												
Increase in stocks, total [a]	3376	3376	...	...	5728	5728	...	...	4081	4081	...	...
Gross fixed capital formation, total	142204	123381	...	18823	153776	134006	...	19770	168059	148914	...	19145
1 Residential buildings [b]	21519	16065	...	5454	23475	18375	...	5100	22576	17963	...	4613
2 Non-residential buildings	18005	14287	...	3718	20311	16158	...	4153	22034	18032	...	4002
3 Other construction [c]	46160	38190	...	7970	50179	41290	...	8889	53563	44988	...	8575
4 Land improvement and plantation and orchard development	...	...	...	...	...	...	...	...	...	...	...	...
5 Producers' durable goods	56520	54839	...	1681	59811	58183	...	1628	69886	67931	...	1955
A Transport equipment	8212	7352	...	860	8468	8043	...	425	10129	9676	...	453
B Machinery and equipment	48308	47487	...	821	51343	50140	...	1203	59757	58255	...	1502
6 Breeding stock, dairy cattle, etc.	...	...	...	...	...	...	...	...	...	...	...	...
Total gross capital formation [d]	145580	126757	...	18823	159504	139734	...	19770	172140	152995	...	19145

	1992 Total	1992 Total private	1992 Public enterprises	1992 General government	1993 Total	1993 Total private	1993 Public enterprises	1993 General government	1994 Total	1994 Total private	1994 Public enterprises	1994 General government
At constant prices of: 1990												
Increase in stocks, total [a]	8453	8453	...	...	2224	2224	...	...	20058	20058	...	...
Gross fixed capital formation, total	183480	163336	...	20144	190259	162198	...	28061	220171	187314	...	32857
1 Residential buildings [b]	23024	17770	...	5254	23785	18843	...	4942	25953	21102	...	4851
2 Non-residential buildings	20502	17084	...	3418	20098	15658	...	4440	21541	18998	...	2543

China, Hong Kong SAR

	1992				1993				1994			
	Total	Total private	Public enterprises	General government	Total	Total private	Public enterprises	General government	Total	Total private	Public enterprises	General government
	At constant prices of: 1990												
3 Other construction [c]	55115	45472	...	9643	59265	43103	...	16162	70135	48012	...	22123
4 Land improvement and plantation and orchard development	...	...	...	...	...	...	...	...	...	...	...	...
5 Producers' durable goods	84839	83010	...	1829	87111	84594	...	2517	102542	99202	...	3340
A Transport equipment	12618	11936	...	682	12823	12330	...	493	13160	12225	...	935
B Machinery and equipment	72221	71074	...	1147	74288	72264	...	2024	89382	86977	...	2405
6 Breeding stock, dairy cattle, etc.	...	...	...	...	...	...	...	...	...	...	...	...
Total gross capital formation [d]	191933	171789	...	20144	192483	164422	...	28061	240229	207372	...	32857

	1995				1996				1997			
	Total	Total private	Public enterprises	General government	Total	Total private	Public enterprises	General government	Total	Total private	Public enterprises	General government
	At constant prices of: 1990												
Increase in stocks, total [a]	40103	40103	...	...	9608	9608	...	...	3703	3703	...	...
Gross fixed capital formation, total	243800	203715	...	40085	270146	223187	...	46959	313295	268607	...	44688
1 Residential buildings [b]	24083	18273	...	5810	27646	20564	...	7082	34079	26906	...	7173
2 Non-residential buildings	23040	19540	...	3500	24109	20055	...	4054	28601	24173	...	4428
3 Other construction [c]	68449	42450	...	25999	75078	46552	...	28526	82298	57972	...	24326
4 Land improvement and plantation and orchard development	...	...	...	...	...	...	...	...	...	...	...	...
5 Producers' durable goods	128228	123452	...	4776	143313	136016	...	7297	168317	159556	...	8761
A Transport equipment	24710	23634	...	1076	26056	24650	...	1406	17539	15795	...	1744
B Machinery and equipment	103518	99818	...	3700	117257	111366	...	5891	150778	143761	...	7017
6 Breeding stock, dairy cattle, etc.	...	...	...	...	...	...	...	...	...	...	...	...
Total gross capital formation [d]	283903	243818	...	40085	279754	232795	...	46959	316998	272310	...	44688

a Refer to "Changes in inventories".
b Item "Residential buildings" includes also combined residential and non-residential buildings.
c Item "other construction" includes transfer costs of land and buildings and real estate developer's margin.
d Column "Public Enterprises" is included in column "General Government".

4.1 Derivation of value added by kind of activity, in current prices

Million Hong Kong dollars

	1986			1987			1988			1989		
	Gross output	Intermediate consumption	Value added	Gross output	Intermediate consumption	Value added	Gross output	Intermediate consumption	Value added	Gross output	Intermediate consumption	Value added
	All producers											
1 Agriculture, hunting, forestry and fishing	3457	2149	1308	3584	2250	1334	3764	2347	1417	3913	2527	1386
2 Mining and quarrying	589	243	346	466	209	257	418	189	229	437	213	224
3 Manufacturing	241266	174430	66836	300424	219711	80713	340463	250428	90035	348161	251991	96170
A Manufacture of food, beverages and tobacco	...	...	...	...	...	...	...	...	...	...	...	...
B Textile, wearing apparel and leather industries	94524	66682	27843	113999	80922	33077	118812	84639	34174	127820	91101	36719
C Manufacture of wood and wood products, including furniture	...	...	...	...	...	...	...	...	...	...	...	...

China, Hong Kong SAR

Million Hong Kong dollars

	1986			1987			1988			1989		
	Gross output	Intermediate consumption	Value added	Gross output	Intermediate consumption	Value added	Gross output	Intermediate consumption	Value added	Gross output	Intermediate consumption	Value added
D Manufacture of paper and paper products, printing and publishing	...	...	...	...	...	...	...	...	...	...	...	...
E Manufacture of chemicals and chemical petroleum, coal, rubber and plastic products	22634	15975	6660	25507	18976	6531	27358	20090	7268	26865	19352	7513
F Manufacture of non-metallic mineral products, except products of petroleum and coal	...	...	...	...	...	...	...	...	...	...	...	...
G Basic metal industries	...	...	...	...	...	...	...	...	...	...	...	...
H Manufacture of fabricated metal products, machinery and equipment	53002	39693	13309	71853	54729	17124	83688	64531	19157	78181	59114	19067
I Other manufacturing industries	71105	52080	19025	89065	65084	23982	110604	81168	29436	115295	82424	32871
4 Electricity, gas and water	12008	3623	8385	13510	3820	9691	14327	4128	10199	16016	5156	10860
5 Construction	30967	16714	14253	36762	19738	17024	44264	23605	20658	53559	27820	25738
6 Wholesale and retail trade, restaurants and hotels	122236	56216	66020	160538	71289	89249	203627	93834	109793	241620	116871	124749
A Wholesale and retail trade	101787	48799	52989	135109	62296	72812	173058	83192	89866	204258	104052	100206
B Restaurants and hotels	20449	7417	13032	25429	8993	16436	30569	10642	19927	37362	12819	24543
7 Transport, storage and communication	53417	29225	24192	63780	32087	31693	77457	37452	40005	89256	44602	44654
A Transport and storage	45071	26385	18686	53559	28375	25184	64840	32748	32092	74272	38961	35310
B Communication	8346	2840	5506	10221	3712	6510	12617	4704	7914	14985	5641	9344
8 Finance, insurance, real estate and business services	101575	21234	80340	129241	27675	101566	160100	33871	126229	189426	40595	148831
A Financial institutions	27624	9262	18362	36048	12281	23767	40249	14192	26057	46966	17185	29781
B Insurance	3208	982	2226	4013	1186	2827	5104	1543	3560	6166	1896	4269
C Real estate and business services	70743	10990	59753	89179	14208	74971	114748	18136	96612	136295	21514	114780
Real estate, except dwellings	24925	4654	20271	32413	5680	26733	43933	7118	36815	54459	9105	45354
Dwellings	31615	1581	30034	37746	1887	35859	45701	2285	43416	54246	2712	51534
9 Community, social and personal services	39180	17731	21450	42809	19287	23521	49985	22783	27202	56082	26115	29966
Statistical discrepancy [a]	...	...	...	...	...	−2752	...	...	−4684	...	...	−465
Total, Industries	604695	321565	283130	751114	396066	355048	894405	468637	425767	998470	515890	482578
Producers of government services	24138	7110	17028	27188	8080	19108	31688	9724	21964	38087	12015	26072
Other producers	13710	4781	8928	15897	5515	10382	18841	7005	11836	23090	9005	14085
Total	642543	333456	309086	794199	409661	384538	944934	485366	459567	1059647	536910	522735
less: Imputed bank service charge [b]	...	−13079	13079	...	−17743	17743	...	−21313	21313	...	−23800	23800
Import duties	...	...	...	...	...	...	...	...	...	...	...	...
Value added tax	1341	...	1341	...	...	...	...	...	...	...	...	...
Other adjustments [c]	15212	...	15212	20445	...	20445	21450	...	21450	25390	...	25390
Total	659096	346535	312561	...	...	384488	966384	506679	455022	1085037	560710	523861

China, Hong Kong SAR

	1990 Gross output	1990 Intermediate consumption	1990 Value added	1991 Gross output	1991 Intermediate consumption	1991 Value added	1992 Gross output	1992 Intermediate consumption	1992 Value added	1993 Gross output	1993 Intermediate consumption	1993 Value added
All producers												
1 Agriculture, hunting, forestry and fishing	3872	2440	1432	3796	2355	1441	3705	2237	1468	3696	2085	1612
2 Mining and quarrying	402	192	210	405	183	222	368	163	205	413	216	197
3 Manufacturing	341986	243634	98352	338692	241469	97223	337928	238164	99764	316271	223688	92582
A Manufacture of food, beverages and tobacco	...	...	...	...	...	...	...	...	...	...	...	...
B Textile, wearing apparel and leather industries	123468	88361	35107	123947	89776	34171	118567	83791	34776	106930	77388	29541
C Manufacture of wood and wood products, including furniture	...	...	...	...	...	...	...	...	...	...	...	...
D Manufacture of paper and paper products, printing and publishing	...	...	...	...	...	...	...	...	...	...	...	...
E Manufacture of chemicals and chemical petroleum, coal, rubber and plastic products	20981	14517	6464	16645	11294	5351	16035	11135	4900	11198	7314	3884
F Manufacture of non-metallic mineral products, except products of petroleum and coal	...	...	...	...	...	...	...	...	...	...	...	...
G Basic metal industries	...	...	...	...	...	...	...	...	...	...	...	...
H Manufacture of fabricated metal products, machinery and equipment	68705	51352	17353	66686	48957	17729	67698	49126	18572	63896	46679	17218
I Other manufacturing industries	128831	89403	39428	131415	91443	39972	135628	94112	41516	134247	92308	41939
4 Electricity, gas and water	18105	5493	12612	20350	6830	13521	22969	7332	15637	24906	7315	17591
5 Construction	61270	31050	30220	70368	35709	34659	74589	37252	37337	87655	44565	43089
6 Wholesale and retail trade, restaurants and hotels	291627	150904	140722	333528	170244	163284	345387	154626	190760	413632	189170	224462
A Wholesale and retail trade	251331	136125	115206	289677	153582	136096	293180	134759	158421	356145	167695	188450
B Restaurants and hotels	40296	14780	25516	43850	16662	27188	52207	19867	32339	57487	21475	36012
7 Transport, storage and communication	106319	53392	52927	114839	54235	60604	135648	64422	71227	155300	76307	78993
A Transport and storage	88347	46643	41705	92468	45854	46614	108652	54362	54291	120534	61166	59368
B Communication	17972	6750	11222	22370	8380	13990	26996	10060	16936	34766	15141	19625
8 Finance, insurance, real estate and business services	222217	49833	172384	269610	57442	212169	323671	63807	259864	379692	75280	304412
A Financial institutions	55851	21250	34600	78945	24803	54142	95017	25415	69602	113269	29997	83272
B Insurance	6910	2355	4555	8224	2807	5418	9806	3196	6609	12764	3563	9201
C Real estate and business services	159456	26228	133228	182440	29833	152609	218849	35196	183653	253659	41720	211939
Real estate, except dwellings	64521	10452	54068	72335	12154	60181	89666	14108	75558	107646	16065	91581
Dwellings	62375	3119	59257	72497	3625	68873	85201	4260	80941	94592	4730	89862
9 Community, social and personal services	62166	29721	32444	66155	30683	35472	76463	35337	41125	102157	51464	50693
Statistical discrepancy [a]	...	...	−6511	...	...	675	...	...	−1562	...	...	14016
Total, Industries	1107964	566659	541303	1217743	599150	618595	1320728	603340	717387	1483722	670091	813631
Producers of government services	45554	14313	31241	54303	16030	38273	67391	18812	48579	76543	21578	54965
Other producers	27977	10334	17643	32879	12331	20548	35346	14348	20999	40581	15831	24750
Total	1181495	591306	590187	1304925	627511	677416	1423464	636500	786965	1600846	707500	893346

China, Hong Kong SAR

	1990			1991			1992			1993		
	Gross output	Intermediate consumption	Value added	Gross output	Intermediate consumption	Value added	Gross output	Intermediate consumption	Value added	Gross output	Intermediate consumption	Value added
less: Imputed bank service charge [b]	...	–30741	30741	...	–45902	45902	...	–54846	54846	...	–63177	63177
Import duties	...	...	...	...	...	...	...	...	...	...	...	...
Value added tax	...	...	...	...	...	...	...	...	...	...	...	...
Other adjustments [c]	29614	...	29614	36323	...	36323	48777	...	48777	53278	...	53278
Total	1211109	622047	582549	1341248	673413	668512	1472241	691346	779335	1654124	770677	897463

	1994			1995			1996			1997		
	Gross output	Intermediate consumption	Value added	Gross output	Intermediate consumption	Value added	Gross output	Intermediate consumption	Value added	Gross output	Intermediate consumption	Value added
All producers												
1 Agriculture, hunting, forestry and fishing	3734	2138	1596	3666	2212	1453	3727	2283	1444	...	...	...
2 Mining and quarrying	476	227	249	636	319	317	682	371	311	...	...	...
3 Manufacturing	298081	210727	87354	301307	216537	84770	283595	200826	82769	...	...	...
A Manufacture of food, beverages and tobacco	...	...	...	...	...	...	...	...	...	...	...	...
B Textile, wearing apparel and leather industries	94316	68853	25463	85899	63409	22490	79300	58773	20527	...	...	...
C Manufacture of wood and wood products, including furniture	...	...	...	...	...	...	...	...	...	...	...	...
D Manufacture of paper and paper products, printing and publishing	...	...	...	...	...	...	...	...	...	...	...	...
E Manufacture of chemicals and chemical petroleum, coal, rubber and plastic products	8607	6042	2566	8459	6012	2447	6919	4625	2294	...	...	...
F Manufacture of non-metallic mineral products, except products of petroleum and coal	...	...	...	...	...	...	...	...	...	...	...	...
G Basic metal industries	...	...	...	...	...	...	...	...	...	...	...	...
H Manufacture of fabricated metal products, machinery and equipment	58601	41091	17510	68654	50178	18476	61882	44910	16972	...	...	...
I Other manufacturing industries	136557	94741	41815	138295	96938	41357	135494	92518	42976	...	...	...
4 Electricity, gas and water	28731	6555	22175	30470	6892	23578	34242	7253	26989	...	...	...
5 Construction	95599	49274	46325	119170	64409	54761	134284	69227	65058	...	...	...
6 Wholesale and retail trade, restaurants and hotels	466858	217691	249167	498727	228207	270520	542496	241219	301277	...	...	...
A Wholesale and retail trade	402633	192708	209925	433157	201603	231554	473567	214171	259396	...	...	...
B Restaurants and hotels	64225	24984	39242	65571	26604	38967	68929	27049	41881	...	...	...
7 Transport, storage and communication	174763	82653	92109	193958	91759	102199	211707	100620	111087	...	...	...
A Transport and storage	135247	65274	69973	148205	72444	75761	155994	74799	81195	...	...	...
B Communication	39515	17379	22136	45753	19315	26438	55713	25820	29893	...	...	...
8 Finance, insurance, real estate and business services	464983	94979	370005	483015	100097	382918	545355	113271	432084	...	...	...
A Financial institutions	125998	37213	88785	134096	39609	94487	159110	46809	112300	...	...	...
B Insurance	16106	4238	11868	16601	4778	11824	16166	5061	11104	...	...	...
C Real estate and business services	322879	53527	269352	332317	55710	276607	370079	61400	308679	...	...	...

China, Hong Kong SAR

	1994			1995			1996			1997		
	Gross output	Intermediate consumption	Value added	Gross output	Intermediate consumption	Value added	Gross output	Intermediate consumption	Value added	Gross output	Intermediate consumption	Value added
Real estate, except dwellings	139499	21801	117698	122742	22262	100480	140586	24841	115745	...	...	...
Dwellings	121746	6087	115659	142035	7102	134933	155312	7766	147546	...	...	...
9 Community, social and personal services	120768	60882	59886	141753	70053	71700	159923	78080	81843	...	...	...
Statistical discrepancy [a]	...	...	4427	...	...	8056	...	...	−463	...	...	...
Total, Industries	1653993	725127	928866	1772702	780485	992216	1916011	813150	1102862	...	...	...
Producers of government services	88265	25142	63123	99809	28497	71312	110834	30819	80015	...	...	...
Other producers	46256	17972	28284	53171	20227	32944	59148	22039	37109	...	...	...
Total	1788514	768241	1020273	1925682	829209	1096472	2085993	866008	1219986	...	...	...
less: Imputed bank service charge [b]	...	−70101	70101	...	−80358	80358	...	−89356	89356	...	...	...
Import duties	...	...	...	...	...	...	...	...	...	...	...	...
Value added tax	...	...	...	...	...	...	...	...	...	...	...	...
Other adjustments [c]	56286	...	56286	52974	...	52974	62442	...	62442	...	...	...
Total	1844800	838342	1010885	1978656	837244	1077145	2148435	874943	1192609	...	...	...

a The estimates shown refers to the difference between production estimate and expenditure estimate.
b FISIM
c Refers to taxes on production and imports.

4.3 Cost components of value added

Million Hong Kong dollars

	1986						1987					
	Compensation of employees	Capital consumption	Net operating surplus	Indirect taxes	less: Subsidies received	Value added	Compensation of employees	Capital consumption	Net operating surplus	Indirect taxes	less: Subsidies received	Value added
All producers													
1 Agriculture, hunting, forestry and fishing	433	...	876	...	...	1308	476	...	859	...	...	1334
2 Mining and quarrying	74	...	272	...	...	346	66	...	191	...	...	257
3 Manufacturing	42199	...	24638	...	...	66836	48536	...	32177	...	...	80713
A Manufacture of food, beverages and tobacco	...	...	...	...	...	...	...	...	...	...	...	...
B Textile, wearing apparel and leather industries	19142	...	8701	...	...	27843	21892	...	11185	...	...	33077
C Manufacture of wood and wood products, including furniture	...	...	...	...	...	...	...	...	...	...	...	...
D Manufacture of paper and paper products, printing and publishing	...	...	...	...	...	...	...	...	...	...	...	...
E Manufacture of chemicals and chemical petroleum, coal, rubber and plastic products	4038	...	2622	...	...	6660	4170	...	2361	...	...	6531
F Manufacture of non-metallic mineral products, except products of petroleum and coal	...	...	...	...	...	...	...	...	...	...	...	...
G Basic metal industries	...	...	...	...	...	...	...	...	...	...	...	...
H Manufacture of fabricated metal products, machinery and equipment	7797	...	5512	...	...	13309	9140	...	7984	...	...	17124

China, Hong Kong SAR

Million Hong Kong dollars

	1986						1987					
	Compensation of employees	Capital consumption	Net operating surplus	Indirect taxes	less: Subsidies received	Value added	Compensation of employees	Capital consumption	Net operating surplus	Indirect taxes	less: Subsidies received	Value added
1 Other manufacturing industries	11222	...	7803	...	...	19025	13334	...	10648	...	...	23982
4 Electricity, gas and water	1743	...	6642	...	...	8385	1952	...	7739	...	...	9691
5 Construction	12344	...	1909	...	...	14253	15015	...	2008	...	...	17024
6 Wholesale and retail trade, restaurants and hotels	32772	...	33248	...	...	66020	40637	...	48612	...	...	89249
A Wholesale and retail trade	23773	...	29216	...	...	52989	29804	...	43008	...	...	72812
B Restaurants and hotels	8999	...	4033	...	...	13032	10833	...	5604	...	...	16436
7 Transport, storage and communication	11399	...	12792	...	...	24192	13541	...	18152	...	...	31693
A Transport and storage	9261	...	9424	...	...	18686	11039	...	14144	...	...	25184
B Communication	2138	...	3368	...	...	5506	2502	...	4008	...	...	6510
8 Finance, insurance, real estate and business services	18312	...	62028	...	...	80340	22852	...	78714	...	...	101566
A Financial institutions	8682	...	9680	...	...	18362	10777	...	12990	...	...	23767
B Insurance	1101	...	1124	...	...	2226	1516	...	1311	...	...	2827
C Real estate and business services	8529	...	51224	...	...	59753	10559	...	64413	...	...	74971
Real estate, except dwellings	2994	...	17277	...	...	20271	3350	...	23384	...	...	26733
Dwellings	...	...	30034	...	...	30034	...	...	35859	...	...	35859
9 Community, social and personal services [a]	10722	...	10728	...	...	21450	12004	...	11517	...	...	23521
Total, Industries	129998	...	153133	...	...	283130	155079	...	199969	...	...	355048
Producers of government services	17028	...	–	...	...	17028	19108	...	–	...	...	19108
Other producers	8928	...	–	...	...	8928	10382	...	–	...	...	10382
Total	155954	...	153133	...	...	309086	184569	...	199969	...	...	384538
less: Imputed bank service charge	...	...	13079	...	...	13079	...	...	17743	...	...	17743
Import duties	...	...	...	...	...	...	...	...	...	...	...	...
Value added tax	...	...	...	...	...	1341	...	...	...	...	...	−2752
Other adjustments [c]	...	...	...	...	...	15212	...	...	...	...	...	20445
Total [d]	155954	...	140054	15212	...	312561	184569	...	182226	20445	...	384488

	1988						1989					
	Compensation of employees	Capital consumption	Net operating surplus	Indirect taxes	less: Subsidies received	Value added	Compensation of employees	Capital consumption	Net operating surplus	Indirect taxes	less: Subsidies received	Value added
All producers												
1 Agriculture, hunting, forestry and fishing	532	...	886	...	...	1417	607	...	779	...	...	1386
2 Mining and quarrying	69	...	160	...	...	229	72	...	152	...	...	224
3 Manufacturing	53076	...	36959	...	...	90035	56718	...	39451	...	...	96170
A Manufacture of food, beverages and tobacco	...	...	...	...	...	...	...	...	...	...	...	...
B Textile, wearing apparel and leather industries	22979	...	11196	...	...	34174	24483	...	12236	...	...	36719
C Manufacture of wood and wood products, including furniture	...	...	...	...	...	...	...	...	...	...	...	...
D Manufacture of paper and paper products, printing and publishing	...	...	...	...	...	...	...	...	...	...	...	...

China, Hong Kong SAR

	1988						1989					
	Compensation of employees	Capital consumption	Net operating surplus	Indirect taxes	less: Subsidies received	Value added	Compensation of employees	Capital consumption	Net operating surplus	Indirect taxes	less: Subsidies received	Value added
E Manufacture of chemicals and chemical petroleum, coal, rubber and plastic products	4223	...	3045	...	...	7268	4081	...	3432	...	...	7513
F Manufacture of non-metallic mineral products, except products of petroleum and coal	...	...	...	...	...	...	...	...	...	...	...	...
G Basic metal industries	...	...	...	...	...	...	...	...	...	...	...	...
H Manufacture of fabricated metal products, machinery and equipment	10132	...	9025	...	...	19157	10413	...	8653	...	...	19067
I Other manufacturing industries	15742	...	13694	...	...	29436	17741	...	15130	...	...	32871
4 Electricity, gas and water	2159	...	8040	...	...	10199	2497	...	8363	...	...	10860
5 Construction	17747	...	2912	...	...	20658	20958	...	4781	...	...	25738
6 Wholesale and retail trade, restaurants and hotels	50716	...	59077	...	...	109793	61172	...	63577	...	...	124749
A Wholesale and retail trade	38099	...	51767	...	...	89866	45051	...	55155	...	...	100206
B Restaurants and hotels	12616	...	7310	...	...	19927	16121	...	8422	...	...	24543
7 Transport, storage and communication	16468	...	23538	...	...	40005	19787	...	24867	...	...	44654
A Transport and storage	13504	...	18587	...	...	32092	16140	...	19171	...	...	35310
B Communication	2964	...	4950	...	...	7914	3647	...	5696	...	...	9344
8 Finance, insurance, real estate and business services	28780	...	97450	...	...	126229	35136	...	113695	...	...	148831
A Financial institutions	13246	...	12811	...	...	26057	16768	...	13013	...	...	29781
B Insurance	2022	...	1539	...	...	3560	2707	...	1563	...	...	4269
C Real estate and business services	13512	...	83100	...	...	96612	15661	...	99119	...	...	114780
Real estate, except dwellings	4365	...	32450	...	...	36815	4786	...	40568	...	...	45354
Dwellings	...	...	43416	...	...	43416	...	...	51534	...	...	51534
9 Community, social and personal services [a]	13483	...	13719	...	...	27202	15394	...	14573	...	...	29966
Statistical discrepancy [b]	...	...	...	...	...	–4684	...	...	...	...	...	–465
Total, Industries	183030	...	242741	...	...	425767	212341	...	270238	...	...	482578
Producers of government services	21964	...	–	...	...	21964	26072	...	–	...	...	26072
Other producers	11836	...	–	...	...	11836	14085	...	–	...	...	14085
Total	216828	...	242741	...	...	459567	252498	...	270238	...	...	522735
less: Imputed bank service charge	...	...	21313	...	...	21313	...	...	23800	...	...	23800
Import duties	...	...	...	...	...	...	...	...	...	...	...	...
Value added tax	...	...	...	...	...	...	...	...	...	...	...	...
Other adjustments [c]	...	...	...	...	...	21450	...	...	...	...	...	25390
Total [d]	216828	...	221427	21450	...	455022	252498	...	246437	25390	...	523861

	1990						1991					
	Compensation of employees	Capital consumption	Net operating surplus	Indirect taxes	less: Subsidies received	Value added	Compensation of employees	Capital consumption	Net operating surplus	Indirect taxes	less: Subsidies received	Value added
All producers												
1 Agriculture, hunting, forestry and fishing	607	...	826	...	...	1432	661	...	780	...	...	1441
2 Mining and quarrying	77	...	133	...	...	210	72	...	150	...	...	222

China, Hong Kong SAR

	1990						1991					
	Compensation of employees	Capital consumption	Net operating surplus	Indirect taxes	less: Subsidies received	Value added	Compensation of employees	Capital consumption	Net operating surplus	Indirect taxes	less: Subsidies received	Value added
3 Manufacturing	57592	...	40759	...	...	98352	55652	...	41571	...	...	97223
A Manufacture of food, beverages and tobacco	...	...	...	...	...	...	...	...	...	...	...	...
B Textile, wearing apparel and leather industries	23946	...	11162	...	...	35107	23043	...	11128	...	...	34171
C Manufacture of wood and wood products, including furniture	...	...	...	...	...	...	...	...	...	...	...	...
D Manufacture of paper and paper products, printing and publishing	...	...	...	...	...	...	...	...	...	...	...	...
E Manufacture of chemicals and chemical petroleum, coal, rubber and plastic products	3534	...	2930	...	...	6464	2974	...	2377	...	...	5351
F Manufacture of non-metallic mineral products, except products of petroleum and coal	...	...	...	...	...	...	...	...	...	...	...	...
G Basic metal industries	...	...	...	...	...	...	...	...	...	...	...	...
H Manufacture of fabricated metal products, machinery and equipment	9294	...	8059	...	...	17353	8938	...	8790	...	...	17729
I Other manufacturing industries	20820	...	18608	...	...	39428	20697	...	19275	...	...	39972
4 Electricity, gas and water	3153	...	9459	...	...	12612	3625	...	9896	...	...	13521
5 Construction	24797	...	5423	...	...	30220	27480	...	7179	...	...	34659
6 Wholesale and retail trade, restaurants and hotels	72513	...	68210	...	...	140722	85834	...	77450	...	...	163284
A Wholesale and retail trade	54361	...	60846	...	...	115206	65492	...	70603	...	...	136096
B Restaurants and hotels	18152	...	7364	...	...	25516	20342	...	6847	...	...	27188
7 Transport, storage and communication	24790	...	28137	...	...	52927	26452	...	34152	...	...	60604
A Transport and storage	20139	...	21565	...	...	41705	21680	...	24933	...	...	46614
B Communication	4650	...	6572	...	...	11222	4771	...	9219	...	...	13990
8 Finance, insurance, real estate and business services	41943	...	130441	...	...	172384	49277	...	162892	...	...	212169
A Financial institutions	20064	...	14536	...	...	34600	23609	...	30533	...	...	54142
B Insurance	3198	...	1357	...	...	4555	3752	...	1666	...	...	5418
C Real estate and business services	18681	...	114548	...	...	133228	21916	...	130693	...	...	152609
Real estate, except dwellings	6163	...	47906	...	...	54068	7655	...	52526	...	...	60181
Dwellings	...	...	59257	...	...	59257	...	...	68873	...	...	68873
9 Community, social and personal services [a]	16482	...	15962	...	...	32444	18128	...	17344	...	...	35472
Statistical discrepancy [b]	...	...	...	...	...	−6511	...	...	...	...	...	675
Total, Industries	241954	...	299350	...	...	541303	267181	...	351414	...	...	618595
Producers of government services	31241	...	−	...	...	31241	38273	...	−	...	...	38273
Other producers	17643	...	−	...	...	17643	20548	...	−	...	...	20548
Total	290838	...	299350	...	...	590187	326002	...	351414	...	...	677416
less: Imputed bank service charge	...	...	30741	...	...	30741	...	...	45902	...	...	45902
Import duties	...	...	...	...	...	...	...	...	...	...	...	...
Value added tax	...	...	...	...	...	...	...	...	...	...	...	...
Other adjustments [c]	...	...	...	...	...	29614	...	...	...	...	...	36323
Total [d]	290838	...	268608	29614	...	582549	326002	...	305512	36323	...	668512

China, Hong Kong SAR

	1992						1993					
	Compensation of employees	Capital consumption	Net operating surplus	Indirect taxes	less: Subsidies received	Value added	Compensation of employees	Capital consumption	Net operating surplus	Indirect taxes	less: Subsidies received	Value added
All producers												
1 Agriculture, hunting, forestry and fishing	603	...	865	...	...	1468	658	...	954	...	...	1612
2 Mining and quarrying	81	...	124	...	...	205	95	...	102	...	...	197
3 Manufacturing	55155	...	44610	...	...	99764	52567	...	40015	...	...	92582
A Manufacture of food, beverages and tobacco	...	...	...	...	...	...	...	...	...	...	...	...
B Textile, wearing apparel and leather industries	21832	...	12944	...	...	34776	19270	...	10271	...	...	29541
C Manufacture of wood and wood products, including furniture	...	...	...	...	...	...	...	...	...	...	...	...
D Manufacture of paper and paper products, printing and publishing	...	...	...	...	...	...	...	...	...	...	...	...
E Manufacture of chemicals and chemical petroleum, coal, rubber and plastic products	2848	...	2052	...	...	4900	2149	...	1735	...	...	3884
F Manufacture of non-metallic mineral products, except products of petroleum and coal	...	...	...	...	...	...	...	...	...	...	...	...
G Basic metal industries	...	...	...	...	...	...	...	...	...	...	...	...
H Manufacture of fabricated metal products, machinery and equipment	8840	...	9733	...	...	18572	8492	...	8725	...	...	17218
I Other manufacturing industries	21635	...	19881	...	...	41516	22656	...	19283	...	...	41939
4 Electricity, gas and water	4115	...	11522	...	...	15637	4603	...	12987	...	...	17591
5 Construction	30023	...	7313	...	...	37337	33449	...	9640	...	...	43089
6 Wholesale and retail trade, restaurants and hotels	98254	...	92507	...	...	190760	116664	...	107798	...	...	224462
A Wholesale and retail trade	74264	...	84157	...	...	158421	90351	...	98099	...	...	188450
B Restaurants and hotels	23990	...	8349	...	...	32339	26313	...	9699	...	...	36012
7 Transport, storage and communication	31978	...	39249	...	...	71227	36149	...	42844	...	...	78993
A Transport and storage	25804	...	28486	...	...	54291	29120	...	30248	...	...	59368
B Communication	6174	...	10762	...	...	16936	7029	...	12596	...	...	19625
8 Finance, insurance, real estate and business services	56820	...	203044	...	...	259864	64933	...	239479	...	...	304412
A Financial institutions	27020	...	42582	...	...	69602	30512	...	52760	...	...	83272
B Insurance	4480	...	2129	...	...	6609	5111	...	4090	...	...	9201
C Real estate and business services	25319	...	158333	...	...	183653	29310	...	182629	...	...	211939
Real estate, except dwellings	7944	...	67613	...	...	75558	10355	...	81226	...	...	91581
Dwellings	...	...	80941	...	...	80941	...	...	89862	...	...	89862
9 Community, social and personal services [a]	22686	...	18439	...	...	41125	29198	...	21495	...	...	50693
Statistical discrepancy [b]	...	...	...	...	...	−1562	...	...	...	...	...	14016
Total, Industries	299715	...	417673	...	...	717387	338317	...	475314	...	...	813631
Producers of government services	48579	...	−	...	...	48579	54965	...	−	...	...	54965
Other producers	20999	...	−	...	...	20999	24750	...	−	...	...	24750
Total	369292	...	417673	...	...	786965	418032	...	475314	...	...	893346

China, Hong Kong SAR

	1992						1993					
	Compensation of employees	Capital consumption	Net operating surplus	Indirect taxes	less: Subsidies received	Value added	Compensation of employees	Capital consumption	Net operating surplus	Indirect taxes	less: Subsidies received	Value added
less: Imputed bank service charge	...	...	54846	...	...	54846	...	...	63177	...	...	63177
Import duties	...	...	...	...	...	...	...	...	...	...	...	...
Value added tax	...	...	...	...	...	...	...	...	...	...	...	...
Other adjustments [c]	...	...	...	...	...	48777	...	...	...	...	...	53278
Total [d]	369292	...	362826	48777	...	779335	418032	...	412137	53278	...	897463

	1994						1995					
	Compensation of employees	Capital consumption	Net operating surplus	Indirect taxes	less: Subsidies received	Value added	Compensation of employees	Capital consumption	Net operating surplus	Indirect taxes	less: Subsidies received	Value added

All producers

1 Agriculture, hunting, forestry and fishing	510	...	1086	...	...	1596	509	...	944	...	...	1453
2 Mining and quarrying	114	...	135	...	...	249	119	...	198	...	...	317
3 Manufacturing	50184	...	37170	...	...	87354	48270	...	36501	...	...	84770
A Manufacture of food, beverages and tobacco	...	...	...	...	...	...	...	...	...	...	...	...
B Textile, wearing apparel and leather industries	17343	...	8119	...	...	25463	14576	...	7914	...	...	22490
C Manufacture of wood and wood products, including furniture	...	...	...	...	...	...	...	...	...	...	...	...
D Manufacture of paper and paper products, printing and publishing	...	...	...	...	...	...	...	...	...	...	...	...
E Manufacture of chemicals and chemical petroleum, coal, rubber and plastic products	1538	...	1028	...	...	2566	1341	...	1106	...	...	2447
F Manufacture of non-metallic mineral products, except products of petroleum and coal	...	...	...	...	...	...	...	...	...	...	...	...
G Basic metal industries	...	...	...	...	...	...	...	...	...	...	...	...
H Manufacture of fabricated metal products, machinery and equipment	8067	...	9444	...	...	17510	7983	...	10493	...	...	18476
I Other manufacturing industries	23236	...	18579	...	...	41815	24370	...	16987	...	...	41357
4 Electricity, gas and water	5105	...	17071	...	...	22175	5742	...	17836	...	...	23578
5 Construction	35499	...	10826	...	...	46325	42192	...	12569	...	...	54761
6 Wholesale and retail trade, restaurants and hotels	129495	...	119672	...	...	249167	145289	...	125231	...	...	270520
A Wholesale and retail trade	101733	...	108192	...	...	209925	116428	...	115125	...	...	231554
B Restaurants and hotels	27762	...	11480	...	...	39242	28861	...	10106	...	...	38967
7 Transport, storage and communication	41370	...	50740	...	...	92109	47663	...	54537	...	...	102199
A Transport and storage	33287	...	36687	...	...	69973	38082	...	37679	...	...	75761
B Communication	8083	...	14053	...	...	22136	9581	...	16858	...	...	26438
8 Finance, insurance, real estate and business services	78182	...	291823	...	...	370005	86892	...	296026	...	...	382918
A Financial institutions	35951	...	52833	...	...	88785	40003	...	54484	...	...	94487
B Insurance	6285	...	5583	...	...	11868	7269	...	4555	...	...	11824
C Real estate and business services	35946	...	233407	...	...	269352	39621	...	236987	...	...	276607

China, Hong Kong SAR

	1994							1995						
	Compensation of employees	Capital consumption	Net operating surplus	Indirect taxes	less: Subsidies received	Value added	Compensation of employees	Capital consumption	Net operating surplus	Indirect taxes	less: Subsidies received	Value added
Real estate, except dwellings	12539	...	105158	...	...	117698	12902	...	87579	...	...	100480
Dwellings	...	...	115659	...	...	115659	...	...	134933	...	...	134933
9 Community, social and personal services [a]	31899	...	27987	...	...	59886	40274	...	31426	...	...	71700
Statistical discrepancy [b]	...	...	...	...	...	4427	...	...	...	...	...	8056
Total, Industries	372357	...	556509	...	...	928866	416950	...	575268	...	...	992216
Producers of government services	63123	...	...	...	...	63123	71312	...	—	...	...	71312
Other producers	28284	...	...	...	...	28284	32944	...	...	...	...	32944
Total	463764	...	556509	...	...	1020273	521206	...	575268	...	...	1096472
less: Imputed bank service charge	...	...	70101	...	...	70101	...	...	80358	...	...	80358
Import duties	...	...	...	...	...	...	...	...	...	...	...	...
Value added tax	...	...	...	...	...	...	...	...	...	...	...	...
Other adjustments [c]	...	...	...	...	...	56286	...	...	...	...	...	52974
Total [d]	463764	...	486408	56286	...	1010885	521206	...	494910	52974	...	1077145

	1996							1997						
	Compensation of employees	Capital consumption	Net operating surplus	Indirect taxes	less: Subsidies received	Value added	Compensation of employees	Capital consumption	Net operating surplus	Indirect taxes	less: Subsidies received	Value added
All producers												
1 Agriculture, hunting, forestry and fishing	483	...	961	...	...	1444	...	...	...	...	...	...
2 Mining and quarrying	123	...	187	...	...	311	...	...	...	...	...	...
3 Manufacturing	45857	...	36912	...	...	82769	...	...	...	...	...	...
A Manufacture of food, beverages and tobacco	...	...	...	...	...	...	...	...	...	...	...	...
B Textile, wearing apparel and leather industries	12763	...	7764	...	...	20527	...	...	...	...	...	...
C Manufacture of wood and wood products, including furniture	...	...	...	...	...	...	...	...	...	...	...	...
D Manufacture of paper and paper products, printing and publishing	...	...	...	...	...	...	...	...	...	...	...	...
E Manufacture of chemicals and chemical petroleum, coal, rubber and plastic products	1282	...	1012	...	...	2294	...	...	...	...	...	...
F Manufacture of non-metallic mineral products, except products of petroleum and coal	...	...	...	...	...	...	...	...	...	...	...	...
G Basic metal industries	...	...	...	...	...	...	...	...	...	...	...	...
H Manufacture of fabricated metal products, machinery and equipment	7554	...	9418	...	...	16972	...	...	...	...	...	...
I Other manufacturing industries	24257	...	18719	...	...	42976	...	...	...	...	...	...
4 Electricity, gas and water	6015	...	20974	...	...	26989	...	...	...	...	...	...
5 Construction	50139	...	14919	...	...	65058	...	...	...	...	...	...
6 Wholesale and retail trade, restaurants and hotels	153633	...	147644	...	...	301277	...	...	...	...	...	...
A Wholesale and retail trade	123925	...	135471	...	...	259396	...	...	...	...	...	...
B Restaurants and hotels	29708	...	12173	...	...	41881	...	...	...	...	...	...

China, Hong Kong SAR

	1996						1997					
	Compensation of employees	Capital consumption	Net operating surplus	Indirect taxes	less: Subsidies received	Value added	Compensation of employees	Capital consumption	Net operating surplus	Indirect taxes	less: Subsidies received	Value added
7 Transport, storage and communication	51213	...	59874	...	...	111087	...	...	...	...	...	...
A Transport and storage	40497	...	40698	...	...	81195	...	...	...	...	...	...
B Communication	10716	...	19176	...	...	29893	...	...	...	...	...	...
8 Finance, insurance, real estate and business services	103391	...	328693	...	...	432084	...	...	...	...	...	...
A Financial institutions	48206	...	64094	...	...	112300	...	...	...	...	...	...
B Insurance	8048	...	3056	...	...	11104	...	...	...	...	...	...
C Real estate and business services	47137	...	261542	...	...	308679	...	...	...	...	...	...
Real estate, except dwellings	15801	...	99944	...	...	115745	...	...	...	...	...	...
Dwellings	–	...	147546	...	...	147546	...	...	...	...	...	...
9 Community, social and personal services [a]	46744	...	35099	...	...	81843	...	...	...	...	...	...
Statistical discrepancy [b]	...	...	...	...	...	–463	...	...	...	...	...	...
Total, Industries	457598	...	645263	...	...	1102862	...	...	...	...	...	...
Producers of government services	80015	...	–	...	...	80015	...	...	...	...	...	...
Other producers	37109	...	–	...	...	37109	...	...	...	...	...	...
Total	574723	...	645263	...	...	1219986	...	...	...	...	...	...
less: Imputed bank service charge	–	...	89356	...	...	89356	...	...	...	...	...	...
Import duties	...	...	...	...	...	...	...	...	...	...	...	...
Value added tax	...	...	...	...	...	...	...	...	...	...	...	...
Other adjustments [c]	...	...	...	...	...	62442	...	...	...	...	...	...
Total [d]	574723	...	555907	62442	...	1192609	...	...	...	...	...	...

a FISIM
b The estimates shown refers to the difference between production estimate and expenditure estimate.
c Refers to taxes on production and imports.
d Includes goods and services tax (V.A.T.).

Colombia

General note

The preparation of national accounts statistics in Colombia is undertaken by the Departamento Administrativo Nacional de Estadística (DANE), Bogotá. Official estimates together with some methodological notes are published in *Cuentas Nacionales de Colombia* (Revision 3). The estimates are generally in accordance with the classifications and definitions recommended in the United Nations System of National Accounts (1968 SNA). The following tables have been prepared from successive replies to the United Nations National Accounts Questionnaire. When the scope and coverage of the estimates differ for conceptual or statistical reasons from the definitions and classifications recommended in SNA, a footnote is indicated to the relevant tables.

Gross domestic product

Gross domestic product is estimated mainly through the production approach.

Expenditures on the gross domestic product

The expenditure approach is used to estimate government final consumption expenditure, exports and imports of goods and services, part of increase in stocks and gross fixed capital formation in construction. For other gross fixed capital formation, the commodity-flow approach is used. Private final consumption expenditure and part of increase in stocks are obtained as a residual. The estimates of government final consumption expenditures are based on official sources such as Informe Financiero de la Contraloría General de la República. The estimates of private consumption expenditure are obtained as a residual except for the benchmark year 1970 which were based on results from the family budget survey conducted that year. The estimates for changes in stocks are based on information obtained from various sources such as manufacturing surveys, commercial census, and the Federación Nacional de Cafeteros. For gross fixed capital formation, the c.i.f. values of imported capital goods in the foreign trade statistics are adjusted to include customs duties, other taxes and transport and insurance costs. Adjustments are also made for trade margins and installation costs on goods passing through trade channels.

For domestic production, estimates are based on manufacturing surveys. Estimates of capital formation in construction are obtained as by-product in the calculation of the construction sectors contribution to gross domestic product whereas investments in the government sector is obtained from the government accounts. The estimates of exports and imports of goods are derived from foreign trade statistics while that of services are derived from the balance of payments. For the constant price estimates, current values of government expenditure and gross fixed capital formation estimates are deflated by appropriate price indexes. Estimates of private consumption expenditure at constant prices are obtained as a residual. No specific information is available for the remaining expenditure items.

Cost structure of the gross domestic product

The estimates of compensation of employees are obtained in the process of estimating value added by industrial origin. The estimates are obtained from the statistical surveys held in 1970 and from accounting data. In the case of agriculture, hunting, forestry and fishing, the estimates are based on projections from census data on employment and statistics of average wages and salaries. Depreciation of assets owned by general government are not included in the estimates. Operating surplus is obtained as a residual and no information is available for the estimates of consumption of fixed capital and of net indirect taxes.

Gross domestic product by kind of activity

The table of gross domestic product by kind of economic activity is prepared at market prices, i.e. producers' values. The production approach is used to estimate value added of almost all industries. The income approach is used to estimate the value added of producers of government services and some private services, while the expenditure approach is used for ownership of dwellings. Gross output of the trade sector is estimated by the commodity-flow approach. For agriculture, the gross value of production is obtained by multiplying the output of each commodity by the price paid to producers. The production and price data are derived from agricultural sample surveys and from various concerned institutions. The Federación Nacional de Cafeteros supplies information on data for coffee. For livestock, the estimates are based on statistics of government controlled slaughterings and net exports with rough estimates made for uncontrolled slaughterings. Data for the petroleum industry are obtained directly from the oil companies. Information on the output and value of minerals is available from censuses of mines and concerned institutions. For manufacturing, results of surveys carried out by the Departamento Administrativo Nacional de Estadística are used. The estimates are projected by applying volume and price indexes to both output and input.

The basic data for electricity, gas and water are obtained from concerned enterprises and surveys. Coefficients calculated from these surveys are used to estimate value added of plants not covered. For urban construction, estimates are derived from building permits issued while rural construction estimates are based on an estimation of economic life of existing constructions and on demographic data. Estimates of public construction are obtained from the government records. For the trade sector, value added is based on estimates of the flow of goods through trade

Colombia

channels. The gross margins are based on data provided by the Banco de la República or recalculated from the Commercial Census 1967. The mark-ups are kept constant over the period of analysis. For transport, estimates are based on information provided by the Banco de la República. Data to measure the contribution of the communication sector are obtained by direct inquiries. Estimates for the financial institutions are obtained directly from the enterprises concerned through the Superintendencia Bancaria. The contribution of the government sector is measured by the wages and salaries paid to employees. Value added of other private services is estimated by the Banco de la República using the results of the census of services in 1970. Constant input-output ratios have been assumed. For the constant price estimates, value added of the majority of industries is extrapolated by quantity index for output. For ownership of dwellings and producers of government services, value added is deflated by an index of rents and an index of wages and salaries, respectively.

1.1 Expenditure on the gross domestic product, in current prices

Thousand million Columbian pesos

	1986	1987	1988	1989	1990	1991	1992	1993	1994	1995	1996	1997
1 Government final consumption expenditure	666	868	1182	1597	2076	2685	3965	5108	7653	11054	...	...
2 Private final consumption expenditure [a]	4479	5919	7714	9943	13270	17348	23077	30454	39254	49273	...	...
3 Gross capital formation	1222	1765	2580	3021	3752	4164	5763	9300	13489	16134	...	...
A Increase in stocks	18	227	292	288	387	354	552	1049	1616	1650	...	...
B Gross fixed capital formation	1204	1537	2288	2733	3365	3810	5212	8251	11873	14484	...	...
Residential buildings	167	245	310	396	459	657	1004	1343	1890	2065	...	...
Non-residential buildings	33	64	98	111	128	173	237	356	516	614	...	...
Other construction and land improvement, etc.	547	508	858	956	1078	1268	1636	2592	4021	5210	...	...
Other	457	721	1023	1270	1700	1712	2334	3960	5445	6595	...	...
4 Exports of goods and services	1365	1588	2059	2866	4390	5902	6470	7871	9674	12441	...	...
5 less: Imports of goods and services	944	1317	1803	2300	3260	3992	5760	8835	12087	15392	...	...
equals: Gross domestic product	6788	8824	11731	15127	20228	26107	33515	43898	57982	73511	...	...

a Item "Private final consumption expenditure" excludes direct purchases abroad by resident households and direct purchases in the domestic market by non-resident households.

1.2 Expenditure on the gross domestic product, in constant prices

Thousand million Columbian pesos

	1986	1987	1988	1989	1990	1991	1992	1993	1994	1995	1996	1997
At constant prices of: 1975												
1 Government final consumption expenditure	65	68	75	79	82	84	93	97	111	120	...	...
2 Private final consumption expenditure [a]	437	453	470	485	500	508	523	555	588	614	...	...
3 Gross capital formation	107	117	126	117	116	106	151	209	264	275	...	...
A Increase in stocks	6	15	14	10	13	9	42	60	84	89	...	...
B Gross fixed capital formation	101	101	113	107	103	97	109	148	180	186	...	...
Residential buildings	16	17	17	17	16	18	22	23	27	25	...	...
Non-residential buildings	3	4	5	4	4	4	4	5	6	6	...	...
Other construction and land improvement, etc.	40	31	37	33	29	26	27	33	42	45	...	...
Other	42	50	54	53	55	48	56	87	105	110	...	...
4 Exports of goods and services	111	119	120	130	152	171	180	191	191	219	...	...
5 less: Imports of goods and services	97	102	109	106	114	118	167	229	285	308	...	...
equals: Gross domestic product	622	655	682	705	735	750	780	822	870	921	...	...

a Item "Private final consumption expenditure" excludes direct purchases abroad by resident households and direct purchases in the domestic market by non-resident households.

Colombia

1.3 Cost components of the gross domestic product

Thousand million Columbian pesos

	1986	1987	1988	1989	1990	1991	1992	1993	1994	1995	1996	1997
1 Indirect taxes, net	799	1033	1254	1595	1990	2461	3236	4761	6843	8791	...	...
A Indirect taxes	838	1076	1314	1666	2099	2610	3408	5044	7222	9194	...	...
B less: Subsidies	39	43	59	71	109	149	173	283	379	403	...	...
2 Consumption of fixed capital	...	...	...	...	...	...	...	...	...	...	...	...
3 Compensation of employees paid by resident producers to ..	2575	3351	4466	5788	7555	9846	13483	17510	23528	30489	...	...
A Resident households	2560	3329	4455	5771	7519	9761	13421	17434	23412	30359	...	...
B Rest of the world	16	22	11	17	36	85	62	76	116	131	...	...
4 Operating surplus [a]	3414	4440	6011	7742	10682	13799	16796	21627	27611	34230	...	...
equals: Gross domestic product ..	6788	8824	11731	15127	20228	26107	33515	43898	57982	73511	...	...

a Item "Operating surplus" includes consumption of fixed capital.

1.4 General government current receipts and disbursements

Thousand million Columbian pesos

	1986	1987	1988	1989	1990	1991	1992	1993	1994	1995	1996	1997
Receipts												
1 Operating surplus	3	−209	−54	−72	−120	20	−48	−194	−106	223	...	...
2 Property and entrepreneurial income	80	129	178	259	419	549	805	1178	2029	2765	...	...
3 Taxes, fees and contributions .	1250	1656	2164	2795	3671	5315	6914	9305	13307	17182	...	...
A Indirect taxes	838	1076	1314	1666	2099	2610	3408	5044	7222	9194	...	...
B Direct taxes	204	303	496	633	885	1770	2150	2562	3309	4108	...	...
C Social security contributions	193	257	336	467	650	867	1237	1562	2557	3518	...	...
D Compulsory fees, fines and penalties	16	20	19	29	37	68	119	137	218	362	...	...
4 Other current transfers	281	370	498	650	812	1182	1705	2572	3804	5217	...	...
Total current receipts of general government	1614	1946	2787	3632	4782	7066	9376	12861	19034	25387	...	...
Disbursements												
1 Government final consumption expenditure	666	868	1182	1597	2076	2685	3965	5108	7653	11054	...	...
2 Property income	97	129	193	251	399	472	527	864	949	1210	...	...
3 Subsidies	39	43	59	71	109	149	173	283	379	403	...	...
4 Other current transfers	460	607	810	1103	1439	2008	2831	4078	6307	8778	...	...
A Social security benefits	105	141	191	265	359	502	694	1037	1613	1874	...	...
B Social assistance grants	68[a]	87[a]	111[a]	161[a]	223[a]	299[a]	395[a]	467	702	1145	...	...
C Other	287	380	509	677	857	1207	1742	2574	3992	5760	...	...
5 Net saving	352	298	542	610	759	1752	1881	2529	3746	3941	...	...
Total current disbursements and net saving of general government	1614	1946	2787	3632	4782	7066	9376	12861	19034	25387	...	...

a Item "Social assistance grants" refers to health only.

Colombia

1.5 Current income and outlay of corporate and quasi-corporate enterprises, summary

Thousand million Columbian pesos

	1986	1987	1988	1989	1990	1991	1992	1993	1994	1995	1996	1997
Receipts												
1 Operating surplus	1278	1860	2436	3295	4694	5472	6849	8957	11398	13606	...	...
2 Property and entrepreneurial income received	692	902	1336	1895	2522	3393	4129	5620	7897	11786	...	...
3 Current transfers	101	143	238	347	457	710	1190	1450	1946	2572	...	...
Total current receipts	2072	2905	4010	5537	7673	9575	12169	16026	21240	27965	...	...
Disbursements												
1 Property and entrepreneurial income	1221	1600	2148	3104	4220	5534	6800	8792	12314	16848	...	...
2 Direct taxes and other current payments to general government	134	203	370	481	695	1451	1789	2086	2712	3398	...	...
3 Other current transfers	120	170	293	390	522	805	1284	1722	2278	3021	...	...
4 Net saving	596	932	1200	1562	2236	1785	2296	3426	3936	4698	...	...
Total current disbursements and net saving	2072	2905	4010	5537	7673	9575	12169	16026	21240	27965	...	...

1.6 Current income and outlay of households and non-profit institutions

Thousand million Columbian pesos

	1986	1987	1988	1989	1990	1991	1992	1993	1994	1995	1996	1997
Receipts												
1 Compensation of employees	2563	3333	4460	5777	7528	9780	13438	17454	23435	30384	...	...
2 Operating surplus of private unincorporated enterprises	2133	2789	3629	4520	6108	8308	9995	12864	16320	20401	...	...
3 Property and entrepreneurial income	413	516	690	958	1302	1798	2247	2995	4120	4934	...	...
4 Current transfers	477	683	886	1160	1626	2543	3411	4409	5508	7114	...	...
A Social security benefits	186	248	331	474	653	924	1317	1844	2800	3643	...	...
B Social assistance grants											...	...
C Other	291	435	555	686	974	1619	2094	2566	2708	3471	...	...
Total current receipts	5586	7322	9666	12415	16565	22429	29091	37722	49382	62832	...	...
Disbursements												
1 Private final consumption expenditure	4479	5919	7714	9943	13270	17348	23077	30454	39254	49273	...	...
2 Property income	157	229	343	513	673	898	1093	1388	2217	3447	...	...
3 Direct taxes and other current transfers n.e.c. to general government	278	377	481	648	877	1254	1717	2175	3372	4590	...	...
A Social security contributions	193	257	336	467	650	867	1237	1562	2557	3518	...	...
B Direct taxes	76	109	134	164	207	359	416	552	712	898	...	...
C Fees, fines and penalties	9	11	11	17	20	28	63	61	104	174	...	...
4 Other current transfers	127	176	231	318	419	546	1013	1079	1460	1982	...	...
5 Net saving	545	620	898	993	1326	2383	2192	2627	3080	3540	...	...
Total current disbursements and net saving	5586	7322	9666	12415	16565	22429	29091	37722	49382	62832	...	...

Colombia

1.7 External transactions on current account, summary

Thousand million Columbian pesos

	1986	1987	1988	1989	1990	1991	1992	1993	1994	1995	1996	1997
Payments to the rest of the world												
1 Imports of goods and services	944	1317	1803	2300	3260	3992	5760	8835	12087	15392	...	...
2 Factor income to rest of the world	336	481	565	883	1259	1495	1605	1765	2193	3038	...	...
A Compensation of employees	16	22	11	18	37	85	62	76	116	131	...	...
B Property and entrepreneurial income	320	459	554	865	1222	1410	1543	1689	2077	2907	...	...
3 Current transfers to the rest of the world	4	5	9	11	8	29	93	167	160	166	...	...
4 Surplus of the nation on current transactions	271	85	60	143	570	1755	605	−718	−2727	−3956	...	...
Payments to the rest of the world and surplus of the nation on current transfers	1555	1888	2437	3337	5097	7271	8064	10048	11712	14640	...	...
Receipts from the rest of the world												
1 Exports of goods and services	1365	1588	2059	2866	4390	5902	6470	7871	9674	12441	...	...
2 Factor income from rest of the world	34	52	81	116	183	265	321	458	666	912	...	...
A Compensation of employees	3	4	5	6	9	18	17	20	22	25	...	...
B Property and entrepreneurial income	31	48	76	110	174	247	304	438	643	887	...	...
3 Current transfers from rest of the world	156	248	297	355	524	1103	1273	1718	1372	1287	...	...
Receipts from the rest of the world on current transactions	1555	1888	2437	3337	5097	7271	8064	10048	11712	14640	...	...

1.8 Capital transactions of the nation, summary

Thousand million Columbian pesos

	1986	1987	1988	1989	1990	1991	1992	1993	1994	1995	1996	1997
Finance of gross capital formation												
Gross saving	1493	1850	2640	3165	4322	5920	6369	8582	10761	12179	...	...
1 Consumption of fixed capital	...	...	...	...	...	...	...	...	...	...	...	...
2 Net saving [a]	1493	1850	2640	3165	4322	5920	6369	8582	10761	12179	...	...
A General government	352	298	542	610	759	1752	1881	2529	3746	3941	...	...
B Corporate and quasi-corporate enterprises	596	932	1200	1562	2236	1785	2296	3426	3936	4698	...	...
C Other	545	620	898	993	1327	2383	2192	2627	3080	3540	...	...
less: Surplus of the nation on current transactions	271	85	60	143	570	1755	605	−718	−2727	−3956	...	...
Finance of gross capital formation	...	...	...	3022	3752	4164	5763	9300	13489	16134	...	...
Gross capital formation												
Increase in stocks	18	227	292	288	387	354	552	1049	1616	1650	...	...
Gross fixed capital formation	1204	1537	2288	2733	3364	3810	5212	8251	11873	14484	...	...
1 General government	203	280	421	564	671	808	1103	1691	2922	3781	...	...
2 Corporate and quasi-corporate enterprises	747	875	1360	1536	1946	2042	2714	4513	6190	7655	...	...
3 Other	255	382	507	633	747	960	1394	2047	2761	3048	...	...
Gross capital formation	1222	1765	2580	3022	3752	4164	5763	9300	13489	16134	...	...

[a] Item "Net saving" includes consumption of fixed capital.

Colombia

1.10 Gross domestic product by kind of activity, in current prices

Thousand million Columbian pesos

	1986	1987	1988	1989	1990	1991	1992	1993	1994	1995	1996	1997
1 Agriculture, hunting, forestry and fishing	1186	1594	1965	2429	3284	4445	5188	5952	7465	9246	...	...
2 Mining and quarrying	332	578	722	1158	1884	2141	2274	2444	2582	3570	...	...
3 Manufacturing	1526	1793	2482	3159	4035	5332	6494	8786	11353	13633	...	...
4 Electricity, gas and water	151	201	271	377	509	691	882	1343	1836	2358	...	...
5 Construction	447	495	776	894	1001	1312	1828	2866	4387	5500	...	...
6 Wholesale and retail trade, restaurants and hotels	921	1240	1684	2154	2861	3763	5160	7393	9665	12439	...	...
7 Transport, storage and communication	527	713	969	1270	1843	2515	3462	4398	5731	7168	...	...
8 Finance, insurance, real estate and business services	766	985	1323	1668	2255	2978	3758	4960	7037	9397	...	...
9 Community, social and personal services	332	431	555	743	987	1348	1797	2359	3161	4216	...	...
Total, Industries	6188	8030	10746	13852	18659	24525	30844	40501	53218	67528	...	...
Producers of government services	547	714	932	1239	1607	1972	3119	3947	5509	7343	...	...
Other producers	...	...	...	...	...	...	...	...	...	...	...	...
Subtotal	6736	8743	11679	15091	20266	26497	33962	44448	58727	74870	...	...
less: Imputed bank service charge	156	227	369	474	657	986	1121	1563	2226	3194	...	...
plus: Import duties	208	308	421	510	619	596	674	1013	1481	1834	...	...
plus: Value added tax	...	...	...	...	...	...	...	...	...	...	...	...
plus: Other adjustments	...	...	...	...	...	...	...	...	...	...	...	...
equals: Gross domestic product	6788	8824	11731	15127	20228	26107	33515	43898	57982	73511	...	...

1.11 Gross domestic product by kind of activity, in constant prices

Thousand million Columbian pesos

	1986	1987	1988	1989	1990	1991	1992	1993	1994	1995	1996	1997
At constant prices of: 1975												
1 Agriculture, hunting, forestry and fishing	133	141	145	151	160	167	164	169	171	178	...	...
2 Mining and quarrying	22	28	29	32	34	34	33	32	33	40	...	...
3 Manufacturing	132	140	143	151	157	159	166	168	171	175	...	...
4 Electricity, gas and water	6	7	7	8	8	8	8	9	10	10	...	...
5 Construction	27	24	27	25	22	22	24	28	33	35	...	...
6 Wholesale and retail trade, restaurants and hotels	74	77	81	82	85	85	87	95	101	109	...	...
7 Transport, storage and communication	56	57	59	61	64	66	69	72	76	80	...	...
8 Finance, insurance, real estate and business services	87	92	99	101	107	113	117	123	139	150	...	...
9 Community, social and personal services	29	31	32	32	33	34	35	36	38	40	...	...
Total, Industries	566	597	622	644	670	687	701	732	771	816	...	...
Producers of government services	52	56	60	62	64	64	72	72	74	80	...	...
Other producers	...	...	...	...	...	...	...	...	...	...	...	...
Subtotal	618	653	682	707	734	751	773	804	845	896	...	...
less: Imputed bank service charge	14	17	21	21	20	22	21	24	28	34	...	...
plus: Import duties	18	19	20	19	21	21	29	43	54	59	...	...
plus: Value added tax	...	...	...	...	...	...	...	...	...	...	...	...
plus: Other adjustments	...	...	...	...	...	...	...	...	...	...	...	...
equals: Gross domestic product	622	655	682	705	735	750	780	822	870	921	...	...

Colombia

1.12 Relations among national accounting aggregates

Thousand million Columbian pesos

	1986	1987	1988	1989	1990	1991	1992	1993	1994	1995	1996	1997
Gross domestic product	6788	8824	11731	15127	20228	26107	33515	43898	57982	73511	...	...
plus: Net factor income from the rest of the world	–302	–429	–484	–766	–1075	–1229	–1284	–1307	–1527	–2125	...	...
Factor income from rest of the world	34	52	81	116	183	265	321	458	666	912	...	...
less: Factor income to the rest of the world	336	481	565	882	1258	1494	1605	1765	2193	3038	...	...
equals: Gross national product	6486	8395	11248	14361	19153	24878	32231	42592	56455	71385	...	...
less: Consumption of fixed capital	...	...	...	...	...	...	...	...	...	...	...	...
equals: National income [a]	6486	8395	11248	14361	19153	24878	32231	42592	56455	71385	...	...
plus: Net current transfers from the rest of the world	152	243	288	344	516	1074	1180	1552	1213	1121	...	...
Current transfers from rest of the world	156	248	297	355	524	1103	1273	1718	1372	1287	...	...
less: Current transfers to the rest of the world	4	5	9	11	8	29	93	167	160	166	...	...
equals: National disposable income [b]	6638	8638	11536	14705	19669	25952	33411	44143	57668	72506	...	...
less: Final consumption	5145	6788	8896	11539	15347	20032	27042	35562	46906	60328	...	...
equals: Net saving [c]	1493	1850	2640	3165	4322	5920	6369	8582	10761	12179	...	...
less: Surplus of the nation on current transactions	271	85	60	143	570	1756	605	–718	–2727	–3956	...	...
equals: Net capital formation [d]	1222	1765	2580	3023	3752	4164	5763	9300	13489	16134	...	...

a Item "National income" includes consumption of fixed capital.
b Item "National disposable income" includes consumption of fixed capital.
c Item "Net saving" includes consumption of fixed capital.
d Includes consumption of fixed capital.

2.1 Government final consumption expenditure by function, in current prices

Thousand million Columbian pesos

	1986	1987	1988	1989	1990	1991	1992	1993	1994	1995	1996	1997
1 General public services	207	268	355	470	640	798	1171	1456	2774	...	...	...
2 Defence	74	99	150	210	252	309	430	521	751	...	...	...
3 Public order and safety	...	...	...	...	...	...	...	...	...	...	...	...
4 Education	197	256	333	426	546	721	985	1227	1603	...	...	...
5 Health	62	84	113	158	205	253	304	561	1091	...	...	...
6 Social security and welfare	37	48	69	102	150	199	353	421	661	...	...	...
7 Housing and community amenities	4	6	7	9	12	17	23	30	28	...	...	...
8 Recreational, cultural and religious affairs	7	7	10	13	19	23	31	47	68	...	...	...
9 Economic services	77	99	142	205	251	343	658	825	651	...	...	...
10 Other functions	1	2	3	4	3	20	11	19	25	...	...	...
Total government final consumption expenditures	666	868	1182	1597	2076	2685	3965	5108	7653	...	...	...

Colombia

2.3 Total government outlays by function and type

Thousand million Columbian pesos

1986

	Final consumption expenditures Total	Compensation of employees	Other	Subsidies	Other current transfers and property income	Total current disbursements	Gross capital formation	Other capital outlays	Total outlays
1 General public services	207	180	28	–	15	222	24	1	247
2 Defence	74	48	25	–	–	74	1	–	75
3 Public order and safety	...	...	...	...	...	...	...	...	...
4 Education	197	182	15	4	4	205	18	–	223
5 Health	62	42	21	–	2	65	10	–	75
6 Social security and welfare	37	75	–38	–	107	144	16	2	162
7 Housing and community amenities	4	3	1	2	–	6	11	3	20
8 Recreational, cultural and religious affairs	7	5	2	1	1	8	5	–	13
9 Economic services	77	80	–3	33	29	138	68	27	233
10 Other functions	1	–	1	–	67	68	–	–	68
Total	666	614	52	39	224	930	153	33	1115

1987

	Final consumption expenditures Total	Compensation of employees	Other	Subsidies	Other current transfers and property income	Total current disbursements	Gross capital formation	Other capital outlays	Total outlays
1 General public services	268	227	41	–	23	290	27	4	321
2 Defence	99	64	35	–	–	99	–	–	99
3 Public order and safety	...	...	...	...	...	...	...	...	...
4 Education	256	240	16	1	4	262	22	1	284
5 Health	84	57	27	–	4	88	14	–	103
6 Social security and welfare	48	98	–49	–	145	193	23	1	218
7 Housing and community amenities	6	4	2	1	–	7	14	1	22
8 Recreational, cultural and religious affairs	7	6	1	1	2	10	5	–	14
9 Economic services	99	104	–5	41	40	180	162	37	379
10 Other functions	2	–	2	–	84	86	–	–	86
Total	868	799	69	43	303	1214	267	44	1525

1988

	Final consumption expenditures Total	Compensation of employees	Other	Subsidies	Other current transfers and property income	Total current disbursements	Gross capital formation	Other capital outlays	Total outlays
1 General public services	355	293	62	–	33	388	45	4	437
2 Defence	150	84	67	–	–	150	–	–	150
3 Public order and safety	...	...	...	...	...	...	...	...	...
4 Education	333	310	22	1	8	341	32	–	373
5 Health	113	75	38	–	4	117	18	–	136
6 Social security and welfare	69	127	–57	–	197	266	38	1	305
7 Housing and community amenities	7	6	1	3	2	12	18	–	30
8 Recreational, cultural and religious affairs	10	8	2	1	2	13	13	1	27

Colombia

1988

	Final consumption expenditures Total	Compensation of employees	Other	Subsidies	Other current transfers and property income	Total current disbursements	Gross capital formation	Other capital outlays	Total outlays
9 Economic services	142	141	1	54	54	250	275	51	576
10 Other functions	3	–	3	–	122	125	–	–	125
Total	1182	1044	139	59	422	1663	438	59	2160

1989

	Total	Compensation of employees	Other	Subsidies	Other current transfers and property income	Total current disbursements	Gross capital formation	Other capital outlays	Total outlays
1 General public services	470	390	...	–	...	...	58	...	575
2 Defence	210	109	...	...	...	...	1	...	211
3 Public order and safety	...	...	...	...	...	...	...	...	...
4 Education	426	401	...	4	...	...	37	...	477
5 Health	158	105	...	–	...	...	21	...	185
6 Social security and welfare	102	171	...	–	...	...	39	...	429
7 Housing and community amenities	9	8	...	...	...	...	31	...	44
8 Recreational, cultural and religious affairs	13	11	...	–	...	...	17	...	35
9 Economic services	205	190	...	66	...	...	359	...	751
10 Other functions	4	–	...	...	...	...	–	...	156
Total	1597	1386	...	71	...	...	564	...	2863

1990

	Total	Compensation of employees	Other	Subsidies	Other current transfers and property income	Total current disbursements	Gross capital formation	Other capital outlays	Total outlays
1 General public services	640	508	...	1	...	...	73	...	790
2 Defence	252	143	...	...	...	...	2	...	254
3 Public order and safety	...	...	...	...	...	...	...	...	...
4 Education	546	509	...	2	...	...	44	...	604
5 Health	205	132	...	–	...	...	27	...	238
6 Social security and welfare	150	239	...	–	...	...	49	...	587
7 Housing and community amenities	12	10	...	–	...	...	41	...	64
8 Recreational, cultural and religious affairs	19	14	...	–	...	...	24	...	55
9 Economic services	251	246	...	105	...	...	410	...	952
10 Other functions	3	...	...	...	...	...	–	...	246
Total	2076	1802	...	109	...	...	671	...	3789

1991

	Total	Compensation of employees	Other	Subsidies	Other current transfers and property income	Total current disbursements	Gross capital formation	Other capital outlays	Total outlays
1 General public services	798	616	...	1	...	...	95	...	998
2 Defence	309	172	...	...	...	...	14	...	325
3 Public order and safety	...	...	...	...	...	...	...	...	...
4 Education	721	640	...	2	...	...	67	...	804
5 Health	253	160	...	–	...	...	24	...	296

Colombia

| | 1991 ||||||||
| | Final consumption expenditures || | Subsidies | Other current transfers and property income | Total current disbursements | Gross capital formation | Other capital outlays | Total outlays |
	Total	Compensation of employees	Other						
6 Social security and welfare	199	319	...	4	...	...	68	...	806
7 Housing and community amenities	17	12	...	36	...	...	51	...	115
8 Recreational, cultural and religious affairs	23	16	...	1	...	...	36	...	69
9 Economic services	343	293	...	106	...	...	454	...	1286
10 Other functions	20	...	...	...	...	...	–	...	321
Total	2685	2230	...	149	...	...	808	...	5019

2.5 Private final consumption expenditure by type and purpose, in current prices

Thousand million Columbian pesos

	1986	1987	1988	1989	1990	1991	1992	1993	1994	1995	1996	1997
Final consumption expenditure of resident households												
1 Food, beverages and tobacco	1650	2102	2702	3454	4602	6003	7931	...	...	...	...	...
A Food	1371	1739	2251	2870	3812	5030	6615	...	...	...	...	...
B Non-alcoholic beverages	47	68	84	109	154	196	266	...	...	...	...	...
C Alcoholic beverages	183	239	296	388	525	636	862	...	...	...	...	...
D Tobacco	49	56	71	82	111	141	188	...	...	...	...	...
2 Clothing and footwear	272	364	489	582	668	782	1035	...	...	...	...	...
3 Gross rent, fuel and power	528	654	817	1053	1376	1819	2316	...	...	...	...	...
A Fuel and power	98	126	167	233	315	423	519	...	...	...	...	...
B Other	429	528	651	820	1061	1396	1797	...	...	...	...	...
4 Furniture, furnishings and household equipment and operation	254	349	490	631	841	1003	1328	...	...	...	...	...
A Household operation	135	183	253	339	466	544	754	...	...	...	...	...
B Other	118	166	236	292	375	459	574	...	...	...	...	...
5 Medical care and health expenses	280	377	486	656	885	1084	1487	...	...	...	...	...
6 Transport and communication	637	883	1210	1551	2252	3119	4285	...	...	...	...	...
A Personal transport equipment	200	281	384	465	601	784	1067	...	...	...	...	...
B Other	437	602	826	1086	1651	2335	3218	...	...	...	...	...
7 Recreational, entertainment, education and cultural services	258	351	454	604	788	995	1261	...	...	...	...	...
A Education	72	94	122	167	223	299	402	...	...	...	...	...
B Other	187	257	332	437	565	696	859	...	...	...	...	...
8 Miscellaneous goods and services	557	755	1036	1344	1826	2512	3528	...	...	...	...	...
A Personal care	47	61	87	120	168	206	271	...	...	...	...	...
B Expenditures in restaurants, cafes and hotels	405	549	736	955	1300	1876	2682	...	...	...	...	...
C Other	105	144	214	269	358	430	575	...	...	...	...	...
Total final consumption expenditure in the domestic market by households, of which	4436	5835	7684	9876	13238	17317	23171	...	...	...	...	...
plus: Direct purchases abroad by resident households	130	177	177	210	262	361	385	...	...	...	...	...
less: Direct purchases in the domestic market by non-resident households	87	93	148	143	230	330	373	...	...	...	...	...

Colombia

Thousand million Columbian pesos

	1986	1987	1988	1989	1990	1991	1992	1993	1994	1995	1996	1997
equals: Final consumption expenditure of resident households [a]	4479	5919	7714	9943	13270	17348	23183	...	...	...	...	...

a Item "Final consumption expenditure of resident households" includes consumption expenditure of private non-profit institutions serving households.

2.6 Private final consumption expenditure by type and purpose, in constant prices

Thousand million Columbian pesos

	1986	1987	1988	1989	1990	1991	1992	1993	1994	1995	1996	1997
At constant prices of: 1975												
Final consumption expenditure of resident households												
1 Food, beverages and tobacco	175	178	186	194	201	201	210	...	...	...	...	...
A Food	151	154	162	170	176	176	184	...	...	...	...	...
B Non-alcoholic beverages	4	4	4	4	5	4	5	...	...	...	...	...
C Alcoholic beverages	15	16	15	16	16	17	18	...	...	...	...	...
D Tobacco	5	5	4	4	4	4	4	...	...	...	...	...
2 Clothing and footwear	27	28	28	30	30	29	32	...	...	...	...	...
3 Gross rent, fuel and power	54	57	59	61	63	65	66	...	...	...	...	...
A Fuel and power	6	6	6	6	7	7	7	...	...	...	...	...
B Other	49	51	53	54	56	58	59	...	...	...	...	...
4 Furniture, furnishings and household equipment and operation	24	25	27	27	28	29	30	...	...	...	...	...
A Household operation	12	12	13	13	14	15	16	...	...	...	...	...
B Other	12	13	14	14	14	14	15	...	...	...	...	...
5 Medical care and health expenses	23	25	25	26	27	28	30	...	...	...	...	...
6 Transport and communication	56	58	61	63	64	66	69	...	...	...	...	...
A Personal transport equipment	15	17	18	17	17	17	19	...	...	...	...	...
B Other	41	42	43	46	47	49	50	...	...	...	...	...
7 Recreational, entertainment, education and cultural services	27	29	29	30	31	32	32	...	...	...	...	...
A Education	7	7	7	8	8	8	8	...	...	...	...	...
B Other	20	22	22	23	23	24	24	...	...	...	...	...
8 Miscellaneous goods and services	50	52	54	54	57	58	60	...	...	...	...	...
A Personal care	5	5	5	6	6	6	7	...	...	...	...	...
B Expenditures in restaurants, cafes and hotels	36	37	38	38	39	40	41	...	...	...	...	...
C Other	10	10	11	10	11	11	12	...	...	...	...	...
Total final consumption expenditure in the domestic market by households, of which	437	453	470	485	500	508	529	...	...	...	...	...
plus: Direct purchases abroad by resident households	16	16	12	11	12	12	12	...	...	...	...	...
less: Direct purchases in the domestic market by non-resident households	7	7	9	7	9	10	11	...	...	...	...	...
equals: Final consumption expenditure of resident households [a]	445	462	473	489	502	509	530	...	...	...	...	...

a Item "Final consumption expenditure of resident households" includes consumption expenditure of private non-profit institutions serving households.

Colombia

3.12 General government income and outlay account: total and subsectors

Thousand million Columbian pesos

	1986					1987				
	Total government	Central government	State or provincial government	Local government	Social security funds	Total government	Central government	State or provincial government	Local government	Social security funds

Receipts

1 Operating surplus	3	1	...	1	1	−209	−211	...	1	1
2 Property and entrepreneurial income	80	35	...	31	14	129	68	...	44	16
A Withdrawals from public quasi-corporations	5	...	...	5	...	6	...	...	6	...
B Interest	48	31	...	4	13	69	47	...	6	16
C Dividends	8	3	...	5	−	10	5	...	5	−
D Net land rent and royalties	19	1	...	17	−	43	16	...	27	−
3 Taxes, fees and contributions	1250	887	...	168	195	1656	1167	...	229	260
A Indirect taxes	838	676	...	161	...	1076	857	...	219	...
B Direct taxes	204	197	...	5	2	303	293	...	7	3
Income	182	182	...	...	...	276	276	...	...	...
Other	22	15	...	5	2	27	17	...	7	3
C Social security contributions	193	...	...	...	193	257	...	...	...	257
D Fees, fines and penalties	16	14	...	2	1	20	17	...	3	−
4 Other current transfers	281	46	...	226	9	370	64	...	295	11
A Casualty insurance claims	−	−	...	−	−	−	−	...	−	−
B Transfers from other government subsectors	220	2	...	210	8	283	3	...	270	10
C Transfers from rest of the world	8	8	...	−	...	12	12	...	−	...
D Other transfers, except imputed	10	7	...	3	−	11	7	...	3	−
E Imputed unfunded employee pension and welfare contributions	44	29	...	14	1	64	42	...	21	1
Total current receipts	1614	968	...	426	219	1946	1088	...	569	289

Disbursements

1 Government final consumption expenditure	666	330	...	321	15	868	433	...	416	19
2 Property income	97	86	...	11	−	129	111	...	17	−
A Interest	97	86	...	11	−	129	111	...	17	−
B Net land rent and royalties	...	...	...	...	...	...	...	...	...	...
3 Subsidies	39	37	...	2	−	43	39	...	4	−
4 Other current transfers	460	261	...	23	176	607	341	...	35	232
A Casualty insurance premiums, net	...	...	...	...	...	...	...	...	...	...
B Transfers to other government subsectors	220	217	...	3	1	283	279	...	3	1
C Social security benefits	105	...	...	...	105	141	...	...	...	141
D Social assistance grants	68	...	...	...	68	87	...	...	...	87
E Unfunded employee welfare benefits	44	29	...	14	1	64	42	...	21	1
F Transfers to private non-profit institutions serving households	21	13	...	7	1	30	18	...	11	2
G Other transfers n.e.c.	...	...	...	...	...	...	...	...	...	...

Colombia

Thousand million Columbian pesos

	1986					1987				
	Total govern-ment	Central govern-ment	State or provincial govern-ment	Local govern-ment	Social security funds	Total govern-ment	Central govern-ment	State or provincial govern-ment	Local govern-ment	Social security funds
H Transfers to rest of the world	2	2	...	–	–	2	2	...	–	–
Net saving	352	255	...	69	29	298	164	...	96	37
Total current disbursements and net saving	1614	968	...	426	219	1946	1088	...	569	289

	1988					1989				
	Total govern-ment	Central govern-ment	State or provincial govern-ment	Local govern-ment	Social security funds	Total govern-ment	Central govern-ment	State or provincial govern-ment	Local govern-ment	Social security funds

Receipts

1 Operating surplus	–54	–57	...	1	2	–72	–75	...	1	1
2 Property and entrepreneurial income	178	98	...	60	21	259	132	...	97	30
A Withdrawals from public quasi-corporations	9	...	...	9	...	11	...	...	11	...
B Interest	87	58	...	8	21	116	74	...	13	28
C Dividends	19	12	...	6	–	21	11	...	8	1
D Net land rent and royalties	64	27	...	37	–	112	47	...	65	–
3 Taxes, fees and contributions	2164	1529	...	294	342	2796	1936	...	385	475
A Indirect taxes	1314	1034	...	279	...	1666	1305	...	361	...
B Direct taxes	496	480	...	11	5	633	609	...	17	7
Income	455	455	...	...	...	575	575	...	...	...
Other	41	25	...	11	5	59	35	...	17	7
C Social security contributions	336	...	...	...	336	467	...	...	...	467
D Fees, fines and penalties	19	14	...	4	1	29	22	...	6	1
4 Other current transfers	498	80	...	403	15	649	79	...	549	22
A Casualty insurance claims	–	–	...	–	–	...	...	...	...	...
B Transfers from other government subsectors	385	4	...	367	14	522	4	...	498	20
C Transfers from rest of the world	15	15	...	–	...	2	2	...	–	...
D Other transfers, except imputed	13	6	...	7	–	14	4	...	10	–
E Imputed unfunded employee pension and welfare contributions	85	55	...	29	1	112	69	...	41	2
Total current receipts	2787	1649	...	758	380	3632	2072	...	1032	528

Disbursements

1 Government final consumption expenditure	1182	612	...	547	24	1597	830	...	731	35
2 Property income	193	168	...	24	1	251	215	...	34	1
A Interest	193	168	...	24	1	251	215	...	34	1
B Net land rent and royalties	...	...	...	...	...	...	...	...	...	...
3 Subsidies	59	49	...	10	–	71	60	...	11	–
4 Other current transfers	810	455	...	48	307	1104	604	...	66	434
A Casualty insurance premiums, net	...	...	...	...	...	...	...	...	...	...
B Transfers to other government subsectors	385	380	...	4	1	522	516	...	4	1
C Social security benefits	191	...	...	...	191	265	...	...	...	265
D Social assistance grants	111	...	...	...	111	161	...	...	...	161

Colombia

	1988					1989				
	Total govern-ment	Central govern-ment	State or provincial govern-ment	Local govern-ment	Social security funds	Total govern-ment	Central govern-ment	State or provincial govern-ment	Local govern-ment	Social security funds
E Unfunded employee welfare benefits	85	55	...	29	1	112	69	...	41	2
F Transfers to private non-profit institutions serving households	34	16	...	15	3	40	15	...	21	4
G Other transfers n.e.c.	...	...	...	...	...	...	...	...	...	...
H Transfers to rest of the world	4	4	...	–	–	5	5	...	–	–
Net saving	542	365	...	130	47	610	363	...	191	57
Total current disbursements and net saving	2787	1649	...	758	380	3632	2072	...	1032	528

	1990					1991				
	Total govern-ment	Central govern-ment	State or provincial govern-ment	Local govern-ment	Social security funds	Total govern-ment	Central govern-ment	State or provincial govern-ment	Local govern-ment	Social security funds

Receipts

1 Operating surplus	−121	−124	...	2	2	20	14	...	2	3
2 Property and entrepreneurial income	419	198	...	181	40	549	271	...	208	70
A Withdrawals from public quasi-corporations	14	...	...	14	...	19	...	...	19	...
B Interest	190	128	...	23	38	268	164	...	36	68
C Dividends	76	58	...	16	2	111	92	...	18	2
D Net land rent and royalties	139	11	...	128	...	151	16	...	135	...
3 Taxes, fees and contributions	3672	2495	...	518	659	5315	3786	...	651	879
A Indirect taxes	2100	1611	...	488	...	2610	1993	...	617	...
B Direct taxes	885	858	...	19	8	1770	1737	...	23	10
Income	772	772	...	...	...	1659	1659	...	...	...
Other	113	86	...	19	8	110	78	...	23	10
C Social security contributions	650	...	...	...	650	867	...	...	...	867
D Fees, fines and penalties	37	26	...	11	1	68	56	...	11	1
4 Other current transfers	812	93	...	706	13	1182	129	...	1011	41
A Casualty insurance claims	...	...	...	...	...	...	...	...	...	...
B Transfers from other government subsectors	651	6	...	634	10	986	11	...	938	36
C Transfers from rest of the world	2	2	...	–	...	26	26	...	–	...
D Other transfers, except imputed	22	6	...	16	–	31	10	...	22	–
E Imputed unfunded employee pension and welfare contributions	137	79	...	55	3	138	82	...	51	4
Total current receipts	4782	2663	...	1406	713	7066	4201	...	1872	993

Disbursements

1 Government final consumption expenditure	2076	1089	...	942	46	2685	1432	...	1189	64
2 Property income	399	339	...	58	1	471	389	...	81	1
A Interest	399	339	...	58	1	471	389	...	81	1
B Net land rent and royalties	...	...	...	...	...	...	...	...	...	...
3 Subsidies	109	92	...	17	...	149	134	...	16	...
4 Other current transfers	1439	745	...	98	596	2008	1091	...	104	814
A Casualty insurance premiums, net	...	...	...	...	...	...	...	...	...	...

Colombia

	1990					1991				
	Total govern-ment	Central govern-ment	State or provincial govern-ment	Local govern-ment	Social security funds	Total govern-ment	Central govern-ment	State or provincial govern-ment	Local govern-ment	Social security funds
B Transfers to other government subsectors	651	643	...	6	2	986	973	...	10	3
C Social security benefits	360	...	...	...	360	502	...	...	...	502
D Social assistance grants	223	...	...	...	223	299	...	...	...	299
E Unfunded employee welfare benefits	137	79	...	55	3	138	82	...	51	4
F Transfers to private non-profit institutions serving households	62	17	...	37	8	75	29	...	42	5
G Other transfers n.e.c.	...	...	...	...	...	...	...	...	...	...
H Transfers to rest of the world	7	7	...	–	–	8	8	...	–	–
Net saving	759	397	...	291	70	1752	1155	...	482	115
Total current disbursements and net saving	4782	2663	...	1406	713	7066	4201	...	1872	993

	1992					1993				
	Total govern-ment	Central govern-ment	State or provincial govern-ment	Local govern-ment	Social security funds	Total govern-ment	Central govern-ment	State or provincial govern-ment	Local govern-ment	Social security funds

Receipts

1 Operating surplus	–24	–28	...	4	–	...	...	...	...	...
2 Property and entrepreneurial income	752	404	...	259	90	...	...	...	...	...
A Withdrawals from public quasi-corporations	25	...	...	25	...	...	...	...	...	...
B Interest	330	197	...	46	87	...	...	...	...	...
C Dividends	160	135	...	22	3	...	...	...	...	...
D Net land rent and royalties	236	71	...	165	...	...	...	...	...	...
3 Taxes, fees and contributions	6768	4710	...	910	1148	...	...	...	...	...
A Indirect taxes	3366	2500	...	866	...	...	...	...	...	...
B Direct taxes	2135	2091	...	31	14	...	...	...	...	...
Income	2039	2039	...	...	...	...	...	...	...	...
Other	96	52	...	31	14	...	...	...	...	...
C Social security contributions	1133	...	...	...	1133	...	...	...	...	...
D Fees, fines and penalties	134	119	...	13	2	...	...	...	...	...
4 Other current transfers	1844	181	...	1598	64	...	...	...	...	...
A Casualty insurance claims	...	...	...	...	...	...	...	...	...	...
B Transfers from other government subsectors	1566	7	...	1501	57	...	...	...	...	...
C Transfers from rest of the world	31	31	...	–	...	...	...	...	...	...
D Other transfers, except imputed	48	21	...	26	–	...	...	...	...	...
E Imputed unfunded employee pension and welfare contributions	199	122	...	71	7	...	...	...	...	...
Total current receipts	9340	5266	...	2771	1302	...	...	...	...	...

Disbursements

1 Government final consumption expenditure	3656	2020	...	1543	93	...	...	...	...	...
2 Property income	682	576	...	104	2	...	...	...	...	...
A Interest	682	576	...	104	2	...	...	...	...	...
B Net land rent and royalties	...	...	...	...	...	...	...	...	...	...

Colombia

	1992					1993				
	Total govern-ment	Central govern-ment	State or provincial govern-ment	Local govern-ment	Social security funds	Total govern-ment	Central govern-ment	State or provincial govern-ment	Local govern-ment	Social security funds
3 Subsidies	119	98	...	21	...	...	...	...	...	...
4 Other current transfers	3052	1730	...	130	1191	...	...	...	...	...
A Casualty insurance premiums, net	...	...	...	...	...	...	...	...	...	...
B Transfers to other government subsectors	1566	1556	...	7	2	...	...	...	...	...
C Social security benefits	730	...	...	...	730	...	...	...	...	...
D Social assistance grants	445	...	...	...	445	...	...	...	...	...
E Unfunded employee welfare benefits	199	122	...	71	7	...	...	...	...	...
F Transfers to private non-profit institutions serving households	102	43	...	52	8	...	...	...	...	...
G Other transfers n.e.c.	...	...	...	...	...	...	...	...	...	...
H Transfers to rest of the world	9	9	...	–	–	...	...	...	...	...
Net saving	1832	843	...	973	17	...	...	...	...	...
Total current disbursements and net saving	9340	5266	...	2771	1302	...	...	...	...	...

3.13 General government capital accumulation account: total and subsectors

Thousand million Columbian pesos

	1986					1987				
	Total govern-ment	Central govern-ment	State or provincial govern-ment	Local govern-ment	Social security funds	Total govern-ment	Central govern-ment	State or provincial govern-ment	Local govern-ment	Social security funds
Finance of gross accumulation										
1 Gross saving	352	255	...	69	29	298	164	...	96	37
2 Capital transfers	–19	–41	...	6	15	–26	–52	...	6	20
A From other government subsectors	...	–15	...	...	15	...	–20	...	...	20
B From other resident sectors	...	...	...	...	...	...	...	...	...	...
C From rest of the world	–19	–25	...	6	...	–26	–32	...	6	...
Finance of gross accumulation	333	214	...	75	44	272	112	...	103	57
Gross accumulation										
1 Gross capital formation	153	63	...	77	12	267	128	...	121	19
A Increase in stocks	–50	–51	...	...	2	–12	–17	...	...	5
B Gross fixed capital formation	203	115	...	77	11	280	145	...	121	14
2 Purchases of land, net	3	1	...	1	1	6	4	...	1	1
3 Purchases of intangible assets, net	...	...	...	...	...	...	...	...	...	...
4 Capital transfers	...	...	...	...	...	...	...	...	...	...
Net lending	177	151	...	–4	30	–1	–19	...	–20	38
Gross accumulation	333	214	...	75	44	272	112	...	103	57

Colombia

	1988					1989				
	Total govern-ment	Central govern-ment	State or provincial govern-ment	Local govern-ment	Social security funds	Total govern-ment	Central govern-ment	State or provincial govern-ment	Local govern-ment	Social security funds
Finance of gross accumulation										
1 Gross saving	542	365	...	130	47	610	363	...	191	57
2 Capital transfers	−14	−48	...	5	29	41	−1	...	4	38
Finance of gross accumulation	528	317	...	135	76	651	362	...	194	95
Gross accumulation										
1 Gross capital formation	438	235	...	173	30	555	281	...	233	41
A Increase in stocks	17	8	...	...	10	−9	−21	...	...	12
B Gross fixed capital formation	421	228	...	173	20	564	302	...	233	29
Own account	29	10	...	19	...	...	...	...	...	...
Other	392	218	...	154	20	...	...	...	...	...
2 Purchases of land, net	10	8	...	−	1	21	18	...	1	2
3 Purchases of intangible assets, net	...	...	...	...	...	...	...	...	...	...
4 Capital transfers	...	...	...	...	...	...	...	...	...	...
Net lending	80	73	...	−39	45	74	63	...	−41	52
Gross accumulation	528	317	...	135	76	651	362	...	194	95

	1990					1991				
	Total govern-ment	Central govern-ment	State or provincial govern-ment	Local govern-ment	Social security funds	Total govern-ment	Central govern-ment	State or provincial govern-ment	Local govern-ment	Social security funds
Finance of gross accumulation										
1 Gross saving	759	397	...	291	70	1752	1155	...	482	115
2 Capital transfers	11	−47	...	−21	79	−139	−185	...	−25	71
Finance of gross accumulation	770	351	...	270	150	1613	971	...	457	186
Gross accumulation										
1 Gross capital formation	642	265	...	327	50	957	392	...	488	77
A Increase in stocks	−29	−40	...	...	11	149	135	...	...	14
B Gross fixed capital formation	671	305	...	327	39	808	257	...	488	62
2 Purchases of land, net	15	8	...	3	3	17	9	...	4	5
3 Purchases of intangible assets, net	...	...	...	...	...	...	...	...	...	...
4 Capital transfers	...	...	...	...	...	...	...	...	...	...
Net lending	113	77	...	−60	96	640	570	...	−35	104
Gross accumulation	770	351	...	270	150	1613	971	...	457	186

	1992					1993				
	Total govern-ment	Central govern-ment	State or provincial govern-ment	Local govern-ment	Social security funds	Total govern-ment	Central govern-ment	State or provincial govern-ment	Local govern-ment	Social security funds
Finance of gross accumulation										
1 Gross saving	1832	843	...	973	17	...	...	...	...	...
2 Capital transfers	−160	−187	...	−14	41	...	...	...	...	...
Finance of gross accumulation	1672	656	...	959	57	...	...	...	...	...
Gross accumulation										
1 Gross capital formation	1007	232	...	663	112	...	...	...	...	...
A Increase in stocks	11	−9	...	...	21	...	...	...	...	...

Colombia

	1992					1993				
	Total government	Central government	State or provincial government	Local government	Social security funds	Total government	Central government	State or provincial government	Local government	Social security funds
B Gross fixed capital formation	995	242	...	663	91	...	...	...	...	...
2 Purchases of land, net	21	10	...	4	7	...	...	...	...	...
3 Purchases of intangible assets, net	...	...	...	...	...	...	...	...	...	...
4 Capital transfers	...	...	...	...	...	...	...	...	...	...
Net lending	645	414	...	292	−61	...	...	...	...	...
Gross accumulation	1672	656	...	959	57	...	...	...	...	...

3.22 Corporate and quasi-corporate enterprise income and outlay account: total and sectors

Thousand million Columbian pesos

	1986			1987			1988			1989		
	Total	Non-financial	Financial	Total	Non-financial	Financial	Total	Non-financial	Financial	Total	Non-financial	Financial
Receipts												
1 Operating surplus	1278	1372	−94	1860	1974	−114	2436	2631	−195	3295	3533	−238
2 Property and entrepreneurial income	692	119	573	902	168	734	1336	253	1083	1896	339	1557
A Withdrawals from quasi-corporate enterprises	2	1	1	4	2	3	5	3	2	3	...	3
B Interest	651	99	552	807	139	668	1212	216	996	1774	284	1490
C Dividends	38	18	20	90	27	63	119	33	85	114	51	63
D Net land rent and royalties	1	1	...	1	1	–	1	–	–	4	4	–
3 Current transfers	101	70	32	143	96	47	238	153	85	347	219	128
A Casualty insurance claims	12	11	1	21	20	1	54	52	2	86	83	2
B Casualty insurance premiums, net, due to be received by insurance companies	19	...	19	31	...	31	68	...	68	102	...	102
C Current transfers from rest of the world	...	...	...	...	...	...	...	...	...	...	...	...
D Other transfers except imputed	...	...	...	...	...	...	...	...	...	...	...	...
E Imputed unfunded employee pension and welfare contributions	70	59	12	91	76	14	115	101	14	159	136	23
Total current receipts	2072	1561	510	2905	2238	667	4010	3037	973	5537	4091	1446
Disbursements												
1 Property and entrepreneurial income	1221	806	416	1600	1098	502	2148	1430	718	3104	2057	1047
A Withdrawals from quasi-corporations	61	61	–	114	114	...	131	131	–	241	241	–
Public	...	5	...	...	6	...	...	9	...	...	...	...
Private	...	56	...	...	108	...	...	122	...	...	...	...
B Interest	914	515	399	1130	644	486	1536	837	699	2215	1208	1007
C Dividends	226	209	16	311	295	16	415	396	19	531	492	39
D Net land rent and royalties	20	20	...	45	45	...	66	66	–	117	117	–
2 Direct taxes and other current transfers n.e.c. to general government	134	117	17	203	179	23	370	345	25	481	432	49
A Direct taxes	127	112	15	194	173	21	362	339	23	470	423	46
B Fines, fees, penalties and other current transfers n.e.c.	7	5	2	8	6	2	8	6	2	11	9	2
3 Other current transfers	120	82	38	170	116	54	293	182	111	390	253	137

Colombia

Thousand million Columbian pesos

	1986 Total	1986 Non-financial	1986 Financial	1987 Total	1987 Non-financial	1987 Financial	1988 Total	1988 Non-financial	1988 Financial	1989 Total	1989 Non-financial	1989 Financial
A Casualty insurance premiums, net	12	11	1	21	20	1	54	52	2	85	81	4
B Casualty insurance claims liability of insurance companies	19	...	19	31	...	31	68	...	68	102	...	102
C Transfers to private non-profit institutions	...	...	...	...	...	...	...	...	...	...	...	...
D Unfunded employee pension and welfare benefits	70	59	12	91	76	14	115	101	14	159	136	23
E Social assistance grants	...	...	...	...	...	...	...	...	...	...	...	...
F Other transfers n.e.c.	...	...	...	...	...	...	...	...	...	...	...	...
G Transfers to rest of the world [a]	19	12	7	28	20	7	56	29	26	44	36	8
Net saving	596	557	39	932	844	87	1200	1080	119	1562	1348	214
Total current disbursements and net saving	2072	1561	510	2905	2238	667	4010	3037	973	5537	4091	1446

	1990 Total	1990 Non-financial	1990 Financial	1991 Total	1991 Non-financial	1991 Financial	1992 Total	1992 Non-financial	1992 Financial	1993 Total	1993 Non-financial	1993 Financial
Receipts												
1 Operating surplus	4694	4897	-202	5472	5988	-516	6849	7387	-538	...	...	...
2 Property and entrepreneurial income	2522	472	2050	3393	641	2752	4129	836	3294	...	...	...
A Withdrawals from quasi-corporate enterprises	34	...	34	45	...	45	49	...	49	...	...	...
B Interest	2305	353	1951	3149	517	2631	3779	657	3123	...	...	...
C Dividends	166	102	65	183	107	76	289	167	122	...	...	...
D Net land rent and royalties	17	17	–	16	16	–	12	12	–	...	...	...
3 Current transfers	457	279	178	710	412	298	1190	653	537	...	...	...
A Casualty insurance claims	98	91	7	166	156	11	304	291	13	...	...	...
B Casualty insurance premiums, net, due to be received by insurance companies	142	...	142	248	...	248	489	...	489	...	...	...
C Current transfers from rest of the world	...	...	...	...	...	...	...	...	...	...	...	...
D Other transfers except imputed	...	...	...	...	...	...	...	...	...	...	...	...
E Imputed unfunded employee pension and welfare contributions	217	189	28	296	257	39	396	362	34	...	...	...
Total current receipts	7673	5648	2025	9575	7041	2534	12169	8877	3292	...	...	...
Disbursements												
1 Property and entrepreneurial income	4204	2883	1321	5534	3739	1795	6800	4530	2271	...	...	...
A Withdrawals from quasi-corporations	383	383	...	475	456	19	652	630	23	...	...	...
B Interest	2861	1588	1272	3773	2131	1643	4426	2370	2056	...	...	...
C Dividends	803	754	49	1115	982	133	1445	1253	192	...	...	...
D Net land rent and royalties	158	158	–	170	170	–	277	277	–	...	...	...
2 Direct taxes and other current transfers n.e.c. to general government	695	644	51	1450	1346	105	1789	1664	125	...	...	...
A Direct taxes	678	633	45	1411	1326	85	1733	1618	116	...	...	...
B Fines, fees, penalties and other current transfers n.e.c.	17	11	6	40	20	20	56	46	10	...	...	...
3 Other current transfers	521	322	199	806	459	347	1284	705	578	...	...	...

Colombia

	1990			1991			1992			1993		
	Total	Non-financial	Financial	Total	Non-financial	Financial	Total	Non-financial	Financial	Total	Non-financial	Financial
A Casualty insurance premiums, net	103	98	6	178	161	17	231	292	17	...	...	...
B Casualty insurance claims liability of insurance companies	142	...	142	248	...	248	489	...	489	...	...	...
C Transfers to private non-profit institutions	...	...	...	...	...	...	...	...	...	...	...	...
D Unfunded employee pension and welfare benefits	217	189	28	296	257	39	396	362	34	...	...	...
E Social assistance grants	...	...	...	...	...	...	...	...	...	...	...	...
F Other transfers n.e.c.	...	...	...	...	...	...	...	...	...	...	...	...
G Transfers to rest of the world [a]	59	36	23	84	42	43	88	51	37	...	...	...
Net saving	2253	1799	454	1785	1498	287	2296	1978	318	...	...	...
Total current disbursements and net saving	7673	5648	2025	9575	7041	2534	12169	8877	3292	...	...	...

[a] Item "Transfers to the rest of the world" refers to net current transfers n. e. c.

3.23 Corporate and quasi-corporate enterprise capital accumulation account: total and sectors

Thousand million Columbian pesos

	1986			1987			1988			1989		
	Total	Non-financial	Financial	Total	Non-financial	Financial	Total	Non-financial	Financial	Total	Non-financial	Financial
Finance of gross accumulation												
1 Gross saving	596	557	39	932	844	87	1200	1080	119	1562	1348	214
2 Capital transfers [a]	33	30	3	34	34	–	–47	34	–81	–43	30	–74
Finance of gross accumulation	629	587	42	966	878	88	1153	1115	38	1519	1378	140
Gross accumulation												
1 Gross capital formation	768	741	26	1034	998	36	1436	1394	42	1673	1624	49
A Increase in stocks	21	21	–	158	149	9	76	69	7	138	117	21
B Gross fixed capital formation	747	720	26	875	849	27	1360	1325	35	1536	1507	29
2 Purchases of land, net	11	11	–	17	13	5	11	5	6	16	6	9
3 Purchases of intangible assets, net	–	–	...	–	–	...	...	...	...	...	...	...
4 Capital transfers	...	...	...	...	...	...	...	...	...	...	...	...
Net lending	–150	–166	16	–85	–133	47	–294	–284	–10	–170	–252	81
Gross accumulation	629	587	42	966	878	88	1153	1115	38	1519	1378	140

	1990			1991			1992			1993		
	Total	Non-financial	Financial	Total	Non-financial	Financial	Total	Non-financial	Financial	Total	Non-financial	Financial
Finance of gross accumulation												
1 Gross saving	2236	1799	437	1785	1498	287	2006	1604	402	...	...	...
2 Capital transfers [a]	–70	79	–148	192	119	73	207	157	51	...	...	...
Finance of gross accumulation	2167	1878	289	1977	1616	361	2213	1761	453	...	...	...
Gross accumulation												
1 Gross capital formation	2185	2087	98	2153	2018	135	2883	2694	189	...	...	...
A Increase in stocks	239	225	14	111	76	35	57	29	28	...	...	...
B Gross fixed capital formation	1946	1862	84	2042	1943	100	2826	2665	160	...	...	...
2 Purchases of land, net	101	97	4	169	151	18	192	163	28	...	...	...

Colombia

	1990 Total	1990 Non-financial	1990 Financial	1991 Total	1991 Non-financial	1991 Financial	1992 Total	1992 Non-financial	1992 Financial	1993 Total	1993 Non-financial	1993 Financial
3 Purchases of intangible assets, net	...	...	...	...	...	...	...	...	...	...	...	...
4 Capital transfers	...	...	...	...	...	...	...	...	...	...	...	...
Net lending	−119	−306	187	−345	−553	208	−861	−1096	236	...	...	...
Gross accumulation	2167	1878	289	1977	1616	361	2213	1761	453	...	...	...

a Capital transfers received are recorded net of capital transfers paid.

3.33 Household and private unincorporated enterprise capital accumulation account
Thousand million Columbian pesos

	1986	1987	1988	1989	1990	1991	1992	1993	1994	1995	1996	1997
Finance of gross accumulation												
1 Gross saving	545	620	898	993	1326	2383	2363	...	...	...	...	...
2 Capital transfers	−14	−8	61	2	58	−53	−47	...	...	...	...	...
Total finance of gross accumulation	531	612	959	995	1385	2329	2316	...	...	...	...	...
Gross accumulation												
1 Gross capital formation	301	464	705	793	924	1054	1818	...	...	...	...	...
A Increase in stocks	46	81	198	159	177	94	424	...	...	...	...	...
B Gross fixed capital formation	255	382	507	633	747	960	1394	...	...	...	...	...
2 Purchases of land, net	−14	−23	−21	−37	−115	−186	−213	...	...	...	...	...
3 Purchases of intangibles, net	−	−	...	...	...	...	...	...	...	...	...	...
4 Capital transfers	...	...	...	...	...	...	...	...	...	...	...	...
Net lending	244	172	275	239	576	1461	710	...	...	...	...	...
Total gross accumulation	531	612	959	995	1385	2329	2316	...	...	...	...	...

4.1 Derivation of value added by kind of activity, in current prices
Thousand million Columbian pesos

	1986 Gross output	1986 Intermediate consumption	1986 Value added	1987 Gross output	1987 Intermediate consumption	1987 Value added	1988 Gross output	1988 Intermediate consumption	1988 Value added	1989 Gross output	1989 Intermediate consumption	1989 Value added
All producers												
1 Agriculture, hunting, forestry and fishing	1473	287	1186	1983	388	1594	2484	519	1965	3105	676	2429
A Agriculture and hunting [a]	1411	283	1128	1900	383	1517	2378	512	1866	2969	667	2302
B Forestry and logging	28	1	27	37	2	36	51	2	49	66	3	63
C Fishing [a]	34	3	31	45	4	42	55	5	50	70	6	64
2 Mining and quarrying	408	76	332	707	129	578	898	176	722	1404	246	1158
3 Manufacturing	3992	2466	1526	5062	3269	1793	6809	4327	2482	8853	5693	3159
A Manufacture of food, beverages and tobacco	1962	1215	748	2130	1475	655	2769	1827	942	3571	2421	1150
B Textile, wearing apparel and leather industries	360	203	157	492	277	215	708	386	322	947	520	427
C Manufacture of wood and wood products, including furniture	57	28	28	80	40	40	116	57	59	155	76	79
D Manufacture of paper and paper products, printing and publishing	206	128	78	279	172	107	377	240	137	488	311	177

Colombia

Thousand million Columbian pesos

	1986 Gross output	1986 Intermediate consumption	1986 Value added	1987 Gross output	1987 Intermediate consumption	1987 Value added	1988 Gross output	1988 Intermediate consumption	1988 Value added	1989 Gross output	1989 Intermediate consumption	1989 Value added
E Manufacture of chemicals and chemical petroleum, coal, rubber and plastic products	773	527	246	1137	771	366	1460	1037	422	1937	1378	559
F Manufacture of non-metallic mineral products, except products of petroleum and coal	150	75	75	214	104	110	301	148	153	396	192	204
G Basic metal industries	...	...	...	...	...	...	...	...	...	...	...	...
H Manufacture of fabricated metal products, machinery and equipment	437	269	167	668	402	266	989	594	395	1233	742	491
I Other manufacturing industries	47	21	27	61	27	34	89	38	51	125	53	72
4 Electricity, gas and water	210	59	151	279	78	201	375	104	271	521	144	377
5 Construction	744	297	447	815	320	495	1265	490	776	1458	564	894
6 Wholesale and retail trade, restaurants and hotels [b]	965	269	695	1280	347	934	1742	469	1273	2210	601	1609
A Wholesale and retail trade	965	269	695	1280	347	934	1742	469	1273	2210	601	1609
B Restaurants and hotels	...	...	...	...	...	...	...	...	...	...	...	...
7 Transport, storage and communication	839	311	527	1126	414	713	1516	546	969	1974	705	1269
A Transport and storage	718	276	442	977	369	609	1299	482	818	1668	614	1054
B Communication	121	36	85	149	45	104	216	64	152	306	90	215
8 Finance, insurance, real estate and business services	916	150	766	1181	195	985	1603	280	1323	2016	348	1668
A Financial institutions [c]	520	120	399	696	159	537	1012	232	780	1274	286	989
B Insurance												
C Real estate and business services [c]	397	30	367	485	36	448	591	49	543	742	63	680
Real estate, except dwellings	...	...	...	...	...	...	...	...	...	...	...	...
Dwellings	397	30	367	485	36	448	591	49	543	742	63	680
9 Community, social and personal services [b]	796	238	558	1054	317	738	1380	415	965	1822	533	1289
A Sanitary and similar services	...	...	...	...	...	...	...	...	...	...	...	...
B Social and related community services	...	...	...	...	...	...	...	...	...	...	...	...
C Recreational and cultural services	...	...	...	...	...	...	...	...	...	...	...	...
D Personal and household services	796	238	558	1054	317	738	1380	415	965	1822	533	1289
Total, Industries	10342	4154	6188	13487	5458	8030	18072	7326	10746	23363	9510	13852
Producers of government services	699	152	547	918	205	714	1249	317	932	1685	448	1239
Other producers	...	...	...	...	...	...	...	...	...	...	...	...
Total	11042	4306	6736	14405	5662	8743	19321	7642	11679	25048	9958	15091
less: Imputed bank service charge	...	−156	156	...	−227	227	...	−369	369	...	−474	474
Import duties	208	...	208	308	...	308	421	...	421	510	...	510
Value added tax	...	...	...	...	...	...	...	...	...	...	...	...
Other adjustments	...	...	...	...	...	...	...	...	...	...	...	...
Total	11250	4462	6788	14713	5889	8824	19742	8011	11731	25558	10432	15127

Colombia

	1990 Gross output	1990 Intermediate consumption	1990 Value added	1991 Gross output	1991 Intermediate consumption	1991 Value added	1992 Gross output	1992 Intermediate consumption	1992 Value added	1993 Gross output	1993 Intermediate consumption	1993 Value added
All producers												
1 Agriculture, hunting, forestry and fishing	4209	925	3284	5588	1144	4444	6557	1361	5196	...	...	...
A Agriculture and hunting [a]	4033	914	3119	5342	1128	4214	6237	1343	4895	...	...	...
B Forestry and logging	83	3	80	112	4	108	134	5	128	...	...	...
C Fishing [a]	93	8	85	133	11	123	186	13	173	...	...	...
2 Mining and quarrying	2258	374	1884	2602	461	2141	3084	736	2348	...	...	...
3 Manufacturing	11700	7665	4035	14697	9365	5332	17894	11454	6440	...	...	...
A Manufacture of food, beverages and tobacco	4782	3348	1434	6128	4103	2025	6514	4245	2269	...	...	...
B Textile, wearing apparel and leather industries	1278	707	571	1661	913	747	2013	1132	881	...	...	...
C Manufacture of wood and wood products, including furniture	192	94	98	236	116	120	...	...	...	...	...	...
D Manufacture of paper and paper products, printing and publishing	642	414	228	822	514	307	...	...	...	...	...	...
E Manufacture of chemicals and chemical petroleum, coal, rubber and plastic products	2595	1850	745	3286	2292	994	...	...	...	...	...	...
F Manufacture of non-metallic mineral products, except products of petroleum and coal	498	245	253	625	300	325	...	...	...	...	...	...
G Basic metal industries	...	...	...	...	...	...	...	...	...	...	...	...
H Manufacture of fabricated metal products, machinery and equipment	1544	934	610	1748	1043	704	...	...	...	...	...	...
I Other manufacturing industries	169	73	96	191	82	109	...	...	...	...	...	...
4 Electricity, gas and water	709	200	509	953	262	691	1185	301	884	...	...	...
5 Construction	1650	649	1001	2083	770	1312	2877	994	1883	...	...	...
6 Wholesale and retail trade, restaurants and hotels [b]	2924	805	2119	3645	1020	2625	4654	1330	3324	...	...	...
A Wholesale and retail trade	2924	805	2119	3645	1020	2625	4654	1330	3324	...	...	...
B Restaurants and hotels	...	...	...	...	...	...	...	...	...	...	...	...
7 Transport, storage and communication	2858	1015	1843	3876	1361	2515	5267	1810	3457	...	...	...
A Transport and storage	2425	887	1538	3282	1189	2093	4486	1585	2901	...	...	...
B Communication	433	128	305	594	172	422	781	225	556	...	...	...
8 Finance, insurance, real estate and business services	2740	486	2254	3616	637	2978	4627	831	3796	...	...	...
A Financial institutions [c]	1789	405	1384	2366	534	1832	3031	701	2330	...	...	...
B Insurance										...	...	...
C Real estate and business services [c]	951	81	870	1249	103	1146	1597	130	1467	...	...	...
Real estate, except dwellings	...	...	...	...	...	...	...	...	...	...	...	...
Dwellings	951	81	870	1249	103	1146	1597	130	1467	...	...	...
9 Community, social and personal services [b]	2448	719	1729	3411	924	2487	4860	1215	3645	...	...	...
A Sanitary and similar services	...	...	...	...	...	...	...	...	...	...	...	...
B Social and related community services	...	...	...	...	...	...	...	...	...	...	...	...

Colombia

	1990 Gross output	1990 Intermediate consumption	1990 Value added	1991 Gross output	1991 Intermediate consumption	1991 Value added	1992 Gross output	1992 Intermediate consumption	1992 Value added	1993 Gross output	1993 Intermediate consumption	1993 Value added
C Recreational and cultural services	...	...	...	...	...	...	...	...	...	...	...	...
D Personal and household services	2448	719	1729	3411	924	2487	4860	1215	3645	...	...	...
Total, Industries	31496	12838	18658	40471	15944	24525	51005	20032	30973	...	...	...
Producers of government services	2199	592	1607	2880	907	1972	3924	1208	2715	...	...	...
Other producers	...	...	...	...	...	...	...	...	...	...	...	...
Total	33695	13430	20265	43351	16851	26497	54929	21240	33688	...	...	...
less: Imputed bank service charge	...	−657	657	...	−986	986	...	−1199	1199	...	...	...
Import duties	619	...	619	596	...	596	653	...	653	...	...	...
Value added tax	...	...	...	...	...	...	...	...	...	...	...	...
Other adjustments	...	...	...	...	...	...	...	...	...	...	...	...
Total	34314	14087	20227	43947	17837	26107	55582	22439	33142	...	...	...

a Hunting is included in item "Fishing".
b Restaurants and hotels are included in item "Community, social and personal services".
c Business services are included in the financial institutions.

4.2 Derivation of value added by kind of activity, in constant prices

Thousand million Columbian pesos

	1986 Gross output	1986 Intermediate consumption	1986 Value added	1987 Gross output	1987 Intermediate consumption	1987 Value added	1988 Gross output	1988 Intermediate consumption	1988 Value added	1989 Gross output	1989 Intermediate consumption	1989 Value added
At constant prices of: 1975												
All producers												
1 Agriculture, hunting, forestry and fishing	162	29	133	172	31	141	177	31	145	184	32	151
A Agriculture and hunting [a]	156	28	127	166	30	136	170	31	139	177	32	146
B Forestry and logging	3	–	3	3	–	3	3	–	3	3	–	3
C Fishing [a]	3	–	3	3	–	3	3	–	3	3	–	3
2 Mining and quarrying	32	10	22	40	13	28	42	13	29	47	15	32
3 Manufacturing	364	232	132	382	242	140	392	250	143	410	259	151
A Manufacture of food, beverages and tobacco	171	115	55	169	114	55	169	115	53	179	122	57
B Textile, wearing apparel and leather industries	38	22	16	40	23	17	44	25	18	47	27	20
C Manufacture of wood and wood products, including furniture	5	2	3	5	3	3	6	3	3	6	3	3
D Manufacture of paper and paper products, printing and publishing	22	13	9	25	14	10	25	15	10	26	15	11
E Manufacture of chemicals and chemical petroleum, coal, rubber and plastic products	69	45	24	78	50	27	78	51	27	81	52	28
F Manufacture of non-metallic mineral products, except products of petroleum and coal	13	6	7	14	6	8	15	7	9	16	7	9
G Basic metal industries	...	...	...	...	...	...	...	...	...	...	...	...

Colombia

Thousand million Columbian pesos

	1986 Gross output	1986 Intermediate consumption	1986 Value added	1987 Gross output	1987 Intermediate consumption	1987 Value added	1988 Gross output	1988 Intermediate consumption	1988 Value added	1989 Gross output	1989 Intermediate consumption	1989 Value added
At constant prices of: 1975												
H Manufacture of fabricated metal products, machinery and equipment	41	25	15	47	29	18	52	32	20	51	31	20
I Other manufacturing industries	4	2	2	4	2	2	4	2	2	4	2	2
4 Electricity, gas and water	11	4	6	12	4	7	12	5	7	13	5	8
5 Construction	58	31	27	52	27	24	58	31	27	53	28	25
6 Wholesale and retail trade, restaurants and hotels [b]	84	26	58	88	27	61	93	28	64	94	28	66
A Wholesale and retail trade	84	26	58	88	27	61	93	28	64	94	28	66
B Restaurants and hotels	...	...	...	...	...	...	...	...	...	...	...	...
7 Transport, storage and communication	81	26	56	84	26	57	87	27	59	89	28	61
A Transport and storage	68	22	45	70	23	47	72	23	48	73	23	49
B Communication	14	4	10	14	4	10	15	4	11	16	4	12
8 Finance, insurance, real estate and business services	103	16	87	108	16	92	117	18	99	119	18	101
A Financial institutions [c]	55	12	43	59	13	46	66	14	51	66	14	52
B Insurance	...	...	...	...	...	...	...	...	...	...	...	...
C Real estate and business services [c]	47	3	44	49	3	46	51	4	47	53	4	49
Real estate, except dwellings	...	...	...	...	...	...	...	...	...	...	...	...
Dwellings	47	3	44	49	3	46	51	4	47	53	4	49
9 Community, social and personal services [b]	71	26	45	74	27	47	75	27	48	76	27	49
A Sanitary and similar services	...	...	...	...	...	...	...	...	...	...	...	...
B Social and related community services	...	...	...	...	...	...	...	...	...	...	...	...
C Recreational and cultural services	...	...	...	...	...	...	...	...	...	...	...	...
D Personal and household services	71	26	45	74	27	47	75	27	48	76	27	49
Total, Industries	965	399	566	1011	413	597	1053	431	622	1084	440	644
Producers of government services	68	15	52	72	16	56	79	19	60	84	21	62
Other producers	...	...	...	...	...	...	...	...	...	...	...	...
Total	1033	414	618	1083	430	653	1132	450	682	1168	461	707
less: Imputed bank service charge	...	−14	14	...	−17	17	...	−21	21	...	−21	21
Import duties	18	...	18	19	...	19	20	...	20	19	...	19
Value added tax	...	...	...	...	...	...	...	...	...	...	...	...
Other adjustments	...	...	...	...	...	...	...	...	...	...	...	...
Total	1050	428	622	1101	446	655	1152	470	682	1187	482	705

Colombia

	1990 Gross output	1990 Intermediate consumption	1990 Value added	1991 Gross output	1991 Intermediate consumption	1991 Value added	1992 Gross output	1992 Intermediate consumption	1992 Value added	1993 Gross output	1993 Intermediate consumption	1993 Value added
At constant prices of: 1975												
All producers												
1 Agriculture, hunting, forestry and fishing	195	35	160	204	37	167	201	37	164	...	...	...
A Agriculture and hunting [a]	189	34	154	197	36	160	194	36	157	...	...	...
B Forestry and logging	3	–	3	3	–	3	3	–	3	...	...	...
C Fishing [a]	3	–	3	4	–	3	4	–	3	...	...	...
2 Mining and quarrying	50	16	34	50	16	34	53	20	33	...	...	...
3 Manufacturing	434	277	157	436	277	159	457	289	168	...	...	...
A Manufacture of food, beverages and tobacco	196	133	62	193	131	62	199	133	66	...	...	...
B Textile, wearing apparel and leather industries	49	28	21	51	29	22	53	31	22	...	...	...
C Manufacture of wood and wood products, including furniture	6	3	3	6	3	3	6	3	3	...	...	...
D Manufacture of paper and paper products, printing and publishing	27	16	11	28	17	11	30	18	12	...	...	...
E Manufacture of chemicals and chemical petroleum, coal, rubber and plastic products	85	56	29	87	57	30	91	60	31	...	...	...
F Manufacture of non-metallic mineral products, except products of petroleum and coal	16	7	9	17	7	9	17	8	10	...	...	...
G Basic metal industries	...	...	...	...	...	...	...	...	...	...	...	...
H Manufacture of fabricated metal products, machinery and equipment	51	32	20	50	31	19	56	35	21	...	...	...
I Other manufacturing industries	5	2	2	4	2	2	4	2	2	...	...	...
4 Electricity, gas and water	13	5	8	14	5	8	13	5	8	...	...	...
5 Construction	48	26	22	48	26	22	52	28	24	...	...	...
6 Wholesale and retail trade, restaurants and hotels [b]	98	30	68	97	30	68	102	32	71	...	...	...
A Wholesale and retail trade	98	30	68	97	30	68	102	32	71	...	...	...
B Restaurants and hotels	...	...	...	...	...	...	...	...	...	...	...	...
7 Transport, storage and communication	93	29	64	96	30	66	102	32	69	...	...	...
A Transport and storage	75	24	50	76	25	51	81	27	54	...	...	...
B Communication	18	5	13	19	5	14	20	5	15	...	...	...
8 Finance, insurance, real estate and business services	127	20	107	133	21	113	139	22	117	...	...	...
A Financial institutions [c]	73	16	57	77	17	61	82	18	64	...	...	...
B Insurance	...	...	...	...	...	...	...	...	...	...	...	...
C Real estate and business services [c]	54	4	50	56	4	52	57	4	53	...	...	...
Real estate, except dwellings	...	...	...	...	...	...	...	...	...	...	...	...
Dwellings	54	4	50	56	4	52	57	4	53	...	...	...
9 Community, social and personal services [b]	79	29	50	81	30	52	84	31	53	...	...	...
A Sanitary and similar services												

Colombia

	1990			1991			1992			1993		
	Gross output	Intermediate consumption	Value added	Gross output	Intermediate consumption	Value added	Gross output	Intermediate consumption	Value added	Gross output	Intermediate consumption	Value added

At constant prices of: 1975

B Social and related community services	...	...	...	...	...	...	...	...	...	...	...	...
C Recreational and cultural services	...	...	...	...	...	...	...	...	...	...	...	...
D Personal and household services	79	29	50	81	30	52	84	31	53	...	...	...
Total, Industries	1137	466	670	1158	471	687	1202	496	706	...	...	...
Producers of government services	87	22	64	91	27	64	97	30	67	...	...	...
Other producers	...	...	...	...	...	...	...	...	...	...	...	...
Total	1223	489	734	1249	498	751	1299	526	773	...	...	...
less: Imputed bank service charge	...	−20	20	...	−22	22	...	−23	23	...	...	...
Import duties	21	...	21	21	...	21	29	...	29	...	...	...
Value added tax	...	...	...	...	...	...	...	...	...	...	...	...
Other adjustments	...	...	...	...	...	...	...	...	...	...	...	...
Total	1245	509	735	1270	520	750	1328	549	779	...	...	...

a Hunting is included in item "Fishing".
b Restaurants and hotels are included in item "Community, social and personal services".
c Business services are included in the financial institutions.

4.3 Cost components of value added

Thousand million Columbian pesos

	1986						1987					
	Compensation of employees	Capital consumption	Net operating surplus	Indirect taxes	less: Subsidies received	Value added	Compensation of employees	Capital consumption	Net operating surplus	Indirect taxes	less: Subsidies received	Value added

All producers

1 Agriculture, hunting, forestry and fishing	419	...	769	−2	...	1186	583	...	1011	−	...	1594
A Agriculture and hunting [a]	411	...	718	−2	...	1128	573	...	944	−	...	1517
B Forestry and logging	6	...	22	−	...	27	7	...	28	−	...	36
C Fishing [a]	2	...	29	−	...	31	2	...	39	−	...	42
2 Mining and quarrying	53	...	274	5	...	332	71	...	500	6	...	578
3 Manufacturing	438	...	655	432	...	1526	585	...	687	521	...	1793
A Manufacture of food, beverages and tobacco	119	...	308	321	...	748	151	...	137	366	...	655
B Textile, wearing apparel and leather industries	91	...	59	8	...	157	115	...	89	11	...	215
C Manufacture of wood and wood products, including furniture	14	...	14	1	...	28	18	...	20	2	...	40
D Manufacture of paper and paper products, printing and publishing	27	...	47	5	...	78	35	...	65	6	...	107
E Manufacture of chemicals and chemical petroleum, coal, rubber and plastic products	71	...	114	61	...	246	100	...	187	79	...	366
F Manufacture of non-metallic mineral products, except products of petroleum and coal	32	...	37	6	...	75	42	...	59	9	...	110
G Basic metal industries	...	...	...	...	...	...	...	...	...	...	...	...

Colombia

Thousand million Columbian pesos

	1986						1987					
	Compensation of employees	Capital consumption	Net operating surplus	Indirect taxes	less: Subsidies received	Value added	Compensation of employees	Capital consumption	Net operating surplus	Indirect taxes	less: Subsidies received	Value added
H Manufacture of fabricated metal products, machinery and equipment	73	...	66	28	...	167	108	...	114	44	...	266
I Other manufacturing industries	12	...	12	2	...	27	15	...	16	3	...	34
4 Electricity, gas and water	48	...	104	–	...	151	64	...	137	–	...	201
5 Construction	196	...	229	22	...	447	202	...	268	25	...	495
6 Wholesale and retail trade, restaurants and hotels [b]	138	...	493	64	...	695	175	...	680	78	...	934
A Wholesale and retail trade	138	...	493	64	...	695	175	...	680	78	...	934
B Restaurants and hotels	...	...	...	...	...	...	...	...	...	...	...	...
7 Transport, storage and communication	234	...	283	10	...	527	308	...	388	17	...	713
A Transport and storage	180	...	260	2	...	442	249	...	352	7	...	609
B Communication	54	...	23	8	...	85	59	...	35	9	...	104
8 Finance, insurance, real estate and business services	235	...	487	44	...	766	303	...	626	56	...	985
A Financial institutions [c]	235	...	144	21	...	399	303	...	208	26	...	537
B Insurance	...	...	...	...	...	...	...	...	...	...	...	...
C Real estate and business services [c]	...	...	344	23	...	367	...	...	418	30	...	448
Real estate, except dwellings	...	...	...	...	...	...	...	...	...	...	...	...
Dwellings	...	...	344	23	...	367	...	...	418	30	...	448
9 Community, social and personal services [b]	271	...	276	11	...	558	353	...	370	15	...	738
A Sanitary and similar services	...	...	...	...	...	...	...	...	...	...	...	...
B Social and related community services	...	...	...	...	...	...	...	...	...	...	...	...
C Recreational and cultural services	...	...	...	...	...	...	...	...	...	...	...	...
D Personal and household services	271	...	276	11	...	558	353	...	370	15	...	738
Total, Industries [de]	2032	...	3570	586	...	6188	2645	...	4667	718	...	8030
Producers of government services	543	...	...	4	...	547	706	...	...	7	...	714
Other producers	...	...	...	...	...	...	...	...	...	...	...	...
Total [de]	2575	...	3570	591	...	6736	3351	...	4667	725	...	8743
less: Imputed bank service charge	...	...	156	...	...	156	...	...	227	...	...	227
Import duties	...	...	...	208	...	208	...	...	...	308	...	308
Value added tax	...	...	...	...	...	...	...	...	...	...	...	...
Other adjustments	...	...	...	...	...	...	...	...	...	...	...	...
Total [de]	2575	...	3414	799	...	6788	3351	...	4440	1033	...	8824

Colombia

	1988						1989					
	Compensation of employees	Capital consumption	Net operating surplus	Indirect taxes	less: Subsidies received	Value added	Compensation of employees	Capital consumption	Net operating surplus	Indirect taxes	less: Subsidies received	Value added

All producers

1 Agriculture, hunting, forestry and fishing	782	...	1182	1	...	1965	1022	...	1400	6	...	2429
A Agriculture and hunting [a]	769	...	1096	1	...	1866	1006	...	1290	6	...	2302
B Forestry and logging	10	...	39	–	...	49	13	...	50	–	...	63
C Fishing [a]	3	...	47	–	...	50	4	...	60	–	...	64
2 Mining and quarrying	99	...	605	17	...	722	130	...	996	31	...	1158
3 Manufacturing	754	...	1203	526	...	2482	996	...	1519	644	...	3159
A Manufacture of food, beverages and tobacco	193	...	439	311	...	942	250	...	539	360	...	1150
B Textile, wearing apparel and leather industries	152	...	156	13	...	322	204	...	208	16	...	427
C Manufacture of wood and wood products, including furniture	26	...	30	4	...	59	35	...	39	5	...	79
D Manufacture of paper and paper products, printing and publishing	44	...	84	8	...	137	57	...	107	13	...	177
E Manufacture of chemicals and chemical petroleum, coal, rubber and plastic products	120	...	198	105	...	422	165	...	251	144	...	559
F Manufacture of non-metallic mineral products, except products of petroleum and coal	57	...	84	12	...	153	72	...	115	17	...	204
G Basic metal industries	...	...	...	...	...	...	...	...	...	...	...	...
H Manufacture of fabricated metal products, machinery and equipment	141	...	186	68	...	395	184	...	223	84	...	491
I Other manufacturing industries	22	...	25	4	...	51	29	...	37	6	...	72
4 Electricity, gas and water	88	...	187	–5	...	271	117	...	258	2	...	377
5 Construction	289	...	453	34	...	776	318	...	531	46	...	894
6 Wholesale and retail trade, restaurants and hotels [b]	231	...	918	124	...	1273	298	...	1132	179	...	1609
A Wholesale and retail trade	231	...	918	124	...	1273	298	...	1132	179	...	1609
B Restaurants and hotels	...	...	...	...	...	...	...	...	...	...	...	...
7 Transport, storage and communication	406	...	535	29	...	969	520	...	705	44	...	1269
A Transport and storage	325	...	477	15	...	818	411	...	619	24	...	1054
B Communication	81	...	58	13	...	152	110	...	86	19	...	215
8 Finance, insurance, real estate and business services	437	...	804	82	...	1323	551	...	1014	102	...	1668
A Financial institutions [c]	437	...	302	41	...	780	551	...	394	42	...	988
B Insurance	...	...	...	...	...	...	...	...	...	...	...	...
C Real estate and business services [c]	...	...	502	40	...	543	...	...	620	60	...	680
Real estate, except dwellings	...	...	...	...	...	...	...	...	...	...	...	...
Dwellings	...	...	502	40	...	543	...	...	620	60	...	680
9 Community, social and personal services [b]	456	...	492	18	...	965	610	...	661	19	...	1289
A Sanitary and similar services	...	...	...	...	...	...	...	...	...	...	...	...
B Social and related community services	...	...	...	...	...	...	...	...	...	...	...	...

416

Colombia

	1988						1989					
	Compensation of employees	Capital consumption	Net operating surplus	Indirect taxes	less: Subsidies received	Value added	Compensation of employees	Capital consumption	Net operating surplus	Indirect taxes	less: Subsidies received	Value added
C Recreational and cultural services	...	...	...	...	...	...	...	...	...	...	...	...
D Personal and household services	456	...	492	18	...	965	610	...	661	19	...	1289
Total, Industries [de]	3542	...	6380	825	...	10746	4562	...	8216	1073	...	13852
Producers of government services	924	...	...	8	...	932	1226	...	...	13	...	1239
Other producers	...	...	...	...	...	...	...	...	...	...	...	...
Total [de]	4466	...	6380	833	...	11679	5788	...	8216	1086	...	15091
less: Imputed bank service charge	...	...	369	...	...	369	...	...	474	...	...	474
Import duties	...	...	...	421	...	421	...	...	...	510	...	510
Value added tax	...	...	...	...	...	...	...	...	...	...	...	...
Other adjustments	...	...	...	...	...	...	...	...	...	...	...	...
Total [de]	4466	...	6011	1254	...	11731	5788	...	7742	1596	...	15127

	1990						1991					
	Compensation of employees	Capital consumption	Net operating surplus	Indirect taxes	less: Subsidies received	Value added	Compensation of employees	Capital consumption	Net operating surplus	Indirect taxes	less: Subsidies received	Value added

All producers

1 Agriculture, hunting, forestry and fishing	1337	...	1942	5	...	3284	1762	...	2670	13	...	4445
A Agriculture and hunting [a]	1316	...	1798	5	...	3119	1733	...	2468	13	...	4214
B Forestry and logging	16	...	64	...	...	80	22	...	86	...	...	108
C Fishing [a]	5	...	80	...	...	85	7	...	116	...	...	123
2 Mining and quarrying	171	...	1629	84	...	1884	211	...	1865	65	...	2141
3 Manufacturing	1306	...	1981	748	...	4035	1691	...	2664	977	...	5332
A Manufacture of food, beverages and tobacco	337	...	705	392	...	1434	444	...	1085	495	...	2024
B Textile, wearing apparel and leather industries	259	...	303	9	...	571	352	...	379	19	...	750
C Manufacture of wood and wood products, including furniture	46	...	46	6	...	98	55	...	58	7	...	120
D Manufacture of paper and paper products, printing and publishing	73	...	139	16	...	228	89	...	197	21	...	307
E Manufacture of chemicals and chemical petroleum, coal, rubber and plastic products	222	...	325	198	...	745	293	...	411	289	...	993
F Manufacture of non-metallic mineral products, except products of petroleum and coal	93	...	140	20	...	253	119	...	181	25	...	325
G Basic metal industries	...	...	...	...	...	...	...	...	...	...	...	...
H Manufacture of fabricated metal products, machinery and equipment	238	...	272	100	...	610	296	...	294	114	...	704
I Other manufacturing industries	38	...	51	7	...	96	43	...	59	7	...	109
4 Electricity, gas and water	158	...	349	2	...	509	212	...	470	8	...	690
5 Construction	365	...	581	55	...	1001	461	...	778	73	...	1312
6 Wholesale and retail trade, restaurants and hotels [b]	390	...	1496	233	...	2119	491	...	1714	419	...	2624
A Wholesale and retail trade	390	...	1496	233	...	2119	491	...	1714	419	...	2624

Colombia

	1990						1991					
	Compensation of employees	Capital consumption	Net operating surplus	Indirect taxes	less: Subsidies received	Value added	Compensation of employees	Capital consumption	Net operating surplus	Indirect taxes	less: Subsidies received	Value added
B Restaurants and hotels	...	...	...	...	...	...	...	...	...	...	...	...
7 Transport, storage and communication	737	...	1043	63	...	1843	968	...	1480	67	...	2515
A Transport and storage	589	...	913	36	...	1538	772	...	1292	29	...	2093
B Communication	148	...	130	27	...	305	196	...	188	38	...	422
8 Finance, insurance, real estate and business services	690	...	1428	136	...	2254	986	...	1811	181	...	2978
A Financial institutions [c]	690	...	635	59	...	1384	986	...	773	73	...	1832
B Insurance	...	...	...	...	...	...	...	...	...	...	...	...
C Real estate and business services [c]	...	...	793	77	...	870	...	...	1038	108	...	1146
Real estate, except dwellings	...	...	...	...	...	...	...	...	...	...	...	...
Dwellings	...	...	793	77	...	870	...	...	1038	108	...	1146
9 Community, social and personal services [b]	816	...	890	23	...	1729	1116	...	1333	39	...	2488
A Sanitary and similar services	...	...	...	...	...	...	...	...	...	...	...	...
B Social and related community services	...	...	...	...	...	...	...	...	...	...	...	...
C Recreational and cultural services	...	...	...	...	...	...	...	...	...	...	...	...
D Personal and household services	816	...	890	23	...	1729	1116	...	1333	39	...	2488
Total, Industries [de]	5970	...	11339	1349	...	18658	7898	...	14785	1842	...	24525
Producers of government services	1585	...	...	22	...	1607	1949	...	...	23	...	1972
Other producers	...	...	...	...	...	...	...	...	...	...	...	...
Total [de]	7555	...	11339	1371	...	20265	9847	...	14785	1865	...	26497
less: Imputed bank service charge	...	...	657	...	...	657	...	...	986	...	...	986
Import duties	...	...	...	620	...	620	...	...	...	596	...	596
Value added tax	...	...	...	...	...	...	...	...	...	...	...	...
Other adjustments	...	...	...	...	...	...	...	...	...	...	...	...
Total [de]	7555	...	10682	1991	...	20228	9847	...	13799	2461	...	26107

	1992						1993					
	Compensation of employees	Capital consumption	Net operating surplus	Indirect taxes	less: Subsidies received	Value added	Compensation of employees	Capital consumption	Net operating surplus	Indirect taxes	less: Subsidies received	Value added
All producers												
1 Agriculture, hunting, forestry and fishing	2132	...	3040	17	...	5188	2565	...	3354	33	...	5952
A Agriculture and hunting	2095[a]	...	2776[a]	17[a]	...	4889[a]	2522	...	3065	33	...	5620
B Forestry and logging	26	...	102	...	...	128	33	...	127	—	...	160
C Fishing	10[a]	...	161[a]	...	...	171[a]	10	...	162	—	...	172
2 Mining and quarrying	306	...	1940	27	...	2274	392	...	1990	63	...	2444
3 Manufacturing	2326	...	2937	1231	...	6494	3054	...	3928	1645	...	8627
A Manufacture of food, beverages and tobacco	594	...	1181	585	...	2360	768	...	1618	786	...	3172
B Textile, wearing apparel and leather industries	469	...	383	23	...	875	570	...	435	28	...	1033
C Manufacture of wood and wood products, including furniture	72	...	68	9	...	149	106	...	84	12	...	202

418

Colombia

	1992						1993					
	Compensation of employees	Capital consumption	Net operating surplus	Indirect taxes	less: Subsidies received	Value added	Compensation of employees	Capital consumption	Net operating surplus	Indirect taxes	less: Subsidies received	Value added
D Manufacture of paper and paper products, printing and publishing	125	...	253	25	...	402	159	...	290	30	...	479
E Manufacture of chemicals and chemical petroleum, coal, rubber and plastic products	401	...	491	348	...	1240	530	...	836	451	...	1817
F Manufacture of non-metallic mineral products, except products of petroleum and coal	166	...	241	30	...	436	244	...	357	40	...	640
G Basic metal industries	...	...	...	...	...	...	...	...	...	...	...	...
H Manufacture of fabricated metal products, machinery and equipment	445	...	260	197	...	902	677	...	309	299	...	1284
I Other manufacturing industries	55	...	60	14	...	130	...	...	...	...	...	...
4 Electricity, gas and water	268	...	614	—	...	882	402	...	946	−5	...	1343
5 Construction	618	...	1107	103	...	1828	877	...	1854	135	...	2866
6 Wholesale and retail trade, restaurants and hotels	635[b]	...	2069[b]	646[b]	...	3351[b]	881	...	2361	1042	...	4284
A Wholesale and retail trade	635	...	2069	646	...	3351	881	...	2361	1042	...	4284
B Restaurants and hotels	...	...	...	...	...	...	...	...	...	...	...	...
7 Transport, storage and communication	1329	...	1997	135	...	3462	1628	...	2466	303	...	4398
A Transport and storage	1075	...	1782	54	...	2911	1297	...	2166	197	...	3660
B Communication	254	...	215	81	...	551	331	...	301	106	...	738
8 Finance, insurance, real estate and business services	1252	...	2195	311	...	3758	1615	...	2953	392	...	4960
A Financial institutions	1252[c]	...	878[c]	154[c]	...	2284[c]	1615	...	1182	204	...	3001
B Insurance	...	...	...	...	...	...	...	...	...	...	...	...
C Real estate and business services	...	...	1317[c]	157[c]	...	1473[c]	...	...	1771	188	...	1959
Real estate, except dwellings	...	...	...	...	...	...	...	...	...	...	...	...
Dwellings	...	...	1317	157	...	1473	...	...	1771	188	...	1959
9 Community, social and personal services	1533[b]	...	2018[b]	56[b]	...	3607[b]	2128	...	3268	71	...	5468
A Sanitary and similar services	...	...	...	...	...	...	...	...	...	...	...	...
B Social and related community services	...	...	...	...	...	...	...	...	...	...	...	...
C Recreational and cultural services	...	...	...	...	...	...	...	...	...	...	...	...
D Personal and household services	1533	...	2018	56	...	3607	2128	...	3268	71	...	5468
Total, Industries [de]	10440	...	18017	2518	...	30975	...	...	...	...	...	...
Producers of government services	3084	...	...	35	...	3119	3894	...	...	53	...	3947
Other producers	...	...	...	...	...	...	...	...	...	...	...	...
Total	13483[de]	...	17917[de]	2562[de]	...	33962[de]	17510	...	23190	3748	...	44448
less: Imputed bank service charge	...	...	1121	...	...	1121	...	...	1563	...	...	1563
Import duties	...	...	...	674	...	674	...	...	...	1013	...	1013
Value added tax	...	...	...	...	...	...	...	...	...	...	...	...
Other adjustments	...	...	...	...	...	...	...	...	...	...	...	...
Total	13483[de]	...	16796[de]	3235[de]	...	33515[de]	17510	...	21627	4761	...	43898

Colombia

	1994						1995					
	Compensation of employees	Capital consumption	Net operating surplus	Indirect taxes	less: Subsidies received	Value added	Compensation of employees	Capital consumption	Net operating surplus	Indirect taxes	less: Subsidies received	Value added

All producers

1 Agriculture, hunting, forestry and fishing	3316	...	4144	4	...	7465	4155	...	4999	92	...	9246
A Agriculture and hunting	3267	...	3834	5	...	7105	4107	...	4643	92	...	8842
B Forestry and logging	40	...	156	–	...	196	34	...	131	–	...	164
C Fishing	10	...	154	–	...	164	14	...	225	–	...	239
2 Mining and quarrying	477	...	1999	105	...	2582	668	...	2711	191	...	3570
3 Manufacturing	4119	...	4725	2509	...	11353	5048	...	5415	2947	...	13390
A Manufacture of food, beverages and tobacco	1028	...	2128	1294	...	4450	1330	...	2672	1519	...	5520
B Textile, wearing apparel and leather industries	653	...	403	43	...	1099	777	...	390	69	...	1236
C Manufacture of wood and wood products, including furniture	158	...	91	16	...	266	187	...	89	19	...	295
D Manufacture of paper and paper products, printing and publishing	219	...	354	43	...	615	281	...	426	55	...	763
E Manufacture of chemicals and chemical petroleum, coal, rubber and plastic products	701	...	908	665	...	2274	902	...	1050	796	...	2748
F Manufacture of non-metallic mineral products, except products of petroleum and coal	333	...	452	54	...	839	418	...	483	64	...	965
G Basic metal industries	...	...	...	...	...	...	...	...	...	...	...	...
H Manufacture of fabricated metal products, machinery and equipment	927	...	319	371	...	1618	1134	...	306	424	...	1864
I Other manufacturing industries	100	...	70	23	...	193	...	...	...	...	...	...
4 Electricity, gas and water	544	...	1316	−23	...	1836	687	...	1763	−92	...	2358
5 Construction	1353	...	2833	201	...	4387	1796	...	3451	253	...	5500
6 Wholesale and retail trade, restaurants and hotels	1188	...	2902	1253	...	5342	1470	...	3173	2137	...	6779
A Wholesale and retail trade	1188	...	2902	1253	...	5342	1470	...	3173	2137	...	6779
B Restaurants and hotels	...	...	...	...	...	...	...	...	...	...	...	...
7 Transport, storage and communication	2100	...	3114	517	...	5731	2996	...	3673	498	...	7168
A Transport and storage	1655	...	2711	375	...	4741	2400	...	3104	299	...	5803
B Communication	445	...	403	142	...	991	596	...	570	200	...	1365
8 Finance, insurance, real estate and business services	2089	...	4365	583	...	7037	2471	...	6317	608	...	9397
A Financial institutions	2089	...	2059	263	...	4411	...	...	...	...	...	...
B Insurance	...	...	...	...	...	...	...	...	...	...	...	...
C Real estate and business services	...	...	...	...	...	...	...	...	...	...	...	...
Real estate, except dwellings	...	...	...	...	...	...	...	...	...	...	...	...
Dwellings	...	...	2306	320	...	2626	...	...	...	...	...	...
9 Community, social and personal services	2921	...	4438	124	...	7484	3877	...	5844	154	...	9875
A Sanitary and similar services	...	...	...	...	...	...	...	...	...	...	...	...
B Social and related community services	...	...	...	...	...	...	...	...	...	...	...	...

Colombia

	1994						1995					
	Compensation of employees	Capital consumption	Net operating surplus	Indirect taxes	less: Subsidies received	Value added	Compensation of employees	Capital consumption	Net operating surplus	Indirect taxes	less: Subsidies received	Value added
C Recreational and cultural services	...	...	...	...	...	...	...	...	...	...	...	...
D Personal and household services	2921	...	4438	124	...	7484	...	...	...	...	...	...
Total, Industries	...	...	...	...	...	...	...	...	...	...	...	...
Producers of government services	5421	...	...	88	...	5509	7204	...	–	139	...	7343
Other producers	...	...	...	...	...	...	...	...	...	...	...	...
Total	23528	...	29837	5362	...	58727	30489	...	37424	6957	...	74870
less: Imputed bank service charge	...	...	2226	...	...	2226	...	...	3194	...	...	3194
Import duties	...	...	...	1481	...	1481	...	...	...	1834	...	1834
Value added tax	...	...	...	...	...	...	...	...	...	...	...	...
Other adjustments	...	...	...	...	...	...	...	...	...	...	...	...
Total	23528	...	27611	6843	...	57982	30489	...	34230	8791	...	73511

a Hunting is included in item "Fishing".
b Restaurants and hotels are included in item "Community, social and personal services".
c Business services are included in the financial institutions.
d Column 4 refers to indirect taxes less subsidies received.
e Column "Consumption of fixed capital" is included in column "Net operating surplus".

Comoros

Source

The estimates was extracted from the publication *Comptes Economiques du Territoire des Comoros*.

General note

The estimates shown have been prepared in accordance with the United Nations System of National Accounts (1968 SNA) so far as existing data would permit.

1.1 Expenditure on the gross domestic product, in current prices

Million Comoro francs

	1986	1987	1988	1989	1990	1991	1992	1993	1994	1995	1996	1997
1 Government final consumption expenditure	15552	16112	16771	17508	17074	17510	...	...	...	...	...	...
2 Private final consumption expenditure	41557	44030	46231	49334	52916	56030	...	...	...	...	...	...
3 Gross capital formation	13370	14904	13493	12028	13388	11268	...	...	...	...	...	...
A Increase in stocks	1597	4155	2681	2886	5280	2780	...	...	...	...	...	...
B Gross fixed capital formation	11773	10749	10812	9142	8108	8488	...	...	...	...	...	...
4 Exports of goods and services	9139	9000	11114	9435	7754	10763	...	...	...	...	...	...
5 less: Imports of goods and services	23348	25011	25813	24908	24762	26323	...	...	...	...	...	...
equals: Gross domestic product	56270	59035	61796	63397	66370	69248	...	...	...	...	...	...

1.10 Gross domestic product by kind of activity, in current prices

Million Comoro francs

	1986	1987	1988	1989	1990	1991	1992	1993	1994	1995	1996	1997
1 Agriculture, hunting, forestry and fishing	21049	22418	24390	25923	27491	28992	...	...	...	...	...	...
2 Mining and quarrying	...	...	...	...	...	...	...	...	...	...	...	...
3 Manufacturing	2062	2210	2373	2533	2793	2986	...	...	...	...	...	...
4 Electricity, gas and water	551	543	476	508	587	622	...	...	...	...	...	...
5 Construction	4673	3499	2948	2227	2105	1940	...	...	...	...	...	...
6 Wholesale and retail trade, restaurants and hotels	14517	15551	16148	16250	17080	17871	...	...	...	...	...	...
7 Transport, storage and communication	1855	2053	2287	2532	2782	2999	...	...	...	...	...	...
8 Finance, insurance, real estate and business services	2258	2401	2586	2746	3024	3249	...	...	...	...	...	...
9 Community, social and personal services	282	312	326	353	380	407	...	...	...	...	...	...
Total, Industries	47247	48987	51534	53072	56242	59066	...	...	...	...	...	...
Producers of government services	10181	11249	11548	11659	11750	12047	...	...	...	...	...	...
Other producers	...	...	...	...	...	...	...	...	...	...	...	...
Subtotal	57428	60236	63082	64731	67992	71113	...	...	...	...	...	...
less: Imputed bank service charge	1158	1201	1286	1329	1622	1865	...	...	...	...	...	...

Comoros

Million Comoro francs

	1986	1987	1988	1989	1990	1991	1992	1993	1994	1995	1996	1997
plus: Import duties	...	...	...	...	...	...	...	...	...	...	...	...
plus: Value added tax	...	...	...	...	...	...	...	...	...	...	...	...
plus: Other adjustments	...	...	...	...	...	...	...	...	...	...	...	...
equals: Gross domestic product	56270	59035	61796	63397	66370	69248	...	...	...	...	...	...

1.11 Gross domestic product by kind of activity, in constant prices

Million Comoro francs

	1986	1987	1988	1989	1990	1991	1992	1993	1994	1995	1996	1997
At constant prices of: 1990												
1 Agriculture, hunting, forestry and fishing	24166	24964	26030	26752	27491	28564	...	...	...	...	...	...
2 Mining and quarrying	...	...	...	...	...	...	...	...	...	...	...	...
3 Manufacturing	2370	2469	2622	2655	2793	2879	...	...	...	...	...	...
4 Electricity, gas and water	461	521	570	520	587	627	...	...	...	...	...	...
5 Construction	5576	4013	3250	2327	2105	1851	...	...	...	...	...	...
6 Wholesale and retail trade, restaurants and hotels	16385	16996	17590	16927	17080	17317	...	...	...	...	...	...
7 Transport, storage and communication	2094	2244	2491	2638	2782	2906	...	...	...	...	...	...
8 Finance, insurance, real estate and business services	2549	2524	2817	2860	3024	3148	...	...	...	...	...	...
9 Community, social and personal services	318	341	355	368	380	394	...	...	...	...	...	...
Total, Industries	53919	54172	55725	55047	56242	57686	...	...	...	...	...	...
Producers of government services	11491	12294	12580	12145	11750	11673	...	...	...	...	...	...
Other producers	...	...	...	...	...	...	...	...	...	...	...	...
Subtotal	65410	66466	68305	67192	67992	69359	...	...	...	...	...	...
less: Imputed bank service charge	1307	1313	1401	1383	1622	1807	...	...	...	...	...	...
plus: Import duties	...	...	...	...	...	...	...	...	...	...	...	...
plus: Value added tax	...	...	...	...	...	...	...	...	...	...	...	...
plus: Other adjustments	...	...	...	...	...	...	...	...	...	...	...	...
equals: Gross domestic product	64103	65153	66904	65809	66370	67552	...	...	...	...	...	...

Costa Rica

Source

Reply to the United Nations National Accounts Questionnaire from the Banco Central de Costa Rica, Departamento de Estudios Económicos, Sección Cuentas Nacionales, San José. Official estimates are published in *Cifras de Cuentas Nacionales de Costa Rica*.

General note

The estimates shown in the following tables have been prepared in accordance with the United Nations System of National Accounts (1968 SNA) so far as the existing data would permit.

1.1 Expenditure on the gross domestic product, in current prices

Million Costa Rican colones

	1986	1987	1988	1989	1990	1991	1992	1993	1994	1995	1996	1997
1 Government final consumption expenditure	37951	42652	54630	72283	94948	111876	144448	178453	226635	278761	...	...
2 Private final consumption expenditure	144381	176475	215794	256923	321143	411105	544609	648463	779307	978513	...	...
3 Gross capital formation	62162	77170	85569	113233	143492	173581	265515	319602	349963	422913	...	...
A Increase in stocks	16139	20857	19358	26009	26421	37483	77197	71067	92200	118546	...	...
B Gross fixed capital formation	46023	56313	66211	87224	117071	136098	188318	248535	257763	304367	...	...
4 Exports of goods and services	77280	90005	118998	148435	178763	264505	342873	412478	514146	678265	...	...
5 less: Imports of goods and services	75195	101767	125247	164963	215499	270903	391167	489737	563749	699066	...	...
equals: Gross domestic product	246579	284533	349743	425911	522848	690164	906278	1069259	1306302	1659385	...	...

1.2 Expenditure on the gross domestic product, in constant prices

Million Costa Rican colones

	1986	1987	1988	1989	1990	1991	1992	1993	1994	1995	1996	1997
At constant prices of: 1966												
1 Government final consumption expenditure	1225	1252	1290	1335	1362	1349	1388	1472	1516	1516	...	...
2 Private final consumption expenditure	6413	6652	6795	7144	7440	7369	7974	8491	8831	9008	...	...
3 Gross capital formation	2665	2756	2562	2753	2953	2559	3551	4006	3837	3612	...	...
A Increase in stocks	546	420	311	155	−21	−34	395	131	304	220	...	...
B Gross fixed capital formation	2119	2336	2251	2598	2974	2593	3156	3875	3533	3392	...	...
4 Exports of goods and services	3865	4674	5019	5826	6286	6845	7682	8556	9169	9805	...	...
5 less: Imports of goods and services	3841	4517	4476	5233	5796	5601	7106	8181	8362	8567	...	...
equals: Gross domestic product	10326	10818	11190	11824	12244	12521	13489	14344	14992	15374	...	...

Costa Rica

1.3 Cost components of the gross domestic product

Million Costa Rican colones

	1986	1987	1988	1989	1990	1991	1992	1993	1994	1995	1996	1997
1 Indirect taxes, net	33642	39127	44584	54846	64587	89339	132254	140446	...	...	...	...
A Indirect taxes	36271	41994	49156	61042	71816	99591	141187	153801	...	...	...	...
B less: Subsidies	2629	2867	4572	6196	7229	10252	8933	13355	...	...	...	...
2 Consumption of fixed capital	6130	7114	8919	10621	13217	18361	22224	25739	...	...	...	...
3 Compensation of employees paid by resident producers to ..	112753	134065	166356	209002	264395	326928	429695	518404	...	...	...	...
4 Operating surplus	94054	104228	129884	151441	180649	255536	322105	384670	...	...	...	...
equals: Gross domestic product ..	246579	284533	349743	425911	522848	690164	906278	1069259	...	...	...	...

1.4 General government current receipts and disbursements

Million Costa Rican colones

	1986	1987	1988	1989	1990	1991	1992	1993	1994	1995	1996	1997
Receipts												
1 Operating surplus	...	...	...	...	...	...	...	...	...	...	...	...
2 Property and entrepreneurial income	3273	4767	7426	9581	10495	14691	15025	18628	...	...	...	...
3 Taxes, fees and contributions .	60573	71562	85309	105543	131544	175814	241083	283754	...	...	...	...
A Indirect taxes	36271	41994	49156	61042	71816	99591	141187	153801	...	...	...	...
B Direct taxes	5696	6317	8236	9507	11820	14545	19016	26942	...	...	...	...
C Social security contributions	17896	21801	26432	32878	44027	54447	71260	90544	...	...	...	...
D Compulsory fees, fines and penalties	710	1450	1485	2116	3880	7230	9620	12467	...	...	...	...
4 Other current transfers	3444	4377	7493	7145	6487	7645	9420	15403	...	...	...	...
Total current receipts of general government	67289	80706	100227	122270	148526	198151	265527	317786	...	...	...	...
Disbursements												
1 Government final consumption expenditure	37951	42652	54630	72283	94948	111876	144448	178453	...	...	...	...
2 Property income	5253	6716	11343	14971	25895	33449	46573	47616	...	...	...	...
A Interest	5253	6716	11343	14971	25895	33449	46573	47616	...	...	...	...
B Net land rent and royalties ..	...	...	...	...	...	...	...	...				
3 Subsidies	2629	2867	4572	6196	7229	10252	8933	13355	...	...	...	...
4 Other current transfers	8539	14874	16078	17350	24202	29198	28449	40135	...	...	...	...
A Social security benefits	3590	3892	5113	6491	8532	11363	14371	17357	...	...	...	...
B Social assistance grants	165	182	206	283	313	386	394	569	...	...	...	...
C Other	4783	10800	10759	10576	15358	17449	13684	22209	...	...	...	...
5 Net saving	12918	13597	13604	11470	–3748	13375	37125	38227	...	...	...	...
Total current disbursements and net saving of general government	67289	80706	100227	122270	148526	198151	265527	317786	...	...	...	...

Costa Rica

1.7 External transactions on current account, summary

Million Costa Rican colones

	1986	1987	1988	1989	1990	1991	1992	1993	1994	1995	1996	1997
Payments to the rest of the world												
1 Imports of goods and services	75195	101768	125247	164963	215499	270903	391167	489737	563749	...	...	...
A Imports of merchandise, c.i.f.	58843	78204	94750	125560	165422	207265	296849	374133	437866	...	...	...
B Other	16352	23564	30497	39403	50077	63638	94318	115604	125883	...	...	...
2 Factor income to rest of the world	18587	22265	30073	41492	34729	37289	44561	50224	53889	...	...	...
A Compensation of employees	294	540	491	775	516	1184	1128	1567	1884	...	...	...
B Property and entrepreneurial income	18293	21725	29582	40717	34213	36105	43433	48658	52005	...	...	...
3 Current transfers to the rest of the world	603	703	856	334	368	427	752	883	1256	...	...	...
4 Surplus of the nation on current transactions	−9453	−24130	−22766	−37984	−48189	−15592	−55866	−90506	−45913	...	...	...
Payments to the rest of the world and surplus of the nation on current transfers	84932	100606	133409	168805	202407	293027	380614	450338	572981	...	...	...
Receipts from the rest of the world												
1 Exports of goods and services	77280	90005	118998	148435	178763	264505	342873	412478	514146	...	...	...
A Exports of merchandise, f.o.b.	60838	69505	87846	108779	124681	182918	233492	265907	330182	...	...	...
B Other	16442	20500	31152	39656	54082	81587	109381	146571	183964	...	...	...
2 Factor income from rest of the world	3488	3649	4412	10752	13217	18361	22224	25739	30556	...	...	...
A Compensation of employees	966	1099	1533	1777	2247	3187	3773	4401	5260	...	...	...
B Property and entrepreneurial income	2522	2550	2879	8974	10970	15174	18451	21338	25296	...	...	...
3 Current transfers from rest of the world	4164	6952	10000	9618	10427	10161	15517	12121	28279	...	...	...
Receipts from the rest of the world on current transactions	84932	100606	133409	168805	202407	293027	380614	450338	572981	...	...	...

1.8 Capital transactions of the nation, summary

Million Costa Rican colones

	1986	1987	1988	1989	1990	1991	1992	1993	1994	1995	1996	1997
Finance of gross capital formation												
Gross saving	52709	53039	62802	75249	95302	157988	209649	229095	304050	394495	...	...
1 Consumption of fixed capital	6130	7114	8919	10621	13217	18361	22224	25739	30556	38898	...	...
2 Net saving	46579	45926	53883	64628	82085	139627	187425	203356	273494	355597	...	...
A General government	12918	13596	13604	11470	...	...	...	...	...	...	...	...
B Corporate and quasi-corporate enterprises [a]	−8340	−3537	−5137	−8785	...	...	...	...	...	...	...	...
Public	−8340	−3537	−5137	−8785	...	...	...	...	...	...	...	...
Private	...	...	...	...	...	...	...	...	...	...	...	...
C Other [a]	42001	35866	45416	61943	...	...	...	...	...	...	...	...
less: Surplus of the nation on current transactions	−9453	−24130	−22766	−37984	−48189	−15592	−55866	−90506	−45913	−28418	...	...
Finance of gross capital formation	62162	77170	85569	113233	143492	173581	265515	319602	349963	422913	...	...
Gross capital formation												

Costa Rica

Million Costa Rican colones

	1986	1987	1988	1989	1990	1991	1992	1993	1994	1995	1996	1997
Increase in stocks	16139	20857	19358	26009	26421	37483	77197	71067	92200	118546	...	...
Gross fixed capital formation	46023	56313	66211	87224	117071	136098	188318	248535	257763	304367	...	...
1 General government	5997	4871	5351	7623	...	...	...	...	...	...	...	...
2 Corporate and quasi-corporate enterprises	8375	7698	9073	11623	...	...	...	...	...	...	...	...
A Public	8375	7698	9073	11623	...	...	...	...	...	...	...	...
B Private	...	...	...	...	...	...	...	...	...	...	...	...
3 Other	31651	43744	51787	67978	...	...	...	...	...	...	...	...
Gross capital formation	62162	77170	85569	113233	143492	173581	265515	319602	349963	422913	...	...

a Item "Other" include private corporate and quasi-corporate enterprises.

1.10 Gross domestic product by kind of activity, in current prices

Million Costa Rican colones

	1986	1987	1988	1989	1990	1991	1992	1993	1994	1995	1996	1997
1 Agriculture, hunting, forestry and fishing	51530	51417	62774	73344	82544	119627	147910	171589	216216	288432	...	...
2 Mining and quarrying	52573	60698	74397	86688	101328	137469	185616	206877	243044	308423	...	...
3 Manufacturing											...	...
4 Electricity, gas and water	7413	8598	10292	13437	16227	24210	31960	39610	47104	56478	...	...
5 Construction	8127	9160	10544	14455	16796	19549	23294	29283	35446	37785	...	...
6 Wholesale and retail trade, restaurants and hotels	47367	58505	70592	83087	105048	139459	193292	222302	263561	335777	...	...
7 Transport, storage and communication	11639	14069	17367	20949	26484	35884	48034	58023	69340	88755	...	...
8 Finance, insurance, real estate and business services	24522	31071	39424	49691	64398	76525	96771	121611	152382	194180	...	...
9 Community, social and personal services [a]	11829	14756	18380	24260	32103	44623	60403	75242	92396	116973	...	...
Total, Industries	215000	248273	303769	365910	444928	597347	787280	924537	1119489	1426803	...	...
Producers of government services	31580	36260	45974	60001	77920	92818	118999	144723	186814	232583	...	...
Other producers	...	...	...	...	...	...	...	...	...	...	...	...
Subtotal	246580	284533	349743	425911	522848	690164	906278	1069259	1306302	1659385	...	...
less: Imputed bank service charge	...	...	...	...	...	...	...	...	...	...	...	...
plus: Import duties	...	...	...	...	...	...	...	...	...	...	...	...
plus: Value added tax	...	...	...	...	...	...	...	...	...	...	...	...
plus: Other adjustments	...	...	...	...	...	...	...	...	...	...	...	...
equals: Gross domestic product	246580	284533	349743	425911	522848	690164	906278	1069259	1306302	1659385	...	...

a Item "Other producers" is included in item "Community, social and personal services".

1.11 Gross domestic product by kind of activity, in constant prices

Million Costa Rican colones

	1986	1987	1988	1989	1990	1991	1992	1993	1994	1995	1996	1997
At constant prices of: 1966												
1 Agriculture, hunting, forestry and fishing	1971	2053	2148	2308	2365	2513	2614	2676	2762	2854	...	...
2 Mining and quarrying	2299	2425	2478	2563	2629	2685	2961	3151	3261	3365	...	...
3 Manufacturing											...	...
4 Electricity, gas and water	308	332	340	357	380	397	421	445	478	496	...	...
5 Construction	453	458	458	515	503	466	478	556	591	520	...	...
6 Wholesale and retail trade, restaurants and hotels	1768	1839	1863	1962	2057	2061	2319	2493	2617	2696	...	...

Costa Rica

Million Costa Rican colones

	1986	1987	1988	1989	1990	1991	1992	1993	1994	1995	1996	1997
At constant prices of: 1966												
7 Transport, storage and communication	770	838	909	994	1061	1092	1245	1378	1484	1573	...	...
8 Finance, insurance, real estate and business services	1344	1413	1494	1580	1663	1689	1799	1936	2033	2062	...	...
9 Community, social and personal services [a]	435	456	477	502	526	550	573	607	637	650	...	...
Total, Industries	9347	9815	10167	10780	11184	11452	12408	13242	13862	14215	...	...
Producers of government services	979	1003	1023	1044	1059	1070	1081	1102	1130	1159	...	...
Other producers	...	...	...	...	...	...	...	...	...	...	...	...
Subtotal	10326	10818	11190	11824	12244	12521	13489	14344	14992	15374	...	...
less: Imputed bank service charge	...	...	...	...	...	...	...	...	...	...	...	...
plus: Import duties	...	...	...	...	...	...	...	...	...	...	...	...
plus: Value added tax	...	...	...	...	...	...	...	...	...	...	...	...
plus: Other adjustments	...	...	...	...	...	...	...	...	...	...	...	...
equals: Gross domestic product	10326	10818	11190	11824	12244	12521	13489	14344	14992	15374	...	...

[a] Item "Other producers" is included in item "Community, social and personal services".

1.12 Relations among national accounting aggregates

Million Costa Rican colones

	1986	1987	1988	1989	1990	1991	1992	1993	1994	1995	1996	1997
Gross domestic product	246579	284533	349743	425911	522848	690164	906278	1069259	1306302	1659385	...	...
plus: Net factor income from the rest of the world	−15098	−18616	−25661	−30740	−21480	−21819	−27268	−31921	−20334	−33393	...	...
Factor income from rest of the world	3489	3649	4412	10752	...	...	...	...	...	...	...	...
less: Factor income to the rest of the world	18587	22265	30073	41492	...	...	...	...	...	...	...	...
equals: Gross national product	231481	265917	324082	395171	501368	668345	879010	1037338	1285967	1625992	...	...
less: Consumption of fixed capital	6130	7114	8919	10621	13217	18361	22224	25739	30556	38898	...	...
equals: National income	225351	258803	315163	384550	488151	649983	856786	1011598	1255412	1587094	...	...
plus: Net current transfers from the rest of the world	3560	6249	9144	9284	10026	12625	19696	18674	24024	25777	...	...
equals: National disposable income	228911	265052	324306	393834	498177	662609	876482	1030272	1279436	1612871	...	...
less: Final consumption	182332	219127	270423	329206	416092	522981	689057	826916	1005941	1257274	...	...
equals: Net saving	46579	45925	53883	64628	82085	139627	187425	203356	273494	355597	...	...
less: Surplus of the nation on current transactions	−9453	−24130	−22766	−37984	−48189	−15592	−55866	−90506	−45913	−28418	...	...
equals: Net capital formation	56032	70056	76650	102612	130275	155219	243291	293863	319407	384015	...	...

2.9 Gross capital formation by kind of activity of owner, ISIC major divisions, in current prices

Million Costa Rican colones

	1986			1987			1988			1989		
	Total gross capital formation	Increase in stocks	Gross fixed capital formation	Total gross capital formation	Increase in stocks	Gross fixed capital formation	Total gross capital formation	Increase in stocks	Gross fixed capital formation	Total gross capital formation	Increase in stocks	Gross fixed capital formation
All producers												
1 Agriculture, hunting, forestry and fishing	3197	−792	3989	6098	−299	6397	7642	−191	7834	11385	837	10548
2 Mining and quarrying	21399	12008	9391	23437	11420	12017	26729	12996	13733	36618	18125	18493

Costa Rica

Million Costa Rican colones

	1986			1987			1988			1989		
	Total gross capital formation	Increase in stocks	Gross fixed capital formation	Total gross capital formation	Increase in stocks	Gross fixed capital formation	Total gross capital formation	Increase in stocks	Gross fixed capital formation	Total gross capital formation	Increase in stocks	Gross fixed capital formation
3 Manufacturing												
4 Electricity, gas and water	6029	517	5512	5072	383	4689	6225	556	5669	6112	–479	6591
5 Construction	1285	–	1285	3434	–	3434	1975	–	1975	3155	–	3155
6 Wholesale and retail trade, restaurants and hotels	5328	3751	1577	9693	7553	2140	7908	5087	2821	12086	8343	3743
7 Transport, storage and communication	8989	353	8636	10392	455	9937	12225	233	11992	14478	–892	15370
8 Finance, insurance, real estate and business services	7917	34	7883	10859	102	10757	14321	39	14282	18686	129	18557
9 Community, social and personal services	1753	–	1753	2071	–	2071	2554	–	2554	3147	–	3147
Total industries	55897	15871	40026	71056	19614	51442	79579	18720	60860	105667	26063	79604
Producers of government services	6265	268	5997	6114	1243	4871	5990	639	5351	7566	–54	7620
Private non-profit institutions serving households	...	...	...	...	...	...	...	...	...	...	...	...
Total	62162	16139	46023	77170	20857	56313	85569	19358	66211	113233	26009	87224

	1990			1991			1992			1993		
	Total gross capital formation	Increase in stocks	Gross fixed capital formation	Total gross capital formation	Increase in stocks	Gross fixed capital formation	Total gross capital formation	Increase in stocks	Gross fixed capital formation	Total gross capital formation	Increase in stocks	Gross fixed capital formation
All producers												
1 Agriculture, hunting, forestry and fishing	15381	1061	14320	17518	319	17198	29482	4258	25224	33753	4588	29165
2 Mining and quarrying	42206	12303	29903	52997	21835	31162	88792	44279	44513	87951	28485	59466
3 Manufacturing												
4 Electricity, gas and water	10321	337	9984	13035	1833	11202	17045	1335	15710	25404	579	24825
5 Construction	4471	...	4471	6455	...	6455	8750	...	8750	12253	...	12253
6 Wholesale and retail trade, restaurants and hotels	16224	11587	4637	18437	11322	7115	35727	25093	10634	48734	36131	12603
7 Transport, storage and communication	22420	441	21979	26198	753	25445	38579	299	38280	52183	495	51688
8 Finance, insurance, real estate and business services	19581	112	19469	20809	48	20762	24630	52	24578	30696	40	30656
9 Community, social and personal services	4407	...	4407	5044	...	5044	7053	...	7053	9334	...	9334
Total industries	135011	25841	109170	160493	36110	124383	250058	75316	174742	300308	70318	229990
Producers of government services	8481	580	7901	13088	1373	11715	15457	1881	13576	19294	749	18545
Private non-profit institutions serving households	...	...	...	...	...	...	...	...	...	...	...	...
Total	143492	26421	117071	173581	37483	136098	265515	77197	188318	319602	71067	248535

2.17 Exports and imports of goods and services, detail

Million Costa Rican colones

	1986	1987	1988	1989	1990	1991	1992	1993	1994	1995	1996	1997
Exports of goods and services												
1 Exports of merchandise, f.o.b.	60838	69505	87846	108779	124681	182918	233492	265907	330182	...	...	...
2 Transport and communication	1232	1570	2039	2496	3591	5946	7626	8632	10834	...	...	...
3 Insurance service charges	357	371	603	702	994	1380	1625	1866	2120	...	...	...
4 Other commodities	5658	7888	12231	15721	19086	27167	32382	41820	48315	...	...	...

Costa Rica

Million Costa Rican colones

		1986	1987	1988	1989	1990	1991	1992	1993	1994	1995	1996	1997
5	Adjustments of merchandise exports to change-of-ownership basis	...	...	...	...	...	...	...	...	...	...	...	...
6	Direct purchases in the domestic market by non-residential households	9196	10670	16279	20738	30411	47094	67748	94253	122695	...	...	...
7	Direct purchases in the domestic market by extraterritorial bodies	...	...	...	...	...	...	...	...	...	...	...	...
	Total exports of goods and services	77280	90005	118998	148435	178763	264505	342873	412478	514146	...	...	...

Imports of goods and services

		1986	1987	1988	1989	1990	1991	1992	1993	1994	1995	1996	1997
1	Imports of merchandise, c.i.f.	58843	78204	94750	125560	165422	207265	296849	374133	437866	...	...	...
	A Imports of merchandise, f.o.b.	52805	69782	84936	111691	147671	185092	265123	333936	390823			
	B Transport of services on merchandise imports	6038	8422	9814	13869	17751	22173	31726	40197	47043			
	C Insurance service charges on merchandise imports	...	...	...	...	...	...	...	...	...			
2	Adjustments of merchandise imports to change-of-ownership basis	...	...	...	...	...	...	...	...	...			
3	Other transport and communication	1092	1357	2195	2423	3582	6056	6525	10840	12562	...	...	...
4	Other insurance service charges	...	...	...	...	...	...	...	...	...			
5	Other commodities [a]	10214	15958	21903	26423	31193	37399	55101	64753	62227			
6	Direct purchases abroad by government	5046	6249	6399	10557	15302	20183	32692	40011	51094	...	...	...
7	Direct purchases abroad by resident households										...	...	...
	Total imports of goods and services	75195	101768	125247	164963	215499	270903	391167	489737	563749	...	...	...
	Balance of goods and services	2085	–11763	–6249	–16528	–36736	–6398	–48294	–77259	–49603	...	...	...
	Total imports and balance of goods and services	77280	90005	118998	148435	178763	264505	342873	412478	514146	...	...	...

a Item "Other commodities" relates to non-factor services.

4.3 Cost components of value added

Million Costa Rican colones

		\multicolumn{6}{c}{1986}	\multicolumn{6}{c}{1987}
		Compensation of employees	Capital consumption	Net operating surplus	Indirect taxes	less: Subsidies received	Value added	Compensation of employees	Capital consumption	Net operating surplus	Indirect taxes	less: Subsidies received	Value added

All producers

		Comp.	Cap.	Net op.	Ind. tax	Subs.	Val. added	Comp.	Cap.	Net op.	Ind. tax	Subs.	Val. added
1	Agriculture, hunting, forestry and fishing	16318	650	...	...	...	51530	19533	727	...	...	...	51417
2	Mining and quarrying	16335	1383	...	...	...	52573	19101	1601	...	...	...	60698
3	Manufacturing												
4	Electricity, gas and water	1820	972	...	...	...	7413	2165	1135	...	...	...	8598
5	Construction	6914	284	...	...	...	8127	7742	317	...	...	...	9160
6	Wholesale and retail trade, restaurants and hotels	19015	454	...	...	...	47367	23778	527	...	...	...	58505
7	Transport, storage and communication	5837	797	...	...	...	11639	6743	914	...	...	...	14069
8	Finance, insurance, real estate and business services	7157	1386	...	...	...	24522	8687	1644	...	...	...	31071

Costa Rica

Million Costa Rican colones

	\multicolumn{6}{c	}{1986}	\multicolumn{6}{c	}{1987}
	Compensation of employees	Capital consumption	Net operating surplus	Indirect taxes	less: Subsidies received	Value added	Compensation of employees	Capital consumption	Net operating surplus	Indirect taxes	less: Subsidies received	Value added
9 Community, social and personal services [a]	7777	204	...	...	...	11829	10057	250	...	...	...	14756
Total, Industries	81173	6130	94054	36271	2629	214999	97806	7114	104228	41994	2867	248273
Producers of government services	31580	...	...	...	...	31580	36260	...	...	...	...	36260
Other producers	...	...	...	...	...	...	...	...	...	...	...	...
Total	112753	6130	94054	36271	2629	246579	134065	7114	104228	41994	2867	284533
less: Imputed bank service charge	...	...	...	...	...	...	...	...	...	...	...	...
Import duties	...	...	...	...	...	...	...	...	...	...	...	...
Value added tax	...	...	...	...	...	...	...	...	...	...	...	...
Other adjustments	...	...	...	...	...	...	...	...	...	...	...	...
Total	112753	6130	94054	36271	2629	246579	134065	7114	104228	41994	2867	284533

	\multicolumn{6}{c	}{1988}	\multicolumn{6}{c	}{1989}
	Compensation of employees	Capital consumption	Net operating surplus	Indirect taxes	less: Subsidies received	Value added	Compensation of employees	Capital consumption	Net operating surplus	Indirect taxes	less: Subsidies received	Value added

All producers

1 Agriculture, hunting, forestry and fishing	24239	887	...	...	...	62774	30666	1052	...	...	...	73344
2 Mining and quarrying	23651	2017	...	...	...	74397	27692	2332	...	...	...	86688
3 Manufacturing												
4 Electricity, gas and water	2597	1422	...	...	...	10292	3336	1740	...	...	...	13437
5 Construction	8975	352	...	...	...	10544	11947	351	...	...	...	14455
6 Wholesale and retail trade, restaurants and hotels	28815	667	...	...	...	70592	35908	793	...	...	...	83087
7 Transport, storage and communication	8545	1152	...	...	...	17367	10819	1326	...	...	...	20949
8 Finance, insurance, real estate and business services	11346	2091	...	...	...	39424	13949	2626	...	...	...	49690
9 Community, social and personal services [a]	12215	331	...	...	...	18380	14684	402	...	...	...	24260
Total, Industries	120382	8919	129884	49156	4572	303769	149001	10621	151441	61042	6196	365910
Producers of government services	45974	...	...	...	...	45974	60001	...	...	...	...	60001
Other producers	...	...	...	...	...	...	...	...	...	...	...	...
Total	166356	8919	129884	49156	4572	349743	209002	10621	151441	61042	6196	425911
less: Imputed bank service charge	...	...	...	...	...	...	...	...	...	...	...	...
Import duties	...	...	...	...	...	...	...	...	...	...	...	...
Value added tax	...	...	...	...	...	...	...	...	...	...	...	...
Other adjustments	...	...	...	...	...	...	...	...	...	...	...	...
Total	166356	8919	129884	49156	4572	349743	209002	10621	151441	61042	6196	425911

	\multicolumn{6}{c	}{1990}	\multicolumn{6}{c	}{1991}
	Compensation of employees	Capital consumption	Net operating surplus	Indirect taxes	less: Subsidies received	Value added	Compensation of employees	Capital consumption	Net operating surplus	Indirect taxes	less: Subsidies received	Value added

All producers

1 Agriculture, hunting, forestry and fishing	38736	1315	...	...	...	82544	49785	1832	...	...	...	119627
2 Mining and quarrying	33142	2973	...	...	...	101328	43889	4195	...	...	...	137469
3 Manufacturing												

Costa Rica

	1990						1991					
	Compensation of employees	Capital consumption	Net operating surplus	Indirect taxes	less: Subsidies received	Value added	Compensation of employees	Capital consumption	Net operating surplus	Indirect taxes	less: Subsidies received	Value added
4 Electricity, gas and water	4269	2184	...	...	...	16227	6314	2924	...	...	...	24210
5 Construction	14118	401	...	...	...	16796	16399	587	...	...	...	19549
6 Wholesale and retail trade, restaurants and hotels	44535	925	...	...	...	105048	53875	1418	...	...	...	139459
7 Transport, storage and communication	14215	1638	...	...	...	26484	18781	2279	...	...	...	35884
8 Finance, insurance, real estate and business services	18656	3252	...	...	...	64398	22897	4351	...	...	...	76525
9 Community, social and personal services [a]	18804	530	...	...	...	32103	22170	774	...	...	...	44623
Total, Industries	186475	13217	180649	71816	7229	444928	234110	18360	255536	99591	10252	597347
Producers of government services	77920	...	...	...	...	77920	92818	...	...	...	...	92818
Other producers	...	...	...	...	...	...	...	...	...	...	...	...
Total	264395	13217	180649	71816	7229	522848	326928	18361	255536	99591	10252	690164
less: Imputed bank service charge	...	...	...	...	...	...	...	...	...	...	...	...
Import duties	...	...	...	...	...	...	...	...	...	...	...	...
Value added tax	...	...	...	...	...	...	...	...	...	...	...	...
Other adjustments	...	...	...	...	...	...	...	...	...	...	...	...
Total	264395	13217	180649	71816	7229	522848	326928	18361	255536	99591	10252	690164

	1992						1993					
	Compensation of employees	Capital consumption	Net operating surplus	Indirect taxes	less: Subsidies received	Value added	Compensation of employees	Capital consumption	Net operating surplus	Indirect taxes	less: Subsidies received	Value added

All producers

1 Agriculture, hunting, forestry and fishing	66046	2322	...	...	...	147910	75353	2782	...	...	...	171589
2 Mining and quarrying	62466	4992	...	...	...	185616	72587	5736	...	...	...	206877
3 Manufacturing												
4 Electricity, gas and water	8726	3580	31960	...	...	31960	10222	4088	396100	...	...	39610
5 Construction	19354	508	...	...	...	23294	24860	625	...	...	...	29283
6 Wholesale and retail trade, restaurants and hotels	70471	1805	...	...	...	193292	89309	2197	...	...	...	222302
7 Transport, storage and communication	24648	2706	...	...	...	48034	28451	3101	...	...	...	58023
8 Finance, insurance, real estate and business services	29188	5334	...	...	...	96771	38916	6001	...	...	...	121611
9 Community, social and personal services [a]	29797	977	...	...	...	60403	33983	1210	...	...	...	75242
Total, Industries	310696	22224	322105	141187	8933	787280	373681	25739	384670	153801	13355	924537
Producers of government services	118999	...	...	...	...	118999	144723	...	...	...	...	144723
Other producers	...	...	...	...	...	...	...	...	...	...	...	...
Total	429695	22224	322105	141187	8933	906278	518404	25739	384670	153801	13355	1069259
less: Imputed bank service charge	...	...	...	...	...	...	...	...	...	...	...	...
Import duties	...	...	...	...	...	...	...	...	...	...	...	...
Value added tax	...	...	...	...	...	...	...	...	...	...	...	...
Other adjustments	...	...	...	...	...	...	...	...	...	...	...	...
Total	429695	22224	322105	141187	8933	906278	518404	25739	384670	153801	13355	1069259

a Item "Other producers" is included in item "Community, social and personal services".

Côte d'Ivoire

Source

Reply to the United Nations National Accounts Questionnaire and communication from the Institut National de la Statistique, Abidjan. The official estimates are published annually in *Comptes de la Nation*.

General note

The official estimates of Côte d'Ivoire have been adjusted by the Institut National de la Statistique in accordance with the United Nations System of National Accounts (1968 SNA) so far as the existing data would permit.

1.1 Expenditure on the gross domestic product, in current prices

Hundred million CFA francs

	1986	1987	1988	1989	1990	1991	1992	1993	1994	1995	1996	1997
1 Government final consumption expenditure	4798	4940	5224	5682	4938	4843	5149	4841	...	...	...	...
2 Private final consumption expenditure	19843	20174	20352	21408	20919	21436	21376	21565	...	...	...	...
3 Gross capital formation	3830	3740	3870	2770	1970	2180	1590	2450	...	...	...	...
A Increase in stocks	80	170	360	−440	−530	−360	−920	140	...	...	...	...
B Gross fixed capital formation	3750	3570	3510	3210	2500	2540	2510	2310	...	...	...	...
4 Exports of goods and services	12528	10135	9310	9970	9310	8880	9420	8460	...	...	...	...
5 less: Imports of goods and services	9572	8980	8520	9050	7970	7990	8300	8140	...	...	...	...
Statistical discrepancy	313	291	294	310	223	251	295	284	...	...	...	...
equals: Gross domestic product	31740	30300	30530	31090	29390	29600	29530	29460	...	...	...	...

1.2 Expenditure on the gross domestic product, in constant prices

Hundred million CFA francs

	1986	1987	1988	1989	1990	1991	1992	1993	1994	1995	1996	1997
At constant prices of: 1986												
1 Government final consumption expenditure	4800	4870	5070	5350	4380	3820	4120	3970	...	...	...	...
2 Private final consumption expenditure	20140	20460	20520	20490	20080	20670	20880	20650	...	...	...	...
A Households	20080	20400	20450	20410	20030	20640	20830	20600	...	...	...	...
B Private non-profit institutions serving households	60	60	70	70	50	30	50	50	...	...	...	...
3 Gross capital formation	3830	3040	2750	1260	20	1550	1200	2860	...	...	...	...
A Increase in stocks	80	−390	−410	−1740	−2380	−910	−1220	450	...	...	...	...
B Gross fixed capital formation	3750	3430	3160	3000	2400	2460	2420	2410	...	...	...	...
4 Exports of goods and services	12530	12290	12060	13990	15480	14270	14240	12730	...	...	...	...
5 less: Imports of goods and services	9570	9050	8440	8180	7400	7760	7950	7800	...	...	...	...
equals: Gross domestic product	31720	31610	31960	32910	32550	32560	32480	32410	...	...	...	...

Cote d'Ivoire

1.3 Cost components of the gross domestic product

Hundred million CFA francs

	1986	1987	1988	1989	1990	1991	1992	1993	1994	1995	1996	1997
1 Indirect taxes, net	...	...	...	...	...	...	...	...	...	...	...	...
A Indirect taxes	...	...	...	...	...	...	...	...	...	...	...	...
B less: Subsidies [a]	587	606	961	457	855	215	267	353	...	...	...	...
2 Consumption of fixed capital	...	...	...	...	...	...	...	...	...	...	...	...
3 Compensation of employees paid by resident producers to ..	9896	10777	10962	10992	10539	10475	10389	10203	...	...	...	...
A Resident households	9777	10720	10901	10932	10469	10408	10332	10150	...	...	...	...
B Rest of the world	119	57	61	60	70	67	57	53	...	...	...	...
4 Operating surplus	15228	14156	15504	16166	15722	14794	14795	15744	...	...	...	...
A Corporate and quasi-corporate enterprises	3608	2951	3603	3568	3532	2495	2817	3563	...	...	...	...
B Private unincorporated enterprises	...	...	...	...	...	...	...	...	...	...	...	...
C General government	−5	−11	−12	−8	−8	−10	–	–	...	...	...	...
equals: Gross domestic product ..	31717	30317	30540	31130	29393	29600	29520	29460	...	...	...	...

[a] Item "Subsidies" includes the profit or loss of the Marketing Board.

1.7 External transactions on current account, summary

Hundred million CFA francs

	1986	1987	1988	1989	1990	1991	1992	1993	1994	1995	1996	1997
Payments to the rest of the world												
1 Imports of goods and services	9570	8980	8520	9050	7970	7990	8300	8140	...	...	...	...
A Imports of merchandise, c.i.f.	7240	7040	6630	7110	6090	6170	6200	6100	...	...	...	...
B Other	2330	1940	1890	1940	1880	1820	2100	2040	...	...	...	...
2 Factor income to rest of the world	2516	3142	3290	3903	4002	4130	3831	3393	...	...	...	...
A Compensation of employees	119	57	61	60	70	67	57	53	...	...	...	...
B Property and entrepreneurial income	2397	3085	3229	3843	3932	4063	3774	3340	...	...	...	...
3 Current transfers to the rest of the world	1399	1721	1705	1663	1482	1307	1242	1269	...	...	...	...
Statistical discrepancy	1174	3452	3993	3842	3539	4344	2867	3605	...	...	...	...
4 Surplus of the nation on current transactions	−610	−2860	−3402	−3419	−3060	−3638	−2509	−3245	...	...	...	...
Payments to the rest of the world and surplus of the nation on current transfers	14049	14435	14106	15039	13933	14133	13731	13162	...	...	...	...
Receipts from the rest of the world												
1 Exports of goods and services	12530	10140	9310	9970	9310	8880	9420	8460	...	...	...	...
A Exports of merchandise, f.o.b.	11440	9090	8290	8990	8360	7930	8460	7500	...	...	...	...
B Other	1090	1050	1020	980	960	960	980	950	...	...	...	...
2 Factor income from rest of the world	146	284	288	309	260	258	337	369	...	...	...	...
A Compensation of employees	115	173	198	235	202	200	279	312	...	...	...	...
B Property and entrepreneurial income	31	111	90	74	58	58	58	57	...	...	...	...
3 Current transfers from rest of the world	460	649	742	982	996	691	1081	681	...	...	...	...
Statistical discrepancy	913	3362	3766	3778	3367	4304	2893	3652	...	...	...	...

Cote d'Ivoire

Hundred million CFA francs

	1986	1987	1988	1989	1990	1991	1992	1993	1994	1995	1996	1997
Receipts from the rest of the world on current transactions	14049	14435	14106	15039	13933	14133	13731	13162	...	...	...	...

1.8 Capital transactions of the nation, summary

Hundred million CFA francs

	1986	1987	1988	1989	1990	1991	1992	1993	1994	1995	1996	1997
Finance of gross capital formation												
Gross saving	3218	682	412	−661	479	−1896	−1013	−919	...	...	...	...
less: Surplus of the nation on current transactions	...	...	...	...	...	...	...	...	...	...	...	...
Finance of gross capital formation	...	...	...	...	...	...	...	...	...	...	...	...
Gross capital formation												
Increase in stocks	80	170	360	−440	−530	−360	−920	140	...	...	...	...
Gross fixed capital formation	3750	3570	3510	3210	2500	2540	2510	2310	...	...	...	...
1 General government	1233	1539	1440	1362	1054	1020	1128	1089	...	...	...	...
2 Corporate and quasi-corporate enterprises	2043	1531	1588	1397	1069	1146	1095	1063	...	...	...	...
3 Other	473	499	479	453	377	372	285	157	...	...	...	...
Gross capital formation	3830	3740	3870	2770	1970	2180	1590	2450	...	...	...	...

1.9 Gross domestic product by institutional sectors of origin

Hundred million CFA francs

	1986	1987	1988	1989	1990	1991	1992	1993	1994	1995	1996	1997
Domestic factor incomes originating												
1 General government	3278	3655	3787	4074	3813	3699	3802	3586	...	...	...	...
2 Corporate and quasi-corporate enterprises	13305	11594	11085	10571	10681	10412	10146	10482	...	...	...	...
A Non-financial	12163	10436	9929	9320	9055	8957	9017	9151	...	...	...	...
B Financial	1142	1158	1155	1251	1626	1455	1129	1331	...	...	...	...
3 Households and private unincorporated enterprises	14051	13980	14644	15563	14498	14941	14776	14907	...	...	...	...
4 Non-profit institutions serving households	98	129	129	135	101	90	123	143	...	...	...	...
subtotal: Domestic factor incomes [a]	30732	29358	29645	30343	29093	29142	28847	29118	...	...	...	...
Indirect taxes, net	...	...	...	...	...	...	...	...	...	...	...	...
A Indirect taxes	...	...	...	...	...	...	...	...	...	...	...	...
B less: Subsidies [b]	587	606	961	457	855	215	267	353	...	...	...	...
Consumption of fixed capital	...	...	...	...	...	...	...	...	...	...	...	...
Gross domestic product	...	...	...	...	...	...	...	...	...	...	...	...

a Item "Domestic factor incomes" includes consumption of fixed capital.   b Item "Subsidies" includes the profit or loss of the Marketing Board.

1.10 Gross domestic product by kind of activity, in current prices

Hundred million CFA francs

	1986	1987	1988	1989	1990	1991	1992	1993	1994	1995	1996	1997
1 Agriculture, hunting, forestry and fishing	9020	8840	9780	10190	9560	9850	10040	10280	...	...	...	...
2 Mining and quarrying	390	280	200	80	90	60	60	50	...	...	...	...
3 Manufacturing	4910	5060	5290	5250	5450	4980	4930	4820	...	...	...	...

Côte d'Ivoire

Hundred million CFA francs

	1986	1987	1988	1989	1990	1991	1992	1993	1994	1995	1996	1997
4 Electricity, gas and water	700	630	660	680	680	770	700	630	...	...	...	...
5 Construction	770	810	760	750	580	620	600	590	...	...	...	...
6 Wholesale and retail trade, restaurants and hotels [a]	6890	5070	4360	3910	3390	3770	3610	3630	...	...	...	...
7 Transport, storage and communication	2280	2460	2400	2420	2370	2310	2530	2660	...	...	...	...
8 Finance, insurance, real estate and business services	2430	2440	2270	2830	3050	2950	2340	2650	...	...	...	...
9 Community, social and personal services	80	80	90	90	90	100	100	110	...	...	...	...
Statistical discrepancy	...	17	10	40	...	...	–10	...	...	...	...	...
Total, Industries	27470	25687	25820	26240	25260	25410	24900	25420	...	...	...	...
Producers of government services	3180	3540	3690	3980	3730	3640	3830	3570	...	...	...	...
Other producers	100	130	130	130	100	90	110	130	...	...	...	...
Subtotal	30750	29357	29640	30350	29090	29140	28840	29120	...	...	...	...
less: Imputed bank service charge	1080	1030	960	1160	1210	1000	1010	1180	...	...	...	...
plus: Import duties	2070	1990	1860	1940	1510	1460	1690	1520	...	...	...	...
plus: Value added tax	...	...	...	...	...	...	...	...	...	...	...	...
plus: Other adjustments	...	...	...	...	...	...	...	...	...	...	...	...
equals: Gross domestic product	31717	30317	30540	31130	29390	29600	29520	29460	...	...	...	...

a Item "Wholesale and retail trade, restaurants and hotels" includes the profit or loss of the Marketing Board.

1.11 Gross domestic product by kind of activity, in constant prices

Hundred million CFA francs

	1986	1987	1988	1989	1990	1991	1992	1993	1994	1995	1996	1997
At constant prices of: 1986												
1 Agriculture, hunting, forestry and fishing	9020	8950	9490	10100	10590	10740	10940	10910	...	...	...	...
2 Mining and quarrying	390	340	270	100	100	70	80	70	...	...	...	...
3 Manufacturing	4910	4970	5100	5280	4970	4940	5250	5260	...	...	...	...
4 Electricity, gas and water	700	720	750	790	770	790	610	660	...	...	...	...
5 Construction	770	700	680	710	560	640	710	700	...	...	...	...
6 Wholesale and retail trade, restaurants and hotels	6890	6560	6270	6460	6380	6340	6260	6000	...	...	...	...
7 Transport, storage and communication	2280	2340	2310	2470	2540	2690	2680	2630	...	...	...	...
8 Finance, insurance, real estate and business services	2430	2480	2510	2660	3080	2970	2480	2870	...	...	...	...
9 Community, social and personal services	80	80	90	90	90	100	100	100	...	...	...	...
Total, Industries	27470	27160	27490	28690	29070	29250	29100	29190	...	...	...	...
Producers of government services	3180	3490	3580	3750	3310	2870	2780	2830	...	...	...	...
Other producers	100	100	110	120	80	70	90	90	...	...	...	...
Subtotal	30750	30750	31180	32560	32460	32190	31970	32110	...	...	...	...
less: Imputed bank service charge	1080	1030	960	1160	1210	1000	1010	1170	...	...	...	...
plus: Import duties	2070	1930	1730	1520	1290	1340	1560	1450	...	...	...	...
plus: Value added tax	...	...	...	...	...	...	...	...	...	...	...	...
plus: Other adjustments	...	...	...	...	...	...	...	...	...	...	...	...
equals: Gross domestic product	31740	31650	31950	32920	32540	32530	32520	32390	...	...	...	...

Cote d'Ivoire

1.12 Relations among national accounting aggregates

Hundred million CFA francs

	1986	1987	1988	1989	1990	1991	1992	1993	1994	1995	1996	1997
Gross domestic product	31720	30320	30540	31130	29390	29600	29520	29460	...	...	...	...
plus: Net factor income from the rest of the world	−2370	−2858	−3002	−3594	−3742	−3872	−3494	−3024	...	...	...	...
Factor income from rest of the world	146	284	288	309	260	258	337	369	...	...	...	...
less: Factor income to the rest of the world	2516	3142	3290	3903	4002	4130	3831	3393	...	...	...	...
equals: Gross national product	29350	27462	27538	27536	25648	25728	26026	26436	...	...	...	...
less: Consumption of fixed capital	...	...	...	...	...	...	...	...	...	...	...	...
equals: National income	...	...	...	...	...	...	...	...	...	...	...	...
plus: Net current transfers from the rest of the world	−939	−1072	−963	−681	−486	−616	−161	−588	...	...	...	...
Current transfers from rest of the world	460	649	742	982	996	691	1081	681	...	...	...	...
less: Current transfers to the rest of the world	1399	1721	1705	1663	1482	1307	1242	1269	...	...	...	...
equals: National disposable income	28411	26390	26575	26855	25162	25244	25865	25848	...	...	...	...
less: Final consumption	24641	25114	25576	27090	25857	26279	26525	26406	...	...	...	...
Statistical discrepancy	−550	−590	−590	−420	−480	−460	−350	−360	...	...	...	...
equals: Net saving	3221	684	407	−659	−1173	−1497	−1014	−918	...	...	...	...
less: Surplus of the nation on current transactions	−610	−2860	−3402	−3419	−3060	−3637	−2509	−3238	...	...	...	...
equals: Net capital formation	3831	3544	3809	2760	1887	2140	1495	2320	...	...	...	...

Croatia

Source

Reply to the United Nations National Accounts Questionnaire from the Central Bureau of Statistics and its respective publications. The official estimates and detailed description on the concepts, sources and methods of estimation used in the compilation of national accounts estimates are published in *National Accounts of the Republic of Croatia* and the *Statistical Yearbook of the Republic of Croatia*.

General note

The estimates shown in the following tables have been prepared in accordance with the System of Material Product Balances (MPS). Gross social product and the elements of its initial distribution are calculated according to the so-called real or production method, except for the non-agricultural private sector where the personal or earnings method is used.

1.1 Expenditure on the gross domestic product, in current prices

Million Croatian dinars

	1986	1987	1988	1989	1990	1991	1992	1993	1994	1995	1996	1997
1 Government final consumption expenditure	...	...	...	...	...	104	644	9158	25738	28917	29154	32183
2 Private final consumption expenditure	...	...	...	...	...	293	1560	24639	46575	62882	65367	74599
A Households	...	...	...	...	...	...	...	...	...	27756	27475	30189
B Private non-profit institutions serving households	...	...	...	...	...	...	...	...	...	1161	1679	1994
3 Gross capital formation	...	...	...	...	...	57	355	5668	15191	17313	23689	34757
A Increase in stocks	...	...	...	...	...	...	...	...	2981	1916	1559	4822
B Gross fixed capital formation	...	...	...	...	...	57	355	5668	12210	15398	22089	29936
Residential buildings	...	...	...	...	...	...	...	...	2352	2874	5747	...
Non-residential buildings	...	...	...	...	...	...	...	...	1413	2043	2911	...
Other construction and land improvement, etc.	...	...	...	...	...	...	...	...	3209	4013	5038	...
Other	...	...	...	...	...	...	...	...	5236	6467	8394	...
4 Exports of goods and services	...	...	...	...	...	343	1614	20434	40086	37951	43402	51743
5 less: Imports of goods and services	...	...	...	...	—	355	1466	20896	40149	48681	53631	70378
equals: Gross domestic product	...	...	...	...	281	441	2707	39003	87441	98382	107981	122905

1.10 Gross domestic product by kind of activity, in current prices

Million Croatian dinars

	1986	1987	1988	1989	1990	1991	1992	1993	1994	1995	1996	1997
1 Agriculture, hunting, forestry and fishing	...	...	...	...	27	43	66	4570	8255	8413	9059	9688
2 Mining and quarrying	...	...	...	...	73[a]	117[a]	700[a]	10107[a]	19927[a]	238	235	646
3 Manufacturing	...	...	...	...	...	...	...	...	...	19178	19660	22791
4 Electricity, gas and water	...	...	...	...	1[b]	2[b]	7[b]	86[b]	151[b]	3023	3411	3676
5 Construction	...	...	...	...	15	19	87	1636	3717	4625	5965	7437
6 Wholesale and retail trade, restaurants and hotels	...	...	...	...	46	63	391	4630	10773	11552	13853	16317

Croatia

Million Croatian dinars

	1986	1987	1988	1989	1990	1991	1992	1993	1994	1995	1996	1997
7 Transport, storage and communication	...	...	...	...	21	38	160	2007	5999	7805	8022	9092
8 Finance, insurance, real estate and business services	...	...	...	...	15	36	321	2687	5738	11765	13315	14694
9 Community, social and personal services	...	...	...	...	15	40	329	3882	5599	1980	2141	2488
Total, Industries	...	...	...	...	213	357	2060	29604	59664	68580	75662	86828
Producers of government services	...	...	...	...	45	63	275	4761	13225	12528	15198	17855
Other producers	...	...	...	...	...	...	...	...	...	...	...	...
Subtotal	...	...	...	...	258	420	2335	34365	72889	81108	90860	104682
less: Imputed bank service charge	...	...	...	...	...	...	...	...	...	...	...	...
plus: Import duties	...	...	...	...	8	19	100	1236	3582	4148	4185	4974
plus: Value added tax	...	...	...	...	22	25	193	4988	12347	15351	15709	17012
plus: Other adjustments [c]	...	...	...	...	–8	–23	–214	–1586	–1872	–2241	–2794	–3788
equals: Gross domestic product	...	...	...	...	281	441	2707	39003	87441	98382	107981	122905

a Includes item "Manufacturing".
b "Electricity and gas" are not included in this item.
c Financial Intermediation Services Indirectly Measured (FISIM).

1.11 Gross domestic product by kind of activity, in constant prices

Thousand Croatian dinars

	1986	1987	1988	1989	1990	1991	1992	1993	1994	1995	1996	1997
		At constant prices of: 1990										
1 Agriculture, hunting, forestry and fishing	...	...	...	39883	27263	24543	23120	21458	19674	19474	...	...
2 Mining and quarrying [a]	...	...	...	114118	73330	53084	39145	35046	37219	35170	...	...
3 Manufacturing	...	...	...	...	...	...	...	...	...	...	...	...
4 Electricity, gas and water [b]	...	...	...	5914	938	630	255	198	200	236	...	...
5 Construction	...	...	...	15853	15198	9621	5932	6376	7191	8405	...	...
6 Wholesale and retail trade, restaurants and hotels	...	...	...	28862	45551	28630	26550	21328	23921	28208	...	...
7 Transport, storage and communication	...	...	...	20758	21427	14396	13995	10318	12831	12936	...	...
8 Finance, insurance, real estate and business services	...	...	...	9918	14893	17348	16028	15562	17554	18346	...	...
9 Community, social and personal services	...	...	...	19872	14859	13576	14865	14297	14126	14400	...	...
Total, Industries	...	...	...	255179	213460	161828	139890	124583	132716	137175	...	...
Producers of government services	...	...	...	46712	44737	46045	42115	42362	42494	45655	...	...
Other producers	...	...	...	...	...	...	...	...	...	...	...	...
Subtotal	...	...	...	301891	258197	207872	182006	166945	175209	182830	...	...
less: Imputed bank service charge	...	...	...	...	...	...	...	...	...	...	...	...
plus: Import duties	...	...	...	...	7920	6038	6842	7933	8752	11411	...	...
plus: Value added tax	...	...	...	...	22462	16436	13047	10789	12497	15474	...	...
plus: Other adjustments [c]	...	...	...	...	–8035	–7328	–6445	–5902	–6141	–6391	...	...
equals: Gross domestic product	...	...	...	301891	280544	221381	195450	179764	190317	203323	215522	229531

a Includes item "Manufacturing".
b "Electricity and gas" are not included in this item.
c Financial Intermediation Services Indirectly Measured (FISIM).

Cuba

Source

Correspondence from the Oficina Nacional de Estadísticas, Habana.

General note

The estimates shown in the following tables have been prepared in accordance with the United Nations System of National Accounts (1968 SNA).

1.1 Expenditure on the gross domestic product, in current prices

Million Cuban pesos

	1986	1987	1988	1989	1990	1991	1992	1993	1994	1995	1996	1997
1 Government final consumption expenditure	5902	5786	6032	6103	6090	5412	5187	5341	5235	5302	5522	...
2 Private final consumption expenditure	10241	10294	10559	10845	10589	9650	9100	9350	13047	15327	16101	...
3 Gross capital formation	4703	4132	4560	5063	4872	2274	976	965	1006	1525	1621	–
A Increase in stocks	–247	–260	–78	137	56	–1402	–1351	–1100	–567	–161	–637	...
B Gross fixed capital formation	4950	4392	4638	4925	4816	3676	2326	2065	1573	1686	2258	...
4 Exports of goods and services	5843	5948	6079	5993	5940	3563	2522	1992	2542	2913	3564	...
5 less: Imports of goods and services	8061	7940	8183	8608	8030	4723	2717	2373	2791	3458	4173	...
Statistical discrepancy	–215	–140	–66	–166	183	70	–162	–180	159	128	180	...
equals: Gross domestic product	18413	18080	18981	19230	19645	16248	14905	15095	19198	21737	22815	...

1.2 Expenditure on the gross domestic product, in constant prices

Million Cuban pesos

	1986	1987	1988	1989	1990	1991	1992	1993	1994	1995	1996	1997
At constant prices of: 1981												
1 Government final consumption expenditure	5496	5361	5581	5602	5576	4993	4732	4682	4592	4564	4747	...
2 Private final consumption expenditure	8442	8606	8803	8942	8353	7498	6160	5462	5772	5857	6086	...
3 Gross capital formation	4813	4327	4753	5234	5084	2752	1147	692	705	954	1172	...
A Increase in stocks	...	...	...	...	41	–1256	–1207	–983	–506	–316	–569	...
B Gross fixed capital formation	4813	4327	4753	5234	5044	4008	2354	1675	1212	1270	1741	...
4 Exports of goods and services	6258	6153	6185	5873	5663	5463	5140	3859	4211	4393	5474	...
5 less: Imports of goods and services	5789	5689	5868	6066	5732	3603	1972	1865	2223	2479	3080	...
Statistical discrepancy	–	–	–1	–	64	–127	–196	–53	–189	–105	–180	...
equals: Gross domestic product	19220	18758	19453	19586	19008	16976	15010	12777	12868	13184	14218	14572

Cuba

1.10 Gross domestic product by kind of activity, in current prices

Million Cuban pesos

	1986	1987	1988	1989	1990	1991	1992	1993	1994	1995	1996	1997
1 Agriculture, hunting, forestry and fishing	2004	2004	2133	2146	2248	1822	1625	1268	1331	1313	1548	...
2 Mining and quarrying	136	128	133	150	120	113	136	114	116	176	332	...
3 Manufacturing	4848	4548	4869	4754	4644	4211	4406	4478	6827	8244	8367	...
4 Electricity, gas and water	387	460	483	504	498	468	381	307	332	461	484	...
5 Construction	1224	1046	1152	1264	1430	1006	749	738	795	891	1176	...
6 Wholesale and retail trade, restaurants and hotels	4481	4349	4387	4490	4845	3030	2225	2461	4089	4972	4774	...
7 Transport, storage and communication	1266	1352	1395	1374	1220	1033	845	741	784	845	1000	...
8 Finance, insurance, real estate and business services	420	414	435	456	485	502	454	507	464	447	488	...
9 Community, social and personal services	3647	3778	3996	4093	4154	4063	4041	4234	4136	4117	4221	...
Total, Industries	18413	18080	18981	19230	19645	16248	14863	14848	18873	21468	22392	...
Producers of government services	...	...	...	...	...	...	...	...	...	...	...	...
Other producers	...	...	...	...	...	...	...	...	...	...	...	...
Subtotal	18413	18080	18981	19230	19645	16248	14863	14848	18873	21468	22392	...
less: Imputed bank service charge	...	...	...	...	...	...	...	...	...	...	...	...
plus: Import duties	...	...	...	...	...	...	42	247	325	269	423	...
plus: Value added tax	...	...	...	...	...	...	...	...	...	...	...	...
plus: Other adjustments	...	...	...	...	...	...	...	...	...	...	...	...
equals: Gross domestic product	18413	18080	18981	19230	19645	16248	14905	15095	19198	21737	22815	...

1.11 Gross domestic product by kind of activity, in constant prices

Million Cuban pesos

	1986	1987	1988	1989	1990	1991	1992	1993	1994	1995	1996	1997
At constant prices of: 1981												
1 Agriculture, hunting, forestry and fishing	1813	1852	1916	1924	1756	1335	1197	925	879	916	1075	1074
2 Mining and quarrying	114	119	117	123	92	82	106	96	98	152	177	182
3 Manufacturing	4869	4691	4943	4887	4640	4200	3507	3104	3341	3555	3835	4155
4 Electricity, gas and water	367	391	414	452	455	426	378	335	350	384	398	422
5 Construction	1205	1085	1207	1350	1508	1085	604	386	384	412	538	556
6 Wholesale and retail trade, restaurants and hotels [a]	5661	5271	5224	5151	4936	4396	4050	2936	2935	2985	3251	3176
7 Transport, storage and communication	1283	1319	1363	1353	1202	1059	912	733	709	748	813	845
8 Finance, insurance, real estate and business services	533	533	550	585	603	639	544	513	492	484	519	544
9 Community, social and personal services [b]	3374	3497	3720	3762	3816	3753	3713	3748	3681	3548	3611	3619
Total, Industries	19220	18758	19453	19586	19008	16976	15010	12777	12868	13184	14218	14572
Producers of government services	...	...	...	...	...	...	...	...	...	...	...	...
Other producers	...	...	...	...	...	...	...	...	...	...	...	...
Subtotal	...	...	...	...	...	...	...	...	...	...	...	...
less: Imputed bank service charge	...	...	...	...	...	...	...	...	...	...	...	...
plus: Import duties	...	...	...	...	...	...	...	...	...	...	...	...

Cuba

Million Cuban pesos

	1986	1987	1988	1989	1990	1991	1992	1993	1994	1995	1996	1997
At constant prices of: 1981												
plus: Value added tax	...	...	...	...	...	...	...	...	...	...	...	...
plus: Other adjustments	...	...	...	...	...	...	...	...	...	...	...	...
equals: Gross domestic product	19220	18758	19453	19586	19008	16976	15010	12777	12868	13184	14218	14572

a Includes import duties.   b Includes "Producers of Government Services" and "Other Producers".

Cyprus

General note

The preparation of national accounts statistics in Cyprus is undertaken by the Department of Statistics and Research, Ministry of Finance, Nicosia. The official estimates are published annually in the *Economic Report* and the *Statistical Abstract*, issued by the same Department. Information on concepts, sources and methods of estimation used can be found in the *History and Analysis of the Methodology of National Accounts in Cyprus*, published in 1977 and covers the period 1960–1975 and the *New National Accounts of Cyprus 1976–1983*, published in 1985 and covers the years 1976 and after. The estimates are generally in accordance with the classifications and definitions of the United Nations System of National Accounts (1968 SNA). For the years 1950–1975, the 1958 SNA was used and since 1976 the 1968 SNA. To compare national accounts estimates based on the 1968 SNA and those based on the 1958 SNA the following differences should be taken into consideration: (a) under the 1968 SNA, rents are treated as intermediate inputs instead of value added, (b) operating surplus is not equal to profits as it includes property income paid to owners, and (c) GDP is at market prices (instead of the factor cost pricing), under the 1958 SNA. The following tables have been prepared from successive replies to the United Nations National Accounts Questionnaire. Where the scope and coverage of the estimates differ for conceptual or statistical reasons from the definitions and classifications recommended in the SNA, a footnote is indicated to the relevant tables.

Gross domestic product

Prior to 1976, gross domestic product was estimated through a combination of the income and the production methods. Since 1976, GDP is solely estimated through the production method.

Expenditures on the gross domestic product

The expenditure method is used to estimate all the components of the expenditure account (i.e. government and private final consumption expenditure, capital formation, stocks and imports and exports of goods and services). Sources of data are the treasury report for government financial accounts, the publications of the Department of Statistics and Research on industry, agriculture, services, imports and exports which provide annual data. The Central Bank of Cyprus provides detailed data on balance of payments and its components. For constant price estimates the total cost of living allowance index is used to deflate wages and salaries in government final consumption expenditure and partial price indices from the retail price index are used to deflate the private final consumption expenditure. For the other expenditure items, various price deflators are used.

Cost structure of the gross domestic product

Separate estimates for compensation of employees and operating surplus were not available prior to 1976. Since 1976, separate estimates for compensation of employees and operating surplus are compiled from annual production surveys and other secondary sources. These estimates are published in the *Economic Report*. The estimate of consumption of fixed capital is based on a fixed percentage (10.5 per cent) of the gross national product. An effort is being made to calculate consumption of fixed capital based on the existing capital stock. Net indirect taxes are available in the *Financial Report*, issued by the Treasury Department.

Gross domestic product by kind of activity

Agricultural estimates were based mainly on ad hoc inquiries of the Ministry of Agriculture and Natural Resources for years prior to 1969. From 1969 to 1974, estimates were derived from area sample surveys conducted twice a year. From 1975, the area sample was replaced by an annual survey of crop and livestock holders. Data on fishing and forestry are supplied by the fisheries and forestry departments respectively. Estimates for mining and quarrying, manufacturing and electricity, gas and water are derived from the annual industrial production surveys and the censuses of industrial production held every five years since 1956. Construction sector consists of public and private construction. Public construction estimates are compiled from the annual financial report of the Treasury Department and the annual reports of semi-government organizations and local government authorities. For private construction the data are derived from the annual construction surveys conducted since 1978 and based on the building permits. While since 1987, an additional survey is conducted through building contractors. In addition, ad hoc inquiries are undertaken for collecting data on inputs, labour, materials, investments etc. supplementing the surveys data. Prior to 1978, the same surveys were conducted every three years. Prior to 1981, wholesale and retail trade estimates were based on gross trade margins, calculated through the commodity flow method. Since the 1981 Census of Wholesale and Retail, estimates are derived from an annual survey. For transport, prior to 1980, estimates were based on extrapolation of value added by using indices of the number of buses in use and bus fares, rented cars and fares as well as the number of taxis and their revenues. For lorry transport, estimates were based on the transport margins derived from the commodity flow method. Estimates for port services and civil aviation were compiled from the annual financial report of the Treasury Department and for Cyprus Airways data were obtained regularly from their annual report. For storage, data were compiled from ad hoc inquiries collected through the agricultural surveys and later by conducting special surveys. For communication, estimates were obtained for postal services from the financial report and for the Cyprus Telecommunication Authority data were compiled from its annual report. Since 1980 estimates are based on annual surveys on all activities of the transport sector.

Data on financial institutions are collected by the Central Bank of Cyprus. Data on insurance activities are extracted from the records of the Office of the Supervisor of Insurance Companies and ad hoc surveys conducted by the Department of Statistics and Research. Data on real estate are based on land and buildings transfer fees and ad hoc surveys. Data on business services are derived from annual surveys. The main source of information for public administration and defence and public services is the annual financial report of the Treasury Department and annual returns submitted by the local authorities. Estimates for the private services are derived from the annual services survey. For the constant price estimates, the double deflation method is used for all items of agricultural outputs and inputs to arrive at value added estimates. Special price deflators for each category and or product items are constructed for both the output and inputs. Prior to 1976, value added was deflated by using a combination of indices for the remaining industries. Quantity indices for mining and quarrying, manufacturing and construction, price indices for wholesale and retail trade, base year average prices for electricity, gas and water, employment and wage rate indices for all the other services sectors. Since 1976, double deflation method of output and inputs is used. For producers of government services, the cost of living allowance index is used to deflate their value added which comprises mainly of compensation of employees.

1.1 Expenditure on the gross domestic product, in current prices

Ten thousand Cyprus pounds

	1986	1987	1988	1989	1990	1991	1992	1993	1994	1995	1996	1997
1 Government final consumption expenditure	22990	29570	33250	36070	44310	49330	59070	55250	60810	65500	74500	...
2 Private final consumption expenditure	97920	105980	121020	134330	153220	175410	193900	193400	210300	237700	254800	...
A Households	96660	104500	119380	132450	151090	172970	191100	190200	206700	233700	250200	...
B Private non-profit institutions serving households	1260	1480	1640	1880	2130	2440	2780	3180	3570	4000	4600	...
3 Gross capital formation	41500	45450	54800	69720	69120	69120	89050	78880	93000	105000	109700	...
A Increase in stocks	3100	3660	5720	7580	6230	4100	9460	4760	18000	28000	29000	...
B Gross fixed capital formation	38400	41790	49080	62140	62890	65020	79590	74120	75000	77000	80700	...
Residential buildings	15020	15130	17070	19040	21870	24420	25940	26370	27300	28600	31500	...
Non-residential buildings	6850	7940	9710	11200	12150	13380	16130	12200	12000	11800	13000	...
Other construction and land improvement, etc.	6570	7930	7100	8050	8410	8990	9500	13040	14400	14700	12400	...
Other	9960	10790	15200	23850	20460	18230	28020	22510	21300	21900	23800	...
4 Exports of goods and services	72100	84180	95920	116140	131680	126080	153460	154900	173500	185100	193900	...
5 less: Imports of goods and services	77920	89490	106790	135130	145630	152690	188190	156210	175550	200000	220900	...
Statistical discrepancy	3470	2390	1040	4460	2900	200	3000	1200	2800	4200	2200	...
equals: Gross domestic product	160060	178080	199240	225620	255600	267500	310300	327500	364900	397600	414300	...

1.2 Expenditure on the gross domestic product, in constant prices

Ten thousand Cyprus pounds

	1986	1987	1988	1989	1990	1991	1992	1993	1994	1995	1996	1997
	At constant prices of: 1985											
1 Government final consumption expenditure	21600	27640	29990	30570	35900	37310	42450	36390	37880	39000	43600	...
2 Private final consumption expenditure	96220	101460	112120	119860	130590	144300	148800	141500	147400	163000	169500	...
A Households	94990	99970	110550	118200	128780	142300	146700	139200	144900	160300	166600	...
B Private non-profit institutions serving households	1230	1490	1570	1650	1820	1900	2060	2250	2500	2700	2900	...
3 Gross capital formation	40450	43050	48960	59250	56470	53900	66800	55800	63700	69500	70600	...
A Increase in stocks	3000	3740	5480	7060	5730	3610	7700	3980	14400	21800	21900	...

Cyprus

Ten thousand Cyprus pounds

	1986	1987	1988	1989	1990	1991	1992	1993	1994	1995	1996	1997
	At constant prices of: 1985											
B Gross fixed capital formation	37450	39310	43480	52190	50740	50300	59100	51800	49300	47700	48700	...
Residential buildings	14770	14580	15400	16080	17450	18610	18580	18000	17900	17800	19000	...
Non-residential buildings	6730	7630	8740	9450	9720	10140	11550	8430	7900	7400	7900	...
Other construction and land improvement, etc.	6460	7540	6440	6780	6710	6690	6800	8900	9600	9500	7700	...
Other	9490	9560	12900	19880	16860	14900	22100	16500	13900	13000	14100	...
4 Exports of goods and services	71020	80750	91800	107180	115470	106400	125100	123000	132800	138400	143000	...
5 less: Imports of goods and services	78060	88690	99920	120280	127230	129200	153700	125200	136100	151800	162300	...
Statistical discrepancy	2490	360	−4780	−4000	−4360	−4400	−1700	−2100	−3000	−1800	−3000	...
equals: Gross domestic product	153720	164570	178170	192580	206840	208300	227800	229400	242700	256300	261400	...

1.3 Cost components of the gross domestic product

Ten thousand Cyprus pounds

	1986	1987	1988	1989	1990	1991	1992	1993	1994	1995	1996	1997
1 Indirect taxes, net	13790	15050	16500	19280	22270	22630	26080	21800	23500	25500	24500	...
A Indirect taxes	15520	17190	19930	23250	24940	25220	29450	25400	26700	29500	28900	...
B less: Subsidies	1730	2140	3430	3970	2670	2590	3370	3640	3150	4000	4400	...
2 Consumption of fixed capital	17030	18950	21170	24060	27300	28600	33000	34900	38700	42200	43800	...
3 Compensation of employees paid by resident producers to	129240	144040	161570	182280	206000	216300	251200	270800	302700	329900	346000	...
4 Operating surplus												...
equals: Gross domestic product	160060	178080	199240	225620	255600	267500	310300	327500	364900	397600	414300	...

1.7 External transactions on current account, summary

Ten thousand Cyprus pounds

	1986	1987	1988	1989	1990	1991	1992	1993	1994	1995	1996	1997
Payments to the rest of the world												
1 Imports of goods and services	77920	89490	106790	135130	145630	152690	188190	156210	175550	...	...	...
A Imports of merchandise, c.i.f.	66120	75820	92180	118990	127460	131790	164900	131240	147830	...	...	...
B Other	11800	13670	14610	16140	18170	20900	23290	24970	27720	...	...	...
2 Factor income to rest of the world	6650	6850	7880	8540	9920	10720	10560	9870	10390	...	...	...
A Compensation of employees	360	350	510	480	550	850	1070	1220	1660	...	...	...
B Property and entrepreneurial income	6290	6500	7370	8060	9370	9870	9490	8650	8730	...	...	...
3 Current transfers to the rest of the world	150	130	150	170	190	250	250	270	500	...	...	...
Statistical discrepancy	...	...	...	...	...	−130	...	...	...	...	...	...
4 Surplus of the nation on current transactions	−1360	−790	−5770	−13170	−7670	−20120	−29210	4970	3150	...	...	...
Payments to the rest of the world and surplus of the nation on current transfers	83360	95680	109050	130670	148080	143410	169790	171320	189590	...	...	...
Receipts from the rest of the world												
1 Exports of goods and services	72100	84180	95920	116140	131680	126080	153460	155170	173610	...	...	...
A Exports of merchandise, f.o.b.	25780	29560	32810	38940	43110	43830	43860	42720	47180	...	...	...
B Other	46320	54620	63110	77200	88570	82250	109600	112450	126430	...	...	...

Cyprus

Ten thousand Cyprus pounds

	1986	1987	1988	1989	1990	1991	1992	1993	1994	1995	1996	1997
2 Factor income from rest of the world	8760	9260	10130	12080	14090	15200	14440	14210	13830	...	...	...
A Compensation of employees	5100	5420	5870	6030	6560	6820	7010	7330	7520	...	...	...
B Property and entrepreneurial income	3660	3840	4260	6050	7530	8380	7430	6880	6310	...	...	...
3 Current transfers from rest of the world	2500	2240	2920	2450	2300	2130	1890	1940	2150	...	...	...
Receipts from the rest of the world on current transactions	83360	95680	109050	130670	148080	143410	169790	171320	189590	...	...	...

1.10 Gross domestic product by kind of activity, in current prices

Ten thousand Cyprus pounds

	1986	1987	1988	1989	1990	1991	1992	1993	1994	1995	1996	1997
1 Agriculture, hunting, forestry and fishing	11730	13230	14320	15640	17530	16560	17760	18380	17780	20000	18900	...
2 Mining and quarrying	750	670	710	620	670	760	840	1030	1200	1100	1100	...
3 Manufacturing	24050	27370	30870	33170	36180	37980	41690	41600	44900	46600	47700	...
4 Electricity, gas and water	3720	3910	4400	4640	5180	5560	6100	6710	7070	8400	8900	...
5 Construction	15650	17000	18920	21550	24230	27220	30680	31250	32260	33400	34800	...
6 Wholesale and retail trade, restaurants and hotels	30390	34640	38630	46870	54650	53280	65200	63800	73200	80500	81200	...
7 Transport, storage and communication	15590	16800	18220	20580	23090	23300	26390	26700	30600	32800	34200	...
8 Finance, insurance, real estate and business services	23060	25470	28540	32330	39100	42500	49700	52100	59400	65700	71800	...
9 Community, social and personal services	7890	9010	10460	12180	13980	16140	19390	22700	25700	28500	32400	...
Total, Industries	132830	148100	165070	187580	214700	223300	257700	264300	292100	317000	331000	...
Producers of government services	20090	21820	24090	26170	29580	33260	37130	42410	46750	50700	53700	...
Other producers	910	980	1140	1330	1610	1870	2130	2450	2680	3300	3700	...
Subtotal	153830	170900	190300	215080	245900	258500	297000	309100	341500	371000	388400	...
less: Imputed bank service charge	4080	4270	4790	5760	7470	8130	9610	8900	10300	11200	11800	...
plus: Import duties	10310	11450	13730	16300	17180	17120	19250	16000	16800	18600	17800	...
plus: Value added tax	...	...	...	...	...	...	3650	11230	16860	19700	19800	...
plus: Other adjustments	...	...	...	...	...	...	...	...	...	−500	...	...
equals: Gross domestic product	160060	178080	199240	225620	255600	267500	310300	327500	364900	397600	414300	...

1.11 Gross domestic product by kind of activity, in constant prices

Ten thousand Cyprus pounds

	1986	1987	1988	1989	1990	1991	1992	1993	1994	1995	1996	1997
At constant prices of: 1985												
1 Agriculture, hunting, forestry and fishing	11040	11420	12670	13090	13190	11500	13800	14200	12300	14500	14300	...
2 Mining and quarrying	710	670	660	520	570	590	650	900	1000	1000	900	...
3 Manufacturing	23260	25130	26850	27550	28660	29000	29500	27700	28700	29000	28300	...
4 Electricity, gas and water	3980	4600	5190	5690	6220	6320	7100	7800	8300	9500	10100	...
5 Construction	14910	15370	15980	17020	17870	18710	19630	18500	18300	18100	18000	...
6 Wholesale and retail trade, restaurants and hotels	28790	31690	35020	39960	44240	43100	49100	47300	52400	55700	55200	...
7 Transport, storage and communication	14360	15130	16580	19010	20400	19600	21400	23200	26100	26700	27500	...
8 Finance, insurance, real estate and business services	22500	24000	25810	27990	32400	33900	37700	38200	41500	44900	47400	...

Cyprus

Ten thousand Cyprus pounds

	1986	1987	1988	1989	1990	1991	1992	1993	1994	1995	1996	1997
At constant prices of: 1985												
9 Community, social and personal services	7320	7900	8730	9820	10440	11300	12500	13700	14600	15500	16900	...
Total, Industries	126870	135910	147490	160650	174000	174000	191400	191400	203100	214800	218500	...
Producers of government services	18980	19890	21280	22000	23550	24680	26060	27600	28600	29700	30800	...
Other producers	870	1030	1080	1210	1350	1500	1600	1800	1800	2100	2300	...
Subtotal	146720	156830	169850	183860	199000	200200	219100	220800	233500	246600	251500	...
less: Imputed bank service charge	3890	3920	4280	4920	6050	6300	7200	6350	7100	7500	7700	...
plus: Import duties	10890	11660	12600	13640	14680	15100	16600	15900	17200	18200	18600	...
plus: Value added tax	...	...	...	...	...	...	...	...	...	...	...	...
plus: Other adjustments	...	...	...	...	...	...	...	...	...	...	...	...
equals: Gross domestic product	153720	164570	178170	192580	207500	208900	228600	230200	243500	257200	262300	...

1.12 Relations among national accounting aggregates

Ten thousand Cyprus pounds

	1986	1987	1988	1989	1990	1991	1992	1993	1994	1995	1996	1997
Gross domestic product	160060	178040	199240	225620	255600	267500	310300	327500	364900	397600	414300	...
plus: Net factor income from the rest of the world	2110	2410	2630	3500	4160	4480	4000	4700	4100	4600	3100	...
Factor income from rest of the world	8760	9260	10130	12040	14080	15200	14450	14500	14500	15200	14600	...
less: Factor income to the rest of the world	6650	6850	7500	8540	9920	10720	10500	9800	10390	10600	11500	...
equals: Gross national product	162170	180490	201870	229120	259700	272000	314300	332200	369000	402200	417400	...
less: Consumption of fixed capital	17030	18950	21170	24060	27300	28600	33000	34900	38700	42200	43800	...
equals: National income	145140	161540	180700	205060	232500	243400	281300	297300	330300	359900	373600	...
plus: Net current transfers from the rest of the world	2350	2110	2770	2280	2100	2000	1640	1670	1650	1300	1500	...
Current transfers from rest of the world	2500	2240	2920	2450	2300	2300	1890	1940	2150	2100	2000	...
less: Current transfers to the rest of the world	150	130	150	170	190	250	250	270	500	800	500	...
equals: National disposable income	147490	163650	183470	207340	234600	245500	282900	299000	331900	361200	375100	...
less: Final consumption	120910	135550	154270	170400	197530	224740	252900	248700	271100	303200	329300	...
Statistical discrepancy	−3470	−2390	−1340	−4490	−2900	−200	−3000	−1200	−2800	−4200	−2200	...
equals: Net saving	23110	25710	27860	32450	34100	20500	27000	49100	58000	53800	43700	...
less: Surplus of the nation on current transactions	−1360	−790	−5770	−13210	−7690	−20120	−29100	5100	3600	−9000	−22300	...
equals: Net capital formation	24470	26500	33630	45660	41800	40600	56100	44000	54300	62700	66000	...

2.1 Government final consumption expenditure by function, in current prices

Ten thousand Cyprus pounds

	1986	1987	1988	1989	1990	1991	1992	1993	1994	1995	1996	1997
1 General public services	3150	3520	3860	4240	4890	5610	6110	7170	7170	...	...	...
2 Defence [a]	1700	6470	7670	8170	12690	13080	19090	9010	9870	...	...	...
3 Public order and safety	3210	3460	3690	3990	4220	4860	5160	5620	5740	...	...	...
4 Education	5240	5750	6440	6990	7730	8730	9640	10910	12380	...	...	...
5 Health	2690	2980	3220	3610	4010	4540	5590	6480	7050	...	...	...
6 Social security and welfare	3250	3570	4140	4420	5570	6300	6880	8290	9770	...	...	...

Cyprus

Ten thousand Cyprus pounds

	1986	1987	1988	1989	1990	1991	1992	1993	1994	1995	1996	1997
7 Housing and community amenities	1000	1010	1250	1270	1540	1710	2160	2290	2640	...	...	...
8 Recreational, cultural and religious affairs	170	190	210	240	280	340	320	450	440	...	...	...
9 Economic services	2570	2620	2770	3130	3360	4140	4110	5020	5740	...	...	...
A Fuel and energy	–	–	–	–	–	–	–	–	–	...	...	...
B Agriculture, hunting, forestry and fishing	890	950	1030	1120	1180	1300	1370	1550	1880	...	...	...
C Mining (except fuels), manufacturing and construction	330	330	340	380	400	420	540	510	600	...	...	...
D Transportation and communication	110	110	80	100	110	110	140	150	180	...	...	...
E Other economic affairs	1240	1230	1320	1530	1670	2310	2060	2810	3080	...	...	...
10 Other functions	10	–	–	10	20	20	10	10	10	...	...	...
Total government final consumption expenditures	22990	29570	33250	36070	44310	49330	59070	55250	60810	...	...	...

a Beginning 1986, item "Defence" includes military expenditure of government.

2.5 Private final consumption expenditure by type and purpose, in current prices

Ten thousand Cyprus pounds

	1986	1987	1988	1989	1990	1991	1992	1993	1994	1995	1996	1997
Final consumption expenditure of resident households												
1 Food, beverages and tobacco	35720	40170	45270	49480	53820	58450	68090	69040	75000	80100	83200	...
A Food	29140	32340	35970	37660	39820	43840	49580	50260	53900	59000	60800	...
B Non-alcoholic beverages	1400	1580	1750	2730	4200	4450	4950	5540	6800	5500	6100	...
C Alcoholic beverages	2730	3130	3820	5240	5420	5300	6900	6770	7300	8300	8900	...
D Tobacco	2450	3120	3730	3860	4390	4860	6660	6470	7000	7400	7400	...
2 Clothing and footwear	13080	13580	14490	17330	20930	23910	26240	24400	23000	26600	27300	...
3 Gross rent, fuel and power	10970	11620	12410	13670	15010	16710	18440	20110	21300	23000	24900	...
A Fuel and power	1800	1830	1910	2230	2660	3170	3520	3760	3630	4200	4500	...
B Other	9170	9790	10500	11440	12350	13540	14920	16300	17720	18800	20300	...
4 Furniture, furnishings and household equipment and operation	13600	15560	17200	19600	21430	23180	28950	28240	31300	33700	35100	...
A Household operation	4050	4500	4830	5150	5800	6880	7560	7780	8900	9800	10500	...
B Other	9550	11060	12370	14450	15630	16300	21390	20400	22400	23900	24600	...
5 Medical care and health expenses	3620	4410	5140	5670	6420	7070	8220	9420	11100	12600	15400	...
6 Transport and communication	19760	20890	26100	30710	33510	37760	42220	38330	42600	49400	46700	...
A Personal transport equipment	6300	6410	9520	11160	11750	14740	15900	15200	12950	17700	14900	...
B Other	13460	14480	16580	19550	21760	23020	26320	23100	29700	31700	31800	...
7 Recreational, entertainment, education and cultural services	8890	9890	11810	14030	16820	17690	21400	22300	25800	28400	31900	...
A Education	1410	1650	1940	2300	2840	3300	4000	4200	5800	6400	7100	...
B Other	7480	8240	9870	11730	13980	14390	17390	18120	20000	22000	24800	...
8 Miscellaneous goods and services	20670	24780	29620	36930	44490	41630	53440	53250	61440	62100	63500	...
A Personal care	1880	2310	2680	3330	3850	4260	5410	6070	6600	7900	8500	...
B Expenditures in restaurants, cafes and hotels	14520	17680	21560	26460	31340	27150	37400	36300	42680	42000	41000	...
C Other	4270	4790	5380	7140	9300	10220	10630	10900	12070	12200	14000	...
Statistical discrepancy [a]	–	–	–	–	–	–	–	...	...	...	...	...

Cyprus

Ten thousand Cyprus pounds

	1986	1987	1988	1989	1990	1991	1992	1993	1994	1995	1996	1997
Total final consumption expenditure in the domestic market by households, of which	126310	140900	162020	187420	212430	226400	267000	265100	291600	315900	327900	...
A Durable goods	16360	17860	22480	26410	29120	32510	36730	31070	34500	40300	38000	...
B Semi-durable goods	22500	24520	27020	32420	37740	42430	48970	46870	47400	52700	54700	...
C Non-durable goods	47710	53290	59930	66390	73490	80000	92000	94070	102100	109900	116100	...
D Services	39740	45230	52590	62210	72080	71460	89300	93100	107600	113000	119100	...
plus: Direct purchases abroad by resident households	4180	4600	5200	5430	6660	7240	8190	8780	9850	12100	13700	...
less: Direct purchases in the domestic market by non-resident households	32650	39240	46450	58070	66600	58770	80820	81880	91590	91600	88400	...
equals: Final consumption expenditure of resident households [b]	96660	104490	119380	132450	151090	172970	191100	190200	206800	233700	250200	...

Final consumption expenditures by private non-profit organisations serving households

	1986	1987	1988	1989	1990	1991	1992	1993	1994	1995	1996	1997
1 Research and science	...	...	...	...	...	...	...	...	...	...	...	...
2 Education	...	...	...	...	...	...	...	...	...	...	...	...
3 Medical and other health services	...	...	...	...	...	...	...	...	...	...	...	...
4 Welfare services	70	70	70	90	100	120	140	170	200	300	300	...
5 Recreational and related cultural services	380	570	640	700	760	870	1050	1230	1390	1300	1700	...
6 Religious organisations	430	450	480	550	660	750	790	870	960	1000	1000	...
7 Professional and labour organisations serving households	360	370	410	490	550	630	720	820	900	1100	1300	...
8 Miscellaneous	20	30	40	50	60	70	80	100	110	200	200	...
equals: Final consumption expenditures by private non-profit organisations serving households	1260	1480	1640	1880	2130	2440	2780	3180	3570	4000	4600	...
Private final consumption expenditure	97920	105980	121020	134330	153220	175410	193900	193400	210300	237700	254800	...

a Item "Statistical discrepancy" represents unclassified estimates. b Beginning 1976, the components do not add up to the total. The difference refers to changes in stocks.

2.6 Private final consumption expenditure by type and purpose, in constant prices

Ten thousand Cyprus pounds

	1986	1987	1988	1989	1990	1991	1992	1993	1994	1995	1996	1997

At constant prices of: 1985

Final consumption expenditure of resident households

	1986	1987	1988	1989	1990	1991	1992	1993	1994	1995	1996	1997
1 Food, beverages and tobacco	34830	38260	41550	43320	45290	45830	49300	48400	49500	52600	52400	...
A Food	28370	30680	32770	32390	32680	33640	35700	35810	36100	39500	38800	...
B Non-alcoholic beverages	1360	1500	1600	2480	3670	3750	3840	4130	4900	3900	4300	...
C Alcoholic beverages	2680	3010	3500	4650	4810	4380	4760	4380	4620	5200	5300	...
D Tobacco	2420	3070	3680	3800	4130	4060	4980	4130	3900	4100	4100	...
2 Clothing and footwear	12640	12750	12810	14450	16340	18470	19000	16400	14800	16600	16000	...
3 Gross rent, fuel and power	11340	11970	12790	13540	14040	14760	15900	16500	16700	17100	17700	...
A Fuel and power	2620	2980	3510	3800	3980	4250	5200	5400	5200	5600	5900	...
B Other	8720	8990	9280	9740	10060	10510	10800	11200	11500	11600	11900	...
4 Furniture, furnishings and household equipment and operation	13300	15010	16180	17890	18980	19910	23200	21310	23000	24100	24900	...
A Household operation	3940	4300	4490	4700	5130	5760	6000	5670	6310	6700	7100	...
B Other	9360	10710	11690	13190	13850	14150	17200	15640	16700	17500	17900	...

Cyprus

Ten thousand Cyprus pounds

	1986	1987	1988	1989	1990	1991	1992	1993	1994	1995	1996	1997
At constant prices of: 1985												
5 Medical care and health expenses	3510	4100	4670	4960	5280	5460	5900	6380	7120	7700	9100	...
6 Transport and communication	19860	20490	24890	29180	31020	33500	36300	31200	33500	38600	36300	...
A Personal transport equipment	6060	5660	8020	9130	10010	12850	13600	9020	10000	13800	11800	...
B Other	13800	14830	16870	20050	21010	20600	22700	22300	23600	24800	24600	...
7 Recreational, entertainment, education and cultural services	8770	9520	10980	12550	14230	14270	15600	15100	16700	17700	19100	...
A Education	1500	1670	1830	2050	2370	2580	2860	2800	3600	3700	3800	...
B Other	7270	7850	9150	10500	11860	11690	12670	12300	13200	14000	15400	...
8 Miscellaneous goods and services	19830	22720	26220	31460	35870	34100	40000	38800	43400	42800	43600	...
A Personal care	1790	2100	2370	2790	3080	3310	3930	4180	4400	5100	5300	...
B Expenditures in restaurants, cafes and hotels	13820	16070	18850	22050	24410	21700	27140	25800	29600	28400	27800	...
C Other	4220	4550	5000	6620	8380	9000	8900	8700	9300	9300	10500	...
Statistical discrepancy	–	–	–	–	–	–	–	–	–	–	–	...
Total final consumption expenditure in the domestic market by households, of which	124090	134830	150090	167350	181050	186300	205100	194100	204700	217100	218900	...
A Durable goods	16070	16940	20620	23730	26320	29600	31900	25700	27500	32200	30700	...
B Semi-durable goods	21750	23010	24240	27730	30680	34000	36800	33100	32200	35100	34900	...
C Non-durable goods	48120	53040	58310	62300	65490	66490	71800	70800	72900	77600	79300	...
D Services	38150	41830	46920	53590	58560	56300	64600	64400	71900	72300	74000	...
plus: Direct purchases abroad by resident households	4140	4430	4840	4870	5720	5910	6280	6420	6880	8200	9100	...
less: Direct purchases in the domestic market by non-resident households	32080	37540	43030	51850	56760	48400	62200	59960	64300	62900	59000	...
equals: Final consumption expenditure of resident households [a]	94990	99970	110550	118200	128780	142300	146700	139200	145000	160500	166900	...

Final consumption expenditures by private non-profit organisations serving households

	1986	1987	1988	1989	1990	1991	1992	1993	1994	1995	1996	1997
1 Research and science	...	...	...	...	...	...	...	...	...	...	...	...
2 Education	...	...	...	...	...	...	...	...	...	...	...	...
3 Medical and other health services	...	...	...	...	...	...	...	...	...	...	...	...
4 Welfare services	60	50	60	60	70	90	90	90	100	100	100	...
5 Recreational and related cultural services	390	640	680	670	660	780	740	840	940	800	900	...
6 Religious organisations	420	420	440	470	600	620	670	690	720	800	800	...
7 Professional and labour organisations serving households	340	350	360	400	440	490	510	560	720	800	900	...
8 Miscellaneous	20	30	30	50	50	60	50	70	80	200	200	...
equals: Final consumption expenditures by private non-profit organisations serving households	1230	1490	1570	1650	1820	2040	2060	2250	2500	2600	2800	...
Private final consumption expenditure	96220	101460	112120	119850	130600	144200	148800	141500	147400	163000	169600	...

a Beginning 1976, the components do not add up to the total. The difference refers to changes in stocks.

Cyprus

2.11 Gross fixed capital formation by kind of activity of owner, ISIC divisions, in current prices

Ten thousand Cyprus pounds

	1986	1987	1988	1989	1990	1991	1992	1993	1994	1995	1996	1997
All producers												
1 Agriculture, hunting, forestry and fishing	4310	4980	3470	3130	2980	2650	2560	2910	3260	3200	3100	...
A Agriculture and hunting	4200	4860	3320	2970	2820	2520	2460	2820	3170	3100	3000	...
B Forestry and logging	40	60	60	60	60	60	60	50	50	100	100	...
C Fishing	70	60	90	100	100	70	40	40	40	–	–	...
2 Mining and quarrying	70	40	50	90	160	140	300	250	300	200	100	...
A Coal mining	...	...	...	...	...	...	...	...	...	...	...	...
B Crude petroleum and natural gas production	...	...	...	...	...	...	...	...	...	...	...	...
C Metal ore mining	20	20	–	–	20	–	–	–	–	–	–	...
D Other mining	50	20	50	90	140	140	300	250	300	200	100	...
3 Manufacturing	3140	3710	4360	5100	5070	5180	5500	5080	5200	6100	6200	...
A Manufacturing of food, beverages and tobacco	1050	1040	1550	1690	1230	1390	1690	1630	1800	2300	1900	...
B Textile, wearing apparel and leather industries	490	820	760	910	940	810	650	410	310	200	200	...
C Manufacture of wood and wood products, including furniture	210	280	440	410	300	370	390	410	300	300	300	...
D Manufacture of paper and paper products, printing and publishing	190	310	320	390	580	630	420	500	400	400	600	...
E Manufacture of chemicals and chemical petroleum, coal, rubber and plastic products	270	390	520	570	730	690	690	710	710	600	1200	...
F Manufacture of non-metallic mineral products, except products of petroleum and coal	300	330	310	370	570	530	880	810	980	800	1000	...
G Basic metal industries	...	...	...	...	...	...	...	...	...	...	...	...
H Manufacture of fabricated metal products, machinery and equipment	580	490	390	620	600	630	630	510	400	1300	900	...
I Other manufacturing industries	50	50	70	140	120	130	150	100	400	300	200	...
4 Electricity, gas and water	900	1400	2850	1600	1920	2800	6900	3210	4300	3000	4000	...
A Electricity, gas and steam	680	1050	2540	1200	1640	2050	6110	2610	3650	2300	2400	...
B Water works and supply	220	350	310	400	280	750	790	600	600	700	1600	...
5 Construction	990	760	1560	1420	1740	1350	1720	2190	1640	1700	1500	...
6 Wholesale and retail trade, restaurants and hotels	6130	7380	8640	10770	11630	12120	14410	10880	9930	11700	10800	...
A Wholesale and retail trade	3020	3680	4560	4900	5310	5250	6520	4540	4950	6900	6300	...
B Restaurants and hotels	3110	3700	4080	5870	6320	6870	7890	6340	4980	4800	4500	...
7 Transport, storage and communication	4680	5050	6020	15880	10180	8430	13430	14110	12640	10200	11400	...
A Transport and storage	2880	3700	4650	14490	8930	7100	11950	11480	8980	8000	8500	...
B Communication	1800	1350	1370	1390	1250	1330	1480	2630	3660	2200	2900	...
8 Finance, insurance, real estate and business services	15580	15770	18060	20270	23710	26580	27960	28810	29600	31900	35200	...
A Financial institutions	220	250	580	710	960	1180	1200	1580	1300	2100	2500	...
B Insurance	90	140	160	140	250	280	320	350	370	500	500	...
C Real estate and business services	15270	15380	17320	19420	22500	25120	26400	26900	27900	29400	32300	...

Cyprus

Ten thousand Cyprus pounds

	1986	1987	1988	1989	1990	1991	1992	1993	1994	1995	1996	1997
Real estate, except dwellings	20	–	20	100	80	60	80	60	60	...	...	...
Dwellings	15020	15130	17070	19040	21870	24600	25900	26400	27300	28600	31500	...
9 Community, social and personal services	770	1020	1310	1690	2210	2480	2640	3380	4100	4000	3100	...
Statistical discrepancy	...	200	...	...	...	...	...	...	...	...	...	...
Total industries	36570	40310	46320	59950	59600	61700	75420	70820	70900	72000	75400	...
Producers of government services	780	1120	2290	1740	2830	2770	3400	2750	3400	4100	4500	...
Private non-profit institutions serving households	450	360	470	450	460	520	770	600	690	900	800	...
Statistical discrepancy	600	–	–	–	–	–	–	–	–	–	–	...
Total	38400	41790	49080	62140	62890	65020	79590	74100	75000	77000	80700	...

2.12 Gross fixed capital formation by kind of activity of owner, ISIC divisions, in constant prices

Ten thousand Cyprus pounds

	1986	1987	1988	1989	1990	1991	1992	1993	1994	1995	1996	1997
At constant prices of: 1985 **All producers**												
1 Agriculture, hunting, forestry and fishing	4190	4690	3120	2680	2460	2050	1900	2000	2170	2100	2000	...
2 Mining and quarrying	60	40	40	80	130	110	230	170	160	100	100	...
3 Manufacturing	3030	3430	3660	4150	3930	3790	3900	3300	3100	3500	3500	...
4 Electricity, gas and water	860	1290	2520	1360	1370	2000	5100	2120	2800	1800	2300	...
5 Construction	930	670	1340	1170	1400	900	1200	1400	1000	1000	900	...
6 Wholesale and retail trade, restaurants and hotels	5980	6970	7610	9050	9310	9300	10700	7600	6700	7500	6800	...
A Wholesale and retail trade	...	...	4000	4100	4200	4000	4800	3100	3200	4200	3800	...
B Restaurants and hotels	...	...	3600	5000	5100	5300	5800	4500	3500	3300	3000	...
7 Transport, storage and communication	4520	4580	5180	13110	8160	6490	10200	9800	8500	6800	7000	...
8 Finance, insurance, real estate and business services	15410	15370	16430	17320	19400	20700	20800	20300	20100	21000	22700	...
9 Community, social and personal services	740	920	1110	1400	1830	1990	2200	2400	2900	2700	2000	...
Total industries	35720	37960	41010	50320	47990	47400	56300	49200	47500	46300	47200	...
Producers of government services	750	1010	2050	1500	2380	2300	2400	2000	2300	2700	2900	...
Private non-profit institutions serving households	440	340	420	370	370	410	560	400	450	600	500	...
Statistical discrepancy	540	–	–	–	–	–	–	–	–	–	–	...
Total	37450	39310	43480	52190	50740	50000	59200	51600	50200	49500	50600	...

2.17 Exports and imports of goods and services, detail

Ten thousand Cyprus pounds

	1986	1987	1988	1989	1990	1991	1992	1993	1994	1995	1996	1997
Exports of goods and services												
1 Exports of merchandise, f.o.b.	25780	29560	32810	38940	43110	43830	43860	42720	47180	55100	64400	63700
2 Transport and communication	8100	9200	9450	10580	11850	12420	14160	14930	16840	17300	18300	18000
3 Insurance service charges	70	70	70	70	70	70	70	80	80	100	100	100
4 Other commodities	12490	13280	14990	17550	19200	21960	25770	27400	28100	31300	32900	36000

Cyprus

Ten thousand Cyprus pounds

	1986	1987	1988	1989	1990	1991	1992	1993	1994	1995	1996	1997
5 Adjustments of merchandise exports to change-of-ownership basis	...	...	...	...	...	...	...	...	...	...	...	...
6 Direct purchases in the domestic market by non-residential households	32650	39240	46450	58070	57500	47800	69600	69800	81300	81300	78300	83900
7 Direct purchases in the domestic market by extraterritorial bodies	...	...	...	...	...	...	...	...	...	...	...	...
Statistical discrepancy	–6990	–7170	...	...	...	...	...	...	...	...	...	...
Total exports of goods and services	72100	84180	95920	116140	131680	126080	153460	154900	173500	185100	193900	201700

Imports of goods and services

	1986	1987	1988	1989	1990	1991	1992	1993	1994	1995	1996	1997
1 Imports of merchandise, c.i.f.	66120	75820	92180	118990	127460	131790	164880	131240	147830	166600	185300	189500
A Imports of merchandise, f.o.b.	59510	68260	82960	107890	114700	118610	148400	118100	133050	149900	166700	170500
B Transport of services on merchandise imports	5950	6800	8300	9990	11500	11860	14800	11800	13300	15000	16700	17100
C Insurance service charges on merchandise imports	660	760	920	1110	1250	1320	1700	1300	1480	1700	1900	1900
2 Adjustments of merchandise imports to change-of-ownership basis	...	...	...	...	...	...	...	...	...	...	...	...
3 Other transport and communication	4050	4730	4820	5370	5920	7260	8010	8750	9640	11500	11200	10400
4 Other insurance service charges	...	...	...	...	...	...	...	...	...	...	...	...
5 Other commodities	2650	3300	3520	4140	4100	4760	5200	5420	5960	7000	7400	7300
6 Direct purchases abroad by government	...	...	...	...	...	...	...	...	...	...	...	...
7 Direct purchases abroad by resident households	4180	4600	5200	5430	8100	8900	10100	10800	12100	14900	17000	19800
Statistical discrepancy	920	1020	...	...	...	...	...	...	...	...	...	...
Total imports of goods and services	77920	89490	106790	135130	145630	152690	188190	156210	175550	200000	220900	226900
Balance of goods and services	–5820	–5310	–10870	–18990	–13950	–26610	–34730	–1300	–2100	–14900	–27000	–25200
Total imports and balance of goods and services	72100	84180	95920	116140	131680	126080	153460	154900	173600	185100	193900	201700

4.1 Derivation of value added by kind of activity, in current prices

Ten thousand Cyprus pounds

	1986 Gross output	1986 Intermediate consumption	1986 Value added	1987 Gross output	1987 Intermediate consumption	1987 Value added	1988 Gross output	1988 Intermediate consumption	1988 Value added	1989 Gross output	1989 Intermediate consumption	1989 Value added
All producers												
1 Agriculture, hunting, forestry and fishing	20390	8660	11730	22160	8930	13230	23990	9670	14320	25670	10030	15640
A Agriculture and hunting	19630	8580	11050	21370	8820	12540	23120	9560	13560	24670	9870	14800
B Forestry and logging	160	40	120	200	70	130	210	70	140	250	80	170
C Fishing	600	40	560	590	40	560	660	40	620	750	80	670
2 Mining and quarrying	1450	700	750	1410	740	670	1430	720	710	1280	660	620
A Coal mining	–	–	–	–	–	–	–	–	–	–	–	–
B Crude petroleum and natural gas production	–	–	–	–	–	–	–	–	–	–	–	–
C Metal ore mining	100	70	30	160	110	50	180	110	70	140	100	40

Cyprus

Ten thousand Cyprus pounds

	1986 Gross output	1986 Intermediate consumption	1986 Value added	1987 Gross output	1987 Intermediate consumption	1987 Value added	1988 Gross output	1988 Intermediate consumption	1988 Value added	1989 Gross output	1989 Intermediate consumption	1989 Value added
D Other mining	1350	630	720	1250	630	620	1250	610	640	1140	560	580
3 Manufacturing	67090	43040	24050	75260	47870	27390	83920	53050	30870	91600	58430	33170
A Manufacture of food, beverages and tobacco	19230	12280	6950	20640	12970	7670	22240	13910	8330	23950	14840	9110
B Textile, wearing apparel and leather industries	14050	8650	5400	17470	10730	6740	20010	12280	7730	20530	12630	7900
C Manufacture of wood and wood products, including furniture	6210	3460	2750	6340	3470	2870	6700	3670	3030	7070	3880	3190
D Manufacture of paper and paper products, printing and publishing	3720	2280	1440	4180	2560	1620	5040	3170	1870	5470	3440	2030
E Manufacture of chemicals and chemical petroleum, coal, rubber and plastic products	9330	7350	1980	10580	8320	2260	11830	9000	2830	12950	10100	2850
F Manufacture of non-metallic mineral products, except products of petroleum and coal	4690	2730	1960	5280	2980	2300	5930	3290	2640	7260	4220	3040
G Basic metal industries	...	–	–	–	–	–	–	–	–	–	–	–
H Manufacture of fabricated metal products, machinery and equipment	8140	5170	2970	8760	5540	3220	10000	6300	3700	11820	7670	4150
I Other manufacturing industries	1720	1120	600	2010	1300	710	2170	1430	740	2550	1650	900
4 Electricity, gas and water	6390	2670	3720	6760	2850	3910	6960	2560	4400	7730	3090	4640
A Electricity, gas and steam	5250	2190	3060	5480	2300	3180	5600	2010	3590	6250	2520	3730
B Water works and supply	1140	480	660	1280	550	730	1360	550	810	1480	570	910
5 Construction	30550	14900	15650	33310	16310	17000	36930	18010	18920	41870	20320	21550
6 Wholesale and retail trade, restaurants and hotels	46140	15750	30390	52320	17680	34640	58760	20130	38630	71380	24510	46870
A Wholesale and retail trade	26890	8250	18640	28960	8790	20170	30580	9650	20930	36100	11280	24820
B Restaurants and hotels	19250	7500	11750	23360	8890	14470	28180	10480	17700	35280	13230	22050
Restaurants	9010	3840	5170	10780	4560	6220	13090	5480	7610	16290	7050	9240
Hotels and other lodging places	10240	3660	6580	12580	4330	8250	15090	5000	10090	18990	6180	12810
7 Transport, storage and communication	23290	7700	15590	25200	8410	16800	26900	8680	18220	29690	9110	20580
A Transport and storage	18650	7250	11400	20120	7920	12200	21240	8190	13050	22900	8560	14340
B Communication	4640	450	4190	5080	490	4600	5660	490	5170	6790	630	6160
8 Finance, insurance, real estate and business services	28140	5080	23060	30630	5220	25410	34380	5840	28540	39220	6890	32330
A Financial institutions	5940	1170	4770	6450	1240	5210	7450	1390	6060	8560	1800	6760
B Insurance	1320	400	920	1690	450	1240	2000	470	1530	1970	520	1450
C Real estate and business services	20880	3510	17370	22490	3530	18960	24930	3980	20950	28690	4570	24120
Real estate, except dwellings	7670	760	6900	8220	810	7420	9040	940	8100	10980	1120	9860
Dwellings	8520	1040	7480	9120	1110	8010	9840	1210	8630	10730	1360	9370
9 Community, social and personal services	10560	2670	7890	11900	2890	9010	13730	3270	10460	16660	4480	12180
A Sanitary and similar services	140	30	110	180	50	130	200	50	150	240	40	200
B Social and related community services [a]	3500	790	2710	4130	990	3140	4940	1170	3770	5940	1490	4450
Educational services	1540	310	1230	1770	370	1400	2100	430	1670	2620	550	2070

Cyprus

Ten thousand Cyprus pounds

	1986			1987			1988			1989		
	Gross output	Intermediate consumption	Value added	Gross output	Intermediate consumption	Value added	Gross output	Intermediate consumption	Value added	Gross output	Intermediate consumption	Value added
Medical, dental, other health and veterinary services	1770	430	1340	2110	550	1560	2550	650	1900	2990	830	2160
C Recreational and cultural services	2540	870	1670	2680	840	1840	3050	930	2120	3800	1320	2480
D Personal and household services	4380	980	3400	4910	1010	3900	5540	1120	4420	6680	1630	5050
Total, Industries	234000	101170	132830	258950	110890	148060	287000	121930	165070	325100	137520	187580
Producers of government services	23710	3620	20090	26390	4570	21820	28910	4820	24090	31560	5390	26170
Other producers	1370	460	910	1570	590	980	1830	690	1140	1920	590	1330
Total	259080	105250	153830	286990	116130	170860	317740	127440	190300	358580	143500	215080
less: Imputed bank service charge	...	−4080	4080	...	−4270	4270	...	−4790	4790	...	−5760	5760
Import duties	10310	...	10310	11450	...	11450	13730	...	13730	16300	...	16300
Value added tax	...	...	...	...	...	...	...	...	...	...	...	...
Other adjustments	...	...	...	...	...	...	...	...	...	...	...	...
Total	269390	109330	160060	298440	120400	178040	331470	132230	199240	374880	149260	225620

	1990			1991			1992			1993		
	Gross output	Intermediate consumption	Value added	Gross output	Intermediate consumption	Value added	Gross output	Intermediate consumption	Value added	Gross output	Intermediate consumption	Value added

All producers

1 Agriculture, hunting, forestry and fishing	27870	10340	17530	27130	10570	16560	29710	11950	17760	30720	12340	18380
A Agriculture and hunting	26610	10130	16480	25940	10370	15570	28440	11730	16710	29390	12110	17280
B Forestry and logging	320	100	220	280	80	200	270	80	190	290	70	220
C Fishing	940	110	830	910	120	790	1000	140	860	1040	160	880
2 Mining and quarrying	1350	680	670	1430	670	760	1580	740	840	1890	860	1030
A Coal mining	−	...	−	−	...	−	−	...	−	−	...	−
B Crude petroleum and natural gas production	−	...	−	−	...	−	−	...	−	−	...	−
C Metal ore mining	60	30	30	40	30	10	40	20	20	40	10	30
D Other mining	1290	650	640	1390	640	750	1540	720	820	1850	850	1000
3 Manufacturing	100080	63900	36180	105410	67430	37980	110890	69200	41690	107300	65600	41600
A Manufacture of food, beverages and tobacco	25970	16130	9840	27180	16960	10220	30890	18680	12210	30950	18330	12600
B Textile, wearing apparel and leather industries	22770	14060	8710	23880	14980	8900	23950	14730	9220	18700	11200	7500
C Manufacture of wood and wood products, including furniture	7810	4380	3430	8370	4650	3720	9160	5140	4020	9340	5210	4130
D Manufacture of paper and paper products, printing and publishing	6910	4440	2470	6470	3930	2540	6990	4060	2930	6910	4030	2880
E Manufacture of chemicals and chemical petroleum, coal, rubber and plastic products	13740	10740	3000	15410	11960	3450	15040	11240	3800	15490	11260	4230
F Manufacture of non-metallic mineral products, except products of petroleum and coal	7880	4570	3310	8150	4750	3400	8800	5130	3670	9500	5300	4200
G Basic metal industries	−	−	−	−	−	−	−	−	−	−	−	−

Cyprus

	1990 Gross output	1990 Intermediate consumption	1990 Value added	1991 Gross output	1991 Intermediate consumption	1991 Value added	1992 Gross output	1992 Intermediate consumption	1992 Value added	1993 Gross output	1993 Intermediate consumption	1993 Value added
H Manufacture of fabricated metal products, machinery and equipment	12290	7740	4550	13110	8190	4920	13180	8230	4950	13500	8300	5200
I Other manufacturing industries	2710	1840	870	2840	2010	830	2880	1990	890	2890	2010	880
4 Electricity, gas and water	8710	3530	5180	9410	3850	5560	10320	4220	6100	10990	4280	6710
A Electricity, gas and steam	7020	2880	4140	7960	3290	4670	8500	3550	4950	9000	3540	5460
B Water works and supply	1690	650	1040	1450	540	890	1820	670	1150	1990	740	1250
5 Construction	46610	22380	24230	51550	24330	27220	56960	26280	30680	57180	25930	31250
6 Wholesale and retail trade, restaurants and hotels	82600	27950	54650	79750	26470	53280	98000	32800	65200	96600	32800	63800
A Wholesale and retail trade	40960	12390	28570	43690	12620	31070	49330	14170	35160	51300	15400	35900
B Restaurants and hotels	41640	15560	26080	36060	13850	22210	48670	18630	30040	45300	17360	27940
Restaurants	19200	8300	10890	17370	7610	9760	23370	10140	13230	22010	9510	12500
Hotels and other lodging places	22440	7250	15200	18690	6240	12450	25300	8490	16810	23290	7850	15440
7 Transport, storage and communication	33660	10570	23090	34000	10700	23300	40210	13820	26390	41200	14500	26700
A Transport and storage	25890	9990	15900	25830	9920	15910	31660	12920	18740	33400	13550	19850
B Communication	7770	580	7190	8170	780	7390	8550	900	7650	7740	890	6850
8 Finance, insurance, real estate and business services	47500	8400	39100	51900	9400	42500	61000	11300	49700	64800	12510	52100
A Financial institutions	11900	2400	9500	13300	2900	10400	15800	3800	12100	15500	4320	10900
B Insurance	2480	700	1780	2650	710	1940	3670	900	2770	4140	1000	3140
C Real estate and business services	33100	5280	27800	36000	5800	30200	41500	6620	34800	45200	7190	38000
Real estate, except dwellings	13100	1280	11800	13600	1230	12400	16400	1490	14900	17400	1520	15900
Dwellings	11710	1480	10230	12760	1650	11110	14030	1810	12220	15300	1970	13330
9 Community, social and personal services	19090	5110	13980	21930	5790	16140	26040	6650	19390	30530	8000	22700
A Sanitary and similar services	250	40	210	400	50	350	590	50	540	700	60	640
B Social and related community services [a]	6840	1800	5040	8000	2060	5940	9390	2260	7130	11180	2590	8590
Educational services	3030	610	2420	3540	720	2820	4150	830	3320	4930	920	4010
Medical, dental, other health and veterinary services	3420	1060	2360	3990	1170	2820	4680	1260	3420	5620	1490	4130
C Recreational and cultural services	4360	1480	2880	4790	1600	3190	5560	1780	3780	6450	2190	4260
D Personal and household services	7640	1790	5850	8740	2080	6660	10500	2560	7940	12200	3160	9040
Total, Industries	367500	152800	214700	382500	159200	223300	434800	177100	257700	441700	176760	264300
Producers of government services	35550	5970	29580	40510	7250	33260	44270	7140	37130	50890	8480	42410
Other producers	2300	740	1610	2750	880	1870	3110	980	2130	3610	1160	2450
Total	405400	159500	245900	425800	167300	258500	482200	185200	297000	496200	187100	309100
less: Imputed bank service charge	...	−7490	7470	...	−8130	8130	...	−9610	9610	...	−8900	8900
Import duties	17180	...	17180	17120	...	17120	19250	...	19200	16160	...	16000
Value added tax	...	...	...	...	...	...	3650	...	3650	11230	...	11230
Other adjustments	...	...	...	...	...	...	...	...	...	...	...	...
Total	422600	167000	255600	442900	175400	267500	505200	194800	310300	523600	196000	327500

Cyprus

	1994 Gross output	1994 Intermediate consumption	1994 Value added	1995 Gross output	1995 Intermediate consumption	1995 Value added	1996 Gross output	1996 Intermediate consumption	1996 Value added	1997 Gross output	1997 Intermediate consumption	1997 Value added
	All producers											
1 Agriculture, hunting, forestry and fishing	30710	12930	17780	34600	14600	20000	34600	15700	18900	...	...	...
A Agriculture and hunting	29240	12670	16570	33200	14300	18900	32900	15200	17700	...	...	...
B Forestry and logging	280	80	200	300	100	200	300	100	200	...	...	...
C Fishing	1190	180	1010	1100	200	900	1400	300	1100	...	...	...
2 Mining and quarrying	2100	910	1200	2000	900	1100	1900	800	1100	...	...	...
A Coal mining	–	...	–	–	–	–	–	–	–	...	...	...
B Crude petroleum and natural gas production	–	...	–	–	–	–	–	–	–	...	...	...
C Metal ore mining	–	–	–	–	–	–	–	–	–	...	...	...
D Other mining	2100	910	1200	2000	900	1100	1900	800	1100	...	...	...
3 Manufacturing	115300	70400	44900	123300	76700	46600	126500	78800	47700	...	...	...
A Manufacture of food, beverages and tobacco	34300	20400	13900	37500	22500	15000	39400	23600	15800	...	...	...
B Textile, wearing apparel and leather industries	17700	10200	7500	18300	11100	7200	16900	10300	6600	...	...	...
C Manufacture of wood and wood products, including furniture	10100	5600	4500	11000	6200	4800	11000	6200	4800	...	...	...
D Manufacture of paper and paper products, printing and publishing	7560	4420	3200	8500	5100	3400	8800	5300	3500	...	...	...
E Manufacture of chemicals and chemical petroleum, coal, rubber and plastic products	17500	12800	4700	17800	12900	4900	19200	14000	5200	...	...	...
F Manufacture of non-metallic mineral products, except products of petroleum and coal	10700	6000	4700	11800	6900	4900	12300	7200	5100	...	...	...
G Basic metal industries	–	–	–	–	–	–	–	–	–	...	...	...
H Manufacture of fabricated metal products, machinery and equipment	14300	8700	5600	15200	9500	5700	15600	9900	5700	...	...	...
I Other manufacturing industries	3100	2200	900	3200	2300	900	3200	2200	1000	...	...	...
4 Electricity, gas and water	11850	4780	7070	13500	5100	8400	14500	5600	8900	...	...	...
A Electricity, gas and steam	9580	3960	5620	10800	4300	6500	11700	4800	6900	...	...	...
B Water works and supply	2270	820	1450	2700	800	1900	2800	800	2000	...	...	...
5 Construction	58510	26250	32260	60400	27000	33400	63000	28200	34800	...	...	...
6 Wholesale and retail trade, restaurants and hotels	110300	37100	73200	121900	41400	80500	123200	42000	81200	...	...	...
A Wholesale and retail trade	58600	17400	41200	66500	19800	46700	69000	20800	48200	...	...	...
B Restaurants and hotels	51660	19620	32040	55500	21700	33800	54200	21200	33000	...	...	...
Restaurants	25150	10610	14540	...	...	...	...	...	...	...	...	...
Hotels and other lodging places	26510	9010	17500	...	...	...	...	...	...	...	...	...
7 Transport, storage and communication	47000	16400	30600	50000	17200	32800	52300	18100	34200	...	...	...
A Transport and storage	38400	15500	22900	40400	16100	24300	40700	16100	24600	...	...	...
B Communication	8700	1000	7650	9600	1200	8400	11600	2000	9600	...	...	...
8 Finance, insurance, real estate and business services	73700	14300	59400	81600	15900	65700	89900	18100	71800	...	...	...
A Financial institutions	18000	4800	13200	20700	5100	15600	23000	6200	16800	...	...	...
B Insurance	4720	1130	3590	4000	1300	2700	5500	1300	4200	...	...	...

Cyprus

	1994 Gross output	1994 Intermediate consumption	1994 Value added	1995 Gross output	1995 Intermediate consumption	1995 Value added	1996 Gross output	1996 Intermediate consumption	1996 Value added	1997 Gross output	1997 Intermediate consumption	1997 Value added
C Real estate and business services	51000	8370	42600	56900	9600	47300	61300	10400	50900	...	...	...
Real estate, except dwellings	20200	1920	18300	23000	2300	20700	24400	2400	22000	...	...	...
Dwellings	16590	2120	14470	17600	2300	15300	18800	2500	16300	...	...	...
9 Community, social and personal services	35600	9370	25700	40300	11800	28500	45700	13300	32400	...	...	...
A Sanitary and similar services	820	70	750	1000	100	1000	1100	100	1000	...	...	...
B Social and related community services [a]	13600	3100	10400	15500	3700	11800	17400	3800	13600	...	...	...
Educational services	5770	1110	4660	...	...	...	...	...	...	...	...	...
Medical, dental, other health and veterinary services	6550	1750	4800	...	...	...	...	...	...	...	...	...
C Recreational and cultural services	6830	2440	4300	6600	2400	4200	8300	3600	4700	...	...	...
D Personal and household services	14360	3760	10200	17100	5600	11500	18900	5800	13100	...	...	...
Total, Industries	485100	193000	292100	527500	210500	317000	551600	220600	331000	...	...	...
Producers of government services	55540	8790	46750	60200	9500	50700	63800	10100	53700	...	...	...
Other producers	4000	1390	2700	4700	1400	3300	5300	1600	3700	...	...	...
Total	544700	203200	341500	592500	221500	371000	620800	232300	388400	...	...	...
less: Imputed bank service charge	...	−10300	10300	...	−11200	11200	...	−11800	11800	...	...	...
Import duties	16800	...	16800	18600	...	18600	17800	...	17800	...	...	...
Value added tax	16900	...	16860	19200	...	19200	19800	...	19800	...	...	...
Other adjustments	...	...	...	...	...	...	...	...	...	...	...	...
Total	578400	213500	364900	630300	232700	397600	658400	244100	414300	...	...	...

a Social and related community services include in addition to educational and health services also the services of commercial and professional associations, welfare institutions and other social and related community services.

Cyprus

4.2 Derivation of value added by kind of activity, in constant prices

Ten thousand Cyprus pounds

	1986 Gross output	1986 Intermediate consumption	1986 Value added	1987 Gross output	1987 Intermediate consumption	1987 Value added	1988 Gross output	1988 Intermediate consumption	1988 Value added	1989 Gross output	1989 Intermediate consumption	1989 Value added
At constant prices of: 1985 **All producers**												
1 Agriculture, hunting, forestry and fishing	20020	8980	11040	20630	9210	11420	22270	9600	12670	23080	9990	13090
A Agriculture and hunting	19330	8890	10440	19960	9110	10850	21580	9490	12090	22330	9840	12490
B Forestry and logging	170	50	120	190	60	130	190	50	140	210	60	150
C Fishing	520	40	480	480	40	440	500	60	440	540	90	450
2 Mining and quarrying	1470	760	710	1480	810	670	1450	790	660	1240	720	520
A Coal mining	–	–	–	–	–	–	–	–	–	–	–	–
B Crude petroleum and natural gas production	–	–	–	–	–	–	–	–	–	–	–	–
C Metal ore mining	110	80	30	150	110	40	160	120	40	130	110	20
D Other mining	1360	680	680	1330	700	630	1290	670	620	1110	610	500
3 Manufacturing	71020	47760	23260	78180	53050	25130	84170	57320	26850	87330	59780	27550
A Manufacture of food, beverages and tobacco	18900	12470	6430	20240	13310	6930	21200	13910	7290	21830	14310	7520
B Textile, wearing apparel and leather industries	14460	8840	5620	17420	10940	6480	19020	12250	6770	18850	12270	6580
C Manufacture of wood and wood products, including furniture	6090	3410	2680	5960	3270	2690	6040	3280	2760	6110	3330	2780
D Manufacture of paper and paper products, printing and publishing	3730	2380	1350	4030	2600	1430	4690	2980	1710	4910	3120	1790
E Manufacture of chemicals and chemical petroleum, coal, rubber and plastic products	13080	11170	1910	14380	12380	2000	16100	13640	2460	16330	13730	2600
F Manufacture of non-metallic mineral products, except products of petroleum and coal	4940	3110	1830	5700	3720	1980	6070	4040	2030	7260	4890	2370
G Basic metal industries	–	–	–	–	–	–	–	–	–	–	–	–
H Manufacture of fabricated metal products, machinery and equipment	8110	5280	2830	8500	5530	2970	8910	5770	3140	9600	6480	3120
I Other manufacturing industries	1710	1100	610	1950	1300	650	2140	1450	690	2440	1650	790
4 Electricity, gas and water	8750	4770	3980	9730	5130	4600	10770	5580	5190	11620	5930	5690
A Electricity, gas and steam	7630	4230	3400	8550	4550	4000	9580	4990	4590	10350	5310	5040
B Water works and supply	1120	540	580	1180	580	600	1190	590	600	1270	620	650
5 Construction	30030	15120	14910	31970	16600	15370	33190	17210	15980	35210	18190	17020
6 Wholesale and retail trade, restaurants and hotels	44660	15870	28790	49010	17320	31690	54180	19160	35020	62420	22460	39960
A Wholesale and retail trade	26360	8300	18060	27750	8630	19120	29470	9240	20230	33340	10410	22930
B Restaurants and hotels	18300	7570	10730	21260	8690	12570	24710	9920	14790	29080	12050	17030
Restaurants	8530	3810	4720	9890	4400	5490	11740	5100	6640	14150	6300	7850
Hotels and other lodging places	9770	3760	6010	11370	4290	7080	12970	4820	8150	14930	5750	9180
7 Transport, storage and communication	22670	8310	14360	24280	9150	15130	25740	9160	16580	28050	9040	19010
A Transport and storage	18100	7850	10250	19270	8660	10610	20170	8670	11500	21360	8520	12840

Cyprus

Ten thousand Cyprus pounds

	1986			1987			1988			1989		
	Gross output	Intermediate consumption	Value added	Gross output	Intermediate consumption	Value added	Gross output	Intermediate consumption	Value added	Gross output	Intermediate consumption	Value added
At constant prices of: 1985											
B Communication	4570	460	4110	5010	490	4520	5570	490	5080	6690	520	6170
8 Finance, insurance, real estate and business services	27390	4890	22500	28900	4900	24000	31070	5260	25810	33910	5920	27990
A Financial institutions	5880	1090	4790	6200	1120	5080	6930	1200	5730	7670	1510	6160
B Insurance	1300	360	940	1630	410	1220	1870	420	1450	1770	440	1330
C Real estate and business services	20210	3440	16770	21070	3370	17700	22270	3640	18630	24470	3970	20500
Real estate, except dwellings	7470	710	6760	7720	740	6980	8160	810	7350	9460	930	8530
Dwellings	8090	1010	7080	8390	1030	7360	8480	1060	7420	8750	1110	7640
9 Community, social and personal services	10100	2780	7320	10850	2950	7900	12020	3290	8730	14100	4280	9820
A Sanitary and similar services	140	20	120	160	50	110	160	40	120	180	40	140
B Social and related community services	3330	800	2530	3700	970	2730	4100	1110	2990	4770	1370	3400
Educational services	1470	310	1160	1570	360	1210	1720	410	1310	2080	500	1580
Medical, dental, other health and veterinary services	1720	430	1290	1910	540	1370	2180	620	1560	2430	770	1660
C Recreational and cultural services	2530	960	1570	2640	910	1730	3020	1020	2000	3650	1310	2340
D Personal and household services	4100	1000	3100	4350	1020	3330	4740	1120	3620	5500	1560	3940
Total, Industries	236110	109240	126870	255030	119120	135910	274860	127370	147490	296960	136310	160650
Producers of government services	22810	3830	18980	24530	4640	19890	25880	4600	21280	26860	4860	22000
Other producers	1340	470	870	1620	590	1030	1750	670	1080	1730	520	1210
Total	260260	113540	146720	281180	124350	156830	302490	132640	169850	325550	141690	183860
less: Imputed bank service charge	...	−3890	3890	...	−3920	3920	...	−4280	4280	...	−4920	4920
Import duties	10890	...	10890	11660	...	11660	12600	...	12600	13640	...	13640
Value added tax	...	...	...	...	...	...	...	...	...	...	...	...
Other adjustments	...	...	...	...	...	...	...	...	...	...	...	...
Total	271150	117430	153720	292840	128270	164570	315090	136920	178170	339190	146610	192580

	1990			1991			1992			1993		
	Gross output	Intermediate consumption	Value added	Gross output	Intermediate consumption	Value added	Gross output	Intermediate consumption	Value added	Gross output	Intermediate consumption	Value added
At constant prices of: 1985											
All producers											
1 Agriculture, hunting, forestry and fishing	23220	10030	13190	21200	9840	11500	24400	10730	13800	25010	10910	14200
A Agriculture and hunting	22280	9840	12440	20400	9670	10800	23500	10550	13000	24080	10690	13390
B Forestry and logging	220	60	160	190	60	130	180	50	130	190	60	130
C Fishing	720	130	590	630	110	520	700	130	570	740	160	580
2 Mining and quarrying	1260	690	570	1240	600	590	1330	600	650	1560	780	780
A Coal mining	−	−	−	−	−	−	−	−	−	−	−	−
B Crude petroleum and natural gas production	−	−	−	−	−	−	−	−	−	−	−	−
C Metal ore mining	50	30	20	40	30	10	30	20	10	30	10	20
D Other mining	1210	660	550	1200	620	580	1300	600	700	1530	770	760

Cyprus

	1990 Gross output	1990 Intermediate consumption	1990 Value added	1991 Gross output	1991 Intermediate consumption	1991 Value added	1992 Gross output	1992 Intermediate consumption	1992 Value added	1993 Gross output	1993 Intermediate consumption	1993 Value added
At constant prices of: 1985												
3 Manufacturing	91630	62970	28660	94500	65620	29000	96400	66900	29500	92200	64490	27700
A Manufacture of food, beverages and tobacco	22830	14920	7910	23030	15110	7920	25200	16630	8600	24200	16140	8100
B Textile, wearing apparel and leather industries	20410	13500	6910	20500	13610	6900	19760	13360	6400	16010	10760	5250
C Manufacture of wood and wood products, including furniture	6330	3460	2870	6470	3600	2870	6560	3680	2880	6530	3820	2710
D Manufacture of paper and paper products, printing and publishing	5750	3900	1850	5270	3400	1870	5640	3690	1950	5470	3590	1880
E Manufacture of chemicals and chemical petroleum, coal, rubber and plastic products	16370	13740	2630	18690	16000	2690	18340	15600	2740	19410	16590	2820
F Manufacture of non-metallic mineral products, except products of petroleum and coal	7610	5090	2520	7700	5070	2630	7870	5200	2670	7870	5090	2780
G Basic metal industries	–	...	–	–	...	–	–	...	–	–	...	–
H Manufacture of fabricated metal products, machinery and equipment	9720	6610	3110	10200	6970	3230	10250	6870	3380	9880	6590	3290
I Other manufacturing industries	2610	1750	860	2730	1860	870	2860	1930	930	2810	1910	900
4 Electricity, gas and water	12640	6420	6220	12800	6400	6400	14800	7700	7100	15800	8090	7800
A Electricity, gas and steam	11270	5740	5530	11700	5920	5780	13600	6960	6600	14500	7340	7200
B Water works and supply	1370	680	690	1150	610	540	1290	660	630	1420	750	670
5 Construction	37090	19220	17870	38800	20190	18710	40580	20950	19630	38400	19770	18500
6 Wholesale and retail trade, restaurants and hotels	68670	24430	44240	64700	21660	43100	74600	25600	49100	72000	24800	47300
A Wholesale and retail trade	35890	10880	25010	36400	10400	26000	39800	11330	28500	40700	11700	28900
B Restaurants and hotels	32780	13550	19230	28360	11260	17100	34940	14320	20620	31410	13030	18380
Restaurants	15910	7090	8820	13400	6040	7360	15900	7590	8310	14400	6940	7460
Hotels and other lodging places	16870	6460	10410	14960	5220	9740	19040	6730	12310	17010	6090	10920
7 Transport, storage and communication	30400	10000	20400	29200	9630	19600	33600	12100	21400	35600	12370	23200
A Transport and storage	22810	9440	13370	21450	8950	12500	25350	11440	13910	27900	11650	16200
B Communication	7590	560	7030	7920	680	7240	8330	740	7590	7840	720	7000
8 Finance, insurance, real estate and business services	39200	6800	32400	40900	7090	33900	45700	8000	37700	46600	8400	38200
A Financial institutions	10200	2000	8200	10900	2300	8600	12400	2700	9700	11700	2900	8800
B Insurance	2130	570	1560	2170	550	1620	2850	650	2200	3110	710	2400
C Real estate and business services	26900	4280	22600	28000	4400	23600	30500	4800	25700	31800	5020	26800
Real estate, except dwellings	10700	1020	9700	10800	950	9800	12200	1080	11100	12400	880	11500
Dwellings	9030	1130	7900	9310	1170	8140	9580	1180	8400	9900	1190	8710
9 Community, social and personal services	15050	4610	10440	16300	5000	11300	18200	5500	12500	20440	6500	13800
A Sanitary and similar services	150	30	120	240	40	200	330	40	290	360	50	310
B Social and related community services	5120	1580	3540	5630	1710	3500	6000	1810	4100	6920	2040	4880
Educational services	2250	530	1720	2460	590	1870	2680	650	2030	2950	720	2230

Cyprus

	1990			1991			1992			1993		
	Gross output	Intermediate consumption	Value added	Gross output	Intermediate consumption	Value added	Gross output	Intermediate consumption	Value added	Gross output	Intermediate consumption	Value added

At constant prices of: 1985

Medical, dental, other health and veterinary services	2580	940	1640	2840	990	1850	2990	1030	1960	3590	1170	2420
C Recreational and cultural services	3930	1370	2560	4300	1450	2800	4780	1610	3100	5220	1780	3440
D Personal and household services	5850	1630	4220	6350	1800	4550	7160	2150	5010	7940	2560	5300
Statistical discrepancy	...	...	...	−240	−730	...	−210	−180	...	190	...	...
Total, Industries	319200	145200	174000	319400	145300	174200	349400	157900	191600	347700	156300	191500
Producers of government services	28720	5170	23550	30610	6000	24600	31490	5500	26060	33700	6060	27600
Other producers	2000	650	1300	2200	720	1500	2300	770	1600	2700	890	1800
Total	349900	151000	198900	352200	152100	200200	383200	164300	219200	384200	163300	220800
less: Imputed bank service charge	...	−6050	6050	...	−6300	6300	...	−7200	7200	...	−6500	6500
Import duties	14680	...	14680	15100	...	15100	16600	...	16600	15900	...	15900
Value added tax	...	...	...	...	...	...	...	...	...	...	...	...
Other adjustments	...	...	...	...	...	...	...	...	...	...	...	...
Total	364600	157100	207500	367400	158400	208900	399700	171500	228600	400200	169900	230200

	1994			1995			1996			1997		
	Gross output	Intermediate consumption	Value added	Gross output	Intermediate consumption	Value added	Gross output	Intermediate consumption	Value added	Gross output	Intermediate consumption	Value added

At constant prices of: 1985

All producers

1 Agriculture, hunting, forestry and fishing	23100	10800	12300	26600	12200	14400	26500	12400	14100	...	...	...
A Agriculture and hunting	22100	10600	11500	25700	12000	13700	25500	12100	13400	...	...	...
B Forestry and logging	170	50	120	200	100	100	200	100	100	...	...	...
C Fishing	770	190	580	700	100	600	800	200	600	...	...	...
2 Mining and quarrying	1800	840	1000	1700	800	900	1600	700	900	...	...	...
A Coal mining	−	−	−	−	−	−	−	−	−	...	...	...
B Crude petroleum and natural gas production	−	−	−	−	−	−	−	−	−	...	...	...
C Metal ore mining	−	−	−	−	−	−	−	−	−	...	...	...
D Other mining	1800	840	1000	1700	800	900	1600	700	900	...	...	...
3 Manufacturing	96500	67700	28700	99100	70200	29000	97000	68700	28400	...	...	...
A Manufacture of food, beverages and tobacco	25790	17080	8710	26800	18100	8700	26000	17600	8500	...	...	...
B Textile, wearing apparel and leather industries	14800	9600	5150	14700	9700	5000	13300	8800	4500	...	...	...
C Manufacture of wood and wood products, including furniture	6800	3940	2810	7100	4200	2900	6800	4100	2700	...	...	...
D Manufacture of paper and paper products, printing and publishing	5940	3900	2040	6200	4100	2100	6300	4200	2100	...	...	...
E Manufacture of chemicals and chemical petroleum, coal, rubber and plastic products	21800	18800	2800	21400	18400	3100	21400	18300	3100	...	...	...
F Manufacture of non-metallic mineral products, except products of petroleum and coal	8500	5700	2800	9400	6500	2900	9300	6400	2900	...	...	...

Cyprus

	1994 Gross output	1994 Intermediate consumption	1994 Value added	1995 Gross output	1995 Intermediate consumption	1995 Value added	1996 Gross output	1996 Intermediate consumption	1996 Value added	1997 Gross output	1997 Intermediate consumption	1997 Value added
At constant prices of: 1985												
G Basic metal industries	–	...	–	–	–	–	–	–	–	...	...	...
H Manufacture of fabricated metal products, machinery and equipment	10000	6710	3350	10400	6900	3500	10800	7100	3700	...	...	...
I Other manufacturing industries	2900	2000	910	3000	2200	900	3000	2100	900	...	...	...
4 Electricity, gas and water	16700	8410	8500	18200	8500	9600	19300	9200	10100	...	...	...
A Electricity, gas and steam	15500	7700	7800	16600	7600	8900	17600	8200	9300	...	...	...
B Water works and supply	1500	780	720	1700	800	800	1800	900	900	...	...	...
5 Construction	38090	19900	18100	37800	19800	18000	37900	19900	18000	...	...	...
6 Wholesale and retail trade, restaurants and hotels	79000	26500	52400	85100	29300	55800	84300	29100	55200	...	...	...
A Wholesale and retail trade	44100	12700	31400	48700	14000	34700	49300	14200	35100	...	...	...
B Restaurants and hotels	34990	14000	21000	36500	15300	21200	35100	14800	20200	...	...	...
Restaurants	16170	7420	8750	18600	8700	9900	18400	8800	9600	...	...	...
Hotels and other lodging places	18820	6640	12180	17900	6600	11300	16700	6100	10600	...	...	...
7 Transport, storage and communication	40100	13900	26200	41000	14300	26700	42300	14800	27500	...	...	...
A Transport and storage	31500	13200	18300	31600	13300	18300	30900	12900	17900	...	...	...
B Communication	8700	790	7800	9500	1000	8500	11500	1800	9700	...	...	...
8 Finance, insurance, real estate and business services	50900	9300	41500	54700	9900	44800	58400	10900	47500	...	...	...
A Financial institutions	13100	3000	10100	14700	3100	11600	15900	3600	12300	...	...	...
B Insurance	3410	770	2640	2800	800	2000	3800	900	2900	...	...	...
C Real estate and business services	34400	5620	28800	37200	6000	31200	38700	6400	32300	...	...	...
Real estate, except dwellings	13800	1200	12600	15100	1300	13800	15500	1400	14100	...	...	...
Dwellings	10250	1210	9040	10600	1300	9300	10900	1300	9600	...	...	...
9 Community, social and personal services	22400	7700	14700	24400	8800	15600	26600	9600	17000	...	...	...
A Sanitary and similar services	500	50	350	600	100	500	600	100	500	...	...	...
B Social and related community services	7600	2270	5300	8200	2600	5600	8800	2900	6000	...	...	...
Educational services	3190	820	2370	...	...	...	...	...	...	...	...	...
Medical, dental, other health and veterinary services	3790	1270	2520	...	...	...	...	...	...	...	...	...
C Recreational and cultural services	5270	2000	3300	5000	2000	3100	5900	2300	3500	...	...	...
D Personal and household services	9000	3200	5800	10500	4000	6500	11300	4200	7100	...	...	...
Statistical discrepancy	...	350	...	...	200	...	200	200	...	...	...	...
Total, Industries	368600	165400	203200	388700	174000	214800	394100	175500	218600	...	...	...
Producers of government services	34770	6130	28640	36200	6600	29600	37400	6600	30800	...	...	...
Other producers	2700	1000	1670	3000	1000	2000	3300	1200	2100	...	...	...
Total	406100	172600	233500	427900	181600	246400	434700	183300	251500	...	...	...
less: Imputed bank service charge	...	−7100	7100	...	−7500	7500	...	−7700	7700	...	...	...
Import duties	17200	...	17200	18200	...	18200	18600	...	18600	...	...	...
Value added tax	...	...	...	...	...	...	...	...	...	...	...	...
Other adjustments	...	...	...	...	...	...	...	...	...	...	...	...
Total	423300	179700	243500	446000	188700	257200	453200	191000	262300	...	...	...

Czech Republic

Source

Reply to the United Nations National Accounts Questionnaire from the Czech Statistical Office.

General note

The estimates shown in the following tables have been prepared in accordance with the System of National Accounts (SNA) so far as the existing data would permit.

1.1 Expenditure on the gross domestic product, in current prices

Million koruna

	1986	1987	1988	1989	1990	1991	1992	1993	1994	1995	1996	1997
1 Government final consumption expenditure [a]	...	106800	108364	112897	112610	134740	163087	221566	255540	281494	323600	334000
2 Private final consumption expenditure	...	233339	242886	251264	284824	318900	442776	496306	571547	667557	771900	847200
A Households	...	233339	242886	251264	284824	318900	439235	490477	564044	657993	760300	834100
B Private non-profit institutions serving households	...	...	...	...	...	...	3541	5829	7503	9564	11600	13100
3 Gross capital formation	143068	145026	140905	140510	162528	214177	226333	274143	346066	459392	544500	558900
A Increase in stocks	12739	19908	4694	4079	13235	48921	−14951	−11700	6146	16940	39000	52000
B Gross fixed capital formation	130329	125118	136211	136431	149293	165256	241284	285843	339920	442452	505500	506900
Residential buildings	...	11924	15704	14233	15401	16978	...	...	...	...	...	...
Non-residential buildings	...						...	...	...	...	...	...
Other construction and land improvement, etc.	...	57652	59224	65819	78173	84921	...	...	...	...	...	...
Other	...	55542	61283	56379	55719	63357	...	...	...	...	...	...
4 Exports of goods and services	...	9908	21293	19894	7360	412276	465236	523592	607964	755819	818800	949400
5 less: Imports of goods and services	...					363500	450587	511537	632454	815537	926200	1040000
equals: Gross domestic product	483000	495073[b]	513448[b]	524565[b]	567322[b]	716593[b]	846845[b]	1004070[b]	1148663[b]	1348725[b]	1532600	1649500

a The consumption expenditure of the private non-profit institutions serving households is included in item "Government final consumption expenditure".   b All figures in 1992-1995 based on quarterly national accounts. 1987-1991 derived from MPS data.

1.2 Expenditure on the gross domestic product, in constant prices

Million koruna

	1986	1987	1988	1989	1990	1991	1992	1993	1994	1995	1996	1997
		At constant prices of: 1984							1994			
1 Government final consumption expenditure [a]	...	100900	98000	102500	103400	94100	91200	89900	89000 / 255500	250300	260600	255000
2 Private final consumption expenditure	...	225100	234000	237400	253200	181100	206600	210900	225900 / 571500	611500	654800	666200
A Households	...	225100	234000	237400	253200	181100	206600	210900	225900 / 564000	603100	645500	656100
B Private non-profit institutions serving households	...	...	...	...	...	...	...	...	7500	8400	9300	10100
3 Gross capital formation	...	147900	140600	143600	148900	126700	103100	92200	124700 / 346100	426100	481500	470700

464

Czech Republic

Million koruna

	1986	1987	1988	1989	1990	1991	1992	1993	1994	1995	1996	1997
At constant prices of:	1984								1994			
A Increase in stocks	...	20100	4600	3800	12100	14100	−19500	−21000	−8100 6200	14900	34700	45600
B Gross fixed capital formation	...	127800	136000	139800	136800	112600	122600	113200	132800 339900	411200	446800	425100
4 Exports of goods and services	...	4100	15200	26400	−1800	239000	255200	277200	274900 608000	705600	743900	819900
5 less: Imports of goods and services	...	...	...	...	...	208800	251600	267900	303300 632500	771900	871400	930000
equals: Gross domestic product	475300	478000	487800	509900	503700	432100	404500	402300	411200 1148600	1221600	1269400	1281800

a The consumption expenditure of the private non-profit institutions serving households is included in item "Government final consumption expenditure".

1.3 Cost components of the gross domestic product

Million koruna

	1986	1987	1988	1989	1990	1991	1992	1993	1994	1995	1996	1997
1 Indirect taxes, net	...	...	...	...	...	...	80970	118173	131186	152534	...	...
A Indirect taxes	...	...	...	...	...	...	124458	151574	172835	195097	...	...
B less: Subsidies	...	...	...	...	...	...	43488	33401	41649	42563	...	...
2 Consumption of fixed capital	...	...	...	...	...	...	179752	216972	261581	262902	...	...
3 Compensation of employees paid by resident producers to	...	...	...	...	...	...	377640	462377	549748	654149	...	...
A Resident households	...	...	...	...	...	...	377599	460414	546004	648332	...	...
B Rest of the world	...	...	...	...	...	...	41	1963	3744	5817	...	...
4 Operating surplus	...	...	...	...	...	...	208483	206548	206148	279140	...	...
A Corporate and quasi-corporate enterprises	...	...	...	...	...	...	112154	91784	88765	143590	...	...
B Private unincorporated enterprises	...	...	...	...	...	...	98783	113413	117381	136259	...	...
C General government	...	...	...	...	...	...	−2454	1351	2	−709	...	...
equals: Gross domestic product	...	...	...	...	...	...	846845	1004070	1148663	1348725	1532600	1649500

1.4 General government current receipts and disbursements

Million koruna

	1986	1987	1988	1989	1990	1991	1992	1993	1994	1995	1996	1997
Receipts												
1 Operating surplus	...	...	...	...	...	...	−2454	1351	2	−709	...	...
2 Property and entrepreneurial income	...	...	...	...	...	...	4605	11904	11093	15291	...	...
3 Taxes, fees and contributions	...	...	...	...	...	...	381748	423860	482088	556643	...	...
A Indirect taxes	...	...	...	...	...	...	124458	151574	172835	195097	...	...
B Direct taxes	...	...	...	...	...	...	150702	117147	121353	139380	...	...
C Social security contributions	...	...	...	...	...	...	106588	155139	187900	222166	...	...
D Compulsory fees, fines and penalties	...	...	...	...	...	...	...	...	...	...	...	...
4 Other current transfers	...	...	...	...	...	...	47057	41211	47253	4736	...	...
Total current receipts of general government	...	...	...	...	...	...	430956	478326	540436	575961	...	...
Disbursements												
1 Government final consumption expenditure	...	...	...	...	...	...	163087	221566	255540	281494	...	...
A Compensation of employees	...	...	...	...	...	...	60978	75292	93136	107136	...	...

Czech Republic

Million koruna

	1986	1987	1988	1989	1990	1991	1992	1993	1994	1995	1996	1997
B Consumption of fixed capital	...	...	...	...	...	...	28641	36115	43801	42624	...	...
C Purchases of goods and services, net	...	...	...	...	...	...	...	...	...	...	...	...
D less: Own-account fixed capital formation	...	...	...	...	...	...	...	...	...	...	...	...
E Indirect taxes paid, net	...	...	...	...	...	...	...	...	...	...	...	...
2 Property income	...	...	...	...	...	...	12329	18160	16653	16341	...	...
A Interest	...	...	...	...	...	...	12329	18158	16653	16341	...	...
B Net land rent and royalties	...	...	...	...	...	...	...	2	...	...	...	...
3 Subsidies	...	...	...	...	...	...	43488	33401	41649	42563	...	...
4 Other current transfers	...	...	...	...	...	...	163346	165894	194842	172739	...	...
A Social security benefits	...	...	...	...	...	...	108700	120698	138296	158091	...	...
B Social assistance grants	...	...	...	...	...	...	...	...	...	...	...	...
C Other	...	...	...	...	...	...	54646	45196	56546	14648	...	...
5 Net saving	...	...	...	...	...	...	48706	39305	31752	62824	...	...
Total current disbursements and net saving of general government	...	...	...	...	...	...	430956	478326	540436	575961	...	...

1.5 Current income and outlay of corporate and quasi-corporate enterprises, summary

Million koruna

	1986	1987	1988	1989	1990	1991	1992	1993	1994	1995	1996	1997
Receipts												
1 Operating surplus	...	...	...	...	...	...	112154	91784	88765	143590	...	...
2 Property and entrepreneurial income received	...	...	...	...	...	...	150257	184133	202468	233797	...	...
3 Current transfers	...	...	...	...	...	...	29107	37465	35787	61858	...	...
Total current receipts	...	...	...	...	...	...	291518	313382	327020	439245	...	...
Disbursements												
1 Property and entrepreneurial income	...	...	...	...	...	...	169557	207780	230224	295155	...	...
2 Direct taxes and other current payments to general government	...	...	...	...	...	...	94037	73167	62564	66375	...	...
3 Other current transfers	...	...	...	...	...	...	26278	45259	43319	63473	...	...
4 Net saving	...	...	...	...	...	...	1646	−12824	−9087	14242	...	...
Total current disbursements and net saving	...	...	...	...	...	...	291518	313382	327020	439245	...	...

1.6 Current income and outlay of households and non-profit institutions

Million koruna

	1986	1987	1988	1989	1990	1991	1992	1993	1994	1995	1996	1997
Receipts												
1 Compensation of employees	...	...	...	...	...	...	382316	465438	552618	653778	...	...
A From resident producers	...	...	...	...	...	...	377599	460414	546004	648332	...	...
B From rest of the world	...	...	...	...	...	...	4717	5024	6614	5446	...	...
2 Operating surplus of private unincorporated enterprises	...	...	...	...	...	...	98783	113413	117381	136259	...	...
3 Property and entrepreneurial income	...	...	...	...	...	...	32431	37804	52985	80570	...	...
4 Current transfers	...	...	...	...	...	...	129525	160797	188396	228994	...	...
A Social security benefits	...	...	...	...	...	...	92285	105737	125374	148628	...	...

Czech Republic

Million koruna

	1986	1987	1988	1989	1990	1991	1992	1993	1994	1995	1996	1997
B Social assistance grants	...	...	...	...	...	...	16895	16127	14301	11329	...	...
C Other	...	...	...	...	...	...	20345	38933	48721	69037	...	...
Total current receipts	...	...	...	...	...	...	643055	777452	911380	1099601	...	...

Disbursements

	1986	1987	1988	1989	1990	1991	1992	1993	1994	1995	1996	1997
1 Private final consumption expenditure	...	...	...	...	...	...	442776	496306	571547	667557	...	...
2 Property income	...	...	...	...	...	...	4466	15222	23382	24932	...	...
3 Direct taxes and other current transfers n.e.c. to general government	...	...	...	...	...	...	163733	200255	247823	301435	...	...
A Social security contributions	...	...	...	...	...	...	106520	155974	189596	228573	...	...
B Direct taxes	...	...	...	...	...	...	56665	43816	57540	72017	...	...
C Fees, fines and penalties	...	...	...	...	...	...	548	465	687	845	...	...
4 Other current transfers	...	...	...	...	...	...	14823	23949	28681	37899	...	...
5 Net saving	...	...	...	...	...	...	17257	41720	39947	67778	...	...
Total current disbursements and net saving	...	...	...	...	...	...	643055	777452	911380	1099601	...	...

1.7 External transactions on current account, summary

Million koruna

	1986	1987	1988	1989	1990	1991	1992	1993	1994	1995	1996	1997
Payments to the rest of the world												
1 Imports of goods and services	...	...	...	...	...	...	450587	511537	632454	815537	926200	1040000
2 Factor income to rest of the world	...	...	...	...	...	...	10491	21210	25456	39274	...	...
A Compensation of employees	...	...	...	...	...	...	41	1963	3744	5817	...	...
B Property and entrepreneurial income	...	...	...	...	...	...	10450	19247	21712	33457	...	...
3 Current transfers to the rest of the world	...	...	...	...	...	...	7545	7156	6761	3179	...	...
4 Surplus of the nation on current transactions	...	...	...	...	...	...	21028	11030	–21873	–51646	...	...
Payments to the rest of the world and surplus of the nation on current transfers	...	...	...	...	...	...	489651	550933	642798	806344	...	...
Receipts from the rest of the world												
1 Exports of goods and services	...	...	...	...	...	...	465236	523592	607964	755819	818800	949400
2 Factor income from rest of the world	...	...	...	...	...	...	16108	16950	24613	32133	...	...
A Compensation of employees	...	...	...	...	...	...	4717	5024	6614	5446	...	...
B Property and entrepreneurial income	...	...	...	...	...	...	11391	11926	17999	26687	...	...
3 Current transfers from rest of the world	...	...	...	...	...	...	8307	10391	10221	18392	...	...
Receipts from the rest of the world on current transactions	...	...	...	...	...	...	489651	550933	642798	806344	...	...

Czech Republic

1.8 Capital transactions of the nation, summary

Million koruna

	1986	1987	1988	1989	1990	1991	1992	1993	1994	1995	1996	1997
Finance of gross capital formation												
Gross saving	...	...	...	...	...	...	247361	285173	324193	407746	...	...
1 Consumption of fixed capital	...	...	...	...	...	...	179752	216972	261581	262902	...	...
A General government	...	...	...	...	...	...	28641	36115	43801	42624	...	...
B Corporate and quasi-corporate enterprises	...	...	...	...	...	...	129347	154916	188407	180237	...	...
C Other	...	...	...	...	...	...	21764	25941	29373	40041	...	...
2 Net saving	...	...	...	...	...	...	67609	68201	62612	144844	...	...
A General government	...	...	...	...	...	...	48706	39305	31752	62824	...	...
B Corporate and quasi-corporate enterprises	...	...	...	...	...	...	1646	−12824	−9087	14242	...	...
C Other	...	...	...	...	...	...	17257	41720	39947	67778	...	...
less: Surplus of the nation on current transactions	...	...	...	...	...	...	21028	11030	−21873	−51646	...	...
Finance of gross capital formation	...	...	...	...	...	...	226333	274143	346066	459392	...	...
Gross capital formation												
Increase in stocks	...	...	...	...	...	...	−14951	−11700	6146	16940	39000	52000
Gross fixed capital formation	...	...	...	...	...	...	241284	285843	339920	442452	505500	506900
1 General government	...	...	...	...	...	...	31974	34144	63699	76855	...	...
2 Corporate and quasi-corporate enterprises	...	...	...	...	...	...	188647	215135	250166	336458	...	...
3 Other	...	...	...	...	...	...	20663	36564	26055	29139	...	...
Gross capital formation	...	...	...	...	...	...	226333	274143	346066	459392	544500	558900

1.9 Gross domestic product by institutional sectors of origin

Million koruna

	1986	1987	1988	1989	1990	1991	1992	1993	1994	1995	1996	1997
Domestic factor incomes originating												
1 General government	...	...	...	...	...	...	58524	76643	93138	106427	...	...
2 Corporate and quasi-corporate enterprises	...	...	...	...	...	...	404899	422435	481640	612666	...	...
A Non-financial	...	...	...	...	...	...	404245	422006	490321	628371	...	...
B Financial	...	...	...	...	...	...	654	429	−8681	−15705	...	...
3 Households and private unincorporated enterprises	...	...	...	...	...	...	121327	167830	177661	210431	...	...
4 Non-profit institutions serving households	...	...	...	...	...	...	1373	2017	3457	3765	...	...
subtotal: Domestic factor incomes	...	...	...	...	...	...	586123	668925	755896	933289	...	...
Indirect taxes, net	...	...	...	...	...	...	80970	118173	131186	152534	...	...
A Indirect taxes	...	...	...	...	...	...	124458	151574	172835	195097	...	...
B less: Subsidies	...	...	...	...	...	...	43488	33401	41649	42563	...	...
Consumption of fixed capital	...	...	...	...	...	...	179752	216972	261581	262902	...	...
Gross domestic product	...	...	...	...	...	...	846845	1004070	1148663	1348725	1532600	1649500

Czech Republic

1.10 Gross domestic product by kind of activity, in current prices

Million koruna	1986	1987	1988	1989	1990	1991	1992	1993	1994	1995	1996	1997
1 Agriculture, hunting, forestry and fishing	...	33304	32866	46476	41436	39902	38259	49434	47196	57666	...	...
2 Mining and quarrying	...	...	...	...	...	...	30900	11145	17045	12542	...	...
3 Manufacturing	...	207386	214765	219462	222679	314916	256570	245217	272676	333514	...	...
4 Electricity, gas and water	...	...	...	...	...	...	48393	52803	58195	77553	...	...
5 Construction	...	39074	41442	41166	46224	44981	44870	68013	82269	101586	...	...
6 Wholesale and retail trade, restaurants and hotels	...	60269	63589	60008	74878	75180	98530	137936	175891	188124	...	...
7 Transport, storage and communication	...	26789	26839	25325	24508	29144	57362	72897	77535	92791	...	...
8 Finance, insurance, real estate and business services	...	25599	24251	30080	30242	68709	119590	191852	203254	220433	...	...
9 Community, social and personal services	...	18069	18327	20089	25406	35343	38113	63762	75761	87270	...	...
Total, Industries	...	410490	422079	442606	465373	608175	732587	893059	1009822	1171479	...	...
Producers of government services	...	42835	44581	46565	47318	53573	46809	40038	48231	56592	...	...
Other producers	...	2557	2672	2885	2354	1987	18860	18461	25368	31946	...	...
Subtotal	...	455882	469332	492056	515045	663735	798256	951558	1083421	1260017	...	...
less: Imputed bank service charge	...	13794	12498	14985	15721	45279	48970	61952	68669	66856	...	...
plus: Import duties [a]	...	3218	3785	5585	4886	17109	22443	19557	27304	30524	...	...
plus: Value added tax [b]	...	51719	55528	44427	64613	81028	—	81021	89461	99862	...	...
plus: Other adjustments	...	−1952[c]	−2699[c]	−2518[c]	−1501[c]	...	75116[d]	13886[d]	17146[d]	25178[d]	...	...
equals: Gross domestic product	483000	495073[e]	513448[e]	524565[e]	567322[e]	716593[e]	846845[e]	1004070[e]	1148663[e]	1348725[e]	1532600	1649500

a Item "Import duties" refers to the differences between retail and import prices. Beginning 1991, it includes customs and import tax.
b Item "value added tax" refers to turnover tax till 1992. Beginning 1992 equals net taxes less subidies.
c Subsidies in 1987-1991
d Taxes on domestic products less subsidies on domestic products (excluding VAT).
e All figures in 1992-1995 based on quarterly national accounts. 1987-1991 derived from MPS data.

1.12 Relations among national accounting aggregates

Million koruna	1986	1987	1988	1989	1990	1991	1992	1993	1994	1995	1996	1997
Gross domestic product	...	...	...	...	...	...	846845	1004070[a]	1148663[a]	1348725	1532600	1649500
plus: Net factor income from the rest of the world	...	...	...	...	...	...	5617	−4260	−843	−7141	...	...
Factor income from rest of the world	...	...	...	...	...	...	16108	16950	24613	32133	...	...
less: Factor income to the rest of the world	...	...	...	...	...	...	10491	21210	25456	39274	...	...
equals: Gross national product	...	...	...	...	...	...	852462	999810	1147820	1341584	...	...
less: Consumption of fixed capital	...	...	...	...	...	...	179752	216972	261581	262902	...	...
equals: National income	...	...	...	...	...	...	672710	782838	886239	1078682	...	...
plus: Net current transfers from the rest of the world	...	...	...	...	...	...	762	3235	3460	15213	...	...
Current transfers from rest of the world	...	...	...	...	...	...	8307	10391	10221	18392	...	...
less: Current transfers to the rest of the world	...	...	...	...	...	...	7545	7156	6761	3179	...	...
equals: National disposable income	...	...	...	...	...	...	673472	786073	889699	1093895	...	...
less: Final consumption	...	...	351250	364161	397434	453640	605863	717872	827087	949051	1095500	1181200
equals: Net saving	...	...	...	...	...	...	67609	68201	62612	144844	...	...
less: Surplus of the nation on current transactions	...	...	...	...	...	...	21028	11030	−21873	−51646	...	...
equals: Net capital formation	...	...	...	...	...	...	46581	57171	84485	196490	...	...

a In 1993, 1994 excluding FISIM

Denmark

General note

The preparation of national accounts statistics in Denmark is undertaken by the Danmarks Statistik, Copenhagen. The official estimates are published three times annually in *Statistiske Efterretninger (Nationalregnskab. Offentlige Finanser, Betalingsbalance)* and in more detail, in the annual publication *Nationalregnskabsstatistik*. The following presentation of sources and methods is mainly based on a report prepared by the Statistical Office of the European Communities in 1976 entitled *Base statistics needed for the ESA accounts and tables: present situation and prospects for improvements* and on *Input-output tabeller for Danmark 1966* published by Danmarks Statistik in 1973. The estimates are generally in accordance with the classifications and definitions recommended in the United Nations System of National Accounts (1968 SNA). The following tables have been prepared from successive replies to the United Nations National Accounts Questionnaire. When the scope and coverage of the estimates differ for conceptual or statistical reasons from the definitions and classifications recommended in SNA, a footnote is indicated to the relevant tables.

Gross domestic product

Gross domestic product is estimated mainly through the production approach.

Expenditures on the gross domestic product

The expenditure approach is used to estimate government final consumption expenditure, increase in stocks and exports and imports of goods and services. The commodity-flow approach is used for private final consumption expenditure and gross fixed capital formation. The estimates of government consumption expenditure are mainly based on the accounts of the central and local government and on social security funds. The estimates of private consumption expenditure, using the commodity-flow method, have a time-lag of two years. Therefore, short-term estimates are made, using turnover statistics for the retail trade. This is supplemented by family budget surveys which are conducted every five years. Changes in stocks are estimated on the basis of inventory statistics. For gross fixed capital formation, information is classified by product and by ownership branch. The valuation is made net of deductible value added tax. Estimates of investments in buildings are based partly on data available on construction starts, work under construction and work completed and partly on information from accounting data. Estimates of investments in machinery and equipment are based on production and foreign trade statistics adjusted to include gross margins, duties etc. Exports and imports of goods and services are estimated mainly form the balance-of-payments and foreign trade statistics. Special surveys are available for shipping and for payments to and receipts from the rest of the world by Danish enterprises. For the constant price estimates, price indexes arrived at for the supply of goods and services, broken down into 4,000 groups, are used for all components of Gross domestic product by expenditure type except that of exports for which the indexes for domestic output are used.

Cost structure of the gross domestic product

Data on the compensation of employees are taken directly from the annual surveys on current transactions. For consumption of fixed capital, only rough estimates are made. Total indirect taxes and subsidies are obtained from government accounts. Operating surplus is estimated as a residual.

Gross domestic product by kind of activity

The table of gross domestic product by kind of economic activity is prepared in factor values. The production approach is used to estimate the value added of almost all industries. The income approach is used to estimate the value added of producers of government services, parts of business services and other private services. The gross output of the trade sector is primarily estimated by means of the commodity-flow approach. The estimates of agricultural production are based on product-by-product data in terms of volume and prices which are obtained from the annual agricultural statistics. The estimates of gross output are supplemented by survey data on total costs and cost structure. For forestry and fishing, the main sources used are the annual agricultural reports and the annual reports of the Ministry of Fisheries. For manufacturing, estimates are based on an annual survey covering all enterprises employing 20 or more persons and on a quarterly survey on the turnover of 4,000 products. Censuses taken in 1966 and 1975 provide a product-by-product breakdown of intermediate inputs. The value added tax returns of enterprises are used to make estimates for small enterprises and services not covered by direct surveys.

For electricity, gas and water, the estimates are based on annual electricity statistics, accounting statistics of the municipalities and on local government reports, respectively. For private construction, various sources are used such as an annual accounting survey and investment statistics. Construction in the public sector is estimated from government accounts. The estimates of gross trade and transport margins are based on data obtained from a sample survey of trade enterprises adjusted for under coverage, mark-ups and other non-available margins. Another method used is to estimate the size of the gross margins of each commodity and its share in the distributive channel. These estimates are partly based on information from the Price Direc-

Denmark

torate. For restaurants and hotels, value added tax statistics are used. For the transport sector, the information is taken from the accounts of the enterprises concerned except road transport which makes use of the value added tax returns. For the financial sector, the balance sheets and complete accounts of the companies' current transactions are used. A benchmark survey of housing rents is carried out every five years. For intervening years, changes in the average rent and total stock of residential buildings are used. Rents of rented dwellings are used for the imputation of rents of owner-occupied dwellings.

Value added tax statistics, population census and accounting data of advertising services are used for the business services sector. The main sources for the producers of government services are the account of the central and local government and social security funds. For other services, value added tax statistics are used except for professions like doctors and dentists, for which social security data are used. For the constant price estimates, double deflation is used. The data are deflated by means of a price index related to each of the 4,000 groups of goods and services. The price indexes are applied to domestic output as well as imports.

1.1 Expenditure on the gross domestic product, in current prices

Million Danish kroner

	1986	1987	1988	1989	1990	1991	1992	1993	1994	1995	1996	1997
1 Government final consumption expenditure	159359	176214	188487	196546	202504	211201	219099	230298	238547	243905	255268	...
2 Private final consumption expenditure	366747	377878	388806	403894	415032	430202	447075	458714	498335	519122	543971	...
A Households	363338	374135	384819	399687	409998	424927	441463	451959	491029	511208	535352	...
B Private non-profit institutions serving households	3409	3743	3987	4207	5034	5275	5612	6756	7306	7913	8620	...
3 Gross capital formation	143386	132958	130738	140838	138440	136026	131603	124416	135635	164656	170171	...
A Increase in stocks	5016	–5075	–1488	1885	–917	–667	–2220	–6320	147	11620	1274	...
B Gross fixed capital formation	138370	138033	132226	138953	139357	136693	133823	130736	135488	153036	168897	...
Residential buildings	33429	33846	32288	30960	28026	25308	25776	24725	27873	31345	...	...
Non-residential buildings	23078	27211	26973	24630	24657	23268	23939	21388	22034	23209	...	...
Other construction and land improvement, etc.	17247	17235	18421	21139	22582	20277	22577	21641	18150	20596	...	...
Other	64617	59742	54543	62224	64092	67840	61531	63992	66657	76807	...	...
4 Exports of goods and services	213559	220084	238915	264909	283575	306006	309395	301843	327013	339037	350806	...
5 less: Imports of goods and services	216555	207226	214892	238936	240442	255567	251142	240966	273818	297640	306289	...
Statistical discrepancy	...	...	...	...	...	...	1	1	–2	–1	1	...
equals: Gross domestic product	666496	699908	732054	767251	799109	827868	856031	874306	925710	969079	1013928	...

1.2 Expenditure on the gross domestic product, in constant prices

Million Danish kroner

	1986	1987	1988	1989	1990	1991	1992	1993	1994	1995	1996	1997
At constant prices of: 1980												
1 Government final consumption expenditure	108205	110873	111920	111234	110752	110588	111062	114405	116670	117283	120050	...
2 Private final consumption expenditure	243583	239929	237481	236539	236644	239429	243897	248722	265820	271542	278579	...
A Households	241352	237660	235163	234187	233967	236691	241029	245455	262273	267822	274673	...
B Private non-profit institutions serving households	2231	2269	2318	2352	2677	2738	2868	3267	3547	3720	3906	...
3 Gross capital formation	94682	85932	82205	86198	82318	77803	72408	67811	73220	86777	89254	...
A Increase in stocks	2506	–2771	–603	2559	139	292	–1840	–2686	1397	7223	3747	...
B Gross fixed capital formation	92176	88703	82808	83639	82179	77511	74248	70497	71823	79554	85507	...
Residential buildings	21475	20780	18817	17149	14804	13079	12601	11692	13055	14279	...	...
Non-residential buildings	15226	17284	16369	14226	13743	12559	12058	10618	10860	11342	...	...
Other construction and land improvement, etc.	11982	11178	11337	12333	12715	11007	12093	11252	9270	10223	...	...

Denmark

Million Danish kroner

	1986	1987	1988	1989	1990	1991	1992	1993	1994	1995	1996	1997
At constant prices of: 1980												
Other	43493	39461	36285	39931	40918	40866	37495	37405	38208	43214	...	...
4 Exports of goods and services	154453	162295	174922	182193	194833	209792	212634	210992	228205	235786	241167	...
5 less: Imports of goods and services	159457	156265	158606	165718	167669	174594	175934	170714	192675	207284	211553	...
Statistical discrepancy	...	...	...	...	...	...	...	1	1	1	2	...
equals: Gross domestic product	441466	442764	447922	450446	456878	463018	464067	471217	491241	504105	517499	...

1.3 Cost components of the gross domestic product

Million Danish kroner

	1986	1987	1988	1989	1990	1991	1992	1993	1994	1995	1996	1997
1 Indirect taxes, net	110820	113962	114213	113248	113167	115735	113586	117659	132897	139485	151262	...
A Indirect taxes	130880	135973	139553	140203	141521	144461	148456	153181	168387	175261	188180	...
B less: Subsidies	20060	22011	25340	26955	28354	28726	34870	35522	35490	35776	36918	...
2 Consumption of fixed capital	94568	103154	109911	117169	122672	129079	135290	139200	141800	143731	143816	...
3 Compensation of employees paid by resident producers to	356230	388891	407106	422094	439262	452933	466982	469873	488303	515160	538113	...
A Resident households	355526	388244	406362	421263	438342	452000	466018	468838	487036	513990	536864	...
B Rest of the world	704	647	744	831	921	932	964	1035	1267	1170	1249	...
4 Operating surplus	104879	93901	100826	114740	124008	130121	140173	147574	162710	170703	180737	...
equals: Gross domestic product	666497	699908	732056	767251	799109	827868	856031	874306	925710	969079	1013928	...

1.4 General government current receipts and disbursements

Million Danish kroner

	1986	1987	1988	1989	1990	1991	1992	1993	1994	1995	1996	1997
Receipts												
1 Operating surplus	–	–	–	–	–	–	–	–	–	–	...	...
2 Property and entrepreneurial income	32654	31369	34127	37849	38390	37902	45754	47437	43538	38346	...	...
3 Taxes, fees and contributions	337759	359647	377223	387762	388490	403559	420020	439412	480109	497188	...	...
A Indirect taxes	130879	135974	139552	140201	141523	144461	148456	153184	168387	175261	...	...
B Direct taxes	195466	208943	226248	235426	233268	245202	256682	270170	294610	304709	...	...
C Social security contributions	10619	13798	10228	10843	12325	12571	13599	14545	15650	15966	...	...
D Compulsory fees, fines and penalties	795	932	1195	1292	1374	1325	1283	1513	1462	1252	...	...
4 Other current transfers	18189	20721	21640	20885	22083	23441	23883	27711	27284	27191	...	...
Total current receipts of general government	388602	411737	432990	446496	448963	464902	489657	514560	550931	562725	...	...
Disbursements												
1 Government final consumption expenditure	159359	176214	188487	196546	202504	211201	219099	230298	238547	243904	...	...
A Compensation of employees	114398	125773	136347	142219	146755	152411	157954	162880	168752	173776	...	...
B Consumption of fixed capital	5412	5997	6420	7025	7542	7912	8558	9036	9650	10055	...	...
C Purchases of goods and services, net	38578	43243	44891	46464	47391	50064	51670	56473	58202	58349	...	...
D less: Own-account fixed capital formation	...	...	...	...	...	...	...	...	...	...	...	...
E Indirect taxes paid, net	971	1201	829	838	816	814	917	1909	1943	1724	...	...
2 Property income	58692	57746	58305	57464	58505	61078	58489	67812	66306	64776	...	...
A Interest	58692	57746	58305	57464	58505	61078	58489	67812	66306	64776	...	...

Denmark

Million Danish kroner

	1986	1987	1988	1989	1990	1991	1992	1993	1994	1995	1996	1997
B Net land rent and royalties	...	...	...	...	...	...	...	...	...	...	...	...
3 Subsidies	20060	22011	25340	26955	28354	28726	34874	35522	35490	35776	...	...
4 Other current transfers	117881	128971	144268	158595	164644	178361	188533	201108	228635	233384	...	...
A Social security benefits	103307	113716	126956	140360	147423	157661	167768	178451	204116	208520	...	...
B Social assistance grants											...	...
C Other	14574	15255	17312	18235	17221	20701	20765	22657	24520	24864		
5 Net saving	32610	26795	16590	6936	−5044	−14464	−11338	−20180	−18048	−15114	...	...
Total current disbursements and net saving of general government	388602	411737	432990	446496	448963	464902	489657	514560	550930	562726	...	...

1.5 Current income and outlay of corporate and quasi-corporate enterprises, summary

Million Danish kroner

	1986	1987	1988	1989	1990	1991	1992	1993	1994	1995	1996	1997
Receipts												
1 Operating surplus	29773	21506	25929	29917	35093	37013	44340	49716	63922	...	...	...
2 Property and entrepreneurial income received	27621	33071	29736	23568	23669	18768	11017	15200	14022	...	...	...
3 Current transfers	26978	29720	32767	31953	35957	37221	39032	43370	47777	...	...	...
Statistical discrepancy	...	...	...	−	−	−	−	−	...	...	...	...
Total current receipts	84372	84297	88432	85438	94719	93002	94389	108286	125721	...	...	...
Disbursements												
1 Property and entrepreneurial income	...	...	...	...	...	...	...	...	...	...	...	...
2 Direct taxes and other current payments to general government	27220	24982	26404	26849	20895	21548	22890	29874	28494	...	...	...
3 Other current transfers	25327	27611	30066	29480	29232	31168	31413	37448	38774	...	...	...
Statistical discrepancy	3651	3914	4351	4197	5247	4785	5068	5426	9127	...	...	...
4 Net saving	28174	27790	27611	24912	39345	35501	35018	35538	49326	...	...	...
Total current disbursements and net saving	84372	84297	88432	85438	94719	93002	94389	108286	125721	...	...	...

1.6 Current income and outlay of households and non-profit institutions

Million Danish kroner

	1986	1987	1988	1989	1990	1991	1992	1993	1994	1995	1996	1997
Receipts												
1 Compensation of employees	356440	389186	407367	422355	439556	454786	469035	471949	486747	...	...	...
2 Operating surplus of private unincorporated enterprises	75105	72394	74896	84823	88916	93108	95831	98519	105196	...	...	...
3 Property and entrepreneurial income	−29200	−34886	−34170	−36101	−38140	−31537	−32708	−26055	−24895	...	...	...
4 Current transfers	117316	128882	143831	157358	166441	178234	190355	205892	231145	...	...	...
A Social security benefits	105215	115522	128887	141245	148847	159142	169699	181912	207107	...	...	...
B Social assistance grants	...	...	...	...	...	...	...	...	...	...	...	...
C Other	12101	13360	14944	16113	17594	19092	20656	23980	24038	...	...	...
Statistical discrepancy	3651	3914	4351	4197	5247	4785	5068	5426	9127	...	...	...
Total current receipts	523312	559490	596275	632632	662020	699376	727581	755731	807320	...	...	...
Disbursements												
1 Private final consumption expenditure	366747	377878	388806	403894	415032	430201	447075	458807	497775	...	...	...

Denmark

Million Danish kroner

	1986	1987	1988	1989	1990	1991	1992	1993	1994	1995	1996	1997
2 Property income	...	...	...	...	...	...	...	...	...	...	...	...
3 Direct taxes and other current transfers n.e.c. to general government	188384	208001	221920	231592	239255	250791	263483	272890	301851	...	...	...
A Social security contributions	20137	24039	22076	23015	26882	27137	29691	32594	37590	...	...	...
B Direct taxes	168247	183962	199844	208577	212373	223654	233792	240296	264261	...	...	...
C Fees, fines and penalties	...	...	...	...	...	...	...	...	...	...	...	...
4 Other current transfers [a]	17310	19108	21019	20833	22187	23385	24612	28762	28598	...	...	...
5 Net saving	–49129	–45497	–35470	–23687	–14454	–5001	–7589	–4728	–20904	...	...	...
Total current disbursements and net saving	523312	559490	596275	632632	662020	699376	727581	755731	807320	...	...	...

[a] Item "Other current transfers" includes item "Fees, fines and penalties".

1.7 External transactions on current account, summary

Million Danish kroner

	1986	1987	1988	1989	1990	1991	1992	1993	1994	1995	1996	1997
Payments to the rest of the world												
1 Imports of goods and services	216555	207226	214892	238936	240442	255567	251142	238970	272290	290751	...	...
A Imports of merchandise, c.i.f.	184388	173651	175786	195705	196348	208642	204675	190858	218803	236445	...	...
B Other	32167	33575	39106	43231	44094	46925	46467	48112	53487	54306	...	...
2 Factor income to rest of the world	46612	48430	55479	68885	75124	96349	131880	181236	176602	187459	...	...
A Compensation of employees	704	647	744	831	921	932	964	1036	1266	1170	...	...
B Property and entrepreneurial income	45908	47783	54735	68054	74203	95417	130916	180200	175336	186289	...	...
3 Current transfers to the rest of the world	15029	14807	16225	15579	15309	17151	15490	18892	21072	19663	...	...
A Indirect taxes to supranational organizations	2260	2201	2383	2639	2475	7609	7199	6810	6996	7415	...	...
B Other current transfers	12769	12606	13842	12940	12834	9542	8291	12082	14076	12248	...	...
4 Surplus of the nation on current transactions	–36215	–20603	–9429	–11342	4077	9088	19785	26403	16542	6053	...	...
Payments to the rest of the world and surplus of the nation on current transfers	241981	249860	277167	312058	334952	378155	418297	465501	486506	503926	...	...
Receipts from the rest of the world												
1 Exports of goods and services	213559	220084	238915	264909	283574	306006	309395	300169	327820	330448	...	...
A Exports of merchandise, f.o.b.	171723	175132	186333	208544	221412	235165	243988	235798	260947	269076	...	...
B Other	41836	44952	52582	56365	62162	70841	65407	64371	66873	61372	...	...
2 Factor income from rest of the world	19119	20863	27746	38015	40831	62257	99509	153327	147833	162835	...	...
A Compensation of employees	914	942	1005	1092	1214	2786	3018	3122	2925	3077	...	...
B Property and entrepreneurial income	18205	19921	26741	36923	39617	59471	96491	150205	144908	159758	...	...
3 Current transfers from rest of the world	9303	8913	10505	9135	10546	9892	9392	12006	10853	10643	...	...
A Subsidies from supranational organisations	8424	9837	9362	8828	9415	9714	9382	11363	10504	10244	...	...
B Other current transfers	879	–924	1143	307	1131	178	10	643	349	399	...	...
Receipts from the rest of the world on current transactions	241981	249860	277166	312059	334951	378155	418296	465502	486506	503926	...	...

Denmark

1.8 Capital transactions of the nation, summary

Million Danish kroner

	1986	1987	1988	1989	1990	1991	1992	1993	1994	1995	1996	1997
Finance of gross capital formation												
Gross saving	107171	112356	121309	129496	142517	145114	151387	150500	149830	172398	178475	...
1 Consumption of fixed capital	94568	103154	109911	117169	122672	129079	135290	139200	141800	143731	143816	...
A General government	5412	5997	6420	7025	7542	7912	8558	9036	9650	10055	...	...
B Corporate and quasi-corporate enterprises	57262	62121	67291	71714	75517	80535	84023	86220	87408	...	...	...
C Other	31894	35036	36200	38430	39613	40632	42710	43944	44765	...	...	...
2 Net saving	12603	9202	11398	12327	19845	16035	16097	11300	8030	28667	34659	...
A General government	32610	26795	16590	6936	–5044	–14464	–11338	–20178	–18047	–15116	...	...
B Corporate and quasi-corporate enterprises	28174	27790	27611	24912	39345	35501	35018	35538	49326	...	...	...
C Other	–49129	–45497	–35470	–23687	–14454	–5001	–7589	–4728	–20904	...	...	...
less: Surplus of the nation on current transactions	–36215	–20603	–9429	–11342	4077	9088	19785	26083	14198	7743	8304	...
Finance of gross capital formation	143386	132959	130738	140838	138440	136026	131602	124417	135632	164655	170171	...
Gross capital formation												
Increase in stocks	5016	–5075	–1488	1885	–917	–667	–2220	–6320	147	11620	1274	...
Gross fixed capital formation	138370	138033	132226	138953	139357	136693	133823	130736	135488	153036	168897	...
1 General government	13869	15581	16836	16618	15570	12966	19639	18947	19913	19657	...	...
2 Corporate and quasi-corporate enterprises	80178	80990	81509	85325	89219	90033	80560	79943	84277	...	...	...
3 Other	44323	41462	33881	37010	34568	33694	33624	32381	33841	...	...	...
Gross capital formation	143386	132958	130738	140838	138440	136026	131603	124416	135635	164656	170171	...

1.9 Gross domestic product by institutional sectors of origin

Million Danish kroner

	1986	1987	1988	1989	1990	1991	1992	1993	1994	1995	1996	1997
Domestic factor incomes originating												
subtotal: Domestic factor incomes	461109	482792	507932	536834	563270	583054	607155	617447	651013	685863	718850	...
Indirect taxes, net	110820	113962	114213	113248	113167	115735	113586	117659	132897	139485	151262	...
A Indirect taxes	130880	135973	139553	140203	141521	144461	148456	153181	168387	175261	188180	...
B less: Subsidies	20060	22011	25340	26955	28354	28726	34870	35522	35490	35776	36918	...
Consumption of fixed capital	94568	103154	109911	117169	122672	129079	135290	139200	141800	143731	143816	...
Gross domestic product	666497	699908	732056	767251	799109	827868	856031	874306	925710	969079	1013928	...

1.10 Gross domestic product by kind of activity, in current prices

Million Danish kroner

	1986	1987	1988	1989	1990	1991	1992	1993	1994	1995	1996	1997
1 Agriculture, hunting, forestry and fishing	30005	27339	27593	31669	30301	29614	29239	27785	30311	34999	...	...
2 Mining and quarrying	5328	5389	4460	6259	7299	6889	7440	7106	7670	7225	...	...
3 Manufacturing	111703	113870	119875	123572	129919	134238	140426	144121	155655	165985	...	...
4 Electricity, gas and water	8509	9228	9935	11726	12511	14752	15395	15425	16049	16172	...	...
5 Construction	37686	43331	42939	40728	40601	38331	42382	41289	41416	45493	...	...

Denmark

Million Danish kroner

	1986	1987	1988	1989	1990	1991	1992	1993	1994	1995	1996	1997
6 Wholesale and retail trade, restaurants and hotels	88351	87952	86348	91443	95467	99765	105264	105489	110494	111092	...	...
7 Transport, storage and communication	44770	48016	53232	58283	62373	65423	69411	71010	73886	75533	...	...
8 Finance, insurance, real estate and business services	100890	107232	114889	127777	135951	139211	136018	143609	152742	158240	...	...
9 Community, social and personal services	27773	30341	32897	33692	35352	37082	40268	41241	44432	46528	...	...
Total, Industries	455014	472697	492166	525149	549775	565306	585844	597076	632654	661264	...	...
Producers of government services	119810	131770	142766	149244	154296	160323	166511	171916	178402	183932	...	...
Other producers	3702	4009	4125	4350	4994	5300	5565	6421	7005	7227	...	...
Subtotal [a]	578526	608476	639058	678744	709065	730930	757919	775414	818061	852423	...	...
less: Imputed bank service charge	22850	22530	21215	24741	23123	18797	15474	18679	25326	24185	...	...
plus: Import duties	...	...	...	...	...	...	...	...	...	...	...	...
plus: Value added tax	...	...	...	...	...	...	...	...	...	...	...	...
plus: Other adjustments [b]	110820	113963	114211	113246	113169	115736	113586	117659	132897	139485	...	...
equals: Gross domestic product	666496	699909	732053	767248	799111	827868	856032	874393	925632	967723	...	...
memorandum item: Mineral fuels and power	13011	13569	13366	17238	18993	20256	21288	20745	21638	21535	...	...

a Gross domestic product in factor values.
b Item "Other adjustments" relates to indirect taxes less subsidies and import duties.

1.11 Gross domestic product by kind of activity, in constant prices

Million Danish kroner

	1986	1987	1988	1989	1990	1991	1992	1993	1994	1995	1996	1997
At constant prices of: 1980												
1 Agriculture, hunting, forestry and fishing	22368	21311	23447	25274	25486	25082	22694	24806	25978	27633	...	...
2 Mining and quarrying	7841	10075	10242	12402	12671	15293	16531	18095	19642	20048	...	...
3 Manufacturing	72921	69933	71036	71869	71130	71058	71669	72463	73841	75878	...	...
4 Electricity, gas and water	6528	6355	6544	6397	6903	8638	7764	7912	7973	8605	...	...
5 Construction	25486	26573	24749	23045	22054	20447	20456	19421	19247	20544	...	...
6 Wholesale and retail trade, restaurants and hotels	56545	57106	57273	55377	57446	59115	58830	59510	60641	61047	...	...
7 Transport, storage and communication	26816	30349	32489	34130	37578	38177	40690	42111	44963	47570	...	...
8 Finance, insurance, real estate and business services	64293	65132	65967	68775	69702	67664	63406	64985	67523	67119	...	...
9 Community, social and personal services	17696	17248	17535	17108	17072	17060	17799	17732	18826	19553	...	...
Total, Industries	300493	304083	309282	314377	320041	322535	319838	327035	338632	347995	...	...
Producers of government services	82950	83398	84769	84689	84599	83907	84641	85397	87532	88821	...	...
Other producers	2401	2403	2429	2451	2734	2826	2935	3275	3562	3597	...	...
Subtotal [a]	385844	389884	396480	401518	407375	409267	407414	415706	429726	440414	...	...
less: Imputed bank service charge	15291	14359	12854	14233	12874	10014	8100	10922	12595	11540	...	...
plus: Import duties	...	...	...	...	...	...	...	...	...	...	...	...
plus: Value added tax	...	...	...	...	...	...	...	...	...	...	...	...
plus: Other adjustments [b]	70916	67240	64295	63160	62379	63764	64753	66402	74023	75297	...	...
equals: Gross domestic product	441469	442765	447921	450444	456879	463018	464067	471187	491154	504170	...	...
memorandum item: Mineral fuels and power	14319	16445	16878	19055	19928	24085	24469	25394	27407	28916	...	...

a Gross domestic product in factor values.
b Item "Other adjustments" relates to indirect taxes less subsidies and import duties.

Denmark

1.12 Relations among national accounting aggregates

Million Danish kroner

	1986	1987	1988	1989	1990	1991	1992	1993	1994	1995	1996	1997
Gross domestic product	666496	699908	732055	767251	799109	827868	856031	874306	925710	969079	1013928	...
plus: Net factor income from the rest of the world	−27493	−27567	−27733	−30870	−34293	−34092	−32371	−27909	−28769	−24624	−24981	...
Factor income from rest of the world	19119	20863	27746	38015	40831	62257	99509	153327	147833	162835	225162	...
less: Factor income to the rest of the world	46612	48430	55479	68885	75124	96349	131880	181236	176602	187459	250142	...
equals: Gross national product	639004	672342	704322	736381	764816	793776	823659	846397	896940	944455	988947	...
less: Consumption of fixed capital	94568	103154	109911	117169	122672	129079	135290	139200	141800	143731	143816	...
equals: National income	544436	569188	594411	619212	642144	664697	688369	707197	755140	800724	845131	...
plus: Net current transfers from the rest of the world	−5726	−5894	−5720	−6444	−4763	−7259	−6098	−6885	−10228	−9030	−11232	...
Current transfers from rest of the world	9303	8913	10505	9135	10546	9892	9392	12008	10895	10633	10141	...
less: Current transfers to the rest of the world	15029	14807	16225	15579	15309	17151	15490	18892	21123	19663	21374	...
equals: National disposable income	538709	563293	588691	612768	637381	657438	682272	700312	744912	791694	833899	...
less: Final consumption	526106	554092	577293	600440	617536	641403	666174	689012	736882	763027	799239	...
equals: Net saving	12603	9202	11398	12327	19845	16035	16097	11300	8030	28667	34659	...
less: Surplus of the nation on current transactions	−36215	−20603	−9429	−11342	4077	9088	19785	26083	14198	7743	8304	...
equals: Net capital formation	48818	29805	20827	23669	15768	6947	−3688	−14783	−6168	20924	26355	...

2.5 Private final consumption expenditure by type and purpose, in current prices

Million Danish kroner

	1986	1987	1988	1989	1990	1991	1992	1993	1994	1995	1996	1997
Final consumption expenditure of resident households												
1 Food, beverages and tobacco	81641	81422	84341	86726	87274	89961	94635	94500	97893	102071	...	...
A Food	55594	55859	58263	60905	60679	63062	66534	66197	69137	73202	...	...
B Non-alcoholic beverages	2016	2067	2182	2397	2417	2383	2770	3298	3793	4169	...	...
C Alcoholic beverages	12851	12764	13121	12794	12838	12863	13172	12324	12661	12906	...	...
D Tobacco	11180	10731	10774	10630	11339	11652	12160	12681	12302	11794	...	...
2 Clothing and footwear	22117	22089	21803	21799	22333	23341	23029	23573	26018	26731	...	...
3 Gross rent, fuel and power	90374	98045	102108	107837	114187	120736	125670	130456	134841	138586	...	...
A Fuel and power	22875	25034	23210	22757	23527	25190	26350	27507	27866	28524	...	...
B Other	67498	73011	78898	85080	90660	95546	99320	102949	106975	110062	...	...
4 Furniture, furnishings and household equipment and operation	25010	24790	26129	26048	26346	27338	27402	27620	29758	29922	...	...
A Household operation	6178	6092	6526	6723	6870	7212	7326	7414	7189	7510	...	...
B Other	18831	18698	19603	19325	19476	20126	20076	20207	22569	22412	...	...
5 Medical care and health expenses	5788	6933	7848	8409	9155	9031	9320	10015	10162	10675	...	...
6 Transport and communication	64437	63875	61714	62359	62981	65824	67825	69525	88177	91707	...	...
A Personal transport equipment	23417	19539	14830	13889	14776	16327	16403	16051	29715	28496	...	...
B Other	41020	44336	46883	48470	48205	49497	51422	53474	58462	63211	...	...
7 Recreational, entertainment, education and cultural services	35629	36048	37003	40062	41825	43879	46160	47192	50393	54211	...	...

Denmark

Million Danish kroner

	1986	1987	1988	1989	1990	1991	1992	1993	1994	1995	1996	1997
A Education	5488	5919	6598	7090	7490	7899	8725	8749	9420	11040	...	...
B Other	30141	30129	30405	32972	34335	35980	37435	38443	40974	43171	...	...
8 Miscellaneous goods and services	36945	39103	41848	44567	45460	47139	50025	50303	54485	56766	...	...
A Personal care	5300	5731	6149	6512	6744	6978	7354	7251	7433	7769	...	...
B Expenditures in restaurants, cafes and hotels	19622	20638	22064	23668	24130	24716	26426	26860	28281	28917	...	...
C Other	12023	12734	13635	14387	14585	15445	16244	16193	18772	20080	...	...
Total final consumption expenditure in the domestic market by households, of which	361942	372306	382794	397806	409559	427249	444066	453184	491728	510668	...	...
A Durable goods	46492	41351	37251	36785	37737	40046	40739	40912	57240	55308	...	...
B Semi-durable goods	54865	57214	57976	58618	60105	63090	64585	65313	70510	73903	...	...
C Non-durable goods	126601	129103	130804	133492	134928	139107	144928	148221	152657	159997	...	...
D Services	133985	144638	156764	168912	176790	185005	193813	198739	211321	221461	...	...
plus: Direct purchases abroad by resident households	17089	18810	20558	20736	23114	21886	23229	22001	23144	24359	...	...
less: Direct purchases in the domestic market by non-resident households	15693	16981	18533	18855	22676	24208	25831	22769	23855	23202	...	...
equals: Final consumption expenditure of resident households	363338	374135	384819	399688	409997	424926	441464	452416	491018	511826	...	...

Final consumption expenditures by private non-profit organisations serving households

	1986	1987	1988	1989	1990	1991	1992	1993	1994	1995	1996	1997
1 Research and science	...	...	...	...	...	...	...	...	...	...	...	...
2 Education	...	...	...	...	...	...	...	...	...	...	...	...
3 Medical and other health services	...	...	...	...	...	...	...	...	...	...	...	...
4 Welfare services	...	...	...	...	...	...	...	...	...	...	...	...
5 Recreational and related cultural services	...	...	...	...	...	...	...	...	...	...	...	...
6 Religious organisations	...	...	...	...	...	...	...	...	...	...	...	...
7 Professional and labour organisations serving households	...	...	...	...	...	...	...	...	...	...	...	...
8 Miscellaneous	...	...	...	...	...	...	...	...	...	...	...	...
equals: Final consumption expenditures by private non-profit organisations serving households	3409	3743	3987	4207	5034	5275	5612	6756	7306	7913	...	...
Private final consumption expenditure	366747	377878	388806	403895	415031	430201	447076	459172	498324	519739	...	...

2.6 Private final consumption expenditure by type and purpose, in constant prices

Million Danish kroner

	1986	1987	1988	1989	1990	1991	1992	1993	1994	1995	1996	1997

At constant prices of: 1980

Final consumption expenditure of resident households

	1986	1987	1988	1989	1990	1991	1992	1993	1994	1995	1996	1997
1 Food, beverages and tobacco	55561	54897	55310	54977	54564	55983	57740	57893	59527	60540	...	...
A Food	37916	37881	38368	38492	37890	39260	40518	40307	41916	43145	...	...
B Non-alcoholic beverages	1093	1074	1071	1156	1127	1130	1273	1545	1797	1884	...	...
C Alcoholic beverages	8951	8756	8797	8429	8370	8591	9040	8835	8893	9009	...	...
D Tobacco	7601	7186	7074	6900	7176	7002	6909	7205	6921	6502	...	...
2 Clothing and footwear	14841	14350	13646	13444	13810	13940	13297	13527	14652	15126	...	...
3 Gross rent, fuel and power	57748	58311	58171	57669	57831	58693	58868	59874	60289	60789	...	...

Denmark

Million Danish kroner

	1986	1987	1988	1989	1990	1991	1992	1993	1994	1995	1996	1997
At constant prices of: 1980												
A Fuel and power	15724	15764	15148	14258	14083	14661	14674	15549	15880	16274	...	...
B Other	42024	42548	43023	43411	43748	44031	44194	44325	44409	44515	...	...
4 Furniture, furnishings and household equipment and operation	15945	15214	15470	14801	14519	14724	14500	14705	15665	15299	...	...
A Household operation	3985	3714	3778	3715	3718	3853	3900	3914	3666	3715	...	...
B Other	11961	11500	11692	11086	10801	10871	10600	10791	11999	11584	...	...
5 Medical care and health expenses	3756	4234	4524	4687	4811	4622	4656	5034	5132	5345	...	...
6 Transport and communication	43827	40717	37112	36393	36220	36840	37589	39094	48315	48517	...	...
A Personal transport equipment	17263	13237	9556	8724	8875	9528	9443	9321	16969	16000	...	...
B Other	26564	27480	27556	27669	27345	27312	28146	29773	31345	32517	...	...
7 Recreational, entertainment, education and cultural services	24796	23978	24184	25426	26139	27303	28696	29448	31013	32304	...	...
A Education	3620	3545	3737	3830	3913	3925	4200	4182	4400	5047	...	...
B Other	21175	20434	20447	21596	22225	23378	24496	25267	26613	27258	...	...
8 Miscellaneous goods and services	23753	24096	24802	25542	25299	25890	26967	26840	27988	28099	...	...
A Personal care	3201	3283	3381	3541	3525	3866	4177	4045	4010	4038	...	...
B Expenditures in restaurants, cafes and hotels	12541	12758	13185	13648	13466	13584	14204	14443	14566	14415	...	...
C Other	8011	8056	8236	8353	8308	8440	8586	8351	9412	9645	...	...
Total final consumption expenditure in the domestic market by households, of which	240227	235797	233218	232939	233192	237994	242314	246414	262580	266018	...	...
A Durable goods	33775	28332	24736	24241	24543	25873	26706	27407	36953	35229	...	...
B Semi-durable goods	35492	35322	34314	34067	34122	34994	34693	34790	36640	37806	...	...
C Non-durable goods	85895	85199	84946	83934	83651	85738	87766	90616	92686	94444	...	...
D Services	85065	86944	89222	90697	90877	91390	93149	93601	96301	98538	...	...
plus: Direct purchases abroad by resident households	11480	12711	13250	12284	13818	12297	12991	12394	12721	14465	...	...
less: Direct purchases in the domestic market by non-resident households	10354	10848	11305	11037	13044	13600	14276	12652	13060	12736	...	...
equals: Final consumption expenditure of resident households	241352	237660	235163	234187	233967	236691	241029	246156	262240	267747	...	...

Final consumption expenditures by private non-profit organisations serving households

	1986	1987	1988	1989	1990	1991	1992	1993	1994	1995	1996	1997
1 Research and science	...	...	...	...	...	...	...	...	...	...	...	...
2 Education	...	...	...	...	...	...	...	...	...	...	...	...
3 Medical and other health services	...	...	...	...	...	...	...	...	...	...	...	...
4 Welfare services	...	...	...	...	...	...	...	...	...	...	...	...
5 Recreational and related cultural services	...	...	...	...	...	...	...	...	...	...	...	...
6 Religious organisations	...	...	...	...	...	...	...	...	...	...	...	...
7 Professional and labour organisations serving households	...	...	...	...	...	...	...	...	...	...	...	...
8 Miscellaneous	...	...	...	...	...	...	...	...	...	...	...	...
equals: Final consumption expenditures by private non-profit organisations serving households	2231	2269	2318	2352	2677	2738	2868	3267	3547	3720	...	...
Private final consumption expenditure	243583	239929	237481	236539	236644	239429	243897	249423	265787	271467	...	...

Denmark

2.11 Gross fixed capital formation by kind of activity of owner, ISIC divisions, in current prices

Million Danish kroner

	1986	1987	1988	1989	1990	1991	1992	1993	1994	1995	1996	1997
All producers												
1 Agriculture, hunting, forestry and fishing	7552	6504	5799	7252	8433	6549	7124	5494	6974	7611	...	...
A Agriculture and hunting	6657	5695	5079	6577	7593	5704	6324	...	...	...	...	...
B Forestry and logging	156	143	142	144	114	124	94	...	...	...	...	...
C Fishing	740	666	577	532	726	721	706	...	...	...	...	...
2 Mining and quarrying	2002	1315	1089	1323	1905	2609	2883	3494	3366	4085	...	...
A Coal mining	...	...	...	...	...	...	...	...	...	...	...	...
B Crude petroleum and natural gas production	1788	1166	902	1170	1763	2301	2593	...	...	...	...	...
C Metal ore mining	...	...	...	...	...	...	...	...	...	...	...	...
D Other mining	214	149	187	153	142	308	290	...	...	...	...	...
3 Manufacturing	20942	19738	19491	20036	20209	22428	20234	18538	18264	20543	...	...
A Manufacturing of food, beverages and tobacco	3723	3859	4306	4010	3897	4907	4437	...	...	...	...	...
B Textile, wearing apparel and leather industries	902	771	779	904	706	600	501	...	...	...	...	...
C Manufacture of wood and wood products, including furniture	1204	976	900	1131	1305	1129	1228	...	...	...	...	...
D Manufacture of paper and paper products, printing and publishing	2673	2590	2394	2313	1844	2352	1498	...	...	...	...	...
E Manufacture of chemicals and chemical petroleum, coal, rubber and plastic products	3276	3159	3340	3732	3526	4341	3955	...	...	...	...	...
F Manufacture of non-metallic mineral products, except products of petroleum and coal	1513	1686	1598	1059	1341	1092	785	...	...	...	...	...
G Basic metal industries	234	202	187	235	303	354	441	...	...	...	...	...
H Manufacture of fabricated metal products, machinery and equipment	6951	5980	5542	6216	6635	6940	6756	...	...	...	...	...
I Other manufacturing industries	465	515	444	435	652	713	632	...	...	...	...	...
4 Electricity, gas and water	7980	7650	8006	9043	9623	7828	7541	6377	5108	7387	...	...
5 Construction	4751	4091	3572	3651	3915	3432	3513	3214	3949	4713	...	...
6 Wholesale and retail trade, restaurants and hotels	8524	8327	8721	8782	8794	7515	7559	...	...	...	...	...
A Wholesale and retail trade	8524	8327	8721	8782	8794	7515	7559	...	...	...	...	...
B Restaurants and hotels	...	...	...	...	...	...	...	...	...	...	...	...
7 Transport, storage and communication	19605	17896	19296	24481	24797	28186	25242	...	...	...	...	...
A Transport and storage	15642	13421	14152	19278	20548	24783	20818	...	...	...	...	...
B Communication	3963	4474	5145	5203	4249	3403	4424	...	...	...	...	...
8 Finance, insurance, real estate and business services	36219	37509	36520	33281	31270	29722	28111	...	...	...	...	...
A Financial institutions	2632	3488	4061	2149	3021	4155	2069	...	...	...	...	...
B Insurance								...	...	...	...	...
C Real estate and business services	33587	34021	32459	31132	28249	25567	26042	...	...	...	...	...
Real estate, except dwellings	...	...	...	...	...	...	...	...	...	...	...	...

Denmark

Million Danish kroner

	1986	1987	1988	1989	1990	1991	1992	1993	1994	1995	1996	1997
Dwellings	33587	34021	32459	31132	28249	25567	26042	...	...	...	...	...
9 Community, social and personal services	1076	1114	1200	1158	1738	1197	1389	...	...	...	...	...
A Sanitary and similar services	...	...	...	...	...	...	...	...	...	...	...	...
B Social and related community services	...	...	...	...	...	...	...	...	...	...	...	...
C Recreational and cultural services	1076	1114	1200	1158	1738	1197	1389	...	...	...	...	...
D Personal and household services	...	...	...	...	...	...	...	...	...	...	...	...
Statistical discrepancy	15652	18175	11388	13253	12975	11406	11818	...	...	...	...	...
Total industries	124304	122318	115083	122261	123660	120872	115415	113060	114852	132455	...	...
Producers of government services	14066	15715	17143	16692	15698	15821	18408	18686	19863	19501	...	...
Private non-profit institutions serving households	...	...	...	...	...	...	...	...	...	...	...	...
Total	138370	138033	132226	138953	139358	136693	133823	131746	134715	151956	...	...

2.12 Gross fixed capital formation by kind of activity of owner, ISIC divisions, in constant prices

Million Danish kroner

	1986	1987	1988	1989	1990	1991	1992	1993	1994	1995	1996	1997
At constant prices of: 1980												
All producers												
1 Agriculture, hunting, forestry and fishing	4841	3995	3427	4224	4785	3500	3709	2822	3411	3719	...	...
A Agriculture and hunting	4251	3469	2954	3820	4305	3035	3246	...	...	...	...	...
B Forestry and logging	96	86	84	81	66	67	48	...	...	...	...	...
C Fishing	494	440	389	324	413	399	416	...	...	...	...	...
2 Mining and quarrying	1320	823	674	785	1079	1411	1550	1801	1704	2018	...	...
A Coal mining	...	...	...	...	...	...	...	...	...	...	...	...
B Crude petroleum and natural gas production	1171	722	548	686	991	1235	1389	...	...	...	...	...
C Metal ore mining	...	...	...	...	...	...	...	...	...	...	...	...
D Other mining	149	100	126	99	88	175	161	...	...	...	...	...
3 Manufacturing	13664	12324	11993	11899	11567	12487	10937	9566	9232	10160	...	...
A Manufacturing of food, beverages and tobacco	2416	2367	2578	2300	2181	2616	2265	...	...	...	...	...
B Textile, wearing apparel and leather industries	602	498	500	555	422	338	268	...	...	...	...	...
C Manufacture of wood and wood products, including furniture	817	650	585	698	769	622	699	...	...	...	...	...
D Manufacture of paper and paper products, printing and publishing	1559	1443	1350	1290	983	1301	746	...	...	...	...	...
E Manufacture of chemicals and chemical petroleum, coal, rubber and plastic products	2150	1946	1988	2095	1896	2303	2033	...	...	...	...	...
F Manufacture of non-metallic mineral products, except products of petroleum and coal	1016	1069	1003	613	757	586	423	...	...	...	...	...
G Basic metal industries	139	118	111	131	173	200	249	...	...	...	...	...

Denmark

Million Danish kroner

	1986	1987	1988	1989	1990	1991	1992	1993	1994	1995	1996	1997
At constant prices of: 1980												
H Manufacture of fabricated metal products, machinery and equipment	4662	3913	3608	3986	4052	4156	3950	...	...	...	...	...
I Other manufacturing industries	301	320	271	231	334	363	303	...	...	...	...	...
4 Electricity, gas and water	5446	4900	4944	5292	5488	4314	4106	3372	2648	3757	...	...
5 Construction	3202	2650	2292	2198	2247	1832	1870	1645	1952	2269	...	...
6 Wholesale and retail trade, restaurants and hotels	5720	5426	5625	5576	5521	4439	4187	...	...	...	...	...
A Wholesale and retail trade	5720	5426	5625	5576	5521	4439	4187	...	...	...	...	...
B Restaurants and hotels	...	...	...	...	...	...	...	...	...	...	...	...
7 Transport, storage and communication	13233	11767	12376	14700	14753	15617	14523	...	...	...	...	...
A Transport and storage	10262	8579	9017	11437	12124	13631	11839	...	...	...	...	...
B Communication	2971	3189	3359	3264	2629	1985	2684	...	...	...	...	...
8 Finance, insurance, real estate and business services	23442	23290	21746	18958	17340	16150	14249	...	...	...	...	...
A Financial institutions	1870	2405	2810	1686	2389	2913	1488	...	...	...	...	...
B Insurance	...	...	...	...	...	...	...	...	...	...	...	...
C Real estate and business services	21572	20885	18936	17272	14951	13237	12761	...	...	...	...	...
Real estate, except dwellings	...	...	...	...	...	...	...	...	...	...	...	...
Dwellings	21572	20885	18936	17272	14951	13237	12761	...	...	...	...	...
9 Community, social and personal services	799	834	917	836	1177	807	926	...	...	...	...	...
A Sanitary and similar services	...	...	...	...	...	...	...	...	...	...	...	...
B Social and related community services	...	...	...	...	...	...	...	...	...	...	...	...
C Recreational and cultural services	799	834	917	836	1177	807	926	...	...	...	...	...
D Personal and household services	...	...	...	...	...	...	...	...	...	...	...	...
Statistical discrepancy	11257	12840	8528	9510	9300	8369	8416	...	...	...	...	...
Total industries	82924	78849	72521	73977	73257	68925	64473	61230	61302	69414	...	...
Producers of government services	9252	9854	10287	9661	8922	8585	9775	9738	10091	9644	...	...
Private non-profit institutions serving households	...	...	...	...	...	...	...	...	...	...	...	...
Total	92176	88703	82808	83638	82179	77510	74248	70968	71393	79058	...	...

2.17 Exports and imports of goods and services, detail

Million Danish kroner

	1986	1987	1988	1989	1990	1991	1992	1993	1994	1995	1996	1997
Exports of goods and services												
1 Exports of merchandise, f.o.b.	171723	175132	186333	208544	221412	235165	243988	235798	260947	269076	...	...
2 Transport and communication	22213	22076	27534	33716	33585	39596	36843	42389	46227	44870	...	...
A In respect of merchandise imports	255	260	322	285	720	748	720	520	560	560	...	...
B Other	21958	21816	27212	33431	32865	38848	36123	41869	45667	44310	...	...
3 Insurance service charges	−1008	−877	−900	−814	72	−428	−561	−1220	1973	−2388	...	...
4 Other commodities	4938	6772	7415	4608	5829	7465	3294	433	−5182	−4313	...	...

Denmark

Million Danish kroner

	1986	1987	1988	1989	1990	1991	1992	1993	1994	1995	1996	1997
5 Adjustments of merchandise exports to change-of-ownership basis	...	...	...	...	...	...	...	...	...	...	...	...
6 Direct purchases in the domestic market by non-residential households	15693	16981	18533	18855	22676	24208	25831	22769	23855	23202	...	...
7 Direct purchases in the domestic market by extraterritorial bodies	...	...	...	...	...	...	...	...	...	...	...	...
Total exports of goods and services	213559	220084	238915	264909	283574	306006	309395	300169	327820	330448	...	...
Imports of goods and services												
1 Imports of merchandise, c.i.f.	184388	173651	175786	195705	196348	208642	204675	190858	218803	236445	...	...
A Imports of merchandise, f.o.b. [a]	177578	167205	169200	188406	189023	200861	197004	183642	210520	227467	...	...
B Transport of services on merchandise imports	6810	6446	6586	7299	7325	7781	7671	7216	8283	8978	...	...
By residents	255	260	322	285	720	748	720	520	560	560	...	...
By non-residents	6555	6186	6264	7014	6605	7033	6951	6696	7723	8418	...	...
C Insurance service charges on merchandise imports	...	...	...	...	...	...	...	...	...	...	...	...
2 Adjustments of merchandise imports to change-of-ownership basis	...	...	...	...	...	...	...	...	...	...	...	...
3 Other transport and communication	13935	14012	17955	21698	20299	23827	22080	25717	29497	28601	...	...
4 Other insurance service charges	...	...	...	...	...	...	...	...	...	...	...	...
5 Other commodities	1143	753	593	797	681	1212	1158	1390	846	1346	...	...
6 Direct purchases abroad by government	...	...	...	...	...	...	...	...	...	...	...	...
7 Direct purchases abroad by resident households	17089	18810	20558	20736	23114	21886	23229	22001	23144	24359	...	...
Total imports of goods and services	216555	207226	214892	238936	240442	255567	251142	238970	272290	290751	...	...
Balance of goods and services	–2996	12858	24023	25973	43132	50439	58253	61199	55530	39697	...	...
Total imports and balance of goods and services	213559	220084	238915	264909	283574	306006	309395	300169	327820	330448	...	...

[a] Item "Insurance service charges in respect of merchandise imports" is included in item "Import of merchandise, f.o.b.".

3.12 General government income and outlay account: total and subsectors

Million Danish kroner

	1986					1987				
	Total government	Central government	State or provincial government	Local government	Social security funds	Total government	Central government	State or provincial government	Local government	Social security funds
Receipts										
1 Operating surplus	–	–	...	–	–	–	–	...	–	–
2 Property and entrepreneurial income	32654	19861	...	4672	8121	31369	19078	...	3975	8316
A Withdrawals from public quasi-corporations	7371	5854	...	1480	37	4458	3266	...	1139	53
B Interest	24530	13342	...	3104	8084	26389	15322	...	2804	8263
C Dividends										
D Net land rent and royalties	753	665	...	88	–	522	490	...	32	–
3 Taxes, fees and contributions	337759	237476	...	92450	7833	359647	247293	...	103857	8497

Denmark

Million Danish kroner

	1986					1987				
	Total govern-ment	Central govern-ment	State or provincial govern-ment	Local govern-ment	Social security funds	Total govern-ment	Central govern-ment	State or provincial govern-ment	Local govern-ment	Social security funds
A Indirect taxes	130879	124441	...	6438	–	135974	127267	...	8715	–
B Direct taxes	195466	109475	...	85991	–	208943	113820	...	95115	–
C Social security contributions	10619	2786	...	–	7833	13798	5301	...	–	8497
D Fees, fines and penalties	795	774	...	21	–	932	905	...	27	–
4 Other current transfers	18189	22812	...	94205	26475	20721	25743	...	97108	28055
A Casualty insurance claims	...	...	...	...	...	...	...	...	...	...
B Transfers from other government subsectors	...	9678	...	89223	26402	...	10546	...	91632	28007
C Transfers from rest of the world	9146	9140	...	6	–	10741	10734	...	7	–
D Other transfers, except imputed	2762	475	...	2214	73	2920	407	...	2465	48
E Imputed unfunded employee pension and welfare contributions	6281	3519	...	2762	–	7060	4056	...	3004	–
Total current receipts	388602	280149	...	191327	42429	411737	292114	...	204940	44868

Disbursements

1 Government final consumption expenditure	159359	48866	...	109281	1212	176214	53683	...	121230	1301
2 Property income	58692	55962	...	2729	1	57746	55041	...	2703	2
A Interest	58692	55962	...	2729	1	57746	55041	...	2703	2
B Net land rent and royalties	...	...	...	...	...	...	...	...	...	...
3 Subsidies	20060	17032	...	2959	69	22011	18751	...	3136	124
4 Other current transfers	117881	139191	...	70586	33407	128971	147234	...	75416	36506
A Casualty insurance premiums, net	...	...	...	...	...	...	...	...	...	...
B Transfers to other government subsectors	...	115625	...	3368	6310	...	119639	...	2979	7567
C Social security benefits	103307	9404	...	66806	27097	113716	12723	...	72054	28939
D Social assistance grants	...	...	...	...	...	...	...	...	...	...
E Unfunded employee welfare benefits	–					–				
F Transfers to private non-profit institutions serving households	616	204	...	412	–	582	199	...	383	–
G Other transfers n.e.c.	...	...	...	...	...	...	...	...	...	...
H Transfers to rest of the world	13958	13958	...	–	–	14673	14673	...	–	–
Net saving	32610	19098	...	5772	7740	26795	17405	...	2455	6935
Total current disbursements and net saving	388602	280149	...	191327	42429	411737	292114	...	204940	44868

	1988					1989				
	Total govern-ment	Central govern-ment	State or provincial govern-ment	Local govern-ment	Social security funds	Total govern-ment	Central govern-ment	State or provincial govern-ment	Local govern-ment	Social security funds

Receipts

1 Operating surplus	–	–	...	–	–	–	–	...	–	–
2 Property and entrepreneurial income	34127	21396	...	3494	9237	37849	23904	...	4105	9840
A Withdrawals from public quasi-corporations	5953	4749	...	1122	82	9056	7345	...	1636	75
B Interest	27625	16125	...	2345	9155	28276	16072	...	2439	9765

Denmark

	1988					1989				
	Total govern-ment	Central govern-ment	State or provincial govern-ment	Local govern-ment	Social security funds	Total govern-ment	Central govern-ment	State or provincial govern-ment	Local govern-ment	Social security funds
C Dividends										
D Net land rent and royalties	549	522	...	27	–	517	487	...	30	–
3 Taxes, fees and contributions	377223	254202	...	113196	9825	387762	260133	...	117098	10531
A Indirect taxes	139552	130583	...	8969	–	140201	131083	...	9118	–
B Direct taxes	226248	122045	...	104203	–	235426	127467	...	107959	–
C Social security contributions	10228	403	...	–	9825	10843	312	...	–	10531
D Fees, fines and penalties	1195	1171	...	24	–	1292	1271	...	21	–
4 Other current transfers	21640	26783	...	102376	31004	20885	27224	...	109461	35253
A Casualty insurance claims	...	...	...	...	...	...	...	...	...	...
B Transfers from other government subsectors	...	11466	...	96092	30965	...	12521	...	103327	35205
C Transfers from rest of the world	10395	10390	...	5	–	9430	9425	...	5	–
D Other transfers, except imputed	3576	433	...	3104	39	3219	404	...	2767	48
E Imputed unfunded employee pension and welfare contributions	7669	4494	...	3175	–	8236	4874	...	3362	–
Total current receipts	432990	302381	...	219066	50066	446496	311261	...	230664	55624

Disbursements

	Total	Central	State	Local	SS	Total	Central	State	Local	SS
1 Government final consumption expenditure	188487	58267	...	128712	1508	196546	60329	...	134592	1625
2 Property income	58305	55523	...	2773	9	57464	54526	...	2922	16
A Interest	58305	55523	...	2773	9	57464	54526	...	2922	16
B Net land rent and royalties	...	...	...	...	...	...	...	...	...	...
3 Subsidies	25340	21791	...	3388	161	26955	23197	...	3514	244
4 Other current transfers	144268	161025	...	81659	40107	158595	175186	...	89105	45357
A Casualty insurance premiums, net	...	...	...	...	...	...	...	...	...	...
B Transfers to other government subsectors	...	127057	...	3203	8263	...	138532	...	3164	9357
C Social security benefits	126956	17143	...	77969	31844	140360	19004	...	85356	36000
D Social assistance grants	...	...	...	...	...	...	...	...	...	...
E Unfunded employee welfare benefits	–					–				
F Transfers to private non-profit institutions serving households	736	249	...	487	–	848	263	...	585	–
G Other transfers n.e.c.	...	...	...	...	...	...	...	...	...	...
H Transfers to rest of the world	16576	16576	...	–	–	17387	17387	...	–	–
Net saving	16590	5775	...	2534	8281	6936	–1977	...	531	8382
Total current disbursements and net saving	432990	302381	...	219066	50066	446496	311261	...	230664	55624

	1990					1991				
	Total govern-ment	Central govern-ment	State or provincial govern-ment	Local govern-ment	Social security funds	Total govern-ment	Central govern-ment	State or provincial govern-ment	Local govern-ment	Social security funds

Receipts

1 Operating surplus	–	–	...	–	–	–	–	...	–	–
2 Property and entrepreneurial income	38390	23625	...	4293	10472	37902	21786	...	5016	11098

Denmark

	1990					1991				
	Total government	Central government	State or provincial government	Local government	Social security funds	Total government	Central government	State or provincial government	Local government	Social security funds
A Withdrawals from public quasi-corporations	6054	4457	...	1522	75	5376	2813	...	2530	33
B Interest	31671	18531	...	2743	10397	31808	18281	...	2461	11065
C Dividends										
D Net land rent and royalties	665	637	...	28	–	718	693	...	25	–
3 Taxes, fees and contributions	388490	256556	...	119991	11943	403559	266507	...	124851	12201
A Indirect taxes	141523	132632	...	8891	–	144461	135771	...	8690	–
B Direct taxes	233268	122184	...	111084	–	245202	129054	...	116148	–
C Social security contributions	12325	382	...	–	11943	12571	370	...	–	12201
D Fees, fines and penalties	1374	1358	...	16	–	1325	1312	...	13	–
4 Other current transfers	22083	27879	...	115663	37325	23441	29634	...	120754	41844
A Casualty insurance claims	...	...	...	...	...	...	...	...	...	...
B Transfers from other government subsectors	...	12215	...	109313	37256	...	12814	...	114205	41772
C Transfers from rest of the world	9980	9975	...	5	–	10669	10663	...	7	–
D Other transfers, except imputed	3685	639	...	2977	69	3750	735	...	2943	72
E Imputed unfunded employee pension and welfare contributions	8418	5050	...	3368	–	9021	5422	...	3599	–
Total current receipts	448963	308060	...	239947	59740	464902	317927	...	250621	65143

Disbursements

	Total government	Central government	State or provincial government	Local government	Social security funds	Total government	Central government	State or provincial government	Local government	Social security funds
1 Government final consumption expenditure	202504	61936	...	138705	1863	211201	64406	...	144933	1862
2 Property income	58505	55486	...	3002	17	61078	58016	...	3044	18
A Interest	58505	55486	...	3002	17	61078	58016	...	3044	18
B Net land rent and royalties	...	...	...	...	...	...	...	...	...	...
3 Subsidies	28354	24279	...	3550	525	28726	23878	...	4080	768
4 Other current transfers	164644	182783	...	93742	46903	178361	196689	...	98750	51713
A Casualty insurance premiums, net	...	...	...	...	...	...	...	...	...	...
B Transfers to other government subsectors	...	146569	...	3154	9061	...	155976	...	3425	9390
C Social security benefits	147423	19550	...	90031	37842	157661	20566	...	94772	42323
D Social assistance grants	...	...	...	...	...	...	...	...	...	...
E Unfunded employee welfare benefits	–					–				
F Transfers to private non-profit institutions serving households	922	365	...	557	–	1151	597	...	553	–
G Other transfers n.e.c.	...	...	...	...	...	...	...	...	...	...
H Transfers to rest of the world	16299	16299	...	–	–	19550	19550	...	–	–
Net saving	–5044	–16424	...	948	10432	–14464	–25061	...	–186	10782
Total current disbursements and net saving	448963	308060	...	239947	59740	464902	317928	...	250621	65143

Denmark

	1992					1993				
	Total government	Central government	State or provincial government	Local government	Social security funds	Total government	Central government	State or provincial government	Local government	Social security funds

Receipts

	1992					1993				
1 Operating surplus	–	–	...	–	–	–	–	...	–	–
2 Property and entrepreneurial income	45754	28741	...	4945	12069	47437	30604	...	4842	11992
A Withdrawals from public quasi-corporations	10868	8611	...	2225	32	8908	6922	...	2033	–46
B Interest	34136	19410	...	2690	12036	37747	22930	...	2779	12039
C Dividends										
D Net land rent and royalties	750	720	...	30	–	782	751	...	30	–
3 Taxes, fees and contributions	420020	275981	...	130824	13216	439412	289948	...	135310	14154
A Indirect taxes	148456	139469	...	8987	–	153184	142483	...	10701	–
B Direct taxes	256682	134867	...	121816	–	270170	145584	...	124586	–
C Social security contributions	13599	383	...	–	13216	14545	391	...	–	14154
D Fees, fines and penalties	1283	1262	...	21	–	1513	1490	...	23	–
4 Other current transfers	23883	30898	...	127032	46036	27711	36625	...	134203	51694
A Casualty insurance claims	...	...	...	...	...	...	...	...	...	...
B Transfers from other government subsectors	...	13920	...	120202	45959	...	16323	...	126892	51595
C Transfers from rest of the world	10352	10345	...	7	–	12894	12886	...	8	–
D Other transfers, except imputed	3953	925	...	2952	77	4816	1533	...	3183	99
E Imputed unfunded employee pension and welfare contributions	9579	5708	...	3871	–	10002	5882	...	4120	–
Total current receipts	489657	335620	...	262801	71321	514560	357177	...	274355	77840

Disbursements

	1992					1993				
1 Government final consumption expenditure	219099	66820	...	149934	2344	230298	70531	...	157322	2479
2 Property income	58489	55274	...	3197	18	67812	64426	...	3341	11
A Interest	58489	55274	...	3197	18	67812	64426	...	3341	11
B Net land rent and royalties	...	...	...	...	...	...	...	...	...	...
3 Subsidies	34874	29486	...	4453	935	35522	29607	...	4919	996
4 Other current transfers	188533	208253	...	103257	57073	201108	222894	...	108431	64594
A Casualty insurance premiums, net	...	...	...	...	...	...	...	...	...	...
B Transfers to other government subsectors	...	166132	...	3374	10544	...	178487	...	3941	12382
C Social security benefits	167768	21975	...	99264	46529	178451	22541	...	103699	52212
D Social assistance grants	...	...	...	...	...	...	...	...	...	...
E Unfunded employee welfare benefits	–					–				
F Transfers to private non-profit institutions serving households	1339	719	...	619	–	1674	884	...	790	–
G Other transfers n.e.c.	...	...	...	...	...	...	...	...	...	...
H Transfers to rest of the world	19426	19426	...	–	–	20983	20983	...	–	–
Net saving	–11338	–24215	...	1959	10950	–20180	–30281	...	342	9759
Total current disbursements and net saving	489657	335618	...	262800	71320	514560	357177	...	274355	77839

Denmark

	1994					1995				
	Total government	Central government	State or provincial government	Local government	Social security funds	Total government	Central government	State or provincial government	Local government	Social security funds
Receipts										
1 Operating surplus	–	–	...	–	–	–	–	...	–	–
2 Property and entrepreneurial income	43538	28354	...	3819	11366	38346	22836	...	3779	11732
A Withdrawals from public quasi-corporations	7445	5785	...	1721	–62	2475	795	...	1486	194
B Interest	35312	21817	...	2069	11427	35070	21268	...	2264	11537
C Dividends										
D Net land rent and royalties	781	752	...	29	–	801	773	...	28	–
3 Taxes, fees and contributions	480109	316195	...	148680	15234	497188	324362	...	157314	15512
A Indirect taxes	168387	157736	...	10651	–	175261	164876	...	10385	–
B Direct taxes	294610	156604	...	138006	–	304709	157794	...	146915	–
C Social security contributions	15650	416	...	–	15234	15966	454	...	–	15512
D Fees, fines and penalties	1462	1439	...	23	–	1252	1238	...	14	–
4 Other current transfers	27284	35750	...	149185	50167	27191	33472	...	152038	45451
A Casualty insurance claims	...	...	...	...	...	...	...	...	...	...
B Transfers from other government subsectors	...	16588	...	141146	50084	...	14791	...	143645	45333
C Transfers from rest of the world	11487	11479	...	9	–	11473	11464	...	10	–
D Other transfers, except imputed	4521	1456	...	2982	83	5261	1908	...	3235	118
E Imputed unfunded employee pension and welfare contributions	11275	6226	...	5048	–	10456	5309	...	5147	–
Total current receipts	550931	380299	...	301684	76767	562725	380670	...	313131	72695
Disbursements										
1 Government final consumption expenditure	238547	73784	...	162031	2755	243904	71996	...	169032	2901
2 Property income	66306	63155	...	3120	9	64776	61597	...	3135	19
A Interest	66306	63155	...	3120	9	64776	61597	...	3135	19
B Net land rent and royalties	...	...	...	...	...	...	...	...	...	...
3 Subsidies	35490	29773	...	4887	830	35776	30398	...	4925	452
4 Other current transfers	228635	244890	...	128152	63411	233384	248596	...	129206	59351
A Casualty insurance premiums, net	...	...	...	...	...	...	...	...	...	...
B Transfers to other government subsectors	...	191229	...	4181	12407	...	188978	...	2401	12390
C Social security benefits	204116	30050	...	123061	51004	208520	35726	...	125833	46961
D Social assistance grants	...	...	...	...	...	...	...	...	...	...
E Unfunded employee welfare benefits	–					–				
F Transfers to private non-profit institutions serving households	2161	1252	...	909	–	2546	1573	...	973	–
G Other transfers n.e.c.	...	...	...	...	...	...	...	...	...	...
H Transfers to rest of the world	22359	22359	...	–	–	22318	22318	...	–	–
Net saving	–18048	–31304	...	3494	9762	–15114	–31918	...	6831	9973
Total current disbursements and net saving	550930	380298	...	301684	76767	562726	380669	...	313129	72696

Denmark

3.13 General government capital accumulation account: total and subsectors

Million Danish kroner

	1986					1987				
	Total government	Central government	State or provincial government	Local government	Social security funds	Total government	Central government	State or provincial government	Local government	Social security funds
Finance of gross accumulation									
1 Gross saving	38022	20340	...	9927	7755	32792	18834	...	7008	6950
A Consumption of fixed capital	5412	1242	...	4155	15	5997	1429	...	4553	15
B Net saving	32610	19098	...	5772	7740	26795	17405	...	2455	6935
2 Capital transfers	2364	2186	...	1492	–	3010	2796	...	309	35
A From other government subsectors	...	2	...	1312	–	...	2	...	128	–
B From other resident sectors	1986	1806	...	180	–	2615	2399	...	181	35
C From rest of the world	378	378	...	–	–	395	395	...	–	–
Finance of gross accumulation	40386	22526	...	11419	7755	35802	21630	...	7317	6985
Gross accumulation									
1 Gross capital formation	13129	2873	...	10238	18	14799	3947	...	10839	13
A Increase in stocks	–740	–740	...	–	–	–782	–782	...	–	–
B Gross fixed capital formation	13869	3613	...	10238	18	15581	4729	...	10839	13
Own account	...	...	...	...	...	...	...	...	...	...
Other	13869	3613	...	10238	18	15581	4729	...	10839	13
2 Purchases of land, net	–2352	–310	...	–2001	–41	–2248	–108	...	–2140	–
3 Purchases of intangible assets, net										
4 Capital transfers	6949	5557	...	1422	1284	6363	3441	...	2044	1008
A To other government subsectors	...	1312	...	2	–	...	128	...	2	–
B To other resident sectors	6283	3579	...	1420	1284	6245	3195	...	2042	1008
C To the rest of the world	666	666	...	–	–	118	118	...	–	–
Net lending	22660	14406	...	1760	6494	16888	14350	...	–3426	5964
Gross accumulation	40386	22526	...	11419	7755	35802	21630	...	7317	6985

	1988					1989				
	Total government	Central government	State or provincial government	Local government	Social security funds	Total government	Central government	State or provincial government	Local government	Social security funds
Finance of gross accumulation									
1 Gross saving	23010	7280	...	7436	8294	13961	–307	...	5881	8387
A Consumption of fixed capital	6420	1505	...	4902	13	7025	1670	...	5350	5
B Net saving	16590	5775	...	2534	8281	6936	–1977	...	531	8382
2 Capital transfers	2804	2545	...	267	42	2715	2494	...	198	76
A From other government subsectors	...	3	...	47	–	...	2	...	51	–
B From other resident sectors	2547	2285	...	220	42	2480	2257	...	147	76
C From rest of the world	257	257	...	–	–	235	235	...	–	–
Finance of gross accumulation	25814	9825	...	7703	8336	16676	2187	...	6079	8463
Gross accumulation									
1 Gross capital formation	15992	4143	...	11849	–	16084	4351	...	11730	3
A Increase in stocks	–844	–844	...	–	–	–534	–534	...	–	–

Denmark

	1988					1989				
	Total government	Central government	State or provincial government	Local government	Social security funds	Total government	Central government	State or provincial government	Local government	Social security funds
B Gross fixed capital formation	16836	4987	...	11849	–	16618	4885	...	11730	3
Own account	...	...	...	...	...	...	...	...	...	...
Other	16836	4987	...	11849	–	16618	4885	...	11730	3
2 Purchases of land, net	–2369	38	...	–2407	–	–2925	–3	...	–2922	–
3 Purchases of intangible assets, net										
4 Capital transfers	7849	3922	...	3089	888	7630	4249	...	2623	811
A To other government subsectors	...	47	...	3	–	...	51	...	2	–
B To other resident sectors	7723	3749	...	3086	888	7555	4123	...	2621	811
C To the rest of the world	126	126	...	–	–	75	75	...	–	–
Net lending	4342	1722	...	–4828	7448	–4113	–6410	...	–5352	7649
Gross accumulation	25814	9825	...	7703	8336	16676	2187	...	6079	8463

	1990					1991				
	Total government	Central government	State or provincial government	Local government	Social security funds	Total government	Central government	State or provincial government	Local government	Social security funds

Finance of gross accumulation

1 Gross saving	2498	–14594	...	6655	10437	–6552	–23190	...	5852	10785
A Consumption of fixed capital	7542	1830	...	5707	5	7912	1871	...	6038	3
B Net saving	–5044	–16424	...	948	10432	–14464	–25061	...	–186	10782
2 Capital transfers	5332	4824	...	544	60	6345	5865	...	498	95
A From other government subsectors	...	–	...	96	–	...	3	...	110	–
B From other resident sectors	5021	4513	...	448	60	5963	5480	...	388	95
C From rest of the world	311	311	...	–	–	382	382	...	–	–
Finance of gross accumulation	7830	–9770	...	7199	10497	–207	–17325	...	6350	10880

Gross accumulation

1 Gross capital formation	15983	5209	...	10770	4	13159	2600	...	10559	–
A Increase in stocks	413	413	...	–	–	192	192	...	–	–
B Gross fixed capital formation	15570	4796	...	10770	4	12967	2408	...	10559	–
Own account	...	...	...	...	...	...	...	...	...	...
Other	15570	4796	...	10770	4	12967	2408	...	10559	–
2 Purchases of land, net	–3203	27	...	–3230	–	–2832	31	...	–2863	–
3 Purchases of intangible assets, net										
4 Capital transfers	7131	4484	...	1818	925	6992	4067	...	2009	1028
A To other government subsectors	...	96	...	–	–	...	110	...	3	–
B To other resident sectors	7052	4309	...	1818	925	6881	3846	...	2006	1028
C To the rest of the world	79	79	...	–	–	111	111	...	–	–
Net lending	–12081	–19490	...	–2159	9568	–17527	–24023	...	–3356	9852
Gross accumulation	7830	–9770	...	7199	10497	–208	–17325	...	6349	10880

Denmark

	1992					1993				
	Total govern-ment	Central govern-ment	State or provincial govern-ment	Local govern-ment	Social security funds	Total govern-ment	Central govern-ment	State or provincial govern-ment	Local govern-ment	Social security funds
Finance of gross accumulation										
1 Gross saving	−2780	−22097	...	8396	10953	−11144	−28013	...	7106	9763
A Consumption of fixed capital	8558	2118	...	6437	3	9036	2268	...	6764	4
B Net saving	−11338	−24215	...	1959	10950	−20180	−30281	...	342	9759
2 Capital transfers	3802	3184	...	655	30	4249	3787	...	520	66
A From other government subsectors	...	–	...	68	–	...	–	...	124	–
B From other resident sectors	3372	2755	...	587	30	3740	3278	...	396	66
C From rest of the world	429	429	...	–	–	509	509	...	–	–
Finance of gross accumulation	1022	−18913	...	9051	10983	−6895	−24226	...	7626	9829
Gross accumulation										
1 Gross capital formation	19772	7796	...	11956	19	18941	6179	...	12759	4
A Increase in stocks	133	133	...	–	–	−6	−6	...	–	–
B Gross fixed capital formation	19639	7663	...	11956	19	18947	6185	...	12759	4
Own account	...	...	...	...	...	...	...	...	...	...
Other	19639	7663	...	11956	19	18947	6185	...	12759	4
2 Purchases of land, net	−2440	30	...	−2471	–	−1866	56	...	−1922	–
3 Purchases of intangible assets, net										
4 Capital transfers	8333	4928	...	2160	1313	9976	5643	...	2559	1898
A To other government subsectors	...	68	...	–	–	...	124	...	–	–
B To other resident sectors	8121	4648	...	2160	1313	9915	5458	...	2559	1898
C To the rest of the world	212	212	...	–	–	61	61	...	–	–
Net lending	−24642	−31667	...	−2595	9651	−33946	−36104	...	−5770	7928
Gross accumulation	1023	−18913	...	9050	10983	−6895	−24226	...	7626	9830

	1994					1995				
	Total govern-ment	Central govern-ment	State or provincial govern-ment	Local govern-ment	Social security funds	Total govern-ment	Central govern-ment	State or provincial govern-ment	Local govern-ment	Social security funds
Finance of gross accumulation										
1 Gross saving	−8398	−28816	...	10652	9766	−5059	−29210	...	14174	9977
A Consumption of fixed capital	9650	2488	...	7158	4	10055	2708	...	7343	4
B Net saving	−18048	−31304	...	3494	9762	−15114	−31918	...	6831	9973
2 Capital transfers	4072	3573	...	828	58	13658	9391	...	4766	57
A From other government subsectors	...	–	...	387	–	...	2	...	554	–
B From other resident sectors	3682	3182	...	441	58	13192	8923	...	4212	57
C From rest of the world	391	391	...	–	–	466	466	...	–	–
Finance of gross accumulation	−4326	−25243	...	11480	9824	8599	−19819	...	18940	10034
Gross accumulation										
1 Gross capital formation	19664	6732	...	12929	3	19194	6694	...	12497	3
A Increase in stocks	−249	−249	...	–	–	−463	−463	...	–	–
B Gross fixed capital formation	19913	6981	...	12929	3	19657	7157	...	12497	3
Own account	...	...	...	...	...	...	...	...	...	...
Other	19913	6981	...	12929	3	19657	7157	...	12497	3

Denmark

	1994					1995				
	Total govern-ment	Central govern-ment	State or provincial govern-ment	Local govern-ment	Social security funds	Total govern-ment	Central govern-ment	State or provincial govern-ment	Local govern-ment	Social security funds
2 Purchases of land, net	–1731	239	...	–1970	–	–1067	155	...	–1221	–
3 Purchases of intangible assets, net										
4 Capital transfers	9473	6130	...	2279	1451	9188	5860	...	2412	1472
A To other government sub-sectors	...	387	...	–	–	...	554	...	2	–
B To other resident sectors	9061	5331	...	2279	1451	8153	4271	...	2409	1472
C To the rest of the world	412	411	...	–	–	1035	1034	...	1	–
Net lending	–31732	–38344	...	–1758	8370	–18716	–32527	...	5252	8559
Gross accumulation	–4326	–25243	...	11480	9824	8599	–19818	...	18940	10034

3.21 Corporate and quasi-corporate enterprise production account: total and sectors
Million Danish kroner

	1987				1988				1989			
	Corporate and quasi-corporate enterprises			Adden-dum: total including unincor-porated	Corporate and quasi-corporate enterprises			Adden-dum: total including unincor-porated	Corporate and quasi-corporate enterprises			Adden-dum: total including unincor-porated
	Total	Non-financial	Financial		Total	Non-financial	Financial		Total	Non-financial	Financial	
Gross output												
Gross output	667809	633912	33897	...	692436	658205	34231	...	740626	701206	39420	...
Gross input												
Intermediate consumption	368026	333296	34730	...	379972	345931	34041	...	410431	371615	38816	...
1 Imputed bank service charge ..	22530	–	22530	...	21215	–	21215	...	24741	–	24741	...
2 Other intermediate consump-tion	345496	333296	12200	...	358757	345931	12826	...	385690	371615	14075	...
subtotal: Value added	299783	300616	–833	...	312464	312274	190	...	330195	329591	604	...
1 Indirect taxes, net	–2205	–2445	240	...	–4040	–5188	1148	...	–5880	–6876	996	...
A Indirect taxes	5421	5126	295	...	6242	4853	1389	...	6173	4897	1276	...
B less: Subsidies	7626	7571	55	...	10282	10041	241	...	12053	11773	280	...
2 Consumption of fixed capital .	62121	60306	1815	...	67291	65241	2050	...	71714	69568	2146	...
3 Compensation of employees ...	218361	198924	19437	...	223284	22834	20450	...	234444	212915	21529	...
4 Net operating surplus	21506	43831	–22325	...	25929	229387	–23458	...	29917	53984	–24067	...
Gross input	667809	633912	33897	...	692436	658205	34231	...	740626	701206	39420	...

	1990				1991				1992			
	Corporate and quasi-corporate enterprises			Adden-dum: total including unincor-porated	Corporate and quasi-corporate enterprises			Adden-dum: total including unincor-porated	Corporate and quasi-corporate enterprises			Adden-dum: total including unincor-porated
	Total	Non-financial	Financial		Total	Non-financial	Financial		Total	Non-financial	Financial	
Gross output												
Gross output	768949	730659	38290	...	793983	760722	33261	...	814409	785273	29136	...
Gross input												
Intermediate consumption	417575	379133	38442	...	427282	393268	34014	...	433701	403042	30659	...
1 Imputed bank service charge ..	23123	–	23123	...	18797	–	18797	...	15474	–	15474	...
2 Other intermediate consump-tion	394452	379133	15319	...	408485	393268	15217	...	418227	403042	15185	...
subtotal: Value added	351374	351526	–152	...	366701	367454	–753	...	380708	382231	–1523	...
1 Indirect taxes, net	–5831	–7205	1374	...	–4719	–6625	1906	...	–8464	–10659	2195	...
A Indirect taxes	6677	5002	1675	...	7497	5375	2122	...	7911	5508	2403	...

Denmark

	1990				1991				1992			
	Corporate and quasi-corporate enterprises			Addendum: total including unincorporated	Corporate and quasi-corporate enterprises			Addendum: total including unincorporated	Corporate and quasi-corporate enterprises			Addendum: total including unincorporated
	Total	Non-financial	Financial		Total	Non-financial	Financial		Total	Non-financial	Financial	
B less: Subsidies	12508	12207	301	...	12216	12000	216	...	16375	16167	208	...
2 Consumption of fixed capital	75517	73173	2344	...	80535	77807	2728	...	84023	81301	2722	...
3 Compensation of employees	246595	223485	23110	...	253872	229677	24195	...	260809	235960	24849	...
4 Net operating surplus	35093	62073	−26980	...	37013	66595	−29582	...	44340	75629	−31289	...
Gross input	768949	730659	38290	...	793983	760722	33261	...	814409	785273	29136	...

	1993				1994				1995			
	Corporate and quasi-corporate enterprises			Addendum: total including unincorporated	Corporate and quasi-corporate enterprises			Addendum: total including unincorporated	Corporate and quasi-corporate enterprises			Addendum: total including unincorporated
	Total	Non-financial	Financial		Total	Non-financial	Financial		Total	Non-financial	Financial	
Gross output												
Gross output	818788	783885	34903	...	867096	823634	43462	...	...	...	...	...
Gross input												
Intermediate consumption	432670	395669	37001	...	457177	411239	45938	...	...	...	...	...
1 Imputed bank service charge	18679	−	18679	...	25326	−	25326	...	...	...	...	...
2 Other intermediate consumption	413991	395669	18322	...	431851	411239	20612	...	...	...	...	...
subtotal: Value added	386118	388216	−2098	...	409919	412395	−2476	...	...	...	...	...
1 Indirect taxes, net	−6298	−8615	2317	...	−7101	−9440	2339	...	...	...	...	...
A Indirect taxes	9296	6699	2597	...	9614	7040	2574	...	...	...	...	...
B less: Subsidies	15594	15314	280	...	16715	16480	235	...	...	...	...	...
2 Consumption of fixed capital	86220	83420	2800	...	87408	84556	2852	...	...	...	...	...
3 Compensation of employees	256480	231950	24530	...	265690	241150	24540	...	...	...	...	...
4 Net operating surplus	49716	81461	−31745	...	63922	96129	−32207	...	...	...	...	...
Gross input	818788	783885	34903	...	867096	823634	43462	...	...	...	...	...

3.22 Corporate and quasi-corporate enterprise income and outlay account: total and sectors

Million Danish kroner

	1986			1987			1988			1989		
	Total	Non-financial	Financial	Total	Non-financial	Financial	Total	Non-financial	Financial	Total	Non-financial	Financial
Receipts												
1 Operating surplus [a]	29773	48945	−19172	21506	43831	−22325	25929	49387	−23458	29917	53984	−24067
2 Property and entrepreneurial income	27621	−14973	42594	33071	−10431	43502	29736	−13461	43197	23568	−19509	43077
3 Current transfers	26978	3938	23040	29720	4466	25254	32767	4923	27844	31953	4788	27165
A Casualty insurance claims	4484	4424	60	4991	4920	71	5474	5395	79	5345	5270	75
B Casualty insurance premiums, net, due to be received by insurance companies	12153	−	12153	13413	−	13413	14297	−	14297	13687	−	13687
C Current transfers from rest of the world	...	...	...	...	...	...	...	...	...	...	...	...
D Other transfers except imputed	10341	−486	10827	11316	−454	11770	12996	−472	13468	12921	−482	13403
E Imputed unfunded employee pension and welfare contributions												
Total current receipts	84372	37910	46462	84297	37866	46431	88432	40849	47583	85438	39263	46175

Disbursements

Denmark

Million Danish kroner

		1986			1987			1988			1989	
	Total	Non-financial	Financial	Total	Non-financial	Financial	Total	Non-financial	Financial	Total	Non-financial	Financial
1 Property and entrepreneurial income	...	...	...	...	...	...	...	...	...	...	...	...
2 Direct taxes and other current transfers n.e.c. to general government	27220	10155	17065	24982	14861	10121	26404	13315	13089	26849	10531	16318
3 Other current transfers	25327	7246	18081	27611	7796	19815	30066	8188	21878	29480	7740	21740
A Casualty insurance premiums, net	4484	4424	60	4991	4920	71	5474	5395	79	5345	5270	75
B Casualty insurance claims liability of insurance companies	12153	–	12153	13413	–	13413	14297	–	14297	13687	–	13687
C Transfers to private non-profit institutions	...	...	...	...	...	...	...	...	...	...	...	...
D Unfunded employee pension and welfare benefits	...	...	...	...	...	...	...	...	...	...	...	...
E Social assistance grants	...	...	...	...	...	...	...	...	...	...	...	...
F Other transfers n.e.c.	8690	2822	5868	9207	2876	6331	10295	2793	7502	10448	2470	7978
G Transfers to rest of the world	...	...	...	...	...	...	...	...	...	...	...	...
Statistical discrepancy [b]	3651	–	3651	3914	–	3914	4351	–	4351	4197	–	4197
Net saving	28174	20509	7665	27790	15209	12581	27611	19346	8265	24912	20992	3920
Total current disbursements and net saving	84372	37910	46462	84297	37866	46431	88432	40849	47583	85438	39263	46175

		1990			1991			1992			1993	
	Total	Non-financial	Financial	Total	Non-financial	Financial	Total	Non-financial	Financial	Total	Non-financial	Financial

Receipts

1 Operating surplus [a]	35093	62073	–26980	37013	66595	–29582	44340	75629	–31289	49716	81461	–31745
2 Property and entrepreneurial income	23669	–18280	41949	18768	–19143	37911	11017	–21885	32902	15200	–19815	35015
3 Current transfers	35957	5769	30188	37221	5924	31297	39032	5632	33400	43370	5369	38001
A Casualty insurance claims	5282	5204	78	6791	6701	90	6703	6591	112	6923	6789	134
B Casualty insurance premiums, net, due to be received by insurance companies	14245	–	14245	16641	–	16641	17196	–	17196	19818	–	19818
C Current transfers from rest of the world	...	...	...	...	...	...	...	...	...	...	...	...
D Other transfers except imputed	16430	565	15865	13789	–777	14566	15133	–959	16092	16629	–1420	18049
E Imputed unfunded employee pension and welfare contributions												
Total current receipts	94719	49562	45157	93002	53376	39626	94389	59376	35013	108286	67015	41271

Disbursements

1 Property and entrepreneurial income	...	...	...	...	...	...	...	...	...	...	...	...
2 Direct taxes and other current transfers n.e.c. to general government	20895	10168	10727	21548	11790	9758	22890	11345	11545	29874	15742	14132
3 Other current transfers	29232	5597	23635	31168	4656	26512	31413	3081	28332	37448	4873	32575
A Casualty insurance premiums, net	5282	5204	78	6791	6701	90	6703	6591	112	6923	6789	134
B Casualty insurance claims liability of insurance companies	14245	–	14245	16641	–	16641	17196	–	17196	19818	–	19818
C Transfers to private non-profit institutions	...	...	...	...	...	...	...	...	...	...	...	...

Denmark

	1990			1991			1992			1993		
	Total	Non-financial	Financial	Total	Non-financial	Financial	Total	Non-financial	Financial	Total	Non-financial	Financial
D Unfunded employee pension and welfare benefits	...	...	...	...	...	...	...	...	...	...	...	...
E Social assistance grants	...	...	...	...	...	...	...	...	...	...	...	...
F Other transfers n.e.c.	9705	393	9312	7736	−2045	9781	7514	−3510	11024	10707	−1916	12623
G Transfers to rest of the world	...	...	...	...	...	...	...	...	...	...	...	...
Statistical discrepancy [b]	5247	–	5247	4785	–	4785	5068	–	5068	5426	–	5426
Net saving	39345	33797	5548	35501	36930	−1429	35018	44950	−9932	35538	46400	−10862
Total current disbursements and net saving	94719	49562	45157	93002	53376	39626	94389	59376	35013	108286	67015	41271

	1994			1995			1996			1997		
	Total	Non-financial	Financial	Total	Non-financial	Financial	Total	Non-financial	Financial	Total	Non-financial	Financial
Receipts												
1 Operating surplus [a]	63922	96129	−32207	...	...	...	...	...	...	...	...	...
2 Property and entrepreneurial income	14022	−34104	48126	...	...	...	...	...	...	...	...	...
3 Current transfers	47777	6492	41285	...	...	...	...	...	...	...	...	...
A Casualty insurance claims	7476	7369	107	...	...	...	...	...	...	...	...	...
B Casualty insurance premiums, net, due to be received by insurance companies	19238	–	19238	...	...	...	...	...	...	...	...	...
C Current transfers from rest of the world	...	...	...	...	...	...	...	...	...	...	...	...
D Other transfers except imputed	21063	−877	21940	...	...	...	...	...	...	...	...	...
E Imputed unfunded employee pension and welfare contributions				...	...	...	...	...	...	...	...	...
Total current receipts	125721	68517	57204	...	...	...	...	...	...	...	...	...
Disbursements												
1 Property and entrepreneurial income	...	...	...	...	...	...	...	...	...	...	...	...
2 Direct taxes and other current transfers n.e.c. to general government	28494	14124	14370	...	...	...	...	...	...	...	...	...
3 Other current transfers	38774	6616	32158	...	...	...	...	...	...	...	...	...
A Casualty insurance premiums, net	7476	7369	107	...	...	...	...	...	...	...	...	...
B Casualty insurance claims liability of insurance companies	19238	–	19238	...	...	...	...	...	...	...	...	...
C Transfers to private non-profit institutions	...	...	...	...	...	...	...	...	...	...	...	...
D Unfunded employee pension and welfare benefits	...	...	...	...	...	...	...	...	...	...	...	...
E Social assistance grants	...	...	...	...	...	...	...	...	...	...	...	...
F Other transfers n.e.c.	12060	−753	12813	...	...	...	...	...	...	...	...	...
G Transfers to rest of the world	...	...	...	...	...	...	...	...	...	...	...	...
Statistical discrepancy [b]	9127	–	9127	...	...	...	...	...	...	...	...	...
Net saving	49326	47777	1549	...	...	...	...	...	...	...	...	...
Total current disbursements and net saving	125721	68517	57204	...	...	...	...	...	...	...	...	...

a Item "Property and entrepreneurial income" received is net of item "Property income" paid.

b Item "Statistical discrepancy" refers to change in the actuarial reserves for pensions.

Denmark

3.23 Corporate and quasi-corporate enterprise capital accumulation account: total and sectors

Million Danish kroner

	1986 Total	1986 Non-financial	1986 Financial	1987 Total	1987 Non-financial	1987 Financial	1988 Total	1988 Non-financial	1988 Financial	1989 Total	1989 Non-financial	1989 Financial
Finance of gross accumulation												
1 Gross saving	85436	76114	9322	89911	75515	14396	94902	84587	10315	96626	90560	6066
A Consumption of fixed capital	57262	55605	1657	62121	60306	1815	67291	65241	2050	71714	69568	2146
B Net saving	28174	20509	7665	27790	15209	12581	27611	19346	8265	24912	20992	3920
2 Capital transfers	5262	5262	–	5072	5072	–	6310	6310	–	5811	5811	–
Finance of gross accumulation	90698	81376	9322	94983	80587	14396	101212	90897	10315	102437	96371	6066
Gross accumulation												
1 Gross capital formation	86246	81930	4316	77169	72743	4426	80114	75713	4401	87214	84876	2338
A Increase in stocks	6068	6068	–	–3821	–3821	–	–1395	–1395	–	1889	1889	–
B Gross fixed capital formation	80178	75862	4316	80990	76564	4426	81509	77108	4401	85325	82987	2338
2 Purchases of land, net	1505	1505	–	1421	1421	–	1404	1404	–	1467	1467	–
3 Purchases of intangible assets, net												
4 Capital transfers	196	195	1	368	214	154	107	92	15	88	80	8
Net lending	2751	–2254	5005	16025	6209	9816	19587	13688	5899	13668	9948	3720
Gross accumulation	90698	81376	9322	94983	80587	14396	101212	90897	10315	102437	96371	6066

	1990 Total	1990 Non-financial	1990 Financial	1991 Total	1991 Non-financial	1991 Financial	1992 Total	1992 Non-financial	1992 Financial	1993 Total	1993 Non-financial	1993 Financial
Finance of gross accumulation												
1 Gross saving	114862	106970	7892	116036	114737	1299	119041	126251	–7210	121758	129820	–8062
A Consumption of fixed capital	75517	73173	2344	80535	77807	2728	84023	81301	2722	86220	83420	2800
B Net saving	39345	33797	5548	35501	36930	–1429	35018	44950	–9932	35538	46400	–10862
2 Capital transfers	5146	5146	–	5089	5089	–	5619	5619	–	6314	6314	–
Finance of gross accumulation	120008	112116	7892	121125	119826	1299	124660	131870	–7210	128072	136134	–8062
Gross accumulation												
1 Gross capital formation	87848	84633	3215	88999	84593	4406	79049	78573	476	72937	73037	–100
A Increase in stocks	–1371	–1371	–	–1034	–1034	–	–1511	–1511	–	–7006	–7006	–
B Gross fixed capital formation	89219	86004	3215	90033	85627	4406	80560	80084	476	79943	80043	–100
2 Purchases of land, net	1709	1709	–	1445	1445	–	1191	1191	–	905	905	–
3 Purchases of intangible assets, net												
4 Capital transfers	333	247	86	384	383	1	124	124	–	174	149	25
Net lending	30118	25527	4591	30297	33405	–3108	44296	51982	–7686	54056	62043	–7987
Gross accumulation	120008	112116	7892	121125	119826	1299	124660	131870	–7210	128072	136134	–8062

	1994 Total	1994 Non-financial	1994 Financial	1995 Total	1995 Non-financial	1995 Financial	1996 Total	1996 Non-financial	1996 Financial	1997 Total	1997 Non-financial	1997 Financial
Finance of gross accumulation												
1 Gross saving	136734	132333	4401	...	...	...	...	...	...	...	...	...
A Consumption of fixed capital	87408	84556	2852	...	...	...	...	...	...	...	...	...
B Net saving	49326	47777	1549	...	...	...	...	...	...	...	...	...

Denmark

	1994 Total	1994 Non-financial	1994 Financial	1995 Total	1995 Non-financial	1995 Financial	1996 Total	1996 Non-financial	1996 Financial	1997 Total	1997 Non-financial	1997 Financial
2 Capital transfers	5529	5529	–	...	...	...	...	...	...	...	...	...
Finance of gross accumulation	142263	137862	4401	...	...	...	...	...	...	...	...	...
Gross accumulation												
1 Gross capital formation	84654	84485	169	...	...	...	...	...	...	...	...	...
A Increase in stocks	377	377	–	...	...	...	...	...	...	...	...	...
B Gross fixed capital formation	84277	84108	169	...	...	...	...	...	...	...	...	...
2 Purchases of land, net	908	908		...	...	...	...	...	...	...	...	...
3 Purchases of intangible assets, net				...	...	...	...	...	...	...	...	...
4 Capital transfers	168	168	–	...	...	...	...	...	...	...	...	...
Net lending	56533	52301	4232	...	...	...	...	...	...	...	...	...
Gross accumulation	142263	137862	4401	...	...	...	...	...	...	...	...	...

3.31 Household and private unincorporated enterprise production account

Million Danish kroner

	1986	1987	1988	1989	1990	1991	1992	1993	1994	1995	1996	1997
Gross output												
A Owner-occupied housing	...	...	...	...	...	...	...	...	...	...	...	...
B Own-account fixed capital formation	...	...	...	...	...	...	302202	312590	323195	...	...	...
C Other subsistence output	...	...	...	...	...	...	...	...	...	...	...	...
Gross output	258098	264961	270470	283353	288791	293476	302202	312590	323195	...	...	...
Gross input												
Intermediate consumption	108716	110918	111631	114583	114726	113901	117807	121806	123729	...	...	...
subtotal: Value added	149382	154043	158839	168770	174065	179575	184395	190784	199466	...	...	...
1 Indirect taxes net liability of unincorporated enterprises	542	1856	268	86	–375	–814	–2366	–2187	–2845	...	...	...
A Indirect taxes	4658	5951	5755	5986	5886	5734	5757	7088	7061	...	...	...
B less: Subsidies	4116	4095	5487	5900	6261	6548	8123	9275	9906	...	...	...
2 Consumption of fixed capital	31894	35036	36200	38430	39613	40632	42710	43944	44765	...	...	...
3 Compensation of employees	41841	44757	47475	45431	45911	46649	48220	50508	52350	...	...	...
4 Net operating surplus	75105	72394	74896	84823	88916	93108	95831	98519	105196	...	...	...
Gross input	258098	264961	270470	283353	288791	293476	302202	312590	323195	...	...	...

3.32 Household and private unincorporated enterprise income and outlay account

Million Danish kroner

	1986	1987	1988	1989	1990	1991	1992	1993	1994	1995	1996	1997
Receipts												
1 Compensation of employees	356440	389186	407367	422355	439556	454786	469035	471949	486747	...	...	...
2 Operating surplus of private unincorporated enterprises	75105	72394	74896	84823	88916	93108	95831	98519	105196	...	...	...
3 Property and entrepreneurial income	–29200	–34886	–34170	–36101	–38140	–31537	–32708	–26055	–24895	...	...	...
4 Current transfers	117316	128882	143831	157358	166441	178234	190355	205892	231145	...	...	...
A Casualty insurance claims	7523	8252	8640	8172	8786	9643	10224	12607	11527	...	...	...
B Social security benefits	105215	115522	128887	141245	148847	159142	169699	181912	207107	...	...	...
C Social assistance grants										...	...	...

Denmark

Million Danish kroner

	1986	1987	1988	1989	1990	1991	1992	1993	1994	1995	1996	1997
D Unfunded employee pension and welfare benefits										...	...	...
E Transfers from general government	...	...	...	...	...	...	...	...	...	...	...	...
F Transfers from rest of the world	...	...	...	...	...	...	...	...	...	...	...	...
G Other transfers n.e.c. [a]	4578	5108	6304	7941	8808	9449	10432	11373	12511	...	...	...
Statistical discrepancy	3651	3914	4351	4197	5247	4785	5068	5426	9127	...	...	...
Total current receipts	523312	559490	596275	632632	662020	699376	727581	755731	807320	...	...	...
Disbursements												
1 Final consumption expenditure	366747	377878	388806	403894	415032	430201	447075	458807	497775	...	...	...
2 Property income	...	...	...	...	...	...	...	...	...	...	...	...
3 Direct taxes and other current transfers n.e.c. to general government	188384	208001	221920	231592	239255	250791	263483	272890	301851	...	...	...
A Social security contributions	20137	24039	22076	23015	26882	27137	29691	32594	37590	...	...	...
B Direct taxes	168247	183962	199844	208577	212373	223654	233792	240296	264261	...	...	...
C Fees, fines and penalties	...	...	...	...	...	...	...	...	...	...	...	...
4 Other current transfers	17310	19108	21019	20833	22187	23385	24612	28762	28598	...	...	...
A Net casualty insurance premiums	7523	8252	8640	8172	8786	9643	10224	12607	11527	...	...	...
B Transfers to private non-profit institutions serving households	...	...	...	...	...	...	...	...	...	...	...	...
C Transfers to rest of the world	...	...	...	...	...	...	...	...	...	...	...	...
D Other current transfers, except imputed [b]	3506	3796	4710	4425	4983	4721	4809	6153	6106	...	...	...
E Imputed employee pension and welfare contributions	6281	7060	7669	8236	8418	9021	9579	10002	10965	...	...	...
Net saving	−49129	−45497	−35470	−23687	−14454	−5001	−7589	−4728	−20904	...	...	...
Total current disbursements and net saving	523312	559490	596275	632632	662020	699376	727581	755731	807320	...	...	...

a Includes items "Transfers from general government" and "transfers from the rest of the world".

b Includes items "Transfers to private non-profit institutions serving households" and "Transfers to the rest of the world".

3.33 Household and private unincorporated enterprise capital accumulation account

Million Danish kroner

	1986	1987	1988	1989	1990	1991	1992	1993	1994	1995	1996	1997
Finance of gross accumulation												
1 Gross saving	−17235	−10461	730	14743	25159	35631	35121	39216	23861	...	...	...
A Consumption of fixed capital	31894	35036	36200	38430	39613	40632	42710	43944	44765	...	...	...
B Net saving	−49129	−45497	−35470	−23687	−14454	−5001	−7589	−4728	−20904	...	...	...
2 Capital transfers	1426	1926	1955	3253	2540	2193	2796	3788	3814	...	...	...
Total finance of gross accumulation	−15809	−8535	2685	17996	27699	37824	37917	43004	27675	...	...	...
Gross accumulation												
1 Gross capital formation	44011	40990	34632	37540	34611	33869	32783	32462	33799	...	...	...
A Increase in stocks	−312	−472	751	530	43	175	−841	81	−42	...	...	...
B Gross fixed capital formation	44323	41462	33881	37010	34568	33694	33624	32381	33841	...	...	...
2 Purchases of land, net	847	827	965	1458	1494	1387	1249	961	868	...	...	...

Denmark

Million Danish kroner

	1986	1987	1988	1989	1990	1991	1992	1993	1994	1995	1996	1997
3 Purchases of intangibles, net ..										...	...	...
4 Capital transfers	2651	2901	3120	2960	5049	6432	3721	4106	4104	...	...	...
Net lending	−63318	−53253	−36032	−23962	−13455	−3864	164	5475	−11096	...	...	...
Total gross accumulation	−15809	−8535	2685	17996	27699	37824	37917	43004	27675	...	...	...

3.51 External transactions, current account: detail

Million Danish kroner

	1986	1987	1988	1989	1990	1991	1992	1993	1994	1995	1996	1997
Payments to the rest of the world												
1 Imports of goods and services	216555	207226	214892	238936	240442	255567	251142	238970	272290	290751	...	...
A Imports of merchandise, c.i.f.	184388	173651	175786	195705	196348	208642	204675	190858	218803	236445	...	...
B Other	32167	33575	39106	43231	44094	46925	46467	48112	53487	54306	...	...
2 Factor income to rest of the world	46612	48430	55479	68885	75124	96349	131880	181236	176602	187459	...	...
A Compensation of employees	704	647	744	831	921	932	964	1036	1266	1170	...	...
B Property and entrepreneurial income	45908	47783	54735	68054	74203	95417	130916	180200	175336	186289	...	...
3 Current transfers to the rest of the world	15029	14807	16225	15579	15309	17151	15490	18892	21072	19663	...	...
A Indirect taxes by general government to supranational organizations	2260	2201	2383	2639	2475	7609	7199	6810	6996	7415	...	...
B Other current transfers	12769	12606	13842	12940	12834	9542	8291	12082	14076	12248	...	...
4 Surplus of the nation on current transactions	−36215	−20603	−9429	−11342	4077	9088	19785	26403	16542	6053	...	...
Payments to the rest of the world and surplus of the nation on current transfers	241981	249860	277167	312058	334952	378155	418297	465501	486506	503926	...	...
Receipts from the rest of the world												
1 Exports of goods and services	213559	220084	238915	264909	283574	306006	309395	300169	327820	330448	...	...
A Exports of merchandise, f.o.b.	171723	175132	186333	208544	221412	235165	243988	235798	260947	269076	...	...
B Other	41836	44952	52582	56365	62162	70841	65407	64371	66873	61372	...	...
2 Factor income from rest of the world	19119	20863	27746	38015	40831	62257	99509	153327	147833	162835	...	...
A Compensation of employees	914	942	1005	1092	1214	2786	3018	3122	2925	3077	...	...
B Property and entrepreneurial income	18205	19921	26741	36923	39617	59471	96491	150205	144908	159758	...	...
3 Current transfers from rest of the world	9303	8913	10505	9135	10546	9892	9392	12006	10853	10643	...	...
A Subsidies to general government from supranational organizations	8424	9837	9362	8828	9415	9714	9382	11363	10504	10244	...	...
B Other current transfers	879	−924	1143	307	1131	178	10	643	349	399	...	...
Receipts from the rest of the world on current transfers	241981	249860	277166	312059	334951	378155	418296	465502	486506	503926	...	...

Denmark

3.52 External transactions, capital accumulation account

Million Danish kroner

	1986	1987	1988	1989	1990	1991	1992	1993	1994	1995	1996	1997
Finance of gross accumulation
1 Surplus of the nation on current transactions	−36215	−20603	−9429	−11342	4077	9088	19785	26403	16542	6053	...	...
2 Capital transfers from rest of the world	782	994	784	1736	859	781	723	843	937	1091	...	...
Total finance of gross accumulation	−35433	−19609	−8645	−9606	4936	9869	20508	27246	17479	7144	...	...
Gross accumulation
1 Capital transfers to the rest of the world	1526	618	790	635	354	963	683	599	1032	1450	...	...
2 Purchases of intangible assets, n.e.c., net, from rest of the world	...	...	...	...	...	...	...	...	...	...	...	...
Net lending to the rest of the world	−36959	−20227	−9435	−10240	4582	8906	19824	26648	16443	5692	...	...
Total gross accumulation	−35433	−19609	−8645	−9605	4936	9869	20507	27247	17475	7142	...	...

4.1 Derivation of value added by kind of activity, in current prices

Million Danish kroner

	1986			1987			1988			1989		
	Gross output	Intermediate consumption	Value added	Gross output	Intermediate consumption	Value added	Gross output	Intermediate consumption	Value added	Gross output	Intermediate consumption	Value added
All producers
1 Agriculture, hunting, forestry and fishing	59056	29051	30005	56415	29077	27339	56546	28953	27593	61386	29718	31669
A Agriculture and hunting	53953	27176	26777	51403	27219	24184	51637	27055	24582	56245	27802	28444
B Forestry and logging	1057	41	1016	993	16	977	1043	42	1001	1105	46	1059
C Fishing	4046	1834	2212	4019	1842	2178	3866	1856	2010	4036	1870	2166
2 Mining and quarrying	7057	1730	5328	7321	1932	5389	6233	1773	4460	8211	1952	6259
A Coal mining	...	...	...	...	...	...	...	...	...	...	...	...
B Crude petroleum and natural gas production	5531	1272	4259	5803	1448	4355	4783	1349	3434	6707	1526	5181
C Metal ore mining	...	...	...	...	...	...	...	...	...	...	...	...
D Other mining	1526	458	1069	1518	484	1034	1450	424	1026	1504	426	1078
3 Manufacturing	321215	209513	111703	316251	202381	113870	326865	206991	119875	345220	221649	123572
A Manufacture of food, beverages and tobacco	98267	74026	24241	95317	70847	24470	96262	71027	25235	99739	74403	25337
B Textile, wearing apparel and leather industries	17653	11291	6362	17269	10939	6330	16901	10661	6241	16743	10733	6010
C Manufacture of wood and wood products, including furniture	16637	10354	6283	16299	10075	6223	16465	10210	6256	18105	11236	6869
D Manufacture of paper and paper products, printing and publishing	30954	18892	12062	32577	19732	12845	33497	20264	13232	34495	20850	13645
E Manufacture of chemicals and chemical petroleum, coal, rubber and plastic products	41764	28153	13611	42369	28138	14232	43831	28324	15506	47191	30805	16386

Denmark

Million Danish kroner

	1986 Gross output	1986 Intermediate consumption	1986 Value added	1987 Gross output	1987 Intermediate consumption	1987 Value added	1988 Gross output	1988 Intermediate consumption	1988 Value added	1989 Gross output	1989 Intermediate consumption	1989 Value added
F Manufacture of non-metallic mineral products, except products of petroleum and coal	12548	6700	5848	12372	6434	5938	12077	6462	5616	12363	6714	5649
G Basic metal industries	4136	2784	1353	3668	2340	1327	3992	2557	1435	4638	3027	1611
H Manufacture of fabricated metal products, machinery and equipment	94197	54609	39588	91319	51326	39994	98405	54924	43481	105926	61011	44915
I Other manufacturing industries	5059	2704	2355	5061	2550	2511	5435	2562	2873	6020	2870	3150
4 Electricity, gas and water	20354	11846	8509	20797	11569	9228	20191	10257	9935	22216	10490	11726
A Electricity, gas and steam	19203	11507	7696	19627	11191	8436	19022	9873	9149	21007	10068	10939
B Water works and supply	1151	339	813	1170	378	792	1169	384	786	1209	422	787
5 Construction	90535	52849	37686	97883	54552	43331	96913	53975	42939	96906	56178	40728
6 Wholesale and retail trade, restaurants and hotels	127436	39085	88351	128962	41009	87952	128120	41772	86348	134958	43515	91443
A Wholesale and retail trade	109342	28838	80504	110211	30378	79833	108461	30627	77834	114705	32161	82543
B Restaurants and hotels	18094	10247	7847	18751	10631	8119	19659	11145	8514	20253	11354	8900
7 Transport, storage and communication	84967	40197	44770	90879	42863	48016	99633	46401	53232	110759	52476	58283
A Transport and storage	70262	34945	35317	73642	36092	37550	81577	39652	41925	91704	45980	45724
B Communication	14705	5252	9453	17237	6771	10466	18056	6749	11307	19055	6496	12559
8 Finance, insurance, real estate and business services	149249	48359	100890	162043	54812	107232	173648	58759	114889	187902	60125	127777
A Financial institutions	28401	8132	20269	28437	10128	18310	28129	11356	16773	32629	12058	20572
B Insurance	4419	2644	1775	5460	2312	3148	6102	2617	3485	6791	3012	3778
C Real estate and business services	116429	37583	78846	128146	42372	85774	139417	44786	94631	148482	45055	103427
Real estate, except dwellings	...	...	...	...	...	...	...	...	...	...	...	...
Dwellings	66826	18378	48448	72336	21025	51311	78214	22393	55820	84399	22181	62218
9 Community, social and personal services	42616	14842	27773	47577	17236	30341	49834	16936	32897	51253	17562	33692
A Sanitary and similar services	...	...	...	...	...	...	...	...	...	...	...	...
B Social and related community services	8180	1467	6712	8597	1571	7026	9681	1525	8155	9884	1626	8258
Educational services	693	205	488	754	238	516	865	121	744	875	258	617
Medical, dental, other health and veterinary services	7487	1262	6224	7843	1333	6510	8816	1404	7411	9009	1368	7641
C Recreational and cultural services	6859	1638	5221	7456	1710	5746	7703	1861	5842	8729	2367	6363
D Personal and household services	27577	11737	15840	31524	13955	17569	32450	13550	18900	32640	13569	19071
Total, Industries	902483	447469	455014	928130	455434	472697	957984	465818	492166	1018812	493663	525149
Producers of government services	174715	54905	119810	192846	61076	131770	206736	63970	142766	216260	67016	149244
Other producers	4257	555	3702	4640	631	4009	4924	798	4125	5167	816	4350
Total [a]	1081456	502930	578526	1125616	517141	608476	1169643	530586	639058	1240239	561495	678744
less: Imputed bank service charge	...	−22850	22850	...	−22530	22530	...	−21215	21215	...	−24741	24741
Import duties	...	...	...	...	...	...	...	...	...	...	...	...
Value added tax	...	...	...	...	...	...	...	...	...	...	...	...

Denmark

Million Danish kroner

	1986			1987			1988			1989		
	Gross output	Intermediate consumption	Value added	Gross output	Intermediate consumption	Value added	Gross output	Intermediate consumption	Value added	Gross output	Intermediate consumption	Value added
Other adjustments [b]	110820	...	110820	113963	...	113963	114211	...	114211	113246	...	113246
Total	1192276	525780	666496	1239579	539671	699909	1283854	551801	732053	1353485	586236	767248
memorandum item: Mineral fuels and power	34177	21165	13011	34032	20462	13569	31254	17888	13366	37120	19881	17238

	1990			1991			1992			1993		
	Gross output	Intermediate consumption	Value added	Gross output	Intermediate consumption	Value added	Gross output	Intermediate consumption	Value added	Gross output	Intermediate consumption	Value added
All producers												
1 Agriculture, hunting, forestry and fishing	60077	29776	30301	58505	28891	29614	58627	29387	29239	55635	27852	27785
A Agriculture and hunting	55144	27949	27194	53256	27092	26164	53363	27579	25784	51601	26139	25463
B Forestry and logging	1156	36	1121	1208	−30	1238	1127	−37	1163	882	−28	910
C Fishing	3777	1791	1986	4041	1829	2212	4137	1845	2292	3152	1741	1412
2 Mining and quarrying	9373	2076	7299	9591	2701	6889	10020	2580	7440	10508	3403	7106
A Coal mining	...	...	...	...	...	...	...	...	...	...	...	...
B Crude petroleum and natural gas production	7946	1633	6314	8205	2214	5990	8506	2094	6412	8633	2747	5886
C Metal ore mining	...	...	...	...	...	...	...	...	...	...	...	...
D Other mining	1427	443	985	1386	487	899	1514	486	1028	1875	656	1220
3 Manufacturing	356613	226694	129919	365509	231271	134238	378599	238173	140426	372792	228672	144121
A Manufacture of food, beverages and tobacco	101213	74532	26681	105285	76563	28721	110912	80758	30154	108529	77185	31344
B Textile, wearing apparel and leather industries	16860	10828	6032	17043	10761	6282	17771	11409	6362	16716	10920	5796
C Manufacture of wood and wood products, including furniture	19315	12036	7279	19999	12372	7628	21287	13057	8229	21808	13206	8602
D Manufacture of paper and paper products, printing and publishing	35480	21350	14130	36016	21498	14518	36125	20957	15169	35167	19846	15322
E Manufacture of chemicals and chemical petroleum, coal, rubber and plastic products	49345	31789	17556	50371	33045	17327	52342	33204	19138	52116	32213	19903
F Manufacture of non-metallic mineral products, except products of petroleum and coal	12457	6700	5757	12582	6926	5656	12393	6717	5677	11965	6013	5951
G Basic metal industries	4507	2843	1664	4248	2632	1616	3958	2419	1539	3555	2247	1309
H Manufacture of fabricated metal products, machinery and equipment	110935	63431	47504	113127	64151	48975	117400	66870	50529	116662	64693	51969
I Other manufacturing industries	6501	3185	3316	6838	3323	3515	6411	2782	3629	6274	2349	3925
4 Electricity, gas and water	23166	10655	12511	26395	11643	14752	26091	10695	15395	26460	11035	15425
A Electricity, gas and steam	21971	10220	11751	25118	11191	13927	24808	10235	14573	25083	10570	14513
B Water works and supply	1195	435	760	1277	452	825	1283	460	822	1377	465	912
5 Construction	96359	55757	40601	90624	52293	38331	95294	52911	42382	91883	50594	41289
6 Wholesale and retail trade, restaurants and hotels	140124	44656	95467	147490	47725	99765	152977	47713	105264	154777	49287	105489
A Wholesale and retail trade	119439	33153	86286	125830	35520	90310	129921	34784	95137	131662	37081	94580
B Restaurants and hotels	20685	11503	9181	21660	12205	9455	23056	12929	10127	23115	12206	10909
7 Transport, storage and communication	112707	50334	62373	123728	58306	65423	125904	56494	69411	135183	64173	71010

Denmark

	1990			1991			1992			1993		
	Gross output	Intermediate consumption	Value added	Gross output	Intermediate consumption	Value added	Gross output	Intermediate consumption	Value added	Gross output	Intermediate consumption	Value added
A Transport and storage	92575	44513	48062	102575	51214	51362	103360	49716	53645	111771	56568	55202
B Communication	20132	5821	14311	21153	7092	14061	22544	6778	15766	23412	7605	15808
8 Finance, insurance, real estate and business services	199696	63746	135951	203222	64011	139211	202585	66568	136018	214233	70624	143609
A Financial institutions	30963	13059	17905	27095	13199	13896	24006	13112	10895	29947	15895	14052
B Insurance	7326	3634	3692	6166	3925	2241	5127	4267	860	4956	4645	311
C Real estate and business services	161407	47053	114354	169961	46887	123074	173452	49189	124263	179330	50084	129246
Real estate, except dwellings	...	...	...	...	...	...	...	...	...	...	...	...
Dwellings	89922	21655	68267	94757	21211	73546	98544	23039	75505	102111	25109	77003
9 Community, social and personal services	53612	18261	35352	56121	19038	37082	59889	19620	40268	62652	21409	41241
A Sanitary and similar services	...	...	...	...	...	...	...	...	...	...	...	...
B Social and related community services	10503	1732	8772	11109	1865	9244	12130	1899	10230	12524	2127	10396
Educational services	964	283	681	1007	306	701	1040	233	806	1063	337	726
Medical, dental, other health and veterinary services	9539	1449	8091	10102	1559	8543	11090	1666	9424	11461	1790	9670
C Recreational and cultural services	9077	2404	6673	10031	2623	7408	11291	2966	8325	12531	3742	8789
D Personal and household services	34032	14125	19907	34981	14550	20430	36468	14755	21713	37597	15540	22056
Total, Industries	1051728	501953	549775	1081184	515878	565306	1109984	524140	585844	1124123	527047	597076
Producers of government services	223879	69583	154296	234844	74521	160323	244370	77859	166511	257831	85915	171916
Other producers	6012	1018	4994	6276	975	5300	6626	1061	5565	7784	1363	6421
Total [a]	1281619	572554	709065	1322304	591374	730930	1360980	603060	757919	1389738	614324	775414
less: Imputed bank service charge	...	−23123	23123	...	−18797	18797	...	−15474	15474	...	−18679	18679
Import duties	...	...	...	...	...	...	...	...	...	...	...	...
Value added tax	...	...	...	...	...	...	...	...	...	...	...	...
Other adjustments [b]	113169	–	113169	115736	–	115736	113586	–	113586	117659	–	117659
Total	1394788	595677	799111	1438040	610171	827868	1474566	618534	856032	1507397	633003	874393
memorandum item: Mineral fuels and power	39408	20415	18993	42598	22342	20256	42066	20778	21288	42324	21579	20745

	1994			1995			1996			1997		
	Gross output	Intermediate consumption	Value added	Gross output	Intermediate consumption	Value added	Gross output	Intermediate consumption	Value added	Gross output	Intermediate consumption	Value added

All producers

1 Agriculture, hunting, forestry and fishing	54708	24397	30311	57904	22906	34999	...	...	...	...	...	...
A Agriculture and hunting	50482	22539	27943	53625	21427	32198	...	...	...	...	...	...
B Forestry and logging	925	−57	982	835	−71	906	...	...	...	...	...	...
C Fishing	3301	1915	1386	3444	1550	1895	...	...	...	...	...	...
2 Mining and quarrying	10705	3036	7670	10407	3183	7225	...	...	...	...	...	...
A Coal mining	...	...	...	...	...	...	...	...	...	...	...	...
B Crude petroleum and natural gas production	8709	2465	6245	8347	2558	5789	...	...	...	...	...	...
C Metal ore mining	...	...	...	...	...	...	...	...	...	...	...	...
D Other mining	1996	571	1425	2060	625	1436	...	...	...	...	...	...

Denmark

	1994			1995			1996			1997		
	Gross output	Intermediate consumption	Value added	Gross output	Intermediate consumption	Value added	Gross output	Intermediate consumption	Value added	Gross output	Intermediate consumption	Value added
3 Manufacturing	396711	241056	155655	425521	259535	165985	...	...	...	...	...	...
A Manufacture of food, beverages and tobacco	107130	77226	29904	105473	74709	30764	...	...	...	...	...	...
B Textile, wearing apparel and leather industries	17900	11279	6621	19032	12409	6622	...	...	...	...	...	...
C Manufacture of wood and wood products, including furniture	26278	15772	10506	27098	16595	10502	...	...	...	...	...	...
D Manufacture of paper and paper products, printing and publishing	38220	21134	17086	45789	25250	20540	...	...	...	...	...	...
E Manufacture of chemicals and chemical petroleum, coal, rubber and plastic products	56097	34088	22009	61024	37968	23056	...	...	...	...	...	...
F Manufacture of non-metallic mineral products, except products of petroleum and coal	13757	6353	7404	14812	7305	7507	...	...	...	...	...	...
G Basic metal industries	4161	2601	1560	5007	2964	2043	...	...	...	...	...	...
H Manufacture of fabricated metal products, machinery and equipment	126807	70492	56315	140734	79973	60761	...	...	...	...	...	...
I Other manufacturing industries	6361	2111	4250	6552	2362	4190	...	...	...	...	...	...
4 Electricity, gas and water	26414	10365	16049	26768	10596	16172	...	...	...	...	...	...
A Electricity, gas and steam	25008	9882	15125	25270	10134	15136	...	...	...	...	...	...
B Water works and supply	1406	483	924	1498	462	1036	...	...	...	...	...	...
5 Construction	93770	52354	41416	102557	57064	45493	...	...	...	...	...	...
6 Wholesale and retail trade, restaurants and hotels	161586	51092	110494	164285	53194	111092	...	...	...	...	...	...
A Wholesale and retail trade	136139	37814	98325	139105	40542	98563	...	...	...	...	...	...
B Restaurants and hotels	25447	13278	12169	25180	12652	12529	...	...	...	...	...	...
7 Transport, storage and communication	142441	68556	73886	139138	63606	75533	...	...	...	...	...	...
A Transport and storage	117013	60480	56534	114370	55225	59146	...	...	...	...	...	...
B Communication	25428	8076	17352	24768	8381	16387	...	...	...	...	...	...
8 Finance, insurance, real estate and business services	229816	77074	152742	237992	79752	158240	...	...	...	...	...	...
A Financial institutions	37347	17553	19794	35706	15777	19929	...	...	...	...	...	...
B Insurance	6114	5398	716	6286	5622	664	...	...	...	...	...	...
C Real estate and business services	186355	54123	132232	196000	58353	137647	...	...	...	...	...	...
Real estate, except dwellings	...	...	...	...	...	...	...	...	...	...	...	...
Dwellings	106041	26891	79150	109026	29028	79998	...	...	...	...	...	...
9 Community, social and personal services	65952	21520	44432	68752	22225	46528	...	...	...	...	...	...
A Sanitary and similar services	...	...	...	...	...	...	...	...	...	...	...	...
B Social and related community services	12728	2076	10653	12879	2101	10779	...	...	...	...	...	...
Educational services	1079	294	785	1114	289	825	...	...	...	...	...	...
Medical, dental, other health and veterinary services	11649	1782	9868	11765	1812	9954	...	...	...	...	...	...
C Recreational and cultural services	13532	3413	10118	14310	3896	10414	...	...	...	...	...	...

Denmark

	1994 Gross output	1994 Intermediate consumption	1994 Value added	1995 Gross output	1995 Intermediate consumption	1995 Value added	1996 Gross output	1996 Intermediate consumption	1996 Value added	1997 Gross output	1997 Intermediate consumption	1997 Value added
D Personal and household services	39692	16031	23661	41563	16228	25335	...	...	...	...	...	...
Total, Industries	1182101	549447	632654	1233322	572058	661264	...	...	...	...	...	...
Producers of government services	267415	89013	178402	276600	92668	183932	...	...	...	...	...	...
Other producers	8346	1341	7005	8967	1741	7227	...	...	...	...	...	...
Total [a]	1457862	639801	818061	1518889	666467	852423	...	...	...	...	...	...
less: Imputed bank service charge	...	−25326	25326	...	−24185	24185	...	...	...	...	...	...
Import duties	...	...	...	...	...	...	...	...	...	...	...	...
Value added tax	...	...	...	...	...	...	...	...	...	...	...	...
Other adjustments [b]	132897	...	132897	139485	...	139485	...	...	...	...	...	...
Total	1590759	665127	925632	1658374	690652	967723	...	...	...	...	...	...
memorandum item: Mineral fuels and power	41931	20293	21638	42508	20973	21535	...	...	...	...	...	...

a Gross domestic product in factor values.   b Item "Other adjustments" refers to indirect taxes net of subsidies.

4.2 Derivation of value added by kind of activity, in constant prices

Million Danish kroner

	1986 Gross output	1986 Intermediate consumption	1986 Value added	1987 Gross output	1987 Intermediate consumption	1987 Value added	1988 Gross output	1988 Intermediate consumption	1988 Value added	1989 Gross output	1989 Intermediate consumption	1989 Value added
At constant prices of: 1980 **All producers**												
1 Agriculture, hunting, forestry and fishing	45107	22739	22368	45144	23833	21311	46523	23076	23447	47542	22268	25274
A Agriculture and hunting	41509	21329	20180	41608	22413	19196	43139	21684	21455	44117	20915	23202
B Forestry and logging	709	6	703	677	−4	680	682	−3	685	711	−1	712
C Fishing	2889	1404	1485	2859	1424	1435	2702	1395	1307	2714	1354	1360
2 Mining and quarrying	8937	1096	7841	11273	1199	10075	11369	1127	10242	13518	1117	12402
A Coal mining	...	...	...	...	...	...	...	...	...	...	...	...
B Crude petroleum and natural gas production	7959	778	7180	10340	866	9474	10500	836	9664	12662	846	11817
C Metal ore mining	...	...	...	...	...	...	...	...	...	...	...	...
D Other mining	978	318	661	933	333	601	869	291	578	856	271	585
3 Manufacturing	227611	154687	72921	221655	151721	69933	223939	152903	71036	224677	152807	71869
A Manufacture of food, beverages and tobacco	74076	56290	17786	72836	55576	17260	72500	54629	17871	70434	52825	17610
B Textile, wearing apparel and leather industries	12139	7728	4410	11650	7671	3978	11084	7509	3575	10879	7360	3519
C Manufacture of wood and wood products, including furniture	10867	6830	4036	10332	6617	3715	10294	6602	3691	10613	6946	3666
D Manufacture of paper and paper products, printing and publishing	19538	12278	7259	19512	12490	7022	19127	12429	6698	18615	12106	6509
E Manufacture of chemicals and chemical petroleum, coal, rubber and plastic products	34352	25873	8479	35165	26345	8820	36267	27329	8938	36540	27440	9100

Denmark

Million Danish kroner

	1986 Gross output	1986 Intermediate consumption	1986 Value added	1987 Gross output	1987 Intermediate consumption	1987 Value added	1988 Gross output	1988 Intermediate consumption	1988 Value added	1989 Gross output	1989 Intermediate consumption	1989 Value added
At constant prices of: 1980												
F Manufacture of non-metallic mineral products, except products of petroleum and coal	7895	4535	3360	7622	4495	3127	7206	4379	2828	7134	4228	2906
G Basic metal industries	3073	2205	868	2779	1926	853	2907	1892	1015	3217	1966	1251
H Manufacture of fabricated metal products, machinery and equipment	62299	37014	25285	58554	34785	23769	61190	36345	24845	63690	38057	25633
I Other manufacturing industries	3372	1934	1438	3205	1816	1389	3364	1789	1575	3555	1879	1675
4 Electricity, gas and water	15355	8826	6528	15714	9359	6355	15299	8755	6544	14867	8471	6397
A Electricity, gas and steam	14643	8607	6035	15012	9079	5933	14611	8481	6130	14195	8197	5999
B Water works and supply	712	219	493	702	280	422	688	274	414	672	274	398
5 Construction	59650	34164	25486	60816	34242	26573	58094	33345	24749	55485	32440	23045
6 Wholesale and retail trade, restaurants and hotels	83702	27156	56545	84299	27193	57106	84646	27372	57273	82629	27252	55377
A Wholesale and retail trade	72086	19815	52270	72729	19711	53018	72736	19745	52991	70758	19703	51055
B Restaurants and hotels	11616	7341	4275	11570	7482	4088	11910	7627	4282	11871	7549	4322
7 Transport, storage and communication	56178	29362	26816	60838	30490	30349	64694	32205	32489	67821	33691	34130
A Transport and storage	47079	25818	21260	50030	26186	23845	54007	28023	25984	57321	29812	27509
B Communication	9099	3544	5556	10808	4304	6504	10687	4182	6505	10500	3879	6621
8 Finance, insurance, real estate and business services	95386	31094	64293	97698	32566	65132	98411	32444	65967	100649	31875	68775
A Financial institutions	19006	5171	13835	18125	6028	12096	17043	6030	11013	18771	6134	12637
B Insurance	2786	1645	1142	3220	1360	1860	3355	1303	2052	3499	1454	2045
C Real estate and business services	73594	24278	49316	76353	25178	51176	78013	25111	52902	78379	24287	54093
Real estate, except dwellings	...	...	...	...	...	...	...	...	...	...	...	...
Dwellings	41613	11994	29619	42147	12160	29986	42630	12110	30520	43043	11518	31525
9 Community, social and personal services	27580	9885	17696	28247	10998	17248	28360	10825	17535	27662	10554	17108
A Sanitary and similar services	...	...	...	...	...	...	...	...	...	...	...	...
B Social and related community services	5446	987	4460	5341	999	4342	5733	1106	4627	5638	1064	4574
Educational services	452	144	308	447	151	296	479	170	309	463	163	300
Medical, dental, other health and veterinary services	4994	843	4152	4894	848	4046	5254	936	4318	5175	901	4274
C Recreational and cultural services	4667	1088	3579	4803	1155	3648	4917	1199	3718	5134	1478	3656
D Personal and household services	17467	7810	9657	18103	8844	9258	17710	8520	9190	16890	8012	8878
Total, Industries	619504	319011	300493	625683	321601	304083	631333	322051	309282	634849	320472	314377
Producers of government services	118471	35521	82950	121219	37821	83398	122665	37897	84769	122360	37671	84689
Other producers	2759	358	2401	2780	377	2403	2821	392	2429	2846	395	2451
Total [a]	740733	354889	385844	749682	359799	389884	756819	360340	396480	760055	358537	401518
less: Imputed bank service charge	...	−15291	15291	...	−14359	14359	...	−12854	12854	...	−14233	14233
Import duties	...	...	...	...	...	...	...	...	...	...	...	...
Value added tax	...	...	...	...	...	...	...	...	...	...	...	...
Other adjustments [b]	70916	...	70916	67240	...	67240	64295	...	64295	63160	...	63160

506

Denmark

Million Danish kroner

	1986			1987			1988			1989		
	Gross output	Intermediate consumption	Value added	Gross output	Intermediate consumption	Value added	Gross output	Intermediate consumption	Value added	Gross output	Intermediate consumption	Value added

At constant prices of: 1980

Total	811649	370180	441469	816922	374158	442765	821114	373194	447921	823215	372770	450444
memorandum item: Mineral fuels and power	35104	20785	14319	37770	21324	16445	37966	21088	16878	40250	21196	19055

	1990			1991			1992			1993		
	Gross output	Intermediate consumption	Value added	Gross output	Intermediate consumption	Value added	Gross output	Intermediate consumption	Value added	Gross output	Intermediate consumption	Value added

At constant prices of: 1980

All producers

1 Agriculture, hunting, forestry and fishing	49156	23671	25486	47803	22722	25082	46266	23572	22694	49289	24483	24806
A Agriculture and hunting	46131	22419	23712	44744	21431	23313	43006	22240	20766	46822	23354	23468
B Forestry and logging	719	−1	721	827	—	828	738	−3	741	568	−5	573
C Fishing	2306	1253	1053	2232	1291	941	2522	1335	1187	1899	1134	765
2 Mining and quarrying	13886	1215	12671	16802	1508	15293	17945	1414	16531	19940	1845	18095
A Coal mining	...	...	...	...	...	...	...	...	...	...	...	...
B Crude petroleum and natural gas production	13117	935	12182	16078	1210	14867	17175	1124	16051	18896	1454	17442
C Metal ore mining	...	...	...	...	...	...	...	...	...	...	...	...
D Other mining	769	280	489	724	298	426	770	290	480	1044	391	653
3 Manufacturing	227278	156147	71130	230887	159828	71058	236200	164532	71669	235914	163449	72463
A Manufacture of food, beverages and tobacco	73725	55362	18364	77902	57892	20010	80214	59726	20488	82974	62547	20426
B Textile, wearing apparel and leather industries	10359	7152	3207	10235	7018	3217	10378	7460	2918	9677	6903	2774
C Manufacture of wood and wood products, including furniture	10733	7130	3603	10793	7330	3463	11313	7764	3550	11723	7644	4079
D Manufacture of paper and paper products, printing and publishing	18386	12026	6360	18180	11966	6214	17667	11709	5958	17174	11231	5943
E Manufacture of chemicals and chemical petroleum, coal, rubber and plastic products	36405	27211	9195	37038	28230	8808	39030	29300	9730	38735	29034	9701
F Manufacture of non-metallic mineral products, except products of petroleum and coal	6854	4149	2705	6732	4133	2599	6547	3925	2622	6134	3459	2675
G Basic metal industries	3100	1935	1164	2907	1862	1044	2839	1759	1080	2573	1618	955
H Manufacture of fabricated metal products, machinery and equipment	63996	39102	24893	63240	39350	23890	64689	41114	23575	63583	39550	24033
I Other manufacturing industries	3720	2080	1639	3860	2047	1813	3523	1775	1748	3341	1463	1877
4 Electricity, gas and water	15605	8701	6903	18804	10166	8638	17278	9513	7764	18121	10209	7912
A Electricity, gas and steam	14974	8435	6538	18181	9897	8284	16671	9235	7435	17479	9932	7547
B Water works and supply	631	266	365	623	269	354	607	278	329	642	277	365
5 Construction	52910	30856	22054	48457	28010	20447	48349	27893	20456	45577	26157	19421
6 Wholesale and retail trade, restaurants and hotels	84942	27496	57446	87221	28106	59115	87615	28786	58830	87438	27928	59510
A Wholesale and retail trade	73183	19840	53343	75220	20345	54875	75258	20111	55147	75295	20012	55283
B Restaurants and hotels	11759	7656	4103	12001	7761	4240	12357	8675	3683	12143	7916	4227

Denmark

	1990			1991			1992			1993		
	Gross output	Intermediate consumption	Value added	Gross output	Intermediate consumption	Value added	Gross output	Intermediate consumption	Value added	Gross output	Intermediate consumption	Value added
At constant prices of: 1980												
7 Transport, storage and communication	70199	32622	37578	73905	35727	38177	74800	34110	40690	79819	37709	42111
A Transport and storage	59509	29188	30322	62907	31690	31216	63491	30314	33177	68052	33465	34587
B Communication	10690	3434	7256	10998	4037	6961	11309	3796	7513	11767	4244	7524
8 Finance, insurance, real estate and business services	102493	32791	69702	100030	32367	67664	95505	32100	63406	99125	34141	64985
A Financial institutions	17239	6359	10880	14435	5958	8478	12567	5567	7000	15465	6371	9094
B Insurance	3714	1664	2050	2851	1723	1128	2321	1737	584	2155	1946	209
C Real estate and business services	81540	24768	56772	82744	24686	58058	80617	24796	55822	81505	25824	55682
Real estate, except dwellings	...	...	...	...	...	...	...	...	...	...	...	...
Dwellings	43371	11049	32322	43657	11141	32516	43834	11331	32504	43943	12324	31620
9 Community, social and personal services	27873	10803	17072	28081	11021	17060	28882	11082	17799	29506	11774	17732
A Sanitary and similar services	...	...	...	...	...	...	...	...	...	...	...	...
B Social and related community services	5810	1103	4708	5985	1134	4851	6314	1150	5163	6454	1218	5236
Educational services	502	178	325	510	182	329	507	144	363	516	184	332
Medical, dental, other health and veterinary services	5308	925	4383	5475	952	4522	5807	1006	4800	5938	1034	4904
C Recreational and cultural services	5231	1463	3769	5592	1635	3957	6157	1794	4363	6927	2111	4816
D Personal and household services	16832	8237	8595	16504	8252	8252	16411	8138	8273	16125	8445	7680
Total, Industries	644344	324303	320041	651989	329454	322535	652839	333001	319838	664728	337693	327035
Producers of government services	122386	37787	84599	122854	38947	83907	123902	39261	84641	127978	42581	85397
Other producers	3163	429	2734	3216	390	2826	3339	404	2935	3740	465	3275
Total [a]	769893	362518	407375	778059	368791	409267	780080	372666	407414	796445	380739	415706
less: Imputed bank service charge	–	–12874	12874	–	–10014	10014	–	–8100	8100	–	–10922	10922
Import duties	...	...	...	...	...	...	...	...	...	...	...	...
Value added tax	...	...	...	...	...	...	...	...	...	...	...	...
Other adjustments [b]	62379	–	62379	63764	–	63764	64753	–	64753	66402	–	66402
Total	832272	375392	456879	841823	378805	463018	844833	380766	464067	862847	391661	471187
memorandum item: Mineral fuels and power	40698	20770	19928	47291	23206	24085	47465	22997	24469	49723	24329	25394

Denmark

	1994 Gross output	1994 Intermediate consumption	1994 Value added	1995 Gross output	1995 Intermediate consumption	1995 Value added	1996 Gross output	1996 Intermediate consumption	1996 Value added	1997 Gross output	1997 Intermediate consumption	1997 Value added

At constant prices of: 1980

All producers

1 Agriculture, hunting, forestry and fishing	48792	22814	25978	50289	22657	27633	...	...	...	...	...	...
A Agriculture and hunting	45886	21492	24394	47620	21609	26012	...	...	...	...	...	...
B Forestry and logging	565	–3	568	520	–1	521	...	...	...	...	...	...
C Fishing	2341	1325	1016	2149	1049	1100	...	...	...	...	...	...
2 Mining and quarrying	21512	1871	19642	22022	1975	20048	...	...	...	...	...	...
A Coal mining	...	...	...	...	...	...	...	...	...	...	...	...
B Crude petroleum and natural gas production	20475	1470	19005	20969	1530	19439	...	...	...	...	...	...
C Metal ore mining	...	...	...	...	...	...	...	...	...	...	...	...
D Other mining	1037	401	637	1053	445	609	...	...	...	...	...	...
3 Manufacturing	245838	171999	73841	255999	180121	75878	...	...	...	...	...	...
A Manufacture of food, beverages and tobacco	80437	60792	19645	77123	58643	18481	...	...	...	...	...	...
B Textile, wearing apparel and leather industries	10134	7337	2797	10546	7890	2656	...	...	...	...	...	...
C Manufacture of wood and wood products, including furniture	13960	9376	4584	14216	9584	4631	...	...	...	...	...	...
D Manufacture of paper and paper products, printing and publishing	18255	11997	6258	20199	13446	6753	...	...	...	...	...	...
E Manufacture of chemicals and chemical petroleum, coal, rubber and plastic products	42383	31800	10584	45793	34676	11118	...	...	...	...	...	...
F Manufacture of non-metallic mineral products, except products of petroleum and coal	6382	3787	2595	6683	4253	2429	...	...	...	...	...	...
G Basic metal industries	3165	1986	1179	3577	2167	1410	...	...	...	...	...	...
H Manufacture of fabricated metal products, machinery and equipment	67907	43567	24341	74568	48000	26568	...	...	...	...	...	...
I Other manufacturing industries	3215	1357	1858	3294	1462	1832	...	...	...	...	...	...
4 Electricity, gas and water	18597	10625	7973	19421	10816	8605	...	...	...	...	...	...
A Electricity, gas and steam	17980	10343	7638	18808	10552	8256	...	...	...	...	...	...
B Water works and supply	617	282	335	613	264	349	...	...	...	...	...	...
5 Construction	45573	26326	19247	48468	27924	20544	...	...	...	...	...	...
6 Wholesale and retail trade, restaurants and hotels	90078	29437	60641	90753	29706	61047	...	...	...	...	...	...
A Wholesale and retail trade	76937	20469	56468	78088	21277	56811	...	...	...	...	...	...
B Restaurants and hotels	13141	8968	4173	12665	8429	4236	...	...	...	...	...	...
7 Transport, storage and communication	84245	39282	44963	85287	37717	47570	...	...	...	...	...	...
A Transport and storage	71583	34861	36722	71900	33304	38596	...	...	...	...	...	...
B Communication	12662	4421	8241	13387	4413	8974	...	...	...	...	...	...
8 Finance, insurance, real estate and business services	102272	34749	67523	102929	35810	67119	...	...	...	...	...	...
A Financial institutions	18573	7051	11522	17086	6305	10781	...	...	...	...	...	...
B Insurance	2629	2031	598	2727	2192	535	...	...	...	...	...	...
C Real estate and business services	81070	25667	55403	83116	27313	55803	...	...	...	...	...	...

Denmark

	1994 Gross output	1994 Intermediate consumption	1994 Value added	1995 Gross output	1995 Intermediate consumption	1995 Value added	1996 Gross output	1996 Intermediate consumption	1996 Value added	1997 Gross output	1997 Intermediate consumption	1997 Value added
At constant prices of: 1980												
Real estate, except dwellings	...	...	...	...	...	...	...	...	...	...	...	...
Dwellings	44022	12254	31768	44113	13206	30907	...	...	...	...	...	...
9 Community, social and personal services	30738	11913	18826	31554	12001	19553	...	...	...	...	...	...
A Sanitary and similar services	...	...	...	...	...	...	...	...	...	...	...	...
B Social and related community services	6400	1170	5230	6376	1153	5223	...	...	...	...	...	...
Educational services	507	144	363	507	136	371	...	...	...	...	...	...
Medical, dental, other health and veterinary services	5893	1026	4867	5869	1017	4852	...	...	...	...	...	...
C Recreational and cultural services	7549	2169	5380	8172	2363	5809	...	...	...	...	...	...
D Personal and household services	16789	8574	8216	17006	8485	8521	...	...	...	...	...	...
Total, Industries	687644	349012	338632	706720	358725	347995	...	...	...	...	...	...
Producers of government services	130749	43217	87532	133001	44180	88821	...	...	...	...	...	...
Other producers	4009	446	3562	4181	584	3597	...	...	...	...	...	...
Total [a]	822401	392675	429726	843902	403489	440414	...	...	...	...	...	...
less: Imputed bank service charge	...	−12595	12595	...	−11540	11540	...	...	...	...	...	...
Import duties	...	...	...	...	...	...	...	...	...	...	...	...
Value added tax	...	...	...	...	...	...	...	...	...	...	...	...
Other adjustments [b]	74023	...	74023	75297	...	75297	...	...	...	...	...	...
Total	896424	405270	491154	919199	415029	504170	...	...	...	...	...	...
memorandum item: Mineral fuels and power	52548	25142	27407	55576	26660	28916	...	...	...	...	...	...

a Gross domestic product in factor values.   b Item "Other adjustments" refers to indirect taxes net of subsidies.

4.3 Cost components of value added

Million Danish kroner

	1986 Compensation of employees	1986 Capital consumption	1986 Net operating surplus	1986 Indirect taxes	1986 less: Subsidies received	1986 Value added	1987 Compensation of employees	1987 Capital consumption	1987 Net operating surplus	1987 Indirect taxes	1987 less: Subsidies received	1987 Value added
All producers												
1 Agriculture, hunting, forestry and fishing	5511	...	24494	...	...	30005	5778	...	21560	...	...	27339
A Agriculture and hunting	3970	...	22807	...	...	26777	4205	...	19979	...	...	24184
B Forestry and logging	528	...	488	...	...	1016	554	...	423	...	...	977
C Fishing	1013	...	1199	...	...	2212	1019	...	1158	...	...	2178
2 Mining and quarrying	577	...	4750	...	...	5328	675	...	4714	...	...	5389
A Coal mining	...	...	...	...	...	...	...	...	...	...	...	...
B Crude petroleum and natural gas production	320	...	3938	...	...	4259	376	...	3979	...	...	4355
C Metal ore mining	...	...	...	...	...	...	...	...	...	...	...	...
D Other mining	257	...	812	...	...	1069	299	...	735	...	...	1034
3 Manufacturing	79046	...	32656	...	...	111703	83313	...	30557	...	...	113870

Denmark

Million Danish kroner

	1986 Compensation of employees	1986 Capital consumption	1986 Net operating surplus	1986 Indirect taxes	1986 less: Subsidies received	1986 Value added	1987 Compensation of employees	1987 Capital consumption	1987 Net operating surplus	1987 Indirect taxes	1987 less: Subsidies received	1987 Value added
A Manufacture of food, beverages and tobacco	14212	...	10030	...	...	24241	15112	...	9358	...	...	24470
B Textile, wearing apparel and leather industries	4686	...	1675	...	...	6362	4768	...	1562	...	...	6330
C Manufacture of wood and wood products, including furniture	4675	...	1608	...	...	6283	4831	...	1392	...	...	6223
D Manufacture of paper and paper products, printing and publishing	9214	...	2847	...	...	12062	10129	...	2716	...	...	12845
E Manufacture of chemicals and chemical petroleum, coal, rubber and plastic products	7710	...	5901	...	...	13611	8612	...	5620	...	...	14232
F Manufacture of non-metallic mineral products, except products of petroleum and coal	3618	...	2230	...	...	5848	3970	...	1968	...	...	5938
G Basic metal industries	1050	...	303	...	...	1353	1064	...	263	...	...	1327
H Manufacture of fabricated metal products, machinery and equipment	32489	...	7099	...	...	39588	33358	...	6636	...	...	39994
I Other manufacturing industries	1392	...	963	...	...	2355	1469	...	1042	...	...	2511
4 Electricity, gas and water	3024	...	5485	...	...	8509	3320	...	5908	...	...	9228
A Electricity, gas and steam	2627	...	5069	...	...	7696	2900	...	5536	...	...	8436
B Water works and supply	397	...	416	...	...	813	420	...	372	...	...	792
5 Construction	28243	...	9444	...	...	37686	31031	...	12300	...	...	43331
6 Wholesale and retail trade, restaurants and hotels	48105	...	40245	...	...	88351	52293	...	35659	...	...	87952
A Wholesale and retail trade	42860	...	37644	...	...	80504	46429	...	33404	...	...	79833
B Restaurants and hotels	5245	...	2601	...	...	7847	5864	...	2255	...	...	8119
7 Transport, storage and communication	25543	...	19227	...	...	44770	28059	...	19959	...	...	48016
A Transport and storage	19616	...	15701	...	...	35317	21337	...	16214	...	...	37550
B Communication	5927	...	3526	...	...	9453	6722	...	3745	...	...	10466
8 Finance, insurance, real estate and business services	34279	...	66611	...	...	100890	39497	...	67734	...	...	107232
A Financial institutions	12395	...	7874	...	...	20269	14021	...	4289	...	...	18310
B Insurance	4314	...	−2539	...	...	1775	5416	...	−2269	...	...	3148
C Real estate and business services	17570	...	61276	...	...	78846	20060	...	65714	...	...	85774
Real estate, except dwellings	...	...	...	...	...	...	...	...	...	...	...	...
Dwellings	1929	...	46519	...	...	48448	2074	...	49237	...	...	51311
9 Community, social and personal services	13946	...	13827	...	...	27773	15280	...	15060	...	...	30341
A Sanitary and similar services	...	...	...	...	...	...	...	...	...	...	...	...
B Social and related community services	1949	...	4763	...	...	6712	2039	...	4987	...	...	7026
Educational services	49	...	439	...	...	488	51	...	465	...	...	516
Medical, dental, other health and veterinary services	1900	...	4324	...	...	6224	1988	...	4522	...	...	6510
C Recreational and cultural services	3198	...	2023	...	...	5221	3274	...	2472	...	...	5746

Denmark

Million Danish kroner

	1986					1987				
	Compensation of employees	Capital consumption	Net operating surplus	Indirect taxes	less: Subsidies received	Value added	Compensation of employees	Capital consumption	Net operating surplus	Indirect taxes	less: Subsidies received	Value added
D Personal and household services	8799	...	7041	...	...	15840	9967	...	7601	...	...	17569
Total, Industries [a]	238273	...	216741	...	...	455014	259246	...	213451	...	...	472697
Producers of government services	114398	...	5412	...	...	119810	125773	...	5997	...	...	131770
Other producers	3558	...	144	...	...	3702	3872	...	137	...	...	4009
Total [ab]	356230	...	222297	...	...	578526	388891	...	219585	...	...	608476
less: Imputed bank service charge	...	...	22850	...	...	22850	...	...	22530	...	...	22530
Import duties	...	...	...	...	...	...	...	...	...	...	...	...
Value added tax	...	...	...	...	...	...	...	...	...	...	...	...
Other adjustments	...	...	...	130880	20060	110820	...	...	...	135974	22011	113963
Total [a]	356230	...	199447	130880	20060	666496	388891	...	197055	135974	22011	699909

	1988					1989				
	Compensation of employees	Capital consumption	Net operating surplus	Indirect taxes	less: Subsidies received	Value added	Compensation of employees	Capital consumption	Net operating surplus	Indirect taxes	less: Subsidies received	Value added

All producers

1 Agriculture, hunting, forestry and fishing	5860	...	21733	...	...	27593	6116	...	25553	...	...	31669
A Agriculture and hunting	4278	...	20304	...	...	24582	4505	...	23939	...	...	28444
B Forestry and logging	577	...	424	...	...	1001	572	...	487	...	...	1059
C Fishing	1005	...	1005	...	...	2010	1039	...	1127	...	...	2166
2 Mining and quarrying	580	...	3879	...	...	4460	593	...	5666	...	...	6259
A Coal mining	...	...	...	...	...	...	...	...	...	...	...	...
B Crude petroleum and natural gas production	276	...	3157	...	...	3434	288	...	4893	...	...	5181
C Metal ore mining	...	...	...	...	...	...	...	...	...	...	...	...
D Other mining	304	...	722	...	...	1026	305	...	773	...	...	1078
3 Manufacturing	84439	...	35436	...	...	119875	87296	...	36275	...	...	123572
A Manufacture of food, beverages and tobacco	15371	...	9864	...	...	25235	15356	...	9980	...	...	25337
B Textile, wearing apparel and leather industries	4462	...	1779	...	...	6241	4437	...	1573	...	...	6010
C Manufacture of wood and wood products, including furniture	4853	...	1402	...	...	6256	5169	...	1700	...	...	6869
D Manufacture of paper and paper products, printing and publishing	10588	...	2644	...	...	13232	10848	...	2797	...	...	13645
E Manufacture of chemicals and chemical petroleum, coal, rubber and plastic products	8797	...	6710	...	...	15506	9336	...	7050	...	...	16386
F Manufacture of non-metallic mineral products, except products of petroleum and coal	3845	...	1771	...	...	5616	3776	...	1872	...	...	5649
G Basic metal industries	1058	...	377	...	...	1435	1127	...	484	...	...	1611
H Manufacture of fabricated metal products, machinery and equipment	33964	...	9517	...	...	43481	35602	...	9313	...	...	44915
I Other manufacturing industries	1501	...	1372	...	...	2873	1645	...	1506	...	...	3150
4 Electricity, gas and water	3553	...	6381	...	...	9935	3773	...	7954	...	...	11726

Denmark

	1988 Compensation of employees	1988 Capital consumption	1988 Net operating surplus	1988 Indirect taxes	1988 less: Subsidies received	1988 Value added	1989 Compensation of employees	1989 Capital consumption	1989 Net operating surplus	1989 Indirect taxes	1989 less: Subsidies received	1989 Value added
A Electricity, gas and steam	3094	...	6055	...	...	9149	3291	...	7649	...	...	10939
B Water works and supply	459	...	326	...	...	786	482	...	305	...	...	787
5 Construction	31378	...	11561	...	...	42939	30361	...	10367	...	...	40728
6 Wholesale and retail trade, restaurants and hotels	53572	...	32775	...	...	86348	55689	...	35754	...	...	91443
A Wholesale and retail trade	47534	...	30299	...	...	77834	49314	...	33229	...	...	82543
B Restaurants and hotels	6038	...	2476	...	...	8514	6375	...	2525	...	...	8900
7 Transport, storage and communication	29529	...	23702	...	...	53232	30270	...	28014	...	...	58283
A Transport and storage	22293	...	19632	...	...	41925	23297	...	22427	...	...	45724
B Communication	7236	...	4070	...	...	11307	6973	...	5587	...	...	12559
8 Finance, insurance, real estate and business services	42056	...	72834	...	...	114889	44737	...	83040	...	...	127777
A Financial institutions	15068	...	1706	...	...	16773	15890	...	4682	...	...	20572
B Insurance	5383	...	−1898	...	...	3485	5639	...	−1861	...	...	3778
C Real estate and business services	21605	...	73026	...	...	94631	23208	...	80219	...	...	103427
Real estate, except dwellings	...	...	...	...	...	...	...	...	...	...	...	...
Dwellings	2163	...	53658	...	...	55820	2292	...	59927	...	...	62218
9 Community, social and personal services	15663	...	17235	...	...	32897	16681	...	17010	...	...	33692
A Sanitary and similar services	...	...	...	...	...	...	...	...	...	...	...	...
B Social and related community services	2184	...	5972	...	...	8155	2471	...	5787	...	...	8258
Educational services	58	...	686	...	...	744	60	...	557	...	...	617
Medical, dental, other health and veterinary services	2126	...	5286	...	...	7411	2411	...	5230	...	...	7641
C Recreational and cultural services	3568	...	2274	...	...	5842	4030	...	2332	...	...	6363
D Personal and household services	9911	...	8989	...	...	18900	10180	...	8891	...	...	19071
Total, Industries [a]	266632	...	225534	...	...	492166	275516	...	249633	...	...	525149
Producers of government services	136347	...	6419	...	...	142766	142219	...	7025	...	...	149244
Other producers	4127	...	−2	...	...	4125	4359	...	−9	...	...	4350
Total [ab]	407106	...	231952	...	...	639058	422094	...	256650	...	...	678744
less: Imputed bank service charge	...	...	21215	...	...	21215	...	...	24741	...	...	24741
Import duties	...	...	...	...	...	...	...	...	...	...	...	...
Value added tax	...	...	...	...	...	...	...	...	...	...	...	...
Other adjustments	...	...	...	139551	25340	114211	...	...	...	140201	26955	113246
Total [a]	407106	...	210737	139551	25340	732053	422094	...	231909	140201	26955	767248

Denmark

	1990						1991					
	Compensation of employees	Capital consumption	Net operating surplus	Indirect taxes	less: Subsidies received	Value added	Compensation of employees	Capital consumption	Net operating surplus	Indirect taxes	less: Subsidies received	Value added

All producers

1 Agriculture, hunting, forestry and fishing	6056	...	24246	...	...	30301	6250	...	23364	...	...	29614
A Agriculture and hunting	4535	...	22660	...	...	27194	4595	...	21569	...	...	26164
B Forestry and logging	559	...	562	...	...	1121	601	...	637	...	...	1238
C Fishing	962	...	1024	...	...	1986	1054	...	1158	...	...	2212
2 Mining and quarrying	583	...	6716	...	...	7299	627	...	6262	...	...	6889
A Coal mining	...	...	...	...	...	...	...	...	...	...	...	...
B Crude petroleum and natural gas production	293	...	6021	...	...	6314	339	...	5652	...	...	5990
C Metal ore mining	...	...	...	...	...	...	...	...	...	...	...	...
D Other mining	290	...	695	...	...	985	288	...	610	...	...	899
3 Manufacturing	91862	...	38057	...	...	129919	93562	...	40674	...	...	134238
A Manufacture of food, beverages and tobacco	15952	...	10729	...	...	26681	16355	...	12366	...	...	28721
B Textile, wearing apparel and leather industries	4432	...	1600	...	...	6032	4361	...	1920	...	...	6282
C Manufacture of wood and wood products, including furniture	5489	...	1790	...	...	7279	5638	...	1990	...	...	7628
D Manufacture of paper and paper products, printing and publishing	11322	...	2809	...	...	14130	11550	...	2968	...	...	14518
E Manufacture of chemicals and chemical petroleum, coal, rubber and plastic products	9852	...	7704	...	...	17556	10295	...	7032	...	...	17327
F Manufacture of non-metallic mineral products, except products of petroleum and coal	3838	...	1919	...	...	5757	3856	...	1799	...	...	5656
G Basic metal industries	1139	...	525	...	...	1664	1147	...	469	...	...	1616
H Manufacture of fabricated metal products, machinery and equipment	38038	...	9466	...	...	47504	38452	...	10523	...	...	48975
I Other manufacturing industries	1800	...	1515	...	...	3316	1908	...	1607	...	...	3515
4 Electricity, gas and water	3854	...	8657	...	...	12511	3999	...	10754	...	...	14752
A Electricity, gas and steam	3404	...	8347	...	...	11751	3540	...	10387	...	...	13927
B Water works and supply	450	...	310	...	...	760	459	...	367	...	...	825
5 Construction	30252	...	10349	...	...	40601	29433	...	8898	...	...	38331
6 Wholesale and retail trade, restaurants and hotels	58043	...	37424	...	...	95467	59735	...	40030	...	...	99765
A Wholesale and retail trade	51381	...	34905	...	...	86286	52807	...	37503	...	...	90310
B Restaurants and hotels	6662	...	2519	...	...	9181	6928	...	2527	...	...	9455
7 Transport, storage and communication	31324	...	31049	...	...	62373	32650	...	32773	...	...	65423
A Transport and storage	24286	...	23776	...	...	48062	25651	...	25711	...	...	51362
B Communication	7038	...	7273	...	...	14311	6999	...	7062	...	...	14061
8 Finance, insurance, real estate and business services	48358	...	87593	...	...	135951	50441	...	88770	...	...	139211
A Financial institutions	16593	...	1312	...	...	17905	17489	...	-3593	...	...	13896
B Insurance	6518	...	-2826	...	...	3692	6706	...	-4465	...	...	2241
C Real estate and business services	25247	...	89107	...	...	114354	26246	...	96828	...	...	123074

Denmark

	1990						1991					
	Compensation of employees	Capital consumption	Net operating surplus	Indirect taxes	less: Subsidies received	Value added	Compensation of employees	Capital consumption	Net operating surplus	Indirect taxes	less: Subsidies received	Value added
Real estate, except dwellings	...	...	...	...	...	...	...	...	...	...	...	...
Dwellings	2302	...	65964	...	...	68267	2385	...	71161	...	...	73546
9 Community, social and personal services	17474	...	17878	...	...	35352	18789	...	18294	...	...	37082
A Sanitary and similar services	...	...	...	...	...	...	...	...	...	...	...	...
B Social and related community services	2677	...	6095	...	...	8772	2744	...	6501	...	...	9244
Educational services	66	...	615	...	...	681	69	...	633	...	...	701
Medical, dental, other health and veterinary services	2611	...	5480	...	...	8091	2675	...	5868	...	...	8543
C Recreational and cultural services	4210	...	2463	...	...	6673	4388	...	3020	...	...	7408
D Personal and household services	10587	...	9320	...	...	19907	11657	...	8773	...	...	20430
Total, Industries [a]	287804	...	261971	...	...	549775	295487	...	269819	...	...	565306
Producers of government services	146755	...	7541	...	...	154296	152411	...	7912	...	...	160323
Other producers	4703	...	291	...	...	4994	5035	...	266	...	...	5300
Total [ab]	439262	...	269803	...	...	709065	452933	...	277997	...	...	730930
less: Imputed bank service charge	...	...	23123	...	...	23123	...	...	18797	...	...	18797
Import duties	...	...	...	...	...	...	...	...	...	...	...	...
Value added tax	...	...	...	...	...	...	...	...	...	...	...	...
Other adjustments	...	...	...	141523	28354	113169	...	...	...	144462	28726	115736
Total [a]	439262	...	246680	141523	28354	799111	452933	...	259200	144462	28726	827868

	1992						1993					
	Compensation of employees	Capital consumption	Net operating surplus	Indirect taxes	less: Subsidies received	Value added	Compensation of employees	Capital consumption	Net operating surplus	Indirect taxes	less: Subsidies received	Value added

All producers

1 Agriculture, hunting, forestry and fishing	6410	...	22830	...	...	29239	5950	...	21834	...	...	27785
A Agriculture and hunting	4826	...	20959	...	...	25784	4641	...	20822	...	...	25463
B Forestry and logging	589	...	574	...	...	1163	512	...	398	...	...	910
C Fishing	995	...	1297	...	...	2292	797	...	614	...	...	1412
2 Mining and quarrying	662	...	6778	...	...	7440	686	...	6420	...	...	7106
A Coal mining	...	...	...	...	...	...	...	...	...	...	...	...
B Crude petroleum and natural gas production	355	...	6057	...	...	6412	...	...	...	...	...	5886
C Metal ore mining	...	...	...	...	...	...	...	...	...	...	...	...
D Other mining	307	...	721	...	...	1028	...	...	...	...	...	1220
3 Manufacturing	95951	...	44476	...	...	140426	93018	...	51102	...	...	144121
A Manufacture of food, beverages and tobacco	16727	...	13427	...	...	30154	16430	...	14915	...	...	31344
B Textile, wearing apparel and leather industries	4414	...	1948	...	...	6362	4152	...	1644	...	...	5796
C Manufacture of wood and wood products, including furniture	5964	...	2266	...	...	8229	5960	...	2642	...	...	8602
D Manufacture of paper and paper products, printing and publishing	11746	...	3422	...	...	15169	11391	...	3930	...	...	15322

Denmark

	1992						1993					
	Compensation of employees	Capital consumption	Net operating surplus	Indirect taxes	less: Subsidies received	Value added	Compensation of employees	Capital consumption	Net operating surplus	Indirect taxes	less: Subsidies received	Value added
E Manufacture of chemicals and chemical petroleum, coal, rubber and plastic products	11234	...	7905	...	...	19138	11298	...	8605	...	...	19903
F Manufacture of non-metallic mineral products, except products of petroleum and coal	3729	...	1948	...	...	5677	3555	...	2396	...	...	5951
G Basic metal industries	1156	...	383	...	...	1539	1014	...	294	...	...	1309
H Manufacture of fabricated metal products, machinery and equipment	39193	...	11336	...	...	50529	37301	...	14668	...	...	51969
I Other manufacturing industries	1788	...	1841	...	...	3629	1917	...	2008	...	...	3925
4 Electricity, gas and water	4223	...	11172	...	...	15395	4210	...	11215	...	...	15425
A Electricity, gas and steam	3755	...	10818	...	...	14573	...	...	...	...	...	14513
B Water works and supply	468	...	354	...	...	822	...	...	...	...	...	912
5 Construction	30384	...	11998	...	...	42382	30534	...	10755	...	...	41289
6 Wholesale and retail trade, restaurants and hotels	61444	...	43821	...	...	105264	61416	...	44074	...	...	105489
A Wholesale and retail trade	54261	...	40877	...	...	95137	53935	...	40645	...	...	94580
B Restaurants and hotels	7183	...	2944	...	...	10127	7481	...	3429	...	...	10909
7 Transport, storage and communication	33582	...	35829	...	...	69411	33165	...	37845	...	...	71010
A Transport and storage	26379	...	27266	...	...	53645	26056	...	29146	...	...	55202
B Communication	7203	...	8563	...	...	15766	7109	...	8699	...	...	15808
8 Finance, insurance, real estate and business services	51422	...	84597	...	...	136018	51957	...	91653	...	...	143609
A Financial institutions	17545	...	−6650	...	...	10895	...	...	...	...	...	14052
B Insurance	7304	...	−6443	...	...	860	...	...	...	...	...	311
C Real estate and business services	26573	...	97690	...	...	124263	27426	...	101820	...	...	129246
Real estate, except dwellings	...	...	...	...	...	...	...	...	...	...	...	...
Dwellings	2515	...	72990	...	...	75505	2438	...	74565	...	...	77003
9 Community, social and personal services	19662	...	20606	...	...	40268	20564	...	20679	...	...	41241
A Sanitary and similar services	...	...	...	...	...	...	...	...	...	...	...	...
B Social and related community services	2928	...	7302	...	...	10230	3104	...	7293	...	...	10396
Educational services	70	...	736	...	...	806	...	...	...	...	...	726
Medical, dental, other health and veterinary services	2858	...	6566	...	...	9424	...	...	...	...	...	9670
C Recreational and cultural services	4598	...	3727	...	...	8325	4792	...	3998	...	...	8789
D Personal and household services	12136	...	9577	...	...	21713	12668	...	9388	...	...	22056
Total, Industries [a]	303738	...	282106	...	...	585844	301499	...	295577	...	...	597076
Producers of government services	157953	...	8558	...	...	166511	162880	...	9036	...	...	171916
Other producers	5291	...	274	...	...	5565	5494	...	927	...	...	6421
Total [ab]	466982	...	290938	...	...	757919	469873	...	305540	...	...	775414
less: Imputed bank service charge	...	...	15474	...	...	15474	...	...	18679	...	...	18679
Import duties	...	...	...	...	...	...	...	...	...	...	...	...

Denmark

	1992						1993					
	Compensation of employees	Capital consumption	Net operating surplus	Indirect taxes	less: Subsidies received	Value added	Compensation of employees	Capital consumption	Net operating surplus	Indirect taxes	less: Subsidies received	Value added
Value added tax	...	...	...	...	...	...	...	...	...	...	...	...
Other adjustments	...	...	...	148456	34870	113586	...	...	...	153181	35522	117659
Total [a]	466982	...	275464	148456	34870	856032	469873	...	286861	153181	35522	874393

	1994						1995					
	Compensation of employees	Capital consumption	Net operating surplus	Indirect taxes	less: Subsidies received	Value added	Compensation of employees	Capital consumption	Net operating surplus	Indirect taxes	less: Subsidies received	Value added
All producers												
1 Agriculture, hunting, forestry and fishing	6088	...	24223	...	...	30311	6333	...	28665	...	...	34999
A Agriculture and hunting	4767	...	23176	...	...	27943	5028	...	27169	...	...	32198
B Forestry and logging	567	...	415	...	...	982	526	...	380	...	...	906
C Fishing	754	...	632	...	...	1386	779	...	1116	...	...	1895
2 Mining and quarrying	698	...	6972	...	...	7670	727	...	6498	...	...	7225
A Coal mining	...	...	...	...	...	...	...	...	...	...	...	...
B Crude petroleum and natural gas production	...	...	...	...	...	6245	...	...	...	...	...	5789
C Metal ore mining	...	...	...	...	...	...	...	...	...	...	...	...
D Other mining	...	...	...	...	...	1425	...	...	...	...	...	1436
3 Manufacturing	96794	...	58862	...	...	155655	103863	...	62123	...	...	165985
A Manufacture of food, beverages and tobacco	16873	...	13031	...	...	29904	17545	...	13219	...	...	30764
B Textile, wearing apparel and leather industries	4182	...	2439	...	...	6621	4120	...	2502	...	...	6622
C Manufacture of wood and wood products, including furniture	6888	...	3618	...	...	10506	7381	...	3121	...	...	10502
D Manufacture of paper and paper products, printing and publishing	11349	...	5737	...	...	17086	11806	...	8734	...	...	20540
E Manufacture of chemicals and chemical petroleum, coal, rubber and plastic products	11532	...	10477	...	...	22009	12578	...	10478	...	...	23056
F Manufacture of non-metallic mineral products, except products of petroleum and coal	3781	...	3623	...	...	7404	4117	...	3390	...	...	7507
G Basic metal industries	1077	...	483	...	...	1560	1213	...	831	...	...	2043
H Manufacture of fabricated metal products, machinery and equipment	39167	...	17149	...	...	56315	43062	...	17699	...	...	60761
I Other manufacturing industries	1945	...	2305	...	...	4250	2041	...	2149	...	...	4190
4 Electricity, gas and water	4200	...	11849	...	...	16049	4423	...	11748	...	...	16172
A Electricity, gas and steam	...	...	...	...	...	15125	...	...	...	...	...	15136
B Water works and supply	...	...	...	...	...	924	...	...	...	...	...	1036
5 Construction	32837	...	8580	...	...	41416	35468	...	10024	...	...	45493
6 Wholesale and retail trade, restaurants and hotels	63818	...	46676	...	...	110494	69029	...	42063	...	...	111092
A Wholesale and retail trade	56041	...	42284	...	...	98325	60687	...	37876	...	...	98563
B Restaurants and hotels	7777	...	4392	...	...	12169	8342	...	4187	...	...	12529
7 Transport, storage and communication	34301	...	39584	...	...	73886	36000	...	39533	...	...	75533
A Transport and storage	26954	...	29580	...	...	56534	28462	...	30684	...	...	59146

Denmark

	1994							1995					
	Compensation of employees	Capital consumption	Net operating surplus	Indirect taxes	less: Subsidies received	Value added	Compensation of employees	Capital consumption	Net operating surplus	Indirect taxes	less: Subsidies received	Value added
B Communication	7347	...	10004	...	...	17352	7538	...	8849	...	...	16387
8 Finance, insurance, real estate and business services	53684	...	99058	...	...	152742	56522	...	101719	...	...	158240
A Financial institutions	...	...	...	...	...	19794	...	...	...	...	...	19929
B Insurance	...	...	...	...	...	716	...	...	...	...	...	664
C Real estate and business services	29022	...	103210	...	...	132232	31483	...	106165	...	...	137647
Real estate, except dwellings	...	...	...	...	...	...	...	...	...	...	...	...
Dwellings	2529	...	76622	...	...	79150	2633	...	77366	...	...	79998
9 Community, social and personal services	21684	...	22749	...	...	44432	23143	...	23385	...	...	46528
A Sanitary and similar services	...	...	...	...	...	...	...	...	...	...	...	...
B Social and related community services	3283	...	7370	...	...	10653	3484	...	7295	...	...	10779
Educational services	...	...	...	...	...	785	...	...	...	...	...	825
Medical, dental, other health and veterinary services	...	...	...	...	...	9868	...	...	...	...	...	9954
C Recreational and cultural services	4975	...	5144	...	...	10118	5332	...	5082	...	...	10414
D Personal and household services	13426	...	10235	...	...	23661	14327	...	11008	...	...	25335
Total, Industries	314102[a]	...	318552[a]	...	...	632654[a]	335509	...	325755	...	...	661264
Producers of government services	168752	...	9650	...	...	178402	173776	...	10156	...	...	183932
Other producers	5449	...	1557	...	...	7005	5874	...	1353	...	...	7227
Total	488303[ab]	...	329758[ab]	...	...	818061[ab]	515160	...	337263	...	...	852423
less: Imputed bank service charge	...	...	25326	...	...	25326	...	...	24185	...	...	24185
Import duties	...	...	...	...	...	...	...	...	...	...	...	...
Value added tax	...	...	...	...	...	...	...	...	...	...	...	...
Other adjustments	...	...	...	168387	35490	132897	...	...	...	175261	35776	139485
Total	488303[a]	...	304432[a]	168387[a]	35490[a]	925632[a]	515160	...	313078	175261	35776	967723

a Column "Consumption of fixed capital" is included in column "Net operating surplus".
b Gross domestic product in factor values.

Dominica

Source

Reply to the United Nations National Accounts Questionnaire from the Ministry of Finance, Trade and Industry, Roseau.

General note

The estimates shown in the following tables have been prepared in accordance with the United Nations System of National Accounts (1968 SNA) so far as the existing data would permit.

1.1 Expenditure on the gross domestic product, in current prices

Thousand East Caribbean dollars

	1986	1987	1988	1989	1990	1991	1992	1993	1994	1995	1996	1997
1 Government final consumption expenditure	62070	68150	75030	86710	91860	95670	...	...	...	...	...	...
2 Private final consumption expenditure	188900	224470	259000	302160	289370	341860	...	...	...	...	...	...
3 Gross capital formation	67510	79330	120570	170670	184200	197650	...	...	...	...	...	...
A Increase in stocks	–	–	–	6500	4950	5150	...	...	...	...	...	...
B Gross fixed capital formation	67510	79330	120570	164170	179250	192500	...	...	...	...	...	...
Residential buildings	30380	37070	54120	64210	72420	74830	...	...	...	...	...	...
Non-residential buildings							...	...	...	...	...	...
Other construction and land improvement, etc.							...	...	...	...	...	...
Other	37130	42260	66450	99960	106830	117670	...	...	...	...	...	...
4 Exports of goods and services	148320	162620	190640	173430	226010	222280	...	...	...	...	...	...
5 less: Imports of goods and services	164200	195300	252000	310250	339900	378630	...	...	...	...	...	...
equals: Gross domestic product	302600	339270	393240	422720	451540	478830	511500	...	...	...	...	...

1.10 Gross domestic product by kind of activity, in current prices

Thousand East Caribbean dollars

	1986	1987	1988	1989	1990	1991	1992	1993	1994	1995	1996	1997
1 Agriculture, hunting, forestry and fishing	76640	82590	95900	89550	96920	101610	...	...	...	...	...	...
2 Mining and quarrying	1380	1760	2570	2910	3080	3810	...	...	...	...	...	...
3 Manufacturing	16880	18250	20990	24530	26430	27430	...	...	...	...	...	...
4 Electricity, gas and water	6680	7390	8970	10040	11180	12930	...	...	...	...	...	...
5 Construction	11820	14420	21050	24970	28160	29100	...	...	...	...	...	...
6 Wholesale and retail trade, restaurants and hotels	28850	34050	37980	43590	48700	52550	...	...	...	...	...	...
7 Transport, storage and communication	34350	41760	49520	53810	59840	64800	...	...	...	...	...	...
8 Finance, insurance, real estate and business services	30010	33050	40100	47270	55160	58470	...	...	...	...	...	...
9 Community, social and personal services	2660	2910	3080	3630	3900	4210	...	...	...	...	...	...
Total, Industries	209270	236180	280160	300300	333370	354910	...	...	...	...	...	...

Dominica

Thousand East Caribbean dollars

	1986	1987	1988	1989	1990	1991	1992	1993	1994	1995	1996	1997
Producers of government services	54360	57630	59520	66980	69010	72500	...	...	...	...	...	...
Other producers	...	...	...	...	...	...	...	...	...	...	...	...
Subtotal [a]	263630	293810	339680	367280	402380	427410	...	...	...	...	...	...
less: Imputed bank service charge	10360	12050	15390	21110	28110	29520	...	...	...	...	...	...
plus: Import duties	...	...	...	...	...	...	...	...	...	...	...	...
plus: Value added tax	...	...	...	...	...	...	...	...	...	...	...	...
plus: Other adjustments [b]	49330	57510	68950	76550	77270	80940	...	...	...	...	...	...
equals: Gross domestic product	302600	339270	393240	422720	451540	478830	...	...	...	...	...	...

a Gross domestic product in factor values.
b Item "Other adjustments" refers to indirect taxes net of subsidies.

1.11 Gross domestic product by kind of activity, in constant prices

Thousand East Caribbean dollars

	1986	1987	1988	1989	1990	1991	1992	1993	1994	1995	1996	1997
	At constant prices of: 1977											
1 Agriculture, hunting, forestry and fishing	36500	38340	40650	34810	38050	38670	...	...	...	...	...	...
2 Mining and quarrying	920	1120	1380	1460	1490	1530	...	...	...	...	...	...
3 Manufacturing	9280	9830	10830	11480	11820	11580	...	...	...	...	...	...
4 Electricity, gas and water	2400	2570	2740	2920	3240	4040	...	...	...	...	...	...
5 Construction	8750	9860	12880	13590	15820	15660	...	...	...	...	...	...
6 Wholesale and retail trade, restaurants and hotels	15600	17350	18840	20540	21920	22190	...	...	...	...	...	...
7 Transport, storage and communication	10210	11690	12800	13490	14280	14840	...	...	...	...	...	...
8 Finance, insurance, real estate and business services	12450	12890	13650	14320	14870	15530	...	...	...	...	...	...
9 Community, social and personal services	1270	1310	1360	1440	1490	1520	...	...	...	...	...	...
Total, Industries	97380	104960	115130	114050	122980	125560	...	...	...	...	...	...
Producers of government services	24210	24820	25560	25870	26700	27500	...	...	...	...	...	...
Other producers	...	...	...	...	...	...	...	...	...	...	...	...
Subtotal [a]	121590	129780	140690	139920	149680	153060	...	...	...	...	...	...
less: Imputed bank service charge	4090	4290	5260	6010	6960	7410	...	...	...	...	...	...
plus: Import duties	...	...	...	...	...	...	...	...	...	...	...	...
plus: Value added tax	...	...	...	...	...	...	...	...	...	...	...	...
plus: Other adjustments [b]	22880	25610	28800	29610	29470	29630	...	...	...	...	...	...
equals: Gross domestic product	140380	151100	164230	163520	172190	175280	...	...	...	...	...	...

a Gross domestic product in factor values.
b Item "Other adjustments" refers to indirect taxes net of subsidies.

Dominican Republic

General note

The preparation of national accounts statistics in Dominican Republic is undertaken by Banco Central de la República Dominicana, Santo Domingo. The official estimates are published in the series *Cuentas Nacionales, Producto Nacional Bruto* which also includes a detailed description of the sources and methods used for the national accounts estimation. The estimates are generally in accordance with the classifications and definitions recommended in the United Nations System of National Accounts (1968 SNA). The following tables have been prepared from successive replies to the United Nations National Accounts Questionnaire. When the scope and coverage of the estimates differ for conceptual or statistical reasons from the definitions and classifications recommended in SNA, a footnote is indicated to the relevant tables.

Gross domestic product

Gross domestic product is estimated mainly through the production approach.

Expenditures on the gross domestic product

The expenditure approach is used to estimate government final consumption expenditure, increase in stocks and exports and imports of goods and services. Gross fixed capital formation is mainly estimated by the commodity-flow method, whereas private final consumption expenditure is taken as a residual, which also includes changes in stocks which could not be computed directly. Government consumption expenditure data for the central government is obtained from the Ministry of Finance and the National Budget Office. For gross fixed capital formation, import statistics are utilized for capital goods such as machinery, equipment and transport and communication equipment, since no such products are produced locally. To the import values are added customs duties, surcharges, mark-ups, etc. The data on exports and imports of goods and services are taken from the publication on balance of payments, prepared by the Central Bank. For the calculation of constant prices, price deflation is used for government consumption expenditure. Compensation of employees is deflated by means of the cost of living index, whereas for government purchases and sales general price indexes are used. Constant value of private consumption expenditure is obtained as a residual. The value of construction is deflated by a construction costs index. In the case of rural dwellings base-year prices are multiplied by number of dwellings built. The import price index is used as a deflator for exports and imports of goods and services.

Cost structure of the gross domestic product

The data on indirect taxes and subsidies are based on the annual reports of the Ministry of Finance and on information from the Treasury and the National Budget Office.

Gross domestic product by kind of activity

The production approach is the basic method of estimation used for most sectors. The income approach is used for trade, transport and communication, finance, general government and other services. In agriculture, gross output is estimated by multiplying the quantities harvested by the average price paid to the producers. Quantity data are available from the agricultural censuses of 1950, 1960 and 1970 and from estimates by the Banco Agrícola, the Ministry of Agriculture and others. Own-account consumption is included in the production series. Data on the volume of livestock production is provided by the Ministry of Agriculture, which also estimates the quantity of unreported slaughter and herd changes in livestock. The basic information for calculating gross output of the mining and quarrying sector is obtained directly from the reports on production and sales of enterprises. For manufacturing, the main source of information is the series of annual bulletins of industrial statistics. The value of construction for 1960, which is taken as a benchmark, is extrapolated by means of a value index. This index is a combination of a price index of construction costs and an index of main materials used.

Value added is obtained by applying to gross output a coefficient representing the ratio of gross factor income. Data for the trade sector are available from the first national trade census carried out in 1955, and from total wholesale and retail sales figures published periodically by the National Statistical Office. Wages and salaries are calculated by combining average remunerations series with sectoral employment series. The Dominican merchant marine and the Dominican airline provide the data needed to estimate incomes, inputs and value added for shipping and air transport. For land transport the information obtained include data from transport enterprises and surveys among owners of trucks and taxis. For financial institutions the estimates are based on complete accounting information which is available for all banks and finance companies and most insurance companies. Value added of ownership of dwellings is taken as the difference between gross rents paid or imputed based on census data and the inputs for maintenance, upkeep and management and property taxes. For public administration and defence, data are obtained from government authorities, publications and from independent institutions. For other private services, data on the number of persons employed and mean income are used. The benchmark

Dominican Republic

data are extrapolated according to a specially constructed income index.

For the computation of constant prices, the value added for agriculture is estimated by a revaluation at base-year prices of the harvested quantities. In the case of livestock products, estimates of annual changes in average meat yield per animal are utilized. For mining and quarrying, value added is estimated by revaluating the different minerals at their respective 1962 prices. Value added of manufacturing is extrapolated by a quantity index of output. Current values of public and private construction are deflated by means of an index of construction costs. Wholesale and retail sales of locally produced and imported goods are deflated using the respective price indexes. For transport, storage and communication, value added is extrapolated by quantity index of output. For financial institutions, value added is extrapolated by quantity indicators of personnel employed. For ownership of dwellings the indicator used is the number of urban and rural dwellings. Value added for public administration, defence and other services is extrapolated by an indicator of the number of personnel employed.

1.1 Expenditure on the gross domestic product, in current prices

Million Dominican pesos

	1986	1987	1988	1989	1990	1991	1992	1993	1994	1995	1996	1997
1 Government final consumption expenditure	1297	1205	1783	1824	2308	4074	5681	6865	...	...	...	...
2 Private final consumption expenditure	11606	14542	19096	31237	51577	82539	91274	92742	...	...	...	...
3 Gross capital formation [a]	3577	5437	8123	11605	13398	17019	23721	26955	...	...	...	...
A Increase in stocks [a]	85	118	89	100	120	127	150	195	...	...	...	...
B Gross fixed capital formation	3492	5319	8034	11505	13278	16892	23571	26760	...	...	...	...
4 Exports of goods and services [b]	4041	5847	11000	13149	16903	24569	26558	28269	...	...	...	...
5 less: Imports of goods and services [b]	4741	7495	11649	15422	19318	28131	34865	34259	...	...	...	...
equals: Gross domestic product	15780	19536	28353	42393	64867	100070	112369	120572	...	...	...	...

a Item "Gross capital formation" includes only increase of stocks of mining, manufacturing, peanuts, raw tobacco and beans.
b Beginning 1984, estimates were converted from dollars to pesos by using the annual average exchange rates fixed by the Central Bank.

1.2 Expenditure on the gross domestic product, in constant prices

Million Dominican pesos

	1986	1987	1988	1989	1990	1991	1992	1993	1994	1995	1996	1997
At constant prices of: 1970												
1 Government final consumption expenditure	386	318	349	349	351	385	407	410	...	...	...	...
2 Private final consumption expenditure	2489	2737	2689	2697	2471	2552	2633	2649	...	...	...	...
3 Gross capital formation [a]	617	783	858	946	783	702	942	1004	...	...	...	...
A Increase in stocks [a]	26	40	25	20	17	33	36	45	...	...	...	...
B Gross fixed capital formation	591	743	833	927	766	670	907	958	...	...	...	...
4 Exports of goods and services [b]	581	696	722	763	874	885	1012	1028	...	...	...	...
5 less: Imports of goods and services [b]	708	829	831	803	724	741	917	891	...	...	...	...
equals: Gross domestic product	3365	3706	3786	3952	3755	3784	4077	4199	...	...	...	...

a Item "Gross capital formation" includes only increase of stocks of mining, manufacturing, peanuts, raw tobacco and beans.
b The estimates of imports and exports of goods and services are deflated by imports and exports price indexes.

Dominican Republic

1.3 Cost components of the gross domestic product

Million Dominican pesos

	1986	1987	1988	1989	1990	1991	1992	1993	1994	1995	1996	1997
1 Indirect taxes, net	1569	1986	2948	3857	4288	6565	12619	14639	...	...	...	...
A Indirect taxes	1571	1986	2948	3857	4374	6773	12815	14810	...	...	...	...
B less: Subsidies	2	–	–	–	87	208	196	172	...	...	...	...
2 Consumption of fixed capital	939	1162	1687	2522	3860	5954	6686	7174				
3 Compensation of employees paid by resident producers to ..	13272	16388	23717	36014	56719	87551	93064	98759	...	...	...	...
4 Operating surplus									...	...	...	...
equals: Gross domestic product ..	15780	19536	28353	42393	64867	100070	112369	120572	...	...	...	...

1.7 External transactions on current account, summary

Million Dominican pesos

	1986	1987	1988	1989	1990	1991	1992	1993	1994	1995	1996	1997
Payments to the rest of the world												
1 Imports of goods and services	4741	7495	11649	15422	19318	28131	34865	34259	...	...	...	...
2 Factor income to rest of the world	1122	1615	1950	1376	2225	3815	3161	4811	...	...	...	...
3 Current transfers to the rest of the world	...	...	...	...	...	...	...	...	...	...	...	...
4 Surplus of the nation on current transactions	–952	–1984	–310	–1140	–517	–1405	–5381	–4613	...	...	...	...
Payments to the rest of the world and surplus of the nation on current transfers	4911	7127	13289	15657	21026	30542	32645	34458	...	...	...	...
Receipts from the rest of the world												
1 Exports of goods and services	4041	5847	11000	13149	16903	24569	26558	28269	...	...	...	...
2 Factor income from rest of the world	48	43	51	68	918	1110	690	668	...	...	...	...
3 Current transfers from rest of the world	821	1236	2238	2441	3206	4862	5397	5520	...	...	...	...
Receipts from the rest of the world on current transactions	4911	7127	13289	15657	21026	30542	32645	34458	...	...	...	...

1.10 Gross domestic product by kind of activity, in current prices

Million Dominican pesos

	1986	1987	1988	1989	1990	1991	1992	1993	1994	1995	1996	1997
1 Agriculture, hunting, forestry and fishing	2589	3655	5173	7558	11157	17813	19627	21060	...	...	...	...
2 Mining and quarrying	607	1043	1397	1997	2660	3974	3374	3621	...	...	...	...
3 Manufacturing [ab]	2739	2866	3979	5866	8757	13504	15824	16979	...	...	...	...
4 Electricity, gas and water	122	127	138	143	260	441	598	641	...	...	...	...
5 Construction	1100	1771	2786	4044	5189	7102	9209	9881	...	...	...	...
6 Wholesale and retail trade, restaurants and hotels [c]	2485	3069	3946	6049	8887	13748	15795	16948	...	...	...	...
7 Transport, storage and communication	1296	1050	1520	2307	4216	6693	7761	8328	...	...	...	...
8 Finance, insurance, real estate and business services [d]	1693	2074	2995	7066	11352	17754	18600	19958	...	...	...	...
9 Community, social and personal services [cd]	1474	1924	3670	3299	6682	10275	12085	12968	...	...	...	...

Dominican Republic

Million Dominican pesos

	1986	1987	1988	1989	1990	1991	1992	1993	1994	1995	1996	1997
Total, Industries	14105	17579	25604	38329	59159	91305	102874	110383	...	...	...	...
Producers of government services	1675	1957	2749	4064	5708	8765	9495	10188	...	...	...	...
Other producers	...	...	...	...	...	...	...	...	...	...	...	...
Subtotal	15780	19536	28353	42393	64867	100070	112369	120572	...	...	...	...
less: Imputed bank service charge	...	...	...	...	...	...	...	...	...	...	...	...
plus: Import duties	...	...	...	...	...	...	...	...	...	...	...	...
plus: Value added tax	...	...	...	...	...	...	...	...	...	...	...	...
plus: Other adjustments	...	...	...	...	...	...	...	...	...	...	...	...
equals: Gross domestic product	15780	19536	28353	42393	64867	100070	112369	120572	...	...	...	...

a Item "Manufacturing" includes handicrafts.
b Repair services are included in item "Manufacturing".
c Restaurants and hotels are included in item "Community, social and personal services".
d Business services are included in item "Community, social and personal services".

1.11 Gross domestic product by kind of activity, in constant prices

Million Dominican pesos

	1986	1987	1988	1989	1990	1991	1992	1993	1994	1995	1996	1997
At constant prices of: 1970												
1 Agriculture, hunting, forestry and fishing	528	544	537	549	502	523	554	558	...	...	...	...
2 Mining and quarrying	120	151	140	139	117	112	91	57	...	...	...	...
3 Manufacturing [ab]	598	674	670	701	672	684	762	779	...	...	...	...
4 Electricity, gas and water	63	70	68	62	56	59	76	88	...	...	...	...
5 Construction	222	297	307	348	281	246	306	337	...	...	...	...
6 Wholesale and retail trade, restaurants and hotels [c]	588	655	683	695	645	665	724	767	...	...	...	...
7 Transport, storage and communication	249	309	311	332	332	351	402	429	...	...	...	...
8 Finance, insurance, real estate and business services [d]	351	370	398	434	449	452	455	454	...	...	...	...
9 Community, social and personal services [cd]	314	321	332	345	344	338	346	356	...	...	...	...
Total, Industries	3034	3391	3446	3604	3396	3430	3716	3826	...	...	...	...
Producers of government services	332	315	340	349	359	354	361	373	...	...	...	...
Other producers	...	...	...	...	...	...	...	...	...	...	...	...
Subtotal	3365	3706	3786	3952	3755	3784	4077	4199	...	...	...	...
less: Imputed bank service charge	...	...	...	...	...	...	...	...	...	...	...	...
plus: Import duties	...	...	...	...	...	...	...	...	...	...	...	...
plus: Value added tax	...	...	...	...	...	...	...	...	...	...	...	...
plus: Other adjustments	...	...	...	...	...	...	...	...	...	...	...	...
equals: Gross domestic product	3365	3706	3786	3952	3755	3784	4077	4199	...	...	...	...

a Item "Manufacturing" includes handicrafts.
b Repair services are included in item "Manufacturing".
c Restaurants and hotels are included in item "Community, social and personal services".
d Business services are included in item "Community, social and personal services".

Dominican Republic

1.12 Relations among national accounting aggregates

Million Dominican pesos

	1986	1987	1988	1989	1990	1991	1992	1993	1994	1995	1996	1997
Gross domestic product	15780	19536	28353	42393	64867	100070	112369	120572	...	...	...	...
plus: Net factor income from the rest of the world [a]	−1074	−1572	−1899	−1308	−1308	−2705	−3035	−4953	...	...	...	...
equals: Gross national product	14706	17964	26454	41085	63559	97365	109334	115619	...	...	...	...
less: Consumption of fixed capital	939	1162	1687	2522	3860	5954	6686	7174	...	...	...	...
equals: National income	13767	16802	24767	38563	59699	91411	102648	108445	...	...	...	...
plus: Net current transfers from the rest of the world [a,b]	821	1236	2238	2441	3206	4862	5397	5520	...	...	...	...
equals: National disposable income	14589	18038	27005	41004	62905	96273	108045	113965	...	...	...	...
less: Final consumption	12903	15747	20879	33061	53884	86613	96955	99607	...	...	...	...
Statistical discrepancy	...	...	...	...	...	...	564	810	...	...	...	...
equals: Net saving	1686	2291	6126	7943	9021	9660	11654	15168	...	...	...	...
less: Surplus of the nation on current transactions [a]	−952	−1984	−310	−1140	−517	−1405	−5381	−4613	...	...	...	...
equals: Net capital formation [c]	2638	4275	6436	9083	9538	11065	17035	19781	...	...	...	...

[a] Beginning 1984, estimates were converted from dollars to pesos by using the annual average exchange rates fixed by the Central Bank.

[b] Item "Net current transfers from the rest of the world" includes mainly net interest receipts.

[c] Item "Gross capital formation" includes only increase of stocks of mining, manufacturing, peanuts, raw tobacco and beans.

Ecuador

Source

Reply to the United Nations National Accounts Questionnaire from the Subgerencia de Cuentas Nacionales, Banco Central del Ecuador, Quito. The official estimates are published annually in *Memoria del Gerente General del Banco Central del Ecuador*.

General note

The estimates shown in the following tables have been prepared in accordance with the United Nations System of National Accounts (1968 SNA) so far as the existing data would permit.

1.1 Expenditure on the gross domestic product, in current prices

Thousand million Ecuadoran sucres

	1986	1987	1988	1989	1990	1991	1992	1993	1994	1995	1996	1997
1 Government final consumption expenditure	167	230	347	485	706	936	1407	2117	...	...	...	...
2 Private final consumption expenditure	926	1269	2087	3706	5622	8432	13148	19374	...	...	...	...
A Households	926	1269	2087	3706	5622	8432	13148	19374	...	...	...	...
B Private non-profit institutions serving households	...	...	...	...	...	...	...	...	...	...	...	...
3 Gross capital formation	288	407	649	1070	1435	2726	4117	5787	...	...	...	...
A Increase in stocks	28	–	6	–1	–77	309	333	330	...	...	...	...
B Gross fixed capital formation	260	407	643	1071	1512	2416	3785	5457	...	...	...	...
Residential buildings	31	41	75	98	144	241	347	502	...	...	...	...
Non-residential buildings	35	43	62	112	189	291	464	619	...	...	...	...
Other construction and land improvement, etc.	73	126	163	304	354	554	784	1275	...	...	...	...
Other	121	197	343	556	826	1330	2189	3060	...	...	...	...
4 Exports of goods and services	315	432	859	1520	2686	3858	6119	7184	...	...	...	...
5 less: Imports of goods and services	313	544	922	1611	2246	3655	5378	7011	...	...	...	...
equals: Gross domestic product	1383	1795	3020	5170	8204	12296	19414	27451	...	...	...	...

1.2 Expenditure on the gross domestic product, in constant prices

Million Ecuadoran sucres

	1986	1987	1988	1989	1990	1991	1992	1993	1994	1995	1996	1997
At constant prices of: 1975												
1 Government final consumption expenditure	20904	21245	21562	20980	21431	20950	20289	20036	...	...	...	...
2 Private final consumption expenditure	111397	114115	116312	119225	122259	125264	128107	131332	...	...	...	...
A Households	111397	114115	116312	119225	122259	125264	128107	131332	...	...	...	...
B Private non-profit institutions serving households	...	...	...	...	...	...	...	...	...	...	...	...
3 Gross capital formation	28816	27915	26876	27656	23449	30452	30084	28836	...	...	...	...
A Increase in stocks	3139	1115	1411	2405	–512	3850	1650	94	...	...	...	...

Ecuador

Million Ecuadoran sucres

	1986	1987	1988	1989	1990	1991	1992	1993	1994	1995	1996	1997
	At constant prices of: 1975											
B Gross fixed capital formation	25677	26800	25465	25251	23961	26602	28434	28742	...	...	...	...
Residential buildings	14367	14982	13017	13175	11559	3077	2783	2536	...	...	...	...
Non-residential buildings	...	...	...	...	...	3208	3357	2986	...	...	...	...
Other construction and land improvement, etc.	...	...	...	...	...	5788	5440	5905	...	...	...	...
Other	11310	11818	12448	12076	12402	14529	16854	17315	...	...	...	...
4 Exports of goods and services	42944	36027	47235	46440	51159	56523	61940	64552	...	...	...	...
5 less: Imports of goods and services	34925	40286	36243	38106	36692	42551	42984	43309	...	...	...	...
equals: Gross domestic product	169136	159016	175742	176195	181531	190638	197436	201447	...	...	...	...

1.3 Cost components of the gross domestic product

Thousand million Ecuadoran sucres

	1986	1987	1988	1989	1990	1991	1992	1993	1994	1995	1996	1997
1 Indirect taxes, net	156	205	357	694	1133	1443	2308	3271	...	...	...	...
A Indirect taxes	191	229	397	761	1279	1706	2626	3649	...	...	...	...
B less: Subsidies	34	24	40	67	146	263	318	378	...	...	...	...
2 Consumption of fixed capital	...	...	...	...	...	...	...	...	...	...	...	...
3 Compensation of employees paid by resident producers to	302	401	550	787	1115	1566	2461	3968	...	...	...	...
A Resident households	298	394	540	765	1075	1510	2354	3836	...	...	...	...
B Rest of the world	4	7	10	22	40	56	106	132	...	...	...	...
4 Operating surplus [a]	925	1189	2113	3690	5955	9287	14645	20212	...	...	...	...
A Corporate and quasi-corporate enterprises [b]	218	214	432	574	1068	1416	2264	2078	...	...	...	...
B Private unincorporated enterprises [c]	705	971	1677	3117	4889	7873	12383	18138	...	...	...	...
C General government	2	4	4	−1	−2	−2	−2	−4	...	...	...	...
equals: Gross domestic product	1383	1795	3020	5170	8204	12296	19414	27451	...	...	...	...

a Item "Operating surplus" includes consumption of fixed capital.
b Beginning 1976, item "Corporate and quasi-corporate enterprises" includes quasi-corporate enterprises that up to 1975 were included with households.
c Item "Private unincorporated enterprises" relates to households.

1.4 General government current receipts and disbursements

Thousand million Ecuadoran sucres

	1986	1987	1988	1989	1990	1991	1992	1993	1994	1995	1996	1997
Receipts												
1 Operating surplus	2	4	4	−1	−2	−2	−2	−3	...	...	...	...
2 Property and entrepreneurial income	29	31	61	105	235	232	301	383	...	...	...	...
3 Taxes, fees and contributions	299	339	593	1091	1870	2588	3843	5383	...	...	...	...
A Indirect taxes	191	229	397	761	1279	1706	2626	3649	...	...	...	...
B Direct taxes	70	63	112	179	373	555	721	1051	...	...	...	...
C Social security contributions	33	41	72	131	197	297	457	625	...	...	...	...
D Compulsory fees, fines and penalties	5	6	11	20	21	30	39	58	...	...	...	...
4 Other current transfers	62	71	95	156	260	345	457	676	...	...	...	...
Total current receipts of general government	393	444	752	1351	2363	3161	4599	6439	...	...	...	...
Disbursements												

Ecuador

Thousand million Ecuadoran sucres

	1986	1987	1988	1989	1990	1991	1992	1993	1994	1995	1996	1997
1 Government final consumption expenditure	167	230	347	485	706	936	1407	2117	...	...	...	...
2 Property income	57	57	78	175	332	337	499	543	...	...	...	...
A Interest	57	57	78	175	332	337	499	543	...	...	...	...
B Net land rent and royalties	–	–	–	–	–	–	–	...	...	...	...	...
3 Subsidies	34	24	40	67	146	263	318	378	...	...	...	...
4 Other current transfers	61	88	121	204	351	475	759	1029	...	...	...	...
A Social security benefits	22	40	55	88	141	204	375	469	...	...	...	...
B Social assistance grants	3	4	6	11	...	...	...	...	...	...	...	...
C Other	36	44	60	105	...	...	...	...	...	...	...	...
5 Net saving [a]	74	45	165	420	829	1148	1616	2371	...	...	...	...
Total current disbursements and net saving of general government	393	444	752	1351	2363	3159	4599	6438	...	...	...	...

a Item "Net saving" includes consumption of fixed capital.

1.5 Current income and outlay of corporate and quasi-corporate enterprises, summary

Thousand million Ecuadoran sucres

	1986	1987	1988	1989	1990	1991	1992	1993	1994	1995	1996	1997
Receipts												
1 Operating surplus [a]	218	214	432	574	1068	1416	2264	2077	...	...	...	...
2 Property and entrepreneurial income received	144	205	296	432	703	1177	1984	2756	...	...	...	...
3 Current transfers	11	19	29	42	74	130	226	384	...	...	...	...
Total current receipts	373	439	758	1048	1845	2723	4474	5217	...	...	...	...
Disbursements												
1 Property and entrepreneurial income	246	322	475	750	1238	1838	2913	3561	...	...	...	...
2 Direct taxes and other current payments to general government	60	50	96	142	325	479	592	833	...	...	...	...
3 Other current transfers	39	47	66	106	148	230	352	600	...	...	...	...
4 Net saving [b]	28	21	122	50	135	176	617	223	...	...	...	...
Total current disbursements and net saving	373	439	758	1048	1845	2723	4474	5217	...	...	...	...

a Item "Operating surplus" includes consumption of fixed capital. b Item "Net saving" includes consumption of fixed capital.

1.6 Current income and outlay of households and non-profit institutions

Thousand million Ecuadoran sucres

	1986	1987	1988	1989	1990	1991	1992	1993	1994	1995	1996	1997
Receipts												
1 Compensation of employees	298	394	541	767	1078	1515	2361	3844	...	...	...	...
A From resident producers	298	394	540	765	1075	1510	2354	3836	...	...	...	...
B From rest of the world	–	1	1	2	3	5	7	8	...	...	...	...
2 Operating surplus of private unincorporated enterprises	705	971	1677	3117	4889	7873	12383	18138	...	...	...	...
3 Property and entrepreneurial income	62	84	87	126	213	351	908	995	...	...	...	...
4 Current transfers	41	90	119	203	325	480	845	1159	...	...	...	...
A Social security benefits	22	40	55	88	141	204	375	469	...	...	...	...
B Social assistance grants									...	...	...	...
C Other	19	51	64	115	184	276	470	690	...	...	...	...
Total current receipts	1107	1540	2424	4213	6505	10219	16498	24135	...	...	...	...

Ecuador

Thousand million Ecuadoran sucres

	1986	1987	1988	1989	1990	1991	1992	1993	1994	1995	1996	1997
Disbursements												
1 Private final consumption expenditure	926	1269	2087	3706	5622	8432	13147	19375	...	...	...	...
2 Property income	40	58	90	103	173	270	612	1003	...	...	...	...
3 Direct taxes and other current transfers n.e.c. to general government	49	61	100	188	266	404	625	899	...	...	...	...
A Social security contributions	33	41	72	131	197	297	457	625	...	...	...	...
B Direct taxes	13	16	22	45	56	86	143	234	...	...	...	...
C Fees, fines and penalties	3	3	5	12	13	21	25	40	...	...	...	...
4 Other current transfers	13	20	29	41	78	129	231	357	...	...	...	...
5 Net saving [a]	79	132	119	175	366	985	1884	2501	...	...	...	...
Total current disbursements and net saving	1107	1540	2424	4213	6505	10220	16498	24135	...	...	...	...

a Item "Net saving" includes consumption of fixed capital.

1.7 External transactions on current account, summary

Thousand million Ecuadoran sucres

	1986	1987	1988	1989	1990	1991	1992	1993	1994	1995	1996	1997
Payments to the rest of the world												
1 Imports of goods and services	313	544	922	1611	2246	3655	5378	7011	...	...	...	...
A Imports of merchandise, c.i.f.	243	448	725	1318	1811	3053	4465	5816	...	...	...	...
B Other	70	96	197	293	435	602	913	1195	...	...	...	...
2 Factor income to rest of the world	116	126	212	400	656	777	992	1165	...	...	...	...
A Compensation of employees	4	7	10	22	40	56	106	132	...	...	...	...
B Property and entrepreneurial income	112	119	203	378	616	721	886	1033	...	...	...	...
3 Current transfers to the rest of the world	4	6	10	18	34	44	84	100	...	...	...	...
4 Surplus of the nation on current transactions	−107	−209	−243	−425	−106	−414	−2	−692	...	...	...	...
Payments to the rest of the world and surplus of the nation on current transfers	325	467	901	1604	2830	4062	6452	7584	...	...	...	...
Receipts from the rest of the world												
1 Exports of goods and services	315	432	859	1520	2686	3858	6119	7184	...	...	...	...
A Exports of merchandise, f.o.b.	250	348	673	1221	2251	3214	5075	5813	...	...	...	...
B Other	65	83	186	299	435	644	1044	1371	...	...	...	...
2 Factor income from rest of the world	4	4	6	16	27	41	61	66	...	...	...	...
A Compensation of employees	–	1	1	2	3	5	7	8	...	...	...	...
B Property and entrepreneurial income	3	3	5	14	24	37	54	58	...	...	...	...
3 Current transfers from rest of the world	6	32	37	69	117	163	272	334	...	...	...	...
Receipts from the rest of the world on current transactions	325	467	901	1604	2830	4062	6452	7584	...	...	...	...

Ecuador

1.8 Capital transactions of the nation, summary

Thousand million Ecuadoran sucres

	1986	1987	1988	1989	1990	1991	1992	1993	1994	1995	1996	1997
Finance of gross capital formation												
Gross saving	181	198	406	645	1330	2311	4115	5096	...	...	...	...
1 Consumption of fixed capital	200	315	542	935	1416	2026	3007	4368	...	...	...	...
2 Net saving	–19	–117	–136	–290	–86	285	1108	728	...	...	...	...
less: Surplus of the nation on current transactions	–107	–209	–243	–425	–105	–415	–2	–691	...	...	...	...
Finance of gross capital formation	288	407	649	1070	1435	2726	4117	5787	...	...	...	...
Gross capital formation												
Increase in stocks	28	–	6	–1	–77	309	333	330	...	...	...	...
Gross fixed capital formation	260	407	643	1071	1512	2417	3784	5457	...	...	...	...
1 General government	82	116	165	237	328	470	754	996	...	...	...	...
2 Corporate and quasi-corporate enterprises	133	226	366	639	790	1367	2127	3169	...	...	...	...
A Public	45	51	96	236	219	435	691	1137	...	...	...	...
B Private	88	175	270	403	571	932	1436	2032	...	...	...	...
3 Other	45	65	112	194	395	580	903	1292	...	...	...	...
Gross capital formation	288	407	649	1070	1435	2726	4117	5787	...	...	...	...

1.9 Gross domestic product by institutional sectors of origin

Thousand million Ecuadoran sucres

	1986	1987	1988	1989	1990	1991	1992	1993	1994	1995	1996	1997
Domestic factor incomes originating												
1 General government	128	169	237	311	444	586	950	1518	...	...	...	...
2 Corporate and quasi-corporate enterprises	441	538	957	1459	2358	3191	5191	6526	...	...	...	...
A Non-financial	415	485	860	1375	2227	2950	4803	5796	...	...	...	...
Public	152	160	300	627	1190	1471	2632	3669	...	...	...	...
Private	263	325	560	748	1037	1480	2171	2127	...	...	...	...
B Financial	26	52	97	84	131	241	388	730	...	...	...	...
Public	6	27	58	27	34	87	138	186	...	...	...	...
Private	20	25	39	57	97	154	250	544	...	...	...	...
3 Households and private unincorporated enterprises	779	1064	1802	3302	5101	8161	12812	18799	...	...	...	...
4 Non-profit institutions serving households	...	...	...	...	...	...	...	...	...	...	...	...
subtotal: Domestic factor incomes [a,b]	1347	1771	2997	5072	7903	11938	18953	26843	...	...	...	...
Indirect taxes, net [c]	64	77	121	196	450	646	951	1486	...	...	...	...
A Indirect taxes	64	77	121	196	450	646	951	1486	...	...	...	...
B less: Subsidies	–	–	–	–	–	–	–	...	...	...	...	...
Consumption of fixed capital	...	...	...	...	...	...	...	...	...	...	...	...
Statistical discrepancy [d]	–29	–54	–98	–97	–149	–288	–490	–878	...	...	...	...
Gross domestic product	1383	1795	3020	5170	8204	12296	19413	27451	...	...	...	...

a Item "Domestic factor incomes" includes consumption of fixed capital.
b Item "Domestic factor incomes" includes net indirect taxes other than import duties.
c Item "Indirect taxes, net" refers to import duties only.
d Item "Statistical discrepancy" relates to imputed bank service charges.

Ecuador

1.10 Gross domestic product by kind of activity, in current prices

Thousand million Ecuadoran sucres

	1986	1987	1988	1989	1990	1991	1992	1993	1994	1995	1996	1997
1 Agriculture, hunting, forestry and fishing	209	275	433	722	1100	1762	2466	3323	...	...	...	...
2 Mining and quarrying [a]	138	123	297	605	1218	1368	2440	2942	...	...	...	...
3 Manufacturing [a]	274	350	645	1090	1588	2554	4280	5969	...	...	...	...
4 Electricity, gas and water	6	7	2	4	−15	−13	23	76	...	...	...	...
5 Construction	67	99	140	236	329	556	882	1340	...	...	...	...
6 Wholesale and retail trade, restaurants and hotels	247	363	611	1119	1737	2723	4168	5551	...	...	...	...
7 Transport, storage and communication	126	170	296	461	708	1064	1505	2450	...	...	...	...
8 Finance, insurance, real estate and business services	105	151	244	334	502	857	1393	2255	...	...	...	...
9 Community, social and personal services	57	77	115	215	331	537	943	1564	...	...	...	...
Total, Industries	1229	1615	2782	4785	7498	11408	18100	25470	...	...	...	...
Producers of government services	113	148	205	272	387	504	813	1309	...	...	...	...
Other producers	6	8	10	14	19	26	40	65	...	...	...	...
Subtotal	1347	1771	2997	5072	7903	11938	18953	26844	...	...	...	...
less: Imputed bank service charge	29	54	98	97	149	288	490	879	...	...	...	...
plus: Import duties	64	77	121	196	215	280	339	537	...	...	...	...
plus: Value added tax	...	...	...	...	234	366	612	949	...	...	...	...
plus: Other adjustments	...	...	...	...	...	...	...	...	...	...	...	...
equals: Gross domestic product	1383	1795	3020	5170	8204	12296	19414	27451	...	...	...	...

[a] Petroleum refining is included in item "Crude petroleum and natural gas production".

1.11 Gross domestic product by kind of activity, in constant prices

Million Ecuadoran sucres

	1986	1987	1988	1989	1990	1991	1992	1993	1994	1995	1996	1997
	At constant prices of: 1975											
1 Agriculture, hunting, forestry and fishing	26656	27323	29416	30230	32080	33988	35154	34555	...	...	...	...
2 Mining and quarrying [a]	24513	11107	23964	21642	21442	23251	24599	27298	...	...	...	...
3 Manufacturing [a]	28241	28729	29312	27858	28055	28951	29989	30731	...	...	...	...
4 Electricity, gas and water	2232	2616	2721	2899	2781	2841	2919	2980	...	...	...	...
5 Construction	6841	7011	6024	6264	5333	5274	5256	5032	...	...	...	...
6 Wholesale and retail trade, restaurants and hotels	24793	25397	25925	26470	27469	28557	29420	29919	...	...	...	...
7 Transport, storage and communication	12571	12829	13620	14700	15362	16289	17223	17992	...	...	...	...
8 Finance, insurance, real estate and business services	18579	21095	22679	19188	19589	20806	21479	23455	...	...	...	...
9 Community, social and personal services	9773	10067	10082	10388	10434	10757	11112	11264	...	...	...	...
Total, Industries	154199	146174	163743	159639	162545	170714	177151	183226	...	...	...	...
Producers of government services	14898	15002	15617	15636	16015	16169	16114	15754	...	...	...	...
Other producers	735	756	778	800	819	844	864	881	...	...	...	...
Subtotal	169832	161932	180138	176075	179379	187727	194129	199861	...	...	...	...
less: Imputed bank service charge	4934	7122	8510	4692	4881	5661	5984	7811	...	...	...	...

Ecuador

Million Ecuadoran sucres

	1986	1987	1988	1989	1990	1991	1992	1993	1994	1995	1996	1997
At constant prices of: 1975												
plus: Import duties	4238	4206	4114	4812	3624	4815	5324	5369	...	...	...	...
plus: Value added tax	...	...	...	...	3409	3757	3967	4028	...	...	...	...
plus: Other adjustments	...	...	...	...	...	...	...	...	...	...	...	...
equals: Gross domestic product	169136	159016	175742	176195	181531	190638	197436	201447	...	...	...	...

a Petroleum refining is included in item "Crude petroleum and natural gas production".

1.12 Relations among national accounting aggregates

Thousand million Ecuadoran sucres

	1986	1987	1988	1989	1990	1991	1992	1993	1994	1995	1996	1997
Gross domestic product	1383	1795	3020	5170	8204	12296	19414	27451	...	...	...	...
plus: Net factor income from the rest of the world	–112	–122	–207	–384	–629	–737	–931	–1098	...	...	...	...
Factor income from rest of the world	4	4	6	16	27	41	61	66	...	...	...	...
less: Factor income to the rest of the world	116	126	212	400	656	778	992	1164	...	...	...	...
equals: Gross national product	1272	1272	2813	4786	7575	11559	18483	26353	...	...	...	...
less: Consumption of fixed capital	200	315	542	935	1416	2026	3007	4368	...	...	...	...
equals: National income	1072	1357	2271	3851	6159	9533	15476	21985	...	...	...	...
plus: Net current transfers from the rest of the world	2	25	27	50	83	119	187	234	...	...	...	...
Current transfers from rest of the world	6	32	37	69	117	163	273	334	...	...	...	...
less: Current transfers to the rest of the world	4	6	10	18	34	44	84	100	...	...	...	...
equals: National disposable income	1074	1382	2298	3901	6242	9652	15663	22219	...	...	...	...
less: Final consumption	1093	1500	2434	4191	6328	9367	14555	21491	...	...	...	...
equals: Net saving	–19	–118	–136	–290	–86	285	1108	728	...	...	...	...
less: Surplus of the nation on current transactions	–107	–209	–243	–425	–106	–415	–2	–691	...	...	...	...
equals: Net capital formation	88	91	107	135	20	700	1110	1419	...	...	...	...

2.1 Government final consumption expenditure by function, in current prices

Thousand million Ecuadoran sucres

	1986	1987	1988	1989	1990	1991	1992	1993	1994	1995	1996	1997
1 General public services	27	38	48	68	101	131	192	...	...	...	...	...
2 Defence	21	30	69	83	113	151	238	...	...	...	...	...
3 Public order and safety	11	14	29	36	55	72	109	...	...	...	...	...
4 Education	57	85	101	134	214	281	402	...	...	...	...	...
5 Health	11	14	21	31	37	46	59	...	...	...	...	...
6 Social security and welfare	9	12	19	27	48	63	117	...	...	...	...	...
7 Housing and community amenities	5	7	12	20	34	50	64	...	...	...	...	...
8 Recreational, cultural and religious affairs	–	1	1	1	2	3	3	...	...	...	...	...
9 Economic services	27	41	56	70	108	150	241	...	...	...	...	...
A Fuel and energy	5	6	10	–	1	1	36	...	...	...	...	...
B Agriculture, hunting, forestry and fishing	7	10	12	19	30	40	53	...	...	...	...	...
C Mining (except fuels), manufacturing and construction	3	6	7	9	14	18	28	...	...	...	...	...

Ecuador

Thousand million Ecuadoran sucres

	1986	1987	1988	1989	1990	1991	1992	1993	1994	1995	1996	1997
D Transportation and communication	11	17	23	35	57	79	111	...	...	...	...	...
E Other economic affairs	2	2	4	6	7	12	13	...	...	...	...	...
10 Other functions	9	4	17	54	66	63	73	...	...	...	...	...
Total government final consumption expenditures [a]	178	245	372	524	777	1009	1498	...	...	...	...	...

[a] Government final consumption expenditure in this table includes compensation of employees and intermediate consumption of the following departmental enterprises: electricity, gas and steam, water works and supply and medical and other health services.

2.3 Total government outlays by function and type

Thousand million Ecuadoran sucres

1986

	Final consumption expenditures Total	Compensation of employees	Other	Subsidies	Other current transfers and property income	Total current disbursements	Gross capital formation	Other capital outlays	Total outlays
1 General public services	27	...	...	...	1	28	3	–	31
2 Defence	21	...	...	...	–	22	–	...	22
3 Public order and safety	11	...	...	...	–	11	1	...	12
4 Education	57	...	...	...	1	58	8	–	67
5 Health	11	...	...	...	9	20	5	–	25
6 Social security and welfare	9	...	...	...	19	28	2	1	31
7 Housing and community amenities	5	...	...	–	–	5	14	2	21
8 Recreational, cultural and religious affairs	–	...	...	...	–	–	–	–	1
9 Economic services	27	...	...	34	1	62	48	3	113
A Fuel and energy	5	...	...	28	–	33	12	–	45
B Agriculture, hunting, forestry and fishing	7	...	...	5	–	12	5	–	17
C Mining (except fuels), manufacturing and construction	3	...	...	–	–	3	–	–	3
D Transportation and communication	11	...	...	1	–	12	23	2	38
E Other economic affairs	2	...	...	–	–	2	8	–	11
10 Other functions	9	...	...	...	52	62	1	–	62
Total [abc]	178	...	...	34	83	296	82	7	385

1987

	Final consumption expenditures Total	Compensation of employees	Other	Subsidies	Other current transfers and property income	Total current disbursements	Gross capital formation	Other capital outlays	Total outlays
1 General public services	38	...	...	...	–	39	4	–	43
2 Defence	30	...	...	...	–	30	–	...	30
3 Public order and safety	14	...	...	...	–	14	1	...	15
4 Education	85	...	...	...	2	87	12	–	100
5 Health	14	...	...	...	12	26	8	1	35
6 Social security and welfare	12	...	...	...	30	43	3	1	46
7 Housing and community amenities	7	...	...	–	–	7	21	3	31
8 Recreational, cultural and religious affairs	1	...	...	...	–	1	–	–	1
9 Economic services	41	...	...	24	1	66	68	1	135

Ecuador

1987

	Final consumption expenditures: Total	Compensation of employees	Other	Subsidies	Other current transfers and property income	Total current disbursements	Gross capital formation	Other capital outlays	Total outlays
A Fuel and energy	6	...	...	17	–	23	22	–	46
B Agriculture, hunting, forestry and fishing	10	...	...	5	–	14	5	–	20
C Mining (except fuels), manufacturing and construction	6	...	...	–	–	6	–	–	6
D Transportation and communication	17	...	...	2	–	19	29	1	48
E Other economic affairs	2	...	...	1	–	3	11	–	15
10 Other functions	4	...	...	...	55	59	–	–	59
Total [abc]	245	...	...	24	101	371	117	6	495

1988

	Final consumption expenditures: Total	Compensation of employees	Other	Subsidies	Other current transfers and property income	Total current disbursements	Gross capital formation	Other capital outlays	Total outlays
1 General public services	48	...	...	–	1	48	5	–	54
2 Defence	69	...	...	...	–	69	–	–	69
3 Public order and safety	29	...	...	...	–	29	2	–	31
4 Education	101	...	...	...	3	104	16	–	120
5 Health	21	...	...	...	2	23	12	–	35
6 Social security and welfare	19	...	...	...	3	22	4	–	25
7 Housing and community amenities	12	...	...	–	–	12	21	14	47
8 Recreational, cultural and religious affairs	1	...	...	...	–	1	1	–	2
9 Economic services	56	...	...	17	1	75	102	1	178
A Fuel and energy	10	...	...	13	–	23	27	–	50
B Agriculture, hunting, forestry and fishing	12	...	...	–	–	12	6	1	19
C Mining (except fuels), manufacturing and construction	7	...	...	–	–	7	1	–	8
D Transportation and communication	23	...	...	3	–	27	40	–	67
E Other economic affairs	4	...	...	2	–	5	28	–	33
10 Other functions	17	...	...	...	76	92	–	–	92
Total [abc]	372	...	...	17	85	475	163	15	653

1989

	Final consumption expenditures: Total	Compensation of employees	Other	Subsidies	Other current transfers and property income	Total current disbursements	Gross capital formation	Other capital outlays	Total outlays
1 General public services	68	...	...	–	1	69	9	–	78
2 Defence	83	...	...	...	–	83	–	–	83
3 Public order and safety	36	...	...	...	–	37	4	–	40
4 Education	134	...	...	...	5	139	32	–	172
5 Health	31	...	...	...	3	35	20	–	55
6 Social security and welfare	27	...	...	...	5	32	6	–	38
7 Housing and community amenities	20	...	...	–	–	20	27	54	101

Ecuador

1989

	Final consumption expenditures Total	Compensation of employees	Other	Subsidies	Other current transfers and property income	Total current disbursements	Gross capital formation	Other capital outlays	Total outlays
8 Recreational, cultural and religious affairs	1	...	...	...	–	1	1	–	2
9 Economic services	70	...	...	67	1	138	139	30	307
A Fuel and energy	–	...	...	62	–	62	–	27	89
B Agriculture, hunting, forestry and fishing	19	...	...	–	–	19	10	1	30
C Mining (except fuels), manufacturing and construction	9	...	...	–	1	10	1	...	11
D Transportation and communication	35	...	...	4	1	40	70	2	112
E Other economic affairs	6	...	...	1	–	7	58	1	66
10 Other functions	54	...	...	...	172	226	–	–	226
Total [abc]	524	...	...	67	188	780	237	84	1101

1990

	Final consumption expenditures Total	Compensation of employees	Other	Subsidies	Other current transfers and property income	Total current disbursements	Gross capital formation	Other capital outlays	Total outlays
1 General public services	101	...	...	–	2	103	14	–	117
2 Defence	113	...	...	...	–	113	–	–	113
3 Public order and safety	55	...	...	...	1	55	8	–	63
4 Education	214	...	...	...	9	222	38	–	260
5 Health	37	...	...	...	6	43	37	–	79
6 Social security and welfare	48	...	...	...	7	54	10	–	65
7 Housing and community amenities	34	...	...	...	2	37	48	19	103
8 Recreational, cultural and religious affairs	2	...	...	...	–	2	1	–	2
9 Economic services	108	...	...	130	3	241	173	64	479
A Fuel and energy	1	...	...	124	–	125	–	61	186
B Agriculture, hunting, forestry and fishing	30	...	...	–	–	30	15	1	46
C Mining (except fuels), manufacturing and construction	14	...	...	–	1	15	2	–	16
D Transportation and communication	57	...	...	4	1	63	120	1	184
E Other economic affairs	7	...	...	2	–	9	36	1	46
10 Other functions	66	...	...	...	327	393	2	–	395
Total [abc]	777	...	...	131	356	1263	329	84	1677

1991

	Final consumption expenditures Total	Compensation of employees	Other	Subsidies	Other current transfers and property income	Total current disbursements	Gross capital formation	Other capital outlays	Total outlays
1 General public services	131	...	...	...	2	133	18	...	151
2 Defence	151	...	...	...	–	151	...	...	151
3 Public order and safety	72	...	...	...	1	73	8	...	81
4 Education	281	...	...	...	12	293	49	...	342
5 Health	46	...	...	...	75	121	56	...	177

Ecuador

	1991							
	Final consumption expenditures			Subsidies	Other current transfers and property income	Total current disburse-ments	Gross capital formation	Other capital outlays	Total outlays
	Total	Compensation of employees	Other						
6 Social security and welfare	63	...	...	...	143	206	14	...	220
7 Housing and community amenities	50	...	...	...	50	100	71	...	171
8 Recreational, cultural and religious affairs	3	...	...	...	–	3	1	...	4
9 Economic services	150	...	...	...	396	546	257	...	803
A Fuel and energy	1	...	...	...	364	365	1	...	366
B Agriculture, hunting, forestry and fishing	40	...	...	...	3	43	23	...	66
C Mining (except fuels), manufacturing and construction	18	...	...	...	1	19	2	...	21
D Transportation and communication	79	...	...	...	24	103	160	...	263
E Other economic affairs	12	...	...	...	5	17	71	...	88
10 Other functions	63	...	...	...	334	397	2	...	399
Total [abc]	1009	...	...	...	1013	2022	476	...	2498

	1992							
	Final consumption expenditures			Subsidies	Other current transfers and property income	Total current disburse-ments	Gross capital formation	Other capital outlays	Total outlays
	Total	Compensation of employees	Other						
1 General public services	192	...	...	...	4	196	46	...	242
2 Defence	238	...	...	...	1	239	...	...	239
3 Public order and safety	109	...	...	...	1	110	7	...	117
4 Education	402	...	...	...	19	421	78	...	499
5 Health	59	...	...	...	157	216	123	...	339
6 Social security and welfare	117	...	...	...	240	357	23	...	380
7 Housing and community amenities	64	...	...	...	104	168	94	...	262
8 Recreational, cultural and religious affairs	3	...	...	...	...	3	1	...	4
9 Economic services	241	...	...	...	495	736	387	...	1123
A Fuel and energy	36	...	...	...	434	470	81	...	551
B Agriculture, hunting, forestry and fishing	53	...	...	...	1	54	27	...	81
C Mining (except fuels), manufacturing and construction	28	...	...	...	2	30	2	...	32
D Transportation and communication	111	...	...	...	47	158	235	...	393
E Other economic affairs	13	...	...	...	11	24	42	...	66
10 Other functions	73	...	...	...	494	567	1	...	568
Total [abc]	1498	...	...	...	1515	3013	760	...	3773

a Government final consumption expenditure in this table includes compensation of employees and intermediate consumption of the following departmental enterprises: electricity, gas and steam, water works and supply and medical and other health services.

b Column 5 (Other current transfers and property income) includes current transfers n.e.c. and social security benefits. Column 8 (Other capital outlays) includes purchases of land, net, capital transfers and increase in stocks.

c Beginning 1984, the estimates of total gross fixed capital formation (column 9) shown in this table is different from the estimates shown in table 3.13. This is because some functions of the general government which are included in the detailed account of table 3.13 could not be allocated to the items included in this table.

Ecuador

2.5 Private final consumption expenditure by type and purpose, in current prices

Thousand million Ecuadoran sucres

	1986	1987	1988	1989	1990	1991	1992	1993	1994	1995	1996	1997
Final consumption expenditure of resident households												
1 Food, beverages and tobacco	348	453	759	1435	2181	3277	5088	7326	...	...	...	...
A Food	290	374	632	1203	1831	2730	4251	6052	...	...	...	...
B Non-alcoholic beverages	17	22	34	59	85	131	209	311	...	...	...	...
C Alcoholic beverages	26	34	56	103	164	251	391	622	...	...	...	...
D Tobacco	15	23	36	71	101	165	237	341	...	...	...	...
2 Clothing and footwear	105	142	248	394	567	838	1243	1790	...	...	...	...
3 Gross rent, fuel and power [a]	63	82	117	193	288	443	664	1011	...	...	...	...
A Fuel and power [a]	13	18	25	43	65	107	172	269	...	...	...	...
B Other	50	64	92	151	224	336	492	742	...	...	...	...
4 Furniture, furnishings and household equipment and operation	67	106	178	300	438	626	942	1285	...	...	...	...
5 Medical care and health expenses	38	54	87	154	230	354	594	893	...	...	...	...
6 Transport and communication [a]	114	163	257	451	720	1078	1666	2690	...	...	...	...
7 Recreational, entertainment, education and cultural services	...	...	...	...	...	...	...	...	...	...	...	...
8 Miscellaneous goods and services	192	272	444	791	1215	1835	2982	4460	...	...	...	...
A Personal care	...	...	...	...	...	...	...	...	...	...	...	...
B Expenditures in restaurants, cafes and hotels	34	45	68	131	232	357	575	851	...	...	...	...
C Other	158	226	376	660	983	1478	2407	3609	...	...	...	...
Total final consumption expenditure in the domestic market by households, of which	927	1271	2089	3719	5639	8451	13179	19455	...	...	...	...
plus: Direct purchases abroad by resident households	–2	–2	–2	–12	–17	–19	–32	–81	...	...	...	...
less: Direct purchases in the domestic market by non-resident households	–	–	–	–	–	–	–	...	...	...	...	...
equals: Final consumption expenditure of resident households [b]	926	1269	2087	3706	5622	8432	13147	19374	...	...	...	...

a Fuel is included in item "Transport and communication".
b Item "Final consumption expenditure of resident households" includes consumption expenditure of private non-profit institutions serving households.

2.6 Private final consumption expenditure by type and purpose, in constant prices

Million Ecuadoran sucres

	1986	1987	1988	1989	1990	1991	1992	1993	1994	1995	1996	1997
At constant prices of: 1975												
Final consumption expenditure of resident households												
1 Food, beverages and tobacco	37052	37693	38645	39332	39512	40067	40841	42048	...	...	...	...
A Food	31276	31869	32870	33405	33594	34089	34709	35712	...	...	...	...
B Non-alcoholic beverages	1518	1496	1497	1525	1567	1574	1623	1662	...	...	...	...
C Alcoholic beverages	3267	3337	3400	3525	3470	3546	3629	3781	...	...	...	...
D Tobacco	991	991	878	877	881	858	880	893	...	...	...	...
2 Clothing and footwear	11653	11783	12073	12298	12623	12782	13130	13441	...	...	...	...
3 Gross rent, fuel and power [a]	12822	13395	13744	14221	14806	15865	15826	16150	...	...	...	...
A Fuel and power [a]	3004	3263	3347	3566	3828	4162	4321	4392	...	...	...	...

Ecuador

Million Ecuadoran sucres

	1986	1987	1988	1989	1990	1991	1992	1993	1994	1995	1996	1997
At constant prices of: 1975												
B Other	9818	10132	10397	10655	10978	11703	11505	10758	...	...	...	...
4 Furniture, furnishings and household equipment and operation	6330	6510	6585	6655	6747	6553	7096	7240	...	...	...	...
5 Medical care and health expenses	4866	5412	5142	4965	5081	5212	5368	5470	...	...	...	...
6 Transport and communication [a]	12585	12842	13701	14456	15468	16028	16486	17098	...	...	...	...
7 Recreational, entertainment, education and cultural services	...	...	...	...	...	...	...	...	...	...	...	...
8 Miscellaneous goods and services	26127	26581	26680	27741	28421	29029	29738	30435	...	...	...	...
A Personal care	...	...	...	...	...	...	...	...	...	...	...	...
B Expenditures in restaurants, cafes and hotels	5074	5263	5464	5668	5825	5956	6094	6215	...	...	...	...
C Other	21053	21318	21216	22073	22596	23073	23644	24220	...	...	...	...
Total final consumption expenditure in the domestic market by households, of which	111435	114216	116570	119668	122658	125536	128485	131882	...	...	...	...
plus: Direct purchases abroad by resident households	−38	−101	−258	−443	−399	−272	−378	−550	...	...	...	...
less: Direct purchases in the domestic market by non-resident households	−	−	−	−	−	−	−	−	...	...	...	...
equals: Final consumption expenditure of resident households [b]	111397	114115	116312	119225	122259	125264	128107	131332	...	...	...	...

a Fuel is included in item "Transport and communication".
b Item "Final consumption expenditure of resident households" includes consumption expenditure of private non-profit institutions serving households.

2.7 Gross capital formation by type of good and owner, in current price

Thousand million Ecuadoran sucres

	1986 Total	1986 Total private	1986 Public enterprises	1986 General government	1987 Total	1987 Total private	1987 Public enterprises	1987 General government	1988 Total	1988 Total private	1988 Public enterprises	1988 General government
Increase in stocks, total	28	21	6	1	−	−7	6	1	6	−5	10	2
Gross fixed capital formation, total	260	136	42	82	407	244	47	115	643	388	90	165
1 Residential buildings	31	31	...	−	41	41	...	−	75	75	...	−
2 Non-residential buildings	35	22	1	12	43	22	1	20	62	33	1	28
3 Other construction	73	2	13	59	126	10	31	85	163	5	35	123
4 Land improvement and plantation and orchard development	...	...	...	...	...	...	...	...	...	...	...	...
5 Producers' durable goods	115	76	28	11	190	164	15	10	333	266	54	13
6 Breeding stock, dairy cattle, etc.	6	6	−	−	7	7	−	−	10	10	−	−
Total gross capital formation	288	157	48	83	407	237	53	117	649	382	100	166

Ecuador

	1989				1990				1991			
	Total	Total private	Public enterprises	General government	Total	Total private	Public enterprises	General government	Total	Total private	Public enterprises	General government
Increase in stocks, total	-1	-38	36	2	-77	-185	103	4	309	192	112	5
Gross fixed capital formation, total	1071	603	230	237	1512	966	219	328	2416	1511	435	470
1 Residential buildings	98	97	...	1	144	144	...	–	241	241	...	–
2 Non-residential buildings	112	67	1	45	189	116	11	61	291	182	14	95
3 Other construction	304	6	127	171	354	8	114	232	554	5	219	330
4 Land improvement and plantation and orchard development	...	...	...	...	...	...	...	...	...	...	...	...
5 Producers' durable goods	536	414	102	21	799	671	94	34	1286	1039	202	45
6 Breeding stock, dairy cattle, etc.	20	20	–	–	27	27	...	–	44	44	...	–
Total gross capital formation	1070	565	266	239	1435	781	323	332	2725	1703	547	475

	1992				1993				1994			
	Total	Total private	Public enterprises	General government	Total	Total private	Public enterprises	General government	Total	Total private	Public enterprises	General government
Increase in stocks, total	333	198	126	9	330	157	161	12	...	...	...	...
Gross fixed capital formation, total	3784	2339	691	754	5457	3324	1137	996	...	...	...	...
1 Residential buildings	347	347	...	–	502	502	...	...	...	...	...	...
2 Non-residential buildings	464	264	36	164	619	411	24	184	...	...	...	...
3 Other construction	784	6	281	497	1275	10	540	725	...	...	...	...
4 Land improvement and plantation and orchard development	...	...	...	...	...	...	...	...	...	...	...	...
5 Producers' durable goods	2132	1665	374	93	2971	2311	573	87	...	...	...	...
6 Breeding stock, dairy cattle, etc.	57	57	...	–	90	90	...	...	...	...	...	...
Total gross capital formation	4117	2537	817	763	5787	3481	1298	1008	...	...	...	...

2.8 Gross capital formation by type of good and owner, in constant prices

Million Ecuadoran sucres

	1986				1987				1988			
	Total	Total private	Public enterprises	General government	Total	Total private	Public enterprises	General government	Total	Total private	Public enterprises	General government
	At constant prices of: 1975											
Increase in stocks, total	3139	...	...	...	1115	...	...	...	1411	...	...	...
Gross fixed capital formation, total	25677	13712	3924	8041	26800	15983	3030	7787	25465	15398	3344	6723
1 Residential buildings	14367	6001	1396	6970	14982	5710	2129	7143	13017	5317	1467	6233
2 Non-residential buildings												
3 Other construction												
4 Land improvement and plantation and orchard development												
5 Producers' durable goods	10677	7079	2527	1071	11121	9577	901	643	11772	9405	1877	490
6 Breeding stock, dairy cattle, etc.	633	632	1	–	697	696	–	1	676	676	–	–
Total gross capital formation	28816	...	...	...	27915	...	...	...	26876	...	...	...

Ecuador

	1989				1990				1991			
	Total	Total private	Public enterprises	General government	Total	Total private	Public enterprises	General government	Total	Total private	Public enterprises	General government
	At constant prices of: 1975												
Increase in stocks, total	2405	...	...	...	–512	...	...	...	3850	...	...	...
Gross fixed capital formation, total	25251	14268	5201	5782	23961	14436	4344	5181	26602	17034	4572	4996
1 Residential buildings	13175	4763	3079	5333	11559	...	...	4646	3077	3077	...	...
2 Non-residential buildings									3208	2013	149	1046
3 Other construction									5788	52	2289	3447
4 Land improvement and plantation and orchard development												
5 Producers' durable goods	11366	8795	2122	449	11660	...	...	535	13754	11117	2134	503
6 Breeding stock, dairy cattle, etc.	710	710	–	–	742	...	...	–	775	775	...	–
Total gross capital formation	27656	...	...	...	23449	...	...	...	30452	...	...	...

	1992				1993				1994			
	Total	Total private	Public enterprises	General government	Total	Total private	Public enterprises	General government	Total	Total private	Public enterprises	General government
	At constant prices of: 1975												
Increase in stocks, total	1650	...	...	...	94	...	...	...	...	...	...	...
Gross fixed capital formation, total	28434	18071	5011	5352	28742	18216	5780	4746	...	...	...	...
1 Residential buildings	2783	2783	...	...	2536	2536	...	...	...	...	...	...
2 Non-residential buildings	3357	1907	262	1188	2986	1984	117	885	...	...	...	...
3 Other construction	5440	44	1953	3443	5905	48	2499	3358	...	...	...	...
4 Land improvement and plantation and orchard development									...	...	...	...
5 Producers' durable goods	16117	12600	2796	721	16499	12832	3164	503	...	...	...	...
6 Breeding stock, dairy cattle, etc.	737	737	...	...	816	816	...	...	...	...	...	...
Total gross capital formation	30084	...	...	...	28836	...	...	...	...	...	...	...

2.17 Exports and imports of goods and services, detail

Thousand million Ecuadoran sucres

	1986	1987	1988	1989	1990	1991	1992	1993	1994	1995	1996	1997
Exports of goods and services													
1 Exports of merchandise, f.o.b.	250	348	673	1221	2251	3214	5075	5813	...	...	...	...
2 Transport and communication	34	45	100	173	250	389	658	828	...	...	...	...
3 Insurance service charges	–	1	–	1	1	1	...	3	...	...	...	...
4 Other commodities	1	1	1	3	5	11	28	41	...	...	...	...
5 Adjustments of merchandise exports to change-of-ownership basis	–	–	–	–	–	–	...	...	...	...	...	...
6 Direct purchases in the domestic market by non-residential households	26	33	78	109	159	214	314	409	...	...	...	...
7 Direct purchases in the domestic market by extraterritorial bodies	3	4	7	13	20	29	43	90	...	...	...	...
Total exports of goods and services [a]	315	432	859	1520	2686	3858	6119	7184	...	...	...	...

Imports of goods and services

Ecuador

Thousand million Ecuadoran sucres

	1986	1987	1988	1989	1990	1991	1992	1993	1994	1995	1996	1997
1 Imports of merchandise, c.i.f.	243	448	725	1318	1811	3053	4465	5816	...	...	...	...
2 Adjustments of merchandise imports to change-of-ownership basis	...	...	...	...	...	...	...	...	...	...	...	...
3 Other transport and communication	25	32	70	98	142	222	339	414	...	...	...	...
4 Other insurance service charges	5	6	8	26	40	34	21	89	...	...	...	...
5 Other commodities	11	19	32	49	74	108	198	250	...	...	...	...
6 Direct purchases abroad by government	1	3	5	11	16	14	29	42	...	...	...	...
7 Direct purchases abroad by resident households	28	36	82	110	162	224	326	400	...	...	...	...
Total imports of goods and services	313	544	922	1611	2246	3655	5378	7011	...	...	...	...
Balance of goods and services	2	−112	−63	−91	440	203	741	173	...	...	...	...
Total imports and balance of goods and services [a]	315	432	859	1520	2686	3858	6119	7184	...	...	...	...

a Data for this table have not been revised, therefore, data for some years are not comparable with those of other tables.

3.11 General government production account: total and subsectors

Thousand million Ecuadoran sucres

	1986 Total government	1986 Central government	1986 State or provincial government	1986 Local government	1986 Social security funds	1987 Total government	1987 Central government	1987 State or provincial government	1987 Local government	1987 Social security funds
Gross output										
1 Sales	29	18	...	2	8	40	27	...	3	11
2 Services produced for own use	8	5	...	3	–	11	8	...	3	–
3 Own account capital formation	168	142	...	20	5	231	199	...	25	7
Gross output [a]	204	165	...	25	14	282	233	...	31	18
Gross input										
Intermediate consumption	76	65	...	7	4	113	98	...	9	6
subtotal: Value added	128	100	...	18	10	169	135	...	23	12
1 Indirect taxes, net	...	...	...	...	...	...	...	...	...	...
2 Consumption of fixed capital	...	...	...	...	...	...	...	...	...	...
3 Compensation of employees	125	98	...	18	10	165	131	...	23	12
4 Net operating surplus [b]	2	3	...	–	...	4	4	...	–	...
Gross input [a]	204	165	...	25	14	282	233	...	31	18

	1988 Total government	1988 Central government	1988 State or provincial government	1988 Local government	1988 Social security funds	1989 Total government	1989 Central government	1989 State or provincial government	1989 Local government	1989 Social security funds
Gross output										
1 Sales	62	42	...	2	18	83	50	...	3	18
2 Services produced for own use	19	15	...	4	–	37	30	...	7	–
3 Own account capital formation	348	301	...	35	12	486	412	...	59	12
Gross output [a]	430	358	...	42	30	605	491	...	69	30
Gross input										
Intermediate consumption	192	173	...	10	9	295	259	...	19	9
subtotal: Value added	237	185	...	32	21	311	233	...	50	21

Ecuador

	1988					1989				
	Total government	Central government	State or provincial government	Local government	Social security funds	Total government	Central government	State or provincial government	Local government	Social security funds
1 Indirect taxes, net	...	...	...	...	...	...	...	...	...	...
2 Consumption of fixed capital	...	...	...	...	...	...	...	...	...	...
3 Compensation of employees	233	181	...	32	21	312	234	...	50	21
4 Net operating surplus [b]	4	4	...	–	...	–1	–1	...	–	...
Gross input [a]	430	358	...	42	30	605	491	...	69	30

	1990					1991				
	Total government	Central government	State or provincial government	Local government	Social security funds	Total government	Central government	State or provincial government	Local government	Social security funds
Gross output										
1 Sales	126	73	...	6	47	174	98	...	8	68
2 Services produced for own use	65	48	...	17	–	70	53	...	17	–
3 Own account capital formation	709	596	...	88	25	939	773	...	131	35
Gross output [a]	901	717	...	111	72	1184	924	...	156	104
Gross input										
Intermediate consumption	457	392	...	34	31	594	502	...	50	43
subtotal: Value added	444	325	...	78	41	589	422	...	106	61
1 Indirect taxes, net	...	...	...	...	...	...	...	...	...	...
2 Consumption of fixed capital	...	...	...	...	...	...	...	...	...	...
3 Compensation of employees	446	327	...	78	41	591	424	...	106	61
4 Net operating surplus [b]	–2	1	...	–	...	–2	–2	...	–	...
Gross input [a]	901	717	...	111	72	1184	924	...	156	104

	1992					1993				
	Total government	Central government	State or provincial government	Local government	Social security funds	Total government	Central government	State or provincial government	Local government	Social security funds
Gross output										
1 Sales	305	151	...	13	141	...	...	...	...	...
2 Services produced for own use	86	63	...	23	–	...	...	...	...	...
3 Own account capital formation	1396	1166	...	167	64	...	...	...	...	...
Gross output [a]	1787	1379	...	202	205	...	...	...	...	...
Gross input										
Intermediate consumption	799	632	...	68	99	...	...	...	...	...
subtotal: Value added	988	748	...	134	106	...	...	...	...	...
1 Indirect taxes, net	...	...	...	...	...	...	...	...	...	...
2 Consumption of fixed capital	...	...	...	...	...	...	...	...	...	...
3 Compensation of employees	990	750	...	134	106	...	...	...	...	...
4 Net operating surplus [b]	–2	–2	...	–	...	...	...	...	...	...
Gross input [a]	1787	1379	...	202	205	...	...	...	...	...

a Data for this table have not been revised, therefore, data for some years are not comparable with those of other tables. b Item "Operating surplus" includes consumption of fixed capital.

Ecuador

3.12 General government income and outlay account: total and subsectors

Thousand million Ecuadoran sucres

	1986					1987				
	Total government	Central government	State or provincial government	Local government	Social security funds	Total government	Central government	State or provincial government	Local government	Social security funds

Receipts

1 Operating surplus	2	3	...	–	–	4	4	...	–	–
2 Property and entrepreneurial income	29	17	...	1	11	31	16	...	1	14
A Withdrawals from public quasi-corporations	...	...	...	...	...	...	...	...	...	...
B Interest	12	1	...	1	10	15	1	...	1	14
C Dividends	1	1	...	–	–	3	3	...	–	–
D Net land rent and royalties	16	16	...	–	–	13	12	...	–	–
3 Taxes, fees and contributions	299	253	...	12	34	339	287	...	11	41
A Indirect taxes	191	182	...	9	–	229	221	...	8	–
B Direct taxes	70	67	...	3	–	63	62	...	2	–
Income	69	67	...	2	–	62	61	...	1	–
Other	1	–	...	1	–	1	–	...	1	–
C Social security contributions	33	–	...	–	33	41	–	...	–	41
D Fees, fines and penalties	5	4	...	1	–	6	5	...	1	–
4 Other current transfers	62	31	...	31	1	71	29	...	41	1
A Casualty insurance claims	...	...	...	...	...	...	...	...	...	...
B Transfers from other government subsectors	30	–	...	30	–	38	–	...	37	–
C Transfers from rest of the world	3	3	...	–	–	3	3	...	–	–
D Other transfers, except imputed	25	24	...	1	–	24	21	...	3	–
E Imputed unfunded employee pension and welfare contributions	5	4	...	1	1	6	5	...	1	1
Total current receipts	393	304	...	45	45	444	336	...	53	56

Disbursements

1 Government final consumption expenditure	167	142	...	19	5	230	198	...	25	7
2 Property income	57	51	...	2	5	57	53	...	2	2
A Interest	57	51	...	2	5	57	53	...	2	2
B Net land rent and royalties	–	–	...	–	–	–	–	...	–	–
3 Subsidies	34	34	...	–	–	24	24	...	–	–
4 Other current transfers	61	37	...	1	23	88	46	...	2	40
A Casualty insurance premiums, net	...	...	...	...	...	...	...	...	...	...
B Transfers to other government subsectors	30	30	...	–	–	38	37	...	–	–
C Social security benefits	22	–	...	–	22	40	–	...	–	40
D Social assistance grants	3	2	...	–	–	4	4	...	1	–
E Unfunded employee welfare benefits	5	4	...	1	1	6	5	...	1	1
F Transfers to private non-profit institutions serving households	...	...	...	...	...	...	...	...	...	...
G Other transfers n.e.c.	–	–	...	–	–	–	–	...	–	–

Ecuador

Thousand million Ecuadoran sucres

	1986					1987				
	Total government	Central government	State or provincial government	Local government	Social security funds	Total government	Central government	State or provincial government	Local government	Social security funds
H Transfers to rest of the world	1	1	...	–	–	1	1	...	–	–
Net saving [a]	74	40	...	22	12	45	13	...	24	7
Total current disbursements and net saving	393	304	...	45	45	444	336	...	53	56

	1988					1989				
	Total government	Central government	State or provincial government	Local government	Social security funds	Total government	Central government	State or provincial government	Local government	Social security funds

Receipts

1 Operating surplus	4	4	...	–	–	–1	–1	...	–	–
2 Property and entrepreneurial income	61	37	...	2	21	105	77	...	4	24
A Withdrawals from public quasi-corporations	...	...	...	...	...	...	...	...	...	...
B Interest	19	1	...	1	17	27	1	...	3	23
C Dividends	5	–	...	–	4	2	1	...	–	1
D Net land rent and royalties	37	36	...	1	–	76	76	...	1	–
3 Taxes, fees and contributions	593	502	...	18	73	1091	931	...	27	132
A Indirect taxes	397	384	...	13	–	761	741	...	20	–
B Direct taxes	112	109	...	3	–	179	174	...	4	–
Income	110	109	...	1	–	175	174	...	2	–
Other	2	–	...	2	–	3	–	...	3	–
C Social security contributions	72	–	...	–	72	131	–	...	–	131
D Fees, fines and penalties	11	9	...	2	–	20	16	...	3	–
4 Other current transfers	95	40	...	53	1	156	62	...	92	2
A Casualty insurance claims	...	...	...	...	...	...	...	...	...	...
B Transfers from other government subsectors	...	...	...	...	...	...	...	...	...	...
C Transfers from rest of the world	3	3	...	–	–	5	5	...	–	–
D Other transfers, except imputed	...	...	...	...	...	...	...	...	...	...
E Imputed unfunded employee pension and welfare contributions	9	6	...	1	1	15	8	...	5	2
Total current receipts	752	584	...	73	95	1351	1070	...	123	157

Disbursements

1 Government final consumption expenditure	347	301	...	34	12	485	411	...	58	16
2 Property income	78	74	...	2	2	175	170	...	2	3
A Interest	78	74	...	2	2	175	170	...	2	3
B Net land rent and royalties	–	–	...	–	–	–	–	...	–	–
3 Subsidies	40	40	...	–	–	67	67	...	–	–
4 Other current transfers	121	62	...	2	57	204	107	...	8	89
A Casualty insurance premiums, net	...	...	...	...	...	...	...	...	...	...
B Transfers to other government subsectors	...	...	...	...	...	...	...	...	...	...
C Social security benefits	55	–	...	–	55	88	–	...	–	88
D Social assistance grants	...	...	...	...	...	...	...	...	...	...

Ecuador

	1988					1989				
	Total govern-ment	Central govern-ment	State or provincial govern-ment	Local govern-ment	Social security funds	Total govern-ment	Central govern-ment	State or provincial govern-ment	Local govern-ment	Social security funds
E Unfunded employee welfare benefits	9	6	...	1	1	15	8	...	5	2
F Transfers to private non-profit institutions serving households	...	...	...	...	...	...	...	...	...	...
G Other transfers n.e.c.	...	...	...	...	...	...	...	...	...	...
H Transfers to rest of the world	1	1	...	–	–	2	2	...	–	–
Net saving [a]	165	106	...	34	25	420	314	...	56	49
Total current disbursements and net saving	752	584	...	73	95	1351	1070	...	123	157

	1990					1991				
	Total govern-ment	Central govern-ment	State or provincial govern-ment	Local govern-ment	Social security funds	Total govern-ment	Central govern-ment	State or provincial govern-ment	Local govern-ment	Social security funds

Receipts

1 Operating surplus	–2	–1	...	...	–	–2	–2	...	–	–
2 Property and entrepreneurial income	235	194	...	8	33	232	171	...	7	54
A Withdrawals from public quasi-corporations	...	...	...	...	...	...	...	...	...	...
B Interest	39	2	...	5	31	57	2	...	5	50
C Dividends	5	3	...	1	1	8	4	...	...	4
D Net land rent and royalties	191	189	...	2	–	167	166	...	2	–
3 Taxes, fees and contributions	1870	1619	...	53	198	2588	2202	...	88	298
A Indirect taxes	1279	1243	...	36	–	1706	1645	...	61	–
B Direct taxes	373	361	...	12	–	555	535	...	20	–
Income	367	361	...	6	–	542	534	...	8	–
Other	6	...	...	6	–	13	1	...	12	–
C Social security contributions	197	–	...	–	197	297	...	...	–	297
D Fees, fines and penalties	21	15	...	5	1	30	22	...	7	1
4 Other current transfers	260	89	...	167	3	345	118	...	221	6
A Casualty insurance claims	...	...	...	...	...	...	...	...	...	...
B Transfers from other government subsectors	...	...	...	...	...	...	...	...	...	...
C Transfers from rest of the world	7	7	...	...	–	3	1	...	2	–
D Other transfers, except imputed	232	71	...	161	...	313	103	...	210	...
E Imputed unfunded employee pension and welfare contributions	21	11	...	7	3	29	14	...	9	6
Total current receipts	2363	1902	...	228	233	3161	2489	...	314	357

Disbursements

1 Government final consumption expenditure	706	596	...	85	25	935	773	...	127	35
2 Property income	332	325	...	1	5	338	330	...	4	4
A Interest	332	325	...	1	5	338	330	...	4	4
B Net land rent and royalties	...	...	...	...	...	...	...	...	...	...
3 Subsidies	146	146	...	–	–	263	263	...	–	–
4 Other current transfers	351	191	...	15	144	475	246	...	19	210
A Casualty insurance premiums, net	...	...	...	...	...	...	...	...	...	...

Ecuador

	1990					1991				
	Total govern-ment	Central govern-ment	State or provincial govern-ment	Local govern-ment	Social security funds	Total govern-ment	Central govern-ment	State or provincial govern-ment	Local govern-ment	Social security funds
B Transfers to other government subsectors	...	...	...	...	...	...	...	...	...	...
C Social security benefits	141	–	...	–	141	204	–	...	–	204
D Social assistance grants	...	...	...	...	...	...	...	...	...	...
E Unfunded employee welfare benefits	21	11	...	7	3	29	14	...	9	6
F Transfers to private non-profit institutions serving households	185	176	...	9	...	...	...	...	...	...
G Other transfers n.e.c.	...	...	...	...	...	237	227	...	10	...
H Transfers to rest of the world	4	4	...	–	...	5	5	...	–	...
Net saving [a]	829	644	...	126	59	1149	876	...	163	108
Total current disbursements and net saving	2363	1902	...	228	233	3160	2489	...	314	357

	1992					1993				
	Total govern-ment	Central govern-ment	State or provincial govern-ment	Local govern-ment	Social security funds	Total govern-ment	Central govern-ment	State or provincial govern-ment	Local govern-ment	Social security funds

Receipts

1 Operating surplus	–2	–2	...	–	–	–3	–3	...	...	...
2 Property and entrepreneurial income	301	206	...	8	87	383	279	...	9	95
A Withdrawals from public quasi-corporations	...	...	...	...	...	...	...	...	...	...
B Interest	84	2	...	5	77	91	3	...	6	82
C Dividends	16	5	...	...	11	20	7	...	–	13
D Net land rent and royalties	201	199	...	2	–	271	269	...	2	...
3 Taxes, fees and contributions	3843	3254	...	131	458	5383	4592	...	163	628
A Indirect taxes	2626	2534	...	92	–	3649	3528	...	121	...
B Direct taxes	721	692	...	29	–	1051	1021	...	30	...
Income	701	691	...	10	–	1034	1020	...	14	...
Other	20	1	...	19	–	17	1	...	16	...
C Social security contributions	457	–	...	–	457	625	...	...	...	625
D Fees, fines and penalties	39	28	...	10	1	58	43	...	12	3
4 Other current transfers	457	149	...	301	7	676	218	...	450	8
A Casualty insurance claims	...	...	...	...	...	...	...	...	...	...
B Transfers from other government subsectors	289	...	...	289	...	597	161	...	436	...
C Transfers from rest of the world	14	13	...	1	–	17	16	...	1	...
D Other transfers, except imputed	112	112	...	...	...	...	...	...	...	...
E Imputed unfunded employee pension and welfare contributions	41	24	...	11	6	62	41	...	13	8
Total current receipts	4599	3607	...	439	553	6439	5085	...	622	732

Disbursements

1 Government final consumption expenditure	1407	1174	...	163	70	2117	1800	...	212	105
2 Property income	499	488	...	6	5	543	518	...	8	17
A Interest	499	488	...	6	5	543	518	...	8	17
B Net land rent and royalties	...	...	...	...	...	...	...	...	...	...

Ecuador

	1992					1993				
	Total govern-ment	Central govern-ment	State or provincial govern-ment	Local govern-ment	Social security funds	Total govern-ment	Central govern-ment	State or provincial govern-ment	Local govern-ment	Social security funds
3 Subsidies	318	318	...	–	–	378	378	...	...	...
4 Other current transfers	757	352	...	24	382	1030	...	...	...	477
A Casualty insurance premiums, net	...	...	...	...	...	...	...	...	...	...
B Transfers to other government subsectors	...	...	...	...	...	...	...	...	...	...
C Social security benefits	375	–	...	–	375	469	...	...	...	469
D Social assistance grants	...	...	...	...	...	...	...	...	...	...
E Unfunded employee welfare benefits	41	23	...	11	7	61	41	...	13	8
F Transfers to private non-profit institutions serving households	334	334	...	...	...	...	...	...	...	...
G Other transfers n.e.c.	...	...	...	...	...	...	...	...	...	...
H Transfers to rest of the world	8	8	...	–	...	...	...	...	...	...
Net saving [a]	1616	1275	...	248	93	2371	1869	...	374	128
Total current disbursements and net saving	4599	3607	...	439	553	6439	5085	...	622	732

a Item "Net saving" includes consumption of fixed capital.

3.13 General government capital accumulation account: total and subsectors

Thousand million Ecuadoran sucres

	1986					1987				
	Total govern-ment	Central govern-ment	State or provincial govern-ment	Local govern-ment	Social security funds	Total govern-ment	Central govern-ment	State or provincial govern-ment	Local govern-ment	Social security funds
Finance of gross accumulation										
1 Gross saving	74	40	...	22	12	45	13	...	24	7
2 Capital transfers	...	...	...	...	...	...	...	...	...	...
Finance of gross accumulation	74	40	...	22	12	45	13	...	24	7
Gross accumulation										
1 Gross capital formation	83	58	...	22	3	117	88	...	25	4
A Increase in stocks	1	...	...	...	1	1	...	...	...	1
B Gross fixed capital formation	82	58	...	22	2	115	88	...	25	3
2 Purchases of land, net	–	–	...	–	–	–	–	...	–	–
3 Purchases of intangible assets, net	...	...	...	...	...	...	...	...	...	...
4 Capital transfers	5	4	...	1	–	4	2	...	2	–
A To other government subsectors	...	...	...	...	...	...	...	...	...	...
B To other resident sectors	5	4	...	1	...	4	2	...	2	...
C To the rest of the world	...	...	...	...	...	...	...	...	...	...
Net lending [a]	–14	–22	...	–	9	–76	–77	...	–2	3
Gross accumulation	74	40	...	22	12	45	13	...	24	7

Ecuador

	1988					1989				
	Total govern-ment	Central govern-ment	State or provincial govern-ment	Local govern-ment	Social security funds	Total govern-ment	Central govern-ment	State or provincial govern-ment	Local govern-ment	Social security funds
Finance of gross accumulation											
1 Gross saving	165	106	...	34	25	420	314	...	56	49
2 Capital transfers	...	...	...	...	...	...	...	...	...	...
Finance of gross accumulation	165	106	...	34	25	420	314	...	56	49
Gross accumulation											
1 Gross capital formation	166	136	...	27	3	239	196	...	38	5
A Increase in stocks	2	1	...	...	–	2	1	...	...	–
B Gross fixed capital formation	165	134	...	27	3	237	195	...	38	5
2 Purchases of land, net	–	–	...	–	–	–1	–	...	–	–
3 Purchases of intangible assets, net	...	...	...	...	...	...	...	...	...	...
4 Capital transfers	13	10	...	3	–	82	78	...	4	–
A To other government sub-sectors	...	...	...	...	...	...	...	...	...	...
B To other resident sectors	13	10	...	3	...	82	78	...	4	...
C To the rest of the world	...	...	...	...	...	...	...	...	...	...
Net lending [a]	–13	–40	...	5	21	100	41	...	15	44
Gross accumulation	165	106	...	34	25	420	314	...	56	49

	1990					1991				
	Total govern-ment	Central govern-ment	State or provincial govern-ment	Local govern-ment	Social security funds	Total govern-ment	Central govern-ment	State or provincial govern-ment	Local govern-ment	Social security funds
Finance of gross accumulation											
1 Gross saving	829	644	...	126	59	1149	876	...	165	108
2 Capital transfers	...	...	...	...	...	...	...	...	...	...
Finance of gross accumulation	829	644	...	126	59	1149	876	...	165	108
Gross accumulation											
1 Gross capital formation	332	235	...	84	12	475	331	...	123	21
A Increase in stocks	4	4	...	...	...	5	5	...	...	...
B Gross fixed capital formation	328	232	...	84	12	470	326	...	123	21
2 Purchases of land, net	–1	...	...	–1	...	–1	...	...	–2	–
3 Purchases of intangible assets, net	...	...	...	...	...	...	...	...	...	...
4 Capital transfers	89	83	...	6	–	177	168	...	9	–
A To other government sub-sectors	...	...	...	...	...	...	...	...	...	...
B To other resident sectors	89	83	...	6	–	173	165	...	8	–
C To the rest of the world	...	...	...	...	...	...	...	...	...	...
Net lending [a]	409	325	...	37	47	497	377	...	34	87
Gross accumulation	829	644	...	126	59	1149	876	...	165	108

Ecuador

	1992					1993				
	Total govern-ment	Central govern-ment	State or provincial govern-ment	Local govern-ment	Social security funds	Total govern-ment	Central govern-ment	State or provincial govern-ment	Local govern-ment	Social security funds
	Finance of gross accumulation									
1 Gross saving	1616	1275	...	248	93	2371	1869	...	374	128
2 Capital transfers	...	...	...	...	...	...	...	...	...	...
Finance of gross accumulation	1616	1275	...	248	93	2371	1869	...	374	128
	Gross accumulation									
1 Gross capital formation	762	508	...	179	75	1009	758	...	230	20
A Increase in stocks	9	8	...	–	...	13	11	...	1	...
B Gross fixed capital formation	753	500	...	178	75	996	747	...	229	20
2 Purchases of land, net	1	1	...	...	–	1	1	...	...	...
3 Purchases of intangible assets, net	...	...	...	...	...	...	...	...	...	...
4 Capital transfers	276	261	...	15	...	417	413	...	4	...
Net lending [a]	577	505	...	54	18	944	697	...	140	108
Gross accumulation	1616	1275	...	248	93	2371	1869	...	374	128

a Net lending of the capital accumulation account and the capital finance account have not been reconciled and are different due to different statistical sources.

3.21 Corporate and quasi-corporate enterprise production account: total and sectors

Thousand million Ecuadoran sucres

	1986				1987				1988			
	Corporate and quasi-corporate enterprises			Adden-dum: total including unincor-porated	Corporate and quasi-corporate enterprises			Adden-dum: total including unincor-porated	Corporate and quasi-corporate enterprises			Adden-dum: total including unincor-porated
	Total	Non-financial	Financial		Total	Non-financial	Financial		Total	Non-financial	Financial	
	Gross output											
1 Output for sale	1004	986	18	...	1322	1298	24	...	2329	2282	47	...
2 Imputed bank service charge	29	–	29	...	54	–	54	...	98	–	98	...
3 Own-account fixed capital formation	...	...	...	...	...	...	...	...	...	...	...	...
Gross output [a]	1032	986	46	...	1376	1298	78	...	2426	2282	144	...
	Gross input											
Intermediate consumption	620	571	49	...	892	813	79	...	1567	1422	145	...
1 Imputed bank service charge	29	–	29	...	54	–	54	...	98	–	98	...
2 Other intermediate consumption	591	571	20	...	838	813	25	...	1469	1422	47	...
subtotal: Value added [a]	412	415	–3	...	484	485	–1	...	859	860	–1	...
1 Indirect taxes, net	77	75	2	...	109	107	2	...	202	200	2	...
A Indirect taxes	112	110	2	...	133	132	2	...	243	241	2	...
B less: Subsidies	34	34	–	...	24	24	–	...	40	40	–	...
2 Consumption of fixed capital	...	...	...	...	...	...	...	...	...	...	...	...
3 Compensation of employees	117	93	25	...	161	124	37	...	224	169	55	...
4 Net operating surplus [b]	218	247	–29	...	214	254	–40	...	432	491	–58	...
Gross input [a]	1032	986	46	...	1376	1298	78	...	2426	2282	144	...

Ecuador

	1989				1990				1991			
	Corporate and quasi-corporate enterprises			Addendum: total including unincorporated	Corporate and quasi-corporate enterprises			Addendum: total including unincorporated	Corporate and quasi-corporate enterprises			Addendum: total including unincorporated
	Total	Non-financial	Financial		Total	Non-financial	Financial		Total	Non-financial	Financial	
Gross output												
1 Output for sale	3947	3879	68	...	6320	6210	110	...	7928	7783	145	...
2 Imputed bank service charge	97	–	97	...	149	–	149	...	288	–	288	...
3 Own-account fixed capital formation	...	...	...	...	...	...	...	...	...	...	...	...
Gross output [a]	4044	3879	165	...	6469	6210	259	...	8216	7783	433	...
Gross input												
Intermediate consumption	2682	2504	178	...	4259	3983	276	...	5311	4846	465	...
1 Imputed bank service charge	97	–	97	...	149	–	149	...	288	–	288	...
2 Other intermediate consumption	2585	2504	81	...	4111	3983	128	...	5023	4846	177	...
subtotal: Value added [a]	1362	1375	–14	...	2209	2227	–17	...	2905	2937	–32	...
1 Indirect taxes, net	446	441	5	...	646	638	8	...	768	757	11	...
A Indirect taxes	513	508	5	...	792	784	8	...	1029	1019	11	...
B less: Subsidies	67	67	–	...	146	146	–	...	261	261	–	...
2 Consumption of fixed capital	...	...	...	...	...	...	...	...	...	...	...	...
3 Compensation of employees	342	258	84	...	495	363	131	...	687	478	209	...
4 Net operating surplus [b]	574	677	–103	...	1068	1225	–157	...	1450	1702	–252	...
Gross input [a]	4044	3879	165	...	6469	6210	259	...	8216	7783	433	...

	1992				1993				1994			
	Corporate and quasi-corporate enterprises			Addendum: total including unincorporated	Corporate and quasi-corporate enterprises			Addendum: total including unincorporated	Corporate and quasi-corporate enterprises			Addendum: total including unincorporated
	Total	Non-financial	Financial		Total	Non-financial	Financial		Total	Non-financial	Financial	
Gross output												
1 Output for sale	14650	14451	199	...	...	...	...	...	...	...	...	...
2 Imputed bank service charge	446	–	446	...	...	...	...	...	...	...	...	...
3 Own-account fixed capital formation	...	...	...	...	...	...	...	...	...	...	...	...
Gross output [a]	15096	14451	644	...	...	...	...	...	...	...	...	...
Gross input												
Intermediate consumption	9999	9250	749	...	...	...	...	...	...	...	...	...
1 Imputed bank service charge	446	...	446	...	...	...	...	...	...	...	...	...
2 Other intermediate consumption	9553	9250	303	...	...	...	...	...	...	...	...	...
subtotal: Value added [a]	5097	5201	–104	...	...	...	...	...	...	...	...	...
1 Indirect taxes, net	1206	1188	18	...	...	...	...	...	...	...	...	...
A Indirect taxes	1509	1491	18	...	...	...	...	...	...	...	...	...
B less: Subsidies	303	303	–	...	...	...	...	...	...	...	...	...
2 Consumption of fixed capital	...	...	...	...	...	...	...	...	...	...	...	...
3 Compensation of employees	1130	762	369	...	...	...	...	...	...	...	...	...
4 Net operating surplus [b]	2761	3252	–491	...	...	...	...	...	...	...	...	...
Gross input [a]	15096	14451	644	...	...	...	...	...	...	...	...	...

a Data for this table have not been revised, therefore, data for some years are not comparable with those of other tables. b Item "Operating surplus" includes consumption of fixed capital.

Ecuador

3.22 Corporate and quasi-corporate enterprise income and outlay account: total and sectors

Thousand million Ecuadoran sucres

	1986 Total	1986 Non-financial	1986 Financial	1987 Total	1987 Non-financial	1987 Financial	1988 Total	1988 Non-financial	1988 Financial	1989 Total	1989 Non-financial	1989 Financial
Receipts												
1 Operating surplus [a]	218	247	−29	214	254	−40	432	491	−58	574	677	−103
2 Property and entrepreneurial income	144	25	119	205	34	171	296	40	256	432	56	376
A Withdrawals from quasi-corporate enterprises	...	...	...	...	...	...	...	...	...	...	...	...
B Interest	140	23	117	200	30	169	288	35	253	414	45	368
C Dividends	4	3	1	6	4	2	8	5	3	18	11	8
D Net land rent and royalties	−	−	−	−	−	−	−	−	−	−	−	−
3 Current transfers	11	8	3	19	14	5	29	20	9	42	27	15
A Casualty insurance claims	3	3	−	5	5	−	8	8	−	14	13	1
B Casualty insurance premiums, net, due to be received by insurance companies	1	−	1	2	−	2	4	−	4	7	−	7
C Current transfers from rest of the world	...	...	...	...	...	...	...	...	...	...	...	...
D Other transfers except imputed	...	...	...	...	...	...	...	...	...	...	...	...
E Imputed unfunded employee pension and welfare contributions	7	5	2	12	9	3	17	12	5	21	14	7
Total current receipts	373	280	93	439	302	137	758	551	207	1048	760	288
Disbursements												
1 Property and entrepreneurial income	246	154	92	322	200	122	475	314	161	750	465	285
A Withdrawals from quasi-corporations	−	−	−	1	−	1	1	1	1	2	1	1
Public	...	...	...	...	...	...	...	...	...	...	...	...
Private	−	−	−	1	−	1	1	1	1	2	1	1
B Interest	184	95	89	248	132	116	327	171	156	524	248	276
C Dividends [b]	37	35	3	50	45	5	91	88	4	124	116	8
D Net land rent and royalties	24	24	−	23	23	−	55	55	−	100	100	−
2 Direct taxes and other current transfers n.e.c. to general government	60	58	1	50	48	1	96	93	3	142	138	4
A Direct taxes	57	56	1	47	46	1	90	89	1	134	131	3
On income	57	56	1	46	46	1	89	88	1	133	130	3
Other	−	−	−	−	−	−	1	1	−	1	1	−
B Fines, fees, penalties and other current transfers n.e.c.	2	2	−	3	2	−	6	4	1	8	7	1
3 Other current transfers	39	28	11	47	28	19	66	46	20	106	88	19
A Casualty insurance premiums, net	3	3	−	5	5	−	9	9	−	15	14	1
B Casualty insurance claims liability of insurance companies	1	−	1	2	−	2	4	−	4	7	−	7
C Transfers to private non-profit institutions	...	...	...	...	...	...	...	...	...	...	...	...
D Unfunded employee pension and welfare benefits	7	5	2	12	9	3	17	12	5	21	14	7
E Social assistance grants	27	19	8	28	14	13	36	25	11	...	...	...
F Other transfers n.e.c.	...	...	...	...	...	...	...	...	...	63	59	4

Ecuador

Thousand million Ecuadoran sucres

	1986			1987			1988			1989		
	Total	Non-financial	Financial	Total	Non-financial	Financial	Total	Non-financial	Financial	Total	Non-financial	Financial
G Transfers to rest of the world	...	...	...	...	...	...	...	...	...	...	...	...
Net saving [c]	28	40	−12	21	25	−5	122	98	23	50	69	−19
Total current disbursements and net saving	373	280	93	439	302	137	758	551	207	1048	760	288

	1990			1991			1992			1993		
	Total	Non-financial	Financial	Total	Non-financial	Financial	Total	Non-financial	Financial	Total	Non-financial	Financial
Receipts												
1 Operating surplus [a]	1068	1225	−157	1416	1679	−263	2264	2749	−485	2077	2865	−788
2 Property and entrepreneurial income	703	105	597	1177	180	997	1984	243	1741	2756	356	2400
A Withdrawals from quasi-corporate enterprises	...	...	...	...	...	...	...	...	...	...	...	...
B Interest	681	95	586	1141	160	981	1949	222	1727	2715	330	2385
C Dividends	22	11	11	36	20	16	35	21	14	41	26	15
D Net land rent and royalties	...	–	–	...	–	–	...	–	–	...	...	...
3 Current transfers	74	48	26	130	87	43	226	132	94	384	203	181
A Casualty insurance claims	25	23	1	37	35	2	56	52	4	77	66	11
B Casualty insurance premiums, net, due to be received by insurance companies	12	–	12	21	–	21	42	–	42	51	...	51
C Current transfers from rest of the world	...	...	...	...	...	...	...	...	...	...	...	...
D Other transfers except imputed	...	...	...	...	...	...	1	...	...	1	1	...
E Imputed unfunded employee pension and welfare contributions	37	25	12	72	52	20	128	80	48	256	137	119
Total current receipts	1845	1379	467	2723	1946	777	4474	3124	1350	5217	3425	1793
Disbursements												
1 Property and entrepreneurial income	1238	781	457	1838	1109	729	2913	1629	1284	3562	1997	1565
A Withdrawals from quasi-corporations	3	1	1	5	2	3	8	2	6	11	2	9
Public	...	...	...	...	...	...	...	...	...	...	...	...
Private	3	1	1	5	2	3	8	2	6	9	...	9
B Interest	817	374	444	1346	645	701	2269	1031	1238	2705	1198	1507
C Dividends [b]	191	179	12	270	245	25	365	325	40	475	426	49
D Net land rent and royalties	227	227	–	217	217	–	271	271	–	371	371	...
2 Direct taxes and other current transfers n.e.c. to general government	325	319	5	479	469	10	592	576	16	833	811	22
A Direct taxes	317	313	4	470	461	9	578	567	11	816	797	19
On income	315	311	4	466	457	9	572	561	11	810	791	19
Other	2	2	–	4	4	...	6	6	...	6	6	...
B Fines, fees, penalties and other current transfers n.e.c.	8	7	1	9	8	1	14	9	5	17	14	3
3 Other current transfers	148	115	32	230	177	53	352	246	106	600	336	264
A Casualty insurance premiums, net	18	16	1	27	25	2	52	47	5	90	67	23
B Casualty insurance claims liability of insurance companies	12	–	12	21	–	21	42	–	42	51	–	51
C Transfers to private non-profit institutions	...	...	...	...	...	...	...	...	...	...	...	...

Ecuador

	1990			1991			1992			1993		
	Total	Non-financial	Financial	Total	Non-financial	Financial	Total	Non-financial	Financial	Total	Non-financial	Financial
D Unfunded employee pension and welfare benefits	37	25	12	72	52	20	128	80	48	256	137	119
E Social assistance grants	...	...	...	...	...	...	...	...	...	...	...	...
F Other transfers n.e.c.	80	74	6	110	100	10	130	119	11	203	132	71
G Transfers to rest of the world	...	...	...	...	...	...	...	...	...	...	...	...
Net saving [c]	135	163	−28	176	191	−15	617	673	−56	223	281	−58
Total current disbursements and net saving	1845	1379	467	2723	1946	777	4474	3124	1350	5218	3425	1793

a Item "Operating surplus" includes consumption of fixed capital.
b Item "Dividends" includes profit-sharing by employees.
c Item "Net saving" includes consumption of fixed capital.

3.23 Corporate and quasi-corporate enterprise capital accumulation account: total and sectors

Thousand million Ecuadoran sucres

	1986			1987			1988			1989		
	Total	Non-financial	Financial	Total	Non-financial	Financial	Total	Non-financial	Financial	Total	Non-financial	Financial
Finance of gross accumulation												
1 Gross saving	28	40	−12	21	25	−5	122	98	23	50	69	−19
2 Capital transfers [a]	3	5	−2	2	4	−2	9	13	−4	77	85	−8
Finance of gross accumulation ...	31	45	−14	23	30	−7	131	112	19	127	154	−27
Gross accumulation												
1 Gross capital formation	155	136	20	226	208	18	370	328	42	665	613	53
A Increase in stocks	22	12	10	1	−6	7	4	−23	28	26	−4	30
B Gross fixed capital formation	133	124	9	226	214	12	366	351	15	639	616	23
2 Purchases of land, net	9	6	3	10	8	2	12	9	3	14	12	2
3 Purchases of intangible assets, net	1	1	−	2	2	−	5	5	−	9	9	−
4 Capital transfers	...	...	...	...	...	...	...	...	...	...	...	...
Net lending [b]	−135	−98	−37	−216	−188	−27	−257	−231	−26	−561	−479	−82
Gross accumulation	31	45	−14	23	30	−7	131	112	19	127	154	−27

	1990			1991			1992			1993		
	Total	Non-financial	Financial	Total	Non-financial	Financial	Total	Non-financial	Financial	Total	Non-financial	Financial
Finance of gross accumulation												
1 Gross saving	135	163	−28	177	192	−15	617	673	−56	223	281	−58
2 Capital transfers [a]	85	94	−9	176	180	−4	272	273	−1	423	377	46
Finance of gross accumulation ...	220	257	−37	353	372	−19	889	946	−57	645	657	−12
Gross accumulation												
1 Gross capital formation	769	696	73	1622	1551	71	2431	2352	79	3519	3455	64
A Increase in stocks	−21	−73	52	256	221	35	304	267	37	350	323	27
B Gross fixed capital formation	790	769	21	1366	1330	36	2127	2085	42	3169	3132	37
2 Purchases of land, net	38	31	7	46	43	3	79	54	25	82	68	14
3 Purchases of intangible assets, net	16	16	−	20	20	−	24	24	−	33	33	−
4 Capital transfers	...	...	...	...	...	...	...	...	...	...	...	...
Net lending [b]	−602	−486	−116	−1335	−1242	−93	−1644	−1484	−160	−2989	−2899	−90
Gross accumulation	220	257	−37	353	372	−19	889	946	−57	645	657	−12

a Capital transfers received are recorded net of capital transfers paid.
b Net lending of the capital accumulation account and the capital finance account have not been reconciled and are different due to different statistical sources.

Ecuador

3.24 Corporate and quasi-corporate enterprise capital finance account: total and sectors

Thousand million Ecuadoran sucres

	1986			1987			1988			1989		
	Total	Non-financial	Financial	Total	Non-financial	Financial	Total	Non-financial	Financial	Total	Non-financial	Financial

Acquisition of financial assets

1 Gold and SDRs	17	–	17	–4	–	–4	13	–	13	–31	...	–31
2 Currency and transferable deposits	12	10	2	16	15	1	28	31	–3	60	43	17
3 Other deposits	–11	10	–21	59	36	23	122	36	86	174	24	150
4 Bills and bonds, short-term	...	...	...	...	...	...	...	...	...	...	...	...
5 Bonds, long-term [a]	9	1	9	50	23	27	46	17	29	19	8	11
6 Corporate equity securities	17	8	9	4	–2	6	21	9	12	41	14	27
7 Short-term loans, n.e.c.	79	10	70	78	19	60	207	66	141	275	36	239
8 Long-term loans, n.e.c.	46	–	46	66	–	66	47	–1	48	76	38	38
9 Trade credits and advances	100	63	37	224	148	76	321	294	27	433	361	71
10 Other receivables	12	10	2	5	1	4	19	8	11	27	20	7
11 Other assets	...	...	...	...	...	...	...	...	...	...	...	...
Total acquisitions of financial assets	282	111	171	497	238	259	824	460	364	1075	545	529

Incurrence of liabilities

1 Currency and transferable deposits	40	–	40	56	–	56	146	–	146	232	–	232
2 Other deposits	71	3	68	100	20	80	239	33	206	316	74	242
3 Bills and bonds, short-term	...	...	...	...	...	...	...	...	...	...	...	...
4 Bonds, long-term [a]	7	1	5	41	–1	42	16	–	16	–2	1	–2
5 Corporate equity securities	47	26	21	45	27	18	73	48	26	109	82	27
6 Short-term loans, n.e.c.	19	21	–2	49	44	5	129	67	62	175	182	–7
7 Long-term loans, n.e.c.	56	9	46	93	71	22	–64	31	–95	97	42	55
8 Net equity of households in life insurance and pension fund reserves	1	–	1	1	–	1	2	–	2	3	–	3
9 Proprietors' net additions to the accumulation of quasi-corporations	...	...	...	...	...	...	...	...	...	...	...	...
10 Trade credits and advances	...	...	...	...	...	...	...	...	...	...	...	...
11 Other accounts payable	...	...	...	...	...	...	...	...	...	...	...	...
12 Other liabilities [b]	...	...	...	...	...	...	...	...	...	...	...	–27
Total incurrence of liabilities	429	224	205	710	427	283	1097	707	390	1593	988	605
Net lending [c]	–147	–113	–34	–213	–189	–24	–273	–247	–26	–518	–443	–76
Incurrence of liabilities and net lending	282	111	171	497	238	259	824	460	364	1075	545	529

	1990			1991			1992			1993		
	Total	Non-financial	Financial	Total	Non-financial	Financial	Total	Non-financial	Financial	Total	Non-financial	Financial

Acquisition of financial assets

1 Gold and SDRs	63	...	63	8	...	8	–110	...	–110	–47	...	–47
2 Currency and transferable deposits	178	135	43	245	190	55	263	207	56	26	...	26
3 Other deposits	356	109	246	344	166	178	317	68	249	1198	...	1198
4 Bills and bonds, short-term	...	...	...	...	...	...	...	...	...	...	...	...
5 Bonds, long-term [a]	–11	...	–11	43	33	10	175	65	110	52	...	52
6 Corporate equity securities	38	21	17	82	55	27	142	86	56	47	...	47
7 Short-term loans, n.e.c.	452	151	301	543	21	522	904	29	875	1720	...	1720

Ecuador

	1990 Total	1990 Non-financial	1990 Financial	1991 Total	1991 Non-financial	1991 Financial	1992 Total	1992 Non-financial	1992 Financial	1993 Total	1993 Non-financial	1993 Financial
8 Long-term loans, n.e.c.	192	76	116	1244	87	1157	2662	188	2474	4051	...	4051
9 Trade credits and advances	847	642	205	1384	1220	164	1962	1652	310	369	...	369
10 Other receivables	48	32	16	134	118	16	146	85	61	51	...	51
11 Other assets	...	...	...	...	...	...	...	...	...	...	...	...
Total acquisitions of financial assets	2163	1166	997	4026	1889	2137	6462	2380	4082	7466	...	7466

Incurrence of liabilities

	Total	Non-fin	Fin	Total	Non-fin	Fin	Total	Non-fin	Fin	Total	Non-fin	Fin
1 Currency and transferable deposits	476	–	476	540	–	540	754	...	754	1335	...	1335
2 Other deposits	647	86	561	769	84	685	1312	117	1195	1423	...	1423
3 Bills and bonds, short-term	...	...	...	...	...	...	...	...	...	...	...	...
4 Bonds, long-term [a]	69	1	68	1	13	–12	262	6	256	76	...	76
5 Corporate equity securities	205	148	57	432	356	76	316	182	134	326	...	326
6 Short-term loans, n.e.c.	371	363	8	484	465	19	814	730	84	197	...	197
7 Long-term loans, n.e.c.	68	200	–132	1185	365	820	2261	609	1652	3481	...	3481
8 Net equity of households in life insurance and pension fund reserves	43	–	4	45	38	7	57	47	...	...	...	...
9 Proprietors' net additions to the accumulation of quasi-corporations	...	...	...	...	...	...	...	...	...	...	...	...
10 Trade credits and advances	...	...	...	...	...	...	...	...	...	...	...	...
11 Other accounts payable	...	...	...	...	...	...	...	...	...	...	...	...
12 Other liabilities [b]	–62	...	–62	–78	...	–78	–149	...	–149	–52	...	–52
Total incurrence of liabilities	2744	1632	1112	5432	3207	2225	7887	3619	4268	7563	...	7563
Net lending [c]	–581	–466	–115	–1405	–1317	–88	–1424	–1239	–185	–97	...	–97
Incurrence of liabilities and net lending	2163	1166	997	4035	1889	2145	6462	2380	4082	7466	...	7466

a Item "Bonds, long-term" includes short-term bonds.
b Item "Other liabilities" refers to gold and SDRS.
c Net lending of the capital accumulation account and the capital finance account have not been reconciled and are different due to different statistical sources.

3.31 Household and private unincorporated enterprise production account

Thousand million Ecuadoran sucres

	1986	1987	1988	1989	1990	1991	1992	1993	1994	1995	1996	1997
Gross output												
1 Output for sale	1209	1690	2818	5112	7915	13156	18728	...	...	...	...	...
2 Non-marketed output	6	8	10	14	19	26	40	...	...	...	...	...
Gross output	1215	1698	2828	5126	7934	13182	18768	...	...	...	...	...
Gross input												
Intermediate consumption	436	634	1026	1824	2832	5124	6413	...	...	...	...	...
subtotal: Value added	779	1064	1802	3302	5101	8058	12356	...	...	...	...	...
1 Indirect taxes net liability of unincorporated enterprises	15	18	33	52	37	58	76	...	...	...	...	...
A Indirect taxes	15	18	33	52	37	61	92	...	...	...	...	...
B less: Subsidies	...	...	...	...	...	2	16	...	...	...	...	...
2 Consumption of fixed capital	...	...	...	...	...	...	...	...	...	...	...	...
3 Compensation of employees	59	75	92	133	174	285	383	...	...	...	...	...
4 Net operating surplus	705	971	1677	3117	4889	7714	11896	...	...	...	...	...
Gross input	1215	1698	2828	5126	7934	13182	18768	...	...	...	...	...

Ecuador

3.32 Household and private unincorporated enterprise income and outlay account

Thousand million Ecuadoran sucres

	1986	1987	1988	1989	1990	1991	1992	1993	1994	1995	1996	1997
Receipts												
1 Compensation of employees	298	394	541	767	1078	1515	2361	3844	...	...	...	...
A Wages and salaries	272	...	...	...	946	1295	2016	3247	...	...	...	...
B Employers' contributions for social security	15	...	...	...	74	119	177	279	...	...	...	...
C Employers' contributions for private pension and welfare plans	12	...	...	...	58	101	168	318	...	...	...	...
2 Operating surplus of private unincorporated enterprises	705	971	1677	3117	4889	7873	12383	18138	...	...	...	...
3 Property and entrepreneurial income	62	84	87	126	213	351	908	995	...	...	...	...
A Withdrawals from private quasi-corporations	...	...	...	...	...	...	...	...	...	...	...	...
B Interest	47	64	61	86	144	254	781	840	...	...	...	...
C Dividends	13	18	24	37	64	90	117	141	...	...	...	...
D Net land rent and royalties	1	2	3	3	5	7	10	14	...	...	...	...
4 Current transfers	41	90	119	203	325	480	845	1159	...	...	...	...
A Casualty insurance claims	1	2	4	6	12	18	57	51	...	...	...	...
B Social security benefits	22	40	55	88	141	204	375	469	...	...	...	...
C Social assistance grants	...	...	...	...	...	...	...	...	...	...	...	...
D Unfunded employee pension and welfare benefits	12	18	26	36	58	101	169	318	...	...	...	...
E Transfers from general government	...	...	...	...	24	28	44	54	...	...	...	...
F Transfers from rest of the world	...	...	...	...	...	...	...	...	...	...	...	...
G Other transfers n.e.c.	6	31	34	73	89	129	200	267	...	...	...	...
Total current receipts	1107	1540	2424	4213	6505	10218	16498	24135	...	...	...	...
Disbursements												
1 Final consumption expenditure	926	1269	2087	3706	5622	8432	13147	19375	...	...	...	...
2 Property income	40	58	90	103	173	270	612	1003	...	...	...	...
A Interest	40	58	90	103	173	270	612	1003	...	...	...	...
B Net land rent and royalties	...	...	...	...	...	...	...	...	...	...	...	...
3 Direct taxes and other current transfers n.e.c. to general government	49	61	100	188	266	404	625	899	...	...	...	...
A Social security contributions	33	41	72	131	197	297	457	625	...	...	...	...
B Direct taxes	13	16	22	45	56	86	143	234	...	...	...	...
Income taxes	12	16	21	42	52	78	130	224	...	...	...	...
Other	1	1	1	2	4	8	13	10	...	...	...	...
C Fees, fines and penalties	3	3	5	12	13	21	25	40	...	...	...	...
4 Other current transfers	13	20	29	41	78	129	231	357	...	...	...	...
A Net casualty insurance premiums	1	2	3	5	19	28	61	38	...	...	...	...
B Transfers to private non-profit institutions serving households	...	...	...	...	...	...	...	...	...	...	...	...
C Transfers to rest of the world	...	...	...	...	...	...	...	...	...	...	...	...

Ecuador

Thousand million Ecuadoran sucres

	1986	1987	1988	1989	1990	1991	1992	1993	1994	1995	1996	1997
D Other current transfers, except imputed	...	...	...	...	...	...	1	1	...	...	...	...
E Imputed employee pension and welfare contributions	12	18	26	36	58	101	169	318	...	...	...	...
Net saving	79	132	119	175	366	985	1884	2501	...	...	...	...
Total current disbursements and net saving	1107	1540	2424	4213	6505	10220	16498	24135	...	...	...	...

3.33 Household and private unincorporated enterprise capital accumulation account

Thousand million Ecuadoran sucres

	1986	1987	1988	1989	1990	1991	1992	1993	1994	1995	1996	1997
Finance of gross accumulation												
1 Gross saving	79	132	119	175	366	985	1884	2501	...	...	...	...
2 Capital transfers	2	2	3	5	4	2	4	−3	...	...	...	...
A From resident sectors	...	...	...	...	...	...	...	−3	...	...	...	...
B From rest of the world	...	...	...	...	...	...	...	...	...	...	...	...
Total finance of gross accumulation	80	134	122	180	370	987	1888	2498	...	...	...	...
Gross accumulation												
1 Gross capital formation	50	63	112	166	335	627	924	1260	...	...	...	...
A Increase in stocks	5	−2	−	−29	−60	47	21	−33	...	...	...	...
B Gross fixed capital formation	45	65	112	194	395	580	903	1293	...	...	...	...
Owner-occupied housing	31	41	...	...	...	...	...	...	...	...	...	...
Other gross fixed capital formation	14	24	...	...	...	...	...	...	...	...	...	...
2 Purchases of land, net	−9	−10	−11	−13	−36	−45	−80	−83	...	...	...	...
3 Purchases of intangibles, net	...	...	...	...	...	...	...	...	...	...	...	...
4 Capital transfers	...	...	...	...	...	...	...	...	...	...	...	...
Net lending	40	80	21	28	71	405	1044	1321	...	...	...	...
Total gross accumulation	80	134	122	180	370	987	1888	2498	...	...	...	...

3.34 Household and private unincorporated enterprise capital finance account

Thousand million Ecuadoran sucres

	1986	1987	1988	1989	1990	1991	1992	1993	1994	1995	1996	1997
Acquisition of financial assets												
1 Gold	...	...	...	...	...	143	...	...	...	...	...	...
2 Currency and transferable deposits	23	17	103	101	150	485	395	...	...	...	...	...
3 Other deposits	50	107	102	193	315	...	872	...	...	...	...	...
4 Bills and bonds, short-term	...	...	...	...	...	...	...	...	...	...	...	...
5 Bonds, long-term	2	4	−14	−20	67	−54	158	...	...	...	...	...
6 Corporate equity securities	6	14	15	4	21	49	22	...	...	...	...	...
7 Short-term loans, n.e.c.	...	...	...	...	...	...	...	...	...	...	...	...
8 Long-term loans, n.e.c.	...	...	...	...	...	...	...	...	...	...	...	...
9 Trade credits and advances	−	−	−	−	...	...	...	...	...	...	...	...
10 Net equity of households in life insurance and pension fund reserves	13	19	23	44	96	110	114	...	...	...	...	...
11 Proprietors' net additions to the accumulation of quasi-corporations	...	...	...	...	...	...	...	...	...	...	...	...

Ecuador

Thousand million Ecuadoran sucres

	1986	1987	1988	1989	1990	1991	1992	1993	1994	1995	1996	1997
12 Other	...	...	...	...	...	...	...	...	...	...	...	...
Total acquisitions of financial assets	94	161	229	322	649	733	1561	...	...	...	...	...
Incurrence of liabilities												
1 Short-term loans, n.e.c.	25	33	63	76	132	128	240	...	...	...	...	...
2 Long-term loans, n.e.c.	36	32	41	101	117	168	286	...	...	...	...	...
3 Trade credits and advances	...	...	...	...	...	...	...	...	...	...	...	...
4 Other accounts payable	−34	11	87	32	231	−40	475	...	...	...	...	...
5 Other liabilities	...	...	...	...	...	...	...	...	...	...	...	...
Total incurrence of liabilities	27	75	191	209	480	257	1001	...	...	...	...	...
Net lending	67	85	38	113	170	476	560	...	...	...	...	...
Incurrence of liabilities and net lending	94	161	229	322	649	733	1561	...	...	...	...	...

3.51 External transactions, current account: detail

Thousand million Ecuadoran sucres

	1986	1987	1988	1989	1990	1991	1992	1993	1994	1995	1996	1997
Payments to the rest of the world												
1 Imports of goods and services	313	544	922	1611	2246	3655	5378	7012	...	...	...	...
A Imports of merchandise, c.i.f.	243	448	725	1318	1811	3053	4465	5816	...	...	...	...
B Other	70	96	197	293	435	602	913	1196	...	...	...	...
2 Factor income to rest of the world	116	126	212	400	656	778	991	1164	...	...	...	...
A Compensation of employees	4	7	10	22	40	56	106	132	...	...	...	...
B Property and entrepreneurial income	112	119	203	378	616	722	885	1032	...	...	...	...
3 Current transfers to the rest of the world	4	6	10	18	34	44	84	100	...	...	...	...
A Indirect taxes by general government to supranational organizations	...	...	...	...	...	...	...	...	...	...	...	...
B Other current transfers	4	6	10	18	34	44	84	100	...	...	...	...
By general government	1	...	...	...	...	...	...	...	...	...	...	...
By other resident sectors	3	...	...	...	...	...	...	...	...	...	...	...
4 Surplus of the nation on current transactions	−107	−209	−243	−425	−106	−415	−2	−692	...	...	...	...
Payments to the rest of the world and surplus of the nation on current transfers	325	467	901	1604	2830	4062	6451	7584	...	...	...	...
Receipts from the rest of the world												
1 Exports of goods and services	315	432	859	1520	2686	3858	6119	7184	...	...	...	...
A Exports of merchandise, f.o.b.	250	348	673	1221	2251	3214	5075	5813	...	...	...	...
B Other	65	83	186	299	435	644	1044	1371	...	...	...	...
2 Factor income from rest of the world	4	4	6	16	27	42	61	66	...	...	...	...
A Compensation of employees	—	1	1	2	3	5	7	8	...	...	...	...
B Property and entrepreneurial income	3	3	5	14	24	37	54	58	...	...	...	...
3 Current transfers from rest of the world	6	32	37	69	117	163	272	334	...	...	...	...

Ecuador

Thousand million Ecuadoran sucres

	1986	1987	1988	1989	1990	1991	1992	1993	1994	1995	1996	1997
A Subsidies to general government from supranational organizations	...	...	...	...	...	...	...	...	...	...	...	...
B Other current transfers	6	32	37	69	117	163	272	334	...	...	...	...
To general government	3	3	...	...	...	...	...	...	...	...	...	...
To other resident sectors	3	28	...	...	...	...	...	...	...	...	...	...
Receipts from the rest of the world on current transfers	325	467	901	1604	2830	4063	6452	7584	...	...	...	...

3.52 External transactions, capital accumulation account

Thousand million Ecuadoran sucres

	1986	1987	1988	1989	1990	1991	1992	1993	1994	1995	1996	1997
Finance of gross accumulation												
1 Surplus of the nation on current transactions	−107	−209	−243	−425	−106	−415	−2	−692	...	...	...	...
2 Capital transfers from rest of the world	–	–	–	–	–	1	1	1	...	...	...	...
A By general government	...	...	...	...	...	...	...	...	...	...	...	...
B By other resident sectors	–	–	–	–	–	–	–	...	...	...	...	...
Total finance of gross accumulation	−107	−209	−243	−425	−106	−414	−1	−691	...	...	...	...
Gross accumulation												
1 Capital transfers to the rest of the world	...	...	...	...	...	...	...	...	...	...	...	...
2 Purchases of intangible assets, n.e.c., net, from rest of the world	1	2	5	9	16	19	23	33	...	...	...	...
Net lending to the rest of the world [a]	−109	−212	−249	−433	−122	−433	−24	−724	...	...	...	...
Total gross accumulation	−107	−209	−243	−425	−106	−414	−1	−691	...	...	...	...

[a] Net lending of the capital accumulation account and the capital finance account have not been reconciled and are different due to different statistical sources.

3.53 External transactions, capital finance account

Thousand million Ecuadoran sucres

	1986	1987	1988	1989	1990	1991	1992	1993	1994	1995	1996	1997
Acquisition of foreign financial assets												
1 Gold and SDRs	5	–	−18	−25	−80	−103	−89	−64	...	...	...	...
2 Currency and transferable deposits	1	–	1	2	4	3	3	93	...	...	...	...
3 Other deposits	10	−7	36	18	−10	15	43	−92	...	...	...	...
4 Bills and bonds, short-term	–	–	–	–	–	–	–	...	...	...	...	...
5 Bonds, long-term [a]	–	–	–	–	–	–	–	...	...	...	...	...
6 Corporate equity securities	8	14	27	27	45	62	98	128	...	...	...	...
7 Short-term loans, n.e.c.	−20	2	66	−8	92	78	157	250	...	...	...	...
8 Long-term loans	59	113	56	262	−3	103	−190	641	...	...	...	...
9 Proprietors' net additions to accumulation of quasi-corporate, non-resident enterprises	...	...	...	...	...	...	...	...	...	...	...	...
10 Trade credits and advances	26	95	203	186	243	719	639	563	...	...	...	...
11 Other [b]	...	...	–	61	157	–	–	...	...	...	...	...
Total acquisitions of foreign financial assets	90	216	371	522	448	877	661	1519	...	...	...	...

Ecuador

Thousand million Ecuadoran sucres

	1986	1987	1988	1989	1990	1991	1992	1993	1994	1995	1996	1997
Incurrence of foreign liabilities												
1 Currency and transferable deposits	15	−10	9	−30	45	−18	−49	−59	...	...	...	...
2 Other deposits	−32	20	47	87	156	12	26	912	...	...	...	...
3 Bills and bonds, short-term	−	−	−	−	−	−	−	...	...	...	...	...
4 Bonds, long-term [a]	−	−	−	1	2	3	16	−6	...	...	...	...
5 Corporate equity securities	2	2	5	8	8	18	29	78	...	...	...	...
6 Short-term loans, n.e.c.	−1	−6	−	3	2	...	−	1	...	...	...	...
7 Long-term loans	...	...	...	...	...	...	...	...	...	...	...	...
8 Non-resident proprietors' net additions to accumulation of resident quasi-corporate enterprises	...	...	...	...	...	...	...	...	...	...	...	...
9 Trade credits and advances	11	34	54	122	110	268	247	27	...	...	...	...
10 Other [b]	−5	−18	−	−	−	−	−	...	...	...	...	...
Total incurrence of liabilities	−10	21	115	193	323	283	269	953	...	...	...	...
Statistical discrepancy	...	...	...	...	3	161	369	−158	...	...	...	...
Net lending [c]	100	195	256	330	122	433	24	724	...	...	...	...
Total incurrence of liabilities and net lending	90	216	371	522	448	877	662	1519	...	...	...	...

a Item "Bonds, long-term" includes short-term bonds.
b Item "Other" refers to other receivables/payables and accounting discrepancies.
c Net lending of the capital accumulation account and the capital finance account have not been reconciled and are different due to different statistical sources.

4.1 Derivation of value added by kind of activity, in current prices

Thousand million Ecuadoran sucres

	1986			1987			1988			1989		
	Gross output	Intermediate consumption	Value added	Gross output	Intermediate consumption	Value added	Gross output	Intermediate consumption	Value added	Gross output	Intermediate consumption	Value added
All producers												
1 Agriculture, hunting, forestry and fishing	255	46	209	338	64	275	553	120	433	932	211	722
A Agriculture and hunting	209	37	171	254	49	205	426	95	332	723	165	558
B Forestry and logging	15	3	12	26	4	22	39	7	33	61	12	49
C Fishing	31	6	26	58	11	48	87	19	68	149	34	115
2 Mining and quarrying	244	106	138	293	170	123	610	313	297	1215	610	605
A Coal mining	...	...	...	...	...	...	...	...	...	...	...	...
B Crude petroleum and natural gas production [a]	228	101	128	270	162	108	558	297	261	1144	583	562
C Metal ore mining	...	...	...	...	...	...	...	...	...	...	...	...
D Other mining [b]	15	5	10	23	8	15	52	16	36	70	27	43
3 Manufacturing	765	491	274	1035	685	350	1790	1145	645	3042	1953	1090
A Manufacture of food, beverages and tobacco	376	232	143	497	308	188	827	475	352	1480	831	649
B Textile, wearing apparel and leather industries	111	64	47	147	87	60	265	163	103	435	276	160
C Manufacture of wood and wood products, including furniture	46	34	11	71	57	15	106	85	21	161	130	31
D Manufacture of paper and paper products, printing and publishing	42	26	17	63	37	26	116	68	48	201	121	81

Ecuador

Thousand million Ecuadoran sucres

	1986 Gross output	1986 Intermediate consumption	1986 Value added	1987 Gross output	1987 Intermediate consumption	1987 Value added	1988 Gross output	1988 Intermediate consumption	1988 Value added	1989 Gross output	1989 Intermediate consumption	1989 Value added
E Manufacture of chemicals and chemical petroleum, coal, rubber and plastic products	55	44	11	74	63	11	126	105	21	224	186	38
F Manufacture of non-metallic mineral products, except products of petroleum and coal	81	50	30	104	72	31	202	142	60	292	222	70
G Basic metal industries												
H Manufacture of fabricated metal products, machinery and equipment	40	32	8	60	51	9	105	88	17	180	155	25
I Other manufacturing industries	14	8	7	20	10	10	42	19	23	68	32	36
4 Electricity, gas and water	24	18	6	37	29	7	52	50	2	93	89	4
5 Construction	163	96	67	239	140	99	342	202	140	594	358	236
6 Wholesale and retail trade, restaurants and hotels	392	146	247	564	201	363	955	344	611	1710	591	1119
A Wholesale and retail trade	346	112	234	502	156	346	860	270	590	1526	454	1072
B Restaurants and hotels	47	34	13	62	44	18	95	74	21	184	136	47
7 Transport, storage and communication	200	74	126	279	109	170	483	187	296	814	353	461
A Transport and storage	187	68	119	265	101	164	458	169	289	761	318	443
B Communication	12	6	7	14	8	6	25	17	8	53	35	18
8 Finance, insurance, real estate and business services	145	40	105	205	54	151	340	96	244	501	166	334
A Financial institutions	46	20	26	78	25	52	144	47	97	165	81	84
B Insurance												
C Real estate and business services	99	20	79	128	29	99	195	49	147	336	85	251
9 Community, social and personal services	82	25	57	116	39	77	184	69	115	337	123	215
A Sanitary and similar services	...	...	...	...	...	...	...	...	...	...	...	...
B Social and related community services	...	...	...	...	...	...	...	...	...	...	...	...
C Recreational and cultural services	...	...	...	...	...	...	...	...	...	...	...	...
D Personal and household services	82	25	57	116	39	77	184	69	115	337	123	215
Total, Industries	2270	1041	1229	3107	1492	1615	5307	2525	2782	9239	4454	4785
Producers of government services	176	63	113	242	94	148	367	162	205	523	251	272
Other producers	6	...	6	8	...	8	10	...	10	14	...	14
Total	2451	1104	1347	3356	1586	1771	5684	2687	2997	9776	4704	5072
less: Imputed bank service charge	...	−29	29	...	−54	54	...	−98	98	...	−97	97
Import duties	64	...	64	77	...	77	121	...	121	196	...	196
Value added tax	...	...	...	...	...	...	...	...	...	...	...	...
Other adjustments	...	...	...	...	...	...	...	...	...	...	...	...
Total	2516	1132	1383	3434	1639	1795	5805	2785	3020	9972	4802	5170

Of which general government:

1 Agriculture, hunting, forestry and fishing	...	...	...	...	...	...	...	...	...	...	...	...
2 Mining and quarrying	...	...	...	...	...	...	...	...	...	...	...	...

Ecuador

Thousand million Ecuadoran sucres

	1986 Gross output	1986 Intermediate consumption	1986 Value added	1987 Gross output	1987 Intermediate consumption	1987 Value added	1988 Gross output	1988 Intermediate consumption	1988 Value added	1989 Gross output	1989 Intermediate consumption	1989 Value added
3 Manufacturing	...	...	...	...	...	...	...	...	...	...	...	...
4 Electricity, gas and water	5	2	4	7	2	5	9	3	6	–	–	–
5 Construction	15	9	6	22	13	9	35	18	17	53	30	23
6 Wholesale and retail trade, restaurants and hotels	...	...	...	...	...	...	...	...	...	...	...	...
7 Transport, storage and communication	...	...	...	...	...	...	...	...	...	...	...	...
8 Finance, insurance, real estate and business services	...	...	...	...	...	...	...	...	...	...	...	...
9 Community, social and personal services	8	3	5	11	4	7	18	7	11	29	14	15
Total, industries of general government	29	14	15	40	19	21	62	28	34	83	44	38
Producers of government services	176	63	113	242	94	148	367	162	205	523	251	272
Total, general government	204	76	128	282	113	169	430	190	239	605	295	311

	1990 Gross output	1990 Intermediate consumption	1990 Value added	1991 Gross output	1991 Intermediate consumption	1991 Value added	1992 Gross output	1992 Intermediate consumption	1992 Value added	1993 Gross output	1993 Intermediate consumption	1993 Value added

All producers

	1990 GO	1990 IC	1990 VA	1991 GO	1991 IC	1991 VA	1992 GO	1992 IC	1992 VA	1993 GO	1993 IC	1993 VA
1 Agriculture, hunting, forestry and fishing	1417	317	1100	2253	491	1762	3237	771	2466	4368	1045	3323
A Agriculture and hunting	1077	244	834	1725	378	1347	2406	589	1817	3274	803	2471
B Forestry and logging	94	17	77	144	25	119	233	40	193	347	61	286
C Fishing	245	57	189	385	89	296	597	142	455	747	181	566
2 Mining and quarrying	2338	1120	1218	2682	1314	1368	4539	2099	2440	5245	2303	2942
A Coal mining	...	...	...	...	...	...	...	...	...	...	...	...
B Crude petroleum and natural gas production [a]	2232	1079	1153	2547	1253	1294	4335	2003	2332	4939	2157	2782
C Metal ore mining	...	...	...	...	...	...	...	...	...	...	...	...
D Other mining [b]	107	41	65	134	60	74	204	96	108	306	146	160
3 Manufacturing	4584	2996	1588	7100	4546	2554	11279	6999	4280	15917	9948	5969
A Manufacture of food, beverages and tobacco	2246	1233	1013	3502	1880	1622	5552	2838	2714	7628	3920	3708
B Textile, wearing apparel and leather industries	634	441	193	933	659	274	1376	957	419	1916	1320	596
C Manufacture of wood and wood products, including furniture	248	218	30	382	336	46	612	533	79	846	737	109
D Manufacture of paper and paper products, printing and publishing	313	177	137	520	248	272	963	440	523	1381	639	742
E Manufacture of chemicals and chemical petroleum, coal, rubber and plastic products	322	295	28	498	460	38	829	757	72	1215	1122	93
F Manufacture of non-metallic mineral products, except products of petroleum and coal	446	330	116	664	475	189	1049	733	316	1623	1132	491
G Basic metal industries												
H Manufacture of fabricated metal products, machinery and equipment	271	254	17	463	434	29	695	661	34	1031	969	62

562

Ecuador

	1990 Gross output	1990 Intermediate consumption	1990 Value added	1991 Gross output	1991 Intermediate consumption	1991 Value added	1992 Gross output	1992 Intermediate consumption	1992 Value added	1993 Gross output	1993 Intermediate consumption	1993 Value added
1 Other manufacturing industries	103	49	54	140	56	84	202	80	122	276	109	167
4 Electricity, gas and water	138	153	–15	224	237	–13	402	379	23	636	560	76
5 Construction	830	501	329	1260	704	556	1912	1030	882	2837	1497	1340
6 Wholesale and retail trade, restaurants and hotels	2660	924	1737	4161	1438	2723	6433	2264	4169	8981	3430	5551
A Wholesale and retail trade	2341	717	1625	3667	1112	2555	5635	1765	3870	7796	2699	5097
B Restaurants and hotels	319	207	112	494	326	168	798	499	299	1185	731	454
7 Transport, storage and communication	1271	563	708	1885	821	1064	2855	1350	1505	4534	2084	2450
A Transport and storage	1174	500	675	1720	705	1015	2594	1162	1432	4101	1792	2309
B Communication	96	63	33	165	116	49	261	188	73	433	292	141
8 Finance, insurance, real estate and business services	760	258	502	1232	375	857	2002	609	1393	3208	953	2255
A Financial institutions	251	128	124	419	178	241	692	303	389	1228	498	730
B Insurance												
C Real estate and business services	509	131	378	814	197	617	1310	306	1004	1980	455	1525
9 Community, social and personal services	511	180	331	797	260	537	1334	391	943	2111	547	1564
A Sanitary and similar services	...	...	...	...	...	...	...	...	...	...	...	...
B Social and related community services	...	...	...	...	...	...	...	...	...	...	...	...
C Recreational and cultural services	...	...	...	...	...	...	...	...	...	...	...	...
D Personal and household services	511	180	331	797	260	537	1334	391	943	2111	547	1564
Total, Industries	14510	7012	7498	21594	10186	11408	33993	15892	18101	47837	22367	25470
Producers of government services	775	388	387	1010	506	504	1498	685	813	2281	972	1309
Other producers	19	...	19	26	...	26	40	...	40	65	...	65
Total	15303	7400	7903	22630	10692	11938	35531	16577	18954	50183	23339	26844
less: Imputed bank service charge	...	–149	149	...	–288	288	...	–491	491	...	–878	878
Import duties	215	...	215	280	...	280	339	...	339	537	...	537
Value added tax	234	...	234	366	...	366	612	...	612	949	...	949
Other adjustments	...	...	...	...	...	...	...	...	...	...	...	...
Total	15753	7548	8204	23276	10980	12296	36482	17068	19414	51669	24217	27452

Of which general government:

	1990 Gross output	1990 Intermediate consumption	1990 Value added	1991 Gross output	1991 Intermediate consumption	1991 Value added	1992 Gross output	1992 Intermediate consumption	1992 Value added	1993 Gross output	1993 Intermediate consumption	1993 Value added
1 Agriculture, hunting, forestry and fishing	...	...	...	...	...	...	...	...	...	...	...	...
2 Mining and quarrying	...	...	...	...	...	...	...	...	...	...	...	...
3 Manufacturing	...	...	...	...	...	...	...	...	...	...	...	...
4 Electricity, gas and water	1	1	–	1	1	–	1	1	–	1	2	–1
5 Construction	79	44	35	107	60	47	168	95	73	258	147	111
6 Wholesale and retail trade, restaurants and hotels	...	...	...	...	...	...	...	...	...	...	...	...
7 Transport, storage and communication	...	...	...	...	...	...	...	...	...	...	...	...
8 Finance, insurance, real estate and business services	...	...	...	...	...	...	...	...	...	...	...	...
9 Community, social and personal services	46	23	23	67	31	36	145	81	64	163	64	99

Ecuador

	1990			1991			1992			1993		
	Gross output	Intermediate consumption	Value added	Gross output	Intermediate consumption	Value added	Gross output	Intermediate consumption	Value added	Gross output	Intermediate consumption	Value added
Total, industries of general government	126	68	58	175	92	83	314	177	137	422	213	209
Producers of government services	775	388	387	1010	506	504	1498	685	813	2281	972	1309
Total, general government	901	456	445	1185	598	587	1812	862	950	2703	1185	1518

a Petroleum refining is included in item "Crude petroleum and natural gas production".
b Items "Coal mining" and "Metal ore mining" are included in item "Other mining".

4.2 Derivation of value added by kind of activity, in constant prices

Million Ecuadoran sucres

	1986			1987			1988			1989		
	Gross output	Intermediate consumption	Value added	Gross output	Intermediate consumption	Value added	Gross output	Intermediate consumption	Value added	Gross output	Intermediate consumption	Value added

At constant prices of: 1975

All producers

1 Agriculture, hunting, forestry and fishing	32462	5806	26656	33453	6130	27323	36090	6674	29416	37217	6987	30230
A Agriculture and hunting	26379	4794	21585	26033	5003	21030	27916	5439	22477	29170	5742	23428
B Forestry and logging	2172	293	1879	2235	300	1935	2326	312	2014	2260	313	1947
C Fishing	3911	719	3192	5185	827	4358	5848	923	4925	5787	932	4855
2 Mining and quarrying	40556	16043	24513	26737	15630	11107	43318	19354	23964	40280	18638	21642
A Coal mining	...	...	...	...	...	...	...	...	...	...	...	...
B Crude petroleum and natural gas production [a]	38981	15633	23348	25130	15205	9925	41322	18825	22497	38336	18122	20214
C Metal ore mining	...	...	...	...	...	...	...	...	...	...	...	...
D Other mining [b]	1575	410	1165	1607	425	1182	1996	529	1467	1944	516	1428
3 Manufacturing	88460	60219	28241	90609	61880	28729	93420	64108	29312	93558	65700	27858
A Manufacture of food, beverages and tobacco	39794	29024	10770	41582	30507	11075	42482	31753	10729	42266	32480	9786
B Textile, wearing apparel and leather industries	14031	8095	5936	14013	8069	5944	14818	8452	6366	15598	9012	6586
C Manufacture of wood and wood products, including furniture	6331	4653	1678	6348	4667	1681	6146	4698	1448	5882	4473	1409
D Manufacture of paper and paper products, printing and publishing	5037	3045	1992	5203	3121	2082	5542	3345	2197	5581	3506	2075
E Manufacture of chemicals and chemical petroleum, coal, rubber and plastic products	7451	5595	1856	7309	5519	1790	7013	5267	1746	7560	5490	2070
F Manufacture of non-metallic mineral products, except products of petroleum and coal	9130	5515	3615	8855	5521	3334	9712	5901	3811	8533	5760	2773
G Basic metal industries												
H Manufacture of fabricated metal products, machinery and equipment	4499	3397	1102	4914	3663	1251	5210	3854	1356	5670	4115	1555
I Other manufacturing industries	2187	895	1292	2385	813	1572	2497	838	1659	2468	864	1604
4 Electricity, gas and water	4843	2611	2232	5378	2762	2616	5590	2869	2721	5775	2876	2899
5 Construction	17142	10301	6841	17448	10437	7011	15118	9094	6024	15556	9292	6264

Ecuador

Million Ecuadoran sucres

	1986 Gross output	1986 Intermediate consumption	1986 Value added	1987 Gross output	1987 Intermediate consumption	1987 Value added	1988 Gross output	1988 Intermediate consumption	1988 Value added	1989 Gross output	1989 Intermediate consumption	1989 Value added
At constant prices of: 1975												
6 Wholesale and retail trade, restaurants and hotels	41450	16657	24793	42349	16952	25397	43423	17498	25925	44488	18018	26470
A Wholesale and retail trade	34360	12481	21879	35058	12794	22264	35766	13118	22648	36602	13412	23190
B Restaurants and hotels	7090	4176	2914	7291	4158	3133	7657	4380	3277	7886	4606	3280
7 Transport, storage and communication	21537	8966	12571	21966	9137	12829	23187	9567	13620	24843	10143	14700
A Transport and storage	18206	8127	10079	18488	8253	10235	19010	8499	10511	19911	8881	11030
B Communication	3331	839	2492	3478	884	2594	4177	1068	3109	4932	1262	3670
8 Finance, insurance, real estate and business services	23568	4989	18579	26252	5157	21095	28198	5519	22679	24843	5655	19188
A Financial institutions	7098	2479	4619	9284	2568	6716	10924	2894	8030	7088	2958	4130
B Insurance												
C Real estate and business services	16470	2510	13960	16968	2589	14379	17274	2625	14649	17755	2697	15058
9 Community, social and personal services	12648	2875	9773	13049	2982	10067	13075	2993	10082	13475	3087	10388
A Sanitary and similar services	...	...	...	...	...	...	...	...	...	...	...	...
B Social and related community services	...	...	...	...	...	...	...	...	...	...	...	...
C Recreational and cultural services	...	...	...	...	...	...	...	...	...	...	...	...
D Personal and household services	12648	2875	9773	13049	2982	10067	13075	2993	10082	13475	3087	10388
Total, Industries	282666	128467	154199	277241	131067	146174	301419	137676	163743	300035	140396	159639
Producers of government services	21757	6859	14898	22015	7013	15002	22817	7200	15617	22248	6612	15636
Other producers	735	...	735	756	...	756	778	...	778	800	...	800
Total	305158	135326	169832	300012	138080	161932	325014	144876	180138	323083	147008	176075
less: Imputed bank service charge	...	−4934	4934	...	−7122	7122	...	−8510	8510	...	−4692	4692
Import duties	4238	...	4238	4206	...	4206	4114	...	4114	4812	...	4812
Value added tax	...	...	...	...	...	...	...	...	...	...	...	...
Other adjustments	...	...	...	...	...	...	...	...	...	...	...	...
Total	309396	140260	169136	304218	145202	159016	329128	153386	175742	327895	151700	176195
Of which general government:												
1 Agriculture, hunting, forestry and fishing	...	...	...	...	...	...	...	...	...	...	...	...
2 Mining and quarrying	...	...	...	...	...	...	...	...	...	...	...	...
3 Manufacturing	...	...	...	...	...	...	...	...	...	...	...	...
4 Electricity, gas and water	...	...	...	...	...	...	...	...	...	...	...	...
5 Construction	...	...	...	...	...	...	...	...	...	...	...	...
6 Wholesale and retail trade, restaurants and hotels	...	...	...	...	...	...	...	...	...	...	...	...
7 Transport, storage and communication	...	...	...	...	...	...	...	...	...	...	...	...
8 Finance, insurance, real estate and business services	...	...	...	...	...	...	...	...	...	...	...	...
9 Community, social and personal services	...	...	...	...	...	...	...	...	...	...	...	...
Total, industries of general government	...	...	...	...	...	...	...	...	...	...	...	...

Ecuador

Million Ecuadoran sucres

	1986			1987			1988			1989		
	Gross output	Intermediate consumption	Value added	Gross output	Intermediate consumption	Value added	Gross output	Intermediate consumption	Value added	Gross output	Intermediate consumption	Value added

At constant prices of: 1975

Producers of government services	21757	6859	14898	22015	7013	15002	22817	7200	15617	22248	6612	15636
Total, general government	...	...	...	...	...	...	...	...	...	...	...	...

	1990			1991			1992			1993		
	Gross output	Intermediate consumption	Value added	Gross output	Intermediate consumption	Value added	Gross output	Intermediate consumption	Value added	Gross output	Intermediate consumption	Value added

At constant prices of: 1975

All producers

	Gross output	Int. cons.	Value added	Gross output	Int. cons.	Value added	Gross output	Int. cons.	Value added	Gross output	Int. cons.	Value added
1 Agriculture, hunting, forestry and fishing	39431	7351	32080	41991	8003	33988	43387	8233	35154	42882	8327	34555
A Agriculture and hunting	30757	6000	24757	32469	6495	25974	33519	6697	26822	33562	6901	26661
B Forestry and logging	2174	303	1871	2317	324	1993	2403	335	2068	2500	347	2153
C Fishing	6500	1048	5452	7205	1184	6021	7465	1201	6264	6820	1079	5741
2 Mining and quarrying	41297	19855	21442	43467	20216	23251	45868	21269	24599	48144	20846	27298
A Coal mining	...	...	...	...	...	...	...	...	...	...	...	...
B Crude petroleum and natural gas production [a]	39335	19329	20006	41441	19669	21772	43794	20709	23085	46018	20272	25746
C Metal ore mining	...	...	...	...	...	...	...	...	...	...	...	...
D Other mining [b]	1962	526	1436	2026	547	1479	2074	560	1514	2126	574	1552
3 Manufacturing	97164	69109	28055	103109	74158	28951	107368	77379	29989	109657	78926	30731
A Manufacture of food, beverages and tobacco	43741	34073	9668	46136	36356	9780	47901	37827	10074	48146	37952	10194
B Textile, wearing apparel and leather industries	15865	9425	6440	16077	9648	6429	16176	9843	6333	16400	9985	6415
C Manufacture of wood and wood products, including furniture	6104	4700	1404	6594	5102	1492	6862	5322	1540	7151	5544	1607
D Manufacture of paper and paper products, printing and publishing	6223	3704	2519	6464	3898	2566	6809	4102	2707	6939	4212	2727
E Manufacture of chemicals and chemical petroleum, coal, rubber and plastic products	7654	5780	1874	8163	6190	1973	8508	6470	2038	8911	6773	2138
F Manufacture of non-metallic mineral products, except products of petroleum and coal	8898	5974	2924	9689	6510	3179	10563	7002	3561	11173	7390	3783
G Basic metal industries												
H Manufacture of fabricated metal products, machinery and equipment	6059	4555	1504	7365	5543	1822	7815	5868	1947	8119	6101	2018
I Other manufacturing industries	2620	898	1722	2621	911	1710	2734	945	1789	2818	969	1849
4 Electricity, gas and water	6025	3244	2781	6583	3742	2841	6778	3859	2919	6971	3991	2980
5 Construction	14375	9042	5333	14445	9171	5274	14403	9147	5256	14077	9045	5032
6 Wholesale and retail trade, restaurants and hotels	46715	19246	27469	49073	20516	28557	50971	21551	29420	52215	22296	29919
A Wholesale and retail trade	38672	14440	24232	40777	15440	25337	42448	16323	26125	43478	16814	26664
B Restaurants and hotels	8043	4806	3237	8296	5076	3220	8523	5228	3295	8737	5482	3255
7 Transport, storage and communication	26049	10687	15362	27704	11415	16289	29243	12020	17223	30606	12614	17992
A Transport and storage	20341	9141	11200	20970	9558	11412	21861	9981	11880	22582	10377	12205

Ecuador

	1990			1991			1992			1993		
	Gross output	Intermediate consumption	Value added	Gross output	Intermediate consumption	Value added	Gross output	Intermediate consumption	Value added	Gross output	Intermediate consumption	Value added
	At constant prices of: 1975										
B Communication	5708	1546	4162	6734	1857	4877	7382	2039	5343	8024	2237	5787
8 Finance, insurance, real estate and business services	25334	5745	19589	26774	5968	20806	27865	6386	21479	30338	6883	23455
A Financial institutions	7264	2976	4288	8198	3088	5110	8728	3404	5324	10559	3753	6806
B Insurance												
C Real estate and business services	18070	2769	15301	18576	2880	15696	19137	2982	16155	19779	3130	16649
9 Community, social and personal services	13559	3125	10434	14028	3271	10757	14508	3396	11112	14723	3459	11264
A Sanitary and similar services	...	...	...	...	...	...	...	...	...	...	...	...
B Social and related community services	...	...	...	...	...	...	...	...	...	...	...	...
C Recreational and cultural services	...	...	...	...	...	...	...	...	...	...	...	...
D Personal and household services	13559	3125	10434	14028	3271	10757	14508	3396	11112	14723	3459	11264
Total, Industries	309949	147404	162545	327174	156460	170714	340391	163240	177151	349613	166387	183226
Producers of government services	23032	7017	16015	22591	6422	16169	21961	5847	16114	21747	5993	15754
Other producers	819	...	819	844	...	844	864	...	864	881	...	881
Total	333800	154421	179379	350609	162882	187727	363216	169087	194129	372241	172380	199861
less: Imputed bank service charge	...	−4881	4881	...	−5661	5661	...	−5984	5984	...	−7811	7811
Import duties	3624	...	3624	4815	...	4815	5324	...	5324	5369	...	5369
Value added tax	3409	...	3409	3757	...	3757	3967	...	3967	4028	...	4028
Other adjustments	...	...	...	...	...	...	...	...	...	...	...	...
Total	340833	159302	181531	359181	168543	190638	372507	175071	197436	381638	180191	201447
Of which general government:												
1 Agriculture, hunting, forestry and fishing	...	...	...	...	...	...	...	...	...	...	...	...
2 Mining and quarrying	...	...	...	...	...	...	...	...	...	...	...	...
3 Manufacturing	...	...	...	...	...	...	...	...	...	...	...	...
4 Electricity, gas and water	...	...	...	...	...	...	...	...	...	...	...	...
5 Construction	...	...	...	...	...	...	...	...	...	...	...	...
6 Wholesale and retail trade, restaurants and hotels	...	...	...	...	...	...	...	...	...	...	...	...
7 Transport, storage and communication	...	...	...	...	...	...	...	...	...	...	...	...
8 Finance, insurance, real estate and business services	...	...	...	...	...	...	...	...	...	...	...	...
9 Community, social and personal services	...	...	...	...	...	...	...	...	...	...	...	...
Total, industries of general government	...	...	...	...	...	...	...	...	...	...	...	...
Producers of government services	23032	7017	16015	22591	6422	16169	21961	5847	16114	21747	5993	15754
Total, general government	...	...	...	...	...	...	...	...	...	...	...	...

a Petroleum refining is included in item "Crude petroleum and natural gas production".

b Items "Coal mining" and "Metal ore mining" are included in item "Other mining".

Ecuador

4.3 Cost components of value added

Thousand million Ecuadoran sucres

	\multicolumn{5}{c	}{1986}		\multicolumn{5}{c	}{1987}	
	Compensation of employees	Capital consumption	Net operating surplus	Indirect taxes	less: Subsidies received	Value added	Compensation of employees	Capital consumption	Net operating surplus	Indirect taxes	less: Subsidies received	Value added
All producers												
1 Agriculture, hunting, forestry and fishing	17	...	191	1	...	209	25	...	248	1	...	275
A Agriculture and hunting	16	...	155	1	...	171	24	...	180	1	...	205
B Forestry and logging	–	...	12	–	...	12	–	...	21	–	...	22
C Fishing	1	...	25	–	...	26	1	...	47	–	...	48
2 Mining and quarrying	12	...	83	43	...	138	15	...	42	66	...	123
A Coal mining	...	...	...	...	...	...	...	...	...	...	...	...
B Crude petroleum and natural gas production [a]	8	...	76	43	...	128	10	...	32	66	...	108
C Metal ore mining	...	...	...	...	...	...	...	...	...	...	...	...
D Other mining [b]	3	...	7	–	...	10	5	...	9	–	...	15
3 Manufacturing	37	...	208	29	...	274	48	...	262	40	...	350
A Manufacture of food, beverages and tobacco	9	...	120	14	...	143	12	...	155	21	...	188
B Textile, wearing apparel and leather industries	9	...	34	3	...	47	13	...	43	4	...	60
C Manufacture of wood and wood products, including furniture	3	...	8	–	...	11	4	...	10	–	...	15
D Manufacture of paper and paper products, printing and publishing	2	...	14	1	...	17	3	...	22	1	...	26
E Manufacture of chemicals and chemical petroleum, coal, rubber and plastic products	4	...	3	4	...	11	5	...	1	5	...	11
F Manufacture of non-metallic mineral products, except products of petroleum and coal	6	...	22	3	...	30	7	...	20	4	...	31
G Basic metal industries												
H Manufacture of fabricated metal products, machinery and equipment	3	...	2	3	...	8	4	...	1	4	...	9
I Other manufacturing industries	1	...	6	–	...	7	1	...	9	1	...	10
4 Electricity, gas and water	7	...	–2	1	...	6	9	...	–4	2	...	7
5 Construction	25	...	41	1	...	67	32	...	66	1	...	99
6 Wholesale and retail trade, restaurants and hotels	26	...	215	6	...	247	34	...	324	5	...	363
A Wholesale and retail trade	22	...	207	5	...	234	29	...	313	4	...	346
B Restaurants and hotels	4	...	8	1	...	13	5	...	12	1	...	18
7 Transport, storage and communication	17	...	105	3	...	126	23	...	142	5	...	170
A Transport and storage	13	...	104	2	...	119	18	...	143	4	...	164
B Communication	4	...	2	1	...	7	6	...	–1	1	...	6
8 Finance, insurance, real estate and business services	30	...	68	7	...	105	43	...	101	7	...	151
A Financial institutions	25	...	–1	2	...	26	37	...	14	2	...	52
B Insurance												

Ecuador

Thousand million Ecuadoran sucres

	1986						1987					
	Compensation of employees	Capital consumption	Net operating surplus	Indirect taxes	less: Subsidies received	Value added	Compensation of employees	Capital consumption	Net operating surplus	Indirect taxes	less: Subsidies received	Value added
C Real estate and business services	5	...	69	5	...	79	7	...	87	5	...	99
9 Community, social and personal services	12	...	44	–	...	57	16	...	60	1	...	77
A Sanitary and similar services	...	...	...	...	...	...	...	...	...	...	...	...
B Social and related community services	...	...	...	...	...	...	...	...	...	...	...	...
C Recreational and cultural services	...	...	...	...	...	...	...	...	...	...	...	...
D Personal and household services	12	...	44	–	...	57	16	...	60	1	...	77
Total, Industries [cd]	183	...	954	92	...	1229	246	...	1243	127	...	1615
Producers of government services	113	...	...	...	...	113	148	...	...	...	...	148
Other producers	6	...	...	...	...	6	8	...	...	...	...	8
Total [cd]	302	...	954	92	...	1347	401	...	1243	127	...	1771
less: Imputed bank service charge	...	...	29	...	...	29	...	...	54	...	...	54
Import duties	...	...	...	64	...	64	...	...	...	77	...	77
Value added tax	...	...	...	...	...	...	...	...	...	...	...	...
Other adjustments	...	...	...	...	...	...	...	...	...	...	...	...
Total [cd]	302	...	925	156	...	1383	401	...	1189	205	...	1795

Of which general government:

1 Agriculture, hunting, forestry and fishing	...	...	...	...	...	...	...	...	...	...	...	...
2 Mining and quarrying	...	...	...	...	...	...	...	...	...	...	...	...
3 Manufacturing	...	...	...	...	...	...	...	...	...	...	...	...
4 Electricity, gas and water	1	...	2	...	...	4	2	...	4	...	...	5
5 Construction	6	...	...	...	...	6	9	...	...	...	...	9
6 Wholesale and retail trade, restaurants and hotels	...	...	...	...	...	...	...	...	...	...	...	...
7 Transport, storage and communication	...	...	...	...	...	...	...	...	...	...	...	...
8 Finance, insurance, real estate and business services	...	...	...	...	...	...	...	...	...	...	...	...
9 Community, social and personal services	5	...	...	...	...	5	7	...	...	...	...	7
Total, industries of general government	12	...	2	...	...	15	17	...	4	...	...	21
Producers of government services	113	...	...	...	...	113	148	...	...	...	...	148
Total, general government	125	...	2	...	...	128	165	...	4	...	...	169

	1988						1989					
	Compensation of employees	Capital consumption	Net operating surplus	Indirect taxes	less: Subsidies received	Value added	Compensation of employees	Capital consumption	Net operating surplus	Indirect taxes	less: Subsidies received	Value added

All producers

1 Agriculture, hunting, forestry and fishing	36	...	395	3	...	433	55	...	663	4	...	722
A Agriculture and hunting	34	...	296	2	...	332	52	...	502	4	...	558
B Forestry and logging	–	...	32	–	...	33	–	...	48	–	...	49

Ecuador

	1988						1989					
	Compensation of employees	Capital consumption	Net operating surplus	Indirect taxes	less: Subsidies received	Value added	Compensation of employees	Capital consumption	Net operating surplus	Indirect taxes	less: Subsidies received	Value added
C Fishing	1	...	67	–	...	68	2	...	113	–	...	115
2 Mining and quarrying	22	...	144	131	...	297	38	...	249	318	...	605
A Coal mining	...	...	...	...	...	...	...	...	...	...	...	...
B Crude petroleum and natural gas production [a]	15	...	115	131	...	261	27	...	217	318	...	562
C Metal ore mining	...	...	...	...	...	...	...	...	...	...	...	...
D Other mining [b]	7	...	29	–	...	36	11	...	32	–	...	43
3 Manufacturing	64	...	514	66	...	645	93	...	886	110	...	1090
A Manufacture of food, beverages and tobacco	16	...	302	35	...	352	24	...	567	58	...	649
B Textile, wearing apparel and leather industries	17	...	78	8	...	103	24	...	122	13	...	160
C Manufacture of wood and wood products, including furniture	5	...	15	1	...	21	7	...	22	1	...	31
D Manufacture of paper and paper products, printing and publishing	4	...	43	1	...	48	6	...	72	2	...	81
E Manufacture of chemicals and chemical petroleum, coal, rubber and plastic products	7	...	6	8	...	21	9	...	16	13	...	38
F Manufacture of non-metallic mineral products, except products of petroleum and coal	9	...	44	7	...	60	13	...	47	11	...	70
G Basic metal industries												
H Manufacture of fabricated metal products, machinery and equipment	6	...	5	6	...	17	8	...	7	10	...	25
I Other manufacturing industries	1	...	22	1	...	23	1	...	33	1	...	36
4 Electricity, gas and water	12	...	−13	3	...	2	17	...	−17	4	...	4
5 Construction	40	...	96	3	...	140	59	...	172	5	...	236
6 Wholesale and retail trade, restaurants and hotels	44	...	559	8	...	611	63	...	1037	19	...	1119
A Wholesale and retail trade	38	...	546	6	...	590	54	...	1002	15	...	1072
B Restaurants and hotels	6	...	13	2	...	21	9	...	35	4	...	47
7 Transport, storage and communication	31	...	256	10	...	296	46	...	397	18	...	461
A Transport and storage	23	...	258	7	...	289	32	...	397	14	...	443
B Communication	8	...	−3	2	...	8	14	...	–	4	...	18
8 Finance, insurance, real estate and business services	64	...	168	11	...	244	97	...	220	18	...	334
A Financial institutions	55	...	39	2	...	97	84	...	−5	5	...	84
B Insurance												
C Real estate and business services	9	...	129	9	...	147	13	...	225	13	...	251
9 Community, social and personal services	22	...	91	1	...	115	32	...	180	2	...	215
A Sanitary and similar services	...	...	...	...	...	...	...	...	...	...	...	...
B Social and related community services	...	...	...	...	...	...	...	...	...	...	...	...
C Recreational and cultural services	...	...	...	...	...	...	...	...	...	...	...	...
D Personal and household services	22	...	91	1	...	115	32	...	180	2	...	215

Ecuador

	1988						1989					
	Compensation of employees	Capital consumption	Net operating surplus	Indirect taxes	less: Subsidies received	Value added	Compensation of employees	Capital consumption	Net operating surplus	Indirect taxes	less: Subsidies received	Value added
Total, Industries [cd]	335	...	2211	236	...	2782	500	...	3787	498	...	4785
Producers of government services	205	...	...	...	...	205	272	...	...	...	...	272
Other producers	10	...	...	...	...	10	14	...	...	...	...	14
Total [cd]	550	...	2211	236	...	2997	787	...	3787	498	...	5072
less: Imputed bank service charge	...	...	98	...	...	98	...	...	97	...	...	97
Import duties	...	...	...	121	...	121	...	...	...	196	...	196
Value added tax	...	...	...	...	...	...	...	...	...	...	...	...
Other adjustments	...	...	...	...	...	...	...	...	...	...	...	...
Total [cd]	550	...	2113	357	...	3020	787	...	3690	694	...	5170

Of which general government:

	Comp.	Cap.	Net op.	Ind. tax	less Sub	VA	Comp.	Cap.	Net op.	Ind. tax	less Sub	VA
1 Agriculture, hunting, forestry and fishing	...	...	...	...	...	...	...	...	...	...	...	...
2 Mining and quarrying	...	...	...	...	...	...	...	...	...	...	...	...
3 Manufacturing	...	...	...	...	...	...	...	...	...	...	...	...
4 Electricity, gas and water	2	...	4	...	...	6	1	...	−1	...	...	−
5 Construction	17	...	...	...	...	17	23	...	...	...	...	23
6 Wholesale and retail trade, restaurants and hotels	...	...	...	...	...	...	...	...	...	...	...	...
7 Transport, storage and communication	...	...	...	...	...	...	...	...	...	...	...	...
8 Finance, insurance, real estate and business services	...	...	...	...	...	...	...	...	...	...	...	...
9 Community, social and personal services	11	...	...	...	...	11	15	...	...	...	...	15
Total, industries of general government	30	...	4	...	...	34	39	...	−1	...	...	38
Producers of government services	205	...	...	...	...	205	272	...	...	...	...	272
Total, general government	235	...	4	...	...	239	312	...	−1	...	...	311

	1990						1991					
	Compensation of employees	Capital consumption	Net operating surplus	Indirect taxes	less: Subsidies received	Value added	Compensation of employees	Capital consumption	Net operating surplus	Indirect taxes	less: Subsidies received	Value added

All producers

1 Agriculture, hunting, forestry and fishing	80	...	1015	5	...	1100	116	...	1635	10	...	1762
A Agriculture and hunting	76	...	753	5	...	834	111	...	1227	9	...	1347
B Forestry and logging	1	...	76	−	...	77	1	...	116	1	...	118
C Fishing	3	...	186	−	...	189	4	...	292	−	...	296
2 Mining and quarrying	61	...	610	547	...	1218	93	...	715	559	...	1368
A Coal mining	...	...	...	...	...	...	...	...	...	...	...	...
B Crude petroleum and natural gas production [a]	47	...	559	547	...	1153	73	...	662	559	...	1294
C Metal ore mining	...	...	...	...	...	...	...	...	...	...	...	...
D Other mining [b]	14	...	51	−	...	65	20	...	53	−	...	73
3 Manufacturing	126	...	1400	62	...	1588	176	...	2257	122	...	2554
A Manufacture of food, beverages and tobacco	31	...	928	54	...	1013	42	...	1470	110	...	1622
B Textile, wearing apparel and leather industries	34	...	157	2	...	193	49	...	221	4	...	274

Ecuador

	1990						1991					
	Compensation of employees	Capital consumption	Net operating surplus	Indirect taxes	less: Subsidies received	Value added	Compensation of employees	Capital consumption	Net operating surplus	Indirect taxes	less: Subsidies received	Value added
C Manufacture of wood and wood products, including furniture	10	...	19	1	...	30	14	...	31	1	...	46
D Manufacture of paper and paper products, printing and publishing	8	...	128	1	...	137	11	...	260	1	...	272
E Manufacture of chemicals and chemical petroleum, coal, rubber and plastic products	13	...	14	1	...	28	18	...	18	2	...	38
F Manufacture of non-metallic mineral products, except products of petroleum and coal	17	...	97	2	...	116	23	...	163	3	...	189
G Basic metal industries												
H Manufacture of fabricated metal products, machinery and equipment	11	...	5	1	...	17	15	...	13	1	...	29
I Other manufacturing industries	2	...	52	–	...	54	3	...	81	–	...	84
4 Electricity, gas and water	23	...	–40	2	...	–15	33	...	–49	3	...	–13
5 Construction	80	...	245	4	...	329	111	...	439	6	...	556
6 Wholesale and retail trade, restaurants and hotels	83	...	1632	21	...	1736	117	...	2569	37	...	2723
A Wholesale and retail trade	71	...	1533	20	...	1624	100	...	2419	36	...	2555
B Restaurants and hotels	12	...	99	1	...	112	17	...	150	1	...	168
7 Transport, storage and communication	63	...	628	17	...	708	93	...	951	20	...	1064
A Transport and storage	45	...	623	7	...	675	64	...	944	7	...	1015
B Communication	18	...	5	10	...	33	29	...	7	13	...	49
8 Finance, insurance, real estate and business services	148	...	330	23	...	501	234	...	588	34	...	857
A Financial institutions	131	...	–16	8	...	124	209	...	25	6	...	240
B Insurance												
C Real estate and business services	17	...	346	15	...	378	25	...	563	28	...	616
9 Community, social and personal services	45	...	284	2	...	331	62	...	470	4	...	537
A Sanitary and similar services	...	...	...	...	...	...	...	...	...	...	...	...
B Social and related community services	...	...	...	...	...	...	...	...	...	...	...	...
C Recreational and cultural services	...	...	...	...	...	...	...	...	...	...	...	...
D Personal and household services	45	...	284	3	...	331	62	...	470	4	...	536
Total, Industries [cd]	709	...	6104	683	...	7496	1035	...	9578	795	...	11408
Producers of government services	387	...	...	...	...	387	504	...	...	...	...	504
Other producers	19	...	...	...	...	19	26	...	...	...	...	26
Total [cd]	1115	...	6104	683	...	7902	1565	...	9578	795	...	11938
less: Imputed bank service charge	...	...	149	...	...	149	...	...	288	...	...	288
Import duties	...	...	...	215	...	215	...	...	...	280	...	280
Value added tax	...	...	...	234	...	234	...	...	...	366	...	366
Other adjustments	...	...	...	...	...	...	...	...	...	...	...	...
Total [cd]	1115	...	5955	1132	...	8202	1565	...	9290	1441	...	12296

Ecuador

	1990						1991					
	Compensation of employees	Capital consumption	Net operating surplus	Indirect taxes	less: Subsidies received	Value added	Compensation of employees	Capital consumption	Net operating surplus	Indirect taxes	less: Subsidies received	Value added

Of which general government:

1 Agriculture, hunting, forestry and fishing	...	...	...	...	...	...	...	...	...	...	...	...
2 Mining and quarrying	...	...	...	...	...	...	...	...	...	...	...	...
3 Manufacturing	...	...	...	...	...	...	...	...	...	...	...	...
4 Electricity, gas and water	2	...	–2	...	...	—	2	...	–2	...	...	2
5 Construction	35	...	...	...	...	35	47	...	...	...	...	47
6 Wholesale and retail trade, restaurants and hotels	...	...	...	...	...	...	...	...	...	...	...	...
7 Transport, storage and communication	...	...	...	...	...	...	...	...	...	...	...	...
8 Finance, insurance, real estate and business services	...	...	...	...	...	...	...	...	...	...	...	...
9 Community, social and personal services	23	...	...	...	...	23	36	...	...	...	...	36
Total, industries of general government	60	...	–2	...	...	58	85	...	–2	...	...	83
Producers of government services	387	...	...	...	...	387	504	...	...	...	...	504
Total, general government	446	...	–2	...	...	445	589	...	–2	...	...	587

	1992						1993					
	Compensation of employees	Capital consumption	Net operating surplus	Indirect taxes	less: Subsidies received	Value added	Compensation of employees	Capital consumption	Net operating surplus	Indirect taxes	less: Subsidies received	Value added

All producers

1 Agriculture, hunting, forestry and fishing	204	...	2244	17	...	2465	380	...	2924	18	...	3322
A Agriculture and hunting	196	...	1605	16	...	1817	365	...	2089	17	...	2471
B Forestry and logging	1	...	191	1	...	193	2	...	283	1	...	286
C Fishing	7	...	448	—	...	455	12	...	553	...	...	565
2 Mining and quarrying	120	...	1311	1009	...	2440	142	...	1414	1386	...	2942
A Coal mining	...	...	...	...	...	...	...	...	...	...	...	...
B Crude petroleum and natural gas production [a]	90	...	1233	1009	...	2332	90	...	1306	1386	...	2782
C Metal ore mining	...	...	...	...	...	...	...	...	...	...	...	...
D Other mining [b]	30	...	78	—	...	108	52	...	108	...	...	160
3 Manufacturing	261	...	3830	190	...	4281	438	...	5270	257	...	5965
A Manufacture of food, beverages and tobacco	64	...	2479	171	...	2714	107	...	3365	236	...	3708
B Textile, wearing apparel and leather industries	73	...	339	6	...	418	124	...	465	7	...	596
C Manufacture of wood and wood products, including furniture	22	...	56	2	...	80	37	...	70	2	...	109
D Manufacture of paper and paper products, printing and publishing	16	...	505	3	...	523	26	...	714	2	...	742
E Manufacture of chemicals and chemical petroleum, coal, rubber and plastic products	24	...	45	4	...	72	46	...	43	3	...	92
F Manufacture of non-metallic mineral products, except products of petroleum and coal	35	...	278	1	...	317	56	...	429	5	...	490

Ecuador

	1992						1993					
	Compensation of employees	Capital consumption	Net operating surplus	Indirect taxes	less: Subsidies received	Value added	Compensation of employees	Capital consumption	Net operating surplus	Indirect taxes	less: Subsidies received	Value added
G Basic metal industries												
H Manufacture of fabricated metal products, machinery and equipment	23	...	10	1	...	34	36	...	24	1	...	61
I Other manufacturing industries	4	...	118	1	...	123	6	...	160	1	...	167
4 Electricity, gas and water	45	...	−27	4	...	22	61	...	10	5	...	76
A Electricity, gas and steam	...	...	...	...	...	...	61	...	10	5	...	76
B Water works and supply	...	...	...	...	...	...	...	...	...	...	...	...
5 Construction	161	...	712	8	...	881	266	...	1065	9	...	1340
6 Wholesale and retail trade, restaurants and hotels	175	...	3938	55	...	4168	274	...	5272	4	...	5550
A Wholesale and retail trade	148	...	3667	54	...	3869	228	...	4865	3	...	5096
B Restaurants and hotels	27	...	271	1	...	299	46	...	407	1	...	454
7 Transport, storage and communication	133	...	1358	14	...	1505	200	...	2251	−2	...	2449
A Transport and storage	91	...	1344	−3	...	1432	128	...	2208	−28	...	2308
B Communication	42	...	14	17	...	73	72	...	43	26	...	141
8 Finance, insurance, real estate and business services	405	...	933	53	...	1393	1227	...	509	146	...	2255
A Financial institutions	370	...	6	12	...	388	614	...	69	47	...	730
B Insurance												
C Real estate and business services	36	...	927	41	...	1004	613	...	813	99	...	1525
9 Community, social and personal services	102	...	836	5	...	943	169	...	1394	1	...	1564
A Sanitary and similar services	...	...	...	...	...	...	...	...	...	...	...	...
B Social and related community services	...	...	...	...	...	...	...	...	...	...	...	...
C Recreational and cultural services	...	...	...	...	...	...	...	...	...	...	...	...
D Personal and household services	102	...	836	5	...	943	169	...	1394	1	...	1564
Statistical discrepancy	...	...	...	...	...	...	...	...	...	...	...	7
Total, Industries [cd]	1606	...	15135	1355	...	18098	3157	...	20090	1824	...	25470
Producers of government services	813	...	...	...	...	813	1309	...	...	...	...	1309
Other producers	40	...	...	...	...	40	65	...	...	...	...	65
Total [cd]	2459	...	15135	1355	...	18951	3968	...	21090	1784	...	26844
less: Imputed bank service charge	...	...	490	...	...	490	...	...	878	...	...	878
Import duties	...	...	...	339	...	339	...	...	...	537	...	537
Value added tax	...	...	...	612	...	612	...	...	...	949	...	949
Other adjustments	...	...	...	...	...	...	...	...	...	...	...	...
Total [cd]	2459	...	14645	2306	...	19412	3968	...	20212	3272	...	27452

Of which general government:

1 Agriculture, hunting, forestry and fishing	...	...	...	...	...	...	...	...	...	...	...	...
2 Mining and quarrying	...	...	...	...	...	...	...	...	...	...	...	...
3 Manufacturing	...	...	...	...	...	...	...	...	...	...	...	...
4 Electricity, gas and water	2	...	−2	...	...	...	2	...	−3	...	...	...
5 Construction	74	...	...	...	...	74	112	...	...	...	...	112
6 Wholesale and retail trade, restaurants and hotels	...	...	...	...	...	...	...	...	...	...	...	...

Ecuador

	1992							1993						
	Compensation of employees	Capital consumption	Net operating surplus	Indirect taxes	less: Subsidies received	Value added	Compensation of employees	Capital consumption	Net operating surplus	Indirect taxes	less: Subsidies received	Value added
7 Transport, storage and communication	...	...	...	...	...	...	...	...	...	...	...	...
8 Finance, insurance, real estate and business services	...	...	...	...	...	...	...	...	...	...	...	...
9 Community, social and personal services	64	...	...	...	...	64	99	...	...	...	...	99
Total, industries of general government	140	...	–2	...	...	138	214	...	–3	...	...	211
Producers of government services	813	...	...	...	...	813	1309	...	...	...	...	1309
Total, general government	953	...	–2	...	...	951	1523	...	–3	...	...	1520

a Petroleum refining is included in item "Crude petroleum and natural gas production".
b Items "Coal mining" and "Metal ore mining" are included in item "Other mining".
c Column 4 refers to indirect taxes less subsidies received.
d Column "Consumption of fixed capital" is included in column "Net operating surplus".

Egypt

General note

The preparation of national accounts statistics in Egypt is undertaken by the Central Agency for Public Mobilization and Statistics (CAPMAS), Cairo. Official estimates are published in the annual *Statistical Yearbook* published by the same agency. The estimates are generally in accordance with the classifications and definitions recommended in the United Nations System of National Accounts (1968 SNA). The following tables have been prepared from successive replies to the United Nations National Accounts Questionnaire. When the scope and coverage of the estimates differ for conceptual or statistical reasons from the definitions and classifications recommended in SNA, a footnote is indicated to the relevant tables.

Gross domestic product

Gross domestic product is estimated mainly through the production approach.

Expenditures on the gross domestic product

All components of gross domestic product by expenditure type are estimated through the expenditure approach. The estimates of government final consumption expenditure are based on government budgets and accounts. For private consumption expenditures, the estimates are based on family budgets and household expenditure surveys. CAPMAS prepares data on inventories of cotton, covering both commercial stocks and stocks of spinning industry. Other sources of information for changes in stocks include data collected regularly by the Ministry of Supply. For gross fixed capital formation, the government sector is estimated directly together with government consumption expenditure. The private sector estimate is obtained by deducting the government estimate from total capital formation. Capital formation in machinery and equipment is estimated through the commodity-flow approach using information on domestic production, imports and exports of capital goods. The estimates of exports and imports of merchandise are generally based on foreign trade statistics. The estimates of GDP by expenditure type in constant prices are prepared on the basis of official index numbers of prices and quantities.

Cost structure of the gross domestic product

The estimates of wages and salaries are based on government accounts and on various sectoral surveys. No specific information is available for operating surplus, which is computed as a gross estimate, i.e., including consumption of fixed capital. Indirect taxes and subsidies are separately available for all economic units in the compulsory standard accounts for public enterprises and in the economic surveys for the private sector.

Gross domestic product by kind of activity

The table of gross domestic product by kind of economic activity is prepared in factor values. The production approach is used to estimate value added of most industries. The income approach is used to estimate value added of community, social and personal services. The Ministry of Agriculture collects, through annual sample surveys, data on crop area, yield and crop-cutting. Livestock data are obtained through special censuses every two years and prices received by farmers are collected annually. The estimated acreage of each of the main crops is multiplied by average productivity of the basic area of measurement. The gross output is evaluated at farm-gate prices and estimates of intermediate consumption are based on data collected from the co-operative societies and from censuses. For the industrial activity sector, annual statistics on industrial production, capital formation, employment, wages and salaries are available for industrial establishments with ten workers or more which form the organized sector of the economy. For the non-organized sector, estimates are made by using data from industrial censuses and by studying the cost-structure of each industry, productivity and degree of mechanization.

The output of construction is estimated indirectly from the input side by means of employment data and data on intermediate consumption. The value of gross output and components of value added are obtained by using the relationship between available data on intermediate consumption and primary inputs in organized enterprises and applying this relationship on the estimated intermediate consumption of this industry. For trade, annual basic statistics are available for establishments with five or more workers, while those with less than five workers are covered by sample surveys conducted every three years. Estimates for restaurants are made by using data on establishments, wages and salaries, working hours and data from sample surveys. Estimates for hotels are obtained through annual questionnaires. Data on input, output and other elements of large-scale transport are available through annual accounts. For unorganized transport, estimates are based on information on the number of establishments and workers, on wages and salaries and on other sources. Indicators such as input ratios are used to estimate value added. Gross output and input of public financial institutions and insurance companies are based on data collected annually. The estimates of real estate, business services, and imputed rents of owner-occupied dwellings are based on family budget surveys. The government accounts provide information to estimate government services. Annual data are available for non-profit institutions serving households. For the service activities of unincorpo-

Egypt

rated enterprises, gross output and inputs are estimated by using available censuses of establishments, wages and salaries statistics.

The constant prices of GDP by kind of economic activity are estimated on the basis of official index numbers of prices and quantities such as wholesale prices, consumer prices and quantities of imported and exported merchandise.

1.1 Expenditure on the gross domestic product, in current prices

Million Egyptian pounds — Fiscal year beginning 1 July

	1986	1987	1988	1989	1990	1991	1992	1993	1994	1995	1996	1997
1 Government final consumption expenditure	6632	7728	8621	9671	11010	12130	...	...	...	...	...	...
2 Private final consumption expenditure	34800	42317	50653	62911	84048	110026	...	...	...	...	...	...
3 Gross capital formation	15778	22076	23614	27335	23964	24617	...	...	...	...	...	...
A Increase in stocks	1526	1919	3405	4845	−655	200	...	...	...	...	...	...
B Gross fixed capital formation	14252	20157	20209	22490	24619	24417	...	...	...	...	...	...
4 Exports of goods and services	6476	10688	13741	19274	30943	40122	...	...	...	...	...	...
5 less: Imports of goods and services	11740	21699	24843	31450	39822	50705	...	...	...	...	...	...
equals: Gross domestic product [a]	51946	61109	71785	87741	110143	136190	...	...	...	...	...	...

a Data in this table have not been revised, therefore they are not comparable with the data in other tables.

1.10 Gross domestic product by kind of activity, in current prices

Million Egyptian pounds — Fiscal year beginning 1 July

	1986	1987	1988	1989	1990	1991	1992	1993	1994	1995	1996	1997
1 Agriculture, hunting, forestry and fishing	10111	11216	13046	15834	17823	20675	...	...	...	...	...	...
2 Mining and quarrying [a]	1873	2589	2408	3921	10986	13342	...	...	...	...	...	...
3 Manufacturing	8137	10633	12675	14669	17417	21409	...	...	...	...	...	...
4 Electricity, gas and water [b]	528	675	775	1033	1435	2009	...	...	...	...	...	...
5 Construction	2822	3242	3804	4490	5226	6076	...	...	...	...	...	...
6 Wholesale and retail trade, restaurants and hotels	11306	12849	14787	17832	21744	26658	...	...	...	...	...	...
7 Transport, storage and communication	4043	5004	5873	7484	10822	14172	...	...	...	...	...	...
8 Finance, insurance, real estate and business services	851	971	1101	1285	1475	1677	...	...	...	...	...	...
9 Community, social and personal services [c]	9094	11207	12785	14793	16416	19467	...	...	...	...	...	...
Total, Industries	48765	58386	67254	81341	103344	125485	...	...	...	...	...	...
Producers of government services	4549	...	...	...	...	...	...	...	...	...	...	...
Other producers	...	...	...	...	...	...	...	...	...	...	...	...
Subtotal [d]	48765	58386	67254	81341	103344	125485	...	...	...	...	...	...
less: Imputed bank service charge	...	...	...	...	...	...	...	...	...	...	...	...
plus: Import duties	...	...	...	...	...	...	...	...	...	...	...	...
plus: Value added tax	...	...	...	...	...	...	...	...	...	...	...	...
plus: Other adjustments [e]	3181	2723	4532	6400	6799	10705	...	...	...	...	...	...
equals: Gross domestic product	51946	61109	71785	87741	110143	136190	...	...	...	...	...	...

a Item "Mining and quarrying" refers to oil and its products.
b Item "Electricity, gas and water" refers to electricity only. Gas and water are included in item "Community, social and personal services".
c Item "Other producers" is included in item "Community, social and personal services".
d Gross domestic product in factor values.
e Item "Other adjustments" refers to indirect taxes net of subsidies.

Egypt

1.11 Gross domestic product by kind of activity, in constant prices

Million Egyptian pounds — Fiscal year beginning 1 July

	1986	1987	1988	1989	1990	1991	1992	1993	1994	1995	1996	1997
At constant prices of:	1981 / 1986 / 1991 / 1996											
1 Agriculture, hunting, forestry and fishing	4670 / 8640	8903	9141	9440	9820	21680	22220	23072	23741	24470	42325	43968
2 Mining and quarrying	3867	—	—	—	...	...	...	...	...	...	...	...
3 Manufacturing	4129 / 8676	9303	9771	10292	10863	34738	35570	37640	39452	41335	59237	63634
4 Electricity, gas and water [a]	241 / 518	557	600	648	724	2220	2296	2382	2525	2658	4220	4608
5 Construction	1242 / 1989	2117	2256	2381	2514	6735	6800	7079	7485	7898	12750	13707
6 Wholesale and retail trade, restaurants and hotels [b]	3728 / 10045	10498	10601	11804	12062	28771	29634	30480	32456	34558	54857	58715
7 Transport, storage and communication	2840 / 3756	3977	4279	4678	4992	14835	14860	15112	15422	16116	22695	23860
8 Finance, insurance, real estate and business services [c]	2500 / 820	898	983	1104	1258	12646	2878	3027	3207	3351	5290	5638
9 Community, social and personal services [d]	1303 / 1842	1922	2018	2112	2225	22078	22955	23857	25068	26334	43416	45760
Statistical discrepancy	299	...	...	...	...	...	...	...	...	...	...	...
Total, Industries	24817	...	...	...	...	...	...	...	...	...	...	...
Producers of government services	4599	4894	5170	5451	5719	87	9832	10217	10667	11150	19061	20092
Other producers	...	...	...	...	...	...	...	...	...	...	...	...
Subtotal [e]	27957 / 40885	43069	45419	47911	50177	131057	134335	139622	146149	153369	239500	254252
less: Imputed bank service charge	...	...	...	...	...	...	...	...	...	...	...	...

Egypt

Million Egyptian pounds												**Fiscal year beginning 1 July**
	1986	1987	1988	1989	1990	1991	1992	1993	1994	1995	1996	1997
At constant prices of: 1981												
1986												
1991												
1996												
plus: Import duties	...	...	...	...	...	...	...	...	...	...	...	...
plus: Value added tax	...	...	...	...	...	...	...	...	...	...	...	...
plus: Other adjustments	...	...	...	...	...	...	...	...	...	...	...	...
equals: Gross domestic product	...	...	...	...	...	...	...	...	...	...	...	...

a Item "Electricity, gas and water" refers to electricity only. Gas and water are included in item "Community, social and personal services".
b Includes finance and insurance.
c Includes gas and water.
d Item "Other producers" is included in item "Community, social and personal services".
e Gross domestic product in factor values.

El Salvador

General note

The preparation of national accounts statistics in El Salvador is undertaken by the Departamento de Investigaciones Económicas del Banco Central, San Salvador. The official estimates are published monthly in *Revista Mensual*. A detailed description of the sources and methods used for the national accounts estimation is contained in *Metodología de Cuentas Nacionales de los Países Centroamericanos* published by the Consejo Monetario Centroamericano Secretaría Ejecutiva in October 1976. The estimates are generally in accordance with the classifications and definitions recommended in the United Nations System of National Accounts (1968 SNA). The following tables have been prepared from successive replies to the United Nations National Accounts Questionnaire. When the scope and coverage of the estimates differ for conceptual or statistical reasons from the definitions and classifications recommended in SNA, a footnote is indicated to the relevant tables.

Gross domestic product

Gross domestic product is estimated mainly through the production approach.

Expenditures on the gross domestic product

The expenditure approach is used to estimate government final consumption expenditure, increase in stocks, and exports and imports of goods and services. The commodity-flow approach supplemented by the expenditure approach is used for private final consumption expenditure and gross fixed capital formation. The estimates of government consumption expenditure are obtained directly from government sources. For private consumption expenditure, the commodity-flow approach is used with adjustments made for distribution and other costs which are included in the retail value. The estimates of increase in stocks are based on information on stored agricultural products, the stocks of the manufacturing and trade industries and the stocks of public construction. Private capital formation is estimated on the basis of data on domestically produced and imported capital goods and on statistics of construction and repair work. The imports data are adjusted to include import duties, trade margins and installation costs. For public expenditure on capital formation, data are obtained from official sources. Data on exports and imports of goods and services are obtained from the balance of payments. Export data on coffee are obtained from the Compañía Salvadoreña de Café, while other merchandise data are furnished by the Dirección General de Estadística y Censos. Gross domestic product by expenditure at constant prices is not estimated.

Cost structure of the gross domestic product

Compensation of employees, combined with operating surplus, is obtained as a residual. The estimates of net indirect taxes are derived from the government accounts. No specific information is available on how consumption of fixed capital is estimated.

Gross domestic product by kind of activity

The table of gross domestic product by kind of economic activity is prepared at market prices, i.e. producers values. The production approach is used to estimate value added of most industries. The income approach is used for domestic services and public administration and defence while an indirect method is used for the trade sector. The agricultural data, which are provided by Ministerio de Agricultura y Ganadería, are obtained through various periodic surveys. Data on the coffee harvest are supplied by the Compañía Salvadoreña de Café while coffee prices are taken from the Compañía de Café's export prices. Information on the production of cotton is provided by the Cooperativa Algodonera Salvadoreña Ltda. The gross value of production is calculated by applying producers' prices to the quantity of each commodity produced. For the livestock sector, information is obtained from the Dirección General de Estadística y Censos, external trade data and through direct studies on prices. Value added of forestry and logging is estimated by means of indirect methods. For the mining and quarrying sector, the estimates are based on 1961 census figures combined with a volume index constructed from square-meter construction data and on price index.

The gross value of production in manufacturing is based on the results of annual surveys and industrial censuses held every five years. Estimates for small-scale manufacturing is extrapolated from census data. The estimates for electricity are based on industrial census results and on information furnished by the concerned agencies. For private construction, the information is obtained from the Dirección General de Estadística y Censos. The basic sources include permits issued for urban construction. Rural population figures are used to determine the number of new dwellings in rural areas. The estimates for public construction are obtained from concerned institutions. For both public and private constructions, intermediate consumption is determined by using a fixed percentage of gross value of production. Gross output of the trade sector is determined on the basis of the values of domestic and imported goods marketed. The gross value of production of domestic goods and the c.i.f. values of imported goods are adjusted for changes in stocks and trade margin are added. An estimate of inputs, which is made from survey based on percentages for electricity, transport, etc., is

El Salvador

deducted from the total gross value of production to arrive at value added. Estimates of restaurants and hotels are interpolated and extrapolated on the basis of census figures.

The enterprises concerned with road transport are classified into international, inter-departmental, urban and interurban transport. A sample from each category is taken in order to obtain average figures for estimating receipts per ton, which are multiplied by quantity figures to arrive at gross value of production and value added. For railways, air transport and communication, information is obtained directly from concerned companies. The estimates of the financial sector are based on financial statements furnished by the banks and insurance companies. Imputation is made for service charges by deducting interest from investment income. The estimate of ownership of dwellings are based on the number of urban and rural dwellings obtained from the population censuses and rents data from surveys, and using the cost of living index as an inflator. Ten per cent of the gross value of production are deducted for inputs. The estimates of government services are based on information published by the Ministerio de Hacienda. For other services such as education, hospitals, religion, the estimates are obtained from concerned institutions or from publications such as Indicadores Económicas and Boletín Estadistico. For domestic services, the annual average wages for four regional areas of the country are applied to an estimate of the number of persons engaged. The latter is based on the 1961 census figures and average growth rates while the wage is estimated annually, applying the cost of living index.

For the constant price estimates, value added for the agricultural, electricity, trade, transport and financial sectors is estimated by using volume or quantity indexes. Double deflation is used for the manufacturing sector. Price deflation is used for mining and quarrying, construction, restaurants and hotels and government services. For domestic services, wages paid in the base year are applied to the number employed in the current year.

1.1 Expenditure on the gross domestic product, in current prices

Million Salvadoran colones

	1986	1987	1988	1989	1990	1991	1992	1993	1994	1995	1996	1997
1 Government final consumption expenditure	2803	3181	3484	3930	3618	4236	4670	5237	5762	...	...	...
2 Private final consumption expenditure	15206	18744	22153	26729	32435	37463	44082	52781	61685	...	...	...
3 Gross capital formation	2619	2861	3501	4940	5058	6563	9235	11270	13977	...	...	...
A Increase in stocks	26	−297	45	646	54	107	673	452	768	...	...	...
B Gross fixed capital formation	2594	3158	3456	4293	5004	6456	8562	10818	13209	...	...	...
Residential buildings	537	637	644	841	...	...	...	...	...	...	...	...
Non-residential buildings	110	146	231	181	...	...	...	...	...	...	...	...
Other construction and land improvement, etc.	425	633	781	938	...	...	...	...	...	...	...	...
Other	1522	1742	1800	2333	...	...	...	...	...	...	...	...
4 Exports of goods and services	4875	4395	4327	4267	6770	7332	8019	11822	14104	...	...	...
5 less: Imports of goods and services	5740	6040	6099	7636	11394	13000	16165	20588	24915	...	...	...
equals: Gross domestic product	19763	23141	27366	32230	36487	42594	49841	60522	70613	...	...	...

1.2 Expenditure on the gross domestic product, in constant prices

Million Salvadoran colones

	1986	1987	1988	1989	1990	1991	1992	1993	1994	1995	1996	1997
At constant prices of: 1962												
1990												
1 Government final consumption expenditure	511	526	539	533	538					...	...	...
					3618	3731	3763	3815	3915			
2 Private final consumption expenditure	2245	2259	2275	2330	2377					...	...	...
					32435	33422	36195	39331	42602			
3 Gross capital formation	385	368	446	551	390					...	...	...
					5058	5932	7602	8314	9423			
A Increase in stocks	5	−46	16	81	2					...	...	...
					54	120	736	439	629			
B Gross fixed capital formation	380	415	430	469	388					...	...	...
					5004	5812	6866	7875	8794			
4 Exports of goods and services	566	637	577	499	719					...	...	...
					6770	6738	7176	9225	9787			

El Salvador

Million Salvadoran colones

	1986	1987	1988	1989	1990	1991	1992	1993	1994	1995	1996	1997
	At constant prices of: 1962											
			1990									
5 less: Imports of goods and services	694	697	693	735	738					...	...	...
					11394	12032	14093	17042	19476			
equals: Gross domestic product ..	3013	3094	3144	3177	3285					...	...	...
					36487	37791	40643	43643	46251			

1.3 Cost components of the gross domestic product

Million Salvadoran colones

	1986	1987	1988	1989	1990	1991	1992	1993	1994	1995	1996	1997
1 Indirect taxes, net	2014	1764	1680	1649	2285	2847	3609	4678	...	...	...	...
A Indirect taxes	2056	1806	1724	1699	2337	2867	3636	4700	...	...	...	...
B less: Subsidies	42	42	44	50	52	20	27	22	...	...	...	...
2 Consumption of fixed capital	815	955	1129	1329	...	...	...	...	...	...	...	...
3 Compensation of employees paid by resident producers to ..	16934	20422	24557	29252	12425	13831	15427	19352	...	...	...	...
4 Operating surplus					21778	25916	30805	36492	...	...	...	...
equals: Gross domestic product ..	19763	23141	27366	32230	36487	42594	49841	60522	...	...	...	...

1.4 General government current receipts and disbursements

Million Salvadoran colones

	1986	1987	1988	1989	1990	1991	1992	1993	1994	1995	1996	1997
Receipts												
1 Operating surplus	...	...	...	...	−5	2	15	...	...	...	...	...
2 Property and entrepreneurial income	...	...	...	...	358	411	450	...	...	...	...	...
3 Taxes, fees and contributions .	...	...	...	...	4177	5209	6525	...	...	...	...	...
A Indirect taxes	...	...	...	...	2337	2867	3636	...	...	...	...	...
B Direct taxes	...	...	...	...	951	1273	1656	...	...	...	...	...
C Social security contributions	...	...	...	...	793	934	1028	...	...	...	...	...
D Compulsory fees, fines and penalties	...	...	...	...	96	135	205	...	...	...	...	...
4 Other current transfers	...	...	...	...	834	1235	1936	...	...	...	...	...
Total current receipts of general government	...	...	...	...	5364	6857	8926	...	...	...	...	...
Disbursements												
1 Government final consumption expenditure	...	...	...	...	3618	4236	4670	...	...	...	...	...
2 Property income	...	...	...	...	473	543	1075	...	...	...	...	...
3 Subsidies	...	...	...	...	52	20	27	...	...	...	...	...
4 Other current transfers	...	...	...	...	768	...	...	...	...	...	...	...
A Social security benefits	...	...	...	...	224	...	...	...	...	...	...	...
B Social assistance grants	...	...	...	...	534	...	...	...	...	...	...	...
C Other	...	...	...	...	10	...	...	...	...	...	...	...
5 Net saving	...	...	...	...	454	...	...	...	...	...	...	...
Total current disbursements and net saving of general government	...	...	...	...	5364	...	...	...	...	...	...	...

El Salvador

1.7 External transactions on current account, summary

Million Salvadoran colones	1986	1987	1988	1989	1990	1991	1992	1993	1994	1995	1996	1997
Payments to the rest of the world												
1 Imports of goods and services	5740	6040	6099	7636	11394	13000	16165	20588	24915	...	...	...
A Imports of merchandise, c.i.f.	4674	4972	5035	6503	9594	11276	14216	18582	22523	...	...	...
B Other	1066	1068	1064	1133	1800	1724	1950	2006	2393	...	...	...
2 Factor income to rest of the world	675	721	710	757	1084	1376	1781	1272	1173	...	...	...
3 Current transfers to the rest of the world	12	12	12	12	164	123	124	22	22	...	...	...
4 Surplus of the nation on current transactions	583	696	262	−988	−1567	−1541	−2197	−667	−371	...	...	...
Payments to the rest of the world and surplus of the nation on current transfers	7011	7469	7082	7417	11075	12958	15874	21215	25739	...	...	...
Receipts from the rest of the world												
1 Exports of goods and services	4875	4395	4327	4267	6770	7332	8019	11822	14104	...	...	...
A Exports of merchandise, f.o.b.	3775	2955	3044	2786	4419	4716	5001	8930	10931	...	...	...
B Other	1101	1440	1283	1481	2351	2616	3018	2892	3173	...	...	...
2 Factor income from rest of the world	203	196	200	230	114	230	175	293	368	...	...	...
3 Current transfers from rest of the world	1932	2878	2555	2921	4191	5396	7680	9100	11267	...	...	...
Receipts from the rest of the world on current transactions	7011	7469	7082	7418	11075	12958	15874	21215	25739	...	...	...

1.8 Capital transactions of the nation, summary

Million Salvadoran colones	1986	1987	1988	1989	1990	1991	1992	1993	1994	1995	1996	1997
Finance of gross capital formation												
Gross saving	3202	3556	3763	3952	3490	5021	7038	10603	13606	...	...	...
1 Consumption of fixed capital	815	955	1129	1329	...	...	...	...	...	...	...	...
A General government	...	...	...	...	454	966	1930	...	...	...	...	...
B Corporate and quasi-corporate enterprises	...	...	...	...	3036	4055	5108	...	...	...	...	...
Public	...	...	...	...	490	305	449	...	...	...	...	...
Private	...	...	...	...	2546	3750	4659	...	...	...	...	...
C Other	...	...	...	...	...	...	...	...	...	...	...	...
2 Net saving	2387	2601	2634	2623	...	...	...	...	...	...	...	...
less: Surplus of the nation on current transactions	583	696	262	−988	−1567	−1541	−2197	−667	−371	...	...	...
Finance of gross capital formation	2619	2861	3501	4940	5057	6563	9235	11270	13977	...	...	...
Gross capital formation												
Increase in stocks	26	−297	45	646	54	107	673	...	...	...	...	...
Gross fixed capital formation	2594	3158	3456	4293	5003	6456	8562	...	...	...	...	...
1 General government	90	103	129	256	475	620	712	...	...	...	...	...
2 Corporate and quasi-corporate enterprises	2504	3055	3327	4037	4528	5835	7850	...	...	...	...	...

El Salvador

Million Salvadoran colones	1986	1987	1988	1989	1990	1991	1992	1993	1994	1995	1996	1997
A Public	...	...	...	...	486	390	2147	...	...	...	...	...
B Private	...	...	...	...	4042	5445	5703	...	...	...	...	...
3 Other	...	...	...	...	...	...	...	...	...	...	...	...
Gross capital formation	2619	2861	3501	4940	5057	6563	9235	11270	13977	...	...	...

1.10 Gross domestic product by kind of activity, in current prices

Million Salvadoran colones	1986	1987	1988	1989	1990	1991	1992	1993	1994	1995	1996	1997
1 Agriculture, hunting, forestry and fishing	3969	3199	3801	3767	6240	7292	7090	8431	9847	...	...	...
2 Mining and quarrying	27	38	47	58	138	167	198	247	328	...	...	...
3 Manufacturing	3086	4045	4808	5836	7923	9410	11876	13549	15775	...	...	...
4 Electricity, gas and water	418	497	535	606	426	307	464	604	739	...	...	...
5 Construction	547	711	815	984	1268	1476	2199	2642	3258	...	...	...
6 Wholesale and retail trade, restaurants and hotels [a]	5627	7275	8721	10831	6621	8032	9429	11304	13736	...	...	...
7 Transport, storage and communication	816	1061	1206	1416	2678	2839	3822	4539	5283	...	...	...
8 Finance, insurance, real estate and business services	1503	1822	2299	2688	6197	7074	8117	9328	10666	...	...	...
9 Community, social and personal services [bc]	1794	2286	2749	3330	2241	2711	3245	3685	4266	...	...	...
Statistical discrepancy	...	...	...	...	...	...	...	...	−406	...	...	...
Total, Industries	17786	20934	24981	29516	33732	39308	46440	54328	63492	...	...	...
Producers of government services	1977	2207	2385	2714	2693	3094	3311	3777	4185	...	...	...
Other producers	...	...	...	...	...	...	...	...	...	...	...	...
Subtotal	19763	23141	27366	32230	36425	42402	49751	58104	67677	...	...	...
less: Imputed bank service charge	...	...	...	...	609	780	1073	1446	1730	...	...	...
plus: Import duties	...	...	...	...	...	...	...	...	...	...	...	...
plus: Value added tax	...	...	...	...	672	972	1163	3864	4666	...	...	...
plus: Other adjustments	...	...	...	...	...	...	...	...	...	...	...	...
equals: Gross domestic product	19763	23141	27366	32230	36487	42594	49841	60522	70613	...	...	...

a Restaurants and hotels are included in item "Community, social and personal services".
b Refers to all other services.
c Beginning 1990, relates to rents of owner-occupied dwellings.

1.11 Gross domestic product by kind of activity, in constant prices

Million Salvadoran colones	1986	1987	1988	1989	1990	1991	1992	1993	1994	1995	1996	1997
At constant prices of: 1962 / 1990												
1 Agriculture, hunting, forestry and fishing	720	735	728	731	785 / 6240	6223	6723	6550	6393	...	...	...
2 Mining and quarrying	4	5	5	5	5 / 138	151	159	176	195	...	...	...
3 Manufacturing	528	544	560	574	592 / 7923	8392	9219	9079	9740	...	...	...
4 Electricity, gas and water	116	118	120	121	128 / 426	210	221	242	258	...	...	...
5 Construction	93	104	112	116	101 / 1268	1398	1489	1542	1719	...	...	...
6 Wholesale and retail trade, restaurants and hotels [a]	491	498	500	517	533 / 6621	7087	7900	8409	9129	...	...	...

El Salvador

Million Salvadoran colones

	1986	1987	1988	1989	1990	1991	1992	1993	1994	1995	1996	1997
	At constant prices of: 1962				1990							
7 Transport, storage and communication	180	183	187	189	201 2678	2804	3068	3272	3439	...	...	...
8 Finance, insurance, real estate and business services	249	255	262	255	261 6197	6315	6592	6768	7093	...	...	...
9 Community, social and personal services [b]	202	205	208	211	214 2241[c]	2306[c]	2379[c]	2446[c]	2575[c]	...	...	...
Total, Industries	2583	2647	2681	2719	2820 33732	34885	37750	38482	40541	...	...	...
Producers of government services	430	447	463	458	465 2693	2709	2615	2624	2693	...	...	...
Other producers	...	...	...	...	...	...	...	...	...	...	...	...
Subtotal	3013	3094	3144	3177	3285 36425	37595	40365	41106	43234	...	...	...
less: Imputed bank service charge	...	...	...	...	609	597	736	940	996	...	...	...
plus: Import duties	...	...	...	...	...	...	...	...	...	...	...	...
plus: Value added tax	...	...	...	...	672	793	1014	3476	4013	...	...	...
plus: Other adjustments	...	...	...	...	...	...	...	...	...	...	...	...
equals: Gross domestic product	3013	3094	3144	3177	3285 36487	37791	40643	43643	46251	...	...	...

a Restaurants and hotels are included in item "Community, social and personal services".
b Refers to all other services.
c Beginning 1990, relates to rents of owner-occupied dwellings.

1.12 Relations among national accounting aggregates

Million Salvadoran colones

	1986	1987	1988	1989	1990	1991	1992	1993	1994	1995	1996	1997
Gross domestic product	19763	23141	27366	32230	36487	42594	49841	60522	70613	...	...	...
plus: Net factor income from the rest of the world	−472	−525	−509	−527	−971	−1208	−1615	−719	−442	...	...	...
Factor income from rest of the world	203	196	200	230	...	...	...	...	...	...	...	...
less: Factor income to the rest of the world	675	721	710	757	...	...	...	...	...	...	...	...
equals: Gross national product	19291	22616	26857	31703	35516	41386	48226	59803	70171	...	...	...
less: Consumption of fixed capital	815	955	1129	1329	...	...	...	...	...	...	...	...
equals: National income	18476	21661	25728	30374	35516	41386	48226	59803	70171	...	...	...
plus: Net current transfers from the rest of the world	1920	2866	2543	2909	4027	5334	7564	8818	10882	...	...	...
Current transfers from rest of the world	1932	2878	2555	2921	...	...	...	...	...	...	...	...
less: Current transfers to the rest of the world	12	12	12	12	...	...	...	...	...	...	...	...
equals: National disposable income	20396	24527	28271	33283	39543	46720	55790	68621	81053	...	...	...
less: Final consumption	18009	21925	25637	30659	36053	41699	48752	58018	67447	...	...	...
equals: Net saving	2387	2602	2634	2623	3490	5021	7038	10603	13606	...	...	...
less: Surplus of the nation on current transactions	583	696	262	−988	−1567	−1541	−2197	−667	−371	...	...	...
equals: Net capital formation	1804	1906	2372	3611	5058	6563	9235	11270	13977	...	...	...

El Salvador

4.1 Derivation of value added by kind of activity, in current prices

Million Salvadoran colones

	1986 Gross output	1986 Intermediate consumption	1986 Value added	1987 Gross output	1987 Intermediate consumption	1987 Value added	1988 Gross output	1988 Intermediate consumption	1988 Value added	1989 Gross output	1989 Intermediate consumption	1989 Value added
All producers												
1 Agriculture, hunting, forestry and fishing	4952	983	3969	4233	1035	3198	4924	1123	3801	5149	1382	3767
A Agriculture and hunting	4781	958	3823	4062	1012	3050	4689	1105	3584	4907	1362	3545
B Forestry and logging	56	–	56	62	–	62	66	–	66	69	–	69
C Fishing	115	25	90	109	23	86	169	18	151	173	20	153
2 Mining and quarrying	40	13	27	56	18	38	68	21	47	85	27	58
A Coal mining	...	...	...	...	...	...	...	...	...	...	...	...
B Crude petroleum and natural gas production	...	...	...	...	...	...	...	...	...	...	...	...
C Metal ore mining	40	13	27	56	18	38	68	21	47	85	27	58
D Other mining	...	...	...	...	...	...	...	...	...	...	...	...
3 Manufacturing	7586	4500	3086	9180	5135	4045	11321	6513	4808	14141	8305	5836
A Manufacture of food, beverages and tobacco	3951	2226	1725	4844	2562	2282	5943	3200	2743	7622	4302	3320
B Textile, wearing apparel and leather industries	904	553	351	1111	657	454	1403	855	548	1746	1071	675
C Manufacture of wood and wood products, including furniture	187	72	115	227	75	152	285	101	184	369	143	226
D Manufacture of paper and paper products, printing and publishing	241	154	87	295	173	122	371	232	139	467	294	173
E Manufacture of chemicals and chemical petroleum, coal, rubber and plastic products	1362	938	424	1517	993	524	1836	1262	574	2100	1426	674
F Manufacture of non-metallic mineral products, except products of petroleum and coal	273	118	155	335	130	205	496	252	244	553	242	311
G Basic metal industries	230	162	68	282	183	99	301	171	130	464	312	152
H Manufacture of fabricated metal products, machinery and equipment	262	166	96	335	204	131	403	244	159	503	310	193
I Other manufacturing industries	176	111	65	233	156	77	283	196	87	317	205	112
4 Electricity, gas and water	543	125	418	637	140	497	686	151	535	776	170	606
A Electricity, gas and steam	...	...	370	...	...	440	...	...	473	686	150	536
B Water works and supply	...	...	48	...	...	57	...	...	62	90	20	70
5 Construction	1098	551	547	1447	736	711	1658	843	815	1960	976	984
6 Wholesale and retail trade, restaurants and hotels	5987	360	5627	7770	495	7275	9314	593	8721	11567	735	10832
A Wholesale and retail trade	5987	360	5627	7770	495	7275	9314	593	8721	11567	735	10832
B Restaurants and hotels	...	...	...	...	...	...	...	...	...	...	...	...
7 Transport, storage and communication	1203	387	816	1554	493	1061	1763	557	1206	2082	666	1416
8 Finance, insurance, real estate and business services	1703	200	1503	2089	267	1822	2629	330	2299	3072	384	2688
A Financial institutions	665	101	564	784	144	640	947	168	779	981	186	795
B Insurance												

El Salvador

Million Salvadoran colones

	1986 Gross output	1986 Intermediate consumption	1986 Value added	1987 Gross output	1987 Intermediate consumption	1987 Value added	1988 Gross output	1988 Intermediate consumption	1988 Value added	1989 Gross output	1989 Intermediate consumption	1989 Value added
C Real estate and business services	1039	100	939	1305	123	1182	1682	162	1520	2091	198	1893
9 Community, social and personal services	2678	884	1794	3391	1104	2287	4074	1325	2749	4900	1570	3330
Total, Industries	25792	8006	17786	30357	9423	20934	36437	11456	24981	43733	14217	29516
Producers of government services	2803	826	1977	3181	974	2207	3484	1099	2385	3930	1216	2714
Other producers	...	...	...	...	...	...	...	...	...	...	...	...
Total	28595	8832	19763	33538	10397	23141	39921	12555	27366	47664	15434	32230
less: Imputed bank service charge	...	...	...	...	...	...	...	...	...	...	...	...
Import duties	...	...	...	...	...	...	...	...	...	...	...	...
Value added tax	...	...	...	...	...	...	...	...	...	...	...	...
Other adjustments	...	...	...	...	...	...	...	...	...	...	...	...
Total	...	...	...	...	...	...	...	...	...	...	...	...

	1990 Gross output	1990 Intermediate consumption	1990 Value added	1991 Gross output	1991 Intermediate consumption	1991 Value added	1992 Gross output	1992 Intermediate consumption	1992 Value added	1993 Gross output	1993 Intermediate consumption	1993 Value added
All producers												
1 Agriculture, hunting, forestry and fishing	8603	2363	6240	9888	2595	7292	10162	3071	7090	11719	3288	8431
A Agriculture and hunting	7954	2269	5685	9062	2492	6570	9250	2949	6301	10743	3149	7594
B Forestry and logging	388	11	377	528	11	517	587	13	574	587	14	573
C Fishing	261	83	178	298	92	206	324	109	215	389	125	264
2 Mining and quarrying	178	40	138	216	49	167	256	58	198	308	62	247
A Coal mining	...	...	...	...	...	...	...	...	...	...	...	...
B Crude petroleum and natural gas production	...	...	...	...	...	...	...	...	...	...	...	...
C Metal ore mining	178	40	138	216	49	167	256	58	198	308	62	247
D Other mining	...	...	...	...	...	...	...	...	...	...	...	...
3 Manufacturing	18629	10705	7923	21911	12501	9410	25798	13923	11876	28577	15029	13549
A Manufacture of food, beverages and tobacco	7742	4557	3185	8741	5341	3400	10052	5813	4239	10783	5980	4803
B Textile, wearing apparel and leather industries	3044	1756	1288	3610	2098	1512	4245	2317	1928	4579	2479	2101
C Manufacture of wood and wood products, including furniture	206	97	109	261	121	139	299	138	161	377	164	213
D Manufacture of paper and paper products, printing and publishing	1219	656	564	1496	734	763	1786	863	923	2091	975	1116
E Manufacture of chemicals and chemical petroleum, coal, rubber and plastic products	3804	2385	1418	4602	2729	1873	5497	3041	2457	5936	3362	2574
F Manufacture of non-metallic mineral products, except products of petroleum and coal	637	281	356	785	349	436	950	432	518	1183	526	657
G Basic metal industries	813	455	358	933	522	411	1116	608	508	1273	716	556
H Manufacture of fabricated metal products, machinery and equipment	610	338	272	777	394	383	904	449	455	1019	502	517

El Salvador

	1990 Gross output	1990 Intermediate consumption	1990 Value added	1991 Gross output	1991 Intermediate consumption	1991 Value added	1992 Gross output	1992 Intermediate consumption	1992 Value added	1993 Gross output	1993 Intermediate consumption	1993 Value added
1 Other manufacturing industries	553	181	372	707	214	493	949	262	687	1337	326	1011
4 Electricity, gas and water	624	199	426	868	561	307	1134	670	464	1466	862	604
A Electricity, gas and steam	456	153	303	680	493	187	913	585	328	1176	755	422
B Water works and supply	168	46	122	188	68	120	221	85	136	290	108	183
5 Construction	2712	1444	1268	3255	1779	1476	4290	2091	2199	5049	2407	2642
6 Wholesale and retail trade, restaurants and hotels	8943	2322	6621	10780	2748	8032	12930	3501	9429	15237	3933	11304
A Wholesale and retail trade	7025	1474	5551	8279	1707	6572	9803	2264	7538	11398	2543	8855
B Restaurants and hotels	1918	848	1070	2501	1041	1461	3127	1237	1891	3839	1390	2449
7 Transport, storage and communication	4226	1549	2678	4726	1887	2839	6122	2300	3822	7101	2562	4539
8 Finance, insurance, real estate and business services	6852	655	6197	7916	842	7074	9088	971	8117	10552	1224	9328
A Financial institutions	1076	282	793	1294	400	894	1630	446	1184	2148	644	1505
B Insurance												
C Real estate and business services	5776	372	5404	6622	441	6181	7458	525	6933	8404	581	7823
Real estate, except dwellings	1521	243	1279	1882	297	1585	2362	357	2005	2754	381	2373
Dwellings	4255	130	4125	4740	145	4596	5096	168	4928	5650	200	5450
9 Community, social and personal services	3038	797	2241	3640	929	2711	4353	1108	3245	4928	1243	3685
A Sanitary and similar services	...	...	...	...	...	...	...	...	...	...	...	...
B Social and related community services	2255	797	1458	2747	929	1818	3402	1108	2294	3885	1243	2643
C Recreational and cultural services	...	...	...	...	...	...	...	...	...	...	...	...
D Personal and household services	783	–	783	893	–	893	951	–	951	1043	–	1043
Total, Industries	53805	20074	33732	63199	23891	39308	74132	27693	46440	84936	30609	54328
Producers of government services	3673	980	2693	4304	1210	3094	4812	1500	3311	5401	1625	3777
Other producers	...	...	...	...	...	...	...	...	...	...	...	...
Total	57478	21054	36425	67503	25100	42402	78944	29193	49751	90338	32233	58104
less: Imputed bank service charge	...	–609	609	...	–780	780	...	–1073	1073	...	–1446	1446
Import duties	...	–672	672	...	–972	972	...	–1163	1163	...	–3864	3864
Value added tax	...	...	...	...	...	...	...	...	...	...	...	...
Other adjustments	...	...	...	...	...	...	...	...	...	...	...	...
Total	57478	20991	36487	67503	24908	42594	78944	29103	49841	90338	29815	60522

Equatorial Guinea

Source

Reply to the United Nations National Accounts Questionnaire from the Ministerio de Planificación y Desarrollo Económico, Dirección General de Estadística, Malabo. The official estimates and information on concepts, sources and methods of estimation can be found in *Las Cuentas Nacionales de Guinea Ecuatorial* published in July 1987.

General note

The estimates shown in the following tables have been prepared in accordance with the United Nations System of National Accounts (1968 SNA) so far as the existing data would permit. The monetary unit was ekwele. On 2 January 1985, the ekwele was replaced by CFA francs. Four bipkwele are equivalent to one CFA franc.

1.1 Expenditure on the gross domestic product, in current prices

Million CFA francs

	1986	1987	1988	1989	1990	1991	1992	1993	1994	1995	1996	1997
1 Government final consumption expenditure	7240	5210	7804	9397	6765	6696	...	...	...	...	...	...
2 Private final consumption expenditure	28754	26630	29096	22956	23593	35225	...	...	...	...	...	...
3 Gross capital formation	6966	10844	10448	8278	13963	7434	...	...	...	...	...	...
A Increase in stocks	−624	654	−685	−7	−1365	−1091	...	...	...	...	...	...
B Gross fixed capital formation	7590	10190	11133	8285	15328	8525	...	...	...	...	...	...
Residential buildings	3079	3004	4293	3492	4993	4502	...	...	...	...	...	...
Non-residential buildings							...	...	...	...	...	...
Other construction and land improvement, etc.							...	...	...	...	...	...
Other	4511	7186	6840	4793	10335	4023	...	...	...	...	...	...
4 Exports of goods and services	12092	18568	19187	17083	26483	13174	...	...	...	...	...	...
5 less: Imports of goods and services	17847	21930	23786	15458	26455	16100	...	...	...	...	...	...
equals: Gross domestic product	37205	39322	42749	42256	44349	46429	...	...	...	...	...	...

1.2 Expenditure on the gross domestic product, in constant prices

Million CFA francs

	1986	1987	1988	1989	1990	1991	1992	1993	1994	1995	1996	1997
	At constant prices of: 1985											
1 Government final consumption expenditure	5583	3202	4588	5612	...	...	...	...	...	...	...	...
2 Private final consumption expenditure	29390	26158	29432	25845	...	...	...	...	...	...	...	...
3 Gross capital formation	6224	7677	7236	6593	...	...	...	...	...	...	...	...
A Increase in stocks	−595	666	−1066	−143	...	...	...	...	...	...	...	...
B Gross fixed capital formation	6819	7011	8302	6736	...	...	...	...	...	...	...	...
4 Exports of goods and services	9194	16408	14637	13081	...	...	...	...	...	...	...	...
5 less: Imports of goods and services	13104	13371	13704	10106	...	...	...	...	...	...	...	...
equals: Gross domestic product	37286	40074	42189	41025	...	...	...	...	...	...	...	...

Equatorial Guinea

1.10 Gross domestic product by kind of activity, in current prices

Million CFA francs

	1986	1987	1988	1989	1990	1991	1992	1993	1994	1995	1996	1997
1 Agriculture, hunting, forestry and fishing	22108	23146	22361	22991	22924	23328	...	...	...	...	...	...
2 Mining and quarrying	...	...	...	...	...	...	...	...	...	...	...	...
3 Manufacturing	471	857	532	545	556	597	...	...	...	...	...	...
4 Electricity, gas and water	762	685	1119	1277	1469	1358	...	...	...	...	...	...
5 Construction	1248	1465	1907	1496	1638	1299	...	...	...	...	...	...
6 Wholesale and retail trade, restaurants and hotels	2926	3370	4735	3597	3266	3319	...	...	...	...	...	...
7 Transport, storage and communication	878	632	760	823	923	855	...	...	...	...	...	...
8 Finance, insurance, real estate and business services	886	918	947	966	989	1005	...	...	...	...	...	...
9 Community, social and personal services	2970	3086	3658	3997	5572	5817	...	...	...	...	...	...
Total, Industries	32249	34161	36019	35692	37337	37578	...	...	...	...	...	...
Producers of government services	2892	3283	5201	5256	5428	6354	...	...	...	...	...	...
Other producers	...	...	...	...	...	...	...	...	...	...	...	...
Subtotal	35141	37444	41220	40948	42765	43932	...	...	...	...	...	...
less: Imputed bank service charge	...	...	...	...	...	...	...	...	...	...	...	...
plus: Import duties	2064	1878	1529	1309	1585	2497	...	...	...	...	...	...
plus: Value added tax	...	...	...	...	...	...	...	...	...	...	...	...
plus: Other adjustments	...	...	...	...	...	...	...	...	...	...	...	...
equals: Gross domestic product	37205	39322	42749	42257	44350	46429	...	...	...	...	...	...

Estonia

Source

Reply to the United Nations National Accounts Questionnaire from the State Statistical Office of Estonia, Tallinn. The official estimates for the years 1980–1990 are published in *National Accounts in Estonia*.

General note

The estimates shown in the following tables have been prepared in accordance with the United Nations *Comparison of the System of National Accounts and the System of Balances of the National Economy, Part 1: Conceptual Relationships for the years 1980–1990*. For the years beginning 1991, the estimates are in accordance with the United Nations *System of National Accounts 1993*. The shift from the Soviet rouble to the Estonian national currency (kroon) was made on June 20, 1992 at the rate of 10 roubles = 1 kroon. From this date, the kroon has been the only legal currency in Estonia.

1.1 Expenditure on the gross domestic product, in current prices

Million Estonian kroons

	1986	1987	1988	1989	1990	1991	1992	1993	1994	1995	1996	1997
1 Government final consumption expenditure	86	90	89	89	105	241	1775 2084	4474	6790	10350	12632	14879
2 Private final consumption expenditure	329	351	352	387	514	1055	8480	...	...	24910	31845	37990
A Households	329	351	352	387	514	1002	7698	...	...	24703	31492	37586
B Private non-profit institutions serving households	...	...	...	...	...	53	782 97			207	353	404
3 Gross capital formation	168	166	189	210	241	448	3738 3518	...	...	9544	14579	19420
A Increase in stocks	7	3	20	25	52	90	983 763	541	739	−1032	564	2193
B Gross fixed capital formation	161	163	169	185	190	357	2755 2755	...	...	10576	14015	17227
4 Exports of goods and services	284	300	328	340	335	584	7893 7893	15197	22486	29451	35186	50238
5 less: Imports of goods and services	350	363	383	384	398	495	7631 7121	16125	25739	32736	41229	57661
Statistical discrepancy	–	–	–	–	–	–	–	...	...	−814	−567	214
equals: Gross domestic product	516	544	576	642	798	1832	14255 12889	21610	29645	40705	52446	65080

Estonia

1.2 Expenditure on the gross domestic product, in constant prices

Million Estonian kroons

	1986	1987	1988	1989	1990	1991	1992	1993	1994	1995	1996	1997
At constant prices of:	1980					1991						
1 Government final consumption expenditure	84	89	88	86	93	241	224	...	...	...	...	...
2 Private final consumption expenditure	305	320	322	343	390	1055	844	...	...	...	...	...
A Households	305	320	322	343	390	1002	757	...	...	...	...	...
B Private non-profit institutions serving households	...	...	...	...	...	53	87	...	...	...	...	...
3 Gross capital formation	128	123	132	134	132	448	304	...	...	...	...	...
A Increase in stocks	5	2	12	15	24	91	89	...	...	...	...	...
B Gross fixed capital formation	123	121	120	119	108	357	215	...	...	...	...	...
4 Exports of goods and services	252	265	288	289	214	584	607	...	...	...	...	...
5 less: Imports of goods and services	311	316	325	307	319	495	408	...	...	...	...	...
equals: Gross domestic product	458	480	505	546	510	441 / 1832	1571	...	...	...	...	...

1.3 Cost components of the gross domestic product

Million Estonian kroons

	1986	1987	1988	1989	1990	1991	1992	1993	1994	1995	1996	1997
1 Indirect taxes, net	4	−1	−5	2	50	211	1283 / 1384	2810	4272	5580	7334	9660
A Indirect taxes	73	71	72	78	100	252	1607 / 1604	3026	4559	5891	7725	10054
B less: Subsidies	69	72	77	76	50	41	324 / 220	216	287	311	391	394
2 Consumption of fixed capital	102	112	116	122	127	102	637 / 640	2699	3346	4527	5651	7145
3 Compensation of employees paid by resident producers to	255	265	286	328	421	860	6021 / 6257	11384	16992	23146	27910	33128
A Resident households	...	...	...	...	...	860	6021 / 6257	11383	16986	23113	27901	33115
B Rest of the world	...	...	...	...	...	...	...	1	6	33	9	13
4 Operating surplus	155	169	179	191	200	659	6314 / 4877	5167	5658	8239	12682	16173
A Corporate and quasi-corporate enterprises	...	...	...	...	...	537	...	...	...	...	...	...
B Private unincorporated enterprises	...	...	...	...	...	122	...	...	...	...	...	...
C General government	...	...	...	...	...	...	...	...	...	...	...	...
Statistical discrepancy	...	...	...	...	...	...	−269	−450	−623	−787	−1131	−1026

Estonia

Million Estonian kroons	1986	1987	1988	1989	1990	1991	1992	1993	1994	1995	1996	1997
equals: Gross domestic product	516	544	576	642	798	1832	14255 12889	21610	29645	40705	52446	65080

1.4 General government current receipts and disbursements

Million Estonian kroons	1986	1987	1988	1989	1990	1991	1992	1993	1994	1995	1996	1997
Receipts												
1 Operating surplus	...	...	...	...	...	–	156	...	...	...	...	...
2 Property and entrepreneurial income	...	...	...	...	...	2	58	76	108	56	157	...
3 Taxes, fees and contributions	...	...	...	...	...	635	4364	8750	12656	16223	19799	...
A Indirect taxes	...	...	...	...	...	252	1607	3026	4559	5891	7725	...
B Direct taxes	...	...	...	...	...	257	1576	2964	3743	4643	5245	...
C Social security contributions	...	...	...	...	...	126	1170	2760	4184	5624	6741	...
D Compulsory fees, fines and penalties	...	...	...	...	...	–	11	58	189	65	88	...
4 Other current transfers	...	...	...	...	...	3	2347	1578	1886	2178	2148	...
Statistical discrepancy	...	...	...	...	...	...	–156	...	...	...	...	...
Total current receipts of general government	...	...	...	...	...	640	6769	10462	14668	18457	22104	...
Disbursements												
1 Government final consumption expenditure	...	...	...	...	...	241	1775	4474	6790	10350	12632	...
A Compensation of employees	...	...	...	...	...	97	815	1982	3279	5059	6253	...
B Consumption of fixed capital	...	...	...	...	...	6	75	558	710	993	1079	...
C Purchases of goods and services, net	...	...	...	...	...	138	881	...	...	...	...	...
D less: Own-account fixed capital formation	...	...	...	...	...	–	–	...	...	...	...	...
E Indirect taxes paid, net	...	...	...	...	...	–	4	...	...	...	...	...
2 Property income	...	...	...	...	...	1	9	44	76	90	223	...
A Interest	...	...	...	...	...	1	9	44	71	90	223	...
B Net land rent and royalties	...	...	...	...	...	–	–	–	5	–	–	...
3 Subsidies	...	...	...	...	...	41	324	216	287	311	391	...
4 Other current transfers	...	...	...	...	...	165	2828	2882	4463	5818	7093	...
A Social security benefits	...	...	...	...	...	165	375	559	619	833	1004	...
B Social assistance grants	...	...	...	...	...	–	–	567	551	618	925	...
C Other	...	...	...	...	...	–	2453	1756	3293	4367	5164	...
5 Net saving	...	...	...	...	...	193	1833	2846	3052	1888	1765	...
Total current disbursements and net saving of general government	...	...	...	...	...	640	6769	10462	14668	18457	22104	...

Estonia

1.5 Current income and outlay of corporate and quasi-corporate enterprises, summary

Million Estonian kroons

	1986	1987	1988	1989	1990	1991	1992	1993	1994	1995	1996	1997
Receipts												
1 Operating surplus	...	...	...	...	...	537	4689	2321	1703	2526	4869	...
2 Property and entrepreneurial income received	...	...	...	...	...	6	130	146	350	752	560	...
3 Current transfers	...	...	...	...	...	1	23	37	276	232	339	...
Statistical discrepancy	...	...	...	...	...	−10	...	...	...	...	...	...
Total current receipts	...	...	...	...	...	534	4842	2504	2329	3510	5768	...
Disbursements												
1 Property and entrepreneurial income	...	...	...	...	...	21	471	1144	1963	2204	2346	...
2 Direct taxes and other current payments to general government	...	...	...	...	...	132	717	1005	1169	1030	858	...
3 Other current transfers	...	...	...	...	...	2	1114	246	371	829	2751	...
4 Net saving	...	...	...	...	...	379	2540	109	−1174	−553	−187	...
Total current disbursements and net saving	...	...	...	...	...	534	4842	2504	2329	3510	5768	...

1.6 Current income and outlay of households and non-profit institutions

Million Estonian kroons

	1986	1987	1988	1989	1990	1991	1992	1993	1994	1995	1996	1997
Receipts												
1 Compensation of employees	...	...	...	...	...	720	6464	11383	17022	23127	27920	...
A From resident producers	...	...	...	...	...	...	6021	11383	16986	23113	27901	...
B From rest of the world	...	...	...	...	...	...	443	−	36	14	19	...
2 Operating surplus of private unincorporated enterprises	...	...	...	...	...	122	1469	2625	3607	5055	6521	...
3 Property and entrepreneurial income	...	...	...	...	...	14	117	203	453	812	777	...
4 Current transfers	...	...	...	...	...	171	2482	2810	4007	5678	8397	...
A Social security benefits	...	...	...	...	...	165	283	559	619	833	1004	...
B Social assistance grants	...	...	...	...	...	−	92	567	551	618	925	...
C Other	...	...	...	...	...	6	2107	1683	2837	4227	6468	...
Total current receipts	...	...	...	...	...	1027	10532	17021	25089	34672	43615	...
Disbursements												
1 Private final consumption expenditure	...	...	...	...	...	1055	8480	...	...	24910	31844	...
2 Property income	...	...	...	...	...	...	...	82	107	109	282	...
3 Direct taxes and other current transfers n.e.c. to general government	...	...	...	...	...	246	2027	4665	6721	9256	11134	...

Estonia

Million Estonian kroons	1986	1987	1988	1989	1990	1991	1992	1993	1994	1995	1996	1997
A Social security contributions	...	...	...	...	...	127	1170	2760	4184	5624	6741	...
B Direct taxes	...	...	...	...	...	119	857	1887	2515	3593	4354	...
C Fees, fines and penalties	...	...	...	...	...	...	...	18	22	39	39	...
4 Other current transfers	...	...	...	...	...	11	242	84	153	265	294	...
Statistical discrepancy	...	...	...	...	...	−136	...	...	...	...	...	...
5 Net saving	...	...	...	...	...	−149	−216	...	...	132	61	...
Total current disbursements and net saving	...	...	...	...	...	1027	10532	17021	15089	34672	43615	...

1.7 External transactions on current account, summary

Million Estonian kroons	1986	1987	1988	1989	1990	1991	1992	1993	1994	1995	1996	1997
Payments to the rest of the world												
1 Imports of goods and services	...	...	...	...	...	...	7631	16125	25739	32736	41229	57661
A Imports of merchandise, c.i.f.	...	...	...	...	...	...	5922	12688	20445	27044	34121	47526
B Other	...	...	...	...	...	...	1709	3437	5294	5692	7108	10135
2 Factor income to rest of the world	...	...	...	...	...	...	83	541	861	700	1326	3605
A Compensation of employees	...	...	...	...	...	...	−	1	6	33	9	13
B Property and entrepreneurial income	...	...	...	...	...	...	83	540	855	667	1317	3592
By general government	...	...	...	...	...	...	−	...	...	...	...	...
By corporate and quasi-corporate enterprises	...	...	...	...	...	...	38	...	...	...	...	...
By other	...	...	...	...	...	...	45	...	...	...	...	...
3 Current transfers to the rest of the world	...	...	...	...	...	...	680	43	73	94	197	257
A Indirect taxes to supranational organizations	...	...	...	...	...	...	...	...	...	...	...	...
B Other current transfers	...	...	...	...	...	...	...	43	73	94	197	257
4 Surplus of the nation on current transactions	...	...	...	...	...	...	1326	279	−2145	−1811	−4807	−7813
Payments to the rest of the world and surplus of the nation on current transfers	...	...	...	...	...	...	9720	16988	24528	31719	37945	53710
Receipts from the rest of the world												
1 Exports of goods and services	...	...	...	...	...	...	7893	15197	22486	29451	35186	50238
A Exports of merchandise, f.o.b.	...	...	...	...	...	...	5549	10763	15829	19428	21833	31871
B Other	...	...	...	...	...	...	2345	4434	6657	10023	13353	18367
2 Factor income from rest of the world	...	...	...	...	...	...	448	356	483	727	1352	1594
A Compensation of employees	...	...	...	...	...	...	443	−	36	14	19	23
B Property and entrepreneurial income	...	...	...	...	...	...	5	356	447	713	1333	1571

Estonia

Million Estonian kroons

	1986	1987	1988	1989	1990	1991	1992	1993	1994	1995	1996	1997
By general government	...	...	...	...	...	...	–	...	...	...	...	...
By corporate and quasi-corporate enterprises	...	...	...	...	...	...	2	...	...	...	...	...
By other	...	...	...	...	...	...	3	...	...	...	...	...
3 Current transfers from rest of the world	...	...	...	...	...	...	1379	1435	1559	1541	1407	1878
Receipts from the rest of the world on current transactions	...	...	...	...	...	...	9720	16988	24528	31719	37945	53710

1.8 Capital transactions of the nation, summary

Million Estonian kroons

	1986	1987	1988	1989	1990	1991	1992	1993	1994	1995	1996	1997
Finance of gross capital formation												
Gross saving	102	102	135	166	178	532	5062	...	...			
							5062			6919	9205	11821
1 Consumption of fixed capital	102	112	116	122	127	102	637					
							640	2699	3346	4527	5651	7145
A General government	...	...	...	...	...	6	75					
							75	558	710	993	1079	1067
B Corporate and quasi-corporate enterprises	...	...	...	...	...	87	543					
							543	2047	2491	3344	4294	5637
C Other	...	...	...	...	...	9	19					
							22	94	145	190	278	441
2 Net saving	–	–9	19	44	52	430	...	...	...			
										2392	3554	4676
A General government	...	...	...	...	...	193	1833					...
							1833	2846	3052	1888	1765	
B Corporate and quasi-corporate enterprises	...	...	...	...	...	386	2503					...
							2503	109	–1174	–553	–187	
C Other	...	...	...	...	...	–149	89	...	...			...
							86			1057	1976	
less: Surplus of the nation on current transactions	–66	–64	–54	–44	–63	84	1324					
							1544	279	–2146	–1811	–4807	–7813
Statistical discrepancy	–	–	–	–	–	–	–	...	...	814	567	–214
Finance of gross capital formation	168	166	189	210	241	448	3738	...	...			
							3518			9544	14579	19420
Gross capital formation												
Increase in stocks	7	3	20	25	52	90	983					
							763	541	739	–1032	564	2193
Gross fixed capital formation	161	163	169	185	190	358	2755	...	...			
							2755			10576	14015	17227
1 General government	...	...	...	...	...	63	504					...
							504	1071	1476	1952	2740	
2 Corporate and quasi-corporate enterprises	...	...	...	...	...	279	2131					...
							2131	3591	5431	7244	9520	

Estonia

Million Estonian kroons	1986	1987	1988	1989	1990	1991	1992	1993	1994	1995	1996	1997
3 Other	...	...	...	...	...	16	120 120	...	...	1380	1755	...
Gross capital formation	168	166	189	210	241	448	3738 3518	...	...	9544	14579	19420

1.9 Gross domestic product by institutional sectors of origin

Million Estonian kroons	1986	1987	1988	1989	1990	1991	1992	1993	1994	1995	1996	1997
Domestic factor incomes originating												
1 General government	...	...	...	...	...	97	815 993	1982	3279	5059	6253	6912
2 Corporate and quasi-corporate enterprises	...	...	...	...	...	1158	10027 8491	11189	14571	19678	25188	31568
A Non-financial	...	...	...	...	...	1144	9797 8208	11189	14571	19678	25188	31568
B Financial	...	...	...	...	...	14	230 283	482	754	1217	2050	2707
3 Households and private unincorporated enterprises	...	...	...	...	...	122	1474 1631	2861	3989	5355	6998	7996
4 Non-profit institutions serving households	...	...	...	...	...	2	19 19	37	57	76	103	118
subtotal: Domestic factor incomes	...	...	...	...	...	1379	12335 11134	16551	22649	31385	40592	49301
Indirect taxes, net	...	...	...	...	...	211	1283 1384	2810	4272	5580	7334	9660
A Indirect taxes	...	...	...	...	...	252	1607 1604	3026	4559	5891	7725	10054
B less: Subsidies	...	...	...	...	...	41	324 220	216	287	311	391	394
Consumption of fixed capital	...	...	...	...	...	102	637 640	2699	3346	4527	5651	7145
Statistical discrepancy	...	...	...	...	...	140	– −269	−450	−623	−787	−1131	−1026
Gross domestic product	...	...	...	...	...	1832	14255 12889	21610	29645	40705	52446	65080

1.10 Gross domestic product by kind of activity, in current prices

Million Estonian kroons	1986	1987	1988	1989	1990	1991	1992	1993	1994	1995	1996	1997
1 Agriculture, hunting, forestry and fishing	110	107	112	127	125	310	1779 1647	2178	2714	2876	3535	4071
2 Mining and quarrying	...	...	...	...	...	30	349 310	367	478	601	728	725
3 Manufacturing	205	213	218	230	316	599	4084 2773	3770	5022	6385	7784	9805
4 Electricity, gas and water	...	...	...	...	...	31	614 537	714	870	1441	1899	2087
5 Construction	40	42	46	52	57	111	654 603	1301	1684	2161	2735	3136
6 Wholesale and retail trade, restaurants and hotels	38	42	43	52	64	147	2064 1980	3633	4389	6435	8623	10924
7 Transport, storage and communication	29	34	39	41	51	114	1698 1715	2456	3060	3831	5070	6745

Estonia

Million Estonian kroons

	1986	1987	1988	1989	1990	1991	1992	1993	1994	1995	1996	1997
8 Finance, insurance, real estate and business services	...	...	...	...	...	44	999 1076	2017	3059	4796	6722	8820
9 Community, social and personal services	94	106	119	141	184	162	312 620	1052	1552	2496	3112	3661
Total, Industries	516	544	576	642	798	1548	12553 11261	17488	22828	31022	40208	49974
Producers of government services	...	...	...	...	...	103	869 960	2311	3651	5471	6751	7435
Other producers						...	...	...	...	...	...	...
Subtotal	516	544	576	642	798	1651	13422 12221	19799	26479	36493	46959	57409
less: Imputed bank service charge	...	...	...	...	...	...	269	450	623	787	1131	1026
plus: Import duties	...	...	...	...	...	...	...	...	...	...	...	...
plus: Value added tax	...	...	...	...	...	...	...	...	...	...	...	...
plus: Other adjustments	...	...	...	...	...	181	833 937	2261	3789	4999	6618	8697
equals: Gross domestic product	516	544	576	642	798	1832	14255 12889	21610	29645	40705	52446	65080

1.11 Gross domestic product by kind of activity, in constant prices

Million Estonian kroons

	1986	1987	1988	1989	1990	1991	1992	1993	1994	1995	1996	1997
At constant prices of:	1980											
			1991									
				1993								
					1995							
1 Agriculture, hunting, forestry and fishing	55	54	53	58	48	34 310	238 2526	3080	2794	2876	2813	2937
2 Mining and quarrying	...	...	...	...	...	30	33 520	686	645	601	646	724
3 Manufacturing	208	218	228	224	212	188 599	426 5385	6010	5806	6385	6560	7848
4 Electricity, gas and water	...	...	...	...	...	31	27 900	1473	1492	1441	1504	1457
5 Construction	38	39	41	46	36	34 111	51 1076	2003	1891	2161	2374	2596
6 Wholesale and retail trade, restaurants and hotels	39	42	42	52	48	39 147	205 3175	5732	5793	6435	7036	7949

Estonia

Million Estonian kroons	1986	1987	1988	1989	1990	1991	1992	1993	1994	1995	1996	1997
At constant prices of:	1980											
		1991										
			1993									
				1995								
7 Transport, storage and communication	25	28	32	32	30	22 / 114	170 / 2339	3973	3995	3831	4111	4634
8 Finance, insurance, real estate and business services	...	...	...	...	...	44	65 / 2129	4971	4850	4796	4926	5713
9 Community, social and personal services	93	100	109	135	135	124 / 162	72 / 1382	2443	2438	2496	2614	2653
Statistical discrepancy		...	...	...	...	...	...	...				
Total, Industries	458	480	505	546	510	441 / 1548	1286 / 19432	– 30371	– 29703	– 31022	– 32584	– 36511
Producers of government services	...	...	...	...	...	103	118 / 2209	5344	5389	5471	5482	5600
Other producers	...	...	...	...	...	...	...					
Subtotal	458	480	505	546	510	441 / 1651	1404 / 21641	– 35715	– 35094	– 36493	– 38066	– 42111
less: Imputed bank service charge	...	...	...	...	...	...	361	727	775	787	850	980
plus: Import duties	...	...	...	...	...	...	...					
plus: Value added tax	...	...	...	...	...	...	...	–	–	–	–	–
plus: Other adjustments	...	...	...	...	...	181	168 / 2471	4840	4712	4999	5110	6014
equals: Gross domestic product	458	480	505	546	510	441 / 1832	1571 / 23751	39827	39031	40705	42326	47146
memorandum item: Mineral fuels and power	...	...	...	...	...	...	...	–	–	–	–	–

599

Estonia

1.12 Relations among national accounting aggregates

Million Estonian kroons

	1986	1987	1988	1989	1990	1991	1992	1993	1994	1995	1996	1997
Gross domestic product	516	544	576	642	798	1832	14255	21610	29645	40705	52446	65080
plus: Net factor income from the rest of the world	...	...	...	...	...	...	365	-186	-378	28	26	-2011
Factor income from rest of the world	...	...	...	...	...	...	448	355	483	728	1352	1594
less: Factor income to the rest of the world	...	...	...	...	...	...	83	541	861	700	1326	3605
equals: Gross national product	516	544	576	642	798	1832	14620	21424	29267	40733	52472	63069
less: Consumption of fixed capital	102	112	116	122	127	102	637	21424 / 2699	29267 / 3346	40733 / 4527	52472 / 5651	63069 / 7145
equals: National income	414	432	460	520	671	1730	13983	18725	25921	36206	46821	55924
plus: Net current transfers from the rest of the world	...	...	...	...	...	...	701	1392	1486	1447	1210	1620
Current transfers from rest of the world	...	...	...	...	...	...	1381	1435	1559	1541	1407	1878
less: Current transfers to the rest of the world	...	...	...	...	...	...	680	43	73	94	197	258
equals: National disposable income	414	432	460	520	671	1730	14684	20117	27407	37653	48031	57544
less: Final consumption	414	441	441	476	620	1296	10255	...	...	35260	44477	52869
Statistical discrepancy	...	...	...	...	...	...	...	...	...	...	...	...
equals: Net saving	–	-9	19	44	52	434	4429	– ...	...	2393	3554	4675
less: Surplus of the nation on current transactions	-66	-64	-54	-44	-63	84	1328	279	-2146	-1811	-4807	-7813
Statistical discrepancy	–	–	–	–	–	...	...	...	...	...	...	...
equals: Net capital formation	66	54	74	88	114	350	3101	...	...	5017	8928	12275

2.1 Government final consumption expenditure by function, in current prices

Million Estonian kroons

	1986	1987	1988	1989	1990	1991	1992	1993	1994	1995	1996	1997
1 General public services	...	...	...	...	...	...	217 / 217	539	874	1157	1394	...
2 Defence	...	...	...	...	...	...	44 / 44	153	294	462	587	...
3 Public order and safety	...	...	...	...	...	...	176 / 176	520	847	1162	1481	...
4 Education	...	...	...	...	...	...	711 / 711	1521	1984	2876	3516	...
5 Health	...	...	...	...	...	...	43 / 352	576	1121	1827	2186	...

600

Estonia

Million Estonian kroons

	1986	1987	1988	1989	1990	1991	1992	1993	1994	1995	1996	1997
6 Social security and welfare	...	...	...	...	...	...	64 64	183	292	403	516	...
7 Housing and community amenities	...	...	...	...	...	...	– –	313	388	538	526	...
8 Recreational, cultural and religious affairs	...	...	...	...	...	...	115 115	212	326	597	706	...
9 Economic services	...	...	...	...	...	...	404 405	457	601	1175	1390	...
A Fuel and energy	...	...	...	...	...	...	...	...	16	2	14	...
B Agriculture, hunting, forestry and fishing	...	...	...	...	...	...	...	257	259	447	587	...
C Mining (except fuels), manufacturing and construction	...	...	...	...	...	...	...	...	13	30	37	...
D Transportation and communication	...	...	...	...	...	...	...	77	221	515	589	...
E Other economic affairs	...	...	...	...	...	...	...	94	121	181	163	...
10 Other functions	...	...	...	...	...	...	...	...	63	153	330	...
Total government final consumption expenditures	...	...	...	...	...	...	1775 2084	4474	6790	10350	12632	14879

4.1 Derivation of value added by kind of activity, in current prices

Million Estonian kroons

	1990 Gross output	1990 Intermediate consumption	1990 Value added	1991 Gross output	1991 Intermediate consumption	1991 Value added	1992 Gross output	1992 Intermediate consumption	1992 Value added	1993 Gross output	1993 Intermediate consumption	1993 Value added
All producers												
1 Agriculture, hunting, forestry and fishing	...	...	...	609	300	310	3784 3901	2005 2254	1779 1647	5838	3660	2178
A Agriculture and hunting	...	...	...	519	248	271	3347 3584	1725 2024	1622 1560	5521	3461	2060
B Forestry and logging	...	...	...	8	5	3	114	70	44			
C Fishing	...	...	...	83	48	35	322 317	209 230	113 87	317	199	118
2 Mining and quarrying	...	...	...	48	19	30	600 580	251 270	349 310	731	364	367
3 Manufacturing	...	...	...	1533	934	599	10912 10208	6828 7435	4084 2773	12821	9051	3770
4 Electricity, gas and water	...	...	...	109	78	31	1980 1955	1367 1418	614 537	2535	1821	714
5 Construction	...	...	...	254	143	111	1593 1690	939 1087	654 603	3446	2145	1301
6 Wholesale and retail trade, restaurants and hotels	...	...	...	230	82	147	2978 3190	914 1210	2064 1980	7528	3895	3633
A Wholesale and retail trade ..	...	...	...	177	44	133	2611 2824	754 1051	1857 1773	6773	3414	3359
B Restaurants and hotels	...	...	...	53	38	15	367 366	159 159	207 207	755	482	273
7 Transport, storage and communication	...	...	...	216	103	114	4032 3884	2334 2169	1698 1715	6292	3836	2456
A Transport and storage	...	...	...	198	99	99	3776	2244	1532	...	...	...
B Communication	...	...	...	18	3	14	256	90	165	...	...	...
8 Finance, insurance, real estate and business services	...	...	...	91	47	44	1496 1731	497 655	998 1076	3699	1682	2017
A Financial institutions	...	...	...	18	5	14	312 416	95 119	217 297	776	216	560

Estonia

Million Estonian kroons

	1990 Gross output	1990 Intermediate consumption	1990 Value added	1991 Gross output	1991 Intermediate consumption	1991 Value added	1992 Gross output	1992 Intermediate consumption	1992 Value added	1993 Gross output	1993 Intermediate consumption	1993 Value added
B Insurance	...	...	...	2	–	1	23	4	19			
C Real estate and business services	...	...	...	71	41	30	1160 / 1315	398 / 536	762 / 779	2923	1466	1457
9 Community, social and personal services	...	...	...	366	204	162	1500 / 1178	1185 / 558	316 / 620	1848	796	1052
Total, Industries	...	...	...	3457	1910	1548	28875 / 28317	16319 / 17056	12556 / 11261	44738	27250	17488
Producers of government services	...	...	...	243	140	103	1813 / 1752	948 / 792	866 / 960	3832	1521	2311
Other producers	...	...	...	...	...	...	...	...	...	...	...	...
Total	...	...	...	3701	2050	1651	30688 / 30069	17266 / 17848	13422 / 12221	48570	28771	19799
less: Imputed bank service charge	...	...	...	...	...	...	...	269	–269	...	450	–450
Import duties	...	...	...	...	...	...	...	...	...	...	...	...
Value added tax	...	...	...	...	...	...	...	...	...	...	...	...
Other adjustments	...	...	...	181	...	181	833 / 937	...	833 / 937	2261	...	2261
Total	...	...	...	3882	2050	1832	31521 / 31006	17266 / 18117	14255 / 12889	50831	29221	21610

Of which general government:

	1990	1991	1992	1993 G	1993 IC	1993 VA
1 Agriculture, hunting, forestry and fishing	...	...	...	260	116	144
2 Mining and quarrying	...	...	...	...	...	...
3 Manufacturing	...	...	...	...	...	...
4 Electricity, gas and water	...	...	...	...	...	...
5 Construction	...	...	...	...	...	...
6 Wholesale and retail trade, restaurants and hotels	...	...	...	...	...	...
7 Transport, storage and communication	...	...	...	77	49	28
8 Finance, insurance, real estate and business services	...	...	...	313	286	27
9 Community, social and personal services	...	...	...	343	178	165
Total, industries of general government	...	...	...	993	629	364
Producers of government services	...	...	...	3575	1391	2184
Total, general government	...	...	...	4568	2020	2548

	1994 Gross output	1994 Intermediate consumption	1994 Value added	1995 Gross output	1995 Intermediate consumption	1995 Value added	1996 Gross output	1996 Intermediate consumption	1996 Value added	1997 Gross output	1997 Intermediate consumption	1997 Value added
All producers												
1 Agriculture, hunting, forestry and fishing	7125	4411	2714	8192	5316	2876	9527	5993	3534	11301	7230	4071
A Agriculture and hunting	5883	3703	2180	6392	4164	2228	7392	4670	2722	7983	5135	2848
B Forestry and logging	876	496	380	1325	850	475	1569	959	610	2552	1623	929
C Fishing	366	212	154	475	302	173	566	364	202	766	472	294

Estonia

	1994 Gross output	1994 Intermediate consumption	1994 Value added	1995 Gross output	1995 Intermediate consumption	1995 Value added	1996 Gross output	1996 Intermediate consumption	1996 Value added	1997 Gross output	1997 Intermediate consumption	1997 Value added
2 Mining and quarrying	979	501	478	1224	622	602	1542	814	728	1800	1075	725
3 Manufacturing	17210	12188	5022	23498	17113	6385	27481	19697	7784	35117	25312	9805
4 Electricity, gas and water	3353	2483	870	4551	3110	1441	5658	3759	1899	6418	4331	2087
A Electricity, gas and steam	3344	2470	874	...	...	...	...	...	...	...	...	...
B Water works and supply	...	...	...	...	...	...	...	...	...	...	...	...
5 Construction	4789	3105	1684	7683	5522	2161	9805	7069	2736	11935	8800	3135
6 Wholesale and retail trade, restaurants and hotels	9936	5547	4389	13742	7307	6435	18193	9570	8623	23172	12248	10924
A Wholesale and retail trade	8939	4861	4078	12582	6566	6016	16667	8632	8035	21434	11255	10179
B Restaurants and hotels	997	686	311	1160	741	419	1526	938	588	1738	993	745
7 Transport, storage and communication	9188	6128	3060	12341	8510	3831	14482	9412	5070	18072	11328	6744
8 Finance, insurance, real estate and business services	6351	3292	3059	9692	4896	4796	12959	6237	6722	17878	9057	8821
A Financial institutions	1125	277	848	1635	313	1322	2613	386	2227	4004	998	3006
B Insurance												
C Real estate and business services	5226	3015	2211	8057	4583	3474	10346	5851	4495	13874	8059	5815
9 Community, social and personal services	2690	1138	1552	4595	2100	2495	6158	3046	3112	7345	3684	3661
Total, Industries	61621	38793	22828	85518	54496	31022	105805	65597	40208	133038	83065	49973
Producers of government services	5929	2278	3651	8860	3389	5471	11037	4286	6751	12847	5411	7436
Other producers	...	...	...	...	...	...	...	...	...	...	...	...
Total	67550	41071	26479	94378	57885	36493	116842	69883	46959	145885	88476	57409
less: Imputed bank service charge	...	623	−623	...	787	−787	...	1131	−1131	...	1026	−1026
Import duties	...	...	...	...	...	...	...	...	...	...	...	...
Value added tax	...	...	...	...	...	...	...	...	...	...	...	...
Other adjustments	3789	...	3789	4999	...	4999	6618	...	6618	8697	...	8697
Total	71339	41694	29645	99377	58672	40705	123460	71014	52446			
memorandum item: Mineral fuels and power	...	...	...	...	...	...	...	...	...	154582	89502	65080

Of which general government:

	1994 Gross output	1994 Intermediate consumption	1994 Value added	1995 Gross output	1995 Intermediate consumption	1995 Value added	1996 Gross output	1996 Intermediate consumption	1996 Value added	1997 Gross output	1997 Intermediate consumption	1997 Value added
1 Agriculture, hunting, forestry and fishing	284	73	211	509	274	235	650	316	334	675	330	345
2 Mining and quarrying	...	...	...	...	...	...	...	...	...	...	...	...
3 Manufacturing	...	...	...	...	...	...	...	...	...	...	...	...
4 Electricity, gas and water	...	...	...	...	...	...	...	...	...	...	...	...
5 Construction	...	...	...	...	...	...	...	...	...	...	...	...
6 Wholesale and retail trade, restaurants and hotels	...	...	...	...	...	...	...	...	...	...	...	...
7 Transport, storage and communication	228	183	45	594	450	144	674	500	174	734	550	184
8 Finance, insurance, real estate and business services	400	356	44	542	461	81	560	466	94	841	741	100
9 Community, social and personal services	526	279	247	1000	538	462	1306	820	486	1631	1118	513
Total, industries of general government	1438	891	547	2645	1723	922	3190	2102	1088	3881	2739	1142
Producers of government services	5547	2075	3472	8276	3103	5173	10212	3883	6329	11903	4964	6939
Total, general government	6985	2966	4019	10921	4826	6095	13402	5985	7417	15784	7703	8081

Estonia

4.2 Derivation of value added by kind of activity, in constant prices

Million Estonian kroons

	1990 Gross output	1990 Intermediate consumption	1990 Value added	1991 Gross output	1991 Intermediate consumption	1991 Value added	1992 Gross output	1992 Intermediate consumption	1992 Value added	1993 Gross output	1993 Intermediate consumption	1993 Value added
At constant prices of:	1991	1993	1995									
All producers												
1 Agriculture, hunting, forestry and fishing	...	...	...	609	300	310	504 / 6298	266 / 3771	238 / 2527	8842	5762	3080
A Agriculture and hunting	...	...	...	519	248	271	451	232	218	7481	4875	2606
B Forestry and logging	...	...	...	8	5	3	17	10	7	947	624	323
C Fishing	...	...	...	83	48	35	36	23	13	414	263	151
2 Mining and quarrying	...	...	...	48	19	30	48 / 1038	15 / 518	33 / 520	1398	712	686
3 Manufacturing	...	...	...	1533	934	599	1144 / 18286	719 / 12902	426 / 5384	21766	15756	6010
4 Electricity, gas and water	...	...	...	109	78	31	128 / 3247	101 / 2348	27 / 899	4727	3254	1473
5 Construction	...	...	...	254	143	111	112 / 2864	61 / 1787	51 / 1077	6797	4794	2003
6 Wholesale and retail trade, restaurants and hotels	...	...	...	230	82	147	290 / 5965	85 / 2790	205 / 3175	12612	6880	5732
A Wholesale and retail trade	...	...	...	177	44	133	249 / 5297	72 / 2416	177 / 2881	11333	6060	5273
B Restaurants and hotels	...	...	...	53	38	15	42 / 668	14 / 374	28 / 294	1279	820	459
7 Transport, storage and communication	...	...	...	216	103	114	377 / 5929	206 / 3590	170 / 2339	13788	9815	3973
A Transport and storage	...	...	...	198	99	99	356	198	159	...	...	...
B Communication	...	...	...	18	3	14	20	8	12	...	...	...
8 Finance, insurance, real estate and business services	...	...	...	91	47	44	105 / 3779	40 / 1650	65 / 2129	10406	5435	4971
A Financial institutions	...	...	...	18	5	14	41	12	29	1541	308	1233
B Insurance	...	...	...	2	–	1	3	1	3	...	...	...
C Real estate and business services	...	...	...	71	41	30	61	27	33	8865	5127	3738
9 Community, social and personal services	...	...	...	366	204	162	290 / 2498	218 / 1116	72 / 1382	4687	2245	2442
Total, Industries	...	...	...	3457	1910	1548	2997 / 49904	1711 / 30472	1286 / 19432	85023	54653	30370

604

Estonia

Million Estonian kroons

	1990			1991			1992			1993		
	Gross output	Intermediate consumption	Value added	Gross output	Intermediate consumption	Value added	Gross output	Intermediate consumption	Value added	Gross output	Intermediate consumption	Value added
	At constant prices of: 1991 1993 1995												
Producers of government services	...	...	...	243	140	103	275 3509	158 1300	118 2209			
....										8638	3294	5344
Other producers	...	...	...	...	...	...	...	...	...	...	...	...
Total	...	...	...	3701	2050	1651	3272 53413	1869 31772	1404 21641	93661	57947	35714
less: Imputed bank service charge	...	...	...	...	...	...	...	...	...		727	−727
Import duties	...	...	...	...	...	...	...	...	...	...	...	...
Value added tax	...	...	...	...	...	...	...	...	...	...	...	...
Other adjustments	...	...	...	181 2339	...	181 2339	168	...	168	4840	...	4840
Total	...	...	...	3882	2050	1832	3440 55752	1869 31772	1571 23980	98501	58674	39827
Of which general government:												
1 Agriculture, hunting, forestry and fishing	...	...	...	...	...	...	...	...	...	515	300	215
2 Mining and quarrying	...	...	...	...	...	...	...	...	...	...	...	...
3 Manufacturing	...	...	...	...	...	...	...	...	...	...	...	...
4 Electricity, gas and water	...	...	...	...	...	...	...	...	...	...	...	...
5 Construction	...	...	...	...	...	...	...	...	...	...	...	...
6 Wholesale and retail trade, restaurants and hotels	...	...	...	...	...	...	...	...	...	...	...	...
7 Transport, storage and communication	...	...	...	...	...	...	...	...	...	576	436	140
8 Finance, insurance, real estate and business services	...	...	...	...	...	...	...	...	...	525	447	78
9 Community, social and personal services	...	...	...	...	...	...	...	...	...	973	522	451
Total, industries of general government	...	...	...	...	...	...	...	...	...	2589	1705	884
Producers of government services	...	...	...	...	...	...	...	...	...	8192	3071	5121
Total, general government	...	...	...	...	...	...	...	...	...	10781	4776	6005

Estonia

	1994			1995			1996			1997		
	Gross output	Intermediate consumption	Value added	Gross output	Intermediate consumption	Value added	Gross output	Intermediate consumption	Value added	Gross output	Intermediate consumption	Value added

At constant prices of: 1995

All producers

1 Agriculture, hunting, forestry and fishing	8001	5206	2795	8192	5316	2876	8023	5209	2814	8400	5463	2937
A Agriculture and hunting	6562	4272	2290	6392	4164	2228	5974	3894	2080	5837	3806	2031
B Forestry and logging	1054	689	365	1325	850	475	1500	966	534	1990	1293	697
C Fishing	385	245	140	475	302	173	549	349	200	573	364	209
2 Mining and quarrying	1314	669	645	1224	622	602	1316	670	646	1475	751	724
3 Manufacturing	21341	15536	5805	23498	17113	6385	24159	17599	6560	29496	21648	7848
4 Electricity, gas and water	4721	3229	1492	4552	3110	1442	4761	3257	1504	4672	3214	1458
5 Construction	6662	4771	1891	7683	5522	2161	8259	5885	2374	9086	6490	2596
6 Wholesale and retail trade, restaurants and hotels	12412	6618	5794	13742	7307	6435	15236	8201	7035	17629	9680	7949
A Wholesale and retail trade	11134	5800	5334	12582	6566	6016	13946	7376	6570	16232	8788	7444
B Restaurants and hotels	1278	818	460	1160	741	419	1290	825	465	1397	892	505
7 Transport, storage and communication	13358	9363	3995	12341	8510	3831	12921	8810	4111	14428	9795	4633
8 Finance, insurance, real estate and business services	9937	5086	4851	9692	4897	4795	9871	4945	4926	11420	5707	5713
A Financial institutions	1614	312	1302	1635	314	1321	1767	339	1428	2043	390	1653
B Insurance	...	...	...	...	...	...	...	...	...	...	...	...
C Real estate and business services	8323	4774	3549	8057	4583	3474	8104	4606	3498	9377	5317	4060
9 Community, social and personal services	4467	2030	2437	4595	2100	2495	4842	2228	2614	4951	2298	2653
Total, Industries	82213	52508	29705	85519	54497	31022	89388	56804	32584	101557	65046	...
Producers of government services	8704	3315	5389	8860	3389	5471	8885	3403	5482	9073	3473	5600
Other producers	...	...	...	...	...	...	...	...	...	...	...	...
Total	90917	55823	35094	94379	57886	36493	98273	60207	38066	110630	68519	42111
less: Imputed bank service charge	...	775	−775	...	787	−787	...	850	−850	...	...	...
Import duties	...	...	...	...	...	...	...	...	...	...	...	...
Value added tax	...	...	...	...	...	...	...	...	...	...	...	...
Other adjustments	4712	...	4712	4999	...	4999	5110	...	5110	...	...	...
Total	95629	56598	39031	99378	58673	40705	103383	61057	42326	...	...	...

Of which general government:

1 Agriculture, hunting, forestry and fishing	524	298	226	509	274	235	507	272	235	507	272	235
2 Mining and quarrying	...	...	...	...	...	...	...	...	...	...	...	...
3 Manufacturing	...	...	...	...	...	...	...	...	...	...	...	...
4 Electricity, gas and water	...	...	...	...	...	...	...	...	...	...	...	...
5 Construction	...	...	...	...	...	...	...	...	...	...	...	...
6 Wholesale and retail trade, restaurants and hotels												
7 Transport, storage and communication	582	440	142	594	450	144	595	451	144	595	451	144
8 Finance, insurance, real estate and business services	530	451	79	542	461	81	542	461	81	542	461	81
9 Community, social and personal services	984	527	457	1000	538	462	1002	540	462	1002	540	462
Total, industries of general government	2620	1716	904	2645	1723	922	2646	1724	922	2646	1724	922

Estonia

	1994			1995			1996			1997		
	Gross output	Intermediate consumption	Value added	Gross output	Intermediate consumption	Value added	Gross output	Intermediate consumption	Value added	Gross output	Intermediate consumption	Value added
	At constant prices of: 1995										
Producers of government services	8225	3076	5149	8275	3102	5173	8246	3093	5153	8421	3157	5264
Total, general government	10845	4792	6053	10920	4825	6095	10892	4817	6075	11067	4881	6186

4.3 Cost components of value added

Million Estonian kroons

	1992							1993					
	Compensation of employees	Capital consumption	Net operating surplus	Indirect taxes	less: Subsidies received	Value added	Compensation of employees	Capital consumption	Net operating surplus	Indirect taxes	less: Subsidies received	Value added
	All producers											
1 Agriculture, hunting, forestry and fishing	...	...	...	...	...	1647	1028	233	865	53	...	2179
A Agriculture and hunting	...	...	...	...	...	1250	776	178	854	36	...	1844
B Forestry and logging	...	...	...	...	...	...	156	33	13	15	...	217
C Fishing	...	...	...	...	...	87	96	22	-2	2	...	118
2 Mining and quarrying	...	...	...	...	...	310	289	66	-5	17	...	367
3 Manufacturing	...	...	...	...	...	2773	2710	690	266	104	...	3770
4 Electricity, gas and water	...	...	...	...	...	537	483	205	1	25	...	714
5 Construction	...	...	...	...	...	603	827	86	329	59	...	1301
6 Wholesale and retail trade, restaurants and hotels	...	...	...	...	...	1980	1226	182	2067	158	...	3633
A Wholesale and retail trade	...	...	...	...	...	1773	1020	137	2055	148	...	3360
B Restaurants and hotels	...	...	...	...	...	207	206	45	12	10	...	273
7 Transport, storage and communication	...	...	...	...	...	1715	1499	559	354	44	...	2456
8 Finance, insurance, real estate and business services	...	...	...	...	...	1076	1021	173	751	72	...	2017
A Financial institutions	...	...	...	...	...	297	261	49	229	21	...	560
B Insurance												
C Real estate and business services	...	...	...	...	...	779	760	124	522	51	...	1457
9 Community, social and personal services	...	...	...	...	...	620	471	78	493	10	...	1052
Total, Industries	...	...	...	...	...	11261	9554	2272	5121	542	...	17489
Producers of government services	...	...	...	...	...	960	1830	427	46	8	...	2311
Other producers	...	...	...	...	...	...	...	...	...	...	...	...
Total	6257	640	4877	447	...	12221	11384	2699	5167	550	...	800
less: Imputed bank service charge	...	...	...	...	269	−269 [a]	...	...	...	...	450 [a]	450
Import duties	...	...	...	...	...	...	...	...	...	...	...	...
Value added tax	...	...	...	...	...	...	...	...	...	...	...	...

Estonia

Million Estonian kroons

	1992						1993					
	Compensation of employees	Capital consumption	Net operating surplus	Indirect taxes	less: Subsidies received	Value added	Compensation of employees	Capital consumption	Net operating surplus	Indirect taxes	less: Subsidies received	Value added
Other adjustments	...	...	...	1157[b]	220[c]	937	...	...	...	2477[b]	217[c]	2260
Total	6257	640	4877	1604	489	12889	11384	2699	5167	3027	667	21610

Of which general government:

1 Agriculture, hunting, forestry and fishing	...	...	...	...	...	...	69	75	–	–	...	144
2 Mining and quarrying	...	...	...	...	...	...	...	...	...	...	...	...
3 Manufacturing	...	...	...	...	...	...	...	...	...	...	...	...
4 Electricity, gas and water	...	...	...	...	...	...	...	...	...	...	...	...
5 Construction	...	...	...	...	...	...	...	...	...	...	...	...
6 Wholesale and retail trade, restaurants and hotels	...	...	...	...	...	...	...	...	...	...	...	...
7 Transport, storage and communication	...	...	...	...	...	...	21	7	–	–	...	28
8 Finance, insurance, real estate and business services	...	...	...	...	...	...	21	6	–	–	...	27
9 Community, social and personal services	...	...	...	...	...	...	116	49	–	1	...	166
Total, industries of general government	...	...	...	...	...	...	227	137	...	1	...	365
Producers of government services							1756	420	–	7		2183
Total, general government	...	...	...	...	...	...	1983	558	...	8	...	2548

	1994						1995					
	Compensation of employees	Capital consumption	Net operating surplus	Indirect taxes	less: Subsidies received	Value added	Compensation of employees	Capital consumption	Net operating surplus	Indirect taxes	less: Subsidies received	Value added

All producers

1 Agriculture, hunting, forestry and fishing	1288	321	1016	89	...	2714	1510	280	950	136	...	2876
A Agriculture and hunting	998	252	888	42	...	2180	1096	194	898	40	...	2228
B Forestry and logging	207	44	84	45	...	380	287	60	34	94	...	475
C Fishing	83	25	44	2	...	154	127	26	18	2	...	173
2 Mining and quarrying	412	55	–4	15	...	478	518	56	5	22	...	601
3 Manufacturing	3847	845	224	106	...	5022	5083	991	211	100	...	6385
4 Electricity, gas and water	675	229	–57	24	...	871	948	240	221	33	...	1442
5 Construction	1127	87	444	26	...	1684	1424	142	570	25	...	2161
6 Wholesale and retail trade, restaurants and hotels	245	312	1546	80	...	4389	2868	689	2791	87	...	6435
A Wholesale and retail trade	2198	257	1545	78	...	4078	2524	607	2801	84	...	6016
B Restaurants and hotels	253	55	1	2	...	311	344	82	–10	3	...	419
7 Transport, storage and communication	2014	645	330	70	...	3059	2844	835	85	67	...	3831
8 Finance, insurance, real estate and business services	1451	208	1354	47	...	3060	2366	333	2030	67	...	4796
A Financial institutions	405	71	352	20	...	848	559	80	659	23	...	1321
B Insurance												
C Real estate and business services	1046	137	1002	27	...	2212	1807	253	1371	44	...	3475

Estonia

	1994						1995					
	Compensation of employees	Capital consumption	Net operating surplus	Indirect taxes	less: Subsidies received	Value added	Compensation of employees	Capital consumption	Net operating surplus	Indirect taxes	less: Subsidies received	Value added
9 Community, social and personal services	698	91	747	15	...	1551	1029	174	1273	19	...	2495
Total, Industries	13963	2793	5600	472	...	22828	18590	3740	8136	556	...	31022
Producers of government services	3029	553	58	11	...	3651	4556	787	103	25	...	5471
Other producers	...	...	...	...	...	...	...	...	...	...	...	...
Total	16992	3346	5658	483	...	26479	23146	4527	8239	581	...	36493
less: Imputed bank service charge	...	...	...	...	623[a]	−623	...	...	...	...	787[a]	−787
Import duties	...	...	...	...	...	...	...	...	...	...	...	...
Value added tax	...	...	...	...	...	...	...	...	...	...	...	...
Other adjustments	...	...	...	4076[b]	287[c]	3789	...	...	...	5310[b]	311[c]	4999
Total	16992	3346	5658	4559	910	29645	23146	4527	8239	5891	1098	40705

Of which general government:

	1994						1995					
1 Agriculture, hunting, forestry and fishing	103	90	–	18	...	211	184	32	–	19	...	235
2 Mining and quarrying	...	...	...	...	...	...	...	...	...	...	...	...
3 Manufacturing	...	...	...	...	...	...	...	...	...	...	...	...
4 Electricity, gas and water	...	...	...	...	...	...	...	...	...	...	...	...
5 Construction	...	...	...	...	...	...	...	...	...	...	...	...
6 Wholesale and retail trade, restaurants and hotels	...	...	...	...	...	...	...	...	...	...	...	...
7 Transport, storage and communication	35	10	–	–	...	45	98	46	–	...	...	144
8 Finance, insurance, real estate and business services	36	8	–	–	...	44	52	29	–	...	...	81
9 Community, social and personal services	187	59	–	1	...	247	341	121	–	–	...	462
Total, industries of general government	361	167	–	19	...	547	675	228	–	19	...	922
Producers of government services	2918	543	–	11	...	3472	4384	765	–	24	...	5173
Total, general government	3279	710	–	30	...	4019	5059	993	...	43	...	6095

	1996						1997					
	Compensation of employees	Capital consumption	Net operating surplus	Indirect taxes	less: Subsidies received	Value added	Compensation of employees	Capital consumption	Net operating surplus	Indirect taxes	less: Subsidies received	Value added

All producers

1 Agriculture, hunting, forestry and fishing	1820	286	1324	105	...	3535	1957	416	1540	158	...	4071
A Agriculture and hunting	1324	206	1140	53	...	2723	1376	305	1082	85	...	2848
B Forestry and logging	344	50	168	47	...	609	391	69	401	68	...	929
C Fishing	152	30	16	5	...	203	190	42	57	5	...	294
2 Mining and quarrying	626	61	9	32	...	728	689	70	−108	74	...	725
3 Manufacturing	5831	1123	737	93	...	7784	6743	1429	1516	117	...	9805
4 Electricity, gas and water	1075	336	438	50	...	1899	1309	507	212	59	...	2087
5 Construction	1460	193	1043	39	...	2735	1962	253	862	59	...	3136
6 Wholesale and retail trade, restaurants and hotels	3880	920	3738	85	...	8623	4844	1193	4765	122	...	10924
A Wholesale and retail trade	3393	811	3751	80	...	8035	4336	1065	4660	118	...	10179
B Restaurants and hotels	487	109	−13	5	...	588	508	128	105	4	...	745
7 Transport, storage and communication	3332	1091	550	97	...	5070	3881	1422	1295	146	...	6744

Estonia

	1996						1997					
	Compensation of employees	Capital consumption	Net operating surplus	Indirect taxes	less: Subsidies received	Value added	Compensation of employees	Capital consumption	Net operating surplus	Indirect taxes	less: Subsidies received	Value added
8 Finance, insurance, real estate and business services	2991	546	3080	105	...	6722	3964	757	3971	129	...	8821
A Financial institutions	758	135	1292	42	...	2227	1079	261	1629	37	...	3006
B Insurance												
C Real estate and business services	2233	411	1788	63	...	4495	2885	496	2342	92	...	5815
9 Community, social and personal services	1205	232	1616	59	...	3112	1439	233	1949	40	...	3661
Total, Industries	22220	4788	12535	665	...	40208	26788	6280	16002	904	...	49974
Producers of government services	5690	863	147	51	...	6751	6341	865	171	58	...	7435
Other producers	...	...	...	...	...	...	...	...	...	...	...	...
Total	27910	5651	12682	716	...	46959	33129	7145	16173	962	...	57409
less: Imputed bank service charge	...	...	...	...	1131[a]	−1131	...	...	...	...	1026[a]	−1026
Import duties	...	...	...	...	...	...	...	...	...	...	...	...
Value added tax	...	...	...	...	...	...	...	...	...	...	...	...
Other adjustments	...	...	...	7009[b]	391[c]	6618	...	...	...	9091[b]	394[c]	8697
Total	27910	5651	12682	7725	1522	52446	33129	7145	16173	10053	1420	65080

Of which general government:

	1996						1997					
1 Agriculture, hunting, forestry and fishing	262	35	–	37	...	334	265	34	–	46	...	345
2 Mining and quarrying	...	...	...	...	...	...	...	...	...	...	...	...
3 Manufacturing	...	...	...	...	...	...	...	...	...	...	...	...
4 Electricity, gas and water	...	...	...	...	...	...	...	...	...	...	...	...
5 Construction	...	...	...	...	...	...	...	...	...	...	...	...
6 Wholesale and retail trade, restaurants and hotels	...	...	...	...	...	...	...	...	...	...	...	...
7 Transport, storage and communication	125	50	–	–	...	175	135	49	–	–	...	184
8 Finance, insurance, real estate and business services	62	31	–	–	...	93	69	31	–	–	...	100
9 Community, social and personal services	355	131	–	–	...	486	382	130	–	–	...	512
Total, industries of general government	804	247	–	37	...	1088	851	244	...	46	...	1141
Producers of government services	5449	832	–	48	...	6329	6061	823	–	56	...	6940
Total, general government	6253	1079	–	85	...	7417	6912	1067	–	102	...	8081

a Financial Intermediation Services Indirectly Measured (FISIM).
b Indirect taxes on product = VAT + excise tax + customs services fee + local sales tax.
c Subsidies.

Ethiopia

General note

The preparation of national accounts statistics in Ethiopia is undertaken by the Central Statistical Office, Addis Ababa. The official estimates with methodological notes are published annually in the *Statistical Abstract*. The estimates are generally in accordance with the classifications and definitions recommended in the United Nations Systems of National Accounts (1968 SNA). The following tables have been prepared from successive replies to the United Nations national accounts questionnaire. The Ethiopian fiscal year which is from June to July has been used for all estimates except the external transactions table. When the scope and coverage of the estimates differ for conceptual or statistical reasons from the definitions and classifications recommended in SNA, a footnote is indicated to the relevant tables. The following tables contain data for Ethiopia from 1993.

Gross domestic product

Gross domestic product is estimated mainly through the production approach.

Expenditures on the gross domestic product

The expenditure approach is used to estimate government final consumption expenditure and exports and imports of goods and services. This approach, in combination with the commodity-flow approach, is also used for estimating gross fixed capital formation. Private consumption expenditure is obtained as a residual which also includes increase in stocks. Government final consumption expenditure, consisting of compensation of employees and net purchases of goods and services, is obtained from the annual budgetary revenue and expenditure report, from the Ministry of Finance and from municipalities. These sources are also used for estimating the public sectors capital formation in building and construction. The estimates of private construction in urban areas are based on building permits which are adjusted for timing by taking the average of the last two years and adding 5 per cent for underreporting. Other urban private construction is estimated by applying the ratio of per capita consumption expenditure in Addis Ababa to the per capita consumption expenditure in other urban areas. Construction in the rural areas is estimated by multiplying the assumed number of tukuls built in a given year by an assumed average cost per tukul. For capital formation in machinery and equipment, import statistics are used. To the import values are added import duties, transport costs, trade margins and installation costs. The data on exports and imports of goods and services are obtained from the external trade statistics. Gross domestic product by expenditure type at constant prices is not estimated.

Cost structure of the gross domestic product

The cost-structure of the gross domestic product is not estimated.

Gross domestic product by kind of activity

The table of gross domestic product by kind of economic activity is prepared in factor values. The production approach is used to estimate value added of most industries. The income approach is also used in measuring the output of the modern sectors of the economy such as the industrial activity and the services sectors. The estimates of the value added of agriculture for the benchmark years 1961–1963 are based on various sources such as population figures, assumed per capita consumption of food grains and wholesale prices. Recent years' estimates are also based on qualitative crop surveys and surveys on cultivated area. The net output by type of plant product is multiplied by wholesale prices adjusted for trade and transport margins. The 1961–1963 benchmark estimates of livestock production were based on the number of livestock by type, on gross output and on value added. For subsequent years, gross output and value added are derived by applying growth factors linked to the population growth rate. For forestry, the sources include the Forestry Department, the survey of wood-working industries, family budget studies in 1967/68 and the annual surveys of manufacturing industries. Value added is derived by deducting 10 per cent from gross value of production of industrial wood and firewood.

The Ministry of Mines and the annual budgetary reports provide data for the mining sector. The value of production is estimated by multiplying the quantity produced of each mineral product by its average price. The source of data for large-scale manufacturing is the annual surveys of manufacturing industries. Value added is obtained by deducting the cost of inputs of raw materials, fuel and energy from the gross value of production. For small-scale manufacturing and handicraft, value added is derived by assuming that the growth rate is half of the one observed for output of large-scale manufacturing. Data for electricity are obtained from annual returns to questionnaires submitted to concerned enterprises. Data on the number of building permits issued, the 1968 household expenditure survey and population estimates are used to estimate the value of construction in the private sector. The total value of Addis Ababa building permits is adjusted for timing and under-reporting. Work done in other towns is estimated by applying the ratio of per capita consumption expenditure in Addis Ababa to the per capita consumption expenditure in other towns.

For the public sector, data are obtained from the budgetary revenue and expenditure reports as well as from questionnaires sent to municipalities and public agencies. The gross trade margin of imported goods is estimated at 15 per cent of the value of imports based on the 1963 trade inquiry. Similar assumptions are made for locally produced goods. Value added in the transport sector is based on the annual reports of concerned enterprises for the railway, water and air transports. For road transport, data on passenger or ton kilometres, registration statistics, and passenger fares and freight rates are used. For the financial institutions, the profit and loss statement and the annual reports of concerned institutions are used. Benchmark estimates for 1961–1963 are available for ownership of dwellings. The gross rental income of the urban areas is obtained by multiplying the total number of housing units by assumed actual and imputed average annual rental rates, while for the rural areas the total number of "tukuls" is multiplied by the assumed average value per "tukul". Value added of public administration and defence is equal to total wages and salaries paid to government employees, including payment in kind. The sources of data include annual reports and questionnaires sent to different agencies. For other government services such as education and health, value added is based on government reports. Value added per student enrolled in non-governmental schools is estimated as two-thirds of the value added per student in government schools. The value of domestic services is obtained by multiplying the number of employees by assumed average pay rates.

For the constant price estimates, the current net output of plant products in the agricultural sector is revalued at base-year producer prices. For livestock, water supply and construction, value added at current factor costs is assumed to be equal to the value added at constant factor costs. Price indexes are used to deflate the current value added of mining and quarrying, small-scale manufacturing, trade, finance and most of the services sectors. For large-scale manufacturing, electricity, transport and domestic services, value added is extrapolated by volume indexes.

1.1 Expenditure on the gross domestic product, in current prices

Million Ethiopian birr — Fiscal year ending 7 July

	1986	1987	1988	1989	1990	1991	1992	1993	1994	1995	1996	1997
1 Government final consumption expenditure	...	...	...	...	...	...	...	2819	3155	3675	4035	...
2 Private final consumption expenditure	...	...	...	...	...	...	...	22209	23774	28137	31240	...
3 Gross capital formation	...	...	...	...	...	...	...	3792	4294	5569	7170	...
A Increase in stocks	...	...	...	...	...	...	...	...	...	...	...	...
B Gross fixed capital formation	...	...	...	...	...	...	...	3792	4294	5569	7170	...
4 Exports of goods and services	...	...	...	...	...	...	...	2223	3223	4899	5244	...
5 less: Imports of goods and services	...	...	...	...	...	...	...	4521	6091	8217	9572	...
equals: Gross domestic product	...	...	...	...	...	...	...	26521	28355	34063	38117	...

Ethiopia (Former)

General note

The preparation of national accounts statistics in Ethiopia is undertaken by the Central Statistical Office, Addis Ababa. The official estimates with methodological notes are published annually in the *Statistical Abstract*. The estimates are generally in accordance with the classifications and definitions recommended in the United Nations Systems of National Accounts (1968 SNA). The following tables have been prepared from successive replies to the United Nations national accounts questionnaire. The Ethiopian fiscal year which is from June to July has been used for all estimates except the external transactions table. When the scope and coverage of the estimates differ for conceptual or statistical reasons from the definitions and classifications recommended in SNA, a footnote is indicated to the relevant tables. The former Ethiopia includes data up to 1993.

Gross domestic product

Gross domestic product is estimated mainly through the production approach.

Expenditures on the gross domestic product

The expenditure approach is used to estimate government final consumption expenditure and exports and imports of goods and services. This approach, in combination with the commodity-flow approach, is also used for estimating gross fixed capital formation. Private consumption expenditure is obtained as a residual which also includes increase in stocks. Government final consumption expenditure, consisting of compensation of employees and net purchases of goods and services, is obtained from the annual budgetary revenue and expenditure report, from the Ministry of Finance and from municipalities. These sources are also used for estimating the public sectors capital formation in building and construction. The estimates of private construction in urban areas are based on building permits which are adjusted for timing by taking the average of the last two years and adding 5 per cent for underreporting. Other urban private construction is estimated by applying the ratio of per capita consumption expenditure in Addis Ababa to the per capita consumption expenditure in other urban areas. Construction in the rural areas is estimated by multiplying the assumed number of tukuls built in a given year by an assumed average cost per tukul. For capital formation in machinery and equipment, import statistics are used. To the import values are added import duties, transport costs, trade margins and installation costs. The data on exports and imports of goods and services are obtained from the external trade statistics. Gross domestic product by expenditure type at constant prices is not estimated.

Cost structure of the gross domestic product

The cost-structure of the gross domestic product is not estimated.

Gross domestic product by kind of activity

The table of gross domestic product by kind of economic activity is prepared in factor values. The production approach is used to estimate value added of most industries. The income approach is also used in measuring the output of the modern sectors of the economy such as the industrial activity and the services sectors. The estimates of the value added of agriculture for the benchmark years 1961–1963 are based on various sources such as population figures, assumed per capita consumption of food grains and wholesale prices. Recent years' estimates are also based on qualitative crop surveys and surveys on cultivated area. The net output by type of plant product is multiplied by wholesale prices adjusted for trade and transport margins. The 1961–1963 benchmark estimates of livestock production were based on the number of livestock by type, on gross output and on value added. For subsequent years, gross output and value added are derived by applying growth factors linked to the population growth rate. For forestry, the sources include the Forestry Department, the survey of wood-working industries, family budget studies in 1967/68 and the annual surveys of manufacturing industries. Value added is derived by deducting 10 per cent from gross value of production of industrial wood and firewood.

The Ministry of Mines and the annual budgetary reports provide data for the mining sector. The value of production is estimated by multiplying the quantity produced of each mineral product by its average price. The source of data for large-scale manufacturing is the annual surveys of manufacturing industries. Value added is obtained by deducting the cost of inputs of raw materials, fuel and energy from the gross value of production. For small-scale manufacturing and handicraft, value added is derived by assuming that the growth rate is half of the one observed for output of large-scale manufacturing. Data for electricity are obtained from annual returns to questionnaires submitted to concerned enterprises. Data on the number of building permits issued, the 1968 household expenditure survey and population estimates are used to estimate the value of construction in the private sector. The total value of Addis Ababa building permits is adjusted for timing and under-reporting. Work done in other towns is estimated by applying the ratio of per capita consumption expenditure in Addis Ababa to the per capita consumption expenditure in other towns.

For the public sector, data are obtained from the budgetary revenue and expenditure reports as well as from questionnaires sent to municipalities and public agencies. The gross trade mar-

Ethiopia (Former)

gin of imported goods is estimated at 15 per cent of the value of imports based on the 1963 trade inquiry. Similar assumptions are made for locally produced goods. Value added in the transport sector is based on the annual reports of concerned enterprises for the railway, water and air transports. For road transport, data on passenger or ton kilometres, registration statistics, and passenger fares and freight rates are used. For the financial institutions, the profit and loss statement and the annual reports of concerned institutions are used. Benchmark estimates for 1961–1963 are available for ownership of dwellings. The gross rental income of the urban areas is obtained by multiplying the total number of housing units by assumed actual and imputed average annual rental rates, while for the rural areas the total number of "tukuls" is multiplied by the assumed average value per "tukul". Value added of public administration and defence is equal to total wages and salaries paid to government employees, including payment in kind. The sources of data include annual reports and questionnaires sent to different agencies. For other government services such as education and health, value added is based on government reports. Value added per student enrolled in non-governmental schools is estimated as two-thirds of the value added per student in government schools. The value of domestic services is obtained by multiplying the number of employees by assumed average pay rates.

For the constant price estimates, the current net output of plant products in the agricultural sector is revalued at base-year producer prices. For livestock, water supply and construction, value added at current factor costs is assumed to be equal to the value added at constant factor costs. Price indexes are used to deflate the current value added of mining and quarrying, small-scale manufacturing, trade, finance and most of the services sectors. For large-scale manufacturing, electricity, transport and domestic services, value added is extrapolated by volume indexes.

1.1 Expenditure on the gross domestic product, in current prices

Million birr — Fiscal year ending 7 July

	1986	1987	1988	1989	1990	1991	1992	1993	1994	1995	1996	1997
1 Government final consumption expenditure	2152	2288	2757	3129	3296	3048	2108	...	...	...	...	...
2 Private final consumption expenditure	11161	12127	11342	12324	13813	16771	18059	...	...	...	...	...
3 Gross capital formation	2317	2338	3187	2362	1585	1410	1911	...	...	...	...	...
A Increase in stocks	...	...	...	...	...	...	...	...	...	...	...	...
B Gross fixed capital formation	2317	2338	3187	2362	1585	1410	1911	...	...	...	...	...
4 Exports of goods and services	1371	1290	1303	1542	1391	1124	938	...	...	...	...	...
5 less: Imports of goods and services	2508	2541	2592	2484	2213	2538	2223	...	...	...	...	...
equals: Gross domestic product	14493	15502	15997	16873	17872	19815	20792	...	...	...	...	...

1.10 Gross domestic product by kind of activity, in current prices

Million birr — Fiscal year ending 7 July

	1986	1987	1988	1989	1990	1991	1992	1993	1994	1995	1996	1997
1 Agriculture, hunting, forestry and fishing	4370	4362	4308	4595	4700	5040	6311	...	...	...	...	...
2 Mining and quarrying	15	12	14	14	22	37	40	...	...	...	...	...
3 Manufacturing	1059	1268	1255	1287	1265	1264	1138	...	...	...	...	...
4 Electricity, gas and water	110	135	144	159	171	182	163	...	...	...	...	...
5 Construction	416	444	442	440	416	394	346	...	...	...	...	...
6 Wholesale and retail trade, restaurants and hotels [a]	1036	1057	1080	1120	1098	1152	1280	...	...	...	...	...
7 Transport, storage and communication	724	701	719	783	826	876	678	...	...	...	...	...
8 Finance, insurance, real estate and business services [b]	614	678	758	746	753	958	988	...	...	...	...	...
9 Community, social and personal services [ab]	603	654	676	708	748	788	690	...	...	...	...	...
Total, Industries	8948	9311	9397	9852	10000	10690	11634	...	...	...	...	...
Producers of government services	869	916	1175	1277	1437	1605	990	...	...	...	...	...
Other producers	...	...	...	...	...	...	...	...	...	...	...	...

Ethiopia (Former)

Million birr   **Fiscal year ending 7 July**

	1986	1987	1988	1989	1990	1991	1992	1993	1994	1995	1996	1997
Subtotal [c]	9817	10227	10572	11129	11436	12295	12544	...	...	...	...	...
less: Imputed bank service charge	...	...	...	...	...	...	...	...	...	...	...	...
plus: Import duties	...	...	...	...	...	...	...	...	...	...	...	...
plus: Value added tax	...	...	...	...	...	...	...	...	...	...	...	...
plus: Other adjustments [d]	1088	1172	1329	1242	1097	1037	964	...	...	...	...	...
equals: Gross domestic product [e]	10905	11399	11901	12371	12533	13332	13508	...	...	...	...	...

a Restaurants and hotels are included in item "Community, social and personal services".
b Business services are included in item "Community, social and personal services".
c Gross domestic product in factor values.
d Item "Other adjustments" refers to indirect taxes net of subsidies
e The data in this table has not been updated.

1.11 Gross domestic product by kind of activity, in constant prices

Million birr   **Fiscal year ending 7 July**

	1986	1987	1988	1989	1990	1991	1992	1993	1994	1995	1996	1997
At constant prices of: 1981												
1 Agriculture, hunting, forestry and fishing	3481	4009	3924	4011	4020	4043	6702	...	...	...	...	...
2 Mining and quarrying	14	11	13	13	20	40	48	...	...	...	...	...
3 Manufacturing	1041	1096	1115	1137	1089	902	1370	...	...	...	...	...
4 Electricity, gas and water	86	92	99	102	107	102	169	...	...	...	...	...
5 Construction	375	390	378	360	322	258	355	...	...	...	...	...
6 Wholesale and retail trade, restaurants and hotels [a]	939	1013	1026	1050	1005	913	1753	...	...	...	...	...
7 Transport, storage and communication	526	527	570	578	592	527	751	...	...	...	...	...
8 Finance, insurance, real estate and business services [b]	580	646	717	694	692	690	844	...	...	...	...	...
9 Community, social and personal services [ab]	475	501	522	539	555	571	1025	...	...	...	...	...
Total, Industries	7515	8284	8364	8484	8403	8044	13019	...	...	...	...	...
Producers of government services	722	740	829	858	898	935	1013	...	...	...	...	...
Other producers	...	...	...	...	...	...	...	...	...	...	...	...
Subtotal [c]	8237	9024	9193	9342	9301	8979	14032	...	...	...	...	...
less: Imputed bank service charge	...	...	...	...	...	...	...	...	...	...	...	...
plus: Import duties	...	...	...	...	...	...	...	...	...	...	...	...
plus: Value added tax	...	...	...	...	...	...	...	...	...	...	...	...
plus: Other adjustments	...	...	...	...	...	...	...	...	...	...	...	...
equals: Gross domestic product [cd]	8237	9024	9193	9342	9301	8979	14032	...	...	...	...	...

a Restaurants and hotels are included in item "Community, social and personal services".
b Business services are included in item "Community, social and personal services".
c Gross domestic product in factor values.
d The data in this table has not been updated.

Fiji

General note

The preparation of national accounts statistics in Fiji is undertaken by the Bureau of Statistics, Suva. The official estimates together with methodological notes are published in a series of reports entitled *National Accounts Studies*. The third volume of this series, *The National Accounts of Fiji* contains a detailed description of the sources and methods used for the national accounts estimation. The estimates are generally in accordance with the classifications and definitions recommended in the United Nations System of National Accounts (1968 SNA). The following tables have been prepared from successive replies to the United Nations National Accounts Questionnaire. When the scope and coverage of the estimates differ for conceptual or statistical reasons from the definitions and classifications recommended in SNA, a footnote is indicated to the relevant tables.

Gross domestic product

Gross domestic product is estimated mainly through the production approach.

Expenditures on the gross domestic product

All components of gross domestic product by expenditure type are estimated through the expenditure approach except private final consumption expenditure which is mostly based on the commodity-flow approach. The estimates of government final consumption expenditure are based on the annual report *An Economic and Functional Classification of Government Accounts*. For private consumption expenditure estimates, all imported items valued at landed cost from foreign trade statistics and producers' values from industrial censuses are grossed up by margins established in the 1970 Census of Distribution and Services. Special estimates are made for those items after consumer expenditure, such as food, electricity, gas and water, medical services and recreations, which are not covered by the commodity-flow approach. For these estimates data from the household budget survey in 1972, income tax statistics and the 1970 census of distribution are used. Estimates of gross capital formation for the private industry are based on surveys of capital investment, for government industry and producers of government services the estimates are derived from government account and for the producers of private non-profit services to households from the 1970/1971 survey of non-profit making institutions. Value of imports and exports of goods and services are obtained from the balance of payments and annual shipping and aircraft statistics. For the constant price estimates, the current values of expenditure items are deflated by various price indexes such as consumer price index, index of rural produce prices, implicit price index of value added of building and construction, trade index of exports, etc.

Cost structure of the gross domestic product

Estimates of the cost-structure of gross domestic product are made from the various sectoral surveys and taxation data. Estimates of indirect taxes and subsidies are based on government accounts.

Gross domestic product by kind of activity

The table of gross domestic product by kind of economic activity is prepared at market price, i.e. producers' values. The production approach is used to estimate value added of most industries, such as agriculture, mining, manufacturing, electricity, gas and water, construction, and for the trade sector in combination with the commodity-flow approach. The income approach is used to estimate value added of restaurants and hotels and most of the subsectors of the service industries. For agricultural sector, the total output of sugarcane and copra are estimated from material inputs revealed by annual industrial censuses. The benchmark estimates of substance output is based on the 1968 Agricultural Census, the 1965 Rural-Urban Household Expenditure Survey and Bureau of Statistics data. The annual increases are based on estimates of population growth and an index of rural produce prices. For other agricultural produce gross output is based on 1968 and 1972 household budget surveys and intermediate consumption is based on case studies. The gross output and intermediate consumption of the industrial activity sectors are based on annual industrial censuses carried out since 1970. Estimates of gross output, intermediate consumption and compensation of employees of private construction are obtained from annual censuses of building and construction conducted annually since 1970. Government bodies engaged in construction are covered through their annual reports and operating budgets. For the trade sector, the estimates are based on statistics from the Inland Revenue Departments and on the Census of Distribution 1970. The producers' values and c.i.f. import values are grossed up by the margin established in the 1970 Census of Distribution. Banking estimates are obtained from income tax statistics while insurance estimates are derived from annual surveys.

Imputed rent per urban household is derived from the household budget survey in 1968, grossed up by the consumer price index for rent and the growth in urban population. For rural areas, an estimated rent has been assumed in 1968 and grossed up annually by a rural price factor and growth in rural population. Estimates for producers of government services are based on the operating budgets and government accounts and finance. Other services estimates are derived from income tax statistics, the

Fiji

1970/71 survey of non-profit institutions and 1970 Census of Distribution and Services.

For the constant price estimates, the general approach used for the major crops of agriculture, industrial activity, transport, insurance and private services is extrapolated. Value added is extrapolated by production indexes. Price deflation is used for construction, trade, restaurants and hotels, real estate, banking and producers of government services, the current value being deflated by various price indexes such as consumer price index, index of wage rates, etc.

1.1 Expenditure on the gross domestic product, in current prices

Million Fiji dollars

	1986	1987	1988	1989	1990	1991	1992	1993	1994	1995	1996	1997
1 Government final consumption expenditure	267	269	263	305	346	357	415	467	441	451	481	...
2 Private final consumption expenditure	873	960	1094	1274	1443	1582	1683	1802	1902	1987	2058	...
3 Gross capital formation	266	234	204	236	363	322	277	399	371	367	328	...
A Increase in stocks	51	4	13	25	35	28	30	38	41	30	41	...
B Gross fixed capital formation	215	230	191	211	328	294	247	361	330	337	287	...
4 Exports of goods and services	609	664	894	1099	1234	1170	1213	1321	1508	1532	1769	...
5 less: Imports of goods and services	577	616	815	1059	1330	1236	1264	1499	1588	1630	1756	...
Statistical discrepancy	24	–46	–53	6	–77	–153	–22	32	40	92	96	...
equals: Gross domestic product	1462[a]	1465[a]	1588	1861	1980	2042	2302	2522	2674	2799	2976	...

a Data in this table have not been revised, therefore they are not comparable with the data in other tables.

1.3 Cost components of the gross domestic product

Million Fiji dollars

	1986	1987	1988	1989	1990	1991	1992	1993	1994	1995	1996	1997
1 Indirect taxes, net	136	136	155	200	206	240	298	358	383	395	416	...
A Indirect taxes	137	136	155	200	206	240	298	358	383	395	416	...
B less: Subsidies	1	–	–	–	–	–	–	–	–	–	–	...
2 Consumption of fixed capital	103	111	119	138	154	168	183	183	183	192	204	...
3 Compensation of employees paid by resident producers to	641	612	661	766	783	810	843	861	946	996	1063	...
4 Operating surplus	582	606	653	757	838	823	978	1120	1162	1217	1293	...
equals: Gross domestic product	1462	1465	1588	1861	1980	2042	2302	2522	2674	2799	2976	...

1.4 General government current receipts and disbursements

Million Fiji dollars

	1986	1987	1988	1989	1990	1991	1992	1993	1994	1995	1996	1997
Receipts												
1 Operating surplus	...	...	...	...	...	...	...	...	...	...	...	...
2 Property and entrepreneurial income	25	32	41	36	16	18	22	21	23	29	...	...
3 Taxes, fees and contributions	300	288	321	409	486	498	536	584	631	676	...	...
A Indirect taxes	137	137	155	199	238	237	293	353	380	398	...	...
B Direct taxes	144	135	147	185	218	229	207	192	206	225	...	...
C Social security contributions	–	–	–	–	–	–	–	–	–	–	...	...
D Compulsory fees, fines and penalties	19	16	19	25	30	32	36	39	45	53	...	...
4 Other current transfers	56	39	53	32	39	51	46	55	53	41	...	...

Fiji

Million Fiji dollars

	1986	1987	1988	1989	1990	1991	1992	1993	1994	1995	1996	1997
Total current receipts of general government	381	359	415	477	...	...	...	...	...	...	...	...
Disbursements												
1 Government final consumption expenditure	267	269	264	305	346	357	415	467	441	451	...	...
2 Property income	51	59	71	69	70	71	70	74	76	76	...	...
A Interest	51	59	71	69	70	71	70	74	76	76	...	...
B Net land rent and royalties	–	–	–	–	–	–	–	–	–	–	...	...
3 Subsidies	1	–	–	–	–	–	–	–	–	–	...	...
4 Other current transfers	43	48	50	56	...	...	...	...	...	...	...	...
A Social security benefits	4	6	6	23	...	...	...	...	...	...	...	...
B Social assistance grants					...	...	...	...	...	...	...	...
C Other	39	42	44	33	...	...	...	...	...	...	...	...
5 Net saving	19	–17	30	47	...	...	...	...	...	...	...	...
Total current disbursements and net saving of general government	381	359	415	477	...	...	...	...	...	...	...	...

1.7 External transactions on current account, summary

Million Fiji dollars

	1986	1987	1988	1989	1990	1991	1992	1993	1994	1995	1996	1997
Payments to the rest of the world												
1 Imports of goods and services	577	616	815	1059	1330	1236	1259	1487	...	...	...	...
2 Factor income to rest of the world	56	82	88	112	108	105	119	96	...	...	...	...
A Compensation of employees	–	–	–	–	–	–	–	–	...	...	...	...
B Property and entrepreneurial income	56	82	88	112	108	105	119	96	...	...	...	...
3 Current transfers to the rest of the world	33	46	36	65	71	87	80	85	...	...	...	...
4 Surplus of the nation on current transactions	–8	–23	46	52	–86	–16	–4	–87	...	...	...	...
Payments to the rest of the world and surplus of the nation on current transfers	659	722	985	1288	1423	1412	1454	1581	...	...	...	...
Receipts from the rest of the world												
1 Exports of goods and services	609	664	894	1163	1310	1279	1316	1425	...	...	...	...
2 Factor income from rest of the world	22	34	53	76	73	76	79	82	...	...	...	...
A Compensation of employees	8	9	19	34	32	28	34	40	...	...	...	...
B Property and entrepreneurial income	14	25	34	42	41	48	45	42	...	...	...	...
3 Current transfers from rest of the world	28	24	37	50	40	55	60	73	...	...	...	...
Receipts from the rest of the world on current transactions	659	722	984	1289	1423	1410	1455	1580	...	...	...	...

1.8 Capital transactions of the nation, summary

Million Fiji dollars

	1986	1987	1988	1989	1990	1991	1992	1993	1994	1995	1996	1997
Finance of gross capital formation												
Gross saving	282	166	196	295	274	236	287	312	...	...	...	...

Fiji

Million Fiji dollars

	1986	1987	1988	1989	1990	1991	1992	1993	1994	1995	1996	1997
1 Consumption of fixed capital	103	111	119	138	154	168	183	183	...	...	...	...
2 Net saving	179	55	77	157	120	68	104	129	...	...	...	...
less: Surplus of the nation on current transactions	−7	−23	46	52	−86	−16	−4	−87	...	...	...	...
Statistical discrepancy	−23	45	54	12	−3	41	20	−15	...	...	...	...
Finance of gross capital formation	266	234	204	257	357	293	311	384	...	...	...	...
Gross capital formation												
Increase in stocks	51	4	13	25	35	26	30	40	...	...	...	...
Gross fixed capital formation	215	230	191	232	322	267	281	344	...	...	...	...
Gross capital formation	266	234	204	257	357	293	311	384	...	...	...	...

1.10 Gross domestic product by kind of activity, in current prices

Million Fiji dollars

	1986	1987	1988	1989	1990	1991	1992	1993	1994	1995	1996	1997
1 Agriculture, hunting, forestry and fishing	277	306	280	326	...	...	...	...	...	...	...	...
2 Mining and quarrying	18	31	62	56	...	...	...	...	...	...	...	...
3 Manufacturing	137	157	137	175	...	...	...	...	...	...	...	...
4 Electricity, gas and water	48	44	52	55	...	...	...	...	...	...	...	...
5 Construction	64	50	60	66	...	...	...	...	...	...	...	...
6 Wholesale and retail trade, restaurants and hotels	223	209	282	379	...	...	...	...	...	...	...	...
7 Transport, storage and communication	132	133	163	169	...	...	...	...	...	...	...	...
8 Finance, insurance, real estate and business services	182	182	197	216	...	...	...	...	...	...	...	...
9 Community, social and personal services	169	153	165	179	...	...	...	...	...	...	...	...
Total, Industries	1250	1265	1397	1621	...	...	...	...	...	...	...	...
Producers of government services	113	105	90	105	...	...	...	...	...	...	...	...
Other producers	27	29	30	33	...	...	...	...	...	...	...	...
Subtotal [a]	1391	1399	1518	1759	...	...	...	...	...	...	...	...
less: Imputed bank service charge	65	70	85	98	...	...	...	...	...	...	...	...
plus: Import duties	...	...	...	...	...	...	...	...	...	...	...	...
plus: Value added tax	...	...	...	...	...	...	...	...	...	...	...	...
plus: Other adjustments [b]	136	136	155	200	...	...	...	...	...	...	...	...
equals: Gross domestic product [c]	1462	1465	1588	1861	...	...	...	...	...	...	...	...

a Gross domestic product in factor values.
b Item "Other adjustments" refers to indirect taxes net of subsidies.
c Data in this table have not been revised, therefore they are not comparable with the data in other tables.

1.11 Gross domestic product by kind of activity, in constant prices

Million Fiji dollars

	1986	1987	1988	1989	1990	1991	1992	1993	1994	1995	1996	1997
At constant prices of: 1977												
1 Agriculture, hunting, forestry and fishing	186	174	170	190	182	179	185	186	373	360	363	324
2 Mining and quarrying	1	1	2	2	2	1	2	2	46	47	61	63
3 Manufacturing	95	84	83	93	99	104	103	108	268	268	277	267
4 Electricity, gas and water	9	9	10	10	11	11	12	12	68	71	77	79
5 Construction	39	29	31	34	37	46	57	43	78	82	84	82

Fiji

Million Fiji dollars

	1986	1987	1988	1989	1990	1991	1992	1993	1994	1995	1996	1997
	At constant prices of: 1977												
6 Wholesale and retail trade, restaurants and hotels	136	117	130	161	183	173	169	183	273	300	308	310
7 Transport, storage and communication	90	88	95	111	120	120	127	133	204	223	235	245
8 Finance, insurance, real estate and business services	98	95	96	99	106	111	116	120	255	261	263	249
9 Community, social and personal services	130	135	133	139	141	143	147	150	336	328	327	365
Statistical discrepancy	...	...	...	...	30	...	...	...	...	...	...	...
Total, Industries	784	732	750	839	911	888	918	937	1901	1940	1995	1984
Producers of government services	...	...	...	...	...	...	...	...	...	...	...	...
Other producers	...	...	...	...	...	...	...	...	...	...	...	...
Subtotal [a]	784	732	750	839	911	888	918	937	...	...	...	...
less: Imputed bank service charge	24	22	23	24	29	32	34	36	...	...	...	...
plus: Import duties	...	...	...	...	...	...	...	...	...	...	...	...
plus: Value added tax	...	...	...	...	...	...	...	...	...	...	...	...
plus: Other adjustments [b]	73	69	66	83	91	91	100	100	...	...	...	...
equals: Gross domestic product	833	779	793	898	973	947	984	1001	...	...	...	...

a Gross domestic product in factor values.   b Item "Other adjustments" refers to indirect taxes net of subsidies.

1.12 Relations among national accounting aggregates

Million Fiji dollars

	1986	1987	1988	1989	1990	1991	1992	1993	1994	1995	1996	1997
Gross domestic product	1462	1465	1587	1861	2045	2176	2377	2540	...	...	...	...
plus: Net factor income from the rest of the world	−34	−48	−35	−36	−35	−29	−40	−14	...	...	...	...
Factor income from rest of the world	22	34	53	76	73	76	79	82	...	...	...	...
less: Factor income to the rest of the world	56	82	88	112	108	105	119	96	...	...	...	...
equals: Gross national product	1427	1417	1552	1825	2010	2147	2337	2526	...	...	...	...
less: Consumption of fixed capital	103	111	119	138	154	168	183	183	...	...	...	...
equals: National income	1324	1306	1433	1687	1856	1979	2154	2343	...	...	...	...
plus: Net current transfers from the rest of the world	−5	−22	1	−15	−31	−32	−20	−12	...	...	...	...
Current transfers from rest of the world	28	24	37	50	40	55	60	73	...	...	...	...
less: Current transfers to the rest of the world	33	46	36	65	71	87	80	85	...	...	...	...
equals: National disposable income	1319	1284	1434	1672	1825	1947	2134	2331	...	...	...	...
less: Final consumption	1140	1229	1358	1515	1706	1881	2029	2203	...	...	...	...
equals: Net saving	179	55	77	157	119	66	105	128	...	...	...	...
less: Surplus of the nation on current transactions	−8	−23	46	52	−86	−16	−4	−87	...	...	...	...
Statistical discrepancy	−23	46	54	15	−2	41	20	−15	...	...	...	...
equals: Net capital formation	164	124	85	120	203	123	129	200	...	...	...	...

Fiji

2.1 Government final consumption expenditure by function, in current prices

Million Fiji dollars

	1986	1987	1988	1989	1990	1991	1992	1993	1994	1995	1996	1997
1 General public services	74	75	87	88	104	91	104	131	113	121	...	...
2 Defence	15	26	28	37	39	39	44	46	45	45	...	...
3 Public order and safety	...	...	...	...	...	...	...	...	...	...	...	...
4 Education	70	69	63	78	86	93	102	116	112	112	...	...
5 Health	32	31	28	33	40	44	49	54	58	58	...	...
6 Social security and welfare	1	1	1	1	1	1	1	1	1	1	...	...
7 Housing and community amenities	5	3	4	6	5	6	8	9	10	10	...	...
8 Recreational, cultural and religious affairs	2	3	3	4	4	4	6	7	7	7	...	...
9 Economic services	67	60	50	57	67	79	101	103	94	97	...	...
A Fuel and energy	–	–	–	–	–	–	–	–	–	–	...	...
B Agriculture, hunting, forestry and fishing	16	9	8	7	7	9	9	10	...	...	...	...
C Mining (except fuels), manufacturing and construction	20	18	12	12	14	17	19	24	...	...	...	...
D Transportation and communication	16	15	12	16	18	23	30	26	...	...	...	...
E Other economic affairs	15	17	18	22	28	31	43	44	...	...	...	...
10 Other functions	...	...	...	...	...	...	...	...	...	...	...	...
Total government final consumption expenditures	266	268	264	304	346	357	415	467	441	451	...	...

2.5 Private final consumption expenditure by type and purpose, in current prices

Million Fiji dollars

	1986	1987	1988	1989	1990	1991	1992	1993	1994	1995	1996	1997
Final consumption expenditure of resident households											
1 Food, beverages and tobacco	281	289	342	370	403	439	496	557	...	...	...	...
A Food	216	225	263	281	299	329	388	439	...	...	...	...
B Non-alcoholic beverages	16	13	17	28	30	32	31	37	...	...	...	...
C Alcoholic beverages	29	31	38	42	45	53	46	48	...	...	...	...
D Tobacco	20	20	24	19	29	25	31	32	...	...	...	...
2 Clothing and footwear	50	49	111	103	105	111	149	159	...	...	...	...
3 Gross rent, fuel and power	125	127	130	148	167	186	170	179	...	...	...	...
4 Furniture, furnishings and household equipment and operation	74	83	85	103	99	111	147	147	...	...	...	...
5 Medical care and health expenses	16	16	23	24	26	28	...	...	...	...	...	...
6 Transport and communication	111	120	123	146	155	165	...	...	...	...	...	...
7 Recreational, entertainment, education and cultural services	37	36	44	52	51	51	...	...	...	...	...	...
8 Miscellaneous goods and services	49	60	69	87	97	104	...	...	...	...	...	...
Statistical discrepancy	92	102	104	103	115	150	...	...	...	...	...	...
Total final consumption expenditure in the domestic market by households, of which	835	882	1031	1137	1217	1345	...	...	...	...	...	...
A Durable goods	35	47	43	64	64	73	...	...	...	...	...	...
B Semi-durable goods	78	75	145	151	159	166	...	...	...	...	...	...

Fiji

Million Fiji dollars

	1986	1987	1988	1989	1990	1991	1992	1993	1994	1995	1996	1997
C Non-durable goods	453	483	551	604	655	734	...	...	...	...	...	...
D Services	269	277	292	318	339	372	...	...	...	...	...	...
plus: Direct purchases abroad by resident households	27	66	50	60	60	60	...	...	...	...	...	...
less: Direct purchases in the domestic market by non-resident households	–	–	–	–	–	–	...	...	...	...	...	...
equals: Final consumption expenditure of resident households	862	948	1081	1197	1277	1405	...	...	...	...	...	...

Final consumption expenditures by private non-profit organisations serving households

	1986	1987	1988	1989	1990	1991	1992	1993	1994	1995	1996	1997
1 Research and science	...	...	...	...	...	...	...	...	...	...	...	...
2 Education	...	...	...	...	...	...	...	...	...	...	...	...
3 Medical and other health services	...	...	...	...	...	...	...	...	...	...	...	...
4 Welfare services	...	...	...	...	...	...	...	...	...	...	...	...
5 Recreational and related cultural services	...	...	...	...	...	...	...	...	...	...	...	...
6 Religious organisations	...	...	...	...	...	...	...	...	...	...	...	...
7 Professional and labour organisations serving households	...	...	...	...	...	...	...	...	...	...	...	...
8 Miscellaneous	...	...	...	...	...	...	...	...	...	...	...	...
equals: Final consumption expenditures by private non-profit organisations serving households	11	12	12	13	15	16	...	...	...	...	...	...
Statistical discrepancy	...	...	...	...	74	63	...	...	...	...	...	...
Private final consumption expenditure	873	960	1093	1210	1366	1484	1522	1545	...	...	...	...

2.6 Private final consumption expenditure by type and purpose, in constant prices

Million Fiji dollars

	1986	1987	1988	1989	1990	1991	1992	1993	1994	1995	1996	1997

At constant prices of: 1977

Final consumption expenditure of resident households

	1986	1987	1988	1989	1990	1991	1992	1993	1994	1995	1996	1997
1 Food, beverages and tobacco	147	140	150	158	152	156	...	...	...	...	...	...
A Food	116	113	119	125	114	121	...	...	...	...	...	...
B Non-alcoholic beverages	9	7	8	10	10	10	...	...	...	...	...	...
C Alcoholic beverages	14	13	15	17	16	18	...	...	...	...	...	...
D Tobacco	8	7	8	6	12	7	...	...	...	...	...	...
2 Clothing and footwear	20	18	28	29	30	32	...	...	...	...	...	...
3 Gross rent, fuel and power	51	54	55	57	62	61	...	...	...	...	...	...
4 Furniture, furnishings and household equipment and operation	46	47	45	49	44	46	...	...	...	...	...	...
5 Medical care and health expenses	7	6	8	8	8	7	...	...	...	...	...	...
6 Transport and communication	63	68	68	77	79	77	...	...	...	...	...	...
7 Recreational, entertainment, education and cultural services	18	17	20	22	20	18	...	...	...	...	...	...
8 Miscellaneous goods and services	25	29	27	30	31	31	...	...	...	...	...	...
Statistical discrepancy	52	47	48	48	49	67	...	...	...	...	...	...

Fiji

Million Fiji dollars

	1986	1987	1988	1989	1990	1991	1992	1993	1994	1995	1996	1997
	At constant prices of: 1977											
Total final consumption expenditure in the domestic market by households, of which	429	426	449	478	475	495	...	...	...	...	...	...
A Durable goods	23	28	24	31	29	36	...	...	...	...	...	...
B Semi-durable goods	36	30	42	47	49	42	...	...	...	...	...	...
C Non-durable goods	240	231	241	254	248	271	...	...	...	...	...	...
D Services	130	137	142	146	149	146	...	...	...	...	...	...
plus: Direct purchases abroad by resident households	15	34	22	26	24	22	...	...	...	...	...	...
less: Direct purchases in the domestic market by non-resident households	...	...	...	...	...	...	...	...	...	...	...	...
equals: Final consumption expenditure of resident households	444	460	471	504	499	517	...	...	...	...	...	...
Final consumption expenditures by private non-profit organisations serving households												
1 Research and science	...	...	...	...	...	...	...	...	...	...	...	...
2 Education	...	...	...	...	...	...	...	...	...	...	...	...
3 Medical and other health services	...	...	...	...	...	...	...	...	...	...	...	...
4 Welfare services	...	...	...	...	...	...	...	...	...	...	...	...
5 Recreational and related cultural services	...	...	...	...	...	...	...	...	...	...	...	...
6 Religious organisations	...	...	...	...	...	...	...	...	...	...	...	...
7 Professional and labour organisations serving households	...	...	...	...	...	...	...	...	...	...	...	...
8 Miscellaneous	...	...	...	...	...	...	...	...	...	...	...	...
equals: Final consumption expenditures by private non-profit organisations serving households	6	6	6	6	...	...	...	...	...	...	...	...
Statistical discrepancy	...	...	6	43	6	6	...	...	...	...	...	...
Private final consumption expenditure	450	466	483	553	505	523	...	...	...	...	...	...

Finland

Source

Reply to the United Nations National Accounts Questionnaire from the Central Statistical Office, Helsinki. Official estimates are published annually in *Tilastotiedotus Kansantalouden Tilinpito* (Statistical Report, National Accounting) issued by the same office. Information on concepts, sources and methods of estimation utilized can be found in *Heikki Sourama-Olli Saariaho, Kansantalouden tilinipito, Rakenne, Maaritelmat ja luokitukset*, Central Statistical Office of Finland, Studies No. 63, Helsinki, 1980.

General note

The estimates shown in the following tables have been prepared by the Central Statistical Office in accordance with the United Nations System of National Accounts (1968 SNA) so far as the existing data would permit.

1.1 Expenditure on the gross domestic product, in current prices

Million Finish markkaa

	1986	1987	1988	1989	1990	1991	1992	1993	1994	1995	1996	1997
1 Government final consumption expenditure	72849	80046	87199	96019	108535	118719	118453	112190	114001	119795	126457	129996
2 Private final consumption expenditure	194007	211534	232580	254588	269754	274709	272114	275252	284425	298201	313690	329147
A Households	186830	203783	223918	245058	259157	263886	261136	264379	273649	287106	302013	316884
B Private non-profit institutions serving households	7177	7751	8662	9530	10597	10823	10978	10873	10776	11095	11677	12263
3 Gross capital formation	80697	91652	112264	142572	142068	100563	82120	67314	82078	90485	89866	107715
A Increase in stocks	−2211	−889	3006	6424	2924	−9498	−5833	−3880	7892	5396	−2169	2868
B Gross fixed capital formation	82908	92541	109258	136148	139144	110061	87953	71194	74186	85089	92035	104847
Residential buildings	20074	21882	28395	38241	38410	29791	22127	17713	18359	19197	19133	...
Non-residential buildings	20226	22670	26848	32792	35822	30179	21112	14186	14322	16852	18503	...
Other construction and land improvement, etc.	10261	10529	10669	12632	13781	13510	12176	10911	11080	12249	13121	...
Other	32347	37460	43346	52483	51131	36581	32538	28384	30425	36791	41775	...
4 Exports of goods and services	95634	100048	108750	116702	118828	109289	128272	159438	182530	207242	218929	247678
5 less: Imports of goods and services	89898	97775	109866	125996	126600	112422	121878	133450	150043	161080	171555	192632
Statistical discrepancy	1705	1350	3414	3113	2845	10	−2303	1653	−1999	−4780	−3360	202
equals: Gross domestic product	354994	386855	434341	486998	515430	490868	476778	482397	510992	549863	574027	622106

1.2 Expenditure on the gross domestic product, in constant prices

Million Finish markkaa

	1986	1987	1988	1989	1990	1991	1992	1993	1994	1995	1996	1997
At constant prices of: 1990												
1 Government final consumption expenditure	95792	99878	102132	104526	108535	111256	108799	103028	102728	104645	108197	108995
2 Private final consumption expenditure	234000	246163	258821	269879	269754	260031	247363	240177	244761	255968	264872	273700
A Households	224238	236228	248631	259445	259157	249612	236968	230026	234728	245857	254584	263090
B Private non-profit institutions serving households	9762	9935	10190	10434	10597	10419	10395	10151	10033	10111	10288	10610

Finland

Million Finish markkaa

	1986	1987	1988	1989	1990	1991	1992	1993	1994	1995	1996	1997
	At constant prices of: 1990											
3 Gross capital formation	107087	113746	129337	153032	142068	101398	86166	70834	82141	89598	87353	103113
A Increase in stocks	−2620	−1321	2967	7978	2924	−9567	−6071	−3694	7491	6542	−2195	2662
B Gross fixed capital formation	109707	115067	126370	145054	139144	110965	92237	74528	74650	83056	89548	100451
Residential buildings	29342	29676	34256	40739	38410	30442	25545	22083	21116	20394	20383	...
Non-residential buildings	28262	29032	31496	35065	35822	31774	24724	17783	16952	18663	20877	...
Other construction and land improvement, etc.	12958	12732	12136	13396	13781	13064	11986	10683	10549	11318	12174	...
Other	39145	43627	48482	55854	51131	35685	29982	23979	26033	32681	36570	...
4 Exports of goods and services	108673	111632	115761	117241	118828	110965	122059	142459	161376	174580	185360	209172
5 less: Imports of goods and services	96281	105175	116898	127311	126600	111755	112989	113842	128411	137327	143611	158689
Statistical discrepancy	−2665	−1327	−1434	−2003	2845	7116	10605	13915	14745	14026	17151	14241
equals: Gross domestic product	446606	464917	487719	515364	515430	479011	462003	456571	477340	501490	519322	550532

1.3 Cost components of the gross domestic product

Million Finish markkaa

	1986	1987	1988	1989	1990	1991	1992	1993	1994	1995	1996	1997
1 Indirect taxes, net	41008	45704	55396	61878	63269	57556	54615	55180	58344	58501	66568	...
A Indirect taxes	52316	57388	66667	75595	78025	74730	71643	71556	74200	76678	83211	...
B less: Subsidies	11308	11684	11271	13717	14756	17174	17028	16376	15856	18177	16643	...
2 Consumption of fixed capital	52202	57102	63366	71813	79512	82170	81892	83819	85480	87027	87698	...
3 Compensation of employees paid by resident producers to	196548	213873	236454	264582	288768	289775	273616	258075	263775	281440	294728	...
A Resident households	196480	213805	236379	264519	288660	289619	273514	257943	263631	281284	294560	...
B Rest of the world	68	68	75	63	108	156	102	132	144	156	168	...
4 Operating surplus	65236	70176	79125	88725	83881	61367	66655	85323	103393	122895	127928	...
A Corporate and quasi-corporate enterprises	21236	28014	33981	38300	30919	12257	17970	32970	47289	65765	69944	...
B Private unincorporated enterprises	43947	42130	45072	50355	52918	49261	48810	52516	56326	57560	58422	...
C General government	53	32	72	70	44	−151	−125	−163	−222	−430	−438	...
equals: Gross domestic product	354994	386855	434341	486998	515430	490868	476778	482397	510992	549863	576922	...

1.4 General government current receipts and disbursements

Million Finish markkaa

	1986	1987	1988	1989	1990	1991	1992	1993	1994	1995	1996	1997
	Receipts											
1 Operating surplus	53	32	72	70	44	−151	−125	−163	−222	−430	−438	...
2 Property and entrepreneurial income	11790	12387	13666	16211	19786	23010	25422	27873	23504	27492	28432	...
3 Taxes, fees and contributions	152101	158341	191102	214797	237177	232536	226366	221804	246276	255380	277219	...
A Indirect taxes	52316	57388	66667	75595	78025	74730	71643	71556	74200	75649	82227	...
B Direct taxes	63127	61308	74454	82179	92741	88138	82270	74900	87815	94555	109489	...
C Social security contributions	34931	37809	46999	53108	63356	66806	69566	72847	81472	82194	82549	...
D Compulsory fees, fines and penalties	1727	1836	2982	3915	3055	2862	2887	2501	2789	2982	2954	...
4 Other current transfers	6729	7342	3745	4021	4472	1977	2180	2386	2103	7364	6624	...
Total current receipts of general government	170673	178102	208585	235099	261479	257372	253843	251900	271661	289806	311837	...

Finland

Million Finish markkaa

	1986	1987	1988	1989	1990	1991	1992	1993	1994	1995	1996	1997
Disbursements												
1 Government final consumption expenditure	72849	80046	87199	96019	108535	118719	118453	112190	114001	119795	126579	...
A Compensation of employees	50885	55765	61032	67522	75449	84015	84141	79669	79638	83520	87850	...
B Consumption of fixed capital	3918	4448	5037	5671	6673	6743	6631	6787	7377	8100	8267	...
C Purchases of goods and services, net	18027	19813	21108	22804	26387	27936	27658	25715	26968	28158	30402	...
D less: Own-account fixed capital formation	...	...	...	...	...	...	...	...	...	...	...	...
E Indirect taxes paid, net	19	20	22	22	26	25	23	19	18	17	60	...
2 Property income	6195	6571	7201	7260	7511	9598	12608	22335	26153	29240	33111	...
A Interest	6185	6559	7186	7240	7487	9570	12583	22284	26105	29178	33024	...
B Net land rent and royalties	10	12	15	18	20	21	19	50	48	58	83	...
3 Subsidies	11308	11684	11271	13717	14756	17174	17028	16376	15856	18177	16643	...
4 Other current transfers	59347	65476	70864	77735	90227	106482	123238	132839	138582	143723	146463	...
A Social security benefits	38936	42486	49136	53787	62387	77566	89081	89754	90905	91304	94267	...
B Social assistance grants	7913	8871	9273	9929	11779	15745	20546	28412	33653	34286	32417	...
C Other	12498	14119	12455	14019	16061	13171	13611	14673	14024	18133	19779	...
5 Net saving	20974	14325	32050	40368	40450	5399	−17484	−31840	−22931	−21129	−10959	...
Total current disbursements and net saving of general government	170673	178102	208585	235099	261479	257372	253843	251900	271661	289806	311837	...

1.5 Current income and outlay of corporate and quasi-corporate enterprises, summary

Million Finish markkaa

	1986	1987	1988	1989	1990	1991	1992	1993	1994	1995	1996	1997
Receipts												
1 Operating surplus	21236	28014	33981	38300	30919	12257	17970	32970	47289	65765	69944	...
2 Property and entrepreneurial income received	45046	51974	67272	93778	116619	118373	111058	89917	72921	67090	57664	...
3 Current transfers [a,b]	14662	15581	17534	19086	18147	17380	21134	18664	24104	24148	23044	...
Total current receipts	80944	95569	118787	151164	165685	148010	150162	141551	144314	157003	150652	...
Disbursements												
1 Property and entrepreneurial income	59587	67489	82857	112685	139390	146498	144474	120017	92701	89023	79966	...
2 Direct taxes and other current payments to general government	5469	4482	5995	7197	10458	10045	8196	2853	3848	11469	16618	...
3 Other current transfers [b]	15266	15911	18181	21037	18604	19771	24835	23152	24866	25454	23257	...
4 Net saving	622	7687	11754	10245	−2767	−28304	−27343	−4471	22899	31057	30811	...
Total current disbursements and net saving	80944	95569	118787	151164	165685	148010	150162	141551	144314	157003	150652	...

a Includes adjustments from the financial institutions sector. b All transfers include reinvested earnings.

1.6 Current income and outlay of households and non-profit institutions

Million Finish markkaa

	1986	1987	1988	1989	1990	1991	1992	1993	1994	1995	1996	1997
Receipts												
1 Compensation of employees	196900	214194	236874	264901	288978	289915	273736	258111	263817	281476	294776	...
A From resident producers	196480	213805	236379	264519	288660	289619	273514	257943	263631	281284	294560	...
B From rest of the world	420	389	495	382	318	296	222	168	186	192	216	...

Finland

Million Finish markkaa

	1986	1987	1988	1989	1990	1991	1992	1993	1994	1995	1996	1997
2 Operating surplus of private unincorporated enterprises	43947	42130	45072	50355	52918	49261	48810	52516	56326	57560	58422	...
3 Property and entrepreneurial income	13016	14823	17932	22028	25258	28610	31580	26821	21405	24594	25119	...
4 Current transfers	68397	74991	82559	90492	101575	117647	135349	144089	151418	152440	153771	...
A Social security benefits [a]	40044	43577	50542	55271	64096	79391	91147	91996	93397	94061	97065	...
B Social assistance grants	8275	9171	9594	10279	12279	16325	21176	29002	34293	35022	32921	...
C Other	20078	22243	22423	24942	25200	21931	23026	23091	23728	23357	23785	...
Total current receipts	322260	346138	382437	427776	468729	485433	489475	481537	492966	516070	532088	...

Disbursements

	1986	1987	1988	1989	1990	1991	1992	1993	1994	1995	1996	1997
1 Private final consumption expenditure	194007	211534	232580	254588	269754	274709	272114	275252	284425	298201	314451	...
2 Property income	12006	13458	17599	23487	28908	30606	30915	25512	20556	19852	16446	...
3 Direct taxes and other current transfers n.e.c. to general government	96056	98498	121008	135450	152796	151659	150269	151177	172687	172874	183408	...
A Social security contributions	36527	39706	49437	56383	67248	70474	72993	75993	85428	86440	87682	...
B Direct taxes	57802	56956	68589	75152	82493	78323	74389	72683	84470	83452	92772	...
C Fees, fines and penalties	1727	1836	2982	3915	3055	2862	2887	2501	2789	2982	2954	...
4 Other current transfers	15212	16309	14073	15866	16066	13848	15460	14477	14040	13862	13788	...
5 Net saving	4979	6339	−2823	−1615	1205	14611	20717	15119	1258	11281	3995	...
Total current disbursements and net saving	322260	346138	382437	427776	468729	485433	489475	481537	492966	516070	532088	...

a Does not include social assistance grants from financial institutions.

1.7 External transactions on current account, summary

Million Finish markkaa

	1986	1987	1988	1989	1990	1991	1992	1993	1994	1995	1996	1997
Payments to the rest of the world												
1 Imports of goods and services	89898	97775	109866	125996	126600	112422	121878	133450	150043	161080	171115	...
A Imports of merchandise, c.i.f.	76736	81867	91232	104400	101967	86348	93188	101559	118684	125451	138106	...
B Other	13162	15908	18634	21596	24633	26074	28690	31891	31359	35629	33009	...
2 Factor income to rest of the world	12560	13599	16864	22318	28960	31006	32491	36446	32007	31788	33084	...
A Compensation of employees	68	68	75	63	108	156	102	132	144	156	168	...
B Property and entrepreneurial income	12492	13531	16789	22255	28852	30850	32389	36314	31863	31632	32916	...
3 Current transfers to the rest of the world	5217	5616	7301	7126	6981	7897	8280	8524	8389	13369	14336	...
A Indirect taxes to supranational organizations	...	...	...	...	...	...	...	...	...	1029	984	...
B Other current transfers [a]	5217	5616	7301	7126	6981	7897	8280	8524	8389	12340	13352	...
4 Surplus of the nation on current transactions	−3625	−7549	−11331	−24874	−26513	−26697	−22035	−6340	6627	22531	22031	...
Payments to the rest of the world and surplus of the nation on current transfers	104050	109441	122700	130566	136028	124628	140614	172080	197066	228768	240566	...
Receipts from the rest of the world												
1 Exports of goods and services	95634	100048	108750	116702	118828	109289	128272	159438	182530	207242	217494	...
A Exports of merchandise, f.o.b.	81066	83826	91313	98265	99750	91100	105809	132550	152022	172820	182436	...
B Other	14568	16222	17437	18437	19078	18189	22463	26888	30508	34422	35058	...

Finland

Million Finish markkaa

	1986	1987	1988	1989	1990	1991	1992	1993	1994	1995	1996	1997
2 Factor income from rest of the world	4976	5586	8497	11222	15024	14437	12674	13229	10469	12885	14824	...
A Compensation of employees	420	389	495	382	318	296	222	168	186	192	216	...
B Property and entrepreneurial income	4556	5197	8002	10840	14706	14141	12452	13061	10283	12693	14608	...
3 Current transfers from rest of the world	3440	3807	5453	2642	2176	902	−332	−587	4067	8641	8249	...
A Subsidies from supranational organisations	...	...	...	...	...	...	...	...	...	...	...	...
B Other current transfers [a]	3440	3807	5453	2642	2176	902	−332	−587	4067	8641	8249	...
Receipts from the rest of the world on current transactions	104050	109441	122700	130566	136028	124628	140614	172080	197066	228768	240567	...

a All transfers include reinvested earnings.

1.8 Capital transactions of the nation, summary

Million Finish markkaa

	1986	1987	1988	1989	1990	1991	1992	1993	1994	1995	1996	1997
Finance of gross capital formation												
Gross saving	78777	85453	104347	120811	118400	73876	57782	62627	86706	108236	111545	...
1 Consumption of fixed capital	52202	57102	63366	71813	79512	82170	81892	83819	85480	87027	87698	...
A General government	4470	5067	5696	6294	7383	7481	7401	7391	7948	8611	8736	...
B Corporate and quasi-corporate enterprises	29543	32164	35236	39918	43637	45657	47525	49744	49574	49223	49612	...
C Other	18189	19871	22434	25601	28492	29032	26966	26684	27958	29193	29350	...
2 Net saving	26575	28351	40981	48998	38888	−8294	−24110	−21192	1226	21209	23847	...
A General government	20974	14325	32050	40368	40450	5399	−17484	−31840	−22931	−21129	−10959	...
B Corporate and quasi-corporate enterprises	622	7687	11754	10245	−2767	−28304	−27343	−4471	22899	31057	30811	...
C Other	4979	6339	−2823	−1615	1205	14611	20717	15119	1258	11281	3995	...
less: Surplus of the nation on current transactions	−3625	−7549	−11331	−24874	−26513	−26697	−22035	−6340	6627	22531	22031	...
Statistical discrepancy	−1705	−1350	−3414	−3113	−2845	−10	2303	−1653	1999	4780	5989	...
Finance of gross capital formation	80697	91652	112264	142572	142068	100563	82120	67314	82078	90485	95503	...
Gross capital formation												
Increase in stocks	−2211	−889	3006	6424	2924	−9498	−5833	−3880	7892	5396	2971	...
Gross fixed capital formation	82908	92541	109258	136148	139144	110061	87953	71194	74186	85089	92532	...
1 General government	11948	14171	15846	15119	18464	18285	16601	13305	14644	14540	15585	...
2 Corporate and quasi-corporate enterprises	42268	47106	55234	70457	69697	53198	42192	33291	35244	44244	50477	...
3 Other	28692	31264	38178	50572	50983	38578	29160	24598	24298	26305	26470	...
Gross capital formation	80697	91652	112264	142572	142068	100563	82120	67314	82078	90485	95503	...

1.9 Gross domestic product by institutional sectors of origin

Million Finish markkaa

	1986	1987	1988	1989	1990	1991	1992	1993	1994	1995	1996	1997
Domestic factor incomes originating												
subtotal: Domestic factor incomes	261784	284049	315579	353307	372649	351142	340271	343398	367168	404335	422656	...
Indirect taxes, net	41008	45704	55396	61878	63269	57556	54615	55180	58344	58501	66568	...
A Indirect taxes	52316	57388	66667	75595	78025	74730	71643	71556	74200	76678	83211	...
B less: Subsidies	11308	11684	11271	13717	14756	17174	17028	16376	15856	18177	16643	...

Finland

Million Finish markkaa	1986	1987	1988	1989	1990	1991	1992	1993	1994	1995	1996	1997
Consumption of fixed capital	52202	57102	63366	71813	79512	82170	81892	83819	85480	87027	87698	...
Gross domestic product	354994	386855	434341	486998	515430	490868	476778	482397	510992	549863	576922	...

1.10 Gross domestic product by kind of activity, in current prices

Million Finish markkaa	1986	1987	1988	1989	1990	1991	1992	1993	1994	1995	1996	1997
1 Agriculture, hunting, forestry and fishing	24239	22612	24739	28077	29043	24073	21468	22081	25264	21920	20207	21670
2 Mining and quarrying	1227	1246	1603	2037	1733	1729	1800	1687	1936	1958	1857	1968
3 Manufacturing	78197	87145	95972	105225	105383	89667	92426	101816	112737	128831	126264	142162
4 Electricity, gas and water	9522	10018	10065	9245	9504	11059	11003	11334	12281	12984	13641	13934
5 Construction	25199	27461	32940	42035	43467	36962	26041	20998	23303	28329	29236	34374
6 Wholesale and retail trade, restaurants and hotels	40958	45712	50944	56344	57971	52144	48409	47401	50827	52969	55474	59524
7 Transport, storage and communication	25424	27251	30136	33591	36406	36126	36484	37260	39114	41624	43939	47846
8 Finance, insurance, real estate and business services	49118	53993	60135	68820	78211	78829	75503	84143	86874	92551	100577	106634
9 Community, social and personal services	7404	8412	9245	10650	12082	12355	12738	12659	12664	13223	14055	14790
Total, Industries	261288	283850	315779	356024	373800	342944	325872	339379	365000	394389	405247	442902
Producers of government services	54822	60233	66091	73215	82148	90783	90795	86475	87033	91637	96170	99006
Other producers	6140	6609	7507	8240	9164	9378	9558	9593	9535	10083	10541	11102
Subtotal	322250	350692	389377	437479	465112	443105	426225	435447	461568	496109	511958	553010
less: Imputed bank service charge	8989	10576	12180	14873	17000	15329	10513	14205	14396	14142	13347	14917
plus: Import duties [a]	41733	46739	57144	64392	67318	63092	61066	61155	63820	67896	75416	84013
plus: Value added tax	...	...	...	...	...	...	...	...	...	...	...	...
plus: Other adjustments	...	...	...	...	...	...	...	...	...	...	...	...
equals: Gross domestic product	354994	386855	434341	486998	515430	490868	476778	482397	510992	549863	574027	622106

[a] Item "Import duties" includes commodity indirect taxes net of subsidies.

1.11 Gross domestic product by kind of activity, in constant prices

Million Finish markkaa	1986	1987	1988	1989	1990	1991	1992	1993	1994	1995	1996	1997
At constant prices of: 1990												
1 Agriculture, hunting, forestry and fishing	27158	24981	26363	28333	29043	25808	25532	26658	29251	28013	26910	29295
2 Mining and quarrying	1376	1416	1538	1705	1733	1597	1562	1521	1696	1778	1770	1974
3 Manufacturing	92536	98019	102024	106104	105383	93911	95751	100938	113551	124453	128159	141270
4 Electricity, gas and water	8470	9076	9322	9324	9504	9798	9752	10165	10751	10588	11534	11525
5 Construction	35274	35725	38998	44490	43467	38446	32702	27994	27448	28597	29913	33824
6 Wholesale and retail trade, restaurants and hotels	48474	51863	54734	59062	57971	50785	44803	42333	44530	46118	47873	50543
7 Transport, storage and communication	27509	29472	31336	34325	36406	35048	34872	35996	37577	39677	41945	45849
8 Finance, insurance, real estate and business services	66140	69585	72796	76971	78211	75542	72046	75064	76563	79732	85401	86262
9 Community, social and personal services	10522	10812	11002	11596	12082	11374	11163	10890	10541	10931	11486	11958
Total, Industries	317459	330949	348113	371910	373800	342309	328183	331559	351908	369887	384991	412500
Producers of government services	74732	77311	79314	80915	82148	83140	81329	77651	77491	78648	80112	81397

Finland

Million Finish markkaa

	1986	1987	1988	1989	1990	1991	1992	1993	1994	1995	1996	1997
At constant prices of: 1990												
Other producers	8600	8605	8860	9064	9164	8917	8949	8950	8796	9018	9093	9409
Subtotal	400791	416865	436287	461889	465112	434366	418461	418160	438195	457553	474196	503306
less: Imputed bank service charge	12270	13679	15169	16943	17000	17343	14339	15585	15545	15230	15630	16555
plus: Import duties [a]	58085	61731	66601	70418	67318	61988	57881	53996	54690	59167	60756	63781
plus: Value added tax	...	...	...	...	...	...	...	...	...	...	...	...
plus: Other adjustments	...	...	...	...	...	...	...	...	...	...	...	...
equals: Gross domestic product	446606	464917	487719	515364	515430	479011	462003	456571	477340	501490	519322	550532

[a] Item "Import duties" includes commodity indirect taxes net of subsidies.

1.12 Relations among national accounting aggregates

Million Finish markkaa

	1986	1987	1988	1989	1990	1991	1992	1993	1994	1995	1996	1997
Gross domestic product	354994	386855	434341	486998	515430	490868	476778	482397	510992	549863	576922	...
plus: Net factor income from the rest of the world	−7584	−8013	−8367	−11096	−13936	−16569	−19817	−23217	−21538	−18903	−18260	...
Factor income from rest of the world	4976	5586	8497	11222	15024	14437	12674	13229	10469	12885	14824	...
less: Factor income to the rest of the world	12560	13599	16864	22318	28960	31006	32491	36446	32007	31788	33084	...
equals: Gross national product	347410	378842	425974	475902	501494	474299	456961	459180	489454	530960	558662	...
less: Consumption of fixed capital	52202	57102	63366	71813	79512	82170	81892	83819	85480	87027	87698	...
equals: National income	295208	321740	362608	404089	421982	392129	375069	375361	403974	443933	470964	...
plus: Net current transfers from the rest of the world	−1777	−1809	−1848	−4484	−4805	−6995	−8612	−9111	−4322	−4728	−6087	...
Current transfers from rest of the world [a]	3440	3807	5453	2642	2176	902	−332	−587	4067	8641	8249	...
less: Current transfers to the rest of the world [a]	5217	5616	7301	7126	6981	7897	8280	8524	8389	13369	14336	...
equals: National disposable income	293431	319931	360760	399605	417177	385134	366457	366250	399652	439205	464877	...
less: Final consumption	266856	291580	319779	350607	378289	393428	390567	387442	398426	417996	441030	...
equals: Net saving	26575	28351	40981	48998	38888	−8294	−24110	−21192	1226	21209	23847	...
less: Surplus of the nation on current transactions	−3625	−7549	−11331	−24874	−26513	−26697	−22035	−6340	6627	22531	22031	...
Statistical discrepancy	−1705	−1350	−3414	−3113	−2845	−10	2303	−1653	1999	4780	5989	...
equals: Net capital formation	28495	34550	48898	70759	62556	18393	228	−16505	−3402	3458	7805	...

[a] All transfers include reinvested earnings.

2.1 Government final consumption expenditure by function, in current prices

Million Finish markkaa

		1986	1987	1988	1989	1990	1991	1992	1993	1994	1995	1996	1997
1	General public services	6655	7503	8237	9070	10033	11123	10842	10039	9531	9283	9983	...
2	Defence	5824	6203	6573	6820	7498	8200	9489	8661	9448	9063	10023	...
3	Public order and safety	4094	4414	4838	5230	5813	6526	6492	6085	6275	6462	6700	...
4	Education	18528	20405	22432	24862	27276	29708	29585	28287	29721	32696	33912	...
5	Health	16616	18077	19354	21494	24546	26522	26129	24511	24177	25543	26936	...
6	Social security and welfare	10963	12172	13562	15269	17718	19494	18829	17212	17432	18724	20269	...
7	Housing and community amenities	2271	2474	2639	2857	3250	3544	3299	3136	2827	2889	2983	...
8	Recreational, cultural and religious affairs	2625	2916	3151	3464	3883	4149	3976	3982	4066	4307	4630	...

Finland

Million Finish markkaa	1986	1987	1988	1989	1990	1991	1992	1993	1994	1995	1996	1997
9 Economic services	4861	5388	6010	6583	8203	9134	9259	9413	9997	10421	10303	...
10 Other functions	412	494	403	370	315	319	553	864	527	407	840	...
Total government final consumption expenditures	72849	80046	87199	96019	108535	118719	118453	112190	114001	119795	126579	...

2.2 Government final consumption expenditure by function, in constant prices

Million Finish markkaa

	1986	1987	1988	1989	1990	1991	1992	1993	1994	1995	1996	1997
At constant prices of: 1990												
1 General public services	8793	9377	9592	9861	10033	10495	10098	9448	8821	8235	8520	...
2 Defence	7225	7297	7290	7233	7498	7578	8612	7681	8399	7999	8769	...
3 Public order and safety	5561	5584	5630	5688	5813	5891	5765	5523	5617	5655	5691	...
4 Education	24318	25358	26024	26709	27276	28217	27530	26238	27172	29261	29968	...
5 Health	21887	22799	23248	23713	24546	24460	23535	22155	21510	21886	22517	...
6 Social security and welfare	14603	15408	16107	16950	17718	18451	17250	15730	15452	15961	16865	...
7 Housing and community amenities	3009	3111	3131	3140	3250	3308	3012	2848	2544	2514	2510	...
8 Recreational, cultural and religious affairs	3501	3673	3758	3801	3883	3941	3709	3669	3669	3709	3880	...
9 Economic services	6392	6694	6900	7039	8203	8606	8762	8944	9067	9063	8824	...
10 Other functions	503	577	452	392	315	309	526	792	477	362	728	...
Total government final consumption expenditures	95792	99878	102132	104526	108535	111256	108799	103028	102728	104645	108272	...

2.5 Private final consumption expenditure by type and purpose, in current prices

Million Finish markkaa

	1986	1987	1988	1989	1990	1991	1992	1993	1994	1995	1996	1997
Final consumption expenditure of resident households												
1 Food, beverages and tobacco	48266	50720	53846	57080	59013	61262	61305	60332	60616	58586	58265	...
A Food	35651	36826	38428	40020	40903	42011	41885	41898	42460	40276	39876	
B Non-alcoholic beverages	919	993	1112	1204	1285	1311	1358	1235	1336	1429	1499	
C Alcoholic beverages	7778	8495	9590	10618	11405	12026	11885	11403	11198	11311	11612	
D Tobacco	3918	4406	4716	5238	5420	5914	6177	5796	5622	5570	5278	
2 Clothing and footwear	10527	11938	12939	13850	14397	14058	12515	12149	12430	13494	13728	
3 Gross rent, fuel and power	34381	36041	38764	42479	47253	53589	58053	64917	68033	70339	75026	
A Fuel and power	7491	8319	8223	8554	9972	10881	11235	13205	13701	13028	14762	
B Other	26890	27722	30541	33925	37281	42708	46818	51712	54332	57311	60264	
4 Furniture, furnishings and household equipment and operation	13027	14407	15821	17063	17264	16608	15583	15247	15627	16836	17995	
A Household operation	2084	2231	2356	2538	2695	2983	3026	3413	3542	3858	4089	
B Other	10943	12176	13465	14525	14569	13625	12557	11834	12085	12978	13906	
5 Medical care and health expenses	7459	8361	9479	10399	11580	12666	13385	13998	14376	15420	16598	
6 Transport and communication	30154	33734	39144	43401	43553	39278	37226	37643	39875	43454	47028	
A Personal transport equipment	11433	13279	16651	18313	15894	11173	8537	7571	9547	11342	13276	
B Other	18721	20455	22493	25088	27659	28105	28689	30072	30328	32112	33752	
7 Recreational, entertainment, education and cultural services	17334	19162	20929	23100	24563	24932	24229	25076	25663	27547	29020	
8 Miscellaneous goods and services	23290	26345	29369	33214	35417	35448	33967	32859	35646	38517	41939	...
A Personal care	3415	3731	4057	4469	4947	5247	5334	5254	5250	5589	5839	...

Finland

Million Finish markkaa

	1986	1987	1988	1989	1990	1991	1992	1993	1994	1995	1996	1997
B Expenditures in restaurants, cafes and hotels	13371	14895	16825	18830	20201	19890	19129	18296	19039	20502	21601	...
C Other	6504	7719	8487	9915	10269	10311	9504	9309	11357	12426	14499	...
Total final consumption expenditure in the domestic market by households, of which	184438	200708	220291	240586	253040	257841	256263	262221	272266	284193	299599	...
A Durable goods	23232	26258	31115	33922	31366	25135	20527	19048	21794	24705	27812	...
B Semi-durable goods	18822	21105	23020	24884	25872	25835	23777	23105	23977	25743	26396	...
C Non-durable goods	72528	77314	81886	87115	93138	97808	98446	100651	102039	101057	103804	...
D Services	69856	76031	84270	94665	102664	109063	113513	119417	124456	132688	141587	...
plus: Direct purchases abroad by resident households	5587	6811	7907	8969	10767	11089	10962	9237	8697	10450	10559	...
less: Direct purchases in the domestic market by non-resident households	3195	3736	4280	4497	4650	5044	6089	7079	7314	7537	7338	...
equals: Final consumption expenditure of resident households	186830	203783	223918	245058	259157	263886	261136	264379	273649	287106	302820	...

Final consumption expenditures by private non-profit organisations serving households

	1986	1987	1988	1989	1990	1991	1992	1993	1994	1995	1996	1997
1 Research and science	96	103	114	140	164	177	196	209	188	193	217	...
2 Education	1381	1428	1556	1691	1869	1899	2029	1936	1873	1692	1793	...
3 Medical and other health services	754	899	1021	1125	1225	1243	1126	1211	1232	1328	1357	...
4 Welfare services	362	384	477	506	585	604	554	592	553	595	626	...
5 Recreational and related cultural services	897	947	1089	1256	1405	1444	1475	1440	1465	1579	1667	...
6 Religious organisations	2010	2209	2392	2631	2899	2919	2933	2883	2929	3022	3133	...
7 Professional and labour organisations serving households	886	938	1061	1171	1305	1359	1332	1283	1256	1336	1434	...
8 Miscellaneous	791	843	952	1010	1145	1178	1333	1319	1280	1350	1404	...
equals: Final consumption expenditures by private non-profit organisations serving households	7177	7751	8662	9530	10597	10823	10978	10873	10776	11095	11631	...
Private final consumption expenditure	194007	211534	232580	254588	269754	274709	272114	275252	284425	298201	314451	...

2.6 Private final consumption expenditure by type and purpose, in constant prices

Million Finish markkaa

	1986	1987	1988	1989	1990	1991	1992	1993	1994	1995	1996	1997

At constant prices of: 1990

Final consumption expenditure of resident households

	1986	1987	1988	1989	1990	1991	1992	1993	1994	1995	1996	1997
1 Food, beverages and tobacco	55921	57151	58417	59895	59013	58578	57777	56637	56677	57963	58154	...
A Food	39321	39863	40914	41407	40903	40932	40770	41001	41346	42644	42982	...
B Non-alcoholic beverages	1164	1177	1279	1307	1285	1243	1292	1189	1333	1514	1590	...
C Alcoholic beverages	9997	10331	10643	11313	11405	11102	10501	9940	9716	9794	9992	...
D Tobacco	5439	5780	5581	5868	5420	5301	5214	4507	4282	4011	3590	...
2 Clothing and footwear	12032	13216	14108	14572	14397	13507	11623	10865	10887	11605	11750	...
3 Gross rent, fuel and power	41084	42942	44210	45456	47253	49090	50184	52331	53887	54592	56005	...
A Fuel and power	8628	9411	9327	9263	9972	10625	10541	10934	11278	10518	11115	...
B Other	32456	33531	34883	36193	37281	38465	39643	41397	42609	44074	44890	...
4 Furniture, furnishings and household equipment and operation	15494	16438	17350	17873	17264	15948	14505	13669	13783	14546	15396	...

Finland

Million Finish markkaa

	1986	1987	1988	1989	1990	1991	1992	1993	1994	1995	1996	1997
At constant prices of: 1990												
A Household operation	2816	2780	2778	2782	2695	2796	2749	2824	2898	3080	3190	...
B Other	12678	13658	14572	15091	14569	13152	11756	10845	10885	11466	12206	...
5 Medical care and health expenses	10251	10873	11165	11268	11580	11700	11622	11396	11237	11819	12546	...
6 Transport and communication	37521	39670	43570	46067	43553	38247	35132	33109	34509	36952	39676	...
A Personal transport equipment	13811	14737	17597	18667	15894	11236	8131	6613	7852	8985	10707	...
B Other	23710	24933	25973	27400	27659	27011	27001	26496	26657	27967	28969	...
7 Recreational, entertainment, education and cultural services	20718	21622	22771	24010	24563	23949	22199	22333	22732	24115	25153	...
8 Miscellaneous goods and services	28825	31140	33243	35500	35417	33321	31168	29900	31640	33226	35890	...
A Personal care	3998	4224	4496	4725	4947	4866	4772	4623	4644	4817	5036	...
B Expenditures in restaurants, cafes and hotels	16961	18054	19110	20147	20201	18568	17569	16856	17413	18030	18756	...
C Other	7866	8862	9637	10628	10269	9887	8827	8421	9583	10379	12098	...
Total final consumption expenditure in the domestic market by households, of which	221846	233052	244834	254641	253040	244340	234210	230240	235352	244818	254570	...
A Durable goods	27269	28958	32869	34627	31366	24896	19479	17158	18835	21280	24376	...
B Semi-durable goods	21595	23335	24914	25974	25872	24829	21974	20523	20959	22396	22891	...
C Non-durable goods	85607	88826	90903	92918	93138	93620	92522	90767	91455	92317	93085	...
D Services	87375	91933	96148	101122	102664	100995	100235	101792	104103	108825	114218	...
plus: Direct purchases abroad by resident households	6406	7664	8675	9611	10767	10101	8577	6481	6232	7909	7454	...
less: Direct purchases in the domestic market by non-resident households	4014	4488	4878	4807	4650	4829	5819	6695	6856	6870	6577	...
equals: Final consumption expenditure of resident households	224238	236228	248631	259445	259157	249612	236968	230026	234728	245857	255447	...

Final consumption expenditures by private non-profit organisations serving households

	1986	1987	1988	1989	1990	1991	1992	1993	1994	1995	1996	1997
1 Research and science	136	137	140	160	164	170	188	193	175	181	191	...
2 Education	1841	1792	1798	1822	1869	1830	1913	1790	1728	1532	1569	...
3 Medical and other health services	1075	1194	1277	1271	1225	1186	1064	1140	1218	1280	1242	...
4 Welfare services	509	514	561	560	585	577	515	521	475	502	473	...
5 Recreational and related cultural services	1192	1200	1278	1385	1405	1399	1400	1367	1403	1474	1522	...
6 Religious organisations	2724	2817	2767	2851	2899	2804	2780	2707	2652	2674	2691	...
7 Professional and labour organisations serving households	1234	1217	1265	1286	1305	1317	1265	1192	1165	1214	1268	...
8 Miscellaneous	1051	1064	1104	1099	1145	1136	1270	1241	1217	1254	1270	...
equals: Final consumption expenditures by private non-profit organisations serving households	9762	9935	10190	10434	10597	10419	10395	10151	10033	10111	10226	...
Private final consumption expenditure	234000	246163	258821	269879	269754	260031	247363	240177	244761	255968	265673	...

Finland

2.11 Gross fixed capital formation by kind of activity of owner, ISIC divisions, in current prices
Million Finish markkaa

	1986	1987	1988	1989	1990	1991	1992	1993	1994	1995	1996	1997
All producers												
1 Agriculture, hunting, forestry and fishing	6165	5856	6332	7149	7106	5549	3977	3602	3712	3881	4459	...
A Agriculture and hunting	4480	4133	4418	5063	5080	3751	2279	2084	2168	2245	2700	...
B Forestry and logging	1571	1604	1786	1954	1892	1670	1590	1426	1444	1541	1670	...
C Fishing	114	119	128	132	134	128	108	92	100	95	89	...
2 Mining and quarrying	312	241	227	375	278	173	136	122	176	410	385	...
A Coal mining	...	...	...	...	...	...	...	...	...	...	...	...
B Crude petroleum and natural gas production	...	...	...	...	...	...	...	...	...	...	...	...
C Metal ore mining	100	17	21	73	31	26	13	34	13	14	57	...
D Other mining	212	224	206	302	247	147	123	88	163	396	328	...
3 Manufacturing	14037	17647	15341	21822	21770	15888	14102	12759	14091	18821	21551	...
A Manufacturing of food, beverages and tobacco	1452	1994	1547	2120	2311	1967	2689	1512	1518	1747	1946	...
B Textile, wearing apparel and leather industries	391	495	−48	412	399	180	153	229	189	338	215	...
C Manufacture of wood and wood products, including furniture [a]	666	681	771	1376	1334	1026	788	826	1065	1111	808	...
D Manufacture of paper and paper products, printing and publishing	4596	5675	5977	8310	8223	6314	5031	4571	4255	4762	9143	...
E Manufacture of chemicals and chemical petroleum, coal, rubber and plastic products	1856	2963	2412	2791	2791	1964	2004	2096	1798	3045	2011	...
F Manufacture of non-metallic mineral products, except products of petroleum and coal	704	719	644	866	1154	463	314	333	372	451	429	...
G Basic metal industries	1140	1530	1116	1368	967	962	675	666	935	2109	2202	...
H Manufacture of fabricated metal products, machinery and equipment	2928	3269	2831	4061	4219	2758	2155	2412	3773	4998	4555	...
I Other manufacturing industries [a]	304	321	91	518	372	254	293	114	186	260	242	...
4 Electricity, gas and water	4339	4432	4143	5777	5434	5957	4901	4077	4872	4886	4769	...
A Electricity, gas and steam	3792	3866	3602	5188	4812	5151	4305	3507	4279	4312	4163	...
B Water works and supply	547	566	541	589	622	806	596	570	593	574	606	...
5 Construction	1160	1600	2334	2916	2856	1865	374	131	611	927	1074	...
6 Wholesale and retail trade, restaurants and hotels	6697	8011	7473	12767	12401	9482	7255	5380	5248	5510	6098	...
A Wholesale and retail trade	6147	7410	6889	10949	10821	8164	6604	5015	5010	5264	5791	...
B Restaurants and hotels	550	601	584	1818	1580	1318	651	365	238	246	307	...
Restaurants	219	270	297	570	563	559	287	164	60	96	134	...
Hotels and other lodging places	331	331	287	1248	1017	759	364	201	178	150	173	...
7 Transport, storage and communication	6835	7127	8186	10920	10223	6900	8007	7456	6659	8965	9833	...
A Transport and storage	4678	4665	5384	7877	6969	4005	5482	4976	3908	5507	6039	...
B Communication	2157	2462	2802	3043	3254	2895	2525	2480	2751	3458	3794	...
8 Finance, insurance, real estate and business services	29392	31188	46794	56083	56845	42204	29341	21274	21788	24177	25388	...
A Financial institutions [b]	1921	1531	−802	1783	753	927	351	−968	894	−1481	−637	...

Finland

Million Finish markkaa

	1986	1987	1988	1989	1990	1991	1992	1993	1994	1995	1996	1997
B Insurance	387	–39	678	259	825	529	1042	–197	192	388	109	...
C Real estate and business services	27084	29696	46918	54041	55267	40748	27948	22439	20702	25270	25916	...
Real estate, except dwellings	4580	5122	14716	11687	12919	8020	3440	2926	595	2948	3502	...
Dwellings	20762	22661	29375	39468	39701	30937	23138	18563	19334	20190	20035	...
9 Community, social and personal services	1711	1768	1956	2516	3277	3169	2503	2264	1937	2036	2239	...
A Sanitary and similar services	953	921	946	1144	1433	1389	1208	1093	913	965	983	...
B Social and related community services	216	267	330	398	493	418	312	224	292	320	333	...
Educational services	91	106	120	131	165	104	82	75	76	96	96	...
Medical, dental, other health and veterinary services	88	115	131	170	216	210	136	81	143	148	153	...
C Recreational and cultural services	457	482	562	811	1177	1163	860	840	630	646	815	...
D Personal and household services	85	98	118	163	174	199	123	107	102	105	108	...
Total industries	70648	77870	92786	120325	120190	91187	70596	57065	59094	69613	75796	...
Producers of government services	11281	13371	15046	14295	17286	17067	15897	12811	13994	14296	15632	...
Private non-profit institutions serving households	979	1300	1426	1528	1668	1807	1460	1318	1098	1180	1104	...
Total	82908	92541	109258	136148	139144	110061	87953	71194	74186	85089	92532	...

a Furniture is included in item "Other manufacturing industries".　　b Item "Financial institutions" include activities auxiliary to financial intermediation and insurance.

2.12 Gross fixed capital formation by kind of activity of owner, ISIC divisions, in constant prices

Million Finish markkaa

	1986	1987	1988	1989	1990	1991	1992	1993	1994	1995	1996	1997
At constant prices of: 1990												
All producers												
1 Agriculture, hunting, forestry and fishing	7596	6951	7160	7617	7106	5506	3907	3446	3506	3942	4493	...
A Agriculture and hunting	5473	4844	4966	5387	5080	3760	2273	2018	2032	2402	2884	...
B Forestry and logging	1987	1971	2054	2090	1892	1619	1534	1349	1388	1458	1531	...
C Fishing	136	136	140	140	134	127	100	79	86	82	78	...
2 Mining and quarrying	386	286	251	393	278	168	130	115	162	386	333	...
A Coal mining	...	...	...	...	...	...	...	...	...	...	...	...
B Crude petroleum and natural gas production	...	...	...	...	...	...	...	...	...	...	...	...
C Metal ore mining	127	20	23	76	31	25	13	32	12	14	48	...
D Other mining	259	266	228	317	247	143	117	83	150	372	285	...
3 Manufacturing	17761	21473	17847	23903	21770	15579	13373	11423	12427	16998	18610	...
A Manufacturing of food, beverages and tobacco	1880	2459	1854	2337	2311	1947	2626	1381	1320	1522	1712	...
B Textile, wearing apparel and leather industries	504	612	–15	459	399	176	144	190	160	289	171	...
C Manufacture of wood and wood products, including furniture [a]	777	773	844	1466	1334	1030	757	783	975	1036	741	...
D Manufacture of paper and paper products, printing and publishing	6392	7630	7393	9314	8223	6054	4573	3948	3526	4087	7352	...

Finland

Million Finish markkaa

	1986	1987	1988	1989	1990	1991	1992	1993	1994	1995	1996	1997
	\multicolumn{12}{c}{At constant prices of: 1990}
E Manufacture of chemicals and chemical petroleum, coal, rubber and plastic products	2177	3336	2601	2989	2791	1960	1974	1954	1664	2878	1898	...
F Manufacture of non-metallic mineral products, except products of petroleum and coal	898	866	725	944	1154	458	300	309	329	398	359	...
G Basic metal industries	1316	1712	1216	1475	967	944	621	555	797	1845	1908	...
H Manufacture of fabricated metal products, machinery and equipment	3459	3718	3119	4362	4219	2754	2075	2201	3484	4695	4236	...
I Other manufacturing industries [a]	358	367	110	557	372	256	303	102	172	248	233	...
4 Electricity, gas and water	5557	5397	4725	6155	5434	5797	4720	3869	4543	4676	4562	...
A Electricity, gas and steam	4847	4696	4100	5526	4812	5019	4129	3305	3943	4092	3947	...
B Water works and supply	710	701	625	629	622	778	591	564	600	584	615	...
5 Construction	1314	1831	2589	3067	2856	1777	336	48	511	834	897	...
6 Wholesale and retail trade, restaurants and hotels	8671	9634	8388	13530	12401	9594	7359	5221	5212	5562	6229	...
A Wholesale and retail trade	7946	8903	7722	11591	10821	8250	6669	4828	4975	5312	5907	...
B Restaurants and hotels	725	731	666	1939	1580	1344	690	393	237	250	322	...
Restaurants	276	320	335	606	563	558	284	158	32	79	124	...
Hotels and other lodging places	449	411	331	1333	1017	786	406	235	205	171	198	...
7 Transport, storage and communication	8246	8253	9267	11477	10223	6815	7582	6484	6165	8444	9269	...
A Transport and storage	5777	5516	6246	8333	6969	3939	5130	4186	3584	5192	5634	...
B Communication	2469	2737	3021	3144	3254	2876	2452	2298	2581	3252	3635	...
8 Finance, insurance, real estate and business services	41867	41095	55029	59487	56845	43451	33736	26201	24837	25549	27334	...
A Financial institutions [b]	2405	1748	−1066	1861	753	918	329	−1351	969	−1559	−710	...
B Insurance	515	−64	775	271	825	551	1194	−271	192	393	96	...
C Real estate and business services	38947	39411	55320	57355	55267	41982	32213	27823	23676	26715	27948	...
Real estate, except dwellings	6539	6562	16784	12288	12919	8548	4163	3857	867	2958	3883	...
Dwellings	30303	30672	35406	42051	39701	31648	26728	23147	22246	21440	21339	...
9 Community, social and personal services	2170	2105	2192	2649	3277	3160	2585	2313	1991	2128	2396	...
A Sanitary and similar services	1235	1127	1077	1210	1433	1371	1219	1096	939	1004	1023	...
B Social and related community services	272	309	364	415	493	417	305	209	265	293	314	...
Educational services	119	124	131	137	165	102	76	66	62	89	93	...
Medical, dental, other health and veterinary services	108	133	144	177	216	211	135	77	133	133	137	...
C Recreational and cultural services	561	557	620	852	1177	1171	940	905	687	724	951	...
D Personal and household services	102	112	131	172	174	201	121	103	100	107	108	...
Total industries	93568	97025	107448	128278	120190	91847	73728	59120	59354	68519	74123	...
Producers of government services	14821	16421	17275	15149	17286	17243	16899	13890	14107	13338	14742	...
Private non-profit institutions serving households	1318	1621	1647	1627	1668	1875	1610	1518	1189	1199	1139	...
Total	109707	115067	126370	145054	139144	110965	92237	74528	74650	83056	90004	...

a Furniture is included in item "Other manufacturing industries".   b Item "Financial institutions" include activities auxiliary to financial intermediation and insurance.

Finland

2.13 Stocks of reproducible fixed assets, by type of good and owner, in current prices

Million Finish markkaa

1986

	Total Gross	Total Net	Total private Gross	Total private Net	Public enterprises Gross	Public enterprises Net	General government Gross	General government Net
1 Residential buildings	592739	402834	592739	402834	...	...	–	–
2 Non-residential buildings	476898	309019	324357	204567	...	...	152541	104452
3 Other construction [a]	328822	207423	197334	111425	...	...	131488	95998
4 Land improvement and plantation and orchard development	...	...	...	...	...	...	...	...
5 Producers' durable goods	421033	231309	406839	222843	...	...	14194	8466
6 Breeding stock, dairy cattle, etc.	...	...	...	...	...	...	...	...
Total	1819492	1150585	1521269	941669	...	...	298223	208916

1987

	Total Gross	Total Net	Total private Gross	Total private Net	Public enterprises Gross	Public enterprises Net	General government Gross	General government Net
1 Residential buildings	658269	443540	658269	443540	...	...	–	–
2 Non-residential buildings	537107	346618	364151	229060	...	...	172956	117558
3 Other construction [a]	349484	218794	208190	116279	...	...	141294	102515
4 Land improvement and plantation and orchard development	...	...	...	...	...	...	...	...
5 Producers' durable goods	454247	251236	438074	241402	...	...	16173	9834
6 Breeding stock, dairy cattle, etc.	...	...	...	...	...	...	...	...
Total	1999107	1260188	1668684	1030281	...	...	330423	229907

1988

	Total Gross	Total Net	Total private Gross	Total private Net	Public enterprises Gross	Public enterprises Net	General government Gross	General government Net
1 Residential buildings	758574	507819	758574	507819	...	...	–	–
2 Non-residential buildings	605831	389709	409716	257207	...	...	196115	132502
3 Other construction [a]	379085	235442	223733	123566	...	...	155352	111876
4 Land improvement and plantation and orchard development	...	...	...	...	...	...	...	...
5 Producers' durable goods	494634	275926	476447	264729	...	...	18187	11197
6 Breeding stock, dairy cattle, etc.	...	...	...	...	...	...	...	...
Total	2238124	1408896	1868470	1153321	...	...	369654	255575

1989

	Total Gross	Total Net	Total private Gross	Total private Net	Public enterprises Gross	Public enterprises Net	General government Gross	General government Net
1 Residential buildings	893624	596077	893624	596077	...	...	–	–
2 Non-residential buildings	694575	446541	474176	299381	...	...	220399	147160
3 Other construction [a]	417144	257498	247331	136023	...	...	169813	121475
4 Land improvement and plantation and orchard development	...	...	...	...	...	...	...	...
5 Producers' durable goods	555770	313729	535573	301129	...	...	20197	12600
6 Breeding stock, dairy cattle, etc.	...	...	...	...	...	...	...	...
Total	2561113	1613845	2150704	1332610	...	...	410409	281235

1990

	Total Gross	Total Net	Total private Gross	Total private Net	Public enterprises Gross	Public enterprises Net	General government Gross	General government Net
1 Residential buildings	988585	655831	988585	655831	...	...	–	–
2 Non-residential buildings	771330	494624	528540	334169	...	...	242790	160455
3 Other construction [a]	454128	278519	242449	128029	...	...	211679	150490

Finland

| | 1990 |||||||
| | Total || Total private || Public enterprises || General government ||
	Gross	Net	Gross	Net	Gross	Net	Gross	Net
4 Land improvement and plantation and orchard development	...	...	...	...	...	...	...	...
5 Producers' durable goods	610976	345493	587811	330959	...	...	23165	14534
6 Breeding stock, dairy cattle, etc.	...	...	...	...	...	...	...	...
Total	2825019	1774467	2347385	1448988	...	...	477634	325479

| | 1991 |||||||
| | Total || Total private || Public enterprises || General government ||
	Gross	Net	Gross	Net	Gross	Net	Gross	Net
1 Residential buildings	993384	652504	993384	652504	...	...	–	–
2 Non-residential buildings	759965	484225	522413	328774	...	...	237552	155451
3 Other construction [a]	477656	290961	253521	132632	...	...	224135	158329
4 Land improvement and plantation and orchard development	...	...	...	...	...	...	...	...
5 Producers' durable goods	642192	356453	616814	340638	...	...	25378	15815
6 Breeding stock, dairy cattle, etc.	...	...	...	...	...	...	...	...
Total	2873197	1784143	2386132	1454548	...	...	487065	329595

| | 1992 |||||||
| | Total || Total private || Public enterprises || General government ||
	Gross	Net	Gross	Net	Gross	Net	Gross	Net
1 Residential buildings	900978	581615	900978	581615	...	...	–	–
2 Non-residential buildings	699925	439485	480280	298103	...	...	219645	141382
3 Other construction [a]	477732	286886	250419	128497	...	...	227313	158389
4 Land improvement and plantation and orchard development	...	...	...	...	...	...	...	...
5 Producers' durable goods	636800	339087	608886	321985	...	...	27914	17102
6 Breeding stock, dairy cattle, etc.	...	...	...	...	...	...	...	...
Total	2715435	1647073	2240563	1330200	...	...	474872	316873

| | 1993 |||||||
| | Total || Total private || Public enterprises || General government ||
	Gross	Net	Gross	Net	Gross	Net	Gross	Net
1 Residential buildings	845853	538018	845853	538018	...	...	–	–
2 Non-residential buildings	666545	411463	456800	278251	...	...	209745	133212
3 Other construction [a]	474856	283374	244852	124483	...	...	230004	158891
4 Land improvement and plantation and orchard development	...	...	...	...	...	...	...	...
5 Producers' durable goods	681786	349330	651043	331148	...	...	30743	18182
6 Breeding stock, dairy cattle, etc.	...	...	...	...	...	...	...	...
Total	2669040	1582185	2198548	1271900	...	...	470492	310285

Finland

	1994							
	Total		Total private		Public enterprises		General government	
	Gross	Net	Gross	Net	Gross	Net	Gross	Net
1 Residential buildings	931242	583295	931242	583295	...	...	–	–
2 Non-residential buildings	701549	425614	470367	280795	...	...	231182	144819
3 Other construction [a]	492155	293558	236950	118856	...	...	255205	174702
4 Land improvement and plantation and orchard development	...	...	...	...	...	...	...	...
5 Producers' durable goods	676559	335918	643837	317155	...	...	32722	18763
6 Breeding stock, dairy cattle, etc.	...	...	...	...	...	...	...	...
Total	2801505	1638385	2282396	1300101	...	...	519109	338284

	1995							
	Total		Total private		Public enterprises		General government	
	Gross	Net	Gross	Net	Gross	Net	Gross	Net
1 Residential buildings	1028001	633819	1028001	633819	...	...	–	–
2 Non-residential buildings	745544	445560	487328	286378	...	...	258216	159182
3 Other construction [a]	513715	305556	236278	117380	...	...	277437	188176
4 Land improvement and plantation and orchard development	...	...	...	...	...	...	...	...
5 Producers' durable goods	661183	323445	626711	304055	...	...	34472	19390
6 Breeding stock, dairy cattle, etc.	...	...	...	...	...	...	...	...
Total	2948443	1708380	2378318	1341632	...	...	570125	366748

	1996							
	Total		Total private		Public enterprises		General government	
	Gross	Net	Gross	Net	Gross	Net	Gross	Net
1 Residential buildings	1034826	628065	1034826	628065	...	...	–	–
2 Non-residential buildings	752054	443247	491005	284629	...	...	261049	158618
3 Other construction [a]	523564	309093	239400	118163	...	...	284164	190930
4 Land improvement and plantation and orchard development	...	...	...	...	...	...	...	...
5 Producers' durable goods	669215	324774	633059	304713	...	...	36156	20061
6 Breeding stock, dairy cattle, etc.	...	...	...	...	...	...	...	...
Total	2979659	1705179	2398290	1335570	...	...	581369	369609

a Item "Land improvement and plantation and orchard development" is included in item "Other construction".

2.14 Stocks of reproducible fixed assets, by type of good and owner, in constant prices

Million Finish markkaa

	1986							
	Total		Total private		Public enterprises		General government	
	Gross	Net	Gross	Net	Gross	Net	Gross	Net

At constant prices of: 1990

1 Residential buildings	862793	586367	862793	586367	...	...	–	–
2 Non-residential buildings	662623	429975	449578	284092	...	...	213045	145883
3 Other construction [a]	418866	264302	250342	141286	...	...	168524	123016
4 Land improvement and plantation and orchard development	...	...	...	...	...	...	...	...
5 Producers' durable goods	509857	279794	494051	270370	...	...	15806	9424
6 Breeding stock, dairy cattle, etc.	...	...	...	...	...	...	...	...
Total	2454139	1560438	2056764	1282115	...	...	397375	278323

Finland

1987

	Total Gross	Total Net	Total private Gross	Total private Net	Public enterprises Gross	Public enterprises Net	General government Gross	General government Net
At constant prices of: 1990								
1 Residential buildings	888352	598570	888352	598570	...	...	–	–
2 Non-residential buildings	686255	443255	465084	292926	...	...	221171	150329
3 Other construction [a]	427713	267842	254134	141959	...	...	173579	125883
4 Land improvement and plantation and orchard development	...	...	...	...	...	...	...	...
5 Producers' durable goods	529901	292442	512407	281806	...	...	17494	10636
6 Breeding stock, dairy cattle, etc.	...	...	...	...	...	...	...	...
Total	2532221	1602109	2119977	1315261	...	...	412244	286848

1988

	Total Gross	Total Net	Total private Gross	Total private Net	Public enterprises Gross	Public enterprises Net	General government Gross	General government Net
At constant prices of: 1990								
1 Residential buildings	918370	614793	918370	614793	...	...	–	–
2 Non-residential buildings	712178	458409	481996	302890	...	...	230182	155519
3 Other construction [a]	435763	270615	257367	142165	...	...	178396	128450
4 Land improvement and plantation and orchard development	...	...	...	...	...	...	...	...
5 Producers' durable goods	554180	308585	534876	296700	...	...	19304	11885
6 Breeding stock, dairy cattle, etc.	...	...	...	...	...	...	...	...
Total	2620491	1652402	2192609	1356548	...	...	427882	295854

1989

	Total Gross	Total Net	Total private Gross	Total private Net	Public enterprises Gross	Public enterprises Net	General government Gross	General government Net
At constant prices of: 1990								
1 Residential buildings	954727	636834	954727	636834	...	...	–	–
2 Non-residential buildings	741475	476491	505753	319103	...	...	235722	157388
3 Other construction [a]	444866	274471	264327	145342	...	...	180539	129129
4 Land improvement and plantation and orchard development	...	...	...	...	...	...	...	...
5 Producers' durable goods	585232	330330	564289	317263	...	...	20943	13067
6 Breeding stock, dairy cattle, etc.	...	...	...	...	...	...	...	...
Total	2726300	1718126	2289096	1418542	...	...	437204	299584

1990

	Total Gross	Total Net	Total private Gross	Total private Net	Public enterprises Gross	Public enterprises Net	General government Gross	General government Net
At constant prices of: 1990								
1 Residential buildings	988585	655831	988585	655831	...	...	–	–
2 Non-residential buildings	771330	494624	528540	334169	...	...	242790	160455
3 Other construction [a]	454128	278519	242449	128029	...	...	211679	150490
4 Land improvement and plantation and orchard development	...	...	...	...	...	...	...	...
5 Producers' durable goods	610976	345493	587811	330959	...	...	23165	14534
6 Breeding stock, dairy cattle, etc.	...	...	...	...	...	...	...	...
Total	2825019	1774467	2347385	1448988	...	...	477634	325479

Finland

1991

	Total Gross	Total Net	Total private Gross	Total private Net	Public enterprises Gross	Public enterprises Net	General government Gross	General government Net
At constant prices of: 1990								
1 Residential buildings	1014278	666228	1014278	666228	...	...	–	–
2 Non-residential buildings	796925	508047	546874	344416	...	...	250051	163631
3 Other construction [a]	462434	281660	244747	127891	...	...	217687	153769
4 Land improvement and plantation and orchard development	...	...	...	...	...	...	...	...
5 Producers' durable goods	620659	344083	595498	328402	...	...	25161	15681
6 Breeding stock, dairy cattle, etc.	...	...	...	...	...	...	...	...
Total	2894296	1800018	2401397	1466937	...	...	492899	333081

1992

	Total Gross	Total Net	Total private Gross	Total private Net	Public enterprises Gross	Public enterprises Net	General government Gross	General government Net
At constant prices of: 1990								
1 Residential buildings	1032048	666226	1032048	666226	...	...	–	–
2 Non-residential buildings	811360	509786	554501	344451	...	...	256859	165335
3 Other construction [a]	466734	280623	243421	124942	...	...	223313	155681
4 Land improvement and plantation and orchard development	...	...	...	...	...	...	...	...
5 Producers' durable goods	579620	308446	553039	292148	...	...	26581	16298
6 Breeding stock, dairy cattle, etc.	...	...	...	...	...	...	...	...
Total	2889762	1765081	2383009	1427767	...	...	506753	337314

1993

	Total Gross	Total Net	Total private Gross	Total private Net	Public enterprises Gross	Public enterprises Net	General government Gross	General government Net
At constant prices of: 1990								
1 Residential buildings	1048795	667102	1048795	667102	...	...	–	–
2 Non-residential buildings	822351	508158	559859	341452	...	...	262492	166706
3 Other construction [a]	472057	281039	243862	123386	...	...	228195	157653
4 Land improvement and plantation and orchard development	...	...	...	...	...	...	...	...
5 Producers' durable goods	572420	293451	544781	277084	...	...	27639	16367
6 Breeding stock, dairy cattle, etc.	...	...	...	...	...	...	...	...
Total	2915623	1749750	2397297	1409024	...	...	518326	340726

1994

	Total Gross	Total Net	Total private Gross	Total private Net	Public enterprises Gross	Public enterprises Net	General government Gross	General government Net
At constant prices of: 1990								
1 Residential buildings	1064276	666623	1064276	666623	...	...	–	–
2 Non-residential buildings	832180	505431	564314	337634	...	...	267866	167797
3 Other construction [a]	476990	281245	243796	121561	...	...	233194	159684
4 Land improvement and plantation and orchard development	...	...	...	...	...	...	...	...
5 Producers' durable goods	565777	281100	536927	264519	...	...	28850	16581
6 Breeding stock, dairy cattle, etc.	...	...	...	...	...	...	...	...
Total	2939223	1734399	2409313	1390337	...	...	529910	344062

Finland

	1995								
	Total		Total private		Public enterprises		General government	
	Gross	Net	Gross	Net	Gross	Net	Gross	Net
At constant prices of: 1990								
1 Residential buildings	1078700	665078	1078700	665078	...	...	–	–
2 Non-residential buildings	844393	505153	572299	337417	...	...	272094	167736
3 Other construction [a]	482440	282147	244408	120648	...	...	238032	161499
4 Land improvement and plantation and orchard development	...	...	...	...	...	...	...	...
5 Producers' durable goods	564614	276055	534205	258913	...	...	30409	17142
6 Breeding stock, dairy cattle, etc.	...	...	...	...	...	...	...	...
Total	2970147	1728433	2429612	1382056	...	...	540535	346377

	1996								
	Total		Total private		Public enterprises		General government	
	Gross	Net	Gross	Net	Gross	Net	Gross	Net
At constant prices of: 1990								
1 Residential buildings	1092741	663215	1092741	663215	...	...	–	–
2 Non-residential buildings	857603	505954	580779	337752	...	...	276824	168202
3 Other construction [a]	488375	283679	245556	120474	...	...	242819	163205
4 Land improvement and plantation and orchard development	...	...	...	...	...	...	...	...
5 Producers' durable goods	565306	274331	533163	256441	...	...	32143	17890
6 Breeding stock, dairy cattle, etc.	...	...	...	...	...	...	...	...
Total	3004025	1727179	2452239	1377882	...	...	551786	349297

a Item "Land improvement and plantation and orchard development" is included in item "Other construction".

2.15 Stocks of reproducible fixed assets, by kind of activity, in current prices

Million Finish markkaa

	1986		1987		1988		1989		1990		1991	
	Gross	Net	Gross	Net	Gross	Net	Gross	Net	Gross	Net	Gross	Net
1 Residential buildings	592739	402834	658269	443540	758574	507819	893624	596077	988585	655831	993384	652504
2 Non-residential buildings	476898	309019	537107	346618	605831	389709	694575	446541	771330	494624	759965	484225
A Industries	308085	193423	345537	216308	388545	242712	449993	282860	501635	315833	495647	310523
1 Agriculture	32320	17523	33901	18611	36042	19970	38875	21742	42260	23903	43208	24582
2 Mining and quarrying	1668	844	1821	904	1948	934	2123	995	2261	1038	2111	935
3 Manufacturing	88335	53637	98881	59572	106743	62399	120083	69779	131542	75971	127070	72601
4 Electricity, gas and water	17604	10922	19630	12070	21567	13045	23968	14302	25908	15238	25226	14775
5 Construction	6615	4430	7387	4865	8326	5423	9382	6022	10449	6659	10283	6489
6 Wholesale and retail trade	59565	36097	67027	40414	73403	43309	84286	50016	93664	55615	91730	54221
7 Transport and communication	12708	8776	14025	9535	15719	10524	19075	12701	21212	13981	21255	13721
8 Finance, etc.	78519	53905	90856	62284	111492	78305	137156	97415	157480	112332	157971	112121
9 Community, social and personal services	10751	7289	12009	8053	13305	8803	15045	9888	16859	11096	16793	11078
B Producers of government services	152541	104452	172956	117558	196115	132502	220399	147160	242790	160455	237552	155451
C Other producers	16272	11144	18614	12752	21171	14495	24183	16521	26905	18336	26766	18251
3 Other construction [a]	328822	207423	349484	218794	379085	235442	417144	257498	454128	278519	477656	290961
A Industries	195769	110391	206512	115170	221865	122327	245249	134640	240147	126497	251091	131020
1 Agriculture	62607	31454	65132	32131	69015	33596	74962	36007	80814	38200	83035	38683
2 Mining and quarrying	1375	816	1450	845	1577	899	1710	954	1820	986	1878	987
3 Manufacturing	14381	7687	15118	7984	16208	8374	17543	8906	18764	9351	19632	9618

Finland

Million Finish markkaa

	1986 Gross	1986 Net	1987 Gross	1987 Net	1988 Gross	1988 Net	1989 Gross	1989 Net	1990 Gross	1990 Net	1991 Gross	1991 Net
4 Electricity, gas and water	57064	32111	60506	33807	65832	36424	72626	40091	78936	43393	83671	45762
5 Construction	18	15	19	15	22	16	24	18	28	21	30	22
6 Wholesale and retail trade	1085	669	1176	726	1243	739	1418	850	1587	954	1703	1016
7 Transport and communication	43617	28006	46489	29586	49629	31303	56606	35769	35806	20468	37539	21275
8 Finance, etc.	–	–	–	–	50	49	54	53	58	54	60	55
9 Community, social and personal services	15622	9633	16622	10076	18289	10927	20306	11992	22334	13070	23543	13602
B Producers of government services	131488	95998	141294	102515	155352	111876	169813	121475	211679	150490	224135	158329
C Other producers	1565	1034	1678	1109	1868	1239	2082	1383	2302	1532	2430	1612
4 Land improvement and development and plantation and orchard development	...	...	...	...	...	...	...	...	...	...	...	...
5 Producers' durable goods	421033	231309	454247	251236	494634	275926	555770	313729	610976	345493	642192	356453
A Industries	404398	221431	435351	239815	473419	262945	532153	299100	583990	328694	612687	338205
1 Agriculture	41889	20774	43347	21139	44717	21642	46738	22587	49033	23390	46969	21518
2 Mining and quarrying	4445	2506	4697	2577	4925	2634	5285	2809	5567	2892	5722	2873
3 Manufacturing	171283	95902	187602	105899	205493	116837	229590	131819	252052	144924	271469	153726
4 Electricity, gas and water	42935	27218	46657	29058	50388	30820	55251	33434	60279	35904	64338	37776
5 Construction	12068	6282	12634	6604	13889	7468	16031	8937	18016	10081	18704	10029
6 Wholesale and retail trade	43882	23604	48913	26885	54459	30690	62406	36244	70261	41241	74672	43044
7 Transport and communication	67900	32658	66974	32138	69691	33806	80505	40153	85804	43419	84029	41729
8 Finance, etc.	14747	9534	18444	12016	22889	14979	28269	18341	33513	21172	36015	21127
9 Community, social and personal services	5249	2953	6083	3499	6968	4069	8078	4776	9465	5671	10769	6383
B Producers of government services	14194	8466	16173	9834	18187	11197	20197	12600	23165	14534	25378	15815
C Other producers	2441	1412	2723	1587	3028	1784	3420	2029	3821	2265	4127	2433
6 Breeding stock, dairy cattle, etc.	...	...	...	...	...	...	...	...	...	...	...	...
Total	1819492	1150585	1999107	1260188	2238124	1408896	2561113	1613845	2825019	1774467	2873197	1784143

	1992 Gross	1992 Net	1993 Gross	1993 Net	1994 Gross	1994 Net	1995 Gross	1995 Net	1996 Gross	1996 Net	1997 Gross	1997 Net
1 Residential buildings	900978	581615	845853	538018	931242	583295	1028001	633819	1034826	628065	...	...
2 Non-residential buildings	699925	439485	666545	411463	701549	425614	745544	445560	752054	443247	...	...
A Industries	455359	281225	432722	262031	443782	263075	457466	266693	460801	264966	...	...
1 Agriculture	41113	23570	40897	23292	41770	23591	37604	21034	37589	20920	...	...
2 Mining and quarrying	1811	768	1653	670	1667	642	1818	722	1757	668	...	...
3 Manufacturing	115148	64714	108303	59796	113265	61483	122941	66393	124620	66952	...	...
4 Electricity, gas and water	22822	13116	21513	12182	22591	12633	24485	13615	24653	13573	...	...
5 Construction	9148	5551	8346	4825	8258	4608	8324	4541	8354	4452	...	...
6 Wholesale and retail trade	83415	48617	78556	44893	78358	43808	78264	42798	78058	41832	...	...
7 Transport and communication	19519	12328	19768	12230	20323	12363	20461	12287	20580	12266	...	...
8 Finance, etc.	146736	102317	138481	94215	141889	93783	147381	94867	148481	93558	...	...
9 Community, social and personal services	15647	10244	15205	9928	15661	10164	16188	10436	16709	10745	...	...
B Producers of government services	219645	141382	209745	133212	231182	144819	258216	159182	261049	158618	...	...
C Other producers	24921	16878	24078	16220	26585	17720	29862	19685	30204	19663	...	...
3 Other construction [a]	477732	286886	474856	283374	492155	293558	513715	305556	523564	309093	...	...
A Industries	247964	126883	242348	122842	234417	117191	233667	115658	236739	116417	...	...

Finland

	1992 Gross	1992 Net	1993 Gross	1993 Net	1994 Gross	1994 Net	1995 Gross	1995 Net	1996 Gross	1996 Net	1997 Gross	1997 Net
1 Agriculture	81807	36977	74558	33138	71366	31027	71384	30376	72574	30217	...	...
2 Mining and quarrying	1790	913	1779	891	1720	856	1694	832	1718	846	...	...
3 Manufacturing	19009	9080	18820	8782	17937	8143	17370	7633	17101	7305	...	...
4 Electricity, gas and water	81781	44246	81861	43881	79154	42039	78514	41510	79131	41740	...	...
5 Construction	31	22	32	21	31	20	31	18	31	17	...	...
6 Wholesale and retail trade	1712	1008	1724	992	1677	938	1659	903	1670	886	...	...
7 Transport and communication	38137	21238	39680	21840	39313	21468	39954	21965	41288	23067	...	...
8 Finance, etc.	59	52	59	51	60	51	56	45	56	44	...	...
9 Community, social and personal services	23638	13347	23835	13246	23159	12649	23005	12376	23170	12295	...	...
B Producers of government services	227313	158389	230004	158891	255205	174702	277437	188176	284164	190930	...	...
C Other producers	2455	1614	2504	1641	2533	1665	2611	1722	2661	1746	...	...
4 Land improvement and development and plantation and orchard development	...	...	...	...	...	...	...	...	...	...	...	...
5 Producers' durable goods	636800	339087	681786	349330	676559	335918	661183	323445	669215	324774	...	...
A Industries	604551	319489	646553	328634	639047	314555	622019	301559	628404	302278	...	...
1 Agriculture	43265	18637	43811	17735	41109	15975	32744	12677	31105	12239	...	...
2 Mining and quarrying	4802	2152	4818	2071	4581	1917	4611	1952	4727	2065	...	...
3 Manufacturing	258996	140419	275519	145195	277540	142776	275449	139859	284899	143869	...	...
4 Electricity, gas and water	67247	37657	73092	39728	76058	40480	77227	39967	78235	39281	...	...
5 Construction	18080	8826	18142	7965	17310	6943	16332	6224	15825	5733	...	...
6 Wholesale and retail trade	76035	42514	82000	43497	77431	39233	75324	36795	74473	35419	...	...
7 Transport and communication	87667	43261	98160	47572	95747	45389	92320	43715	92861	44109	...	...
8 Finance, etc.	36844	19461	38566	18287	36861	15710	36286	14869	34839	14374	...	...
9 Community, social and personal services	11615	6562	12445	6584	12410	6132	11726	5501	11440	5189	...	...
B Producers of government services	27914	17102	30743	18182	32722	18763	34472	19390	36156	20061	...	...
C Other producers	4335	2496	4490	2514	4790	2600	4692	2496	4655	2435	...	...
6 Breeding stock, dairy cattle, etc.	...	...	...	...	...	...	...	...	...	...	...	...
Total	2715435	1647073	2669040	1582185	2801505	1638385	2948443	1708380	2979659	1705179	...	...

a Item "Land improvement and plantation and orchard development" is included in item "Other construction".

2.16 Stocks of reproducible fixed assets, by kind of activity, in constant prices

Million Finish markkaa

	1986 Gross	1986 Net	1987 Gross	1987 Net	1988 Gross	1988 Net	1989 Gross	1989 Net	1990 Gross	1990 Net	1991 Gross	1991 Net
At constant prices of: 1990												
1 Residential buildings	862793	586367	888352	598570	918370	614793	954727	636834	988585	655831	1014278	666228
2 Non-residential buildings	662623	429975	686255	443255	712178	458409	741475	476491	771330	494624	796925	508047
A Industries	426850	268529	441283	276619	457148	285878	479890	301435	501635	315833	518700	325204
1 Agriculture	40461	21934	41026	22522	41394	22935	41753	23352	42260	23903	42608	24238
2 Mining and quarrying	2330	1180	2327	1156	2287	1096	2271	1064	2261	1038	2222	984
3 Manufacturing	123376	74911	126444	76180	125284	73237	128429	74632	131542	75971	133758	76419
4 Electricity, gas and water	24586	15254	25103	15435	25314	15311	25634	15296	25908	15238	26554	15552
5 Construction	9238	6188	9446	6221	9772	6365	10035	6440	10449	6659	10824	6830
6 Wholesale and retail trade	83190	50414	85712	51680	86153	50831	90145	53492	93664	55615	96559	57074

Finland

Million Finish markkaa

	1986 Gross	1986 Net	1987 Gross	1987 Net	1988 Gross	1988 Net	1989 Gross	1989 Net	1990 Gross	1990 Net	1991 Gross	1991 Net
At constant prices of: 1990												
7 Transport and communication	17652	12217	18241	12433	18742	12558	20431	13609	21212	13981	21599	13955
8 Finance, etc.	111003	76252	117621	80688	132576	93206	145089	102966	157480	112332	166886	118481
9 Community, social and personal services	15014	10179	15363	10304	15626	10339	16103	10584	16859	11096	17690	11671
B Producers of government services	213045	145883	221171	150329	230182	155519	235722	157388	242790	160455	250051	163631
C Other producers	22728	15563	23801	16307	24848	17012	25863	17668	26905	18336	28174	19212
3 Other construction [a]	418866	264302	427713	267842	435763	270615	444866	274471	454128	278519	462434	281660
A Industries	248320	139951	252047	140578	255209	140734	262099	143862	240147	126497	242392	126329
1 Agriculture	80729	40655	80896	40118	80970	39540	80979	38940	80814	38200	80570	37414
2 Mining and quarrying	1775	1052	1798	1046	1816	1034	1827	1019	1820	986	1807	952
3 Manufacturing	18567	9925	18753	9905	18721	9676	18755	9521	18764	9351	18778	9197
4 Electricity, gas and water	73669	41455	75051	41934	76054	42080	77641	42859	78936	43393	80029	43771
5 Construction	23	19	24	19	25	19	26	19	28	21	29	21
6 Wholesale and retail trade	1401	865	1459	900	1436	855	1516	909	1587	954	1649	984
7 Transport and communication	51989	33544	53449	34158	55000	34849	59589	37719	35806	20468	36665	20761
8 Finance, etc.	–	–	–	–	58	57	58	56	58	54	58	53
9 Community, social and personal services	20167	12436	20617	12498	21129	12624	21708	12820	22334	13070	22807	13176
B Producers of government services	168524	123016	173579	125883	178396	128450	180539	129129	211679	150490	217687	153769
C Other producers	2022	1335	2087	1381	2158	1431	2228	1480	2302	1532	2355	1562
4 Land improvement and development and plantation and orchard development	...	...	...	...	...	...	...	...	...	...	...	...
5 Producers' durable goods	509857	279794	529901	292442	554180	308585	585232	330330	610976	345493	620659	344083
A Industries	491216	268733	509349	280025	531561	294749	560722	315149	583990	328694	591432	326005
1 Agriculture	49779	24687	49186	23966	49001	23677	49290	23811	49033	23390	47331	21679
2 Mining and quarrying	5291	2980	5333	2924	5372	2872	5525	2936	5567	2892	5514	2769
3 Manufacturing	209947	117079	220178	123890	230767	131000	242624	139258	252052	144924	255880	144935
4 Electricity, gas and water	53183	33709	54873	34176	56451	34530	58629	35481	60279	35904	61968	36383
5 Construction	13791	7178	14184	7413	15258	8204	16852	9392	18016	10081	18047	9677
6 Wholesale and retail trade	54132	29131	56982	31321	60681	34201	65820	38237	70261	41241	72484	41785
7 Transport and communication	81379	39189	81034	38907	81624	39592	84241	42030	85804	43419	84757	42052
8 Finance, etc.	17349	11215	20647	13449	24825	16245	29355	19045	33513	21172	34982	20522
9 Community, social and personal services	6365	3565	6932	3979	7582	4428	8386	4959	9465	5671	10469	6203
B Producers of government services	15806	9424	17494	10636	19304	11885	20943	13067	23165	14534	25161	15681
C Other producers	2835	1637	3058	1781	3315	1951	3567	2114	3821	2265	4066	2397
6 Breeding stock, dairy cattle, etc.	...	...	...	...	...	...	...	...	...	...	...	...
Total	2454139	1560438	2532221	1602109	2620491	1652402	2726300	1718126	2825019	1774467	2894296	1800018

Finland

	1992 Gross	1992 Net	1993 Gross	1993 Net	1994 Gross	1994 Net	1995 Gross	1995 Net	1996 Gross	1996 Net	1997 Gross	1997 Net
At constant prices of: 1990												
1 Residential buildings	1032048	666226	1048795	667102	1064276	666623	1078700	665078	1092741	663215	...	...
2 Non-residential buildings	811360	509786	822351	508158	832180	505431	844393	505153	857603	505954	...	...
A Industries	525354	324712	529723	321151	533490	317087	540832	316675	548750	316902	...	...
1 Agriculture	41690	23895	41586	23677	41478	23418	41396	23150	41653	23177	...	...
2 Mining and quarrying	2118	898	2068	838	2009	773	2059	819	2001	761	...	...
3 Manufacturing	134675	75690	135547	74841	136462	74076	139231	75192	141937	76256	...	...
4 Electricity, gas and water	26692	15341	26925	15247	27218	15221	27729	15419	28078	15459	...	...
5 Construction	10700	6492	10445	6039	10400	5803	10523	5740	10629	5664	...	...
6 Wholesale and retail trade	97562	56864	98320	56188	98688	55172	98942	54105	99311	53221	...	...
7 Transport and communication	21995	13885	22482	13978	22913	14025	23435	14166	24133	14478	...	...
8 Finance, etc.	171620	119667	173318	117917	174674	115847	177229	114998	179931	114323	...	...
9 Community, social and personal services	18302	11980	19032	12426	19648	12752	20288	13086	21077	13563	...	...
B Producers of government services	256859	165335	262492	166706	267866	167797	272094	167736	276824	168202	...	...
C Other producers	29147	19739	30136	20301	30824	20547	31467	20742	32029	20850	...	...
3 Other construction [a]	466734	280623	472057	281039	476990	281245	482440	282147	488375	283679	...	...
A Industries	241023	123366	241407	121778	241296	119932	241856	118991	242955	118793	...	...
1 Agriculture	79189	35787	78532	34699	77655	33458	76691	32219	75626	30987	...	...
2 Mining and quarrying	1773	906	1770	890	1776	886	1777	875	1805	890	...	...
3 Manufacturing	18562	8867	18450	8611	18246	8283	17947	7883	17687	7554	...	...
4 Electricity, gas and water	79865	43209	80256	43020	80523	42766	81110	42882	81832	43165	...	...
5 Construction	30	21	31	21	32	20	32	19	32	18	...	...
6 Wholesale and retail trade	1671	985	1691	973	1705	954	1714	932	1727	916	...	...
7 Transport and communication	36791	20506	37251	20528	37741	20648	38761	21348	40227	22502	...	...
8 Finance, etc.	58	51	58	50	58	49	58	47	58	46	...	...
9 Community, social and personal services	23084	13034	23368	12986	23560	12868	23766	12786	23961	12715	...	...
B Producers of government services	223313	155681	228195	157653	233194	159684	238032	161499	242819	163205	...	...
C Other producers	2398	1576	2455	1608	2500	1629	2552	1657	2601	1681	...	...
4 Land improvement and development and plantation and orchard development	...	...	...	...	...	...	...	...	...	...	...	...
5 Producers' durable goods	579620	308446	572420	293451	565777	281100	564614	276055	565306	274331	...	...
A Industries	548890	289760	540505	274691	532561	262149	529721	256528	528565	254036	...	...
1 Agriculture	42219	18183	38954	15770	35879	13951	33360	12879	31308	12276	...	...
2 Mining and quarrying	4409	1977	4166	1791	3973	1659	3894	1653	3838	1676	...	...
3 Manufacturing	225805	122464	223797	118054	222419	114607	223389	113769	225494	114243	...	...
4 Electricity, gas and water	61311	34332	61642	33509	62568	33303	62942	32575	63076	31671	...	...
5 Construction	16396	8004	15157	6654	14135	5667	13462	5124	12677	4586	...	...
6 Wholesale and retail trade	71435	39978	71230	37967	71190	36280	71285	34998	71530	34167	...	...
7 Transport and communication	81669	40300	80340	38834	78491	37174	78022	37094	77803	37260	...	...
8 Finance, etc.	34772	18374	34111	16208	32830	14011	32354	13246	31924	13182	...	...
9 Community, social and personal services	10874	6148	11108	5904	11076	5497	11013	5190	10915	4975	...	...
B Producers of government services	26581	16298	27639	16367	28850	16581	30409	17142	32143	17890	...	...
C Other producers	4149	2388	4276	2393	4366	2370	4484	2385	4598	2405	...	...

Finland

	1992		1993		1994		1995		1996		1997	
	Gross	Net	Gross	Net	Gross	Net	Gross	Net	Gross	Net	Gross	Net
At constant prices of: 1990												
6 Breeding stock, dairy cattle, etc.	...	...	...	...	...	...	...	...	...	...	...	...
Total	2889762	1765081	2915623	1749750	2939223	1734399	2970147	1728433	3004025	1727179	...	...

a Item "Land improvement and plantation and orchard development" is included in item "Other construction".

2.17 Exports and imports of goods and services, detail

Million Finish markkaa

	1986	1987	1988	1989	1990	1991	1992	1993	1994	1995	1996	1997
Exports of goods and services												
1 Exports of merchandise, f.o.b. [a]	81066	83826	91313	98265	99750	91100	105809	132550	152022	172820	182436	...
2 Transport and communication	5757	6387	7026	7662	8347	7508	8643	10430	11385	11900	12404	...
A In respect of merchandise imports [b]	861	870	963	1060	1091	974	1085	1300	1444	1739	...	...
B Other	4896	5517	6063	6602	7256	6534	7558	9130	9941	10161	...	...
3 Insurance service charges	−121	−313	−575	−603	−816	−1190	−1650	−1468	−616	−573	−553	...
A In respect of merchandise imports [b]	−	−	−	−	−	−	−	−	−	−	−	...
B Other	−121	−313	−575	−603	−816	−1190	−1650	−1468	−616	−573	−553	...
4 Other commodities	5628	6292	6535	6625	6779	6745	9196	10646	12323	15472	15869	...
5 Adjustments of merchandise exports to change-of-ownership basis	...	...	...	...	...	...	...	...	...	...	...	...
6 Direct purchases in the domestic market by non-residential households	3195	3736	4280	4497	4650	5045	6089	7079	7314	7537	7338	...
7 Direct purchases in the domestic market by extraterritorial bodies	109	120	171	256	118	81	184	201	101	86	...	...
Total exports of goods and services	95634	100048	108750	116702	118828	109289	128272	159438	182530	207242	217494	...
Imports of goods and services												
1 Imports of merchandise, c.i.f. [a]	76736	81867	91232	104400	101967	86348	93188	101559	118684	125451	138106	...
2 Adjustments of merchandise imports to change-of-ownership basis	...	...	...	...	...	...	...	...	...	...	...	...
3 Other transport and communication	2160	2610	3338	3869	4363	3974	4360	5646	5862	6029	5529	...
4 Other insurance service charges	294	274	94	172	−288	−37	23	184	166	469	9	...
5 Other commodities	4857	5921	7120	8393	9571	10647	12964	16200	15755	18357	16399	...
6 Direct purchases abroad by government	264	294	176	194	221	401	382	624	879	324	513	...
7 Direct purchases abroad by resident households	5587	6811	7907	8969	10767	11089	10962	9237	8697	10450	10559	...
Total imports of goods and services	89898	97775	109866	125996	126600	112422	121878	133450	150043	161080	171115	...
Balance of goods and services	5736	2273	−1116	−9294	−7772	−3133	6394	25988	32487	46162	46379	...
Total imports and balance of goods and services	95634	100048	108750	116702	118828	109289	128272	159438	182530	207242	217494	...

a Exports and imports of merchandise are recorded on the basis of the crossing of frontiers. No data are available on the basis of changes in the ownership of the goods.

b Insurance service charges in respect of merchandise imports are included in transport and communication in respect of merchandise imports.

Finland

3.12 General government income and outlay account: total and subsectors

Million Finish markkaa

	1986					1987				
	Total government	Central government	State or provincial government	Local government	Social security funds	Total government	Central government	State or provincial government	Local government	Social security funds
Receipts											
1 Operating surplus	53	74	...	−21	–	32	65	...	−33	–
2 Property and entrepreneurial income	11790	2977	...	2047	6766	12387	3204	...	2061	7122
A Withdrawals from public quasi-corporations	1004	390	...	614	–	1265	599	...	666	–
B Interest	9883	2269	...	1028	6586	10056	2202	...	930	6924
C Dividends	502	316	...	6	180	604	400	...	6	198
D Net land rent and royalties	401	2	...	399	–	462	3	...	459	–
3 Taxes, fees and contributions	152101	84018	...	33157	34926	158341	85754	...	34778	37809
A Indirect taxes	52316	52316	...	–	–	57388	57388	...	–	–
B Direct taxes	63127	30015	...	33112	–	61308	26580	...	34728	–
Income	62776	30015	...	32761	–	60934	26580	...	34354	–
Other	351	–	...	351	–	374	–	...	374	–
C Social security contributions	34931	5	...	–	34926	37809	–	...	–	37809
D Fees, fines and penalties	1727	1682	...	45	–	1836	1786	...	50	–
4 Other current transfers	6729	2365	...	27811	8780	7342	2651	...	30629	10670
A Casualty insurance claims	38	–	...	19	19	31	–	...	11	20
B Transfers from other government subsectors	–	479	...	23299	8449	–	534	...	25752	10322
C Transfers from rest of the world	–	–	...	–	–	–	–	...	–	–
D Other transfers, except imputed	310	69	...	–	241	320	70	...	–	250
E Imputed unfunded employee pension and welfare contributions	6381	1817	...	4493	71	6991	2047	...	4866	78
Total current receipts	170673	89434	...	62994	50472	178102	91674	...	67435	55601
Disbursements											
1 Government final consumption expenditure	72849	21423	...	49594	1832	80046	23767	...	54283	1996
2 Property income	6195	4667	...	1419	109	6571	4868	...	1612	91
A Interest	6185	4665	...	1411	109	6559	4866	...	1602	91
B Net land rent and royalties	10	2	...	8	–	12	2	...	10	–
3 Subsidies	11308	10833	...	475	–	11684	11182	...	502	–
4 Other current transfers	59347	43704	...	7986	39884	65476	49291	...	9169	43624
A Casualty insurance premiums, net	62	–	...	43	19	58	–	...	38	20
B Transfers to other government subsectors	–	29513	...	2167	547	–	33673	...	2290	645
C Social security benefits	38936	2600	...	–	36336	42486	2795	...	–	39691
D Social assistance grants	7913	3618	...	1877	2418	8871	3830	...	2416	2625
E Unfunded employee welfare benefits	7315	4200	...	3073	42	8108	4566	...	3494	48
F Transfers to private non-profit institutions serving households	3147	2287	...	826	34	3550	2577	...	931	42
G Other transfers n.e.c.	785	297	...	–	488	956	403	...	–	553

Finland

Million Finish markkaa

	1986					1987				
	Total government	Central government	State or provincial government	Local government	Social security funds	Total government	Central government	State or provincial government	Local government	Social security funds
H Transfers to rest of the world	1189	1189	...	–	–	1447	1447	...	–	–
Net saving	20974	8807	...	3520	8647	14325	2566	...	1869	9890
Total current disbursements and net saving	170673	89434	...	62994	50472	178102	91674	...	67435	55601

	1988					1989				
	Total government	Central government	State or provincial government	Local government	Social security funds	Total government	Central government	State or provincial government	Local government	Social security funds

Receipts

1 Operating surplus	72	53	...	19	–	70	82	...	–12	–
2 Property and entrepreneurial income	13666	3347	...	2278	8041	16211	4351	...	2626	9234
A Withdrawals from public quasi-corporations	1304	449	...	855	–	1374	481	...	893	–
B Interest	11149	2435	...	919	7795	13301	3244	...	1184	8873
C Dividends	715	460	...	9	246	995	623	...	11	361
D Net land rent and royalties	498	3	...	495	–	541	3	...	538	–
3 Taxes, fees and contributions	191102	104280	...	39823	46999	214797	118223	...	43537	53037
A Indirect taxes	66667	66667	...	–	–	75595	75595	...	–	–
B Direct taxes	74454	34691	...	39763	–	82179	38708	...	43471	–
Income	74073	34691	...	39382	–	81777	38708	...	43069	–
Other	381	–	...	381	–	402	–	...	402	–
C Social security contributions	46999	–	...	–	46999	53108	71	...	–	53037
D Fees, fines and penalties	2982	2922	...	60	–	3915	3849	...	66	–
4 Other current transfers	3745	3103	...	29537	10838	4021	3301	...	33026	10702
A Casualty insurance claims	28	–	...	8	20	29	–	...	8	21
B Transfers from other government subsectors	–	645	...	28616	10472	–	698	...	32002	10308
C Transfers from rest of the world	–	–	...	–	–	–	–	...	–	–
D Other transfers, except imputed	387	127	...	–	260	427	148	...	–	279
E Imputed unfunded employee pension and welfare contributions	3330	2331	...	913	86	3565	2455	...	1016	94
Total current receipts	208585	110783	...	71657	65878	235099	125957	...	79177	72973

Disbursements

1 Government final consumption expenditure	87199	26131	...	58876	2192	96019	28097	...	65622	2300
2 Property income	7201	5283	...	1769	149	7260	5018	...	1987	255
A Interest	7186	5281	...	1756	149	7240	5016	...	1972	252
B Net land rent and royalties	15	2	...	13	–	18	2	...	15	1
3 Subsidies	11271	10712	...	559	–	13717	13053	...	664	–
4 Other current transfers	70864	53960	...	6664	49973	77735	59284	...	7487	53972
A Casualty insurance premiums, net	61	–	...	41	20	62	–	...	41	21
B Transfers to other government subsectors	–	36633	...	2445	655	–	39769	...	2588	651
C Social security benefits	49136	3015	...	–	46121	53787	3518	...	–	50269
D Social assistance grants	9273	4206	...	2578	2489	9929	4511	...	3137	2281

Finland

	1988					1989				
	Total government	Central government	State or provincial government	Local government	Social security funds	Total government	Central government	State or provincial government	Local government	Social security funds
E Unfunded employee welfare benefits	5635	4971	...	610	54	6214	5508	...	642	64
F Transfers to private non-profit institutions serving households	3924	2875	...	990	59	4370	3227	...	1079	64
G Other transfers n.e.c.	1071	496	...	–	575	1203	581	...	–	622
H Transfers to rest of the world	1764	1764	...	–	–	2170	2170	...	–	–
Net saving	32050	14697	...	3789	13564	40368	20505	...	3417	16446
Total current disbursements and net saving	208585	110783	...	71657	65878	235099	125957	...	79177	72973

	1990					1991				
	Total government	Central government	State or provincial government	Local government	Social security funds	Total government	Central government	State or provincial government	Local government	Social security funds

Receipts

1 Operating surplus	44	118	...	–74	–	–151	–18	...	–133	–
2 Property and entrepreneurial income	19786	5772	...	2720	11294	23010	6472	...	3124	13414
A Withdrawals from public quasi-corporations	1443	617	...	826	–	1931	745	...	1186	–
B Interest	16531	4431	...	1258	10842	19227	5101	...	1231	12895
C Dividends	1125	723	...	11	391	1064	625	...	13	426
D Net land rent and royalties	687	1	...	625	61	788	1	...	694	93
3 Taxes, fees and contributions	237177	124298	...	51078	61801	232536	124203	...	48188	60145
A Indirect taxes	78025	78025	...	–	–	74730	74730	...	–	–
B Direct taxes	92741	41741	...	51000	–	88138	40064	...	48074	–
Income	92287	41741	...	50546	–	87643	40064	...	47579	–
Other	454	–	...	454	–	495	–	...	495	–
C Social security contributions	63356	1555	...	–	61801	66806	6661	...	–	60145
D Fees, fines and penalties	3055	2977	...	78	–	2862	2748	...	114	–
4 Other current transfers	4472	3605	...	37209	11379	1977	1394	...	40824	21832
A Casualty insurance claims	49	–	...	19	30	43	–	...	14	29
B Transfers from other government subsectors	–	699	...	36092	10930	–	940	...	39656	21477
C Transfers from rest of the world	1	1	...	–	–	1	1	...	–	–
D Other transfers, except imputed	535	215	...	–	320	602	276	...	–	326
E Imputed unfunded employee pension and welfare contributions	3887	2690	...	1098	99	1331	177	...	1154	–
Total current receipts	261479	133793	...	90933	84474	257372	132051	...	92003	95391

Disbursements

1 Government final consumption expenditure	108535	31824	...	74014	2697	118719	36592	...	79158	2969
2 Property income	7511	4912	...	2316	283	9598	6378	...	2965	255
A Interest	7487	4910	...	2299	278	9570	6375	...	2950	245
B Net land rent and royalties	20	2	...	17	1	21	3	...	15	3
3 Subsidies	14756	13999	...	757	–	17174	16402	...	772	–
4 Other current transfers	90227	68766	...	8994	60188	106482	85313	...	10228	73014
A Casualty insurance premiums, net	75	–	...	45	30	72	–	...	43	29

Finland

	1990					1991				
	Total govern-ment	Central govern-ment	State or provincial govern-ment	Local govern-ment	Social security funds	Total govern-ment	Central govern-ment	State or provincial govern-ment	Local govern-ment	Social security funds
B Transfers to other government subsectors	–	44207	...	2707	807	–	57395	...	3030	1648
C Social security benefits	62387	6458	...	–	55929	77566	12379	...	–	65187
D Social assistance grants	11779	5054	...	4317	2408	15745	5549	...	5149	5047
E Unfunded employee welfare benefits	7029	6257	...	694	78	3085	2266	...	727	92
F Transfers to private non-profit institutions serving households	4995	3693	...	1231	71	5404	4051	...	1279	74
G Other transfers n.e.c.	1528	663	...	–	865	1664	727	...	–	937
H Transfers to rest of the world	2434	2434	...	–	–	2946	2946	...	–	–
Net saving	40450	14292	...	4852	21306	5399	–12634	...	–1120	19153
Total current disbursements and net saving	261479	133793	...	90933	84474	257372	132051	...	92003	95391

	1992					1993				
	Total govern-ment	Central govern-ment	State or provincial govern-ment	Local govern-ment	Social security funds	Total govern-ment	Central govern-ment	State or provincial govern-ment	Local govern-ment	Social security funds

Receipts

1 Operating surplus	–125	–19	...	–106	–	–163	141	...	–304	–
2 Property and entrepreneurial income	25422	6802	...	3906	14714	27873	9016	...	4592	14265
A Withdrawals from public quasi-corporations	1983	459	...	1524	–	2697	760	...	1937	–
B Interest	22074	6042	...	1638	14394	23848	8002	...	1785	14061
C Dividends	555	300	...	15	240	400	250	...	16	134
D Net land rent and royalties	810	1	...	729	80	928	4	...	854	70
3 Taxes, fees and contributions	226366	117261	...	46196	62909	221804	108464	...	47208	66132
A Indirect taxes	71643	71643	...	–	–	71556	71556	...	–	–
B Direct taxes	82270	36201	...	46069	–	74900	27822	...	47078	–
Income	81728	36201	...	45527	–	72668	27822	...	44846	–
Other	542	–	...	542	–	2232	–	...	2232	–
C Social security contributions	69566	6657	...	–	62909	72847	6715	...	–	66132
D Fees, fines and penalties	2887	2760	...	127	–	2501	2371	...	130	–
4 Other current transfers	2180	1727	...	41349	24493	2386	1309	...	42518	41179
A Casualty insurance claims	43	–	...	7	36	39	–	...	10	29
B Transfers from other government subsectors	–	1029	...	40206	24154	–	840	...	41258	40522
C Transfers from rest of the world	136	136	...	–	–	1	1	...	–	–
D Other transfers, except imputed	685	382	...	–	303	1096	468	...	–	628
E Imputed unfunded employee pension and welfare contributions	1316	180	...	1136	–	1250	–	...	1250	–
Total current receipts	253843	125771	...	91345	102116	251900	118930	...	94014	121576

Disbursements

1 Government final consumption expenditure	118453	38399	...	77223	2831	112190	36039	...	73153	2998
2 Property income	12608	8687	...	3563	358	22335	17907	...	4004	424
A Interest	12583	8687	...	3546	350	22284	17879	...	3984	421
B Net land rent and royalties	19	–	...	17	2	50	28	...	20	2

Finland

	1992					1993				
	Total govern-ment	Central govern-ment	State or provincial govern-ment	Local govern-ment	Social security funds	Total govern-ment	Central govern-ment	State or provincial govern-ment	Local govern-ment	Social security funds
3 Subsidies	17028	16218	...	810	–	16376	15454	...	922	–
4 Other current transfers	123238	90036	...	12247	86344	132839	97316	...	13803	104340
A Casualty insurance premiums, net	76	–	...	40	36	78	–	...	49	29
B Transfers to other government subsectors	–	58794	...	4234	2361	–	70014	...	8633	3973
C Social security benefits	89081	13766	...	–	75315	89754	8470	...	–	81284
D Social assistance grants	20546	7039	...	6054	7453	28412	7244	...	3201	17967
E Unfunded employee welfare benefits	3297	2575	...	722	–	3524	2861	...	663	–
F Transfers to private non-profit institutions serving households	5270	4000	...	1197	73	6099	4769	...	1257	73
G Other transfers n.e.c.	2462	1356	...	–	1106	2730	1716	...	–	1014
H Transfers to rest of the world	2506	2506	...	–	–	2242	2242	...	–	–
Net saving	–17484	–27569	...	–2498	12583	–31840	–47786	...	2132	13814
Total current disbursements and net saving	253843	125771	...	91345	102116	251900	118930	...	94014	121576

	1994					1995				
	Total govern-ment	Central govern-ment	State or provincial govern-ment	Local govern-ment	Social security funds	Total govern-ment	Central govern-ment	State or provincial govern-ment	Local govern-ment	Social security funds

Receipts

1 Operating surplus	–222	64	...	–286	–	–430	–132	...	–298	–
2 Property and entrepreneurial income	23504	6916	...	4138	12450	27492	9299	...	4286	13907
A Withdrawals from public quasi-corporations	2143	445	...	1698	–	1865	338	...	1527	–
B Interest	19764	6100	...	1509	12155	23278	8049	...	1827	13402
C Dividends	566	329	...	17	220	1326	868	...	23	435
D Net land rent and royalties	1031	42	...	914	75	1023	44	...	909	70
3 Taxes, fees and contributions	246276	116770	...	54362	75144	255380	123869	...	55591	75920
A Indirect taxes	74200	74196	...	4	–	75649	75643	...	6	–
B Direct taxes	87815	33577	...	54238	–	94555	39100	...	55455	–
Income	85197	33577	...	51620	–	91931	39100	...	52831	–
Other	2618	–	...	2618	–	2624	–	...	2624	–
C Social security contributions	81472	6328	...	–	75144	82194	6274	...	–	75920
D Fees, fines and penalties	2789	2669	...	120	–	2982	2852	...	130	–
4 Other current transfers	2103	1015	...	40263	49886	7364	6200	...	40571	49840
A Casualty insurance claims	32	–	...	9	23	13	–	...	8	5
B Transfers from other government subsectors	–	811	...	39005	49245	–	720	...	39218	49309
C Transfers from rest of the world	15	15	...	–	–	5407	5367	...	40	–
D Other transfers, except imputed	807	189	...	–	618	639	113	...	–	526
E Imputed unfunded employee pension and welfare contributions	1249	–	...	1249	–	1305	–	...	1305	–
Total current receipts	271661	124765	...	98477	137480	289806	139236	...	100150	139667

Disbursements

652

Finland

	1994					1995				
	Total govern-ment	Central govern-ment	State or provincial govern-ment	Local govern-ment	Social security funds	Total govern-ment	Central govern-ment	State or provincial govern-ment	Local govern-ment	Social security funds
1 Government final consumption expenditure	114001	37515	...	73335	3151	119795	37867	...	78746	3182
2 Property income	26153	22405	...	3452	296	29240	25878	...	3130	232
A Interest	26105	22379	...	3430	296	29178	25842	...	3108	228
B Net land rent and royalties	48	26	...	22	–	58	36	...	22	–
3 Subsidies	15856	15082	...	774	–	18177	17395	...	782	–
4 Other current transfers	138582	99823	...	14062	113758	143723	104140	...	13868	114962
A Casualty insurance premiums, net	91	–	...	68	23	64	–	...	59	5
B Transfers to other government subsectors	–	76289	...	8671	4101	–	77012	...	8309	3926
C Social security benefits	90905	8701	...	–	82204	91304	9042	...	–	82262
D Social assistance grants	33653	3454	...	3590	26609	34286	2397	...	3813	28076
E Unfunded employee welfare benefits	3620	2980	...	640	–	3745	3122	...	623	–
F Transfers to private non-profit institutions serving households	6095	4929	...	1090	76	6373	5240	...	1060	73
G Other transfers n.e.c.	2129	1381	...	3	745	1797	1173	...	4	620
H Transfers to rest of the world	2089	2089	...	–	–	6154	6154	...	–	–
Net saving	–22931	–50060	...	6854	20275	–21129	–46044	...	3624	21291
Total current disbursements and net saving	271661	124765	...	98477	137480	289806	139236	...	100150	139667

	1996					1997				
	Total govern-ment	Central govern-ment	State or provincial govern-ment	Local govern-ment	Social security funds	Total govern-ment	Central govern-ment	State or provincial govern-ment	Local govern-ment	Social security funds
Receipts										
1 Operating surplus	–438	–70	...	–368	–	...	...	...	...	...
2 Property and entrepreneurial income	28432	8819	...	4651	14962	...	...	...	...	...
A Withdrawals from public quasi-corporations	1958	256	...	1702	–	...	...	...	...	...
B Interest	23100	6978	...	1931	14191	...	...	...	...	...
C Dividends	2292	1527	...	64	701	...	...	...	...	...
D Net land rent and royalties	1082	58	...	954	70	...	...	...	...	...
3 Taxes, fees and contributions	277219	137993	...	62647	76579	...	...	...	...	...
A Indirect taxes	82227	82222	...	5	–	...	...	...	...	...
B Direct taxes	109489	47058	...	62431	–	...	...	...	...	...
Income	106907	47058	...	59849	–	...	...	...	...	...
Other	2582	–	...	2582	–	...	...	...	...	...
C Social security contributions	82549	5884	...	86	76579	...	...	...	...	...
D Fees, fines and penalties	2954	2829	...	125	–	...	...	...	...	...
4 Other current transfers	6624	5424	...	33903	46898	...	...	...	...	...
A Casualty insurance claims	29	–	...	8	21	...	...	...	...	...
B Transfers from other government subsectors	–	697	...	32537	46367	...	...	...	...	...
C Transfers from rest of the world	4641	4580	...	61	–	...	...	...	...	...
D Other transfers, except imputed	657	147	...	–	510	...	...	...	...	...

Finland

	1996					1997				
	Total govern-ment	Central govern-ment	State or provincial govern-ment	Local govern-ment	Social security funds	Total govern-ment	Central govern-ment	State or provincial govern-ment	Local govern-ment	Social security funds
E Imputed unfunded employee pension and welfare contributions	1297	–	...	1297	–	...	...	...	...	...
Total current receipts	311837	152166	...	100833	138439	...	...	...	...	...
Disbursements										
1 Government final consumption expenditure	126579	39178	...	84007	3394	...	...	...	...	...
2 Property income	33111	30230	...	2626	255	...	...	...	...	...
A Interest	33024	30188	...	2585	251	...	...	...	...	...
B Net land rent and royalties	83	42	...	41	...	...	...	...	...	...
3 Subsidies	16643	15936	...	707	...	...	...	...	...	...
4 Other current transfers	146463	101163	...	9215	115686	...	...	...	...	...
A Casualty insurance premiums, net	82	...	...	61	21	...	...	...	...	...
B Transfers to other government subsectors	...	72847	...	3012	3742	...	...	...	...	...
C Social security benefits	94267	9314	...	...	84953	...	...	...	...	...
D Social assistance grants	32417	2285	...	4348	25784	...	...	...	...	...
E Unfunded employee welfare benefits	3878	3272	...	606	...	...	...	...	...	...
F Transfers to private non-profit institutions serving households	6787	5526	...	1183	78	...	...	...	...	...
G Other transfers n.e.c.	2295	1182	...	5	1108	...	...	...	...	...
H Transfers to rest of the world	6737	6737	...	...	...	...	...	...	...	...
Net saving	–10959	–34341	...	4278	19104	...	...	...	...	...
Total current disbursements and net saving	311837	152166	...	100833	138439	...	...	...	...	...

3.13 General government capital accumulation account: total and subsectors

Million Finish markkaa

	1986					1987				
	Total govern-ment	Central govern-ment	State or provincial govern-ment	Local govern-ment	Social security funds	Total govern-ment	Central govern-ment	State or provincial govern-ment	Local govern-ment	Social security funds
Finance of gross accumulation										
1 Gross saving	25444	10188	...	6472	8784	19392	4128	...	5214	10050
A Consumption of fixed capital	4470	1381	...	2952	137	5067	1562	...	3345	160
B Net saving	20974	8807	...	3520	8647	14325	2566	...	1869	9890
2 Capital transfers [a]	–539	–1971	...	1432	–	–588	–2221	...	1633	–
A From other government subsectors	–	–1436	...	1436	–	–	–1637	...	1637	–
B From other resident sectors	–539	–535	...	–4	–	–588	–584	...	–4	–
C From rest of the world	–	–	...	–	–	–	–	...	–	–
Finance of gross accumulation	24905	8217	...	7904	8784	18804	1907	...	6847	10050
Gross accumulation										
1 Gross capital formation	12298	4670	...	7462	166	14449	5414	...	8576	459
A Increase in stocks	350	350	...	–	–	278	278	...	–	–

Finland

Million Finish markkaa

	1986					1987				
	Total govern-ment	Central govern-ment	State or provincial govern-ment	Local govern-ment	Social security funds	Total govern-ment	Central govern-ment	State or provincial govern-ment	Local govern-ment	Social security funds
B Gross fixed capital formation	11948	4320	...	7462	166	14171	5136	...	8576	459
2 Purchases of land, net	572	225	...	347	–	386	130	...	256	–
3 Purchases of intangible assets, net	...	...	...	...	...	...	...	...	...	...
4 Capital transfers	...	...	...	...	...	...	...	...	...	...
Net lending	12035	3322	...	95	8618	3969	–3637	...	–1985	9591
Gross accumulation	24905	8217	...	7904	8784	18804	1907	...	6847	10050

	1988					1989				
	Total govern-ment	Central govern-ment	State or provincial govern-ment	Local govern-ment	Social security funds	Total govern-ment	Central govern-ment	State or provincial govern-ment	Local govern-ment	Social security funds

Finance of gross accumulation

1 Gross saving	37746	16433	...	7560	13753	46662	22333	...	7659	16670
A Consumption of fixed capital	5696	1736	...	3771	189	6294	1828	...	4242	224
B Net saving	32050	14697	...	3789	13564	40368	20505	...	3417	16446
2 Capital transfers [a]	–3277	–5052	...	1775	–	–870	–2876	...	2006	–
A From other government subsectors	–	–1780	...	1780	–	–	–2012	...	2012	–
B From other resident sectors	–3277	–3272	...	–5	–	–870	–864	...	–6	–
C From rest of the world	–	–	...	–	–	–	–	...	–	–
Finance of gross accumulation	34469	11381	...	9335	13753	45792	19457	...	9665	16670

Gross accumulation

1 Gross capital formation	16129	5770	...	8928	1431	15212	5728	...	9469	15
A Increase in stocks	283	283	...	–	–	93	93	...	–	–
B Gross fixed capital formation	15846	5487	...	8928	1431	15119	5635	...	9469	15
2 Purchases of land, net	705	218	...	487	–	26	131	...	–105	–
3 Purchases of intangible assets, net	...	...	...	...	...	...	...	...	...	...
4 Capital transfers	...	...	...	...	...	...	...	...	...	...
Net lending	17635	5393	...	–80	12322	30554	13598	...	301	16655
Gross accumulation	34469	11381	...	9335	13753	45792	19457	...	9665	16670

	1990					1991				
	Total govern-ment	Central govern-ment	State or provincial govern-ment	Local govern-ment	Social security funds	Total govern-ment	Central govern-ment	State or provincial govern-ment	Local govern-ment	Social security funds

Finance of gross accumulation

1 Gross saving	47833	16691	...	9596	21546	12880	–10173	...	3664	19389
A Consumption of fixed capital	7383	2399	...	4744	240	7481	2461	...	4784	236
B Net saving	40450	14292	...	4852	21306	5399	–12634	...	–1120	19153
2 Capital transfers [a]	–757	–3098	...	2341	–	–1202	–3478	...	2276	–
A From other government subsectors	–	–2347	...	2347	–	–	–2283	...	2283	–
B From other resident sectors	–757	–751	...	–6	–	–903	–896	...	–7	–
C From rest of the world	–	–	...	–	–	–299	–299	...	–	–
Finance of gross accumulation	47076	13593	...	11937	21546	11678	–13651	...	5940	19389

Finland

	1990					1991				
	Total govern-ment	Central govern-ment	State or provincial govern-ment	Local govern-ment	Social security funds	Total govern-ment	Central govern-ment	State or provincial govern-ment	Local govern-ment	Social security funds

Gross accumulation

1 Gross capital formation	18641	7218	...	11243	180	18661	8232	...	10215	214
A Increase in stocks	177	177	...	–	–	376	376	...	–	–
B Gross fixed capital formation	18464	7041	...	11243	180	18285	7856	...	10215	214
2 Purchases of land, net	362	156	...	206	–	213	157	...	54	2
3 Purchases of intangible assets, net	...	...	...	...	...	...	...	...	...	...
4 Capital transfers	...	...	...	...	...	...	...	...	...	...
Net lending	27692	6219	...	488	20985	–7367	–22040	...	–4329	19002
Gross accumulation	47076	13593	...	11937	21546	11678	–13651	...	5940	19389

	1992					1993				
	Total govern-ment	Central govern-ment	State or provincial govern-ment	Local govern-ment	Social security funds	Total govern-ment	Central govern-ment	State or provincial govern-ment	Local govern-ment	Social security funds

Finance of gross accumulation

1 Gross saving	–10083	–25037	...	2143	12811	–24449	–45098	...	6608	14041
A Consumption of fixed capital	7401	2532	...	4641	228	7391	2688	...	4476	227
B Net saving	–17484	–27569	...	–2498	12583	–31840	–47786	...	2132	13814
2 Capital transfers [a]	–896	–3021	...	2125	–	–544	–1925	...	1381	–
A From other government subsectors	–	–2130	...	2130	–	–	–1386	...	1386	–
B From other resident sectors	–896	–891	...	–5	–	–544	–539	...	–5	–
C From rest of the world	–	–	...	–	–	–	–	...	–	–
Finance of gross accumulation	–10979	–28058	...	4268	12811	–24993	–47023	...	7989	14041

Gross accumulation

1 Gross capital formation	16734	8089	...	8153	492	13652	7147	...	6081	424
A Increase in stocks	133	133	...	–	–	347	347	...	–	–
B Gross fixed capital formation	16601	7956	...	8153	492	13305	6800	...	6081	424
2 Purchases of land, net	179	219	...	–40	–	61	48	...	13	–
3 Purchases of intangible assets, net	...	...	...	...	...	...	...	...	...	...
4 Capital transfers	...	...	...	...	...	...	...	...	...	...
Net lending	–27892	–36366	...	–3845	12319	–38706	–54218	...	1895	13617
Gross accumulation	–10979	–28058	...	4268	12811	–24993	–47023	...	7989	14041

	1994					1995				
	Total govern-ment	Central govern-ment	State or provincial govern-ment	Local govern-ment	Social security funds	Total govern-ment	Central govern-ment	State or provincial govern-ment	Local govern-ment	Social security funds

Finance of gross accumulation

1 Gross saving	–14983	–47154	...	11646	20525	–12518	–42888	...	8800	21570
A Consumption of fixed capital	7948	2906	...	4792	250	8611	3156	...	5176	279
B Net saving	–22931	–50060	...	6854	20275	–21129	–46044	...	3624	21291
2 Capital transfers [a]	–1357	–2810	...	1453	–	–421	–1941	...	1520	–
A From other government subsectors	–	–1458	...	1458	–	–	–1530	...	1530	–
B From other resident sectors	–1357	–1352	...	–5	–	–702	–692	...	–10	–

Finland

	1994					1995				
	Total govern-ment	Central govern-ment	State or provincial govern-ment	Local govern-ment	Social security funds	Total govern-ment	Central govern-ment	State or provincial govern-ment	Local govern-ment	Social security funds
C From rest of the world	–	–	...	–	–	281	281	...	–	–
Finance of gross accumulation	–16340	–49964	...	13099	20525	–12939	–44829	...	10320	21570
Gross accumulation											
1 Gross capital formation	14933	7776	...	6394	763	15106	7937	...	7033	136
A Increase in stocks	289	289	...	–	–	566	566	...	–	–
B Gross fixed capital formation	14644	7487	...	6394	763	14540	7371	...	7033	136
2 Purchases of land, net	312	190	...	113	9	302	277	...	17	8
3 Purchases of intangible assets, net	...	...	...	...	...	...	...	...	...	...
4 Capital transfers	...	...	...	...	...	...	...	...	...	...
Net lending	–31585	–57930	...	6592	19753	–28347	–53043	...	3270	21426
Gross accumulation	–16340	–49964	...	13099	20525	–12939	–44829	...	10320	21570

	1996					1997				
	Total govern-ment	Central govern-ment	State or provincial govern-ment	Local govern-ment	Social security funds	Total govern-ment	Central govern-ment	State or provincial govern-ment	Local govern-ment	Social security funds
Finance of gross accumulation											
1 Gross saving	–2223	–31080	...	9477	19380	...	...	...	...	...
A Consumption of fixed capital	8736	3261	...	5199	276	...	...	...	...	...
B Net saving	–10959	–34341	...	4278	19104	...	...	...	...	...
2 Capital transfers [a]	–1615	–3182	...	1043	524	...	...	...	...	...
A From other government subsectors	–	–1577	...	1053	524	...	...	...	...	...
B From other resident sectors	–1871	–1861	...	–10	–	...	...	...	...	...
C From rest of the world	256	256	...	–	–	...	...	...	...	...
Finance of gross accumulation	–3838	–34262	...	10520	19904	...	...	...	...	...
Gross accumulation											
1 Gross capital formation	15592	7546	...	7933	113	...	...	...	...	...
A Increase in stocks	7	7	...	–	–	...	...	...	...	...
B Gross fixed capital formation	15585	7539	...	7933	113	...	...	...	...	...
2 Purchases of land, net	475	280	...	195	–	...	...	...	...	...
3 Purchases of intangible assets, net	...	...	...	...	...	...	...	...	...	...
4 Capital transfers	...	...	...	...	...	...	...	...	...	...
Net lending	–19905	–42088	...	2392	19791	...	...	...	...	...
Gross accumulation	–3838	–34262	...	10520	19904	...	...	...	...	...

a Capital transfers received are recorded net of capital transfers paid.

Finland

3.14 General government capital finance account: total and subsectors

Million Finish markkaa

| | \multicolumn{5}{c|}{1986} | \multicolumn{5}{c}{1987} |
	Total government	Central government	State or provincial government	Local government	Social security funds	Total government	Central government	State or provincial government	Local government	Social security funds
Acquisition of financial assets										
1 Gold and SDRs	...	...	...	...	...	...	...	...	...	...
2 Currency and transferable deposits	6577	7775	...	−295	−903	2412	1929	...	188	295
3 Other deposits	−1790	−2249	...	−159	618	−1611	−1208	...	−750	347
4 Bills and bonds, short-term	...	...	...	...	...	...	...	...	...	...
5 Bonds, long-term	934	121	...	−83	896	646	−53	...	−81	780
A Corporations	...	121	...	–	...	...	−53	...	–	...
B Other government subsectors	...	–	...	−83	...	...	–	...	−81	...
C Rest of the world	...	–	...	–	...	...	–	...	–	...
6 Corporate equity securities	3002	837	...	1773	392	4340	1017	...	1688	1635
7 Short-term loans, n.e.c.	328	−218	...	343	203	1238	3	...	−1179	2414
8 Long-term loans, n.e.c.	10079	1872	...	1107	7100	5881	2078	...	723	3080
A Mortgages	...	798	...	264	17	...	...	...	...	...
B Other	...	1074	...	843	7083	...	...	...	...	...
9 Other receivables	1851	1259	...	79	513	2000	279	...	1000	721
10 Other assets	880	304	...	576	–	166	−394	...	560	–
Total aquisition of financial assets	21861	9701	...	3341	8819	15072	3651	...	2149	9272
Incurrence of liabilities										
1 Currency and transferable deposits	...	...	...	...	...	...	...	...	...	...
2 Other deposits	...	...	...	...	...	...	...	...	...	...
3 Bills and bonds, short-term	−1	–	...	−18	17	−25	2	...	−25	−2
4 Bonds, long-term	4700	4345	...	355	41	7130	7094	...	36	89
5 Short-term loans, n.e.c.	−852	−762	...	−131	−244	702	761	...	−148	210
6 Long-term loans, n.e.c.	1293	84	...	1453	288	2162	−772	...	2724	49
7 Other payables	3683	2713	...	682	–	−758	−1058	...	251	–
8 Other liabilities	1208	–	...	1208	–	1200	–	...	1200	–
Total incurrence of liabilities	10031	6380	...	3549	102	10411	6027	...	4038	346
Statistical discrepancy [a]	−205	−1	...	−303	99	692	1261	...	96	−665
Net lending	12035	3322	...	95	8618	3969	−3637	...	−1985	9591
Incurrence of liabilities and net worth	21861	9701	...	3341	8819	15072	3651	...	2149	9272

| | \multicolumn{5}{c|}{1988} | \multicolumn{5}{c}{1989} |
	Total government	Central government	State or provincial government	Local government	Social security funds	Total government	Central government	State or provincial government	Local government	Social security funds
Acquisition of financial assets										
1 Gold and SDRs	...	...	...	...	...	...	...	...	...	...
2 Currency and transferable deposits	−232	−965	...	248	485	−1377	−482	...	232	−1127
3 Other deposits	770	1191	...	14	−435	3322	3234	...	−453	541
4 Bills and bonds, short-term	...	...	...	...	...	...	...	...	...	...
5 Bonds, long-term	2800	−58	...	–	2858	502	18	...	–	484

Finland

	1988					1989				
	Total govern-ment	Central govern-ment	State or provincial govern-ment	Local govern-ment	Social security funds	Total govern-ment	Central govern-ment	State or provincial govern-ment	Local govern-ment	Social security funds
A Corporations	...	−58	...	–	...	...	18	...	–	...
B Other government subsectors	...	–	...	–	...	...	–	...	–	...
C Rest of the world	...	–	...	–	...	...	–	...	–	...
6 Corporate equity securities	7491	1015	...	1469	5007	7124	1055	...	2077	3992
7 Short-term loans, n.e.c.	9824	6158	...	860	2806	5791	3628	...	357	1806
8 Long-term loans, n.e.c.	4380	1069	...	589	2722	14212	2424	...	533	11255
9 Other receivables	1760	209	...	464	1087	4302	616	...	2007	1679
10 Other assets	466	74	...	392	–	1118	501	...	617	–
Total aquisition of financial assets	27259	8693	...	4036	14530	34994	10994	...	5370	18630

Incurrence of liabilities

	1988					1989				
1 Currency and transferable deposits	...	...	...	...	...	...	...	...	...	...
2 Other deposits	...	...	...	...	...	...	...	...	...	...
3 Bills and bonds, short-term	−8	–	...	20	−28	16	–	...	9	7
4 Bonds, long-term	2339	2128	...	211	660	−585	−720	...	135	159
5 Short-term loans, n.e.c.	1917	712	...	545	696	−120	−1333	...	1054	1
6 Long-term loans, n.e.c.	2018	−989	...	2311	683	954	−548	...	1501	591
7 Other payables	1545	748	...	114	4	1633	459	...	583	–
8 Other liabilities	1155	–	...	1151	–	1778	–	...	1778	–
Total incurrence of liabilities	8966	2599	...	4352	2015	3676	−2142	...	5060	758
Statistical discrepancy [a]	658	701	...	−236	193	764	−462	...	9	1217
Net lending	17635	5393	...	−80	12322	30554	13598	...	301	16655
Incurrence of liabilities and net worth	27259	8693	...	4036	14530	34994	10994	...	5370	18630

	1990					1991				
	Total govern-ment	Central govern-ment	State or provincial govern-ment	Local govern-ment	Social security funds	Total govern-ment	Central govern-ment	State or provincial govern-ment	Local govern-ment	Social security funds

Acquisition of financial assets

	1990					1991				
1 Gold and SDRs	...	...	...	...	...	...	...	...	...	...
2 Currency and transferable deposits	4073	3792	...	412	−131	−8266	−9385	...	216	903
3 Other deposits	−3199	−4004	...	−232	1037	−2947	−1317	...	−769	−861
4 Bills and bonds, short-term	...	...	...	...	...	...	...	...	...	...
5 Bonds, long-term	187	−105	...	–	292	878	−121	...	–	999
A Corporations	...	−105	...	–	...	...	−121	...	–	...
B Other government subsectors	...	–	...	–	...	...	–	...	–	...
C Rest of the world	...	–	...	–	...	...	–	...	–	...
6 Corporate equity securities	10059	5276	...	3632	1151	3703	373	...	1568	1762
7 Short-term loans, n.e.c.	5091	2039	...	1730	1322	7444	4221	...	682	2541
8 Long-term loans, n.e.c.	20863	4772	...	730	15361	23717	7178	...	2407	14132
9 Other receivables	365	−714	...	−30	1109	4043	39	...	402	3602
10 Other assets	−1313	−2042	...	729	–	−300	−638	...	338	–
Total aquisition of financial assets	36126	9014	...	6971	20141	28272	350	...	4844	23078

Incurrence of liabilities

	1990					1991				
1 Currency and transferable deposits	185	185	...	...	...	59	59	...	...	...

Finland

	1990					1991				
	Total govern-ment	Central govern-ment	State or provincial govern-ment	Local govern-ment	Social security funds	Total govern-ment	Central govern-ment	State or provincial govern-ment	Local govern-ment	Social security funds
2 Other deposits	...	...	...	...	...	...	...	...	...	...
3 Bills and bonds, short-term	85	–	...	109	–24	11	–	...	11	–
4 Bonds, long-term	1188	1256	...	–68	386	22629	21341	...	1288	1849
5 Short-term loans, n.e.c.	1122	145	...	591	–1134	8023	4774	...	1400	68
6 Long-term loans, n.e.c.	4006	2743	...	2397	230	4229	–1036	...	5197	3005
7 Other payables	2131	–735	...	2636	30	2647	–417	...	59	–
8 Other liabilities	2037	–	...	2007	–	567	–	...	567	–
Total incurrence of liabilities	10754	3594	...	7672	–512	38165	24721	...	8522	4922
Statistical discrepancy [a]	–2320	–799	...	–1189	–332	–2526	–2331	...	651	–846
Net lending	27692	6219	...	488	20985	–7367	–22040	...	–4329	19002
Incurrence of liabilities and net worth	36126	9014	...	6971	20141	28272	350	...	4844	23078

	1992					1993				
	Total govern-ment	Central govern-ment	State or provincial govern-ment	Local govern-ment	Social security funds	Total govern-ment	Central govern-ment	State or provincial govern-ment	Local govern-ment	Social security funds

Acquisition of financial assets

1 Gold and SDRs	...	...	...	...	...	...	...	...	...	...
2 Currency and transferable deposits	–374	–1278	...	149	755	1698	1140	...	539	19
3 Other deposits	311	–3	...	854	–540	–350	–	...	–1455	1105
4 Bills and bonds, short-term	...	...	...	...	...	...	...	...	...	...
5 Bonds, long-term	21870	16502	...	–	5368	12706	1633	...	–	11073
A Corporations	...	16502	...	–	...	...	1633	...	–	...
B Other government subsectors	...	...	...	–	...	...	–	...	–	...
C Rest of the world	...	–	...	–	...	...	–	...	–	...
6 Corporate equity securities	6735	5030	...	416	1289	9350	6110	...	1899	1341
7 Short-term loans, n.e.c.	3479	4111	...	217	–849	29844	17485	...	3247	9112
8 Long-term loans, n.e.c.	14302	7153	...	3299	3850	–4130	4567	...	1109	–9806
9 Other receivables	8425	3188	...	2236	3001	2830	938	...	–1819	3711
10 Other assets	–1595	–1114	...	–481	–	–1629	–170	...	–1459	–
Total aquisition of financial assets	53153	33589	...	6690	12874	50319	31703	...	2061	16555

Incurrence of liabilities

1 Currency and transferable deposits	74	74	...	...	...	342	342	...	...	...
2 Other deposits	...	...	...	...	...	...	...	...	...	...
3 Bills and bonds, short-term	–66	–	...	–66	–	–74	1	...	–76	1
4 Bonds, long-term	59749	56385	...	3364	–	73272	71538	...	1734	–
5 Short-term loans, n.e.c.	9980	11151	...	–260	–911	10291	8844	...	–935	2382
6 Long-term loans, n.e.c.	9395	2269	...	6654	472	3848	3704	...	437	–293
7 Other payables	1157	483	...	–491	1165	376	672	...	–586	290
8 Other liabilities	379	–	...	369	10	605	–	...	596	9
Total incurrence of liabilities	80668	70362	...	9570	736	88660	85101	...	1170	2389
Statistical discrepancy [a]	377	–407	...	965	–181	365	820	...	–1004	549
Net lending	–27892	–36366	...	–3845	12319	–38706	–54218	...	1895	13617
Incurrence of liabilities and net worth	53153	33589	...	6690	12874	50319	31703	...	2061	16555

Finland

	1994					1995				
	Total government	Central government	State or provincial government	Local government	Social security funds	Total government	Central government	State or provincial government	Local government	Social security funds

Acquisition of financial assets

1 Gold and SDRs	...	...	...	...	...	...	...	...	...	...
2 Currency and transferable deposits	2409	1388	...	1489	–468	139	–2665	...	44	2760
3 Other deposits	1288	...	...	1495	–207	2229	...	...	–542	2771
4 Bills and bonds, short-term	...	...	...	...	...	...	...	...	...	...
5 Bonds, long-term	16670	–846	...	–	17516	21354	–4036	...	–136	25526
A Corporations	...	–846	...	–	...	...	–4036	...	–	...
B Other government subsectors	...	–	...	–	...	...	–	...	–	...
C Rest of the world	...	–	...	–	...	...	–	...	–	...
6 Corporate equity securities	10710	4719	...	1158	4833	7955	8277	...	1395	–1717
7 Short-term loans, n.e.c.	14320	7324	...	1040	5956	–11899	–8533	...	–74	–3292
8 Long-term loans, n.e.c.	–9851	1428	...	541	–11820	2292	7280	...	530	–5518
9 Other receivables	348	823	...	816	–1291	–15	823	...	–341	–497
10 Other assets	852	–189	...	1041	–	1091	97	...	994	–
Total aquisition of financial assets	36746	14647	...	7580	14519	23146	1243	...	1870	20033

Incurrence of liabilities

1 Currency and transferable deposits	18	18	...	...	...	76	76	...	...	...
2 Other deposits	...	...	...	...	...	...	...	...	...	...
3 Bills and bonds, short-term	–	–	...	–	–	...	...	...	...	...
4 Bonds, long-term	58966	58921	...	45	–	47195	47937	...	–742	...
5 Short-term loans, n.e.c.	10009	11909	...	202	–2102	3356	4571	...	224	–1439
6 Long-term loans, n.e.c.	–280	2630	...	–2382	–528	–1395	1955	...	–3080	–270
7 Other payables	–300	–797	...	2559	–2062	–764	–809	...	67	–22
8 Other liabilities	779	–	...	774	5	1261	...	...	1241	20
Total incurrence of liabilities	69192	72681	...	1198	–4687	49729	53730	...	–2290	–1711
Statistical discrepancy [a]	–861	–104	...	–210	–547	1764	556	...	890	318
Net lending	–31585	–57930	...	6592	19753	–28347	–53043	...	3270	21426
Incurrence of liabilities and net worth	36746	14647	...	7580	14519	23146	1243	...	1870	20033

[a] Statistical discrepancy refers to adjustment made in order to reconcile the net lending of the Capital Accumulation Account and the Capital Finance Account.

3.22 Corporate and quasi-corporate enterprise income and outlay account: total and sectors

Million Finish markkaa

	1986			1987			1988			1989		
	Total	Non-financial	Financial	Total	Non-financial	Financial	Total	Non-financial	Financial	Total	Non-financial	Financial

Receipts

1 Operating surplus	21236	27120	–5884	28014	34470	–6456	33981	43570	–9589	38300	49591	–11291
2 Property and entrepreneurial income	45046	9050	35996	51974	9802	42172	67272	12794	54478	93778	17918	75860
A Withdrawals from quasi-corporate enterprises	–	–	–	–	–	–	–	–	–	–	–	–
B Interest	43096	7722	35374	49430	7999	41431	63274	9911	53363	88981	14537	74444
C Dividends	1801	1187	614	2364	1633	731	3795	2693	1102	4566	3156	1410
D Net land rent and royalties ..	149	141	8	180	170	10	203	190	13	231	225	6
3 Current transfers [a]	14662	4453	10209	15581	5271	10310	17534	5960	11574	19086	5547	13539

Finland

Million Finish markkaa

	1986			1987			1988			1989		
	Total	Non-financial	Financial	Total	Non-financial	Financial	Total	Non-financial	Financial	Total	Non-financial	Financial
A Casualty insurance claims ..	3843	2719	1124	3643	2634	1009	4198	3215	983	5086	3945	1141
B Casualty insurance premiums, net, due to be received by insurance companies [a] ..	7472	–	7472	7386	–	7386	7960	–	7960	9610	–	9610
C Current transfers from rest of the world	298	298	...	1087	1087	...	1541	1368	173	–434	75	–509
D Other transfers except imputed	1935	339	1596	2289	392	1897	2832	394	2438	3699	424	3275
E Imputed unfunded employee pension and welfare contributions	1114	1097	17	1176	1158	18	1003	983	20	1125	1103	22
Total current receipts	80944	40623	40321	95569	49543	46026	118787	62324	56463	151164	73056	78108

Disbursements

	Total	Non-financial	Financial	Total	Non-financial	Financial	Total	Non-financial	Financial	Total	Non-financial	Financial
1 Property and entrepreneurial income	59587	31357	28230	67489	33948	33541	82857	39164	43693	112685	49585	63100
A Withdrawals from quasi-corporations	2700	2700	–	3037	3037	–	3289	3289	–	3746	3746	–
Public	1004	1004	–	1265	1265	–	1304	1304	–	1374	1374	–
Private	1696	1696	–	1772	1772	–	1985	1985	–	2372	2372	–
B Interest	51507	24152	27355	58026	25648	32378	71234	28873	42361	98584	37080	61504
C Dividends	4100	3230	870	4984	3827	1157	6760	5434	1326	8587	6996	1591
D Net land rent and royalties ..	1280	1275	5	1442	1436	6	1574	1568	6	1768	1763	5
2 Direct taxes and other current transfers n.e.c. to general government	5469	4660	809	4482	3529	953	5995	5062	933	7197	6051	1146
A Direct taxes	5232	4660	572	4235	3529	706	5738	5062	676	6925	6051	874
On income	5145	4581	564	4148	3450	698	5650	4983	667	6823	5958	865
Other	87	79	8	87	79	8	88	79	9	102	93	9
B Fines, fees, penalties and other current transfers n.e.c.	237	...	237	247	...	247	257	...	257	272	...	272
3 Other current transfers	15266	5446	9820	15911	6223	9688	18181	7447	10734	21037	7970	13067
A Casualty insurance premiums, net	3815	2691	1124	3612	2603	1009	4159	3176	983	5040	3899	1141
B Casualty insurance claims liability of insurance companies	7472	–	7472	7386	–	7386	7960	–	7960	9610	–	9610
C Transfers to private non-profit institutions	483	452	31	531	481	50	625	579	46	693	637	56
D Unfunded employee pension and welfare benefits	2242	2208	34	2437	2400	37	2467	2428	39	2694	2651	43
E Social assistance grants	1108	–	1108	1091	–	1091	1406	–	1406	1484	–	1484
F Other transfers n.e.c. [b]	51	–	51	115	–	115	300	–	300	733	–	733
G Transfers to rest of the world [c]	95	95	–	739	739	–	1264	1264	–	783	783	–
Net saving	622	–840	1462	7687	5843	1844	11754	10651	1103	10245	9450	795
Total current disbursements and net saving	80944	40623	40321	95569	49543	46026	118787	62324	56463	151164	73056	78108

	1990			1991			1992			1993		
	Total	Non-financial	Financial	Total	Non-financial	Financial	Total	Non-financial	Financial	Total	Non-financial	Financial

Receipts

	Total	Non-financial	Financial	Total	Non-financial	Financial	Total	Non-financial	Financial	Total	Non-financial	Financial
1 Operating surplus	30919	40872	–9953	12257	23840	–11583	17970	28184	–10214	32970	42312	–9342
2 Property and entrepreneurial income	116619	22262	94357	118373	24138	94235	111058	24303	86755	89917	20696	69221
A Withdrawals from quasi-corporate enterprises	–	–	–	–	–	–	–	–	–	–	–	–

Finland

	1990 Total	1990 Non-financial	1990 Financial	1991 Total	1991 Non-financial	1991 Financial	1992 Total	1992 Non-financial	1992 Financial	1993 Total	1993 Non-financial	1993 Financial
B Interest	111469	18718	92751	112777	20047	92730	106213	20667	85546	85329	17046	68283
C Dividends	4889	3314	1575	5264	3851	1413	4587	3394	1193	4330	3401	929
D Net land rent and royalties	261	230	31	332	240	92	258	242	16	258	249	9
3 Current transfers [a]	18147	3987	14160	17380	2051	15329	21134	2949	18185	18664	1835	16829
A Casualty insurance claims	5614	3974	1640	6110	4161	1949	8394	6108	2286	7832	6300	1532
B Casualty insurance premiums, net, due to be received by insurance companies [a]	9670	–	9670	10738	–	10738	13296	–	13296	12425	–	12425
C Current transfers from rest of the world	–1777	–711	–1066	–3918	–2867	–1051	–5750	–4901	–849	–6415	–6095	–320
D Other transfers except imputed	4460	568	3892	4234	566	3668	4406	979	3427	4475	1329	3146
E Imputed unfunded employee pension and welfare contributions	180	156	24	216	191	25	788	763	25	347	301	46
Total current receipts	165685	67121	98564	148010	50029	97981	150162	55436	94726	141551	64843	76708

Disbursements

	1990 Total	1990 Non-financial	1990 Financial	1991 Total	1991 Non-financial	1991 Financial	1992 Total	1992 Non-financial	1992 Financial	1993 Total	1993 Non-financial	1993 Financial
1 Property and entrepreneurial income	139390	60813	78577	146498	67216	79282	144474	67663	76811	120017	63183	56834
A Withdrawals from quasi-corporations	4116	4116	–	4190	4190	–	4101	4101	–	4612	4612	–
Public	1443	1443	–	1931	1931	–	1983	1983	–	2697	2697	–
Private	2673	2673	–	2259	2259	–	2118	2118	–	1915	1915	–
B Interest	123589	46627	76962	130634	52317	78317	131885	55455	76430	106969	50357	56612
C Dividends	9805	8192	1613	9501	8536	965	6446	6065	381	5972	5750	222
D Net land rent and royalties	1880	1878	2	2173	2173	–	2042	2042	–	2464	2464	–
2 Direct taxes and other current transfers n.e.c. to general government	10458	8515	1943	10045	8876	1169	8196	7453	743	2853	1657	1196
A Direct taxes	10127	8505	1622	9709	8856	853	7814	7373	441	2059	1560	499
On income	10013	8401	1612	9584	8742	842	7669	7240	429	1154	698	456
Other	114	104	10	125	114	11	145	133	12	905	862	43
B Fines, fees, penalties and other current transfers n.e.c.	331	10	321	336	20	316	382	80	302	794	97	697
3 Other current transfers	18604	4514	14090	19771	4402	15369	24835	6383	18452	23152	6775	16377
A Casualty insurance premiums, net	5562	3922	1640	6072	4123	1949	8358	6072	2286	7789	6257	1532
B Casualty insurance claims liability of insurance companies	9670	–	9670	10738	–	10738	13296	–	13296	12425	–	12425
C Transfers to private non-profit institutions	766	700	66	683	627	56	500	460	40	213	186	27
D Unfunded employee pension and welfare benefits	613	566	47	522	471	51	771	715	56	329	253	76
E Social assistance grants	1709	–	1709	1825	–	1825	2066	–	2066	2242	–	2242
F Other transfers n.e.c. [b]	957	–	957	849	–	849	600	–	600	23	–	23
G Transfers to rest of the world [c]	–673	–674	1	–918	–819	–99	–756	–864	108	131	79	52
Net saving	–2767	–6721	3954	–28304	–30465	2161	–27343	–26063	–1280	–4471	–6772	2301
Total current disbursements and net saving	165685	67121	98564	148010	50029	97981	150162	55436	94726	141551	64843	76708

Finland

	1994 Total	1994 Non-financial	1994 Financial	1995 Total	1995 Non-financial	1995 Financial	1996 Total	1996 Non-financial	1996 Financial	1997 Total	1997 Non-financial	1997 Financial
Receipts												
1 Operating surplus	47289	56380	−9091	65765	73457	−7692	69944	75425	−5481	...	...	...
2 Property and entrepreneurial income	72921	16395	56526	67090	16991	50099	57664	15918	41746	...	...	...
A Withdrawals from quasi-corporate enterprises	−	−	−	−	−	−	−	−	−	...	...	...
B Interest	66939	11438	55501	60405	11572	48833	48450	8464	39986	...	...	...
C Dividends	5711	4693	1018	6413	5152	1261	8868	7108	1760	...	...	...
D Net land rent and royalties	271	264	7	272	267	5	346	346	−	...	...	...
3 Current transfers [a]	24104	7311	16793	24148	9496	14652	23044	6595	16449	...	...	...
A Casualty insurance claims	7449	5472	1977	7002	6474	528	6077	4950	1127	...	...	...
B Casualty insurance premiums, net, due to be received by insurance companies [a]	11563	−	11563	11434	−	11434	9683	−	9683	...	...	...
C Current transfers from rest of the world	−268	462	−730	491	2074	−1583	1071	604	467	...	...	...
D Other transfers except imputed	4943	987	3956	5153	907	4246	6170	1026	5144	...	...	...
E Imputed unfunded employee pension and welfare contributions	417	390	27	68	41	27	43	15	28	...	...	...
Total current receipts	144314	80086	64228	157003	99944	57059	150652	97938	52714	...	...	...
Disbursements												
1 Property and entrepreneurial income	92701	50095	42606	89023	52212	36811	79966	51062	28904	...	...	...
A Withdrawals from quasi-corporations	4281	4281	−	4352	4352	−	4544	4544	−	...	...	...
Public	2143	2143	−	1865	1865	−	1958	1958	−	...	...	...
Private	2138	2138	−	2487	2487	−	2586	2586	−	...	...	...
B Interest	78213	36106	42107	71450	35340	36110	56018	27995	28023	...	...	...
C Dividends	7720	7221	499	10615	9914	701	16247	15366	881	...	...	...
D Net land rent and royalties	2487	2487	−	2606	2606	−	3157	3157	−	...	...	...
2 Direct taxes and other current transfers n.e.c. to general government	3848	2492	1356	11469	10000	1469	16618	14818	1800	...	...	...
A Direct taxes	3122	2491	631	10907	9991	916	16057	14798	1259	...	...	...
On income	2051	1472	579	9832	8969	863	14996	13786	1210	...	...	...
Other	1071	1019	52	1075	1022	53	1061	1012	49	...	...	...
B Fines, fees, penalties and other current transfers n.e.c.	726	1	725	562	9	553	561	20	541	...	...	...
3 Other current transfers	24866	7662	17204	25454	9498	15956	23257	7716	15541	...	...	...
A Casualty insurance premiums, net	7405	5428	1977	6952	6424	528	6026	4899	1127	...	...	...
B Casualty insurance claims liability of insurance companies	11563	−	11563	11434	−	11434	9683	−	9683	...	...	...
C Transfers to private non-profit institutions	255	248	7	553	538	15	772	729	43	...	...	...
D Unfunded employee pension and welfare benefits	388	329	59	94	35	59	86	25	61	...	...	...
E Social assistance grants	2492	−	2492	2757	−	2757	2798	−	2798	...	...	...
F Other transfers n.e.c. [b]	1143	−	1143	1063	−	1063	1773	−	1773	...	...	...
G Transfers to rest of the world [c]	1620	1657	−37	2601	2501	100	2119	2063	56	...	...	...
Net saving	22899	19837	3062	31057	28234	2823	30811	24342	6469	...	...	...

Finland

	1994			1995			1996			1997		
	Total	Non-financial	Financial	Total	Non-financial	Financial	Total	Non-financial	Financial	Total	Non-financial	Financial
Total current disbursements and net saving	144314	80086	64228	157003	99944	57059	150652	97938	52714	...	...	...

a Includes adjustments from the financial institutions sector.
b Item "Other transfers n.e.c." refers to transfers to households.
c Item "Transfers to the rest of the world" includes re-invested earnings.

3.23 Corporate and quasi-corporate enterprise capital accumulation account: total and sectors

Million Finish markkaa

	1986			1987			1988			1989		
	Total	Non-financial	Financial	Total	Non-financial	Financial	Total	Non-financial	Financial	Total	Non-financial	Financial
Finance of gross accumulation												
1 Gross saving	30165	27660	2505	39851	36796	3055	46990	44530	2460	50163	47825	2338
A Consumption of fixed capital	29543	28500	1043	32164	30953	1211	35236	33879	1357	39918	38375	1543
B Net saving	622	−840	1462	7687	5843	1844	11754	10651	1103	10245	9450	795
2 Capital transfers [a]	205	205	–	215	215	–	1383	236	1147	420	414	6
A From resident sectors	205	205	–	215	215	–	1383	236	1147	420	414	6
B From rest of the world	...	...	...	...	...	...	...	...	...	...	...	...
Finance of gross accumulation	30370	27865	2505	40066	37011	3055	48373	44766	3607	50583	48239	2344
Gross accumulation												
1 Gross capital formation	39958	37681	2277	46898	45507	1391	58361	59085	−724	76118	74010	2108
A Increase in stocks	−2310	−2310	–	−208	−208	–	3127	3127	–	5661	5661	–
B Gross fixed capital formation	42268	39991	2277	47106	45715	1391	55234	55958	−724	70457	68349	2108
2 Purchases of land, net	370	200	170	409	401	8	1619	1609	10	1245	1176	69
3 Purchases of intangible assets, net	–	–	–	–	–	–	–	−714	714	–	–	–
4 Capital transfers	...	...	...	...	...	...	...	...	...	...	...	...
Net lending	−9958	−10016	58	−7241	−8897	1656	−11607	−15214	3607	−26780	−26947	167
Gross accumulation	30370	27865	2505	40066	37011	3055	48373	44766	3607	50583	48239	2344

	1990			1991			1992			1993		
	Total	Non-financial	Financial	Total	Non-financial	Financial	Total	Non-financial	Financial	Total	Non-financial	Financial
Finance of gross accumulation												
1 Gross saving	40870	35196	5674	17353	13411	3942	20182	19693	489	45273	41162	4111
A Consumption of fixed capital	43637	41917	1720	45657	43876	1781	47525	45756	1769	49744	47934	1810
B Net saving	−2767	−6721	3954	−28304	−30465	2161	−27343	−26063	−1280	−4471	−6772	2301
2 Capital transfers [a]	528	515	13	594	2092	−1498	493	488	5	405	517	−112
A From resident sectors	528	515	13	594	2092	−1498	493	488	5	405	517	−112
B From rest of the world	...	...	...	...	...	...	...	...	...	...	...	...
Finance of gross accumulation	41398	35711	5687	17947	15503	2444	20675	20181	494	45678	41679	3999
Gross accumulation												
1 Gross capital formation	72118	70589	1529	43403	41889	1514	37494	36061	1433	28703	29650	−947
A Increase in stocks	2421	2421	–	−9795	−9795	–	−4698	−4698	–	−4588	−4588	–
B Gross fixed capital formation	69697	68168	1529	53198	51684	1514	42192	40759	1433	33291	34238	−947
2 Purchases of land, net	972	905	67	98	−17	115	−8	304	−312	−340	60	−400
3 Purchases of intangible assets, net	−381	−381	–	−171	−171	–	–	–	–	–	–	–
4 Capital transfers	...	...	...	...	...	...	...	...	...	...	...	...
Net lending	−31311	−35402	4091	−25383	−26198	815	−16811	−16184	−627	17315	11969	5346

Finland

	1990			1991			1992			1993		
	Total	Non-financial	Financial	Total	Non-financial	Financial	Total	Non-financial	Financial	Total	Non-financial	Financial
Gross accumulation	41398	35711	5687	17947	15503	2444	20675	20181	494	45678	41679	3999

	1994			1995			1996			1997		
	Total	Non-financial	Financial	Total	Non-financial	Financial	Total	Non-financial	Financial	Total	Non-financial	Financial
Finance of gross accumulation											
1 Gross saving	72473	67650	4823	80280	75757	4523	80423	72382	8041	...	...	...
A Consumption of fixed capital	49574	47813	1761	49223	47523	1700	49612	48040	1572	...	...	...
B Net saving	22899	19837	3062	31057	28234	2823	30811	24342	6469	...	...	...
2 Capital transfers [a]	1830	2372	−542	1027	1554	−527	2497	656	1841	...	...	...
A From resident sectors	1830	2372	−542	1027	1554	−527	2497	656	1841	...	...	...
B From rest of the world	...	...	...	...	...	...	...	...	...	...	...	...
Finance of gross accumulation	74303	70022	4281	81307	77311	3996	82920	73038	9882	...	...	...
Gross accumulation											
1 Gross capital formation	43262	42140	1122	49734	50654	−920	53432	53975	−543	...	...	...
A Increase in stocks	8018	8018	−	5490	5490	−	2955	2955	−	...	...	...
B Gross fixed capital formation	35244	34122	1122	44244	45164	−920	50477	51020	−543	...	...	...
2 Purchases of land, net	−209	−793	584	340	191	149	162	105	57	...	...	...
3 Purchases of intangible assets, net	−	−	−	−	−	−	−	−	−	...	...	...
4 Capital transfers	...	...	...	...	...	...	...	...	...	...	...	...
Net lending	31250	28675	2575	31233	26466	4767	29326	18958	10368	...	...	...
Gross accumulation	74303	70022	4281	81307	77311	3996	82920	73038	9882	...	...	...

a Capital transfers received are recorded net of capital transfers paid.

3.24 Corporate and quasi-corporate enterprise capital finance account: total and sectors

Million Finish markkaa

	1986			1987			1988			1989		
	Total	Non-financial	Financial	Total	Non-financial	Financial	Total	Non-financial	Financial	Total	Non-financial	Financial
Acquisition of financial assets											
1 Gold and SDRs	92	−	92	46	−	46	364	−	364	−4	−	−4
2 Currency and transferable deposits	7999	1044	6955	19396	367	19029	6653	326	6327	−18142	−7070	−11072
3 Other deposits	711	−244	955	7213	3775	3438	22086	10414	11672	18648	11770	6878
4 Bills and bonds, short-term	−141	−	−141	754	−	754	8730	−	8730	7343	−	7343
A Corporate and quasi-corporate, resident	−1399	−	−1399	1683	−	1683	7415	−	7415	8279	−	8279
B Government	−20	−	−20	−22	−	−22	18	−	18	9	−	9
C Rest of the world	1278	−	1278	−908	−	−908	1297	−	1297	−945	−	−945
5 Bonds, long-term	13585	795	12790	4786	1340	3446	4997	1789	3208	10065	3157	6908
A Corporate, resident	...	795	...	...	1340	...	...	1789	...	...	3157	...
B Government	...	−	...	...	−	...	...	−	...	...	−	...
C Rest of the world	...	−	...	...	−	...	...	−	...	...	−	...
6 Corporate equity securities	9724	4161	5563	18009	10404	7605	23271	11964	11307	24614	17845	6769
7 Short-term loans, n.e.c.	30106	7371	22735	27552	14094	13458	60621	20942	39679	74403	10431	63972
8 Long-term loans, n.e.c.	31050	266	30784	48121	149	47972	75050	2627	72423	53486	3245	50241
A Mortgages	...	−	...	...	−	...	...	−	...	...	−	...
B Other	...	266	...	...	149	...	...	2627	...	...	3245	...
9 Trade credits and advances	−1486	−1767	281	7652	7304	348	11789	11409	380	7293	5539	1754
10 Other receivables	2574	1475	1099	2447	347	2100	10229	4332	5897	9269	3442	5827

Finland

Million Finish markkaa

	1986 Total	1986 Non-financial	1986 Financial	1987 Total	1987 Non-financial	1987 Financial	1988 Total	1988 Non-financial	1988 Financial	1989 Total	1989 Non-financial	1989 Financial
11 Other assets	–	–	–	–	–	–	–	–	–	–	–	–
Total acquisitions of financial assets	94214	13101	81113	135976	37780	98196	223790	63803	159987	186975	48359	138616

Incurrence of liabilities

	Total	Non-financial	Financial	Total	Non-financial	Financial	Total	Non-financial	Financial	Total	Non-financial	Financial
1 Currency and transferable deposits	19026	–	19026	36379	–	36379	15990	–	15990	–6061	–	–6061
2 Other deposits	9796	12	9784	18764	–4	18768	51824	100	51724	34160	95	34065
3 Bills and bonds, short-term	–1678	–4239	2561	1803	682	1121	6481	–322	6803	6734	–395	7129
4 Bonds, long-term	17473	5077	12396	12702	2936	9766	21932	3526	18406	27952	2879	25073
5 Corporate equity securities	9595	7069	2526	16933	13723	3210	23989	16982	7007	21816	18139	3677
6 Short-term loans, n.e.c.	33778	7915	25863	17046	11037	6009	65833	21919	43914	65191	9549	55642
7 Long-term loans, n.e.c.	20844	18592	2252	28304	15654	12650	30622	27355	3267	38423	34018	4405
8 Net equity of households in life insurance and pension fund reserves	2322	–	2322	2828	–	2828	2519	–	2519	2839	–	2839
9 Proprietors' net additions to the accumulation of quasi-corporations	880	880	–	166	166	–	466	466	–	1118	1118	–
10 Trade credits and advances	–2388	–3144	756	9217	9223	–6	9093	8616	477	10384	8964	1420
11 Other accounts payable	405	–2575	2980	6376	596	5780	8250	3014	5236	12601	5577	7024
12 Other liabilities	...	...	...	...	...	...	...	...	...	...	...	...
Total incurrence of liabilities	110053	29587	80466	150518	54013	96505	236999	81656	155343	215157	79944	135213
Statistical discrepancy [a]	–5881	–6470	589	–7301	–7336	35	–1602	–2639	1037	–1402	–4638	3236
Net lending	–9958	–10016	58	–7241	–8897	1656	–11607	–15214	3607	–26780	–26947	167
Incurrence of liabilities and net lending	94214	13101	81113	135976	37780	98196	223790	63803	159987	186975	48359	138616

	1990 Total	1990 Non-financial	1990 Financial	1991 Total	1991 Non-financial	1991 Financial	1992 Total	1992 Non-financial	1992 Financial	1993 Total	1993 Non-financial	1993 Financial

Acquisition of financial assets

	Total	Non-financial	Financial	Total	Non-financial	Financial	Total	Non-financial	Financial	Total	Non-financial	Financial
1 Gold and SDRs	–300	–	–300	239	–	239	–217	–	–217	–123	–	–123
2 Currency and transferable deposits	20644	–800	21444	–8264	824	–9088	–3433	150	–3583	9341	5125	4216
3 Other deposits	–12116	–2951	–9165	–2468	2668	–5136	163	–7336	7499	–18087	2193	–20280
4 Bills and bonds, short-term	–4136	–	–4136	–8628	–	–8628	–2188	–	–2188	–19042	–	–19042
A Corporate and quasi-corporate, resident	–4620	–	–4620	...	–	...	...	–	...	...	–	...
B Government	109	–	109	...	–	...	...	–	...	...	–	...
C Rest of the world	375	–	375	...	–	...	...	–	...	...	–	...
5 Bonds, long-term	5554	6369	–815	10448	–2233	12681	3404	–686	4090	14677	4095	10582
A Corporate, resident	...	6369	...	...	–2233	...	...	–686	...	...	4095	...
B Government	...	–	...	...	–	...	...	–	...	...	–	...
C Rest of the world	...	–	...	...	–	...	...	–	...	...	–	...
6 Corporate equity securities	32315	26700	5615	26180	11178	15002	2288	13395	–11107	8106	3493	4613
7 Short-term loans, n.e.c.	–18308	–1451	–16857	36515	12716	23799	–4755	16200	–20955	31481	–6247	37728
8 Long-term loans, n.e.c.	77211	13046	64165	36426	13736	22690	12117	9643	2474	–18171	–4404	–13767
A Mortgages	...	–	...	...	–	...	...	–	...	...	–	...
B Other	...	13046	...	...	13736	...	...	9643	...	...	–4404	...
9 Trade credits and advances	–6345	–5601	–744	–11348	–10807	–541	–8819	–8568	–251	–2535	–1821	–714
10 Other receivables	9167	1463	7704	4652	3884	768	2833	1054	1779	–2768	–1299	–1469
11 Other assets	–	–	–	–	–	–	–	–	–	–	–	–
Total acquisitions of financial assets	103686	36775	66911	83752	31966	51786	1393	23852	–22459	2879	1135	1744

Finland

	1990			1991			1992			1993		
	Total	Non-financial	Financial	Total	Non-financial	Financial	Total	Non-financial	Financial	Total	Non-financial	Financial

Incurrence of liabilities

	Total	Non-fin	Fin	Total	Non-fin	Fin	Total	Non-fin	Fin	Total	Non-fin	Fin
1 Currency and transferable deposits	23980	–	23980	–8110	–	–8110	4574	–	4574	–7395	–	–7395
2 Other deposits	–5906	165	–6071	3123	435	2688	5427	–167	5594	–27435	362	–27797
3 Bills and bonds, short-term	–5327	4031	–9358	–6949	–2793	–4156	–1865	–3944	2079	–13982	–6348	–7634
4 Bonds, long-term	33141	2322	30819	29921	5400	24521	9878	2064	7814	–9458	7900	–17358
5 Corporate equity securities	23838	22027	1811	23707	12750	10957	6044	7825	–1781	23207	13993	9214
6 Short-term loans, n.e.c.	–10539	–8659	–1880	11179	6187	4992	–33027	–5460	–27567	37675	–7669	45344
7 Long-term loans, n.e.c.	86059	73143	12916	55921	43393	12528	16389	32872	–16483	–25107	–21557	–3550
8 Net equity of households in life insurance and pension fund reserves	2804	–	2804	3269	–	3269	4101	–	4101	5252	–	5252
9 Proprietors' net additions to the accumulation of quasi-corporations	–1313	–1313	–	–300	–300	–	–1595	–1595	–	–1629	–1629	–
10 Trade credits and advances	–7524	–6737	–787	–11010	–9947	–1063	–1697	–2652	955	163	858	–695
11 Other accounts payable	7845	2983	4862	4802	2594	2208	9881	6464	3417	1330	4297	–2967
12 Other liabilities	...	...	...	...	...	...	...	...	...	...	...	...
Total incurrence of liabilities	147058	87962	59096	105553	57719	47834	18110	35407	–17297	–17379	–9793	–7586
Statistical discrepancy [a]	–12061	–15785	3724	3582	445	3137	94	4629	–4535	2943	–1041	3984
Net lending	–31311	–35402	4091	–25383	–26198	815	–16811	–16184	–627	17315	11969	5346
Incurrence of liabilities and net lending	103686	36775	66911	83752	31966	51786	1393	23852	–22459	2879	1135	1744

	1994			1995			1996			1997		
	Total	Non-financial	Financial	Total	Non-financial	Financial	Total	Non-financial	Financial	Total	Non-financial	Financial

Acquisition of financial assets

	Total	Non-fin	Fin	Total	Non-fin	Fin	Total	Non-fin	Fin	Total	Non-fin	Fin
1 Gold and SDRs	772	–	772	–314	–	–314	...	...	...	...	...	...
2 Currency and transferable deposits	31023	2525	28498	12366	3488	8878	...	...	...	...	...	...
3 Other deposits	2604	–2466	5070	6006	2239	3767	...	...	...	...	...	...
4 Bills and bonds, short-term	–	–	–	...	–	...	...	...	...	...	...	...
A Corporate and quasi-corporate, resident	...	–	...	...	–	...	...	...	...	...	...	...
B Government	...	–	...	...	–	...	...	...	...	...	...	...
C Rest of the world	...	–	...	...	–	...	...	...	...	...	...	...
5 Bonds, long-term	–6561	–1036	–5525	11734	1222	10512	...	...	...	...	...	...
A Corporate, resident	...	–1036	...	...	1222	...	...	...	...	...	...	...
B Government	...	–	...	...	–	...	...	...	...	...	...	...
C Rest of the world	...	–	...	...	–	...	...	...	...	...	...	...
6 Corporate equity securities	7018	–514	7532	–6022	–2889	–3133	...	...	...	...	...	...
7 Short-term loans, n.e.c.	11830	–4069	15899	–17522	–701	–16821	...	...	...	...	...	...
8 Long-term loans, n.e.c.	–32902	–6406	–26496	–13498	–3020	–10478	...	...	...	...	...	...
A Mortgages	...	–	...	...	–	...	...	...	...	...	...	...
B Other	...	–6406	...	...	–3020	...	...	...	...	...	...	...
9 Trade credits and advances	5956	3151	2805	4423	120	4303	...	...	...	...	...	...
10 Other receivables	9112	7051	2061	4687	13217	–8530	...	...	...	...	...	...
11 Other assets	–	–	–	–	–	–	...	...	...	...	...	...
Total acquisitions of financial assets	28852	–1764	30616	1860	13676	–11816	...	...	...	...	...	...

Incurrence of liabilities

	Total	Non-fin	Fin	Total	Non-fin	Fin	Total	Non-fin	Fin	Total	Non-fin	Fin
1 Currency and transferable deposits	5854	–	5854	23898	–	23898	...	...	...	...	...	...

Finland

	1994			1995			1996			1997		
	Total	Non-financial	Financial	Total	Non-financial	Financial	Total	Non-financial	Financial	Total	Non-financial	Financial
2 Other deposits	–4398	–1411	–2987	9636	–466	10102	...	...	...	...	...	...
3 Bills and bonds, short-term	–	–	–	...	...	...	...	...	...	...	...	...
4 Bonds, long-term	–19601	–3745	–15856	–29715	–4797	–24918	...	...	...	...	...	...
5 Corporate equity securities	23478	11000	12478	5672	5417	255	...	...	...	...	...	...
6 Short-term loans, n.e.c.	15892	–3478	19370	–26935	150	–27085	...	...	...	...	...	...
7 Long-term loans, n.e.c.	–35703	–29348	–6355	–4820	–4008	–812	...	...	...	...	...	...
8 Net equity of households in life insurance and pension fund reserves	3583	–	3583	4242	–	4242	...	...	...	...	...	...
9 Proprietors' net additions to the accumulation of quasi-corporations	852	852	–	1091	1091	–	...	...	...	...	...	...
10 Trade credits and advances	6352	5088	1264	1068	–1288	2356	...	...	...	...	...	...
11 Other accounts payable	6573	–439	7012	–4073	–645	–3428	...	...	...	...	...	...
12 Other liabilities	...	...	...	...	...	...	...	...	...	...	...	...
Total incurrence of liabilities	2882	–21481	24363	–19936	–4546	–15390	...	...	...	...	...	...
Statistical discrepancy [a]	–5280	–8958	3678	–9437	–8244	–1193	...	...	...	...	...	...
Net lending	31250	28675	2575	31233	26466	4767	...	...	...	...	...	...
Incurrence of liabilities and net lending	28852	–1764	30616	1860	13676	–11816	...	...	...	...	...	...

a Statistical discrepancy refers to adjustment made in order to reconcile the net lending of the Capital Accumulation Account and the Capital Finance Account.

3.32 Household and private unincorporated enterprise income and outlay account

Million Finish markkaa

	1986	1987	1988	1989	1990	1991	1992	1993	1994	1995	1996	1997
Receipts												
1 Compensation of employees	196900	214194	236874	264901	288978	289915	273736	258111	263817	281476	294776	...
A Wages and salaries	160309	174395	192161	213839	229910	229721	216736	202714	204302	219428	231278	...
B Employers' contributions for social security	36591	39799	44713	51062	59068	60194	57000	55397	59515	62048	63498	...
C Employers' contributions for private pension and welfare plans	...	...	...	...	...	...	...	...	...	...	...	...
2 Operating surplus of private unincorporated enterprises	46207	45090	48870	56236	58535	54701	53031	56103	60587	62444	63202	...
3 Property and entrepreneurial income	12405	14179	17196	21172	24270	27543	30652	25979	20326	23365	24008	...
A Withdrawals from private quasi-corporations	1696	1772	1985	2372	2673	2259	2118	1915	2138	2487	2586	...
B Interest	9388	10961	13605	16838	19024	22084	26210	21305	15210	16604	15802	...
C Dividends	975	1073	1194	1513	2124	2705	1825	2254	2462	3646	4930	...
D Net land rent and royalties	346	373	412	449	449	495	499	505	516	628	690	...
4 Current transfers	60753	66668	73325	80298	90182	106114	124099	132480	139583	139986	140459	...
A Casualty insurance claims	1802	2056	2394	3268	3044	3143	3475	3227	3272	3596	3045	...
B Social security benefits	40044	43577	50542	55271	64096	79391	91147	91996	93397	94061	97065	...
C Social assistance grants	8275	9171	9594	10279	12279	16325	21176	29002	34293	35022	32921	...
D Unfunded employee pension and welfare benefits	9795	10807	8395	9227	7989	4002	4478	4267	4427	4275	4422	...
E Transfers from general government	353	447	550	677	839	992	1416	1243	919	754	748	...
F Transfers from rest of the world	412	474	1529	820	953	1385	1787	2702	2107	1190	460	...
G Other transfers n.e.c.	72	136	321	756	982	876	620	43	1168	1088	1798	...
Total current receipts	316265	340131	376265	422607	461965	478273	481518	472673	484313	507271	522445	...

Finland

Million Finish markkaa

	1986	1987	1988	1989	1990	1991	1992	1993	1994	1995	1996	1997
Disbursements												
1 Final consumption expenditure	186830	203783	223918	245058	259157	263886	261136	264379	273649	287106	302820	...
2 Property income	10269	11646	15402	20797	25528	26689	26550	21628	16967	16084	12960	...
A Interest	10033	11387	15129	20505	25242	26367	26230	21238	16530	15551	12418	...
B Net land rent and royalties	236	259	273	292	286	322	320	390	437	533	542	...
3 Direct taxes and other current transfers n.e.c. to general government	95806	98260	120749	135143	152414	151251	149857	150670	172057	172234	182763	...
A Social security contributions	36527	39706	49437	56383	67248	70474	72993	75993	85428	86440	87682	...
B Direct taxes	57552	56718	68330	74845	82111	77915	73977	72176	83840	82812	92127	...
Income taxes	57472	56638	68251	74751	82007	77801	73844	71425	82973	81942	91266	...
Other	80	80	79	94	104	114	133	751	867	870	861	...
C Fees, fines and penalties	1727	1836	2982	3915	3055	2862	2887	2501	2789	2982	2954	...
4 Other current transfers	14302	15403	13003	14660	14581	12151	13679	12737	12410	12120	12245	...
A Net casualty insurance premiums	1802	2056	2394	3268	3044	3143	3475	3227	3272	3596	3045	...
B Transfers to private non-profit institutions serving households	3494	3697	4061	4450	4890	4660	4664	4767	4916	4969	5187	...
C Transfers to rest of the world	1109	1054	1727	1727	2015	2210	2804	2796	2208	1822	2309	...
D Other current transfers, except imputed	...	...	...	...	...	...	...	...	...	...	...	...
E Imputed employee pension and welfare contributions	7897	8596	4821	5215	4632	2138	2736	1947	2014	1733	1704	...
Net saving	9058	11039	3193	6949	10285	24296	30296	23259	9230	19727	11657	...
Total current disbursements and net saving	316265	340131	376265	422607	461965	478273	481518	472673	484313	507271	522445	...

3.33 Household and private unincorporated enterprise capital accumulation account

Million Finish markkaa

	1986	1987	1988	1989	1990	1991	1992	1993	1994	1995	1996	1997
Finance of gross accumulation												
1 Gross saving	22121	25153	18766	24041	29103	43471	48236	41006	27500	38284	30308	...
A Consumption of fixed capital	13063	14114	15573	17092	18818	19175	17940	17747	18270	18557	18651	...
B Net saving	9058	11039	3193	6949	10285	24296	30296	23259	9230	19727	11657	...
2 Capital transfers	47	–15	1367	–105	–394	–467	–514	–234	–619	–504	–787	...
A From resident sectors	47	–15	1367	–105	–394	–467	–514	–234	–619	–504	–787	...
B From rest of the world	...	...	...	...	...	...	...	...	...	...	...	...
Total finance of gross accumulation	22168	25138	20133	23936	28709	43004	47722	40772	26881	37780	29521	...
Gross accumulation												
1 Gross capital formation	19476	19487	23377	31138	30907	24354	17587	16015	14860	16004	17579	...
A Increase in stocks	–251	–959	–404	670	326	–79	–1268	361	–415	–660	9	...
B Gross fixed capital formation	19727	20446	23781	30468	30581	24433	18855	15654	15275	16664	17570	...
2 Purchases of land, net	–1179	–1030	–2639	–1433	–1530	–394	–244	240	–176	–660	–671	...
3 Purchases of intangibles, net	–	–	–	–	–	–	–	–	–	–	–	...
4 Capital transfers	...	...	...	...	...	...	...	...	...	...	...	...

Finland

Million Finish markkaa	1986	1987	1988	1989	1990	1991	1992	1993	1994	1995	1996	1997
Net lending	3871	6681	−605	−5769	−668	19044	30379	24517	12197	22436	12613	...
Total gross accumulation	22168	25138	20133	23936	28709	43004	47722	40772	26881	37780	29521	...

3.34 Household and private unincorporated enterprise capital finance account

Million Finish markkaa

	1986	1987	1988	1989	1990	1991	1992	1993	1994	1995	1996	1997
Acquisition of financial assets												
1 Gold	...	...	...	...	...	...	...	...	...	...	...	...
2 Currency and transferable deposits	−227	372	499	1144	78	1010	1883	625	3274	7531	...	...
3 Other deposits	10391	14603	28773	11080	6801	9295	1994	−4004	−6612	1401	...	...
4 Bills and bonds, short-term	...	...	...	...	...	...	...	...	...	...	...	...
5 Bonds, long-term	3077	8386	4351	1229	1200	3600	5453	4888	1503	5795	...	...
6 Corporate equity securities	4500	5096	7008	9591	3450	3300	4720	6900	2533	3059	...	...
7 Short-term loans, n.e.c.	−17	60	117	−123	44	−13	29	−38	–	2	...	...
8 Long-term loans, n.e.c.	–	–	–	–	–	–	–	–	−39	−136	...	...
A Mortgages	...	...	...	...	...	...	–	–	–	–	...	...
B Other	–	–	–	–	–	–	–	–	−39	−136	...	...
9 Trade credits and advances	20	256	−280	488	−203	−168	4101	200	−81	48	...	...
10 Net equity of households in life insurance and pension fund reserves	2322	2828	2519	2839	2804	3269	−40	5252	3583	4242	...	...
11 Proprietors' net additions to the accumulation of quasi-corporations	–	–	–	–	–	–	–	–	–	–	...	...
12 Other	212	94	94	−273	1486	−312	288	90	−1335	−3254	...	...
Total acquisitions of financial assets	20278	31695	43081	25975	15660	19981	18428	13913	2826	18688	...	...
Incurrence of liabilities												
1 Short-term loans, n.e.c.	509	1741	2389	3908	2641	1224	−2030	−3201	–	...	...	...
2 Long-term loans, n.e.c.	13800	21532	38547	22111	8158	3383	−4570	−8735	−9973	−8745	...	...
A Mortgages	8764	...	...	...	...	...	...	...	...	...	...	...
B Other	5036	...	...	...	...	...	...	...	...	...	...	...
3 Trade credits and advances	502	−98	891	9	−296	−1083	−715	115	353	69	...	...
4 Other accounts payable	−113	1529	378	867	300	642	814	−391	−1760	4752	...	...
5 Other liabilities	...	...	...	...	...	...	...	...	...	...	...	...
Total incurrence of liabilities	14698	24704	42205	26895	10803	4166	−6501	−12212	−11380	−3924	...	...
Statistical discrepancy	1709	310	1481	4849	5525	−3229	−5450	1608	2009	176	...	...
Net lending	3871	6681	−605	−5769	−668	19044	30379	24517	12197	22436	...	...
Incurrence of liabilities and net lending	20278	31695	43081	25975	15660	19981	18428	13913	2826	18688	...	...

3.42 Private non-profit institutions serving households: income and outlay account

Million Finish markkaa

	1986	1987	1988	1989	1990	1991	1992	1993	1994	1995	1996	1997
Receipts												
1 Operating surplus	−2260	−2960	−3798	−5881	−5617	−5440	−4221	−3587	−4261	−4884	−4780	...
2 Property and entrepreneurial income	611	644	736	856	988	1067	928	842	1079	1229	1111	...
A Withdrawals from quasi-corporations	–	–	–	–	–	–	–	–	–	–	–	...

Finland

Million Finish markkaa

	1986	1987	1988	1989	1990	1991	1992	1993	1994	1995	1996	1997
B Interest	269	298	323	376	508	619	619	563	687	713	563	...
C Dividends	311	312	372	436	432	400	259	229	328	450	482	...
D Net land rent and royalties	31	34	41	44	48	48	50	50	64	66	66	...
3 Current transfers	7644	8323	9234	10194	11393	11533	11250	11609	11835	12454	13312	...
A Casualty insurance claims	110	107	127	146	166	184	173	173	213	191	179	...
B Current transfers from general government	3147	3550	3924	4370	4995	5404	5270	6099	6095	6373	6787	...
C Other transfers from resident sectors	3981	4232	4690	5147	5661	5348	5169	4981	5173	5524	5962	...
D Current transfers received from the rest of the world	4	5	5	6	6	6	6	6	6	6	20	...
E Imputed unfunded employee pension and welfare contributions	402	429	488	525	565	591	632	350	348	360	364	...
Total current receipts	5995	6007	6172	5169	6764	7160	7957	8864	8653	8799	9643	...
Disbursements												
1 Final consumption expenditures	7177	7751	8662	9530	10597	10823	10978	10873	10776	11095	11631	...
A Compensation of employees	...	...	...	...	...	...	...	...	...	...	...	...
B Consumption of fixed capital	...	...	...	...	...	...	...	...	...	...	...	...
C Purchases of goods and services, net	7177	7751	8662	9530	10597	10823	10978	10873	10776	11095	11631	...
Purchases	7177	7751	8662	9530	10597	10823	10978	10873	10776	11095	11631	...
less: Sales	–	–	–	–	–	–	–	–	–	–	–	...
2 Property income [a]	1737	1812	2197	2690	3380	3917	4365	3884	3589	3768	3486	...
A Interest	1597	1672	2035	2524	3163	3707	4182	3691	3395	3528	3253	...
B Net land rent and royalties	127	129	146	149	198	186	165	193	194	240	233	...
3 Direct taxes and other transfers to general government	250	238	259	307	382	408	412	507	630	640	645	...
A Direct taxes	250	238	259	307	382	408	412	507	630	640	645	...
B Fees, fines and penalties	–	–	–	–	–	–	–	–	–	–	–	...
4 Other current transfers	910	906	1070	1206	1485	1697	1781	1740	1630	1742	1543	...
A Net casualty insurance premiums	110	114	130	153	171	189	173	173	213	191	179	...
B Social assistance grants	362	300	321	350	500	580	630	590	640	736	504	...
C Unfunded employee pension and welfare benefits	238	262	293	319	347	395	410	414	419	436	458	...
D Current transfers to the rest of the world	102	132	171	202	233	235	240	323	108	104	124	...
E Other current transfers n.e.c.	98	98	155	182	234	298	328	240	250	275	278	...
Net saving	–4079	–4700	–6016	–8564	–9080	–9685	–9579	–8140	–7972	–8446	–7662	...
Total current disbursements	5995	6007	6172	5169	6764	7160	7957	8864	8653	8799	9643	...

a Item "Property income" includes dividends.

3.43 Private non-profit institutions serving households: capital accumulation account

Million Finish markkaa

	1986	1987	1988	1989	1990	1991	1992	1993	1994	1995	1996	1997
Finance of gross accumulation												
1 Gross saving	1047	1057	845	–55	594	172	–553	797	1716	2190	3037	...
A Consumption of fixed capital	5126	5757	6861	8509	9674	9857	9026	8937	9688	10636	10699	...
B Net saving	–4079	–4700	–6016	–8564	–9080	–9685	–9579	–8140	–7972	–8446	–7662	...
2 Capital transfers [a]	287	388	527	555	623	776	917	373	146	179	161	...

Finland

Million Finish markkaa

	1986	1987	1988	1989	1990	1991	1992	1993	1994	1995	1996	1997
A From resident sectors	287	388	527	555	623	776	917	373	146	179	161	...
Private	–	–	–	–	–	–	–	–	–	–	–	...
Public	287	388	527	555	623	776	917	373	146	179	161	...
B From rest of the world	–	–	–	–	–	–	–	–	–	–	–	...
Finance of gross accumulation	1334	1445	1372	500	1217	948	364	1170	1862	2369	3198	...

Gross accumulation

	1986	1987	1988	1989	1990	1991	1992	1993	1994	1995	1996	1997
1 Gross capital formation	8965	10818	14397	20104	20402	14145	10305	8944	9023	9641	8900	...
A Increase in stocks	–	–	–	–	–	–	–	–	–	–	–	...
B Gross fixed capital formation	8965	10818	14397	20104	20402	14145	10305	8944	9023	9641	8900	...
2 Purchases of land, net	237	235	315	162	196	83	73	39	73	18	34	...
3 Purchases of intangible assets, net	...	...	...	...	...	...	...	...	...	...	...	...
4 Capital transfers	...	...	...	...	...	...	...	...	...	...	...	...
Net lending	–7868	–9608	–13340	–19766	–19381	–13280	–10014	–7813	–7234	–7290	–5736	...
Gross accumulation	1334	1445	1372	500	1217	948	364	1170	1862	2369	3198	...

a Capital transfers received are recorded net of capital transfers paid.

3.44 Private non-profit institutions serving households: capital finance account

Million Finish markkaa

	1986	1987	1988	1989	1990	1991	1992	1993	1994	1995	1996	1997
Acquisition of financial assets												
1 Gold	...	...	...	...	...	...	...	...	...	...	...	...
2 Currency and transferable deposits	176	126	92	6	175	644	240	–567	557	1235	...	...
3 Other deposits	281	365	370	101	1957	331	67	–34	90	–	...	...
4 Bills and bonds, short-term	...	...	...	...	...	...	...	...	...	...	...	...
5 Bonds, long-term	31	40	49	–5	7	316	588	55	80	–	...	...
A Corporate, resident	31	40	49	–5	7	316	588	55	80	–	...	...
B Government	...	...	...	...	...	...	...	...	...	...	...	...
C Rest of the world	–	–	–	–	–	–	–	–	–	–	...	...
6 Corporate equity securities	330	251	401	392	143	135	609	17	748	–302	...	...
7 Short-term loans, n.e.c.	–32	205	173	473	–1331	111	274	44	71	653	...	...
8 Long-term loans, n.e.c.	64	127	178	–19	40	1	77	–12	76	–1	...	...
9 Other receivables	88	204	45	170	82	113	171	53	–48	1305	...	...
10 Proprietors' net additions to the accumulation of quasi-corporations	–	–	–	–	–	–	–	–	–	–	...	...
11 Other assets	–	–	–	–	–	–	–	–	–	–	...	...
Total acquisitions of financial assets	938	1318	1308	1118	1073	1651	2026	–444	1574	2890	...	...
Incurrence of liabilities												
1 Short-term loans	88	297	229	284	302	–6	–191	330	10	5	...	...
2 Long-term loans	2223	3643	5045	6075	5872	7800	4502	1421	3931	2864	...	...
3 Other liabilities	6161	6502	8596	13270	12448	6976	7780	5320	4867	4576	...	...
Total incurrence of liabilities	8472	10442	13870	19629	18622	14770	12091	7071	8808	7445	...	...
Statistical discrepancy [a]	334	484	778	1255	1832	161	–51	298	–	2735	...	...
Net lending	–7868	–9608	–13340	–19766	–19381	–13280	–10014	–7813	–7234	–7290	...	...
Total incurrence of liabilities and net lending	938	1318	1308	1118	1073	1651	2026	–444	1574	2890	...	...

a Statistical discrepancy refers to adjustment made in order to reconcile the net lending of the Capital Accumulation Account and the Capital Finance Account.

Finland

3.51 External transactions, current account: detail

Million Finish markkaa

	1986	1987	1988	1989	1990	1991	1992	1993	1994	1995	1996	1997
Payments to the rest of the world												
1 Imports of goods and services	89898	97775	109866	125996	126600	112422	121878	133450	150043	161080	171115	...
A Imports of merchandise, c.i.f.	76736	81867	91232	104400	101967	86348	93188	101559	118684	125451	138106	...
B Other	13162	15908	18634	21596	24633	26074	28690	31891	31359	35629	33009	...
2 Factor income to rest of the world	12560	13599	16864	22318	28960	31006	32491	36446	32007	31788	33084	...
A Compensation of employees	68	68	75	63	108	156	102	132	144	156	168	...
B Property and entrepreneurial income	12492	13531	16789	22255	28852	30850	32389	36314	31863	31632	32916	...
3 Current transfers to the rest of the world	5217	5616	7301	7126	6981	7897	8280	8524	8389	13369	14336	...
A Indirect taxes by general government to supranational organizations	...	...	...	...	...	...	...	...	...	1029	984	...
B Other current transfers	5217	5616	7301	7126	6981	7897	8280	8524	8389	12340	13352	...
By general government	1189	1447	1764	2170	2434	2946	2506	2242	2089	6154	6737	...
By other resident sectors [a]	4028	4169	5537	4956	4547	4951	5774	6282	6300	6186	6615	...
4 Surplus of the nation on current transactions	−3625	−7549	−11331	−24874	−26513	−26697	−22035	−6340	6627	22531	22031	...
Payments to the rest of the world and surplus of the nation on current transfers	104050	109441	122700	130566	136028	124628	140614	172080	197066	228768	240566	...
Receipts from the rest of the world												
1 Exports of goods and services	95634	100048	108750	116702	118828	109289	128272	159438	182530	207242	217494	...
A Exports of merchandise, f.o.b.	81066	83826	91313	98265	99750	91100	105809	132550	152022	172820	182436	...
B Other	14568	16222	17437	18437	19078	18189	22463	26888	30508	34422	35058	...
2 Factor income from rest of the world	4976	5586	8497	11222	15024	14437	12674	13229	10469	12885	14824	...
A Compensation of employees	420	389	495	382	318	296	222	168	186	192	216	...
B Property and entrepreneurial income	4556	5197	8002	10840	14706	14141	12452	13061	10283	12693	14608	...
3 Current transfers from rest of the world	3440	3807	5453	2642	2176	902	−332	−587	4067	8641	8249	...
A Subsidies to general government from supranational organizations	...	...	...	...	...	...	...	...	...	...	...	...
B Other current transfers	3440	3807	5453	2642	2176	902	−332	−587	4067	8641	8249	...
To general government	–	–	–	–	1	1	136	1	15	5407	4641	...
To other resident sectors [a]	3440	3807	5453	2642	2175	901	−468	−588	4052	3234	3608	...
Receipts from the rest of the world on current transfers	104050	109441	122700	130566	136028	124628	140614	172080	197066	228768	240567	...

a All transfers include reinvested earnings.

Finland

3.53 External transactions, capital finance account

Million Finish markkaa

	1986	1987	1988	1989	1990	1991	1992	1993	1994	1995	1996	1997
Acquisition of foreign financial assets												
1 Gold and SDRs	92	46	364	−4	−300	239	−217	−123	772	−314	...	...
2 Currency and transferable deposits	4597	18420	3700	−13017	18544	−8152	−6670	−1525	30668	−2383	...	...
3 Other deposits	−203	1806	175	−1009	−651	1550	1468	−2110	1768	−	...	...
4 Bills and bonds, short-term	1278	−1364	1297	−945	375	−1107	827	−3187	−	−	...	...
5 Bonds, long-term	4124	2097	1878	−1003	−281	−2	321	1549	−4625	3685	...	...
6 Corporate equity securities	3585	4352	7511	8979	8299	2653	1593	11693	11029	7393	...	...
7 Short-term loans, n.e.c.	8085	3350	4264	11230	−1045	8710	3654	8460	−855	−5493	...	...
A Subsidiaries abroad	−	−	−	−	−	−	−	−	−	−	...	...
B Other	8085	3350	4264	11230	−1045	8710	3654	8460	−855	−5493	...	...
8 Long-term loans	1232	1397	3552	8995	13910	1538	2438	7986	4249	−1875	...	...
A Subsidiaries abroad	620	...	...	...	...	...	...	...	...	...	...	...
B Other	612	...	...	...	...	...	...	...	...	...	...	...
9 Proprietors' net additions to accumulation of quasi-corporate, non-resident enterprises	−	−	−	−	−	−	−	−	−	−	...	...
10 Trade credits and advances	−441	−1339	1235	−507	1663	2696	1385	1885	1213	3839	...	...
11 Other	1042	126	2754	2618	1880	−	100	−2662	2518	13570	...	...
Total acquisitions of foreign financial assets	23391	28891	26730	15337	42394	8125	4899	21966	46737	18422	...	...
Incurrence of foreign liabilities												
1 Currency and transferable deposits	9098	32493	12678	−709	17739	−1327	−338	−19675	−723	320	...	...
2 Other deposits	−	−	−	−	−	462	−	−	−	...	...	...
3 Bills and bonds, short-term	−89	301	1128	164	125	−	4360	−7070	−	−	...	...
4 Bonds, long-term	8791	8126	14010	14578	27109	37238	38261	32988	22986	−17868	...	...
5 Corporate equity securities	2755	1117	2879	4044	437	177	1639	16443	19284	13646	...	...
A Subsidiaries of non-resident incorporated units	1623	...	...	...	...	...	...	...	...	...	...	...
B Other	1037	...	...	...	...	...	...	...	...	...	...	...
6 Short-term loans, n.e.c.	13529	−4780	5171	2086	8739	−13462	−22357	−4009	−2134	1420	...	...
A Subsidiaries of non-residents	−	−	−	−	−	−	−	−	−	...	...	...
B Other	13529	−4780	5171	2086	8739	−13462	−22357	−4009	−2134	1420	...	...
7 Long-term loans	−1922	2854	118	8874	19882	12795	2030	1775	3003	−7258	...	...
8 Non-resident proprietors' net additions to accumulation of resident quasi-corporate enterprises	−	−	−	−	−	−	−	−	−	...	...	...
9 Trade credits and advances	−1633	−558	−238	1379	626	1247	8329	4183	3012	−1216	...	...
10 Other	530	2702	1000	4329	1274	3	40	−1543	−1186	11328	...	...
Total incurrence of liabilities	31059	42255	36746	34745	75931	37133	31964	23092	44242	372	...	...
Statistical discrepancy [a]	−4043	−5815	1315	5466	−7024	−2012	−5030	5214	−4132	−4762	...	...
Net lending	−3625	−7549	−11331	−24874	−26513	−26996	−22035	−6340	6627	22812	...	...
Total incurrence of liabilities and net lending [b]	23391	28891	26730	15337	42394	8125	4899	21966	46737	18422	...	...

a Statistical discrepancy refers to adjustment made in order to reconcile the net lending of the Capital Accumulation Account and the Capital Finance Account.
b "Total incurrence of liabilities" includes allocated Special Drawing Rights.

Finland

4.1 Derivation of value added by kind of activity, in current prices

Million Finish markkaa

	1986 Gross output	1986 Intermediate consumption	1986 Value added	1987 Gross output	1987 Intermediate consumption	1987 Value added	1988 Gross output	1988 Intermediate consumption	1988 Value added	1989 Gross output	1989 Intermediate consumption	1989 Value added
All producers												
1 Agriculture, hunting, forestry and fishing	36924	12685	24239	35794	13182	22612	37706	12967	24739	41534	13457	28077
A Agriculture and hunting	25534	11509	14025	23466	11949	11517	23627	11662	11965	26541	12095	14446
B Forestry and logging	10685	968	9717	11561	1008	10553	13180	1040	12140	14196	1126	13070
C Fishing	705	208	497	767	225	542	899	265	634	797	236	561
2 Mining and quarrying	2579	1352	1227	2521	1275	1246	2966	1363	1603	3550	1513	2037
A Coal mining	...	...	...	...	...	...	...	...	...	...	...	...
B Crude petroleum and natural gas production	...	...	...	...	...	...	...	...	...	...	...	...
C Metal ore mining	599	335	264	583	331	252	880	340	540	1155	356	799
D Other mining	1980	1017	963	1938	944	994	2086	1023	1063	2395	1157	1238
3 Manufacturing	229931	151734	78197	245807	158662	87145	267323	171351	95972	293085	187860	105225
A Manufacture of food, beverages and tobacco	44300	34084	10216	44793	34326	10467	47484	36052	11432	49047	37265	11782
B Textile, wearing apparel and leather industries	12198	7076	5122	11788	6572	5216	10972	6156	4816	10266	5588	4678
C Manufacture of wood and wood products, including furniture [a]	13510	9618	3892	14560	9866	4694	15747	10545	5202	18684	12511	6173
D Manufacture of paper and paper products, printing and publishing	50489	33496	16993	54432	35259	19173	61820	38822	22998	66708	42795	23913
E Manufacture of chemicals and chemical petroleum, coal, rubber and plastic products	27530	18397	9133	29746	20352	9394	29795	20157	9638	33323	21978	11345
F Manufacture of non-metallic mineral products, except products of petroleum and coal	7044	3832	3212	8220	4389	3831	9020	4593	4427	10381	5284	5097
G Basic metal industries	14906	11467	3439	15261	11547	3714	19101	14373	4728	21887	16023	5864
H Manufacture of fabricated metal products, machinery and equipment	54661	31103	23558	61231	33481	27750	66856	37423	29433	75676	42891	32785
I Other manufacturing industries [a]	5293	2661	2632	5776	2870	2906	6528	3230	3298	7113	3525	3588
4 Electricity, gas and water	28475	18953	9522	29198	19180	10018	29234	19169	10065	29125	19880	9245
A Electricity, gas and steam	27372	18663	8709	28051	18881	9170	27976	18861	9115	27791	19542	8249
B Water works and supply	1103	290	813	1147	299	848	1258	308	950	1334	338	996
5 Construction	59168	33969	25199	64546	37085	27461	76380	43440	32940	96303	54268	42035
6 Wholesale and retail trade, restaurants and hotels	71169	30211	40958	79106	33394	45712	88455	37511	50944	98739	42395	56344
A Wholesale and retail trade	56745	21941	34804	63074	24221	38853	70329	27196	43133	78450	30622	47828
B Restaurants and hotels	14424	8270	6154	16032	9173	6859	18126	10315	7811	20289	11773	8516
Restaurants	9970	5796	4174	11137	6457	4680	12615	7286	5329	14078	8371	5707
Hotels and other lodging places	4454	2474	1980	4895	2716	2179	5511	3029	2482	6211	3402	2809
7 Transport, storage and communication	42595	17171	25424	46391	19140	27251	51609	21473	30136	57906	24315	33591
A Transport and storage	33713	15231	18482	36354	16927	19427	40433	18960	21473	45896	21501	24395

Finland

Million Finish markkaa

	1986 Gross output	1986 Intermediate consumption	1986 Value added	1987 Gross output	1987 Intermediate consumption	1987 Value added	1988 Gross output	1988 Intermediate consumption	1988 Value added	1989 Gross output	1989 Intermediate consumption	1989 Value added
B Communication	8882	1940	6942	10037	2213	7824	11176	2513	8663	12010	2814	9196
8 Finance, insurance, real estate and business services	81714	32596	49118	90720	36727	53993	102183	42048	60135	116409	47589	68820
A Financial institutions [b]	14943	4689	10254	17441	5812	11629	19743	6821	12922	23299	7988	15311
B Insurance	2767	1523	1244	3526	1493	2033	2649	1747	902	2195	1609	586
C Real estate and business services	64004	26384	37620	69753	29422	40331	79791	33480	46311	90915	37992	52923
Real estate, except dwellings	12238	7158	5080	13669	7934	5735	15860	8743	7117	17712	9600	8112
Dwellings	29069	8470	20599	29970	9105	20865	32788	9899	22889	36230	10690	25540
9 Community, social and personal services	12557	5153	7404	14245	5833	8412	15744	6499	9245	18008	7358	10650
A Sanitary and similar services	1496	531	965	1739	604	1135	1942	660	1282	2328	764	1564
B Social and related community services	4741	1573	3168	5267	1765	3502	5777	1974	3803	6517	2312	4205
Educational services	520	172	348	543	184	359	612	213	399	748	281	467
Medical, dental, other health and veterinary services	2894	906	1988	3274	1034	2240	3633	1163	2470	4060	1327	2733
C Recreational and cultural services	4444	2326	2118	5166	2680	2486	5728	3015	2713	6570	3357	3213
D Personal and household services	1876	723	1153	2073	784	1289	2297	850	1447	2593	925	1668
Total, Industries	565112	303824	261288	608328	324478	283850	671600	355821	315779	754659	398635	356024
Producers of government services	82781	27959	54822	91019	30786	60233	99400	33309	66091	109702	36487	73215
Other producers	10568	4428	6140	11349	4740	6609	12676	5169	7507	13987	5747	8240
Total	658461	336211	322250	710696	360004	350692	783676	394299	389377	878348	440869	437479
less: Imputed bank service charge	...	−8989	8989	...	−10576	10576	...	−12180	12180	...	−14873	14873
Import duties [c]	41733	...	41733	46739	...	46739	57144	...	57144	64392	...	64392
Value added tax	...	...	...	...	...	...	...	...	...	...	...	...
Other adjustments	...	...	...	...	...	...	...	...	...	...	...	...
Total	700194	345200	354994	757435	370580	386855	840820	406479	434341	942740	455742	486998

	1990 Gross output	1990 Intermediate consumption	1990 Value added	1991 Gross output	1991 Intermediate consumption	1991 Value added	1992 Gross output	1992 Intermediate consumption	1992 Value added	1993 Gross output	1993 Intermediate consumption	1993 Value added
All producers												
1 Agriculture, hunting, forestry and fishing	42589	13546	29043	36886	12813	24073	34435	12967	21468	34980	12899	22081
A Agriculture and hunting	27545	12143	15402	24865	11531	13334	22781	11635	11146	23623	11530	12093
B Forestry and logging	14216	1158	13058	11210	1043	10167	10683	1046	9637	10349	1072	9277
C Fishing	828	245	583	811	239	572	971	286	685	1008	297	711
2 Mining and quarrying	3454	1721	1733	3287	1558	1729	3334	1534	1800	3225	1538	1687
A Coal mining	...	...	...	...	...	...	...	...	...	...	...	...
B Crude petroleum and natural gas production	...	...	...	...	...	...	...	...	...	...	...	...
C Metal ore mining	765	329	436	681	290	391	625	272	353	582	285	297
D Other mining	2689	1392	1297	2606	1268	1338	2709	1262	1447	2643	1253	1390
3 Manufacturing	297738	192355	105383	265223	175556	89667	269231	176805	92426	292201	190385	101816
A Manufacture of food, beverages and tobacco	51329	38938	12391	50991	37848	13143	50034	36879	13155	50677	37092	13585

Finland

		1990			1991			1992			1993		
		Gross output	Intermediate consumption	Value added	Gross output	Intermediate consumption	Value added	Gross output	Intermediate consumption	Value added	Gross output	Intermediate consumption	Value added
B	Textile, wearing apparel and leather industries	9415	5334	4081	7636	4242	3394	7030	3796	3234	7098	3896	3202
C	Manufacture of wood and wood products, including furniture [a]	19280	12719	6561	14869	10402	4467	14754	9709	5045	16606	10495	6111
D	Manufacture of paper and paper products, printing and publishing	64367	42350	22017	59495	41113	18382	60356	40579	19777	64961	42294	22667
E	Manufacture of chemicals and chemical petroleum, coal, rubber and plastic products	36444	24598	11846	33913	22889	11024	34431	23759	10672	37711	26041	11670
F	Manufacture of non-metallic mineral products, except products of petroleum and coal	10770	5653	5117	8932	4824	4108	7443	4135	3308	6948	3783	3165
G	Basic metal industries	19377	14755	4622	17791	13526	4265	20928	15567	5361	23769	17250	6519
H	Manufacture of fabricated metal products, machinery and equipment	79548	44393	35155	65324	37374	27950	68468	39246	29222	78912	46498	32414
I	Other manufacturing industries [a]	7208	3615	3593	6272	3338	2934	5787	3135	2652	5519	3036	2483
4	Electricity, gas and water	32719	23215	9504	33918	22859	11059	35111	24108	11003	37472	26138	11334
A	Electricity, gas and steam	31253	22863	8390	32339	22453	9886	33429	23681	9748	35704	25685	10019
B	Water works and supply	1466	352	1114	1579	406	1173	1682	427	1255	1768	453	1315
5	Construction	102189	58722	43467	88306	51344	36962	69004	42963	26041	56951	35953	20998
6	Wholesale and retail trade, restaurants and hotels	103550	45579	57971	97476	45332	52144	92035	43626	48409	89360	41959	47401
A	Wholesale and retail trade	81761	32964	48797	76335	32786	43549	71845	31229	40616	70206	30067	40139
B	Restaurants and hotels	21789	12615	9174	21141	12546	8595	20190	12397	7793	19154	11892	7262
	Restaurants	15106	8905	6201	14819	8891	5928	14137	8794	5343	13471	8466	5005
	Hotels and other lodging places	6683	3710	2973	6322	3655	2667	6053	3603	2450	5683	3426	2257
7	Transport, storage and communication	62011	25605	36406	60994	24868	36126	61240	24756	36484	63243	25983	37260
A	Transport and storage	48814	22407	26407	47167	21390	25777	46992	21126	25866	48975	22086	26889
B	Communication	13197	3198	9999	13827	3478	10349	14248	3630	10618	14268	3897	10371
8	Finance, insurance, real estate and business services	129306	51095	78211	130960	52131	78829	125262	49759	75503	136851	52708	84143
A	Financial institutions [b]	26320	8201	18119	24078	8476	15602	19186	7736	11450	23123	8632	14491
B	Insurance	3204	1225	1979	3486	1104	2382	2894	1361	1533	4127	1230	2897
C	Real estate and business services	99782	41669	58113	103396	42551	60845	103182	40662	62520	109601	42846	66755
	Real estate, except dwellings	19762	11103	8659	20910	12380	8530	20523	12793	7730	20799	13390	7409
	Dwellings	39962	11737	28225	45621	12494	33127	49745	12361	37384	54835	13726	41109
9	Community, social and personal services	20208	8126	12082	20515	8160	12355	20950	8212	12738	20835	8176	12659
A	Sanitary and similar services	2629	830	1799	2698	802	1896	2955	878	2077	3030	930	2100
B	Social and related community services	7098	2531	4567	7384	2640	4744	7194	2556	4638	6970	2435	4535
	Educational services	785	307	478	763	281	482	772	282	490	863	315	548
	Medical, dental, other health and veterinary services	4546	1523	3023	4929	1653	3276	4792	1608	3184	4548	1521	3027
C	Recreational and cultural services	7556	3761	3795	7259	3617	3642	7599	3712	3887	7741	3772	3969

Finland

	1990			1991			1992			1993		
	Gross output	Intermediate consumption	Value added	Gross output	Intermediate consumption	Value added	Gross output	Intermediate consumption	Value added	Gross output	Intermediate consumption	Value added
D Personal and household services	2925	1004	1921	3174	1101	2073	3202	1066	2136	3094	1039	2055
Total, Industries	793764	419964	373800	737565	394621	342944	710602	384730	325872	735118	395739	339379
Producers of government services	123834	41686	82148	136377	45594	90783	137645	46850	90795	153628	67153	86475
Other producers	15304	6140	9164	15604	6226	9378	15657	6099	9558	15783	6190	9593
Total	932902	467790	465112	889546	446441	443105	863904	437679	426225	904529	469082	435447
less: Imputed bank service charge	...	−17000	17000	...	−15329	15329	...	−10513	10513	...	−14205	14205
Import duties [c]	67318	...	67318	63092	...	63092	61066	...	61066	61155	...	61155
Value added tax	...	...	...	...	...	...	...	...	...	...	...	...
Other adjustments	...	...	...	...	...	...	...	...	...	...	...	...
Total	1000220	484790	515430	952638	461770	490868	924970	448192	476778	965684	483287	482397

	1994			1995			1996			1997		
	Gross output	Intermediate consumption	Value added	Gross output	Intermediate consumption	Value added	Gross output	Intermediate consumption	Value added	Gross output	Intermediate consumption	Value added

All producers

1 Agriculture, hunting, forestry and fishing	38026	12762	25264	32703	10783	21920	31158	10769	20389	...	...	...
A Agriculture and hunting	24295	11320	12975	17726	9342	8384	17010	9313	7697	...	...	...
B Forestry and logging	12712	1142	11570	14145	1197	12948	13359	1199	12160	...	...	...
C Fishing	1019	300	719	832	244	588	789	257	532	...	...	...
2 Mining and quarrying	3523	1587	1936	3816	1858	1958	3852	1900	1952	...	...	...
A Coal mining	...	...	...	...	...	...	...	...	...	...	...	...
B Crude petroleum and natural gas production	...	...	...	...	...	...	...	...	...	...	...	...
C Metal ore mining	584	305	279	561	378	183	580	410	170	...	...	...
D Other mining	2939	1282	1657	3255	1480	1775	3272	1490	1782	...	...	...
3 Manufacturing	326149	213412	112737	382076	253245	128831	394354	265143	129211	...	...	...
A Manufacture of food, beverages and tobacco	49922	37039	12883	47327	34774	12553	49581	36931	12650	...	...	...
B Textile, wearing apparel and leather industries	7920	4356	3564	8045	4450	3595	8218	4630	3588	...	...	...
C Manufacture of wood and wood products, including furniture [a]	20624	13037	7587	21201	14363	6838	20540	14557	5983	...	...	...
D Manufacture of paper and paper products, printing and publishing	73013	47085	25928	92988	60664	32324	87816	58584	29232	...	...	...
E Manufacture of chemicals and chemical petroleum, coal, rubber and plastic products	40901	27532	13369	42480	29281	13199	45706	32362	13344	...	...	...
F Manufacture of non-metallic mineral products, except products of petroleum and coal	7499	4035	3464	7963	4346	3617	8660	4785	3875	...	...	...
G Basic metal industries	25857	18851	7006	30574	22209	8365	29869	22772	7097	...	...	...
H Manufacture of fabricated metal products, machinery and equipment	94317	58044	36273	124360	79011	45349	136500	86075	50425	...	...	...
I Other manufacturing industries [a]	6096	3433	2663	7138	4147	2991	7464	4447	3017	...	...	...
4 Electricity, gas and water	38921	26640	12281	41941	28957	12984	47398	33757	13641	...	...	...
A Electricity, gas and steam	37096	26203	10893	39996	28509	11487	45444	33304	12140	...	...	...

Finland

	1994			1995			1996			1997		
	Gross output	Intermediate consumption	Value added	Gross output	Intermediate consumption	Value added	Gross output	Intermediate consumption	Value added	Gross output	Intermediate consumption	Value added
B Water works and supply	1825	437	1388	1945	448	1497	1954	453	1501	...	...	...
5 Construction	57077	33774	23303	62457	34128	28329	64759	35539	29220	...	...	...
6 Wholesale and retail trade, restaurants and hotels	94197	43370	50827	97308	44339	52969	101632	46158	55474	...	...	...
A Wholesale and retail trade	74259	31081	43178	76548	31677	44871	79908	32957	46951	...	...	...
B Restaurants and hotels	19938	12289	7649	20760	12662	8098	21724	13201	8523	...	...	...
Restaurants	14010	8745	5265	14500	9019	5481	15195	9421	5774	...	...	...
Hotels and other lodging places	5928	3544	2384	6260	3643	2617	6529	3780	2749	...	...	...
7 Transport, storage and communication	66613	27499	39114	70595	28971	41624	75258	30966	44292	...	...	...
A Transport and storage	52180	23374	28806	54957	24366	30591	57587	25506	32081	...	...	...
B Communication	14433	4125	10308	15638	4605	11033	17671	5460	12211	...	...	...
8 Finance, insurance, real estate and business services	144311	57437	86874	152923	60372	92551	163043	63117	99926	...	...	...
A Financial institutions [b]	24934	10244	14690	23254	8669	14585	23262	8351	14911	...	...	...
B Insurance	3268	1293	1975	4422	1441	2981	6074	1366	4708	...	...	...
C Real estate and business services	116109	45900	70209	125247	50262	74985	133707	53400	80307	...	...	...
Real estate, except dwellings	21185	14021	7164	22109	14286	7823	23121	15021	8100	...	...	...
Dwellings	57498	15055	42443	60466	16970	43496	63731	18005	45726	...	...	...
9 Community, social and personal services	20800	8136	12664	21779	8556	13223	23149	9097	14052	...	...	...
A Sanitary and similar services	3363	1043	2320	3698	1202	2496	4031	1310	2721	...	...	...
B Social and related community services	6782	2405	4377	7107	2544	4563	7521	2694	4827	...	...	...
Educational services	806	298	508	862	328	534	905	348	557	...	...	...
Medical, dental, other health and veterinary services	4382	1490	2892	4557	1549	3008	4858	1652	3206	...	...	...
C Recreational and cultural services	7700	3696	4004	8070	3823	4247	8635	4090	4545	...	...	...
D Personal and household services	2955	992	1963	2904	987	1917	2962	1003	1959	...	...	...
Total, Industries	789617	424617	365000	865598	471209	394389	904603	496446	408157	...	...	...
Producers of government services	156733	69700	87033	164995	73358	91637	175342	79165	96177	...	...	...
Other producers	15630	6095	9535	16566	6483	10083	17260	6699	10561	...	...	...
Total	961980	500412	461568	1047159	551050	496109	1097205	582310	514895	...	...	...
less: Imputed bank service charge	...	−14396	14396	...	−14142	14142	...	−13347	13347	...	...	...
Import duties [c]	63820	...	63820	67896	...	67896	75374	...	75374	...	...	...
Value added tax	...	...	...	...	...	...	...	...	...	...	...	...
Other adjustments	...	...	...	...	...	...	...	...	...	...	...	...
Total	1025800	514808	510992	1115055	565192	549863	1172579	595657	576922	...	...	...

a Furniture is included in item "Other manufacturing industries".
b Item "Financial institutions" include activities auxiliary to financial intermediation and insurance.
c Item "Import duties" includes commodity indirect taxes net of subsidies.

Finland

4.2 Derivation of value added by kind of activity, in constant prices

Million Finish markkaa

	1986 Gross output	1986 Intermediate consumption	1986 Value added	1987 Gross output	1987 Intermediate consumption	1987 Value added	1988 Gross output	1988 Intermediate consumption	1988 Value added	1989 Gross output	1989 Intermediate consumption	1989 Value added

At constant prices of: 1990

All producers

1 Agriculture, hunting, forestry and fishing	40870	13712	27158	39290	14309	24981	40391	14028	26363	42438	14105	28333
A Agriculture and hunting	27122	12379	14743	24595	12964	11631	24843	12628	12215	26593	12654	13939
B Forestry and logging	12992	1160	11832	13942	1169	12773	14639	1186	13453	15019	1222	13797
C Fishing	756	173	583	753	176	577	909	214	695	826	229	597
2 Mining and quarrying	2766	1390	1376	2832	1416	1416	3060	1522	1538	3360	1655	1705
A Coal mining	...	...	...	...	...	...	...	...	...	...	...	...
B Crude petroleum and natural gas production	...	...	...	...	...	...	...	...	...	...	...	...
C Metal ore mining	645	294	351	692	316	376	766	344	422	835	358	477
D Other mining	2121	1096	1025	2140	1100	1040	2294	1178	1116	2525	1297	1228
3 Manufacturing	266057	173521	92536	279938	181919	98019	289969	187945	102024	298593	192489	106104
A Manufacture of food, beverages and tobacco	48928	37568	11360	49757	38066	11691	50586	38520	12066	50551	38334	12217
B Textile, wearing apparel and leather industries	13610	7720	5890	13050	7434	5616	11734	6680	5054	10578	6007	4571
C Manufacture of wood and wood products, including furniture [a]	17120	11373	5747	18009	11916	6093	19069	12607	6462	20821	13711	7110
D Manufacture of paper and paper products, printing and publishing	56637	37350	19287	59154	38906	20248	63076	41487	21589	64621	42505	22116
E Manufacture of chemicals and chemical petroleum, coal, rubber and plastic products	30087	20318	9769	32834	22264	10570	34337	23114	11223	34927	23151	11776
F Manufacture of non-metallic mineral products, except products of petroleum and coal	8626	4533	4093	9681	5092	4589	9908	5207	4701	10785	5666	5119
G Basic metal industries	16888	12874	4014	17455	13298	4157	18273	13893	4380	18879	14358	4521
H Manufacture of fabricated metal products, machinery and equipment	67738	38571	29167	73223	41545	31678	75686	42780	32906	79856	44957	34899
I Other manufacturing industries [a]	6423	3214	3209	6775	3398	3377	7300	3657	3643	7575	3800	3775
4 Electricity, gas and water	29108	20638	8470	31293	22217	9076	32093	22771	9322	32069	22745	9324
A Electricity, gas and steam	27749	20312	7437	29892	21880	8012	30656	22426	8230	30617	22396	8221
B Water works and supply	1359	326	1033	1401	337	1064	1437	345	1092	1452	349	1103
5 Construction	81892	46618	35274	83141	47416	35725	90112	51114	38998	102703	58213	44490
6 Wholesale and retail trade, restaurants and hotels	89606	41132	48474	95454	43591	51863	100573	45839	54734	106590	47528	59062
A Wholesale and retail trade	70958	30092	40866	75716	31904	43812	79893	33593	46300	84832	34729	50103
B Restaurants and hotels	18648	11040	7608	19738	11687	8051	20680	12246	8434	21758	12799	8959
Restaurants	12887	7769	5118	13707	8264	5443	14389	8674	5715	15094	9041	6053
Hotels and other lodging places	5761	3271	2490	6031	3423	2608	6291	3572	2719	6664	3758	2906
7 Transport, storage and communication	47690	20181	27509	51466	21994	29472	54904	23568	31336	59455	25130	34325

Finland

Million Finish markkaa

	1986			1987			1988			1989		
	Gross output	Intermediate consumption	Value added	Gross output	Intermediate consumption	Value added	Gross output	Intermediate consumption	Value added	Gross output	Intermediate consumption	Value added

At constant prices of: 1990

	Gross 86	IC 86	VA 86	Gross 87	IC 87	VA 87	Gross 88	IC 88	VA 88	Gross 89	IC 89	VA 89
A Transport and storage	38384	18002	20382	41079	19546	21533	43484	20857	22627	47083	22170	24913
B Communication	9306	2179	7127	10387	2448	7939	11420	2711	8709	12372	2960	9412
8 Finance, insurance, real estate and business services	104946	38806	66140	111876	42291	69585	119343	46547	72796	127494	50523	76971
A Financial institutions [b]	21634	5571	16063	23574	6655	16919	24983	7523	17460	27102	8459	18643
B Insurance	2988	1394	1594	3163	1365	1798	2918	1470	1448	3020	1421	1599
C Real estate and business services	80324	31841	48483	85139	34271	50868	91442	37554	53888	97372	40643	56729
Real estate, except dwellings	14899	7775	7124	15924	8446	7478	17417	9387	8030	18637	10264	8373
Dwellings	34858	10775	24083	36113	11147	24966	37413	11379	26034	38685	11490	27195
9 Community, social and personal services	17173	6651	10522	17907	7095	10812	18438	7436	11002	19462	7866	11596
A Sanitary and similar services	1998	644	1354	2193	708	1485	2290	738	1552	2530	799	1731
B Social and related community services	6791	2138	4653	6916	2243	4673	6857	2359	4498	7075	2484	4591
Educational services	759	220	539	747	232	515	764	254	510	837	307	530
Medical, dental, other health and veterinary services	4189	1289	2900	4359	1353	3006	4313	1422	2891	4427	1474	2953
C Recreational and cultural services	5889	2996	2893	6208	3238	2970	6594	3396	3198	7050	3619	3431
D Personal and household services	2495	873	1622	2590	906	1684	2697	943	1754	2807	964	1843
Total, Industries	680108	362649	317459	713197	382248	330949	748883	400770	348113	792164	420254	371910
Producers of government services	108898	34166	74732	113617	36306	77311	116483	37169	79314	119459	38544	80915
Other producers	14143	5543	8600	14339	5734	8605	14718	5858	8860	15156	6092	9064
Total	803149	402358	400791	841153	424288	416865	880084	443797	436287	926779	464890	461889
less: Imputed bank service charge	...	−12270	12270	...	−13679	13679	...	−15169	15169	...	−16943	16943
Import duties [c]	58085	...	58085	61731	...	61731	66601	...	66601	70418	...	70418
Value added tax	...	...	...	...	...	...	...	...	...	...	...	...
Other adjustments	...	...	...	...	...	...	...	...	...	...	...	...
Total	861234	414628	446606	902884	437967	464917	946685	458966	487719	997197	481833	515364

	1990			1991			1992			1993		
	Gross output	Intermediate consumption	Value added	Gross output	Intermediate consumption	Value added	Gross output	Intermediate consumption	Value added	Gross output	Intermediate consumption	Value added

At constant prices of: 1990

All producers

1 Agriculture, hunting, forestry and fishing	42589	13546	29043	38005	12197	25808	37547	12015	25532	38209	11551	26658
A Agriculture and hunting	27545	12143	15402	25462	10955	14507	23435	10713	12722	23624	10251	13373
B Forestry and logging	14216	1158	13058	11714	998	10716	13138	1015	12123	13618	1015	12603
C Fishing	828	245	583	829	244	585	974	287	687	967	285	682
2 Mining and quarrying	3454	1721	1733	3158	1561	1597	3163	1601	1562	3064	1543	1521
A Coal mining	...	...	...	...	...	...	...	...	...	...	...	...
B Crude petroleum and natural gas production	...	...	...	...	...	...	...	...	...	...	...	...
C Metal ore mining	765	329	436	745	320	425	662	284	378	621	267	354

Finland

	1990 Gross output	1990 Intermediate consumption	1990 Value added	1991 Gross output	1991 Intermediate consumption	1991 Value added	1992 Gross output	1992 Intermediate consumption	1992 Value added	1993 Gross output	1993 Intermediate consumption	1993 Value added
At constant prices of: 1990												
D Other mining	2689	1392	1297	2413	1241	1172	2501	1317	1184	2443	1276	1167
3 Manufacturing	297738	192355	105383	270553	176642	93911	276489	180738	95751	290171	189233	100938
A Manufacture of food, beverages and tobacco	51329	38938	12391	50567	38429	12138	50675	38348	12327	51689	38966	12723
B Textile, wearing apparel and leather industries	9415	5334	4081	7617	4305	3312	7016	3959	3057	6876	3891	2985
C Manufacture of wood and wood products, including furniture [a]	19280	12719	6561	15298	10120	5178	15943	10609	5334	18153	12133	6020
D Manufacture of paper and paper products, printing and publishing	64367	42350	22017	61555	40759	20796	62091	41278	20813	65864	44028	21836
E Manufacture of chemicals and chemical petroleum, coal, rubber and plastic products	36444	24598	11846	34993	23836	11157	35759	24426	11333	36684	24967	11717
F Manufacture of non-metallic mineral products, except products of petroleum and coal	10770	5653	5117	9070	4745	4325	7882	4099	3783	7346	3808	3538
G Basic metal industries	19377	14755	4622	19133	14635	4498	21307	16324	4983	22465	17187	5278
H Manufacture of fabricated metal products, machinery and equipment	79548	44393	35155	66000	36647	29353	69878	38720	31158	75356	41387	33969
I Other manufacturing industries [a]	7208	3615	3593	6320	3166	3154	5938	2975	2963	5738	2866	2872
4 Electricity, gas and water	32719	23215	9504	33868	24070	9798	33711	23959	9752	35305	25140	10165
A Electricity, gas and steam	31253	22863	8390	32421	23722	8699	32275	23614	8661	33894	24801	9093
B Water works and supply	1466	352	1114	1447	348	1099	1436	345	1091	1411	339	1072
5 Construction	102189	58722	43467	90173	51727	38446	76788	44086	32702	65538	37544	27994
6 Wholesale and retail trade, restaurants and hotels	103550	45579	57971	91540	40755	50785	83049	38246	44803	78681	36348	42333
A Wholesale and retail trade	81761	32964	48797	71512	29176	42336	64163	27172	36991	60480	25590	34890
B Restaurants and hotels	21789	12615	9174	20028	11579	8449	18886	11074	7812	18201	10758	7443
Restaurants	15106	8905	6201	13896	8187	5709	13116	7829	5287	12547	7554	4993
Hotels and other lodging places	6683	3710	2973	6132	3392	2740	5770	3245	2525	5654	3204	2450
7 Transport, storage and communication	62011	25605	36406	58693	23645	35048	57593	22721	34872	59289	23293	35996
A Transport and storage	48814	22407	26407	45203	20343	24860	43673	19285	24388	45201	19786	25415
B Communication	13197	3198	9999	13490	3302	10188	13920	3436	10484	14088	3507	10581
8 Finance, insurance, real estate and business services	129306	51095	78211	125749	50207	75542	119469	47423	72046	124277	49213	75064
A Financial institutions [b]	26320	8201	18119	25123	8112	17011	20743	7285	13458	21734	7761	13973
B Insurance	3204	1225	1979	3564	1071	2493	3944	1275	2669	4236	1072	3164
C Real estate and business services	99782	41669	58113	97062	41024	56038	94782	38863	55919	98307	40380	57927
Real estate, except dwellings	19762	11103	8659	20669	12009	8660	21491	12142	9349	22211	12405	9806
Dwellings	39962	11737	28225	41361	12136	29225	42387	12037	30350	44204	13084	31120
9 Community, social and personal services	20208	8126	12082	19213	7839	11374	18805	7642	11163	18383	7493	10890
A Sanitary and similar services	2629	830	1799	2468	740	1728	2495	786	1709	2400	805	1595
B Social and related community services	7098	2531	4567	6647	2439	4208	6140	2264	3876	5832	2108	3724
Educational services	785	307	478	691	265	426	689	260	429	786	288	498

Finland

	1990			1991			1992			1993		
	Gross output	Intermediate consumption	Value added	Gross output	Intermediate consumption	Value added	Gross output	Intermediate consumption	Value added	Gross output	Intermediate consumption	Value added

At constant prices of: 1990

Medical, dental, other health and veterinary services	4546	1523	3023	4360	1509	2851	3970	1395	2575	3659	1279	2380
C Recreational and cultural services	7556	3761	3795	7094	3613	3481	7182	3597	3585	7289	3619	3670
D Personal and household services	2925	1004	1921	3004	1047	1957	2988	995	1993	2862	961	1901
Total, Industries	793764	419964	373800	730952	388643	342309	706614	378431	328183	712917	381358	331559
Producers of government services	123834	41686	82148	127716	44576	83140	126381	45052	81329	122295	44644	77651
Other producers	15304	6140	9164	15003	6086	8917	14812	5863	8949	14668	5718	8950
Total	932902	467790	465112	873671	439305	434366	847807	429346	418461	849880	431720	418160
less: Imputed bank service charge	...	−17000	17000	...	−17343	17343	...	−14339	14339	...	−15585	15585
Import duties [c]	67318	...	67318	61988	...	61988	57881	...	57881	53996	...	53996
Value added tax	...	...	...	...	...	...	...	...	...	...	...	...
Other adjustments	...	...	...	...	...	...	...	...	...	...	...	...
Total	1000220	484790	515430	935659	456648	479011	905688	443685	462003	903876	447305	456571

	1994			1995			1996			1997		
	Gross output	Intermediate consumption	Value added	Gross output	Intermediate consumption	Value added	Gross output	Intermediate consumption	Value added	Gross output	Intermediate consumption	Value added

At constant prices of: 1990

All producers

1 Agriculture, hunting, forestry and fishing	40790	11539	29251	40596	12583	28013	39044	12262	26782	...	...	...
A Agriculture and hunting	24224	10166	14058	23703	11143	12560	23249	10882	12367	...	...	...
B Forestry and logging	15646	1102	14544	15946	1160	14786	14810	1089	13721	...	...	...
C Fishing	920	271	649	947	280	667	985	291	694	...	...	...
2 Mining and quarrying	3457	1761	1696	3633	1855	1778	3556	1817	1739	...	...	...
A Coal mining	...	...	...	...	...	...	...	...	...	...	...	...
B Crude petroleum and natural gas production	...	...	...	...	...	...	...	...	...	...	...	...
C Metal ore mining	626	269	357	608	261	347	615	264	351	...	...	...
D Other mining	2831	1492	1339	3025	1594	1431	2941	1553	1388	...	...	...
3 Manufacturing	322209	208658	113551	346533	222080	124453	358233	229558	128675	...	...	...
A Manufacture of food, beverages and tobacco	51446	38741	12705	52640	39783	12857	54892	41596	13296	...	...	...
B Textile, wearing apparel and leather industries	7442	4221	3221	7092	4001	3091	6936	3910	3026	...	...	...
C Manufacture of wood and wood products, including furniture [a]	20939	14019	6920	20473	13708	6765	20808	13879	6929	...	...	...
D Manufacture of paper and paper products, printing and publishing	71786	48073	23713	73124	48835	24289	70462	46976	23486	...	...	...
E Manufacture of chemicals and chemical petroleum, coal, rubber and plastic products	41536	28514	13022	41838	28531	13307	43500	29900	13600	...	...	...
F Manufacture of non-metallic mineral products, except products of petroleum and coal	7899	4094	3805	7997	4171	3826	8429	4404	4025	...	...	...
G Basic metal industries	23843	18172	5671	25013	18974	6039	27719	21144	6575	...	...	...

Finland

	1994 Gross output	1994 Intermediate consumption	1994 Value added	1995 Gross output	1995 Intermediate consumption	1995 Value added	1996 Gross output	1996 Intermediate consumption	1996 Value added	1997 Gross output	1997 Intermediate consumption	1997 Value added
At constant prices of: 1990												
H Manufacture of fabricated metal products, machinery and equipment	91027	49676	41351	111465	60505	50960	118313	64039	54274	...	...	...
I Other manufacturing industries [a]	6291	3148	3143	6891	3572	3319	7174	3710	3464	...	...	...
4 Electricity, gas and water	37416	26665	10751	36814	26226	10588	40454	28873	11581	...	...	...
A Electricity, gas and steam	35964	26316	9648	35363	25877	9486	38970	28516	10454	...	...	...
B Water works and supply	1452	349	1103	1451	349	1102	1484	357	1127	...	...	...
5 Construction	64213	36765	27448	66919	38322	28597	69969	40091	29878	...	...	...
6 Wholesale and retail trade, restaurants and hotels	81968	37438	44530	84885	38767	46118	88050	40177	47873	...	...	...
A Wholesale and retail trade	63125	26364	36761	65471	27351	38120	67966	28372	39594	...	...	...
B Restaurants and hotels	18843	11074	7769	19414	11416	7998	20084	11805	8279	...	...	...
Restaurants	12969	7772	5197	13358	8012	5346	13874	8314	5560	...	...	...
Hotels and other lodging places	5874	3302	2572	6056	3404	2652	6210	3491	2719	...	...	...
7 Transport, storage and communication	62391	24814	37577	65988	26311	39677	69738	27654	42084	...	...	...
A Transport and storage	47886	21195	26691	50301	22370	27931	52200	23197	29003	...	...	...
B Communication	14505	3619	10886	15687	3941	11746	17538	4457	13081	...	...	...
8 Finance, insurance, real estate and business services	129425	52862	76563	135019	55287	79732	141808	56762	85046	...	...	...
A Financial institutions [b]	22536	9115	13421	21390	7704	13686	22249	7307	14942	...	...	...
B Insurance	3880	1079	2801	4141	1174	2967	5660	1092	4568	...	...	...
C Real estate and business services	103009	42668	60341	109488	46409	63079	113899	48363	65536	...	...	...
Real estate, except dwellings	22571	12663	9908	23332	12528	10804	24083	12816	11267	...	...	...
Dwellings	45398	13590	31808	46759	14493	32266	47741	14899	32842	...	...	...
9 Community, social and personal services	17919	7378	10541	18742	7811	10931	19741	8255	11486	...	...	...
A Sanitary and similar services	2562	904	1658	2844	1067	1777	3098	1113	1985	...	...	...
B Social and related community services	5537	2030	3507	5764	2166	3598	6010	2299	3711	...	...	...
Educational services	726	268	458	786	310	476	824	329	495	...	...	...
Medical, dental, other health and veterinary services	3423	1216	2207	3524	1269	2255	3696	1358	2338	...	...	...
C Recreational and cultural services	7179	3546	3633	7513	3665	3848	7963	3887	4076	...	...	...
D Personal and household services	2641	898	1743	2621	913	1708	2670	956	1714	...	...	...
Total, Industries	759788	407880	351908	799129	429242	369887	830593	445449	385144	...	...	...
Producers of government services	123547	46056	77491	126209	47561	78648	130586	50473	80113	...	...	...
Other producers	14411	5615	8796	14966	5948	9018	15193	6103	9090	...	...	...
Total	897746	459551	438195	940304	482751	457553	976372	502025	474347	...	...	...
less: Imputed bank service charge	...	−15545	15545	...	−15230	15230	...	−15630	15630	...	...	...
Import duties [c]	54690	...	54690	59167	...	59167	60778	...	60778	...	...	...
Value added tax	...	...	...	...	...	...	...	...	...	...	...	...
Other adjustments	...	...	...	...	...	...	...	...	...	...	...	...
Total	952436	475096	477340	999471	497981	501490	1037150	517655	519495	...	...	...

a Furniture is included in item "Other manufacturing industries".
b Item "Financial institutions" include activities auxiliary to financial intermediation and insurance.
c Item "Import duties" includes commodity indirect taxes net of subsidies.

Finland

4.3 Cost components of value added

Million Finish markkaa

	1986						1987					
	Compensation of employees	Capital consumption	Net operating surplus	Indirect taxes	less: Subsidies received	Value added	Compensation of employees	Capital consumption	Net operating surplus	Indirect taxes	less: Subsidies received	Value added
All producers												
1 Agriculture, hunting, forestry and fishing	4293	5830	16013	198	2095	24239	4391	6067	14232	207	2285	22612
A Agriculture and hunting	1699	4106	10082	166	2028	14025	1690	4260	7611	173	2217	11517
B Forestry and logging	2563	1589	5579	10	24	9717	2668	1669	6236	10	30	10553
C Fishing	31	135	352	22	43	497	33	138	385	24	38	542
2 Mining and quarrying	700	294	261	9	37	1227	651	315	316	10	46	1246
A Coal mining	...	...	...	...	...	...	...	...	...	...	...	...
B Crude petroleum and natural gas production	...	...	...	...	...	...	...	...	...	...	...	...
C Metal ore mining	270	167	−143	2	32	264	245	173	−138	2	30	252
D Other mining	430	127	404	7	5	963	406	142	454	8	16	994
3 Manufacturing	48785	10275	18926	977	766	78197	51892	11239	23924	1032	942	87145
A Manufacture of food, beverages and tobacco	5611	1261	3292	100	48	10216	6019	1390	3014	104	60	10467
B Textile, wearing apparel and leather industries	3762	470	910	60	80	5122	3718	505	1028	62	97	5216
C Manufacture of wood and wood products, including furniture [a]	3051	673	141	75	48	3892	3182	711	776	87	62	4694
D Manufacture of paper and paper products, printing and publishing	10236	3185	3523	225	176	16993	10904	3469	4764	241	205	19173
E Manufacture of chemicals and chemical petroleum, coal, rubber and plastic products	4119	1282	3688	91	47	9133	4588	1409	3360	98	61	9394
F Manufacture of non-metallic mineral products, except products of petroleum and coal	1937	406	858	27	16	3212	2125	456	1239	32	21	3831
G Basic metal industries	2106	698	590	66	21	3439	2124	769	780	64	23	3714
H Manufacture of fabricated metal products, machinery and equipment	16312	2056	5185	303	298	23558	17494	2267	8053	310	374	27750
I Other manufacturing industries [a]	1651	244	739	30	32	2632	1738	263	910	34	39	2906
4 Electricity, gas and water	3316	3249	2981	42	66	9522	3491	3508	3053	44	78	10018
A Electricity, gas and steam	3020	2789	2925	39	64	8709	3194	3019	2968	40	51	9170
B Water works and supply	296	460	56	3	2	813	297	489	85	4	27	848
5 Construction	18663	1297	5039	217	17	25199	20753	1367	5178	181	18	27461
6 Wholesale and retail trade, restaurants and hotels	27606	4568	8285	586	87	40958	30657	5097	9399	677	118	45712
A Wholesale and retail trade	22989	4113	7187	546	31	34804	25591	4612	8064	629	43	38853
B Restaurants and hotels	4617	455	1098	40	56	6154	5066	485	1335	48	75	6859
Restaurants	3207	249	706	28	16	4174	3563	261	845	33	22	4680
Hotels and other lodging places	1410	206	392	12	40	1980	1503	224	490	15	53	2179
7 Transport, storage and communication	13893	6368	4934	285	56	25424	15228	6502	5279	293	51	27251
A Transport and storage	9581	4869	3810	278	56	18482	10407	4877	3909	285	51	19427
B Communication	4312	1499	1124	7	–	6942	4821	1625	1370	8	–	7824
8 Finance, insurance, real estate and business services	17419	14805	16746	253	105	49118	19968	16760	17129	248	112	53993

Finland

Million Finish markkaa

	1986						1987					
	Compensation of employees	Capital consumption	Net operating surplus	Indirect taxes	less: Subsidies received	Value added	Compensation of employees	Capital consumption	Net operating surplus	Indirect taxes	less: Subsidies received	Value added
A Financial institutions [b]	5935	866	3501	16	64	10254	6921	1014	3735	16	57	11629
B Insurance	1362	184	−301	2	3	1244	1485	206	344	2	4	2033
C Real estate and business services	10122	13755	13546	235	38	37620	11562	15540	13050	230	51	40331
Real estate, except dwellings	2141	1126	1754	59	–	5080	2344	1374	1964	53	–	5735
Dwellings	–	11886	8613	112	12	20599	–	13224	7558	97	14	20865
9 Community, social and personal services	4031	1120	2353	78	178	7404	4465	1261	2803	107	224	8412
A Sanitary and similar services	387	686	−101	15	22	965	459	761	−90	19	14	1135
B Social and related community services	1520	134	1536	23	45	3168	1684	155	1684	32	53	3502
Educational services	256	73	35	–	16	348	267	81	25	5	19	359
Medical, dental, other health and veterinary services	793	45	1127	23	–	1988	904	52	1257	27	–	2240
C Recreational and cultural services	1605	237	367	17	108	2118	1759	283	576	23	155	2486
D Personal and household services	519	63	551	23	3	1153	563	62	633	33	2	1289
Total, Industries	138706	47806	75538	2645	3407	261288	151496	52116	81313	2799	3874	283850
Producers of government services	50885	3918	–	19	–	54822	55765	4448	–	20	–	60233
Other producers	5644	478	–	18	–	6140	6051	538	–	20	–	6609
Total	195235	52202	75538	2682	3407	322250	213312	57102	81313	2839	3874	350692
less: Imputed bank service charge	...	...	8989	...	...	8989	...	...	10576	...	...	10576
Import duties	...	...	...	...	...	...	...	...	...	...	...	...
Value added tax	...	...	...	...	...	...	...	...	...	...	...	...
Other adjustments [c]	1313	...	−1313	49634	7901	41733	561	...	−561	54549	7810	46739
Total	196548	52202	65236	52316	11308	354994	213873	57102	70176	57388	11684	386855

	1988						1989					
	Compensation of employees	Capital consumption	Net operating surplus	Indirect taxes	less: Subsidies received	Value added	Compensation of employees	Capital consumption	Net operating surplus	Indirect taxes	less: Subsidies received	Value added

All producers

1 Agriculture, hunting, forestry and fishing	4845	6358	16109	191	2764	24739	4955	6743	20060	214	3895	28077
A Agriculture and hunting	1977	4384	8138	155	2689	11965	2021	4611	11450	174	3810	14446
B Forestry and logging	2834	1834	7495	11	34	12140	2897	1991	8205	12	35	13070
C Fishing	34	140	476	25	41	634	37	141	405	28	50	561
2 Mining and quarrying	659	336	626	18	36	1603	641	356	1053	21	34	2037
A Coal mining	...	...	...	...	...	...	...	...	...	...	...	...
B Crude petroleum and natural gas production	...	...	...	...	...	...	...	...	...	...	...	...
C Metal ore mining	224	180	159	5	28	540	201	184	433	7	26	799
D Other mining	435	156	467	13	8	1063	440	172	620	14	8	1238
3 Manufacturing	55420	12301	28563	820	1132	95972	60073	13614	31660	943	1065	105225
A Manufacture of food, beverages and tobacco	6563	1502	3350	90	73	11432	6921	1637	3176	104	56	11782
B Textile, wearing apparel and leather industries	3621	527	756	39	127	4816	3452	556	711	44	85	4678

Finland

	1988							1989					
	Compensation of employees	Capital consumption	Net operating surplus	Indirect taxes	less: Subsidies received	Value added	Compensation of employees	Capital consumption	Net operating surplus	Indirect taxes	less: Subsidies received	Value added
C Manufacture of wood and wood products, including furniture [a]	3312	746	1156	70	82	5202	3868	804	1502	82	83	6173
D Manufacture of paper and paper products, printing and publishing	11744	3925	7376	187	234	22998	12926	4540	6427	215	195	23913
E Manufacture of chemicals and chemical petroleum, coal, rubber and plastic products	4831	1550	3254	75	72	9638	5313	1683	4355	87	93	11345
F Manufacture of non-metallic mineral products, except products of petroleum and coal	2317	503	1603	30	26	4427	2594	552	1953	36	38	5097
G Basic metal industries	2194	822	1701	37	26	4728	2350	889	2610	43	28	5864
H Manufacture of fabricated metal products, machinery and equipment	18882	2450	8281	263	443	29433	20580	2659	9704	301	459	32785
I Other manufacturing industries [a]	1956	276	1086	29	49	3298	2069	294	1222	31	28	3588
4 Electricity, gas and water	3797	3807	2501	47	87	10065	4040	4166	1042	55	58	9245
A Electricity, gas and steam	3490	3279	2361	44	59	9115	3719	3588	923	51	32	8249
B Water works and supply	307	528	140	3	28	950	321	578	119	4	26	996
5 Construction	23784	1492	7446	247	29	32940	28151	1712	11957	289	74	42035
6 Wholesale and retail trade, restaurants and hotels	34475	5639	10290	702	162	50944	39146	6387	10249	838	276	56344
A Wholesale and retail trade	28751	5127	8657	643	45	43133	32711	5821	8640	770	114	47828
B Restaurants and hotels	5724	512	1633	59	117	7811	6435	566	1609	68	162	8516
Restaurants	4024	269	1029	41	34	5329	4492	288	927	47	47	5707
Hotels and other lodging places	1700	243	604	18	83	2482	1943	278	682	21	115	2809
7 Transport, storage and communication	16943	6834	6115	329	85	30136	18961	7592	6769	365	96	33591
A Transport and storage	11532	5079	4626	321	85	21473	13053	5683	5395	355	91	24395
B Communication	5411	1755	1489	8	–	8663	5908	1909	1374	10	5	9196
8 Finance, insurance, real estate and business services	23457	19530	16861	463	176	60135	26908	23276	18354	546	264	68820
A Financial institutions [b]	8070	1135	3779	17	79	12922	8726	1282	5344	17	58	15311
B Insurance	1678	234	−1007	2	5	902	1860	275	−1546	3	6	586
C Real estate and business services	13709	18161	14089	444	92	46311	16322	21719	14556	526	200	52923
Real estate, except dwellings	2706	1771	2494	146	–	7117	3094	2401	2459	160	2	8112
Dwellings	–	15216	7560	146	33	22889	–	17876	7517	198	51	25540
9 Community, social and personal services	4964	1421	2996	115	251	9245	5703	1601	3411	154	219	10650
A Sanitary and similar services	507	843	−81	18	5	1282	609	929	18	26	18	1564
B Social and related community services	1888	180	1758	38	61	3803	2186	212	1853	50	96	4205
Educational services	300	89	26	6	22	399	365	98	28	9	33	467
Medical, dental, other health and veterinary services	1021	64	1353	32	–	2470	1163	79	1454	41	4	2733
C Recreational and cultural services	1923	333	609	31	183	2713	2181	395	669	39	71	3213
D Personal and household services	646	65	710	28	2	1447	727	65	871	39	34	1668

Finland

	1988						1989					
	Compensation of employees	Capital consumption	Net operating surplus	Indirect taxes	less: Subsidies received	Value added	Compensation of employees	Capital consumption	Net operating surplus	Indirect taxes	less: Subsidies received	Value added
Total, Industries	168344	57718	91507	2932	4722	315779	188578	65447	104555	3425	5981	356024
Producers of government services	61032	5037	–	22	–	66091	67522	5671	–	22	–	73215
Other producers	6876	611	–	20	–	7507	7525	695	–	20	–	8240
Total	236252	63366	91507	2974	4722	389377	263625	71813	104555	3467	5981	437479
less: Imputed bank service charge	...	...	12180	...	...	12180	...	...	14873	...	...	14873
Import duties	...	...	...	...	...	...	...	...	...	...	...	...
Value added tax	...	...	...	...	...	...	...	...	...	...	...	...
Other adjustments [c]	202	...	−202	63693	6549	57144	957	...	−957	72128	7736	64392
Total	236454	63366	79125	66667	11271	434341	264582	71813	88725	75595	13717	486998

	1990						1991					
	Compensation of employees	Capital consumption	Net operating surplus	Indirect taxes	less: Subsidies received	Value added	Compensation of employees	Capital consumption	Net operating surplus	Indirect taxes	less: Subsidies received	Value added
All producers												
1 Agriculture, hunting, forestry and fishing	5109	7215	20832	151	4264	29043	5180	7260	16752	145	5264	24073
A Agriculture and hunting	2173	4909	12392	110	4182	15402	2435	4826	11119	105	5151	13334
B Forestry and logging	2898	2164	8016	11	31	13058	2704	2290	5215	10	52	10167
C Fishing	38	142	424	30	51	583	41	144	418	30	61	572
2 Mining and quarrying	659	381	714	15	36	1733	671	386	696	13	37	1729
A Coal mining	...	...	...	...	...	...	...	...	...	...	...	...
B Crude petroleum and natural gas production	...	...	...	...	...	...	...	...	...	...	...	...
C Metal ore mining	168	190	89	3	14	436	177	185	42	3	16	391
D Other mining	491	191	625	12	22	1297	494	201	654	10	21	1338
3 Manufacturing	64538	14935	26493	589	1172	105383	60912	15779	13699	540	1263	89667
A Manufacture of food, beverages and tobacco	7458	1784	3147	62	60	12391	7380	1846	3925	56	64	13143
B Textile, wearing apparel and leather industries	3189	587	372	23	90	4081	2721	586	153	19	85	3394
C Manufacture of wood and wood products, including furniture [a]	4084	865	1653	55	96	6561	3474	898	125	52	82	4467
D Manufacture of paper and paper products, printing and publishing	13936	5118	3039	138	214	22017	13665	5641	−829	132	227	18382
E Manufacture of chemicals and chemical petroleum, coal, rubber and plastic products	5785	1824	4252	65	80	11846	5828	1896	3322	61	83	11024
F Manufacture of non-metallic mineral products, except products of petroleum and coal	2927	611	1591	22	34	5117	2623	643	860	22	40	4108
G Basic metal industries	2670	959	988	32	27	4622	2565	992	699	31	22	4265
H Manufacture of fabricated metal products, machinery and equipment	22325	2874	10324	171	539	35155	20634	2962	4823	145	614	27950
I Other manufacturing industries [a]	2164	313	1127	21	32	3593	2022	315	621	22	46	2934
4 Electricity, gas and water	4449	4535	530	54	64	9504	4590	4766	1743	51	91	11059
A Electricity, gas and steam	4091	3913	373	50	37	8390	4202	4111	1593	48	68	9886
B Water works and supply	358	622	157	4	27	1114	388	655	150	3	23	1173

Finland

	1990						1991					
	Compensation of employees	Capital consumption	Net operating surplus	Indirect taxes	less: Subsidies received	Value added	Compensation of employees	Capital consumption	Net operating surplus	Indirect taxes	less: Subsidies received	Value added
5 Construction	30780	1946	10622	194	75	43467	27903	2061	6876	174	52	36962
6 Wholesale and retail trade, restaurants and hotels	42044	7203	8457	563	296	57971	40207	7568	4143	511	285	52144
A Wholesale and retail trade ..	34923	6563	6921	520	130	48797	33469	6892	2785	473	70	43549
B Restaurants and hotels	7121	640	1536	43	166	9174	6738	676	1358	38	215	8595
Restaurants	4944	318	957	30	48	6201	4674	338	951	27	62	5928
Hotels and other lodging places	2177	322	579	13	118	2973	2064	338	407	11	153	2667
7 Transport, storage and communication	20915	7835	7413	371	128	36406	20381	8011	7580	396	242	36126
A Transport and storage	14578	5756	5841	353	121	26407	13931	5828	5846	380	208	25777
B Communication	6337	2079	1572	18	7	9999	6450	2183	1734	16	34	10349
8 Finance, insurance, real estate and business services	29907	26202	21982	458	338	78211	30164	26837	21824	415	411	78829
A Financial institutions [b]	9236	1421	7517	17	72	18119	9293	1466	4909	16	82	15602
B Insurance	2069	317	–405	3	5	1979	2037	332	16	3	6	2382
C Real estate and business services	18602	24464	14870	438	261	58113	18834	25039	16899	396	323	60845
Real estate, except dwellings	3347	2926	2241	147	2	8659	3372	3115	1918	129	4	8530
Dwellings	–	19845	8372	114	106	28225	–	20067	13082	99	121	33127
9 Community, social and personal services	6546	1808	3850	136	258	12082	6658	1972	3910	137	322	12355
A Sanitary and similar services	690	1014	83	28	16	1799	697	1069	114	30	14	1896
B Social and related community services	2524	245	1871	40	113	4567	2576	274	2021	40	167	4744
Educational services	380	107	24	5	38	478	344	110	88	5	65	482
Medical, dental, other health and veterinary services	1394	95	1504	35	5	3023	1487	111	1648	35	5	3276
C Recreational and cultural services	2524	474	850	31	84	3795	2527	542	645	30	102	3642
D Personal and household services	808	75	1046	37	45	1921	858	87	1130	37	39	2073
Total, Industries	204947	72060	100893	2531	6631	373800	196666	74640	77223	2382	7967	342944
Producers of government services	75449	6673	–	26	–	82148	84015	6743	–	25	–	90783
Other producers	8360	779	–	25	–	9164	8567	787	–	24	–	9378
Total	288756	79512	100893	2582	6631	465112	289248	82170	77223	2431	7967	443105
less: Imputed bank service charge	...	...	17000	...	...	17000	...	...	15329	...	...	15329
Import duties	...	...	...	...	...	...	...	...	...	...	...	...
Value added tax	...	...	...	...	...	...	...	...	...	...	...	...
Other adjustments [c]	12	...	–12	75443	8125	67318	527	...	–527	72299	9207	63092
Total	288768	79512	83881	78025	14756	515430	289775	82170	61367	74730	17174	490868

	1992						1993					
	Compensation of employees	Capital consumption	Net operating surplus	Indirect taxes	less: Subsidies received	Value added	Compensation of employees	Capital consumption	Net operating surplus	Indirect taxes	less: Subsidies received	Value added
All producers												
1 Agriculture, hunting, forestry and fishing	4701	7133	15084	135	5585	21468	4447	7109	15235	130	4840	22081
A Agriculture and hunting	2287	4735	9504	99	5479	11146	2154	4717	9870	93	4741	12093
B Forestry and logging	2367	2251	5060	9	50	9637	2245	2226	4831	8	33	9277

Finland

	1992						1993					
	Compensation of employees	Capital consumption	Net operating surplus	Indirect taxes	less: Subsidies received	Value added	Compensation of employees	Capital consumption	Net operating surplus	Indirect taxes	less: Subsidies received	Value added
C Fishing	47	147	520	27	56	685	48	166	534	29	66	711
2 Mining and quarrying	642	371	809	12	34	1800	611	368	731	10	33	1687
A Coal mining	...	...	...	...	...	...	...	...	...	...	...	...
B Crude petroleum and natural gas production	...	...	...	...	...	...	...	...	...	...	...	...
C Metal ore mining	172	162	27	2	10	353	160	146	–1	2	10	297
D Other mining	470	209	782	10	24	1447	451	222	732	8	23	1390
3 Manufacturing	57142	16611	19651	488	1466	92426	56420	17568	29212	491	1875	101816
A Manufacture of food, beverages and tobacco	7167	1978	4037	51	78	13155	6846	2096	4673	48	78	13585
B Textile, wearing apparel and leather industries	2267	595	449	17	94	3234	2149	599	500	15	61	3202
C Manufacture of wood and wood products, including furniture [a]	3156	929	987	48	75	5045	3263	960	1999	54	165	6111
D Manufacture of paper and paper products, printing and publishing	12996	6022	846	119	206	19777	12791	6468	3622	122	336	22667
E Manufacture of chemicals and chemical petroleum, coal, rubber and plastic products	5606	1961	3154	55	104	10672	5778	2066	3886	63	123	11670
F Manufacture of non-metallic mineral products, except products of petroleum and coal	2170	661	496	20	39	3308	1897	684	638	18	72	3165
G Basic metal industries	2620	1062	1684	28	33	5361	2669	1119	2797	32	98	6519
H Manufacture of fabricated metal products, machinery and equipment	19394	3081	7387	131	771	29222	19379	3242	10334	121	662	32414
I Other manufacturing industries [a]	1766	322	611	19	66	2652	1648	334	763	18	280	2483
4 Electricity, gas and water	4572	4907	1561	46	83	11003	4144	5123	2166	51	150	11334
A Electricity, gas and steam	4195	4255	1318	43	63	9748	3776	4468	1841	48	114	10019
B Water works and supply	377	652	243	3	20	1255	368	655	325	3	36	1315
5 Construction	23122	2110	711	158	60	26041	19017	2108	–190	140	77	20998
6 Wholesale and retail trade, restaurants and hotels	36904	7728	3780	462	465	48409	34615	8206	4487	431	338	47401
A Wholesale and retail trade	30749	7046	2615	428	222	40616	28866	7519	3537	402	185	40139
B Restaurants and hotels	6155	682	1165	34	243	7793	5749	687	950	29	153	7262
Restaurants	4335	349	705	24	70	5343	4004	360	664	21	44	5005
Hotels and other lodging places	1820	333	460	10	173	2450	1745	327	286	8	109	2257
7 Transport, storage and communication	20007	8345	8051	359	278	36484	19286	9195	8613	402	236	37260
A Transport and storage	13529	6013	6223	345	244	25866	13349	6695	6683	389	227	26889
B Communication	6478	2332	1828	14	34	10618	5937	2500	1930	13	9	10371
8 Finance, insurance, real estate and business services	28333	25175	21970	371	346	75503	26901	24304	32956	331	349	84143
A Financial institutions [b]	8673	1460	1425	14	122	11450	8122	1461	5093	12	197	14491
B Insurance	1994	337	–793	3	8	1533	1961	349	591	3	7	2897
C Real estate and business services	17666	23378	21338	354	216	62520	16818	22494	27272	316	145	66755
Real estate, except dwellings	3674	3041	907	117	9	7730	3688	3020	601	102	2	7409
Dwellings	–	18361	18933	90	–	37384	–	17332	23700	77	–	41109

Finland

	1992						1993					
	Compensation of employees	Capital consumption	Net operating surplus	Indirect taxes	less: Subsidies received	Value added	Compensation of employees	Capital consumption	Net operating surplus	Indirect taxes	less: Subsidies received	Value added
9 Community, social and personal services	6648	2091	4209	123	333	12738	6343	2248	4168	123	223	12659
A Sanitary and similar services	716	1095	254	27	15	2077	711	1143	272	28	54	2100
B Social and related community services	2576	301	1923	36	198	4638	2373	329	1916	35	118	4535
Educational services	333	117	114	3	77	490	345	129	117	3	46	548
Medical, dental, other health and veterinary services	1496	124	1549	33	18	3184	1329	131	1546	32	11	3027
C Recreational and cultural services	2539	598	819	27	96	3887	2548	657	779	26	41	3969
D Personal and household services	817	97	1213	33	24	2136	711	119	1201	34	10	2055
Total, Industries	182071	74471	75826	2154	8650	325872	171784	76229	97378	2109	8121	339379
Producers of government services	84141	6631	–	23	–	90795	79669	6787	–	19	–	86475
Other producers	8746	790	–	22	–	9558	8772	803	–	18	–	9593
Total	274958	81892	75826	2199	8650	426225	260225	83819	97378	2146	8121	435447
less: Imputed bank service charge	...	...	10513	...	...	10513	...	...	14205	...	...	14205
Import duties	...	...	...	...	...	...	...	...	...	...	...	...
Value added tax	...	...	...	...	...	...	...	...	...	...	...	...
Other adjustments [c]	–1342	...	1342	69444	8378	61066	–2150	...	2150	69410	8255	61155
Total	273616	81892	66655	71643	17028	476778	258075	83819	85323	71556	16376	482397

	1994						1995					
	Compensation of employees	Capital consumption	Net operating surplus	Indirect taxes	less: Subsidies received	Value added	Compensation of employees	Capital consumption	Net operating surplus	Indirect taxes	less: Subsidies received	Value added
All producers													
1 Agriculture, hunting, forestry and fishing	4452	6785	18390	137	4500	25264	4619	5893	19766	128	8486	21920
A Agriculture and hunting	2210	4542	10557	83	4417	12975	2080	3694	10923	80	8393	8384
B Forestry and logging	2198	2096	7299	6	29	11570	2482	2062	8429	6	31	12948
C Fishing	44	147	534	48	54	719	57	137	414	42	62	588
2 Mining and quarrying	600	352	1004	9	29	1936	666	350	961	9	28	1958
A Coal mining	...	...	...	...	...	...	...	...	...	...	...	...
B Crude petroleum and natural gas production	...	...	...	...	...	...	...	...	...	...	...	...
C Metal ore mining	155	130	1	2	9	279	140	121	–72	2	8	183
D Other mining	445	222	1003	7	20	1657	526	229	1033	7	20	1775
3 Manufacturing	60498	17872	35297	319	1249	112737	68668	17960	43150	307	1254	128831
A Manufacture of food, beverages and tobacco	6803	2145	3936	39	40	12883	7115	2124	3316	37	39	12553
B Textile, wearing apparel and leather industries	2168	594	842	13	53	3564	2289	573	762	13	42	3595
C Manufacture of wood and wood products, including furniture [a]	3734	974	2946	28	95	7587	4028	950	1932	21	93	6838
D Manufacture of paper and paper products, printing and publishing	13172	6548	6365	72	229	25928	14029	6582	11868	69	224	32324
E Manufacture of chemicals and chemical petroleum, coal, rubber and plastic products	6037	2095	5291	30	84	13369	6644	2131	4476	29	81	13199

Finland

	1994						1995					
	Compensation of employees	Capital consumption	Net operating surplus	Indirect taxes	less: Subsidies received	Value added	Compensation of employees	Capital consumption	Net operating surplus	Indirect taxes	less: Subsidies received	Value added
F Manufacture of non-metallic mineral products, except products of petroleum and coal	1941	690	855	17	39	3464	2045	701	893	17	39	3617
G Basic metal industries	2855	1146	3049	13	57	7006	3162	1168	4076	13	54	8365
H Manufacture of fabricated metal products, machinery and equipment	22016	3340	11256	97	436	36273	27343	3398	14997	93	482	45349
I Other manufacturing industries [a]	1772	340	757	10	216	2663	2013	333	830	15	200	2991
4 Electricity, gas and water	4169	5192	3020	31	131	12281	4232	5286	3564	30	128	12984
A Electricity, gas and steam	3800	4546	2620	27	100	10893	3850	4640	3069	26	98	11487
B Water works and supply	369	646	400	4	31	1388	382	646	495	4	30	1497
5 Construction	17827	2009	3407	126	66	23303	19305	1908	7061	120	65	28329
6 Wholesale and retail trade, restaurants and hotels	34766	7870	8126	414	349	50827	36698	7675	8466	389	259	52969
A Wholesale and retail trade	29014	7219	6716	388	159	43178	30612	7053	6921	364	79	44871
B Restaurants and hotels	5752	651	1410	26	190	7649	6086	622	1545	25	180	8098
Restaurants	3975	329	1003	19	61	5265	4224	308	990	18	59	5481
Hotels and other lodging places	1777	322	407	7	129	2384	1862	314	555	7	121	2617
7 Transport, storage and communication	19830	8884	10295	351	246	39114	20952	8708	11923	291	250	41624
A Transport and storage	13682	6378	8641	341	236	28806	14753	6147	9648	282	239	30591
B Communication	6148	2506	1654	10	10	10308	6199	2561	2275	9	11	11033
8 Finance, insurance, real estate and business services	27503	26008	33526	300	463	86874	29044	28001	35612	286	392	92551
A Financial institutions [b]	7682	1421	5875	10	298	14690	7226	1321	6265	9	236	14585
B Insurance	2065	365	−455	3	3	1975	2398	398	185	3	3	2981
C Real estate and business services	17756	24222	28106	287	162	70209	19420	26282	29162	274	153	74985
Real estate, except dwellings	3733	3050	302	83	4	7164	3651	3086	1010	80	4	7823
Dwellings	–	19120	23256	67	–	42443	–	21166	22265	65	–	43496
9 Community, social and personal services	6339	2252	4237	139	303	12664	6642	2211	4495	131	256	13223
A Sanitary and similar services	782	1126	463	32	83	2320	827	1108	600	30	69	2496
B Social and related community services	2386	337	1755	38	139	4377	2438	342	1866	36	119	4563
Educational services	358	123	78	3	54	508	378	119	83	3	49	534
Medical, dental, other health and veterinary services	1300	141	1430	35	14	2892	1333	150	1501	33	9	3008
C Recreational and cultural services	2505	665	863	29	58	4004	2711	643	913	27	47	4247
D Personal and household services	666	124	1156	40	23	1963	666	118	1116	38	21	1917
Total, Industries	175984	77224	117302	1826	7336	365000	190826	77992	134998	1691	11118	394389
Producers of government services	79638	7377	–	18	–	87033	83520	8100	–	17	–	91637
Other producers	8640	879	–	16	–	9535	9133	935	–	15	–	10083
Total	264262	85480	117302	1860	7336	461568	283479	87027	134998	1723	11118	496109
less: Imputed bank service charge	...	...	14396	...	...	14396	...	...	14142	...	...	14142
Import duties	...	...	...	...	...	...	...	...	...	...	...	...
Value added tax	...	...	...	...	...	...	...	...	...	...	...	...
Other adjustments [c]	−487	...	487	72340	8520	63820	69935	...	2039	74955	7059	...
Total	263775	85480	103393	74200	15856	510992	281440	87027	122895	76678	18177	549863

Finland

	1996						1997					
	Compensation of employees	Capital consumption	Net operating surplus	Indirect taxes	less: Subsidies received	Value added	Compensation of employees	Capital consumption	Net operating surplus	Indirect taxes	less: Subsidies received	Value added
	All producers												
1 Agriculture, hunting, forestry and fishing	4267	5775	18590	127	8370	20389	...	...	...	...	...	...
A Agriculture and hunting	1984	3527	10346	79	8239	7697	...	...	...	...	...	...
B Forestry and logging	2225	2116	7845	6	32	12160	...	...	...	...	...	...
C Fishing	58	132	399	42	99	532	...	...	...	...	...	...
2 Mining and quarrying	670	354	943	10	25	1952	...	...	...	...	...	...
A Coal mining	...	...	...	...	...	...	...	...	...	...	...	...
B Crude petroleum and natural gas production	...	...	...	...	...	...	...	...	...	...	...	...
C Metal ore mining	135	109	−68	1	7	170	...	...	...	...	...	...
D Other mining	535	245	1011	9	18	1782	...	...	...	...	...	...
3 Manufacturing	70846	18556	40694	348	1233	129211	...	...	...	...	...	...
A Manufacture of food, beverages and tobacco	7114	2162	3373	41	40	12650	...	...	...	...	...	...
B Textile, wearing apparel and leather industries	2252	547	819	14	44	3588	...	...	...	...	...	...
C Manufacture of wood and wood products, including furniture [a]	3921	967	1166	23	94	5983	...	...	...	...	...	...
D Manufacture of paper and paper products, printing and publishing	14098	6826	8444	74	210	29232	...	...	...	...	...	...
E Manufacture of chemicals and chemical petroleum, coal, rubber and plastic products	6789	2179	4421	32	77	13344	...	...	...	...	...	...
F Manufacture of non-metallic mineral products, except products of petroleum and coal	2051	726	1119	19	40	3875	...	...	...	...	...	...
G Basic metal industries	3321	1262	2550	14	50	7097	...	...	...	...	...	...
H Manufacture of fabricated metal products, machinery and equipment	29277	3561	17949	116	478	50425	...	...	...	...	...	...
I Other manufacturing industries [a]	2023	326	853	15	200	3017	...	...	...	...	...	...
4 Electricity, gas and water	4339	5369	4020	34	121	13641	...	...	...	...	...	...
A Electricity, gas and steam	3940	4717	3547	29	93	12140	...	...	...	...	...	...
B Water works and supply	399	652	473	5	28	1501	...	...	...	...	...	...
5 Construction	20025	1892	7227	133	57	29220	...	...	...	...	...	...
6 Wholesale and retail trade, restaurants and hotels	38358	7590	9297	456	227	55474	...	...	...	...	...	...
A Wholesale and retail trade	31896	6988	7701	429	63	46951	...	...	...	...	...	...
B Restaurants and hotels	6462	602	1596	27	164	8523	...	...	...	...	...	...
Restaurants	4511	293	1006	19	55	5774	...	...	...	...	...	...
Hotels and other lodging places	1951	309	590	8	109	2749	...	...	...	...	...	...
7 Transport, storage and communication	21399	8704	14069	380	260	44292	...	...	...	...	...	...
A Transport and storage	15065	6098	10797	371	250	32081	...	...	...	...	...	...
B Communication	6334	2606	3272	9	10	12211	...	...	...	...	...	...
8 Finance, insurance, real estate and business services	31162	28005	40763	317	321	99926	...	...	...	...	...	...
A Financial institutions [b]	7195	1166	6677	11	138	14911	...	...	...	...	...	...
B Insurance	2320	406	1981	4	3	4708	...	...	...	...	...	...

Finland

	1996						1997					
	Compensation of employees	Capital consumption	Net operating surplus	Indirect taxes	less: Subsidies received	Value added	Compensation of employees	Capital consumption	Net operating surplus	Indirect taxes	less: Subsidies received	Value added
C Real estate and business services	21647	26433	32105	302	180	80307	...	...	...	...	...	...
Real estate, except dwellings	3894	3088	1038	83	3	8100	...	...	...	...	...	...
Dwellings	–	21335	24341	66	16	45726	...	...	...	...	...	...
9 Community, social and personal services	6901	2195	5030	165	239	14052	...	...	...	...	...	...
A Sanitary and similar services	877	1109	755	39	59	2721	...	...	...	...	...	...
B Social and related community services	2502	346	2057	44	122	4827	...	...	...	...	...	...
Educational services	394	114	96	4	51	557	...	...	...	...	...	...
Medical, dental, other health and veterinary services	1358	157	1660	40	9	3206	...	...	...	...	...	...
C Recreational and cultural services	2845	624	1082	33	39	4545	...	...	...	...	...	...
D Personal and household services	677	116	1136	49	19	1959	...	...	...	...	...	...
Total, Industries	197967	78440	140633	1970	10853	408157	...	...	...	...	...	...
Producers of government services	87850	8267	–	60	–	96177	...	...	...	...	...	...
Other producers	9553	991	–	17	–	10561	...	...	...	...	...	...
Total	295370	87698	140633	2047	10853	514895	...	...	...	...	...	...
less: Imputed bank service charge	...	...	13347	...	...	13347	...	...	...	...	...	...
Import duties	...	...	...	...	...	...	...	...	...	...	...	...
Value added tax	...	...	...	...	...	...	...	...	...	...	...	...
Other adjustments [c]	76016	...	642	81164	5790	...	...	...	...	...	...	...
Total	294728	87698	127928	83211	16643	576922	...	...	...	...	...	...

a Furniture is included in item "Other manufacturing industries".
b Item "Financial institutions" include activities auxiliary to financial intermediation and insurance.
c Includes import duties.

France

General note

The preparation of national accounts statistics in France is undertaken by the Institut national de la statistique et des études économiques (INSEE), Paris, with the cooperation of some other administrative bodies. The official estimates are published in *Comptes et indicateurs économiques—Rapport sur les Comptes de la Nation*, which is issued annually in June in the *INSEE-Résultats* series. The estimates are generally in accordance with the classifications and definitions recommended in the United Nations System of National Accounts (1968 SNA). However, it is worth noting that they are elaborated according to French classifications and guidelines of the *Système Elargi de Comptabilité Nationale*, which is the French version of the *European System of Integrated Economic Accounts* (ESA). Input-output tables valued at market prices are an integral part of the French national accounts and are published every year at the same time. When the scope and coverage of the estimates differ for conceptual or statistical reasons from the definitions and classifications recommended in SNA, a footnote is indicated to the relevant tables.

Gross domestic product

Gross domestic product (GDP) is estimated through three different approaches: the production, the expenditure and the income approach, which are used to derived GDP by kind of economic activity, by expenditure and by cost structure, respectively. The input-output table allows a partial synthesis between the production and the expenditure approaches. The final synthesis is based on the production accounts by industry. It actually concerns a part of the national economy only: some accounts (government and private non-profit administrations, financial institutions, insurance companies, large public corporations) which are integratedly built for the industries and for the corresponding sectors are taken to be final and are not questioned at this stage. Reconciling estimates relating to industries and to sectors is performed by distributing value added discrepancies among them or adjusting the global value added estimate: in this case, the distribution of total supply between intermediate consumption and final uses is revised and/or production accounts are corrected for institutional sectors which are considered to be questionable.

Expenditures on the gross domestic product

For each commodity of the input-output table classification, a commodity-flow balance is built, generally by aggregating and completing balances elaborated at a more detailed level of the classification. Sources allowing the household private consumption to be estimated are infra-annual inquiries on production combined with foreign trade data at a very detailed level of the classification, households surveys and specific informations relating to such expenses as health or dwelling. Estimates relating to goods are compared with informations about the retail trade turnover. Gross fixed capital formation estimates proceed from the commodity flow balances compared with informations originating in the investors business accounts at a rather aggregated level. Changes in producers stocks come from the breakdown, by product, of stocks held at the beginning and at the end of the year by enterprises and from an estimate of the holding gains accruing on goods held in stock. Users and trade stocks are estimated by composing intermediate and households consumptions estimates in the commodity flows. Foreign trade comes from the customs statistics and the balance of payments services exchanges, completed by some ad-hoc sources.

Cost structure of the gross domestic product

Three basic sources are used to estimate the cost-components of the different institutional sectors. First, individual accounting data which are not adjusted: government administrations, large public corporations, financial institutions and insurance companies. Second, data on firms (non-financial corporations excluding large public corporations and private unincorporated non-agricultural enterprises) originating from fiscal informations which are adjusted to take into account absences, tax cheating and evading and made consistent with corresponding data obtain from the first source. Third, statistics not originating in the centralization of individual accounting data: unincorporated agricultural enterprises, some productions of households (rental services of dwellings, self consumption of agricultural products, domestic services), private non-profit institutions.

Gross domestic product by kind of activity

The estimates of the production of non-financial and non-agricultural firms by industry, except large public national firm start from the sales as reported in the firms' fiscal returns. The part of the production which is not properly reported in the sales—inter-establishment deliveries, production for own capital formation, subcontracting and processing of customers owned materials—is added up in order to obtain non-stocked production estimates. Accounting data of financial institutions, insurance companies and large public corporations which are processed separately make it possible to estimate the output of the corresponding industries. Agriculture production indirectly estimated from products sources while trade output is estimated from trade margins by product and type of use. The estimates of the production of government industries come from data supplied by concerned units. Non-market services output is obtained as the sum of the costs. With the exception of some rows or columns, or

France

more generally of some cells, of the intermediate consumptions table, the intermediate consumptions are calculated, for current year in an indirect way, that is, the principle consists in projecting the preceding year table assuming that the technical coefficients remain unchanged at constant prices. The adding up of the estimates in row, i.e., the projected total intermediate consumption for each product, is compared with the intermediate demand as estimated from the commodity-flow balances (see gross domestic product by expenditure).

1.1 Expenditure on the gross domestic product, in current prices

Million French francs

	1986	1987	1988	1989	1990	1991	1992	1993	1994	1995	1996	1997
1 Government final consumption expenditure	959509	1004657	1058400	1106075	1170435	1238998	1320450	1402898	1438634	1476381	1539007	1573054
2 Private final consumption expenditure	3062808	3249514	3444407	3671748	3878580	4055649	4208087	4309128	4461087	4605910	4783518	4877929
A Households	3049520	3235582	3429508	3655793	3861322	4037525	4189535	4290741	4442335	4586648	4763486	4857296
B Private non-profit institutions serving households	13288	13932	14899	15955	17258	18124	18552	18387	18752	19262	20032	20633
3 Gross capital formation	994673	1075447	1228608	1373822	1462303	1457983	1376437	1213460	1328878	1398584	1343708	1365605
A Increase in stocks	17156	20679	40295	59270	70945	21061	−28972	−97933	−3223	23749	−28345	−22483
B Gross fixed capital formation	977517	1054768	1188313	1314552	1391358	1436922	1405409	1311393	1332101	1374835	1372053	1388088
Residential buildings	268128	283307	308052	331217	344902	353182	349074	327160	338151	346829	348681	351950
Non-residential buildings	283324	304266	345184	379770	404248	434344	442069	424524	407394	405229	389774	392335
Other construction and land improvement, etc.												
Other	426065	467195	535077	603565	642208	649396	614266	559709	586556	622777	633598	643803
4 Exports of goods and services	1074095	1101383	1221304	1411087	1467972	1538062	1588103	1556368	1684130	1802974	1897678	2168498
5 less: Imports of goods and services	1021789	1094349	1217627	1403052	1469802	1514461	1493531	1404767	1523075	1621458	1692180	1848001
equals: Gross domestic product	5069296	5336652	5735092	6159680	6509488	6776231	6999546	7077087	7389654	7662391	7871731	8137085

1.2 Expenditure on the gross domestic product, in constant prices

Million French francs

	1986	1987	1988	1989	1990	1991	1992	1993	1994	1995	1996	1997
At constant prices of: 1980												
1 Government final consumption expenditure	585855	602353	622838	625494	638447	656280	678707	702495	710191	709994	728357	736965
2 Private final consumption expenditure	1894291	1948459	2012059	2073624	2129872	2158815	2187838	2191318	2221464	2258256	2302913	2322782
A Households	1886019	1939871	2003042	2064262	2119975	2148656	2177695	2181485	2211542	2248287	2292804	2312433
B Private non-profit institutions serving households	8272	8588	9017	9362	9897	10159	10143	9833	9922	9969	10109	10349
3 Gross capital formation	656419	690068	757943	824667	852684	826608	783764	676876	746737	774525	745621	752521
A Increase in stocks	23251	26306	30494	39969	45652	19174	−1181	−55661	4859	14263	−10931	−5508
B Gross fixed capital formation	633168	663762	727449	784698	807032	807434	784945	732537	741878	760262	756552	758029
Residential buildings	177377	181141	191270	201810	204507	200186	193848	178441	183382	186211	183032	181460
Non-residential buildings	188960	196935	217083	233647	242246	250734	252018	238885	228116	224218	211918	209426
Other construction and land improvement, etc.												
Other	266831	285686	319096	349241	360279	356514	339079	315211	330380	349833	361602	367143
4 Exports of goods and services	686413	707373	764552	842590	887719	924058	969313	965383	1023016	1087815	1144339	1283234
5 less: Imports of goods and services	718342	773744	840080	908005	963623	992992	1005293	969825	1034392	1087178	1119733	1205773
equals: Gross domestic product	3104636	3174509	3317312	3458370	3545099	3572769	3614329	3566247	3667016	3743412	3801497	3889729

France

1.3 Cost components of the gross domestic product

Million French francs

	1986	1987	1988	1989	1990	1991	1992	1993	1994	1995	1996	1997
1 Indirect taxes, net	627563	667420	747551	796725	846942	851103	861506	865322	930400	976588	1008334	1053325
A Indirect taxes	785542	836125	891710	934229	983429	995345	1015800	1035458	1102813	1155070	1221100	1275264
B less: Subsidies	157979	168705	144159	137504	136487	144242	154294	170136	172413	178482	212766	221939
2 Consumption of fixed capital	631975	673500	725034	776143	828961	880117	905901	925815	954624	983997	1000996	1031616
3 Compensation of employees paid by resident producers to ..	2708114	2821197	2976425	3161614	3371797	3531792	3668567	3738938	3829366	3980473	4115718	4221754
A Resident households	2688804	2804228	2956067	3146024	3354073	3511656	3645556	3717196	3807223	3962234	4100545	4208684
B Rest of the world	19310	16969	20358	15590	17724	20136	23011	21742	22143	18239	15173	13070
4 Operating surplus	1101644	1174535	1286082	1425198	1461788	1513219	1563572	1547012	1675265	1721333	1746683	1830390
A Corporate and quasi-corporate enterprises	368361	414130	493672	545243	506886	535948	527515	502699	607966	595206	600395	650076
B Private unincorporated enterprises [a]	732714	756472	794645	885146	944150	979219	1032804	1039174	1076889	1125719	1157672	1183790
C General government	569	3933	−2235	−5191	10752	−1948	3253	5139	−9590	408	−11384	−3476
Statistical discrepancy	...	...	...	...	...	...	...	...	−1	...	...	...
equals: Gross domestic product	5069296	5336652	5735092	6159680	6509488	6776231	6999546	7077087	7389654	7662391	7871731	8137085

[a] Private unincorporated enterprises includes households.

1.4 General government current receipts and disbursements

Million French francs

	1986	1987	1988	1989	1990	1991	1992	1993	1994	1995	1996	1997
Receipts												
1 Operating surplus	569	3933	−2235	−5191	10752	−1948	3253	5139	−9590	408	−11384	−3476
2 Property and entrepreneurial income	73895	66531	62550	70708	80021	78550	76849	75013	60594	57702	60724	59213
3 Taxes, fees and contributions	2170224	2310033	2439819	2616467	2769595	2875589	2953964	3029483	3165409	3312903	3510047	3660696
A Indirect taxes [a]	736494	781946	829419	873123	922814	926557	950891	977592	1042367	1091294	1165980	1218894
B Direct taxes	469768	499110	514221	553220	581504	632890	630157	651780	694958	730258	778620	863736
C Social security contributions	955257	1019205	1086937	1179692	1253800	1304210	1360258	1387017	1414447	1479478	1550742	1558420
D Compulsory fees, fines and penalties	8705	9772	9242	10432	11477	11932	12658	13094	13637	11873	14705	19646
4 Other current transfers	134054	142355	171395	159181	164123	195912	204995	210721	210665	222245	235499	238207
Total current receipts of general government	2378742	2522852	2671529	2841165	3024491	3148103	3239061	3320356	3427078	3593258	3794886	3954640
Disbursements												
1 Government final consumption expenditure	959509	1004657	1058400	1106075	1170435	1238998	1320450	1402898	1438634	1476381	1539007	1573054
A Compensation of employees	712439	733702	763439	799813	841269	886661	941529	994326	1032223	1076909	1119811	1146314
B Consumption of fixed capital	77663	83510	90288	97715	105885	115546	123868	131454	138100	146713	152733	156581
C Purchases of goods and services, net	153324	170706	187572	190105	203423	215910	232428	252743	242345	225793	237740	241310
D less: Own-account fixed capital formation	...	...	...	...	...	...	...	...	...	...	...	...
E Indirect taxes paid, net	16083	16739	17101	18442	19858	20881	22625	24375	25966	26966	28723	28849
2 Property income	145927	147570	152362	168485	191321	208554	237383	261616	279655	308419	314994	306834
A Interest	145859	147497	152287	168366	191222	208442	237253	261476	279463	308323	314900	306742
B Net land rent and royalties	68	73	75	119	99	112	130	140	192	96	94	92
3 Subsidies	118625	117683	102041	102657	101086	102748	112922	110256	118667	124946	159281	169078

France

Million French francs	1986	1987	1988	1989	1990	1991	1992	1993	1994	1995	1996	1997
4 Other current transfers	1212164	1269650	1350189	1425546	1520469	1635045	1746594	1870762	1921452	1986793	2067084	2149891
A Social security benefits	880391	913086	978761	1039064	1107756	1183483	1262220	1337635	1361993	1408506	1471932	1532519
B Social assistance grants	129284	130718	138284	143098	152362	163752	172695	194283	212281	219640	214243	219742
C Other	202489	225846	233144	243384	260351	287810	311679	338844	347178	358647	380909	397630
5 Net saving	−57483	−16708	8537	38402	41180	−37242	−178288	−325176	−331330	−303281	−285480	−244217
Total current disbursements and net saving of general government	2378742	2522852	2671529	2841165	3024491	3148103	3239061	3320356	3427078	3593258	3794886	3954640

a Net of indirect taxes to supranational organizations.

1.5 Current income and outlay of corporate and quasi-corporate enterprises, summary

Million French francs	1986	1987	1988	1989	1990	1991	1992	1993	1994	1995	1996	1997
Receipts												
1 Operating surplus	368361	414130	493672	545243	506886	535948	527515	502699	607966	595206	600395	650076
2 Property and entrepreneurial income received	1155200	1161873	1286828	1489734	1663361	1842918	1926488	2089111	1805532	1887912	1850534	1858060
3 Current transfers	280272	305376	313287	318409	370217	381647	400190	418186	424579	469385	440934	440883
Total current receipts	1803833	1881379	2093787	2353386	2540464	2760513	2854193	3009996	2838077	2952503	2891863	2949019
Disbursements												
1 Property and entrepreneurial income	1216143	1230903	1340292	1574577	1768150	2003767	2077652	2231136	1938176	2017570	1982163	2005516
2 Direct taxes and other current payments to general government	136134	150124	162539	180722	186607	168871	146728	147829	162962	176122	185484	218405
3 Other current transfers	294334	308091	343499	340248	386143	403073	424783	440280	439793	479973	480096	477027
4 Net saving	157222	192261	247457	257839	199564	184802	205030	190751	297146	278838	244120	248071
Total current disbursements and net saving	1803833	1881379	2093787	2353386	2540464	2760513	2854193	3009996	2838077	2952503	2891863	2949019

1.6 Current income and outlay of households and non-profit institutions

Million French francs	1986	1987	1988	1989	1990	1991	1992	1993	1994	1995	1996	1997
Receipts												
1 Compensation of employees	2700561	2816655	2972468	3161822	3370516	3531133	3664892	3737354	3827608	3984477	4120343	4231878
A From resident producers	2688804	2804228	2956067	3146024	3354073	3511656	3645556	3717196	3807223	3962234	4100545	4208684
B From rest of the world	11757	12427	16401	15798	16443	19477	19336	20158	20385	22243	19798	23194
2 Operating surplus of private unincorporated enterprises	732714	756472	794645	885146	944150	979219	1032804	1039174	1076888	1125719	1157672	1183790
3 Property and entrepreneurial income	306159	329982	349034	422604	460835	532224	552831	553075	530711	576616	577239	616785
4 Current transfers	1386675	1440181	1543753	1627775	1749096	1860171	1982828	2102342	2153647	2233702	2317108	2381053
A Social security benefits	896206	930719	999470	1061412	1131617	1209285	1289790	1367969	1395965	1442474	1511231	1573248
B Social assistance grants	131665	133238	140997	146029	155572	167145	176176	197747	215838	223289	218047	223670
C Other	358804	376224	403286	420334	461907	483741	516862	536626	541844	567939	587830	584135
Total current receipts	5126109	5343290	5659900	6097347	6524597	6902747	7233355	7431945	7588854	7920514	8172362	8413506
Disbursements												
1 Private final consumption expenditure	3062808	3249514	3444407	3671748	3878580	4055649	4208087	4309128	4461087	4605910	4783518	4877929
2 Property income	182239	187838	213448	250163	275549	278999	295079	279055	230214	231024	224558	218019

France

Million French francs

	1986	1987	1988	1989	1990	1991	1992	1993	1994	1995	1996	1997
3 Direct taxes and other current transfers n.e.c. to general government	1317128	1402602	1475078	1595046	1695219	1816203	1893700	1945287	2006288	2096812	2215704	2283788
A Social security contributions	979420	1048753	1119307	1217772	1294247	1346155	1403743	1434403	1467218	1537088	1614980	1626078
B Direct taxes	331724	347117	348497	368774	391866	460760	480032	500363	528039	549480	588254	640783
C Fees, fines and penalties	5984	6732	7274	8500	9106	9288	9925	10521	11031	10244	12470	16927
4 Other current transfers	277099	286446	297139	311250	344988	358805	384404	404956	410453	432658	442968	441497
5 Net saving	286835	216890	229828	269140	330261	393091	452085	493519	480812	554110	505614	592273
Total current disbursements and net saving	5126109	5343290	5659900	6097347	6524597	6902747	7233355	7431945	7588854	7920514	8172362	8413506

1.7 External transactions on current account, summary

Million French francs

	1986	1987	1988	1989	1990	1991	1992	1993	1994	1995	1996	1997
Payments to the rest of the world												
1 Imports of goods and services	1021789	1094349	1217627	1403052	1469802	1514461	1493531	1404767	1523075	1621458	1692180	1848001
A Imports of merchandise, c.i.f.	893847	952251	1063873	1229621	1273885	1302876	1268897	1171952	1283565	1383901	1430825	1563648
B Other	127942	142098	153754	173431	195917	211585	224634	232815	239510	237557	261355	284353
2 Factor income to rest of the world	190134	184380	202977	247784	295867	367291	403149	451799	412193	405112	392724	440958
A Compensation of employees	19310	16969	20358	15590	17724	20136	23011	21742	22143	18239	15173	13070
B Property and entrepreneurial income	170824	167411	182619	232194	278143	347155	380138	430057	390050	386873	377551	427888
3 Current transfers to the rest of the world	128709	137175	158742	161310	163981	193977	195557	210192	214974	218681	232190	241194
A Indirect taxes to supranational organizations	49048	54179	62291	61106	60615	68788	64909	57866	60446	63776	55120	56370
B Other current transfers	79661	82996	96451	100204	103366	125189	130648	152326	154528	154905	177070	184824
4 Surplus of the nation on current transactions	23876	−9504	−17752	−32298	−62337	−37215	8291	71449	72374	115080	121542	262138
Payments to the rest of the world and surplus of the nation on current transfers	1364508	1406400	1561594	1779848	1867313	2038514	2100528	2138207	2222616	2360331	2438636	2792291
Receipts from the rest of the world												
1 Exports of goods and services	1074095	1101383	1221304	1411087	1467972	1538062	1588103	1556368	1684130	1802974	1897678	2168498
A Exports of merchandise, f.o.b.	860303	886740	992606	1135583	1173049	1218530	1247213	1203283	1310041	1429458	1496475	1713321
B Other	213792	214643	228698	275504	294923	319532	340890	353085	374089	373516	401203	455177
2 Factor income from rest of the world	173526	171913	191330	237813	263783	329004	345528	395607	359227	374333	364131	454771
A Compensation of employees	11757	12427	16401	15798	16443	19477	19336	20158	20385	22243	19798	23194
B Property and entrepreneurial income	161769	159486	174929	222015	247340	309527	326192	375449	338842	352090	344333	431577
3 Current transfers from rest of the world	116887	133104	148960	130948	135558	171448	166897	186232	179259	183024	176827	169022
A Subsidies from supranational organisations	39354	51022	42118	34847	35401	41494	41372	59880	53746	53536	53485	52861
B Other current transfers	77533	82082	106842	96101	100157	129954	125525	126352	125513	129488	123342	116161
Receipts from the rest of the world on current transactions	1364508	1406400	1561594	1779848	1867313	2038514	2100528	2138207	2222616	2360331	2438636	2792291

France

1.8 Capital transactions of the nation, summary

Million French francs

	1986	1987	1988	1989	1990	1991	1992	1993	1994	1995	1996	1997
Finance of gross capital formation												
Gross saving	1018549	1065943	1210856	1341524	1399966	1420768	1384728	1284909	1401252	1513664	1465250	1627743
1 Consumption of fixed capital	631975	673500	725034	776143	828961	880117	905901	925815	954624	983997	1000996	1031616
A General government	88614	95049	102336	110785	119557	129829	138983	146975	153935	159945	171554	173461
B Corporate and quasi-corporate enterprises	370246	392148	417385	439559	475522	518085	542157	551162	566743	584275	586754	602886
C Other	173115	186303	205313	225799	233882	232203	224761	227678	233946	239777	242688	255269
2 Net saving	386574	392443	485822	565381	571005	540651	478827	359094	446628	529667	464254	596127
A General government	−57483	−16708	8537	38402	41180	−37242	−178288	−325176	−331330	−303281	−285480	−244217
B Corporate and quasi-corporate enterprises	157222	192261	247457	257839	199564	184802	205030	190751	297145	278838	244120	248071
C Other	286835	216890	229828	269140	330261	393091	452085	493519	480813	554110	505614	592273
less: Surplus of the nation on current transactions	23876	−9504	−17752	−32298	−62337	−37215	8291	71449	72374	115080	121542	262138
Finance of gross capital formation	994673	1075447	1228608	1373822	1462303	1457983	1376437	1213460	1328878	1398584	1343708	1365605
Gross capital formation												
Increase in stocks	17156	20679	40295	59270	70945	21061	−28972	−97933	−3223	23749	−28345	−22483
Gross fixed capital formation	977517	1054768	1188313	1314552	1391358	1436922	1405409	1311393	1332101	1374835	1372053	1388088
1 General government	152435	161760	188556	205077	212033	230440	242317	241521	241442	242092	227460	230075
2 Corporate and quasi-corporate enterprises	475315	525833	595681	655612	706495	738335	721711	657241	665423	691497	698933	701810
3 Other	349767	367175	404076	453863	472830	468147	441381	412631	425236	441246	445660	456203
Gross capital formation	994673	1075447	1228608	1373822	1462303	1457983	1376437	1213460	1328878	1398584	1343708	1365605

1.9 Gross domestic product by institutional sectors of origin

Million French francs

	1986	1987	1988	1989	1990	1991	1992	1993	1994	1995	1996	1997
Domestic factor incomes originating												
1 General government	731510	755915	779105	813899	871844	905459	967211	1023066	1045964	1101457	1133533	1168948
2 Corporate and quasi-corporate enterprises	2152300	2286812	2482333	2667976	2784296	2923055	2994577	2985604	3140343	3224978	3310457	3430255
A Non-financial	2125522	2263031	2474535	2669008	2814249	2939374	3006686	3011770	3083431	3212841	3300523	3425651
B Financial [a]	26778	23781	7798	−1032	−29953	−16319	−12109	−26166	56912	12137	9934	4604
3 Households and private unincorporated enterprises	914116	940604	987840	1090799	1162204	1200564	1254094	1261106	1301799	1358385	1400867	1434951
4 Non-profit institutions serving households [b]	11832	12401	13229	14138	15241	15933	16257	16174	16525	16986	17544	17990
subtotal: Domestic factor incomes	3809758	3995732	4262507	4586812	4833585	5045011	5232139	5285950	5504631	5701806	5862401	6052144
Indirect taxes, net	627563	667420	747551	796725	846942	851103	861506	865322	930400	976588	1008334	1053325
A Indirect taxes	785542	836125	891710	934229	983429	995345	1015800	1035458	1102813	1155070	1221100	1275264
B less: Subsidies	157979	168705	144159	137504	136487	144242	154294	170136	172413	178482	212766	221939
Consumption of fixed capital	631975	673500	725034	776143	828961	880117	905901	925815	954624	983997	1000996	1031616
Statistical discrepancy	...	...	...	...	...	...	...	...	−1	...	...	...
Gross domestic product	5069296	5336652	5735092	6159680	6509488	6776231	6999546	7077087	7389654	7662391	7871731	8137085

a Financial of Corporate and quasi-corporate enterprises refers to net of imputed bank service charges. b Net of operating surplus.

France

1.10 Gross domestic product by kind of activity, in current prices

Million French francs

	1986	1987	1988	1989	1990	1991	1992	1993	1994	1995	1996	1997
1 Agriculture, hunting, forestry and fishing	189495	189002	191278	215282	221865	204699	197741	165859	177863	181919	182668	183447
2 Mining and quarrying	35657	34723	30772	31738	29754	31200	32945	31662	31943	32872	33733	32507
3 Manufacturing	1120100	1143222	1242136	1324621	1394503	1409777	1402737	1380297	1423067	1478907	1501761	1569662
4 Electricity, gas and water	118093	122784	126454	128259	138739	153795	165111	171619	173396	180035	186297	183046
5 Construction	262953	278086	309643	320643	335812	357518	363316	357982	342298	347231	336231	347464
6 Wholesale and retail trade, restaurants and hotels	747077	797082	854082	928578	990699	1031337	1060452	1080595	1107301	1158139	1173035	1193013
7 Transport, storage and communication	310759	322383	334976	357487	378473	397426	414513	414197	427443	435618	441300	460900
8 Finance, insurance, real estate and business services	977594	1086928	1198252	1322401	1390152	1471222	1539073	1570139	1697018	1738757	1783123	1860715
9 Community, social and personal services	256333	276677	306334	335181	363473	385027	420555	443280	458920	475294	490030	504354
Total, Industries	4018061	4250887	4593927	4964190	5243470	5442001	5596443	5615630	5839249	6028772	6128178	6335108
Producers of government services	845325	873976	913641	961363	1015534	1076801	1146244	1211348	1261469	1320310	1377060	1412597
Other producers												
Subtotal	4863386	5124863	5507568	5925553	6259004	6518802	6742687	6826978	7100718	7349082	7505238	7747705
less: Imputed bank service charge	223272	246505	262490	279423	278020	269336	274663	275227	263132	271846	253998	256291
plus: Import duties [a]	8976	9667	10747	11030	10946	11954	10644	10271	9658	9926	8476	9252
plus: Value added tax	420379	449074	479572	502698	517561	514827	520879	515065	542410	575229	612015	636419
plus: Other adjustments	–173	–447	–305	–178	–3	–16	–1	–	–	–	–	–
equals: Gross domestic product	5069296	5336652	5735092	6159680	6509488	6776231	6999546	7077087	7389654	7662391	7871731	8137085

a Item "Import duties" includes also value added tax (VAT) on products.

1.11 Gross domestic product by kind of activity, in constant prices

Million French francs

	1986	1987	1988	1989	1990	1991	1992	1993	1994	1995	1996	1997
At constant prices of: 1980												
1 Agriculture, hunting, forestry and fishing	139457	141354	140801	145962	148989	143700	159587	146795	147338	146915	155188	154288
2 Mining and quarrying	20745	21054	20275	19729	18338	20771	21357	21842	20865	21755	22581	20632
3 Manufacturing	667256	661095	700521	736640	750400	736204	722278	699825	732057	761300	775151	813334
4 Electricity, gas and water	77261	81682	83221	82712	84444	88838	91573	92224	93092	96269	98811	99379
5 Construction	185861	187684	202688	212123	217515	218195	213137	201497	195817	196698	188057	185376
6 Wholesale and retail trade, restaurants and hotels	443225	448663	457080	476416	492158	493593	492420	483270	484831	494599	499293	506853
7 Transport, storage and communication	198339	209271	228695	246655	259184	268722	275763	275717	284274	291302	301192	311870
8 Finance, insurance, real estate and business services	566336	601553	623157	649334	650680	656998	662012	658108	685066	695070	687646	702348
9 Community, social and personal services	160419	165288	174073	185046	196265	202460	212248	217104	218111	221417	224400	226686
Total, Industries	2458899	2517644	2630511	2754617	2817973	2829481	2850375	2796382	2861451	2925325	2952319	3020766
Producers of government services	505807	512351	526532	531650	539211	553844	568275	580589	594640	601668	617735	625513
Other producers												
Subtotal	2964706	3029995	3157043	3286267	3357184	3383325	3418650	3376971	3456091	3526993	3570054	3646279
less: Imputed bank service charge	131917	140115	143561	145827	138811	129690	126896	122902	112466	114659	105751	104829

France

Million French francs	1986	1987	1988	1989	1990	1991	1992	1993	1994	1995	1996	1997
At constant prices of: 1980												
plus: Import duties [a]	8482	9437	10318	11127	11878	12422	12590	12523	13304	14303	14957	15412
plus: Value added tax	263514	275354	293687	306977	315001	306865	310001	299671	310087	316775	322237	332867
plus: Other adjustments	−149	−162	−175	−174	−153	−153	−16	−16	–	–	–	–
equals: Gross domestic product	3104636	3174509	3317312	3458370	3545099	3572769	3614329	3566247	3667016	3743412	3801497	3889729

[a] Item "Import duties" includes also value added tax (VAT) on products.

1.12 Relations among national accounting aggregates

Million French francs	1986	1987	1988	1989	1990	1991	1992	1993	1994	1995	1996	1997
Gross domestic product	5069296	5336652	5735092	6159680	6509488	6776231	6999546	7077087	7389654	7662391	7871731	8137085
plus: Net factor income from the rest of the world	−16608	−12467	−11647	−9971	−32084	−38287	−57621	−56192	−52966	−30779	−28593	13813
Factor income from rest of the world	173526	171913	191330	237813	263783	329004	345528	395607	359227	374333	364131	454771
less: Factor income to the rest of the world	190134	184380	202977	247784	295867	367291	403149	451799	412193	405112	392724	440958
equals: Gross national product	5052688	5324185	5723445	6149709	6477404	6737944	6941925	7020895	7336688	7631612	7843138	8150898
less: Consumption of fixed capital	631975	673500	725034	776143	828961	880117	905901	925815	954624	983997	1000996	1031616
equals: National income	4420713	4650685	4998411	5373566	5648443	5857827	6036024	6095080	6382064	6647615	6842142	7119282
plus: Net current transfers from the rest of the world	−11822	−4071	−9782	−30362	−28423	−22529	−28660	−23960	−35715	−35657	−55363	−72172
Current transfers from rest of the world	116887	133104	148960	130948	135558	171448	166897	186232	179259	183024	176827	169022
less: Current transfers to the rest of the world	128709	137175	158742	161310	163981	193977	195557	210192	214974	218681	232190	241194
equals: National disposable income	4408891	4646614	4988629	5343204	5620020	5835298	6007364	6071120	6346349	6611958	6786779	7047110
less: Final consumption	4022317	4254171	4502807	4777823	5049015	5294647	5528537	5712026	5899721	6082291	6322525	6450983
equals: Net saving	386574	392443	485822	565381	571005	540651	478827	359094	446628	529667	464254	596127
less: Surplus of the nation on current transactions	23876	−9504	−17752	−32298	−62337	−37215	8291	71449	72374	115080	121542	262138
equals: Net capital formation	362698	401947	503574	597679	633342	577866	470536	287645	374254	414587	342712	333989

2.1 Government final consumption expenditure by function, in current prices

Million French francs	1986	1987	1988	1989	1990	1991	1992	1993	1994	1995	1996	1997
1 General public services	129631	132760	138014	144190	139482	150803	159269	169928	...	...	...	...
2 Defence	153648	162885	182210	180818	194531	194360	209551	221640	...	...	...	...
3 Public order and safety	43522	45947	47865	50682	54108	57580	61268	65316	...	...	...	...
4 Education	249379	255929	266166	280022	303876	324163	346573	365286	...	...	...	...
5 Health	156086	168687	172667	188635	201866	215280	228484	243227	...	...	...	...
6 Social security and welfare	75293	75112	83781	83802	88188	92206	97695	104876	...	...	...	...
7 Housing and community amenities	58538	62372	65245	70796	73561	81280	88594	96585	...	...	...	...
8 Recreational, cultural and religious affairs	28944	30757	31935	34728	37311	40139	43066	44803	...	...	...	...
9 Economic services	62597	67828	66803	68961	73526	76667	79113	83425	...	...	...	...
A Fuel and energy	...	...	...	...	...	...	...	...	...	...	...	...
B Agriculture, hunting, forestry and fishing	...	...	...	...	...	...	...	...	...	...	...	...
C Mining (except fuels), manufacturing and construction	...	...	...	...	...	...	...	...	...	...	...	...

France

Million French francs

	1986	1987	1988	1989	1990	1991	1992	1993	1994	1995	1996	1997
D Transportation and communication	28170	32549	30026	29911	33090	35192	36671	38395	...	...	...	...
E Other economic affairs	34427	35279	36777	39050	40436	41475	42442	45030	...	...	...	...
10 Other functions	1871	2380	3714	3441	3986	6520	6837	7812	...	...	...	...
Total government final consumption expenditures	959509	1004657	1058400	1106075	1170435	1238998	1320450	1402898	...	...	...	...

2.3 Total government outlays by function and type

Million French francs

1986

	Final consumption expenditures – Total	Compensation of employees	Other	Subsidies	Other current transfers and property income	Total current disbursements	Gross capital formation	Other capital outlays	Total outlays
1 General public services	129631	92731	36900	2729	40551	172911	21074	4151	198136
2 Defence	153648	82287	71361	2489	1440	157577	1392	5468	164437
3 Public order and safety	43522	34445	9077	46	946	44514	3412	352	48278
4 Education	249379	219899	29480	1995	8483	259857	20207	2624	282688
5 Health	156086	127727	28359	3809	191321	351216	13063	1730	366009
6 Social security and welfare	75293	76359	–1066	4922	943190	1023405	4163	4485	1032053
7 Housing and community amenities	58538	28703	29835	28118	28471	115127	43294	15252	173673
8 Recreational, cultural and religious affairs	28944	15453	13491	824	4702	34470	16561	1307	52338
9 Economic services	62597	33405	29192	72938	10763	146298	26759	17613	190670
A Fuel and energy	...	...	...	...	...	...	...	...	...
B Agriculture, hunting, forestry and fishing	...	...	...	...	...	...	...	...	...
C Mining (except fuels), manufacturing and construction	...	...	...	...	...	...	...	...	...
D Transportation and communication	28170	12804	15366	20365	1127	49662	17302	4656	71620
E Other economic affairs	34427	20601	13826	52573	9636	96636	9457	12957	119050
10 Other functions	1871	1430	441	755	128224	130850	2510	15728	149088
Total	959509	712439	247070	118625	1358091	2436225	152435	68710	2657370

1987

	Final consumption expenditures – Total	Compensation of employees	Other	Subsidies	Other current transfers and property income	Total current disbursements	Gross capital formation	Other capital outlays	Total outlays
1 General public services	132760	89465	43295	2293	47228	182281	22854	7410	212545
2 Defence	162885	83522	79363	2644	2436	167965	1690	–1009	168646
3 Public order and safety	45947	35709	10238	44	1152	47143	3888	388	51419
4 Education	255929	226545	29384	2318	9808	268055	20279	2787	291121
5 Health	168687	137250	31437	4438	197339	370464	14606	1846	386916
6 Social security and welfare	75112	78061	–2949	4853	985686	1065651	4750	3565	1073966
7 Housing and community amenities	62372	30675	31697	25641	29743	117756	45572	16094	179422
8 Recreational, cultural and religious affairs	30757	16182	14575	498	5230	36485	15085	1407	52977
9 Economic services	67828	34715	33113	74159	11519	153506	30359	22512	206377
A Fuel and energy	...	...	...	...	...	...	...	...	...

France

1987

	Final consumption expenditures Total	Compensation of employees	Other	Subsidies	Other current transfers and property income	Total current disbursements	Gross capital formation	Other capital outlays	Total outlays
B Agriculture, hunting, forestry and fishing	...	...	...	...	...	...	...	...	...
C Mining (except fuels), manufacturing and construction	...	...	...	...	...	...	...	...	...
D Transportation and communication	32549	14480	18069	20954	1139	54642	19909	5095	79646
E Other economic affairs	35279	20235	15044	53205	10380	98864	10450	17417	126731
10 Other functions	2380	1578	802	795	127079	130254	2677	18010	150941
Total	1004657	733702	270955	117683	1417220	2539560	161760	73010	2774330

1988

	Final consumption expenditures Total	Compensation of employees	Other	Subsidies	Other current transfers and property income	Total current disbursements	Gross capital formation	Other capital outlays	Total outlays
1 General public services	138014	94715	43299	2533	56399	196946	27211	21350	245507
2 Defence	182210	85420	96790	2300	1420	185930	1917	3771	191618
3 Public order and safety	47865	36729	11136	3752	714	52331	4716	364	57411
4 Education	266166	235885	30281	2224	10062	278452	22792	2131	303375
5 Health	172667	140408	32259	4751	206404	383822	15130	1841	400793
6 Social security and welfare	83781	85612	−1831	5334	1047238	1136353	5157	3564	1145074
7 Housing and community amenities	65245	31844	33401	22129	31658	119032	52765	18717	190514
8 Recreational, cultural and religious affairs	31935	16781	15154	866	5319	38120	20338	1307	59765
9 Economic services	66803	32999	33804	57792	14639	139234	34740	8133	182107
A Fuel and energy	...	...	...	...	...	...	...	...	...
B Agriculture, hunting, forestry and fishing	...	...	...	...	...	...	...	...	...
C Mining (except fuels), manufacturing and construction	...	...	...	...	...	...	...	...	...
D Transportation and communication	30026	12416	17610	20911	1414	52351	22615	5242	80208
E Other economic affairs	36777	20583	16194	36881	13225	86883	12125	2891	101899
10 Other functions	3714	3046	668	360	128698	132772	3790	22259	158821
Total	1058400	763439	294961	102041	1502551	2662992	188556	83437	2934985

1989

	Final consumption expenditures Total	Compensation of employees	Other	Subsidies	Other current transfers and property income	Total current disbursements	Gross capital formation	Other capital outlays	Total outlays
1 General public services	144190	98277	45913	2509	53050	199749	29019	12951	241719
2 Defence	180818	87622	93196	2166	1436	184420	2230	6814	193464
3 Public order and safety	50682	38568	12114	44	447	51173	5849	212	57234
4 Education	280022	247843	32179	3191	9489	292702	26896	2123	321721
5 Health	188635	151969	36666	4972	218426	412033	16767	1777	430577
6 Social security and welfare	83802	86526	−2724	5376	1108982	1198160	4979	5385	1208524
7 Housing and community amenities	70796	33826	36970	20805	27960	119561	59126	21252	199939
8 Recreational, cultural and religious affairs	34728	18070	16658	996	9908	45632	18616	2538	66786

France

1989

	Final consumption expenditures Total	Compensation of employees	Other	Subsidies	Other current transfers and property income	Total current disbursements	Gross capital formation	Other capital outlays	Total outlays
9 Economic services	68961	33897	35064	62585	14880	146426	37253	9481	193160
A Fuel and energy	...	...	...	...	...	...	...	...	...
B Agriculture, hunting, forestry and fishing	...	...	...	...	...	...	...	...	...
C Mining (except fuels), manufacturing and construction	...	...	...	...	...	...	...	...	...
D Transportation and communication	29911	12266	17645	23541	1403	54855	24851	7680	87386
E Other economic affairs	39050	21631	17419	39044	13477	91571	12402	1801	105774
10 Other functions	3441	3215	226	13	149453	152907	4342	24670	181919
Total	1106075	799813	306262	102657	1594031	2802763	205077	87203	3095043

1990

	Final consumption expenditures Total	Compensation of employees	Other	Subsidies	Other current transfers and property income	Total current disbursements	Gross capital formation	Other capital outlays	Total outlays
1 General public services	139482	101022	38460	3028	56735	199245	29488	26563	255296
2 Defence	194531	90524	104007	2528	1511	198570	1917	7024	207511
3 Public order and safety	54108	40422	13686	39	13053	67200	4374	19261	90835
4 Education	303876	267830	36046	3480	11219	318575	30183	1942	350700
5 Health	201866	161390	40476	5323	249924	457113	18582	2195	477890
6 Social security and welfare	88188	87286	902	5580	1166082	1259850	4930	4634	1269414
7 Housing and community amenities	73561	34575	38986	18661	29683	121905	56981	23196	202082
8 Recreational, cultural and religious affairs	37311	19016	18295	887	11265	49463	19592	2539	71594
9 Economic services	73526	35844	37682	61552	16125	151203	39650	29892	220745
A Fuel and energy	...	...	...	...	...	...	...	...	...
B Agriculture, hunting, forestry and fishing	...	...	...	...	...	...	...	...	...
C Mining (except fuels), manufacturing and construction	...	...	...	...	...	...	...	...	...
D Transportation and communication	33090	13223	19867	21924	1630	56644	26386	7808	90838
E Other economic affairs	40436	22621	17815	39628	14495	94559	13264	22084	129907
10 Other functions	3986	3360	626	16	168691	172693	4684	30412	207789
Total	1170435	841269	329166	101086	1711790	2983311	212033	129080	3324424

1991

	Final consumption expenditures Total	Compensation of employees	Other	Subsidies	Other current transfers and property income	Total current disbursements	Gross capital formation	Other capital outlays	Total outlays
1 General public services	150803	103872	46931	3291	66212	220306	31607	11546	263459
2 Defence	194360	95366	98994	2579	1686	198625	1256	8658	208539
3 Public order and safety	57580	42944	14636	32	12423	70035	4576	2215	76826
4 Education	324163	284916	39247	4547	11355	340065	35610	406	376081
5 Health	215280	169067	46213	6349	266307	487936	21159	2535	511630
6 Social security and welfare	92206	93131	–925	7543	1246617	1346366	6423	5127	1357916

France

1991

	Final consumption expenditures Total	Compensation of employees	Other	Subsidies	Other current transfers and property income	Total current disbursements	Gross capital formation	Other capital outlays	Total outlays
7 Housing and community amenities	81280	35138	46142	19709	31715	132704	62507	31691	226902
8 Recreational, cultural and religious affairs	40139	20389	19750	955	10515	51609	21770	2349	75728
9 Economic services	76667	36130	40537	57733	18432	152832	39479	22206	214517
A Fuel and energy	...	...	...	...	...	...	...	...	...
B Agriculture, hunting, forestry and fishing	...	...	...	...	...	...	...	...	...
C Mining (except fuels), manufacturing and construction	...	...	...	...	...	...	...	...	...
D Transportation and communication	35192	12971	22221	20883	1792	57867	27609	8604	94080
E Other economic affairs	41475	23159	18316	36850	16640	94965	11870	13602	120437
10 Other functions	6520	5708	812	12	190154	196686	4095	28144	228925
Total	1238998	886661	352337	102748	1843599	3185345	230440	113022	3528807

1992

	Final consumption expenditures Total	Compensation of employees	Other	Subsidies	Other current transfers and property income	Total current disbursements	Gross capital formation	Other capital outlays	Total outlays
1 General public services	159269	110434	48835	3557	68986	231812	30161	14306	276279
2 Defence	209551	98866	110685	2122	1669	213342	3343	990	217675
3 Public order and safety	61268	45505	15763	274	18558	80100	4988	3430	88518
4 Education	346573	303960	42613	4784	15201	366558	38660	471	405689
5 Health	228484	180356	48128	8057	263280	499821	23117	2555	525493
6 Social security and welfare	97695	98321	–626	6718	1356034	1460447	7296	12542	1480285
7 Housing and community amenities	88594	37715	50879	21099	33301	142994	64889	35889	243772
8 Recreational, cultural and religious affairs	43066	21973	21093	1028	13221	57315	22369	2545	82229
9 Economic services	79113	38325	40788	64907	15088	159108	42380	20371	221859
A Fuel and energy	...	...	...	...	...	...	...	...	...
B Agriculture, hunting, forestry and fishing	...	...	...	...	...	...	...	...	...
C Mining (except fuels), manufacturing and construction	...	...	...	...	...	...	...	...	...
D Transportation and communication	36671	13778	22893	22687	1500	60858	29446	8553	98857
E Other economic affairs	42442	24547	17895	42220	13588	98250	12934	11818	123002
10 Other functions	6837	6074	763	618	216586	224041	4612	34096	262749
Total	1320450	941529	378921	112922	1983977	3417349	242317	124085	3783751

1993

	Final consumption expenditures Total	Compensation of employees	Other	Subsidies	Other current transfers and property income	Total current disbursements	Gross capital formation	Other capital outlays	Total outlays
1 General public services	169928	115294	54634	23939	76915	270782	28899	23956	323637
2 Defence	221640	104220	117420	2710	1209	225559	1249	–14071	212737
3 Public order and safety	65316	48506	16810	35	13824	79175	5362	2951	87488
4 Education	365286	320353	44933	5744	16756	387786	39797	–891	426692

France

	1993							
	Final consumption expenditures			Subsidies	Other current transfers and property income	Total current disbursements	Gross capital formation	Other capital outlays	Total outlays
	Total	Compensation of employees	Other						
5 Health	243227	192033	51194	8885	485169	737281	24319	2653	764253
6 Social security and welfare	104876	104458	418	8760	1243132	1356768	6410	13469	1376647
7 Housing and community amenities	96585	40169	56416	18235	38268	153088	66127	42920	262135
8 Recreational, cultural and religious affairs	44803	23161	21642	2782	12945	60530	21876	3163	85569
9 Economic services	83425	39740	43685	39151	166543	289119	43010	17497	349626
A Fuel and energy	...	...	...	...	...	...	...	...	...
B Agriculture, hunting, forestry and fishing	...	...	...	...	...	...	...	...	...
C Mining (except fuels), manufacturing and construction	...	...	...	...	...	...	...	...	...
D Transportation and communication	38395	14381	24014	292	1827	40514	30273	6212	76999
E Other economic affairs	45030	25359	19671	38859	164716	248605	12737	11285	272627
10 Other functions	7812	6392	1420	21	90684	98517	4069	27197	129783
Total	1402898	994326	408572	110256	2132378	3645532	241521	116362	4003415

2.5 Private final consumption expenditure by type and purpose, in current prices

Million French francs

	1986	1987	1988	1989	1990	1991	1992	1993	1994	1995	1996	1997
Final consumption expenditure of resident households												
1 Food, beverages and tobacco	623560	646863	672382	709369	743698	769674	778589	794892	811678	835188	848748	871002
A Food	509730	528628	547656	577486	603019	622930	624279	626904	635559	650469	657210	673415
B Non-alcoholic beverages	15430	16296	17131	18606	21278	22792	23463	24653	25580	27427	28221	29475
C Alcoholic beverages	64017	65477	67905	71188	76001	78957	81335	86913	86537	88989	91115	92862
D Tobacco	34383	36462	39690	42089	43400	44995	49512	56422	64002	68303	72202	75250
2 Clothing and footwear [a]	218764	226660	232664	241271	252991	257842	261097	257224	251785	247044	247907	252815
3 Gross rent, fuel and power	571375	604634	644247	688292	733360	803783	851589	906219	947727	999059	1060822	1092825
A Fuel and power	148789	141755	133463	135902	144635	164037	162878	164083	158367	164274	179769	175107
B Other	422586	462879	510784	552390	588725	639746	688711	742136	789360	834785	881053	917718
4 Furniture, furnishings and household equipment and operation	254969	268124	284086	297066	307973	315632	319915	323161	328984	338461	349029	356646
A Household operation	80124	83850	88686	93782	97916	104861	110625	114602	118575	125014	132946	139726
B Other	174845	184274	195400	203284	210057	210771	209290	208559	210409	213447	216083	216920
5 Medical care and health expenses	270716	284184	311542	340028	367837	393009	418388	440599	455674	472658	485100	498021
6 Transport and communication	501845	545823	577636	624266	655844	662920	685967	679001	725314	748428	796387	789464
A Personal transport equipment	124556	140101	149484	165108	168806	155216	161982	142109	160383	159206	177944	146226
B Other	377289	405722	428152	459158	487038	507704	523985	536892	564931	589222	618443	643238
7 Recreational, entertainment, education and cultural services	220494	238155	255153	277347	294010	304270	323170	325732	336414	342652	352128	360780
A Education	14467	16967	18789	21323	21167	21669	23549	24191	26167	25650	26571	27533
B Other	206027	221188	236364	256024	272843	282601	299621	301541	310247	317002	325557	333247
8 Miscellaneous goods and services	409379	440803	475216	516915	548704	580295	609309	623411	644188	658656	677315	701916
A Personal care [a]	53063	57983	63129	68789	73650	78391	83091	85454	87009	88214	90110	92527

France

Million French francs

	1986	1987	1988	1989	1990	1991	1992	1993	1994	1995	1996	1997
B Expenditures in restaurants, cafes and hotels	200733	215735	235227	257656	277819	295644	306977	314691	324317	331216	340565	352934
C Other	155583	167085	176860	190470	197235	206260	219241	223266	232862	239226	246640	256455
Total final consumption expenditure in the domestic market by households, of which	3071102	3255246	3452926	3694554	3904417	4087425	4248024	4350239	4501764	4642146	4817436	4923469
A Durable goods	250825	274648	295255	315919	325584	309625	314990	292109	311910	313169	332081	300503
B Semi-durable goods	472428	494899	516467	544382	571453	588900	600286	593636	600068	613473	621078	634032
C Non-durable goods	1113117	1147280	1187160	1260091	1327938	1391897	1415832	1452791	1480168	1529844	1582835	1622513
D Services	1234732	1338419	1454044	1574162	1679442	1797003	1916916	2011703	2109618	2185660	2281442	2366421
plus: Direct purchases abroad by resident households	45113	51328	58000	64162	66576	69835	74060	73143	77012	81097	90250	96180
less: Direct purchases in the domestic market by non-resident households	66695	70992	81418	102923	109671	119735	132549	132641	136441	136595	144200	162353
equals: Final consumption expenditure of resident households	3049520	3235582	3429508	3655793	3861322	4037525	4189535	4290741	4442335	4586648	4763486	4857296

Final consumption expenditures by private non-profit organisations serving households

	1986	1987	1988	1989	1990	1991	1992	1993	1994	1995	1996	1997
1 Research and science	...	...	...	...	...	...	...	...	...	...	...	...
2 Education	...	...	...	...	...	...	...	...	...	...	...	...
3 Medical and other health services	...	...	...	...	...	...	...	...	...	...	...	...
4 Welfare services	...	...	...	...	...	...	...	...	...	...	...	...
5 Recreational and related cultural services	...	...	...	...	...	...	...	...	...	...	...	...
6 Religious organisations	...	...	...	...	...	...	...	...	...	...	...	...
7 Professional and labour organisations serving households	...	...	...	...	...	...	...	...	...	...	...	...
8 Miscellaneous	...	...	...	...	...	...	...	...	...	...	...	...
equals: Final consumption expenditures by private non-profit organisations serving households	13288	13932	14899	15955	17258	18124	18552	18387	18752	19262	20032	20633
Private final consumption expenditure	3062808	3249514	3444407	3671748	3878580	4055649	4208087	4309128	4461087	4605910	4783518	4877929

a Personal effects are included in item "Clothing and footwear".

2.6 Private final consumption expenditure by type and purpose, in constant prices

Million French francs

	1986	1987	1988	1989	1990	1991	1992	1993	1994	1995	1996	1997

At constant prices of: 1980

Final consumption expenditure of resident households

	1986	1987	1988	1989	1990	1991	1992	1993	1994	1995	1996	1997
1 Food, beverages and tobacco	380978	387976	395200	400249	404756	407267	408089	412040	413176	418016	418279	420738
A Food	311833	318254	323954	326946	329386	331294	332345	334029	335782	339461	339740	342424
B Non-alcoholic beverages	9346	9567	10266	11580	12977	13371	13273	13783	14341	15365	15648	16100
C Alcoholic beverages	39328	39500	40429	40801	41011	40721	40721	43456	42821	43281	43340	43347
D Tobacco	20471	20655	20551	20922	21382	21881	21750	20772	20232	19909	19551	18867
2 Clothing and footwear [a]	130997	129361	128457	129565	131910	130159	128493	125317	122015	119037	118340	120089
3 Gross rent, fuel and power	345566	355874	361046	367889	377790	395790	404154	412121	416597	430618	447728	453028
A Fuel and power	93341	94114	89488	89281	90399	99083	98763	98987	95341	98767	105373	101857
B Other	252225	261760	271558	278608	287391	296707	305391	313134	321256	331851	342355	351171
4 Furniture, furnishings and household equipment and operation	157412	160728	167190	169824	170560	168696	166504	165438	166790	168978	170294	171982

France

Million French francs

	1986	1987	1988	1989	1990	1991	1992	1993	1994	1995	1996	1997
At constant prices of: 1980												
A Household operation	46061	46945	48884	50052	50726	52067	53473	54267	55258	56954	58942	60643
B Other	111351	113783	118306	119772	119834	116629	113031	111171	111532	112024	111352	111339
5 Medical care and health expenses	183496	188712	202304	218954	237289	250867	262114	273127	276024	280096	284566	289722
6 Transport and communication	310825	325426	338833	352783	361031	355419	363291	350785	364600	369817	385337	380022
A Personal transport equipment	75784	82485	86637	92735	94196	84171	86506	74140	83882	82145	91796	76980
B Other	235041	242941	252196	260048	266835	271248	276785	276645	280718	287672	293541	303042
7 Recreational, entertainment, education and cultural services	142217	149589	160763	171795	181072	183331	187307	186647	192610	197382	201558	209189
A Education	8310	9173	9602	10337	9691	9412	9797	9681	10241	9804	10014	10247
B Other	133907	140416	151161	161458	171381	173919	177510	176966	182369	187578	191544	198942
8 Miscellaneous goods and services	247843	253949	262841	274920	278986	283378	287791	285889	288960	291183	292281	298635
A Personal care [a]	30604	31659	33112	34680	35457	35944	36578	36344	36511	36636	36731	36973
B Expenditures in restaurants, cafes and hotels	114887	115598	119505	124686	127293	128835	128702	127377	128338	128055	128732	131257
C Other	102352	106692	110224	115554	116236	118599	122511	122168	124111	126492	126818	130405
Total final consumption expenditure in the domestic market by households, of which	1899334	1951615	2016634	2085979	2143394	2174907	2207743	2211364	2240772	2275127	2318383	2343405
A Durable goods	168722	180341	193699	203711	210729	199244	201126	187660	201065	203609	214901	206101
B Semi-durable goods	287767	289595	293926	301550	307522	306688	304362	297230	297592	301040	300918	306535
C Non-durable goods	698900	713715	729414	747787	764029	782224	789502	799039	799574	813997	824421	830473
D Services	743945	767964	799595	832931	861114	886751	912753	927435	942541	956481	978143	1000296
plus: Direct purchases abroad by resident households	27839	30662	33671	35954	36185	36744	38054	36738	37886	39229	42801	45028
less: Direct purchases in the domestic market by non-resident households	41154	42406	47263	57671	59604	62995	68102	66617	67116	66069	68380	76000
equals: Final consumption expenditure of resident households	1886019	1939871	2003042	2064262	2119975	2148656	2177695	2181485	2211542	2248287	2292804	2312433

Final consumption expenditures by private non-profit organisations serving households

	1986	1987	1988	1989	1990	1991	1992	1993	1994	1995	1996	1997
1 Research and science	...	...	...	...	...	...	...	...	...	...	...	...
2 Education	...	...	...	...	...	...	...	...	...	...	...	...
3 Medical and other health services	...	...	...	...	...	...	...	...	...	...	...	...
4 Welfare services	...	...	...	...	...	...	...	...	...	...	...	...
5 Recreational and related cultural services	...	...	...	...	...	...	...	...	...	...	...	...
6 Religious organisations	...	...	...	...	...	...	...	...	...	...	...	...
7 Professional and labour organisations serving households	...	...	...	...	...	...	...	...	...	...	...	...
8 Miscellaneous	...	...	...	...	...	...	...	...	...	...	...	...
equals: Final consumption expenditures by private non-profit organisations serving households	8272	8588	9017	9362	9897	10159	10143	9833	9922	9969	10109	10349
Private final consumption expenditure	1894291	1948459	2012059	2073624	2129872	2158815	2187838	2191318	2221464	2258256	2302913	2322782

a Personal effects are included in item "Clothing and footwear".

France

2.9 Gross capital formation by kind of activity of owner, ISIC major divisions, in current prices

Million French francs

	1986 Total gross capital formation	1986 Increase in stocks	1986 Gross fixed capital formation	1987 Total gross capital formation	1987 Increase in stocks	1987 Gross fixed capital formation	1988 Total gross capital formation	1988 Increase in stocks	1988 Gross fixed capital formation	1989 Total gross capital formation	1989 Increase in stocks	1989 Gross fixed capital formation
All producers												
1 Agriculture, hunting, forestry and fishing	31698	1972	29726	26284	−3252	29536	31518	−3266	34784	45270	5492	39778
2 Mining and quarrying	1141	–	1141	801	−140	941	864	−282	1146	451	−607	1058
3 Manufacturing	150478	−8208	158686	163115	−8321	171436	206393	11236	195157	241461	24839	216622
4 Electricity, gas and water	51766	2807	48959	48969	2135	46834	45728	134	45594	44241	−1251	45492
5 Construction	26427	2882	23545	29825	4320	25505	34999	5222	29777	34071	−1962	36033
6 Wholesale and retail trade, restaurants and hotels	96685	14792	81893	123095	24641	98454	116088	17439	98649	139845	27108	112737
7 Transport, storage and communication	78724	−46	78770	84358	−1069	85427	101832	598	101234	109221	7	109214
8 Finance, insurance, real estate and business services	382690	−40	382730	411596	1586	410010	473238	8311	464927	522162	5937	516225
9 Community, social and personal services	32040	868	31172	36972	986	35986	42761	903	41858	46274	−65	46339
Total industries	851649	15027	836622	925015	20886	904129	1053421	40295	1013126	1182996	59498	1123498
Producers of government services	140680	2129	138551	147975	−207	148182	172559	–	172559	188013	−228	188241
Private non-profit institutions serving households	2344	–	2344	2457	–	2457	2628	–	2628	2813	–	2813
Total	994673	17156	977517	1075447	20679	1054768	1228608	40295	1188313	1373822	59270	1314552

	1990 Total gross capital formation	1990 Increase in stocks	1990 Gross fixed capital formation	1991 Total gross capital formation	1991 Increase in stocks	1991 Gross fixed capital formation	1992 Total gross capital formation	1992 Increase in stocks	1992 Gross fixed capital formation	1993 Total gross capital formation	1993 Increase in stocks	1993 Gross fixed capital formation
All producers												
1 Agriculture, hunting, forestry and fishing	43330	1601	41729	26898	−11845	38743	35745	270	35475	...	...	32757
2 Mining and quarrying	307	−481	788	323	−304	627	1064	491	573	...	...	41
3 Manufacturing	275162	36761	238401	240950	7082	233868	197005	−14242	211247	...	...	170197
4 Electricity, gas and water	42174	−1623	43797	44633	−239	44872	52538	338	52200	...	...	52819
5 Construction	37892	5460	32432	36626	1117	35509	25521	−5043	30564	...	...	28701
6 Wholesale and retail trade, restaurants and hotels	130402	17286	113116	130395	13017	117378	115848	−2500	118348	...	...	106503
7 Transport, storage and communication	120176	1174	119002	135208	375	134833	127261	−895	128156	...	...	119424
8 Finance, insurance, real estate and business services	559016	10533	548483	571504	10388	561116	548448	−6803	555251	...	...	516739
9 Community, social and personal services	53148	−587	53735	52121	−176	52297	44040	−1707	45747	...	...	56991
Total industries	1261607	70124	1191483	1238658	19415	1219243	1147470	−30091	1177561	...	...	1084172
Producers of government services	197660	821	196839	216134	1646	214488	225689	1109	224580	...	...	223982
Private non-profit institutions serving households	3036	–	3036	3191	–	3191	3278	10	3268	...	...	3239
Total	1462303	70945	1391358	1457983	21061	1436922	1376437	−28972	1405409	...	...	1311393

France

	1994			1995			1996			1997		
	Total gross capital formation	Increase in stocks	Gross fixed capital formation	Total gross capital formation	Increase in stocks	Gross fixed capital formation	Total gross capital formation	Increase in stocks	Gross fixed capital formation	Total gross capital formation	Increase in stocks	Gross fixed capital formation
	All producers											
1 Agriculture, hunting, forestry and fishing	...	...	36836	...	...	41073	...	...	43455	...	...	43243
2 Mining and quarrying	...	...	–15	...	...	–7017	...	...	396	...	...	334
3 Manufacturing	...	...	179896	...	...	183867	...	...	192114	...	...	193386
4 Electricity, gas and water	...	...	48440	...	...	49264	...	...	50534	...	...	48834
5 Construction	...	...	28173	...	...	26443	...	...	25096	...	...	24920
6 Wholesale and retail trade, restaurants and hotels	...	...	111170	...	...	119177	...	...	119781	...	...	118117
7 Transport, storage and communication	...	...	104576	...	...	110099	...	...	101876	...	...	108039
8 Finance, insurance, real estate and business services	...	...	539610	...	...	565513	...	...	565144	...	...	576899
9 Community, social and personal services	...	...	56749	...	...	58949	...	...	59552	...	...	58386
Total industries	...	...	1105435	...	...	1147368	...	...	1157948	...	...	1172158
Producers of government services	...	...	223359	...	...	224069	...	...	210571	...	...	212291
Private non-profit institutions serving households	...	...	3307	...	...	3398	...	...	3534	...	...	3639
Total	...	...	1332101	...	...	1374835	...	...	1372053	...	...	1388088

2.11 Gross fixed capital formation by kind of activity of owner, ISIC divisions, in current prices

Million French francs

	1986	1987	1988	1989	1990	1991	1992	1993	1994	1995	1996	1997
	All producers											
1 Agriculture, hunting, forestry and fishing	29726	29536	34784	39778	41729	38743	35475	32757	36836	41073	43455	43243
2 Mining and quarrying	1141	941	1146	1058	788	627	573	41	–15	–7017	396	334
A Coal mining	1141	941	1146	1058	788	627	573	41	–15	–7017	396	334
B Crude petroleum and natural gas production	...	...	...	...	...	...	...	...	...	...	...	...
C Metal ore mining	...	...	...	...	...	...	...	...	...	...	...	...
D Other mining	...	...	...	...	...	...	...	...	...	...	...	...
3 Manufacturing	158686	171436	195157	216622	238401	233868	211247	170197	179896	183867	192114	193386
A Manufacturing of food, beverages and tobacco	21919	23450	28988	34100	32600	35078	35248	28837	28724	24379	25226	24728
B Textile, wearing apparel and leather industries	6893	7630	9307	9379	9869	8558	7984	6072	6473	6758	6881	6523
C Manufacture of wood and wood products, including furniture	5812	6672	7781	9365	9523	9590	8491	5743	6006	5722	5789	5496
D Manufacture of paper and paper products, printing and publishing	12697	14431	15948	18534	21013	20359	16572	11552	11842	14046	15345	15190
E Manufacture of chemicals and chemical petroleum, coal, rubber and plastic products	30708	33887	36780	41001	47671	45603	42383	38355	39095	41585	44417	44392
F Manufacture of non-metallic mineral products, except products of petroleum and coal	8145	8863	11534	13177	11063	9706	6575	8882	10136	12848	13179	13908
G Basic metal industries	14295	14062	13637	14112	14554	13762	13148	9389	10994	9385	9477	10000

France

Million French francs

	1986	1987	1988	1989	1990	1991	1992	1993	1994	1995	1996	1997
H Manufacture of fabricated metal products, machinery and equipment	58217	62441	71182	76954	92108	91212	80846	61367	66626	69144	71800	73149
I Other manufacturing industries	...	...	...	...	...	...	...	...	...	...	...	...
4 Electricity, gas and water	48959	46834	45594	45492	43797	44872	52200	52819	48440	49264	50534	48834
5 Construction	23545	25505	29777	36033	32432	35509	30564	28701	28173	26443	25096	24920
6 Wholesale and retail trade, restaurants and hotels	81893	98454	98649	112737	113116	117378	118348	106503	111170	119177	119781	118117
A Wholesale and retail trade	60728	71875	70426	81513	80358	82203	84061	78573	83720	90814	91499	90349
B Restaurants and hotels	21165	26579	28223	31224	32758	35175	34287	27930	27450	28363	28282	27768
7 Transport, storage and communication	78770	85427	101234	109214	119002	134833	128156	119424	104576	110099	101876	108039
A Transport and storage	53211	59086	75286	79456	87581	96126	99185	86486	78535	83712	77653	81056
B Communication	25559	26341	25948	29758	31421	38707	28971	32938	26041	26387	24223	26983
8 Finance, insurance, real estate and business services	382730	410010	464927	516225	548483	561116	555251	516739	539610	565513	565144	576899
A Financial institutions	18546	20987	24340	22575	23844	29645	9315	8411	10900	6103	11884	15608
B Insurance	4484	4636	4391	6168	8194	7045	5453	3792	−3979	5280	2794	3074
C Real estate and business services	359700	384387	436196	487482	516445	524426	540483	504536	532689	554130	550466	558217
Real estate, except dwellings	45569	45978	63817	70953	85104	93157	106037	100869	106183	122445	123027	121155
Dwellings	314131	338409	372379	416529	431341	431269	434446	403667	426506	431685	427439	437062
9 Community, social and personal services	31172	35986	41858	46339	53735	52297	45747	56991	56749	58949	59552	58386
Total industries	836622	904129	1013126	1123498	1191483	1219243	1177561	1084172	1105435	1147368	1157948	1172158
Producers of government services	138551	148182	172559	188241	196839	214488	224580	223982	223359	224069	210571	212291
Private non-profit institutions serving households	2344	2457	2628	2813	3036	3191	3268	3239	3307	3398	3534	3639
Total	977517	1054768	1188313	1314552	1391358	1436922	1405409	1311393	1332101	1374835	1372053	1388088

2.12 Gross fixed capital formation by kind of activity of owner, ISIC divisions, in constant prices

Million French francs

	1986	1987	1988	1989	1990	1991	1992	1993	1994	1995	1996	1997
At constant prices of: 1980												
All producers												
1 Agriculture, hunting, forestry and fishing	18452	17311	19781	22202	22636	20116	18475	17179	19098	20467	20963	20660
2 Mining and quarrying	737	592	696	620	455	357	322	23	−1	−3797	231	197
A Coal mining	737	592	696	620	455	357	322	23	−1	−3797	231	197
B Crude petroleum and natural gas production	...	...	...	...	...	...	...	...	...	...	...	...
C Metal ore mining	...	...	...	...	...	...	...	...	...	...	...	...
D Other mining	...	...	...	...	...	...	...	...	...	...	...	...
3 Manufacturing	99177	104487	116128	124282	133506	126827	112966	91269	95859	97100	100098	99962
A Manufacturing of food, beverages and tobacco	13796	14368	17274	19549	18243	19255	18693	15345	15154	12641	12861	12510
B Textile, wearing apparel and leather industries	4282	4642	5517	5336	5489	4587	4318	3250	3438	3532	3543	3338
C Manufacture of wood and wood products, including furniture	3624	4024	4598	5366	5320	5225	4536	3058	3160	2968	2941	2801

France

Million French francs

	1986	1987	1988	1989	1990	1991	1992	1993	1994	1995	1996	1997
At constant prices of: 1980												
D Manufacture of paper and paper products, printing and publishing	7914	8786	9487	10600	11723	10983	8870	6236	6344	7444	8026	7878
E Manufacture of chemicals and chemical petroleum, coal, rubber and plastic products	19331	20780	21996	23660	26798	24701	22877	20664	20962	22176	23458	23146
F Manufacture of non-metallic mineral products, except products of petroleum and coal	5141	5456	6939	7635	6260	5297	3550	4806	5471	6813	6935	7307
G Basic metal industries	8962	8546	8092	8084	8165	7468	6986	4935	5767	4880	4845	5084
H Manufacture of fabricated metal products, machinery and equipment	36127	37885	42225	44052	51508	49311	43136	32975	35563	36646	37489	37898
I Other manufacturing industries	...	...	...	...	...	...	...	...	...	...	...	...
4 Electricity, gas and water	31924	29556	28072	27299	25570	25290	28911	29008	26413	26419	26634	25504
5 Construction	15104	15903	18163	21122	18562	19612	16545	15621	15158	13907	13118	13271
6 Wholesale and retail trade, restaurants and hotels	52587	61442	60269	66709	65066	65557	64411	58136	60032	63344	63364	62260
A Wholesale and retail trade	38969	44818	42947	48108	46145	46019	45569	42816	45044	48036	48223	47518
B Restaurants and hotels	13618	16624	17322	18601	18921	19538	18842	15320	14988	15308	15141	14742
7 Transport, storage and communication	49964	52598	59707	64565	67986	74639	70218	64868	56471	58256	53685	58094
A Transport and storage	33466	36047	43817	46609	49474	52325	53607	45693	41007	42563	39397	41358
B Communication	16498	16551	15890	17956	18512	22314	16611	19175	15464	15693	14288	16736
8 Finance, insurance, real estate and business services	250756	260977	286904	310323	319527	316238	313384	290385	303767	318199	321097	321475
A Financial institutions	11437	12868	14657	13402	14013	16925	6636	6282	8470	5100	11019	13555
B Insurance	2977	2990	2747	3786	4907	4031	3169	2209	–1767	3098	2777	2857
C Real estate and business services	236342	245119	269500	293135	300607	295282	303579	281894	297064	310001	307301	305063
Real estate, except dwellings	28875	29305	40252	43230	52182	56664	65145	63231	66478	78743	80942	80021
Dwellings	207467	215814	229248	249905	248425	238618	238434	218663	230586	231258	226359	225042
9 Community, social and personal services	20344	22867	26387	28630	32503	30738	27201	33937	33715	35318	35893	35244
Total industries	539045	565733	616107	665752	685811	679374	652433	600426	610512	629213	635083	636667
Producers of government services	92557	96428	109663	117174	119337	126141	130557	130173	129385	129008	119350	119195
Private non-profit institutions serving households	1566	1601	1679	1772	1884	1919	1955	1938	1981	2041	2119	2167
Total	633168	663762	727449	784698	807032	807434	784945	732537	741878	760262	756552	758029

2.17 Exports and imports of goods and services, detail

Million French francs

	1986	1987	1988	1989	1990	1991	1992	1993	1994	1995	1996	1997
Exports of goods and services												
1 Exports of merchandise, f.o.b.	860303	886740	992606	1135583	1173049	1218530	1247213	1203283	1310041	1429458	1496475	1713321
2 Transport and communication	49486	50045	53717	59151	59532	61673	60610	61286	62315	63517	62382	67757
3 Insurance service charges	1946	2622	2505	1999	1634	1993	2090	2604	2992	3356	3144	3024
4 Other commodities	95665	90984	91058	111431	124086	136131	145641	156554	172341	170048	191477	222043
5 Adjustments of merchandise exports to change-of-ownership basis	...	...	...	...	...	...	...	...	...	...	...	...

France

Million French francs

	1986	1987	1988	1989	1990	1991	1992	1993	1994	1995	1996	1997
6 Direct purchases in the domestic market by non-residential households	66695	70992	81418	102923	109671	119735	132549	132641	136441	136595	144200	162353
7 Direct purchases in the domestic market by extraterritorial bodies	...	...	...	...	...	...	...	...	...	...	...	...
Total exports of goods and services	1074095	1101383	1221304	1411087	1467972	1538062	1588103	1556368	1684130	1802974	1897678	2168498

Imports of goods and services

	1986	1987	1988	1989	1990	1991	1992	1993	1994	1995	1996	1997
1 Imports of merchandise, c.i.f.	893847	952251	1063873	1229621	1273885	1302876	1268897	1171952	1283565	1383901	1430825	1563648
2 Adjustments of merchandise imports to change-of-ownership basis	...	...	...	...	...	...	...	...	...	...	...	...
3 Other transport and communication	26416	27358	29920	32048	35285	36546	36782	37480	34239	35886	35484	40351
4 Other insurance service charges	2614	4570	6091	4448	3880	4812	4362	6687	4460	4130	7220	5661
5 Other commodities	53799	58842	59743	72773	90176	100392	109430	115505	123799	116444	128401	142161
6 Direct purchases abroad by government	...	...	...	...	...	...	...	...	...	...	...	...
7 Direct purchases abroad by resident households	45113	51328	58000	64162	66576	69835	74060	73143	77012	81097	90250	96180
Total imports of goods and services	1021789	1094349	1217627	1403052	1469802	1514461	1493531	1404767	1523075	1621458	1692180	1848001
Balance of goods and services	52306	7034	3677	8035	–1830	23601	94572	151601	161055	181516	205498	320497
Total imports and balance of goods and services	1074095	1101383	1221304	1411087	1467972	1538062	1588103	1556368	1684130	1802974	1897678	2168498

3.11 General government production account: total and subsectors

Million French francs

	1986 Total government	1986 Central government	1986 State or provincial government	1986 Local government	1986 Social security funds	1987 Total government	1987 Central government	1987 State or provincial government	1987 Local government	1987 Social security funds
Gross output										
1 Sales	...	...	...	...	...	...	...	...	...	...
2 Services produced for own use	959509	546752	...	222347	190410	1004657	568344	...	234465	201848
3 Own account capital formation	188450	53732	...	95240	39478	202236	62372	...	100195	39669
Gross output	1147959	600484	...	317587	229888	1206893	630716	...	334660	241517
Gross input										
Intermediate consumption	323592	159925	...	103667	60000	348597	178536	...	108314	61747
subtotal: Value added	824367	440559	...	213920	169888	858296	452180	...	226346	179770
1 Indirect taxes, net	4243	–3971	...	–1227	9441	7332	–1092	...	–1396	9820
A Indirect taxes	16896	5968	...	1487	9441	17764	6330	...	1614	9820
B less: Subsidies	12653	9939	...	2714	–	10432	7422	...	3010	–
2 Consumption of fixed capital	88614	21050	...	59015	8549	95049	22139	...	63858	9052
3 Compensation of employees	730941	422429	...	156614	151898	751982	427176	...	163908	160898
4 Net operating surplus	569	1051	...	–482	–	3933	3957	...	–24	–
Gross input	1147959	600484	...	317587	229888	1206893	630716	...	334660	241517

France

	1988					1989				
	Total govern-ment	Central govern-ment	State or provincial govern-ment	Local govern-ment	Social security funds	Total govern-ment	Central govern-ment	State or provincial govern-ment	Local govern-ment	Social security funds
Gross output										
1 Sales	...	...	...	...	...	...	...	...	...	...
2 Services produced for own use	1058400	599978	...	248677	209745	1106075	618302	...	263353	224420
3 Own account capital formation	212173	63449	...	107452	41272	219595	66020	...	110953	42622
Gross output	1270573	663427	...	356129	251017	1325670	684322	...	374306	267042
Gross input										
Intermediate consumption	379578	200752	...	114374	64452	387824	200282	...	119375	68167
subtotal: Value added	890995	462675	...	241755	186565	937846	484040	...	254931	198875
1 Indirect taxes, net	9554	312	...	−1145	10387	13162	2997	...	−1116	11281
A Indirect taxes	18196	5984	...	1825	10387	19542	6238	...	2023	11281
B less: Subsidies	8642	5672	...	2970	—	6380	3241	...	3139	—
2 Consumption of fixed capital	102336	23391	...	69319	9626	110785	25239	...	75316	10230
3 Compensation of employees	781340	441342	...	173446	166552	819090	461007	...	180719	177364
4 Net operating surplus	−2235	−2370	...	135	—	−5191	−5203	...	12	—
Gross input	1270573	663427	...	356129	251017	1325670	684322	...	374306	267042

	1990					1991				
	Total govern-ment	Central govern-ment	State or provincial govern-ment	Local govern-ment	Social security funds	Total govern-ment	Central govern-ment	State or provincial govern-ment	Local govern-ment	Social security funds
Gross output										
1 Sales	...	...	...	...	...	...	...	...	...	...
2 Services produced for own use	1170435	645966	...	285474	238995	1238998	677839	...	309007	252152
3 Own account capital formation	245453	87768	...	112772	44913	243915	77248	...	119365	47302
Gross output	1415888	733734	...	398246	283908	1482913	755087	...	428372	299454
Gross input										
Intermediate consumption	408146	206447	...	128149	73550	431431	216091	...	136992	78348
subtotal: Value added	1007742	527287	...	270097	210358	1051482	538996	...	291380	221106
1 Indirect taxes, net	16341	4857	...	−837	12321	16194	3674	...	−527	13047
A Indirect taxes	21220	6562	...	2337	12321	22673	6758	...	2868	13047
B less: Subsidies	4879	1705	...	3174	—	6479	3084	...	3395	—
2 Consumption of fixed capital	119557	26784	...	81869	10904	129829	28572	...	89450	11807
3 Compensation of employees	861092	483624	...	190335	187133	907407	507480	...	203675	196252
4 Net operating surplus	10752	12022	...	−1270	—	−1948	−730	...	−1218	—
Gross input	1415888	733734	...	398246	283908	1482913	755087	...	428372	299454

	1992					1993				
	Total govern-ment	Central govern-ment	State or provincial govern-ment	Local govern-ment	Social security funds	Total govern-ment	Central govern-ment	State or provincial govern-ment	Local govern-ment	Social security funds
Gross output										
1 Sales	...	...	...	...	...	...	...	...	...	...
2 Services produced for own use	1320450	720676	...	333174	266600	1402898	765498	...	353452	283948
3 Own account capital formation	263333	86638	...	126503	50192	279962	94302	...	131834	53826
Gross output	1583783	807314	...	459677	316792	1682860	859800	...	485286	337774
Gross input										
Intermediate consumption	459821	229457	...	148414	81950	494372	249033	...	157411	87928
subtotal: Value added	1123962	577857	...	311263	234842	1188488	610767	...	327875	249846

France

	1992					1993				
	Total govern-ment	Central govern-ment	State or provincial govern-ment	Local govern-ment	Social security funds	Total govern-ment	Central govern-ment	State or provincial govern-ment	Local govern-ment	Social security funds
1 Indirect taxes, net	17768	4177	...	–392	13983	18447	4078	...	–602	14971
A Indirect taxes	24524	7376	...	3165	13983	26283	8222	...	3090	14971
B less: Subsidies	6756	3199	...	3557	–	7836	4144	...	3692	–
2 Consumption of fixed capital	138983	30314	...	96026	12643	146975	31478	...	102112	13385
3 Compensation of employees	963958	537884	...	217858	208216	1017927	567426	...	229011	221490
4 Net operating surplus	3253	5482	...	–2229	–	5139	7785	...	–2646	–
Gross input	1583783	807314	...	459677	316792	1682860	859800	...	485286	337774

	1994					1995				
	Total govern-ment	Central govern-ment	State or provincial govern-ment	Local govern-ment	Social security funds	Total govern-ment	Central govern-ment	State or provincial govern-ment	Local govern-ment	Social security funds

Gross output

1 Sales	...	...	...	...	...	...	...	...	...	...
2 Services produced for own use	1438634	773726	...	372402	292506	1476381	776648	...	392849	306884
3 Own account capital formation	267218	71770	...	137844	57604	281129	80513	...	139833	60783
Gross output	1705852	845496	...	510246	350110	1757510	857161	...	532682	367667

Gross input

Intermediate consumption	484209	226278	...	166731	91200	473234	206899	...	172045	94290
subtotal: Value added	1221643	619218	...	343515	258910	1284276	650262	...	360637	273377
1 Indirect taxes, net	21744	6479	...	–451	15716	22874	6854	...	–488	16508
A Indirect taxes	27932	8864	...	3352	15716	29050	9044	...	3498	16508
B less: Subsidies	6188	2385	...	3803	–	6176	2190	...	3986	–
2 Consumption of fixed capital	153935	32114	...	107643	14178	159945	30818	...	114061	15066
3 Compensation of employees	1055554	587153	...	239385	229016	1101049	608431	...	250815	241803
4 Net operating surplus	–9590	–6528	...	–3062	–	408	4159	...	–3751	–
Gross input	1705852	845496	...	510246	350110	1757510	857161	...	532682	367667

	1996					1997				
	Total govern-ment	Central govern-ment	State or provincial govern-ment	Local govern-ment	Social security funds	Total govern-ment	Central govern-ment	State or provincial govern-ment	Local govern-ment	Social security funds

Gross output

1 Sales	...	...	...	...	...	...	...	...	...	...
2 Services produced for own use	1539007	796805	...	422200	320002	1573054	804427	...	444018	324609
3 Own account capital formation	288791	83178	...	141796	63817	299504	89808	...	145078	64618
Gross output	1827798	879983	...	563996	383819	1872558	894235	...	589096	389227

Gross input

Intermediate consumption	500241	222346	...	179815	98080	508164	215631	...	193036	99497
subtotal: Value added	1327557	657637	...	384181	285739	1364394	678604	...	396060	289730
1 Indirect taxes, net	22470	5151	...	117	17202	21985	4366	...	135	17484
A Indirect taxes	31209	9668	...	4339	17202	31259	9270	...	4505	17484
B less: Subsidies	8739	4517	...	4222	–	9274	4904	...	4370	–
2 Consumption of fixed capital	171554	34650	...	121885	15019	173461	34183	...	123631	15647
3 Compensation of employees	1144917	624588	...	266811	253518	1172424	638353	...	277472	256599
4 Net operating surplus	–11384	–6752	...	–4632	–	–3476	1702	...	–5178	–
Gross input	1827798	879983	...	563996	383819	1872558	894235	...	589096	389227

France

3.12 General government income and outlay account: total and subsectors

Million French francs

		1986				1987				
		Total government	Central government	State or provincial government	Local government	Social security funds	Total government	Central government	State or provincial government	Local government	Social security funds

Receipts

1	Operating surplus	569	1051	...	–482	–	3933	3957	...	–24	–
2	Property and entrepreneurial income	73895	43365	...	8505	22025	66531	39166	...	9038	18327
	A Withdrawals from public quasi-corporations	21917	21917	...	–	–	20359	20359	...	–	–
	B Interest	38076	14333	...	4215	19528	32501	12021	...	4498	15982
	C Dividends	10727	5414	...	2816	2497	10814	5505	...	2964	2345
	D Net land rent and royalties	3175	1701	...	1474	–	2857	1281	...	1576	–
3	Taxes, fees and contributions	2170224	1013604	...	197700	958920	2310033	1079811	...	208811	1021411
	A Indirect taxes	736494	610075	...	108497	17922	781946	650164	...	113376	18406
	B Direct taxes	469768	382490	...	87020	258	499110	406037	...	92876	197
	Income	321469	321469	...	–	–	349285	349285	...	–	–
	Other	148299	61021	...	87020	258	149825	56752	...	92876	197
	C Social security contributions	955257	14517	...	–	940740	1019205	16397	...	–	1002808
	D Fees, fines and penalties	8705	6522	...	2183	–	9772	7213	...	2559	–
4	Other current transfers	134054	3055	...	143103	114673	142355	–8534	...	153099	130088
	A Casualty insurance claims	572	–	...	452	120	620	–	...	471	149
	B Transfers from other government subsectors	...	–101900	...	130196	98481	...	–118095	...	139395	110998
	C Transfers from rest of the world	8052	7775	...	–	277	10337	10007	...	–	330
	D Other transfers, except imputed	29583	8859	...	8435	12289	32601	8919	...	9020	14662
	E Imputed unfunded employee pension and welfare contributions	95847	88321	...	4020	3506	98797	90635	...	4213	3949
	Total current receipts	2378742	1061075	...	348826	1095618	2522852	1114400	...	370924	1169826

Disbursements

1	Government final consumption expenditure	959509	546752	...	222347	190410	1004657	568344	...	234465	201848
2	Property income	145927	95608	...	45063	5256	147570	95255	...	46824	5491
	A Interest	145859	95540	...	45063	5256	147497	95182	...	46824	5491
	B Net land rent and royalties	68	68	...	–	–	73	73	...	–	–
3	Subsidies	118625	106217	...	8035	4373	117683	104109	...	8666	4908
4	Other current transfers	1212164	383598	...	49692	905651	1269650	407788	...	51608	942552
	A Casualty insurance premiums, net	1161	56	...	853	252	1217	18	...	925	274
	B Transfers to other government subsectors	...	111684	...	3831	11262	...	115200	...	3855	13243
	C Social security benefits	880391	–	...	–	880391	913086	–	...	–	913086
	D Social assistance grants	129284	109435	...	19849	–	130718	110130	...	20588	–
	E Unfunded employee welfare benefits	101205	93679	...	4020	3506	107413	99251	...	4213	3949
	F Transfers to private non-profit institutions serving households	7493	3809	...	3061	623	7927	4155	...	3202	570
	G Other transfers n.e.c.	57426	33648	...	18078	5700	71034	45007	...	18825	7202

France

Million French francs

	1986					1987				
	Total government	Central government	State or provincial government	Local government	Social security funds	Total government	Central government	State or provincial government	Local government	Social security funds
H Transfers to rest of the world	35204	31287	...	–	3917	38255	34027	...	–	4228
Net saving	–57483	–71100	...	23689	–10072	–16708	–61096	...	29361	15027
Total current disbursements and net saving	2378742	1061075	...	348826	1095618	2522852	1114400	...	370924	1169826

	1988					1989				
	Total government	Central government	State or provincial government	Local government	Social security funds	Total government	Central government	State or provincial government	Local government	Social security funds

Receipts

1 Operating surplus	–2235	–2370	...	135	–	–5191	–5203	...	12	–
2 Property and entrepreneurial income	62550	34874	...	9714	17962	70708	41181	...	10650	18877
A Withdrawals from public quasi-corporations	15456	15456	...	–	–	18299	18299	...	–	–
B Interest	31403	11364	...	4580	15459	33389	11156	...	5241	16992
C Dividends	12487	6706	...	3278	2503	15428	10117	...	3426	1885
D Net land rent and royalties	3204	1348	...	1856	–	3592	1609	...	1983	–
3 Taxes, fees and contributions	2439819	1121948	...	229322	1088549	2616467	1194046	...	243216	1179205
A Indirect taxes	829419	684088	...	127313	18018	873123	717269	...	137123	18731
B Direct taxes	514221	415118	...	98967	136	553220	449973	...	102979	268
Income	360707	360707	...	–	–	392324	392324	...	–	–
Other	153514	54411	...	98967	136	160896	57649	...	102979	268
C Social security contributions	1086937	16542	...	–	1070395	1179692	19486	...	–	1160206
D Fees, fines and penalties	9242	6200	...	3042	–	10432	7318	...	3114	–
4 Other current transfers	171395	9158	...	163288	142128	159181	–10764	...	177576	135970
A Casualty insurance claims	619	–	...	495	124	190	–	...	151	39
B Transfers from other government subsectors	...	–124181	...	148374	118986	...	–135558	...	162854	116305
C Transfers from rest of the world	14214	13285	...	–	929	13288	12998	...	–	290
D Other transfers, except imputed	53031	25433	...	9894	17704	39469	14884	...	10010	14575
E Imputed unfunded employee pension and welfare contributions	103531	94621	...	4525	4385	106234	96912	...	4561	4761
Total current receipts	2671529	1163610	...	402459	1248639	2841165	1219260	...	431454	1334052

Disbursements

1 Government final consumption expenditure	1058400	599978	...	248677	209745	1106075	618302	...	263353	224420
2 Property income	152362	99146	...	47779	5437	168485	113143	...	49780	5562
A Interest	152287	99071	...	47779	5437	168366	113024	...	49780	5562
B Net land rent and royalties	75	75	...	–	–	119	119	...	–	–
3 Subsidies	102041	88576	...	8319	5146	102657	88054	...	8705	5898
4 Other current transfers	1350189	425699	...	56857	1010812	1425546	437108	...	60475	1071564
A Casualty insurance premiums, net	1321	29	...	1020	272	811	18	...	632	161
B Transfers to other government subsectors	...	124584	...	3849	14746	...	123099	...	4117	16385
C Social security benefits	978761	–	...	–	978761	1039064	–	...	–	1039064
D Social assistance grants	138284	116549	...	21735	–	143098	121851	...	21247	–

France

	1988					1989				
	Total government	Central government	State or provincial government	Local government	Social security funds	Total government	Central government	State or provincial government	Local government	Social security funds
E Unfunded employee welfare benefits	111384	102474	...	4525	4385	116735	107413	...	4561	4761
F Transfers to private non-profit institutions serving households	9918	5707	...	3689	522	10180	5242	...	4368	570
G Other transfers n.e.c.	61619	31947	...	22039	7633	67422	35971	...	25550	5901
H Transfers to rest of the world	48902	44409	...	–	4493	48236	43514	...	–	4722
Net saving	8537	–49789	...	40827	17499	38402	–37347	...	49141	26608
Total current disbursements and net saving	2671529	1163610	...	402459	1248639	2841165	1219260	...	431454	1334052

	1990					1991				
	Total government	Central government	State or provincial government	Local government	Social security funds	Total government	Central government	State or provincial government	Local government	Social security funds

Receipts

1 Operating surplus	10752	12022	...	–1270	–	–1948	–730	...	–1218	–
2 Property and entrepreneurial income	80021	49590	...	12500	17931	78550	46681	...	13133	18736
A Withdrawals from public quasi-corporations	20918	20918	...	–	–	18935	18935	...	–	–
B Interest	35508	13795	...	5774	15939	37068	14046	...	6251	16771
C Dividends	20115	13580	...	4543	1992	18344	11870	...	4509	1965
D Net land rent and royalties	3480	1297	...	2183	–	4203	1830	...	2373	–
3 Taxes, fees and contributions	2769595	1249868	...	267575	1252152	2875589	1288655	...	281509	1305425
A Indirect taxes	922814	746757	...	156912	19145	926557	742532	...	163951	20074
B Direct taxes	581504	474502	...	106793	209	632890	518820	...	113837	233
Income	415280	415280	...	–	–	463221	463221	...	–	–
Other	166224	59222	...	106793	209	169669	55599	...	113837	233
C Social security contributions	1253800	21002	...	–	1232798	1304210	19092	...	–	1285118
D Fees, fines and penalties	11477	7607	...	3870	–	11932	8211	...	3721	–
4 Other current transfers	164123	–23185	...	188047	136448	195912	–31542	...	207558	160648
A Casualty insurance claims	722	–	...	562	160	698	–	...	562	136
B Transfers from other government subsectors	...	–149065	...	171331	114921	...	–183161	...	188247	135666
C Transfers from rest of the world	12523	12422	...	1	100	27644	27643	...	1	–
D Other transfers, except imputed	40041	12349	...	11448	16244	49595	16220	...	13718	19657
E Imputed unfunded employee pension and welfare contributions	110837	101109	...	4705	5023	117975	107756	...	5030	5189
Total current receipts	3024491	1288295	...	466852	1406531	3148103	1303064	...	500982	1484809

Disbursements

1 Government final consumption expenditure	1170435	645966	...	285474	238995	1238998	677839	...	309007	252152
2 Property income	191321	134227	...	51633	5461	208554	146732	...	55645	6177
A Interest	191222	134128	...	51633	5461	208442	146620	...	55645	6177
B Net land rent and royalties	99	99	...	–	–	112	112	...	–	–
3 Subsidies	101086	85671	...	9415	6000	102748	85267	...	10031	7450
4 Other current transfers	1520469	444437	...	69874	1143345	1635045	473056	...	74668	1228073
A Casualty insurance premiums, net	1552	25	...	1189	338	1686	23	...	1339	324

France

	1990					1991				
	Total government	Central government	State or provincial government	Local government	Social security funds	Total government	Central government	State or provincial government	Local government	Social security funds
B Transfers to other government subsectors	...	114214	...	4982	17991	...	115910	...	4789	20053
C Social security benefits	1107756	—	...	—	1107756	1183483	—	...	—	1183483
D Social assistance grants	152362	129480	...	22882	—	163752	139385	...	24367	—
E Unfunded employee welfare benefits	122330	112602	...	4705	5023	127242	117023	...	5030	5189
F Transfers to private non-profit institutions serving households	11329	5732	...	4933	664	12221	6099	...	5406	716
G Other transfers n.e.c.	76999	39578	...	31179	6242	80590	36137	...	33733	10720
H Transfers to rest of the world	48141	42806	...	4	5331	66071	58479	...	4	7588
Net saving	41180	−22006	...	50456	12730	−37242	−79830	...	51631	−9043
Total current disbursements and net saving	3024491	1288295	...	466852	1406531	3148103	1303064	...	500982	1484809

	1992					1993				
	Total government	Central government	State or provincial government	Local government	Social security funds	Total government	Central government	State or provincial government	Local government	Social security funds

Receipts

1 Operating surplus	3253	5482	...	−2229	—	5139	7785	...	−2646	—
2 Property and entrepreneurial income	76849	46209	...	13372	17268	75013	45301	...	12602	17110
A Withdrawals from public quasi-corporations	18426	18426	...	—	—	19325	19325	...	—	—
B Interest	37885	15372	...	6575	15938	39972	18222	...	5860	15890
C Dividends	16742	11147	...	4265	1330	12314	6935	...	4159	1220
D Net land rent and royalties	3796	1264	...	2532	—	3402	819	...	2583	—
3 Taxes, fees and contributions	2953964	1298176	...	293405	1362383	3029483	1320581	...	314439	1394463
A Indirect taxes	950891	762556	...	167493	20842	977592	774005	...	176414	27173
B Direct taxes	630157	508012	...	121834	311	651780	517791	...	133654	335
Income	454976	454976	...	—	—	469019	469019	...	—	—
Other	175181	53036	...	121834	311	182761	48772	...	133654	335
C Social security contributions	1360258	19028	...	—	1341230	1387017	20062	...	—	1366955
D Fees, fines and penalties	12658	8580	...	4078	—	13094	8723	...	4371	—
4 Other current transfers	204995	−43160	...	220822	184509	210721	−66948	...	229877	205958
A Casualty insurance claims	833	—	...	656	177	880	—	...	703	177
B Transfers from other government subsectors	...	−199320	...	198981	157515	...	−227148	...	206543	178771
C Transfers from rest of the world	20585	20008	...	577	—	21255	20767	...	488	—
D Other transfers, except imputed	57169	20519	...	15255	21395	53983	16104	...	16568	21311
E Imputed unfunded employee pension and welfare contributions	126408	115633	...	5353	5422	134603	123329	...	5575	5699
Total current receipts	3239061	1306707	...	525370	1564160	3320356	1306719	...	554272	1617531

Disbursements

1 Government final consumption expenditure	1320450	720676	...	333174	266600	1402898	765498	...	353452	283948
2 Property income	237383	168363	...	59573	9447	261616	183951	...	62972	14693
A Interest	237253	168233	...	59573	9447	261476	183811	...	62972	14693
B Net land rent and royalties	130	130	...	—	—	140	140	...	—	—

France

	1992					1993				
	Total govern-ment	Central govern-ment	State or provincial govern-ment	Local govern-ment	Social security funds	Total govern-ment	Central govern-ment	State or provincial govern-ment	Local govern-ment	Social security funds
3 Subsidies	112922	94111	...	10100	8711	110256	90235	...	10202	9819
4 Other current transfers	1746594	511148	...	81966	1310656	1870762	552397	...	86653	1389878
A Casualty insurance premiums, net	1883	27	...	1460	396	1983	48	...	1545	390
B Transfers to other government subsectors	...	131139	...	5631	20406	...	131608	...	5480	21078
C Social security benefits	1262220	–	...	–	1262220	1337635	4	...	–	1337631
D Social assistance grants	172695	146654	...	26041	–	194283	166228	...	28055	–
E Unfunded employee welfare benefits	133851	123076	...	5353	5422	140632	129358	...	5575	5699
F Transfers to private non-profit institutions serving households	14810	7710	...	6180	920	15375	8635	...	5948	792
G Other transfers n.e.c.	91988	41530	...	37297	13161	99282	44712	...	40046	14524
H Transfers to rest of the world	69147	61012	...	4	8131	81572	71804	...	4	9764
Net saving	–178288	–187591	...	40557	–31254	–325176	–285362	...	40993	–80807
Total current disbursements and net saving	3239061	1306707	...	525370	1564160	3320356	1306719	...	554272	1617531

	1994					1995				
	Total govern-ment	Central govern-ment	State or provincial govern-ment	Local govern-ment	Social security funds	Total govern-ment	Central govern-ment	State or provincial govern-ment	Local govern-ment	Social security funds

Receipts

1 Operating surplus	–9590	–6528	...	–3062	–	408	4159	...	–3751	–
2 Property and entrepreneurial income	60594	35846	...	12270	12478	57702	33885	...	12335	11482
A Withdrawals from public quasi-corporations	1812	1812	...	–	–	–	–	...	–	–
B Interest	35223	19220	...	5354	10649	37209	21656	...	5360	10193
C Dividends	19583	13539	...	4215	1829	16717	11072	...	4356	1289
D Net land rent and royalties	3976	1275	...	2701	–	3776	1157	...	2619	–
3 Taxes, fees and contributions	3165409	1411861	...	333533	1420015	3312903	1486225	...	341531	1485147
A Indirect taxes	1042367	832569	...	183202	26596	1091294	880044	...	182874	28376
B Direct taxes	694958	549037	...	145561	360	730258	576054	...	153838	366
Income	502101	502101	...	–	–	523404	523404	...	–	–
Other	192857	46936	...	145561	360	206854	52650	...	153838	366
C Social security contributions	1414447	21388	...	–	1393059	1479478	23073	...	–	1456405
D Fees, fines and penalties	13637	8867	...	4770	–	11873	7054	...	4819	–
4 Other current transfers	210665	–55046	...	238198	231925	222245	–61352	...	254049	237593
A Casualty insurance claims	878	–	...	702	176	1317	–	...	1059	258
B Transfers from other government subsectors	...	–216971	...	213364	208019	...	–231218	...	229489	209774
C Transfers from rest of the world	18922	18164	...	758	–	21278	20685	...	593	–
D Other transfers, except imputed	50690	15377	...	17550	17763	53662	15888	...	16875	20899
E Imputed unfunded employee pension and welfare contributions	140175	128384	...	5824	5967	145988	133293	...	6033	6662
Total current receipts	3427078	1386133	...	580939	1664418	3593258	1462917	...	604164	1734222

Disbursements

France

	1994					1995				
	Total govern-ment	Central govern-ment	State or provincial govern-ment	Local govern-ment	Social security funds	Total govern-ment	Central govern-ment	State or provincial govern-ment	Local govern-ment	Social security funds
1 Government final consumption expenditure	1438634	773726	...	372402	292506	1476381	776648	...	392849	306884
2 Property income	279655	209473	...	62483	7699	308419	232924	...	63919	11576
A Interest	279463	209281	...	62483	7699	308323	232828	...	63919	11576
B Net land rent and royalties	192	192	...	–	–	96	96	...	–	–
3 Subsidies	118667	98259	...	10609	9799	124946	103864	...	10831	10251
4 Other current transfers	1921452	616239	...	97836	1411789	1986793	630586	...	102109	1462143
A Casualty insurance premiums, net	2249	49	...	1760	440	2777	62	...	2183	532
B Transfers to other government subsectors	...	174714	...	7818	21880	...	174524	...	9816	23705
C Social security benefits	1361993	–	...	–	1361993	1408506	–	...	–	1408506
D Social assistance grants	212281	181779	...	30502	–	219640	187619	...	32021	–
E Unfunded employee welfare benefits	145681	133890	...	5824	5967	153602	140907	...	6033	6662
F Transfers to private non-profit institutions serving households	15794	8654	...	6373	767	15998	8653	...	6719	626
G Other transfers n.e.c.	97293	40409	...	45559	11325	104629	48305	...	45281	11043
H Transfers to rest of the world	86161	76744	...	–	9417	81641	70516	...	56	11069
Net saving	–331330	–311564	...	37609	–57375	–303281	–281105	...	34456	–56632
Total current disbursements and net saving	3427078	1386133	...	580939	1664418	3593258	1462917	...	604164	1734222

	1996					1997				
	Total govern-ment	Central govern-ment	State or provincial govern-ment	Local govern-ment	Social security funds	Total govern-ment	Central govern-ment	State or provincial govern-ment	Local govern-ment	Social security funds

Receipts

1 Operating surplus	–11384	–6752	...	–4632	–	–3476	1702	...	–5178	–
2 Property and entrepreneurial income	60724	35891	...	12842	11991	59213	33334	...	13158	12721
A Withdrawals from public quasi-corporations	–	–	...	–	–	–	–	...	–	–
B Interest	40699	24790	...	5704	10205	41492	24141	...	5828	11523
C Dividends	15973	9814	...	4373	1786	13533	7853	...	4482	1198
D Net land rent and royalties	4052	1287	...	2765	–	4188	1340	...	2848	–
3 Taxes, fees and contributions	3510047	1554235	...	376927	1578885	3660696	1692483	...	398729	1569484
A Indirect taxes	1165980	917688	...	200788	47504	1218894	963844	...	212844	42206
B Direct taxes	778620	603732	...	170283	4605	863736	683931	...	177874	1931
Income	558434	558434	...	–	–	638365	638365	...	–	–
Other	220186	45298	...	170283	4605	225371	45566	...	177874	1931
C Social security contributions	1550742	23966	...	–	1526776	1558420	33073	...	–	1525347
D Fees, fines and penalties	14705	8849	...	5856	–	19646	11635	...	8011	–
4 Other current transfers	235499	–86831	...	248753	232053	238207	–152067	...	263601	296509
A Casualty insurance claims	1358	–	...	1128	230	1098	–	...	852	246
B Transfers from other government subsectors	...	–269138	...	222683	204931	...	–343182	...	239084	273934
C Transfers from rest of the world	27354	26449	...	905	–	30655	29732	...	923	–
D Other transfers, except imputed	54931	16775	...	17944	20212	48268	16358	...	16426	15484

France

	1996					1997				
	Total government	Central government	State or provincial government	Local government	Social security funds	Total government	Central government	State or provincial government	Local government	Social security funds
E Imputed unfunded employee pension and welfare contributions	151856	139083	...	6093	6680	158186	145025	...	6316	6845
Total current receipts	3794886	1496543	...	633890	1822929	3954640	1575452	...	670310	1878714
Disbursements											
1 Government final consumption expenditure	1539007	796805	...	422200	320002	1573054	804427	...	444018	324609
2 Property income	314994	245877	...	61602	7515	306834	243742	...	55413	7679
A Interest	314900	245783	...	61602	7515	306742	243650	...	55413	7679
B Net land rent and royalties	94	94	...	–	–	92	92	...	–	–
3 Subsidies	159281	137088	...	11871	10322	169078	144399	...	14774	9905
4 Other current transfers	2067084	583435	...	107549	1534576	2149891	616940	...	111160	1591627
A Casualty insurance premiums, net	3145	66	...	2398	681	2043	21	...	1569	453
B Transfers to other government subsectors	...	119611	...	10537	28328	...	128599	...	10781	30456
C Social security benefits	1471932	–	...	–	1471932	1532519	9696	...	–	1522823
D Social assistance grants	214243	180980	...	33263	–	219742	184169	...	35573	–
E Unfunded employee welfare benefits	158374	145601	...	6093	6680	162645	149484	...	6316	6845
F Transfers to private non-profit institutions serving households	17834	10546	...	6756	532	19543	11541	...	7459	543
G Other transfers n.e.c.	108555	46641	...	48394	13520	112122	47076	...	49351	15695
H Transfers to rest of the world	93001	79990	...	108	12903	101277	86354	...	111	14812
Net saving	−285480	−266662	...	30668	−49486	−244217	−234056	...	44945	−55106
Total current disbursements and net saving	3794886	1496543	...	633890	1822929	3954640	1575452	...	670310	1878714

3.13 General government capital accumulation account: total and subsectors

Million French francs

	1986					1987				
	Total government	Central government	State or provincial government	Local government	Social security funds	Total government	Central government	State or provincial government	Local government	Social security funds
Finance of gross accumulation											
1 Gross saving	31131	−50050	...	82704	−1523	78341	−38957	...	93219	24079
A Consumption of fixed capital	88614	21050	...	59015	8549	95049	22139	...	63858	9052
B Net saving	−57483	−71100	...	23689	−10072	−16708	−61096	...	29361	15027
2 Capital transfers	51614	23806	...	25000	2808	56036	26640	...	26584	2812
A From other government subsectors	...	...	...	...	...	...	...	...	...	...
B From other resident sectors	23018	18771	...	2668	1579	25956	21724	...	2767	1465
C From rest of the world	28596	5035	...	22332	1229	30080	4916	...	23817	1347
Finance of gross accumulation	82745	−26244	...	107704	1285	134377	−12317	...	119803	26891
Gross accumulation											
1 Gross capital formation	159504	36833	...	109013	13658	160326	29094	...	115655	15577
A Increase in stocks	7069	7079	...	−10	–	−1434	−1459	...	25	–

France

Million French francs

	1986					1987				
	Total government	Central government	State or provincial government	Local government	Social security funds	Total government	Central government	State or provincial government	Local government	Social security funds
B Gross fixed capital formation	152435	29754	...	109023	13658	161760	30553	...	115630	15577
2 Purchases of land, net	2805	852	...	918	1035	1381	905	...	283	193
3 Purchases of intangible assets, net	78	17	...	61	–	119	21	...	98	–
4 Capital transfers	58758	46873	...	10416	1469	72944	60459	...	11458	1027
Net lending	–138400	–110819	...	–12704	–14877	–100393	–102796	...	–7691	10094
Gross accumulation	82745	–26244	...	107704	1285	134377	–12317	...	119803	26891

	1988					1989				
	Total government	Central government	State or provincial government	Local government	Social security funds	Total government	Central government	State or provincial government	Local government	Social security funds

Finance of gross accumulation

1 Gross saving	110873	–26398	...	110146	27125	149187	–12108	...	124457	36838
A Consumption of fixed capital	102336	23391	...	69319	9626	110785	25239	...	75316	10230
B Net saving	8537	–49789	...	40827	17499	38402	–37347	...	49141	26608
2 Capital transfers	66229	33047	...	30391	2791	67879	30742	...	34417	2720
A From other government subsectors	...	...	...	...	...	...	...	...	...	...
B From other resident sectors	32625	27742	...	3461	1422	30880	25173	...	4155	1552
C From rest of the world	33604	5305	...	26930	1369	36999	5569	...	30262	1168
Finance of gross accumulation	177102	6649	...	140537	29916	217066	18634	...	158874	39558

Gross accumulation

1 Gross capital formation	188144	34523	...	137358	16263	204989	37397	...	149872	17720
A Increase in stocks	–412	–488	...	76	–	–88	–107	...	19	–
B Gross fixed capital formation	188556	35011	...	137282	16263	205077	37504	...	149853	17720
2 Purchases of land, net	1612	1095	...	354	163	4324	2862	...	1348	114
3 Purchases of intangible assets, net	165	25	...	140	–	239	36	...	203	–
4 Capital transfers	82072	67944	...	13034	1094	82728	64944	...	16229	1555
Net lending	–94891	–96938	...	–10349	12396	–75214	–86605	...	–8778	20169
Gross accumulation	177102	6649	...	140537	29916	217066	18634	...	158874	39558

	1990					1991				
	Total government	Central government	State or provincial government	Local government	Social security funds	Total government	Central government	State or provincial government	Local government	Social security funds

Finance of gross accumulation

1 Gross saving	160737	4778	...	132325	23634	92587	–51258	...	141081	2764
A Consumption of fixed capital	119557	26784	...	81869	10904	129829	28572	...	89450	11807
B Net saving	41180	–22006	...	50456	12730	–37242	–79830	...	51631	–9043
2 Capital transfers	79287	39627	...	37256	2404	103797	62666	...	38311	2820
A From other government subsectors	...	...	...	...	...	...	...	...	...	...
B From other resident sectors	37081	33044	...	3269	768	59857	54977	...	3528	1352
C From rest of the world	42206	6583	...	33987	1636	43940	7689	...	34783	1468
Finance of gross accumulation	240024	44405	...	169581	26038	196384	11408	...	179392	5584

France

	1990					1991				
	Total government	Central government	State or provincial government	Local government	Social security funds	Total government	Central government	State or provincial government	Local government	Social security funds

Gross accumulation

1 Gross capital formation	229662	57454	...	153096	19112	238936	48251	...	167907	22778
A Increase in stocks	17629	17587	...	42	–	8496	8459	...	37	–
B Gross fixed capital formation	212033	39867	...	153054	19112	230440	39792	...	167870	22778
2 Purchases of land, net	3467	1209	...	1814	444	4289	1165	...	2673	451
3 Purchases of intangible assets, net	429	130	...	299	–	341	–59	...	400	–
4 Capital transfers	107555	87163	...	18892	1500	99896	75751	...	22603	1542
Net lending	–101089	–101551	...	–4520	4982	–147078	–113700	...	–14191	–19187
Gross accumulation	240024	44405	...	169581	26038	196384	11408	...	179392	5584

	1992					1993				
	Total government	Central government	State or provincial government	Local government	Social security funds	Total government	Central government	State or provincial government	Local government	Social security funds

Finance of gross accumulation

1 Gross saving	–39305	–157277	...	136583	–18611	–178201	–253884	...	143105	–67422
A Consumption of fixed capital	138983	30314	...	96026	12643	146975	31478	...	102112	13385
B Net saving	–178288	–187591	...	40557	–31254	–325176	–285362	...	40993	–80807
2 Capital transfers	118892	74103	...	41757	3032	105434	57833	...	44390	3211
A From other government subsectors	...	...	...	...	...	...	...	...	...	...
B From other resident sectors	72045	66756	...	4210	1079	54642	49862	...	3517	1263
C From rest of the world	46847	7347	...	37547	1953	50792	7971	...	40873	1948
Finance of gross accumulation	79587	–83174	...	178340	–15579	–72767	–196051	...	187495	–64211

Gross accumulation

1 Gross capital formation	246417	45874	...	175163	25380	230589	31476	...	173362	25751
A Increase in stocks	4100	4062	...	38	–	–10932	–10972	...	40	–
B Gross fixed capital formation	242317	41812	...	175125	25380	241521	42448	...	173322	25751
2 Purchases of land, net	5515	1246	...	3409	860	5347	1669	...	3110	568
3 Purchases of intangible assets, net	501	64	...	437	–	471	6	...	465	–
4 Capital transfers	113969	81998	...	24153	7818	121476	88874	...	25737	6865
Net lending	–286815	–212356	...	–24822	–49637	–430650	–318076	...	–15179	–97395
Gross accumulation	79587	–83174	...	178340	–15579	–72767	–196051	...	187495	–64211

	1994					1995				
	Total government	Central government	State or provincial government	Local government	Social security funds	Total government	Central government	State or provincial government	Local government	Social security funds

Finance of gross accumulation

1 Gross saving	–177395	–279450	...	145252	–43197	–143336	–250287	...	148517	–41566
A Consumption of fixed capital	153935	32114	...	107643	14178	159945	30818	...	114061	15066
B Net saving	–331330	–311564	...	37609	–57375	–303281	–281105	...	34456	–56632
2 Capital transfers	113657	66147	...	44144	3366	105099	58472	...	42702	3925
A From other government subsectors	...	...	...	...	...	...	...	...	...	...
B From other resident sectors	63324	58579	...	3306	1439	55954	50822	...	3212	1920

France

	1994					1995				
	Total government	Central government	State or provincial government	Local government	Social security funds	Total government	Central government	State or provincial government	Local government	Social security funds
C From rest of the world	50333	7568	...	40838	1927	49145	7650	...	39490	2005
Finance of gross accumulation ...	−63738	−213303	...	189396	−39831	−38237	−191815	...	191219	−37641

Gross accumulation

	Total	Central	State/prov	Local	Social	Total	Central	State/prov	Local	Social
1 Gross capital formation	234117	32045	...	175001	27071	246847	42257	...	176819	27771
A Increase in stocks	−7325	−7368	...	43	–	4755	4711	...	44	–
B Gross fixed capital formation	241442	39413	...	174958	27071	242092	37546	...	176775	27771
2 Purchases of land, net	4852	1048	...	3577	227	6413	2688	...	3649	76
3 Purchases of intangible assets, net	539	107	...	432	–	457	3	...	454	–
4 Capital transfers	137952	109352	...	25609	2991	120863	89842	...	27792	3229
Net lending	−441198	−355855	...	−15223	−70120	−412817	−326605	...	−17495	−68717
Gross accumulation	−63738	−213303	...	189396	−39831	−38237	−191815	...	191219	−37641

	1996					1997				
	Total government	Central government	State or provincial government	Local government	Social security funds	Total government	Central government	State or provincial government	Local government	Social security funds

Finance of gross accumulation

	Total	Central	State/prov	Local	Social	Total	Central	State/prov	Local	Social
1 Gross saving	−113926	−232012	...	152553	−34467	−70756	−199873	...	168576	−39459
A Consumption of fixed capital	171554	34650	...	121885	15019	173461	34183	...	123631	15647
B Net saving	−285480	−266662	...	30668	−49486	−244217	−234056	...	44945	−55106
2 Capital transfers	102264	56105	...	42632	3527	146962	99924	...	44018	3020
A From other government subsectors	...	...	...	...	...	...	...	...	...	...
B From other resident sectors	53270	48141	...	3583	1546	95818	91668	...	4150	–
C From rest of the world	48994	7964	...	39049	1981	51144	8256	...	39868	3020
Finance of gross accumulation ...	−11662	−175907	...	195185	−30940	76206	−99949	...	212594	−36439

Gross accumulation

	Total	Central	State/prov	Local	Social	Total	Central	State/prov	Local	Social
1 Gross capital formation	232199	45028	...	158965	28206	231861	43400	...	159841	28620
A Increase in stocks	4739	4699	...	40	–	1786	1745	...	41	–
B Gross fixed capital formation	227460	40329	...	158925	28206	230075	41655	...	159800	28620
2 Purchases of land, net	5139	1281	...	3686	172	5160	1148	...	3866	146
3 Purchases of intangible assets, net	635	9	...	626	–	639	–	...	639	–
4 Capital transfers	116001	84380	...	28471	3150	119771	88419	...	30671	681
Net lending	−365636	−306605	...	3437	−62468	−281225	−232916	...	17577	−65886
Gross accumulation	−11662	−175907	...	195185	−30940	76206	−99949	...	212594	−36439

France

3.14 General government capital finance account: total and subsectors

Million French francs

	1986					1987				
	Total government	Central government	State or provincial government	Local government	Social security funds	Total government	Central government	State or provincial government	Local government	Social security funds

Acquisition of financial assets

1 Gold and SDRs	−116	−116	...	...	...	−20	−20	...	...	...
2 Currency and transferable deposits	−17383	−13064	...	2770	−7089	75710	78909	...	8535	−11734
3 Other deposits	−7790	−558	...	−366	−6866	−2790	1706	...	−644	−3852
4 Bills and bonds, short-term	−	...	...	...	−	2069	...	...	...	2069
5 Bonds, long-term	6680	4769	...	845	1066	3976	2005	...	388	1583
6 Corporate equity securities	55928	50474	...	−	5454	−34422	−48327	...	−	13905
7 Short-term loans, n.e.c.	−2190	−6487	...	4587	−290	45969	18522	...	9379	18068
8 Long-term loans, n.e.c.	−23296	−23296	...	−	...	5239	5239	...	−	...
9 Other receivables	127	...	...	127	...	127	...	...	127	...
10 Other assets	33282	23110	...	5991	4181	33456	23516	...	2165	7775
Total aquisition of financial assets	45242	34832	...	13954	−3544	129314	81550	...	19950	27814

Incurrence of liabilities

1 Currency and transferable deposits	−14542	−14542	...	...	1039	41392	41392	...	...	168
2 Other deposits	−7545	−8584	...	−	...	2936	2768	...	−	...
3 Bills and bonds, short-term	38364	38364	...	...	...	60608	60608	...	...	...
4 Bonds, long-term	112416	111649	...	767	−	15087	18849	...	−3762	−
5 Short-term loans, n.e.c.	20396	21184	...	−5295	4507	76130	71762	...	998	3370
6 Long-term loans, n.e.c.	29997	1344	...	27539	1114	36000	1081	...	33708	1211
7 Other payables	111	101	...	10	...	−	−	...	−	...
8 Other liabilities	4445	−3865	...	3637	4673	−2446	−12114	...	−3303	12971
Total incurrence of liabilities	183642	145651	...	26658	11333	229707	184346	...	27641	17720
Net lending	−138400	−110819	...	−12704	−14877	−100393	−102796	...	−7691	10094
Incurrence of liabilities and net worth	45242	34832	...	13954	−3544	129314	81550	...	19950	27814

	1988					1989				
	Total government	Central government	State or provincial government	Local government	Social security funds	Total government	Central government	State or provincial government	Local government	Social security funds

Acquisition of financial assets

1 Gold and SDRs	291	291	...	...	...	115	115	...	...	...
2 Currency and transferable deposits	−54678	−47713	...	−5332	−1633	44962	34374	...	6085	4503
3 Other deposits	−2195	2007	...	995	−5197	−215	42	...	−244	−13
4 Bills and bonds, short-term	1663	−	...	...	1663	−3130	−	...	...	−3130
5 Bonds, long-term	4803	267	...	222	4314	2703	−931	...	1767	1867
6 Corporate equity securities	5185	287	...	−	4898	17919	6987	...	−	10932
7 Short-term loans, n.e.c.	48458	18815	...	6654	22989	48290	30300	...	−693	18683
8 Long-term loans, n.e.c.	9957	9957	...	−	...	2592	2592	...	−	...
9 Other receivables	130	...	...	130	...	−1017	...	...	−1017	...
10 Other assets	28097	12099	...	13204	2794	40735	24260	...	8742	7733
Total aquisition of financial assets	41711	−3990	...	15873	29828	152954	97739	...	14640	40575

France

	1988					1989				
	Total govern-ment	Central govern-ment	State or provincial govern-ment	Local govern-ment	Social security funds	Total govern-ment	Central govern-ment	State or provincial govern-ment	Local govern-ment	Social security funds

Incurrence of liabilities

1 Currency and transferable deposits	−2283	−2283	...	...	151	19590	19590	...	...	153
2 Other deposits	4667	4516	...	−	...	−189	−342	...	−	...
3 Bills and bonds, short-term	15541	15541	...	...	...	70018	70018	...	...	...
4 Bonds, long-term	60599	62167	...	−2350	782	71977	76362	...	−2454	−1931
5 Short-term loans, n.e.c.	−3680	−12856	...	5004	4172	32677	22232	...	2416	8029
6 Long-term loans, n.e.c.	35058	10594	...	23149	1315	17716	−1381	...	19886	−789
7 Other payables	−	−	...	−	...	−	−	...	−	...
8 Other liabilities	26700	15269	...	419	11012	16379	−2135	...	3570	14944
Total incurrence of liabilities	136602	92948	...	26222	17432	228168	184344	...	23418	20406
Net lending	−94891	−96938	...	−10349	12396	−75214	−86605	...	−8778	20169
Incurrence of liabilities and net worth	41711	−3990	...	15873	29828	152954	97739	...	14640	40575

	1990					1991				
	Total govern-ment	Central govern-ment	State or provincial govern-ment	Local govern-ment	Social security funds	Total govern-ment	Central govern-ment	State or provincial govern-ment	Local govern-ment	Social security funds

Acquisition of financial assets

1 Gold and SDRs	12244	−619	...	2218	10645	4243	−23	...	43	4223
2 Currency and transferable deposits	2534	−4980	...	1864	5650	−20225	−27490	...	−8755	16020
3 Other deposits	−503	−183	...	−442	122	1801	−491	...	103	2189
4 Bills and bonds, short-term	−602	−	...	...	−602	383	383	...	−	−
5 Bonds, long-term	7402	1762	...	141	5499	3036	−404	...	1941	1499
6 Corporate equity securities	5788	3931	...	−	1857	6855	3374	...	−	3481
7 Short-term loans, n.e.c.	−19292	−16026	...	8300	−11566	−3710	−4235	...	16638	−16113
8 Long-term loans, n.e.c.	−3135	−3135	...	−	...	1553	1553	...	−	−
9 Other receivables	31311	...	...	929	...	33393	−	...	−75	−
10 Other assets	929	13409	...	13217	4685	−75	19153	...	15530	−1290
Total aquisition of financial assets	36676	−5841	...	26227	16290	27254	−8180	...	25425	10009

Incurrence of liabilities

1 Currency and transferable deposits	2586	2586	...	...	−	−10284	−10284	...	−	−
2 Other deposits	351	215	...	−	136	−10866	−11004	...	−	138
3 Bills and bonds, short-term	29700	29700	...	...	...	7400	7400	...	−	−
4 Bonds, long-term	85978	89310	...	−1400	−1932	90789	91747	...	−451	−507
5 Short-term loans, n.e.c.	−13343	−29332	...	9723	6266	46930	20687	...	8860	17383
6 Long-term loans, n.e.c.	41588	19541	...	22851	−804	25600	581	...	26797	−1778
7 Other payables	−	−	...	−	−	−	−	...	−	−
8 Other liabilities	−9095	−16310	...	−427	7642	24265	5895	...	4410	13960
Total incurrence of liabilities	137765	95710	...	30747	11308	173834	105022	...	39616	29196
Statistical discrepancy	...	...	...	...	...	498	498	...	−	−
Net lending	−101089	−101551	...	−4520	4982	−147078	−113700	...	−14191	−19187
Incurrence of liabilities and net worth	36676	−5841	...	26227	16290	27254	−8180	...	25425	10009

France

	1992					1993				
	Total govern-ment	Central govern-ment	State or provincial govern-ment	Local govern-ment	Social security funds	Total govern-ment	Central govern-ment	State or provincial govern-ment	Local govern-ment	Social security funds

Acquisition of financial assets

1 Gold and SDRs	19089	4233	...	1922	12934	−254	−394	...	−1864	2004
2 Currency and transferable deposits	25310	51806	...	−5751	−20745	58905	60427	...	−457	−1065
3 Other deposits	3054	515	...	−1	2540	3229	3572	...	−423	80
4 Bills and bonds, short-term	4854	749	...	–	4105	−3545	418	...	–	−3963
5 Bonds, long-term	4285	4124	...	4	157	8688	12903	...	1776	−5991
6 Corporate equity securities	−6960	−9439	...	–	2479	−47594	−43307	...	–	−4287
7 Short-term loans, n.e.c.	20748	9428	...	5815	5505	−41721	−49395	...	8127	−453
8 Long-term loans, n.e.c.	9381	9381	...	–	–	22540	22540	...	–	–
9 Other receivables	269	–	...	269	–	70	–	...	70	–
10 Other assets	74353	32753	...	14965	26635	68681	40840	...	17865	9976
Total aquisition of financial assets	154383	103550	...	17223	33610	68999	47604	...	25094	−3699

Incurrence of liabilities

1 Currency and transferable deposits	−6824	−6824	...	–	–	10693	10693	...	–	–
2 Other deposits	−8450	−8841	...	–	391	1244	844	...	–	400
3 Bills and bonds, short-term	157700	157700	...	–	–	75488	75488	...	–	–
4 Bonds, long-term	132378	131286	...	−974	2066	315734	311479	...	2217	2038
5 Short-term loans, n.e.c.	50355	22646	...	−3801	31510	43423	−21722	...	452	64693
6 Long-term loans, n.e.c.	42116	−5745	...	34270	13591	23058	−4206	...	25699	1565
7 Other payables	–	–	...	–	–	–	–	...	–	–
8 Other liabilities	73923	25684	...	12550	35689	30009	−6896	...	11905	25000
Total incurrence of liabilities	441198	315906	...	42045	83247	499649	365680	...	40273	93696
Statistical discrepancy	–	–	...	–	–	–	–	...	–	–
Net lending	−286815	−212356	...	−24822	−49637	−430650	−318076	...	−15179	−97395
Incurrence of liabilities and net worth	154383	103550	...	17223	33610	68999	47604	...	25094	−3699

	1994					1995				
	Total govern-ment	Central govern-ment	State or provincial govern-ment	Local govern-ment	Social security funds	Total govern-ment	Central govern-ment	State or provincial govern-ment	Local govern-ment	Social security funds

Acquisition of financial assets

1 Gold and SDRs	−471	−26	...	401	−846	−450	26	...	−625	149
2 Currency and transferable deposits	−80235	−75036	...	8361	−13560	−35171	−57053	...	10589	11293
3 Other deposits	−1586	149	...	387	−2122	−3116	−2700	...	−204	−212
4 Bills and bonds, short-term	191	191	...	–	–	−960	−12	...	–	−948
5 Bonds, long-term	8168	3777	...	168	4223	2836	4553	...	162	−1879
6 Corporate equity securities	−32895	−35739	...	–	2844	41437	11862	...	–	29575
7 Short-term loans, n.e.c.	51004	11819	...	21918	17267	192965	82522	...	−1759	112202
8 Long-term loans, n.e.c.	−3496	−3496	...	–	–	−4868	−4868	...	–	–
9 Other receivables	66	–	...	66	–	−207	–	...	−207	–
10 Other assets	80603	44447	...	12814	23342	17990	8299	...	10375	−684
Total aquisition of financial assets	21349	−53914	...	44115	31148	210456	42629	...	18331	149496

Incurrence of liabilities

1 Currency and transferable deposits	25048	25048	...	–	–	8348	8348	...	–	–

France

	1994					1995				
	Total govern-ment	Central govern-ment	State or provincial govern-ment	Local govern-ment	Social security funds	Total govern-ment	Central govern-ment	State or provincial govern-ment	Local govern-ment	Social security funds
2 Other deposits	7485	7083	...	–	402	–1289	–1641	...	–	352
3 Bills and bonds, short-term	139417	139417	...	–	–	144443	144443	...	–	–
4 Bonds, long-term	221898	203207	...	16168	2523	221921	225056	...	–3135	–
5 Short-term loans, n.e.c.	79402	–4155	...	7512	76045	198781	1007	...	7740	190034
6 Long-term loans, n.e.c.	–74129	–95268	...	25359	–4220	24971	–3480	...	23673	4778
7 Other payables	–	–	...	–	–	–	–	...	–	–
8 Other liabilities	63426	26609	...	10299	26518	26098	–4499	...	7548	23049
Total incurrence of liabilities	462547	301941	...	59338	101268	623273	369234	...	35826	218213
Statistical discrepancy	–	–	...	–	–	–	–	...	...	...
Net lending	–441198	–355855	...	–15223	–70120	–412817	–326605	...	–17495	–68717
Incurrence of liabilities and net worth	21349	–53914	...	44115	31148	210456	42629	...	18331	149496

	1996					1997				
	Total govern-ment	Central govern-ment	State or provincial govern-ment	Local govern-ment	Social security funds	Total govern-ment	Central govern-ment	State or provincial govern-ment	Local govern-ment	Social security funds
Acquisition of financial assets										
1 Gold and SDRs	5205	2628	...	2577	–	14279	14279	...	–	–
2 Currency and transferable deposits	–48561	–37728	...	6824	–17657	79033	46706	...	9890	22437
3 Other deposits	12116	11332	...	358	426	–2306	–4306	...	2000	–
4 Bills and bonds, short-term	–4416	–5872	...	–	1456	3560	4060	...	–	–500
5 Bonds, long-term	7191	5619	...	110	1462	–18054	–16704	...	650	–2000
6 Corporate equity securities	13703	7011	...	–	6692	–17803	3189	...	–	–20992
7 Short-term loans, n.e.c.	94717	21181	...	1119	72417	61797	62302	...	–100	–405
8 Long-term loans, n.e.c.	–761	–761	...	–	–	–15840	–15840	...	–	–
9 Other receivables	71	–	...	71	–	–	–	...	–	–
10 Other assets	3252	–18163	...	12491	8924	–8844	–12570	...	3726	–
Total aquisition of financial assets	82517	–14753	...	23550	73720	95822	81116	...	16166	–1460
Incurrence of liabilities										
1 Currency and transferable deposits	21943	21943	...	–	–	23090	23090	...	–	–
2 Other deposits	–2526	–2910	...	–	384	3790	3790	...	–	–
3 Bills and bonds, short-term	113522	113522	...	–	–	146396	146396	...	–	–
4 Bonds, long-term	329378	331048	...	–1668	–2	166224	167082	...	–858	–
5 Short-term loans, n.e.c.	–68160	–168893	...	9952	90781	56385	6304	...	160	49921
6 Long-term loans, n.e.c.	13010	–1998	...	9494	5514	–19142	–18429	...	–713	–
7 Other payables	–	–	...	–	–	–	–	...	–	–
8 Other liabilities	40986	–860	...	2335	39511	304	–14201	...	–	14505
Total incurrence of liabilities	448153	291852	...	20113	136188	377047	314032	...	–1411	64426
Statistical discrepancy	–	–	...	...	...	–	–	...	...	...
Net lending	–365636	–306605	...	3437	–62468	–281225	–232916	...	17577	–65886
Incurrence of liabilities and net worth	82517	–14753	...	23550	73720	95822	81116	...	16166	–1460

France

3.21 Corporate and quasi-corporate enterprise production account: total and sectors

Million French francs

	1986				1987				1988			
	Corporate and quasi-corporate enterprises			Addendum: total including unincorporated	Corporate and quasi-corporate enterprises			Addendum: total including unincorporated	Corporate and quasi-corporate enterprises			Addendum: total including unincorporated
	Total	Non-financial	Financial		Total	Non-financial	Financial		Total	Non-financial	Financial	
Gross output												
1 Output for sale	5646862	5432402	214460	7108691	6016416	5746459	269957	7516451	6568672	6261923	306749	8159309
2 Imputed bank service charge	223272	–	223272	223272	246505	–	246505	246505	262490	–	262490	262490
3 Own-account fixed capital formation	...	...	...	...	...	...	...	...	...	...	...	...
Gross output	5870134	5432402	437732	7359821	6262921	5746459	516462	7791266	6831162	6261923	569239	8452116
Gross input												
Intermediate consumption	3160602	2778130	382472	3557190	3389816	2933328	456488	3784959	3698231	3182211	516020	4112701
1 Imputed bank service charge	223272	–	223272	223272	246505	–	246505	246505	262490	–	262490	262490
2 Other intermediate consumption	2937330	2778130	159200	3333918	3143311	2933328	209983	3538454	3435741	3182211	253530	3850211
subtotal: Value added	2709532	2654272	55260	3802631	2873105	2813131	59974	4006307	3132931	3079712	53219	4339415
1 Indirect taxes, net	186986	171857	15129	194059	194145	172359	21786	201711	233213	203613	29600	247895
A Indirect taxes	306111	261819	44292	339212	324673	277394	47279	359537	342924	293909	49015	383107
B less: Subsidies	119125	89962	29163	145153	130528	105035	25493	157826	109711	90296	19415	135212
2 Consumption of fixed capital	370246	356893	13353	542156	392148	377741	14407	577180	417385	401564	15821	621347
3 Compensation of employees	1783939	1660900	123039	1964628	1872682	1743656	129026	2056059	1988661	1853199	135462	2181057
4 Net operating surplus	368361	464622	–96261	1101788	414130	519375	–105245	1171357	493672	621336	–127664	1289116
Gross input	5870134	5432402	437732	7359821	6262921	5746459	516462	7791266	6831162	6261923	569239	8452116

	1989				1990				1991			
	Corporate and quasi-corporate enterprises			Addendum: total including unincorporated	Corporate and quasi-corporate enterprises			Addendum: total including unincorporated	Corporate and quasi-corporate enterprises			Addendum: total including unincorporated
	Total	Non-financial	Financial		Total	Non-financial	Financial		Total	Non-financial	Financial	
Gross output												
1 Output for sale	7287030	6882157	404873	9022769	7761722	7261957	499765	9576439	8174198	7583438	590760	1000785[a]
2 Imputed bank service charge	279423	–	279423	279423	278020	–	278020	278020	269336	–	269336	269336
3 Own-account fixed capital formation	...	...	...	...	...	...	...	...	...	...	...	...
Gross output	7566453	6882157	684296	9334374	8039742	7261957	777785	9888681	8443534	7583438	860096	1031597[a]
Gross input												
Intermediate consumption	4200466	3564394	636072	4641750	4493121	3738878	754243	4932305	4709756	3891367	818389	5135644
1 Imputed bank service charge	279423	–	279423	279423	278020	–	278020	278020	269336	–	269336	269336
2 Other intermediate consumption	3921043	3564394	356649	4362327	4215101	3738878	476223	4654285	4440420	3891367	549053	4866308
subtotal: Value added	3365987	3317763	48224	4692624	3546621	3523079	23542	4956376	3733778	3692071	41707	5180326
1 Indirect taxes, net	258452	226547	31905	269919	286803	252273	34530	301995	292638	255382	37256	308037
A Indirect taxes	362190	312514	49676	400865	390170	338187	51983	433600	401985	350457	51528	445784
B less: Subsidies	103738	85967	17771	130946	103367	85914	17453	131605	109347	95075	14272	137747
2 Consumption of fixed capital	439559	422208	17351	663930	475522	456557	18965	707881	518085	497315	20770	748670
3 Compensation of employees	2122733	1980227	142506	2327549	2277410	2127376	150034	2494580	2387107	2229700	157407	2607505
4 Net operating surplus	545243	688781	–143538	1431226	506886	686873	–179987	1451920	535948	709674	–173726	1516114
Gross input	7566453	6882157	684296	9334374	8039742	7261957	777785	9888681	8443534	7583438	860096	1031597[a]

France

	1992				1993				1994			
	Corporate and quasi-corporate enterprises			Addendum: total including unincor- porated	Corporate and quasi-corporate enterprises			Addendum: total including unincor- porated	Corporate and quasi-corporate enterprises			Addendum: total including unincor- porated
	Total	Non-financial	Financial		Total	Non-financial	Financial		Total	Non-financial	Financial	
Gross output												
1 Output for sale	8527386	7743506	783880	1040598[a]	8799746	7620996	1178750	1064715[a]	9199269	7932796	1266473	1112378[a]
2 Imputed bank service charge	274663	–	274663	274663	275227	–	275227	275227	263132	–	263132	263132
3 Own-account fixed capital formation	...	...	...	...	...	...	...	...	...	...	...	...
Gross output	8802049	7743506	1058543	1071795[a]	9074973	7620996	1453977	1096161[a]	9462401	7932796	1529605	1143189[a]
Gross input												
Intermediate consumption	4959760	3946249	1013511	5391930	5203777	3785567	1418210	5616338	5379677	3970870	1408807	5834333
1 Imputed bank service charge	274663	–	274663	274663	275227	–	275227	275227	263132	–	263132	263132
2 Other intermediate consumption	4685097	3946249	738848	5117267	4928550	3785567	1142983	5341111	5116545	3970870	1145675	5571201
subtotal: Value added	3842289	3797257	45032	5326018	3871196	3835429	35767	5345270	4082724	3961926	120798	5597555
1 Indirect taxes, net	305555	269189	36366	312107	334430	293678	40752	321431	375638	332960	42678	356478
A Indirect taxes	417944	366516	51428	459644	443011	389731	53280	483731	481332	427880	53452	522703
B less: Subsidies	112389	97327	15062	147537	108581	96053	12528	162300	105694	94920	10774	166225
2 Consumption of fixed capital	542157	521382	20775	765240	551162	529981	21181	777129	566743	545535	21208	798935
3 Compensation of employees	2467062	2304007	163055	2687361	2482905	2313233	169672	2703807	2532377	2362041	170336	2756229
4 Net operating surplus	527515	702679	–175164	1561310	502699	698537	–195838	1542903	607966	721390	–113424	1685913
Gross input	8802049	7743506	1058543	1071795[a]	9074973	7620996	1453977	1096161[a]	9462401	7932796	1529605	1143189[a]

	1995				1996				1997			
	Corporate and quasi-corporate enterprises			Addendum: total including unincor- porated	Corporate and quasi-corporate enterprises			Addendum: total including unincor- porated	Corporate and quasi-corporate enterprises			Addendum: total including unincor- porated
	Total	Non-financial	Financial		Total	Non-financial	Financial		Total	Non-financial	Financial	
Gross output												
1 Output for sale	9845748	8255042	1590706	1182501[a]	1052762[a]	8350455	2177166	1258600[a]	1136816[a]	8653656	2714502	1349417[a]
2 Imputed bank service charge	271846	–	271846	271846	253998	–	253998	253998	256291	–	256291	256291
3 Own-account fixed capital formation	...	...	...	...	...	...	...	...	...	...	...	...
Gross output	1011759[a]	8255042	1862552	1214625[a]	1078162[a]	8350455	2431164	1289542[a]	1162445[a]	8653656	2970793	1381010[a]
Gross input												
Intermediate consumption	5914060	4131069	1782991	6372207	6493316	4143788	2349528	6991285	7189062	4302079	2886983	7703150
1 Imputed bank service charge	271846	–	271846	271846	253998	–	253998	253998	256291	–	256291	256291
2 Other intermediate consumption	5642214	4131069	1511145	6100361	6239318	4143788	2095530	6737287	6932771	4302079	2630692	7446859
subtotal: Value added	4203534	4123973	79561	5774047	4288303	4206667	81636	5904132	4435387	4351577	83810	6106950
1 Indirect taxes, net	394281	346919	47362	368445	391092	341737	49355	365255	402246	345938	56308	385548
A Indirect taxes	500985	444281	56704	540751	529973	470530	59443	569282	554711	487355	67356	598213
B less: Subsidies	106704	97362	9342	172306	138881	128793	10088	204027	152465	141417	11048	212665
2 Consumption of fixed capital	584275	564213	20062	822239	586754	564407	22347	827553	602886	579988	22898	856196
3 Compensation of employees	2629772	2456351	173421	2861339	2710062	2531720	178342	2952111	2780179	2598042	182137	3030146
4 Net operating surplus	595206	756490	–161284	1722024	600395	768803	–168408	1759213	650076	827609	–177533	1835060
Gross input	1011759[a]	8255042	1862552	1214625[a]	1078162[a]	8350455	2431164	1289542[a]	1162445[a]	8653656	2970793	1381010[a]

a Estimates in ten millions.

France

3.22 Corporate and quasi-corporate enterprise income and outlay account: total and sectors

Million French francs

	1986 Total	1986 Non-financial	1986 Financial	1987 Total	1987 Non-financial	1987 Financial	1988 Total	1988 Non-financial	1988 Financial	1989 Total	1989 Non-financial	1989 Financial
Receipts												
1 Operating surplus	368361	464622	−96261	414130	519375	−105245	493672	621336	−127664	545243	688781	−143538
2 Property and entrepreneurial income	1155200	110029	1045171	1161873	118390	1043483	1286828	146384	1140444	1489734	185524	1304210
A Withdrawals from quasi-corporate enterprises	−	−	−	−	−	−	−	−	−	−	−	−
B Interest	1049881	38929	1010952	1050717	42370	1008347	1141120	44863	1096257	1299340	51938	1247402
C Dividends	97915	63707	34208	102910	67786	35124	135767	91580	44187	182193	125385	56808
D Net land rent and royalties	7404	7393	11	8246	8234	12	9941	9941	−	8201	8201	−
3 Current transfers	280272	148203	132069	305376	149417	155959	313287	163627	149660	318409	160387	158022
A Casualty insurance claims	25374	24804	570	25846	25231	615	32456	31844	612	22586	22066	520
B Casualty insurance premiums, net, due to be received by insurance companies	88758	−	88758	94949	−	94949	100094	−	100094	97603	−	97603
C Current transfers from rest of the world	...	...	...	...	...	...	...	...	...	...	...	...
D Other transfers except imputed	114160	73787	40373	131451	73487	57964	127174	80764	46410	140912	83837	57075
E Imputed unfunded employee pension and welfare contributions	51980	49612	2368	53130	50699	2431	53563	51019	2544	57308	54484	2824
Total current receipts	1803833	722854	1080979	1881379	787182	1094197	2093787	931347	1162440	2353386	1034692	1318694
Disbursements												
1 Property and entrepreneurial income	1216143	421334	794809	1230903	445506	785397	1340292	476634	863658	1574577	566730	1007847
A Withdrawals from quasi-corporations	21917	21917	−	20359	20359	−	15456	15456	−	18299	18299	−
B Interest	978228	255103	723125	947868	256423	691445	1018032	265183	752849	1156343	306355	849988
C Dividends [a]	199731	128047	71684	244749	150797	93952	285110	174301	110809	380787	222928	157859
D Net land rent and royalties	16267	16267	−	17927	17927	−	21694	21694	−	19148	19148	−
2 Direct taxes and other current transfers n.e.c. to general government	136134	95849	40285	150124	108752	41372	162539	119551	42988	180722	132980	47742
A Direct taxes	133526	93241	40285	147305	105933	41372	160820	117832	42988	178949	131207	47742
On income	36756	17003	19753	37804	18336	19468	38389	18897	19492	38973	18980	19993
Other	96770	76238	20532	109501	87597	21904	122431	98935	23496	139976	112227	27749
B Fines, fees, penalties and other current transfers n.e.c.	2608	2608	−	2819	2819	−	1719	1719	−	1773	1773	−
3 Other current transfers	294334	140946	153388	308091	141234	166857	343499	151385	192114	340248	156241	184007
A Casualty insurance premiums, net	28987	28461	526	28600	28013	587	31147	30553	594	25570	24940	630
B Casualty insurance claims liability of insurance companies	107332	−	107332	113902	−	113902	119957	−	119957	118591	−	118591
C Transfers to private non-profit institutions	1366	1366	−	1282	1282	−	1315	1315	−	1376	1376	−
D Unfunded employee pension and welfare benefits	93719	67443	26276	98847	69339	29508	106687	73005	33682	112953	76629	36324
E Social assistance grants	...	...	...	...	...	...	...	...	...	...	...	...
F Other transfers n.e.c.	62930	43676	19254	65460	42600	22860	84393	46512	37881	81758	53296	28462
G Transfers to rest of the world	...	...	...	...	...	...	...	...	...	...	...	...

France

Million French francs

	1986 Total	1986 Non-financial	1986 Financial	1987 Total	1987 Non-financial	1987 Financial	1988 Total	1988 Non-financial	1988 Financial	1989 Total	1989 Non-financial	1989 Financial
Net saving	157222	64725	92497	192261	91690	100571	247457	183777	63680	257839	178741	79098
Total current disbursements and net saving	1803833	722854	1080979	1881379	787182	1094197	2093787	931347	1162440	2353386	1034692	1318694

	1990 Total	1990 Non-financial	1990 Financial	1991 Total	1991 Non-financial	1991 Financial	1992 Total	1992 Non-financial	1992 Financial	1993 Total	1993 Non-financial	1993 Financial
Receipts												
1 Operating surplus	506886	686873	−179987	535948	709674	−173726	527515	702679	−175164	502699	698537	−195838
2 Property and entrepreneurial income	1663361	215112	1448249	1842918	268293	1574625	1926488	304524	1621964	2089111	351729	1737382
A Withdrawals from quasi-corporate enterprises	–	–	–	–	–	–	–	–	–	–	–	–
B Interest	1446307	59241	1387066	1583492	77004	1506488	1632366	80629	1551737	1753797	92439	1661358
C Dividends	206690	145507	61183	246688	178551	68137	280060	209833	70227	322071	246047	76024
D Net land rent and royalties	10364	10364	–	12738	12738	–	14062	14062	–	13243	13243	–
3 Current transfers	370217	179748	190469	381647	190460	191187	400190	198485	201705	418186	204556	213630
A Casualty insurance claims	32284	31491	793	37306	36538	768	42111	41249	862	44963	44097	866
B Casualty insurance premiums, net, due to be received by insurance companies	125562	–	125562	129052	–	129052	147095	–	147095	154538	–	154538
C Current transfers from rest of the world	...	...	...	...	...	...	...	...	...	...	...	...
D Other transfers except imputed	151661	90512	61149	151660	93437	58223	142718	92219	50499	150132	95312	54820
E Imputed unfunded employee pension and welfare contributions	60710	57745	2965	63629	60485	3144	68266	65017	3249	68553	65147	3406
Total current receipts	2540464	1081733	1458731	2760513	1168427	1592086	2854193	1205688	1648505	3009996	1254822	1755174
Disbursements												
1 Property and entrepreneurial income	1768150	634580	1133570	2003767	701770	1301997	2077652	768106	1309546	2231136	804613	1426523
A Withdrawals from quasi-corporations	20918	20918	–	18935	18935	–	18426	18426	–	19325	19325	–
B Interest	1293040	340914	952126	1466514	377302	1089212	1492343	427797	1064546	1646237	422548	1223689
C Dividends [a]	432168	250724	181444	494518	281733	212785	541345	296345	245000	540529	337695	202834
D Net land rent and royalties	22024	22024	–	23800	23800	–	25538	25538	–	25045	25045	–
2 Direct taxes and other current transfers n.e.c. to general government	186607	136215	50392	168871	122965	45906	146728	99193	47535	147829	97391	50438
A Direct taxes	184376	133984	50392	166342	120436	45906	144243	96708	47535	145494	95056	50438
On income	42039	20736	21303	43013	22139	20874	45249	24275	20974	46053	26898	19155
Other	142337	113248	29089	123329	98297	25032	98994	72433	26561	99441	68158	31283
B Fines, fees, penalties and other current transfers n.e.c.	2231	2231	–	2529	2529	–	2485	2485	–	2335	2335	–
3 Other current transfers	386143	171476	214667	403073	186726	216347	424783	195237	229546	440280	204349	235931
A Casualty insurance premiums, net	34587	33776	811	41030	40236	794	46651	45755	896	48668	47748	920
B Casualty insurance claims liability of insurance companies	145984	–	145984	149534	–	149534	169966	–	169966	176929	–	176929
C Transfers to private non-profit institutions	1558	1558	–	1218	1218	–	1227	1227	–	1247	1247	46306
D Unfunded employee pension and welfare benefits	118589	81024	37565	123773	83899	39874	130515	87866	42649	134720	88414	–
E Social assistance grants	...	...	...	...	...	...	...	...	...	...	...	...
F Other transfers n.e.c.	85425	55118	30307	87518	61373	26145	76424	60389	16035	78716	66940	11776

France

	1990			1991			1992			1993		
	Total	Non-financial	Financial	Total	Non-financial	Financial	Total	Non-financial	Financial	Total	Non-financial	Financial
G Transfers to rest of the world	...	...	...	...	...	...	...	...	...	...	...	...
Net saving	199564	139462	60102	184802	156966	27836	205030	143152	61878	190751	148469	42282
Total current disbursements and net saving	2540464	1081733	1458731	2760513	1168427	1592086	2854193	1205688	1648505	3009996	1254822	1755174

	1994			1995			1996			1997		
	Total	Non-financial	Financial	Total	Non-financial	Financial	Total	Non-financial	Financial	Total	Non-financial	Financial
Receipts											
1 Operating surplus	607966	721390	–113424	595206	756490	–161284	600395	768803	–168408	650076	827609	–177533
2 Property and entrepreneurial income	1805532	320890	1484642	1887912	358602	1529310	1850534	382741	1467793	1858060	417665	1440395
A Withdrawals from quasi-corporate enterprises	–	–	–	–	–	–	–	–	–	–	–	–
B Interest	1482696	70794	1411902	1529992	79468	1450524	1452372	71133	1381239	1399854	68952	1330902
C Dividends	308104	235364	72740	341791	263005	78786	387334	300780	86554	444439	334946	109493
D Net land rent and royalties	14732	14732	–	16129	16129	–	10828	10828	–	13767	13767	–
3 Current transfers	424579	207650	216929	469385	218157	251228	440934	195050	245884	440883	196909	243974
A Casualty insurance claims	45328	44457	871	55252	54168	1084	50357	49371	986	49144	48165	979
B Casualty insurance premiums, net, due to be received by insurance companies	154228	–	154228	177976	–	177976	168058	–	168058	167373	–	167373
C Current transfers from rest of the world	...	...	...	...	...	...	...	...	...	...	...	...
D Other transfers except imputed	156009	97503	58506	164786	95960	68826	149519	76005	73514	158291	86015	72276
E Imputed unfunded employee pension and welfare contributions	69014	65690	3324	71371	68029	3342	73000	69674	3326	66075	62729	3346
Total current receipts	2838077	1249930	1588147	2952503	1333249	1619254	2891863	1346594	1545269	2949019	1442183	1506836
Disbursements											
1 Property and entrepreneurial income	1938176	737915	1200261	2017570	782823	1234747	1982163	799165	1182998	2005516	858719	1146797
A Withdrawals from quasi-corporations	1812	1812	–	–	–	–	–	–	–	–	–	–
B Interest	1375606	351370	1024236	1419701	358339	1061362	1351007	332584	1018423	1297008	305661	991347
C Dividends [a]	532785	356760	176025	569847	396462	173385	608124	443549	164575	683039	527589	155450
D Net land rent and royalties	27973	27973	–	28022	28022	–	23032	23032	–	25469	25469	–
2 Direct taxes and other current transfers n.e.c. to general government	162962	113541	49421	176122	128034	48088	185484	134954	50530	218405	155921	62484
A Direct taxes	160609	111188	49421	174728	126640	48088	183479	132949	50530	216069	153585	62484
On income	46792	27932	18860	54976	30216	24760	52224	35655	16569	52499	34821	17678
Other	113817	83256	30561	119752	96424	23328	131255	97294	33961	163570	118764	44806
B Fines, fees, penalties and other current transfers n.e.c.	2353	2353	–	1394	1394	–	2005	2005	–	2336	2336	...
3 Other current transfers	439793	200487	239306	479973	213213	266760	480096	219083	261013	477027	209117	267910
A Casualty insurance premiums, net	47596	46679	917	58723	57622	1101	54368	53330	1038	55064	54030	1034
B Casualty insurance claims liability of insurance companies	175174	–	175174	197645	–	197645	184951	–	184951	184212	–	184212
C Transfers to private non-profit institutions	1293	1293	50428	1360	1360	53084	1350	1350	57093	1397	1397	59398
D Unfunded employee pension and welfare benefits	140516	90088	–	145337	92253	–	151766	94673	–	147740	88342	–
E Social assistance grants	...	...	...	...	...	...	...	...	...	...	...	...

France

	1994			1995			1996			1997		
	Total	Non-financial	Financial	Total	Non-financial	Financial	Total	Non-financial	Financial	Total	Non-financial	Financial
F Other transfers n.e.c.	75214	62427	12787	76908	61978	14930	87661	69730	17931	88614	65348	23266
G Transfers to rest of the world	...	...	...	...	...	...	...	...	...	...	...	...
Net saving	297146	197987	99159	278838	209179	69659	244120	193392	50728	248071	218426	29645
Total current disbursements and net saving	2838077	1249930	1588147	2952503	1333249	1619254	2891863	1346594	1545269	2949019	1442183	1506836

a Item "Dividends" includes profit-sharing by employees.

3.23 Corporate and quasi-corporate enterprise capital accumulation account: total and sectors

Million French francs

	1986			1987			1988			1989		
	Total	Non-financial	Financial	Total	Non-financial	Financial	Total	Non-financial	Financial	Total	Non-financial	Financial
Finance of gross accumulation												
1 Gross saving	527468	421618	105850	584409	469431	114978	664842	585341	79501	697398	600949	96449
A Consumption of fixed capital	370246	356893	13353	392148	377741	14407	417385	401564	15821	439559	422208	17351
B Net saving	157222	64725	92497	192261	91690	100571	247457	183777	63680	257839	178741	79098
2 Capital transfers	39633	34274	5359	39133	33327	5806	37169	30979	6190	46583	40556	6027
Finance of gross accumulation	567101	455892	111209	623542	502758	120784	702011	616320	85691	743981	641505	102476
Gross accumulation												
1 Gross capital formation	482524	456061	26463	549126	519681	29445	640236	606031	34205	709476	674350	35126
A Increase in stocks	7209	7370	−161	23293	23507	−214	44555	44540	15	53864	53858	6
B Gross fixed capital formation	475315	448691	26624	525833	496174	29659	595681	561491	34190	655612	620492	35120
2 Purchases of land, net	8407	7501	906	14416	13423	993	20887	19867	1020	29932	28604	1328
3 Purchases of intangible assets, net	16395	16380	15	16948	16948	–	22140	22140	–	17317	17317	–
4 Capital transfers	29099	12046	17053	28085	14898	13187	28345	13613	14732	34618	12775	21843
Net lending	30676	−36096	66772	14967	−62192	77159	−9597	−45331	35734	−47362	−91541	44179
Gross accumulation	567101	455892	111209	623542	502758	120784	702011	616320	85691	743981	641505	102476

	1990			1991			1992			1993		
	Total	Non-financial	Financial	Total	Non-financial	Financial	Total	Non-financial	Financial	Total	Non-financial	Financial
Finance of gross accumulation												
1 Gross saving	675086	596019	79067	702887	654281	48606	747187	664534	82653	741913	678450	63463
A Consumption of fixed capital	475522	456557	18965	518085	497315	20770	542157	521382	20775	551162	529981	21181
B Net saving	199564	139462	60102	184802	156966	27836	205030	143152	61878	190751	148469	42282
2 Capital transfers	50463	43990	6473	57967	51299	6668	70123	60718	9405	92331	82733	9598
Finance of gross accumulation	725549	640009	85540	760854	705580	55274	817310	725252	92058	834244	761183	73061
Gross accumulation												
1 Gross capital formation	761191	721635	39556	764889	720792	44097	693767	672972	20795	580665	563045	17620
A Increase in stocks	54696	54664	32	26554	26476	78	−27944	−27803	−141	−76576	−76553	−23
B Gross fixed capital formation	706495	666971	39524	738335	694316	44019	721711	700775	20936	657241	639598	17643
2 Purchases of land, net	35893	34162	1731	39371	37938	1433	32487	31032	1455	16448	15651	797
3 Purchases of intangible assets, net	19810	19810	–	27353	27353	–	44225	44225	–	55746	55746	–
4 Capital transfers	37015	13698	23317	60682	15513	45169	74423	18867	55556	80939	20041	60898
Net lending	−128360	−149296	20936	−131441	−96016	−35425	−27592	−41844	14252	100446	106700	−6254
Gross accumulation	725549	640009	85540	760854	705580	55274	817310	725252	92058	834244	761183	73061

France

	1994			1995			1996			1997		
	Total	Non-financial	Financial	Total	Non-financial	Financial	Total	Non-financial	Financial	Total	Non-financial	Financial
	Finance of gross accumulation											
1 Gross saving	863889	743522	120367	863113	773392	89721	830874	757799	73075	850957	798414	52543
A Consumption of fixed capital	566743	545535	21208	584275	564213	20062	586754	564407	22347	602886	579988	22898
B Net saving	297146	197987	99159	278838	209179	69659	244120	193392	50728	248071	218426	29645
2 Capital transfers	104721	94333	10388	150268	122000	28268	141733	121886	19847	144736	123478	21258
Finance of gross accumulation	968610	837855	130755	1013381	895392	117989	972607	879685	92922	995693	921892	73801
	Gross accumulation											
1 Gross capital formation	676023	661109	14914	710997	692582	18415	663899	641021	22878	679803	652792	27011
A Increase in stocks	10600	10600	–	19500	19500	–	–35034	–35034	–	–22007	–22007	–
B Gross fixed capital formation	665423	650509	14914	691497	673082	18415	698933	676055	22878	701810	674799	27011
2 Purchases of land, net	16250	16183	67	18710	17473	1237	18406	17744	662	18267	17643	624
3 Purchases of intangible assets, net	59418	59418	–	62044	62044	–	61775	61775	–	61275	61275	–
4 Capital transfers	111227	21424	89803	151508	21623	129885	133943	31755	102188	167610	70340	97270
Net lending	105692	79721	25971	70122	101670	–31548	94584	127390	–32806	68738	119842	–51104
Gross accumulation	968610	837855	130755	1013381	895392	117989	972607	879685	92922	995693	921892	73801

3.24 Corporate and quasi-corporate enterprise capital finance account: total and sectors

Million French francs

	1986			1987			1988			1989		
	Total	Non-financial	Financial	Total	Non-financial	Financial	Total	Non-financial	Financial	Total	Non-financial	Financial
	Acquisition of financial assets											
1 Gold and SDRs	3613	–2753	6366	–787	5334	–6121	–26111	1415	–27526	15917	12188	3729
2 Currency and transferable deposits	101179	15293	85886	57877	17053	40824	21504	–2505	24009	172548	37438	135110
3 Other deposits	283586	16728	266858	404007	13993	390014	239164	13775	225389	439510	58384	381126
4 Bills and bonds, short-term	93696	14417	79279	212424	92691	119733	161447	6534	154913	291727	81706	210021
5 Bonds, long-term	263211	2032	261179	197808	7153	190655	271247	43790	227457	171793	841	170952
6 Corporate equity securities	212301	88162	124139	270828	144582	126246	265622	158106	107516	292261	198217	94044
7 Short-term loans, n.e.c.	127261	69708	57553	427928	6161	421767	209437	117074	92363	689864	216028	473836
8 Long-term loans, n.e.c.	214367	–	214367	351735	–	351735	388106	–	388106	427018	–	427018
9 Trade credits and advances	78978	71865	7113	140635	146018	–5383	264917	262885	2032	187306	175176	12130
10 Other receivables	4548	4450	98	4923	4830	93	5083	4979	104	–11399	–10994	–405
11 Other assets	...	...	...	...	...	...	...	...	...	...	...	...
Total acquisitions of financial assets	1382740	279902	1102838	2067378	437815	1629563	1800416	606053	1194363	2676545	768984	1907561
	Incurrence of liabilities											
1 Currency and transferable deposits	154888	–	154888	194716	–	194716	4677	–	4677	269085	–	269085
2 Other deposits	366609	11333	355276	547182	22907	524275	375617	30594	345023	561472	23828	537644
3 Bills and bonds, short-term	68647	22413	46234	169883	15638	154245	191605	20872	170733	255892	66081	189811
4 Bonds, long-term	166899	44309	122590	175415	22176	153239	222405	47043	175362	187965	35274	152691
5 Corporate equity securities	458144	177091	281053	348230	159578	188652	422984	157964	265020	480830	221183	259647
6 Short-term loans, n.e.c.	–23203	–47388	24185	256092	41500	214592	125584	103183	22401	426507	179682	246825
7 Long-term loans, n.e.c.	–10758	31064	–41822	88590	90309	–1719	145527	136843	8684	213809	211742	2067
8 Net equity of households in life insurance and pension fund reserves	67527	–	67527	81541	–	81541	124415	–	124415	163763	–	163763

France

Million French francs

	1986 Total	1986 Non-financial	1986 Financial	1987 Total	1987 Non-financial	1987 Financial	1988 Total	1988 Non-financial	1988 Financial	1989 Total	1989 Non-financial	1989 Financial
9 Proprietors' net additions to the accumulation of quasi-corporations	...	...	...	...	...	...	...	...	...	...	...	...
10 Trade credits and advances	78498	78071	427	155612	156099	–487	187645	176509	11136	184527	165801	18726
11 Other accounts payable	21725	–	21725	24634	–	24634	14679	–	14679	21632	–	21632
12 Other liabilities	...	...	...	...	...	...	...	...	...	...	...	...
Total incurrence of liabilities	1348976	316893	1032083	2041895	508207	1533688	1815138	673008	1142130	2765482	903591	1861891
Statistical discrepancy [a]	3088	–895	3983	10516	–8200	18716	–5125	–21624	16499	–9651	–11142	1491
Net lending	30676	–36096	66772	14967	–62192	77159	–9597	–45331	35734	–79286	–123465	44179
Incurrence of liabilities and net lending	1382740	279902	1102838	2067378	437815	1629563	1800416	606053	1194363	2676545	768984	1907561

	1990 Total	1990 Non-financial	1990 Financial	1991 Total	1991 Non-financial	1991 Financial	1992 Total	1992 Non-financial	1992 Financial	1993 Total	1993 Non-financial	1993 Financial
Acquisition of financial assets												
1 Gold and SDRs	118474	13283	105191	–1644	22780	–24424	–14524	5701	–20225	44302	31766	12536
2 Currency and transferable deposits	–57258	42113	–99371	–77066	–63346	–13720	–12361	–6637	–5724	102834	33521	69313
3 Other deposits	403448	46798	356650	110981	–14576	125557	367094	78572	288522	359350	15760	343590
4 Bills and bonds, short-term	355293	35544	319749	202805	19714	183091	447359	80197	367162	15552	–3327	18879
5 Bonds, long-term	185584	14937	170647	223283	–14130	237413	152021	–15959	167980	467302	19248	448054
6 Corporate equity securities	446625	363194	83431	279078	194208	84870	382025	267564	114461	460236	198640	261596
7 Short-term loans, n.e.c.	153726	12392	141334	551548	334438	217110	596684	12366	584318	380497	25961	354536
8 Long-term loans, n.e.c.	392756	–	392756	224192	–	224192	127001	–	127001	–17841	–	–17841
9 Trade credits and advances	156874	162461	–5587	154351	139453	14898	34683	25846	8837	–106598	–140496	33898
10 Other receivables	11781	11502	279	8457	8391	66	8201	8035	166	3524	3463	61
11 Other assets	...	...	...	...	...	...	...	...	...	...	...	...
Total acquisitions of financial assets	2167303	702224	1465079	1675985	626932	1049053	2088183	455685	1632498	1709158	184536	1524622
Incurrence of liabilities												
1 Currency and transferable deposits	–8194	–	–8194	–104718	–	–104718	128600	–	128600	157070	–	157070
2 Other deposits	595019	25593	569426	201371	78922	122449	279419	78154	201265	415773	104750	311023
3 Bills and bonds, short-term	421953	27977	393976	208821	6805	202016	304253	16880	287373	18580	–17314	35894
4 Bonds, long-term	195458	70932	124526	204998	60682	144316	206798	51519	155279	189101	51302	137799
5 Corporate equity securities	546052	221602	324450	500112	242032	258080	498240	233764	264476	454675	217710	236965
6 Short-term loans, n.e.c.	506	141413	–140907	357410	106524	250886	342212	7100	335112	178071	–198122	376193
7 Long-term loans, n.e.c.	199734	199880	–146	148977	141478	7499	71882	65954	5928	29752	20705	9047
8 Net equity of households in life insurance and pension fund reserves	165866	–	165866	184748	–	184748	210150	–	210150	264462	–	264462
9 Proprietors' net additions to the accumulation of quasi-corporations	...	...	...	...	...	...	...	...	...	...	...	...
10 Trade credits and advances	148466	149222	–756	92910	84465	8445	68470	56586	11884	–110591	–104837	–5754
11 Other accounts payable	17780	–	17780	11082	–	11082	20619	–	20619	14548	–	14548
12 Other liabilities	...	...	...	...	...	...	...	...	...	...	...	...
Total incurrence of liabilities	2282640	836619	1446021	1805711	720908	1084803	2130643	509957	1620686	1611441	74194	1537247
Statistical discrepancy [a]	13023	14901	–1878	1715	2040	–325	–14868	–12428	–2440	–2729	3642	–6371
Net lending	–128360	–149296	20936	–131441	–96016	–35425	–27592	–41844	14252	100446	106700	–6254
Incurrence of liabilities and net lending	2167303	702224	1465079	1675985	626932	1049053	2088183	455685	1632498	1709158	184536	1524622

France

	1994			1995			1996			1997		
	Total	Non-financial	Financial	Total	Non-financial	Financial	Total	Non-financial	Financial	Total	Non-financial	Financial

Acquisition of financial assets

1 Gold and SDRs	−9301	13390	−22691	−25965	−31166	5201	−27710	−45658	17948	73461	12089	61372
2 Currency and transferable deposits	92091	31246	60845	134115	39977	94138	147112	61137	85975	99707	23808	75899
3 Other deposits	254771	152878	101893	498446	70356	428090	73624	17626	55998	423052	20426	402626
4 Bills and bonds, short-term	95832	61329	34503	8923	47414	−38491	138126	−26982	165108	195731	75700	120031
5 Bonds, long-term	470579	67979	402600	305389	2255	303134	609811	70921	538890	415085	−35845	450930
6 Corporate equity securities	435821	214101	221720	265055	208209	56846	457347	279121	178226	569814	287023	282791
7 Short-term loans, n.e.c.	−241545	−10560	−230985	322509	89173	233336	109764	82910	26854	545060	96150	448910
8 Long-term loans, n.e.c.	−110188	−	−110188	262945	−	262945	3018	−	3018	−41213	−	−41213
9 Trade credits and advances	339104	335064	4040	156177	131868	24309	182724	168910	13814	70384	49963	20421
10 Other receivables	3189	3148	41	4346	4423	−77	3228	3164	64	3060	3000	60
11 Other assets	...	...	...	...	...	...	...	...	...	...	...	...
Total acquisitions of financial assets	1330353	868575	461778	1931940	562509	1369431	1697044	611149	1085895	2354141	532314	1821827

Incurrence of liabilities

1 Currency and transferable deposits	−44082	−	−44082	137327	−	137327	49838	−	49838	213893	−	213893
2 Other deposits	612171	161573	450598	745071	70592	674479	450259	68278	381981	762925	34988	727937
3 Bills and bonds, short-term	−110888	−7472	−103416	−44409	17186	−61595	−16493	50350	−66843	26373	−1401	27774
4 Bonds, long-term	30355	20094	10261	−45612	−2308	−43304	−54546	28782	−83328	−18386	17312	−35698
5 Corporate equity securities	318510	256370	62140	97411	257997	−160586	362601	295768	66833	441069	331443	109626
6 Short-term loans, n.e.c.	−252552	−608	−251944	290688	−7265	297953	291561	−61923	353484	482476	81341	401135
7 Long-term loans, n.e.c.	−23265	−6026	−17239	186260	−26915	213175	−79513	−53492	−26021	−90116	−62108	−28008
8 Net equity of households in life insurance and pension fund reserves	297039	−	297039	323113	−	323113	412976	−	412976	454769	−	454769
9 Proprietors' net additions to the accumulation of quasi-corporations	...	...	...	...	...	...	...	...	...	...	...	...
10 Trade credits and advances	396381	373041	23340	153365	159816	−6451	187888	160597	27291	9349	21000	−11651
11 Other accounts payable	8446	−	8446	7086	−	7086	13742	−	13742	11453	−	11453
12 Other liabilities	...	...	...	...	...	...	...	...	...	...	...	...
Total incurrence of liabilities	1232115	796972	435143	1850300	469103	1381197	1618313	488360	1129953	2293805	422575	1871230
Statistical discrepancy [a]	−7454	−8118	664	11518	−8264	19782	−15853	−4601	−11252	−8402	−10103	1701
Net lending	105692	79721	25971	70122	101670	−31548	94584	127390	−32806	68738	119842	−51104
Incurrence of liabilities and net lending	1330353	868575	461778	1931940	562509	1369431	1697044	611149	1085895	2354141	532314	1821827

a Statistical discrepancy refers to adjustment made in order to reconcile the net lending of the Capital Accumulation Account and the Capital Finance Account.

3.31 Household and private unincorporated enterprise production account

Million French francs

	1986	1987	1988	1989	1990	1991	1992	1993	1994	1995	1996	1997
Gross output												
1 Output for sale	1461829	1500035	1590637	1735739	1814717	1833654	1873213	1840779	1919984	1975077	2054674	2121914
2 Non-marketed output	27858	28310	30317	32182	34222	38782	42686	45856	49503	53583	59124	63737
Gross output	1489687	1528345	1620954	1767921	1848939	1872436	1915899	1886635	1969487	2028660	2113798	2185651
Gross input												
Intermediate consumption	396588	395143	414470	441284	439184	425888	432170	412561	454656	458147	497969	514088
subtotal: Value added	1093099	1133202	1206484	1326637	1409755	1446548	1483729	1474074	1514831	1570513	1615829	1671563

France

Million French francs	1986	1987	1988	1989	1990	1991	1992	1993	1994	1995	1996	1997
1 Indirect taxes net liability of unincorporated enterprises	7073	7566	14682	11467	15192	15399	6552	–12999	–19160	–25836	–25837	–16698
A Indirect taxes	33101	34864	40183	38675	43430	43799	41700	40720	41371	39766	39309	43502
B less: Subsidies	26028	27298	25501	27208	28238	28400	35148	53719	60531	65602	65146	60200
2 Consumption of fixed capital	171910	185032	203962	224371	232359	230585	223083	225967	232192	237964	240799	253310
3 Compensation of employees	180689	183377	192396	204816	217170	220398	220299	220902	223852	231567	242049	249967
4 Net operating surplus	733427	757227	795444	885983	945034	980166	1033795	1040204	1077947	1126818	1158818	1184984
Gross input	1489687	1528345	1620954	1767921	1848939	1872436	1915899	1886635	1969487	2028660	2113798	2185651

3.32 Household and private unincorporated enterprise income and outlay account

Million French francs	1986	1987	1988	1989	1990	1991	1992	1993	1994	1995	1996	1997
Receipts												
1 Compensation of employees	2700561	2816655	2972468	3161822	3370516	3531133	3664892	3737354	3827608	3984477	4120343	4231878
A Wages and salaries	1945807	2024989	2138217	2273162	2429113	2548018	2637166	2687274	2752394	2856544	2940714	3026845
B Employers' contributions for social security	606927	639739	677157	725118	769856	801511	833052	846924	866025	910574	954773	980772
C Employers' contributions for private pension and welfare plans	147827	151927	157094	163542	171547	181604	194674	203156	209189	217359	224856	224261
2 Operating surplus of private unincorporated enterprises	733427	757227	795444	885983	945034	980166	1033795	1040204	1077947	1126818	1158818	1184984
3 Property and entrepreneurial income	305074	328844	347817	421301	459426	530744	551315	551572	529176	575039	575599	615096
A Withdrawals from private quasi-corporations	...	...	...	...	...	...	...	...	...	...	...	...
B Interest	186774	182014	194686	217873	243522	275413	273234	310948	294534	336286	340738	350510
C Dividends	101706	133614	135977	185134	197632	237421	259783	222795	216075	219526	214721	243227
D Net land rent and royalties	16594	13216	17154	18294	18272	17910	18298	17829	18567	19227	20140	21359
4 Current transfers	1361872	1414309	1514816	1597992	1716527	1826103	1945663	2064557	2115039	2194883	2275415	2337501
A Casualty insurance claims	87659	92703	98518	99963	117240	121831	137112	142740	141764	153634	147194	147151
B Social security benefits	896206	930719	999470	1061412	1131617	1209285	1289790	1367969	1395965	1442474	1511231	1573248
C Social assistance grants	131665	133238	140997	146029	155572	167145	176176	197747	215838	223289	218047	223670
D Unfunded employee pension and welfare benefits	169348	177833	185234	194374	204525	212428	223001	230447	237103	247074	254386	252068
E Transfers from general government	...	...	...	...	...	...	...	...	...	...	...	...
F Transfers from rest of the world	6207	6628	6523	7276	8094	9085	10354	10300	12100	12828	12554	12717
G Other transfers n.e.c.	70787	73188	84074	88938	99479	106329	109230	115354	112269	115584	132003	128647
Total current receipts	5100934	5317035	5630545	6067098	6491503	6868146	7195665	7393687	7549770	7881217	8130175	8369459
Disbursements												
1 Final consumption expenditure	3049520	3235582	3429508	3655793	3861322	4037525	4189535	4290741	4442335	4586648	4763486	4857296
2 Property income	182139	187733	213336	250043	275419	278862	294939	278916	230072	230878	224406	217862
A Interest	166994	176375	198130	233927	259818	264232	280660	265863	216701	217424	211027	204030
B Net land rent and royalties	15145	11358	15206	16116	15601	14630	14279	13053	13371	13454	13379	13832
3 Direct taxes and other current transfers n.e.c. to general government	1317028	1402493	1474957	1594920	1695081	1816055	1893540	1945105	2006163	2096601	2215464	2283538
A Social security contributions	979420	1048753	1119307	1217772	1294247	1346155	1403743	1434403	1467218	1537088	1614980	1626078
B Direct taxes	331624	347008	348376	368648	391728	460612	479872	500181	527914	549269	588014	640533
Income taxes	223547	238662	237206	251000	271238	338187	354266	368002	386586	401875	425405	472878

France

Million French francs

	1986	1987	1988	1989	1990	1991	1992	1993	1994	1995	1996	1997
Other	108077	108346	111170	117648	120490	122425	125606	132179	141328	147394	162609	167655
C Fees, fines and penalties	5984	6732	7274	8500	9106	9288	9925	10521	11031	10244	12470	16927
4 Other current transfers	273631	282771	293252	307107	340476	354089	379499	400020	405442	427501	437654	436039
A Net casualty insurance premiums	62662	67487	71124	72020	89190	92673	105302	110128	109195	120309	115461	116759
B Transfers to private non-profit institutions serving households	15825	16534	17572	18108	19511	20461	20940	20974	21337	21239	22299	22389
C Transfers to rest of the world	15525	14736	14249	14205	15142	15565	16305	15648	14955	15681	15664	16855
D Other current transfers, except imputed	31792	32087	33213	39232	45086	43786	42278	50114	50766	52913	59374	55775
E Imputed employee pension and welfare contributions	147827	151927	157094	163542	171547	181604	194674	203156	209189	217359	224856	224261
Net saving	278616	208456	219492	259235	319205	381615	438152	478905	465758	539589	489165	574724
Total current disbursements and net saving	5100934	5317035	5630545	6067098	6491503	6868146	7195665	7393687	7549770	7881217	8130175	8369459

3.33 Household and private unincorporated enterprise capital accumulation account

Million French francs

	1986	1987	1988	1989	1990	1991	1992	1993	1994	1995	1996	1997
Finance of gross accumulation												
1 Gross saving	450526	393488	423454	483606	551564	612200	661235	704872	697950	777553	729964	828034
A Consumption of fixed capital	171910	185032	203962	224371	232359	230585	223083	225967	232192	237964	240799	253310
B Net saving	278616	208456	219492	259235	319205	381615	438152	478905	465758	539589	489165	574724
2 Capital transfers	10920	13778	30673	23180	20098	24055	27950	29185	27678	33601	27987	26836
Total finance of gross accumulation	461446	407266	454127	506786	571662	636255	689185	734057	725628	811154	757951	854870
Gross accumulation												
1 Gross capital formation	349295	362483	396472	455335	467110	449595	431580	397575	413996	435888	442559	448738
A Increase in stocks	2878	–1180	–3848	5494	–1380	–13989	–5128	–10425	–6512	–501	1950	–2262
B Gross fixed capital formation	346417	363663	400320	449841	468490	463584	436708	408000	420508	436389	440609	451000
2 Purchases of land, net	–11265	–15853	–22559	–34319	–39428	–43731	–38075	–21867	–21176	–25199	–23624	–23508
3 Purchases of intangibles, net	–16473	–17067	–22305	–17556	–20239	–27694	–44726	–56217	–59957	–62501	–62410	–61914
4 Capital transfers	18979	20974	24613	26546	29466	32363	31018	30503	32749	30567	34602	42299
Net lending	120910	56729	77906	76780	134753	225722	309388	384063	360016	432399	366824	449255
Total gross accumulation	461446	407266	454127	506786	571662	636255	689185	734057	725628	811154	757951	854870

3.34 Household and private unincorporated enterprise capital finance account

Million French francs

	1986	1987	1988	1989	1990	1991	1992	1993	1994	1995	1996	1997
Acquisition of financial assets												
1 Gold	–8241	–1008	6741	–3658	–1009	–1328	–	–719	–264	–807	–3178	10000
2 Currency and transferable deposits	65500	46128	58965	66187	37993	–30320	26299	–17711	10937	42540	–31515	15195
3 Other deposits	67021	153174	143344	73123	53525	99074	72336	232124	268848	338815	265682	270124
4 Bills and bonds, short-term	–	7168	7163	–8624	3530	8468	9596	17917	2371	–5177	–19725	–50
5 Bonds, long-term	18111	–29971	–14960	–18767	–9150	19363	18931	67740	8424	–10488	–14936	–116023
6 Corporate equity securities	188604	131481	173869	191263	149771	237437	95556	–31690	–122985	–272134	–144846	–104170
7 Short-term loans, n.e.c.	6255	20266	–53904	9719	–28848	–74991	–14688	–39409	–57127	363	30944	72988

France

Million French francs

	1986	1987	1988	1989	1990	1991	1992	1993	1994	1995	1996	1997
8 Long-term loans, n.e.c.	...	...	...	...	...	...	...	...	...	...	...	...
9 Trade credits and advances	−7930	−1282	24146	28614	3688	−2921	9930	7497	37954	9275	25623	−12598
10 Net equity of households in life insurance and pension fund reserves	67527	81541	124415	163763	165866	184748	210150	264462	297039	323113	412976	454769
11 Proprietors' net additions to the accumulation of quasi-corporations	...	...	...	...	...	...	...	...	...	...	...	...
12 Other	17677	20003	10545	33849	5198	3153	12457	11611	6309	4270	10737	8383
Total acquisitions of financial assets	414524	427500	480324	535469	380564	442683	440567	511822	451506	429770	531762	598618

Incurrence of liabilities

1 Short-term loans, n.e.c.	134150	145650	85032	237066	55076	92120	152614	91770	43940	−76413	77106	40398
2 Long-term loans, n.e.c.	136041	213701	207169	177500	153213	55373	22509	−39471	18707	27980	79504	62389
3 Trade credits and advances	21006	15510	97481	31543	44456	67448	−72571	58982	−1458	32997	2907	35000
4 Other accounts payable	...	...	...	...	...	...	...	...	...	...	...	...
5 Other liabilities	82	−5	797	−898	1519	−439	993	−1230	−469	−112	184	100
Total incurrence of liabilities	291279	374856	390479	445211	254264	214502	103545	110051	60720	−15548	159701	137887
Statistical discrepancy [a]	2335	−4085	11939	13478	−8453	2459	27634	17708	30770	12919	5237	11476
Net lending	120910	56729	77906	76780	134753	225722	309388	384063	360016	432399	366824	449255
Incurrence of liabilities and net lending	414524	427500	480324	535469	380564	442683	440567	511822	451506	429770	531762	598618

a Statistical discrepancy refers to adjustment made in order to reconcile the net lending of the Capital Accumulation Account and the Capital Finance Account.

3.41 Private non-profit institutions serving households: production account

Million French francs

	1986	1987	1988	1989	1990	1991	1992	1993	1994	1995	1996	1997
Gross output												
1 Sales	15918	16699	17738	18858	20187	21044	21439	21564	22085	22755	23323	23829
2 Non-marketed output	13288	13932	14899	15955	17258	18124	18552	18387	18752	19262	20032	20633
Gross output	29206	30631	32637	34813	37445	39168	39991	39951	40837	42017	43355	44462
Gross input												
Intermediate consumption	16090	16876	17969	19153	20579	21510	21947	21958	22449	23104	23804	24392
subtotal: Value added	13116	13755	14668	15660	16866	17658	18044	17993	18388	18913	19551	20070
1 Indirect taxes, net	79	83	88	94	102	107	109	108	110	114	118	121
2 Consumption of fixed capital	1205	1271	1351	1428	1523	1618	1678	1711	1754	1813	1889	1959
3 Compensation of employees	12545	13156	14028	14975	16125	16880	17248	17204	17583	18085	18690	19184
4 Net operating surplus	−713	−755	−799	−837	−884	−947	−991	−1030	−1059	−1099	−1146	−1194
Gross input	29206	30631	32637	34813	37445	39168	39991	39951	40837	42017	43355	44462

3.42 Private non-profit institutions serving households: income and outlay account

Million French francs

	1986	1987	1988	1989	1990	1991	1992	1993	1994	1995	1996	1997
Receipts												
1 Operating surplus	−713	−755	−799	−837	−884	−947	−991	−1030	−1059	−1099	−1146	−1194
2 Property and entrepreneurial income	1085	1138	1217	1303	1409	1480	1516	1503	1535	1577	1640	1689
A Withdrawals from quasi-corporations	–	–	–	–	–	–	–	–	–	–	–	–
B Interest	1085	1138	1217	1303	1409	1480	1516	1503	1535	1577	1640	1689

France

Million French francs

	1986	1987	1988	1989	1990	1991	1992	1993	1994	1995	1996	1997
C Dividends	–	–	–	–	–	–	–	–	–	–	–	–
D Net land rent and royalties	–	–	–	–	–	–	–	–	–	–	–	–
3 Current transfers	24803	25872	28937	29783	32569	34068	37165	37785	38608	38819	41693	43552
A Casualty insurance claims	119	129	132	119	171	168	188	189	184	222	210	223
B Current transfers from general government	7493	7927	9918	10180	11329	12221	14810	15375	15794	15998	17834	19543
C Other transfers from resident sectors	17191	17816	18887	19484	21069	21679	22167	22221	22630	22599	23649	23786
D Current transfers received from the rest of the world	–	–	–	–	–	–	–	–	–	–	–	–
E Imputed unfunded employee pension and welfare contributions	...	...	...	...	...	...	...	...	...	...	...	...
Total current receipts	25175	26255	29355	30249	33094	34601	37690	38258	39084	39297	42187	44047

Disbursements

	1986	1987	1988	1989	1990	1991	1992	1993	1994	1995	1996	1997
1 Final consumption expenditures	13288	13932	14899	15955	17258	18124	18552	18387	18752	19262	20032	20633
2 Property income	100	105	112	120	130	137	140	139	142	146	152	157
A Interest	100	105	112	120	130	137	140	139	142	146	152	157
B Net land rent and royalties	...	...	...	...	...	...	...	...	...	...	...	...
3 Direct taxes and other transfers to general government	100	109	121	126	138	148	160	182	125	211	240	250
A Direct taxes	...	...	...	...	...	148	160	182	125	211	240	250
B Fees, fines and penalties	...	...	...	...	...	...	...	...	...	...	...	...
4 Other current transfers	3468	3675	3887	4143	4512	4716	4905	4936	5011	5157	5314	5458
A Net casualty insurance premiums	89	106	108	102	147	135	162	172	157	190	182	182
B Social assistance grants	...	...	...	...	...	...	...	...	...	...	...	...
C Unfunded employee pension and welfare benefits	2879	3019	3229	3458	3740	3928	4022	3986	4070	4181	4348	4478
D Current transfers to the rest of the world	...	...	...	...	...	...	...	...	...	...	...	...
E Other current transfers n.e.c.	500	550	550	583	625	653	721	778	784	786	784	798
Net saving	8219	8434	10336	9905	11056	11476	13933	14614	15054	14521	16449	17549
Total current disbursements	25175	26255	29355	30249	33094	34601	37690	38258	39084	39297	42187	44047

3.43 Private non-profit institutions serving households: capital accumulation account

Million French francs

	1986	1987	1988	1989	1990	1991	1992	1993	1994	1995	1996	1997

Finance of gross accumulation

	1986	1987	1988	1989	1990	1991	1992	1993	1994	1995	1996	1997
1 Gross saving	9424	9705	11687	11333	12579	13094	15611	16325	16808	16334	18338	19508
A Consumption of fixed capital	1205	1271	1351	1428	1523	1618	1678	1711	1754	1813	1889	1959
B Net saving	8219	8434	10336	9905	11056	11476	13933	14614	15054	14521	16449	17549
2 Capital transfers	1739	1855	2354	2618	3357	4221	4405	4523	5013	5397	5135	5082
Finance of gross accumulation	11163	11560	14041	13951	15936	17315	20016	20848	21821	21731	23473	24590

Gross accumulation

	1986	1987	1988	1989	1990	1991	1992	1993	1994	1995	1996	1997
1 Gross capital formation	3350	3512	3756	4022	4340	4563	4673	4631	4728	4857	5051	5203
A Increase in stocks	–	–	–	–	–	–	–	–	–	–	–	–
B Gross fixed capital formation	3350	3512	3756	4022	4340	4563	4673	4631	4728	4857	5051	5203
2 Purchases of land, net	53	56	60	63	68	71	73	72	74	76	79	81

France

Million French francs

	1986	1987	1988	1989	1990	1991	1992	1993	1994	1995	1996	1997
3 Purchases of intangible assets, net	–	–	–	–	–	–	–	–	–	–	–	–
4 Capital transfers	291	304	325	348	376	395	404	400	408	419	436	449
Net lending	7469	7688	9900	9518	11152	12286	14866	15745	16611	16379	17907	18857
Gross accumulation	11163	11560	14041	13951	15936	17315	20016	20848	21821	21731	23473	24590

3.44 Private non-profit institutions serving households: capital finance account

Million French francs

	1986	1987	1988	1989	1990	1991	1992	1993	1994	1995	1996	1997
Acquisition of financial assets												
1 Gold	...	...	...	...	...	...	...	...	...	...	...	...
2 Currency and transferable deposits	223	7680	903	1000	409	–2073	4500	3335	10245	4179	46	4236
3 Other deposits	1110	1083	–99	152	233	–	–11	–6514	708	3853	–907	5865
4 Bills and bonds, short-term	...	...	...	...	...	...	...	...	...	...	...	...
5 Bonds, long-term	–	–	9579	3902	13395	–1967	12825	4052	3318	2597	1466	348
6 Corporate equity securities	...	...	...	...	...	...	...	...	...	...	...	...
7 Short-term loans, n.e.c.	–220	1081	–310	1581	–2667	13684	27818	10724	14824	10578	22869	9879
8 Long-term loans, n.e.c.	...	...	...	...	–	–1360	1955	919	192	–4555	–374	380
9 Other receivables	19	18	29	–187	15	13	34	13	10	5	14	10
10 Proprietors' net additions to the accumulation of quasi-corporations	...	...	...	...	...	...	...	...	...	...	...	...
11 Other assets	6463	1420	2184	4320	1230	6921	–29637	7170	–19179	–1	–	40
Total acquisitions of financial assets	7595	11282	12286	10768	12615	15218	17484	19699	10118	16656	23114	20758
Incurrence of liabilities												
1 Short-term loans	–97	3514	1401	768	1044	2325	2499	2833	–3173	–623	6625	934
2 Long-term loans	155	–32	978	400	244	500	–	1097	–3341	896	–1530	967
3 Other liabilities	68	112	7	82	175	107	119	24	21	4	112	–
Total incurrence of liabilities	126	3594	2386	1250	1463	2932	2618	3954	–6493	277	5207	1901
Net lending	7469	7688	9900	9518	11152	12286	14866	15745	16611	16379	17907	18857
Total incurrence of liabilities and net lending	7595	11282	12286	10768	12615	15218	17484	19699	10118	16656	23114	20758

3.51 External transactions, current account: detail

Million French francs

	1986	1987	1988	1989	1990	1991	1992	1993	1994	1995	1996	1997
Payments to the rest of the world												
1 Imports of goods and services	1021789	1094349	1217627	1403052	1469802	1514461	1493531	1404767	1523075	1621458	1692180	1848001
A Imports of merchandise, c.i.f.	893847	952251	1063873	1229621	1273885	1302876	1268897	1171952	1283565	1383901	1430825	1563648
B Other	127942	142098	153754	173431	195917	211585	224634	232815	239510	237557	261355	284353
2 Factor income to rest of the world	190134	184380	202977	247784	295867	367291	403149	451799	412193	405112	392724	440958
A Compensation of employees	19310	16969	20358	15590	17724	20136	23011	21742	22143	18239	15173	13070
B Property and entrepreneurial income	170824	167411	182619	232194	278143	347155	380138	430057	390050	386873	377551	427888
3 Current transfers to the rest of the world	128709	137175	158742	161310	163981	193977	195557	210192	214974	218681	232190	241194

France

Million French francs

	1986	1987	1988	1989	1990	1991	1992	1993	1994	1995	1996	1997
A Indirect taxes by general government to supranational organizations	49048	54179	62291	61106	60615	68788	64909	57866	60446	63776	55120	56370
B Other current transfers	79661	82996	96451	100204	103366	125189	130648	152326	154528	154905	177070	184824
4 Surplus of the nation on current transactions	23876	−9504	−17752	−32298	−62337	−37215	8291	71449	72374	115080	121542	262138
Payments to the rest of the world and surplus of the nation on current transfers	1364508	1406400	1561594	1779848	1867313	2038514	2100528	2138207	2222616	2360331	2438636	2792291

Receipts from the rest of the world

	1986	1987	1988	1989	1990	1991	1992	1993	1994	1995	1996	1997
1 Exports of goods and services	1074095	1101383	1221304	1411087	1467972	1538062	1588103	1556368	1684130	1802974	1897678	2168498
A Exports of merchandise, f.o.b.	860303	886740	992606	1135583	1173049	1218530	1247213	1203283	1310041	1429458	1496475	1713321
B Other	213792	214643	228698	275504	294923	319532	340890	353085	374089	373516	401203	455177
2 Factor income from rest of the world	173526	171913	191330	237813	263783	329004	345528	395607	359227	374333	364131	454771
A Compensation of employees	11757	12427	16401	15798	16443	19477	19336	20158	20385	22243	19798	23194
B Property and entrepreneurial income	161769	159486	174929	222015	247340	309527	326192	375449	338842	352090	344333	431577
3 Current transfers from rest of the world	116887	133104	148960	130948	135558	171448	166897	186232	179259	183024	176827	169022
A Subsidies to general government from supranational organizations	39354	51022	42118	34847	35401	41494	41372	59880	53746	53536	53485	52861
B Other current transfers	77533	82082	106842	96101	100157	129954	125525	126352	125513	129488	123342	116161
Receipts from the rest of the world on current transfers	1364508	1406400	1561594	1779848	1867313	2038514	2100528	2138207	2222616	2360331	2438636	2792291

3.52 External transactions, capital accumulation account

Million French francs

	1986	1987	1988	1989	1990	1991	1992	1993	1994	1995	1996	1997

Finance of gross accumulation

	1986	1987	1988	1989	1990	1991	1992	1993	1994	1995	1996	1997
1 Surplus of the nation on current transactions	23876	−9504	−17752	−32298	−62337	−37215	8291	71449	72374	115080	121542	262138
2 Capital transfers from rest of the world	907	1268	6338	1879	6046	6949	11617	9413	1531	921	1929	847
Total finance of gross accumulation	24783	−8236	−11414	−30419	−56291	−30266	19908	80862	73905	116001	123471	262985

Gross accumulation

	1986	1987	1988	1989	1990	1991	1992	1993	1994	1995	1996	1997
1 Capital transfers to the rest of the world	4128	12773	5268	5859	27253	10245	10061	11258	32784	9918	9792	7360
2 Purchases of intangible assets, n.e.c., net, from rest of the world	...	...	...	...	...	...	...	...	...	...	...	...
Net lending to the rest of the world	20655	−21009	−16682	−36278	−83544	−40511	9847	69604	41121	106083	113679	255625
Total gross accumulation	24783	−8236	−11414	−30419	−56291	−30266	19908	80862	73905	116001	123471	262985

France

3.53 External transactions, capital finance account

Million French francs

	1986	1987	1988	1989	1990	1991	1992	1993	1994	1995	1996	1997
Acquisition of foreign financial assets											
1 Gold and SDRs	–8176	–1407	–17563	8826	128448	2632	–6267	39959	–12499	–25656	–33703	42526
2 Currency and transferable deposits	19336	–22507	–6068	25298	14270	–24181	10037	–43261	8892	9567	27014	31298
3 Other deposits	46224	225527	147195	296564	248100	–4943	247620	200923	204275	229699	3518	81983
4 Bills and bonds, short-term	–897	740	2092	2874	3166	30982	50173	–39384	13464	403	67375	118127
5 Bonds, long-term	33441	7360	19934	28598	43470	38607	59056	136487	110545	68206	173971	177790
6 Corporate equity securities	46895	67137	82783	131624	151624	141595	108484	87931	71928	48605	99808	166266
7 Short-term loans, n.e.c.	3900	16114	–5716	59379	83675	10160	129699	–3813	–95695	198640	20053	207641
8 Long-term loans	–1477	9093	15259	17578	–5982	–1435	17014	1093	–32299	17791	–6182	17737
9 Proprietors' net additions to accumulation of quasi-corporate, non-resident enterprises	...	...	...	...	...	...	...	...	...	...	...	...
10 Trade credits and advances	5209	27410	33645	37174	43093	22827	49885	44568	68915	42243	80254	110003
11 Other	915	687	1334	238	242	1011	1169	875	1265	712	548	–
Total acquisitions of foreign financial assets	145370	330154	272895	608153	710106	217255	666870	425378	338791	590210	432656	953371
Incurrence of foreign liabilities											
1 Currency and transferable deposits	6731	26614	–28852	25728	23723	–8138	77233	–26231	–45643	11145	23693	14896
2 Other deposits	61443	220166	148062	344379	388286	–26733	77109	28521	300721	135371	100920	152063
3 Bills and bonds, short-term	12418	9570	38965	48811	96598	35547	50317	24760	–56401	97651	50419	90105
4 Bonds, long-term	24754	26049	41848	132811	141070	90679	210170	93540	–127691	–55819	–154729	45822
5 Corporate equity securities	48317	47480	51512	107109	82097	104653	108285	150930	95673	101080	113336	149615
6 Short-term loans, n.e.c.	4040	2256	–1060	6943	24039	37458	72680	11998	19398	99791	92134	107609
7 Long-term loans	–37113	–9622	5928	–2607	–824	3270	17139	10830	–643	–179	3032	28888
8 Non-resident proprietors' net additions to accumulation of resident quasi-corporate enterprises	...	...	...	...	...	...	...	...	...	...	...	...
9 Trade credits and advances	–1567	21969	26134	8730	33992	15813	30497	46242	88803	71266	100548	105674
10 Other	269	250	226	624	99	545	827	205	137	–616	240	–
Total incurrence of liabilities	119292	344732	282763	672528	789080	253094	644257	340795	274354	459690	329593	694672
Statistical discrepancy [a]	5423	6431	6814	–28097	4570	4672	12766	14979	23316	24437	–10616	3074
Net lending	20655	–21009	–16682	–36278	–83544	–40511	9847	69604	41121	106083	113679	255625
Total incurrence of liabilities and net lending	145370	330154	272895	608153	710106	217255	666870	425378	338791	590210	432656	953371

a Statistical discrepancy refers to adjustment made in order to reconcile the net lending of the Capital Accumulation Account and the Capital Finance Account.

4.1 Derivation of value added by kind of activity, in current prices

Thousand million French francs

	1986			1987			1988			1989		
	Gross output	Intermediate consumption	Value added	Gross output	Intermediate consumption	Value added	Gross output	Intermediate consumption	Value added	Gross output	Intermediate consumption	Value added
All producers											
1 Agriculture, hunting, forestry and fishing	404	214	189	402	213	189	411	220	191	434	218	215
A Agriculture and hunting	381	209	172	378	208	170	385	215	171	405	213	192

France

Thousand million French francs

	1986 Gross output	1986 Intermediate consumption	1986 Value added	1987 Gross output	1987 Intermediate consumption	1987 Value added	1988 Gross output	1988 Intermediate consumption	1988 Value added	1989 Gross output	1989 Intermediate consumption	1989 Value added
B Forestry and logging	14	1	13	16	1	14	17	2	16	19	2	17
C Fishing	8	4	5	9	4	5	9	4	5	9	4	6
2 Mining and quarrying	84	48	36	72	37	35	67	37	31	70	39	32
A Coal mining	16	11	5	13	9	4	12	9	3	12	9	3
B Crude petroleum and natural gas production	52	29	23	43	20	23	39	19	20	41	21	20
C Metal ore mining	4	2	2	3	2	2	4	2	2	3	2	2
D Other mining	12	6	6	12	6	6	13	7	6	14	7	7
3 Manufacturing	2919	1799	1120	3001	1857	1143	3243	2001	1242	3552	2228	1325
A Manufacture of food, beverages and tobacco	522	375	147	520	376	144	547	393	155	585	415	170
B Textile, wearing apparel and leather industries	206	122	84	207	124	83	207	126	81	215	132	83
C Manufacture of wood and wood products, including furniture	79	46	32	84	50	35	91	54	37	98	59	39
D Manufacture of paper and paper products, printing and publishing	201	123	78	215	130	84	235	144	91	258	161	96
E Manufacture of chemicals and chemical petroleum, coal, rubber and plastic products	553	326	226	557	336	221	597	353	244	658	404	254
F Manufacture of non-metallic mineral products, except products of petroleum and coal	94	49	45	100	52	48	110	57	53	118	63	55
G Basic metal industries	203	144	58	197	140	58	223	153	69	250	173	77
H Manufacture of fabricated metal products, machinery and equipment	1022	593	428	1079	628	450	1190	700	491	1322	794	528
I Other manufacturing industries	40	20	20	40	20	20	43	22	20	47	26	21
4 Electricity, gas and water	181	63	118	190	67	123	194	68	126	208	79	128
5 Construction	574	311	263	612	334	278	679	369	310	736	415	321
6 Wholesale and retail trade, restaurants and hotels	1030	283	747	1098	300	797	1188	334	854	1296	367	929
A Wholesale and retail trade	834	207	627	887	222	665	959	250	709	1040	276	764
B Restaurants and hotels	196	76	120	210	78	132	229	83	145	256	92	164
7 Transport, storage and communication	454	143	311	474	151	322	498	163	335	540	182	357
A Transport and storage	319	124	195	332	131	201	361	142	220	393	161	232
B Communication	135	19	115	142	21	121	137	21	115	147	22	125
8 Finance, insurance, real estate and business services	1394	417	978	1599	513	1087	1787	589	1198	2075	753	1322
A Financial institutions	...	...	218	...	...	245	...	...	251	...	...	255
B Insurance	...	...	51	...	...	51	...	...	53	...	...	61
C Real estate and business services	...	...	709	...	...	791	...	...	895	...	...	1007
Real estate, except dwellings	...	...	37	...	...	40	...	...	41	...	...	44
Dwellings	...	...	329	...	...	362	...	...	401	...	...	436
9 Community, social and personal services	356	100	256	386	109	277	423	117	306	464	128	335
A Sanitary and similar services	...	...	...	...	...	...	...	...	...	...	...	...

France

Thousand million French francs

	1986			1987			1988			1989		
	Gross output	Intermediate consumption	Value added	Gross output	Intermediate consumption	Value added	Gross output	Intermediate consumption	Value added	Gross output	Intermediate consumption	Value added
B Social and related community services	...	...	150	...	...	158	...	...	178	...	...	193
Educational services	...	...	17	...	...	18	...	...	21	...	...	24
Medical, dental, other health and veterinary services	...	...	133	...	...	140	...	...	156	...	...	169
C Recreational and cultural services	...	...	99	...	...	110	...	...	118	...	...	131
D Personal and household services	...	...	7	...	...	9	...	...	10	...	...	11
Total, Industries	7395	3377	4018	7833	3582	4251	8491	3897	4594	9374	4410	4964
Producers of government services	1142	297	845	1196	322	874	1264	351	914	1320	359	961
Other producers	...	...	...	...	...	...	...	...	...	...	...	...
Total	8537	3674	4863	9029	3904	5125	9755	4248	5508	10695	4769	5926
less: Imputed bank service charge	...	−223	223	...	−247	247	...	−262	262	...	−279	279
Import duties [a]	9	...	9	10	...	10	11	...	11	11	...	11
Value added tax	420	...	420	449	...	449	480	...	480	503	...	503
Other adjustments	–	...	–	–	...	–	–	...	–	–	...	–
Total	8966	3897	5069	9487	4150	5337	10245	4510	5735	11208	5049	6160

	1990			1991			1992			1993		
	Gross output	Intermediate consumption	Value added	Gross output	Intermediate consumption	Value added	Gross output	Intermediate consumption	Value added	Gross output	Intermediate consumption	Value added

All producers

1 Agriculture, hunting, forestry and fishing	439	217	222	433	229	205	424	226	198	375	209	166
A Agriculture and hunting	410	211	199	405	223	182	397	220	177	352	203	149
B Forestry and logging	19	2	17	19	2	17	17	2	16	14	2	13
C Fishing	9	4	5	9	4	5	9	4	5	8	4	4
2 Mining and quarrying	71	41	30	79	47	31	77	44	33	74	43	32
A Coal mining	12	9	3	11	8	3	11	8	2	9	8	2
B Crude petroleum and natural gas production	43	24	19	50	30	21	49	26	23	49	26	23
C Metal ore mining	3	2	1	2	1	1	3	2	1	2	2	1
D Other mining	14	7	6	15	8	7	15	8	7	14	7	7
3 Manufacturing	3700	2305	1395	3738	2328	1410	3735	2332	1403	3569	2189	1380
A Manufacture of food, beverages and tobacco	606	427	179	623	439	184	633	442	191	626	421	205
B Textile, wearing apparel and leather industries	219	132	87	214	129	85	211	127	84	194	116	78
C Manufacture of wood and wood products, including furniture	107	63	44	108	63	45	108	61	46	103	57	46
D Manufacture of paper and paper products, printing and publishing	273	168	105	283	170	113	284	171	113	276	161	114
E Manufacture of chemicals and chemical petroleum, coal, rubber and plastic products	685	421	264	694	423	271	685	423	263	687	417	270

France

	1990 Gross output	1990 Intermediate consumption	1990 Value added	1991 Gross output	1991 Intermediate consumption	1991 Value added	1992 Gross output	1992 Intermediate consumption	1992 Value added	1993 Gross output	1993 Intermediate consumption	1993 Value added
F Manufacture of non-metallic mineral products, except products of petroleum and coal	124	66	58	128	69	59	125	68	57	118	64	54
G Basic metal industries	230	159	71	212	149	64	204	143	62	181	125	56
H Manufacture of fabricated metal products, machinery and equipment	1406	843	563	1428	861	567	1436	872	564	1335	803	531
I Other manufacturing industries	50	26	24	49	26	23	49	26	23	48	24	24
4 Electricity, gas and water	220	81	139	241	87	154	253	88	165	262	91	172
5 Construction	781	445	336	823	465	358	822	458	363	787	429	358
6 Wholesale and retail trade, restaurants and hotels	1374	383	991	1434	403	1031	1481	421	1060	1498	417	1081
A Wholesale and retail trade	1098	286	811	1140	299	840	1172	314	858	1183	312	871
B Restaurants and hotels	276	97	179	295	104	191	309	107	202	315	105	210
7 Transport, storage and communication	571	193	378	610	212	397	641	226	415	642	228	414
A Transport and storage	413	170	243	433	184	249	451	191	259	443	193	250
B Communication	158	22	136	177	28	148	190	35	155	199	34	164
8 Finance, insurance, real estate and business services	2294	904	1390	2474	1003	1471	2754	1215	1539	3199	1629	1570
A Financial institutions	...	...	245	...	...	248	...	...	262	...	...	252
B Insurance	...	...	42	...	...	49	...	...	42	...	...	43
C Real estate and business services	...	...	1103	...	...	1174	...	...	1235	...	...	1276
Real estate, except dwellings	...	...	49	...	...	53	...	...	55	...	...	58
Dwellings	...	...	471	...	...	511	...	...	555	...	...	598
9 Community, social and personal services	497	134	363	530	145	385	582	162	421	609	165	443
A Sanitary and similar services	...	...	...	...	...	...	...	...	...	...	...	...
B Social and related community services	...	...	211	...	...	226	...	...	239	...	...	251
Educational services	...	...	26	...	...	27	...	...	29	...	...	30
Medical, dental, other health and veterinary services	...	...	185	...	...	198	...	...	210	...	...	221
C Recreational and cultural services	...	...	141	...	...	149	...	...	162	...	...	170
D Personal and household services	...	...	12	...	...	13	...	...	13	...	...	14
Total, Industries	9947	4703	5243	10362	4920	5442	10768	5172	5596	11016	5400	5616
Producers of government services	1395	380	1016	1476	399	1077	1573	427	1146	1669	458	1211
Other producers	...	...	...	...	...	...	...	...	...	...	...	...
Total	11342	5083	6259	11838	5319	6519	12342	5599	6743	12684	5857	6827
less: Imputed bank service charge	...	−278	278	...	−269	269	...	−275	275	...	−275	275
Import duties [a]	11	...	11	12	...	12	11	...	11	10	...	10
Value added tax	518	...	518	515	...	515	521	...	521	515	...	515
Other adjustments	−	...	−	−	...	−	−	...	−	−	...	−
Total	11871	5361	6509	12365	5589	6776	12873	5874	7000	13210	6133	7077

France

	1994			1995			1996			1997		
	Gross output	Intermediate consumption	Value added	Gross output	Intermediate consumption	Value added	Gross output	Intermediate consumption	Value added	Gross output	Intermediate consumption	Value added
All producers												
1 Agriculture, hunting, forestry and fishing	391	214	178	395	213	182	397	215	183	404	220	183
A Agriculture and hunting	365	208	157	368	207	161	371	209	163	377	214	163
B Forestry and logging	18	2	17	19	2	18	18	2	16	18	2	16
C Fishing	8	4	4	7	4	3	8	4	4	8	4	4
2 Mining and quarrying	74	42	32	75	42	33	79	45	34	80	48	33
A Coal mining	9	7	2	9	7	2	8	6	2	7	6	2
B Crude petroleum and natural gas production	49	26	23	50	26	24	55	30	25	57	33	24
C Metal ore mining	2	1	–	1	1	–	1	1	–	2	1	–
D Other mining	14	8	7	15	8	7	14	8	7	15	8	7
3 Manufacturing	3758	2335	1423	3944	2465	1479	3976	2474	1502	4166	2597	1570
A Manufacture of food, beverages and tobacco	636	430	206	651	442	208	665	447	218	690	460	230
B Textile, wearing apparel and leather industries	202	123	78	200	123	77	188	116	71	187	118	70
C Manufacture of wood and wood products, including furniture	109	63	46	115	66	49	113	64	49	114	65	49
D Manufacture of paper and paper products, printing and publishing	290	174	116	313	191	122	303	178	124	305	178	127
E Manufacture of chemicals and chemical petroleum, coal, rubber and plastic products	716	439	277	749	458	291	781	482	299	835	517	318
F Manufacture of non-metallic mineral products, except products of petroleum and coal	125	68	57	130	71	59	124	68	56	126	70	56
G Basic metal industries	203	140	62	216	150	66	208	144	64	223	155	68
H Manufacture of fabricated metal products, machinery and equipment	1425	869	556	1517	935	581	1541	946	595	1628	1003	625
I Other manufacturing industries	51	25	25	53	28	26	55	29	26	58	31	28
4 Electricity, gas and water	267	94	173	276	96	180	285	98	186	280	97	183
5 Construction	790	447	342	798	451	347	779	443	336	789	442	347
6 Wholesale and retail trade, restaurants and hotels	1542	435	1107	1601	443	1158	1625	452	1173	1653	460	1193
A Wholesale and retail trade	1220	330	890	1274	339	935	1291	346	946	1310	351	958
B Restaurants and hotels	322	105	217	327	105	223	334	107	227	343	108	235
7 Transport, storage and communication	667	239	427	680	244	436	696	255	441	728	267	461
A Transport and storage	462	204	258	472	208	264	482	217	265	510	229	281
B Communication	205	36	170	208	36	171	214	38	176	218	39	180
8 Finance, insurance, real estate and business services	3340	1643	1697	3762	2024	1739	4413	2629	1783	5048	3187	1861
A Financial institutions	...	...	312	...	...	294	...	...	275	...	...	282
B Insurance	...	...	56	...	...	44	...	...	47	...	...	44
C Real estate and business services	...	...	1329	...	...	1401	...	...	1461	...	...	1534
9 Community, social and personal services	628	169	459	645	170	475	666	176	490	682	177	504
Total, Industries	11457	5618	5839	12176	6147	6029	12916	6788	6128	13831	7496	6335

France

	1994			1995			1996			1997		
	Gross output	Intermediate consumption	Value added	Gross output	Intermediate consumption	Value added	Gross output	Intermediate consumption	Value added	Gross output	Intermediate consumption	Value added
Producers of government services	1721	460	1261	1770	450	1320	1850	473	1377	1896	483	1413
Other producers	...	...	...	...	...	...	...	...	...	...	...	...
Total	13179	6078	7101	13946	6597	7349	14767	7261	7505	15727	7979	7748
less: Imputed bank service charge	...	−263	263	...	−272	272	...	−254	254	...	−256	256
Import duties [a]	10	...	10	10	...	10	8	...	8	9	...	9
Value added tax	542	...	542	575	...	575	612	...	612	636	...	636
Other adjustments	–	...	–	–	...	–	–	...	–	–	...	–
Total	13731	6341	7390	14531	6869	7662	15387	7515	7872	16373	8236	8137

a Item "Import duties" includes also value added tax (VAT) on products.

4.2 Derivation of value added by kind of activity, in constant prices

Thousand million French francs

	1986			1987			1988			1989		
	Gross output	Intermediate consumption	Value added	Gross output	Intermediate consumption	Value added	Gross output	Intermediate consumption	Value added	Gross output	Intermediate consumption	Value added

At constant prices of: 1980

All producers

1 Agriculture, hunting, forestry and fishing	275	135	139	282	140	141	283	142	141	284	138	146
A Agriculture and hunting	260	132	128	266	137	129	267	139	128	268	135	133
B Forestry and logging	11	1	10	11	1	10	12	1	11	12	1	11
C Fishing	4	2	2	4	2	2	4	2	2	4	3	2
2 Mining and quarrying	52	31	21	52	31	21	51	31	20	51	31	20
A Coal mining	11	8	3	10	7	3	9	7	3	9	6	2
B Crude petroleum and natural gas production	32	19	13	33	19	14	31	19	13	32	20	12
C Metal ore mining	2	1	1	2	1	1	3	1	1	2	1	1
D Other mining	7	4	3	7	4	3	8	4	4	8	4	4
3 Manufacturing	1884	1216	667	1912	1250	661	2014	1314	701	2115	1379	737
A Manufacture of food, beverages and tobacco	345	253	92	349	261	87	359	269	90	367	270	97
B Textile, wearing apparel and leather industries	128	77	51	125	78	48	123	77	46	125	79	46
C Manufacture of wood and wood products, including furniture	53	32	21	56	34	22	59	35	23	61	37	24
D Manufacture of paper and paper products, printing and publishing	122	79	43	126	83	43	135	88	47	141	93	48
E Manufacture of chemicals and chemical petroleum, coal, rubber and plastic products	385	260	125	387	263	124	410	276	135	431	289	142
F Manufacture of non-metallic mineral products, except products of petroleum and coal	59	30	29	61	32	29	65	34	31	68	37	32
G Basic metal industries	138	100	37	137	101	36	146	107	39	151	110	41
H Manufacture of fabricated metal products, machinery and equipment	629	372	258	647	385	262	691	413	278	742	448	294

France

Thousand million French francs

	1986 Gross output	1986 Intermediate consumption	1986 Value added	1987 Gross output	1987 Intermediate consumption	1987 Value added	1988 Gross output	1988 Intermediate consumption	1988 Value added	1989 Gross output	1989 Intermediate consumption	1989 Value added
At constant prices of: 1980												
1 Other manufacturing industries	24	14	11	24	13	10	25	14	11	28	16	12
4 Electricity, gas and water	117	40	77	123	41	82	125	42	83	131	48	83
5 Construction	384	198	186	396	208	188	427	224	203	452	240	212
6 Wholesale and retail trade, restaurants and hotels	619	176	443	635	186	449	659	202	457	691	214	476
A Wholesale and retail trade	506	129	377	521	138	383	543	152	391	568	161	407
B Restaurants and hotels	113	47	66	113	48	65	116	50	66	123	53	70
7 Transport, storage and communication	286	88	198	302	93	209	329	101	229	354	108	247
A Transport and storage	193	76	117	205	80	124	222	87	135	236	94	142
B Communication	93	12	81	98	13	85	108	14	93	119	14	105
8 Finance, insurance, real estate and business services	820	254	566	904	302	602	961	338	623	1064	415	649
A Financial institutions	...	...	125	...	...	134	...	...	128	...	...	121
B Insurance	...	...	21	...	...	20	...	...	20	...	...	20
C Real estate and business services	...	...	421	...	...	448	...	...	475	...	...	509
Real estate, except dwellings	...	...	26	...	...	28	...	...	28	...	...	30
Dwellings	...	...	200	...	...	208	...	...	216	...	...	222
9 Community, social and personal services	223	62	160	231	66	165	242	68	174	257	72	185
A Sanitary and similar services	...	...	...	...	...	...	...	...	...	...	...	...
B Social and related community services	...	...	99	...	...	102	...	...	110	...	...	119
Educational services	...	...	10	...	...	10	...	...	11	...	...	11
Medical, dental, other health and veterinary services	...	...	90	...	...	93	...	...	99	...	...	107
C Recreational and cultural services	...	...	57	...	...	59	...	...	60	...	...	62
D Personal and household services	...	...	4	...	...	4	...	...	4	...	...	4
Total, Industries	4660	2201	2459	4836	2318	2518	5091	2461	2631	5400	2645	2755
Producers of government services	694	189	506	713	201	512	739	212	527	741	209	532
Other producers	...	...	...	...	...	...	...	...	...	...	...	...
Total	5355	2390	2965	5549	2519	3030	5830	2673	3157	6141	2855	3286
less: Imputed bank service charge	...	−132	132	...	−140	140	...	−144	144	...	−146	146
Import duties [a]	8	...	8	9	...	9	10	...	10	11	...	11
Value added tax	264	...	264	275	...	275	294	...	294	307	...	307
Other adjustments	−	...	−	−	...	−	−	...	−	−	...	−
Total	5626	2522	3105	5834	2659	3175	6134	2817	3317	6459	3001	3458

France

	1990			1991			1992			1993		
	Gross output	Intermediate consumption	Value added	Gross output	Intermediate consumption	Value added	Gross output	Intermediate consumption	Value added	Gross output	Intermediate consumption	Value added

At constant prices of: 1980

All producers

1 Agriculture, hunting, forestry and fishing	289	140	149	286	143	144	299	140	160	285	138	147
A Agriculture and hunting	273	136	137	270	138	132	284	135	148	270	134	137
B Forestry and logging	12	2	10	12	2	10	12	2	10	10	2	8
C Fishing	4	3	2	4	3	2	4	2	2	4	3	1
2 Mining and quarrying	51	32	18	55	35	21	56	34	21	55	33	22
A Coal mining	8	6	2	8	6	2	8	6	2	8	5	3
B Crude petroleum and natural gas production	33	21	12	37	23	14	37	23	15	38	23	15
C Metal ore mining	2	1	1	2	1	1	2	1	1	2	1	1
D Other mining	8	4	4	8	4	4	8	4	4	7	4	3
3 Manufacturing	2173	1423	750	2181	1445	736	2185	1463	722	2106	1406	700
A Manufacture of food, beverages and tobacco	379	282	97	389	290	99	390	294	96	391	291	100
B Textile, wearing apparel and leather industries	126	78	48	122	77	45	121	76	45	113	71	42
C Manufacture of wood and wood products, including furniture	64	38	26	62	38	25	61	37	24	58	35	23
D Manufacture of paper and paper products, printing and publishing	146	98	49	148	101	47	149	103	46	148	103	45
E Manufacture of chemicals and chemical petroleum, coal, rubber and plastic products	443	297	146	449	305	144	455	314	141	461	315	146
F Manufacture of non-metallic mineral products, except products of petroleum and coal	70	38	32	70	38	32	68	37	31	64	35	29
G Basic metal industries	147	106	41	144	105	39	143	105	38	131	96	35
H Manufacture of fabricated metal products, machinery and equipment	770	469	300	768	474	294	770	480	290	714	444	270
I Other manufacturing industries	28	16	12	28	16	12	28	16	11	27	16	11
4 Electricity, gas and water	134	50	84	143	54	89	145	53	92	147	54	92
5 Construction	467	249	218	472	254	218	463	249	213	436	235	201
6 Wholesale and retail trade, restaurants and hotels	712	220	492	720	227	494	726	233	492	712	229	483
A Wholesale and retail trade	586	165	420	592	170	422	596	175	421	585	173	412
B Restaurants and hotels	126	54	72	128	57	72	130	58	72	128	56	71
7 Transport, storage and communication	371	112	259	389	121	269	404	129	276	405	129	276
A Transport and storage	243	98	145	247	102	145	254	106	148	250	107	143
B Communication	129	14	114	143	19	124	150	22	128	155	22	132
8 Finance, insurance, real estate and business services	1135	484	651	1177	520	657	1274	612	662	1430	772	658
A Financial institutions	...	...	105	...	...	99	...	...	96	...	...	94
B Insurance	...	...	20	...	...	24	...	...	26	...	...	23
C Real estate and business services	...	...	526	...	...	534	...	...	541	...	...	542
Real estate, except dwellings	...	...	32	...	...	34	...	...	35	...	...	36

France

	1990			1991			1992			1993		
	Gross output	Intermediate consumption	Value added	Gross output	Intermediate consumption	Value added	Gross output	Intermediate consumption	Value added	Gross output	Intermediate consumption	Value added
At constant prices of: 1980													
Dwellings	...	...	229	...	...	237	...	...	244	...	...	252
9 Community, social and personal services	271	74	196	283	80	202	300	88	212	306	89	217
A Sanitary and similar services	...	...	...	...	...	...	...	...	...	...	...	...
B Social and related community services	...	...	128	...	...	134	...	...	139	...	...	144
Educational services	...	...	12	...	...	12	...	...	12	...	...	12
Medical, dental, other health and veterinary services	...	...	116	...	...	123	...	...	127	...	...	132
C Recreational and cultural services	...	...	64	...	...	66	...	...	67	...	...	67
D Personal and household services	...	...	4	...	...	4	...	...	4	...	...	4
Total, Industries	5603	2785	2818	5708	2879	2829	5852	3001	2850	5882	3086	2796
Producers of government services	756	217	539	775	222	554	802	233	568	828	248	581
Other producers	...	...	...	...	...	...	...	...	...	...	...	...
Total	6359	3002	3357	6483	3100	3383	6653	3234	3419	6710	3333	3377
less: Imputed bank service charge	...	−139	139	...	−130	130	...	−127	127	...	−123	123
Import duties [a]	12	...	12	12	...	12	13	...	13	13	...	13
Value added tax	315	...	315	307	...	307	310	...	310	300	...	300
Other adjustments	–	...	–	–	...	–	–	...	–	–	...	–
Total	6685	3140	3545	6803	3230	3573	6976	3361	3614	7022	3456	3566

	1994			1995			1996			1997		
	Gross output	Intermediate consumption	Value added	Gross output	Intermediate consumption	Value added	Gross output	Intermediate consumption	Value added	Gross output	Intermediate consumption	Value added
At constant prices of: 1980													
All producers													
1 Agriculture, hunting, forestry and fishing	289	142	147	290	143	147	299	143	155	301	147	154
A Agriculture and hunting	275	138	137	275	139	136	284	139	145	286	142	144
B Forestry and logging	11	2	9	11	2	9	11	2	9	11	2	9
C Fishing	4	2	2	4	2	1	4	2	1	4	2	2
2 Mining and quarrying	53	32	21	54	33	22	57	35	23	56	35	21
A Coal mining	7	4	3	7	4	3	6	4	2	6	4	2
B Crude petroleum and natural gas production	37	23	14	38	24	15	42	26	16	41	26	15
C Metal ore mining	2	1	1	1	1	1	1	1	1	1	1	1
D Other mining	8	4	3	8	4	3	7	4	3	8	4	3
3 Manufacturing	2199	1467	732	2275	1514	761	2310	1535	775	2416	1603	813
A Manufacture of food, beverages and tobacco	397	295	102	405	303	102	414	309	105	425	313	112
B Textile, wearing apparel and leather industries	117	74	43	115	73	42	107	69	38	107	70	37
C Manufacture of wood and wood products, including furniture	61	37	24	62	38	25	61	37	24	62	38	24
D Manufacture of paper and paper products, printing and publishing	156	108	48	156	108	48	155	107	47	159	109	50

France

	1994 Gross output	1994 Intermediate consumption	1994 Value added	1995 Gross output	1995 Intermediate consumption	1995 Value added	1996 Gross output	1996 Intermediate consumption	1996 Value added	1997 Gross output	1997 Intermediate consumption	1997 Value added
At constant prices of: 1980												
E Manufacture of chemicals and chemical petroleum, coal, rubber and plastic products	474	326	148	486	331	155	500	345	155	527	364	163
F Manufacture of non-metallic mineral products, except products of petroleum and coal	67	37	30	69	38	31	66	36	29	67	37	30
G Basic metal industries	139	101	38	142	104	39	141	102	40	153	110	43
H Manufacture of fabricated metal products, machinery and equipment	760	472	288	812	503	309	835	511	325	885	543	342
I Other manufacturing industries	27	16	11	28	17	11	30	18	12	31	19	12
4 Electricity, gas and water	148	55	93	152	56	96	157	59	99	157	57	99
5 Construction	434	238	196	436	239	197	420	232	188	417	231	185
6 Wholesale and retail trade, restaurants and hotels	719	234	485	733	238	495	739	239	499	749	242	507
A Wholesale and retail trade	592	179	414	606	183	423	612	183	428	621	186	435
B Restaurants and hotels	127	56	71	127	55	71	127	56	71	128	56	72
7 Transport, storage and communication	418	134	284	429	137	291	441	140	301	457	145	312
A Transport and storage	262	111	150	269	114	155	275	116	159	286	120	165
B Communication	157	23	134	159	23	136	166	24	142	171	25	147
8 Finance, insurance, real estate and business services	1449	764	685	1611	916	695	1849	1162	688	2072	1370	702
A Financial institutions	...	...	107	...	...	98	...	...	84	...	...	83
B Insurance	...	...	24	...	...	23	...	...	21	...	...	19
C Real estate and business services	...	...	553	...	...	574	...	...	584	...	...	601
9 Community, social and personal services	307	89	218	309	88	221	315	91	224	318	92	227
Total, Industries	6017	3155	2861	6289	3364	2925	6588	3635	2952	6942	3922	3021
Producers of government services	841	246	595	843	241	602	866	248	618	877	252	626
Other producers	...	...	...	...	...	...	...	...	...	...	...	...
Total	6858	3402	3456	7132	3605	3527	7454	3884	3570	7819	4173	3646
less: Imputed bank service charge	...	−112	112	...	−115	115	...	−106	106	...	−105	105
Import duties [a]	13	...	13	14	...	14	15	...	15	15	...	15
Value added tax	310	...	310	317	...	317	322	...	322	333	...	333
Other adjustments	–	...	–	–	...	–	–	...	–	–	...	–
Total	7181	3514	3667	7463	3719	3743	7791	3989	3801	8168	4278	3890

[a] Item "Import duties" includes also value added tax (VAT) on products.

France

4.3 Cost components of value added

Million French francs

	1986 Compensation of employees	1986 Capital consumption	1986 Net operating surplus	1986 Indirect taxes	1986 less: Subsidies received	1986 Value added	1987 Compensation of employees	1987 Capital consumption	1987 Net operating surplus	1987 Indirect taxes	1987 less: Subsidies received	1987 Value added
All producers												
1 Agriculture, hunting, forestry and fishing	29685	...	164899	5524	10613	189495	31073	...	163263	6256	11590	189002
A Agriculture and hunting	23445	...	152802	5196	9507	171936	24433	...	150207	5850	10541	169949
B Forestry and logging	3674	...	9901	173	989	12759	3638	...	11201	182	995	14026
C Fishing	2566	...	2196	155	117	4800	3002	...	1855	224	54	5027
2 Mining and quarrying	22434	...	18740	1913	7429	35657	22240	...	17923	1816	7256	34723
A Coal mining	10078	...	1966	433	7382	5095	9188	...	1648	368	7204	4000
B Crude petroleum and natural gas production	7629	...	13959	1197	16	22769	8339	...	13570	1168	18	23059
C Metal ore mining	1287	...	792	69	3	2145	1161	...	661	65	4	1883
D Other mining	3440	...	2023	214	28	5648	3552	...	2044	215	30	5781
3 Manufacturing	702594	...	325928	124843	33266	1120100	713583	...	344042	124642	39045	1143222
A Manufacture of food, beverages and tobacco	80326	...	65911	19173	18171	147239	81126	...	67472	20145	25050	143693
B Textile, wearing apparel and leather industries	58594	...	23315	2991	491	84409	58133	...	22687	3011	608	83223
C Manufacture of wood and wood products, including furniture	20846	...	10349	1469	240	32424	21733	...	11613	1513	267	34592
D Manufacture of paper and paper products, printing and publishing	54033	...	21061	4083	780	78397	56928	...	24930	2805	627	84036
E Manufacture of chemicals and chemical petroleum, coal, rubber and plastic products	96644	...	56694	73778	828	226288	98363	...	50377	73483	808	221415
F Manufacture of non-metallic mineral products, except products of petroleum and coal	27148	...	15779	1949	136	44741	28386	...	17957	1930	192	48081
G Basic metal industries	36908	...	18992	2816	348	58368	36413	...	18571	2831	251	57564
H Manufacture of fabricated metal products, machinery and equipment	315589	...	106810	17985	12160	428224	320005	...	123279	18306	11112	450478
I Other manufacturing industries	12506	...	7017	599	112	20010	12496	...	7156	618	130	20140
4 Electricity, gas and water	36937	...	69437	13781	2062	118093	38671	...	71630	14861	2378	122784
5 Construction	175239	...	81553	9593	3432	262953	182204	...	90159	9524	3801	278086
6 Wholesale and retail trade, restaurants and hotels	383437	...	316669	72724	25753	747077	410751	...	334432	83544	31645	797082
A Wholesale and retail trade	319973	...	260481	68930	22561	626823	341779	...	271836	79502	28185	664932
B Restaurants and hotels	63464	...	56188	3794	3192	120254	68972	...	62596	4042	3460	132150
7 Transport, storage and communication	184702	...	140984	9238	24165	310759	189049	...	148888	9149	24703	322383
A Transport and storage	127197	...	84815	7416	24145	195283	131630	...	86786	7448	24683	201181
B Communication	57505	...	56169	1822	20	115476	57419	...	62102	1701	20	121202
8 Finance, insurance, real estate and business services	327084	...	611345	84685	45520	977594	356403	...	679406	92193	41074	1086928
A Financial institutions	...	...	...	...	...	217918	...	...	...	...	...	245189
B Insurance	...	...	...	...	...	50760	...	...	...	...	...	50712

France

Million French francs

	1986						1987					
	Compensation of employees	Capital consumption	Net operating surplus	Indirect taxes	less: Subsidies received	Value added	Compensation of employees	Capital consumption	Net operating surplus	Indirect taxes	less: Subsidies received	Value added
C Real estate and business services	...	...	...	...	...	708916	...	...	...	...	...	791027
Real estate, except dwellings	...	...	...	...	...	36916	...	...	...	...	...	40471
Dwellings	...	...	...	...	...	329475	...	...	...	...	...	362049
9 Community, social and personal services	95225	...	149181	17493	5566	256333	104324	...	160771	18348	6766	276677
A Sanitary and similar services	...	...	...	...	...	...	...	...	...	...	...	...
B Social and related community services	...	...	...	...	...	149524	...	...	...	...	...	157912
Educational services	...	...	...	...	...	16814	...	...	...	...	...	18401
Medical, dental, other health and veterinary services	...	...	...	...	...	132710	...	...	...	...	...	139511
C Recreational and cultural services	...	...	...	...	...	99364	...	...	...	...	...	110066
D Personal and household services	...	...	...	...	...	7445	...	...	...	...	...	8699
Total, Industries	1957337	...	1878736	339794	157806	4018061	2048298	...	2010514	360333	168258	4250887
Producers of government services	750777	...	78155	16393	...	845325	772899	...	84026	17051	...	873976
Other producers	...	...	...	...	...	...	...	...	...	...	...	...
Total	2708114	...	1956891	356187	157806	4863386	2821197	...	2094540	377384	168258	5124863
less: Imputed bank service charge	...	...	223272	...	...	223272	...	...	246505	...	...	246505
Import duties	...	...	...	8976	...	8976	...	...	...	9667	...	9667
Value added tax	...	...	...	420379	...	420379	...	...	...	449074	...	449074
Other adjustments	...	...	...	...	173	−173	...	...	...	...	447	−447
Total [a]	2708114	...	1733619	785542	157979	5069296	2821197	...	1848035	836125	168705	5336652

	1988						1989					
	Compensation of employees	Capital consumption	Net operating surplus	Indirect taxes	less: Subsidies received	Value added	Compensation of employees	Capital consumption	Net operating surplus	Indirect taxes	less: Subsidies received	Value added

All producers

1 Agriculture, hunting, forestry and fishing	32222	...	161845	8439	11228	191278	33442	...	186601	6528	11289	215282
A Agriculture and hunting	24918	...	147627	8074	10113	170506	25842	...	170555	6127	10170	192354
B Forestry and logging	3763	...	12881	140	1050	15734	3783	...	14503	144	1030	17400
C Fishing	3541	...	1337	225	65	5038	3817	...	1543	257	89	5528
2 Mining and quarrying	20150	...	11698	2246	3322	30772	19804	...	13421	1882	3369	31738
A Coal mining	6807	...	−1006	375	3284	2892	6046	...	79	307	3258	3174
B Crude petroleum and natural gas production	8505	...	9610	1589	13	19691	8774	...	10375	1277	82	20344
C Metal ore mining	1147	...	742	63	2	1950	960	...	538	56	2	1552
D Other mining	3691	...	2352	219	23	6239	4024	...	2429	242	27	6668
3 Manufacturing	734214	...	415747	125742	33567	1242136	774755	...	453801	127088	31023	1324621
A Manufacture of food, beverages and tobacco	84795	...	70509	20391	20989	154706	89197	...	78678	21392	18927	170340
B Textile, wearing apparel and leather industries	57413	...	21515	2945	439	81434	57915	...	22697	2968	452	83128
C Manufacture of wood and wood products, including furniture	22841	...	13025	1667	190	37343	24143	...	13450	1693	222	39064

France

	1988						1989					
	Compensation of employees	Capital consumption	Net operating surplus	Indirect taxes	less: Subsidies received	Value added	Compensation of employees	Capital consumption	Net operating surplus	Indirect taxes	less: Subsidies received	Value added
D Manufacture of paper and paper products, printing and publishing	60616	...	28223	3145	563	91421	63206	...	30481	3337	639	96385
E Manufacture of chemicals and chemical petroleum, coal, rubber and plastic products	102630	...	68555	73482	861	243806	108315	...	73591	73144	849	254201
F Manufacture of non-metallic mineral products, except products of petroleum and coal	29453	...	21756	2043	128	53124	30641	...	22824	2039	171	55333
G Basic metal industries	36869	...	30101	2652	189	69433	36018	...	38454	2613	217	76868
H Manufacture of fabricated metal products, machinery and equipment	327048	...	154991	18743	10126	490656	352055	...	165922	19272	9443	527806
I Other manufacturing industries	12549	...	7072	674	82	20213	13265	...	7704	630	103	21496
4 Electricity, gas and water	39933	...	72766	16072	2317	126454	42184	...	71241	17143	2309	128259
5 Construction	197431	...	106113	9945	3846	309643	210088	...	103099	11546	4090	320643
6 Wholesale and retail trade, restaurants and hotels	442081	...	345382	91757	25138	854082	469972	...	378437	100816	20647	928578
A Wholesale and retail trade	365960	...	277069	87330	21492	708867	385290	...	299010	96095	15966	764429
B Restaurants and hotels	76121	...	68313	4427	3646	145215	84682	...	79427	4721	4681	164149
7 Transport, storage and communication	197532	...	152554	9445	24555	334976	209303	...	164451	9676	25943	357487
A Transport and storage	138416	...	97410	8230	24538	219518	147054	...	102713	8406	25923	232250
B Communication	59116	...	55144	1215	17	115458	62249	...	61738	1270	20	125237
8 Finance, insurance, real estate and business services	393503	...	737276	101021	33548	1198252	433842	...	815354	104801	31596	1322401
A Financial institutions	...	...	...	...	...	250530	...	...	...	...	...	254529
B Insurance	...	...	...	...	...	53135	...	...	...	...	...	60507
C Real estate and business services	...	...	...	...	...	894587	...	...	...	...	...	1007365
Real estate, except dwellings	...	...	...	...	...	41310	...	...	...	...	...	44136
Dwellings	...	...	...	...	...	400531	...	...	...	...	...	435826
9 Community, social and personal services	113988	...	179385	19294	6333	306334	123945	...	196053	22243	7060	335181
A Sanitary and similar services	...	...	...	...	...	...	...	...	...	...	...	...
B Social and related community services	...	...	...	...	...	177737	...	...	...	...	...	193172
Educational services	...	...	...	...	...	21393	...	...	...	...	...	23895
Medical, dental, other health and veterinary services	...	...	...	...	...	156344	...	...	...	...	...	169277
C Recreational and cultural services	...	...	...	...	...	118398	...	...	...	...	...	130659
D Personal and household services	...	...	...	...	...	10199	...	...	...	...	...	11350
Total, Industries	2171054	...	2182766	383961	143854	4593927	2317335	...	2382458	401723	137326	4964190
Producers of government services	805371	...	90840	17430	...	913641	844279	...	98306	18778	...	961363
Other producers	...	...	...	...	...	...	...	...	...	...	...	...
Total	2976425	...	2273606	401391	143854	5507568	3161614	...	2480764	420501	137326	5925553
less: Imputed bank service charge	...	...	262490	...	...	262490	...	...	279423	...	...	279423
Import duties	...	...	...	10747	...	10747	...	...	...	11030	...	11030

France

	1988						1989					
	Compensation of employees	Capital consumption	Net operating surplus	Indirect taxes	less: Subsidies received	Value added	Compensation of employees	Capital consumption	Net operating surplus	Indirect taxes	less: Subsidies received	Value added
Value added tax	...	...	...	479572	...	479572	...	...	...	502698	...	502698
Other adjustments	...	...	...	...	305	−305	...	...	...	...	178	−178
Total [a]	2976425	...	2011116	891710	144159	5735092	3161614	...	2201341	934229	137504	6159680

	1990						1991					
	Compensation of employees	Capital consumption	Net operating surplus	Indirect taxes	less: Subsidies received	Value added	Compensation of employees	Capital consumption	Net operating surplus	Indirect taxes	less: Subsidies received	Value added

All producers

1 Agriculture, hunting, forestry and fishing	35060	...	192736	8628	14559	221865	35985	...	175933	6881	14100	204699
A Agriculture and hunting	26819	...	177681	8229	13375	199354	27553	...	161149	6371	12927	182146
B Forestry and logging	3864	...	14436	152	1111	17341	3630	...	14600	253	1116	17367
C Fishing	4377	...	619	247	73	5170	4802	...	184	257	57	5186
2 Mining and quarrying	19378	...	11922	1686	3231	29754	19208	...	13017	1914	2939	31200
A Coal mining	5606	...	189	311	3188	2918	4622	...	619	299	2876	2664
B Crude petroleum and natural gas production	8758	...	9656	1075	19	19470	9477	...	9972	1294	26	20717
C Metal ore mining	946	...	−45	45	1	945	740	...	−22	43	3	758
D Other mining	4068	...	2122	255	23	6421	4369	...	2448	278	34	7061
3 Manufacturing	818074	...	468378	140752	32702	1394503	845372	...	457542	144056	37193	1409777
A Manufacture of food, beverages and tobacco	91566	...	82409	25532	20600	178907	92804	...	90222	23843	22840	184029
B Textile, wearing apparel and leather industries	59321	...	25199	3146	420	87246	58955	...	23079	3232	522	84744
C Manufacture of wood and wood products, including furniture	25942	...	16563	2100	198	44407	26277	...	17224	1717	224	44994
D Manufacture of paper and paper products, printing and publishing	67425	...	34745	3683	637	105216	72763	...	37776	4179	2068	112650
E Manufacture of chemicals and chemical petroleum, coal, rubber and plastic products	112803	...	73740	77885	708	263720	118313	...	72446	80894	981	270672
F Manufacture of non-metallic mineral products, except products of petroleum and coal	32018	...	23647	2303	181	57788	33273	...	23664	2494	214	59217
G Basic metal industries	39587	...	28091	3123	193	70608	39489	...	21706	3012	416	63791
H Manufacture of fabricated metal products, machinery and equipment	374679	...	175809	22281	9674	563095	388261	...	164831	23790	9727	567155
I Other manufacturing industries	14733	...	8175	699	91	23516	15237	...	6594	895	201	22525
4 Electricity, gas and water	44763	...	76162	19706	1892	138739	48389	...	85539	21844	1977	153795
5 Construction	219136	...	107336	13019	3679	335812	234563	...	113991	12923	3959	357518
6 Wholesale and retail trade, restaurants and hotels	504537	...	401008	104443	19289	990699	522838	...	426913	105830	24244	1031337
A Wholesale and retail trade	411374	...	315290	99237	14556	811345	425443	...	332791	101271	19179	840326
B Restaurants and hotels	93163	...	85718	5206	4733	179354	97395	...	94122	4559	5065	191011
7 Transport, storage and communication	219612	...	172348	11108	24595	378473	227118	...	181693	12161	23546	397426
A Transport and storage	153437	...	104265	9753	24586	242869	156960	...	105564	10345	23540	249329
B Communication	66175	...	68083	1355	9	135604	70158	...	76129	1816	6	148097
8 Finance, insurance, real estate and business services	489845	...	816849	112888	29430	1390152	521330	...	857557	118789	26454	1471222

France

	1990						1991					
	Compensation of employees	Capital consumption	Net operating surplus	Indirect taxes	less: Subsidies received	Value added	Compensation of employees	Capital consumption	Net operating surplus	Indirect taxes	less: Subsidies received	Value added
A Financial institutions	...	...	...	...	...	245401	...	...	...	...	...	248090
B Insurance	...	...	...	...	...	41953	...	...	...	...	...	48870
C Real estate and business services	...	...	...	...	...	1102798	...	...	...	...	...	1174262
Real estate, except dwellings	...	...	...	...	...	48627	...	...	...	...	...	52927
Dwellings	...	...	...	...	...	470863	...	...	...	...	...	510793
9 Community, social and personal services	132702	...	215398	22480	7107	363473	137658	...	234270	22913	9814	385027
A Sanitary and similar services	...	...	...	...	...	...	...	...	...	...	...	...
B Social and related community services	...	...	209614	...	...	211037	...	...	224346	...	...	225657
Educational services	...	...	...	...	...	26040	...	...	...	...	...	27484
Medical, dental, other health and veterinary services	...	...	...	...	...	184997	...	...	...	...	...	198173
C Recreational and cultural services	...	...	141456	...	...	140536	...	...	150317	...	...	149205
D Personal and household services	...	...	12405	...	...	11900	...	...	12807	...	...	12607
Total, Industries	2483107	...	2462137	434710	136484	5243470	2592461	...	2546455	447311	144226	5442001
Producers of government services	888690	...	106632	20212	...	1015534	939331	...	116217	21253	...	1076801
Other producers	...	...	...	...	...	...	...	...	...	...	...	...
Total	3371797	...	2568769	454922	136484	6259004	3531792	...	2662672	468564	144226	6518802
less: Imputed bank service charge	...	...	278020	...	...	278020	...	...	269336	...	...	269336
Import duties	...	...	...	10946	...	10946	...	...	...	11954	...	11954
Value added tax	...	...	...	517561	...	517561	...	...	...	514827	...	514827
Other adjustments	...	...	...	...	3	−3	...	...	...	...	16	−16
Total [a]	3371797	...	2290749	983429	136487	6509488	3531792	...	2393336	995345	144242	6776231

	1992						1993					
	Compensation of employees	Capital consumption	Net operating surplus	Indirect taxes	less: Subsidies received	Value added	Compensation of employees	Capital consumption	Net operating surplus	Indirect taxes	less: Subsidies received	Value added

All producers

1 Agriculture, hunting, forestry and fishing	36304	...	175136	5692	19391	197741	...	...	...	...	...	165859
A Agriculture and hunting	28323	...	162007	5190	18175	177345	...	...	...	...	...	148954
B Forestry and logging	3711	...	12825	265	1170	15631	...	...	...	...	...	12649
C Fishing	4270	...	304	237	46	4765	...	...	...	...	...	4256
2 Mining and quarrying	18493	...	15368	1951	2868	32945	...	...	...	...	...	31662
A Coal mining	4610	...	217	219	2777	2269	...	...	...	...	...	1832
B Crude petroleum and natural gas production	9066	...	12466	1423	42	22913	...	...	...	...	...	22641
C Metal ore mining	567	...	215	21	2	801	...	...	...	...	...	571
D Other mining	4250	...	2470	288	47	6962	...	...	...	...	...	6618
3 Manufacturing	847810	...	446935	145919	37926	1402737	...	...	...	...	...	1380297
A Manufacture of food, beverages and tobacco	97211	...	89860	24402	20839	190634	...	...	...	...	...	205436
B Textile, wearing apparel and leather industries	57902	...	23648	3232	554	84228	...	...	...	...	...	78179

France

	1992						1993					
	Compensation of employees	Capital consumption	Net operating surplus	Indirect taxes	less: Subsidies received	Value added	Compensation of employees	Capital consumption	Net operating surplus	Indirect taxes	less: Subsidies received	Value added
C Manufacture of wood and wood products, including furniture	26960	...	17788	1861	272	46337	...	...	...	...	...	45848
D Manufacture of paper and paper products, printing and publishing	74800	...	37148	4120	3063	113005	...	...	...	...	...	114220
E Manufacture of chemicals and chemical petroleum, coal, rubber and plastic products	113247	...	68895	81815	1296	262661	...	...	...	...	...	270453
F Manufacture of non-metallic mineral products, except products of petroleum and coal	32505	...	22632	2610	261	57485	...	...	...	...	...	54424
G Basic metal industries	36214	...	22796	2790	288	61512	...	...	...	...	...	56190
H Manufacture of fabricated metal products, machinery and equipment	392800	...	158189	24147	11178	563958	...	...	...	...	...	531464
I Other manufacturing industries	16171	...	5979	942	175	22917	...	...	...	...	...	24083
4 Electricity, gas and water	49881	...	94721	22598	2089	165111	...	...	...	...	...	171619
5 Construction	241471	...	111413	14758	4326	363316	...	...	...	...	...	357982
6 Wholesale and retail trade, restaurants and hotels	542660	...	427702	113551	23461	1060452	...	...	...	...	...	1080595
A Wholesale and retail trade	441897	...	327232	107707	18786	858050	...	...	...	...	...	870890
B Restaurants and hotels	100763	...	100470	5844	4675	202402	...	...	...	...	...	209705
7 Transport, storage and communication	242088	...	182984	13035	23594	414513	...	...	...	...	...	414197
A Transport and storage	165619	...	106084	11075	23587	259191	...	...	...	...	...	250103
B Communication	76469	...	76900	1960	7	155322	...	...	...	...	...	164094
8 Finance, insurance, real estate and business services	533180	...	918684	115809	28600	1539073	...	...	...	...	...	1570139
A Financial institutions	...	...	...	...	...	262230	...	...	...	...	...	251553
B Insurance	...	...	...	...	...	41966	...	...	...	...	...	42916
C Real estate and business services	...	...	...	...	...	1234877	...	...	...	...	...	1275670
Real estate, except dwellings	...	...	...	...	...	55110	...	...	...	...	...	58021
Dwellings	...	...	...	...	...	554588	...	...	...	...	...	597929
9 Community, social and personal services	158025	...	246638	27930	12038	420555	...	...	...	...	...	443280
A Sanitary and similar services	...	...	...	...	...	...	...	...	...	...	...	...
B Social and related community services	...	...	...	...	...	238747	...	...	...	...	...	250934
Educational services	...	...	...	...	...	28671	...	...	...	...	...	30208
Medical, dental, other health and veterinary services	...	...	...	...	...	210076	...	...	...	...	...	220726
C Recreational and cultural services	...	...	...	...	...	162161	...	...	...	...	...	169893
D Personal and household services	...	...	...	...	...	13390	...	...	...	...	...	14274
Total, Industries	2669912	...	2619581	461243	154293	5596443	...	...	...	...	170136	5615630
Producers of government services	998655	...	124555	23034	...	1146244	...	...	...	...	...	1211348
Other producers	...	...	...	...	...	...	...	...	...	...	...	...
Total	3668567	...	2744136	484277	154293	6742687	3738938	...	2748054	510122	170136	6826978

France

	1992						1993					
	Compensation of employees	Capital consumption	Net operating surplus	Indirect taxes	less: Subsidies received	Value added	Compensation of employees	Capital consumption	Net operating surplus	Indirect taxes	less: Subsidies received	Value added
less: Imputed bank service charge	...	...	274663	...	...	274663	...	...	275227	...	...	275227
Import duties	...	...	...	10644	...	10644	...	...	...	10271	...	10271
Value added tax	...	...	...	520879	...	520879	...	...	...	515065	...	515065
Other adjustments	...	...	...	...	1	−1	...	...	...	...	−	−
Total [a]	3668567	...	2469473	1015800	154294	6999546	3738938	...	2472827	1035458	170136	7077087

	1994						1995					
	Compensation of employees	Capital consumption	Net operating surplus	Indirect taxes	less: Subsidies received	Value added	Compensation of employees	Capital consumption	Net operating surplus	Indirect taxes	less: Subsidies received	Value added

All producers

1 Agriculture, hunting, forestry and fishing	...	...	...	...	...	177863	...	...	...	...	...	181919
A Agriculture and hunting	...	...	...	...	...	157083	...	...	...	...	...	161040
B Forestry and logging	...	...	...	...	...	16608	...	...	...	...	...	17568
C Fishing	...	...	...	...	...	4172	...	...	...	...	...	3311
2 Mining and quarrying	...	...	...	...	...	31943	...	...	...	...	...	32872
A Coal mining	...	...	...	...	...	2032	...	...	...	...	...	2011
B Crude petroleum and natural gas production	...	...	...	...	...	22761	...	...	...	...	...	23699
C Metal ore mining	...	...	...	...	...	383	...	...	...	...	...	274
D Other mining	...	...	...	...	...	6767	...	...	...	...	...	6888
3 Manufacturing	...	...	...	...	...	1423067	...	...	...	...	...	1478907
A Manufacture of food, beverages and tobacco	...	...	...	...	...	205600	...	...	...	...	...	208439
B Textile, wearing apparel and leather industries	...	...	...	...	...	78289	...	...	...	...	...	76996
C Manufacture of wood and wood products, including furniture	...	...	...	...	...	46019	...	...	...	...	...	48663
D Manufacture of paper and paper products, printing and publishing	...	...	...	...	...	116193	...	...	...	...	...	121897
E Manufacture of chemicals and chemical petroleum, coal, rubber and plastic products	...	...	...	...	...	277020	...	...	...	...	...	290513
F Manufacture of non-metallic mineral products, except products of petroleum and coal	...	...	...	...	...	56756	...	...	...	...	...	58973
G Basic metal industries	...	...	...	...	...	62472	...	...	...	...	...	66451
H Manufacture of fabricated metal products, machinery and equipment	...	...	...	...	...	555510	...	...	...	...	...	581471
I Other manufacturing industries	...	...	...	...	...	25208	...	...	...	...	...	25504
4 Electricity, gas and water	...	...	...	...	...	173396	...	...	...	...	...	180035
5 Construction	...	...	...	...	...	342298	...	...	...	...	...	347231
6 Wholesale and retail trade, restaurants and hotels	...	...	...	...	...	1107301	...	...	...	...	...	1158139
A Wholesale and retail trade	...	...	...	...	...	890362	...	...	...	...	...	935407
B Restaurants and hotels	...	...	...	...	...	216939	...	...	...	...	...	222732
7 Transport, storage and communication	...	...	...	...	...	427443	...	...	...	...	...	435618
A Transport and storage	...	...	...	...	...	257605	...	...	...	...	...	264427

France

	1994						1995					
	Compensation of employees	Capital consumption	Net operating surplus	Indirect taxes	less: Subsidies received	Value added	Compensation of employees	Capital consumption	Net operating surplus	Indirect taxes	less: Subsidies received	Value added
B Communication	...	...	...	...	...	169838	...	...	...	...	...	171191
8 Finance, insurance, real estate and business services	...	...	...	...	...	1697018	...	...	...	...	...	1738757
A Financial institutions	...	...	...	...	...	312194	...	...	...	...	...	293607
B Insurance	...	...	...	...	...	55793	...	...	...	...	...	44131
C Real estate and business services	...	...	...	...	...	1329031	...	...	...	...	...	1401019
9 Community, social and personal services	...	...	...	...	...	458920	...	...	...	...	...	475294
Total, Industries	...	...	...	...	172413	5839249	...	...	...	...	178482	6028772
Producers of government services	...	...	...	...	...	1261469	...	...	...	...	...	1320310
Other producers	...	...	...	...	...	...	...	...	...	...	...	...
Total	3829366	...	2893021	550745	172413	7100718	3980473	...	2977176	569915	178482	7349082
less: Imputed bank service charge	...	...	263132	...	...	263132	...	...	271846	...	...	271846
Import duties	...	...	...	9658	...	9658	...	...	...	9926	...	9926
Value added tax	...	...	...	542410	...	542410	...	...	...	575229	...	575229
Other adjustments	...	...	...	...	...	—	...	...	...	...	...	—
Total [a]	3829366	...	2629889	1102813	172413	7389654	3980473	...	2705330	1155070	178482	7662391

	1996						1997					
	Compensation of employees	Capital consumption	Net operating surplus	Indirect taxes	less: Subsidies received	Value added	Compensation of employees	Capital consumption	Net operating surplus	Indirect taxes	less: Subsidies received	Value added
All producers													
1 Agriculture, hunting, forestry and fishing	...	...	...	...	...	182668	...	...	...	...	...	183447
A Agriculture and hunting	...	...	...	...	...	162882	...	...	...	...	...	163115
B Forestry and logging	...	...	...	...	...	16032	...	...	...	...	...	16380
C Fishing	...	...	...	...	...	3754	...	...	...	...	...	3952
2 Mining and quarrying	...	...	...	...	...	33733	...	...	...	...	...	32507
A Coal mining	...	...	...	...	...	1733	...	...	...	...	...	1655
B Crude petroleum and natural gas production	...	...	...	...	...	25067	...	...	...	...	...	23532
C Metal ore mining	...	...	...	...	...	276	...	...	...	...	...	469
D Other mining	...	...	...	...	...	6657	...	...	...	...	...	6851
3 Manufacturing	...	...	...	...	...	1501761	...	...	...	...	...	1569662
A Manufacture of food, beverages and tobacco	...	...	...	...	...	217873	...	...	...	...	...	229771
B Textile, wearing apparel and leather industries	...	...	...	...	...	71063	...	...	...	...	...	69666
C Manufacture of wood and wood products, including furniture	...	...	...	...	...	48650	...	...	...	...	...	48507
D Manufacture of paper and paper products, printing and publishing	...	...	...	...	...	124240	...	...	...	...	...	126922
E Manufacture of chemicals and chemical petroleum, coal, rubber and plastic products	...	...	...	...	...	298784	...	...	...	...	...	318199
F Manufacture of non-metallic mineral products, except products of petroleum and coal	...	...	...	...	...	55974	...	...	...	...	...	55613

France

	1996						1997					
	Compensation of employees	Capital consumption	Net operating surplus	Indirect taxes	less: Subsidies received	Value added	Compensation of employees	Capital consumption	Net operating surplus	Indirect taxes	less: Subsidies received	Value added
G Basic metal industries	...	...	...	...	...	63962	...	...	...	...	...	68188
H Manufacture of fabricated metal products, machinery and equipment	...	...	...	...	...	595052	...	...	...	...	...	624916
I Other manufacturing industries	...	...	...	...	...	26163	...	...	...	...	...	27880
4 Electricity, gas and water	...	...	...	...	...	186297	...	...	...	...	...	183046
5 Construction	...	...	...	...	...	336231	...	...	...	...	...	347464
6 Wholesale and retail trade, restaurants and hotels	...	...	...	...	...	1173035	...	...	...	...	...	1193013
A Wholesale and retail trade	...	...	...	...	...	945839	...	...	...	...	...	958494
B Restaurants and hotels	...	...	...	...	...	227196	...	...	...	...	...	234519
7 Transport, storage and communication	...	...	...	...	...	441300	...	...	...	...	...	460900
A Transport and storage	...	...	...	...	...	265179	...	...	...	...	...	281094
B Communication	...	...	...	...	...	176121	...	...	...	...	...	179806
8 Finance, insurance, real estate and business services	...	...	...	...	...	1783123	...	...	...	...	...	1860715
A Financial institutions	...	...	...	...	...	275263	...	...	...	...	...	282117
B Insurance	...	...	...	...	...	46566	...	...	...	...	...	44237
C Real estate and business services	...	...	...	...	...	1461294	...	...	...	...	...	1534361
9 Community, social and personal services	...	...	...	...	...	490030	...	...	...	...	...	504354
Total, Industries	...	...	...	...	212766	6128178	...	...	...	...	221939	6335108
Producers of government services	...	...	...	...	...	1377060	...	...	...	...	...	1412597
Other producers	...	...	...	...	...	...	...	...	...	...	...	...
Total	4115718	...	3001677	600609	212766	7505238	4221754	...	3118297	629593	221939	7747705
less: Imputed bank service charge	...	...	253998	...	...	253998	...	...	256291	...	...	256291
Import duties	...	...	...	8476	...	8476	...	...	...	9252	...	9252
Value added tax	...	...	...	612015	...	612015	...	...	...	636419	...	636419
Other adjustments	...	...	...	...	...	–	...	...	...	...	...	–
Total [a]	4115718	...	2747679	1221100	212766	7871731	4221754	...	2862006	1275264	221939	8137085

a Column "Consumption of fixed capital" is included in column "Net operating surplus".

French Guiana

Source

Reply to the United Nations National Accounts Questionnaire from the Institut national de la statistique et des études économiques (INSEE), Paris.

General note

The estimates shown in the following tables have been prepared by INSEE in accordance with the United Nations System of National Accounts (1968 SNA) so far as the existing data would permit.

1.1 Expenditure on the gross domestic product, in current prices

Million French francs

	1986	1987	1988	1989	1990	1991	1992	1993	1994	1995	1996	1997
1 Government final consumption expenditure	1405	1573	1779	2027	2285	2548	2728	...	...	...	...	...
2 Private final consumption expenditure	2404	2835	3329	3837	4201	4447	4698	...	...	...	...	...
3 Gross capital formation	1243	1304	1777	2620	3109	3111	2575	...	...	...	...	...
A Increase in stocks	24	11	52	90	−12	114	118	...	...	...	...	...
B Gross fixed capital formation	1219	1292	1725	2530	3121	2997	2457	...	...	...	...	...
4 Exports of goods and services	1239	1194	3721	4034	4391	6004	5220	...	...	...	...	...
5 less: Imports of goods and services	3373	3225	5677	6834	7461	8707	7246	...	...	...	...	...
equals: Gross domestic product	2918	3681	4929	5684	6526	7404	7976	...	...	...	...	...

1.3 Cost components of the gross domestic product

Million French francs

	1986	1987	1988	1989	1990	1991	1992	1993	1994	1995	1996	1997
1 Indirect taxes, net	266	368	488	550	667	626	657	...	...	...	...	...
A Indirect taxes	441	489	602	650	803	824	792	...	...	...	...	...
B less: Subsidies [a]	175	121	114	100	136	198	135	...	...	...	...	...
2 Consumption of fixed capital	...	...	...	...	...	...	...	...	...	...	...	...
3 Compensation of employees paid by resident producers to	2248	2672	3116	3715	4200	4489	4869	...	...	...	...	...
4 Operating surplus	404	641	1326	1419	1659	2289	2450	...	...	...	...	...
equals: Gross domestic product	2918	3681	4929	5684	6526	7404	7976	...	...	...	...	...

a Includes subsidies from the rest of the world.

1.4 General government current receipts and disbursements

Million French francs

	1986	1987	1988	1989	1990	1991	1992	1993	1994	1995	1996	1997
Receipts												
1 Operating surplus	...	...	...	...	...	...	...	...	...	...	...	...
2 Property and entrepreneurial income	14	11	10	22	16	16	15	...	...	...	...	...

French Guiana

Million French francs

	1986	1987	1988	1989	1990	1991	1992	1993	1994	1995	1996	1997
3 Taxes, fees and contributions	1325	1456	1730	1924	2175	2424	2419	...	...	...	...	...
4 Other current transfers	1412	1647	1689	1950	2370	2543	2830	...	...	...	...	...
Total current receipts of general government	2750	3114	3429	3897	4561	4983	5264	...	...	...	...	...

Disbursements

	1986	1987	1988	1989	1990	1991	1992	1993	1994	1995	1996	1997
1 Government final consumption expenditure	1405	1573	1779	2027	2285	2548	2728	...	...	...	...	...
2 Property income	50	61	79	107	134	154	179	...	...	...	...	...
3 Subsidies	24	16	22	26	25	40	28	...	...	...	...	...
4 Other current transfers	848	1011	1034	1140	1289	1461	1574	...	...	...	...	...
5 Net saving	423	454	514	596	828	779	755	...	...	...	...	...
Total current disbursements and net saving of general government	2750	3114	3429	3897	4561	4983	5264	...	...	...	...	...

1.7 External transactions on current account, summary

Million French francs

	1986	1987	1988	1989	1990	1991	1992	1993	1994	1995	1996	1997

Payments to the rest of the world

	1986	1987	1988	1989	1990	1991	1992	1993	1994	1995	1996	1997
1 Imports of goods and services	3373	3225	5677	6834	7461	8707	7246	...	...	...	...	...
2 Factor income to rest of the world	−251	83	560	180	315	634	730	...	...	...	...	...
A Compensation of employees	...	...	...	...	...	...	...	...	...	...	...	...
B Property and entrepreneurial income	−251	83	560	180	315	634	730	...	...	...	...	...
3 Current transfers to the rest of the world	20	22	24	28	52	32	32	...	...	...	...	...
4 Surplus of the nation on current transactions	−180	−199	−555	−898	−825	−474	332	...	...	...	...	...
Payments to the rest of the world and surplus of the nation on current transfers	2962	3130	5706	6145	7003	8899	8340	...	...	...	...	...

Receipts from the rest of the world

	1986	1987	1988	1989	1990	1991	1992	1993	1994	1995	1996	1997
1 Exports of goods and services	1239	1194	3721	4034	4391	6004	5220	...	...	...	...	...
2 Factor income from rest of the world	154	184	200	160	194	203	183	...	...	...	...	...
A Compensation of employees	...	...	...	...	...	...	...	...	...	...	...	...
B Property and entrepreneurial income	154	184	200	160	194	203	183	...	...	...	...	...
3 Current transfers from rest of the world	1569	1752	1786	1951	2418	2692	2937	...	...	...	...	...
Receipts from the rest of the world on current transactions	2962	3130	5706	6145	7003	8899	8340	...	...	...	...	...

1.8 Capital transactions of the nation, summary

Million French francs

	1986	1987	1988	1989	1990	1991	1992	1993	1994	1995	1996	1997

Finance of gross capital formation

	1986	1987	1988	1989	1990	1991	1992	1993	1994	1995	1996	1997
Gross saving	1064	1105	1223	1722	2284	2637	2907	...	...	...	...	...
less: Surplus of the nation on current transactions	−180	−199	−555	−898	−825	−474	332	...	...	...	...	...
Finance of gross capital formation	1243	1304	1777	2620	3109	3111	2575	...	...	...	...	...

French Guiana

Million French francs

	1986	1987	1988	1989	1990	1991	1992	1993	1994	1995	1996	1997
Gross capital formation												
Increase in stocks	24	11	52	90	−12	114	118	...	...	...	...	...
Gross fixed capital formation	1219	1292	1725	2530	3121	2997	2457	...	...	...	...	...
1 General government	475	597	737	812	911	1091	1111	...	...	...	...	...
2 Corporate and quasi-corporate enterprises	549	486	749	1353	1704	1468	990	...	...	...	...	...
3 Other	196	209	240	365	506	438	356	...	...	...	...	...
Gross capital formation	1243	1304	1777	2620	3109	3111	2575	...	...	...	...	...

1.10 Gross domestic product by kind of activity, in current prices

Million French francs

	1986	1987	1988	1989	1990	1991	1992	1993	1994	1995	1996	1997
1 Agriculture, hunting, forestry and fishing	245	285	439	605	651	546	578	...	...	...	...	...
2 Mining and quarrying	171	208	257	398	492	564	726	...	...	...	...	...
3 Manufacturing	...	...	...	...	...	...	...	...	...	...	...	...
4 Electricity, gas and water	30	30	36	73	46	34	47	...	...	...	...	...
5 Construction	340	336	479	761	828	891	868	...	...	...	...	...
6 Wholesale and retail trade, restaurants and hotels	413	481	577	672	874	970	961	...	...	...	...	...
7 Transport, storage and communication	−130	214	707	388	498	908	921	...	...	...	...	...
8 Finance, insurance, real estate and business services	439	534	619	704	806	937	1185	...	...	...	...	...
9 Community, social and personal services	348	417	466	632	681	782	835	...	...	...	...	...
Total, Industries	1856	2505	3581	4234	4876	5634	6122	...	...	...	...	...
Producers of government services	1070	1168	1315	1401	1522	1685	1856	...	...	...	...	...
Other producers	32	36	42	50	55	66	74	...	...	...	...	...
Subtotal	2957	3708	4938	5684	6453	7385	8052	...	...	...	...	...
less: Imputed bank service charge	274	295	347	372	378	417	458	...	...	...	...	...
plus: Import duties	234	268	338	371	451	436	383	...	...	...	...	...
plus: Value added tax	−	−	−	−	...	...	...	...	...	...	...	...
plus: Other adjustments	...	...	...	...	...	...	...	...	...	...	...	...
equals: Gross domestic product	2918	3681	4929	5684	6526	7404	7976	...	...	...	...	...

1.12 Relations among national accounting aggregates

Million French francs

	1986	1987	1988	1989	1990	1991	1992	1993	1994	1995	1996	1997
Gross domestic product	2918	3681	4929	5684	6526	7404	7976	...	...	...	...	...
plus: Net factor income from the rest of the world	405	102	−361	−20	−122	−431	−547	...	...	...	...	...
Factor income from rest of the world	154	184	200	160	193	203	183	...	...	...	...	...
less: Factor income to the rest of the world	−251	83	560	180	315	634	730	...	...	...	...	...
equals: Gross national product	3324	3783	4569	5663	6405	6973	7429	...	...	...	...	...
less: Consumption of fixed capital	...	...	...	...	...	...	...	...	...	...	...	...
equals: National income	3324	3783	4569	5663	6405	6973	7429	...	...	...	...	...

French Guiana

Million French francs

	1986	1987	1988	1989	1990	1991	1992	1993	1994	1995	1996	1997
plus: Net current transfers from the rest of the world	1548	1730	1762	1923	2366	2660	2905	...	...	...	...	...
Current transfers from rest of the world	1569	1752	1786	1951	2418	2692	2937	...	...	...	...	...
less: Current transfers to the rest of the world	20	22	24	28	52	32	32	...	...	...	...	...
equals: National disposable income	4872	5513	6330	7586	8771	9633	10334	...	...	...	...	...
less: Final consumption	3809	4408	5108	5864	6487	6995	7427	...	...	...	...	...
equals: Net saving	1063	1105	1222	1722	2284	2637	2907	...	...	...	...	...
less: Surplus of the nation on current transactions	−180	−199	−555	−898	−825	−474	332	...	...	...	...	...
equals: Net capital formation	1243	1304	1777	2620	3109	3111	2575	...	...	...	...	...

French Polynesia

Source

Reply to the United Nations National Accounts Questionnaire from the Institut national de la statistique et des études économiques (INSEE), Paris. Official estimates and descriptions are published by the same Institut in *Comptes Economiques de la Polynésie Française*.

General note

The estimates shown in the following tables have been adjusted by INSEE in accordance with the United Nations System of National Accounts (1968 SNA) so far as the existing data would permit.

1.1 Expenditure on the gross domestic product, in current prices

Million CFP francs

	1986	1987	1988	1989	1990	1991	1992	1993	1994	1995	1996	1997
1 Government final consumption expenditure	104685	99216	110051	115339	117199	120023	150180	126127	...	...	...	...
2 Private final consumption expenditure	143944	174387	169289	167249	179451	194906	200854	202563	...	...	...	...
3 Gross capital formation	89389	48792	53005	65882	58022	55722	52531	52958	...	...	...	...
A Increase in stocks	1078	42	–836	520	169	–583	8	–536	...	...	...	...
B Gross fixed capital formation	88311	48750	53841	65362	57853	56305	52523	53494	...	...	...	...
4 Exports of goods and services	21575	24125	23218	24860	27318	28391	25982	34523	...	...	...	...
5 less: Imports of goods and services	92658	90554	87487	91663	91926	93831	86018	86905	...	...	...	...
Statistical discrepancy	...	...	...	...	...	...	–29264	...	...	...	...	...
equals: Gross domestic product	266935	255966	268076	281667	290064	305211	314265	329266	...	...	...	...

1.4 General government current receipts and disbursements

Million CFP francs

	1986	1987	1988	1989	1990	1991	1992	1993	1994	1995	1996	1997
Receipts												
1 Operating surplus	...	...	...	...	...	...	...	...	...	...	...	...
2 Property and entrepreneurial income	1258	518	45	–215	–277	–650	–36	233	...	...	...	...
3 Taxes, fees and contributions	54423	59772	56386	60540	67480	73108	74090	75912	...	...	...	...
A Indirect taxes	40921	44672	41908	42493	48039	51174	49927	51492	...	...	...	...
B Direct taxes									...	...	...	...
C Social security contributions	13502	15100	14478	18047	19441	21934	24163	24420	...	...	...	...
D Compulsory fees, fines and penalties	...	...	...	...	...				...	...	...	...
4 Other current transfers	144736	135938	153520	158474	163797	...	...	...	...	...	...	...
Total current receipts of general government	200417	196228	209951	218799	224913							
Disbursements												
1 Government final consumption expenditure	104685	99216	110051	115339	117199	120023	150180	126127	...	...	...	...

French Polynesia

Million CFP francs

	1986	1987	1988	1989	1990	1991	1992	1993	1994	1995	1996	1997
A Compensation of employees	60554	62394	70141	73796	77637	80686	83044	86035	...	...	...	...
B Consumption of fixed capital	...	...	...	...	...	...	...	...	...	...	...	...
C Purchases of goods and services, net	...	...	...	...	...	...	...	...	...	...	...	...
D less: Own-account fixed capital formation	...	...	...	...	...	...	...	...	...	...	...	...
E Indirect taxes paid, net	...	...	...	...	...	...	...	...	...	...	...	...
2 Property income	2852	1792	2043	2406	3167	4543	4596	5012	...	...	...	...
A Interest	2852	1792	2043	2406	3167	4543	4596	5012	...	...	...	...
B Net land rent and royalties	...	...	...	...	...	...	...	...	...	...	...	...
3 Subsidies	2829	2760	3154	3327	3680	2510	1799	2418	...	...	...	...
4 Other current transfers	63726	66268	71238	74822	77561	...	...	...	...	...	...	...
5 Net saving [a]	26325	26192	23465	22905	23306	...	...	...	...	...	...	...
Total current disbursements and net saving of general government	200417	196228	209951	218799	224913	...	...	...	...	...	...	...

a Item "Net saving" includes consumption of fixed capital.

1.5 Current income and outlay of corporate and quasi-corporate enterprises, summary

Million CFP francs

	1986	1987	1988	1989	1990	1991	1992	1993	1994	1995	1996	1997
Receipts												
1 Operating surplus	128832	96095	96939	98485	95081	96454	97468	109646	...	...	...	...
2 Property and entrepreneurial income received	2852	1274	1998	2621	3444	5193	4632	4779	...	...	...	...
3 Current transfers	...	...	...	...	...	...	...	...	...	...	...	...
Total current receipts [a]	131684	97369	98937	101106	98525	101647	102100	114425	...	...	...	...
Disbursements												
1 Property and entrepreneurial income	50718	40774	41415	45620	53114	45981	46534	48262	...	...	...	...
2 Direct taxes and other current payments to general government	10801	9166	8064	7567	9453	9339	9849	12655	...	...	...	...
3 Other current transfers	3708	5660	6079	6220	6520	6494	8039	10290	...	...	...	...
Statistical discrepancy	...	...	...	...	...	...	20	...	...	...	...	...
1 Net saving [b]	66457	41769	43379	41699	29438	39833	37658	43218	...	...	...	...
Total current disbursements and net saving [a]	131684	97369	98937	101106	98525	101647	102100	114425	...	...	...	...

a Private unincorporated enterprises are included in corporate and quasi-corporate enterprises.
b Item "Net saving" includes consumption of fixed capital.

1.6 Current income and outlay of households and non-profit institutions

Million CFP francs

	1986	1987	1988	1989	1990	1991	1992	1993	1994	1995	1996	1997
Receipts												
1 Compensation of employees	96924	114155	127846	135545	142587	149573	156836	161989	...	...	...	...
2 Operating surplus of private unincorporated enterprises	...	...	...	...	...	...	...	...	...	...	...	...
3 Property and entrepreneurial income	50718	44394	45225	49390	57024	49491	51914	56152	...	...	...	...
4 Current transfers	31116	29420	30913	32658	35309	38261	41540	43403	...	...	...	...
Total current receipts	178758	187969	203984	217593	234920	237325	250290	261544	...	...	...	...

French Polynesia

Million CFP francs

	1986	1987	1988	1989	1990	1991	1992	1993	1994	1995	1996	1997
Disbursements												
1 Private final consumption expenditure	143944	174387	169289	167249	179451	194906	200854	202563	...	...	...	...
2 Property income	...	...	...	...	...	...	...	...	...	...	...	...
3 Direct taxes and other current transfers n.e.c. to general government	2350	2130	1877	2009	1951	2075	2461	3208	...	...	...	...
4 Other current transfers	5214	6646	7173	7885	10156	10793	11567	12701	...	...	...	...
5 Net saving [a]	27250	4806	25645	40450	43362	29551	35408	43072	...	...	...	...
Total current disbursements and net saving	178758	187969	203984	217593	234920	237325	250290	261544	...	...	...	...

a Item "Net saving" includes consumption of fixed capital.

1.7 External transactions on current account, summary

Million CFP francs

	1986	1987	1988	1989	1990	1991	1992	1993	1994	1995	1996	1997
Payments to the rest of the world												
1 Imports of goods and services	92658	90554	87487	91663	91926	93831	86018	86905	...	...	...	...
2 Factor income to rest of the world	...	...	...	...	...	...	...	...	...	...	...	...
3 Current transfers to the rest of the world	—	...	...	...	...	...	...	...	...	...	...	...
4 Surplus of the nation on current transactions	30643	24214	40307	40620	46045	50456	51964	66042	...	...	...	...
Payments to the rest of the world and surplus of the nation on current transfers	123301	114768	127794	132283	137971	144287	137982	152947	...	...	...	...
Receipts from the rest of the world												
1 Exports of goods and services	21575	24125	23218	24860	27318	28391	25982	34523	...	...	...	...
2 Factor income from rest of the world	...	...	...	...	...	...	...	...	...	...	...	...
3 Current transfers from rest of the world	101726	90643	104576	107423	110653	115896	112000	118424	...	...	...	...
Receipts from the rest of the world on current transactions	123301	114768	127794	132283	137971	144287	137982	152947	...	...	...	...

1.8 Capital transactions of the nation, summary

Million CFP francs

	1986	1987	1988	1989	1990	1991	1992	1993	1994	1995	1996	1997
Finance of gross capital formation												
Gross saving	120032	72767	92489	105054	96106	...	...	...	...	...	...	...
1 Consumption of fixed capital	...	...	...	...	...	...	...	...	...	...	...	...
2 Net saving [a]	120032	72767	92489	105054	96106	...	...	...	...	...	...	...
A General government	26325	26192	23465	22905	23306	...	...	...	...	...	...	...
B Corporate and quasi-corporate enterprises	66457	41769	43379	41699	29438	39833	37658	43218	...	...	...	...
C Other	27250	4806	25645	40450	43362	29551	35408	43072	...	...	...	...
less: Surplus of the nation on current transactions	30643	24214	40307	40620	46045	50456	51964	66042	...	...	...	...
Statistical discrepancy	...	239	823	1448	7961	...	...	...	...	...	...	...
Finance of gross capital formation	89389	48792	53005	65882	58022	55722	52531	52958	...	...	...	...

French Polynesia

Million CFP francs

	1986	1987	1988	1989	1990	1991	1992	1993	1994	1995	1996	1997
Gross capital formation												
Increase in stocks	1078	42	–836	520	169	–583	8	–536	...	...	...	...
Gross fixed capital formation	88311	48750	53841	65362	57853	56305	52523	53494	...	...	...	...
1 General government	20588	25703	30550	31653	29608	28593	22264	22654	...	...	...	...
2 Corporate and quasi-corporate enterprises	48373	14159	15442	22750	18962	17151	19358	17199	...	...	...	...
3 Other	19350	8888	7849	10959	9283	10561	10901	13641	...	...	...	...
Gross capital formation	89389	48792	53005	65882	58022	55722	52531	52958	...	...	...	...

a Item "Net saving" includes consumption of fixed capital.

1.10 Gross domestic product by kind of activity, in current prices

Million CFP francs

	1986	1987	1988	1989	1990	1991	1992	1993	1994	1995	1996	1997
1 Agriculture, hunting, forestry and fishing	9249	10401	11170	12439	13097	12420	11851	12872	...	...	...	...
2 Mining and quarrying	...	...	...	...	...	...	...	...	...	...	...	...
3 Manufacturing [a]	23490	17886	19701	20235	21191	22849	23716	22034	...	...	...	...
4 Electricity, gas and water [a]	2525	3704	4080	4328	5157	5414	6593	6917	...	...	...	...
5 Construction	30396	15556	15169	18646	17973	17535	18393	18735	...	...	...	...
6 Wholesale and retail trade, restaurants and hotels	...	65255	61897	64184	67632				...	...	...	...
7 Transport, storage and communication	17391	75433	79894	81392	84436				...	...	...	...
8 Finance, insurance, real estate and business services	...					...	...	...	...	...	...	...
9 Community, social and personal services	...					...	...	...	...	...	...	...
Total, Industries	200222	188235	191911	201224	204575	215642	221618	233632	...	...	...	...
Producers of government services	65901	66912	75307	79536	84527	88542	91652	94557	...	...	...	...
Other producers	812	819	858	907	962	1027	995	1077	...	...	...	...
Subtotal	266935	255966	268076	281667	290064	305211	314265	329266	...	...	...	...
less: Imputed bank service charge	...	...	...	...	...	...	...	...	...	...	...	...
plus: Import duties	...	...	...	...	...	...	...	...	...	...	...	...
plus: Value added tax	...	...	...	...	...	...	...	...	...	...	...	...
plus: Other adjustments	...	...	...	...	...	...	...	...	...	...	...	...
equals: Gross domestic product	266935	255966	268076	281667	290064	305211	314265	329266	...	...	...	...

a Manufacturing of energy-generating products is included in item "Electricity, gas and water".

Gabon

Source

Reply to the United Nations National Accounts Questionnaire from the Direction de la Statistique et des Etudes Economiques, Libreville. The official estimates which conform to the 1968 United Nations System of National Accounts are published annually by the same office in *Comptes Economiques*.

General note

The estimates shown in the following tables have been prepared by the Direction de la Statistique et des Etudes Economiques in accordance with the United Nations System of National Accounts (1968 SNA) so far as the existing data would permit.

1.1 Expenditure on the gross domestic product, in current prices

Million CFA francs

	1986	1987	1988	1989	1990	1991	1992	1993	1994	1995	1996	1997
1 Government final consumption expenditure	303900	242200	220600	215387	...	...	...	...	...	...	...	...
2 Private final consumption expenditure	562100	496300	487900	565201	...	...	...	...	...	...	...	...
3 Gross capital formation	543482	272500	367300	271672	...	...	...	...	...	...	...	...
4 Exports of goods and services	475822	421200	377700	587000	...	...	...	...	...	...	...	...
5 less: Imports of goods and services	684200	411600	439900	471200	...	...	...	...	...	...	...	...
equals: Gross domestic product	1201100	1020600	1013600	1168066	1344400	1494500	1533100	1565200	...	...	...	...

Gambia

Source

Reply to the United Nations National Accounts Questionnaire from the Central Statistics Department, Ministry of Economic Planning and Industrial Development, Banjul. The official estimates are published in *Sources and Methods of Estimates of National Income at Current Prices in The Gambia* (1985), *Estimates of National Income at Constant Prices in The Gambia*, and *National Accounts of The Gambia*.

General note

The estimates shown in the following tables have been prepared in accordance with the United Nations System of National Accounts (1968 SNA) so far as the existing data would permit.

1.1 Expenditure on the gross domestic product, in current prices

Thousand Gambian dalasis — Fiscal year beginning 1 July

	1986	1987	1988	1989	1990	1991	1992	1993	1994	1995	1996	1997
1 Government final consumption expenditure	186983	243563	264206	316700	380500	379700	404900	490400	...	...	...	...
2 Private final consumption expenditure	...	...	...	1794700	2157600	2443100	2500700	2534500	...	...	...	...
3 Gross capital formation	...	...	344220	468885	469298	530918	688935	878054	...	...	...	...
A Increase in stocks	...	...	...	...	...	...	...	...	...	...	...	...
B Gross fixed capital formation [a]	103542	126128	344220	468885	469298	530918	688935	878054	...	...	...	...
Residential buildings	19771	48041	114852	212797	237691	261495	223579	267388	...	...	...	...
Non-residential buildings									...	...	...	...
Other construction and land improvement, etc.	57146	30811	64187	64286	32145	33709	91989	63221	...	...	...	...
Other	26625	47276	165181	191802	199462	235714	373367	547445	...	...	...	...
4 Exports of goods and services [b]	763944	790065	1010752	975200	1134500	1322500	1389800	1186400	...	...	...	...
5 less: Imports of goods and services [c]	839972	843460	1066492	1291900	1514900	1756300	1906500	1846000	...	...	...	...
equals: Gross domestic product	1461656	1601020	1898087	2263661	2627040	2919904	3077811	3243457	...	...	...	...

a The estimates refer to central government capital formation only.
b Item "Exports of goods and services" includes net travel and tourism income.
c Item "Imports of goods and services" includes net freight and insurance.

1.10 Gross domestic product by kind of activity, in current prices

Thousand Gambian dalasis — Fiscal year beginning 1 July

	1986	1987	1988	1989	1990	1991	1992	1993	1994	1995	1996	1997
1 Agriculture, hunting, forestry and fishing	460883	489670	481140	591688	591094	659227	571641	666105	...	...	...	...
2 Mining and quarrying	311	342	373	405	486	600	636	706	...	...	...	...
3 Manufacturing	25688	57881	80268	122720	150431	162596	175862	168559	...	...	...	...
4 Electricity, gas and water	12494	14320	14994	7419	24011	25638	30000	31650	...	...	...	...
5 Construction	70294	53928	84204	122504	118623	130101	144312	148364	...	...	...	...
6 Wholesale and retail trade, restaurants and hotels	515250	565057	747507	843795	1045251	1157328	1293014	1262891	...	...	...	...

Gambia

Thousand Gambian dalasis	1986	1987	1988	1989	1990	1991	1992	1993	1994	1995	1996	1997
7 Transport, storage and communication	133011	161281	190574	222027	280264	321523	345771	411027	...	...	...	...
8 Finance, insurance, real estate and business services	168752	176887	187737	202251	216659	249575	267480	314736	...	...	...	...
9 Community, social and personal services	28136	29998	34207	41910	48501	60114	56635	62284	...	...	...	...
Total, Industries	1414819	1549364	1821004	2154719	2475320	2766702	2885351	3066322	...	...	...	...
Producers of government services	95150	111656	146229	174151	191529	195202	214836	229920	...	...	...	...
Other producers	...	...	...	...	...	...	...	...	...	...	...	...
Subtotal	1509969	1661020	1967233	2328870	2666849	2961904	3100187	3296242	...	...	...	...
less: Imputed bank service charge	48313	60000	69146	65209	39809	42000	22376	52785	...	...	...	...
plus: Import duties	...	...	...	...	...	...	...	...	...	...	...	...
plus: Value added tax	...	...	...	...	...	...	...	...	...	...	...	...
plus: Other adjustments	...	...	...	...	...	...	...	...	...	...	...	...
equals: Gross domestic product	1461656	1601020	1898087	2263661	2627040	2919904	3077811	3243457	...	...	...	...

1.11 Gross domestic product by kind of activity, in constant prices

Thousand Gambian dalasis	1986	1987	1988	1989	1990	1991	1992	1993	1994	1995	1996	1997
At constant prices of: 1976												
1 Agriculture, hunting, forestry and fishing	121370	120158	116983	127101	109248	123531	106069	119580	...	...	...	...
2 Mining and quarrying	172	178	184	190	209	230	253	278	...	...	...	...
3 Manufacturing	30709	34365	31635	33104	32880	32712	34334	36022	...	...	...	...
4 Electricity, gas and water	2260	2486	2404	2517	3100	3162	3414	3585	...	...	...	...
5 Construction	27611	19756	24901	29238	26952	28077	30323	31536	...	...	...	...
6 Wholesale and retail trade, restaurants and hotels	143446	143273	156339	158061	170235	175299	183560	188067	...	...	...	...
7 Transport, storage and communication	53127	63160	67373	72837	81986	86652	92608	105673	...	...	...	...
8 Finance, insurance, real estate and business services	43952	45232	46653	48804	49703	50938	52302	58108	...	...	...	...
9 Community, social and personal services	9180	9372	9625	10195	10354	11757	10976	11544	...	...	...	...
Total, Industries	431827	437980	456097	482047	484667	512358	513837	554393	...	...	...	...
Producers of government services	48500	50682	54900	54900	56500	57630	58679	60229	...	...	...	...
Other producers	...	...	...	...	...	...	...	...	...	...	...	...
Subtotal	480327	488662	510997	536947	541167	569988	572516	614622	...	...	...	...
less: Imputed bank service charge	10950	12092	12572	10761	6022	5671	5715	10574	...	...	...	...
plus: Import duties	...	...	...	...	...	...	...	...	...	...	...	...
plus: Value added tax	...	...	...	...	...	...	...	...	...	...	...	...
plus: Other adjustments	...	...	...	...	...	...	...	...	...	...	...	...
equals: Gross domestic product	469377	476570	498425	526186	535145	564317	566801	604048	...	...	...	...

1.12 Relations among national accounting aggregates

Thousand Gambian dalasis	1986	1987	1988	1989	1990	1991	1992	1993	1994	1995	1996	1997
Gross domestic product	1461656	1601020	1898087	2263661	2627040	2919904	3077811	3243457	...	...	...	...
plus: Net factor income from the rest of the world	−134800	−93900	−80200	−94700	−64300	−48800	−40200	−49200	...	...	...	...

Gambia

Thousand Gambian dalasis	1986	1987	1988	1989	1990	1991	1992	1993	1994	1995	1996	1997
equals: Gross national product	1326900	1507100	1817900	2168961	2562740	2871104	3037611	3194257	...	...	...	...
less: Consumption of fixed capital	161600	189000	213200	250930	297927	341822	379175	417193	...	...	...	...
equals: National income	1165300	1318100	1604700	1918031	2264813	2529282	2658536	2777064	...	...	...	...
plus: Net current transfers from the rest of the world [a]	347400	386400	369700	429200	447000	506300	474500	514700	...	...	...	...
equals: National disposable income [b]	1512700	1704500	1974400	2347231	2711813	3035582	3133036	3291764	...	...	...	...
less: Final consumption	...	...	...	2111400	2538100	2822800	2905600	3024900	...	...	...	...
equals: Net saving	...	...	...	235831	173713	212782	227436	266864	...	...	...	...
less: Surplus of the nation on current transactions	...	...	...	17876	2342	23686	−82324	−193997	...	...	...	...
equals: Net capital formation	...	...	...	217955	171371	189096	309760	460861	...	...	...	...

a Item "Net current transfers from the rest of the world" includes mainly net interest receipts.
b Item "National disposable income" includes unrequited private transfers and official transfers.

2.1 Government final consumption expenditure by function, in current prices

Thousand Gambian dalasis	1986	1987	1988	1989	1990	1991	1992	1993	1994	1995	1996	1997
1 General public services	177283	256275	152961	153778	179915	178219	...	...	...	...	...	...
2 Defence	...	...	...	...	...	...	...	...	...	...	...	...
3 Public order and safety	...	...	...	...	...	...	...	...	...	...	...	...
4 Education [a]	29916	33131	49956	67841	105635	101530	...	...	...	...	...	...
5 Health	14198	56251	24379	41191	52191	45733	...	...	...	...	...	...
6 Social security and welfare	197	240	422	347	438	560	...	...	...	...	...	...
7 Housing and community amenities	18118	32654	23366	24015	24446	30962	...	...	...	...	...	...
8 Recreational, cultural and religious affairs	...	...	...	...	...	...	...	...	...	...	...	...
9 Economic services	152988	139468	144284	165929	152451	194056	...	...	...	...	...	...
A Fuel and energy	...	...	...	...	...	...	...	...	...	...	...	...
B Agriculture, hunting, forestry and fishing	71411	60291	36608	32090	48147	59927	...	...	...	...	...	...
C Mining (except fuels), manufacturing and construction	14923	7231	7398	29237	15092	16398	...	...	...	...	...	...
D Transportation and communication	47030	64159	75807	67323	30402	84663	...	...	...	...	...	...
E Other economic affairs	19624	7787	24471	37279	58810	33068	...	...	...	...	...	...
10 Other functions	73334	118879	165385	205923	303797	253260	...	...	...	...	...	...
Total government final consumption expenditures [b,c]	466034	636898	560753	659024	818873	804320	...	...	...	...	...	...

a Item "Education" includes item "Recreational, cultural and religious affairs".
b Data in this table have not been revised, therefore they are not comparable with the data in other tables.
c Only central government data are included in the general government estimates.

Georgia

Source

Reply to the United Nations National Accounts questionnaire by the State Department For Statistics.

General note

The estimates shown in the following tables have been prepared in accordance with the United Nations System of National Accounts so far as the existing data would permit.

1.1 Expenditure on the gross domestic product, in current prices

Hundred million lari

	1986	1987	1988	1989	1990	1991	1992	1993	1994	1995	1996	1997
1 Government final consumption expenditure	...	...	...	...	25	36	215	12130	1190120	3	3	...
2 Private final consumption expenditure	...	...	...	...	95	113	1505	294560	1786108[a]	31	46	...
A Households	...	...	...	...	91	109	1350	277080	1607731[a]	28	41	...
B Private non-profit institutions serving households	...	...	...	...	3	3	155	17480	1783770	3	5	...
3 Gross capital formation	...	...	...	...	46	54	349	3040	3028380	9	9	...
A Increase in stocks	...	...	...	...	10	17	105	910	1083080	2	2	...
B Gross fixed capital formation	...	...	...	...	35	37	244	2130	1945300	7	7	...
4 Exports of goods and services	...	...	...	...	60	53	685	53170	4218170	5	6	...
5 less: Imports of goods and services	...	...	...	...	68	60	1371	93330	8135810	11	10	...
Statistical discrepancy	...	...	...	...	−7	−5	1	6310	−95610	–	−2	...
equals: Gross domestic product	...	...	...	...	150	191	1383	275880	1806633[a]	37	53	64

a Estimates in thousand millions.

1.3 Cost components of the gross domestic product

Hundred million lari

	1986	1987	1988	1989	1990	1991	1992	1993	1994	1995	1996	1997
1 Indirect taxes, net	...	...	...	...	13	18	25	15670	395380	2	2	3
A Indirect taxes	...	...	...	...	27	29	105	16390	422490	2	2	3
B less: Subsidies	...	...	...	...	15	11	80	720	27110	–	–	–
2 Consumption of fixed capital	...	...	...	...	23	25	135	28790	2353710	4	6	8
3 Compensation of employees paid by resident producers to	...	...	...	...	72	103	379	42580	3760250	14	14	15
A Resident households	...	...	...	...	72	103	379	42570	3721620	14	14	14
B Rest of the world	...	...	...	...	...	...	–	10	38630	–	–	–
4 Operating surplus	...	...	...	...	42	46	584	190300	1175230[a]	17	32	40
A Corporate and quasi-corporate enterprises	...	...	...	...	11	9	−59	30900	2866410	5	9	10
B Private unincorporated enterprises	...	...	...	...	31	37	637	134000	8615100	12	23	30
C General government	...	...	...	...	–	–	5	25400	270790	–	–	–
Statistical discrepancy	...	...	...	...	−1	−1	260	−1460	−195310	–	–	−1
equals: Gross domestic product	...	...	...	...	150	191	1383	275880	1806633[a]	37	53	64

a Estimates in thousand millions.

Georgia

1.4 General government current receipts and disbursements

Hundred million lari

	1986	1987	1988	1989	1990	1991	1992	1993	1994	1995	1996	1997
Receipts												
1 Operating surplus	...	...	...	...	–	–	5	25400	270790	–	...	...
2 Property and entrepreneurial income	...	...	...	...	7	12	69	3570	155070	1	...	...
3 Taxes, fees and contributions	...	...	...	...	38	34	114	17000	436890	3	...	...
A Indirect taxes	...	...	...	...	27	29	105	16390	422490	2	...	...
B Direct taxes	...	...	...	...	5	5	9	610	14400	–	...	...
C Social security contributions	...	...	...	...	6	27	71	11310	1522550	3	...	...
D Compulsory fees, fines and penalties	...	...	...	...	...	...	...	...	...	...	...	...
4 Other current transfers	...	...	...	...	2	2	3	...	473340	1	...	...
Total current receipts of general government	...	...	...	...	46	48	192	45970	1336090	4	...	...
Disbursements												
1 Government final consumption expenditure	...	...	...	...	25	36	215	12130	1190120	3	...	...
A Compensation of employees	...	...	...	...	15	22	113	5460	227610	1	...	...
B Consumption of fixed capital	...	...	...	...	3	3	13	2400	157780	–	...	...
C Purchases of goods and services, net	...	...	...	...	5	5	51	1020	725530	3	...	...
D less: Own-account fixed capital formation	...	...	...	...	6	6	32	320	75870	2	...	...
E Indirect taxes paid, net	...	...	...	...	7	12	69	3570	155070	1	...	...
2 Property income	...	...	...	...	6	8	68	570	9070	–	...	...
A Interest	...	...	...	...	6	8	68	570	9070	–	...	...
B Net land rent and royalties	...	...	...	...	...	...	...	...	...	...	...	...
3 Subsidies	...	...	...	...	15	11	80	720	27110	–	...	...
4 Other current transfers	...	...	...	...	13	19	54	1670	660270	2	...	...
A Social security benefits	...	...	...	...	13	18	50	1620	105190	1	...	...
B Social assistance grants	...	...	...	...	...	...	...	...	79970	–	...	...
C Other	...	...	...	...	–	1	4	50	475110	1	...	...
Statistical discrepancy	...	...	...	...	–13	–27	–225	30880	–550480	–1	...	...
Total current disbursements and net saving of general government	...	...	...	...	46	48	192	45970	1336090	4	...	...

1.5 Current income and outlay of corporate and quasi-corporate enterprises, summary

Hundred million lari

	1986	1987	1988	1989	1990	1991	1992	1993	1994	1995	1996	1997
Receipts												
1 Operating surplus	...	...	...	...	11	9	–59	30900	2866410	5	...	...
2 Property and entrepreneurial income received	...	...	...	...	6	9	174	2080	360630	–	...	...
3 Current transfers	...	...	...	...	2	4	7	3390	543740	1	...	...
Total current receipts	...	...	...	...	19	22	123	36370	3770780	5	...	...
Disbursements												
1 Property and entrepreneurial income	...	...	...	...	17	24	145	3530	335080	–	...	...

Georgia

Hundred million lari	1986	1987	1988	1989	1990	1991	1992	1993	1994	1995	1996	1997
2 Direct taxes and other current payments to general government	...	...	...	...	3	6	69	4080	1553810	3	...	...
3 Other current transfers	...	...	...	...	5	7	24	3780	770	–	...	...
4 Net saving	...	...	...	...	–6	–15	–116	24980	1881120	2	...	...
Total current disbursements and net saving	...	...	...	...	19	22	123	36370	3770780	5	...	...

1.6 Current income and outlay of households and non-profit institutions

Hundred million lari	1986	1987	1988	1989	1990	1991	1992	1993	1994	1995	1996	1997
Receipts												
1 Compensation of employees	...	...	...	...	72	103	389	43650	3724110	14	...	...
A From resident producers	...	...	...	...	72	103	379	42570	3721620	14	...	...
B From rest of the world	...	...	...	...	–	–	10	1080	2490	–	...	...
2 Operating surplus of private unincorporated enterprises	...	...	...	...	31	37	637	134000	8615100	12	...	...
3 Property and entrepreneurial income	...	...	...	...	4	5	126	6220	290	–	...	...
4 Current transfers	...	...	...	...	19	24	227	19720	636760	2	...	...
A Social security benefits	...	...	...	...	13	19	68	2190	106910	1	...	...
B Social assistance grants	...	...	...	...	...	...	...	...	...	...	...	...
C Other	...	...	...	...	6	5	159	17530	529850	1	...	...
Total current receipts	...	...	...	...	127	169	1378	203590	1297626[a]	28	...	...
Disbursements												
1 Private final consumption expenditure	...	...	...	...	91	109	1350	277080	1607731[a]	28	...	...
2 Property income	...	...	...	...	–	–	–	...	6960	–	...	...
3 Direct taxes and other current transfers n.e.c. to general government	...	...	...	...	10	32	89	11370	45040	–	...	...
A Social security contributions	...	...	...	...	6	27	71	11310	1960	...	...	...
B Direct taxes	...	...	...	...	4	6	17	60	43080	–	...	...
C Fees, fines and penalties	...	...	...	...	...	...	...	...	...	...	...	...
4 Other current transfers	...	...	...	...	2	2	4	40	520	...	...	...
5 Net saving	...	...	...	...	23	25	–65	–84900	–3153570	–	...	...
Total current disbursements and net saving	...	...	...	...	127	169	1378	203590	1297626[a]	28	...	...

a Estimates in thousand millions.

1.8 Capital transactions of the nation, summary

Hundred million lari	1986	1987	1988	1989	1990	1991	1992	1993	1994	1995	1996	1997
Finance of gross capital formation												
Gross saving	...	...	...	...	31	43	–110	–21100	–387340	4	...	...
1 Consumption of fixed capital	...	...	...	...	23	25	135	28790	2353710	4	...	...
A General government	...	...	...	...	3	3	13	2400	157780	–	...	...
B Corporate and quasi-corporate enterprises	...	...	...	...	21	22	122	26390	2195930	4	...	...
C Other	...	...	...	...	...	...	...	...	...	...	...	...
2 Net saving	...	...	...	...	8	18	–245	–49890	–2741050	–	...	...

Georgia

Hundred million lari

	1986	1987	1988	1989	1990	1991	1992	1993	1994	1995	1996	1997
A General government	...	...	...	...	−1	18	−55	39	959	2	...	...
B Corporate and quasi-corporate enterprises	...	...	...	...	−10	−20	−304	18	1961	2	...	...
C Other	...	...	...	...	19	20	114	−49947	−2743970	−4	...	...
less: Surplus of the nation on current transactions	...	...	...	...	−7	−6	−459	−30450	−3320110	−5	...	...
Statistical discrepancy	...	...	...	...	7	5	−1	−6310	95610	−	...	...
Finance of gross capital formation	...	...	...	...	46	54	349	3040	3028380	9	...	...
Gross capital formation												
Increase in stocks	...	...	...	...	10	17	105	910	1083080	2	...	...
Gross fixed capital formation	...	...	...	...	35	37	244	2130	1945300	7	...	...
1 General government	...	...	...	...	6	6	32	−	76	2	...	...
2 Corporate and quasi-corporate enterprises	...	...	...	...	25	25	162	1	1	3	...	...
3 Other	...	...	...	...	5	7	50	2128	1945223	2	...	...
Gross capital formation	...	...	...	...	46	54	349	3040	3028380	9	...	...

1.9 Gross domestic product by institutional sectors of origin

Hundred million lari

	1986	1987	1988	1989	1990	1991	1992	1993	1994	1995	1996	1997
Domestic factor incomes originating												
1 General government	...	...	...	...	15	22	118	30860	498400	1	...	...
2 Corporate and quasi-corporate enterprises	...	...	...	...	11	9	−59	30900	2866410	5	...	...
A Non-financial	...	...	...	...	11	10	−116	27480	2651290	4	...	...
B Financial	...	...	...	...	−	−1	57	3420	215120	−	...	...
3 Households and private unincorporated enterprises	...	...	...	...	72	103	389	43650	3724110	14	...	...
4 Non-profit institutions serving households	...	...	...	...	16	15	514	127470	8423630	11	...	...
subtotal: Domestic factor incomes	...	...	...	...	114	149	962	232880	1551255[a]	31	...	...
Indirect taxes, net	...	...	...	...	13	18	25	15670	395380	2	...	...
A Indirect taxes	...	...	...	...	27	29	105	16390	422490	2	...	...
B less: Subsidies	...	...	...	...	15	11	80	720	27110	−	...	...
Consumption of fixed capital	...	...	...	...	23	25	135	28790	2353710	4	...	...
Statistical discrepancy	...	...	...	...	−1	−1	260	−1460	−195310	−	...	...
Gross domestic product	...	...	...	...	150	191	1383	275880	1806633[a]	37	...	...

a Estimates in thousand millions.

1.10 Gross domestic product by kind of activity, in current prices

Hundred million lari

	1986	1987	1988	1989	1990	1991	1992	1993	1994	1995	1996	1997
1 Agriculture, hunting, forestry and fishing	...	...	...	...	45	51	757	182850	1164842[a]	15	16	18
2 Mining and quarrying	...	...	...	...	4	6	21	2664	177974	−	1	1
3 Manufacturing	...	...	...	...	21	32	108	13764	919534	2	3	4
4 Electricity, gas and water	...	...	...	...	9	13	45	5772	385611	1	1	2
5 Construction	...	...	...	...	13	15	93	2250	307240	1	2	3
6 Wholesale and retail trade, restaurants and hotels	...	...	...	...	9	11	24	18680	1495100	10	12	14

Georgia

Hundred million lari

	1986	1987	1988	1989	1990	1991	1992	1993	1994	1995	1996	1997
7 Transport, storage and communication	...	...	...	...	11	13	57	9850	920800	3	3	6
8 Finance, insurance, real estate and business services	...	...	...	...	3	3	93	8080	470650	–	2	3
9 Community, social and personal services	...	...	...	...	28	34	175	18350	1555330	2	9	10
Total, Industries	...	...	...	...	142	179	1373	262260	1788066[a]	35	51	61
Producers of government services	...	...	...	...	...	...	...	...	...	...	...	...
Other producers	...	...	...	...	...	...	...	...	...	...	...	...
Subtotal	...	...	...	...	142	179	1373	262260	1788066[a]	35	51	61
less: Imputed bank service charge	...	...	...	...	1	1	7	1430	195310	–	...	...
plus: Import duties	...	...	...	...	5	4	15	14110	198510	–	–	1
plus: Value added tax	...	...	...	...	1	–	–	560	118600	2	1	2
plus: Other adjustments	...	...	...	...	2	9	1	380	63870	–	–	1
equals: Gross domestic product	...	...	...	...	150	191	1383	275880	1806633[a]	37	53	64

a Estimates in thousand millions.

1.12 Relations among national accounting aggregates

Hundred million lari

	1986	1987	1988	1989	1990	1991	1992	1993	1994	1995	1996	1997
Gross domestic product	...	...	...	...	150	191	1383	275880	1806633[a]	37	53	64
plus: Net factor income from the rest of the world	...	...	...	...	–	–	90	–4040	–131260	–1	1	2
Factor income from rest of the world	...	...	...	...	–	–	107	2110	2900	–	1	2
less: Factor income to the rest of the world	...	...	...	...	–	–	17	6150	134160	1	–	1
equals: Gross national product	...	...	...	...	150	191	1473	271840	1793507[a]	36	54	66
less: Consumption of fixed capital	...	...	...	...	23	25	135	28790	2353710	4	6	8
equals: National income	...	...	...	...	126	167	1338	243050	1558136[a]	32	48	58
plus: Net current transfers from the rest of the world	...	...	...	...	1	–	138	13750	728790	1	1	3
Current transfers from rest of the world	...	...	...	...	2	–	138	13750	728790	1	1	3
less: Current transfers to the rest of the world	...	...	...	...	–	–	–	–	–	–	–	–
equals: National disposable income	...	...	...	...	128	167	1475	256800	1631015[a]	34	49	61
less: Final consumption	...	...	...	...	120	148	1720	306690	1905120[a]	34	49	64
equals: Net saving	...	...	...	...	8	18	–245	–49890	–2741050	–	–1	–3
less: Surplus of the nation on current transactions	...	...	...	...	–7	–6	–459	–30450	–3320110	–5	–2	–7
Statistical discrepancy	...	...	...	...	7	5	–1	–6310	95610	–	2	–
equals: Net capital formation	...	...	...	...	22	29	214	–25750	674670	5	3	3

a Estimates in thousand millions.

Georgia

2.1 Government final consumption expenditure by function, in current prices

Hundred million lari

	1986	1987	1988	1989	1990	1991	1992	1993	1994	1995	1996	1997
1 General public services	...	...	...	...	...	...	...	...	...	...	...	...
2 Defence	...	...	...	...	10	10	38	230	64640	–	...	...
3 Public order and safety	...	...	...	...	–	2	41	990	119710	1	...	...
4 Education	...	...	...	...	6	10	53	690	57040	–	...	...
5 Health	...	...	...	...	4	5	33	70	37930	–	...	...
6 Social security and welfare	...	...	...	...	–	–	1	60	107630	–	...	...
7 Housing and community amenities	...	...	...	...	...	...	...	...	...	...	...	...
8 Recreational, cultural and religious affairs	...	...	...	...	–	2	12	20	14850	–	...	...
9 Economic services	...	...	...	...	2	2	23	3680	757060	–	...	...
A Fuel and energy	...	...	...	...	...	...	...	...	...	...	...	...
B Agriculture, hunting, forestry and fishing	...	...	...	...	1	1	15	2530	745580	–	...	...
C Mining (except fuels), manufacturing and construction	...	...	...	...	...	...	...	...	...	...	...	...
D Transportation and communication	...	...	...	...	2	2	8	1150	11480	–	...	...
E Other economic affairs	...	...	...	...	...	...	...	...	...	...	...	...
10 Other functions	...	...	...	...	3	4	14	6390	31260	–	...	...
Total government final consumption expenditures	...	...	...	...	25	36	215	12130	1190120	3	...	...

Germany

Source

Reply to the United Nations National Accounts Questionnaire from the Federal Statistical Office, Wiesbaden. The estimates are in close accordance with the classifications and definitions recommended in the United Nations System of National Accounts (1968 SNA).

General note

The official estimates are published in the monthly bulletin *Wirtschaft und Statistik*. Detailed data as well as description of the sources and methods used for the national accounts estimation are published annually in Fachserie 18 *Volkswirtschaftliche Gesamtrechnungen*, Reihe 1 *Konten und Standaqrdtabellen*' The following tables have been prepared from successive replies to the United Nations National Accounts Questionnaire. When the scope and coverage of the estimates differ for conceptual or statistical reasons from the definitions and classifications recommended in SNA, a footnote is indicated to the relevant tables.

1.1 Expenditure on the gross domestic product, in current prices

Million Deutsche marks

	1986	1987	1988	1989	1990	1991	1992	1993	1994	1995	1996	1997
1 Government final consumption expenditure	...	...	...	...	...	556720	616350	634860	658580	686550	705110	703400
2 Private final consumption expenditure	...	...	...	...	...	1630330	1755510	1829260	1906020	1975310	2046350	2095230
A Households	...	...	...	...	...	1592830	1712550	1782490	1856900	1920870	1986660	2034360
B Private non-profit institutions serving households	...	...	...	...	...	37500	42960	46770	49120	54440	59690	60870
3 Gross capital formation	...	...	...	...	...	668820	707640	681800	742570	753880	729330	770510
A Increase in stocks	...	...	...	...	...	12810	−1720	−9210	16400	18270	5890	47580
B Gross fixed capital formation	...	...	...	...	...	656010	709360	691010	726170	735610	723440	722930
Residential buildings	...	...	...	...	...	168160	195390	212760	243740	251770	250530	249180
Non-residential buildings [a]	...	...	...	...	...	181080	212180	216770	224310	221510	205000	194270
Other construction and land improvement, etc.	...	...	...	...	...	...	...	...	...	...	...	...
Other	...	...	...	...	...	306770	301790	261480	258120	262330	267910	279480
4 Exports of goods and services	...	...	...	...	...	727120	732300	697570	756960	821240	866180	971790
5 less: Imports of goods and services	...	...	...	...	...	729390	733200	679790	735930	794180	823470	916930
equals: Gross domestic product	...	...	...	...	...	2853600	3078600	3163700	3328200	3442800	3523500	3624000

a Including item "other construction and land improvement etc.".

1.2 Expenditure on the gross domestic product, in constant prices

Million Deutsche marks

	1986	1987	1988	1989	1990	1991	1992	1993	1994	1995	1996	1997
	At constant prices of: 1991											
1 Government final consumption expenditure	...	...	...	...	...	556720	579370	576640	588890	600530	616910	612730
2 Private final consumption expenditure	...	...	...	...	...	1630330	1676380	1678700	1698960	1730200	1757550	1765720
A Households	...	...	...	...	...	1592830	1636200	1637680	1658450	1686310	1711100	1719170

Germany

Million Deutsche marks

	1986	1987	1988	1989	1990	1991	1992	1993	1994	1995	1996	1997
At constant prices of: 1991												
B Private non-profit institutions serving households	...	...	...	...	...	37500	40180	41020	40510	43890	46450	46550
3 Gross capital formation	...	...	...	...	...	668820	679830	637710	683520	682510	660120	698320
A Increase in stocks	...	...	...	...	...	12810	560	–3800	19360	18540	4050	41850
B Gross fixed capital formation	...	...	...	...	...	656010	679270	641510	664160	663970	656070	656470
Residential buildings	...	...	...	...	...	168160	184020	191360	213500	214830	213660	212140
Non-residential buildings [a]	...	...	...	...	...	181080	199100	196630	199700	194140	182440	174210
Other construction and land improvement, etc.	...	...	...	...	...	...	...	...	...	...	...	...
Other	...	...	...	...	...	306770	296150	253520	250960	255000	259970	270120
4 Exports of goods and services	...	...	...	...	...	727120	724880	688650	742800	791840	832510	924790
5 less: Imports of goods and services	...	...	...	...	...	729390	744060	699800	753970	808880	832490	900160
equals: Gross domestic product	...	...	...	...	...	2853600	2916400	2881900	2960200	2996200	3034600	3101400

a Including item "other construction and land improvement etc.".

1.3 Cost components of the gross domestic product

Million Deutsche marks

	1986	1987	1988	1989	1990	1991	1992	1993	1994	1995	1996	1997
1 Indirect taxes, net	...	...	...	...	...	293510	330000	347660	374740	375910	379510	392910
A Indirect taxes	...	...	...	...	...	358460	389840	409560	443820	447400	449540	459770
B less: Subsidies	...	...	...	...	...	64950	59840	61900	69080	71490	70030	66860
2 Consumption of fixed capital	...	...	...	...	...	361150	393840	420610	435440	451710	460990	471500
3 Compensation of employees paid by resident producers to	...	...	...	...	...	1607850	1739280	1776880	1823890	1884980	1904520	1909260
A Resident households	...	...	...	...	...	1602870	1732830	1770220	1817110	1877090	1896270	1900860
B Rest of the world	...	...	...	...	...	4980	6450	6660	6780	7890	8250	8400
4 Operating surplus	...	...	...	...	...	591090	615480	618550	694130	730200	778480	850330
A Corporate and quasi-corporate enterprises	...	...	...	...	...	591090	615480	618550	694130	730200	778480	850330
B Private unincorporated enterprises	...	...	...	...	...	...	...	...	...	...	...	...
C General government	...	...	...	...	...	...	...	...	...	...	...	...
equals: Gross domestic product	...	...	...	...	...	2853600	3078600	3163700	3328200	3442800	3523500	3624000

1.4 General government current receipts and disbursements

Million Deutsche marks

	1986	1987	1988	1989	1990	1991	1992	1993	1994	1995	1996	1997
Receipts												
1 Operating surplus	...	...	...	...	...	...	...	...	...	...	...	...
2 Property and entrepreneurial income	...	...	...	...	...	37250	48870	47530	50560	39590	37100	...
3 Taxes, fees and contributions	...	...	...	...	...	1190230	1310850	1359150	1439740	1499760	1510820	...
A Indirect taxes	...	...	...	...	...	358460	389840	409560	443820	447310	452190	...
B Direct taxes	...	...	...	...	...	330760	364900	363350	367670	391350	368700	...
C Social security contributions	...	...	...	...	...	484320	531660	563710	603840	635810	665000	...
D Compulsory fees, fines and penalties	...	...	...	...	...	16690	24450	22530	24410	25290	24930	...
4 Other current transfers	...	...	...	...	...	42680	44970	45780	50900	53270	56090	...

Germany

Million Deutsche marks

	1986	1987	1988	1989	1990	1991	1992	1993	1994	1995	1996	1997
Total current receipts of general government	...	...	...	...	...	1270160	1404690	1452460	1541200	1592620	1604010	...

Disbursements

	1986	1987	1988	1989	1990	1991	1992	1993	1994	1995	1996	1997
1 Government final consumption expenditure	...	...	...	...	...	556720	616350	634860	658580	686540	702660	...
A Compensation of employees	...	...	...	...	...	297030	326970	342110	347990	357350	360280	...
B Consumption of fixed capital	...	...	...	...	...	20050	21890	23530	24540	25550	26200	...
C Purchases of goods and services, net	...	...	...	...	...	239750	267610	269340	286170	303760	316300	...
D less: Own-account fixed capital formation	...	...	...	...	...	460	470	470	470	470	470	...
E Indirect taxes paid, net	...	...	...	...	...	350	350	350	350	350	350	...
2 Property income	...	...	...	...	...	75690	99360	103300	110460	129850	129740	...
A Interest	...	...	...	...	...	75690	99360	103300	110460	129850	129740	...
B Net land rent and royalties	...	...	...	...	...	...	...	...	...	...	...	...
3 Subsidies	...	...	...	...	...	64950	59840	61900	69080	71020	69120	...
4 Other current transfers	...	...	...	...	...	556790	605500	658720	695670	732390	747020	...
A Social security benefits	...	...	...	...	...	351830	396070	434550	453510	482330	509080	...
B Social assistance grants	...	...	...	...	...	82660	89750	96550	102950	106300	92460	...
C Other	...	...	...	...	...	123300	119680	127620	139210	143760	14480	...
5 Net saving	...	...	...	...	...	16010	23640	−6320	7410	−27180	−44530	...
Total current disbursements and net saving of general government	...	...	...	...	...	1270160	1404690	1452460	1541200	1592620	1604010	...

1.5 Current income and outlay of corporate and quasi-corporate enterprises, summary

Million Deutsche marks

	1986	1987	1988	1989	1990	1991	1992	1993	1994	1995	1996	1997

Receipts

	1986	1987	1988	1989	1990	1991	1992	1993	1994	1995	1996	1997
1 Operating surplus	...	...	...	...	...	591090	615480	618550	695540	747660	794410	...
2 Property and entrepreneurial income received	...	...	...	...	...	592450	653520	667370	666030	669820	671880	...
3 Current transfers [a]	...	...	...	...	...	130810	143580	146700	148440	154900	158420	...
Total current receipts [a]	...	...	...	...	...	1314350	1412580	1432620	1510010	1572380	1624710	...

Disbursements

	1986	1987	1988	1989	1990	1991	1992	1993	1994	1995	1996	1997
1 Property and entrepreneurial income	...	...	...	...	...	1131140	1231320	1263520	1328770	1347410	1398070	...
2 Direct taxes and other current payments to general government [a]	...	...	...	...	...	47520	54700	50850	44170	44060	53790	...
3 Other current transfers [a]	...	...	...	...	...	118390	129190	140330	136390	139590	143990	...
4 Net saving [a]	...	...	...	...	...	17300	−2630	−22080	680	41320	28860	...
Total current disbursements and net saving [a]	...	...	...	...	...	1314350	1412580	1432620	1510010	1572380	1624710	...

a Corporate enterprises only

Germany

1.6 Current income and outlay of households and non-profit institutions

Million Deutsche marks

	1986	1987	1988	1989	1990	1991	1992	1993	1994	1995	1996	1997
Receipts												
1 Compensation of employees	...	...	...	...	...	1611640	1741220	1777890	1822730	1882390	1900350	...
A From resident producers	...	...	...	...	...	1602870	1732830	1770220	1815700	1876050	1894110	...
B From rest of the world	...	...	...	...	...	8770	8390	7670	7030	6340	6240	...
2 Operating surplus of private unincorporated enterprises	...	...	...	...	...	...	...	...	...	...	...	...
3 Property and entrepreneurial income [a]	...	...	...	...	...	632030	681140	696150	754270	793740	832820	...
4 Current transfers	...	...	...	...	...	596210	663020	720620	753130	795060	814810	...
A Social security benefits	...	...	...	...	...	346670	390640	428750	448030	475290	501770	...
B Social assistance grants	...	...	...	...	...	80850	87940	94730	101190	104560	90710	...
C Other	...	...	...	...	...	168690	184440	197140	203910	215210	222330	...
Total current receipts	...	...	...	...	...	2839880	3085380	3194660	3330130	3471190	3547980	...
Disbursements												
1 Private final consumption expenditure	...	...	...	...	...	1630330	1755510	1829260	1906020	1979190	2045400	...
2 Property income	...	...	...	...	...	30190	35790	40140	39880	40740	39890	...
3 Direct taxes and other current transfers n.e.c. to general government	...	...	...	...	...	780350	861090	894020	946210	1002270	997930	...
A Social security contributions	...	...	...	...	...	482800	529650	561520	601600	633170	662120	...
B Direct taxes	...	...	...	...	...	285610	318290	317930	327290	350390	317300	...
C Fees, fines and penalties	...	...	...	...	...	11940	13150	14570	17320	18710	18510	...
4 Other current transfers	...	...	...	...	...	158050	174500	176630	187240	196480	201010	...
5 Net saving	...	...	...	...	...	240960	258490	254610	250780	252510	263750	...
Total current disbursements and net saving [a]	...	...	...	...	...	2839880	3085380	3194660	3330130	3471190	3547980	...

a Including undistributed profits of unincorporated enterprises.

1.7 External transactions on current account, summary

Million Deutsche marks

	1986	1987	1988	1989	1990	1991	1992	1993	1994	1995	1996	1997
Payments to the rest of the world												
1 Imports of goods and services [a]	...	...	...	...	...	729390	733200	679790	735930	790870	814110	...
A Imports of merchandise, c.i.f. [b]	...	...	...	...	...	600960	593670	533940	580710	625930	641110	...
B Other	...	...	...	...	...	128430	139530	145850	155220	164940	173000	...
2 Factor income to rest of the world	...	...	...	...	...	93390	108300	121890	131860	151790	162110	...
A Compensation of employees	...	...	...	...	...	4980	6450	6660	6780	7890	8340	...
B Property and entrepreneurial income	...	...	...	...	...	88410	101850	115230	125080	143900	153770	...
By general government	...	...	...	...	...	13670	17600	26260	29620	22800	22650	...
By corporate and quasi-corporate enterprises	...	...	...	...	...	74740	84250	88970	95460	121100	131120	...
By other	...	...	...	...	...	...	...	...	...	...	...	...
3 Current transfers to the rest of the world [c]	...	...	...	...	...	80510	73860	77990	82900	82810	81260	...

Germany

Million Deutsche marks

	1986	1987	1988	1989	1990	1991	1992	1993	1994	1995	1996	1997
A Indirect taxes to supranational organizations	...	...	...	...	...	...	...	...	...	...	...	...
B Other current transfers	...	...	...	...	...	80510	73860	77990	82900	82810	81260	...
4 Surplus of the nation on current transactions	...	...	...	...	...	−33400	−34300	−34980	−48260	−48370	−40760	...
Payments to the rest of the world and surplus of the nation on current transfers	...	...	...	...	...	869890	881060	844690	902430	977100	1016720	...

Receipts from the rest of the world

	1986	1987	1988	1989	1990	1991	1992	1993	1994	1995	1996	1997
1 Exports of goods and services [a]	...	...	...	...	...	727120	732300	697570	756960	818010	857140	...
A Exports of merchandise, f.o.b.	...	...	...	...	...	630550	636950	602300	662150	715030	746180	...
B Other	...	...	...	...	...	96570	95350	95270	94810	102980	110960	...
2 Factor income from rest of the world	...	...	...	...	...	121890	127300	126990	123860	135390	134110	...
A Compensation of employees	...	...	...	...	...	8770	8390	7670	7030	6340	6240	...
B Property and entrepreneurial income	...	...	...	...	...	113120	118910	119320	116830	129050	127870	...
By general government	...	...	...	...	...	300	230	240	340	290	290	...
By corporate and quasi-corporate enterprises	...	...	...	...	...	96890	104110	107100	103470	115000	113840	...
By other	...	...	...	...	...	15930	14570	11980	13020	13760	13740	...
3 Current transfers from rest of the world [c]	...	...	...	...	...	20880	21460	20130	21610	23700	25470	...
A Subsidies from supranational organisations	...	...	...	...	...	...	...	...	...	...	...	...
B Other current transfers	...	...	...	...	...	20880	21460	20130	21610	23700	25470	...
Receipts from the rest of the world on current transactions	...	...	...	...	...	869890	881060	844690	902430	977100	1016720	...

a Exports and imports of goods for purposes of repair and improvement are reduced to the value of these services.
b Imports of merchandise, f.o.b. rather than c.i.f.
c Indirect taxes paid to and subsidies received from supranational organizations are included in "Current transfers".

1.8 Capital transactions of the nation, summary

Million Deutsche marks

	1986	1987	1988	1989	1990	1991	1992	1993	1994	1995	1996	1997

Finance of gross capital formation

	1986	1987	1988	1989	1990	1991	1992	1993	1994	1995	1996	1997
Gross saving	...	...	...	...	...	635420	673340	646820	695020	710080	694930	749250
1 Consumption of fixed capital	...	...	...	...	...	361150	393840	420610	435440	451710	460990	471500
A General government	...	...	...	...	...	20050	21890	23530	24540	25550	26180	26660
B Corporate and quasi-corporate enterprises [a]	...	...	...	...	...	336290	366810	391610	405210	420260	428830	438740
C Other	...	...	...	...	...	4810	5140	5470	5690	5900	5980	6100
2 Net saving	...	...	...	...	...	274270	279500	226210	259580	258370	233940	277750
A General government	...	...	...	...	...	16010	23640	−6320	7900	−25630	−42730	−28120
B Corporate and quasi-corporate enterprises	...	...	...	...	...	17300	−2630	−22080	900	29860	10610	46030
C Other [a]	...	...	...	...	...	240960	258490	254610	250780	254140	266060	259840
less: Surplus of the nation on current transactions	...	...	...	...	...	−33400	−34300	−34980	−47550	−43800	−34400	−21260
Finance of gross capital formation	...	...	...	...	...	668820	707640	681800	742570	753880	729330	770510

Gross capital formation

	1986	1987	1988	1989	1990	1991	1992	1993	1994	1995	1996	1997
Increase in stocks	...	...	...	...	...	12810	−1720	−9210	16400	18270	5890	47580
Gross fixed capital formation	...	...	...	...	...	656010	709360	691010	726170	735610	723440	722930

Germany

Million Deutsche marks	1986	1987	1988	1989	1990	1991	1992	1993	1994	1995	1996	1997
1 General government	...	...	...	...	...	72920	85300	85450	86270	82880	77580	72610
2 Corporate and quasi-corporate enterprises [a]	...	...	...	...	...	583090	624060	605560	639900	652730	645860	650320
3 Other	...	...	...	...	...	...	...	...	...	...	...	...
Gross capital formation	...	...	...	...	...	668820	707640	681800	742570	753880	729330	770510

a Including private non-profit organizations

1.9 Gross domestic product by institutional sectors of origin

Million Deutsche marks	1986	1987	1988	1989	1990	1991	1992	1993	1994	1995	1996	1997
Domestic factor incomes originating												
1 General government	...	...	...	...	...	297030	326970	342110	347990	358890	362990	363580
2 Corporate and quasi-corporate enterprises [a]	...	...	...	...	...	1837120	1954720	1975220	2086910	2167240	2226380	2300460
A Non-financial	...	...	...	...	...	1835210	1953670	1972410	2079870	2160030	2221370	2294260
B Financial [a]	...	...	...	...	...	1910	1050	2810	7040	7210	5010	...
3 Households and private unincorporated enterprises	...	...	...	...	...	...	...	...	...	...	...	...
4 Non-profit institutions serving households	...	...	...	...	...	...	...	...	...	...	...	...
subtotal: Domestic factor incomes	...	...	...	...	...	2198940	2354760	2395430	2518020	2615180	2683000	2759590
Indirect taxes, net	...	...	...	...	...	293510	330000	347660	374740	375910	379510	392910
A Indirect taxes	...	...	...	...	...	358460	389840	409560	443820	447400	449540	459770
B less: Subsidies	...	...	...	...	...	64950	59840	61900	69080	71490	70030	66860
Consumption of fixed capital	...	...	...	...	...	361150	393840	420610	435440	451710	460990	471500
Gross domestic product	...	...	...	...	...	2853600	3078600	3163700	3328200	3442800	3523500	3624000

a Net of imputed output of bank services.

1.10 Gross domestic product by kind of activity, in current prices

Million Deutsche marks	1986	1987	1988	1989	1990	1991	1992	1993	1994	1995	1996	1997
1 Agriculture, hunting, forestry and fishing	...	...	...	...	...	41040	40610	36480	36060	35850	37490	...
2 Mining and quarrying	...	...	...	...	...	...	...	...	...	...	...	...
3 Manufacturing [abc]	...	...	...	...	...	825300	835840	787440	809920	826300	836920	...
4 Electricity, gas and water	...	...	...	...	...	...	...	...	...	...	...	...
5 Construction [b]	...	...	...	...	...	161810	191020	200270	216460	222500	216490	...
6 Wholesale and retail trade, restaurants and hotels	...	...	...	...	...	...	...	...	...	...	...	...
7 Transport, storage and communication	...	...	...	...	...	154400	164420	168230	173280	180240	178240	...
8 Finance, insurance, real estate and business services [d]	...	...	...	...	...	322090	362030	402270	435400	461250	489790	...
9 Community, social and personal services	...	...	...	...	...	...	...	...	...	...	...	...
Total, Industries	...	...	...	...	...	2369780	2550370	2604010	2741110	2852030	2927270	...
Producers of government services	...	...	...	...	...	317430	349210	365990	372880	383250	386830	...
Other producers	...	...	...	...	...	69630	78250	83610	88850	94970	99690	...
Subtotal	...	...	...	...	...	2756840	2977830	3053610	3202840	3330250	3413790	...
less: Imputed bank service charge	...	...	...	...	...	117100	129290	135550	139680	137150	139990	...
plus: Import duties	...	...	...	...	...	30100	31110	28530	30150	31090	30490	...

Germany

Million Deutsche marks

	1986	1987	1988	1989	1990	1991	1992	1993	1994	1995	1996	1997
plus: Value added tax	...	...	...	...	...	183760	198950	217110	234890	235410	237210	...
plus: Other adjustments	...	...	...	...	...	...	...	...	...	...	...	...
equals: Gross domestic product	...	...	...	...	...	2853600	3078600	3163700	3328200	3459600	3541500	...

a Item "quarrying" is included in item "manufacturing".
b Item "manufacturing" includes "Structural steel erection".
c Item "publishing" is included in item "community, social and personal services".
d Item "real estate and buisness services" except item "dwelings" is included in item "community, social and personal services".

1.11 Gross domestic product by kind of activity, in constant prices

Million Deutsche marks

	1986	1987	1988	1989	1990	1991	1992	1993	1994	1995	1996	1997
				At constant prices of: 1991								
1 Agriculture, hunting, forestry and fishing	...	...	...	...	...	41040	48110	45570	43830	44900	45480	...
2 Mining and quarrying	...	...	...	...	...	...	...	...	...	...	...	...
3 Manufacturing [abc]	...	...	...	...	...	825300	805390	747480	767870	777920	779130	...
4 Electricity, gas and water	...	...	...	...	...	...	...	...	...	...	...	...
5 Construction [b]	...	...	...	...	...	161810	172970	171720	180640	179820	173300	...
6 Wholesale and retail trade, restaurants and hotels	...	...	...	...	...	...	...	...	...	...	...	...
7 Transport, storage and communication	...	...	...	...	...	154400	161260	163930	169780	175470	181520	...
8 Finance, insurance, real estate and business services [d]	...	...	...	...	...	322090	327720	343650	357710	369630	390500	...
9 Community, social and personal services	...	...	...	...	...	...	...	...	...	...	...	...
Total, Industries	...	...	...	...	...	2369780	2421120	2392170	2460700	2518910	2570060	...
Producers of government services	...	...	...	...	...	317430	320790	320710	322690	321610	320980	...
Other producers	...	...	...	...	...	69630	73340	75540	78650	81240	83720	...
Subtotal	...	...	...	...	...	2756840	2815250	2788420	2862040	2921760	2974760	...
less: Imputed bank service charge	...	...	...	...	...	117100	119740	124710	131410	136360	148040	...
plus: Import duties	...	...	...	...	...	30100	29620	27150	27050	28050	27630	...
plus: Value added tax	...	...	...	...	...	183760	191270	191040	202520	200350	200150	...
plus: Other adjustments	...	...	...	...	...	...	...	...	...	...	...	...
equals: Gross domestic product	...	...	...	...	...	2853600	2916400	2881900	2960200	3013800	3054500	...

a Item "quarrying" is included in item "manufacturing".
b Item "manufacturing" includes "Structural steel erection".
c Item "publishing" is included in item "community, social and personal services".
d Item "real estate and buisness services" except item "dwelings" is included in item "community, social and personal services".

1.12 Relations among national accounting aggregates

Million Deutsche marks

	1986	1987	1988	1989	1990	1991	1992	1993	1994	1995	1996	1997
Gross domestic product	...	...	...	...	...	2853600	3078600	3163700	3328200	3442800	3523500	3624000
plus: Net factor income from the rest of the world	...	...	...	...	...	28500	19000	5100	–8000	–16200	–26000	–23900
Factor income from rest of the world	...	...	...	...	...	121890	127300	126990	123860	119200	113300	127980
less: Factor income to the rest of the world	...	...	...	...	...	93390	108300	121890	131860	135400	139300	151880
equals: Gross national product	...	...	...	...	...	2882100	3097600	3168800	3320200	3426600	3497500	3600100
less: Consumption of fixed capital	...	...	...	...	...	361150	393840	420610	435440	451710	460990	471500
equals: National income	...	...	...	...	...	2520950	2703760	2748190	2884760	2974890	3036510	3128600

Germany

Million Deutsche marks	1986	1987	1988	1989	1990	1991	1992	1993	1994	1995	1996	1997
plus: Net current transfers from the rest of the world [a]	...	...	...	...	...	–59630	–52400	–57860	–60580	–54660	–51110	–52220
Current transfers from rest of the world	...	...	...	...	...	20880	21460	20130	22220	24560	26330	27620
less: Current transfers to the rest of the world	...	...	...	...	...	80510	73860	77990	82800	79220	77440	79840
equals: National disposable income	...	...	...	...	...	2461320	2651360	2690330	2824180	2920230	2985400	3076380
less: Final consumption	...	...	...	...	...	2187050	2371860	2464120	2564600	2661860	2751460	2798630
equals: Net saving	...	...	...	...	...	274270	279500	226210	259580	258370	233940	277750
less: Surplus of the nation on current transactions	...	...	...	...	...	–33400	–34300	–34980	–47550	–43800	–34400	–21260
equals: Net capital formation	...	...	...	...	...	307670	313800	261190	307130	302170	268340	299010

[a] Indirect taxes paid to and subsidies received from supranational organizations are included in "Current transfers".

2.1 Government final consumption expenditure by function, in current prices

Million Deutsche marks	1986	1987	1988	1989	1990	1991	1992	1993	1994	1995	1996	1997
1 General public services	...	...	...	...	...	60150	65300	68750	68730	70320	...	...
2 Defence	...	...	...	...	...	53490	54620	51320	48490	48410	...	...
3 Public order and safety	...	...	...	...	...	42010	46700	50200	52560	55150	...	...
4 Education	...	...	...	...	...	108210	112330	118060	121630	127510	...	...
5 Health	...	...	...	...	...	175930	199730	200460	215930	226570	...	...
6 Social security and welfare	...	...	...	...	...	68150	83030	91140	96450	103070	...	...
7 Housing and community amenities	...	...	...	...	...	9910	10760	9850	9440	10010	...	...
8 Recreational, cultural and religious affairs	...	...	...	...	...	15210	17360	17480	17130	17300	...	...
9 Economic services	...	...	...	...	...	23660	26520	27600	28220	28200	...	...
A Fuel and energy	...	...	...	...	...	110	110	130	120	80	...	...
B Agriculture, hunting, forestry and fishing	...	...	...	...	...	3100	3260	3560	3600	3510	...	...
C Mining (except fuels), manufacturing and construction	...	...	...	...	...	350	300	330	240	210	...	...
D Transportation and communication	...	...	...	...	...	14900	16250	16880	17520	17430	...	...
E Other economic affairs	...	...	...	...	...	5200	6600	6700	6740	6970	...	...
10 Other functions	...	...	...	...	...	–	–	–	...	...	...	...
Total government final consumption expenditures	...	...	...	...	...	556720	616350	634860	658580	686540	...	...

2.3 Total government outlays by function and type

Million Deutsche marks

1991

	Final consumption expenditures			Subsidies	Other current transfers and property income	Total current disbursements	Gross capital formation	Other capital outlays	Total outlays
	Total	Compensation of employees	Other						
1 General public services	60150	41670	18480	2150	55750	118050	5570	10640	134260
2 Defence	53490	29900	23590	–	1160	54650	180	120	54950
3 Public order and safety	42010	34440	7570	10	90	42110	3630	150	45890
4 Education	108210	83990	24220	160	9020	117390	9980	1080	128450
5 Health	175930	38780	137150	130	640	176700	6500	2810	186010

Germany

Million Deutsche marks

1991

	Final consumption expenditures			Subsidies	Other current transfers and property income	Total current disbursements	Gross capital formation	Other capital outlays	Total outlays
	Total	Compensation of employees	Other						
6 Social security and welfare	68150	30360	37790	1160	473300	542610	3040	3600	549250
7 Housing and community amenities	9910	15730	−5820	5070	130	15110	17950	6190	39250
8 Recreational, cultural and religious affairs	15210	9170	6040	1080	3170	19460	4360	1490	25310
9 Economic services	23660	12990	10670	55190	13530	92380	21710	40920	155010
A Fuel and energy	110	–	110	9280	–	9390	–	970	10360
B Agriculture, hunting, forestry and fishing	3100	1860	1240	20270	100	23470	310	2080	25860
C Mining (except fuels), manufacturing and construction	350	–	350	1480	–	1830	–	2460	4290
D Transportation and communication	14900	8390	6510	13460	–	28360	19490	21710	69560
E Other economic affairs	5200	2740	2460	10700	13430	29330	1910	13700	44940
10 Other functions	–	–	–	–	75690	75690	–	–	75690
Total	556720	297030	259690	64950	632480	1254150	72920	67000	1394070

1992

	Final consumption expenditures			Subsidies	Other current transfers and property income	Total current disbursements	Gross capital formation	Other capital outlays	Total outlays
	Total	Compensation of employees	Other						
1 General public services	65300	45060	20240	2300	47140	114740	5900	7180	127820
2 Defence	54620	30630	23990	–	1140	55760	220	110	56090
3 Public order and safety	46700	38780	7920	30	110	46840	4100	140	51080
4 Education	112330	87350	24980	110	9300	121740	10260	1230	133230
5 Health	199730	41730	158000	130	570	200430	7680	3030	211140
6 Social security and welfare	83030	40670	42360	1090	526890	611010	4750	3830	619590
7 Housing and community amenities	10760	17350	−6590	4620	160	15540	21360	6110	43010
8 Recreational, cultural and religious affairs	17360	10790	6570	1160	2390	20910	5040	1750	27700
9 Economic services	26520	14610	11910	50400	17800	94720	25990	34450	155160
A Fuel and energy	110	–	110	9780	–	9890	–	1150	11040
B Agriculture, hunting, forestry and fishing	3260	2050	1210	16230	120	19610	280	2100	21990
C Mining (except fuels), manufacturing and construction	300	–	300	1940	–	2240	10	1630	3880
D Transportation and communication	16250	9330	6920	11370	–	27620	22890	13480	63990
E Other economic affairs	6600	3230	3370	11080	17680	35360	2810	16090	54260
10 Other functions	–	–	–	–	99360	99360	–	–	99360
Total	616350	326970	289380	59840	704860	1381050	85300	57830	1524180

Germany

1993

	Final consumption expenditures — Total	Compensation of employees	Other	Subsidies	Other current transfers and property income	Total current disbursements	Gross capital formation	Other capital outlays	Total outlays
1 General public services	68750	47510	21240	2210	49780	120740	5900	5890	132530
2 Defence	51320	29490	21830	—	990	52310	160	70	52540
3 Public order and safety	50200	41700	8500	40	110	50350	4230	130	54710
4 Education	118060	92010	26050	210	9590	127860	11140	1200	140200
5 Health	200460	44780	155680	190	590	201240	8010	3130	212380
6 Social security and welfare	91140	43160	47980	1160	577610	669910	5270	4280	679460
7 Housing and community amenities	9850	17620	−7770	4370	170	14390	20400	4930	39720
8 Recreational, cultural and religious affairs	17480	10840	6640	1500	2410	21390	5090	1670	28150
9 Economic services	27600	15000	12600	52220	17470	97290	25250	33580	156120
A Fuel and energy	130	10	120	8730	—	8860	—	1680	10540
B Agriculture, hunting, forestry and fishing	3560	2160	1400	19040	120	22720	280	2200	25200
C Mining (except fuels), manufacturing and construction	330	—	330	1440	—	1770	—	980	2750
D Transportation and communication	16880	9670	7210	12970	10	29860	22160	13800	65820
E Other economic affairs	6700	3160	3540	10040	17340	34080	2810	14920	51810
10 Other functions	—	—	—	—	103300	103300	—	—	103300
Total	634860	342110	292750	61900	762020	1458780	85450	54880	1599110

1994

	Final consumption expenditures — Total	Compensation of employees	Other	Subsidies	Other current transfers and property income	Total current disbursements	Gross capital formation	Other capital outlays	Total outlays
1 General public services	68730	48280	20450	6350	53310	128390	5740	4190	138320
2 Defence	48490	28340	20150	—	880	49370	100	40	49510
3 Public order and safety	52560	43790	8770	20	130	52710	4260	140	57110
4 Education	121630	94660	26970	260	9590	131480	11960	1100	144540
5 Health	215930	45550	170380	280	500	216710	8380	2970	228060
6 Social security and welfare	96450	43660	52790	1200	610120	707770	4960	3950	716680
7 Housing and community amenities	9440	17600	−8160	6570	210	16220	19850	5130	41200
8 Recreational, cultural and religious affairs	17130	10680	6450	1570	2290	20990	5070	1640	27700
9 Economic services	28220	15440	12780	52830	18640	99690	25950	26620	152260
A Fuel and energy	120	20	100	9200	—	9320	—	1670	10990
B Agriculture, hunting, forestry and fishing	3600	2280	1320	16540	90	20230	300	2170	22700
C Mining (except fuels), manufacturing and construction	240	—	240	1190	—	1430	—	970	2400
D Transportation and communication	17520	10000	7520	16210	2600	36330	23020	7780	67130
E Other economic affairs	6740	3140	3600	9690	15950	32380	2630	14030	49040
10 Other functions	...	—	—	—	110460	110460	—	—	110460
Total	658580	348000	310580	69080	806130	1533790	86270	45780	1665840

Germany

	1995								
	Final consumption expenditures			Subsidies	Other current transfers and property income	Total current disburse- ments	Gross capital formation	Other capital outlays	Total outlays
	Total	Compen- sation of employ- ees	Other						
1 General public services	70320	49490	20830	5910	52920	129150	5600	5550	140300
2 Defence	48410	28220	20190	–	220	48630	100	40	48770
3 Public order and safety	55150	45680	9470	20	160	55330	3940	200	59470
4 Education	127510	99090	28420	610	9750	137870	11450	1250	150570
5 Health	226570	46660	179910	540	540	227650	8160	3450	239260
6 Social security and welfare	103070	44850	58220	1170	645590	749830	5890	3110	758830
7 Housing and community amenities	10010	17690	–7680	5710	250	15970	18710	5710	40390
8 Recreational, cultural and religious affairs	17300	10510	6790	2050	2440	21790	4540	2070	28400
9 Economic services	28200	15160	13040	55010	20520	103730	24700	262700	391130
A Fuel and energy	80	10	70	8830	–	8910	–	1370	10280
B Agriculture, hunting, for- estry and fishing	3510	2200	1310	16100	80	19690	260	2340	22290
C Mining (except fuels), manufacturing and con- struction	210	–	210	1440	–	1650	–	770	2420
D Transportation and communication	17430	9840	7590	17140	2380	36950	21770	9580	68300
E Other economic affairs	6970	3110	3860	11500	18060	36530	2670	248640	287840
10 Other functions	...	–	–	–	129850	129850	–	–	129850
Total	686540	357350	329190	71020	862240	1619800	83090	284080	1986970

2.5 Private final consumption expenditure by type and purpose, in current prices

Million Deutsche marks

	1986	1987	1988	1989	1990	1991	1992	1993	1994	1995	1996	1997
Final consumption expenditure of resident households												
1 Food, beverages and tobacco [a]	...	...	...	...	...	339770	354270	357770	362490	372200	375130	...
A Food [b]	...	...	...	...	...	308470	323100	326070	328800	338190	340950	...
B Non-alcoholic beverages	...	...	...	...	...	...	...	...	...	...	...	...
C Alcoholic beverages	...	...	...	...	...	...	...	...	...	...	...	...
D Tobacco	...	...	...	...	...	31300	31170	31700	33690	34010	34180	...
2 Clothing and footwear	...	...	...	...	...	127550	133540	137150	134230	135690	136780	...
3 Gross rent, fuel and power [cd]	...	...	...	...	...	305130	338380	378600	406700	438050	469910	...
A Fuel and power [d]	...	...	...	...	...	67590	68940	72540	71150	72240	74420	...
B Other	...	...	...	...	...	237540	269440	306060	335550	365810	395490	...
4 Furniture, furnishings and household equipment and operation [c]	...	...	...	...	...	150070	162770	168980	173300	172610	172510	...
5 Medical care and health expenses	...	...	...	...	...	51660	58690	63140	67090	70300	73790	...
6 Transport and communication [d]	...	...	...	...	...	288130	302540	293430	307860	319110	335110	...
A Personal transport equip- ment	...	...	...	...	...	102390	105230	92960	97010	102090	112360	...
B Other [d]	...	...	...	...	...	185740	197310	200470	210850	217020	222750	...
7 Recreational, entertainment, education and cultural services	...	...	...	...	...	164850	176790	181320	184700	188890	191380	...
8 Miscellaneous goods and services [a]	...	...	...	...	...	142110	154460	165700	176900	185650	190890	...
A Personal care	...	...	...	...	...	31440	33380	34920	35130	36390	37130	...

Germany

Million Deutsche marks

	1986	1987	1988	1989	1990	1991	1992	1993	1994	1995	1996	1997
B Expenditures in restaurants, cafes and hotels	...	...	...	...	...	...	...	...	...	...	...	...
C Other	...	...	...	...	...	...	...	...	...	...	...	...
Total final consumption expenditure in the domestic market by households, of which	...	...	...	...	...	1569270	1681440	1746090	1813270	1882500	1945500	...
plus: Direct purchases abroad by resident households	...	...	...	...	...	60430	65280	68290	74090	73170	74520	...
less: Direct purchases in the domestic market by non-resident households	...	...	...	...	...	36870	34170	31890	30460	31090	32110	...
equals: Final consumption expenditure of resident households	...	...	...	...	...	1592830	1712550	1782490	1856900	1924580	1987910	...

Final consumption expenditures by private non-profit organisations serving households

	1986	1987	1988	1989	1990	1991	1992	1993	1994	1995	1996	1997
1 Research and science	...	...	...	...	...	...	...	...	...	...	...	...
2 Education	...	...	...	...	...	...	...	...	...	...	...	...
3 Medical and other health services	...	...	...	...	...	...	...	...	...	...	...	...
4 Welfare services	...	...	...	...	...	...	...	...	...	...	...	...
5 Recreational and related cultural services	...	...	...	...	...	...	...	...	...	...	...	...
6 Religious organisations	...	...	...	...	...	...	...	...	...	...	...	...
7 Professional and labour organisations serving households	...	...	...	...	...	...	...	...	...	...	...	...
8 Miscellaneous	...	...	...	...	...	...	...	...	...	...	...	...
equals: Final consumption expenditures by private non-profit organisations serving households	...	...	...	...	...	37500	42960	46770	49120	54610	57490	...
Private final consumption expenditure	...	...	...	...	...	1630330	1755510	1829260	1906020	1979190	2045400	...

a Expenditure in restaurants and cafes is included in item "Food, beverages and tobacco", expenditure in hotels, etc., is included in item "Miscellaneous goods and services".
b Including beverages.
c Indoor repairs and upkeep paid for by tenants are included in household equipment and operation.
d Fuel for personal transport equipment is included in item "Transport and communication".

2.6 Private final consumption expenditure by type and purpose, in constant prices

Million Deutsche marks

	1986	1987	1988	1989	1990	1991	1992	1993	1994	1995	1996	1997
At constant prices of: 1991												

Final consumption expenditure of resident households

	1986	1987	1988	1989	1990	1991	1992	1993	1994	1995	1996	1997
1 Food, beverages and tobacco [a]	...	...	...	...	...	339770	342090	338780	338400	342840	342970	...
A Food [b]	...	...	...	...	...	308470	312620	310220	308430	313280	313460	...
B Non-alcoholic beverages	...	...	...	...	...	...	...	...	...	...	...	...
C Alcoholic beverages	...	...	...	...	...	...	...	...	...	...	...	...
D Tobacco	...	...	...	...	...	31300	29470	28560	29970	29560	29510	...
2 Clothing and footwear	...	...	...	...	...	127550	129520	129640	125380	125810	125970	...
3 Gross rent, fuel and power [cd]	...	...	...	...	...	305130	313580	325710	335070	347690	361910	...
A Fuel and power [d]	...	...	...	...	...	67590	67500	70030	68930	70390	73520	...
B Other	...	...	...	...	...	237540	246080	255680	266140	277300	288390	...
4 Furniture, furnishings and household equipment and operation [c]	...	...	...	...	...	150070	157280	158880	159990	156970	155480	...
5 Medical care and health expenses	...	...	...	...	...	51660	59660	61370	61750	63500	64970	...

Germany

Million Deutsche marks

	1986	1987	1988	1989	1990	1991	1992	1993	1994	1995	1996	1997
At constant prices of: 1991												
6 Transport and communication [d]	...	...	...	...	...	288130	290240	271020	275630	282710	291570	...
A Personal transport equipment	...	...	...	...	...	102390	101520	85240	88810	92590	101490	...
B Other [d]	...	...	...	...	...	185740	188720	185780	186820	190120	190080	...
7 Recreational, entertainment, education and cultural services	...	...	...	...	...	164850	168280	167290	166560	167210	167430	...
8 Miscellaneous goods and services [a]	...	...	...	...	...	142110	144300	145930	149720	153190	154620	...
A Personal care	...	...	...	...	...	31440	32120	32220	31790	32330	32700	...
B Expenditures in restaurants, cafes and hotels	...	...	...	...	...	...	...	...	...	...	...	...
C Other	...	...	...	...	...	...	...	...	...	...	...	...
Total final consumption expenditure in the domestic market by households, of which	...	...	...	...	...	1569270	1604950	1598620	1612500	1639920	1664920	...
plus: Direct purchases abroad by resident households	...	...	...	...	...	60430	64000	68380	73310	74230	71430	...
less: Direct purchases in the domestic market by non-resident households	...	...	...	...	...	36870	32750	29320	27360	26980	27550	...
equals: Final consumption expenditure of resident households	...	...	...	...	...	1592830	1636200	1637680	1658450	1687170	1708800	...

Final consumption expenditures by private non-profit organisations serving households

	1986	1987	1988	1989	1990	1991	1992	1993	1994	1995	1996	1997
1 Research and science	...	...	...	...	...	...	...	...	...	...	...	...
2 Education	...	...	...	...	...	...	...	...	...	...	...	...
3 Medical and other health services	...	...	...	...	...	...	...	...	...	...	...	...
4 Welfare services	...	...	...	...	...	...	...	...	...	...	...	...
5 Recreational and related cultural services	...	...	...	...	...	...	...	...	...	...	...	...
6 Religious organisations	...	...	...	...	...	...	...	...	...	...	...	...
7 Professional and labour organisations serving households	...	...	...	...	...	...	...	...	...	...	...	...
8 Miscellaneous	...	...	...	...	...	...	...	...	...	...	...	...
equals: Final consumption expenditures by private non-profit organisations serving households	...	...	...	...	...	37500	40180	41020	40510	43970	44740	...
Private final consumption expenditure	...	...	...	...	...	1630330	1676380	1678700	1698960	1731140	1753540	...

[a] Expenditure in restaurants and cafes is included in item "Food, beverages and tobacco", expenditure in hotels, etc., is included in item "Miscellaneous goods and services".
[b] Including beverages.
[c] Indoor repairs and upkeep paid for by tenants are included in household equipment and operation.
[d] Fuel for personal transport equipment is included in item "Transport and communication".

2.11 Gross fixed capital formation by kind of activity of owner, ISIC divisions, in current prices

Million Deutsche marks

	1986	1987	1988	1989	1990	1991	1992	1993	1994	1995	1996	1997
All producers												
1 Agriculture, hunting, forestry and fishing	...	...	...	...	...	14360	13880	11870	11580	12200	12200	...
2 Mining and quarrying [a]	...	...	...	...	...	2830	3500	2880	2310	2840	2750	...
3 Manufacturing	...	...	...	...	...	133800	133350	110540	102560	109520	110620	...
4 Electricity, gas and water	...	...	...	...	...	27850	35640	36580	41720	33010	35100	...

Germany

Million Deutsche marks

	1986	1987	1988	1989	1990	1991	1992	1993	1994	1995	1996	1997
5 Construction [b]	...	...	...	...	...	12100	14130	14020	13860	13160	12210	...
6 Wholesale and retail trade, restaurants and hotels	...	...	...	...	...	...	...	...	...	...	...	...
A Wholesale and retail trade	...	...	...	...	...	41370	45810	41080	41070	39000	29440	...
B Restaurants and hotels	...	...	...	...	...	...	...	...	...	...	...	...
7 Transport, storage and communication	...	...	...	...	...	60980	65010	65700	62710	55460	...	...
8 Finance, insurance, real estate and business services	...	...	...	...	...	168340	194530	207340	233940	246840	247130	...
A Financial institutions	...	...	...	...	...	8720	11450	11660	11730	13840	13110	...
B Insurance	...	...	...	...	...	6210	6110	5230	5460	3740	3640	...
C Real estate and business services [c]	...	...	...	...	...	153410	176970	190450	216750	229260	230380	...
Real estate, except dwellings	...	...	...	...	...	...	...	...	...	...	...	...
Dwellings	...	...	...	...	...	153410	176970	190450	216750	229260	230380	...
9 Community, social and personal services	...	...	...	...	...	...	...	...	...	...	...	...
Total industries	...	...	...	...	...	584820	626520	608320	642400	662060	657110	...
Producers of government services	...	...	...	...	...	73200	85720	85990	87260	83760	78860	...
Private non-profit institutions serving households	...	...	...	...	...	8030	9010	9190	9340	9490	9040	...
Statistical discrepancy [d]	...	...	...	...	...	-10040	-11890	-12490	-12830	-13330	-14710	...
Total	...	...	...	...	...	656010	709360	691010	726170	741980	730300	...

a Item "quarrying" is included in item "manufacture of non-metalic mineral products" except item "products of petroleum and coal".
b Item "structural steel erection" is included in item "manufacture of fabricated metal products, machinery and equipment".
c Item "real estate and buisness services" except item "dwelings" is included in item "community, social and personal services".
d Relating to adjustment for net purchases of used capital goods.

2.12 Gross fixed capital formation by kind of activity of owner, ISIC divisions, in constant prices

Million Deutsche marks

	1986	1987	1988	1989	1990	1991	1992	1993	1994	1995	1996	1997
At constant prices of: 1991												
All producers												
1 Agriculture, hunting, forestry and fishing	...	...	...	...	...	14360	13250	11090	10680	11070	10970	...
2 Mining and quarrying [a]	...	...	...	...	...	2830	3380	2720	2200	2720	2620	...
3 Manufacturing	...	...	...	...	...	133800	128780	103900	95820	102140	102940	...
4 Electricity, gas and water	...	...	...	...	...	27850	34060	34310	39000	30470	32240	...
5 Construction [b]	...	...	...	...	...	12100	13730	13390	13160	12460	11540	...
6 Wholesale and retail trade, restaurants and hotels	...	...	...	...	...	...	...	...	...	...	...	...
A Wholesale and retail trade	...	...	...	...	...	41370	44280	38870	38880	36750	27190	...
B Restaurants and hotels	...	...	...	...	...	...	...	...	...	...	...	...
7 Transport, storage and communication	...	...	...	...	...	60980	63120	63500	60380	53150	...	...
8 Finance, insurance, real estate and business services	...	...	...	...	...	168340	183730	187330	206210	212030	211810	...
A Financial institutions	...	...	...	...	...	8720	11140	11210	11360	13010	12300	...
B Insurance	...	...	...	...	...	6210	5900	4890	5020	3440	3350	...
C Real estate and business services [c]	...	...	...	...	...	153410	166690	171230	189830	195580	196160	...
Real estate, except dwellings	...	...	...	...	...	...	...	...	...	...	...	...
Dwellings	...	...	...	...	...	153410	166690	171230	189830	195580	196160	...

Germany

Million Deutsche marks

	1986	1987	1988	1989	1990	1991	1992	1993	1994	1995	1996	1997
At constant prices of: 1991												
9 Community, social and personal services	...	...	...	...	...	...	...	...	...	...	...	...
Total industries	...	...	...	...	...	584820	601030	566110	589060	598590	595840	...
Producers of government services	...	...	...	...	...	73200	81080	78650	78590	74660	70730	...
Private non-profit institutions serving households	...	...	...	...	...	8030	8560	8410	8380	8320	7990	...
Statistical discrepancy [d]	...	...	...	...	...	−10040	−11400	−11660	−11870	−12200	−13270	...
Total	...	...	...	...	...	656010	679270	641510	664160	669370	661290	...

a Item "quarrying" is included in item "manufacture of non-metalic mineral products" except item "products of petroleum and coal".
b Item "structural steel erection" is included in item "manufacture of fabricated metal products, machinery and equipment".
c Item "real estate and buisness services" except item "dwelings" is included in item "community, social and personal services".
d Relating to adjustment for net purchases of used capital goods.

2.13 Stocks of reproducible fixed assets, by type of good and owner, in current prices

Thousand million Deutsche marks

1991

	Total Gross	Total Net	Total private Gross	Total private Net	Public enterprises Gross	Public enterprises Net	General government Gross	General government Net
1 Residential buildings	5720[a]	3903[a]	5720	3903	...	...	−	−
2 Non-residential buildings	...	...	...	...	...	...	...	...
3 Other construction	4571[a]	2933[a]	3676	2329	...	...	895	604
4 Land improvement and plantation and orchard development	...	...	...	...	...	...	...	...
5 Producers' durable goods	2747[a]	1506[a]	2628	1442	...	...	119	64
6 Breeding stock, dairy cattle, etc.	...	...	...	...	...	...	...	...
Total	13038[a]	8341[a]	12024	7674	...	...	1014	668

1992

	Total Gross	Total Net	Total private Gross	Total private Net	Public enterprises Gross	Public enterprises Net	General government Gross	General government Net
1 Residential buildings	6175[a]	4198[a]	6175	4198	...	...	−	−
2 Non-residential buildings	...	...	...	...	...	...	...	...
3 Other construction	4930[a]	3162[a]	3968	2515	...	...	962	646
4 Land improvement and plantation and orchard development	...	...	...	...	...	...	...	...
5 Producers' durable goods	2914[a]	1609[a]	2786	1538	...	...	128	71
6 Breeding stock, dairy cattle, etc.	...	...	...	...	...	...	...	...
Total	14019[a]	8969[a]	12929	8252	...	...	1091	717

1993

	Total Gross	Total Net	Total private Gross	Total private Net	Public enterprises Gross	Public enterprises Net	General government Gross	General government Net
1 Residential buildings	6522[a]	4421[a]	6522	4421	...	...	−	−
2 Non-residential buildings	...	...	...	...	...	...	...	...
3 Other construction	5172[a]	3315[a]	4159	2638	...	...	1013	677
4 Land improvement and plantation and orchard development	...	...	...	...	...	...	...	...
5 Producers' durable goods	3017[a]	1651[a]	2883	1575	...	...	135	75
6 Breeding stock, dairy cattle, etc.	...	...	...	...	...	...	...	...
Total	14712[a]	9387[a]	13564	8635	...	...	1148	753

Germany

	1994							
	Total		Total private		Public enterprises		General government	
	Gross	Net	Gross	Net	Gross	Net	Gross	Net
1 Residential buildings	6865[a]	4645[a]	6865	4645	...	...	–	–
2 Non-residential buildings	...	...	...	...	...	...	...	...
3 Other construction	5420[a]	3471[a]	4361	2768	...	...	1058	704
4 Land improvement and plantation and orchard development	...	...	...	...	...	...	...	...
5 Producers' durable goods	3089[a]	1671[a]	2950	1593	...	...	139	77
6 Breeding stock, dairy cattle, etc.	...	...	...	...	...	...	...	...
Total	15373[a]	9787[a]	14176	9006	...	...	1197	781

	1995							
	Total		Total private		Public enterprises		General government	
	Gross	Net	Gross	Net	Gross	Net	Gross	Net
1 Residential buildings	7167[a]	4840[a]	7167	4840	...	...	–	–
2 Non-residential buildings	...	...	...	...	...	...	...	...
3 Other construction	5599[a]	3585[a]	4501	2859	...	...	1098	726
4 Land improvement and plantation and orchard development	...	...	...	...	...	...	...	...
5 Producers' durable goods	3150[a]	1688[a]	3006	1609	...	...	144	79
6 Breeding stock, dairy cattle, etc.	...	...	...	...	...	...	...	...
Total	15916[a]	10113[a]	14674	9308	...	...	1242	805

	1996							
	Total		Total private		Public enterprises		General government	
	Gross	Net	Gross	Net	Gross	Net	Gross	Net
1 Residential buildings	7365[a]	4963[a]	7365	4963	...	...	–	–
2 Non-residential buildings	...	...	...	...	...	...	...	...
3 Other construction	5677[a]	3624[a]	4561	2891	...	...	1116	733
4 Land improvement and plantation and orchard development	...	...	...	...	...	...	...	...
5 Producers' durable goods	3214[a]	1709[a]	3068	1629	...	...	146	80
6 Breeding stock, dairy cattle, etc.	...	...	...	...	...	...	...	...
Total	16257[a]	10296[a]	14994	9483	...	...	1263	813

[a] Value recorded at the beginning of the year (opening stock).

2.14 Stocks of reproducible fixed assets, by type of good and owner, in constant prices

Thousand million Deutsche marks

	1991							
	Total		Total private		Public enterprises		General government	
	Gross	Net	Gross	Net	Gross	Net	Gross	Net
At constant prices of: 1991								
1 Residential buildings	5575[a]	3803[a]	5575	3803	...	...	–	–
2 Non-residential buildings	...	...	...	...	...	...	...	...
3 Other construction	4466[a]	2865[a]	3595	2277	...	...	871	587
4 Land improvement and plantation and orchard development	...	...	...	...	...	...	...	...
5 Producers' durable goods	2722[a]	1493[a]	2605	1429	...	...	117	63
6 Breeding stock, dairy cattle, etc.	...	...	...	...	...	...	...	...
Total	12764[a]	8161[a]	11775	7510	...	...	989	651

Germany

1992

	Total Gross	Total Net	Total private Gross	Total private Net	Public enterprises Gross	Public enterprises Net	General government Gross	General government Net
At constant prices of: 1991								
1 Residential buildings	5725[a]	3892[a]	5725	3892	...	...	–	–
2 Non-residential buildings	...	...	...	...	...	...	...	...
3 Other construction	4601[a]	2948[a]	3709	2349	...	...	892	599
4 Land improvement and plantation and orchard development	...	...	...	...	...	...	...	...
5 Producers' durable goods	2854[a]	1576[a]	2729	1507	...	...	125	69
6 Breeding stock, dairy cattle, etc.	...	...	...	...	...	...	...	...
Total	13180[a]	8417[a]	12163	7749	...	...	1017	668

1993

	Total Gross	Total Net	Total private Gross	Total private Net	Public enterprises Gross	Public enterprises Net	General government Gross	General government Net
At constant prices of: 1991								
1 Residential buildings	5870[a]	3978[a]	5870	3978	...	...	–	–
2 Non-residential buildings	...	...	...	...	...	...	...	...
3 Other construction	4720[a]	3022[a]	3808	2413	...	...	912	609
4 Land improvement and plantation and orchard development	...	...	...	...	...	...	...	...
5 Producers' durable goods	2932[a]	1604[a]	2802	1531	...	...	130	73
6 Breeding stock, dairy cattle, etc.	...	...	...	...	...	...	...	...
Total	13522[a]	8604[a]	12480	7922	...	...	1042	682

1994

	Total Gross	Total Net	Total private Gross	Total private Net	Public enterprises Gross	Public enterprises Net	General government Gross	General government Net
At constant prices of: 1991								
1 Residential buildings	6033[a]	4080[a]	6033	4080	...	...	–	–
2 Non-residential buildings	...	...	...	...	...	...	...	...
3 Other construction	4839[a]	3096[a]	3908	2477	...	...	931	618
4 Land improvement and plantation and orchard development	...	...	...	...	...	...	...	...
5 Producers' durable goods	3002[a]	1624[a]	2868	1549	...	...	134	75
6 Breeding stock, dairy cattle, etc.	...	...	...	...	...	...	...	...
Total	13874[a]	8799[a]	12809	8106	...	...	1065	693

1995

	Total Gross	Total Net	Total private Gross	Total private Net	Public enterprises Gross	Public enterprises Net	General government Gross	General government Net
At constant prices of: 1991								
1 Residential buildings	6202[a]	4185[a]	6202	4185	...	...	–	–
2 Non-residential buildings	...	...	...	...	...	...	...	...
3 Other construction	4952[a]	3164[a]	4003	2538	...	...	949	627
4 Land improvement and plantation and orchard development	...	...	...	...	...	...	...	...
5 Producers' durable goods	3061[a]	1640[a]	2923	1564	...	...	138	76
6 Breeding stock, dairy cattle, etc.	...	...	...	...	...	...	...	...
Total	14214[a]	8989[a]	13127	8286	...	...	1087	703

Germany

	1996							
	Total		Total private		Public enterprises		General government	
	Gross	Net	Gross	Net	Gross	Net	Gross	Net
	At constant prices of: 1991							
1 Residential buildings	6370[a]	4288[a]	6370	4288	...	...	–	–
2 Non-residential buildings	...	...	...	...	...	...	...	...
3 Other construction	5056[a]	3222[a]	4089	2588	...	...	967	634
4 Land improvement and plantation and orchard development	...	...	...	...	...	...	...	...
5 Producers' durable goods	3121[a]	1659[a]	2981	1583	...	...	140	76
6 Breeding stock, dairy cattle, etc.	...	...	...	...	...	...	...	...
Total	14547[a]	9169[a]	13440	8459	...	...	1107	710

a Value recorded at the beginning of the year (opening stock).

2.15 Stocks of reproducible fixed assets, by kind of activity, in current prices

Thousand million Deutsche marks

	1991		1992		1993		1994		1995		1996	
	Gross	Net	Gross	Net	Gross	Net	Gross	Net	Gross	Net	Gross	Net
1 Residential buildings [a]	5720	3903	6175	4198	6522	4421	6865	4645	7167	4840	7365	4963
2 Non-residential buildings	...	...	...	...	...	...	...	...	...	...	...	...
3 Other construction [abc]	4571	2933	4930	3162	5172	3315	5420	3471	5599	3585	5677	3624
A Industries [a]	3449	2170	3723	2345	3900	2459	4090	2581	4219	2666	4276	2697
1 Agriculture [a]	270	145	285	152	291	154	303	159	305	159	308	159
2 Mining and quarrying	...	...	...	...	...	...	...	...	...	...	...	...
3 Manufacturing [ad]	713	367	757	390	770	396	780	398	778	394	...	...
4 Electricity, gas and water	...	...	...	...	...	...	...	...	...	...	...	...
5 Construction [a]	56	34	61	36	64	38	68	41	71	43	...	...
6 Wholesale and retail trade [a]	370	246	403	268	424	282	448	296	466	308	...	...
7 Transport and communication [a]	530	303	571	328	594	341	614	351	629	357	...	...
8 Finance, etc. [a]	204	149	224	163	243	176	257	185	264	189	...	...
9 Community, social and personal services [a]	809	595	890	654	964	707	1051	773	1128	833	...	...
B Producers of government services [ae]	895	604	962	646	1013	677	1058	704	1098	726	1116	733
C Other producers [a]	227	159	245	170	260	179	272	187	282	193	285	194
4 Land improvement and development and plantation and orchard development	...	...	...	...	...	...	...	...	...	...	...	...
5 Producers' durable goods [a]	2747	1506	2914	1609	3017	1651	3089	1671	3150	1688	3214	1709
A Industries [a]	2601	1428	2758	1524	2854	1560	2921	1578	2977	1593	3038	1614
1 Agriculture [a]	166	84	170	86	169	85	168	83	166	81	...	...
2 Mining and quarrying	...	...	...	...	...	...	...	...	...	...	...	...
3 Manufacturing [ad]	1043	566	1101	600	1132	608	1144	603	1147	598	...	...
4 Electricity, gas and water	...	...	...	...	...	...	...	...	...	...	...	...
5 Construction [a]	56	31	63	36	67	39	72	41	75	42	...	...
6 Wholesale and retail trade [a]	146	84	164	96	176	103	186	107	194	108	...	...
7 Transport and communication [a]	335	181	347	189	359	198	371	205	381	209	...	...
8 Finance, etc. [a]	45	27	50	30	54	32	56	33	62	36	...	...
9 Community, social and personal services [a]	549	324	597	350	627	357	652	364	677	375	...	...
B Producers of government services [a]	119	64	128	71	135	75	139	77	144	79	146	80

Germany

Thousand million Deutsche marks

	1991 Gross	1991 Net	1992 Gross	1992 Net	1993 Gross	1993 Net	1994 Gross	1994 Net	1995 Gross	1995 Net	1996 Gross	1996 Net
C Other producers [a]	27	14	28	15	29	15	29	15	29	15	30	16
6 Breeding stock, dairy cattle, etc.	...	...	...	...	...	...	...	...	...	...	...	...
Total [af]	13038	8341	14019	8969	14712	9387	15373	9787	15916	10113	16257	10296

a Value recorded at the beginning of the year (opening stock).
b Including item "Non-residential buildings".
c Includes item "Land improvement and plantation and orchard development".
d Item "quarrying" is included in item "manufacturing"
e Item "Producers of government services" does not include government civil engineering works.
f Public civil engineering is not contained in the data of this table.

2.16 Stocks of reproducible fixed assets, by kind of activity, in constant prices

Thousand million Deutsche marks

	1991 Gross	1991 Net	1992 Gross	1992 Net	1993 Gross	1993 Net	1994 Gross	1994 Net	1995 Gross	1995 Net	1996 Gross	1996 Net
At constant prices of: 1991												
1 Residential buildings [a]	5575	3803	5725	3892	5870	3978	6033	4080	6202	4185	6370	4288
2 Non-residential buildings	...	...	...	...	...	...	...	...	...	...	...	...
3 Other construction [abc]	4466	2865	4601	2948	4720	3022	4839	3096	4952	3164	5056	3222
A Industries [a]	3372	2122	3480	2190	3572	2250	3666	2311	3755	2368	3836	2416
1 Agriculture [a]	267	143	267	143	267	141	267	140	268	139	268	138
2 Mining and quarrying	...	...	...	...	...	...	...	...	...	...	...	...
3 Manufacturing [ad]	697	359	707	364	705	362	697	355	687	348	...	...
4 Electricity, gas and water	...	...	...	...	...	...	...	...	...	...	...	...
5 Construction [a]	55	33	57	34	58	35	61	37	63	38	...	...
6 Wholesale and retail trade [a]	361	240	376	251	388	257	400	264	412	271	...	...
7 Transport and communication [a]	518	296	535	307	549	314	563	321	573	324	...	...
8 Finance, etc. [a]	199	145	207	151	218	157	226	163	233	167	...	...
9 Community, social and personal services [a]	790	582	830	609	877	644	933	686	993	732	...	...
B Producers of government services [ae]	871	587	892	599	912	609	931	618	949	627	967	634
C Other producers [a]	223	156	229	159	236	163	242	166	248	169	253	172
4 Land improvement and development and plantation and orchard development	...	...	...	...	...	...	...	...	...	...	...	...
5 Producers' durable goods [a]	2722	1493	2854	1576	2932	1604	3002	1624	3061	1640	3121	1659
A Industries [a]	2578	1415	2702	1493	2775	1517	2840	1535	2896	1550	2953	1569
1 Agriculture [a]	162	82	161	82	159	79	157	77	154	75	...	...
2 Mining and quarrying	...	...	...	...	...	...	...	...	...	...	...	...
3 Manufacturing [ad]	1032	560	1072	584	1085	582	1092	575	1099	572	...	...
4 Electricity, gas and water	...	...	...	...	...	...	...	...	...	...	...	...
5 Construction [a]	56	30	61	35	66	38	70	40	73	41	...	...
6 Wholesale and retail trade [a]	145	83	160	94	173	101	184	106	192	107	...	...
7 Transport and communication [a]	335	181	349	191	365	202	379	210	387	212	...	...
8 Finance, etc. [a]	45	27	51	30	55	32	59	34	64	37	...	...
9 Community, social and personal services [a]	545	322	586	343	611	347	634	353	662	366	...	...
B Producers of government services [a]	117	63	125	69	130	73	134	75	138	76	140	76
C Other producers [a]	27	14	27	14	27	14	28	14	28	14	28	14
6 Breeding stock, dairy cattle, etc.	...	...	...	...	...	...	...	...	...	...	...	...
Total [af]	12764	8161	13180	8417	13522	8604	13874	8799	14214	8989	14547	9169

Germany

Thousand million Deutsche marks

	1991		1992		1993		1994		1995		1996	
	Gross	Net	Gross	Net	Gross	Net	Gross	Net	Gross	Net	Gross	Net

At constant prices of: 1991

a Value recorded at the beginning of the year (opening stock).
b Item "Land improvement and plantation and orchard development" is included in item "Other construction".
c Including item "Non-residential buildings".
d Quarrying is included in item "Manufacturing".
e Item "Producers of government services" does not include government civil engineering works.
f Public civil engineering is not contained in the data of this table.

2.17 Exports and imports of goods and services, detail

Million Deutsche marks

	1986	1987	1988	1989	1990	1991	1992	1993	1994	1995	1996	1997
Exports of goods and services												
1 Exports of merchandise, f.o.b.	...	...	...	...	...	630550	636950	602300	662150	715030	746180	...
2 Transport and communication	...	...	...	...	...	59700	61180	63380	64350	71890	78850	...
3 Insurance service charges	...	...	...	...	...	...	...	...	...	...	...	...
4 Other commodities	...	...	...	...	...	...	...	...	...	...	...	...
5 Adjustments of merchandise exports to change-of-ownership basis	...	...	...	...	...	...	...	...	...	...	...	...
6 Direct purchases in the domestic market by non-residential households	...	...	...	...	...	36870	34170	31890	30460	31090	32110	...
7 Direct purchases in the domestic market by extraterritorial bodies	...	...	...	...	...	...	...	...	...	...	...	...
Total exports of goods and services [a]	...	...	...	...	...	727120	732300	697570	756960	818010	857140	...
Imports of goods and services												
1 Imports of merchandise, c.i.f.	...	...	...	...	...	600960	593670	533940	580710	625930	641110	...
A Imports of merchandise, f.o.b.	...	...	...	...	...	600960	593670	533940	580710	625930	641110	...
B Transport of services on merchandise imports	...	...	...	...	...	...	...	...	...	...	...	...
C Insurance service charges on merchandise imports	...	...	...	...	...	...	...	...	...	...	...	...
2 Adjustments of merchandise imports to change-of-ownership basis	...	...	...	...	...	...	...	...	...	...	...	...
3 Other transport and communication	...	...	...	...	...	68000	74250	77560	81130	91770	98480	...
4 Other insurance service charges	...	...	...	...	...	...	...	...	...	...	...	...
5 Other commodities	...	...	...	...	...	...	...	...	...	...	...	...
6 Direct purchases abroad by government	...	...	...	...	...	...	...	...	...	...	...	...
7 Direct purchases abroad by resident households	...	...	...	...	...	60430	65280	68290	74090	73170	74520	...
Total imports of goods and services [a]	...	...	...	...	...	729390	733200	679790	735930	790870	814110	...
Balance of goods and services	...	...	...	...	...	−2270	−900	17780	21030	27140	43030	...
Total imports and balance of goods and services	...	...	...	...	...	727120	732300	697570	756960	818010	857140	...

a Exports and imports of goods for purposes of repair and improvement are reduced to the value of these services.

Germany

3.11 General government production account: total and subsectors

Million Deutsche marks

	1990					1991				
	Total govern-ment	Central govern-ment	State or provincial govern-ment	Local govern-ment	Social security funds	Total govern-ment	Central govern-ment	State or provincial govern-ment	Local govern-ment	Social security funds
Gross output											
1 Sales	...	...	...	...	...	92530	4710	22610	65120	90
2 Services produced for own use	...	...	...	...	...	556720	80580	172870	114260	189010
3 Own account capital formation	...	...	...	...	...	460	–	220	240	–
Gross output	...	...	...	...	...	649710	85290	195700	179620	189100
Gross input											
Intermediate consumption	...	...	...	...	...	332280	40410	43200	78540	170130
subtotal: Value added	...	...	...	...	...	317430	44880	152500	101080	18970
1 Indirect taxes, net	...	...	...	...	...	350	–	180	160	10
A Indirect taxes	...	...	...	...	...	350	–	180	160	10
B less: Subsidies	...	...	...	...	...	...	...	...	...	...
2 Consumption of fixed capital	...	...	...	...	...	20050	1290	6390	11620	750
3 Compensation of employees	...	...	...	...	...	297030	43590	145930	89300	18210
4 Net operating surplus	...	...	...	...	...	...	...	...	...	...
Gross input	...	...	...	...	...	649710	85290	195700	179620	189100

	1992					1993				
	Total govern-ment	Central govern-ment	State or provincial govern-ment	Local govern-ment	Social security funds	Total govern-ment	Central govern-ment	State or provincial govern-ment	Local govern-ment	Social security funds
Gross output											
1 Sales	104840	5670	25480	73610	80	111120	4770	26400	79780	170
2 Services produced for own use	616350	83890	188490	126040	217930	634860	83240	201120	130180	220320
3 Own account capital formation	470	–	220	250	–	470	–	220	250	–
Gross output	721660	89560	214190	199900	218010	746450	88010	227740	210210	220490
Gross input											
Intermediate consumption	372450	42240	46320	87750	196140	380460	40280	49060	94090	197030
subtotal: Value added	349210	47320	167870	112150	21870	365990	47730	178680	116120	23460
1 Indirect taxes, net	350	–	180	160	10	350	–	180	160	10
A Indirect taxes	350	–	180	160	10	350	–	180	160	10
B less: Subsidies	...	...	...	...	...	...	...	...	...	...
2 Consumption of fixed capital	21890	1440	7000	12610	840	23530	1550	7500	13540	940
3 Compensation of employees	326970	45880	160690	99380	21020	342110	46180	171000	102420	22510
4 Net operating surplus	...	...	...	...	...	...	...	...	...	...
Gross input	721660	89560	214190	199900	218010	746450	88010	227740	210210	220490

	1994					1995				
	Total govern-ment	Central govern-ment	State or provincial govern-ment	Local govern-ment	Social security funds	Total govern-ment	Central govern-ment	State or provincial govern-ment	Local govern-ment	Social security funds
Gross output											
1 Sales	116390	4590	27480	83950	370	119800	4920	28300	86280	300
2 Services produced for own use	658580	80260	208170	132310	237840	686540	79840	217050	137190	252460
3 Own account capital formation	470	–	220	250	–	470	–	220	250	–
Gross output	775440	84850	235870	216510	238210	806810	84760	245570	223720	252760
Gross input											

Germany

	1994					1995				
	Total govern-ment	Central govern-ment	State or provincial govern-ment	Local govern-ment	Social security funds	Total govern-ment	Central govern-ment	State or provincial govern-ment	Local govern-ment	Social security funds
Intermediate consumption	402560	37340	51190	100280	213750	423560	37220	53460	105730	227150
subtotal: Value added	372880	47510	184680	116230	24460	383250	47540	192110	117990	25610
1 Indirect taxes, net	350	–	180	160	10	350	–	180	160	10
A Indirect taxes	350	–	180	160	10	350	–	180	160	10
B less: Subsidies	...	...	...	...	...	...	...	...	...	...
2 Consumption of fixed capital	24540	1600	7830	14100	1010	25550	1630	8170	14680	1070
3 Compensation of employees	347990	45910	176670	101970	23440	357350	45910	183760	103150	24530
4 Net operating surplus	...	...	...	...	...	...	...	...	...	...
Gross input	775440	84850	235870	216510	238210	806810	84760	245570	223720	252760

	1996					1997				
	Total govern-ment	Central govern-ment	State or provincial govern-ment	Local govern-ment	Social security funds	Total govern-ment	Central govern-ment	State or provincial govern-ment	Local govern-ment	Social security funds
Gross output										
1 Sales	122030	5680	28490	87610	250	...	...	...	...	...
2 Services produced for own use	702660	80280	220700	133750	267930	...	...	...	...	...
3 Own account capital formation	470	–	220	250	–	...	...	...	...	...
Gross output	825160	85960	249410	221610	268180	...	...	...	...	...
Gross input										
Intermediate consumption	438330	38190	53750	104130	242260	...	...	...	...	...
subtotal: Value added	386830	47770	195660	117480	25920	...	...	...	...	...
1 Indirect taxes, net	350	–	180	160	10	...	...	...	...	...
A Indirect taxes	350	–	180	160	10	...	...	...	...	...
B less: Subsidies	...	...	...	...	...	...	...	...	...	...
2 Consumption of fixed capital	26200	1660	8390	15000	1150	...	...	...	...	...
3 Compensation of employees	360280	46110	187090	102320	24760	...	...	...	...	...
4 Net operating surplus	...	...	...	...	...	...	...	...	...	...
Gross input	825160	85960	249410	221610	268180	...	...	...	...	...

3.12 General government income and outlay account: total and subsectors

Million Deutsche marks

	1991					1992				
	Total govern-ment	Central govern-ment	State or provincial govern-ment	Local govern-ment	Social security funds	Total govern-ment	Central govern-ment	State or provincial govern-ment	Local govern-ment	Social security funds
Receipts										
1 Operating surplus	...	...	...	...	...	...	...	...	...	...
2 Property and entrepreneurial income	37250	19260	120	7990	10850	48870	29230	–780	9490	11960
3 Taxes, fees and contributions	1190230	368560	248940	87700	485030	1310850	407370	275240	96130	532110
A Indirect taxes	358460	222220	91800	44440	–	389840	240530	101470	47840	–
B Direct taxes	330760	145200	148720	36840	–	364900	159190	164310	41400	–
Income	317800	...	...	...	...	350720	...	...	...	...
Other	12960	...	...	...	...	14180	...	...	...	...
C Social security contributions	484320	–	–	...	484320	531660	–	–	...	531660
D Fees, fines and penalties	16690	1140	8420	6420	710	24450	7650	9460	6890	450
4 Other current transfers	42680	18670	94120	72410	76840	44970	21530	96110	77540	83600

Germany

Million Deutsche marks

	1991					1992				
	Total government	Central government	State or provincial government	Local government	Social security funds	Total government	Central government	State or provincial government	Local government	Social security funds
A Casualty insurance claims ..	1770	–	–	420	1350	1960	–	–	420	1540
B Transfers from other government subsectors	–	1870	74350	69030	74110	–	4800	74570	73840	80600
C Transfers from rest of the world	12190	11750	440	–	–	11770	11380	390	–	–
D Other transfers, except imputed	...	...	...	...	...	...	...	...	...	...
E Imputed unfunded employee pension and welfare contributions	28720	5050	19330	2960	1380	31240	5350	21150	3280	1460
Total current receipts	1270160	406490	343180	168100	572720	1404690	458130	370570	183160	627670

Disbursements

	Total	Central	State/prov	Local	Social sec	Total	Central	State/prov	Local	Social sec
1 Government final consumption expenditure	556720	80580	172870	114260	189010	616350	83890	188490	126040	217930
2 Property income	75690	44200	24140	8290	30	99360	64830	26150	9360	50
A Interest	75690	44200	24140	8290	30	99360	64830	26150	9360	50
B Net land rent and royalties ..	...	...	...	...	...	...	...	...	...	...
3 Subsidies	64950	39580	18530	3980	2860	59840	35190	15270	4400	4980
4 Other current transfers	556790	268530	118660	30810	358150	605500	269040	129560	35360	405350
A Casualty insurance premiums, net	5120	4700	–	420	–	5480	5060	–	420	–
B Transfers to other government subsectors	–	144600	66050	5520	3190	–	150100	72560	6640	4510
C Social security benefits	346670	–	–	–	346670	390640	–	–	–	390640
D Social assistance grants	80850	50220	16480	14150	–	87940	53900	17920	15790	330
E Unfunded employee welfare benefits	41920	9610	24710	6220	1380	44680	10280	26600	6340	1460
F Transfers to private non-profit institutions serving households	19640	3720	9950	4480	1490	22540	2730	11000	6150	2660
G Other transfers n.e.c.	...	...	...	...	...	...	...	...	...	...
H Transfers to rest of the world	62590	55680	1470	20	5420	54220	46970	1480	20	5750
Net saving	16010	–26400	8980	10760	22670	23640	5180	11100	8000	–640
Total current disbursements and net saving	1270160	406490	343180	168100	572720	1404690	458130	370570	183160	627670

	1993					1994				
	Total government	Central government	State or provincial government	Local government	Social security funds	Total government	Central government	State or provincial government	Local government	Social security funds

Receipts

1 Operating surplus	...	...	...	...	...	...	...	...	...	...
2 Property and entrepreneurial income	47530	27980	–580	9860	11170	50560	32920	–1420	10100	9800
3 Taxes, fees and contributions .	1359150	402860	292710	99340	564240	1439740	427200	305290	102760	604490
A Indirect taxes	409560	246900	113190	49470	–	443820	270120	123210	50490	–
B Direct taxes	363350	151780	168900	42670	–	367670	154260	170030	43380	–
Income	348710	...	...	...	...	353130	...	...	...	...
Other	14640	...	...	...	...	14540	...	...	...	...
C Social security contributions	563710	–	–	...	563710	603840	–	–	...	603840
D Fees, fines and penalties	22530	4180	10620	7200	530	24410	2820	12050	8890	650
4 Other current transfers	45780	27680	95490	84570	103400	50900	35480	95270	87020	98170

Germany

	1993					1994				
	Total govern-ment	Central govern-ment	State or provincial govern-ment	Local govern-ment	Social security funds	Total govern-ment	Central govern-ment	State or provincial govern-ment	Local govern-ment	Social security funds
A Casualty insurance claims	2090	–	–	440	1650	2260	–	–	480	1780
B Transfers from other government subsectors	–	11980	72440	80740	100200	–	17030	70430	82800	94780
C Transfers from rest of the world	11050	10370	680	–	–	11460	11200	260	–	–
D Other transfers, except imputed	...	...	...	...	...	...	...	...	...	...
E Imputed unfunded employee pension and welfare contributions	32640	5330	22370	3390	1550	37180	7250	24580	3740	1610
Total current receipts	1452460	458520	387620	193770	678810	1541200	495600	399140	199880	712460

Disbursements

1 Government final consumption expenditure	634860	83240	201120	130180	220320	658580	80260	208170	132310	237840
2 Property income	103300	64470	29490	10160	80	110460	71840	29030	10280	150
A Interest	103300	64470	29490	10160	80	110460	71840	29030	10280	150
B Net land rent and royalties	...	...	...	...	...	...	...	...	...	...
3 Subsidies	61900	36700	15400	5040	4760	69080	42150	16500	5560	4870
4 Other current transfers	658720	295360	144150	40000	444570	695670	301410	153490	42930	462880
A Casualty insurance premiums, net	5710	5270	–	440	–	3190	2710	–	480	–
B Transfers to other government subsectors	–	167510	85890	7610	4350	–	159010	94420	8510	3100
C Social security benefits	428750	–	–	–	428750	447030	–	–	–	447030
D Social assistance grants	94730	59190	16790	18250	500	101190	64560	15800	20230	600
E Unfunded employee welfare benefits	47280	10970	28120	6640	1550	57400	19880	29040	6870	1610
F Transfers to private non-profit institutions serving households	25140	2990	11870	7050	3230	25810	2560	12810	6830	3610
G Other transfers n.e.c.	...	...	...	...	...	...	...	...	...	...
H Transfers to rest of the world	57110	49430	1480	10	6190	61050	52690	1420	10	6930
Net saving	–6320	–21250	–2540	8390	9080	7410	–60	–8050	8800	6720
Total current disbursements and net saving	1452460	458520	387620	193770	678810	1541200	495600	399140	199880	712460

Germany

	1995					1996				
	Total government	Central government	State or provincial government	Local government	Social security funds	Total government	Central government	State or provincial government	Local government	Social security funds

Receipts

1 Operating surplus	...	...	...	...	...	...	...	...	...	...
2 Property and entrepreneurial income	39590	21850	−880	10390	8990	37100	19920	−1030	10500	8470
3 Taxes, fees and contributions	1499760	438270	319990	104480	637020	1510820	412770	327580	103980	666490
A Indirect taxes	447310	258410	138660	50240	–	452190	244560	153380	54250	–
B Direct taxes	391350	178920	168770	43660	–	368700	167990	161490	39220	–
Income	375760	...	...	...	...	351950	...	...	...	...
Other	15590	...	...	...	...	16750	...	...	...	...
C Social security contributions	635810	–	–	...	635810	665000	–	–	...	665000
D Fees, fines and penalties	25290	940	12560	10580	1210	24930	220	12710	10510	1490
4 Other current transfers	53270	29960	77380	86820	98980	56090	31670	84290	88470	110680
A Casualty insurance claims	2340	–	–	440	1900	2280	–	–	440	1840
B Transfers from other government subsectors	–	10690	51180	82640	95360	–	10590	57150	84170	107110
C Transfers from rest of the world	12920	12360	560	–	–	14620	14060	560	–	–
D Other transfers, except imputed	...	...	...	...	...	...	...	...	...	...
E Imputed unfunded employee pension and welfare contributions	38010	6910	25640	3740	1720	39190	7020	26580	3860	1730
Total current receipts	1592620	490080	396490	201690	744990	1604010	464360	410840	202950	785640

Disbursements

1 Government final consumption expenditure	686540	79840	217050	137190	252460	702660	80280	220700	133750	267930
2 Property income	129850	86940	32370	11060	240	129740	85140	33960	11170	230
A Interest	129850	86940	32370	11060	240	129740	85140	33960	11170	230
B Net land rent and royalties	...	...	...	...	...	...	...	...	...	...
3 Subsidies	71020	43280	16250	5990	5500	69120	37360	19760	6360	5640
4 Other current transfers	732390	283120	148690	48330	492120	747020	284120	153410	49720	518790
A Casualty insurance premiums, net	2930	2490	–	440	–	2620	2180	–	440	–
B Transfers to other government subsectors	–	136690	87810	12350	3020	–	153290	90220	12510	3000
C Social security benefits	475290	–	–	–	475290	501770	–	–	–	501770
D Social assistance grants	104560	68380	15300	20390	490	90710	54050	15610	20700	350
E Unfunded employee welfare benefits	61100	21460	30930	6990	1720	63030	21800	32330	7170	1730
F Transfers to private non-profit institutions serving households	27980	2450	13240	8150	4140	29700	2480	13820	8890	4510
G Other transfers n.e.c.	...	...	...	...	...	...	...	...	...	...
H Transfers to rest of the world	60530	51650	1410	10	7460	59190	50320	1430	10	7430
Net saving	−27180	−3100	−17870	−880	−5330	−44530	−22540	−16990	1950	−6950
Total current disbursements and net saving	1592620	490080	396490	201690	744990	1604010	464360	410840	202950	785640

Germany

3.13 General government capital accumulation account: total and subsectors

Million Deutsche marks

	1991					1992				
	Total govern-ment	Central govern-ment	State or provincial govern-ment	Local govern-ment	Social security funds	Total govern-ment	Central govern-ment	State or provincial govern-ment	Local govern-ment	Social security funds
Finance of gross accumulation											
1 Gross saving	36060	−25110	15370	22380	23420	45530	6620	18100	20610	200
A Consumption of fixed capital	20050	1290	6390	11620	750	21890	1440	7000	12610	840
B Net saving	16010	−26400	8980	10760	22670	23640	5180	11100	8000	−640
2 Capital transfers	9170	810	28660	35270	30	10360	250	27190	34650	30
A From other government subsectors	–	670	24410	30490	30	–	160	22340	29230	30
B From other resident sectors	8330	70	3480	4780	–	9180	30	3730	5420	–
C From rest of the world	840	70	770	–	–	1180	60	1120	–	–
Finance of gross accumulation	45230	−24300	44030	57650	23450	55890	6870	45290	55260	230
Gross accumulation											
1 Gross capital formation	72920	9200	15040	47030	1650	85300	10850	16160	56300	1990
A Increase in stocks	–	–	–	–	–	–	–	–	–	–
B Gross fixed capital formation	72920	9200	15040	47030	1650	85300	10850	16160	56300	1990
Own account	460	–	220	240	–	470	–	220	250	–
Other	72460	9200	14820	46790	1650	84830	10850	15940	56050	1990
2 Purchases of land, net	2110	160	620	1180	150	1910	550	360	810	190
3 Purchases of intangible assets, net	...	...	...	...	...	...	...	...	...	...
4 Capital transfers	64890	59630	52380	8180	300	55920	44710	54860	7860	250
A To other government subsectors	–	24740	29690	1080	90	–	21580	28940	1160	80
B To other resident sectors	58450	28450	22690	7100	210	52100	19310	25920	6700	170
C To the rest of the world	6440	6440	–	–	–	3820	3820	–	–	–
Net lending	−94690	−93290	−24010	1260	21350	−87240	−49240	−26090	−9710	−2200
Gross accumulation	45230	−24300	44030	57650	23450	55890	6870	45290	55260	230

	1993					1994				
	Total govern-ment	Central govern-ment	State or provincial govern-ment	Local govern-ment	Social security funds	Total govern-ment	Central govern-ment	State or provincial govern-ment	Local govern-ment	Social security funds
Finance of gross accumulation											
1 Gross saving	17210	−19700	4960	21930	10020	31950	1540	−220	22900	7730
A Consumption of fixed capital	23530	1550	7500	13540	940	24540	1600	7830	14100	1010
B Net saving	−6320	−21250	−2540	8390	9080	7410	−60	−8050	8800	6720
2 Capital transfers	11330	260	26330	35940	30	13800	1080	25920	33170	20
A From other government subsectors	–	190	21230	29780	30	–	150	19770	26450	20
B From other resident sectors	10060	30	3870	6160	–	11800	110	4970	6720	–
C From rest of the world	1270	40	1230	–	–	2000	820	1180	–	–
Finance of gross accumulation	28540	−19440	31290	57870	10050	45750	2620	25700	56070	7750
Gross accumulation											
1 Gross capital formation	85450	10250	15900	57180	2120	86270	10230	16500	57360	2180
A Increase in stocks	–	–	–	–	–	–	–	–	–	–

Germany

	1993					1994				
	Total government	Central government	State or provincial government	Local government	Social security funds	Total government	Central government	State or provincial government	Local government	Social security funds
B Gross fixed capital formation	85450	10250	15900	57180	2120	86270	10230	16500	57360	2180
Own account	470	–	220	250	–	470	–	220	250	–
Other	84980	10250	15680	56930	2120	85800	10230	16280	57110	2180
2 Purchases of land, net	1340	430	400	270	240	130	–150	390	–220	110
3 Purchases of intangible assets, net	...	...	...	...	...	...	...	...	...	...
4 Capital transfers	53540	42010	55460	7050	250	45650	33400	53140	5380	120
A To other government sub-sectors	–	20360	29490	1260	120	–	18820	26150	1330	90
B To other resident sectors	49520	17630	25970	5790	130	41640	10570	26990	4050	30
C To the rest of the world	4020	4020	–	–	–	4010	4010	–	–	–
Net lending	–111790	–72130	–40470	–6630	7440	–86300	–40860	–44330	–6450	5340
Gross accumulation	28540	–19440	31290	57870	10050	45750	2620	25700	56070	7750

	1995					1996				
	Total government	Central government	State or provincial government	Local government	Social security funds	Total government	Central government	State or provincial government	Local government	Social security funds

Finance of gross accumulation

1 Gross saving	–1630	–1470	–9700	13800	–4260	–18330	–20880	–8600	16950	–5800
A Consumption of fixed capital	25550	1630	8170	14680	1070	26200	1660	8390	15000	1150
B Net saving	–27180	–3100	–17870	–880	–5330	–44530	–22540	–16990	1950	–6950
2 Capital transfers	18810	7320	32920	33950	20	16090	1120	35530	33840	20
A From other government subsectors	–	1270	26650	27460	20	–	210	26750	27440	20
B From other resident sectors	17560	5780	5290	6490	–	13320	210	6710	6400	–
C From rest of the world	1250	270	980	–	–	2770	700	2070	–	–
Finance of gross accumulation	17180	5850	23220	47750	–4240	–2240	–19760	26930	50790	–5780

Gross accumulation

1 Gross capital formation	83090	10400	16490	52790	3410	77830	10300	15980	48330	3220
A Increase in stocks	–	–	–	–	–	–	–	–	–	–
B Gross fixed capital formation	83090	10400	16490	52790	3410	77830	10300	15980	48330	3220
Own account	470	–	220	250	–	470	–	220	250	–
Other	82620	10400	16270	52540	3410	77360	10300	15760	48080	3220
2 Purchases of land, net	30	–160	500	–380	70	–950	–780	240	–620	210
3 Purchases of intangible assets, net	...	...	...	...	...	...	...	...	...	...
4 Capital transfers	284050	278310	54120	5750	1270	45170	39360	55240	4790	200
A To other government sub-sectors	–	25590	27170	1430	1210	–	25590	27210	1510	110
B To other resident sectors	278080	246750	26950	4320	60	41320	9920	28030	3280	90
C To the rest of the world	5970	5970	–	–	–	3850	3850	–	–	–
Net lending	–349990	–282700	–47890	–10410	–8990	–124290	–68640	–44530	–1710	–9410
Gross accumulation	17180	5850	23220	47750	–4240	–2240	–19760	26930	50790	–5780

Germany

3.21 Corporate and quasi-corporate enterprise production account: total and sectors

Million Deutsche marks

	1991				1992				1993			
	\multicolumn{3}{c	}{Corporate and quasi-corporate enterprises}	Addendum: total including unincorporated	\multicolumn{3}{c	}{Corporate and quasi-corporate enterprises}	Addendum: total including unincorporated	\multicolumn{3}{c	}{Corporate and quasi-corporate enterprises}	Addendum: total including unincorporated
	Total	Non-financial	Financial		Total	Non-financial	Financial		Total	Non-financial	Financial	
Gross output													
Gross output	6388180[a]	6168490	219690	...	6706240[a]	6465620	240620	...	6697260[a]	6441740	255520	...
Gross input													
Intermediate consumption	4134170[a]	3936780	197390	...	4284720[a]	4069240	215480	...	4216730[a]	3991210	225520	...
1 Imputed bank service charge	117100[a]	–	117100	...	129290[a]	–	129290	...	135550[a]	–	135550	...
2 Other intermediate consumption	4017070[a]	3936780	80290	...	4155430[a]	4069240	86190	...	4081180[a]	3991210	89970	...
subtotal: Value added	2252680[a]	2230380	22300	...	2421080[a]	2395940	25140	...	2468460[a]	2438190	30270	...
1 Indirect taxes, net	79270[a]	65910	13360	...	99550[a]	83440	16110	...	101630[a]	83070	18560	...
A Indirect taxes	144220[a]	130860	13360	...	159390[a]	143280	16110	...	163530[a]	144970	18560	...
B less: Subsidies	64950[a]	64950	–	...	59840[a]	59840	–	...	61900[a]	61900	–	...
2 Consumption of fixed capital	336290[a]	329260	7030	...	366810[a]	358830	7980	...	391610[a]	382710	8900	...
3 Compensation of employees	1246030[a]	1176670	69360	...	1339240[a]	1262200	77040	...	1356670[a]	1275760	80910	...
4 Net operating surplus	591090[a]	658540	–67450	...	615480[a]	691470	–75990	...	618550[a]	696650	–78100	...
Gross input	6386850[a]	6167160	219690	...	6705800[a]	6465180	240620	...	6685190[a]	6429400	255790	...

	1994				1995				1996			
	\multicolumn{3}{c	}{Corporate and quasi-corporate enterprises}	Addendum: total including unincorporated	\multicolumn{3}{c	}{Corporate and quasi-corporate enterprises}	Addendum: total including unincorporated	\multicolumn{3}{c	}{Corporate and quasi-corporate enterprises}	Addendum: total including unincorporated
	Total	Non-financial	Financial		Total	Non-financial	Financial		Total	Non-financial	Financial	
Gross output													
Gross output	7000100[a]	6728130	271970	...	7267920[a]	6986860	281060	...	...	...	...	...
Gross input													
Intermediate consumption	4383410[a]	4149190	234220	...	4570340[a]	4333290	237050	...	4580480	4337080	243400	...
1 Imputed bank service charge	139680[a]	–	139680	...	137150[a]	–	137150	...	139990	–	139990	...
2 Other intermediate consumption	4243730[a]	4149190	94540	...	4433190[a]	4333290	99900	...	4440490	4337080	103410	...
subtotal: Value added	2601430[a]	2563470	37960	...	2714880[a]	2672400	42480	...	2787280	2743570	43710	...
1 Indirect taxes, net	109310[a]	87910	21400	...	109400[a]	84290	25110	...	114980	89010	25970	...
A Indirect taxes	178390[a]	156990	21400	...	180420[a]	155310	25110	...	184100	158130	25970	...
B less: Subsidies	69080[a]	69080	–	...	71020[a]	71020	–	...	69120	69120	–	...
2 Consumption of fixed capital	405210[a]	395690	9520	...	420260[a]	410020	10240	...	429360	418610	10750	...
3 Compensation of employees	1391370[a]	1307820	83550	...	1437560[a]	1350770	86790	...	1448530	1361010	87520	...
4 Net operating surplus	695540[a]	772050	–76510	...	747660[a]	827320	–79660	...	794410	874940	–80530	...
Gross input	6984840[a]	6712660	272180	...	7285220[a]	7005690	279530	...	7367760	7080650	287110	...

a Excluding private non-profit organizations.

3.22 Corporate and quasi-corporate enterprise income and outlay account: total and sectors

Million Deutsche marks

	1990			1991			1992			1993		
	Total	Non-financial	Financial	Total	Non-financial	Financial	Total	Non-financial	Financial	Total	Non-financial	Financial
Receipts												
1 Operating surplus [a]	...	...	...	591090	658540	–67450	615480	691470	–75990	618550	696650	–78100

Germany

Million Deutsche marks

	1990 Total	1990 Non-financial	1990 Financial	1991 Total	1991 Non-financial	1991 Financial	1992 Total	1992 Non-financial	1992 Financial	1993 Total	1993 Non-financial	1993 Financial
2 Property and entrepreneurial income	...	...	...	592450	82980	509470	653520	89790	563730	667370	91550	575820
A Withdrawals from quasi-corporate enterprises	...	...	...	8400	7710	690	8550	7820	730	8780	7970	810
B Interest [b]	...	...	...	536580	48030	488550	599820	58070	541750	606760	56650	550110
C Dividends	...	...	...	47470	27240	20230	45150	23900	21250	51830	26930	24900
D Net land rent and royalties	...	...	...	...	...	...	...	...	...	...	...	...
3 Current transfers	...	...	...	130810	45810	85420	143580	49690	94350	146700	45040	101970
A Casualty insurance claims	...	...	...	9750	9210	540	10250	9740	510	11490	10840	650
B Casualty insurance premiums, net, due to be received by insurance companies	...	...	...	70670	–	70670	78330	–	78330	86570	–	86570
C Current transfers from rest of the world	...	...	...	...	...	...	...	...	...	...	...	...
D Other transfers except imputed	...	...	...	216980	4700	212280	239620	5060	234560	249360	5270	244090
E Imputed unfunded employee pension and welfare contributions	...	...	...	3080	–	69970	3320	–	76690	3240	–	70880
Total current receipts	...	...	...	1314350	787330	527440	1412580	830950	582090	1432620	833240	599690

Disbursements

	1990 Total	1990 Non-financial	1990 Financial	1991 Total	1991 Non-financial	1991 Financial	1992 Total	1992 Non-financial	1992 Financial	1993 Total	1993 Non-financial	1993 Financial
1 Property and entrepreneurial income	...	...	...	1131140	741540	389600	1231320	792410	438910	1263520	820480	443040
A Withdrawals from quasi-corporations	...	...	...	...	...	–	...	...	–	...	...	–
B Interest [b]	...	...	...	595020	221110	373910	663350	249080	414270	687030	269230	417800
C Dividends	...	...	...	...	...	–	...	...	–	...	...	–
D Net land rent and royalties	...	...	...	...	...	...	...	...	...	...	...	...
2 Direct taxes and other current transfers n.e.c. to general government	...	...	...	47520	35750	11770	54700	42010	12690	50850	36560	14290
A Direct taxes	...	...	...	42770	31000	11770	43400	30710	12690	42890	28600	14290
B Fines, fees, penalties and other current transfers n.e.c.	...	...	...	4750	4750	–	11300	11300	–	7960	7960	–
3 Other current transfers	...	...	...	118390	38040	80770	129190	40600	89050	140330	43410	97230
A Casualty insurance premiums, net	...	...	...	10750	10210	540	11410	10900	510	12770	12120	650
B Casualty insurance claims liability of insurance companies	...	...	...	70670	–	70670	78330	–	78330	86570	–	86570
C Transfers to private non-profit institutions	...	...	...	...	...	...	...	...	...	...	...	...
D Unfunded employee pension and welfare benefits	...	...	...	29880	27810	2070	31890	29680	2210	33470	31280	2190
E Social assistance grants	...	...	...	7510	20	7490	8020	20	8000	7830	10	7820
F Other transfers n.e.c.	...	...	...	...	...	...	...	...	...	...	...	...
G Transfers to rest of the world	...	...	...	...	...	...	...	...	...	...	...	...
Net saving [a]	...	...	...	17300	–28000	45300	–2630	–44070	41440	–22080	–67210	45130
Total current disbursements and net saving	...	...	...	1314350	787330	527440	1412580	830950	582090	1432620	833240	599690

Germany

	1994 Total	1994 Non-financial	1994 Financial	1995 Total	1995 Non-financial	1995 Financial	1996 Total	1996 Non-financial	1996 Financial	1997 Total	1997 Non-financial	1997 Financial
Receipts												
1 Operating surplus [a]	695540	772050	–76510	747660	827320	–79660	794410	874940	–80530	...	...	...
2 Property and entrepreneurial income	666030	98650	567380	669820	92830	576990	671880	85720	586160	...	...	...
A Withdrawals from quasi-corporate enterprises	8970	8100	870	9260	8280	980	9450	8410	1040	...	...	...
B Interest [b]	579810	48250	531560	603780	60960	542820	606880	58050	548830	...	...	...
C Dividends	77250	42300	34950	56780	23590	33190	55550	19260	36290	...	...	...
D Net land rent and royalties	...	...	...	...	...	...	...	...	...	...	...	...
3 Current transfers	148440	43390	105300	154900	46620	108560	158420	46360	110000	...	...	...
A Casualty insurance claims	11300	10580	720	11040	10280	760	...	...	...	...	...	...
B Casualty insurance premiums, net, due to be received by insurance companies	89910	–	89910	90640	–	90640	...	...	...	...	...	...
C Current transfers from rest of the world	...	...	...	...	...	...	...	...	...	...	...	...
D Other transfers except imputed	263730	2710	261020	276070	2490	273580	...	2180	...	...	...	...
E Imputed unfunded employee pension and welfare contributions	3260	–	75910	3740	80	77010	...	30	...	...	...	...
Total current receipts	1510010	914090	596170	1572380	966770	605890	1624710	1007020	615630	...	...	...
Disbursements												
1 Property and entrepreneurial income	1328770	897280	431490	1347410	912660	434750	1398070	956010	442060	...	...	...
A Withdrawals from quasi-corporations	...	...	–	...	...	–	...	...	...	...	...	...
B Interest [b]	659740	259890	399850	675660	263850	411810	688770	271430	417340	...	...	...
C Dividends	...	...	–	...	...	–	...	...	...	...	...	...
D Net land rent and royalties	...	...	...	...	...	...	...	...	...	...	...	...
2 Direct taxes and other current transfers n.e.c. to general government	44170	30020	14150	44060	28430	15630	53790	37270	16520	...	...	...
A Direct taxes	37080	22930	14150	37480	21850	15630	47370	30850	16520	...	...	...
B Fines, fees, penalties and other current transfers n.e.c.	7090	7090	–	6580	6580	–	6420	6420	–	...	...	...
3 Other current transfers	136390	35920	100720	139590	37840	102030	143990	38950	102980	...	...	...
A Casualty insurance premiums, net	12750	12030	720	12500	11740	760	...	...	...	...	...	...
B Casualty insurance claims liability of insurance companies	89910	–	89910	90640	–	90640	...	...	...	...	...	...
C Transfers to private non-profit institutions	...	...	...	...	...	...	...	...	...	...	...	...
D Unfunded employee pension and welfare benefits	26090	23880	2210	28390	26090	2300	29270	26940	2330	...	...	...
E Social assistance grants	7890	10	7880	8340	10	8330	8660	10	8650	...	...	...
F Other transfers n.e.c.	...	...	...	...	...	...	...	...	...	...	...	...
G Transfers to rest of the world	...	...	...	...	...	...	...	...	...	...	...	...
Net saving [a]	680	–49130	49810	41320	–12160	53480	28860	–25210	54070	...	...	...
Total current disbursements and net saving	1510010	914090	596170	1572380	966770	605890	1624710	1007020	615630	...	...	...

a Including undistributed profits of unincorporated enterprises. b Including net land rent, etc.

Germany

3.23 Corporate and quasi-corporate enterprise capital accumulation account: total and sectors

Million Deutsche marks

	1990			1991			1992			1993		
	Total	Non-financial	Financial	Total	Non-financial	Financial	Total	Non-financial	Financial	Total	Non-financial	Financial
Finance of gross accumulation												
1 Gross saving	...	...	...	358400	306070	52330	369320	319900	49420	375000	320970	54030
A Consumption of fixed capital	...	...	...	341100	334070	7030	371950	363970	7980	397080	388180	8900
B Net saving	...	...	...	17300	−28000	45300	−2630	−44070	41440	−22080	−67210	45130
2 Capital transfers	...	...	...	102790	102790	–	97260	97260	–	98010	98010	–
A From resident sectors	...	...	...	102790	102790	–	97260	97260	–	98010	98010	–
B From rest of the world	...	...	...	...	...	...	...	...	...	...	...	...
Finance of gross accumulation [a]	...	...	...	461190	408860	52330	466580	417160	49420	473010	418980	54030
Gross accumulation												
1 Gross capital formation	...	...	...	595900	580960	14940	622340	604880	17460	596350	579520	16830
A Increase in stocks	...	...	...	12810	12800	10	−1720	−1620	−100	−9210	−9150	−60
B Gross fixed capital formation	...	...	...	583090	568160	14930	624060	606500	17560	605560	588670	16890
2 Purchases of land, net	...	...	...	−2110	−2380	270	−1910	−2380	470	−1340	−1920	580
3 Purchases of intangible assets, net	...	...	...	25900	19760	6140	29790	22690	7100	24410	15270	9140
4 Capital transfers	...	...	...	25900	20060	5840	30070	22860	7210	24810	15270	9540
A To resident sectors	...	...	...	25900	20060	5840	30070	22860	7210	24810	15270	9540
B To the rest of the world	...	...	...	...	...	...	...	...	...	...	...	...
Net lending	...	...	...	−158500	−189780	31280	−183920	−208200	24280	−146810	−173890	27080
Gross accumulation [a]	...	...	...	461190	408860	52330[b]	466580	417160	49420[b]	473010	418980	54030[b]

	1994			1995			1996			1997		
	Total	Non-financial	Financial	Total	Non-financial	Financial	Total	Non-financial	Financial	Total	Non-financial	Financial
Finance of gross accumulation												
1 Gross saving	411580	352250	59330	467480	403760	63720	464230	399410	64820	...	...	...
A Consumption of fixed capital	410900	401380	9520	426160	415920	10240	435370	424620	10750	...	...	...
B Net saving	680	−49130	49810	41320	−12160	53480	28860	−25210	54070	...	...	...
2 Capital transfers	90810	90810	–	328460	328460	–	92440	92440	–	...	...	...
A From resident sectors	90810	90810	–	328460	328460	–	92440	92440	–	...	...	...
B From rest of the world	...	...	...	...	...	...	...	...	...	...	...	...
Finance of gross accumulation [a]	502390	443060	59330	795940	732220	63720	556670	491850	64820	...	...	...
Gross accumulation												
1 Gross capital formation	656300	639140	17160	683640	665980	17660	672580	655780	16800	...	...	...
A Increase in stocks	16400	16430	−30	24750	24670	80	20110	20060	50	...	...	...
B Gross fixed capital formation	639900	622710	17190	658890	641310	17580	652470	635720	16750	...	...	...
2 Purchases of land, net	−130	−180	50	−30	−990	960	950	−10	960	...	...	...
3 Purchases of intangible assets, net	22440	17860	4580	32270	23840	8430	...	...	...	...	...	...
4 Capital transfers	23900	18830	5070	38400	27730	10670	44520	33020	11500	...	...	...
A To resident sectors	23900	18830	5070	38400	27730	10670	44520	33020	11500	...	...	...
B To the rest of the world	...	...	...	...	...	...	...	...	...	...	...	...
Net lending	−177680	−214730	37050	73930	39500	34430	−161380	−196940	35560	...	...	...
Gross accumulation [a]	502390	443060	59330[b]	795940	732220	63720[b]	556670	491850	64820	...	...	...

a Including private non-profit institutions.   b Including private non-profit organizations

Germany

3.32 Household and private unincorporated enterprise income and outlay account

Million Deutsche marks

	1986	1987	1988	1989	1990	1991	1992	1993	1994	1995	1996	1997
Receipts												
1 Compensation of employees	...	...	...	...	...	1611640	1741220	1777890	1822730	1882390	1900350	...
A Wages and salaries	...	...	...	...	...	1313560	1417700	1450870	1471810	1514180	1524340	...
B Employers' contributions for social security	...	...	...	...	...	228110	246830	256150	273950	285720	292430	...
C Employers' contributions for private pension and welfare plans	...	...	...	...	...	69970	76690	70870	76970	82490	83580	...
2 Operating surplus of private unincorporated enterprises	...	...	...	...	...	...	...	...	...	...	...	...
3 Property and entrepreneurial income	...	...	...	...	...	632030	681140	696150	754270	793740	832820	...
A Withdrawals from private quasi-corporations	...	...	...	...	...	451080	476130	483800	534380	579170	619960	...
B Interest [a]	...	...	...	...	...	163830	187010	192250	189040	193400	191960	...
C Dividends	...	...	...	...	...	17120	18000	20100	30850	21170	20900	...
D Net land rent and royalties	...	...	...	...	...	...	...	...	...	...	...	...
4 Current transfers	...	...	...	...	...	596210	663020	720620	753130	795060	814810	...
A Casualty insurance claims	...	...	...	...	...	58500	65510	72370	75660	76460	79340	...
B Social security benefits	...	...	...	...	...	346670	390640	428750	448030	475290	501770	...
C Social assistance grants	...	...	...	...	...	80850	87940	94730	101190	104560	90710	...
D Unfunded employee pension and welfare benefits	...	...	...	...	...	72420	77250	81460	84240	90470	93480	...
E Transfers from general government	...	...	...	...	...	19640	22540	25140	25810	27980	29700	...
F Transfers from rest of the world	...	...	...	...	...	3580	3430	3280	3460	3430	2760	...
G Other transfers n.e.c.	...	...	...	...	...	14550	15710	14890	14740	16870	17050	...
Total current receipts [b]	...	...	...	...	...	2839880	3085380	3194660	3330130	3471190	3547980	...
Disbursements												
1 Final consumption expenditure	...	...	...	...	...	1630330	1755510	1829260	1906020	1979190	2045400	...
A Market purchases	...	...	...	...	...	1592830	1712550	1782490	1856900	1924580	1987910	...
B Gross rents of owner-occupied housing	...	...	...	...	...	...	...	...	...	...	...	...
C Consumption from own-account production	...	...	...	...	...	37500	42960	46770	49120	54610	57490	...
2 Property income	...	...	...	...	...	30190	35790	40140	39880	40740	39890	...
A Interest	...	...	...	...	...	30190	35790	40140	39880	40740	39890	...
Consumer debt	...	...	...	...	...	30190	35790	40140	39880	40740	39890	...
Mortgages	...	...	...	...	...	...	...	...	...	...	...	...
Other	...	...	...	...	...	...	...	...	...	...	...	...
B Net land rent and royalties	...	...	...	...	...	...	...	...	...	...	...	...
3 Direct taxes and other current transfers n.e.c. to general government	...	...	...	...	...	780350	861090	894020	946210	1002270	997930	...
A Social security contributions	...	...	...	...	...	482800	529650	561520	601600	633170	662120	...
B Direct taxes	...	...	...	...	...	285610	318290	317930	327290	350390	317300	...
Income taxes	...	...	...	...	...	279380	310860	310080	319370	342650	309580	...
Other	...	...	...	...	...	6230	7430	7850	7920	7740	7720	...
C Fees, fines and penalties	...	...	...	...	...	11940	13150	14570	17320	18710	18510	...

Germany

Million Deutsche marks

	1986	1987	1988	1989	1990	1991	1992	1993	1994	1995	1996	1997
4 Other current transfers	...	...	...	...	...	158050	174500	176630	187240	196480	201010	...
A Net casualty insurance premiums	...	...	...	...	...	58900	66120	73030	76320	77350	80050	...
B Transfers to private non-profit institutions serving households	...	...	...	...	...	...	...	...	...	...	...	...
C Transfers to rest of the world	...	...	...	...	...	16510	18220	19370	20230	20430	20320	...
D Other current transfers, except imputed	...	...	...	...	...	12670	13470	13360	13720	16210	17060	...
E Imputed employee pension and welfare contributions	...	...	...	...	...	69970	76690	70870	76970	82490	83580	...
Net saving	...	...	...	...	...	240960	258490	254610	250780	252510	263750	...
Total current disbursements and net saving [b]	...	...	...	...	...	2839880	3085380	3194660	3330130	3471190	3547980	...

  a Including net land rent, etc.   b Including private non-profit institutions.

3.33 Household and private unincorporated enterprise capital accumulation account

Million Deutsche marks

	1986	1987	1988	1989	1990	1991	1992	1993	1994	1995	1996	1997
Finance of gross accumulation												
1 Gross saving	...	...	...	...	...	240960	258490	254610	250780	252510	263750	...
A Consumption of fixed capital	...	...	...	...	...	...	...	...	...	...	...	...
B Net saving [a]	...	...	...	...	...	240960	258490	254610	250780	252510	263750	...
2 Capital transfers	...	...	...	...	...	22510	25670	18980	17800	26340	27530	...
A From resident sectors	...	...	...	...	...	22490	25650	18960	17770	26320	27510	...
B From rest of the world	...	...	...	...	...	20	20	20	30	20	20	...
Total finance of gross accumulation	...	...	...	...	...	263470	284160	273590	268580	278850	291280	...
Gross accumulation												
1 Gross capital formation	...	...	...	...	...	...	...	...	...	...	...	...
2 Purchases of land, net	...	...	...	...	...	...	...	...	...	...	...	...
3 Purchases of intangibles, net	...	...	...	...	...	...	...	...	...	...	...	...
4 Capital transfers	...	...	...	...	...	49750	50490	53270	55500	56520	58190	...
A To resident sectors	...	...	...	...	...	49260	49920	52700	54840	55860	57430	...
B To the rest of the world	...	...	...	...	...	490	570	570	660	660	760	...
Net lending	...	...	...	...	...	213720	233670	220320	213080	222330	233090	...
Total gross accumulation	...	...	...	...	...	263470	284160	273590	268580	278850	291280	...

  a Excluding undistributed profits of unincorporated enterprises.

3.51 External transactions, current account: detail

Million Deutsche marks

	1986	1987	1988	1989	1990	1991	1992	1993	1994	1995	1996	1997
Payments to the rest of the world												
1 Imports of goods and services [a]	...	...	...	...	...	729390	733200	679790	735930	790870	814110	...
A Imports of merchandise, c.i.f. [b]	...	...	...	...	...	600960	593670	533940	580710	625930	641110	...
B Other	...	...	...	...	...	128430	139530	145850	155220	164940	173000	...
2 Factor income to rest of the world	...	...	...	...	...	93390	108300	121890	131860	151790	162110	...
A Compensation of employees	...	...	...	...	...	4980	6450	6660	6780	7890	8340	...

Germany

Million Deutsche marks

	1986	1987	1988	1989	1990	1991	1992	1993	1994	1995	1996	1997
B Property and entrepreneurial income	...	...	...	...	...	88410	101850	115230	125080	143900	153770	...
By general government	...	...	...	...	...	13670	17600	26260	29620	22800	22650	...
By corporate and quasi-corporate enterprises	...	...	...	...	...	74740	84250	88970	95460	121100	131120	...
By other	...	...	...	...	...	...	...	...	...	...	...	...
3 Current transfers to the rest of the world	...	...	...	...	...	80510	73860	77990	82900	82810	81260	...
A Indirect taxes by general government to supranational organizations	...	...	...	...	...	...	...	...	...	...	...	...
B Other current transfers	...	...	...	...	...	80510	73860	77990	82900	82810	81260	...
By general government	...	...	...	...	...	62590	54220	57110	61050	60530	59190	...
By other resident sectors	...	...	...	...	...	17920	19640	20880	21850	22280	22070	...
4 Surplus of the nation on current transactions	...	...	...	...	...	−33400	−34300	−34980	−48260	−48370	−40760	...
Payments to the rest of the world and surplus of the nation on current transfers	...	...	...	...	...	869890	881060	844690	902430	977100	1016720	...

Receipts from the rest of the world

	1986	1987	1988	1989	1990	1991	1992	1993	1994	1995	1996	1997
1 Exports of goods and services [a]	...	...	...	...	...	727120	732300	697570	756960	818010	857140	...
A Exports of merchandise, f.o.b.	...	...	...	...	...	630550	636950	602300	662150	715030	746180	...
B Other	...	...	...	...	...	96570	95350	95270	94810	102980	110960	...
2 Factor income from rest of the world	...	...	...	...	...	121890	127300	126990	123860	135390	134110	...
A Compensation of employees	...	...	...	...	...	8770	8390	7670	7030	6340	6240	...
B Property and entrepreneurial income	...	...	...	...	...	113120	118910	119320	116830	129050	127870	...
By general government	...	...	...	...	...	300	230	240	340	290	290	...
By corporate and quasi-corporate enterprises	...	...	...	...	...	96890	104110	107100	103470	115000	113840	...
By other	...	...	...	...	...	15930	14570	11980	13020	13760	13740	...
3 Current transfers from rest of the world	...	...	...	...	...	20880	21460	20130	21610	23700	25470	...
A Subsidies to general government from supranational organizations	...	...	...	...	...	...	...	...	...	...	...	...
B Other current transfers	...	...	...	...	...	20880	21460	20130	21610	23700	25470	...
To general government	...	...	...	...	...	16090	16990	15770	17000	19040	21530	...
To other resident sectors	...	...	...	...	...	4790	4470	4360	4610	4660	3940	...
Receipts from the rest of the world on current transfers	...	...	...	...	...	869890	881060	844690	902430	977100	1016720	...

[a] Exports and imports of goods for purposes of repair and improvement are reduced to the value of these services.

[b] Imports of merchandise are recorded F.O.B.

3.52 External transactions, capital accumulation account

Million Deutsche marks

	1986	1987	1988	1989	1990	1991	1992	1993	1994	1995	1996	1997
Finance of gross accumulation												
1 Surplus of the nation on current transactions	...	...	...	...	...	−33400	−34300	−34980	−48260	−48370	−40760	...
2 Capital transfers from rest of the world	...	...	...	...	...	860	1200	1290	2030	1270	2790	...
A By general government	...	...	...	...	...	840	1180	1270	2000	1250	2770	...
B By other resident sectors	...	...	...	...	...	20	20	20	30	20	20	...

Germany

Million Deutsche marks

	1986	1987	1988	1989	1990	1991	1992	1993	1994	1995	1996	1997
Total finance of gross accumulation	...	...	...	...	...	−32540	−33100	−33690	−46230	−47100	−37970	...

Gross accumulation

	1986	1987	1988	1989	1990	1991	1992	1993	1994	1995	1996	1997
1 Capital transfers to the rest of the world	...	...	...	...	...	6930	4390	4590	4670	6630	14610	...
A By general government	...	...	...	...	...	6440	3820	4020	4010	5970	3850	...
B By other resident sectors	...	...	...	...	...	490	570	570	660	660	10760	...
2 Purchases of intangible assets, n.e.c., net, from rest of the world	...	...	...	...	...	...	...	...	...	...	...	...
Net lending to the rest of the world	...	...	...	...	...	−39470	−37490	−38280	−50900	−53730	−52580	...
Total gross accumulation	...	...	...	...	...	−32540	−33100	−33690	−46230	−47100	−37970	...

4.1 Derivation of value added by kind of activity, in current prices

Million Deutsche marks

	1991 Gross output	1991 Intermediate consumption	1991 Value added	1992 Gross output	1992 Intermediate consumption	1992 Value added	1993 Gross output	1993 Intermediate consumption	1993 Value added	1994 Gross output	1994 Intermediate consumption	1994 Value added
All producers												
1 Agriculture, hunting, forestry and fishing	82910	41870	41040	81420	40810	40610	75940	39460	36480	76370	40310	36060
2 Mining and quarrying	...	...	...	...	...	...	...	...	...	...	...	...
3 Manufacturing	2270360	1445060	825300	2278830	1442990	835840	2135230	1347790	787440	2211790	1401870	809920
4 Electricity, gas and water	...	...	...	...	...	...	...	...	...	...	...	...
5 Construction [a]	338780	176970	161810	400590	209570	191020	426010	225740	200270	470080	253620	216460
6 Wholesale and retail trade, restaurants and hotels	...	...	...	...	...	...	...	...	...	...	...	...
A Wholesale and retail trade	1830630	1568110	262520	1885100	1608350	276750	1860810	1574930	285880	1912070	1606990	305080
B Restaurants and hotels	...	...	...	...	...	...	...	...	...	...	...	...
7 Transport, storage and communication	303900	149500	154400	329010	164590	164420	336410	168180	168230	351630	178350	173280
8 Finance, insurance, real estate and business services	457230	135140	322090	510060	148030	362030	561850	159580	402270	607740	172340	435400
A Financial institutions	149890	40570	109320	164500	43420	121080	175130	46580	128550	180080	49230	130850
B Insurance	69800	39720	30080	76120	42770	33350	80660	43390	37270	92100	45310	46790
C Real estate and business services [b]	237540	54850	182690	269440	61840	207600	306060	69610	236450	335560	77800	257760
Real estate, except dwellings	...	...	...	...	...	...	...	...	...	...	...	...
Dwellings	237540	54850	182690	269440	61840	207600	306060	69610	236450	335560	77800	257760
9 Community, social and personal services	...	...	...	...	...	...	...	...	...	...	...	...
Total, Industries	6386850	4017070	2369780	6705800	4155430	2550370	6685190	4081180	2604010	6984840	4243730	2741110
Producers of government services	649710	332280	317430	721660	372450	349210	746450	380460	365990	775440	402560	372880
Other producers	99140	29510	69630	111350	33100	78250	118910	35300	83610	126390	37540	88850
Total	7135700	4378860	2756840	7538810	4560980	2977830	7550550	4496940	3053610	7886670	4683830	3202840
less: Imputed bank service charge	...	−117100	117100	...	−129290	129290	...	−135550	135550	...	−139680	139680
Import duties	...	...	30100	...	...	31110	...	...	28530	...	...	30150
Value added tax	...	...	183760	...	...	198950	...	...	217110	...	...	234890
Other adjustments	...	...	...	...	...	...	...	...	...	...	...	...

Germany

Million Deutsche marks

	1991 Gross output	1991 Intermediate consumption	1991 Value added	1992 Gross output	1992 Intermediate consumption	1992 Value added	1993 Gross output	1993 Intermediate consumption	1993 Value added	1994 Gross output	1994 Intermediate consumption	1994 Value added
Total	7135700	4495960	2853600	7538810	4690270	3078600	7550550	4632490	3163700	7886670	4823510	3328200
memorandum item: Mineral fuels and power	3457400	...	...	...	...	...	...	...	...	...	...	...

	1995 Gross output	1995 Intermediate consumption	1995 Value added	1996 Gross output	1996 Intermediate consumption	1996 Value added	1997 Gross output	1997 Intermediate consumption	1997 Value added	Gross output	Intermediate consumption	Value added

All producers

	Gross output	Interm. consumption	Value added	Gross output	Interm. consumption	Value added						
1 Agriculture, hunting, forestry and fishing	77550	41700	35850	80490	43000	37490	...	...	...	...	...	...
2 Mining and quarrying	...	...	...	...	...	...	...	...	...	...	...	...
3 Manufacturing	2330960	1504660	826300	2336300	1499380	836920	...	...	...	...	...	...
4 Electricity, gas and water	...	...	...	...	...	...	...	...	...	...	...	...
5 Construction [a]	478940	256440	222500	461020	244530	216490	...	...	...	...	...	...
6 Wholesale and retail trade, restaurants and hotels	...	...	...	...	...	...	...	...	...	...	...	...
A Wholesale and retail trade	1962920	1655410	307510	1972260	1658840	313420	...	...	...	...	...	...
B Restaurants and hotels	...	...	...	...	...	...	...	...	...	...	...	...
7 Transport, storage and communication	359900	179660	180240	360920	182680	178240	...	...	...	...	...	...
8 Finance, insurance, real estate and business services	645340	184090	461250	682600	192810	489790	...	...	...	...	...	...
A Financial institutions	177520	50380	127140	183230	53360	129870	...	...	...	...	...	...
B Insurance	102010	49520	52490	103880	50050	53830	...	...	...	...	...	...
C Real estate and business services [b]	365810	84190	281620	395490	89400	306090	...	...	...	...	...	...
Real estate, except dwellings	...	...	...	...	...	...	...	...	...	...	...	...
Dwellings	365810	84190	281620	395490	89400	306090	...	...	...	...	...	...
9 Community, social and personal services	...	...	...	...	...	...	...	...	...	...	...	...
Total, Industries	7285220	4433190	2852030	7367760	4440490	2927270	...	...	...	...	...	...
Producers of government services	806810	423560	383250	825160	438330	386830	...	...	...	...	...	...
Other producers	135100	40130	94970	141630	41940	99690	...	...	...	...	...	...
Total	8227130	4896880	3330250	8334550	4920760	3413790	...	...	...	...	...	...
less: Imputed bank service charge	...	−137150	137150	...	−139990	139990	...	...	...	...	...	...
Import duties	...	...	31090	...	...	30490	...	...	...	...	...	...
Value added tax	...	...	235410	...	...	237210	...	...	...	...	...	...
Other adjustments	...	...	...	...	...	...	...	...	...	...	...	...
Total	8227130	5034030	3459600	8334550	5060750	3541500	...	...	...	...	...	...

a Item "structural steel erection" is included in item "manufacture of fabricated metal products, machinery and equipment".

b Item "real estate and buisness services" except item "dwelings" is included in item "community, social and personal services".

Germany

4.2 Derivation of value added by kind of activity, in constant prices

Million Deutsche marks

	1991 Gross output	1991 Intermediate consumption	1991 Value added	1992 Gross output	1992 Intermediate consumption	1992 Value added	1993 Gross output	1993 Intermediate consumption	1993 Value added	1994 Gross output	1994 Intermediate consumption	1994 Value added
At constant prices of: 1991												
All producers												
1 Agriculture, hunting, forestry and fishing	82910	41870	41040	88670	40560	48110	84900	39330	45570	83730	39900	43830
2 Mining and quarrying [a,b]	263740	173600	...	258350	171590	...	257100	171520	...	257190	172520	...
3 Manufacturing	2270360	1445060	825300	2245600	1440210	805390	2095600	1348120	747480	2154200	1386330	767870
4 Electricity, gas and water	...	...	...	...	...	...	...	...	...	...	...	...
5 Construction [c]	338780	176970	161810	376650	203680	172970	386440	214720	171720	416900	236260	180640
6 Wholesale and retail trade, restaurants and hotels [d]	1831240	1569490	...	1859430	1595300	...	1828570	1568940	...	1836270	1576250	...
A Wholesale and retail trade	1830630	1568110	262520	1859290	1593700	265590	1832260	1570210	262050	1846420	1583320	263100
B Restaurants and hotels	...	...	...	...	...	...	...	...	...	...	...	...
7 Transport, storage and communication	303900	149500	154400	321390	160130	161260	323480	159550	163930	336690	166910	169780
8 Finance, insurance, real estate and business services	457230	135140	322090	470780	143060	327720	491220	147570	343650	512490	154780	357710
A Financial institutions [e]	219690	80290	109320	224700	83820	110250	235540	85630	115730	246350	88500	120210
B Insurance [e]	...	...	30080	...	...	30630	...	...	34180	...	...	37640
C Real estate and business services [f]	237540	54850	182690	246080	59240	186840	255680	61940	193740	266140	66280	199860
Real estate, except dwellings	...	...	...	...	...	...	...	...	...	...	...	...
Dwellings	237540	54850	182830	246080	59240	186680	255680	61940	192140	266140	66280	198070
9 Community, social and personal services [d,f,g]	839300	326820	...	913370	360050	...	945200	373010	...	980860	387760	...
Total, Industries	6386850	4017070	2369780	6534100	4112980	2421120	6416200	4024030	2392170	6588480	4127780	2460700
Producers of government services [h]	748850	361790	317430	781470	387340	320790	782480	386230	320710	798120	396780	322690
Other producers	...	...	69630	...	...	73340	...	...	75540	...	...	78650
Total	7135700	4378860	2756840	7315570	4500320	2815250	7198680	4410260	2788420	7386600	4524560	2862040
less: Imputed bank service charge	...	−117100	117100	...	−119740	119740	...	−124710	124710	...	−131410	131410
Import duties	...	...	30100	...	...	29620	...	...	27150	...	...	27050
Value added tax	...	...	183760	...	...	191270	...	...	191040	...	...	202520
Other adjustments	...	...	...	...	...	...	...	...	...	...	...	...
Total	7135700	4495960	2853600	7315570	4620060	2916400	7198680	4534970	2881900	7386600	4655970	2960200

	1995 Gross output	1995 Intermediate consumption	1995 Value added	1996 Gross output	1996 Intermediate consumption	1996 Value added	1997 Gross output	1997 Intermediate consumption	1997 Value added	Gross output	Intermediate consumption	Value added
At constant prices of: 1991												
All producers												
1 Agriculture, hunting, forestry and fishing	85090	40190	44900	85400	39920	45480	...	...	...	...	...	...
2 Mining and quarrying [a,b]	265640	178940	...	278010	187550	...	...	...	...	...	...	...
3 Manufacturing	2226990	1449070	777920	2229860	1450730	779130	...	...	...	...	...	...
4 Electricity, gas and water	...	...	...	...	...	...	...	...	...	...	...	...
5 Construction [c]	415660	235840	179820	400120	226820	173300	...	...	...	...	...	...
6 Wholesale and retail trade, restaurants and hotels [d]	1852900	1590510	...	...	...	...	...	...	...	...	...	...

Germany

	1995 Gross output	1995 Intermediate consumption	1995 Value added	1996 Gross output	1996 Intermediate consumption	1996 Value added	1997 Gross output	1997 Intermediate consumption	1997 Value added	Gross output	Intermediate consumption	Value added
	At constant prices of: 1991											
A Wholesale and retail trade..	1867150	1600730	266420	1874990	1606280	268710	...	...	...	...	...	...
B Restaurants and hotels	...	...	...	...	...	...	...	...	...	...	...	...
7 Transport, storage and communication	343470	168000	175470	351750	170230	181520	...	...	...	...	...	...
8 Finance, insurance, real estate and business services	531580	161950	369630	557850	167350	390500	...	...	...	...	...	...
A Financial institutions [e]	254280	91530	124370	269460	93500	135470	...	...	...	...	...	...
B Insurance [e]	...	...	38380	...	...	40490	...	...	...	...	...	...
C Real estate and business services [f]	277300	70420	206880	288390	73850	214540	...	...	...	...	...	...
Real estate, except dwellings	...	...	...	...	...	...	...	...	...	...	...	...
Dwellings	277300	70420	204950	288390	73850	...	...	...	...	...	...	...
9 Community, social and personal services [dfg]	1019780	401730	...	1055140	414180	...	...	...	...	...	...	...
Total, Industries	6755360	4236450	2518910	6833120	4263060	2570060	...	...	...	...	...	...
Producers of government services [h]	813830	410980	321610	826410	421710	320980	...	...	...	...	...	...
Other producers	...	...	81240	...	...	83720	...	...	...	...	...	...
Total	7569190	4647430	2921760	7659530	4684770	2974760	...	...	...	...	...	...
less: Imputed bank service charge	...	–136360	136360	...	–148040	148040	...	...	...	...	...	...
Import duties	...	...	28050	...	...	27630	...	...	...	...	...	...
Value added tax	...	...	200350	...	...	200150	...	...	...	...	...	...
Other adjustments	...	...	...	...	...	...	...	...	...	...	...	...
Total	7569190	4783790	3013800	7659530	4832810	3054500	...	...	...	...	...	...

a Gross output and intermediate consumption of electricity, gas and water are included in item "Mining and quarrying".
b "Quarrying" is included in item "Manufacture of non-metallic mineral products".
c Item "structural steel erection" is included in item "manufacture of fabricated metal products, etc."
d Gross output and intermediate consumption of restaurants and hotels are included in item "Community, social and personal services".
e Gross output and intermediate consumption of insurance are included in item "Financial institutions".
f Item "real estate and buisness services" except item "dwelings" is included in item "community, social and personal services".
g Publishing is included in item "Community, social and personal services".
h Gross output and intermediate consumption of "Other producers" are included in item "Producers of government services".

4.3 Cost components of value added

Million Deutsche marks

	1990 Compensation of employees	1990 Capital consumption	1990 Net operating surplus	1990 Indirect taxes	1990 less: Subsidies received	1990 Value added	1991 Compensation of employees	1991 Capital consumption	1991 Net operating surplus	1991 Indirect taxes	1991 less: Subsidies received	1991 Value added
All producers												
1 Agriculture, hunting, forestry and fishing	...	...	...	...	...	...	16200	14080	17550	–6790[a]	...	41040
2 Mining and quarrying	...	...	...	...	...	...	...	...	...	...	...	...
3 Manufacturing	...	...	...	...	...	...	579930	91260	87630	66480[a]	...	825300
4 Electricity, gas and water	...	...	...	...	...	...	...	...	...	...	...	...
5 Construction [b]	...	...	...	...	...	...	110450	6770	42000	2590[a]	...	161810
6 Wholesale and retail trade, restaurants and hotels	...	...	...	...	...	...	...	...	...	...	...	...
A Wholesale and retail trade..	...	...	...	...	...	...	164640	18790	76980	2110[a]	...	262520
B Restaurants and hotels	...	...	...	...	...	...	...	...	...	...	...	...

Germany

Million Deutsche marks

	1990						1991					
	Compensation of employees	Capital consumption	Net operating surplus	Indirect taxes	less: Subsidies received	Value added	Compensation of employees	Capital consumption	Net operating surplus	Indirect taxes	less: Subsidies received	Value added
7 Transport, storage and communication	...	...	...	...	...	...	98490	38360	26800	-9250[a]	...	154400
8 Finance, insurance, real estate and business services[c]	...	...	...	...	...	...	69360	82350	49650	13720[a]	...	322090
A Financial institutions	...	...	...	...	...	...	...	...	...	...	...	109320
B Insurance	...	...	...	...	...	...	...	...	...	...	...	30080
C Real estate and business services[d]	...	...	...	...	...	...	...	75320	...	360[a]	...	182690
9 Community, social and personal services	...	...	...	...	...	...	...	...	...	...	...	...
Total, Industries	...	...	...	...	...	...	1246030	336290	708190	79270[a]	...	2369780
Producers of government services	...	...	...	...	...	...	297030	20050	...	350[a]	...	317430
Other producers	...	...	...	...	...	...	64790	4810	...	30[a]	...	69630
Total	...	...	...	...	...	...	1607850	361150	708190	79650[a]	...	2756840
less: Imputed bank service charge	...	...	...	...	...	...	...	...	117100	...	...	117100
Import duties	...	...	...	...	...	...	...	...	...	30100[a]	...	30100
Value added tax	...	...	...	...	...	...	...	...	...	183760[a]	...	183760
Other adjustments	...	...	...	...	...	...	...	...	...	...	...	...
Total	...	...	...	...	...	...	1607850	361150	591090	293510[a]	...	2853600

	1992						1993					
	Compensation of employees	Capital consumption	Net operating surplus	Indirect taxes	less: Subsidies received	Value added	Compensation of employees	Capital consumption	Net operating surplus	Indirect taxes	less: Subsidies received	Value added

All producers

1 Agriculture, hunting, forestry and fishing	14350	14760	16920	-5420[a]	...	40610	14500	14990	15990	-9000[a]	...	36480
2 Mining and quarrying	...	...	...	...	...	...	...	...	...	...	...	...
3 Manufacturing	598190	98430	66960	72260[a]	...	835840	573380	103910	36230	73920[a]	...	787440
4 Electricity, gas and water	...	...	...	...	...	...	...	...	...	...	...	...
5 Construction[b]	126720	7680	53230	3390[a]	...	191020	136700	8440	51720	3410[a]	...	200270
6 Wholesale and retail trade, restaurants and hotels	...	...	...	...	...	...	...	...	...	...	...	...
A Wholesale and retail trade	183610	21410	68020	3710[a]	...	276750	193780	23680	64300	4120[a]	...	285880
B Restaurants and hotels	...	...	...	...	...	...	...	...	...	...	...	...
7 Transport, storage and communication	107860	41340	22700	-7480[a]	...	164420	111130	43800	22430	-9130[a]	...	168230
8 Finance, insurance, real estate and business services[c]	77040	90030	53300	19820[a]	...	362030	80910	97160	57450	23400[a]	...	402270
A Financial institutions	...	...	...	...	...	121080	...	...	...	...	...	128550
B Insurance	...	...	...	...	...	33350	...	...	...	...	...	37270
C Real estate and business services[d]	...	82050	...	3710[a]	...	207600	...	88260	...	4840[a]	...	236450
9 Community, social and personal services	...	...	...	...	...	...	...	...	...	...	...	...
Total, Industries	1339240	366810	744770	99550[a]	...	2550370	1356670	391610	754100	101630[a]	...	2604010
Producers of government services	326970	21890	...	350[a]	...	349210	342110	23530	...	350[a]	...	365990
Other producers	73070	5140	...	40[a]	...	78250	78100	5470	...	40[a]	...	83610
Total	1739280	393840	744770	99940[a]	...	2977830	1776880	420610	754100	102020[a]	...	3053610
less: Imputed bank service charge	...	...	129290	...	...	129290	...	...	135550	...	...	135550

Germany

	1992						1993					
	Compensation of employees	Capital consumption	Net operating surplus	Indirect taxes	less: Subsidies received	Value added	Compensation of employees	Capital consumption	Net operating surplus	Indirect taxes	less: Subsidies received	Value added
Import duties	...	...	...	31110[a]	...	31110	...	...	...	28530[a]	...	28530
Value added tax	...	...	...	198950[a]	...	198950	...	...	...	217110[a]	...	217110
Other adjustments	...	...	...	...	...	...	...	...	...	...	...	...
Total	1739280	393840	615480	330000[a]	...	3078600	1776880	420610	618550	347660[a]	...	3163700

	1994						1995					
	Compensation of employees	Capital consumption	Net operating surplus	Indirect taxes	less: Subsidies received	Value added	Compensation of employees	Capital consumption	Net operating surplus	Indirect taxes	less: Subsidies received	Value added
All producers											
1 Agriculture, hunting, forestry and fishing	14900	15040	16930	−10810[a]	...	36060	15400	15070	16280	−10900[a]	...	35850
2 Mining and quarrying	...	...	...	...	...	...	...	...	...	...	...	...
3 Manufacturing	576450	104750	45160	83560[a]	...	809920	593790	105710	44160	82640[a]	...	826300
4 Electricity, gas and water	...	...	...	...	...	...	...	...	...	...	...	...
5 Construction [b]	148650	9060	55070	3680[a]	...	216460	151520	9570	58620	2790[a]	...	222500
6 Wholesale and retail trade, restaurants and hotels	...	...	...	...	...	...	...	...	...	...	...	...
A Wholesale and retail trade	195610	25180	76910	7380[a]	...	305080	200210	26560	73580	7160[a]	...	307510
B Restaurants and hotels	...	...	...	...	...	...	...	...	...	...	...	...
7 Transport, storage and communication	111840	45620	31570	−15750[a]	...	173280	109070	47400	40150	−16380[a]	...	180240
8 Finance, insurance, real estate and business services [c]	83550	102680	63170	25230[a]	...	435400	86790	108970	57490	28790[a]	...	461250
A Financial institutions	...	...	...	...	...	130850	...	...	...	...	...	127140
B Insurance	...	...	...	...	...	46790	...	...	...	...	...	52490
C Real estate and business services [d]	...	93160	...	3830[a]	...	257760	...	98730	...	3680[a]	...	281620
9 Community, social and personal services	...	...	...	...	...	...	...	...	...	...	...	...
Total, Industries	1391370	405210	835220	109310[a]	...	2741110	1437560	420260	884810	109400[a]	...	2852030
Producers of government services	347990	24540	...	350[a]	...	372880	357350	25550	...	350[a]	...	383250
Other producers	83120	5690	...	40[a]	...	88850	89030	5900	...	40[a]	...	94970
Total	1822480	435440	835220	109700[a]	...	3202840	1883940	451710	884810	109790[a]	...	3330250
less: Imputed bank service charge	...	...	139680	...	...	139680	...	...	137150	...	...	137150
Import duties	...	...	...	30150[a]	...	30150	...	...	...	31090[a]	...	31090
Value added tax	...	...	...	234890[a]	...	234890	...	...	...	235410[a]	...	235410
Other adjustments	...	...	...	...	...	...	...	...	...	...	...	...
Total	1822480	435440	695540	374740[a]	...	3328200	1883940	451710	747660	376290[a]	...	3459600

	1996						1997					
	Compensation of employees	Capital consumption	Net operating surplus	Indirect taxes	less: Subsidies received	Value added	Compensation of employees	Capital consumption	Net operating surplus	Indirect taxes	less: Subsidies received	Value added
All producers											
1 Agriculture, hunting, forestry and fishing	15180	...	...	...	...	37490	...	...	...	...	...	...
2 Mining and quarrying	...	...	...	...	...	...	...	...	...	...	...	...
3 Manufacturing	594660	...	...	...	...	836920	...	...	...	...	...	...
4 Electricity, gas and water	...	...	...	...	...	...	...	...	...	...	...	...
5 Construction [b]	145550	...	...	...	...	216490	...	...	...	...	...	...

Germany

	1996						1997					
	Compensation of employees	Capital consumption	Net operating surplus	Indirect taxes	less: Subsidies received	Value added	Compensation of employees	Capital consumption	Net operating surplus	Indirect taxes	less: Subsidies received	Value added
6 Wholesale and retail trade, restaurants and hotels	...	...	...	...	...	...	...	...	...	...	...	...
A Wholesale and retail trade ..	203770	...	...	...	...	313420	...	...	...	...	...	...
B Restaurants and hotels	...	...	...	...	...	...	...	...	...	...	...	...
7 Transport, storage and communication	107630	...	...	...	...	178240	...	...	...	...	...	...
8 Finance, insurance, real estate and business services [c]	87520	...	...	...	...	489790	...	...	...	...	...	...
A Financial institutions	...	...	...	...	...	129870	...	...	...	...	...	...
B Insurance	...	...	...	...	...	53830	...	...	...	...	...	...
C Real estate and business services [d]	...	...	...	...	...	306090	...	...	...	...	...	...
9 Community, social and personal services	...	...	...	...	...	...	...	...	...	...	...	...
Total, Industries	1448530	429360	934400	114980	...	2927270	...	...	...	...	...	...
Producers of government services	360280	26200	...	350	...	386830	...	...	...	...	...	...
Other producers	93640	6010	...	40	...	99690	...	...	...	...	...	...
Total	1902450	461570	934400	115370	...	3413790	...	...	...	...	...	...
less: Imputed bank service charge	...	...	139990	...	...	139990	...	...	...	...	...	...
Import duties	...	...	...	30490	...	30490	...	...	...	...	...	...
Value added tax	...	...	...	237210	...	237210	...	...	...	...	...	...
Other adjustments	...	...	...	...	...	...	...	...	...	...	...	...
Total	1902450	461570	794410	383070	...	3541500	...	...	...	...	...	...

  a Column 4 refers to indirect taxes less subsidies received.
  b Structural steel erection is included in item "Manufacture of fabricated metal products, machinery and equipment".
  c Column 1 and column 3 excluding item "dwellings"
  d "Real estate and Business services" except item "Dwellings" is included in item "community, social and personal services".

Germany, Federal Republic (Former)

General note

The preparation of national accounts statistics in the Federal Republic of Germany was undertaken by the Federal Statistical Office, Wiesbaden. The official estimates were published in the monthly bulletin *Wirtschaft und Statistik*. Detailed data as well as description of the sources and methods used for the national accounts estimation were published annually in Fachserie 18 *Volkswirtschaftliche Gesamtrechnungen*, Reihe 1 *Konten und Standardtabellen*. The estimates are in close accordance with the classifications and definitions recommended in the United Nations System of National Accounts (1968 SNA). The following tables have been prepared from successive replies to the United Nations National Accounts Questionnaire. Estimates shown include the relevant data relating to Berlin, for which separate data were not supplied. When the scope and coverage of the estimates differ for conceptual or statistical reasons from the definitions and classifications recorded in SNA, a footnote is indicated to the relevant tables. As a general principle, the statistical units in the case of the data provided in the ISIC classification are institutional units (e.g., enterprises). Only the ownership of dwellings (including owner-occupied housing) is shown in a functional delimitation and fully allocated to the enterprise sector. The enterprise sector comprises all enterprises, i.e. also those which according to SNA should be shown in the sector of private households or general government, respectively.

Gross domestic product

The main approach used to estimate GDP is the production approach.

Expenditures on the gross domestic product

The expenditure approach is used to estimate all components of GDP by expenditure type except gross fixed capital formation which is calculated mainly by the commodity-flow approach. Government final consumption expenditure is based on records from all sectors of general government. Private final consumption expenditure is estimated mainly from data on retail sales. Data for certain base years are derived mainly from censuses (trade census 1979, crafts census 1977, industrial production census (1979). Annual data are liked with these base year data by means of current turnover and other supply statistics. The estimates of gross fixed capital formation are based on quarterly production reports, monthly construction reports, statistics on building activity and the previously mentioned censuses. Exports and imports of goods are based on foreign trade statistics, while exports and imports of services are obtained mainly from the Central Bank. For the calculation of constant prices, price deflation is used for all expenditure groups.

Cost structure of the gross domestic product

Compensation of employees is calculated from three sources: social security statistics, census data extrapolated by current data and taxation statistics. Capital consumption is calculated at constant prices and at current replacement costs according to the perpetual inventory method. Indirect taxes and subsidies are taken directly from the general government accounts. Operating surplus is then obtained as a residual.

Gross domestic product by kind of activity

The table of GDP by kind of economic activity is prepared at market prices, i.e. producers' values. The production approach is used to estimate value added of most industries. The income approach is used to estimate value added of domestic services, private non-profit institutions and producers of government services. The value of agricultural production is defined as the difference between primary gross production and internally used quantities, times average prices, or, as the sum of sales, change in livestock and other stocks, own-account consumption, investment of exports. The basic statistics used are mainly data on utilization of agricultural production. Inputs are derived from bookkeeping records, foreign trade statistics and production and sales statistics from suppliers of agricultural input goods. The main sources for estimating mining and quarrying, manufacturing, electricity, gas and water and construction are the censuses of production industries, which provide benchmark data, and annual data taken from several sources. Data on intermediate consumption for these sectors are taken from the censuses and cost-structure statistics. For trade, the benchmark estimates are mainly based on the trade censuses 1979. Output is extrapolated by turnover data, while input is estimated from trade census, cost-structure statistics and annual trade reports. For the transport sector, cost-structure statistics are used to estimate parts of output and intermediate consumption for most subsectors. Turnover tax statistics are utilized for preparing the current output estimates.

Banking statistics, collected by central bank, and insurance statistics, collected by Federal Supervisory Board, provide the basis for estimating output and financial institutions including insurance. Input is estimated on the basis of bank company reports and insurance company reports. Rents are estimated separately for three different categories: old, medium and new buildings. The rents are based on data from censuses of buildings and dwellings which include owner-occupied dwellings. The data are extrapolated by quantity and price indexes. The data used to estimate value added of government services, are mainly based on receipts and expenditure statistics of general government. For private non-profit institutions output is estimated as the sum of

Germany, Federal Republic (Former)

costs for wages and salaries, estimated capital consumption and indirect taxes.

Double deflation is used in the calculations of constant prices, for all sectors except transport and real estate business services. Output of most sectors is deflated by producer price indexes. However, for most agricultural products, current quantities are multiplied by base year prices; for some transport and communication services, output is extrapolated by quantity indexes; and for insurance and business services, extrapolation is used. Deflation by purchase price indexes or specially constructed input indexes is done for almost all sectors. For trade, and partly for transportation and communication, however, constant input-output ratios are assumed.

1.1 Expenditure on the gross domestic product, in current prices

Million Deutsche marks

	1986	1987	1988	1989	1990	1991	1992	1993	1994	1995	1996	1997
1 Government final consumption expenditure	382550	397280	412380	418820	444070	467160	505480	513950	527660	...	...	...
2 Private final consumption expenditure	1066430	1108020	1153690	1220950	1320710	1446970	1536510	1591580	1646340	...	...	...
A Households	1042340	1082150	1126620	1192120	1289980	1412760	1498580	1550620	1603910	...	...	...
B Private non-profit institutions serving households	24090	25870	27070	28830	30730	34210	37930	40960	42430	...	...	...
3 Gross capital formation	376400	385220	420200	464530	519270	582030	577710	521160	562980	...	...	...
A Increase in stocks	2920	−560	10300	16010	11490	17770	−4940	−17010	12990	...	...	...
B Gross fixed capital formation	373480	385780	409900	448520	507780	564260	582650	538170	549990	...	...	...
Residential buildings	101830	102580	108610	117930	135860	151430	170110	177740	197320	...	...	...
Non-residential buildings	110780	113770	118830	127120	137350	147890	157370	149150	148670			
Other construction and land improvement, etc.										...	...	...
Other	160870	169430	182460	203470	234570	264940	255170	211280	204000	...	...	...
4 Exports of goods and services	580540	576610	619830	701430	778900	885730	940380	924700	1002050	...	...	...
5 less: Imports of goods and services	480630	476650	510120	581290	636950	734290	747080	705090	765630	...	...	...
equals: Gross domestic product	1925290	1990480	2095980	2224440	2426000	2647600	2813000	2846300	2973400	...	...	...

1.2 Expenditure on the gross domestic product, in constant prices

Million Deutsche marks

	1986	1987	1988	1989	1990	1991	1992	1993	1994	1995	1996	1997
At constant prices of: 1991												
1 Government final consumption expenditure	445840	452710	462330	454880	465030	467160	487890	485920	492770	...	...	...
2 Private final consumption expenditure	1189950	1230610	1264340	1300150	1370010	1446970	1477960	1480000	1488840	...	...	...
A Households	1162020	1201180	1234370	1269200	1337920	1412760	1442110	1443300	1452610	...	...	...
B Private non-profit institutions serving households	27930	29430	29970	30950	32090	34210	35850	36700	36230	...	...	...
3 Gross capital formation	438590	441630	473900	508740	547370	582030	558060	494580	530280	...	...	...
A Increase in stocks	4300	−610	12130	18080	15020	17770	−3060	−10460	19850	...	...	...
B Gross fixed capital formation	434290	442240	461770	490660	532350	564260	561120	505040	510430	...	...	...
Residential buildings	124580	123050	127620	133870	145240	151430	161050	161570	175620	...	...	...
Non-residential buildings	133600	135160	138500	143980	146190	147890	149530	137590	135420			
Other construction and land improvement, etc.										...	...	...
Other	176110	184030	195650	212810	240920	264940	250540	205880	199390	...	...	...
4 Exports of goods and services	609300	611700	645250	710920	789050	885730	928220	908610	977390	...	...	...
5 less: Imports of goods and services	497580	518250	544820	590290	651060	734290	757830	724610	782480	...	...	...
equals: Gross domestic product	2186100	2218400	2301000	2384400	2520400	2647600	2694300	2644500	2706800	...	...	...

Germany, Federal Republic (Former)

1.3 Cost components of the gross domestic product

Million Deutsche marks

	1986	1987	1988	1989	1990	1991	1992	1993	1994	1995	1996	1997
1 Indirect taxes, net	194860	200700	209370	231550	253390	292020	321590	335090	359590	...	...	...
A Indirect taxes	236170	245500	257110	278330	302220	337530	365360	380170	408520	...	...	...
B less: Subsidies	41310	44800	47740	46780	48830	45510	43770	45080	48930	...	...	...
2 Consumption of fixed capital	243690	252300	263090	279450	303010	332890	359700	379290	388630	...	...	...
3 Compensation of employees paid by resident producers to ..	1074440	1119350	1163780	1216250	1315520	1430300	1528650	1543340	1564310	...	...	...
A Resident households	1072240	1117010	1161220	1213390	1308100	1410270	1501280	1514520	1534720	...	...	...
B Rest of the world	2200	2340	2560	2860	7420	20030	27370	28820	29590	...	...	...
4 Operating surplus	412300	418130	459740	497190	554080	592390	603060	588580	660870	...	...	...
A Corporate and quasi-corporate enterprises	412300	418130	459740	497190	554080	592390	603060	588580	660870	...	...	...
B Private unincorporated enterprises	...	...	...	...	...	...	...	...	...	...	...	...
C General government	...	...	...	...	...	...	...	...	...	...	...	...
equals: Gross domestic product ..	1925290	1990480	2095980	2224440	2426000	2647600	2813000	2846300	2973400	...	...	...

1.4 General government current receipts and disbursements

Million Deutsche marks

	1986	1987	1988	1989	1990	1991	1992	1993	1994	1995	1996	1997
Receipts												
1 Operating surplus	...	...	...	...	...	...	...	...	...	...	...	...
2 Property and entrepreneurial income	32830	26040	19020	30580	33310	34780	46120	43670	47090	...	...	...
3 Taxes, fees and contributions .	796710	828050	865110	929240	969130	1089010	1174210	1207960	1265630	...	...	...
A Indirect taxes	236170	245500	257110	278330	302220	337530	365360	380170	408520	...	...	...
B Direct taxes	237040	245940	255410	281760	271000	316020	342010	336040	334180	...	...	...
C Social security contributions	313390	325900	341090	356940	382770	421050	451850	475550	504800	...	...	...
D Compulsory fees, fines and penalties	10110	10710	11500	12210	13140	14410	14990	16200	18130	...	...	...
4 Other current transfers	36750	36210	39460	38890	40600	46170	49190	49170	52070	...	...	...
Total current receipts of general government	866290	890300	923590	998710	1043040	1169960	1269520	1300800	1364790	...	...	...
Disbursements												
1 Government final consumption expenditure	382550	397280	412380	418820	444070	467160	505480	513950	527660	...	...	...
A Compensation of employees	203300	211500	216920	222840	236290	252960	271040	280300	283780	...	...	...
B Consumption of fixed capital	13570	14070	14690	15550	16660	18010	19380	20530	21130	...	...	...
C Purchases of goods and services, net	165810	171860	180920	180590	191300	196360	215240	213300	222930	...	...	...
D less: Own-account fixed capital formation	380	400	400	410	430	420	430	430	430	...	...	...
E Indirect taxes paid, net	250	250	250	250	250	250	250	250	250	...	...	...
2 Property income	56130	56780	58940	59590	62390	73500	83020	90520	101380	...	...	...
A Interest	56130	56780	58940	59590	62390	73500	83020	90520	101380	...	...	...
B Net land rent and royalties ..	...	...	...	...	...	...	...	...	...	...	...	...
3 Subsidies	41310	44800	47740	46780	48830	45510	43770	45080	48930	...	...	...
4 Other current transfers	353850	371390	392530	409620	472900	573590	614250	656440	677860	...	...	...
A Social security benefits	220980	232050	245000	254320	269050	283750	302990	329580	345750	...	...	...

Germany, Federal Republic (Former)

Million Deutsche marks

	1986	1987	1988	1989	1990	1991	1992	1993	1994	1995	1996	1997
B Social assistance grants	52980	55500	55950	58350	60280	63930	68680	75580	77500	...	...	...
C Other	79890	83840	91580	96950	143570	225910	242580	251280	254610	...	...	...
5 Net saving	32450	20050	12000	63900	14850	10200	23000	−5190	8960	...	...	...
Total current disbursements and net saving of general government	866290	890300	923590	998710	1043040	1169960	1269520	1300800	1364790	...	...	...

1.5 Current income and outlay of corporate and quasi-corporate enterprises, summary

Million Deutsche marks

	1986	1987	1988	1989	1990	1991	1992	1993	1994	1995	1996	1997
Receipts												
1 Operating surplus	396010	391110	455810	487410	553530	536460	524760	474970	...	...	...	...
2 Property and entrepreneurial income received	321560	322020	337490	379110	458960	531520	600800	619400	...	...	...	...
3 Current transfers [a]	90830	97210	101940	107740	120120	128880	141070	143770	...	...	...	...
Total current receipts [ab]	808400	810340	895240	974260	1132610	1196860	1266630	1238140	...	...	...	...
Disbursements												
1 Property and entrepreneurial income	652050	650720	697680	774110	908130	995260	1078730	1073310	...	...	...	...
2 Direct taxes and other current payments to general government [a]	40860	36580	39840	45870	41500	45020	45150	44130	36810	...	...	...
3 Other current transfers [a]	82270	87400	92920	99400	108560	116900	127240	138110	...	...	...	...
4 Net saving [a]	33220	35640	64800	54880	74420	39680	15510	−17410	11790	...	...	...
Total current disbursements and net saving [ab]	808400	810340	895240	974260	1132610	1196860	1266630	1238140	48600	...	...	...

a Current income and outlay of corporate and quasi-corporate enterprises refers to corporate enterprises only.   b Data in this table refer to the non-consolidated receipts and disbursements.

1.6 Current income and outlay of households and non-profit institutions

Million Deutsche marks

	1986	1987	1988	1989	1990	1991	1992	1993	1994	1995	1996	1997
Receipts												
1 Compensation of employees	1079490	1124700	1169380	1221890	1317100	1422240	1515070	1529090	1548880	...	...	...
A From resident producers	1072240	1117010	1161220	1213390	1308100	1410270	1501280	1514520	1534720	...	...	...
B From rest of the world	7250	7690	8160	8500	9000	11970	13790	14570	14160	...	...	...
2 Operating surplus of private unincorporated enterprises	...	...	...	...	...	...	...	...	...	...	...	...
3 Property and entrepreneurial income [a]	377480	384090	424700	462490	521920	612530	646350	662740	...	...	...	...
4 Current transfers	392360	412890	433310	453310	480370	504340	542890	586740	...	...	...	...
A Social security benefits	220980	232050	245000	254320	269050	283750	302990	329580	345750	...	...	...
B Social assistance grants	52980	55500	55950	58350	60280	63930	68680	75580	77500	...	...	...
C Other	118400	125340	132360	140640	151040	156660	171220	181580	106860	...	...	...
Total current receipts	1849330	1921680	2027390	2137690	2319390	2539110	2704310	2778570	...	...	...	...
Disbursements												
1 Private final consumption expenditure	1066430	1108020	1153690	1220950	1320710	1446970	1536510	1591580	1646340	...	...	...
2 Property income	17930	17480	18170	19460	22100	25880	31540	36920	...	...	...	...
3 Direct taxes and other current transfers n.e.c. to general government	517070	543280	564250	602060	619360	696250	749850	768820	...	...	...	...

Germany, Federal Republic (Former)

Million Deutsche marks

	1986	1987	1988	1989	1990	1991	1992	1993	1994	1995	1996	1997
A Social security contributions	312750	325220	340330	356100	380450	414750	443160	466210	494880	...	...	...
B Direct taxes	196270	209430	214670	236340	228590	270530	295020	290180	294120	...	...	...
C Fees, fines and penalties	8050	8630	9250	9620	10320	10970	11670	12430		...	...	...
4 Other current transfers	114920	120360	125750	131680	145190	147700	162170	162620		...	...	...
5 Net saving	132980	132540	165530	163540	212030	222310	224240	218630	213900	...	...	...
Total current disbursements and net saving [a]	1849330	1921680	2027390	2137690	2319390	2539110	2704310	2778570		...	...	...

a Item "Property and entrepreneurial income" includes undistributed profits of unincorporated enterprises.

1.7 External transactions on current account, summary

Million Deutsche marks

	1986	1987	1988	1989	1990	1991	1992	1993	1994	1995	1996	1997
Payments to the rest of the world												
1 Imports of goods and services [a]	480630	476650	510120	581290	636950	734290	747080	705090	765630	...	...	...
A Imports of merchandise, c.i.f. [b]	390690	383890	411770	475320	521240	603560	603460	552720	604500	...	...	...
B Other	89940	92760	98350	105970	115710	130730	143620	152370	161130	...	...	...
2 Factor income to rest of the world	45670	48390	56020	62200	82890	102960	122700	135940	143440	...	...	...
A Compensation of employees	2200	2340	2560	2860	7420	20030	27370	28820	29590	...	...	...
B Property and entrepreneurial income	43470	46050	53460	59340	75470	82930	95330	107120	113850	...	...	...
By general government	9790	11590	11670	11340	12640	14030	17610	26210	25470	...	...	...
By corporate and quasi-corporate enterprises	33680	34460	41790	48000	62830	68900	77720	80910	88380	...	...	...
By other	...	...	...	...	...	...	...	...	...	...	...	...
3 Current transfers to the rest of the world [c]	44650	44980	51170	55640	100830	183700	197410	203580	202410	...	...	...
A Indirect taxes to supranational organizations	...	...	...	...	...	...	...	...	...	...	...	...
B Other current transfers	44650	44980	51170	55640	100830	183700	197410	203580	202410	...	...	...
4 Surplus of the nation on current transactions	82230	82330	89150	107020	85040	23050	44740	54160	60300	...	...	...
Payments to the rest of the world and surplus of the nation on current transfers	653180	652350	706460	806150	905710	1044000	1111930	1098770	1171780	...	...	...
Receipts from the rest of the world												
1 Exports of goods and services [a]	580540	576610	619830	701430	778900	885730	940380	924700	1002050	...	...	...
A Exports of merchandise, f.o.b.	508960	506850	548020	616360	663700	743940	804480	793200	875340	...	...	...
B Other	71580	69760	71810	85070	115200	141790	135900	131500	126710	...	...	...
2 Factor income from rest of the world	56480	60910	68040	86860	105490	123160	130800	133140	127240	...	...	...
A Compensation of employees	7250	7690	8160	8500	9000	11970	13790	14570	14160	...	...	...
B Property and entrepreneurial income	49230	53220	59880	78360	96490	111190	117010	118570	113080	...	...	...
By general government	120	90	120	140	230	300	230	240	340	...	...	...
By corporate and quasi-corporate enterprises	41580	45460	49120	62540	80690	94020	100900	105140	99060	...	...	...
By other	7530	7670	10640	15680	15570	16870	15880	13190	13680	...	...	...
3 Current transfers from rest of the world [c]	16160	14830	18590	17860	21320	35110	40750	40930	42490	...	...	...
A Subsidies from supranational organisations	...	...	...	...	...	...	...	...	...	...	...	...

Germany, Federal Republic (Former)

Million Deutsche marks	1986	1987	1988	1989	1990	1991	1992	1993	1994	1995	1996	1997
B Other current transfers	16160	14830	18590	17860	21320	35110	40750	40930	42490	...	...	...
Receipts from the rest of the world on current transactions	653180	652350	706460	806150	905710	1044000	1111930	1098770	1171780	...	...	...

a Exports and imports of goods for purposes of repair and improvement are reduced to the value of these services.
b Imports of merchandise, f.o.b. rather than c.i.f.
c Indirect taxes paid to and subsidies received from supranational organizations are included in "Current transfers".

1.8 Capital transactions of the nation, summary

Million Deutsche marks

	1986	1987	1988	1989	1990	1991	1992	1993	1994	1995	1996	1997
Finance of gross capital formation												
Gross saving	458630	467550	509350	571550	604310	605080	622450	575320	623280	...	...	...
1 Consumption of fixed capital	243690	252300	263090	279450	303010	332890	359700	379290	388630	...	...	...
A General government	13570	14070	14690	15550	16660	18010	19380	20530	21130	...	...	...
B Corporate and quasi-corporate enterprises	230120	238230	248400	263900	286350	314880	340310	358760	367500	...	...	...
C Other	...	...	...	...	...	...	...	...	...	...	...	...
2 Net saving	214940	215250	246260	292100	301300	272190	262750	196030	234650	...	...	...
A General government	32450	20050	12000	63900	14850	10200	23000	−5190	8960	...	...	...
B Corporate and quasi-corporate enterprises	33220	35640	64800	54880	74420	39680	15510	−17410	11790	...	...	...
C Other	149270	159560	169460	173320	212030	222310	224240	218630	213900	...	...	...
less: Surplus of the nation on current transactions	82230	82330	89150	107020	85040	23050	44740	54160	60300	...	...	...
Finance of gross capital formation	376400	385220	420200	464530	519270	582030	577710	521160	562980	...	...	...
Gross capital formation												
Increase in stocks	2920	−560	10300	16010	11490	17770	−4940	−17010	12990	...	...	...
Gross fixed capital formation	373480	385780	409900	448520	507780	564260	582650	538170	549990	...	...	...
1 General government	45310	46000	47500	50990	54160	58440	62670	61320	59930	...	...	...
2 Corporate and quasi-corporate enterprises [a]	328170	339780	362400	397530	453620	505820	519980	476850	490060	...	...	...
3 Other	...	...	...	...	...	...	...	...	...	...	...	...
Gross capital formation	376400	385220	420200	464530	519270	582030	577710	521160	562980	...	...	...

a Including gross fixed capital formation of private non-profit organizations.

1.9 Gross domestic product by institutional sectors of origin

Million Deutsche marks

	1986	1987	1988	1989	1990	1991	1992	1993	1994	1995	1996	1997
Domestic factor incomes originating												
1 General government	203300	211500	216920	222840	236290	252960	271040	280300	283780	...	...	...
2 Corporate and quasi-corporate enterprises [a]	1240570	1280390	1358760	1440710	1579330	1709830	1794770	1781950	1868460	...	...	...
A Non-financial	1237670	1277470	1354160	1433580	1575410	1706480	1792480	1774770		...	...	...
B Financial [a]	2900	2920	4600	7130	3920	3350	2290	7180		...	...	...
3 Households and private unincorporated enterprises	2530	2530	2520	2520	2630	2860	2960	3040	3150	...	...	...
4 Non-profit institutions serving households	40340	43060	45320	47370	51350	57040	62950	66630	69790	...	...	...
subtotal: Domestic factor incomes	1486740	1537480	1623520	1713440	1869600	2022690	2131710	2131920	2225180	...	...	...
Indirect taxes, net	194860	200700	209370	231550	253390	292020	321590	335090	359590	...	...	...

Germany, Federal Republic (Former)

Million Deutsche marks

	1986	1987	1988	1989	1990	1991	1992	1993	1994	1995	1996	1997
A Indirect taxes	236170	245500	257110	278330	302220	337530	365360	380170	408520	...	...	...
B less: Subsidies	41310	44800	47740	46780	48830	45510	43770	45080	48930	...	...	...
Consumption of fixed capital	243690	252300	263090	279450	303010	332890	359700	379290	388630	...	...	...
Gross domestic product	1925290	1990480	2095980	2224440	2426000	2647600	2813000	2846300	2973400	...	...	...

a Financial of Corporate and quasi-corporate enterprises refers to net of imputed bank service charges.

1.10 Gross domestic product by kind of activity, in current prices

Million Deutsche marks

	1986	1987	1988	1989	1990	1991	1992	1993	1994	1995	1996	1997
1 Agriculture, hunting, forestry and fishing	34000	30240	33720	37210	36740	34080	33730	29880	...	...	...	...
2 Mining and quarrying [a]	13580	12780	11180	11740	11390	12450	12660	12650	...	...	...	...
3 Manufacturing [abc]	620440	624690	652670	686010	741550	790660	799090	746310	765980	...	...	...
4 Electricity, gas and water	52330	55890	56660	57560	58840	61620	63680	63180	...	...	...	...
5 Construction [b]	100130	101680	106250	114660	127620	137250	152390	152700	162710	...	...	...
6 Wholesale and retail trade, restaurants and hotels	186050	193910	204470	214350	244650	277060	286890	283170	...	...	...	...
7 Transport, storage and communication	107310	111110	116870	125710	134200	143810	153650	155280	158970	...	...	...
8 Finance, insurance, real estate and business services [d]	239910	243520	257080	273460	288850	318010	350080	387100	415870	...	...	...
9 Community, social and personal services [cd]	256790	279570	309070	338680	386990	444610	505510	541670	...	...	...	...
Total, Industries	1610540	1653390	1747970	1859380	2030830	2219550	2357680	2371940	2476950	...	...	...
Producers of government services	217120	225820	231860	238640	253200	271220	290670	301080	305160	...	...	...
Other producers	46420	49280	51670	53920	58300	64570	70890	74920	78350	...	...	...
Subtotal	1874080	1928490	2031500	2151940	2342330	2555340	2719240	2747940	2860460	...	...	...
less: Imputed bank service charge	83690	82270	85150	88410	96280	111240	124070	132330	134620	...	...	...
plus: Import duties	17020	19150	19530	23380	24980	29280	30270	27670	29290	...	...	...
plus: Value added tax	117880	125110	130100	137530	154970	174220	187560	203020	218270	...	...	...
plus: Other adjustments	...	...	...	...	...	...	...	...	...	...	...	...
equals: Gross domestic product	1925290	1990480	2095980	2224440	2426000	2647600	2813000	2846300	2973400	...	...	...

a Quarrying is included in item "Manufacturing".
b Structural steel erection is included in item "Manufacturing".
c Publishing is included in item "Community, social and personal services".
d Business services and real estate except dwellings are included in item "Community, social and personal services".

1.11 Gross domestic product by kind of activity, in constant prices

Million Deutsche marks

	1986	1987	1988	1989	1990	1991	1992	1993	1994	1995	1996	1997
At constant prices of: 1991												
1 Agriculture, hunting, forestry and fishing	35150	32090	34480	34970	36430	34080	41390	37960	...	...	...	...
2 Mining and quarrying [a]	12630	12690	11770	12680	11210	12450	11900	11850	...	...	...	...
3 Manufacturing [abc]	689570	677000	698640	722600	762270	790660	768920	707450	723560	...	...	...
4 Electricity, gas and water	51360	54300	54910	56830	58170	61620	61380	59680	...	...	...	...
5 Construction [b]	126620	124560	127110	132460	136790	137250	140570	135270	139600	...	...	...
6 Wholesale and retail trade, restaurants and hotels	212370	216440	223520	233180	251400	277060	276900	270480	...	...	...	...
7 Transport, storage and communication	109390	113920	121770	127850	137630	143810	150670	150370	152770	...	...	...
8 Finance, insurance, real estate and business services [d]	266700	276310	287570	297550	310100	318010	324960	341260	357610	...	...	...

Germany, Federal Republic (Former)

Million Deutsche marks

	1986	1987	1988	1989	1990	1991	1992	1993	1994	1995	1996	1997
At constant prices of: 1991												
9 Community, social and personal services [c,d]	306300	324480	349890	370510	405800	444610	477980	496500	...	...	...	...
Total, Industries	1810090	1831790	1909660	1988630	2109800	2219550	2254670	2210820	2261920	...	...	...
Producers of government services	255610	258960	261700	262620	266910	271220	277140	279400	280930	...	...	...
Other producers	54150	55790	57470	59120	61570	64570	67350	69150	71400	...	...	...
Subtotal	2119850	2146540	2228830	2310370	2438280	2555340	2599160	2559370	2614250	...	...	...
less: Imputed bank service charge	86920	91570	95480	98870	105400	111240	114910	121060	125000	...	...	...
plus: Import duties	19010	21900	22080	23970	25900	29280	28860	26350	27950	...	...	...
plus: Value added tax	134160	141530	145570	148930	161620	174220	181190	179840	189600	...	...	...
plus: Other adjustments	...	...	...	...	...	...	...	...	...			
equals: Gross domestic product	2186100	2218400	2301000	2384400	2520400	2647600	2694300	2644500	2706800	...	...	...

a Quarrying is included in item "Manufacturing".
b Structural steel erection is included in item "Manufacturing".
c Publishing is included in item "Community, social and personal services".
d Business services and real estate except dwellings are included in item "Community, social and personal services".

1.12 Relations among national accounting aggregates

Million Deutsche marks

	1986	1987	1988	1989	1990	1991	1992	1993	1994	1995	1996	1997
Gross domestic product	1925290	1990480	2095980	2224440	2426000	2647600	2813000	2846300	2973400	...	...	...
plus: Net factor income from the rest of the world	10810	12520	12020	24660	22600	20200	8100	−2800	−16200	...	...	...
Factor income from rest of the world	56480	60910	68040	86860	105490	123160	130800	133140	127240	...	...	...
less: Factor income to the rest of the world	45670	48390	56020	62200	82890	102960	122700	135940	143440	...	...	...
equals: Gross national product	1936100	2003000	2108000	2249100	2448600	2667800	2821100	2843500	2957200	...	...	...
less: Consumption of fixed capital	243690	252300	263090	279450	303010	332890	359700	379290	388630	...	...	...
equals: National income	1692410	1750700	1844910	1969650	2145590	2334910	2461400	2464210	2568570	...	...	...
plus: Net current transfers from the rest of the world [a]	−28490	−30150	−32580	−37780	−79510	−148590	−156660	−162650	−159920	...	...	...
Current transfers from rest of the world	16160	14830	18590	17860	21320	35110	40750	40930	...	...	...	...
less: Current transfers to the rest of the world	44650	44980	51170	55640	100830	183700	197410	203580	...	...	...	...
equals: National disposable income	1663920	1720550	1812330	1931870	2066080	2186320	2304740	2301560	2408650	...	...	...
less: Final consumption	1448980	1505300	1566070	1639770	1764780	1914130	2041990	2105530	2174000	...	...	...
equals: Net saving	214940	215250	246260	292100	301300	272190	262750	196030	234650	...	...	...
less: Surplus of the nation on current transactions	82230	82330	89150	107020	85040	23050	44740	54160	60300	...	...	...
equals: Net capital formation	132710	132920	157110	185080	216260	249140	218010	141870	174350	...	...	...

a Indirect taxes paid to and subsidies received from supranational organizations are included in "Current transfers".

Germany, Federal Republic (Former)

2.1 Government final consumption expenditure by function, in current prices

Million Deutsche marks

	1986	1987	1988	1989	1990	1991	1992	1993	1994	1995	1996	1997
1 General public services	39510	42210	42290	43740	46130	...	...	...	...	...	...	...
2 Defence	51290	52300	52480	53790	52730	...	...	...	...	...	...	...
3 Public order and safety	29500	30790	31740	32990	35300	...	...	...	...	...	...	...
4 Education	74810	76370	77700	80060	84070	...	...	...	...	...	...	...
5 Health	115190	119940	129650	126010	136500	...	...	...	...	...	...	...
6 Social security and welfare	39830	41710	44260	47510	53160	...	...	...	...	...	...	...
7 Housing and community amenities	6160	6630	6490	6310	6380	...	...	...	...	...	...	...
8 Recreational, cultural and religious affairs	9130	9690	10020	10450	11140	...	...	...	...	...	...	...
9 Economic services	17130	17640	17750	17960	18660	...	...	...	...	...	...	...
A Fuel and energy	120	100	110	90	90	...	...	...	...	...	...	...
B Agriculture, hunting, forestry and fishing	2240	2270	2260	2330	2420	...	...	...	...	...	...	...
C Mining (except fuels), manufacturing and construction	210	220	250	200	210	...	...	...	...	...	...	...
D Transportation and communication	10710	10960	11040	11220	11590	...	...	...	...	...	...	...
E Other economic affairs	3850	4090	4090	4120	4350	...	...	...	...	...	...	...
10 Other functions	–	–	–	–	–	...	...	...	...	...	...	...
Total government final consumption expenditures	382550	397280	412380	418820	444070	...	...	...	...	...	...	...

2.3 Total government outlays by function and type

Million Deutsche marks

	\multicolumn{8}{c}{1986}
	Final consumption expenditures			Subsidies	Other current transfers and property income	Total current disbursements	Gross capital formation	Other capital outlays	Total outlays
	Total	Compensation of employees	Other						
1 General public services	39510	...	...	1670	24590	65770	2550	6130	74450
2 Defence	51290	...	...	–	1270	52560	250	230	53040
3 Public order and safety	29500	...	...	–	40	29540	2230	60	31830
4 Education	74810	...	...	100	5150	80060	5780	510	86350
5 Health	115190	...	...	140	270	115600	4480	1960	122040
6 Social security and welfare	39830	...	...	1070	313820	354720	1390	4880	360990
7 Housing and community amenities	6160	...	...	3580	90	9830	10450	3000	23280
8 Recreational, cultural and religious affairs	9130	...	...	690	1430	11250	2870	1180	15300
9 Economic services	17130	...	...	34060	7190	58380	15310	14030	87720
A Fuel and energy	120	...	...	5100	–	5220	–	860	6080
B Agriculture, hunting, forestry and fishing	2240	...	...	14830	40	17110	230	930	18270
C Mining (except fuels), manufacturing and construction	210	...	...	170	–	380	–	450	830
D Transportation and communication	10710	...	...	7180	–	17890	13940	6900	38730
E Other economic affairs	3850	...	...	6780	7150	17780	1140	4890	23810

Germany, Federal Republic (Former)

Million Deutsche marks

	1986								
	Final consumption expenditures			Subsidies	Other current transfers and property income	Total current disburse-ments	Gross capital formation	Other capital outlays	Total outlays
	Total	Compen-sation of employ-ees	Other						
10 Other functions	–	...	...	–	56130	56130	–	–	56130
Total	382550	...	...	41310	409980	833840	45310	31980	911130

	1987								
	Final consumption expenditures			Subsidies	Other current transfers and property income	Total current disburse-ments	Gross capital formation	Other capital outlays	Total outlays
	Total	Compen-sation of employ-ees	Other						
1 General public services	42210	...	...	1850	25620	69680	2690	5590	77960
2 Defence	52300	...	...	–	1310	53610	250	200	54060
3 Public order and safety	30790	...	...	–	40	30830	2530	60	33420
4 Education	76370	...	...	90	5430	81890	5850	570	88310
5 Health	119940	...	...	160	290	120390	4440	2030	126860
6 Social security and welfare	41710	...	...	870	328600	371180	1250	4700	377130
7 Housing and community amenities	6630	...	...	3210	80	9920	10990	2910	23820
8 Recreational, cultural and religious affairs	9690	...	...	770	1520	11980	3040	1210	16230
9 Economic services	17640	...	...	37850	8500	63990	14960	15040	93990
A Fuel and energy	100	...	...	8290	–	8390	–	1210	9600
B Agriculture, hunting, forestry and fishing	2270	...	...	15360	40	17670	220	990	18880
C Mining (except fuels), manufacturing and construction	220	...	...	160	–	380	–	490	870
D Transportation and communication	10960	...	...	7110	10	18080	13590	6990	38660
E Other economic affairs	4090	...	...	6930	8450	19470	1150	5360	25980
10 Other functions	–	...	...	–	56780	56780	–	–	56780
Total	397280	...	...	44800	428170	870250	46000	32310	948560

	1988								
	Final consumption expenditures			Subsidies	Other current transfers and property income	Total current disburse-ments	Gross capital formation	Other capital outlays	Total outlays
	Total	Compen-sation of employ-ees	Other						
1 General public services	42290	...	...	1900	31120	75310	2840	5090	83240
2 Defence	52480	...	...	–	1300	53780	250	180	54210
3 Public order and safety	31740	...	...	–	40	31780	2500	130	34410
4 Education	77700	...	...	70	5650	83420	6060	380	89860
5 Health	129650	...	...	150	350	130150	4700	2050	136900
6 Social security and welfare	44260	...	...	1000	342180	387440	1420	4220	393080
7 Housing and community amenities	6490	...	...	2650	100	9240	11520	2950	23710
8 Recreational, cultural and religious affairs	10020	...	...	790	1570	12380	3170	1130	16680
9 Economic services	17750	...	...	41180	10220	69150	15040	14970	99160
A Fuel and energy	110	...	...	8040	–	8150	–	760	8910
B Agriculture, hunting, forestry and fishing	2260	...	...	17480	40	19780	210	1030	21020
C Mining (except fuels), manufacturing and construction	250	...	...	480	–	730	–	490	1220

Germany, Federal Republic (Former)

1988

	Final consumption expenditures Total	Compensation of employees	Other	Subsidies	Other current transfers and property income	Total current disbursements	Gross capital formation	Other capital outlays	Total outlays
D Transportation and communication	11040	...	...	7460	–	18500	13740	6760	39000
E Other economic affairs	4090	...	...	7720	10180	21990	1090	5930	29010
10 Other functions	–	...	...	–	58940	58940	–	–	58940
Total	412380	...	...	47740	451470	911590	47500	31100	990190

1989

	Final consumption expenditures Total	Compensation of employees	Other	Subsidies	Other current transfers and property income	Total current disbursements	Gross capital formation	Other capital outlays	Total outlays
1 General public services	43740	...	...	1830	31840	77410	3110	5320	85840
2 Defence	53790	...	...	–	1460	55250	220	180	55650
3 Public order and safety	32990	...	...	–	50	33040	2670	70	35780
4 Education	80060	...	...	50	5900	86010	6510	480	93000
5 Health	126010	...	...	130	380	126520	4800	2170	133490
6 Social security and welfare	47510	...	...	870	357730	406110	1560	4320	411990
7 Housing and community amenities	6310	...	...	2770	90	9170	12890	3050	25110
8 Recreational, cultural and religious affairs	10450	...	...	860	1600	12910	3440	1200	17550
9 Economic services	17960	...	...	40270	10570	68800	15790	15400	99990
A Fuel and energy	90	...	...	9680	–	9770	–	710	10480
B Agriculture, hunting, forestry and fishing	2330	...	...	14320	50	16700	230	1140	18070
C Mining (except fuels), manufacturing and construction	200	...	...	1020	–	1220	–	860	2080
D Transportation and communication	11220	...	...	7580	–	18800	14390	6540	39730
E Other economic affairs	4120	...	...	7670	10520	22310	1170	6150	29630
10 Other functions	–	...	...	–	59590	59590	–	–	59590
Total	418820	...	...	46780	469210	934810	50990	32190	1017990

1990

	Final consumption expenditures Total	Compensation of employees	Other	Subsidies	Other current transfers and property income	Total current disbursements	Gross capital formation	Other capital outlays	Total outlays
1 General public services	46130	...	...	2000	77400	125530	3330	9000	137860
2 Defence	52730	...	...	–	1360	54090	180	150	54420
3 Public order and safety	35300	...	...	–	60	35360	2750	110	38220
4 Education	84070	...	...	50	6530	90650	7160	710	98520
5 Health	136500	...	...	120	430	137050	4840	2240	144130
6 Social security and welfare	53160	...	...	970	374140	428270	1840	2200	432310
7 Housing and community amenities	6380	...	...	3340	80	9800	14140	3800	27740
8 Recreational, cultural and religious affairs	11140	...	...	920	1710	13770	3500	1260	18530
9 Economic services	18660	...	...	41430	11190	71280	16420	15340	103040
A Fuel and energy	90	...	...	9380	–	9470	–	660	10130
B Agriculture, hunting, forestry and fishing	2420	...	...	14490	60	16970	210	1380	18560

Germany, Federal Republic (Former)

	1990								
	Final consumption expenditures			Subsidies	Other current transfers and property income	Total current disburse-ments	Gross capital formation	Other capital outlays	Total outlays
	Total	Compensation of employees	Other						
C Mining (except fuels), manufacturing and construction	210	...	...	750	–	960	–	940	1900
D Transportation and communication	11590	...	...	7980	10	19580	14930	6070	40580
E Other economic affairs	4350	...	...	8830	11120	24300	1280	6290	31870
10 Other functions	–	...	...	–	62390	62390	–	–	62390
Total	444070	...	...	48830	535290	1028190	54160	34810	1117160

2.5 Private final consumption expenditure by type and purpose, in current prices

Million Deutsche marks

	1986	1987	1988	1989	1990	1991	1992	1993	1994	1995	1996	1997
Final consumption expenditure of resident households												
1 Food, beverages and tobacco [a]	236670	241060	247360	262310	285500	301090	309950	310400	312450	...	...	...
A Food	214200	218550	224300	238110	258400	275080	284120	284100	284700	...	...	...
B Non-alcoholic beverages										...	...	...
C Alcoholic beverages										...	...	...
D Tobacco	22470	22510	23060	24200	27100	26010	25830	26300	27750	...	...	...
2 Clothing and footwear	88630	91720	92830	95580	107040	118010	120600	122380	119370	...	...	...
3 Gross rent, fuel and power [bc]	225450	228720	234150	246560	264260	288730	309800	337110	362020	...	...	...
A Fuel and power [c]	55180	50440	46600	47790	51220	58920	58420	60370	60620	...	...	...
B Other	170270	178280	187550	198770	213040	229810	251380	276740	301400	...	...	...
4 Furniture, furnishings and household equipment and operation [b]	90570	96120	102040	109300	120950	134460	143000	145910	146960	...	...	...
5 Medical care and health expenses	33990	35680	38100	40300	44010	49150	53860	57300	60590	...	...	...
6 Transport and communication [c]	160460	170610	179590	197370	222160	254570	263040	255520	262080	...	...	...
A Personal transport equipment	57670	63570	64450	66890	75500	88280	87450	77950	80060	...	...	...
B Other [c]	102790	107040	115140	130480	146660	166290	175590	177570	182020	...	...	...
7 Recreational, entertainment, education and cultural services	104000	108200	114770	119780	134260	146390	155920	157800	159980	...	...	...
8 Miscellaneous goods and services [a]	87600	92030	98780	106340	115360	127730	136920	147590	156080	...	...	...
A Personal care	19380	20510	21800	22580	24220	26070	27200	27770	27840	...	...	...
B Expenditures in restaurants, cafes and hotels	...	...	...	...	...	...	...	...	...	...	...	...
C Other	...	...	...	...	...	...	...	...	...	...	...	...
Total final consumption expenditure in the domestic market by households, of which	1027370	1064140	1107620	1177540	1293540	1420130	1493090	1534010	1579530	...	...	...
plus: Direct purchases abroad by resident households	42380	45240	47790	49130	54270	59790	66070	71590	75510	...	...	...
less: Direct purchases in the domestic market by non-resident households	27410	27230	28790	34550	57830	67160	60580	54980	51130	...	...	...
equals: Final consumption expenditure of resident households	1042340	1082150	1126620	1192120	1289980	1412760	1498580	1550620	1603910	...	...	...

Germany, Federal Republic (Former)

Million Deutsche marks

	1986	1987	1988	1989	1990	1991	1992	1993	1994	1995	1996	1997

Final consumption expenditures by private non-profit organisations serving households

	1986	1987	1988	1989	1990	1991	1992	1993	1994	1995	1996	1997
1 Research and science	...	...	...	...	...	...	...	...	...	...	...	...
2 Education	...	...	...	...	...	...	...	...	...	...	...	...
3 Medical and other health services	...	...	...	...	...	...	...	...	...	...	...	...
4 Welfare services	...	...	...	...	...	...	...	...	...	...	...	...
5 Recreational and related cultural services	...	...	...	...	...	...	...	...	...	...	...	...
6 Religious organisations	...	...	...	...	...	...	...	...	...	...	...	...
7 Professional and labour organisations serving households	...	...	...	...	...	...	...	...	...	...	...	...
8 Miscellaneous	...	...	...	...	...	...	...	...	...	...	...	...
equals: Final consumption expenditures by private non-profit organisations serving households	24090	25870	27070	28830	30730	34210	37930	40960	42430	...	...	...
Private final consumption expenditure	1066430	1108020	1153690	1220950	1320710	1446970	1536510	1591580	1646340	...	...	...

a Expenditure in restaurants and cafes is included in item "Food, beverages and tobacco", expenditure in hotels, etc., is included in item "Miscellaneous goods and services".
b Indoor repairs and upkeep paid for by tenants are included in household equipment and operation.
c Fuel for personal transport equipment is included in item "Transport and communication".

2.6 Private final consumption expenditure by type and purpose, in constant prices

Million Deutsche marks

At constant prices of: 1991

Final consumption expenditure of resident households

	1986	1987	1988	1989	1990	1991	1992	1993	1994	1995	1996	1997
1 Food, beverages and tobacco [a]	254350	260740	266440	276680	293020	301090	300470	294770	292230	...	...	...
A Food	229260	235470	241120	251110	265760	275080	276000	271060	267610	...	...	...
B Non-alcoholic beverages										...	...	...
C Alcoholic beverages										...	...	...
D Tobacco	25090	25270	25320	25570	27260	26010	24470	23710	24620			
2 Clothing and footwear	95310	97530	97330	98940	109390	118010	117170	115710	111430			
3 Gross rent, fuel and power [b,c]	254540	259890	262300	265690	275630	288730	296460	306940	317040			
A Fuel and power [c]	57150	56660	53530	51060	53200	58920	58260	59350	59490			
B Other	197390	203230	208770	214630	222430	229810	238200	247590	257550			
4 Furniture, furnishings and household equipment and operation [b]	99160	104100	109050	114850	124400	134460	138450	137270	135530			
5 Medical care and health expenses	39270	40290	42120	42680	45830	49150	52080	53430	53870			
6 Transport and communication [c]	186900	196850	204180	213940	234540	254570	252420	236640	235120			
A Personal transport equipment	66940	71770	70640	71360	78570	88280	84190	71300	73100			
B Other [c]	119960	125080	133540	142580	155970	166290	168230	165340	162020			
7 Recreational, entertainment, education and cultural services	110820	114650	120350	124570	136440	146390	150040	147630	146680	...	...	...
8 Miscellaneous goods and services [a]	101800	103900	109800	115350	121950	127730	128590	130620	132840	...	...	...
A Personal care	21170	22180	23230	23670	24890	26070	26220	25760	25370	...	...	...
B Expenditures in restaurants, cafes and hotels	...	...	...	...	...	...	...	...	...	...	...	...
C Other	...	...	...	...	...	...	...	...	...	...	...	...

Germany, Federal Republic (Former)

Million Deutsche marks

	1986	1987	1988	1989	1990	1991	1992	1993	1994	1995	1996	1997
At constant prices of: 1991												
Total final consumption expenditure in the domestic market by households, of which	1142150	1177950	1211570	1252700	1341200	1420130	1435680	1423010	1424740	...	...	...
plus: Direct purchases abroad by resident households	51110	53830	54550	53310	56400	59790	64660	71050	73870	...	...	...
less: Direct purchases in the domestic market by non-resident households	31240	30600	31750	36810	59680	67160	58230	50760	46000	...	...	...
equals: Final consumption expenditure of resident households	1162020	1201180	1234370	1269200	1337920	1412760	1442110	1443300	1452610	...	...	...

Final consumption expenditures by private non-profit organisations serving households

	1986	1987	1988	1989	1990	1991	1992	1993	1994	1995	1996	1997
1 Research and science	...	...	...	...	...	...	...	...	...	...	...	...
2 Education	...	...	...	...	...	...	...	...	...	...	...	...
3 Medical and other health services	...	...	...	...	...	...	...	...	...	...	...	...
4 Welfare services	...	...	...	...	...	...	...	...	...	...	...	...
5 Recreational and related cultural services	...	...	...	...	...	...	...	...	...	...	...	...
6 Religious organisations	...	...	...	...	...	...	...	...	...	...	...	...
7 Professional and labour organisations serving households	...	...	...	...	...	...	...	...	...	...	...	...
8 Miscellaneous	...	...	...	...	...	...	...	...	...	...	...	...
equals: Final consumption expenditures by private non-profit organisations serving households	27930	29430	29970	30950	32090	34210	35850	36700	36230	...	...	...
Private final consumption expenditure	1189950	1230610	1264340	1300150	1370010	1446970	1477960	1480000	1488840	...	...	...

a Expenditure in restaurants and cafes is included in item "Food, beverages and tobacco", expenditure in hotels, etc., is included in item "Miscellaneous goods and services".
b Indoor repairs and upkeep paid for by tenants are included in household equipment and operation.
c Fuel for personal transport equipment is included in item "Transport and communication".

2.11 Gross fixed capital formation by kind of activity of owner, ISIC divisions, in current prices

Million Deutsche marks

	1986	1987	1988	1989	1990	1991	1992	1993	1994	1995	1996	1997
All producers												
1 Agriculture, hunting, forestry and fishing	9730	9750	10290	11320	12430	13130	12630	10800	10560	...	...	...
A Agriculture and hunting [a]	9200	9130	9550	10560	11590	12260	11750	10050	9820	...	...	...
B Forestry and logging [a]	530	620	740	760	840	870	880	750	740	...	...	...
C Fishing	...	...	...	...	...	...	...	...	...	...	...	...
2 Mining and quarrying [b]	3060	2740	3140	2690	2180	2030	2620	1950	1780	...	...	...
A Coal mining	2380	2250	2610	2040	1530	1300	1670	1210		...	...	...
B Crude petroleum and natural gas production	...	...	...	...	...	...	...	...	...	...	...	...
C Metal ore mining	...	...	...	...	...	...	...	...	...	...	...	...
D Other mining	...	...	...	...	...	...	...	...	...	...	...	...
3 Manufacturing	74160	79050	81800	91840	105850	115710	109860	85310	77630	...	...	...
A Manufacturing of food, beverages and tobacco	6260	7010	7610	8480	10000	12690	12790	10990		...	...	...
B Textile, wearing apparel and leather industries	2380	2440	2560	2840	3130	3020	2610	1950		...	...	...

Germany, Federal Republic (Former)

Million Deutsche marks

	1986	1987	1988	1989	1990	1991	1992	1993	1994	1995	1996	1997
C Manufacture of wood and wood products, including furniture	1370	1520	1950	2210	2690	3090	3440	2770	...	...	...	...
D Manufacture of paper and paper products, printing and publishing [c]	4200	4470	5970	6420	6830	7410	6950	5910	...	...	...	...
E Manufacture of chemicals and chemical petroleum, coal, rubber and plastic products	13660	15490	15710	17600	19820	20640	20040	15760	...	...	...	...
F Manufacture of non-metallic mineral products, except products of petroleum and coal [b]	2910	3120	3740	4600	5190	5870	6150	5390	...	...	...	...
G Basic metal industries	5880	5640	5760	6170	7450	8070	8080	6000	...	...	...	...
H Manufacture of fabricated metal products, machinery and equipment [d]	37140	38900	38010	42900	50160	54280	49200	36070	...	...	...	...
I Other manufacturing industries	360	460	490	620	580	640	600	470	...	...	...	...
4 Electricity, gas and water	20990	20670	20220	20070	20180	20730	24320	24160	24730	...	...	...
A Electricity, gas and steam	19250	18990	18310	17990	18060	18560	21640	21480	...	...	...	...
B Water works and supply	1740	1680	1910	2080	2120	2170	2680	2680	...	...	...	...
5 Construction [d]	4730	4980	5280	6420	7790	8940	10330	10000	8740	...	...	...
6 Wholesale and retail trade, restaurants and hotels	19820	22500	26950	29240	32800	40120	43750	38620	...	...	...	...
A Wholesale and retail trade	17070	19660	24010	26190	29570	36970	40510	35380	34090	...	...	...
B Restaurants and hotels	2750	2840	2940	3050	3230	3150	3240	3240	...	...	...	...
7 Transport, storage and communication	36120	35970	36400	39280	41990	45470	43540	41890	...	...	...	...
A Transport and storage	19210	18460	18410	20060	22340	23730	22840	22550	13340	...	...	...
B Communication	16910	17510	17990	19220	19650	21740	20700	19340	...	...	...	...
8 Finance, insurance, real estate and business services	102320	101900	108380	117870	136090	152110	170390	175180	191700	...	...	...
A Financial institutions	5910	5330	5530	5500	6080	8080	10360	9920	10780	...	...	...
B Insurance	2850	2310	3650	4560	5810	6150	6070	5910	4900	...	...	...
C Real estate and business services [e]	93560	94260	99200	107810	124200	137880	153960	159350	176020	...	...	...
Real estate, except dwellings	...	...	...	...	...	...	...	...	...	...	...	...
Dwellings	93560	94260	99200	107810	124200	137880	153960	159350	176020	...	...	...
9 Community, social and personal services [ce]	58580	64240	72750	82740	98290	111380	106110	92110	...	...	...	...
Educational services	...	...	...	...	...	...	...	...	...	...	...	...
Medical, dental, other health and veterinary services	9450	10430	11060	12070	14220	15120	14360	12290	...	...	...	...
Total industries	329510	341800	365210	401470	457600	509620	523550	480020	492900	...	...	...
Producers of government services	45480	46200	47720	51250	54430	58670	62980	61580	60590	...	...	...
Private non-profit institutions serving households	5530	5720	5990	6280	6660	7180	7770	7740	7630	...	...	...
Statistical discrepancy [f]	−7040	−7940	−9020	−10480	−10910	−11210	−11650	−11170	−11130	...	...	...
Total	373480	385780	409900	448520	507780	564260	582650	538170	549990	...	...	...

a Hunting and fishing are included in item "Forestry and logging".
b Quarrying is included in item "Manufacture of non-metallic mineral products except products of petroleum and coal".
c Publishing is included in item "Community, social and personal services".
d Structural steel erection is included in item "Manufacture of fabricated metal products, machinery and equipment".
e Business services and real estate except dwellings are included in item "Community, social and personal services".
f Item "Statistical discrepancy" relates to adjustment for net purchases of used capital goods.

Germany, Federal Republic (Former)

2.12 Gross fixed capital formation by kind of activity of owner, ISIC divisions, in constant prices

Ten million Deutsche marks

At constant prices of: 1991

All producers

		1986	1987	1988	1989	1990	1991	1992	1993	1994	1995	1996	1997
1	Agriculture, hunting, forestry and fishing	1109	1103	1142	1226	1294	1313	1210	1016	975	...	...	...
	A Agriculture and hunting [a]	1048	1032	1059	1143	1207	1226	1126	945	908	...	...	...
	B Forestry and logging [a]	61	71	83	83	87	87	84	71	67	...	...	...
	C Fishing	...	...	...	...	...	...	...	...	...	...	...	...
2	Mining and quarrying [b]	339	300	339	280	223	203	254	186	172	...	...	...
	A Coal mining	262	246	282	212	156	130	162	116	...	...	...	...
	B Crude petroleum and natural gas production	...	...	...	...	...	...	...	...	...	...	...	...
	C Metal ore mining	...	...	...	...	...	...	...	...	...	...	...	...
	D Other mining	...	...	...	...	...	...	...	...	...	...	...	...
3	Manufacturing	8427	8853	8986	9793	10974	11571	10674	8141	7481	...	...	...
	A Manufacturing of food, beverages and tobacco	729	802	844	911	1045	1269	1232	1033				
	B Textile, wearing apparel and leather industries	271	272	279	304	324	302	250	185				
	C Manufacture of wood and wood products, including furniture	155	170	218	239	282	309	332	264	...	...	...	...
	D Manufacture of paper and paper products, printing and publishing [c]	462	481	639	673	701	741	686	575	...	...	...	...
	E Manufacture of chemicals and chemical petroleum, coal, rubber and plastic products	1569	1745	1732	1876	2051	2064	1944	1502	...	...	...	...
	F Manufacture of non-metallic mineral products, except products of petroleum and coal [b]	330	349	414	495	541	587	595	512	...	...	...	...
	G Basic metal industries	665	628	631	650	768	807	783	570	...	...	...	...
	H Manufacture of fabricated metal products, machinery and equipment [d]	4205	4356	4176	4579	5203	5428	4794	3456				
	I Other manufacturing industries	41	50	53	66	59	64	58	44	...	...	...	...
4	Electricity, gas and water	2371	2306	2215	2152	2092	2073	2349	2303	2321	...	...	...
	A Electricity, gas and steam	2169	2112	1999	1924	1870	1856	2093	2052				
	B Water works and supply	202	194	216	228	222	217	256	251	...	...	...	...
5	Construction [d]	540	557	577	684	808	894	1010	967	841	...	...	...
6	Wholesale and retail trade, restaurants and hotels	2281	2545	2987	3148	3414	4012	4235	3678	...	...	...	...
	A Wholesale and retail trade	1963	2221	2658	2814	3076	3697	3922	3372	3227	...	...	...
	B Restaurants and hotels	318	324	329	334	338	315	313	306	...	...	...	...
7	Transport, storage and communication	4058	4011	3993	4222	4364	4547	4273	4101	...	...	...	...
	A Transport and storage	2202	2097	2046	2175	2337	2373	2214	2166	1280	...	...	...
	B Communication	1856	1914	1947	2047	2027	2174	2059	1935	...	...	...	...
8	Finance, insurance, real estate and business services	12421	12147	12662	13309	14505	15211	16174	15992	17164	...	...	...
	A Financial institutions	647	579	596	573	621	808	1010	957	1045	...	...	...
	B Insurance	327	263	411	498	607	615	586	557	461	...	...	...
	C Real estate and business services [e]	11447	11305	11655	12238	13277	13788	14578	14478	15658	...	...	...

Germany, Federal Republic (Former)

Ten million Deutsche marks

	1986	1987	1988	1989	1990	1991	1992	1993	1994	1995	1996	1997
At constant prices of: 1991												
Real estate, except dwellings	...	...	...	...	...	...	...	...	...	...	...	...
Dwellings	11447	11305	11655	12238	13277	13788	14578	14478	15658	...	...	...
9 Community, social and personal services [c,e]	6631	7217	8082	8947	10239	11138	10303	8747	...	...	...	...
Educational services	...	...	...	...	...	...	...	...	...	...	...	...
Medical, dental, other health and veterinary services	1030	1130	1212	1298	1478	1512	1408	1177	...	...	...	...
Total industries	38177	39039	40983	43761	47913	50962	50482	45131	45819	...	...	...
Producers of government services	5408	5408	5496	5728	5765	5867	6007	5702	5558	...	...	...
Private non-profit institutions serving households	662	673	689	702	704	718	743	714	694	...	...	...
Statistical discrepancy [f]	−818	−896	−991	−1125	−1147	−1121	−1120	−1043	−1028	...	...	...
Total	43429	44224	46177	49066	53235	56426	56112	50504	51043	...	...	...

a Hunting and fishing are included in item "Forestry and logging".
b Quarrying is included in item "Manufacture of non-metallic mineral products except products of petroleum and coal".
c Publishing is included in item "Community, social and personal services".
d Structural steel erection is included in item "Manufacture of fabricated metal products, machinery and equipment".
e Business services and real estate except dwellings are included in item "Community, social and personal services".
f Item "Statistical discrepancy" relates to adjustment for net purchases of used capital goods.

2.13 Stocks of reproducible fixed assets, by type of good and owner, in current prices

Ten million Deutsche marks

1986

	Total Gross	Total Net	Total private Gross	Total private Net	Public enterprises Gross	Public enterprises Net	General government Gross	General government Net
1 Residential buildings	379098	268216	379098	268216	...	...	...	...
2 Non-residential buildings	...	...	...	...	...	...	...	...
3 Other construction	286984	190178	228908	149253	...	...	58076	40925
4 Land improvement and plantation and orchard development	...	...	...	...	...	...	...	...
5 Producers' durable goods	191761	101311	182983	96842	...	...	8778	4469
6 Breeding stock, dairy cattle, etc.	...	...	...	...	...	...	...	...
Total [a,b]	857843	559705	790989	514311	...	...	66854	45394

1987

	Total Gross	Total Net	Total private Gross	Total private Net	Public enterprises Gross	Public enterprises Net	General government Gross	General government Net
1 Residential buildings	395100	277651	395100	277651	...	...	...	...
2 Non-residential buildings	...	...	...	...	...	...	...	...
3 Other construction	299875	197579	239292	155145	...	...	60583	42434
4 Land improvement and plantation and orchard development	...	...	...	...	...	...	...	...
5 Producers' durable goods	198020	104837	188988	100214	...	...	9032	4623
6 Breeding stock, dairy cattle, etc.	...	...	...	...	...	...	...	...
Total [a,b]	892995	580067	823380	533010	...	...	69615	47057

1988

	Total Gross	Total Net	Total private Gross	Total private Net	Public enterprises Gross	Public enterprises Net	General government Gross	General government Net
1 Residential buildings	415150	289831	415150	289831	...	...	...	...
2 Non-residential buildings	...	...	...	...	...	...	...	...
3 Other construction	316055	207110	252361	162772	...	...	63694	44338

Germany, Federal Republic (Former)

| | 1988 ||||||||
| | Total || Total private || Public enterprises || General government ||
	Gross	Net	Gross	Net	Gross	Net	Gross	Net
4 Land improvement and plantation and orchard development	...	...	...	...	...	...	...	...
5 Producers' durable goods	207201	110198	197757	105343	...	...	9444	4855
6 Breeding stock, dairy cattle, etc.	...	...	...	...	...	...	...	...
Total [ab]	938406	607139	865268	557946	...	...	73138	49193

| | 1989 ||||||||
| | Total || Total private || Public enterprises || General government ||
	Gross	Net	Gross	Net	Gross	Net	Gross	Net
1 Residential buildings	443002	307371	443002	307371	...	...	...	...
2 Non-residential buildings	...	...	...	...	...	...	...	...
3 Other construction	339171	221090	271054	174004	...	...	68117	47086
4 Land improvement and plantation and orchard development	...	...	...	...	...	...	...	...
5 Producers' durable goods	221339	117714	211432	112565	...	...	9907	5149
6 Breeding stock, dairy cattle, etc.	...	...	...	...	...	...	...	...
Total [ab]	1003512	646175	925488	593940	...	...	78024	52235

| | 1990 ||||||||
| | Total || Total private || Public enterprises || General government ||
	Gross	Net	Gross	Net	Gross	Net	Gross	Net
1 Residential buildings	483937	333971	483937	333971	...	...	...	...
2 Non-residential buildings	...	...	...	...	...	...	...	...
3 Other construction	371019	240687	297053	189906	...	...	73966	50781
4 Land improvement and plantation and orchard development	...	...	...	...	...	...	...	...
5 Producers' durable goods	237345	127817	227037	122405	...	...	10308	5412
6 Breeding stock, dairy cattle, etc.	...	...	...	...	...	...	...	...
Total [ab]	1092301	702475	1008027	646282	...	...	84274	56193

| | 1991 ||||||||
| | Total || Total private || Public enterprises || General government ||
	Gross	Net	Gross	Net	Gross	Net	Gross	Net
1 Residential buildings	529334	363443	529334	363443	...	...	...	...
2 Non-residential buildings	...	...	...	...	...	...	...	...
3 Other construction	403877	260855	323414	205995	...	...	80463	54860
4 Land improvement and plantation and orchard development	...	...	...	...	...	...	...	...
5 Producers' durable goods	255819	139499	244862	133665	...	...	10957	5834
6 Breeding stock, dairy cattle, etc.	...	...	...	...	...	...	...	...
Total [ab]	1189030	763797	1097610	703103	...	...	91420	60694

Germany, Federal Republic (Former)

	1992 Total Gross	1992 Total Net	1992 Total private Gross	1992 Total private Net	1992 Public enterprises Gross	1992 Public enterprises Net	1992 General government Gross	1992 General government Net
1 Residential buildings	570246	389741	570246	389741	...	...	...	...
2 Non-residential buildings	...	...	...	...	...	...	...	...
3 Other construction	433490	278776	347372	220469	...	...	86118	58307
4 Land improvement and plantation and orchard development	...	...	...	...	...	...	...	...
5 Producers' durable goods	268804	146693	257256	140485	...	...	11548	6208
6 Breeding stock, dairy cattle, etc.	...	...	...	...	...	...	...	...
Total [a,b]	1272540	815210	1174874	750695	...	...	97666	64515

	1993 Total Gross	1993 Total Net	1993 Total private Gross	1993 Total private Net	1993 Public enterprises Gross	1993 Public enterprises Net	1993 General government Gross	1993 General government Net
1 Residential buildings	601482	409095	601482	409095	...	...	...	...
2 Non-residential buildings	...	...	...	...	...	...	...	...
3 Other construction	452598	289438	362426	228857	...	...	90172	60581
4 Land improvement and plantation and orchard development	...	...	...	...	...	...	...	...
5 Producers' durable goods	275130	147756	263207	141354	...	...	11923	6402
6 Breeding stock, dairy cattle, etc.	...	...	...	...	...	...	...	...
Total [a,b]	1329210	846289	1227115	779306	...	...	102095	66983

	1994 Total Gross	1994 Total Net	1994 Total private Gross	1994 Total private Net	1994 Public enterprises Gross	1994 Public enterprises Net	1994 General government Gross	1994 General government Net
1 Residential buildings	631467	427756	631467	427756	...	...	...	...
2 Non-residential buildings	...	...	...	...	...	...	...	...
3 Other construction	471342	299693	377626	237247	...	...	93716	62446
4 Land improvement and plantation and orchard development	...	...	...	...	...	...	...	...
5 Producers' durable goods	277691	146555	265610	140150	...	...	12081	6405
6 Breeding stock, dairy cattle, etc.	...	...	...	...	...	...	...	...
Total [a,b]	1380500	874004	1274703	805153	...	...	105797	68851

a Column "Public enterprises" is included in column "Total private".   b Value recorded at the beginning of the year (opening stock).

2.14 Stocks of reproducible fixed assets, by type of good and owner, in constant prices

Ten million Deutsche marks

	1986 Total Gross	1986 Total Net	1986 Total private Gross	1986 Total private Net	1986 Public enterprises Gross	1986 Public enterprises Net	1986 General government Gross	1986 General government Net
At constant prices of: 1991								
1 Residential buildings	460272	325644	460272	325644	...	...	...	...
2 Non-residential buildings	...	...	...	...	...	...	...	...
3 Other construction	345821	229101	275413	179521	...	...	70408	49580
4 Land improvement and plantation and orchard development	...	...	...	...	...	...	...	...
5 Producers' durable goods	215239	112932	205610	108003	...	...	9629	4929
6 Breeding stock, dairy cattle, etc.	...	...	...	...	...	...	...	...
Total [a,b]	1021332	667677	941295	613168	...	...	80037	54509

Germany, Federal Republic (Former)

1987

	Total Gross	Total Net	Total private Gross	Total private Net	Public enterprises Gross	Public enterprises Net	General government Gross	General government Net
	At constant prices of: 1991							
1 Residential buildings	470367	330540	470367	330540	...	...	...	...
2 Non-residential buildings	...	...	...	...	...	...	...	...
3 Other construction	355214	233962	283189	183550	...	...	72024	50412
4 Land improvement and plantation and orchard development	...	...	...	...	...	...	...	...
5 Producers' durable goods	219990	115598	210171	110552	...	...	9819	5046
6 Breeding stock, dairy cattle, etc.	...	...	...	...	...	...	...	...
Total [ab]	1045571	680100	963727	624642	...	...	81843	55458

1988

	Total Gross	Total Net	Total private Gross	Total private Net	Public enterprises Gross	Public enterprises Net	General government Gross	General government Net
	At constant prices of: 1991							
1 Residential buildings	480759	335631	480759	335631	...	...	...	...
2 Non-residential buildings	...	...	...	...	...	...	...	...
3 Other construction	364839	238990	291201	187767	...	...	73638	51223
4 Land improvement and plantation and orchard development	...	...	...	...	...	...	...	...
5 Producers' durable goods	225614	119036	215629	113889	...	...	9985	5147
6 Breeding stock, dairy cattle, etc.	...	...	...	...	...	...	...	...
Total [ab]	1071212	693657	987589	637287	...	...	83623	56370

1989

	Total Gross	Total Net	Total private Gross	Total private Net	Public enterprises Gross	Public enterprises Net	General government Gross	General government Net
	At constant prices of: 1991							
1 Residential buildings	491678	341144	491678	341144	...	...	...	...
2 Non-residential buildings	...	...	...	...	...	...	...	...
3 Other construction	374699	244241	299432	192212	...	...	75267	52029
4 Land improvement and plantation and orchard development	...	...	...	...	...	...	...	...
5 Producers' durable goods	232499	123649	222294	118345	...	...	10205	5304
6 Breeding stock, dairy cattle, etc.	...	...	...	...	...	...	...	...
Total [ab]	1098876	709034	1013404	651701	...	...	85472	57333

1990

	Total Gross	Total Net	Total private Gross	Total private Net	Public enterprises Gross	Public enterprises Net	General government Gross	General government Net
	At constant prices of: 1991							
1 Residential buildings	503576	347524	503576	347524	...	...	...	...
2 Non-residential buildings	...	...	...	...	...	...	...	...
3 Other construction	384679	249553	307871	196821	...	...	76808	52732
4 Land improvement and plantation and orchard development	...	...	...	...	...	...	...	...
5 Producers' durable goods	241942	130293	231459	124789	...	...	10483	5504
6 Breeding stock, dairy cattle, etc.	...	...	...	...	...	...	...	...
Total [ab]	1130197	727370	1042906	669134	...	...	87291	58236

Germany, Federal Republic (Former)

	1991							
	Total		Total private		Public enterprises		General government	
	Gross	Net	Gross	Net	Gross	Net	Gross	Net
	At constant prices of: 1991							
1 Residential buildings	515920	354233	515920	354233	...	...	...	...
2 Non-residential buildings	...	...	...	...	...	...	...	...
3 Other construction	394764	254934	316416	201516	...	...	78348	53418
4 Land improvement and plantation and orchard development	...	...	...	...	...	...	...	...
5 Producers' durable goods	253537	138255	242688	132479	...	...	10849	5776
6 Breeding stock, dairy cattle, etc.	...	...	...	...	...	...	...	...
Total [a,b]	1164221	747422	1075024	688228	...	...	89197	59194

	1992							
	Total		Total private		Public enterprises		General government	
	Gross	Net	Gross	Net	Gross	Net	Gross	Net
	At constant prices of: 1991							
1 Residential buildings	528985	361541	528985	361541	...	...	...	...
2 Non-residential buildings	...	...	...	...	...	...	...	...
3 Other construction	404898	260354	325011	206266	...	...	79887	54088
4 Land improvement and plantation and orchard development	...	...	...	...	...	...	...	...
5 Producers' durable goods	263275	143675	252038	137634	...	...	11237	6041
6 Breeding stock, dairy cattle, etc.	...	...	...	...	...	...	...	...
Total [a,b]	1197158	765570	1106034	705441	...	...	91124	60129

	1993							
	Total		Total private		Public enterprises		General government	
	Gross	Net	Gross	Net	Gross	Net	Gross	Net
	At constant prices of: 1991							
1 Residential buildings	541876	368554	541876	368554	...	...	...	...
2 Non-residential buildings	...	...	...	...	...	...	...	...
3 Other construction	413835	264622	332525	209995	...	...	81309	54627
4 Land improvement and plantation and orchard development	...	...	...	...	...	...	...	...
5 Producers' durable goods	267897	143872	256371	137684	...	...	11526	6188
6 Breeding stock, dairy cattle, etc.	...	...	...	...	...	...	...	...
Total [a,b]	1223608	777048	1130772	716233	...	...	92835	60815

	1994							
	Total		Total private		Public enterprises		General government	
	Gross	Net	Gross	Net	Gross	Net	Gross	Net
	At constant prices of: 1991							
1 Residential buildings	555869	376546	555869	376546	...	...	...	...
2 Non-residential buildings	...	...	...	...	...	...	...	...
3 Other construction	422644	268728	340002	213661	...	...	82642	55067
4 Land improvement and plantation and orchard development	...	...	...	...	...	...	...	...
5 Producers' durable goods	271183	143121	259535	136946	...	...	11648	6175
6 Breeding stock, dairy cattle, etc.	...	...	...	...	...	...	...	...
Total [a,b]	1249696	788395	1155406	727153	...	...	94290	61242

a Column "Public enterprises" is included in column "Total private".   b Value recorded at the beginning of the year (opening stock).

Germany, Federal Republic (Former)

2.15 Stocks of reproducible fixed assets, by kind of activity, in current prices

Ten million Deutsche marks

	1986 Gross	1986 Net	1987 Gross	1987 Net	1988 Gross	1988 Net	1989 Gross	1989 Net	1990 Gross	1990 Net	1991 Gross	1991 Net
1 Residential buildings	379098	268216	395100	277651	415150	289831	443002	307371	483937	333971	529334	363443
2 Non-residential buildings	...	...	...	...	...	...	...	...	...	...	...	...
3 Other construction [a,b]	286984	190178	299875	197579	316055	207110	339171	221090	371019	240687	403877	260855
A Industries	213311	137883	223000	143352	235306	150513	252688	160910	276937	175669	301630	190688
1 Agriculture	17447	9292	17831	9431	18302	9614	19328	10079	20770	10770	21866	11259
2 Mining and quarrying [c]	2318	1231	2360	1236	2417	1249	2431	1240	2495	1257	2553	1265
3 Manufacturing [c]	45329	23327	46611	23768	48322	24402	51291	25703	55407	27625	59432	29494
4 Electricity, gas and water	25952	18785	27131	19467	28661	20395	30578	21590	33403	23399	36297	25218
5 Construction	3266	2060	3359	2079	3486	2118	3713	2220	4026	2372	4345	2528
6 Wholesale and retail trade	23560	16044	24578	16601	26084	17543	28121	18843	31062	20729	34403	22960
7 Transport and communication	33727	20469	35452	21363	37470	22374	39861	23559	43281	25304	46637	26940
8 Finance, etc.	13492	10141	14096	10508	14988	11107	16320	12027	17976	13179	19787	14458
9 Community, social and personal services	48220	36534	51582	38899	55576	41711	61045	45649	68517	51034	76310	56566
B Producers of government services [d]	58076	40925	60583	42434	63694	44338	68117	47086	73966	50781	80463	54860
C Other producers	15597	11370	16292	11793	17055	12259	18366	13094	20116	14237	21784	15307
4 Land improvement and development and plantation and orchard development	...	...	...	...	...	...	...	...	...	...	...	...
5 Producers' durable goods	191761	101311	198020	104837	207201	110198	221339	117714	237345	127817	255819	139499
A Industries	180658	95704	186614	99056	195311	104149	208955	111327	224424	121088	242169	132298
1 Agriculture	13518	6572	13536	6575	13639	6650	14031	6861	14788	7319	15432	7742
2 Mining and quarrying [c]	3472	1839	3524	1842	3643	1898	3716	1915	3680	1873	3688	1843
3 Manufacturing [c]	72706	37898	75211	39459	78689	41476	84333	44335	90400	48153	97241	52423
4 Electricity, gas and water	16096	8657	16668	8962	17314	9237	18085	9451	18469	9511	18806	9555
5 Construction	4487	1995	4432	1988	4367	1996	4440	2084	4656	2310	5014	2618
6 Wholesale and retail trade	9846	4903	10235	5218	10858	5712	11596	6221	12571	6949	13970	7945
7 Transport and communication	24336	12944	24825	13138	25531	13466	26812	14072	28324	14970	29887	15951
8 Finance, etc.	3158	1851	3277	1902	3488	2021	3748	2154	4060	2364	4469	2624
9 Community, social and personal services	33039	19045	34906	19972	37782	21693	42194	24234	47476	27639	53662	31597
B Producers of government services	8778	4469	9032	4623	9444	4855	9907	5149	10308	5412	10957	5834
C Other producers	2325	1138	2374	1158	2446	1194	2477	1238	2613	1317	2693	1367
6 Breeding stock, dairy cattle, etc.	...	...	...	...	...	...	...	...	...	...	...	...
Total [e,f]	857843	559705	892995	580067	938406	607139	1003512	646175	1092301	702475	1189030	763797

	1992 Gross	1992 Net	1993 Gross	1993 Net	1994 Gross	1994 Net	1995 Gross	1995 Net	1996 Gross	1996 Net	1997 Gross	1997 Net
1 Residential buildings	570246	389741	601482	409095	631467	427756	...	...	...	...	...	...
2 Non-residential buildings	...	...	...	...	...	...	...	...	...	...	...	...
3 Other construction [a,b]	433490	278776	452598	289438	471342	299693	...	...	...	...	...	...
A Industries	323972	204140	337782	211786	352018	219644	...	...	...	...	...	...
1 Agriculture	23038	11788	23884	12133	24607	12404	...	...	...	...	...	...
2 Mining and quarrying [c]	2573	1257	2497	1203	...	...	...	...	...	...	...	...
3 Manufacturing [c]	62601	30898	63770	31155	...	...	...	...	...	...	...	...
4 Electricity, gas and water	38902	26843	40480	27736	...	...	...	...	...	...	...	...

Germany, Federal Republic (Former)

	1992 Gross	1992 Net	1993 Gross	1993 Net	1994 Gross	1994 Net	1995 Gross	1995 Net	1996 Gross	1996 Net	1997 Gross	1997 Net
5 Construction	4636	2675	4871	2810	...	...	...	...	...	...	...	...
6 Wholesale and retail trade	37462	24989	39327	26082	...	...	...	...	...	...	...	...
7 Transport and communication	49547	28285	50887	28656	...	...	...	...	...	...	...	...
8 Finance, etc.	21610	15749	22998	16686	...	...	...	...	...	...	...	...
9 Community, social and personal services	83603	61656	89068	65325	...	...	...	...	...	...	...	...
B Producers of government services [d]	86118	58307	90172	60581	93716	62446	...	...	...	...	...	...
C Other producers	23400	16329	24644	17071	25608	17603	...	...	...	...	...	...
4 Land improvement and development and plantation and orchard development	...	...	...	...	...	...	...	...	...	...	...	...
5 Producers' durable goods	268804	146693	275130	147756	277691	146555	...	...	...	...	...	...
A Industries	254477	139065	260384	139910	262793	138711	...	...	...	...	...	...
1 Agriculture	15818	7965	15828	7907	15761	7796	...	...	...	...	...	...
2 Mining and quarrying [c]	3680	1840	3564	1759	...	...	...	...	...	...	...	...
3 Manufacturing [c]	101670	54802	103207	54530	...	...	...	...	...	...	...	...
4 Electricity, gas and water	19046	9640	19166	9649	...	...	...	...	...	...	...	...
5 Construction	5434	2964	5759	3171	...	...	...	...	...	...	...	...
6 Wholesale and retail trade	15418	8923	16560	9509	...	...	...	...	...	...	...	...
7 Transport and communication	30502	16249	30864	16367	...	...	...	...	...	...	...	...
8 Finance, etc.	4891	2883	5221	3043	...	...	...	...	...	...	...	...
9 Community, social and personal services	58018	33799	60215	33975	...	...	...	...	...	...	...	...
B Producers of government services	11548	6208	11923	6402	12081	6405	...	...	...	...	...	...
C Other producers	2779	1420	2823	1444	2817	1439	...	...	...	...	...	...
6 Breeding stock, dairy cattle, etc.	...	...	...	...	...	...	...	...	...	...	...	...
Total [ef]	1272540	815210	1329210	846289	1380500	874004	...	...	...	...	...	...

a Item "Land improvement and plantation and orchard development" is included in item "Other construction".
b Item "Non-residential buildings" is included in item "Other construction".
c Quarrying is included in item "Manufacturing".
d Item "Producers of government services" does not include government civil engineering works.
e Value recorded at the beginning of the year (opening stock).
f Public underground construction is not contained in the data of this table (Stocks of Reproducible Fixed Assets by kind of activity).

2.16 Stocks of reproducible fixed assets, by kind of activity, in constant prices

Ten million Deutsche marks

	1986 Gross	1986 Net	1987 Gross	1987 Net	1988 Gross	1988 Net	1989 Gross	1989 Net	1990 Gross	1990 Net	1991 Gross	1991 Net
At constant prices of: 1991												
1 Residential buildings	460272	325644	470367	330540	480759	335631	491678	341144	503576	347524	515920	354233
2 Non-residential buildings	...	...	...	...	...	...	...	...	...	...	...	...
3 Other construction [ab]	345821	229101	355214	233962	364839	238990	374699	244241	384679	249553	394764	254934
A Industries	256487	165741	263787	169522	271311	173487	279048	177679	287004	182052	295059	186509
1 Agriculture	21331	11353	21381	11302	21428	11249	21476	11199	21546	11172	21585	11115
2 Mining and quarrying [c]	2730	1455	2734	1437	2734	1417	2658	1359	2579	1299	2499	1238
3 Manufacturing [c]	54931	28240	55575	28301	56147	28315	56802	28458	57490	28660	58112	28841
4 Electricity, gas and water	30487	22063	31434	22552	32423	23071	33451	23616	34483	24154	35504	24669
5 Construction	3974	2507	4020	2488	4065	2470	4120	2463	4183	2465	4248	2472
6 Wholesale and retail trade	28492	19408	29235	19752	30221	20330	31237	20927	32285	21544	33635	22449

Germany, Federal Republic (Former)

Ten million Deutsche marks

	1986		1987		1988		1989		1990		1991	
	Gross	Net	Gross	Net	Gross	Net	Gross	Net	Gross	Net	Gross	Net
At constant prices of: 1991												
7 Transport and communication	39614	24021	41064	24723	42356	25270	43592	25764	44680	26122	45628	26358
8 Finance, etc.	16348	12283	16781	12506	17332	12840	17921	13205	18542	13594	19264	14076
9 Community, social and personal services	58580	44411	61563	46461	64605	48525	67791	50688	71216	53042	74584	55291
B Producers of government services [d]	70408	49580	72024	50412	73638	51223	75267	52029	76808	52732	78348	53418
C Other producers	18926	13780	19403	14028	19890	14280	20384	14533	20867	14769	21357	15007
4 Land improvement and development and plantation and orchard development	...	...	...	...	...	...	...	...	...	...	...	...
5 Producers' durable goods	215239	112932	219990	115598	225614	119036	232499	123649	241942	130293	253537	138255
A Industries	202982	106698	207540	109246	212996	112579	219659	117028	228814	123456	240030	131130
1 Agriculture	15434	7463	15243	7358	15089	7307	15022	7346	15013	7431	15071	7560
2 Mining and quarrying [c]	3849	2025	3871	2008	3928	2030	3866	1993	3738	1903	3640	1819
3 Manufacturing [c]	83160	43001	84811	44093	86636	45215	88985	46784	92362	49198	96231	51874
4 Electricity, gas and water	17888	9566	18323	9781	18586	9839	18708	9779	18721	9640	18697	9497
5 Construction	5183	2282	4954	2198	4760	2147	4684	2199	4756	2359	4942	2580
6 Wholesale and retail trade	11007	5449	11211	5675	11584	6046	12065	6477	12787	7069	13833	7865
7 Transport and communication	27131	14315	27432	14395	27760	14517	28221	14803	28921	15280	29895	15964
8 Finance, etc.	3213	1875	3379	1951	3576	2058	3778	2172	4087	2379	4474	2628
9 Community, social and personal services	36117	20722	38316	21787	41077	23420	44330	25475	48429	28197	53247	31343
B Producers of government services	9629	4929	9819	5046	9985	5147	10205	5304	10483	5504	10849	5776
C Other producers	2628	1305	2631	1306	2633	1310	2635	1317	2645	1333	2658	1349
6 Breeding stock, dairy cattle, etc.	...	...	...	...	...	...	...	...	...	...	...	...
Total [ef]	1021332	667677	1045571	680100	1071212	693657	1098876	709034	1130197	727370	1164221	747422

	1992		1993		1994		1995		1996		1997	
	Gross	Net	Gross	Net	Gross	Net	Gross	Net	Gross	Net	Gross	Net
At constant prices of: 1991												
1 Residential buildings	528985	361541	541876	368554	555869	376546	...	...	...	...	...	...
2 Non-residential buildings	...	...	...	...	...	...	...	...	...	...	...	...
3 Other construction [ab]	404898	260354	413835	264622	422644	268728	...	...	...	...	...	...
A Industries	303142	191005	310163	194504	317158	197958	...	...	...	...	...	...
1 Agriculture	21632	11069	21654	11000	21661	10919	...	...	...	...	...	...
2 Mining and quarrying [c]	2419	1182	2315	1115	...	...	...	...	...	...	...	...
3 Manufacturing [c]	58576	28918	58598	28642	...	...	...	...	...	...	...	...
4 Electricity, gas and water	36646	25292	37792	25908	...	...	...	...	...	...	...	...
5 Construction	4334	2501	4468	2578	...	...	...	...	...	...	...	...
6 Wholesale and retail trade	35006	23356	36036	23909	...	...	...	...	...	...	...	...
7 Transport and communication	46502	26554	47154	26568	...	...	...	...	...	...	...	...
8 Finance, etc.	20069	14629	20799	15097	...	...	...	...	...	...	...	...
9 Community, social and personal services	77958	57504	81347	59687	...	...	...	...	...	...	...	...
B Producers of government services [d]	79887	54088	81309	54627	82642	55067	...	...	...	...	...	...
C Other producers	21869	15261	22363	15491	22844	15703	...	...	...	...	...	...
4 Land improvement and development and plantation and orchard development	...	...	...	...	...	...	...	...	...	...	...	...

Germany, Federal Republic (Former)

	1992 Gross	1992 Net	1993 Gross	1993 Net	1994 Gross	1994 Net	1995 Gross	1995 Net	1996 Gross	1996 Net	1997 Gross	1997 Net
At constant prices of: 1991												
5 Producers' durable goods	263275	143675	267897	143872	271183	143121	...	...	...	...	...	...
A Industries	249368	136270	253703	136319	256880	135590	...	...	...	...	...	...
1 Agriculture	15036	7571	14848	7417	14648	7245	...	...	...	...	...	...
2 Mining and quarrying [c]	3572	1786	3439	1697	...	...	...	...	...	...	...	...
3 Manufacturing [c]	99191	53458	99719	52673	...	...	...	...	...	...	...	...
4 Electricity, gas and water	18795	9509	18812	9463	...	...	...	...	...	...	...	...
5 Construction	5247	2862	5480	3018	...	...	...	...	...	...	...	...
6 Wholesale and retail trade	15069	8715	16070	9222	...	...	...	...	...	...	...	...
7 Transport and communication	30528	16279	31116	16530	...	...	...	...	...	...	...	...
8 Finance, etc.	4932	2907	5351	3118	...	...	...	...	...	...	...	...
9 Community, social and personal services	56998	33183	58868	33181	...	...	...	...	...	...	...	...
B Producers of government services	11237	6041	11526	6188	11648	6175	...	...	...	...	...	...
C Other producers	2670	1364	2668	1365	2655	1356	...	...	...	...	...	...
6 Breeding stock, dairy cattle, etc.	...	...	...	...	...	...	...	...	...	...	...	...
Total [ef]	1197158	765570	1223608	777048	1249696	788395	...	...	...	...	...	...

a Item "Land improvement and plantation and orchard development" is included in item "Other construction".
b Item "Non-residential buildings" is included in item "Other construction".
c Quarrying is included in item "Manufacturing".
d Item "Producers of government services" does not include government civil engineering works.
e Value recorded at the beginning of the year (opening stock).
f Public underground construction is not contained in the data of this table (Stocks of Reproducible Fixed Assets by kind of activity).

2.17 Exports and imports of goods and services, detail

Million Deutsche marks

	1986	1987	1988	1989	1990	1991	1992	1993	1994	1995	1996	1997
Exports of goods and services												
1 Exports of merchandise, f.o.b.	508960	506850	548020	616360	663700	743940	804480	793200	875340	...	...	...
2 Transport and communication	44170	42530	43020	50520	57370	74630	75320	76520	75580	...	...	...
3 Insurance service charges	...	...	...	...	...	...	...	...	...	...	...	...
4 Other commodities	...	...	...	...	...	...	...	...	...	...	...	...
5 Adjustments of merchandise exports to change-of-ownership basis	...	...	...	...	...	...	...	...	...	...	...	...
6 Direct purchases in the domestic market by non-residential households	27410	27230	28790	34550	57830	67160	60580	54980	51130	...	...	...
7 Direct purchases in the domestic market by extraterritorial bodies	...	...	...	...	...	...	...	...	...	...	...	...
Total exports of goods and services [a]	580540	576610	619830	701430	778900	885730	940380	924700	1002050	...	...	...
Imports of goods and services												
1 Imports of merchandise, c.i.f.	390690	383890	411770	475320	521240	603560	603460	552720	604500	...	...	...
A Imports of merchandise, f.o.b.	390690	383890	411770	475320	521240	603560	603460	552720	604500	...	...	...
B Transport of services on merchandise imports	...	...	...	...	...	...	...	...	...	...	...	...
C Insurance service charges on merchandise imports	...	...	...	...	...	...	...	...	...	...	...	...

Germany, Federal Republic (Former)

Million Deutsche marks

	1986	1987	1988	1989	1990	1991	1992	1993	1994	1995	1996	1997
2 Adjustments of merchandise imports to change-of-ownership basis	...	...	...	...	...	...	...	...	...	...	...	...
3 Other transport and communication	47560	47520	50560	56840	61440	70940	77550	80780	85620	...	...	...
4 Other insurance service charges	...	...	...	...	...	...	...	...	...	...	...	...
5 Other commodities	...	...	...	...	...	...	...	...	...	...	...	...
6 Direct purchases abroad by government	...	...	...	...	...	...	...	...	...	...	...	...
7 Direct purchases abroad by resident households	42380	45240	47790	49130	54270	59790	66070	71590	75510	...	...	...
Total imports of goods and services [a]	480630	476650	510120	581290	636950	734290	747080	705090	765630	...	...	...
Balance of goods and services	99910	99960	109710	120140	141950	151440	193300	219610	236420	...	...	...
Total imports and balance of goods and services	580540	576610	619830	701430	778900	885730	940380	924700	1002050	...	...	...

a Exports and imports of goods for purposes of repair and improvement are reduced to the value of these services.

3.11 General government production account: total and subsectors

Million Deutsche marks

	\multicolumn{5}{c}{1986}	\multicolumn{5}{c}{1987}
	Total government	Central government	State or provincial government	Local government	Social security funds	Total government	Central government	State or provincial government	Local government	Social security funds
Gross output										
1 Sales	57990	2640	14410	40880	60	60380	2510	14900	42900	70
2 Services produced for own use	382550	71140	118910	68470	124030	397280	73110	123270	71390	129510
3 Own account capital formation	380	–	180	200	–	400	–	190	210	–
Gross output	440920	73780	133500	109550	124090	458060	75620	138360	114500	129580
Gross input										
Intermediate consumption	223800	39070	25200	48310	111220	232240	39740	26360	50050	116090
subtotal: Value added	217120	34710	108300	61240	12870	225820	35880	112000	64450	13490
1 Indirect taxes, net	250	–	120	120	10	250	–	120	120	10
A Indirect taxes	250	–	120	120	10	250	–	120	120	10
B less: Subsidies	...	...	...	...	...	...	...	...	...	...
2 Consumption of fixed capital	13570	890	4170	7960	550	14070	920	4340	8240	570
3 Compensation of employees	203300	33820	104010	53160	12310	211500	34960	107540	56090	12910
4 Net operating surplus	...	...	...	...	...	...	...	...	...	...
Gross input	440920	73780	133500	109550	124090	458060	75620	138360	114500	129580

	\multicolumn{5}{c}{1988}	\multicolumn{5}{c}{1989}
	Total government	Central government	State or provincial government	Local government	Social security funds	Total government	Central government	State or provincial government	Local government	Social security funds
Gross output										
1 Sales	63650	3190	15490	44890	80	66170	3100	16180	46830	60
2 Services produced for own use	412380	72940	126640	72910	139890	418820	75270	130790	76210	136550
3 Own account capital formation	400	–	190	210	–	410	–	190	220	–
Gross output	476430	76130	142320	118010	139970	485400	78370	147160	123260	136610
Gross input										
Intermediate consumption	244570	39380	27370	51820	126000	246760	40340	29570	54690	122160

Germany, Federal Republic (Former)

	1988					1989				
	Total government	Central government	State or provincial government	Local government	Social security funds	Total government	Central government	State or provincial government	Local government	Social security funds
subtotal: Value added	231860	36750	114950	66190	13970	238640	38030	117590	68570	14450
1 Indirect taxes, net	250	–	120	120	10	250	–	120	120	10
A Indirect taxes	250	–	120	120	10	250	–	120	120	10
B less: Subsidies	...	...	...	...	...	...	...	...	...	...
2 Consumption of fixed capital	14690	970	4560	8570	590	15550	1040	4850	9050	610
3 Compensation of employees	216920	35780	110270	57500	13370	222840	36990	112620	59400	13830
4 Net operating surplus	...	...	...	...	...	...	...	...	...	...
Gross input	476430	76130	142320	118010	139970	485400	78370	147160	123260	136610

	1990					1991				
	Total government	Central government	State or provincial government	Local government	Social security funds	Total government	Central government	State or provincial government	Local government	Social security funds
Gross output										
1 Sales	74880	6480	17460	50870	70	90320	14460	19470	56250	140
2 Services produced for own use	444070	74780	138950	82260	148080	467160	64530	146880	90190	165560
3 Own account capital formation	430	–	200	230	–	420	–	200	220	–
Gross output	519380	81260	156610	133360	148150	557900	78990	166550	146660	165700
Gross input										
Intermediate consumption	266180	41500	32250	59730	132700	286680	38270	34020	65870	148520
subtotal: Value added	253200	39760	124360	73630	15450	271220	40720	132530	80790	17180
1 Indirect taxes, net	250	–	120	120	10	250	–	120	120	10
A Indirect taxes	250	–	120	120	10	250	–	120	120	10
B less: Subsidies	...	...	...	...	...	...	...	...	...	...
2 Consumption of fixed capital	16660	1110	5210	9680	660	18010	1220	5640	10430	720
3 Compensation of employees	236290	38650	119030	63830	14780	252960	39500	126770	70240	16450
4 Net operating surplus	...	...	...	...	...	...	...	...	...	...
Gross input	519380	81260	156610	133360	148150	557900	78990	166550	146660	165700

	1992					1993				
	Total government	Central government	State or provincial government	Local government	Social security funds	Total government	Central government	State or provincial government	Local government	Social security funds
Gross output										
1 Sales	97190	13890	21010	62070	220	101790	13330	22290	65870	300
2 Services produced for own use	505480	67740	157300	97030	183410	513950	66910	163040	101240	182760
3 Own account capital formation	430	–	200	230	–	430	–	200	230	–
Gross output	603100	81630	178510	159330	183630	616170	80240	185530	167340	183060
Gross input										
Intermediate consumption	312430	39420	35950	72310	164750	315090	37660	37280	76650	163500
subtotal: Value added	290670	42210	142560	87020	18880	301080	42580	148250	90690	19560
1 Indirect taxes, net	250	–	120	120	10	250	–	120	120	10
A Indirect taxes	250	–	120	120	10	250	–	120	120	10
B less: Subsidies	...	...	...	...	...	...	...	...	...	...
2 Consumption of fixed capital	19380	1330	6070	11190	790	20530	1430	6420	11830	850
3 Compensation of employees	271040	40880	136370	75710	18080	280300	41150	141710	78740	18700
4 Net operating surplus	...	...	...	...	...	...	...	...	...	...
Gross input	603100	81630	178510	159330	183630	616170	80240	185530	167340	183060

Germany, Federal Republic (Former)

	1994					1995				
	Total govern-ment	Central govern-ment	State or provincial govern-ment	Local govern-ment	Social security funds	Total govern-ment	Central govern-ment	State or provincial govern-ment	Local govern-ment	Social security funds
	Gross output									
1 Sales	108210	12620	23730	71380	480	...	...	...	...	...
2 Services produced for own use	527660	64620	166030	100200	196810	...	...	...	...	...
3 Own account capital formation	430	–	200	230	–	...	...	...	...	...
Gross output	636300	77240	189960	171810	197290	...	...	...	...	...
	Gross input									
Intermediate consumption	331140	34960	39280	79690	177210	...	...	...	...	...
subtotal: Value added	305160	42280	150680	92120	20080	...	...	...	...	...
1 Indirect taxes, net	250	–	120	120	10	...	...	...	...	...
A Indirect taxes	250	–	120	120	10	...	...	...	...	...
B less: Subsidies	...	...	...	...	...	...	...	...	...	...
2 Consumption of fixed capital	21130	1450	6590	12200	890	...	...	...	...	...
3 Compensation of employees	283780	40830	143970	79800	19180	...	...	...	...	...
4 Net operating surplus	...	...	...	...	...	...	...	...	...	...
Gross input	636300	77240	189960	171810	197290	...	...	...	...	...

3.12 General government income and outlay account: total and subsectors

Million Deutsche marks

	1986					1987				
	Total govern-ment	Central govern-ment	State or provincial govern-ment	Local govern-ment	Social security funds	Total govern-ment	Central govern-ment	State or provincial govern-ment	Local govern-ment	Social security funds
	Receipts									
1 Operating surplus	...	...	...	...	...	...	...	...	...	...
2 Property and entrepreneurial income	32830	20660	2150	5510	5560	26040	15070	1010	5400	5560
3 Taxes, fees and contributions	796710	240180	178130	64620	313780	828050	250540	185110	66260	326140
A Indirect taxes	236170	140360	61590	34220	–	245500	147540	64300	33660	–
B Direct taxes	237040	99820	111090	26130	–	245940	103000	114910	28030	–
Income	227440	...	...	...	...	235850	...	...	...	...
Other	9600	...	...	...	...	10090	...	...	...	...
C Social security contributions	313390	–	–	–	313390	325900	–	–	–	325900
D Fees, fines and penalties	10110	–	5450	4270	390	10710	–	5900	4570	240
4 Other current transfers	36750	16240	41690	38360	44260	36210	15200	43280	40340	46490
A Casualty insurance claims	1450	–	–	280	1170	1470	–	–	260	1210
B Transfers from other government subsectors	...	940	25130	35700	42030	...	890	26450	37630	44130
C Transfers from rest of the world	11290	11080	210	–	...	10090	9980	110	–	...
D Other transfers, except imputed	...	...	...	...	...	...	...	...	...	...
E Imputed unfunded employee pension and welfare contributions	24010	4220	16350	2380	1060	24650	4330	16720	2450	1150
Total current receipts	866290	277080	221970	108490	363600	890300	280810	229400	112000	378190
	Disbursements									
1 Government final consumption expenditure	382550	71140	118910	68470	124030	397280	73110	123270	71390	129510

Germany, Federal Republic (Former)

Million Deutsche marks

	1986					1987				
	Total government	Central government	State or provincial government	Local government	Social security funds	Total government	Central government	State or provincial government	Local government	Social security funds
2 Property income	56130	30680	19560	6920	20	56780	31310	19700	6740	30
A Interest	56130	30680	19560	6920	20	56780	31310	19700	6740	30
B Net land rent and royalties	...	...	...	...	...	...	...	...	...	...
3 Subsidies	41310	28380	10160	1840	930	44800	31100	10550	1970	1180
4 Other current transfers	353850	138960	69090	20900	228700	371390	144700	73230	22120	240440
A Casualty insurance premiums, net	3910	3630	–	280	–	4050	3790	–	260	–
B Transfers to other government subsectors	–	65210	33950	3400	1240	–	68280	35810	3600	1410
C Social security benefits	220980	–	–	–	220980	232050	–	–	–	232050
D Social assistance grants	52980	35220	8100	9660	–	55500	36400	8880	10220	–
E Unfunded employee welfare benefits	32830	8180	18820	4770	1060	34330	8360	19830	4990	1150
F Transfers to private non-profit institutions serving households	12170	1640	6600	2610	1320	13330	1820	7110	2810	1590
G Other transfers n.e.c.	...	...	...	...	...	...	...	...	...	...
H Transfers to rest of the world	30980	25080	1620	180	4100	32130	26050	1600	240	4240
Net saving	32450	7920	4250	10360	9920	20050	590	2650	9780	7030
Total current disbursements and net saving	866290	277080	221970	108490	363600	890300	280810	229400	112000	378190

	1988					1989				
	Total government	Central government	State or provincial government	Local government	Social security funds	Total government	Central government	State or provincial government	Local government	Social security funds

Receipts

1 Operating surplus	...	...	...	...	...	...	...	...	...	...
2 Property and entrepreneurial income	19020	8360	240	5620	5670	30580	18690	280	5970	6510
3 Taxes, fees and contributions	865110	260850	192500	70450	341310	929240	287180	209390	75400	357270
A Indirect taxes	257110	153550	66920	36640	–	278330	168440	71070	38820	–
B Direct taxes	255410	107300	119220	28890	–	281760	118740	131610	31410	–
Income	245280	...	...	...	...	270850	...	...	...	...
Other	10130	...	...	...	...	10910	...	...	...	...
C Social security contributions	341090	–	–	–	341090	356940	–	–	–	356940
D Fees, fines and penalties	11500	–	6360	4920	220	12210	–	6710	5170	330
4 Other current transfers	39460	17660	44920	41660	50040	38890	16390	47620	43380	54200
A Casualty insurance claims	1560	–	–	320	1240	1550	–	–	320	1230
B Transfers from other government subsectors	...	910	27500	38790	47620	...	930	29680	40410	51680
C Transfers from rest of the world	12470	12300	170	–	...	11130	10850	280	–	...
D Other transfers, except imputed	...	...	...	...	...	...	...	...	...	...
E Imputed unfunded employee pension and welfare contributions	25430	4450	17250	2550	1180	26210	4610	17660	2650	1290
Total current receipts	923590	286870	237660	117730	397020	998710	322260	257290	124750	417980

Disbursements

1 Government final consumption expenditure	412380	72940	126640	72910	139890	418820	75270	130790	76210	136550

Germany, Federal Republic (Former)

	1988					1989				
	Total govern-ment	Central govern-ment	State or provincial govern-ment	Local govern-ment	Social security funds	Total govern-ment	Central govern-ment	State or provincial govern-ment	Local govern-ment	Social security funds
2 Property income	58940	32740	20390	6650	30	59590	32470	21150	6810	30
A Interest	58940	32740	20390	6650	30	59590	32470	21150	6810	30
B Net land rent and royalties	...	...	...	...	...	...	...	...	...	...
3 Subsidies	47740	33990	10530	2010	1210	46780	32250	11450	2100	980
4 Other current transfers	392530	154170	75770	23480	253930	409620	163070	80350	25640	263260
A Casualty insurance premiums, net	4080	3760	–	320	–	4160	3840	–	320	–
B Transfers to other government subsectors	–	72810	36830	3800	1380	–	78500	38590	4190	1420
C Social security benefits	245000	–	–	–	245000	254320	–	–	–	254320
D Social assistance grants	55950	35740	9300	10910	–	58350	36590	9960	11800	–
E Unfunded employee welfare benefits	35510	8460	20700	5170	1180	37010	8640	21720	5360	1290
F Transfers to private non-profit institutions serving households	14150	1890	7400	2990	1870	14540	2100	7760	3190	1490
G Other transfers n.e.c.	...	...	...	...	...	...	...	...	...	...
H Transfers to rest of the world	37840	31510	1540	290	4500	41240	33400	2320	780	4740
Net saving	12000	–6970	4330	12680	1960	63900	19200	13550	13990	17160
Total current disbursements and net saving	923590	286870	237660	117730	397020	998710	322260	257290	124750	417980

	1990					1991				
	Total govern-ment	Central govern-ment	State or provincial govern-ment	Local govern-ment	Social security funds	Total govern-ment	Central govern-ment	State or provincial govern-ment	Local govern-ment	Social security funds

Receipts

1 Operating surplus	...	...	...	...	...	...	...	...	...	...
2 Property and entrepreneurial income	33310	19690	–410	6450	8540	34780	18120	20	7100	10490
3 Taxes, fees and contributions	969130	297120	211710	77200	383100	1089010	347020	236750	83480	421760
A Indirect taxes	302220	183450	77790	40980	–	337530	208010	86750	42770	–
B Direct taxes	271000	113670	126650	30680	–	316020	139010	142030	34980	–
Income	259850	...	...	...	...	303860	...	...	...	...
Other	11150	...	...	...	...	12160	...	...	...	...
C Social security contributions	382770	–	–	–	382770	421050	–	–	–	421050
D Fees, fines and penalties	13140	–	7270	5540	330	14410	–	7970	5730	710
4 Other current transfers	40600	16600	50360	45800	55800	46170	20900	56370	50410	66590
A Casualty insurance claims	1600	–	–	330	1270	1730	–	–	420	1310
B Transfers from other government subsectors	...	730	31400	42640	53190	...	1810	35300	47080	63910
C Transfers from rest of the world	11310	11060	250	–	...	16130	14320	1810	–	...
D Other transfers, except imputed	...	...	...	...	...	...	...	...	...	...
E Imputed unfunded employee pension and welfare contributions	27690	4810	18710	2830	1340	28310	4770	19260	2910	1370
Total current receipts	1043040	333410	261660	129450	447440	1169960	386040	293140	140990	498840

Disbursements

1 Government final consumption expenditure	444070	74780	138950	82260	148080	467160	64530	146880	90190	165560
2 Property income	62390	34150	21850	7320	30	73500	42380	24000	8040	30

Germany, Federal Republic (Former)

	1990					1991				
	Total govern-ment	Central govern-ment	State or provincial govern-ment	Local govern-ment	Social security funds	Total govern-ment	Central govern-ment	State or provincial govern-ment	Local govern-ment	Social security funds
A Interest	62390	34150	21850	7320	30	73500	42380	24000	8040	30
B Net land rent and royalties	...	...	...	...	...	...	...	...	...	...
3 Subsidies	48830	33380	12000	2350	1100	45510	30310	11440	2570	1190
4 Other current transfers	472900	211740	84570	26880	277670	573590	275230	103680	29020	313760
A Casualty insurance premiums, net	4530	4200	–	330	–	4980	4560	–	420	–
B Transfers to other government subsectors	–	81390	41050	4360	1160	–	95680	45850	5300	1270
C Social security benefits	269050	–	–	–	269050	283750	–	–	–	283750
D Social assistance grants	60280	37140	10290	12850	–	63930	38860	11930	13140	–
E Unfunded employee welfare benefits	39100	9030	22960	5770	1340	41670	9560	24590	6150	1370
F Transfers to private non-profit institutions serving households	15720	2790	8300	3550	1080	16830	2620	9090	3990	1130
G Other transfers n.e.c.	...	...	...	...	...	...	...	...	...	...
H Transfers to rest of the world	84220	77190	1970	20	5040	162430	123950	12220	20	26240
Net saving	14850	–20640	4290	10640	20560	10200	–26410	7140	11170	18300
Total current disbursements and net saving	1043040	333410	261660	129450	447440	1169960	386040	293140	140990	498840

	1992					1993				
	Total govern-ment	Central govern-ment	State or provincial govern-ment	Local govern-ment	Social security funds	Total govern-ment	Central govern-ment	State or provincial govern-ment	Local govern-ment	Social security funds

Receipts

1 Operating surplus	...	...	...	...	...	...	...	...	...	...
2 Property and entrepreneurial income	46120	27770	–20	8010	11310	43670	25840	20	8220	10540
3 Taxes, fees and contributions	1174210	374090	257940	89960	452220	1207960	369970	269940	92050	476000
A Indirect taxes	365360	224730	94960	45670	–	380170	229500	104170	46500	–
B Direct taxes	342010	149360	154240	38410	–	336040	140470	156480	39090	–
Income	328880	...	...	...	...	322580	...	...	...	...
Other	13130	...	...	...	...	13460	...	...	...	...
C Social security contributions	451850	–	–	–	451850	475550	–	–	–	475550
D Fees, fines and penalties	14990	–	8740	5880	370	16200	–	9290	6460	450
4 Other current transfers	49190	24630	59790	54950	67400	49170	30360	58120	60020	78340
A Casualty insurance claims	1850	–	–	420	1430	1930	–	–	440	1490
B Transfers from other government subsectors	...	4800	36890	51350	64540	...	11500	34520	56330	75320
C Transfers from rest of the world	17220	14910	2310	–	...	16150	13950	2200	–	...
D Other transfers, except imputed	...	...	...	...	...	...	...	...	...	...
E Imputed unfunded employee pension and welfare contributions	30120	4920	20590	3180	1430	31090	4910	21400	3250	1530
Total current receipts	1269520	426490	317710	152920	530930	1300800	426170	328080	160290	564880

Disbursements

1 Government final consumption expenditure	505480	67740	157300	97030	183410	513950	66910	163040	101240	182760
2 Property income	83020	49520	25550	8850	50	90520	54880	26950	9580	60
A Interest	83020	49520	25550	8850	50	90520	54880	26950	9580	60

Germany, Federal Republic (Former)

	1992					1993				
	Total government	Central government	State or provincial government	Local government	Social security funds	Total government	Central government	State or provincial government	Local government	Social security funds
B Net land rent and royalties ..	...	...	...	...	...	...	...	...	...	...
3 Subsidies	43770	27600	11960	3020	1190	45080	29820	10570	3800	890
4 Other current transfers	614250	276830	114210	33460	347330	656440	292760	128130	39270	373950
A Casualty insurance premiums, net	5460	5040	–	420	–	5710	5270	–	440	–
B Transfers to other government subsectors	–	97200	52500	6650	1230	–	104160	64070	8210	1230
C Social security benefits	302990	–	–	–	302990	329580	–	–	–	329580
D Social assistance grants	68680	41390	12820	14470	–	75580	44520	13290	17770	–
E Unfunded employee welfare benefits	44550	10280	26540	6300	1430	46970	10960	27880	6600	1530
F Transfers to private non-profit institutions serving households	18610	2490	9370	5600	1150	19910	2380	10020	6240	1270
G Other transfers n.e.c.	...	...	...	...	...	...	...	...	...	...
H Transfers to rest of the world	173960	120430	12980	20	40530	178690	125470	12870	10	40340
Net saving	23000	4800	8690	10560	–1050	–5190	–18200	–610	6400	7220
Total current disbursements and net saving	1269520	426490	317710	152920	530930	1300800	426170	328080	160290	564880

	1994					1995				
	Total government	Central government	State or provincial government	Local government	Social security funds	Total government	Central government	State or provincial government	Local government	Social security funds

Receipts

1 Operating surplus	...	...	...	...	...	...	...	...	...	...
2 Property and entrepreneurial income	47090	30400	200	8320	9010	...	...	...	...	...
3 Taxes, fees and contributions .	1265630	390240	276640	93430	505320	...	...	...	...	...
A Indirect taxes	408520	250120	111830	46570	–	...	...	...	...	...
B Direct taxes	334180	140120	154900	39160	–	...	...	...	...	...
Income	320830	...	...	...	...	...	...	...	...	...
Other	13350	...	...	...	...	...	...	...	...	...
C Social security contributions	504800	–	–	–	504800	...	...	...	...	...
D Fees, fines and penalties	18130	–	9910	7700	520	...	...	...	...	...
4 Other current transfers	52070	37010	58940	61720	76580	...	...	...	...	...
A Casualty insurance claims ..	1990	–	–	490	1500	...	...	...	...	...
B Transfers from other government subsectors	...	16320	34590	57770	73500	...	...	...	...	...
C Transfers from rest of the world	15360	13870	1490	–	...	...	...	...	...	...
D Other transfers, except imputed	...	...	...	...	...	...	...	...	...	...
E Imputed unfunded employee pension and welfare contributions	34720	6820	22860	3460	1580	...	...	...	...	...
Total current receipts	1364790	457650	335780	163470	590910	...	...	...	...	...

Disbursements

1 Government final consumption expenditure	527660	64620	166030	100200	196810	...	...	...	...	...
2 Property income	101380	65060	27500	9600	60	...	...	...	...	...
A Interest	101380	65060	27500	9600	60	...	...	...	...	...
B Net land rent and royalties ..	...	...	...	...	...	...	...	...	...	...

… Germany, Federal Republic (Former)

	1994					1995				
	Total government	Central government	State or provincial government	Local government	Social security funds	Total government	Central government	State or provincial government	Local government	Social security funds
3 Subsidies	48930	34080	10050	4040	760	...	...	...	...	...
4 Other current transfers	677860	292610	134680	41880	390870	...	...	...	...	...
A Casualty insurance premiums, net	610	120	–	490	–	...	...	...	...	...
B Transfers to other government subsectors	–	101470	70650	9100	960	...	...	...	...	...
C Social security benefits	345750	–	–	–	345750	...	...	...	...	...
D Social assistance grants	77500	45890	12450	19160	–	...	...	...	...	...
E Unfunded employee welfare benefits	56920	20060	28640	6640	1580	...	...	...	...	...
F Transfers to private non-profit institutions serving households	21150	2400	10730	6480	1540	...	...	...	...	...
G Other transfers n.e.c.	...	...	...	...	...	...	...	...	...	...
H Transfers to rest of the world	175930	122670	12210	10	41040	...	...	...	...	...
Net saving	8960	1280	–2480	7750	2410	...	...	...	...	...
Total current disbursements and net saving	1364790	457650	335780	163470	590910	...	...	...	...	...

3.13 General government capital accumulation account: total and subsectors

Million Deutsche marks

	1986					1987				
	Total government	Central government	State or provincial government	Local government	Social security funds	Total government	Central government	State or provincial government	Local government	Social security funds
Finance of gross accumulation											
1 Gross saving	46020	8810	8420	18320	10470	34120	1510	6990	18020	7600
A Consumption of fixed capital	13570	890	4170	7960	550	14070	920	4340	8240	570
B Net saving	32450	7920	4250	10360	9920	20050	590	2650	9780	7030
2 Capital transfers	5870	320	10690	17040	30	6350	240	11550	17640	30
A From other government subsectors	–	210	8520	13450	30	–	140	8990	13950	30
B From other resident sectors	5710	20	2100	3590	–	6160	20	2450	3690	–
C From rest of the world	160	90	70	–	–	190	80	110	–	–
Finance of gross accumulation	51890	9130	19110	35360	10500	40470	1750	18540	35660	7630
Gross accumulation											
1 Gross capital formation	45310	6070	9560	28580	1100	46000	6120	9690	29250	940
A Increase in stocks	–	–	–	–	–	–	–	–	–	–
B Gross fixed capital formation	45310	6070	9560	28580	1100	46000	6120	9690	29250	940
Own account	380	–	180	200	–	400	–	190	210	–
Other	44930	6070	9380	28380	1100	45600	6120	9500	29040	940
2 Purchases of land, net	1980	410	390	1180	–	1990	480	360	1130	20
3 Purchases of intangible assets, net	...	...	...	...	...	...	...	...	...	...
4 Capital transfers	30000	22740	24060	5140	270	30320	23080	25120	5120	110
A To other government subsectors	–	7930	13270	900	110	–	8430	13680	890	110
B To other resident sectors	27650	12490	10760	4240	160	28060	12390	11440	4230	–
C To the rest of the world	2350	2320	30	–	–	2260	2260	–	–	–

Germany, Federal Republic (Former)

Million Deutsche marks

	1986					1987				
	Total government	Central government	State or provincial government	Local government	Social security funds	Total government	Central government	State or provincial government	Local government	Social security funds
Net lending	−25400	−20090	−14900	460	9130	−37840	−27930	−16630	160	6560
Gross accumulation	51890	9130	19110	35360	10500	40470	1750	18540	35660	7630

	1988					1989				
	Total government	Central government	State or provincial government	Local government	Social security funds	Total government	Central government	State or provincial government	Local government	Social security funds

Finance of gross accumulation

1 Gross saving	26690	−6000	8890	21250	2550	79450	20240	18400	23040	17770
A Consumption of fixed capital	14690	970	4560	8570	590	15550	1040	4850	9050	610
B Net saving	12000	−6970	4330	12680	1960	63900	19200	13550	13990	17160
2 Capital transfers	6670	200	11630	17710	30	6480	270	13960	18450	30
A From other government subsectors	–	120	8940	13810	30	–	100	11570	14530	30
B From other resident sectors	6520	10	2610	3900	–	6220	20	2280	3920	–
C From rest of the world	150	70	80	–	–	260	150	110	–	–
Finance of gross accumulation	33360	−5800	20520	38960	2580	85930	20510	32360	41490	17800

Gross accumulation

1 Gross capital formation	47500	6160	9730	30580	1030	50990	6540	10550	32960	940
A Increase in stocks	–	–	–	–	–	–	–	–	–	–
B Gross fixed capital formation	47500	6160	9730	30580	1030	50990	6540	10550	32960	940
Own account	400	–	190	210	–	410	–	190	220	–
Other	47100	6160	9540	30370	1030	50580	6540	10360	32740	940
2 Purchases of land, net	1410	190	430	730	60	1380	250	330	790	10
3 Purchases of intangible assets, net	...	...	...	...	...	...	...	...	...	...
4 Capital transfers	29690	22360	25260	4860	110	30810	25340	26830	4780	90
A To other government subsectors	–	8240	13530	1020	110	–	10910	14250	980	90
B To other resident sectors	27200	11630	11730	3840	–	27910	11530	12580	3800	–
C To the rest of the world	2490	2490	–	–	–	2900	2900	–	–	–
Net lending	−45240	−34510	−14900	2790	1380	2750	−11620	−5350	2960	16760
Gross accumulation	33360	−5800	20520	38960	2580	85930	20510	32360	41490	17800

	1990					1991				
	Total government	Central government	State or provincial government	Local government	Social security funds	Total government	Central government	State or provincial government	Local government	Social security funds

Finance of gross accumulation

1 Gross saving	31510	−19530	9500	20320	21220	28210	−25190	12780	21600	19020
A Consumption of fixed capital	16660	1110	5210	9680	660	18010	1220	5640	10430	720
B Net saving	14850	−20640	4290	10640	20560	10200	−26410	7140	11170	18300
2 Capital transfers	7720	720	15520	19740	20	7930	800	16590	20870	30
A From other government subsectors	–	530	12110	15620	20	–	660	13400	16270	30
B From other resident sectors	7470	10	3340	4120	–	7790	70	3120	4600	–
C From rest of the world	250	180	70	–	–	140	70	70	–	–
Finance of gross accumulation	39230	−18810	25020	40060	21240	36140	−24390	29370	42470	19050

Germany, Federal Republic (Former)

	1990					1991				
	Total govern-ment	Central govern-ment	State or provincial govern-ment	Local govern-ment	Social security funds	Total govern-ment	Central govern-ment	State or provincial govern-ment	Local govern-ment	Social security funds

Gross accumulation

1 Gross capital formation	54160	7010	11100	34990	1060	58440	7420	11620	37930	1470
A Increase in stocks	–	–	–	–	–	–	–	–	–	–
B Gross fixed capital formation	54160	7010	11100	34990	1060	58440	7420	11620	37930	1470
Own account	430	–	200	230	–	420	–	200	220	–
Other	53730	7010	10900	34760	1060	58020	7420	11420	37710	1470
2 Purchases of land, net	1370	200	310	820	40	1460	170	390	850	50
3 Purchases of intangible assets, net	...	...	...	...	...	...	...	...	...	...
4 Capital transfers	33440	27470	28670	5480	100	66150	61320	29240	5590	360
A To other government sub-sectors	–	11820	15330	1060	70	–	13210	16000	1060	90
B To other resident sectors	27410	9630	13330	4420	30	39750	21930	13240	4530	50
C To the rest of the world	6030	6020	10	–	–	26400	26180	–	–	220
Net lending	–49740	–53490	–15060	–1230	20040	–89910	–93300	–11880	–1900	17170
Gross accumulation	39230	–18810	25020	40060	21240	36140	–24390	29370	42470	19050

	1992					1993				
	Total govern-ment	Central govern-ment	State or provincial govern-ment	Local govern-ment	Social security funds	Total govern-ment	Central govern-ment	State or provincial govern-ment	Local govern-ment	Social security funds

Finance of gross accumulation

1 Gross saving	42380	6130	14760	21750	–260	15340	–16770	5810	18230	8070
A Consumption of fixed capital	19380	1330	6070	11190	790	20530	1430	6420	11830	850
B Net saving	23000	4800	8690	10560	–1050	–5190	–18200	–610	6400	7220
2 Capital transfers	8970	350	17760	22220	30	9540	300	16610	22860	40
A From other government subsectors	–	140	14090	17130	30	–	160	12850	17220	40
B From other resident sectors	8620	30	3500	5090	–	9300	30	3630	5640	–
C From rest of the world	350	180	170	–	–	240	110	130	–	–
Finance of gross accumulation	51350	6480	32520	43970	–230	24880	–16470	22420	41090	8110

Gross accumulation

1 Gross capital formation	62670	8540	11700	40820	1610	61320	7810	11520	40330	1660
A Increase in stocks	–	–	–	–	–	–	–	–	–	–
B Gross fixed capital formation	62670	8540	11700	40820	1610	61320	7810	11520	40330	1660
Own account	430	–	200	230	–	430	–	200	230	–
Other	62240	8540	11500	40590	1610	60890	7810	11320	40100	1660
2 Purchases of land, net	1270	350	360	480	80	970	250	400	130	190
3 Purchases of intangible assets, net	...	...	...	...	...	...	...	...	...	...
4 Capital transfers	51610	47140	30210	5170	480	49850	44390	30160	5210	360
A To other government sub-sectors	–	13410	16830	1070	80	–	12130	16930	1130	80
B To other resident sectors	26120	8600	13380	4100	40	25300	7900	13230	4080	90
C To the rest of the world	25490	25130	–	–	360	24550	24360	–	–	190
Net lending	–64200	–49550	–9750	–2500	–2400	–87260	–68920	–19660	–4580	5900
Gross accumulation	51350	6480	32520	43970	–230	24880	–16470	22420	41090	8110

Germany, Federal Republic (Former)

	1994					1995				
	Total govern-ment	Central govern-ment	State or provincial govern-ment	Local govern-ment	Social security funds	Total govern-ment	Central govern-ment	State or provincial govern-ment	Local govern-ment	Social security funds

Finance of gross accumulation

1 Gross saving	30090	2730	4110	19950	3300	...	...	...	...	...
A Consumption of fixed capital	21130	1450	6590	12200	890	...	...	...	...	...
B Net saving	8960	1280	−2480	7750	2410	...	...	...	...	...
2 Capital transfers	10320	260	17640	21480	30	...	...	...	...	...
A From other government subsectors	−	140	13230	15690	30	...	...	...	...	...
B From other resident sectors	9990	100	4100	5790	−	...	...	...	...	...
C From rest of the world	330	20	310	−	−	...	...	...	...	...
Finance of gross accumulation	40410	2990	21750	41430	3330	...	...	...	...	...

Gross accumulation

1 Gross capital formation	59930	7970	11250	38950	1760	...	...	...	...	...
A Increase in stocks	−	−	−	−	−	...	...	...	...	...
B Gross fixed capital formation	59930	7970	11250	38950	1760	...	...	...	...	...
Own account	430	−	200	230	−	...	...	...	...	...
Other	59500	7970	11050	38720	1760	...	...	...	...	...
2 Purchases of land, net	−80	−360	300	−70	50	...	...	...	...	...
3 Purchases of intangible assets, net	...	...	...	...	...	...	...	...	...	...
4 Capital transfers	39480	35310	28850	4150	260	...	...	...	...	...
A To other government subsectors	−	12500	15400	1110	80	...	...	...	...	...
B To other resident sectors	21840	5340	13450	3040	10	...	...	...	...	...
C To the rest of the world	17640	17470	−	−	170	...	...	...	...	...
Net lending	−58920	−39930	−18650	−1600	1260	...	...	...	...	...
Gross accumulation	40410	2990	21750	41430	3330	...	...	...	...	...

3.14 General government capital finance account: total and subsectors

Million Deutsche marks

	1986					1987				
	Total govern-ment	Central govern-ment	State or provincial govern-ment	Local govern-ment	Social security funds	Total govern-ment	Central govern-ment	State or provincial govern-ment	Local govern-ment	Social security funds

Acquisition of financial assets

1 Gold and SDRs	−	−	...	...	−	−	−	...	...	−
2 Currency and transferable deposits	−2010	−910	...	...	−1100	3670	3590	...	...	80
3 Other deposits	12590	4700	...	...	7890	5300	5360	...	...	−60
4 Bills and bonds, short-term	20	20	...	...	−	−40	−40	...	...	−
5 Bonds, long-term	170	−20	...	...	190	1630	−200	...	...	1830
6 Corporate equity securities	160	160	...	...	−	−2160	−2160	...	...	−
7 Short-term loans, n.e.c.	1210	180	...	...	1030	1300	500	...	...	800
8 Long-term loans, n.e.c.	4210	3050	...	...	1160	4800	950	...	...	3850
9 Other receivables	...	...	...	...	...	...	...	...	...	...
10 Other assets	80	80	...	...	−	280	280	...	...	−
Total aquisition of financial assets [a]	16430	7260	...	...	9170	14780	8280	...	...	6500

Germany, Federal Republic (Former)

Million Deutsche marks

	1986					1987				
	Total government	Central government	State or provincial government	Local government	Social security funds	Total government	Central government	State or provincial government	Local government	Social security funds

Incurrence of liabilities

1 Currency and transferable deposits	–	–	...	...	–	–	–	...	...	–
2 Other deposits	–	–	...	...	–	–	–	...	...	–
3 Bills and bonds, short-term	–1820	–1820	...	...	–	–3200	–3200	...	...	–
4 Bonds, long-term	51190	51190	...	...	–	49910	49910	...	...	–
5 Short-term loans, n.e.c.	2560	2540	...	...	20	–920	–860	...	...	–60
6 Long-term loans, n.e.c.	–10090	–10120	...	...	30	6820	6830	...	...	–10
7 Other payables	...	...	...	...	...	...	...	...	...	...
8 Other liabilities	–	–	...	...	–	–	–	...	...	–
Total incurrence of liabilities	41840	41790	...	...	50	52610	52680	...	...	–70
Net lending	–25410	–34530	...	...	9120	–37830	–44400	...	...	6570
Incurrence of liabilities and net worth [a]	16430	7260	...	...	9170	14780	8280	...	...	6500

	1988					1989				
	Total government	Central government	State or provincial government	Local government	Social security funds	Total government	Central government	State or provincial government	Local government	Social security funds

Acquisition of financial assets

1 Gold and SDRs	–	–	...	...	–	–	–	...	...	–
2 Currency and transferable deposits	–50	–210	...	...	160	6240	4930	...	...	1310
3 Other deposits	6310	6020	...	...	290	10510	5460	...	...	5050
4 Bills and bonds, short-term	–30	–30	...	...	–	–20	–20	...	...	–
5 Bonds, long-term	1650	200	...	...	1450	2900	900	...	...	2000
6 Corporate equity securities	–2020	–2020	...	...	–	1230	1230	...	...	–
7 Short-term loans, n.e.c.	2290	730	...	...	1560	5180	–1460	...	...	6640
8 Long-term loans, n.e.c.	4360	6260	...	...	–1900	8080	6060	...	...	2020
9 Other receivables	...	...	...	...	...	...	...	...	...	...
10 Other assets	60	60	...	...	–	80	80	...	...	–
Total aquisition of financial assets [a]	12570	11010	...	...	1560	34200	17180	...	...	17020

Incurrence of liabilities

1 Currency and transferable deposits	–	–	...	...	–	–	–	...	...	–
2 Other deposits	–	–	...	...	–	–	–	...	...	–
3 Bills and bonds, short-term	–60	–60	...	...	–	7210	7210	...	...	–
4 Bonds, long-term	42940	42940	...	...	–	26210	26210	...	...	–
5 Short-term loans, n.e.c.	1540	1580	...	...	–40	490	440	...	...	50
6 Long-term loans, n.e.c.	12860	12860	...	...	–	–5070	–5060	...	...	–10
7 Other payables	...	...	...	...	...	...	...	...	...	...
8 Other liabilities	–	–	...	...	–	–	–	...	...	–
Total incurrence of liabilities	57280	57320	...	...	–40	28840	28800	...	...	40
Net lending	–44710	–46310	...	...	1600	5360	–11620	...	...	16980
Incurrence of liabilities and net worth [a]	12570	11010	...	...	1560	34200	17180	...	...	17020

Germany, Federal Republic (Former)

	1990					1991				
	Total government	Central government	State or provincial government	Local government	Social security funds	Total government	Central government	State or provincial government	Local government	Social security funds

Acquisition of financial assets

1 Gold and SDRs	–	–	...	...	–	...	...	...	...	...
2 Currency and transferable deposits	8340	7260	...	...	1080	...	...	...	...	...
3 Other deposits	11660	4140	...	...	7520	...	...	...	...	...
4 Bills and bonds, short-term	200	200	...	...	–	...	...	...	...	...
5 Bonds, long-term	3300	600	...	...	2700	...	...	...	...	...
6 Corporate equity securities	1260	1260	...	...	–	...	...	...	...	...
7 Short-term loans, n.e.c.	8180	2510	...	...	5670	...	...	...	...	...
8 Long-term loans, n.e.c.	8980	5730	...	...	3250	...	...	...	...	...
9 Other receivables	...	...	...	...	...	...	...	...	...	...
10 Other assets	50	50	...	...	–	...	...	...	...	...
Total aquisition of financial assets [a]	41970	21750	...	...	20220	...	...	...	...	...

Incurrence of liabilities

1 Currency and transferable deposits	–	–	...	...	–	...	...	...	...	...
2 Other deposits	–	–	...	...	–	...	...	...	...	...
3 Bills and bonds, short-term	8380	8380	...	...	–	...	...	...	...	...
4 Bonds, long-term	76740	76740	...	...	–	...	...	...	...	...
5 Short-term loans, n.e.c.	740	900	...	...	–160	...	...	...	...	...
6 Long-term loans, n.e.c.	7310	7200	...	...	110	...	...	...	...	...
7 Other payables	...	...	...	...	...	...	...	...	...	...
8 Other liabilities	–	–	...	...	–	...	...	...	...	...
Total incurrence of liabilities	93170	93220	...	...	–50	...	...	...	...	...
Net lending	–51200	–71470	...	...	20270	...	...	...	...	...
Incurrence of liabilities and net worth [a]	41970	21750	...	...	20220	...	...	...	...	...

a Data in this table have not been revised, therefore they are not comparable with the data in other tables.

3.21 Corporate and quasi-corporate enterprise production account: total and sectors

Million Deutsche marks

	1986				1987				1988			
	Corporate and quasi-corporate enterprises			Addendum: total including unincorporated	Corporate and quasi-corporate enterprises			Addendum: total including unincorporated	Corporate and quasi-corporate enterprises			Addendum: total including unincorporated
	Total	Non-financial	Financial		Total	Non-financial	Financial		Total	Non-financial	Financial	

Gross output

Gross output [a]	4327510	4174440	153070	...	4375560	4224780	150780	...	4617530	4457780	159750	...

Gross input

Intermediate consumption	2800660	2664410	136250	...	2804440	2670220	134220	...	2954710	2814580	140130	...
1 Imputed bank service charge	83690	–	83690	...	82270	–	82270	...	85150	–	85150	...
2 Other intermediate consumption	2716970	2664410	52560	...	2722170	2670220	51950	...	2869560	2814580	54980	...
subtotal: Value added	1526850	1510030	16820	...	1571120	1554560	16560	...	1662820	1643200	19620	...
1 Indirect taxes, net	59680	50490	9190	...	56160	47500	8660	...	59460	49640	9820	...
A Indirect taxes	100990	91800	9190	...	100960	92300	8660	...	107200	97380	9820	...
B less: Subsidies	41310	41310	–	...	44800	44800	–	...	47740	47740	–	...
2 Consumption of fixed capital	226600	221870	4730	...	234570	229590	4980	...	244600	239400	5200	...

Germany, Federal Republic (Former)

Million Deutsche marks

	1986				1987				1988			
	Corporate and quasi-corporate enterprises			Addendum: total including unincorporated	Corporate and quasi-corporate enterprises			Addendum: total including unincorporated	Corporate and quasi-corporate enterprises			Addendum: total including unincorporated
	Total	Non-financial	Financial		Total	Non-financial	Financial		Total	Non-financial	Financial	
3 Compensation of employees	828270	781250	47020	...	862260	812150	50110	...	899020	846650	52370	...
4 Net operating surplus	412300	456420	−44120	...	418130	465320	−47190	...	459740	507510	−47770	...
Gross input [a]	4327510	4174440	153070	...	4375560	4224780	150780	...	4617530	4457780	159750	...

	1989				1990				1991			
	Corporate and quasi-corporate enterprises			Addendum: total including unincorporated	Corporate and quasi-corporate enterprises			Addendum: total including unincorporated	Corporate and quasi-corporate enterprises			Addendum: total including unincorporated
	Total	Non-financial	Financial		Total	Non-financial	Financial		Total	Non-financial	Financial	

Gross output

Gross output [a]	4962520	4794020	168500	...	5405620	5223250	182370	...	5905090	5694780	210320	...

Gross input

Intermediate consumption	3191550	3046010	145540	...	3471070	3308920	162150	...	3796790	3609430	187360	...
1 Imputed bank service charge	88410	−	88410	...	96280	−	96280	...	111240	−	111240	...
2 Other intermediate consumption	3103140	3046010	57130	...	3374790	3308920	65870	...	3685550	3609430	76120	...
subtotal: Value added	1770970	1748010	22960	...	1934550	1914330	20220	...	2108310	2085350	22960	...
1 Indirect taxes, net	70360	60150	10210	...	73160	63020	10140	...	88240	75550	12690	...
A Indirect taxes	117140	106930	10210	...	121990	111850	10140	...	133750	121060	12690	...
B less: Subsidies	46780	46780	−	...	48830	48830	−	...	45510	45510	−	...
2 Consumption of fixed capital	259900	254280	5620	...	282060	275900	6160	...	310240	303320	6920	...
3 Compensation of employees	943520	888660	54860	...	1025250	964350	60900	...	1117440	1050840	66600	...
4 Net operating surplus	497190	544920	−47730	...	554080	611010	−56980	...	592390	655640	−63250	...
Gross input [a]	4962520	4794020	168500	...	5405620	5223200	182370	...	5905100	5694780	210320	...

	1992				1993				1994			
	Corporate and quasi-corporate enterprises			Addendum: total including unincorporated	Corporate and quasi-corporate enterprises			Addendum: total including unincorporated	Corporate and quasi-corporate enterprises			Addendum: total including unincorporated
	Total	Non-financial	Financial		Total	Non-financial	Financial		Total	Non-financial	Financial	

Gross output

Gross output [a]	6135050	5903760	231290	...	6042880	5791650	251230	...	6277450	...	...	...

Gross input

Intermediate consumption	3901440	3695730	205710	...	3803270	3585760	217510	...	3935120	...	...	...
1 Imputed bank service charge	124070	−	124070	...	132330	−	132330	...	...	...	...	...
2 Other intermediate consumption	3777370	3695730	81640	...	3670940	3585760	85180	...	...	...	...	...
subtotal: Value added	2233610	2208030	25580	...	2239610	2205890	33720	...	2342330	...	...	...
1 Indirect taxes, net	103470	87970	15500	...	104110	86170	17940	...	111740	−48930	...	...
A Indirect taxes	147240	131740	15500	...	149190	131250	17940	...	160670	...	...	...
B less: Subsidies	43770	43770	−	...	45080	45080	−	...	48930	48930	...	...
2 Consumption of fixed capital	335370	327580	7790	...	353550	344950	8600	...	362130	...	...	...
3 Compensation of employees	1191700	1118580	73120	...	1193370	1116890	76480	...	1207590	1129100	78490	...
4 Net operating surplus	603060	673890	−70830	...	588580	657880	−69300	...	...	...	...	...
Gross input [a]	6135040	5903760	231290	...	6042880	5791650	251230	...	5616580	1080170	78490	...

a The estimates of this table exclude private non-profit organizations.

Germany, Federal Republic (Former)

3.22 Corporate and quasi-corporate enterprise income and outlay account: total and sectors
Million Deutsche marks

	1986 Total	1986 Non-financial	1986 Financial	1987 Total	1987 Non-financial	1987 Financial	1988 Total	1988 Non-financial	1988 Financial	1989 Total	1989 Non-financial	1989 Financial
Receipts												
1 Operating surplus [a]	396010	440130	–44120	391110	438300	–47190	455810	503580	–47770	487410	535140	–47730
2 Property and entrepreneurial income	321560	43110	278450	322020	43020	279000	337490	45350	292140	379110	50340	328770
A Withdrawals from quasi-corporate enterprises	7220	6690	530	7270	6720	550	8030	7420	610	8040	7460	580
B Interest [b]	286750	18360	268390	287180	18040	269140	302170	22180	279990	343820	30200	313620
C Dividends	27590	18060	9530	27570	18260	9310	27290	15750	11540	27250	12680	14570
D Net land rent and royalties	...	...	...	...	...	...	...	...	...	...	...	...
3 Current transfers	90830	34400	56430	97210	37010	60200	101940	37680	64260	107740	39110	68630
A Casualty insurance claims	6760	6450	310	7240	6910	330	7500	7180	320	8210	7890	320
B Casualty insurance premiums, net, due to be received by insurance companies	46940	–	46940	49680	–	49680	53130	–	53130	56960	–	56960
C Current transfers from rest of the world	...	...	...	...	...	...	...	...	...	...	...	...
D Other transfers except imputed	9880	3630	6250	10810	3790	7020	11370	3760	7610	12000	3840	8160
E Imputed unfunded employee pension and welfare contributions	27250	24320	2930	29480	26310	3170	29940	26740	3200	30570	27380	3190
Total current receipts	808400	517640	290760	810340	518330	292010	895240	586610	308630	974260	624590	349670
Disbursements												
1 Property and entrepreneurial income	652050	448560	203490	650720	450940	199780	697680	495560	202120	774110	529180	244930
A Withdrawals from quasi-corporations	273850	273850	...	281390	281390	...	315830	315830	...	336910	336910	...
B Interest [b]	317140	131630	185510	315550	128850	186700	327660	131390	196270	375570	146800	228770
C Dividends	61060	43080	17980	53780	40700	13080	54190	48340	5850	61630	45470	16160
D Net land rent and royalties	...	...	...	...	...	...	...	...	...	...	...	...
2 Direct taxes and other current transfers n.e.c. to general government	40860	30910	9950	36580	27520	9060	39840	29650	10190	45870	37330	8540
A Direct taxes	38800	28850	9950	34500	25440	9060	37590	27400	10190	43280	34740	8540
B Fines, fees, penalties and other current transfers n.e.c.	2060	2060	–	2080	2080	–	2250	2250	–	2590	2590	–
3 Other current transfers	82270	29080	53190	87400	30980	56420	92920	32460	60460	99400	34420	64980
A Casualty insurance premiums, net	7720	7410	310	8240	7910	330	8620	8300	320	9410	9090	320
B Casualty insurance claims liability of insurance companies	46940	–	46940	49680	–	49680	53130	–	53130	56960	–	56960
C Transfers to private non-profit institutions	...	...	...	...	...	...	...	...	...	...	...	...
D Unfunded employee pension and welfare benefits	23030	21530	1500	24570	22930	1640	25720	24020	1700	26960	25180	1780
E Social assistance grants	4580	140	4440	4910	140	4770	5450	140	5310	6070	150	5920
F Other transfers n.e.c.	...	...	...	...	...	...	...	...	...	...	...	...
G Transfers to rest of the world	...	...	...	...	...	...	...	...	...	...	...	...
Net saving	33220	9090	24130	35640	8890	26750	64800	28940	35860	54880	23660	31220
Total current disbursements and net saving	808400	517640	290760	810340	518330	292010	895240	586610	308630	974260	624590	349670

Germany, Federal Republic (Former)

	1990 Total	1990 Non-financial	1990 Financial	1991 Total	1991 Non-financial	1991 Financial	1992 Total	1992 Non-financial	1992 Financial	1993 Total	1993 Non-financial	1993 Financial
Receipts												
1 Operating surplus [a]	553530	610460	−56930	536460	599710	−63250	524760	595590	−70830	474970	544270	−69300
2 Property and entrepreneurial income	458960	71300	387660	531520	85370	446150	600800	97350	503450	619400	96990	522410
A Withdrawals from quasi-corporate enterprises	8190	7570	620	8320	7670	650	8470	7780	690	8700	7930	770
B Interest [b]	414610	41700	372910	484360	53590	430770	550100	62320	487780	564100	58440	505660
C Dividends	36160	22030	14130	38840	24110	14730	42230	27250	14980	46600	30620	15980
D Net land rent and royalties	...	...	...	...	...	...	...	...	...	...	...	...
3 Current transfers	120120	43440	76680	128880	45580	83300	141070	49370	91700	143770	44650	99120
A Casualty insurance claims	8910	8580	330	9400	8860	360	9860	9350	510	11020	10370	650
B Casualty insurance premiums, net, due to be received by insurance companies	63430	–	63430	69080	–	69080	76360	–	76360	84360	–	84360
C Current transfers from rest of the world	...	...	...	...	...	...	...	...	...	...	...	...
D Other transfers except imputed	13150	4200	8950	14230	4560	9670	15060	5040	10020	14870	5270	9600
E Imputed unfunded employee pension and welfare contributions	34630	30660	3970	36170	31980	4190	39790	34980	4810	33520	29010	4510
Total current receipts	1132610	725200	407410	1196860	730660	466200	1266630	742310	524320	1238140	685910	552230
Disbursements												
1 Property and entrepreneurial income	908130	611940	296190	995260	656830	338430	1078730	688700	390030	1073310	673860	399450
A Withdrawals from quasi-corporations	377200	377200	...	393510	393510	...	385740	385740	...	362950	362950	...
B Interest [b]	452800	172790	280010	527680	204250	323430	604820	237930	366890	624540	248030	376510
C Dividends	78130	61950	16180	74070	59070	15000	88170	65030	23140	85820	62880	22940
D Net land rent and royalties	...	...	...	...	...	...	...	...	...	...	...	...
2 Direct taxes and other current transfers n.e.c. to general government	41500	33500	8000	45020	34480	10540	45150	33580	11570	44130	30970	13160
A Direct taxes	38680	30680	8000	41580	31040	10540	41830	30260	11570	40360	27200	13160
B Fines, fees, penalties and other current transfers n.e.c.	2820	2820	–	3440	3440	–	3320	3320	–	3770	3770	–
3 Other current transfers	108560	36270	72290	116900	38250	78650	127240	40560	86680	138110	43360	94750
A Casualty insurance premiums, net	10100	9770	330	10700	10160	540	11290	10780	510	12590	11940	650
B Casualty insurance claims liability of insurance companies	63430	–	63430	69080	–	69080	76360	–	76360	84360	–	84360
C Transfers to private non-profit institutions	...	...	...	...	...	...	...	...	...	...	...	...
D Unfunded employee pension and welfare benefits	28510	26340	2170	29980	27910	2070	31990	29780	2210	33610	31420	2190
E Social assistance grants	6520	160	6360	7140	180	6960	7600	–	7600	7550	–	7550
F Other transfers n.e.c.	...	...	...	...	...	...	...	...	...	...	...	...
G Transfers to rest of the world	...	...	...	...	...	...	...	...	...	...	...	...
Net saving	74420	43490	30930	39680	1100	38580	15510	−20530	36040	−17410	−62280	44870
Total current disbursements and net saving	1132610	725200	407410	1196860	730660	466200	1266630	742310	524320	1238140	685910	552230

Germany, Federal Republic (Former)

	1994			1995			1996			1997		
	Total	Non-financial	Financial	Total	Non-financial	Financial	Total	Non-financial	Financial	Total	Non-financial	Financial

Receipts

A Casualty insurance claims ..	...	...	...	...	...	...	...	...	...	...	...	...
B Casualty insurance premiums, net, due to be received by insurance companies	...	—	...	...	...	...	...	...	...	...	...	...
C Current transfers from rest of the world	...	...	...	...	...	...	...	...	...	...	...	...
D Other transfers except imputed	9720	120	9600	...	...	...	...	...	...	...	...	...
E Imputed unfunded employee pension and welfare contributions	31510	26950	4560	...	...	...	...	...	...	...	...	...
Total current receipts	...	...	...	...	...	...	...	...	...	...	...	...

Disbursements

1 Property and entrepreneurial income	...	...	...	...	...	...	...	...	...	...	...	...
2 Direct taxes and other current transfers n.e.c. to general government	36810	23240	13570	...	...	...	...	...	...	...	...	...
A Direct taxes	32730	19160	13570	...	...	...	...	...	...	...	...	...
B Fines, fees, penalties and other current transfers n.e.c.	4080	4080	—	...	...	...	...	...	...	...	...	...
3 Other current transfers	...	28910	18490	...	...	...	...	...	...	...	...	...
A Casualty insurance premiums, net	...	...	...	...	...	...	...	...	...	...	...	...
B Casualty insurance claims liability of insurance companies	...	—	...	...	...	...	...	...	...	...	...	...
C Transfers to private non-profit institutions	...	...	...	...	...	...	...	...	...	...	...	...
D Unfunded employee pension and welfare benefits	...	...	...	...	...	...	...	...	...	...	...	...
E Social assistance grants	...	...	...	...	...	...	...	...	...	...	...	...
F Other transfers n.e.c.	...	...	...	...	...	...	...	...	...	...	...	...
G Transfers to rest of the world	...	...	...	...	...	...	...	...	...	...	...	...
Net saving	11790	...	...	...	...	...	...	...	...	...	...	...
Total current disbursements and net saving	48600	52150	32060	...	...	...	...	...	...	...	...	...

a Including undistributed profits of unincorporated enterprises.   b Item "Interest" includes item "Net land rent and royalties".

3.23 Corporate and quasi-corporate enterprise capital accumulation account: total and sectors

Million Deutsche marks

	1986			1987			1988			1989		
	Total	Non-financial	Financial	Total	Non-financial	Financial	Total	Non-financial	Financial	Total	Non-financial	Financial

Finance of gross accumulation

1 Gross saving	263340	234480	28860	273870	242140	31730	313200	272140	41060	318780	281940	36840
A Consumption of fixed capital	230120	225390	4730	238230	233250	4980	248400	243200	5200	263900	258280	5620
B Net saving	33220	9090	24130	35640	8890	26750	64800	28940	35860	54880	23660	31220
2 Capital transfers	65280	65280	—	68910	68910	—	67490	67490	—	67240	67240	—
A From resident sectors	65280	65280	—	68910	68910	—	67490	67490	—	67240	67240	—
B From rest of the world	...	...	...	...	...	...	...	...	...	...	...	...
Finance of gross accumulation [a]	328620	299760	28860	342780	311050	31730	380690	339630	41060	386020	349180	36840

Germany, Federal Republic (Former)

Million Deutsche marks

	1986 Total	1986 Non-financial	1986 Financial	1987 Total	1987 Non-financial	1987 Financial	1988 Total	1988 Non-financial	1988 Financial	1989 Total	1989 Non-financial	1989 Financial
Gross accumulation												
1 Gross capital formation	331090	322530	8560	339220	331660	7560	372700	363420	9280	413540	403620	9920
A Increase in stocks	2920	3120	–200	–560	–480	–80	10300	10200	100	16010	16150	–140
B Gross fixed capital formation	328170	319410	8760	339780	332140	7640	362400	353220	9180	397530	387470	10060
2 Purchases of land, net	–1980	–2230	250	–1990	–2170	180	–1410	–1080	–330	–1380	–960	–420
3 Purchases of intangible assets, net	...	...	...	...	...	...	...	...	...	...	...	...
4 Capital transfers	20970	13940	7030	19270	15050	4220	19760	14690	5070	19320	14380	4940
A To resident sectors	20970	13940	7030	19270	15050	4220	19760	14690	5070	19320	14380	4940
B To the rest of the world	...	...	...	...	...	...	...	...	...	...	...	...
Net lending	–21460	–34480	13020	–13720	–33490	19770	–10360	–37400	27040	–45460	–67860	22400
Gross accumulation [a]	328620	299760	28860	342780	311050	31730	380690	339630	41060	386020	349180	36840

	1990 Total	1990 Non-financial	1990 Financial	1991 Total	1991 Non-financial	1991 Financial	1992 Total	1992 Non-financial	1992 Financial	1993 Total	1993 Non-financial	1993 Financial
Finance of gross accumulation												
1 Gross saving	360770	323680	37090	354560	309060	45500	355830	312000	43830	341350	287880	53470
A Consumption of fixed capital	286350	280190	6160	314880	307960	6920	340310	332530	7790	358760	350160	8600
B Net saving	74420	43490	30930	39680	1100	38580	15510	–20530	36040	–17410	–62280	44870
2 Capital transfers	70070	70070	–	83440	83440	–	70600	70600	–	72780	72780	–
A From resident sectors	70070	70070	–	83440	83440	–	70600	70600	–	72780	72780	–
B From rest of the world	...	...	...	...	...	...	...	...	...	...	...	...
Finance of gross accumulation [a]	430840	393750	37090	438000	392500	45500	426430	380900	43890	414130	360660	53470
Gross accumulation												
1 Gross capital formation	465110	453280	11830	523590	509350	14240	515040	498710	16330	459840	444040	15800
A Increase in stocks	11490	11550	–60	17770	17760	10	–4940	–4840	–100	–17010	–16980	–30
B Gross fixed capital formation	453620	441730	11890	505820	491590	14230	519980	503550	16430	476850	461020	15830
2 Purchases of land, net	–1370	–1320	–50	–1460	–1670	210	–1270	–1640	370	–970	–1290	320
3 Purchases of intangible assets, net	...	...	...	...	...	...	...	...	...	...	...	...
4 Capital transfers	20330	18250	2080	25330	19520	5810	29210	22310	6900	23680	14580	9100
A To resident sectors	20330	18250	2080	25330	19520	5810	29210	22310	6900	23680	14580	9100
B To the rest of the world	...	...	...	...	...	...	...	...	...	...	...	...
Net lending	–53230	–76460	23230	–109460	–134700	25240	–116550	–136780	20230	–68420	–96670	28250
Gross accumulation [a]	430840	393750	37090	438000	392500	45500	426430	380900	43890	414130	360660	53470

	1994 Total	1994 Non-financial	1994 Financial	1995 Total	1995 Non-financial	1995 Financial	1996 Total	1996 Non-financial	1996 Financial	1997 Total	1997 Non-financial	1997 Financial
Finance of gross accumulation												
1 Gross saving	379290	...	...	...	...	...	...	...	...	...	...	...
A Consumption of fixed capital	367500	...	...	...	...	...	...	...	...	...	...	...
B Net saving	11790	...	...	...	...	...	...	...	...	...	...	...
2 Capital transfers	70500	70500	–	...	...	...	...	...	...	...	...	...
A From resident sectors	70500	70500	–	...	...	...	...	...	...	...	...	...
B From rest of the world	...	...	...	...	...	...	...	...	...	...	...	...
Finance of gross accumulation	...	...	...	...	...	...	...	...	...	...	...	...

Germany, Federal Republic (Former)

	1994			1995			1996			1997		
	Total	Non-financial	Financial	Total	Non-financial	Financial	Total	Non-financial	Financial	Total	Non-financial	Financial
Gross accumulation												
1 Gross capital formation	490060	...	...	...	...	...	...	...	...	...	...	...
A Increase in stocks	...	...	...	...	...	...	...	...	...	...	...	...
B Gross fixed capital formation	490060	...	...	...	...	...	...	...	...	...	...	...
2 Purchases of land, net	80	...	...	...	...	...	...	...	...	...	...	...
3 Purchases of intangible assets, net	...	...	...	...	...	...	...	...	...	...	...	...
4 Capital transfers	23630	14820	8810	...	...	...	...	...	...	...	...	...
A To resident sectors	23630	14820	8810	...	...	...	...	...	...	...	...	...
B To the rest of the world	...	...	...	...	...	...	...	...	...	...	...	...
Net lending	...	...	...	...	...	...	...	...	...	...	...	...
Gross accumulation	...	...	...	...	...	...	...	...	...	...	...	...

a Capital accumulation account of corporate and quasi-corporate enterprise includes private non-profit organizations.

3.24 Corporate and quasi-corporate enterprise capital finance account: total and sectors

Million Deutsche marks

	1986			1987			1988			1989		
	Total	Non-financial	Financial	Total	Non-financial	Financial	Total	Non-financial	Financial	Total	Non-financial	Financial
Acquisition of financial assets												
1 Gold and SDRs	−1000	−	−1000	12500	−	12500	−7900	−	−7900	−4600	−	−4600
2 Currency and transferable deposits	23610	19840	3770	19270	14760	4510	20420	16160	4260	31140	18980	12160
3 Other deposits	114320	21230	93090	62420	18460	43960	75420	15140	60280	136140	31640	104500
4 Bills and bonds, short-term	7470	−390	7860	23560	250	23310	−20520	−110	−20410	12280	3140	9140
5 Bonds, long-term	36550	−1600	38150	51350	3980	47370	51210	2780	48430	37500	3780	33720
6 Corporate equity securities	13320	−810	14130	13870	4410	9460	17420	10700	6720	13630	280	13350
7 Short-term loans, n.e.c.	−800	6530	−7330	−27200	−270	−26930	87320	7220	80100	106200	27040	79160
8 Long-term loans, n.e.c.	94840	6540	88300	122450	10070	112380	110130	9750	100380	129860	11000	118860
9 Trade credits and advances	520	520	−	−1210	−1210	−	16160	16160	−	15000	15000	−
10 Other receivables	...	...	...	...	...	...	...	...	...	...	...	...
11 Other assets	3140	3140	−	3080	3080	−	−	−	−	1330	1330	−
Total acquisitions of financial assets [a]	291970	55000	236970	280090	53530	226560	349660	77800	271860	478480	112190	366290
Incurrence of liabilities												
1 Currency and transferable deposits	36400	−	36400	31790	−	31790	53460	−	53460	71900	−	71900
2 Other deposits	122070	−	122070	119530	−	119530	89500	−	89500	122630	−	122630
3 Bills and bonds, short-term	−3560	−	−3560	−770	−500	−270	−910	−500	−410	−1120	−410	−710
4 Bonds, long-term	36240	6790	29450	39340	10820	28520	−7720	3240	−10960	52530	−20	52550
5 Corporate equity securities	16390	12450	3940	11910	9000	2910	7530	5270	2260	19350	13530	5820
6 Short-term loans, n.e.c.	−23400	−12220	−11180	−34090	−11740	−22350	81110	18220	62890	91340	51370	39970
7 Long-term loans, n.e.c.	77750	77680	70	67580	67290	290	69960	70000	−40	101760	101630	130
8 Net equity of households in life insurance and pension fund reserves	48010	10120	37890	49480	12130	37350	53030	10570	42460	54850	10300	44550
9 Proprietors' net additions to the accumulation of quasi-corporations	...	...	...	...	...	...	...	...	...	...	...	...
10 Trade credits and advances	−4630	−4630	−	680	680	−	7750	7750	−	4710	4710	−
11 Other accounts payable	...	...	...	...	...	...	...	...	...	...	...	...

Germany, Federal Republic (Former)

Million Deutsche marks

	1986 Total	1986 Non-financial	1986 Financial	1987 Total	1987 Non-financial	1987 Financial	1988 Total	1988 Non-financial	1988 Financial	1989 Total	1989 Non-financial	1989 Financial
12 Other liabilities	8850	–	8850	9040	–	9040	5990	–	5990	8600	–	8600
Total incurrence of liabilities	314120	90190	223930	294490	87680	206810	359700	114550	245150	526550	181110	345440
Net lending	−22150	−35190	13040	−14400	−34150	19750	−10040	−36750	26710	−48070	−68920	20850
Incurrence of liabilities and net lending [a]	291970	55000	236970	280090	53530	226560	349660	77800	271860	478480	112190	366290

	1990 Total	1990 Non-financial	1990 Financial	1991 Total	1991 Non-financial	1991 Financial	1992 Total	1992 Non-financial	1992 Financial	1993 Total	1993 Non-financial	1993 Financial
Acquisition of financial assets												
1 Gold and SDRs	1500	–	1500	...	...	...	...	...	...	...	...	...
2 Currency and transferable deposits	31470	22470	9000	...	...	...	...	...	...	...	...	...
3 Other deposits	62090	29860	32230	...	...	...	...	...	...	...	...	...
4 Bills and bonds, short-term	15650	6380	9270	...	...	...	...	...	...	...	...	...
5 Bonds, long-term	133350	38560	94790	...	...	...	...	...	...	...	...	...
6 Corporate equity securities	51470	32810	18660	...	...	...	...	...	...	...	...	...
7 Short-term loans, n.e.c.	164310	37030	127280	...	...	...	...	...	...	...	...	...
8 Long-term loans, n.e.c.	197270	16010	181260	...	...	...	...	...	...	...	...	...
9 Trade credits and advances	4150	4150	–	...	...	...	...	...	...	...	...	...
10 Other receivables	...	...	...	...	...	...	...	...	...	...	...	...
11 Other assets	1510	1510	–	...	...	...	...	...	...	...	...	...
Total acquisitions of financial assets [a]	662770	188780	473990	...	...	...	...	...	...	...	...	...
Incurrence of liabilities												
1 Currency and transferable deposits	117650	–	117650	...	...	...	...	...	...	...	...	...
2 Other deposits	166280	–	166280	...	...	...	...	...	...	...	...	...
3 Bills and bonds, short-term	−1250	−1590	340	...	...	...	...	...	...	...	...	...
4 Bonds, long-term	87070	7300	79770	...	...	...	...	...	...	...	...	...
5 Corporate equity securities	28020	21990	6030	...	...	...	...	...	...	...	...	...
6 Short-term loans, n.e.c.	90960	60580	30380	...	...	...	...	...	...	...	...	...
7 Long-term loans, n.e.c.	108610	108760	−150	...	...	...	...	...	...	...	...	...
8 Net equity of households in life insurance and pension fund reserves	53500	10320	43180	...	...	...	...	...	...	...	...	...
9 Proprietors' net additions to the accumulation of quasi-corporations	...	...	...	...	...	...	...	...	...	...	...	...
10 Trade credits and advances	7310	7310	–	...	...	...	...	...	...	...	...	...
11 Other accounts payable	...	...	...	...	...	...	...	...	...	...	...	...
12 Other liabilities	7260	–	7260	...	...	...	...	...	...	...	...	...
Total incurrence of liabilities	665410	214670	450740	...	...	...	...	...	...	...	...	...
Net lending	−2640	−25890	23250	...	...	...	...	...	...	...	...	...
Incurrence of liabilities and net lending [a]	662770	188780	473990	...	...	...	...	...	...	...	...	...

a Data in this table have not been revised, therefore they are not comparable with the data in other tables.

Germany, Federal Republic (Former)

3.32 Household and private unincorporated enterprise income and outlay account

Million Deutsche marks

	1986	1987	1988	1989	1990	1991	1992	1993	1994	1995	1996	1997
Receipts												
1 Compensation of employees	1079490	1124700	1169380	1221890	1317100	1422240	1515070	1529090	1548880	...	...	...
A Wages and salaries	876630	912810	948870	992810	1069650	1154690	1228200	1241330	1247000	...	...	...
B Employers' contributions for social security	147720	153610	160940	168020	180180	197850	211150	218340	230790	...	...	...
C Employers' contributions for private pension and welfare plans	55140	58280	59570	61060	67270	69700	75720	69420	71090	...	...	...
2 Operating surplus of private unincorporated enterprises	...	...	...	...	...	...	...	...	...	...	...	...
3 Property and entrepreneurial income	393770	411110	428630	472270	521920	612530	646350	662740	...	...	...	...
A Withdrawals from private quasi-corporations	282920	301140	311730	338650	369560	441120	455570	467860	...	...	...	...
B Interest	99770	99020	102730	117380	133520	154370	172570	176190	...	...	...	...
C Dividends	11080	10950	14170	16240	18840	17040	18210	18690	...	...	...	...
D Net land rent and royalties	...	...	...	...	...	...	...	...	...	...	...	...
4 Current transfers	392360	412890	433310	453310	480370	504340	542890	586740	...	...	...	...
A Casualty insurance claims	38250	40470	43510	46380	51390	51260	57500	63680	...	...	...	...
B Social security benefits	220980	232050	245000	254320	269050	283750	302990	329580	345750	...	...	...
C Social assistance grants	52980	55500	55950	58350	60280	63930	68680	75580	77500	...	...	...
D Unfunded employee pension and welfare benefits	58120	61280	63740	66620	70430	74760	79840	83070	85710	...	...	...
E Transfers from general government	12170	13330	14150	14540	15720	16830	18610	19910	21150	...	...	...
F Transfers from rest of the world	1540	1340	1450	2900	2190	1720	2140	1800	...	...	...	...
G Other transfers n.e.c.	8320	8920	9510	10200	11310	12090	13130	13120	...	...	...	...
Total current receipts	1865620	1948700	2031320	2147470	2319390	2539110	2704310	2778570	...	...	...	...
Disbursements												
1 Final consumption expenditure	1066430	1108020	1153690	1220950	1320710	1446970	1536510	1591580	1646340	...	...	...
A Market purchases	1042340	1082150	1126620	1192120	1289980	1412760	1498580	1550620	1603910	...	...	...
B Gross rents of owner-occupied housing	...	...	...	...	...	...	...	...	...	...	...	...
C Consumption from own-account production	24090	25870	27070	28830	30730	34210	37930	40960	42430	...	...	...
2 Property income	17930	17480	18170	19460	22100	25880	31540	36920	...	...	...	...
A Interest	17930	17480	18170	19460	22100	25880	31540	36920	...	...	...	...
Consumer debt	17930	17480	18170	19460	22100	25880	31540	36920	...	...	...	...
Mortgages	...	...	...	...	...	...	...	...	...	...	...	...
Other	...	...	...	...	...	...	...	...	...	...	...	...
B Net land rent and royalties	...	...	...	...	...	...	...	...	...	...	...	...
3 Direct taxes and other current transfers n.e.c. to general government	517070	543280	564250	602060	619360	696250	749850	768820	...	...	...	...
A Social security contributions	312750	325220	340330	356100	380450	414750	443160	466210	494880	...	...	...
B Direct taxes	196270	209430	214670	236340	228590	270530	295020	290180	294120	...	...	...
Income taxes	191070	204760	210090	231200	223770	265080	288660	283510	287390	...	...	...
Other	5200	4670	4580	5140	4820	5450	6360	6670	6730	...	...	...
C Fees, fines and penalties	8050	8630	9250	9620	10320	10970	11670	12430	...	...	...	...

Germany, Federal Republic (Former)

Million Deutsche marks

	1986	1987	1988	1989	1990	1991	1992	1993	1994	1995	1996	1997
4 Other current transfers	114920	120360	125750	131680	145190	147700	162170	162620	...	...	...	...
A Net casualty insurance premiums	38710	40930	43910	46850	51810	51530	57780	63900	...	...	...	...
B Transfers to private non-profit institutions serving households	...	...	...	...	...	...	...	...	...	...	...	...
C Transfers to rest of the world	12560	11750	12150	12960	14340	13810	15480	16310	...	...	...	...
D Other current transfers, except imputed	8510	9400	10120	10810	11770	12660	13190	12990	9600	...	...	...
E Imputed employee pension and welfare contributions	55140	58280	59570	61060	67270	69700	75720	69420	71090	...	...	...
Net saving	149270	159560	169460	173320	212030	222310	224240	218630	213900	...	...	...
Total current disbursements and net saving	1865620	1948700	2031320	2147470	2319390	2539110	2704310	2778570	...	...	...	...

3.33 Household and private unincorporated enterprise capital accumulation account

Million Deutsche marks

	1986	1987	1988	1989	1990	1991	1992	1993	1994	1995	1996	1997
Finance of gross accumulation												
1 Gross saving	149270	159560	169460	173320	212030	222310	224240	218630	213900	...	...	...
A Consumption of fixed capital	...	...	...	...	...	...	...	...	...	...	...	...
B Net saving	149270	159560	169460	173320	212030	222310	224240	218630	213900	...	...	...
2 Capital transfers	20980	18850	19930	18410	16580	22410	25230	18420	18010	...	...	...
A From resident sectors	20940	18820	19900	18360	16550	22380	25210	18400	17980	...	...	...
B From rest of the world	40	30	30	50	30	30	20	20	30	...	...	...
Total finance of gross accumulation	170250	178410	189390	191730	228610	244720	249470	237050	231910	...	...	...
Gross accumulation												
1 Gross capital formation	...	...	...	...	...	...	...	...	...	...	...	...
2 Purchases of land, net	...	...	...	...	...	...	...	...	...	...	...	...
3 Purchases of intangibles, net	...	...	...	...	...	...	...	...	...	...	...	...
4 Capital transfers	43780	47070	47440	45010	46860	49020	49660	52070	54050	...	...	...
A To resident sectors	43310	46560	46950	44590	46350	48530	49100	51500	53000	...	...	...
B To the rest of the world	470	510	490	420	510	490	560	570	1050	...	...	...
Net lending	126470	131340	141950	146720	181750	195700	199810	184980	177860	...	...	...
Total gross accumulation	170250	178410	189390	191730	228610	244720	249470	237050	231910	...	...	...

3.34 Household and private unincorporated enterprise capital finance account

Million Deutsche marks

	1986	1987	1988	1989	1990	1991	1992	1993	1994	1995	1996	1997
Acquisition of financial assets												
1 Gold	–	–	–	–	–	...	...	...	...	...	...	...
2 Currency and transferable deposits	13290	13750	23270	7630	16370	...	...	...	...	...	...	...
3 Other deposits	58710	43390	22530	39010	48350	...	...	...	...	...	...	...
4 Bills and bonds, short-term	–290	–1050	–300	3650	5830	...	...	...	...	...	...	...
5 Bonds, long-term	8020	26380	48020	62620	75630	...	...	...	...	...	...	...
6 Corporate equity securities	3640	5910	2540	–6990	–2820	...	...	...	...	...	...	...
7 Short-term loans, n.e.c.	–	–	–	–	–	...	...	...	...	...	...	...

Germany, Federal Republic (Former)

Million Deutsche marks

	1986	1987	1988	1989	1990	1991	1992	1993	1994	1995	1996	1997
8 Long-term loans, n.e.c.	330	180	20	40	40	...	...	...	...	...	...	...
9 Trade credits and advances	–	–	–	–	–	...	...	...	...	...	...	...
10 Net equity of households in life insurance and pension fund reserves	48010	49480	53030	54850	53500	...	...	...	...	...	...	...
11 Proprietors' net additions to the accumulation of quasi-corporations	...	...	...	...	...	...	...	...	...	...	...	...
12 Other	5460	5490	5790	7010	5580	...	...	...	...	...	...	...
Total acquisitions of financial assets	137170	143530	154900	167820	202480	...	...	...	...	...	...	...
Incurrence of liabilities												
1 Short-term loans, n.e.c.	120	–730	10	4680	5250	...	...	...	...	...	...	...
2 Long-term loans, n.e.c.	9880	12300	12960	16360	18550	...	...	...	...	...	...	...
3 Trade credits and advances	–	–	–	–	–	...	...	...	...	...	...	...
4 Other accounts payable	...	...	...	...	...	...	...	...	...	...	...	...
5 Other liabilities	–	–	–	–	–	...	...	...	...	...	...	...
Total incurrence of liabilities	10000	11570	12970	21040	23800	...	...	...	...	...	...	...
Net lending	127170	131960	141930	146780	178680	...	...	...	...	...	...	...
Incurrence of liabilities and net lending	137170	143530	154900	167820	202480	...	...	...	...	...	...	...

3.41 Private non-profit institutions serving households: production account

Million Deutsche marks

	1986	1987	1988	1989	1990	1991	1992	1993	1994	1995	1996	1997
Gross output												
1 Sales	39050	41160	43180	44640	48920	54050	59230	61850	65120	...	...	...
2 Non-marketed output	24090	25870	27070	28830	30730	34210	37930	40960	42430	...	...	...
A Services produced for own use	24090	25870	27070	28830	30730	34210	37930	40960	42430	...	...	...
B Own-account fixed capital formation	...	...	...	...	...	...	...	...	...	...	...	...
Gross output	63140	67030	70250	73470	79650	88260	97160	102810	107550	...	...	...
Gross input												
Intermediate consumption	19250	20280	21100	22070	23980	26550	29230	30930	32350	...	...	...
subtotal: Value added	43890	46750	49150	51400	55670	61710	67930	71880	75200	...	...	...
1 Indirect taxes, net	30	30	30	30	30	30	40	40	40	...	...	...
2 Consumption of fixed capital	3520	3660	3800	4000	4290	4640	4940	5210	5370	...	...	...
3 Compensation of employees	40340	43060	45320	47370	51350	57040	62950	66630	69790	...	...	...
A To residents	40340	43060	45320	47370	51350	57040	62950	66630	69790	...	...	...
B To the rest of the world	...	...	...	...	...	...	...	...	...	...	...	...
4 Net operating surplus	...	...	...	...	...	...	...	...	...	...	...	...
Gross input	63140	67030	70250	73470	79650	88260	97160	102810	107550	...	...	...

Germany, Federal Republic (Former)

3.51 External transactions, current account: detail

Million Deutsche marks

	1986	1987	1988	1989	1990	1991	1992	1993	1994	1995	1996	1997
Payments to the rest of the world												
1 Imports of goods and services [a]	480630	476650	510120	581290	636950	734290	747080	705090	765630	...	...	...
A Imports of merchandise, c.i.f. [b]	390690	383890	411770	475320	521240	603560	603460	552720	604500	...	...	...
B Other	89940	92760	98350	105970	115710	130730	143620	152370	161130	...	...	...
2 Factor income to rest of the world	45670	48390	56020	62200	82890	102960	122700	135940	143440	...	...	...
A Compensation of employees	2200	2340	2560	2860	7420	20030	27370	28820	29590	...	...	...
B Property and entrepreneurial income	43470	46050	53460	59340	75470	82930	95330	107120	113850	...	...	...
By general government	9790	11590	11670	11340	12640	14030	17610	26210	25470	...	...	...
By corporate and quasi-corporate enterprises	33680	34460	41790	48000	62830	68900	77720	80910	88380	...	...	...
By other	...	...	...	...	...	...	...	...	...	...	...	...
3 Current transfers to the rest of the world	44650	44980	51170	55640	100830	183700	197410	203580	202410	...	...	...
A Indirect taxes by general government to supranational organizations	...	...	...	...	...	...	...	...	...	...	...	...
B Other current transfers	44650	44980	51170	55640	100830	183700	197410	203580	202410	...	...	...
By general government	30980	32130	37840	41240	84220	162430	173960	178690	175930	...	...	...
By other resident sectors	13670	12850	13330	14400	16610	21270	23450	24890	26480	...	...	...
4 Surplus of the nation on current transactions	82230	82330	89150	107020	85040	23050	44740	54160	60300	...	...	...
Payments to the rest of the world and surplus of the nation on current transfers	653180	652350	706460	806150	905710	1044000	1111930	1098770	1171780	...	...	...
Receipts from the rest of the world												
1 Exports of goods and services [a]	580540	576610	619830	701430	778900	885730	940380	924700	1002050	...	...	...
A Exports of merchandise, f.o.b.	508960	506850	548020	616360	663700	743940	804480	793200	875340	...	...	...
B Other	71580	69760	71810	85070	115200	141790	135900	131500	126710	...	...	...
2 Factor income from rest of the world	56480	60910	68040	86860	105490	123160	130800	133140	127240	...	...	...
A Compensation of employees	7250	7690	8160	8500	9000	11970	13790	14570	14160	...	...	...
B Property and entrepreneurial income	49230	53220	59880	78360	96490	111190	117010	118570	113080	...	...	...
By general government	120	90	120	140	230	300	230	240	340	...	...	...
By corporate and quasi-corporate enterprises	41580	45460	49120	62540	80690	94020	100900	105140	99060	...	...	...
Branch profits and earnings of subsidiaries	...	...	...	...	...	...	...	...	...	...	...	...
Other	...	...	...	...	15570	16870	15880	13190	13680	...	...	...
By other	7530	7670	10640	15680	15570	16870	15880	13190	13680	...	...	...
3 Current transfers from rest of the world	16160	14830	18590	17860	21320	35110	40750	40930	42490	...	...	...
A Subsidies to general government from supranational organizations	...	...	...	...	...	...	...	...	...	...	...	...
B Other current transfers	16160	14830	18590	17860	21320	35110	40750	40930	42490	...	...	...
To general government	13900	12780	16380	14110	17360	26340	31070	30990	32610	...	...	...
To other resident sectors	2260	2050	2210	3750	3960	8770	9680	9940	9880	...	...	...

Germany, Federal Republic (Former)

Million Deutsche marks

	1986	1987	1988	1989	1990	1991	1992	1993	1994	1995	1996	1997
Receipts from the rest of the world on current transfers	653180	652350	706460	806150	905710	1044000	1111930	1098770	1171780	...	...	...

a Exports and imports of goods for purposes of repair and improvement are reduced to the value of these services.
b Imports of merchandise, f.o.b. rather than c.i.f.

3.52 External transactions, capital accumulation account

Million Deutsche marks

	1986	1987	1988	1989	1990	1991	1992	1993	1994	1995	1996	1997
Finance of gross accumulation												
1 Surplus of the nation on current transactions	82230	82330	89150	107020	85040	23050	44740	54160	60300	...	...	...
2 Capital transfers from rest of the world	200	220	180	310	280	170	370	260	360	...	...	...
A By general government	160	190	150	260	250	140	350	240	330	...	...	...
B By other resident sectors	40	30	30	50	30	30	20	20	30	...	...	...
Total finance of gross accumulation	82430	82550	89330	107330	85320	23220	45110	54420	60660	...	...	...
Gross accumulation												
1 Capital transfers to the rest of the world	2820	2770	2980	3320	6540	26890	26050	25120	18690	...	...	...
A By general government	2350	2260	2490	2900	6030	26400	25490	24550	17640	...	...	...
B By other resident sectors	470	510	490	420	510	490	560	570	1050	...	...	...
2 Purchases of intangible assets, n.e.c., net, from rest of the world	...	...	...	...	...	...	...	...	...	...	...	...
Net lending to the rest of the world	79610	79780	86350	104010	78780	−3670	19060	29300	41970	...	...	...
Total gross accumulation	82430	82550	89330	107330	85320	23220	45110	54420	60660	...	...	...

3.53 External transactions, capital finance account

Million Deutsche marks

	1986	1987	1988	1989	1990	1991	1992	1993	1994	1995	1996	1997
Acquisition of foreign financial assets												
1 Gold and SDRs	−1000	12500	−7900	−4600	1500	...	...	...	...	...	...	...
2 Currency and transferable deposits	7780	890	1960	7910	6000	...	...	...	...	...	...	...
3 Other deposits	82520	16280	30250	94450	23230	...	...	...	...	...	...	...
4 Bills and bonds, short-term	12390	25980	−19820	9760	15320	...	...	...	...	...	...	...
5 Bonds, long-term	16390	25090	67730	46780	76600	...	...	...	...	...	...	...
6 Corporate equity securities	15890	4390	13740	14720	20510	...	...	...	...	...	...	...
7 Short-term loans, n.e.c.	14580	8770	8550	35360	90010	...	...	...	...	...	...	...
8 Long-term loans	20000	31550	14530	25590	74800	...	...	...	...	...	...	...
9 Proprietors' net additions to accumulation of quasi-corporate, non-resident enterprises	...	...	...	...	...	...	...	...	...	...	...	...
10 Trade credits and advances	520	−1210	16160	15000	4150	...	...	...	...	...	...	...
11 Other	–	–	–	–	–	...	...	...	...	...	...	...
Total acquisitions of foreign financial assets [a]	169070	124240	125200	244970	312120	...	...	...	...	...	...	...

Germany, Federal Republic (Former)

Million Deutsche marks

	1986	1987	1988	1989	1990	1991	1992	1993	1994	1995	1996	1997
Incurrence of foreign liabilities												
1 Currency and transferable deposits	9300	–4010	11780	34810	67450	...	...	...	...	...	...	...
2 Other deposits	18980	24710	15500	31400	67410	...	...	...	...	...	...	...
3 Bills and bonds, short-term	–200	–490	70	–50	770	...	...	...	...	...	...	...
4 Bonds, long-term	59070	35000	2090	22490	28110	...	...	...	...	...	...	...
5 Corporate equity securities	15170	–1340	3320	26210	–1370	...	...	...	...	...	...	...
6 Short-term loans, n.e.c.	–6550	–1070	1610	20510	14480	...	...	...	...	...	...	...
7 Long-term loans	–1860	–9220	–4220	640	2950	...	...	...	...	...	...	...
8 Non-resident proprietors' net additions to accumulation of resident quasi-corporate enterprises	...	...	...	...	...							
9 Trade credits and advances	–4630	680	7750	4710	7310	...	...	...	...	...	...	...
10 Other	180	190	150	190	130	...	...	...	...	...	...	...
Total incurrence of liabilities	89460	44450	38050	140910	187240	...	...	...	...	...	...	...
Net lending	79610	79790	87150	104060	124880	...	...	...	...	...	...	...
Total incurrence of liabilities and net lending [a]	169070	124240	125200	244970	312120	...	...	...	...	...	...	...

a Data in this table have not been revised, therefore they are not comparable with the data in other tables.

4.1 Derivation of value added by kind of activity, in current prices

Million Deutsche marks

	1986 Gross output	1986 Intermediate consumption	1986 Value added	1987 Gross output	1987 Intermediate consumption	1987 Value added	1988 Gross output	1988 Intermediate consumption	1988 Value added	1989 Gross output	1989 Intermediate consumption	1989 Value added
All producers												
1 Agriculture, hunting, forestry and fishing	69480	35480	34000	64160	33920	30240	67330	33610	33720	72000	34790	37210
A Agriculture and hunting [a]	60480	31560	28920	54990	29900	25090	57690	29550	28140	61630	30110	31520
B Forestry and logging [a]	9000	3920	5080	9170	4020	5150	9640	4060	5580	10370	4680	5690
C Fishing	...	...	...	...	...	...	...	...	...	...	...	...
2 Mining and quarrying [b]	33720	20140	13580	31060	18280	12780	30280	19100	11180	31360	19620	11740
A Coal mining	27640	16390	11250	25750	14980	10770	24780	15660	9120	24570	15540	9030
B Crude petroleum and natural gas production	...	...	...	...	...	...	...	...	...	...	...	...
C Metal ore mining	...	...	...	...	...	...	...	...	...	...	...	...
D Other mining	6080	3750	2330	5310	3300	2010	5500	3440	2060	6790	4080	2710
3 Manufacturing	1632040	1011600	620440	1637530	1012840	624690	1730900	1078230	652670	1872590	1186580	686010
A Manufacture of food, beverages and tobacco	221970	156000	65970	217980	151890	66090	220420	154110	66310	230260	162190	68070
B Textile, wearing apparel and leather industries	74320	47850	26470	74470	47800	26670	75920	49080	26840	79900	52680	27220
C Manufacture of wood and wood products, including furniture	46360	28650	17710	48570	29800	18770	51780	31760	20020	55320	34620	20700
D Manufacture of paper and paper products, printing and publishing [c]	65650	38150	27500	68250	39330	28920	72040	42920	29120	77550	47650	29900
E Manufacture of chemicals and chemical petroleum, coal, rubber and plastic products	320470	199940	120530	314570	202980	111590	333300	211300	122000	361700	234490	127210

875

Germany, Federal Republic (Former)

Million Deutsche marks

	1986 Gross output	1986 Intermediate consumption	1986 Value added	1987 Gross output	1987 Intermediate consumption	1987 Value added	1988 Gross output	1988 Intermediate consumption	1988 Value added	1989 Gross output	1989 Intermediate consumption	1989 Value added
F Manufacture of non-metallic mineral products, except products of petroleum and coal [b]	54470	31090	23380	55020	31280	23740	58750	33400	25350	62660	36220	26440
G Basic metal industries	126640	79770	46870	116810	71890	44920	133070	85380	47690	152050	100430	51620
H Manufacture of fabricated metal products, machinery and equipment [d]	712860	425320	287540	732130	432710	299420	775450	464830	310620	842490	512460	330030
I Other manufacturing industries	9300	4830	4470	9730	5160	4570	10170	5450	4720	10660	5840	4820
4 Electricity, gas and water	166150	113820	52330	155980	100090	55890	155830	99170	56660	164680	107120	57560
A Electricity, gas and steam	159530	110970	48560	150180	97860	52320	148530	96110	52420	157610	104330	53280
B Water works and supply	6620	2850	3770	5800	2230	3570	7300	3060	4240	7070	2790	4280
5 Construction [d]	199250	99120	100130	203120	101440	101680	214720	108470	106250	233710	119050	114660
6 Wholesale and retail trade, restaurants and hotels	1313880	1127830	186050	1320960	1127050	193910	1377260	1172790	204470	1461840	1247490	214350
A Wholesale and retail trade	1253340	1091070	162270	1257160	1088730	168430	1310120	1132330	177790	1390060	1204520	185540
B Restaurants and hotels	60540	36760	23780	63800	38320	25480	67140	40460	26680	71780	42970	28810
7 Transport, storage and communication	199700	92390	107310	206930	95820	111110	218190	101320	116870	235750	110040	125710
A Transport and storage	148080	84140	63940	152680	86730	65950	161290	91970	69320	174790	99970	74820
B Communication	51620	8250	43370	54250	9090	45160	56900	9350	47550	60960	10070	50890
8 Finance, insurance, real estate and business services	323340	83430	239910	329060	85540	243520	347300	90220	257080	367270	93810	273460
A Financial institutions	106890	28970	77920	104410	28630	75780	108910	29730	79180	114510	31090	83420
B Insurance	46180	23590	22590	46370	23320	23050	50840	25250	25590	53990	26040	27950
C Real estate and business services [e]	170270	30870	139400	178280	33590	144690	187550	35240	152310	198770	36680	162090
Real estate, except dwellings	...	...	...	...	...	...	...	...	...	...	...	...
Dwellings	170270	30870	139400	178280	33590	144690	187550	35240	152310	198770	36680	162090
9 Community, social and personal services [ce]	389950	133160	256790	426760	147190	279570	475720	166650	309070	523320	184640	338680
Educational services	...	...	...	...	...	...	...	...	...	...	...	...
Medical, dental, other health and veterinary services	61160	18420	42740	62180	18640	43540	69330	21200	48130	68700	20660	48040
Total, Industries	4327510	2716970	1610540	4375560	2722170	1653390	4617530	2869560	1747970	4962520	3103140	1859380
Producers of government services	440920	223800	217120	458060	232240	225820	476430	244570	231860	485400	246760	238640
Other producers	65670	19250	46420	69560	20280	49280	72770	21100	51670	75990	22070	53920
Total	4834100	2960020	1874080	4903180	2974690	1928490	5166730	3135230	2031500	5523910	3371970	2151940
less: Imputed bank service charge	...	−83690	83690	...	−82270	82270	...	−85150	85150	...	−88410	88410
Import duties	17020	...	17020	19150	...	19150	19530	...	19530	23380	...	23380
Value added tax	117880	...	117880	125110	...	125110	130100	...	130100	137530	...	137530
Other adjustments	...	...	...	...	...	...	...	...	...	...	...	...
Total	4969000	3043710	1925290	5047440	3056960	1990480	5316360	3220380	2095980	5684820	3460380	2224440

Germany, Federal Republic (Former)

	1990 Gross output	1990 Intermediate consumption	1990 Value added	1991 Gross output	1991 Intermediate consumption	1991 Value added	1992 Gross output	1992 Intermediate consumption	1992 Value added	1993 Gross output	1993 Intermediate consumption	1993 Value added
All producers												
1 Agriculture, hunting, forestry and fishing	72660	35920	36740	69440	35360	34080	68430	34700	33730	62490	32610	29880
A Agriculture and hunting [a]	58420	29500	28920	58320	29580	28740	57410	29030	28380	51720	27190	24530
B Forestry and logging [a]	14240	6420	7820	11120	5780	5340	11020	5670	5350	10770	5420	5350
C Fishing	...	...	...	...	...	...	...	...	...	...	...	...
2 Mining and quarrying [b]	30760	19370	11390	32170	19720	12450	31690	19030	12660	30910	18260	12650
A Coal mining	23470	14800	8670	23750	14570	9180	23740	14470	9270	22640	13300	9340
B Crude petroleum and natural gas production	...	...	...	...	...	...	...	...	...	...	...	...
C Metal ore mining	...	...	...	...	...	...	...	...	...	...	...	...
D Other mining	7290	4570	2720	8420	5150	3270	7950	4560	3390	8270	4960	3310
3 Manufacturing	2005610	1264060	741550	2150060	1359400	790660	2156210	1357120	799090	2004040	1257730	746310
A Manufacture of food, beverages and tobacco	247040	168780	78260	268170	186060	82110	271620	188270	83350	264820	179220	85600
B Textile, wearing apparel and leather industries	83070	55120	27950	84990	57210	27780	81780	54070	27710	75440	49890	25550
C Manufacture of wood and wood products, including furniture	60620	37780	22840	66240	40270	25970	69710	42100	27610	68630	41110	27520
D Manufacture of paper and paper products, printing and publishing [c]	86780	52660	34120	94380	57290	37090	92830	55410	37420	86790	51150	35640
E Manufacture of chemicals and chemical petroleum, coal, rubber and plastic products	377120	244750	132370	397240	259170	138070	397500	252900	144600	382920	239300	143620
F Manufacture of non-metallic mineral products, except products of petroleum and coal [b]	65980	37950	28030	71740	41650	30090	76700	44640	32060	77710	44900	32810
G Basic metal industries	150550	96040	54510	146650	91370	55280	141990	88030	53960	121060	75340	45720
H Manufacture of fabricated metal products, machinery and equipment [d]	923050	564760	358290	1009120	620070	389050	1012540	625740	386800	915500	570850	344650
I Other manufacturing industries	11400	6220	5180	11530	6310	5220	11540	5960	5580	11170	5970	5200
4 Electricity, gas and water	173420	114580	58840	186730	125110	61620	186970	123290	63680	188710	125530	63180
A Electricity, gas and steam	165150	110780	54370	178640	121280	57360	178110	119120	58990	180640	122120	58520
B Water works and supply	8270	3800	4470	8090	3830	4260	8860	4170	4690	8070	3410	4660
5 Construction [d]	262380	134760	127620	286660	149410	137250	315540	163150	152390	317460	164760	152700
6 Wholesale and retail trade, restaurants and hotels	1603810	1359160	244650	1768170	1491110	277060	1802270	1515380	286890	1760980	1477810	283170
A Wholesale and retail trade	1524670	1312120	212550	1683790	1441000	242790	1714180	1463340	250840	1671220	1424850	246370
B Restaurants and hotels	79140	47040	32100	84380	50110	34270	88090	52040	36050	89760	52960	36800
7 Transport, storage and communication	259840	125640	134200	277210	133400	143810	299820	146170	153650	303740	148460	155280
A Transport and storage	193010	111870	81140	207640	121470	86170	221580	130770	90810	221080	130320	90760
B Communication	66830	13770	53060	69570	11930	57640	78240	15400	62840	82660	18140	64520
8 Finance, insurance, real estate and business services	395410	106560	288850	440130	122120	318010	482670	132590	350080	527970	140870	387100
A Financial institutions	125750	34760	90990	142070	37350	104720	156970	39870	117100	168790	42860	125930
B Insurance	56620	31110	25510	68250	38770	29480	74320	41770	32550	82440	42320	40120
C Real estate and business services [e]	213040	40690	172350	229810	46000	183810	251380	50950	200430	276740	55690	221050

Germany, Federal Republic (Former)

	1990			1991			1992			1993		
	Gross output	Intermediate consumption	Value added	Gross output	Intermediate consumption	Value added	Gross output	Intermediate consumption	Value added	Gross output	Intermediate consumption	Value added
Real estate, except dwellings	...	...	...	...	...	...	...	...	...	...	...	...
Dwellings	213040	40690	172350	229810	46000	183810	251380	50950	200430	276740	55690	221050
9 Community, social and personal services [ce]	601730	214740	386990	694530	249920	444610	791450	285940	505510	846580	304910	541670
Educational services	...	...	...	...	...	...	...	...	...	...	...	...
Medical, dental, other health and veterinary services	75270	22590	52680	83720	25240	58480	93470	28360	65110	97040	29420	67620
Total, Industries	5405620	3374790	2030830	5905100	3685550	2219550	6135050	3777370	2357680	6042880	3670940	2371940
Producers of government services	519380	266180	253200	557900	286680	271220	603100	312430	290670	616170	315090	301080
Other producers	82280	23980	58300	91120	26550	64570	100120	29230	70890	105850	30930	74920
Total	6007280	3664950	2342330	6554120	3998780	2555340	6838270	4119030	2719240	6764900	4016960	2747940
less: Imputed bank service charge	...	−96280	96280	...	−111240	111240	...	−124070	124070	...	−132330	132330
Import duties	24980	...	24980	29280	...	29280	30270	...	30270	27670	...	27670
Value added tax	154970	...	154970	174220	...	174220	187560	...	187560	203020	...	203020
Other adjustments	...	...	...	...	...	...	...	...	...	...	...	...
Total	6187230	3761230	2426000	6757620	4110020	2647600	7056100	4243100	2813000	6995590	4149290	2846300

	1994			1995			1996			1997		
	Gross output	Intermediate consumption	Value added	Gross output	Intermediate consumption	Value added	Gross output	Intermediate consumption	Value added	Gross output	Intermediate consumption	Value added
All producers												
1 Agriculture, hunting, forestry and fishing	...	...	...	...	...	...	...	...	...	...	...	...
2 Mining and quarrying	...	...	...	...	...	...	...	...	...	...	...	...
3 Manufacturing	...	...	765980	...	...	...	...	...	...	...	...	...
4 Electricity, gas and water	...	...	...	...	...	...	...	...	...	...	...	...
5 Construction [d]	...	...	162710	...	...	...	...	...	...	...	...	...
6 Wholesale and retail trade, restaurants and hotels	...	...	...	...	...	...	...	...	...	...	...	...
A Wholesale and retail trade	...	...	250180	...	...	...	...	...	...	...	...	...
B Restaurants and hotels	...	...	...	...	...	...	...	...	...	...	...	...
7 Transport, storage and communication	...	...	158970	...	...	...	...	...	...	...	...	...
8 Finance, insurance, real estate and business services	...	...	415870	...	...	...	...	...	...	...	...	...
A Financial institutions	...	...	...	...	...	...	...	...	...	...	...	...
B Insurance	...	...	...	...	...	...	...	...	...	...	...	...
C Real estate and business services [e]	...	...	240430	...	...	...	...	...	...	...	...	...
Real estate, except dwellings	...	...	...	...	...	...	...	...	...	...	...	...
Dwellings	...	...	240430	...	...	...	...	...	...	...	...	...
9 Community, social and personal services	...	...	...	...	...	...	...	...	...	...	...	...
Total, Industries	6277450	3800500	2476950	...	...	...	...	...	...	...	...	...
Producers of government services	636300	331140	305160	...	...	...	...	...	...	...	...	...
Other producers	110700	32350	78350	...	...	...	...	...	...	...	...	...
Total	7024450	4163990	2860460	...	...	...	...	...	...	...	...	...

Germany, Federal Republic (Former)

	1994			1995			1996			1997		
	Gross output	Intermediate consumption	Value added	Gross output	Intermediate consumption	Value added	Gross output	Intermediate consumption	Value added	Gross output	Intermediate consumption	Value added
less: Imputed bank service charge	...	−134620	134620	...	...	...	...	...	...	...	...	...
Import duties	29290	...	29290	...	...	...	...	...	...	...	...	...
Value added tax	218270	...	218270	...	...	...	...	...	...	...	...	...
Other adjustments	...	...	...	...	...	...	...	...	...	...	...	...
Total	7272010	4298610	2973400	...	...	...	...	...	...	...	...	...

a Hunting and fishing are included in item "Forestry and logging".
b Quarrying is included in item "Manufacture of non-metallic mineral products except products of petroleum and coal".
c Publishing is included in item "Community, social and personal services".
d Structural steel erection is included in item "Manufacture of fabricated metal products, machinery and equipment".
e Business services and real estate except dwellings are included in item "Community, social and personal services".

4.2 Derivation of value added by kind of activity, in constant prices

Million Deutsche marks

	1986			1987			1988			1989		
	Gross output	Intermediate consumption	Value added	Gross output	Intermediate consumption	Value added	Gross output	Intermediate consumption	Value added	Gross output	Intermediate consumption	Value added

At constant prices of: 1991

All producers

1 Agriculture, hunting, forestry and fishing	71070	35920	35150	68280	36190	32090	70450	35970	34480	70610	35640	34970
A Agriculture and hunting [a]	...	...	29930	...	...	26820	...	...	28970	...	...	29560
B Forestry and logging [a]	...	...	5220	...	...	5270	...	...	5510	...	...	5410
C Fishing	...	...	...	...	...	...	...	...	...	...	...	...
2 Mining and quarrying [bc]	188260	124270	12630	193790	126800	12690	192150	125470	11770	201690	132180	12680
A Coal mining	...	...	11170	...	...	10620	...	...	9450	...	...	9650
B Crude petroleum and natural gas production	...	...	...	...	...	...	...	...	...	...	...	...
C Metal ore mining	...	...	...	...	...	...	...	...	...	...	...	...
D Other mining	...	...	1460	...	...	2070	...	...	2320	...	...	3030
3 Manufacturing	1767860	1078290	689570	1781330	1104330	677000	1856670	1158030	698640	1939080	1216480	722600
A Manufacture of food, beverages and tobacco	...	...	75660	...	...	72880	...	...	72860	...	...	72500
B Textile, wearing apparel and leather industries	...	...	27870	...	...	27760	...	...	27740	...	...	28130
C Manufacture of wood and wood products, including furniture	...	...	21930	...	...	22280	...	...	22810	...	...	22980
D Manufacture of paper and paper products, printing and publishing [d]	...	...	30740	...	...	32040	...	...	31780	...	...	32130
E Manufacture of chemicals and chemical petroleum, coal, rubber and plastic products	...	...	142100	...	...	129490	...	...	137340	...	...	138100
F Manufacture of non-metallic mineral products, except products of petroleum and coal [b]	...	...	26090	...	...	26030	...	...	27400	...	...	28610
G Basic metal industries	...	...	47070	...	...	45540	...	...	46780	...	...	49280
H Manufacture of fabricated metal products, machinery and equipment [e]	...	...	313440	...	...	316240	...	...	327000	...	...	345670
I Other manufacturing industries	...	...	4670	...	...	4740	...	...	4930	...	...	5200

Germany, Federal Republic (Former)

Million Deutsche marks

	1986			1987			1988			1989		
	Gross output	Intermediate consumption	Value added	Gross output	Intermediate consumption	Value added	Gross output	Intermediate consumption	Value added	Gross output	Intermediate consumption	Value added

At constant prices of: 1991

4 Electricity, gas and water [c]	...	...	51360	...	...	54300	...	...	54910	...	...	56830
A Electricity, gas and steam	...	...	47100	...	...	50470	...	...	50310	...	...	52560
B Water works and supply	...	...	4260	...	...	3830	...	...	4600	...	...	4270
5 Construction [e]	242400	115780	126620	242520	117960	124560	251330	124220	127110	264890	132430	132460
6 Wholesale and retail trade, restaurants and hotels [f]	1343670	1159450	212370	1370910	1183640	216440	1414710	1220660	223520	1435100	1232950	233180
A Wholesale and retail trade	...	...	184220	...	...	187270	...	...	194050	...	...	202150
B Restaurants and hotels	...	...	28150	...	...	29170	...	...	29470	...	...	31030
7 Transport, storage and communication	207900	98510	109390	218680	104760	113920	234640	112870	121770	245400	117550	127850
A Transport and storage	...	...	64800	...	...	67280	...	...	72060	...	...	74870
B Communication	...	...	44590	...	...	46640	...	...	49710	...	...	52980
8 Finance, insurance, real estate and business services	359790	93090	266700	371790	95480	276310	387550	99980	287570	400100	102550	297550
A Financial institutions [g]	162400	56620	82530	168560	56630	85960	178780	59570	90220	185470	60380	94790
B Insurance [g]	...	...	23250	...	...	25970	...	...	28990	...	...	30300
C Real estate and business services [h]	197390	36470	160920	203230	38850	164380	208770	40410	168360	214630	42170	172460
Real estate, except dwellings	...	...	...	...	...	...	...	...	...	...	...	...
Dwellings	...	...	160920	...	...	164380	...	...	168360	...	...	172460
9 Community, social and personal services [dfh]	529410	194960	306300	564410	210760	324480	611600	232240	349890	650800	249260	370510
Educational services	...	...	...	...	...	...	...	...	...	...	...	...
Medical, dental, other health and veterinary services	...	...	49210	...	...	49060	...	...	53420	...	...	51710
Total, Industries	4710360	2900270	1810090	4811710	2979920	1831790	5019100	3109440	1909660	5207670	3219040	1988630
Producers of government services [i]	593680	283920	255610	603390	288640	258960	617170	298000	261700	612570	290830	262620
Other producers [i]	...	...	54150	...	...	55790	...	...	57470	...	...	59120
Total	5304040	3184190	2119850	5415100	3268560	2146540	5636270	3407440	2228830	5820240	3509870	2310370
less: Imputed bank service charge	...	-86920	86920	...	-91570	91570	...	-95480	95480	...	-98870	98870
Import duties	...	...	19010	...	...	21900	...	...	22080	...	...	23970
Value added tax	...	...	134160	...	...	141530	...	...	145570	...	...	148930
Other adjustments	...	...	...	...	...	...	...	...	...	...	...	...
Total	5304040	3271110	2186100	5415100	3360130	2218400	5636270	3502920	2301000	5820240	3608740	2384400

	1990			1991			1992			1993		
	Gross output	Intermediate consumption	Value added	Gross output	Intermediate consumption	Value added	Gross output	Intermediate consumption	Value added	Gross output	Intermediate consumption	Value added

At constant prices of: 1991

All producers

1 Agriculture, hunting, forestry and fishing	74020	37590	36430	69440	35360	34080	75790	34400	41390	70570	32610	37960
A Agriculture and hunting [a]	...	...	29610	...	...	28740	...	...	36120	...	...	32680
B Forestry and logging [a]	...	...	6820	...	...	5340	...	...	5270	...	...	5280
C Fishing	...	...	...	...	...	...	...	...	...	...	...	...
2 Mining and quarrying [bc]	207770	138390	11210	218900	144830	12450	219060	145780	11900	217920	146390	11850
A Coal mining	...	...	8510	...	...	9180	...	...	8520	...	...	8360

Germany, Federal Republic (Former)

	1990 Gross output	1990 Intermediate consumption	1990 Value added	1991 Gross output	1991 Intermediate consumption	1991 Value added	1992 Gross output	1992 Intermediate consumption	1992 Value added	1993 Gross output	1993 Intermediate consumption	1993 Value added
At constant prices of: 1991												
B Crude petroleum and natural gas production	...	...	...	...	...	...	...	...	...	...	...	...
C Metal ore mining	...	...	...	...	...	...	...	...	...	...	...	...
D Other mining	...	...	2700	...	...	3270	...	...	3380	...	...	3490
3 Manufacturing	2049080	1286810	762270	2150060	1359400	790660	2124990	1356070	768920	1969920	1262470	707450
A Manufacture of food, beverages and tobacco	...	...	79130	...	...	82110	...	...	77510	...	...	76680
B Textile, wearing apparel and leather industries	...	...	28320	...	...	27780	...	...	26510	...	...	23940
C Manufacture of wood and wood products, including furniture	...	...	23850	...	...	25970	...	...	26280	...	...	25610
D Manufacture of paper and paper products, printing and publishing [d]	...	...	35260	...	...	37090	...	...	36650	...	...	34690
E Manufacture of chemicals and chemical petroleum, coal, rubber and plastic products	...	...	140690	...	...	138070	...	...	138670	...	...	137030
F Manufacture of non-metallic mineral products, except products of petroleum and coal [b]	...	...	28950	...	...	30090	...	...	30400	...	...	30090
G Basic metal industries	...	...	53350	...	...	55280	...	...	55220	...	...	49260
H Manufacture of fabricated metal products, machinery and equipment [e]	...	...	367370	...	...	389050	...	...	372400	...	...	325230
I Other manufacturing industries	...	...	5350	...	...	5220	...	...	5280	...	...	4920
4 Electricity, gas and water [c]	...	...	58170	...	...	61620	...	...	61380	...	...	59680
A Electricity, gas and steam	...	...	53450	...	...	57360	...	...	56950	...	...	55820
B Water works and supply	...	...	4720	...	...	4260	...	...	4430	...	...	3860
5 Construction [e]	279980	143190	136790	286660	149410	137250	298880	158310	140570	291200	155930	135270
6 Wholesale and retail trade, restaurants and hotels [f]	1554390	1336270	251400	1683790	1441000	277060	1693100	1449840	276900	1650170	1412640	270480
A Wholesale and retail trade	...	...	218120	...	...	242790	...	...	243260	...	...	237530
B Restaurants and hotels	...	...	33280	...	...	34270	...	...	33640	...	...	32950
7 Transport, storage and communication	268470	130840	137630	277210	133400	143810	292880	142210	150670	291560	141190	150370
A Transport and storage	...	...	81720	...	...	86170	...	...	88120	...	...	88650
B Communication	...	...	55910	...	...	57640	...	...	62550	...	...	61720
8 Finance, insurance, real estate and business services	423160	113060	310100	440130	122120	318010	454670	129710	324960	475080	133820	341260
A Financial institutions [g]	200730	68280	100720	210320	76120	104720	216470	79400	106930	227490	81000	113130
B Insurance [g]	...	...	31730	...	...	29480	...	...	30140	...	...	33360
C Real estate and business services [h]	222430	44780	177650	229810	46000	183810	238200	50310	187890	247590	52820	194770
Real estate, except dwellings	...	...	...	...	...	...	...	...	...	...	...	...
Dwellings	222430	44780	177650	229810	46000	183810	238200	50310	187890	247590	52820	194770
9 Community, social and personal services [dfh]	715850	276770	405800	778910	300030	444610	839110	327490	477980	865610	336160	496500
Educational services	...	...	...	...	...	...	...	...	...	...	...	...
Medical, dental, other health and veterinary services	...	...	54490	...	...	58480	...	...	64360	...	...	68060
Total, Industries	5572720	3462920	2109800	5905100	3685550	2219550	5998480	3743810	2254670	5832030	3621210	2210820

Germany, Federal Republic (Former)

	1990			1991			1992			1993		
	Gross output	Intermediate consumption	Value added	Gross output	Intermediate consumption	Value added	Gross output	Intermediate consumption	Value added	Gross output	Intermediate consumption	Value added

At constant prices of: 1991

Producers of government services [i]	632000	303520	266910	649020	313230	271220	674520	330030	277140	675280	326730	279400
Other producers [i]	...	...	61570	...	...	64570	...	...	67350	...	...	69150
Total	6204720	3766440	2438280	6554120	3998780	2555340	6673000	4073840	2599160	6507310	3947940	2559370
less: Imputed bank service charge	...	−105400	105400	...	−111240	111240	...	−114910	114910	...	−121060	121060
Import duties	...	...	25900	...	...	29280	...	...	28860	...	...	26350
Value added tax	...	...	161620	...	...	174220	...	...	181190	...	...	179840
Other adjustments	...	...	...	...	...	...	...	...	...	...	...	...
Total	6204720	3871840	2520400	6554120	4110020	2647600	6673000	4188750	2694300	6507310	4069000	2644500

	1994			1995			1996			1997		
	Gross output	Intermediate consumption	Value added	Gross output	Intermediate consumption	Value added	Gross output	Intermediate consumption	Value added	Gross output	Intermediate consumption	Value added

At constant prices of: 1991

All producers

1 Agriculture, hunting, forestry and fishing	...	...	...	...	...	...	...	...	...	...	...	...
2 Mining and quarrying	...	...	...	...	...	...	...	...	...	...	...	...
3 Manufacturing	...	...	723560	...	...	...	...	...	...	...	...	...
4 Electricity, gas and water	...	...	...	...	...	...	...	...	...	...	...	...
5 Construction [e]	...	...	139600	...	...	...	...	...	...	...	...	...
6 Wholesale and retail trade, restaurants and hotels	...	...	...	...	...	...	...	...	...	...	...	...
A Wholesale and retail trade	...	...	235430	...	...	...	...	...	...	...	...	...
B Restaurants and hotels	...	...	...	...	...	...	...	...	...	...	...	...
7 Transport, storage and communication	...	...	152770	...	...	...	...	...	...	...	...	...
8 Finance, insurance, real estate and business services	...	...	357610	...	...	...	...	...	...	...	...	...
A Financial institutions	...	...	...	...	...	...	...	...	...	...	...	...
B Insurance	...	...	...	...	...	...	...	...	...	...	...	...
C Real estate and business services [h]	...	...	200980	...	...	...	...	...	...	...	...	...
Real estate, except dwellings	...	...	...	...	...	...	...	...	...	...	...	...
Dwellings	...	...	200980	...	...	...	...	...	...	...	...	...
9 Community, social and personal services	...	...	...	...	...	...	...	...	...	...	...	...
Total, Industries	5977240	3715320	2261920	...	...	...	...	...	...	...	...	...
Producers of government services [i]	686380	334050	280930	...	...	...	...	...	...	...	...	...
Other producers [i]	...	...	71400	...	...	...	...	...	...	...	...	...
Total	6663620	4049370	2614250	...	...	...	...	...	...	...	...	...
less: Imputed bank service charge	...	−125000	125000	...	...	...	...	...	...	...	...	...
Import duties	...	...	27950	...	...	...	...	...	...	...	...	...
Value added tax	...	...	189600	...	...	...	...	...	...	...	...	...
Other adjustments	...	...	...	...	...	...	...	...	...	...	...	...
Total	6663620	4174370	2706800	...	...	...	...	...	...	...	...	...

Germany, Federal Republic (Former)

	1994			1995			1996			1997		
	Gross output	Intermediate consumption	Value added	Gross output	Intermediate consumption	Value added	Gross output	Intermediate consumption	Value added	Gross output	Intermediate consumption	Value added

At constant prices of: 1991

a Hunting and fishing are included in item "Forestry and logging".
b Quarrying is included in item "Manufacture of non-metallic mineral products except products of petroleum and coal".
c Gross output and intermediate consumption of electricity, gas and water are included in item "Mining and quarrying".
d Publishing is included in item "Community, social and personal services".
e Structural steel erection is included in item "Manufacture of fabricated metal products, machinery and equipment".
f Gross output and intermediate consumption of restaurants and hotels are included in item "Community, social and personal services".
g Gross output and intermediate consumption of insurance are included in item "Financial institutions".
h Business services and real estate except dwellings are included in item "Community, social and personal services".
i Gross output and intermediate consumption of "Other producers" are included in item "Producers of government services".

4.3 Cost components of value added

Million Deutsche marks

	1986						1987					
	Compensation of employees	Capital consumption	Net operating surplus	Indirect taxes	less: Subsidies received	Value added	Compensation of employees	Capital consumption	Net operating surplus	Indirect taxes	less: Subsidies received	Value added
All producers													
1 Agriculture, hunting, forestry and fishing	7120	10980	19780	−3880	...	34000	6950	10940	15610	−3260	...	30240
A Agriculture and hunting [a]	3750	10320	18680	−3830	...	28920	3580	10270	14490	−3250	...	25090
B Forestry and logging [a]	3370	660	1100	−50	...	5080	3370	670	1120	−10	...	5150
C Fishing	...	...	...	...	...	...	...	...	...	...	...	...
2 Mining and quarrying [b]	13360	2910	−350	−2340	...	13580	13410	2970	210	−3810	...	12780
A Coal mining	11980	2280	−610	−2400	...	11250	12030	2320	280	−3860	...	10770
B Crude petroleum and natural gas production	...	...	...	...	...	...	...	...	...	...	...	...
C Metal ore mining	...	...	...	...	...	...	...	...	...	...	...	...
D Other mining	1380	630	260	60	...	2330	1380	650	−70	50	...	2010
3 Manufacturing	407390	62960	102310	47780	...	620440	425350	64550	89320	45470	...	624690
A Manufacture of food, beverages and tobacco	27830	7010	14560	16570	...	65970	28680	7100	13990	16320	...	66090
B Textile, wearing apparel and leather industries	18630	2630	4660	550	...	26470	18780	2650	4660	580	...	26670
C Manufacture of wood and wood products, including furniture	13630	1840	1950	290	...	17710	13900	1820	2750	300	...	18770
D Manufacture of paper and paper products, printing and publishing [c]	18070	3220	5590	620	...	27500	18630	3400	6250	640	...	28920
E Manufacture of chemicals and chemical petroleum, coal, rubber and plastic products	60830	11760	24980	22960	...	120530	64540	12080	13560	21410	...	111590
F Manufacture of non-metallic mineral products, except products of petroleum and coal [b]	14410	3510	4770	690	...	23380	14970	3490	4590	690	...	23740
G Basic metal industries	33590	6990	5610	680	...	46870	33300	6560	4520	540	...	44920
H Manufacture of fabricated metal products, machinery and equipment [d]	218120	25670	38450	5300	...	287540	230190	27100	37260	4870	...	299420
I Other manufacturing industries	2280	330	1740	120	...	4470	2360	350	1740	120	...	4570
4 Electricity, gas and water	18850	13580	18580	1320	...	52330	19950	14080	21200	660	...	55890
A Electricity, gas and steam	17370*	12410	17550	1230	...	48560	18680	12890	20180	570	...	52320
B Water works and supply	1480	1170	1030	90	...	3770	1270	1190	1020	90	...	3570

Germany, Federal Republic (Former)

Million Deutsche marks

	1986						1987					
	Compensation of employees	Capital consumption	Net operating surplus	Indirect taxes	less: Subsidies received	Value added	Compensation of employees	Capital consumption	Net operating surplus	Indirect taxes	less: Subsidies received	Value added
5 Construction [d]	67580	5300	25460	1790	...	100130	67770	5240	27050	1620	...	101680
6 Wholesale and retail trade, restaurants and hotels	120020	14590	51290	150	...	186050	124820	15030	53670	390	...	193910
A Wholesale and retail trade	107080	12560	43210	−580	...	162270	111800	12920	44060	−350	...	168430
B Restaurants and hotels	12940	2030	8080	730	...	23780	13020	2110	9610	740	...	25480
7 Transport, storage and communication	66180	26640	20230	−5740	...	107310	68850	27530	19900	−5170	...	111110
A Transport and storage	42700	15720	11210	−5690	...	63940	44470	15850	10760	−5130	...	65950
B Communication	23480	10920	9020	−50	...	43370	24380	11680	9140	−40	...	45160
8 Finance, insurance, real estate and business services [e]	47020	55840	39570	11270	...	239910	50110	58420	35080	10940	...	243520
A Financial institutions	34660	3450	35150	4660	...	77920	36980	3620	30970	4210	...	75780
B Insurance	12360	1280	4420	4530	...	22590	13130	1360	4110	4450	...	23050
C Real estate and business services [f]	...	51110	...	2080	...	139400	...	53440	...	2280	...	144690
Real estate, except dwellings	...	...	...	...	...	...	...	...	...	...	...	...
Dwellings	...	51110	...	2080	...	139400	...	53440	...	2280	...	144690
9 Community, social and personal services [cef]	80750	33800	219120	9330	...	256790	85050	35810	238360	9320	...	279570
Educational services	...	...	...	...	...	...	...	...	...	...	...	...
Medical, dental, other health and veterinary services	14910	6250	21720	−140	...	42740	15430	6570	21740	−200	...	43540
Total, Industries [g]	828270	226600	495990	59680	...	1610540	862260	234570	500400	56160	...	1653390
Producers of government services	203300	13570	−	250	...	217120	211500	14070	−	250	...	225820
Other producers	42870	3520	−	30	...	46420	45590	3660	−	30	...	49280
Total [g]	1074440	243690	495990	59960	...	1874080	1119350	252300	500400	56440	...	1928490
less: Imputed bank service charge	...	...	83690	...	...	83690	...	...	82270	...	...	82270
Import duties	...	...	...	17020	...	17020	...	...	...	19150	...	19150
Value added tax	...	...	...	117880	...	117880	...	...	...	125110	...	125110
Other adjustments	...	...	...	...	...	...	...	...	...	...	...	...
Total [g]	1074440	243690	412300	194860	...	1925290	1119350	252300	418130	200700	...	1990480

	1988						1989					
	Compensation of employees	Capital consumption	Net operating surplus	Indirect taxes	less: Subsidies received	Value added	Compensation of employees	Capital consumption	Net operating surplus	Indirect taxes	less: Subsidies received	Value added
All producers												
1 Agriculture, hunting, forestry and fishing	7070	11000	20040	−4390	...	33720	7090	11210	23210	−4300	...	37210
A Agriculture and hunting [a]	3590	10310	18590	−4350	...	28140	3540	10500	21710	−4230	...	31520
B Forestry and logging [a]	3480	690	1450	−40	...	5580	3550	710	1500	−70	...	5690
C Fishing	...	...	...	...	...	...	...	...	...	...	...	...
2 Mining and quarrying [b]	13020	3030	−600	−4270	...	11180	12750	3470	290	−4770	...	11740
A Coal mining	11660	2370	−600	−4310	...	9120	11480	2790	−190	−5050	...	9030
B Crude petroleum and natural gas production	...	...	...	...	...	...	...	...	...	...	...	...
C Metal ore mining	...	...	...	...	...	...	...	...	...	...	...	...
D Other mining	1360	660	−	40	...	2060	1270	680	480	280	...	2710
3 Manufacturing	440000	66890	97410	48370	...	652670	461680	70690	100100	53540	...	686010

884

Germany, Federal Republic (Former)

	1988						1989					
	Compensation of employees	Capital consumption	Net operating surplus	Indirect taxes	less: Subsidies received	Value added	Compensation of employees	Capital consumption	Net operating surplus	Indirect taxes	less: Subsidies received	Value added
A Manufacture of food, beverages and tobacco	28720	7260	13500	16830	...	66310	29580	7530	12960	18000	...	68070
B Textile, wearing apparel and leather industries	18980	2700	4560	600	...	26840	19200	2750	4640	630	...	27220
C Manufacture of wood and wood products, including furniture	14830	1830	2980	380	...	20020	15470	1860	2930	440	...	20700
D Manufacture of paper and paper products, printing and publishing [c]	19460	3600	5480	580	...	29120	20720	3880	4760	540	...	29900
E Manufacture of chemicals and chemical petroleum, coal, rubber and plastic products	68040	12610	17830	23520	...	122000	70400	13350	16780	26680	...	127210
F Manufacture of non-metallic mineral products, except products of petroleum and coal [b]	15890	3510	5140	810	...	25350	16450	3620	5440	930	...	26440
G Basic metal industries	34150	6280	6490	770	...	47690	35550	6530	8570	970	...	51620
H Manufacture of fabricated metal products, machinery and equipment [d]	237500	28720	39650	4750	...	310620	251680	30760	42380	5210	...	330030
I Other manufacturing industries	2430	380	1780	130	...	4720	2630	410	1640	140	...	4820
4 Electricity, gas and water	20940	14740	19380	1600	...	56660	21100	15370	19020	2070	...	57560
A Electricity, gas and steam	19380	13510	18050	1480	...	52420	19570	14090	17670	1950	...	53280
B Water works and supply	1560	1230	1330	120	...	4240	1530	1280	1350	120	...	4280
5 Construction [d]	71330	5180	27980	1760	...	106250	75490	5220	31980	1970	...	114660
6 Wholesale and retail trade, restaurants and hotels	131720	15730	58100	−1080	...	204470	139190	16750	56280	2130	...	214350
A Wholesale and retail trade	117390	13550	48680	−1830	...	177790	123890	14470	45880	1300	...	185540
B Restaurants and hotels	14330	2180	9420	750	...	26680	15300	2280	10400	830	...	28810
7 Transport, storage and communication	71220	28690	22430	−5470	...	116870	73380	30060	27300	−5030	...	125710
A Transport and storage	46340	16130	12280	−5430	...	69320	47990	16570	15260	−5000	...	74820
B Communication	24880	12560	10150	−40	...	47550	25390	13490	12040	−30	...	50890
8 Finance, insurance, real estate and business services [e]	52370	61070	37380	12830	...	257080	54860	64860	40680	13420	...	273460
A Financial institutions	38400	3770	32300	4710	...	79180	40060	4030	35490	3840	...	83420
B Insurance	13970	1430	5080	5110	...	25590	14800	1590	5190	6370	...	27950
C Real estate and business services [f]	...	55870	...	3010	...	152310	...	59240	...	3210	...	162090
Real estate, except dwellings	...	...	...	...	...	...	...	...	...	...	...	...
Dwellings	...	55870	...	3010	...	152310	...	59240	...	3210	...	162090
9 Community, social and personal services [cef]	91350	38270	262770	10110	...	309070	97980	42270	286740	11330	...	338680
Educational services	...	...	...	...	...	...	...	...	...	...	...	...
Medical, dental, other health and veterinary services	15920	6810	25560	−160	...	48130	17080	7330	23760	−130	...	48040
Total, Industries [g]	899020	244600	544890	59460	...	1747970	943520	259900	585600	70360	...	1859380
Producers of government services	216920	14690	−	250	...	231860	222840	15550	−	250	...	238640
Other producers	47840	3800	−	30	...	51670	49890	4000	−	30	...	53920
Total [g]	1163780	263090	544890	59740	...	2031500	1216250	279450	585600	70640	...	2151940
less: Imputed bank service charge	...	...	85150	...	...	85150	...	...	88410	...	...	88410

Germany, Federal Republic (Former)

	1988						1989					
	Compensation of employees	Capital consumption	Net operating surplus	Indirect taxes	less: Subsidies received	Value added	Compensation of employees	Capital consumption	Net operating surplus	Indirect taxes	less: Subsidies received	Value added
Import duties	...	...	...	19530	...	19530	...	...	...	23380	...	23380
Value added tax	...	...	...	130100	...	130100	...	...	...	137530	...	137530
Other adjustments	...	...	...	...	...	...	...	...	...	...	...	...
Total [g]	1163780	263090	459740	209370	...	2095980	1216250	279450	497190	231550	...	2224440

	1990						1991					
	Compensation of employees	Capital consumption	Net operating surplus	Indirect taxes	less: Subsidies received	Value added	Compensation of employees	Capital consumption	Net operating surplus	Indirect taxes	less: Subsidies received	Value added

All producers

1 Agriculture, hunting, forestry and fishing	7430	11870	22020	−4580	...	36740	7960	12410	17610	−3900	...	34080
A Agriculture and hunting [a]	3610	11080	18680	−4450	...	28920	3910	11570	16890	−3860	...	28740
B Forestry and logging [a]	3820	790	3340	−130	...	7820	4050	840	530	−50	...	5340
C Fishing	...	...	...	...	...	...	...	...	...	...	...	...
2 Mining and quarrying [b]	13320	3550	−1040	−4440	...	11390	13270	3440	−80	−4180	...	12450
A Coal mining	12010	2840	−1440	−4740	...	8670	11970	2690	−940	−4540	...	9180
B Crude petroleum and natural gas production	...	...	...	...	...	...	...	...	...	...	...	...
C Metal ore mining	...	...	...	...	...	...	...	...	...	...	...	...
D Other mining	1310	710	400	300	...	2720	1300	750	860	360	...	3270
3 Manufacturing	499730	76070	111000	54750	...	741550	534980	83140	111160	61380	...	790660
A Manufacture of food, beverages and tobacco	31980	7950	19810	18520	...	78260	35570	8630	16910	21000	...	82110
B Textile, wearing apparel and leather industries	19460	2890	5010	590	...	27950	19840	3070	4250	620	...	27780
C Manufacture of wood and wood products, including furniture	16560	1980	3830	470	...	22840	18360	2180	4900	530	...	25970
D Manufacture of paper and paper products, printing and publishing [c]	22850	4230	6290	750	...	34120	25210	4660	6410	810	...	37090
E Manufacture of chemicals and chemical petroleum, coal, rubber and plastic products	74960	14230	16060	27120	...	132370	78820	15320	12380	31550	...	138070
F Manufacture of non-metallic mineral products, except products of petroleum and coal [b]	17280	3840	5950	960	...	28030	18550	4190	6410	940	...	30090
G Basic metal industries	38590	6860	7910	1150	...	54510	40270	7230	6880	900	...	55280
H Manufacture of fabricated metal products, machinery and equipment [d]	275220	33650	44380	5040	...	358290	295410	37380	51370	4890	...	389050
I Other manufacturing industries	2830	440	1760	150	...	5180	2950	480	1650	140	...	5220
4 Electricity, gas and water	22040	16140	18780	1880	...	58840	24570	16870	17660	2520	...	61620
A Electricity, gas and steam	20410	14780	17380	1800	...	54370	23070	15430	16340	2520	...	57360
B Water works and supply	1630	1360	1400	80	...	4470	1500	1440	1320	−	...	4260
5 Construction [d]	84050	5470	35720	2380	...	127620	89980	5940	38670	2660	...	137250
6 Wholesale and retail trade, restaurants and hotels	152280	18190	71470	2710	...	244650	170780	20360	81200	4720	...	277060
A Wholesale and retail trade	135340	15760	59660	1790	...	212550	151810	17750	69460	3770	...	242790
B Restaurants and hotels	16940	2430	11810	920	...	32100	18970	2610	11740	950	...	34270
7 Transport, storage and communication	77890	32260	29260	−5210	...	134200	85400	35020	27660	−4270	...	143810

Germany, Federal Republic (Former)

	1990							1991					
	Compensation of employees	Capital consumption	Net operating surplus	Indirect taxes	less: Subsidies received	Value added	Compensation of employees	Capital consumption	Net operating surplus	Indirect taxes	less: Subsidies received	Value added
A Transport and storage	52210	17490	16610	−5170	...	81140	57500	18870	14060	−4260	...	86170
B Communication	25680	14770	12650	−40	...	53060	27900	16150	13600	−10	...	57640
8 Finance, insurance, real estate and business services [e] .	60900	70670	39300	13050	...	288850	66600	77710	47990	15860	...	318010
A Financial institutions	45090	4380	37690	3830	...	90990	48610	4890	45940	5280	...	104720
B Insurance	15810	1780	1610	6310	...	25510	17990	2030	2050	7410	...	29480
C Real estate and business services [f]	...	64510	...	2910	...	172350	...	70790	...	3170	...	183810
Real estate, except dwellings	...	...	...	...	...	...	...	...	...	...	...	...
Dwellings	...	64510	...	2910	...	172350	...	70790	...	3170	...	183810
9 Community, social and personal services [cef]	107610	47840	323850	12620	...	386990	123900	55350	361760	13450	...	444610
Educational services	...	...	...	...	...	...	...	...	...	...	...	...
Medical, dental, other health and veterinary services	17860	8090	26900	−170	...	52680	20610	9070	29000	−200	...	58480
Total, Industries [g]	1025250	282060	650360	73160	...	2030830	1117440	310240	703630	88240	...	2219550
Producers of government services	236290	16660	−	250	...	253200	252960	18010	−	250	...	271220
Other producers	53980	4290	−	30	...	58300	59900	4640	−	30	...	64570
Total [g]	1315520	303010	650360	73440	...	2342330	1430300	332890	703630	88520	...	2555340
less: Imputed bank service charge	...	...	96280	...	...	96280	...	...	111240	...	...	111240
Import duties	...	...	...	24980	...	24980	...	...	...	29280	...	29280
Value added tax	...	...	...	154970	...	154970	...	...	...	174220	...	174220
Other adjustments	...	...	...	...	...	...	...	...	...	...	...	...
Total [g]	1315520	303010	554080	253390	...	2426000	1430300	332890	592390	292020	...	2647600

	1992							1993					
	Compensation of employees	Capital consumption	Net operating surplus	Indirect taxes	less: Subsidies received	Value added	Compensation of employees	Capital consumption	Net operating surplus	Indirect taxes	less: Subsidies received	Value added

All producers

1 Agriculture, hunting, forestry and fishing	8310	13000	16360	−3940	...	33730	8390	13180	15700	−7390	...	29880
A Agriculture and hunting [a] ...	3990	12110	15140	−3720	...	28380	3930	12260	...	...	...	24530
B Forestry and logging [a]	4320	890	200	−70	...	5350	4460	920	...	...	...	5350
C Fishing	...	...	...	...	...	...	...	...	...	...	...	...
2 Mining and quarrying [b]	13730	3510	−950	−3630	...	12660	12850	3550	−190	−3560	...	12650
A Coal mining	12550	2710	−1880	−4110	...	9270	11690	2720	−1090	−3980	...	9340
B Crude petroleum and natural gas production	...	...	...	...	...	...	...	...	...	...	...	...
C Metal ore mining	...	...	...	...	...	...	...	...	...	...	...	...
D Other mining	1180	800	930	480	...	3390	1160	830	900	420	...	3310
3 Manufacturing	556310	88800	86340	67640	...	799090	534220	92370	51670	68050	...	746310
A Manufacture of food, beverages and tobacco	37120	9260	15880	21090	...	83350	37360	9690	16980	21570	...	85600
B Textile, wearing apparel and leather industries	19620	3180	4240	670	...	27710	18320	3220	3370	640	...	25550
C Manufacture of wood and wood products, including furniture	18990	2370	5580	670	...	27610	19360	2490	5030	640	...	27520
D Manufacture of paper and paper products, printing and publishing [c]	26380	4980	5230	830	...	37420	26010	5240	3720	670	...	35640

Germany, Federal Republic (Former)

	1992						1993					
	Compensation of employees	Capital consumption	Net operating surplus	Indirect taxes	less: Subsidies received	Value added	Compensation of employees	Capital consumption	Net operating surplus	Indirect taxes	less: Subsidies received	Value added
E Manufacture of chemicals and chemical petroleum, coal, rubber and plastic products	82420	16220	8900	37060	...	144600	82110	16690	5940	38880	...	143620
F Manufacture of non-metallic mineral products, except products of petroleum and coal [b]	19650	4510	6760	1140	...	32060	20310	4720	6680	1100	...	32810
G Basic metal industries	40180	7530	5500	750	...	53960	36570	8160	450	540	...	45720
H Manufacture of fabricated metal products, machinery and equipment [d]	308990	40240	32290	5280	...	386800	291340	41630	7790	3890	...	344650
I Other manufacturing industries	2960	510	1960	150	...	5580	2840	530	1710	120	...	5200
4 Electricity, gas and water	26340	17520	17740	2080	...	63680	26900	17920	15840	2520	...	63180
A Electricity, gas and steam	24310	15980	16730	1970	...	58990	25150	16320	14620	2430	...	58520
B Water works and supply	2030	1540	1010	110	...	4690	1750	1600	1220	90	...	4660
5 Construction [d]	97180	6490	45240	3480	...	152390	100220	7020	42190	3270	...	152700
6 Wholesale and retail trade, restaurants and hotels	187470	22710	70130	6580	...	286890	193830	24720	58420	6200	...	283170
A Wholesale and retail trade	165580	19960	59780	5520	...	250840	172440	21890	46830	5210	...	246370
B Restaurants and hotels	21890	2750	10350	1060	...	36050	21390	2830	11590	990	...	36800
7 Transport, storage and communication	91470	36880	29090	−3790	...	153650	92750	38070	29090	−4630	...	155280
A Transport and storage	61300	19880	13440	−3810	...	90810	61730	20340	13350	−4660	...	90760
B Communication	30170	17000	15650	20	...	62840	31020	17730	15740	30	...	64520
8 Finance, insurance, real estate and business services [e]	73120	84570	53240	19110	...	350080	76480	90760	63030	22630	...	387100
A Financial institutions	53010	5510	52730	5850	...	117100	56050	6080	57180	6620	...	125930
B Insurance	20110	2280	510	9650	...	32550	20430	2520	5850	11320	...	40120
C Real estate and business services [f]	...	76780	...	3610	...	200430	...	82160	...	4690	...	221050
Real estate, except dwellings	...	...	...	...	...	...	...	...	...	...	...	...
Dwellings	...	76780	...	3610	...	200430	...	82160	...	4690	...	221050
9 Community, social and personal services [cef]	137770	61890	409950	15940	...	505510	147730	65960	445160	17020	...	541670
Educational services	...	...	...	...	...	...	...	...	...	...	...	...
Medical, dental, other health and veterinary services	22880	9800	32620	−190	...	65110	24870	10250	32690	−190	...	67620
Total, Industries [g]	1191700	335370	727140	103470	...	2357680	1193370	353550	720910	104110	...	2371940
Producers of government services	271040	19380	–	250	...	290670	280300	20530	–	250	...	301080
Other producers	65910	4940	–	40	...	70890	69670	5210	–	40	...	74920
Total [g]	1528650	359700	727130	103760	...	2719240	1543340	379290	720910	104400	...	2747940
less: Imputed bank service charge	...	...	124070	...	...	124070	...	...	132330	...	...	132330
Import duties	...	...	...	30270	...	30270	...	...	...	27670	...	27670
Value added tax	...	...	...	187560	...	187560	...	...	...	203020	...	203020
Other adjustments	...	...	...	...	...	...	...	...	...	...	...	...
Total [g]	1528650	359700	603060	321590	...	2813000	1543340	379290	588580	335090	...	2846300

Germany, Federal Republic (Former)

	1994						1995					
	Compensation of employees	Capital consumption	Net operating surplus	Indirect taxes	less: Subsidies received	Value added	Compensation of employees	Capital consumption	Net operating surplus	Indirect taxes	less: Subsidies received	Value added
All producers												
1 Agriculture, hunting, forestry and fishing	8580	...	...	...	...	...	...	...	...	...	...	...
2 Mining and quarrying	...	...	...	...	...	...	...	...	...	...	...	...
3 Manufacturing	529360	...	...	...	...	765980	...	...	...	...	...	...
4 Electricity, gas and water	...	...	...	...	...	...	...	...	...	...	...	...
5 Construction [d]	105940	...	...	...	...	162710	...	...	...	...	...	...
6 Wholesale and retail trade, restaurants and hotels	...	...	...	...	...	...	...	...	...	...	...	...
A Wholesale and retail trade	175640	...	...	...	...	250180	...	...	...	...	...	...
B Restaurants and hotels	...	...	...	...	...	...	...	...	...	...	...	...
7 Transport, storage and communication	91900	...	...	...	...	158970	...	...	...	...	...	...
8 Finance, insurance, real estate and business services [e]	78490	...	...	...	...	415870	...	...	...	...	...	...
A Financial institutions	...	...	...	...	...	...	...	...	...	...	...	...
B Insurance	...	...	...	...	...	...	...	...	...	...	...	...
C Real estate and business services [f]	...	...	...	...	...	240430	...	...	...	...	...	...
Real estate, except dwellings	...	...	...	...	...	...	...	...	...	...	...	...
Dwellings	...	...	...	...	...	240430	...	...	...	...	...	...
9 Community, social and personal services	...	...	...	...	...	...	...	...	...	...	...	...
Total, Industries [g]	1207590	362130	795490	111740	...	2476950	...	...	...	...	...	...
Producers of government services	283780	21130	–	250	...	305160	...	...	...	...	...	...
Other producers	72940	5370	–	40	...	78350	...	...	...	...	...	...
Total [g]	1564310	388630	795490	112030	...	2860460	...	...	...	...	...	...
less: Imputed bank service charge	...	...	134620	...	...	134620	...	...	...	...	...	...
Import duties	...	...	...	29290	...	29290	...	...	...	...	...	...
Value added tax	...	...	...	218270	...	218270	...	...	...	...	...	...
Other adjustments	...	...	...	...	...	...	...	...	...	...	...	...
Total [g]	1564310	388630	660870	359590	...	2973400	...	...	...	...	...	...

a Hunting and fishing are included in item "Forestry and logging".
b Quarrying is included in item "Manufacture of non-metallic mineral products except products of petroleum and coal".
c Publishing is included in item "Community, social and personal services".
d Structural steel erection is included in item "Manufacture of fabricated metal products, machinery and equipment".
e Dwelling is excluded from columns 1 and 3 of item "Finance, insurance, real estate and business services" and is included in columns 1 and 3 of item "Community, social and personal services".
f Business services and real estate except dwellings are included in item "Community, social and personal services".
g Column 4 refers to indirect taxes less subsidies received.

Ghana

General note

The preparation of national accounts statistics in Ghana is undertaken by the Central Bureau of Statistics, Accra. The official estimates are published by the bureau in the *Economic Survey*. A detailed description of the sources and methods used for the national accounts estimation is contained in the publications *Sources and Methods of Estimation of National Income at Current Prices in Ghana* and *National Income of Ghana at Constant Prices*. The estimates are generally in accordance with the classifications and definitions recommended in the United Nations System of National Accounts (1968 SNA). Work relating to input-output analysis is being done at present. The following tables have been prepared from successive replies to the United Nations National Accounts Questionnaire. When the scope and coverage of the estimates differ for conceptual or statistical reasons from the definitions and classifications recommended in SNA, a footnote is indicated to the relevant tables.

Gross domestic product

Gross domestic product is estimated mainly through the production approach.

Expenditures on the gross domestic product

Gross fixed capital formation is estimated by using the commodity-flow approach. A combination of commodity-flow and expenditure approach is used for increase in stock. Private consumption expenditure is treated as a residual. Gross fixed capital formation is classified according to type of capital goods and not according to kind of economic activity. The estimates of increase in stocks are mainly based on special inquiries into the stocks held by selected kinds of producers and distributors. Adjustment is made to arrive at estimates on the equivalent of physical changes in the stocks, valued at average market prices during the period of account. Government consumption expenditure is estimated on a cash basis from government records. These records are reclassified according to government purposes. It is feasible to distinguish between acquisition for military purposes and for civilian purposes which exclude durable goods. Sales of goods and services by government to the public are subtracted from total expenditure. Exports and imports of goods and services are mainly estimated from foreign trade statistics of merchandise trade supplemented by information from the Central Bank. For the constant price estimates, no specific information is available for government consumption expenditure, but wages and salaries paid by government are extrapolated by index numbers of employment. For gross capital formation, current values are deflated by appropriate price indexes. In the case of commodity trade, current values are deflated by Paasche indexes of prices specially prepared for this purpose. Private consumption expenditure is obtained as a residual.

1.1 Expenditure on the gross domestic product, in current prices

Million Ghanaian cedis

	1986	1987	1988	1989	1990	1991	1992	1993	1994	1995	1996	1997
1 Government final consumption expenditure	56600	74700	104800	145500	222000	294200	400100	...	...	...	...	...
2 Private final consumption expenditure	415400	610400	834300	1186700	1736100	2159400	2544300	...	...	...	...	...
3 Gross capital formation [a]	47800	77900	114900	192000	249100	328000	388000	...	...	...	...	...
A Increase in stocks [a]	300	600	800	1000	1400	1600	1900	...	...	...	...	...
B Gross fixed capital formation	47500	77300	114100	191000	247700	326400	386100	...	...	...	...	...
4 Exports of goods and services	81800	157800	217700	292000	312600	404700	482900	...	...	...	...	...
5 less: Imports of goods and services	90400	174700	220600	398900	488000	611500	806400	...	...	...	...	...
equals: Gross domestic product	511400	746000	1051200	1417200	2031700	2574800	3008800	...	...	...	...	...

a Cocoa is valued at cost to the Ghana Cocoa Marketing Board. Stocks of other export commodities, including minerals, are valued at export prices.

Greece

General note

The preparation of national accounts statistics in Greece is undertaken by the National Accounts Service, Ministry of National Economy, Athens. Official estimates are published in a series of reports entitled *National Accounts of Greece*. The estimates are generally in accordance with the classifications and definitions recommended in the United Nations System of National Accounts (1968 SNA). The following tables have been prepared from successive replies to the United Nations National Accounts Questionnaire. When the scope and coverage of the estimates differ for conceptual or statistical reasons from the definitions and classifications recommended in SNA, a footnote is indicated to the relevant tables.

Gross domestic product

Gross domestic product is estimated mainly through the production approach.

Expenditures on the gross domestic product

The expenditure approach is used to estimate government final consumption expenditure and exports and imports of goods and services. This approach, in combination with the commodity-flow approach, is also used to estimate gross capital formation. Private final consumption expenditure is estimated on the basis of the direct expenditure approach. The estimates of government final consumption expenditure are obtained from the accounts of the different government units. For private consumption expenditure, sources include the household budget surveys, tax statistics and other statistical sources. In estimating increase in stocks, delayed information from the manufacturing and mining surveys is used to supplement the commodity-flow method. Estimates of investments in private buildings are based on building permits that have been issued, while for the public sector construction, estimates are derived from government budgetary accounts and replies from public enterprises and public funds. Information from the annual manufacturing and mining surveys as well as investments by large industrial units, public enterprises and public funds are used for machinery and equipment. Own-account construction is covered by information on loans granted for such construction works.

For exports and imports of goods and services, foreign trade statistics based on the special trade principle are used. For the constant price estimates, price indices are used to deflate the wages and salaries of government employees. For the private expenditure, the annual quantities of food, fuel, light and water charges are multiplied by average base-year prices. Expenditure on other private goods and services are deflated by appropriate price indexes. Value added of residential and non-residential buildings is extrapolated by specially constructed indicators. For other components of gross capital formation, price deflation is used. The base-year values of exports and imports of merchandise are extrapolated by volume indexes while other goods and services are deflated by mean value index of exports and imports.

Cost structure of the gross domestic product

Estimates of compensation of employees for various services such as finance, insurance and transport are estimated by using data derived from questionnaires sent to them by the National Accounts Service. For manufacturing and mining, data are derived from the annual industrial surveys. The employers' contributions are estimated by using data derived from statements of the social insurance funds. Capital consumption is estimated as a percentage of the corresponding capital stock figure for each industry and type of assists. The current-price estimates of capital stock and depreciation are calculated on a replacement cost basis. The estimates of indirect taxes and subsidies are obtained from government accounts. Operating surplus is calculated as a residual.

Gross domestic product by kind of activity

The table of gross domestic product by kind of economic activity is prepared in factor values. The production approach is used to estimate value added of most industries. The income approach is used for lignite mining, electricity, gas and water and parts of the service sectors such as transportation, communication, health and education, and miscellaneous services. For agricultural and animal breeding, the estimate of production is based on annual surveys conducted by the National Statistical Office of Greece. Intermediate consumption estimates are based on data taken from various sources such as Ministry of Agriculture and the Public Power Corporation. Agricultural product prices refer to prices obtained by farmers. The estimates of mining and quarrying and manufacturing are based on the annual survey of industrial establishments. The information from the survey is available within 2–3 years, meanwhile, value added is extrapolated by the index of industrial production and the wholesale price index. Value added of electricity, gas and water is estimated on the basis of annual questionnaires sent to the concerned enterprises.

For construction, gross value is obtained from investment data of buildings and other construction to which values of military construction and repairs are added. The estimates of gross trade margins for agricultural products are based on traded quantities valued at the difference between consumers' and producers' prices. For industrial and imported products, percentages of gross trade margins are applied to the traded values at current prices.

Greece

Intermediate consumption estimates are based on a survey conducted in 1970 for the compilation of the input-output table. Value added of transport and communication and finance and insurance services is based on data compiled through questionnaires sent to the concerned enterprises. For ownership of dwellings, the estimation of real or imputed rent is carried out at constant prices, based on the number of dwelling rooms existing and the average annual rent expenditure in a benchmark year. These data are obtained from dwelling censuses and household budget surveys. Estimates concerning government services are obtained from general government accounts. For private health and educational services, only wages and salaries data are available. Value added of hotels is based on surveys conducted every three years by the National Accounts Service, while that of restaurants is based on data obtained from household budget surveys. For other services, employment data as well as data on average remuneration per person employed or data derived from taxation returns are used.

For the constant price estimates, double deflation is used for agriculture and electricity. For water, construction, transport and hotels, value added is extrapolated by quantity indicators. For the remaining sectors of the industries, price deflation is used.

1.1 Expenditure on the gross domestic product, in current prices

Thousand million Greek drachmas

	1986	1987	1988	1989	1990	1991	1992	1993	1994	1995	1996	1997
1 Government final consumption expenditure	1067	1225	1530	1819	2251	2555	2925	3201	3494	3945	...	...
2 Private final consumption expenditure	3719	4356	5153	6158	7498	9112	10669	12148	13662	15172	...	...
3 Gross capital formation	1093	1103	1464	1839	2101	2612	2907	3100	3401	3794	...	...
A Increase in stocks	75	28	145	148	29	236	211	190	220	203	...	...
B Gross fixed capital formation	1018	1075	1318	1690	2072	2376	2696	2910	3181	3591	...	...
Residential buildings	248	287	329	403	555	560	551	604	636	707	...	...
Non-residential buildings	125	141	195	221	267	293	321	353	419	465	...	...
Other construction and land improvement, etc.	246	215	266	337	376	528	632	646	639	793	...	...
Other	399	432	528	729	874	995	1192	1306	1487	1627	...	...
4 Exports of goods and services [a]	1233	1537	1801	2019	2279	2906	3438	3709	4364	4876	...	...
5 less: Imports of goods and services	1703	1993	2291	2810	3445	4253	4898	5419	6103	6478	...	...
Statistical discrepancy	106	45	−84	−220	−132	−42	−209	21	46	−186	...	...
equals: Gross domestic product	5515	6272	7572	8805	10551	12889	14832	16760	18864	21123	...	...

a Exclude income from ocean-going cargo ships under Greek flag or ownership. However, remittances actually received by the bank of Greece from persons engaged in these enterprises are included in factor income from the rest of the world.

1.2 Expenditure on the gross domestic product, in constant prices

Thousand million Greek drachmas

	1986	1987	1988	1989	1990	1991	1992	1993	1994	1995	1996	1997
At constant prices of: 1970												
1 Government final consumption expenditure	82	82	87	90	92	94	95	95	95	96	...	...
2 Private final consumption expenditure	361	365	378	395	403	412	420	421	427	434	...	...
3 Gross capital formation	86	76	93	96	95	100	101	98	101	105	...	...
A Increase in stocks	9	2	13	8	−1	8	8	7	7	6	...	...
B Gross fixed capital formation	77	73	80	88	96	92	93	91	93	98	...	...
Residential buildings	19	20	21	22	25	21	18	18	17	17	...	...
Non-residential buildings	10	10	12	12	12	11	11	10	11	11	...	...
Other construction and land improvement, etc.	15	12	13	14	13	16	17	15	14	16	...	...
Other	33	32	34	41	46	44	47	48	51	54	...	...
4 Exports of goods and services [a]	113	131	143	144	146	170	183	184	198	202	...	...

Greece

Thousand million Greek drachmas

	1986	1987	1988	1989	1990	1991	1992	1993	1994	1995	1996	1997
At constant prices of: 1970												
5 less: Imports of goods and services	135	157	170	188	209	236	251	257	271	262	...	...
Statistical discrepancy	8	15	4	17	24	29	24	26	26	12	...	...
equals: Gross domestic product	514	512	535	554	550	569	572	567	575	586	...	...

a Exclude income from ocean-going cargo ships under Greek flag or ownership. However, remittances actually received by the bank of Greece from persons engaged in these enterprises are included in factor income from the rest of the world.

1.3 Cost components of the gross domestic product

Thousand million Greek drachmas

	1986	1987	1988	1989	1990	1991	1992	1993	1994	1995	1996	1997
1 Indirect taxes, net	642	794	952	967	1332	1817	2301	2401	2885	3306	...	...
A Indirect taxes	1001	1165	1314	1430	1922	2499	3067	3414	3960	4327	...	...
B less: Subsidies	359	371	362	464	591	682	766	1013	1075	1021	...	...
2 Consumption of fixed capital	505	578	662	793	942	1108	1276	1447	1602	1755	...	...
3 Compensation of employees paid by resident producers to [a]	2165	2436	2978	3600	4376	4936	5455	6035	6898	7930	...	...
A Resident households [a]	2157	2425	2965	3581	4356	4915	5422	5977	6850	7870	...	...
B Rest of the world	8	10	14	19	19	22	33	58	48	59	...	...
4 Operating surplus [a]	2202	2464	2981	3445	3901	5027	5800	6877	7479	8132	...	...
equals: Gross domestic product	5515	6272	7572	8805	10551	12889	14832	16760	18864	21123	...	...

a Compensation of employees paid by resident producers to resident households excludes wages paid to agricultural workers which are included in item "Operating surplus".

1.4 General government current receipts and disbursements

Thousand million Greek drachmas

	1986	1987	1988	1989	1990	1991	1992	1993	1994	1995	1996	1997
Receipts												
1 Operating surplus	...	...	...	...	...	...	...	...	...	...	...	...
2 Property and entrepreneurial income	91	113	96	126	195	225	439	488	636	778	...	...
3 Taxes, fees and contributions	1848	2142	2460	2767	3654	4577	5457	6245	7549	8527	...	...
A Indirect taxes [a]	911	1091	1228	1325	1805	2322	2874	3146	3661	4000	...	...
B Direct taxes [b]	336	378	449	465	651	811	898	1033	1454	1821	...	...
C Social security contributions	601	672	784	978	1198	1444	1685	2066	2434	2706	...	...
D Compulsory fees, fines and penalties	...	...	...	...	...	...	...	...	...	...	...	...
4 Other current transfers	18	18	23	28	35	88	53	66	158	193	...	...
Total current receipts of general government	1956	2273	2580	2922	3885	4890	5949	6799	8342	9498	...	...
Disbursements												
1 Government final consumption expenditure	1067	1225	1530	1819	2251	2555	2925	3201	3494	3945	...	...
A Compensation of employees	730	840	1032	1282	1584	1799	1970	...	...	...	...	...
B Consumption of fixed capital	...	...	...	...	...	...	...	...	...	...	...	...
C Purchases of goods and services, net	...	...	...	...	...	...	...	...	...	...	...	...
D less: Own-account fixed capital formation	...	...	...	...	...	...	...	...	...	...	...	...
E Indirect taxes paid, net	...	...	...	...	...	...	...	...	...	...	...	...
2 Property income	316	449	592	729	1193	1564	1927	2535	3036	3310	...	...

Greece

Thousand million Greek drachmas

	1986	1987	1988	1989	1990	1991	1992	1993	1994	1995	1996	1997
3 Subsidies [c]	154	152	122	144	176	151	138	180	171	163	...	...
4 Other current transfers	826	940	1103	1364	1612	2040	2270	2673	3232	3595	...	...
A Social security benefits	821	936	1098	1359	1607	2034	2263	2662	3215	3577	...	...
B Social assistance grants	...	...	...	...	...	...	...	...	...	...	...	...
C Other	5	4	5	5	6	6	7	11	17	17	...	...
5 Net saving	−407	−493	−767	−1134	−1348	−1420	−1311	−1790	−1591	−1515	...	...
Total current disbursements and net saving of general government	1956	2273	2580	2922	3885	4890	5949	6799	8342	9498	...	...

a Excludes indirect taxes from the rest of the world.
b Item "Fees, fines and penalties" is included in item "Direct taxes".
c Excludes subsidies from the rest of the world.

1.6 Current income and outlay of households and non-profit institutions

Thousand million Greek drachmas

	1986	1987	1988	1989	1990	1991	1992	1993	1994	1995	1996	1997
Receipts												
1 Compensation of employees [a]	2204	2480	3007	3628	4405	4983	5525	6166	6998	8040	...	...
A From resident producers [a]	2157	2425	2965	3581	4356	4915	5422	5977	6850	7870	...	...
B From rest of the world	47	55	42	47	48	68	103	189	148	170	...	...
2 Operating surplus of private unincorporated enterprises	...	...	...	...	...	...	...	...	...	...	...	...
3 Property and entrepreneurial income [b]	2238	2592	3290	3814	4638	5978	6784	8448	9187	9777	...	...
4 Current transfers	958	1122	1343	1585	1879	2427	2710	3219	3825	4186	...	...
A Social security benefits	821	936	1098	1359	1607	2034	2263	2662	3215	3577	...	...
B Social assistance grants	...	...	...	...	...	...	...	...	...	...	...	...
C Other	137	186	245	226	272	393	447	556	610	609	...	...
Total current receipts	5400	6194	7640	9028	10921	13388	15019	17833	20011	22004	...	...
Disbursements												
1 Private final consumption expenditure	3719	4356	5153	6158	7498	9112	10669	12148	13662	15172	...	...
2 Property income	...	...	...	...	...	...	...	...	...	...	...	...
3 Direct taxes and other current transfers n.e.c. to general government	854	950	1132	1322	1665	1964	2201	2659	3188	3677	...	...
A Social security contributions	601	672	784	978	1198	1444	1685	2066	2434	2706	...	...
B Direct taxes	253	278	348	344	466	520	516	593	754	971	...	...
C Fees, fines and penalties	...	...	...	...	...	...	...	...	...	...	...	...
4 Other current transfers	18	18	23	28	35	88	53	66	158	193	...	...
Statistical discrepancy	106	45	−84	−220	−132	−42	−209	21	46	−186	...	...
1 Net saving	704	825	1416	1738	1857	2267	2305	2939	2957	3149	...	...
Total current disbursements and net saving	5400	6194	7640	9028	10921	13388	15019	17833	20011	22004	...	...

a Compensation of employees paid by resident producers to resident households excludes wages paid to agricultural workers which are included in item "Operating surplus".
b Beginning 1975, item "Property and entrepreneurial income" includes savings of corporations.

Greece

1.7 External transactions on current account, summary

Thousand million Greek drachmas

	1986	1987	1988	1989	1990	1991	1992	1993	1994	1995	1996	1997
Payments to the rest of the world												
1 Imports of goods and services	1703	1993	2291	2810	3445	4253	4898	5419	6103	6478	...	...
A Imports of merchandise, c.i.f.	1538	1830	2061	2520	3093	3818	4351	...	...	...	...	...
B Other	165	163	230	290	353	436	547	...	...	...	...	...
2 Factor income to rest of the world	199	218	254	315	324	392	483	541	571	704	...	...
A Compensation of employees	8	10	14	19	19	22	33	...	...	...	...	...
B Property and entrepreneurial income	191	208	241	295	305	371	449	...	...	...	...	...
3 Current transfers to the rest of the world	95	77	91	111	123	183	200	279	316	344	...	...
A Indirect taxes to supranational organizations	90	73	86	105	118	177	193	268	299	327	...	...
B Other current transfers	5	4	5	5	6	6	7	11	17	17	...	...
4 Surplus of the nation on current transactions	−291	−192	−153	−441	−649	−657	−637	−505	−432	−405	...	...
Payments to the rest of the world and surplus of the nation on current transfers	1707	2097	2484	2794	3243	4172	4944	5734	6558	7121	...	...
Receipts from the rest of the world												
1 Exports of goods and services [a]	1233	1537	1801	2019	2279	2906	3438	3709	4364	4876	...	...
A Exports of merchandise, f.o.b.	790	955	1083	1231	1268	1580	1816	...	...	...	...	...
B Other	443	582	717	788	1011	1326	1622	...	...	...	...	...
2 Factor income from rest of the world	132	155	198	230	278	342	431	636	679	778	...	...
A Compensation of employees	47	48	42	47	48	68	103	155	...	...	...	...
B Property and entrepreneurial income	84	107	156	182	230	274	328	480	...	...	...	...
3 Current transfers from rest of the world	343	405	485	546	686	925	1075	1389	1514	1467	...	...
A Subsidies from supranational organisations	205	219	240	320	414	531	628	833	904	858	...	...
B Other current transfers	137	186	245	226	272	393	447	556	610	609	...	...
Receipts from the rest of the world on current transactions	1707	2097	2484	2794	3243	4172	4944	5734	6558	7121	...	...

a Exclude income from ocean-going cargo ships under Greek flag or ownership. However, remittances actually received by the bank of Greece from persons engaged in these enterprises are included in factor income from the rest of the world.

1.8 Capital transactions of the nation, summary

Thousand million Greek drachmas

	1986	1987	1988	1989	1990	1991	1992	1993	1994	1995	1996	1997
Finance of gross capital formation												
Gross saving	802	911	1311	1398	1452	1955	2269	2595	2969	3389	...	...
1 Consumption of fixed capital	505	578	662	793	942	1108	1276	1447	1602	1755	...	...
2 Net saving	297	333	650	604	509	847	994	1149	1367	1634	...	...
A General government	−407	−493	−767	−1134	−1348	−1420	−1311	−1790	−1591	−1515	...	...
B Corporate and quasi-corporate enterprises	...	...	...	...	...	...	...	...	...	...	...	...
C Other [a]	704	825	1416	1738	1857	2267	2305	2939	2957	3149	...	...

Greece

Thousand million Greek drachmas

	1986	1987	1988	1989	1990	1991	1992	1993	1994	1995	1996	1997
less: Surplus of the nation on current transactions	−291	−192	−153	−441	−649	−657	−637	−505	−432	−405	...	...
Finance of gross capital formation	1093	1103	1464	1839	2101	2612	2907	3100	3401	3794	...	...
Gross capital formation												
Increase in stocks	75	28	145	148	29	236	211	190	220	203	...	...
Gross fixed capital formation	1018	1075	1318	1690	2072	2376	2696	2910	3181	3591	...	...
1 General government	228	202	243	296	326	485	601	607	663	811	...	...
2 Corporate and quasi-corporate enterprises [b]	157	139	156	218	238	284	348	437	465	515	...	...
A Public	157	139	156	218	238	284	348	437	465	515	...	...
B Private	...	...	...	...	...	...	...	...	...	...	...	...
3 Other [b]	634	734	919	1176	1507	1607	1747	1866	2053	2266	...	...
Gross capital formation	1093	1103	1464	1839	2101	2612	2907	3100	3401	3794	...	...

a Beginning 1975, item "Corporate and quasi-corporate enterprises" is included in item "Other".   b Private corporate and quasi-corporate enterprises are included in item "Other".

1.9 Gross domestic product by institutional sectors of origin

Thousand million Greek drachmas

	1986	1987	1988	1989	1990	1991	1992	1993	1994	1995	1996	1997
Domestic factor incomes originating												
subtotal: Domestic factor incomes	4368	4900	5959	7045	8277	9963	11255	12913	14377	16062	...	...
Indirect taxes, net	642	794	952	967	1332	1817	2301	2401	2885	3306	...	...
A Indirect taxes	1001	1165	1314	1430	1922	2499	3067	3414	3960	4327	...	...
B less: Subsidies	359	371	362	464	591	682	766	1013	1075	1021	...	...
Consumption of fixed capital	505	578	662	793	942	1108	1276	1447	1602	1755	...	...
Gross domestic product	5515	6272	7572	8805	10551	12889	14832	16760	18864	21123	...	...

1.10 Gross domestic product by kind of activity, in current prices

Thousand million Greek drachmas

	1986	1987	1988	1989	1990	1991	1992	1993	1994	1995	1996	1997
1 Agriculture, hunting, forestry and fishing	788	865	1087	1279	1337	1819	1853	1983	2387	2539	...	...
2 Mining and quarrying	79	99	108	118	141	157	162	173	186	214	...	...
3 Manufacturing	907	971	1149	1347	1511	1736	1941	2220	2400	2483	...	...
4 Electricity, gas and water	140	156	174	186	253	292	340	377	405	434	...	...
5 Construction	335	348	445	542	676	784	846	946	1009	1103	...	...
6 Wholesale and retail trade, restaurants and hotels [a]	657	725	853	997	1156	1381	1650	1975	2163	2455	...	...
7 Transport, storage and communication [b]	373	443	525	585	702	788	894	1016	1143	1309	...	...
8 Finance, insurance, real estate and business services [c]	383	458	568	683	851	1121	1369	1625	1735	2001	...	...
9 Community, social and personal services [acd]	675	795	957	1182	1450	1702	2050	2471	2788	3327	...	...
Total, Industries	4337	4860	5865	6919	8078	9780	11106	12785	14216	15865	...	...
Producers of government services	536	618	755	919	1141	1291	1425	1574	1763	1952	...	...
Other producers	...	...	...	...	...	...	...	...	...	...	...	...
Subtotal [e]	4873	5478	6621	7838	9219	11072	12531	14359	15979	17817	...	...
less: Imputed bank service charge	...	...	...	...	...	...	...	...	...	...	...	...

Greece

Thousand million Greek drachmas

	1986	1987	1988	1989	1990	1991	1992	1993	1994	1995	1996	1997
plus: Import duties	...	...	...	...	...	...	...	...	...	...	...	...
plus: Value added tax	...	...	...	...	...	...	...	...	...	...	...	...
plus: Other adjustments [f]	642	794	952	967	1332	1817	2301	2401	2885	3306	...	...
equals: Gross domestic product	5515	6272	7572	8805	10551	12889	14832	16760	18864	21123	...	...

a Restaurants and hotels are included in item "Community, social and personal services".
b Exclude income from ocean-going cargo ships under Greek flag or ownership. However, remittances actually received by the bank of Greece from persons engaged in these enterprises are included in factor income from the rest of the world.
c Business services are included in item "Community, social and personal services".
d Item "Other producers" is included in item "Community, social and personal services".
e Gross domestic product in factor values.
f Item "Other adjustments" refers to indirect taxes net of subsidies.

1.11 Gross domestic product by kind of activity, in constant prices

Thousand million Greek drachmas

	1986	1987	1988	1989	1990	1991	1992	1993	1994	1995	1996	1997
At constant prices of: 1970												
1 Agriculture, hunting, forestry and fishing	62	59	63	63	54	63	61	60	64	61	...	...
2 Mining and quarrying	8	8	9	9	9	9	9	9	9	9	...	...
3 Manufacturing	89	87	91	93	91	90	89	85	86	87	...	...
4 Electricity, gas and water	17	19	20	21	20	22	23	24	25	25	...	...
5 Construction	24	24	26	27	28	27	26	26	25	25	...	...
6 Wholesale and retail trade, restaurants and hotels [a]	57	57	60	62	63	65	65	62	62	63	...	...
7 Transport, storage and communication [b]	49	49	53	56	56	57	60	63	64	69	...	...
8 Finance, insurance, real estate and business services [c]	59	60	62	65	68	71	75	76	77	80	...	...
9 Community, social and personal services [acd]	49	50	52	54	56	55	58	60	61	65	...	...
Total, Industries	415	413	435	450	444	459	466	465	472	484	...	...
Producers of government services	42	42	42	45	44	45	42	42	42	40	...	...
Other producers	...	...	...	...	...	...	...	...	...	...	...	...
Subtotal [e]	457	455	477	495	488	505	509	506	513	524	...	...
less: Imputed bank service charge	...	...	...	...	...	...	...	...	...	...	...	...
plus: Import duties	...	...	...	...	...	...	...	...	...	...	...	...
plus: Value added tax	...	...	...	...	...	...	...	...	...	...	...	...
plus: Other adjustments [f]	57	57	57	59	62	65	63	60	62	62	...	...
equals: Gross domestic product	514	512	535	554	550	569	572	567	575	586	...	...

a Restaurants and hotels are included in item "Community, social and personal services".
b Exclude income from ocean-going cargo ships under Greek flag or ownership. However, remittances actually received by the bank of Greece from persons engaged in these enterprises are included in factor income from the rest of the world.
c Business services are included in item "Community, social and personal services".
d Item "Other producers" is included in item "Community, social and personal services".
e Gross domestic product in factor values.
f Item "Other adjustments" refers to indirect taxes net of subsidies.

Greece

1.12 Relations among national accounting aggregates

Thousand million Greek drachmas

	1986	1987	1988	1989	1990	1991	1992	1993	1994	1995	1996	1997
Gross domestic product	5515	6272	7572	8805	10551	12889	14832	16760	18864	21123	...	...
plus: Net factor income from the rest of the world	−68	−63	−57	−85	−46	−50	−52	94	108	74	...	...
Factor income from rest of the world	132	155	198	230	278	342	431	636	679	778	...	...
less: Factor income to the rest of the world	199	218	254	315	324	392	483	541	571	704	...	...
equals: Gross national product	5447	6209	7516	8720	10505	12838	14780	16855	18973	21196	...	...
less: Consumption of fixed capital	505	578	662	793	942	1108	1276	1447	1602	1755	...	...
equals: National income	4942	5631	6854	7926	9562	11730	13505	15408	17371	19442	...	...
plus: Net current transfers from the rest of the world	247	328	394	435	563	741	874	1111	1198	1123	...	...
Current transfers from rest of the world	343	405	485	546	686	925	1075	1389	1514	1467	...	...
less: Current transfers to the rest of the world	95	77	91	111	123	183	200	279	316	344	...	...
equals: National disposable income	5189	5958	7248	8362	10125	12471	14379	16519	18569	20564	...	...
less: Final consumption	4786	5581	6682	7977	9748	11667	13594	15349	17156	19117	...	...
Statistical discrepancy	−106	−45	84	220	132	42	209	−21	−46	186	...	...
equals: Net saving	297	333	650	604	509	847	994	1149	1367	1634	...	...
less: Surplus of the nation on current transactions	−291	−192	−153	−441	−649	−657	−637	−505	−432	−405	...	...
equals: Net capital formation	588	525	802	1045	1158	1504	1631	1654	1799	2039	...	...

2.5 Private final consumption expenditure by type and purpose, in current prices

Thousand million Greek drachmas

	1986	1987	1988	1989	1990	1991	1992	1993	1994	1995	1996	1997
Final consumption expenditure of resident households												
1 Food, beverages and tobacco	1515	1772	2061	2436	2947	3514	4019	4605	5335	5785	...	...
A Food	1259	1463	1662	1975	2346	2781	3145	3587	4157	4561	...	...
B Non-alcoholic beverages	41	48	60	71	89	107	126	157	173	191	...	...
C Alcoholic beverages	99	125	151	172	231	278	325	372	401	425	...	...
D Tobacco	115	136	188	218	281	348	423	489	603	608	...	...
2 Clothing and footwear	350	418	502	589	694	829	881	977	1029	1018	...	...
3 Gross rent, fuel and power	419	515	624	721	891	1156	1406	1709	1941	2214	...	...
A Fuel and power	118	145	156	164	203	245	290	308	323	395	...	...
B Other	301	370	467	557	688	912	1116	1401	1618	1818	...	...
4 Furniture, furnishings and household equipment and operation	324	392	453	532	637	738	843	932	1041	1167	...	...
A Household operation	113	144	173	205	251	307	364	414	470	533	...	...
B Other	212	248	280	327	385	431	480	518	570	634	...	...
5 Medical care and health expenses	147	163	183	214	263	339	430	529	652	769	...	...
6 Transport and communication	556	597	700	844	1092	1380	1717	1858	1909	2135	...	...
A Personal transport equipment	140	125	144	214	290	394	537	456	384	429	...	...
B Other	416	472	555	629	802	986	1180	1402	1525	1705	...	...

Greece

Thousand million Greek drachmas

	1986	1987	1988	1989	1990	1991	1992	1993	1994	1995	1996	1997
7 Recreational, entertainment, education and cultural services	229	273	329	383	439	541	595	671	754	853	...	...
A Education	23	26	32	38	47	62	80	97	104	117	...	...
B Other	206	248	298	345	392	479	515	574	650	735	...	...
8 Miscellaneous goods and services	363	455	542	631	770	895	1166	1384	1662	1873	...	...
A Personal care	69	86	100	115	141	177	217	257	306	321	...	...
B Expenditures in restaurants, cafes and hotels	231	289	344	402	484	547	715	857	1041	1209	...	...
C Other	62	80	97	114	145	170	233	269	314	344	...	...
Total final consumption expenditure in the domestic market by households, of which	3902	4587	5394	6350	7733	9393	11057	12664	14323	15814	...	...
A Durable goods	325	339	378	487	602	719	886	815	768	835	...	...
B Semi-durable goods	507	614	739	869	1033	1231	1389	1548	1683	1721	...	...
C Non-durable goods	1965	2306	2664	3114	3823	4564	5271	6075	6975	7653	...	...
D Services	1105	1327	1612	1879	2275	2878	3511	4226	4897	5605	...	...
plus: Direct purchases abroad by resident households	69	69	105	133	173	186	227	231	272	307	...	...
less: Direct purchases in the domestic market by non-resident households	252	299	346	325	409	467	615	747	933	949	...	...
equals: Final consumption expenditure of resident households [a]	3719	4356	5153	6158	7498	9112	10669	12148	13662	15172	...	...

a Item "Final consumption expenditure of resident households" includes consumption expenditure of private non-profit institutions serving households.

2.6 Private final consumption expenditure by type and purpose, in constant prices

Thousand million Greek drachmas

	1986	1987	1988	1989	1990	1991	1992	1993	1994	1995	1996	1997
At constant prices of: 1970												
Final consumption expenditure of resident households												
1 Food, beverages and tobacco	135	140	144	144	144	146	148	151	157	158	...	...
A Food	98	101	105	105	104	105	107	111	116	118	...	...
B Non-alcoholic beverages	3	3	4	4	4	4	5	5	5	5	...	...
C Alcoholic beverages	13	14	15	15	16	16	16	15	16	15	...	...
D Tobacco	21	21	20	20	20	21	20	20	20	19	...	...
2 Clothing and footwear	29	28	29	29	29	30	27	27	26	24	...	...
3 Gross rent, fuel and power	63	65	67	69	71	74	76	78	80	81	...	...
A Fuel and power	12	13	13	13	13	14	15	15	15	16	...	...
B Other	51	53	54	56	58	59	61	63	65	65	...	...
4 Furniture, furnishings and household equipment and operation	28	28	29	30	31	30	30	30	30	31	...	...
A Household operation	9	10	10	10	10	11	11	11	11	11	...	...
B Other	19	18	19	20	20	19	19	19	19	20	...	...
5 Medical care and health expenses	12	12	12	12	12	12	13	13	15	17	...	...
6 Transport and communication	57	55	58	63	67	72	76	71	70	73	...	...
A Personal transport equipment	10	8	8	11	14	19	22	16	13	15	...	...
B Other	47	47	49	52	53	53	54	55	56	58	...	...
7 Recreational, entertainment, education and cultural services	22	21	22	24	24	25	25	27	27	27	...	...
A Education	2	2	2	2	2	2	2	2	2	2	...	...
B Other	20	19	20	22	22	23	23	25	24	24	...	...

Greece

Thousand million Greek drachmas

	1986	1987	1988	1989	1990	1991	1992	1993	1994	1995	1996	1997
At constant prices of: 1970												
8 Miscellaneous goods and services	30	31	32	32	34	33	36	36	38	38	...	...
A Personal care	6	6	6	6	7	7	7	7	8	8	...	...
B Expenditures in restaurants, cafes and hotels	19	19	20	20	21	20	21	21	22	22	...	...
C Other	5	6	6	6	7	7	8	8	8	8	...	...
Total final consumption expenditure in the domestic market by households, of which	375	381	392	404	412	422	432	435	443	448	...	...
A Durable goods	29	26	27	31	35	38	42	37	34	35	...	...
B Semi-durable goods	43	43	45	46	47	47	47	47	47	44	...	...
C Non-durable goods	180	188	194	196	197	200	204	209	217	222	...	...
D Services	122	123	127	131	133	136	139	142	146	148	...	...
plus: Direct purchases abroad by resident households	6	5	7	7	8	7	7	7	7	7	...	...
less: Direct purchases in the domestic market by non-resident households	19	20	20	17	17	17	19	21	23	21	...	...
equals: Final consumption expenditure of resident households [a]	361	365	378	395	403	412	420	421	427	434	...	...

[a] Item "Final consumption expenditure of resident households" includes consumption expenditure of private non-profit institutions serving households.

2.7 Gross capital formation by type of good and owner, in current price

Thousand million Greek drachmas

	1986 Total	1986 Total private	1986 Public enterprises	1986 General government	1987 Total	1987 Total private	1987 Public enterprises	1987 General government	1988 Total	1988 Total private	1988 Public enterprises	1988 General government
Increase in stocks, total	75	75	9	–8	28	22	7	–	145	133	12	–
1 Goods producing industries	73	68	4	...	44	38	6	...	137	131	6	...
2 Wholesale and retail trade	–7	–7	–	...	5	5	–	...	6	6	–	...
3 Other, except government stocks	17	13	5	...	–21	–21	1	...	2	–4	6	...
4 Government stocks	–8	...	...	–8	–	...	...	–	–	...	...	–
Gross fixed capital formation, total	1018	634	157	228	1075	734	139	202	1318	919	156	243
1 Residential buildings	248	240	7	2	287	278	8	1	329	318	11	1
2 Non-residential buildings	125	77	10	38	141	97	8	35	195	138	10	47
3 Other construction	228	20	53	155	198	15	50	133	246	24	62	159
4 Land improvement and plantation and orchard development [a]	17	2	–	15	17	3	–	15	20	4	–	16
5 Producers' durable goods	399	294	88	18	432	341	73	17	528	436	73	20
A Transport equipment	90	82	7	1	90	88	1	1	94	92	1	1
B Machinery and equipment	309	212	81	17	342	254	72	17	434	344	71	19
6 Breeding stock, dairy cattle, etc.	...	...	...	...	...	...	...	...	...	...	...	...
Total gross capital formation	1093	708	166	219	1103	756	146	201	1464	1052	168	243

Greece

	1989				1990				1991			
	Total	Total private	Public enterprises	General government	Total	Total private	Public enterprises	General government	Total	Total private	Public enterprises	General government
Increase in stocks, total	148	127	21	–	29	3	26	–	236	204	32	–
1 Goods producing industries	115	104	11	...	47	37	10	...	220	209	12	...
2 Wholesale and retail trade	21	21	–	...	–39	–39	–	...	–5	–5	–	...
3 Other, except government stocks	13	3	10	...	21	5	16	...	21	–	21	...
4 Government stocks	–	...	...	–	–	...	...	–	–	...	...	–
Gross fixed capital formation, total	1690	1176	218	296	2072	1507	238	326	2376	1612	284	485
1 Residential buildings	403	391	12	1	555	539	15	1	560	542	16	1
2 Non-residential buildings	221	156	11	54	267	192	9	66	293	196	17	81
3 Other construction	311	26	84	201	349	27	87	235	498	25	124	349
4 Land improvement and plantation and orchard development [a]	26	5	–	21	27	6	–	21	33	4	–	29
5 Producers' durable goods	729	598	111	19	874	743	127	4	995	844	126	26
A Transport equipment	143	132	11	–	216	202	14	–	250	235	15	–
B Machinery and equipment	586	467	100	19	658	541	113	3	745	609	111	26
6 Breeding stock, dairy cattle, etc.	...	...	...	...	...	...	...	...	...	...	...	...
Total gross capital formation	1839	1304	239	296	2101	1510	264	326	2612	1816	316	485

	1992				1993				1994			
	Total	Total private	Public enterprises	General government	Total	Total private	Public enterprises	General government	Total	Total private	Public enterprises	General government
Increase in stocks, total	211	229	39	–	190	...	...	...	220	...	...	...
1 Goods producing industries	232	218	15	...	...	...	...	...	...	...	...	...
2 Wholesale and retail trade	7	7	–	...	...	...	...	...	...	...	...	...
3 Other, except government stocks	28	4	24	...	...	...	...	...	...	...	...	...
4 Government stocks	...	...	...	–	...	...	...	...	...	...	...	...
Gross fixed capital formation, total	2696	1747	326	601	2910	...	...	...	3181	...	...	...
1 Residential buildings	551	542	16	1	604	...	...	...	636	...	...	...
2 Non-residential buildings	321	192	14	111	353	...	...	...	419	...	...	...
3 Other construction	557	28	132	397	...	...	...	...	...	...	...	...
4 Land improvement and plantation and orchard development [a]	63	6	–	57	...	...	...	...	...	...	...	...
5 Producers' durable goods	1192	980	164	34	1306	...	...	...	1487	...	...	...
A Transport equipment	304	274	17	–	311	...	...	...	339	...	...	...
B Machinery and equipment	889	706	148	34	995	...	...	...	1147	...	...	...
6 Breeding stock, dairy cattle, etc.	...	...	...	...	...	...	...	...	...	...	...	...
Total gross capital formation	2907	1976	365	601	3100	...	...	...	3401	...	...	...

	1995				1996				1997			
	Total	Total private	Public enterprises	General government	Total	Total private	Public enterprises	General government	Total	Total private	Public enterprises	General government
Increase in stocks, total	203	...	...	...	...	...	...	...	...	...	...	...
Gross fixed capital formation, total	3591	...	...	...	...	...	...	...	...	...	...	...
1 Residential buildings	707	...	...	...	...	...	...	...	...	...	...	...
2 Non-residential buildings	465	...	...	...	...	...	...	...	...	...	...	...
3 Other construction	...	...	...	...	...	...	...	...	...	...	...	...

Greece

	1995				1996				1997			
	Total	Total private	Public enterprises	General government	Total	Total private	Public enterprises	General government	Total	Total private	Public enterprises	General government
4 Land improvement and plantation and orchard development	...	...	...	...	...	...	...	...	...	...	...	...
5 Producers' durable goods	1627	...	...	...	...	...	...	...	...	...	...	...
A Transport equipment	386	...	...	...	...	...	...	...	...	...	...	...
B Machinery and equipment	1241	...	...	...	...	...	...	...	...	...	...	...
6 Breeding stock, dairy cattle, etc.	...	...	...	...	...	...	...	...	...	...	...	...
Total gross capital formation	3794	...	...	...	...	...	...	...	...	...	...	...

a Item "Land improvement and plantation and orchard development" includes outlays on land improvement and transfer costs on purchases and sales of agricultural land only.

2.8 Gross capital formation by type of good and owner, in constant prices

Thousand million Greek drachmas

	1986				1987				1988			
	Total	Total private	Public enterprises	General government	Total	Total private	Public enterprises	General government	Total	Total private	Public enterprises	General government
At constant prices of: 1970												
Increase in stocks, total	9	9	1	−1	2	2	–	–	13	12	1	–
1 Goods producing industries	6	6	–	...	5	4	–	...	12	12	–	...
2 Wholesale and retail trade	–	–	–	...	1	1	–	...	1	1	–	...
3 Other, except government stocks	4	3	–	...	−4	−4	–	...	–	–	–	...
4 Government stocks	−1	...	...	−1	–	...	...	–	–	...	...	–
Gross fixed capital formation, total	77	51	12	14	73	52	9	11	80	58	9	12
1 Residential buildings	19	19	1	–	20	19	1	–	21	20	1	–
2 Non-residential buildings	10	6	1	3	10	7	1	2	12	9	1	3
3 Other construction	14	1	4	9	11	1	3	7	12	1	3	7
4 Land improvement and plantation and orchard development [a]	1	–	–	1	1	–	–	1	1	–	–	1
5 Producers' durable goods	33	24	7	1	32	25	5	1	34	28	5	1
A Transport equipment	9	8	1	–	7	7	–	–	7	6	–	–
B Machinery and equipment	25	17	7	1	24	18	5	1	28	22	5	1
6 Breeding stock, dairy cattle, etc.	...	...	...	...	...	...	...	...	...	...	...	...
Total gross capital formation	86	59	13	14	76	54	10	11	93	70	10	12

	1989				1990				1991			
	Total	Total private	Public enterprises	General government	Total	Total private	Public enterprises	General government	Total	Total private	Public enterprises	General government
At constant prices of: 1970												
Increase in stocks, total	8	7	1	–	−1	−3	1	–	8	7	1	–
1 Goods producing industries	5	4	1	...	2	2	–	...	8	7	–	...
2 Wholesale and retail trade	2	2	–	...	−4	−4	–	...	–	–	–	...
3 Other, except government stocks	1	–	1	...	1	–	1	...	1	–	1	...
4 Government stocks	–	...	...	–	–	...	...	–	–	...	...	–
Gross fixed capital formation, total	88	64	11	13	96	73	11	12	92	66	11	15
1 Residential buildings	22	21	1	–	25	24	1	–	21	20	1	–
2 Non-residential buildings	12	8	1	3	12	9	–	3	11	7	1	3
3 Other construction	13	1	4	8	12	1	4	8	15	1	4	10

Greece

	1989				1990				1991			
	Total	Total private	Public enterprises	General government	Total	Total private	Public enterprises	General government	Total	Total private	Public enterprises	General government

At constant prices of: 1970

4 Land improvement and plantation and orchard development [a]	1	–	–	1	1	–	–	1	1	–	–	1
5 Producers' durable goods	41	33	6	1	46	40	7	–	44	37	6	1
A Transport equipment	9	8	1	–	11	11	1	–	11	10	1	–
B Machinery and equipment	32	25	5	1	35	29	6	–	33	27	5	1
6 Breeding stock, dairy cattle, etc.	...	...	...	...	...	...	...	...	...	...	...	...
Total gross capital formation	96	71	13	13	95	71	12	12	100	73	12	15

	1992				1993				1994			
	Total	Total private	Public enterprises	General government	Total	Total private	Public enterprises	General government	Total	Total private	Public enterprises	General government

At constant prices of: 1970

Increase in stocks, total	8	9	1	–	7	...	...	...	7	...	...	...
1 Goods producing industries	9	8	1	...	...	...	...	...	...	...	...	...
2 Wholesale and retail trade	–	–	–	...	...	...	...	...	...	...	...	...
3 Other, except government stocks	1	–	1	...	...	...	...	...	...	...	...	...
4 Government stocks	...	...	...	–	...	...	...	...	...	...	...	...
Gross fixed capital formation, total	93	65	12	17	91	...	...	...	93	...	...	...
1 Residential buildings	18	18	1	–	18	...	...	...	17	...	...	...
2 Non-residential buildings	11	6	–	4	10	...	...	...	11	...	...	...
3 Other construction	15	1	4	10	...	...	...	...	...	...	...	...
4 Land improvement and plantation and orchard development [a]	2	–	–	2	...	...	...	...	...	...	...	...
5 Producers' durable goods	47	39	7	1	48	...	...	...	51	...	...	...
A Transport equipment	12	11	1	–	11	...	...	...	10	...	...	...
B Machinery and equipment	35	28	6	1	37	...	...	...	41	...	...	...
6 Breeding stock, dairy cattle, etc.	...	...	...	...	...	...	...	...	...	...	...	...
Total gross capital formation	101	74	13	17	98	...	...	...	101	...	...	...

	1995				1996				1997			
	Total	Total private	Public enterprises	General government	Total	Total private	Public enterprises	General government	Total	Total private	Public enterprises	General government

At constant prices of: 1970

Increase in stocks, total	6	...	...	...	...	...	...	...	...	...	...	...
Gross fixed capital formation, total	98	...	...	...	...	...	...	...	...	...	...	...
1 Residential buildings	17	...	...	...	...	...	...	...	...	...	...	...
2 Non-residential buildings	11	...	...	...	...	...	...	...	...	...	...	...
3 Other construction	...	...	...	...	...	...	...	...	...	...	...	...
4 Land improvement and plantation and orchard development	...	...	...	...	...	...	...	...	...	...	...	...
5 Producers' durable goods	54	...	...	...	...	...	...	...	...	...	...	...
A Transport equipment	11	...	...	...	...	...	...	...	...	...	...	...
B Machinery and equipment	43	...	...	...	...	...	...	...	...	...	...	...
6 Breeding stock, dairy cattle, etc.	...	...	...	...	...	...	...	...	...	...	...	...
Total gross capital formation	105	...	...	...	...	...	...	...	...	...	...	...

[a] Item "Land improvement and plantation and orchard development" includes outlays on land improvement and transfer costs on purchases and sales of agricultural land only.

Greece

2.9 Gross capital formation by kind of activity of owner, ISIC major divisions, in current prices

Thousand million Greek drachmas

	1986			1987			1988			1989		
	Total gross capital formation	Increase in stocks	Gross fixed capital formation	Total gross capital formation	Increase in stocks	Gross fixed capital formation	Total gross capital formation	Increase in stocks	Gross fixed capital formation	Total gross capital formation	Increase in stocks	Gross fixed capital formation
All producers												
1 Agriculture, hunting, forestry and fishing	56	16	40	26	–8	34	83	35	48	31	–28	59
2 Mining and quarrying	28	7	21	26	–3	29	31	–	31	35	1	34
3 Manufacturing	213	46	168	237	49	188	333	97	236	419	130	288
4 Electricity, gas and water	63	4	59	55	6	49	72	6	66	105	11	94
5 Construction	...	...	...	...	...	...	...	...	...	...	...	...
6 Wholesale and retail trade, restaurants and hotels [a]	–7	–7	...	5	5	...	6	6	...	21	21	...
7 Transport, storage and communication	135	18	118	105	–20	124	144	3	141	220	13	207
8 Finance, insurance, real estate and business services [b]	247	–	247	285	–1	286	327	–1	329	403	–	403
9 Community, social and personal services [ab]	138	...	138	162	...	162	225	...	225	309	...	309
Total industries [c]	874	83	791	902	29	873	1221	145	1075	1543	148	1394
Producers of government services [c]	219	–8	228	201	–	202	243	–	243	296	–	296
Private non-profit institutions serving households	...	...	...	...	...	...	...	...	...	...	...	...
Total [d]	1093	75	1018	1103	28	1075	1464	145	1318	1839	148	1690

	1990			1991			1992			1993		
	Total gross capital formation	Increase in stocks	Gross fixed capital formation	Total gross capital formation	Increase in stocks	Gross fixed capital formation	Total gross capital formation	Increase in stocks	Gross fixed capital formation	Total gross capital formation	Increase in stocks	Gross fixed capital formation
All producers												
1 Agriculture, hunting, forestry and fishing	22	–50	72	149	83	66	188	105	83	...	...	...
2 Mining and quarrying	35	–	36	36	–	36	48	3	45	...	...	...
3 Manufacturing	427	88	339	482	125	357	499	110	389	...	...	...
4 Electricity, gas and water	113	10	103	107	12	96	138	15	123	...	...	...
5 Construction	...	...	...	...	...	...	...	...	...	...	...	...
6 Wholesale and retail trade, restaurants and hotels [a]	–39	–39	...	–5	–5	...	7	7	...	...	...	...
7 Transport, storage and communication	311	21	290	393	21	372	449	28	421	...	...	...
8 Finance, insurance, real estate and business services [b]	554	–	554	559	–	559	558	–	558	...	...	...
9 Community, social and personal services [ab]	351	...	351	410	...	410	454	...	454	...	...	...
Total industries [c]	1774	29	1745	2131	236	1895	2341	268	2074	...	...	...
Producers of government services [c]	326	–	326	485	–	485	601	–	601	...	...	...
Private non-profit institutions serving households	...	...	...	...	...	...	...	...	...	...	...	...
Total [d]	2101	29	2072	2617	236	2381	2942	268	2675	...	...	...

a Gross fixed capital formation of item "Wholesale and retail trade, restaurants and hotels" is included in item "Community, social and personal services".
b Only ownership of dwellings is included in Gross fixed capital formation, all other activities are included in item "Community, social and personal services".
c Beginning 1979, gross fixed capital formation and increase in stocks of public enterprises are included in item "Total industries".
d Data in this series has been revised. The breakdown, if any, may not add up to the total.

Greece

2.10 Gross capital formation by kind of activity of owner, ISIC major divisions, in constant prices

Thousand million Greek drachmas

	1986 Total gross capital formation	1986 Increase in stocks	1986 Gross fixed capital formation	1987 Total gross capital formation	1987 Increase in stocks	1987 Gross fixed capital formation	1988 Total gross capital formation	1988 Increase in stocks	1988 Gross fixed capital formation	1989 Total gross capital formation	1989 Increase in stocks	1989 Gross fixed capital formation
At constant prices of: 1970 **All producers**												
1 Agriculture, hunting, forestry and fishing	5	2	3	3	1	2	8	5	3	–	–3	3
2 Mining and quarrying	2	1	2	2	–	2	2	–	2	2	–	2
3 Manufacturing	17	4	13	17	3	13	21	6	15	23	7	16
4 Electricity, gas and water	5	–	5	4	–	3	4	–	4	5	1	5
5 Construction	...	...	...	...	...	...	...	...	...	...	...	...
6 Wholesale and retail trade, restaurants and hotels [a]	–	–	...	1	1	...	1	1	...	3	3	...
7 Transport, storage and communication	14	4	11	6	–4	10	10	–	9	13	1	12
8 Finance, insurance, real estate and business services [b]	19	–	19	20	–	20	21	–	21	22	–	22
9 Community, social and personal services [ab]	11	...	11	11	...	11	14	...	14	17	...	17
Total industries [c]	73	9	63	64	2	62	80	13	68	83	8	75
Producers of government services [c]	14	–1	14	11	–	11	12	–	12	13	–	13
Private non-profit institutions serving households	...	...	...	...	...	...	...	...	...	...	...	...
Total [d]	86	9	77	76	2	73	93	13	80	96	8	88

	1990 Total gross capital formation	1990 Increase in stocks	1990 Gross fixed capital formation	1991 Total gross capital formation	1991 Increase in stocks	1991 Gross fixed capital formation	1992 Total gross capital formation	1992 Increase in stocks	1992 Gross fixed capital formation	1993 Total gross capital formation	1993 Increase in stocks	1993 Gross fixed capital formation
At constant prices of: 1970 **All producers**												
1 Agriculture, hunting, forestry and fishing	1	–3	4	5	2	3	7	4	3	...	...	...
2 Mining and quarrying	2	–	2	1	–	1	2	–	2	...	...	...
3 Manufacturing	22	4	18	21	5	16	19	4	15	...	...	...
4 Electricity, gas and water	5	–	5	4	–	4	5	1	4	...	...	...
5 Construction	...	...	...	...	...	...	...	...	...	...	...	...
6 Wholesale and retail trade, restaurants and hotels [a]	–4	–4	...	–	–	...	–	–	...	...	...	...
7 Transport, storage and communication	16	1	16	16	1	16	17	1	16	...	...	...
8 Finance, insurance, real estate and business services [b]	25	–	25	21	–	21	19	–	19	...	...	...
9 Community, social and personal services [ab]	16	...	16	17	...	17	17	...	17	...	...	...
Total industries [c]	83	–1	84	85	8	77	87	10	76	...	...	...
Producers of government services [c]	12	–	12	15	–	15	17	–	17	...	...	...
Private non-profit institutions serving households	...	...	...	...	...	...	...	...	...	...	...	...
Total [d]	95	–1	96	100	8	92	103	10	93	...	...	...

a Gross fixed capital formation of item "Wholesale and retail trade, restaurants and hotels" is included in item "Community, social and personal services".
b Only ownership of dwellings is included in Gross fixed capital formation, all other activities are included in item "Community, social and personal services".
c Beginning 1979, gross fixed capital formation and increase in stocks of public enterprises are included in item "Total industries".
d Data in this series has been revised. The breakdown, if any, may not add up to the total.

Greece

2.11 Gross fixed capital formation by kind of activity of owner, ISIC divisions, in current prices

Thousand million Greek drachmas

	1986	1987	1988	1989	1990	1991	1992	1993	1994	1995	1996	1997
All producers												
1 Agriculture, hunting, forestry and fishing	40	34	48	59	72	66	83	...	...	...	...	...
2 Mining and quarrying	21	29	31	34	36	36	45	...	...	...	...	...
3 Manufacturing	168	188	236	288	339	357	389	...	...	...	...	...
4 Electricity, gas and water	59	49	66	94	103	96	123	...	...	...	...	...
A Electricity, gas and steam	54	46	62	90	97	88	115	...	...	...	...	...
B Water works and supply	5	4	4	3	6	7	8	...	...	...	...	...
5 Construction	...	...	...	...	...	...	...	...	...	...	...	...
6 Wholesale and retail trade, restaurants and hotels	...	...	...	...	...	...	...	...	...	...	...	...
7 Transport, storage and communication	118	124	141	207	290	372	421	...	...	...	...	...
A Transport and storage	97	100	108	162	227	278	314	...	...	...	...	...
B Communication	20	24	33	46	63	94	108	...	...	...	...	...
8 Finance, insurance, real estate and business services	247	286	329	403	554	559	558	...	...	...	...	...
A Financial institutions	...	...	...	...	...	...	...	...	...	...	...	...
B Insurance	...	...	...	...	...	...	...	...	...	...	...	...
C Real estate and business services	247	286	329	403	554	559	558	...	...	...	...	...
Real estate, except dwellings	...	...	...	...	...	...	...	...	...	...	...	...
Dwellings	247	286	329	403	554	559	558	...	...	...	...	...
9 Community, social and personal services	138	162	225	309	351	410	454	...	...	...	...	...
A Sanitary and similar services	...	...	...	...	...	...	...	...	...	...	...	...
B Social and related community services	11	12	9	14	22	29	36	...	...	...	...	...
Educational services	–	–	1	–	1	–	–	...	...	...	...	...
Medical, dental, other health and veterinary services	11	12	9	14	21	29	36	...	...	...	...	...
C Recreational and cultural services	1	2	2	2	2	5	8	...	...	...	...	...
D Personal and household services	127	148	214	293	328	376	410	...	...	...	...	...
Total industries	791	873	1075	1394	1745	1895	2074	...	...	...	...	...
Producers of government services	228	202	243	296	326	485	601	...	...	...	...	...
Private non-profit institutions serving households	...	...	...	...	...	...	...	...	...	...	...	...
Total [a]	1018	1075	1318	1690	2072	2381	2675	...	...	...	...	...

a Data in this series has been revised. The breakdown, if any, may not add up to the total.

Greece

2.12 Gross fixed capital formation by kind of activity of owner, ISIC divisions, in constant prices

Thousand million Greek drachmas

	1986	1987	1988	1989	1990	1991	1992	1993	1994	1995	1996	1997
At constant prices of: 1970												
All producers												
1 Agriculture, hunting, forestry and fishing	3	2	3	3	4	3	3	...	...	...	...	...
2 Mining and quarrying	2	2	2	2	2	1	2	...	...	...	...	...
3 Manufacturing	13	13	15	16	18	16	15	...	...	...	...	...
4 Electricity, gas and water	5	3	4	5	5	4	4	...	...	...	...	...
A Electricity, gas and steam	5	3	4	5	5	4	4	...	...	...	...	...
B Water works and supply	–	–	–	–	–	–	–	...	...	...	...	...
5 Construction	...	...	...	...	...	...	...	...	...	...	...	...
6 Wholesale and retail trade, restaurants and hotels	...	...	...	...	...	...	...	...	...	...	...	...
7 Transport, storage and communication	11	10	9	12	16	16	16	...	...	...	...	...
A Transport and storage	9	8	7	10	13	12	13	...	...	...	...	...
B Communication	2	2	2	2	3	4	4	...	...	...	...	...
8 Finance, insurance, real estate and business services	19	20	21	22	25	21	19	...	...	...	...	...
A Financial institutions	...	...	...	...	...	...	...	...	...	...	...	...
B Insurance	...	...	...	...	...	...	...	...	...	...	...	...
C Real estate and business services	19	20	21	22	25	21	19	...	...	...	...	...
Real estate, except dwellings	...	...	...	...	...	...	...	...	...	...	...	...
Dwellings	19	20	21	22	25	21	19	...	...	...	...	...
9 Community, social and personal services	11	11	14	17	16	17	17	...	...	...	...	...
A Sanitary and similar services	...	...	...	...	...	...	...	...	...	...	...	...
B Social and related community services	1	1	1	1	1	1	1	...	...	...	...	...
Educational services	–	–	–	–	–	–	–	...	...	...	...	...
Medical, dental, other health and veterinary services	1	1	1	1	1	1	1	...	...	...	...	...
C Recreational and cultural services	–	–	–	–	–	–	–	...	...	...	...	...
D Personal and household services	10	10	13	16	15	16	15	...	...	...	...	...
Total industries	63	62	68	75	84	77	76	...	...	...	...	...
Producers of government services	14	11	12	13	12	15	17	...	...	...	...	...
Private non-profit institutions serving households	...	...	...	...	...	...	...	...	...	...	...	...
Total	77	73	80	88	96	92	93	...	...	...	...	...

Greece

2.17 Exports and imports of goods and services, detail

Thousand million Greek drachmas

	1986	1987	1988	1989	1990	1991	1992	1993	1994	1995	1996	1997
Exports of goods and services												
1 Exports of merchandise, f.o.b. [a]	790	955	1083	1231	1268	1580	1816	...	...	...	...	...
2 Transport and communication	187	278	369	454	596	845	998	...	...	...	...	...
3 Insurance service charges								...	...	...	...	...
4 Other commodities								...	...	...	...	...
5 Adjustments of merchandise exports to change-of-ownership basis	...	...	...	...	...	...	...	...	...	...	...	...
6 Direct purchases in the domestic market by non-residential households	252	299	346	325	409	467	615	747	933	949	...	...
7 Direct purchases in the domestic market by extraterritorial bodies	4	5	3	9	6	14	10	12	16	17	...	...
Total exports of goods and services	1233	1537	1801	2019	2279	2906	3438	3709	4364	4876	...	...
Imports of goods and services												
1 Imports of merchandise, c.i.f.	1538	1830	2061	2520	3093	3818	4351	...	...	...	...	...
A Imports of merchandise, f.o.b.	1361	1620	1824	2256	...	...	...	...	...	...	...	...
B Transport of services on merchandise imports	177	210	237	293	...	...	...	...	...	...	...	...
C Insurance service charges on merchandise imports	...	...	...	...	...	...	...	...	...	...	...	...
2 Adjustments of merchandise imports to change-of-ownership basis	...	...	...	...	...	...	...	...	...	...	...	...
3 Other transport and communication	77	75	100	124	141	210	273	...	...	...	...	...
4 Other insurance service charges								...	...	...	...	...
5 Other commodities								...	...	...	...	...
6 Direct purchases abroad by government	19	19	25	32	38	40	47	73	82	79	...	...
7 Direct purchases abroad by resident households	69	69	105	133	173	186	227	231	272	307	...	...
Total imports of goods and services	1703	1993	2291	2810	3445	4253	4898	5419	6103	6478	...	...
Balance of goods and services	−470	−457	−490	−791	−1166	−1348	−1460	−1710	−1738	−1602	...	...
Total imports and balance of goods and services	1233	1537	1801	2019	2279	2906	3438	3709	4364	4876	...	...

[a] Exclude income from ocean-going cargo ships under Greek flag or ownership. However, remittances actually received by the bank of Greece from persons engaged in these enterprises are included in factor income from the rest of the world.

Greece

3.12 General government income and outlay account: total and subsectors

Thousand million Greek drachmas

	1986					1987				
	Total government	Central government	State or provincial government	Local government	Social security funds	Total government	Central government	State or provincial government	Local government	Social security funds

Receipts

1 Operating surplus	...	...	...	...	...	...	...	...	...	...
2 Property and entrepreneurial income	91	6	...	42	42	113	5	...	46	62
3 Taxes, fees and contributions	1848	1137	...	44	666	2142	1360	...	49	732
A Indirect taxes	911	830	...	16	65	1091	1014	...	18	60
B Direct taxes	336[a]	308	...	28	–	378[a]	347	...	32	–
Income	253	225	...	28	...	278	246	...	32	...
Other	83	83	...	–	...	100	100	...	–	...
C Social security contributions	601	–	...	–	601	672	–	...	–	672
D Fees, fines and penalties	...	...	...	...	...	...	...	...	...	...
4 Other current transfers	18	18	...	180	44	18	16	...	226	129
A Casualty insurance claims	...	...	...	...	...	...	...	...	...	...
B Transfers from other government subsectors	...	4	...	176	44	...	3	...	221	129
C Transfers from rest of the world	–	–	...	–	...	–	–	...	–	...
D Other transfers, except imputed	18	14	...	4	...	18	13	...	5	...
E Imputed unfunded employee pension and welfare contributions	...	...	...	...	...	...	...	...	...	...
Total current receipts	1956	1161	...	266[b]	753	2273	1382	...	321[b]	923

Disbursements

1 Government final consumption expenditure	1067	738	...	230	100	1225	850	...	272	103
2 Property income	316	295	...	–	21	449	408	...	–	41
3 Subsidies	154	154	...	–	...	152	152	...	–	...
4 Other current transfers	826	277	...	15	757	940	406	...	15	872
A Casualty insurance premiums, net	...	...	...	...	...	...	...	...	...	...
B Transfers to other government subsectors	...	220	...	4	–	...	350	...	3	–
C Social security benefits	821	52	...	11	757	936	52	...	12	872
D Social assistance grants	...	...	...	...	...	...	...	...	...	...
E Unfunded employee welfare benefits	...	...	...	...	...	...	...	...	...	...
F Transfers to private non-profit institutions serving households	...	...	...	...	...	...	...	...	...	...
G Other transfers n.e.c.	...	...	...	...	...	...	...	...	...	...
H Transfers to rest of the world	5	5	...	–	...	4	4	...	–	...
Net saving	–407	–303	...	21[b]	–126	–493	–434	...	34[b]	–93
Total current disbursements and net saving	1956	1161	...	266[b]	753	2273	1382	...	321[b]	923

Greece

	1988					1989				
	Total government	Central government	State or provincial government	Local government	Social security funds	Total government	Central government	State or provincial government	Local government	Social security funds
Receipts										
1 Operating surplus	...	...	...	...	...	...	...	...	...	...
2 Property and entrepreneurial income	96	−28	...	54	71	126	−31	...	58	99
3 Taxes, fees and contributions	2460	1552	...	60	849	2767	1654	...	65	1049
A Indirect taxes	1228	1141	...	21	65	1325	1231	...	23	71
B Direct taxes	449[a]	410	...	39	–	465[a]	422	...	42	–
Income	348	309	...	39	...	344	302	...	42	...
Other	101	101	...	–	...	120	120	...	–	...
C Social security contributions	784	–	...	–	784	978	–	...	–	978
D Fees, fines and penalties	...	...	...	...	...	...	...	...	...	...
4 Other current transfers	23	22	...	301	245	28	23	...	436	313
A Casualty insurance claims	...	...	...	...	...	...	...	...	...	...
B Transfers from other government subsectors	...	4	...	295	245	...	5	...	426	313
C Transfers from rest of the world	–	–	...	–	...	–	–	...	–	...
D Other transfers, except imputed	23	18	...	6	...	28	18	...	10	...
E Imputed unfunded employee pension and welfare contributions	...	...	...	...	...	...	...	...	...	...
Total current receipts	2580	1545	...	415[b]	1164	2922	1645	...	560[b]	1461
Disbursements										
1 Government final consumption expenditure	1530	1038	...	351	141	1819	1242	...	424	153
2 Property income	592	549	...	–	43	729	631	...	–	97
3 Subsidies	122	122	...	–	...	144	144	...	–	...
4 Other current transfers	1103	604	...	18	1025	1364	836	...	26	1247
A Casualty insurance premiums, net	...	...	...	...	...	...	...	...	...	...
B Transfers to other government subsectors	...	540	...	4	–	...	739	...	5	–
C Social security benefits	1098	59	...	14	1025	1359	92	...	21	1247
D Social assistance grants	...	...	...	...	...	...	...	...	...	...
E Unfunded employee welfare benefits	...	...	...	...	...	...	...	...	...	...
F Transfers to private non-profit institutions serving households	...	...	...	...	...	...	...	...	...	...
G Other transfers n.e.c.	...	...	...	...	...	...	...	...	...	...
H Transfers to rest of the world	5	5	...	–	...	5	5	...	–	...
Net saving	−767	−768	...	46[b]	−44	−1134	−1207	...	110[b]	−37
Total current disbursements and net saving	2580	1545	...	415[b]	1164	2922	1645	...	560[b]	1461

Greece

	1990					1991				
	Total government	Central government	State or provincial government	Local government	Social security funds	Total government	Central government	State or provincial government	Local government	Social security funds

Receipts

1 Operating surplus	...	...	...	...	...	...	...	...	...	...
2 Property and entrepreneurial income	195	−17	...	65	147	225	12	...	79	134
3 Taxes, fees and contributions	3654	2304	...	68	1283	4577	2897	...	79	1600
A Indirect taxes	1805	1698	...	22	84	2322	2136	...	29	157
B Direct taxes [a]	651	606	...	46	–	811	761	...	50	–
Income	466	420	...	46	...	520	470	...	50	...
Other	185	185	...	–	...	291	291	...	–	...
C Social security contributions	1198	–	...	–	1198	1444	–	...	–	1444
D Fees, fines and penalties	...	...	...	...	...	...	...	...	...	...
4 Other current transfers	35	30	...	500	362	88	84	...	560	338
A Casualty insurance claims	...	...	...	...	...	...	...	...	...	...
B Transfers from other government subsectors	...	6	...	489	362	...	7	...	549	338
C Transfers from rest of the world	–	–	...	–	...	–	–	...	–	...
D Other transfers, except imputed	35	24	...	11	...	88	77	...	11	...
E Imputed unfunded employee pension and welfare contributions	...	...	...	...	...	...	...	...	...	...
Total current receipts	3885	2317	...	634[b]	1792	4890	2993	...	719[b]	2072

Disbursements

1 Government final consumption expenditure	2251	1510	...	522	219	2555	1711	...	594	250
2 Property income	1193	1164	...	–	29	1564	1561	...	–	3
3 Subsidies	176	176	...	–	...	151	151	...	–	...
4 Other current transfers	1612	978	...	16	1476	2040	1079	...	18	1837
A Casualty insurance premiums, net	...	...	...	...	...	...	...	...	...	...
B Transfers to other government subsectors	...	852	...	6	1	...	887	...	7	1
C Social security benefits	1607	120	...	11	1476	2034	186	...	12	1837
D Social assistance grants	...	...	...	...	...	...	...	...	...	...
E Unfunded employee welfare benefits	...	...	...	...	...	...	...	...	...	...
F Transfers to private non-profit institutions serving households	...	...	...	...	...	...	...	...	...	...
G Other transfers n.e.c.	...	...	...	...	...	...	...	...	...	...
H Transfers to rest of the world	6	6	...	–	...	6	6	...	–	...
Net saving	−1348	−1511	...	95[b]	68	−1420	−1509	...	107[b]	−18
Total current disbursements and net saving	3885	2317	...	634[b]	1792	4890	2993	...	719[b]	2072

Greece

	1992					1993				
	Total government	Central government	State or provincial government	Local government	Social security funds	Total government	Central government	State or provincial government	Local government	Social security funds

Receipts

1 Operating surplus	...	...	...	...	...	...	...	...	...	...
2 Property and entrepreneurial income	439	176	...	93	170	488	100	...	194	194
3 Taxes, fees and contributions	5457	3480	...	90	1888	6245	3833	...	110	2302
A Indirect taxes	2874	2637	...	35	202	3146	2863	...	47	236
B Direct taxes [a]	898	843	...	55	–	1033	970	...	63	–
Income	516	461	...	55	...	593	530	...	63	...
Other	383	383	...	–	...	440	440	...	–	...
C Social security contributions	1685	–	...	–	1685	2066	–	...	–	2066
D Fees, fines and penalties	...	...	...	...	...	...	...	...	...	...
4 Other current transfers	53	48	...	613	382	66	114	...	497	451
A Casualty insurance claims	...	...	...	...	...	...	...	...	...	...
B Transfers from other government subsectors	...	9	...	600	382	...	63	...	482	451
C Transfers from rest of the world	–	–	...	...	...	–	–	...	–	...
D Other transfers, except imputed	53	40	...	13	...	66	51	...	15	...
E Imputed unfunded employee pension and welfare contributions	...	...	...	...	...	...	...	...	...	...
Total current receipts	5949	3704	...	796[b]	2439	6799	4047	...	801[b]	2947

Disbursements

1 Government final consumption expenditure	2925	1959	...	657	310	3201	2172	...	694	335
2 Property income	1927	1903	...	–	24	2535	2460	...	–	75
3 Subsidies	138	138	...	–	...	180	180	...	–	...
4 Other current transfers	2270	1148	...	20	2092	2673	1110	...	76	2483
A Casualty insurance premiums, net	...	...	...	...	...	...	...	...	...	...
B Transfers to other government subsectors	...	982	...	8	1	...	933	...	62	1
C Social security benefits	2263	159	...	13	2091	2662	166	...	14	2483
D Social assistance grants	...	...	...	...	...	...	...	...	...	...
E Unfunded employee welfare benefits	...	...	...	...	...	...	...	...	...	...
F Transfers to private non-profit institutions serving households	...	...	...	...	...	...	...	...	...	...
G Other transfers n.e.c.	...	...	...	...	...	...	...	...	...	...
H Transfers to rest of the world	7	7	...	–	...	11	11	...	–	...
Net saving	–1311	–1444	...	119[b]	14	–1790	–1875	...	31[b]	54
Total current disbursements and net saving	5949	3704	...	796[b]	2439	6799	4047	...	801[b]	2947

Greece

	1994					1995				
	Total government	Central government	State or provincial government	Local government	Social security funds	Total government	Central government	State or provincial government	Local government	Social security funds

Receipts

1 Operating surplus	...	...	...	...	...	...	...	...	...	...
2 Property and entrepreneurial income	636	156	...	155	325	778	221	...	173	384
3 Taxes, fees and contributions	7549	4705	...	130	2714	8527	5489	...	107	2931
A Indirect taxes	3661	3325	...	56	280	4000	3759	...	16	225
B Direct taxes	1454[a]	1380[a]	...	74[a]	–[a]	1821	1730[a]	...	91[a]	–[a]
Income	754	680	...	74	...	971	880	...	91	...
Other	700	700	...	–	...	850	850	...	–	...
C Social security contributions	2434	–	...	–	2434	2706	–	...	–	2706
D Fees, fines and penalties	...	...	...	...	...	...	...	...	...	...
4 Other current transfers	158	158	...	609	568	193	182	...	761	690
A Casualty insurance claims	...	...	...	...	...	...	...	...	...	...
B Transfers from other government subsectors	...	18	...	591	568	...	20	...	730	690
C Transfers from rest of the world	–	–	...	–	...	–	–	...	–	...
D Other transfers, except imputed	158	140	...	18	...	193	162	...	31	...
E Imputed unfunded employee pension and welfare contributions	...	...	...	...	...	...	...	...	...	...
Total current receipts	8342	5019	...	894[b]	3607	9498	5893	...	1040[b]	4005

Disbursements

1 Government final consumption expenditure	3494	2371	...	757	366	3945	2787	...	824	334
2 Property income	3036	3033	...	–	3	3310	3260	...	–	50
3 Subsidies	171	171	...	–	...	163	163	...	–	...
4 Other current transfers	3232	1386	...	47	2976	3595	1717	...	56	3261
A Casualty insurance premiums, net	...	...	...	...	...	...	...	...	...	...
B Transfers to other government subsectors	...	1159	...	17	1	...	1420	...	20	–
C Social security benefits	3215	210	...	30	2975	3577	280	...	36	3261
D Social assistance grants	...	...	...	...	...	...	...	...	...	...
E Unfunded employee welfare benefits	...	...	...	...	...	...	...	...	...	...
F Transfers to private non-profit institutions serving households	...	...	...	...	...	...	...	...	...	...
G Other transfers n.e.c.	...	...	...	...	...	...	...	...	...	...
H Transfers to rest of the world	17	17	...	–	...	17	17	...	–	...
Net saving	−1591	−1942	...	89[b]	262	−1515	−2035	...	160	360
Total current disbursements and net saving	8342	5019	...	894[b]	3607	9498	5893	...	1040	4005

a Item "Fees, fines and penalties" is included in item "Direct taxes". b Column "Local government" includes all public funds.

Greece

3.32 Household and private unincorporated enterprise income and outlay account

Thousand million Greek drachmas

	1986	1987	1988	1989	1990	1991	1992	1993	1994	1995	1996	1997
Receipts												
1 Compensation of employees	2204	2480	3007	3628	4405	4983	5525	6166	6998	8040	...	...
2 Operating surplus of private unincorporated enterprises	...	...	...	...	...	...	...	...	...	...	...	...
3 Property and entrepreneurial income	2238	2592	3290	3814	4638	5978	6784	8448	9187	9777	...	...
4 Current transfers	958	1122	1343	1585	1879	2427	2710	3219	3825	4186	...	...
A Casualty insurance claims	...	...	...	...	...	...	...	...	...	...	...	...
B Social security benefits	821	936	1098	1359	1607	2034	2263	2662	3215	3577	...	...
C Social assistance grants	...	...	...	...	...	...	...	...	...	...	...	...
D Unfunded employee pension and welfare benefits	...	...	...	...	...	...	...	...	...	...	...	...
E Transfers from general government	...	...	...	...	...	...	...	...	...	...	...	...
F Transfers from rest of the world	137	186	245	226	272	393	447	556	610	609	...	...
G Other transfers n.e.c.	...	...	...	...	...	...	...	...	...	...	...	...
Total current receipts	5400	6194	7640	9028	10921	13388	15019	17833	20011	22004	...	...
Disbursements												
1 Final consumption expenditure	3719	4356	5153	6158	7498	9112	10669	12148	13662	15172	...	...
2 Property income	...	...	...	...	...	...	...	...	...	...	...	...
3 Direct taxes and other current transfers n.e.c. to general government	854	950	1132	1322	1665	1964	2201	2659	3188	3677	...	...
A Social security contributions	601	672	784	978	1198	1444	1685	2066	2434	2706	...	...
B Direct taxes	253	278	348	344	466	520	516	593	754	971	...	...
C Fees, fines and penalties	...	...	...	...	...	...	...	...	...	...	...	...
4 Other current transfers	18	18	23	28	35	88	53	66	158	193	...	...
A Net casualty insurance premiums	...	...	...	...	...	...	...	...	...	...	...	...
B Transfers to private non-profit institutions serving households	...	...	...	...	...	...	...	...	...	...	...	...
C Transfers to rest of the world	–	–	–	–	–	–	–	–	–	–	...	...
D Other current transfers, except imputed	18	18	23	28	35	88	53	66	158	193	...	...
E Imputed employee pension and welfare contributions	...	...	...	...	...	...	...	...	...	...	...	...
Statistical discrepancy	106	45	-84	-211	-350	-42	-209	21	46	-186	...	...
Net saving	704	825	1416	1729	2075	2267	2305	2939	2957	3149	...	...
Total current disbursements and net saving	5400	6194	7640	9028	10921	13388	15019	17833	20011	22004	...	...

Greece

3.51 External transactions, current account: detail

Thousand million Greek drachmas

	1986	1987	1988	1989	1990	1991	1992	1993	1994	1995	1996	1997
Payments to the rest of the world												
1 Imports of goods and services	1703	1993	2291	2810	3445	4253	4898	5419	6103	6478	...	...
A Imports of merchandise, c.i.f.	1538	1830	2061	2520	3093	3818	4351	...	...	...	...	...
B Other	165	163	230	290	353	436	547	...	...	...	...	...
2 Factor income to rest of the world	199	218	254	315	324	392	483	541	571	704	...	...
A Compensation of employees	8	10	14	19	19	22	33	...	...	...	...	...
B Property and entrepreneurial income	191	208	241	295	305	371	449	...	...	...	...	...
3 Current transfers to the rest of the world	95	77	91	111	123	183	200	279	316	344	...	...
A Indirect taxes by general government to supranational organizations	90	73	86	105	118	177	193	268	299	327	...	...
B Other current transfers	5	4	5	5	6	6	7	11	17	17	...	...
By general government	5	4	5	5	6	6	7	11	17	17	...	...
By other resident sectors	–	–	–	–	–	–	–	–	–	–	...	...
4 Surplus of the nation on current transactions	–291	–192	–153	–441	–649	–657	–637	–505	–432	–405	...	...
Payments to the rest of the world and surplus of the nation on current transfers	1707	2097	2484	2794	3243	4172	4944	5734	6558	7121	...	...
Receipts from the rest of the world												
1 Exports of goods and services [a]	1233	1537	1801	2019	2279	2906	3438	3709	4364	4876	...	...
A Exports of merchandise, f.o.b.	790	955	1083	1231	1268	1580	1816	...	...	...	...	...
B Other	443	582	717	788	1011	1326	1622	...	...	...	...	...
2 Factor income from rest of the world	132	155	198	230	278	342	431	636	679	778	...	...
A Compensation of employees	47	48	42	47	48	68	103	155	...	...	...	...
B Property and entrepreneurial income	84	107	156	182	230	274	328	480	...	...	...	...
3 Current transfers from rest of the world	343	405	485	546	686	925	1075	1389	1514	1467	...	...
A Subsidies to general government from supranational organizations	205	219	240	320	414	531	628	833	904	858	...	...
B Other current transfers	137	186	245	226	272	393	447	556	610	609	...	...
To general government	–	–	–	–	–	–	–	–	–	–	...	...
To other resident sectors	137	186	245	226	272	393	447	556	610	609	...	...
Receipts from the rest of the world on current transfers	1707	2097	2484	2794	3243	4172	4944	5734	6558	7121	...	...

a Exclude income from ocean-going cargo ships under Greek flag or ownership. However, remittances actually received by the bank of Greece from persons engaged in these enterprises are included in factor income from the rest of the world.

Greece

3.52 External transactions, capital accumulation account

Thousand million Greek drachmas

	1986	1987	1988	1989	1990	1991	1992	1993	1994	1995	1996	1997
Finance of gross accumulation												
1 Surplus of the nation on current transactions	−291	−192	−153	−441	−649	−657	−637	−505	−432	−405	...	...
2 Capital transfers from rest of the world	56	58	65	92	142	180	298	352	329	433	...	...
Total finance of gross accumulation	−235	−134	−87	−349	−508	−476	−339	−153	−103	27	...	...
Gross accumulation												
1 Capital transfers to the rest of the world	1	2	2	3	3	4	5	5	6	6	...	...
A By general government	1	2	2	3	3	4	5	5	6	6	...	...
B By other resident sectors	...	...	...	...	...	...	...	...	...	...	...	...
2 Purchases of intangible assets, n.e.c., net, from rest of the world	...	...	...	...	...	...	...	...	...	...	...	...
Statistical discrepancy	...	...	...	...	...	...	...	...	...	−9	...	...
Net lending to the rest of the world	−237	−136	−90	−352	−511	−481	−344	−159	−109	31	...	...
Total gross accumulation	−235	−134	−87	−349	−508	−476	−339	−153	−103	27	...	...

Grenada

Source

National Income Estimates of Grenada (St. George's).

General note

The estimates shown in the following tables have been prepared in accordance with the United Nations System of National Accounts so far as the existing data would permit.

1.1 Expenditure on the gross domestic product, in current prices

Million E.C. dollars

	1986	1987	1988	1989	1990	1991	1992	1993	1994	1995	1996	1997
1 Government final consumption expenditure	81	77	83	88	111	107	115	...	...	...	...	...
2 Private final consumption expenditure	262	295	320	340	351	393	384	...	...	...	...	...
3 Gross capital formation	116	150	168	196	228	248	200	...	...	...	...	...
A Increase in stocks	−1	8	7	15	17	21	12	...	...	...	...	...
B Gross fixed capital formation	117	142	160	181	210	227	187	...	...	...	...	...
4 Exports of goods and services	163	174	181	185	240	257	223	...	...	...	...	...
5 less: Imports of goods and services	272	290	303	318	389	437	344	...	...	...	...	...
equals: Gross domestic product	350	406	449	491	541	567	578	...	...	...	...	...

1.10 Gross domestic product by kind of activity, in current prices

Million E.C. dollars

	1986	1987	1988	1989	1990	1991	1992	1993	1994	1995	1996	1997
1 Agriculture, hunting, forestry and fishing	53	70	72	74	71	69	...	...	...	...	...	...
2 Mining and quarrying	1	1	1	1	2	2	...	...	...	...	...	...
3 Manufacturing	13	16	18	21	23	24	...	...	...	...	...	...
4 Electricity, gas and water	8	9	10	12	13	14	...	...	...	...	...	...
5 Construction	23	28	34	40	44	48	...	...	...	...	...	...
6 Wholesale and retail trade, restaurants and hotels	55	61	67	74	82	90	...	...	...	...	...	...
7 Transport, storage and communication	38	42	49	55	60	66	...	...	...	...	...	...
8 Finance, insurance, real estate and business services	34	36	39	41	43	44	...	...	...	...	...	...
9 Community, social and personal services	12	12	12	13	13	13	...	...	...	...	...	...
Total, Industries [a]	237	275	303	311	351	371	...	...	...	...	...	...
Producers of government services	59	60	63	82	89	92	...	...	...	...	...	...
Other producers	...	...	...	...	...	...	...	...	...	...	...	...
Subtotal	295	335	366	393	440	463	...	...	...	...	...	...
less: Imputed bank service charge	13	15	16	17	18	19	...	...	...	...	...	...

Grenada

Million E.C. dollars

	1986	1987	1988	1989	1990	1991	1992	1993	1994	1995	1996	1997
plus: Import duties	...	...	...	...	...	...	...	...	...	...	...	...
plus: Value added tax	...	...	...	...	...	...	...	...	...	...	...	...
plus: Other adjustments [b]	68	86	98	115	119	123	...	...	...	...	...	...
equals: Gross domestic product	350	406	449	491	541	567	...	...	...	...	...	...

a Gross domestic product in factor values.   b Item "Other adjustments" refers to indirect taxes net of subsidies.

1.11 Gross domestic product by kind of activity, in constant prices

Million E.C. dollars

	1986	1987	1988	1989	1990	1991	1992	1993	1994	1995	1996	1997
At constant prices of: 1984												
1 Agriculture, hunting, forestry and fishing	42	45	46	48	47	47	...	...	...	...	...	...
2 Mining and quarrying	1	1	1	1	1	1	...	...	...	...	...	...
3 Manufacturing	12	14	15	17	18	19	...	...	...	...	...	...
4 Electricity, gas and water	5	6	6	7	8	8	...	...	...	...	...	...
5 Construction	22	26	29	34	37	39	...	...	...	...	...	...
6 Wholesale and retail trade, restaurants and hotels	49	51	54	58	62	64	...	...	...	...	...	...
7 Transport, storage and communication	33	36	40	43	47	50	...	...	...	...	...	...
8 Finance, insurance, real estate and business services	30	31	31	32	33	34	...	...	...	...	...	...
9 Community, social and personal services	11	11	11	11	11	11	...	...	...	...	...	...
Total, Industries [a]	205	221	235	251	266	274	...	...	...	...	...	...
Producers of government services	54	54	54	54	55	56	...	...	...	...	...	...
Other producers	...	...	...	...	...	...	...	...	...	...	...	...
Subtotal	259	275	289	305	320	330	...	...	...	...	...	...
less: Imputed bank service charge	12	13	13	13	14	14	...	...	...	...	...	...
plus: Import duties	...	...	...	...	...	...	...	...	...	...	...	...
plus: Value added tax	...	...	...	...	...	...	...	...	...	...	...	...
plus: Other adjustments [b]	61	...	...	...	...	...	...	...	...	...	...	...
equals: Gross domestic product	308	262	276	292	307	316	...	...	...	...	...	...

a Gross domestic product in factor values.   b Item "Other adjustments" refers to indirect taxes net of subsidies.

Guadeloupe

Source

Reply to the United Nations National Accounts Questionnaire from the Institut national de la statistique et des études économiques (INSEE), Paris. Official estimates and descriptions are published by INSEE in *Comptes Economiques de la Guadeloupe*.

General note

The estimates shown in the following tables have been adjusted by INSEE in accordance with the United Nations System of National Accounts (1968 SNA) so far as the existing data would permit.

1.1 Expenditure on the gross domestic product, in current prices

Million French francs

	1986	1987	1988	1989	1990	1991	1992	1993	1994	1995	1996	1997
1 Government final consumption expenditure	3577	3814	4074	4450	4680	5085	5263	...	...	...	...	...
2 Private final consumption expenditure	9868	10905	11818	12683	14112	14332	15121	...	...	...	...	...
3 Gross capital formation	2316	3307	3477	4222	5316	5580	5231	...	...	...	...	...
A Increase in stocks	−74	251	−98	112	161	166	227	...	...	...	...	...
B Gross fixed capital formation	2390	3056	3576	4109	5155	5413	5004	...	...	...	...	...
4 Exports of goods and services	819	698	1036	784	744	998	803	...	...	...	...	...
5 less: Imports of goods and services	5621	6430	7380	8077	9651	9580	8447	...	...	...	...	...
equals: Gross domestic product	10958	12294	13025	14062	15200	16415	17972	...	...	...	...	...

1.3 Cost components of the gross domestic product

Million French francs

	1986	1987	1988	1989	1990	1991	1992	1993	1994	1995	1996	1997
1 Indirect taxes, net	1136	1411	1720	1698	1939	2003	1948	...	...	...	...	...
A Indirect taxes	1501	1723	1962	2123	2184	2308	2283	...	...	...	...	...
B less: Subsidies [a]	364	312	242	425	245	305	334	...	...	...	...	...
2 Consumption of fixed capital	...	...	...	...	...	...	...	...	...	...	...	...
3 Compensation of employees paid by resident producers to ..	7590	8342	9311	10117	11319	12664	14003	...	...	...	...	...
4 Operating surplus [b]	2231	2540	1994	2248	1942	1748	2021	...	...	...	...	...
equals: Gross domestic product	10958	12294	13025	14062	15200	16415	17972	...	...	...	...	...

a Includes subsidies from the rest of the world.   b Item "Operating surplus" includes consumption of fixed capital.

Guadeloupe

1.4 General government current receipts and disbursements

Million French francs

	1986	1987	1988	1989	1990	1991	1992	1993	1994	1995	1996	1997
Receipts												
1 Operating surplus	–	–	–	–	...	...	...	...	...	...	...	...
2 Property and entrepreneurial income	49	43	42	53	39	108	58	...	...	...	...	...
3 Taxes, fees and contributions	4327	4985	5609	5985	5979	7136	7134	...	...	...	...	...
4 Other current transfers	4060	4184	4236	5283	5620	5736	6478	...	...	...	...	...
Total current receipts of general government	8436	9212	9887	11321	11638	12980	13671	...	...	...	...	...
Disbursements												
1 Government final consumption expenditure	3577	3814	4074	4450	4680	5085	5263	...	...	...	...	...
2 Property income	250	252	349	338	386	368	390	...	...	...	...	...
3 Subsidies	73	80	156	166	126	156	171	...	...	...	...	...
4 Other current transfers	3958	4380	4547	5078	5194	5942	6452	...	...	...	...	...
5 Net saving	578	688	761	1290	1252	1428	1394	...	...	...	...	...
Total current disbursements and net saving of general government	8436	9212	9887	11321	11638	12980	13670	...	...	...	...	...

1.7 External transactions on current account, summary

Million French francs

	1986	1987	1988	1989	1990	1991	1992	1993	1994	1995	1996	1997
Payments to the rest of the world												
1 Imports of goods and services	5621	6430	7380	8077	9651	9580	8447	...	...	...	...	...
2 Factor income to rest of the world	608	680	744	705	783	807	826	...	...	...	...	...
A Compensation of employees	–	–	–	–	–	–	–	...	...	...	...	...
B Property and entrepreneurial income	608	680	744	705	783	807	826	...	...	...	...	...
3 Current transfers to the rest of the world	82	92	100	96	94	103	105	...	...	...	...	...
4 Surplus of the nation on current transactions	–914	–1862	–2538	–2158	–3616	–3327	–1604	...	...	...	...	...
Payments to the rest of the world and surplus of the nation on current transfers	5396	5340	5686	6720	6913	7163	7773	...	...	...	...	...
Receipts from the rest of the world												
1 Exports of goods and services	819	698	1036	784	744	998	803	...	...	...	...	...
2 Factor income from rest of the world	192	253	294	368	402	252	294	...	...	...	...	...
A Compensation of employees	–	–	–	–	–	–	–	...	...	...	...	...
B Property and entrepreneurial income	192	253	294	368	402	252	294	...	...	...	...	...
3 Current transfers from rest of the world	4385	4388	4357	5567	5767	5913	6675	...	...	...	...	...
Receipts from the rest of the world on current transactions	5396	5340	5686	6720	6913	7163	7773	...	...	...	...	...

Guadeloupe

1.8 Capital transactions of the nation, summary

Million French francs

	1986	1987	1988	1989	1990	1991	1992	1993	1994	1995	1996	1997
Finance of gross capital formation												
Gross saving	1401	1445	939	2064	1700	2253	3627	...	...	...	...	...
less: Surplus of the nation on current transactions	−914	−1862	−2538	−2158	−3616	−3327	−1604	...	...	...	...	...
Finance of gross capital formation	2316	3307	3477	4222	5316	5580	5231	...	...	...	...	...
Gross capital formation												
Increase in stocks	−74	251	−98	112	161	166	227	...	...	...	...	...
Gross fixed capital formation	2390	3056	3576	4109	5155	5413	5004	...	...	...	...	...
1 General government	861	972	848	1066	1410	1645	1332	...	...	...	...	...
2 Corporate and quasi-corporate enterprises	1117	1514	1934	2108	2561	2596	2595	...	...	...	...	...
3 Other	413	570	794	935	1184	1172	1078	...	...	...	...	...
Gross capital formation	2316	3307	3477	4222	5316	5580	5232	...	...	...	...	...

1.10 Gross domestic product by kind of activity, in current prices

Million French francs

	1986	1987	1988	1989	1990	1991	1992	1993	1994	1995	1996	1997
1 Agriculture, hunting, forestry and fishing	1095	1167	1311	1177	1011	1192	1207	...	...	...	...	...
2 Mining and quarrying	548	615	688	758	812	1000	1238	...	...	...	...	...
3 Manufacturing								...	...	...	...	...
4 Electricity, gas and water	−12	60	90	39	152	224	308	...	...	...	...	...
5 Construction	538	626	646	949	1118	1145	1164	...	...	...	...	...
6 Wholesale and retail trade, restaurants and hotels	1806	2061	2099	2500	2758	2693	2908	...	...	...	...	...
7 Transport, storage and communication	652	739	774	773	882	984	1415	...	...	...	...	...
8 Finance, insurance, real estate and business services	990	1283	1361	1374	1712	1891	2023	...	...	...	...	...
9 Community, social and personal services	1581	1696	1796	2031	2040	2294	2588	...	...	...	...	...
Total, Industries	7197	8246	8766	9602	10485	11425	12850	...	...	...	...	...
Producers of government services	3195	3448	3729	4058	4235	4534	4770	...	...	...	...	...
Other producers	279	282	270	282	316	320	348	...	...	...	...	...
Subtotal	10671	11977	12764	13941	15036	16278	17968	...	...	...	...	...
less: Imputed bank service charge	628	795	972	1160	1222	1535	1311	...	...	...	...	...
plus: Import duties	430	537	614	664	723	738	699	...	...	...	...	...
plus: Value added tax	485	575	620	616	664	934	616	...	...	...	...	...
plus: Other adjustments	...	...	...	...	...	...	...	...	...	...	...	...
equals: Gross domestic product	10958	12294	13025	14062	15200	16415	17972	...	...	...	...	...

Guadeloupe

1.12 Relations among national accounting aggregates

Million French francs

	1986	1987	1988	1989	1990	1991	1992	1993	1994	1995	1996	1997
Gross domestic product	10958	12294	13025	14062	15200	16415	17972	...	...	...	...	...
plus: Net factor income from the rest of the world	−416	−427	−450	−336	−381	−555	−531	...	...	...	...	...
Factor income from rest of the world	192	253	294	368	402	252	294	...	...	...	...	...
less: Factor income to the rest of the world	608	680	744	705	783	807	826	...	...	...	...	...
equals: Gross national product	10542	11866	12575	13726	14819	15860	17441	...	...	...	...	...
less: Consumption of fixed capital	...	...	...	...	...	...	...	...	...	...	...	...
equals: National income	...	...	...	...	...	...	...	...	...	...	...	...
plus: Net current transfers from the rest of the world	4303	4297	4257	5471	5673	5810	6570	...	...	...	...	...
Current transfers from rest of the world	4385	4388	4357	5567	5767	5913	6675	...	...	...	...	...
less: Current transfers to the rest of the world	82	92	100	96	94	103	105	...	...	...	...	...
equals: National disposable income	...	...	...	...	...	...	...	...	...	...	...	...
less: Final consumption	13444	14718	15892	17133	18792	19417	20384	...	...	...	...	...
equals: Net saving	...	...	...	...	...	...	...	...	...	...	...	...
less: Surplus of the nation on current transactions	−914	−1862	−2538	−2158	−3616	−3327	−1604	...	...	...	...	...
equals: Net capital formation	...	...	...	...	...	...	...	...	...	...	...	...

Guatemala

Source

Reply to the United Nations National Accounts Questionnaire from the Banco de Guatemala, Guatemala City. The official estimates are published in *Boletín Estadístico del Banco de Guatemala*.

General note

The estimates shown in the following tables have been prepared in accordance with the United Nations System of National Accounts (1968 SNA) so far as the existing data would permit.

1.1 Expenditure on the gross domestic product, in current prices

Million Guatemalan quetzales

	1986	1987	1988	1989	1990	1991	1992	1993	1994	1995	1996	1997
1 Government final consumption expenditure	1124	1400	1640	1870	2324	2714	3481	4151	4468	4692	4851	5323
2 Private final consumption expenditure	12847	14989	17289	19837	28692	39693	45899	54165	63893	72900	83072	93804
3 Gross capital formation	1636	2464	2814	3201	4668	6762	9893	11080	11709	12820	12113	14927
A Increase in stocks	43	275	67	−54	213	1002	1448	745	1087	460	−614	−1052
B Gross fixed capital formation	1593	2188	2747	3255	4455	5760	8445	10334	10622	12360	12727	15979
Residential buildings	190	227	306	376	431	667	977	1170	1281	1435	1423	1589
Non-residential buildings												
Other construction and land improvement, etc.	327	418	531	620	866	999	1533	1786	1762	2165	2522	2318
Other	1076	1544	1911	2259	3158	4094	5935	7378	7579	8761	8782	11072
4 Exports of goods and services	2542	2807	3308	4099	6776	8349	9483	11613	13170	16400	17005	19342
5 less: Imports of goods and services	2311	3948	4507	5323	8143	10216	14771	16765	18571	21656	21562	25454
equals: Gross domestic product	15838	17711	20545	23685	34317	47302	53985	64243	74669	85157	95479	107943

1.2 Expenditure on the gross domestic product, in constant prices

Million Guatemalan quetzales

	1986	1987	1988	1989	1990	1991	1992	1993	1994	1995	1996	1997
At constant prices of: 1958												
1 Government final consumption expenditure	243	260	273	283	293	298	314	339	350	354	354	374
2 Private final consumption expenditure	2284	2373	2470	2544	2606	2706	2843	2959	3103	3266	3357	3491
3 Gross capital formation	237	314	310	311	307	377	488	460	468	462	393	456
A Increase in stocks	8	47	10	−8	21	80	103	49	66	26	−34	−56
B Gross fixed capital formation	229	266	300	319	286	297	385	412	401	436	427	512
Residential buildings	31	34	41	45	36	41	54	56	58	60	55	59
Non-residential buildings												
Other construction and land improvement, etc.	70	80	91	96	93	92	119	119	112	127	135	161
Other	127	152	168	178	157	164	212	236	232	249	237	292

Guatemala

Million Guatemalan quetzales

	1986	1987	1988	1989	1990	1991	1992	1993	1994	1995	1996	1997
At constant prices of: 1958												
4 Exports of goods and services	390	414	437	495	528	502	544	596	616	694	754	831
5 less: Imports of goods and services	214	316	328	347	344	369	506	527	554	596	555	663
equals: Gross domestic product	2940	3044	3163	3288	3390	3514	3684	3828	3983	4180	4303	4488

1.7 External transactions on current account, summary

Million Guatemalan quetzales

	1986	1987	1988	1989	1990	1991	1992	1993	1994	1995	1996	1997
Payments to the rest of the world												
1 Imports of goods and services	2311	3948	4507	5323	8143	10216	14771	16765	18571	21656	21562	25454
A Imports of merchandise, c.i.f.	2101	3575	4048	4677	7090	9312	13113	14660	16021	19129	19160	23381
B Other	210	374	459	646	1053	904	1658	2105	2551	2527	2402	2073
2 Factor income to rest of the world	509	549	546	585	867	981	1055	999	1096	1196	1645	1847
A Compensation of employees	...	...	...	...	...	...	...	...	...	...	...	...
B Property and entrepreneurial income	509	549	546	585	867	981	1055	999	1096	1196	1645	1847
By general government	414	430	432	398	662	757	865	693	723	642	856	808
By corporate and quasi-corporate enterprises	26	62	73	128	102	127	85	163	229	230	245	268
By other	69	56	41	59	103	97	105	144	144	324	542	771
3 Current transfers to the rest of the world	2	6	9	15	46	85	82	46	46	100	89	134
4 Surplus of the nation on current transactions	–40	–1136	–1087	–1055	–1201	–1078	–3691	–3957	–3674	–2970	–2379	–3321
Payments to the rest of the world and surplus of the nation on current transfers	2782	3367	3975	4868	7855	10205	12217	13853	16039	19981	20917	24114
Receipts from the rest of the world												
1 Exports of goods and services	2542	2807	3308	4099	6776	8349	9483	11613	13170	16400	17005	19342
A Exports of merchandise, f.o.b.	2286	2416	2791	3209	5209	6187	6649	7689	8929	11566	12523	14482
B Other	256	392	518	890	1566	2162	2834	3924	4241	4834	4482	4859
2 Factor income from rest of the world	73	76	75	42	40	465	629	145	240	269	245	439
A Compensation of employees	...	...	...	...	...	...	...	...	...	...	...	...
B Property and entrepreneurial income	73	76	75	42	40	465	629	145	240	269	245	439
By general government	72	76	67	31	28	112	120	137	178	201	157	288
By corporate and quasi-corporate enterprises	–	–	4	8	11[a]	350[a]	508[a]	6	54	40	81	81
By other	–	–	4	2	–	2	1	2	8	28	7	68
3 Current transfers from rest of the world	167	484	592	727	1040	1392	2105	2095	2629	2954	3306	3811
Receipts from the rest of the world on current transactions	2782	3367	3975	4868	7855	10205	12217	13853	16039	19981	20917	24114

[a] For the years 1990-1992, property and entrepreneurial income received by the corporate and quasi-corporate enterprises from the rest of the world includes bank service charges.

Guatemala

1.8 Capital transactions of the nation, summary

Million Guatemalan quetzales

	1986	1987	1988	1989	1990	1991	1992	1993	1994	1995	1996	1997
Finance of gross capital formation												
Gross saving	1596	1327	1728	2146	3468	5684	6202	7123	8035	8850	9734	11606
less: Surplus of the nation on current transactions	−40	−1136	−1087	−1055	−1201	−1078	−3691	−3957	−3674	−2970	−2379	−3321
Finance of gross capital formation	1636	2464	2814	3201	4668	6762	9893	11080	11709	12820	12113	14927
Gross capital formation												
Increase in stocks	43	275	67	−54	213	1002	1448	745	1087	460	−614	−1052
Gross fixed capital formation	1593	2188	2747	3255	4455	5760	8445	10334	10622	12360	12727	15979
1 General government	249	325	428	500	688	758	1250	1471	1404	1751	2048	2790
2 Corporate and quasi-corporate enterprises	1344	1863	2319	2755	3767	5003	7196	8863	9218	10609	10679	13189
3 Other												
Gross capital formation	1636	2464	2814	3201	4668	6762	9893	11080	11709	12820	12113	14927

1.11 Gross domestic product by kind of activity, in constant prices

Million Guatemalan quetzales

	1986	1987	1988	1989	1990	1991	1992	1993	1994	1995	1996	1997
At constant prices of: 1958												
1 Agriculture, hunting, forestry and fishing	753	782	818	843	877	904	931	952	975	1010	1035	1064
2 Mining and quarrying	8	8	9	9	8	9	12	13	14	16	19	24
3 Manufacturing	468	477	488	499	510	522	539	555	571	590	601	617
4 Electricity, gas and water	63	68	74	80	85	88	100	110	116	126	133	153
5 Construction	51	59	68	73	67	68	86	83	83	90	93	102
6 Wholesale and retail trade, restaurants and hotels	731	753	776	803	816	850	888	924	977	1036	1065	1105
7 Transport, storage and communication	211	221	230	254	270	286	307	322	336	361	374	396
8 Finance, insurance, real estate and business services	269	276	286	297	310	324	338	355	373	398	417	436
9 Community, social and personal services	186	190	196	201	208	212	219	226	234	243	251	260
Total, Industries	2741	2834	2944	3059	3152	3265	3421	3541	3680	3870	3988	4157
Producers of government services	200	210	218	229	238	248	262	288	303	309	315	331
Other producers	...	...	...	...	...	...	...	...	...	...	...	...
Subtotal	2940	3044	3163	3288	3390	3514	3684	3828	3983	4179	4303	4488
less: Imputed bank service charge	...	...	...	...	...	...	...	...	...	...	...	...
plus: Import duties	...	...	...	...	...	...	...	...	...	...	...	...
plus: Value added tax	...	...	...	...	...	...	...	...	...	...	...	...
plus: Other adjustments	...	...	...	...	...	...	...	...	...	...	...	...
equals: Gross domestic product	2940	3044	3163	3288	3390	3514	3684	3828	3983	4179	4303	4488

Guatemala

1.12 Relations among national accounting aggregates

Million Guatemalan quetzales

	1986	1987	1988	1989	1990	1991	1992	1993	1994	1995	1996	1997
Gross domestic product	15838	17711	20545	23685	34317	47302	53985	64243	74669	85157	95479	107943
plus: Net factor income from the rest of the world	−436	−472	−471	−544	−828	−517	−426	−854	−856	−926	−1400	−1408
Factor income from rest of the world	73	76	75	42	40	465	629	145	240	269	245	439
less: Factor income to the rest of the world	509	549	546	585	867	981	1055	999	1096	1196	1645	1847
equals: Gross national product	15402	17239	20074	23141	33489	46786	53560	63389	73813	84231	94079	106535
less: Consumption of fixed capital	...	...	...	...	...	...	...	...	...	...	...	...
equals: National income	15402	17239	20074	23141	33489	46786	53560	63389	73813	84231	94079	106535
plus: Net current transfers from the rest of the world	165	477	583	712	994	1306	2023	2049	2583	2854	3217	3677
Current transfers from rest of the world	167	484	592	727	1040	1392	2105	2095	2629	2954	3306	3811
less: Current transfers to the rest of the world	2	6	9	15	46	85	82	46	46	100	89	134
equals: National disposable income	15567	17716	20656	23853	34483	48092	55583	65438	76396	87085	97296	120212
less: Final consumption	13971	16389	18929	21707	31016	42407	49381	58316	68361	77235	87562	91252
equals: Net saving	1596	1327	1728	2146	3468	5684	6202	7123	8035	9850	9734	11606
less: Surplus of the nation on current transactions	−40	−1136	−1087	−1055	−1201	−1078	−3691	−3957	−3674	−2970	−2379	−3321
equals: Net capital formation	1636	2464[a]	2814[a]	3201[a]	4668[a]	6762[a]	9893[a]	11080[a]	11709[a]	12820[a]	12113[a]	14927[a]

[a] Includes consumption of fixed capital.

2.11 Gross fixed capital formation by kind of activity of owner, ISIC divisions, in current prices

Million Guatemalan quetzales

	1986	1987	1988	1989	1990	1991	1992	1993	1994	1995	1996	1997
All producers												
1 Agriculture, hunting, forestry and fishing	129	165	186	229	401	497	645	785	823	936	944	1183
2 Mining and quarrying	...	...	...	...	...	...	...	...	...	...	...	...
3 Manufacturing	874	1191	1499	1774	2464	3042	4349	5414	5551	6456	6514	8164
4 Electricity, gas and water	...	...	...	...	...	...	...	...	...	...	...	...
5 Construction	190	227	306	376	431	667	977	1170	1281	1435	1423	1589
6 Wholesale and retail trade, restaurants and hotels	...	...	...	...	...	...	...	...	...	...	...	...
7 Transport, storage and communication	152	280	327	376	470	797	1224	1494	1562	1782	1798	2253
8 Finance, insurance, real estate and business services	...	...	...	...	...	...	...	...	...	...	...	...
9 Community, social and personal services	...	...	...	...	...	...	...	...	...	...	...	...
Total industries	1344	1863	2319	2755	3767	5003	7196	8863	9218	10609	10679	13189
Producers of government services	249	325	428	500	688	758	1250	1471	1404	1751	2048	2790
Private non-profit institutions serving households	...	...	...	...	...	...	...	...	...	...	...	...
Total	1593	2188	2747	3255	4455	5760	8445	10334	10622	12360	12727	15979

Guatemala

2.17 Exports and imports of goods and services, detail

Million Guatemalan quetzales

	1986	1987	1988	1989	1990	1991	1992	1993	1994	1995	1996	1997
Exports of goods and services												
1 Exports of merchandise, f.o.b.	2286	2416	2791	3209	5209	6187	6649	7689	8929	11556	...	...
2 Transport and communication	16	22	44	69	82	121	136	194	229	309	...	...
A In respect of merchandise imports	–	–	1	6	29	34	11	25	38	79	...	...
B Other	16	22	43	63	52	88	125	169	191	230	...	...
3 Insurance service charges	1	2	6	19	26	28	61	25	31	48	...	...
A In respect of merchandise imports	–	–	1	4	2	–	2	15	8	11	...	...
B Other	–	1	5	15	25	28	59	10	23	37	...	...
4 Other commodities	107	181	147	268	766	1097	1494	2353	2576	3020	...	...
5 Adjustments of merchandise exports to change-of-ownership basis	...	...	...	...	...	...	...	...	...	...	...	...
6 Direct purchases in the domestic market by non-residential households	64	126	161	310	507	731	963	1153	1181	1234	...	...
7 Direct purchases in the domestic market by extraterritorial bodies	68	61	160	224	185	186	179	198	224	222	...	...
Total exports of goods and services	2542	2807	3308	4099	6776	8349	9483	11613	13170	16390	...	...
Imports of goods and services												
1 Imports of merchandise, c.i.f.	2101	3575	4048	4677	7090	9312	13113	14660	16021	19129	...	...
A Imports of merchandise, f.o.b.	1920	3293	3674	4231	6950	8445	12058	13446	14669	17619	...	...
B Transport of services on merchandise imports	172	267	354	423	89	819	999	1150	1280	1430	...	...
By residents	...	...	...	...	...	...	...	...	...	...	...	...
By non-residents	172	267	354	423	89	819	999	1150	1280	1430	...	...
C Insurance service charges on merchandise imports	10	15	20	24	50	48	56	64	72	80	...	...
By residents	...	...	...	...	...	...	...	...	...	...	...	...
By non-residents	10	15	20	24	50	48	56	64	72	80	...	...
2 Adjustments of merchandise imports to change-of-ownership basis	...	...	...	...	...	...	...	...	...	...	...	...
3 Other transport and communication	19	26	42	55	62	70	89	157	194	189	...	...
4 Other insurance service charges	12	9	17	28	21	25	43	90	108	104	...	...
5 Other commodities	108	223	102	151	455	162	827	984	1132	1283	...	...
6 Direct purchases abroad by government	37	35	49	60	88	142	165	215	249	130	...	...
7 Direct purchases abroad by resident households	34	81	248	352	428	504	534	660	868	821	...	...
Total imports of goods and services	2311	3948	4507	5323	8143	10216	14771	16765	18571	21656	...	...
Balance of goods and services	231	−1141	−1198	−1224	−1367	−1867	−5289	−5152	−5401	−5266	...	...
Total imports and balance of goods and services	2542	2807	3308	4099	6776	8349	9483	11613	13170	16390	...	...

Guinea-Bissau

Source

Reply to the United Nations National Accounts Questionnaire from the Ministerio do Plano, Bissau.

General note

The estimates shown in the following tables have been prepared in accordance with the United Nations System of National Accounts (1968 SNA) so far as the existing data would permit.

1.1 Expenditure on the gross domestic product, in current prices

Million Ginea-Bissau pesos

	1986	1987	1988	1989	1990	1991	1992	1993	1994	1995	1996	1997
1 Government final consumption expenditure	6423	10776	20134	46925	58013	108032	163100	...	...	...	...	...
2 Private final consumption expenditure	41844	82375	160420	351049	514670	860458	1700380	...	...	...	...	...
A Households	41844	82375	160420	351049	514670	860458	1700380	...	...	...	...	...
B Private non-profit institutions serving households	...	...	...	...	...	...	...					
3 Gross capital formation	9967	21785	49864	72534	75136	96820	405660	...	...	...	...	...
A Increase in stocks	582	879	192	6337	4591	7695	...					
B Gross fixed capital formation	9385	20906	49672	66197	70546	89125	...					
4 Exports of goods and services	2211	13788	22666	28924	61211	114568	125010	...	...	...	...	...
5 less: Imports of goods and services	13472	36349	81134	140557	198937	324894	864140	...	...	...	...	...
equals: Gross domestic product	46973	92375	171949	358875	510094	854985	1530010	...	...	...	...	...

1.2 Expenditure on the gross domestic product, in constant prices

Million Ginea-Bissau pesos

	1986	1987	1988	1989	1990	1991	1992	1993	1994	1995	1996	1997
	At constant prices of: 1986											
1 Government final consumption expenditure	6423	5756	6207	6486	6299	6252	...	...	...	...	...	...
2 Private final consumption expenditure	41844	44264	49493	50556	52281	53791	...	...	...	...	...	...
A Households	41844	44264	49493	50556	52281	53791	...	...	...	...	...	...
B Private non-profit institutions serving households	...	...	...	...	...	...						
3 Gross capital formation	9967	11711	15384	14579	14431	14568	...	...	...	...	...	...
A Increase in stocks	582	496	53	277	344	295	...					
B Gross fixed capital formation	9385	11214	15331	14302	14087	14273	...					
4 Exports of goods and services	2211	7394	7002	7816	8590	9142	...	...	...	...	...	...
5 less: Imports of goods and services	13472	19502	25038	24003	24337	24772	...	...	...	...	...	...
equals: Gross domestic product	46973	49623	53047	55434	57263	58981	...	...	...	...	...	...

Guinea-Bissau

1.10 Gross domestic product by kind of activity, in current prices

Million Ginea-Bissau pesos

	1986	1987	1988	1989	1990	1991	1992	1993	1994	1995	1996	1997
1 Agriculture, hunting, forestry and fishing	21997	47096	78470	160016	227508	382400	...	...	...	...	...	...
2 Mining and quarrying	31	15	57	28465	41930	72556	...	...	...	...	...	...
3 Manufacturing	6959	7026	11763				...	...	...	...	...	...
4 Electricity, gas and water	16	640	1809				...	...	...	...	...	...
5 Construction	2621	4266	10947	34645	50937	71874	...	...	...	...	...	...
6 Wholesale and retail trade, restaurants and hotels	9267	22874	48341	92338	131250	220356	...	...	...	...	...	...
7 Transport, storage and communication	1337	3550	6375	12824	18874	33364	...	...	...	...	...	...
8 Finance, insurance, real estate and business services	248	1264	5264	11697	16626	27914	...	...	...	...	...	...
9 Community, social and personal services							...	...	...	...	...	...
Total, Industries	42476	86731	163026	339985	487125	808464	...	...	...	...	...	...
Producers of government services	4497	5644	8923	18891	22969	46522	...	...	...	...	...	...
Other producers	...	...	...	...	...	...	...	...	...	...	...	...
Subtotal	46973	92375	171949	358875	510094	854985	...	...	...	...	...	...
less: Imputed bank service charge	...	...	...	...	...	...	...	...	...	...	...	...
plus: Import duties	...	...	...	...	...	...	...	...	...	...	...	...
plus: Value added tax	...	...	...	...	...	...	...	...	...	...	...	...
plus: Other adjustments	...	...	...	...	...	...	...	...	...	...	...	...
equals: Gross domestic product	46973	92375	171949	358875	510094	854985	...	...	...	...	...	...

1.11 Gross domestic product by kind of activity, in constant prices

Million Ginea-Bissau pesos

	1986	1987	1988	1989	1990	1991	1992	1993	1994	1995	1996	1997
At constant prices of: 1986												
1 Agriculture, hunting, forestry and fishing	21997	24313	26630	27883	28918	29785	...	...	...	...	...	...
2 Mining and quarrying	31	10	5729	5932	5841	5780	...	...	...	...	...	...
3 Manufacturing	6959	6077	...				...	...	...	...	...	...
4 Electricity, gas and water	16	577	...				...	...	...	...	...	...
5 Construction	2621	1348	1804	1774	1890	1946	...	...	...	...	...	...
6 Wholesale and retail trade, restaurants and hotels	9267	10091	10928	11752	12598	13271	...	...	...	...	...	...
7 Transport, storage and communication	1337	1413	1538	1663	1718	1828	...	...	...	...	...	...
8 Finance, insurance, real estate and business services	248	1054	1220	1330	1432	1416	...	...	...	...	...	...
9 Community, social and personal services							...	...	...	...	...	...
Total, Industries	42476	44883	47849	50334	52397	54026	...	...	...	...	...	...
Producers of government services	4497	4740	5199	5100	4867	4954	...	...	...	...	...	...
Other producers	...	...	...	...	...	...	...	...	...	...	...	...
Subtotal	46973	49623	53047	55434	57263	58981	...	...	...	...	...	...
less: Imputed bank service charge	...	...	...	...	...	...	...	...	...	...	...	...
plus: Import duties	...	...	...	...	...	...	...	...	...	...	...	...
plus: Value added tax	...	...	...	...	...	...	...	...	...	...	...	...
plus: Other adjustments	...	...	...	...	...	...	...	...	...	...	...	...
equals: Gross domestic product	46973	49623	53047	55434	57263	58981	...	...	...	...	...	...

Guyana

Source

Reply to the United Nations National Accounts Questionnaire from the Statistical Bureau, Georgetown. Official estimates have been published by the Statistical Bureau in *Annual Statistical Abstract*.

General note

The estimates shown in the following tables have been prepared in accordance with the United Nations System of National Accounts (1968 SNA) so far as the existing data would permit.

1.1 Expenditure on the gross domestic product, in current prices

Million Guyana dollars

	1986	1987	1988	1989	1990	1991	1992	1993	1994	1995	1996	1997
1 Government final consumption expenditure	876	952	1162	1701	2133	4610	6383	7377	...	...	...	...
2 Private final consumption expenditure	1000	1715	2279	5987	9537	2150	2352	2913	...	...	...	...
3 Gross capital formation	586	1123	890	3536	6624	13746	25113	30118	...	...	...	...
A Increase in stocks	–	–	–	–	–	–	–	–	...	...	...	...
B Gross fixed capital formation	586	1123	890	3536	6624	13746	25113	30118	...	...	...	...
4 Exports of goods and services	1092	...	...	...	...	...	...	...	...	...	...	...
5 less: Imports of goods and services	1335	...	...	...	...	...	...	...	...	...	...	...
equals: Gross domestic product	2219	3357	4137	10330	15665	38966	46734	56647	...	...	...	...

1.10 Gross domestic product by kind of activity, in current prices

Million Guyana dollars

	1986	1987	1988	1989	1990	1991	1992	1993	1994	1995	1996	1997
1 Agriculture, hunting, forestry and fishing	544	1090	1085	4278	5973	15790	20467	21686	...	...	...	...
2 Mining and quarrying	116	171	360	1027	1392	5252	4549	8150	...	...	...	...
3 Manufacturing	188	234	311	555	713	1454	1760	1977	...	...	...	...
4 Electricity, gas and water									...	...	...	...
5 Construction [a]	124	148	246	434	620	1170	1405	1673	...	...	...	...
6 Wholesale and retail trade, restaurants and hotels [b]	134	162	290	500	915	1738	2016	2323	...	...	...	...
7 Transport, storage and communication	139	198	299	546	1056	2112	2312	2645	...	...	...	...
8 Finance, insurance, real estate and business services [c]	134	191	250	687	1661	3115	3650	3922	...	...	...	...
9 Community, social and personal services [bc]	55	72	125	225	310	553	664	746	...	...	...	...
Total, Industries	1434	2266	2966	8252	12640	31184	36823	43122	...	...	...	...
Producers of government services	387	585	633	822	1175	2438	3568	3996	...	...	...	...
Other producers	...	...	...	...	...	...	...	...	...	...	...	...
Subtotal [d]	1821	2851	3599	9074	13815	33622	40391	47118	...	...	...	...

Guyana

Million Guyana dollars

	1986	1987	1988	1989	1990	1991	1992	1993	1994	1995	1996	1997
less: Imputed bank service charge	...	...	...	...	...	...	...	...	...	...	...	...
plus: Import duties	...	...	...	...	...	...	...	...	...	...	...	...
plus: Value added tax	...	...	...	...	...	...	...	...	...	...	...	...
plus: Other adjustments [e]	399	506	538	1256	1850	5344	6343	9529	...	...	...	...
equals: Gross domestic product	2220	3357	4137	10330	15665	38966	46734	56647	...	...	...	...

a Item "Construction" includes engineering and sewage services.
b Restaurants and hotels are included in item "Community, social and personal services".
c Business services are included in item "Community, social and personal services".
d Gross domestic product in factor values.
e Item "Other adjustments" refers to indirect taxes net of subsidies.

1.11 Gross domestic product by kind of activity, in constant prices

Million Guyana dollars

	1986	1987	1988	1989	1990	1991	1992	1993	1994	1995	1996	1997
At constant prices of:	1977 / 1988											
1 Agriculture, hunting, forestry and fishing	223 / 1057	1023	936	909	784	881	1095	1160	...	...	...	...
2 Mining and quarrying	68 / 368	370	360	266	314	381	337	502	...	...	...	...
3 Manufacturing	93 / 499	478	460	426	370	409	488	505	...	...	...	...
4 Electricity, gas and water									...	...	...	...
5 Construction [a]	60 / 232	245	246	241	246	251	256	265	...	...	...	...
6 Wholesale and retail trade, restaurants and hotels [b]	58 / 259	275	290	278	287	301	316	338	...	...	...	...
7 Transport, storage and communication	63 / 257	289	299	284	290	290	299	317	...	...	...	...
8 Finance, insurance, real estate and business services [c]	59 / 232	249	250	259	266	266	270	280	...	...	...	...
9 Community, social and personal services [bc]	20 / 116	122	125	125	128	131	134	139	...	...	...	...
Total, Industries	644 / 3020	3051	2966	2788	2685	2910	3195	3507	...	...	...	...
Producers of government services	187 / 644	644	634	634	634	609	597	597	...	...	...	...
Other producers	...	...	...	...	...	...	...	...	...	...	...	...
Subtotal [d]	831 / 3664	3695	3600	3422	3319	3519	3792	4104	...	...	...	...
less: Imputed bank service charge	...	...	...	...	...	...	...	...	...	...	...	...
plus: Import duties	...	...	...	...	...	...	...	...	...	...	...	...
plus: Value added tax	...	...	...	...	...	...	...	...	...	...	...	...
plus: Other adjustments	...	...	...	...	...	...	...	...	...	...	...	...
equals: Gross domestic product	...	...	...	...	...	...	...	...	...	...	...	...

a Item "Construction" includes engineering and sewage services.
b Restaurants and hotels are included in item "Community, social and personal services".
c Business services are included in item "Community, social and personal services".
d Gross domestic product in factor values.

Haiti

Source

Reply to the United Nations National Accounts Questionnaire from the Institut Haitien de Statistique, Port-au-Prince. The official estimates are published by the Institut in *Le Bulletin de Statistique, Supplément Annuel de l'Institut*.

General note

The estimates shown in the following tables have been prepared in accordance with the United Nations System of National Accounts (1968 SNA) so far as the existing data would permit.

1.1 Expenditure on the gross domestic product, in current prices

Million Haitian gourdes — Fiscal year ending 30 September

	1986	1987	1988	1989	1990	1991	1992	1993	1994	1995	1996	1997
1 Government final consumption expenditure	10472	9156	9579	10081	11661	13755	15321	21344	31310	38063	45374	53699
2 Private final consumption expenditure												
3 Gross capital formation	1620	1545	1500	1791	1866	2221	1376	1487	1857	4867	6279	6432
A Increase in stocks	...	...	...	...	...	...	...	...	...	...	...	...
B Gross fixed capital formation	1620	1545	1500	1791	1866	2221	1376	1487	1857	4867	6279	6432
4 Exports of goods and services	2340	2860	2542	2143	2371	2609	1346	1912	1942	3845	4112	4694
5 less: Imports of goods and services	3245	3767	3766	2688	2830	4395	3022	4849	4173	11568	12532	13036
equals: Gross domestic product	11188	9794	9855	11327	13068	14190	15020	19894	30936	35207	43234	51789

1.2 Expenditure on the gross domestic product, in constant prices

Million Haitian gourdes — Fiscal year ending 30 September

	1986	1987	1988	1989	1990	1991	1992	1993	1994	1995	1996	1997
At constant prices of: 1976												
1 Government final consumption expenditure	4759	4725	4969	4778	4729	4647	4675	5354	4921	5825	5820	5887
2 Private final consumption expenditure												
3 Gross capital formation	987	997	955	901	866	835	500	463	430	811	799	787
A Increase in stocks	...	...	...	...	...	...	...	...	...	...	...	...
B Gross fixed capital formation	987	997	955	901	866	835	500	463	430	811	799	787
4 Exports of goods and services	1259	1536	1496	1186	1343	1465	764	796	670	1011	1078	1161
5 less: Imports of goods and services	1930	2220	2144	1531	1610	1605	1301	2087	1870	3313	3246	3333
equals: Gross domestic product	5075	5037	5275	5334	5329	5342	4638	4525	4150	4334	4451	4502

Haiti

1.7 External transactions on current account, summary

Million Haitian gourdes	1986	1987	1988	1989	1990	1991	1992	1993	1994	1995	1996	1997
Payments to the rest of the world												
1 Imports of goods and services	3245	3767	3766	2688	2830	4395	3022	4849	4173	11568	12422	13036
2 Factor income to rest of the world	...	131	167	151	148	272	74	160	126	445	172	221
3 Current transfers to the rest of the world	267	285	304	317	321	433	...	...	...	...	...	...
4 Surplus of the nation on current transactions	−246	−158	−395	198	248	−226	−380	−963	78	−144	−798	−1264
Payments to the rest of the world and surplus of the nation on current transfers	...	4026	3841	3354	3547	4874	2716	4046	4377	11869	11796	11993
Receipts from the rest of the world												
1 Exports of goods and services	2340	2860	2542	2143	2371	2609	1346	1912	1942	3845	4383	4694
2 Factor income from rest of the world	...	26	31	22	23	40	...	...	...	...	...	...
3 Current transfers from rest of the world	1026	1140	1268	1189	1153	2239	1370	2134	2435	8024	7413	7299
Receipts from the rest of the world on current transactions	...	4026	3841	3354	3547	4888	2716	4046	4377	11869	11796	11993

1.8 Capital transactions of the nation, summary

Million Haitian gourdes	1986	1987	1988	1989	1990	1991	1992	1993	1994	1995	1996	1997
Finance of gross capital formation												
Gross saving	1375	1387	1078	1954	2452	1995	995	523	1935	3990	4092	4176
1 Consumption of fixed capital	257	246	239	285	297	351	256	264	329	775	1000	1025
2 Net saving	1117	1141	839	1669	2155	1644	740	259	1607	3214	3091	3151
less: Surplus of the nation on current transactions	−246	−158	−395	198	248	−226	−380	−963	78	−144	−798	−1264
Statistical discrepancy	...	...	27	35	−338	...	...	...	...	733	1389	992
Finance of gross capital formation	1620	1545	1500	1791	1866	2221	1376	1487	1857	4867	6279	6432
Gross capital formation												
Increase in stocks	...	...	...	...	...	...	...	...	...	...	...	...
Gross fixed capital formation	1620	1545	1500	1791	1866	2221	1376	1487	1857	4867	6279	6432
Gross capital formation	1620	1545	1500	1791	1866	2221	1376	1487	1857	4867	6279	6432

1.11 Gross domestic product by kind of activity, in constant prices

Million Haitian gourdes	1986	1987	1988	1989	1990	1991	1992	1993	1994	1995	1996	1997
At constant prices of: 1976												
1 Agriculture, hunting, forestry and fishing	1670	1688	1914	1914	1869	1932	1919	1748	1551	1395	1390	1356
2 Mining and quarrying	5	8	8	7	7	7	6	7	6	7	8	9
3 Manufacturing	814	783	776	787	806	660	357	310	285	312	322	324
4 Electricity, gas and water	47	49	54	56	56	51	41	42	29	38	43	42
5 Construction	308	315	320	323	310	321	250	318	303	398	467	520

Haiti

Million Haitian gourdes	1986	1987	1988	1989	1990	1991	1992	1993	1994	1995	1996	1997
At constant prices of: 1976												
6 Wholesale and retail trade, restaurants and hotels	912	902	900	900	901	870	611	585	481	598	600	604
7 Transport, storage and communication	88	99	105	108	113	106	97	92	87	93	96	97
8 Finance, insurance, real estate and business services	290	291	278	283	290	314	323	330	336	343	351	358
9 Community, social and personal services	202	177	176	186	193	180	186	202	196	211	210	211
Statistical discrepancy	...	...	−189	...	...	...	...	...	...	...	...	...
Total, Industries	4336	4313	4531	4564	4545	4441	3790	3633	3275	3395	3487	3521
Producers of government services	596	605	645	653	670	755	774	799	817	812	821	820
Other producers	...	...	...	...	...	...	...	...	...	...	...	...
Subtotal	4932	4918	5176	5217	5215	5196	4564	4432	4091	4207	4308	4341
less: Imputed bank service charge	...	...	...	...	...	...	...	...	...	...	...	...
plus: Import duties	143	119	99	118	113	146	74	93	58	127	143	161
plus: Value added tax	...	...	...	...	...	...	...	...	...	...	...	...
plus: Other adjustments	...	...	...	...	...	...	...	...	...	...	...	...
equals: Gross domestic product	5075	5037	5275	5334	5329	5342	4638	4525	4150	4334	4451	4502

1.12 Relations among national accounting aggregates

Million Haitian gourdes	1986	1987	1988	1989	1990	1991	1992	1993	1994	1995	1996	1997
Gross domestic product	11188	9794	9855	11327	13068	14190	15020	19894	30936	35207	43234	51789
plus: Net factor income from the rest of the world	−100	−105	−136	−128	−125	−232	−74	−160	−126	−445	−172	−221
Factor income from rest of the world	...	26	31	23	23	40	...	...	...	...	...	...
less: Factor income to the rest of the world	...	131	167	151	148	272	74	160	126	445	172	221
equals: Gross national product	11088	9689	9719	11199	12943	13958	14946	19734	30810	34762	43062	51568
less: Consumption of fixed capital	257	246	239	285	297	351	256	264	329	775	1000	1025
equals: National income	10831	9443	9480	10914	12646	13607	14690	19470	30481	33987	42062	50543
plus: Net current transfers from the rest of the world	759	855	965	872	832	1806	1370	2134	2436	8024	7413	7299
Current transfers from rest of the world	1026	1140	1268	1189	1153	2239	1370	2134	2436	8024	7413	7299
less: Current transfers to the rest of the world	267	285	303	317	321	433	...	...	...	...	...	...
equals: National disposable income	11590	10298	10445	11786	13478	15413	16060	21604	32917	42011	49475	57842
less: Final consumption	10472	9156	9579	10081	11661	13755	15321	21344	31310	38063	45374	53699
equals: Net saving	1117	1141	866	1705	1817	1658	739	260	1607	3948	4101	4143
less: Surplus of the nation on current transactions	−246	−158	−395	198	248	−226	−380	−963	78	−144	−798	−1264
Statistical discrepancy	...	...	...	...	...	...	...	...	...	...	380	...
equals: Net capital formation	1363	1299	1261	1507	1569	1884	1119	1223	1529	4092	5279	5407

Honduras

General note

The preparation of national accounts statistics in Honduras is undertaken by the Departamento de Estudios Económicos, Banco Central de Honduras, Tegucigalpa, D.C. The official estimates are published in *Cuentas Nacionales*. A detailed description of sources and methods used for the national accounts estimation is found in *Metodologíia de cuentas nacionales de los paises centroamericanos* issued by the Consejo Monetario Centroamericano in October 1976. The estimates are generally in accordance with the classifications and definitions recommended in the United Nations System of National Accounts (1968 SNA) so far as the existing data would permit. The following tables have been prepared from successive replies to the United Nations National Accounts Questionnaire. When the scope and coverage of the estimates differ for conceptual or statistical reasons from the definitions and classifications recommended in SNA, a footnote is indicated to the relevant tables.

Gross domestic product

Gross domestic product is estimated mainly through the production approach.

Expenditures on the gross domestic product

The expenditure approach is used to estimate government final consumption expenditure and exports and imports of goods and services. The commodity-flow approach is used for private final consumption expenditure and for gross capital formation. Government final consumption expenditure is estimated on the basis of government accounts. Changes in stocks are estimated on the basis of information obtained from various sectors such as the banana industry, the mines, the petroleum sector and the trade enterprises. Private investment consists of gross value of production in the construction sector, plus imports and domestic production of capital goods which are adjusted to purchasers' values. Public investment is estimated from public sector data on settlements by type of construction and classes of machinery and equipment. The estimates of exports and imports of goods and services are based on the balance of payment data. Private consumption expenditure is estimated as a residual. For the constant price estimates, private final consumption expenditure is estimated as a residual while all other items of GDP by expenditure type are deflated by various price indexes.

Cost structure of the gross domestic product

Estimates of labour income are derived from sources such as censuses and surveys, supplemented by information on wages and salaries paid by various government agencies and other public bodies. Estimates of profits of enterprises and professional incomes are obtained from the Dirección General del Impuesto sobre la Renta. Estimates of interest and dividend payments received by household and private non-profit institutions are derived as a residual. Indirect taxes and subsidies are estimated on the basis of government sources. For consumption of fixed capital, no specific information is available.

Gross domestic product by kind of activity

The table of gross domestic product by kind of economic activity is prepared in factor values. The production approach is used to estimate value added of most industries. The income approach is, however, used to estimate value added of producers of government services, part of the transport sectors and other private services. For the agricultural crop production, information is obtained directly from the most important export enterprises while for other products, estimates are obtained from consumption per capita data adjusted for exports and imports. Surveys are conducted to obtain information on basic production of grains. Agricultural censuses were held in 1953, 1965 and 1974. The Instituto Hondureño del Café provides complete information for coffee production. The banana companies in the northern zone are visited annually while for the rest of the country, consumption per capita data are taken into account together with prices collected from native producers. Livestock production information is gathered from the most important producers with adjustments made for clandestine or uncontrolled transaction. Inputs are estimated as 30 percent of the gross value of production. The production in the forestry sector is calculated as a function of household and industrial consumption of firewood, and extrapolated by an index. The estimates of fishing are calculated on the basis of information from the Dirección General de Pesca, the foreign trade statistics and per capita consumption data. For metal mining, the statistical information is obtained directly while estimates for non-metallic mineral are based on inputs used in the construction sector using certain coefficients derived from analysis of construction costs. The estimates of manufacturing are based on censuses, surveys and sample data provided by the Dirección General de Industrias and the Departamento de Estudios Industriales. Information on electricity, gas and water is obtained directly from concerned enterprises. The data available cover gross values of production, aggregated values, physical production, installed capacity and personal occupation.

Information on public construction is taken directly from the municipalities. Based on the information obtained from them, a sample is taken from which the growth of private construction can be measured. The population and housing censuses are also taken into account for dwellings. For the trade sector, the estimates are based on the gross value of agricultural and industrial

Honduras

production by item. The value of imports and exports are estimated from foreign trade statistics and information received from the Direccion de Tributación Directa. In estimating road transport, information on registered vehicles for rental is used. Data on income and expenditure by type of vehicle, depreciation and profits are obtained. Information for financial institutions is obtained from the Superintendencia de Bancos, which provides financial statements for all banks in the system and insurance companies. The estimates of ownership of dwellings are based on census information for 1949, 1961 and 1974 covering the number of dwellings and the average rents paid and imputed. For producers of government services, information is obtained directly from the Contaduría General de la Nación and the Asesoría Técnica Municipal. For private services, use is made of employment data, classified by type of service rendered and data on average wages and salaries from other information sources. For domestic services, data on employment and wages are basis for estimating the value added with 75 per cent added to the cash figures for board and lodging as wages and salaries in kind.

For the constant price estimates, value added of the agricultural sector is either extrapolated by quantity indexes for output or deflated by price indexes. For the industrial activity sector, trade, transport and storage, financial institutions and insurance and private services, value added is extrapolated by quantity index. For the remaining sectors, current values are deflated by various price indexes.

1.1 Expenditure on the gross domestic product, in current prices

Million Honduran lempiras

	1986	1987	1988	1989	1990	1991	1992	1993	1994	1995	1996	1997
1 Government final consumption expenditure	1087	1181	1308	1475	1621	1769	2171	2405	2780	3495	4556	5377
2 Private final consumption expenditure	5606	5916	6245	7226	8379	11021	12520	14717	18114	23818	31093	39643
3 Gross capital formation	1055	1446	1942	1978	2881	4022	4881	7614	10861	11836	14510	18318
A Increase in stocks	10	314	513	94	348	926	679	1079	2751	2842	3400	3893
B Gross fixed capital formation	1045	1132	1429	1884	2533	3096	4202	6535	8110	8994	11110	14425
4 Exports of goods and services	2025	1907	2432	3204	4664	5632	6048	7869	11498	16391	22435	28417
5 less: Imports of goods and services	2156	2145	2676	3549	5008	6130	6820	9916	14391	18033	24821	30670
equals: Gross domestic product	7617	8305	9251	10334	12537	16314	18800	22689	28862	37507	47774	61084

1.2 Expenditure on the gross domestic product, in constant prices

Million Honduran lempiras

	1986	1987	1988	1989	1990	1991	1992	1993	1994	1995	1996	1997
At constant prices of: 1978												
1 Government final consumption expenditure	563	597	651	669	579	520	587	532	505	491	517	507
2 Private final consumption expenditure	3164	3212	3279	3452	3464	3637	3716	3879	3897	3963	4179	4425
3 Gross capital formation	596	777	994	957	988	1165	1310	1693	1817	1871	1761	1754
A Increase in stocks	5	147	230	37	111	286	194	177	303	574	422	280
B Gross fixed capital formation	591	630	764	920	877	879	1116	1516	1514	1297	1339	1474
4 Exports of goods and services	1527	1564	1550	1629	1637	1604	1732	1713	1540	1749	1890	1908
5 less: Imports of goods and services	1390	1421	1527	1546	1502	1592	1711	1832	1852	1926	1973	1936
equals: Gross domestic product	4460	4729	4947	5161	5166	5334	5634	5985	5907	6148	6374	6658

1.3 Cost components of the gross domestic product

Million Honduran lempiras

	1986	1987	1988	1989	1990	1991	1992	1993	1994	1995	1996	1997
1 Indirect taxes, net	811	944	1033	1078	1381	2339	2669	3194	4092	4881	6603	8212
A Indirect taxes	880	983	1059	1098	1674	2381	2717	3314	4230	4976	6733	8332
B less: Subsidies	69	39	26	20	293	42	48	120	138	95	130	120

Honduras

Million Honduran lempiras

	1986	1987	1988	1989	1990	1991	1992	1993	1994	1995	1996	1997
2 Consumption of fixed capital	534	571	608	654	872	1115	1214	1372	1707	2258	2798	3335
3 Compensation of employees paid by resident producers to ..	3771	4021	4366	4746	5636	6644	8166	9197	11036	14304	17708	20352
4 Operating surplus	2501	2769	3244	3856	4648	6216	6751	8926	12027	16064	20665	29185
equals: Gross domestic product ..	7617	8305	9251	10334	12537	16314	18800	22689	28862	37507	47774	61084

1.7 External transactions on current account, summary

Million Honduran lempiras

	1986	1987	1988	1989	1990	1991	1992	1993	1994	1995	1996	1997
Payments to the rest of the world												
1 Imports of goods and services	2156	2145	2676	3549	5008	6130	6820	9916	14391	18033	24821	30670
A Imports of merchandise, c.i.f.	2025	2008	2375	3126	4441	5405	6028	8789	12915	16315	22589	27998
B Other	131	137	301	423	567	725	792	1127	1476	1718	2232	2672
2 Factor income to rest of the world	444	498	601	781	1180	1566	1931	1606	2028	2839	3467	3644
3 Current transfers to the rest of the world	25	26	31	36	51	54	57	8	10	11	14	16
4 Surplus of the nation on current transactions	–234	–328	–261	–509	–230	–932	–1433	–2126	–2942	–1675	–2223	–1314
Payments to the rest of the world and surplus of the nation on current transfers	2391	2341	3047	3857	6009	6818	7375	9404	13487	19208	26079	33016
Receipts from the rest of the world												
1 Exports of goods and services	2025	1907	2432	3204	4664	5632	6048	7869	11498	16391	22435	28417
A Exports of merchandise, f.o.b.	1808	1661	2090	2725	4002	4539	4656	5925	8560	12289	16658	19963
B Other	217	246	342	479	662	1093	1392	1944	2939	4102	5778	8454
2 Factor income from rest of the world	24	23	31	41	44	67	72	108	202	306	390	527
3 Current transfers from rest of the world	342	411	584	612	1301	1119	1256	1427	1786	2511	3254	4072
Receipts from the rest of the world on current transactions	2391	2341	3047	3857	6009	6818	7375	9404	13486	19208	26079	33016

1.8 Capital transactions of the nation, summary

Million Honduran lempiras

	1986	1987	1988	1989	1990	1991	1992	1993	1994	1995	1996	1997
Finance of gross capital formation												
Gross saving	821	1118	1682	1469	2651	3090	3449	5488	7950	10134	12284	16757
1 Consumption of fixed capital	534	571	608	654	872	1115	1214	1372	1707	2258	2798	3335
2 Net saving	287	547	1074	815	1779	1975	2235	4116	6243	7876	9486	13422
less: Surplus of the nation on current transactions	–234	–328	–261	–509	–230	–932	–1432	–2127	–2942	–1675	–2223	–1314
Statistical discrepancy	...	...	...	...	...	...	...	...	–31	27	...	247
Finance of gross capital formation	1055	1446	1942	1978	2881	4022	4881	7614	10861	11836	14510	18318
Gross capital formation												
Increase in stocks	10	314	513	94	348	926	679	1079	2751	2842	3400	3893
Gross fixed capital formation	1045	1132	1429	1884	2533	3096	4202	6535	8110	8994	11110	14425
1 General government	447	425	467	589	823	1168	1948	2824	3202	3757	3835	3496

Honduras

Million Honduran lempiras

	1986	1987	1988	1989	1990	1991	1992	1993	1994	1995	1996	1997
2 Corporate and quasi-corporate enterprises	598	707	962	1295	1710	1928	2254	3711	4908	5237	7275	10929
3 Other	...	...	...	...	...	...	...	...	...	...	...	...
Gross capital formation	1055	1446	1942	1978	2881	4022	4881	7614	10861	11836	14510	18318

1.10 Gross domestic product by kind of activity, in current prices

Million Honduran lempiras

	1986	1987	1988	1989	1990	1991	1992	1993	1994	1995	1996	1997
1 Agriculture, hunting, forestry and fishing	1400	1539	1742	1951	2503	3178	3286	4014	6030	7026	9188	11971
2 Mining and quarrying	114	83	126	158	191	206	308	369	454	629	763	920
3 Manufacturing	972	1070	1244	1389	1823	2367	2875	3456	4275	5818	7455	9535
4 Electricity, gas and water	229	236	241	276	353	497	530	589	939	1778	2540	3263
5 Construction	286	302	365	464	574	745	1061	1457	1465	1791	1900	2268
6 Wholesale and retail trade, restaurants and hotels	915	961	1027	1089	1289	1567	1762	2056	2555	3919	4903	6264
7 Transport, storage and communication	462	509	567	648	703	909	1048	1116	1309	1546	1824	2557
8 Finance, insurance, real estate and business services	1033	1129	1259	1433	1616	2015	2370	2816	3646	4839	5995	8002
9 Community, social and personal services	787	880	963	1075	1290	1441	1704	2113	2550	3372	4174	5196
Total, Industries	6198	6709	7534	8483	10342	12925	14944	17986	23223	30714	38742	49976
Producers of government services	608	652	684	773	814	1050	1187	1509	1547	1912	2429	2896
Other producers	...	...	...	...	...	...	...	...	...	...	...	...
Subtotal [a]	6806	7361	8218	9256	11156	13975	16131	19495	24770	32626	41171	52872
less: Imputed bank service charge	...	...	...	...	...	...	...	...	...	...	...	...
plus: Import duties	...	...	...	...	...	...	...	...	...	...	...	...
plus: Value added tax	...	...	...	...	...	...	...	...	...	...	...	...
plus: Other adjustments [b]	811	944	1033	1078	1381	2339	2669	3194	4092	4881	6603	8212
equals: Gross domestic product	7617	8305	9251	10334	12537	16314	18800	22689	28862	37507	47774	61084

a Gross domestic product in factor values.   b Item "Other adjustments" refers to indirect taxes net of subsidies.

1.11 Gross domestic product by kind of activity, in constant prices

Million Honduran lempiras

	1986	1987	1988	1989	1990	1991	1992	1993	1994	1995	1996	1997
At constant prices of: 1978												
1 Agriculture, hunting, forestry and fishing	1072	1161	1155	1271	1285	1364	1413	1404	1415	1540	1578	1629
2 Mining and quarrying	83	51	69	78	72	75	83	86	83	96	103	108
3 Manufacturing	606	646	678	704	709	721	765	813	798	842	881	935
4 Electricity, gas and water	82	96	108	113	128	129	130	140	130	149	172	185
5 Construction	177	184	211	242	218	212	284	344	282	264	234	240
6 Wholesale and retail trade, restaurants and hotels	507	517	531	507	503	514	529	572	572	604	631	653
7 Transport, storage and communication	334	348	372	396	411	423	441	456	443	477	498	532
8 Finance, insurance, real estate and business services	505	536	587	625	648	690	736	796	840	893	939	1005
9 Community, social and personal services	360	384	406	410	406	380	406	451	449	449	446	459
Total, Industries	3726	3923	4117	4346	4380	4508	4787	5062	5013	5314	5482	5746

Honduras

Million Honduran lempiras

	1986	1987	1988	1989	1990	1991	1992	1993	1994	1995	1996	1997
At constant prices of: 1978												
Producers of government services	314	329	331	341	291	280	291	334	281	269	275	273
Other producers	...	...	...	...	...	...	...	...	...	...	...	...
Subtotal [a]	4040	4252	4448	4687	4671	4788	5078	5396	5294	5583	5757	6019
less: Imputed bank service charge	...	...	...	...	...	...	...	...	...	...	...	...
plus: Import duties	...	...	...	...	...	...	...	...	...	...	...	...
plus: Value added tax	...	...	...	...	...	...	...	...	...	...	...	...
plus: Other adjustments [b]	420	477	499	474	495	546	556	589	613	565	617	639
equals: Gross domestic product	4460	4729	4947	5161	5166	5334	5634	5985	5907	6148	6374	6658

a Gross domestic product in factor values.   b Item "Other adjustments" refers to indirect taxes net of subsidies.

1.12 Relations among national accounting aggregates

Million Honduran lempiras

	1986	1987	1988	1989	1990	1991	1992	1993	1994	1995	1996	1997
Gross domestic product	7617	8305	9251	10334	12537	16314	18800	22689	28862	37507	47774	61084
plus: Net factor income from the rest of the world	–420	–475	–570	–740	–1136	–1499	–1859	–1498	–1826	–2533	–3081	–3117
Factor income from rest of the world	24	23	31	41	44	67	72	108	202	306	390	527
less: Factor income to the rest of the world	444	498	601	781	1180	1566	1931	1606	2028	2839	3471	3644
equals: Gross national product	7197	7830	8681	9594	11401	14815	16941	21191	27036	34974	44693	57967
less: Consumption of fixed capital	534	571	608	654	872	1115	1214	1372	1707	2258	2798	3335
equals: National income	6663	7259	8073	8940	10529	13700	15727	19819	25329	32716	41895	54632
plus: Net current transfers from the rest of the world	317	385	554	576	1250	1065	1199	1419	1776	2500	3240	4056
Current transfers from rest of the world	342	411	584	612	1301	1119	1256	1427	1786	2511	3254	4072
less: Current transfers to the rest of the world	25	26	31	36	51	54	57	8	10	11	14	16
equals: National disposable income	6980	7644	8627	9516	11779	14765	16926	21238	27105	35216	45135	58688
less: Final consumption	6693	7097	7553	8701	10000	12790	14691	17122	20894	27313	35649	45019
Statistical discrepancy	...	...	...	...	...	...	...	...	32	–27	...	–247
equals: Net saving	287	547	1074	815	1779	1975	2235	4116	6243	7876	9486	13422
less: Surplus of the nation on current transactions	–234	–328	–260	–509	–230	–932	–1432	–2127	–2942	–1675	–2223	–1314
Statistical discrepancy	...	...	...	...	...	...	...	...	–32	27	...	247
equals: Net capital formation	521	875	1335	1324	2009	2907	3667	6243	9154	9578	11712	14983

2.1 Government final consumption expenditure by function, in current prices

Million Honduran lempiras

	1986	1987	1988	1989	1990	1991	1992	1993	1994	1995	1996	1997
1 General public services	468	413	325	410	440	460	617	667	791	973	1183	1669
2 Defence	211	245	254	265	248	251	284	258	287	332	373	395
3 Public order and safety	...	...	...	...	...	...	...	...	...	...	...	...
4 Education	315	366	402	430	507	552	688	804	961	1367	1672	1894
5 Health	120	141	244	270	328	386	454	569	624	716	1256	1340
6 Social security and welfare	...	...	...	...	...	...	...	...	...	...	...	...
7 Housing and community amenities	...	...	...	...	...	...	...	...	...	...	...	...

Honduras

Million Honduran lempiras

	1986	1987	1988	1989	1990	1991	1992	1993	1994	1995	1996	1997
8 Recreational, cultural and religious affairs	...	...	...	...	...	...	...	...	...	...	...	...
9 Economic services	...	...	...	...	...	...	...	...	...	...	...	...
10 Other functions	183	206	83	100	98	120	128	107	118	107	72	79
Total government final consumption expenditures	1087	1181	1308	1475	1621	1769	2171	2405	2781	3495	4556	5377

2.17 Exports and imports of goods and services, detail

Million Honduran lempiras

	1986	1987	1988	1989	1990	1991	1992	1993	1994	1995	1996	1997
Exports of goods and services												
1 Exports of merchandise, f.o.b.	1808	1661	2090	2725	4002	4539	4657	5925	8560	12289	16658	19963
2 Transport and communication	...	...	106	153	203	355	393	490	693	822	1131	1352
A In respect of merchandise imports	...	...	21	29	43	49	50	59	90	109	165	195
B Other	...	...	85	124	160	306	343	431	603	713	966	1157
3 Insurance service charges	...	...	...	...	...	...	...	...	...	...	...	...
A In respect of merchandise imports	...	...	2	3	4	5	5	12	12	39	30	38
B Other	...	...	...	...	...	...	...	...	...	...	...	...
4 Other commodities	...	...	234	323	456	737	994	1442	2233	3241	4616	7064
5 Adjustments of merchandise exports to change-of-ownership basis	...	...	...	...	...	...	...	...	...	...	...	...
6 Direct purchases in the domestic market by non-residential households	...	...	...	...	...	...	...	...	...	...	...	...
7 Direct purchases in the domestic market by extraterritorial bodies	...	...	...	...	...	...	...	...	...	...	...	...
Total exports of goods and services	2025	1907	2432	3204	4664	5632	6048	7869	11498	16391	22435	28417
Imports of goods and services												
1 Imports of merchandise, c.i.f.	2025	2008	2375	3126	4441	5405	6028	8790	12915	16315	22589	27998
A Imports of merchandise, f.o.b.	1759	1743	2170	2858	4054	4928	5496	8014	11778	14878	20597	25537
B Transport of services on merchandise imports	266	265	188	246	354	434	485	717	1053	1333	1840	2258
C Insurance service charges on merchandise imports			17	22	33	43	47	59	84	104	152	203
2 Adjustments of merchandise imports to change-of-ownership basis	...	...	...	...	...	...	...	...	...	...	...	...
3 Other transport and communication	...	...	28	70	74	114	124	285	454	571	772	875
4 Other insurance service charges	...	...	59	86	112	135	150	77	63	63	101	137
5 Other commodities	131	137	214	267	381	477	519	765	959	1084	1359	1660
6 Direct purchases abroad by government	...	...	...	...	...	...	...	...	...	...	...	...
7 Direct purchases abroad by resident households	...	...	...	...	...	...	...	...	...	...	...	...
Total imports of goods and services	2156	2145	2676	3549	5008	6130	6820	9916	14391	18033	24821	30670
Balance of goods and services	−131	−238	−244	−345	−344	−498	−772	−2047	−2893	−1642	−2386	−2253
Total imports and balance of goods and services	2025	1907	2432	3204	4664	5632	6048	7869	11498	16391	22435	28417

Hungary

General note

The compilation of national accounts statistics in Hungary is undertaken by the Hungarian Central Statistical Office. The official estimates are published in the *Statisztikai Evkonyv* (Statistical Yearbook). Detailed data are published in the series of *National Accounts, Hungary*. The most relevant long-time series were published in the *Nepgazdasagi merlegek 1947–1988* and *National Accounts, Hungary, 1991–1994*. The description of the sources and methods used for the national accounts estimation are published in the joint OECD/HCSO publication: *National Accounts for Hungary—Sources, Methods and Estimations*. From 1991 the estimations are in accordance with the 1993 SNA and ISIC Rev.3 (sources and methods concerning the earlier periods are described in previous UN national accounts publications). As a general rule the statistical units are institutional units. Only the government production is shown by establishments. When the scope and coverage of the estimates differ for conceptual or statistical reasons from the definitions and classifications recommended in 1993 SNA, a footnote is indicated to the relevant tables.

Substantial changes were introduced in the compilation of national accounts from 1991. The most important ones are as follows: (a) the output of financial intermediaries was measured on cost level before the revision, presently the service charges are accounted as the output of this sector; (b) owner-occupied dwellings are valued on imputed market rents (prior to 1991 they were accounted on costs); (c) consumption of fixed capital in the government sector is based on replacement cost (prior to 1991 they were based on historical costs); (d) financial leasing and capital contribution in kind are included in gross fixed capital formation. The base years for the constant price estimations are 1976, 1988 and 1991. (For every base year two data series are given. Some methodological changes were introduced in the base year as well.)

Gross domestic product

Gross domestic product is estimated from three approaches: production, expenditure and cost structure (income side). The main approach used for the estimation of GDP is the production approach.

Expenditures on the gross domestic product

The expenditure approach is used to estimate all expenditure type components of GDP. Government final consumption expenditure is based on records from all subsectors of general government. Private final consumption expenditure is estimated mainly from household budget survey and partly from trade statistics. The main sources for estimation of gross fixed capital formation are the investment surveys. Exports and imports of goods are based on customs declaration, while exports and imports of services are obtained from the balance of payments. For the calculation of constant prices, price deflation is used for all expenditure groups.

Cost structure of the gross domestic product

Compensation of employees is estimated from tax declarations of corporations, income tax declarations, labour surveys, financial data for general government and social security statistics. Taxes and subsidies on products are taken directly from the general government accounts.

Gross domestic product by kind of activity

The table of value added by kind of activity is prepared at basic prices. The main sources of the estimation at current prices are: financial tax reports of corporations, state budget, income tax statistics, agricultural statistics, reports of financial intermediaries and nonprofit surveys. Double deflation is used for the calculations at constant prices, except agriculture and trade margin. Government production is an exception where the cost elements are deflated.

Hungary

1.1 Expenditure on the gross domestic product, in current prices

Million Hungarian forints

	1986	1987	1988	1989	1990	1991	1992	1993	1994	1995	1996	1997
1 Government final consumption expenditure	219335	239078	289989 320663[a]	363075[a]	457973[a]	590932[a] 641400	780600	1013500	1145400	1368100	...	...
2 Private final consumption expenditure	592144	665723	721924 716366[b]	844251[b]	1046338[b]	1303792[b] 1370200	1696900	2117800	2533400	2995300	...	...
A Households	...	...	...	...	...	1354100	1670800	2061500	2458300	2911900	...	...
B Private non-profit institutions serving households	...	...	...	...	...	16100	26100	56300	75100	83400	...	...
3 Gross capital formation	292739	327484	358947 364678	458103	530433	480748 510900	473000	708100	968600	1252200	...	...
A Increase in stocks	31561	23947	63375 53877[c]	85615[c]	129915[c]	39880[c] −12000	−111700	38100	90100	192600	...	...
B Gross fixed capital formation	261178	303537	295572 310801	372488	400518	440868 522900	584700	670000	878500	1059600	...	...
4 Exports of goods and services	431585	464391	530395 530395[d]	620857[d]	650704[d]	834913[d] 818400	925300	937000	1262500	1914800	...	...
5 less: Imports of goods and services	447003	470306	491738 491738[e]	563453[e]	596135[e]	901981[e] 842600	933200	1228100	1545100	2036600	...	...
Statistical discrepancy					−12075		...	...	...	...	...	...
equals: Gross domestic product	1088800	1226370	1409517 1440364	1710758	2089313	2308404 2498300	2942600	3548300	4364800	5493800	...	...

a Until 1991 item "Government final consumption expenditure" includes health, social and cultural expenditure of enterprises and final consumption expenditure of non-profit institutions, and gross output of financial services and insurance is valued at cost level.
b Item "Private final consumption expenditure" covers total final consumption expenditure in domestic market of households. From 1988 to 1991, consumption from own-account production is evaluated at basic prices. The wage-like part of the business travel cost (i.e. per diem) is treated as private consumption expenditure.
c Until 1991 item "Increase in stocks" includes gains or losses arising from fluctuations in prices.
d Until 1991 Item "Exports of goods and services" excludes direct purchases in the domestic market by non-resident households.
e Until 1991 item "Imports of goods and services" excludes direct purchases abroad by resident households, except purchase of cars by Hungarian individuals for own use.

1.2 Expenditure on the gross domestic product, in constant prices

Million Hungarian forints

	1986	1987	1988	1989	1990	1991	1992	1993	1994	1995	1996	1997
At constant prices of:	1981		1988			1991						
1 Government final consumption expenditure	166519	168736	171802 332448[a]	327428[a]	324958[a]	316217[a] 641352	634547	696763	645267	625500	...	...
2 Private final consumption expenditure	433166	450521	430098 716366[b]	730158[b]	704454[b]	659129[b] 1370193	1389355	1437281	1439968	1915800	...	...
A Households	...	...	...	...	...	1354114	1366495	1397064	1394690	1290300	...	...
B Private non-profit institutions serving households	...	...	...	...	...	16079	22860	40217	45278	43000	...	...

Hungary

Million Hungarian forints

	1986	1987	1988	1989	1990	1991	1992	1993	1994	1995	1996	1997
At constant prices of:	1981											
			1988									
				1991								
3 Gross capital formation	202581	208997	202201								...	...
			360742	365214	349747	276224						
						510994	406963	538602	645186	686000		
A Increase in stocks	7246	−5560	7214								...	...
			49941	32685	40947	−376						
						−11951	−102179	19119	60922	127000		
B Gross fixed capital formation	195335	214557	194987								...	...
			310801	332529	308800	276600						
						522945	509142	519483	584264	559000		
4 Exports of goods and services	373406	391140	416375								...	...
			530395[c]	536815[c]	508132[c]	492506[c]						
						818407	835607	750882	853903	968400		
5 less: Imports of goods and services	343653	353668	355315								...	...
			491738[d]	500737[d]	479425[d]	505353[d]						
						842627	844708	1015714	1105548	1097700		
Statistical discrepancy	...	...	...	...	...		...	...	...	...	...	...
						1719						
equals: Gross domestic product	832019	865726	865161								...	...
			1448213	1458878	1407866	1240442						
							2498319	2421764	2407814	2478776	2515500	

a Until 1991 item "Government final consumption expenditure" includes health, social and cultural expenditure of enterprises and final consumption expenditure of non-profit institutions, and gross output of financial services and insurance is valued at cost level.

b Item "Private final consumption expenditure" covers total final consumption expenditure in domestic market of households. From 1988 to 1991, consumption from own-account production is evaluated at basic prices. The wage-like part of the business travel cost (i.e. per diem) is treated as private consumption expenditure.

c Until 1991 Item "Exports of goods and services" excludes direct purchases in the domestic market by non-resident households.

d Until 1991 item "Imports of goods and services" excludes direct purchases abroad by resident households, except purchase of cars by Hungarian individuals for own use.

1.3 Cost components of the gross domestic product

Million Hungarian forints

	1986	1987	1988	1989	1990	1991	1992	1993	1994	1995	1996	1997
1 Indirect taxes, net	37765	61247	160767								...	...
				201854	287302	299179						
						369684	453844	555145	633164			
A Indirect taxes	257378	300052	377938								...	...
				403308	464339	443917						
						465826	515596	619387	739256			
B less: Subsidies	219613	238805	217171								...	...
				201454	177037	144738						
						96142	61752	64242	106092			
2 Consumption of fixed capital	116956	124776	132739									
				154395[a]	163878[a]	185789[a]	...	...	...			
3 Compensation of employees paid by resident producers to	503221	548142	695106								...	...
				891472	1118021	1350900						
						1385824	1606072	1906150	2216124	2507900		
4 Operating surplus	418574	477000	402869								...	...
				463037	509138	472536						
						850550	983395	1211407	1714605			
A Corporate and quasi-corporate enterprises	281317	330109	254668								...	...
				303326	307016	204752						
						368703	336543	464856	778483			
B Private unincorporated enterprises	134434	143200	144253								...	...
				155082	194636	259493						
						363003	499128	584557	738755			
C General government	2823	3691	3948								...	...
				4629	7486	8291						
						118844	147724	161994	197367			
Statistical discrepancy	12284	15205	18036								...	...
				−[b]	10974[b]							
							−107739[b]	−100643[b]	−124440[b]	−199082[b]		

Hungary

Million Hungarian forints

	1986	1987	1988	1989	1990	1991	1992	1993	1994	1995	1996	1997
equals: Gross domestic product ..	1088800	1226370	1409517	1710758	2089313	2308404 / 2498319	2942668	3548262	4364811	5493800	...	...

a Until 1991 Item "Consumption of fixed capital" was estimated on the basis of the charges actually made by producers.

b Item "Statistical discrepancy" refers to the difference between own-account agricultural production valued at approximated basic values and final consumption of goods from own-account production valued at consumer prices. From 1989 to 1991, own-account agricultural production is valued at purchasers' prices, as in the case of private final consumption.

1.5 Current income and outlay of corporate and quasi-corporate enterprises, summary

Million Hungarian forints

	1986	1987	1988	1989	1990	1991	1992	1993	1994	1995	1996	1997
Receipts												
1 Operating surplus	...	...	...	...	...	368703	336543	464856	778483	...	...	...
2 Property and entrepreneurial income received	...	...	...	...	...	731536	737931	673359	907094	...	...	...
3 Current transfers	...	...	...	...	...	44169	46280	45884	43171	...	...	...
Total current receipts	...	...	...	...	...	1144408	1120754	1184099	1728748	...	...	...
Disbursements												
1 Property and entrepreneurial income	...	...	...	...	...	846874	822720	737117	956917	...	...	...
2 Direct taxes and other current payments to general government	...	...	...	...	...	87612	64075	71774	114671	...	...	...
3 Other current transfers	...	...	...	...	...	44422	69528	73423	91165	...	...	...
Statistical discrepancy	...	...	...	...	...	107739	100643	124440	199082	...	...	...
4 Net saving	...	...	...	...	...	57761	63788	177345	366913	...	...	...
Total current disbursements and net saving	...	...	...	...	...	1144408	1120754	1184099	1728748	...	...	...

1.9 Gross domestic product by institutional sectors of origin

Million Hungarian forints

	1986	1987	1988	1989	1990	1991	1992	1993	1994	1995	1996	1997
Domestic factor incomes originating												
1 General government	98694	109676	140530	199847	261544	332472 / 435778	551199	663364	811665	...	...	...
2 Corporate and quasi-corporate enterprises	683281	765075	801568	965523	1117754	1149284 / 1452814	1509679	1792426	2234094	...	...	...
A Non-financial	672356	754822	787296	946562	1092095	1118755 / 1350999	1400535	1646831	1988969	...	...	...
B Financial	10925	10253	14272	18961	25659	30529 / 101815	109144	145595	245125	...	...	...
3 Households and private unincorporated enterprises	139820	150391	155877	189139	247861	341680 / 401469	550238	655811	830533	...	...	...
4 Non-profit institutions serving households	...	...	...	...	...	8930	13153	30726	43142	...	...	...
subtotal: Domestic factor incomes	921795	1025142	1097975	1354509	1627159	1823436 / 2298991	2624269	3142327	3919434	...	...	...
Indirect taxes, net	37765	61247	160767	201854	287302	299179 / 369684	453844	555145	633164	...	...	...

Hungary

Million Hungarian forints

	1986	1987	1988	1989	1990	1991	1992	1993	1994	1995	1996	1997
A Indirect taxes	257378	300052	377938	403308	464339	443917 / 465826	515594	619387	739256	...	...	...
B less: Subsidies	219613	238805	217171	201454	177037	144738 / 96142	61752	64242	106092	...	...	...
Consumption of fixed capital	116956	124776	132739	154395	163878	185789	...	...	...	...	...	...
Statistical discrepancy	12284	15205	18036	...	10974		−170356	−135445	−149210	−187787	...	...
Gross domestic product	1088800	1226370	1409517	1710758	2089313	2308404 / 2498319	2942668	3548262	4364811	...	...	...

1.10 Gross domestic product by kind of activity, in current prices

Million Hungarian forints

	1986	1987	1988	1989	1990	1991	1992	1993	1994	1995	1996	1997
1 Agriculture, hunting, forestry and fishing	182569	189222	209454 / 209781[a]	235893[a]	261236[a]	230593[a] / 195138	189879	206095	262271	351100	...	...
2 Mining and quarrying	56512	56360	55446 / 55446	51754	60772	71923 / 81813	32210	20094	20048	23200	...	...
3 Manufacturing	275451	308902	327184 / 327317[b]	416202[b]	436523[b]	496464[b] / 494217	583044	688401	848241	1125500	...	...
4 Electricity, gas and water	44750[c]	54293[c]	64501[c] / 64796	68300	83457	76787 / 90486	102003	115923	125265	166900	...	...
5 Construction	78966	92233	96775 / 102316	115394	125436	121929 / 123500	153892	167392	201455	238700	...	...
6 Wholesale and retail trade, restaurants and hotels	107977	128107	125857 / 127804	159513	266560	329674 / 355643	341615	417535	493793	607100	...	...
7 Transport, storage and communication	86250	94425	101170 / 101399	124406	143539	185374 / 209907	245244	276967	333774	480700	...	...
8 Finance, insurance, real estate and business services	59926	70275	86511 / 95175[d]	116420[d]	145007[d]	179521[d] / 336630	426409	557773	770283	904700	...	...
9 Community, social and personal services	8280	9430	15220 / 15075	19331	22915	27561 / 411657	549973	692147	864304	987100	...	...
Total, Industries	900681	1003247	1082118 / 1099109[e]	1307213[e]	1545445[e]	1719826[e] / 2298991	2624269	3142327	3919434	4885000	...	...
Producers of government services	96538	107092	131957 / 163849[f]	190423[f]	251058[f]	319369[f]	...	...	...	...	...	...
Other producers	...	...	...	...	...	...	...	...	...	...	...	...
Subtotal	997219	1110339	1214075 / 1262958	1497636	1796503	2039195 / 2298991	2624269	3142327	3919434	4885000	...	...
less: Imputed bank service charge	...	...	...	...	...	...	...	...	...	...	...	...
plus: Import duties	79297	100826	177406 / 177406[g]	213122[g]	292810[g]	269209[g] / 307067[h]	419042[h]	530375[h]	644459[h]	...	...	...
plus: Value added tax	...	...	...	...	...	...	...	...	...	...	...	...
plus: Other adjustments	12284	15205	18036	...	...		−107739	−100643	−124440	−199082	...	...

Hungary

Million Hungarian forints

	1986	1987	1988	1989	1990	1991	1992	1993	1994	1995	1996	1997
equals: Gross domestic product ..	1088800	1226370	1409517 1440364	1710758	2089313	2308404 2498319	2942668	3548262	4364811	5493800	...	...

a Until 1991 item "Agriculture, hunting, forestry and fishing" includes operation of irrigation systems and veterinary services. From 1988 to 1991, the operation of irrigation systems is included in item "Electricity, gas and water".
b Until 1991 item "Manufacturing" includes gas.
c For the years before 1988, item "Electricity, gas and water" excludes gas and operation of irrigation systems.
d Until 1991 gross output of finance, insurance and that of owner-occupied housing are estimated at cost level.

e Until 1991 all types of repair services are included in the relevant industries.
f Until 1991 item "Producers of government services" includes non-profit institutions.
g Until 1991 item "Import duties" refers to all net taxes on commodities and are excluded from the value added of industries.
h Until 1991 item "Import duties" include "other adjustments". After 1991 it includes Financial Intermediation Services Indirectly Measured (FISIM).

1.11 Gross domestic product by kind of activity, in constant prices

Million Hungarian forints

	1986	1987	1988	1989	1990	1991	1992	1993	1994	1995	1996	1997
At constant prices of:	1981											
			1988									
						1991						
1 Agriculture, hunting, forestry and fishing	157851	153117	165153 210153[a]	207618[a]	197943[a]	181672[a] 195138	162865	149971	149302	...	...	...
2 Mining and quarrying	40166	40020	39085 55446	50220	44898	36593 81813	30110	16929	14811	...	...	...
3 Manufacturing	224478	233086	229450 327771[b]	324148[b]	295482[b]	240906[b] 494217	502102	531907	567760	...	...	...
4 Electricity, gas and water	24996[c]	25914[c]	25968[c] 64812	64945	65643	56159 90486	89861	91647	96034	...	...	...
5 Construction	49914	53815	50846 102846	111370	86996	73956 123500	125793	118849	124481	...	...	...
6 Wholesale and retail trade, restaurants and hotels	71279	75244	65483 128008	126301	141165	129387 355643	298218	286745	275614	...	...	...
7 Transport, storage and communication	68010	71045	71975 101632	108621	100655	89153 209907	200779	189845	192463	...	...	...
8 Finance, insurance, real estate and business services	44663	50113	50674 96221[d]	99236[d]	108511[d]	104596[d] 336630	329849	349240	391196	...	...	...
9 Community, social and personal services	6141	6998	7940 15075	14265	13794	13123 411657	442834	459289	476494	...	...	...
Total, Industries	687498	709352	706574 1101964[e]	1106724[e]	1055087[e]	925545[e] 2298991	2182411	2194422	2288155	...	...	...
Producers of government services	73081	75367	75911 168843[f]	173676[f]	176806[f]	174660[f]	...	...	...	...	...	...
Other producers	...	...	...	...	...	...	...	...	...	...	...	...
Subtotal	760579	784719	782485 1270807	1280400	1231893	1100205 2298991	2182411	2194422	2288155	...	...	...
less: Imputed bank service charge	...	...	...	...	...	...	...	...	...	...	...	...
plus: Import duties	71440	81007	82676 177406[g]	178478[g]	175973[g]	140237[g] 307067[h]	319869[h]	298918[h]	307728[h]	...	...	...
plus: Value added tax												
plus: Other adjustments	...	...	...	...	...	–107739	–80514	–85526	–117107	...	...	...

Hungary

Million Hungarian forints

	1986	1987	1988	1989	1990	1991	1992	1993	1994	1995	1996	1997
			At constant prices of: 1981									
			1988									
			1991									
equals: Gross domestic product ..	832019	865726	865161							...	...	...
			1448213	1458878	1407866	1240442						
						2498319	2421766	2407814	2478776			

a Until 1991 item "Agriculture, hunting, forestry and fishing" includes operation of irrigation systems and veterinary services. From 1988 to 1991, the operation of irrigation systems is included in item "Electricity, gas and water".
b Until 1991 item "Manufacturing" includes gas.
c For the years before 1988, item "Electricity, gas and water" excludes gas and operation of irrigation systems.
d Until 1991 gross output of finance, insurance and that of owner-occupied housing are estimated at cost level.
e Until 1991 all types of repair services are included in the relevant industries.
f Until 1991 item "Producers of government services" includes non-profit institutions.
g Until 1991 item "Import duties" refers to all net taxes on commodities and are excluded from the value added of industries.
h Until 1991 item "Import duties" include "other adjustments". After 1991 it includes Financial Intermediation Services Indirectly Measured (FISIM).

2.5 Private final consumption expenditure by type and purpose, in current prices

Million Hungarian forints

		1986	1987	1988	1989	1990	1991	1992	1993	1994	1995	1996	1997
	Final consumption expenditure of resident households												
1	Food, beverages and tobacco ..	277533	307677	341257							...	...	...
				326037[a]	376878[a]	460627[a]	533651[a]						
							535403	641884	770609	917981			
A	Food	188589	212418	234455							...	...	...
					225133	262462	316758	368377					
								369879	448538	547490	658387		
B	Non-alcoholic beverages	7874	8592	9844							...	...	...
					9844	10949	12316	16300					
								16300	22064	28056	37498		
C	Alcoholic beverages	65565	67577	74055							...	...	...
					68157	76944	97322	112327					
								112577	128360	143013	160833		
D	Tobacco	15505	19090	22903							...	...	...
					22903	26523	34231	36647					
								36647	42922	52050	61263		
2	Clothing and footwear	57872	64586	63856							...	...	...
					63856	69585	82490	97087					
								97167	117820	139312	159263		
3	Gross rent, fuel and power	54594	61968	70974							...	...	...
					78836	89064	111897	156382					
								234245[b]	290713[b]	350385[b]	419275[b]		
A	Fuel and power	27195	31216	34075							...	...	...
					34075	38655	48006	79560					
								79560	100744	120833	136039		
B	Other	27399	30752	36899							...	...	...
					44761	50409	63891	76822					
								154685	189969	229552	283236		
4	Furniture, furnishings and household equipment and operation	53771	62171	64301							...	...	...
					62837[c]	76853[c]	88230[c]	114028[c]					
								114028	137739	162840	189329		
A	Household operation	11815	12850	13821							...	...	...
					12357	14519	17898	25609					
								25609	31407	38709	47618		
B	Other	41956	49321	50480							...	...	...
					50480	62334	70332	88419					
								88419	106332	124131	141711		
5	Medical care and health expenses	4190	4528	5172							...	...	...
					9099	11403	15203	19521					
								19903	27956	35370	46968		
6	Transport and communication	61229	70012	77755							...	...	...
					77755	97407	134627	198141					
								198841	252279	319386	361802		
A	Personal transport equipment	15626	19174	19073							...	...	...
					19073	24206	35422	47555					
								47555	71916	88641	81051		
B	Other	45603	50838	58682							...	...	...
					58682[d]	73201[d]	99205[d]	150586[d]					
								151286	180363	230745	280751		

Hungary

Million Hungarian forints

	1986	1987	1988	1989	1990	1991	1992	1993	1994	1995	1996	1997
7 Recreational, entertainment, education and cultural services	42419	48176	45385 45518	60323	68565	85721 92589	114103	146473	185711	...	...	...
A Education	6337	6531	6600 5937	6000	7950	8795 9385	11664	14946	22785	...	...	...
B Other	36082	41645	38785 39581	54323	60615	76926 83204	102439	131527	162926	...	...	...
8 Miscellaneous goods and services	40536	46605	53224 52428	62738	84699	99261 99233	134190	178466	230663	...	...	...
A Personal care	9112	10819	12601 12601	14004	17456	20617 20617	24997	32040	37375	...	...	...
B Expenditures in restaurants, cafes and hotels	6407	7801	10316 11088	12240	15714	14300 14300	21300	23400	29641	...	...	...
C Other	25017	27985	30307 28739	36494	51529	64344 69431	91612	123026	163647	...	...	...
Total final consumption expenditure in the domestic market by households, of which	592144	665723	721924 716366[e]	844251[e]	1046338[e]	1303792[e] 1391409	1716684	2102841	2510992	...	...	...
A Durable goods	57212	69795	67894 67894	91068	105753	132800 132800	174642	210250	221976	...	...	...
B Semi-durable goods	102118	114896	116152 116001	132438	163400	206839 206919	250496	303367	347893	...	...	...
C Non-durable goods	347687	386309	428588 413368	482405	601103	749863 751615	917472	1113437	1318133	...	...	...
D Services	85127	94723	109290 119103	138340	176082	214290 300075	374074	475787	622990	...	...	...
plus: Direct purchases abroad by resident households	...	...	...	...	...	...	...	...	...	...	...	...
less: Direct purchases in the domestic market by non-resident households	8514	14023	−8382 −8382	−35200	−5740	40283 37295	45882	41351	52734	...	...	...
equals: Final consumption expenditure of resident households	583630	651700	730306 724748[f]	879451[f]	1052078[f]	1303792[f] 1354114	1670802	2061490	2458258	...	...	...

Final consumption expenditures by private non-profit organisations serving households

	1986	1987	1988	1989	1990	1991	1992	1993	1994	1995	1996	1997
1 Research and science	...	...	...	...	...	...	...	...	...	...	...	...
2 Education	...	...	...	...	...	...	...	...	...	...	...	...
3 Medical and other health services	...	...	...	...	...	...	...	...	...	...	...	...
4 Welfare services	...	...	...	...	...	...	...	...	...	...	...	...
5 Recreational and related cultural services	...	...	...	...	...	...	...	...	...	...	...	...
6 Religious organisations	...	...	...	...	...	...	...	...	...	...	...	...
7 Professional and labour organisations serving households	...	...	...	...	...	...	...	...	...	...	...	...
8 Miscellaneous	...	...	...	...	...	...	...	...	...	...	...	...

Hungary

Million Hungarian forints

	1986	1987	1988	1989	1990	1991	1992	1993	1994	1995	1996	1997
equals: Final consumption expenditures by private non-profit organisations serving households	...	...	...	...	...	16079	26076	56284	75128	...	...	...
Private final consumption expenditure	592144	665723	721924 / 716366	844252	1046338	1303792 / 1370193	1696878	2117774	2533386	...	...	...

a Until 1991 item "Food, beverages and tobacco" includes expenditure in restaurants, cafes and hotels.
b Gross rent of owner-occupied housing is evaluated at imputed market rents but not until 1991.
c Until 1991 service for insurance of household property is not taken into account.
d Until 1991 service charges on insurance of personal transport equipment is not taken into account.
e Item "Private final consumption expenditure" covers total final consumption expenditure in domestic market of households. From 1988 to 1991, consumption from own-account production is evaluated at basic prices. The wage-like part of the business travel cost (i.e. per diem) is treated as private consumption expenditure.
f Before 1988, some benefits (like meal contributions of the employers) were accounted as part of social benefit in kind, and was included in the government consumption. From 1988 to 1991, they are being accounted as part of labour income and are being included in the (purchased) private final consumption.

2.6 Private final consumption expenditure by type and purpose, in constant prices

Million Hungarian forints

	1986	1987	1988	1989	1990	1991	1992	1993	1994	1995	1996	1997
At constant prices of:			1981 / 1988 / 1991									

Final consumption expenditure of resident households

	1986	1987	1988	1989	1990	1991	1992	1993	1994	1995	1996	1997
1 Food, beverages and tobacco	209016	209637	204174 / 326037[a]	328046[a]	301274[a]	289799[a] / 535403	537096	522588	509913	...	...	...
A Food	141594	145469	141602 / 225133	226250	206172	201626 / 369879	374178	363868	353342	...	...	...
B Non-alcoholic beverages	6189	6435	6180 / 9844	9573	8447	9503 / 16300	19022	19440	20587	...	...	...
C Alcoholic beverages	48462	45263	43627 / 68157	68982	66010	60048 / 112577	109668	105839	103379	...	...	...
D Tobacco	12771	12470	12765 / 22903	23241	20645	18622 / 36647	34228	33441	32605	...	...	...
2 Clothing and footwear	38613	39459	32802 / 63856	58771	56521	50025 / 97167	95868	97205	95531	...	...	...
3 Gross rent, fuel and power	39553	42033	42709 / 78836	81534	83294	79634 / 234245[b]	231153[b]	234956[b]	242640[b]	...	...	...
A Fuel and power	18619	20115	19778 / 34075	34996	36470	34271 / 79560	70712	70535	72338	...	...	...
B Other	20934	21918	22931 / 44761	46538	46824	45363 / 154685	160441	164421	170302	...	...	...
4 Furniture, furnishings and household equipment and operation	40120	43765	39769 / 62837[c]	64376[c]	58656[c]	55573[c] / 114028	113460	115247	117374	...	...	...
A Household operation	8812	9125	8189 / 12357	11357	10560	10704 / 25609	25701	26840	28021	...	...	...
B Other	31308	34640	31580 / 50480	53019	48096	44869 / 88419	87759	88407	89353	...	...	...
5 Medical care and health expenses	3544	3750	3694 / 9099	8147	8942	8203 / 19903	18217	16441	16234	...	...	...

Hungary

Million Hungarian forints

	1986	1987	1988	1989	1990	1991	1992	1993	1994	1995	1996	1997
At constant prices of:	1981											
			1988									
						1991						
6 Transport and communication	42193	47091	48754			77003				...	...	...
			77755	82057	86051	198841	208998	223985	216904			
A Personal transport equipment	12073	14757	14661			19756				...	...	...
			19073	19146	22173	47555	64869	70889	57052			
B Other	30120	32334	34093			57247[d]				...	...	...
			58682[d]	62911[d]	63878[d]	151286	144129	153096	159852			
7 Recreational, entertainment, education and cultural services	33334	37357	32593			47656				...	...	...
			45518	53311	50968	92589	92574	92242	90901			
A Education	4855	5008	4842			4621				...	...	...
			5937	5536	5378	9385	10167	9356	12100			
B Other	28479	32349	27751			43035				...	...	...
			39581	47775	45590	83204	82407	82886	78801			
8 Miscellaneous goods and services	26793	27429	25603			51236				...	...	...
			52428	53916	58791	99233	103380	112145	121061			
A Personal care	6331	6678	6481			10822				...	...	...
			12601	12044	12325	20617	20073	20123	18858			
B Expenditures in restaurants, cafes and hotels	3173	3181	3168			10080				...	...	...
			11088	10487	11248	14300	16200	14450	16910			
C Other	17289	17570	15954			30334				...	...	...
			28739	31385	35218	64316	67107	77572	85293			
Total final consumption expenditure in the domestic market by households, of which	433166	450521	430098			659129[e]				...	...	...
			716366	730158[e]	704497[e]	1391409	1400746	1414809	1410558			
A Durable goods	44898	53665	47531			71692				...	...	...
			67894	79341	76537	132800	153108	164965	153390			
B Semi-durable goods	69866	72325	62842			100974				...	...	...
			116001	111739	111347	206919	200192	203137	197675			
C Non-durable goods	259550	263594	258111			375567				...	...	...
			413368	417214	392837	751615	741278	728461	716082			
D Services	58852	60937	61614			110896				...	...	...
			119103	121864	123776	300075	306168	318246	343411			
plus: Direct purchases abroad by resident households	...	...	...	...	...	...	...	...	...	...	...	...
less: Direct purchases in the domestic market by non-resident households	...	...	...	...	...	37295	34251	17745	15868	...	...	...
equals: Final consumption expenditure of resident households	433166	450521	430098			659129[f]				...	...	...
			716366[f]	730158[f]	704497[f]	1354114	1366495	1397064	1394690			

Final consumption expenditures by private non-profit organisations serving households

	1986	1987	1988	1989	1990	1991	1992	1993	1994	1995	1996	1997
1 Research and science	...	...	...	...	...	...	...	...	...	...	...	...
2 Education	...	...	...	...	...	...	...	...	...	...	...	...
3 Medical and other health services	...	...	...	...	...	...	...	...	...	...	...	...
4 Welfare services	...	...	...	...	...	...	...	...	...	...	...	...

Hungary

Million Hungarian forints

	1986	1987	1988	1989	1990	1991	1992	1993	1994	1995	1996	1997
At constant prices of:	1981											
	1988											
	1991											
5 Recreational and related cultural services	...	...	...	...	...	...	...	...	...	...	...	...
6 Religious organisations	...	...	...	...	...	...	...	...	...	...	...	...
7 Professional and labour organisations serving households	...	...	...	...	...	...	...	...	...	...	...	...
8 Miscellaneous	...	...	...	...	...	...	...	...	...	...	...	...
equals: Final consumption expenditures by private non-profit organisations serving households	...	...	...	...	...		16079	22860	40217	45278	...	...
Statistical discrepancy	...	...	...	...	-43	...	...	...	...	...	...	...
Private final consumption expenditure	433166	450521	430098							...	...	...
			716366	730158	704454	659129						
						1370193	1389355	1437281	1439968			

a Until 1991 item "Food, beverages and tobacco" includes goods consumed in restaurants, cafes, hotels, hospitals, other medical institutions and schools.
b Gross rent of owner-occupied housing is evaluated at imputed market rents but not until 1991.
c Until 1991 service for insurance of household property is not taken into account.
d Until 1991 service charges on insurance of personal transport equipment is not taken into account.
e Item "Private final consumption expenditure" covers total final consumption expenditure in domestic market of households. From 1988 to 1991, consumption from own-account production is evaluated at basic prices. The wage-like part of the business travel cost (i.e. per diem) is treated as private consumption expenditure.
f Before 1988, some benefits (like meal contributions of the employers) were accounted as part of social benefit in kind, and was included in the government consumption. From 1988 to 1991, they are being accounted as part of labour income and are being included in the (purchased) private final consumption.

4.1 Derivation of value added by kind of activity, in current prices

Million Hungarian forints

	1986			1987			1988			1989		
	Gross output	Intermediate consumption	Value added	Gross output	Intermediate consumption	Value added	Gross output	Intermediate consumption	Value added	Gross output	Intermediate consumption	Value added
All producers												
1 Agriculture, hunting, forestry and fishing	470893	288324	182569	500916	311694	189222	533831	324377	209454			
							534158[a]	324377[a]	209781[a]	601587[a]	365694[a]	235893[a]
A Agriculture and hunting	449036	274569	174467	477066	296896	180170	508842	308953	199889			
							509111	308953	200158	572998	348430	224568
B Forestry and logging	21857	13755	8102	23850	14798	9052	24989	15424	9565			
							25047	15424	9623	28589	17264	11325
C Fishing	...	...	...	...	...	...	...	...	...	...	...	...
2 Mining and quarrying	96011	39499	56512	97333	40973	56360	95023	39577	55446			
							95023	39577	55446	97243	45489	51754
3 Manufacturing	1196501	921050	275451	1284749	975847	308902	1347062	1019878	327184			
							1347195	1019878	327317	1578524	1162322	416202
A Manufacture of food, beverages and tobacco	224816	213703	11113	242209	226898	15311	253574	232729	20845			
							256418	233735	22683	311538	277133	34405
B Textile, wearing apparel and leather industries	174627	124856	49771	188390	135651	52739	195257	143009	52248			
							204919	146426	58493	230363	160954	69409
C Manufacture of wood and wood products, including furniture												

Hungary

Million Hungarian forints

	1986 Gross output	1986 Intermediate consumption	1986 Value added	1987 Gross output	1987 Intermediate consumption	1987 Value added	1988 Gross output	1988 Intermediate consumption	1988 Value added	1989 Gross output	1989 Intermediate consumption	1989 Value added
D Manufacture of paper and paper products, printing and publishing												
E Manufacture of chemicals and chemical petroleum, coal, rubber and plastic products	255761	211588	44173	267720	210565	57155	286327 287513[b]	221724 222144[b]	64603 65369[b]	325966[b]	240752[b]	85214[b]
F Manufacture of non-metallic mineral products, except products of petroleum and coal	43185	27726	15459	47688	30328	17360	48679 48863	31613 31678	17066 17185	54127	34893	19234
G Basic metal industries	111621	100482	11139	117326	104833	12493	136603 136956	114746 114871	21857 22085	181497	141284	40213
H Manufacture of fabricated metal products, machinery and equipment	348097	226846	121251	378483	249616	128867	377015 389865	253939 258473	123076 131392	456429	297224	159205
I Other manufacturing industries	38394	15849	22545	42933	17956	24977	49607 22661	22118 12551	27489 10110	18604	10082	8522
4 Electricity, gas and water	114723[c]	69973[c]	44750[c]	128785[c]	74492[c]	54293[c]	136433[c] 136728	71932[c] 71932	64501[c] 64796	146103	77803	68300
A Electricity, gas and steam	80958	51961	28997	91606	54632	36974	101956 101958	54419 54419	47537 47539	106871	59256	47615
B Water works and supply	33765	18012	15753	37179	19860	17319	34477 34770	17513 17513	16964 17257	39232	18547	20685
5 Construction	189115	110149	78966	210487	118254	92233	226943 232541	130168 130225	96775 102316	273509	158115	115394
6 Wholesale and retail trade, restaurants and hotels	186321	78344	107977	220658	92551	128107	229567 233278	103710 105474	125857 127804	281810	122297	159513
7 Transport, storage and communication	152323	66073	86250	167880	73455	94425	183244 183473	82074 82074	101170 101399	215766	91360	124406
A Transport and storage	131237	60409	70828	143286	67045	76241	156529 156758	74456 74456	82073 82302	182234	82612	99622
B Communication	21086	5664	15422	24594	6410	18184	26715 26715	7618 7618	19097 19097	33532	8748	24784
8 Finance, insurance, real estate and business services	126329	66403	59926	149561	79286	70275	188910 199606[d]	102399 104431[d]	86511 95175[d]	233754[d]	117334[d]	116420[d]
A Financial institutions	13741	4668	9073	18977	6570	12407	29025 28982	10667 10667	18358 18315	38836	14171	24665
B Insurance												
C Real estate and business services	112588	61735	50853	130584	72716	57868	159885 170624	91732 93764	68153 76860	194918	103163	91755
9 Community, social and personal services	20179	11899	8280	22565	13135	9430	33415 33140[e]	18195 18065[e]	15220 15075[e]	44687[e]	25356[e]	19331[e]
Total, Industries	2552395	1651714	900681	2782934	1779687	1003247	2974428 2995142[f]	1892310 1896033[f]	1082118 1099109[f]	3472983[f]	2165770[f]	1307213[f]
Producers of government services	202267	105729	96538	220095	113003	107092	253701 285241[g]	121744 121392[g]	131957 163849[g]	323467[g]	133044[g]	190423[g]
Other producers	...	...	...	...	...	...	...	...	...	...	...	...
Total	2754662	1757443	997219	3003029	1892690	1110339	3228129 3280383	2014054 2017425	1214075 1262958	3796450	2298814	1497636
less: Imputed bank service charge	...	...	...	...	...	...	...	...	...	...	...	...
Import duties	79297	...	79297	100826	...	100826	177406 177406[h]	...	177406 177406[h]	213122[h]	...	213122[h]
Value added tax	...	...	...	...	...	...	...	...	...	...	...	...
Other adjustments	12284	–	12284	15205	–	15205	18036	–	18036	...	–	–
Total	2846243	1757443	1088800	3119060	1892690	1226370	3423571 3457789	2014054 2017425	1409517 1440364	4009572	2298814	1710758

Hungary

	1990			1991			1992			1993		
	Gross output	Intermediate consumption	Value added	Gross output	Intermediate consumption	Value added	Gross output	Intermediate consumption	Value added	Gross output	Intermediate consumption	Value added

All producers

1 Agriculture, hunting, forestry and fishing	693829[a]	432593[a]	261236[a]	657026[a] 546443	426433[a] 351305	230593[a] 195138	541140	351261	189879	569506	363411	206095
A Agriculture and hunting	662043	412728	249315	625853 522062	406987 334379	218866 187683	516604	339177	177427	542308	349281	193027
B Forestry and logging	31786	19865	11921	31173 22619	19446 15754	11727 6865	22831	10973	11858	25156	12646	12510
C Fishing	...	...	...	1762	1172	590	1705	1111	594	2042	1484	558
2 Mining and quarrying	105455	44683	60772	121276 145438	49353 63625	71923 81813	66565	34355	32210	48285	28191	20094
A Coal mining	...	...	...	47486	25049	22437	45389	21831	23558	22518	14654	7864
B Crude petroleum and natural gas production	...	...	...	83699	29427	54272	9620	5899	3721	12323	6377	5946
C Metal ore mining	...	...	...	8225	5626	2599	5623	2798	2825	6166	2634	3532
D Other mining	...	...	...	6028	3523	2505	5933	3827	2106	7279	4526	2753
3 Manufacturing	1751103	1314580	436523	1844783 1861385	1348319 1367168	496464 494217	1912527	1329483	583044	2110030	1421629	688401
A Manufacture of food, beverages and tobacco	399493	345552	53941	441080 520776	352272 404744	88808 116032	524658	400605	124053	578946	436633	142313
B Textile, wearing apparel and leather industries	248166	168347	79819	255404 130012	169068 85887	86336 44125	136773	79655	57118	151638	85296	66342
C Manufacture of wood and wood products, including furniture				71784	47165	24619	99003	62837	36166	99556	60879	38677
D Manufacture of paper and paper products, printing and publishing				102186	74874	27312	115640	83530	32110	124703	83689	41014
E Manufacture of chemicals and chemical petroleum, coal, rubber and plastic products	385530[b]	297564[b]	87966[b]	457974[b] 408358	351847[b] 301648	106127[b] 106710	417610	272515	145095	463261	288161	175100
F Manufacture of non-metallic mineral products, except products of petroleum and coal	67003	43731	23272	68775 67225	46792 46106	21983 21119	70874	46270	24604	77796	47928	29868
G Basic metal industries	188978	154504	34474	154792 140722	132019 120938	22773 19784	103186	87237	15949	90819	74685	16134
H Manufacture of fabricated metal products, machinery and equipment	439586	292923	146663	435207 216145	280083 140441	155124 75704	235349	151656	83693	252362	162215	90147
I Other manufacturing industries	22347	11959	10388	31551 204177	16238 145365	15313 58812	209434	145178	64256	270949	182143	88806
4 Electricity, gas and water	176641	93184	83457	217541 311119	140754 220633	76787 90486	294846	192843	102003	326571	210648	115923
A Electricity, gas and steam	133699	72865	60834	168939 272862	117824 203132	51115 69730	256774	175703	81071	283860	190842	93018
B Water works and supply	42942	20319	22623	48602 38257	22930 17501	25672 20756	38072	17140	20932	42711	19806	22905
5 Construction	286733	161297	125436	291103 275590	169174 152090	121929 123500	334857	180965	153892	364662	197270	167392
6 Wholesale and retail trade, restaurants and hotels	460613	194053	266560	604944 672729	275270 317086	329674 355643	796118	454503	341615	859572	442037	417535
7 Transport, storage and communication	249043	105504	143539	318529 348212	133155 138305	185374 209907	439484	194240	245244	492117	215150	276967
A Transport and storage	204199	93629	110570	251017 281904	115351 120576	135666 161328	347379	160030	187349	372659	174653	198006
B Communication	44844	11875	32969	67512 66308	17804 17729	49708 48579	92105	34210	57895	119458	40497	78961
8 Finance, insurance, real estate and business services	297679[d]	152672[d]	145007[d]	390042[d] 533679	210521[d] 197049	179521[d] 336630	658852	232443	426409	830054	272281	557773

	1990			1991			1992			1993		
	Gross output	Interme-diate consump-tion	Value added	Gross output	Interme-diate consump-tion	Value added	Gross output	Interme-diate consump-tion	Value added	Gross output	Interme-diate consump-tion	Value added
A Financial institutions	61000	25724	35276	90761 152155	46783 50340	43978 101815	163984	54840	109144	209264	63669	145595
B Insurance												
C Real estate and business services	236679	126948	109731	299281 381524	163738 146709	135543 234815	494868	177603	317265	620790	208612	412178
9 Community, social and personal services	58333[e]	35418[e]	22915[e]	73996[e] 629556	46435[e] 217899	27561[e] 411657	841809	291836	549973	1136298	444151	692147
Total, Industries	4079429[f]	2533984[f]	1545445[f]	4519240[f] 5324151	2799414[f] 3025160	1719826[f] 2298991	5886198	3261929	2624269	6737095	3594768	3142327
Producers of government services[g]	417904	166846	251058	517201	197832	319369	...	...	...	...	...	...
Other producers	...	...	...	...	...	...	...	...	...	...	...	...
Total	4497333	2700830	1796503	5036441 5324151	2997246 3025160	2039195 2298991	5886198	3261929	2624269	6737095	3594768	3142327
less: Imputed bank service charge	...	...	...	...	...	...	...	...	...	...	...	...
Import duties	292810[h]	...	292810[h]	269209[h] 307067	...	269209[h] 307067	419042	...	419042	530375	...	530375
Value added tax	...	...	...	...	...	...	...	...	...	...	...	...
Other adjustments	...	–	–	...	– 107739	– –107739	...	100643	–100643	...	124440	–124440
Total	4790143	2700830	2089313	5305650 5631218	2997246 3132899	2308404 2498319	6305240	3362572	2942668	7267470	3719208	3548262

	1994			1995			1996			1997		
	Gross output	Interme-diate consump-tion	Value added	Gross output	Interme-diate consump-tion	Value added	Gross output	Interme-diate consump-tion	Value added	Gross output	Interme-diate consump-tion	Value added
All producers												
1 Agriculture, hunting, forestry and fishing	688495	426224	262271	...	...	...	...	...	...	...	...	...
A Agriculture and hunting	660740	412624	248116	...	...	...	...	...	...	...	...	...
B Forestry and logging	25572	12231	13341	...	...	...	...	...	...	...	...	...
C Fishing	2183	1369	814	...	...	...	...	...	...	...	...	...
2 Mining and quarrying	49154	29106	20048	...	...	...	...	...	...	...	...	...
A Coal mining	19313	13668	5645	...	...	...	...	...	...	...	...	...
B Crude petroleum and natural gas production	14017	6557	7460	...	...	...	...	...	...	...	...	...
C Metal ore mining	5368	2682	2686	...	...	...	...	...	...	...	...	...
D Other mining	10456	6199	4257	...	...	...	...	...	...	...	...	...
3 Manufacturing	2561976	1713735	848241	...	...	...	...	...	...	...	...	...
A Manufacture of food, beverages and tobacco	706270	539176	167094	...	...	...	...	...	...	...	...	...
B Textile, wearing apparel and leather industries	164737	85154	79583	...	...	...	...	...	...	...	...	...
C Manufacture of wood and wood products, including furniture	114775	66875	47900	...	...	...	...	...	...	...	...	...
D Manufacture of paper and paper products, printing and publishing	155173	101406	53767	...	...	...	...	...	...	...	...	...
E Manufacture of chemicals and chemical petroleum, coal, rubber and plastic products	544813	344890	199923	...	...	...	...	...	...	...	...	...

Hungary

	1994 Gross output	1994 Intermediate consumption	1994 Value added	1995 Gross output	1995 Intermediate consumption	1995 Value added	1996 Gross output	1996 Intermediate consumption	1996 Value added	1997 Gross output	1997 Intermediate consumption	1997 Value added
F Manufacture of non-metallic mineral products, except products of petroleum and coal	99852	58081	41771	...	...	...	...	...	...	...	...	...
G Basic metal industries	111198	90371	20827	...	...	...	...	...	...	...	...	...
H Manufacture of fabricated metal products, machinery and equipment	314673	205615	109058	...	...	...	...	...	...	...	...	...
I Other manufacturing industries	350485	222167	128318	...	...	...	...	...	...	...	...	...
4 Electricity, gas and water	334558	209293	125265	...	...	...	...	...	...	...	...	...
A Electricity, gas and steam	289596	189665	99931	...	...	...	...	...	...	...	...	...
B Water works and supply	44962	19628	25334	...	...	...	...	...	...	...	...	...
5 Construction	472411	270956	201455	...	...	...	...	...	...	...	...	...
6 Wholesale and retail trade, restaurants and hotels	1030862	537069	493793	...	...	...	...	...	...	...	...	...
7 Transport, storage and communication	599261	265487	333774	...	...	...	...	...	...	...	...	...
A Transport and storage	439124	202563	236561	...	...	...	...	...	...	...	...	...
B Communication	160137	62924	97213	...	...	...	...	...	...	...	...	...
8 Finance, insurance, real estate and business services	1120229	349946	770283	...	...	...	...	...	...	...	...	...
A Financial institutions	326080	80955	245125	...	...	...	...	...	...	...	...	...
B Insurance				...	...	...	...	...	...	...	...	...
C Real estate and business services	794149	268991	525158	...	...	...	...	...	...	...	...	...
9 Community, social and personal services	1318302	453998	864304	...	...	...	...	...	...	...	...	...
Total, Industries	8175248	4255814	3919434	...	...	...	...	...	...	...	...	...
Producers of government services	...	...	...	...	...	...	...	...	...	...	...	...
Other producers	...	...	...	...	...	...	...	...	...	...	...	...
Total	8175248	4255814	3919434	...	...	...	...	...	...	...	...	...
less: Imputed bank service charge	...	...	...	...	...	...	...	...	...	...	...	...
Import duties	644459	...	644459	...	...	...	...	...	...	...	...	...
Value added tax	...	...	...	...	...	...	...	...	...	...	...	...
Other adjustments	...	199082	–199082	...	...	...	...	...	...	...	...	...
Total	8819707	4454896	4364811	...	...	...	...	...	...	...	...	...

a Until 1991 item "Agriculture, hunting, forestry and fishing" includes operation of irrigation systems and veterinary services. From 1988 to 1991, the operation of irrigation systems is included in item "Electricity, gas and water".
b Until 1991 item "Manufacturing" includes gas.
c For the years before 1988, item "Electricity, gas and water" excludes gas and operation of irrigation systems.
d Until 1991 gross output of finance, insurance and that of owner-occupied housing are estimated at cost level.
e Until 1991 services - except trade, transport, restaurants, hotels, storage, communications, sanitary and community services - are included in item "Finance, insurance, real estate and business services"
f Until 1991 all types of repair services are included in the relevant industries.
g Until 1991 item "Producers of government services" includes non-profit institutions.
h Until 1991 item "Import duties" refers to all net taxes on commodities and are excluded from the value added of industries.

Hungary

4.2 Derivation of value added by kind of activity, in constant prices

Million Hungarian forints

	1986 Gross output	1986 Intermediate consumption	1986 Value added	1987 Gross output	1987 Intermediate consumption	1987 Value added	1988 Gross output	1988 Intermediate consumption	1988 Value added	1989 Gross output	1989 Intermediate consumption	1989 Value added
At constant prices of:	1981											
							1988					
All producers												
1 Agriculture, hunting, forestry and fishing	401389	243538	157851	406457	253340	153117	410555	245402	165153			
							534530[a]	324377[a]	210153[a]	516442[a]	308824[a]	207618[a]
A Agriculture and hunting	382106	231422	150684	386566	240797	145769	389819	232149	157670			
							509482	308953	200529	491407	293390	198017
B Forestry and logging	19283	12116	7167	19891	12543	7348	20736	13253	7483			
							25048	15424	9624	25035	15434	9601
C Fishing	...	...	...	...	...	...	...	...	...	...	...	...
2 Mining and quarrying	70162	29996	40166	70057	30037	40020	67525	28440	39085			
							95023	39577	55446	89964	39744	50220
3 Manufacturing	992550	768072	224478	1030136	797050	233086	1029247	799797	229450			
							1347649	1019878	327771	1338608	1014460	324148
A Manufacture of food, beverages and tobacco	201294	178742	22552	207337	183354	23983	203084	178908	24176			
							256418	233735	22683	260098	237274	22824
B Textile, wearing apparel and leather industries	141994	101021	40973	145540	103924	41616	145112	105112	40000			
							204946	146426	58520	198411	140309	58102
C Manufacture of wood and wood products, including furniture												
D Manufacture of paper and paper products, printing and publishing												
E Manufacture of chemicals and chemical petroleum, coal, rubber and plastic products	222132	183935	38197	235052	194534	40518	238245	197275	40970			
							287513[b]	222144[b]	65369[b]	277239[b]	216977[b]	60262[b]
F Manufacture of non-metallic mineral products, except products of petroleum and coal	34375	22750	11625	36704	24572	12132	36898	24817	12081			
							48863	31678	17185	47833	31365	16468
G Basic metal industries	91241	81610	9631	92279	81721	10558	96603	84425	12178			
							136956	114871	22085	142182	118924	23258
H Manufacture of fabricated metal products, machinery and equipment	270277	185246	85031	281231	193417	87814	277700	193523	84177			
							389931	258473	131458	396980	260898	136082
I Other manufacturing industries	31237	14768	16469	31993	15528	16465	31605	15737	15868			
							23022	12551	10471	15865	8713	7152
4 Electricity, gas and water	77657[c]	52661[c]	24996[c]	80277[c]	54363[c]	25914[c]	80034[c]	54066[c]	25968[c]			
							136744	71932	64812	137159	72214	64945
A Electricity, gas and steam	53328	39105	14223	54940	40156	14784	54857	39895	14962			
							101958	54419	47539	103576	55684	47892
B Water works and supply	24329	13556	10773	25337	14207	11130	25177	14171	11006			
							34786	17513	17273	33583	16530	17053
5 Construction	138454	88540	49914	145288	91473	53815	142842	91996	50846			
							233071	130225	102846	249466	138096	111370
6 Wholesale and retail trade, restaurants and hotels	135205	63926	71279	145295	70051	75244	137820	72337	65483			
							233482	105474	128008	234076	107775	126301
7 Transport, storage and communication	123383	55373	68010	129523	58478	71045	133323	61348	71975			
							183706	82074	101632	190767	82146	108621
A Transport and storage	109613	49147	60466	110232	53550	56682	112879	55813	57066			
							156991	74456	82535	160691	74402	86289
B Communication	13770	6226	7544	19291	4928	14363	20444	5535	14909			
							26715	7618	19097	30076	7744	22332
8 Finance, insurance, real estate and business services	93792	49129	44663	105892	55779	50113	114971	64297	50674			
							200652[d]	104431[d]	96221[d]	200891[d]	101655[d]	99236[d]

Hungary

Million Hungarian forints

	1986 Gross output	1986 Intermediate consumption	1986 Value added	1987 Gross output	1987 Intermediate consumption	1987 Value added	1988 Gross output	1988 Intermediate consumption	1988 Value added	1989 Gross output	1989 Intermediate consumption	1989 Value added
	At constant prices of: 1981 / 1988											
A Financial institutions	11105	3937	7168	14396	5298	9098	16940 / 29549	5937 / 10667	11003 / 18882	33144	11908	21236
B Insurance												
C Real estate and business services	82687	45192	37495	91496	50481	41015	98031 / 171103	58360 / 93764	39671 / 77339	167747	89747	78000
9 Community, social and personal services	16020	9879	6141	17780	10782	6998	18742 / 33140	10802 / 18065	7940 / 15075	36182	21917	14265
Total, Industries	2048612	1361114	687498	2130705	1421353	709352	2135059 / 2997997[e]	1428485 / 1896033[e]	706574 / 1101964[e]	2993555[e]	1886831[e]	1106724[e]
Producers of government services	154085	81004	73081	158296	82929	75367	155697 / 290235[f]	79786 / 121392[f]	75911 / 168843[f]	287868[f]	114192[f]	173676[f]
Other producers	...	...	...	...	...	...	...	...	...	...	...	...
Total	2202697	1442118	760579	2289001	1504282	784719	2290756 / 3288232	1508271 / 2017425	782485 / 1270807	3281423	2001023	1280400
less: Imputed bank service charge	...	...	...	...	...	...	...	...	...	...	...	...
Import duties	71440	–	71440	81007	–	81007	82676 / 177406[g]	– / –[g]	82676 / 177406[g]	178478[g]	–[g]	178478[g]
Value added tax												
Other adjustments												
Total	2274137	1442118	832019	2370008	1504282	865726	2373432 / 3465638	1508271 / 2017425	865161 / 1448213	3459901	2001023	1458878

	1990 Gross output	1990 Intermediate consumption	1990 Value added	1991 Gross output	1991 Intermediate consumption	1991 Value added	1992 Gross output	1992 Intermediate consumption	1992 Value added	1993 Gross output	1993 Intermediate consumption	1993 Value added
	At constant prices of: 1988 / 1991											
All producers												
1 Agriculture, hunting, forestry and fishing	474371[a]	276428[a]	197943[a]	408385[a] / 546443	226713[a] / 351305	181672[a] / 195138	486182	323317	162865	434540	284569	149971
A Agriculture and hunting	450152	261303	188849	387046 / 522062	213465 / 334379	173581 / 187683	463980	312316	151664	412484	272841	139643
B Forestry and logging	24219	15125	9094	21339 / 22619	13248 / 15754	8091 / 6865	20650	9979	10671	20418	10533	9885
C Fishing	...	...	...	1762	1172	590	1552	1022	530	1638	1195	443
2 Mining and quarrying	75010	30112	44898	60996 / 145438	24403 / 63625	36593 / 81813	61776	31666	30110	41078	24149	16929
A Coal mining	...	...	...	47486	25049	22437	42635	20379	22256	20079	12740	7339
B Crude petroleum and natural gas production	...	...	...	83699	29427	54272	8449	5368	3081	10139	5505	4634
C Metal ore mining	...	...	...	8225	5626	2599	5945	2645	3300	5831	2309	3522
D Other mining	...	...	...	6028	3523	2505	4747	3274	1473	5029	3595	1434
3 Manufacturing	1218438	922956	295482	974486 / 1861385	733580 / 1367168	240906 / 494217	1688087	1185985	502102	1711480	1179573	531907
A Manufacture of food, beverages and tobacco	255911	234155	21756	235695 / 520776	216761 / 404744	18934 / 116032	461950	355284	106666	450516	351086	99430
B Textile, wearing apparel and leather industries	178182	124842	53340	142948 / 130012	97296 / 85887	45652 / 44125	119472	72522	46950	123317	73820	49497
C Manufacture of wood and wood products, including furniture				71784	47165	24619	84401	55668	28733	77888	49329	28559

Hungary

	1990			1991			1992			1993		
	Gross output	Intermediate consumption	Value added	Gross output	Intermediate consumption	Value added	Gross output	Intermediate consumption	Value added	Gross output	Intermediate consumption	Value added
	At constant prices of: 1988			1991								
D Manufacture of paper and paper products, printing and publishing				102186	74874	27312	102446	74405	28041	99775	69229	30546
E Manufacture of chemicals and chemical petroleum, coal, rubber and plastic products	262853[b]	203017[b]	59836[b]	221344[b] 408358	161277[b] 301648	60067[b] 106710	378355	245777	132578	397111	247558	149553
F Manufacture of non-metallic mineral products, except products of petroleum and coal	47965	31239	16726	33202 67225	23003 46106	10199 21119	62965	42213	20752	62523	40193	22330
G Basic metal industries	122551	104047	18504	79878 140722	70085 120938	9793 19784	100654	82156	18498	86023	67686	18337
H Manufacture of fabricated metal products, machinery and equipment	334582	217185	117397	244283 216145	156677 140441	87606 75704	205489	134451	71038	209330	136954	72376
I Other manufacturing industries	16394	8471	7923	17136 204177	8481 145365	8655 58812	172355	123509	48846	204997	143718	61279
4 Electricity, gas and water	137065	71422	65643	124634 311119	68475 220633	56159 90486	268891	179030	89861	275760	184113	91647
A Electricity, gas and steam	106039	56615	49424	98763 272862	56149 203132	42614 69730	237400	164516	72884	247498	170020	77478
B Water works and supply	31026	14807	16219	25871 38257	12326 17501	13545 20756	31491	14514	16977	28262	14093	14169
5 Construction	196983	109987	86996	163213 275590	89257 152090	73956 123500	284093	158300	125793	272127	153278	118849
6 Wholesale and retail trade, restaurants and hotels	268520	127355	141165	257299 672729	127912 317086	129387 355643	660933	362715	298218	611068	324323	286745
7 Transport, storage and communication	174537	73882	100655	150414 348212	61261 138305	89153 209907	362006	161227	200779	347319	157474	189845
A Transport and storage	142497	65581	76916	116083 281904	52372 120576	63711 161328	285344	132538	152806	268284	129444	138840
B Communication	32040	8301	23739	34331 66308	8889 17729	25442 48579	76662	28689	47973	79035	28030	51005
8 Finance, insurance, real estate and business services	221660[d]	113149[d]	108511[d]	222496[d] 533679	117900[d] 197049	104596[d] 336630	515974	186125	329849	536158	186918	349240
A Financial institutions	41444	17056	24388	50133 152155	23003 50340	27130 101815	131187	44226	86962	143824	44837	98987
B Insurance												
C Real estate and business services	180216	96093	84123	172363 381524	94897 146709	77466 234815	384786	141899	242887	392334	142081	250253
9 Community, social and personal services	37257	23463	13794	35238 629556	22115 217899	13123 411657	676617	233783	442834	772538	313249	459289
Total, Industries	2803841[e]	1748754[e]	1055087[e]	2397161[e] 5324151	1471616[e] 3025160	925545[e] 2298991	5004558	2822147	2182411	5002068	2807646	2194422
Producers of government services [f]	289027	112221	176806	270378	95718	174660	...	...	...	...	...	...
Other producers	...	...	...	...	...	...	...	...	...	...	...	...
Total	3092868	1860975	1231893	2667539 5324151	1567334 3025160	1100205 2298991	5004558	2822147	2182411	5002068	2807646	2194422
less: Imputed bank service charge	...	...	...	...	...	...	...	...	...	...	...	...
Import duties	175973[g]	_[g]	175973[g]	140237[g] 307067	_[g]	140237[g] 307067	319869		319869	298918		298918
Value added tax				...	...	...	...	...	...	...	...	...
Other adjustments				... 107739		... −107739	80514		−80514	85526		−85526
Total	3268841	1860975	1407866	2807776 5631218	1567334 3132899	1240442 2498319	5324427	2902661	2421766	5300986	2893172	2407814

Hungary

	1994			1995			1996			1997		
	Gross output	Intermediate consumption	Value added	Gross output	Intermediate consumption	Value added	Gross output	Intermediate consumption	Value added	Gross output	Intermediate consumption	Value added

At constant prices of: 1991

All producers

	Gross output	Intermediate consumption	Value added
1 Agriculture, hunting, forestry and fishing	433454	284152	149302
A Agriculture and hunting	413496	274143	139353
B Forestry and logging	18499	9027	9472
C Fishing	1459	982	477
2 Mining and quarrying	37694	22883	14811
A Coal mining	15817	10848	4969
B Crude petroleum and natural gas production	11286	5441	5845
C Metal ore mining	4389	2115	2274
D Other mining	6202	4479	1723
3 Manufacturing	1836750	1268990	567760
A Manufacture of food, beverages and tobacco	465904	367487	98417
B Textile, wearing apparel and leather industries	121767	66701	55066
C Manufacture of wood and wood products, including furniture	80941	48773	32168
D Manufacture of paper and paper products, printing and publishing	110087	75545	34542
E Manufacture of chemicals and chemical petroleum, coal, rubber and plastic products	417106	272665	144441
F Manufacture of non-metallic mineral products, except products of petroleum and coal	69973	44573	25400
G Basic metal industries	95777	74748	21029
H Manufacture of fabricated metal products, machinery and equipment	235754	156880	78874
I Other manufacturing industries	239441	161618	77823
4 Electricity, gas and water	274827	178793	96034
A Electricity, gas and steam	249222	166081	83141
B Water works and supply	25605	12712	12893
5 Construction	308656	184175	124481
6 Wholesale and retail trade, restaurants and hotels	613384	337770	275614
7 Transport, storage and communication	358845	166382	192463
A Transport and storage	270394	129103	141291
B Communication	88451	37279	51172
8 Finance, insurance, real estate and business services	601801	210605	391196
A Financial institutions	175019	48168	126851
B Insurance			
C Real estate and business services	426782	162437	264345
9 Community, social and personal services	740526	264032	476494

Hungary

	1994 Gross output	1994 Intermediate consumption	1994 Value added	1995 Gross output	1995 Intermediate consumption	1995 Value added	1996 Gross output	1996 Intermediate consumption	1996 Value added	1997 Gross output	1997 Intermediate consumption	1997 Value added
	At constant prices of: 1991											
Total, Industries	5205937	2917782	2288155	...	...	...	...	...	...	...	...	...
Producers of government services	...	...	...	...	...	...	...	...	...	...	...	...
Other producers	...	...	...	...	...	...	...	...	...	...	...	...
Total	5205937	2917782	2288155	...	...	...	...	...	...	...	...	...
less: Imputed bank service charge	...	...	...	...	...	...	...	...	...	...	...	...
Import duties	307728	...	307728	...	...	...	...	...	...	...	...	...
Value added tax	...	...	...	...	...	...	...	...	...	...	...	...
Other adjustments	...	117107	–117107	...	...	...	...	...	...	...	...	...
Total	5513665	3034889	2478776	...	...	...	...	...	...	...	...	...

a Until 1991 item "Agriculture, hunting, forestry and fishing" includes operation of irrigation systems and veterinary services. From 1988 to 1991, the operation of irrigation systems is included in item "Electricity, gas and water".
b Until 1991 item "Manufacturing" includes gas.
c For the years before 1988, item "Electricity, gas and water" excludes gas and operation of irrigation systems.
d Until 1991 gross output of finance, insurance and that of owner-occupied housing are estimated at cost level.
e Until 1991 all types of repair services are included in the relevant industries.
f Until 1991 item "Producers of government services" includes non-profit institutions.
g Until 1991 item "Import duties" refers to all net taxes on commodities and are excluded from the value added of industries.

Iceland

General note

The preparation of national accounts statistics in Iceland is undertaken by the National Economic Institute, Reykjavik. The official estimates are published once or twice a year in The Icelandic Economy and in more detail but irregularly in a special series *National Accounts Publications*. A detailed description of the sources and methods is found in that series on national accounts especially in No. 13. The estimates shown in the following tables have been prepared in accordance with the United Nations System of National Accounts.

Gross domestic product

Gross domestic product is estimated mainly through the expenditure approach. The production approach is used in estimating GDP by kind of economic activity as well as cost-structure of GDP as described below. The difference between the two methods is explicitly presented as statistical discrepancy on the cost components side of GDP.

Expenditures on the gross domestic product

All components of gross domestic product by expenditure type are estimated through the expenditure approach. Government final consumption expenditure is mainly based on government accounts. Estimates of private consumption expenditure are based on various sources. A vital source is the import of consumer goods plus import duties and trade and transport margin. The Agricultural Production Board is the source for the estimate of consumption of domestically produced agricultural products. A considerable part of the consumption of services is derived from the Industrial Statistics and the Family Expenditure Survey which is used as a weight in consumer price index. Gross capital formation is based on import of investment goods, direct inquiries to the main constructors and domestical producers of investment goods and government accounts. Exports and imports of goods and services are estimated from foreign trade statistics and balance of payment statistics. Price deflation is used for most of the expenditure items in arriving at constant prices. Various price indices are used.

Cost structure of the gross domestic product

See below.

Gross domestic product by kind of activity

The production approach is used to estimate both cost-structure of domestic product and gross domestic product by kind of activity. The main source are the annual accounts of enterprises. From the tax assessments data a sample of establishments is drawn from almost every single branch of industry. The sample is drawn from the tax records presenting the total value of wages and salaries of all employees and calculated income of self-employed. These amounts are classified by enterprises and establishments within each enterprise which enables breakdown by activity within enterprises. A sample of annual reports of enterprises, including operating accounts and balance sheets, are compiled from tax authorities. After processing these sources the samples are blown-up according to the total value of wages and salaries statistics on turnover as well as other vital administrative registers in each branch of industry.

The operating account as presented in operating accounts of the firms is not suitable for national accounting purposes. One reason is the price increases during the year and therefore adjustments are made for the effects of inflation on the valuation of stocks at the beginning and the end of a year. By introducing a new concept "stock appreciation", an attempt is made to correct the value of the stocks at the beginning and end of each year in such a way that both items are revalued at the annual average prices instead of prices at the beginning and end of year. By doing this the increase in stocks during the year is valued at the annual average prices and that value item replaces the former increase in stocks valued at prices in the beginning and the end of year respectively.

For the constant price estimates the general approach for almost all industries is the deflation of the gross output or extrapolation of base year value of output. Double-deflation is not used except in the case of the fishing industry.

Iceland

1.1 Expenditure on the gross domestic product, in current prices

Million Icelandic kronur

	1986	1987	1988	1989	1990	1991	1992	1993	1994	1995	1996	1997
1 Government final consumption expenditure	28776	38981	50537	60341	69989	78157	80375	84818	89424	94080	100358	...
2 Private final consumption expenditure	99196	133557	161068	190254	223176	248366	248339	248182	256949	272708	296840	...
3 Gross capital formation	27163	38860	47418	50555	65856	75282	69103	65193	65850	68235	85550	...
A Increase in stocks [a]	−3748	−3779	−3080	−8143	−4247	−891	−486	1016	−26	2285	−1202	...
B Gross fixed capital formation	30911	42639	50498	58698	70103	76173	69589	64177	65876	65950	86752	...
Residential buildings	6923	9303	12586	15936	18666	19104	18912	18212	18667	17338	18935	...
Non-residential buildings	7639	11108	12481	14849	15552	16397	16259	16157	15417	15538	20045	...
Other construction and land improvement, etc.	6140	8203	9979	12243	13514	16237	13325	13887	13135	12855	15285	...
Other	10208	14025	15452	15670	22371	24435	21093	15921	18656	20219	32488	...
4 Exports of goods and services	61961	71681	81721	106282	124936	125671	121597	135694	157436	161250	176147	...
5 less: Imports of goods and services	55880	73965	84100	99240	119556	130491	121782	122466	134631	144725	173727	...
equals: Gross domestic product	161217	209114	256645	308192	364401	396985	397632	411421	435028	451548	485168	...

a Item "Increase in stocks" includes stocks of export products only.

1.2 Expenditure on the gross domestic product, in constant prices

Million Icelandic kronur

	1986	1987	1988	1989	1990	1991	1992	1993	1994	1995	1996	1997
At constant prices of:	1980											
					1990							
1 Government final consumption expenditure	3646	3884	4065	4187	4370 / 69989	72192	71580	73240	75937	76924	77693	...
2 Private final consumption expenditure	11332	13165	12664	12136	12196 / 223176	232382	222012	212064	215992	225154	239464	...
3 Gross capital formation	3755	4624	4818	4280	4354 / 65856	72663	63513	57154	55773	56588	68448	...
A Increase in stocks [a]	−201	−75	130	−40	−96 / −4247	1126	34	925	136	2528	48	...
B Gross fixed capital formation	3956	4698	4689	4320	4450 / 70103	71537	63479	56229	55637	54060	68400	...
Residential buildings	853	974	1118	1149	1143 / 18666	17755	17162	16174	16176	14578	15161	...
Non-residential buildings	940	1162	1108	1070	966 / 15552	15257	14786	14354	13366	13053	16245	...
Other construction and land improvement, etc.	792	874	888	886	818 / 13514	15186	12161	12369	11416	10807	12469	...
Other	1371	1689	1574	1215	1523 / 22371	23340	19371	13332	14679	15623	24526	...
4 Exports of goods and services	7092	7324	7060	7268	7266 / 124936	117537	115269	123465	135763	132800	145533	...
5 less: Imports of goods and services	6549	8073	7702	6912	6981 / 119556	126361	116287	106313	110733	114903	133968	...
Statistical discrepancy	...	...	...	...								...
equals: Gross domestic product	19276	20924	20905	20959	21204 / 364401	368413	356087	359610	372732	376563	397170	...

a Item "Increase in stocks" includes stocks of export products only.

Iceland

1.3 Cost components of the gross domestic product

Million Icelandic kronur

	1986	1987	1988	1989	1990	1991	1992	1993	1994	1995	1996	1997
1 Indirect taxes, net	30550	42332	52217	59317	66214	71624	70489	66505	69397	72881	79757	...
A Indirect taxes	35823	48320	61324	72152	79167	83943	83714	77009	79004	82373	89811	...
B less: Subsidies	5273	5988	9107	12835	12953	12319	13225	10504	9607	9492	10054	...
2 Consumption of fixed capital	19668	23435	28905	37308	43692	47933	50881	54144	56453	57702	59911	...
3 Compensation of employees paid by resident producers to ..	74425	109930	136181	153447	175063	201642	203831	203471	211092	224677	247300	...
A Resident households	74336	109755	135850	152928	174381	200759	203108	202769	210560	224312	246994	...
B Rest of the world	89	175	331	519	682	883	723	702	532	365	306	...
4 Operating surplus	25345	29639	32830	45283	59835	57621	61754	64268	74212	69622	70989	...
Statistical discrepancy [a]	11229	3779	6511	12836	19597	18164	10678	23034	23874	26665	27211	...
equals: Gross domestic product ..	161217	209114	256645	308192	364401	396984	397633	411422	435028	451547	485168	...

a The estimates shown refers to the difference between production estimate and expenditure estimate.

1.4 General government current receipts and disbursements

Million Icelandic kronur

	1986	1987	1988	1989	1990	1991	1992	1993	1994	1995	1996	1997
Receipts												
1 Operating surplus	...	...	...	...	...	...	...	...	...	...	...	...
2 Property and entrepreneurial income	4134	5123	6134	8597	8786	10465	11000	10563	11557	12058	11579	...
3 Taxes, fees and contributions	50226	65691	89969	106878	122369	137472	139271	136965	142123	150701	166512	...
A Indirect taxes	35824	48320	61323	72153	79152	83943	83714	77009	79004	82373	89811	...
B Direct taxes	12296	14448	25267	30442	38430	42663	43789	48198	50509	54974	61187	...
C Social security contributions	1996	2729	3137	4033	4532	10489	11322	11386	12181	13067	15132	...
D Compulsory fees, fines and penalties	110	194	242	250	255	377	446	372	429	287	382	...
4 Other current transfers	–	–	–	–	–	–	–	–	–	–	–	...
Total current receipts of general government	54360	70814	96103	115475	131155	147937	150271	147528	153680	162759	178091	...
Disbursements												
1 Government final consumption expenditure	28777	38980	50536	60341	69989	78157	80375	84818	89424	94080	100358	...
A Compensation of employees	17054	24789	32627	37823	43289	48929	50399	53076	56319	59420	65252	...
B Consumption of fixed capital	948	1151	1357	1680	2029	2319	2454	2600	2705	2843	3049	...
C Purchases of goods and services, net	10774	13041	16552	20838	24672	26909	27522	29142	30400	31816	32057	...
D less: Own-account fixed capital formation	...	...	...	...	...	...	...	...	...	...	...	...
E Indirect taxes paid, net	...	...	...	...	...	...	...	...	...	...	...	...
2 Property income	4434	5132	8290	11207	12903	14717	14508	15381	16805	18673	17913	...
A Interest	4434	5132	8290	11207	12903	14717	14508	15381	16805	18673	17913	...
B Net land rent and royalties	...	...	...	...	...	...	...	...	...	...	...	...
3 Subsidies	5273	5988	9106	12835	12953	12320	13225	10504	9606	9492	10055	...
4 Other current transfers	8462	11610	17490	21081	25604	28775	30295	32764	33821	36147	37097	...
A Social security benefits	5431	7625	10162	12406	14445	16182	17824	19204	19922	21312	21102	...
B Social assistance grants	1909	2467	5058	5404	7729	8483	8641	9504	9513	10078	11034	...
C Other	1122	1518	2270	3271	3430	4110	3830	4056	4386	4757	4961	...
5 Net saving	7413	9106	10682	10011	9706	13970	11867	4061	4024	4366	12668	...

Iceland

Million Icelandic kronur

	1986	1987	1988	1989	1990	1991	1992	1993	1994	1995	1996	1997
Total current disbursements and net saving of general government	54359	70816	96104	115475	131155	147939	150270	147528	153680	162758	178091	...

1.7 External transactions on current account, summary

Million Icelandic kronur

	1986	1987	1988	1989	1990	1991	1992	1993	1994	1995	1996	1997
Payments to the rest of the world												
1 Imports of goods and services	55880	73965	84100	99240	119556	130491	121782	122466	134631	144725	173727	...
A Imports of merchandise, c.i.f.	45910	61237	68723	80250	96621	104129	96895	91307	102541	113614	135994	...
B Other	9970	12728	15377	18990	22935	26362	24887	31159	32090	31111	37733	...
2 Factor income to rest of the world	7042	7281	9461	15087	17320	15584	14682	15803	18948	18257	18349	...
A Compensation of employees	89	175	331	519	682	883	723	702	532	365	306	...
B Property and entrepreneurial income [a]	6953	7106	9130	14568	16638	14701	13959	15101	18416	17892	18043	...
3 Current transfers to the rest of the world	72	–76	57	340	200	510	269	211	626	306	464	...
A Indirect taxes to supranational organizations	...	...	...	...	...	...	...	...	...	...	...	...
B Other current transfers	72	–76	57	340	200	510	269	211	626	306	464	...
4 Surplus of the nation on current transactions	707	–7007	–8942	–4462	–7669	–15974	–9365	3196	8734	3717	–8892	...
Payments to the rest of the world and surplus of the nation on current transfers	63701	74163	84676	110205	129407	130611	127368	141676	162939	167005	183648	...
Receipts from the rest of the world												
1 Exports of goods and services	61961	71681	81721	106282	124936	125671	121597	135694	157436	161250	176147	...
A Exports of merchandise, f.o.b.	44968	53053	61667	80072	92452	91560	87833	94658	112654	116607	125690	...
B Other	16993	18628	20054	26210	32484	34111	33764	41036	44782	44643	50457	...
2 Factor income from rest of the world	1740	2482	2955	3923	4471	4940	5771	5982	5503	5755	7501	...
A Compensation of employees	1013	1589	1998	2306	2658	2994	3037	3175	2993	3260	4242	...
B Property and entrepreneurial income [a]	727	893	957	1617	1813	1946	2734	2807	2510	2495	3259	...
3 Current transfers from rest of the world	–	–	–	–	–	–	–	–	–	–	–	...
A Subsidies from supranational organisations	...	...	...	...	...	...	...	...	...	...	...	...
B Other current transfers	–	–	–	–	–	–	–	–	–	–	–	...
Receipts from the rest of the world on current transactions	63701	74163	84676	110205	129407	130611	127368	141676	162939	167005	183648	...

a Item "Property and entrepreneurial income" paid/received refers to interest payments.

1.8 Capital transactions of the nation, summary

Million Icelandic kronur

	1986	1987	1988	1989	1990	1991	1992	1993	1994	1995	1996	1997
Finance of gross capital formation												
Gross saving	28053	31853	38477	46093	58187	59308	59738	68390	74584	71951	76659	...
1 Consumption of fixed capital	19668	23435	28905	37308	43692	47933	50881	54144	56453	57702	59911	...
A General government	948	1151	1357	1680	2029	2319	2454	2600	2705	2843	3049	...

Iceland

Million Icelandic kronur	1986	1987	1988	1989	1990	1991	1992	1993	1994	1995	1996	1997
B Corporate and quasi-corporate enterprises	...	...	...	...	...	...	...	...	...	...	...	...
C Other	...	...	...	...	...	...	...	...	...	...	...	...
2 Net saving	8385	8418	9571	8785	14495	11375	8857	14246	18131	14249	16748	...
A General government	7413	9104	10682	10011	9707	13972	11867	4061	4022	4366	12668	...
B Corporate and quasi-corporate enterprises	...	...	...	...	...	...	...	...	...	...	...	...
C Other	...	...	...	...	...	...	...	...	...	...	...	...
less: Surplus of the nation on current transactions	890	–7007	–8942	–4462	–7669	–15974	–9365	3196	8734	3717	–8892	...
Statistical discrepancy	...	–	–	–	–	–	–	–	–	–	–	...
Finance of gross capital formation	27163	38860	47418	50555	65856	75282	69103	65194	65850	68234	85551	...

Gross capital formation

	1986	1987	1988	1989	1990	1991	1992	1993	1994	1995	1996	1997
Increase in stocks [a]	–3748	–3779	–3080	–8143	–4247	–891	–486	1016	–26	2285	–1202	...
Gross fixed capital formation	30911	42639	50498	58698	70103	76173	69589	64177	65876	65950	86752	...
1 General government	4800	7294	10348	12630	14378	16228	16016	17746	17647	13714	15416	...
2 Corporate and quasi-corporate enterprises	...	...	...	...	...	...	...	...	...	...	...	...
3 Other	...	...	...	...	...	...	...	...	...	...	...	...
Gross capital formation	27163	38860	47418	50555	65856	75282	69103	65193	65850	68235	85550	...

a Item "Increase in stocks" includes stocks of export products only.

1.9 Gross domestic product by institutional sectors of origin

Million Icelandic kronur	1986	1987	1988	1989	1990	1991	1992	1993	1994	1995	1996	1997
Domestic factor incomes originating												
subtotal: Domestic factor incomes	99770	139568	169011	198731	233586	258486	264654	267149	285102	296797	320990	...
Indirect taxes, net	30550	42332	52217	59317	66214	71624	70489	66505	69397	72881	79757	...
A Indirect taxes	35823	48320	61324	72152	79167	83943	83714	77009	79004	82373	89811	...
B less: Subsidies	5273	5988	9107	12835	12953	12319	13225	10504	9607	9492	10054	...
Consumption of fixed capital	19668	23435	28905	37308	43692	47933	50881	54144	56453	57702	59911	...
Statistical discrepancy	11229	3779	6511	12836	20908	18941	11608	23623	24076	24167	24512	...
Gross domestic product	161217	209114	256645	308192	364400	396984	397632	411421	435028	451547	485170	...

1.10 Gross domestic product by kind of activity, in current prices

Million Icelandic kronur	1986	1987	1988	1989	1990	1991	1992	1993	1994	1995	1996	1997
1 Agriculture, hunting, forestry and fishing	15848	21105	25184	29251	34975	38922	37959	39301	39627	42485	...	...
2 Mining and quarrying	...	...	...	...	...	...	...	...	...	...	...	...
3 Manufacturing	24077	32736	37689	43739	47560	51746	52559	52455	59088	59005	...	...
4 Electricity, gas and water	6106	6447	9142	10929	11767	11967	12711	13491	13526	14824	...	...
5 Construction	10305	14594	16340	19927	22781	24152	24919	24049	23151	23606	...	...
6 Wholesale and retail trade, restaurants and hotels	13795	19402	21090	26609	37082	40827	43087	42379	45530	46680	...	...
7 Transport, storage and communication	9397	12415	15257	16933	21386	22469	22746	23716	27286	27796	...	...
8 Finance, insurance, real estate and business services	20111	29194	38462	47486	52251	58743	61434	63542	65080	65152	...	...

Iceland

Million Icelandic kronur

	1986	1987	1988	1989	1990	1991	1992	1993	1994	1995	1996	1997
9 Community, social and personal services	5711	8465	11129	12756	15195	17144	18479	18011	19210	19899	...	...
Total, Industries	105350	144357	174295	207631	242996	265969	273894	276945	292498	299448	...	...
Producers of government services [a]	17524	25248	33082	38461	44144	51423	53027	55849	59195	62448	...	...
Other producers	1056	1484	2097	2649	3871	4156	4105	4285	4348	4984	...	...
Subtotal	123930	171089	209473	248741	291011	321548	331025	337080	356040	366880	...	...
less: Imputed bank service charge	4493	8085	11557	12702	12422	14352	14559	15197	14283	14878	...	...
plus: Import duties	–	–	–	–	–	–	–	–	–	–	...	...
plus: Value added tax	...	...	...	...	...	...	...	...	...	...	...	...
plus: Other adjustments [b]	41779	46111	58728	72153	85811	89788	81166	89539	93271	99546	...	...
equals: Gross domestic product	161216	209114	256645	308192	364400	396984	397633	411421	435029	451548	...	...

a Beginning 1980, all accrued pension liabilities of central government employees are included even if they had not become effective. Thus, the estimates of "Producers of government services" beginning 1980 are not comparable with those of previous years.

b Item "Other adjustments" includes import duties, other indirect taxes less subsidies as well as residual error between production and expenditure approaches.

1.11 Gross domestic product by kind of activity, in constant prices

Million Icelandic kronur

	1986	1987	1988	1989	1990	1991	1992	1993	1994	1995	1996	1997
At constant prices of:	1980				1990							
1 Agriculture, hunting, forestry and fishing	1629	1817	1855	1804	1843 34975	32609	32494	34006	33077	32769	...	...
2 Mining and quarrying	...	...	...	...		...	...	...	...	...	...	...
3 Manufacturing	2563	2772	2583	2490	2421 47560	48379	46672	46066	47578	48215	...	...
4 Electricity, gas and water	802	813	852	870	875 11767	11916	12169	12652	12672	12984	...	...
5 Construction	1123	1276	1263	1274	1258 22781	23364	21427	20836	20373	18970	...	...
6 Wholesale and retail trade, restaurants and hotels	1579	1826	1775	1677	1745 37082	38423	36778	35242	36085	37567	...	...
7 Transport, storage and communication	1233	1386	1366	1331	1422 21387	21384	20945	21090	22339	23381	...	...
8 Finance, insurance, real estate and business services	3006	3183	3308	3331	3339 52251	52647	52189	51801	53374	53903	...	...
9 Community, social and personal services	667	737	747	731	723 15195	15710	15707	15843	16495	16774	...	...
Total, Industries	12603	13811	13749	13509	13626 242996	244433	238381	237535	241994	244564	...	...
Producers of government services [a]	2351	2560	2732	2814	2952 44145	45826	45577	46935	48894	49155	...	...
Other producers	167	177	191	197	204 3871	3857	3773	3917	4019	4346	...	...
Subtotal	15121	16548	16673	16520	16782 291012	294116	287731	288388	294907	298064	...	...
less: Imputed bank service charge	838	877	946	925	909 12422	12562	12251	12110	11828	11833	...	...
plus: Import duties	...	...	...	...	...	...	...	...	...	...	...	...
plus: Value added tax	...	...	...	...	...	...	...	...	...	...	...	...
plus: Other adjustments	...	...	...	...	85811 15873	86860	80608	83333	89652	90332	...	...
equals: Gross domestic product	14283	15672	15727	15595	364401	368414	356088	359610	372731	376564	...	...

a Beginning 1980, all accrued pension liabilities of central government employees are included even if they had not become effective. Thus, the estimates of "Producers of government services" beginning 1980 are not comparable with those of previous years.

Iceland

1.12 Relations among national accounting aggregates

Million Icelandic kronur

	1986	1987	1988	1989	1990	1991	1992	1993	1994	1995	1996	1997
Gross domestic product	161217	209114	256645	308192	364401	396984	397632	411421	435028	451547	485168	...
plus: Net factor income from the rest of the world	−5302	−4799	−6506	−11164	−12849	−10644	−8911	−9821	−13445	−12502	−10848	...
Factor income from rest of the world	1740	2482	2955	3923	4471	4940	5771	5982	5503	5755	7501	
less: Factor income to the rest of the world	7042	7281	9461	15087	17320	15584	14682	15803	18948	18257	18349	...
equals: Gross national product	155915	204315	250138	297028	351552	386341	388721	401600	421583	439045	474320	...
less: Consumption of fixed capital	19668	23435	28905	37308	43692	47933	50881	54144	56453	57702	59911	...
equals: National income	136247	180880	221233	259720	307860	338408	337840	347456	365130	381343	414410	...
plus: Net current transfers from the rest of the world	111	76	−57	−340	−200	−510	−269	−211	−626	−306	−464	...
Current transfers from rest of the world	−	−	−	−	−	−	−	−	−	−	−	...
less: Current transfers to the rest of the world	−111	−76	57	340	200	510	269	211	626	306	464	...
equals: National disposable income	136358	180956	221176	259380	307660	337897	337571	347245	364504	381037	413946	...
less: Final consumption	127972	172538	211605	250595	293165	326523	328714	333000	346373	366788	397198	...
Statistical discrepancy	−	−	−	−	−	−	−	−	−	−	−	...
equals: Net saving	8385	8418	9571	8785	14495	11375	8857	14246	18131	14249	16748	...
less: Surplus of the nation on current transactions	890	−7007	−8942	−4462	−7669	−15974	−9365	3196	8734	3717	−8892	...
Statistical discrepancy	−	−	−	−	−	−	−	−	−	−	−	...
equals: Net capital formation	7495	15425	18513	13248	22164	27349	18222	11050	9397	10532	25640	...

2.1 Government final consumption expenditure by function, in current prices

Million Icelandic kronur

		1986	1987	1988	1989	1990	1991	1992	1993	1994	1995	1996	1997
1	General public services	1863	2739	3715	4372	5772	6471	6448	6769	7288	7589	7993	...
2	Defence	...	...	...	...	−	...	...	...	...	...	...	...
3	Public order and safety	2031	2856	3641	3891	4442	5028	5112	5384	5403	5860	6199	...
4	Education	5791	8051	10350	12280	13764	15438	15951	16398	17017	18167	21172	...
5	Health	10165	13673	17957	21526	24008	26547	26544	27180	28312	29908	31871	...
6	Social security and welfare	1640	2370	3285	3777	4625	5668	6149	6556	7118	7683	8130	...
7	Housing and community amenities	747	1054	1295	1712	2104	2552	2905	3314	3536	3615	3659	...
8	Recreational, cultural and religious affairs	1123	1417	1887	2444	2965	3467	3763	4481	4835	4913	5167	...
9	Economic services	3252	4066	4743	5962	6944	7308	7602	8391	8925	9042	8951	...
	A Fuel and energy	179	279	274	298	230	255	266	218	244	251	198	...
	B Agriculture, hunting, forestry and fishing	576	800	901	980	1262	1619	1619	1775	1582	1692	1805	...
	C Mining (except fuels), manufacturing and construction	75	116	161	155	203	232	263	238	390	298	430	...
	D Transportation and communication	2127	2477	2899	3881	4484	4414	4656	5079	5282	5479	5110	...
	E Other economic affairs	296	394	508	648	765	787	799	1081	1427	1323	1409	...
10	Other functions	2167	2755	3663	4378	5367	5680	5901	6345	6990	7304	7216	...
	Total government final consumption expenditures	28778	38981	50536	60340	69989	78157	80375	84818	89424	94080	100359	...

Iceland

2.2 Government final consumption expenditure by function, in constant prices

Million Icelandic kronur

	1986	1987	1988	1989	1990	1991	1992	1993	1994	1995	1996	1997
	At constant prices of: 1990											
1 General public services	3804	4384	4803	4861	5772	5985	5746	5837	6185	6219	6510	...
2 Defence	–	–	–	...	...	...	...	...	...	...	...	...
3 Public order and safety	4131	4497	4627	4302	4442	4635	4542	4648	4587	4784	5049	...
4 Education	11754	12588	13062	13541	13763	14221	14160	14158	14450	14807	17243	...
5 Health	20940	22279	23427	24041	24008	24564	23674	23434	24027	24515	25956	...
6 Social security and welfare	3308	3644	4091	4134	4625	5209	5444	5666	6046	6237	6621	...
7 Housing and community amenities	1533	1719	1692	1916	2104	2365	2595	2855	3001	2969	2980	...
8 Recreational, cultural and religious affairs	2294	2243	2415	2711	2965	3203	3353	3865	4104	4012	4208	...
9 Economic services	6718	6696	6223	6684	6943	6765	6784	7232	7573	7428	7289	...
A Fuel and energy	361	437	342	328	230	234	235	189	207	203	161	...
B Agriculture, hunting, forestry and fishing	1173	1269	1149	1085	1261	1495	1440	1531	1343	1382	1470	...
C Mining (except fuels), manufacturing and construction	149	172	196	167	203	212	232	206	331	241	350	...
D Transportation and communication	4426	4179	3874	4379	4484	4100	4169	4373	4479	4521	4161	...
E Other economic affairs	608	639	663	724	765	725	709	933	1211	1081	1147	...
10 Other functions	4364	4414	4825	4938	5367	5245	5281	5545	5986	6015	5839	...
Total government final consumption expenditures	58845	62464	65167	67128	69989	72192	71579	73240	75959	76985	81696	...

2.3 Total government outlays by function and type

Million Icelandic kronur

	1986								
	Final consumption expenditures				Other current transfers and property income	Total current disbursements	Gross capital formation	Other capital outlays	Total outlays
	Total	Compensation of employees	Other	Subsidies					
1 General public services	1863	1214	649	–	108	1970	67	11	2048
2 Defence	...	–	–	–	–	–	–	–	–
3 Public order and safety	2031	1486	545	–	27	2058	97	38	2193
4 Education	5791	4458	1333	–	114	5905	572	1013	7490
5 Health	10165	4917	5248	–	–	10165	457	110	10732
6 Social security and welfare	1640	1454	186	–	7483	9122	392	102	9616
7 Housing and community amenities	747	419	328	–	–	747	83	1649	2479
8 Recreational, cultural and religious affairs	1123	716	407	215	673	2011	878	236	3124
9 Economic services	3252	1385	1867	5057	54	8363	2315	7012	17689
A Fuel and energy	179	160	19	869	6	1054	19	5330	6403
B Agriculture, hunting, forestry and fishing	576	396	180	3540	24	4139	302	830	5271
C Mining (except fuels), manufacturing and construction	75	83	–9	233	1	308	21	210	538
D Transportation and communication	2127	598	1529	315	–	2442	1962	277	4681
E Other economic affairs	296	148	148	101	23	420	12	366	797
10 Other functions	2167	1005	1162	–	4436	6603	–61	–83	6460

Iceland

Million Icelandic kronur

1986

	Final consumption expenditures — Total	Compensation of employees	Other	Subsidies	Other current transfers and property income	Total current disbursements	Gross capital formation	Other capital outlays	Total outlays
Total	28778	17054	11724	5273	12894	46945	4801	10086	61832

1987

	Final consumption expenditures — Total	Compensation of employees	Other	Subsidies	Other current transfers and property income	Total current disbursements	Gross capital formation	Other capital outlays	Total outlays
1 General public services	2739	1782	957	–	139	2878	176	17	3071
2 Defence	...	–	–	–	–	–	–	–	–
3 Public order and safety	2856	2137	719	–	42	2898	174	55	3126
4 Education	8051	6359	1692	–	144	8195	840	738	9773
5 Health	13673	7429	6244	–	16	13688	618	112	14418
6 Social security and welfare	2370	2097	273	–	10302	12672	638	112	13422
7 Housing and community amenities	1054	569	485	–	–	1054	128	1390	2572
8 Recreational, cultural and religious affairs	1417	1019	398	363	884	2664	1048	104	3817
9 Economic services	4066	1947	2120	5625	78	9769	3166	2387	15322
A Fuel and energy	279	218	61	793	5	1078	12	484	1574
B Agriculture, hunting, forestry and fishing	800	563	237	3989	41	4830	599	806	6236
C Mining (except fuels), manufacturing and construction	116	127	–11	366	1	482	7	539	1028
D Transportation and communication	2477	815	1662	340	–	2817	2532	275	5623
E Other economic affairs	394	223	171	137	32	562	16	283	861
10 Other functions	2755	1449	1306	–	5139	7893	506	–168	8231
Total	38981	24788	14194	5988	16743	61711	7294	4747	73753

1988

	Final consumption expenditures — Total	Compensation of employees	Other	Subsidies	Other current transfers and property income	Total current disbursements	Gross capital formation	Other capital outlays	Total outlays
1 General public services	3715	2307	1408	–	327	4042	459	21	4522
2 Defence	...	–	–	–	–	–	–	–	–
3 Public order and safety	3641	2709	932	–	42	3683	240	61	3983
4 Education	10350	8217	2133	–	222	10572	1449	1399	13419
5 Health	17957	9974	7983	–	184	18141	645	141	18927
6 Social security and welfare	3285	2911	374	–	15473	18758	983	110	19852
7 Housing and community amenities	1295	706	589	–	–	1295	106	1867	3268
8 Recreational, cultural and religious affairs	1887	1311	576	716	1160	3763	1605	130	5497
9 Economic services	4743	2440	2303	8391	66	13199	4269	3374	20842
A Fuel and energy	274	236	38	700	1	975	9	267	1251
B Agriculture, hunting, forestry and fishing	901	650	251	6694	13	7608	607	1383	9598
C Mining (except fuels), manufacturing and construction	161	168	–7	362	21	544	6	397	947

Iceland

1988

	Final consumption expenditures			Subsidies	Other current transfers and property income	Total current disburse-ments	Gross capital formation	Other capital outlays	Total outlays
	Total	Compensation of employees	Other						
D Transportation and communication	2899	1100	1799	419	–	3318	3610	351	7279
E Other economic affairs	508	286	222	216	30	754	38	976	1768
10 Other functions	3663	2053	1610	–	8305	11968	593	–200	12361
Total	50536	32627	17909	9107	25778	85421	10348	6903	102672

1989

	Final consumption expenditures			Subsidies	Other current transfers and property income	Total current disburse-ments	Gross capital formation	Other capital outlays	Total outlays
	Total	Compensation of employees	Other						
1 General public services	4372	2718	1654	–	520	4892	579	10	5480
2 Defence	...	–	–	–	–	–	–	–	–
3 Public order and safety	3891	2855	1036	–	56	3948	264	53	4264
4 Education	12280	9598	2682	–	259	12539	1648	1658	15845
5 Health	21526	11560	9966	–	176	21701	775	160	22635
6 Social security and welfare	3777	3477	300	–	18132	21909	1200	92	23200
7 Housing and community amenities	1712	837	875	–	1	1712	180	1319	3212
8 Recreational, cultural and religious affairs	2444	1633	811	948	1761	5153	1923	136	7212
9 Economic services	5962	2773	3189	11886	172	18020	4521	9909	32451
A Fuel and energy	298	251	47	865	3	1167	12	3569	4747
B Agriculture, hunting, forestry and fishing	980	690	290	9499	36	10515	284	1830	12629
C Mining (except fuels), manufacturing and construction	155	185	–30	465	18	638	15	518	1171
D Transportation and communication	3881	1316	2565	672	–	4554	4175	1121	9849
E Other economic affairs	648	331	317	385	115	1148	36	2872	4056
10 Other functions	4378	2373	2005	–	11212	15590	1540	–243	16886
Total	60340	37823	22517	12835	32287	105462	12630	13093	131185

1990

	Final consumption expenditures			Subsidies	Other current transfers and property income	Total current disburse-ments	Gross capital formation	Other capital outlays	Total outlays
	Total	Compensation of employees	Other						
1 General public services	5772	3401	2371	–	505	6277	921	–	7198
2 Defence	–	–	–	–	–	–	–	–	–
3 Public order and safety	4442	3269	1173	–	71	4513	216	74	4803
4 Education	13764	10675	3089	–	246	14010	1742	2033	17784
5 Health	24008	12722	11286	–	206	24214	787	83	25084
6 Social security and welfare	4625	4218	407	–	22512	27137	1545	–169	28513
7 Housing and community amenities	2104	850	1254	–	1	2105	169	622	2897
8 Recreational, cultural and religious affairs	2965	1975	990	884	1967	5816	1764	275	7855
9 Economic services	6944	3223	3721	12069	91	19104	5577	6516	31196
A Fuel and energy	230	226	4	868	5	1102	10	851	1963
B Agriculture, hunting, forestry and fishing	1262	883	379	9859	27	11148	476	2560	14184

Iceland

1990

	Final consumption expenditures Total	Compensation of employees	Other	Subsidies	Other current transfers and property income	Total current disbursements	Gross capital formation	Other capital outlays	Total outlays
C Mining (except fuels), manufacturing and construction	203	222	−19	324	20	547	14	1013	1574
D Transportation and communication	4484	1393	3091	694	−	5178	5049	1035	11262
E Other economic affairs	765	499	266	325	40	1129	29	1057	2214
10 Other functions	5367	2955	2412	−	12908	18275	1656	34	19965
Total	69989	43288	26701	12953	38507	121449	14378	9468	145295

1991

	Final consumption expenditures Total	Compensation of employees	Other	Subsidies	Other current transfers and property income	Total current disbursements	Gross capital formation	Other capital outlays	Total outlays
1 General public services	6471	3637	2834	−	622	7093	932	60	8084
2 Defence	...	−	−	−	−	−	−	−	−
3 Public order and safety	5028	3735	1293	−	93	5121	232	82	5435
4 Education	15438	12072	3366	−	295	15732	2202	2258	20192
5 Health	26547	14326	12221	−	346	26893	920	134	27946
6 Social security and welfare	5668	5143	525	−	25048	30716	1561	−127	32150
7 Housing and community amenities	2552	1145	1407	−	3	2555	78	951	3585
8 Recreational, cultural and religious affairs	3467	2169	1298	1197	2178	6842	1448	718	9007
9 Economic services	7308	3735	3574	11123	187	18617	6771	7574	32962
A Fuel and energy	255	231	24	933	6	1194	21	320	1535
B Agriculture, hunting, forestry and fishing	1619	1110	510	8521	42	10183	438	2872	13492
C Mining (except fuels), manufacturing and construction	232	265	−33	261	29	521	7	404	932
D Transportation and communication	4414	1493	2921	743	−	5157	6261	1265	12683
E Other economic affairs	787	635	152	665	109	1561	45	2714	4320
10 Other functions	5680	2968	2712	−	14719	20399	2085	37	22521
Total	78157	48930	29228	12319	43491	133967	16228	11686	161881

1992

	Final consumption expenditures Total	Compensation of employees	Other	Subsidies	Other current transfers and property income	Total current disbursements	Gross capital formation	Other capital outlays	Total outlays
1 General public services	6448	3771	2677	−	519	6967	784	5	7756
2 Defence	...	−	−	−	−	−	−	−	−
3 Public order and safety	5112	3781	1331	−	115	5227	339	62	5627
4 Education	15951	12446	3505	−	324	16275	2485	1937	20696
5 Health	26544	14357	12187	−	246	26791	663	306	27759
6 Social security and welfare	6149	5641	508	−	26689	32838	1873	−173	34538
7 Housing and community amenities	2905	1292	1613	−	16	2920	282	926	4128
8 Recreational, cultural and religious affairs	3763	2213	1550	1147	2279	7189	1773	384	9345
9 Economic services	7602	3875	3727	12078	107	19788	6570	6084	32442

Iceland

1992

	Final consumption expenditures - Total	Compensation of employees	Other	Subsidies	Other current transfers and property income	Total current disbursements	Gross capital formation	Other capital outlays	Total outlays
A Fuel and energy	266	233	33	1095	6	1366	–	170	1537
B Agriculture, hunting, forestry and fishing	1619	1148	471	9239	20	10877	547	2022	13447
C Mining (except fuels), manufacturing and construction	263	281	–19	283	26	571	22	501	1094
D Transportation and communication	4656	1563	3093	759	–	5414	5919	929	12262
E Other economic affairs	799	650	149	704	56	1559	82	2461	4102
10 Other functions	5901	3023	2878	–	14509	20410	1247	–3	21654
Total	80375	50399	29976	13225	44804	138404	16016	9526	163946

1993

	Final consumption expenditures - Total	Compensation of employees	Other	Subsidies	Other current transfers and property income	Total current disbursements	Gross capital formation	Other capital outlays	Total outlays
1 General public services	6769	3896	2873	–	692	7461	203	49	7713
2 Defence	...	–	–	–	–	–	–	–	–
3 Public order and safety	5384	4014	1370	–	101	5485	294	97	5876
4 Education	16398	12555	3843	–	345	16743	2413	1599	20755
5 Health	27180	14985	12195	–	245	27425	680	384	28488
6 Social security and welfare	6556	6112	444	–	28927	35483	1622	–11	37093
7 Housing and community amenities	3314	1313	2001	–	21	3336	68	1032	4436
8 Recreational, cultural and religious affairs	4481	2686	1795	1296	2241	8018	2596	528	11142
9 Economic services	8391	4096	4295	9208	191	17790	8237	3674	29701
A Fuel and energy	218	234	–16	1111	6	1336	10	114	1460
B Agriculture, hunting, forestry and fishing	1775	1180	595	6580	18	8372	499	1354	10225
C Mining (except fuels), manufacturing and construction	238	288	–50	286	36	561	15	331	906
D Transportation and communication	5079	1686	3393	538	26	5643	7678	1023	14344
E Other economic affairs	1081	708	373	694	104	1879	35	852	2767
10 Other functions	6345	3420	2925	–	15381	21726	1633	2	23361
Total	84818	53076	31742	10504	48145	143466	17747	7353	168567

1994

	Final consumption expenditures - Total	Compensation of employees	Other	Subsidies	Other current transfers and property income	Total current disbursements	Gross capital formation	Other capital outlays	Total outlays
1 General public services	7288	4273	3015	–	621	7909	241	85	8235
2 Defence	...	–	–	–	–	–	–	–	–
3 Public order and safety	5403	3953	1450	–	103	5506	836	62	6403
4 Education	17017	13112	3905	–	337	17353	2576	1305	21235
5 Health	28312	15589	12723	–	330	28643	728	291	29662
6 Social security and welfare	7118	6240	878	–	29650	36768	1143	–112	37799
7 Housing and community amenities	3536	1728	1808	–	15	3552	193	1199	4943

Iceland

1994

	Final consumption expenditures Total	Compensation of employees	Other	Subsidies	Other current transfers and property income	Total current disbursements	Gross capital formation	Other capital outlays	Total outlays
8 Recreational, cultural and religious affairs	4835	3226	1609	1318	2524	8677	2293	463	11433
9 Economic services	8925	4396	4529	8289	227	17440	8384	5990	31814
A Fuel and energy	244	245	−1	1122	7	1373	13	144	1530
B Agriculture, hunting, forestry and fishing	1582	1161	421	5520	40	7143	456	1326	8925
C Mining (except fuels), manufacturing and construction	390	292	98	363	64	817	13	428	1259
D Transportation and communication	5282	1812	3470	707	39	6027	7513	916	14455
E Other economic affairs	1427	886	541	577	77	2081	388	3176	5645
10 Other functions	6990	3802	3188	_	16819	23810	1253	435	25497
Total	89424	56319	33105	9607	50626	149657	17647	9717	177021

1995

	Final consumption expenditures Total	Compensation of employees	Other	Subsidies	Other current transfers and property income	Total current disbursements	Gross capital formation	Other capital outlays	Total outlays
1 General public services	7589	4340	3249	_	778	8367	284	56	8706
2 Defence	...	−	−	−	−	−	−	−	−
3 Public order and safety	5860	4124	1736	_	113	5973	733	43	6749
4 Education	18167	13734	4433	_	301	18468	2396	1197	22061
5 Health	29908	16843	13065	_	459	30367	657	218	31242
6 Social security and welfare	7683	6847	836	_	31671	39354	1432	−84	40701
7 Housing and community amenities	3615	1760	1855	_	23	3638	110	729	4476
8 Recreational, cultural and religious affairs	4913	3404	1509	1377	2551	8840	1183	492	10516
9 Economic services	9042	4449	4593	8115	252	17409	6870	3946	28225
A Fuel and energy	251	253	−2	1144	8	1403	12	26	1440
B Agriculture, hunting, forestry and fishing	1692	1155	537	5565	38	7295	475	1050	8819
C Mining (except fuels), manufacturing and construction	298	301	−3	292	68	658	9	369	1036
D Transportation and communication	5479	1832	3647	659	38	6176	6149	1298	13623
E Other economic affairs	1323	908	415	455	101	1879	226	1203	3308
10 Other functions	7304	3921	3383	_	18673	25977	49	294	26321
Total	94080	59420	34660	9492	54820	158393	13714	6891	178997

1996

	Final consumption expenditures Total	Compensation of employees	Other	Subsidies	Other current transfers and property income	Total current disbursements	Gross capital formation	Other capital outlays	Total outlays
1 General public services	7993	4712	3281	_	794	8787	388	85	9260
2 Defence	...	−	−	−	−	−	−	−	−
3 Public order and safety	6199	4610	1589	_	116	6316	600	53	6969
4 Education	21172	16629	4543	_	378	21550	3151	1186	25887
5 Health	31871	18197	13674	_	487	32358	534	221	33112

Iceland

	1996							
	Final consumption expenditures			Subsidies	Other current transfers and property income	Total current disburse- ments	Gross capital formation	Other capital outlays	Total outlays
	Total	Compen- sation of employ- ees	Other						
6 Social security and welfare	8130	7222	908	–	32482	40612	1492	–137	41968
7 Housing and community amenities	3659	1830	1829	–	19	3678	170	575	4423
8 Recreational, cultural and religious affairs	5167	3382	1785	1436	2598	9201	958	610	10769
9 Economic services	8951	4795	4156	8619	224	17793	8225	5622	31640
A Fuel and energy	198	263	–65	1069	9	1275	6	26	1307
B Agriculture, hunting, forestry and fishing	1805	1331	474	5970	51	7826	484	1089	9399
C Mining (except fuels), manufacturing and construction	430	302	128	354	20	804	6	431	1241
D Transportation and communication	5110	1878	3232	941	39	6090	7711	2905	16706
E Other economic affairs	1409	1021	388	285	105	1799	18	1171	2988
10 Other functions	7216	3835	3381	–	17913	25129	–103	–186	24840
Total	100359	65211	35148	10054	55011	165424	15416	8029	188869

2.4 Composition of general government social security benefits and social assistance grants to households
Million Icelandic kronur

	1986		1987		1988		1989		1990		1991	
	Social security benefits	Social assistance grants	Social security benefits	Social assistance grants	Social security benefits	Social assistance grants	Social security benefits	Social assistance grants	Social security benefits	Social assistance grants	Social security benefits	Social assistance grants
1 Education benefits	...	114	...	144	...	222	...	259	...	246	...	295
2 Health benefits	...	–	...	16	...	184	...	176	...	206	...	346
3 Social security and welfare benefits	5431	1795	7625	2308	10162	4652	12406	4969	14445	7276	16182	7839
A Social security	5431	1443	7625	1881	10162	4269	12406	3440	14445	6657	16182	7365
Temporary sickness	121	...	152	...	177	...	209	...	186	...	220	...
Old age and permanent disability	4110	...	5755	...	7583	...	8844	...	10168	...	11664	...
Unemployment	189	...	234	...	348	...	876	...	1066	...	957	...
Family assistance	515	1443	738	1881	1122	4269	1395	3440	1795	6657	1918	7365
Other	496	...	747	...	932	...	1082	...	1229	...	1423	...
B Welfare	...	352	...	427	...	383	...	1529	...	619	...	474
4 Housing and community amenities	...	–	...	–	...	–	...	1	...	1	...	3
5 Recreation and cultural benefits	...	...	...	...	...	...	...	...	...	...	...	–
6 Other	...	...	...	...	...	...	...	...	...	...	...	...
Total	5431	1909	7625	2467	10162	5058	12406	5404	14445	7729	16182	8483

	1992		1993		1994		1995		1996		1997	
	Social security benefits	Social assistance grants	Social security benefits	Social assistance grants	Social security benefits	Social assistance grants	Social security benefits	Social assistance grants	Social security benefits	Social assistance grants	Social security benefits	Social assistance grants
1 Education benefits	...	324	...	345	...	337	...	301	...	378	...	...
2 Health benefits	...	246	...	245	...	330	...	459	...	487	...	...
3 Social security and welfare benefits	17824	8055	19204	8898	19922	8831	21312	9294	21102	10150	...	...
A Social security	17824	7304	19204	7652	19922	7454	21312	7886	21102	...	...	...
Temporary sickness	221	...	224	...	234	...	247	...	181	...	...	...

Iceland

| | 1992 || 1993 || 1994 || 1995 || 1996 || 1997 ||
	Social security benefits	Social assistance grants	Social security benefits	Social assistance grants	Social security benefits	Social assistance grants	Social security benefits	Social assistance grants	Social security benefits	Social assistance grants	Social security benefits	Social assistance grants
Old age and permanent disability	12351	...	13300	...	13798	...	14624	...	15176	...	...	...
Unemployment	1824	...	2596	...	2913	...	3335	...	2984	...	...	...
Family assistance	2008	7304	1493	7652	1436	7454	1456	7886	1377	8339	...	...
Other	1420	...	1591	...	1541	...	1651	...	1384	...	...	...
B Welfare	...	751	...	1246	...	1377	...	1408	...	1811	...	...
4 Housing and community amenities	...	16	...	16	...	15	...	23	...	...	...	...
5 Recreation and cultural benefits	...	–	...	–	...	–	...	–	...	–	...	...
6 Other	...	–	...	–	...	–	...	–	...	...	...	...
Total	17824	8641	19204	9504	19922	9513	21312	10077	21102	11034	...	...

2.5 Private final consumption expenditure by type and purpose, in current prices

Million Icelandic kronur

	1986	1987	1988	1989	1990	1991	1992	1993	1994	1995	1996	1997
Final consumption expenditure of resident households											
1 Food, beverages and tobacco	22997	29915	38097	48835	56808	59910	61046	61667	60979	63517	67301	...
A Food	16652	21338	27578	34579	40555	42150	43181	43337	42204	44212	47028	...
B Non-alcoholic beverages	2180	3140	3899	5258	6291	7024	7036	6891	6794	7317	7861	...
C Alcoholic beverages	2257	2988	3629	5440	6035	6527	6507	6976	7148	7275	7590	...
D Tobacco	1909	2449	2991	3557	3928	4208	4322	4464	4834	4713	4823	...
2 Clothing and footwear	9445	12361	13981	15368	17426	19864	19322	18098	19500	20488	21353	...
3 Gross rent, fuel and power	17914	21320	26062	32572	39304	43147	43850	45276	47028	48837	50175	...
A Fuel and power	2709	3004	3804	4502	5500	6082	6400	6879	7135	7362	7574	...
B Other	15205	18315	22258	28071	33804	37066	37450	38397	39893	41475	42600	...
4 Furniture, furnishings and household equipment and operation	9752	13802	14361	16345	17694	20131	19244	18257	19926	21167	23533	...
A Household operation	3572	4808	4409	5276	6221	6797	6661	7135	7641	8348	8907	...
B Other	6179	8994	9952	11069	11473	13334	12583	11122	12285	12819	14626	...
5 Medical care and health expenses	1668	2092	2801	3522	3877	4161	4654	5474	5748	5892	6489	...
6 Transport and communication	15985	23087	25610	26929	30875	37051	35038	34666	35150	40454	47874	...
A Personal transport equipment	12847	19098	20434	20570	23602	28946	26531	25933	25802	10882	15425	...
B Other	3138	3989	5176	6359	7274	8105	8507	8733	9348	29572	32450	...
7 Recreational, entertainment, education and cultural services	8211	11482	16143	19509	22931	25148	25464	26162	28392	30322	33082	...
A Education	431	573	1682	2103	2512	2512	2841	3115	3300	3520	3751	...
B Other	7780	10909	14461	17406	20419	22636	22623	23047	25093	26802	29331	...
8 Miscellaneous goods and services	10196	14406	18479	21410	26432	29953	30959	30084	32930	35841	38283	...
A Personal care	1719	2303	3239	4020	4893	5831	5847	5865	6297	6930	7498	...
B Expenditures in restaurants, cafes and hotels	6082	8588	11244	12673	15694	17689	18397	17712	19784	21584	23016	...
C Other	2394	3516	3996	4717	5845	6433	6715	6507	6850	7327	7769	...
Total final consumption expenditure in the domestic market by households, of which	96169	128465	155534	184490	215347	239365	239577	239685	249652	266518	288090	...
plus: Direct purchases abroad by resident households	5632	8581	10348	12196	16635	17685	16886	18261	17892	18194	20472	...

Iceland

Million Icelandic kronur

	1986	1987	1988	1989	1990	1991	1992	1993	1994	1995	1996	1997
less: Direct purchases in the domestic market by non-resident households	2604	3489	4814	6432	8806	8684	8124	9764	10595	12004	11722	...
equals: Final consumption expenditure of resident households	99196[a]	133557[a]	161068	190254	223176	248366	248339	248182	256949	272708	296840	...

a Item "Final consumption expenditure of resident households" includes consumption expenditure of private non-profit institutions serving households.

2.6 Private final consumption expenditure by type and purpose, in constant prices

Million Icelandic kronur

	1986	1987	1988	1989	1990	1991	1992	1993	1994	1995	1996	1997
	At constant prices of: 1980											
					1990							

Final consumption expenditure of resident households

	1986	1987	1988	1989	1990	1991	1992	1993	1994	1995	1996	1997
1 Food, beverages and tobacco	2447	2752	2669	2893	2884 / 56808	57638	56815	55459	55341	56250	58126	...
A Food	1725	1928	1864	1975	1953 / 40555	41038	40891	39824	39707	40427	41724	...
B Non-alcoholic beverages	215	268	261	279	319 / 6291	6602	6476	6284	6179	6404	6704	...
C Alcoholic beverages	285	315	318	409	394 / 6035	6063	5629	5705	5739	5823	6073	...
D Tobacco	223	240	226	230	218 / 3928	3935	3819	3646	3717	3595	3625	...
2 Clothing and footwear	977	1047	984	921	875 / 17426	18091	16837	15590	16772	17566	18303	...
3 Gross rent, fuel and power	2133	2171	2220	2272	2335 / 39304	39699	40111	40310	40898	41518	42344	...
A Fuel and power	294	298	304	311	330 / 5500	5252	5319	5345	5422	5633	5742	...
B Other	1839	1872	1916	1962	2005 / 33804	34447	34792	34966	35476	35884	36602	...
4 Furniture, furnishings and household equipment and operation	1284	1542	1306	1209	1076 / 17694	19045	17293	16271	17434	18331	19827	...
A Household operation	425	483	369	356	361 / 6221	6522	6007	6199	6447	6969	7240	...
B Other	858	1059	937	853	714 / 11473	12524	11286	10072	10986	11363	12587	...
5 Medical care and health expenses	174	190	190	190	180 / 3877	3851	3788	3870	3960	4149	4315	...
6 Transport and communication	2216	2889	2466	1932	2003 / 30875	34036	30505	27886	27507	31172	35499	...
A Personal transport equipment	1830	2476	2069	1522	1592 / 8337	11157	7809	6368	6032	7938	10954	...
B Other	387	413	397	410	411 / 22539	22879	22697	21517	21476	23234	24544	...
7 Recreational, entertainment, education and cultural services	810	960	1195	1199	1205 / 22931	23973	22265	21702	22763	23965	25404	...
A Education	38	38	87	89	89 / 2512	2513	2538	2564	2589	2719	2800	...
B Other	772	922	1108	1110	1116 / 20419	21459	19726	19138	20173	21246	22603	...
8 Miscellaneous goods and services	1052	1187	1224	1227	1278 / 26432	27351	26576	24627	25986	27990	29471	...
A Personal care	151	175	241	261	263 / 4893	5509	5399	5059	5298	5709	6065	...
B Expenditures in restaurants, cafes and hotels	606	654	669	648	687 / 15694	15936	15504	14098	15121	16415	17400	...
C Other	295	358	314	317	328 / 5845	5906	5673	5470	5567	5866	6006	...
Total final consumption expenditure in the domestic market by households, of which	11093	12737	12253	11844	11836 / 215347	223684	214190	205716	210660	220941	233289	...

Iceland

Million Icelandic kronur

	1986	1987	1988	1989	1990	1991	1992	1993	1994	1995	1996	1997
	At constant prices of: 1980 / 1990											
plus: Direct purchases abroad by resident households	534	761	774	690	811 / 16635	16812	15116	14700	14243	14130	15619	...
less: Direct purchases in the domestic market by non-resident households	296	333	363	397	451 / 8806	8114	7293	8351	8911	9918	9444	...
equals: Final consumption expenditure of resident households [a]	11332	13165	12664	12136	12196 / 223176	232382	222012	212064	215992	225154	239464	...

a Item "Final consumption expenditure of resident households" includes consumption expenditure of private non-profit institutions serving households.

2.11 Gross fixed capital formation by kind of activity of owner, ISIC divisions, in current prices

Million Icelandic kronur

	1986	1987	1988	1989	1990	1991	1992	1993	1994	1995	1996	1997
All producers												
1 Agriculture, hunting, forestry and fishing	4946	6605	8381	5799	4248	4854	7568	4029	5276	3152	7716	...
A Agriculture and hunting	1258	1653	1593	1584	1537	1943	1618	1884	1804	1606	2542	...
B Forestry and logging	...	...	...	...	...	...	...	...	...	...	...	...
C Fishing	3688	4952	6788	4216	2711	2911	5950	2146	3471	1546	5174	
2 Mining and quarrying	4815	5701	6180	7130	7116	8055	6839	7098	7776	9280	18516	...
3 Manufacturing												...
4 Electricity, gas and water	1739	2107	3532	5443	6526	7101	3857	3513	3044	3496	5137	
A Electricity, gas and steam	1529	1867	3212	5073	5921	6381	3308	2949	2582	2949	4631	...
B Water works and supply	210	240	320	370	605	720	549	564	462	548	506	...
5 Construction [a]	764	1164	1305	1377	1744	2473	1562	1528	1274	1749	2624	...
6 Wholesale and retail trade, restaurants and hotels [bc]	4234	6950	6693	6535	7033	6998	7043	6776	7474	8597	10751	...
7 Transport, storage and communication	3124	4925	3311	6185	11945	12814	9241	5988	5734	7301	8183	
A Transport and storage	2321	3809	2559	5280	10941	11348	7387	3952	2825	4642	5465	
B Communication	802	1116	752	905	1003	1466	1854	2036	2909	2659	2718	...
8 Finance, insurance, real estate and business services [bcd]	6923	9303	12586	15936	18666	19104	18912	18212	18667	17338	18935	...
A Financial institutions	...	...	...	...	...	...	...	...	...	...	...	
B Insurance	...	...	...	...	...	...	...	...	...	...	...	
C Real estate and business services	6923	9303	12586	15936	18666	19104	18912	18212	18667	17338	18935	
Real estate, except dwellings	...	...	...	...	...	...	...	...	...	...	...	
Dwellings	6923	9303	12586	15936	18666	19104	18912	18212	18667	17338	18935	
9 Community, social and personal services	...	...	...	...	...	...	...	...	...	...	...	
Total industries	26545	36755	41988	48406	57278	61398	55021	47144	49246	50914	71862	
Producers of government services	4365	5884	8510	10293	12825	14775	14568	17033	16630	15036	14890	...
Private non-profit institutions serving households	...	...	...	...	...	...	...	...	...	...	...	...
Total	30911	42639	50498	58698	70103	76173	69589	64177	65876	65949	86752	...

a Item "Construction" includes machinery only.
b Finance, insurance and business services are included in item "Wholesale and retail trade, restaurants and hotels".
c Computers in all economic activities are included in item "Wholesale and retail trade".
d Real estate refers to owner-occupied dwellings and rent only.

Iceland

2.12 Gross fixed capital formation by kind of activity of owner, ISIC divisions, in constant prices

Million Icelandic kronur

	1986	1987	1988	1989	1990	1991	1992	1993	1994	1995	1996	1997
At constant prices of:			1980									
					1990							
All producers												
1 Agriculture, hunting, forestry and fishing	641	748	795	433	277							...
					4248	4611	6965	3440	4210	2469	5897	
A Agriculture and hunting	167	198	158	119	105							...
					1537	1859	1494	1638	1493	1254	2045	
B Forestry and logging	...	...	...	...	...	...	...	...	...	...	...	
C Fishing	474	550	637	314	172							...
					2711	2752	5471	1802	2718	1216	3852	
2 Mining and quarrying	586	614	562	513	448							...
					7116	7636	6263	6059	6310	7362	14336	
3 Manufacturing												...
4 Electricity, gas and water	215	221	315	395	416							...
					6526	6653	3506	3105	2628	2931	4113	
A Electricity, gas and steam	189	196	286	368	382							
					5921	5984	3008	2604	2228	2471	3701	
B Water works and supply	26	25	28	27	34							...
					605	669	498	501	401	460	412	
5 Construction [a]	87	122	140	115	143							...
					1744	2371	1439	1265	980	1332	1939	
6 Wholesale and retail trade, restaurants and hotels [bc]	604	835	681	512	532							...
					7033	6582	6428	5843	6094	6848	8299	
7 Transport, storage and communication	419	570	334	468	766							...
					11945	12172	8449	5168	4781	5880	6463	
A Transport and storage	292	420	247	385	684							
					10941	10810	6766	3423	2410	3756	4358	
B Communication	127	150	87	83	82							...
					1003	1362	1682	1745	2371	2124	2105	
8 Finance, insurance, real estate and business services [bcd]	853	974	1118	1149	1143							...
					18666	17755	17161	16174	16176	14578	15161	
A Financial institutions	...	...	...	...	...	...	...	...	...	...	...	...
B Insurance	...	...	...	...	...	...	...	...	...	...	...	...
C Real estate and business services	853	974	1118	1149	1143							...
					18666	17755	17161	16174	16176	14578	15161	
Real estate, except dwellings	...	...	...	...	...	...	...	...	...	...	...	
Dwellings	853	974	1118	1149	1143							...
					18666	17755	17161	16174	16176	14578	15161	
9 Community, social and personal services	...	...	...	...	...	...	...	...	...	...	...	
Total industries	3405	4085	3945	3585	3725							...
					57278	57780	50212	41053	41180	41400	56208	
Producers of government services	551	614	744	735	725							...
					12825	13757	13267	15176	14456	12660	12192	
Private non-profit institutions serving households	...	...	...	...	...	...	...	...	...	...	...	
Total	3956	4698	4689	4320	4450							...
					70103	71537	63479	56229	55637	54060	68400	

a Item "Construction" includes machinery only.
b Finance, insurance and business services are included in item "Wholesale and retail trade, restaurants and hotels".
c Computers in all economic activities are included in item "Wholesale and retail trade".
d Real estate refers to owner-occupied dwellings and rent only.

Iceland

2.13 Stocks of reproducible fixed assets, by type of good and owner, in current prices

Million Icelandic kronur

	\multicolumn{8}{c}{1986}
	Total		Total private		Public enterprises		General government	
	Gross	Net	Gross	Net	Gross	Net	Gross	Net
1 Residential buildings	...	183742	...	183742	...	–	...	–
2 Non-residential buildings	...	111033	...	67710	...	3232	...	40092
3 Other construction	...	112220	...	2629	...	70422	...	39169
4 Land improvement and plantation and orchard development	...	11634	...	11634	...	–	...	–
5 Producers' durable goods	...	74831	...	70663	...	4167	...	–
A Transport equipment	...	14560	...	14560	...	–	...	–
Passenger cars	...	...	...	...	...	–	...	–
Other	...	14560	...	14560	...	–	...	–
B Machinery and equipment	...	60271	...	56103	...	4167	...	–
6 Breeding stock, dairy cattle, etc.	...	5040	...	5040	...	...	...	...
Statistical discrepancy	...	–	...	–	...	–	...	–
Total	...	498500	...	341418	...	77821	...	79261

	\multicolumn{8}{c}{1987}
	Total		Total private		Public enterprises		General government	
	Gross	Net	Gross	Net	Gross	Net	Gross	Net
1 Residential buildings	...	220167	...	220167	...	–	...	–
2 Non-residential buildings	...	137766	...	84416	...	3955	...	49395
3 Other construction	...	137511	...	4159	...	83138	...	50214
4 Land improvement and plantation and orchard development	...	14272	...	14272	...	–	...	–
5 Producers' durable goods	...	88814	...	83408	...	5406	...	–
A Transport equipment	...	16000	...	16000	...	–	...	–
Passenger cars	...	...	...	...	...	–	...	–
Other	...	16000	...	16000	...	–	...	–
B Machinery and equipment	...	72814	...	67408	...	5406	...	–
6 Breeding stock, dairy cattle, etc.	...	6209	...	6209	...	...	...	...
Statistical discrepancy	...	–	...	–	...	–	...	–
Total	...	604739	...	412631	...	92499	...	99609

	\multicolumn{8}{c}{1988}
	Total		Total private		Public enterprises		General government	
	Gross	Net	Gross	Net	Gross	Net	Gross	Net
1 Residential buildings	...	265465	...	265465	...	...	...	...
2 Non-residential buildings	...	169488	...	103121	...	4605	...	61761
3 Other construction	...	166982	...	5983	...	98286	...	62713
4 Land improvement and plantation and orchard development	...	18073	...	18073	...	...	...	...
5 Producers' durable goods	...	110909	...	104563	...	6347	...	–
A Transport equipment	...	19406	...	19406	...	–	...	–
Passenger cars	...	...	...	...	...	...	...	...
Other	...	19406	...	19406	...	...	...	...
B Machinery and equipment	...	91503	...	85156	...	6347	...	...
6 Breeding stock, dairy cattle, etc.	...	7593	...	7593	...	...	...	...
Total	...	738510	...	504798	...	109238	...	124474

Iceland

1989

	Total Gross	Total Net	Total private Gross	Total private Net	Public enterprises Gross	Public enterprises Net	General government Gross	General government Net
1 Residential buildings	...	334786	...	334786	...	...	...	...
2 Non-residential buildings	...	217051	...	130701	...	5831	...	80519
3 Other construction	...	208066	...	7948	...	122324	...	77794
4 Land improvement and plantation and orchard development	...	21681	...	21681	...	...	...	...
5 Producers' durable goods	...	144226	...	136353	...	7873	...	–
A Transport equipment	...	26524	...	26524	...	–	...	–
Passenger cars	...	...	...	...	...	...	...	...
Other	...	26524	...	26524	...	...	...	...
B Machinery and equipment	...	117702	...	109830	...	7873	...	...
6 Breeding stock, dairy cattle, etc.	...	8964	...	8964	...	...	...	...
Total	...	934774	...	640433	...	136028	...	158313

1990

	Total Gross	Total Net	Total private Gross	Total private Net	Public enterprises Gross	Public enterprises Net	General government Gross	General government Net
1 Residential buildings	...	403167	...	403167	...	...	...	...
2 Non-residential buildings	...	254548	...	141213	...	6072	...	107262
3 Other construction	...	251447	...	9345	...	142078	...	100024
4 Land improvement and plantation and orchard development	...	22984	...	22984	...	...	...	...
5 Producers' durable goods	...	172558	...	163153	...	9406	...	–
A Transport equipment	...	35867	...	35867	...	–	...	–
Passenger cars	...	...	...	...	...	...	...	...
Other	...	35867	...	35867	...	...	...	...
B Machinery and equipment	...	136692	...	127286	...	9406	...	...
6 Breeding stock, dairy cattle, etc.	...	10223	...	10223	...	...	...	...
Total	...	1114927	...	750085	...	157556	...	207286

1991

	Total Gross	Total Net	Total private Gross	Total private Net	Public enterprises Gross	Public enterprises Net	General government Gross	General government Net
1 Residential buildings	...	442068	...	442068	...	...	...	...
2 Non-residential buildings	...	281123	...	153281	...	6513	...	121329
3 Other construction	...	274568	...	9872	...	154808	...	109887
4 Land improvement and plantation and orchard development	...	24214	...	24214	...	...	...	...
5 Producers' durable goods	...	188693	...	178300	...	10393	...	–
A Transport equipment	...	42403	...	42403	...	–	...	–
Passenger cars	...	...	...	...	...	...	...	...
Other	...	42403	...	42403	...	...	...	...
B Machinery and equipment	...	146290	...	135897	...	10393	...	...
6 Breeding stock, dairy cattle, etc.	...	10318	...	10318	...	...	...	...
Total	...	1220984	...	818053	...	171714	...	231216

1992

	Total Gross	Total Net	Total private Gross	Total private Net	Public enterprises Gross	Public enterprises Net	General government Gross	General government Net
1 Residential buildings	...	460342	...	460342	...	...	...	...
2 Non-residential buildings	...	294727	...	158169	...	6635	...	129923
3 Other construction	...	282694	...	9677	...	158537	...	114479

Iceland

1992

	Total Gross	Total Net	Total private Gross	Total private Net	Public enterprises Gross	Public enterprises Net	General government Gross	General government Net
4 Land improvement and plantation and orchard development	...	25186	...	25186	...	...	...	...
5 Producers' durable goods	...	197669	...	186293	...	11376	...	—
A Transport equipment	...	43632	...	43632	...	—	...	—
Passenger cars	...	...	...	...	...	...	...	...
Other	...	43632	...	43632	...	...	...	...
B Machinery and equipment	...	154037	...	142661	...	11376	...	...
6 Breeding stock, dairy cattle, etc.	...	10483	...	10483	...	...	...	...
Total	...	1271101	...	850150	...	176548	...	244402

1993

	Total Gross	Total Net	Total private Gross	Total private Net	Public enterprises Gross	Public enterprises Net	General government Gross	General government Net
1 Residential buildings	...	476819	...	476819	...	...	...	...
2 Non-residential buildings	...	308813	...	163401	...	6677	...	138735
3 Other construction	...	293030	...	9443	...	162167	...	121421
4 Land improvement and plantation and orchard development	...	26540	...	26540	...	...	...	...
5 Producers' durable goods	...	211075	...	198235	...	12840	...	—
A Transport equipment	...	44761	...	44761	...	—	...	—
Passenger cars	...	...	...	...	...	...	...	...
Other	...	44761	...	44761	...	...	...	...
B Machinery and equipment	...	166314	...	153474	...	12840	...	...
6 Breeding stock, dairy cattle, etc.	...	10385	...	10385	...	...	...	...
Total	...	1326662	...	884823	...	181684	...	260156

1994

	Total Gross	Total Net	Total private Gross	Total private Net	Public enterprises Gross	Public enterprises Net	General government Gross	General government Net
1 Residential buildings	...	495127	...	495127	...	...	...	...
2 Non-residential buildings	...	322075	...	167554	...	6791	...	147730
3 Other construction	...	302394	...	9226	...	164911	...	128257
4 Land improvement and plantation and orchard development	...	27603	...	27603	...	...	...	...
5 Producers' durable goods	...	223369	...	208407	...	14963	...	—
A Transport equipment	...	43717	...	43717	...	—	...	—
Passenger cars	...	...	...	...	...	...	...	...
Other	...	43717	...	43717	...	...	...	...
B Machinery and equipment	...	179652	...	164690	...	14963	...	...
6 Breeding stock, dairy cattle, etc.	...	10512	...	10512	...	...	...	...
Total	...	1381080	...	918429	...	186665	...	275987

1995

	Total Gross	Total Net	Total private Gross	Total private Net	Public enterprises Gross	Public enterprises Net	General government Gross	General government Net
1 Residential buildings	...	514883	...	514883	...	...	...	...
2 Non-residential buildings	...	337660	...	173280	...	6924	...	157456
3 Other construction	...	312252	...	9090	...	168502	...	134660
4 Land improvement and plantation and orchard development	...	28453	...	28453	...	...	...	...
5 Producers' durable goods	...	224606	...	208313	...	16293	...	—
A Transport equipment	...	41941	...	41941	...	—	...	—

Iceland

	1995						
	Total		Total private		Public enterprises		General government	
	Gross	Net	Gross	Net	Gross	Net	Gross	Net
Passenger cars	...	...	...	...	...	...	...	...
Other	...	41941	...	41941	...	...	...	...
B Machinery and equipment	...	182665	...	166372	...	16293	...	...
6 Breeding stock, dairy cattle, etc.	...	10864	...	10864	...	...	...	...
Total	...	1428718	...	944883	...	191719	...	292116

	1996						
	Total		Total private		Public enterprises		General government	
	Gross	Net	Gross	Net	Gross	Net	Gross	Net
1 Residential buildings	...	546099	...	546099	...	...	...	...
2 Non-residential buildings	...	357482	...	183452	...	7008	...	167023
3 Other construction	...	322863	...	8913	...	173972	...	139979
4 Land improvement and plantation and orchard development	...	28890	...	28890	...	...	...	...
5 Producers' durable goods	...	240822	...	222950	...	17872	...	—
A Transport equipment	...	40784	...	40784	...	—	...	...
Passenger cars	...	...	...	...	...	...	...	...
Other	...	40784	...	40784	...	...	...	...
B Machinery and equipment	...	200038	...	182166	...	17872	...	...
6 Breeding stock, dairy cattle, etc.	...	10827	...	10827	...	...	...	...
Total	...	1506983	...	1001131	...	198852	...	307002

2.14 Stocks of reproducible fixed assets, by type of good and owner, in constant prices

Million Icelandic kronur

	1986						
	Total		Total private		Public enterprises		General government	
	Gross	Net	Gross	Net	Gross	Net	Gross	Net
At constant prices of: 1980							
1 Residential buildings	...	17176	...	17176	...	—	...	—
2 Non-residential buildings	...	14081	...	8855	...	221	...	5005
3 Other construction	...	14092	...	—	...	8828	...	5264
4 Land improvement and plantation and orchard development	...	1293	...	1293	...	—	...	—
5 Producers' durable goods	...	9825	...	8865	...	960	...	—
A Transport equipment	...	1768	...	1768	...	—	...	—
Passenger cars	...	901	...	901	...	—	...	—
Other	...	867	...	867	...	—	...	—
B Machinery and equipment	...	8058	...	7098	...	960	...	—
6 Breeding stock, dairy cattle, etc.	...	...	...	...	...	...	...	...
Total	...	56467	...	36189	...	10009	...	10269

	1987						
	Total		Total private		Public enterprises		General government	
	Gross	Net	Gross	Net	Gross	Net	Gross	Net
At constant prices of: 1980							
1 Residential buildings	...	17558	...	17558	...	—	...	—
2 Non-residential buildings	...	14904	...	9429	...	239	...	5236
3 Other construction	...	14225	...	—	...	8860	...	5364
4 Land improvement and plantation and orchard development	...	1290	...	1290	...	—	...	—
5 Producers' durable goods	...	10606	...	9569	...	1038	...	—

Iceland

1987

	Total Gross	Total Net	Total private Gross	Total private Net	Public enterprises Gross	Public enterprises Net	General government Gross	General government Net
At constant prices of: 1980								
A Transport equipment	...	1775	...	1775	...	–	...	–
Passenger cars	...	968	...	968	...	–	...	–
Other	...	807	...	807	...	–	...	–
B Machinery and equipment	...	8832	...	7794	...	1038	...	–
6 Breeding stock, dairy cattle, etc.	...	...	...	...	...	...	...	...
Total	...	58583	...	37846	...	10137	...	10600

1988

	Total Gross	Total Net	Total private Gross	Total private Net	Public enterprises Gross	Public enterprises Net	General government Gross	General government Net
At constant prices of: 1980								
1 Residential buildings	...	18017	...	18017	...	–	...	–
2 Non-residential buildings	...	15650	...	9852	...	246	...	5552
3 Other construction	...	14379	...	–	...	8879	...	5500
4 Land improvement and plantation and orchard development	...	1284	...	1284	...	–	...	–
5 Producers' durable goods	...	11309	...	10250	...	1060	...	–
A Transport equipment	...	1831	...	1831	...	–	...	–
Passenger cars	...	1023	...	1023	...	–	...	–
Other	...	808	...	808	...	–	...	–
B Machinery and equipment	...	9478	...	8419	...	1060	...	–
6 Breeding stock, dairy cattle, etc.	...	...	...	...	...	...	...	...
Total	...	60639	...	39403	...	10185	...	11052

1989

	Total Gross	Total Net	Total private Gross	Total private Net	Public enterprises Gross	Public enterprises Net	General government Gross	General government Net
At constant prices of: 1980								
1 Residential buildings	...	18485	...	18485	...	–	...	–
2 Non-residential buildings	...	16282	...	10154	...	257	...	5871
3 Other construction	...	14590	...	–	...	8977	...	5613
4 Land improvement and plantation and orchard development	...	1277	...	1277	...	–	...	–
5 Producers' durable goods	...	11472	...	10399	...	1073	...	–
A Transport equipment	...	1909	...	1909	...	–	...	–
Passenger cars	...	997	...	997	...	–	...	–
Other	...	912	...	912	...	–	...	–
B Machinery and equipment	...	9563	...	8490	...	1073	...	–
6 Breeding stock, dairy cattle, etc.	...	...	...	...	...	...	...	...
Total	...	62106	...	40315	...	10307	...	11484

1990

	Total Gross	Total Net	Total private Gross	Total private Net	Public enterprises Gross	Public enterprises Net	General government Gross	General government Net
At constant prices of: 1990								
1 Residential buildings	...	403219	...	403219	...	–	...	–
2 Non-residential buildings	...	254609	...	141192	...	6152	...	107265
3 Other construction	...	251444	...	9342	...	142078	...	100024
4 Land improvement and plantation and orchard development	...	23042	...	23042	...	–	...	–
5 Producers' durable goods	...	172599	...	163188	...	9411	...	–
A Transport equipment	...	35856	...	35856	...	–	...	–

Iceland

	1990							
	Total		Total private		Public enterprises		General government	
	Gross	Net	Gross	Net	Gross	Net	Gross	Net
At constant prices of: 1990								
Passenger cars	...	...	...	...	...	–	...	–
Other	...	35856	...	35856	...	–	...	–
B Machinery and equipment	...	136743	...	127332	...	9411	...	–
6 Breeding stock, dairy cattle, etc.	...	10223	...	10223	...	...	...	...
Total	...	1115136	...	750206	...	157641	...	207289

	1991							
	Total		Total private		Public enterprises		General government	
	Gross	Net	Gross	Net	Gross	Net	Gross	Net
At constant prices of: 1990								
1 Residential buildings	...	410894	...	410894	...	...	...	...
2 Non-residential buildings	...	261771	...	142877	...	6133	...	112762
3 Other construction	...	256249	...	9172	...	144474	...	102602
4 Land improvement and plantation and orchard development	...	23251	...	23251	...	...	...	...
5 Producers' durable goods	...	179459	...	169763	...	9696	...	–
A Transport equipment	...	40620	...	40620	...	–	...	–
Passenger cars	...	...	...	...	...	...	...	...
Other	...	40620	...	40620	...	...	...	...
B Machinery and equipment	...	138839	...	129143	...	9696	...	...
6 Breeding stock, dairy cattle, etc.	...	10008	...	10008	...	...	...	...
Total	...	1141632	...	765965	...	160303	...	215364

	1992							
	Total		Total private		Public enterprises		General government	
	Gross	Net	Gross	Net	Gross	Net	Gross	Net
At constant prices of: 1990								
1 Residential buildings	...	417783	...	417783	...	...	...	...
2 Non-residential buildings	...	268297	...	144302	...	6094	...	117901
3 Other construction	...	257797	...	8777	...	144187	...	104833
4 Land improvement and plantation and orchard development	...	23519	...	23519	...	...	...	...
5 Producers' durable goods	...	181520	...	171177	...	10344	...	–
A Transport equipment	...	40187	...	40187	...	–	...	–
Passenger cars	...	...	...	...	...	...	...	...
Other	...	40187	...	40187	...	...	...	...
B Machinery and equipment	...	141333	...	130989	...	10344	...	...
6 Breeding stock, dairy cattle, etc.	...	10005	...	10005	...	...	...	...
Total	...	1158921	...	775563	...	160625	...	222734

	1993							
	Total		Total private		Public enterprises		General government	
	Gross	Net	Gross	Net	Gross	Net	Gross	Net
At constant prices of: 1990								
1 Residential buildings	...	423512	...	423512	...	...	...	...
2 Non-residential buildings	...	274247	...	145034	...	6000	...	123213
3 Other construction	...	259643	...	8383	...	142656	...	108604
4 Land improvement and plantation and orchard development	...	23691	...	23691	...	...	...	...
5 Producers' durable goods	...	177050	...	166063	...	10986	...	–
A Transport equipment	...	37329	...	37329	...	–	...	–
Passenger cars	...	...	...	...	...	...	...	...

Iceland

| | 1993 ||||||||
| | Total || Total private || Public enterprises || General government ||
	Gross	Net	Gross	Net	Gross	Net	Gross	Net
At constant prices of: 1990								
Other	...	37329	...	37329	...	...	...	...
B Machinery and equipment	...	139721	...	128734	...	10986	...	...
6 Breeding stock, dairy cattle, etc.	...	9854	...	9854	...	...	...	...
Total	...	1167997	...	776537	...	159642	...	231817

| | 1994 ||||||||
| | Total || Total private || Public enterprises || General government ||
	Gross	Net	Gross	Net	Gross	Net	Gross	Net
At constant prices of: 1990								
1 Residential buildings	...	429101	...	429101	...	...	...	...
2 Non-residential buildings	...	279080	...	145114	...	5947	...	128018
3 Other construction	...	260538	...	7998	...	140623	...	111917
4 Land improvement and plantation and orchard development	...	23853	...	23853	...	...	...	...
5 Producers' durable goods	...	174459	...	162299	...	12160	...	—
A Transport equipment	...	34065	...	34065	...	—	...	—
Passenger cars	...	...	...	...	...	...	...	...
Other	...	34065	...	34065	...	...	...	...
B Machinery and equipment	...	140394	...	128233	...	12160	...	...
6 Breeding stock, dairy cattle, etc.	...	10020	...	10020	...	...	...	...
Total	...	1177051	...	778385	...	158730	...	239935

| | 1995 ||||||||
| | Total || Total private || Public enterprises || General government ||
	Gross	Net	Gross	Net	Gross	Net	Gross	Net
At constant prices of: 1990								
1 Residential buildings	...	432951	...	432951	...	...	...	...
2 Non-residential buildings	...	283506	...	145427	...	5873	...	132206
3 Other construction	...	260869	...	7632	...	139407	...	113831
4 Land improvement and plantation and orchard development	...	23998	...	23998	...	...	...	...
5 Producers' durable goods	...	173503	...	160516	...	12987	...	—
A Transport equipment	...	32105	...	32105	...	—	...	—
Passenger cars	...	...	...	...	...	...	...	...
Other	...	32105	...	32105	...	...	...	...
B Machinery and equipment	...	141398	...	128412	...	12987	...	...
6 Breeding stock, dairy cattle, etc.	...	10134	...	10134	...	...	...	...
Total	...	1184961	...	780658	...	158267	...	246037

| | 1996 ||||||||
| | Total || Total private || Public enterprises || General government ||
	Gross	Net	Gross	Net	Gross	Net	Gross	Net
At constant prices of: 1990								
1 Residential buildings	...	437288	...	437288	...	...	...	...
2 Non-residential buildings	...	291038	...	149257	...	5767	...	136015
3 Other construction	...	262875	...	7265	...	140116	...	115494
4 Land improvement and plantation and orchard development	...	24167	...	24167	...	...	...	...
5 Producers' durable goods	...	180886	...	167062	...	13824	...	—
A Transport equipment	...	30335	...	30335	...	—	...	—
Passenger cars	...	...	...	...	...	...	...	...

Iceland

	1996						
	Total		Total private		Public enterprises		General government	
	Gross	Net	Gross	Net	Gross	Net	Gross	Net
At constant prices of: 1990								
Other	...	30335	...	30335	...	...	...	...
B Machinery and equipment	...	150551	...	136727	...	13824	...	...
6 Breeding stock, dairy cattle, etc.	...	10042	...	10042	...	...	...	...
Total	...	1206296	...	795081	...	159707	...	251509

2.15 Stocks of reproducible fixed assets, by kind of activity, in current prices

Million Icelandic kronur

	1986		1987		1988		1989		1990		1991	
	Gross	Net	Gross	Net	Gross	Net	Gross	Net	Gross	Net	Gross	Net
1 Residential buildings	...	183742	...	220167	...	265465	...	334786	...	403167	...	442068
2 Non-residential buildings	...	111033	...	137766	...	169488	...	217051	...	254548	...	281123
A Industries	...	70941	...	88371	...	107726	...	136532	...	147286	...	159794
1 Agriculture	...	9369	...	10821	...	12703	...	15708	...	16029	...	16565
2 Mining and quarrying	...	–	...	–	...	...	...	...	...	...	...	...
3 Manufacturing	...	27973	...	33988	...	40633	...	50568	...	53097	...	56723
4 Electricity, gas and water	...	–	...	–	...	...	...	...	...	...	...	...
5 Construction	...	–	...	–	...	–	...	...	...	...	...	...
6 Wholesale and retail trade	...	31288	...	40672	...	50910	...	65843	...	73550	...	81490
7 Transport and communication	...	2311	...	2890	...	3480	...	4413	...	4610	...	5015
8 Finance, etc.	...	...	...	...	...	...	...	...	...	...	...	...
9 Community, social and personal services	...	–	...	–	...	...	...	...	...	...	...	...
Statistical discrepancy	...	–	...	–	...	...	...	...	...	...	...	...
B Producers of government services	...	40092	...	49395	...	61761	...	80519	...	107262	...	121329
C Other producers	...	–	...	–	...	...	...	...	...	...	...	...
3 Other construction	...	112220	...	137511	...	166982	...	208066	...	251447	...	274568
A Industries	...	73051	...	87297	...	104269	...	130272	...	151423	...	164681
1 Agriculture	...	2629	...	4159	...	5983	...	7948	...	9345	...	9872
2 Mining and quarrying	...	...	...	...	...	...	...	...	...	...	...	...
3 Manufacturing	...	–	...	–	...	...	...	...	...	...	...	...
4 Electricity, gas and water	...	55204	...	63759	...	74946	...	93013	...	104842	...	113682
5 Construction	...	...	...	...	...	...	...	...	...	...	...	...
6 Wholesale and retail trade	...	–	...	–	...	...	...	...	...	...	...	...
7 Transport and communication	...	15218	...	19379	...	23340	...	29312	...	37236	...	41126
8 Finance, etc.	...	...	...	...	...	...	...	...	...	...	...	...
9 Community, social and personal services	...	–	...	–	...	...	...	...	...	...	...	...
Statistical discrepancy	...	–	...	–	...	...	...	...	...	...	...	...
B Producers of government services	...	39169	...	50214	...	62713	...	77794	...	100024	...	109887
C Other producers	...	–	...	–	...	...	...	...	...	...	...	...
4 Land improvement and development and plantation and orchard development	...	11634	...	14272	...	18073	...	21681	...	22984	...	24214
5 Producers' durable goods	...	74831	...	88814	...	110909	...	144226	...	172558	...	188693
A Industries	...	74831	...	88814	...	110909	...	144226	...	172558	...	188693
1 Agriculture	...	27395	...	32541	...	42242	...	53960	...	62965	...	65865

Iceland

Million Icelandic kronur

	1986		1987		1988		1989		1990		1991	
	Gross	Net	Gross	Net	Gross	Net	Gross	Net	Gross	Net	Gross	Net
2 Mining and quarrying	...	–	...	–	...	...	...	...	...	...	...	...
3 Manufacturing	...	19094	...	22520	...	27506	...	35724	...	43183	...	46243
4 Electricity, gas and water	...	–	...	–	...	...	...	...	...	...	...	...
5 Construction	...	5214	...	5993	...	6290	...	8253	...	8872	...	10338
6 Wholesale and retail trade	...	–	...	–	...	...	...	...	...	...	...	...
7 Transport and communication	...	18164	...	20800	...	24977	...	33433	...	44134	...	51695
8 Finance, etc.	...	–	...	–	...	...	...	...	...	...	...	...
9 Community, social and personal services	...	–	...	–	...	...	...	...	...	...	...	...
Statistical discrepancy	...	4963	...	6959	...	9894	...	12856	...	13405	...	14552
B Producers of government services	...	–	...	–	...	...	...	...	...	...	...	...
C Other producers	...	–	...	–	...	...	...	...	...	...	...	...
6 Breeding stock, dairy cattle, etc.	...	5040	...	6209	...	7593	...	8964	...	10223	...	10318
Statistical discrepancy	...	–	...	–	...	–	...	–	...	–	...	–
Total	...	498500	...	604739	...	738510	...	934774	...	1114927	...	1220984

	1992		1993		1994		1995		1996		1997	
	Gross	Net	Gross	Net	Gross	Net	Gross	Net	Gross	Net	Gross	Net
1 Residential buildings	...	460342	...	476819	...	495127	...	514883	...	546099	...	...
2 Non-residential buildings	...	294727	...	308813	...	322075	...	337660	...	357482	...	...
A Industries	...	164804	...	170078	...	174345	...	180204	...	190460	...	...
1 Agriculture	...	16210	...	16963	...	16893	...	16980	...	17165	...	...
2 Mining and quarrying	...	...	...	...	...	...	...	...	...	...	...	...
3 Manufacturing	...	57687	...	58563	...	59268	...	60448	...	65191	...	...
4 Electricity, gas and water	...	...	...	...	...	...	...	...	...	...	...	...
5 Construction	...	...	...	...	...	...	...	...	...	...	...	...
6 Wholesale and retail trade	...	85771	...	89332	...	92811	...	97243	...	102456	...	...
7 Transport and communication	...	5135	...	5221	...	5373	...	5533	...	5648	...	...
8 Finance, etc.	...	...	...	...	...	...	...	...	...	...	...	...
9 Community, social and personal services	...	...	...	...	...	...	...	...	...	...	...	...
B Producers of government services	...	129923	...	138735	...	147730	...	157456	...	167023	...	...
C Other producers	...	...	...	...	...	...	...	...	...	...	...	...
3 Other construction	...	282694	...	293030	...	302394	...	312252	...	322863	...	...
A Industries	...	168215	...	171610	...	174137	...	177592	...	182885	...	...
1 Agriculture	...	9677	...	9443	...	9226	...	9090	...	8913	...	...
2 Mining and quarrying	...	...	...	...	...	...	...	...	...	...	...	...
3 Manufacturing	...	...	...	...	...	...	...	...	...	...	...	...
4 Electricity, gas and water	...	114742	...	116766	...	117857	...	118548	...	121256	...	...
5 Construction	...	...	...	...	...	...	...	...	...	...	...	...
6 Wholesale and retail trade	...	...	...	...	...	...	...	...	...	...	...	...
7 Transport and communication	...	43795	...	45401	...	47054	...	49954	...	52716	...	...
8 Finance, etc.	...	...	...	...	...	...	...	...	...	...	...	...
9 Community, social and personal services	...	...	...	...	...	...	...	...	...	...	...	...
B Producers of government services	...	114479	...	121421	...	128257	...	134660	...	139979	...	...
C Other producers	...	...	...	...	...	...	...	...	...	...	...	...

Iceland

	1992 Gross	1992 Net	1993 Gross	1993 Net	1994 Gross	1994 Net	1995 Gross	1995 Net	1996 Gross	1996 Net	1997 Gross	1997 Net
4 Land improvement and development and plantation and orchard development	...	25186	...	26540	...	27603	...	28453	...	28890	...	...
5 Producers' durable goods	...	197669	...	211075	...	223369	...	224606	...	240822	...	...
A Industries	...	197669	...	211075	...	223369	...	224606	...	240822	...	...
1 Agriculture	...	69800	...	73416	...	78505	...	76048	...	79134	...	...
2 Mining and quarrying	...	...	...	...	...	...	...	...	...	...	...	...
3 Manufacturing	...	47731	...	51910	...	55311	...	57420	...	65720	...	...
4 Electricity, gas and water	...	...	...	...	...	...	...	...	...	...	...	...
5 Construction	...	10702	...	11657	...	11937	...	11997	...	13132	...	...
6 Wholesale and retail trade	...	...	...	...	...	...	...	...	...	...	...	...
7 Transport and communication	...	53923	...	56519	...	57617	...	57226	...	57587	...	...
8 Finance, etc.	...	...	...	...	...	...	...	...	...	...	...	...
9 Community, social and personal services	...	...	...	...	...	...	...	...	...	...	...	...
Statistical discrepancy	...	15513	...	17572	...	19999	...	21916	...	25250	...	...
B Producers of government services	...	...	...	...	...	...	...	...	...	...	...	...
C Other producers	...	...	...	...	...	...	...	...	...	...	...	...
6 Breeding stock, dairy cattle, etc.	...	10483	...	10385	...	10512	...	10864	...	10827	...	...
Statistical discrepancy	...	–	...	–	...	–	...	–	...	–	...	...
Total	...	1271101	...	1326662	...	1381080	...	1428718	...	1506983	...	...

2.16 Stocks of reproducible fixed assets, by kind of activity, in constant prices

Million Icelandic kronur

	1986 Gross	1986 Net	1987 Gross	1987 Net	1988 Gross	1988 Net	1989 Gross	1989 Net	1990 Gross	1990 Net	1991 Gross	1991 Net
At constant prices of: 1980 / 1990												
1 Residential buildings	...	17176	...	17558	...	18017	...	18485	...	403219	...	410894
2 Non-residential buildings	...	14081	...	14904	...	15650	...	16282	...	254609	...	261771
A Industries	...	9075	...	9668	...	10098	...	10411	...	147344	...	149009
1 Agriculture	...	1641	...	1748	...	1844	...	1873	...	16029	...	15851
2 Mining and quarrying	...	–	...	–	...	–	...	–	...	–	...	...
3 Manufacturing	...	3373	...	3437	...	3497	...	3544	...	53155	...	52762
4 Electricity, gas and water	...	–	...	–	...	–	...	–	...	–	...	...
5 Construction	...	–	...	–	...	–	...	–	...	–	...	...
6 Wholesale and retail trade	...	3841	...	4244	...	4510	...	4736	...	73550	...	75735
7 Transport and communication	...	221	...	239	...	246	...	257	...	4610	...	4661
8 Finance, etc.	...	–	...	–	...	–	...	–	...	–	...	...
9 Community, social and personal services	...	–	...	–	...	–	...	–	...	–	...	...
Statistical discrepancy	...	–	...	–	...	–	...	–	...	–	...	...
B Producers of government services	...	5005	...	5236	...	5552	...	5871	...	107265	...	112762

Iceland

Million Icelandic kronur

	1986 Gross	1986 Net	1987 Gross	1987 Net	1988 Gross	1988 Net	1989 Gross	1989 Net	1990 Gross	1990 Net	1991 Gross	1991 Net
	At constant prices of: 1980								1990			
C Other producers	...	–	...	–	...	–	...	–	...	–	...	...
3 Other construction	...	14092	...	14225	...	14379	...	14590	...	251444	...	256249
A Industries	...	8828	...	8860	...	8879	...	8977	...	151420	...	153647
1 Agriculture	...	–	...	–	...	–	...	–	...	9342	...	9172
2 Mining and quarrying	...	–	...	–	...	–	...	–	...	–	...	...
3 Manufacturing	...	–	...	–	...	–	...	–	...	–	...	...
4 Electricity, gas and water	...	6841	...	6720	...	6699	...	6759	...	104842	...	106253
5 Construction	...	–	...	–	...	–	...	–	...	–	...	...
6 Wholesale and retail trade	...	–	...	–	...	–	...	–	...	–	...	...
7 Transport and communication	...	1987	...	2140	...	2180	...	2218	...	37236	...	38221
8 Finance, etc.	...	–	...	–	...	–	...	–	...	–	...	...
9 Community, social and personal services	...	–	...	–	...	–	...	–	...	–	...	...
Statistical discrepancy	...	–	...	–	...	–	...	–	...	–	...	...
B Producers of government services	...	5264	...	5364	...	5500	...	5613	...	100024	...	102602
C Other producers	...	–	...	–	...	–	...	–	...	–	...	...
4 Land improvement and development and plantation and orchard development	...	1293	...	1290	...	1284	...	1277	...	23042	...	23251
5 Producers' durable goods	...	9825	...	10606	...	11309	...	11472	...	172599	...	179459
A Industries	...	9825	...	10606	...	11309	...	11472	...	172599	...	179459
1 Agriculture	...	3291	...	3601	...	3952	...	3985	...	63005	...	62091
2 Mining and quarrying	...	–	...	–	...	–	...	–	...	–	...	...
3 Manufacturing	...	2354	...	2500	...	2579	...	2613	...	43195	...	44247
4 Electricity, gas and water	...	–	...	–	...	–	...	–	...	–	...	...
5 Construction	...	586	...	620	...	667	...	682	...	8872	...	9912
6 Wholesale and retail trade	...	–	...	–	...	–	...	–	...	–	...	...
7 Transport and communication	...	2728	...	2813	...	2891	...	2982	...	44123	...	49257
8 Finance, etc.	...	–	...	–	...	–	...	–	...	–	...	...
9 Community, social and personal services	...	–	...	–	...	–	...	–	...	–	...	...
Statistical discrepancy	...	866	...	1072	...	1220	...	1210	...	13405	...	13952
B Producers of government services	...	–	...	–	...	–	...	–	...	–	...	...
C Other producers	...	–	...	–	...	–	...	–	...	–	...	...
6 Breeding stock, dairy cattle, etc.	...	–	...	–	...	–	...	–	...	10223	...	10008
Statistical discrepancy	...	–	...	–	...	–	...	–	10005	–	9854	–

Iceland

Million Icelandic kronur

	1986		1987		1988		1989		1990		1991	
	Gross	Net	Gross	Net	Gross	Net	Gross	Net	Gross	Net	Gross	Net
	At constant prices of: 1980								1990			
Total	...	56467	...	58583	...	60639	...	62106	...	1115136	...	1141632

	1992		1993		1994		1995		1996		1997	
	Gross	Net	Gross	Net	Gross	Net	Gross	Net	Gross	Net	Gross	Net
	At constant prices of: 1990											
1 Residential buildings	...	417783	...	423512	...	429101	...	432951	...	437288	...	...
2 Non-residential buildings	...	268297	...	274247	...	279080	...	283506	...	291038	...	...
A Industries	...	150396	...	151034	...	151062	...	151300	...	155023	...	...
1 Agriculture	...	15602	...	15351	...	14912	...	14524	...	14245	...	...
2 Mining and quarrying	...	...	...	...	...	...	...	...	...	...	...	...
3 Manufacturing	...	52300	...	51708	...	51069	...	50481	...	52745	...	...
4 Electricity, gas and water	...	...	...	...	...	...	...	...	...	...	...	...
5 Construction	...	...	...	...	...	...	...	...	...	...	...	...
6 Wholesale and retail trade	...	77832	...	79335	...	80427	...	81649	...	83433	...	...
7 Transport and communication	...	4662	...	4640	...	4655	...	4645	...	4600	...	...
8 Finance, etc.	...	...	...	...	...	...	...	...	...	...	...	...
9 Community, social and personal services	...	...	...	...	...	...	...	...	...	...	...	...
B Producers of government services	...	117901	...	123213	...	128018	...	132206	...	136015	...	...
C Other producers	...	...	...	...	...	...	...	...	...	...	...	...
3 Other construction	...	257797	...	259643	...	260538	...	260869	...	262875	...	...
A Industries	...	152964	...	151038	...	148621	...	147039	...	147381	...	...
1 Agriculture	...	8777	...	8383	...	7998	...	7632	...	7265	...	...
2 Mining and quarrying	...	...	...	...	...	...	...	...	...	...	...	...
3 Manufacturing	...	...	...	...	...	...	...	...	...	...	...	...
4 Electricity, gas and water	...	104446	...	102329	...	99841	...	97780	...	97004	...	...
5 Construction	...	...	...	...	...	...	...	...	...	...	...	...
6 Wholesale and retail trade	...	...	...	...	...	...	...	...	...	...	...	...
7 Transport and communication	...	39740	...	40327	...	40782	...	41627	...	43113	...	...
8 Finance, etc.	...	...	...	...	...	...	...	...	...	...	...	...
9 Community, social and personal services	...	...	...	...	...	...	...	...	...	...	...	...
B Producers of government services	...	104833	...	108604	...	111917	...	113831	...	115494	...	...
C Other producers	...	...	...	...	...	...	...	...	...	...	...	...
4 Land improvement and development and plantation and orchard development	...	23519	...	23691	...	23853	...	23998	...	24167	...	...
5 Producers' durable goods	...	181520	...	177050	...	174459	...	173503	...	180886	...	...
A Industries	...	181520	...	177050	...	174459	...	173503	...	180886	...	...
1 Agriculture	...	63924	...	61915	...	60975	...	58789	...	59499	...	...
2 Mining and quarrying	...	...	...	...	...	...	...	...	...	...	...	...
3 Manufacturing	...	43909	...	43554	...	43564	...	44603	...	49691	...	...
4 Electricity, gas and water	...	...	...	...	...	...	...	...	...	...	...	...
5 Construction	...	9864	...	9649	...	9182	...	9137	...	9706	...	...
6 Wholesale and retail trade	...	...	...	...	...	...	...	...	...	...	...	...
7 Transport and communication	...	49525	...	47384	...	45354	...	44282	...	43328	...	...

Iceland

	1992 Gross	1992 Net	1993 Gross	1993 Net	1994 Gross	1994 Net	1995 Gross	1995 Net	1996 Gross	1996 Net	1997 Gross	1997 Net
At constant prices of: 1990												
8 Finance, etc.	...	...	...	...	...	...	...	...	...	...	...	...
9 Community, social and personal services	...	...	...	...	...	...	...	...	...	...	...	...
Statistical discrepancy	...	14297	...	14547	...	15384	...	16692	...	18662	...	...
B Producers of government services	...	...	...	...	...	...	...	...	...	...	...	...
C Other producers	...	...	...	...	...	...	...	...	...	...	...	...
6 Breeding stock, dairy cattle, etc.	...	10005	...	9854	...	10020	...	10134	...	10042	...	...
Statistical discrepancy	10020	–	10134	–	10042	–	...	–	...	–	...	...
Total	...	1158921	...	1167997	...	1177051	...	1184961	...	1206296	...	...

2.17 Exports and imports of goods and services, detail

Million Icelandic kronur

	1986	1987	1988	1989	1990	1991	1992	1993	1994	1995	1996	1997
Exports of goods and services												
1 Exports of merchandise, f.o.b.	44968	53053	61667	80072	92452	91560	87833	94658	112654	116607	125690	...
2 Transport and communication	16993	18628	20054	26210	32484	34111	33764	41036	44781	44643	50457	...
3 Insurance service charges												...
4 Other commodities												...
5 Adjustments of merchandise exports to change-of-ownership basis	...	...	...	...	...	...	...	...	...	...	...	...
6 Direct purchases in the domestic market by non-residential households	...	...	...	...	...	...	...	...	...	...	...	...
7 Direct purchases in the domestic market by extraterritorial bodies	...	...	...	...	...	...	...	...	...	...	...	...
Total exports of goods and services	61961	71681	81721	106282	124936	125671	121597	135694	157436	161250	176147	...
Imports of goods and services												
1 Imports of merchandise, c.i.f.	45910	61237	68723	80250	96621	104129	96895	91307	102541	113614	135994	...
A Imports of merchandise, f.o.b.	40988	55020	61996	72603	87652	94634	87909	82386	92993	103251	124489	...
B Transport of services on merchandise imports	4922	6217	6727	7647	8969	9495	8986	8921	9548	10363	11505	...
C Insurance service charges on merchandise imports												...
2 Adjustments of merchandise imports to change-of-ownership basis	...	...	...	...	...	...	...	...	...	...	...	...
3 Other transport and communication	9970	12728	15377	18990	22935	26362	24887	31159	32090	31111	37733	...
4 Other insurance service charges												...
5 Other commodities												...
6 Direct purchases abroad by government												...
7 Direct purchases abroad by resident households	...	...	...	...	...	...	...	...	...	...	...	...
Total imports of goods and services	55880	73965	84100	99240	119556	130491	121782	122466	134631	144725	173727	...
Balance of goods and services	6081	–2284	–2379	7042	5380	–4820	–185	13228	22805	16525	2420	...

Iceland

Million Icelandic kronur

	1986	1987	1988	1989	1990	1991	1992	1993	1994	1995	1996	1997
Total imports and balance of goods and services	61961	71681	81721	106282	124936	125671	121597	135694	157436	161250	176147	...

3.12 General government income and outlay account: total and subsectors

Million Icelandic kronur

	1986					1987				
	Total government	Central government	State or provincial government	Local government	Social security funds	Total government	Central government	State or provincial government	Local government	Social security funds
Receipts										
1 Operating surplus	–	–	...	–	–	...	...	...	–	–
2 Property and entrepreneurial income	4134	3247	...	843	44	5123	3763	...	1308	52
A Withdrawals from public quasi-corporations	516	370	...	146	...	560	353	...	207	...
B Interest	3455	2872	...	539	44	4360	3403	...	905	52
C Dividends	16	1	...	15	...	15	1	...	14	...
D Net land rent and royalties	147	4	...	143	...	188	6	...	182	...
3 Taxes, fees and contributions	50226	40384	...	9842	...	65691	52846	...	12845	...
A Indirect taxes	35824	31194	...	4630	...	48320	42468	...	5852	...
B Direct taxes	12296	7084	...	5212	...	14448	7455	...	6993	...
Income	11362	6150	...	5212	...	13210	6217	...	6993	...
Other	934	934	...	–	...	1238	1238	...	–	...
C Social security contributions	1996	1996	...	...	...	2729	2729	...	...	...
D Fees, fines and penalties	110	110	...	...	...	194	194	...	...	...
4 Other current transfers	–	–	...	52	11623	–	–	...	73	13738
A Casualty insurance claims	–	...	...	...	...	...	...	...	...	...
B Transfers from other government subsectors	–	–	...	52	11623	–	–	...	73	13738
C Transfers from rest of the world	...	...	...	...	...	...	...	...	...	...
D Other transfers, except imputed	...	...	...	...	...	...	...	...	...	...
E Imputed unfunded employee pension and welfare contributions	...	...	...	...	...	...	...	...	...	...
Total current receipts	54360	43631	...	10737	11667	70814	56609	...	14226	13790
Disbursements										
1 Government final consumption expenditure	28777	16517	...	6242	6018	38980	24966	...	8141	5873
2 Property income	4434	3931	...	503	–	5132	4340	...	792	–
A Interest	4434	3931	...	503	–	5132	4340	...	792	–
B Net land rent and royalties	–	–	...	–	...	–	–	...	–	...
3 Subsidies	5273	5064	...	209	–	5988	5727	...	261	–
4 Other current transfers	8462	13261	...	1443	5433	11610	15818	...	1977	7625
A Casualty insurance premiums, net	...	...	...	...	...	...	...	...	...	...
B Transfers to other government subsectors	–	10746	...	929	–	–	12567	...	1244	–
C Social security benefits	5431	–	...	–	5431	7625	–	...	–	7625
D Social assistance grants	1909	1615	...	292	2	2467	2031	...	435	1
E Unfunded employee welfare benefits	...	...	...	...	...	...	...	...	...	...

Iceland

Million Icelandic kronur

	1986					1987				
	Total govern-ment	Central govern-ment	State or provincial govern-ment	Local govern-ment	Social security funds	Total govern-ment	Central govern-ment	State or provincial govern-ment	Local govern-ment	Social security funds
F Transfers to private non-profit institutions serving households	...	...	...	...	...	...	...	...	...	—
G Other transfers n.e.c.	1048	826	...	222	—	1440	1142	...	298	—
H Transfers to rest of the world	74	74	...	—	—	78	78	...	—	—
Net saving	7413	4857	...	2340	216	9106	5759	...	3055	292
Total current disbursements and net saving	54359	43630	...	10737	11667	70816	56610	...	14226	13790

	1988					1989				
	Total govern-ment	Central govern-ment	State or provincial govern-ment	Local govern-ment	Social security funds	Total govern-ment	Central govern-ment	State or provincial govern-ment	Local govern-ment	Social security funds

Receipts

1 Operating surplus	...	...	—	...	...	...	...	—	...	...
2 Property and entrepreneurial income	6134	4427	...	1707	—	8597	6593	...	2004	—
A Withdrawals from public quasi-corporations	757	359	...	398	...	1415	930	...	485	...
B Interest	5083	4032	...	1051	—	6727	5527	...	1200	—
C Dividends	51	28	...	23	...	134	106	...	28	...
D Net land rent and royalties	243	8	...	235	...	321	30	...	291	...
3 Taxes, fees and contributions	89969	72096	...	17873	...	106878	85303	...	21575	...
A Indirect taxes	61323	53459	...	7864	...	72153	62666	...	9487	...
B Direct taxes	25267	15258	...	10009	...	30442	18354	...	12088	...
Income	23680	13671	...	10009	...	27849	15761	...	12088	...
Other	1587	1587	...	...	...	2593	2593	...	...	...
C Social security contributions	3137	3137	...	...	...	4033	4033	...	...	...
D Fees, fines and penalties	242	242	...	...	...	250	250	...	...	...
4 Other current transfers	—	—	...	155	17799	—	—	...	124	21275
A Casualty insurance claims	—	...	...	...	...	—	...	...	...	...
B Transfers from other government subsectors	—	—	...	155	17799	—	—	...	124	21275
C Transfers from rest of the world	...	...	...	...	...	...	...	...	...	...
D Other transfers, except imputed	...	...	...	...	...	...	...	...	...	...
E Imputed unfunded employee pension and welfare contributions	...	...	...	...	...	...	...	...	...	...
Total current receipts	96103	76523	...	19735	17799	115475	91896	...	23703	21275

Disbursements

1 Government final consumption expenditure	50536	32140	...	10934	7462	60341	38049	...	13498	8794
2 Property income	8290	7133	...	1115	42	11207	9644	...	1522	41
A Interest	8290	7133	...	1115	42	11207	9644	...	1522	41
B Net land rent and royalties	—	...	...	...	...	...	...	...	...	...
3 Subsidies	9106	8779	...	327	—	12835	12366	...	469	—
4 Other current transfers	17490	22629	...	2652	10163	21081	26798	...	3275	12407
A Casualty insurance premiums, net	...	...	...	...	...	...	...	...	...	...

Iceland

	1988					1989				
	Total govern-ment	Central govern-ment	State or provincial govern-ment	Local govern-ment	Social security funds	Total govern-ment	Central govern-ment	State or provincial govern-ment	Local govern-ment	Social security funds
B Transfers to other government subsectors	–	16311	...	1643	–	–	19310	...	2089	–
C Social security benefits	10162	–	...	–	10162	12406	–	...	–	12406
D Social assistance grants	5058	4470	...	587	1	5404	4752	...	651	1
E Unfunded employee welfare benefits	...	...	...	...	...	...	...	...	...	...
F Transfers to private non-profit institutions serving households	...	...	...	...	...	...	...	...	...	...
G Other transfers n.e.c.	2175	1753	...	422	–	3118	2583	...	535	–
H Transfers to rest of the world	95	95	...	–	–	153	153	...	–	–
Net saving	10682	5843	...	4707	132	10011	5039	...	4939	33
Total current disbursements and net saving	96104	76524	...	19735	17799	115475	91896	...	23703	21275

	1990					1991				
	Total govern-ment	Central govern-ment	State or provincial govern-ment	Local govern-ment	Social security funds	Total govern-ment	Central govern-ment	State or provincial govern-ment	Local govern-ment	Social security funds

Receipts

1 Operating surplus	...	...	–	...	...	...	...	–	...	...
2 Property and entrepreneurial income	8786	6699	...	1953	134	10465	8150	...	2268	47
A Withdrawals from public quasi-corporations	2633	2041	...	592	...	2747	1895	...	852	...
B Interest	5728	4596	...	998	134	7324	6210	...	1067	47
C Dividends	77	58	...	19	...	28	12	...	16	...
D Net land rent and royalties	348	4	...	344	...	366	33	...	333	...
3 Taxes, fees and contributions	122369	99080	...	23289	...	137472	111178	...	26294	...
A Indirect taxes	79152	69562	...	9590	...	83943	72601	...	11342	...
B Direct taxes	38430	24731	...	13699	...	42663	27711	...	14952	...
Income	35745	22046	...	13699	...	39343	24391	...	14952	...
Other	2685	2685	...	...	...	3320	3320	...	...	...
C Social security contributions	4532	4532	...	...	...	10489	10489	...	...	...
D Fees, fines and penalties	255	255	...	...	...	377	377	...	...	...
4 Other current transfers	–	–	...	1380	24178	–	–	...	1582	27254
A Casualty insurance claims	–	...	...	...	...	–	...	...	...	...
B Transfers from other government subsectors	–	–	...	1380	24178	–	–	...	1582	27254
C Transfers from rest of the world	...	...	...	...	...	...	...	...	...	...
D Other transfers, except imputed	...	...	...	...	...	...	...	...	...	...
E Imputed unfunded employee pension and welfare contributions	...	...	...	...	...	...	...	...	...	...
Total current receipts	131155	105779	...	26622	24312	147937	119328	...	30144	27301

Disbursements

1 Government final consumption expenditure	69989	44741	...	15125	10123	78157	49596	...	17620	10941
2 Property income	12903	11370	...	1533	–	14717	12962	...	1755	–
A Interest	12903	11370	...	1533	–	14717	12962	...	1755	–
B Net land rent and royalties	...	...	...	...	...	...	...	...	...	...

Iceland

	1990					1991				
	Total govern-ment	Central govern-ment	State or provincial govern-ment	Local govern-ment	Social security funds	Total govern-ment	Central govern-ment	State or provincial govern-ment	Local govern-ment	Social security funds
3 Subsidies	12953	12281	...	672	–	12320	11351	...	969	–
4 Other current transfers	25604	34871	...	1845	14446	28775	39767	...	1661	16183
A Casualty insurance premiums, net	...	...	...	...	...	...	...	...	...	...
B Transfers to other government subsectors	–	25332	...	226	–	–	28836	...	–	–
C Social security benefits	14445	–	...	–	14445	16182	–	...	–	16182
D Social assistance grants	7729	6940	...	788	1	8483	7680	...	802	1
E Unfunded employee welfare benefits	...	...	...	...	...	...	...	...	...	...
F Transfers to private non-profit institutions serving households	...	...	...	...	...	...	...	...	...	...
G Other transfers n.e.c.	3113	2282	...	831	–	3711	2852	...	859	–
H Transfers to rest of the world	317	317	...	–	–	399	399	...	–	–
Net saving	9706	2516	...	7447	–257	13970	5653	...	8139	178
Total current disbursements and net saving	131155	105779	...	26622	24312	147939	119329	...	30144	27302

	1992					1993				
	Total govern-ment	Central govern-ment	State or provincial govern-ment	Local govern-ment	Social security funds	Total govern-ment	Central govern-ment	State or provincial govern-ment	Local govern-ment	Social security funds

Receipts

1 Operating surplus	...	...	–	...	...	–	–	–	–	–
2 Property and entrepreneurial income	11000	8446	...	2402	152	10563	8217	...	2254	92
A Withdrawals from public quasi-corporations	3665	2430	...	1235	...	3378	2328	...	1050	...
B Interest	6828	5868	...	808	152	6795	5870	...	833	92
C Dividends	43	17	...	26	...	49	17	...	32	...
D Net land rent and royalties	464	131	...	333	...	341	2	...	339	...
3 Taxes, fees and contributions	139271	111934	...	27337	...	136965	110240	...	26725	...
A Indirect taxes	83714	72144	...	11570	...	77009	70104	...	6905	...
B Direct taxes	43789	28022	...	15767	...	48198	28378	...	19820	...
Income	40426	24659	...	15767	...	44545	24725	...	19820	...
Other	3363	3363	...	...	...	3653	3653	...	...	...
C Social security contributions	11322	11322	...	...	...	11386	11386	...	...	...
D Fees, fines and penalties	446	446	...	...	...	372	372	...	...	...
4 Other current transfers	–	601	...	1743	28311	–	–	...	2016	29368
A Casualty insurance claims	–	...	...	...	...	–	...	...	...	...
B Transfers from other government subsectors	–	601	...	1743	28311	–	–	...	2016	29368
C Transfers from rest of the world	...	...	...	...	...	...	...	...	...	...
D Other transfers, except imputed	...	...	...	...	...	...	...	...	...	...
E Imputed unfunded employee pension and welfare contributions	...	...	...	...	...	...	...	...	...	...
Total current receipts	150271	120981	...	31482	28463	147528	118457	...	30995	29460

Iceland

	1992					1993				
	Total govern-ment	Central govern-ment	State or provincial govern-ment	Local govern-ment	Social security funds	Total govern-ment	Central govern-ment	State or provincial govern-ment	Local govern-ment	Social security funds

Disbursements

1 Government final consumption expenditure	80375	50112	...	19679	10584	84818	53389	...	21373	10056
2 Property income	14508	12875	...	1633	–	15381	13678	...	1703	–
A Interest	14508	12875	...	1633	–	15381	13678	...	1703	–
B Net land rent and royalties	...	...	...	...	...	...	...	...	...	...
3 Subsidies	13225	12227	...	998	–	10504	9526	...	978	–
4 Other current transfers	30295	40831	...	2295	17824	32764	42200	...	2629	19320
A Casualty insurance premiums, net	...	...	...	...	...	...	...	...	...	...
B Transfers to other government subsectors	–	30054	...	601	–	–	30769	...	500	116
C Social security benefits	17824	–	...	–	17824	19204	–	...	–	19204
D Social assistance grants	8641	7696	...	945	–	9504	8110	...	1394	–
E Unfunded employee welfare benefits	...	...	...	...	...	...	...	...	...	...
F Transfers to private non-profit institutions serving households	...	...	...	...	...	...	...	...	...	...
G Other transfers n.e.c.	3473	2724	...	749	–	3684	2949	...	735	–
H Transfers to rest of the world	357	357	...	–	–	372	372	...	–	–
Net saving	11867	4935	...	6877	55	4061	–337	...	4312	84
Total current disbursements and net saving	150270	120980	...	31482	28463	147528	118456	...	30995	29460

	1994					1995				
	Total govern-ment	Central govern-ment	State or provincial govern-ment	Local govern-ment	Social security funds	Total govern-ment	Central govern-ment	State or provincial govern-ment	Local govern-ment	Social security funds

Receipts

1 Operating surplus	–	–	–	–	–	–	–	–	–	–
2 Property and entrepreneurial income	11557	9273	...	2205	79	12058	9183	...	2801	75
A Withdrawals from public quasi-corporations	4105	2882	...	1223	...	4827	2971	...	1856	...
B Interest	7013	6387	...	547	79	6803	6211	...	517	75
C Dividends	30	4	...	26	...	20	–	...	20	...
D Net land rent and royalties	408	–	...	408	...	408	–	...	408	...
3 Taxes, fees and contributions	142123	115023	...	27100	...	150701	121273	...	29428	...
A Indirect taxes	79004	71816	...	7188	...	82373	74115	...	8258	...
B Direct taxes	50509	30597	...	19912	...	54974	33804	...	21170	...
Income	46759	26847	...	19912	...	51085	29915	...	21170	...
Other	3750	3750	...	...	...	3889	3889	...	...	...
C Social security contributions	12181	12181	...	...	...	13067	13067	...	...	...
D Fees, fines and penalties	429	429	...	...	...	287	287	...	...	...
4 Other current transfers	–	–	...	2630	30500	–	–	...	2696	32415
A Casualty insurance claims	–	...	...	...	...	–	...	...	...	...
B Transfers from other government subsectors	–	–	...	2630	30500	–	–	...	2696	32415
C Transfers from rest of the world	...	...	...	...	...	...	...	...	...	...

Iceland

	1994					1995				
	Total govern-ment	Central govern-ment	State or provincial govern-ment	Local govern-ment	Social security funds	Total govern-ment	Central govern-ment	State or provincial govern-ment	Local govern-ment	Social security funds
D Other transfers, except imputed	...	...	...	...	...	...	...	...	...	...
E Imputed unfunded employee pension and welfare contributions	...	...	...	...	...	...	...	...	...	...
Total current receipts	153680	124296	...	31935	30579	162759	130456	...	34925	32490

Disbursements

	1994					1995				
1 Government final consumption expenditure	89424	55257	...	23498	10669	94080	58676	...	24075	11329
2 Property income	16805	14795	...	2010	–	18673	16499	...	2174	–
A Interest	16805	14795	...	2010	–	18673	16499	...	2174	–
B Net land rent and royalties	...	...	...	...	...	...	...	...	...	...
3 Subsidies	9606	8551	...	1055	–	9492	8545	...	947	–
4 Other current transfers	33821	43658	...	3018	20275	36147	47002	...	2704	21552
A Casualty insurance premiums, net	...	...	...	...	...	...	...	...	...	...
B Transfers to other government subsectors	–	32178	...	599	353	–	34871	...	–	240
C Social security benefits	19922	–	...	–	19922	21312	–	...	–	21312
D Social assistance grants	9513	7941	...	1572	–	10078	8235	...	1843	–
E Unfunded employee welfare benefits	...	...	...	...	...	...	...	...	...	...
F Transfers to private non-profit institutions serving households	...	...	...	...	...	...	...	...	...	...
G Other transfers n.e.c.	3981	3134	...	847	–	4309	3448	...	861	–
H Transfers to rest of the world	405	405	...	–	–	448	448	...	–	–
Net saving	4024	2035	...	2354	–365	4366	–268	...	5024	–390
Total current disbursements and net saving	153680	124296	...	31935	30579	162758	130454	...	34924	32491

	1996					1997				
	Total govern-ment	Central govern-ment	State or provincial govern-ment	Local govern-ment	Social security funds	Total govern-ment	Central govern-ment	State or provincial govern-ment	Local govern-ment	Social security funds

Receipts

	1996					1997				
1 Operating surplus	–	–	–	–	–	...	...	...	...	...
2 Property and entrepreneurial income	11579	8821	...	2704	53	...	...	...	...	...
A Withdrawals from public quasi-corporations	4371	2619	...	1752	...	...	...	...	...	...
B Interest	6784	6203	...	528	53	...	...	...	...	...
C Dividends	19	–	...	19	...	...	...	...	...	...
D Net land rent and royalties	405	–	...	405	...	...	...	...	...	...
3 Taxes, fees and contributions	166512	134768	...	31744	...	...	...	...	...	...
A Indirect taxes	89811	81149	...	8662	...	...	...	...	...	...
B Direct taxes	61187	38105	...	23082	...	...	...	...	...	...
Income	57167	34085	...	23082	...	...	...	...	...	...
Other	4020	4020	...	...	...	...	...	...	...	...
C Social security contributions	15132	15132	...	...	...	...	...	...	...	...
D Fees, fines and penalties	382	382	...	...	...	...	...	...	...	...
4 Other current transfers	–	–	...	5579	33541	...	...	...	...	...

Iceland

	1996					1997				
	Total government	Central government	State or provincial government	Local government	Social security funds	Total government	Central government	State or provincial government	Local government	Social security funds
A Casualty insurance claims	–	...	...	...	...	...	...	...	...	...
B Transfers from other government subsectors	–	–	...	5579	33541	...	...	...	...	...
C Transfers from rest of the world	...	...	...	...	...	...	...	...	...	...
D Other transfers, except imputed	...	...	...	...	...	...	...	...	...	...
E Imputed unfunded employee pension and welfare contributions	...	...	...	...	...	...	...	...	...	...
Total current receipts	178091	143589	...	40027	33594	...	...	...	...	...

Disbursements

1 Government final consumption expenditure	100358	59993	...	28054	12311	...	...	...	...	...
2 Property income	17913	15812	...	2101	–	...	...	...	...	...
A Interest	17913	15812	...	2101	–	...	...	...	...	...
B Net land rent and royalties	...	...	...	...	...	...	...	...	...	...
3 Subsidies	10055	8676	...	1379	–	...	...	...	...	...
4 Other current transfers	37097	51980	...	2990	21247	...	...	...	...	...
A Casualty insurance premiums, net	...	...	...	...	...	...	...	...	...	...
B Transfers to other government subsectors	–	38975	...	–	140	...	...	...	...	...
C Social security benefits	21102	–	...	–	21102	...	...	...	...	...
D Social assistance grants	11034	8879	...	2155	–	...	...	...	...	...
E Unfunded employee welfare benefits	...	...	...	...	...	...	...	...	...	...
F Transfers to private non-profit institutions serving households	...	...	...	...	...	...	...	...	...	...
G Other transfers n.e.c.	4506	3671	...	835	–	...	...	...	...	...
H Transfers to rest of the world	455	455	...	–	–	...	...	...	...	...
Net saving	12668	7128	...	5504	36	...	...	...	...	...
Total current disbursements and net saving	178091	143589	...	40028	33594	...	...	...	...	...

3.13 General government capital accumulation account: total and subsectors

Million Icelandic kronur

	1986					1987				
	Total government	Central government	State or provincial government	Local government	Social security funds	Total government	Central government	State or provincial government	Local government	Social security funds

Finance of gross accumulation

1 Gross saving	8361	5568	...	2576	217	10255	6622	...	3342	291
A Consumption of fixed capital	948	711	...	237	–	1151	863	...	288	–
B Net saving	7413	4857	...	2339	217	9104	5759	...	3054	291
2 Capital transfers [a]	192	169	...	638	–	407	371	...	1069	–
A From other government subsectors	–	–	...	615	–	–	–	...	1033	–
B From other resident sectors	192	169	...	23	–	407	371	...	36	–

Iceland

Million Icelandic kronur

	1986					1987				
	Total government	Central government	State or provincial government	Local government	Social security funds	Total government	Central government	State or provincial government	Local government	Social security funds
C From rest of the world	...	...	...	...	...	...	...	...	...	...
Finance of gross accumulation	8553	5737	...	3214	217	10662	6993	...	4411	291
Gross accumulation											
1 Gross capital formation	4800	1874	...	2926	–	7294	3077	...	4217	–
A Increase in stocks	...	...	...	...	...	...	...	...	...	...
B Gross fixed capital formation	4800	1874	...	2926	–	7294	3077	...	4217	–
2 Purchases of land, net	...	...	...	...	...	...	...	...	...	...
3 Purchases of intangible assets, net	...	...	...	...	...	...	...	...	...	...
4 Capital transfers	10278	10488	...	405	–	5154	5769	...	418	–
A To other government subsectors	–	615	...	–	–	–	1033	...	–	–
B To other resident sectors	10278	9873	...	405	–	5154	4736	...	418	–
C To the rest of the world	...	...	...	...	...	...	...	...	...	...
Net lending	–6526	–6625	...	–118	217	–1786	–1852	...	–225	291
Gross accumulation	8552	5737	...	3213	217	10662	6994	...	4410	291

	1988					1989				
	Total government	Central government	State or provincial government	Local government	Social security funds	Total government	Central government	State or provincial government	Local government	Social security funds
Finance of gross accumulation											
1 Gross saving	12039	6861	...	5046	132	11691	6284	...	5374	33
A Consumption of fixed capital	1357	1018	...	339	–	1680	1245	...	435	–
B Net saving	10682	5843	...	4707	132	10011	5039	...	4939	33
2 Capital transfers [a]	518	474	...	1682	–	510	469	...	1981	–
A From other government subsectors	–	–	...	1638	–	–	–	...	1940	–
B From other resident sectors	518	474	...	44	–	510	469	...	41	–
C From rest of the world	...	...	...	...	...	...	...	...	...	...
Finance of gross accumulation	12557	7335	...	6728	132	12201	6753	...	7355	33
Gross accumulation											
1 Gross capital formation	10348	3972	...	6376	–	12630	4444	...	8186	–
A Increase in stocks	...	...	...	...	...	...	...	...	...	...
B Gross fixed capital formation	10348	3972	...	6376	–	12630	4444	...	8186	–
2 Purchases of land, net	...	...	...	...	...	...	...	...	...	...
3 Purchases of intangible assets, net	...	...	...	...	...	...	...	...	...	...
4 Capital transfers	7421	8509	...	550	–	13603	14596	...	947	–
A To other government subsectors	–	1638	...	–	–	–	1940	...	–	–
B To other resident sectors	7421	6871	...	550	–	13603	12656	...	947	–
C To the rest of the world	...	...	...	...	...	...	...	...	...	...
Net lending	–5213	–5147	...	–198	132	–14033	–12288	...	–1778	33
Gross accumulation	12556	7334	...	6728	132	12200	6752	...	7355	33

Iceland

	1990					1991				
	Total government	Central government	State or provincial government	Local government	Social security funds	Total government	Central government	State or provincial government	Local government	Social security funds

Finance of gross accumulation

1 Gross saving	11736	4024	...	7969	–257	16291	7389	...	8724	178
A Consumption of fixed capital	2029	1508	...	521	–	2319	1736	...	583	–
B Net saving	9707	2516	...	7448	–257	13972	5653	...	8141	178
2 Capital transfers [a]	517	468	...	1725	–	711	610	...	1956	–
A From other government subsectors	–	–	...	1676	–	–	–	...	1855	–
B From other resident sectors	517	468	...	49	–	711	610	...	101	–
C From rest of the world	...	...	...	...	...	...	...	...	...	...
Finance of gross accumulation	12253	4492	...	9694	–257	17002	7999	...	10680	178

Gross accumulation

1 Gross capital formation	14378	6338	...	8040	–	16228	7100	...	9128	–
A Increase in stocks	...	...	...	...	...	...	...	...	...	...
B Gross fixed capital formation	14378	6338	...	8040	–	16228	7100	...	9128	–
2 Purchases of land, net	...	...	...	...	...	...	...	...	...	...
3 Purchases of intangible assets, net	...	...	...	...	...	...	...	...	...	...
4 Capital transfers	9980	10198	...	1458	–	12397	12086	...	2166	–
A To other government subsectors	–	1676	...	–	–	–	1855	...	–	–
B To other resident sectors	9980	8522	...	1458	–	12397	10231	...	2166	–
C To the rest of the world	...	...	...	...	...	...	...	...	...	...
Net lending	–12105	–12044	...	196	–257	–11623	–11187	...	–614	178
Gross accumulation	12253	4492	...	9694	–257	17002	7999	...	10680	178

	1992					1993				
	Total government	Central government	State or provincial government	Local government	Social security funds	Total government	Central government	State or provincial government	Local government	Social security funds

Finance of gross accumulation

1 Gross saving	14321	6748	...	7518	55	6661	1580	...	4997	84
A Consumption of fixed capital	2454	1813	...	641	–	2600	1917	...	683	–
B Net saving	11867	4935	...	6877	55	4061	–337	...	4314	84
2 Capital transfers [a]	619	517	...	1904	–	679	531	...	1864	–
A From other government subsectors	–	–	...	1802	–	–	–	...	1716	–
B From other resident sectors	619	517	...	102	–	679	531	...	148	–
C From rest of the world	...	...	...	...	...	...	...	...	...	...
Finance of gross accumulation	14940	7265	...	9422	55	7340	2111	...	6861	84

Gross accumulation

1 Gross capital formation	16016	6434	...	9582	–	17746	8025	...	9721	–
A Increase in stocks	...	...	...	...	...	...	...	...	...	...
B Gross fixed capital formation	16016	6434	...	9582	–	17746	8025	...	9721	–
2 Purchases of land, net	...	...	...	...	...	...	...	...	...	...
3 Purchases of intangible assets, net	...	...	...	...	...	...	...	...	...	...
4 Capital transfers	10145	10394	...	1553	–	8032	7867	...	1881	–

Iceland

	1992					1993				
	Total govern-ment	Central govern-ment	State or provincial govern-ment	Local govern-ment	Social security funds	Total govern-ment	Central govern-ment	State or provincial govern-ment	Local govern-ment	Social security funds
A To other government subsectors	–	1802	...	–	–	–	1716	...	–	–
B To other resident sectors	10145	8592	...	1553	–	8032	6151	...	1881	–
C To the rest of the world	...	...	...	...	...	...	...	...	...	...
Net lending	–11221	–9563	...	–1713	55	–18438	–13781	...	–4741	84
Gross accumulation	14940	7265	...	9422	55	7340	2111	...	6861	84

	1994					1995				
	Total govern-ment	Central govern-ment	State or provincial govern-ment	Local govern-ment	Social security funds	Total govern-ment	Central govern-ment	State or provincial govern-ment	Local govern-ment	Social security funds

Finance of gross accumulation

1 Gross saving	6727	4015	...	3077	–365	7209	1828	...	5771	–390
A Consumption of fixed capital	2705	1981	...	724	–	2843	2096	...	747	–
B Net saving	4022	2034	...	2353	–365	4366	–268	...	5024	–390
2 Capital transfers [a]	749	688	...	1694	...	767	729	...	1479	...
A From other government subsectors	–	–	...	1633	–	–	–	...	1441	–
B From other resident sectors	749	688	...	61	–	767	729	...	38	–
C From rest of the world	...	...	...	...	...	...	...	...	...	...
Finance of gross accumulation	7476	4703	...	4771	–365	7976	2557	...	7250	–390

Gross accumulation

1 Gross capital formation	17647	8290	...	9357	–	13714	7316	...	6398	–
A Increase in stocks	...	...	...	...	...	...	...	...	...	...
B Gross fixed capital formation	17647	8290	...	9357	–	13714	7316	...	6398	–
2 Purchases of land, net	...	...	...	...	...	...	...	...	...	...
3 Purchases of intangible assets, net	...	...	...	...	...	...	...	...	...	...
4 Capital transfers	10465	9854	...	2244	–	7658	6801	...	2298	–
A To other government subsectors	–	1633	...	–	–	–	1441	...	–	–
B To other resident sectors	10465	8221	...	2244	–	7658	5360	...	2298	–
C To the rest of the world	...	...	...	...	...	...	...	...	...	...
Net lending	–20636	–13441	...	–6830	–365	–13396	–11560	...	–1446	–390
Gross accumulation	7476	4703	...	4771	–365	7976	2557	...	7250	–390

	1996					1997				
	Total govern-ment	Central govern-ment	State or provincial govern-ment	Local govern-ment	Social security funds	Total govern-ment	Central govern-ment	State or provincial govern-ment	Local govern-ment	Social security funds

Finance of gross accumulation

1 Gross saving	15717	9382	...	6299	36	...	...	...	...	...
A Consumption of fixed capital	3049	2254	...	795	–	...	...	...	...	...
B Net saving	12668	7128	...	5504	36	...	...	...	...	...
2 Capital transfers [a]	846	817	...	1644	...	...	...	...	...	...
A From other government subsectors	–	–	...	1615	–	...	...	...	...	...
B From other resident sectors	846	817	...	29	–	...	...	...	...	...
C From rest of the world	...	...	...	...	...	...	...	...	...	...
Finance of gross accumulation	16563	10199	...	7943	36	...	...	...	...	...

Iceland

	1996					1997				
	Total government	Central government	State or provincial government	Local government	Social security funds	Total government	Central government	State or provincial government	Local government	Social security funds

Gross accumulation

1 Gross capital formation	15416	8486	...	6930	–	...	...	...	...	...
A Increase in stocks	...	...	...	...	...	...	...	...	...	...
B Gross fixed capital formation	15416	8486	...	6930	–	...	...	...	...	...
2 Purchases of land, net	...	...	...	...	...	...	...	...	...	...
3 Purchases of intangible assets, net	...	...	...	...	...	...	...	...	...	...
4 Capital transfers	8874	9052	...	1437	–	...	...	...	...	...
A To other government sub-sectors	–	1615	...	–	–	...	...	...	...	...
B To other resident sectors	8874	7437	...	1437	–	...	...	...	...	...
C To the rest of the world	...	...	...	...	...	...	...	...	...	...
Net lending	–7728	–7339	...	–425	36	...	...	...	...	...
Gross accumulation	16562	10199	...	7942	36	...	...	...	...	...

a Capital transfers received are recorded net of capital transfers paid.

3.51 External transactions, current account: detail

Million Icelandic kronur

	1986	1987	1988	1989	1990	1991	1992	1993	1994	1995	1996	1997
Payments to the rest of the world													
1 Imports of goods and services	55880	73965	84100	99240	119556	130491	121782	122466	134631	144725	173727	...
A Imports of merchandise, c.i.f.	45910	61237	68723	80250	96621	104129	96895	91307	102541	113614	135994	...
B Other	9970	12728	15377	18990	22935	26362	24887	31159	32090	31111	37733	...
2 Factor income to rest of the world	7042	7281	9461	15087	17320	15584	14682	15803	18948	18257	18349	...
A Compensation of employees	89	175	331	519	682	883	723	702	532	365	306	...
B Property and entrepreneurial income	6953	7106	9130	14568	16638	14701	13959	15101	18416	17892	18043	...
3 Current transfers to the rest of the world	72	–76	57	340	200	510	269	211	626	306	464	...
A Indirect taxes by general government to supranational organizations	...	...	...	...	...	...	...	...	...	...	...	...
B Other current transfers	72	–76	57	340	200	510	269	211	626	306	464	...
By general government	72	–76	57	340	200	510	269	211	626	306	464	...
By other resident sectors	–	–	–	–	–	–	–	–	–	–	–	...
4 Surplus of the nation on current transactions	707	–7007	–8942	–4462	–7669	–15974	–9365	3196	8734	3717	–8892	...
Payments to the rest of the world and surplus of the nation on current transfers	63701	74163	84676	110205	129407	130611	127368	141676	162939	167005	183648	...
Receipts from the rest of the world													
1 Exports of goods and services	61961	71681	81721	106282	124936	125671	121597	135694	157436	161250	176147	...
A Exports of merchandise, f.o.b.	44968	53053	61667	80072	92452	91560	87833	94658	112654	116607	125690	...
B Other	16993	18628	20054	26210	32484	34111	33764	41036	44782	44643	50457	...
2 Factor income from rest of the world	1740	2482	2955	3923	4471	4940	5771	5982	5503	5755	7501	...
A Compensation of employees	1013	1589	1998	2306	2658	2994	3037	3175	2993	3260	4242	...

Iceland

Million Icelandic kronur

	1986	1987	1988	1989	1990	1991	1992	1993	1994	1995	1996	1997
B Property and entrepreneurial income	727	893	957	1617	1813	1946	2734	2807	2510	2495	3259	...
3 Current transfers from rest of the world	–	–	–	–	–	–	–	–	–	–	–	...
A Subsidies to general government from supranational organizations	...	...	...	...	...	...	...	...	...	...	...	...
B Other current transfers	–	–	–	–	–	–	–	–	–	–	–	...
Receipts from the rest of the world on current transfers	63701	74163	84676	110205	129407	130611	127368	141676	162939	167005	183648	...

3.52 External transactions, capital accumulation account

Million Icelandic kronur

	1986	1987	1988	1989	1990	1991	1992	1993	1994	1995	1996	1997
Finance of gross accumulation												
1 Surplus of the nation on current transactions	707	–7007	–8942	–4462	–7669	–15974	–9365	3196	8734	3717	–8892	...
2 Capital transfers from rest of the world	232	–100	15	155	157	135	–171	–41	–429	–286	–32	...
A By general government	–	–	–	–	–	–	–	–	–	–	–	...
B By other resident sectors	232	–100	15	155	157	135	–171	–41	–429	–286	–32	...
Statistical discrepancy	...	...	...	...	...	...	...	...	...	...	3431	...
Total finance of gross accumulation	939	–7107	–8927	–4307	–7512	–15839	–9536	3155	8305	3431	–5493	...
Gross accumulation												
1 Capital transfers to the rest of the world	...	...	...	...	...	...	...	...	...	...	...	...
2 Purchases of intangible assets, n.e.c., net, from rest of the world	...	...	...	...	...	...	...	...	...	...	...	...
Net lending to the rest of the world	939	–7107	–8927	–4307	–7512	–15839	–9536	3155	8305	3431	–5493	...
Total gross accumulation	939	–7107	–8927	–4307	–7512	–15839	–9536	3155	8305	3431	–5493	...

4.1 Derivation of value added by kind of activity, in current prices

Million Icelandic kronur

	1986 Gross output	1986 Intermediate consumption	1986 Value added	1987 Gross output	1987 Intermediate consumption	1987 Value added	1988 Gross output	1988 Intermediate consumption	1988 Value added	1989 Gross output	1989 Intermediate consumption	1989 Value added
All producers												
1 Agriculture, hunting, forestry and fishing	28780	12746	16034	35107	13896	21211	43080	17713	25367	50779	21526	29254
A Agriculture and hunting	8891	3949	4942	10023	3861	6162	11595	5371	6224	13319	6349	6970
B Forestry and logging	...	...	...	...	...	...	...	...	...	...	...	...
C Fishing	19889	8797	11092	25085	10036	15049	31485	12342	19144	37460	15177	22284
2 Mining and quarrying	...	...	...	...	...	...	...	...	...	...	...	...
3 Manufacturing	77452	52901	24551	100081	65694	34386	112952	75138	37814	137846	92567	45279
A Manufacture of food, beverages and tobacco	44786	33552	11234	55685	40643	15043	60057	45948	14109	73578	55953	17626
B Textile, wearing apparel and leather industries	4514	2844	1669	5927	3760	2168	5539	3491	2048	5907	3940	1967

Iceland

Million Icelandic kronur

	1986 Gross output	1986 Intermediate consumption	1986 Value added	1987 Gross output	1987 Intermediate consumption	1987 Value added	1988 Gross output	1988 Intermediate consumption	1988 Value added	1989 Gross output	1989 Intermediate consumption	1989 Value added
C Manufacture of wood and wood products, including furniture	3188	1714	1474	4532	2019	2513	5313	2466	2847	6085	3124	2961
D Manufacture of paper and paper products, printing and publishing	5222	2844	2378	6350	3120	3230	8024	4094	3930	9796	4645	5150
E Manufacture of chemicals and chemical petroleum, coal, rubber and plastic products	4138	2697	1440	5078	3253	1825	6275	3779	2496	7643	4593	3050
F Manufacture of non-metallic mineral products, except products of petroleum and coal	2960	1579	1381	3890	2031	1859	4706	2536	2171	5197	2654	2543
G Basic metal industries	5269	4211	1057	6263	4659	1604	9350	6252	3099	13213	8613	4600
H Manufacture of fabricated metal products, machinery and equipment	5797	2419	3379	9240	3937	5303	9963	3932	6031	12104	5939	6165
I Other manufacturing industries	1579	1041	539	3115	2274	841	3725	2642	1083	4324	3107	1217
4 Electricity, gas and water	10554	4151	6403	11809	4937	6872	15887	5905	9981	18666	6807	11859
A Electricity, gas and steam	10148	3985	6163	11246	4668	6578	15103	5564	9539	17709	6450	11258
B Water works and supply	407	166	241	563	268	294	784	342	442	958	357	601
5 Construction	31258	19932	11326	40629	24783	15845	48563	30575	17988	60063	38274	21789
6 Wholesale and retail trade, restaurants and hotels	36935	10490	26445	52625	14426	38200	66203	19015	47187	77120	20053	57066
A Wholesale and retail trade	30797	7065	23732	43856	10052	33805	54663	13211	41451	64340	14093	50247
B Restaurants and hotels	6138	3425	2713	8769	4374	4395	11540	5804	5736	12780	5961	6819
Restaurants	4465	2587	1878	6243	3426	2817	8667	4743	3924	9713	4708	5005
Hotels and other lodging places	1673	839	834	2526	948	1578	2873	1061	1812	3067	1253	1814
7 Transport, storage and communication	24315	14051	10264	29443	16002	13441	35201	18241	16960	41343	22437	18906
A Transport and storage	21288	13136	8152	25455	14756	10699	29805	16832	12973	34815	20738	14077
B Communication	3026	915	2112	3988	1246	2741	5396	1409	3987	6528	1699	4828
8 Finance, insurance, real estate and business services	32974	10811	22163	45888	14142	31746	59528	18083	41445	72772	21439	51332
A Financial institutions	6416	2134	4282	11650	3141	8509	16731	4505	12226	19663	5126	14538
B Insurance	1562	481	1081	2051	630	1421	2533	856	1677	3697	984	2713
C Real estate and business services	24996	8196	16800	32187	10371	21816	40264	12722	27542	49412	15330	34081
9 Community, social and personal services	12833	5978	6856	17962	7890	10072	22454	9553	12900	26155	11287	14869
A Sanitary and similar services	...	...	...	...	...	...	...	...	...	...	...	...
B Social and related community services	1651	480	1171	2589	623	1966	3743	961	2783	4489	1290	3199
Educational services	...	...	...	...	...	...	...	...	...	...	...	...
Medical, dental, other health and veterinary services	1651	480	1171	2589	623	1966	3743	961	2783	4489	1290	3199
C Recreational and cultural services	3579	1818	1761	5509	2805	2704	7517	3845	3673	9184	4647	4538
D Personal and household services [a]	7603	3680	3924	9864	4462	5402	11193	4748	6445	12482	5350	7132
Total, Industries	255101	131059	124042	333544	161770	171774	403867	194224	209643	484744	234390	250353

Iceland

Million Icelandic kronur

	1986			1987			1988			1989		
	Gross output	Intermediate consumption	Value added	Gross output	Intermediate consumption	Value added	Gross output	Intermediate consumption	Value added	Gross output	Intermediate consumption	Value added
Producers of government services	31663	13614	18049	43253	17243	26010	56720	22634	34086	67952	28328	39625
Other producers	1867	775	1092	2613	1079	1534	3705	1536	2168	4636	1898	2738
Total	288631	145448	143183	379410	180092	199318	464292	218395	245897	557332	264616	292716
less: Imputed bank service charge	_	–4493	4493	_	–8085	8085	_	–11557	11557	_	–12702	12702
Import duties [b]	11297	_	11297	14103	_	14103	15793	_	15793	15341	_	15341
Value added tax	...	...	...	...	...	...	...	...	...	...	...	...
Other adjustments [c]	11229	...	11229	3774	...	3774	6506	...	6506	12836	...	12836
Total	311157	149941	161217	397287	188177	209110	486591	229951	256640	585510	277318	308192

	1990			1991			1992			1993		
	Gross output	Intermediate consumption	Value added	Gross output	Intermediate consumption	Value added	Gross output	Intermediate consumption	Value added	Gross output	Intermediate consumption	Value added
All producers											
1 Agriculture, hunting, forestry and fishing	63048	27458	35590	67639	28187	39452	65121	26940	38181	67792	28310	39482
A Agriculture and hunting	17037	9494	7543	17386	9044	8342	16455	8885	7570	16170	8862	7308
B Forestry and logging	...	...	...	...	...	...	...	...	...	...	...	...
C Fishing	46011	17964	28047	50254	19143	31111	48666	18055	30611	51622	19447	32175
2 Mining and quarrying	...	...	...	...	...	...	...	...	...	...	...	...
3 Manufacturing	157876	107648	50228	169282	114810	54472	165389	111291	54098	164084	110343	53741
A Manufacture of food, beverages and tobacco	90779	66824	23955	99646	72065	27581	97741	70482	27259	97025	69108	27917
B Textile, wearing apparel and leather industries	6557	4287	2270	6331	4022	2309	6290	3848	2442	5892	3633	2259
C Manufacture of wood and wood products, including furniture	5998	3582	2416	6640	3891	2749	6387	3488	2899	5581	3205	2376
D Manufacture of paper and paper products, printing and publishing	10558	5108	5450	12240	5939	6301	12204	6301	5903	12230	6563	5667
E Manufacture of chemicals and chemical petroleum, coal, rubber and plastic products	8988	5523	3465	9706	6067	3639	9192	5237	3955	9010	5183	3827
F Manufacture of non-metallic mineral products, except products of petroleum and coal	5528	3105	2423	6174	3640	2534	5729	3162	2567	5363	3052	2311
G Basic metal industries	12014	9436	2578	10134	8858	1276	9921	8149	1772	11154	9067	2087
H Manufacture of fabricated metal products, machinery and equipment	12141	6064	6077	13154	6724	6430	12572	7013	5559	12267	6948	5319
I Other manufacturing industries	5314	3720	1594	5257	3604	1653	5353	3611	1742	5563	3585	1978
4 Electricity, gas and water	19853	8065	11788	20926	8959	11967	22470	9760	12710	23612	10121	13491
A Electricity, gas and steam	18761	7667	11094	19673	8632	11041	21186	9306	11880	22290	9609	12681
B Water works and supply	1093	399	694	1253	328	925	1285	454	831	1322	512	810
5 Construction	71469	47142	24327	82216	57326	24890	75082	49809	25273	79061	54671	24390
6 Wholesale and retail trade, restaurants and hotels	69719	23286	46433	75954	25544	50410	70982	26976	44006	67550	24381	43169
A Wholesale and retail trade	56670	16163	40507	61140	17443	43697	56279	18743	37536	53080	16260	36820
B Restaurants and hotels	13049	7122	5927	14814	8102	6712	14703	8233	6470	14470	8121	6349
Restaurants	9689	5604	4085	11234	6496	4738	11137	6625	4512	11022	6546	4476

Iceland

	1990			1991			1992			1993		
	Gross output	Intermediate consumption	Value added	Gross output	Intermediate consumption	Value added	Gross output	Intermediate consumption	Value added	Gross output	Intermediate consumption	Value added
Hotels and other lodging places	3361	1519	1842	3580	1605	1975	3566	1608	1958	3448	1575	1873
7 Transport, storage and communication	49009	26293	22716	52075	28892	23183	52063	28657	23406	56381	31899	24482
A Transport and storage	42435	24261	18174	44901	26554	18347	43197	25434	17763	47057	28653	18404
B Communication	6574	2033	4541	7175	2338	4837	8866	3224	5642	9324	3246	6078
8 Finance, insurance, real estate and business services	80877	25834	55043	88407	27347	61060	90409	27537	62872	92578	27821	64757
A Financial institutions	20998	6302	14696	23573	7258	16315	24404	7193	17211	25237	7026	18211
B Insurance	1650	1340	310	2151	1324	827	2439	1453	986	2645	1455	1190
C Real estate and business services	58229	18192	40037	62684	18765	43919	63566	18891	44675	64697	19341	45356
9 Community, social and personal services	29757	13977	15780	32673	15111	17562	33556	14761	18795	34420	16040	18380
A Sanitary and similar services	...	...	...	...	...	...	...	...	...	...	...	...
B Social and related community services	5883	1907	3976	6577	2118	4459	7048	2366	4682	7332	2732	4600
Educational services	...	...	...	...	...	...	...	...	...	...	...	...
Medical, dental, other health and veterinary services	4948	1569	3379	5501	1739	3762	5920	2035	3885	6181	2310	3871
C Recreational and cultural services	10823	5588	5235	11330	5466	5864	11569	5577	5992	12004	5935	6069
D Personal and household services [a]	13051	6481	6570	14767	7526	7241	14940	6817	8123	15085	7373	7712
Total, Industries	541610	279702	261908	589172	306176	282996	575071	295730	279341	585478	303586	281892
Producers of government services	79734	34256	45478	89231	37808	51423	92923	39896	53027	97606	41758	55848
Other producers	6071	2575	3496	6442	2717	3725	6362	2681	3681	6631	2803	3828
Total	627414	316533	310881	684845	346702	338143	674356	338307	336049	689715	348147	341568
less: Imputed bank service charge	–	−12422	12422	–	−14352	14352	–	−14559	14559	–	−15197	15197
Import duties [b]	45082	–	45082	53524	–	53524	63250	–	63250	59840	–	59840
Value added tax	...	...	...	...	...	...	...	...	...	...	...	...
Other adjustments [c]	20860	...	20860	19669	...	19669	12892	...	12892	25210	...	25210
Total	693356	328955	364401	758038	361054	396984	750498	352866	397632	774765	363344	411421

	1994			1995			1996			1997		
	Gross output	Intermediate consumption	Value added	Gross output	Intermediate consumption	Value added	Gross output	Intermediate consumption	Value added	Gross output	Intermediate consumption	Value added

All producers

1 Agriculture, hunting, forestry and fishing	70149	30350	39799	72375	29720	42655	...	...	...	...	...	...
A Agriculture and hunting	17167	9391	7776	16997	9082	7915	...	...	...	...	...	...
B Forestry and logging	...	...	...	...	...	...	...	...	...	...	...	...
C Fishing	52982	20959	32023	55378	20638	34740	...	...	...	...	...	...
2 Mining and quarrying	...	...	...	...	...	...	...	...	...	...	...	...
3 Manufacturing	180248	119944	60304	189285	128935	60350	...	...	...	...	...	...
A Manufacture of food, beverages and tobacco	106945	75422	31523	109090	79239	29851	...	...	...	...	...	...
B Textile, wearing apparel and leather industries	6549	3951	2598	7465	4549	2916	...	...	...	...	...	...

Iceland

	1994 Gross output	1994 Intermediate consumption	1994 Value added	1995 Gross output	1995 Intermediate consumption	1995 Value added	1996 Gross output	1996 Intermediate consumption	1996 Value added	1997 Gross output	1997 Intermediate consumption	1997 Value added
C Manufacture of wood and wood products, including furniture	5710	3490	2220	5764	3463	2301	...	...	...	...	...	...
D Manufacture of paper and paper products, printing and publishing	12659	6280	6379	13419	6844	6575	...	...	...	...	...	...
E Manufacture of chemicals and chemical petroleum, coal, rubber and plastic products	9550	5917	3633	10123	6411	3712	...	...	...	...	...	...
F Manufacture of non-metallic mineral products, except products of petroleum and coal	5866	3183	2683	5922	3370	2552	...	...	...	...	...	...
G Basic metal industries	13796	9640	4156	15106	10963	4143	...	...	...	...	...	...
H Manufacture of fabricated metal products, machinery and equipment	13111	7933	5178	14973	9033	5940	...	...	...	...	...	...
I Other manufacturing industries	6062	4130	1932	7425	5065	2360	...	...	...	...	...	...
4 Electricity, gas and water	24464	10938	13526	25587	10763	14824	...	...	...	...	...	...
A Electricity, gas and steam	23105	10246	12859	24157	10124	14033	...	...	...	...	...	...
B Water works and supply	1359	692	667	1430	639	791	...	...	...	...	...	...
5 Construction	81714	58301	23413	77279	53429	23850	...	...	...	...	...	...
6 Wholesale and retail trade, restaurants and hotels	71911	25442	46469	75816	28293	47523	...	...	...	...	...	...
A Wholesale and retail trade	56333	17041	39292	59299	18815	40484	...	...	...	...	...	...
B Restaurants and hotels	15579	8402	7177	16517	9477	7040	...	...	...	...	...	...
Restaurants	12134	6739	5395	12970	7709	5261	...	...	...	...	...	...
Hotels and other lodging places	3445	1662	1783	3547	1768	1779	...	...	...	...	...	...
7 Transport, storage and communication	61301	31355	29946	65070	34334	30736	...	...	...	...	...	...
A Transport and storage	51451	27563	23888	53938	30260	23678	...	...	...	...	...	...
B Communication	9851	3792	6059	11133	4073	7060	...	...	...	...	...	...
8 Finance, insurance, real estate and business services	97348	30845	66503	100598	33400	67198	...	...	...	...	...	...
A Financial institutions	24813	7296	17517	23523	7657	15866	...	...	...	...	...	...
B Insurance	2433	1452	981	1997	1465	532	...	...	...	...	...	...
C Real estate and business services	70102	22097	48005	75078	24277	50801	...	...	...	...	...	...
9 Community, social and personal services	37331	17757	19574	38450	18271	20179	...	...	...	...	...	...
A Sanitary and similar services	...	...	...	...	...	...	...	...	...	...	...	...
B Social and related community services	7299	2273	5026	7178	2191	4987	...	...	...	...	...	...
C Recreational and cultural services	13922	6963	6959	14344	7297	7047	...	...	...	...	...	...
D Personal and household services [a]	16111	8521	7590	16927	8784	8143	...	...	...	...	...	...
Total, Industries	624467	324932	299535	644460	337144	307316	...	...	...	...	...	...
Producers of government services	104001	44807	59194	109682	47234	62448	...	...	...	...	...	...
Other producers	6740	2841	3899	8957	4605	4352	...	...	...	...	...	...
Total	735208	372580	362628	763098	388984	374114	...	...	...	...	...	...
less: Imputed bank service charge	–	–14283	14283	–	–14878	14878	...	...	...	...	...	...

Iceland

	1994			1995			1996			1997		
	Gross output	Intermediate consumption	Value added	Gross output	Intermediate consumption	Value added	Gross output	Intermediate consumption	Value added	Gross output	Intermediate consumption	Value added
Import duties [b]	60757	–	60757	63843	–	63843	...	...	...	...	...	...
Value added tax	...	...	...	...	...	...	...	...	...	...	...	...
Other adjustments [c]	25925	...	25925	28468	...	28468	...	...	...	...	...	...
Total	821890	386863	435027	855409	403862	451547	...	...	...	...	...	...

a Item "Personal and household services" includes also ISIC-code 96, residents directly employed at the NATO-base.
b Item "Import duties" includes all indirect taxes and subsidies not directly allocated to specified activities.
c Item "Other adjustments" includes residual error between production and expenditure approaches.

4.3 Cost components of value added

Million Icelandic kronur

	1987						1988					
	Compensation of employees	Capital consumption	Net operating surplus	Indirect taxes	less: Subsidies received	Value added	Compensation of employees	Capital consumption	Net operating surplus	Indirect taxes	less: Subsidies received	Value added
All producers											
1 Agriculture, hunting, forestry and fishing	11840	4824	4441	299	192	21211	14339	5259	5586	358	175	25367
A Agriculture and hunting	603	1210	4339	202	192	6162	753	1463	3943	239	175	6224
B Forestry and logging	–	–	–	–	–	–	–	–	–	–	–	–
C Fishing	11236	3614	102	97	–	15049	13586	3797	1643	119	–	19144
2 Mining and quarrying	...	...	...	...	...	...	...	...	...	...	...	...
3 Manufacturing	25575	4600	2561	3982	2332	34386	29674	5207	2808	5384	5259	37814
A Manufacture of food, beverages and tobacco	11510	2380	2074	1115	2036	15043	13504	2732	1096	1643	4866	14109
B Textile, wearing apparel and leather industries	2037	241	–206	255	159	2168	2008	261	–363	306	163	2048
C Manufacture of wood and wood products, including furniture	1563	239	–7	718	–	2513	1659	235	135	820	2	2847
D Manufacture of paper and paper products, printing and publishing	2214	296	353	367	–	3230	2587	334	487	554	32	3930
E Manufacture of chemicals and chemical petroleum, coal, rubber and plastic products	1249	328	72	312	138	1825	1628	454	57	407	49	2496
F Manufacture of non-metallic mineral products, except products of petroleum and coal	915	273	224	447	–	1859	1198	333	116	530	7	2171
G Basic metal industries	1137	554	–170	83	–	1604	1528	523	710	337	–	3099
H Manufacture of fabricated metal products, machinery and equipment	4328	248	131	596	–	5303	4820	290	357	691	126	6031
I Other manufacturing industries	623	40	89	88	–	841	742	45	211	97	13	1083
4 Electricity, gas and water	1360	3688	1400	831	406	6872	1806	4150	3186	1086	246	9981
A Electricity, gas and steam	1327	3562	1264	830	404	6578	1718	4012	2965	1083	238	9539
B Water works and supply	33	126	136	1	2	294	88	138	222	3	8	442
5 Construction	8814	875	4905	1253	2	15845	10514	979	4848	1647	–	17988
6 Wholesale and retail trade, restaurants and hotels	15933	2264	1205	18800	2	38200	19357	2761	–1028	26143	46	47187
A Wholesale and retail trade	13510	1456	1426	17413	2	33805	16497	1768	–750	23982	46	41451
B Restaurants and hotels	2423	807	–221	1386	–	4395	2860	993	–278	2161	–	5736

Iceland

Million Icelandic kronur

	1987						1988					
	Compensation of employees	Capital consumption	Net operating surplus	Indirect taxes	less: Subsidies received	Value added	Compensation of employees	Capital consumption	Net operating surplus	Indirect taxes	less: Subsidies received	Value added
Restaurants	1677	305	−274	1109	−	2817	2037	457	−378	1808	−	3924
Hotels and other lodging places	746	502	53	278	−	1578	824	536	100	353	−	1812
7 Transport, storage and communication	7815	2572	2028	1378	353	13441	9451	2940	2866	2132	430	16960
A Transport and storage	6016	2048	2013	974	353	10699	7275	2328	2303	1497	430	12973
B Communication	1799	524	15	404	−	2741	2177	612	563	635	−	3987
8 Finance, insurance, real estate and business services	8085	7088	14020	2928	376	31746	10927	8643	18893	4579	1596	41445
A Financial institutions	4082	551	3756	496	376	8509	5339	794	7017	672	1596	12226
B Insurance	570	75	−121	897	−	1421	780	94	−573	1376	−	1677
C Real estate and business services	3433	6462	10386	1534	−	21816	4807	7754	12449	2531	−	27542
9 Community, social and personal services	5091	744	2630	2023	416	10072	6526	863	3740	2349	578	12900
A Sanitary and similar services	...	...	...	...	...	...	...	...	...	...	...	...
B Social and related community services	278	49	1561	78	−	1966	463	62	2142	115	−	2783
Educational services	...	...	...	...	...	...	...	...	...	...	...	...
Medical, dental, other health and veterinary services	278	49	1561	78	−	1966	463	62	2142	115	−	2783
C Recreational and cultural services	1730	277	609	503	415	2704	2181	324	1156	590	578	3673
D Personal and household services	3083	418	459	1442	−	5402	3882	476	442	1644	−	6445
Total, Industries	84514	26655	33189	31494	4077	171774	102594	30802	40898	43678	8330	209643
Producers of government services	24054	1154	40	762	−	26010	31660	1361	60	1004	−	34086
Other producers	1362	142	−21	50	−	1534	1926	203	−33	72	−	2168
Total	109930	27951	33208	32307	4077	199318	136181	32366	40926	44754	8330	245897
less: Imputed bank service charge	−	−	8085	−	−	8085	−	−	11557	−	−	11557
Import duties	−	−	−	16013	1910	14103	−	−	−	16570	777	15793
Value added tax	...	...	...	...	...	...	...	...	...	...	...	...
Other adjustments	...	...	...	...	...	...	...	...	...	...	...	...
Total	109930	27951	25123	48320	5988	205336	136181	32366	29370	61324	9107	250134

	1989						1990					
	Compensation of employees	Capital consumption	Net operating surplus	Indirect taxes	less: Subsidies received	Value added	Compensation of employees	Capital consumption	Net operating surplus	Indirect taxes	less: Subsidies received	Value added

All producers

1 Agriculture, hunting, forestry and fishing	16957	5564	6730	484	482	29254	21116	7377	6482	616	−	35591
A Agriculture and hunting	885	1658	4631	278	482	6970	1063	1698	4456	326	−	7543
B Forestry and logging	−	−	−	−	−	−	−	−	−	−	−	−
C Fishing	16072	3906	2099	206	−	22284	20053	5678	2026	290	−	28047
2 Mining and quarrying	...	...	...	...	...	...	...	...	...	...	...	...
3 Manufacturing	32063	6709	4966	7185	5645	45279	33774	7704	6082	2669	−	50229
A Manufacture of food, beverages and tobacco	15247	3534	1697	2582	5435	17626	15501	3956	3037	1460	−	23954
B Textile, wearing apparel and leather industries	1777	372	−336	336	181	1967	1697	435	6	132	−	2270

Iceland

	1989						1990					
	Compensation of employees	Capital consumption	Net operating surplus	Indirect taxes	less: Subsidies received	Value added	Compensation of employees	Capital consumption	Net operating surplus	Indirect taxes	less: Subsidies received	Value added
C Manufacture of wood and wood products, including furniture	1580	242	181	959	–	2961	1994	249	53	121	–	2417
D Manufacture of paper and paper products, printing and publishing	3268	526	826	530	–	5150	3725	722	811	193	–	5451
E Manufacture of chemicals and chemical petroleum, coal, rubber and plastic products	1784	538	154	602	27	3050	1890	609	781	185	–	3465
F Manufacture of non-metallic mineral products, except products of petroleum and coal	1288	332	212	711	–	2543	1560	406	236	223	–	2425
G Basic metal industries	1780	606	1833	380	–	4600	1917	722	–91	30	–	2578
H Manufacture of fabricated metal products, machinery and equipment	4528	500	169	970	2	6165	4451	541	806	279	–	6077
I Other manufacturing industries	811	59	231	115	–	1217	1039	66	444	46	–	1595
4 Electricity, gas and water	2271	5349	3308	1224	293	11859	2730	6775	2262	21	–	11788
A Electricity, gas and steam	2174	5151	3003	1224	293	11258	2555	6591	1932	16	–	11094
B Water works and supply	98	198	305	–	–	601	175	184	330	5	–	694
5 Construction	12528	945	6454	1861	–	21789	14103	948	7730	1546	–	24327
6 Wholesale and retail trade, restaurants and hotels	20930	3021	2658	30471	14	57066	23753	3567	9762	9351	–	46433
A Wholesale and retail trade	17864	2377	1985	28035	14	50247	19695	2879	8910	9024	–	40508
B Restaurants and hotels	3066	644	673	2436	–	6819	4058	689	852	328	–	5927
Restaurants	2217	353	413	2022	–	5005	3033	282	555	215	–	4085
Hotels and other lodging places	849	291	260	414	–	1814	1025	406	297	113	–	1841
7 Transport, storage and communication	10310	3955	2668	2444	472	18906	11511	4204	5671	1329	–	22715
A Transport and storage	7834	2791	2262	1663	472	14077	8721	3030	5137	1287	–	18175
B Communication	2476	1164	406	782	–	4828	2791	1174	534	43	–	4542
8 Finance, insurance, real estate and business services	12357	10629	24500	5154	1308	51332	14645	12727	24879	3680	887	55044
A Financial institutions	5894	830	8393	729	1308	14538	6736	1002	7044	802	887	14697
B Insurance	993	129	206	1386	–	2713	1137	146	–1164	192	–	311
C Real estate and business services	5470	9671	15902	3039	–	34081	6773	11580	18999	2686	–	40038
9 Community, social and personal services	6903	1026	4827	2698	585	14869	7720	1351	6124	586	–	15781
A Sanitary and similar services	...	...	...	...	...	...	...	...	...	...	...	...
B Social and related community services	481	62	2539	117	–	3199	660	140	3044	131	–	3975
Educational services	...	...	...	...	...	...	...	...	...	...	...	...
Medical, dental, other health and veterinary services	481	62	2539	117	–	3199	660	140	3044	131	–	3975
C Recreational and cultural services	2607	455	1374	688	585	4538	2954	666	1456	159	–	5235
D Personal and household services	3816	508	915	1893	–	7132	4107	545	1624	295	–	6571
Total, Industries	114319	37198	56113	51522	8799	250353	129353	44652	68991	19799	887	261908
Producers of government services	36691	1685	86	1164	–	39625	41992	2035	117	1333	375	45102

Iceland

	1989						1990					
	Compen-sation of employ-ees	Capital consump-tion	Net operating surplus	Indirect taxes	less: Subsidies received	Value added	Compen-sation of employ-ees	Capital consump-tion	Net operating surplus	Indirect taxes	less: Subsidies received	Value added
Other producers	2438	249	−38	90	–	2738	3718	91	62	–	–	3871
Total	153447	39132	56161	52775	8799	292716	175062	46778	69171	21132	1263	310880
less: Imputed bank service charge	–	–	12702	–	–	12702	–	–	12422	–	–	12422
Import duties	–	–	–	19377	4036	15341	–	–	–	58035	11690	46345
Value added tax	...	...	...	...	...	...	...	...	...	...	...	...
Other adjustments	...	...	...	...	...	...	...	...	...	...	...	...
Total	153447	39132	43459	72152	12835	295355	175062	46778	56749	79167	12953	344803

	1991						1992					
	Compen-sation of employ-ees	Capital consump-tion	Net operating surplus	Indirect taxes	less: Subsidies received	Value added	Compen-sation of employ-ees	Capital consump-tion	Net operating surplus	Indirect taxes	less: Subsidies received	Value added
All producers												
1 Agriculture, hunting, forestry and fishing	22249	8103	8570	530	–	39452	22208	7545	8206	222	–	38181
A Agriculture and hunting	1049	1917	5179	196	–	8341	1268	1978	4160	165	–	7571
B Forestry and logging	–	–	–	–	–	–	–	–	–	–	–	–
C Fishing	21200	6186	3392	334	–	31112	20940	5568	4046	57	–	30611
2 Mining and quarrying	...	...	...	...	...	...	...	...	...	...	...	...
3 Manufacturing	37996	7687	6063	2727	–	54473	36788	7753	8018	1539	–	54098
A Manufacture of food, beverages and tobacco	17533	3989	4463	1597	–	27582	17092	3949	5241	977	–	27259
B Textile, wearing apparel and leather industries	1887	232	75	114	–	2308	1903	195	291	53	–	2442
C Manufacture of wood and wood products, including furniture	2252	249	131	116	–	2748	2197	250	390	63	–	2900
D Manufacture of paper and paper products, printing and publishing	4417	739	956	189	–	6301	4079	698	1054	71	–	5902
E Manufacture of chemicals and chemical petroleum, coal, rubber and plastic products	2151	699	617	173	–	3640	2259	694	891	111	–	3955
F Manufacture of non-metallic mineral products, except products of petroleum and coal	1846	395	100	194	–	2535	1772	398	289	109	–	2568
G Basic metal industries	1903	828	−1480	24	–	1275	1836	929	−1014	21	–	1772
H Manufacture of fabricated metal products, machinery and equipment	4905	486	772	267	–	6430	4491	478	487	103	–	5559
I Other manufacturing industries	1102	68	429	53	–	1652	1158	163	388	32	–	1741
4 Electricity, gas and water	2935	6532	2500	–	–	11967	3091	6841	2779	–	–	12711
A Electricity, gas and steam	2736	6273	2033	–	–	11042	2879	6537	2465	–	–	11881
B Water works and supply	199	259	468	–	–	926	212	304	315	–	–	831
5 Construction	16397	1119	6636	739	–	24891	15408	1593	7918	353	–	25272
6 Wholesale and retail trade, restaurants and hotels	29352	3731	7744	9582	–	50409	30505	3963	8619	919	–	44006
A Wholesale and retail trade	24068	3102	7175	9352	–	43697	25401	3295	8041	799	–	37536
B Restaurants and hotels	5285	630	569	229	–	6713	5104	668	578	120	–	6470
Restaurants	4057	210	352	119	–	4738	3868	236	367	41	–	4512
Hotels and other lodging places	1227	420	217	111	–	1975	1236	432	211	79	–	1958

Iceland

	1991						1992					
	Compensation of employees	Capital consumption	Net operating surplus	Indirect taxes	less: Subsidies received	Value added	Compensation of employees	Capital consumption	Net operating surplus	Indirect taxes	less: Subsidies received	Value added
7 Transport, storage and communication	13365	5275	3829	715	–	23184	13612	4551	4583	660	–	23406
A Transport and storage	10248	3875	3510	714	–	18347	10330	3541	3272	621	–	17764
B Communication	3117	1400	319	1	–	4837	3282	1010	1311	39	–	5642
8 Finance, insurance, real estate and business services	17989	13832	26922	3390	1073	61060	18432	14356	28646	3229	1792	62871
A Financial institutions	7920	1131	7678	659	1073	16315	8013	1122	9114	754	1792	17211
B Insurance	1354	163	–860	170	–	827	1440	248	–736	34	–	986
C Real estate and business services	8715	12538	20104	2561	–	43918	8979	12986	20269	2441	–	44675
9 Community, social and personal services	8401	1408	7335	418	–	17562	9404	1551	7524	317	–	18796
A Sanitary and similar services	...	...	...	...	...	...	...	...	...	...	...	...
B Social and related community services	707	121	3567	63	–	4458	788	179	3672	42	–	4681
Educational services	...	...	...	...	...	...	...	...	...	...	...	...
Medical, dental, other health and veterinary services	707	121	3567	63	–	4458	788	179	3672	42	–	4681
C Recreational and cultural services	3126	800	1776	160	–	5862	3196	746	1919	131	–	5992
D Personal and household services	4567	486	1992	195	–	7240	5419	626	1933	144	–	8122
Total, Industries	148684	47686	69599	18100	1073	282996	149448	48154	76292	7239	1792	279341
Producers of government services	48966	2326	131	–	432	50991	50440	2461	126	–	423	52604
Other producers	3993	98	65	–	–	4156	3943	97	65	–	–	4105
Total	201642	50111	69795	18100	1505	338143	203831	50712	76482	7239	2215	336049
less: Imputed bank service charge	–	–	14352	–	–	14352	–	–	14559	–	–	14559
Import duties	–	–	–	65843	10814	55029	–	–	–	76475	11010	65465
Value added tax	...	...	...	...	...	...	...	...	...	...	...	...
Other adjustments	...	...	...	...	...	...	...	...	...	...	...	...
Total	201642	50111	55443	83943	12319	378820	203831	50712	61923	83714	13225	386955

	1993						1994					
	Compensation of employees	Capital consumption	Net operating surplus	Indirect taxes	less: Subsidies received	Value added	Compensation of employees	Capital consumption	Net operating surplus	Indirect taxes	less: Subsidies received	Value added

All producers

1 Agriculture, hunting, forestry and fishing	23028	7950	8323	182	–	39483	23416	7798	8413	172	–	39799
A Agriculture and hunting	1257	1977	3912	162	–	7308	1202	2016	4386	172	–	7776
B Forestry and logging	–	–	–	–	–	–	–	–	–	–	–	–
C Fishing	21770	5973	4412	20	–	32175	22215	5782	4027	–	–	32024
2 Mining and quarrying	...	...	...	...	...	...	...	...	...	...	...	...
3 Manufacturing	35865	7558	9032	1286	–	53741	37350	7573	14165	1216	–	60304
A Manufacture of food, beverages and tobacco	17804	3994	5480	639	–	27917	19042	4033	7709	738	–	31522
B Textile, wearing apparel and leather industries	1657	193	362	48	–	2260	1789	214	555	41	–	2599
C Manufacture of wood and wood products, including furniture	1673	204	448	50	–	2375	1524	196	442	58	–	2220

Iceland

	1993 Compensation of employees	1993 Capital consumption	1993 Net operating surplus	1993 Indirect taxes	1993 less: Subsidies received	1993 Value added	1994 Compensation of employees	1994 Capital consumption	1994 Net operating surplus	1994 Indirect taxes	1994 less: Subsidies received	1994 Value added
D Manufacture of paper and paper products, printing and publishing	4166	646	773	81	–	5666	4656	645	983	97	–	6381
E Manufacture of chemicals and chemical petroleum, coal, rubber and plastic products	2271	566	864	126	–	3827	2142	472	935	85	–	3634
F Manufacture of non-metallic mineral products, except products of petroleum and coal	1411	354	496	51	–	2312	1474	373	770	67	–	2684
G Basic metal industries	1656	981	−552	3	–	2088	1671	1116	1369	–	–	4156
H Manufacture of fabricated metal products, machinery and equipment	3978	466	770	104	–	5318	3671	395	1021	91	–	5178
I Other manufacturing industries	1247	154	391	186	–	1978	1382	130	382	39	–	1933
4 Electricity, gas and water	3139	7444	2908	–	–	13491	3286	7537	2703	–	–	13526
A Electricity, gas and steam	2923	7156	2602	–	–	12681	3022	7177	2660	–	–	12859
B Water works and supply	217	288	306	–	–	811	264	360	44	–	–	668
5 Construction	14581	1514	7954	339	–	24388	13945	1507	7699	262	–	23413
6 Wholesale and retail trade, restaurants and hotels	29459	3929	8991	789	–	43168	30912	3790	10828	938	–	46468
A Wholesale and retail trade	24489	3218	8437	675	–	36819	25502	3118	9832	839	–	39291
B Restaurants and hotels	4970	711	555	114	–	6350	5410	672	997	99	–	7178
Restaurants	3669	375	384	48	–	4476	4135	429	775	55	–	5394
Hotels and other lodging places	1301	336	170	66	–	1873	1275	243	221	43	–	1782
7 Transport, storage and communication	13315	4574	5827	767	–	24483	13921	4524	8841	2661	–	29947
A Transport and storage	9878	3494	4302	730	–	18404	10425	3340	7502	2620	–	23887
B Communication	3437	1080	1525	37	–	6079	3496	1184	1339	41	–	6060
8 Finance, insurance, real estate and business services	17798	14438	31306	2932	1718	64756	18171	15661	31248	3027	1603	66504
A Financial institutions	8026	1056	10392	455	1718	18211	7940	1433	9449	299	1603	17518
B Insurance	1466	185	−461	–	–	1190	1491	228	−773	35	–	981
C Real estate and business services	8306	13198	21375	2477	–	45356	8740	14001	22572	2692	–	48005
9 Community, social and personal services	9059	1631	7321	369	–	18380	9557	1740	7913	364	–	19574
A Sanitary and similar services	...	...	...	...	...	...	...	...	...	...	...	...
B Social and related community services	769	215	3594	22	–	4600	919	103	3978	25	–	5025
Educational services	...	...	...	...	...	...	...	...	...	...	...	...
Medical, dental, other health and veterinary services	769	215	3594	22	–	4600	919	103	3978	25	–	5025
C Recreational and cultural services	3374	776	1713	205	–	6068	3831	940	1993	195	–	6959
D Personal and household services	4916	639	2014	143	–	7712	4807	697	1941	145	–	7590
Total, Industries	146244	49037	81664	6665	1718	281892	150558	50130	91810	8640	1603	299535
Producers of government services	53112	2607	130	–	458	55391	56357	2712	126	–	449	58746
Other producers	4115	102	68	–	–	4285	4177	103	68	–	–	4348
Total	203471	51747	81862	6665	2176	341569	211092	52945	92003	8640	2052	362628

Iceland

	1993						1994					
	Compensation of employees	Capital consumption	Net operating surplus	Indirect taxes	less: Subsidies received	Value added	Compensation of employees	Capital consumption	Net operating surplus	Indirect taxes	less: Subsidies received	Value added
less: Imputed bank service charge	–	–	15197	–	–	15197	–	–	14283	–	–	14283
Import duties	–	–	–	70344	8328	62016	–	–	–	70364	7555	62809
Value added tax	...	...	...	...	...	...	...	...	...	...	...	...
Other adjustments	...	...	...	...	...	...	...	...	...	...	...	...
Total	203471	51747	66665	77009	10504	388388	211092	52945	77720	79004	9607	411154

	1995						1996					
	Compensation of employees	Capital consumption	Net operating surplus	Indirect taxes	less: Subsidies received	Value added	Compensation of employees	Capital consumption	Net operating surplus	Indirect taxes	less: Subsidies received	Value added
All producers											
1 Agriculture, hunting, forestry and fishing	24116	7482	10887	170	–	42655	...	...	...	...	...	...
A Agriculture and hunting	1366	1824	4555	170	–	7915	...	...	...	...	...	...
B Forestry and logging	–	–	–	–	–	–	...	...	...	...	...	...
C Fishing	22750	5658	6332	–	–	34740	...	...	...	...	...	...
2 Mining and quarrying	...	...	...	...	...	...	...	...	...	...	...	...
3 Manufacturing	40024	7656	11325	1344	–	60349	...	...	...	...	...	...
A Manufacture of food, beverages and tobacco	19989	4234	4744	884	–	29851	...	...	...	...	...	...
B Textile, wearing apparel and leather industries	1936	206	731	44	–	2917	...	...	...	...	...	...
C Manufacture of wood and wood products, including furniture	1794	121	344	43	–	2302	...	...	...	...	...	...
D Manufacture of paper and paper products, printing and publishing	4887	672	928	89	–	6576	...	...	...	...	...	...
E Manufacture of chemicals and chemical petroleum, coal, rubber and plastic products	2196	478	954	84	–	3712	...	...	...	...	...	...
F Manufacture of non-metallic mineral products, except products of petroleum and coal	1472	402	608	71	–	2553	...	...	...	...	...	...
G Basic metal industries	1691	933	1519	–	–	4143	...	...	...	...	...	...
H Manufacture of fabricated metal products, machinery and equipment	4432	455	962	91	–	5940	...	...	...	...	...	...
I Other manufacturing industries	1628	157	537	38	–	2360	...	...	...	...	...	...
4 Electricity, gas and water	3529	7614	3681	–	–	14824	...	...	...	...	...	...
A Electricity, gas and steam	3225	7240	3568	–	–	14033	...	...	...	...	...	...
B Water works and supply	305	374	112	–	–	791	...	...	...	...	...	...
5 Construction	13912	1412	8282	244	–	23850	...	...	...	...	...	...
6 Wholesale and retail trade, restaurants and hotels	32188	4134	10358	844	–	47524	...	...	...	...	...	...
A Wholesale and retail trade	26618	3469	9626	770	–	40483	676	840	...	...	...	...
B Restaurants and hotels	5570	665	732	73	–	7040	...	...	...	...	...	...
Restaurants	4325	451	443	42	–	5261	...	...	...	...	...	...
Hotels and other lodging places	1245	214	289	31	–	1779	...	...	...	...	...	...
7 Transport, storage and communication	16563	4786	6447	2940	–	30736	...	...	...	...	...	...
A Transport and storage	11941	3478	5369	2888	–	23676	...	...	...	...	...	...

Iceland

	1995						1996					
	Compensation of employees	Capital consumption	Net operating surplus	Indirect taxes	less: Subsidies received	Value added	Compensation of employees	Capital consumption	Net operating surplus	Indirect taxes	less: Subsidies received	Value added
B Communication	4621	1308	1078	52	–	7059	...	...	...	...	...	...
8 Finance, insurance, real estate and business services	19648	16079	29425	3216	1170	67198	...	...	...	...	...	...
A Financial institutions	8557	1054	7115	309	1170	15865	...	...	...	...	...	...
B Insurance	1555	239	–1300	38	–	532	...	...	...	...	...	...
C Real estate and business services	9536	14786	23610	2869	–	50801	...	...	...	...	...	...
9 Community, social and personal services	10573	1711	7615	280	–	20179	...	...	...	...	...	...
A Sanitary and similar services	...	...	...	...	...	...	...	...	...	...	...	...
B Social and related community services	1239	135	3594	20	–	4988	...	...	...	...	...	...
Educational services	...	...	...	...	...	...	...	...	...	...	...	...
Medical, dental, other health and veterinary services	1239	135	3594	20	–	4988	...	...	...	...	...	...
C Recreational and cultural services	4199	891	1835	123	–	7048	...	...	...	...	...	...
D Personal and household services	5135	686	2186	137	–	8144	...	...	...	...	...	...
Total, Industries	160553	50876	88019	9038	1170	307316	...	...	...	...	...	...
Producers of government services	59468	2851	129	–	633	61815	...	...	...	...	...	...
Other producers	4656	255	73	–	–	4984	...	...	...	...	...	...
Total	224677	53982	88221	9038	1803	374115	...	...	...	...	...	...
less: Imputed bank service charge	–	–	14878	–	–	14878	...	...	...	...	...	...
Import duties	–	–	–	73335	7689	65646	...	...	...	...	...	...
Value added tax	...	...	...	...	...	...	...	...	...	...	...	...
Other adjustments	...	...	...	...	...	...	...	...	...	...	...	...
Total	224677	53982	73343	82373	9492	424883	...	...	...	...	...	...

India

General note

The preparation of national accounts statistics in India is undertaken by the National Accounts Division of the Central Statistical Organization (CSO), Department of Statistics, Ministry of Planning, New Delhi. Official estimates are published annually in the *National Accounts Statistics*. The sources of data and methodology followed are given in *National Accounts Statistics—Sources and Methods, 1989*. The estimates are generally in accordance with the classifications and definitions recommended in the United Nations System of National Accounts (1968 SNA). The estimates relate to fiscal year beginning 1 April. When the scope and coverage of the estimates differ for conceptual and statistical reasons from the definitions and classifications recommended in SNA, a footnote is indicated to the relevant tables.

Gross domestic product

Gross domestic product is estimated mainly through the production approach for the commodity producing sectors and income approach for the services sectors.

Expenditures on the gross domestic product

The expenditure approach is used to estimate government final consumption expenditure, increase in stocks and exports of goods and services. The commodity-flow approach is used to estimate private final consumption expenditure whereas the estimate of gross fixed capital formation is based on the expenditure approach. Estimates of government consumption expenditure are mainly obtained from budget documents and annual reports of the government bodies. Estimates of private expenditure on goods are obtained from commodity production data adjusted for change in stocks and foreign trade and reduced by intermediate consumption and government final consumption and by the quantities used for capital formation. Private expenditure on services is estimated as the value of the total output for each kind of service reduced by the estimated expenditures on service by government and the business. Estimates of increase in stocks for the public sector and organized (i.e. larger or modern) private industries are based on government budget documents and annual accounts and reports of industries respectively. Estimates of change in stocks of unorganized private industries are based on sample survey data, data on bank advances and margins and on livestock censuses.

For gross fixed capital formation, estimates of construction are compiled using data from a number of sources such as annual survey of industries, dispatches of cement for domestic consumption, sample surveys and government budget documents and the All-India debt and investment surveys. These estimates are extrapolated by the relevant indicators. For machinery and equipment, estimates are based on the annual survey of industries, foreign trade statistics, customs and excise revenue statements, data on trade, transport and other charges collected from leading manufacturing firms. The estimates of exports and imports of goods and services are based on balance of payment statistics supplemented by information supplied by government agencies. For the constant 1980–81 price estimates, private expenditure on goods is extrapolated by quantity indexes. Changes in stocks of livestock, mining and foodgrains are valued at 1980–81 prices. For government expenditure, private expenditure on services, increase in stock for other sectors and gross fixed capital formation, the current values are deflated by relevant price indexes. Import and export of goods and services are not estimated at constant prices.

Cost structure of the gross domestic product

Estimates of compensation of employees are based on budget documents, annual reports of enterprises, income and expenditure accounts of institutions and companies and sample surveys. Estimates of operating surplus are based on most of the sources used for compensation of employees. Consumption of fixed capital is estimated for each industry separately on the basis of estimated value of capital stock and the expected age of various types of assets at the aggregate level by following the perpetual inventory method. The sources include the All-India rural debt and investment surveys, livestock censuses, budget documents and annual accounts. Estimates of indirect taxes and subsidies are based on accounts and annual reports of government bodies.

Gross domestic product by kind of activity

The table of gross domestic product by kind of economic activity is prepared at factor cost. The production approach is used to estimate value added for all commodity producing sectors and moving the benchmark estimates for small-scale manufacturing. Value added of construction is based on a combination of the commodity-flow and expenditure approaches. The income approach is used for all other sectors. The production estimates of principal agricultural crops are based on results of the random sample crop-cutting surveys conducted by the respective state government agencies. The wholesale prices in the primary markets are used to evaluate the total production of each commodity. The annual estimates of livestock products are based on the livestock population by type and the corresponding average yield rates. Intermediate consumption is estimated by using a variety of sources such as the National Sample Survey (NSS), the All-India rural debt and investment survey, and marketing reports. Estimates of the gross output of minerals are based on data avail-

India

able from the Indian Bureau of Mines. For large-scale manufacturing, estimates are prepared for 19 industry groups based on the Annual Surveys of Industries (ASI). Benchmark estimates for the household and non-household small-scale manufacturing and other unorganised portions of trade, transport etc. have been prepared using data on value added per worker derived from the follow-up surveys of economic census of CSO and NSSO and estimated working force. Other years' estimates are extrapolated by means of indicators of physical output or input and prices. Estimates of pucca construction are compiled by the commodity flow approach using data on steel and cement production, foreign trade statistics, customs and excise revenue, etc. The estimates of kutcha construction are based on expenditure data from NSS, debt and investment surveys and other sources. For public sector trade, transport, administration, banks etc., estimates are based on the analysis of budget documents and annual accounts. The estimates of gross rents for urban and rural dwellings are based on the number of dwellings and estimated gross rental value per dwelling obtained from the NSSO surveys on consumer expenditure.

For the constant price estimates, double deflation is used for the agriculture and mining sectors. Current values of large-scale manufacturing and construction are deflated by price indexes. For small-scale manufacturing, electricity, gas and water, trade, transport, ownership of dwellings and other services, value added is extrapolated by quantity indexes. Current price estimates of public administration are deflated with the consumer price index of industrial workers to obtain the constant price estimates.

1.1 Expenditure on the gross domestic product, in current prices

Ten million Indian rupees — Fiscal year beginning 1 April

	1986	1987	1988	1989	1990	1991	1992	1993	1994	1995	1996	1997
1 Government final consumption expenditure	34625	40843	47331	54203	61779	69459	78596	89926	100498	115957	132166	...
2 Private final consumption expenditure	198599	222551	257419	288242	330371	381888	430180	493380	570417	643435	729629	...
3 Gross capital formation [a]	67899	74882	96411	110195	135156	140068	169656	172532	241379	304980	321848	...
A Increase in stocks	5847	2688	10742	7420	11152	3565	10799	217	24972	33386	15865	...
B Gross fixed capital formation [b]	62052	72194	85669	102775	124004	136503	158857	174702	216407	271594	305983	...
Residential buildings	8080	9004	10151	11772	14732	16820	19407	21650	24019	27701	30504	...
Non-residential buildings	6212	7281	9029	11418	13763	15259	18925	18458	22315	30305	37247	...
Other construction and land improvement, etc.	16281	18502	22265	24702	29868	34853	37294	40926	48319	57029	63291	...
Other	31479	37407	44224	54883	65641	69571	83231	93668	121754	156559	174941	...
4 Exports of goods and services	16543	20281	25913	34609	40635	56254	67312	86110	101607	130733	...	...
5 less: Imports of goods and services	22359	25259	32010	40212	48698	56249	73000	85700	104710	144953	...	...
Statistical discrepancy	-2358	-97	718	9784	16291	25379	33174	54501	54301	68812	...	...
equals: Gross domestic product	292949	333201	395782	456821	535534	616799	705918	810749	963492	1118964	1276974	...

a Figures in this table are unadjusted for errors and ommissions/statistical discrepancies and therefore do not tally with figures in tables 1.8, 2.7, and 2.9.   b Figures are based on type of assets and therefore do not tally with figures in tables 2.9 and 2.11 which are based on industry of use.

1.2 Expenditure on the gross domestic product, in constant prices

Ten million Indian rupees — Fiscal year beginning 1 April

	1986	1987	1988	1989	1990	1991	1992	1993	1994	1995	1996	1997
At constant prices of: 1980												
1 Government final consumption expenditure	20849	22660	23868	25215	26059	25912	26779	28495	29034	30441	31997	...
2 Private final consumption expenditure [a]	130262	135129	143468	149738	155454	158179	164585	172322	182385	191973	203174	...
3 Gross capital formation [b]	40171	41786	49577	50684	56885	50633	56894	54353	72446	84912	84418	...
A Increase in stocks	4174	1831	6807	4201	5794	1587	4433	-988	8629	10432	5074	...
B Gross fixed capital formation [c]	35997	39955	42770	46483	51091	49046	52461	55341	63817	74480	79344	...
Residential buildings	3583	3653	3530	3630	3647	3869	4004	4114	4259	4404	4590	...
Non-residential buildings	2903	3109	3578	4186	4741	4665	5362	4834	5373	6548	7559	...
Other construction and land improvement, etc.	8104	8283	9315	9253	10369	10657	10383	10478	11336	12019	12279	...

India

Ten million Indian rupees — Fiscal year beginning 1 April

	1986	1987	1988	1989	1990	1991	1992	1993	1994	1995	1996	1997
At constant prices of: 1980												
Other	21407	24910	26347	29414	32334	29855	32712	35915	42849	51509	54916	...
4 Exports of goods and services	...	...	...	...	...	...	...	...	...	...	...	...
5 less: Imports of goods and services	...	...	...	...	...	...	...	...	...	...	...	...
equals: Gross domestic product	185250	194085	213345	227367	240238	241255	254332	266934	288637	309917	332721	...

a Item "Private consumption expenditure" refers to expenditure in the domestic market only.
b Figures in this table are unadjusted for errors and ommissions/statistical discrepancies and therefore do not tally with figures in tables 2.8 and 2.10.
c Figures are based on type of assets and therefore, do not tally with figures in table 2.10 and 2.12 which are based on industry of use.

1.3 Cost components of the gross domestic product

Ten million Indian rupees — Fiscal year beginning 1 April

	1986	1987	1988	1989	1990	1991	1992	1993	1994	1995	1996	1997
1 Indirect taxes, net	32919	38350	43076	48159	57720	64031	75146	77875	95473	112678	127759	...
A Indirect taxes	42714	49847	57430	66749	76329	86661	95596	101126	121067	142403	164902	...
B less: Subsidies	9795	11497	14354	18590	18609	22630	20450	23251	25594	29725	37143	...
2 Consumption of fixed capital	29823	33341	38921	45646	52195	63079	72946	81552	95339	111586	127182	...
3 Compensation of employees paid by resident producers to												
A Resident households	...	...	...	...	...	...	...	...	...	...	...	...
B Rest of the world	178	380	390	332	320	286	347	1277	1299	1504	...	...
4 Operating surplus	...	...	...	...	...	...	...	...	...	...	...	...
equals: Gross domestic product	292949	333201	395782	456821	535534	616799	705918	810749	963492	1118964	1276974	...

1.4 General government current receipts and disbursements

Ten million Indian rupees — Fiscal year beginning 1 April

	1986	1987	1988	1989	1990	1991	1992	1993	1994	1995	1996	1997
Receipts												
1 Operating surplus	−1313	−1384	−1758	−2269	−2550	−2872	−3443	−3057	−3101	−4686	...	...
2 Property and entrepreneurial income	5687	5845	6008	6964	6575	11642	11100	11358	11289	13734	...	...
3 Taxes, fees and contributions	51225	59050	69468	80608	91354	106263	119529	128364	159353	187607	...	...
A Indirect taxes	42714	49847	57430	66749	76329	86661	95596	101126	121067	142403	...	...
B Direct taxes	7328	8001	10396	11888	12928	17471	20615	22985	30206	37419	...	...
C Social security contributions	...	...	...	...	...	...	...	...	...	...	...	...
D Compulsory fees, fines and penalties	1183	1202	1642	1971	2097	2131	3318	4253	8080	7785	...	...
4 Other current transfers	...	...	...	...	...	...	...	...	...	...	...	...
Total current receipts of general government	55599	63511	73718	85303	95379	115033	127186	136665	167541	196655	...	...
Disbursements												
1 Government final consumption expenditure	34625	40843	47331	54203	61779	69459	78596	89926	100498	115957	...	...
A Compensation of employees	20055	24121	28367	33183	38258	43914	50492	56051	62739	73367	...	...
B Consumption of fixed capital	2264	2623	3049	3537	3901	4650	5305	5893	6686	7719	...	...
C Purchases of goods and services, net	12306	14099	15915	17483	19620	20895	22799	27982	31073	34871	...	...
D less: Own-account fixed capital formation	...	...	...	...	...	...	...	...	...	...	...	...
E Indirect taxes paid, net	...	...	...	...	...	...	...	...	...	...	...	...

India

Ten million Indian rupees	1986	1987	1988	1989	1990	1991	1992	1993	1994	1995	1996	1997
2 Property income	7592	9678	11816	15667	20233	26258	30387	36302	45283	49438	...	...
A Interest [a]	7592	9678	11816	15667	20233	26258	30387	36302	45283	49438	...	...
B Net land rent and royalties	–	–	–	–	–	–	–	–	–	...	...	...
3 Subsidies	9795	11497	14354	18590	18609	22630	20450	23251	25594	29725	...	...
4 Other current transfers	8720	10016	12172	14142	15717	17388	20070	22640	31614	35525	...	...
Statistical discrepancy [b]	844	868	600	166	469	–427	106	366	–507	1189	...	...
1 Net saving	–5977	–9391	–12555	–17465	–21428	–20275	–22423	3582	–34941	–35179	...	...
Total current disbursements and net saving of general government	55599	63511	73718	85303	95379	115033	127186	136665	167541	196655	...	...

[a] Item "Interest" refers to interest on the public debt.
[b] Item "Statistical discrepancy" relates to inter-governmental accounting adjustments.

1.7 External transactions on current account, summary

Ten million Indian rupees	1986	1987	1988	1989	1990	1991	1992	1993	1994	1995	1996	1997
Payments to the rest of the world												
1 Imports of goods and services	22359	25259	32010	40212	48698	56249	73000	85700	104710	144953	...	...
A Imports of merchandise, c.i.f.	22760	25831	34482	40983	50350	51864	69456	79421	106763	140812	...	...
B Other	–401	–572	–2472	–771	–1652	4385	3544	6279	–2053	4141	...	...
2 Factor income to rest of the world	2468	3222	5142	6544	8295	10752	12859	13732	16191	18624	...	...
A Compensation of employees	178	380	390	332	320	286	347	1277	1299	1504	...	...
B Property and entrepreneurial income	2290	2842	4752	6212	7975	10466	12512	12455	14892	17120	...	...
3 Current transfers to the rest of the world	15	34	24	26	26	37	35	68	58	108	...	...
A Indirect taxes to supranational organizations	...	...	...	...	...	...	...	...	...	...	...	...
B Other current transfers	15	34	24	26	26	37	35	68	58	108	...	...
Statistical discrepancy [a]	2573	3449	5967	5314	6894	3567	5488	5529	16183	17315	...	...
4 Surplus of the nation on current transactions	–6355	–6825	–12304	–12279	–18196	–3377	–13816	–4791	–11891	–20780	...	...
Payments to the rest of the world and surplus of the nation on current transfers	21060	25139	30839	39817	45717	67228	77566	100238	125251	160220	...	...
Receipts from the rest of the world												
1 Exports of goods and services	16543	20281	25913	34609	40635	56254	67312	86110	101607	130733	...	...
A Exports of merchandise, f.o.b.	13315	16396	20647	28229	33153	44922	54762	71146	84329	108480	...	...
B Other	3228	3885	5266	6380	7482	11332	12550	14964	17278	22253	...	...
2 Factor income from rest of the world	663	603	646	813	750	675	1056	1389	3108	5140	...	...
A Compensation of employees	9	17	33	113	74	117	35	105	278	302	...	...
B Property and entrepreneurial income	654	586	613	700	676	558	1021	1284	2830	4838	...	...
3 Current transfers from rest of the world	2991	3533	3865	3824	3737	9419	8124	11344	18881	22220	...	...
A Subsidies from supranational organisations	...	...	...	...	...	...	...	...	...	...	...	...
B Other current transfers	2991	3533	3865	3824	3737	9419	8124	11344	18881	22220	...	...
Statistical discrepancy [a]	863	722	415	571	595	880	1074	1395	1655	2127	...	...
Receipts from the rest of the world on current transactions	21060	25139	30839	39817	45717	67228	77566	100238	125251	160220	...	...

[a] Item "Statistical discrepancy" refers to difference of payment and ownership basis of imports and exports of merchandise.

India

1.8 Capital transactions of the nation, summary

Ten million Indian rupees — Fiscal year beginning 1 April

	1986	1987	1988	1989	1990	1991	1992	1993	1994	1995	1996	1997
Finance of gross capital formation												
Gross saving	54801	69631	84668	102370	129999	141251	155225	183710	247087	283003	333816	...
1 Consumption of fixed capital	29823	33341	38921	45646	52195	63079	72946	81552	95339	111586	127182	...
A General government	3901	4447	5144	5932	6492	7673	8699	9601	10800	12425	14029	...
B Corporate and quasi-corporate enterprises	13816	15473	18461	22237	26000	32515	38613	43622	51954	61697	71420	...
Public	9197	10481	12409	14932	17258	21100	24372	26853	31149	35499	39448	...
Private [a]	4619	4992	6052	7305	8742	11415	14241	16769	20805	26198	31972	...
C Other	12106	13421	15316	17477	19703	22891	25634	28329	32585	37464	41733	...
2 Net saving	24978	36290	45747	56724	77804	78172	82279	102158	151748	171417	206634	...
A General government	−5977	−9391	−12555	−17465	−21428	−20275	−22423	−35820	−34941	−35179	−41578	...
B Corporate and quasi-corporate enterprises	1474	2484	5370	8369	9312	11979	5511	16634	23871	33643	30402	...
Public	881	1686	3103	4024	3114	3390	117	3923	10483	12450	12829	...
Private [a]	593	798	2267	4345	6198	8589	5394	12711	13388	21193	17573	...
C Other	29481	43197	52932	65820	89920	86468	99191	121344	162818	172953	217810	...
less: Surplus of the nation on current transactions	−6355	−6825	−12304	−12279	−18196	−3377	−13816	−4791	−11891	−20780	−14669	...
Statistical discrepancy	6743	...	...	...	...	...	...	...	...	...	...	...
Finance of gross capital formation	67899	76456	96972	114649	148195	144628	169041	188501	258978	303783	348485	...
Gross capital formation												
Increase in stocks	5847	2688	10742	7420	11152	3565	10799	2170	24972	33386	15865	...
Gross fixed capital formation	62052	72194	85669	102775	124004	136503	158857	174702	216407	271594	305983	...
1 General government	11857	11462	13714	13072	15101	16608	18854	21264	27292	30289	34138	...
2 Corporate and quasi-corporate enterprises	34023	33332	38398	46281	55981	77124	83236	96622	117449	148663	161057	...
A Public	21829	23109	26152	30790	35075	42129	41263	46289	59916	59595	57656	...
B Private [a]	12194	10223	12246	15491	20906	34995	41973	50333	57533	89068	103401	...
3 Other	16172	27400	33557	43422	52922	42771	56767	56816	71666	92642	110788	...
Statistical discrepancy	...	1574	561	4454	13039	4560	−615	15969	17599	−1197	26637	...
Gross capital formation [b]	67899	76456	96972	114649	148195	144628	169041	188501	258978	303783	348485	...

a Estimates relate to private corporate sector enterprises only.
b Figures in this table are adjusted for errors and ommissions/statistical discrepancies and therefore do not tally with figures in table 1.1.

1.10 Gross domestic product by kind of activity, in current prices

Ten million Indian rupees — Fiscal year beginning 1 April

	1986	1987	1988	1989	1990	1991	1992	1993	1994	1995	1996	1997
1 Agriculture, hunting, forestry and fishing	82413	92379	114073	127051	148001	172771	193045	223705	259064	276852	310144	...
2 Mining and quarrying	6796	7085	9208	10308	11785	12803	14589	16818	18879	20554	20544	...
3 Manufacturing	46166	52865	62863	77076	89160	96305	111044	127646	159713	198348	222609	...
4 Electricity, gas and water	5567	6268	7325	8723	10464	12720	16114	18879	23662	28021	32856	...
5 Construction	15217	17611	20677	23586	28616	32246	36700	40699	47978	58416	68583	...
6 Wholesale and retail trade, restaurants and hotels	34551	38433	45222	52910	61883	70807	82769	98024	118488	142808	167608	...
7 Transport, storage and communication	16537	19938	23872	27731	33913	41004	48892	56096	66680	75365	88605	...
8 Finance, insurance, real estate and business services	22309	24756	28256	33577	38902	49056	52639	67145	78468	94475	108007	...

India

Ten million Indian rupees	1986	1987	1988	1989	1990	1991	1992	1993	1994	1995	1996	1997
9 Community, social and personal services	15541	17568	20352	23567	27981	33615	38730	43912	50507	59366	69611	...
Total, Industries	245097	276903	331848	384529	450705	521327	594522	692924	823439	954205	1088567	...
Producers of government services	14933	17948	20858	24133	27109	31441	36250	39950	44580	52081	60648	...
Other producers	...	...	...	...	...	...	...	...	...	...	...	...
Subtotal [a]	260030	294851	352706	408662	477814	552768	630772	732874	868019	1006286	1149215	...
less: Imputed bank service charge	...	...	...	...	...	...	...	...	...	...	...	...
plus: Import duties	...	...	...	...	...	...	...	...	...	...	...	...
plus: Value added tax	...	...	...	...	...	...	...	...	...	...	...	...
plus: Other adjustments [b]	32919	38350	43076	48159	57720	64031	75146	77875	95473	112678	127759	...
equals: Gross domestic product	292949	333201	395782	456821	535534	616799	705918	810749	963492	1118964	1276974	...

a Gross domestic product in factor values. b Item "Other adjustments" refers to indirect taxes net of subsidies.

1.11 Gross domestic product by kind of activity, in constant prices

Ten million Indian rupees	1986	1987	1988	1989	1990	1991	1992	1993	1994	1995	1996	1997
At constant prices of: 1980												
1 Agriculture, hunting, forestry and fishing	53281	53479	62214	63263	65653	64118	68009	70513	74133	71907	77564	...
2 Mining and quarrying	2978	3080	3542	3801	4207	4362	4412	4488	4751	5151	5138	...
3 Manufacturing	32445	34818	37865	42285	44863	43200	45005	48770	54570	62207	66785	...
4 Electricity, gas and water	3422	3692	4080	4505	4797	5258	5700	6060	6632	7113	7466	...
5 Construction	7537	7777	8379	8807	9833	10047	10386	10484	11134	12216	12851	...
6 Wholesale and retail trade, restaurants and hotels	20852	21801	23385	25231	26580	26827	28653	30923	34647	39968	43313	...
7 Transport, storage and communication	8483	9227	9804	10663	11164	11785	12367	13065	14091	15264	16664	...
8 Finance, insurance, real estate and business services	15916	16871	18416	20403	21700	23972	25084	28210	30232	33152	36045	...
9 Community, social and personal services	9550	9873	10434	11281	12128	12844	13454	14149	14842	15732	16707	...
Total, Industries	154464	160618	178119	190239	200925	202413	213070	226662	245032	262710	282533	...
Producers of government services	8807	9704	10342	11214	11328	11570	12170	12483	12668	13422	14312	...
Other producers	...	...	...	...	...	...	...	...	...	...	...	...
Subtotal [a]	163271	170322	188461	201453	212253	213983	225240	239145	257700	276132	296845	...
less: Imputed bank service charge	...	...	...	...	...	...	...	...	...	...	...	...
plus: Import duties	...	...	...	...	...	...	...	...	...	...	...	...
plus: Value added tax	...	...	...	...	...	...	...	...	...	...	...	...
plus: Other adjustments [b]	21979	23763	24884	25914	27985	27272	29092	27789	30937	33785	35876	...
equals: Gross domestic product	185250	194085	213345	227367	240238	241255	254332	266934	288637	309917	332721	...

a Gross domestic product in factor values. b Item "Other adjustments" refers to indirect taxes net of subsidies.

1.12 Relations among national accounting aggregates

Ten million Indian rupees	1986	1987	1988	1989	1990	1991	1992	1993	1994	1995	1996	1997
Gross domestic product	292949	333201	395782	456821	535534	616799	705918	810749	963492	1118964	1276974	...
plus: Net factor income from the rest of the world	−1805	−2619	−4496	−5731	−7545	−10077	−11803	−12343	−13083	−13484	−13845	...
Factor income from rest of the world	663	603	646	813	750	675	1056	1389	3108	5140	...	...

India

Ten million Indian rupees	1986	1987	1988	1989	1990	1991	1992	1993	1994	1995	1996	1997
less: Factor income to the rest of the world	2468	3222	5142	6544	8295	10752	12859	13732	16191	18624	...	...
equals: Gross national product	291144	330582	391286	451090	527989	606722	694115	798406	950409	1105480	1263129	...
less: Consumption of fixed capital	29823	33341	38921	45646	52195	63079	72946	81552	95339	111586	127182	...
equals: National income	261321	297241	352365	405444	475794	543643	621169	716854	855070	993894	1135947	...
plus: Net current transfers from the rest of the world	2976	3499	3841	3798	3711	9382	8089	11276	18823	22112	41120	...
Current transfers from rest of the world	2991	3533	3865	3824	3737	9419	8124	11344	18881	22220	...	...
less: Current transfers to the rest of the world	15	34	24	26	26	37	35	68	58	108	...	...
equals: National disposable income	264297	300740	356206	409242	479505	553025	629258	728130	873893	1016006	1177067	...
less: Final consumption	233224	263394	304750	342445	392150	451347	508776	583306	670915	759392	861795	...
Statistical discrepancy	−6095	−1056	−5709	10073	−9551	−23506	−38203	−42666	−51230	−85197	−108638	...
equals: Net saving [a]	24978	36290	45747	56724	77804	78172	82279	102158	151748	171417	206634	...
less: Surplus of the nation on current transactions	−6355	−6825	−12304	−12279	−18196	−3377	−13816	−4791	−11891	−20780	−14669	...
Statistical discrepancy	6743	−1574	−561	−4454	−113039	−4560	615	−15969	−17599	1197	−26637	...
equals: Net capital formation	38076	41541	57490	64549	82961	76989	96710	90980	146040	193394	194666	...

a Item "Net Savings" includes retained earnings of foreign controlled rupee companies and branches of foreign companies in India.

2.1 Government final consumption expenditure by function, in current prices

Ten million Indian rupees	1986	1987	1988	1989	1990	1991	1992	1993	1994	1995	1996	1997
1 General public services [a]	6140	7507	8734	10239	11845	14212	16472	17594	20389	23536	...	...
2 Defence	11255	13323	14998	16450	17652	18802	21032	25366	27060	31116	...	...
3 Public order and safety	...	...	...	...	...	...	...	...	...	...	...	...
4 Education	3975	4529	5323	6542	7937	8966	10035	11380	12977	15164	...	...
5 Health	1976	2260	2584	2888	3506	3808	4375	4939	5450	6190	...	...
6 Social security and welfare	835	882	1204	1399	1780	2000	2181	2791	3241	3607	...	...
7 Housing and community amenities	621	680	749	862	1273	1367	1402	1761	2274	2165	...	...
8 Recreational, cultural and religious affairs	247	344	389	437	524	445	512	553	663	736	...	...
9 Economic services	3910	4682	5297	6149	6784	7833	8620	10095	11076	13442	...	...
A Fuel and energy	483	633	776	961	1014	1229	1376	1559	1796	2199	...	...
B Agriculture, hunting, forestry and fishing	1422	1797	1984	2200	2281	2646	2924	3117	3285	3933	...	...
C Mining (except fuels), manufacturing and construction	373	420	501	582	728	619	669	612	581	756	...	...
D Transportation and communication	888	942	1124	1379	1589	1913	2192	3166	3544	4283	...	...
E Other economic affairs	744	890	912	1027	1172	1426	1459	1641	1870	2271	...	...
10 Other functions	117	101	226	126	167	97	276	301	302	449	...	...
Total government final consumption expenditures [bcd]	29076	34308	39504	45092	51468	57530	64848	74755	83432	96405	...	...

a Item "Public order and safety" is included in item "General public services".
b Item "Total government consumption expenditure" includes central and state government but excludes other local authorities. Consumption of fixed capital has also not been accounted for. Therefore, the figures will not tally with figures in tables 1.4, 3.12 and 3.13 to this extent.
c Up to 1980, losses of departmental enterprises are treated as consumption expenditure of the government, whereas, after 1980 they are treated as losses of the government.
d Up to 1980, compensation of employees of the administrative departments includes pension payable to the employees of the departmental enterprises also, whereas, after 1980 it has been allocated to the respective departmental enterprises.

India

2.3 Total government outlays by function and type

Ten million Indian rupees — Fiscal year beginning 1 April

1986

	Final consumption expenditures Total	Compensation of employees	Other	Subsidies	Other current transfers and property income	Total current disbursements	Gross capital formation	Other capital outlays	Total outlays
1 General public services [a]	6140	4681	1459	42	1305	7487	728	161	8376
2 Defence	11255	4529	6726	8	46	11309	57	–	11366
3 Public order and safety	...	...	...	...	...	...	...	...	...
4 Education	3975	3647	328	–	5505	9480	232	73	9785
5 Health	1976	1430	546	–	284	2260	245	16	2521
6 Social security and welfare	835	505	330	161	1116	2112	108	108	2328
7 Housing and community amenities	621	398	223	69	686	1376	1632	471	3479
8 Recreational, cultural and religious affairs	247	128	119	1	188	436	64	6	506
9 Economic services	3910	2253	1657	9480	1684	15074	3344	1409	19827
A Fuel and energy	483	224	259	210	417	1110	763	367	2240
B Agriculture, hunting, forestry and fishing	1422	1059	363	4723	818	6963	725	518	8206
C Mining (except fuels), manufacturing and construction	373	331	42	2932	196	3501	110	210	3821
D Transportation and communication	888	145	743	119	147	1154	1651	284	3089
E Other economic affairs	744	494	250	1496	106	2346	95	30	2471
10 Other functions	117	27	90	14	188	319	37	29	385
Total [bc]	29076	17598	11478	9775	11002	49853	6447	2273	58573

1987

	Final consumption expenditures Total	Compensation of employees	Other	Subsidies	Other current transfers and property income	Total current disbursements	Gross capital formation	Other capital outlays	Total outlays
1 General public services [a]	7507	5728	1779	13	1270	8790	712	219	9721
2 Defence	13323	5695	7628	12	102	13437	60	–	13497
3 Public order and safety	...	...	...	...	...	...	...	...	...
4 Education	4529	4144	385	–	6853	11382	234	117	11733
5 Health	2260	1622	638	1	434	2695	237	22	2954
6 Social security and welfare	882	602	280	301	1416	2599	109	49	2757
7 Housing and community amenities	680	445	235	63	887	1630	1615	737	3982
8 Recreational, cultural and religious affairs	344	156	188	1	224	569	61	10	640
9 Economic services	4682	2709	1973	11062	2051	17795	3570	1463	22828
A Fuel and energy	633	269	364	569	468	1670	974	448	3092
B Agriculture, hunting, forestry and fishing	1797	1259	538	4846	978	7621	689	436	8746
C Mining (except fuels), manufacturing and construction	420	380	40	3433	257	4110	90	201	4401
D Transportation and communication	942	203	739	105	177	1224	1758	365	3347

India

1987

	Final consumption expenditures			Subsidies	Other current transfers and property income	Total current disburse- ments	Gross capital formation	Other capital outlays	Total outlays
	Total	Compen- sation of employ- ees	Other						
E Other economic affairs	890	598	292	2109	171	3170	59	13	3242
10 Other functions	101	25	76	10	274	385	55	53	493
Total [bc]	34308	21126	13182	11463	13511	59282	6653	2670	68605

1988

	Final consumption expenditures			Subsidies	Other current transfers and property income	Total current disburse- ments	Gross capital formation	Other capital outlays	Total outlays
	Total	Compen- sation of employ- ees	Other						
1 General public services [a]	8734	6619	2115	9	1421	10164	886	189	11239
2 Defence	14998	6551	8447	14	108	15120	70	–	15190
3 Public order and safety	...	...	...	...	...	...	...	...	...
4 Education	5323	4834	489	–	8095	13418	310	131	13859
5 Health	2584	1930	654	2	491	3077	273	32	3382
6 Social security and welfare	1204	754	450	293	1543	3040	103	26	3169
7 Housing and community amenities	749	503	246	60	1048	1857	1754	857	4468
8 Recreational, cultural and religious affairs	389	186	203	1	375	765	88	6	859
9 Economic services	5297	3185	2112	13937	2858	22092	3882	1703	27677
A Fuel and energy	776	356	420	573	522	1871	1021	441	3333
B Agriculture, hunting, forestry and fishing	1984	1451	533	5900	1429	9313	730	569	10612
C Mining (except fuels), manufacturing and construction	501	444	57	4403	391	5295	71	284	5650
D Transportation and communication	1124	258	866	72	347	1543	1991	397	3931
E Other economic affairs	912	676	236	2989	169	4070	69	12	4151
10 Other functions	226	23	203	11	332	569	54	45	668
Total [bc]	39504	24585	14919	14327	16271	70102	7420	2989	80511

1989

	Final consumption expenditures			Subsidies	Other current transfers and property income	Total current disburse- ments	Gross capital formation	Other capital outlays	Total outlays
	Total	Compen- sation of employ- ees	Other						
1 General public services [a]	10239	7804	2435	14	1809	12062	907	217	13186
2 Defence	16450	7345	9105	18	123	16591	59	–	16650
3 Public order and safety	...	...	...	...	...	...	...	...	...
4 Education	6542	5912	630	15	9723	16280	400	213	16893
5 Health	2888	2241	647	3	549	3440	294	30	3764
6 Social security and welfare	1399	902	497	625	1796	3820	95	43	3958
7 Housing and community amenities	862	566	296	50	1138	2050	1100	917	4067
8 Recreational, cultural and religious affairs	437	227	210	1	258	696	112	4	812
9 Economic services	6149	3755	2394	17808	3374	27331	3725	3958	35014
A Fuel and energy	961	408	553	850	493	2304	781	469	3554
B Agriculture, hunting, forestry and fishing	2200	1742	458	7191	1388	10779	695	607	12081

India

1989

	Total	Compensation of employees	Other	Subsidies	Other current transfers and property income	Total current disbursements	Gross capital formation	Other capital outlays	Total outlays
C Mining (except fuels), manufacturing and construction	582	514	68	5042	983	6607	81	322	7010
D Transportation and communication	1379	288	1091	816	295	2490	2061	451	5002
E Other economic affairs	1027	803	224	3909	215	5151	107	2109	7367
10 Other functions	126	19	107	10	119	255	30	31	316
Total [bc]	45092	28771	16321	18544	18889	82525	6722	5413	94660

1990

	Total	Compensation of employees	Other	Subsidies	Other current transfers and property income	Total current disbursements	Gross capital formation	Other capital outlays	Total outlays
1 General public services [a]	11845	9365	2480	13	2619	14477	1024	357	15858
2 Defence	17652	7537	10115	19	112	17783	71	–	17854
3 Public order and safety	...	...	...	...	...	...	...	...	...
4 Education	7937	7254	683	–	11193	19130	533	116	19779
5 Health	3506	2768	738	3	590	4099	365	41	4505
6 Social security and welfare	1780	1121	659	813	1960	4553	106	101	4760
7 Housing and community amenities	1273	733	540	2	1333	2608	1642	1391	5641
8 Recreational, cultural and religious affairs	524	244	280	1	251	776	125	14	915
9 Economic services	6784	4141	2643	17690	2998	27472	4537	3708	35717
A Fuel and energy	1014	455	559	725	493	2232	683	457	3372
B Agriculture, hunting, forestry and fishing	2281	1792	489	7509	1599	11389	819	2424	14632
C Mining (except fuels), manufacturing and construction	728	650	78	5019	411	6158	97	337	6592
D Transportation and communication	1589	355	1234	121	250	1960	2814	454	5228
E Other economic affairs	1172	889	283	4316	245	5733	124	36	5893
10 Other functions	167	21	146	15	196	378	64	28	470
Total [bc]	51468	33184	18284	18556	21252	91276	8467	5756	105499

1991

	Total	Compensation of employees	Other	Subsidies	Other current transfers and property income	Total current disbursements	Gross capital formation	Other capital outlays	Total outlays
1 General public services [a]	14212	10883	3329	6	2831	17049	1042	379	18470
2 Defence	18802	9105	9697	22	100	18924	167	–	19091
3 Public order and safety	...	...	...	...	...	...	...	...	...
4 Education	8966	8263	703	1	12266	21233	569	101	21903
5 Health	3808	2988	820	–	671	4479	359	48	4886
6 Social security and welfare	2000	1239	761	785	2202	4987	183	97	5267
7 Housing and community amenities	1367	770	597	8	1812	3187	1863	1711	6761
8 Recreational, cultural and religious affairs	445	268	177	2	290	737	136	20	893
9 Economic services	7833	4619	3214	21747	3434	33014	5207	3238	41459

India

1991

	Total	Compensation of employees	Other	Subsidies	Other current transfers and property income	Total current disbursements	Gross capital formation	Other capital outlays	Total outlays
A Fuel and energy	1229	523	706	4614	621	6464	970	543	7977
B Agriculture, hunting, forestry and fishing	2646	2106	540	9859	1486	13991	928	2028	16947
C Mining (except fuels), manufacturing and construction	619	526	93	4576	497	5692	123	395	6210
D Transportation and communication	1913	419	1494	147	378	2438	3075	221	5734
E Other economic affairs	1426	1045	381	2551	452	4429	111	51	4591
10 Other functions	97	17	80	–	199	296	17	22	335
Total [bc]	57530	38152	19378	22571	23805	103906	9543	5617	119066

1992

	Total	Compensation of employees	Other	Subsidies	Other current transfers and property income	Total current disbursements	Gross capital formation	Other capital outlays	Total outlays
1 General public services [a]	16472	12825	3647	250	3243	19965	1181	262	21408
2 Defence	21032	10160	10872	–	129	21161	157	–	21318
3 Public order and safety	...	...	...	...	...	...	...	...	...
4 Education	10035	9385	650	–	14034	24069	535	106	24710
5 Health	4375	3462	913	–	828	5203	386	25	5614
6 Social security and welfare	2181	1451	730	716	2513	5410	165	133	5708
7 Housing and community amenities	1402	887	515	3	1851	3256	2287	1943	7486
8 Recreational, cultural and religious affairs	512	302	210	3	304	819	146	18	983
9 Economic services	8620	5310	3310	19402	4255	32277	5905	3974	42156
A Fuel and energy	1376	622	754	1927	600	3903	1126	997	6026
B Agriculture, hunting, forestry and fishing	2924	2386	538	10618	1537	15079	1028	2285	18392
C Mining (except fuels), manufacturing and construction	669	615	54	5626	999	7294	105	326	7725
D Transportation and communication	2192	483	1709	231	432	2855	3525	309	6689
E Other economic affairs	1459	1204	255	1000	687	3146	121	57	3324
10 Other functions	219	27	192	9	258	486	25	13	524
Total [bc]	64848	43809	21039	20383	27415	112646	10787	6474	129907

1993

	Total	Compensation of employees	Other	Subsidies	Other current transfers and property income	Total current disbursements	Gross capital formation	Other capital outlays	Total outlays
1 General public services [a]	17594	14376	3218	3	4441	22038	1168	338	23544
2 Defence	25366	10993	14373	24	218	25608	168	–	25776
3 Public order and safety	...	...	...	...	...	...	...	...	...
4 Education	11380	10568	812	–	15445	26825	569	97	27491
5 Health	4939	3967	972	2	897	5238	346	21	6205
6 Social security and welfare	2791	1622	1169	858	2764	6413	182	138	6733
7 Housing and community amenities	1761	1015	746	31	2223	4015	2351	3379	9745

India

1993

	Final consumption expenditures Total	Compensation of employees	Other	Subsidies	Other current transfers and property income	Total current disbursements	Gross capital formation	Other capital outlays	Total outlays
8 Recreational, cultural and religious affairs	553	331	222	15	395	963	116	70	1149
9 Economic services	10095	5771	4324	22245	4030	36370	6685	3933	46988
A Fuel and energy	1559	698	861	2400	739	4698	1305	1251	7254
B Agriculture, hunting, forestry and fishing	3117	2567	550	13340	1764	18221	1066	1404	20691
C Mining (except fuels), manufacturing and construction	612	631	—	5039	694	6345	111	485	6941
D Transportation and communication	3166	528	2638	337	397	3900	4046	746	8692
E Other economic affairs	1641	1347	294	1129	436	3206	157	47	3410
10 Other functions	276	67	209	1	306	583	60	7	650
Total [bc]	74755	48710	26045	23179	30719	128653	11645	7983	148281

1994

	Final consumption expenditures Total	Compensation of employees	Other	Subsidies	Other current transfers and property income	Total current disbursements	Gross capital formation	Other capital outlays	Total outlays
1 General public services [a]	20389	16091	4298	4	10510	30903	1403	358	32664
2 Defence	27060	12319	14741	57	348	27465	69	—	27534
3 Public order and safety	...	...	...	...	...	...	...	...	...
4 Education	12977	11950	1027	...	18199	31176	751	89	32016
5 Health	5450	4419	1031	...	945	6395	456	42	6893
6 Social security and welfare	3241	1887	1354	1335	3248	7824	236	144	8204
7 Housing and community amenities	2274	1134	1140	47	2197	4518	2527	6103	13148
8 Recreational, cultural and religious affairs	663	373	290	6	449	1118	184	34	1336
9 Economic services	11076	6272	4804	24055	4151	39282	8206	4464	51952
A Fuel and energy	1796	777	1019	2338	728	4862	1804	1162	7828
B Agriculture, hunting, forestry and fishing	3285	2684	601	14739	1989	20013	1107	1224	22344
C Mining (except fuels), manufacturing and construction	581	667	−8	5243	715	6539	105	642	7286
D Transportation and communication	3544	588	2956	378	372	4294	4955	941	10190
E Other economic affairs	1870	1556	314	1357	347	3574	235	495	4304
10 Other functions	302	72	230	10	377	689	134	50	873
Total [bc]	83432	54517	28915	25514	40424	149370	13966	11284	174620

1995

	Final consumption expenditures Total	Compensation of employees	Other	Subsidies	Other current transfers and property income	Total current disbursements	Gross capital formation	Other capital outlays	Total outlays
1 General public services [a]	23536	19148	4388	8	10032	33576	1811	402	35789
2 Defence	31116	14305	16811	34	294	31444	109	—	31553
3 Public order and safety	...	...	...	...	...	...	...	...	...
4 Education	15164	14041	1123	51	20748	35963	781	102	36846
5 Health	6190	5125	1065	—	1040	7230	468	57	7755

India

	1995								
	Final consumption expenditures			Subsidies	Other current transfers and property income	Total current disbursements	Gross capital formation	Other capital outlays	Total outlays
	Total	Compensation of employees	Other						
6 Social security and welfare	3607	2172	1435	2073	4098	9778	289	151	10218
7 Housing and community amenities	2165	1240	925	28	3404	5597	2909	6998	15504
8 Recreational, cultural and religious affairs	736	435	301	9	472	1217	203	40	1460
9 Economic services	13442	7441	6001	27430	5457	46329	8833	5807	60969
A Fuel and energy	2199	942	1257	1828	1305	5332	1715	1378	8425
B Agriculture, hunting, forestry and fishing	3933	3155	778	15983	2121	22037	1185	970	24192
C Mining (except fuels), manufacturing and construction	756	789	–3	5905	833	7494	93	1000	8587
D Transportation and communication	4283	760	3523	300	507	5090	5648	826	11564
E Other economic affairs	2271	1795	476	3414	691	6376	192	1633	8201
10 Other functions	449	86	363	_	407	856	175	51	1082
Total [bc]	96405	63993	32412	29633	45952	171990	15578	13608	201176

a Item "Public order and safety" is included in item "General public services".
b Item "Total government consumption expenditure" includes central and state government but excludes other local authorities. Consumption of fixed capital has also not been accounted for. Therefore, the figures will not tally with figures in tables 1.4, 3.12 and 3.13 to this extent.
c Up to 1980, losses of departmental enterprises are treated as consumption expenditure of the government, whereas, after 1980 they are treated as losses of the government.

2.5 Private final consumption expenditure by type and purpose, in current prices

Ten million Indian rupees   Fiscal year beginning 1 April

	1986	1987	1988	1989	1990	1991	1992	1993	1994	1995	1996	1997
Final consumption expenditure of resident households												
1 Food, beverages and tobacco	108488	120644	138592	152447	173756	206883	232654	265633	302442	331601	381449	...
A Food	102188	113823	130711	143290	163290	195195	219016	250973	285635	308695	354056	...
B Non-alcoholic beverages	182	199	231	284	337	421	508	638	894	1174	1410	...
C Alcoholic beverages	2573	2538	2568	2545	2722	2933	3038	3054	3358	4385	4391	...
D Tobacco	3545	4084	5082	6328	7407	8334	10092	10968	12555	17347	21592	...
2 Clothing and footwear	22841	24892	28910	32629	37148	38616	43375	52510	60674	74045	81536	...
3 Gross rent, fuel and power	23984	26684	29300	32424	35641	39121	42776	48421	53704	58045	62199	...
A Fuel and power	9813	11268	12475	13652	15011	16379	17715	20820	23139	24270	25279	...
B Other	14171	15416	16825	18772	20630	22742	25061	27601	30565	33775	36920	...
4 Furniture, furnishings and household equipment and operation	8731	9795	11376	14058	15791	16336	18137	20641	23745	28968	31243	...
A Household operation	3441	4154	4512	5341	6030	6343	7886	8288	9438	11183	12337	...
B Other	5290	5641	6864	8717	9761	9993	10251	12353	14307	17785	18906	...
5 Medical care and health expenses	5355	5923	7264	7622	8261	9029	9868	10984	13092	14222	16201	...
6 Transport and communication	16605	19942	24328	27988	35675	44273	53028	60940	72047	82703	95135	...
A Personal transport equipment	1131	1102	1366	1420	1695	1722	1851	2391	3348	4671	5994	...
B Other	15474	18840	22962	26568	33980	42551	51177	58549	68699	78032	89141	...
7 Recreational, entertainment, education and cultural services	6325	7300	8851	10036	11814	13479	15104	16521	19903	24241	27689	...
A Education	3341	4003	4635	5557	6990	7933	8750	9843	11007	12998	15720	...
B Other	2984	3297	4216	4479	4824	5546	6354	6678	8896	11243	11969	...

India

Ten million Indian rupees	1986	1987	1988	1989	1990	1991	1992	1993	1994	1995	1996	1997
8 Miscellaneous goods and services	7669	8881	10372	12868	14278	17413	20375	23277	29728	35269	39414	...
A Personal care	2278	2664	2879	3830	3832	4508	5722	6238	7307	8469	8304	...
B Expenditures in restaurants, cafes and hotels	1921	2161	2612	3122	3613	4172	4852	5841	7255	9212	10983	...
C Other	3470	4056	4881	5916	6833	8733	9801	11198	15166	17588	20127	...
Total final consumption expenditure in the domestic market by households, of which	199998	224061	258993	290072	332364	385150	435317	498927	575335	649094	734866	
A Durable goods	4729	5083	6130	7284	7926	8294	9950	11317	14885	18529	19739	
B Semi-durable goods	26977	29632	34734	40400	45837	47814	52905	63766	73694	89984	98258	
C Non-durable goods	130193	145871	167945	184655	210995	249905	281896	321627	366906	402906	461598	
D Services	38099	43475	50184	57733	67606	79137	90566	102217	119850	137675	155271	
plus: Direct purchases abroad by resident households	341	467	594	609	649	1659	1118	1475	2502	3521	5502	
less: Direct purchases in the domestic market by non-resident households	1740	1977	2168	2439	2642	4921	6255	7022	7420	9180	10739	...
equals: Final consumption expenditure of resident households [a]	198599	222551	257419	288242	330371	381888	430180	493380	570417	643435	729629	...

a Item "Final consumption expenditure of resident households" includes consumption expenditure of private non-profit institutions serving households.

2.6 Private final consumption expenditure by type and purpose, in constant prices

Ten million Indian rupees	1986	1987	1988	1989	1990	1991	1992	1993	1994	1995	1996	1997

At constant prices of: 1980

Final consumption expenditure of resident households

	1986	1987	1988	1989	1990	1991	1992	1993	1994	1995	1996	1997
1 Food, beverages and tobacco	70105	72021	75816	77752	80085	82210	84513	87294	91673	93567	100402	...
A Food	65925	68038	71721	73515	76073	78022	80078	82973	87178	88158	94559	...
B Non-alcoholic beverages	127	109	118	140	155	154	177	181	232	218	337	...
C Alcoholic beverages	1976	1626	1586	1535	1526	1546	1524	1309	1321	1576	1303	...
D Tobacco	2077	2248	2391	2562	2331	2488	2734	2831	2942	3615	4203	...
2 Clothing and footwear	15992	16384	18063	18384	19062	17963	19039	20928	20677	22555	24194	...
3 Gross rent, fuel and power	15505	16102	16733	17333	17923	18558	19200	19880	20635	21405	22072	...
A Fuel and power	5904	6182	6483	6740	6974	7239	7498	7780	8121	8460	8682	...
B Other	9601	9920	10250	10593	10949	11319	11702	12100	12514	12945	13390	...
4 Furniture, furnishings and household equipment and operation	6297	6424	6555	7396	7771	7326	7542	8066	8591	9540	9890	...
A Household operation	2268	2340	2409	2815	3029	2842	3167	3157	3266	3523	3595	
B Other	4029	4084	4146	4581	4742	4484	4375	4909	5325	6017	6295	
5 Medical care and health expenses	3370	3441	3518	3598	3672	3753	3819	3885	3963	4036	4108	...
6 Transport and communication	9487	10386	11397	12557	13726	14501	15595	16822	18625	20638	21300	...
A Personal transport equipment	756	699	775	748	832	787	800	1014	1322	1691	2024	
B Other	8731	9687	10622	11809	12894	13714	14795	15808	17303	18947	19276	...
7 Recreational, entertainment, education and cultural services	4308	4665	5214	5487	5873	6012	6254	6377	7413	8389	8984	
A Education	1977	2172	2310	2605	2941	2941	2961	3098	3150	3376	3745	
B Other	2331	2493	2904	2882	2932	3071	3293	3279	4263	5013	5239	
8 Miscellaneous goods and services	5198	5706	6172	7231	7342	7856	8623	9070	10808	11843	12224	...
A Personal care	1713	1968	1986	2494	2440	2604	2982	3216	3679	3999	3781	...

India

Ten million Indian rupees — Fiscal year beginning 1 April

	1986	1987	1988	1989	1990	1991	1992	1993	1994	1995	1996	1997
At constant prices of: 1980												
B Expenditures in restaurants, cafes and hotels	1212	1279	1401	1551	1641	1674	1779	1968	2270	2769	3016	...
C Other	2273	2459	2785	3186	3261	3578	3862	3886	4859	5075	5427	...
Total final consumption expenditure in the domestic market by households, of which	130262	135129	143468	149738	155454	158179	164585	172322	182385	191973	203174	...
A Durable goods	3549	3780	4191	4618	4702	4552	5111	5572	7048	8277	8647	...
B Semi-durable goods	19387	19867	21567	22434	23295	22185	23161	25477	25623	27931	29704	...
C Non-durable goods	83837	86580	91333	94233	97433	100145	103563	107204	112765	116180	123557	...
D Services	23489	24902	26377	28453	30024	31297	32750	34069	36949	39585	41266	...
plus: Direct purchases abroad by resident households	...	...	...	...	...	...	...	...	...	...	...	...
less: Direct purchases in the domestic market by non-resident households	...	...	...	...	...	...	...	...	...	...	...	...
equals: Final consumption expenditure of resident households	...	...	...	...	...	...	...	...	...	...	...	...

2.7 Gross capital formation by type of good and owner, in current price

Ten million Indian rupees — Fiscal year beginning 1 April

	1986 Total	1986 Total private	1986 Public enterprises	1986 General government	1987 Total	1987 Total private	1987 Public enterprises	1987 General government	1988 Total	1988 Total private	1988 Public enterprises	1988 General government
Increase in stocks, total	5847	4959	839	49	2688	4200	−1557	45	10742	11243	−293	−208
1 Goods producing industries	−97	...	...	...	2910	...	...	...	12855	...	...	...
A Materials and supplies	...	...	...	...	...	...	...	...	...	...	...	...
B Work in progress	...	...	...	...	...	...	...	...	...	...	...	...
C Livestock, except breeding stocks, dairy cattle, etc.	300	...	...	...	337	...	...	...	165	...	...	...
D Finished goods	...	...	...	...	...	...	...	...	...	...	...	...
2 Wholesale and retail trade	5927	...	...	...	−313	...	...	...	−2309	...	...	...
3 Other, except government stocks	−31	...	...	...	125	...	...	...	176	...	...	...
4 Government stocks	48	...	...	...	−34	...	...	...	20	...	...	...
Gross fixed capital formation, total [a]	62052	28798	21349	11905	72194	37623	19677	14894	85669	45803	21549	18317
1 Residential buildings	8080	7429	–	651	9004	8334	–	670	10151	9394	–	757
2 Non-residential buildings [b]	6212	2437	2047	1728	7281	3381	2181	1719	9029	4593	2339	2097
3 Other construction	16281	2109	5222	8950	18502	3764	4510	10228	22265	5181	5346	11738
4 Land improvement and plantation and orchard development	...	...	...	...	...	...	...	...	...	...	...	...
5 Producers' durable goods	31125	16469	11683	2973	36972	21709	12986	2277	43939	26350	13864	3725
A Transport equipment	7524	4766	1555	1203	8533	6482	1434	617	10958	7951	2131	876
B Machinery and equipment	23601	11703	10128	1770	28439	15227	11552	1660	32981	18399	11733	2849
6 Breeding stock, dairy cattle, etc.	354	354	–	–	435	435	–	–	285	285	–	–
Statistical discrepancy	...	...	2397	−2397	...	...	...	...	...	...	...	...
Statistical discrepancy	...	...	−2397	2397	1574	...	...	...	561	...	...	...
Total gross capital formation	67899	33757	19791	14351	76456[c]	41823[c]	18120[c]	14939[c]	96972[c]	57046[c]	21256[c]	18109[c]

India

	1989				1990				1991			
	Total	Total private	Public enterprises	General government	Total	Total private	Public enterprises	General government	Total	Total private	Public enterprises	General government
Increase in stocks, total	7420	5716	1750	−46	11152	9177	1873	102	3565	5765	−1890	−310
1 Goods producing industries	4828	...	...	...	5622	...	...	...	73	...	...	...
A Materials and supplies	...	...	...	...	...	...	...	...	...	...	...	...
B Work in progress	...	...	...	...	...	...	...	...	...	...	...	...
C Livestock, except breeding stocks, dairy cattle, etc.	215	...	...	...	191	...	...	...	219	...	...	...
D Finished goods	...	...	...	...	...	...	...	...	...	...	...	...
2 Wholesale and retail trade	2426	...	...	...	5000	...	...	...	3565	...	...	...
3 Other, except government stocks	289	...	...	...	445	...	...	...	−53	...	...	...
4 Government stocks	−123	...	...	...	85	...	...	...	−20	...	...	...
Gross fixed capital formation, total [a]	102775	58913	25752	18110	124004	73828	29475	20701	136503	77766	35838	22899
1 Residential buildings	11772	11040	–	732	14732	14116	–	616	16820	15954	–	866
2 Non-residential buildings [b]	11418	6898	2458	2062	13763	8579	2649	2535	15259	10087	2447	2725
3 Other construction	24702	7980	5321	11401	29868	10182	6390	13296	34853	10787	9315	14751
4 Land improvement and plantation and orchard development	...	...	...	...	...	...	...	...	...	...	...	...
5 Producers' durable goods	54553	32665	17973	3915	65129	40439	20436	4254	69027	40394	24076	4557
A Transport equipment	13797	9928	2916	953	16331	12463	2683	1185	16791	11929	3553	1309
B Machinery and equipment	40756	22737	15057	2962	48798	27976	17753	3069	52236	28465	20523	3248
6 Breeding stock, dairy cattle, etc.	330	330	–	–	512	512	...	...	544	544	...	...
Statistical discrepancy	4454	...	...	...	13039	...	...	...	4045	...	...	...
Total gross capital formation [c]	114649	64629	27502	18064	148195	83005	31348	20803	144113	83531	33948	22589

	1992				1993				1994			
	Total	Total private	Public enterprises	General government	Total	Total private	Public enterprises	General government	Total	Total private	Public enterprises	General government
Increase in stocks, total	10799	8153	2661	−15	−2170	−4140	1816	154	24972	25431	19	26
1 Goods producing industries	11656	...	...	...	−3261	...	...	...	12484	...	...	...
A Materials and supplies	...	...	...	...	...	...	...	...	...	...	...	...
B Work in progress	...	...	...	...	...	...	...	...	...	...	...	...
C Livestock, except breeding stocks, dairy cattle, etc.	255	...	...	...	495	...	...	...	609	...	...	...
D Finished goods	...	...	...	...	...	...	...	...	...	...	...	...
2 Wholesale and retail trade	−1192	...	...	...	672	...	...	...	11571	...	...	...
3 Other, except government stocks	265	...	...	...	416	...	...	...	594	...	...	...
4 Government stocks	70	...	...	...	3	...	...	...	323	...	...	...
Gross fixed capital formation, total [a]	158857	98740	32648	27469	174702	107149	36613	30940	216407	129199	49201	38007
1 Residential buildings	19407	18388	–	1019	21650	20572	–	1078	24019	22750	–	1269
2 Non-residential buildings [b]	18925	13348	2604	2973	18458	12099	2578	3781	22315	14840	2909	4566
3 Other construction	37294	12096	7409	17789	40926	12461	8977	19488	48319	12714	10424	25181
4 Land improvement and plantation and orchard development	...	...	...	...	...	...	...	...	...	...	...	...
5 Producers' durable goods	82595	54272	22635	5688	92643	60992	25058	6593	120462	77603	35868	6991
A Transport equipment	18875	14210	2680	1985	24875	18002	4975	1898	31563	25878	3885	1800
B Machinery and equipment	63720	40062	19955	3703	67768	42990	20083	4695	88899	51725	31983	5191
6 Breeding stock, dairy cattle, etc.	636	636	...	...	1025	1025	...	...	1292	1292	...	...
Statistical discrepancy	−615	...	...	...	15969	...	...	...	17599	...	...	...
Total gross capital formation [c]	169041	106893	35309	27454	188501	103009	38429	31094	258978	154630	49002	37747

India

| | 1995 |||| 1996 |||| 1997 ||||
	Total	Total private	Public enterprises	General government	Total	Total private	Public enterprises	General government	Total	Total private	Public enterprises	General government
Increase in stocks, total	33386	34793	−141	11	15865	13444	2373	48	...	...	...	...
1 Goods producing industries	20113	...	...	...	8414	...	...	...	...	...	...	...
A Materials and supplies	...	...	...	...	...	...	...	...	...	...	...	...
B Work in progress	...	...	...	...	...	...	...	...	...	...	...	...
C Livestock, except breeding stocks, dairy cattle, etc.	724	...	...	...	797	...	...	...	...	...	...	...
D Finished goods	...	...	...	...	...	...	...	...	...	...	...	...
2 Wholesale and retail trade	12577	...	...	...	6539	...	...	...	...	...	...	...
3 Other, except government stocks	607	...	...	...	239	...	...	...	...	...	...	...
4 Government stocks	89	...	...	...	181	...	...	...	...	...	...	...
Gross fixed capital formation, total [a]	271594	181710	47043	42841	305983	214189	43656	48138	...	...	...	...
1 Residential buildings	27701	26186	–	1515	30504	28625	–	1879	...	...	...	...
2 Non-residential buildings [b]	30305	21113	3926	5266	37247	27638	3478	6131	...	...	...	...
3 Other construction	57029	16440	12057	28532	63291	23044	9393	30854	...	...	...	...
4 Land improvement and plantation and orchard development	...	...	...	...	...	...	...	...	...	...	...	...
5 Producers' durable goods	155042	116454	31060	7528	173272	133213	30785	9274	...	...	...	...
A Transport equipment	40940	35958	2774	2208	50942	44691	3521	2730	...	...	...	...
B Machinery and equipment	114102	80496	28286	5320	122330	88522	27264	6544	...	...	...	...
6 Breeding stock, dairy cattle, etc.	1517	1517	...	...	1669	1669	...	...	...	...	...	...
Statistical discrepancy	−1197	...	...	...	26637	...	...	...	...	...	...	...
Total gross capital formation [c]	303783	216503	45625	42852	348485	227633	46029	48186	...	...	...	...

a Gross fixed capital formation by kind of activity and by type of goods are prepared independently and therefore, do not always tally.
b Item "Non-residential buildings" includes residential house construction of public enterprises and the private corporate sector.
c Figures in this table are adjusted for errors and ommissions/statistical discrepancies and therefore do not tally with figures in table 1.1.

2.8 Gross capital formation by type of good and owner, in constant prices

Ten million Indian rupees
Fiscal year beginning 1 April

| | 1986 |||| 1987 |||| 1988 ||||
	Total	Total private	Public enterprises	General government	Total	Total private	Public enterprises	General government	Total	Total private	Public enterprises	General government
At constant prices of: 1980												
Increase in stocks, total	4174	3494	645	35	1831	2757	−955	29	6807	7050	−112	−131
1 Goods producing industries	−141	...	...	...	1942	...	...	...	8092	...	...	...
A Materials and supplies	...	...	...	...	...	...	...	...	...	...	...	...
B Work in progress	...	...	...	...	...	...	...	...	...	...	...	...
C Livestock, except breeding stocks, dairy cattle, etc.	175	...	...	...	191	...	...	...	87	...	...	...
D Finished goods	...	...	...	...	...	...	...	...	...	...	...	...
2 Wholesale and retail trade	4301	...	...	...	−169	...	...	...	−1404	...	...	...
3 Other, except government stocks	−19	...	...	...	80	...	...	...	107	...	...	...
4 Government stocks	33	...	...	...	−22	...	...	...	12	...	...	...
Gross fixed capital formation, total [a]	35997	16766	11537	7694	39955	21295	11423	7237	42770	23231	11281	8258
1 Residential buildings	3583	3284	–	299	3653	3371	–	282	3530	3232	–	298
2 Non-residential buildings [b]	2903	1143	954	806	3109	1455	917	737	3578	1834	919	825
3 Other construction	8104	792	2722	4590	8283	1416	2126	4741	9315	2093	2276	4946

India

Ten million Indian rupees   *Fiscal year beginning 1 April*

	1986				1987				1988			
	Total	Total private	Public enterprises	General government	Total	Total private	Public enterprises	General government	Total	Total private	Public enterprises	General government
At constant prices of: 1980												
4 Land improvement and plantation and orchard development	...	...	...	...	...	...	...	...	...	...	...	...
5 Producers' durable goods	21192	11332	7861	1999	24683	14826	8380	1477	26210	15935	8086	2189
A Transport equipment	5141	3280	1049	812	5572	4267	913	392	6483	4801	1192	490
B Machinery and equipment	16051	8052	6812	1187	19111	10559	7467	1085	19727	11134	6894	1699
6 Breeding stock, dairy cattle, etc.	215	215	—	—	227	227	—	—	137	137	—	—
Statistical discrepancy	...	...	...	...	871	...	...	...	280	...	...	...
Total gross capital formation	40171	20260	12182	7729	42657[c]	24052[c]	10468[c]	7266[c]	49857[c]	30281[c]	11169[c]	8127[c]

	1989				1990				1991			
	Total	Total private	Public enterprises	General government	Total	Total private	Public enterprises	General government	Total	Total private	Public enterprises	General government
At constant prices of: 1980												
Increase in stocks, total	4201	3211	1015	−25	5794	4803	943	48	1587	2552	−827	−138
1 Goods producing industries	2744	...	...	...	2875	...	...	...	6	...	...	...
A Materials and supplies	...	...	...	...	...	...	...	...	...	...	...	...
B Work in progress	...	...	...	...	...	...	...	...	...	...	...	...
C Livestock, except breeding stocks, dairy cattle, etc.	91	...	...	...	73	...	...	...	76	...	...	...
D Finished goods	...	...	...	...	...	...	...	...	...	...	...	...
2 Wholesale and retail trade	1365	...	...	...	2653	...	...	...	1616	...	...	...
3 Other, except government stocks	160	...	...	...	223	...	...	...	26	...	...	...
4 Government stocks	−68	...	...	...	43	...	...	...	−61	...	...	...
Gross fixed capital formation, total [a]	46483	26832	12292	7359	51091	30490	12058	7933	49046	28034	13581	7431
1 Residential buildings	3630	3332	—	298	3647	3435	—	212	3869	3605	—	264
2 Non-residential buildings [b]	4186	2550	905	731	4741	2955	907	879	4665	3088	747	830
3 Other construction	9253	2967	2025	4261	10369	3516	2154	4699	10657	3322	2899	4436
4 Land improvement and plantation and orchard development	...	...	...	...	...	...	...	...	...	...	...	...
5 Producers' durable goods	29275	17844	9362	2069	32184	20434	9607	2143	29677	17841	9935	1901
A Transport equipment	7314	5372	1464	478	7981	6204	1231	546	7354	5354	1461	539
B Machinery and equipment	21961	12472	7898	1591	24203	14230	8376	1597	22323	12487	8474	1362
6 Breeding stock, dairy cattle, etc.	139	139	—	—	150	150	...	...	178	178	...	...
Statistical discrepancy	2014	...	...	...	5372	...	...	...	1638	...	...	...
Total gross capital formation [c]	52698	30043	13307	7334	62257	35293	13611	7981	52271	30586	12754	7293

India

	1992				1993				1994			
	Total	Total private	Public enterprises	General government	Total	Total private	Public enterprises	General government	Total	Total private	Public enterprises	General government
	At constant prices of: 1980											
Increase in stocks, total	4433	3358	1089	−14	−988	−1619	582	49	8629	8882	−162	−91
1 Goods producing industries	4863	...	...	...	−1407	...	...	...	4332	...	...	...
A Materials and supplies	...	...	...	...	...	...	...	...	...	...	...	...
B Work in progress	...	...	...	...	...	...	...	...	...	...	...	...
C Livestock, except breeding stocks, dairy cattle, etc.	83	...	...	...	128	...	...	...	149	...	...	...
D Finished goods	...	...	...	...	...	...	...	...	...	...	...	...
2 Wholesale and retail trade	−565	...	...	...	249	...	...	...	3984	...	...	...
3 Other, except government stocks	106	...	...	...	169	...	...	...	162	...	...	...
4 Government stocks	29	...	...	...	1	...	...	...	151	...	...	...
Gross fixed capital formation, total [a]	52461	32953	11252	8256	55341	34426	12189	8726	63817	38619	15401	9797
1 Residential buildings	4004	3717	–	287	4114	3832	–	282	4259	3953	–	306
2 Non-residential buildings [b]	5362	3792	734	836	4834	3171	675	988	5373	3574	700	1099
3 Other construction	10383	3446	2051	4886	10478	3273	2277	4928	11336	3055	2413	5868
4 Land improvement and plantation and orchard development	...	...	...	...	...	...	...	...	...	...	...	...
5 Producers' durable goods	32529	21815	8467	2247	35619	23854	9237	2528	42515	27703	12288	2524
A Transport equipment	7709	5928	1023	758	9912	7357	1849	706	11857	9873	1357	627
B Machinery and equipment	24820	15887	7444	1489	25707	16497	7388	1822	30658	17830	10931	1897
6 Breeding stock, dairy cattle, etc.	183	183	...	...	296	296	...	...	334	334	...	...
Statistical discrepancy	−203	...	...	...	5059	...	...	...	5190	...	...	...
Total gross capital formation [c]	56691	36311	12341	8242	59412	32807	12771	8775	77636	47501	15239	9706

	1995				1996				1997			
	Total	Total private	Public enterprises	General government	Total	Total private	Public enterprises	General government	Total	Total private	Public enterprises	General government
	At constant prices of: 1980											
Increase in stocks, total	10432	10818	−390	4	5074	4345	709	20	...	...	...	...
1 Goods producing industries	5316	...	...	...	2500	...	...	...	...	...	...	...
A Materials and supplies	...	...	...	...	...	...	...	...	...	...	...	...
B Work in progress	...	...	...	...	...	...	...	...	...	...	...	...
C Livestock, except breeding stocks, dairy cattle, etc.	162	...	...	...	174	...	...	...	...	...	...	...
D Finished goods	...	...	...	...	...	...	...	...	...	...	...	...
2 Wholesale and retail trade	3715	...	...	...	2282	...	...	...	...	...	...	...
3 Other, except government stocks	193	...	...	...	239	...	...	...	...	...	...	...
4 Government stocks	28	...	...	...	53	...	...	...	...	...	...	...
Gross fixed capital formation, total [a]	74480	51157	13312	10011	79344	57081	11786	10477	...	...	...	...
1 Residential buildings	4404	4077	–	327	4590	4207	–	383	...	...	...	...
2 Non-residential buildings [b]	6548	4561	848	1139	7559	5597	712	1250	...	...	...	...
3 Other construction	12019	3546	2493	5980	12279	4633	1750	5896	...	...	...	...
4 Land improvement and plantation and orchard development	...	...	...	...	...	...	...	...	...	...	...	...
5 Producers' durable goods	51152	38616	9971	2565	54533	42261	9324	2948	...	...	...	...
A Transport equipment	14415	12787	906	722	17074	15119	1100	855	...	...	...	...
B Machinery and equipment	36737	25829	9065	1843	37459	27142	8224	2093	...	...	...	...

India

	1995				1996				1997			
	Total	Total private	Public enter- prises	General govern- ment	Total	Total private	Public enter- prises	General govern- ment	Total	Total private	Public enter- prises	General govern- ment
At constant prices of: 1980												
6 Breeding stock, dairy cattle, etc.	357	357	...	...	383	383	...	...	...	...	...	...
Statistical discrepancy	−328	...	...	...	6907	...	...	...	...	...	...	...
Total gross capital formation [c]	84584	61975	12922	10015	91325	61426	12495	10497	...	...	...	...

a Gross fixed capital formation by kind of activity and by type of goods are prepared independently and therefore, do not always tally.
b Item "Non-residential buildings" includes residential house construction of public enterprises and the private corporate sector.
c Figures in this table are adjusted for errors and ommissions/statistical discrepancies and therefore do not tally with figures in table 1.2.

2.9 Gross capital formation by kind of activity of owner, ISIC major divisions, in current prices

Ten million Indian rupees Fiscal year beginning 1 April

	1986			1987			1988			1989		
	Total gross capital formation	Increase in stocks	Gross fixed capital formation	Total gross capital formation	Increase in stocks	Gross fixed capital formation	Total gross capital formation	Increase in stocks	Gross fixed capital formation	Total gross capital formation	Increase in stocks	Gross fixed capital formation
All producers												
1 Agriculture, hunting, forestry and fishing	7734	348	7386	9181	353	8828	9984	159	9825	11112	371	10741
2 Mining and quarrying	4459	258	4201	4217	235	3982	4789	310	4479	6304	328	5976
3 Manufacturing	11541	−1059	12600	17086	1876	15210	29859	12673	17186	24862	3968	20894
4 Electricity, gas and water	9513	257	9256	10378	290	10088	11295	−155	11450	12344	223	12121
5 Construction	1044	99	945	1241	156	1085	1134	−132	1266	1892	−61	1953
6 Wholesale and retail trade, restaurants and hotels	7818	5930	1888	1709	−309	2018	296	−2309	2605	5599	2426	3173
7 Transport, storage and communication	7876	−178	8054	8058	108	7950	10644	159	10485	12822	204	12618
8 Finance, insurance, real estate and business services	8959	131	8828	10485	2	10483	12262	−19	12281	14166	37	14129
9 Community, social and personal services	1619	13	1606	1654	11	1643	2075	36	2039	2419	47	2372
Total industries [a]	60563	5799	54764	64009	2722	61287	82338	10722	71616	91520	7543	83977
Producers of government services	5501	48	5453	5508	−34	5542	6224	20	6204	5578	−123	5701
Private non-profit institutions serving households	...	...	...	...	...	...	...	...	...	...	...	...
Statistical discrepancy	1835	...	1835	6939	...	−	8410	...	−	17551	...	−
Total [ab]	67899	5847	62052	76456	2688	66829	96972	10742	77820	114649	7420	89678

	1990			1991			1992			1993		
	Total gross capital formation	Increase in stocks	Gross fixed capital formation	Total gross capital formation	Increase in stocks	Gross fixed capital formation	Total gross capital formation	Increase in stocks	Gross fixed capital formation	Total gross capital formation	Increase in stocks	Gross fixed capital formation
All producers												
1 Agriculture, hunting, forestry and fishing	12853	344	12509	14776	193	14583	18113	305	17808	18708	211	18497
2 Mining and quarrying	6626	161	6465	6336	211	6125	6585	221	6364	6536	−904	7440
3 Manufacturing	31095	4918	26177	30302	−460	30762	48438	11171	37267	40838	−2979	43817
4 Electricity, gas and water	14406	−19	14425	18895	13	18882	18984	−325	19309	22185	144	22041
5 Construction	2211	212	1999	1748	116	1632	2544	284	2260	2779	267	2512
6 Wholesale and retail trade, restaurants and hotels	8792	5000	3792	7507	3565	3942	3008	−1192	4200	5389	672	4717
7 Transport, storage and communication	14333	395	13938	16156	−48	16204	19699	275	19424	24115	416	23699

India

	1990			1991			1992			1993		
	Total gross capital formation	Increase in stocks	Gross fixed capital formation	Total gross capital formation	Increase in stocks	Gross fixed capital formation	Total gross capital formation	Increase in stocks	Gross fixed capital formation	Total gross capital formation	Increase in stocks	Gross fixed capital formation
8 Finance, insurance, real estate and business services	17821	10	17811	21803	15	21788	24137	−15	24152	28528	74	28454
9 Community, social and personal services	2652	46	2606	2598	−20	2618	3011	5	3006	3060	−74	3134
Total industries [a]	110789	11067	99722	120121	3585	116536	144519	10729	133790	152138	−2173	154311
Producers of government services	7513	85	7428	8227	−20	8247	9517	70	9447	10632	3	10629
Private non-profit institutions serving households	...	...	...	...	...	...	...	...	...	...	...	...
Statistical discrepancy	29893	...	–	16280	...	–	15005	...	–	25731	...	–
Total [a,b]	148195	11152	107150	144628	3565	124783	169041	10799	143237	188501	−2170	164940

	1994			1995			1996			1997		
	Total gross capital formation	Increase in stocks	Gross fixed capital formation	Total gross capital formation	Increase in stocks	Gross fixed capital formation	Total gross capital formation	Increase in stocks	Gross fixed capital formation	Total gross capital formation	Increase in stocks	Gross fixed capital formation
	All producers										
1 Agriculture, hunting, forestry and fishing	24520	571	23949	29335	787	28548	31930	685	31245	...	...	...
2 Mining and quarrying	15672	−129	15801	12514	533	11981	7871	−803	8674	...	...	...
3 Manufacturing	74473	12517	61956	94793	18930	75863	93529	7732	85797	...	...	...
4 Electricity, gas and water	21545	−540	22085	24193	16	24177	24130	461	23669	...	...	...
5 Construction	2892	65	2827	3517	−153	3670	4045	339	3706	...	...	...
6 Wholesale and retail trade, restaurants and hotels	17978	11571	6407	20929	12577	8352	15983	6539	9444	...	...	...
7 Transport, storage and communication	25730	−73	25803	29822	−290	30112	35559	242	35317	...	...	...
8 Finance, insurance, real estate and business services	35463	211	35252	42047	391	41656	47816	406	47410	...	...	...
9 Community, social and personal services	4993	456	4537	5891	506	5385	6938	83	6855	...	...	...
Total industries [a]	223266	24649	198617	263041	33297	229744	267801	15684	252117	...	...	...
Producers of government services	14889	323	14566	16475	89	16386	18548	181	18367	...	...	...
Private non-profit institutions serving households	...	...	...	...	...	...	...	...	...	...	...	...
Statistical discrepancy	20823	...	–	24267	...	–	62136	...	–	...	...	...
Total [a,b]	258978	24972	213183	303783	33386	246130	348485	15865	270484	...	...	...

a Gross fixed capital formation by kind of activity and by type of goods are prepared independently and therefore, do not always tally.

b The estimates of "Increase in stocks" and "Gross fixed capital formation" (columns 2 and 3, respectively) are unadjusted for statistical discrepancy and therefore, do not add up to "Gross capital formation" (column 1).

2.10 Gross capital formation by kind of activity of owner, ISIC major divisions, in constant prices

Ten million Indian rupees
Fiscal year beginning 1 April

	1986			1987			1988			1989		
	Total gross capital formation	Increase in stocks	Gross fixed capital formation	Total gross capital formation	Increase in stocks	Gross fixed capital formation	Total gross capital formation	Increase in stocks	Gross fixed capital formation	Total gross capital formation	Increase in stocks	Gross fixed capital formation
	At constant prices of: 1980										
	All producers										
1 Agriculture, hunting, forestry and fishing	4355	208	4147	4778	201	4577	4733	82	4651	4791	177	4614
2 Mining and quarrying	2722	181	2541	2433	165	2268	2547	211	2336	2992	217	2775

India

Ten million Indian rupees — Fiscal year beginning 1 April

	1986 Total gross capital formation	1986 Increase in stocks	1986 Gross fixed capital formation	1987 Total gross capital formation	1987 Increase in stocks	1987 Gross fixed capital formation	1988 Total gross capital formation	1988 Increase in stocks	1988 Gross fixed capital formation	1989 Total gross capital formation	1989 Increase in stocks	1989 Gross fixed capital formation
At constant prices of: 1980												
3 Manufacturing	6740	−779	7519	10159	1288	8871	17007	7955	9052	12264	2243	10021
4 Electricity, gas and water	5731	197	5534	5855	212	5643	5657	−99	5756	5772	133	5639
5 Construction	663	52	611	772	76	696	669	−57	726	995	−25	1020
6 Wholesale and retail trade, restaurants and hotels	5408	4304	1104	999	−167	1166	−50	−1404	1354	2873	1365	1508
7 Transport, storage and communication	4843	−121	4964	4570	69	4501	5382	96	5286	5875	112	5763
8 Finance, insurance, real estate and business services	4114	90	4024	4534	2	4532	4988	−11	4999	5367	21	5346
9 Community, social and personal services	846	9	837	835	7	828	958	22	936	1022	26	996
Total industries [a]	35422	4141	31281	34935	1853	33082	41891	6795	35096	41951	4269	37682
Producers of government services	2983	33	2950	2744	−22	2766	2870	12	2858	2312	−68	2380
Private non-profit institutions serving households	...	...	...	...	...	...	...	...	...	...	...	...
Statistical discrepancy	1766	...	1766	4978	...	−	5096	...	−	8435	...	−
Total [a,b]	40171	4174	35997	42657	1831	35848	49857	6807	37954	52698	4201	40062

	1990 Total gross capital formation	1990 Increase in stocks	1990 Gross fixed capital formation	1991 Total gross capital formation	1991 Increase in stocks	1991 Gross fixed capital formation	1992 Total gross capital formation	1992 Increase in stocks	1992 Gross fixed capital formation	1993 Total gross capital formation	1993 Increase in stocks	1993 Gross fixed capital formation
At constant prices of: 1980												
All producers												
1 Agriculture, hunting, forestry and fishing	5076	151	4925	5212	65	5147	5873	103	5770	5564	22	5542
2 Mining and quarrying	2844	94	2750	2380	111	2269	2223	104	2119	1998	−380	2379
3 Manufacturing	14193	2559	11634	11820	−214	12034	18070	4708	13362	13912	−1186	15098
4 Electricity, gas and water	6151	−10	6161	6932	6	6926	6432	−142	6574	7229	60	7169
5 Construction	1039	81	958	714	38	676	948	90	858	994	78	916
6 Wholesale and retail trade, restaurants and hotels	4323	2653	1670	3139	1616	1523	918	−565	1483	1840	249	1591
7 Transport, storage and communication	6043	193	5850	5993	−23	6016	6739	110	6629	8011	169	7842
8 Finance, insurance, real estate and business services	6345	6	6339	6945	6	6939	7100	−6	7106	7893	27	7866
9 Community, social and personal services	1033	24	1009	872	−9	881	932	2	930	890	−27	917
Total industries [a]	47047	5751	41296	44007	1596	42411	49235	4404	44831	48331	−989	49320
Producers of government services	2839	43	2796	2711	−9	2720	2896	29	2867	2999	1	2998
Private non-profit institutions serving households	...	...	...	...	...	...	...	...	...	...	...	...
Statistical discrepancy	12371	...	−	5553	...	−	4560	...	−	8082	...	−
Total [a,b]	62257	5794	44092	52271	1587	45131	56691	4433	47698	59412	−988	52318

India

	1994			1995			1996			1997		
	Total gross capital formation	Increase in stocks	Gross fixed capital formation	Total gross capital formation	Increase in stocks	Gross fixed capital formation	Total gross capital formation	Increase in stocks	Gross fixed capital formation	Total gross capital formation	Increase in stocks	Gross fixed capital formation

At constant prices of: 1980

All producers

1 Agriculture, hunting, forestry and fishing	6823	137	6686	7587	181	7406	7673	141	7532	...	...	...
2 Mining and quarrying	4932	−51	4983	3461	209	3252	1926	−282	2208	...	...	...
3 Manufacturing	24056	4426	19630	28327	6138	22189	26280	2411	23869	...	...	...
4 Electricity, gas and water	6337	−197	6534	6514	5	6509	6186	151	6035	...	...	...
5 Construction	959	17	942	1107	−37	1144	1181	79	1102	...	...	...
6 Wholesale and retail trade, restaurants and hotels	5962	3984	1978	6088	3715	2373	4833	2282	2551	...	...	...
7 Transport, storage and communication	7918	−16	7934	8499	−84	8583	9728	96	9632	...	...	...
8 Finance, insurance, real estate and business services	9212	71	9141	9936	121	9815	10814	118	10696	...	...	...
9 Community, social and personal services	1376	151	1225	1471	156	1315	1615	25	1590	...	...	...
Total industries [a]	67575	8522	59053	72990	10404	62586	70236	5021	65215	...	...	...
Producers of government services	3847	107	3740	3830	28	3802	3980	53	3927	...	...	...
Private non-profit institutions serving households	...	...	...	...	...	...	...	...	...	...	...	...
Statistical discrepancy	9956	...	−	15191	...	−	17109	...	−	...	...	...
Total [ab]	77636	8629	62793	84584	10432	66388	91325	5074	69142	...	...	...

a Gross fixed capital formation by kind of activity and by type of goods are prepared independently and therefore, do not always tally.
b The estimates of "Increase in stocks" and "Gross fixed capital formation" (columns 2 and 3, respectively) are unadjusted for statistical discrepancy and therefore, do not add up to "Gross capital formation" (column 1).

2.11 Gross fixed capital formation by kind of activity of owner, ISIC divisions, in current prices

Ten million Indian rupees — Fiscal year beginning 1 April

	1986	1987	1988	1989	1990	1991	1992	1993	1994	1995	1996	1997
All producers												
1 Agriculture, hunting, forestry and fishing	7386	8828	9825	10741	12509	14583	17808	18497	23949	28548	31245	...
A Agriculture and hunting	6689	8045	8898	9681	11279	13203	16287	16762	21889	26091	28506	...
B Forestry and logging	244	247	301	355	425	437	473	483	524	619	697	...
C Fishing	453	536	626	705	805	943	1048	1252	1536	1838	2042	...
2 Mining and quarrying	4201	3982	4479	5976	6465	6125	6364	7440	15801	11981	8674	...
3 Manufacturing	12600	15210	17186	20894	26177	30762	37267	43817	61956	75863	85797	...
4 Electricity, gas and water	9256	10088	11450	12121	14425	18882	19309	22041	22085	24177	23669	...
A Electricity, gas and steam	8500	9149	10542	11349	13639	17883	18179	20840	20505	22373	21511	...
B Water works and supply	756	939	908	772	786	999	1130	1201	1580	1804	2158	...
5 Construction	945	1085	1266	1953	1999	1632	2260	2512	2827	3670	3706	...
6 Wholesale and retail trade, restaurants and hotels	1888	2018	2605	3173	3792	3942	4200	4717	6407	8352	9444	...
A Wholesale and retail trade	1290	1310	1705	2007	2684	2700	2716	2840	3866	4863	5480	...
B Restaurants and hotels	598	708	900	1166	1108	1242	1484	1877	2541	3489	3964	...
7 Transport, storage and communication	8054	7950	10485	12618	13938	16204	19424	23699	803	112	35317	...
A Transport and storage	6995	6511	8345	10012	11135	12718	14496	17862	18674	21695	25556	...
B Communication	1059	1439	2140	2606	2803	3486	4928	5837	7129	8417	9761	...
8 Finance, insurance, real estate and business services	8828	10483	12281	14129	17811	21788	24152	28454	35252	41656	47410	...

India

Ten million Indian rupees	1986	1987	1988	1989	1990	1991	1992	1993	1994	1995	1996	1997
A Financial institutions	745	1478	2126	2354	3079	4966	4745	6802	11113	13761	16683	...
B Insurance	...	...	...	...	...	...	...	...	...	...	...	...
C Real estate and business services	8083	9005	10155	11775	14732	16822	19407	21652	24139	27895	30727	...
Real estate, except dwellings	3	1	5	3	–	2	–	2	120	194	223	...
Dwellings [a]	8080	9004	10150	11772	14732	16820	19407	21650	24019	27701	30504	...
9 Community, social and personal services	1606	1643	2039	2372	2606	2618	3006	3134	4537	5385	6855	...
Total industries	54764	61287	71616	83977	99722	116536	133790	154311	198617	229744	252117	...
Producers of government services	5453	5542	6204	5701	7428	8247	9447	10629	14566	16386	18367	...
Private non-profit institutions serving households	...	...	...	...	...	...	...	...	...	...	...	...
Statistical discrepancy	1835	–	–	–	–	–	–	–	–	–	–	...
Total [b]	62052	66829	77820	89678	107150	124783	143237	164940	213183	246130	270484	...

a Item "Dwellings" includes residential house construction of general government.
b Gross fixed capital formation by kind of activity and by type of goods are prepared independently and therefore, do not always tally.

2.12 Gross fixed capital formation by kind of activity of owner, ISIC divisions, in constant prices

Ten million Indian rupees	1986	1987	1988	1989	1990	1991	1992	1993	1994	1995	1996	1997
At constant prices of: 1980												
All producers												
1 Agriculture, hunting, forestry and fishing	4147	4577	4651	4614	4925	5147	5770	5542	6686	7406	7532	...
A Agriculture and hunting	3798	4219	4260	4191	4459	4667	5260	5005	6110	6777	6856	...
B Forestry and logging	129	118	130	137	152	137	135	126	125	136	136	...
C Fishing	220	240	261	286	314	343	375	411	451	493	540	...
2 Mining and quarrying	2541	2268	2336	2775	2750	2269	2119	2379	4983	3252	2208	...
3 Manufacturing	7519	8871	9052	10021	11634	12034	13362	15098	19630	22189	23869	...
4 Electricity, gas and water	5534	5643	5756	5639	6161	6926	6574	7169	6534	6509	6035	...
5 Construction	611	696	726	1020	958	676	858	916	942	1144	1102	...
6 Wholesale and retail trade, restaurants and hotels	1104	1166	1354	1508	1670	1523	1483	1591	1978	2373	2551	...
A Wholesale and retail trade	765	767	897	967	1195	1055	969	971	1209	1403	1505	...
B Restaurants and hotels	339	399	457	541	475	468	514	620	769	970	1046	...
7 Transport, storage and communication	4964	4501	5286	5763	5850	6016	6629	7842	7934	8583	9632	...
A Transport and storage	4353	3706	4238	4622	4706	4777	5048	6049	5872	6436	7319	...
B Communication	611	795	1048	1141	1144	1239	1581	1793	2062	2147	2313	...
8 Finance, insurance, real estate and business services	4024	4532	4999	5346	6339	6939	7106	7866	9141	9815	10696	...
A Financial institutions	439	878	1143	1138	1367	1939	1700	2332	3470	3941	4588	...
B Insurance	...	...	...	...	...	...	...	...	...	...	...	...
C Real estate and business services	3585	3654	3856	4208	4972	5000	5406	5534	5671	5874	6108	...
Real estate, except dwellings	–	–	–	–	–	–	–	–	–	–	–	...
Dwellings [a]	3585	3654	3856	4208	4972	5000	5406	5534	5671	5874	6108	...
9 Community, social and personal services	837	828	936	996	1009	881	930	917	1225	1315	1590	...
Total industries	31281	33082	35096	37682	41296	42411	44831	49320	59053	62586	65215	...
Producers of government services	2950	2766	2858	2380	2796	2720	2867	2998	3740	3802	3927	...

India

Ten million Indian rupees — Fiscal year beginning 1 April

	1986	1987	1988	1989	1990	1991	1992	1993	1994	1995	1996	1997
	At constant prices of: 1980											
Private non-profit institutions serving households	...	...	...	...	...	...	...	...	...	...	...	...
Statistical discrepancy	1766	–	–	–	–	–	–	–	–	–	–	...
Total [b]	35997	35848	37954	40062	44092	45131	47698	52318	62793	66388	69142	...

a Item "Dwellings" includes residential house construction of general government.

b Gross fixed capital formation by kind of activity and by type of goods are prepared independently and therefore, do not always tally.

2.13 Stocks of reproducible fixed assets, by type of good and owner, in current prices

Ten million Indian rupees

1990

	Total Gross	Total Net	Total private Gross	Total private Net	Public enterprises Gross	Public enterprises Net	General government Gross	General government Net
1 Residential buildings	127240	102778	...	...	51191	42817	76049	59961
2 Non-residential buildings	...	...	...	...	...	...	...	...
3 Other construction	1041440	798456	592546	464065	97074	64479	351820	269912
4 Land improvement and plantation and orchard development	...	...	...	...	...	...	...	...
5 Producers' durable goods	...	...	...	...	...	...	...	...
A Transport equipment	46941	25242	...	...	19985	11627	27046	13616
B Machinery and equipment	494086	312148	273276	176553	186764	115780	34045	19815
6 Breeding stock, dairy cattle, etc.	...	...	...	...	...	...	...	...
Total	1709707	1238624	865822	640618	354925	234702	488960	363304

1991

	Total Gross	Total Net	Total private Gross	Total private Net	Public enterprises Gross	Public enterprises Net	General government Gross	General government Net
1 Residential buildings	149840	120317	...	...	60303	50080	89538	70238
2 Non-residential buildings	...	...	...	...	...	...	...	...
3 Other construction	1230041	940300	697928	545136	120406	79883	411707	315281
4 Land improvement and plantation and orchard development	...	...	...	...	...	...	...	...
5 Producers' durable goods	...	...	...	...	...	...	...	...
A Transport equipment	54914	29943	...	...	24512	14684	30403	15259
B Machinery and equipment	596550	369782	322015	202982	233101	143075	41434	23724
6 Breeding stock, dairy cattle, etc.	...	...	...	...	...	...	...	...
Total	2031346	1460343	1019943	748119	438322	287722	573081	424502

1992

	Total Gross	Total Net	Total private Gross	Total private Net	Public enterprises Gross	Public enterprises Net	General government Gross	General government Net
1 Residential buildings	168946	134843	...	...	67946	56013	101000	78829
2 Non-residential buildings	...	...	...	...	...	...	...	...
3 Other construction	1393859	1057534	783425	606953	139665	91517	470769	359063
4 Land improvement and plantation and orchard development	...	...	...	...	...	...	...	...
5 Producers' durable goods	...	...	...	...	...	...	...	...
A Transport equipment	60465	33550	...	...	26879	16510	33586	17039
B Machinery and equipment	698358	435925	376970	243775	272918	164862	48469	27289
6 Breeding stock, dairy cattle, etc.	...	...	...	...	...	...	...	...
Total	2321628	1661851	1160395	850728	507409	328903	653824	482220

India

| | 1993 ||||||||
| | Total || Total private || Public enterprises || General government ||
	Gross	Net	Gross	Net	Gross	Net	Gross	Net
1 Residential buildings	189258	150185	...	...	75719	61922	113539	88263
2 Non-residential buildings	...	...	...	...	...	...	...	...
3 Other construction	1581771	1195296	891613	689725	160873	104282	529286	401288
4 Land improvement and plantation and orchard development	...	...	...	...	...	...	...	...
5 Producers' durable goods	...	...	...	...	...	...	...	...
A Transport equipment	66506	37490	...	...	31291	19570	35215	17920
B Machinery and equipment	778507	477140	433715	274852	292295	172922	52497	29366
6 Breeding stock, dairy cattle, etc.	...	...	...	...	...	...	...	...
Total	2616043	1860111	1325328	964578	560178	358696	730537	536837

| | 1994 ||||||||
| | Total || Total private || Public enterprises || General government ||
	Gross	Net	Gross	Net	Gross	Net	Gross	Net
1 Residential buildings	214124	169041	...	...	25079	69037	129046	100004
2 Non-residential buildings	...	...	...	...	...	...	...	...
3 Other construction	1805349	1359748	1020247	787314	185353	119110	599748	453324
4 Land improvement and plantation and orchard development	...	...	...	...	...	...	...	...
5 Producers' durable goods	...	...	...	...	...	...	...	...
A Transport equipment	73791	41399	...	...	65880	22074	379911	19325
B Machinery and equipment	929896	573121	528610	338353	343431	202823	57856	31946
6 Breeding stock, dairy cattle, etc.	...	...	...	...	...	...	...	...
Total	3023161	2143309	1548857	1125667	649743	413044	824561	604598

| | 1995 ||||||||
| | Total || Total private || Public enterprises || General government ||
	Gross	Net	Gross	Net	Gross	Net	Gross	Net
1 Residential buildings	249321	195959	...	...	98749	79627	150573	116332
2 Non-residential buildings	...	...	...	...	...	...	...	...
3 Other construction	2110995	1584425	197816	923279	219337	139905	693843	521242
4 Land improvement and plantation and orchard development	...	...	...	...	...	...	...	...
5 Producers' durable goods	...	...	...	...	...	...	...	...
A Transport equipment	80471	44519	...	...	39478	23413	40993	21106
B Machinery and equipment	1089881	674727	636869	413464	387904	225897	65108	35366
6 Breeding stock, dairy cattle, etc.	...	...	...	...	...	...	...	...
Total	3530669	2499629	1834685	1336742	745467	468841	950517	694046

| | 1996 ||||||||
| | Total || Total private || Public enterprises || General government ||
	Gross	Net	Gross	Net	Gross	Net	Gross	Net
1 Residential buildings	275463	215514	...	...	108045	86435	167418	129079
2 Non-residential buildings	...	...	...	...	...	...	...	...
3 Other construction	2355599	1749554	1315539	1001842	250843	157479	789217	590233
4 Land improvement and plantation and orchard development	...	...	...	...	...	...	...	...
5 Producers' durable goods	...	...	...	...	...	...	...	...
A Transport equipment	85801	47881	...	...	42071	24943	43730	22938
B Machinery and equipment	1249397	770866	745992	484905	430037	246482	73368	39478
6 Breeding stock, dairy cattle, etc.	...	...	...	...	...	...	...	...
Total	3966259	2783815	2061531	1486747	830996	515340	1073732	781728

India

2.14 Stocks of reproducible fixed assets, by type of good and owner, in constant prices

Ten million Indian rupees

	1990 Total Gross	Net	Total private Gross	Net	Public enterprises Gross	Net	General government Gross	Net
	At constant prices of: 1980							
1 Residential buildings	43815	35392	...	...	17628	14744	26187	20648
2 Non-residential buildings	...	...	...	...	...	...	...	...
3 Other construction	357831	274135	203004	157740	34325	22799	120503	93594
4 Land improvement and plantation and orchard development	...	...	...	...	...	...	...	...
5 Producers' durable goods	...	...	...	...	...	...	...	...
A Transport equipment	21562	11595	...	...	9139	5341	12424	6254
B Machinery and equipment	229975	142258	124476	77473	89232	55318	16267	9468
6 Breeding stock, dairy cattle, etc.	...	...	...	...	...	...	...	...
Total	653184	463379	327479	235213	160324	98202	175381	129964

	1991 Total Gross	Net	Total private Gross	Net	Public enterprises Gross	Net	General government Gross	Net
	At constant prices of: 1980							
1 Residential buildings	45655	3660	...	...	18374	15259	27282	21401
2 Non-residential buildings	...	...	...	...	...	...	...	...
3 Other construction	372804	284202	211332	163417	37083	24600	124389	96186
4 Land improvement and plantation and orchard development	...	...	...	...	...	...	...	...
5 Producers' durable goods	...	...	...	...	...	...	...	...
A Transport equipment	22580	12312	...	...	10079	6038	12501	6274
B Machinery and equipment	247294	151963	133990	83122	96204	59049	17100	9791
6 Breeding stock, dairy cattle, etc.	...	...	...	...	...	...	...	...
Total	688332	485137	345322	246539	161739	104946	181271	133652

	1992 Total Gross	Net	Total private Gross	Net	Public enterprises Gross	Net	General government Gross	Net
	At constant prices of: 1980							
1 Residential buildings	47510	37920	...	...	19107	15752	28403	22168
2 Non-residential buildings	...	...	...	...	...	...	...	...
3 Other construction	388596	294707	220814	170051	38994	25541	128788	99115
4 Land improvement and plantation and orchard development	...	...	...	...	...	...	...	...
5 Producers' durable goods	...	...	...	...	...	...	...	...
A Transport equipment	23070	12800	...	...	10256	6299	12814	6501
B Machinery and equipment	265705	162541	145827	90870	101797	61493	18079	10179
6 Breeding stock, dairy cattle, etc.	...	...	...	...	...	...	...	...
Total	724880	507967	366643	260920	170154	109085	188083	137962

India

	1993							
	Total		Total private		Public enterprises		General government	
	Gross	Net	Gross	Net	Gross	Net	Gross	Net
	At constant prices of: 1980							
1 Residential buildings	49453	39244	...	...	19785	16180	29668	23064
2 Non-residential buildings	...	...	...	...	...	...	...	...
3 Other construction	405466	306035	231102	177366	41125	26645	133239	102024
4 Land improvement and plantation and orchard development	...	...	...	...	...	...	...	...
5 Producers' durable goods	...	...	...	...	...	...	...	...
A Transport equipment	24733	13942	...	...	11638	7278	13095	6664
B Machinery and equipment	286917	174489	160062	100064	107541	63621	19314	10804
6 Breeding stock, dairy cattle, etc.	...	...	...	...	...	...	...	...
Total	766569	533710	391164	277430	180089	113725	195316	142555

	1994							
	Total		Total private		Public enterprises		General government	
	Gross	Net	Gross	Net	Gross	Net	Gross	Net
	At constant prices of: 1980							
1 Residential buildings	51559	40703	...	...	20487	16624	31072	24079
2 Non-residential buildings	...	...	...	...	...	...	...	...
3 Other construction	424782	319574	242813	185964	43337	27827	138632	105783
4 Land improvement and plantation and orchard development	...	...	...	...	...	...	...	...
5 Producers' durable goods	...	...	...	...	...	...	...	...
A Transport equipment	25747	14445	...	...	12519	7702	13228	6743
B Machinery and equipment	315826	193054	178680	112818	117372	69317	19773	10918
6 Breeding stock, dairy cattle, etc.	...	...	...	...	...	...	...	...
Total	817913	567776	421493	298783	193715	121470	202705	147523

	1995							
	Total		Total private		Public enterprises		General government	
	Gross	Net	Gross	Net	Gross	Net	Gross	Net
	At constant prices of: 1980							
1 Residential buildings	53872	42342	...	...	21337	17205	32536	25137
2 Non-residential buildings	...	...	...	...	...	...	...	...
3 Other construction	445517	334025	255614	195435	45543	29027	144360	109562
4 Land improvement and plantation and orchard development	...	...	...	...	...	...	...	...
5 Producers' durable goods	...	...	...	...	...	...	...	...
A Transport equipment	26315	14558	...	...	12910	7656	13405	6902
B Machinery and equipment	345571	212164	200421	128453	124289	72380	20861	11331
6 Breeding stock, dairy cattle, etc.	...	...	...	...	...	...	...	...
Total	871275	603089	456035	323888	204078	126269	211162	152932

	1996							
	Total		Total private		Public enterprises		General government	
	Gross	Net	Gross	Net	Gross	Net	Gross	Net
	At constant prices of: 1980							
1 Residential buildings	56217	43982	...	...	22050	17640	34167	26343
2 Non-residential buildings	...	...	...	...	...	...	...	...
3 Other construction	466032	348267	269322	205650	46931	29448	149778	113169
4 Land improvement and plantation and orchard development	...	...	...	...	...	...	...	...
5 Producers' durable goods	...	...	...	...	...	...	...	...

India

	1996							
	Total		Total private		Public enterprises		General government	
	Gross	Net	Gross	Net	Gross	Net	Gross	Net
At constant prices of: 1980								
A Transport equipment	26855	14986	...	...	13168	7807	13686	7179
B Machinery and equipment	377682	231523	225820	145258	129728	74356	22133	11909
6 Breeding stock, dairy cattle, etc.	...	...	...	...	...	...	...	...
Total	926785	638759	495142	350908	211878	129251	219765	158600

2.17 Exports and imports of goods and services, detail

Ten million Indian rupees — Fiscal year beginning 1 April

	1986	1987	1988	1989	1990	1991	1992	1993	1994	1995	1996	1997
Exports of goods and services												
1 Exports of merchandise, f.o.b.	13315	16396	20647	28229	33153	44922	54762	71146	84329	108480	...	...
2 Transport and communication	688	882	1300	1510	1765	2308	2851	4495	5328	6765	...	...
A In respect of merchandise imports	...	...	...	...	...	...	...	...	...	...	...	...
B Other	688	882	1300	1510	1765	2308	2851	4495	5328	6765	...	...
3 Insurance service charges	83	105	136	198	198	265	459	388	476	600	...	...
A In respect of merchandise imports	...	...	...	...	...	...	...	...	...	...	...	...
B Other	83	105	136	198	198	265	459	388	476	600	...	...
4 Other commodities	1580	1643	2077	2804	3472	4718	4059	4454	5709	7835	...	...
5 Adjustments of merchandise exports to change-of-ownership basis	−863	−722	−415	−571	−595	−880	−1074	−1395	−1655	−2127	...	...
6 Direct purchases in the domestic market by non-residential households	1740	1977	2168	2439	2642	4921	6255	7022	7420	9180	...	...
7 Direct purchases in the domestic market by extraterritorial bodies	27	39	44	20	12	3	205	5	2	2	...	...
Statistical discrepancy	−27	−39	−44	−20	−12	−3	−205	−5	−2	−2	...	...
Total exports of goods and services	16543	20281	25913	34609	40635	56254	67312	86110	101607	130733	...	...
Imports of goods and services												
1 Imports of merchandise, c.i.f.	22760	25831	34482	40983	50350	51864	69456	79421	106763	140812	...	...
2 Adjustments of merchandise imports to change-of-ownership basis	−2573	−3449	−5967	−5314	−6894	−3567	−5488	−5529	−16183	−17315	...	...
3 Other transport and communication	657	989	1292	1516	1698	1982	4616	4746	5243	6460	...	...
4 Other insurance service charges	102	107	95	140	158	307	449	612	567	479	...	...
5 Other commodities	907	1112	1284	2038	2373	3664	2530	4508	5350	10458	...	...
6 Direct purchases abroad by government	165	202	230	240	364	340	319	467	468	538	...	...
7 Direct purchases abroad by resident households	341	467	594	609	649	1659	1118	1475	2502	3521	...	...
Total imports of goods and services	22359	25259	32010	40212	48698	56249	73000	85700	104710	144953	...	...
Balance of goods and services	−5816	−4978	−6097	−5603	−8063	5	−5688	410	−3103	−14220	...	...
Total imports and balance of goods and services	16543	20281	25913	34609	40635	56254	67312	86110	101607	130733	...	...

3.26 Financial transactions of financial institutions: detail

Ten million Indian rupees — Fiscal year beginning 1 April

	1986					1987				
	All financial institutions	Central bank	Other monetary institutions	Insurance	Other financial institutions	All financial institutions	Central bank	Other monetary institutions	Insurance	Other financial institutions

Acquisition of financial assets

1 Gold and SDRs	...	...	...	...	...	...	...	...	...	...
2 Currency and transferable deposits	2420	1	2412	–	7	3856	–	3807	26	23
3 Other deposits	191	–	–437	66	562	1641	–	1110	102	429
4 Bills and bonds, short-term	–10967	–11883	576	–	340	1194	657	238	–	299
5 Bonds, long-term	...	...	...	...	...	...	...	...	...	...
6 Corporate equity securities	24997	14228	7769	1608	1392	15962	3952	7852	1739	2419
7 Short-term loans, n.e.c.	12330	883	6877	483	4087	13512	525	6174	655	6158
8 Long-term loans, n.e.c.										
9 Trade credits and advances	...	...	...	...	...	...	...	...	...	...
10 Other assets	2075	247	1299	454	75	5215	–1152	5422	551	394
Total acquisitions of financial assets	31046	3476	18496	2611	6463	41380	3982	24603	3073	9722

Incurrence of liabilities

1 Currency and transferable deposits	20087	2118	17709	–	260	20156	2216	17527	–	413
2 Other deposits	...	...	...	...	...	...	...	...	...	...
3 Bills and bonds, short-term	...	...	...	...	...	...	...	...	...	...
4 Bonds, long-term	...	...	...	...	...	...	...	...	...	...
5 Corporate equity securities	1568	–	408	57	1103	2507	–	203	1	2303
6 Short-term loans, n.e.c.	1377	–	–79	9	1447	3557	–	1663	–	1894
7 Long-term loans, n.e.c.										
8 Net equity of households in life insurance and pension fund reserves	...	...	...	...	...	...	...	...	...	...
9 Other liabilities	5408	982	–372	2176	2622	12699	1334	4391	2603	4371
Total incurrence of liabilities	28440	3100	17666	2242	5432	38919	3550	23784	2604	8981
Net lending	2606	376	830	369	1031	2461	432	819	469	741
Incurrence of liabilities and net lending	31046	3476	18496	2611	6463	41380	3982	24603	3073	9722

	1988					1989				
	All financial institutions	Central bank	Other monetary institutions	Insurance	Other financial institutions	All financial institutions	Central bank	Other monetary institutions	Insurance	Other financial institutions

Acquisition of financial assets

1 Gold and SDRs	...	...	...	...	...	...	...	...	...	...
2 Currency and transferable deposits	5874	3	5856	31	–16	4500	–1	4442	55	4
3 Other deposits	732	–	21	65	646	1200	–	714	436	50
4 Bills and bonds, short-term	2433	–1002	1504	–	1931	–207	–1810	956	–	647
5 Bonds, long-term	...	...	...	...	...	...	...	...	...	...
6 Corporate equity securities	13642	1636	7330	2025	2651	22320	6698	9604	2553	3465
7 Short-term loans, n.e.c.	23421	2985	12442	1075	6919	24306	1297	13672	1269	8068
8 Long-term loans, n.e.c.										
9 Trade credits and advances	...	...	...	...	...	...	...	...	...	...

India

	1988					1989				
	All financial institutions	Central bank	Other monetary institutions	Insurance	Other financial institutions	All financial institutions	Central bank	Other monetary institutions	Insurance	Other financial institutions
10 Other assets	9841	667	5512	955	2707	9976	−563	6273	797	3469
Total acquisitions of financial assets	55943	4289	32665	4151	14838	62095	5621	35661	5110	15703

Incurrence of liabilities

	All	CB	OMI	Ins	OFI	All	CB	OMI	Ins	OFI
1 Currency and transferable deposits	25459	1550	23843	–	66	34879	4081	29377	–	1421
2 Other deposits	...	...	...	...	...	...	...	...	...	...
3 Bills and bonds, short-term	...	...	...	...	...	...	...	...	...	...
4 Bonds, long-term	...	...	...	...	...	...	...	...	...	...
5 Corporate equity securities	4672	–	327	35	4310	6106	–	731	–	5375
6 Short-term loans, n.e.c.	6972	–	2909	–	4063	5730	–	3149	43	2538
7 Long-term loans, n.e.c.										
8 Net equity of households in life insurance and pension fund reserves	...	...	...	...	...	...	...	...	...	...
9 Other liabilities	16117	2227	4787	3778	5325	11579	984	2341	4093	4161
Total incurrence of liabilities	53220	3777	31866	3813	13764	58294	5065	35598	4136	13495
Net lending	2723	512	799	338	1074	3801	556	63	974	2208
Incurrence of liabilities and net lending	55943	4289	32665	4151	14838	62095	5621	35661	5110	15703

	1990					1991				
	All financial institutions	Central bank	Other monetary institutions	Insurance	Other financial institutions	All financial institutions	Central bank	Other monetary institutions	Insurance	Other financial institutions

Acquisition of financial assets

	All	CB	OMI	Ins	OFI	All	CB	OMI	Ins	OFI
1 Gold and SDRs	...	...	...	...	...	...	...	...	...	...
2 Currency and transferable deposits	3443	−6	3358	86	5	312	2	203	–	107
3 Other deposits	−178	–	−623	−192	637	6903	–	4312	403	2188
4 Bills and bonds, short-term	−7	−1398	1702	–	−311	1898	14	1465	–	419
5 Bonds, long-term	...	...	...	...	...	...	...	...	...	...
6 Corporate equity securities	29941	13987	8613	4464	2877	19851	−7598	14408	4563	8478
7 Short-term loans, n.e.c.	31925	4580	11565	1881	13899	33135	5179	12177	2928	12851
8 Long-term loans, n.e.c.										
9 Trade credits and advances	...	...	...	...	...	...	...	...	...	...
10 Other assets	13132	67	8414	485	4166	29086	14427	10270	836	3553
Total acquisitions of financial assets	78256	17230	33029	6724	21273	91185	12024	42835	8730	27596

Incurrence of liabilities

	All	CB	OMI	Ins	OFI	All	CB	OMI	Ins	OFI
1 Currency and transferable deposits	34910	8560	25792	–	558	48697	14088	34243	–	366
2 Other deposits	...	...	...	...	...	...	...	...	...	...
3 Bills and bonds, short-term	...	...	...	...	...	...	...	...	...	...
4 Bonds, long-term	...	...	...	...	...	...	...	...	...	...
5 Corporate equity securities	5146	–	817	99	4230	9599	–	773	–	8826
6 Short-term loans, n.e.c.	9842	–	2197	–	7645	−1692	–	−5979	–	4287
7 Long-term loans, n.e.c.										
8 Net equity of households in life insurance and pension fund reserves	...	...	...	...	...	...	...	...	...	...
9 Other liabilities	25294	8105	2816	6125	8248	28799	−2054	11517	7585	11751
Total incurrence of liabilities	75192	16665	31622	6224	20681	85403	12034	40554	7585	25230

India

	1990					1991				
	All financial institutions	Central bank	Other monetary institutions	Insurance	Other financial institutions	All financial institutions	Central bank	Other monetary institutions	Insurance	Other financial institutions
Net lending	3064	565	1407	500	592	5782	−10	2281	1145	2366
Incurrence of liabilities and net lending	78256	17230	33029	6724	21273	91185	12024	42835	8730	27596

	1992					1993				
	All financial institutions	Central bank	Other monetary institutions	Insurance	Other financial institutions	All financial institutions	Central bank	Other monetary institutions	Insurance	Other financial institutions

Acquisition of financial assets

1 Gold and SDRs	...	...	...	...	...	...	...	...	...	...
2 Currency and transferable deposits	173	−8	209	1	−29	−137	9	−142	7	−11
3 Other deposits	1417	−	3246	98	−1927	9391	−	8687	155	549
4 Bills and bonds, short-term	3403	633	2614	−	156	1733	14	706	−	1013
5 Bonds, long-term	...	...	...	...	...	...	...	...	...	...
6 Corporate equity securities	39063	11766	14029	5517	7751	33385	−22538	33005	8457	14461
7 Short-term loans, n.e.c.	16967	−5957	10197	2266	10461	4421	2022	−6313	2261	6451
8 Long-term loans, n.e.c.										
9 Trade credits and advances	...	...	...	...	...	...	...	...	...	...
10 Other assets	5217	2287	292	1277	1361	30044	23887	3319	1043	1795
Total acquisitions of financial assets	66240	8721	30587	9159	17773	78837	3394	39262	11923	24258

Incurrence of liabilities

1 Currency and transferable deposits	38241	7422	30346	−	473	48174	5876	40849	−	1449
2 Other deposits	...	...	...	...	...	...	...	...	...	...
3 Bills and bonds, short-term	...	...	...	...	...	...	...	...	...	...
4 Bonds, long-term	...	...	...	...	...	...	...	...	...	...
5 Corporate equity securities	7158	−	707	−	6451	15040	−	5767	108	9165
6 Short-term loans, n.e.c.	8388	−	4938	−	3450	−6126	−	−7984	−50	1908
7 Long-term loans, n.e.c.										
8 Net equity of households in life insurance and pension fund reserves	...	...	...	...	...	...	...	...	...	...
9 Other liabilities	9883	1298	−4775	8291	5069	17036	−4346	1712	10370	9300
Total incurrence of liabilities	63670	8720	31216	8291	15443	74124	1530	40344	10428	21822
Net lending	2570	1	−629	868	2330	4713	1864	−1082	1495	2436
Incurrence of liabilities and net lending	66240	8721	30587	9159	17773	78837	3394	39262	11923	24258

	1994					1995				
	All financial institutions	Central bank	Other monetary institutions	Insurance	Other financial institutions	All financial institutions	Central bank	Other monetary institutions	Insurance	Other financial institutions

Acquisition of financial assets

1 Gold and SDRs	...	...	...	...	...	...	...	...	...	...
2 Currency and transferable deposits	183	−	205	6	−28	492	10	474	1	7
3 Other deposits	9615	−	8783	1009	−177	8496	−	7470	326	700
4 Bills and bonds, short-term	5627	−823	5560	−	890	−612	−1297	588	−	97
5 Bonds, long-term	...	...	...	...	...	...	...	...	...	...
6 Corporate equity securities	44294	4655	16749	10048	12842	32882	7972	12744	12359	−193
7 Short-term loans, n.e.c.	43778	6543	26136	2091	9008	38883	−7171	31311	3033	11710

India

	1994					1995				
	All financial institutions	Central bank	Other monetary institutions	Insurance	Other financial institutions	All financial institutions	Central bank	Other monetary institutions	Insurance	Other financial institutions
8 Long-term loans, n.e.c.										
9 Trade credits and advances	...	...	...	...	...	...	...	...	...	...
10 Other assets	7430	6748	200	1331	–849	17823	1763	10678	1696	3686
Total acquisitions of financial assets	110927	17123	57633	14485	21686	97964	1277	63265	17415	16007
Incurrence of liabilities										
1 Currency and transferable deposits	59880	13846	45538	–	496	34897	–8246	43083	...	60
2 Other deposits	...	...	...	...	...	...	...	...	...	...
3 Bills and bonds, short-term	...	...	...	...	...	...	...	...	...	...
4 Bonds, long-term	...	...	...	...	...	...	...	...	...	...
5 Corporate equity securities	10911	–	4178	–	6733	–911	–	–561	–	–350
6 Short-term loans, n.e.c.	9153	–	6530	–	2623	12784	–	8583	–	4201
7 Long-term loans, n.e.c.										
8 Net equity of households in life insurance and pension fund reserves	...	...	...	...	...	...	...	...	...	...
9 Other liabilities	24490	1782	–919	13577	10050	43079	5913	10242	16189	10735
Total incurrence of liabilities	104434	15628	55327	13577	19902	89849	–2333	61347	16189	14646
Net lending	6493	1495	2306	908	1784	8115	3610	1918	1226	1361
Incurrence of liabilities and net lending	110927	17123	57633	14485	21686	97964	1277	63265	17415	16007

3.51 External transactions, current account: detail

Ten million Indian rupees — Fiscal year beginning 1 April

	1986	1987	1988	1989	1990	1991	1992	1993	1994	1995	1996	1997
Payments to the rest of the world												
1 Imports of goods and services	22359	25259	32010	40212	48698	56249	73000	85700	104710	144953	...	...
A Imports of merchandise, c.i.f.	22760	25831	34482	40983	50350	51864	69456	79421	106763	140812	...	...
B Other	–401	–572	–2472	–771	–1652	4385	3544	6279	–2053	4141	...	...
2 Factor income to rest of the world	2468	3222	5142	6544	8295	10752	12859	13732	16191	18624	...	...
A Compensation of employees	178	380	390	332	320	286	347	1277	1299	1504	...	...
B Property and entrepreneurial income	2290	2842	4752	6212	7975	10466	12512	12455	14892	17120	...	...
3 Current transfers to the rest of the world [a]	15	34	24	26	26	37	35	68	58	108	...	...
A Indirect taxes by general government to supranational organizations	...	...	...	...	...	...	...	...	...	...	...	...
B Other current transfers	15	34	24	26	26	37	35	68	58	108	...	...
By general government	...	...	...	...	...	...	...	...	...	...	...	...
By other resident sectors	15	34	24	26	26	37	35	68	58	108	...	...
Statistical discrepancy [b]	2573	3449	5967	5314	6894	3567	5488	5529	16183	17315	...	...
1 Surplus of the nation on current transactions	–6355	–6825	–12304	–12279	–18196	–3377	–13816	–4791	–11891	–20780	...	...
Payments to the rest of the world and surplus of the nation on current transfers	21060	25139	30839	39817	45717	67228	77566	100238	125251	160220	...	...

India

Ten million Indian rupees   Fiscal year beginning 1 April

	1986	1987	1988	1989	1990	1991	1992	1993	1994	1995	1996	1997
Receipts from the rest of the world												
1 Exports of goods and services	16543	20281	25913	34609	40635	56254	67312	86110	101607	130733	...	...
A Exports of merchandise, f.o.b.	13315	16396	20647	28229	33153	44922	54762	71146	84329	108480	...	...
B Other	3228	3885	5266	6380	7482	11332	12550	14964	17278	22253	...	...
2 Factor income from rest of the world	663	603	646	813	750	675	1056	1389	3108	5140	...	...
A Compensation of employees	9	17	33	113	74	117	35	105	278	302	...	...
B Property and entrepreneurial income	654	586	613	700	676	558	1021	1284	2830	4838	...	...
3 Current transfers from rest of the world [a]	2991	3533	3865	3824	3737	9419	8124	11344	18881	22220	...	...
A Subsidies to general government from supranational organizations	...	...	...	...	...	...	...	...	...	...	...	...
B Other current transfers	2991	3533	3865	3824	3737	9419	8124	11344	18881	22220	...	...
To general government	...	...	...	...	...	...	...	...	...	...	...	...
To other resident sectors	2991	3533	3865	3824	3737	9419	8124	11344	18881	22220	...	...
Statistical discrepancy [b]	863	722	415	571	595	880	1074	1395	1655	2127	...	...
Receipts from the rest of the world on current transfers	21060	25139	30839	39817	45717	67228	77566	100238	125251	160220	...	...

a The estimates of "Transfers to the rest of the world" shown in the government tables represent the current disbursements by the government in the form of contributions to international bodies appearing in the government budget documents, whereas the estimates shown in the external transaction tables represent the current transfer payments/receipts by private bodies to/from other countries as shown in India's overall balance of payments data supplied by the Reserve Bank of India.

b Item "Statistical discrepancy" refers to difference of payment and ownership basis of imports and exports of merchandise.

4.1 Derivation of value added by kind of activity, in current prices

Ten million Indian rupees   Fiscal year beginning 1 April

	1986			1987			1988			1989		
	Gross output	Intermediate consumption	Value added	Gross output	Intermediate consumption	Value added	Gross output	Intermediate consumption	Value added	Gross output	Intermediate consumption	Value added
All producers												
1 Agriculture, hunting, forestry and fishing	108998	26585	82413	121604	29225	92379	147645	33572	114073	163098	36047	127051
A Agriculture and hunting	100062	25657	74405	111632	28117	83515	136423	32320	104103	150030	34583	115447
B Forestry and logging	6398	640	5758	6865	687	6178	7587	759	6828	8692	869	7823
C Fishing	2538	288	2250	3107	421	2686	3635	493	3142	4376	595	3781
2 Mining and quarrying	9855	3059	6796	10561	3476	7085	12875	3667	9208	14231	3923	10308
A Coal mining	3952	2200	1752	4312	2396	1916	5486	2528	2958	5912	2670	3242
B Crude petroleum and natural gas production	4348	554	3794	4566	724	3842	5377	761	4616	5927	827	5100
C Metal ore mining	689	144	545	764	183	581	928	223	705	1078	245	833
D Other mining	866	161	705	919	173	746	1084	155	929	1314	181	1133
3 Manufacturing	...	...	46166	...	...	52865	...	...	62863	...	...	77076
A Manufacture of food, beverages and tobacco	...	...	4411	...	...	4786	...	...	6324	...	...	7703
B Textile, wearing apparel and leather industries	...	...	8802	...	...	9854	...	...	10661	...	...	13563
C Manufacture of wood and wood products, including furniture	...	...	1267	...	...	1335	...	...	1317	...	...	1367

India

Ten million Indian rupees — Fiscal year beginning 1 April

	1986 Gross output	1986 Intermediate consumption	1986 Value added	1987 Gross output	1987 Intermediate consumption	1987 Value added	1988 Gross output	1988 Intermediate consumption	1988 Value added	1989 Gross output	1989 Intermediate consumption	1989 Value added
D Manufacture of paper and paper products, printing and publishing	...	...	1734	...	...	1788	...	...	2069	...	...	2782
E Manufacture of chemicals and chemical petroleum, coal, rubber and plastic products	...	...	7044	...	...	8272	...	...	9888	...	...	11599
F Manufacture of non-metallic mineral products, except products of petroleum and coal	...	...	2039	...	...	2278	...	...	2623	...	...	3303
G Basic metal industries	...	...	3168	...	...	3733	...	...	5798	...	...	6132
H Manufacture of fabricated metal products, machinery and equipment	...	...	11393	...	...	13441	...	...	16168	...	...	20212
I Other manufacturing industries	...	...	6308	...	...	7378	...	...	8015	...	...	10415
4 Electricity, gas and water	...	...	5567	...	...	6268	...	...	7325	...	...	8723
A Electricity, gas and steam	...	...	5006	...	...	5571	...	...	6502	...	...	7752
B Water works and supply	...	...	561	...	...	697	...	...	823	...	...	971
5 Construction	38933	23716	15217	43900	26289	17611	52044	31367	20677	59935	36349	23586
6 Wholesale and retail trade, restaurants and hotels	...	...	34551	...	...	38433	...	...	45222	...	...	52910
A Wholesale and retail trade	...	...	32624	...	...	36265	...	...	42601	...	...	49777
B Restaurants and hotels	...	...	1927	...	...	2168	...	...	2621	...	...	3133
7 Transport, storage and communication	...	...	16537	...	...	19938	...	...	23872	...	...	27731
A Transport and storage	...	...	14555	...	...	17141	...	...	20314	...	...	23748
B Communication	...	...	1982	...	...	2797	...	...	3558	...	...	3983
8 Finance, insurance, real estate and business services	...	...	22309	...	...	24756	...	...	28256	...	...	33577
A Financial institutions	...	...	7364	...	...	8636	...	...	10577	...	...	13042
B Insurance	...	...	2300	...	...	2507	...	...	2836	...	...	4089
C Real estate and business services	...	...	12645	...	...	13613	...	...	14843	...	...	16446
Real estate, except dwellings [a]	...	...	698	...	...	692	...	...	775	...	...	870
Dwellings	...	...	11947	...	...	12921	...	...	14068	...	...	15576
9 Community, social and personal services	...	...	15541	...	...	17568	...	...	20352	...	...	23567
A Sanitary and similar services	...	...	556	...	...	704	...	...	893	...	...	1061
B Social and related community services [b]	...	...	14985	...	...	16864	...	...	19459	...	...	22506
C Recreational and cultural services	...	...	...	...	...	...	...	...	...	...	...	...
D Personal and household services	...	...	...	...	...	...	...	...	...	...	...	...
Total, Industries	...	...	245097	...	...	276903	...	...	331848	...	...	384529
Producers of government services	...	...	14933	...	...	17948	...	...	20858	...	...	24133
Other producers	...	...	...	...	...	...	...	...	...	...	...	...
Total [d]	...	...	260030	...	...	294851	...	...	352706	...	...	408662
less: Imputed bank service charge	...	...	...	...	...	...	...	...	...	...	...	...
Import duties	...	...	...	...	...	...	...	...	...	...	...	...
Value added tax	...	...	...	...	...	...	...	...	...	...	...	...

India

Ten million Indian rupees
Fiscal year beginning 1 April

	1986			1987			1988			1989		
	Gross output	Intermediate consumption	Value added	Gross output	Intermediate consumption	Value added	Gross output	Intermediate consumption	Value added	Gross output	Intermediate consumption	Value added
Other adjustments [e]	...	...	32919	...	...	38350	...	...	43076	...	...	48159
Total	...	...	292949	...	...	333201	...	...	395782	...	...	456821

Of which general government:

	1986			1987			1988			1989		
1 Agriculture, hunting, forestry and fishing	...	...	2888	...	...	3194	...	...	3806	...	...	4334
2 Mining and quarrying	...	...	—	...	...	—	...	...	—	...	...	...
3 Manufacturing	...	...	1479	...	...	1959	...	...	2105	...	...	2161
4 Electricity, gas and water	...	...	588	...	...	653	...	...	679	...	...	724
5 Construction	...	...	1881	...	...	2341	...	...	2840	...	...	3545
6 Wholesale and retail trade, restaurants and hotels	...	...	31	...	...	64	...	...	81	...	...	35
7 Transport, storage and communication	...	...	127	...	...	133	...	...	148	...	...	157
8 Finance, insurance, real estate and business services	...	...	207	...	...	275	...	...	281	...	...	357
9 Community, social and personal services	...	...	6501	...	...	7657	...	...	9144	...	...	10921
Statistical discrepancy	...	...	—	...	...	—	...	...	—	...	...	—
Total, industries of general government	...	...	13702	...	...	16276	...	...	19084	...	...	22234
Producers of government services	...	...	14933	...	...	17948	...	...	20858	...	...	24133
Total, general government	...	...	28635	...	...	34224	...	...	39942	...	...	46367

	1990			1991			1992			1993		
	Gross output	Intermediate consumption	Value added	Gross output	Intermediate consumption	Value added	Gross output	Intermediate consumption	Value added	Gross output	Intermediate consumption	Value added

All producers

	1990			1991			1992			1993		
1 Agriculture, hunting, forestry and fishing	189232	41231	148001	221047	48276	172771	245722	52677	193045	281569	57864	223705
A Agriculture and hunting	174745	39583	135162	205771	46472	159299	228503	50593	177910	261796	55474	206322
B Forestry and logging	9201	920	8281	9322	932	8390	9838	984	8854	10929	1093	9836
C Fishing	5286	728	4558	5954	872	5082	7381	1100	6281	8844	1297	7547
2 Mining and quarrying	15648	3863	11785	17552	4749	12803	20480	5893	14589	24129	7311	16818
A Coal mining	6277	2545	3732	7372	2979	4393	9216	3867	5349	11052	5097	5955
B Crude petroleum and natural gas production	6584	813	5771	6540	1044	5496	7132	1198	5934	8552	1272	7280
C Metal ore mining	1262	305	957	1620	434	1186	1831	483	1348	2069	568	1501
D Other mining	1525	200	1325	2020	292	1728	2301	345	1956	2456	374	2082
3 Manufacturing	...	...	89160	...	...	96305	...	...	111044	...	...	127646
A Manufacture of food, beverages and tobacco	...	...	8248	...	...	9182	...	...	10162	...	...	12444
B Textile, wearing apparel and leather industries	...	...	15799	...	...	16766	...	...	19835	...	...	25439
C Manufacture of wood and wood products, including furniture	...	...	1373	...	...	1294	...	...	2408	...	...	2944
D Manufacture of paper and paper products, printing and publishing	...	...	3165	...	...	3836	...	...	3901	...	...	4678
E Manufacture of chemicals and chemical petroleum, coal, rubber and plastic products	...	...	13798	...	...	15482	...	...	19877	...	...	22968

India

	1990 Gross output	1990 Intermediate consumption	1990 Value added	1991 Gross output	1991 Intermediate consumption	1991 Value added	1992 Gross output	1992 Intermediate consumption	1992 Value added	1993 Gross output	1993 Intermediate consumption	1993 Value added
F Manufacture of non-metallic mineral products, except products of petroleum and coal	...	...	4013	...	...	4868	...	...	4665	...	...	5046
G Basic metal industries	...	...	7727	...	...	8533	...	...	9000	...	...	9971
H Manufacture of fabricated metal products, machinery and equipment	...	...	23261	...	...	24511	...	...	27428	...	...	29158
I Other manufacturing industries	...	...	11776	...	...	11833	...	...	13768	...	...	14998
4 Electricity, gas and water	...	...	10464	...	...	12720	...	...	16114	...	...	18879
A Electricity, gas and steam	...	...	9386	...	...	11455	...	...	14634	...	...	17180
B Water works and supply	...	...	1078	...	...	1265	...	...	1480	...	...	1699
5 Construction	72664	44048	28616	82835	50589	32246	93292	56592	36700	101272	60573	40699
6 Wholesale and retail trade, restaurants and hotels	...	...	61883	...	...	70807	...	...	82769	...	...	98024
A Wholesale and retail trade	...	...	58258	...	...	66621	...	...	77904	...	...	92163
B Restaurants and hotels	...	...	3625	...	...	4186	...	...	4865	...	...	5861
7 Transport, storage and communication	...	...	33913	...	...	41004	...	...	48892	...	...	56096
A Transport and storage	...	...	29189	...	...	35341	...	...	41808	...	...	47283
B Communication	...	...	4724	...	...	5663	...	...	7084	...	...	8813
8 Finance, insurance, real estate and business services	...	...	38902	...	...	49056	...	...	52639	...	...	67145
A Financial institutions	...	...	16742	...	...	23701	...	...	24898	...	...	35911
B Insurance	...	...	4354	...	...	5814	...	...	6334	...	...	7659
C Real estate and business services	...	...	17806	...	...	19541	...	...	21407	...	...	23575
Real estate, except dwellings [a]	...	...	1161	...	...	1286	...	...	1424	...	...	1594
Dwellings	...	...	16645	...	...	18255	...	...	19983	...	...	21981
9 Community, social and personal services	...	...	27981	...	...	33615	...	...	38730	...	...	43912
A Sanitary and similar services	...	...	1197	...	...	1382	...	...	1656	...	...	1862
B Social and related community services [b]	...	...	26784	...	...	32233	...	...	37074	...	...	42050
C Recreational and cultural services	...	...	...	...	...	...	...	...	...	...	...	...
D Personal and household services	...	...	...	...	...	...	...	...	...	...	...	...
Total, Industries	...	...	450705	...	...	521327	...	...	594522	...	...	692924
Producers of government services	...	...	27109	...	...	31441	...	...	36250	...	...	39950
Other producers	...	...	...	...	...	...	...	...	...	...	...	...
Total [d]	...	...	477814	...	...	552768	...	...	630772	...	...	732874
less: Imputed bank service charge	...	...	...	...	...	...	...	...	...	...	...	...
Import duties	...	...	...	...	...	...	...	...	...	...	...	...
Value added tax	...	...	...	...	...	...	...	...	...	...	...	...
Other adjustments [e]	...	...	57720	...	...	64031	...	...	75146	...	...	77875
Total	...	...	535534	...	...	616799	...	...	705918	...	...	810749

Of which general government:

1 Agriculture, hunting, forestry and fishing	...	...	4282	...	...	5183	...	...	5738	...	...	6475

India

	1990 Gross output	1990 Intermediate consumption	1990 Value added	1991 Gross output	1991 Intermediate consumption	1991 Value added	1992 Gross output	1992 Intermediate consumption	1992 Value added	1993 Gross output	1993 Intermediate consumption	1993 Value added
2 Mining and quarrying	...	...	...	...	...	...	...	...	...	...	...	...
3 Manufacturing	...	...	2492	...	...	2847	...	...	3005	...	...	3531
4 Electricity, gas and water	...	...	865	...	...	934	...	...	1200	...	...	1683
5 Construction	...	...	4151	...	...	4647	...	...	5342	...	...	5348
6 Wholesale and retail trade, restaurants and hotels	...	...	45	...	...	38	...	...	−4	...	...	58
7 Transport, storage and communication	...	...	176	...	...	195	...	...	356	...	...	483
8 Finance, insurance, real estate and business services	...	...	382	...	...	468	...	...	609	...	...	678
9 Community, social and personal services	...	...	13135	...	...	14908	...	...	16982	...	...	19103
Statistical discrepancy	...	...	—	...	...	...	...	...	...	...	...	...
Total, industries of general government	...	...	25528	...	...	29220	...	...	33228	...	...	37359
Producers of government services	...	...	27109	...	...	31441	...	...	36250	...	...	39950
Total, general government	...	...	52637	...	...	60661	...	...	69478	...	...	77309

	1994 Gross output	1994 Intermediate consumption	1994 Value added	1995 Gross output	1995 Intermediate consumption	1995 Value added	1996 Gross output	1996 Intermediate consumption	1996 Value added	1997 Gross output	1997 Intermediate consumption	1997 Value added
All producers												
1 Agriculture, hunting, forestry and fishing	324789	65725	259064	348670	71818	276852	...	...	310144	...	...	...
A Agriculture and hunting	302206	63047	239159	324393	68780	255613	...	...	287132	...	...	...
B Forestry and logging	12394	1240	11154	12519	1252	11267	...	...	11293	...	...	...
C Fishing	10189	1438	8751	11758	1786	9972	...	...	11719	...	...	...
2 Mining and quarrying	27124	8245	18879	29780	9226	20554	30057	9513	20544	...	...	...
A Coal mining	12091	5688	6403	13089	6194	6895	13804	6528	7276	...	...	...
B Crude petroleum and natural gas production	9694	1520	8174	10582	1672	8910	9917	1574	8343	...	...	...
C Metal ore mining	2298	548	1750	2691	645	2046	2675	648	2027	...	...	...
D Other mining	3041	489	2552	3418	715	2703	3661	763	2898	...	...	...
3 Manufacturing	...	...	159713	...	...	198348	...	...	222609	...	...	...
A Manufacture of food, beverages and tobacco	...	...	15775	...	...	18918	...	...	20745	...	...	...
B Textile, wearing apparel and leather industries	...	...	31415	...	...	39791	...	...	43762	...	...	...
C Manufacture of wood and wood products, including furniture	...	...	3535	...	...	3955	...	...	3862	...	...	...
D Manufacture of paper and paper products, printing and publishing	...	...	5468	...	...	6925	...	...	7593	...	...	...
E Manufacture of chemicals and chemical petroleum, coal, rubber and plastic products	...	...	27104	...	...	32073	...	...	34739	...	...	...
F Manufacture of non-metallic mineral products, except products of petroleum and coal	...	...	6142	...	...	7942	...	...	9090	...	...	...
G Basic metal industries	...	...	13125	...	...	15070	...	...	20978	...	...	...

India

	1994			1995			1996			1997		
	Gross output	Intermediate consumption	Value added	Gross output	Intermediate consumption	Value added	Gross output	Intermediate consumption	Value added	Gross output	Intermediate consumption	Value added
H Manufacture of fabricated metal products, machinery and equipment	...	...	38485	...	...	50305	...	...	56347	...	...	...
I Other manufacturing industries	...	...	18664	...	...	23369	...	...	25493	...	...	...
4 Electricity, gas and water	...	...	23662	...	...	28021	...	...	32856	...	...	...
A Electricity, gas and steam	...	...	21713	...	...	25716	...	...	30150	...	...	...
B Water works and supply	...	...	1949	...	...	2305	...	...	2706	...	...	...
5 Construction	117651	69672	47979	142373	83957	58416	...	...	68583	...	...	...
6 Wholesale and retail trade, restaurants and hotels	...	...	118488	...	...	142808	...	...	167608	...	...	...
A Wholesale and retail trade	...	...	111208	...	...	133529	...	...	156577	...	...	...
B Restaurants and hotels	...	...	7280	...	...	9279	...	...	11031	...	...	...
7 Transport, storage and communication	...	...	66680	...	...	75365	...	...	88605	...	...	...
A Transport and storage	...	...	55516	...	...	61916	...	...	72924	...	...	...
B Communication	...	...	11164	...	...	13449	...	...	15681	...	...	...
8 Finance, insurance, real estate and business services	...	...	78468	...	...	94475	...	...	108007	...	...	...
A Financial institutions	...	...	44512	...	...	55455	...	...	...	...	...	...
B Insurance	...	...	7691	...	...	9859	...	...	...	...	...	...
C Real estate and business services	...	...	26265	...	...	29161	...	...	32134	...	...	...
Real estate, except dwellings [a]	...	...	2007	...	...	2606	...	...	...	...	...	...
Dwellings	...	...	24258	...	...	26555	...	...	...	...	...	...
9 Community, social and personal services	...	...	50507	...	...	59366	...	...	69611	...	...	...
A Sanitary and similar services	...	...	2079	...	...	2384	...	...	...	...	...	...
B Social and related community services [b]	...	...	48428	...	...	56982	...	...	...	...	...	...
C Recreational and cultural services	...	...	...	...	...	...	...	...	...	...	...	...
D Personal and household services	...	...	...	...	...	...	...	...	...	...	...	...
Total, Industries	...	...	823439	...	...	954205	...	...	1088567[c]	...	...	...
Producers of government services	...	...	44580	...	...	52081	...	...	60648	...	...	...
Other producers	...	...	...	...	...	985787	...	...	...	...	...	...
Total [d]	...	...	868019	...	...	1006286[c]	...	...	1149215[c]	...	...	...
less: Imputed bank service charge	...	...	...	...	...	...	...	...	...	...	...	...
Import duties	...	...	...	...	...	...	...	...	...	...	...	...
Value added tax	...	...	...	...	...	...	...	...	...	...	...	...
Other adjustments [e]	...	...	95473	...	...	112678	...	...	127759	...	...	...
Total	...	...	963492	...	...	1118964[c]	...	...	1276974[c]	...	...	...

Of which general government:

1 Agriculture, hunting, forestry and fishing	...	...	7368	...	...	8465	...	...	...	...	...	...
2 Mining and quarrying	...	...	...	...	...	...	...	...	...	...	...	...
3 Manufacturing	...	...	3919	...	...	3818	...	...	...	...	...	...
4 Electricity, gas and water	...	...	1869	...	...	1886	...	...	...	...	...	...
5 Construction	...	...	6571	...	...	7657	...	...	...	...	...	...

India

	1994			1995			1996			1997		
	Gross output	Intermediate consumption	Value added	Gross output	Intermediate consumption	Value added	Gross output	Intermediate consumption	Value added	Gross output	Intermediate consumption	Value added
6 Wholesale and retail trade, restaurants and hotels	...	...	112	...	...	137	...	...	...	...	...	...
7 Transport, storage and communication	...	...	476	...	...	477	...	...	...	...	...	...
8 Finance, insurance, real estate and business services	...	...	707	...	...	812	...	...	...	...	...	...
9 Community, social and personal services	...	...	21447	...	...	24930	...	...	...	...	...	...
Total, industries of general government	...	...	42469	...	...	48182	...	...	...	...	...	...
Producers of government services	...	...	44580	...	...	52081	...	...	...	...	...	...
Total, general government	...	...	87049	...	...	100263	...	...	...	...	...	...

a Item "Real estate, except dwellings" includes also business services other than legal services.
b Item "Social and related community services" includes legal services and the rest of the community, social and personal services other than sanitary services but excluding repair services which are included under manufacturing.
c Estimates in ten millions.
d Gross domestic product in factor values.
e Item "Other adjustments" refers to indirect taxes net of subsidies.

4.2 Derivation of value added by kind of activity, in constant prices

Ten million Indian rupees
Fiscal year beginning 1 April

	1986			1987			1988			1989		
	Gross output	Intermediate consumption	Value added	Gross output	Intermediate consumption	Value added	Gross output	Intermediate consumption	Value added	Gross output	Intermediate consumption	Value added

At constant prices of: 1980

All producers

1 Agriculture, hunting, forestry and fishing	71986	18705	53281	71796	18317	53479	82687	20473	62214	84250	20987	63263
A Agriculture and hunting	67204	18209	48995	67051	17793	49258	77872	19932	57940	78951	20383	58568
B Forestry and logging	3433	343	3090	3318	332	2986	3267	327	2940	3550	355	3195
C Fishing	1349	153	1196	1427	192	1235	1548	214	1334	1749	249	1500
2 Mining and quarrying	4493	1515	2978	4766	1686	3080	5099	1557	3542	5367	1566	3801
A Coal mining	2092	1165	927	2317	1289	1028	2485	1147	1338	2521	1136	1385
B Crude petroleum and natural gas production	1448	186	1262	1511	238	1273	1641	232	1409	1860	260	1600
C Metal ore mining	380	91	289	368	85	283	392	91	301	400	88	312
D Other mining	573	73	500	570	74	496	581	87	494	586	82	504
3 Manufacturing	...	...	32445	...	...	34818	...	...	37865	...	...	42285
A Manufacture of food, beverages and tobacco	...	...	3107	...	...	3210	...	...	4111	...	...	4448
B Textile, wearing apparel and leather industries	...	...	6796	...	...	6712	...	...	6802	...	...	7616
C Manufacture of wood and wood products, including furniture	...	...	879	...	...	890	...	...	774	...	...	799
D Manufacture of paper and paper products, printing and publishing	...	...	1154	...	...	1150	...	...	1251	...	...	1458
E Manufacture of chemicals and chemical petroleum, coal, rubber and plastic products	...	...	4963	...	...	5528	...	...	6283	...	...	7197

India

Ten million Indian rupees — Fiscal year beginning 1 April

	1986 Gross output	1986 Intermediate consumption	1986 Value added	1987 Gross output	1987 Intermediate consumption	1987 Value added	1988 Gross output	1988 Intermediate consumption	1988 Value added	1989 Gross output	1989 Intermediate consumption	1989 Value added
At constant prices of: 1980												
F Manufacture of non-metallic mineral products, except products of petroleum and coal	...	...	1269	...	...	1388	...	...	1544	...	...	1773
G Basic metal industries	...	...	1813	...	...	1898	...	...	2534	...	...	2381
H Manufacture of fabricated metal products, machinery and equipment	...	...	7770	...	...	8745	...	...	9261	...	...	10298
I Other manufacturing industries	...	...	4694	...	...	5297	...	...	5305	...	...	6315
4 Electricity, gas and water	...	...	3422	...	...	3692	...	...	4080	...	...	4505
A Electricity, gas and steam	...	...	3110	...	...	3336	...	...	3694	...	...	4084
B Water works and supply	...	...	312	...	...	356	...	...	386	...	...	421
5 Construction	18580	11043	7537	18987	11210	7777	20622	12243	8379	21361	12554	8807
6 Wholesale and retail trade, restaurants and hotels	...	...	20852	...	...	21801	...	...	23385	...	...	25231
A Wholesale and retail trade	...	...	19636	...	...	20518	...	...	21979	...	...	23675
B Restaurants and hotels	...	...	1216	...	...	1283	...	...	1406	...	...	1556
7 Transport, storage and communication	...	...	8483	...	...	9227	...	...	9804	...	...	10663
A Transport and storage	...	...	7335	...	...	8006	...	...	8516	...	...	9294
B Communication	...	...	1148	...	...	1221	...	...	1288	...	...	1369
8 Finance, insurance, real estate and business services	...	...	15916	...	...	16871	...	...	18416	...	...	20403
A Financial institutions	...	...	5334	...	...	6033	...	...	7159	...	...	8228
B Insurance	...	...	1358	...	...	1366	...	...	1464	...	...	2041
C Real estate and business services	...	...	9224	...	...	9472	...	...	9793	...	...	10134
Real estate, except dwellings	...	...	494	...	...	449	...	...	466	...	...	492
Dwellings	...	...	8730	...	...	9023	...	...	9327	...	...	9642
9 Community, social and personal services	...	...	9550	...	...	9873	...	...	10434	...	...	11281
A Sanitary and similar services	...	...	316	...	...	360	...	...	419	...	...	462
B Social and related community services [a]	...	...	9234	...	...	9513	...	...	10015	...	...	10819
C Recreational and cultural services	...	...	...	...	...	...	...	...	...	...	...	...
D Personal and household services	...	...	...	...	...	...	...	...	...	...	...	...
Total, Industries	...	...	154464	...	...	160618	...	...	178119	...	...	190239
Producers of government services	...	...	8807	...	...	9704	...	...	10342	...	...	11214
Other producers	...	...	...	...	...	...	...	...	...	...	...	...
Total [b]	...	...	163271	...	...	170322	...	...	188461	...	...	201453
less: Imputed bank service charge	...	...	...	...	...	...	...	...	...	...	...	...
Import duties	...	...	...	...	...	...	...	...	...	...	...	...
Value added tax	...	...	...	...	...	...	...	...	...	...	...	...
Other adjustments [c]	...	...	21979	...	...	23763	...	...	24884	...	...	25914
Total	...	...	185250	...	...	194085	...	...	213345	...	...	227367

India

Ten million Indian rupees — Fiscal year beginning 1 April

	1986 Gross output	1986 Intermediate consumption	1986 Value added	1987 Gross output	1987 Intermediate consumption	1987 Value added	1988 Gross output	1988 Intermediate consumption	1988 Value added	1989 Gross output	1989 Intermediate consumption	1989 Value added

At constant prices of: 1980

Of which general government:

1 Agriculture, hunting, forestry and fishing	...	...	1401	...	...	1429	...	...	1410	...	...	1498
2 Mining and quarrying	...	...	–	...	...	–	...	...	–	...	...	–
3 Manufacturing	...	...	808	...	...	987	...	...	980	...	...	883
4 Electricity, gas and water	...	...	318	...	...	450	...	...	491	...	...	533
5 Construction	...	...	1125	...	...	1284	...	...	1429	...	...	1672
6 Wholesale and retail trade, restaurants and hotels	...	...	16	...	...	33	...	...	35	...	...	19
7 Transport, storage and communication	...	...	69	...	...	64	...	...	63	...	...	61
8 Finance, insurance, real estate and business services	...	...	87	...	...	91	...	...	97	...	...	105
9 Community, social and personal services	...	...	3852	...	...	4158	...	...	4556	...	...	5109
Statistical discrepancy	...	...	–	...	...	–	...	...	–	...	...	–
Total, industries of general government	...	...	7676	...	...	8496	...	...	9061	...	...	9880
Producers of government services	...	...	8807	...	...	9704	...	...	10342	...	...	11214
Total, general government	...	...	16483	...	...	18200	...	...	19403	...	...	21094

	1990 Gross output	1990 Intermediate consumption	1990 Value added	1991 Gross output	1991 Intermediate consumption	1991 Value added	1992 Gross output	1992 Intermediate consumption	1992 Value added	1993 Gross output	1993 Intermediate consumption	1993 Value added

At constant prices of: 1980

All producers

1 Agriculture, hunting, forestry and fishing	87160	21507	65653	86204	22086	64118	90295	22286	68009	93249	22736	70513
A Agriculture and hunting	81885	20894	60991	80868	21470	59398	84979	21652	63327	87847	22085	65762
B Forestry and logging	3450	345	3105	3426	343	3083	3278	328	2950	3201	320	2881
C Fishing	1825	268	1557	1910	273	1637	2038	306	1732	2201	331	1870
2 Mining and quarrying	5732	1525	4207	6098	1736	4362	6262	1850	4412	6500	2012	4488
A Coal mining	2680	1085	1595	2913	1175	1738	3050	1279	1771	3159	1454	1705
B Crude petroleum and natural gas production	1933	236	1697	1943	308	1635	1939	322	1617	2016	288	1728
C Metal ore mining	438	113	325	483	141	342	480	133	347	478	130	348
D Other mining	681	91	590	759	112	647	793	116	677	847	140	707
3 Manufacturing	...	...	44863	...	...	43200	...	...	45005	...	...	48770
A Manufacture of food, beverages and tobacco	...	...	4103	...	...	4051	...	...	4142	...	...	4777
B Textile, wearing apparel and leather industries	...	...	8173	...	...	7906	...	...	8554	...	...	10165
C Manufacture of wood and wood products, including furniture	...	...	794	...	...	736	...	...	697	...	...	711
D Manufacture of paper and paper products, printing and publishing	...	...	1555	...	...	1602	...	...	1368	...	...	1557
E Manufacture of chemicals and chemical petroleum, coal, rubber and plastic products	...	...	7982	...	...	7976	...	...	9040	...	...	9738

India

	1990 Gross output	1990 Intermediate consumption	1990 Value added	1991 Gross output	1991 Intermediate consumption	1991 Value added	1992 Gross output	1992 Intermediate consumption	1992 Value added	1993 Gross output	1993 Intermediate consumption	1993 Value added
At constant prices of: 1980												
F Manufacture of non-metallic mineral products, except products of petroleum and coal	...	...	1940	...	...	2024	...	...	1799	...	...	1775
G Basic metal industries	...	...	2838	...	...	2952	...	...	2830	...	...	2908
H Manufacture of fabricated metal products, machinery and equipment	...	...	10877	...	...	10105	...	...	10353	...	...	10550
I Other manufacturing industries	...	...	6601	...	...	5848	...	...	6221	...	...	6589
4 Electricity, gas and water	...	...	4797	...	...	5258	...	...	5700	...	...	6060
A Electricity, gas and steam	...	...	4368	...	...	4809	...	...	5213	...	...	5541
B Water works and supply	...	...	429	...	...	449	...	...	487	...	...	519
5 Construction	23354	13521	9833	23751	13704	10047	24362	13976	10386	24315	13798	10484
6 Wholesale and retail trade, restaurants and hotels	...	...	26580	...	...	26827	...	...	28653	...	...	30923
A Wholesale and retail trade	...	...	24933	...	...	25147	...	...	26866	...	...	28950
B Restaurants and hotels	...	...	1647	...	...	1680	...	...	1787	...	...	1973
7 Transport, storage and communication	...	...	11164	...	...	11785	...	...	12367	...	...	13065
A Transport and storage	...	...	9707	...	...	10228	...	...	10673	...	...	11151
B Communication	...	...	1457	...	...	1557	...	...	1725	...	...	1914
8 Finance, insurance, real estate and business services	...	...	21700	...	...	23972	...	...	25084	...	...	28210
A Financial institutions	...	...	9327	...	...	10843	...	...	11696	...	...	14184
B Insurance	...	...	1842	...	...	2264	...	...	2165	...	...	2426
C Real estate and business services	...	...	10531	...	...	10865	...	...	11223	...	...	11600
Real estate, except dwellings	...	...	586	...	...	574	...	...	580	...	...	591
Dwellings	...	...	9945	...	...	10291	...	...	10643	...	...	11009
9 Community, social and personal services	...	...	12128	...	...	12844	...	...	13454	...	...	14149
A Sanitary and similar services	...	...	472	...	...	478	...	...	501	...	...	512
B Social and related community services [a]	...	...	11656	...	...	12366	...	...	12953	...	...	13637
C Recreational and cultural services	...	...	...	...	...	...	...	...	...	...	...	...
D Personal and household services	...	...	...	...	...	...	...	...	...	...	...	...
Total, Industries	...	...	200925	...	...	202413	...	...	213070	...	...	226662
Producers of government services	...	...	11328	...	...	11570	...	...	12170	...	...	12483
Other producers	...	...	...	...	...	...	...	...	...	...	...	...
Total [b]	...	...	212253	...	...	213983	...	...	225240	...	...	239145
less: Imputed bank service charge	...	...	...	...	...	...	...	...	...	...	...	...
Import duties	...	...	...	...	...	...	...	...	...	...	...	...
Value added tax	...	...	...	...	...	...	...	...	...	...	...	...
Other adjustments [c]	...	...	27985	...	...	27272	...	...	29092	...	...	27789
Total	...	...	240238	...	...	241255	...	...	254332	...	...	266934

India

	1990			1991			1992			1993		
	Gross output	Intermediate consumption	Value added	Gross output	Intermediate consumption	Value added	Gross output	Intermediate consumption	Value added	Gross output	Intermediate consumption	Value added

At constant prices of: 1980

Of which general government:

1 Agriculture, hunting, forestry and fishing	...	...	1439	...	...	1500	...	...	1476	...	...	1504
2 Mining and quarrying	...	...	–	...	...	–	...	...	–	...	...	–
3 Manufacturing	...	...	938	...	...	969	...	...	891	...	...	979
4 Electricity, gas and water	...	...	567	...	...	593	...	...	628	...	...	670
5 Construction	...	...	1757	...	...	1731	...	...	1786	...	...	1694
6 Wholesale and retail trade, restaurants and hotels	...	...	16	...	...	10	...	...	–1	...	...	12
7 Transport, storage and communication	...	...	59	...	...	57	...	...	89	...	...	109
8 Finance, insurance, real estate and business services	...	...	115	...	...	112	...	...	113	...	...	114
9 Community, social and personal services	...	...	5521	...	...	5520	...	...	5737	...	...	6006
Statistical discrepancy	...	...	–	...	...	...	...	...	...	...	...	...
Total, industries of general government	...	...	10412	...	...	10492	...	...	10719	...	...	11088
Producers of government services	...	...	11328	...	...	11570	...	...	12170	...	...	12483
Total, general government	...	...	21740	...	...	22062	...	...	22889	...	...	23571

	1994			1995			1996			1997		
	Gross output	Intermediate consumption	Value added	Gross output	Intermediate consumption	Value added	Gross output	Intermediate consumption	Value added	Gross output	Intermediate consumption	Value added

At constant prices of: 1980

All producers

1 Agriculture, hunting, forestry and fishing	98137	24004	74133	96443	24536	71907	...	...	77564	...	...	...
A Agriculture and hunting	92539	23333	69206	90693	23830	66863	...	...	72362	...	...	...
B Forestry and logging	3258	326	2932	3250	325	2925	...	...	2930	...	...	...
C Fishing	2340	345	1995	2500	381	2119	...	...	2272	...	...	...
2 Mining and quarrying	6913	2162	4751	7485	2334	5151	7466	2328	5138	...	...	...
A Coal mining	3278	1541	1737	3487	1649	1838	3668	1733	1935	...	...	...
B Crude petroleum and natural gas production	2241	348	1893	2521	402	2119	2329	315	2014	...	...	...
C Metal ore mining	506	124	382	558	134	424	530	127	403	...	...	...
D Other mining	888	149	739	919	149	770	939	153	786	...	...	...
3 Manufacturing	...	...	54570	...	...	62207	...	...	66785	...	...	...
A Manufacture of food, beverages and tobacco	...	...	5485	...	...	6192	...	...	6429	...	...	...
B Textile, wearing apparel and leather industries	...	...	10525	...	...	11660	...	...	12468	...	...	...
C Manufacture of wood and wood products, including furniture	...	...	771	...	...	822	...	...	797	...	...	...
D Manufacture of paper and paper products, printing and publishing	...	...	1802	...	...	2019	...	...	2194	...	...	...
E Manufacture of chemicals and chemical petroleum, coal, rubber and plastic products	...	...	10410	...	...	11466	...	...	11797	...	...	...

India

	1994			1995			1996			1997		
	Gross output	Intermediate consumption	Value added	Gross output	Intermediate consumption	Value added	Gross output	Intermediate consumption	Value added	Gross output	Intermediate consumption	Value added

At constant prices of: 1980

	1994			1995			1996			1997		
F Manufacture of non-metallic mineral products, except products of petroleum and coal	...	...	1991	...	...	2252	...	...	2433	...	...	...
G Basic metal industries	...	...	3476	...	...	3697	...	...	4943	...	...	...
H Manufacture of fabricated metal products, machinery and equipment	...	...	12837	...	...	15625	...	...	16892	...	...	...
I Other manufacturing industries	...	...	7273	...	...	8474	...	...	8832	...	...	...
4 Electricity, gas and water	...	...	6632	...	...	7113	...	...	7466	...	...	...
A Electricity, gas and steam	...	...	6090	...	...	6526	...	...	618	...	...	...
B Water works and supply	...	...	542	...	...	587	...	...	6848	...	...	...
5 Construction	26063	14929	11134	28430	16214	12216	...	...	12851	...	...	...
6 Wholesale and retail trade, restaurants and hotels	...	...	34647	...	...	39968	...	...	43313	...	...	...
A Wholesale and retail trade	...	...	32370	...	...	37188	...	...	40286	...	...	...
B Restaurants and hotels	...	...	2277	...	...	2780	...	...	3027	...	...	...
7 Transport, storage and communication	...	...	14091	...	...	15264	...	...	16664	...	...	...
A Transport and storage	...	...	11869	...	...	12633	...	...	13574	...	...	...
B Communication	...	...	2222	...	...	2631	...	...	3090	...	...	...
8 Finance, insurance, real estate and business services	...	...	30232	...	...	33152	...	...	36045	...	...	...
A Financial institutions	...	...	16014	...	...	18013	...	...	...	...	...	...
B Insurance	...	...	2168	...	...	2621	...	...	...	...	...	...
C Real estate and business services	...	...	12050	...	...	12518	...	...	12965	...	...	...
Real estate, except dwellings	...	...	661	...	...	734	...	...	...	...	...	...
Dwellings	...	...	11389	...	...	11784	...	...	...	...	...	...
9 Community, social and personal services	...	...	14842	...	...	15732	...	...	16707	...	...	...
A Sanitary and similar services	...	...	523	...	...	539	...	...	...	...	...	...
B Social and related community services [a]	...	...	14319	...	...	15193	...	...	...	...	...	...
C Recreational and cultural services	...	...	...	...	...	...	...	...	...	...	...	...
D Personal and household services	...	...	...	...	...	...	...	...	...	...	...	...
Total, Industries	...	...	245032	...	...	262710	...	...	282533	...	...	...
Producers of government services	...	...	12668	...	...	13422	...	...	14312	...	...	...
Other producers	...	...	...	...	...	...	...	...	...	...	...	...
Total [b]	...	...	257700	...	...	276132	...	...	296845	...	...	...
less: Imputed bank service charge	...	...	...	...	...	...	...	...	...	...	...	...
Import duties	...	...	...	...	...	...	...	...	...	...	...	...
Value added tax	...	...	...	...	...	...	...	...	...	...	...	...
Other adjustments [c]	...	...	30937	...	...	33785	...	...	35876	...	...	...
Total	...	...	288637	...	...	309917	...	...	332721	...	...	...

India

	1994			1995			1996			1997		
	Gross output	Intermediate consumption	Value added	Gross output	Intermediate consumption	Value added	Gross output	Intermediate consumption	Value added	Gross output	Intermediate consumption	Value added

At constant prices of: 1980

Of which general government:

1 Agriculture, hunting, forestry and fishing	...	...	1541	...	...	1557	...	...	...	...	...	...
2 Mining and quarrying	...	...	–	...	...	–	...	...	...	...	...	...
3 Manufacturing	...	...	1010	...	...	940	...	...	...	...	...	...
4 Electricity, gas and water	...	...	711	...	...	759	...	...	...	...	...	...
5 Construction	...	...	1891	...	...	2000	...	...	...	...	...	...
6 Wholesale and retail trade, restaurants and hotels	...	...	19	...	...	23	...	...	...	...	...	...
7 Transport, storage and communication	...	...	100	...	...	96	...	...	...	...	...	...
8 Finance, insurance, real estate and business services	...	...	133	...	...	141	...	...	...	...	...	...
9 Community, social and personal services	...	...	6129	...	...	6464	...	...	...	...	...	...
Total, industries of general government	...	...	11533	...	...	11980	...	...	...	...	...	...
Producers of government services	...	...	12668	...	...	13422	...	...	...	...	...	...
Total, general government	...	...	24202	...	...	25402	...	...	...	...	...	...

a Item "Social and related community services" includes legal services and the rest of the community, social and personal services other than sanitary services but excluding repair services which are included under manufacturing.
b Gross domestic product in factor values.
c Item "Other adjustments" refers to indirect taxes net of subsidies.

4.3 Cost components of value added

Ten million Indian rupees — Fiscal year beginning 1 April

	1986						1987					
	Compensation of employees	Capital consumption	Net operating surplus	Indirect taxes	less: Subsidies received	Value added	Compensation of employees	Capital consumption	Net operating surplus	Indirect taxes	less: Subsidies received	Value added

All producers

1 Agriculture, hunting, forestry and fishing	16716	5381	60316	...	...	82413	17962	5941	68476	...	...	92379
A Agriculture and hunting	15572	4959	53874	...	...	74405	16735	5450	61330	...	...	83515
B Forestry and logging	739	101	4918	...	...	5758	740	119	5319	...	...	6178
C Fishing	405	321	1524	...	...	2250	487	372	1827	...	...	2686
2 Mining and quarrying	1970	1641	3185	...	...	6796	2005	1901	3179	...	...	7085
3 Manufacturing	15817	6719	23630	...	...	46166	18295	7357	27213	...	...	52865
4 Electricity, gas and water	2102	3267	198	...	...	5567	2568	3810	–110	...	...	6268
5 Construction	11182	791	3244	...	...	15217	13658	831	3122	...	...	17611
6 Wholesale and retail trade, restaurants and hotels	7367	968	26216	...	...	34551	8197	1052	29184	...	...	38433
A Wholesale and retail trade	6835	684	25105	...	...	32624	7598	743	27924	...	...	36265
B Restaurants and hotels	532	284	1111	...	...	1927	599	309	1260	...	...	2168
7 Transport, storage and communication	7186	4792	4559	...	...	16537	8733	5416	5789	...	...	19938
A Transport and storage	5892	4301	4362	...	...	14555	7115	4833	5193	...	...	17141
B Communication	1294	491	197	...	...	1982	1618	583	596	...	...	2797
8 Finance, insurance, real estate and business services	4373	4139	13797	...	...	22309	5047	4589	15120	...	...	24756

India

Ten million Indian rupees   *Fiscal year beginning 1 April*

	1986							1987						
	Compensation of employees	Capital consumption	Net operating surplus	Indirect taxes	less: Subsidies received	Value added	Compensation of employees	Capital consumption	Net operating surplus	Indirect taxes	less: Subsidies received	Value added
A Financial institutions	4102	201	5361	...	...	9664	4704	261	6178	...	...	11143
B Insurance												
C Real estate and business services	271	3938	8436	...	...	12645	343	4328	8942	...	...	13613
9 Community, social and personal services	11017	646	3878	...	...	15541	12485	729	4354	...	...	17568
Total, Industries [a]	77730	28344	139023	...	...	245097	88950	31626	156327	...	...	276903
Producers of government services	13454	1479	–	...	...	14933	16233	1715	–	...	...	17948
Other producers	...	...	...	...	...	...	...	...	...	...	...	...
Total [b]	91184	29823	139023	...	...	260030	105183	33341	156327	...	...	294851
less: Imputed bank service charge	...	...	...	...	...	...	...	...	...	...	...	...
Import duties	...	...	...	...	...	...	...	...	...	...	...	...
Value added tax	...	...	...	...	...	...	...	...	...	...	...	...
Other adjustments [c]	...	...	...	...	...	32919	...	...	...	...	...	38350
Total	...	...	...	...	...	292949	...	...	...	...	...	333201

Of which general government:

1 Agriculture, hunting, forestry and fishing	723	889	1276	...	...	2888	871	1021	1302	...	...	3194
2 Mining and quarrying	–	–	–	...	...	–	–	–	–	...	...	–
3 Manufacturing	1735	292	–548	...	...	1479	2109	328	–478	...	...	1959
4 Electricity, gas and water	448	666	–526	...	...	588	544	729	–620	...	...	653
5 Construction	1805	76	–	...	...	1881	2259	82	–	...	...	2341
6 Wholesale and retail trade, restaurants and hotels	7	–	24	...	...	31	9	–	55	...	...	64
7 Transport, storage and communication	154	112	–139	...	...	127	177	123	–167	...	...	133
8 Finance, insurance, real estate and business services	88	117	2	...	...	207	137	136	2	...	...	275
9 Community, social and personal services	6219	348	–66	...	...	6501	7340	403	–86	...	...	7657
Total, industries of general government	11179	2500	23	...	...	13702	13446	2822	8	...	...	16276
Producers of government services	13454	1479	–	...	...	14933	16233	1715	–	...	...	17948
Total, general government	24633	3979	23	...	...	28635	29679	4537	8	...	...	34224

	1988						1989					
	Compensation of employees	Capital consumption	Net operating surplus	Indirect taxes	less: Subsidies received	Value added	Compensation of employees	Capital consumption	Net operating surplus	Indirect taxes	less: Subsidies received	Value added

All producers

1 Agriculture, hunting, forestry and fishing	21534	6734	85805	...	...	114073	24061	7768	95222	...	...	127051
A Agriculture and hunting	20001	6134	77968	...	...	104103	22465	7060	85922	...	...	115447
B Forestry and logging	971	139	5718	...	...	6828	915	164	6744	...	...	7823
C Fishing	562	461	2119	...	...	3142	681	544	2556	...	...	3781
2 Mining and quarrying	2569	2297	4342	...	...	9208	2837	2840	4631	...	...	10308
3 Manufacturing	20284	8679	33900	...	...	62863	23752	10232	43092	...	...	77076
4 Electricity, gas and water	3041	4536	–252	...	...	7325	3567	5433	–277	...	...	8723
5 Construction	15391	987	4299	...	...	20677	17743	1202	4641	...	...	23586

India

	1988						1989					
	Compensation of employees	Capital consumption	Net operating surplus	Indirect taxes	less: Subsidies received	Value added	Compensation of employees	Capital consumption	Net operating surplus	Indirect taxes	less: Subsidies received	Value added
6 Wholesale and retail trade, restaurants and hotels	9735	1247	34240	...	...	45222	11286	1471	40153	...	...	52910
A Wholesale and retail trade	9010	881	32710	...	...	42601	10416	1037	38324	...	...	49777
B Restaurants and hotels	725	366	1530	...	...	2621	870	434	1829	...	...	3133
7 Transport, storage and communication	9902	6486	7484	...	...	23872	11300	7759	8672	...	...	27731
A Transport and storage	8197	5763	6354	...	...	20314	9457	6856	7435	...	...	23748
B Communication	1705	723	1130	...	...	3558	1843	903	1237	...	...	3983
8 Finance, insurance, real estate and business services	6054	5105	17097	...	...	28256	7158	5619	20800	...	...	33577
A Financial institutions	5666	364	7383	...	...	13413	6727	489	9915	...	...	17131
B Insurance												
C Real estate and business services	388	4741	9714	...	...	14843	431	5130	10885	...	...	16446
9 Community, social and personal services	14397	849	5106	...	...	20352	16843	994	5730	...	...	23567
Total, Industries [a]	102907	36920	192021	...	...	331848	118547	43318	222664	...	...	384529
Producers of government services	18857	2001	–	...	...	20858	21805	2328	–	...	...	24133
Other producers	...	...	...	...	...	...	...	...	...	...	...	...
Total [b]	121764	38921	192021	...	...	352706	140352	45646	222664	...	...	408662
less: Imputed bank service charge	...	...	...	...	...	...	...	...	...	...	...	...
Import duties	...	...	...	...	...	...	...	...	...	...	...	...
Value added tax	...	...	...	...	...	...	...	...	...	...	...	...
Other adjustments [c]	...	...	...	...	...	43076	...	...	...	...	...	48159
Total	...	...	...	...	...	395782	...	...	...	...	...	456821

Of which general government:

	Compensation of employees	Capital consumption	Net operating surplus	Indirect taxes	less: Subsidies received	Value added	Compensation of employees	Capital consumption	Net operating surplus	Indirect taxes	less: Subsidies received	Value added
1 Agriculture, hunting, forestry and fishing	1026	1170	1610	...	...	3806	1233	1346	1755	...	...	4334
2 Mining and quarrying	–	–	–	...	...	–	–	–	–	...	...	–
3 Manufacturing	2260	382	–537	...	...	2105	2537	454	–830	...	...	2161
4 Electricity, gas and water	598	833	–752	...	...	679	706	951	–933	...	...	724
5 Construction	2748	92	–	...	...	2840	3442	103	–	...	...	3545
6 Wholesale and retail trade, restaurants and hotels	9	–	72	...	...	81	10	–	25	...	...	35
7 Transport, storage and communication	203	129	–184	...	...	148	241	145	–229	...	...	157
8 Finance, insurance, real estate and business services	122	155	4	...	...	281	179	175	3	...	...	357
9 Community, social and personal services	8788	471	–115	...	...	9144	10527	557	–163	...	...	10921
Total, industries of general government	15754	3232	98	...	...	19084	18875	3731	–372	...	...	22234
Producers of government services	18857	2001	–	...	...	20858	21805	2328	–	...	...	24133
Total, general government	34611	5233	98	...	...	39942	40680	6059	–372	...	...	46367

India

	1990						1991					
	Compensation of employees	Capital consumption	Net operating surplus	Indirect taxes	less: Subsidies received	Value added	Compensation of employees	Capital consumption	Net operating surplus	Indirect taxes	less: Subsidies received	Value added

All producers

1 Agriculture, hunting, forestry and fishing	27511	8703	111787	...	...	148001	30635	10413	131723	...	...	172771
A Agriculture and hunting	25745	7903	101514	...	...	135162	28680	9475	121144	...	...	159299
B Forestry and logging	938	186	7157	...	...	8281	1041	223	7126	...	...	8390
C Fishing	828	614	3116	...	...	4558	914	715	3453	...	...	5082
2 Mining and quarrying	3903	3366	4516	...	...	11785	3681	4096	5026	...	...	12803
3 Manufacturing	28055	11973	49132	...	...	89160	31957	14722	49626	...	...	96305
4 Electricity, gas and water	4033	6286	145	...	...	10464	4599	7807	314	...	...	12720
5 Construction	21058	1394	6164	...	...	28616	23609	1598	7039	...	...	32246
6 Wholesale and retail trade, restaurants and hotels	13056	1728	47099	...	...	61883	15080	2104	53623	...	...	70807
A Wholesale and retail trade	12053	1215	44990	...	...	58258	13914	1471	51236	...	...	66621
B Restaurants and hotels	1003	513	2109	...	...	3625	1166	633	2387	...	...	4186
7 Transport, storage and communication	12760	8835	12318	...	...	33913	14614	10506	15884	...	...	41004
A Transport and storage	10755	7780	10654	...	...	29189	12395	9161	13785	...	...	35341
B Communication	2005	1055	1664	...	...	4724	2219	1345	2099	...	...	5663
8 Finance, insurance, real estate and business services	8315	6229	24358	...	...	38902	9511	7443	32102	...	...	49056
A Financial institutions	7698	644	12754	...	...	21096	8801	927	19787	...	...	29515
B Insurance												
C Real estate and business services	617	5585	11604	...	...	17806	710	6516	12315	...	...	19541
9 Community, social and personal services	20239	1092	6650	...	...	27981	24189	1298	8128	...	...	33615
Total, Industries [a]	138931	49606	262168	...	...	450705	157875	59987	303465	...	...	521327
Producers of government services	24520	2589	–	...	...	27109	28349	3092	–	...	...	31441
Other producers	...	...	...	...	...	...	...	...	...	...	...	...
Total [b]	163451	52195	262168	...	...	477814	186224	63079	303465	...	...	552768
less: Imputed bank service charge	...	...	...	...	...	...	...	...	...	...	...	...
Import duties	...	...	...	...	...	...	...	...	...	...	...	...
Value added tax	...	...	...	...	...	...	...	...	...	...	...	...
Other adjustments [c]	...	...	...	...	...	57720	...	...	...	...	...	64031
Total	...	...	...	...	...	535534	...	...	...	...	...	616799

Of which general government:

1 Agriculture, hunting, forestry and fishing	1454	1491	1337	...	...	4282	1654	1748	1781	...	...	5183
2 Mining and quarrying	–	–	–	...	...	–	–	–	–	...	...	–
3 Manufacturing	2698	498	–704	...	...	2492	2953	590	–696	...	...	2847
4 Electricity, gas and water	851	1005	–991	...	...	865	962	1174	–1202	...	...	934
5 Construction	4037	114	–	...	...	4151	4515	132	–	...	...	4647
6 Wholesale and retail trade, restaurants and hotels	11	–	34	...	...	45	13	–	25	...	...	38
7 Transport, storage and communication	294	151	–269	...	...	176	315	171	–291	...	...	195
8 Finance, insurance, real estate and business services	183	195	4	...	...	382	234	231	3	...	...	468
9 Community, social and personal services	12705	595	–165	...	...	13135	14400	711	–203	...	...	14908

India

	1990						1991					
	Compensation of employees	Capital consumption	Net operating surplus	Indirect taxes	less: Subsidies received	Value added	Compensation of employees	Capital consumption	Net operating surplus	Indirect taxes	less: Subsidies received	Value added
Total, industries of general government	22233	4049	−754	...	...	25528	25046	4757	−583	...	...	29220
Producers of government services	24520	2589	—	...	...	27109	28349	3092	—	...	...	31441
Total, general government	46753	6638	−754	...	...	52637	53395	7849	−583	...	...	60661

	1992						1993					
	Compensation of employees	Capital consumption	Net operating surplus	Indirect taxes	less: Subsidies received	Value added	Compensation of employees	Capital consumption	Net operating surplus	Indirect taxes	less: Subsidies received	Value added
All producers												
1 Agriculture, hunting, forestry and fishing	33113	12007	147925	...	...	193045	38979	13229	171497	...	...	223705
A Agriculture and hunting	30934	10961	136015	...	...	177910	36399	12006	157917	...	...	206322
B Forestry and logging	1029	257	7568	...	...	8854	1196	288	8352	...	...	9836
C Fishing	1150	789	4342	...	...	6281	1384	935	5228	...	...	7547
2 Mining and quarrying	4337	4696	5556	...	...	14589	4843	5148	6827	...	...	16818
3 Manufacturing	35940	17376	57728	...	...	111044	38158	19640	69848	...	...	127646
4 Electricity, gas and water	5262	9189	1663	...	...	16114	6178	10287	2414	...	...	18879
5 Construction	26981	1783	7936	...	...	36700	29635	1899	9165	...	...	40699
6 Wholesale and retail trade, restaurants and hotels	17911	2432	62426	...	...	82769	21278	2690	74056	...	...	98024
A Wholesale and retail trade	16547	1682	59675	...	...	77904	19604	1839	70720	...	...	92163
B Restaurants and hotels	1364	750	2751	...	...	4865	1674	851	3336	...	...	5861
7 Transport, storage and communication	16912	12098	19882	...	...	48892	19139	13554	23403	...	...	56096
A Transport and storage	14478	10425	16905	...	...	41808	16428	11575	19280	...	...	47283
B Communication	2434	1673	2977	...	...	7084	2711	1979	4123	...	...	8813
8 Finance, insurance, real estate and business services	10995	8363	33281	...	...	52639	12639	9565	44941	...	...	67145
A Financial institutions	10243	1204	19785	...	...	31232	11813	1526	30231	...	...	43570
B Insurance												
C Real estate and business services	752	7159	13496	...	...	21407	826	8039	14710	...	...	23575
9 Community, social and personal services	27602	1476	9652	...	...	38730	31180	1618	11114	...	...	43912
Total, Industries [a]	179053	69420	346049	...	...	594522	202029	77630	413265	...	...	692924
Producers of government services	32724	3526	—	...	...	36250	36028	3922	—	...	...	39950
Other producers	...	...	...	...	...	...	...	...	...	...	...	...
Total [b]	211777	72946	346049	...	...	630772	238057	81552	413265	...	...	732874
less: Imputed bank service charge	...	...	...	...	...	...	...	...	...	...	...	...
Import duties	...	...	...	...	...	...	...	...	...	...	...	...
Value added tax	...	...	...	...	...	...	...	...	...	...	...	...
Other adjustments [c]	...	...	...	...	...	75146	...	...	...	...	...	77875
Total	...	...	...	...	...	705918	...	...	...	...	...	810749
Of which general government:												
1 Agriculture, hunting, forestry and fishing	1931	1967	1840	...	...	5738	1981	2182	2312	...	...	6475
2 Mining and quarrying	—	—	—	...	...	—	...	...	...	...	...	...
3 Manufacturing	3418	661	−1074	...	...	3005	3704	688	−861	...	...	3531
4 Electricity, gas and water	1101	1324	−1225	...	...	1200	1273	1475	−1065	...	...	1683

India

	1992						1993					
	Compensation of employees	Capital consumption	Net operating surplus	Indirect taxes	less: Subsidies received	Value added	Compensation of employees	Capital consumption	Net operating surplus	Indirect taxes	less: Subsidies received	Value added
5 Construction	5195	147	–	...	...	5342	5198	150	–	...	...	5348
6 Wholesale and retail trade, restaurants and hotels	15	–	–19	...	...	–4	15	–	43	...	...	58
7 Transport, storage and communication	376	197	–217	...	...	356	461	208	–186	...	...	483
8 Finance, insurance, real estate and business services	327	263	19	...	...	609	375	297	6	...	...	678
9 Community, social and personal services	16420	815	–253	...	...	16982	18490	891	–278	...	...	19103
Total, industries of general government	28783	5374	–929	...	...	33228	31497	5891	–29	...	...	37359
Producers of government services	32724	3526	–	...	...	36250	36028	3922	–	...	...	39950
Total, general government	61507	8900	–929	...	...	69478	67525	9813	–29	...	...	77309

	1994						1995					
	Compensation of employees	Capital consumption	Net operating surplus	Indirect taxes	less: Subsidies received	Value added	Compensation of employees	Capital consumption	Net operating surplus	Indirect taxes	less: Subsidies received	Value added

All producers

1 Agriculture, hunting, forestry and fishing	45197	15224	198643	...	...	259064	48691	17764	210397	...	...	276852
A Agriculture and hunting	42201	13763	183195	...	...	239159	45328	16031	194254	...	...	255613
B Forestry and logging	1402	324	9428	...	...	11154	1557	379	9331	...	...	11267
C Fishing	1594	1137	6020	...	...	8751	1806	1354	6812	...	...	9972
2 Mining and quarrying	4958	6345	7576	...	...	18879	6336	7266	6952	...	...	20554
3 Manufacturing	45031	23640	91042	...	...	159713	55029	28231	115088	...	...	198348
4 Electricity, gas and water	6838	11819	5005	...	...	23662	8086	13623	6312	...	...	28021
5 Construction	34982	2148	10848	...	...	47978	42730	2487	13199	...	...	58416
6 Wholesale and retail trade, restaurants and hotels	26170	3161	89157	...	...	118488	32976	3724	106108	...	...	142808
A Wholesale and retail trade	24059	2131	85018	...	...	111208	30191	2480	100858	...	...	133529
B Restaurants and hotels	2111	1030	4139	...	...	7280	2785	1244	5250	...	...	9279
7 Transport, storage and communication	21982	15546	29152	...	...	66680	26116	17931	31318	...	...	75365
A Transport and storage	18856	13098	23562	...	...	55516	22504	14928	24484	...	...	61916
B Communication	3126	2448	5590	...	...	11164	3612	3003	6834	...	...	13449
8 Finance, insurance, real estate and business services	15693	11135	51640	...	...	78468	20270	13238	60967	...	...	94475
A Financial institutions	14604	2127	35472	...	...	52203	18858	2884	43572	...	...	65314
B Insurance												
C Real estate and business services	1089	9008	16168	...	...	26265	1412	10354	17395	...	...	29161
9 Community, social and personal services	35827	1857	12823	...	...	50507	42001	2156	15209	...	...	59366
Total, Industries [a]	236678	90875	495886	...	...	823439	282235	106420	565550	...	...	954205
Producers of government services	40116	4464	–	...	...	44580	46915	5166	–	...	...	52081
Other producers	...	...	...	...	...	...	...	...	...	...	...	...
Total [b]	276794	95339	495886	...	...	868019	329150	111586	565550	...	...	1006286
less: Imputed bank service charge	...	...	...	...	...	...	...	...	...	...	...	...
Import duties	...	...	...	...	...	...	...	...	...	...	...	...
Value added tax	...	...	...	...	...	...	...	...	...	...	...	...
Other adjustments [c]	...	...	...	...	...	95473	...	...	...	...	...	112678

India

	1994						1995					
	Compensation of employees	Capital consumption	Net operating surplus	Indirect taxes	less: Subsidies received	Value added	Compensation of employees	Capital consumption	Net operating surplus	Indirect taxes	less: Subsidies received	Value added
Total	...	...	...	...	...	963492	...	...	...	...	...	1118964

Of which general government:

1 Agriculture, hunting, forestry and fishing	2377	2435	2556	...	...	7368	2812	2795	2858	...	...	8465
2 Mining and quarrying	...	...	...	...	...	...	...	...	...	...	...	...
3 Manufacturing	4070	743	−89	...	...	3919	4450	802	−143	...	...	3818
4 Electricity, gas and water	1124	1663	−91	...	...	1869	1346	1960	142	...	...	1886
5 Construction	6414	157	–	...	...	6571	7492	165	–	...	...	7657
6 Wholesale and retail trade, restaurants and hotels	17	–	95	...	...	112	22	–	114	...	...	136
7 Transport, storage and communication	460	227	−21	...	...	476	523	258	−30	...	...	477
8 Finance, insurance, real estate and business services	360	338	9	...	...	707	408	395	9	...	...	812
9 Community, social and personal services	20862	1007	−422	...	...	21447	24331	1141	−54	...	...	24930
Total, industries of general government	35684	6570	215	...	...	42469	41384	7516	71	...	...	48181
Producers of government services	40116	4464	–	...	...	44580	46915	5166	–	...	...	52081
Total, general government	75800	11034	215	...	...	87049	88299	12682	71	...	...	100262

a Mixed income of self-employed workers is included in column "Compensation of employees".
b Gross domestic product in factor values.
c Item "Other adjustments" refers to indirect taxes net of subsidies.

Indonesia

General note

The preparation of national accounts statistics in Indonesia is undertaken by the Central Bureau of Statistics, Jakarta. The official estimates are generally in accordance with the United Nations System of National Accounts (1968 SNA). The following tables are prepared for the United Nations National Accounts Questionnaire. When the scope and coverage of the estimates differ for conceptual and statistical reasons from the definitions and classifications recommended in the SNA, a footnote is indicated to the relevant tables.

Gross domestic product

Gross domestic product is estimated mainly through the production approach.

Expenditures on the gross domestic product

The expenditure approach is used to estimate government final consumption expenditure, exports and imports of goods and services. Private final consumption expenditure is derived as residual. The commodity-flow approach is used for gross fixed capital formation. The main sources of data for the estimation of central government consumption expenditure are the budgetary accounts of the Department of Finance, while local governments provide data directly to the Central Bureau of Statistics (CBS). Benchmark data for capital formation are based on statistics of imports and domestic production of construction materials and machinery and equipment. For other years, import of machineries and equipments are obtained from import statistics, while domestic production is compiled by using production and implicit price indexes to extrapolate the benchmark estimates. The input-output ratios for buildings and structures have been established for 1971 on the basis of special surveys on construction projects in that year. Other years' estimates are extrapolated by quantity and price indexes of domestic production and imports of construction materials.

Estimates of exports and imports of goods and services are obtained from foreign trade and balance of payment statistics. For the constant price estimates, current values of government expenditure items are deflated by the consumer price index and by the wholesale price index. For gross fixed capital formation referring to buildings and structures, the benchmark values are extrapolated by quantity indicators of domestic production and volume indicators of imports of construction materials. Values of exports and imports are deflated by the corresponding unit value price indexes.

Cost structure of the gross domestic product

Consumption of fixed capital for manufacturing, electricity, gas and water, is estimated from information available at the CBS. For other sectors the estimates are based on the results of special surveys. The main source of data for net indirect taxes are the budgetary accounts of the central and local governments. Compensation of employees together with operating surplus is obtained as a residual.

Gross domestic product by kind of activity

The table on gross domestic product by kind of economic activity is prepared at market prices, i.e. producers' values. The production approach is used to estimate value added of most of the industries. The income approach is used for government and domestic services while gross output of trade and construction is estimated on the basis of the commodity-flow approach. For agriculture, main food crops production is compiled on the basis of information relating to area harvested and average yield for each crop obtained from the CBS. The prices used are based on farm-gate prices obtained from annual surveys. The consumption of vegetables by households is based on per capita consumption estimates derived from the Household Survey 1969/79 and 1976, extrapolated by population and price changes and adding one per cent to cover consumption outside households. For main food crops, commercial and estate crops, the value of intermediate inputs is based on cost-structure surveys. Estimates of livestock, forestry, and fishing are obtained from the departments concerned. For livestock, intermediate inputs are calculated as fixed percentages of gross output. The most important mining commodity is crude petroleum for which production data are available for all enterprises concerned. Estimates of prices and input costs are compiled on the basis of returns furnished by the largest firm. For the base-year 1971, data on output and input structure of manufacturing have been compiled for each industry group from statistics maintained by the CBS and from surveys and other studies undertaken. For other years industrial production indexes are compiled on the basis of output of selected manufactured products. For gross output of construction, the information on imports of construction materials is obtained from commodity imports statistics whereas estimates of domestically produced materials are based on the annual industrial surveys. The average ratios of intermediate inputs to gross output are based on data gathered from surveys.

Gross output of the trade sector is calculated by multiplying estimates of the producers' values of the marketed surplus of agricultural products, domestically produced manufactured goods, selected mining and quarrying products and the cost of imported goods by the percentage distribution mark-ups gathered

Indonesia

from special surveys undertaken in 1971. Estimates for other years are extrapolated by a quantity index of marketed surplus traded and an implicit price index. For railway transport, the annual reports of the State Railway Company constitute the main source of data for estimating gross output, intermediate input and value added. For road transport, gross output and input values are estimated by multiplying the average earning of each type of vehicle by the corresponding number of vehicles. For other transports, estimates are based on cost-structure surveys and data from concerned authorities and companies. The information of gross output and value added of the banking sector is based on the data compiled annually by the Bank of Indonesia supplemented by special inquiries for other financial intermediaries.

Basic data relating to real estate and business services are limited and rough procedures are adopted by using information gathered from the special surveys. For government services, estimates are obtained from current budget expenditure and information furnished by local bodies. Estimates of other services are calculated for the year 1971 as the benchmark year, and estimates of other years are extrapolated by using employment and price indicators.

For the constant price estimates, revaluation is used for the agricultural sector, while value added of public administration and defence, is deflated by a moving average of the consumer price index. In all other sectors value added is extrapolated by various quantity indicators and indexes.

1.1 Expenditure on the gross domestic product, in current prices

Thousand million Indonesian rupiahs

	1986	1987	1988	1989	1990	1991	1992	1993	1994	1995	1996	1997
1 Government final consumption expenditure	11329	11764	12756	15698	18649	20785	24731	29757	31014	35584	40299	42293
2 Private final consumption expenditure	63355	71989	89722	100234	124184	145540	157910	192958	228119	279876	331586	388255
3 Gross capital formation	29025	39146	43171	58479	64790	80029	91511	97213	118708	145118	164025	197263
A Increase in stocks	4243	8166	4815	10773	5032	12541	18737	10546	13327	15900	6372	17994
B Gross fixed capital formation	24782	30980	38356	47706	59758	67488	72774	86667	105381	129218	157653	179269
4 Exports of goods and services	20010	29874	35585	43614	53289	63865	78723	88231	101332	119593	137533	174423
5 less: Imports of goods and services	21036	27956	31566	38443	50046	60249	70481	78383	96953	125657	140812	177898
equals: Gross domestic product	102683	124817	149669	179582	210866	249969	282395	329776	382219	454514	532631	624337

1.2 Expenditure on the gross domestic product, in constant prices

Thousand million Indonesian rupiahs

	1986	1987	1988	1989	1990	1991	1992	1993	1994	1995	1996	1997
At constant prices of:			1983 / 1993									
1 Government final consumption expenditure	9241	9226	9924 / 23080	25458	26689	28094	29702	29757	30443	30851	31681	31740
2 Private final consumption expenditure	50530	52200	54225 / 123144	132330	155094	167455	172640	192958	208062	234245	259719	273593
3 Gross capital formation	27755	27646	26321 / 64766	72737	80652	88372	97427	97213	113425	128239	132490	138767
A Increase in stocks	6333	5049	1120 / 12650	12846	11133	9884	16125	10546	14836	15853	3791	4733
B Gross fixed capital formation	21422	22597	25201 / 52116	59891	69519	78488	81302	86667	98589	112386	128699	134034
4 Exports of goods and services	22460	25745	26016 / 53950	59566	59808	71702	82605	88231	97002	104492	112391	119445
5 less: Imports of goods and services	19906	20299	16504 / 43533	48570	58981	68856	74900	78383	94291	114035	121863	129858
equals: Gross domestic product	90081	94518	99981 / 221407	241521	263262	286765	307474	329776	354641	383792	414419	433685

Indonesia

1.3 Cost components of the gross domestic product

Thousand million Indonesian rupiahs

	1986	1987	1988	1989	1990	1991	1992	1993	1994	1995	1996	1997
1 Indirect taxes, net	6529	7130	9033	12445	13420	15004	17795	20544	...	...	...	...
2 Consumption of fixed capital	5134	6241	7105	8365	9784	11380	13045	14907	...	...	...	...
3 Compensation of employees paid by resident producers to ..	91020	111446	125967	146375	172393	201118	229946	262575	...	...	...	...
4 Operating surplus									...	...	...	...
equals: Gross domestic product ..	102683	124817	142105	167185	195597	227502	260786	298026	...	...	...	...

1.10 Gross domestic product by kind of activity, in current prices

Thousand million Indonesian rupiahs

	1986	1987	1988	1989	1990	1991	1992	1993	1994	1995	1996	1997
1 Agriculture, hunting, forestry and fishing	24871	29116	33651	38894	40930	45636	52746	58963	66072	77696	88041	100349
2 Mining and quarrying	11503	17267	18200	22921	25634	31953	30587	31497	33507	40195	45916	59492
3 Manufacturing	17185	21150	29484	35441	43569	53379	62016	73556	89241	109889	135561	159830
4 Electricity, gas and water	647	747	873	1508	1489	1898	2472	3290	4577	5655	6594	7566
5 Construction	5314	6087	7219	8991	11795	13762	16878	22513	28017	34452	42025	47013
6 Wholesale and retail trade, restaurants and hotels [a]	17122	21048	25345	30415	35824	41981	47144	55298	63559	75839	88878	104433
7 Transport, storage and communication	6407	7443	9884	10936	13362	16968	19714	23249	27353	30795	34926	42232
8 Finance, insurance, real estate and business services [b]	7013	8144	9006	12196	16403	20835	23994	28048	34506	39510	44371	49585
9 Community, social and personal services	4315	4903	6161	6706	7538	8339	9447	10903	12335	14127	16547	20241
Total, Industries	94376	115905	139823	168008	196544	234751	264996	307318	359464	427959	503099	590738
Producers of government services	8307	8912	9846	11574	14322	15218	17399	22458	22755	26555	29532	33599
Other producers	...	...	...	...	...	...	...	...	...	...	...	...
Subtotal	102683	124817	149669	179582	210866	249969	282395	329776	382219	454514	532631	624337
less: Imputed bank service charge	...	...	...	...	...	...	...	...	...	...	...	...
plus: Import duties	...	...	...	...	...	...	...	...	...	...	...	...
plus: Value added tax	...	...	...	...	...	...	...	...	...	...	...	...
plus: Other adjustments	...	...	...	...	...	...	...	...	...	...	...	...
equals: Gross domestic product ..	102683	124817	149669	179582	210866	249969	282395	329776	382219	454514	532631	624337

a Restaurants and hotels are included in item "Community, social and personal services".   b Business services are included in item "Community, social and personal services".

1.11 Gross domestic product by kind of activity, in constant prices

Thousand million Indonesian rupiahs

	1986	1987	1988	1989	1990	1991	1992	1993	1994	1995	1996	1997
At constant prices of: 1983												
1993												
1 Agriculture, hunting, forestry and fishing	19799	20224	21214									
			49073	51476	53056	54583	58002	58963	59291	61885	63743	64149
2 Mining and quarrying	16309	16366	15893									
			23241	24832	26628	29969	30461	31497	33262	35502	37556	38182
3 Manufacturing	14678	16235	18182									
			43516	48426	54211	59941	66042	73556	82649	91637	102259	108631
4 Electricity, gas and water	430	495	549									
			1850	2100	2508	2720	2961	3290	3703	4292	4541	5414

Indonesia

Thousand million Indonesian rupiahs

	1986	1987	1988	1989	1990	1991	1992	1993	1994	1995	1996	1997
	At constant prices of:	1983										
			1993									
5 Construction	4609	4803	5259									
			11499	13022	15226	17487	19664	22513	25858	29198	32924	35037
6 Wholesale and retail trade, restaurants and hotels [a]	13399	14356	15657									
			33963	37714	41725	46669	50344	55298	59504	64231	69372	73161
7 Transport, storage and communication	4668	4939	5212									
			15272	16917	18474	20040	21618	23249	25189	27326	29701	32204
8 Finance, insurance, real estate and business services [b]	6028	6313	6514									
			15574	18317	21479	24309	26164	28048	30901	34313	37401	39184
9 Community, social and personal services	3299	3422	3570									
			8685	8885	9218	9670	10207	10903	11533	12360	13272	14107
Total, Industries	83219	87153	92049									
			202673	221689	242524	265385	285462	307318	331889	360746	391084	410066
Producers of government services	6862	7366	7932									
			18734	19832	20738	21380	22012	22458	22752	23046	23335	23619
Other producers	...	...	...	...	...	...	...	...	...	...	...	...
Subtotal	90081	94518	99981									
			221407	241521	263262	286765	307474	329776	354641	383792	414419	433685
less: Imputed bank service charge	...	...	...	...	...	...	...	...	...	...	...	...
plus: Import duties	...	...	...	...	...	...	...	...	...	...	...	...
plus: Value added tax	...	...	...	...	...	...	...	...	...	...	...	...
plus: Other adjustments	...	...	...	...	...	...	...	...	...	...	...	...
equals: Gross domestic product	90081	94518	99981									
			221407	241521	263262	286765	307474	329776	354641	383792	414419	433685

a Restaurants and hotels are included in item "Community, social and personal services".   b Business services are included in item "Community, social and personal services".

1.12 Relations among national accounting aggregates

Thousand million Indonesian rupiahs

	1986	1987	1988	1989	1990	1991	1992	1993	1994	1995	1996	1997
Gross domestic product	102683	124817	149669	179582	210866	249969	282395	329776	382219	454514	532631	624337
plus: Net factor income from the rest of the world	–4193	–6022	–6922	–8074	–9616	–10913	–12542	–12553	–10248	–13366	–14272	–19118
equals: Gross national product	98490	118795	142747	171508	201250	239056	269853	317223	371971	441148	518359	605219
less: Consumption of fixed capital	5134	6241	7105	8365	9784	11380	13045	...	...	...	...	...
equals: National income	93356	112554	135642	163143	191466	227676	256808	...	...	...	...	...
plus: Net current transfers from the rest of the world	...	...	...	...	...	...	...	...	...	...	...	...
equals: National disposable income	...	...	...	...	...	...	...	...	...	...	...	...
less: Final consumption	74684	83753	102478	115932	142833	166325	182641	222715	259133	315460	371885	430548
equals: Net saving	...	...	...	...	...	...	...	...	...	...	...	...
less: Surplus of the nation on current transactions	...	...	...	...	...	...	...	...	...	...	...	...
equals: Net capital formation	...	...	...	...	...	...	...	...	...	...	...	...

Iran, Islamic Republic of

General note

The preparation of national accounts statistics in Iran is undertaken by the National Accounts Department, Bank Markazi Jomhouri Islami Iran, Tehran. The official estimates are published in the annual bulletin *Bank Markazi Jomhouri Islami Iran, Economic Report and Balance Sheet*. Detailed data as well as description of sources and methods used for national accounts estimation are published in the latest volume of *National Accounts of Iran*. The estimates are generally in accordance with the classifications and definitions recommended in the United Nations System of National Accounts (1968 SNA). Input-output tables have been compiled for the years 1965, 1969, 1973 and 1984. The following tables have been prepared from successive replies to the United Nations National Accounts Questionnaire. When the scope and coverage of the estimates differ for conceptual or statistical reasons from the definitions and classifications recommended in SNA, a footnote is indicated to the relevant tables.

Gross domestic product

Gross domestic product is estimated mainly through the production approach.

Expenditures on the gross domestic product

The expenditure approach is used to estimate all components of gross domestic product by expenditure type except gross fixed capital formation in machinery which is calculated mainly by commodity-flow approach. Estimates for government final consumption expenditure are based on records from all sectors of general government. Private final consumption expenditure is estimated using data from family budget surveys. The estimates of gross fixed capital formation in private construction are derived from annual surveys on construction. The data on investment in construction by the public sector is obtained from the accounts of different government units. The capital formation in machinery and equipment is estimated through commodity-flow approach using information on domestic production, imports and exports of capital goods. The estimates of exports and imports of goods and services are obtained from the balance of payments accounts and foreign trade statistics. For the constant price estimates all items of gross domestic product by expenditure type are deflated by appropriate price indices.

Cost structure of the gross domestic product

The estimates of compensation of employees are obtained in the process of estimating value added by industrial origin. Consumption of fixed capital is estimated according to useful lifetime of different type of capital goods. Operating surplus is obtained as a residual. Estimates of indirect taxes and subsidies are based on government accounts.

Gross domestic product by kind of activity

The table of gross domestic product by kind of economic activity is prepared in factor values. The production approach is used to estimate the value added of most industries. The income approach is used for producers of government services, communication and part of other services. The agricultural estimates are based on annual surveys of agriculture, carried out by Ministry of Agriculture. The estimates are checked using the results of the annual family budget surveys. Data on the production of red meat are based on information supplied by slaughter houses in urban areas and on the results of expenditure surveys in rural areas. The data are then converted to current price estimates by using wholesale price index. Statistics concerning forestry and fishing are obtained from concerned agencies. Mining estimates are based on annual sample surveys and the 1991 Census of Mining. The value added of oil sector is derived from the reports of the Ministry of Oil. The manufacturing estimates for large establishments which employ 10 workers or more are based on the results of the annual surveys of manufacturing. For small establishments, estimates are derived using the sample surveys of 1986 and information from other sources. The estimates of electricity, gas and water are based on information obtained from the government accounts. Estimates for private construction in the urban areas are obtained from the results of Bank Markazi's annual surveys with adjustments made to cover contractors' profits which are not included in the surveys. As for the rural areas, the results of 1973 Survey of Rural Construction by the Statistical Center of Iran are extrapolated using information concerning construction in small towns.

For trade sector the gross margin is calculated using the results or survey of wholesale and retail trade in the urban areas. Estimates for transport sector are generally based on the sample surveys by Bank Markazi Jomhouri Islami Iran and financial statements of the government organizations involved. The value added of financial institutions and insurance is obtained directly from the financial statements of concerned institutions. The estimates for dwellings are based on data obtained from family budget surveys and imputations are made for owner-occupied dwellings. For producers of government services estimates are derived from government accounts. Estimates for social and personal services are based on information from various sources mainly the family budget surveys.

For constant price estimates, the current values are deflated by an appropriate price index for each kind of economic activity.

Iran, Islamic Republic of

1.1 Expenditure on the gross domestic product, in current prices

Thousand million Iranian rials — Fiscal year beginning 21 March

	1986	1987	1988	1989	1990	1991	1992	1993	1994	1995	1996	1997
1 Government final consumption expenditure	2371	2707	3199	3294	4054	5367	6927	13644	16177	23053	31283	...
2 Private final consumption expenditure	10439	12226	14906	18448	24071	31677	41187	51623	71963	108922	143664	...
A Households	10307	12086	14775	18369	23943	31655	41164	51262	71675	108500	143109	...
B Private non-profit institutions serving households	132	139	131	79	127	22	23	361	288	422	555	...
3 Gross capital formation	3593	5079	4253	6600	10490	16650	23507	27157	31118	35004	46271	...
A Increase in stocks	1099	2417	1296	2891	4827	5806	8867	6499[a]	1265[a]	−6507[a]	−13203[a]	...
B Gross fixed capital formation	2494	2662	2957	3709	5663	10844	14640	20658	29853	41511	59474	...
Residential buildings	1269	1318	1315	1572	2030	3051	3833	5408	6608	8914	...	...
Non-residential buildings [b]	826	881	998	1096	1871	3324	4357	6587	8667	11948	...	...
Other construction and land improvement, etc.											...	...
Other	399	463	644	1042	1761	4469	6450	8663	14578	20649	...	...
4 Exports of goods and services	553	837	1514	2773	5395	7439	9864	22617	31909	36747	43828	...
5 less: Imports of goods and services	935	950	1756	3594	6792	9749	12319	21431	22785	24851	32305	...
Statistical discrepancy	207	51	189	266	−573	−1277	−2703	...	...	...	...	...
equals: Gross domestic product	16227	19949	22304	27787	36645	50107	66463	93610	128382	178875	232742	...

a Item "Increase in stocks" includes a statistical discrepancy.   b Including item "other construction and land improvement etc.".

1.2 Expenditure on the gross domestic product, in constant prices

Thousand million Iranian rials — Fiscal year beginning 21 March

	1986	1987	1988	1989	1990	1991	1992	1993	1994	1995	1996	1997
At constant prices of: 1982												
1 Government final consumption expenditure	1508	1403	1396	1189	1337	1450	1552	1820	1899	1955	2073	...
2 Private final consumption expenditure	6544	6141	6172	6327	7564	8281	8725	8928	9124	9358	9644	...
A Households	6460	6075	6120	6298	7523	8277	8720	8866	9090	9323	9608	...
B Private non-profit institutions serving households	84	67	52	29	40	5	5	62	34	35	36	...
3 Gross capital formation	2057	2058	1432	1766	2201	2764	3087	2214	1488	1733	2278	...
A Increase in stocks	411	698	288	549	822	821	1010	81	−718	−544	−169	...
B Gross fixed capital formation	1646	1361	1144	1217	1379	1943	2077	2133	2206	2277	2447	...
Residential buildings	794	665	508	508	493	572	584	573	666	690	...	...
Non-residential buildings	531	451	386	356	425	590	643	697	676	700	...	...
Other construction and land improvement, etc.											...	...
Other	320	245	249	353	461	781	850	863	864	887	...	...
4 Exports of goods and services	1221	1557	1730	1866	2253	2529	2718	3155	3196	2931	2883	...
5 less: Imports of goods and services	946	1006	791	946	1274	1651	1627	1362	822	662	785	...
Statistical discrepancy [a]	−134	214	−470	−421	−1149	−1192	−1576	−1671	−1704	−1574	−1543	...
equals: Gross domestic product	10249	10368	9468	9782	10930	12181	12879	13084	13181	13741	14550	...

a Item "Statistical discrepancy" includes terms of trade adjustment.

Iran, Islamic Republic of

1.3 Cost components of the gross domestic product

Thousand million Iranian rials — Fiscal year beginning 21 March

	1986	1987	1988	1989	1990	1991	1992	1993	1994	1995	1996	1997
1 Indirect taxes, net	613	665	551	758	890	1435	2062	92	−969	−1925	−909	...
A Indirect taxes	799	816	691	998	1410	2130	3220	2348	2792	3085	5712	...
B less: Subsidies	186	151	140	239	520	695	1158	2256	3761	5010	6621	...
2 Consumption of fixed capital	2299	2886	3290	3957	5443	7601	9919	14276	18967	28074	38026	...
3 Compensation of employees paid by resident producers to ..	13109	16347	18275	22807	30884	42348	57185	79242	110384	152726	...	...
4 Operating surplus	...	...	...	...	...	...	...	...	...	...	...	...
Statistical discrepancy	207	51	189	266	−573	−1277	−2703	...	...	...	...	...
equals: Gross domestic product ..	16227	19949	22304	27787	36645	50107	66463	93610	128382	178875	232742	...

1.4 General government current receipts and disbursements

Thousand million Iranian rials — Fiscal year beginning 21 March

	1986	1987	1988	1989	1990	1991	1992	1993	1994	1995	1996	1997
Receipts												
1 Operating surplus	...	...	...	...	...	...	...	...	...	...	...	...
2 Property and entrepreneurial income	450	790	1097	1972	1148	1074	1142	10061	21617	26823	32941	...
3 Taxes, fees and contributions	1595	1686	1696	2036	2903	4325	6311	6460	8358	11752	15620	...
A Indirect taxes	799	816	691	998	1410	2130	3220	2348	2792	3085	5712	...
B Direct taxes	511	563	638	642	955	1396	1991	2616	3854	5649	6162	...
C Social security contributions	281	302	362	389	530	771	1056	1434	1640	2903	3529	...
D Compulsory fees, fines and penalties	5	5	6	8	9	28	44	62	72	115	217	...
4 Other current transfers	281	415	100	111	3061	4308	5070	6336	2108	7998	14097	...
Total current receipts of general government	2325	2891	2892	4118	7112	9707	12523	22857	32083	46573	62658	...
Disbursements												
1 Government final consumption expenditure	2371	2707	3199	3294	4054	5367	6927	13644	16177	23053	31283	...
A Compensation of employees	1927	2182	2466	2607	3092	4193	5487	10578	12464	16791	...	...
B Consumption of fixed capital	...	...	...	...	...	...	...	...	...	...	...	...
C Purchases of goods and services, net	443	526	733	688	963	1174	1439	3066	3713	6262	...	...
D less: Own-account fixed capital formation	...	...	...	...	...	...	...	...	...	...	...	...
E Indirect taxes paid, net	...	...	...	...	...	...	...	...	...	...	...	...
2 Property income	5	4	5	3	3	2	46	20	22	8	1	...
A Interest	5	4	5	3	3	2	46	20	22	8	1	...
B Net land rent and royalties ..	−	−	−	−	...	...	...	...	...	...	...	...
3 Subsidies	186	151	140	239	520	695	1159	2256	3761	5010	6621	...
4 Other current transfers	402	614	772	736	1283	1735	2126	2757	5585	7356	9806	...
A Social security benefits	270	290	349	353	502	981	1227	1328	2546	2727	3540	...
B Social assistance grants												...
C Other	132	323	423	383	780	754	899	1429	3039	4629	6266	...
5 Net saving	−637	−584	−1223	−153	1252	1908	2265	4180	6538	11146	14947	...
Total current disbursements and net saving of general government	2325	2891	2892	4118	7112	9707	12523	22857	32083	46573	62658	...

Iran, Islamic Republic of

1.7 External transactions on current account, summary

Thousand million Iranian rials	1986	1987	1988	1989	1990	1991	1992	1993	1994	1995	1996	1997
Payments to the rest of the world												
1 Imports of goods and services	935	950	1756	3594	6792	9749	12320	21431	22785	24851	32305	...
A Imports of merchandise, c.i.f.	911	931	1729	3494	6624	8617	10717	20600	22503	24110	31516	...
B Other [a]	24	20	28	100	168	1132	1603	831	282	741	789	...
2 Factor income to rest of the world	61	65	177	382	531	991	1044	4178	4081	3111	4366	...
A Compensation of employees	56	61	164	357	505	872	815	3935	3421	1722	2312	...
B Property and entrepreneurial income	5	5	12	25	25	119	229	243	660	1389	2054	...
3 Current transfers to the rest of the world	...	...	...	...	...	...	...	...	...	...	...	...
4 Surplus of the nation on current transactions	−401	−153	−358	−1032	−1660	−1847	−2522	−1299	6109	10017	8704	...
Payments to the rest of the world and surplus of the nation on current transfers	596	863	1574	2944	5662	8893	10842	24310	32975	37979	45375	...
Receipts from the rest of the world												
1 Exports of goods and services	553	837	1514	2773	5395	7439	9864	22617	31909	36747	43828	...
A Exports of merchandise, f.o.b.	70	81	10	27	24	159	101	147	178	615	417	...
B Other [b]	483	756	1504	2746	5371	7280	9763	22470	31731	36132	43411	...
2 Factor income from rest of the world	43	26	60	170	267	1454	978	1693	1066	1232	1547	...
A Compensation of employees	15	12	27	87	120	796	559	1458	826	679	590	...
B Property and entrepreneurial income	28	14	34	84	147	658	419	235	240	553	957	...
3 Current transfers from rest of the world	...	...	...	...	...	...	...	...	...	...	...	...
Receipts from the rest of the world on current transactions	596	863	1574	2944	5662	8893	10842	24310	32975	37979	45375	...

a Item "Other" of Imports of goods and services refers to imports of services only.
b Item "Other" of exports of goods and services includes export of oil.

1.8 Capital transactions of the nation, summary

Thousand million Iranian rials	1986	1987	1988	1989	1990	1991	1992	1993	1994	1995	1996	1997
Finance of gross capital formation												
Gross saving	3192	4926	3895	5568	8829	14803	20985	25857	37227	45021	54975	...
1 Consumption of fixed capital	2299	2886	3290	3957	5443	7601	9919	14276	18967	28074	38026	...
2 Net saving	894	2040	604	1611	3387	7202	11066	11581	18260	16947	16949	...
less: Surplus of the nation on current transactions	−401	−153	−358	−1032	−1660	−1847	−2522	−1299	6109	10017	8704	...
Finance of gross capital formation	3593	5079	4253	6600	10490	16650	23507	27156	31118	35004	46271	...
Gross capital formation												
Increase in stocks	1099	2417	1296	2891	4827	5806	8867	6499	1265	−6507	−13203	...
Gross fixed capital formation	2494	2662	2957	3709	5663	10844	14640	20657	29853	41511	59474	...
1 General government [a]	1094	1100	1201	1424	2616	4240	6003	9971	13349	18779	26232	...

Iran, Islamic Republic of

Thousand million Iranian rials	1986	1987	1988	1989	1990	1991	1992	1993	1994	1995	1996	1997
2 Corporate and quasi-corporate enterprises	...	...	...	...	...	...	...	...	...	...	...	...
3 Other [b]	1401	1562	1756	2285	3046	6604	8637	10686	16504	22732	33242	...
Gross capital formation	3593	5079	4253	6600	10490	16650	23507	27156	31118	35004	46271	...

a Public corporate and quasi corporate enterprises are included in item "General government".   b Private corporate and quasi-corporate enterprises are included in item "Other".

1.10 Gross domestic product by kind of activity, in current prices

Thousand million Iranian rials	1986	1987	1988	1989	1990	1991	1992	1993	1994	1995	1996	1997
1 Agriculture, hunting, forestry and fishing	3753	4891	5209	6670	8419	11222	15392	19446	27273	46892	48911	...
2 Mining and quarrying [a]	747	1005	1100	1845	3967	4251	6189	16990	25069	29952	37542	...
3 Manufacturing	1354	1837	2288	2906	4414	6833	9218	12682	17725	25877	33882	...
4 Electricity, gas and water	163	201	261	305	395	554	834	1079	1322	1855	3465	...
5 Construction	1153	1168	1111	1288	1438	2129	2551	3134	4429	6346	10346	...
6 Wholesale and retail trade, restaurants and hotels	2753	3569	4469	5529	6542	8646	11308	14536	19978	27981	36903	...
7 Transport, storage and communication	1133	1316	1491	1791	2652	4371	5274	6582	8167	11435	13721	...
8 Finance, insurance, real estate and business services	2217	2519	3001	3614	4296	5899	7579	9698	12273	16331	23873	...
9 Community, social and personal services [b]	380	454	560	623	817	1076	1403	1754	2421	3283	4729	...
Total, Industries	13651	16960	19490	24570	32940	44981	59748	85901	118657	169952	213372	...
Producers of government services	2044	2330	2401	2607	3092	4201	5327	8576	11689	16832	20911	...
Other producers	...	...	...	...	...	...	...	...	...	...	...	...
Subtotal	15695	19290	21891	27177	36032	49182	65075	94477	130346	186784	234283	...
less: Imputed bank service charge	81	6	137	148	277	510	674	959	995	659	632	...
plus: Import duties	...	...	...	...	...	...	...	...	...	...	...	...
plus: Value added tax	...	...	...	...	...	...	...	...	...	...	...	...
plus: Other adjustments [c]	613	665	551	758	890	1435	2062	92	-969	-7250	-909	...
equals: Gross domestic product	16227	19949	22304	27787	36645	50107	66463	93610	128382	178875	232742	...

a Oil production is included in item "Mining and quarrying".   b Item "Other producers" is included in item "Community, social and personal services".   c Item "Other adjustments" refers to indirect taxes net of subsidies.

1.11 Gross domestic product by kind of activity, in constant prices

Thousand million Iranian rials	1986	1987	1988	1989	1990	1991	1992	1993	1994	1995	1996	1997
At constant prices of: 1982												
1 Agriculture, hunting, forestry and fishing	2651	2716	2648	2746	2968	3120	3352	3536	3606	3739	3818	...
2 Mining and quarrying [a]	1465	1664	1811	1948	2328	2585	2626	2722	2576	2602	2645	...
3 Manufacturing	1148	1276	1302	1418	1644	1940	2002	1992	2061	2181	2294	...
4 Electricity, gas and water	174	193	186	207	247	285	309	339	377	400	421	...
5 Construction	649	550	433	426	438	508	549	562	597	629	690	...
6 Wholesale and retail trade, restaurants and hotels	1045	1042	1008	1069	1136	1258	1325	1370	1374	1309	1400	...
7 Transport, storage and communication	786	643	600	655	796	926	1032	1113	1180	1288	1160	...
8 Finance, insurance, real estate and business services	1362	1300	1269	1305	1392	1512	1630	1707	1760	1866	2023	...

Iran, Islamic Republic of

Thousand million Iranian rials	1986	1987	1988	1989	1990	1991	1992	1993	1994	1995	1996	Fiscal year beginning 21 March 1997
At constant prices of: 1982												
9 Community, social and personal services [b]	236	262	282	267	299	329	353	360	368	334	411	...
Total, Industries	9515	9646	9540	10040	11247	12463	13178	13701	13899	14348	14862	...
Producers of government services	1226	1093	871	805	876	922	1003	1194	1203	1160	1327	...
Other producers	...	...	...	...	...	...	...	...	...	...	...	...
Subtotal	10741	10739	10410	10846	12124	13385	14181	14895	15102	15508	16189	...
less: Imputed bank service charge	48	3	50	46	78	121	131	153	117	52	40	...
plus: Import duties	...	...	...	...	...	...	...	...	...	...	...	...
plus: Value added tax	...	...	...	...	...	...	...	...	...	...	...	...
plus: Other adjustments [c]	387	348	234	267	265	356	401	13	−100	−146	−55	...
equals: Gross domestic product [d]	11080	11085	10594	11067	12311	13620	14451	14755	14885	15310	16094	...

a Oil production is included in item "Mining and quarrying".
b Item "Other producers" is included in item "Community, social and personal services".
c Item "Other adjustments" refers to indirect taxes net of subsidies.
d Gross domestic product in factor values.

1.12 Relations among national accounting aggregates

Thousand million Iranian rials	1986	1987	1988	1989	1990	1991	1992	1993	1994	1995	1996	Fiscal year beginning 21 March 1997
Gross domestic product	16227	19949	22304	27787	36645	50107	66463	93610	128382	178875	232741	...
plus: Net factor income from the rest of the world	−19	−39	−116	−212	−264	463	−67	−2485	−3015	−1879	−2819	...
Factor income from rest of the world	43	26	60	170	267	1454	978	1693	1066	1232	1547	...
less: Factor income to the rest of the world	61	65	177	382	531	991	1044	4178	4081	3111	4366	...
equals: Gross national product	16208	19910	22188	27575	36381	50570	66396	91125	125367	176996	229923	...
less: Consumption of fixed capital	2299	2886	3290	3957	5443	7601	9919	14276	18967	28074	38026	...
equals: National income	13910	17024	18897	23619	30939	42969	56477	76849	106400	148922	191896	...
plus: Net current transfers from the rest of the world	...	...	...	...	...	...	...	...	...	...	...	...
equals: National disposable income	13910	17024	18897	23619	30939	42969	56477	76849	106400	148922	191896	...
less: Final consumption	12809	14933	18104	21742	28125	37044	48113	65268	88140	131975	174947	...
Statistical discrepancy	−207	−51	−189	−266	573	1277	2703	...	...	...	...	...
equals: Net saving	894	2040	604	1611	3387	7202	11067	11581	18260	16947	16949	...
less: Surplus of the nation on current transactions	−401	−153	−358	−1032	−1660	−1847	−2522	−1299	6109	10017	8704	...
equals: Net capital formation	1294	2193	963	2644	5047	9049	13589	12880	12151	6930	8245	...

2.1 Government final consumption expenditure by function, in current prices

Thousand million Iranian rials	1986	1987	1988	1989	1990	1991	1992	1993	1994	1995	1996	Fiscal year beginning 21 March 1997
1 General public services	91	87	111	128	133	186	130	386	375	357	...	...
2 Defence	867	1099	1345	1117	1124	1205	1323	2007	3303	4731	...	...
3 Public order and safety	145	136	145	156	228	357	353	470	464	477	...	...
4 Education	586	561	673	808	1049	1434	1742	2692	2664	2587	...	...
5 Health	162	152	209	276	301	416	539	877	869	1413	...	...
6 Social security and welfare	198	214	227	274	388	521	451	835	828	2026	...	...
7 Housing and community amenities	14	9	10	12	14	39	233	344	346	1072	...	...

Iran, Islamic Republic of

Thousand million Iranian rials	1986	1987	1988	1989	1990	1991	1992	1993	1994	1995	1996	1997
8 Recreational, cultural and religious affairs	41	37	44	48	68	120	135	334	336	511	...	...
9 Economic services	109	214	236	200	293	393	1213	4018	3986	6111	...	...
10 Other functions [a]	158	200	197	274	458	696	808	1681	3006	3768	...	...
Total government final consumption expenditures	2371	2707	3199	3294	4054	5367	6927	13644	16177	23053	...	...

[a] Beginning 1985, the estimates of "Other functions" exclude municipalities and social security fund.

2.2 Government final consumption expenditure by function, in constant prices

Thousand million Iranian rials	1986	1987	1988	1989	1990	1991	1992	1993	1994	1995	1996	1997
At constant prices of: 1982												
1 General public services	55	41	42	41	38	51	25	40	29	30	...	...
2 Defence	600	639	702	500	505	328	486	535	542	405	...	...
3 Public order and safety	88	64	54	49	65	97	67	49	40	41	...	...
4 Education	354	267	252	256	298	391	331	283	212	221	...	...
5 Health	98	72	78	87	85	114	102	92	100	121	...	...
6 Social security and welfare	120	102	85	87	110	141	86	88	70	173	...	...
7 Housing and community amenities	8	4	4	4	4	11	44	36	32	91	...	...
8 Recreational, cultural and religious affairs	25	18	17	15	19	32	26	35	29	44	...	...
9 Economic services	66	102	88	63	83	107	231	421	479	522	...	...
10 Other functions [a]	96	95	73	87	130	178	154	241	366	308	...	...
Total government final consumption expenditures	1508	1403	1396	1189	1337	1450	1552	1820	1899	1956	...	...

[a] Beginning 1985, the estimates of "Other functions" exclude municipalities and social security fund.

2.5 Private final consumption expenditure by type and purpose, in current prices

Thousand million Iranian rials	1986	1987	1988	1989	1990	1991	1992	1993	1994	1995	1996	1997
Final consumption expenditure of resident households												
1 Food, beverages and tobacco [a]	4834	5736	7023	8573	10204	11259	14493	18439	26866	42140	56979	...
2 Clothing and footwear	851	1136	1658	2220	2823	4077	5275	5715	7491	11766	15049	...
3 Gross rent, fuel and power	2641	2913	3529	4319	5969	9490	12027	15817	19750	27413	31474	...
4 Furniture, furnishings and household equipment and operation	552	678	695	1020	1530	2138	2744	3639	4977	7590	9618	...
5 Medical care and health expenses	380	488	580	624	924	1315	2025	2115	3675	5479	6272	...
6 Transport and communication	617	721	746	853	1210	1710	2334	2999	4451	7083	11389	...
7 Recreational, entertainment, education and cultural services	155	175	202	261	400	660	1023	1218	1944	3094	3248	...
8 Miscellaneous goods and services	278	239	342	500	883	1006	1243	1320	2521	3935	9080	...
Total final consumption expenditure in the domestic market by households, of which	10307	12086	14775	18369	23943	31655	41164	51262	71675	108500	143109	...
A Durable goods	341	380	331	432	613	1374	2131	2640	3654	4918	6440	...
B Semi-durable goods	1179	1510	2100	2929	3394	5255	6673	7368	9948	16685	22039	...
C Non-durable goods	5526	6591	7986	9672	12833	13336	17406	22156	32018	50493	66545	...
D Services	3261	3605	4357	5336	7104	11690	14954	19098	26055	36404	48085	...
plus: Direct purchases abroad by resident households	...	...	...	...	...	...	...	...	...	...	...	...

Iran, Islamic Republic of

Thousand million Iranian rials	1986	1987	1988	1989	1990	1991	1992	1993	1994	1995	1996	1997
less: Direct purchases in the domestic market by non-resident households	...	...	...	...	...	...	...	...	...	...	...	...
equals: Final consumption expenditure of resident households	10307	12086	14775	18369	23943	31655	41164	51262	71675	108500	143109	...

Final consumption expenditures by private non-profit organisations serving households

	1986	1987	1988	1989	1990	1991	1992	1993	1994	1995	1996	1997
1 Research and science	...	...	...	...	...	...	...	...	...	...	...	...
2 Education	...	...	...	...	...	...	...	...	...	...	...	...
3 Medical and other health services	...	...	...	...	...	...	...	...	...	...	...	...
4 Welfare services	...	...	...	...	...	...	...	...	...	...	...	...
5 Recreational and related cultural services	...	...	...	...	...	...	...	...	...	...	...	...
6 Religious organisations	...	...	...	...	...	...	...	...	...	...	...	...
7 Professional and labour organisations serving households	...	...	...	...	...	...	...	...	...	...	...	...
8 Miscellaneous	...	...	...	...	...	...	...	...	...	...	...	...
equals: Final consumption expenditures by private non-profit organisations serving households	132	139	131	79	127	22	23	361	288	422	554	...
Private final consumption expenditure	10439	12226	14906	18448	24071	31677	41187	51623	71963	108922	143664	...

a Item "Food, beverages and tobacco" includes expenditure in restaurants, cafes and hotels.

2.6 Private final consumption expenditure by type and purpose, in constant prices

Thousand million Iranian rials	1986	1987	1988	1989	1990	1991	1992	1993	1994	1995	1996	1997

At constant prices of: 1982

Final consumption expenditure of resident households

	1986	1987	1988	1989	1990	1991	1992	1993	1994	1995	1996	1997
1 Food, beverages and tobacco [a]	2920	2838	2956	3075	3463	3138	3229	3341	3466	3446	3923	...
2 Clothing and footwear	638	632	610	630	666	865	983	911	829	786	718	...
3 Gross rent, fuel and power	1667	1510	1569	1507	1927	2517	2566	2813	2880	3085	2642	...
4 Furniture, furnishings and household equipment and operation	350	276	186	241	334	455	519	595	568	547	577	...
5 Medical care and health expenses	263	330	370	345	460	525	525	372	450	508	437	...
6 Transport and communication	391	332	255	270	319	357	410	411	408	436	592	...
7 Recreational, entertainment, education and cultural services	54	42	37	46	74	130	196	190	193	190	155	...
8 Miscellaneous goods and services	178	116	137	185	279	290	293	233	296	325	564	...
Total final consumption expenditure in the domestic market by households, of which	6460	6075	6120	6298	7523	8277	8721	8866	9090	9323	9608	...
A Durable goods	207	151	89	109	144	299	394	402	388	342	...	...
B Semi-durable goods	827	779	735	812	937	1127	1262	1184	1083	1132	...	...
C Non-durable goods	3365	3265	3344	3454	4065	3674	3832	3973	4118	4199	...	...
D Services	2061	1880	1952	1923	2377	3177	3233	3307	3501	3650	...	...
plus: Direct purchases abroad by resident households	...	...	...	...	...	...	...	...	...	...	...	...
less: Direct purchases in the domestic market by non-resident households	...	...	...	...	...	...	...	...	...	...	...	...

Iran, Islamic Republic of

Thousand million Iranian rials   **Fiscal year beginning 21 March**

	1986	1987	1988	1989	1990	1991	1992	1993	1994	1995	1996	1997
At constant prices of: 1982												
equals: Final consumption expenditure of resident households	6460	6075	6120	6298	7523	8277	8721	8866	9090	9323	9608	...

Final consumption expenditures by private non-profit organisations serving households

	1986	1987	1988	1989	1990	1991	1992	1993	1994	1995	1996	1997
1 Research and science	...	...	...	...	...	...	...	...	...	...	...	...
2 Education	...	...	...	...	...	...	...	...	...	...	...	...
3 Medical and other health services	...	...	...	...	...	...	...	...	...	...	...	...
4 Welfare services	...	...	...	...	...	...	...	...	...	...	...	...
5 Recreational and related cultural services	...	...	...	...	...	...	...	...	...	...	...	...
6 Religious organisations	...	...	...	...	...	...	...	...	...	...	...	...
7 Professional and labour organisations serving households	...	...	...	...	...	...	...	...	...	...	...	...
8 Miscellaneous	...	...	...	...	...	...	...	...	...	...	...	...
equals: Final consumption expenditures by private non-profit organisations serving households	84	67	52	29	40	5	5	62	34	35	36	...
Private final consumption expenditure	6544	6141	6172	6327	7564	8282	8726	8928	9124	9358	9644	...

a Item "Food, beverages and tobacco" includes expenditure in restaurants, cafes and hotels.

2.11 Gross fixed capital formation by kind of activity of owner, ISIC divisions, in current prices

Thousand million Iranian rials   **Fiscal year beginning 21 March**

	1986	1987	1988	1989	1990	1991	1992	1993	1994	1995	1996	1997
All producers												
1 Agriculture, hunting, forestry and fishing	138	169	214	240	425	643	710	1002	1162	2058	...	...
2 Mining and quarrying [a,b]	137	89	122	176	212	635	506	713	1342	2095	...	...
3 Manufacturing [b]	156	197	272	356	624	1504	2453	3462	7631	9244	...	...
4 Electricity, gas and water [c]	164	168	149	205	349	869	956	1349	2168	3240	...	...
5 Construction	15	13	17	26	60	329	351	496	268	370	...	...
6 Wholesale and retail trade, restaurants and hotels	...	...	...	...	...	...	...	...	...	...	...	...
7 Transport, storage and communication	286	338	417	583	778	1768	2375	3350	3798	6546	...	...
8 Finance, insurance, real estate and business services	1269	1318	1315	1572	2030	3051	3833	5408	6608	8914	...	...
9 Community, social and personal services	329	371	451	552	1184	2045	3456	4877	6876	9044	...	...
Total industries	2494	2662	2957	3709	5663	10844	14640	20657	29853	41511	...	...
Producers of government services	...	...	...	...	...	...	...	...	...	...	...	...
Private non-profit institutions serving households	...	...	...	...	...	...	...	...	...	...	...	...
Total	2494	2662	2957	3709	5663	10844	14640	20657	29853	41511	...	...

a Item "Mining and quarrying" refers only to oil and gas production.
b Mining is included in item "Manufacturing".
c Item "Electricity, gas and water" excludes gas.

Iran, Islamic Republic of

2.12 Gross fixed capital formation by kind of activity of owner, ISIC divisions, in constant prices

Thousand million Iranian rials — Fiscal year beginning 21 March

	1986	1987	1988	1989	1990	1991	1992	1993	1994	1995	1996	1997
At constant prices of: 1982												
All producers												
1 Agriculture, hunting, forestry and fishing	94	87	83	78	109	124	109	104	95	119	...	...
2 Mining and quarrying [a,b]	90	46	47	58	48	111	73	74	100	116	...	...
3 Manufacturing [b]	111	102	105	118	155	262	331	354	462	417	...	...
4 Electricity, gas and water [c]	110	87	57	68	84	152	130	137	144	161	...	...
5 Construction	12	7	7	9	16	57	46	49	16	16	...	...
6 Wholesale and retail trade, restaurants and hotels	...	...	...	...	...	...	...	...	...	...	...	...
7 Transport, storage and communication	206	176	161	195	191	308	325	343	251	301	...	...
8 Finance, insurance, real estate and business services	794	665	508	508	493	572	584	573	666	690	...	...
9 Community, social and personal services	229	192	175	183	283	357	479	499	472	457	...	...
Total industries	1646	1361	1144	1217	1379	1943	2077	2133	2206	2277	...	...
Producers of government services	...	...	...	...	...	...	...	...	...	...	...	...
Private non-profit institutions serving households	...	...	...	...	...	...	...	...	...	...	...	...
Total	1646	1361	1144	1217	1379	1943	2077	2133	2206	2277	...	...

a Item "Mining and quarrying" refers only to oil and gas production.
b Mining is included in item "Manufacturing".
c Item "Electricity, gas and water" excludes gas.

Iraq

General note

The preparation of national accounts statistics in Iraq is undertaken by the Central Statistical Organization, Baghdad. The following presentation of sources and methods is mainly based on information contained in a handbook entitled *Technical Note on the Estimation of National Income of the Republic of Iraq, 1962–1965*. The estimates are generally in accordance with the classifications and definitions recommended in the United Nations System of National Accounts (1968 SNA). The following tables have been prepared from successive replies to the United Nations National Accounts Questionnaire. When the scope and coverage of the estimates differ for conceptual or statistical reasons from the definitions and classifications recommended in SNA, a footnote is indicated to the relevant tables.

Gross domestic product

Gross domestic product is estimated mainly through the production approach.

Expenditures on the gross domestic product

The expenditure approach is used to estimate government final consumption expenditure, increase in stocks, and exports and imports of goods and services. This approach, in combination with the commodity-flow approach is used for gross fixed capital formation. The commodity-flow approach is used for private consumption expenditure. The estimates of government final consumption expenditure, consisting of wages, salaries and allowances and intermediate consumption of goods and services are obtained from the final accounts of the concerned bodies. The estimates of private final consumption expenditure is obtained as a residual for some years, while family budget surveys are used for other years. The data used for the estimation of increase in stocks are obtained from the final accounts of the establishments of the trade, transport and communication sectors. The industrial surveys provide data for the manufacturing industries. The gross fixed capital formation is classified according to economic activities and kinds of assets. Data are obtained from various sources such as the ordinary budget, actual expenditure on the development planning budget, reports and surveys. Foreign trade statistics provide data on imports of capital goods in c.i.f. values. Exports and imports of goods and services are estimated from foreign trade statistics and balance of payments data. Gross domestic product by expenditure type at constant prices is not estimated.

Cost structure of the gross domestic product

The estimates of compensation of employees in the socialist sector are obtained from the final accounts of the government and companies. For the private sector, the data are obtained from service surveys and internal trade surveys. Operating surplus is obtained as a residual. The depreciation estimates are prepared according to kinds of fixed assets and are based on the estimates of fixed capital formation, taking into consideration the prices of fixed assets and the average age of each kind of asset. The data on indirect taxes and subsidies are obtained from the actual accounts of the government or from the final accounts of the establishments of the socialist sector.

Gross domestic product by kind of activity

The table of gross domestic product by kind of economic activity is prepared in factor values. The production approach is used to estimate the value added of most industries. The income approach is used for transport and storage, private services and producers of government services. The commodity-flow approach is used to estimate gross output of the trade sector. Data on areas cultivated, average yield, quantity and value of each crop are obtained from the Central Statistical Organization (CSO) while prices are based on a production survey. The production of various types of vegetables is estimated from data of the Ministry of Agriculture, and the valuation is made by using farm prices collected by the CSO. The results of the 1971 Agricultural Census are used for estimating the value of fruit production. Intermediate consumption of these agricultural crops are estimated individually. The estimation of livestock products is based on sample surveys. The quantity of meat is estimated by multiplying the number of animals slaughtered in the abattoirs by the average weight of the animals. The number of animals slaughtered outside the abattoirs is estimated on the basis of data on exports of skins and guts. The estimate of the output of crude oil, natural gas and sulphur is based on the final accounts of the producing companies, from which data on the quantity and value of production and other factors of the value added are obtained.

The data on manufacturing are obtained from the annual and quarterly industrial surveys which collect data on the number of establishments and employees, wages and salaries, quantity and value of inputs, increase in stocks and capital formation. The data for electricity, gas and water are obtained from the balance sheets and final accounts of the concerned establishments and from the Industrial Department of the CSO. The value added in the construction sector is based on the reports of the CSO and data on fixed capital formation which are based on the national development planning budget. The data used to estimate value added in the trade sector are taken from government final accounts, the internal trade survey and the hotel survey. For restaurants and hotels, a survey of services and hotels comprising the number of employees and establishments, wages and salaries, revenue, purchases, etc. is used. The final accounts of public establishments and the reports issued by the CSO are the basis for estimating transport and communication. The gross value of output is obtained by adding intermediate consumption to value added. Data on banking, insurance and other financing establishments have been obtained directly from concerned establishments. The services survey is used for the value added of real estate services. For ownership of dwellings, rents are imputed based on the rent survey conducted by the Ministry of Finance and the family budget surveys. For government services, estimates are based on final government accounts and balance-sheets and final accounts of semi-governmental institutions.

The services survey and the family budget surveys are used for estimating private services, GDP by kind of economic activity at constant prices, taking 1964, 1969 and 1974 as base years.

1.1 Expenditure on the gross domestic product, in current prices

Million Iraqi dinars

	1986	1987	1988	1989	1990	1991	1992	1993	1994	1995	1996	1997
1 Government final consumption expenditure	5253	5674	6260	5990	6142	7033	...	...	...	...	...	...
2 Private final consumption expenditure	8398	9204	10101	11232	11760	9611	...	...	...	...	...	...
3 Gross capital formation	2868	3534	4278	3988	5243	3809	...	...	...	...	...	...
A Increase in stocks	−991	−124	−118	−2317	−977	520	...	...	...	...	...	...
B Gross fixed capital formation	3859	3657	4397	6306	6220	3289	...	...	...	...	...	...
Residential buildings	...	671	999	2356	2772	902	...	...	...	...	...	...
Non-residential buildings	...	1141	1232	902	311	837	...	...	...	...	...	...
Other construction and land improvement, etc.	...	1044	998	1414	...	...	...	...	...	...	...	...
Other	...	801	1168	1635	...	...	...	...	...	...	...	...
4 Exports of goods and services	2418	4087	3826	4483	4305	548	...	...	...	...	...	...
5 less: Imports of goods and services	3874	4598	4433	4667	4154	1062	...	...	...	...	...	...
equals: Gross domestic product	15063	17901	20032	21026	23297	19940	...	...	...	...	...	...

1.3 Cost components of the gross domestic product

Million Iraqi dinars

	1986	1987	1988	1989	1990	1991	1992	1993	1994	1995	1996	1997
1 Indirect taxes, net	411	301	600	618	448	−1374	...	...	...	...	...	...
A Indirect taxes	783	708	1020	1035	1025	486	...	...	...	...	...	...
B less: Subsidies	372	408	419	417	576	1859	...	...	...	...	...	...
2 Consumption of fixed capital	1304	1584	1749	1837	2056	1918	...	...	...	...	...	...
3 Compensation of employees paid by resident producers to	5151	5697	6301	6705	7855	8990	...	...	...	...	...	...
4 Operating surplus	8197	10319	11382	11866	12937	10405	...	...	...	...	...	...
equals: Gross domestic product	15063	17901	20032	21026	23297	19940	...	...	...	...	...	...

1.10 Gross domestic product by kind of activity, in current prices

Million Iraqi dinars

	1986	1987	1988	1989	1990	1991	1992	1993	1994	1995	1996	1997
1 Agriculture, hunting, forestry and fishing [a]	2174	2519	2834	3346	4613	6047	20844	45463	304002	1255760	...	...
2 Mining and quarrying	2181	3595	3639	3895	3331	149	230	92	−329	−2026	...	...
3 Manufacturing [abc]	1756	2071	2641	2694	2059	1274	5620	8012	23098	87515	...	...
4 Electricity, gas and water [c]	220	298	326	269	248	162	181	460	1042	256	...	...
5 Construction	1374	1431	1528	1418	1693	812	2259	7822	9543	27119	...	...

Iraq

Million Iraqi dinars

	1986	1987	1988	1989	1990	1991	1992	1993	1994	1995	1996	1997
6 Wholesale and retail trade, restaurants and hotels [bc]	1916	2183	2524	2376	3455	3608	15190	35798	195920	203557	...	...
7 Transport, storage and communication	1104	1270	1295	1533	2104	2646	5947	19163	106739	515782	...	...
8 Finance, insurance, real estate and business services [d]	1648	1789	1981	2385	2781	3150	4692	15538	30630	78711	...	...
9 Community, social and personal services [d]	198	200	230	305	292	490	764	1691	6227	37110	...	...
Total, Industries	12571	15355	16998	18221	20575	18339	55728	134040	676872	2203783	...	...
Producers of government services	2848	3228	3557	3599	4116	5335	7209	12873	44731	116888	...	...
Other producers											...	...
Subtotal [e]	15419	18583	20556	21820	24691	23675	62936	146912	721603	2320671	...	...
less: Imputed bank service charge	767	983	1123	1413	1550	1872	2824	5142	11851	30399	...	...
plus: Import duties	...	...	...	...	...	...	...	...	...	...	...	...
plus: Value added tax	...	...	...	...	...	...	...	...	...	...	...	...
plus: Other adjustments [f]	411	301	600	618	448	−1374	−1988	−10855	−17832	−106934	...	...
equals: Gross domestic product	15063	17901	20032	21026	23297	19940	57360	112142	612174	2551763	...	...

a Agricultural services and related activities such as cotton ginning and pressing are included in item "Manufacturing".
b Distribution of petroleum products is included in item "Wholesale and retail trade".
c Gas distribution is included in item "Wholesale and retail trade".
d Business services are included in item "Community, social and personal services".
e Gross domestic product in factor values.
f Item "Other adjustments" refers to indirect taxes net of subsidies.

1.11 Gross domestic product by kind of activity, in constant prices

Million Iraqi dinars

	1986	1987	1988	1989	1990	1991	1992	1993	1994	1995	1996	1997
At constant prices of: 1975												
1 Agriculture, hunting, forestry and fishing [a]	496	454	484	536	575	405	...	...	...	...	...	...
2 Mining and quarrying	1747	2793	2898	2460	2253	54	...	...	...	...	...	...
3 Manufacturing [abc]	577	787	739	616	475	345	...	...	...	...	...	...
4 Electricity, gas and water [c]	85	87	97	113	94	49	...	...	...	...	...	...
5 Construction	566	543	535	458	514	95	...	...	...	...	...	...
6 Wholesale and retail trade, restaurants and hotels [bc]	631	618	686	608	798	291	...	...	...	...	...	...
7 Transport, storage and communication	358	360	352	392	486	213	...	...	...	...	...	...
8 Finance, insurance, real estate and business services [d]	594	577	608	670	706	469	...	...	...	...	...	...
9 Community, social and personal services [d]	64	57	63	78	68	40	...	...	...	...	...	...
Total, Industries	5117	6277	6462	5932	5968	1960	...	...	...	...	...	...
Producers of government services	922	915	967	921	883	390	...	...	...	...	...	...
Other producers	...	...	...	...	...	...	...	...	...	...	...	...
Subtotal [e]	6039	7191	7429	6853	6851	2351	...	...	...	...	...	...
less: Imputed bank service charge	248	279	305	361	358	151	...	...	...	...	...	...
plus: Import duties	...	...	...	...	...	...	...	...	...	...	...	...
plus: Value added tax	...	...	...	...	...	...	...	...	...	...	...	...
plus: Other adjustments	...	...	...	...	...	...	...	...	...	...	...	...
equals: Gross domestic product [e]	5791	6913	7124	6492	6493	2200	...	...	...	...	...	...

a Agricultural services and related activities such as cotton ginning and pressing are included in item "Manufacturing".
b Distribution of petroleum products is included in item "Wholesale and retail trade".
c Gas distribution is included in item "Wholesale and retail trade".
d Business services are included in item "Community, social and personal services".
e Gross domestic product in factor values.

Iraq

1.12 Relations among national accounting aggregates

Million Iraqi dinars

	1986	1987	1988	1989	1990	1991	1992	1993	1994	1995	1996	1997
Gross domestic product	15063	17901	20032	21026	23297	19940	...	...	...	...	...	...
plus: Net factor income from the rest of the world	−692	−705	−700	−704	−774	−650	...	...	...	...	...	...
Factor income from rest of the world	40	24	41	37	...	...	...	...	...	...	...	...
less: Factor income to the rest of the world	732	728	741	742	...	...	...	...	...	...	...	...
equals: Gross national product	14371	17196	19332	20321	22523	19289	...	...	...	...	...	...
less: Consumption of fixed capital	1304	1584	1749	1837	2056	1918	...	...	...	...	...	...
equals: National income	13067	15612	17583	18485	20467	17371	...	...	...	...	...	...
plus: Net current transfers from the rest of the world	−89	−84	−19	−149	−49	123	...	...	...	...	...	...
equals: National disposable income	12978	15528	17564	18336	20417	17494	...	...	...	...	...	...
less: Final consumption	13650	14878	16361	17223	17902	16644	...	...	...	...	...	...
equals: Net saving	−673	650	1203	1113	2515	849	...	...	...	...	...	...
less: Surplus of the nation on current transactions	−2237	−1300	−1326	−1038	−672	−1042	...	...	...	...	...	...
equals: Net capital formation	1564	1950	2529	2151	3187	1891	...	...	...	...	...	...

2.11 Gross fixed capital formation by kind of activity of owner, ISIC divisions, in current prices

Million Iraqi dinars

	1986	1987	1988	1989	1990	1991	1992	1993	1994	1995	1996	1997
All producers												
1 Agriculture, hunting, forestry and fishing	416	335	437	472	376	178	858	2061	2959	7729	...	...
2 Mining and quarrying	181	215	379	608	385	134	63	291	91	127	...	...
3 Manufacturing	283	153	148	913	1014	710	1504	3857	3564	10519	...	...
4 Electricity, gas and water	493	357	403	434	312	242	451	1042	1258	1639	...	...
5 Construction	22	21	38	51	58	15	46	92	140	224	...	...
6 Wholesale and retail trade, restaurants and hotels [a]	103	46	61	224	58	59	55	523	731	1388	...	...
7 Transport, storage and communication	727	263	187	310	289	261	384	1079	512	706	...	...
8 Finance, insurance, real estate and business services [b]	546	522	899	2252	2711	864	5718	5575	5299	23573	...	...
9 Community, social and personal services [a,b]	3	4	5	5	5	5	15	15	55	197	...	...
Total industries	2775	1915	2557	5268	5206	2468	9095	14535	14608	46102	...	...
Producers of government services	597	1742	1840	1037	1014	821	1687	17256	7845	11273	...	...
Private non-profit institutions serving households	...	...	...	...	...	...	...	...	...	...	...	...
Total	3372[c]	3658[c]	4397[c]	6306[c]	6220[c]	3289[c]	10782	31791	22453	57375	...	...

a Restaurants and hotels are included in item "Community, social and personal services".
b Business services are included in item "Community, social and personal services".
c Data for this table have not been revised, therefore, data for some years are not comparable with those of other tables.

Iraq

2.12 Gross fixed capital formation by kind of activity of owner, ISIC divisions, in constant prices
Million Iraqi dinars

	1986	1987	1988	1989	1990	1991	1992	1993	1994	1995	1996	1997
At constant prices of: 1988												
All producers												
1 Agriculture, hunting, forestry and fishing	491	364	437	436	254	73	...	...	...	...	...	...
2 Mining and quarrying	191	224	379	572	237	59	...	...	...	...	...	...
3 Manufacturing	327	165	148	849	638	456	...	...	...	...	...	...
4 Electricity, gas and water	572	386	403	402	185	153	...	...	...	...	...	...
5 Construction	30	22	38	48	33	12	...	...	...	...	...	...
6 Wholesale and retail trade, restaurants and hotels	121	49	61	206	35	27	...	...	...	...	...	...
7 Transport, storage and communication	486	282	187	287	202	118	...	...	...	...	...	...
8 Finance, insurance, real estate and business services	641	565	899	2077	1430	292	...	...	...	...	...	...
9 Community, social and personal services	4	5	5	4	2	3	...	...	...	...	...	...
Total industries	2863	2062	2557	4881	3016	1193	...	...	...	...	...	...
Producers of government services	1293	1878	1840	960	684	481	...	...	...	...	...	...
Private non-profit institutions serving households	...	...	...	...	...	...	...	...	...	...	...	...
Total	4156	3940	4396	5840	3700	1674	...	...	...	...	...	...

Ireland

General note

The preparation of national accounts statistics in Ireland is undertaken by the Central Statistics Office, Cork. The official estimates are published annually in *National Income and Expenditure*. The following presentation of sources and methods is mainly based on a report entitled *Basic statistics needed for the ESA accounts and tables: present situation and prospects for improvements* prepared by the Statistical Office of the European Communities in 1976 and on information received from Ireland's Central Statistics Office. The estimates are generally in accordance with the classifications and definitions recommended in the United Nations System of National Accounts (1968 SNA). The following tables have been prepared from successive replies to the United Nations National Accounts Questionnaire. When the scope and coverage of the estimates differ for conceptual or statistical reasons from the definitions and classifications recommended in SNA, a footnote is indicated to the relevant tables.

Gross domestic product

Gross domestic product is estimated mainly through the income approach.

Expenditures on the gross domestic product

The expenditure approach is used to estimate government final consumption expenditure, increase in stocks, and exports and imports of goods and services. The commodity-flow approach is used to estimate private final consumption expenditure and gross fixed capital formation except in the case of building and construction and government capital formation. Government final consumption expenditure is estimated from the accounts of the various government bodies such as the ministries, the local authorities and health boards, extrabudgetary funds and the Industrial Development Authority. Data on private consumption expenditure are also estimated from Household Budget Inquiries. *Largescale Household Budget Inquiries* were carried out in 1951–52, 1965–66, 1973 and 1980. The 1951–52 and 1965–66 surveys were restricted to urban areas. *Smallscale Annual Household Budget Surveys* were undertaken in 1974–1979 and 1981. These were restricted to urban areas for 1974–1979 but covered urban and rural areas in 1981. Estimates of transactions in goods and services are obtained from the censuses of industrial production and the statistics of imports and exports of merchandise. The goods are valued at national average retail prices where volume data are available. Otherwise, they are aggregated at appropriate producers' or import prices and adjusted for distribution costs. In building up the stock figures, industrial stocks from stocks inquiries and censuses of industrial production, and stockpiles of strategic commodities from the Department of Agriculture.

Investment in building and construction is estimated through the use of data from the production surveys. Estimates of locally produced goods are obtained from production census data minus exports plus distribution margins. Estimates of imported goods are obtained from detailed import returns. The estimates of imports and exports of goods and services are obtained from balance-of-payments, special studies and surveys. For the constant price estimates, direct revaluation at base-year prices is used for items of private final consumption expenditure where quantity data are available. For all other components of GDP by expenditure type, price deflation is used.

Cost structure of the gross domestic product

Estimates of compensation of employees are based on wage rates and number of farm worker for the agricultural sector, censuses of industrial production for the industrial sectors, surveys conducted at intervals and updated by indexes of earnings for the trade sector, annual surveys conducted among the relevant companies for the transport, credit and insurance sectors and salary rates and number of employees for the other market services. Operating surplus is calculated from returns made to the revenue authorities and from government accounts. Depreciation is based on the perpetual inventory method for the agricultural sector. For private enterprises, it is taken as the income tax wear-and-tear and other allowances. Indirect taxes and subsidies are estimated from the government accounts.

Gross domestic product by kind of activity

The table of gross domestic product by kind of economic activity is prepared in factor values. The income approach is used to estimate the value added of all industries except agriculture, for which the production approach is used. Annual estimates of agricultural output are calculated on a commodity basis for crops, livestock and livestock products. The data on quantities and values are obtained from various sources such as Department of Agriculture and Central Statistics Office. The total quantities purchased and amounts paid by the purchasers for important agricultural items such as wheat and barley are available from various inquiries and adjusted for marketing margins and transport costs. For live exports, f.o.b. export value less an allowance for marketing margins, is taken as the output value. For the remaining items market prices are used as the basis for evaluation. Input data are obtained through the Department of Agriculture for fertilizers. Data for seeds are compiled indirectly from acreages and seedling rates. Own-account consumption of food and fuel is evaluated at agricultural prices. For mining, quarrying and

Ireland

manufacturing enterprises employing more than three persons, the estimates are based on annual censuses. Quarterly surveys of turnover and employment are conducted for manufacturing. For small-scale manufacturing, the number of persons engaged, which is derived as the difference between population census data and data from the production census, interpolated for intercensal years and projected forward, are multiplied by average income per person.

The estimates of electricity, gas and water and of construction are based on annual inquiries. For trade, censuses of distribution provide benchmark data for turnover, purchase of products, wages and salaries and intermediate inputs. For intervening years, monthly turnover figures from a sample of 2,500 establishments are used together with annual estimates of the number of employees and trends in earnings. For restaurants and hotels, annual surveys and revenue data are used. Transport is mainly provided by public enterprises and data are obtained from published accounts. Data obtained from annual reports, direct surveys on wages and salaries and revenue statistics are used for the estimates of the financial sector. For real estate and business services, data from population census, imputed average income and revenue accounts are used. The imputed rent of owner-occupied dwellings is taken as the average rent paid for similar dwellings in similar locations. Estimates of other private services are based on the results of inquiries into wages and salaries and on trends in operating surplus taken from revenue data. Data on government services are obtained from the government accounts.

For the constant price estimates, double deflation is used for agriculture. Value added of all other economic activity sectors of GDP is extrapolated by a quantity index.

1.1 Expenditure on the gross domestic product, in current prices

Million Irish pounds

	1986	1987	1988	1989	1990	1991	1992	1993	1994	1995	1996	1997
1 Government final consumption expenditure	3542 3542	3575	3540	3670	4067	4481	4842	5219	5579	5949	6244	...
2 Private final consumption expenditure	12138 12138	12845	13937	15449	15992	16825	17966	18713	20400	21695	23318	...
3 Gross capital formation	3536 3574	3481	3686	4644	5847	5520	4888	4826	5448	6526	7913	...
A Increase in stocks	142 142	11	−150	176	663	604	−195	−151	−140	124	330	...
B Gross fixed capital formation	3393 3432	3469	3836	4468	5184	4916	5083	4977	5588	6402	7583	...
Residential buildings	882 920	910	904	1046	1224	1287	1496	1401	1835	2140	2644	...
Non-residential buildings [a]	919 919	871	1044	1136	1563	1627	1572	1499	1542	1842	2234	...
Other construction and land improvement, etc.	...	...	...	...	...	...	...	...	...	...	...	...
Other	1592 1592	1688	1888	2286	2397	2002	2014	2076	2211	2420	2706	...
4 Exports of goods and services	10352 10377	11855	13653	16159	16153	16958	18859	21988	25248	30755	33740	...
5 less: Imports of goods and services	9860 9929	10681	11921	14359	14533	15084	15920	17631	20612	24671	27024	...
equals: Gross domestic product	18874 19703	21075	22894	25563	27525	28700	30635	33115	36063	40254	44190	...

a Including item "other construction and land improvement etc.".

1.2 Expenditure on the gross domestic product, in constant prices

Million Irish pounds

	1986	1987	1988	1989	1990	1991	1992	1993	1994	1995	1996	1997
	At constant prices of: 1985 1990											
1 Government final consumption expenditure	3388 4322	4112	3908	3858	4067	4185	4288	4311	4519	4697	4832	...
2 Private final consumption expenditure	10811 13712	14168	14804	15769	15992	16340	17008	17385	18450	19232	20438	...
3 Gross capital formation	3449 4246	3948	3993	4724	5847	5390	4610	4394	4787	5592	6745	...
A Increase in stocks	157 256	3	−158	152	663	622	−183	−143	−209	78	354	...
B Gross fixed capital formation	3292 3990	3944	4151	4572	5184	4768	4793	4537	4996	5514	6391	...

Ireland

Million Irish pounds

	1986	1987	1988	1989	1990	1991	1992	1993	1994	1995	1996	1997
At constant prices of: 1985 / 1990												
Residential buildings	823 / 1237	1168	1071	1166	1224	1250	1393	1285	1641	1826	2139	...
Non-residential buildings [a]	879 / 1138	1048	1149	1192	1563	1583	1495	1389	1393	1607	1925	...
Other construction and land improvement, etc.	...	...	...	...	...	...	...	...	...	...	...	...
Other	1590 / 1674	1760	1930	2214	2397	1935	1906	1864	1962	2080	2328	...
4 Exports of goods and services	11048 / 10862	12352	13467	14856	16153	17006	19311	21165	24165	28893	31801	
5 less: Imports of goods and services	10982 / 10944	11620	12189	13830	14533	14730	15740	16704	18994	21817	24062	...
Statistical discrepancy	− / −421	−168	...	...	...	...	...	...	...	...	...	...
equals: Gross domestic product	17714 / 21777	22793	23982	25376	27525	28192	29477	30551	32927	36598	39754	...

a Including item "other construction and land improvement etc.".

1.3 Cost components of the gross domestic product

Million Irish pounds

	1986	1987	1988	1989	1990	1991	1992	1993	1994	1995	1996	1997
1 Indirect taxes, net	1988 / 2172	2298	2353	3197	2836	2873	3308	3223	3964	4377	4356	...
A Indirect taxes	3475 / 3475	3672	3965	4377	4446	4511	4781	4901	5590	6063	6503	...
B less: Subsidies	1488 / 1303	1375	1612	1180	1610	1638	1474	1678	1626	1686	2147	...
2 Consumption of fixed capital	1835 / 1885	2062	2140	2384	2615	2846	2979	3157	3488	3848	4303	...
3 Compensation of employees paid by resident producers to	10255 / 10265	10797	11260	12019	12995	13850	14806	16023	17091	18341	19700	
A Resident households	10255 / 10265	10797	11260	12019	12995	13850	14806	16023	17091	18341	19700	...
B Rest of the world	− / −	−	−	−	−	−	−	−	−	−	−	...
4 Operating surplus	4796 / 5381	5918	7141	7962	9078	9131	9542	10712	11520	13687	15830	...
equals: Gross domestic product	18874 / 19703	21075	22894	25563	27525	28701	30635	33115	36063	40254	44190	...

1.4 General government current receipts and disbursements

Million Irish pounds

	1986	1987	1988	1989	1990	1991	1992	1993	1994	1995	1996	1997
Receipts												
1 Operating surplus	177 / 177	167	214	143	120	141	150	169	191	213	...	...
2 Property and entrepreneurial income	332 / 332	370	314	287	346	427	441	445	357	311	...	...
3 Taxes, fees and contributions	7470 / 7470	8005	8920	9156	9785	10302	11102	11955	13247	13799	...	...
A Indirect taxes [a]	3191 / 3191	3344	3672	4046	4133	4164	4443	4496	5161	5580	...	...
B Direct taxes	2880 / 2880	3179	3641	3385	3776	4120	4490	5081	5599	5635	...	...
C Social security contributions	1398 / 1398	1483	1607	1724	1876	2018	2169	2378	2487	2584	...	...
D Compulsory fees, fines and penalties	...	...	...	...	...	...	...	...	...	...	...	...
4 Other current transfers	158 / 158	238	181	170	215	366	338	369	353	296	...	...

Ireland

Million Irish pounds

	1986	1987	1988	1989	1990	1991	1992	1993	1994	1995	1996	1997
Total current receipts of general government	8137 8137	8779	9629	9756	10465	11236	12030	12938	14147	14620	...	...

Disbursements

	1986	1987	1988	1989	1990	1991	1992	1993	1994	1995	1996	1997
1 Government final consumption expenditure [a]	3542 3542	3575	3539	3670	4067	4479	4842	5219	5579	5949	...	...
A Compensation of employees	2335 2335	2419	2514	2609	2817	3101	3356	3675	3823	3984	...	...
B Consumption of fixed capital	141 141	150	158	168	177	185	193	201	210	223	...	...
C Purchases of goods and services, net	...	...	...	...	...	...	...	...	...	...	...	...
D less: Own-account fixed capital formation	...	...	...	...	...	...	...	...	...	...	...	...
E Indirect taxes paid, net	...	...	...	...	...	...	...	...	...	...	...	...
2 Property income	1758 1758	1944	1957	1967	2125	2148	2116	2142	2051	2016	...	...
3 Subsidies	569 385	576	706	325	314	325	359	446	386	439	...	...
4 Other current transfers	3635 3819	3980	4156	4116	4336	4771	5228	5663	6072	6442	...	...
A Social security benefits	1303 1303	1339	1323	1307	1336	1448	1562	1613	1620	1868	...	...
B Social assistance grants	1898 2082	2188	2359	2326	2500	2744	3029	3301	3603	3668	...	...
C Other	434 434	452	474	484	499	578	637	749	850	907	...	...
5 Net saving	−1367 −1367	−1296	−730	−322	−377	−487	−515	−532	59	−226	...	...
Total current disbursements and net saving of general government	8137 8137	8779	9629	9756	10465	11236	12030	12938	14147	14620	...	...

[a] Item "Fees, fines and penalties" is included in item "Indirect taxes" or is offset against item "Final consumption expenditure".

1.7 External transactions on current account, summary

Million Irish pounds

	1986	1987	1988	1989	1990	1991	1992	1993	1994	1995	1996	1997

Payments to the rest of the world

	1986	1987	1988	1989	1990	1991	1992	1993	1994	1995	1996	1997
1 Imports of goods and services	9860 9929	10681	11921	14359	14533	15084	15920	17631	20612	24671	27024	...
A Imports of merchandise, c.i.f.	8745 8745	9137	10048	12114	12294	12609	13004	14633	17028	20239	21884	...
B Other	1115 1183	1544	1873	2245	2240	2475	2916	2998	3584	4432	5140	...
2 Factor income to rest of the world	2705 2769	2899	3690	4578	4873	4737	5029	5697	6630	8155	9479	...
A Compensation of employees	− −	−	−	−	−	−	−	−	−	−	−	...
B Property and entrepreneurial income	2705 2769	2899	3690	4578	4873	4737	5029	5697	6630	8155	9479	...
3 Current transfers to the rest of the world	374 374	378	363	372	439	523	532	646	728	769	841	...
A Indirect taxes to supranational organizations	284 284	329	294	331	313	347	338	405	429	482	423	...
B Other current transfers	90 90	50	69	41	126	176	194	241	299	287	418	...
4 Surplus of the nation on current transactions	−540 −642	−47	138	−270	−48	691	988	1764	1283	1806	1682	...
Payments to the rest of the world and surplus of the nation on current transfers	12399 12429	13912	16112	19039	19797	21035	22470	25737	29253	35400	39027	...

Ireland

Million Irish pounds

	1986	1987	1988	1989	1990	1991	1992	1993	1994	1995	1996	1997
Receipts from the rest of the world												
1 Exports of goods and services	10352 10377	11855	13653	16159	16153	16958	18859	21988	25248	30755	33740	...
A Exports of merchandise, f.o.b.	9181 9181	10447	12073	14358	14091	14675	16505	19460	22424	27698	30300	...
B Other	1171 1197	1408	1580	1801	2062	2283	2354	2529	2824	3057	3440	...
2 Factor income from rest of the world	748 752	787	1147	1472	1794	1945	1834	1794	2121	2766	3093	...
A Compensation of employees	16 16	16	135	144	146	149	157	172	183	181	190	...
B Property and entrepreneurial income	732 736	771	1012	1329	1647	1796	1677	1622	1938	2585	2903	...
3 Current transfers from rest of the world	1300 1300	1270	1312	1408	1851	2131	1777	1954	1883	1879	2194	...
A Subsidies from supranational organisations	918 918	799	906	854	1295	1313	1114	1232	1240	1247	1549	...
B Other current transfers	381 381	471	406	553	556	818	663	723	644	633	645	...
Receipts from the rest of the world on current transactions	12399 12429	13912	16112	19039	19797	21035	22470	25737	29253	35400	39027	...

1.8 Capital transactions of the nation, summary

Million Irish pounds

	1986	1987	1988	1989	1990	1991	1992	1993	1994	1995	1996	1997
Finance of gross capital formation												
Gross saving	2995 2932	3434	3824	4374	5799	6212	5876	6589	6731	8332	9595	...
1 Consumption of fixed capital	1835 1885	2062	2140	2384	2615	2846	2979	3157	3488	3848	4303	...
A General government	141 141	150	158	168	177	185	193	201	210	223	...	...
B Corporate and quasi-corporate enterprises	1694 1744	1913	1982	2217	2439	2661	2786	2956	3277	3625	...	...
C Other	...	...	...	...	...	...	...	...	...	...	...	...
2 Net saving	1160 1046	1372	1684	1990	3183	3365	2897	3432	3243	4483	5292	...
A General government	−1367 −1367	−1296	−730	−322	−377	−487	−515	−532	6	−226	...	...
B Corporate and quasi-corporate enterprises	2527 2414	2667	2413	2312	3560	3852	3412	3964	3237	4709	...	...
C Other	...	...	...	...	...	...	...	...	...	...	...	...
less: Surplus of the nation on current transactions	−540 −642	−47	138	−270	−48	691	988	1764	1283	1806	1682	...
Statistical discrepancy			...	...	...	...	...	...	...	...	...	...
Finance of gross capital formation	3536 3574	− 3481	3686	4644	5847	5520	4888	4826	5448	6526	7913	...
Gross capital formation												
Increase in stocks	142 142	11	−150	176	663	604	−195	−151	−140	124	330	...
Gross fixed capital formation	3393 3432	3469	3836	4468	5184	4916	5083	4977	5588	6402	7583	...
1 General government	693 693	555	411	462	570	620	630	724	832	871	...	...
2 Corporate and quasi-corporate enterprises	2700 2738	2915	3425	4006	4615	4296	4453	4253	4756	5531	...	...
3 Other	...	...	...	...	...	...	...	...	...	...	...	...
Gross capital formation	3536 3574	3481	3686	4644	5847	5520	4888	4826	5448	6526	7913	...

Ireland

1.9 Gross domestic product by institutional sectors of origin

Million Irish pounds

	1986	1987	1988	1989	1990	1991	1992	1993	1994	1995	1996	1997
Domestic factor incomes originating												
subtotal: Domestic factor incomes	15051 15645	16715	18401	19981	22073	22981	24348	26734	28611	32029	35530	...
Indirect taxes, net	1988 2172	2298	2353	3197	2836	2873	3308	3223	3964	4377	4356	...
A Indirect taxes	3475 3475	3672	3965	4377	4446	4511	4781	4901	5590	6063	6503	...
B less: Subsidies	1488 1303	1375	1612	1180	1610	1638	1474	1678	1626	1686	2147	...
Consumption of fixed capital	1835 1885	2062	2140	2384	2615	2846	2979	3157	3488	3848	4303	...
Gross domestic product	18874 19703	21075	22894	25563	27525	28700	30635	33115	36063	40254	44190	...

1.10 Gross domestic product by kind of activity, in current prices

Million Irish pounds

	1986	1987	1988	1989	1990	1991	1992	1993	1994	1995	1996	1997
1 Agriculture, hunting, forestry and fishing	1532 1532	1804	2004	2164	1975	1919	2127	2182	2032	2065	...	...
2 Mining and quarrying	5891	6215	6754	7641	8218	8739	9408	10165	11399	...	...	...
3 Manufacturing										...	...	...
4 Electricity, gas and water										...	...	...
5 Construction	968 1026	1041	1066	1112	1304	1360	1393	1511	1634	1814	...	...
6 Wholesale and retail trade, restaurants and hotels	1916 2003	2194	2267	2788	3229	3117	3061	3640	3751	4325	...	...
7 Transport, storage and communication	982 1009	1142	1310	1370	1460	1573	1604	1673	1839	2010	...	...
8 Finance, insurance, real estate and business services	1067 1147	1204	1374	1406	1480	1704	2055	2299	2397	2695	...	...
9 Community, social and personal services	2261 2641	2800	3273	3856	4262	4482	4662	5045	5618	5964	...	...
Total, Industries	14332 15248	16399	18032	20305	21964	22954	24502	26719	29088	32887	...	...
Producers of government services	3117 3029	3200	3272	3416	3683	3960	4305	4814	5048	5387	...	...
Other producers											...	...
Subtotal	17448 18277	19599	21304	23721	25646	26913	28808	31533	34136	38274	...	...
less: Imputed bank service charge	804 804	828	965	976	993	1094	1235	1419	1493	1770	...	...
plus: Import duties	678 678	691	791	873	903	870	884	746	814	864	...	...
plus: Value added tax	1551 1551	1612	1764	1944	1969	2012	2179	2255	2605	2887	...	...
plus: Other adjustments	...	...	...	...	...	...	...	...	...	...	...	...
equals: Gross domestic product	18874 19703	21074	22894	25562	27525	28701	30635	33115	36063	40254	...	...

Ireland

1.12 Relations among national accounting aggregates

Million Irish pounds

	1986	1987	1988	1989	1990	1991	1992	1993	1994	1995	1996	1997
Gross domestic product	18874 19703	21075	22894	25563	27525	28700	30635	33115	36063	40255	44190	...
plus: Net factor income from the rest of the world	−1957 −2017	−2112	−2543	−3105	−3080	−2791	−3196	−3902	−4509	−5389	−6387	...
Factor income from rest of the world	748 752	787	1147	1472	1794	1945	1834	1794	2121	2766	3093	...
less: Factor income to the rest of the world	2705 2769	2899	3690	4578	4873	4737	5029	5697	6630	8155	9479	...
equals: Gross national product	16917 17686	18962	20351	22457	24445	25909	27439	29213	31554	34865	37804	...
less: Consumption of fixed capital	1835 1885	2062	2140	2384	2615	2846	2979	3157	3488	3848	4303	...
equals: National income	15082 15801	16900	18211	20073	21830	23063	24460	26055	28066	31017	33500	...
plus: Net current transfers from the rest of the world	926 926	892	949	1036	1412	1608	1245	1309	1156	1110	1353	...
Current transfers from rest of the world	1300 1300	1270	1312	1408	1851	2131	1777	1954	1883	1879	2194	...
less: Current transfers to the rest of the world	374 374	378	363	372	439	523	532	646	728	769	841	...
equals: National disposable income	16008 16727	17792	19160	21109	23242	24672	25705	27364	29222	32127	34854	...
less: Final consumption	14847 15680	16420	17476	19119	20059	21306	22808	23932	25979	27644	29562	...
equals: Net saving	1160 1046	1372	1684	1990	3183	3365	2897	3432	3243	4483	5292	...
less: Surplus of the nation on current transactions	−540 −642	−47	138	−270	−48	691	988	1764	1283	1806	1682	...
Statistical discrepancy	− −		...	...	...	...	...	...	...	...	...	...
equals: Net capital formation	1700 1689	1418	1546	2260	3232	2674	1909	1668	1960	2677	3609	...

2.5 Private final consumption expenditure by type and purpose, in current prices

Million Irish pounds

	1986	1987	1988	1989	1990	1991	1992	1993	1994	1995	1996	1997
Final consumption expenditure of resident households												
1 Food, beverages and tobacco	4511 4496	4753	4884	5362	5440	5727	6104	6299	6724	7028	7308	...
A Food	2498 2493	2671	2541	2844	2824	2940	3108	3249	3365	3395	3375	...
B Non-alcoholic beverages	156 185	181	199	227	208	206	234	223	253	262	306	...
C Alcoholic beverages	1338 1260	1329	1568	1694	1800	1888	2033	2091	2303	2464	2689	...
D Tobacco	518 559	572	576	596	608	693	729	735	803	908	937	...
2 Clothing and footwear	798 882	907	921	1038	1039	1100	1152	1228	1292	1293	1517	...
3 Gross rent, fuel and power	1323 1666	1728	2204	2411	2529	2740	2853	3032	3262	3370	3609	...
A Fuel and power	654 653	671	649	731	743	808	776	819	889	856	935	...
B Other	669 1013	1056	1555	1680	1786	1932	2077	2213	2373	2514	2675	...
4 Furniture, furnishings and household equipment and operation	802 864	878	976	1130	1067	1119	1143	1170	1278	1334	1439	...
A Household operation	298 328	326	383	460	421	429	448	468	558	554	592	...

Ireland

Million Irish pounds

	1986	1987	1988	1989	1990	1991	1992	1993	1994	1995	1996	1997
B Other	504 536	552	593	670	646	690	694	702	720	780	847	...
5 Medical care and health expenses	451 451	491	536	564	602	661	728	781	837	901	960	...
6 Transport and communication	1386 1550	1607	1732	1999	2162	2180	2314	2419	2723	2960	3230	...
A Personal transport equipment	373 376	374	441	585	659	536	546	569	715	785	918	...
B Other	1012 1174	1234	1291	1414	1503	1644	1768	1850	2007	2175	2311	...
7 Recreational, entertainment, education and cultural services	1087 1258	1420	1516	1711	1833	1942	2130	2267	2451	2777	3034	...
A Education	323 399	439	560	595	625	650	728	801	886	1020	1076	...
B Other	764 859	980	956	1116	1208	1292	1402	1465	1564	1758	1958	...
8 Miscellaneous goods and services	929 1030	1169	1295	1421	1623	1728	1827	1920	2165	2380	2700	...
A Personal care [a]	224 247	264	254	239	275	366	364	336	420	464	528	...
B Expenditures in restaurants, cafes and hotels	180 222	247	345	378	432	483	525	576	650	716	815	...
C Other	524 560	658	696	804	916	878	938	1008	1095	1199	1358	...
Total final consumption expenditure in the domestic market by households, of which	11287 12195	12952	14065	15635	16294	17198	18251	19115	20731	22042	23797	...
plus: Direct purchases abroad by resident households	511 436	457	526	565	573	567	664	689	871	1028	1064	...
less: Direct purchases in the domestic market by non-resident households	492 492	564	655	751	876	939	949	1090	1202	1375	1543	...
equals: Final consumption expenditure of resident households [b]	11305 12138	12845	13937	15449	15992	16825	17966	18713	20400	21695	23318	...

a Item "Personal care" excludes services of barbers, beauty shops etc.   b Item "Final consumption expenditure of resident households" includes consumption expenditure of private non-profit institutions serving households.

2.6 Private final consumption expenditure by type and purpose, in constant prices

Million Irish pounds

	1986	1987	1988	1989	1990	1991	1992	1993	1994	1995	1996	1997
At constant prices of: 1985 1995 1990												

Final consumption expenditure of resident households

	1986	1987	1988	1989	1990	1991	1992	1993	1994	1995	1996	1997
1 Food, beverages and tobacco	4196 4226 	4403	4490 5160	5441	5440	5589	5776	5864	6002	6070	6166	...
A Food	2371 2378 	2489	2499 2678	2870	2824	2905	3043	3182	3184	3118	3060	...
B Non-alcoholic beverages	128 153 	192	211 209	231	208	201	226	219	244	247	281	...
C Alcoholic beverages	1225 1185 	1229	1297 1682	1747	1800	1829	1881	1864	1958	2043	2174	...
D Tobacco	472 510 	494	483 591	594	608	656	626	598	617	662	651	...
2 Clothing and footwear	768 849 	865	947 954	1053	1039	1083	1113	1180	1226	1240	1471	...

1094

Ireland

Million Irish pounds

	1986	1987	1988	1989	1990	1991	1992	1993	1994	1995	1996	1997
At constant prices of:	1985											
			1995									
			1990									
3 Gross rent, fuel and power	1318											...
	1665	1705	1724									
			2376	2474	2529	2637	2666	2760	2894	2938	3081	
A Fuel and power	684											...
	680	712	732									
			663	740	743	796	769	809	882	856	915	
B Other	635											...
	985	992	992									
			1714	1734	1786	1841	1897	1951	2012	2083	2166	
4 Furniture, furnishings and household equipment and operation	786											...
	848	847	995									
			1033	1150	1067	1096	1103	1136	1212	1245	1324	
A Household operation	290											...
	320	309	374									
			409	467	421	417	431	456	524	502	526	
B Other	496											...
	528	539	621									
			624	683	646	679	672	680	688	743	798	
5 Medical care and health expenses	431											...
	431	420	419									
			579	588	602	622	643	657	672	703	730	
6 Transport and communication	1387											...
	1579	1588	1726									
			1821	2034	2162	2130	2253	2299	2561	2741	2948	
A Personal transport equipment	352											...
	354	327	396									
			466	590	659	535	545	540	666	707	819	
B Other	1036											...
	1225	1261	1329									
			1355	1444	1503	1595	1709	1760	1894	2035	2129	
7 Recreational, entertainment, education and cultural services	1016											...
	1179	1281	1279									
			1603	1748	1833	1886	2020	2118	2264	2564	2867	
A Education	281											...
	347	354	344									
			602	615	625	630	684	742	802	900	934	
B Other	734											...
	832	927	935									
			1001	1133	1208	1256	1336	1376	1462	1664	1933	
8 Miscellaneous goods and services	890											...
	986	1090	1173									
			1383	1460	1623	1674	1717	1760	1930	2059	2282	
A Personal care [a]	216											...
	239	249	246									
			272	246	275	355	343	313	383	409	453	
B Expenditures in restaurants, cafes and hotels	171											...
	211	228	257									
			371	391	432	460	477	504	548	581	640	
C Other	503											...
	537	614	669									
			740	823	916	859	897	943	1000	1069	1190	
Total final consumption expenditure in the domestic market by households, of which	10793											...
	11764	12199	12754									
			14910	15947	16294	16718	17292	17774	18761	19562	20870	
plus: Direct purchases abroad by resident households	492											...
	420	427	481									
			599	597	573	532	608	621	777	885	908	
less: Direct purchases in the domestic market by non-resident households	474											...
	474	527	599									
			704	776	876	910	892	1010	1088	1214	1340	
equals: Final consumption expenditure of resident households [b]	10811											...
	11710	12099	12636									
			14804	15769	15992	16340	17008	17385	18450	19232	20438	

a Item "Personal care" excludes services of barbers, beauty shops etc. b Item "Final consumption expenditure of resident households" includes consumption expenditure of private non-profit institutions serving households.

Ireland

2.11 Gross fixed capital formation by kind of activity of owner, ISIC divisions, in current prices

Million Irish pounds

	1986	1987	1988	1989	1990	1991	1992	1993	1994	1995	1996	1997
All producers												
1 Agriculture, hunting, forestry and fishing	247 / 247	310	431	541	574	464	494	380	459	585	682	...
A Agriculture and hunting	222 / 222	275	385	465	517	411	448	340	413	533	631	...
B Forestry and logging	3 / 3	3	8	30	29	31	26	25	32	34	36	...
C Fishing	22 / 22	32	38	47	29	22	20	15	14	18	16	...
2 Mining and quarrying	27 / 25	34	42	50	75	38	37	28	46	77	93	...
3 Manufacturing	653 / 655	630	698	844	896	837	945	845	877	977	1122	...
A Manufacturing of food, beverages and tobacco	223 / 224	207	199	232	242	196	202	179	206	...	...	
B Textile, wearing apparel and leather industries	31 / 31	29	39	38	42	18	20	30	23	...	...	
C Manufacture of wood and wood products, including furniture	18 / 18	12	17	22	26	18	26	25	33	...	...	
D Manufacture of paper and paper products, printing and publishing	32 / 33	39	53	47	69	35	41	39	34	...	...	
E Manufacture of chemicals and chemical petroleum, coal, rubber and plastic products	113 / 113	124	156	146	207	228	329	228	234	...	...	
F Manufacture of non-metallic mineral products, except products of petroleum and coal	49 / 49	47	34	97	77	66	29	12	16	...	...	...
G Basic metal industries	10 / 11	10	16	9	5	10	8	6	4	...	...	
H Manufacture of fabricated metal products, machinery and equipment	176 / 177	163	186	253	228	267	288	326	326	...	...	
I Other manufacturing industries	...	...	...	...	...	...	...	...	...	...	...	
4 Electricity, gas and water	198 / 198	156	178	123	157	210	235	278	257	265	284	...
5 Construction	89 / 89	67	75	113	135	96	92	92	120	119	155	...
6 Wholesale and retail trade, restaurants and hotels	180 / 180	179	297	367	466	345	292	272	352	332	435	...
A Wholesale and retail trade	180 / 180	179	297	367	466	345	292	272	352	332	435	
B Restaurants and hotels	...	...	...	...	...	...	...	...	...	...	...	
7 Transport, storage and communication	441 / 441	458	473	601	747	695	674	840	756	827	914	...
A Transport and storage	304 / 304	334	339	446	586	544	512	637	571	682	712	...
B Communication	136 / 136	124	134	155	161	151	162	203	185	145	202	...
8 Finance, insurance, real estate and business services	1028 / 1066	1084	1091	1271	1473	1474	1614	1549	2007	2352	2901	...
A Financial institutions	146 / 146	174	187	225	249	188	118	148	172	212	258	...
B Insurance	...	...	...	...	...	...	...	...	...	...	...	
C Real estate and business services	882 / 920	910	904	1046	1224	1287	1496	1401	1835	2140	2644	...

Ireland

Million Irish pounds

	1986	1987	1988	1989	1990	1991	1992	1993	1994	1995	1996	1997
Real estate, except dwellings	...	...	...	...	...	...	...	...	...	...	...	...
Dwellings	882 920	910	904	1046	1224	1287	1496	1401	1835	2140	2644	...
9 Community, social and personal services [a]	435 435	450	430	414	459	612	600	584	567	706	805	...
A Sanitary and similar services [b]	257 257	263	281	273	323	467	422	408	376	476	558	...
B Social and related community services	178 178	186	150	141	136	145	178	176	191	230	247	...
Educational services	93 93	87	56	45	58	79	100	104	108	116	138	...
Medical, dental, other health and veterinary services	85 85	99	94	96	78	66	78	72	83	114	109	...
C Recreational and cultural services	...	...	...	...	...	...	...	...	...	...	...	...
D Personal and household services	...	...	...	...	...	...	...	...	...	...	...	...
Statistical discrepancy	–	...	...	...	...	...	...	...	...	...	...	...
Total industries	3298 3336	3367	3716	4325	4981	4772	4982	4869	5442	6240	7390	...
Producers of government services [c]	96 96	102	120	143	203	144	101	108	146	163	194	...
Private non-profit institutions serving households	...	...	...	...	...	...	...	...	...	...	...	...
Total	3393 3432	3469	3836	4468	5184	4916	5083	4977	5588	6402	7583	...

a Item "Private non-profit institutions serving households" is included in item "Community, social and personal services".
b Items "Restaurants and hotels", "Recreational and cultural services" and "Personal and household services" are included in item "Sanitary and similar services".
c Item "Producers of Government Services" includes public administration and defence only. All other activities of government are included in the corresponding industries.

2.12 Gross fixed capital formation by kind of activity of owner, ISIC divisions, in constant prices

Million Irish pounds

	1986	1987	1988	1989	1990	1991	1992	1993	1994	1995	1996	1997
At constant prices of:	1985 1985 1990											

All producers

	1986	1987	1988	1989	1990	1991	1992	1993	1994	1995	1996	1997
1 Agriculture, hunting, forestry and fishing	245 245	301	364 436	523	574	452	478	345	408	506	591	...
A Agriculture and hunting	220 220	257	340 388	445	517	400	434	309	366	461	...	...
B Forestry and logging	3 3	2	2 8	31	29	30	25	23	29	30	...	...
C Fishing	22 22	42	22 40	47	29	22	19	13	12	15	...	...
2 Mining and quarrying	27 25	34	38 44	49	75	37	35	26	41	63	77	...
3 Manufacturing	652 654	626	677 722	819	896	806	885	754	769	823	947	...
A Manufacturing of food, beverages and tobacco	223 223	206	192 206	225	242	193	188	155	176	...	...	...

Ireland

Million Irish pounds

		1986	1987	1988	1989	1990	1991	1992	1993	1994	1995	1996	1997
		At constant prices of:	1985										
				1985									
				1990									
B	Textile, wearing apparel and leather industries	31 31	29	38 40	37	42	17	18	26	20	...	...	...
C	Manufacture of wood and wood products, including furniture	18 18	12	16 17	22	26	17	25	22	28	...	...	...
D	Manufacture of paper and paper products, printing and publishing	32 33	38	51 54	45	69	35	39	34	29	...	...	...
E	Manufacture of chemicals and chemical petroleum, coal, rubber and plastic products	112 113	123	151 162	141	207	224	307	198	200	...	...	...
F	Manufacture of non-metallic mineral products, except products of petroleum and coal	49 49	46	33 35	94	77	48	31	31	34	...	...	...
G	Basic metal industries	10 11	10	15 16	9	5	10	8	5	4	...	...	...
H	Manufacture of fabricated metal products, machinery and equipment	176 177	162	180 192	245	228	262	269	283	278	...	...	...
I	Other manufacturing industries	...	...	...	...	...	...	...	...	...	...	...	...
4	Electricity, gas and water	194 194	155	161 191	125	157	203	223	255	236	231	250	...
5	Construction	89 89	66	65 77	109	135	93	86	83	105	100	131	...
6	Wholesale and retail trade, restaurants and hotels	173 173	164	191 326	382	466	338	280	253	324	305	384	...
A	Wholesale and retail trade ..	173 173	164	191 326	382	466	338	280	253	324	305	384	...
B	Restaurants and hotels	...	...	...	...	...	...	...	...	...	...	...	...
7	Transport, storage and communication	426 426	433	425 505	611	747	674	641	771	678	721	786	...
A	Transport and storage	293 293	314	305 365	456	586	531	492	593	519	601	...	...
B	Communication	133 133	119	121 141	155	161	143	149	178	159	120	...	...
8	Finance, insurance, real estate and business services	969 1028	1005	920 1265	1388	1473	1431	1503	1417	1793	2008	2361	...
A	Financial institutions	146 146	173	196 194	222	249	181	110	132	152	182	...	...
B	Insurance	...	...	...	...	...	...	...	...	...	...	...	...
C	Real estate and business services	823 882	832	724 1071	1166	1224	1250	1393	1285	1641	1826	...	...
	Real estate, except dwellings	...	...	...	...	...	...	...	...	...	...	...	...

Ireland

Million Irish pounds

	1986	1987	1988	1989	1990	1991	1992	1993	1994	1995	1996	1997
At constant prices of:	1985											
	1985											
	1990											
Dwellings	823										...	...
	882	832	724									
			1071	1166	1224	1250	1393	1285	1641	1826		
9 Community, social and personal services	424											...
	424	432	379									
			454	418	459	593	567	534	510	612	697	
A Sanitary and similar services	252										...	...
	251	255	248									
			295	276	323	453	399	372	337	412		
B Social and related community services	173										...	...
	173	177	131									
			160	143	136	141	168	162	173	200		
Educational services	89										...	...
	89	82	49									
			61	47	58	76	94	96	96	99		
Medical, dental, other health and veterinary services	83										...	...
	83	95	82									
			98	96	78	64	74	66	76	102		
C Recreational and cultural services	...	...	...	...	...	...	...	...	...	...	...	...
D Personal and household services	...	...	...	...	...	...	...	...	...	...	...	...
Total industries	3199											...
	3258	3217	3221									
			4021	4426	4981	4628	4697	4437	4863	5371	6223	
Producers of government services	93											...
	93	96	106									
			130	146	203	141	96	100	133	143	168	
Private non-profit institutions serving households	...	...	...	...	...	...	...	...	...	...	...	...
Total	3292											...
	3351	3313	3327									
			4151	4572	5184	4768	4794	4538	4996	5514	6391	

2.17 Exports and imports of goods and services, detail

Million Irish pounds

	1986	1987	1988	1989	1990	1991	1992	1993	1994	1995	1996	1997
Exports of goods and services												
1 Exports of merchandise, f.o.b.	9181											...
	9181	10447	12073	14358	14091	14675	16505	19460	22424	27698	30300	
2 Transport and communication [a]	679											...
	704	844	925	1050	1186	1344	1405	1439	1622	1682	1896	
A In respect of merchandise imports [b]	69											...
	69	70	61	64	67	69	69	66	66	70	82	
B Other	610											...
	635	774	863	985	1119	1275	1336	1373	1556	1612	1815	
3 Insurance service charges	...	...	...	...	...	...	...	...	...	...	...	...
4 Other commodities	...	...	...	...	...	...	...	...	...	...	...	...
5 Adjustments of merchandise exports to change-of-ownership basis	...	...	...	...	...	...	...	...	...	...	...	...
6 Direct purchases in the domestic market by non-residential households	492											...
	492	564	655	751	876	939	949	1090	1202	1375	1543	
7 Direct purchases in the domestic market by extraterritorial bodies	...	...	...	...	...	...	...	...	...	...	...	...

Ireland

Million Irish pounds

	1986	1987	1988	1989	1990	1991	1992	1993	1994	1995	1996	1997
Total exports of goods and services	10352 10377	11855	13653	16159	16153	16958	18859	21988	25248	30755	33740	...

Imports of goods and services

	1986	1987	1988	1989	1990	1991	1992	1993	1994	1995	1996	1997
1 Imports of merchandise, c.i.f.	8745 8745	9137	10048	12114	12294	12609	13004	14633	17028	20239	21884	...
2 Adjustments of merchandise imports to change-of-ownership basis	...	...	...	...	...	...	...	...	...	...	...	...
3 Other transport and communication [a]	604 747	1087	1347	1680	1667	1908	2252	2309	2713	3403	4076	...
4 Other insurance service charges	...	...	...	...	...	...	...	...	...	...	...	...
5 Other commodities	...	...	...	...	...	...	...	...	...	...	...	...
6 Direct purchases abroad by government	...	...	...	...	...	...	...	...	...	...	...	...
7 Direct purchases abroad by resident households	511 436	457	526	565	573	567	664	689	871	1028	1064	...
Total imports of goods and services	9860 9929	10681	11921	14359	14533	15084	15920	17631	20612	24671	27024	...
Balance of goods and services	491 449	1174	1732	1800	1619	1874	2939	4357	4636	6085	6716	...
Total imports and balance of goods and services	10352 10377	11855	13653	16159	16153	16958	18859	21988	25248	30755	33740	...

a Item "Transport and communication" includes all services.
b Item "Direct purchases in the domestic market by non-residential households" refers to governmental and other services.

3.12 General government income and outlay account: total and subsectors

Million Irish pounds

	1986					1987				
	Total government	Central government	State or provincial government	Local government	Social security funds	Total government	Central government	State or provincial government	Local government	Social security funds

Receipts

1 Operating surplus	177	9	...	168	...	167	–6	...	172	...
2 Property and entrepreneurial income	332	576	...	77	3	370	636	...	81	4
3 Taxes, fees and contributions	7470	6227	...	275	968	8005	6705	...	292	1009
A Indirect taxes [a]	3191	3025	...	167	...	3344	3160	...	184	...
B Direct taxes	2880	2880	...	...	...	3179	3179	...	...	...
Income	2796	2796	...	...	...	3092	3092	...	...	...
Other	85	85	...	...	...	86	86	...	...	...
C Social security contributions	1398	322	...	108	968	1483	366	...	108	1009
D Fees, fines and penalties	...	...	...	...	...	...	...	...	...	...
4 Other current transfers	158	158	...	2017	410	238	238	...	2089	402
A Casualty insurance claims	...	...	...	...	...	...	...	...	...	...
B Transfers from other government subsectors	...	1	...	2017	410	...	–	...	2089	401
C Transfers from rest of the world	158	158	...	...	–	238	237	...	...	–
D Other transfers, except imputed	...	...	...	...	...	...	...	...	...	...
E Imputed unfunded employee pension and welfare contributions	...	...	...	...	...	...	...	...	...	...
Total current receipts	8137	6971	...	2537	1381	8779	7573	...	2634	1414

Ireland

Million Irish pounds

	1986					1987				
	Total govern-ment	Central govern-ment	State or provincial govern-ment	Local govern-ment	Social security funds	Total govern-ment	Central govern-ment	State or provincial govern-ment	Local govern-ment	Social security funds
Disbursements										
1 Government final consumption expenditure [a]	3542	1787	...	1693	62	3575	1876	...	1632	67
2 Property income	1758	1734	...	348	...	1944	1893	...	402	...
3 Subsidies	385	385	...	–	...	576	576	...	–	...
4 Other current transfers	3819	4315	...	629	1303	3980	4482	...	649	1339
A Casualty insurance premiums, net	...	...	...	...	...	...	...	...	...	...
B Transfers to other government subsectors	...	2428	...	1	...	...	2490	...	–	...
C Social security benefits	1303	...	...	...	1303	1339	...	...	...	1339
D Social assistance grants	2082	1501	...	581	...	2188	1583	...	606	...
E Unfunded employee welfare benefits	...	...	...	...	...	...	...	...	...	...
F Transfers to private non-profit institutions serving households	385	337	...	48	...	404	361	...	43	...
G Other transfers n.e.c.	...	...	...	...	...	...	...	...	...	...
H Transfers to rest of the world	49	49	...	...	...	48	48	...	...	...
Net saving	−1367	−1250	...	−134	16	−1296	−1254	...	−49	8
Total current disbursements and net saving	8137	6971	...	2537	1381	8779	7573	...	2634	1414

	1988					1989				
	Total govern-ment	Central govern-ment	State or provincial govern-ment	Local govern-ment	Social security funds	Total govern-ment	Central govern-ment	State or provincial govern-ment	Local govern-ment	Social security funds
Receipts										
1 Operating surplus	214	16	...	197	–	143	−26	...	169	–
2 Property and entrepreneurial income	314	313	...	85	2	287	282	...	86	3
3 Taxes, fees and contributions	8920	7533	...	312	1075	9156	7620	...	364	1172
A Indirect taxes [a]	3672	3478	...	194	...	4046	3816	...	230	...
B Direct taxes	3641	3641	...	...	...	3385	3385	...	...	...
Income	3530	3530	...	...	...	3276	3276	...	...	...
Other	112	112	...	...	...	110	110	...	...	...
C Social security contributions	1607	414	...	118	1075	1724	419	...	134	1172
D Fees, fines and penalties	...	...	...	...	...	...	...	...	...	...
4 Other current transfers	181	182	...	1800	305	170	170	...	1814	224
A Casualty insurance claims	...	...	...	...	...	...	...	...	...	...
B Transfers from other government subsectors	...	1	...	1800	305	...	–	...	1814	224
C Transfers from rest of the world	181	181	...	...	–	170	170	...	...	–
D Other transfers, except imputed	...	...	...	...	...	...	...	...	...	...
E Imputed unfunded employee pension and welfare contributions	...	...	...	...	...	...	...	...	...	...
Total current receipts	9629	8044	...	2395	1382	9756	8047	...	2433	1398

Ireland

	1988					1989				
	Total government	Central government	State or provincial government	Local government	Social security funds	Total government	Central government	State or provincial government	Local government	Social security funds

Disbursements

1 Government final consumption expenditure [a]	3539	1807	...	1663	70	3670	1871	...	1726	72
2 Property income	1957	1927	...	117	...	1967	1938	...	114	...
3 Subsidies	706	706	...	–	...	325	325	...	–	...
4 Other current transfers	4156	4257	...	682	1323	4116	4189	...	659	1307
A Casualty insurance premiums, net	...	...	...	...	...	...	...	...	...	...
B Transfers to other government subsectors	...	2105	...	1	...	...	2038	...	–	...
C Social security benefits	1323	...	...	...	1323	1307	...	...	...	1307
D Social assistance grants	2359	1716	...	643	...	2326	1706	...	620	...
E Unfunded employee welfare benefits	...	...	...	...	...	...	...	...	...	...
F Transfers to private non-profit institutions serving households	401	362	...	39	...	421	382	...	39	...
G Other transfers n.e.c.	...	...	...	...	...	...	...	...	...	...
H Transfers to rest of the world	73	73	...	...	...	63	63	...	...	...
Net saving	–730	–653	...	–67	–10	–322	–277	...	–65	19
Total current disbursements and net saving	9629	8045	...	2395	1382	9756	8047	...	2433	1398

	1990					1991				
	Total government	Central government	State or provincial government	Local government	Social security funds	Total government	Central government	State or provincial government	Local government	Social security funds

Receipts

1 Operating surplus	120	–37	...	156	–	141	–11	...	152	–
2 Property and entrepreneurial income	346	335	...	88	4	427	412	...	88	2
3 Taxes, fees and contributions	9785	8119	...	386	1280	10302	8530	...	388	1385
A Indirect taxes [a]	4133	3893	...	240	...	4164	3913	...	251	...
B Direct taxes	3776	3776	...	...	...	4120	4120	...	...	...
Income	3656	3656	...	...	...	3971	3971	...	...	...
Other	120	120	...	...	...	149	149	...	...	...
C Social security contributions	1876	450	...	146	1280	2018	497	...	137	1385
D Fees, fines and penalties	...	...	...	...	...	...	...	...	...	...
4 Other current transfers	215	215	...	1982	76	366	366	...	2185	148
A Casualty insurance claims	...	...	...	...	...	...	...	...	...	...
B Transfers from other government subsectors	...	–	...	1982	76	...	–	...	2185	148
C Transfers from rest of the world	215	215	...	...	–	366	366	...	...	–
D Other transfers, except imputed	...	...	...	...	...	...	...	...	...	...
E Imputed unfunded employee pension and welfare contributions	...	...	...	...	...	...	...	...	...	...
Total current receipts	10465	8632	...	2611	1361	11236	9297	...	2813	1535

Ireland

	1990					1991				
	Total govern-ment	Central govern-ment	State or provincial govern-ment	Local govern-ment	Social security funds	Total govern-ment	Central govern-ment	State or provincial govern-ment	Local govern-ment	Social security funds

Disbursements

1 Government final consumption expenditure [a]	4067	2036	...	1952	79	4479	2268	...	2126	84
2 Property income	2125	2114	...	92	...	2148	2125	...	99	...
3 Subsidies	314	314	...	–	...	325	325	...	–	...
4 Other current transfers	4336	4355	...	702	1336	4771	4905	...	751	1448
A Casualty insurance premiums, net	...	...	...	...	...	...	...	...	...	...
B Transfers to other government subsectors	...	2058	...	–	...	...	2333	...	–	...
C Social security benefits	1336	...	...	...	1336	1448	...	...	...	1448
D Social assistance grants	2500	1847	...	653	...	2744	2042	...	702	...
E Unfunded employee welfare benefits	...	...	...	...	...	...	...	...	...	...
F Transfers to private non-profit institutions serving households	449	400	...	49	...	479	430	...	49	...
G Other transfers n.e.c.	...	...	...	...	...	...	...	...	...	...
H Transfers to rest of the world	50	50	...	...	...	99	99	...	...	...
Net saving	–377	–188	...	–135	–54	–487	–326	...	–163	2
Total current disbursements and net saving	10465	8632	...	2612	1361	11236	9297	...	2813	1535

	1992					1993				
	Total govern-ment	Central govern-ment	State or provincial govern-ment	Local govern-ment	Social security funds	Total govern-ment	Central govern-ment	State or provincial govern-ment	Local govern-ment	Social security funds

Receipts

1 Operating surplus	150	–8	...	158	–	169	–4	...	173	–
2 Property and entrepreneurial income	441	420	...	89	16	445	428	...	89	1
3 Taxes, fees and contributions	11102	9203	...	415	1485	11955	9907	...	440	1608
A Indirect taxes [a]	4443	4175	...	268	...	4496	4219	...	278	...
B Direct taxes	4490	4490	...	...	...	5081	5081	...	...	...
Income	4308	4308	...	...	...	4919	4919	...	...	...
Other	182	182	...	...	...	162	162	...	...	...
C Social security contributions	2169	537	...	147	1485	2378	608	...	162	1608
D Fees, fines and penalties	...	...	...	...	...	...	...	...	...	...
4 Other current transfers	338	337	...	2438	160	369	369	...	2704	107
A Casualty insurance claims	...	...	...	...	...	...	...	...	...	...
B Transfers from other government subsectors	...	–	...	2438	160	...	–	...	2704	107
C Transfers from rest of the world	338	337	...	...	–	369	369	...	...	–
D Other transfers, except imputed	...	...	...	...	...	...	...	...	...	...
E Imputed unfunded employee pension and welfare contributions	...	...	...	...	...	...	...	...	...	...
Total current receipts	12030	9952	...	3100	1661	12938	10700	...	3406	1716

Ireland

	1992					1993				
	Total govern-ment	Central govern-ment	State or provincial govern-ment	Local govern-ment	Social security funds	Total govern-ment	Central govern-ment	State or provincial govern-ment	Local govern-ment	Social security funds
Disbursements										
1 Government final consumption expenditure [a]	4842	2452	...	2297	94	5219	2550	...	2568	101
2 Property income	2116	2100	...	101	...	2142	2110	...	105	...
3 Subsidies	359	359	...	—	...	446	446	...	—	...
4 Other current transfers	5228	5424	...	839	1562	5663	5939	...	922	1613
A Casualty insurance premiums, net	...	...	...	...	...	...	...	...	...	...
B Transfers to other government subsectors	...	2598	...	—	...	...	2811	...	—	...
C Social security benefits	1562	...	...	...	1562	1613	...	...	...	1613
D Social assistance grants	3029	2251	...	778	...	3301	2452	...	849	...
E Unfunded employee welfare benefits	...	...	...	...	...	...	...	...	...	...
F Transfers to private non-profit institutions serving households	529	468	...	61	...	594	521	...	73	...
G Other transfers n.e.c.	...	...	...	...	...	...	...	...	...	...
H Transfers to rest of the world	108	108	...	...	...	155	155	...	...	...
Net saving	−515	−383	...	−137	5	−532	−345	...	−189	2
Total current disbursements and net saving	12030	9952	...	3100	1661	12938	10700	...	3406	1716

	1994					1995				
	Total govern-ment	Central govern-ment	State or provincial govern-ment	Local govern-ment	Social security funds	Total govern-ment	Central govern-ment	State or provincial govern-ment	Local govern-ment	Social security funds
Receipts										
1 Operating surplus	191	−2	...	193	—	213	−1	...	214	—
2 Property and entrepreneurial income	357	327	...	95	—	311	275	...	90	—
3 Taxes, fees and contributions	13247	11098	...	465	1685	13799	11560	...	495	1744
A Indirect taxes [a]	5161	4859	...	302	...	5580	5259	...	321	...
B Direct taxes	5599	5599	...	...	...	5635	5635	...	...	...
Income	5410	5410	...	...	...	5439	5439	...	...	...
Other	189	189	...	...	...	196	196	...	...	...
C Social security contributions	2487	640	...	163	1685	2584	666	...	174	1744
D Fees, fines and penalties	...	...	...	...	...	...	...	...	...	...
4 Other current transfers	353	352	...	3022	48	296	296	...	3161	220
A Casualty insurance claims	...	...	...	...	...	...	...	...	...	...
B Transfers from other government subsectors	...	—	...	3022	48	...	—	...	3161	220
C Transfers from rest of the world	353	352	...	...	—	296	296	...	...	—
D Other transfers, except imputed	...	...	...	...	...	...	...	...	...	...
E Imputed unfunded employee pension and welfare contributions	...	...	...	...	...	...	...	...	...	...
Total current receipts	14147	11775	...	3775	1733	14620	12130	...	3960	1965

Ireland

	1994					1995				
	Total government	Central government	State or provincial government	Local government	Social security funds	Total government	Central government	State or provincial government	Local government	Social security funds

Disbursements

1 Government final consumption expenditure [a]	5579	2700	...	2773	106	5949	2860	...	2997	91
2 Property income	2051	2026	...	91	...	2016	1988	...	83	...
3 Subsidies	386	386	...	–	...	439	439	...	–	...
4 Other current transfers	6072	6510	...	1012	1620	6442	6850	...	1106	1868
A Casualty insurance premiums, net	...	...	...	...	...	...	...	...	...	...
B Transfers to other government subsectors	...	3070	...	–	...	...	3381	...	–	...
C Social security benefits	1620	...	...	...	1620	1868	...	...	...	1868
D Social assistance grants	3603	2690	...	912	...	3668	2689	...	979	...
E Unfunded employee welfare benefits	...	...	...	...	...	...	...	...	...	...
F Transfers to private non-profit institutions serving households	657	558	...	99	...	700	572	...	127	...
G Other transfers n.e.c.	...	...	...	...	...	...	...	...	...	...
H Transfers to rest of the world	193	193	...	...	...	207	207	...	...	...
Net saving	59	152	...	–100	7	–226	–5	...	–226	5
Total current disbursements and net saving	14147	11775	...	3775	1733	14620	12133	...	3960	1965

a Item "Fees, fines and penalties" is included in item "Indirect taxes" or is offset against item "Final consumption expenditure".

3.13 General government capital accumulation account: total and subsectors

Million Irish pounds

	1986					1987				
	Total government	Central government	State or provincial government	Local government	Social security funds	Total government	Central government	State or provincial government	Local government	Social security funds

Finance of gross accumulation

1 Gross saving	–1226	–1188	...	–55	16	–1146	–1189	...	35	8
A Consumption of fixed capital	141	62	...	79	...	150	65	...	84	...
B Net saving	–1367	–1250	...	–134	16	–1296	–1254	...	–49	8
2 Capital transfers [a]	–103	–369	...	266	...	–79	–384	...	305	...
A From other government subsectors	...	–208	...	208	...	...	–211	...	211	...
B From other resident sectors	–196	–254	...	58	...	–191	–284	...	94	...
C From rest of the world	93	93	...	...	...	112	112	...	...	...
Finance of gross accumulation	–1329	–1556	...	211	16	–1225	–1573	...	340	8

Gross accumulation

1 Gross capital formation	693	163	...	530	...	555	156	...	399	...
A Increase in stocks	...	...	...	...	...	...	...	...	...	...
B Gross fixed capital formation	693	163	...	530	...	555	156	...	399	...
2 Purchases of land, net	...	...	...	...	...	...	...	...	...	...
3 Purchases of intangible assets, net	...	...	...	...	...	...	...	...	...	...
4 Capital transfers	...	...	...	...	...	...	...	...	...	...

Ireland

Million Irish pounds

	1986					1987				
	Total govern-ment	Central govern-ment	State or provincial govern-ment	Local govern-ment	Social security funds	Total govern-ment	Central govern-ment	State or provincial govern-ment	Local govern-ment	Social security funds
Net lending	−2023	−1720	...	−319	16	−1780	−1729	...	−59	8
Gross accumulation	−1329	−1557	...	211	16	−1225	−1573	...	340	8

	1988					1989				
	Total govern-ment	Central govern-ment	State or provincial govern-ment	Local govern-ment	Social security funds	Total govern-ment	Central govern-ment	State or provincial govern-ment	Local govern-ment	Social security funds

Finance of gross accumulation

1 Gross saving	−571	−584	...	23	−10	−155	−204	...	30	19
A Consumption of fixed capital	158	69	...	89	...	168	73	...	95	...
B Net saving	−730	−653	...	−67	−10	−322	−277	...	−65	19
2 Capital transfers [a]	−21	−398	...	376	...	14	−433	...	446	...
A From other government subsectors	...	−279	...	279	...	...	−333	...	333	...
B From other resident sectors	−135	−232	...	97	...	−100	−214	...	114	...
C From rest of the world	114	114	...	...	...	114	114	...	...	...
Finance of gross accumulation	−593	−982	...	399	−10	−141	−637	...	476	19

Gross accumulation

1 Gross capital formation	411	117	...	294	...	463	88	...	375	...
A Increase in stocks	...	...	...	...	...	...	...	...	...	...
B Gross fixed capital formation	411	117	...	294	...	463	88	...	375	...
2 Purchases of land, net	...	...	...	...	...	...	...	...	...	...
3 Purchases of intangible assets, net	...	...	...	...	...	...	...	...	...	...
4 Capital transfers	...	...	...	...	...	...	...	...	...	...
Net lending	−1004	−1099	...	106	−10	−604	−724	...	102	19
Gross accumulation	−593	−982	...	399	−10	−141	−637	...	476	19

	1990					1991				
	Total govern-ment	Central govern-ment	State or provincial govern-ment	Local govern-ment	Social security funds	Total govern-ment	Central govern-ment	State or provincial govern-ment	Local govern-ment	Social security funds

Finance of gross accumulation

1 Gross saving	−200	−112	...	−34	−54	−301	−246	...	−57	2
A Consumption of fixed capital	177	76	...	101	...	185	79	...	106	...
B Net saving	−377	−188	...	−135	−54	−487	−326	...	−163	2
2 Capital transfers [a]	151	−333	...	484	...	263	−256	...	519	...
A From other government subsectors	...	−333	...	333	...	...	−378	...	378	...
B From other resident sectors	−98	−249	...	151	...	−88	−230	...	141	...
C From rest of the world	249	249	...	...	...	352	352	...	...	...
Finance of gross accumulation	−49	−445	...	450	−54	−38	−502	...	462	2

Gross accumulation

1 Gross capital formation	570	132	...	437	...	621	128	...	493	...
A Increase in stocks	...	...	...	...	...	...	...	...	...	...
B Gross fixed capital formation	570	132	...	437	...	621	128	...	493	...
2 Purchases of land, net	...	...	...	...	...	...	...	...	...	...

Ireland

	1990					1991			
	Total govern-ment	Central govern-ment	State or provincial govern-ment	Local govern-ment	Social security funds	Total govern-ment	Central govern-ment	State or provincial govern-ment	Local govern-ment	Social security funds
3 Purchases of intangible assets, net	...	...	...	...	...	...	...	...	...	...
4 Capital transfers	...	...	...	...	...	...	...	...	...	...
Net lending	−619	−578	...	13	−54	−659	−630	...	−31	2
Gross accumulation	−49	−445	...	450	−54	−38	−502	...	462	2

	1992					1993			
	Total govern-ment	Central govern-ment	State or provincial govern-ment	Local govern-ment	Social security funds	Total govern-ment	Central govern-ment	State or provincial govern-ment	Local govern-ment	Social security funds

Finance of gross accumulation

1 Gross saving	−322	−301	...	−26	5	−331	−260	...	−72	2
A Consumption of fixed capital	193	82	...	111	...	201	85	...	116	...
B Net saving	−515	−383	...	−137	5	−532	−345	...	−189	2
2 Capital transfers [a]	205	−319	...	524	...	267	−436	...	703	...
A From other government subsectors	...	−406	...	406	...	...	−559	...	559	...
B From other resident sectors	−154	−272	...	118	...	−167	−311	...	144	...
C From rest of the world	359	359	...	...	...	434	434	...	...	...
Finance of gross accumulation	−117	−620	...	498	5	−64	−696	...	631	2

Gross accumulation

1 Gross capital formation	630	122	...	508	...	724	145	...	579	...
A Increase in stocks	...	...	...	...	...	...	...	...	...	...
B Gross fixed capital formation	630	122	...	508	...	724	145	...	579	...
2 Purchases of land, net	...	...	...	...	...	...	...	...	...	...
3 Purchases of intangible assets, net	...	...	...	...	...	...	...	...	...	...
4 Capital transfers	...	...	...	...	...	...	...	...	...	...
Net lending	−747	−742	...	−10	5	−788	−841	...	52	2
Gross accumulation	−117	−620	...	498	5	−64	−696	...	631	2

	1994					1995			
	Total govern-ment	Central govern-ment	State or provincial govern-ment	Local govern-ment	Social security funds	Total govern-ment	Central govern-ment	State or provincial govern-ment	Local govern-ment	Social security funds

Finance of gross accumulation

1 Gross saving	269	241	...	21	7	−2	89	...	−97	5
A Consumption of fixed capital	210	89	...	122	...	223	94	...	129	...
B Net saving	59	152	...	−100	7	−226	−5	...	−226	5
2 Capital transfers [a]	8	−799	...	807	...	152	−735	...	886	...
A From other government subsectors	...	−581	...	581	...	...	−691	...	691	...
B From other resident sectors	−214	−440	...	226	...	−356	−551	...	195	...
C From rest of the world	222	222	...	...	...	508	508	...	...	...
Finance of gross accumulation	277	−558	...	828	7	149	−645	...	789	5

Gross accumulation

1 Gross capital formation	832	175	...	657	...	873	174	...	699	...
A Increase in stocks	...	...	...	...	...	...	...	...	...	...

Ireland

	1994					1995				
	Total govern-ment	Central govern-ment	State or provincial govern-ment	Local govern-ment	Social security funds	Total govern-ment	Central govern-ment	State or provincial govern-ment	Local govern-ment	Social security funds
B Gross fixed capital formation	832	175	...	657	...	873	174	...	699	...
2 Purchases of land, net	...	...	...	...	...	...	...	...	...	...
3 Purchases of intangible assets, net	...	...	...	...	...	...	...	...	...	...
4 Capital transfers	...	...	...	...	...	...	...	...	...	...
Net lending	−556	−733	...	171	7	−724	−819	...	90	5
Gross accumulation	277	−558	...	828	7	149	−645	...	789	5

a Capital transfers received are recorded net of capital transfers paid.

3.51 External transactions, current account: detail

Million Irish pounds

	1986	1987	1988	1989	1990	1991	1992	1993	1994	1995	1996	1997
Payments to the rest of the world												
1 Imports of goods and services	9860 9929	10681	11921	14359	14533	15084	15920	17631	20612	24671	27024	...
A Imports of merchandise, c.i.f.	8745 8745	9137	10048	12114	12294	12609	13004	14633	17028	20239	21884	...
B Other	1115 1183	1544	1873	2245	2240	2475	2916	2998	3584	4432	5140	...
2 Factor income to rest of the world	2705 2769	2899	3690	4578	4873	4737	5029	5697	6630	8155	9479	...
A Compensation of employees	– –	–	–	–	–	–	–	–	–	–	–	...
B Property and entrepreneurial income	2705 2769	2899	3690	4578	4873	4737	5029	5697	6630	8155	9479	...
3 Current transfers to the rest of the world	374 374	378	363	372	439	523	532	646	728	769	841	...
A Indirect taxes by general government to supranational organizations	284 284	329	294	331	313	347	338	405	429	482	423	...
B Other current transfers	90 90	50	69	41	126	176	194	241	299	287	418	...
By general government	67 67	26	18	19	62	109	114	162	207	209	343	...
By other resident sectors	22 22	24	51	22	64	67	79	79	92	78	74	...
4 Surplus of the nation on current transactions	−540 −642	−47	138	−270	−48	691	988	1764	1283	1806	1682	...
Payments to the rest of the world and surplus of the nation on current transfers	12399 12429	13912	16112	19039	19797	21035	22470	25737	29253	35400	39027	...
Receipts from the rest of the world												
1 Exports of goods and services	10352 10377	11855	13653	16159	16153	16958	18859	21988	25248	30755	33740	...
A Exports of merchandise, f.o.b.	9181 9181	10447	12073	14358	14091	14675	16505	19460	22424	27698	30300	...
B Other	1171 1197	1408	1580	1801	2062	2283	2354	2529	2824	3057	3440	...
2 Factor income from rest of the world	748 752	787	1147	1472	1794	1945	1834	1794	2121	2766	3093	...
A Compensation of employees	16 16	16	135	144	146	149	157	172	183	181	190	...
B Property and entrepreneurial income	732 736	771	1012	1329	1647	1796	1677	1622	1938	2585	2903	...
3 Current transfers from rest of the world	1300 1300	1270	1312	1408	1851	2131	1777	1954	1883	1879	2194	...

Ireland

Million Irish pounds	1986	1987	1988	1989	1990	1991	1992	1993	1994	1995	1996	1997
A Subsidies to general government from supranational organizations	918 / 918	799	906	854	1295	1313	1114	1232	1240	1247	1549	...
B Other current transfers	381 / 381	471	406	553	556	818	663	723	644	633	645	...
To general government	56 / 56	80	64	62	228	474	414	484	383	367	366	...
To other resident sectors	325 / 325	391	341	491	328	344	249	238	261	265	279	...
Receipts from the rest of the world on current transfers	12399 / 12429	13912	16112	19039	19797	21035	22470	25737	29253	35400	39027	...

3.52 External transactions, capital accumulation account

Million Irish pounds	1986	1987	1988	1989	1990	1991	1992	1993	1994	1995	1996	1997
Finance of gross accumulation												
1 Surplus of the nation on current transactions	−540 / −642	−47	138	−270	−48	691	988	1764	1283	1806	1682	...
2 Capital transfers from rest of the world	100 / 100	119	162	162	290	438	523	573	312	571	549	...
Total finance of gross accumulation	−441 / −542	72	300	−108	242	1130	1512	2337	1594	2377	2232	...
Gross accumulation												
1 Capital transfers to the rest of the world	69 / 69	132	100	90	61	60	60	60	60	60	60	...
2 Purchases of intangible assets, n.e.c., net, from rest of the world	...	...	...	...	...	...	...	...	...	...	...	...
Net lending to the rest of the world	−509 / −611	−60	200	−198	181	1070	1452	2277	1534	2317	2172	...
Total gross accumulation	−441 / −542	72	300	−108	242	1130	1512	2337	1594	2377	2232	...

4.3 Cost components of value added

Million Irish pounds	1986 Compensation of employees	Capital consumption	Net operating surplus	Indirect taxes	less: Subsidies received	Value added	1987 Compensation of employees	Capital consumption	Net operating surplus	Indirect taxes	less: Subsidies received	Value added
All producers												
1 Agriculture, hunting, forestry and fishing	142 / 142	313 / 313	1196 / 1196	39 / 39	158 / 158	1532 / 1532	150	321	1458	46	172	1804
2 Mining and quarrying	2900	382	2088	860	625	5605	...	...	...	...	...	...
3 Manufacturing							...	...	...	...	...	...
4 Electricity, gas and water							...	...	...	...	...	...
5 Construction	800 / 844	18 / 20	149 / 161	1 / 1	— / —	968 / 1026	844	26	170	1	—	1041
6 Wholesale and retail trade, restaurants and hotels	1290 / 1262	188 / 188	717 / 831	95 / 95	373 / 373	1916 / 2003	1331	207	897	109	349	2194
A Wholesale and retail trade	1005 / 1005	155 / 155	626 / 729	76 / 76	373 / 373	1489 / 1592	1059	170	780	88	349	1748
B Restaurants and hotels	285 / 258	33 / 33	90 / 102	20 / 20	— / —	427 / 411	272	36	116	22	—	446
7 Transport, storage and communication	616 / 628	175 / 175	266 / 281	26 / 26	102 / 102	982 / 1009	644	187	389	29	108	1142

Ireland

Million Irish pounds

	1986						1987					
	Compensation of employees	Capital consumption	Net operating surplus	Indirect taxes	less: Subsidies received	Value added	Compensation of employees	Capital consumption	Net operating surplus	Indirect taxes	less: Subsidies received	Value added
A Transport and storage	392	97	143	23	102	553						
	403	97	157	23	102	579	410	97	239	27	108	665
B Communication	225	79	124	2	–	429						
	225	79	124	2	–	430	235	90	150	3	–	477
8 Finance, insurance, real estate and business services	664	169	165	69	–	1067						
	664	158	256	69	–	1147	759	153	214	78	–	1204
9 Community, social and personal services	890	450	1017	134	230	2261						
	908	461	1183	134	46	2641	1003	536	1152	155	46	2800
Total, Industries	7301	1694	5600	1224	1488	14332						
	7399	1744	6185	1224	1303	15248	7769	1913	6746	1346	1375	16399
Producers of government services	2954	141	–	22	–	3117						
	2866	141	–	22	–	3029	3028	150	–	23	–	3200
Other producers												
Total	10255	1835	5600	1246	1488	17448						
	10264	1885	6185	1246	1303	18277	10797	2063	6746	1369	1375	19599
less: Imputed bank service charge	...	...	804	...	...	804	...	...	...	...	...	...
			804			804			828			828
Import duties	...	...	...	678	...	678	...	...	...	...	...	...
				678		678				691		691
Value added tax	...	...	...	1551	...	1551	...	...	...	...	...	...
				1551		1551				1612		1612
Other adjustments	...	...	...	...	...	...	...	...	...	...	...	...
Total	10255	1835	4796	3475	1488	18874						
	10264	1885	5381	3475	1303	19703	10797	2063	5918	3672	1375	21074

	1988						1989					
	Compensation of employees	Capital consumption	Net operating surplus	Indirect taxes	less: Subsidies received	Value added	Compensation of employees	Capital consumption	Net operating surplus	Indirect taxes	less: Subsidies received	Value added

All producers

1 Agriculture, hunting, forestry and fishing	163	331	1720	49	257	2004	187	350	1803	52	227	2164
2 Mining and quarrying	...	...	...	...	...	...	...	...	...	...	...	...
3 Manufacturing	...	...	...	...	...	...	...	...	...	...	...	...
4 Electricity, gas and water	...	...	...	...	...	...	...	...	...	...	...	...
5 Construction	831	28	205	2	–	1066	851	25	234	2	–	1112
6 Wholesale and retail trade, restaurants and hotels	1456	210	1078	114	591	2267	1548	227	1086	136	210	2788
A Wholesale and retail trade	1166	171	964	91	591	1802	1249	180	959	108	210	2287
B Restaurants and hotels	289	38	114	23	–	465	300	47	127	27	–	501
7 Transport, storage and communication	772	198	419	32	112	1310	829	237	379	37	112	1370
A Transport and storage	512	96	250	29	112	775	549	105	195	34	112	770
B Communication	261	102	169	3	–	535	280	132	184	3	–	600
8 Finance, insurance, real estate and business services	842	182	254	96	–	1374	891	195	207	113	–	1406
9 Community, social and personal services	983	552	1616	174	53	3273	1103	626	1944	239	56	3856
Total, Industries	8154	1982	8106	1403	1612	18032	8778	2217	8938	1550	1178	20305
Producers of government services	3106	159	–	8	–	3272	3241	168	–	10	2	3416
Other producers												
Total	11260	2140	8106	1411	1612	21304	12019	2384	8938	1560	1180	23721
less: Imputed bank service charge	...	...	965	...	...	965	...	...	976	...	...	976
Import duties	...	...	...	791	...	791	...	...	...	873	...	873
Value added tax	...	...	...	1764	...	1764	...	...	...	1944	...	1944

Ireland

	1988						1989					
	Compensation of employees	Capital consumption	Net operating surplus	Indirect taxes	less: Subsidies received	Value added	Compensation of employees	Capital consumption	Net operating surplus	Indirect taxes	less: Subsidies received	Value added
Other adjustments	...	...	...	...	...	...	...	...	...	...	...	...
Total	11260	2140	7141	3966	1612	22894	12019	2384	7962	4377	1180	25562

	1990						1991					
	Compensation of employees	Capital consumption	Net operating surplus	Indirect taxes	less: Subsidies received	Value added	Compensation of employees	Capital consumption	Net operating surplus	Indirect taxes	less: Subsidies received	Value added

All producers

1 Agriculture, hunting, forestry and fishing	194	369	1777	52	417	1975	203	378	1629	53	344	1919
2 Mining and quarrying	...	...	...	...	...	...	...	...	...	...	...	...
3 Manufacturing	...	...	...	...	...	...	...	...	...	...	...	...
4 Electricity, gas and water	...	...	...	...	...	...	...	...	...	...	...	...
5 Construction	992	31	280	2	–	1304	1047	44	268	2	–	1360
6 Wholesale and retail trade, restaurants and hotels	1667	239	1707	142	526	3229	1839	236	1643	147	747	3117
A Wholesale and retail trade	1336	199	1537	112	526	2659	1464	172	1482	117	747	2487
B Restaurants and hotels	331	40	171	30	–	571	375	65	161	30	–	631
7 Transport, storage and communication	880	260	395	39	114	1460	961	287	399	39	113	1573
A Transport and storage	577	121	186	35	114	806	655	132	199	35	113	909
B Communication	302	138	210	4	–	654	306	155	200	4	–	664
8 Finance, insurance, real estate and business services	925	217	228	110	–	1480	972	264	366	103	–	1704
9 Community, social and personal services	1240	704	2136	243	61	4262	1325	747	2217	244	51	4482
Total, Industries	9500	2439	10071	1562	1608	21964	10082	2661	10226	1620	1635	22954
Producers of government services	3495	177	–	13	2	3683	3768	185	–	9	2	3960
Other producers												
Total	12995	2616	10071	1574	1610	25646	13850	2846	10226	1629	1638	26913
less: Imputed bank service charge	...	...	993	...	...	993	...	...	1094	...	...	1094
Import duties	...	...	...	903	...	903	...	...	...	870	...	870
Value added tax	...	...	...	1969	...	1969	...	...	...	2012	...	2012
Other adjustments	...	...	...	...	...	...	...	...	...	...	...	...
Total	12995	2616	9078	4446	1610	27525	13850	2846	9131	4511	1638	28701

	1992						1993					
	Compensation of employees	Capital consumption	Net operating surplus	Indirect taxes	less: Subsidies received	Value added	Compensation of employees	Capital consumption	Net operating surplus	Indirect taxes	less: Subsidies received	Value added

All producers

1 Agriculture, hunting, forestry and fishing	218	377	1900	50	418	2127	220	377	1944	56	416	2182
2 Mining and quarrying	...	...	...	...	...	...	...	...	...	...	...	...
3 Manufacturing	...	...	...	...	...	...	...	...	...	...	...	...
4 Electricity, gas and water	...	...	...	...	...	...	...	...	...	...	...	...
5 Construction	1045	35	311	2	–	1393	1135	39	335	2	–	1511
6 Wholesale and retail trade, restaurants and hotels	2054	200	1021	162	375	3061	2240	215	1419	172	406	3640
A Wholesale and retail trade	1647	157	832	127	375	2388	1786	164	1212	133	406	2890
B Restaurants and hotels	407	43	189	34	–	673	454	51	208	38	–	750

Ireland

	1992						1993					
	Compensation of employees	Capital consumption	Net operating surplus	Indirect taxes	less: Subsidies received	Value added	Compensation of employees	Capital consumption	Net operating surplus	Indirect taxes	less: Subsidies received	Value added
7 Transport, storage and communication	980	294	399	42	112	1604	1040	309	396	44	115	1673
A Transport and storage	665	133	185	38	112	909	678	122	201	40	115	925
B Communication	315	161	214	4	–	695	362	187	195	4	–	748
8 Finance, insurance, real estate and business services	1074	277	593	111	–	2055	1097	268	831	104	–	2299
9 Community, social and personal services	1417	775	2279	265	73	4662	1628	838	2424	259	104	5045
Total, Industries	10706	2787	10778	1703	1471	24502	11420	2957	12131	1886	1675	26719
Producers of government services	4100	193	–	15	3	4305	4603	200	–	14	3	4814
Other producers												
Total	14806	2979	10778	1718	1474	28808	16023	3157	12131	1899	1678	31533
less: Imputed bank service charge	...	...	1235	...	...	1235	...	...	1419	...	...	1419
Import duties	...	...	...	884	...	884	...	...	...	746	...	746
Value added tax	...	...	...	2179	...	2179	...	...	...	2255	...	2255
Other adjustments	...	...	...	...	...	...	...	...	...	...	...	...
Total	14806	2979	9542	4781	1474	30635	16023	3157	10712	4901	1678	33115

	1994						1995					
	Compensation of employees	Capital consumption	Net operating surplus	Indirect taxes	less: Subsidies received	Value added	Compensation of employees	Capital consumption	Net operating surplus	Indirect taxes	less: Subsidies received	Value added

All producers

1 Agriculture, hunting, forestry and fishing	220	385	2063	45	681	2032	226	407	2212	53	833	2065
2 Mining and quarrying	...	...	...	...	...	...	...	...	...	...	...	...
3 Manufacturing	...	...	...	...	...	...	...	...	...	...	...	...
4 Electricity, gas and water	...	...	...	...	...	...	...	...	...	...	...	...
5 Construction	1236	38	358	2	–	1634	1356	35	420	2	–	1814
6 Wholesale and retail trade, restaurants and hotels	2366	192	1166	187	160	3751	2547	222	1401	192	36	4325
A Wholesale and retail trade	1872	150	914	146	160	2922	2020	172	1134	155	36	3446
B Restaurants and hotels	494	42	252	41	–	829	526	50	266	36	–	879
7 Transport, storage and communication	1109	394	396	50	110	1839	1167	432	468	53	110	2010
A Transport and storage	735	126	214	45	110	1011	785	148	219	48	110	1090
B Communication	374	268	182	4	–	828	383	284	249	5	–	920
8 Finance, insurance, real estate and business services	1126	321	839	111	–	2397	1221	313	1054	107	–	2695
9 Community, social and personal services	1810	957	2599	321	69	5618	2021	1076	2601	343	77	5964
Total, Industries	12264	3278	13013	2158	1624	29088	13190	3625	15457	2299	1684	32887
Producers of government services	4828	210	–	12	2	5048	5151	223	–	14	2	5387
Other producers												
Total	17091	3488	13013	2170	1626	34136	18341	3848	15457	2312	1686	38274
less: Imputed bank service charge	...	...	1493	...	...	1493	...	...	1770	...	...	1770
Import duties	...	...	...	814	...	814	...	...	...	864	...	864
Value added tax	...	...	...	2605	...	2605	...	...	...	2887	...	2887
Other adjustments	...	...	...	...	...	...	...	...	...	...	...	...
Total	17091	3488	11520	5590	1626	36063	18341	3848	13687	6063	1686	40254

Israel

General note

The preparation of national accounts statistics in Israel is undertaken by the Central Bureau of Statistics. The official estimates are published annually by the Bureau in the *Statistical Abstract of Israel* and in the May supplement to the *Monthly Bulletin of Statistics*. A detailed description of the sources and methods used for the national accounts estimates is found in *Israel's National Income and Expenditure 1950–1962* published in 1964. Another edition of this publication for the years 1950–1968 published in 1970 included a description of the principal changes made in the methods of estimation. The estimates are generally in accordance with the classifications and definitions recommended in the United Nations Systems of National Accounts (1968 SNA). Input-output tables have been published in *Input-Output Tables 1988*. The following tables have been prepared from successive replies to the United Nations National Accounts Questionnaire. When the scope and coverage of the estimates differ for conceptual or statistical reasons from the definitions and classifications recommended in SNA, a footnote is indicated to the relevant tables.

Gross domestic product

Gross domestic product is estimated mainly through the expenditure approach.

Expenditures on the gross domestic product

The expenditure approach is used to estimate government final consumption expenditure and exports and imports of goods and services. This approach, in combination with the commodity-flow approach, is used for private final consumption expenditure and gross capital formation. General government consumption expenditure is estimated on the basis of activity reports of the Accountant-General and the Budget Provision supplemented by data from the Ministry of Finance. Expenditure of the local authorities and national institutions is estimated on the basis of financial statements and budget proposals. Private expenditure estimates on food, beverages and tobacco are based on data concerning quantities produced and marketed and on consumer prices, while estimates of expenditure on housing and business services, consumption of industrial products and other food products are based on family expenditure surveys held every five or six years. For the intervening years, estimates are computed by extrapolating year-to-year changes by the commodity-flow approach. Estimates of increase in stocks in agriculture, fuel and government strategic stocks are prepared by multiplying quantity changes in inventory stocks by their average prices. Regular quarterly and annual surveys are used to estimate inventory changes for industry and wholesale trade. The data obtained are adjusted to approximate the value of the physical change in stocks.

Building and construction works are estimated either from financial data on investment in building carried out by general government and major enterprises or by multiplying data on the areas under construction by the average cost per square meter for each type of construction. The estimates of imported machinery and equipment are based on the foreign trade statistics using the customs tariff description to identify the relevant items, while estimates of locally produced goods are based on a monthly report of sales by product obtained from a sample of the producers. The estimates of exports and imports of goods and services are based on foreign trade statistics and balance of payments data. Data pertaining to trade with the administered territories are a gross evaluation based on a sample enumeration of movement of goods through the official transit points. For the constant price estimates, government wages and salaries are extrapolated using changes in the number of employees. Government purchases of goods and services are deflated by relevant components of the consumer or wholesale price index. Price deflation is also used for most of the items of private expenditure, gross fixed capital formation and exports and imports of goods and services. For private food consumption and inventory changes in agriculture, fuel supplies, and government strategic stocks, estimates are computed by multiplying current quantities by prices in the base year.

Cost structure of the gross domestic product

The estimates of wages and salaries are based either on surveys of the industrial and construction branches, surveys of parts of the transportation branch and surveys of government and private non-profit institutions and services or on employers' reports to the National Insurance Institute and estimates of supplementary payments. The estimate of consumption of fixed capital was calculated at replacement cost. Estimates of indirect taxes are based on the financial reports of the government and the local authorities. Operating surplus is obtained as a residual.

Gross domestic product by kind of activity

The table of gross domestic product by kind of economic activity is prepared in net factor values. Net indirect taxes are estimated as totals only and not by industry. The production approach is used to estimate value added of the agricultural sector, the mining, quarrying and manufacturing sectors and the construction industry. For other sectors, the income approach is used. Estimates for recent years have been extrapolated by using the production approach. For the agricultural sector, data on output and input are based on the agricultural statistics series prepared by the Central Bureau of Statistics. For mining and quarrying and manufacturing, estimates are based on industrial surveys carried out annually. For years not covered by industrial surveys estimates are interpolated and extrapolated using current production indices. The Israel Electric Corporation and the Water Authority Commission supply data for their respective utility. For the construction industry a fixed ratio is assumed between input and output at constant prices and differences between the price movements of inputs and outputs are taken into account.

Benchmark estimates for wholesale and retail trade have been based on a survey held in 1976/77. Extrapolation for other years is based on changes in sales to final users. The value added of the hotel industry is estimated by changes in revenue and inputs using data obtained from special surveys. For transport and communication, estimates are based on annual reports of the concerned establishments and on surveys of the trucking industry. Estimates for the financing and insurance industries are based on consolidated reports prepared by the supervisor of banks and the supervisor of insurance. Benchmark estimate for residential rent for 1986 has been based on the family expenditure survey, extrapolated by the change in the value of inventories of dwellings. Estimates of government services are based on reports of the Accountant-General, the national institutions and local authorities as well as on data obtained from the Budget Provisions, and from the Ministry of Finance. For other services, estimates are derived from a sample of income tax files, indirect tax data, manpower data and data on *qibbutz* personal services.

Gross domestic product by kind of economic activity is not estimated at constant prices.

1.1 Expenditure on the gross domestic product, in current prices

Million new shekels

	1986	1987	1988	1989	1990	1991	1992	1993	1994	1995	1996	1997
1 Government final consumption expenditure	13645	19358	22199	25108	31745	40115	45783	53188	62634	77199	90547	99480
2 Private final consumption expenditure	27800	36391	44257	53168	64745	81484	97915	116475	142478	161217	186598	209328
A Households	27145	35511	43235	52012	63378	79819	95945	114264	139413	157790	182812	205159
B Private non-profit institutions serving households	655	881	1022	1156	1367	1665	1969	2211	3065	3427	3786	4169
3 Gross capital formation	8452	10958	12889	14811	20656	34240	40205	46990	54234	64896	74144	73694
A Increase in stocks	401	−336	113	258	422	1960	2137	4505	2220	3506	3201	667
B Gross fixed capital formation	8051	11294	12776	14554	20234	32280	38068	42485	52014	61390	70943	73027
Residential buildings	2136	2959	3625	4618	6476	13134	14443	12012	13737	18851	21378	23176
Non-residential buildings	754	1093	1387	1834	2332	3063	4396	6155	7789	9823	11759	12054
Other construction and land improvement, etc.	613	915	1146	1342	1928	2693	3545	4869	5070	5890	7100	7635
Other	4549	6328	6618	6760	9498	13390	15683	19450	25418	26826	30706	30162
4 Exports of goods and services	16944	21566	23716	30411	35739	39472	48712	60026	75952	83167	93978	106974
5 less: Imports of goods and services	19132	26806	27936	33932	41711	52170	60741	78385	94362	110563	124685	133806
Statistical discrepancy	...	...	...	...	...	−100	...	...	−2999	...	...	...
equals: Gross domestic product	47709	61467	75125	89567	111174	143041	171874	198294	237937	275917	320581	355670

1.2 Expenditure on the gross domestic product, in constant prices

Million new shekels

	1986	1987	1988	1989	1990	1991	1992	1993	1994	1995	1996	1997
	At constant prices of:	1980										
			1986									
					1990							
										1995		
1 Government final consumption expenditure	43 13646	16115	15737	14380	15486 31743	33049	33514	34921	34861	34968 77198	81620	82856
2 Private final consumption expenditure	84 27799	30284	31651	31769	33534 64746	69411	74931	80408	88060	94365 161219	169311	176087

Israel

Million new shekels

	1986	1987	1988	1989	1990	1991	1992	1993	1994	1995	1996	1997
At constant prices of: 1980												
1986												
1990												
1995												
A Households	82 27144	29606	31021	31112	32866 63378	67925	73371	78874	86279	92653 157792	165989	172649
B Private non-profit institutions serving households	2 655	679	631	657	668 1368	1486	1560	1535	1781	1712 3427	3322	3438
3 Gross capital formation	28 8449	8854	9111	8914	11170 20656	29308	30822	32462	35200	38889 64897	70223	65602
A Increase in stocks	3 401	−357	47	140	422 422	1326	976	2094	801	1388 3507	3136	645
B Gross fixed capital formation	25 8049	9211	9063	8774	10748 20234	27982	29846	30368	34398	37501 61391	67087	64957
Residential buildings	7 2136	2317	2367	2530	2955 6477	11256	11255	8613	8957	11194 18851	19765	19814
Non-residential buildings	2 754	868	919	985	1129 2331	2580	3329	4250	4914	5542 9827	10906	10316
Other construction and land improvement, etc.	2 613	746	744	760	934 1929	2292	2710	3462	3324	3542 5886	6539	6503
Other	13 4547	5279	5033	4498	5732 9498	11855	12552	14044	17204	17222 26827	29877	28324
4 Exports of goods and services	63 16943	18735	18333	19045	19400 35739	34798	39748	43648	49224	54577 83167	87344	93590
5 less: Imports of goods and services	77 19133	22801	22336	21310	23105 41711	47260	50811	58419	64612	70242 110563	118991	122841
equals: Gross domestic product	141 47705	51188	52496	52798	56485 111173	119306	128205	133020	142733	152557 275919	289507	295294

1.3 Cost components of the gross domestic product

Million new shekels

	1986	1987	1988	1989	1990	1991	1992	1993	1994	1995	1996	1997
1 Indirect taxes, net	8242	10848	12195	13476	17811	24789	30046	33784	39656	47579	56587	63123
A Indirect taxes	10195	13337	15207	16539	21115	28597	34980	38598	44998	52396	61274	67866
B less: Subsidies [a]	1953	2489	3012	3063	3304	3808	4934	4814	5342	4817	4687	4743
2 Consumption of fixed capital	7136	8882	10455	12971	15661	19189	22061	26281	31474	37049	42892	49073
3 Compensation of employees paid by resident producers to	23431	31357	38674	46638	55957	69722	84047	98425	122211	144182	168356	189741
A Resident households	22665	30194	37502	45205	54204	67834	81250	95778	119365	139863	162548	182624
B Rest of the world	766	1163	1172	1433	1753	1888	2797	2647	2846	4319	5808	7117
4 Operating surplus	8898	10380	13800	16483	21744	29341	35725	39807	44596	47106	52746	55532

Israel

Million new shekels

	1986	1987	1988	1989	1990	1991	1992	1993	1994	1995	1996	1997
Statistical discrepancy	...	...	...	...	...	...	...	...	...	...	...	−1799
equals: Gross domestic product	47707	61467	75125	89567	111174	143041	171874	198294	237937	275917	320581	355670

a Beginning 1975, item "Subsidies" includes subsidy component in government loans to industries.

1.4 General government current receipts and disbursements

Million new shekels

	1986	1987	1988	1989	1990	1991	1992	1993	1994	1995	1996	1997
Receipts												
1 Operating surplus	...	...	...	...	...	...	...	...	...	...	...	...
2 Property and entrepreneurial income	898	995	1479	1919	2732	3646	3862	3156	3105	5453	4613	4718
3 Taxes, fees and contributions	20430	25670	30144	33113	40545	51846	63140	73271	89667	105963	120083	138605
A Indirect taxes	10195	13337	15207	16539	21115	28597	34980	38598	44998	52396	61274	67866
B Direct taxes	7335	8842	10795	11597	13404	15989	19930	25041	33013	37312	39767	48249
C Social security contributions	2714	3188	3773	4505	5461	6605	7403	8676	10564	14958	17410	20486
D Compulsory fees, fines and penalties	186	303	369	472	565	655	827	956	1092	1297	1632	2004
4 Other current transfers	6818	6052	6213	7235	9245	12134	12729	13967	14420	14623	17539	19268
Total current receipts of general government	28146	32717	37836	42267	52523	67626	79731	90394	107192	126039	142235	162591
Disbursements												
1 Government final consumption expenditure	13643	19358	22199	25108	31745	40015	45783	53188	62634	77199	90547	99480
A Compensation of employees	7099	9086	11937	14565	18034	22935	26885	30856	39882	47105	54491	59794
B Consumption of fixed capital	737	955	1176	1442	1654	2031	2328	2666	3008	3482	3875	4331
C Purchases of goods and services, net	5807	9317	9086	9102	12057	15049	16570	19666	19745	26612	32181	35355
D less: Own-account fixed capital formation	...	...	...	...	...	...	...	...	...	...	...	...
E Indirect taxes paid, net	...	...	...	...	...	...	...	...	...	...	...	...
2 Property income [a]	5387	6091	6838	8212	9720	11334	12382	13773	15641	18564	19132	21762
3 Subsidies	1953	2489	3012	3063	3304	3808	4934	4814	5342	4817	4687	4743
4 Other current transfers	4375	5695	7128	9089	11866	15206	17970	21046	25009	30659	36913	42317
5 Net saving	2788	−916	−1341	−3205	−4113	−2736	−1338	−2427	−1434	−5200	−9044	−5711
Total current disbursements and net saving of general government	28146	32717	37836	42267	52523	67626	79731	90394	107192	126039	142235	162591

a Item "Property income" relates to interest on public debt.

1.7 External transactions on current account, summary

Million new shekels

	1986	1987	1988	1989	1990	1991	1992	1993	1994	1995	1996	1997
Payments to the rest of the world												
1 Imports of goods and services	19135	26806	27936	33932	41711	52170	60741	78385	94362	110563	124685	133806
A Imports of merchandise, c.i.f.	15429	21998	22481	26537	32749	41608	48474	62067	73478	86825	97123	102368
B Other	3706	4808	5455	7395	8962	10562	12267	16318	20884	23738	27562	31438
2 Factor income to rest of the world	4505	5077	5402	6564	7282	7764	9081	9242	10798	13687	16112	18639
A Compensation of employees	766	1163	1172	1433	1753	1889	2803	2649	2852	4337	5762	6762

Israel

Million new shekels

	1986	1987	1988	1989	1990	1991	1992	1993	1994	1995	1996	1997
B Property and entrepreneurial income	3739	3914	4230	5131	5529	5875	6278	6593	7946	9350	10350	11877
By general government	2000	2186	2401	2570	2733	3069	3409	3783	4563	5079	5420	6061
By corporate and quasi-corporate enterprises	1739	1728	1829	2561	2796	2806	2869	2810	3383	4271	4930	5816
By other												
3 Current transfers to the rest of the world	164	312	295	269	382	539	721	810	690	756	890	939
4 Surplus of the nation on current transactions	2414	−1257	−642	1799	1310	−1737	−830	−5603	−8311	−15258	−17119	−11998
Payments to the rest of the world and surplus of the nation on current transfers	26217	30938	32991	42564	50685	58736	69713	82834	97539	109748	124568	141386

Receipts from the rest of the world

	1986	1987	1988	1989	1990	1991	1992	1993	1994	1995	1996	1997
1 Exports of goods and services	16943	21566	23716	30411	35739	39472	48712	60026	72952	83167	93978	106974
A Exports of merchandise, f.o.b.	11665	14742	16435	21215	25431	27503	33002	41494	51460	57633	65848	75129
B Other	5278	6824	7281	9196	10308	11969	15710	18532	21492	25534	28130	31845
2 Factor income from rest of the world	1374	1545	1796	2674	3250	3937	3995	3580	3577	4696	5330	6498
A Compensation of employees	144	203	205	238	232	353	374	510	452	213	220	243
B Property and entrepreneurial income	1230	1341	1591	2436	3019	3584	3621	3070	3125	4483	5110	6255
By general government	431	458	574	884	1198	1732	1532	1073	671	1386	1557	2715
By corporate and quasi-corporate enterprises	799	883	1017	1552	1821	1852	2089	1997	2454	3097	3553	3540
By other												
3 Current transfers from rest of the world	7900	7827	7479	9477	11695	15327	17001	19225	21010	21885	25260	27914
Receipts from the rest of the world on current transactions	26217	30938	32991	42562	50685	58736	69713	82831	97539	109748	124568	141386

1.8 Capital transactions of the nation, summary

Million new shekels

	1986	1987	1988	1989	1990	1991	1992	1993	1994	1995	1996	1997
Finance of gross capital formation												
Gross saving	10866	9701	13024	16273	21552	32020	39549	42116	45877	49638	57030	61695
1 Consumption of fixed capital	7136	8882	10455	12971	15661	19189	22061	26281	31474	37049	42892	49073
A General government	737	955	1176	1442	1654	2030	2328	2666	3008	3482	3875	4331
B Corporate and quasi-corporate enterprises	6399	7927	9279	11529	14007	17159	19734	23615	28466	33567	39017	44742
C Other	...	...	...	...	...	...	...	...	...	...	...	...
2 Net saving	3730	819	2568	3302	5891	12831	17488	15835	14403	12589	14138	12622
A General government	2788	−916	−564	−3542	−4526	−3219	−1164	−1696	−1479	−5200	−9039	−5711
B Corporate and quasi-corporate enterprises	942	1735	3132	6844	10417	16050	18652	17531	15882	17789	23177	18333
C Other												
less: Surplus of the nation on current transactions	2414	−1257	135	1462	895	−2220	−656	−4874	−8356	−15258	−17114	−11998
Finance of gross capital formation	8452	10958	12889	14811	20657	34240	40205	46990	54233	64896	74144	73693
Gross capital formation												
Increase in stocks	401	−336	113	258	422	1960	2138	4505	2220	3506	3201	667
Gross fixed capital formation	8051	11294	12776	14554	20234	32280	38068	42485	52014	61390	70943	73027
Gross capital formation	8452	10958	12889	14811	20656	34240	40205	46990	54234	64896	74144	73694

Israel

1.10 Gross domestic product by kind of activity, in current prices

Million new shekels

	1986	1987	1988	1989	1990	1991	1992	1993	1994	1995	1996	1997
1 Agriculture, hunting, forestry and fishing	1519	1778	1899	2119	2549	2648	3375	3302	4137	4310 / 4619	4828 / 4792	5009 / 4971
2 Mining and quarrying [a]	7079	9630	11327	14184	16982	20520	24901	28931	33383	36359 / 36359	38579 / 41491	41709 / 47280
3 Manufacturing	...	...	...	...	...	...	...	...	...	...	...	...
4 Electricity, gas and water	515	672	826	900	962	1120	1392	1618	1810	2229 / 2229	21710 / 2344	22440 / 2557
5 Construction	1610	2244	2987	3652	4983	7875	9524	10444	12722	16416 / 16416	19124	2060
6 Wholesale and retail trade, restaurants and hotels	4464	5744	6411	7471	8723	10553	13166	15267	18029	21505 / 23373	27448 / 26632	30085 / 28862
7 Transport, storage and communication	2595	3446	4784	5477	6403	7793	9003	10340	11823	13766 / 14670	15015 / 15201	16711 / 15709
8 Finance, insurance, real estate and business services	6969	9986	12169	15396	18727	24124	29189	35884	44449	52630 / 51736	64433 / 63859	73596 / 71687
9 Community, social and personal services	1241	1822	2287	2824	3410	3982	4759	5840	7094	8384 / 6210	7309 / 7168	8021 / 8176
Statistical discrepancy [b]	997	794	705	568	569	578	534	471	418	363 / 363	295	189
Total, Industries	26989	36116	43395	52591	63308	79193	95843	112097	133865	155962 / 155975	179322 / 180906	197571 / 181491
Producers of government services	7324	9434	12361	15433	18663	23473	27500	31638	41022	48360 / 48360	56864 / 55927	62793 / 61159
Other producers	...	...	...	...	...	...	...	...	...	...	295	189
Subtotal	34313	45550	55756	68024	81971	102666	123343	143735	174887	204322 / 204335	236481 / 236833	260552 / 242650
less: Imputed bank service charge	1600	2614	3289	3915	4164	5382	5835	6064	6611	8757 / 8757	10520 / 10520	12364 / 11285
plus: Import duties	...	...	...	...	...	...	...	...	...	...	...	...
plus: Value added tax	...	...	...	...	...	...	...	...	...	...	...	...
plus: Other adjustments [c]	–388	–1199	7	–988	–314	1234	1779	595	–1972	–4286 / –4291	–3364 / –5211	–3738 / –6433
equals: Gross domestic product [d]	32325	41738	52474	63121	77701	99063	119772	138239	166807	191289 / 191289	222597 / 221102	244450 / 243479

a Includes Manufacturing.
b Item "Statistical discrepancy" relates to subsidy component in government loans to the business sector (on domestic production and exports) which could not be classified by industry.
c Item "Other adjustments" includes errors and omissions.
d Net domestic product in factor values rather than gross domestic product.

1.12 Relations among national accounting aggregates

Million new shekels

	1986	1987	1988	1989	1990	1991	1992	1993	1994	1995	1996	1997
Gross domestic product	47707	61467	75125	89567	111174	143041	171874	198294	237937	275917	320581	355670
plus: Net factor income from the rest of the world	–3130	–3532	–3606	–3890	–4031	–3827	–5085	–5662	–7221	–8991	–10782	–12141
Factor income from rest of the world	1374	1545	1796	2674	3250	3937	3996	3580	3577	4696	5330	6498
less: Factor income to the rest of the world	4504	5077	5402	6564	7281	7764	9081	9242	10798	13687	16112	18639
equals: Gross national product	44577	57935	71519	85677	107143	139214	166789	192632	230716	266926	309799	343529
less: Consumption of fixed capital	7136	8882	10455	12971	15661	19189	22061	26281	31474	37049	42892	49073
equals: National income	37441	49053	61064	72706	91482	120025	144728	166351	199242	229877	266907	294456
plus: Net current transfers from the rest of the world	7736	7515	7184	9208	11313	14788	16280	18415	20320	21128	24370	26975
Current transfers from rest of the world	7900	7827	7479	9477	11695	15327	17001	19225	21010	21885	25260	27914

Israel

Million new shekels

	1986	1987	1988	1989	1990	1991	1992	1993	1994	1995	1996	1997
less: Current transfers to the rest of the world	164	312	295	269	382	539	721	810	690	757	890	939
equals: National disposable income	45177	56568	68248	81914	102795	134813	161008	184766	219562	251005	291277	321431
less: Final consumption	41443	55749	66456	78276	96490	121499	143697	169663	205112	238417	277145	308808
equals: Net saving	3734	819	1792	3638	6305	13314	17311	15103	14450	12589	14133	12623
less: Surplus of the nation on current transactions	2414	−1257	−652	1798	1310	−1737	−833	−5606	−8310	−15258	−17119	−11998
equals: Net capital formation	1320	2076	2444	1840	4995	15051	18144	20709	22760	27847	31252	24621

2.3 Total government outlays by function and type

Million new shekels

1992

	Final consumption expenditures			Subsidies	Other current transfers and property income	Total current disbursements	Gross capital formation	Other capital outlays	Total outlays
	Total	Compensation of employees	Other						
1 General public services	3675	1710	1966	...	136	3811	298	70	4179
2 Defence	18952	7203	11749	...	47	18999	15	...	19014
3 Public order and safety	2221	1488	733	...	28	2249	168	1	2418
4 Education	10397	7560	2837	1	423	10821	1063	26	11910
5 Health	4085	4067	18	...	1341	5426	309	5	5740
6 Social security and welfare	1654	785	869	1	14902	16556	114	10	16680
7 Housing and community amenities	1376	576	800	888	194	2458	1443	5583	9485
8 Recreational, cultural and religious affairs	1632	935	697	3	474	2108	646	103	2858
9 Economic services	1445	478	967	4040	158	5643	1577	1866	9086
A Fuel and energy	44	15	29	128	...	172	214	44	430
B Agriculture, hunting, forestry and fishing	310	181	129	292	40	642	278	357	1277
C Mining (except fuels), manufacturing and construction	81	34	47	1625	1	1707	2	1084	2794
D Transportation and communication	685	134	551	775	7	1467	921	216	2604
E Other economic affairs	324	114	210	1220	110	1654	162	165	1981
10 Other functions	346	289	57	2	12648	12996	265	8	13269
Total [a]	45783	25090	20692	4934	30352	81069	5899	7672	94640

1993

	Final consumption expenditures			Subsidies	Other current transfers and property income	Total current disbursements	Gross capital formation	Other capital outlays	Total outlays
	Total	Compensation of employees	Other						
1 General public services	4207	2031	2176	...	212	4419	328	68	4814
2 Defence	22355	7853	14502	...	52	22407	29	—	22436
3 Public order and safety	2630	1765	865	...	32	2662	241	2	2905
4 Education	12101	9065	3036	...	493	12594	1474	20	14088
5 Health	4347	4544	−197	...	1721	6068	505	7	6580
6 Social security and welfare	1926	908	1018	...	17393	19319	132	12	19463
7 Housing and community amenities	1594	690	904	954	20	2568	1365	4492	8426
8 Recreational, cultural and religious affairs	1957	1117	840	1	781	2740	846	174	3760

Israel

1993

	Final consumption expenditures			Subsidies	Other current transfers and property income	Total current disbursements	Gross capital formation	Other capital outlays	Total outlays
	Total	Compensation of employees	Other						
9 Economic services	1725	515	1211	3866	71	5662	2167	2860	10689
A Fuel and energy	59	17	42	232	–	291	164	74	529
B Agriculture, hunting, forestry and fishing	309	179	131	345	11	665	293	551	1510
C Mining (except fuels), manufacturing and construction	77	42	35	1198	2	1277	3	1775	3055
D Transportation and communication	899	159	740	746	9	1654	1482	191	3327
E Other economic affairs	381	118	263	1345	49	1775	225	269	2269
10 Other functions	344	317	27	–	14038	14382	73	283	14738
Total [a]	53188	28805	24382	4814	34819	92821	7160	7918	107899

1994

	Final consumption expenditures			Subsidies	Other current transfers and property income	Total current disbursements	Gross capital formation	Other capital outlays	Total outlays
	Total	Compensation of employees	Other						
1 General public services	4964	2498	2467	–	179	5142	418	89	5649
2 Defence	23220	9779	13441	–	45	23265	39	–	23304
3 Public order and safety	3377	2284	1093	–	37	3414	346	2	3760
4 Education	14658	11218	3440	–	598	15256	1785	23	17064
5 Health	6130	6441	–311	–	2135	8265	620	16	8901
6 Social security and welfare	2950	1438	1511	–	20986	23937	170	14	24122
7 Housing and community amenities	2295	967	1328	1042	13	3350	1353	2705	7408
8 Recreational, cultural and religious affairs	2719	1550	1169	1	720	3440	899	195	4534
9 Economic services	1987	675	1312	4297	76	6361	2793	3150	12304
A Fuel and energy	66	24	42	428	–	494	267	100	861
B Agriculture, hunting, forestry and fishing	386	228	158	501	11	899	423	260	1581
C Mining (except fuels), manufacturing and construction	100	47	53	1109	–	1209	3	2198	3410
D Transportation and communication	968	230	738	737	9	1714	1890	224	3828
E Other economic affairs	467	146	321	1523	55	2046	210	368	2624
10 Other functions	334	368	–34	2	15861	16196	–195	492	16494
Total [a]	62634	37218	25416	5342	40650	108626	8228	6686	123540

Israel

	1995								
	Final consumption expenditures			Subsidies	Other current transfers and property income	Total current disbursements	Gross capital formation	Other capital outlays	Total outlays
	Total	Compensation of employees	Other						
1 General public services	6153	3166	2987	–	420	6573	533	101	7207
2 Defence	25036	11591	13445	–	55	25091	46	–	25137
3 Public order and safety	4185	2796	1389	–	34	4219	393	2	4614
4 Education	18507	14273	4235	–	734	19241	2369	26	21636
5 Health	12267	6720	5547	–	2300	14567	789	7	15363
6 Social security and welfare	3067	1466	1601	1	25673	28740	210	13	28963
7 Housing and community amenities	2424	1036	1388	1119	17	3559	1400	2573	7532
8 Recreational, cultural and religious affairs	2967	1672	1294	9	935	3910	1042	138	5090
9 Economic services	2340	803	1537	3687	84	6110	2948	4099	13156
A Fuel and energy	74	29	45	422	–	496	264	67	827
B Agriculture, hunting, forestry and fishing	458	266	192	387	5	850	485	450	1784
C Mining (except fuels), manufacturing and construction	125	57	68	1006	–	1131	4	2866	4001
D Transportation and communication	1106	279	827	762	10	1878	1976	219	4073
E Other economic affairs	577	172	405	1110	69	1756	219	497	2472
10 Other functions	253	435	–182	1	18971	19229	–61	521	19689
Total [a]	77199	43958	33241	4817	49223	131239	9669	7480	148388

	1996								
	Final consumption expenditures			Subsidies	Other current transfers and property income	Total current disbursements	Gross capital formation	Other capital outlays	Total outlays
	Total	Compensation of employees	Other						
1 General public services	7074	3663	3411	–	444	7518	618	196	8332
2 Defence	29581	12908	16673	–	62	29643	46	264	29953
3 Public order and safety	5053	3333	1720	–	38	5091	391	2	5484
4 Education	21934	16893	5041	–	722	22656	2662	28	25347
5 Health	14277	7803	6474	–	2791	17068	876	131	18074
6 Social security and welfare	3556	1713	1843	1	31483	35039	227	13	35279
7 Housing and community amenities	2772	1189	1583	1248	22	4042	1631	3091	8763
8 Recreational, cultural and religious affairs	3379	1897	1481	9	882	4270	1107	185	5564
9 Economic services	2631	934	1698	3430	141	6202	3244	4286	13732
A Fuel and energy	96	33	63	394	–	490	280	82	851
B Agriculture, hunting, forestry and fishing	530	312	219	292	8	830	540	803	2173
C Mining (except fuels), manufacturing and construction	145	62	83	853	47	1045	4	2726	3775
D Transportation and communication	1224	333	891	1067	8	2299	2181	176	4656
E Other economic affairs	635	194	442	824	78	1538	239	499	2277
10 Other functions	290	507	–217	–1	19460	19750	73	–194	19628
Total [a]	90547	50840	39707	4687	56045	151279	10875	8002	170156

a Total government expenditure.

Israel

2.5 Private final consumption expenditure by type and purpose, in current prices

Million new shekels

	1986	1987	1988	1989	1990	1991	1992	1993	1994	1995	1996	1997
Final consumption expenditure of resident households												
1 Food, beverages and tobacco [a]	7615	9574	11614	14173	16389	19896	23342	26480	31951	35412	40983	45438
A Food	6705	8335	10042	12259	13894	16682	19587	21828	26288	29144	33746	37206
B Non-alcoholic beverages	523	786	971	1196	1528	1839	2064	2501	2860	3308	3694	4007
C Alcoholic beverages	167	210	261	294	411	544	664	793	1294	1407	1621	1960
D Tobacco	390	433	506	624	785	1119	1380	1668	1906	1969	2389	2755
2 Clothing and footwear	1956	2802	2960	2939	3310	3914	4886	6242	7481	8734	8901	8936
3 Gross rent, fuel and power	5407	6684	8212	11027	14427	18751	22044	26617	33053	38797	46442	53312
A Fuel and power	544	613	736	1094	1362	1669	2173	2369	2800	3340	3958	4655
B Other	4863	6071	7476	9933	13065	17082	19871	24243	30253	35457	42484	48657
4 Furniture, furnishings and household equipment and operation	3137	4173	4930	5547	6796	8392	9880	11703	13495	16384	18987	21839
A Household operation	843	1261	1651	1938	2335	2728	3084	3588	3935	4555	5359	6041
B Other	2294	2912	3279	3609	4461	5664	6796	8115	9560	11829	13627	15798
5 Medical care and health expenses	1545	2194	2734	3564	4357	5546	7220	8780	10690	7733	8882	9445
6 Transport and communication	3262	4440	5562	5750	7290	9738	12996	15120	18058	21570	24620	27191
A Personal transport equipment	889	1322	2056	1393	1860	2798	4394	4742	5708	6976	7512	6887
B Other	2373	3118	3506	4357	5430	6940	8602	10378	12350	14594	17108	20304
7 Recreational, entertainment, education and cultural services	1979	2770	3323	4034	4793	5911	7403	9679	12256	14857	16970	18708
A Education	756	1090	1362	1748	2185	2727	3286	4301	5102	6509	7616	8556
B Other	1223	1680	1961	2286	2608	3184	4117	5378	7154	8348	9354	10152
8 Miscellaneous goods and services	2733	3724	4619	5726	6480	7797	9606	11068	13165	15220	17565	19244
A Personal care	837	1144	1409	1715	1915	2267	2656	3202	3901	4265	5147	5451
B Expenditures in restaurants, cafes and hotels	1094	1500	1767	2154	2324	2610	3454	3856	4662	5598	6178	6863
C Other	802	1080	1443	1857	2241	2920	3496	4010	4602	5357	6240	6930
Statistical discrepancy	...	...	...	...	...	...	...	–5	...	...	...	...
Total final consumption expenditure in the domestic market by households, of which	27635	36361	43954	52760	63841	79945	97377	115683	140151	158704	183351	204114
A Durable goods	...	...	...	...	6321	8462	11190	12856	15268	18805	21139	22686
B Semi-durable goods	...	...	...	...	...	...	...	...	...	...	...	...
C Non-durable goods	...	...	...	...	...	...	...	...	...	...	...	...
D Services	...	...	...	...	18091	22410	27903	33902	41199	43740	50095	57271
plus: Direct purchases abroad by resident households	1148[b]	1550[b]	1735[b]	2364[b]	2785[b]	3368	3868	5093	6836	8253	8993	10756
less: Direct purchases in the domestic market by non-resident households	1638	2401	2453	3176	3248	3493	5300	6513	7574	9167	9532	9711
equals: Final consumption expenditure of resident households	27145	35510	43236	51948	63378	79819	95945	114264	139413	157790	182812	205159
Final consumption expenditures by private non-profit organisations serving households												
1 Research and science	18	21	24	23	26	35	41	44	54	57	68	73
2 Education	80	103	93	101	108	140	169	202	257	294	345	375
3 Medical and other health services	150	170	335	393	295	261	269	342	478	504	585	668

Israel

Million new shekels

	1986	1987	1988	1989	1990	1991	1992	1993	1994	1995	1996	1997
4 Welfare services [c]	135	163	177	191	200	270	323	338	413	485	582	633
5 Recreational and related cultural services	117	166	175	201	245	329	406	462	594	700	790	859
6 Religious organisations [c]	...	17	19	23	24	33	42	47	57	67	80	87
7 Professional and labour organisations serving households	155	241	200	223	469	596	703	775	1212	1321	1337	1474
8 Miscellaneous	...	...	...	...	...	...	16	...	...	...	...	...
equals: Final consumption expenditures by private non-profit organisations serving households	655	881	1022	1156	1367	1665	1969	2211	3065	3427	3786	4169
Statistical discrepancy	...	...	...	66	...	...	...	...	...	...	...	...
Private final consumption expenditure	27800	36391	44256	53170	64745	81484	97915	116475	142478	161217	186598	209328

a The sum of the components of item "Food, beverages and tobacco" is greater than the totals shown because the sum has been adjusted for the expenditure included in other items of the national accounts.

b For the years 1983-1990, the estimates for this item include taxes on purchase of foreign currencies by residents for travel abroad.

c Item "Religious organizations" is included in item "Welfare services".

2.6 Private final consumption expenditure by type and purpose, in constant prices

Million new shekels

	1986	1987	1988	1989	1990	1991	1992	1993	1994	1995	1996	1997
At constant prices of: 1980												
1986												
1990												
1995												

Final consumption expenditure of resident households

	1986	1987	1988	1989	1990	1991	1992	1993	1994	1995	1996	1997
1 Food, beverages and tobacco [a]	23 7615	8227	8650	8762	9191 16389	17280	17984	19340	21004	22375 35414	37131	37995
A Food	20 6705	7142	7327	7370	7684 13894	14696	15367	16384	17463	18551 29145	30538	31110
B Non-alcoholic beverages	2 523	658	715	756	867 1528	1643	1551	1810	2040	2228 3308	3603	3831
C Alcoholic beverages	1 167	162	170	165	194 411	392	454	513	795	840 1408	1485	1611
D Tobacco	1 390	419	561	594	572 785	799	883	881	955	1021 1968	1936	1880
2 Clothing and footwear	5 1956	2468	2344	2228	2425 3310	3571	4058	4896	5610	6093 8734	8368	8282
3 Gross rent, fuel and power	16 5407	5556	5725	5895	6043 14427	14865	15893	16616	17205	17788 38797	40453	42354
A Fuel and power	2 544	587	650	704	723 1362	1444	1771	1861	1969	2093 3340	3575	3846

Israel

Million new shekels

	1986	1987	1988	1989	1990	1991	1992	1993	1994	1995	1996	1997
At constant prices of:	1980											
	1986											
	1990											
	1995											
B Other	14 863 / 4863	4969	5075	5191	5320 / 13065	13421	14122	14755	15236	15695 / 35457	36878	38508
4 Furniture, furnishings and household equipment and operation	12 / 3137	3405	3480	3437	3864 / 6796	7278	7965	8823	9569	10970 / 16384	17557	18938
A Household operation	2 / 843	913	953	934	986 / 2335	2374	2483	2735	2807	2995 / 4555	4883	5113
B Other	10 / 2294	2492	2527	2503	2878 / 4461	4904	5482	6088	6762	7975 / 11829	12674	13825
5 Medical care and health expenses	4 / 1545	1715	1784	1925	2061 / 4357	4568	5081	5580	6159	6624 / 7733	8133	7916
6 Transport and communication	10 / 3262	3771	4187	3832	4069 / 7291	8383	10403	10526	11655	12817 / 21570	22533	23138
A Personal transport equipment	2 / 889	1113	1379	880	1086 / 1860	2714	4010	3452	3833	4169 / 6976	7343	6702
B Other	7 / 2373	2658	2808	2952	2983 / 5431	5669	6393	7074	7822	8648 / 14594	15190	16436
7 Recreational, entertainment, education and cultural services	5 / 1979	2190	2207	2215	2255 / 4793	5058	5712	6430	7334	8184 / 14857	15409	15410
A Education	2 / 756	834	839	878	898 / 2185	2299	2513	2732	2886	3216 / 6509	6860	6945
B Other	3 / 1223	1356	1368	1337	1357 / 2608	2759	3199	3698	4448	4968 / 8348	8549	8465
8 Miscellaneous goods and services	8 / 2733	2975	3037	3198	3261 / 6480	6804	7517	7826	8531	9052 / 15220	15920	16121
A Personal care	3 / 837	907	946	1005	1027 / 1915	2007	2179	2438	2796	2815 / 4265	4757	4806
B Expenditures in restaurants, cafes and hotels	3 / 1094	1213	1176	1212	1206 / 2324	2245	2635	2563	2773	3071 / 5598	5575	5551
C Other	2 / 802	855	915	981	1028 / 2241	2552	2703	2825	2962	3166 / 5357	5588	5764
Statistical discrepancy	...	...	...	...	...	...	...	...	10	...	...	...
Total final consumption expenditure in the domestic market by households, of which	83 / 27634	30308	31416	31493	33170 / 63841	67809	74613	80038	87070	93903 / 158705	165504	170154

1124

Israel

Million new shekels

	1986	1987	1988	1989	1990	1991	1992	1993	1994	1995	1996	1997
At constant prices of:	1980											
	1986											
	1990											
	1995											
plus: Direct purchases abroad by resident households	4 1148[b]	1229[b]	1310[b]	1503[b]	1464[b] 2785	2901	2912	3320	4080	4478 8253	9115	10296
less: Direct purchases in the domestic market by non-resident households	4 1638	1932	1707	1884	1770 3248	2786	4154	4484	4871	5729 9167	8630	7801
equals: Final consumption expenditure of resident households	82 27144	29606	31020	31112	32864 63378	67925	73371	78874	86279	92653 157792	165989	172649

Final consumption expenditures by private non-profit organisations serving households

	1986	1987	1988	1989	1990	1991	1992	1993	1994	1995	1996	1997
1 Research and science	– 18	20	22	25	26 26	30	33	34	38	39 72	75	71
2 Education	– 80	83	64	69	74 109	117	126	127	148	156 281	294	280
3 Medical and other health services	– 150	145	117	107	92 295	304	321	286	312	320 504	524	569
4 Welfare services [c]	– 135	142	151	165	177 201	229	247	245	270	267 525	548	522
5 Recreational and related cultural services	– 117	125	122	135	138 246	294	296	312	367	368 668	697	664
6 Religious organisations [c]	...	...	...	...	24	27	29	28	31	28 56	59	56
7 Professional and labour organisations serving households	– 155	163	155	156	159 468	485	508	505	616	535 1321	1125	1277
8 Miscellaneous	...	...	...	...	...	...	...	...	...	...	...	...
equals: Final consumption expenditures by private non-profit organisations serving households	2 655	679	631	651	667 1368	1486	1560	1535	1781	1712 3427	3322	3438
Private final consumption expenditure	84 27799	30284	31651	31769	33534 64746	69411	74931	80408	88060	94365 161219	169311	176087

a The sum of the components of item "Food, beverages and tobacco" is greater than the totals shown because the sum has been adjusted for the expenditure included in other items of the national accounts.
b For the years 1983-1990, the estimates for this item include taxes on purchase of foreign currencies by residents for travel abroad.
c Item "Religious organizations" is included in item "Welfare services".

Israel

2.11 Gross fixed capital formation by kind of activity of owner, ISIC divisions, in current prices

Million new shekels

	1986	1987	1988	1989	1990	1991	1992	1993	1994	1995	1996	1997
All producers												
1 Agriculture, hunting, forestry and fishing	277	397	355	295	344	473	577	711	788	1025 / 1056	1052	1012
2 Mining and quarrying [a]	1869	2437	2259	2740	3606	4893	5928	8266	10883	12861 / 12748	14297	13211
3 Manufacturing	...	...	...	...	...	...	...	...	...	...	...	...
4 Electricity, gas and water [b]	406	537	729	990	1557	1682	1993	2983	3308	3228 / 3238	3967	5276
5 Construction [c]	46	88	115	113	243	703	566	799	1015	1170 / 1208	1036	987
6 Wholesale and retail trade, restaurants and hotels [d]	1798	2343	2739	3245	4157	5439	6861	8368	10063	11804 / 11748	14269	14844
7 Transport, storage and communication	1520	2532	2952	2552	3849	5958	7700	9345	12220	12448 / 12535	14942	14523
8 Finance, insurance, real estate and business services	2136	2959	3625	4618	6476	13134	14443	12012	13737	18851 / 8851	21378	23176
9 Community, social and personal services	...	...	...	...	...	...	...	...	...	...	...	...
Total industries	8051	11294	12776	14554	20234	32279	38068	42485	52014	61389 / 61387	70943	73029
Producers of government services	...	...	...	...	...	...	...	...	...	...	...	...
Private non-profit institutions serving households	...	...	...	...	...	...	...	...	...	...	...	...
Total	8051	11294	12776	14554	20234	32279	38068	42485	52014	61389 / 61387	70943	73029

a Includes item "Manufacturing".
b Item "Electricity, gas and water" includes water projects.
c Item "Construction" includes construction equipment only.
d All services are included in item "Wholesale and retail trade, restaurants and hotels".

2.12 Gross fixed capital formation by kind of activity of owner, ISIC divisions, in constant prices

Million new shekels

	1986	1987	1988	1989	1990	1991	1992	1993	1994	1995	1996	1997
At constant prices of:	1980											
	1986											
	1990											
	1995											
All producers												
1 Agriculture, hunting, forestry and fishing	1 / 277	336	259	182	188 / 344	409	465	544	560	654 / 1055	990	880
2 Mining and quarrying [a]	5 / 1869	2031	1744	1768	2062 / 3606	4246	4638	5881	7306	7985 / 12748	13644	12011
3 Manufacturing	...	...	...	...	...	...	...	...	...	...	...	...
4 Electricity, gas and water [b]	1 / 406	423	517	605	832 / 1557	1456	1565	2146	2219	2017 / 3238	3753	4784

Israel

Million new shekels

	1986	1987	1988	1989	1990	1991	1992	1993	1994	1995	1996	1997
At constant prices of:	1980											
		1986										
			1990									
				1995								
5 Construction [c]	− 46	75	91	77	148 243	614	449	580	704	771 1208	994	924
6 Wholesale and retail trade, restaurants and hotels [d]	5 1798	1837	1925	1960	2273 4157	4654	5278	5952	6698	7207 11749	13425	13096
7 Transport, storage and communication	4 1520	2193	2158	1652	2289 3849	5346	6196	6656	7959	7673 12537	14517	13448
8 Finance, insurance, real estate and business services	7 2136	2317	2367	2530	2955 6477	11256	11255	8613	8957	11195 18851	19785	19814
9 Community, social and personal services	...	...	...	...	...	...	...	...	...	...	...	...
Total industries	25 8051	9210	9063	8774	10748 20234	27982	29846	30373	34403	37504 61389	67087	64957
Producers of government services	...	...	...	...	...	...	...	...	...	...	...	...
Private non-profit institutions serving households	...	...	...	...	...	...	...	...	...	...	...	...
Total	25 8051	9210	9063	8774	10748 20234	27982	29846	30373	34403	37504 61389	67087	64957

a Includes item "Manufacturing".
b Item "Electricity, gas and water" includes water projects.
c Item "Construction" includes construction equipment only.
d All services are included in item "Wholesale and retail trade, restaurants and hotels".

2.17 Exports and imports of goods and services, detail

Million new shekels

	1986	1987	1988	1989	1990	1991	1992	1993	1994	1995	1996	1997
Exports of goods and services												
1 Exports of merchandise, f.o.b.	11664	14742	16435	21215	25431	27503	33002	41494	51460	57633	65848	75129
2 Transport and communication	1881	2388	2525	3296	3926	4721	5428	6640	7464	8425	9100	10164
A In respect of merchandise imports	529	670	582	720	893	1103	1153	1294	1397	1476	1604	1643
B Other	1352	1718	1943	2576	3033	3618	4275	5346	6067	6949	7496	8521
3 Insurance service charges	33	35	42	−17	9	39	16	102	113	141	146	181
A In respect of merchandise imports	15	18	27	29	32	48	49	65	75	87	101	80
B Other	17	17	15	−46	−23	−9	−33	37	38	54	45	101
4 Other commodities	1710	1955	2504	3023	3459	4085	5426	5350	6510	7956	9458	11737
5 Adjustments of merchandise exports to change-of-ownership basis	−	−	−	−	−	−	−	−	...	...	...	...

Israel

Million new shekels

	1986	1987	1988	1989	1990	1991	1992	1993	1994	1995	1996	1997
6 Direct purchases in the domestic market by non-residential households	1638	2401	2154	2814	2819	3015	4710	6307	7254	8819	9171	9459
7 Direct purchases in the domestic market by extraterritorial bodies	16	45	56	80	95	109	130	133	151	193	255	304
Total exports of goods and services	16943	21566	23716	30411	35739	39472	48712	60026	72952	83167	93978	106974
Imports of goods and services												
1 Imports of merchandise, c.i.f.	15429	21998	22481	26537	32749	41608	48474	62067	73478	86825	97123	102368
A Imports of merchandise, f.o.b.	14315	20568	20960	24716	30495	38624	44978	57747	68133	80313	90009	95034
B Transport of services on merchandise imports	1058	1359	1430	1706	2123	2828	3312	4082	5053	6166	6727	6970
By residents	529	670	582	720	893	1103	1153	1294	1397	1476	1604	1643
By non-residents	529	689	848	986	1230	1725	2159	2788	3656	4690	5123	5327
C Insurance service charges on merchandise imports	55	71	91	115	131	156	184	238	292	346	387	364
By residents	15	18	27	29	32	48	49	65	75	87	101	80
By non-residents	40	53	64	86	99	108	135	173	217	259	286	284
2 Adjustments of merchandise imports to change-of-ownership basis	–	–	–	–	–	–	–	–	...	...	...	...
3 Other transport and communication	1352	1718	1943	2576	3033	3618	4275	5346	6067	6949	7946	8521
4 Other insurance service charges	160	212	172	245	431	312	102	580	637	740	856	1002
5 Other commodities	1061	1333	1424	1898	2320	2750	3364	4038	5737	5914	7986	8837
6 Direct purchases abroad by government	108	171	177	240	262	315	401	543	614	656	695	693
7 Direct purchases abroad by resident households	1024	1374	1739	2436	2916	3567	4125	5811	7829	9479	10529	12385
Statistical discrepancy	...	...	...	...	...	...	...	...	...	...	–450	...
Total imports of goods and services	19135	26806	27936	33932	41711	52170	60741	78385	94362	110563	124685	133806
Balance of goods and services	–2191	–5240	–4220	–3521	–5972	–12698	–12029	–18359	–21410	–27396	–30707	–26832
Total imports and balance of goods and services	16943	21566	23716	30411	35739	39472	48712	60026	72952	83167	93978	106974

Italy

General note

The preparation of national accounts statistics in Italy is undertaken by the Instituto Central di Statistica, Rome. The official estimates are published in the *Annuario Statistico Italiano* and in *Compendio Statistico Italiano*. The latter publication is also published in English under the title *Italian Statistical Abstract*. The following presentation on sources and method is based mainly on information prepared by the Statistical Office of the European Communities in 1976 in a report entitled *Basic statistics needed for the ESA accounts and tables: present situation and prospects for improvements*. The estimates are generally in accordance with the definitions and classifications recommended in the United Nations System of National Accounts (1968 SNA). Input-output tables have been published in *Supplemento Straordinario al Bolletiono Mensile di Statistica*. The following tables have been prepared from successive replies to the United Nations National Accounts Questionnaire. When the scope and coverage of the estimates differ for conceptual or statistical reasons from the definitions and classifications recommended in SNA, a footnote is indicated to the relevant tables.

Gross domestic product

Gross domestic product is estimated mainly through the production approach.

Expenditures on the gross domestic product

The expenditure approach is used to estimate government final consumption expenditure, increase in stocks and exports and imports of goods and services. This aproach, in combination with the commodity-flow approach is used to estimate private final consumption expenditure and gross fixed capital formation. For central government, the estimates are based on data obtained from the Bilancio dello Stato. Complete accounts for the other bodies of the general government are available after 39 months and for social security funds, after 27 months, Household consumption expenditure is primarily based on the quarterly surveys of family budgets supplemented by estimates based on commodity-flows. The surveys cover 36,000 households by rotation with 9000 new families each quarter. Surveys carried out by the Banco d'Italia provide consumption data for non-resident households on the domestic market and for residents abroad. The main statistical source used for estimating changes in stocks is the value added surveys conducted for all enterprises in the industrial construction, trade and transport sectors that employ more than 20 persons. The stocks relate to industrial products only.

Data for estimating gross fixed capital formation are obtained through a questionnaire attached to the value-added survey. Government capital expenditure are obtained from government accounts. For construction and building, the Istituto Central di Statistico conducts specific surveys such as surveys on residential buildings and on public works. The estimates of exports and imports of goods and services are based mainly on the balance-of-payments and foreign trade statistics. For the constant price estimates, most of the items of GDP by expenditure type are deflated by appropriate price indexes. Government building depreciation is estimated as a certain percentage of the stock value at constant prices. Private consumption of own-produced food and stock increases of agricultural products are revalued at base-year prices. Gross rent is extrapolated by the number of dwelling units.

Cost structure of the gross domestic product

Compensation of employees is estimated through use of the value-added survey and a survey carried out by the Ministry of Labour and Social Security for the industrial sector, minimum contractual wages and survey of the compensation of permanent employees for the agricultural sector, surveys and inquiries carried out by other institutes for the service sector and other indirect evaluation for sectors not covered by surveys. Information on operating surplus is obtained from the value-added surveys and from actual interest received and paid by the various sectors. Depreciation is valued on the basis of time series of gross fixed capital formation at constant prices by product and by branch of economic activity. Constant prices of 1970 are estimated by using the perpetual inventory method, assuming that the devaluation of the product is constant during its economic life. Estimates of indirect taxes and subsidies are obtained from government sources. Taxes linked to production and imports are broken down by branch according to the type of tax. Data on subsidies are classified by branch on the basis of the recipients indicated in the government budgets.

Gross domestic product by kind of activity

The table of gross domestic product by kind of economic activity is prepared at market prices, i.e., producers' values. The production approach is used to estimate the value added of most of the industries. This is supplemented by the income approach for industries to which the value added surveys are applied. The income approach alone is used for the producers of government services. Statistics on agricultural production prices, etc. are derived from current agricultural surveys. A new survey was carried out in 1975, covering 6,000 farms with complete accounts which produce about 10 per cent of the total output. Crop surveys of major products are conducted annually. Information on gross marketable livestock production is available separately for major items. For forestry, a quarterly survey supplies data on produc-

Italy

tion and prices. Monthly surveys of products unloaded in Italian ports are used for estimating value added of fishing. For the industrial activity sector, the estimates are based on value added surveys and the product surveys. In addition to these surveys, the rapid surveys of large enterprises are also used for manufacturing. The annual value added survey, which covers all enterprises employing more than 20 persons and is available after 15 months, includes transactions in goods and services, distributive transactions and employment data. The survey does not allow product-by-product analysis. The product survey which covers all enterprises employing more than 50 persons and is available after 24 months, is used for compiling input-output tables and is linked with the European Community surveys on industrial activity. The annual rapid survey, covering all enterprises employing more than 250 persons is available within three months. This survey provides information similar to that obtained in the value added surveys. The surveys used for the manufacturing sector are also used for construction. In addition construction estimates are based on the results of surveys on the number of residential buildings, surveys of public works and sample surveys of work in progress on building sites.

For the trade sector, the main source is the value added survey. However, to cover enterprises employing less than 20 persons, an indirect method, which consists in constructing an index of traded consumer goods, capital goods and goods for export, is used for estimating gross output of the trade sector. The value added surveys are also used for the transport sector. Additional information is supplied directly by the relevant firms and public agencies. For the financial institutions, annual surveys are carried out which covers 97 per cent of the activity. Special calculations are made for institutions not covered. Estimates of government services are based on surveys conducted by the social security funds and on data compiled by the Ragioneria generale dello Stato and the Istituto Centrale de Statistic. For other services, the Istituto Central di Statistica carries out a single direct survey of public hospitals. Other market services are valued indirectly, mostly on the basis of the results of family budgets surveys.

For the constant price estimates, price deflation is used for community, social and personal services. Double deflation is used for all the other sectors. Output is either deflated by appropriate indexes or is extrapolated by quantum indexes while input is deflated by price indexes.

1.1 Expenditure on the gross domestic product, in current prices

Thousand million Italian lire

	1986	1987	1988	1989	1990	1991	1992	1993	1994	1995	1996	1997
1 Government final consumption expenditure	147636	165565	186034	200304	230163	251260	265418	273379	280474	284633	305995	318411
2 Private final consumption expenditure	549170	603508	668195	738181	803619	882079	944094	961466	1014471	1089514	1149318	1205745
A Households	546774	601048	665527	735321	800412	878437	940367	957650	1010470	1085224	1144790	1201016
B Private non-profit institutions serving households	2396	2460	2668	2860	3207	3642	3727	3816	4001	4290	4528	4729
3 Gross capital formation	189152	208727	234606	255381	276405	293690	293113	262290	282508	323199	319438	342107
A Increase in stocks	11643	15069	15410	14220	10361	11043	4910	–475	9695	16330	1897	17193
B Gross fixed capital formation	177509	193658	219196	241161	266044	282647	288203	262765	272813	306869	317541	324914
Residential buildings	50220	51099	55686	60064	68240	76057	80089	81731	83091	84593	83807	82111
Non-residential buildings	44669	47390	52495	58449	66851	71814	71763	65116	60002	64703	70891	74116
Other construction and land improvement, etc.	...	...	...	...	...	...	...	...	...	...	...	...
Other	82620	95169	111015	122648	130953	134776	136351	115918	129720	157573	162843	168687
4 Exports of goods and services	181067	191016	207495	238437	262664	271428	295515	355486	399915	491571	499986	532957
5 less: Imports of goods and services	168736	186053	206307	240342	262192	270886	295647	302325	338702	416663	402102	448540
equals: Gross domestic product	898289	982763	1090023	1191961	1310659	1427571	1502493	1550296	1638666	1772254	1872635	1950680

1.2 Expenditure on the gross domestic product, in constant prices

Thousand million Italian lire

	1986	1987	1988	1989	1990	1991	1992	1993	1994	1995	1996	1997
	At constant prices of: 1990											
1 Government final consumption expenditure	212617	219424	225326	227396	230163	233978	236675	237748	236333	233786	234304	232588
2 Private final consumption expenditure	693949	723972	756941	784281	803619	824974	836094	807864	814806	826597	836191	855904

Italy

Thousand million Italian lire

	1986	1987	1988	1989	1990	1991	1992	1993	1994	1995	1996	1997
At constant prices of: 1990												
A Households	691058	721039	753949	781215	800412	821653	832750	804506	811446	823129	832661	852283
B Private non-profit institutions serving households	2891	2933	2992	3066	3207	3321	3344	3358	3360	3468	3530	3621
3 Gross capital formation	235139	247477	256754	265581	276405	274420	270365	229111	238745	255330	251647	266618
A Increase in stocks	14768	17419	10882	8861	10361	6147	7004	−517	7960	8196	3530	17083
B Gross fixed capital formation	220371	230058	245872	256720	266044	268273	263361	229628	230785	247134	248117	249535
Residential buildings	65634	64135	64815	66408	68240	70295	70248	69784	68454	67266	65010	62167
Non-residential buildings	58331	58990	61041	64152	66851	66738	63505	55540	49506	51438	55013	55987
Other construction and land improvement, etc.	...	...	...	...	...	...	...	...	...	...	...	...
Other	96406	106933	120016	126160	130953	131240	129608	104304	112825	128430	128094	131381
4 Exports of goods and services	207708	216863	227704	245208	262664	262990	280762	308303	339908	380865	378403	402887
5 less: Imports of goods and services	184948	207213	219759	239561	262192	270780	290824	265358	283525	310718	305527	341942
equals: Gross domestic product	1164465	1200523	1246966	1282905	1310659	1325582	1333072	1317668	1346267	1385860	1395018	1416055

1.3 Cost components of the gross domestic product

Thousand million Italian lire

	1986	1987	1988	1989	1990	1991	1992	1993	1994	1995	1996	1997
1 Indirect taxes, net	58356	70583	86263	97850	115986	133361	143687	155659	164654	186563	195748	211307
A Indirect taxes	89071	101141	117823	132464	148938	170552	178864	198094	204154	221301	233504	248454
B less: Subsidies	30715	30558	31560	34614	32952	37191	35177	42435	39500	34738	37756	37147
2 Consumption of fixed capital	107975	116878	128224	140643	154886	168539	180407	192379	203505	219765	232605	239390
3 Compensation of employees paid by resident producers to	404065	438837	482553	528340	592391	647792	681573	688223	698174	726045	769780	806110
A Resident households	402961	437468	480562	524719	588020	644715	678954	685026	695473	723689	767207	803211
B Rest of the world	1104	1369	1991	3621	4371	3077	2619	3197	2701	2356	2573	2899
4 Operating surplus	327893	356465	392983	425128	447396	477879	496826	514035	572333	639881	674502	693873
A Corporate and quasi-corporate enterprises	64437	69152	79153	85623	80740	71312	65095	78782	103557	117461	124852	...
B Private unincorporated enterprises	261871	285529	311502	336760	363739	403714	427956	431312	464513	515590	546203	...
C General government	1585	1784	2328	2745	2917	2853	3775	3941	4370	4516	5065	...
equals: Gross domestic product	898289	982763	1090023	1191961	1310659	1427571	1502493	1550296	1638666	1772254	1872635	1950680

1.4 General government current receipts and disbursements

Thousand million Italian lire

	1986	1987	1988	1989	1990	1991	1992	1993	1994	1995	1996	1997
Receipts												
1 Operating surplus	1585	1784	2328	2745	2917	2853	3775	3941	4370	4516	5065	...
2 Property and entrepreneurial income	10787	10547	10902	12072	13762	14636	14931	13876	14512	17852	18427	...
3 Taxes, fees and contributions	308804	344839	388149	444318	497542	553269	589197	650262	650706	701788	783893	...
A Indirect taxes	81743	93240	109076	123867	139465	159022	167660	186611	192173	209490	222644	...
B Direct taxes	115683	130611	145720	170697	189124	207054	221506	250835	244854	260627	284843	...
C Social security contributions	111378	120988	133353	149754	168953	187193	200031	212816	213679	231671	276406	...
D Compulsory fees, fines and penalties	−	−	−	−	−	−	−	−	−	−	−	...
4 Other current transfers	31494	29797	31876	35479	40682	48100	54834	63279	68215	69983	46499	...

Italy

Thousand million Italian lire

	1986	1987	1988	1989	1990	1991	1992	1993	1994	1995	1996	1997
Total current receipts of general government	352670	386967	433255	494614	554903	618858	662737	731358	737803	794139	853884	...
Disbursements												
1 Government final consumption expenditure	147636	165565	186034	200303	230163	251260	265418	273379	280474	285637	306328	...
2 Property income	77645	80037	90866	109074	129601	151010	178345	192685	186160	206606	206383	...
A Interest	77422	79777	90578	108726	129230	150563	177822	192126	185581	206018	205756	...
B Net land rent and royalties	223	260	288	348	371	447	523	559	579	588	627	...
3 Subsidies	26115	24665	24799	27382	26543	28763	27032	33915	32864	28252	28908	...
4 Other current transfers	162554	178745	199155	224084	250642	276622	306781	323803	337300	353910	383818	...
A Social security benefits	154826	170500	189065	209963	238585	261320	290578	302873	319464	336118	360823	
B Social assistance grants												...
C Other	7728	8245	10090	14121	12057	15302	16203	20930	17836	17792	22995	
5 Net saving	-61280	-62045	-67599	-66229	-82046	-88797	-114839	-92424	-98995	-80266	-71553	...
Total current disbursements and net saving of general government	352670	386967	433255	494614	554903	618858	662737	731358	737803	794139	853884	...

1.5 Current income and outlay of corporate and quasi-corporate enterprises, summary

Thousand million Italian lire

	1986	1987	1988	1989	1990	1991	1992	1993	1994	1995	1996	1997
Receipts												
1 Operating surplus	64437	69152	79153	85623	80740	71312	65095	78782	103557	117031	123944	...
2 Property and entrepreneurial income received	150995	148345	161699	190161	216087	235905	274599	272724	263133	301582	310986	...
3 Current transfers	32642	35728	39774	47623	54212	60540	64442	64394	63855	68854	71427	...
Total current receipts	248074	253225	280626	323407	351039	367757	404136	415900	430545	487467	506357	...
Disbursements												
1 Property and entrepreneurial income	166116	164356	177580	205709	233811	256374	294703	286254	274679	313518	319189	...
2 Direct taxes and other current payments to general government	24658	29253	27956	35077	36375	39207	37374	46510	52516	56649	65157	...
3 Other current transfers	28563	33568	37562	43571	50917	58391	63666	65845	68916	70016	72302	...
Statistical discrepancy	7982	6503	7359	8518	8354	9393	6740	6546	5883	7326	5411	...
4 Net saving	20755	19545	30169	30532	21582	4392	1653	10745	28551	39958	44298	...
Total current disbursements and net saving	248074	253225	280626	323407	351039	367757	404136	415900	430545	487467	506357	...

1.6 Current income and outlay of households and non-profit institutions

Thousand million Italian lire

	1986	1987	1988	1989	1990	1991	1992	1993	1994	1995	1996	1997
Receipts												
1 Compensation of employees	407031	440989	484624	529622	592527	648062	681667	688123	698364	728926	768592	...
A From resident producers	402961	437468	480562	524719	588020	644715	678954	685026	695473	723689	767207	...
B From rest of the world	4070	3521	4062	4903	4507	3347	2713	3097	2891	3151	3375	...
2 Operating surplus of private unincorporated enterprises	261871	285529	311502	336760	363739	403714	427956	431312	464513	515590	546203	...
3 Property and entrepreneurial income	96976	101763	113225	130773	148921	170906	201654	209520	194939	217722	216728	...
4 Current transfers	185375	205586	228872	254729	289246	317760	350958	365956	384767	405648	435510	...
A Social security benefits	164181	181782	201440	223955	254478	279044	311112	325144	342604	359289	384570	...

Italy

Thousand million Italian lire

	1986	1987	1988	1989	1990	1991	1992	1993	1994	1995	1996	1997
B Social assistance grants	...	...	...	...	...	...	...	...	...	...	...	...
C Other	21194	23804	27432	30774	34768	38716	39846	40812	42163	46359	50940	...
Statistical discrepancy	10090	9286	10307	11496	11514	12877	10160	9907	8920	11369	11397	...
Total current receipts	961343	1043153	1148530	1263380	1405947	1553319	1672395	1704818	1751503	1879255	1978430	...

Disbursements

	1986	1987	1988	1989	1990	1991	1992	1993	1994	1995	1996	1997
1 Private final consumption expenditure	549170	603508	668195	738181	803619	882079	944094	961466	1014471	1087399	1146551	...
2 Property income	24585	25151	27119	30017	33534	36666	44636	43667	39343	44062	45028	...
3 Direct taxes and other current transfers n.e.c. to general government	203593	223182	251899	285986	321795	355579	384474	417406	406476	436445	497038	...
A Social security contributions	112376	121771	134141	150341	169205	187759	200475	213150	213863	232070	276604	...
B Direct taxes	91217	101411	117758	135645	152590	167820	183999	204256	192613	204375	220434	...
C Fees, fines and penalties	...	...	...	...	...	...	...	...	...	...	...	...
4 Other current transfers	57038	57368	63555	73248	83141	96023	106073	112106	116049	122662	104412	...
Statistical discrepancy	2108	2783	2948	2978	3160	3484	3420	3361	3037	3613	5078	...
5 Net saving	124849	131161	134814	132970	160698	179488	189698	166812	172127	185074	180323	...
Total current disbursements and net saving	961343	1043153	1148530	1263380	1405947	1553319	1672395	1704818	1751503	1879255	1978430	...

1.7 External transactions on current account, summary

Thousand million Italian lire

	1986	1987	1988	1989	1990	1991	1992	1993	1994	1995	1996	1997
Payments to the rest of the world												
1 Imports of goods and services	168736	186053	206307	240342	262192	270886	295647	302325	338702	416663	402102	448540
A Imports of merchandise, c.i.f.	149070	163182	180930	210821	219753	228191	235384	236618	276062	340396	325855	359524
B Other	19666	22871	25377	29521	42439	42695	60263	65707	62640	76267	76247	89016
2 Factor income to rest of the world	18852	18600	22010	30485	41267	48676	60403	74523	73697	82278	85479	99053
A Compensation of employees	1104	1369	1991	3621	4371	3077	2619	3197	2701	2356	2573	2899
B Property and entrepreneurial income	17748	17231	20019	26864	36896	45599	57784	71326	70996	79922	82906	96154
3 Current transfers to the rest of the world	13339	13762	16633	20720	18844	24523	25565	30937	28557	26360	30566	31372
A Indirect taxes to supranational organizations	...	...	...	...	...	...	...	...	...	...	...	...
B Other current transfers	13339	13762	16633	20720	18844	24523	25565	30937	28557	26360	30566	31372
4 Surplus of the nation on current transactions	3147	−3188	−8998	−17466	−21285	−30068	−36194	15222	22573	41018	63243	56490
Payments to the rest of the world and surplus of the nation on current transfers	204074	215227	235952	274081	301018	314017	345421	423007	463529	566319	581390	635455
Receipts from the rest of the world												
1 Exports of goods and services	181067	191016	207495	238437	262664	271428	295515	355486	399915	491571	499986	532957
A Exports of merchandise, f.o.b.	144778	151219	166769	193037	205581	212575	223879	271090	313340	387380	394992	412856
B Other	36289	39797	40726	45400	57083	58853	71636	84396	86575	104191	104994	120101
2 Factor income from rest of the world	12270	11967	14453	20049	23329	26502	34136	48057	46355	56057	62093	78244
A Compensation of employees	4070	3521	4062	4903	4507	3347	2713	3097	2891	3151	3375	3314
B Property and entrepreneurial income	8200	8446	10391	15146	18822	23155	31423	44960	43464	52906	58718	74930

Italy

Thousand million Italian lire	1986	1987	1988	1989	1990	1991	1992	1993	1994	1995	1996	1997
3 Current transfers from rest of the world	10737	12244	14004	15595	15025	16087	15770	19464	17259	18691	19311	24254
A Subsidies from supranational organisations	...	...	...	...	...	...	...	...	...	...	...	...
B Other current transfers	10737	12244	14004	15595	15025	16087	15770	19464	17259	18691	19311	24254
Receipts from the rest of the world on current transactions	204074	215227	235952	274081	301018	314017	345421	423007	463529	566319	581390	635455

1.8 Capital transactions of the nation, summary

Thousand million Italian lire	1986	1987	1988	1989	1990	1991	1992	1993	1994	1995	1996	1997
Finance of gross capital formation												
Gross saving	192299	205539	225608	237915	255120	263622	256919	277512	305081	364217	382681	398597
1 Consumption of fixed capital	107975	116878	128224	140643	154886	168539	180407	192379	203505	219765	232605	239390
A General government	4010	4420	4966	5585	6269	6945	7573	8307	8990	9757	10613	...
B Corporate and quasi-corporate enterprises	44120	47524	51489	56406	62031	67787	72001	76632	80585	86691	91184	...
C Other	59845	64934	71769	78652	86586	93807	100833	107440	113823	123181	129984	...
2 Net saving	84324	88661	97384	97272	100234	95083	76512	85133	101576	144452	150076	159207
A General government	−61280	−62045	−67599	−66229	−82046	−88797	−114839	−92424	−98995	−80265	−71553	...
B Corporate and quasi-corporate enterprises	20755	19545	30169	30532	21582	4392	1653	10745	28551	39958	44298	...
C Other	124849	131161	134814	132970	160698	179488	189698	166812	172127	185074	180323	...
less: Surplus of the nation on current transactions	3147	−3188	−8998	−17466	−21285	−30068	−36194	15222	22573	41018	63243	56490
Finance of gross capital formation	189152	208727	234606	255381	276405	293690	293113	262290	282508	323199	319438	342107
Gross capital formation												
Increase in stocks	11643	15069	15410	14220	10361	11043	4910	−475	9695	16330	1897	17193
Gross fixed capital formation	177509	193658	219196	241161	266044	282647	288203	262765	272813	306869	317541	324914
1 General government	31787	34447	36697	39685	43051	46521	45538	41049	37855	38589	41738	...
2 Corporate and quasi-corporate enterprises	62805	72159	85054	97678	116067	123547	111118	91246	99103	114408	117665	...
3 Other	82917	87052	97445	103798	106926	112579	131547	130470	135855	153184	159762	...
Gross capital formation	189152	208727	234606	255381	276405	293690	293113	262290	282508	323199	319438	342107

1.9 Gross domestic product by institutional sectors of origin

Thousand million Italian lire	1986	1987	1988	1989	1990	1991	1992	1993	1994	1995	1996	1997
Domestic factor incomes originating												
subtotal: Domestic factor incomes	731958	795302	875536	953468	1039787	1125671	1178399	1202258	1270507	1365926	1444282	1499983
Indirect taxes, net	58356	70583	86263	97850	115986	133361	143687	155659	164654	186563	195748	211307
A Indirect taxes	89071	101141	117823	132464	148938	170552	178864	198094	204154	221301	233504	248454
B less: Subsidies	30715	30558	31560	34614	32952	37191	35177	42435	39500	34738	37756	37147
Consumption of fixed capital	107975	116878	128224	140643	154886	168539	180407	192379	203505	219765	232605	239390
Gross domestic product	898289	982763	1090023	1191961	1310659	1427571	1502493	1550296	1638666	1772254	1872635	1950680

Italy

1.10 Gross domestic product by kind of activity, in current prices

Thousand million Italian lire

	1986	1987	1988	1989	1990	1991	1992	1993	1994	1995	1996	1997
1 Agriculture, hunting, forestry and fishing	38604	40053	39330	41605	42133	47847	47321	46108	47527	50844	52763	51332
2 Mining and quarrying	...	...	...	...	...	...	...	...	...	...	...	...
3 Manufacturing [a]	213686	230093	256378	279654	293622	300246	307906	310429	331792	365455	377870	391048
4 Electricity, gas and water	43607	48109	52480	57543	67380	77413	85878	89016	95920	103689	106087	109048
5 Construction	53986	56585	61920	67653	76627	83758	87742	85617	84721	88369	93058	94887
6 Wholesale and retail trade, restaurants and hotels [b]	170312	187748	205632	221626	240691	263026	276203	286649	301889	330983	348572	358361
7 Transport, storage and communication	51246	55453	61823	67706	73761	82647	89594	96675	105342	115078	119944	126692
8 Finance, insurance, real estate and business services [c]	202036	221060	248873	277498	315645	347652	385332	409432	428610	466329	501908	527145
9 Community, social and personal services	...	...	...	...	...	...	...	...	...	...	...	...
Total, Industries	773477	839101	926436	1013285	1109859	1202589	1279976	1323926	1395801	1520747	1600202	1658513
Producers of government services	107328	119749	134948	145587	170808	185924	194937	198468	203439	207838	225204	237018
Other producers	7588	7872	8695	10111	11522	13345	14802	15697	16394	17884	18892	20203
Subtotal	888393	966722	1070079	1168983	1292189	1401858	1489715	1538091	1615634	1746469	1844298	1915734
less: Imputed bank service charge	38175	39013	44496	50780	60721	66270	78718	79889	72807	79139	79350	79117
plus: Import duties	48071	55054	64440	73758	79191	91983	91496	92094	95839	104924	107687	114063
plus: Value added tax	...	...	...	...	...	...	...	...	...	...	...	...
plus: Other adjustments	...	...	...	...	...	...	...	...	...	...	...	...
equals: Gross domestic product [d]	898289	982763	1090023	1191961	1310659	1427571	1502493	1550296	1638666	1772254	1872635	1950680

a Including mining and quarrying.
b Item "Wholesale and retail trade, restaurants and hotels" includes repair services.
c Including Community, social and personal services.
d The branch breakdown used in this table (GDP by kind of activity) is according to the classification NACE/CLIO.

1.11 Gross domestic product by kind of activity, in constant prices

Thousand million Italian lire

	1986	1987	1988	1989	1990	1991	1992	1993	1994	1995	1996	1997
At constant prices of: 1990												
1 Agriculture, hunting, forestry and fishing	44091	45278	43460	43768	42133	45541	46699	45987	46196	46393	47276	47061
2 Mining and quarrying	...	...	...	...	...	...	...	...	...	...	...	...
3 Manufacturing [a]	249694	259719	277749	288519	293622	291594	291651	282497	297973	314112	310315	317357
4 Electricity, gas and water	61051	61801	62649	64151	67380	67922	69709	70940	73335	74113	74121	75010
5 Construction	69425	70338	72315	74661	76627	77619	77284	72926	69672	70244	71691	70960
6 Wholesale and retail trade, restaurants and hotels [b]	212407	221633	230926	235703	240691	243691	245231	241491	246806	254975	255969	260073
7 Transport, storage and communication	61411	63882	68097	71591	73761	76019	78737	81881	85372	89787	93175	96174
8 Finance, insurance, real estate and business services [c]	274239	282617	293978	304799	315645	319487	324676	331161	333627	340210	346071	351117
9 Community, social and personal services	...	...	...	...	...	...	...	...	...	...	...	...
Total, Industries	972318	1005268	1049174	1083192	1109859	1121873	1133987	1126883	1152981	1189834	1198618	1217752
Producers of government services	162483	165075	167471	169186	170808	172282	173179	173170	172877	172252	171481	170645
Other producers	10969	10777	10928	11083	11522	12072	12731	12805	12938	13300	13535	13858
Subtotal	1145770	1181120	1227573	1263461	1292189	1306227	1319897	1312858	1338796	1375386	1383634	1402255

Italy

Thousand million Italian lire

	1986	1987	1988	1989	1990	1991	1992	1993	1994	1995	1996	1997
At constant prices of: 1990												
less: Imputed bank service charge	48290	50694	54524	57820	60721	61973	68851	72540	71028	70362	69652	70489
plus: Import duties	66985	70097	73917	77264	79191	81328	82026	77350	78499	80836	81036	84289
plus: Value added tax	...	...	...	...	...	...	...	...	...	...	...	...
plus: Other adjustments	...	...	...	...	...	...	...	...	...	...	...	...
equals: Gross domestic product [d]	1164465	1200523	1246966	1282905	1310659	1325582	1333072	1317668	1346267	1385860	1395018	1416055

a Including mining and quarrying.
b Item "Wholesale and retail trade, restaurants and hotels" includes repair services.
c Including Community, social and personal services.
d The branch breakdown used in this table (GDP by kind of activity) is according to the classification NACE/CLIO.

1.12 Relations among national accounting aggregates

Thousand million Italian lire

	1986	1987	1988	1989	1990	1991	1992	1993	1994	1995	1996	1997
Gross domestic product	898289	982763	1090023	1191961	1310659	1427571	1502493	1550296	1638666	1772254	1872635	1950680
plus: Net factor income from the rest of the world	−6582	−6633	−7557	−10436	−17938	−22174	−26267	−26466	−27342	−26221	−23386	−20809
Factor income from rest of the world	12270	11967	14453	20049	23329	26502	34136	48057	46355	56057	62093	78244
less: Factor income to the rest of the world	18852	18600	22010	30485	41267	48676	60403	74523	73697	82278	85479	99053
equals: Gross national product	891707	976130	1082466	1181525	1292721	1405397	1476226	1523830	1611324	1746033	1849249	1929871
less: Consumption of fixed capital	107975	116878	128224	140643	154886	168539	180407	192379	203505	219765	232605	239390
equals: National income	783732	859252	954242	1040882	1137835	1236858	1295819	1331451	1407819	1526268	1616644	1690481
plus: Net current transfers from the rest of the world [a]	−2602	−1518	−2629	−5125	−3819	−8436	−9795	−11473	−11298	−7669	−11255	−7118
Current transfers from rest of the world	10737	12244	14004	15595	15025	16087	15770	19464	17259	18691	19311	24254
less: Current transfers to the rest of the world	13339	13762	16633	20720	18844	24523	25565	30937	28557	26360	30566	31372
equals: National disposable income	781130	857734	951613	1035757	1134016	1228422	1286024	1319978	1396521	1518599	1605389	1683363
less: Final consumption	696806	769073	854229	938485	1033782	1133339	1209512	1234845	1294945	1374147	1455313	1524156
equals: Net saving	84324	88661	97384	97272	100234	95083	76512	85133	101576	144452	150076	159207
less: Surplus of the nation on current transactions	3147	−3188	−8998	−17466	−21285	−30068	−36194	15222	22573	41018	63243	56490
equals: Net capital formation	81177	91849	106382	114738	121519	125151	112706	69911	79003	103434	86833	102717

a Item "Net current transfers from the rest of the world" excludes indirect taxes, net to EEC.

2.1 Government final consumption expenditure by function, in current prices

Thousand million Italian lire

	1986	1987	1988	1989	1990	1991	1992	1993	1994	1995	1996	1997
1 General public services	22272	25834	29157	31554	37003	41316	43183	46294	48239	49378	...	...
2 Defence	17877	20247	22950	24438	25312	26901	27802	28964	30117	30164	...	...
3 Public order and safety	14045	15820	17965	19119	22731	24612	26789	28545	29727	30510	...	...
4 Education	42073	46216	51839	56384	64746	67760	72449	71905	73104	75242	...	...
5 Health	27418	32003	35866	39015	46209	53367	56048	57362	58890	59882	...	...
6 Social security and welfare	6532	7068	7775	8255	9896	10662	11182	11641	11953	12010	...	...
7 Housing and community amenities	4589	4951	5478	5878	6593	7324	7580	7941	8455	8993	...	...
8 Recreational, cultural and religious affairs	2091	2302	2624	2762	2997	3582	3634	3864	3982	4245	...	...
9 Economic services	10182	10839	11827	12663	14243	15221	15822	16059	16058	17049	...	...
A Fuel and energy	1030	1132	1308	1367	1512	1584	1578	1685	1724	1842	...	...

Italy

Thousand million Italian lire

	1986	1987	1988	1989	1990	1991	1992	1993	1994	1995	1996	1997
B Agriculture, hunting, forestry and fishing	2087	2171	2454	2738	3215	3249	3339	3433	3363	3506	...	...
C Mining (except fuels), manufacturing and construction	908	969	988	965	1141	1173	1170	1244	1173	1469	...	...
D Transportation and communication	4807	5150	5599	5977	6593	7066	7265	7236	7337	7634	...	...
E Other economic affairs	1350	1417	1478	1616	1782	2149	2470	2461	2461	2598	...	...
10 Other functions	557	285	553	235	433	515	929	804	1278	982	...	...
Total government final consumption expenditures	147636	165565	186034	200303	230163	251260	265418	273379	281803	288455	...	...

2.2 Government final consumption expenditure by function, in constant prices

Thousand million Italian lire

	1986	1987	1988	1989	1990	1991	1992	1993	1994	1995	1996	1997
	At constant prices of: 1990											
1 General public services	52830	55063	56614	57959	59734	61590	63087	64560	65104	65397	...	...
2 Defence	23859	24567	24834	25050	25312	25659	25624	25445	25192	25293	...	...
3 Public order and safety	...	...	...	...	...	...	...	...	...	...	...	...
4 Education	59193	61330	63738	64514	64746	65334	65624	65179	63842	62251	...	...
5 Health	43847	45185	46078	46129	46209	46424	46920	47026	47507	47686	...	...
6 Social security and welfare	9455	9649	9731	9796	9896	10147	10218	10241	10264	10198	...	...
7 Housing and community amenities	6287	6465	6538	6557	6593	6745	6765	6856	6918	7032	...	...
8 Recreational, cultural and religious affairs	2648	2780	2840	2905	2997	3083	3157	3229	3245	3229	...	...
9 Economic services	13817	14051	14331	14237	14243	14506	14436	14482	14576	14549	...	...
A Fuel and energy	...	...	...	...	...	...	...	...	...	...	...	...
B Agriculture, hunting, forestry and fishing	...	...	...	...	...	...	...	...	...	...	...	...
C Mining (except fuels), manufacturing and construction	...	...	...	...	...	...	...	...	...	...	...	...
D Transportation and communication	...	...	...	...	...	...	...	...	...	...	...	...
E Other economic affairs	13817	14051	14331	14237	14243	14506	14436	14482	14576	14549	...	...
10 Other functions	681	334	622	249	433	490	844	730	1065	775	...	...
Total government final consumption expenditures	212617	219424	225326	227396	230163	233978	236675	237748	237713	236410	...	...

2.3 Total government outlays by function and type

Thousand million Italian lire

	1986								
	Final consumption expenditures				Other current transfers and property income	Total current disbursements	Gross capital formation	Other capital outlays	Total outlays
	Total	Compensation of employees	Other	Subsidies					
1 General public services	22272	15052	7220	–	10211	32483	2896	1046	36425
2 Defence	17877	10361	7516	–	–	17877	97	–	17974
3 Public order and safety	14045	11774	2271	–	291	14336	322	–	14658
4 Education	42073	36605	5468	226	1470	43769	2193	234	46196
5 Health	27418	18570	8848	–	18862	46280	1352	57	47689
6 Social security and welfare	6532	4614	1918	–	138331	144863	416	87	145366

Italy

Thousand million Italian lire

1986

	Final consumption expenditures - Total	Compensation of employees	Other	Subsidies	Other current transfers and property income	Total current disbursements	Gross capital formation	Other capital outlays	Total outlays
7 Housing and community amenities	4589	1945	2644	–	1694	6283	6939	1241	14463
8 Recreational, cultural and religious affairs	2091	1345	746	389	961	3441	1168	190	4799
9 Economic services	10182	4846	5336	27078	3884	41144	13432	10248	64824
A Fuel and energy	1030	590	440	327	381	1738	2018	153	3909
B Agriculture, hunting, forestry and fishing	2087	1270	817	1553	474	4114	1647	2212	7973
C Mining (except fuels), manufacturing and construction	908	330	578	4876	543	6327	1605	2542	10474
D Transportation and communication	4807	2123	2684	18955	2062	25824	6737	4925	37486
E Other economic affairs	1350	533	817	1367	424	3141	1425	416	4982
10 Other functions	557	63	494	–	63443	64000	2972	1142	68114
Total	147636	105175	42461	27693	239147	414476	31787	14245	460508

1987

	Final consumption expenditures - Total	Compensation of employees	Other	Subsidies	Other current transfers and property income	Total current disbursements	Gross capital formation	Other capital outlays	Total outlays
1 General public services	25834	17074	8760	–	9963	35797	3215	573	39585
2 Defence	20247	11384	8863	–	–	20247	113	–	20360
3 Public order and safety	15820	13244	2576	–	273	16093	361	–	16454
4 Education	46216	40028	6188	222	1584	48022	2423	273	50718
5 Health	32003	21783	10220	–	22918	54921	1451	23	56395
6 Social security and welfare	7068	5070	1998	–	149665	156733	481	95	157309
7 Housing and community amenities	4951	2057	2894	–	1583	6534	7603	1217	15354
8 Recreational, cultural and religious affairs	2302	1442	860	636	1388	4326	1274	135	5735
9 Economic services	10839	5095	5744	25235	3505	39579	14372	11923	65874
A Fuel and energy	1132	625	507	252	288	1672	1986	286	3944
B Agriculture, hunting, forestry and fishing	2171	1293	878	2030	443	4644	1909	2787	9340
C Mining (except fuels), manufacturing and construction	969	341	628	4514	488	5971	1687	2865	10523
D Transportation and communication	5150	2248	2902	16624	1886	23660	7098	5506	36264
E Other economic affairs	1417	588	829	1815	400	3632	1692	479	5803
10 Other functions	285	90	195	–	66325	66610	3154	812	70576
Total	165565	117267	48298	26093	257204	448862	34447	15051	498360

1988

	Final consumption expenditures - Total	Compensation of employees	Other	Subsidies	Other current transfers and property income	Total current disbursements	Gross capital formation	Other capital outlays	Total outlays
1 General public services	29157	19622	9535	–	11696	40853	3499	561	44913
2 Defence	22950	12889	10061	–	–	22950	123	–	23073
3 Public order and safety	17965	15075	2890	–	276	18241	343	–	18584

Italy

	1988								
	Final consumption expenditures			Subsidies	Other current transfers and property income	Total current disbursements	Gross capital formation	Other capital outlays	Total outlays
	Total	Compensation of employees	Other						
4 Education	51839	45130	6709	237	1532	53608	2833	247	56688
5 Health	35866	24283	11583	–	27160	63026	1608	23	64657
6 Social security and welfare	7775	5527	2248	–	164720	172495	549	49	173093
7 Housing and community amenities	5478	2300	3178	–	1614	7092	7782	1377	16251
8 Recreational, cultural and religious affairs	2624	1558	1066	659	1408	4691	1489	198	6378
9 Economic services	11827	5638	6189	25681	3193	40701	15192	12907	68800
A Fuel and energy	1308	684	624	302	194	1804	1609	255	3668
B Agriculture, hunting, forestry and fishing	2454	1492	962	1923	399	4776	2055	2836	9667
C Mining (except fuels), manufacturing and construction	988	363	625	4620	459	6067	1593	3333	10993
D Transportation and communication	5599	2442	3157	17825	1665	25089	8131	5826	39046
E Other economic affairs	1478	657	821	1011	476	2965	1804	657	5426
10 Other functions	553	114	439	–	76768	77321	3279	1171	81771
Total	186034	132136	53898	26577	288367	500978	36697	16533	554208

	1989								
	Final consumption expenditures			Subsidies	Other current transfers and property income	Total current disbursements	Gross capital formation	Other capital outlays	Total outlays
	Total	Compensation of employees	Other						
1 General public services	31554	20718	10836	–	15263	46817	4021	872	51710
2 Defence	24438	14495	9943	–	–	24438	118	–	24556
3 Public order and safety	19119	16097	3022	–	290	19409	358	2	19769
4 Education	56384	48810	7574	274	1640	58298	3165	310	61773
5 Health	39015	25856	13159	–	29367	68382	1855	45	70282
6 Social security and welfare	8255	5972	2283	–	183855	192110	634	46	192790
7 Housing and community amenities	5878	2439	3439	–	1511	7389	8465	1696	17550
8 Recreational, cultural and religious affairs	2762	1680	1082	766	1491	5019	1715	256	6990
9 Economic services	12663	6159	6504	28797	3182	44642	15782	12637	73061
A Fuel and energy	1367	718	649	348	149	1864	1293	549	3706
B Agriculture, hunting, forestry and fishing	2738	1689	1049	2473	403	5614	1907	2856	10377
C Mining (except fuels), manufacturing and construction	965	360	605	5181	476	6622	1590	3737	11949
D Transportation and communication	5977	2631	3346	20000	1661	27638	9041	5055	41734
E Other economic affairs	1616	761	855	795	493	2904	1951	440	5295
10 Other functions	235	105	130	–	94457	94692	3572	1848	100112
Total	200303	142331	57972	29837	331056	561196	39685	17712	618593

Italy

1990

		Final consumption expenditures			Other current transfers and property income	Total current disbursements	Gross capital formation	Other capital outlays	Total outlays
		Total	Compensation of employees	Other	Subsidies				
1	General public services	37003	24893	12110	–	13216	50219	4099	1018	55336
2	Defence	25312	16629	8683	–	–	25312	118	–	25430
3	Public order and safety	22731	19501	3230	–	296	23027	356	–	23383
4	Education	64746	56228	8518	294	2020	67060	3454	270	70784
5	Health	46209	30627	15582	–	34307	80516	2576	79	83171
6	Social security and welfare	9896	7427	2469	–	207486	217382	681	75	218138
7	Housing and community amenities	6593	2698	3895	–	1704	8297	8681	1907	18885
8	Recreational, cultural and religious affairs	2997	1883	1114	698	1713	5408	1828	366	7602
9	Economic services	14243	7008	7235	28585	3265	46093	18121	17423	81637
A	Fuel and energy	1512	777	735	340	75	1927	1364	717	4008
B	Agriculture, hunting, forestry and fishing	3215	1968	1247	2585	402	6202	1810	2710	10722
C	Mining (except fuels), manufacturing and construction	1141	438	703	4416	545	6102	1853	4381	12336
D	Transportation and communication	6593	2996	3597	20294	1611	28498	10858	8999	48355
E	Other economic affairs	1782	829	953	950	632	3364	2236	616	6216
10	Other functions	433	164	269	–	113350	113783	3137	1709	118629
	Total	230163	167058	63105	29577	377357	637097	43051	22847	702995

1991

		Final consumption expenditures			Other current transfers and property income	Total current disbursements	Gross capital formation	Other capital outlays	Total outlays
		Total	Compensation of employees	Other	Subsidies				
1	General public services	41316	27868	13448	–	17932	59248	4740	1190	65178
2	Defence	26901	18025	8876	–	–	26901	165	–	27066
3	Public order and safety	24612	20950	3662	–	303	24915	394	–	25309
4	Education	67760	58408	9352	394	2415	70569	3905	408	74882
5	Health	53367	35635	17732	–	38178	91545	2634	62	94241
6	Social security and welfare	10662	7973	2689	–	227306	237968	756	79	238803
7	Housing and community amenities	7324	2771	4553	–	1749	9073	9234	1911	20218
8	Recreational, cultural and religious affairs	3582	2111	1471	1217	1759	6558	1650	415	8623
9	Economic services	15221	7765	7456	30943	3217	49381	19414	12374	81169
A	Fuel and energy	1584	785	799	290	61	1935	1425	175	3535
B	Agriculture, hunting, forestry and fishing	3249	2093	1156	2304	378	5931	1656	3043	10630
C	Mining (except fuels), manufacturing and construction	1173	494	679	5376	707	7256	1874	4688	13818
D	Transportation and communication	7066	3316	3750	21621	1564	30251	12247	3595	46093
E	Other economic affairs	2149	1077	1072	1352	507	4008	2212	873	7093
10	Other functions	515	249	266	–	130108	130623	3629	1967	136219
	Total	251260	181755	69505	32554	422967	706781	46521	18406	771708

Italy

1992

	Final consumption expenditures Total	Compensation of employees	Other	Subsidies	Other current transfers and property income	Total current disbursements	Gross capital formation	Other capital outlays	Total outlays
1 General public services	43183	28713	14470	_	19299	62482	4521	1853	68856
2 Defence	27802	18657	9145	_	_	27802	156	_	27958
3 Public order and safety	26789	22285	4504	_	349	27138	426	6	27570
4 Education	72449	62606	9843	426	2384	75259	4554	533	80346
5 Health	56048	36763	19285	_	39127	95175	2254	81	97510
6 Social security and welfare	11182	8259	2923	_	255882	267064	834	112	268010
7 Housing and community amenities	7580	2706	4874	_	1760	9340	8913	1771	20024
8 Recreational, cultural and religious affairs	3634	2069	1565	1495	1876	7005	1647	359	9011
9 Economic services	15822	7775	8047	29603	3601	49026	19958	14988	83972
A Fuel and energy	1578	731	847	504	47	2129	1582	617	4328
B Agriculture, hunting, forestry and fishing	3339	2121	1218	2596	414	6349	1725	3020	11094
C Mining (except fuels), manufacturing and construction	1170	487	683	5829	964	7963	1976	4785	14724
D Transportation and communication	7265	3293	3972	19568	1724	28557	12392	5722	46671
E Other economic affairs	2470	1143	1327	1106	452	4028	2283	844	7155
10 Other functions	929	415	514	_	155048	155977	2275	729	158981
Total	265418	190248	75170	31524	479326	776268	45538	20432	842238

1993

	Final consumption expenditures Total	Compensation of employees	Other	Subsidies	Other current transfers and property income	Total current disbursements	Gross capital formation	Other capital outlays	Total outlays
1 General public services	46294	29405	16889	_	24365	70659	4469	1871	76999
2 Defence	28964	19498	9466	_	_	28964	167	_	29131
3 Public order and safety	28545	23721	4824	_	388	28933	430	6	29369
4 Education	71905	61890	10015	406	2631	74942	4309	659	79910
5 Health	57362	37405	19957	_	37475	94837	2000	52	96889
6 Social security and welfare	11641	8326	3315	_	270075	281716	638	118	282472
7 Housing and community amenities	7941	2618	5323	_	2008	9949	7304	2500	19753
8 Recreational, cultural and religious affairs	3864	2142	1722	1596	2109	7569	1600	592	9761
9 Economic services	16059	7716	8343	33287	4450	53796	17971	20166	91933
A Fuel and energy	1685	708	977	552	61	2298	1424	1240	4962
B Agriculture, hunting, forestry and fishing	3433	2175	1258	2972	456	6861	1527	3527	11915
C Mining (except fuels), manufacturing and construction	1244	505	739	5298	941	7483	1861	6971	16315
D Transportation and communication	7236	3313	3923	22972	2489	32697	11015	7067	50779
E Other economic affairs	2461	1015	1446	1493	503	4457	2144	1361	7962
10 Other functions	804	400	404	_	168493	169297	2407	9342	181046
Total	273379	193121	80258	35289	511994	820662	41295	35306	897263

Italy

1994

		Final consumption expenditures			Other current transfers and property income	Total current disburse-ments	Gross capital formation	Other capital outlays	Total outlays
		Total	Compen-sation of employ-ees	Other	Subsidies				
1	General public services	48239	29528	18711	–	21338	69577	4409	1507	75493
2	Defence	30117	20854	9263	–	–	30117	211	–	30328
3	Public order and safety	29727	24670	5057	–	434	30161	465	7	30633
4	Education	73104	62644	10460	383	2323	75810	4002	337	80149
5	Health	58890	38216	20674	–	35975	94865	1723	53	96641
6	Social security and welfare	11953	8268	3685	–	288290	300243	571	136	300950
7	Housing and community amenities	8455	2571	5884	–	1480	9935	6841	2124	18900
8	Recreational, cultural and religious affairs	3982	2153	1829	1489	2639	8110	1570	376	10056
9	Economic services	16058	7632	8426	34947	3203	54208	15727	15608	85543
	A Fuel and energy	1724	704	1020	513	26	2263	1283	232	3778
	B Agriculture, hunting, forestry and fishing	3363	2154	1209	2478	397	6238	1437	2987	10662
	C Mining (except fuels), manufacturing and construction	1173	487	686	6781	899	8853	1627	4184	14664
	D Transportation and communication	7337	3238	4099	23752	1596	32685	9478	7166	49329
	E Other economic affairs	2461	1049	1412	1423	285	4169	1902	1039	7110
10	Other functions	1278	366	912	–	158496	159774	2725	3890	166389
	Total	281803	196902	84901	36819	514178	832800	38244	24038	895082

1995

		Final consumption expenditures			Other current transfers and property income	Total current disburse-ments	Gross capital formation	Other capital outlays	Total outlays
		Total	Compen-sation of employ-ees	Other	Subsidies				
1	General public services	49378	30368	19010	–	24289	73667	4823	1388	79878
2	Defence	30164	21337	8827	–	–	30164	223	–	30387
3	Public order and safety	30510	25387	5123	–	431	30941	506	7	31454
4	Education	75242	64129	11113	388	2473	78103	4302	327	82732
5	Health	59882	39234	20648	–	34016	93898	1896	53	95847
6	Social security and welfare	12010	8510	3500	–	303885	315895	664	137	316696
7	Housing and community amenities	8993	2622	6371	–	1634	10627	7669	2421	20717
8	Recreational, cultural and religious affairs	4245	2242	2003	1520	3029	8794	1754	392	10940
9	Economic services	17049	8067	8982	30671	3586	51306	15453	15434	82193
	A Fuel and energy	1842	710	1132	519	35	2396	1481	111	3988
	B Agriculture, hunting, forestry and fishing	3506	2251	1255	2246	406	6158	1533	3197	10888
	C Mining (except fuels), manufacturing and construction	1469	670	799	5443	795	7707	1682	7660	17049
	D Transportation and communication	7634	3369	4265	21311	2019	30964	8811	3333	43108
	E Other economic affairs	2598	1067	1531	1152	331	4081	1946	1133	7160
10	Other functions	982	458	524	–	177290	178272	2611	1712	182595
	Total	288455	202354	86101	32579	550633	871667	39901	21871	933439

Italy

2.5 Private final consumption expenditure by type and purpose, in current prices

Thousand million Italian lire

	1986	1987	1988	1989	1990	1991	1992	1993	1994	1995	1996	1997
Final consumption expenditure of resident households												
1 Food, beverages and tobacco	134325	141023	148061	158031	167953	179965	189316	195106	202021	213653	220331	221797
A Food	115751	121565	127366	135899	144364	154338	162453	165133	170484	179903	184272	184580
B Non-alcoholic beverages	1815	2090	2383	2660	3129	3554	3865	4097	4259	4621	4961	5047
C Alcoholic beverages	7205	7547	7760	8126	8747	9397	9766	9891	9983	10393	11178	11318
D Tobacco	9554	9821	10552	11346	11713	12676	13232	15985	17295	18736	19920	20852
2 Clothing and footwear	56313	63880	70854	77301	81054	88202	92620	88365	93834	101082	101526	106841
3 Gross rent, fuel and power	79129	86585	94890	105404	117657	136389	147991	160907	175110	194098	209912	221306
A Fuel and power	20344	21319	22545	24718	27939	34880	34874	37335	35964	40072	41103	41187
B Other	58785	65266	72345	80686	89718	101509	113117	123572	139146	154026	168809	180119
4 Furniture, furnishings and household equipment and operation	50707	55737	62219	69826	75795	84157	88353	88687	94504	101544	103499	107365
A Household operation	14589	15726	16981	18457	20058	21988	23329	23140	25193	27210	28742	29700
B Other	36118	40011	45238	51369	55737	62169	65024	65547	69311	74334	74757	77665
5 Medical care and health expenses	31073	36364	41901	46586	54157	59806	64732	68864	71511	72215	77151	81626
6 Transport and communication	68701	75370	83597	92594	99423	105588	115970	112837	122101	134159	144348	162938
A Personal transport equipment	21562	25183	29463	33716	35374	35524	39865	31050	33884	36984	38993	50874
B Other	47139	50187	54134	58878	64049	70064	76105	81787	88217	97175	105355	112064
7 Recreational, entertainment, education and cultural services	47809	51588	59308	67462	73191	78850	83906	85559	90124	95925	99439	103318
A Education	3996	4506	5093	5760	6239	7028	7290	7711	8044	8428	9033	9298
B Other	43813	47082	54215	61702	66952	71822	76616	77848	82080	87497	90406	94020
8 Miscellaneous goods and services	88986	100262	112908	125273	138757	154031	163470	169805	180026	195489	210725	218461
A Personal care	15576	18190	20282	22621	25207	27446	28851	30087	32142	33923	36270	38120
B Expenditures in restaurants, cafes and hotels	51431	57631	64135	70088	77493	86875	91754	94835	102362	112589	122228	126758
C Other	21979	24441	28491	32564	36057	39710	42865	44883	45522	48977	52227	53583
Total final consumption expenditure in the domestic market by households, of which	557043	610809	673738	742477	807987	886988	946358	970130	1029231	1108165	1166931	1223652
A Durable goods	199802	212239	225343	243489	263085	287533	301908	313018	322433	343051	357995	365706
B Semi-durable goods	105262	117729	132527	146595	156955	170695	180318	178987	189447	203326	208153	219164
C Non-durable goods	62165	70017	80871	92152	98220	104623	111587	102438	108515	115723	119347	131066
D Services	189815	210824	234997	260241	289727	324137	352545	375688	408836	446065	481436	507717
plus: Direct purchases abroad by resident households	4704	6310	8270	9316	11891	14506	22360	22151	19554	23868	24118	28121
less: Direct purchases in the domestic market by non-resident households	14973	16071	16481	16472	19466	23057	28351	34631	38315	46809	46259	50757
equals: Final consumption expenditure of resident households	546774	601048	665527	735321	800412	878437	940367	957650	1010470	1085224	1144790	1201016
Final consumption expenditures by private non-profit organisations serving households												
1 Research and science	...	...	...	...	...	...	...	...	...	...	...	...
2 Education	...	...	...	...	...	...	...	...	...	...	...	...
3 Medical and other health services	...	...	...	...	...	...	...	...	...	...	...	...
4 Welfare services	...	...	...	...	...	...	...	...	...	...	...	...

Italy

Thousand million Italian lire

	1986	1987	1988	1989	1990	1991	1992	1993	1994	1995	1996	1997
5 Recreational and related cultural services	...	...	...	...	...	...	...	...	...	...	...	...
6 Religious organisations	...	...	...	...	...	...	...	...	...	...	...	...
7 Professional and labour organisations serving households	...	...	...	...	...	...	...	...	...	...	...	...
8 Miscellaneous	...	...	...	...	...	...	...	...	...	...	...	...
equals: Final consumption expenditures by private non-profit organisations serving households	2396	2460	2668	2860	3207	3642	3727	3816	4001	4290	4528	4729
Private final consumption expenditure	549170	603508	668195	738181	803619	882079	944094	961466	1014471	1089514	1149318	1205745

2.6 Private final consumption expenditure by type and purpose, in constant prices

Thousand million Italian lire

	1986	1987	1988	1989	1990	1991	1992	1993	1994	1995	1996	1997

At constant prices of: 1990

Final consumption expenditure of resident households

	1986	1987	1988	1989	1990	1991	1992	1993	1994	1995	1996	1997
1 Food, beverages and tobacco	163877	165109	166847	167815	167953	168689	168661	168860	168434	167531	165480	165960
A Food	139519	141383	143111	143923	144364	145065	145614	145452	145371	144568	142483	142967
B Non-alcoholic beverages	2213	2460	2689	2892	3129	3272	3397	3487	3545	3636	3659	3728
C Alcoholic beverages	9273	9196	9021	8869	8747	8638	8448	8215	8077	8011	7974	7839
D Tobacco	12872	12070	12026	12131	11713	11714	11202	11706	11441	11316	11364	11426
2 Clothing and footwear	71198	76068	79857	81795	81054	83786	84020	77339	79512	82304	79488	81595
3 Gross rent, fuel and power	107469	110421	112775	114960	117657	121715	121763	121732	122470	125240	127639	127132
A Fuel and power	25944	26736	26774	27069	27939	30192	29132	29109	27314	29234	29784	29240
B Other	81525	83685	86001	87891	89718	91523	92631	92623	95156	96006	97855	97892
4 Furniture, furnishings and household equipment and operation	63817	66575	70380	73857	75795	79394	79542	76604	79074	80963	79458	80840
A Household operation	17890	18249	18824	19422	20058	20928	21275	20450	21645	22623	23360	24119
B Other	45927	48326	51556	54435	55737	58466	58267	56154	57429	58340	56098	56721
5 Medical care and health expenses	42717	45937	47410	49836	54157	56328	57927	57744	58081	57713	59595	60940
6 Transport and communication	82130	86292	92278	97431	99423	100120	105217	96705	98981	102056	105819	117639
A Personal transport equipment	25725	28626	32188	35040	35374	34356	37000	26537	26796	27107	27327	36013
B Other	56405	57666	60090	62391	64049	65764	68217	70168	72185	74949	78492	81626
7 Recreational, entertainment, education and cultural services	59217	61555	66024	70828	73191	74694	75671	74474	76363	78392	78718	80800
A Education	5355	5597	5887	6187	6239	6445	6342	6359	6395	6409	6599	6627
B Other	53862	55958	60137	64641	66952	68249	69329	68115	69968	71983	72119	74173
8 Miscellaneous goods and services	113671	120788	127992	132540	138757	144916	145523	144432	146518	150759	155724	157160
A Personal care	20000	21733	22736	23831	25207	25820	25706	25447	26195	26456	27303	27969
B Expenditures in restaurants, cafes and hotels	68043	71815	74534	75560	77493	80573	79294	78153	80585	84104	87359	88130
C Other	25628	27240	30722	33149	36057	38523	40523	40832	39738	40199	41062	41061
Total final consumption expenditure in the domestic market by households, of which	704096	732745	763563	789062	807987	829642	838324	817890	829433	844958	851921	872066
A Durable goods	245173	249811	254146	259019	263085	267572	269891	269787	268765	271073	272791	275153
B Semi-durable goods	129875	138239	147972	154093	156955	162694	164011	156975	160755	165097	162152	166861
C Non-durable goods	72373	78319	87140	95051	98220	101534	104951	91512	92281	93482	93183	101157
D Services	256675	266376	274306	280899	289727	297842	299472	299616	307632	315306	323795	328895

Italy

Thousand million Italian lire

	1986	1987	1988	1989	1990	1991	1992	1993	1994	1995	1996	1997
At constant prices of: 1990												
plus: Direct purchases abroad by resident households	5562	7381	9051	9639	11891	13661	19717	16266	13574	14769	15574	17759
less: Direct purchases in the domestic market by non-resident households	18600	19087	18665	17486	19466	21650	25291	29650	31561	36598	34834	37542
equals: Final consumption expenditure of resident households	691058	721039	753949	781215	800412	821653	832750	804506	811446	823129	832661	852283

Final consumption expenditures by private non-profit organisations serving households

	1986	1987	1988	1989	1990	1991	1992	1993	1994	1995	1996	1997
1 Research and science	...	...	...	...	...	...	...	...	...	...	...	...
2 Education	...	...	...	...	...	...	...	...	...	...	...	...
3 Medical and other health services	...	...	...	...	...	...	...	...	...	...	...	...
4 Welfare services	...	...	...	...	...	...	...	...	...	...	...	...
5 Recreational and related cultural services	...	...	...	...	...	...	...	...	...	...	...	...
6 Religious organisations	...	...	...	...	...	...	...	...	...	...	...	...
7 Professional and labour organisations serving households	...	...	...	...	...	...	...	...	...	...	...	...
8 Miscellaneous	...	...	...	...	...	...	...	...	...	...	...	...
equals: Final consumption expenditures by private non-profit organisations serving households	2891	2933	2992	3066	3207	3321	3344	3358	3360	3468	3530	3621
Private final consumption expenditure	693949	723972	756941	784281	803619	824974	836094	807864	814806	826597	836191	855904

2.11 Gross fixed capital formation by kind of activity of owner, ISIC divisions, in current prices

Thousand million Italian lire

	1986	1987	1988	1989	1990	1991	1992	1993	1994	1995	1996	1997
All producers												
1 Agriculture, hunting, forestry and fishing	11825	12355	14901	15310	14901	15301	15205	14752	16605	18216	20847	...
2 Mining and quarrying	...	...	...	...	...	...	...	...	...	...	...	...
3 Manufacturing [a]	29662	34419	40466	46785	49661	51643	49886	42632	46683	...	...	...
A Manufacturing of food, beverages and tobacco	2993	3466	4101	4492	4547	4891	5827	6133	6126	...	...	...
B Textile, wearing apparel and leather industries	3982	4312	5016	5321	6024	5875	5017	3814	5165	...	...	...
C Manufacture of wood and wood products, including furniture												
D Manufacture of paper and paper products, printing and publishing	...	...	...	...	...	...	...	...	...	...	...	...
E Manufacture of chemicals and chemical petroleum, coal, rubber and plastic products	...	...	...	...	...	...	...	...	...	...	...	...
F Manufacture of non-metallic mineral products, except products of petroleum and coal	2135	3003	3652	4743	4697	4741	4686	3514	3991	...	...	...
G Basic metal industries	2450	2170	2026	2711	4120	4516	3753	2224	2286	...	...	...

Italy

Thousand million Italian lire

	1986	1987	1988	1989	1990	1991	1992	1993	1994	1995	1996	1997
H Manufacture of fabricated metal products, machinery and equipment	9981	12043	14468	16599	17082	17848	17223	15692	17199	...	...	...
I Other manufacturing industries	...	...	...	...	...	...	...	...	...	...	...	...
4 Electricity, gas and water	11073	11037	10727	11609	12351	15047	17364	16025	13619	...	...	...
5 Construction	4816	4984	5370	6513	6568	7196	7630	5773	5984	...	...	...
6 Wholesale and retail trade, restaurants and hotels [b]	15300	15107	18733	21469	22920	23340	23392	23047	23692	...	...	...
A Wholesale and retail trade	12770	12389	15038	16597	18144	18809	18348	18525	18603	...	...	...
B Restaurants and hotels	2530	2718	3695	4872	4776	4531	5044	4522	5089	...	...	...
7 Transport, storage and communication	17340	21749	24792	28561	34071	35425	35872	30184	31051	...	...	...
A Transport and storage	11677	15082	16964	18874	21131	21332	23260	20177	21374	...	...	...
B Communication	5663	6667	7828	9687	12940	14093	12612	10007	9677	...	...	...
8 Finance, insurance, real estate and business services	69064	72920	82925	87590	99668	107522	113183	107540	113568	...	...	...
9 Community, social and personal services										...	...	...
Total industries	159080	172571	197914	217837	240140	255474	262532	239951	251102	282875	294784	...
Producers of government services	18426	21092	21288	23319	25903	27173	25672	22811	21711	23306	24381	...
Private non-profit institutions serving households	...	...	...	...	...	...	...	...	...	...	...	...
Total	177506	193663	219202	241156	266043	282647	288204	262762	272813	306181	319165	...

a Including mining and quarrying.
b Item "Wholesale and retail trade, restaurants and hotels" includes repair services.

2.12 Gross fixed capital formation by kind of activity of owner, ISIC divisions, in constant prices

Thousand million Italian lire

	1986	1987	1988	1989	1990	1991	1992	1993	1994	1995	1996	1997
At constant prices of: 1990												
All producers												
1 Agriculture, hunting, forestry and fishing	15066	14909	17010	16401	14901	14265	13563	12622	13660	14295	15796	...
2 Mining and quarrying	...	...	...	...	...	...	...	...	...	...	...	...
3 Manufacturing [a]	35530	39216	44433	48981	49661	49834	46535	37933	40259	...	...	...
A Manufacturing of food, beverages and tobacco	3607	3960	4512	4707	4547	4705	5397	5407	5246	...	...	...
B Textile, wearing apparel and leather industries	4789	4939	5516	5583	6024	5655	4670	3393	4452	...	...	...
C Manufacture of wood and wood products, including furniture	...	...	...	...	...	...	...	...	...	...	...	...
D Manufacture of paper and paper products, printing and publishing	...	...	...	...	...	...	...	...	...	...	...	...
E Manufacture of chemicals and chemical petroleum, coal, rubber and plastic products	...	...	...	...	...	...	...	...	...	...	...	...
F Manufacture of non-metallic mineral products, except products of petroleum and coal	2554	3419	4006	4961	4697	4576	4376	3136	3444	...	...	...
G Basic metal industries	2925	2470	2219	2822	4120	4390	3538	2008	1986	...	...	...

Italy

Thousand million Italian lire

	1986	1987	1988	1989	1990	1991	1992	1993	1994	1995	1996	1997
At constant prices of: 1990												
H Manufacture of fabricated metal products, machinery and equipment	11948	13681	15897	17403	17082	17193	16008	13881	15198	...	...	...
I Other manufacturing industries	...	...	...	...	...	...	...	...	...	...	...	...
4 Electricity, gas and water	13741	13033	12070	12292	12351	14404	16132	14310	11695	...	...	...
5 Construction	5843	5742	5898	6824	6568	6915	7052	5080	5074	...	...	...
6 Wholesale and retail trade, restaurants and hotels	18515	17389	20563	22422	22920	22471	21854	20510	20383	...	...	...
A Wholesale and retail trade	15509	14298	16527	17354	18144	18062	17031	16402	15889	...	...	...
B Restaurants and hotels	3006	3091	4036	5068	4776	4409	4823	4108	4494	...	...	...
7 Transport, storage and communication	20930	25387	27381	29937	34071	34004	33289	26746	26359	...	...	...
A Transport and storage	14339	17835	18882	19914	21131	20255	21271	17553	17650	...	...	...
B Communication	6591	7552	8499	10023	12940	13749	12018	9193	8709	...	...	...
8 Finance, insurance, real estate and business services	87625	88841	94340	94788	99668	100795	101648	92500	95017	...	...	...
9 Community, social and personal services										...	...	...
Total industries	197250	204517	221695	231645	240140	242688	240073	209701	212447	227833	230394	...
Producers of government services	23120	25541	24176	25067	25903	25586	23289	19926	18338	18826	19225	...
Private non-profit institutions serving households	...	...	...	...	...	...	...	...	...	...	...	...
Total	220370	230058	245871	256712	266043	268274	263362	229627	230785	246659	249619	...

a Including mining and quarrying.

3.11 General government production account: total and subsectors

Thousand million Italian lire

	1986					1987				
	Total government	Central government	State or provincial government	Local government	Social security funds	Total government	Central government	State or provincial government	Local government	Social security funds
Gross output										
1 Sales	6913	2703	...	3496	714	7688	3266	...	3613	809
2 Services produced for own use	147840	80913	...	62971	3956	165791	90362	...	71189	4240
3 Own account capital formation	...	...	...	...	...	...	...	...	...	...
Gross output	154753	83616	...	66467	4670	173479	93628	...	74802	5049
Gross input										
Intermediate consumption	42875	17203	...	24141	1531	48695	20094	...	27050	1551
subtotal: Value added	111878	66413	...	42326	3139	124784	73534	...	47752	3498
1 Indirect taxes, net	1108	1108	...	–	–	1313	1313	...	–	–
A Indirect taxes	1108	1108	...	–	–	1313	1313	...	–	–
B less: Subsidies	–	–	...	–	–	–	–	...	–	–
2 Consumption of fixed capital	4010	1982	...	1882	146	4420	2185	...	2073	162
3 Compensation of employees	105175	62796	...	39940	2439	117267	69404	...	45157	2706
4 Net operating surplus	1585	527	...	504	554	1784	632	...	522	630
Gross input	154753	83616	...	66467	4670	173479	93628	...	74802	5049

Italy

	1988					1989				
	Total govern-ment	Central govern-ment	State or provincial govern-ment	Local govern-ment	Social security funds	Total govern-ment	Central govern-ment	State or provincial govern-ment	Local govern-ment	Social security funds

Gross output

1 Sales	9325	4073	...	4291	961	10891	4593	...	5162	1136
2 Services produced for own use	186253	102307	...	79436	4510	200507	109766	...	85799	4942
3 Own account capital formation	...	...	...	...	...	...	...	...	...	...
Gross output	195578	106380	...	83727	5471	211398	114359	...	90961	6078

Gross input

Intermediate consumption	54432	22547	...	30152	1733	58634	23177	...	33608	1849
subtotal: Value added	141146	83833	...	53575	3738	152764	91182	...	57353	4229
1 Indirect taxes, net	1716	1716	...	–	–	2103	2103	...	–	–
A Indirect taxes	1716	1716	...	–	–	2103	2103	...	–	–
B less: Subsidies	–	–	...	–	–	–	–	...	–	–
2 Consumption of fixed capital .	4966	2454	...	2330	182	5585	2763	...	2618	204
3 Compensation of employees ...	132136	78765	...	50576	2795	142331	85344	...	53875	3112
4 Net operating surplus	2328	898	...	669	761	2745	972	...	860	913
Gross input	195578	106380	...	83727	5471	211398	114359	...	90961	6078

	1990					1991				
	Total govern-ment	Central govern-ment	State or provincial govern-ment	Local govern-ment	Social security funds	Total govern-ment	Central govern-ment	State or provincial govern-ment	Local govern-ment	Social security funds

Gross output

1 Sales	11639	5078	...	5326	1235	12843	5098	...	6297	1448
2 Services produced for own use	230377	125091	...	99216	6070	251490	133225	...	111836	6429
3 Own account capital formation	...	...	...	...	...	...	...	...	...	...
Gross output	242016	130169	...	104542	7305	264333	138323	...	118133	7877

Gross input

Intermediate consumption	63328	23122	...	38133	2073	70042	24404	...	43305	2333
subtotal: Value added	178688	107047	...	66409	5232	194291	113919	...	74828	5544
1 Indirect taxes, net	2444	2444	...	–	–	2738	2738	...	–	–
A Indirect taxes	2444	2444	...	–	–	2738	2738	...	–	–
B less: Subsidies	–	–	...	–	–	–	–	...	–	–
2 Consumption of fixed capital .	6269	3100	...	2940	229	6945	3434	...	3257	254
3 Compensation of employees ...	167058	100497	...	62535	4026	181755	107128	...	70496	4131
4 Net operating surplus	2917	1006	...	934	977	2853	619	...	1075	1159
Gross input	242016	130169	...	104542	7305	264333	138323	...	118133	7877

	1992					1993				
	Total govern-ment	Central govern-ment	State or provincial govern-ment	Local govern-ment	Social security funds	Total govern-ment	Central govern-ment	State or provincial govern-ment	Local govern-ment	Social security funds

Gross output

1 Sales	15167	6346	...	7244	1577	15996	6707	...	7581	1708
2 Services produced for own use	265664	143547	...	115316	6801	273612	148677	...	117824	7111
3 Own account capital formation	...	...	...	...	...	...	...	...	...	...
Gross output	280831	149893	...	122560	8378	289608	155384	...	125405	8819

Gross input

Intermediate consumption	75608	26690	...	46312	2606	79923	29359	...	47620	2944
subtotal: Value added	205223	123203	...	76248	5772	209685	126025	...	77785	5875

Italy

	1992					1993				
	Total government	Central government	State or provincial government	Local government	Social security funds	Total government	Central government	State or provincial government	Local government	Social security funds
1 Indirect taxes, net	3627	3627	...	–	–	4316	4316	...	–	–
A Indirect taxes	3627	3627	...	–	–	4316	4316	...	–	–
B less: Subsidies	–	–	...	–	–	–	–	...	–	–
2 Consumption of fixed capital	7573	3749	...	3547	277	8307	4106	...	3897	304
3 Compensation of employees	190248	114708	...	71286	4254	193121	116721	...	72174	4226
4 Net operating surplus	3775	1119	...	1415	1241	3941	882	...	1714	1345
Gross input	280831	149893	...	122560	8378	289608	155384	...	125405	8819

	1994					1995				
	Total government	Central government	State or provincial government	Local government	Social security funds	Total government	Central government	State or provincial government	Local government	Social security funds

Gross output

1 Sales	16758	6807	...	8127	1628	18539	7699	...	8489	1710
2 Services produced for own use	280767	145862	...	128959	7275	285923	148380	...	133236	7119
3 Own account capital formation	...	...	...	...	...	...	...	...	...	...
Gross output	297525	152669	...	137086	8903	304462	156079	...	141725	8829

Gross input

Intermediate consumption	82371	31227	...	49839	3154	82440	30452	...	51808	2918
subtotal: Value added	215154	121442	...	87247	5749	222022	125627	...	89917	5911
1 Indirect taxes, net	4348	4348	...	–	–	5167	5063	...	–	–
A Indirect taxes	4348	4348	...	–	–	5167	5063	...	–	–
B less: Subsidies	–	–	...	–	–	–	–	...	–	–
2 Consumption of fixed capital	8990	4437	...	4210	328	9757	4764	...	4523	353
3 Compensation of employees	197446	111716	...	81037	4149	202582	114878	...	83261	4215
4 Net operating surplus	4370	941	...	2000	1272	4516	922	...	2133	1343
Gross input	297525	152669	...	137086	8903	304462	156079	...	141725	8829

	1996					1997				
	Total government	Central government	State or provincial government	Local government	Social security funds	Total government	Central government	State or provincial government	Local government	Social security funds

Gross output

1 Sales	21770	...	...	...	...	...	...	...	...	...
2 Services produced for own use	306620	...	...	...	...	...	...	...	...	...
3 Own account capital formation	...	...	...	...	...	...	...	...	...	...
Gross output	328390	...	...	...	...	...	...	...	...	...

Gross input

Intermediate consumption	86945	...	...	...	...	...	...	...	...	...
subtotal: Value added	241445	...	...	...	...	...	...	...	...	...
1 Indirect taxes, net	7154	...	...	...	...	...	...	...	...	...
A Indirect taxes	7154	...	...	...	...	...	...	...	...	...
B less: Subsidies	–	...	...	...	...	...	...	...	...	...
2 Consumption of fixed capital	10613	...	...	...	...	...	...	...	...	...
3 Compensation of employees	218613	...	...	...	...	...	...	...	...	...
4 Net operating surplus	5065	...	...	...	...	...	...	...	...	...
Gross input	328390	...	...	...	...	...	...	...	...	...

Italy

3.12 General government income and outlay account: total and subsectors

Thousand million Italian lire

	1986 Total government	1986 Central government	1986 State or provincial government	1986 Local government	1986 Social security funds	1987 Total government	1987 Central government	1987 State or provincial government	1987 Local government	1987 Social security funds
Receipts										
1 Operating surplus	1585	527	...	504	554	1784	632	...	522	630
2 Property and entrepreneurial income	10787	5248	...	2858	2681	10547	5428	...	2409	2710
A Withdrawals from public quasi-corporations	...	...	...	...	...	...	...	...	...	...
B Interest	9512	4631	...	2200	2681	9308	4811	...	1787	2710
C Dividends	...	...	...	...	...	...	...	...	...	...
D Net land rent and royalties [a]	1275	617	...	658	–	1239	617	...	622	–
3 Taxes, fees and contributions	308804	188998	...	11639	108684	344839	214732	...	12712	117939
A Indirect taxes	81743	77224	...	4519	–	93240	88058	...	5182	–
B Direct taxes	115683	109136	...	7064	–	130611	123693	...	7462	–
Income	115683	109136	...	7064	...	130611	123693	...	7462	...
Other	–	–	...	–	...	–	–	...	–	...
C Social security contributions	111378	2638	...	56	108684	120988	2981	...	68	117939
D Fees, fines and penalties	–	–	...	–	–	–	–	...	–	–
4 Other current transfers	31494	63076	...	91007	47667	29797	64043	...	104437	52225
A Casualty insurance claims	...	...	...	...	...	...	...	...	...	...
B Transfers from other government subsectors	...	41666	...	83132	45458	...	45325	...	95655	49928
C Transfers from rest of the world	17154	72	...	148	...	14719	111	...	194	...
D Other transfers, except imputed	14120	8470	...	6918	1766	14773	5202	...	7656	1861
E Imputed unfunded employee pension and welfare contributions	220	12868	...	809	443	305	13405	...	932	436
Total current receipts	352670	257849	...	106008	159586	386967	284835	...	120080	173504
Disbursements										
1 Government final consumption expenditure	147636	80758	...	62922	3956	165565	90191	...	71134	4240
2 Property income	77645	71918	...	6939	897	80037	74493	...	7341	205
A Interest	77422	71871	...	6765	895	79777	74439	...	7139	201
B Net land rent and royalties	223	47	...	174	2	260	54	...	202	4
3 Subsidies	26115	20684	...	7009	...	24665	18648	...	7445	...
4 Other current transfers	162554	156117	...	23622	153588	178745	175713	...	28723	165761
A Casualty insurance premiums, net	...	...	...	...	...	...	...	...	...	...
B Transfers to other government subsectors	...	128555	...	967	41251	...	145571	...	1117	44764
C Social security benefits	154826	23916	...	19020	111890	170500	26254	...	23629	120617
D Social assistance grants										
E Unfunded employee welfare benefits										
F Transfers to private non-profit institutions serving households	1454	433	...	793	228	1949	810	...	887	252
G Other transfers n.e.c.	3774	713	...	2842	219	3976	758	...	3090	128

Italy

Thousand million Italian lire

	1986					1987				
	Total government	Central government	State or provincial government	Local government	Social security funds	Total government	Central government	State or provincial government	Local government	Social security funds
H Transfers to rest of the world	2500	2500	...	–	–	2320	2320	...	–	–
Net saving	–61280	–71628	...	5516	1145	–62045	–74210	...	5437	3298
Total current disbursements and net saving	352670	257849	...	106008	159586	386967	284835	...	120080	173504

	1988					1989				
	Total government	Central government	State or provincial government	Local government	Social security funds	Total government	Central government	State or provincial government	Local government	Social security funds

Receipts

1 Operating surplus	2328	898	...	669	761	2745	972	...	860	913
2 Property and entrepreneurial income	10902	6032	...	1855	3015	12072	6533	...	2102	3437
A Withdrawals from public quasi-corporations	...	...	...	...	...	...	...	...	...	...
B Interest	9479	5349	...	1115	3015	10441	5831	...	1173	3437
C Dividends	...	...	...	...	...	...	...	...	...	...
D Net land rent and royalties [a]	1423	683	...	740	–	1631	702	...	929	–
3 Taxes, fees and contributions	388149	244225	...	14631	129909	444318	279720	...	19441	145889
A Indirect taxes	109076	102834	...	6242	–	123867	115664	...	8203	–
B Direct taxes	145720	138026	...	8310	–	170697	160287	...	11142	–
Income	145720	138026	...	8310	...	170697	160287	...	11142	...
Other	–	–	...	–	...	–	–	...	–	...
C Social security contributions	133353	3365	...	79	129909	149754	3769	...	96	145889
D Fees, fines and penalties	–	–	...	–	–	–	–	...	–	–
4 Other current transfers	31876	60938	...	114319	46738	35479	65964	...	122459	53845
A Casualty insurance claims	...	...	...	...	...	...	...	...	...	...
B Transfers from other government subsectors	...	41153	...	104404	44562	...	45493	...	111027	50269
C Transfers from rest of the world	15592	76	...	180	...	17495	89	...	177	...
D Other transfers, except imputed	16028	5154	...	8664	1774	17718	4277	...	10165	3053
E Imputed unfunded employee pension and welfare contributions	256	14555	...	1071	402	266	16105	...	1090	523
Total current receipts	433255	312093	...	131474	180423	494614	353189	...	144862	204084

Disbursements

1 Government final consumption expenditure	186034	102128	...	79396	4510	200303	109608	...	85753	4942
2 Property income	90866	85430	...	7582	228	109074	103048	...	7946	300
A Interest	90578	85369	...	7356	227	108726	102977	...	7674	295
B Net land rent and royalties	288	61	...	226	1	348	71	...	272	5
3 Subsidies	24799	18964	...	7613	...	27382	20794	...	9043	...
4 Other current transfers	199155	182196	...	33168	174526	224084	201199	...	36783	193623
A Casualty insurance premiums, net	...	...	...	...	...	...	...	...	...	...
B Transfers to other government subsectors	...	148959	...	917	40859	...	161282	...	1257	44982
C Social security benefits	189065	28305	...	27491	133269	209963	32337	...	29521	148105
D Social assistance grants										

Italy

	1988					1989				
	Total govern-ment	Central govern-ment	State or provincial govern-ment	Local govern-ment	Social security funds	Total govern-ment	Central govern-ment	State or provincial govern-ment	Local govern-ment	Social security funds
E Unfunded employee welfare benefits										
F Transfers to private non-profit institutions serving households	2391	872	...	1223	296	2982	910	...	1764	308
G Other transfers n.e.c.	4663	1024	...	3537	102	5367	898	...	4241	228
H Transfers to rest of the world	3036	3036	...	–	–	5772	5772	...	–	–
Net saving	–67599	–76625	...	3715	1159	–66229	–81460	...	5337	5219
Total current disbursements and net saving	433255	312093	...	131474	180423	494614	353189	...	144862	204084

	1990					1991				
	Total govern-ment	Central govern-ment	State or provincial govern-ment	Local govern-ment	Social security funds	Total govern-ment	Central govern-ment	State or provincial govern-ment	Local govern-ment	Social security funds

Receipts

1 Operating surplus	2917	1006	...	934	977	2853	619	...	1075	1159
2 Property and entrepreneurial income	13762	7416	...	2138	4208	14636	8180	...	2048	4408
A Withdrawals from public quasi-corporations	...	...	...	...	...	...	...	...	...	...
B Interest	12034	6614	...	1212	4208	12757	7288	...	1061	4408
C Dividends	...	...	...	...	...	...	...	...	...	...
D Net land rent and royalties [a]	1728	802	...	926	–	1879	892	...	987	–
3 Taxes, fees and contributions .	497542	309629	...	24146	164590	553269	344517	...	27275	182582
A Indirect taxes	139465	130963	...	8502	–	159022	149299	...	9723	–
B Direct taxes	189124	174399	...	15548	–	207054	190714	...	17445	–
Income	189124	174399	...	15548	...	207054	190714	...	17445	...
Other	–	–	...	–	...	–	–	...	–	...
C Social security contributions	168953	4267	...	96	164590	187193	4504	...	107	182582
D Fees, fines and penalties	–	–	...	–	–	–	–	...	–	–
4 Other current transfers	40682	83073	...	129296	69638	48100	88249	...	154515	67701
A Casualty insurance claims ..	...	...	...	...	...	...	...	...	...	...
B Transfers from other government subsectors	...	58534	...	116425	66366	...	59092	...	138757	64516
C Transfers from rest of the world	20032	66	...	228	...	24823	86	...	430	...
D Other transfers, except imputed	20356	5852	...	11566	2614	22761	8024	...	14273	2526
E Imputed unfunded employee pension and welfare contributions	294	18621	...	1077	658	516	21047	...	1055	659
Total current receipts	554903	401124	...	156514	239413	618858	441565	...	184913	255850

Disbursements

1 Government final consumption expenditure	230163	124923	...	99170	6070	251260	133044	...	111787	6429
2 Property income	129601	122480	...	9051	271	151010	141858	...	9780	292
A Interest	129230	122405	...	8764	262	150563	141779	...	9424	280
B Net land rent and royalties ..	371	75	...	287	9	447	79	...	356	12
3 Subsidies	26543	20442	...	9135	...	28763	23348	...	9206	...
4 Other current transfers	250642	223996	...	42392	226402	276622	249641	...	46362	244089
A Casualty insurance premiums, net	...	...	...	...	...	...	...	...	...	...

Italy

	1990					1991				
	Total govern-ment	Central govern-ment	State or provincial govern-ment	Local govern-ment	Social security funds	Total govern-ment	Central govern-ment	State or provincial govern-ment	Local govern-ment	Social security funds
B Transfers to other government subsectors	...	182787	...	866	58495	...	203270	...	732	59468
C Social security benefits	238585	36469	...	34889	167227	261320	39510	...	37757	184053
D Social assistance grants										
E Unfunded employee welfare benefits										
F Transfers to private non-profit institutions serving households	3487	960	...	2141	386	3912	967	...	2568	377
G Other transfers n.e.c.	5814	1024	...	4496	294	6646	1150	...	5305	191
H Transfers to rest of the world	2756	2756	...	–	–	4744	4744	...	–	–
Net saving	–82046	–90717	...	–3234	6670	–88797	–106326	...	7778	5040
Total current disbursements and net saving	554903	401124	...	156514	239413	618858	441565	...	184913	255850

	1992					1993				
	Total govern-ment	Central govern-ment	State or provincial govern-ment	Local govern-ment	Social security funds	Total govern-ment	Central govern-ment	State or provincial govern-ment	Local govern-ment	Social security funds

Receipts

1 Operating surplus	3775	1119	...	1415	1241	3941	882	...	1714	1345
2 Property and entrepreneurial income	14931	7747	...	2269	4915	13876	5946	...	2497	5432
A Withdrawals from public quasi-corporations	...	...	...	...	...	...	...	...	...	...
B Interest	12705	6795	...	995	4915	11980	5477	...	1071	5432
C Dividends	...	...	...	...	...	...	...	...	...	...
D Net land rent and royalties [a]	2226	952	...	1274	–	1896	469	...	1426	–
3 Taxes, fees and contributions	589197	363894	...	31504	195029	650262	403429	...	41491	207363
A Indirect taxes	167660	155862	...	11798	–	186611	166918	...	19693	–
B Direct taxes	221506	203149	...	19587	–	250835	231177	...	21679	–
Income	221506	203149	...	19587	...	250835	231177	...	21679	...
Other	–	–	...	–	...	–	–	...	–	...
C Social security contributions	200031	4883	...	119	195029	212816	5334	...	119	207363
D Fees, fines and penalties	–	–	...	–	–	–	–	...	–	–
4 Other current transfers	54834	90884	...	159596	78494	63279	90130	...	147269	68612
A Casualty insurance claims	...	...	...	...	...	...	...	...	...	...
B Transfers from other government subsectors	...	58724	...	140892	74524	...	51972	...	127550	63672
C Transfers from rest of the world	28295	76	...	306	...	35020	73	...	387	...
D Other transfers, except imputed	26157	7830	...	17283	3182	27799	12302	...	18092	4164
E Imputed unfunded employee pension and welfare contributions	382	24254	...	1115	788	460	25783	...	1240	776
Total current receipts	662737	463644	...	194784	279679	731358	500387	...	192971	282752

Disbursements

1 Government final consumption expenditure	265418	143353	...	115264	6801	273379	148492	...	117776	7111
2 Property income	178345	167366	...	10069	310	192685	180993	...	10702	441
A Interest	177822	167281	...	9658	283	192126	180911	...	10247	416
B Net land rent and royalties	523	85	...	411	27	559	82	...	455	25

1153

Italy

	1992					1993				
	Total government	Central government	State or provincial government	Local government	Social security funds	Total government	Central government	State or provincial government	Local government	Social security funds
3 Subsidies	27032	21318	...	10206	...	33915	23840	...	11449	...
4 Other current transfers	306781	267078	...	47883	267190	323803	252884	...	46548	269967
A Casualty insurance premiums, net	...	...	...	...	...	...	...	...	...	...
B Transfers to other government subsectors	...	215413	...	863	59094	...	191215	...	1195	52805
C Social security benefits	290578	44567	...	38440	207571	302873	49311	...	37079	216483
D Social assistance grants										
E Unfunded employee welfare benefits										
F Transfers to private non-profit institutions serving households	4697	1036	...	3235	426	5216	1269	...	3394	432
G Other transfers n.e.c.	6348	904	...	5345	99	5640	1015	...	4880	247
H Transfers to rest of the world	5158	5158	...	–	–	10074	10074	...	–	–
Net saving	–114839	–135471	...	11362	5378	–92424	–105822	...	6497	5233
Total current disbursements and net saving	662737	463644	...	194784	279679	731358	500387	...	192972	282752

	1994					1995				
	Total government	Central government	State or provincial government	Local government	Social security funds	Total government	Central government	State or provincial government	Local government	Social security funds
Receipts										
1 Operating surplus	4370	941	...	2000	1272	4516	922	...	2133	1343
2 Property and entrepreneurial income	14512	6748	...	2232	4829	17852	8870	...	2325	5103
A Withdrawals from public quasi-corporations	...	...	...	...	...	...	...	...	...	...
B Interest	12376	6245	...	856	4829	12417	6194	...	896	5103
C Dividends	...	...	...	...	...	...	...	...	...	...
D Net land rent and royalties [a]	2136	503	...	1376	–	5435	2676	...	1429	–
3 Taxes, fees and contributions	650706	395401	...	49974	207959	701788	427849	...	51280	222727
A Indirect taxes	192173	164622	...	27636	–	209490	180835	...	28361	–
B Direct taxes	244854	225174	...	22223	–	260627	240235	...	22800	–
Income	244854	225174	...	22223	...	260627	240235	...	22800	...
Other	–	–	...	–	...	–	–	...	–	...
C Social security contributions	213679	5605	...	115	207959	231671	6779	...	119	222727
D Fees, fines and penalties	–	–	...	–	–	–	–	...	–	–
4 Other current transfers	68215	92515	...	155044	80021	69983	97182	...	156428	76159
A Casualty insurance claims	...	...	...	...	...	...	...	...	...	...
B Transfers from other government subsectors	...	51349	...	134061	74591	...	55054	...	134714	72200
C Transfers from rest of the world	37116	108	...	403	...	38158	119	...	473	...
D Other transfers, except imputed	30588	12586	...	19202	4649	31274	12952	...	19827	3222
E Imputed unfunded employee pension and welfare contributions	511	28472	...	1378	781	551	29057	...	1414	737
Total current receipts	737803	495605	...	209250	294081	794139	534823	...	212166	305332

Italy

Disbursements

	1994 Total government	1994 Central government	1994 State or provincial government	1994 Local government	1994 Social security funds	1995 Total government	1995 Central government	1995 State or provincial government	1995 Local government	1995 Social security funds
1 Government final consumption expenditure	280474	145617	...	128911	7275	285637	148150	...	133186	7119
2 Property income	186160	170703	...	10979	467	206606	192429	...	10765	433
A Interest	185581	170618	...	10505	446	206018	192342	...	10266	411
B Net land rent and royalties	579	85	...	474	21	588	87	...	499	22
3 Subsidies	32864	25747	...	11072	...	28252	21553	...	11026	...
4 Other current transfers	337300	271510	...	45804	282724	353910	271710	...	45309	299273
A Casualty insurance premiums, net	...	...	...	...	...	...	...	...	...	...
B Transfers to other government subsectors	...	208583	...	1354	52518	...	206907	...	1311	56181
C Social security benefits	319464	54320	...	35551	229571	336118	56781	...	34947	242374
D Social assistance grants										
E Unfunded employee welfare benefits										
F Transfers to private non-profit institutions serving households	5754	1800	...	4070	447	6630	2307	...	4273	428
G Other transfers n.e.c.	6251	976	...	4829	188	6823	1374	...	4778	290
H Transfers to rest of the world	5831	5831	...	–	–	4339	4341	...	–	...
Net saving	–98995	–117972	...	12485	3615	–80266	–99019	...	11881	–1493
Total current disbursements and net saving	737803	495605	...	209251	294081	794139	534823	...	212167	305332

Receipts

	1996 Total government	1996 Central government	1996 State or provincial government	1996 Local government	1996 Social security funds	1997 Total government	1997 Central government	1997 State or provincial government	1997 Local government	1997 Social security funds
1 Operating surplus	5065	...	...	...	...	...	...	...	...	...
2 Property and entrepreneurial income	18427	...	...	...	...	...	...	...	...	...
A Withdrawals from public quasi-corporations	...	...	...	...	...	...	...	...	...	...
B Interest	11777	...	...	...	...	...	...	...	...	...
C Dividends	...	...	...	...	...	...	...	...	...	...
D Net land rent and royalties [a]	6650	...	...	...	...	...	...	...	...	...
3 Taxes, fees and contributions	783893	...	...	...	...	...	...	...	...	...
A Indirect taxes	222644	...	...	...	...	...	...	...	...	...
B Direct taxes	284843	...	...	...	...	...	...	...	...	...
Income	284843	...	...	...	...	...	...	...	...	...
Other	–	...	...	...	...	...	...	...	...	...
C Social security contributions	276406	...	...	...	...	...	...	...	...	...
D Fees, fines and penalties	–	...	...	...	...	...	...	...	...	...
4 Other current transfers	46499	...	...	...	...	...	...	...	...	...
A Casualty insurance claims	...	...	...	...	...	...	...	...	...	...
B Transfers from other government subsectors	...	...	...	...	...	...	...	...	...	...
C Transfers from rest of the world	40156	...	...	...	...	...	...	...	...	...

Italy

	1996					1997				
	Total govern-ment	Central govern-ment	State or provincial govern-ment	Local govern-ment	Social security funds	Total govern-ment	Central govern-ment	State or provincial govern-ment	Local govern-ment	Social security funds
D Other transfers, except imputed	5766	...	...	...	...	...	...	...	...	...
E Imputed unfunded employee pension and welfare contributions	577	...	...	...	...	...	...	...	...	...
Total current receipts	853884	...	...	...	...	...	...	...	...	...
Disbursements											
1 Government final consumption expenditure	306328	...	...	...	...	...	...	...	...	...
2 Property income	206383	...	...	...	...	...	...	...	...	...
A Interest	205756	...	...	...	...	...	...	...	...	...
B Net land rent and royalties	627	...	...	...	...	...	...	...	...	...
3 Subsidies	28908	...	...	...	...	...	...	...	...	...
4 Other current transfers	383818	...	...	...	...	...	...	...	...	...
A Casualty insurance premiums, net	...	...	...	...	...	...	...	...	...	...
B Transfers to other government subsectors	...	...	...	...	...	...	...	...	...	...
C Social security benefits	360823	...	...	...	...	...	...	...	...	...
D Social assistance grants						...	...	...	...	...
E Unfunded employee welfare benefits						...	...	...	...	...
F Transfers to private non-profit institutions serving households	7700	...	...	...	...	...	...	...	...	...
G Other transfers n.e.c.	7263	...	...	...	...	...	...	...	...	...
H Transfers to rest of the world	8032	...	...	...	...	...	...	...	...	...
Net saving	−71553	...	...	...	...	...	...	...	...	...
Total current disbursements and net saving	853884	...	...	...	...	...	...	...	...	...

a Items "Dividends" and "Casualty insurance claim" are included in item "Net land rent and royalties".

3.13 General government capital accumulation account: total and subsectors

Thousand million Italian lire

	1986					1987				
	Total govern-ment	Central govern-ment	State or provincial govern-ment	Local govern-ment	Social security funds	Total govern-ment	Central govern-ment	State or provincial govern-ment	Local govern-ment	Social security funds
Finance of gross accumulation											
1 Gross saving	−57270	−69646	...	7398	1291	−57625	−72025	...	7510	3460
A Consumption of fixed capital	4010	1982	...	1882	146	4420	2185	...	2073	162
B Net saving	−61280	−71628	...	5516	1145	−62045	−74210	...	5437	3298
2 Capital transfers	17235	1866	...	15369	−	17979	2122	...	15857	−
Finance of gross accumulation	−40035	−67780	...	22767	1291	−39646	−69903	...	23367	3460
Gross accumulation											
1 Gross capital formation	31787	9641	...	20480	1666	34447	9458	...	22768	2221
A Increase in stocks	−	...	...	...	...	−	...	...	...	...
B Gross fixed capital formation	31787	9641	...	20480	1666	34447	9458	...	22768	2221

Italy

Thousand million Italian lire

	1986					1987				
	Total government	Central government	State or provincial government	Local government	Social security funds	Total government	Central government	State or provincial government	Local government	Social security funds
2 Purchases of land, net	70	6	...	64	–	60	5	...	55	–
3 Purchases of intangible assets, net	–	–	...	–	–	–	–	...	–	–
4 Capital transfers	30503	23132	...	5944	–	33719	24448	...	6023	–
Net lending [a]	–102395	–100559	...	–3721	–375	–107872	–103814	...	–5479	1239
Gross accumulation	–40035	–67780	...	22767	1291	–39646	–69903	...	23367	3460

	1988					1989				
	Total government	Central government	State or provincial government	Local government	Social security funds	Total government	Central government	State or provincial government	Local government	Social security funds

Finance of gross accumulation

1 Gross saving	–62633	–74171	...	6045	1341	–60644	–78697	...	7955	5423
A Consumption of fixed capital	4966	2454	...	2330	182	5585	2763	...	2618	204
B Net saving	–67599	–76625	...	3715	1159	–66229	–81460	...	5337	5219
2 Capital transfers	17800	2722	...	15078	–	22754	4001	...	18753	–
Finance of gross accumulation	–44833	–71449	...	21123	1341	–37890	–74696	...	26708	5423

Gross accumulation

1 Gross capital formation	36697	9606	...	25129	1962	39685	9407	...	27839	2439
A Increase in stocks	–	...	...	...	...	–	...	...	...	...
B Gross fixed capital formation	36697	9606	...	25129	1962	39685	9407	...	27839	2439
2 Purchases of land, net	66	5	...	61	–	99	5	...	94	–
3 Purchases of intangible assets, net	–	–	...	–	–	–	–	...	–	–
4 Capital transfers	35177	24570	...	6515	–	39603	28577	...	7320	–
Net lending [a]	–116773	–105630	...	–10582	–621	–117277	–112685	...	–8545	2984
Gross accumulation	–44833	–71449	...	21123	1341	–37890	–74696	...	26708	5423

	1990					1991				
	Total government	Central government	State or provincial government	Local government	Social security funds	Total government	Central government	State or provincial government	Local government	Social security funds

Finance of gross accumulation

1 Gross saving	–75777	–87617	...	–294	6899	–81852	–102892	...	11035	5294
A Consumption of fixed capital	6269	3100	...	2940	229	6945	3434	...	3257	254
B Net saving	–82046	–90717	...	–3234	6670	–88797	–106326	...	7778	5040
2 Capital transfers	22948	2833	...	20115	–	23982	4648	...	19334	–
Finance of gross accumulation	–52829	–84784	...	19821	6899	–57870	–98244	...	30369	5294

Gross accumulation

1 Gross capital formation	43051	10883	...	29446	2722	46521	12854	...	30289	3378
A Increase in stocks	–	...	...	...	...	–	...	...	...	...
B Gross fixed capital formation	43051	10883	...	29446	2722	46521	12854	...	30289	3378
2 Purchases of land, net	90	4	...	86	–	66	3	...	63	–
3 Purchases of intangible assets, net	–	–	...	–	–	–	–	...	–	–
4 Capital transfers	49832	34393	...	7946	–	39624	28150	...	8984	–
Net lending [a]	–145802	–130064	...	–17657	4177	–144081	–139251	...	–8967	1916
Gross accumulation	–52829	–84784	...	19821	6899	–57870	–98244	...	30369	5294

Italy

	1992					1993				
	Total government	Central government	State or provincial government	Local government	Social security funds	Total government	Central government	State or provincial government	Local government	Social security funds

Finance of gross accumulation

1 Gross saving	−107266	−131722	...	14909	5655	−84117	−101716	...	10394	5537
A Consumption of fixed capital	7573	3749	...	3547	277	8307	4106	...	3897	304
B Net saving	−114839	−135471	...	11362	5378	−92424	−105822	...	6497	5233
2 Capital transfers	53441	32022	...	21419	−	32312	12589	...	19882	−
Finance of gross accumulation	−53825	−99700	...	36328	5655	−51805	−89127	...	30276	5537

Gross accumulation

1 Gross capital formation	45538	12410	...	29574	3554	41049	11650	...	27443	2202
A Increase in stocks	−	...	...	...	...	−	...	...	...	...
B Gross fixed capital formation	45538	12410	...	29574	3554	41049	11650	...	27443	2202
2 Purchases of land, net	−84	3	...	−87	−	55	3	...	52	−
3 Purchases of intangible assets, net	−	−	...	−	−	−	−	...	−	−
4 Capital transfers	44375	31584	...	8590	−	61676	45057	...	8550	−
Net lending [a]	−143654	−143697	...	−1749	2101	−154585	−145837	...	−5769	3335
Gross accumulation	−53825	−99700	...	36328	5655	−51805	−89127	...	30276	5537

	1994					1995				
	Total government	Central government	State or provincial government	Local government	Social security funds	Total government	Central government	State or provincial government	Local government	Social security funds

Finance of gross accumulation

1 Gross saving	−90005	−113535	...	16695	3943	−70509	−94255	...	16404	−1140
A Consumption of fixed capital	8990	4437	...	4210	328	9757	4764	...	4523	353
B Net saving	−98995	−117972	...	12485	3615	−80266	−99019	...	11881	−1493
2 Capital transfers	20405	6004	...	13900	−	29363	13858	...	16398	−
Finance of gross accumulation	−69600	−107531	...	30595	3943	−41146	−80397	...	32802	−1140

Gross accumulation

1 Gross capital formation	37855	10291	...	26188	1765	38589	9643	...	27937	2321
A Increase in stocks	−	...	...	...	...	−	...	...	...	...
B Gross fixed capital formation	37855	10291	...	26188	1765	38589	9643	...	27937	2321
2 Purchases of land, net	52	3	...	50	−	84	3	...	52	−
3 Purchases of intangible assets, net	−	−	...	−	−	−	−	...	−	−
4 Capital transfers	50433	28013	...	8677	−	43444	28012	...	8802	−
Net lending [a]	−157940	−145838	...	−4320	2178	−123263	−118055	...	−3989	−3461
Gross accumulation	−69600	−107531	...	30595	3943	−41146	−80397	...	32802	−1140

Italy

	1996					1997				
	Total government	Central government	State or provincial government	Local government	Social security funds	Total government	Central government	State or provincial government	Local government	Social security funds

Finance of gross accumulation

1 Gross saving	−60940	...	...	...	...	...	...	...	...	...
A Consumption of fixed capital	10613	...	...	...	...	...	...	...	...	...
B Net saving	−71553	...	...	...	...	...	...	...	...	...
2 Capital transfers	24449	...	...	...	...	...	...	...	...	...
Finance of gross accumulation	−36491	...	...	...	...	...	...	...	...	...

Gross accumulation

1 Gross capital formation	41738	...	...	...	...	...	...	...	...	...
A Increase in stocks	−	...	...	...	...	...	...	...	...	...
B Gross fixed capital formation	41738	...	...	...	...	...	...	...	...	...
2 Purchases of land, net	69	...	...	...	...	...	...	...	...	...
3 Purchases of intangible assets, net	−	...	...	...	...	...	...	...	...	...
4 Capital transfers	48027	...	...	...	...	...	...	...	...	...
Net lending [a]	−126325	...	...	...	...	...	...	...	...	...
Gross accumulation	−36491	...	...	...	...	...	...	...	...	...

[a] Net lending of the capital accumulation account and the capital finance account have not been reconciled and are different due to different statistical sources.

3.21 Corporate and quasi-corporate enterprise production account: total and sectors

Thousand million Italian lire

	1986				1987				1988			
	Corporate and quasi-corporate enterprises			Addendum: total including unincorporated	Corporate and quasi-corporate enterprises			Addendum: total including unincorporated	Corporate and quasi-corporate enterprises			Addendum: total including unincorporated
	Total	Non-financial	Financial		Total	Non-financial	Financial		Total	Non-financial	Financial	

Gross output

1 Output for sale	732388	706946	25442	...	790210	764790	25420	...	890097	863192	26905	...
2 Imputed bank service charge	38175	...	38175	...	39014	...	39014	...	44497	...	44497	...
3 Own-account fixed capital formation	...	...	...	...	...	...	...	...	...	...	...	...
Gross output	770563	706946	63617	...	829224	764790	64434	...	934594	863192	71402	...

Gross input

Intermediate consumption	449841	396678	53163	...	482347	425682	56665	...	549164	485466	63698	...
1 Imputed bank service charge	38175	−	38175	...	39013	−	39013	...	44496	−	44496	...
2 Other intermediate consumption	411666	396678	14988	...	443334	425682	17652	...	504668	485466	19202	...
subtotal: Value added	320722	310268	10454	...	346877	339108	7769	...	385430	377726	7704	...
1 Indirect taxes, net	12038	8408	3630	...	14619	10502	4117	...	20099	15081	5018	...
A Indirect taxes	33252	29533	3719	...	37118	32959	4159	...	43059	38037	5022	...
B less: Subsidies	21214	21125	89	...	22499	22457	42	...	22960	22956	4	...
2 Consumption of fixed capital	44120	41697	2423	...	47524	44948	2576	...	51489	48692	2797	...
3 Compensation of employees	200127	175945	24182	...	215582	189099	26483	...	234689	205861	28828	...
4 Net operating surplus	64437	84218	−19781	...	69152	94559	−25407	...	79153	108092	−28939	...
Gross input	770563	706946	63617	...	829224	764790	64434	...	934594	863192	71402	...

Italy

| | 1989 |||| 1990 |||| 1991 ||||
| | Corporate and quasi-corporate enterprises ||| Addendum: total including unincorporated | Corporate and quasi-corporate enterprises ||| Addendum: total including unincorporated | Corporate and quasi-corporate enterprises ||| Addendum: total including unincorporated |
	Total	Non-financial	Financial		Total	Non-financial	Financial		Total	Non-financial	Financial	
Gross output												
1 Output for sale	1004032	975036	28996	...	1071292	1038643	32649	...	1113348	1076068	37280	...
2 Imputed bank service charge	50779	...	50779	...	60721	...	60721	...	66270	...	66270	...
3 Own-account fixed capital formation	...	...	...	...	...	...	...	...	...	...	...	...
Gross output	1054811	975036	79775	...	1132013	1038643	93370	...	1179618	1076068	103550	...
Gross input												
Intermediate consumption	629005	555541	73464	...	668281	580387	87894	...	688175	589857	98318	...
1 Imputed bank service charge	50780	–	50780	...	60721	–	60721	...	66270	–	66270	...
2 Other intermediate consumption	578225	555541	22684	...	607560	580387	27173	...	621905	589857	32048	...
subtotal: Value added	425806	419495	6311	...	463732	458256	5476	...	491443	486211	5232	...
1 Indirect taxes, net	23324	17781	5543	...	33618	27349	6269	...	38138	30809	7329	...
A Indirect taxes	47518	41965	5553	...	57247	50931	6316	...	63670	56338	7332	...
B less: Subsidies	24194	24184	10	...	23629	23582	47	...	25532	25529	3	...
2 Consumption of fixed capital	56406	53346	3060	...	62031	58680	3351	...	67787	64240	3547	...
3 Compensation of employees	260453	228982	31471	...	287343	253235	34108	...	314206	276290	37916	...
4 Net operating surplus	85623	119386	−33763	...	80740	118992	−38252	...	71312	114872	−43560	...
Gross input	1054811	975036	79775	...	1132013	1038643	93370	...	1179618	1076068	103550	...

| | 1992 |||| 1993 |||| 1994 ||||
| | Corporate and quasi-corporate enterprises ||| Addendum: total including unincorporated | Corporate and quasi-corporate enterprises ||| Addendum: total including unincorporated | Corporate and quasi-corporate enterprises ||| Addendum: total including unincorporated |
	Total	Non-financial	Financial		Total	Non-financial	Financial		Total	Non-financial	Financial	
Gross output												
1 Output for sale	1168270	1127799	40471	...	1206435	1152846	53589	...	1318750	1263409	55341	...
2 Imputed bank service charge	78718	...	78718	...	79889	...	79889	...	72807	...	72807	...
3 Own-account fixed capital formation	...	...	...	...	...	...	...	...	...	...	...	...
Gross output	1246988	1127799	119189	...	1286324	1152846	133478	...	1391557	1263409	128148	...
Gross input												
Intermediate consumption	730916	613104	117812	...	749616	625233	124383	...	816058	697779	118279	...
1 Imputed bank service charge	78718	–	78718	...	79889	–	79889	...	72807	–	72807	...
2 Other intermediate consumption	652198	613104	39094	...	669727	625233	44494	...	743251	697779	45472	...
subtotal: Value added	516072	514695	1377	...	536708	527613	9095	...	575499	565630	9869	...
1 Indirect taxes, net	48059	39742	8317	...	48970	38922	10048	...	53954	43685	10269	...
A Indirect taxes	71424	63105	8319	...	79344	69294	10050	...	81940	71668	10272	...
B less: Subsidies	23365	23363	2	...	30374	30372	2	...	27986	27983	3	...
2 Consumption of fixed capital	72001	68339	3662	...	76632	72737	3895	...	80585	76695	3890	...
3 Compensation of employees	330917	289032	41885	...	332324	289919	42405	...	337403	293238	44165	...
4 Net operating surplus	65095	117582	−52487	...	78782	126035	−47253	...	103557	152012	−48455	...
Gross input	1246988	1127799	119189	...	1286324	1152846	133478	...	1391557	1263409	128148	...

Italy

	1995				1996				1997			
	Corporate and quasi-corporate enterprises			Addendum: total including unincorporated	Corporate and quasi-corporate enterprises			Addendum: total including unincorporated	Corporate and quasi-corporate enterprises			Addendum: total including unincorporated
	Total	Non-financial	Financial		Total	Non-financial	Financial		Total	Non-financial	Financial	
Gross output												
1 Output for sale	1489085	1433005	56080	...	1525506	1463165	62341	...	...	...	...	...
2 Imputed bank service charge	78446	...	78446	...	81190	...	81190	...	...	...	...	...
3 Own-account fixed capital formation	...	...	...	...	...	...	...	...	...	...	...	...
Gross output	1567531	1433005	134526	...	1606696	1463165	143531	...	...	...	...	...
Gross input												
Intermediate consumption	944856	817579	127277	...	951481	819730	131751	...	...	...	...	...
1 Imputed bank service charge	78446	...	78446	...	81190	...	81190	...	...	...	...	...
2 Other intermediate consumption	866410	817579	48831	...	870291	819730	50561	...	...	...	...	...
subtotal: Value added	622675	615426	7249	...	655215	643435	11780	...	...	...	...	...
1 Indirect taxes, net	65559	54914	10645	...	71948	60088	11860	...	...	...	...	...
A Indirect taxes	89800	79154	10646	...	97439	85577	11862	...	...	...	...	...
B less: Subsidies	24241	24240	1	...	25491	25489	2	...	...	...	...	...
2 Consumption of fixed capital	86691	82520	4171	...	91184	86907	4277	...	...	...	...	...
3 Compensation of employees	352964	306434	46530	...	367231	318511	48720	...	...	...	...	...
4 Net operating surplus	117461	171558	−54097	...	124852	177929	−53077	...	...	...	...	...
Gross input	1567531	1433005	134526	...	1606696	1463165	143531	...	...	...	...	...

3.22 Corporate and quasi-corporate enterprise income and outlay account: total and sectors

Thousand million Italian lire

	1986			1987			1988			1989		
	Total	Non-financial	Financial	Total	Non-financial	Financial	Total	Non-financial	Financial	Total	Non-financial	Financial
Receipts												
1 Operating surplus	64437	84218	−19781	69152	94559	−25407	79153	108092	−28939	85623	119386	−33763
2 Property and entrepreneurial income	150995	18168	132827	148345	18561	129784	161699	18862	142837	190161	21653	168508
A Withdrawals from quasi-corporate enterprises	...	...	...	...	...	...	...	...	...	...	...	...
B Interest	144719	12788	131931	140087	11638	128449	153324	11862	141462	180654	13680	166974
C Dividends	5691	4801	890	7600	6270	1330	7615	6242	1373	8522	7021	1501
D Net land rent and royalties	585	579	6	658	653	5	760	758	2	985	952	33
3 Current transfers	32642	16064	16578	35728	17390	18338	39774	18790	20984	47623	22220	25403
A Casualty insurance claims	4205	2678	1527	4542	3010	1532	4876	3089	1787	6394	4170	2224
B Casualty insurance premiums, net, due to be received by insurance companies	11174	...	11174	12829	...	12829	14723	...	14723	17717	...	17717
C Current transfers from rest of the world	...	...	...	...	...	...	...	...	...	...	...	...
D Other transfers except imputed	1590	1370	220	1633	1403	230	2060	1820	240	2298	2048	250
E Imputed unfunded employee pension and welfare contributions	15673	12016	3657	16724	12977	3747	18115	13881	4234	21214	16002	5212
Total current receipts	248074	118450	129624	253225	130510	122715	280626	145744	134882	323407	163259	160148

Italy

Thousand million Italian lire

	1986 Total	1986 Non-financial	1986 Financial	1987 Total	1987 Non-financial	1987 Financial	1988 Total	1988 Non-financial	1988 Financial	1989 Total	1989 Non-financial	1989 Financial
Disbursements												
1 Property and entrepreneurial income	166116	75266	90850	164356	78137	86219	177580	83906	93674	205709	94329	111380
A Withdrawals from quasi-corporations	11794	11794	...	12801	12801	...	14123	14123	...	14951	14951	...
B Interest	140900	52874	88026	134981	51689	83292	145698	55232	90466	171371	63427	107944
C Dividends	11229	8421	2808	14105	11195	2910	14857	11664	3193	15115	11695	3420
D Net land rent and royalties	2193	2177	16	2469	2452	17	2902	2887	15	4272	4256	16
2 Direct taxes and other current transfers n.e.c. to general government	24658	19243	5415	29253	22825	6428	27956	22515	5441	35077	28259	6818
A Direct taxes	24658	19243	5415	29253	22825	6428	27956	22515	5441	35077	28259	6818
B Fines, fees, penalties and other current transfers n.e.c.	...	...	...	...	...	...	...	...	...	...	...	...
3 Other current transfers	28563	13283	15280	33568	16341	17227	37562	17810	19752	43571	20139	23432
A Casualty insurance premiums, net	4575	2907	1668	5226	3529	1697	6010	4029	1981	7031	4602	2429
B Casualty insurance claims liability of insurance companies	11174	...	11174	12829	...	12829	14723	...	14723	17717	...	17717
C Transfers to private non-profit institutions	1564	...	1564	1707	...	1707	2003	...	2003	2181	...	2181
D Unfunded employee pension and welfare benefits	–	...	...	–	...	...	–	...	...	–	...	...
E Social assistance grants	6974	6311	663	9311	8541	770	9875	9067	808	10964	10127	837
F Other transfers n.e.c.	4276	4065	211	4495	4271	224	4951	4714	237	5678	5410	268
G Transfers to rest of the world	–	...	...	–	...	...	–	...	...	–	...	...
Statistical discrepancy	7982	5885	2097	6503	4629	1874	7359	5038	2321	8518	6097	2421
Net saving	20755	4773	15982	19545	8578	10967	30169	16475	13694	30532	14435	16097
Total current disbursements and net saving	248074	118450	129624	253225	130510	122715	280626	145744	134882	323407	163259	160148

	1990 Total	1990 Non-financial	1990 Financial	1991 Total	1991 Non-financial	1991 Financial	1992 Total	1992 Non-financial	1992 Financial	1993 Total	1993 Non-financial	1993 Financial
Receipts												
1 Operating surplus	80740	118992	–38252	71312	114872	–43560	65095	117582	–52487	78782	126035	–47253
2 Property and entrepreneurial income	216087	21228	194859	235905	23514	212391	274599	26458	248141	272724	25504	247220
A Withdrawals from quasi-corporate enterprises	...	...	...	...	...	...	...	...	...	...	...	...
B Interest	207561	14547	193014	226152	15600	210552	266435	19950	246485	264168	18612	245556
C Dividends	7476	5637	1839	8575	6741	1834	6720	5071	1649	6976	5333	1643
D Net land rent and royalties	1050	1044	6	1178	1173	5	1444	1437	7	1580	1559	21
3 Current transfers	54212	24828	29384	60540	27195	33345	64442	28896	35546	64394	29813	34581
A Casualty insurance claims	7364	4751	2613	8142	4864	3278	8678	5797	2881	8402	6134	2268
B Casualty insurance premiums, net, due to be received by insurance companies	20857	...	20857	24068	...	24068	26098	...	26098	25651	...	25651
C Current transfers from rest of the world	...	...	...	...	...	...	...	...	...	...	...	...
D Other transfers except imputed	2359	2049	310	2970	2582	388	3100	2684	416	3295	2835	460
E Imputed unfunded employee pension and welfare contributions	23632	18028	5604	25360	19749	5611	26566	20415	6151	27046	20844	6202
Total current receipts	351039	165048	185991	367757	165581	202176	404136	172936	231200	415900	181352	234548

Italy

	1990 Total	1990 Non-financial	1990 Financial	1991 Total	1991 Non-financial	1991 Financial	1992 Total	1992 Non-financial	1992 Financial	1993 Total	1993 Non-financial	1993 Financial
Disbursements												
1 Property and entrepreneurial income	233811	105125	128686	256374	116523	139851	294703	131390	163313	286254	125650	160604
A Withdrawals from quasi-corporations	16471	16471	...	18195	18195	...	18711	18711	...	19211	19211	...
B Interest	196412	71886	124526	216730	81001	135729	254074	95570	158504	245808	89704	156104
C Dividends	15603	11463	4140	15672	11572	4100	15803	11017	4786	14469	9997	4472
D Net land rent and royalties	5325	5305	20	5777	5755	22	6115	6092	23	6766	6738	28
2 Direct taxes and other current transfers n.e.c. to general government	36375	28365	8010	39207	29119	10088	37374	26982	10392	46510	33397	13113
A Direct taxes	36375	28365	8010	39207	29119	10088	37374	26982	10392	46510	33397	13113
B Fines, fees, penalties and other current transfers n.e.c.	...	...	...	...	...	...	...	...	...	...	...	...
3 Other current transfers	50917	23836	27081	58391	27120	31271	63666	30697	32969	65845	34314	31531
A Casualty insurance premiums, net	8340	5505	2835	9047	5514	3533	9728	6561	3167	9443	6857	2586
B Casualty insurance claims liability of insurance companies	20857	...	20857	24068	...	24068	26098	...	26098	25651	...	25651
C Transfers to private non-profit institutions	2195	...	2195	2419	...	2419	2936	...	2936	2671	...	2671
D Unfunded employee pension and welfare benefits	−	...	...	−	...	...	−	...	...	−	...	...
E Social assistance grants	12775	11882	893	15017	14137	880	16589	16206	383	17399	17192	207
F Other transfers n.e.c.	6750	6449	301	7840	7469	371	8315	7930	385	10681	10265	416
G Transfers to rest of the world	−	...	...	−	...	...	−	...	...	−	...	...
Statistical discrepancy	8354	6388	1966	9393	5924	3469	6740	4539	2201	6546	3974	2572
Net saving	21582	1334	20248	4392	−13105	17497	1653	−20672	22325	10745	−15983	26728
Total current disbursements and net saving	351039	165048	185991	367757	165581	202176	404136	172936	231200	415900	181352	234548

	1994 Total	1994 Non-financial	1994 Financial	1995 Total	1995 Non-financial	1995 Financial	1996 Total	1996 Non-financial	1996 Financial	1997 Total	1997 Non-financial	1997 Financial
Receipts												
1 Operating surplus	103557	152012	−48455	117031	171558	−54527	123944	177929	−53985	...	...	...
2 Property and entrepreneurial income	263133	26885	236248	301582	32063	269519	310986	33779	277207	...	...	...
A Withdrawals from quasi-corporate enterprises	...	...	...	...	...	...	...	...	...	...	...	...
B Interest	253681	19094	234587	291281	23948	267333	298761	24024	274737	...	...	...
C Dividends	7845	6189	1656	8637	6458	2179	10428	7965	2463	...	...	...
D Net land rent and royalties	1607	1602	5	1664	1657	7	1797	1790	7	...	...	...
3 Current transfers	63855	28308	35547	68854	30142	38712	71427	29842	41585	...	...	...
A Casualty insurance claims	8733	6114	2619	9448	6569	2879	9588	6423	3165	...	...	...
B Casualty insurance premiums, net, due to be received by insurance companies	26644	...	26644	29241	...	29241	31337	...	31337	...	...	...
C Current transfers from rest of the world	...	...	...	...	...	...	...	...	...	...	...	...
D Other transfers except imputed	2974	2504	470	3379	2887	492	3026	2472	554	...	...	...
E Imputed unfunded employee pension and welfare contributions	25504	19690	5814	26786	20686	6100	27476	20947	6529	...	...	...
Total current receipts	430545	207205	223340	487467	233763	253704	506357	241550	264807	...	...	...

Italy

	1994 Total	1994 Non-financial	1994 Financial	1995 Total	1995 Non-financial	1995 Financial	1996 Total	1996 Non-financial	1996 Financial	1997 Total	1997 Non-financial	1997 Financial
Disbursements												
1 Property and entrepreneurial income	274679	119469	155210	313518	132127	181391	319189	131667	187522	...	...	...
A Withdrawals from quasi-corporations	19980	19980	...	21334	21334	...	22278	22278	...	...	...	...
B Interest	231731	80194	151537	265144	88130	177014	271519	88659	182860	...	...	...
C Dividends	15452	11807	3645	18298	13952	4346	16319	11684	4635	...	...	...
D Net land rent and royalties	7516	7488	28	8742	8711	31	9073	9046	27	...	...	...
2 Direct taxes and other current transfers n.e.c. to general government	52516	42618	9898	56649	42560	14089	65157	48711	16446	...	...	...
A Direct taxes	52516	42618	9898	56649	42560	14089	65157	48711	16446	...	...	...
B Fines, fees, penalties and other current transfers n.e.c.	...	...	...	...	...	...	...	...	...	...	...	...
3 Other current transfers	68916	35761	33155	70016	34762	35254	72302	33753	38549	...	...	...
A Casualty insurance premiums, net	9803	6862	2941	10925	7717	3208	11162	7650	3512	...	...	...
B Casualty insurance claims liability of insurance companies	26644	...	26644	29241	...	29241	31337	...	31337	...	...	...
C Transfers to private non-profit institutions	2922	...	2922	2129	...	2129	2997	...	2997	...	...	...
D Unfunded employee pension and welfare benefits	...	...	...	...	...	...	...	...	...	...	...	...
E Social assistance grants	16959	16752	207	16508	16315	193	16392	16208	184	...	...	...
F Other transfers n.e.c.	12588	12147	441	11213	10730	483	10414	9895	519	...	...	...
G Transfers to rest of the world	...	...	...	...	...	...	...	...	...	...	...	...
Statistical discrepancy	5883	2986	2897	7326	4421	2905	5411	4739	672	...	...	...
Net saving	28551	6371	22180	39958	19893	20065	44298	22680	21618	...	...	...
Total current disbursements and net saving	430545	207205	223340	487467	233763	253704	506357	241550	264807	...	...	...

3.23 Corporate and quasi-corporate enterprise capital accumulation account: total and sectors

Thousand million Italian lire

	1986 Total	1986 Non-financial	1986 Financial	1987 Total	1987 Non-financial	1987 Financial	1988 Total	1988 Non-financial	1988 Financial	1989 Total	1989 Non-financial	1989 Financial
Finance of gross accumulation												
1 Gross saving	64875	46470	18405	67069	53526	13543	81658	65167	16491	86938	67781	19157
A Consumption of fixed capital	44120	41697	2423	47524	44948	2576	51489	48692	2797	56406	53346	3060
B Net saving	20755	4773	15982	19545	8578	10967	30169	16475	13694	30532	14435	16097
2 Capital transfers	10034	10034	–	12329	12329	–	14005	14005	–	14732	14732	–
Finance of gross accumulation	74909	56504	18405	79398	65855	13543	95663	79172	16491	101670	82513	19157
Gross accumulation												
1 Gross capital formation	66597	63085	3512	78991	75393	3598	94148	89457	4691	107590	103131	4459
A Increase in stocks	3792	3792	–	6832	6832	–	9094	9094	–	9912	9912	–
B Gross fixed capital formation	62805	59293	3512	72159	68561	3598	85054	80363	4691	97678	93219	4459
2 Purchases of land, net	80	82	–2	171	160	11	364	380	–16	326	319	7
3 Purchases of intangible assets, net	840	840	–	915	915	–	1006	1006	–	1050	1050	–
4 Capital transfers	817	330	487	602	306	296	814	577	237	1483	1285	198

Italy

Thousand million Italian lire

	1986 Total	1986 Non-financial	1986 Financial	1987 Total	1987 Non-financial	1987 Financial	1988 Total	1988 Non-financial	1988 Financial	1989 Total	1989 Non-financial	1989 Financial
Net lending [a]	6575	−7833	14408	−1281	−10919	9638	−669	−12248	11579	−8779	−23272	14493
Gross accumulation	74909	56504	18405	79398	65855	13543	95663	79172	16491	101670	82513	19157

	1990 Total	1990 Non-financial	1990 Financial	1991 Total	1991 Non-financial	1991 Financial	1992 Total	1992 Non-financial	1992 Financial	1993 Total	1993 Non-financial	1993 Financial
Finance of gross accumulation												
1 Gross saving	83613	60014	23599	72179	51135	21044	73654	47667	25987	87377	56754	30623
A Consumption of fixed capital	62031	58680	3351	67787	64240	3547	72001	68339	3662	76632	72737	3895
B Net saving	21582	1334	20248	4392	−13105	17497	1653	−20672	22325	10745	−15983	26728
2 Capital transfers	21576	21576	−	15473	15473	−	16097	16097	−	26290	24240	2050
Finance of gross accumulation	105189	81590	23599	87652	66608	21044	89751	63764	25987	113667	80994	32673
Gross accumulation												
1 Gross capital formation	123976	117661	6315	131863	125885	5978	114381	108329	6052	91094	87244	3850
A Increase in stocks	7909	7909	−	8316	8316	−	3263	3263	−	−152	−152	−
B Gross fixed capital formation	116067	109752	6315	123547	117569	5978	111118	105066	6052	91246	87396	3850
2 Purchases of land, net	260	255	5	243	239	4	271	269	2	176	201	−25
3 Purchases of intangible assets, net	1468	1468	−	1511	1511	−	1656	1656	−	1811	1811	−
4 Capital transfers	926	628	298	2609	2046	563	15761	14173	1588	5263	4347	916
Net lending [a]	−21441	−38422	16981	−48574	−63073	14499	−42318	−60663	18345	15323	−12609	27932
Gross accumulation	105189	81590	23599	87652	66608	21044	89751	63764	25987	113667	80994	32673

	1994 Total	1994 Non-financial	1994 Financial	1995 Total	1995 Non-financial	1995 Financial	1996 Total	1996 Non-financial	1996 Financial	1997 Total	1997 Non-financial	1997 Financial
Finance of gross accumulation												
1 Gross saving	109136	83066	26070	126649	102413	24236	135482	109587	25895	...	...	...
A Consumption of fixed capital	80585	76695	3890	86691	82520	4171	91184	86907	4277	...	...	...
B Net saving	28551	6371	22180	39958	19893	20065	44298	22680	21618	...	...	...
2 Capital transfers	22619	21759	860	19592	19435	157	25487	23995	1492	...	...	...
Finance of gross accumulation	131755	104825	26930	146241	121848	24393	160969	133582	27387	...	...	...
Gross accumulation												
1 Gross capital formation	105778	102649	3129	124837	121402	3435	118516	115458	3058	...	...	...
A Increase in stocks	6675	6675	−	10429	10429	−	851	851	−	...	...	...
B Gross fixed capital formation	99103	95974	3129	114408	110973	3435	117665	114607	3058	...	...	...
2 Purchases of land, net	184	174	10	130	138	−8	133	128	5	...	...	...
3 Purchases of intangible assets, net	1970	1970	−	2054	2054	−	2291	2291	−	...	...	...
4 Capital transfers	1737	1244	493	4858	4177	681	3684	3206	478	...	...	...
Net lending [a]	22086	−1212	23298	14362	−5923	20285	36345	12499	23846	...	...	...
Gross accumulation	131755	104825	26930	146241	121848	24393	160969	133582	27387	...	...	...

a Net lending of the capital accumulation account and the capital finance account have not been reconciled and are different due to different statistical sources.

Italy

3.31 Household and private unincorporated enterprise production account

Thousand million Italian lire

	1986	1987	1988	1989	1990	1991	1992	1993	1994	1995	1996	1997
Gross output												
1 Output for sale	681725	742395	821423	893724	969131	1057554	1115424	1116601	1177162	1288484	1350349	...
2 Non-marketed output	...	...	...	...	...	...	...	...	...	...	...	...
Gross output	681725	742395	821423	893724	969131	1057554	1115424	1116601	1177162	1288484	1350349	...
Gross input												
Intermediate consumption	264107	286347	322416	354091	380083	407700	425722	404792	424988	467087	481509	...
subtotal: Value added	417618	456048	499007	539633	589048	649854	689702	711809	752174	821397	868840	
1 Indirect taxes net liability of unincorporated enterprises	−2861	−403	8	−1335	733	502	505	10279	10513	10393	10139	
A Indirect taxes	6640	7656	8608	9085	10056	12161	12317	22340	22027	21290	22098	
B less: Subsidies	9501	8059	8600	10420	9323	11659	11812	12061	11514	10897	11959	
2 Consumption of fixed capital	59845	64934	71769	78652	86586	93807	100833	107440	113823	123181	129984	
3 Compensation of employees	98763	105988	115728	125556	137990	151831	160408	162778	163325	172233	182514	
4 Net operating surplus	261871	285529	311502	336760	363739	403714	427956	431312	464513	515590	546203	
Gross input	681725	742395	821423	893724	969131	1057554	1115424	1116601	1177162	1288484	1350349	...

3.32 Household and private unincorporated enterprise income and outlay account

Thousand million Italian lire

	1986	1987	1988	1989	1990	1991	1992	1993	1994	1995	1996	1997
Receipts												
1 Compensation of employees	407031	440989	484624	529622	592527	648062	681667	688123	698364	728926	768592	...
A Wages and salaries	294869	321102	352114	378475	422183	462541	483589	485074	493686	511893	534789	...
B Employers' contributions for social security	78978	84477	93996	107660	121250	131587	139165	141823	142242	151197	192016	...
C Employers' contributions for private pension and welfare plans	33184	35410	38514	43487	49094	53934	58913	61226	62436	65836	41787	...
2 Operating surplus of private unincorporated enterprises	261871	285529	311502	336760	363739	403714	427956	431312	464513	515590	546203	
3 Property and entrepreneurial income	96976	101763	113225	130773	148921	170906	201654	209520	194939	217722	216728	...
A Withdrawals from private quasi-corporations	11560	12508	13774	14572	16034	17708	18279	19203	19976	21316	22257	
B Interest	79290	82487	93258	108723	125151	145170	175715	182398	166043	186431	183697	
C Dividends	5117	5453	4762	4879	4280	4571	4386	4204	4537	5521	6200	
D Net land rent and royalties	1009	1315	1431	2599	3456	3457	3274	3715	4383	4454	4574	
4 Current transfers	185375	205586	228872	254729	289246	317760	350958	365956	384767	405648	435510	
A Casualty insurance claims	8305	9662	11451	13265	15822	18897	19897	19050	19984	22053	24243	
B Social security benefits	164181	181782	201440	223955	254478	279044	311112	325144	342604	359289	384570	
C Social assistance grants	...	...	...	...	...	...	...	...	...	...	...	
D Unfunded employee pension and welfare benefits												
E Transfers from general government	...	...	...	...	...	...	...	...	...	...	...	
F Transfers from rest of the world	2817	2681	3308	3248	2933	2158	1951	2376	2034	1905	1888	...
G Other transfers n.e.c.	10072	11461	12673	14261	16013	17661	17998	19386	20145	22401	24809	...
Statistical discrepancy	10090	9286	10307	11496	11514	12877	10160	9907	8920	11369	11397	...
Total current receipts	961343	1043153	1148530	1263380	1405947	1553319	1672395	1704818	1751503	1879255	1978430	...

Italy

Thousand million Italian lire

	1986	1987	1988	1989	1990	1991	1992	1993	1994	1995	1996	1997
Disbursements												
1 Final consumption expenditure	549170	603508	668195	738181	803619	882079	944094	961466	1014471	1087399	1146551	...
2 Property income	24585	25151	27119	30017	33534	36666	44636	43667	39343	44062	45028	...
A Interest	24086	24610	26530	29379	32846	35947	43882	42889	38534	43145	44070	...
B Net land rent and royalties	499	541	589	638	688	719	754	778	809	917	958	...
3 Direct taxes and other current transfers n.e.c. to general government	203593	223182	251899	285986	321795	355579	384474	417406	406476	436445	497038	...
A Social security contributions	112376	121771	134141	150341	169205	187759	200475	213150	213863	232070	276604	...
B Direct taxes	91217	101411	117758	135645	152590	167820	183999	204256	192613	204375	220434	...
C Fees, fines and penalties	...	...	...	...	...	...	...	...	...	...	...	...
4 Other current transfers	57038	57368	63555	73248	83141	96023	106073	112106	116049	122662	104412	...
A Net casualty insurance premiums	7895	8874	10206	12552	14744	17833	18708	17889	18848	20562	22660	...
B Transfers to private non-profit institutions serving households	479	492	534	572	641	728	745	763	800	857	899	...
C Transfers to rest of the world	115	195	735	1187	1361	2148	2268	2065	2186	2328	2574	...
D Other current transfers, except imputed	15365	12397	13566	15450	17301	21380	25439	30163	31779	33820	36492	...
E Imputed employee pension and welfare contributions	33184	35410	38514	43487	49094	53934	58913	61226	62436	65095	41787	...
Statistical discrepancy	2108	2783	2948	2978	3160	3484	3420	3361	3037	3613	5078	...
Net saving	124849	131161	134814	132970	160698	179488	189698	166812	172127	185074	180323	...
Total current disbursements and net saving	961343	1043153	1148530	1263380	1405947	1553319	1672395	1704818	1751503	1879255	1978430	...

3.33 Household and private unincorporated enterprise capital accumulation account

Thousand million Italian lire

	1986	1987	1988	1989	1990	1991	1992	1993	1994	1995	1996	1997
Finance of gross accumulation												
1 Gross saving	184694	196095	206583	211622	247284	273295	290531	274252	285950	308255	310307	...
A Consumption of fixed capital	59845	64934	71769	78652	86586	93807	100833	107440	113823	123181	129984	...
B Net saving	124849	131161	134814	132970	160698	179488	189698	166812	172127	185074	180323	...
2 Capital transfers	4998	5880	6666	6532	8539	5298	8189	18424	16756	11577	7588	...
Total finance of gross accumulation	189692	201975	213249	218154	255823	278593	298720	292676	302706	319832	317895	...
Gross accumulation												
1 Gross capital formation	90768	95289	103761	108106	109378	115306	133194	130147	138875	158022	160069	...
A Increase in stocks	7851	8237	6316	4308	2452	2727	1647	−323	3020	4838	307	...
B Gross fixed capital formation	82917	87052	97445	103798	106926	112579	131547	130470	135855	153184	159762	...
2 Purchases of land, net	−150	−231	−430	−425	−350	−309	−187	−231	−236	−214	−202	...
3 Purchases of intangibles, net	−711	−775	−1140	−1111	−1370	−1277	−1308	−1595	−1603	−2012	−1680	...
4 Capital transfers	944	1409	1876	1732	1300	1555	16285	7273	5487	9477	5054	...
Net lending [a]	98841	106283	109182	109852	146865	163318	150736	157082	160183	154559	154654	...
Total gross accumulation	189692	201975	213249	218154	255823	278593	298720	292676	302706	319832	317895	...

[a] Net lending of the capital accumulation account and the capital finance account have not been reconciled and are different due to different statistical sources.

Italy

3.51 External transactions, current account: detail

Thousand million Italian lire

	1986	1987	1988	1989	1990	1991	1992	1993	1994	1995	1996	1997
Payments to the rest of the world												
1 Imports of goods and services	168736	186053	206307	240342	262192	270886	295647	302325	338702	416663	402102	448540
A Imports of merchandise, c.i.f.	149070	163182	180930	210821	219753	228191	235384	236618	276062	340396	325855	359524
B Other	19666	22871	25377	29521	42439	42695	60263	65707	62640	76267	76247	89016
2 Factor income to rest of the world	18852	18600	22010	30485	41267	48676	60403	74523	73697	82278	85479	99053
A Compensation of employees	1104	1369	1991	3621	4371	3077	2619	3197	2701	2356	2573	2899
B Property and entrepreneurial income	17748	17231	20019	26864	36896	45599	57784	71326	70996	79922	82906	96154
3 Current transfers to the rest of the world	13339	13762	16633	20720	18844	24523	25565	30937	28557	26360	30566	31372
A Indirect taxes by general government to supranational organizations	...	...	...	...	...	...	...	...	...	...	...	...
B Other current transfers	13339	13762	16633	20720	18844	24523	25565	30937	28557	26360	30566	31372
By general government	2500	2320	3036	5772	2756	4744	5158	10074	5831	4339	8032	...
By other resident sectors	10839	11442	13597	14948	16088	19779	20407	20863	22726	22021	22534	...
4 Surplus of the nation on current transactions	3147	−3188	−8998	−17466	−21285	−30068	−36194	15222	22573	41018	63243	56490
Payments to the rest of the world and surplus of the nation on current transfers	204074	215227	235952	274081	301018	314017	345421	423007	463529	566319	581390	635455
Receipts from the rest of the world												
1 Exports of goods and services	181067	191016	207495	238437	262664	271428	295515	355486	399915	491571	499986	532957
A Exports of merchandise, f.o.b.	144778	151219	166769	193037	205581	212575	223879	271090	313340	387380	394992	412856
B Other	36289	39797	40726	45400	57083	58853	71636	84396	86575	104191	104994	120101
2 Factor income from rest of the world	12270	11967	14453	20049	23329	26502	34136	48057	46355	56057	62093	78244
A Compensation of employees	4070	3521	4062	4903	4507	3347	2713	3097	2891	3151	3375	3314
B Property and entrepreneurial income	8200	8446	10391	15146	18822	23155	31423	44960	43464	52906	58718	74930
3 Current transfers from rest of the world	10737	12244	14004	15595	15025	16087	15770	19464	17259	18691	19311	24254
A Subsidies to general government from supranational organizations	...	...	...	...	...	...	...	...	...	...	...	...
B Other current transfers	10737	12244	14004	15595	15025	16087	15770	19464	17259	18691	19311	24254
To general government	220	305	256	266	294	516	382	460	511	551	577	...
To other resident sectors	10517	11939	13748	15329	14731	15571	15388	19004	16748	18140	18734	...
Receipts from the rest of the world on current transfers	204074	215227	235952	274081	301018	314017	345421	423007	463529	566319	581390	635455

Italy

3.52 External transactions, capital accumulation account

Thousand million Italian lire

	1986	1987	1988	1989	1990	1991	1992	1993	1994	1995	1996	1997
Finance of gross accumulation												
1 Surplus of the nation on current transactions	3147	−3188	−8998	−17466	−21285	−30068	−36194	15222	22573	41018	63243	56490
2 Capital transfers from rest of the world	1033	1206	1503	1841	1643	1815	2544	4086	3153	3854	1721	6449
Total finance of gross accumulation	4180	−1982	−7495	−15625	−19642	−28253	−33650	19308	25726	44872	64964	62939
Gross accumulation												
1 Capital transfers to the rest of the world	1030	748	899	641	638	850	1238	1272	1030	1101	965	1146
2 Purchases of intangible assets, n.e.c., net, from rest of the world	129	140	−134	−61	98	234	348	216	367	42	645	−128
Net lending to the rest of the world [a]	3021	−2870	−8260	−16205	−20378	−29337	−35236	17820	24329	43729	63354	61921
Total gross accumulation	4180	−1982	−7495	−15625	−19642	−28253	−33650	19308	25726	44872	64964	62939

a Net lending of the capital accumulation account and the capital finance account have not been reconciled and are different due to different statistical sources.

4.3 Cost components of value added

Thousand million Italian lire

	1986						1987					
	Compensation of employees	Capital consumption	Net operating surplus	Indirect taxes	less: Subsidies received	Value added	Compensation of employees	Capital consumption	Net operating surplus	Indirect taxes	less: Subsidies received	Value added
All producers												
1 Agriculture, hunting, forestry and fishing	11175	...	29815	359	2745	38604	11677	...	31814	418	3856	40053
A Agriculture and hunting	...	...	...	...	...	36616	...	...	...	...	...	37805
B Forestry and logging	...	...	...	...	...	571	...	...	...	...	...	547
C Fishing	...	...	...	...	...	1504	...	...	...	...	...	1701
2 Mining and quarrying	...	...	...	...	...	...	...	...	...	...	...	...
3 Manufacturing [a]	115275	...	96943	7546	6078	213686	123522	...	105280	7775	6484	230093
A Manufacture of food, beverages and tobacco	8672	...	11543	6107	2885	23437	9351	...	12451	6307	3415	24694
B Textile, wearing apparel and leather industries	18410	...	17851	276	303	36234	19516	...	18770	277	294	38269
C Manufacture of wood and wood products, including furniture	5507	...	6364	119	169	11821	5743	...	6749	122	178	12436
D Manufacture of paper and paper products, printing and publishing	6925	...	5586	94	377	12228	7678	...	6142	97	342	13575
E Manufacture of chemicals and chemical petroleum, coal, rubber and plastic products	14523	...	12447	250	135	27085	16275	...	13695	266	130	30106
F Manufacture of non-metallic mineral products, except products of petroleum and coal	7828	...	7022	113	156	14807	8528	...	7966	117	155	16456
G Basic metal industries	5757	...	3834	62	447	9206	5913	...	3691	58	405	9257

Italy

Thousand million Italian lire

	1986					1987				
	Compensation of employees	Capital consumption	Net operating surplus	Indirect taxes	less: Subsidies received	Value added	Compensation of employees	Capital consumption	Net operating surplus	Indirect taxes	less: Subsidies received	Value added
H Manufacture of fabricated metal products, machinery and equipment	46400	...	30993	506	1583	76316	49189	...	34500	512	1550	82651
I Other manufacturing industries	1253	...	1303	19	23	2552	1329	...	1316	19	15	2649
4 Electricity, gas and water	8749	...	14399	20787	328	43607	9505	...	15280	23576	252	48109
A Electricity, gas and steam	8749	...	14399	20787	328	43607	9505	...	15280	23576	252	48109
B Water works and supply	...	...	...	...	...	...	...	...	...	...	...	...
5 Construction	23934	...	30565	561	1074	53986	24794	...	32096	585	890	56585
6 Wholesale and retail trade, restaurants and hotels	43281	...	127595	1689	2253	170312	46978	...	141781	1873	2884	187748
A Wholesale and retail trade	36214	...	107367	1519	2080	143020	39394	...	119041	1694	2713	157416
B Restaurants and hotels	7067	...	20228	170	173	27292	7584	...	22740	179	171	30332
7 Transport, storage and communication	33913	...	34103	668	17438	51246	36710	...	33219	720	15196	55453
A Transport and storage	25534	...	27579	576	15617	38072	27336	...	25818	626	12966	40814
B Communication	8379	...	6524	92	1821	13174	9374	...	7401	94	2230	14639
8 Finance, insurance, real estate and business services	56549	...	136896	9390	799	202036	62128	...	148788	11140	996	221060
9 Community, social and personal services												
Total, Industries	292876	...	470316	41000	30715	773477	315314	...	508258	46087	30558	839101
Producers of government services	103656	...	3672	...	...	107328	115718	...	4031	...	...	119749
Other producers	7533	...	55	...	...	7588	7805	...	67	...	...	7872
Total	404065	...	474043	41000	30715	888393	438837	...	512356	46087	30558	966722
less: Imputed bank service charge	...	...	38175	...	...	38175	...	...	39013	...	...	39013
Import duties	...	...	...	48071	...	48071	...	...	...	55054	...	55054
Value added tax	...	...	...	...	...	...	...	...	...	...	...	...
Other adjustments	...	...	...	...	...	...	...	...	...	...	...	...
Total [bc]	404065	...	435868	89071	30715	898289	438837	...	473343	101141	30558	982763

	1988					1989				
	Compensation of employees	Capital consumption	Net operating surplus	Indirect taxes	less: Subsidies received	Value added	Compensation of employees	Capital consumption	Net operating surplus	Indirect taxes	less: Subsidies received	Value added
All producers												
1 Agriculture, hunting, forestry and fishing	12395	...	30744	479	4288	39330	13317	...	32635	553	4900	41605
A Agriculture and hunting	...	...	...	...	...	37057	...	...	...	...	...	39314
B Forestry and logging	...	...	...	...	...	576	...	...	...	...	...	584
C Fishing	...	...	...	...	...	1697	...	...	...	...	...	1707
2 Mining and quarrying	...	...	...	...	...	...	...	...	...	...	...	...
3 Manufacturing [a]	134902	...	119084	9025	6633	256378	149261	...	127528	9654	6789	279654
A Manufacture of food, beverages and tobacco	10119	...	12974	6946	3475	26564	11047	...	13255	7273	3433	28142
B Textile, wearing apparel and leather industries	20946	...	20656	407	243	41766	22672	...	21808	456	299	44637
C Manufacture of wood and wood products, including furniture	6091	...	7729	215	143	13892	6597	...	8283	230	181	14929
D Manufacture of paper and paper products, printing and publishing	8361	...	7147	144	373	15279	9127	...	7872	162	283	16878

Italy

	1988						1989					
	Compensation of employees	Capital consumption	Net operating surplus	Indirect taxes	less: Subsidies received	Value added	Compensation of employees	Capital consumption	Net operating surplus	Indirect taxes	less: Subsidies received	Value added
E Manufacture of chemicals and chemical petroleum, coal, rubber and plastic products	18035	...	15740	315	167	33923	20149	...	16912	370	152	37279
F Manufacture of non-metallic mineral products, except products of petroleum and coal	9561	...	8738	162	156	18305	11115	...	8966	189	169	20101
G Basic metal industries	6198	...	6016	70	298	11986	6758	...	6709	85	291	13261
H Manufacture of fabricated metal products, machinery and equipment	54176	...	38598	737	1760	91751	60285	...	42132	857	1963	101311
I Other manufacturing industries	1415	...	1486	29	18	2912	1511	...	1591	32	18	3116
4 Electricity, gas and water	10232	...	15931	26619	302	52480	11214	...	16796	29881	348	57543
A Electricity, gas and steam	10232	...	15931	26619	302	52480	11214	...	16796	29881	348	57543
B Water works and supply	...	...	...	...	...	...	...	...	...	...	...	...
5 Construction	27040	...	35102	682	904	61920	29368	...	38640	809	1164	67653
6 Wholesale and retail trade, restaurants and hotels	50128	...	155220	2636	2352	205632	54876	...	166566	2940	2756	221626
A Wholesale and retail trade	42256	...	129643	2426	2119	172206	46431	...	138606	2741	2520	185258
B Restaurants and hotels	7872	...	25577	210	233	33426	8445	...	27960	199	236	36368
7 Transport, storage and communication	39767	...	37239	864	16047	61823	44091	...	40176	984	17545	67706
A Transport and storage	29601	...	29366	768	13485	46250	32912	...	32741	865	15283	51235
B Communication	10166	...	7873	96	2562	15573	11179	...	7435	119	2262	16471
8 Finance, insurance, real estate and business services	69043	...	167786	13078	1034	248873	75680	...	189045	13885	1112	277498
9 Community, social and personal services												
Total, Industries	343507	...	561106	53383	31560	926436	377807	...	611386	58706	34614	1013285
Producers of government services	130427	...	4521	...	...	134948	140506	...	5081	...	...	145587
Other producers	8619	...	76	...	...	8695	10027	...	84	...	...	10111
Total	482553	...	565703	53383	31560	1070079	528340	...	616551	58706	34614	1168983
less: Imputed bank service charge	...	...	44496	...	...	44496	...	...	50780	...	...	50780
Import duties	...	...	...	64440	...	64440	...	...	...	73758	...	73758
Value added tax	...	...	...	...	...	...	...	...	...	...	...	...
Other adjustments	...	...	...	...	...	...	...	...	...	...	...	...
Total [bc]	482553	...	521207	117823	31560	1090023	528340	...	565771	132464	34614	1191961

	1990						1991					
	Compensation of employees	Capital consumption	Net operating surplus	Indirect taxes	less: Subsidies received	Value added	Compensation of employees	Capital consumption	Net operating surplus	Indirect taxes	less: Subsidies received	Value added

All producers

1 Agriculture, hunting, forestry and fishing	13938	...	32331	565	4701	42133	14214	...	38446	632	5445	47847
A Agriculture and hunting	...	...	...	...	...	39859	...	...	...	...	...	45398
B Forestry and logging	...	...	...	...	...	555	...	...	...	...	...	642
C Fishing	...	...	...	...	...	1719	...	...	...	...	...	1866
2 Mining and quarrying	...	...	...	...	...	...	...	...	...	...	...	...
3 Manufacturing [a]	162880	...	126680	10697	6635	293622	174766	...	122144	11022	7686	300246
A Manufacture of food, beverages and tobacco	11983	...	14123	8051	3684	30473	13109	...	15449	8158	4003	32713

Italy

	1990						1991					
	Compensation of employees	Capital consumption	Net operating surplus	Indirect taxes	less: Subsidies received	Value added	Compensation of employees	Capital consumption	Net operating surplus	Indirect taxes	less: Subsidies received	Value added
B Textile, wearing apparel and leather industries	24543	...	21897	495	199	46736	26233	...	21948	533	254	48460
C Manufacture of wood and wood products, including furniture	7158	...	8698	253	123	15986	7782	...	9233	273	154	17134
D Manufacture of paper and paper products, printing and publishing	10041	...	8325	177	439	18104	10863	...	8004	193	335	18725
E Manufacture of chemicals and chemical petroleum, coal, rubber and plastic products	22048	...	15753	402	158	38045	23690	...	14387	436	156	38357
F Manufacture of non-metallic mineral products, except products of petroleum and coal	12046	...	9586	211	124	21719	12399	...	9343	228	141	21829
G Basic metal industries	7017	...	5701	89	396	12411	7364	...	4274	91	406	11323
H Manufacture of fabricated metal products, machinery and equipment	66391	...	41029	983	1490	106913	71546	...	37928	1071	2209	108336
I Other manufacturing industries	1653	...	1568	36	22	3235	1780	...	1578	39	28	3369
4 Electricity, gas and water	12620	...	18533	36567	340	67380	13796	...	21856	42051	290	77413
A Electricity, gas and steam	12620	...	18533	36567	340	67380	13796	...	21856	42051	290	77413
B Water works and supply	...	...	...	...	...	...	...	...	...	...	...	...
5 Construction	33496	...	42832	1003	704	76627	36885	...	46694	1116	937	83758
6 Wholesale and retail trade, restaurants and hotels	60935	...	178658	3301	2203	240691	67596	...	194680	4034	3284	263026
A Wholesale and retail trade	51502	...	147991	3076	1962	200607	57394	...	161609	3780	3075	219708
B Restaurants and hotels	9433	...	30667	225	241	40084	10202	...	33071	254	209	43318
7 Transport, storage and communication	47651	...	42201	1169	17260	73761	51898	...	47252	1328	17831	82647
A Transport and storage	34869	...	34744	1025	15093	55545	37999	...	37489	1164	15238	61414
B Communication	12782	...	7457	144	2167	18216	13899	...	9763	164	2593	21233
8 Finance, insurance, real estate and business services	84340	...	215969	16445	1109	315645	95779	...	235205	18386	1718	347652
9 Community, social and personal services												
Total, Industries	415860	...	657204	69747	32952	1109859	454934	...	706277	78569	37191	1202589
Producers of government services	165103	...	5705	...	...	170808	179613	...	6311	...	...	185924
Other producers	11428	...	94	...	...	11522	13245	...	100	...	...	13345
Total	592391	...	663003	69747	32952	1292189	647792	...	712688	78569	37191	1401858
less: Imputed bank service charge	...	...	60721	...	...	60721	...	...	66270	...	...	66270
Import duties	...	...	...	79191	...	79191	...	...	...	91983	...	91983
Value added tax	...	...	...	...	...	...	...	...	...	...	...	...
Other adjustments	...	...	...	...	...	...	...	...	...	...	...	...
Total [bc]	592391	...	602282	148938	32952	1310659	647792	...	646418	170552	37191	1427571

Italy

	1992					1993				
	Compensation of employees	Capital consumption	Net operating surplus	Indirect taxes	less: Subsidies received	Value added	Compensation of employees	Capital consumption	Net operating surplus	Indirect taxes	less: Subsidies received	Value added

All producers

	Comp.	Cap.	Net op.	Ind. tax	Subs.	VA	Comp.	Cap.	Net op.	Ind. tax	Subs.	VA
1 Agriculture, hunting, forestry and fishing	15673	...	36938	648	5938	47321	14925	...	37670	951	7438	46108
A Agriculture and hunting	...	...	...	...	...	43732	...	...	...	...	...	...
B Forestry and logging	...	...	...	...	...	678	...	...	...	...	...	...
C Fishing	...	...	...	...	...	1959	...	...	...	...	...	...
2 Mining and quarrying	...	...	...	...	...	...	...	...	...	...	...	...
3 Manufacturing [a]	179375	...	123927	11186	6582	307906	177572	...	124099	14656	5898	310429
A Manufacture of food, beverages and tobacco	13723	...	15862	8437	2903	35119	14179	...	16181	10456	2627	38189
B Textile, wearing apparel and leather industries	26546	...	22683	507	280	49456	26078	...	22989	721	322	49466
C Manufacture of wood and wood products, including furniture	7855	...	9627	249	176	17555	7847	...	9812	338	181	17816
D Manufacture of paper and paper products, printing and publishing	11370	...	8346	182	384	19514	11657	...	8433	281	255	20116
E Manufacture of chemicals and chemical petroleum, coal, rubber and plastic products	25187	...	14713	436	151	40185	24929	...	15427	695	224	40827
F Manufacture of non-metallic mineral products, except products of petroleum and coal	12882	...	9929	224	146	22889	13141	...	9134	350	191	22434
G Basic metal industries	7547	...	3787	88	226	11196	7344	...	4917	261	220	12302
H Manufacture of fabricated metal products, machinery and equipment	72460	...	37327	1018	2285	108520	70594	...	35495	1488	1840	105737
I Other manufacturing industries	1805	...	1653	45	31	3472	1803	...	1711	66	38	3542
4 Electricity, gas and water	14477	...	24393	47512	504	85878	14022	...	27176	48390	572	89016
A Electricity, gas and steam	14477	...	24393	47512	504	85878	14022	...	27176	48390	572	89016
B Water works and supply	...	...	...	...	...	...	...	...	...	...	...	...
5 Construction	39393	...	48647	1204	1502	87742	38268	...	47276	1475	1402	85617
6 Wholesale and retail trade, restaurants and hotels	72062	...	203391	4323	3573	276203	75652	...	208394	6058	3455	286649
A Wholesale and retail trade	61009	...	168016	4020	3343	229702	64133	...	171281	5476	3209	237681
B Restaurants and hotels	11053	...	35375	303	230	46501	11519	...	37113	582	246	48968
7 Transport, storage and communication	54919	...	48337	1414	15076	89594	56046	...	59806	2421	21598	96675
A Transport and storage	40552	...	34889	1230	11617	65054	40886	...	43573	1889	16092	70256
B Communication	14367	...	13448	184	3459	24540	15160	...	16233	532	5506	26419
8 Finance, insurance, real estate and business services	102885	...	263368	21081	2002	385332	105196	...	274259	32049	2072	409432
9 Community, social and personal services												
Total, Industries	478784	...	749001	87368	35177	1279976	481681	...	778680	106000	42435	1323926
Producers of government services	188103	...	6834	...	...	194937	190972	...	7496	...	...	198468
Other producers	14686	...	116	...	...	14802	15570	...	127	...	...	15697
Total	681573	...	755951	87368	35177	1489715	688223	...	786303	106000	42435	1538091
less: Imputed bank service charge	...	...	78718	...	...	78718	...	...	79889	...	...	79889
Import duties	...	...	...	91496	...	91496	...	...	...	92094	...	92094

Italy

	1992						1993					
	Compensation of employees	Capital consumption	Net operating surplus	Indirect taxes	less: Subsidies received	Value added	Compensation of employees	Capital consumption	Net operating surplus	Indirect taxes	less: Subsidies received	Value added
Value added tax	...	...	...	...	...	...	...	...	...	...	...	...
Other adjustments	...	...	...	...	...	...	...	...	...	...	...	...
Total [bc]	681573	...	677233	178864	35177	1502493	688223	...	706414	198094	42435	1550296

	1994						1995					
	Compensation of employees	Capital consumption	Net operating surplus	Indirect taxes	less: Subsidies received	Value added	Compensation of employees	Capital consumption	Net operating surplus	Indirect taxes	less: Subsidies received	Value added
All producers												
1 Agriculture, hunting, forestry and fishing	14187	...	39691	800	7151	47527	13949	...	43871	796	7772	50844
2 Mining and quarrying	...	...	...	...	...	...	...	...	...	...	...	...
3 Manufacturing [a]	181217	...	141218	15264	5907	331792	190257	...	164322	15868	4992	365455
A Manufacture of food, beverages and tobacco	14526	...	15015	11574	1881	39234	14950	...	15291	12089	1637	40693
B Textile, wearing apparel and leather industries	27264	...	25788	615	414	53253	28442	...	29741	625	271	58537
C Manufacture of wood and wood products, including furniture	7970	...	10436	280	221	18465	8320	...	11198	286	157	19647
D Manufacture of paper and paper products, printing and publishing	11669	...	9147	254	304	20766	12038	...	10693	254	125	22860
E Manufacture of chemicals and chemical petroleum, coal, rubber and plastic products	25095	...	19129	632	301	44555	26031	...	23858	643	234	50298
F Manufacture of non-metallic mineral products, except products of petroleum and coal	13252	...	9716	314	205	23077	13915	...	10443	319	138	24539
G Basic metal industries	7417	...	7551	248	496	14720	7520	...	12334	261	444	19671
H Manufacture of fabricated metal products, machinery and equipment	72191	...	42584	1293	2040	114028	77118	...	48565	1337	1954	125066
I Other manufacturing industries	1833	...	1852	54	45	3694	1923	...	2199	54	32	4144
4 Electricity, gas and water	14460	...	31321	50749	610	95920	14974	...	33078	56274	637	103689
A Electricity, gas and steam	14460	...	31074	50749	610	95673	14974	...	31884	56274	637	102495
B Water works and supply	...	...	...	...	...	...	...	...	...	...	...	...
5 Construction	37183	...	48242	1393	2097	84721	37036	...	51309	1405	1381	88369
6 Wholesale and retail trade, restaurants and hotels	77169	...	221590	5107	1977	301889	82312	...	245344	5148	1821	330983
A Wholesale and retail trade	65415	...	180187	4575	1356	248821	69560	...	201044	4619	1482	273741
B Restaurants and hotels	11754	...	41403	532	621	53068	12752	...	44300	529	339	57242
7 Transport, storage and communication	55063	...	67664	2268	19653	105342	56474	...	72496	2312	16204	115078
A Transport and storage	40352	...	53122	1774	19059	76189	41572	...	55853	1806	15931	83300
B Communication	14711	...	14542	494	594	29153	14902	...	16643	506	273	31778
8 Finance, insurance, real estate and business services	107316	...	290665	32734	2105	428610	114305	...	319381	34574	1931	466329
9 Community, social and personal services												
Total, Industries	486595	...	840391	108315	39500	1395801	509307	...	929801	116377	34738	1520747
Producers of government services	195324	...	8115	...	...	203439	199019	...	8819	...	...	207838
Other producers	16255	...	139	...	...	16394	17719	...	165	...	...	17884

Italy

	1994						1995					
	Compensation of employees	Capital consumption	Net operating surplus	Indirect taxes	less: Subsidies received	Value added	Compensation of employees	Capital consumption	Net operating surplus	Indirect taxes	less: Subsidies received	Value added
Total	698174	...	848645	108315	39500	1615634	726045	...	938785	116377	34738	1746469
less: Imputed bank service charge	...	...	72807	...	...	72807	...	...	79139	...	...	79139
Import duties	...	...	...	95839	...	95839	...	...	...	104924	...	104924
Value added tax	...	...	...	...	...	...	...	...	...	...	...	...
Other adjustments	...	...	...	...	...	...	...	...	...	...	...	...
Total [bc]	698174	...	775838	204154	39500	1638666	726045	...	859646	221301	34738	1772254

	1996						1997					
	Compensation of employees	Capital consumption	Net operating surplus	Indirect taxes	less: Subsidies received	Value added	Compensation of employees	Capital consumption	Net operating surplus	Indirect taxes	less: Subsidies received	Value added
All producers												
1 Agriculture, hunting, forestry and fishing	13954	...	47534	839	9564	52763	14011	...	46490	952	10121	51332
2 Mining and quarrying	...	...	...	...	...	...	...	...	...	...	...	...
3 Manufacturing [a]	198777	...	168377	16748	6032	377870	207707	...	170665	17519	4843	391048
A Manufacture of food, beverages and tobacco	15435	...	18051	12792	1677	44601	16041	...	18211	13411	1473	46190
B Textile, wearing apparel and leather industries	29543	...	29659	651	339	59514	30569	...	29714	673	267	60689
C Manufacture of wood and wood products, including furniture	8429	...	11000	293	298	19424	8708	...	10150	307	196	18969
D Manufacture of paper and paper products, printing and publishing	12537	...	11680	266	161	24322	12959	...	12523	277	127	25632
E Manufacture of chemicals and chemical petroleum, coal, rubber and plastic products	27370	...	22189	674	206	50027	28705	...	22765	703	180	51993
F Manufacture of non-metallic mineral products, except products of petroleum and coal	14388	...	9645	331	131	24233	14982	...	10540	344	117	25749
G Basic metal industries	7712	...	12602	282	434	20162	8103	...	12862	297	346	20916
H Manufacture of fabricated metal products, machinery and equipment	81390	...	51060	1405	2759	131096	85572	...	51741	1451	2109	136655
I Other manufacturing industries	1973	...	2491	54	27	4491	2068	...	2159	56	28	4255
4 Electricity, gas and water	15405	...	32745	58823	886	106087	15130	...	34637	59906	625	109048
A Electricity, gas and steam	15405	...	−73342	58823	886	...	15130	...	−74411	59906	625	...
B Water works and supply	...	...	...	...	...	...	...	...	...	...	...	...
5 Construction	37504	...	55238	1668	1352	93058	38636	...	55590	1875	1214	94887
6 Wholesale and retail trade, restaurants and hotels	88488	...	256070	5721	1707	348572	93679	...	261417	5809	2544	358361
A Wholesale and retail trade	74762	...	205539	5138	1384	284055	79130	...	209693	5202	2232	291793
B Restaurants and hotels	13726	...	50531	583	323	64517	14549	...	51724	607	312	66568
7 Transport, storage and communication	58502	...	74775	2444	15777	119944	60390	...	79831	2565	16094	126692
A Transport and storage	43096	...	56398	1904	15523	85875	44526	...	59643	1997	15816	90350
B Communication	15406	...	18377	540	254	34069	15864	...	20188	568	278	36342
8 Finance, insurance, real estate and business services	122658	...	342114	39574	2438	501908	129489	...	353597	45765	1706	527145
9 Community, social and personal services												

Italy

	1996						1997					
	Compensation of employees	Capital consumption	Net operating surplus	Indirect taxes	less: Subsidies received	Value added	Compensation of employees	Capital consumption	Net operating surplus	Indirect taxes	less: Subsidies received	Value added
Total, Industries	535288	...	976853	125817	37756	1600202	559042	...	1002227	134391	37147	1658513
Producers of government services	215768	...	9436	...	...	225204	227055	...	9963	...	...	237018
Other producers	18724	...	168	...	...	18892	20013	...	190	...	...	20203
Total	769780	...	986457	125817	37756	1844298	806110	...	1012380	134391	37147	1915734
less: Imputed bank service charge	...	...	79350	...	...	79350	...	...	79117	...	...	79117
Import duties	...	...	...	107687	...	107687	...	...	...	114063	...	114063
Value added tax	...	...	...	...	...	...	...	...	...	...	...	...
Other adjustments	...	...	...	...	...	...	...	...	...	...	...	...
Total [bc]	769780	...	907107	233504	37756	1872635	806110	...	933263	248454	37147	1950680

a Item "Mining and quarrying" is included in item "Manufacturing".
b The branch breakdown used in this table (GDP by kind of activity) is according to the classification NACE/CLIO.
c Column "Consumption of fixed capital" is included in column "Net operating surplus".

Jamaica

Source

Reply to the United Nations National Accounts Questionnaire from the Department of Statistics, Kingston. Official estimates, together with information on concepts, sources and methods of estimation utilized are published annually by the Department in *National Income and Product*.

General note

The estimates have been prepared in accordance with the United Nations System of National Accounts (1968 SNA) so far as the existing data would permit.

1.1 Expenditure on the gross domestic product, in current prices

Million Jamaican dollars

	1986	1987	1988	1989	1990	1991	1992	1993	1994	1995	1996	1997
1 Government final consumption expenditure	2143	2497	3013	3290	4282	5784	7692	13553	16495	23393	31722	...
2 Private final consumption expenditure	8744	10387	12329	15673	18897	27967	45911	67131	89428	120577	142844	...
3 Gross capital formation	2566	3695	4988	6660	8507	12055	24156	34507	43825	58488	70575	...
A Increase in stocks	134	151	123	122	145	231	202	726	326	586	553	...
B Gross fixed capital formation	2432	3545	4865	6538	8362	11824	23953	33781	43499	57901	70022	...
Residential buildings	1146	1598	2330	3275	3415	...	...	...	...	...	...	...
Non-residential buildings						...	...	...	...	...	...	...
Other construction and land improvement, etc.	87	83	274	127	176	...	...	...	...	...	...	...
Other	1198	1863	2262	3137	4770	...	...	...	...	...	...	...
4 Exports of goods and services	7370	8404	9168	11036	15856	24978	50552	57835	83815	100863	111565	...
5 less: Imports of goods and services	6924	8344	10041	13259	17115	25567	51319	67883	93908	123633	137604	...
equals: Gross domestic product	13898	16640	19458	23400	30518	45217	76992	105142	139655	179686	219103	...

1.10 Gross domestic product by kind of activity, in current prices

Million Jamaican dollars

	1986	1987	1988	1989	1990	1991	1992	1993	1994	1995	1996	1997
1 Agriculture, hunting, forestry and fishing	1049	1276	1393	1623	1973	3073	5777	8043	...	...	...	...
2 Mining and quarrying	902	1147	1727	2199	2831	4817	6845	6961	...	...	...	...
3 Manufacturing	2960	3473	3805	4576	5923	8445	14239	17667	...	...	...	...
4 Electricity, gas and water	569	612	601	531	809	810	1836	2193	...	...	...	...
5 Construction	1086	1405	2021	2672	3587	5565	9382	12341	...	...	...	...
6 Wholesale and retail trade, restaurants and hotels	2794	3471	3967	4783	6419	9285	17138	22706	...	...	...	...
7 Transport, storage and communication	1310	1554	1742	2077	2641	3538	5581	7630	...	...	...	...
8 Finance, insurance, real estate and business services	2022	2367	2804	3386	4285	5603	9017	10772	...	...	...	...
9 Community, social and personal services	597	713	767	934	1221	1713	2869	3838	...	...	...	...

Jamaica

Million Jamaican dollars

	1986	1987	1988	1989	1990	1991	1992	1993	1994	1995	1996	1997
Total, Industries	13288	16017	18826	22781	29689	42849	72685	92152	...	...	...	...
Producers of government services	1238	1407	1646	1909	2570	3446	4406	9063	...	...	...	...
Other producers	111	118	148	182	229	274	428	505	...	...	...	...
Subtotal	14638	17542	20621	24872	32489	46568	77519	101720	...	...	...	...
less: Imputed bank service charge	744	919	1190	1530	2012	2410	4980	5935	...	...	...	...
plus: Import duties	...	...	...	...	...	...	...	...	...	...	...	...
plus: Value added tax	...	...	...	...	...	...	...	...	...	...	...	...
plus: Other adjustments	...	...	...	...	...	...	...	...	...	...	...	...
equals: Gross domestic product	13893	16623	19430	23342	30477	44158	72539	95785	...	...	...	...

1.11 Gross domestic product by kind of activity, in constant prices

Million Jamaican dollars

	1986	1987	1988	1989	1990	1991	1992	1993	1994	1995	1996	1997
	At constant prices of: 1974 / 1986											
1 Agriculture, hunting, forestry and fishing	160 / 1049	1103	1065	968	1080	1078	1217	1324	...	...	...	...
2 Mining and quarrying	102 / 902	956	913	1238	1520	1607	1566	1575	...	...	...	...
3 Manufacturing	306 / 2960	3128	3296	3537	3668	3378	3410	3313	...	...	...	...
4 Electricity, gas and water	31 / 569	615	617	685	733	746	778	809	...	...	...	...
5 Construction	107 / 1086	1241	1425	1680	1707	1718	1726	1717	...	...	...	...
6 Wholesale and retail trade, restaurants and hotels	335 / 2794	3101	3131	3237	3387	3462	3645	3791	...	...	...	...
7 Transport, storage and communication	154 / 1310	1465	1532	1592	1647	1719	1803	1939	...	...	...	...
8 Finance, insurance, real estate and business services	372 / 2022	2154	2374	2649	2890	3259	3449	3494	...	...	...	...
9 Community, social and personal services	81 / 597	650	627	676	722	701	709	747	...	...	...	...
Total, Industries	1649 / 13288	14412	14981	16264	17354	17668	18304	18709	...	...	...	...
Producers of government services	322 / 1238	1243	1287	1270	1244	1222	1227	1217	...	...	...	...
Other producers	111	115	119	114	121	114	103	88	...	...	...	...
Subtotal	1971 / 14638	15770	16387	17648	18720	19004	19633	20014	...	...	...	...
less: Imputed bank service charge	104 / 744	804	990	1198	1371	1566	1954	2124	...	...	...	...
plus: Import duties	...	...	...	...	...	...	...	...	...	...	...	...
plus: Value added tax	...	...	...	...	...	...	...	...	...	...	...	...
plus: Other adjustments	...	...	...	...	...	...	...	...	...	...	...	...
equals: Gross domestic product	1867 / 13893	14966	15398	16451	17349	17438	17679	17891	...	...	...	...

Japan

General note

The preparation of national accounts statistics in Japan is undertaken by the Economic Research Institute of the Economic Planning Agency, Tokyo. The official estimates are published in *Annual Report on National Accounts*. The following presentation of sources and methods is mainly based on information from *A System of National Accounts in Japan* published by the Economic Planning Agency. The estimates are generally in accordance with the classifications and definitions recommended in the United Nations System of National Accounts (1968 SNA). The following tables have been prepared from successive replies to the United Nations National Accounts Questionnaire. When the scope and coverage of the estimates differ for conceptual or statistical reasons from the definitions and classifications recommended in SNA, a footnote is indicated to the relevant tables.

Gross domestic product

Gross domestic product is estimated mainly through the production approach.

Expenditures on the gross domestic product

Using the commodity flow method, output, intermediate consumption by industry, household final consumption expenditure, gross capital formation, exports and imports are estimated for each of approximately 2,200 commodities. Shipments estimates are derived directly or indirectly from the statistics such as Crop Survey, Census of Manufactures, Current Production Statistics Survey, Establishment Census and Census of Commerce. The distribution channels and the constant coefficients such as the distribution ratios, the transportation fee rates and the trade margin rates are decided for each of the commodities based on the information of the Input-output Table. Services produced and consumed by the producers of government services and private non-profit services to households are estimated separately based on the settlement of accounts of governments, Survey of Private Non-profit Institutions and so on. Gross domestic expenditure is obtained by adding up final consumption expenditure, gross capital formation, increase in stocks and current external transactions.

Exports and Imports are estimated by the estimation method for external transactions, which rearranges the Balance of Payments in consideration of its consistency with the Balance of Payments. For final consumption expenditure of households, calendar-year figure is estimated by the commodity flow method. Each commodity is classified into one of the elements of a 43-objects x 5-uses matrix. Each element of the matrix corresponds to one of the 4 types of expenditure. Quarterly figures are estimated by distributing the calendar-year figure through expenditure approach which uses Survey of Farm Household Economy, Family Income and Expenditure Survey and National Survey of Family Income and Expenditure. For gross capital formation, quarterly and sectorial figures are estimated by breaking down the calendar-year figure estimated by the commodity flow method, on the basis of the quarterly and sectorial figures estimated through expenditure approach which uses settlements of accounts of government, *Financial Statements of Corporations by Industry* and so on for gross fixed capital formation. For increase in stocks, special accounts for food administration, *Financial Statements of Corporations by Industry* are used. Gross domestic product at constant prices is estimated mainly using price indexes called basic unit deflators which correspond to the approximately 400 commodities aggregated from the approximately 2,200 commodities used for the commodity flow method. Series at constant prices are obtained by dividing the nominal values of the 400 commodities by the basic unit deflators for each demand item. In other words, constant value is estimated using Paasche-type deflator weighted by 400 commodities. Government services and private non-profit services to households are estimated using deflators by activities which correspond respectively to six activities of government services and three activities of private non-profit services to households.

Cost structure of the gross domestic product

Wages and salaries are estimated separately for the three groups of agriculture, forestry and fisheries, government services, and other industries. Concerning the other industries, quarterly cash allowances to employees by industries are calculated by multiplying the per head wage by the number of employees. In this case, the number of employees is based on the *Population Census* conducted every five years and is interpolated in the mid-year of a five-year period by trends observed from the *Labor Force Survey*, while the cash allowances per head is mainly based on the *Monthly Labor Survey*. Cash allowances to officers are estimated by multiplying the number of officers by the difference between the per head allowances of both officers and regular employees, which are obtained from the *Financial Statements of Corporations by Industry*, and the per head allowances of regular employees. Employers' contributions to social security schemes are estimated on the basis of the operational reports of these schemes. Employers' contributions to others and payments in kind are estimated on the basis of settlements of accounts of the central government and local governments data on taxation, business and housing survey data on payments for housing.

The operating surplus is estimated through production approach (value-added method), and is distributed to each institutional sector according to the ratios of operating profits to the total by kind of income-earning subject (after inventory valuation adjustment). The ratios are estimated on the basis of statistical

Japan

data such as *Financial Statements of Corporations by Industry*. Consumption of fixed capital consists of loss from wear and tear (depreciation) and estimated damage from fire, typhoons, floods and other accidents. Depreciation is estimated on the basis of *Financial Statements of Corporations by Industry*, *Financial Statistics of Local Public Enterprises* and so on. Accidental damage is estimated making use of settlements of accounts of insurance companies and so on. Indirect taxes and subsidies are estimated on the basis of settlements of accounts of central and local governments.

Gross domestic product by kind of activity

The gross domestic product by kind of economic activity is prepared at market prices, i.e. producers' values. The output of each of the 82 industry groups is estimated from the "V" table (a make matrix for commodity by activity), of which the control total is given as the output of the 2200 commodities estimated by the commodity flow method. The intermediate input of each industry group is estimated from the "U" table (a use matrix for commodity by activity), in the base year which is compiled from *Input-output Table* and the "V" table, and from the "U" table in the mid-year which is separately compiled from the information of the cost structure estimated for about 4 or 15 items every year. The value added and its component items by industry are estimated by substracting the intermediate input from the output. The output, intermediate input, value added and its component items by the producers of government services and by the producers of private non-profit services to households are separately estimated using the settlement of accounts of government, survey of private non-profit institutions and so on.

Gross domestic product by industry at constant prices is estimated by the double deflation technique. The output by industry is estimated from the "V" table at constant prices which is obtained by dividing the output of each commodity by its output deflator. The intermediate input by industry is estimated from the "U" table at constant prices which is obtained by dividing the intermediate input of each commodity by its input deflator.

1.1 Expenditure on the gross domestic product, in current prices

Thousand million Japanese yen

	1986	1987	1988	1989	1990	1991	1992	1993	1994	1995	1996	1997
1 Government final consumption expenditure	32387	32975	34183	36275	38807	41356	43262	44771	45743	47419	48352	...
2 Private final consumption expenditure	196712	205956	217839	232890	249288	261891	272294	278703	286154	290524	299281	...
A Households	194051	203342	214992	229831	246154	258332	268676	274696	282354	286454	295020	...
B Private non-profit institutions serving households	2661	2614	2848	3059	3135	3559	3618	4007	3799	4069	4261	...
3 Gross capital formation	93059	99813	113532	125250	138897	147451	145014	141053	137341	138157	149549	...
A Increase in stocks	1560	661	2676	2976	2430	3453	1489	620	50	546	1227	...
B Gross fixed capital formation	91499	99152	110856	122274	136467	143998	143525	140433	137291	137611	148322	...
Residential buildings	16568	20301	22927	24045	26397	24985	24041	25175	27154	25631	29102	...
Non-residential buildings	16164	16367	18196	21996	25253	30045	31792	31617	29872	29488	28672	...
Other construction and land improvement, etc.	22698	24385	26698	27905	30565	32901	33990	34508	34350	33684	34802	...
Other	36069	38098	43035	48328	54251	56067	53703	49133	45915	48808	55746	...
4 Exports of goods and services	38090	36210	37483	42352	45920	46722	47341	44197	44410	45393	49700	...
5 less: Imports of goods and services	24791	25195	29065	36768	42872	39121	36891	33343	34387	38272	47022	...
equals: Gross domestic product	335457	349760	373973	399998	430040	458299	471021	475381	479260	483220	499861	...

1.2 Expenditure on the gross domestic product, in constant prices

Thousand million Japanese yen

	1986	1987	1988	1989	1990	1991	1992	1993	1994	1995	1996	1997
	At constant prices of: 1990											
1 Government final consumption expenditure	35962	36524	37375	38113	38681	39452	40224	41170	42154	43546	44214	...
2 Private final consumption expenditure	207669	216413	227860	238703	249139	255410	260708	263744	268801	274368	282355	...
A Households	204808	213617	224889	235627	246155	252093	257386	259995	265332	270631	278483	...
B Private non-profit institutions serving households	2861	2796	2971	3075	2984	3316	3322	3749	3469	3737	3872	...

Japan

Thousand million Japanese yen

	1986	1987	1988	1989	1990	1991	1992	1993	1994	1995	1996	1997
At constant prices of: 1990												
3 Gross capital formation	97173	105158	119234	129146	139120	144656	140465	137096	135259	138466	151846	...
A Increase in stocks	1467	706	2806	3141	2435	3493	1484	827	16	867	1109	...
B Gross fixed capital formation	95707	104453	116428	126006	136685	141163	138981	136269	135243	137600	150736	...
Residential buildings	18631	22495	24958	25393	26643	24521	23184	23860	25771	24275	27453	...
Non-residential buildings	18087	18230	19887	22900	25247	29009	30218	30060	28756	28303	27442	...
Other construction and land improvement, etc.	24012	25770	27658	28531	30557	31535	31916	32495	32461	31475	32457	...
Other	34976	37957	43924	49182	54238	56098	53663	49854	48255	53547	63385	...
4 Exports of goods and services	37434	37232	39441	43044	46012	48426	50816	51500	53865	56787	58772	...
5 less: Imports of goods and services	25358	27771	33584	39822	42966	41628	41337	41229	44880	51274	57173	...
equals: Gross domestic product	352880	367556	390325	409184	429985	446315	450876	452281	455197	461894	480013	...

1.3 Cost components of the gross domestic product

Thousand million Japanese yen

	1986	1987	1988	1989	1990	1991	1992	1993	1994	1995	1996	1997
1 Indirect taxes, net	21535	24961	27469	29053	30568	31116	33996	33728	34537	35690	37475	...
A Indirect taxes	25213	28379	30878	32158	35212	34968	37300	37199	38003	39348	41062	...
B less: Subsidies	3678	3419	3409	3104	4644	3852	3304	3471	3466	3658	3587	...
2 Consumption of fixed capital	46205	48930	52398	58080	62987	68541	72823	74383	75605	77153	79849	...
3 Compensation of employees paid by resident producers to	181278	187757	198284	212422	230313	248301	256885	262899	269534	273964	279433	...
A Resident households	181023	187476	198052	212148	230000	247951	256522	262580	269213	273574	278880	...
B Rest of the world	255	281	232	274	313	350	362	319	321	390	552	...
4 Operating surplus	86101	89142	96965	101293	105992	110744	107509	104012	99041	96790	104813	...
A Corporate and quasi-corporate enterprises	43550	44284	49653	51875	54573	56450	49510	47936	41093	41374	47822	...
B Private unincorporated enterprises	42551	44858	47312	49418	51419	54294	57999	56075	57949	55416	56991	...
C General government	...	...	...	...	...	...	...	...	...	...	...	...
Statistical discrepancy [a]	338	−1030	−1143	−851	179	−403	−192	360	543	−377	−1709	...
equals: Gross domestic product	335457	349760	373973	399998	430040	458299	471021	475381	479260	483220	499861	...

a Item "Other adjustments" refers to inventory valuation adjustment.

1.4 General government current receipts and disbursements

Thousand million Japanese yen

	1986	1987	1988	1989	1990	1991	1992	1993	1994	1995	1996	1997
Receipts												
1 Operating surplus	...	...	...	...	...	...	...	...	...	...	...	...
2 Property and entrepreneurial income	9344	10013	11109	11617	13188	15122	14588	14138	18084	15621	14879	...
3 Taxes, fees and contributions	93970	103111	110997	119870	132987	138965	140754	137237	134480	137975	142290	...
A Indirect taxes	25213	28379	30878	32158	35212	34968	37300	37199	38003	39348	41062	...
B Direct taxes	40639	44615	48329	53901	58367	62253	59519	54761	50363	48243	49526	...
C Social security contributions	27761	29694	31363	33387	38957	41264	43436	44753	45585	49840	51135	...
D Compulsory fees, fines and penalties	357	423	426	424	452	480	498	524	530	544	568	...
4 Other current transfers	543	603	665	749	846	939	1035	1042	1070	1085	1101	...
Total current receipts of general government	103857	113727	122770	132236	147021	155027	156377	152417	153634	154681	158269	...

Japan

Thousand million Japanese yen

	1986	1987	1988	1989	1990	1991	1992	1993	1994	1995	1996	1997
Disbursements												
1 Government final consumption expenditure	32387	32975	34183	36275	38807	41356	43262	44771	45743	47419	48352	...
A Compensation of employees	25355	26061	26952	28346	30136	31656	32995	33997	34696	35689	36518	...
B Consumption of fixed capital	2144	2245	2325	2458	2508	2525	2624	2767	2962	3111	3167	...
C Purchases of goods and services, net	4852	4633	4869	5428	6119	7132	7597	7959	8035	8562	8603	...
D less: Own-account fixed capital formation	...	...	...	...	...	...	...	...	...	...	...	...
E Indirect taxes paid, net	36	37	37	43	44	43	46	47	50	56	64	...
2 Property income	14912	15347	15671	16023	16820	17377	17733	17690	17971	18462	18742	...
A Interest	14797	15225	15537	15871	16645	17180	17512	17455	17719	18192	18465	...
B Net land rent and royalties	115	122	134	151	175	197	221	235	252	270	277	...
3 Subsidies	3678	3419	3409	3104	4644	3852	3304	3471	3466	3658	3587	...
4 Other current transfers	39164	42136	44090	45813	51063	52115	55937	59589	62927	68017	71127	...
A Social security benefits	31476	34235	35922	37389	42370	42954	46229	49433	52382	56875	59652	...
B Social assistance grants	6073	6185	6313	6377	6453	6633	6913	7157	7388	7727	7874	...
C Other	1615	1717	1855	2047	2240	2528	2794	2999	3157	3415	3602	...
5 Net saving	13716	19850	25418	31021	35688	40327	36141	26896	23528	17125	16461	...
Total current disbursements and net saving of general government	103857	113727	122770	132236	147021	155027	156377	152417	153634	154681	158269	...

1.5 Current income and outlay of corporate and quasi-corporate enterprises, summary

Thousand million Japanese yen

	1986	1987	1988	1989	1990	1991	1992	1993	1994	1995	1996	1997
Receipts												
1 Operating surplus	43550	44284	49653	51875	54573	56450	49510	47936	41093	41374	47822	...
2 Property and entrepreneurial income received	96865	102394	112521	132271	159635	169081	152588	137915	127341	122360	114852	...
3 Current transfers	4030	3832	3926	4052	4642	6046	6055	6435	6128	5895	5910	...
Total current receipts	144445	150510	166099	188197	218851	231577	208153	192287	174562	169629	168585	...
Disbursements												
1 Property and entrepreneurial income	110604	113890	123777	145962	176643	189466	168511	152833	141693	132625	121372	...
2 Direct taxes and other current payments to general government	17790	19690	22247	26168	25205	24802	22663	20028	17773	18154	20147	...
3 Other current transfers	5219	5129	5396	5606	6217	7876	7944	8433	8231	10788	13461	...
4 Net saving	10832	11801	14680	10461	10786	9433	9035	10991	6864	8062	13604	...
Total current disbursements and net saving	144445	150510	166099	188197	218851	231577	208153	192287	174561	169629	168585	...

1.6 Current income and outlay of households and non-profit institutions

Thousand million Japanese yen

	1986	1987	1988	1989	1990	1991	1992	1993	1994	1995	1996	1997
Receipts												
1 Compensation of employees	181325	187812	198364	212529	230447	248392	257139	263100	269653	274119	279414	...
A From resident producers	181023	187476	198052	212148	230000	247951	256522	262580	269213	273574	278880	...
B From rest of the world	303	336	312	381	447	441	616	520	441	545	534	...

Japan

Thousand million Japanese yen

	1986	1987	1988	1989	1990	1991	1992	1993	1994	1995	1996	1997
2 Operating surplus of private unincorporated enterprises	42551	44858	47312	49418	51419	54294	57999	56075	57949	55416	56991	...
3 Property and entrepreneurial income	34031	32834	32688	36682	43318	48109	44087	41832	35580	33223	29993	...
4 Current transfers	61362	65112	68937	70942	77951	81430	86491	89935	93912	102580	108031	...
A Social security benefits	31476	34235	35922	37389	42370	42954	46229	49433	52382	56875	59652	...
B Social assistance grants	7930	8228	8545	8677	8844	9146	9429	9602	9876	10232	10531	...
C Other	21957	22649	24470	24876	26737	29331	30833	30901	31655	35473	37848	...
Total current receipts	319270	330617	347302	369571	403134	432226	445716	450943	457094	465339	474428	...

Disbursements

	1986	1987	1988	1989	1990	1991	1992	1993	1994	1995	1996	1997
1 Private final consumption expenditure	196712	205956	217839	232890	249288	261891	272294	278703	286154	290523	299281	...
2 Property income	13542	14007	14648	15842	19880	22370	21006	19183	17519	16282	14134	...
3 Direct taxes and other current transfers n.e.c. to general government	50967	55042	57872	61544	72571	79195	80790	80009	78704	80473	81081	...
A Social security contributions	27761	29694	31363	33387	38957	41264	43436	44753	45585	49840	51135	...
B Direct taxes	22995	25098	26268	27925	33349	37633	37033	34909	32763	30279	29595	...
C Fees, fines and penalties	211	251	240	232	265	298	321	347	356	354	351	...
4 Other current transfers	21775	22652	24398	24657	26501	28796	30162	29953	30536	31443	31430	...
5 Net saving	36274	32959	32544	34637	34893	39973	41464	43095	44182	46617	48502	...
Total current disbursements and net saving	319270	330617	347301	369571	403134	432225	445716	450943	457095	465338	474428	...

1.7 External transactions on current account, summary

Thousand million Japanese yen

	1986	1987	1988	1989	1990	1991	1992	1993	1994	1995	1996	1997
Payments to the rest of the world												
1 Imports of goods and services	24791	25195	29065	36768	42872	39121	36891	33343	34387	38272	47022	...
A Imports of merchandise, c.i.f. [a]	19356	18708	21330	26905	31598	28542	26306	23682	24617	27915	34469	...
B Other	5435	6487	7735	9863	11274	10579	10585	9661	9770	10357	12552	...
2 Factor income to rest of the world	4108	5553	7822	11911	15588	16577	14784	13001	12823	15140	20218	...
A Compensation of employees	255	281	232	274	313	350	362	319	321	390	552	...
B Property and entrepreneurial income	3853	5273	7590	11637	15274	16227	14422	12681	12502	14750	19666	...
3 Current transfers to the rest of the world	292	463	497	475	491	563	674	738	771	875	1632	...
A Indirect taxes to supranational organizations	...	...	...	...	...	...	...	...	...	...	...	...
B Other current transfers	292	463	497	475	491	563	674	738	771	875	1632	...
4 Surplus of the nation on current transactions	14306	12697	10364	8100	5638	10419	14256	14672	13381	10425	7158	...
Payments to the rest of the world and surplus of the nation on current transfers	43497	43908	47748	57254	64589	66680	66605	61754	61362	64711	76030	...
Receipts from the rest of the world												
1 Exports of goods and services	38090	36210	37483	42352	45920	46722	47341	44197	44410	45393	49700	...
A Exports of merchandise, f.o.b.	34575	32490	33398	37372	40651	41465	42082	39164	39348	40260	43566	...
B Other	3515	3720	4085	4980	5269	5257	5259	5033	5061	5133	6134	...

Japan

Thousand million Japanese yen

	1986	1987	1988	1989	1990	1991	1992	1993	1994	1995	1996	1997
2 Factor income from rest of the world	5337	7607	10124	14761	18520	19767	19052	17381	16765	19131	25675	...
A Compensation of employees	303	336	312	381	447	441	616	520	441	545	534	...
B Property and entrepreneurial income	5035	7271	9812	14380	18073	19326	18436	16861	16324	18586	25141	...
3 Current transfers from rest of the world	70	92	141	142	149	191	212	175	187	187	655	...
A Subsidies from supranational organisations	...	...	...	...	...	...	...	...	...	...	...	...
B Other current transfers	70	92	141	142	149	191	212	175	187	187	655	...
Receipts from the rest of the world on current transactions	43497	43908	47748	57254	64589	66680	66605	61754	61362	64711	76030	...

a Imports of merchandise c.i.f. is not estimated in the Balance of Payments in Japan. Therefore, valuation basis is f.o.b.

1.8 Capital transactions of the nation, summary

Thousand million Japanese yen

	1986	1987	1988	1989	1990	1991	1992	1993	1994	1995	1996	1997
Finance of gross capital formation												
Gross saving	107027	113541	125040	134200	144355	158273	159463	155365	150179	148958	158416	...
1 Consumption of fixed capital	46205	48930	52398	58080	62987	68541	72823	74383	75605	77153	79849	...
A General government	2144	2245	2325	2458	2508	2525	2624	2767	2962	3111	3167	...
B Corporate and quasi-corporate enterprises	29490	31475	33966	38309	41923	46168	49317	49971	50484	51558	53788	...
Public	1982	1716	1683	1818	2039	2276	2468	2593	2768	3060	3373	...
Private	27507	29759	32284	36491	39885	43891	46849	47378	47716	48497	50415	...
C Other	14571	15211	16106	17314	18556	19848	20882	21645	22159	22485	22894	...
2 Net saving	60822	64610	72642	76120	81368	89732	86640	80982	74574	71805	78567	...
A General government	13716	19850	25418	31021	35688	40327	36141	26896	23528	17125	16461	...
B Corporate and quasi-corporate enterprises	10832	11801	14680	10461	10786	9433	9035	10991	6864	8062	13604	...
Public	12742	12658	14704	7453	6776	1160	−42	976	−2412	1311	1454	...
Private	−1910	−857	−24	3009	4010	8273	9076	10015	9276	6752	12151	...
C Other	36274	32959	32544	34637	34893	39973	41464	43095	44182	46617	48502	...
less: Surplus of the nation on current transactions	14306	12697	10364	8100	5638	10419	14256	14672	13381	10425	7158	...
Statistical discrepancy	338	−1030	−1143	−851	179	−403	−192	360	543	−377	−1710	...
Finance of gross capital formation	93059	99813	113533	125250	138896	147451	145014	141053	137341	138157	149549	...
Gross capital formation												
Increase in stocks	1560	661	2676	2976	2430	3453	1489	620	50	546	1227	...
Gross fixed capital formation	91499	99152	110856	122274	136467	143998	143525	140433	137291	137611	148322	...
1 General government	16048	17536	18860	19808	21614	23229	26474	30777	31335	30875	33174	...
2 Corporate and quasi-corporate enterprises	51694	54226	61660	70733	81463	87831	83729	76401	71858	74071	79468	...
A Public	6223	6194	6187	6074	6556	7228	8868	9917	9996	10468	10607	...
B Private	45471	48033	55473	64659	74907	80604	74861	66484	61862	63603	68861	...
3 Other	23757	27389	30336	31733	33389	32937	33322	33255	34098	32665	35680	...
Gross capital formation	93059	99813	113532	125250	138897	147451	145014	141053	137341	138157	149549	...

Japan

1.9 Gross domestic product by institutional sectors of origin

Thousand million Japanese yen

	1986	1987	1988	1989	1990	1991	1992	1993	1994	1995	1996	1997
Domestic factor incomes originating												
1 General government	25355	26061	26952	28346	30136	31656	32995	33997	34696	35689	36518	...
2 Corporate and quasi-corporate enterprises	236136	244742	261675	278327	298715	319476	323119	324163	324813	325522	337759	...
3 Households and private unincorporated enterprises												...
4 Non-profit institutions serving households	5889	6096	6622	7043	7454	7913	8279	8750	9066	9543	9969	...
subtotal: Domestic factor incomes	267379	276899	295249	313715	336305	359045	364394	366911	368575	370754	384246	...
Indirect taxes, net	21535	24961	27469	29053	30568	31116	33996	33728	34537	35690	37475	...
A Indirect taxes	25213	28379	30878	32158	35212	34968	37300	37199	38003	39348	41062	...
B less: Subsidies	3678	3419	3409	3104	4644	3852	3304	3471	3466	3658	3587	...
Consumption of fixed capital	46205	48930	52398	58080	62987	68541	72823	74383	75605	77153	79849	...
Statistical discrepancy	338	−1030	−1143	−851	179	−403	−192	360	543	−377	−1709	...
Gross domestic product	335457	349760	373973	399998	430040	458299	471021	475381	479260	483220	499861	...

1.10 Gross domestic product by kind of activity, in current prices

Thousand million Japanese yen

	1986	1987	1988	1989	1990	1991	1992	1993	1994	1995	1996	1997
1 Agriculture, hunting, forestry and fishing	10048	9915	9974	10426	10920	10845	10620	9787	10242	9351	9308	...
2 Mining and quarrying	960	913	964	928	1122	1144	1152	1087	1033	1071	1073	...
3 Manufacturing	95817	98407	105315	112676	121219	128789	127643	121428	117253	119261	121554	...
4 Electricity, gas and water	11283	11238	11239	11082	11242	12070	12535	12821	13424	13733	14130	...
5 Construction	27146	30649	34789	39025	43428	46866	48809	51115	51665	50332	52768	...
6 Wholesale and retail trade, restaurants and hotels [a]	44338	47083	50324	53463	58358	62979	63467	61350	60862	60985	60691	...
7 Transport, storage and communication	22185	23421	25045	27400	28475	29988	30235	30214	30468	31354	33289	...
8 Finance, insurance, real estate and business services	53005	58086	63353	69252	72338	75676	78820	81349	85705	86622	89696	...
9 Community, social and personal services [a]	49050	50406	52780	57612	63624	69493	75269	79192	80373	82333	87233	...
Total, Industries	313833	330117	353784	381863	410725	437850	448550	448343	451025	455041	469741	...
Producers of government services	27535	28342	29314	30847	32688	34224	35665	36812	37708	38856	39749	...
Other producers	6675	6970	7530	8023	8524	9017	9483	10001	10430	10907	11377	...
Subtotal	348042	365430	390627	420733	451938	481090	493698	495156	499163	504804	520867	...
less: Imputed bank service charge	13969	15806	16728	20677	22606	22955	23332	20819	21372	22263	20413	...
plus: Import duties	1046	1166	1217	2252	2733	2874	2894	2549	2676	2861	3163	...
plus: Value added tax	...	...	...	−1458	−2204	−2308	−2047	−1864	−1749	−1806	−2047	...
plus: Other adjustments [b]	338	−1030	−1143	−851	179	−403	−192	360	543	−377	−1709	...
equals: Gross domestic product	335457	349760	373973	399998	430040	458299	471021	475381	479260	483220	499861	...

a Restaurants and hotels are included in item "Community, social and personal services".   b Item "Other adjustments" refers to inventory valuation adjustment.

Japan

1.11 Gross domestic product by kind of activity, in constant prices

Thousand million Japanese yen

	1986	1987	1988	1989	1990	1991	1992	1993	1994	1995	1996	1997
At constant prices of: 1990												
1 Agriculture, hunting, forestry and fishing	10438	10799	10502	10865	10920	10060	10678	9390	10162	9653	9840	...
2 Mining and quarrying	1049	972	976	910	1122	1092	1072	1024	872	861	919	...
3 Manufacturing	94230	98613	106506	113490	121219	127598	125822	120841	119986	126554	129840	...
4 Electricity, gas and water	9299	9466	9976	10444	11242	12003	12081	12044	12412	12649	13888	...
5 Construction	30928	34352	37909	40587	43428	45044	45404	46757	46719	44781	46656	...
6 Wholesale and retail trade, restaurants and hotels	43970	47548	51099	53809	58358	61940	62688	61243	61098	62643	62951	...
7 Transport, storage and communication	22949	23822	25379	27690	28475	29309	29138	29233	29577	29871	32092	...
8 Finance, insurance, real estate and business services	57742	62231	66823	71063	72338	74053	75591	76404	79118	79548	81258	...
9 Community, social and personal services	55387	55245	56599	59376	63624	67240	70499	72902	73529	75589	80585	...
Total, Industries	325992	343048	365770	388233	410725	428340	432973	429839	433472	442148	458028	...
Producers of government services	31497	31983	32319	32599	32688	32378	32677	33162	33800	34460	35109	...
Other producers	7520	7751	8141	8390	8524	8717	9067	9513	9732	10116	10436	...
Subtotal	365010	382782	406230	429222	451938	469435	474717	472514	477004	486724	503574	...
less: Imputed bank service charge	14094	16350	17356	21045	22606	22965	23583	21481	22420	23642	21609	...
plus: Import duties	1120	1331	1478	2535	2733	3140	3349	3290	3708	3999	3926	...
plus: Value added tax	−1445	−1533	−1778	−2000	−2204	−2331	−2175	−2009	−1942	−2044	−2256	...
plus: Other adjustments	2290	1326	1751	473	125	−964	−1433	−32	−1153	−3143	−3621	...
equals: Gross domestic product	352880	367556	390325	409184	429985	446315	450876	452282	455197	461894	480013	...

1.12 Relations among national accounting aggregates

Thousand million Japanese yen

	1986	1987	1988	1989	1990	1991	1992	1993	1994	1995	1996	1997
Gross domestic product	335457	349760	373973	399998	430040	458299	471021	475381	479260	483220	499861	...
plus: Net factor income from the rest of the world	1229	2054	2302	2849	2932	3190	4268	4381	3941	3991	5457	...
Factor income from rest of the world	5337	7607	10124	14761	18520	19767	19052	17381	16765	19131	25675	...
less: Factor income to the rest of the world	4108	5553	7822	11911	15588	16577	14784	13001	12823	15140	20218	...
equals: Gross national product	336686	351814	376275	402848	432972	461489	475288	479762	483202	487212	505318	...
less: Consumption of fixed capital	46205	48930	52398	58080	62987	68541	72823	74383	75605	77153	79849	...
equals: National income [a]	290143	303913	325021	345618	369805	393351	402658	405019	407053	410435	427178	...
plus: Net current transfers from the rest of the world	−222	−372	−356	−333	−343	−372	−461	−563	−583	−688	−977	...
Current transfers from rest of the world	70	92	141	142	149	191	212	175	187	187	655	...
less: Current transfers to the rest of the world	292	463	497	475	491	563	674	738	771	875	1632	...
equals: National disposable income	289921	303542	324664	345285	369463	392979	402196	404457	406470	409747	426201	...
less: Final consumption	229099	238932	252023	269165	288095	303247	315557	323474	331896	337942	347634	...
equals: Net saving	60822	64610	72642	76120	81368	89732	86640	80982	74574	71805	78567	...
less: Surplus of the nation on current transactions	14306	12697	10364	8100	5638	10419	14256	14672	13381	10425	7158	...

Japan

Thousand million Japanese yen

	1986	1987	1988	1989	1990	1991	1992	1993	1994	1995	1996	1997
Statistical discrepancy	338	−1030	−1143	−851	179	−403	−192	360	543	−377	−1710	...
equals: Net capital formation	46854	50883	61135	67169	75910	78910	72191	66670	61735	61004	69700	...

a Item "National income" includes a statistical discrepancy.

2.3 Total government outlays by function and type

Thousand million Japanese yen *Fiscal year beginning 1 April*

1986

	Total (Final consumption)	Compensation of employees	Other	Subsidies	Other current transfers and property income	Total current disbursements	Gross capital formation	Other capital outlays	Total outlays
1 General public services	8859	6761	2098	63	...	...	910	...	...
2 Defence	3094	1551	1543	−	...	...	−	...	...
3 Public order and safety	...	...	...	...	...	...	...	...	...
4 Education	11656	9612	2043	11	...	...	1156	...	...
5 Health	1230	2287	−1057	167	...	...	365	...	...
6 Social security and welfare	1819	1597	221	101	...	...	245	...	...
7 Housing and community amenities	1857	1106	752	631	...	...	3373	...	...
8 Recreational, cultural and religious affairs	758	380	378	16	...	...	515	...	...
9 Economic services	3162	2100	1062	2481	...	...	9674	...	...
10 Other functions	125	102	22	−	...	...	14	...	...
Total	32559	25497	7063	3470	55550	91580	16253	2780	110612

1987

	Total	Compensation of employees	Other	Subsidies	Other current transfers and property income	Total current disbursements	Gross capital formation	Other capital outlays	Total outlays
1 General public services	8933	7013	1920	67	...	...	1287	...	...
2 Defence	3219	1576	1643	−	...	...	−	...	...
3 Public order and safety	...	...	...	...	...	...	...	...	...
4 Education	11961	9841	2120	13	...	...	1159	...	...
5 Health	1267	2374	−1107	172	...	...	435	...	...
6 Social security and welfare	1888	1650	238	140	...	...	275	...	...
7 Housing and community amenities	1936	1170	766	658	...	...	3834	...	...
8 Recreational, cultural and religious affairs	800	397	403	18	...	...	566	...	...
9 Economic services	3116	2101	1015	2406	...	...	10884	...	...
10 Other functions	121	99	22	6	...	...	10	...	...
Total	33241	26220	7021	3481	58097	94818	18451	3382	116651

1988

	Total	Compensation of employees	Other	Subsidies	Other current transfers and property income	Total current disbursements	Gross capital formation	Other capital outlays	Total outlays
1 General public services	9108	7295	1813	129	...	...	1339	...	...
2 Defence	3415	1642	1773	−	...	...	−	...	...
3 Public order and safety	...	...	...	...	...	...	...	...	...
4 Education	12417	10230	2187	14	...	...	1059	...	...
5 Health	1362	2491	−1130	185	...	...	419	...	...

Japan

| | 1988 ||||||||
| | Final consumption expenditures ||| Subsidies | Other current transfers and property income | Total current disburse-ments | Gross capital formation | Other capital outlays | Total outlays |
	Total	Compensation of employees	Other						
6 Social security and welfare	1931	1725	206	260	...	...	284	...	...
7 Housing and community amenities	2036	1169	867	645	...	...	4325	...	...
8 Recreational, cultural and religious affairs	860	416	444	17	...	...	597	...	...
9 Economic services	3228	2167	1062	2140	...	...	10592	...	...
10 Other functions	208	72	136	3	...	...	86	...	...
Total	34565	27208	7357	3392	60323	98280	18701	3973	120955

| | 1989 ||||||||
| | Final consumption expenditures ||| Subsidies | Other current transfers and property income | Total current disburse-ments | Gross capital formation | Other capital outlays | Total outlays |
	Total	Compensation of employees	Other						
1 General public services	9793	7720	2073	131	...	...	1268	...	...
2 Defence	3643	1678	1965	–	...	...	–	...	...
3 Public order and safety	...	...	...	...	...	...	...	...	...
4 Education	12922	10609	2313	16	...	...	1334	...	...
5 Health	1513	2648	–1135	190	...	...	407	...	...
6 Social security and welfare	2155	1873	282	327	...	...	339	...	...
7 Housing and community amenities	2225	1236	989	1249	...	...	4647	...	...
8 Recreational, cultural and religious affairs	934	446	489	25	...	...	747	...	...
9 Economic services	3375	2216	1160	2841	...	...	11392	...	...
10 Other functions	174	77	98	–	...	...	93	...	...
Total	36734	28501	8233	4779	63318	104831	20226	3918	128975

| | 1990 ||||||||
| | Final consumption expenditures ||| Subsidies | Other current transfers and property income | Total current disburse-ments | Gross capital formation | Other capital outlays | Total outlays |
	Total	Compensation of employees	Other						
1 General public services	10614	8281	2333	120	...	...	1773	...	...
2 Defence	3944	1781	2164	–	...	...	–	...	...
3 Public order and safety	...	...	...	...	...	...	...	...	...
4 Education	13693	11323	2371	17	...	...	1308	...	...
5 Health	1691	2858	–1167	217	...	...	516	...	...
6 Social security and welfare	2338	2015	323	212	...	...	423	...	...
7 Housing and community amenities	2431	1328	1103	661	...	...	4819	...	...
8 Recreational, cultural and religious affairs	1023	488	534	20	...	...	1004	...	...
9 Economic services	3592	2358	1234	2154	...	...	11947	...	...
10 Other functions	194	80	114	–	...	...	124	...	...
Total	39520	30511	9009	3401	66701	109622	21914	4630	136166

Japan

1991

	Final consumption expenditures – Total	Compensation of employees	Other	Subsidies	Other current transfers and property income	Total current disbursements	Gross capital formation	Other capital outlays	Total outlays
1 General public services	11378	8698	2681	131	...	...	1715	...	...
2 Defence	4106	1836	2270	–	...	...	–	...	...
3 Public order and safety	...	...	...	...	...	...	...	...	...
4 Education	14207	11788	2419	19	...	...	1945	...	...
5 Health	1874	3047	–1173	239	...	...	591	...	...
6 Social security and welfare	2498	2137	362	146	...	...	495	...	...
7 Housing and community amenities	2663	1409	1254	687	...	...	5410	...	...
8 Recreational, cultural and religious affairs	1110	527	583	26	...	...	1058	...	...
9 Economic services	3748	2449	1300	2039	...	...	12559	...	...
10 Other functions	210	86	125	–	...	...	137	...	...
Total	41795	31976	9819	3287	70491	115573	23910	5212	144695

1992

	Final consumption expenditures – Total	Compensation of employees	Other	Subsidies	Other current transfers and property income	Total current disbursements	Gross capital formation	Other capital outlays	Total outlays
1 General public services	11856	9018	2838	119	...	...	2136	...	...
2 Defence	4238	1929	2309	–	...	...	–	...	...
3 Public order and safety	...	...	...	...	...	...	...	...	...
4 Education	14695	12108	2587	21	...	...	2217	...	...
5 Health	2007	3227	–1220	255	...	...	716	...	...
6 Social security and welfare	2671	2257	414	129	...	...	626	...	...
7 Housing and community amenities	2858	1469	1389	727	...	...	6627	...	...
8 Recreational, cultural and religious affairs	1202	563	639	30	...	...	1244	...	...
9 Economic services	3947	2577	1371	2036	...	...	14326	...	...
10 Other functions	217	89	128	–	...	...	141	...	...
Total	43691	33235	10455	3317	74301	121309	28033	6077	155419

1993

	Final consumption expenditures – Total	Compensation of employees	Other	Subsidies	Other current transfers and property income	Total current disbursements	Gross capital formation	Other capital outlays	Total outlays
1 General public services	12302	9352	2950	119	...	...	2168	...	...
2 Defence	4225	1956	2270	–	...	...	–	...	...
3 Public order and safety	...	...	...	...	...	...	...	...	...
4 Education	14900	12237	2663	22	...	...	2334	...	...
5 Health	2126	3348	–1222	274	...	...	937	...	...
6 Social security and welfare	2859	2353	505	158	...	...	729	...	...
7 Housing and community amenities	3041	1523	1519	766	...	...	7676	...	...
8 Recreational, cultural and religious affairs	1298	596	702	33	...	...	1331	...	...
9 Economic services	4060	2609	1450	2044	...	...	15828	...	...
10 Other functions	228	90	138	–	...	...	156	...	...
Total	45039	34064	10975	3416	77897	126352	31158	6362	163872

Japan

1994

	Total	Compensation of employees	Other	Subsidies	Other current transfers and property income	Total current disbursements	Gross capital formation	Other capital outlays	Total outlays
1 General public services	12535	9646	2889	128	...	...	1988	...	...
2 Defence	4244	1999	2244	–	...	...	–	...	...
3 Public order and safety	...	...	...	...	...	...	...	...	...
4 Education	15248	12492	2756	22	...	...	2108	...	...
5 Health	2134	3456	–1322	291	...	...	879	...	...
6 Social security and welfare	3010	2422	588	220	...	...	619	...	...
7 Housing and community amenities	3235	1565	1670	738	...	...	7646	...	...
8 Recreational, cultural and religious affairs	1371	622	749	41	...	...	1286	...	...
9 Economic services	4158	2666	1492	2041	...	...	15817	...	...
10 Other functions	262	101	161	–	...	...	158	...	...
Total	46197	34969	11228	3482	82399	132078	30501	5465	168043

1995

	Total	Compensation of employees	Other	Subsidies	Other current transfers and property income	Total current disbursements	Gross capital formation	Other capital outlays	Total outlays
1 General public services	13097	9930	3167	142	...	...	2239	...	...
2 Defence	4312	2073	2239	–	...	...	–	...	...
3 Public order and safety	...	...	...	...	...	...	...	...	...
4 Education	15533	12745	2788	23	...	...	2064	...	...
5 Health	2176	3599	–1423	302	...	...	893	...	...
6 Social security and welfare	3145	2489	656	326	...	...	639	...	...
7 Housing and community amenities	3234	1588	1645	753	...	...	7883	...	...
8 Recreational, cultural and religious affairs	1425	643	783	36	...	...	1246	...	...
9 Economic services	4281	2690	1590	2175	...	...	17303	...	...
10 Other functions	470	104	366	–	...	...	251	...	...
Total	47673	35861	11812	3757	87236	138667	32517	6008	177192

1996

	Total	Compensation of employees	Other	Subsidies	Other current transfers and property income	Total current disbursements	Gross capital formation	Other capital outlays	Total outlays
1 General public services	13223	10167	3056	125	...	...	1955	...	...
2 Defence	4398	2093	2305	–	...	...	–	...	...
3 Public order and safety	...	...	...	...	...	...	...	...	...
4 Education	15822	13011	2810	23	...	...	1891	...	...
5 Health	2129	3701	–1572	302	...	...	939	...	...
6 Social security and welfare	3287	2548	739	219	...	...	600	...	...
7 Housing and community amenities	3281	1621	1660	818	...	...	7964	...	...
8 Recreational, cultural and religious affairs	1487	660	827	29	...	...	1163	...	...
9 Economic services	4367	2766	1601	2219	...	...	16655	...	...
10 Other functions	501	105	395	–	...	...	238	...	...
Total	48494	36674	11820	3734	90828	143056	31404	5185	179645

Japan

2.5 Private final consumption expenditure by type and purpose, in current prices

Thousand million Japanese yen

	1986	1987	1988	1989	1990	1991	1992	1993	1994	1995	1996	1997
Final consumption expenditure of resident households												
1 Food, beverages and tobacco	41723	41856	42588	43844	46328	48484	49429	49482	49763	49005	47503	...
2 Clothing and footwear	13196	13970	14522	15469	16392	17279	16895	16266	15162	15160	15236	...
3 Gross rent, fuel and power	36126	37951	40109	43273	46886	50600	54316	57624	61303	64718	67875	...
4 Furniture, furnishings and household equipment and operation	11440	11847	12369	12642	13679	14510	14685	14647	14789	14868	14529	...
5 Medical care and health expenses	20249	21074	21759	22433	23395	24566	26066	27435	28981	30550	31507	...
6 Transport and communication	19316	20822	23318	26337	28881	30058	30533	31129	31677	31920	33833	...
7 Recreational, entertainment, education and cultural services	20395	22240	24491	27285	30694	32461	34103	35346	35996	36349	37272	...
8 Miscellaneous goods and services	30625	32313	33785	35839	36781	37573	39674	40146	41867	40675	43620	...
Total final consumption expenditure in the domestic market by households, of which	193070	202073	212940	227122	243036	255532	265702	272075	279539	283245	291375	...
A Durable goods	12755	14532	17203	19336	21873	22985	22469	22394	22280	23098	23157	...
B Semi-durable goods	23482	24361	25362	27130	29342	30789	30971	30462	29118	28769	28831	...
C Non-durable goods	57791	57653	58385	60144	63649	66433	68279	69050	70062	69753	69402	...
D Services	99041	105526	111991	120513	128171	135324	143983	150170	158079	161626	169985	...
plus: Direct purchases abroad by resident households	1247	1591	2439	3158	3651	3274	3443	3028	3183	3524	4098	...
less: Direct purchases in the domestic market by non-resident households	266	322	387	450	533	475	468	407	367	314	453	...
equals: Final consumption expenditure of resident households	194051	203342	214992	229831	246154	258332	268676	274696	282354	286454	295020	...
Final consumption expenditures by private non-profit organisations serving households												
1 Research and science	...	...	...	...	...	...	...	...	...	...	...	...
2 Education	...	...	...	...	...	...	...	...	...	...	...	...
3 Medical and other health services	...	...	...	...	...	...	...	...	...	...	...	...
4 Welfare services	...	...	...	...	...	...	...	...	...	...	...	...
5 Recreational and related cultural services	...	...	...	...	...	...	...	...	...	...	...	...
6 Religious organisations	...	...	...	...	...	...	...	...	...	...	...	...
7 Professional and labour organisations serving households	...	...	...	...	...	...	...	...	...	...	...	...
8 Miscellaneous	...	...	...	...	...	...	...	...	...	...	...	...
equals: Final consumption expenditures by private non-profit organisations serving households	2661	2614	2848	3059	3135	3559	3618	4007	3799	4069	4261	...
Private final consumption expenditure	196712	205956	217839	232890	249288	261891	272294	278703	286154	290523	299281	...

Japan

2.6 Private final consumption expenditure by type and purpose, in constant prices

Thousand million Japanese yen

	1986	1987	1988	1989	1990	1991	1992	1993	1994	1995	1996	1997
At constant prices of: 1990												
Final consumption expenditure of resident households												
1 Food, beverages and tobacco	43672	44152	44725	45337	46328	46491	47141	46708	46637	46704	45293	...
2 Clothing and footwear	14700	15358	15814	16181	16392	16543	15709	15137	14296	14373	14325	...
3 Gross rent, fuel and power	38977	40433	42108	44435	46886	49297	51699	53670	56045	58178	60353	...
4 Furniture, furnishings and household equipment and operation	11408	11840	12374	12597	13679	14386	14458	14550	15034	15728	15730	...
5 Medical care and health expenses	21312	21706	22353	22785	23395	24428	24846	25677	26703	27911	28517	...
6 Transport and communication	19637	21099	23690	26508	28881	29619	29963	30388	31039	31448	33840	...
7 Recreational, entertainment, education and cultural services	21357	23252	25627	28037	30694	31882	32645	33373	33989	35095	37266	...
8 Miscellaneous goods and services	32702	34222	35489	36674	36781	36604	37842	37484	38223	37220	39456	...
Total final consumption expenditure in the domestic market by households, of which	203764	212062	222180	232552	243036	249248	254304	256988	261966	266657	274779	...
A Durable goods	11352	13319	16315	19119	21873	23124	22736	23033	23733	26072	27422	...
B Semi-durable goods	25325	26084	26905	27959	29342	29810	29345	28704	27670	27723	28132	...
C Non-durable goods	59610	60351	61207	61998	63649	64164	65577	65863	66637	67454	67739	...
D Services	107478	112308	117754	123476	128171	132150	136645	139387	143926	145408	151486	...
plus: Direct purchases abroad by resident households	1325	1897	3116	3538	3652	3304	3528	3391	3710	4269	4129	...
less: Direct purchases in the domestic market by non-resident households	281	341	408	463	533	459	446	384	344	296	425	...
equals: Final consumption expenditure of resident households	204808	213617	224889	235627	246155	252093	257386	259995	265332	270631	278483	...
Final consumption expenditures by private non-profit organisations serving households												
1 Research and science	...	...	...	...	...	...	...	...	...	...	...	...
2 Education	...	...	...	...	...	...	...	...	...	...	...	...
3 Medical and other health services	...	...	...	...	...	...	...	...	...	...	...	...
4 Welfare services	...	...	...	...	...	...	...	...	...	...	...	...
5 Recreational and related cultural services	...	...	...	...	...	...	...	...	...	...	...	...
6 Religious organisations	...	...	...	...	...	...	...	...	...	...	...	...
7 Professional and labour organisations serving households	...	...	...	...	...	...	...	...	...	...	...	...
8 Miscellaneous	...	...	...	...	...	...	...	...	...	...	...	...
equals: Final consumption expenditures by private non-profit organisations serving households	2861	2796	2971	3075	2984	3316	3322	3749	3469	3737	3872	...
Private final consumption expenditure	207669	216413	227860	238703	249139	255410	260708	263744	268801	274368	282355	...

2.7 Gross capital formation by type of good and owner, in current price

Thousand million Japanese yen

	1986				1987				1988			
	Total	Total private	Public enter-prises	General govern-ment	Total	Total private	Public enter-prises	General govern-ment	Total	Total private	Public enter-prises	General govern-ment
Increase in stocks, total	1560	1122	438	–	661	673	–12	–	2676	3052	–376	–
1 Goods producing industries	–352	...	...	...	145	...	...	...	1188	...	...	...
A Materials and supplies	88	...	...	...	92	...	...	...	222	...	...	...
B Work in progress	–358	...	...	...	58	...	...	...	681	...	...	...
C Livestock, except breeding stocks, dairy cattle, etc.	...	...	...	...	...	...	...	...	...	...	...	...
D Finished goods	–82	...	...	...	–5	...	...	...	285	...	...	...
2 Wholesale and retail trade	1912	...	...	...	516	...	...	...	1488	...	...	...
3 Other, except government stocks	...	...	...	...	...	...	...	...	...	...	...	...
4 Government stocks	...	...	...	...	...	...	...	...	...	...	...	...
Gross fixed capital formation, total	91499	69229	6223	16048	99152	75422	6194	17536	110856	85810	6187	18860
1 Residential buildings	16568	15703	865	...	20301	19513	788	...	22927	22126	801	...
2 Non-residential buildings	16164	...	...	...	16367	...	...	...	18196	...	...	...
3 Other construction	18456	...	...	...	20009	...	...	...	22131	...	...	...
4 Land improvement and plantation and orchard development	4242	...	...	...	4376	...	...	...	4568	...	...	...
5 Producers' durable goods	36069	...	...	...	38098	...	...	...	43035	...	...	...
A Transport equipment	6987	...	...	...	7843	...	...	...	8173	...	...	...
B Machinery and equipment	29083	...	...	...	30255	...	...	...	34862	...	...	...
6 Breeding stock, dairy cattle, etc.	...	...	...	...	...	...	...	...	...	...	...	...
Total gross capital formation	93059	70350	6661	16048	99813	76095	6182	17536	113532	88862	5810	18860

	1989				1990				1991			
	Total	Total private	Public enter-prises	General govern-ment	Total	Total private	Public enter-prises	General govern-ment	Total	Total private	Public enter-prises	General govern-ment
Increase in stocks, total	2976	3244	–268	–	2430	2345	85	–	3453	3646	–193	–
1 Goods producing industries	1618	...	...	...	2194	...	...	...	2391	...	...	...
A Materials and supplies	272	...	...	...	226	...	...	...	139	...	...	...
B Work in progress	617	...	...	...	1497	...	...	...	1047	...	...	...
C Livestock, except breeding stocks, dairy cattle, etc.	...	...	...	...	...	...	...	...	...	...	...	...
D Finished goods	729	...	...	...	471	...	...	...	1205	...	...	...
2 Wholesale and retail trade	1456	...	...	...	289	...	...	...	1143	...	...	...
3 Other, except government stocks	...	...	...	...	...	...	...	...	...	...	...	...
4 Government stocks	...	...	...	...	...	...	...	...	...	...	...	...
Statistical discrepancy	–97	...	...	...	–53	...	...	...	–80	...	...	...
Gross fixed capital formation, total	122274	96392	6074	19808	136467	108297	6556	21614	143998	113541	7228	23229
1 Residential buildings	23912	23083	829	...	26146	25218	929	...	24850	23827	1023	...
2 Non-residential buildings	21996	...	...	...	25253	...	...	...	30045	...	...	...
3 Other construction	24460	...	...	...	27617	...	...	...	29662	...	...	...
4 Land improvement and plantation and orchard development	4806	...	...	...	5098	...	...	...	5466	...	...	...
5 Producers' durable goods	48328	...	...	...	54251	...	...	...	56067	...	...	...
A Transport equipment	9000	...	...	...	9687	...	...	...	9953	...	...	...

Japan

	1989				1990				1991			
	Total	Total private	Public enterprises	General government	Total	Total private	Public enterprises	General government	Total	Total private	Public enterprises	General government
B Machinery and equipment ..	39327	...	...	...	44564	...	...	...	46115	...	...	...
6 Breeding stock, dairy cattle, etc.	...	...	...	...	...	...	...	...	...	...	...	...
Statistical discrepancy	−1228	...	...	...	−1900	...	...	...	−2092	...	...	...
Total gross capital formation	125250	99636	5806	19808	138897	110641	6642	21614	147451	117187	7035	23229

	1992				1993				1994			
	Total	Total private	Public enterprises	General government	Total	Total private	Public enterprises	General government	Total	Total private	Public enterprises	General government
Increase in stocks, total	1489	1546	−57	—	620	805	−185	—	50	−154	204	—
1 Goods producing industries	981	...	...	...	164	...	...	...	−640	...	...	...
A Materials and supplies	14	...	...	...	82	...	...	...	26	...	...	...
B Work in progress	374	...	...	...	149	...	...	...	−230	...	...	...
C Livestock, except breeding stocks, dairy cattle, etc.	...	...	...	...	...	...	...	...	...	...	...	...
D Finished goods	593	...	...	...	−67	...	...	...	−435	...	...	...
2 Wholesale and retail trade	542	...	...	...	471	...	...	...	690	...	...	...
3 Other, except government stocks	...	...	...	...	...	...	...	...	...	...	...	...
4 Government stocks	...	...	...	...	...	...	...	...	...	...	...	...
Statistical discrepancy	−34	...	...	...	−15	...	...	...	—	...	...	...
Gross fixed capital formation, total	143525	108183	8868	26474	140433	99738	9917	30777	137291	95960	9996	31335
1 Residential buildings	24040	22803	1236	...	25173	23765	1408	...	27153	25747	1406	...
2 Non-residential buildings	31792	...	...	...	31617	...	...	...	29872	...	...	...
3 Other construction	30400	...	...	...	30686	...	...	...	30467	...	...	...
4 Land improvement and plantation and orchard development	5603	...	...	...	5672	...	...	...	5631	...	...	...
5 Producers' durable goods	53703	...	...	...	49133	...	...	...	45915	...	...	...
A Transport equipment	9548	...	...	...	8771	...	...	...	8285	...	...	...
B Machinery and equipment ..	44155	...	...	...	40363	...	...	...	37631	...	...	...
6 Breeding stock, dairy cattle, etc.	...	...	...	...	...	...	...	...	...	...	...	...
Statistical discrepancy	−2013	...	...	...	−1848	...	...	...	−1748	...	...	...
Total gross capital formation	145014	109729	8811	26474	141053	100543	9733	30777	137341	95806	10200	31335

	1995				1996				1997			
	Total	Total private	Public enterprises	General government	Total	Total private	Public enterprises	General government	Total	Total private	Public enterprises	General government
Increase in stocks, total	546	434	112	—	1227	1032	195	—	...	...	...	...
1 Goods producing industries	1402	...	...	...	693	...	...	...	...	...	...	...
A Materials and supplies	182	...	...	...	59	...	...	...	...	...	...	...
B Work in progress	753	...	...	...	513	...	...	...	...	...	...	...
C Livestock, except breeding stocks, dairy cattle, etc.	...	...	...	...	...	...	...	...	...	...	...	...
D Finished goods	468	...	...	...	121	...	...	...	...	...	...	...
2 Wholesale and retail trade	−846	...	...	...	569	...	...	...	...	...	...	...
3 Other, except government stocks	...	...	...	...	...	...	...	...	...	...	...	...
4 Government stocks	...	...	...	...	...	...	...	...	...	...	...	...
Statistical discrepancy	−10	...	...	...	−35	...	...	...	...	...	...	...
Gross fixed capital formation, total	137611	96269	10468	30875	148322	104541	10607	33174	...	...	...	...
1 Residential buildings	25635	24126	1509	...	29101	27581	1520	...	...	...	...	...
2 Non-residential buildings	29488	...	...	...	28672	...	...	...	...	...	...	...

Japan

	1995				1996				1997			
	Total	Total private	Public enterprises	General government	Total	Total private	Public enterprises	General government	Total	Total private	Public enterprises	General government
3 Other construction	29962	...	...	...	31093	...	...	...	...	...	...	...
4 Land improvement and plantation and orchard development	5518	...	...	...	5722	...	...	...	...	...	...	...
5 Producers' durable goods	48808	...	...	...	55746	...	...	...	...	...	...	...
A Transport equipment	8787	...	...	...	8922	...	...	...	...	...	...	...
B Machinery and equipment	40021	...	...	...	46823	...	...	...	...	...	...	...
6 Breeding stock, dairy cattle, etc.	...	...	...	...	...	...	...	...	...	...	...	...
Statistical discrepancy	−1799	...	...	...	−2011	...	...	...	...	...	...	...
Total gross capital formation	138157	96702	10580	30875	149549	105574	10802	33174	...	...	...	...

2.8 Gross capital formation by type of good and owner, in constant prices

Thousand million Japanese yen

	1986				1987				1988			
	Total	Total private	Public enterprises	General government	Total	Total private	Public enterprises	General government	Total	Total private	Public enterprises	General government
	At constant prices of: 1990											
Increase in stocks, total	1467	1076	391	–	706	712	−6	–	2806	2994	−188	–
1 Goods producing industries	−399	...	...	...	163	...	...	...	1262	...	...	...
A Materials and supplies	88	...	...	...	106	...	...	...	215	...	...	...
B Work in progress	−381	...	...	...	68	...	...	...	748	...	...	...
C Livestock, except breeding stocks, dairy cattle, etc.	...	...	...	...	...	...	...	...	...	...	...	...
D Finished goods	−105	...	...	...	−11	...	...	...	299	...	...	...
2 Wholesale and retail trade	1898	...	...	...	557	...	...	...	1601	...	...	...
3 Other, except government stocks	...	...	...	...	...	...	...	...	...	...	...	...
4 Government stocks	...	...	...	...	...	...	...	...	...	...	...	...
Statistical discrepancy	−32	...	...	...	−14	...	...	...	−58	...	...	...
Gross fixed capital formation, total	95707	71521	6678	17508	104453	78653	6658	19141	116428	89513	6558	20357
1 Residential buildings	18631	17668	963	...	22495	21623	872	...	24958	24088	869	...
2 Non-residential buildings	18087	...	...	...	18230	...	...	...	19887	...	...	...
3 Other construction	19312	...	...	...	20925	...	...	...	22687	...	...	...
4 Land improvement and plantation and orchard development	4700	...	...	...	4845	...	...	...	4971	...	...	...
5 Producers' durable goods	34976	...	...	...	37957	...	...	...	43924	...	...	...
A Transport equipment	6695	...	...	...	7712	...	...	...	8144	...	...	...
B Machinery and equipment	28281	...	...	...	30246	...	...	...	35781	...	...	...
6 Breeding stock, dairy cattle, etc.	...	...	...	...	...	...	...	...	...	...	...	...
Total gross capital formation	97173	72597	7069	17508	105158	79365	6652	19141	119234	92507	6370	20357

	1989				1990				1991			
	Total	Total private	Public enterprises	General government	Total	Total private	Public enterprises	General government	Total	Total private	Public enterprises	General government
	At constant prices of: 1990											
Increase in stocks, total	3141	3221	−80	–	2435	2351	84	–	3493	3687	−194	–
1 Goods producing industries	1703	...	...	...	2195	...	...	...	2418	...	...	...
A Materials and supplies	338	...	...	...	226	...	...	...	154	...	...	...
B Work in progress	632	...	...	...	1497	...	...	...	1050	...	...	...

Japan

	1989				1990				1991			
	Total	Total private	Public enterprises	General government	Total	Total private	Public enterprises	General government	Total	Total private	Public enterprises	General government
At constant prices of: 1990												
C Livestock, except breeding stocks, dairy cattle, etc.	...	...	...	...	...	...	...	...	...	...	...	...
D Finished goods	733	...	...	...	472	...	...	...	1214	...	...	...
2 Wholesale and retail trade	1502	...	...	...	290	...	...	...	1146	...	...	...
3 Other, except government stocks	...	...	...	...	...	...	...	...	...	...	...	...
4 Government stocks	...	...	...	...	...	...	...	...	...	...	...	...
Statistical discrepancy	−64	...	...	...	−50	...	...	...	−71	...	...	...
Gross fixed capital formation, total	126006	99193	6275	20538	136685	108546	6552	21587	141163	111642	6992	22529
1 Residential buildings	25157	24297	860	...	26393	25465	928	...	24293	23304	989	...
2 Non-residential buildings	22900	...	...	...	25247	...	...	...	29009	...	...	...
3 Other construction	25461	...	...	...	27610	...	...	...	28540	...	...	...
4 Land improvement and plantation and orchard development	5006	...	...	...	5097	...	...	...	5254	...	...	...
5 Producers' durable goods	49182	...	...	...	54238	...	...	...	56098	...	...	...
A Transport equipment	9040	...	...	...	9685	...	...	...	9976	...	...	...
B Machinery and equipment	40142	...	...	...	44553	...	...	...	46122	...	...	...
6 Breeding stock, dairy cattle, etc.	...	...	...	...	...	...	...	...	...	...	...	...
Statistical discrepancy	−1699	...	...	...	−1900	...	...	...	−2031	...	...	...
Total gross capital formation	129146	102414	6194	20538	139120	110897	6636	21587	144656	115329	6799	22529

	1992				1993				1994			
	Total	Total private	Public enterprises	General government	Total	Total private	Public enterprises	General government	Total	Total private	Public enterprises	General government
At constant prices of: 1990												
Increase in stocks, total	1484	1545	−61	—	827	969	−142	—	16	−277	292	—
1 Goods producing industries	961	...	...	...	307	...	...	...	−635	...	...	...
A Materials and supplies	−18	...	...	...	145	...	...	...	27	...	...	...
B Work in progress	376	...	...	...	222	...	...	...	−197	...	...	...
C Livestock, except breeding stocks, dairy cattle, etc.	...	...	...	...	...	...	...	...	...	...	...	...
D Finished goods	603	...	...	...	−60	...	...	...	−465	...	...	...
2 Wholesale and retail trade	554	...	...	...	537	...	...	...	651	...	...	...
3 Other, except government stocks	...	...	...	...	...	...	...	...	...	...	...	...
4 Government stocks	...	...	...	...	...	...	...	...	...	...	...	...
Statistical discrepancy	−30	...	...	...	−17	...	...	...	—	...	...	...
Gross fixed capital formation, total	138981	105174	8455	25352	136269	97149	9473	29647	135243	95034	9619	30590
1 Residential buildings	22969	21789	1180	...	23640	22309	1331	...	25533	24195	1337	...
2 Non-residential buildings	30218	...	...	...	30060	...	...	...	28756	...	...	...
3 Other construction	28766	...	...	...	29106	...	...	...	29039	...	...	...
4 Land improvement and plantation and orchard development	5294	...	...	...	5382	...	...	...	5364	...	...	...
5 Producers' durable goods	53663	...	...	...	49854	...	...	...	48255	...	...	...
A Transport equipment	9450	...	...	...	8736	...	...	...	8453	...	...	...
B Machinery and equipment	44213	...	...	...	41118	...	...	...	39802	...	...	...
6 Breeding stock, dairy cattle, etc.	...	...	...	...	...	...	...	...	...	...	...	...
Statistical discrepancy	−1930	...	...	...	−1772	...	...	...	−1703	...	...	...
Total gross capital formation	140465	106719	8394	25352	137096	98118	9331	29647	135259	94757	9911	30590

Japan

	1995				1996				1997			
	Total	Total private	Public enterprises	General government	Total	Total private	Public enterprises	General government	Total	Total private	Public enterprises	General government

At constant prices of: 1990

Increase in stocks, total	867	747	120	–	1109	962	147	–	...	...	...	...
1 Goods producing industries	1745	...	...	...	716	...	...	...	...	...	...	...
A Materials and supplies	238	...	...	...	68	...	...	...	...	...	...	...
B Work in progress	935	...	...	...	516	...	...	...	...	...	...	...
C Livestock, except breeding stocks, dairy cattle, etc.	...	...	...	...	...	...	...	...	...	...	...	...
D Finished goods	572	...	...	...	132	...	...	...	...	...	...	...
2 Wholesale and retail trade	–860	...	...	...	416	...	...	...	...	...	...	...
3 Other, except government stocks	...	...	...	...	...	...	...	...	...	...	...	...
4 Government stocks	...	...	...	...	...	...	...	...	...	...	...	...
Statistical discrepancy	–18	...	...	...	–23	...	...	...	...	...	...	...
Gross fixed capital formation, total	137600	97137	10069	30393	150736	107379	10242	33116	...	...	...	...
1 Residential buildings	24051	22620	1431	...	27199	25762	1437	...	...	...	...	...
2 Non-residential buildings	28303	...	...	...	27442	...	...	...	...	...	...	...
3 Other construction	28298	...	...	...	29305	...	...	...	...	...	...	...
4 Land improvement and plantation and orchard development	5204	...	...	...	5385	...	...	...	...	...	...	...
5 Producers' durable goods	53547	...	...	...	63385	...	...	...	...	...	...	...
A Transport equipment	9107	...	...	...	9187	...	...	...	...	...	...	...
B Machinery and equipment	44440	...	...	...	54198	...	...	...	...	...	...	...
6 Breeding stock, dairy cattle, etc.	...	...	...	...	...	...	...	...	...	...	...	...
Statistical discrepancy	–1803	...	...	...	–1980	...	...	...	...	...	...	...
Total gross capital formation	138466	97884	10189	30393	151846	108341	10389	33116	...	...	...	...

2.15 Stocks of reproducible fixed assets, by kind of activity, in current prices

Thousand million Japanese yen

	1986		1987		1988		1989		1990		1991	
	Gross	Net	Gross	Net	Gross	Net	Gross	Net	Gross	Net	Gross	Net
1 Residential buildings	...	160903	...	172569	...	182424	...	201251	...	217847	...	229165
2 Non-residential buildings	...	161302	...	171082	...	181489	...	201377	...	222664	...	244474
3 Other construction	...	266123	...	282256	...	301954	...	330873	...	362401	...	390901
4 Land improvement and development and plantation and orchard development	...	...	...	...	...	...	...	...	...	...	...	...
5 Producers' durable goods	...	124393	...	130599	...	141445	...	159620	...	178354	...	193079
6 Breeding stock, dairy cattle, etc.	...	...	...	...	...	...	...	...	...	...	...	...
Statistical discrepancy	...	...	...	...	...	...	...	–1391	...	–3597	...	–5883
Total	...	712720	...	756505	...	807311	...	891730	...	977669	...	1051737

	1992		1993		1994		1995		1996		1997	
	Gross	Net	Gross	Net	Gross	Net	Gross	Net	Gross	Net	Gross	Net
1 Residential buildings	...	235235	...	243364	...	249659	...	251902	...	262907	...	...
2 Non-residential buildings	...	261251	...	274887	...	285301	...	292824	...	305842	...	...
3 Other construction	...	412480	...	432614	...	451882	...	469912	...	488618	...	...
4 Land improvement and development and plantation and orchard development	...	...	...	...	...	...	...	...	...	...	...	...
5 Producers' durable goods	...	202633	...	203393	...	197936	...	199381	...	208657	...	...

Japan

	1992 Gross	1992 Net	1993 Gross	1993 Net	1994 Gross	1994 Net	1995 Gross	1995 Net	1996 Gross	1996 Net	1997 Gross	1997 Net
6 Breeding stock, dairy cattle, etc.	...	...	...	...	...	...	...	...	...	...	...	...
Statistical discrepancy	...	−7946	...	−9830	...	−11599	...	−13416	...	−15453	...	...
Total	...	1103654	...	1144429	...	1173179	...	1200603	...	1250570	...	...

2.16 Stocks of reproducible fixed assets, by kind of activity, in constant prices

Thousand million Japanese yen

	1986 Gross	1986 Net	1987 Gross	1987 Net	1988 Gross	1988 Net	1989 Gross	1989 Net	1990 Gross	1990 Net	1991 Gross	1991 Net
	At constant prices of: 1990											
1 Residential buildings	...	183606	...	190931	...	200096	...	208621	...	217847	...	224106
2 Non-residential buildings	...	183624	...	190714	...	199052	...	210025	...	222664	...	238170
3 Other construction	...	304498	...	316654	...	330515	...	345457	...	362401	...	379347
4 Land improvement and development and plantation and orchard development	...	...	...	...	...	...	...	...	...	...	...	...
5 Producers' durable goods	...	122033	...	132077	...	145479	...	160985	...	178354	...	194185
6 Breeding stock, dairy cattle, etc.	...	...	...	...	...	...	...	...	...	...	...	...
Total	...	793761	...	830377	...	875142	...	925088	...	981266	...	1035808

	1992 Gross	1992 Net	1993 Gross	1993 Net	1994 Gross	1994 Net	1995 Gross	1995 Net	1996 Gross	1996 Net	1997 Gross	1997 Net
	At constant prices of: 1990											
1 Residential buildings	...	228725	...	233730	...	240229	...	242158	...	249676	...	...
2 Non-residential buildings	...	254029	...	268826	...	281438	...	288580	...	298811	...	...
3 Other construction	...	395799	...	412050	...	427768	...	439996	...	455723	...	...
4 Land improvement and development and plantation and orchard development	...	...	...	...	...	...	...	...	...	...	...	...
5 Producers' durable goods	...	204738	...	209548	...	211641	...	217318	...	229538	...	...
6 Breeding stock, dairy cattle, etc.	...	...	...	...	...	...	...	...	...	...	...	...
Total	...	1083292	...	1124154	...	1161076	...	1188052	...	1233748	...	...

2.17 Exports and imports of goods and services, detail

Thousand million Japanese yen

	1986	1987	1988	1989	1990	1991	1992	1993	1994	1995	1996	1997
Exports of goods and services												
1 Exports of merchandise, f.o.b. [a]	34575	32490	33398	37372	40651	41465	42082	39164	39348	40260	43566	...
2 Transport and communication	1732	1738	1861	2313	2377	2396	2362	2126	2123	2170	2500	...
A In respect of merchandise imports	...	...	...	...	...	...	...	...	...	...	...	...
B Other	1732	1738	1861	2313	2377	2396	2362	2126	2123	2170	2500	...
3 Insurance service charges	27	42	31	28	9	−35	−22	8	37	28	53	...
A In respect of merchandise imports	...	...	...	...	...	...	...	...	...	...	...	...
B Other	27	42	31	28	9	−35	−22	8	37	28	53	...
4 Other commodities	1107	1318	1537	1901	2100	2195	2229	2238	2251	2345	2852	...
5 Adjustments of merchandise exports to change-of-ownership basis	...	...	...	...	...	...	...	...	...	...	...	...
6 Direct purchases in the domestic market by non-residential households	266	322	387	450	533	475	468	407	367	314	453	...

Japan

Thousand million Japanese yen

	1986	1987	1988	1989	1990	1991	1992	1993	1994	1995	1996	1997
7 Direct purchases in the domestic market by extraterritorial bodies	383	300	270	288	250	227	221	253	284	276	277	...
Total exports of goods and services	38090	36210	37483	42352	45920	46722	47341	44197	44410	45393	49700	...

Imports of goods and services

	1986	1987	1988	1989	1990	1991	1992	1993	1994	1995	1996	1997
1 Imports of merchandise, c.i.f. [b]	19356	18708	21330	26905	31598	28542	26306	23682	24617	27915	34469	...
A Imports of merchandise, f.o.b. [a]	19356	18708	21330	26905	31598	28542	26306	23682	24617	27915	34469	...
B Transport of services on merchandise imports	...	...	...	...	...	...	...	...	...	...	...	...
C Insurance service charges on merchandise imports	...	...	...	...	...	...	...	...	...	...	...	...
2 Adjustments of merchandise imports to change-of-ownership basis	...	...	...	...	...	...	...	...	...	...	...	...
3 Other transport and communication	2018	2414	2648	3215	3582	3637	3538	3287	3314	3459	3860	...
4 Other insurance service charges	142	171	171	174	194	−37	114	210	263	235	208	...
5 Other commodities	1996	2288	2452	3286	3810	3663	3446	3098	2970	3098	4312	...
6 Direct purchases abroad by government	32	22	25	30	37	41	43	38	41	42	75	...
7 Direct purchases abroad by resident households	1247	1591	2439	3158	3651	3274	3443	3028	3183	3524	4098	...
Total imports of goods and services	24791	25195	29065	36768	42872	39121	36891	33343	34387	38272	47022	...
Balance of goods and services	13299	11015	8418	5584	3048	7601	10450	10854	10023	7121	2678	...
Total imports and balance of goods and services	38090	36210	37483	42352	45920	46722	47341	44197	44410	45393	49700	...

a Item "Adjustment of merchandise export/import to change-of-ownership basis" is included in item "Exports/Imports of merchandise, f.o.b.".   b Imports of merchandise c.i.f. is not estimated in the Balance of Payments in Japan. Therefore, valuation basis is f.o.b.

3.12 General government income and outlay account: total and subsectors

Thousand million Japanese yen

	1986 Total government	1986 Central government	1986 State or provincial government	1986 Local government	1986 Social security funds	1987 Total government	1987 Central government	1987 State or provincial government	1987 Local government	1987 Social security funds
Receipts										
1 Operating surplus	...	...	...	...	...	...	...	...	...	...
2 Property and entrepreneurial income	9344	1726	...	1002	6872	10013	2249	...	1010	7186
3 Taxes, fees and contributions	93970	43232	...	25311	28709	103111	47271	...	27965	30034
A Indirect taxes	25213	11792	...	14264	...	28379	13057	...	15669	...
B Direct taxes	40639	31259	...	10875	...	44615	33971	...	12107	...
Income	39161	...	...	...	...	43064	...	...	...	...
Other	1477	...	...	...	...	1550	...	...	...	...
C Social security contributions	27761	−	...	−	28700	29694	−	...	−	30025
D Fees, fines and penalties	357	181	...	171	9	423	243	...	189	9
4 Other current transfers	543	598	...	16270	8757	603	677	...	17014	8788
A Casualty insurance claims	10	5	...	5	−	10	5	...	5	−
B Transfers from other government subsectors	...	108	...	16262	8693	...	134	...	17006	8723

Japan

Thousand million Japanese yen

	1986					1987				
	Total government	Central government	State or provincial government	Local government	Social security funds	Total government	Central government	State or provincial government	Local government	Social security funds
C Transfers from rest of the world	7	11	...	–	...	9	8	...	–	...
D Other transfers, except imputed	519	469	...	...	64	575	525	...	...	64
E Imputed unfunded employee pension and welfare contributions	8	5	...	3	...	8	5	...	3	...
Total current receipts [a]	103857	45556	...	42583	44338	113727	50196	...	45989	46008

Disbursements

1 Government final consumption expenditure	32387	8093	...	23834	632	32975	7995	...	24567	679
2 Property income	14912	11581	...	3593	–	15347	11790	...	3647	3
A Interest	14797	...	...	...	...	15225	...	...	...	...
B Net land rent and royalties	115	...	...	...	...	122	...	...	...	...
3 Subsidies	3678	2601	...	870	...	3419	2567	...	913	...
4 Other current transfers	39164	26494	...	5970	32974	42136	27355	...	6125	35041
A Casualty insurance premiums, net	11	5	...	5	–	11	5	...	5	–
B Transfers to other government subsectors	...	23921	...	1015	127	...	24650	...	1069	144
C Social security benefits	31476	–	...	–	32632	34235	–	...	–	34639
D Social assistance grants	6073	1966	...	4137	...	6185	2058	...	4202	...
E Unfunded employee welfare benefits	8	5	...	3	–	8	5	...	3	–
F Transfers to private non-profit institutions serving households	1517	516	...	810	216	1609	547	...	846	258
G Other transfers n.e.c.	...	...	...	...	...	...	...	...	...	...
H Transfers to rest of the world	80	80	...	–	...	88	89	...	–	...
Net saving	13716	–3213	...	8316	10732	19850	488	...	10738	10286
Total current disbursements and net saving [a]	103857	45556	...	42583	44338	113727	50196	...	45989	46008

	1988					1989				
	Total government	Central government	State or provincial government	Local government	Social security funds	Total government	Central government	State or provincial government	Local government	Social security funds

Receipts

1 Operating surplus	...	...	...	...	...	...	...	...	...	...
2 Property and entrepreneurial income	11109	2685	...	1171	7409	11617	2917	...	1505	7700
3 Taxes, fees and contributions	110997	51684	...	30906	31914	119870	56349	...	32727	34775
A Indirect taxes	30878	14325	...	17314	...	32158	15187	...	17972	...
B Direct taxes	48329	37146	...	13393	...	53901	40946	...	14545	...
Income	46677	...	...	...	...	52142	...	...	...	...
Other	1652	...	...	...	...	1758	...	...	...	...
C Social security contributions	31363	–	...	–	31905	33387	–	...	–	34766
D Fees, fines and penalties	426	213	...	198	9	424	216	...	210	9
4 Other current transfers	665	749	...	17875	10599	749	846	...	21143	10872
A Casualty insurance claims	9	5	...	5	–	9	5	...	5	–
B Transfers from other government subsectors	...	148	...	17867	10528	...	160	...	21135	10794

Japan

	1988					1989				
	Total govern-ment	Central govern-ment	State or provincial govern-ment	Local govern-ment	Social security funds	Total govern-ment	Central govern-ment	State or provincial govern-ment	Local govern-ment	Social security funds
C Transfers from rest of the world	9	6	...	–	...	14	16	...	–	...
D Other transfers, except imputed	638	585	...	...	71	717	660	...	...	78
E Imputed unfunded employee pension and welfare contributions	9	6	...	3	...	9	6	...	3	...
Total current receipts [a]	122770	55117	...	49952	49922	132236	60112	...	55375	53346
Disbursements										
1 Government final consumption expenditure	34183	8332	...	25570	663	36275	8853	...	27172	709
2 Property income	15671	12101	...	3710	2	16023	12432	...	3752	3
A Interest	15537	...	...	...	...	15871	...	...	...	...
B Net land rent and royalties	134	...	...	...	...	151	...	...	...	...
3 Subsidies	3409	2411	...	982	...	3104	3662	...	1117	...
4 Other current transfers	44090	29812	...	6518	36722	45813	33497	...	6663	39060
A Casualty insurance premiums, net	10	5	...	5	–	11	5	...	5	–
B Transfers to other government subsectors	...	27027	...	1359	156	...	30630	...	1294	166
C Social security benefits	35922	–	...	–	36309	37389	–	...	–	38623
D Social assistance grants	6313	2045	...	4240	...	6377	2016	...	4374	...
E Unfunded employee welfare benefits	9	6	...	3	–	9	6	...	3	–
F Transfers to private non-profit institutions serving households	1732	600	...	911	256	1879	682	...	986	270
G Other transfers n.e.c.	...	...	...	...	...	...	...	...	...	...
H Transfers to rest of the world	104	129	...	–	...	148	159	...	–	...
Net saving	25418	2462	...	13171	12535	31021	1666	...	16672	13574
Total current disbursements and net saving [a]	122770	55117	...	49952	49922	132236	60110	...	55375	53346

	1990					1991				
	Total govern-ment	Central govern-ment	State or provincial govern-ment	Local govern-ment	Social security funds	Total govern-ment	Central govern-ment	State or provincial govern-ment	Local govern-ment	Social security funds
Receipts										
1 Operating surplus	...	...	...	...	...	...	...	...	...	...
2 Property and entrepreneurial income	13188	2995	...	2253	8366	15122	2999	...	2541	9376
3 Taxes, fees and contributions	132987	61917	...	34474	39331	138965	63451	...	36144	42218
A Indirect taxes	35212	16548	...	18496	...	34968	17523	...	19476	...
B Direct taxes	58367	45144	...	15754	...	62253	45675	...	16438	...
Income	56495	...	...	...	...	60299	...	...	...	...
Other	1871	...	...	...	...	1954	...	...	...	...
C Social security contributions	38957	–	...	–	39323	41264	–	...	–	42210
D Fees, fines and penalties	452	225	...	224	8	480	253	...	230	8
4 Other current transfers	846	935	...	22566	10437	939	1048	...	23484	11245
A Casualty insurance claims	10	5	...	5	–	10	5	...	5	–
B Transfers from other government subsectors	...	166	...	22558	10341	...	190	...	23476	11145

1201

Japan

	1990					1991				
	Total govern-ment	Central govern-ment	State or provincial govern-ment	Local govern-ment	Social security funds	Total govern-ment	Central govern-ment	State or provincial govern-ment	Local govern-ment	Social security funds
C Transfers from rest of the world	11	11	...	–	...	8	17	...	–	...
D Other transfers, except imputed	817	747	...	...	96	912	830	...	...	100
E Imputed unfunded employee pension and welfare contributions	9	6	...	3	...	10	6	...	3	–
Total current receipts [a]	147021	65846	...	59292	58134	155027	67498	...	62170	62839

Disbursements

1 Government final consumption expenditure	38807	9436	...	29325	759	41356	9892	...	31107	796
2 Property income	16820	13079	...	3909	4	17377	13379	...	4095	4
A Interest	16645	...	...	...	...	17180	...	...	...	...
B Net land rent and royalties	175	...	...	...	...	197	...	...	...	...
3 Subsidies	4644	2265	...	1135	...	3852	2151	...	1136	...
4 Other current transfers	51063	34265	...	6985	41523	52115	36072	...	7427	44325
A Casualty insurance premiums, net	11	6	...	6	–	12	6	...	6	–
B Transfers to other government subsectors	...	31445	...	1437	183	...	33082	...	1519	210
C Social security benefits	42370	–	...	–	40969	42954	–	...	–	43684
D Social assistance grants	6453	1963	...	4513	...	6633	1935	...	4756	...
E Unfunded employee welfare benefits	9	6	...	3	–	10	6	...	3	–
F Transfers to private non-profit institutions serving households	2070	732	...	1026	371	2367	890	...	1142	432
G Other transfers n.e.c.	...	...	...	...	...	...	...	...	...	...
H Transfers to rest of the world	149	114	...	–	...	139	152	...	–	...
Net saving	35688	6800	...	17938	15849	40327	6005	...	18404	17714
Total current disbursements and net saving [a]	147021	65846	...	59292	58134	155027	67498	...	62169	62839

	1992					1993				
	Total govern-ment	Central govern-ment	State or provincial govern-ment	Local govern-ment	Social security funds	Total govern-ment	Central govern-ment	State or provincial govern-ment	Local govern-ment	Social security funds

Receipts

1 Operating surplus	...	...	...	...	...	...	...	...	...	...
2 Property and entrepreneurial income	14588	3015	...	1959	9498	14138	5624	...	1606	9384
3 Taxes, fees and contributions	140754	58121	...	35614	43928	137237	57237	...	34604	45198
A Indirect taxes	37300	18000	...	19241	...	37199	18728	...	18800	...
B Direct taxes	59519	39860	...	16140	...	54761	38235	...	15559	...
Income	57516	...	...	...	...	52720	...	...	...	...
Other	2003	...	...	...	...	2041	...	...	...	...
C Social security contributions	43436	–	...	–	43919	44753	–	...	–	45189
D Fees, fines and penalties	498	261	...	232	9	524	274	...	244	10
4 Other current transfers	1035	1100	...	24710	11685	1042	1159	...	24745	12419
A Casualty insurance claims	10	5	...	5	–	11	6	...	6	–
B Transfers from other government subsectors	...	187	...	24701	11560	...	193	...	24736	12345

Japan

	1992					1993				
	Total govern-ment	Central govern-ment	State or provincial govern-ment	Local govern-ment	Social security funds	Total govern-ment	Central govern-ment	State or provincial govern-ment	Local govern-ment	Social security funds
C Transfers from rest of the world	19	12	...	_	...	16	15	...	_	...
D Other transfers, except imputed	996	890	...	...	125	1005	938	...	...	74
E Imputed unfunded employee pension and welfare contributions	10	7	...	3	_	10	7	...	3	_
Total current receipts [a]	156377	62236	...	62283	65111	152417	64020	...	60955	67001

Disbursements

	Total	Central	State/prov	Local	Social sec	Total	Central	State/prov	Local	Social sec
1 Government final consumption expenditure	43262	10258	...	32595	837	44771	10459	...	33731	850
2 Property income	17733	13082	...	4304	4	17690	12963	...	4589	2
A Interest	17512	...	...	...	...	17455	...	...	...	...
B Net land rent and royalties	221	...	...	...	...	235	...	...	...	...
3 Subsidies	3304	2119	...	1198	...	3471	2164	...	1252	...
4 Other current transfers	55937	37477	...	8151	47731	59589	38353	...	8506	50758
A Casualty insurance premiums, net	12	6	...	6	_	13	6	...	6	_
B Transfers to other government subsectors	...	34400	...	1829	220	...	35167	...	1870	238
C Social security benefits	46229	_	...	_	47067	49433	_	...	_	50082
D Social assistance grants	6913	1929	...	5061	...	7157	1908	...	5307	...
E Unfunded employee welfare benefits	10	7	...	3	_	10	7	...	3	_
F Transfers to private non-profit institutions serving households	2604	961	...	1251	445	2792	1063	...	1320	438
G Other transfers n.e.c.	...	...	...	...	...	...	...	...	...	...
H Transfers to rest of the world	168	175	...	_	...	184	201	...	_	...
Net saving	36141	–701	...	16036	16538	26896	82	...	12876	15392
Total current disbursements and net saving [a]	156377	62236	...	62283	65111	152417	64020	...	60955	67001

	1994					1995				
	Total govern-ment	Central govern-ment	State or provincial govern-ment	Local govern-ment	Social security funds	Total govern-ment	Central govern-ment	State or provincial govern-ment	Local govern-ment	Social security funds

Receipts

	Total	Central	State/prov	Local	Social sec	Total	Central	State/prov	Local	Social sec
1 Operating surplus	...	...	...	...	...	...	...	...	...	...
2 Property and entrepreneurial income	18084	5924	...	1402	9240	15621	4806	...	1111	9753
3 Taxes, fees and contributions	134480	53714	...	33524	46714	137975	54366	...	34691	50346
A Indirect taxes	38003	19162	...	19223	...	39348	19637	...	20009	...
B Direct taxes	50363	34285	...	14047	...	48243	34447	...	14422	...
Income	48220	...	...	...	...	45962	...	...	...	...
Other	2143	...	...	...	...	2281	...	...	...	...
C Social security contributions	45585	_	...	_	46704	49840	_	...	_	50334
D Fees, fines and penalties	530	267	...	253	10	544	283	...	260	12
4 Other current transfers	1070	1201	...	25178	12798	1085	1253	...	26243	13466
A Casualty insurance claims	11	6	...	6	_	12	6	...	6	_
B Transfers from other government subsectors	...	203	...	25169	12731	...	232	...	26234	13404

Japan

	1994					1995				
	Total govern-ment	Central govern-ment	State or provincial govern-ment	Local govern-ment	Social security funds	Total govern-ment	Central govern-ment	State or provincial govern-ment	Local govern-ment	Social security funds
C Transfers from rest of the world	14	14	...	–	...	12	14	...	–	...
D Other transfers, except imputed	1034	971	...	...	68	1050	994	...	...	61
E Imputed unfunded employee pension and welfare contributions	10	7	...	3	–	11	8	...	3	–
Total current receipts	153634[a]	60839[a]	...	60104[a]	68752[a]	154681	60426	...	62045[a]	73565[a]
Disbursements										
1 Government final consumption expenditure	45743	10546	...	34776	875	47419	11034	...	35703	937
2 Property income	17971	13309	...	4953	2	18462	13264	...	5301	1
A Interest	17719	...	...	...	...	18192	...	...	...	...
B Net land rent and royalties	252	...	...	...	...	270	...	...	...	...
3 Subsidies	3466	2196	...	1286	...	3658	2422	...	1335	...
4 Other current transfers	62927	39082	...	9075	54080	68017	40835	...	9611	58094
A Casualty insurance premiums, net	13	6	...	6	–	13	6	...	7	–
B Transfers to other government subsectors	...	35799	...	2056	247	...	37353	...	2242	275
C Social security benefits	52382	–	...	–	53417	56875	–	...	–	57423
D Social assistance grants	7388	1879	...	5630	...	7727	1838	...	5901	...
E Unfunded employee welfare benefits	10	7	...	3	–	11	8	...	3	–
F Transfers to private non-profit institutions serving households	2943	1197	...	1380	416	3174	1392	...	1458	396
G Other transfers n.e.c.	...	...	...	...	...	...	...	...	...	...
H Transfers to rest of the world	190	194	...	–	...	216	238	...	–	...
Net saving	23528	–4294	...	10014	13795	17125	–7129	...	10095	14533
Total current disbursements and net saving[a]	153634	60839	...	60104	68752	154681	60426	...	62045	73565

	1996					1997				
	Total govern-ment	Central govern-ment	State or provincial govern-ment	Local govern-ment	Social security funds	Total govern-ment	Central govern-ment	State or provincial govern-ment	Local govern-ment	Social security funds
Receipts										
1 Operating surplus	...	...	...	...	...	...	...	...	...	...
2 Property and entrepreneurial income	14879	3420	...	1047	9252	...	...	...	...	...
3 Taxes, fees and contributions	142290	55367	...	36086	51906	...	...	...	...	...
A Indirect taxes	41062	19997	...	21371	...	...	...	...	...	...
B Direct taxes	49526	35076	...	14449	...	...	...	...	...	...
Income	47148	...	...	...	...	...	...	...	...	...
Other	2377	...	...	...	...	...	...	...	...	...
C Social security contributions	51135	–	...	–	51894	...	...	...	...	...
D Fees, fines and penalties	568	295	...	265	13	...	...	...	...	...
4 Other current transfers	1101	1309	...	27370	14134	...	...	...	...	...
A Casualty insurance claims	12	6	...	6	–	...	...	...	...	...
B Transfers from other government subsectors	...	270	...	27360	14079	...	...	...	...	...

Japan

	1996					1997				
	Total govern-ment	Central govern-ment	State or provincial govern-ment	Local govern-ment	Social security funds	Total govern-ment	Central govern-ment	State or provincial govern-ment	Local govern-ment	Social security funds
C Transfers from rest of the world	18	18	...	–	...	...	...	...	...	...
D Other transfers, except imputed	1059	1008	...	...	55	...	...	...	...	...
E Imputed unfunded employee pension and welfare contributions	11	7	...	4	–	...	...	...	...	...
Total current receipts	158269	60096	...	64503[a]	75292[a]	...	...	...	...	...
Disbursements										
1 Government final consumption expenditure	48352	11154	...	36375	964	...	...	...	...	...
2 Property income	18742	13312	...	5602	1	...	...	...	...	...
A Interest	18465	...	...	...	...	...	...	...	...	...
B Net land rent and royalties	277	...	...	...	...	...	...	...	...	...
3 Subsidies	3587	2279	...	1455	...	...	...	...	...	...
4 Other current transfers	71127	42451	...	10205	60966	...	...	...	...	...
A Casualty insurance premiums, net	14	7	...	7	–	...	...	...	...	...
B Transfers to other government subsectors	...	38910	...	2493	307	...	...	...	...	...
C Social security benefits	59652	–	...	–	60273	...	...	...	...	...
D Social assistance grants	7874	1775	...	6157	...	...	...	...	...	...
E Unfunded employee welfare benefits	11	7	...	4	–	...	...	...	...	...
F Transfers to private non-profit institutions serving households	3345	1443	...	1546	385	...	...	...	...	...
G Other transfers n.e.c.	...	...	...	...	...	...	...	...	...	...
H Transfers to rest of the world	232	309	...	–	...	...	...	...	...	...
Net saving	16461	–9101	...	10865	13361	...	...	...	...	...
Total current disbursements and net saving[a]	158269	60096	...	64503	75292	...	...	...	...	...

[a] The subsectors of general government, central government, local government, and social security funds refer to fiscal year beginning 1 April.

3.13 General government capital accumulation account: total and subsectors

Thousand million Japanese yen

	1986					1987				
	Total govern-ment	Central govern-ment	State or provincial govern-ment	Local govern-ment	Social security funds	Total govern-ment	Central govern-ment	State or provincial govern-ment	Local govern-ment	Social security funds
Finance of gross accumulation										
1 Gross saving	15860	–2907	...	10159	10744	22095	811	...	12674	10299
A Consumption of fixed capital	2144	307	...	1844	12	2245	323	...	1937	13
B Net saving	13716	–3213	...	8316	10732	19850	488	...	10738	10286
2 Capital transfers[a]	–165	–4364	...	4622	–295	271	–4001	...	4747	–303
A From other government subsectors	...	–5173	...	5225	–52	...	–5256	...	5305	–49
B From other resident sectors	–38	810	...	–603	–243	427	1255	...	–558	–254
C From rest of the world	–127	...	...	...	...	–156	...	...	...	...
Finance of gross accumulation[b]	15695	–7270	...	14781	10449	22366	–3191	...	17421	9995

Japan

Thousand million Japanese yen

	1986					1987				
	Total govern-ment	Central govern-ment	State or provincial govern-ment	Local govern-ment	Social security funds	Total govern-ment	Central govern-ment	State or provincial govern-ment	Local govern-ment	Social security funds
	Gross accumulation									
1 Gross capital formation	16048	2690	...	13491	72	17536	3297	...	15074	80
A Increase in stocks	...	...	...	...	...	...	...	...	...	...
B Gross fixed capital formation	16048	2690	...	13491	72	17536	3297	...	15074	80
2 Purchases of land, net	2781	279	...	2484	16	3220	342	...	3024	16
3 Purchases of intangible assets, net	...	...	...	...	...	...	...	...	...	...
4 Capital transfers	...	...	...	...	...	...	...	...	...	...
Net lending [c]	−3133	−10240	...	−1194	10361	1610	−6829	...	−677	9899
Gross accumulation [b]	15695	−7270	...	14781	10449	22366	−3191	...	17421	9995

	1988					1989				
	Total govern-ment	Central govern-ment	State or provincial govern-ment	Local govern-ment	Social security funds	Total govern-ment	Central govern-ment	State or provincial govern-ment	Local govern-ment	Social security funds
	Finance of gross accumulation									
1 Gross saving	27743	2761	...	15201	12548	33479	1974	...	18847	13588
A Consumption of fixed capital	2325	299	...	2030	13	2458	308	...	2175	14
B Net saving	25418	2462	...	13171	12535	31021	1666	...	16672	13574
2 Capital transfers [a]	530	−3444	...	4138	−316	216	−3440	...	4211	−338
A From other government subsectors	...	−4702	...	4751	−49	...	−4836	...	4884	−48
B From other resident sectors	701	1258	...	−613	−267	462	1396	...	−673	−290
C From rest of the world	−172	...	...	...	...	−247	...	...	...	...
Finance of gross accumulation [b]	28272	−683	...	19339	12232	33695	−1466	...	23058	13250
	Gross accumulation									
1 Gross capital formation	18860	3090	...	15538	74	19808	3139	...	17010	77
A Increase in stocks	...	...	...	...	...	...	...	...	...	...
B Gross fixed capital formation	18860	3090	...	15538	74	19808	3139	...	17010	77
2 Purchases of land, net	3829	416	...	3540	17	3928	274	...	3624	19
3 Purchases of intangible assets, net	...	...	...	...	...	...	...	...	...	...
4 Capital transfers	...	...	...	...	...	...	...	...	...	...
Net lending [c]	5583	−4189	...	261	12141	9959	−4879	...	2423	13154
Gross accumulation [b]	28272	−683	...	19339	12232	33695	−1466	...	23058	13250

	1990					1991				
	Total govern-ment	Central govern-ment	State or provincial govern-ment	Local govern-ment	Social security funds	Total govern-ment	Central govern-ment	State or provincial govern-ment	Local govern-ment	Social security funds
	Finance of gross accumulation									
1 Gross saving	38196	7114	...	20121	15862	42852	6328	...	20596	17729
A Consumption of fixed capital	2508	315	...	2184	14	2525	323	...	2192	15
B Net saving	35688	6800	...	17938	15849	40327	6005	...	18404	17714
2 Capital transfers [a]	224	−4855	...	4011	−381	−1357	−3403	...	4173	−505
A From other government subsectors	...	−4786	...	4837	−51	...	−5202	...	5264	−61

Japan

	1990					1991				
	Total govern-ment	Central govern-ment	State or provincial govern-ment	Local govern-ment	Social security funds	Total govern-ment	Central govern-ment	State or provincial govern-ment	Local govern-ment	Social security funds
B From other resident sectors	659	−68	...	−826	−330	47	1800	...	−1090	−443
C From rest of the world	−435	...	...	...	...	−1405	...	...	...	...
Finance of gross accumulation [b]	38420	2260	...	24132	15481	41495	2925	...	24769	17224

Gross accumulation

1 Gross capital formation	21614	3298	...	18534	83	23229	3530	...	20293	87
A Increase in stocks	...	...	...	...	...	...	...	...	...	...
B Gross fixed capital formation	21614	3298	...	18534	83	23229	3530	...	20293	87
2 Purchases of land, net	4465	363	...	4249	18	5060	348	...	4838	26
3 Purchases of intangible assets, net	...	...	...	...	...	...	...	...	...	...
4 Capital transfers	...	...	...	...	...	...	...	...	...	...
Net lending [c]	12342	−1401	...	1349	15381	13207	−952	...	−362	17111
Gross accumulation [b]	38420	2260	...	24132	15481	41495	2925	...	24769	17224

	1992					1993				
	Total govern-ment	Central govern-ment	State or provincial govern-ment	Local govern-ment	Social security funds	Total govern-ment	Central govern-ment	State or provincial govern-ment	Local govern-ment	Social security funds

Finance of gross accumulation

1 Gross saving	38765	−374	...	18350	16553	29663	402	...	15346	15407
A Consumption of fixed capital	2624	327	...	2314	14	2767	319	...	2470	15
B Net saving	36141	−701	...	16036	16538	26896	82	...	12876	15392
2 Capital transfers [a]	404	−4878	...	5491	−465	−216	−8114	...	8270	−484
A From other government subsectors	...	−6747	...	6807	−59	...	−9823	...	9884	−61
B From other resident sectors	590	1869	...	−1316	−406	−48	1708	...	−1614	−423
C From rest of the world	−186	...	...	...	...	−168	...	...	...	...
Finance of gross accumulation [b]	39169	−5252	...	23842	16088	29447	−7713	...	23616	14923

Gross accumulation

1 Gross capital formation	26474	4355	...	23558	120	30777	5297	...	25706	155
A Increase in stocks	...	...	...	...	...	...	...	...	...	...
B Gross fixed capital formation	26474	4355	...	23558	120	30777	5297	...	25706	155
2 Purchases of land, net	5858	459	...	5579	39	6304	570	...	5735	57
3 Purchases of intangible assets, net	...	...	...	...	...	...	...	...	...	...
4 Capital transfers	...	...	...	...	...	...	...	...	...	...
Net lending [c]	6837	−10067	...	−5295	15928	−7634	−13580	...	−7826	14712
Gross accumulation [b]	39169	−5252	...	23842	16087	29447	−7713	...	23616	14923

	1994					1995				
	Total govern-ment	Central govern-ment	State or provincial govern-ment	Local govern-ment	Social security funds	Total govern-ment	Central govern-ment	State or provincial govern-ment	Local govern-ment	Social security funds

Finance of gross accumulation

1 Gross saving	26490	−3944	...	12664	13811	20236	−6718	...	12810	14551
A Consumption of fixed capital	2962	349	...	2650	16	3111	411	...	2715	18
B Net saving	23528	−4294	...	10014	13795	17125	−7129	...	10095	14533
2 Capital transfers [a]	−507	−8283	...	8081	−533	−1121	−7095	...	6426	−510

Japan

	1994					1995				
	Total govern-ment	Central govern-ment	State or provincial govern-ment	Local govern-ment	Social security funds	Total govern-ment	Central govern-ment	State or provincial govern-ment	Local govern-ment	Social security funds
A From other government subsectors	...	−9600	...	9716	−116	...	−8328	...	8429	−100
B From other resident sectors	−276	1317	...	−1635	−417	−868	1233	...	−2003	−410
C From rest of the world	−231	...	...	...	...	−253	...	...	...	...
Finance of gross accumulation [b]	25983	−12227	...	20745	13278	19116	−13813	...	19235	14041
Gross accumulation										
1 Gross capital formation	31335	4784	...	25579	138	30875	5520	...	26855	142
A Increase in stocks	...	...	...	...	...	...	...	...	...	...
B Gross fixed capital formation	31335	4784	...	25579	138	30875	5520	...	26855	142
2 Purchases of land, net	5716	518	...	4904	43	5825	546	...	5402	60
3 Purchases of intangible assets, net	...	...	...	...	...	...	...	...	...	...
4 Capital transfers	...	...	...	...	...	...	...	...	...	...
Net lending [c]	−11068	−17529	...	−9739	13097	−17584	−19879	...	−13021	13838
Gross accumulation	25983[b]	−12227[b]	...	20745[b]	13278[b]	19116	−13812	...	19235	14041

	1996					1997				
	Total govern-ment	Central govern-ment	State or provincial govern-ment	Local govern-ment	Social security funds	Total govern-ment	Central govern-ment	State or provincial govern-ment	Local govern-ment	Social security funds
Finance of gross accumulation										
1 Gross saving	19628	−8688	...	13610	13379	...	...	...	...	...
A Consumption of fixed capital	3167	413	...	2745	18	...	...	...	...	...
B Net saving	16461	−9101	...	10865	13361	...	...	...	...	...
2 Capital transfers [a]	−2275	−7920	...	6032	−505	...	...	...	...	...
A From other government subsectors	...	−8029	...	8132	−103	...	...	...	...	...
B From other resident sectors	−2082	109	...	−2100	−402	...	...	...	...	...
C From rest of the world	−192	...	...	...	...	...	...	...	...	...
Finance of gross accumulation [b]	17353	−16608	...	19641	12873	...	...	...	...	...
Gross accumulation										
1 Gross capital formation	33174	5139	...	26113	152	...	...	...	...	...
A Increase in stocks	...	...	...	...	...	...	...	...	...	...
B Gross fixed capital formation	33174	5139	...	26113	152	...	...	...	...	...
2 Purchases of land, net	5429	391	...	4758	37	...	...	...	...	...
3 Purchases of intangible assets, net	...	...	...	...	...	...	...	...	...	...
4 Capital transfers	...	...	...	...	...	...	...	...	...	...
Net lending [c]	−21249	−22138	...	−11229	12685	...	...	...	...	...
Gross accumulation	17353	−16608	...	19641	12873	...	...	...	...	...

a Capital transfers received are recorded net of capital transfers paid.
b The subsectors of general government, central government, local government, and social security funds refer to fiscal year beginning 1 April.
c Net lending of the capital accumulation account and the capital finance account have not been reconciled and are different due to different statistical sources.

Japan

3.14 General government capital finance account: total and subsectors

Thousand million Japanese yen

	\multicolumn{5}{c	}{1986}	\multicolumn{5}{c	}{1987}
	Total government	Central government	State or provincial government	Local government	Social security funds	Total government	Central government	State or provincial government	Local government	Social security funds

Acquisition of financial assets

	Total	Central	State/prov	Local	Social	Total	Central	State/prov	Local	Social
1 Gold and SDRs	...	...	...	...	...	...	...	...	...	...
2 Currency and transferable deposits	−237	−13	...	102	−198	473	313	...	−134	360
3 Other deposits	2481	46	...	817	2505	7804	2379	...	2809	2733
4 Bills and bonds, short-term	−1180	2021	...	−	−4	5102	1822	...	−	−
5 Bonds, long-term	1523	436	...	−1	1644	384	−470	...	−	803
6 Corporate equity securities	−232	−2328	...	4	18	−7133	−5028	...	5	31
7 Short-term loans, n.e.c.	5844	5560	...	208	84	1114	554	...	459	315
8 Long-term loans, n.e.c.										
9 Other receivables	...	...	...	...	...	...	...	...	...	...
10 Other assets [a]	11285	5287	...	155	7605	17098	8640	...	334	6529
Total aquisition of financial assets [b]	19484	11009	...	1286	11654	24842	8210	...	3474	10771

Incurrence of liabilities

1 Currency and transferable deposits	...	...	...	...	...	...	...	...	...	...
2 Other deposits	...	...	...	...	...	...	...	...	...	...
3 Bills and bonds, short-term	2811	3362	...	...	...	4201	4714	...	...	...
4 Bonds, long-term	9044	10751	...	62	...	7401	6588	...	−243	...
5 Short-term loans, n.e.c.	8370	6705	...	2650	12	6805	2236	...	3533	11
6 Long-term loans, n.e.c.										
7 Other payables	...	...	...	...	...	...	...	...	...	...
8 Other liabilities	1179	1549	...	−12	...	157	609	...	−12	...
Total incurrence of liabilities	21404	22367	...	2700	12	18564	14147	...	3278	11
Net lending [c]	−1920	−11359	...	−1414	11642	6278	−5937	...	196	10760
Incurrence of liabilities and net worth [b]	19484	11009	...	1286	11654	24842	8210	...	3473	10771

	\multicolumn{5}{c	}{1988}	\multicolumn{5}{c	}{1989}
	Total government	Central government	State or provincial government	Local government	Social security funds	Total government	Central government	State or provincial government	Local government	Social security funds

Acquisition of financial assets

	Total	Central	State/prov	Local	Social	Total	Central	State/prov	Local	Social
1 Gold and SDRs	...	...	...	...	...	...	...	...	...	...
2 Currency and transferable deposits	−133	−314	...	860	−242	431	3072	...	593	−26
3 Other deposits	7130	1571	...	3469	2500	10809	4347	...	4414	2683
4 Bills and bonds, short-term	−1097	189	...	−	−	−2890	−3156	...	−	−1
5 Bonds, long-term	2610	423	...	−1	232	−3532	417	...	−2	−278
6 Corporate equity securities	−2767	−2857	...	6	24	39	22	...	5	12
7 Short-term loans, n.e.c.	130	665	...	196	−445	802	1376	...	348	−67
8 Long-term loans, n.e.c.										
9 Other receivables	...	...	...	...	...	...	...	...	...	...
10 Other assets [a]	11621	5858	...	14	7941	10679	1331	...	168	7896
Total aquisition of financial assets [b]	17496	5536	...	4544	10009	16337	7410	...	5526	10220

Japan

	1988					1989				
	Total govern-ment	Central govern-ment	State or provincial govern-ment	Local govern-ment	Social security funds	Total govern-ment	Central govern-ment	State or provincial govern-ment	Local govern-ment	Social security funds

Incurrence of liabilities

1 Currency and transferable deposits	...	...	...	...	...	...	...	...	...	...
2 Other deposits	...	...	...	...	...	...	...	...	...	...
3 Bills and bonds, short-term	1271	3316	...	...	...	1827	787	...	...	...
4 Bonds, long-term	4732	4979	...	−277	...	887	5902	...	−189	...
5 Short-term loans, n.e.c.	5033	1325	...	3657	18	5715	3531	...	3779	18
6 Long-term loans, n.e.c.										
7 Other payables	...	...	...	...	...	...	...	...	...	...
8 Other liabilities	381	693	...	12	...	−98	169	...	20	...
Total incurrence of liabilities	11417	10314	...	3392	18	8330	10389	...	3610	18
Net lending [c]	6079	−4778	...	1153	9991	8007	−2978	...	1916	10202
Incurrence of liabilities and net worth [b]	17496	5536	...	4545	10009	16337	7411	...	5526	10220

	1990					1991				
	Total govern-ment	Central govern-ment	State or provincial govern-ment	Local govern-ment	Social security funds	Total govern-ment	Central govern-ment	State or provincial govern-ment	Local govern-ment	Social security funds

Acquisition of financial assets

1 Gold and SDRs	...	...	...	...	...	...	...	...	...	...
2 Currency and transferable deposits	190	−3038	...	−257	−530	−78	18	...	475	811
3 Other deposits	10986	4040	...	4096	1768	8600	3906	...	1997	2566
4 Bills and bonds, short-term	−51	784	...	−	19	1094	1487	...	−	−18
5 Bonds, long-term	3046	79	...	−2	342	−183	−702	...	−2	419
6 Corporate equity securities	37	31	...	7	3	80	62	...	13	5
7 Short-term loans, n.e.c.	1267	1373	...	461	113	2079	1448	...	745	437
8 Long-term loans, n.e.c.										
9 Other receivables	...	...	...	...	...	...	...	...	...	...
10 Other assets [a]	18385	5867	...	288	11734	15616	4455	...	308	15569
Total aquisition of financial assets [b]	33858	9135	...	4593	13448	27207	10674	...	3536	19789

Incurrence of liabilities

1 Currency and transferable deposits	...	...	...	...	...	...	...	...	...	...
2 Other deposits	...	...	...	...	...	...	...	...	...	...
3 Bills and bonds, short-term	2805	−2010	...	...	...	−4360	−699	...	...	−
4 Bonds, long-term	6199	3688	...	147	...	5453	5373	...	−817	−
5 Short-term loans, n.e.c.	7514	4886	...	3675	38	7871	4953	...	4545	15
6 Long-term loans, n.e.c.										
7 Other payables	...	...	...	...	...	...	...	...	...	...
8 Other liabilities	471	1307	...	20	...	66	−137	...	12	−
Total incurrence of liabilities	16989	7871	...	3842	38	9029	9489	...	3741	15
Net lending [c]	16869	1264	...	751	13410	18177	1185	...	−205	19774
Incurrence of liabilities and net worth [b]	33858	9135	...	4593	13448	27207	10674	...	3536	19789

Japan

	1992					1993				
	Total government	Central government	State or provincial government	Local government	Social security funds	Total government	Central government	State or provincial government	Local government	Social security funds

Acquisition of financial assets

1 Gold and SDRs	...	...	...	...	...	...	...	...	...	...
2 Currency and transferable deposits	111	766	...	158	−82	−35	2940	...	470	−23
3 Other deposits	6635	5331	...	−274	1943	6206	4878	...	−73	1596
4 Bills and bonds, short-term	2358	1225	...	−	−1	−3688	−3958	...	−	1
5 Bonds, long-term	83	636	...	−1	964	739	912	...	−	965
6 Corporate equity securities	68	53	...	13	2	35	24	...	9	2
7 Short-term loans, n.e.c.	1170	−280	...	631	242	3040	1686	...	507	561
8 Long-term loans, n.e.c.										
9 Other receivables	...	...	...	...	...	...	...	...	...	...
10 Other assets [a]	15390	3609	...	378	11486	15723	4757	...	454	11111
Total aquisition of financial assets [b]	25815	11340	...	905	14554	22020	11239	...	1366	14212

Incurrence of liabilities

1 Currency and transferable deposits	...	...	...	...	...	...	...	...	...	...
2 Other deposits	...	...	...	...	...	...	...	...	...	...
3 Bills and bonds, short-term	1585	721	...	...	−	1588	−288	...	...	−
4 Bonds, long-term	8841	6801	...	3511	−	12036	14258	...	3996	−
5 Short-term loans, n.e.c.	13470	9358	...	3498	−	13521	7782	...	4741	−
6 Long-term loans, n.e.c.										
7 Other payables	...	...	...	...	...	...	...	...	...	...
8 Other liabilities	87	675	...	−5	−	210	939	...	8	−
Total incurence of liabilities	23982	17555	...	7003	−	27356	22691	...	8744	−
Net lending [c]	1832	−6215	...	−6099	14554	−5336	−11452	...	−7378	14212
Incurrence of liabilities and net worth [b]	25815	11340	...	905	14554	22020	11239	...	1366	14212

	1994					1995				
	Total government	Central government	State or provincial government	Local government	Social security funds	Total government	Central government	State or provincial government	Local government	Social security funds

Acquisition of financial assets

1 Gold and SDRs	...	...	...	...	...	...	...	...	...	...
2 Currency and transferable deposits	33	−3639	...	−416	−495	128	1721	...	1110	662
3 Other deposits	1988	2322	...	288	745	4768	3692	...	−2005	2410
4 Bills and bonds, short-term	2974	3752	...	−	−	−849	267	...	−	2
5 Bonds, long-term	2163	1013	...	−	2548	1409	−53	...	−	−618
6 Corporate equity securities	−1	−4	...	−	3	61	22	...	−	40
7 Short-term loans, n.e.c.	1271	4	...	283	152	−526	−199	...	829	−927
8 Long-term loans, n.e.c.										
9 Other receivables	...	...	...	...	...	...	...	...	...	...
10 Other assets [a]	14496	5604	...	475	9042	18505	8798	...	535	7871
Total aquisition of financial assets [b]	22923	9053	...	630	11995	23497	14247	...	469	9438

Incurrence of liabilities

1 Currency and transferable deposits	...	...	...	...	...	...	...	...	...	...
2 Other deposits	...	...	...	...	...	...	...	...	...	...

Japan

	1994					1995				
	Total govern-ment	Central govern-ment	State or provincial govern-ment	Local govern-ment	Social security funds	Total govern-ment	Central govern-ment	State or provincial govern-ment	Local govern-ment	Social security funds
3 Bills and bonds, short-term	798	765	...	...	–	720	5775	...	...	–
4 Bonds, long-term	22656	14122	...	5044	–	26040	18605	...	6098	–
5 Short-term loans, n.e.c.	13944	9403	...	5368	–	12528	4742	...	6363	–
6 Long-term loans, n.e.c.										
7 Other payables	...	...	...	...	...	...	...	...	...	...
8 Other liabilities	106	557	...	–4	–	256	873	...	–10	–
Total incurrence of liabilities	37504	24847	...	10408	–	39544	29994	...	12451	–
Net lending [c]	–14580	–15794	...	–9779	11995	–16047	–15747	...	–11982	9438
Incurrence of liabilities and net worth [b]	22923	9053	...	630	11995	23497	14247	...	469	9438

	1996					1997				
	Total govern-ment	Central govern-ment	State or provincial govern-ment	Local govern-ment	Social security funds	Total govern-ment	Central govern-ment	State or provincial govern-ment	Local govern-ment	Social security funds

Acquisition of financial assets

1 Gold and SDRs	...	...	...	...	...	...	...	...	...	...
2 Currency and transferable deposits	140	–1629	...	–253	109	...	...	...	...	...
3 Other deposits	7180	4740	...	209	2330	...	...	...	...	...
4 Bills and bonds, short-term	474	1614	...	–	3	...	...	...	...	...
5 Bonds, long-term	3335	971	...	–	1163	...	...	...	...	...
6 Corporate equity securities	–41	–8	...	5	–38	...	...	...	...	...
7 Short-term loans, n.e.c.	1654	928	...	644	135	...	...	...	...	...
8 Long-term loans, n.e.c.						...	...	...	...	...
9 Other receivables	...	...	...	...	...	...	...	...	...	...
10 Other assets [a]	7743	–639	...	485	9770	...	...	...	...	...
Total aquisition of financial assets [b]	20484	5976	...	1090	13471	...	...	...	...	...

Incurrence of liabilities

1 Currency and transferable deposits	...	...	...	...	...	...	...	...	...	...
2 Other deposits	...	...	...	...	...	...	...	...	...	...
3 Bills and bonds, short-term	1248	1075	...	...	–	...	...	...	...	...
4 Bonds, long-term	25597	19484	...	4721	–	...	...	...	...	...
5 Short-term loans, n.e.c.	10448	2663	...	7965	–	...	...	...	...	...
6 Long-term loans, n.e.c.						...	...	...	...	...
7 Other payables	...	...	...	...	...	...	...	...	...	...
8 Other liabilities	123	552	...	4	–	...	...	...	...	...
Total incurrence of liabilities	37416	23774	...	12691	–	...	...	...	...	...
Net lending [c]	–16932	–17798	...	–11601	13471	...	...	...	...	...
Incurrence of liabilities and net worth [b]	20484	5976	...	1090	13471	...	...	...	...	...

a Item "Gold and SDRs" is included in item "Other assets".
b The subsectors of general government, central government, local government, and social security funds refer to fiscal year beginning 1 April.
c Net lending of the capital accumulation account and the capital finance account have not been reconciled and are different due to different statistical sources.

3.22 Corporate and quasi-corporate enterprise income and outlay account: total and sectors

Thousand million Japanese yen

	1986 Total	1986 Non-financial	1986 Financial	1987 Total	1987 Non-financial	1987 Financial	1988 Total	1988 Non-financial	1988 Financial	1989 Total	1989 Non-financial	1989 Financial
Receipts												
1 Operating surplus	43550	51857	−8307	44284	54104	−9820	49653	59355	−9702	51875	63047	−11172
2 Property and entrepreneurial income	96865	9024	87841	102394	9553	92841	112521	9942	102578	132271	11313	120958
A Withdrawals from quasi-corporate enterprises	...	...	...	...	...	...	...	...	...	...	...	...
B Interest	91759	6676	85083	95708	5988	89721	105258	5622	99636	121655	5137	116519
C Dividends	4600	1842	2758	6112	2991	3121	6608	3666	2942	9851	5411	4439
D Net land rent and royalties	506	506	–	575	575	–	654	654	–	765	765	–
3 Current transfers	4030	1072	2958	3832	979	2853	3926	1004	2921	4052	1074	2978
A Casualty insurance claims	1081	1019	62	971	922	49	950	938	13	972	1004	−32
B Casualty insurance premiums, net, due to be received by insurance companies	2894	–	2894	2801	–	2801	2906	–	2906	3007	–	3007
C Current transfers from rest of the world	...	...	...	...	...	...	...	...	...	...	...	...
D Other transfers except imputed	...	...	...	...	...	...	...	...	...	...	...	...
E Imputed unfunded employee pension and welfare contributions	55	53	2	60	57	2	69	66	3	73	70	2
Total current receipts	144445	61953	82492	150510	64636	85873	166099	70302	95797	188197	75433	112764
Disbursements												
1 Property and entrepreneurial income	110604	33852	76752	113890	33221	80669	123777	34716	89061	145962	39561	106401
A Withdrawals from quasi-corporations [a]	...	...	–	...	...	–	...	...	–	...	...	–
B Interest	98525	28015	70510	99942	26829	73113	109218	27761	81458	125402	30330	95072
C Dividends	9950	3845	6105	11574	4177	7397	11850	4420	7430	17571	6465	11106
D Net land rent and royalties	2129	1991	137	2373	2215	158	2708	2535	173	2989	2765	223
2 Direct taxes and other current transfers n.e.c. to general government	17790	13667	4123	19690	15336	4353	22247	17813	4434	26168	21126	5042
A Direct taxes	17643	13554	4090	19517	15202	4315	22061	17663	4398	25975	20970	5005
On income	17355	13312	4044	19216	14959	4257	21744	17405	4339	25643	20695	4948
Other	288	242	46	301	243	58	317	258	59	332	276	56
B Fines, fees, penalties and other current transfers n.e.c.	146	114	33	173	134	38	186	149	37	193	156	37
3 Other current transfers	5219	1805	3415	5129	1851	3278	5396	2023	3373	5606	2188	3419
A Casualty insurance premiums, net	1065	1001	63	950	901	50	932	919	14	955	986	−31
B Casualty insurance claims liability of insurance companies	2894	–	2894	2801	–	2801	2906	–	2906	3007	–	3007
C Transfers to private non-profit institutions	...	...	...	...	...	...	...	...	...	...	...	...
D Unfunded employee pension and welfare benefits	55	53	2	60	57	2	69	66	3	73	70	2
E Social assistance grants [b]	1206	750	456	1318	894	425	1489	1039	451	1571	1132	440
F Other transfers n.e.c.	...	...	...	...	...	...	...	...	...	...	...	...
G Transfers to rest of the world	...	...	...	...	...	...	...	...	...	...	...	...

Japan

Thousand million Japanese yen

	1986			1987			1988			1989		
	Total	Non-financial	Financial	Total	Non-financial	Financial	Total	Non-financial	Financial	Total	Non-financial	Financial
Net saving	10832	12629	−1797	11801	14228	−2427	14680	15750	−1071	10461	12559	−2097
Total current disbursements and net saving	144445	61953	82492	150510	64636	85874	166099	70302	95797	188197	75433	112764

	1990			1991			1992			1993		
	Total	Non-financial	Financial	Total	Non-financial	Financial	Total	Non-financial	Financial	Total	Non-financial	Financial
Receipts												
1 Operating surplus	54573	67777	−13203	56450	70600	−14150	49510	65389	−15879	47936	62815	−14878
2 Property and entrepreneurial income	159635	14414	145222	169081	15388	153693	152588	12393	140195	137915	11008	126907
A Withdrawals from quasi-corporate enterprises	...	...	...	...	...	...	...	...	...	...	...	...
B Interest	149337	8052	141285	158474	8729	149745	142320	5924	136396	127719	4705	123014
C Dividends	9387	5451	3936	9595	5647	3948	9193	5394	3799	9010	5117	3893
D Net land rent and royalties	911	911	—	1012	1012	—	1074	1074	—	1186	1186	—
3 Current transfers	4642	1270	3373	6046	1717	4329	6055	1584	4472	6435	1495	4941
A Casualty insurance claims	1159	1195	−36	1654	1637	16	1603	1499	105	1559	1406	153
B Casualty insurance premiums, net, due to be received by insurance companies	3406	—	3406	4311	—	4311	4366	—	4366	4786	—	4786
C Current transfers from rest of the world	...	...	...	...	...	...	...	...	...	...	...	...
D Other transfers except imputed	...	...	...	...	...	...	...	...	...	...	...	...
E Imputed unfunded employee pension and welfare contributions	77	75	2	81	80	1	86	85	1	90	88	1
Total current receipts	218851	83460	135391	231577	87705	143872	208153	79365	128788	192287	75317	116969
Disbursements												
1 Property and entrepreneurial income	176643	50043	126599	189466	55987	133479	168511	50175	118336	152833	45775	107059
A Withdrawals from quasi-corporations [a]	...	...	—	...	...	—	...	...	—	...	...	—
B Interest	157923	41349	116574	170767	46961	123806	150620	40924	109696	135137	36363	98774
C Dividends	15357	5597	9759	15154	5744	9410	13963	5599	8364	13678	5668	8011
D Net land rent and royalties	3363	3097	266	3545	3281	264	3928	3652	276	4018	3744	274
2 Direct taxes and other current transfers n.e.c. to general government	25205	20770	4435	24802	20731	4071	22663	18382	4281	20028	16303	3726
A Direct taxes	25018	20615	4402	24620	20577	4043	22486	18237	4249	19851	16157	3694
On income	24669	20322	4347	24249	20249	4000	22101	17888	4213	19459	15799	3660
Other	349	294	55	371	328	43	384	349	36	393	358	35
B Fines, fees, penalties and other current transfers n.e.c.	187	155	32	182	154	29	177	145	32	177	145	32
3 Other current transfers	6217	2543	3675	7876	3070	4807	7944	2787	5157	8433	2557	5876
A Casualty insurance premiums, net	1144	1178	−35	1629	1611	18	1585	1479	106	1546	1392	154
B Casualty insurance claims liability of insurance companies	3406	—	3406	4311	—	4311	4366	—	4366	4786	—	4786
C Transfers to private non-profit institutions	...	...	...	...	...	...	...	...	...	...	...	...
D Unfunded employee pension and welfare benefits	77	75	2	81	80	1	86	85	1	90	88	1
E Social assistance grants [b]	1591	1289	301	1855	1378	477	1907	1224	684	2011	1077	934
F Other transfers n.e.c.	...	...	...	...	...	...	...	...	...	...	...	...

Japan

	1990			1991			1992			1993		
	Total	Non-financial	Financial	Total	Non-financial	Financial	Total	Non-financial	Financial	Total	Non-financial	Financial
G Transfers to rest of the world	...	...	...	...	...	...	...	...	...	...	...	...
Net saving	10786	10104	682	9433	7918	1515	9035	8020	1014	10991	10683	309
Total current disbursements and net saving	218851	83460	135391	231577	87705	143872	208153	79365	128788	192287	75317	116969

	1994			1995			1996			1997		
	Total	Non-financial	Financial	Total	Non-financial	Financial	Total	Non-financial	Financial	Total	Non-financial	Financial
Receipts												
1 Operating surplus	41093	54852	−13760	41374	56685	−15311	47822	61719	−13897	...	...	...
2 Property and entrepreneurial income	127341	8688	118653	122360	7778	114582	114852	6101	108751	...	...	...
A Withdrawals from quasi-corporate enterprises	...	...	...	...	...	...	...	...	...	...	...	...
B Interest	118467	2934	115532	113728	2119	111609	107500	1686	105814	...	...	...
C Dividends	7588	4468	3120	7298	4325	2973	5882	2946	2937	...	...	...
D Net land rent and royalties	1286	1286	–	1334	1334	–	1469	1469	–	...	...	...
3 Current transfers	6128	1421	4707	5895	1355	4540	5910	1377	4533	...	...	...
A Casualty insurance claims	1497	1330	168	1438	1262	176	1458	1281	177	...	...	...
B Casualty insurance premiums, net, due to be received by insurance companies	4538	–	4538	4363	–	4363	4354	–	4354	...	...	...
C Current transfers from rest of the world	...	...	...	...	...	...	...	...	...	...	...	...
D Other transfers except imputed	...	...	...	...	...	...	...	...	...	...	...	...
E Imputed unfunded employee pension and welfare contributions	93	92	1	95	93	1	98	96	1	...	...	...
Total current receipts	174562	64962	109600	169629	65819	103811	168585	69198	99387	...	...	...
Disbursements												
1 Property and entrepreneurial income	141693	40685	101008	132625	39495	93131	121372	34958	86415	...	...	...
A Withdrawals from quasi-corporations [a]	...	...	–	...	...	–	...	...	–	...	...	...
B Interest	121645	31574	90071	114898	29828	85070	105698	24952	80746	...	...	...
C Dividends	15982	5265	10716	13547	5709	7838	11411	5960	5452	...	...	...
D Net land rent and royalties	4066	3845	220	4179	3957	222	4263	4046	217	...	...	...
2 Direct taxes and other current transfers n.e.c. to general government	17773	15055	2719	18154	15404	2750	20147	17835	2312	...	...	...
A Direct taxes	17599	14905	2694	17964	15242	2722	19931	17644	2287	...	...	...
On income	17159	14498	2662	17481	14796	2685	19435	17188	2247	...	...	...
Other	440	407	33	482	445	37	496	457	39	...	...	...
B Fines, fees, penalties and other current transfers n.e.c.	174	150	25	190	162	28	216	191	25	...	...	...
3 Other current transfers	8231	2295	5936	10788	−970	11758	13461	−3670	17131	...	...	...
A Casualty insurance premiums, net	1476	1308	169	1413	1236	177	1423	1246	178	...	...	...
B Casualty insurance claims liability of insurance companies	4538	–	4538	4363	–	4363	4354	–	4354	...	...	...
C Transfers to private non-profit institutions	...	...	...	...	...	...	...	...	...	...	...	...
D Unfunded employee pension and welfare benefits	93	92	1	95	93	1	98	96	1	...	...	...
E Social assistance grants [b]	2123	895	1228	4918	−2299	7217	7585	−5012	12597	...	...	...

Japan

	1994			1995			1996			1997		
	Total	Non-financial	Financial	Total	Non-financial	Financial	Total	Non-financial	Financial	Total	Non-financial	Financial
F Other transfers n.e.c.	...	...	...	...	...	...	...	...	...	...	...	...
G Transfers to rest of the world	...	...	...	...	...	...	...	...	...	...	...	...
Net saving	6864	6928	–63	8062	11890	–3828	13604	20075	–6471	...	...	...
Total current disbursements and net saving	174561	64962	109600	169629	65819	103811	168585	69198	99387	...	...	...

a Item "Withdrawals from quasi-corporate enterprises" is not included in the income and outlay accounts of the corporate and quasi-corporate enterprise table and household and private unincorporated enterprise table.

b Unrequited current transfers are recorded on a net basis, so that those net estimates are included in item "Social assistance grants".

3.23 Corporate and quasi-corporate enterprise capital accumulation account: total and sectors

Thousand million Japanese yen

	1986			1987			1988			1989		
	Total	Non-financial	Financial	Total	Non-financial	Financial	Total	Non-financial	Financial	Total	Non-financial	Financial
Finance of gross accumulation												
1 Gross saving	40322	41187	–865	43276	44562	–1286	48646	48418	228	48770	49317	–547
A Consumption of fixed capital	29490	28558	932	31475	30334	1141	33966	32668	1299	38309	36758	1551
B Net saving	10832	12629	–1797	11801	14228	–2427	14680	15750	–1071	10461	12559	–2097
2 Capital transfers [a]	1494	1494	–	1422	1422	–	1447	1447	–	1529	1529	–
Finance of gross accumulation	41816	42681	–865	44698	45984	–1286	50093	49865	228	50299	50846	–547
Gross accumulation												
1 Gross capital formation	53096	51908	1188	54811	53347	1464	64269	62305	1964	73600	71084	2517
A Increase in stocks	1401	1401	...	584	584	...	2609	2609	...	2867	2867	...
B Gross fixed capital formation	51694	50507	1188	54226	52762	1464	61660	59696	1964	70733	68217	2517
2 Purchases of land, net	2961	2721	240	5350	5067	283	8437	8062	375	10273	9760	512
3 Purchases of intangible assets, net	...	...	...	...	...	...	...	...	...	...	...	...
4 Capital transfers	...	...	...	...	...	...	...	...	...	...	...	...
Net lending [b]	–14241	–11948	–2293	–15462	–12429	–3033	–22613	–20501	–2111	–33574	–29998	–3575
Gross accumulation	41816	42681	–865	44698	45984	–1286	50093	49865	228	50299	50846	–547

	1990			1991			1992			1993		
	Total	Non-financial	Financial	Total	Non-financial	Financial	Total	Non-financial	Financial	Total	Non-financial	Financial
Finance of gross accumulation												
1 Gross saving	52709	50208	2502	55600	52348	3253	58352	55436	2916	60962	58934	2027
A Consumption of fixed capital	41923	40104	1819	46168	44430	1738	49317	47416	1901	49971	48251	1719
B Net saving	10786	10104	682	9433	7918	1515	9035	8020	1014	10991	10683	309
2 Capital transfers [a]	1692	1692	–	2050	2050	–	2481	2481	–	3095	3095	–
Finance of gross accumulation	54402	51900	2502	57651	54398	3253	60833	57917	2916	64057	62029	2027
Gross accumulation												
1 Gross capital formation	83864	80809	3055	91217	88220	2997	85182	82450	2732	76963	74618	2345
A Increase in stocks	2401	2401	...	3385	3385	–	1453	1453	–	562	562	–
B Gross fixed capital formation	81463	78409	3055	87831	84835	2997	83729	80997	2732	76401	74056	2345
2 Purchases of land, net	12985	12429	556	5012	4458	554	2456	2159	298	–1728	–1930	202
3 Purchases of intangible assets, net	...	...	...	...	...	...	...	...	...	...	...	...
4 Capital transfers	...	...	...	...	...	...	...	...	...	...	...	...

Japan

	1990			1991			1992			1993		
	Total	Non-financial	Financial	Total	Non-financial	Financial	Total	Non-financial	Financial	Total	Non-financial	Financial
Net lending [b]	−42447	−41338	−1109	−38578	−38280	−298	−26806	−26692	−114	−11179	−10659	−519
Gross accumulation	54402	51900	2502	57651	54398	3253	60833	57917	2916	64057	62029	2027

	1994			1995			1996			1997		
	Total	Non-financial	Financial	Total	Non-financial	Financial	Total	Non-financial	Financial	Total	Non-financial	Financial
Finance of gross accumulation												
1 Gross saving	57349	55750	1599	59620	61747	−2127	67392	72436	−5044	...	...	...
A Consumption of fixed capital	50484	48822	1662	51558	49857	1701	53788	52361	1427	...	...	...
B Net saving	6864	6928	−63	8062	11890	−3828	13604	20075	−6471	...	...	...
2 Capital transfers [a]	3326	3326	−	3710	3710	−	4559	3879	680	...	...	...
Finance of gross accumulation	60675	59076	1599	63330	65457	−2127	71951	76314	−4364	...	...	...
Gross accumulation												
1 Gross capital formation	71885	69676	2209	74601	72744	1858	80650	78277	2372	...	...	...
A Increase in stocks	27	27	−	530	530	−	1182	1182	−	...	...	...
B Gross fixed capital formation	71858	69648	2209	74071	72214	1858	79468	77095	2372	...	...	...
2 Purchases of land, net	−7939	−8119	180	−478	−636	158	−5394	−5506	112	...	...	...
3 Purchases of intangible assets, net	...	...	...	...	...	...	...	...	...	...	...	...
4 Capital transfers	...	...	...	...	...	...	...	...	...	...	...	...
Net lending [b]	−3271	−2481	−790	−10793	−6650	−4142	−3305	3543	−6848	...	...	...
Gross accumulation	60674	59076	1599	63330	65457	−2127	71951	76315	−4364	...	...	...

a Capital transfers received are recorded net of capital transfers paid. b Net lending of the capital accumulation account and the capital finance account have not been reconciled and are different due to different statistical sources.

3.24 Corporate and quasi-corporate enterprise capital finance account: total and sectors

Thousand million Japanese yen

	1986			1987			1988			1989		
	Total	Non-financial	Financial	Total	Non-financial	Financial	Total	Non-financial	Financial	Total	Non-financial	Financial
Acquisition of financial assets												
1 Gold and SDRs	...	...	...	...	...	...	...	...	...	...	...	...
2 Currency and transferable deposits	5020	5086	−66	−1057	−1441	384	4873	3590	1284	−9420	−9279	−141
3 Other deposits	17693	17693	−	25522	25522	−	22584	22584	−	25581	25581	−
4 Bills and bonds, short-term	4092	779	3313	−1085	−969	−116	1725	−66	1792	4513	−191	4705
5 Bonds, long-term	28103	541	27561	22566	60	22506	21696	856	20840	8940	−1458	10397
6 Corporate equity securities	13248	349	12899	25992	4866	21126	22910	2918	19992	28510	3349	25161
7 Short-term loans, n.e.c.	52578	−	52578	63823	−	63823	64060	−	64060	88512	−	88512
8 Long-term loans, n.e.c.												
9 Trade credits and advances	−10869	−10869	...	28267	28267	...	17948	17948	...	31447	31447	...
10 Other receivables	...	...	...	...	...	...	...	...	...	...	...	...
11 Other assets [a]	35757	4047	31710	34353	−1200	35553	53194	8356	44838	36651	10156	26495
Total acquisitions of financial assets	145622	17627	127995	198381	55106	143275	208990	56184	152806	214735	59606	155128
Incurrence of liabilities												
1 Currency and transferable deposits	10470	−	10470	6056	−	6056	10705	−	10705	4485	−	4485
2 Other deposits	39444	−	39444	55468	−	55468	56163	−	56163	75119	−	75119
3 Bills and bonds, short-term	96	96	−	−213	−213	−	−613	−613	−	−207	−207	−

Japan

Thousand million Japanese yen

	1986			1987			1988			1989		
	Total	Non-financial	Financial	Total	Non-financial	Financial	Total	Non-financial	Financial	Total	Non-financial	Financial
4 Bonds, long-term	25230	6834	18396	25537	7023	18514	22111	7214	14897	21583	12585	8998
5 Corporate equity securities	2508	2205	303	6145	4125	2020	8444	5226	3218	15011	10124	4887
6 Short-term loans, n.e.c.	34373	25174	9199	31684	26963	4721	37334	32189	5145	51362	41339	10023
7 Long-term loans, n.e.c.												
8 Net equity of households in life insurance and pension fund reserves	15021	–	15021	18350	–	18350	22474	–	22474	24321	–	24321
9 Proprietors' net additions to the accumulation of quasi-corporations	–	–	–	–	–	–	–	–	–	–	–	–
10 Trade credits and advances	–12040	–12040	–	27649	27649	–	15627	15627	–	23154	23154	–
11 Other accounts payable	...	...	...	...	...	...	...	...	...	...	...	...
12 Other liabilities	42544	5895	36649	53124	12728	40396	60491	17639	42852	40375	9262	31113
Total incurrence of liabilities	157647	28165	129482	223798	78274	145524	232737	77282	155454	255203	96257	158946
Net lending [b]	–12026	–10539	–1487	–25417	–23168	–2249	–23747	–21098	–2649	–40468	–36651	–3818
Incurrence of liabilities and net lending	145621	17626	127995	198381	55106	143275	208990	56184	152806	214735	59606	155128

	1990			1991			1992			1993		
	Total	Non-financial	Financial	Total	Non-financial	Financial	Total	Non-financial	Financial	Total	Non-financial	Financial

Acquisition of financial assets

1 Gold and SDRs	...	...	...	...	...	...	...	...	...	...	...	...
2 Currency and transferable deposits	4064	3325	739	8158	9207	–1049	1956	2876	–920	4240	4000	240
3 Other deposits	–4548	–4548	–	–17996	–17996	–	–9103	–9103	–	–8006	–8006	–
4 Bills and bonds, short-term	2740	447	2293	–5637	–447	–5190	–952	773	–1725	5047	27	5021
5 Bonds, long-term	8871	3584	5287	13288	–875	14162	26226	–506	26731	33977	2091	31886
6 Corporate equity securities	9005	3122	5883	–158	–1219	1061	–6438	–748	–5690	2863	–2851	5714
7 Short-term loans, n.e.c.	69589	–	69589	59321	–	59321	39450	–	39450	25285	2	25282
8 Long-term loans, n.e.c.												
9 Trade credits and advances	15157	15157	...	12808	12808	...	–13926	–13926	...	–7382	–7382	...
10 Other receivables	...	...	...	...	...	...	...	...	...	...	...	...
11 Other assets [a]	32549	17659	14890	5752	1242	–667	6483	1129	5354	–6235	1514	–7749
Total acquisitions of financial assets	137428	38747	98681	75536	2721	67639	43696	–19504	63200	49789	–10605	60394

Incurrence of liabilities

1 Currency and transferable deposits	5387	–	5387	11288	–	11288	4863	–	4863	9633	–	9633
2 Other deposits	49279	–	49279	31033	–	31033	25949	–	25949	27177	–	27177
3 Bills and bonds, short-term	–132	–132	–	–158	–158	–	–164	–164	–	–224	–224	–
4 Bonds, long-term	16426	8603	7822	14690	13797	893	15124	5628	9497	9915	3959	5956
5 Corporate equity securities	6242	4438	1804	1437	1278	160	583	465	118	1279	823	456
6 Short-term loans, n.e.c.	37349	41722	–4373	39715	28743	10972	20261	17123	3139	4553	13015	–8462
7 Long-term loans, n.e.c.												
8 Net equity of households in life insurance and pension fund reserves	21404	–	21404	18998	–	18998	20836	–	20836	23112	–	23112
9 Proprietors' net additions to the accumulation of quasi-corporations	–	–	–	–	–	–	–12522	–12522	–	–4230	–4230	–
10 Trade credits and advances	9644	9644	–	7661	7661	–	–12522	–12522	–	–4230	–4230	–
11 Other accounts payable	...	...	...	...	...	...	...	...	...	...	...	...
12 Other liabilities	40940	22171	18769	–11153	–5583	–5570	–1886	2556	–4442	–1313	–5324	4011
Total incurrence of liabilities	186539	86447	100092	113511	45737	67773	73045	13085	59960	69901	8018	61883

Japan

	1990			1991			1992			1993		
	Total	Non-financial	Financial	Total	Non-financial	Financial	Total	Non-financial	Financial	Total	Non-financial	Financial
Net lending [b]	−49111	−47700	−1411	−37975	−43017	−135	−29349	−32589	3240	−20112	−18623	−1489
Incurrence of liabilities and net lending	137429	38747	98681	75536	2721	67639	43696	−19504	63200	49789	−10605	60394

	1994			1995			1996			1997		
	Total	Non-financial	Financial	Total	Non-financial	Financial	Total	Non-financial	Financial	Total	Non-financial	Financial

Acquisition of financial assets

1 Gold and SDRs	...	...	...	...	...	...	...	...	...	...	...	...
2 Currency and transferable deposits	−137	185	−322	4158	3677	480	4793	4640	153	...	...	...
3 Other deposits	1452	1452	−	−2509	−2509	−	−5313	−5313	−	...	...	...
4 Bills and bonds, short-term	−1869	−151	−1718	817	300	517	396	−652	1048	...	...	...
5 Bonds, long-term	17862	−1899	19761	40228	3438	36790	26760	−1414	28174	...	...	...
6 Corporate equity securities	4474	−2584	7058	−2480	−1264	−1217	100	−1606	1705	...	...	...
7 Short-term loans, n.e.c.	18638	−	18638	17250	−	17250	11565	−	11565	...	...	...
8 Long-term loans, n.e.c.										...	...	...
9 Trade credits and advances	3412	3412	...	7009	7009	...	8987	8987	...	...	...	...
10 Other receivables	...	...	...	...	...	...	...	...	...	...	...	...
11 Other assets [a]	5172	5054	118	8260	−3433	11693	20820	17660	3159	...	...	...
Total acquisitions of financial assets	49003	5469	43534	72732	7220	65512	68108	22304	45805	...	...	...

Incurrence of liabilities

1 Currency and transferable deposits	6368	−	6368	21357	−	21357	17531	−	17531	...	...	...
2 Other deposits	25783	−	25783	19785	−	19785	12736	−	12736	...	...	...
3 Bills and bonds, short-term	275	275	−	−275	−275	−	−	−	−	...	...	...
4 Bonds, long-term	−1633	5665	−7299	7251	4788	2463	7697	5894	1802	...	...	...
5 Corporate equity securities	1425	879	546	1000	703	297	3251	1902	1349	...	...	...
6 Short-term loans, n.e.c.	1950	7210	−5260	−3152	3299	−6452	−4007	−4959	952	...	...	...
7 Long-term loans, n.e.c.										...	...	...
8 Net equity of households in life insurance and pension fund reserves	20105	−	20105	19973	−	19973	9705	−	9705	...	...	...
9 Proprietors' net additions to the accumulation of quasi-corporations	−	−	−	−	−	−	−	−	−	...	...	...
10 Trade credits and advances	2355	2355	−	4242	4242	−	7345	7345	−	...	...	...
11 Other accounts payable	...	...	...	...	...	...	...	...	...	...	...	...
12 Other liabilities	619	−8176	8795	17007	2083	14924	19802	9313	10489	...	...	...
Total incurrence of liabilities	57248	8209	49039	87188	14840	72348	74060	19494	54566	...	...	...
Net lending [b]	−8245	−2740	−5505	−14456	−7620	−6835	−5952	2809	−8761	...	...	...
Incurrence of liabilities and net lending	49003	5469	43534	72732	7220	65512	68108	22304	45805	...	...	...

a Item "Gold and SDRs" is included in item "Other assets".   b Net lending of the capital accumulation account and the capital finance account have not been reconciled and are different due to different statistical sources.

3.32 Household and private unincorporated enterprise income and outlay account

Thousand million Japanese yen

	1986	1987	1988	1989	1990	1991	1992	1993	1994	1995	1996	1997
Receipts												
1 Compensation of employees	181325	187812	198364	212529	230447	248392	257139	263100	269653	274119	279414	...
A Wages and salaries	157113	161255	170397	182118	196898	212338	221863	226645	232794	234237	239378	...

Japan

Thousand million Japanese yen

	1986	1987	1988	1989	1990	1991	1992	1993	1994	1995	1996	1997
B Employers' contributions for social security	14618	15386	16267	17768	20076	21430	22564	23162	23379	25482	26171	...
C Employers' contributions for private pension and welfare plans	9595	11171	11700	12642	13473	14624	12712	13293	13481	14400	13866	...
2 Operating surplus of private unincorporated enterprises	42551	44858	47312	49418	51419	54294	57999	56075	57949	55416	56991	...
3 Property and entrepreneurial income	32767	31724	31681	35684	41996	46583	42817	40707	34905	32754	29609	...
A Withdrawals from private quasi-corporations	...	...	...	...	...	...	...	...	...	...	...	...
B Interest	25712	23437	22760	23048	29588	34006	30744	28843	24450	22243	20614	...
C Dividends	5290	6371	6791	10327	9895	9868	9155	8739	7273	7235	5758	...
D Net land rent and royalties	1765	1916	2129	2309	2513	2709	2918	3124	3181	3276	3237	...
4 Current transfers	56759	60238	63543	65067	71608	74650	79347	82578	86296	94313	99371	...
A Casualty insurance claims	1790	1807	1932	2012	2219	2617	2726	3191	3007	2891	2861	...
B Social security benefits	31476	34235	35922	37389	42370	42954	46229	49433	52382	56875	59652	...
C Social assistance grants	7930	8228	8545	8677	8844	9146	9429	9602	9876	10232	10531	...
D Unfunded employee pension and welfare benefits	65	70	81	84	89	94	99	103	107	109	113	...
E Transfers from general government	...	...	...	...	...	...	...	...	...	...	...	...
F Transfers from rest of the world	...	...	...	...	...	...	...	...	...	...	...	...
G Other transfers n.e.c.	15498	15898	17063	16905	18087	19840	20864	20249	20925	24206	26214	...
Total current receipts	313402	324633	340900	362698	395470	423919	437302	442460	448804	456602	465385	...

Disbursements

	1986	1987	1988	1989	1990	1991	1992	1993	1994	1995	1996	1997
1 Final consumption expenditure	194051	203342	214992	229831	246154	258332	268676	274696	282354	286454	295020	...
2 Property income	12599	13077	13724	14878	18681	20961	19641	17952	16426	15254	13260	...
A Interest	12109	12634	13251	14388	18136	20405	19127	17390	15817	14641	12697	...
Consumer debt	1423	1497	1703	1986	2566	3334	3053	3215	3165	3189	2603	...
Mortgages	10685	11137	11548	12402	15570	17071	16073	14176	12652	11452	10094	...
Other												...
B Net land rent and royalties	490	443	472	490	544	556	514	562	609	613	563	...
3 Direct taxes and other current transfers n.e.c. to general government	50967	55042	57872	61544	72571	79195	80790	80009	78704	80473	81081	...
A Social security contributions	27761	29694	31363	33387	38957	41264	43436	44753	45585	49840	51135	...
B Direct taxes	22995	25098	26268	27925	33349	37633	37033	34909	32763	30279	29595	...
Income taxes	21806	23848	24933	26499	31827	36050	35415	33261	31061	28480	27713	...
Other	1189	1250	1335	1426	1522	1583	1619	1648	1703	1799	1882	...
C Fees, fines and penalties	211	251	240	232	265	298	321	347	356	354	351	...
4 Other current transfers	19897	20589	22145	22335	24086	26250	27615	27477	28018	28907	28741	...
A Net casualty insurance premiums	1801	1822	1945	2022	2230	2639	2740	3201	3021	2910	2889	...
B Transfers to private non-profit institutions serving households	2694	2821	3129	3429	3673	3834	4014	4122	4271	4719	4845	...
C Transfers to rest of the world	...	...	...	...	...	...	...	...	...	...	...	...
D Other current transfers, except imputed	15338	15876	16990	16800	18095	19683	20761	20051	20618	21170	20894	...
E Imputed employee pension and welfare contributions	65	70	81	84	89	94	99	103	107	109	113	...
Net saving	35888	32582	32168	34110	33979	39181	40580	42326	43301	45513	47283	...

Japan

Thousand million Japanese yen

	1986	1987	1988	1989	1990	1991	1992	1993	1994	1995	1996	1997
Total current disbursements and net saving	313402	324633	340900	362698	395470	423919	437302	442460	448804	456602	465385	...

3.33 Household and private unincorporated enterprise capital accumulation account

Thousand million Japanese yen

	1986	1987	1988	1989	1990	1991	1992	1993	1994	1995	1996	1997
Finance of gross accumulation												
1 Gross saving	49726	46985	47454	50537	51579	58044	60383	62850	64236	66767	68907	...
A Consumption of fixed capital	13838	14403	15286	16428	17600	18863	19803	20524	20934	21254	21625	...
B Net saving	35888	32582	32168	34110	33979	39181	40580	42326	43301	45513	47283	...
2 Capital transfers [a]	−2067	−2474	−2788	−2660	−3082	−2838	−3845	−3848	−3838	−3657	−3469	...
Total finance of gross accumulation	47659	44512	44666	47878	48497	55206	56538	59002	60398	63109	65438	...
Gross accumulation												
1 Gross capital formation	22853	26283	29066	30398	31847	31392	31704	31724	32526	31073	33990	...
A Increase in stocks	159	77	67	109	30	68	36	58	22	16	45	...
B Gross fixed capital formation	22695	26205	28999	30290	31817	31324	31668	31666	32503	31057	33945	...
2 Purchases of land, net	−5899	−8806	−12489	−14484	−17710	−10018	−8366	−4766	2056	−5591	−122	...
3 Purchases of intangibles, net	...	...	...	...	...	...	...	...	...	...	...	...
4 Capital transfers	...	...	...	...	...	...	...	...	...	...	...	...
Net lending [b]	30706	27035	28089	31963	34360	33832	33200	32043	25816	37627	31570	...
Total gross accumulation	47659	44512	44666	47878	48497	55206	56538	59002	60398	63109	65438	...

a Capital transfers received are recorded net of capital transfers paid.   b Net lending of the capital accumulation account and the capital finance account have not been reconciled and are different due to different statistical sources.

3.34 Household and private unincorporated enterprise capital finance account

Thousand million Japanese yen

	1986	1987	1988	1989	1990	1991	1992	1993	1994	1995	1996	1997
Acquisition of financial assets												
1 Gold	...	...	...	...	...	...	...	...	...	...	...	...
2 Currency and transferable deposits	5733	6702	6063	13441	1106	3168	2738	5349	6348	16912	12428	...
3 Other deposits	19301	20910	25219	37286	40710	40319	26838	29085	21819	17187	10109	...
4 Bills and bonds, short-term	...	...	...	...	...	...	...	...	...	...	...	...
5 Bonds, long-term	3400	6294	−700	5356	2823	−4304	−602	−7298	−5490	−3811	519	...
6 Corporate equity securities	−1553	4607	−1574	−1257	2144	−2905	−254	−1116	−2024	−560	−2086	...
7 Short-term loans, n.e.c.	...	...	...	...	...	...	...	...	...	...	...	...
8 Long-term loans, n.e.c.	...	...	...	...	...	...	...	...	...	...	...	...
9 Trade credits and advances	...	...	...	...	...	...	...	...	...	...	...	...
10 Net equity of households in life insurance and pension fund reserves	14488	17217	20890	22273	18111	14341	15825	18821	16925	19214	14435	...
11 Proprietors' net additions to the accumulation of quasi-corporations	...	...	...	...	...	...	...	...	...	...	...	...
12 Other	2229	1680	430	1825	2209	371	709	669	633	295	1626	...
Total acquisitions of financial assets	43598	57409	50328	78925	67103	50990	45253	45511	38210	49236	37032	...

Japan

Thousand million Japanese yen

	1986	1987	1988	1989	1990	1991	1992	1993	1994	1995	1996	1997
Incurrence of liabilities												
1 Short-term loans, n.e.c.	14543	25491	20585	30990	24384	12207	5625	9448	3454	6596	7360	...
2 Long-term loans, n.e.c.	...	...	...	...	...	...	...	...	...	...	...	...
3 Trade credits and advances	1080	587	2206	8114	5454	5055	−1530	−3351	982	2531	1539	...
4 Other accounts payable	...	...	...	...	...	...	...	...	...	...	...	...
5 Other liabilities	...	...	...	...	–	–	–	–	...	...	...	...
Total incurrence of liabilities	15624	26077	22791	39104	29838	17263	4095	6097	4437	9127	8899	...
Net lending	27975	31332	27537	39821	37266	33727	41158	39414	33774	40109	28132	...
Incurrence of liabilities and net lending	43598	57409	50328	78925	67103	50990	45253	45511	38210	49236	37032	...

3.41 Private non-profit institutions serving households: production account

Thousand million Japanese yen

	1986	1987	1988	1989	1990	1991	1992	1993	1994	1995	1996	1997
Gross output												
A Services produced for own use	2661	2614	2848	3059	3135	3559	3618	4007	3799	4069	4261	...
B Own-account fixed capital formation	...	...	...	...	...	...	...	...	...	...	...	...
Gross output	...	...	...	...	...	...	...	...	...	...	...	...
Gross input												
Intermediate consumption	3731	4016	4253	4489	4836	5066	5473	5742	6007	6168	6482	...
subtotal: Value added	...	...	...	...	...	...	...	...	...	...	...	...
1 Indirect taxes, net	...	...	...	...	...	...	...	...	...	...	...	...
2 Consumption of fixed capital	733	807	820	886	956	985	1079	1121	1225	1231	1270	...
3 Compensation of employees	5889	6096	6622	7043	7454	7913	8279	8750	9066	9543	9969	...
4 Net operating surplus	...	...	...	...	...	...	...	...	...	...	...	...
Gross input	...	...	...	...	...	...	...	...	...	...	...	...

3.42 Private non-profit institutions serving households: income and outlay account

Thousand million Japanese yen

	1986	1987	1988	1989	1990	1991	1992	1993	1994	1995	1996	1997
Receipts												
1 Operating surplus	...	...	...	...	...	...	...	...	...	...	...	...
2 Property and entrepreneurial income	1264	1110	1007	998	1321	1527	1270	1126	675	470	383	...
A Withdrawals from quasi-corporations	...	...	...	...	...	...	...	...	...	...	...	...
B Interest	1171	992	876	799	1140	1347	1115	975	546	349	279	...
C Dividends	57	80	91	159	144	141	118	110	90	82	68	...
D Net land rent and royalties	36	38	40	39	38	38	38	40	39	38	36	...
3 Current transfers	4603	4874	5394	5875	6343	6780	7144	7357	7616	8267	8660	...
A Casualty insurance claims	13	14	14	14	19	31	26	25	22	22	23	...
B Current transfers from general government	1193	1268	1341	1418	1546	1718	1850	1946	2023	2123	2221	...
C Other transfers from resident sectors	3396	3590	4037	4441	4775	5029	5265	5383	5567	6119	6412	...
D Current transfers received from the rest of the world	–	–	–	–	–	–	–	–	–	–	–	...

Japan

Thousand million Japanese yen

	1986	1987	1988	1989	1990	1991	1992	1993	1994	1995	1996	1997
E Imputed unfunded employee pension and welfare contributions	2	2	3	3	3	3	3	3	4	4	4	...
Total current receipts	5868	5984	6402	6873	7664	8307	8414	8483	8291	8736	9044	...

Disbursements

	1986	1987	1988	1989	1990	1991	1992	1993	1994	1995	1996	1997
1 Final consumption expenditures	2661	2614	2848	3059	3135	3559	3618	4007	3799	4069	4261	...
A Compensation of employees	...	...	...	...	...	...	...	...	...	...	...	...
B Consumption of fixed capital	733	807	820	886	956	985	1079	1121	1225	1231	1270	...
C Purchases of goods and services, net	...	...	...	...	...	...	...	...	...	...	...	...
2 Property income	944	930	925	964	1200	1410	1365	1231	1092	1027	873	...
3 Direct taxes and other transfers to general government	...	...	...	...	...	...	...	...	...	...	...	...
4 Other current transfers	1877	2063	2253	2322	2415	2547	2547	2476	2518	2536	2689	...
A Net casualty insurance premiums	18	18	18	19	21	31	28	27	27	27	28	...
B Social assistance grants	1857	2043	2232	2300	2391	2513	2516	2445	2487	2505	2657	...
C Unfunded employee pension and welfare benefits	2	2	3	3	3	3	3	3	4	4	4	...
D Current transfers to the rest of the world	...	...	...	...	...	...	...	...	...	...	...	...
E Other current transfers n.e.c.	...	...	...	...	...	...	...	...	...	...	...	...
Net saving	386	377	377	528	914	791	884	770	880	1104	1219	...
Total current disbursements	5868	5984	6401	6873	7664	8307	8414	8483	8291	8736	9043	...

3.43 Private non-profit institutions serving households: capital accumulation account

Thousand million Japanese yen

	1986	1987	1988	1989	1990	1991	1992	1993	1994	1995	1996	1997

Finance of gross accumulation

	1986	1987	1988	1989	1990	1991	1992	1993	1994	1995	1996	1997
1 Gross saving	1119	1184	1197	1414	1870	1776	1963	1890	2105	2335	2489	...
A Consumption of fixed capital	733	807	820	886	956	985	1079	1121	1225	1231	1270	...
B Net saving	386	377	377	528	914	791	884	770	880	1104	1219	...
2 Capital transfers	610	625	640	668	731	740	774	802	788	815	831	...
Finance of gross accumulation	1729	1809	1836	2082	2600	2516	2737	2692	2893	3151	3320	...

Gross accumulation

	1986	1987	1988	1989	1990	1991	1992	1993	1994	1995	1996	1997
1 Gross capital formation	1062	1184	1337	1443	1572	1613	1654	1588	1595	1608	1736	...
A Increase in stocks	...	...	...	...	...	...	...	...	...	...	...	...
B Gross fixed capital formation	1062	1184	1337	1443	1572	1613	1654	1588	1595	1608	1736	...
2 Purchases of land, net	157	236	224	284	260	−54	52	189	167	244	87	...
3 Purchases of intangible assets, net	...	...	...	...	...	...	...	...	...	...	...	...
4 Capital transfers	...	...	...	...	...	...	...	...	...	...	...	...
Net lending [a]	509	389	275	355	768	957	1031	914	1131	1298	1498	...
Gross accumulation	1729	1809	1836	2082	2601	2516	2737	2692	2893	3151	3320	...

a Net lending of the capital accumulation account and the capital finance account have not been reconciled and are different due to different statistical sources.

Japan

3.44 Private non-profit institutions serving households: capital finance account

Thousand million Japanese yen

	1986	1987	1988	1989	1990	1991	1992	1993	1994	1995	1996	1997
Acquisition of financial assets												
1 Gold	...	...	...	...	...	...	...	...	...	...	...	...
2 Currency and transferable deposits	−45	−63	−99	32	28	41	59	79	124	159	170	...
3 Other deposits	1226	1236	1436	1543	1549	1513	1372	1018	987	178	534	...
4 Bills and bonds, short-term	...	...	...	...	...	...	...	...	...	...	...	...
5 Bonds, long-term	159	132	202	278	304	323	349	475	178	1033	347	...
6 Corporate equity securities	11	11	30	17	11	5	7	9	96	40	−20	...
7 Short-term loans, n.e.c.	184	−60	45	−203	−176	88	104	−45	1555	−90	−6	...
8 Long-term loans, n.e.c.												...
9 Other receivables	...	...	...	...	...	...	...	...	...	...	...	...
10 Proprietors' net additions to the accumulation of quasi-corporations	...	...	...	...	...	...	...	...	...	...	...	...
11 Other assets	102	95	204	−31	139	134	177	37	338	218	57	...
Total acquisitions of financial assets	1637	1351	1818	1637	1856	2102	2068	1574	3278	1538	1082	...
Incurrence of liabilities												
1 Short-term loans	1320	897	1283	1044	1434	1695	1368	758	2115	662	−588	...
2 Long-term loans												...
3 Other liabilities	168	105	212	100	244	147	272	276	169	310	114	...
Total incurrence of liabilities	1487	1003	1494	1144	1677	1841	1640	1035	2284	972	−474	...
Net lending [a]	150	349	324	494	179	261	428	539	994	566	1556	...
Total incurrence of liabilities and net lending	1637	1351	1818	1637	1856	2102	2068	1574	3278	1538	1082	...

a Net lending of the capital accumulation account and the capital finance account have not been reconciled and are different due to different statistical sources.

3.51 External transactions, current account: detail

Thousand million Japanese yen

	1986	1987	1988	1989	1990	1991	1992	1993	1994	1995	1996	1997
Payments to the rest of the world												
1 Imports of goods and services	24791	25195	29065	36768	42872	39121	36891	33343	34387	38272	47022	...
A Imports of merchandise, c.i.f. [a]	19356	18708	21330	26905	31598	28542	26306	23682	24617	27915	34469	...
B Other	5435	6487	7735	9863	11274	10579	10585	9661	9770	10357	12552	...
2 Factor income to rest of the world	4108	5553	7822	11911	15588	16577	14784	13001	12823	15140	20218	...
A Compensation of employees	255	281	232	274	313	350	362	319	321	390	552	...
B Property and entrepreneurial income	3853	5273	7590	11637	15274	16227	14422	12681	12502	14750	19666	...
3 Current transfers to the rest of the world	292	463	497	475	491	563	674	738	771	875	1632	...
A Indirect taxes by general government to supranational organizations	...	...	...	...	...	...	...	...	...	...	...	...
B Other current transfers	292	463	497	475	491	563	674	738	771	875	1632	...
By general government	80	88	104	148	149	139	168	184	190	216	232	...
By other resident sectors	212	375	393	327	342	424	506	554	580	659	1400	...
4 Surplus of the nation on current transactions	14306	12697	10364	8100	5638	10419	14256	14672	13381	10425	7158	...

Japan

Thousand million Japanese yen

	1986	1987	1988	1989	1990	1991	1992	1993	1994	1995	1996	1997
Payments to the rest of the world and surplus of the nation on current transfers	43497	43908	47748	57254	64589	66680	66605	61754	61362	64711	76030	...
Receipts from the rest of the world												
1 Exports of goods and services	38090	36210	37483	42352	45920	46722	47341	44197	44410	45393	49700	...
A Exports of merchandise, f.o.b.	34575	32490	33398	37372	40651	41465	42082	39164	39348	40260	43566	...
B Other	3515	3720	4085	4980	5269	5257	5259	5033	5061	5133	6134	...
2 Factor income from rest of the world	5337	7607	10124	14761	18520	19767	19052	17381	16765	19131	25675	...
A Compensation of employees	303	336	312	381	447	441	616	520	441	545	534	...
B Property and entrepreneurial income	5035	7271	9812	14380	18073	19326	18436	16861	16324	18586	25141	...
3 Current transfers from rest of the world	70	92	141	142	149	191	212	175	187	187	655	...
A Subsidies to general government from supranational organizations	...	...	...	...	...	...	...	...	...	...	...	...
B Other current transfers	70	92	141	142	149	191	212	175	187	187	655	...
To general government	7	9	9	14	11	8	19	16	14	12	18	...
To other resident sectors	63	82	132	128	138	183	193	160	173	175	637	...
Receipts from the rest of the world on current transfers	43497	43908	47748	57254	64589	66680	66605	61754	61362	64711	76030	...

a Imports of merchandise c.i.f. is not estimated in the Balance of Payments in Japan. Therefore, valuation basis is f.o.b.

3.52 External transactions, capital accumulation account

Thousand million Japanese yen

	1986	1987	1988	1989	1990	1991	1992	1993	1994	1995	1996	1997
Finance of gross accumulation												
1 Surplus of the nation on current transactions	14306	12697	10364	8100	5638	10419	14256	14672	13381	10425	7158	...
2 Capital transfers from rest of the world [a]	−127	−156	−172	−247	−435	−1405	−186	−168	−231	−253	−354	...
A By general government	−127	−156	−172	−247	−435	−1405	−186	−168	−231	−253	−354	...
B By other resident sectors	–	–	–	–	–	–	–	–	–	–	–	...
Total finance of gross accumulation	14179	12541	10192	7853	5203	9014	14070	14504	13150	10172	6805	...
Gross accumulation												
1 Capital transfers to the rest of the world	...	...	...	...	...	...	...	...	...	...	...	...
2 Purchases of intangible assets, n.e.c., net, from rest of the world	...	...	...	...	...	...	...	...	...	...	...	...
Net lending to the rest of the world	14179	12541	10192	7853	5203	9014	14070	14504	13150	10172	6805	...
Total gross accumulation	14179	12541	10192	7853	5203	9014	14070	14504	13150	10172	6805	...

a Capital transfers received are recorded net of capital transfers paid.

Japan

4.1 Derivation of value added by kind of activity, in current prices

Thousand million Japanese yen

	1986 Gross output	1986 Intermediate consumption	1986 Value added	1987 Gross output	1987 Intermediate consumption	1987 Value added	1988 Gross output	1988 Intermediate consumption	1988 Value added	1989 Gross output	1989 Intermediate consumption	1989 Value added
All producers												
1 Agriculture, hunting, forestry and fishing	17967	7919	10048	17101	7186	9915	17256	7281	9974	18076	7650	10426
2 Mining and quarrying	1884	923	960	1834	921	913	1933	970	964	2022	1094	928
3 Manufacturing	273941	178124	95817	271939	173532	98407	292177	186862	105315	316146	203470	112676
A Manufacture of food, beverages and tobacco [a]	32262	20677	11585	32054	20341	11712	32635	20994	11641	33281	21609	11672
B Textile, wearing apparel and leather industries [b]	7550	5040	2510	7260	4706	2554	7496	4847	2650	7577	5169	2408
C Manufacture of wood and wood products, including furniture	...	...	...	...	...	...	...	...	...	...	...	...
D Manufacture of paper and paper products, printing and publishing [c]	8061	5501	2560	8288	5549	2739	8810	5844	2966	9591	6264	3327
E Manufacture of chemicals and chemical petroleum, coal, rubber and plastic products [d]	33374	21572	11802	31612	19541	12070	32435	20119	12316	34821	21450	13371
F Manufacture of non-metallic mineral products, except products of petroleum and coal	8436	4910	3527	8470	4748	3722	9080	5034	4046	9557	5300	4258
G Basic metal industries	29273	22270	7003	28853	21362	7491	31692	22916	8776	34024	24536	9488
H Manufacture of fabricated metal products, machinery and equipment	117615	75881	41735	116791	74629	42162	128590	82273	46317	142559	91741	50818
I Other manufacturing industries	37370	22273	15097	38612	22656	15956	41439	24835	16604	44736	27402	17334
4 Electricity, gas and water	17773	6490	11283	17464	6225	11238	17637	6398	11239	17888	6806	11082
5 Construction	60616	33470	27146	66619	35969	30649	73819	39030	34789	81842	42817	39025
6 Wholesale and retail trade, restaurants and hotels	67604	23266	44338	71083	24000	47083	75838	25514	50324	80386	26923	53463
A Wholesale and retail trade	67604	23266	44338	71083	24000	47083	75838	25514	50324	80386	26923	53463
B Restaurants and hotels	...	...	...	...	...	...	...	...	...	...	...	...
7 Transport, storage and communication	33999	11814	22185	35118	11697	23421	37333	12288	25045	40578	13178	27400
8 Finance, insurance, real estate and business services	64849	11844	53005	70928	12842	58086	76058	12705	63353	84968	15716	69252
9 Community, social and personal services [e]	86681	37632	49050	90760	40354	50406	96225	43444	52780	104872	47260	57612
Total, Industries	625314	311482	313833	642845	312727	330117	688276	334492	353784	746777	364914	381863
Producers of government services	38582	11047	27535	39548	11206	28342	41014	11700	29314	43465	12618	30847
Other producers	10406	3731	6675	10985	4016	6970	11782	4253	7530	12511	4489	8023
Total	674302	326260	348042	693378	327948	365430	741072	350446	390627	802753	382020	420733
less: Imputed bank service charge	...	−13969	13969	...	−15806	15806	...	−16728	16728	...	−20677	20677
Import duties	1046	...	1046	1166	...	1166	1217	...	1217	2252	...	2252
Value added tax	...	...	...	...	...	...	...	...	...	−1458	...	−1458
Other adjustments [f]	338	...	338	−1030	...	−1030	−1143	...	−1143	−851	...	−851
Total	675687	340229	335457	693513	343754	349760	741146	367173	373973	802696	402697	399998

Japan

	1990 Gross output	1990 Intermediate consumption	1990 Value added	1991 Gross output	1991 Intermediate consumption	1991 Value added	1992 Gross output	1992 Intermediate consumption	1992 Value added	1993 Gross output	1993 Intermediate consumption	1993 Value added
All producers												
1 Agriculture, hunting, forestry and fishing	18819	7898	10920	18793	7948	10845	18219	7599	10620	16939	7152	9787
2 Mining and quarrying	2162	1041	1122	2184	1039	1144	2192	1040	1152	2066	979	1087
3 Manufacturing	339830	218611	121219	357765	228976	128789	345298	217655	127643	325752	204325	121428
A Manufacture of food, beverages and tobacco [a]	34403	22081	12322	35690	22879	12811	36739	23009	13730	36454	22671	13782
B Textile, wearing apparel and leather industries [b]	7424	4910	2514	7465	4969	2496	7106	4513	2593	6055	3616	2440
C Manufacture of wood and wood products, including furniture	...	...	...	...	...	...	...	...	...	...	...	...
D Manufacture of paper and paper products, printing and publishing [c]	9889	6523	3366	10005	6565	3440	9704	6306	3399	9322	5875	3447
E Manufacture of chemicals and chemical petroleum, coal, rubber and plastic products [d]	37586	24067	13518	39272	24670	14602	38394	23096	15298	36712	21690	15022
F Manufacture of non-metallic mineral products, except products of petroleum and coal	10141	5759	4382	10448	5942	4506	10188	5600	4588	9609	5247	4361
G Basic metal industries	35590	26124	9466	36113	26227	9886	32640	23027	9613	30011	21344	8668
H Manufacture of fabricated metal products, machinery and equipment	156486	100016	56470	167657	107158	60499	160660	102456	58204	149921	95755	54165
I Other manufacturing industries	48313	29131	19181	51115	30566	20549	49867	29649	20218	47669	28127	19542
4 Electricity, gas and water	18901	7659	11242	20157	8087	12070	20755	8221	12535	20835	8014	12821
5 Construction	91157	47730	43428	97407	50541	46866	99134	50325	48809	100454	49339	51115
6 Wholesale and retail trade, restaurants and hotels	87539	29181	58358	94639	31660	62979	95255	31789	63467	91734	30385	61350
A Wholesale and retail trade	87539	29181	58358	94639	31660	62979	95255	31789	63467	91734	30385	61350
B Restaurants and hotels	...	...	...	...	...	...	...	...	...	...	...	...
7 Transport, storage and communication	42792	14318	28475	45031	15042	29988	45215	14980	30235	45513	15299	30214
8 Finance, insurance, real estate and business services	89641	17303	72338	92833	17157	75676	97433	18614	78820	98503	17153	81349
9 Community, social and personal services [e]	114758	51134	63624	125572	56079	69493	134741	59473	75269	137699	58507	79192
Total, Industries	805600	394875	410725	854379	416530	437850	858243	409694	448550	839497	391154	448343
Producers of government services	46475	13787	32688	49249	15025	34224	51656	15991	35665	53646	16835	36812
Other producers	13361	4836	8524	14083	5066	9017	14956	5473	9483	15743	5742	10001
Total	865436	413498	451938	917711	436620	481090	924855	431157	493698	908886	413730	495156
less: Imputed bank service charge	...	−22606	22606	...	−22955	22955	...	−23332	23332	...	−20819	20819
Import duties	2733	...	2733	2874	...	2874	2894	...	2894	2549	...	2549
Value added tax	−2204	...	−2204	−2308	...	−2308	−2047	...	−2047	−1864	...	−1864
Other adjustments [f]	179	...	179	−403	...	−403	−192	...	−192	360	...	360
Total	866144	436104	430040	917874	459575	458299	925509	454489	471021	909930	434549	475381

Japan

	1994 Gross output	1994 Intermediate consumption	1994 Value added	1995 Gross output	1995 Intermediate consumption	1995 Value added	1996 Gross output	1996 Intermediate consumption	1996 Value added	1997 Gross output	1997 Intermediate consumption	1997 Value added
All producers												
1 Agriculture, hunting, forestry and fishing	17659	7416	10242	16358	7007	9351	16125	6817	9308	...	...	...
2 Mining and quarrying	1952	919	1033	1965	893	1071	1978	905	1073	...	...	...
3 Manufacturing	314491	197238	117253	320552	201290	119261	325997	204444	121554	...	...	...
A Manufacture of food, beverages and tobacco [a]	36408	22737	13672	36031	22407	13624	36079	22384	13695	...	...	...
B Textile, wearing apparel and leather industries [b]	5463	3358	2105	5145	3270	1875	4824	3094	1730	...	...	...
C Manufacture of wood and wood products, including furniture	...	...	...	...	...	...	...	...	...	...	...	...
D Manufacture of paper and paper products, printing and publishing [c]	9013	5713	3300	9509	6029	3480	9530	5952	3578	...	...	...
E Manufacture of chemicals and chemical petroleum, coal, rubber and plastic products [d]	35477	20365	15112	36468	21385	15083	37523	22285	15238	...	...	...
F Manufacture of non-metallic mineral products, except products of petroleum and coal	9703	5351	4352	9560	5305	4255	9608	5244	4365	...	...	...
G Basic metal industries	28228	20047	8181	29310	20650	8660	29072	20290	8781	...	...	...
H Manufacture of fabricated metal products, machinery and equipment	144771	93081	51690	149092	95187	53905	153785	97985	55800	...	...	...
I Other manufacturing industries	45429	26587	18842	45437	27058	18380	45576	27210	18366	...	...	...
4 Electricity, gas and water	21657	8233	13424	22135	8402	13733	22534	8405	14130	...	...	...
5 Construction	100214	48549	51665	97562	47230	50332	101789	49021	52768	...	...	...
6 Wholesale and retail trade, restaurants and hotels	91356	30494	60862	92932	31948	60985	93568	32877	60691	...	...	...
A Wholesale and retail trade	91356	30494	60862	92932	31948	60985	93568	32877	60691	...	...	...
B Restaurants and hotels	...	...	...	...	...	...	...	...	...	...	...	...
7 Transport, storage and communication	46500	16033	30468	47913	16559	31354	50637	17348	33289	...	...	...
8 Finance, insurance, real estate and business services	103741	18036	85705	106936	20315	86622	108481	18785	89696	...	...	...
9 Community, social and personal services [e]	141245	60873	80373	145396	63063	82333	153873	66640	87233	...	...	...
Total, Industries	838815	387791	451025	851748	396707	455041	874982	405241	469741	...	...	...
Producers of government services	54781	17073	37708	56912	18056	38856	58315	18566	39749	...	...	...
Other producers	16437	6007	10430	17075	6168	10907	17859	6482	11377	...	...	...
Total	910033	410870	499163	925735	420930	504804	951156	430289	520867	...	...	...
less: Imputed bank service charge	...	−21372	21372	...	−22263	22263	...	−20413	20413	...	...	...
Import duties	2676	...	2676	2861	...	2861	3163	...	3163	...	...	...
Value added tax	−1749	...	−1749	−1806	...	−1806	−2047	...	−2047	...	...	...
Other adjustments [f]	543	...	543	−377	...	−377	−1709	...	−1709	...	...	...
Total	911502	432242	479260	926413	443193	483220	950562	450701	499861	...	...	...

a Item "Manufacture of food, beverages and tobacco" excludes tobacco.
b Item "Textile, wearing apparel and leather industries" refers to textile only.
c Item "Manufacture of paper and paper products, printing and publishing" excludes printing and publishing.
d Item "Manufacture of chemical and chemical petroleum, coal, rubber and plastic products" excludes rubber and plastic products.
e Restaurants and hotels are included in item "Community, social and personal services".
f Item "Other adjustments" refers to inventory valuation adjustment.

Japan

4.2 Derivation of value added by kind of activity, in constant prices

Thousand million Japanese yen

	1986 Gross output	1986 Intermediate consumption	1986 Value added	1987 Gross output	1987 Intermediate consumption	1987 Value added	1988 Gross output	1988 Intermediate consumption	1988 Value added	1989 Gross output	1989 Intermediate consumption	1989 Value added
At constant prices of: 1990												
All producers												
1 Agriculture, hunting, forestry and fishing	18679	8240	10438	18641	7842	10799	18420	7918	10502	18755	7891	10865
2 Mining and quarrying	2004	954	1049	1962	991	972	2041	1064	976	2064	1154	910
3 Manufacturing	276391	182161	94230	282072	183459	98613	304306	197800	106506	321645	208156	113490
A Manufacture of food, beverages and tobacco	33345	21094	12252	33704	21979	11725	34190	22334	11857	34064	22247	11817
B Textile, wearing apparel and leather industries	7810	5201	2610	7585	4886	2699	7717	5097	2620	7518	5235	2283
C Manufacture of wood and wood products, including furniture	...	...	...	...	...	...	...	...	...	...	...	...
D Manufacture of paper and paper products, printing and publishing	8308	5836	2472	8647	6013	2634	9087	6239	2848	9604	6363	3241
E Manufacture of chemicals and chemical petroleum, coal, rubber and plastic products	33086	22322	10764	33551	21531	12019	35184	23197	11987	36503	23314	13188
F Manufacture of non-metallic mineral products, except products of petroleum and coal	8658	5043	3615	8833	5027	3806	9497	5383	4113	9790	5511	4279
G Basic metal industries	32163	24853	7310	32308	24317	7991	34064	25274	8791	34680	25432	9247
H Manufacture of fabricated metal products, machinery and equipment	113803	74608	39195	116686	75732	40953	130801	84238	46563	143729	92407	51322
I Other manufacturing industries	39218	23206	16012	40759	23974	16785	43765	26038	17727	45758	27645	18113
4 Electricity, gas and water	15749	6450	9299	16361	6895	9466	17266	7290	9976	17941	7497	10444
5 Construction	67454	36526	30928	73820	39467	34352	80349	42440	37909	85085	44499	40587
6 Wholesale and retail trade, restaurants and hotels	68549	24580	43970	73131	25584	47548	78188	27089	51099	81453	27644	53809
A Wholesale and retail trade	68549	24580	43970	73131	25584	47548	78188	27089	51099	81453	27644	53809
B Restaurants and hotels	...	...	...	...	...	...	...	...	...	...	...	...
7 Transport, storage and communication	35322	12373	22949	36490	12667	23822	38817	13438	25379	41507	13816	27690
8 Finance, insurance, real estate and business services	70521	12778	57742	76094	13863	62231	80423	13600	66823	87257	16194	71063
9 Community, social and personal services	94967	39581	55387	98313	43068	55245	102931	46333	56599	108129	48753	59376
Total, Industries	649635	323644	325992	676885	333837	343048	722742	356971	365770	763837	375604	388233
Producers of government services	42735	11237	31497	43691	11709	31983	44751	12432	32319	45645	13047	32599
Other producers	11290	3770	7520	11873	4123	7751	12562	4421	8141	12952	4562	8390
Total	703660	338651	365010	732449	349668	382782	780055	373825	406230	822434	393212	429222
less: Imputed bank service charge	...	−14094	14094	...	−16350	16350	...	−17356	17356	...	−21045	21045
Import duties	1120	...	1120	1331	...	1331	1478	...	1478	2535	...	2535
Value added tax	−1445	...	−1445	−1533	...	−1533	−1778	...	−1778	−2000	...	−2000
Other adjustments	2290	...	2290	1326	...	1326	1751	...	1751	473	...	473
Total	705625	352745	352880	733574	366018	367556	781506	391181	390325	823441	414258	409184

Japan

	1990			1991			1992			1993		
	Gross output	Intermediate consumption	Value added	Gross output	Intermediate consumption	Value added	Gross output	Intermediate consumption	Value added	Gross output	Intermediate consumption	Value added

At constant prices of: 1990
All producers

	1990 Gross output	1990 Int. cons.	1990 Value added	1991 Gross output	1991 Int. cons.	1991 Value added	1992 Gross output	1992 Int. cons.	1992 Value added	1993 Gross output	1993 Int. cons.	1993 Value added
1 Agriculture, hunting, forestry and fishing	18819	7898	10920	17970	7910	10060	18303	7625	10678	16659	7269	9390
2 Mining and quarrying	2162	1041	1122	2115	1023	1092	2085	1013	1072	1983	959	1024
3 Manufacturing	339830	218611	121219	356749	229150	127598	349303	223481	125822	337744	216903	120841
A Manufacture of food, beverages and tobacco	34403	22081	12322	35187	22551	12636	35670	22937	12733	35473	22994	12478
B Textile, wearing apparel and leather industries	7424	4910	2514	7284	4905	2379	7115	4615	2500	6423	3904	2519
C Manufacture of wood and wood products, including furniture	...	...	...	...	...	...	...	...	...	...	...	...
D Manufacture of paper and paper products, printing and publishing	9889	6523	3366	9986	6746	3240	9883	6683	3199	9602	6541	3061
E Manufacture of chemicals and chemical petroleum, coal, rubber and plastic products	37586	24067	13518	38778	24731	14047	39892	24525	15367	39879	24849	15031
F Manufacture of non-metallic mineral products, except products of petroleum and coal	10141	5759	4382	10122	5833	4289	9908	5534	4374	9460	5288	4172
G Basic metal industries	35590	26124	9466	36941	27473	9467	35936	26557	9379	35259	26478	8781
H Manufacture of fabricated metal products, machinery and equipment	156485	100016	56470	168610	106907	61704	162551	103060	59491	155360	98364	56996
I Other manufacturing industries	48313	29131	19181	49841	30003	19837	48348	29571	18777	46288	28485	17803
4 Electricity, gas and water	18901	7659	11242	19970	7967	12003	20433	8352	12081	20495	8451	12044
5 Construction	91157	47730	43428	94135	49091	45044	94068	48664	45404	94977	48220	46757
6 Wholesale and retail trade, restaurants and hotels	87539	29181	58358	92912	30972	61940	93353	30665	62688	90461	29218	61243
A Wholesale and retail trade	87539	29181	58358	92912	30972	61940	93353	30665	62688	90461	29218	61243
B Restaurants and hotels	...	...	...	...	...	...	...	...	...	...	...	...
7 Transport, storage and communication	42792	14318	28475	44092	14783	29309	43818	14679	29138	44368	15135	29233
8 Finance, insurance, real estate and business services	89641	17303	72338	90799	16746	74053	93513	17923	75591	92956	16552	76404
9 Community, social and personal services	114758	51134	63624	122319	55078	67240	128504	58004	70499	130274	57372	72902
Total, Industries	805600	394875	410725	841060	412720	428340	843379	410406	432973	829917	400078	429839
Producers of government services	46475	13787	32688	47189	14811	32378	48303	15626	32677	49674	16512	33162
Other producers	13361	4836	8524	13738	5021	8717	14474	5407	9067	15242	5729	9513
Total	865436	413498	451938	901987	432552	469435	906156	431439	474717	894833	422320	472514
less: Imputed bank service charge	...	−22606	22606	...	−22965	22965	...	−23583	23583	...	−21481	21481
Import duties	2733	...	2733	3140	...	3140	3349	...	3349	3290	...	3290
Value added tax	−2204	...	−2204	−2331	...	−2331	−2175	...	−2175	−2009	...	−2009
Other adjustments	125	...	125	−964	...	−964	−1433	...	−1433	−32	...	−32
Total	866089	436104	429985	901832	455517	446315	905899	455022	450876	896082	443801	452282

Japan

	1994			1995			1996			1997		
	Gross output	Intermediate consumption	Value added	Gross output	Intermediate consumption	Value added	Gross output	Intermediate consumption	Value added	Gross output	Intermediate consumption	Value added

At constant prices of: 1990

All producers

1 Agriculture, hunting, forestry and fishing	17808	7646	10162	17024	7371	9653	16748	6908	9840	...	...	...
2 Mining and quarrying	1781	909	872	1745	884	861	1800	882	919	...	...	...
3 Manufacturing	336220	216235	119986	348517	221963	126554	355415	225575	129840	...	...	...
A Manufacture of food, beverages and tobacco	35810	23491	12319	36234	23390	12844	35608	22979	12629	...	...	...
B Textile, wearing apparel and leather industries	5921	3637	2284	5681	3532	2148	5216	3310	1906	...	...	...
C Manufacture of wood and wood products, including furniture	...	...	...	...	...	...	...	...	...	...	...	...
D Manufacture of paper and paper products, printing and publishing	9454	6515	2939	9560	6438	3122	9566	6435	3131	...	...	...
E Manufacture of chemicals and chemical petroleum, coal, rubber and plastic products	39883	24806	15077	40231	25460	14771	41044	25120	15924	...	...	...
F Manufacture of non-metallic mineral products, except products of petroleum and coal	9793	5484	4309	9748	5446	4303	9861	5366	4495	...	...	...
G Basic metal industries	35389	26259	9131	36608	26835	9773	36921	26729	10192	...	...	...
H Manufacture of fabricated metal products, machinery and equipment	155299	98368	56931	165516	102578	62937	172018	107369	64650	...	...	...
I Other manufacturing industries	44672	27675	16997	44939	28283	16656	45180	28268	16912	...	...	...
4 Electricity, gas and water	21566	9154	12412	22063	9414	12649	22907	9019	13888	...	...	...
5 Construction	95364	48645	46719	92447	47666	44781	96127	49470	46656	...	...	...
6 Wholesale and retail trade, restaurants and hotels	90949	29851	61098	94269	31626	62643	95577	32625	62951	...	...	...
A Wholesale and retail trade	90949	29851	61098	94269	31626	62643	95577	32625	62951	...	...	...
B Restaurants and hotels	...	...	...	...	...	...	...	...	...	...	...	...
7 Transport, storage and communication	45724	16146	29577	46601	16730	29871	49298	17206	32092	...	...	...
8 Finance, insurance, real estate and business services	96682	17564	79118	99465	19917	79548	99703	18446	81258	...	...	...
9 Community, social and personal services	133718	60189	73529	138450	62861	75589	146850	66265	80585	...	...	...
Total, Industries	839813	406341	433472	860581	418433	442148	884425	426397	458028	...	...	...
Producers of government services	50823	17023	33800	52637	18177	34460	53791	18681	35109	...	...	...
Other producers	15789	6057	9732	16393	6278	10116	17050	6613	10436	...	...	...
Total	906424	429420	477004	929611	442888	486724	955265	451691	503574	...	...	...
less: Imputed bank service charge	...	−22420	22420	...	−23642	23642	...	−21609	21609	...	...	...
Import duties	3708	...	3708	3999	...	3999	3926	...	3926	...	...	...
Value added tax	−1942	...	−1942	−2044	...	−2044	−2256	...	−2256	...	...	...
Other adjustments	−1153	...	−1153	−3143	...	−3143	−3621	...	−3621	...	...	...
Total	907038	451840	455197	928423	466530	461894	953313	473300	480013	...	...	...

Japan

4.3 Cost components of value added

Thousand million Japanese yen

	1986						1987					
	Compensation of employees	Capital consumption	Net operating surplus	Indirect taxes	less: Subsidies received	Value added	Compensation of employees	Capital consumption	Net operating surplus	Indirect taxes	less: Subsidies received	Value added
All producers												
1 Agriculture, hunting, forestry and fishing	2220	1903	5802	123	...	10048	2219	1799	5758	138	...	9915
2 Mining and quarrying	476	198	281	4	...	960	469	195	243	6	...	913
3 Manufacturing	49679	12836	23329	9973	...	95817	50382	13408	23778	10840	...	98407
A Manufacture of food, beverages and tobacco [a]	4280	668	3062	3576	...	11585	4409	722	2868	3713	...	11712
B Textile, wearing apparel and leather industries [c]	1885	279	212	134	...	2510	1906	282	215	150	...	2554
C Manufacture of wood and wood products, including furniture	...	...	...	...	...	...	...	...	...	...	...	...
D Manufacture of paper and paper products, printing and publishing [d]	1294	488	644	134	...	2560	1344	550	693	151	...	2739
E Manufacture of chemicals and chemical petroleum, coal, rubber and plastic products [e]	3311	1628	4494	2369	...	11802	3446	1719	4389	2517	...	12070
F Manufacture of non-metallic mineral products, except products of petroleum and coal	1889	492	968	178	...	3527	1958	507	1054	203	...	3722
G Basic metal industries	3149	1302	2135	416	...	7003	3096	1385	2538	472	...	7491
H Manufacture of fabricated metal products, machinery and equipment	24760	6266	8140	2569	...	41735	24956	6401	7861	2943	...	42162
I Other manufacturing industries	9111	1714	3675	598	...	15097	9265	1841	4159	691	...	15956
4 Electricity, gas and water	2355	3608	4118	1202	...	11283	2538	3882	3543	1274	...	11238
5 Construction	16266	2218	7908	754	...	27146	16875	2391	10481	903	...	30649
6 Wholesale and retail trade, restaurants and hotels [b]	27826	3148	11054	2310	...	44338	29393	3245	11790	2655	...	47083
A Wholesale and retail trade	27826	3148	11054	2310	...	44338	29393	3245	11790	2655	...	47083
B Restaurants and hotels	...	...	...	...	...	...	...	...	...	...	...	...
7 Transport, storage and communication	15016	3883	3011	275	...	22185	14924	4021	3551	924	...	23421
8 Finance, insurance, real estate and business services	12127	10022	27982	2874	...	53005	13261	10932	30242	3651	...	58086
9 Community, social and personal services [b]	24070	5512	16584	2884	...	49050	25540	6005	15561	3300	...	50406
Total, Industries [f]	150035	43328	100070	20400	...	313833	155600	45878	104948	23691	...	330117
Producers of government services	25355	2144	–	36	...	27535	26061	2245	–	37	...	28342
Other producers	5889	733	–	53	...	6675	6096	807	–	66	...	6970
Total [f]	181278	46205	100070	20489	...	348042	187757	48930	104948	23795	...	365430
less: Imputed bank service charge	...	...	13969	...	...	13969	...	...	15806	...	...	15806
Import duties	...	...	...	1046	...	1046	...	...	...	1166	...	1166
Value added tax	...	...	...	...	...	...	...	...	...	...	...	...
Other adjustments [g]	...	...	...	...	...	338	...	...	...	...	...	−1030
Total [f]	181278	46205	86101	21535	...	335457	187757	48930	89142	24961	...	349760

Japan

	1988						1989					
	Compensation of employees	Capital consumption	Net operating surplus	Indirect taxes	less: Subsidies received	Value added	Compensation of employees	Capital consumption	Net operating surplus	Indirect taxes	less: Subsidies received	Value added

All producers

1 Agriculture, hunting, forestry and fishing	2240	1836	5752	147	...	9974	2188	1830	6054	354	...	10426
2 Mining and quarrying	427	206	311	20	...	964	404	222	269	33	...	928
3 Manufacturing	52944	14095	26530	11746	...	105315	56870	16016	27879	11911	...	112676
A Manufacture of food, beverages and tobacco [a]	4619	755	2463	3804	...	11641	4925	877	2133	3737	...	11672
B Textile, wearing apparel and leather industries [c]	1902	302	283	164	...	2650	1807	343	62	195	...	2408
C Manufacture of wood and wood products, including furniture	...	...	...	...	...	...	...	...	...	...	...	...
D Manufacture of paper and paper products, printing and publishing [d]	1393	603	801	168	...	2966	1486	747	866	228	...	3327
E Manufacture of chemicals and chemical petroleum, coal, rubber and plastic products [e]	3552	1841	4172	2752	...	12316	3821	2022	4532	2996	...	13371
F Manufacture of non-metallic mineral products, except products of petroleum and coal	2122	523	1171	231	...	4046	2249	593	1114	301	...	4258
G Basic metal industries	3135	1473	3624	543	...	8776	3376	1582	3819	711	...	9488
H Manufacture of fabricated metal products, machinery and equipment	26541	6602	9871	3303	...	46317	28922	7503	11567	2827	...	50818
I Other manufacturing industries	9680	1996	4145	783	...	16604	10284	2348	3786	916	...	17334
4 Electricity, gas and water	2680	4099	3222	1238	...	11239	2821	4293	2912	1056	...	11082
5 Construction	18647	2755	12382	1005	...	34789	20673	3060	13689	1603	...	39025
6 Wholesale and retail trade, restaurants and hotels [b]	30408	3445	13474	2997	...	50324	32301	3898	13668	3594	...	53463
A Wholesale and retail trade	30408	3445	13474	2997	...	50324	32301	3898	13668	3594	...	53463
B Restaurants and hotels	...	...	...	...	...	...	...	...	...	...	...	...
7 Transport, storage and communication	15579	4310	4129	1027	...	25045	16637	4734	4594	1436	...	27400
8 Finance, insurance, real estate and business services	14047	11806	33216	4284	...	63353	15068	12958	37264	3961	...	69252
9 Community, social and personal services [b]	27738	6702	14678	3664	...	52780	30071	7726	15641	4173	...	57612
Total, Industries [f]	164710	49253	113693	26128	...	353784	177034	54736	121970	28122	...	381863
Producers of government services	26952	2325	–	37	...	29314	28346	2458	–	43	...	30847
Other producers	6622	820	–	88	...	7530	7043	886	–	94	...	8023
Total [f]	198284	52398	113693	26252	...	390627	212422	58080	121970	28260	...	420733
less: Imputed bank service charge	...	...	16728	...	...	16728	...	...	20677	...	...	20677
Import duties	...	...	...	1217	...	1217	...	...	...	2252	...	2252
Value added tax	...	...	...	...	...	...	...	...	...	−1458	...	−1458
Other adjustments [g]	...	...	...	...	...	−1143	...	...	...	...	...	−851
Total [f]	198284	52398	96965	27469	...	373973	212422	58080	101293	29053	...	399998

Japan

	1990						1991					
	Compensation of employees	Capital consumption	Net operating surplus	Indirect taxes	less: Subsidies received	Value added	Compensation of employees	Capital consumption	Net operating surplus	Indirect taxes	less: Subsidies received	Value added

All producers

1 Agriculture, hunting, forestry and fishing	2299	1989	6399	234	...	10920	2347	2063	6347	87	...	10845
2 Mining and quarrying	379	240	451	52	...	1122	399	276	418	51	...	1144
3 Manufacturing	61691	17406	29125	12997	...	121219	66193	19394	30228	12973	...	128789
A Manufacture of food, beverages and tobacco [a]	5515	1054	1897	3855	...	12322	5959	1119	2169	3564	...	12811
B Textile, wearing apparel and leather industries [c]	1869	269	171	205	...	2514	1921	291	75	210	...	2496
C Manufacture of wood and wood products, including furniture	...	...	...	...	...	...	...	...	...	...	...	...
D Manufacture of paper and paper products, printing and publishing [d]	1562	679	878	247	...	3366	1648	715	822	254	...	3440
E Manufacture of chemicals and chemical petroleum, coal, rubber and plastic products [e]	4001	2163	4209	3144	...	13518	4282	2297	4853	3170	...	14602
F Manufacture of non-metallic mineral products, except products of petroleum and coal	2404	641	1020	317	...	4382	2598	675	901	332	...	4506
G Basic metal industries	3519	1574	3631	741	...	9466	3675	1723	3706	782	...	9886
H Manufacture of fabricated metal products, machinery and equipment	31681	8779	12610	3398	...	56470	34131	10065	12770	3533	...	60499
I Other manufacturing industries	11137	2247	4708	1089	...	19181	11980	2511	4932	1127	...	20549
4 Electricity, gas and water	3019	3882	3291	1050	...	11242	3203	3763	4040	1063	...	12070
5 Construction	22930	3991	14565	1941	...	43428	25320	4417	15113	2016	...	46866
6 Wholesale and retail trade, restaurants and hotels [b]	35021	3835	15269	4234	...	58358	37985	4443	16617	3935	...	62979
A Wholesale and retail trade	35021	3835	15269	4234	...	58358	37985	4443	16617	3935	...	62979
B Restaurants and hotels	...	...	...	...	...	...	...	...	...	...	...	...
7 Transport, storage and communication	17648	5541	4104	1182	...	28475	18679	6105	3351	1854	...	29988
8 Finance, insurance, real estate and business services	16203	14231	38719	3184	...	72338	16916	15266	40198	3295	...	75676
9 Community, social and personal services [b]	33532	8409	16676	5008	...	63624	37690	9303	17386	5113	...	69493
Total, Industries [f]	192722	59523	128598	29882	...	410725	208732	65031	133699	30388	...	437850
Producers of government services	30136	2508	–	44	...	32688	31656	2525	–	43	...	34224
Other producers	7454	956	–	114	...	8524	7913	985	–	119	...	9017
Total [f]	230313	62987	128598	30039	...	451938	248301	68541	133699	30550	...	481090
less: Imputed bank service charge	...	...	22606	...	...	22606	...	...	22955	...	...	22955
Import duties	...	...	...	2733	...	2733	...	...	...	2874	...	2874
Value added tax	...	...	...	–2204	...	–2204	...	...	...	–2308	...	–2308
Other adjustments [g]	...	...	...	...	...	179	...	...	...	...	...	–403
Total [f]	230313	62987	105992	30568	...	430040	248301	68541	110744	31116	...	458299

Japan

	1992						1993					
	Compensation of employees	Capital consumption	Net operating surplus	Indirect taxes	less: Subsidies received	Value added	Compensation of employees	Capital consumption	Net operating surplus	Indirect taxes	less: Subsidies received	Value added
All producers												
1 Agriculture, hunting, forestry and fishing	2339	1987	5964	331	...	10620	2328	1848	5246	365	...	9787
2 Mining and quarrying	386	253	464	50	...	1152	396	245	386	61	...	1087
3 Manufacturing	68056	20665	25069	13852	...	127643	68602	20383	18903	13540	...	121428
A Manufacture of food, beverages and tobacco [a]	6102	1200	2439	3988	...	13730[b]	6339	1271	2156	4015	...	13782
B Textile, wearing apparel and leather industries [c]	1988	292	85	229	...	2593	1951	267	−4	226	...	2440
C Manufacture of wood and wood products, including furniture	...	...	...	...	...	...	...	...	...	...	...	...
D Manufacture of paper and paper products, printing and publishing [d]	1697	737	692	272	...	3399	1740	746	690	271	...	3447
E Manufacture of chemicals and chemical petroleum, coal, rubber and plastic products [e]	4437	2494	4989	3378	...	15298	4575	2589	4410	3447	...	15022
F Manufacture of non-metallic mineral products, except products of petroleum and coal	2709	727	788	364	...	4588	2757	712	543	350	...	4361
G Basic metal industries	3766	1845	3158	844	...	9613	3725	1893	2254	796	...	8668
H Manufacture of fabricated metal products, machinery and equipment	34922	10669	9014	3599	...	58204	34755	10248	5839	3325	...	54165
I Other manufacturing industries	12434	2701	3905	1178	...	20218	12760	2657	3015	1111	...	19542
4 Electricity, gas and water	3303	3855	4214	1163	...	12535	3509	4116	4018	1178	...	12821
5 Construction	26328	5042	15267	2172	...	48809	27809	5549	15618	2139	...	51115
6 Wholesale and retail trade, restaurants and hotels [b]	39358	4679	15117	4314	...	63467	39840	4747	12425	4337	...	61350
A Wholesale and retail trade	39358	4679	15117	4314	...	63467	39840	4747	12425	4337	...	61350
B Restaurants and hotels	...	...	...	...	...	...	...	...	...	...	...	...
7 Transport, storage and communication	19286	6439	2360	2150	...	30235	19897	6558	1685	2075	...	30214
8 Finance, insurance, real estate and business services	17364	16418	41532	3506	...	78820	17411	17151	43072	3716	...	81349
9 Community, social and personal services [b]	39191	9782	20853	5442	...	75269	40360	9899	23478	5454	...	79192
Total, Industries [f]	215610	69120	130841	32979	...	448550[b]	220151	70495	124831	32866	...	448343
Producers of government services	32995	2624	−	46	...	35665	33997	2767	−	47	...	36812
Other producers	8279	1079	−	125	...	9483	8750	1121	−	130	...	10001
Total [f]	256885	72823	130841	33149	...	493698[b]	262899	74383	124831	33043	...	495156
less: Imputed bank service charge	...	...	23332	...	...	23332	...	...	20819	...	...	20819
Import duties	...	...	...	2894	...	2894	...	...	...	2549	...	2549
Value added tax	...	...	...	−2047	...	−2047	...	...	...	−1864	...	−1864
Other adjustments [g]	...	...	...	...	...	−192	...	...	...	...	...	360
Total [f]	256885	72823	107509	33996	...	471021	262899	74383	104012	33728	...	475381

Japan

	1994						1995					
	Compensation of employees	Capital consumption	Net operating surplus	Indirect taxes	less: Subsidies received	Value added	Compensation of employees	Capital consumption	Net operating surplus	Indirect taxes	less: Subsidies received	Value added
All producers													
1 Agriculture, hunting, forestry and fishing	2274	1956	5586	426	...	10242	2252	1857	4809	433	...	9351
2 Mining and quarrying	406	228	345	54	...	1033	382	215	416	58	...	1071
3 Manufacturing	68769	19656	15129	13699	...	117253	69175	19122	16946	14018	...	119261
A Manufacture of food, beverages and tobacco [a]	6719	1289	1521	4143	...	13672	6837	1338	1333	4116	...	13624
B Textile, wearing apparel and leather industries [c]	1832	238	−185	219	...	2105	1791	228	−362	217	...	1875
C Manufacture of wood and wood products, including furniture	...	...	...	...	...	...	...	...	...	...	...	...
D Manufacture of paper and paper products, printing and publishing [d]	1736	738	553	273	...	3300	1726	745	721	287	...	3480
E Manufacture of chemicals and chemical petroleum, coal, rubber and plastic products [e]	4575	2596	4346	3595	...	15112	4614	2558	4224	3686	...	15083
F Manufacture of non-metallic mineral products, except products of petroleum and coal	2868	718	404	361	...	4352	2839	684	364	369	...	4255
G Basic metal industries	3590	1898	1891	802	...	8181	3463	1816	2531	850	...	8660
H Manufacture of fabricated metal products, machinery and equipment	34506	9637	4341	3206	...	51690	34932	9304	6291	3378	...	53905
I Other manufacturing industries	12943	2541	2257	1100	...	18842	12973	2448	1844	1115	...	18380
4 Electricity, gas and water	3695	4347	4170	1213	...	13424	3839	4698	3927	1269	...	13733
5 Construction	29561	5675	14205	2224	...	51665	29665	5439	13013	2214	...	50332
6 Wholesale and retail trade, restaurants and hotels [b]	40272	4430	11549	4611	...	60862	40652	4614	10908	4811	...	60985
A Wholesale and retail trade	40272	4430	11549	4611	...	60862	40652	4614	10908	4811	...	60985
B Restaurants and hotels	...	...	...	...	...	...	...	...	...	...	...	...
7 Transport, storage and communication	20043	6778	1404	2243	...	30468	20713	7185	1070	2386	...	31354
8 Finance, insurance, real estate and business services	17725	18083	46178	3720	...	85705	17991	18827	45968	3835	...	86622
9 Community, social and personal services [b]	43026	10268	21846	5232	...	80373	44063	10852	21995	5422	...	82333
Total, Industries [f]	225771	71418	120413	33422	...	451025	228732	72811	119053	34446[a]	...	455041[g]
Producers of government services	34696	2962	—	50	...	37708	35689	3111	—	56	...	38856
Other producers	9066	1225	—	139	...	10430	9543	1231	—	132	...	10907
Total [f]	269534	75605	120413	33610	...	499163	273964	77153	119053	34635	...	504804
less: Imputed bank service charge	...	...	21372	...	...	21372	...	...	22263	...	...	22263
Import duties	...	...	...	2676	...	2676	...	...	...	2861	...	2861
Value added tax	...	...	...	−1749	...	−1749	...	...	...	−1806	...	−1806
Other adjustments [g]	...	...	...	...	...	543	...	...	...	...	...	−377
Total [f]	269534	75605	99041	34537	...	479260	273964	77153	96790	35690	...	483220

Japan

	1996						1997					
	Compensation of employees	Capital consumption	Net operating surplus	Indirect taxes	less: Subsidies received	Value added	Compensation of employees	Capital consumption	Net operating surplus	Indirect taxes	less: Subsidies received	Value added
All producers												
1 Agriculture, hunting, forestry and fishing	2221	1846	4802	439	...	9308	...	...	...	...	...	...
2 Mining and quarrying	367	223	413	71	...	1073	...	...	...	...	...	...
3 Manufacturing	70495	19272	17229	14558	...	121554	...	...	...	...	...	...
A Manufacture of food, beverages and tobacco [a]	7037	1400	1059	4200	...	13695	...	...	...	...	...	...
B Textile, wearing apparel and leather industries [c]	1803	222	−513	218	...	1730	...	...	...	...	...	...
C Manufacture of wood and wood products, including furniture	...	...	...	...	...	...	...	...	...	...	...	...
D Manufacture of paper and paper products, printing and publishing [d]	1756	756	767	300	...	3578	...	...	...	...	...	...
E Manufacture of chemicals and chemical petroleum, coal, rubber and plastic products [e]	4523	2616	4252	3847	...	15238	...	...	...	...	...	...
F Manufacture of non-metallic mineral products, except products of petroleum and coal	2851	704	426	383	...	4365	...	...	...	...	...	...
G Basic metal industries	3543	1840	2522	877	...	8781	...	...	...	...	...	...
H Manufacture of fabricated metal products, machinery and equipment	35986	9161	7077	3577	...	55800	...	...	...	...	...	...
I Other manufacturing industries	12997	2574	1639	1157	...	18366	...	...	...	...	...	...
4 Electricity, gas and water	3930	5095	3793	1311	...	14130	...	...	...	...	...	...
5 Construction	30207	5423	14777	2362	...	52768	...	...	...	...	...	...
6 Wholesale and retail trade, restaurants and hotels [b]	41439	4816	9511	4924	...	60691	...	...	...	...	...	...
A Wholesale and retail trade	41439	4816	9511	4924	...	60691	...	...	...	...	...	...
B Restaurants and hotels	...	...	...	...	...	...	...	...	...	...	...	...
7 Transport, storage and communication	20802	8020	1939	2529	...	33289	...	...	...	...	...	...
8 Finance, insurance, real estate and business services	17822	19264	48462	4149	...	89696	...	...	...	...	...	...
9 Community, social and personal services [b]	45663	11454	24301	5815	...	87233	...	...	...	...	...	...
Total, Industries [f]	232946	75413	125226	36156	...	469741	...	...	...	...	...	...
Producers of government services	36518	3167	−	64	...	39749	...	...	...	...	...	...
Other producers	9969	1270	−	139	...	11377	...	...	...	...	...	...
Total [f]	279433	79849	125226	36359	...	520867	...	...	...	...	...	...
less: Imputed bank service charge	...	...	20413	...	...	20413	...	...	...	...	...	...
Import duties	...	...	...	3163	...	3163	...	...	...	...	...	...
Value added tax	...	...	...	−2047	...	−2047	...	...	...	...	...	...
Other adjustments	...	...	...	...	...	−1709	...	...	...	...	...	...
Total [f]	279433	79849	104813	37475	...	499861	...	...	...	...	...	...

a Item "Manufacture of food, beverages and tobacco" excludes tobacco.
b Restaurants and hotels are included in item "Community, social and personal services".
c Item "Textile, wearing apparel and leather industries" refers to textile only.
d Item "Manufacture of paper and paper products, printing and publishing" excludes printing and publishing.
e Item "Manufacture of chemical and chemical petroleum, coal, rubber and plastic products" excludes rubber and plastic products.
f Column 4 refers to indirect taxes less subsidies received.
g Item "Other adjustments" refers to inventory valuation adjustment.

Jordan

General note

The preparation of national accounts statistics in Jordan is undertaken by the Department of Statistics, Amman. The annual official estimates together with methodological notes are published in a series of publications entitled *National Accounts*. A comprehensive description of the concepts and definitions underlying the various tables is contained in *The National Accounts 1970-1974*, published in 1976 by the Department of Statistics. The estimates are generally in accordance with the classifications and definitions recommended in the United Nations System of National Accounts (1968 SNA). The following tables have been prepared from successive replies to the United Nations National Accounts Questionnaire. When the scope and coverage of the estimates differ for conceptual or statistical reasons from the definitions and classifications recommended in SNA, a footnote is indicated to the relevant tables.

Gross domestic product

Gross domestic product is estimated mainly through the production approach.

Expenditures on the gross domestic product

All components of gross domestic product by expenditure type are estimated through the expenditure approach except private consumption expenditure and investment in machinery and equipment which are estimated by using the commodity-flow approach. The estimates of government final consumption expenditure are obtained from the records of the Ministry of Finance, National Planning Council and municipalities. The estimates of private final consumption expenditure are built up from studies of the origin and use of the country's economic resources and from the input-output analysis made for the years 1960-1969. Estimates of gross fixed capital formation of the private sector are based on building licence statistics, a special survey and on imports of machinery and equipment, while that of the government sector are mainly obtained from records of the Ministry of Finance. Estimates of increase in stocks are approximate and in most cases based on inquiries in the manufacturing industry. Imports and exports of goods and services are mainly estimated from the external trade statistics. Gross domestic product by expenditure at constant prices is not estimated.

Cost structure of the gross domestic product

The sources and methods applied in estimating the cost-structure components of gross domestic product are based on income estimates. Separate estimates are made for income of agricultural workers, income of skilled labourers, and for income from property and capital assets. Gross operating surplus (i.e. including consumption of fixed capital) is arrived at as a residual.

Gross domestic product by kind of activity

The table of gross domestic product by kind of economic activity is prepared at factor costs. The production approach is used to estimate the value added of most industries, such as agriculture, forestry and fishing, mining and manufacturing, wholesale and retail trade, while the income approach is used for a number of service sectors. Annual agricultural sample surveys are undertaken on a country-wide basis providing production estimates for crops. The quantities obtained from these surveys are valued at farm prices which are assumed to be a certain percentage of the relevant wholesale or retail prices. Livestock estimates are obtained from the municipalities and the Ministry of Reconstruction and Development, adjusted to arrive at a total number of slaughtering for the country. The estimates of industrial production are based on the 1967 and 1974 industrial censuses, balance sheets and income and expenditure statements in 1970, and on analysis of large industrial companies and industrial sample surveys for the remaining years. Value added of private building construction is calculated from cost estimates obtained from special inquiries, while value of public construction is obtained from the records of the Ministry of Finance, National Planning Council and municipalities. Special sample surveys of wholesale and retail trade were conducted in the years 1967-1971 and supplemented by a systematic study of the origin and use of all goods imported and produced in the economy for the year 1975. For passenger and freight transport, the source of information is mainly the records of the authority or the corporation concerned. As for road transport, estimates are based on a survey undertaken in 1974 and on special inquiries.

The estimates for banking are based on returns sent to the Department of Statistics by the various banks. Information on the operation of insurance companies has been collected by means of special surveys undertaken during 1970-1974, covering also information on the activities of foreign exchange dealers. The income arising from ownership of dwellings represents the net rental value of all dwellings based initially on the assessments of the Ministry of Finance. For other services, data are provided by the Ministry of Finance or by the institutions concerned.

Gross domestic product by kind of economic activity at constant prices is not estimated.

Jordan

1.1 Expenditure on the gross domestic product, in current prices

Million Jordanian dinars

	1986	1987	1988	1989	1990	1991	1992	1993	1994	1995	1996	1997
1 Government final consumption expenditure [a]	566	587	604	619	664	742	791	858	990	1081	1200	...
2 Private final consumption expenditure	1718	1670	1626	1635	1976	2040	2648	2711	2774	3023	3323	...
3 Gross capital formation	444	516	532	563	850	738	1209	1423	1451	1547	1801	...
A Increase in stocks	35	67	19	9	156	60	160	119	60	68	84	...
B Gross fixed capital formation [a]	409	448	513	554	694	678	1049	1304	1391	1480	1717	...
Residential buildings	98	105	230	213	300	325	612	892	833	1204	1331	...
Non-residential buildings	189	202	147	169	136	151	199	245	292			...
Other construction and land improvement, etc.										...	...	...
Other	122	141	137	172	258	202	238	166	266	276	386	...
4 Exports of goods and services	634	756	1021	1360	1652	1698	1820	1962	2093	2438	2687	...
5 less: Imports of goods and services	1199	1320	1520	1804	2474	2363	2975	3152	3108	3435	3865	...
Statistical discrepancy	...	...	...	...	...	...	...	...	17	−36	...	...
equals: Gross domestic product	2164	2209	2264	2372	2668	2855	3493	3802	4218	4619	5147	...

a Government final consumption expenditure includes pension payments less employees' pension contributions. Some non-capital development expenditure of the central government is included in other construction of gross domestic fixed capital formation.

1.3 Cost components of the gross domestic product

Million Jordanian dinars

	1986	1987	1988	1989	1990	1991	1992	1993	1994	1995	1996	1997
1 Indirect taxes, net	343	331	318	262	344	350	532	597	666	740	...	...
A Indirect taxes	349	341	333	275	350	354	532	597	666	740	...	...
B less: Subsidies	7	11	16	12	6	5	–	–	–	–	...	...
2 Consumption of fixed capital	197	203	221	238	233	303	324	352	390	441	...	...
3 Compensation of employees paid by resident producers to	802	838	888	934	995	1074	1288	1462	1599	1801	...	...
4 Operating surplus	821	837	838	938	1096	1128	1350	1390	1563	1638	...	...
equals: Gross domestic product	2164	2209	2264	2372	2668	2855	3493	3802	4218	4619	...	...

1.4 General government current receipts and disbursements

Million Jordanian dinars

	1986	1987	1988	1989	1990	1991	1992	1993	1994	1995	1996	1997
Receipts												
1 Operating surplus	64	80	205	296	109	105	111	148	89	67	...	...
2 Property and entrepreneurial income	16 / 34	33	45	24	28	37	37	73	61	68	...	...
3 Taxes, fees and contributions	348 / 489	483	478	449	600	681	966	999	1091	1197	...	...
A Indirect taxes	222 / 349	341	333	275	350	354	532	597	666	740	...	...
B Direct taxes	79 / 48	46	44	52	114	93	110	119	137	152	...	...
C Social security contributions	8 / 45	44	46	48	61	54	62	72	80	90	...	...
D Compulsory fees, fines and penalties	40 / 47	52	56	74	75	179	262	212	208	215	...	...
4 Other current transfers	200 / 244	223	233	380	292	368	325	299	288	296	...	...
Statistical discrepancy	...	...	...	...	...	...	...	52	53	58	...	...

Jordan

Million Jordanian dinars

	1986	1987	1988	1989	1990	1991	1992	1993	1994	1995	1996	1997
Total current receipts of general government	564 831	819	961	1149	1029	1191	1438	1571	1580	1686	...	...

Disbursements

	1986	1987	1988	1989	1990	1991	1992	1993	1994	1995	1996	1997
1 Government final consumption expenditure	461	...	604	619	664	742	791	858	986	1111	...	...
A Compensation of employees	289	...	390	401	418	441	520	576	622	699	...	...
B Consumption of fixed capital	6	...	28	30	31	33	35	43	45	57	...	...
C Purchases of goods and services, net	166	...	226	237	271	331	298	319	405	451	...	...
D less: Own-account fixed capital formation	...	...	41	50	56	64	62	81	86	96	...	...
E Indirect taxes paid, net	...	...	–	–	–	–	–	–	–	–	...	...
2 Property income	...	...	205	296	365	374	355	323	319	347	...	...
A Interest	...	...	205	296	365	374	355	323	319	347	...	...
B Net land rent and royalties	...	...	–	–	–	–	–	–	–	–	...	...
3 Subsidies	8	...	16	12	6	5	–	–	9	–	...	...
4 Other current transfers	191	...	90	100	108	102	136	172	193	217	...	...
A Social security benefits	...	...	11	15	18	18	20	23	28	29	...	...
B Social assistance grants	...	...	6	4	4	8	10	12	16	18	...	...
C Other	...	...	74	82	86	76	106	136	148	171	...	...
Statistical discrepancy	...	...	145	245	38	22	14	65	85	57	...	...
5 Net saving	–96	...	–99	–123	–152	–53	142	153	–11	–46	...	...
Total current disbursements and net saving of general government	564	...	961	1149	1029	1191	1438	1571	1580	1686	...	...

1.7 External transactions on current account, summary

Million Jordanian dinars

	1986	1987	1988	1989	1990	1991	1992	1993	1994	1995	1996	1997

Payments to the rest of the world

	1986	1987	1988	1989	1990	1991	1992	1993	1994	1995	1996	1997
1 Imports of goods and services	1199	1320	1520	1804	2474	2363	2975	3152	3108	3435	...	...
2 Factor income to rest of the world	95	102	137	250	317	330	320	290	279	285	...	...
A Compensation of employees	10	7	7	6	6	5	7	6	8	9	...	...
B Property and entrepreneurial income	84	94	131	244	312	325	313	283	271	276	...	...
3 Current transfers to the rest of the world	79	62	60	54	46	40	58	54	76	95	...	...
4 Surplus of the nation on current transactions	–64	–197	–114	–32	–532	–314	–598	–467	–308	–180	...	...
Payments to the rest of the world and surplus of the nation on current transfers	1308	1286	1604	2077	2306	2418	2755	3029	3155	3635	...	...

Receipts from the rest of the world

	1986	1987	1988	1989	1990	1991	1992	1993	1994	1995	1996	1997
1 Exports of goods and services	634	756	1021	1360	1652	1698	1820	1962	2093	2439	...	...
2 Factor income from rest of the world	77	52	49	59	78	108	134	141	127	168	...	...
A Compensation of employees	42	32	34	36	33	31	57	72	76	87	...	...

Jordan

Million Jordanian dinars	1986	1987	1988	1989	1990	1991	1992	1993	1994	1995	1996	1997
B Property and entrepreneurial income	36	20	15	23	45	78	76	69	51	81	...	...
3 Current transfers from rest of the world	597	479	534	658	576	612	802	926	934	1028	...	...
Receipts from the rest of the world on current transactions	1308	1286	1604	2077	2306	2418	2755	3029	3155	3635	...	...

1.8 Capital transactions of the nation, summary

Million Jordanian dinars	1986	1987	1988	1989	1990	1991	1992	1993	1994	1995	1996	1997
Finance of gross capital formation												
Gross saving	380	318	419	531	318	425	611	956	1143	1375	...	...
1 Consumption of fixed capital	197	203	221	238	233	303	324	352	390	441	...	...
2 Net saving	183	115	198	293	85	122	287	604	753	934	...	...
less: Surplus of the nation on current transactions	−64	−197	−114	−32	−532	−314	−598	−467	−308	−180	...	...
Finance of gross capital formation	444	516	532	563	850	738	1209	1423	1451	1554	...	...
Gross capital formation												
Increase in stocks	35	67	19	9	156	60	160	119	60	159	...	...
Gross fixed capital formation	409	448	513	554	694	678	1049	1304	1391	1395	...	...
Gross capital formation	444	516	532	563	850	738	1209	1423	1451	1554	...	...

1.10 Gross domestic product by kind of activity, in current prices

Million Jordanian dinars	1986	1987	1988	1989	1990	1991	1992	1993	1994	1995	1996	1997
1 Agriculture, hunting, forestry and fishing	112	135	131	140	188	214	248	194	195	173	...	...
2 Mining and quarrying	66	68	78	167	187	156	159	133	127	184	...	...
3 Manufacturing	342	354	323	322	430	435	526	569	784	866	...	...
4 Electricity, gas and water	44	49	51	53	54	62	67	79	85	98	...	...
5 Construction	138	121	114	103	107	127	217	286	302	300	...	...
6 Wholesale and retail trade, restaurants and hotels	284	277	255	179	226	256	288	331	397	442	...	...
7 Transport, storage and communication	284	287	306	370	370	391	457	496	529	582	...	...
8 Finance, insurance, real estate and business services	330	343	390	427	421	492	539	644	679	744	...	...
9 Community, social and personal services	40	41	47	47	52	67	88	90	111	131	...	...
Total, Industries	1640	1676	1695	1808	2034	2200	2588	2822	3208	3521	...	...
Producers of government services	370	388	419	431	449	474	555	619	667	757	...	...
Other producers	26	26	27	31	37	39	46	47	53	56	...	...
Subtotal [a]	2035	2090	2141	2271	2520	2714	3189	3488	3929	4334	...	...
less: Imputed bank service charge	39	39	50	55	40	54	42	66	74	75	...	...
plus: Import duties	...	...	...	...	...	...	...	...	...	...	...	...
plus: Value added tax	...	...	...	...	...	...	...	...	...	...	...	...
plus: Other adjustments [b]	167	158	173	157	188	195	346	380	363	360	...	...
equals: Gross domestic product	2164	2209	2264	2372	2668	2855	3493	3802	4218	4619	...	...

a Gross domestic product in factor values.   b Item "Other adjustments" refers to indirect taxes net of subsidies.

Jordan

1.11 Gross domestic product by kind of activity, in constant prices

Million Jordanian dinars

	1986	1987	1988	1989	1990	1991	1992	1993	1994	1995	1996	1997
	At constant prices of: 1985											
1 Agriculture, hunting, forestry and fishing	105	124	165	124	163	179	210	154	140	138	...	...
2 Mining and quarrying	72	76	70	77	64	54	54	47	48	68	...	...
3 Manufacturing	197	204	165	204	224	221	254	262	337	340	...	...
4 Electricity, gas and water	61	65	63	69	53	56	59	67	70	82	...	...
5 Construction	141	133	108	86	81	89	139	174	194	196	...	...
6 Wholesale and retail trade, restaurants and hotels	271	264	226	77	58	59	65	82	101	108	...	...
7 Transport, storage and communication	275	290	289	280	270	255	278	290	302	328	...	...
8 Finance, insurance, real estate and business services	319	331	368	364	336	370	386	441	472	499	...	...
9 Community, social and personal services	38	38	40	30	31	40	50	51	60	68	...	...
Total, Industries	1479	1524	1494	1312	1279	1323	1494	1569	1724	1828	...	...
Producers of government services	354	381	405	388	386	393	415	452	465	481	...	...
Other producers	26	26	26	24	26	26	30	29	32	33	...	...
Subtotal [a]	1858	1931	1925	1725	1691	1742	1939	2049	2221	2343	...	...
less: Imputed bank service charge	39	40	48	44	28	36	27	42	45	44	...	...
plus: Import duties	...	...	...	...	...	...	...	...	...	...	...	...
plus: Value added tax	...	...	...	...	...	...	...	...	...	...	...	...
plus: Other adjustments [b]	342	333	306	209	246	238	344	374	408	438	...	...
equals: Gross domestic product	2162	2224	2183	1890	1908	1943	2255	2381	2584	2737	...	...

a Gross domestic product in factor values.   b Item "Other adjustments" refers to indirect taxes net of subsidies.

1.12 Relations among national accounting aggregates

Million Jordanian dinars

	1986	1987	1988	1989	1990	1991	1992	1993	1994	1995	1996	1997
Gross domestic product	2164	2209	2264	2372	2668	2855	3493	3802	4218	4619	...	...
plus: Net factor income from the rest of the world	−17	−50	−88	−191	−240	−221	−186	−149	−151	−117	...	...
Factor income from rest of the world	77	52	49	59	78	108	134	141	127	168	...	...
less: Factor income to the rest of the world	95	102	137	250	317	330	320	290	279	285	...	...
equals: Gross national product	2146	2158	2176	2181	2429	2634	3307	3653	4067	4502	...	...
less: Consumption of fixed capital	197	203	221	238	233	303	324	352	390	441	...	...
equals: National income	1949	1955	1955	1942	2195	2331	2983	3300	3676	4061	...	...
plus: Net current transfers from the rest of the world	518	417	474	604	530	572	743	872	858	934	...	...
Current transfers from rest of the world	597	479	534	658	576	612	802	926	934	1028	...	...
less: Current transfers to the rest of the world	79	62	60	54	46	40	58	54	76	95	...	...
equals: National disposable income	2467	2372	2429	2547	2725	2904	3726	4172	4534	4995	...	...
less: Final consumption [a]	2285	2256	2231	2254	2640	2782	3439	3569	3781	4062	...	...
equals: Net saving	183	115	198	293	85	122	287	604	753	934	...	...

Jordan

Million Jordanian dinars

	1986	1987	1988	1989	1990	1991	1992	1993	1994	1995	1996	1997
less: Surplus of the nation on current transactions	−64	−197	−114	−32	−532	−314	−598	−467	−308	−180	...	...
equals: Net capital formation [a]	247	312	312	325	617	436	885	1070	1061	1113	...	...

a Government final consumption expenditure includes pension payments less employees' pension contributions. Some non-capital development expenditure of the central government is included in other construction of gross domestic fixed capital formation.

2.1 Government final consumption expenditure by function, in current prices

Million Jordanian dinars

	1986	1987	1988	1989	1990	1991	1992	1993	1994	1995	1996	1997
1 General public services [a]	302	292	...	...	400	492	517	503	584	667	...	...
2 Defence	...	...	...	...	...	...	...	...	...	...	...	...
3 Public order and safety	...	...	...	...	...	...	...	...	...	...	...	...
4 Education	72	78	...	...	162	160	169	205	201	237	...	...
5 Health	25	26	...	...	74	67	71	95	81	92	...	...
6 Social security and welfare	2	2	...	...	4	5	7	9	10	10	...	...
7 Housing and community amenities	...	...	...	...	...	...	...	...	...	...	...	...
8 Recreational, cultural and religious affairs	...	...	...	...	37	33	31	60	60	62	...	...
9 Economic services	42	42	...	...	...	...	...	...	...	...	...	...
10 Other functions	18	19	...	...	43	48	58	66	50	43	...	...
Total government final consumption expenditures	461	460	...	...	720	805	853	938	986	1111	...	...

a Includes item "Defence" and item "Public order and safety".

2.11 Gross fixed capital formation by kind of activity of owner, ISIC divisions, in current prices

Million Jordanian dinars

	1986	1987	1988	1989	1990	1991	1992	1993	1994	1995	1996	1997
All producers												
1 Agriculture, hunting, forestry and fishing	11	11	8	2	12	17	20	20	18	28	...	...
2 Mining and quarrying	1	6	12	23	10	50	11	13	92	12	...	...
3 Manufacturing	9	42	18	20	13	26	45	31	113	78	...	...
4 Electricity, gas and water	90	56	39	41	24	29	39	58	70	94	...	...
5 Construction	11	10	7	8	3	3	15	20	32	15	...	...
6 Wholesale and retail trade, restaurants and hotels	9	7	3	2	5	10	17	12	22	18	...	...
7 Transport, storage and communication	57	53	43	93	188	62	74	−17	40	56	...	...
8 Finance, insurance, real estate and business services	104	110	238	220	310	334	626	914	710	752	...	...
9 Community, social and personal services	4	5	6	1	3	7	16	18	30	56	...	...
Total industries	296	300	373	410	567	539	864	1068	1127	1107	...	...
Producers of government services	112	147	139	143	124	136	181	235	257	281	...	...
Private non-profit institutions serving households	2	1	1	1	3	3	5	1	7	7	...	...
Total	409	448	513	554	694	678	1049	1304	1391	1395	...	...

Jordan

2.17 Exports and imports of goods and services, detail

Million Jordanian dinars

	1986	1987	1988	1989	1990	1991	1992	1993	1994	1995	1996	1997
Exports of goods and services												
1 Exports of merchandise, f.o.b.	256	318	490	647	691	777	836	871	1003	1241	...	...
2 Transport and communication	91	117	148	157	245	170	224	254	245	292	...	...
3 Insurance service charges	22	21	8	12	2	1	3	1	2	–	...	...
4 Other commodities	75	104	144	229	374	534	443	446	438	447	...	...
5 Adjustments of merchandise exports to change-of-ownership basis	...	...	...	...	...	...	...	...	...	...	...	...
6 Direct purchases in the domestic market by non-residential households	186	196	231	315	340	216	314	390	406	488	...	...
7 Direct purchases in the domestic market by extraterritorial bodies	...	...	...	...	...	...	...	...	...	...	...	...
Total exports of goods and services	630	756	1021	1360	1652	1698	1820	1962	2093	2468	...	...
Imports of goods and services												
1 Imports of merchandise, c.i.f.	848	980	1126	1326	1822	1793	2326	2488	2394	2588	...	...
2 Adjustments of merchandise imports to change-of-ownership basis	...	...	...	...	...	...	...	...	...	...	...	...
3 Other transport and communication	70	86	134	138	232	115	201	207	212	274	...	...
4 Other insurance service charges	...	...	...	...	...	...	...	...	...	...	...	...
5 Other commodities	91	102	81	99	198	263	209	218	226	272	...	...
6 Direct purchases abroad by government	...	...	...	...	...	...	...	...	...	...	...	...
7 Direct purchases abroad by resident households	155	151	178	242	223	192	238	239	275	294	...	...
Total imports of goods and services	1164	1320	1520	1804	2474	2363	2975	3152	3108	3429	...	...
Balance of goods and services	–534	–563	–499	–445	–822	–665	–1155	–1190	–1014	–961	...	...
Total imports and balance of goods and services	630	756	1021	1360	1652	1698	1820	1962	2093	2468	...	...

4.1 Derivation of value added by kind of activity, in current prices

Million Jordanian dinars

	1986			1987			1988			1989		
	Gross output	Intermediate consumption	Value added	Gross output	Intermediate consumption	Value added	Gross output	Intermediate consumption	Value added	Gross output	Intermediate consumption	Value added
All producers												
1 Agriculture, hunting, forestry and fishing	267	156	112	298	164	135	297	166	131	340	200	140
2 Mining and quarrying	134	68	66	128	59	68	162	84	78	286	119	167
3 Manufacturing	805	464	342	889	535	354	922	598	323	1215	892	322
4 Electricity, gas and water	92	48	44	93	44	49	95	44	51	96	43	53
5 Construction	336	198	138	388	267	121	424	310	114	454	351	103
6 Wholesale and retail trade, restaurants and hotels	430	146	284	419	142	277	369	114	255	322	144	179

Jordan

Million Jordanian dinars

	1986			1987			1988			1989		
	Gross output	Intermediate consumption	Value added	Gross output	Intermediate consumption	Value added	Gross output	Intermediate consumption	Value added	Gross output	Intermediate consumption	Value added
7 Transport, storage and communication	514	229	284	516	229	287	550	245	306	654	284	370
8 Finance, insurance, real estate and business services	381	50	330	387	44	343	436	47	390	477	49	427
9 Community, social and personal services	61	21	40	62	21	41	69	22	47	74	27	47
Total, Industries	3020	1380	1640	3181	1505	1676	3324	1629	1695	3919	2111	1808
Producers of government services	600	230	370	624	236	388	645	226	419	668	237	431
Other producers	28	2	26	32	5	26	34	7	27	39	8	31
Total	3648	1612	2035	3837	1746	2090	4003	1862	2141	4626	2355	2271
less: Imputed bank service charge	...	–39	39	...	–39	39	–	–50	50	–	–55	55
Import duties	167	...	167	158	...	158	173	...	173	157	...	157
Value added tax	...	...	...	...	...	...	...	...	...	...	...	...
Other adjustments	...	...	...	...	...	...	...	...	...	...	...	...
Total	3815	1651	2164	3994	1786	2209	4176	1912	2264	4783	2411	2372

	1990			1991			1992			1993		
	Gross output	Intermediate consumption	Value added	Gross output	Intermediate consumption	Value added	Gross output	Intermediate consumption	Value added	Gross output	Intermediate consumption	Value added
All producers												
1 Agriculture, hunting, forestry and fishing	439	251	188	485	271	214	593	345	248	493	299	194
2 Mining and quarrying	292	106	187	278	122	156	275	116	159	240	108	133
3 Manufacturing	1377	947	430	1405	970	435	2012	1487	526	1966	1396	569
4 Electricity, gas and water	100	46	54	119	56	62	140	73	67	169	90	79
5 Construction	499	392	107	533	406	127	854	637	217	1218	933	286
6 Wholesale and retail trade, restaurants and hotels	384	158	226	414	159	256	468	180	288	524	193	331
7 Transport, storage and communication	718	349	370	681	290	391	794	337	457	844	348	496
8 Finance, insurance, real estate and business services	481	60	421	554	62	492	613	74	539	733	89	644
9 Community, social and personal services	79	27	52	106	38	67	132	44	88	140	50	90
Total, Industries	4370	2336	2034	4574	2374	2200	5881	3293	2588	6328	3506	2822
Producers of government services	720	271	449	806	331	474	852	298	555	938	319	619
Other producers	47	10	37	49	10	39	58	11	46	62	16	47
Total	5137	2617	2520	5429	2715	2714	6791	3602	3189	7329	3842	3488
less: Imputed bank service charge	–	–40	40	–	–54	54	–	–42	42	–	–66	66
Import duties	188	–	188	195	–	195	346	–	346	380	–	380
Value added tax	...	...	...	...	...	...	...	...	...	...	...	...
Other adjustments	...	...	...	...	...	...	...	...	...	...	...	...
Total	5325	2657	2668	5624	2769	2855	7137	3644	3493	7710	3908	3802

Jordan

	1994 Gross output	1994 Intermediate consumption	1994 Value added	1995 Gross output	1995 Intermediate consumption	1995 Value added	1996 Gross output	1996 Intermediate consumption	1996 Value added	1997 Gross output	1997 Intermediate consumption	1997 Value added
All producers												
1 Agriculture, hunting, forestry and fishing	551	356	195	572	399	173	...	...	...	...	...	...
2 Mining and quarrying	236	109	127	287	103	184	...	...	...	...	...	...
3 Manufacturing	2542	1758	784	2899	2032	866	...	...	...	...	...	...
4 Electricity, gas and water	190	105	85	209	111	98	...	...	...	...	...	...
5 Construction	1207	905	302	1135	835	300	...	...	...	...	...	...
6 Wholesale and retail trade, restaurants and hotels	612	215	397	678	236	442	...	...	...	...	...	...
7 Transport, storage and communication	881	352	529	959	377	582	...	...	...	...	...	...
8 Finance, insurance, real estate and business services	774	95	679	859	114	744	...	...	...	...	...	...
9 Community, social and personal services	169	58	111	200	69	131	...	...	...	...	...	...
Total, Industries	7163	3955	3208	7796	4275	3521	...	...	...	...	...	...
Producers of government services	1072	405	667	1208	451	757	...	...	...	...	...	...
Other producers	73	20	53	78	22	56	...	...	...	...	...	...
Total	8308	4379	3929	9082	4748	4334	...	...	...	...	...	...
less: Imputed bank service charge	...	−74	74	...	−75	75	...	...	...	...	...	...
Import duties	363	...	363	360	–	360	...	...	...	...	...	...
Value added tax	...	...	...	...	...	...	...	...	...	...	...	...
Other adjustments	...	...	...	...	...	...	...	...	...	...	...	...
Total	8671	4453	4218	9442	4823	4619	...	...	...	...	...	...

4.3 Cost components of value added

Million Jordanian dinars

	1986 Compensation of employees	1986 Capital consumption	1986 Net operating surplus	1986 Indirect taxes	1986 less: Subsidies received	1986 Value added	1987 Compensation of employees	1987 Capital consumption	1987 Net operating surplus	1987 Indirect taxes	1987 less: Subsidies received	1987 Value added
All producers												
1 Agriculture, hunting, forestry and fishing	21	8	85	–	3	112	22	8	108	–	3	135
2 Mining and quarrying	20	14	34	1	4	66	21	14	32	9	8	68
3 Manufacturing	72	43	79	148	–	342	76	45	92	141	–	354
4 Electricity, gas and water	23	15	6	–	...	44	23	17	8	–	...	49
5 Construction	80	22	36	1	...	138	84	17	19	1	...	121
6 Wholesale and retail trade, restaurants and hotels	81	15	178	10	–	284	78	15	177	8	–	277
7 Transport, storage and communication	70	47	158	9	...	284	77	51	149	10	...	287
8 Finance, insurance, real estate and business services	42	5	271	12	...	330	48	5	277	14	...	343
9 Community, social and personal services	21	5	13	1	...	40	21	5	14	1	...	41
Total, Industries [a]	430	175	860	182	7	1640	450	177	876	184	11	1676
Producers of government services	348	22	...	–	...	370	362	26	...	–	...	388
Other producers	25	–	...	–	...	26	26	–	...	–	...	26

Jordan

Million Jordanian dinars

	1986						1987					
	Compensation of employees	Capital consumption	Net operating surplus	Indirect taxes	less: Subsidies received	Value added	Compensation of employees	Capital consumption	Net operating surplus	Indirect taxes	less: Subsidies received	Value added
Total [a]	802	197	860	182	7	2035	838	203	876	184	11	2090
less: Imputed bank service charge	...	...	39	...	...	39	...	...	39	...	...	39
Import duties	...	...	...	167	...	167	...	...	...	158	...	158
Value added tax	...	...	...	...	...	...	...	...	...	...	...	...
Other adjustments	...	...	...	...	...	...	...	...	...	...	...	...
Total [a]	802	197	821	349	7	2164	838	203	837	341	11	2209

	1988						1989					
	Compensation of employees	Capital consumption	Net operating surplus	Indirect taxes	less: Subsidies received	Value added	Compensation of employees	Capital consumption	Net operating surplus	Indirect taxes	less: Subsidies received	Value added

All producers

1 Agriculture, hunting, forestry and fishing	22	9	104	–	4	131	24	11	104	–	–	140
2 Mining and quarrying	24	17	41	3	7	78	26	21	107	16	4	167
3 Manufacturing	83	49	65	126	–	323	92	54	109	68	–	322
4 Electricity, gas and water	25	15	10	–	...	51	26	16	11	–	...	53
5 Construction	82	20	10	1	...	114	89	19	–7	1	...	103
6 Wholesale and retail trade, restaurants and hotels	68	16	171	5	5	255	72	19	90	6	8	179
7 Transport, storage and communication	84	52	159	11	...	306	86	52	221	11	...	370
8 Finance, insurance, real estate and business services	58	7	312	12	...	390	56	7	351	14	...	427
9 Community, social and personal services	25	6	15	1	...	47	30	7	8	1	...	47
Total, Industries [a]	472	191	888	160	16	1695	503	207	993	118	12	1808
Producers of government services	390	28	...	–	...	419	401	30	...	–	...	431
Other producers	26	1	...	–	...	27	30	1	...	–	...	31
Total [a]	888	221	888	160	16	2141	934	238	993	118	12	2271
less: Imputed bank service charge	...	...	50	...	...	50	...	...	55	...	...	55
Import duties	...	...	...	173	...	173	...	...	...	157	...	157
Value added tax	...	...	...	...	...	...	...	...	...	...	...	...
Other adjustments	...	...	...	...	...	...	...	...	...	...	...	...
Total [a]	888	221	838	333	16	2264	934	238	938	275	12	2372

	1990						1991					
	Compensation of employees	Capital consumption	Net operating surplus	Indirect taxes	less: Subsidies received	Value added	Compensation of employees	Capital consumption	Net operating surplus	Indirect taxes	less: Subsidies received	Value added

All producers

1 Agriculture, hunting, forestry and fishing	26	12	150	–	–	188	32	22	159	1	–	214
2 Mining and quarrying	32	19	98	38	–	187	37	27	61	31	–	156
3 Manufacturing	99	56	190	84	–	430	116	58	170	91	–	435
4 Electricity, gas and water	28	16	10	–	–	54	29	22	11	–	–	62
5 Construction	89	20	–3	2	–	107	110	15	1	1	–	127
6 Wholesale and retail trade, restaurants and hotels	74	20	123	15	6	226	79	22	154	6	5	256
7 Transport, storage and communication	99	43	220	8	–	370	95	85	202	8	–	391

Jordan

	1990						1991					
	Compen-sation of employ-ees	Capital consump-tion	Net operating surplus	Indirect taxes	less: Subsidies received	Value added	Compen-sation of employ-ees	Capital consump-tion	Net operating surplus	Indirect taxes	less: Subsidies received	Value added
8 Finance, insurance, real estate and business services	61	7	339	14	–	421	61	8	403	19	–	492
9 Community, social and personal services	33	8	11	1	–	52	35	9	21	1	–	67
Total, Industries [a]	541	201	1136	162	6	2034	595	268	1182	159	5	2200
Producers of government services	418	31	–	–	–	449	441	33	–	–	–	474
Other producers	36	1	–	–	–	37	38	1	–	–	–	39
Total [a]	995	233	1136	162	6	2520	1074	303	1182	159	5	2714
less: Imputed bank service charge	...	...	40	...	...	40	...	...	54	...	...	54
Import duties	...	...	...	188	...	188	...	...	...	195	...	195
Value added tax	...	...	...	...	...	...	...	...	...	...	...	...
Other adjustments	...	...	...	...	...	...	...	...	...	...	...	...
Total [a]	995	233	1096	350	6	2668	1074	303	1128	354	5	2855

	1992						1993					
	Compen-sation of employ-ees	Capital consump-tion	Net operating surplus	Indirect taxes	less: Subsidies received	Value added	Compen-sation of employ-ees	Capital consump-tion	Net operating surplus	Indirect taxes	less: Subsidies received	Value added
All producers												
1 Agriculture, hunting, forestry and fishing	35	24	188	1	–	248	25	22	146	1	–	194
2 Mining and quarrying	41	31	58	29	–	159	44	29	34	26	–	133
3 Manufacturing	147	66	194	119	–	526	159	63	205	142	–	569
4 Electricity, gas and water	32	21	14	–	–	67	36	21	22	–	–	79
5 Construction	159	16	40	2	–	217	215	21	48	2	–	286
6 Wholesale and retail trade, restaurants and hotels	83	22	173	9	–	288	96	22	200	14	–	331
7 Transport, storage and communication	105	88	256	7	–	457	126	103	258	9	–	496
8 Finance, insurance, real estate and business services	75	9	436	18	–	539	90	13	520	22	–	644
9 Community, social and personal services	44	10	32	1	–	88	51	14	24	1	–	90
Total, Industries [a]	723	288	1391	186	–	2588	842	308	1456	216	–	2822
Producers of government services	520	35	–	–	–	555	576	43	–	–	–	619
Other producers	45	1	–	–	–	46	45	2	–	–	–	47
Total [a]	1288	324	1391	186	–	3189	1462	352	1456	216	–	3488
less: Imputed bank service charge	...	...	42	...	...	42	...	...	66	...	...	66
Import duties	...	...	...	346	...	346	...	...	...	380	...	380
Value added tax	...	...	...	...	...	...	...	...	...	...	...	...
Other adjustments	...	...	...	...	...	...	...	...	...	...	...	...
Total [a]	1288	324	1350	532	–	3493	1462	352	1390	597	–	3802

Jordan

	1994						1995					
	Compensation of employees	Capital consumption	Net operating surplus	Indirect taxes	less: Subsidies received	Value added	Compensation of employees	Capital consumption	Net operating surplus	Indirect taxes	less: Subsidies received	Value added
	All producers											
1 Agriculture, hunting, forestry and fishing	31	27	135	1	...	195	54	24	94	1	...	173
2 Mining and quarrying	43	25	34	25	...	127	49	30	79	27	...	184
3 Manufacturing	193	93	276	223	...	784	221	105	254	287	...	866
4 Electricity, gas and water	41	22	21	1	...	85	41	24	33	–	...	98
5 Construction	212	22	66	2	...	302	235	27	36	3	...	300
6 Wholesale and retail trade, restaurants and hotels	102	24	251	20	...	397	107	24	284	28	...	442
7 Transport, storage and communication	135	99	286	9	...	529	144	109	320	10	...	582
8 Finance, insurance, real estate and business services	107	15	537	20	...	679	122	18	582	22	...	744
9 Community, social and personal services	62	16	31	2	...	111	77	20	32	2	...	131
Total, Industries [a]	926	343	1636	302	...	3208	1049	380	1713	379	...	3521
Producers of government services	622	45	–	–	...	667	699	57	–	–	...	757
Other producers	50	3	...	–	...	53	53	3	–	–	...	56
Total [a]	1599	390	1636	303	...	3929	1801	441	1713	380	...	4334
less: Imputed bank service charge	...	...	74	...	...	74	–	–	75	–	...	75
Import duties	...	...	...	363	...	363	–	–	–	360	...	360
Value added tax	...	...	...	...	...	...	...	...	...	...	...	...
Other adjustments	...	...	...	...	...	...	...	...	...	...	...	...
Total [a]	1599	390	1563	666	...	4218	1801	441	1638	740	...	4619

a Column 4 refers to indirect taxes less subsidies received.

كيفية الحصول على منشورات الأمم المتحدة

يمكن الحصول على منشورات الأمم المتحدة من المكتبات ودور التوزيع في جميع أنحاء العالم . استعلم عنها من المكتبة التي تتعامل معها أو اكتب إلى : الأمم المتحدة ، قسم البيع في نيويورك أو في جنيف .

如何购取联合国出版物

联合国出版物在全世界各地的书店和经售处均有发售。请向书店询问或写信到纽约或日内瓦的联合国销售组。

HOW TO OBTAIN UNITED NATIONS PUBLICATIONS

United Nations publications may be obtained from bookstores and distributors throughout the world. Consult your bookstore or write to: United Nations, Sales Section, New York or Geneva.

COMMENT SE PROCURER LES PUBLICATIONS DES NATIONS UNIES

Les publications des Nations Unies sont en vente dans les librairies et les agences dépositaires du monde entier. Informez-vous auprès de votre libraire ou adressez-vous à : Nations Unies, Section des ventes, New York ou Genève.

КАК ПОЛУЧИТЬ ИЗДАНИЯ ОРГАНИЗАЦИИ ОБЪЕДИНЕННЫХ НАЦИЙ

Издания Организации Объединенных Наций можно купить в книжных магазинах и агентствах во всех районах мира. Наводите справки об изданиях в вашем книжном магазине или пишите по адресу: Организация Объединенных Наций, Секция по продаже изданий, Нью-Йорк или Женева.

COMO CONSEGUIR PUBLICACIONES DE LAS NACIONES UNIDAS

Las publicaciones de las Naciones Unidas están en venta en librerías y casas distribuidoras en todas partes del mundo. Consulte a su librero o diríjase a: Naciones Unidas, Sección de Ventas, Nueva York o Ginebra.

Litho in United Nations, New York
23737 — October 2000 — 2,930
ISBN 92-1-161425-2

United Nations publication
Sales No. E.00.XVII.11
ST/ESA/STAT/SER.X/25, Part I

William F. Maag Library
Youngstown State University